ENCYCLOPÆDIA
Britannica
ALMANAC
2003

From the knowledge leader since 1768

ENCYCLOPÆDIA
Britannica
ALMANAC
2003

ENCYCLOPÆDIA BRITANNICA, INC.

Jacob E. Safra, *Chairman of the Board*
Ilan Yeshua, *Chief Executive Officer*

Chicago · London · New Delhi · Paris · Seoul · Sydney · Taipei · Tokyo

Remembering September 11

by Robert G. Kaiser

For years we said we lived in a global village. On September 11, 2001, terrorists bent on wreaking havoc in New York City and Washington DC, proved that this was so. Never before had the world so intimately shared the same tragic disaster. Because the attacks occurred in the morning on the United States East Coast, perhaps 90% of the Earth's population was awake when two airplanes flew into the World Trade Center and another crashed into the Pentagon. Transported to New York by some of the most powerful images ever conveyed by television, billions of people vicariously experienced the horror.

Rare are the events that jolt the entire globe. In truth, there may never have been another that had the impact of September 11. The detonation of the first atomic bomb or the bringing down of the Berlin Wall may have been more important historical events, but neither had an audience as big or as raptly attentive as that on September 11. In part because nearly everyone was jolted, we will need a long time—longer surely than the year that has passed—to grasp the true import of that date. It became a cliché almost immediately afterward that "everything has changed." Giving that phrase real content will take years.

Some of the things that changed were quickly obvious. The United States lost its innocence and its isolation, becoming in just a few days a different kind of global power. For 56 years after World War II, Americans had policed the globe as beneficent gendarmes, trying to keep the world safe for democracy and capitalism. Suddenly on September 11 the mission changed. The goal became to keep America itself safe.

For the first time, other nations rushed to America's side, offering condolences and active assistance. The North Atlantic Treaty Organization invoked Article 5 of its founding treaty, declaring that the terrorist actions constituted an attack against all NATO members, which would respond—as required by the treaty—as if they had been attacked themselves. Article 5 had never before been invoked. In Moscow the young president of Russia phoned the young United States president aboard Air Force One and pledged his country's cooperation for a war against terrorism. Vladimir Putin's call was the first the administration of George W. Bush received from a foreign leader. On September 19 the Organization of American States agreed by acclamation to invoke the Rio Treaty, a mutual defense pact. One after another the countries of the world lined up with the United States. Most did so without evident hesitation, a few because Bush made it so clear, in his speech to Congress on September 20, that the United States expected their support: "Every nation in every region now has a decision to make: Either you are with us or you are with the terrorists."

Ultimately, only Iraq offered sympathy to the terrorists; no other government would take their side. This was a huge change. The nations of the world had never before been so united on an important global issue. The collapse of international factions into a united front against terrorism signaled powerfully that, as United States Secretary of State Colin Powell put it in a speech in Shanghai on October 18, "not only is the Cold War over, the post-Cold War period is also over." Suddenly the world had a new cause and a new sense of shared challenge. Old alignments seemed to disappear.

But that near unanimity among political leaders was not so evident on the streets of the world's cities, towns, and villages. Within hours of the September 11 attacks, cameras caught Palestinians on the West Bank exulting over the terrorists' successes. Posters carrying the likeness of Osama bin Laden blossomed throughout the Muslim world. Public opinion polls and questioning reporters found that citizens of many lands felt sympathy for the terrorists and antipathy for the United States.

In China government officials had to censor Internet discussions, which included much cheering for a blow struck against American arrogance. A poll taken in Bolivia found that Bin Laden was the most admired man in that Andean nation. In Muslim countries certain myths took hold: that it was not the Arabs on board who hijacked the aircraft and flew them into the Pentagon and the WTC but, in fact, Israeli intelligence agents who were responsible for the attacks; that the Americans had no proof that Bin Laden was behind what had happened. One of the ugliest myths, written and repeated time and again in the Arab world, was that several thousand Jews who ordinarily worked in the World Trade Center did not show up for work on September 11—an implication that they had been warned of the attacks. In fact, many of the nearly 3,000 victims in the World Trade Center were Jewish.

These expressions of hostility toward the United States and sympathy for those who killed so many innocent people shocked and alarmed many Americans, who wondered how foreigners could wish them ill. Americans hold their country in a high regard, and many did not realize how ambivalent others could be in their attitudes toward the world's only superpower. Anti-Americanism was nothing new, of course, but this latest strain had special characteristics related to America's overwhelming power and the way it had been used and perceived through the 1990s.

Before September 11, Americans had clearly grown comfortable with their cushy position, above the world's frays. Americans liked being richer than the rest and well-insulated from their tribulations. In 2001 the new United States administration was becoming famous for a go-it-alone approach to international affairs, infuriating allies and rivals by its unilateral policies and decisions and by its reluctance to

> ❝ *We will need a long time to grasp the true import of that date.* ❞

join other nations in collective action. One example was the international effort to do something about global warming by controlling the emissions of "greenhouse gases," especially the carbon monoxide produced by the burning of fossil fuels. On September 11 the international community was preparing for a conference that would complete a final agreement on emissions controls, but the United States, the producer of one-fourth of the world's greenhouse gases, had opted not to participate.

On those occasions when the United States did play an active part in world affairs and did join other countries in some collaborative efforts, it was usually on its own terms. Many Americans considered this reasonable and appropriate. Why should they give others any influence over matters they wanted to, and could, control themselves?

September 11 created a new reality. Beginning with that communication from Russian Pres. Vladimir Putin, President Bush spent most of the first days after the attacks speaking and meeting with foreign leaders, building what he called a new global coalition against terrorism. "We will rally the world," Bush said, and he did just that. A president regarded warily by many world leaders as a unilateralist and a bit of a cowboy was suddenly courting support from every conceivable precinct. On September 24 the House of Representatives voted to release $582 million of the $819 million in back dues to the United Nations. Concerns that just before September 11 dominated American policy suddenly disappeared. So, for example, Uzbekistan, with its corrupt and authoritarian regime that had been held at arm's length by the United States before September 11, became an important ally and a base for American military operations soon afterward.

"Working well with others" became a category on school report cards in the United States in the last generation, but globally, this had not been an American value. George Washington, the founding father, offered his countrymen the vision of a United States totally insulated from foreign entanglements in his famous Farewell Address 205 years before September 11, and that remained a tantalizing goal for many Americans. Washington, of course, could not have imagined the technological changes that would shrink the world in our time. Even Americans who experienced those changes remained reluctant to accept their true implications.

September 11 ended the dream of "fortress America." The 19 Arab terrorists who hijacked four airliners that day obviously were not restrained by any sense that the United States enjoyed special protection from hostile foreign forces. The shock that went through the American population after September 11, all but eliminating air travel and tourism for weeks, also marked a turning point for the American experiment, though it was impossible to explain just how. That might take years to clarify.

The horror planned for September 11 was supposed to be worse, and very nearly was. The fourth hijacked airplane was evidently aimed at the Capitol or the White House in Washington—we may never know its target for certain. A direct hit on either would have been symbolically devastating, adding enormously to the impact of the attacks. But a group of brave and resourceful passengers on United Airlines Flight 93 prevented its hijackers from fulfilling their mission, forcing the plane down in a Pennsylvania farm field, where the lives of everyone on board ended.

The fate of Flight 93 was a demonstration of how the modern global village can function. Passengers on board the flight, who thought they were flying from Newark NJ, to San Francisco, made calls to relatives on the ground with cellular telephones and learned that a hijacked plane already had been flown into the World Trade Center in New York. One of them was Jeremy Glick, 31, sales manager for a technology firm, who told his wife to "have a good life" and promised to go down fighting against the terrorists. Glick and several other passengers, all apparently holed in the galley at the rear of the Boeing 757, were plotting to rush the cockpit of the plane, 110 feet forward of the galley, to disrupt whatever plan their hijackers had in mind. One of the other plotters, Todd Beamer, told a telephone operator whom he had reached via an onboard "airfone" about this plan. The operator heard him shout to his comrades, "Are you guys ready? Let's roll!" The operator then heard screams and sounds of a scuffle before the line went dead. In the next few moments, the plane took a series of sharp turns and then plunged into the Pennsylvania countryside near the town of Shanksville, just south of Johnstown. Somehow, the passengers had disrupted the hijackers and forced the plane to Earth.

In that case the technological wizardry of the age contributed to heroism and a self-sacrifice that may have saved many lives in Washington. This was one example of how the events of September 11 were made possible by modern technology or modern styles of life. Other examples of the same phenomenon were not so uplifting.

Eerily, the terrorists, avowed enemies of secular modernity, were able to have the enormous impact they had by mastering skills and technologies that were part of what they claimed to detest. Their ability to move freely between their countries of origin, principally Saudi Arabia and Egypt, and the flying schools and Internet cafés of the United States they so ardently hated, and then into the cockpits of those four Boeing jetliners, was perhaps the most powerful symbol of what September 11 really represented—on one hand, angry young Arabs who belonged to a movement dedicated to antimodernism and an anti-American crusade; on the other hand, a hypermodern America open to the world, open even to these fanatics who were determined to inflict great harm on the United States. In an age of irony, this ultimate irony: the terrorists could do the damage they did only by acquiring skills from American flying schools, exploiting America's porous airport-security arrangements, and mastering the arts of hiding in plain sight in a society they abhorred. In the real global village of 2001, we were all startled to discover, such trickery was amazingly simple. On September 10, it soon became clear, we had not understood the world we lived in; a month later we understood it a lot better, though far from thoroughly.

The easy, comforting notion of a global village implies that all the world's peoples are intimate neighbors, sharing more than they do not share. But this is not the global village that September 11 revealed so starkly.

> ❝ *'We will rally the world,'* *Bush said, and he* *did just that.* ❞

In the real modern world, different peoples have taken what are sometimes radically different paths and reached very different destinations. In Europe and North America, where technology, education, and tradition produced the greatest wealth, the failure of the Muslim world to match this prosperity was just a fact of modern life, little remarked upon before September 11. Most Muslims lived in relative poverty; some were rich from oil; and almost none, rich or poor, occupied the most modern precincts of the global village. The most modern and successful nation in the Middle East, the center of the Muslim world, was not Muslim at all: Israel. But Israel was a hated symbol to many of its Arab neighbors.

The gulf that divides Muslim, mostly Arab peoples from Europeans and Americans, and also Asians, may be the most significant dividing line in the 21st-century world. Put simply, the secular global economy created by the richer countries gave great benefit to many and was a model to be emulated for many more. South Koreans, Chinese, Cypriots, and Chileans all subscribed to the same broad propositions that animated Americans, Germans, and Japanese: technological progress is good; wealth earned from global trade is desirable; consumerism and the democratization of wealth are goals to be pursued. For most of the adherents of this loose creed, political democracy was also part of the formula: democratic governments, most agreed, were most likely to achieve the prosperity so many were seeking.

> ❝ *Americans remarked on a new mood in the country, a new spirit of cooperation and sharing, and a new recognition of what 'really matters' in their lives.* ❞

Many Muslims and Arabs embraced the rich world's ideals—this is evident from the fact that millions of them have found ways to establish residency in rich countries and pursue new lives in them. The governments and especially the religious establishments of the Arab world, however, were not part of the fledgling consensus joined by so many other nations. No Arab government was a democracy, and no Arab nation was a full participant in the technological revolution of the age. Only a few oil-rich autocracies even took a stab at participation.

The Muslim world has never experienced anything comparable to the enlightenment of the 17th and 18th centuries that prepared the Christian nations of Europe for the Industrial Revolution and modernity. For Muslim fundamentalists—for example, the Wahhabi sect that dominates the religious life of Saudi Arabia—nonparticipation in the modern world is seen as a good thing, a way to avoid pollution of Muslim values by infidels. But such fundamentalists are surrounded by the temptations of the wealthy world, and often by neighbors in their own countries who do not share their disdain for modernity. Tens of thousands of well-to-do Saudis, for example, own houses or apartments in Europe or the United States and happily partake of modern pleasures when visiting those places. Yet at home they support a system that denies such pleasures to most of their countrymen and provides few opportunities for citizens to express themselves or influence their government.

The Arab world differs from the modernized West and Asia in another important respect. When countries get rich, their birthrates decline. Birthrates are so low in the developed European nations that they are all facing shrinkage of their native populations. Japan is in a similar position. Conversely, the Arab countries are experiencing rapid population growth. Saudi Arabia is growing more than 3% a year; Egypt, about 2%. Burgeoning populations aggravate tensions in these societies, none of which is creating opportunities for young people sufficient to satisfy the growing number of working-age citizens.

All of these factors are related to the success Bin Laden and his allies have had in building the al-Qaeda terrorist movement that shook the world on September 11. Obviously, only a tiny fraction of the young men of the Arab and Muslim worlds joined al-Qaeda and other like-minded groups. Might there be many more in the future? The possibility could not be dismissed lightly after September 11.

Americans took comfort from their own response to September 11. The country found many heroes to thank, from those passengers on Flight 93 to the fire fighters and police officers of New York City, so many of whom gave their lives that day in service to their country and community. Americans poured hundreds of millions of dollars into charities to support the victims' families and stoically put up with the practical consequences of the attacks, which included a sharp economic downturn, closures and postponements of various meetings and events, and total disruption of domestic airline travel in the United States. Countless Americans remarked on a new mood in the country, a new spirit of cooperation and sharing, and a new recognition, as many put it, of what "really matters" in their lives.

Still, the healing process was slow. Families who lost loved ones on September 11 had to struggle with painful facts: missing bodies, no arrests of key perpetrators, disputes over how the government and others should compensate them for their loss. The fact that Osama bin Laden was not found, dead or alive, left a large hole in the center of the story. The government arrested many suspects, but only one man, arrested before September 11, was accused of direct involvement in the events of that day, Zacarias Moussaoui. Americans frequently paused to remember their national trauma: the flag from the WTC was solemnly paraded at the opening of the Winter Olympic Games in Salt Lake City; the half-year anniversary of the attacks was marked in numerous ceremonies around the country, and the official ending of the clean-up operation at the WTC site again focused the nation's attention. A new phrase entered the language, "homeland security," and soon a cabinet-level department to look after security from terrorism, given that name, was in the works in Washington. With the signing onto law of the "Patriot Act" in October 2001 a national debate began over due process, privacy issues, and the rights of the government—the FBI and airport security authorities, for example—in dealing with private citizens. Congress, initially totally supportive of the Bush administration, began to raise questions about sensitive issues, including whether government officials should have paid more attention to pre-September 11 warnings of possible terrorist attacks. Internationally, the anti-terrorist coalition held, and produced results, including the arrests of persons associated with al-Qaeda or other terrorist groups. Aftershocks from September 11 were evident in other world trouble spots as well, notably Kashmir, Palestine, and the southern Philippines, where Muslims have been involved in armed conflicts for many years.

One year later it was still too early to know the more profound impact of September 11 and its aftermath.

Would Americans' lost innocence be translated into a real commitment to confronting the underlying problems facing the global village? Or would a quick war on terrorism be followed by a relapse into American exceptionalism and another retreat from international engagement? The terrorists of September 11 challenged the United States to confront the fact that it overwhelms all other nations in its wealth, power, and influence and to accept the responsibilities that accompany such preponderance. The terrorists succeeded in making America the target. Americans would have to choose a response to that new status.

Robert G. Kaiser is an Associate Editor of the Washington Post, *coauthor (with Leonard Downie, Jr.) of* The News About the News: American Journalism in Peril *(2002), and author of several other books on international affairs. This article is adapted from* Britannica Book of the Year 2002.

The XIX Olympic Winter Games
by Melinda C. Shepherd

For 17 days, 8–24 Feb 2002, Salt Lake City, Utah, played host to the XIX Olympic Winter Games. In the years leading up to the event, the scandal-ridden Salt Lake Olympic Committee had faced allegations of official bribery, corruption, and misused funds as well as a change in leadership. The terrorist attacks in the US on 11 Sep 2001 and the subsequent "war on terrorism" had also increased the need for additional costly security measures. Initially, some observers raised concerns that the event would become little more than a display of US strength and patriotism, and some criticized the introduction in the Opening Ceremony of a US flag from New York City's "ground zero," where the destroyed World Trade Center had stood. By the Closing Ceremony, however, International Olympic Committee Pres. Jacques Rogge praised Salt Lake, the largest city ever to host the Winter Olympics, for the "superb games."

Some 2,400 athletes representing 77 national Olympic committees from places as far away (and unlikely) as Cameroon, Kenya, India, Brazil, Iran, Thailand, and Fiji competed for 234 medals in 78 events. Athletes from 25 countries, including Australia and Estonia, took home medals, led by Germany's record 35 (12 gold). The US finished with 34 (10 gold), far exceeding the 13 earned at the 1998 Winter Games in Nagano, Japan. Norway finished third with 24 (11 gold). Fifty-three competitors won more than one medal, notably Norwegian Ole Einar Björndalen, who swept all 4 golds in men's biathlon; Croatian Janica Kostelic, who captured 3 golds and a silver in Alpine skiing; Samppa Lajunen of Finland, who won all 3 Nordic combined events, and Swiss sensation Simon Ammann, who upset the favorites to win both the 90-m and 120-m individual ski jumps. Eight speed skating world records were broken, in-

> **"** *Jacques Rogge praised Salt Lake, the largest city ever to host the Winter Olympics, for the 'superb games.'* **"**

cluding two by Jochem Uytdehaage of The Netherlands and two by Germany's Claudia Pechstein. Men's skeleton, which returned to the Olympics after a 54-year absence, was won by third-generation US Olympian Jim Shea, Jr., just a month after the death of his grandfather, champion speed skater Jack Shea. Two women's events made their first appearance—skeleton and bobsleigh, which was won in an upset by Americans Jill Bakken and Vonetta Flowers, the first black Winter Olympic medalist.

The competitions were not without controversy, however. Several athletes were banned even before the Games began when they failed pre-Olympic drug tests. Three Nordic skiers, Johann Mühlegg of Spain and two Russians, Larisa Lazutina and Olga Danilova, were ejected from the Games on the last day when they tested positive for darbepoetin (a drug designed to increase the production of red blood cells); Mühlegg and Lazutina were stripped of the gold medals they had won that day. (Lazutina had been barred from an earlier race when a blood test showed elevated hemoglobin levels; she was expected to lose her two silver medals as well.) Alpine skier Alain Baxter of Great Britain was later stripped of his slalom bronze medal when it was revealed that he had tested positive for a banned substance he ingested in an over-the-counter cold medication.

Once again, a judging scandal in figure skating captured world headlines. In the pairs competition a French judge initially claimed that she had been pressured to vote for gold medal winners Yelena Berezhnaya and Anton Sikharulidze of Russia over the second-place Canadian pair, Jamie Salé and David Pelletier. Although the judge later recanted her story, after four days of discussions Salé and Pelletier were also awarded gold medals.

See the table of all medalists in the 2002 Winter Games beginning on page XXX. Melinda C. Shepherd is Associate Editor of Encyclopædia Britannica Yearbooks.

Enron—What Happened?

by Christopher O'Leary

In less than a year, Enron Corp. has gone from being considered one of the most innovative companies of the late 20th century to being a byword for corruption and mismanagement.

Enron was formed in July 1985, when Houston Natural Gas merged with InterNorth, a Nebraska-based natural gas company. In its first few years, the new company was simply a natural gas provider but by 1989 it had begun trading natural gas commodities, and in 1994 it began trading electricity. This trading operation was the source of all its future glories and its future problems.

The company introduced a number of revolutionary changes to energy trading, abetted by the changing nature of the energy markets, which were being deregulated in the 1990s and thus opening the door for new power traders and suppliers. Enron tailored electricity and natural gas contracts to reflect the cost of delivery to a specific destination—creating in essence, for the first time, a nationwide (and global) energy trading network. In 1999 Enron launched Enron Online, an Internet-based system that by 2001 was running about $2.5 billion a day in on-line trades.

By century's end, Enron had become one of the most successful companies in the world, having posted a 57% increase in sales between 1996 and 2000, and at its peak was controlling over 25% of the "over the counter" energy trading market—that is, trades done party-to-party, rather than being conducted over an exchange like the New York Mercantile Exchange. Enron shares hit a 52-week high in the last week of 2000, with an $84.87 per share price.

Yet the market had already begun to notice irregularities. Much of Enron's balance sheet did not make sense to analysts, as Enron had begun, by the late 1990s, shuffling much of its debt obligations onto offshore partnerships—many created by chief financial officer Andrew Fastow. At the same time, the company was reporting inaccurate trading revenues. Some of the schemes traders used included serving as a middleman on a contract trade, linking up a buyer and a seller for a future contract, but then booking the entire sale as Enron revenue. Enron was also using its partnerships to sell contracts back and forth to itself and booking revenue each time.

In February 2001 president and chief operating officer Jeffrey Skilling took over as chief executive of Enron, while former CEO Kenneth Lay stayed on as chairman. In August, however, Skilling abruptly resigned and Lay resumed the CEO role. By this point, Lay had received an anonymous memo from Sherron Watkins, an Enron VP who had become worried about the Fastow partnerships, and who warned of possible accounting scandals. Watkins also drafted a series of signed memos to Lay detailing her concerns and met with the chairman.

The house of cards collapsed, suddenly, during October 2001. As rumors about Enron's troubles abounded, the firm shocked investors when on 16 October it announced it was going to post a $638 million loss for the third quarter and take a $1.2 billion reduction in shareholder equity due in part to Fastow's partnerships. At the same time, some officials at Arthur Andersen, Enron's accountant, began shredding documents related to Enron audits.

By 22 October the Securities and Exchange Commission began an inquiry into Enron and the partnerships; a week later it had become a full investigation. By the last week of October, Enron officials became increasingly desperate. Fastow was forced out, while Lay began calling government officials, including Federal Reserve Chairman Alan Greenspan, Treasury Secretary Paul O'Neill, and Commerce Secretary Donald Evans. In some cases, officials said Lay was simply informing them of Enron's troubles, but with Evans Lay was more aggressive. He asked for Evans to intervene with Moody's Investors Service, which was considering downgrading Enron to non-investment grade status. Evans declined.

On 8 November Enron revised its financial statements for the last five years, acknowledging that instead of profits, it actually had posted $586 million in losses. Its stock value began to crater—it would fall below $1 per share by the end of November and would be delisted on 16 Jan 2002.

There was one last ace in the hole for Enron. On 9 November, rival energy trader Dynegy Inc. said it would purchase the company for $8 billion in stock. Yet by the end of the month, Dynegy backed out of the deal, citing Enron's downgrade to "junk bond" status and its continuing financial irregularities—Enron had just disclosed it was trying to restructure a $690 million obligation, for which it was running the risk of defaulting.

The end came on 2 December when Enron, which a year before had been touted as the seventh-largest company in the United States, filed for Chapter 11 bankruptcy protection and sued Dynegy for wrongful termination of the failed acquisition. A month later, Lay resigned and the White House announced the Justice Department had begun a criminal investigation of Enron.

The once-mighty company is in tatters. Its energy trading business was sold off to European bank UBS Warburg in January, its top officials spent the spring of 2002 being subpoenaed to Congressional hearings, and the majority of Enron's employees had lost their jobs, their employee stock plans no longer nest eggs, but almost worthless.

> **"*The once-mighty company is in tatters.*"**

Christopher O'Leary is a Senior Editor for Investment Dealers Digest. *This article is adapted from* Britannica Book of the Year 2003 *(forthcoming).*

Continuing Crisis in Kashmir—A Timeline

In 2001–02 the crisis in the Himalayan region of Kashmir, which has been festering for more than 50 years and has its roots deep in the ethnic, cultural, and religious history of the region, seemed to be propelling India and Pakistan, both nuclear powers, toward war. Here is a review of the history of the contested region.

3rd century BC: Emperor Ashoka introduces Buddhism to Kashmir.

1346: Kashmir comes under Muslim rule.

1819: Kashmir is annexed to the Sikh kingdom of the Punjab.

1846: Kashmir is transferred to the Dogra kingdom of Jammu by the terms of the treaty ending the First Sikh War. Its boundaries are undefined. The state is supported by the British.

1947: The British withdraw from the subcontinent; British India is divided into the sovereign states of India and Pakistan; Hari Singh, maharaja of Kashmir, signs an Instrument of Accession to the Indian

1980: Pakistan attempts to raise the Kashmir issue at international forums, in contravention of the terms of the 1972 Simla accord.

1982: The chief minister of the Indian state of Jammu and Kashmir, Sheikh Muhammad Abdullah, dies and is replaced by his son, Farooq Abdullah. A law is enacted permitting the return of migrants to Kashmir. Pakistan and India agree to form a joint commission to study the problem.

1984: Indian Prime Minister Indira Gandhi is assassinated.

1985: Martial law is lifted in Pakistan.

1986: Indian Prime Minister Rajiv Gandhi forces the

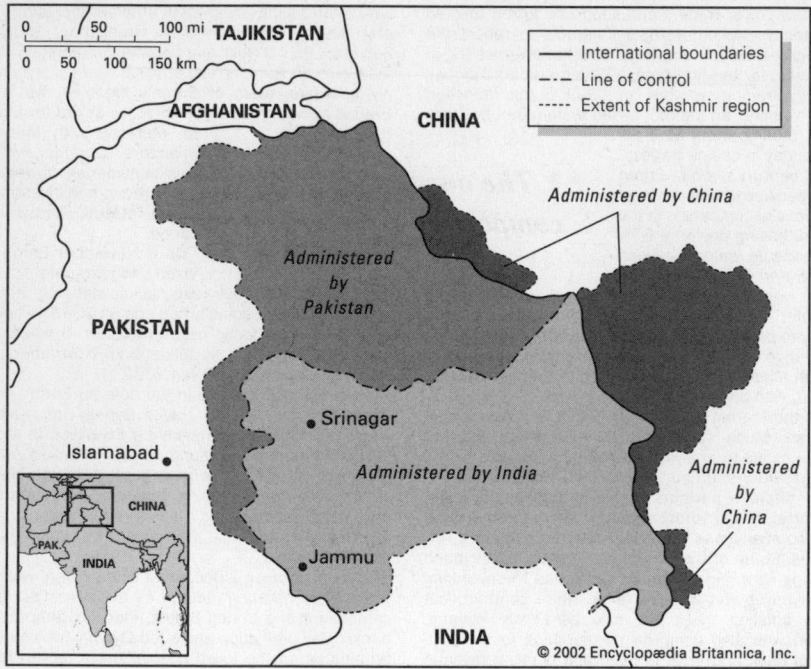

© 2002 Encyclopædia Britannica, Inc.

Map legend:
— International boundaries
—·— Line of control
----- Extent of Kashmir region

Union. Pakistan immediately intervenes, followed by India.

1949: A UN-imposed cease-fire line (the line of control), intended to be temporary, divides the administration of Kashmir between Pakistan and India.

1962: China invades Ladakh.

1965: Warfare over Kashmir breaks out between India and Pakistan.

1966: India and Pakistan sign an agreement to seek peaceful means of resolving their dispute.

1971: War between India and Pakistan leads to the creation of Bangladesh.

1972: A peace accord is signed in Simla, India.

1977: India explodes a nuclear test weapon.

1979: The execution of Pakistani Prime Minister Zulfiqar Ali Bhutto leads to renewed tension over Kashmir.

1986: resignation of Jammu and Kashmir Chief Minister Ghulam Muhammad Shah; Farooq Abdullah, whom Indira Gandhi had removed in 1984, is reinstalled.

1987: Indian and Pakistani troops in the Karakoram Range exchange fire, and scores are killed.

1988: Pakistani Pres. Zia-ul-Haq is killed in an airplane crash.

1989: The daughter of the Indian minister of home affairs is kidnapped by the Jammu and Kashmir Liberation Front and exchanged for five Muslim separatists. Fighting continues over the Siachen Glacier area of the Karakorams.

1990: Violence erupts in Srinagar, Jammu and Kashmir, when Indian troops attempt to enforce a curfew. India accuses Pakistan of supporting Muslim separatists in Kashmir, but the countries finalize an accord, initialed in 1988, in which they agree to share information on troop movements.

1991: Former Indian prime minister Rajiv Gandhi is assassinated. Violence in Kashmir grows.

1994: Pakistan discloses that it possesses nuclear weapons, as has long been suspected. Pakistan closes its embassy in India. India declines third-party mediation on Kashmir. Bloodletting in Kashmir escalates.

1995: India cancels elections in Jammu and Kashmir because of increasing violence. On 11 May, Hindu militants burn down the 535-year-old shrine of Nooruddin Noorani at Charar-i-Sharif.

1996: The BJP, a Hindu nationalist party, comes to power in India. Violence in Kashmir abates as the US urges the parties to talk.

1997: India and Pakistan agree in June to negotiate on the future of Kashmir. In the fall, however, the armies of the two countries again exchange fire across the line of control.

1998: India and Pakistan each detonate nuclear devices in weapons testing. In summer, artillery fire across the line of control is again exchanged. Peace talks are held in October.

1999: Though Pakistan and India are improving bilateral relations, it is discovered in midyear that insurgents from the Pakistani side have been crossing the line of control and infiltrating the Indian area, and the Indian army and air force act to push the intruders back. In the fall, Pakistan agrees to pull back across the line of control. In Pakistan, Pervez Musharraf overthrows Prime Minister Mohammed Nawaz Sharif.

2000: Violence continues throughout the year. India announces a cease-fire for Ramadan and later extends it. In response, Pakistan announces a partial withdrawal of troops.

2001: In May, India ends its cease-fire but invites talks. Talks are held in July but break off abruptly. Violence escalates. In October a militant Islamic group explodes a car bomb at the Legislative Assembly building in Srinagar. On 13 Dec, Muslim terrorists attack the Parliament House in New Delhi and tensions rise to crisis level.

2002: In early spring, India and Pakistan come to the brink of war over Kashmir.

Meltdown in Antarctica

In late winter 2002 scientists reported that large portions of Antarctica's Larsen Ice Shelf were breaking off at an unusually rapid rate. The disintegration of the ice is likely caused by rising temperatures in Antarctica and may be linked to overall global warming. The map shows the changing profile of Antarctica.

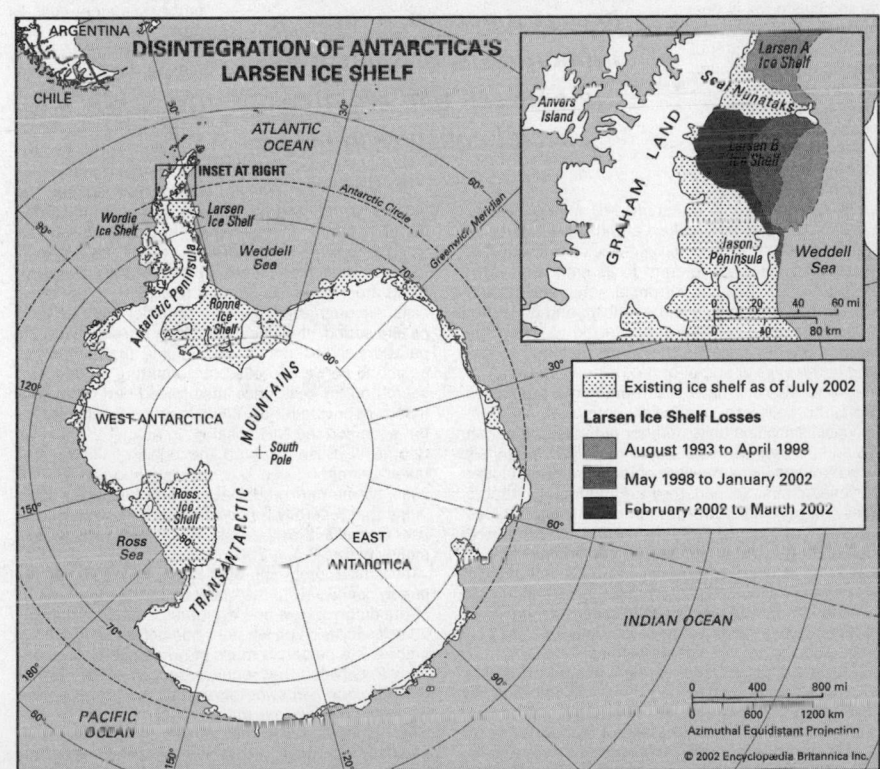

The Science and Ethics of Embryonic Stem Cell Research

by Lori P. Knowles and Erik Parens

At the end of 1998, almost simultaneously, one team of researchers announced that it had isolated human embryonic stem (ES) cells and another announced that it had isolated human embryonic germ (EG) cells. These announcements gave rise both to the promise of great medical benefits and to contentious ethical and policy questions. The medical promise of these cells is the potential to provide an endless supply of transplantable tissue. The ethical and policy questions primarily concern the embryonic and fetal sources of these cells. To understand both the promise and the ethical issues, it is important to understand some basic scientific facts about ES and EG cells.

The announcement of the isolation of ES cells was made by James A. Thomson at the University of Wisconsin at Madison. Thomson and his colleagues isolated ES cells from "spare embryos"—that is, embryos created in a fertility clinic by in vitro fertilization that are no longer needed for transfer to a woman. These embryos, five to seven days old, are called blastocysts. The outer layer of the blastocyst is destined to become the placenta. The remainder of the blastocyst, called the inner cell mass, is destined to become the fetus. Embryonic stem cells are isolated from this inner cell mass.

John Gearhart at Johns Hopkins University in Baltimore MD announced the isolation of EG cells. Gearhart and his colleagues isolated EG cells from five- to nine-week-old aborted fetuses. Such cells are referred to as embryonic germ cells because they come from a small set of stem cells that were set aside in the embryo and prevented from differentiating. They are referred to as embryonic germ cells because they were destined to give rise to the eggs or sperm of the next generation.

ES and EG cells have two remarkable properties. First, the cells are in principle immortal. Whereas most cells divide a finite number of times and perish, ES and EG cells can be cultured to divide indefinitely, which makes them excellent objects for manipulation by researchers. Second, they are pluripotent; that is, they can turn into many—and perhaps all—cell types. All other cells have to some degree differentiated; that is, they have turned into one or another type of cell, such as nerve or muscle or skin. No one has yet successfully directed ES and EG cell differentiation to an extent that would be clinically useful, but the hope is that someday soon these cells will be used to generate specific, transplantable tissues.

Despite the potential for medical benefit offered by ES and EG cells, the origin of these cells raises policy and ethical concerns. In the United States the policy issues primarily concern the use of federal funds for research involving human embryos and fetal tissue. The ethical concerns are primarily related to the moral status of the embryo and the aborted fetus.

Human fetal tissue has been used in research aimed at developing therapies for disorders such as Parkinson's disease by transplanting that tissue into afflicted people. Before 1993, laws in the US prohibited the use of federal funds for this research because the tissue used is obtained from aborted fetuses. In 1993 Pres. Bill Clinton lifted that ban. A number of restrictions exist to ensure that fetal tissue for research is obtained in a manner that respects the women from whom it is taken and that research does not encourage abortion. These restrictions are likely to apply to EG cell research.

First, the physician is required to obtain the woman's informed consent to use fetal tissue removed from her body. Second, to ensure that the possibility of donating tissue to benefit medical science does not influence a woman's decision, the donation of fetal tissue can be discussed only following a decision to terminate the pregnancy. Finally, a woman may not direct that her fetal tissue be used to benefit a particular person.

The policy situation with respect to human embryonic stem cells is more complicated. Currently, US law prohibits federal funding of human embryo research. Consequently, private corporations have taken the lead and funded the research mentioned above that isolated the first human ES and EG cells. Lawyers for the US National Institutes of Health (NIH) in Bethesda MD provided an opinion that under the current law it is legal to fund research on human ES cells so long as federal funds are not used to support the derivation of those cells. Although this legal interpretation may be technically sound, it places the US government in the paradoxical position of withholding funds from research to derive ES cells but permitting funds for research on ES cells once they have been derived by means of private funds. While in office President Clinton endorsed the NIH position. In August 2001 Pres. George W. Bush adopted the position Clinton had taken permitting use but not derivation of ES cell lines, but he narrowed that position further by stipulating that federally funded researchers were only to use ES cells that had been derived with private money before 9 Aug 2001.

The ethical problems associated with ES cells are largely connected to the question of the moral status of the embryo. How one evaluates the act of deriving ES cells depends on whether one believes the human embryo is a person, a mass of human cells, or something in between that requires special consideration. Science cannot answer this question. Currently, most Western countries permit embryo research for specific purposes and within strict limits. They proceed from the view that embryos have neither the moral status of persons nor that of mere cells; because of their special connection with the human

> *How one evaluates the act of deriving embryonic stem cells depends on whether one believes the human embryo is a person, a mass of human cells, or something in between that requires special consideration.*

community, they enjoy an intermediate position that requires that they be treated with special respect.

Many people argue that creating embryos for research does not recognize the special status of the human embryo. Some argue that there is no important moral difference between doing research on embryos originally created for reproduction and doing research on embryos specifically created for that purpose.

Finally, ES cell research implicates the cloning debate. Many countries have policies forbidding the use of cloning, or somatic cell nuclear transfer (SCNT), to create a human being (reproductive cloning). It is possible, however, to use SCNT to create embryos as a source of ES cells. A patient can donate a tissue, and by means of SCNT it is possible to create a source of ES cells with that patient's DNA. Consequently, this research cloning technique offers the potential to create tissues for transplantation that exactly match the recipient's tissues. In July 2002 President Bush's Council on Bioethics issued a report with a majority opinion in favor of a four-year moratorium on attempts to create embryos by cloning for medical research. The majority favored a moratorium to permit time for further study of ethical and scientific controversies surrounding research cloning and to improve regulatory oversight. As of summer 2002 the Senate has been unable to overcome an impasse that would permit it to vote on bills addressing research cloning. Consequently, the future of ES cell research in the US remains uncertain.

ES and EG cell research offers the potential of great medical benefit, but it also raises difficult ethical issues and complicates policy development. This turbulent area of research will surely command our attention well into the new millennium.

Lori P. Knowles is Associate for Law and Bioethics and Erik Parens is Associate for Philosophical Studies at the Hastings Center, Garrison NY. This article is adapted from Britannica Book of the Year 2000.

Election Reform Debate in the US

by Michael Levy

Amid calls for a radical overhaul of the US electoral system and bitterness over his narrow win, George W. Bush was inaugurated as president of the United States on 20 Jan 2001. The 2000 presidential balloting exposed several deficiencies in the conduct of American elections: the possibility that a candidate could win more popular votes than his opponent and still lose the electoral college tally—Bush defeated Al Gore 271-266 despite winning 500,000 fewer votes nationwide; faulty and outdated election equipment—a General Accounting Office audit found that nearly three-fifths of voting sites had problems in 2000; a lack of uniform rules for election recounts; early and incorrect media projections; and confusing ballot design, most notably in Florida, where possibly thousands of people were led to vote mistakenly for a candidate. The election controversy, coupled with the collapse in late 2001 of energy services giant Enron, which had donated large sums of money to both political parties, also gave further impetus to campaign finance reform.

Many proposed election reforms, such as the abolition of the electoral college and the creation of a national holiday for election day, were discarded quickly owing to a lack of support, though in early 2001 momentum in favor of reform suggested that major changes, such as a uniform national poll closing time, would be enacted by year's end. Of the more than 1,500 bills proposed in Congress and in all 50 states, however, few were enacted, as reform efforts were hampered by partisan wrangling.

Receiving the most support were proposals to eliminate punch-card ballot systems, which had led to high rates of uncounted ballots and which tended to be concentrated in poorer areas, in favor of optical scanning systems. Some studies found that as many as two million votes were uncounted nationwide because of faulty election equipment.

Although reform efforts seemed to stall in mid-2001, in December the House of Representatives overwhelmingly approved (362-63) a bill that provided some $2.6 billion in funds to states to modernize election equipment and establish national voting standards, and in April 2002 the Senate passed (99-1) a modified version of the House package, providing about $3.5 billion to the states to implement national standards such as electronically notifying voters of any possible balloting error and allowing persons whose names were not on registration lists, but who claimed that they were registered, to cast a provisional ballot. The bill passed by the Senate, however, was opposed by many groups that supported election reform, such as the American Civil Liberties Union, which claimed that the bill as written would provide an undue obstacle by requiring certain first-time voters to provide photo identification In order to cast a ballot. Because the two versions differed substantially, a conference committee would need to create a compromise bill.

> **" The 2000 presidential balloting exposed several deficiencies in the conduct of American elections. "**

By mid-2002 the future of electoral reform was still uncertain. On the state level the most sweeping election reform package was adopted in Florida, the state that had endured a five-week standoff in the presidential election before Bush was declared the winner by a margin of only 537 votes after the Supreme Court halted a recount. On 9 May 2001 Florida Gov. Jeb Bush, the brother of the president, approved a uniform statewide ballot design and the elimination of punch cards in favor of optical scanners or other advanced technologies by 2002. The new law also established standardized procedures for the review of ballots during manual recounts—a key point of contention between the Gore and Bush camps.

Nevertheless, the US Commission on Civil Rights issued a report a few weeks later that criticized Florida election officials, finding them "grossly

derelict" both before and during the November 2000 standoff. The commission's report, which was criticized by Republicans, also found that African Americans were 10 times more likely than white voters to have their votes uncounted and claimed that the reforms enacted in Florida would not entirely eliminate this disparity.

In late 2001 Enron declared bankruptcy, and, owing to its large financial ties to both political parties (but particularly to the Republicans), support for campaign finance reform gained strength. Although Bush had been equivocal about such reform, the House (240–189) and the Senate (60–40) passed legislation that Bush signed into law in March 2002. The sweeping bill—which significantly modified America's campaign finance system for the first time since the

1970s—banned individuals, unions, and corporations from contributing unlimited amounts of unregulated "soft money," doubled to $2,000 the amount an individual could contribute to a candidate directly, raised contribution ceilings for candidates facing wealthy, self-financed opponents, and prohibited organizations from funding with soft money "issue ad" broadcasts on behalf of federal candidates within 30 days of an election. The changes, which were set to take place after the 2002 midterm elections, promised to radically alter how federal campaigns are conducted in the US. Critics on both sides, however, predicted that either the bill would be struck down by the courts as unconstitutional or the new regulations would be circumvented by the parties and interest groups.

Michael Levy is Associate Editor at Encyclopædia Britannica. This article was adapted from Britannica Book of the Year 2002.

Association Football (Soccer) World Cup 2002

by Jack Rollin

On 30 Jun 2002—with some 69,000 spectators in the stands and an estimated billion fans watching on televisions around the world—Brazil won a record fifth association football (soccer) World Cup title, beating Germany 2–0 in an evenly contested final in Yokohama, Japan. The games, held in several sites throughout Japan and Korea, represented the first time the World Cup had been hosted by two countries. While the organization of the event was generally satisfactory, high prices and poor ticket distribution kept crowds down. Overall attendance at the 64 matches was 2,705,566 (1,438,637 in Japan, 1,266,929 in South Korea). American fans had to cope with live broadcasts of games that came in the middle of the night or the wee hours of the morning.

Shocks abounded in the early stages of the tournament. France, the World Cup titleholder, was stung by Senegal (a former French colony) and then failed to qualify from its group, as did highly touted Argentina, Portugal, and Poland. Home teams South Korea and Japan, however, each unexpectedly headed their sections. The surprises continued as Korea stunned Italy in overtime, the United States played exceedingly well and earned its quarter-final berth, and Senegal—fortunate to survive an exciting 3–3 contest with Uruguay (which trailed 3–0 at halftime)—became only the second African nation to reach the final eight. Yet stripped of such episodes, the overall standard of play disappointed.

Still it was Brazil, patchy but potentially a threat, and the dogged, persistent Germans who survived the mayhem around them to reach the final game. In fact Germany might have taken the lead in the 49th minute. Oliver Neuville's blistering, long-range free-kick was brilliantly finger-tipped onto a post by the

> *66* ***Shocks abounded in the early stages of the tournament.*** *99*

Brazilian goalkeeper Marcos. Gradually Brazil assumed control, and in the 67th minute Ronaldo side-footed the ball in after Oliver Kahn, voted goalkeeper of the tournament, had spilled Rivaldo's shot into his path. Ronaldo added his second goal 12 minutes later after Rivaldo cleverly feinted to allow the ball to run to him. It confirmed Ronaldo as leading World Cup scorer with eight goals.

Belgium won the tournament Fair Play award. The overall tally of penalties was 267 yellow cards, including 16 in one game (both records) and 17 red. Turkey's Hakan Unsal became the 100th player sent off with a red card in a final tournament. There was a general increase in disciplinary actions in penalty areas because of players' shirt-pulling and wrestling while awaiting corners and free-kicks. The level of refereeing and poor interpretation by touchline officials was criticized, notably Spain's having two apparently legitimate goals against South Korea ruled out. The World Cup final match, however, was superbly controlled by the Italian Pierluigi Collina.

Other records were set as well. Among the 161 goals, Turkish player Hakan Sukur hit the fastest in any finals: he scored only 10.8 seconds into the game against South Korea. The worldwide television audience was 45 billion. Paolo Maldini (Italy) completed 2,100 minutes of play over four finals, and Bora Milutinovic, the Yugoslav in charge of the Chinese team, became the first to coach five different countries: Mexico 1986, Costa Rica 1990, United States 1994, and Nigeria 1998. Cafu, the Brazilian captain, became the first to play in three World Cup final matches.

Germany's consolation prize was that it had been named the host of the next World Cup, in 2006.

Jack Rollin is Editor of Rothmans Football Yearbook *and author of* World Cup 1930–1990 *and other books. This article is adapted from* Britannica Book of the Year 2003.

Chronology, July 2001–June 2002

A day-by-day listing of important and interesting events, adapted from Britannica Book of the Year.

July 2001

1 Jul David Trimble resigns as first minister of Northern Ireland, citing as his reason the failure of the Irish Republican Army to disarm.

▸ A US law creating the Tortugas Ecological Reserve underwater off the Dry Tortugas National Park in Florida goes into effect.

2 Jul US Pres. George W. Bush signs an executive order to continue economic sanctions against the Taliban for harboring Osama bin Laden, whom the US blames for the 1998 bombings of the US embassies in Tanzania and Kenya.

▸ The first completely implantable artificial heart, the AbioCor, is placed into a patient on the brink of death, Robert Tools; Tools, however, later suffers a stroke and dies in November.

▸ Mexican Pres. Vicente Fox Quesada marries his spokesperson, Martha Sahagún.

3 Jul In Russia's worst airline disaster since 1996, a Russian passenger liner crashes on its approach to Irkutsk, killing all 143 aboard.

▸ Australia and East Timor agree on a plan to share the oil and gas reserves in the Timor Sea between the two countries, with 90% of the revenues going to East Timor.

▸ Algirdas Brazauskas, head of the Lithuanian Social Democratic Party, becomes prime minister of Lithuania.

4 Jul Scientists from the US and Vietnam agree to cooperate on a study examining environmental damage caused by the use of the herbicide Agent Orange by US forces during the Vietnam War.

▸ Farmers in Klamath Falls OR open irrigation gates that had been closed in April by order of the federal government to protect the endangered suckerfish.

5 Jul The government of Macedonia signs a cease-fire agreement with leaders of the ethnic Albanian rebels who have been fighting in the western part of the country.

▸ Jessie Argobast, an eight-year-old boy, has his arm bitten off by a 2-m (7-ft) bull shark while swimming off the coast of Florida.

▸ The Connecticut Historical Society reveals that a flag discovered in a storage area has been authenticated as one of the flags in the theater box occupied by Pres. Abraham Lincoln on the night he was assassinated.

▸ Hannelore Kohl, wife of former German chancellor Helmut Kohl, in despair over the rare, painful, and untreatable allergy to sunlight she has developed, commits suicide.

6 Jul Scientists at the Stanford (CA) Linear Accelerator Center announce that they have found CP violation (which may explain why more matter than antimatter resulted from the big bang) in the decay of B mesons, confirming results seen only once before.

7 Jul Maoist insurgents in Nepal kill 39 police officers at various security posts throughout the country.

▸ Violence breaks out in Kingston, Jamaica, in the wake of a police raid for illegal weapons and continues for the next three days, leaving at least 25 people dead.

▸ Six people are gored in the first day of an unusually dangerous running of the bulls in Pamplona, Spain.

8 Jul Great Britain's fourth race riot, the worst so far this year, rages for nine hours in the northern town of Bradford.

▸ Officials in Bosnia and Herzegovina say they have found a mass grave containing at least 200 bodies in the village of Liplje.

▸ American tennis star Venus Williams defeats Belgian Justine Henin to win her second consecutive Wimbledon title.

▸ Israeli conductor Daniel Barenboim creates an uproar in Israel when, at the Israel Festival, he conducts the overture to Richard Wagner's *Tristan und Isolde* as an encore piece.

9 Jul An appeals court in Chile rules that August Pinochet Ugarte is too ill to stand trial, effectively ending efforts to try him on human rights abuse charges stemming from his 17-year rule of Chile.

▸ Goran Ivanisevic of Croatia becomes the first wild-card entrant to win a major tennis tournament when he defeats Australian Patrick Rafter at Wimbledon.

10 Jul Sri Lankan Pres. Chandrika Kumaratunga orders Parliament suspended for two months and calls for a referendum on a proposed new constitution that would give more rights to Tamils.

▸ Preeti Shakya, age four, is enthroned as Kumari, the virgin goddess who brings peace and prosperity to Nepal.

▸ Zlatko Lagumdzija, a Bosnian Muslim, is appointed prime minister of Bosnia and Herzegovina, replacing Bozidar Matic, a Bosnian Croat who had resigned on 22 June.

11 Jul The Organization of African Unity votes to dissolve itself after 38 years of existence and transform itself into the African Union, modeled on the European Union.

▸ Police in Washington DC, search the apartment of Rep. Gary Condit of California, looking for clues in the disappearance of Chandra Levy, a Washington intern who was last seen on 30 April.

▸ Four firefighters die in the deadliest wildfire in the US since 1994, in the Okanogan National Forest in Washington.

12 Jul A report issued by Human Rights Watch charges that the human rights record of the opposition to the Taliban in Afghanistan is as bad as that of the Taliban.

▸ France orders the extradition of former high-profile antiwar activist Ira Einhorn to the US, whence he fled in 1981 to avoid being tried for the 1977 murder of his girlfriend, Holly Maddux.

13 Jul Beijing is selected to host the 2008 Olympic Games.

14 Jul Pres. Pervez Musharraf of Pakistan arrives in India for a summit meeting with Indian Prime Minister Atal Bihari Vajpayee to discuss the Kashmir dispute.

▸ The last original episode of the *Bozo's Circus* TV show in the US is broadcast in Chicago.

15 Jul Astronauts aboard the International Space Station install a new entryway that is compatible with NASA spacesuits as well as the Russian spacesuits that the other airlock is able to accommodate.

16 Jul Russian Pres. Vladimir Putin and Chinese Pres. Jiang Zemin sign the first mutual friendship treaty between the two countries in more than 50 years.

▸ Jacque Rogge of Belgium is chosen to replace Juan António Samaranch of Spain as president of the International Olympic Committee.

▸ Talks between Pakistan's Pervez Musharraf and India's Atal Bihari Vajpayee abruptly break off.

▸ Germany asks the Czech Republic to close down a nuclear plant on the border between the countries, contending that the plant is not safe.

▸ The on-line bookseller Amazon.com celebrates the 50th anniversary of the publication of J.D. Salinger's *The Catcher in the Rye* by offering the book at the 1951 price—$3.

▸ Fifteen sea lions in Ecuador's Galápagos National Park are discovered butchered on the beach on San Cristóbal Island.

17 Jul Dragisa Pesic is named by Pres. Vojislav Kostunica to replace Zoran Zizic as prime minister of Yugoslavia.

18 Jul A 60-car train carrying hazardous materials derails in a tunnel under Baltimore MD and catches fire, melting fiber-optic cables and slowing Internet and rail traffic throughout the Middle Atlantic region.

▸ A special train arrives in Vladivostok, Russia, from Moscow as part of a celebration of the centenary of the 9,267-km (5,758-mi)-long Trans-Siberian Railroad, still the longest railway in the world.

19 Jul Indonesia passes a bill granting increased autonomy to the rebellious province of Aceh.

▸ Prime Minister Girija Prasad Koirala of Nepal resigns.

▸ Nearly two-thirds of Argentina's workers participate in a one-day strike, effectively shutting down the country, to protest recently announced austerity measures.

20 Jul Outside the Group of Eight meeting in Genoa, Italy, Carlo Giuliani, one of tens of thousands of protesters, is killed by police in the first death among antiglobalization activists.

QUOTE OF THE MONTH

" *One hundred thousand people don't get upset unless there is a problem in their hearts and spirits.* **"**

—French Pres. Jacques Chirac, speaking about antiglobalization protesters, in Genoa, 20 July

---

▸ The London Stock Exchange goes public.

▸ A public uproar greets a media report about a study commissioned by the Philip Morris tobacco company in the Czech Republic that spells out the savings to public finances brought about by smokers' dying earlier than nonsmokers.

21 Jul The UN Conference on the Illicit Trade in Small Arms and Light Weapons in All Its Aspects approves an agreement, much weakened by the demands of the US, to reduce trafficking in small arms.

▸ Doctors in Murcia, Spain, report that more than 300 people have become ill in the largest known outbreak of Legionnaires disease.

22 Jul David Duval of the US wins his first major golf tournament, against Niclas Fasth of Sweden, at the 130th British Open.

▸ The first of 91.6 million tax-rebate checks authorized in the US budget are mailed out to American taxpayers.

▸ King Gyanendra of Nepal appoints Sher Bahadur Deuba as the new prime minister.

23 Jul Indonesia's legislature votes unanimously to oust Pres. Abdurrahman Wahid in favor of his vice president, Megawati Sukarnoputri.

▸ In Bonn, Germany, 178 nations, not including the US, reach an agreement on the Kyoto Protocol after three days of marathon bargaining.

▸ Burundi Pres. Pierre Buyoya signs an agreement with Hutu politicians to lead the first transitional government under the Arusha accords, designed to end the civil war in Burundi.

24 Jul The Liberation Tigers of Tamil Eelam attack Sri Lanka's international airport at Colombo, destroying or disabling 14 commercial and military aircraft and leaving 20 dead.

▸ A court in Seoul, South Korea, finds seven former executives of the Daewoo Corp. guilty of accounting fraud and sentences them to as much as seven years in prison.

▸ Phase I of the largest rat eradication program in the world is completed on the 106-sq-km (41-sq-mi) sub-Antarctic Campbell Island, believed to be infested with as many as 200,000 Norway rats.

25 Jul The US rejects an international protocol for compliance with the 1972 treaty banning germ warfare, objecting to provisions that it believes would be detrimental to the business community.

▸ Louis G. Spisto, the executive director in New York of the American Ballet Theatre, quits abruptly.

26 Jul The Chinese government says that it has released US residents Gao Zhan and Qin Quangguang to the US two days after having sentenced them both to 10 years' imprisonment for spying.

▸ Congressional Gold Medals are awarded to the 29 Navajo code talkers (only 5 of whom are still living) who were instrumental in the Allied victory over Japan in World War II by relaying military information coded in the Navajo language.

27 Jul Scientists at California's Lawrence Berkeley National Laboratory retract a claim they made in 1999 that they had created a 118th element.

▸ Heeding local farmers who complain of health problems and damaged crops, a judge in Bogotá, Colombia, orders a halt to spraying intended to destroy the coca crop.

▸ United Airlines and US Airways call off their proposed merger as the US Department of Justice threatens to sue to prevent it from taking place.

28 Jul A study finds that the Smithsonian Institution needs about $1.5 million worth of repairs and renovation and blames management problems for much of the deterioration.

29 Jul American Lance Armstrong wins his third consecutive Tour de France bicycle race.

▸ In a nonbinding referendum on the Puerto Rican island of Vieques, 68% vote for an immediate end to US Navy exercises on the island.

30 Jul New rules go into effect in Canada that permit anyone who is terminally ill or suffers from certain chronic illnesses to grow and smoke marijuana for pain relief, provided they have a medical certificate verifying their condition.

▸ The UN Security Council approves a plan to appoint experts to monitor and help enforce an arms embargo against the Taliban in Afghanistan.

31 Jul Prime Minister Atal Bihari Vajpayee shocks the government of India when he offers to resign, but he is immediately persuaded to stay on.

▶ Lava from Mt. Etna in Sicily, Italy, which has been erupting for two weeks, threatens two villages and forces the closing of tourist and scientific facilities.

August 2001

1 Aug The first book is placed in the new Bibliotheca Alexandrina in Egypt, located approximately on the site of the ancient Library at Alexandria.

▶ Azerbaijan adopts the Latin alphabet in place of the Cyrillic for its national language, Azerbaijani.

▶ A new law permitting same-sex partnerships goes into effect in Germany.

2 Aug Former Bosnian Serb general Radislav Krstic is found guilty of genocide by the UN war crimes tribunal in The Hague and is sentenced to 46 years in prison.

▶ Robert S. Mueller is confirmed as the new FBI director.

3 Aug Scientists from the Sloan Digital Sky Survey say they believe they have observed the beginning of star formation.

▶ Thailand's high court acquits Prime Minister Thaksin Shinawatra of financial irregularities.

4 Aug North Korean leader Kim Jong Il and Russian Pres. Vladimir Putin issue a joint statement in which they pledge to combat international terrorism.

▶ Football players Lynn Swann, Nick Buoniconti, Mike Munchak, Jackie Slater, Ron Yary, and Jack Youngblood and coach Marv Levy are inducted into the Pro Football Hall of Fame.

▶ Hundreds of First Nations people gather in Montreal to celebrate the 300th anniversary of the Great Peace of 1701, between the French and the Iroquois.

5 Aug Taliban officials close the Kabul offices of Shelter Now, a Christian relief agency, and arrest 24 of its workers.

▶ Pak Se Ri of South Korea defeats Australian Karrie Webb to win the Women's British Open tennis tournament.

▶ American runner Maurice Green wins his third consecutive world championship in the 100-m sprint.

6 Aug The Irish Republican Army agrees to a method for putting its weapons beyond use.

▶ The publishing house Alfred A. Knopf, Inc., agrees to pay the biggest publishing advance ever, $10 million, to former US president Bill Clinton for his memoirs.

▶ American sprinter Marion Jones loses her first 100-m race since 1997 to Zhanna Pintusevich-Block of Ukraine.

7 Aug Pres. Hugo Bánzer Suárez of Bolivia hands the presidency over to his vice president, Jorge Quiroga Ramírez, because of ill health.

▶ The August 7 Memorial Park is opened on the site of the US embassy in Nairobi, Kenya, to commemorate the victims of the terrorist bombing on 7 Aug 1998.

8 Aug Bayer AG withdraws its anticholesterol drug, Baycol, from the world market after 31 deaths are linked to it.

▶ Kyrgyzstan announces plans to charge Kazakhstan, Tajikistan, and Uzbekistan for using water in rivers that originate in Kyrgyzstan.

▶ Ethiopian runner Haile Gabrselassie loses his first 10,000-m race since 1993 to Charles Kamathi of Kenya.

9 Aug President Bush announces that the US will support stem-cell research, provided it is done only on the 60 existing stem-cell lines.

▶ The US and Mexico agree to a program that will allow many undocumented Mexicans in the US to gain worker permits and work toward permanent residency.

▶ Soldiers overthrow the secessionist government of Said Abeid Abderemanein on Anjouan Island, which had agreed in 2000 to rejoin Comoros.

10 Aug A passenger train strikes a land mine, for which UNITA rebels take responsibility, near Zenza do Itombe, Angola, and more than 250 passengers are killed.

▶ Cambodia's King Norodom Sihanouk signs a law to create a UN-assisted tribunal to try former Khmer Rouge leaders for war crimes.

11 Aug Home rule is restored in Northern Ireland after a one-day suspension to allow a six-week wait before new elections must be called.

▶ China refuses a US offer of $34,576 to defray the costs from the incident wherein a US spy plane and Chinese fighter jet crashed.

12 Aug Two days of heavy rains cause flash flooding and mud slides in northeastern Iran, killing over 100 people, destroying crops, and leaving thousands homeless.

▶ The space shuttle *Discovery* delivers a new three-member crew to the International Space Station for a four-month stay.

13 Aug Government and ethnic Albanian leaders sign a political deal in Macedonia that gives more representation to ethnic Albanians and recognizes Albanian as an official language.

> **QUOTE OF THE MONTH**
>
> *According to the second paragraph of Article 7, I have the right to speak the Albanian language.*
>
> —Arben Xhaferi, ethnic Albanian leader, surprising participants at the signing of a peace agreement in Macedonia by addressing them in Albanian, 13 August

▶ Japanese Prime Minister Junichiro Koizumi visits a Shinto memorial to those who died during World War II, exciting a storm of protest in China and South Korea.

14 Aug Leaders of the 11 African countries with a stake in Air Afrique agree to a restructuring plan whereby the airline will be dissolved and then recreated with Air France holding a majority stake, in order to save the airline from going out of business.

▶ A bill that would have created the Kenya Anticorruption Authority, on which continued financial aid from the IMF is contingent, is defeated in that country's parliament.

▶ New Delhi, India, suffers its heaviest rainfall in 40 years.

▶ Emmanuel Milingo, the Roman Catholic archbishop of Zambia, who had married Maria Sung of South Korea in a mass wedding in May presided over by the Rev. Sun Myung Moon of the Unification

Church, renounces his wife and reconciles with the Roman Catholic Church.

15 Aug A law to give Indian groups greater rights, which has lost support among Indians in the five years since it was drafted, goes into effect in Mexico.

▸ A new civil code granting women equal legal rights with men is passed in Brazil.

16 Aug A six-day auction of the assets of Prince Jefri Bolkiah's defunct construction company in Brunei comes to a close with total sales of $7.8 million, a fraction of the $15 billion the former finance minister had lost.

▸ *The Industry Standard,* a respected financial magazine that focused on the dot-com economy, suspends publication.

17 Aug The first of the NATO peacekeeping troops arrive in Macedonia.

▸ Prime Minister Percival Patterson of Jamaica agrees with opposition leader Edward Seaga to create a strategy to reduce violence in the inner city.

▸ Because of bad weather, American balloonist Steve Fosset halts his fifth attempt to become the first person to circumnavigate the globe solo in a balloon just past the halfway mark, in Brazil.

18 Aug Security bars on windows and inaccessible fire escapes contribute to the death toll when a hotel in Quezon City, Philippines, burns down, killing 73.

▸ Danny Almonte, playing for the Bronx NY Rolando Paulino All-Stars, pitches the first perfect game in the Little League World Series since 1957, though it is later proved that Almonte is 14 years old, two years too old to be eligible to play Little League Baseball, and his team's entire season is struck from the record books.

▸ The 10-day consecration of the Great Stupa of Dharmakaya is completed at Red Feather Lakes CO.

19 Aug Three days of performances, parades, and fireworks celebrating the 800th anniversary of Riga, the capital of Latvia, come to a close.

▸ American David Toms wins the PGA golf championship and sets a new scoring record for a major tournament championship with a score of 265.

20 Aug Government officials from the Dem. Rep. of the Congo, opposition politicians, and rebel leaders begin peace talks in Gaborone, Botswana.

▸ In the Kabylie region of Algeria, 100,000 people demonstrate for greater recognition of the Berber language and culture.

21 Aug Two hundred yachts race in the America's Cup Jubilee regatta over the course of the race that the schooner *America* won 150 years ago, around the Isle of Wight, and victory goes to Gianni Agnelli's *Stealth.*

▸ The 14th-century Orthodox monastery at Lesok, Macedonia, is destroyed by an explosion, apparently the work of ethnic Albanian terrorists.

22 Aug Jesse Helms, the ultraconservative Republican senator from North Carolina, announces that he will retire at the end of his term in 2003.

▸ The Bush administration releases figures showing that the large projected US budget surplus for the next several years has dwindled to a negligible amount.

▸ It is reported that banana fossils dating to 500 BC have been found in Cameroon, where it had been believed that bananas first arrived in the 10th century AD.

23 Aug Pres. George W. Bush says definitively that the US will pull out of the ABM Treaty.

▸ For the first time, an official of the Chinese government acknowledges that the country is facing an AIDS epidemic.

▸ In the most-watched TV show of the summer of 2001, US Rep. Gary Condit of California appears on a prime-time interview with ABC News investigator Connie Chung.

24 Aug It is reported that researchers in Kenya and the US have found that forest elephants and savanna elephants in Africa are in fact two different species, which brings to three the number of living elephant species.

▸ In Provo UT Tom Green is sentenced to five years in prison for bigamy and nonsupport, in spite of the pleas of his five wives.

25 Aug Crown Prince Haakon of Norway marries Mette-Marit Tjessem Høiby, a commoner with a colorful past.

▸ The hero of East Timor's independence struggle, José Alexandre Gusmão, bows to public pressure and agrees to run for president in 2002.

▸ The Bay Area CyberRays defeat the Atlanta Beat to win the Founders Cup in the first championship game of the Women's United Soccer Association.

▸ A Norwegian container vessel rescues from a sinking Indonesian ferry 434 Afghan, Sri Lankan, and Pakistani refugees seeking asylum in Australia.

26 Aug In Williamsport PA Kitasuna of Tokyo, Japan, becomes the 55th champion Little League team when it beats the nine from Apopka FL.

▸ Sammy Sosa of the Chicago Cubs becomes the third player in major league baseball history to reach four 50-home-run seasons, after Babe Ruth and Mark McGwire, before finishing the season with 64.

27 Aug A study is published that suggests that the fine structure constant has increased slightly over the life of the universe, implying that other constants, such as the speed of light, may also have changed over time.

▸ A parade in Chisinau marks the 10th anniversary of Moldova's independence in a month when Ukraine and Belarus also celebrate their 10th anniversaries as independent states.

▸ Tonga's first major exhibition of prehistoric artifacts, most dating to the Lapita era, 3,000 years ago, opens at the Tonga National Museum in Nuku'alofa.

28 Aug The computer company Gateway announces plans to lay off one-quarter of its staff, eliminate most overseas operations, and close one factory and four support centers in the US.

▸ Cuba's central bank says that US coins will not be accepted as currency after 15 October.

29 Aug Australian troops seize the Norwegian container vessel crowded with refugees off Christmas Island to prevent it from landing on Australian territory.

▸ Thirty Nigerian families file suit against the American pharmaceutical Pfizer, Inc., in US federal court, contending that the company illegally experimented on their children during a 1996 meningitis outbreak.

▸ The National Black Sports and Entertainers Hall of Fame inducts its first 24 members in New York City.

30 Aug Voters in East Timor go to the polls for their first free election to select the assembly that will write the constitution for the new nation.

▸ The astonishing wealth of jewelry accumulated by the Nizams of Hyderabad goes on view to the public for the first time at the National Museum in New Delhi.

31 Aug Papua New Guinea signs a peace agreement with rebels in Bougainville after a decade-long civil war.

▸ The ILO releases a report showing that Americans worked the longest hours of any country in the world between 1990 and 2000.

September 2001

1 Sep The Los Angeles Sparks overwhelm the Charlotte Sting to win the WNBA championship.

▸ Tokyo's deadliest fire since 1982, with 44 fatalities, breaks out in a mah-jongg parlor in a red-light district.

2 Sep Hewlett-Packard Co. announces plans to buy Compaq Computer Corp.

3 Sep Israel and the US walk out on the UN World Conference Against Racism.

▸ Fradique de Menezes is inaugurated as the new president of São Tomé and Príncipe.

4 Sep Disney's newest theme park, Tokyo DisneySea, opens in Japan.

▸ An arson fire at the Straw Market engulfs the market and many nearby buildings in the heart of the tourist strip in Nassau, The Bahamas.

▸ Researchers at the University of Wisconsin report inducing human embryonic blood cells to become blood-making cells.

5 Sep Though Azerbaijan says it is illegal, Nagorno-Karabakh, which regards itself as independent, holds elections.

▸ Scientists report that the Chandra X-Ray Observatory has provided evidence of the theorized black hole at the center of the Milky Way Galaxy.

6 Sep The Florida Fish and Wildlife Conservation Commission bans the practice of attracting sharks with bait so that tourists can swim with them.

▸ ABC announces that it will join CBS in broadcasting most of its offerings in the HDTV format.

7 Sep In the first transoceanic telesurgery, surgeons in New York City remove a diseased gall bladder from a woman in Strasbourg, France.

▸ The final tally of last week's election in Fiji shows that Laisenia Qarase was elected prime minister.

8 Sep Tajikistan's minister of culture, Abdurahim Rahimov, is murdered by a gunman outside his home in Dushanbe.

▸ The UN Conference Against Racism produces a declaration that condemns slavery and discrimination against ethnic minorities, refugees, and women.

▸ Venus Williams defeats her sister Serena Williams to win her second straight US Open tennis title.

▸ *Monsoon Wedding,* by Indian director Mira Nair, wins the Golden Lion award at the Venice Film Festival.

9 Sep Suicide bombers fatally attack Ahmad Shah Masoud, the leader of the anti-Taliban opposition in Afghanistan.

▸ Pres. Alyaksandr Lukashenka declares himself the winner of presidential elections in Belarus.

▸ A gala attended by 800 dignitaries marks the opening of the Jewish Museum Berlin, designed by Daniel Libeskind.

▸ Lleyton Hewitt wins the men's title at the US Open tennis finals, defeating Pete Sampras.

10 Sep Tokyo's benchmark Nikkei Stock Average closes at its lowest point since 1984.

▸ A general election in Norway results in the Labor Party's worst showing since 1924.

11 Sep An exceptionally violent typhoon kills five people in Tokyo and causes great damage to roads and rail.

▸ In a coordinated terrorist attack, two hijacked airliners strike the twin towers of the World Trade Center (WTC) in New York City, which subsequently collapse, another strikes the Pentagon near Washington DC, and a fourth crashes in rural Pennsylvania, apparently short of its intended goal; the total death toll is in the vicinity of 3,000.

12 Sep For the first time ever, the governing council of NATO agrees to invoke Article 5 of the NATO charter, which states that an attack against any member is to be regarded as an attack against all.

▸ US authorities say that they have evidence that the hijackers in the 11 September terrorist attacks were followers of Osama bin Laden.

▸ The FAA announces that henceforward knives and other cutting implements will not be allowed on US airline flights.

13 Sep Interest rates plummet when bond markets begin trading in the US for the first time since 11 September.

▸ The FAA allows all airports except Logan in Boston and Reagan National in Washington DC to reopen.

▸ After several days of fighting between Christians and Muslims in Jos, Nigeria, leave hundreds dead, the government promises to intervene.

▸ It is reported that the bacterium that causes stomach ulcers is also responsible for most stomach cancers.

14 Sep The US government releases the names of all 19 hijackers who took part in the 11 September terrorist attacks.

▸ Tropical Storm Gabrielle makes landfall in Florida, causing extensive damage and flooding throughout central Florida.

▸ Musicians who had gathered (and become stranded) in Los Angeles for the canceled Latin Grammy Awards hold an impromptu benefit concert for the Red Cross and the New York Disaster Relief Fund.

15 Sep Pres. Pervez Musharraf pledges Pakistan's support for US efforts to punish those responsible for the 11 September attacks.

▸ A barge collides with a piling of the Queen Isabella Causeway in Texas well before sunrise, causing sections of the bridge to collapse into the water below and a number of vehicles to drive off the edge in the dark.

16 Sep The PGA announces that the Ryder Cup golf tournament, scheduled for later this month, will be postponed to next year.

17 Sep The government of Macedonia reluctantly agrees to accept a small NATO security force to help keep the peace.

▸ General Motors agrees to buy about two-thirds of South Korea's bankrupt Daewoo Motor Co.

18 Sep For the second straight day, Typhoon Nari pounds Taiwan with record rainfalls, causing massive flooding and killing 79 people.

▸ North and South Korea agree on a new round of family visits and work to complete a rail link between them, among other things.

Timeline of a Tragedy

11 Sep 2001
7:59 A.M. American Airlines Flight 11 takes off from Logan International Airport in Boston, bound for Los Angeles.
8:14 A.M. United Airlines Flight 175 takes off from Logan International Airport, bound for Los Angeles.
8:20 A.M. American Airlines Flight 77 takes off from Washington Dulles International Airport in Washington DC, bound for Los Angeles.
8:42 A.M. UA Flight 93 takes off from Newark International Airport in Newark NJ, bound for San Francisco.
8:48 A.M. AA Flight 11 crashes into the WTC north tower.
9:03 A.M. UA Flight 175 crashes into the WTC south tower.
9:40 A.M. AA Flight 77 crashes into the Pentagon.
9:45 A.M. For the first time ever, the US government closes the airspace over the US, as well as all airports to commercial traffic.
9:59 A.M. The WTC south tower collapses.
10:10 A.M. UA Flight 93 crashes near Shanksville PA.
10:28 A.M. The WTC north tower collapses.
5:25 P.M. A third building in the WTC complex, 7 World Trade Center, 47 stories tall, collapses.
10:30 P.M. President Bush addresses the nation from the White House.

12 Sep NATO, for the first time in its history, invokes Article 5, which states that an attack against one member state is an attack against all.
▸ Osama bin Laden is identified by US officials as likely to be connected with the bombings.
14 Sep Congress authorizes President Bush to use all necessary force to retaliate against those responsible for the attacks.
▸ Most US airports are reopened.
▸ US Secretary of State Colin Powell confirms Bin Laden as top suspect.
▸ The US government releases the names of all 19 hijackers.
17 Sep The NYSE opens for the first time since it closed the morning of 11 September.
▸ After a week in abeyance, Major League Baseball resumes playing games.
▸ For the first time ever, the World Bank and the IMF cancel their annual meetings.
19 Sep The Organization of American States invokes the Rio Treaty, a mutual defense pact.
20 Sep President Bush, in a televised speech to the nation, announces the creation of the Office of Homeland Security.
24 Sep The US freezes assets of organizations that are connected with the Taliban or Osama bin Laden.
26 Sep President Bush authorizes two Air Force generals to order threatening commercial airlines shot down.
28 Sep The UN Security Council unanimously adopts a resolution requiring all UN members to take steps to eliminate terrorism.
▸ The Commonwealth cancels its biennial summit.
7 Oct The US begins air strikes in Afghanistan and also begins dropping food packets.

19 Sep The OAS agrees to invoke the Rio Treaty, a hemispheric mutual-defense pact.
▸ United Airlines announces plans to cut 20% of its workforce.

▸ Indonesian Pres. Megawata Sukarnoputri meets with President Bush in Washington DC.
▸ The first of 434 largely Afghan refugees turned away from Australia in late August 2001 land in Nauru, where they will be processed by officials from UNHCR.
20 Sep In his first formal televised address to the nation since his inauguration, President Bush announces plans to create a new cabinet-level office to be called the Office of Homeland Security and to be headed by Tom Ridge.
▸ Rwanda adopts a new national anthem, "Rwanda Nziza," replacing "Rwanda Rwacu," which was felt to have ethnically divisive lyrics.

QUOTE OF THE MONTH

" *As for those that carried out these attacks there are no adequate words of condemnation. Their barbarism will stand as their shame for all eternity.* **"**

—British Prime Minister Tony Blair, in his address to his nation on 11 September

---

21 Sep *America: A Tribute to Heroes,* a benefit show to raise money for relief work in New York City and Washington DC, is broadcast on more than 30 cable and broadcast TV stations in the US and in 200 other countries as well.
▸ A special assembly in Estonia chooses Arnold Ruutel to replace Lennart Meri as president.
▸ The Lasker Awards for medical research are presented in New York City.
22 Sep Deep Space 1, a NASA probe, passes within 2,250 km (1,400 mi) of the nucleus of Comet Borrelly and transmits pictures and other data.
23 Sep Voters in Poland oust Solidarity from the National Assembly and favor the Democratic Left Alliance, the former communist party.
▸ The leftist Social Democratic Party, which has ruled Hamburg, Germany, for 44 years, is voted out in favor of a conservative coalition.
▸ The worst US coal mine disaster since 1984 takes place in Brookwood AL when two methane gas explosions kill 13 miners.
24 Sep President Bush announces that all assets of suspected terrorists will be frozen.
▸ The US House of Representatives votes to release $582 million of the $819 million in back dues that the US owes the UN.
25 Sep Saudi Arabia severs relations with the Taliban rulers of Afghanistan, leaving Pakistan as the only country that recognizes the Taliban as the legitimate government of Afghanistan.
▸ Basketball legend Michael Jordan announces his second comeback from retirement.
▸ General Motors announces that the 2002 model year will be the last in which the Chevrolet Camaro and the Pontiac Firebird are produced.
26 Sep President Bush authorizes two air force generals to order the shooting down of commercial airplanes that appear to be threatening US cities.
▸ A pro-Taliban mob burns down the long-abandoned US embassy building in Kabul, Afghanistan.
27 Sep In Zug, Switzerland, an unhinged man armed with an assault rifle bursts into a cantonal parliament meeting and opens fire, killing 14 legislators.

▸ Ali Ahmeti, political representative of the ethnic Albanian National Liberation Army in Macedonia, gives the rebel force orders to disband.

28 Sep In spite of a 10-day-old truce, a flare-up of violence in Palestinian areas in the Middle East marks the first anniversary of the new *intifadah*.

29 Sep Members of the Free Papua Movement occupy the city of Ilaga in Irian Jaya, in spite of the fact that Indonesia recently granted Irian Jaya autonomy.

▸ American Bernard Hopkins becomes the first unified middleweight boxing champion in 14 years when he knocks out Félix Trinidad in the 12th round in Madison Square Garden in New York City.

30 Sep President Bush approves the disbursement of funds for the covert support of the opponents of the Taliban in Afghanistan.

▸ Japanese runner Naoko Takahashi sets a new world record for women in the Berlin Marathon, running 42.2 km (26.2 mi) in 2:19:46, nearly a full minute faster than the previous record.

October 2001

1 Oct The Swissair Group files for bankruptcy protection for most of its operations.

▸ A car bomb at the Legislative Building in Srinagar, the summer capital of the Indian state of Jammu and Kashmir, leads to a gunfight and the death of 38 people.

▸ Italy's highest court acquits Prime Minister Silvio Berlusconi of having falsified documents.

▸ FOMA, the world's first third-generation high-speed cellular phone service, is launched in Japan.

▸ Condé Nast announces that the November issue of *Mademoiselle* will be the last.

2 Oct NATO says that the US has proved that Osama bin Laden and al-Qaeda are responsible for the 11 Sept 2001 terrorist attacks in the US and that it is therefore prepared to support the US in retaliating against them.

▸ Russia and Iran sign a military accord under which Russia will sell missiles and other weapons to Iran.

▸ President Bush expresses explicit support for the creation of a Palestinian state.

3 Oct A deranged passenger on a Greyhound bus traveling through Tennessee attacks the bus driver, causing the bus to flip over and the death of six passengers.

▸ GlaxoSmithKline announces a national discount program for low-income senior citizens whose health insurance does not cover prescription drugs.

▸ Algeria agrees to give Tamazight, the Berber language, national recognition and promises to punish police brutality against Berbers.

4 Oct A Russian airliner, hit by an errant Ukrainian missile, explodes and crashes into the Black Sea, killing all 76 aboard.

▸ Health officials report that Robert Stevens, a photo editor for the supermarket tabloid *Sun,* has been hospitalized with the first case of pulmonary anthrax in the US since 1976.

▸ The party of Khaleda Zia is victorious in legislative elections in Bangladesh.

▸ San Diego Padres outfielder Rickey Henderson scores his 2,246th career run, breaking the record held by Ty Cobb since 1928.

▸ The WHO urges national governments to devote more resources to mental health.

5 Oct Philippine authorities announce that Mustapha Ting Emmo, a key leader of the militant Abu Sayyaf, has surrendered.

▸ San Francisco Giants slugger Barry Bonds breaks Mark McGwire's single-season home-run record by hitting his 71st and 72nd home runs.

▸ Robert Stevens dies of anthrax.

6 Oct A record 72,554 people watch an ice hockey game between Michigan State University and the University of Michigan.

7 Oct US and British forces launch air strikes against Taliban positions in Afghanistan, as US forces begin dropping food packets in remote and poverty-stricken areas of Afghanistan.

▸ A referendum to move a number of responsibilities from the national government to regional governments passes in Italy.

▸ Railtrack, the company that owns the railroad track in the UK, undergoes bankruptcy reorganization.

▸ Kenyan runner Catherine Ndereba sets a new world record in the women's marathon of 2:18:47 at the Chicago Marathon.

8 Oct It is discovered that a co-worker of Robert Stevens has been exposed to anthrax, and spores are found on Stevens's computer keyboard.

▸ Girma Wolde-Giorgis is elected by the parliament as the second federal president of Ethiopia.

▸ The Nobel Prize for Physiology or Medicine is awarded.

▸ In Italy's worst civilian air disaster in nearly 30 years, a Cessna collides with an SAS airliner on a taxiway in Milan, causing an explosion in which 118 people, including 4 airport workers, are killed.

9 Oct Macedonia grants amnesty to all ethnic Albanian rebels who have disarmed.

▸ The winners of the Nobel Prizes for Physics, Chemistry, and Economic Sciences are announced.

▸ The USO appoints Wayne Newton to succeed Bob Hope as its official celebrity front man.

10 Oct Sri Lankan Pres. Chandrika Kumaratunga dissolves the government and calls for new elections.

▸ The five major US TV news organizations agree to censor tapes of Osama bin Laden to remove inflammatory propaganda and possibly prevent the airing of clandestine signals to operatives.

11 Oct The Nobel Prize for Literature is awarded.

▸ NBC agrees to buy Telemundo Communications Group, the second-biggest Spanish-language broadcaster in the US.

12 Oct The winners of the centennial Nobel Prize for Peace are announced.

▸ US government officials say that they have received credible threats of a possible terrorist attack in the next two days and instruct citizens to be calm but wary.

▸ An assistant to NBC newsman Tom Brokaw is diagnosed with cutaneous anthrax.

▸ Polaroid Corp. files for bankruptcy protection.

13 Oct Officials at the company that owns the *Sun* say that five more employees, in addition to the man who died and two others who were infected with anthrax, have been exposed to anthrax.

▸ A US district court judge appoints Eric D. Green, a specialist in dispute resolution, to mediate between Microsoft and the US Department of Justice.

14 Oct Ireland holds a state funeral for 10 IRA volun-

teers who were hanged by British authorities in 1920 and 1921.

▶ A large monument to controversial nationalist leader Stepan Bandera is unveiled in Drohobych, Ukraine.

15 Oct An anthrax-laden letter addressed to US Senate Majority Leader Tom Daschle is opened by one of his assistants.

▶ Bethlehem Steel Corp. files for bankruptcy protection.

QUOTE OF THE MONTH

❝ *You can not stop us. We have this anthrax. You die now. Are you afraid? Death to America. Death to Israel. Allah is great.* ❞

—text of anthrax-laden letter sent to Sen. Tom Daschle and opened on 15 October

---

▶ *Brill's Content,* a magazine about the media, suspends publication.

▶ New York City Mayor Rudolph Giuliani is knighted by Queen Elizabeth II of Great Britain for his support to British families affected by the 11 Sept 2001 terrorist attacks.

▶ Whoopi Goldberg is awarded the Mark Twain Prize of the Kennedy Center for the Performing Arts in Washington DC.

16 Oct Bayer AG announces that it will triple its production of Cipro, the primary antibiotic for use against anthrax.

▶ Peace talks to end the war in Congo (Kinshasa) begin in Addis Ababa, Ethiopia.

17 Oct Israel's right-wing minister of tourism, Rechavam Ze'evi, is assassinated by members of the PFLP.

▶ After losing in local elections in Norway, Prime Minister Jens Stoltenberg's Labor Party government resigns.

▶ In London the Booker Prize is awarded to Australian author Peter Carey for *True History of the Kelly Gang.*

▶ Daniel S. Goldin announces that he will resign as head of NASA.

18 Oct The men who were convicted in May 2001 of having conspired with Osama bin Laden to bomb the US embassies in Kenya and Tanzania in 1998 are sentenced to life in prison without parole.

▶ Japan's legislature allows Japanese troops to go overseas to provide logistical support to US troops fighting in Afghanistan.

19 Oct US ground forces enter the war in Afghanistan.

▶ Leszek Miller of the Democratic Left Alliance is inaugurated as prime minister of Poland.

▶ Kjell Magne Bondevik, at the head of a center-right coalition, becomes prime minister of Norway.

▶ A wooden fishing boat carrying at least 400 refugees from the Middle East sinks in the Java Sea, drowning all but 44.

▶ An anthrax-laden letter addressed to "the Editor of the New York Post" is found.

20 Oct Investigators say that anthrax spores have been found in the mail room of the US House of Representatives.

▶ President Bush tells the Asian-Pacific Economic Cooperation forum that the 11 September terrorist attacks in the US were meant to disrupt the world economy.

21 Oct The San Jose Earthquakes defeat the Los Angeles Galaxy to win the Major League Soccer championship.

▶ Lloyd Ward is named the new CEO of the USOC.

22 Oct Two postal workers in Washington DC die of pulmonary anthrax, and two others are hospitalized with the same disease.

▶ East Timor's new constituent assembly requests that the UN grant it independence on 20 May 2002.

23 Oct The IRA in Northern Ireland begins putting its weapons verifiably beyond use.

▶ Israel turns down a US request that Israeli forces be withdrawn from Palestinian-controlled areas of the West Bank.

▶ A UN appeals court overturns the conviction by the international war crimes tribunal in The Hague of three Bosnian Croats.

24 Oct A truck accident causes a conflagration in a heavily used tunnel in Bellinzona, Switzerland, that kills 11 people and closes the tunnel to all traffic for several weeks.

▶ Bayer AG agrees to sell Cipro to the US government for half the price it had been charging.

▶ Pope John Paul II apologizes to China for what he calls errors by Roman Catholic missions to China.

25 Oct The US Congress passes an antiterrorism bill that expands the government's rights to use electronic surveillance and to detain immigrants without charges.

▶ Microsoft releases the newest version of its PC operating system, Windows XP.

26 Oct South Africa and Burundi sign an agreement to allow South African peacekeeping troops to protect the transitional government to be established in Burundi.

▶ Bernadine Healy unexpectedly resigns as president of the American Red Cross.

▶ Abdul Haq, an ethnic Pashtun anti-Taliban leader, is executed by the Taliban in Afghanistan.

27 Oct Intel cofounder Gordon Moore and his wife donate $600 million to the California Institute of Technology in the single largest gift ever given to an American university.

▶ The Democratic Alliance, a merger of the two majority-white political parties in South Africa, collapses when former New National Party members pull out.

▶ Tiznow becomes the first horse in 18 years to win the Breeders' Cup race two years in a row.

28 Oct Gunmen enter a Christian church in Bahawalpur, Pakistan, during services and mow down the worshipers, killing 16.

29 Oct The US government again warns that it has credible information that there may be a terrorist attack against the US in the next few days.

▶ The US Supreme Court hears cases outside the Supreme Court building for the first time since 1935 while the courthouse is searched for evidence of anthrax.

30 Oct Jacques Nasser resigns as head of Ford Motor Co. and is replaced by William Clay Ford, Jr.

▶ Nelson O. Oduber is sworn in as prime minister of Aruba.

31 Oct Kathy T. Nguyen, a hospital worker in New York City, mysteriously dies of pulmonary anthrax.

▶ A smaller version of a bridge designed by Leonardo da Vinci opens near Oslo, Norway.

▶ Five women who had been hanged as witches in Salem MA more than 300 years ago are officially exonerated.

November 2001

1 Nov The US recalls its ambassador from Caracas after Venezuelan Pres. Hugo Chávez Frías criticizes the US war in Afghanistan.

▸ A transitional power-sharing government, headed by Pierre Buyoya, is inaugurated in Burundi.

2 Nov Microsoft Corp. and the US government announce an agreement to settle the long-running antitrust lawsuit.

▸ The last issue of the *Atlanta Journal* is published.

▸ King Muhammad VI of Morocco completes a two-day visit to Western Sahara.

3 Nov The ruling People's Action Party wins its ninth consecutive election in Singapore.

▸ The original of the 1931 Norman Rockwell painting *The Barefoot Boy* is exhibited for the first time, at the Solomon R. Guggenheim Museum in New York City.

4 Nov The Arizona Diamondbacks defeat the New York Yankees four games to three to win the Major League Baseball championship.

▸ The twice-delayed Emmy Awards are presented to, among others, the HBO comedy series *Sex and the City* and the NBC drama *The West Wing*.

▸ *Harry Potter and the Philosopher's Stone*, the film version of J.K. Rowling's best-seller, opens in the UK and breaks box-office records.

▸ Hurricane Michelle, the worst storm to hit Cuba in 50 years, makes landfall on the island's south coast.

▸ Enrique Bolaños Geyer of the Constitutionalist Liberal Party is elected president of Nicaragua.

5 Nov IBM announces that it is placing a number of its software tools in the public domain.

6 Nov David Trimble wins reelection as the head of a renewed power-sharing government in Northern Ireland.

▸ The Belgian airline Sabena is declared bankrupt.

▸ Republican Michael R. Bloomberg is elected to succeed Rudolph Giuliani as mayor of New York City.

7 Nov A US court of appeals vacates the $5.3 billion award in the *Exxon Valdez* case and returns the case to the Alaska district court.

▸ The first commercial Concorde flight since a crash in July 2000 takes place.

▸ The Academy of American Poets names John Ashbery the winner of the Wallace Stevens lifetime achievement award.

8 Nov First Minister Henry McLeish of Scotland resigns after financial irregularities are revealed.

9 Nov The fourth ministerial conference of the WTO begins in Doha, Qatar.

▸ With its stock price in free fall, Enron Corp. agrees to be acquired by Dynegy Inc.

10 Nov After 15 years of negotiations, China becomes a member of the WTO.

▸ Anti-Taliban forces capture the stronghold of Mazar-e Sharif in northern Afghanistan.

▸ Australian Prime Minister John Howard is elected to a third term of office.

11 Nov Canada 3000, Canada's second largest airline company, goes out of business.

▸ St. Louis Cardinals slugger Mark McGwire announces his retirement from pro baseball.

▸ Taiwan becomes the 144th member of the WTO.

12 Nov American Airlines Flight 587, en route from New York City to Santo Domingo, Dominican Rep., crashes in a residential neighborhood in New York City, killing all 260 aboard and several on the ground.

▸ The Super-Kamiokande neutrino-detection apparatus at the Kamioka Neutrino Observatory is nearly destroyed in an accident in which thousands of photomultipliers implode in a chain reaction.

13 Nov President Bush signs an executive order permitting foreign nationals suspected of terrorism to by tried by military tribunals with fewer rights than defendants in US civil courts enjoy.

▸ Taliban fighters withdraw from Kabul, the capital of Afghanistan, and anti-Taliban forces move in and take control.

▸ The US Conference of Catholic Bishops elects Wilton D. Gregory as its first African American president.

14 Nov Unification talks between North and South Korea break off abruptly.

▸ Christian aid workers from Shelter Now are abandoned by their Taliban captors and rescued by US military forces.

▸ The National Book Awards are presented.

15 Nov The US Congress agrees on an aviation security bill that will make all airport security screeners federal employees.

▸ Philip Morris, owner of Kraft Foods, Miller Brewing Co., and two major tobacco companies, announces plans to change its name to the Altria Group.

▸ New York Yankees pitcher Roger Clemens wins his sixth Cy Young Award.

16 Nov Investigators sifting through impounded mail discover an anthrax-laden envelope addressed to US Sen. Patrick Leahy.

▸ Chancellor Gerhard Schröder wins a vote to allow German troops to be deployed in the war against terrorism.

▸ Macedonia adopts 15 constitutional amendments to give civil rights to ethnic Albanians.

▸ Miss Nigeria, Agbani Dareno, becomes the first black African to win the Miss World crown.

17 Nov The party of ethnic Albanian nationalist Ibrahim Rugova wins the first democratic legislative election to be held in the Serbian province of Kosovo.

▸ Rains in Austin TX ease up after a week of flooding that kills nine people.

▸ Lennox Lewis defeats Hasim Rahman and retakes the WBC and IBF heavyweight boxing titles.

18 Nov The oil companies Conoco Inc. and Phillips Petroleum Co. announce plans to merge into a company to be known as ConocoPhillips.

▸ Georgi Parvanov of the Socialist Party is elected president of Bulgaria in a runoff election.

19 Nov The Olympic torch is lit in a ceremony at Mt. Olympus in Greece.

▸ Barry Bonds is named the National League MVP for a record fourth time.

20 Nov The Social Democratic Party, led by Prime Minister Poul Nyrup Rasmussen, loses legislative elections in Denmark to Anders Fogh Rasmussen's Liberal Party, which had promised immigration limits.

▸ The insurgent Moro National Liberation Front announces it is abrogating a 1996 peace agreement with the Philippine government.

▸ Seattle Mariners outfielder Ichiro Suzuki, already Rookie of the Year, is named the American League's MVP.

21 Nov Ottilie Lundgren, an elderly woman living alone in rural Connecticut, becomes the fifth person in the US to die of pulmonary anthrax.

▸ P&O Princess Cruises and Royal Caribbean Cruises announce plans to merge to become the world's largest cruise ship company.

▶ Four American food companies sign deals to sell Cuba food in the first trade deals made by American companies with Cuba since 1959.

22 Nov Scientists at the American biotechnology company Advanced Cell Technology, Inc., say they have created 24 normal cow clones.

▶ A landslide kills approximately 80 people illegally working a closed open-pit gold mine in Filadelfia, Colombia.

▶ The first official papal e-mail is sent by Pope John Paul II from a laptop in his office in the Vatican.

▶ Pakistan closes the Taliban embassy in Islamabad.

▶ Jack McConnell is appointed first minister of Scotland.

23 Nov Spain says it will not extradite the eight men it has charged with complicity in the 11 September terrorist attacks without a guarantee that they will be tried in a civilian court rather than by a military tribunal.

▶ Marks & Spencer announces that it is selling Brooks Brothers to Retail Brand Alliance Inc., owner of Casual Corner.

24 Nov The Grand National Assembly of Turkey ratifies changes to the legal code that make women equal to men before the law and no longer subject to their husbands.

▶ Taliban soldiers surrender the city of Kunduz, their last stronghold in northern Afghanistan.

▶ A Crossair jet crashes while coming in to land at the airport in Zürich, killing 24 of the 32 people aboard.

25 Nov Taliban POWs being held in a prison outside Mazar-e Sharif, Afghanistan, begin a revolt; by the time it is put down two days later 450 are dead.

▶ Advanced Cell Technology, Inc., announces that it has successfully cloned a human embryo.

▶ Ricardo Maduro, running on an anticrime platform, is elected president of Honduras.

26 Nov The National Bureau of Economic Research declares that the US economy officially entered a recession in March.

▶ A court orders the closure of TV-6, the last major independent TV station in Russia.

27 Nov The Nepalese army launches an air and ground offensive against Maoist rebels who seek to topple the government.

▶ The Cayman Islands enters an agreement to share information with the US to aid it in uncovering tax violators and money laundering.

28 Nov Dynegy backs out of its deal to buy Enron, saying the energy company failed to disclose the depth of its financial problems.

QUOTE OF THE MONTH

❝ *In hindsight, we made some very bad investments in noncore businesses that performed worse than we ever could have conceived.* ❞

—Enron CEO Kenneth Lay, to investment analysts, 28 November

▶ Chiquita Brands International (formerly the United Fruit Company) files for bankruptcy protection.

▶ The WHO releases a report saying 40 million people worldwide have either HIV or AIDS.

29 Nov Representatives of 30 countries plus the diamond industry agree on a certification process for the diamond trade to prevent diamond profits from supporting armed conflict in Africa.

▶ Officials in Nigeria disclose that a cholera outbreak has killed at least 700 people in the northern part of the country.

▶ Former Beatle George Harrison dies of cancer in Los Angeles.

30 Nov The East African Community, consisting of Kenya, Tanzania, and Uganda, is reestablished after being disbanded in 1977.

▶ The Apartheid Museum opens in Johannesburg, South Africa.

▶ The discovery of the world's smallest reptile, a dwarf gecko 1.0 cm (0.75 in) long, is reported.

December 2001

1 Dec Pres. Chen Shui-bian's Democratic Progressive Party supplants the Kuomintang as the ruling party of Taiwan.

▶ Japanese Crown Prince Naruhito and his wife, Princess Masako, become the parents of a baby girl, later named Princess Aiko.

2 Dec In the largest corporate bankruptcy filing in US history, Enron Corp. files for bankruptcy protection.

▶ The Kennedy Center Honors Gala celebrates the achievements of Julie Andrews, Jack Nicholson, Van Cliburn, Luciano Pavarotti, and Quincy Jones.

▶ France defeats Australia to win its ninth Davis Cup tennis trophy.

3 Dec It is revealed that one of the Taliban prisoners who surrendered after the November uprising in Mazar-e Sharif, is an American, John Walker.

▶ Dean Kamen's long-awaited invention is revealed to be a two-wheeled gyroscopic scooter, the Segway Human Transporter.

4 Dec Turkish Cypriot leader Rauf Denktash and Greek Cypriot leader Glafcos Clerides agree to hold face-to-face peace negotiations.

▶ President Bush freezes the assets of the Holy Land Foundation for Relief and Development, the largest Muslim charity in the US, saying it supports the Palestinian organization Hamas.

▶ The first bridge over the Mekong River opens, connecting eastern and western Cambodia by road for the first time.

5 Dec Four Afghan factions agree to an interim government in Afghanistan.

▶ An Enron spokesman confirms that it paid out $55 million in bonuses just before filing for bankruptcy.

▶ Ranil Wickremesinghe's opposition United National Party wins legislative elections in Sri Lanka.

▶ Owner and former CEO of Sotheby's auction house, A. Alfred Taubman, is convicted of having conspired to fix fees charged to sellers.

6 Dec The name of Newfoundland is officially changed to Newfoundland and Labrador.

7 Dec The Taliban abandons its last stronghold in Afghanistan, Kandahar.

▶ *Here...Now,* choreographed by Judith Jamison as a tribute to runner Florence Griffith Joyner, is debuted by the Alvin Ailey Dance Theater.

8 Dec After a week of rent riots in a slum on the outskirts of Nairobi, Kenya, ethnic group leaders and residents hold a peace rally.

9 Dec The WHO confirms that there is an outbreak of Ebola fever in Gabon.

10 Dec Legislative elections are held in Trinidad and Tobago.

▸ Venezuela suffers a one-day strike against the economic policies of Pres. Hugo Chávez Frías.

11 Dec The US government brings its first indictment in the 11 September terrorist attacks, against Zacarias Moussaoui.

▸ US Attorney General John Ashcroft says the US has broken up the largest operation to smuggle illegal immigrants in history.

▸ The Japan Prizes are awarded to Timothy Berners-Lee, for inventing the World Wide Web, and to Anne McClaren and Andrzej K. Tarkouski, for their work on mammalian embryonic development.

12 Dec Pres. Jiang Zemin of China goes to Myanmar to discuss transportation and trade ties.

▸ The centennial of the first transatlantic telegraph signal is celebrated by a re-creation of the original event, a signal sent from Poldhu in Cornwall, England, to Signal Hill in St. John's, Newfoundland and Labrador.

▸ The last jai alai game is played in Connecticut 29 years after the first fronton opened as a way to bring gambling revenues to the state.

13 Dec Five armed men attack the Parliament House in New Delhi, India; a total of 12 people are killed and 2 more mortally wounded.

▸ Israel announces that it is breaking off contact with Yasir Arafat, characterizing him as "irrelevant."

▸ President Bush formally announces US withdrawal from the 1972 Anti-Ballistic Missile Treaty.

▸ The US releases a videotape that shows Osama bin Laden gloating about the 11 September terrorist attacks in the US.

14 Dec An emergency antiterrorism bill becomes law in Great Britain.

▸ A high court judge in South Africa rules that the government must make available to HIV-positive women a low-cost drug that will reduce the risk of transferring the infection to their babies.

▸ Koloa Talake becomes the new prime minister of Tuvalu.

15 Dec EU leaders agree to set up a constitutional convention to revisit its institution.

▸ Because their original SAT tests were quarantined during the anthrax scare and never reached the Educational Testing Service in New Jersey for scoring, 7,500 high-school students across the US retake their SATs.

▸ Ethnic clashes that last for five days and result in 25 deaths break out in Mendi, Papua New Guinea.

16 Dec The beginning of the three-day Eid al-Fitr festival is celebrated with exceptional enthusiasm in Kabul.

▸ The Philadelphia Orchestra plays its first program in its new home, Verizon Hall.

▸ Calf roper Cody Ohl wins the all-around world championship of the Professional Rodeo Cowboys Association.

▸ The first commercial shipment of food from the US in almost 40 years arrives in Cuba.

17 Dec Armed men storm the National Palace in Port-au-Prince, Haiti, in an unsuccessful coup.

▸ Vivendi Universal of France announces that it will buy the TV and film units of USA Networks Inc.

▸ Portuguese Prime Minister António Guterres announces his resignation.

▸ The new parliament in the Solomon Islands chooses Sir Allan Kemakeza to be prime minister.

▸ Portuguese association football (soccer) player Luis Figo, of the Real Madrid team, is named FIFA World Player of the Year; American Mia Hamm wins the newly established award for women.

18 Dec The death sentence, but not the conviction, of celebrated black activist Mumia Abu-Jamal, who had been convicted in 1982 of killing a police officer in 1981, is overturned in court.

▸ The parliament of France approves a bill to give a bit more autonomy to Corsica.

▸ The WMO says that 2001 will have been the second warmest year on record, behind 1998, with an average surface temperature of 14.42 °C (58 °F).

19 Dec The US federal government indicts Tyson Foods, Inc., the largest meat producer in the US, for smuggling illegal immigrants from Mexico to work in its meat-processing plants.

▸ AT&T agrees to sell its cable television business to Comcast Corp.

▸ Katie Couric and the NBC network sign a television news contract for the highest amount ever, about $60 million over five years.

▸ A botanist in Australia says he has rediscovered a shrub, *Asterolasi buxifolia*, that for 130 years has been believed extinct.

20 Dec After several days of rioting throughout Argentina, Pres. Fernando de la Rúa resigns.

▸ The UN authorizes a security force, to be led by Great Britain, to assist in the transition in Afghanistan.

▸ A series of wildfires, many of them set by teenagers, begin burning in New South Wales, Australia.

▸ Fires from the World Trade Center disaster on 11 Sep 2001 have finally been declared extinguished.

21 Dec India recalls its ambassador to Pakistan and cuts off transportation ties.

▸ Hamas announces that it is suspending the use of suicide attacks in Israel.

▸ The world's fastest rollercoaster, the Dodonpa, with speeds up to 170 km/h (100 mph), opens in Japan.

▸ Ramon Puerta is installed as acting president of Argentina.

22 Dec Hamid Karzai is sworn in as head of the interim government in Afghanistan.

▸ A Paris–Miami flight makes an emergency landing in Boston after passengers and crew subdue a passenger who was attempting to ignite the soles of his shoes, which were filled with explosives.

23 Dec Adolfo Rodríguez Saá is sworn in as interim president of Argentina and immediately announces the suspension of payment on the external debt in the biggest debt default in history.

24 Dec A truce between the new government of Sri Lanka and the Liberation Tigers of Tamil Eelam goes into effect.

▸ Patrick Manning takes office as prime minister of Trinidad and Tobago.

▸ The Adolph Coors Co. says that it will acquire the Carling operation of Bass Brewers from Interbrew.

25 Dec In his annual Christmas address, Pope John Paul II enjoins the faithful to save the children of the world.

26 Dec The Qatar-based television network Al-Jazeera broadcasts excerpts from a videotaped speech by Osama bin Laden in which the alleged terrorist mastermind looks startlingly gaunt and pale.

27 Dec Presidential elections are held in Zambia; Levy Mwanawasa is later declared the winner.

28 Dec The Um-Kalthoum Museum, dedicated to the Egyptian singing star, opens in Cairo.

▸ Bill Cartwright, who played as the center on the Chicago Bulls championship teams in 1991–93, is named head coach of the pro basketball team.

29 Dec Nearly 300 people are killed when a firecracker ignites fireworks stands lining narrow streets in Lima, Peru.

▸ The city of Buffalo NY digs out after a snowstorm that began on 24 December dumped a record 206 cm (6.75 ft) of snow on the city in five days.

30 Dec Adolfo Rodríguez Saá resigns as interim president of Argentina.

▸ Pakistan arrests Hafiz Muhammad Saeed, founder of one of the militant Muslim groups believed to be behind the attack on India's Parliament House.

31 Dec Eduardo Camaño takes the post of acting president of Argentina.

> QUOTE OF THE MONTH
>
> **❝** *It's not enough to choose a president. Argentina is insolvent.* **❞**
>
> —Eduardo Camaño, acting president of Argentina, in a television interview, 31 December

▸ La Scala, Milan's famous opera house, closes for renovation; it is scheduled to reopen in 2004.

January 2002

1 Jan The euro becomes the official currency of Germany, France, Italy, Spain, Greece, Austria, Belgium, Finland, Ireland, Luxembourg, The Netherlands, and Portugal.

▸ A law granting autonomy to the Indonesian province of Iran Jaya (West Papua) goes into effect, and the name of the province officially becomes Papua.

▸ Military conscription officially ends in Spain.

2 Jan Eduardo Duhalde becomes Argentina's fifth president in two weeks when he is sworn in as interim president, to serve until elections in 2003.

▸ US Senate Democrats announce that they plan to conduct hearings into the collapse of Enron.

▸ A former White House pet, a chocolate Labrador named Buddy owned by former US Pres. Bill Clinton, is hit by a car and killed in Chappaqua NY.

3 Jan The Netherlands renationalizes its rail network after years of private ownership during which service had deteriorated.

▸ The heaviest snowfall in many years covers a swath of the southern US, causing hundreds of traffic accidents and leaving 70,000 without electricity.

▸ In the Rose Bowl, the University of Miami (FL) defeats the University of Nebraska 37–14 to win the national college football Division I-A championship.

4 Jan Nathan Ross Chapman becomes the first US serviceman to die in combat in Afghanistan.

▸ Israel seizes a ship loaded with munitions that Israel says, and the captain of the ship later agrees, are destined for the Palestinian National Authority.

▸ Scientists in Scotland reveal that the cloned sheep Dolly has developed arthritis at an unusually early age, although it is unclear if her condition is related to the cloning.

5 Jan A 15-year-old pilot steals a Cessna 172 and crashes it into a 40-story bank building in Tampa FL.

▸ The National Society of Film Critics chooses *Mulholland Dr.* as the best film of 2001, and the American Film Institute, in its first annual award, chooses *The Lord of the Rings: The Fellowship of the Ring* as best film.

6 Jan Argentina decouples the peso from the US dollar, ending a policy that had been followed since 1991.

▸ A UN official says that a disarmament program in Sierra Leone has successfully concluded.

▸ The 67-year-old Griffith Observatory in Los Angeles closes for its first-ever renovations, with plans to reopen in 2005.

7 Jan The worst snowstorm in over three decades drops about 30 cm (12 in) of snow on Jordan and Lebanon.

▸ Scientists present findings that many gamma-ray bursts originated in nearby galaxy clusters and that such bursts may result from supernova explosions.

▸ Lucent Technologies names Patricia F. Russo as its new CEO.

▸ Seminal fashion designer Yves Saint Laurent announces his retirement in Paris.

▸ Apple Computer introduces its new iMac, featuring a flat-panel monitor on an adjustable "neck" attached to a hemispheric base.

▸ The foreign ministers of Myanmar and Thailand begin talks to try to reach an accord on the repatriation to Myanmar of some 400,000 migrant workers registered in Thailand.

8 Jan The US Supreme Court issues a ruling that narrows the scope of the Americans with Disabilities Act, holding that a qualifying disability must limit one's ability to function in everyday life as well as on the job.

▸ Rules issued by the Vatican that require that priests accused of pedophilia be tried by ecclesiastical courts overseen by the Holy See are made public.

▸ Astrophysicist Kenneth Lanzetta presents research indicating that stars originally formed rapidly and profusely, rather than gradually, as has been the assumption.

▸ Major League Soccer eliminates 2 of its 12 teams, the Miami Fusion and the Tampa Bay Mutiny, leaving it with no teams in Florida.

▸ Shortstop Ozzie Smith is elected to the National Baseball Hall of Fame.

9 Jan Pres. Andrés Pastrana Arango of Colombia says that negotiations with FARC have failed and gives the rebel group 48 hours to vacate the area that Colombia had ceded to it during the peace talks.

▸ A US military tanker plane crashes in southwestern Pakistan, killing its seven-member Marine Corps crew, among them the first American woman to die in the conflict in Afghanistan.

10 Jan The US begins bringing al-Qaeda and Taliban prisoners to its naval base at Guantánamo Bay in Cuba, the first 20 of whom land the following day.

▸ Officials of Arthur Andersen, the auditor of the collapsed energy company Enron, disclose that Andersen employees destroyed documents relating to Enron, even after such documents had been subpoenaed by the SEC.

11 Jan Ford Motor announces its biggest cutbacks in 20 years, including the discontinuation of the Lincoln Continental, the Ford Escort, the Mercury Cougar, and the Mercury Villager.

▸ Astronomers say that, if it were possible to view the universe from the outside, it would appear to be a pale green.

12 Jan After several days of violence in Belfast, Northern Ireland, a Roman Catholic mailman is killed, and a Protestant group called the Red Hand Defenders claims responsibility and threatens to kill Catholic schoolteachers throughout the country.

▸ Pakistani Pres. Pervez Musharraf announces broad new restrictions on Muslim extremism, including the banning of five organizations.

13 Jan US Pres. George W. Bush briefly loses consciousness while choking on a pretzel and falls, bruising his face.

▸ After almost 42 years and exactly 17,162 performances, the curtain falls on *The Fantasticks* in the Sullivan Street Playhouse in Greenwich Village, New York City, for the last time.

▸ The winners of the 24th annual Dakar Rally are Hiroshi Masuoka, in a Mitsubishi Pajero, Fabrizio Meoni, on a KTM LC8 950 motorcycle, and Vladimir Chagin, in a Kamaz 49255 truck.

14 Jan The British government announces that the country is officially free of foot-and-mouth disease.

▸ Prime Minister Hamada Madi Bolero of Comoros announces his resignation as the first step toward the creation of a transitional government, and on 17 January Pres. Azali Assoumani also resigns.

15 Jan US and Philippine military officials begin preparing joint operations against Abu Sayyaf, a militant Muslim organization that is believed to have ties to al-Qaeda.

▸ The world's largest drug company, Pfizer, announces plans to make its drugs available to low-income elderly Americans for $15 a month per prescription.

16 Jan Riots break out in Lagos, Nigeria, as the Nigeria Labor Congress begins a general strike to protest an 18% increase in the price of gasoline and diesel fuel and a 40% increase in the price of kerosene.

▸ Pres. Olusegun Obasanjo of Nigeria and Pres. Fradique de Menezes of São Tomé and Príncipe launch the Joint High Authority to manage oil exploration in the disputed Gulf of Guinea.

17 Jan Argentina reopens its stock exchange and replaces the president of the central bank in an effort to gain control over the continuing economic crisis.

▸ Colin Powell makes the first visit by an American secretary of state to Kabul, Afghanistan, since Henry Kissinger visited in 1976.

▸ Mt. Nyiragongo, just outside Goma, Dem. Rep. of the Congo, begins erupting, and the next day almost the entire population of Goma flees as lava destroys much of the city.

18 Jan Pres. Ahmad Tejan Kabbah ceremonially declares that the civil war in Sierra Leone, which began in 1991, has ended.

▸ Newmont Mining, based in Denver CO, becomes the buyer of Normandy Mining of Australia, which will make Newmont the largest gold mining concern in the world.

▸ Israeli tanks surround the headquarters of Palestinian National Authority head Yasir Arafat in the West Bank town of Ramallah, effectively putting him under house arrest.

▸ New rules requiring the screening of all checked luggage go into effect in US airports.

▸ *Talk* magazine, founded two years earlier by former *New Yorker* editor Tina Brown, suspends publication.

19 Jan At the World Cup swimming meet in Paris, Luo Zuejuan of China breaks the world record in the 50-m breaststroke, with a time of 30.47 sec, and Yana Klochkova of Ukraine breaks the record, set in 1993, for the women's 400-m individual medley with a time of 4 min 27.83 sec.

▸ Winning films at the Sundance Film Festival awards ceremony in Park City UT include *Daughter from Danang, Personal Velocity, Amandla! A Revolution in Four Part Harmony,* and *Real Women Have Curves.*

▸ A series of 2,000-year-old erotic frescoes, discovered in 1985 on the walls of a bathhouse in Pompeii, Italy, go on view to the public for the first time since AD 79.

20 Jan A transitional government is formed in Comoros, with Hamada Madi Bolero serving as both prime minister and president.

▸ A new constitution providing for a president to be elected for a seven-year term and a bicameral legislature is approved in a referendum in the Rep. of the Congo.

▸ At the Golden Globe Awards in Beverly Hills CA, best picture honors go to *A Beautiful Mind* and *Moulin Rouge.*

21 Jan It is announced that the US will contribute nearly $300 million to the reconstruction of Afghanistan, close to one-fifth of what the UN estimates will be needed in the first year, and the next day other countries agree to provide a total $4.5 billion.

▸ In the field of children's literature, the Newbery Medal is awarded to Linda Sue Park for *A Single Shard,* and David Wiesner wins the Caldecott Medal for his reworking of *The Three Pigs.*

22 Jan Kmart files for bankruptcy protection in the largest bankruptcy filing ever made by a retail company, though it plans to continue operating its stores.

▸ The Hart Senate Office Building is finally declared free of anthrax contamination and reopens after having been closed since mid-October 2001.

▸ Philip Pullman wins the 2001 Whitbread Book of the Year Award for his young-adult novel *The Amber Spyglass.*

23 Jan Daniel Pearl, a reporter working in Karachi, Pakistan, for *The Wall Street Journal,* is reported missing after he fails to return from a meeting with sources the previous day.

▸ The US government, which has come under criticism for its treatment of al-Qaeda and Taliban prisoners at Guantánamo Bay, suspends transport of prisoners there, as it has run out of space.

▸ A panel of experts working for the National Cancer Institute says that studies that have been relied on as proof that mammograms prevent breast cancer deaths are so seriously flawed that they do not show whether such screening is beneficial.

▸ EMI Records announces that it is paying its recently signed singing star Mariah Carey $28 million to break its contract with her.

▸ Enron chairman and CEO Kenneth L. Lay resigns.

24 Jan Congressional hearings into the Enron collapse begin.

▸ US special operations forces conduct a successful commando raid on what they believe to be a Taliban stronghold in the Afghan town of Uruzgan, but it later tuns out that the raid had mistakenly been against anti-Taliban fighters.

▶ Leaders of 12 world religions gather in Assisi, Italy, to pray for peace in an event organized by Pope John Paul II.

25 Jan India test-fires an intermediate-range nuclear-capable missile, alarming the world community.

26 Jan For the second consecutive year, Jennifer Capriati defeats Martina Hingis to win the Australian Open tennis tournament.

27 Jan News organizations receive e-mail saying missing *Wall Street Journal* reporter Daniel Pearl has been kidnapped.

▶ In Bodh Gaya, India, the Kalchakra festival, one of the largest Buddhist gatherings in the world, is canceled when the Dalai Lama falls ill.

▶ PanCanadian Energy agrees to buy Alberta Energy to create the biggest oil and gas company in Canada, to be called EnCana.

▶ A series of large explosions at a munitions depot in Lagos, Nigeria, causes great damage and panic, and hundreds of people, many of them children, drown while fleeing across canals, while hundreds more are trampled to death.

▶ The first Palestinian woman to act as a suicide bomber strikes in a shopping district in Jerusalem, killing one other person and injuring scores, including a man who had survived the World Trade Center attack on 11 Sep 2001.

▶ Thomas Johansson defeats Marat Safin at the Australian Open tennis tournament to win his first Grand Slam title.

28 Jan The Doha Round of WTO talks begins in Geneva.

▶ Verizon Wireless announces the first commercial 3G wireless service in the US, providing high-speed Internet access on cellular phones to customers on the East Coast, in northern California, and in Salt Lake City UT.

▶ Siim Kallas takes office as prime minister of Estonia, replacing Mart Laar, who resigned over the pace of reform on 8 January.

29 Jan US Pres. George W. Bush delivers his first state of the union address to Congress; highlights of his speech include the creation of a new volunteer agency, the Freedom Corps, and the identification of Iran, Iraq, and North Korea as members of an "axis of evil."

QUOTE OF THE MONTH

❝ *I will not wait on events while dangers gather. I will not stand by as peril draws closer and closer. The United States of America will not permit the world's most dangerous regimes to threaten us with the world's most destructive weapons.* **❞**

—US Pres. George W. Bush in his state of the union message, 29 January

---

▶ Prime Minister Ilir Meta of Albania unexpectedly resigns his post.

▶ Japanese Prime Minister Junichiro Koizumi fires his popular and outspoken foreign minister, Makiko Tanaka.

▶ The state of Nevada declines to reinstate Mike Tyson's boxing license, so that his planned 6 April heavyweight title fight against Lennox Lewis cannot take place, as scheduled, in Las Vegas.

30 Jan Chile announces its plans to buy 10 F-16 fighter jets from the US in the first sale of sophisticated military equipment to a Latin American country approved by the US in over 20 years.

31 Jan The World Economic Forum opens in New York City (rather than its usual venue, Davos, Switzerland), with Irish rock star Bono among its opening-session speakers.

▶ Crossair, the designated successor airline to the bankrupt Swissair, announces plans that will make it Europe's fourth largest international airlines, under the new name Swiss.

▶ Ecuador designates a 557-sq-km (215-sq-mi) area in the Amazon rainforest the Cofán Ecological Reserve after it was declared the most biologically diverse mountain range in the world.

February 2002

1 Feb John Hume, one of the architects of the agreement that led to the power-sharing government in Northern Ireland, is presented with the Gandhi Peace Prize in New Delhi, India.

▶ Japanese Prime Minister Junichiro Koizumi names a second woman, Yoriko Kawaguchi, to be foreign minister in an effort to stem the political damage from his sacking of Makiko Tanaka.

▶ The NCAA punishes the University of Alabama's football program for recruiting violations by banning it from bowl games for two years, putting it on probation for five years, and cutting the number of football scholarships it may offer.

2 Feb In Amsterdam Crown Prince Willem-Alexander of The Netherlands marries Máxima Zorreguieta, an investment banker from Argentina.

▶ Former NFL players Dave Casper, Dan Hampton, Jim Kelly, and John Stallworth and coach George Allen are elected to the Pro Football Hall of Fame.

3 Feb In a dramatic upset, the New England Patriots defeat the St. Louis Rams 20–17 in the final seconds of the NFL's Super Bowl XXXVI.

▶ In response to a recent Supreme Court ruling, the Argentine government offers a new economic plan that will allow the peso to float freely against the US dollar.

4 Feb The eight-year investigation into corruption at the French oil company Elf Aquitaine comes to a close; the trials of the more than 40 people implicated in the investigation are not expected to begin for many months.

▶ Three days of violence between Hausa and Yoruba gangs in Lagos, Nigeria, leave more than 100 people dead.

▶ Some 14,000 teachers go on strike in the Canadian province of Alberta.

5 Feb The World Social Forum, an antiglobalization gathering of some 35,000 attendees, closes in Porto Alegre, Brazil; the summit was more successful in denouncing free trade and US military action than in proposing solutions.

▶ The government of Belgium apologizes for its role in the assassination in 1961 of Patrice Lumumba, the first prime minister of the Dem. Rep. of the Congo.

▸ Major League Baseball Commissioner Bud Selig abandons his plan to eliminate two baseball teams, the Minnesota Twins and the Montreal Expos, for the 2002 season.

▸ Japan's benchmark Nikkei Stock Average closes at 9,475.60, its lowest level since 1983.

6 Feb On the 50th anniversary of her accession to the throne of Great Britain, Queen Elizabeth II opens a cancer hospital.

▸ Democrat Nancy Pelosi of California becomes the first woman to join the leadership of the US House of Representatives when she is sworn in as minority whip.

7 Feb Engulfed in a scandal that broke with the trial of a former priest, John J. Geoghan, for child sexual abuse, the Roman Catholic archdiocese of Boston announces that six priests have been suspended because of similar accusations; this is in addition to two priests who were suspended on 2 February.

▸ The US government says that Taliban prisoners being held at the US military base at Guantánamo Bay in Cuba will be treated in accordance with the guidelines of the Geneva Convention but maintains that al-Qaeda prisoners are still exempt.

8 Feb The XIX Olympic Winter Games open in Salt Lake City UT.

▸ Mullah Wakil Ahmed Muttawakil, the Taliban's foreign minister, surrenders to authorities of the new Afghan government in Kandahar.

▸ The Alqueva dam in the Alentejo region of Portugal begins filling what will be the largest artificial lake in Europe, in spite of the objections of environmentalists.

9 Feb Algerian forces say they have killed Antar Zouabri, the leader of the Armed Islamic Group.

▸ Princess Margaret, the younger sister of the UK's Queen Elizabeth II, dies.

▸ At the Olympic Games, American Derek Parra breaks the world record in the 5,000-m speed skating race, but about 20 minutes later Dutchman Jochem Uytdehaage beats Parra's time.

10 Feb Seven people are ax-murdered in a village near Moscow.

▸ At the Olympic Games, German skater Claudia Pechstein breaks her own world record in the 3,000-m speed skating race.

11 Feb In pairs figure skating at the Olympics, the gold medal goes to Russian skaters Anton Sikharulidze and Yelena Berezhnaya for a performance that most observers believe is inferior to that of Canadians David Pelletier and Jamie Salé, who are awarded the silver medal; a storm of protest ensues.

▸ The Roman Catholic church creates four new dioceses within Russia; the Russian Orthodox Church views this as an attempt to convert Orthodox believers.

▸ NBC agrees to pay $7 million per episode to air a new season of the situation comedy *Friends*, with each of the six cast members receiving $1 million, a record price for a half hour of television.

▸ The World Wildlife Fund Mexico releases information that 74% of the monarch butterflies in one colony and 80% of those in another were killed by a storm in mid-January in the largest die-off of migrating butterflies ever seen.

12 Feb The first day of the Year of the Horse, 4700, is celebrated by Chinese people throughout the world.

▸ In testimony before the Senate Budget Committee, Secretary of State Colin Powell says that the US government is looking at options for engineering the overthrow of Saddam Hussein as ruler of Iraq.

▸ Pakistani authorities arrest Muslim militant Ahmed Omar Sheikh, a leader in Jaish-e-Muhammad, whom they identified on 6 February as their chief suspect in the kidnapping of American journalist Daniel Pearl.

▸ The Westminster Kennel Club Dog Show Best in Show prize is won by Surrey Spice Girl, a miniature poodle.

13 Feb The Lenten season begins in Spain with the traditional "burial of the sardine."

▸ The Scottish Parliament passes the Protection of Wild Mammals Bill, which makes it illegal to hunt wild mammals with dogs, effectively outlawing fox hunting in Scotland.

▸ The day after Pres. Hugo Chávez announced his decision to let the bolívar float, the Venezuelan national currency falls in value by 19% against the dollar.

14 Feb Emir Hamad ibn Isa al-Khalifah, ruler of Bahrain, proclaims himself king at the head of a constitutional monarchy.

▸ As his alternative to the Kyoto Protocol, US Pres. George W. Bush announces a plan to reduce the increase in greenhouse gases by voluntary means.

▸ The International Court of Justice (the World Court) invalidates a Belgian law that gave Belgium the right to try war crimes committed by citizens of any nation against citizens of any nation.

▸ New York City's Metropolitan Opera debuts its version of Prokofiev's *War and Peace,* with its biggest cast ever: 52 soloists, 227 extras, 120 choristers, 41 dancers, and a horse.

15 Feb Authorities are horrified to learn, upon the chance discovery of a skull, that the Tri-State Crematory in Noble GA has been piling bodies in the yard rather than cremating them; by early June, 339 bodies have been found on the crematory grounds.

▸ After the IOC asks the International Skating Union to look into the dispute over the pairs figure skating awards, the ISU determines that the French judge was improperly influenced, and Pelletier and Salé are awarded gold medals of their own.

16 Feb Zimbabwe expels Pierre Schori, the head of a European mission there to observe the presidential election.

▸ Ole Einar Björndalen of Norway becomes the first biathlete to win three Olympic gold medals in the same Games when he wins the 12.5-km competition, having previously won the 20-km and 10-km events.

17 Feb In their deadliest attack to date, Maoist rebels in Nepal kill 129, mostly police officers and soldiers, in Mangalsen.

▸ Responsibility for airport security in the US is transferred to the federal government.

▸ In the Daytona 500 NASCAR race there are nine crashes, one involving 18 cars, and the one-time leader, Sterling Marlin, is sent to the end of the pack for making an unauthorized pit stop; the eventual winner is Ward Burton.

18 Feb George Speight, who led a coup in Fiji in May 2000, pleads guilty to treason and is sentenced to death, which is soon commuted to life in prison.

▸ Point Given, winner of the Preakness and the Belmont stakes, is named Horse of the Year for 2001.

▸ Pentagon officials say plans are being made to disseminate information and disinformation to foreign media organizations through its new Office of

Strategic Influence, established shortly after 11 Sep 2001.

19 Feb Rain and hail lead to floods and mud slides that kill 69 people in La Paz, Bolivia; the storms are the worst La Paz has ever experienced.

20 Feb The worst rail disaster in Egypt's history occurs when a cooking stove on a train overcrowded with people traveling to celebrate the Eid el-Adha holiday catches fire and the train continues traveling for several miles, spreading the fire; more than 370 passengers die.

▸ A videotape that is delivered to Pakistani officials shows that kidnapped reporter Daniel Pearl has been killed.

▸ Jim Shea, Jr., wins the gold medal in men's skeleton and becomes the first third-generation Winter Olympian; his grandfather Jack Shea won two gold medals in speed skating in 1932, and his father, Jim Shea, Sr., had competed in Nordic skiing in 1964.

▸ A rare calendrical triple palindrome occurs at 8:02 PM, when the time and date are, in the European system, 20:02, 20/02/2002; such an occasion last occurred at 11:11 11/11/1111 and will next occur at 21:12 12/21/2112.

21 Feb John Geoghan, a defrocked priest, is sentenced to 9–10 years in prison for sexually molesting a 10-year-old boy; revelations of Geoghan's long history as a child molester and priest have led to calls for Boston's Cardinal Bernard Law to step down.

▸ Sarah Hughes, a 16-year-old American skater, performs a nearly flawless long program to win the Olympic women's figure skating gold medal.

▸ The US citizenship of John Demjanjuk, believed to have been a guard at a Nazi death camp, is revoked for the second time.

22 Feb Jonas Savimbi, head of the rebel group UNITA, is killed by government soldiers in Moxico province, Angola.

▸ With the results of the December 2001 election still unclear, contender Marc Ravalomanana declares himself president of Madagascar.

▸ Prime Minister Ranil Wickremesinghe of Sri Lanka and Velupillai Prabhakaran, leader of the Liberation Tigers of Tamil Eelam, sign a cease-fire agreement.

▸ In its first suit ever against the executive branch, the General Accounting Office sues US Vice Pres. Dick Cheney over his refusal to release to Congress records of his energy task force meetings in 2001.

▸ Japan notifies the International Whaling Commission that it plans to kill 50 more minke whales in 2002 than the previous year and in addition will kill 50 sei whales.

▸ In Washington DC, the Washington Monument is reopened after being closed for 15 months for renovations.

23 Feb FARC guerrillas in Colombia kidnap Ingrid Betancourt, a high-profile presidential candidate.

24 Feb The journal *Nature* releases a paper describing the successful cloning of a cat on 22 Dec 2001.

▸ The annual *hajj*—the pilgrimage to Mecca—held under unusually tight security, concludes without incident.

▸ On the final day of Olympic competition, for the first time in 50 years Canada wins the gold medal in men's ice hockey.

25 Feb A plan for peace in the Middle East proposed by Saudi Arabian Crown Prince Abdullah 'Abd al-'Aziz al-Sa'ud is seized upon eagerly throughout the Western world and by Israelis and Palestinians.

▸ NATO proposes to Russia the creation of a NATO-Russia Council to serve as a parallel organization to NATO's North Atlantic Council.

▸ Representatives from the government, three armed rebel groups, and civic organizations open talks meant to lead to peace and democracy in the Dem. Rep. of the Congo in Sun City, South Africa.

QUOTE OF THE MONTH

❝ A great responsibility is on you to deliver your own country from self-annihilation. ❞

—Ketumile Masere, facilitator, at the opening ceremony for inter-Congolese dialogue, in Sun City, South Africa, 25 February

---

▸ The Philippines celebrates a new national holiday in commemoration of the revolution that toppled Ferdinand Marcos in 1986.

26 Feb US Secretary of Defense Donald Rumsfeld disbands the Office of Strategic Influence after Pres. George W. Bush expresses his opposition to some of its proposed functions.

▸ France begins a planned 1-year celebration of the seminal Romantic writer Victor Hugo, who was born 200 years ago this day.

27 Feb A train carrying Hindu activists from Ayodhya is set on fire by a Muslim mob in Godhra, in Gujarat state, India, killing 58.

▸ At the Grammy Awards in Los Angeles, top winners are Alicia Keys, who wins five Grammys, and the sound track for the movie *O Brother, Where Art Thou?*, which also takes home five awards; record of the year is U2's *Walk On*.

▸ On the centenary of the birth of the writer John Steinbeck, his hometown of Salinas CA holds a tribute.

28 Feb Hindu mobs rampage through Ahmadabad, India, and more than 60 Muslims are killed.

▸ The Convention on the Future of Europe, meant to meet for one full year, is opened in Brussels, Belgium, by Valéry Giscard d'Estaing, who challenges the convention to produce a draft constitution for the European Union.

▸ The journal *Nature* reports that scientists have found that the dinosaur *Tyrannosaurus rex* would have been incapable of running quickly or possibly at all.

▸ The last day that national currencies may be used in the countries of the Euro Zone passes uneventfully; most people had fully switched to euros weeks before.

March 2002

1 Mar The government of India sends armed forces to the city of Ahmadabad in an attempt to contain the violence of Hindu mobs seeking revenge for the Muslim attack on a train.

▸ US government officials confirm reports that a "shadow government," consisting of career executive-branch officials, is being rotated through secret bunkers to assure continuity of government in case of disaster.

2 Mar By means of a satellite television linkup, Pope John Paul II leads prayers in several European cities: Athens, Budapest, Strasbourg, Valencia, Vienna, and Moscow.

3 Mar A referendum in Switzerland results in a narrow go-ahead for the government to apply for membership in the UN.

▶ Austrian skier Stephan Eberharter clinches the men's overall World Cup title, and three days later Michaela Dorfmeister, also of Austria, wins the women's overall title.

4 Mar Ethnic Albanian leader Ibrahim Rugova is elected president of the province of Kosovo.

▶ Murder charges are brought against Foday Sankoh, leader of the Revolutionary United Front rebel group in Sierra Leone, by a war crimes tribunal formed by the UN and by the government of Sierra Leone.

▶ Two days after the declaration of a state of emergency in Madagascar by Pres. Didier Ratsiraka, the members of the alternative government appointed by Marc Ravalomanana take over government buildings as the armed forces stand aside.

5 Mar US Pres. George W. Bush imposes tariffs of as much as 30% on steel imported from Europe, Asia, and South America, to begin on 20 March and last for three years.

▶ In primary elections in California, US Rep. Gary Condit, at the center of a scandal involving missing federal intern Chandra Levy, loses his bid to be the Democratic Party candidate for his seat in Congress to Dennis Cardoza.

6 Mar The head of the US Army Corps of Engineers, Michael Parker, is made to resign after voicing reservations about the $450 million cut in the organization's funds envisioned by the budget proposed by President Bush.

7 Mar Alan Greenspan, head of the US Federal Reserve Board, indicates that he believes that the economic recession has ended.

▶ The scientists who earlier announced that the universe is a pale green revise their findings and declare that the color of the universe is in fact a pale beige.

8 Mar Kmart, which filed for bankruptcy protection in January, announces that it will close 284 stores in 40 states across the US.

▶ Bishop Anthony J. O'Connell of Palm Beach FL admits that he committed sexual abuse in the 1970s and resigns.

9 Mar Newspapers in the US report that a Pentagon document discusses the use of nuclear weapons as a key element in military planning and indicates that possible targets would include Iran, Iraq, Libya, North Korea, and Syria.

▶ The Mont Blanc tunnel between France and Italy, which had been closed since a truck fire took place in it in 1999, reopens.

▶ Mexican authorities arrest Benjamín Arellano Félix, head of Mexico's most powerful drug cartel.

▶ Following a highly contentious election, Melissa Gilbert defeats Valerie Harper for the position of president of the Screen Actors Guild.

10 Mar Denis Sassou-Nguesso is overwhelmingly elected to continue in the presidency of the Rep. of Congo for a term of seven years.

11 Mar As a culmination of observances of the six-month anniversary of the terrorist attacks of 11

Sep 2001, a temporary memorial made of beams of light to illuminate the sky where the World Trade Center stood is lit.

▶ The US Postal Service unveils a new fund-raising stamp bearing the image of New York City firefighters raising an American flag in the rubble of the World Trade Center.

▶ David Letterman announces that he is declining ABC's offer to move his talk show to the ABC network to replace *Nightline* and that he will remain with CBS.

12 Mar Data from the most recent census show that Canada in 2001 had a population of 30,007,094.

▶ Homeland Security chief Tom Ridge unveils a color-coded system for terrorism alerts with specific meanings for local law enforcement agencies; the code has five levels, ranging from a low of green to a high of red, and the present level is declared to be yellow, meaning an elevated risk of a terrorist attack.

▶ The nine members of the Organization of Eastern Caribbean States enact legislation permitting free movement of people among the member states, without requiring the use of a visa or even a passport.

▶ Swiss-born Martin Buser wins the Iditarod Trail Sled Dog Race in 8 days 22 hours 46 minutes, breaking the record set by Doug Swingley in 2000 and becoming the first to finish in under 9 days.

13 Mar Robert Mugabe is declared the winner of the presidential election in Zimbabwe.

▶ Jamil Abdullah Al-Amin, a Muslim cleric who as a prominent black activist in the 1960s was known as H. Rap Brown, is sentenced to life in prison without parole for having murdered a sheriff's deputy in Fulton county, Georgia.

14 Mar Leaders of the two remaining republics in Yugoslavia agree to remake the country into a loose federation called Serbia and Montenegro.

▶ The government of the Dem. Rep. of the Congo pulls out of the peace talks in Sun City, South Africa.

▶ John C. Polkinghorne, an Anglican priest and former particle physicist, is named the winner of the Templeton Prize for Progress Toward Research or Discoveries About Spiritual Realities.

▶ The Whitley Conservation Awards are presented in London to Laury Cullen, for his work in preserving rainforests in Brazil; Carlos Soza, for his work in the Maya Biosphere Reserve in Guatemala; John Mauremootoo, for his work to restore forests in Mauritius; Lourdes Mugica Valdes, for her work involving bird life in Cuba; and Silas Kpanan 'Ayoung Siakor, for his efforts to preserve rainforests in Liberia.

15 Mar Israel pulls its armed forces out of every West Bank town except Bethlehem.

▶ A number of its high-profile clients, including Sara Lee and Abbott Laboratories, sever ties with beleaguered accounting firm Arthur Andersen, as do several of the company's foreign subsidiaries.

▶ A 2-m (7-ft) bronze statue of John Lennon is unveiled at the airport in Liverpool, England, which is renamed the Liverpool John Lennon Airport.

16 Mar The outspoken Roman Catholic archbishop Isaías Duarte Cancino of Colombia is gunned down outside his church in Cali.

17 Mar The Gravity Recovery and Climate Experiment (Grace), sponsored by NASA and the German Aerospace Center, is launched from the Plesetsk Cosmodrome in Russia.

▶ The 17th biannual Arctic Winter Games, held simultaneously in Nuuk, Greenland, and Iqaluit,

Nunavut, open; included are Dene and Inuit games and dog mushing as well as basketball, skating, and skiing.

18 Mar Almost the entire population of Gibraltar turns out to protest the beginning of talks between Great Britain and Spain over the future status of the territory.

▶ The Rock and Roll Hall of Fame in Cleveland inducts Brenda Lee, Isaac Hayes, Gene Pitney, Chet Atkins, and Jim Stewart as well as the bands the Ramones, the Talking Heads, and Tom Petty and the Heartbreakers.

▶ Maud Farris-Luse, recognized by the *Guinness Book of Records* as the oldest living person, dies in Michigan at the age of 115; the crown is now assumed by Japan's Kamato Hongo, age 114.

▶ In the Chinese province of Yunnan, in the mountains near the border with Tibet, the county of Zhongdian officially changes its name to Shangri-La in hopes of drawing increased tourism.

19 Mar The Commonwealth suspends Zimbabwe from membership for a period of one year after concluding that a high level of violence had made the presidential elections unfair.

▶ The CEO of the computer company Hewlett-Packard, Carly S. Fiorina, says she has won a shareholder vote to allow a friendly merger with Compaq Computer.

▶ Scientists say that the Larsen B ice shelf on the east coast of Antarctica, about 3,240 sq km (1,250 sq mi) in extent, has disintegrated with astonishing and unprecedented speed. (See map p.11)

20 Mar On the day of the vernal equinox Farsi-speakers throughout the world celebrate Noruz (Navruz), the traditional solar New Year's Day.

▶ The Bipartisan Campaign Reform Act of 2001 is passed by the US Congress; it is the first major change in campaign finance rules since 1974.

21 Mar Heads of state or government of 50 countries begin two days of addresses before the UN International Conference on Financing for Development, which opened in Monterrey, Mexico, on 18 March; the meeting addressed the funneling of foreign aid to reduce worldwide poverty.

22 Mar The World Meteorological Organization celebrates World Water Day.

▶ The US imposes tariffs that average 29% on softwood lumber imported from Canada, maintaining that Canada illegally subsidizes its lumber industry.

▶ Germany's legislature passes a hotly disputed comprehensive immigration law that is intended to regulate the flow of foreign workers into the country.

▶ A report released in Switzerland states that the Swiss government worked secretly with Nazi Germany and that Switzerland refused refuge to thousands of Jews during World War II though it was aware of the concentration camps.

23 Mar Street Cry, owned by Sheikh Muhammad al-Maktoum and ridden by Jerry Bailey, wins the Dubai World Cup, the world's richest horse race.

▶ More than one million people in Rome demonstrate against government plans to rewrite labor regulations.

24 Mar Shi'ite Muslims in Lebanon, Bahrain, and Iran observe the holiday of Ashura, when they commemorate the death in 670 of the Imam Husayn, son of 'Ali and grandson of Muhammad.

▶ The Academy Awards ceremony, hosted by Whoopi Goldberg, honors among others *A Beautiful Mind*, director Ron Howard, and actors Denzel Washington, Halle Berry, Jim Broadbent, and Jennifer Connelly.

25 Mar A magnitude 6.1 earthquake destroys the densely populated village of Nahrin in northern Afghanistan; about 1,000 people are believed dead.

▶ China launches its third unmanned spacecraft, Shenzhou III, from the Jiuquan Launch Center.

26 Mar Palestinian leader Yasir Arafat chooses not to attend an Arab summit meeting in Beirut, Lebanon, because Israeli Prime Minister Ariel Sharon has indicated he might not permit Arafat to return to the West Bank once he left.

▶ The Finnish telecommunications company Sonera and the Swedish telecommunications company Telia announce that they will merge.

27 Mar A Palestinian suicide bomber detonates himself in a hotel dining room in Netanya, Israel, as 200 people are sitting down to celebrate Passover, and at least 19 people are killed.

▶ A mentally ill man opens fire at a city council meeting in Nanterre, France, killing 8 council members and wounding 19 people.

▶ General Motors announces a plan to revive the Pontiac GTO model; the GTO, made from 1964 until 1974, was the original "muscle car."

28 Mar Leaders at the Beirut Arab League summit agree to a Saudi Arabian proposal to form normal relations with Israel if it will agree to conditions meant to lead to the creation of a Palestinian state, and they also unite in opposing any US military action against Iraq.

▶ Juliusz Paetz, archbishop of Poznan, Poland, resigns; he had been accused of sexually molesting teenage seminarians.

29 Mar The Israeli Army moves into the West Bank town of Ramallah and storms the compound of Palestinian leader Yasir Arafat, imprisoning him in his office.

▶ A Palestinian high school student detonates herself in the entrance to a grocery store in Jerusalem, killing 2 Israelis in addition to herself and wounding at least 30.

▶ Direct commercial flights between Delhi, India, and Beijing, China, resume after a hiatus of 40 years.

30 Mar Great Britain's beloved Elizabeth, the Queen Mother, dies in her sleep at Windsor Palace at the age of 101.

▶ After more than two weeks of secret negotiations, military leaders of the government of Angola and of the UNITA rebel group sign a preliminary cease-fire agreement.

▶ Oxford defeats Cambridge by just two thirds of a length in the 148th Boat Race; Cambridge leads the series 77–70.

31 Mar After a suicide bomber blows himself up in a restaurant in Haifa—killing 14 people, many of them Israeli Arabs—Israeli Prime Minister Ariel Sharon declares that Israel is at war.

QUOTE OF THE MONTH

❝ *The chairman of the Palestinian Authority is an enemy of Israel. He is the enemy of the entire free world.* ❞

—Israeli Prime Minister Ariel Sharon, in his address to the nation, 31 March

April 2002

1 Apr After a weekend in which three French synagogues were set on fire and two other acts of violent anti-Semitism took place, Prime Minister Lionel Jospin calls out 1,100 extra police officers to guard synagogues and Jewish schools, declaring that any acts of anti-Semitism will be firmly pursued by the justice system.

▸ Bishop Brendan Comiskey of the southeastern Irish diocese of Ferns announces his resignation, admitting that he had dealt inadequately with Sean Fortune, a priest who sexually assaulted dozens of boys for a period of about 10 years, before his suicide in 1999.

▸ The NCAA championship in men's basketball is won by the University of Maryland, which defeats Indiana University 64–52; the previous day the University of Connecticut defeated the University of Oklahoma 82–70 in the women's championship.

▸ A team of Indian and British divers discovers what it believes to be the lost city of Seven Pagodas off the coast of Mahabalipuram, India.

▸ *Bel Canto*, a novel by Ann Patchett, wins the 2002 PEN/Faulkner Award for fiction.

2 Apr Israeli forces pursue Palestinian gunmen into Manger Square in Bethlehem, where the Palestinians seek refuge inside the Church of the Nativity.

3 Apr A synagogue in Antwerp, Belgium, is firebombed; earlier in the week a synagogue in Brussels had also been firebombed.

▸ The Israeli army occupies Nablus, giving the army control of every major center in the West Bank except Hebron.

▸ Bayer AG and Exelixis Inc. announce that they have sequenced most of the genome of the tobacco budworm, an agricultural pest.

4 Apr The Israeli army completes its takeover of the West Bank when its tanks roll into Hebron; US Pres. George W. Bush demands that Israel withdraw from the West Bank.

▸ Military leaders of the forces of the government and of UNITA sign a cease-fire agreement in Angola.

▸ Arthur Andersen announces that it has reached an agreement to sell most of its tax business to another Big Five accounting firm, Deloitte & Touche.

▸ A synagogue in the Paris suburb of Le Kremlin-Bicêtre is firebombed.

5 Apr Representatives of the countries of the European Union and 10 Asian countries meet in the Canary Islands to make a plan to try to stem the flow of illegal immigrants to Europe.

▸ A team of Chinese researchers and a Swiss genomics company publish the genomes of two different strains of rice.

▸ Oprah Winfrey announces that she is discontinuing her Oprah's Book Club, which has tremendously boosted the sales of each of its featured books.

6 Apr José Manuel Durão Barroso is sworn in as prime minister of Portugal.

7 Apr Two bombs go off in rapid succession in a nightclub in Villavicencio, Colombia, killing 12 people and injuring dozens more.

▸ US Secretary of State Colin Powell sets off on a peacemaking trip to the Middle East.

8 Apr An international commission announces that the Irish Republican Army has for the second time decommissioned a large quantity of arms.

▸ Algeria's legislature approves a constitutional amendment that makes the Berber language, Tamazight, a national language.

▸ In New York City the winners of the 2002 Pulitzer Prizes are announced: a record seven awards go to the *New York Times*.

9 Apr Mexico's Senate votes not to allow Pres. Vicente Fox to make a planned trip to the US and Canada.

▸ Spain's top investigative magistrate opens an investigation into the country's second-largest bank, Banco Bilbao Vizcaya Argentaria.

▸ David Duncan, a former partner at Arthur Andersen, pleads guilty to obstruction of justice, admitting that he made an effort to destroy documents related to Enron's collapse.

▸ The 72nd James E. Sullivan Award is awarded to Michelle Kwan.

10 Apr Scientists describe research on two unusual stars based on data gathered by the Chandra X-ray Observatory that led them to think that the stars might be made of quarks in a form called strange quark matter.

▸ General Motors and the creditors of Daewoo Motor reach a detailed agreement on the takeover of Daewoo by General Motors.

11 Apr A treaty that creates a permanent International Criminal Court, to be based in The Hague, is signed at the UN headquarters in New York City; the US government boycotts the ceremony.

▸ A truck bomb explodes at a historic synagogue in Djerba, Tunisia, killing 18 people, most of them German tourists.

▸ The Walton Family Charitable Support Foundation, owned by the family that owns the Wal-Mart store chain, donates $300 million to the University of Arkansas; it is the biggest gift ever given to a public university in the US.

> **QUOTE OF THE MONTH**
>
> *They have put themselves outside the law to instigate violence, knowing there is an insurrectional plan, a crazy plan, a diabolic plan, an irrational plan.*
>
> —Venezuelan Pres. Hugo Chávez, 11 April, shortly before being briefly forced from office

12 Apr After pro-Chávez forces fire on anti-Chávez demonstrators in Caracas, Venezuela, some military generals break ranks and Pres. Hugo Chávez is forced from office.

▸ Princeton University announces that it has hired the prominent African American scholar Cornel West away from Harvard University.

13 Apr The Permanent Court of Arbitration in The Hague delimits a 1,000-km (620-mi) stretch of border between Ethiopia and Eritrea, ending a dispute that led to war in 1998–2000.

▸ Scotland defeats Sweden for the women's World Curling Championship; the following day Canada trounces Norway 10–5 for the men's title.

14 Apr In soon-to-be-independent East Timor's first presidential election, José Alexandre ("Xanana")

Gusmão wins by a landslide; the turnout is better than 86%.

▸ Venezuelan Pres. Hugo Chávez resumes his post following popular demonstrations against his ouster and the condemnation of governments throughout the Western Hemisphere.

▸ In winning the London Marathon, American Khalid Khannouchi breaks his own world record; Paula Radcliffe of the UK wins the women's race in the first marathon she has ever entered.

▸ For the third time, Tiger Woods wins the Masters golf tournament in Augusta GA, becoming only the third person ever to win it in two consecutive years.

▸ The retail chain J.C. Penney celebrates its centenary: one hundred years ago this day James Cash Penney opened his first store, the Golden Rule Store, in Kemmerer WY.

15 Apr Pope John Paul II unexpectedly summons all 13 US cardinals to Vatican City to discuss the burgeoning pedophile scandal.

▸ The US Food and Drug Administration approves the use of Botox for cosmetic purposes; Botox injections temporarily paralyze muscles, smoothing wrinkles.

▸ Australian architect Glenn Murcutt is announced as the winner of the 2002 Pritzker Architecture Prize.

▸ The Ruth Lilly Poetry Prize is awarded to German-born American poet Lisel Mueller.

▸ The 106th Boston Marathon is won by Rodgers Rop of Kenya; Margaret Okayo of Kenya breaks the course record for women.

16 Apr A one-day general strike idles 13 million workers in Italy and virtually shuts down the country.

▸ Dutch Prime Minister Wim Kok and his cabinet resign in order to take responsibility for mistakes made by the Dutch government when Dutch peacekeepers were unable to protect the town of Srebrenica, Bosnia and Herzegovina, from being destroyed by Bosnian Serbs in 1995.

17 Apr A court in Madagascar orders a recount of the votes in the disputed presidential election.

▸ South African Pres. Thabo Mbeki announces that, in a change of policy, the government will make universally available the anti-AIDS drug nevirapine, which greatly reduces the chances of an infected mother transmitting the disease to her newborn baby.

▸ The family of the Nigerian dictator Sani Abacha, who died in 1998, agrees to return to Nigeria $1 billion believed to have been plundered from the country by Abacha during his five years in power.

▸ Hewlett-Packard says that independent inspectors have confirmed that the disputed shareholder vote on 19 March was won by those voting with CEO Carly Fiorina in favor of a merger with Compaq Computer.

18 Apr A US fighter pilot in Afghanistan drops a 227-kg (500-pound) bomb on Canadian forces conducting training exercises, killing four Canadian soldiers; the pilot had mistakenly believed he was being fired upon.

▸ After 29 years in exile, the former king of Afghanistan, Muhammad Zahir Shah, returns to Kabul.

▸ The US Senate votes not to allow drilling for oil and gas in the Arctic National Wildlife Refuge; the plan had been the centerpiece of President Bush's energy policy.

▸ Abercrombie & Fitch removes from its shelves a line of T-shirts depicting what it thought were humorous caricatures of Asian Americans; the line,

introduced on 12 April, aroused the ire of Asian Americans and others, who found the stereotypes offensive.

19 Apr New constitutions are announced for each of the two entities making up Bosnia and Herzegovina (the Federation of Bosnia and Herzegovina and Republika Srpska).

▸ The inter-Congolese dialogue in Sun City, South Africa, ends without an agreement on an interim government to end the war in the Dem. Rep. of the Congo.

▸ A US scientist reports that a Japanese computer built to analyze climate change and track weather and earthquake patterns is far faster than the previous fastest computer, built by IBM.

▸ *Science* magazine publishes an article describing the discovery of a new order of insects, Mantophasmatodiea; the wingless mantislike insect order, found in the mountains of Namibia, is the first insect order discovered since 1914, at which time it was believed all insect orders had been identified.

20 Apr A meeting of finance ministers and central bankers of the Group of Seven advanced industrial nations in Washington DC yields an agreement that will allow indebted countries more easily to renegotiate their payment schedules in order to lighten their burden.

21 Apr In a shocking upset, the first round of presidential voting in France winnows the field of 16 candidates to the incumbent, Jacques Chirac, and extreme-right-wing candidate Jean-Marie Le Pen.

▸ Socialist Party candidate Peter Medgyessey is elected to succeed center-right politician Viktor Orban as prime minister of Hungary.

▸ Israel begins a partial withdrawal of its troops from the West Bank cities of Nablus and Ramallah, bringing to a halt its ground invasion.

22 Apr Martti Ahtisaari, a former president of Finland, is appointed to head a UN fact-finding team that is to look into Palestinian allegations of a massacre in the West Bank refugee camp of Jenin.

▸ The US succeeds in orchestrating the ouster of José M. Bustani as director-general of the 145-member Organisation for the Prohibition of Chemical Weapons; no successor is selected.

▸ A. Alfred Taubman, the former head of Sotheby's auction house, is sentenced to a year and a day in prison and fined $7.5 million for leading a price-fixing scheme.

▸ A federal ban on the use of motorized water scooters in US national parks goes into effect.

23 Apr Karen Hughes, counselor to the president of the US and perhaps his most influential adviser, announces her resignation, effective probably in the summer.

24 Apr US cardinals summoned by Pope John Paul II to Rome issue proposals for handling the issue of priests accused of sexual abuse, suggesting dismissal for serial offenders but discretion in cases that are not, in their words, notorious.

▸ As a wildfire near Denver CO doubles in size, the town of Bailey is evacuated.

25 Apr NASA scientists say they have measured the temperature of the coldest white dwarf stars observed by the Hubble Space Telescope in the constellation Scorpius in the Milky Way and concluded that the universe is about 13 billion years old.

▸ A Russian rocket blasts off from the Baikonur Cosmodrome in Kazakhstan carrying among its crew South African Internet millionaire Mark Shuttleworth, the second space tourist and first person from Africa ever to go into space.

▸ During a holiday celebration a bomb explodes in the women's section of a Shi'ite mosque in Bukker, in eastern Pakistan; 12 women and children are killed.

26 Apr Argentine Pres. Eduardo Duhalde, after several attempts, finds a minister of the economy, Roberto Lavagna, who meets with the approval of everyone concerned; Duhalde also partially reopens the banks.

▸ A recently expelled student, Robert Steinhäuser, goes on a shooting spree at a secondary school in Erfurt, Germany, killing 17 people, 13 of them teachers, before turning a gun on himself.

27 Apr Pakistan's Supreme Court rules that the constitution allows Pres. Pervez Musharraf to hold his planned referendum on whether his presidency, which was set to end in October, should be extended for five years; the referendum, held on 30 April, passes resoundingly.

▸ In an auction of Texas longhorn cattle held by Red McCombs outside Johnson City TX, a record price of $59,000 is paid by Vicki Mosser for Day's Feisty Fannie, a heifer that sports horns close to 182 cm (76 in) from tip to tip, making her, in the words of her new owner, "the longest-horned longhorn that's ever been sold."

28 Apr Israel agrees to end the blockade of Palestinian leader Yasir Arafat's compound in the West Bank town of Ramallah, but a few hours later, on the following day, Israeli forces seize control of Hebron.

▸ A pipe bomb explodes in an outdoor market in Vladikavkaz, the capital of Russia's North Ossetian Republic, killing seven.

▸ A storm system roars through the valleys of the Tennessee and Ohio rivers, spawning an exceptionally strong tornado in Maryland and killing four people.

29 Apr The US regains its seat on the United Nations Human Rights Commission; it had unexpectedly lost its seat on the organization, which it helped found, on 3 May 2001.

▸ The High Constitutional Court of Madagascar says that the recount of the vote shows that Marc Ravalomanana won an outright majority and was elected president; the incumbent, Didier Ratsiraka, who had agreed to the recount, does not accept the result.

30 Apr In talks sponsored by the Red Cross, North Korea agrees to allow a search for Japanese citizens whom Japan believes were kidnapped decades ago, and Japan agrees to search for Koreans taken to Japan before 1945.

▸ John W. Sidgmore abruptly replaces Bernard J. Ebbers as president and CEO of WorldCom, the telecommunications and Internet giant Ebbers created.

May 2002

1 May Throughout France more than a million people turn out in May Day demonstrations against right-wing presidential candidate Jean-Marie Le Pen.

▸ A car bomb created by the Basque separatist organization ETA explodes outside a stadium in Madrid where soccer fans were lined up in anticipation of a game.

▸ At the National Magazine Awards ceremony, the big winners are *The Atlantic Monthly* and *The New Yorker*, while awards for general excellence go to *Newsweek*, *Entertainment Weekly*, *Vibe*, *National Geographic Adventure*, and *Print*.

2 May Israeli forces withdraw from Yasir Arafat's compound in Ramallah, and a firefight erupts at the Church of the Nativity in Bethlehem, resulting in some fire damage to the structure.

▸ Erik R. Lindbergh lands his Lancair Columbia 300 airplane at La Bourget airport after a 17-hour trans-Atlantic flight that was a re-creation of the historic New York–Paris flight made by his grandfather, Charles Lindbergh, in 1927.

3 May Eight rural mailboxes in a circular cluster of small towns in northwestern Illinois and northeastern Iowa are found to be booby-trapped with pipe bombs; each bomb is accompanied by a long, obscure antigovernment note.

▸ Russia signs an agreement returning Cam Ranh Bay, after 1979 the largest Soviet naval base outside the Soviet Union, to Vietnam.

▸ A funeral is held in Cape Town, South Africa, for Saartje Baartman, a Khoisan woman who left South Africa in 1810 and was exhibited in France as the "Hottentot Venus" for the rest of her life and after her death; Baartman's remains were returned to South Africa by Paris's Musée de l'Homme.

▸ The Mystery Writers of America, Inc. present their Grand Master award to Robert B. Parker, author of the Spenser novels, and name *Silent Joe*, by T. Jefferson Parker, best novel.

4 May In the 128th running of the Kentucky Derby, a long-shot horse, War Emblem, wins.

5 May Pres. Jacques Chirac defeats Jean-Marie Le Pen in the second round of balloting for president of France.

6 May An anti-immigration advocate with flamboyant views and lifestyle and a leading candidate to become prime minister of The Netherlands, Pim Fortuyn, is assassinated.

▸ Myanmar announces that it is releasing rights activist Daw Aung San Suu Kyi from house arrest and allowing her to engage in political activity.

▸ In its opening weekend in the US, the movie *Spider-Man* smashes box-office records with a take of $115 million; it is the first movie to make more than $100 million in its first weekend.

7 May A suicide bomber explodes his weapon in a gambling and billiards club outside Tel Aviv, Israel, killing 15 and wounding 58; Israeli Prime Minister Ariel Sharon cuts short his visit with US Pres. George W. Bush and returns home the following day.

▸ Lucas Helder, a student at the University of Wisconsin—Stout, is arrested in Nevada on suspicion of responsibility for the pipe bombs found in various rural mailboxes in the Midwest.

8 May Abel Pacheco is inaugurated as the new president of Costa Rica.

▸ A car bomb explodes outside the Sheraton Hotel in Karachi, Pakistan, killing 14 people.

▸ Volkert van der Graaf, a radical animal-rights activist, is arraigned in Amsterdam, in the assassination of politician Pim Fortuyn.

▸ Feyenoord Rotterdam beats Borussia Dortmund of Germany 3–2 in the association football (soccer) UEFA Cup final in Rotterdam, The Netherlands.

9 May A pipe bomb explodes at a military parade in Kaspiysk, in the Russian republic of Dagestan; 42 people are killed.

▶ Two men push into a bank in Mor, Hungary, and open fire with automatic weapons, killing at least six people and deeply shocking a nation unaccustomed to violent crime.

10 May Robert Hanssen, former FBI employee and double agent for the Soviet Union, is sentenced to life in prison without possibility of parole.

▶ After several false starts, the siege of the Church of the Nativity in Jerusalem is lifted with an agreement that many of the Palestinians within be exiled; the siege began on 2 April.

11 May Slovakia defeats Russia 4–3 to win its first world ice hockey championship.

▶ David Beckham, the star captain of the English national soccer team, signs a new contract with Manchester United.

▶ Italian tenor Luciano Pavarotti cancels what would have been his final appearance at the Metropolitan Opera in New York City, pleading illness; he has announced that he will retire this year.

12 May Former US president Jimmy Carter begins a five-day visit with Pres. Fidel Castro of Cuba.

13 May A US official arrives in India on a mission to try to defuse tension between India and Pakistan, which are believed to be on the brink of war.

▶ Sears, Roebuck and Co. announces that it has made a deal to buy mail-order retailer Land's End.

14 May Ahmed Tejan Kabbah is reelected as president of Sierra Leone.

▶ Three Pakistani gunmen open fire on a bus and then the family quarters of a military encampment in the Indian-administered area of Kashmir, killing 32 people.

▶ For the first time in its history, a court in Jordan grants a woman a divorce from her husband; until a new law in January, men could divorce their wives, but not vice versa.

15 May Presidential press secretary Ari Fleischer says that US Pres. George W. Bush was given information in August 2001 that Osama bin Laden was interested in hijacking aircraft in order to attack US interests.

▶ In the Dutch parliamentary elections, Prime Minister Wim Kok's Labour Party wins only 23 seats.

▶ The Gold Medal for Architecture, awarded every six years by the American Academy of Arts and Letters, is presented to Frank O. Gehry in a ceremony in New York City.

▶ Real Madrid defeats Bayer Leverkusen of Germany 2–1 in Glasgow, Scotland, to win the association football (soccer) Champions League final.

16 May *Granma,* the newspaper of the Cuban Communist Party, unexpectedly publishes the full text of a speech by former US president Jimmy Carter in which he is critical of the Cuban government.

▶ Scientists at the University of Hawaii announce that they have discovered 11 new moons orbiting Jupiter, giving it a total of 39.

17 May Bertie Ahern is reelected prime minister of Ireland.

▶ A US proposal to exempt peacekeeping troops from prosecution before the new International Criminal Court is not accepted by the UN Security Council.

▶ The German media giant Bertelsmann agrees to acquire the assets of Napster, a company that developed a World Wide Web file exchange system.

▶ Legislators in Germany rewrite a clause of the Basic Law to require the government to respect the dignity of animals as well as people.

18 May As Indian and Pakistani troops fire at each other across the line of control in Kashmir, India

expels the Pakistani ambassador over the 14 May attack.

▶ The WHO agrees to delay the destruction of the last remaining stocks of smallpox virus, due to be destroyed at the end of the year to prevent the disease from ever occurring again, in order to allow time to develop vaccines and treatments in case some of the virus were to fall into the wrong hands.

▶ Kentucky Derby winner War Emblem wins the Preakness Stakes.

19 May A Palestinian suicide bomber disguised as an Israeli soldier blows himself up in a market in Netanya, killing two people and wounding dozens.

▶ As questions as to whether the US intelligence community should have been able to prevent the terrorist attacks of 11 Sep 2001 are raised in Congress, Vice Pres. Dick Cheney says that there will almost certainly be more al-Qaeda attacks against the US.

▶ Pope John Paul II canonizes Amabile Lucia Visintainer, known as Mother Paulina; she becomes the first Brazilian saint.

▶ Norman Rockwell's *Rosie the Riveter* is auctioned off at Sotheby's for $4.9 million, the highest price ever brought at public auction for a Rockwell painting.

20 May Thousands of people attend the celebration in Dili of the birth of a new nation, East Timor.

21 May A moderate Kashmiri separatist leader, Abdul Ghani Lone, is gunned down in Srinagar in the Indian state of Jammu and Kashmir; it is unclear who the assassin is.

▶ The brokerage firm Merrill Lynch and Co. agrees to pay a $100 million fine to settle a case in which it is accused of publicly promoting stocks of companies with which it wished to do business, while privately denigrating those same stocks.

▶ It is reported that scientists at Hebrew University in Israel have developed a featherless broiler chicken, claiming that broiler chickens tend to produce excessive body heat, so this benefits the chickens, and it of course eliminates the need for plucking.

22 May The skeletal remains of congressional intern Chandra Levy, missing since 30 Apr 2001, are discovered not far from her home in Washington DC's Rock Creek Park; it is later confirmed that she was murdered.

▶ In Birmingham AL former Klansman Bobby Frank Cherry is convicted of four counts of murder in the 1963 bombing of the 16th Street Baptist Church, in which four girls were killed.

▶ Pope John Paul II arrives in Baku, Azerbaijan, an almost wholly Muslim country, for a five-day trip that will also take him to Bulgaria.

▶ Samuel D. Waksal resigns as CEO of ImClone, which is under investigation for having misled investors as to the regulatory status of its anticancer drug Erbitux; meanwhile at the Gap, where stock prices have fallen precipitously of late, Millard S. Drexler unexpectedly resigns as CEO.

23 May FBI director Robert Mueller says that he is ordering an inquiry into complaints by senior Minneapolis agent Coleen Rowley that higher-ups had stymied her office's attempts to investigate suspected terrorist Zacarias Moussaoui before 11 Sep 2001.

▶ Officials in India report that an ongoing nationwide heat wave has killed 1,030 people, mostly in Andhra Pradesh state.

24 May US Pres. George W. Bush and Russian Pres. Vladimir Putin sign a treaty pledging each to deactivate nuclear warheads until, by 2012, there are no more than 2,200 active warheads each.

▸ Amadou Toumani Touré is elected president of Mali.

▸ Sandra Baldwin resigns as president of the US Olympic Committee after admitting that her résumé contained false information.

25 May Lesotho holds parliamentary elections under a proportional representation system new to Africa, in which each voter votes separately for the party of his choice and the district representative.

▸ New Zealand's Canterbury Crusaders defeat Australian rival the ACT Brumbies 31–13 in the rugby Union Super 12 final in Christchurch, New Zealand.

26 May In the race for the presidency of Colombia, Álvaro Uribe Vélez, who campaigned on a strong anti-crime platform, is elected.

▸ Near Webbers Falls OK a river barge bumps into a support of a bridge over the Arkansas River, causing a section of the four-lane Interstate 40 to collapse into the river and a number of vehicles to plunge over the edge.

▸ In the Indianapolis 500 auto race, Paul Tracy is penalized for passing after a yellow caution flag had been flown in the final laps of the race, making Brazilian Hélio Castroneves the first person since 1971 to win two consecutive Indy 500s.

▸ At the 55th Cannes International Film Festival, Roman Polanski's film *The Pianist* wins the Palme d'Or.

27 May In a televised speech to the nation, Pakistani Pres. Pervez Musharraf urges dialogue with India over the Kashmir issue but asserts solidarity with Kashmiris resisting Indian rule, denies that Pakistan supports terrorist attacks across the line of control, and maintains that Pakistan is ready to fight if need be.

QUOTE OF THE MONTH

We do not want war. But if war is thrust upon us, we would respond with full might, and give a befitting reply.

—Pakistani Pres. Pervez Musharraf, in his 27 May address to the nation

---

28 May Both sides officially agree to the establishment of a NATO-Russia Council, permitting Russia to participate in many NATO discussions.

▸ It is reported that Libya has offered to pay $2.7 billion to the survivors of the passengers on Pan Am flight 103, which crashed in Lockerbie, Scotland, in 1988, in return for the lifting of UN and US sanctions against the country.

▸ Palestinian leader Yasir Arafat signs a Basic Law, delineating rights of the people and responsibilities of the government, that was passed by the Palestinian Legislative Council in 1997.

29 May In a Cabinet reshuffle in Great Britain, Alistair Darling is named to replace Stephen Byers as transport secretary after Byers had resigned over, among other things, rail failures, and Paul Boateng becomes the first black member of the British Cabinet when he is named deputy treasury secretary.

▸ Mohammad al-Fayed, owner of the genteelly satirical British magazine *Punch*, announces that he has had to close the magazine owing to lack of revenue and declining subscriptions.

▸ Black Sabbath vocalist Ozzy Osbourne and his family agree to a contract for a second season of MTV's surprise hit television show *The Osbournes*, chronicling everyday life in the rock star's household.

30 May A ceremony is held to mark the conclusion of the cleanup operation at the site of the World Trade Center in New York City.

▸ The Philip Morris Companies agree to sell the Miller Brewing Company to South African Breweries.

▸ The *New England Journal of Medicine* publishes the results of a small study of an experimental drug that appears to stop the progress of Type I diabetes.

31 May Zimbabwe declares an AIDS-related national emergency in order to take advantage of trade rules that permit it to bypass patents and import cheaper generic versions of needed drugs.

▸ In first-round World Cup association football (soccer) play in Seoul, South Korea, the sports world is stunned when Senegal defeats France, the reigning champion.

▸ The Dr. Seuss National Memorial Sculpture Garden, featuring sculptures of the Cat in the Hat, Horton the Elephant, and the Lorax, among others, opens in Springfield MA.

June 2002

1 Jun In a graduation speech at the US Military Academy at West Point, US Pres. George W. Bush declares that the Cold War policies of containment and deterrence are outdated and must be replaced by a policy of preemptive strikes.

2 Jun In rural southwestern Mexico, 16 people are jailed in connection with a massacre of 26 sawmill workers from the village of Santiago Xochiltepec two days previously; the event is believed to stem from a feud, mostly over land, between neighboring villages.

▸ The 56th annual Tony Awards are presented at Radio City Music Hall in New York City; winners include the plays *The Goat, or Who Is Sylvia?*, *Thoroughly Modern Millie*, *Private Lives*, and *Into the Woods* and the actors Alan Bates, Lindsay Duncan, John Lithgow, and Sutton Foster.

3 Jun A rock concert and fireworks show at Buckingham Palace are a high point of the four-day official celebration of Queen Elizabeth II's golden jubilee, commemorating her 50 years on the throne.

▸ Under threat of indictment for tax evasion, Dennis Kozlowski resigns as chairman and CEO of the industrial services manufacturing giant Tyco International Ltd.

4 Jun Japan ratifies the Kyoto Protocol on global warming, improving the document's chances of becoming international law; Japan is the world's fourth-largest emitter of the greenhouse gas carbon dioxide, behind the US, the European Union (all the members of which have ratified the agreement), and Russia.

5 Jun The space shuttle *Endeavour* takes off with a new crew for the International Space Station after a week of delays occasioned by bad weather and faulty equipment.

6 Jun In a nationally televised address, President Bush proposes the creation of a new cabinet post, the Department of Homeland Security, under which would fall the Customs Service, the Secret Service, the Immigration and Naturalization Service, and the Coast Guard, but not the FBI or the CIA.

▶ It is reported that home arts maven Martha Stewart, a close friend of former ImClone CEO Samuel Waksal, sold all her ImClone stock shortly before an unfavorable ruling by the US Food and Drug Administration was made public; on June 12 Waksal is arrested on charges of insider trading.

7 Jun The leaders of Russia, China, Kazakhstan, Uzbekistan, Kyrgyzstan, and Tajikistan sign a charter that creates a new international organization, the Shanghai Cooperation Organization.

8 Jun A government official in India says that Pakistani incursions into the Indian-administered portion of Kashmir have been halted and that this is a promising development; two days later India begins pulling back naval vessels from Pakistan's coast.

▶ Two thousand people in Glenwood Springs CO are evacuated from the path of the fast-moving Coal Seam Fire; another fire ignited on this day in the Pike National Forest near Denver, the Hayman Fire, grows within two days to become the largest wildfire in Colorado's history.

▶ Serena Williams defeats her older sister, Venus, to win the women's French Open tennis title; the following day Albert Costa, of Spain, defeats his countryman Juan Carlos Ferrero to win the men's title.

▶ Kentucky Derby and Preakness winner War Emblem stumbles coming out of the gate at the Belmont Stakes; the winner of the last of the Triple Crown horse races, Sarava, is, at 70–1, the longest-shot horse ever to win the Belmont.

▶ In Memphis TN Lennox Lewis defeats Mike Tyson by a knockout in the eighth round to retain his WBC and IBF heavyweight titles.

▶ Documenta 11, an exposition featuring the work of more than 100 international artists, opens in Kassel, Germany; Documenta is a thorough survey of contemporary art that is mounted every five years.

9 Jun Pak Se Ri of South Korea wins the LPGA Championship by three strokes over veteran Beth Daniel; it is Pak's fourth major title and second LPGA championship in five years.

10 Jun US Attorney General John Ashcroft announces that the Department of Justice has broken up an al-Qaeda plot to detonate a so-called dirty bomb, a radioactive device, in the US with the arrest of former Chicago gang member Jose Padilla, who is using the name Abdullah al-Muhajir.

▶ For the second time in a week, Israeli forces surround the compound of Palestinian leader Yasir Arafat in Ramallah.

▶ The UN FAO begins a four-day World Food Summit in Rome; most of the member countries are represented by agriculture ministers rather than heads of state.

11 Jun Afghanistan's *loya jirga* is officially opened; the council will choose a government to rule Afghanistan for the next two years, until elections are held.

▶ In a castle near Glaslough, Ireland, the former Beatle Sir Paul McCartney marries the former model Heather Mills.

12 Jun The Los Angeles Lakers defeat the New Jersey Nets 113–107 to win the NBA championship for the third year in a row; also for the third time, Shaquille O'Neal is named Most Valuable Player of the finals.

▶ The World Council of Religious Leaders begins a peace conference in Bangkok seeking ways to reduce sectarian conflict; the conference, attended by more than 100 leaders of different religions, is an outgrowth of the Millennium World Peace Summit in 2000.

13 Jun The US formally withdraws from the Antiballistic Missile Treaty, signed in 1972 by US Pres. Richard M. Nixon and Soviet leader Leonid Brezhnev; the following day Russia announces that it is abandoning the 1993 Start II accord.

▶ Afghanistan's *loya jirga* elects Hamid Karzai to lead the transitional government for the next two years; the vote, monitored by the UN, gives Karzai 1,295 votes out of a total of 1,575.

▶ The Detroit Red Wings defeat the Carolina Hurricanes to win the Stanley Cup, the National Hockey League championship, for the third time in six years; the score of the final game is 3–1.

14 Jun A car bomb explodes outside the US consulate in Karachi, Pakistan, killing 12 people and wounding more than 50.

▶ The US Conference of Catholic Bishops meeting in Dallas sets a new policy declaring that any priest who has ever sexually abused a minor may no longer engage in any ministerial duties, although it stops short of requiring that such a priest be defrocked.

15 Jun The 89-year-old Big Five accounting firm Arthur Andersen LLP is found guilty of obstruction of justice by a federal jury in Houston TX and tells the government it will cease auditing public companies by the end of the summer, in effect going out of business.

▶ Rolling Stones vocalist Mick Jagger is awarded a knighthood "for services to popular music" by Queen Elizabeth II.

16 Jun US Pres. George W. Bush directs his top security personnel to develop a doctrine of preemptive action against nations and groups believed to be developing weapons of mass destruction or sponsoring terrorism.

▶ The popular Italian stigmatic Padre Pio da Pietrelcina, who died in 1968, is canonized by Pope John Paul II in a ceremony in St. Peter's Square.

▶ The CEO of Qwest Communications International, Joseph P. Nacchio, is forced to resign; Qwest's accounting practices are being investigated by the SEC.

▶ In the face of massive protests against plans to privatize utilities in Peru, Pres. Alejandro Toledo declares a monthlong state of emergency.

17 Jun Thousands of construction workers walk off the job in Germany in a strike for higher wages; it is the first major strike in the construction sector in more than 50 years.

18 Jun A suicide bomber detonates an explosion on a morning rush-hour bus in Jerusalem, killing at least 19 people; the next day Israel announces that it will begin seizing land held by the Palestinian Authority in retaliation.

19 Jun With the French in the lead, air-traffic controllers throughout Western Europe go on a brief strike to protest European Union plans to bring air-traffic control under a single framework by 2005; nearly 8,000 flights have to be canceled.

20 Jun The day before an EU summit meeting in Seville, the whole of Spain is brought to a near standstill by a 24-hour general strike called by Spain's two largest unions in protest against changes imposed by the conservative government.

▶ The US Supreme Court rules that an evolving national consensus now means that executing the mentally retarded violates the constitutional prohibition of cruel and unusual punishment; it does not, however, define mental retardation.

21 Jun A.Q.M. Badruddoza Chowdhury resigns from the presidency of Bangladesh after being accused by the Bangladesh National Party of disrespecting the party's founder by failing to visit his grave.

▸ In Arizona, the Rodeo Fire, which started three days earlier, threatens the resort town of Show Low, while 14 km (9 mi) away the Chediski Fire is rapidly expanding.

22 Jun A magnitude 6.3 earthquake hits northwestern Iran in the Kazvin region, destroying six villages and killing at least 235 people.

23 Jun In Arizona, the Rodeo and Chediski fires merge, creating the largest wildfire in Arizona's history and passing in size Colorado's giant Hayman Fire; about 121,000 ha (330,000 ac) have been burned in Arizona.

24 Jun US President Bush makes a speech laying out a new Middle East policy, in which he says that, if the Palestinian people end terrorism, reform their economy, establish democracy, and change their leadership, the US will support the creation of a provisional Palestinian state; meanwhile, Israeli forces occupy Ramallah and surround Yasir Arafat's compound.

▸ *Galileo Galilei,* a new one-act opera by composer Philip Glass and director-librettist Mary Zimmerman, has its world premiere at the Goodman Theater in Chicago.

▸ Susan Jaffe gives her farewell performance at the American Ballet Theatre in the title role in *Giselle;* she has danced with the troupe for 22 years.

25 Jun WorldCom, the second-largest US long-distance-communication carrier, says that it overstated its cash flow by more than $3.8 billion during the past five quarters; the following day the SEC files fraud charges against the company.

26 Jun A three-member panel for the US Court of Appeals for the Ninth Circuit, covering California, Alaska, Arizona, Hawaii, Idaho, Montana, Nevada, Oregon, and Washington, rules that the Pledge of Allegiance must not be recited in public schools because the phrase "under God," added to the pledge

in 1954, violates the constitutional prohibition against government support of a particular religion.

27 Jun At the Group of Eight meeting in Calgary AB, a program is announced that will give billions of dollars in aid to African countries that adopt a wide range of reforms in their governments and economies.

> QUOTE OF THE MONTH
>
> **"** *We are satisfied with this commitment.... There is nothing that is human that can be regarded as perfect.* **"**
>
> —Nigerian Pres. Olusegun Obasanjo, in Calgary AB, on the G-8 agreement to provide aid for Africa in return for reforms, 27 June

▸ The US Supreme Court rules that a program in place in Cleveland whereby public school money is given to students in the form of vouchers to be used at the private school of their choice does not violate the separation of church and state, even though some 95% of the vouchers are used to pay tuition at religious schools.

28 Jun The Xerox Corp. announces that, between 1997 and 2001, it overstated its equipment revenue by $6.4 billion and its pretax income by $1.4 billion, a much larger restatement than had been anticipated.

29 Jun A North Korean patrol boat exchanges fire with a South Korean vessel, sinking it; each country blames the other for the incident.

30 Jun The price of a first-class postage stamp in the US rises three cents to $.37.

▸ A part-time firefighter is charged with having started Arizona's Rodeo Fire in order to secure employment; earlier a US Forest Service employee had been charged with setting Colorado's Hayman Fire.

▸ In Yokohama, Japan, Brazil defeats Germany 2–0 to win the World Cup association football (soccer) championship; Ronaldo, who scores both goals, is named most valuable player of the World Cup.

Disasters

Listed here are major disasters between July 2001 and June 2002. The list includes natural and nonmilitary mechanical disasters that claimed 15 or more lives and/or resulted in significant damage to property.

July 2001

3 Jul Near Irkutsk, Russia. An airliner en route from Yekaterinburg in the Ural Mountains to the eastern port city of Vladivostok with 145 persons aboard goes down in a Siberian forest, the disaster is blamed on pilot error; there are no survivors.

early Jul Southern Taiwan, northern Philippines, and Guangdong province, China. Typhoon Utor wreaks havoc in lands touching the South China Sea. The storm kills 1 person in Taiwan, at least 121 persons in the Philippines, and 23 persons in Guangdong.

15 Jul South Korea. A tropical storm—described as the worst to have hit the country in 37 years—sweeps across South Korea, setting off landslides and flooding that leave at least 40 persons dead and 14 missing. Some 34,000 homes are flooded in Seoul and the surrounding area.

17 Jul Shanghai. A massive crane topples over at a shipbuilding plant; at least 36 persons are killed.

21 Jul Near Katoka, Dem. Rep. of the Congo. An overcrowded ferry capsizes in a whirlpool on the Kasai River; some 60 persons drown; the accident occurs at night, and the boat captain who is piloting the craft reportedly is drunk.

22 Jul Off the coast of Karachi, Pakistan. A boat described as old and in poor condition capsizes on the Arabian Sea; 19 family members die.

22 Jul Xuzhou, China. An explosion occurs at a coal mine that had reopened illegally after having been shut down only a month before; 92 miners die.

23 Jul Mansehra, Swat, and Buner districts, Pakistan. Monsoonal rains trigger a series of flash floods that claim the lives of at least 150 persons and wash away hundreds of houses.

24 Jul Near Jinju, South Korea. A tourist bus strikes a telephone pole and plunges down a steep hill; 18 persons are killed, and 25 are injured.

24 Jul Punjab state, India. A bus topples from a road into an irrigation canal after its brakes fail; at least 22 persons are feared dead.

late Jul Southeastern Poland. Heavy flooding and thunderstorms devastate the region. By 26 July, when the Vistula River overflows its banks, at least 26 persons had died.

30 Jul Hua-lien and Nan-t'ou counties, Taiwan. Typhoon Toraji rips through the area, bringing heavy rains that set off landslides and flash floods; by the time the storm recedes, 77 persons have been killed, and 133 are missing and presumed dead.

August 2001

1 Aug Nias Island, Indonesia. Massive landslides and floods strike the island following days of torrential rains; more than 70 persons are confirmed dead, and at least 100 are missing.

6 Aug Erwady, India. A fire at a mental asylum kills at least 26 persons, many of whom had reportedly been chained to their beds; it was unclear what started the blaze.

9 Aug Dhaka, Bangladesh. A faulty fire alarm at a garment factory triggers a stampede; 16 workers, most of them women, are crushed to death in a stairwell; 50 are injured.

10–12 Aug Northeastern Iran. The worst flooding in the region in 200 years inflicts widespread damage. According to figures announced on state television, 181 persons are known to have died, and at least 168 are missing. Some 10,000 persons are displaced by the disaster, which causes an estimated $25 million in damage.

11 Aug Northern Thailand. Flash floods in the mountains of Phetchabun province follow heavy rains and claim the lives of at least 86 persons.

12 Aug Eastern Zambia. A crowded bus overturns and crashes into a ditch, killing at least 38 persons.

15 Aug Near Nairobi, Kenya. An overloaded minibus swerved from a road to avoid hitting another vehicle and plunges into the Mwania River; 23 persons die.

16 Aug Katpadi, India. An accidental explosion at a government-run dynamite factory claims the lives of at least 25 persons and seriously injures 3.

16 Aug Ujani, India. An express train bound for Mumbai (Bombay) strikes and kills 15 persons between stations at Bodhwad and Achaigaon.

18 Aug Quezon City, Philippines. Fire sweeps through a six-story hotel, killing at least 73 persons, many of whom are trapped by security bars on the windows of their rooms; 51 persons are injured. The fire is caused by a short circuit in the ceiling of a stockroom; the hotel's owner, who had been cited for safety violations, is later charged with reckless endangerment.

18 Aug Southern Iran. A head-on collision between a bus and a truck on a highway between Kerman and Sirjan claims the lives of 30 persons and injures at least 20.

19 Aug Donetsk, Ukraine. A methane gas explosion rips through the Zasyadko coal mine, igniting a raging fire and trapping workers; at least 47 miners die and 44 are injured.

21 Aug Near San Nicolas de los Arroyos, Argentina. Some 20 persons are killed when a bus slams into the back of a truck, reportedly after the driver of the bus falls asleep at the wheel.

26 Aug Northern Nigeria. A speeding bus blows a tire and careens off a bridge into a river; 49 persons perish.

late Aug Near Yamoussoukro, Côte d'Ivoire. At least 27 persons die after drinking corn broth contaminated with rat poison; the woman who sold the broth is detained and could face manslaughter charges, but officials describe the poisoning as accidental.

late Aug Nepal. Heavy rains bring on flash floods and landslides across the country; at least 28 persons lose their lives.

September 2001

1 Sep Tokyo. An explosion and fire in a nightclub in the Kabukicho entertainment district claim the lives of 44 persons.

4–5 Sep Kruger National Park, South Africa. A bush fire of unknown origins sweeps through the park, killing 15 villagers and 4 game rangers who are trying to rescue them.

11 Sep Two passenger aircraft leaving Boston's Logan International Airport loaded with fuel for transcontinental flights are hijacked by terrorists and deliberately crashed into the twin towers of the World Trade Center in New York City, killing all aboard as well as thousands more in the buildings, which collapse. A third hijacked airliner is crashed into the Pentagon, the seat of the US military, near Washington DC, while in a fourth, apparently targeted at the Capitol or the White House, a struggle between passengers and hijackers causes the plane to crash near Shanksville PA. In the four aircraft 266 persons die. The total toll on the ground is set at 189 at the Pentagon and as many as 2,550 in lower Manhattan. (See **Chronology** for a timeline of the tragedy.)

12 Sep Mérida, Mexico. A charter plane carrying tourists from a cruise ship to see ancient Mayan ruins crashes shortly after takeoff; 19 persons die, including 16 Americans.

mid-Sep Southern Estonia. About 60 persons die after drinking illegally brewed vodka—contaminated with methyl alcohol—that was being sold in the resort city of Parnu.

16–19 Sep Taiwan. Typhoon Nari pummels the north of the island; flooding, mud slides, and power outages result; at least 94 persons die, including 25 in Taipei.

21 Sep Toulouse, France. A massive explosion at an industrial plant leaves a 15-m (50-ft) crater at the site and claims the lives of at least 29 persons and injures some 2,000; officials state that the blast was likely an accident.

29 Sep Northern Iran. A bus collides head-on with another bus and plummets into an Alborz mountain valley; 20 persons die.

October 2001

4 Oct Over the Black Sea. A Russian airliner en route from Tel Aviv, Israel, to Novosibirsk, Russia, explodes in midair and crashes in the Black Sea, killing all 78 persons aboard the craft. Initial suspicions of terrorism are discounted; the Ukrainian government later acknowledges that a stray surface-to-air missile fired during a Ukrainian air defense exercise had caused the explosion. Ukrainian Defense Minister Oleksandr Kuzmuk resigns over the incident.

8 Oct Milan. A Scandinavian Airlines System passenger jet taking off for Copenhagen from Milan's Linate Airport collides with a small private plane in heavy fog and explodes; 118 persons are killed, including all 114 persons aboard the two planes and 4 airport workers. Investigators blame the absence of ground-level radar at the airport in part. It is Italy's worst aviation disaster.

8–9 Oct Southern Belize. Hurricane Iris—described as the worst storm to hit the country in 40 years—devastates much of the southern region; 22 persons die, at least 3,000 houses are destroyed, and some 12,000 persons are left homeless.

10 Oct Near Calama, Chile. A bus carrying workers to a copper mine collides head-on with a truck, killing 22 persons and injuring 21; a plane carrying investigators to the site also crashes, killing 6.

17 Oct Southern India. A strong storm pummels towns along the coast, killing at least 31 persons, including 16 in Kurnool.

19 Oct Java Sea. An overcrowded fishing boat en route from the Indonesian island of Sumatra to Australia with some 400 illegal immigrants aboard breaks apart and sinks; only 44 persons are rescued.

late Oct Buenavista, Philippines. A bus slams into a house where mourners are gathered for a vigil; at least 21 persons die.

November 2001

early Nov Karnataka state, India. A head-on collision between two trucks claims the lives of at least 22 persons and injures 37.

7 Nov Southern and central Philippines. Tropical Storm Lingling batters the regions, triggering flash floods and uprooting trees with winds as strong as 90 km/h (56 mph); particularly hard hit is the island of Camiguin, where hundreds are forced to flee their homes; at least 68 persons are killed, and dozens are missing.

9 Nov Kerala state, India. A landslide in the village of Amboori claims the lives of approximately 50 persons.

9–17 Nov Northern Algeria. Torrential rain produces heavy flooding in the region; the official death toll is 750 persons, most of whom die in the Bab el Oued neighborhood of Algiers; some 24,000 persons are left homeless, and at least 1,500 houses are destroyed in the capital alone.

12 Nov New York City. American Airlines Flight 587 crashes on takeoff from John F. Kennedy International Airport; the plane, which is headed to Santo Domingo, Dominican Republic, loses its tail in midair and goes down in the borough of Queens, striking several buildings; 260 persons die, including all 255 persons aboard the plane and 5 on the ground. Although no evidence points to terrorism, investigators at year's end are still trying to determine why the tail sheared off the plane.

14 Nov Near Huelva, Spain. A bus carrying retirees on an excursion to caves in the area crashes after the driver loses control of the vehicle on a curve in the road; 19 persons die, and 14 are injured.

16–17 Nov Florida Straits. A twin-engine speedboat carrying some 30 Cubans intent on illegally entering the US capsizes; the US Coast Guard later recovers the boat but no bodies.

18 Nov Lake Tanganyika, Dem. Rep. of the Congo. A collision between two boats as one is preparing to leave shore and another to dock claims the lives of at least 19 persons.

18 Nov Angash, Peru. A bus falls from a mountain road in the central Andes 183 m (600 ft) into a ravine; at least 25 persons die, and 20 are injured.

22 Nov Filadelfia, Colombia. A landslide buries a group of gold miners digging illegally at a condemned mine; about 80 persons are killed, and dozens are missing and feared dead.

24 Nov Near Zürich, Switzerland. A Swiss airplane en route from Berlin to Zürich crashes in a wooded area after encountering some rain and snow as it is making its approach to land; 24 of the 33 persons aboard the plane die.

late Nov Sulawesi Utara province, Indonesia. At least 27 persons die and at least 4 are hospitalized after they drink contaminated homemade liquor.

29 Nov Near Bhola, Bangladesh. A ferryboat sinks on the Tetulia River after colliding with a larger vessel; around 90 persons are missing and feared drowned.

late Nov–early Dec Tamil Nadu state, India. At least 50 persons are reported dead by 1 December from drinking contaminated homemade liquor.

December 2001

2 Dec Near Okhotsk, Russia. A cargo plane crashes following a fire aboard the aircraft; as many as 18 persons are feared killed.

8 Dec Near Taloqan, Afghanistan. Bad weather conditions are blamed in the crash of a helicopter carrying Northern Alliance commandos and captured Taliban fighters; 21 persons die.

14 Dec Southern Jordan. A bus loaded with Muslim pilgrims returning home from Mecca crashes through the fence of a truck depot, slams into other vehicles, and explodes into flames; the driver apparently loses control of the vehicle after a brake failure; all 52 persons aboard the bus die.

16 Dec Near Medellín, Colombia. A small plane crashes in a mountainous area shortly after taking off in rainy weather; all 16 persons aboard die.

17 Dec Southern Italy. A state-run home for the disabled in a remote area of the Apennine Mountains is destroyed in a blaze started by an electrical short circuit; 19 patients are killed; authorities later acknowledge that the home was constructed of flammable material and should have been torn down.

25 Dec Brebes, Indonesia. A head-on collision between two passenger trains crowded with holiday travelers claims the lives of at least 42 persons after the driver of one of the trains reportedly falls asleep and speeds past a stop signal.

late Dec Rio de Janeiro state, Brazil. Torrential rains and mud slides claim the lives of at least 52 persons; more than 30 are missing, and some 2,000 are forced to abandon their homes.

29 Dec Lima, Peru. An explosion at a fireworks shop ignites a blaze that sweeps through a crowded commercial center in Lima's historic district; the explosion is thought to have been caused by a fireworks demonstration that went out of control; at least 290 persons are killed.

30 Dec Jiangxi province, China. An explosion at a fireworks factory destroys a warehouse and 10 workshops; more than 40 persons die.

31 Dec Mpumalanga, South Africa. A truck carrying more than 100 family members on an annual pilgrimage to their ancestral burial ground overturns on a steep gravel road; at least 48 persons die.

January 2002

7 Jan Northern Nigeria. A head-on collision between a bus and a minibus on a road in the village of Durbunde claims the lives of some 50 persons, many of them members of a wedding party.

7 Jan Near Dhaka, Bangladesh. A speeding bus overturns and lands in a water-filled ditch; nearly 30 persons are believed killed.

early Jan Dem. Rep. of the Congo. Heavy rains trigger the collapse of a coltan mine; at least 30 miners are killed.

14 Jan Yunnan and Hunan provinces, China. At least 43 miners die in two separate disasters. A gas explosion in an unlicensed coal pit in Yunnan claims the lives of 25 miners. In Hunan, at least 18 miners are believed to have suffocated following a gas explosion.

17–19 Jan Goma, Dem. Rep. of the Congo. The Mount Nyiragongo volcano 19 km (12 mi) north of Goma erupts, and a river of lava some 50 m (165 ft) wide rolls through the city; hundreds of thousands of persons in the area are displaced, and at least 45 die.

21 Jan Goma. Hot lava sets off an explosion at a gas station in the center of the city; some 50 persons who are looting fuel at the station are killed.

27 Jan Lagos, Nigeria. A fire at a military arms depot sets off a series of huge explosions; bombs, shells, and rockets career into heavily populated neighborhoods, causing thousands of residents to flee their homes; more than 1,000 persons die, many of whom are trampled to death or drowned while trying to cross two canals to safety; government officials maintain that the fire at the arms depot was accidental and not the result of sabotage.

27 Jan Southern Philippines. After experiencing engine trouble and encountering rough seas in the area, a ferry with some 70 persons aboard loses contact with coast guard officials; the boat is presumed to have sunk, and there are no signs of survivors.

late Jan Europe. Winds approaching 200 km/h (120 mph) wreak havoc across the continent. At least 18 persons die, including 8 in Britain, 4 in Poland, and 3 in Germany. Hundreds of thousands are left without electricity, and travel is brought to a standstill in many areas.

28 Jan Southern Colombia. An Ecuadorean airliner reportedly flying in heavy mist crashes on the slopes of the Nevado de Cumbal volcano; all 92 persons aboard the plane are killed.

28 & 31 Jan Central and Southwestern China. A total of 14 miners die in a gas explosion at a coal mine in Hengyang on January 28. Three days later a natural gas leak at a coal mine near the southwestern city of Chongqing causes 13 miners to suffocate; another 8 are missing.

February 2002

Feb Java, Indonesia. Weeks of heavy rains trigger floods and landslides on the island; at least 150 persons perish.

3 Feb Central Turkey. An earthquake of magnitude 6.0 jolts the region; at least 43 persons die, more than 300 others are injured, and some 600 buildings are destroyed.

5 Feb KwaZulu Natal province, South Africa. A collision between a crowded passenger train and a stationary freight train claims the lives of 24 persons, as many as 18 of whom are schoolchildren; cables used in the railroad's signaling system reportedly were vandalized and stolen shortly before the disaster.

6 Feb Northern Afghanistan. During a blizzard, an avalanche of snow blocks an entrance to the Salang Tunnel some 130 km (80 mi) north of Kabul; 4 persons are killed.

12 Feb Western Iran. An Iranian airliner flying in bad weather conditions with 119 persons aboard crashes in mountains near the city of Khorramabad; there are no survivors.

13 Feb Eastern Saudi Arabia. A collision between a bus and a truck on a road near the Saudi–United Arab Emirates border claims the lives of some 40 persons and injures 10 others. The bus was carrying Muslims to Mecca on the annual pilgrimage known as the hajj.

mid-Feb Peru. At least 38 persons die in separate traffic disasters. A bus traveling to Desaguadero in the south of the country overturns, and at least 23 persons are killed. In the northeastern province of Ancash, a truck overturns, killing 15.

18 Feb Tangshan, China. A fire, probably caused by an electrical short circuit, destroys an illegal videogame parlor; at least 17 persons die.

19 Feb La Paz, Bolivia. A devastating storm—the most destructive in the history of the Bolivian capital—sets off a series of flash floods and mud slides; 69 persons die, at least 100 are injured, and hundreds are left homeless.

19 Feb Chitwan, Nepal. A passenger bus en route from Kathmandu to Dhankuta falls from a highway into a stream; at least 40 persons perish.

20 Feb Near Cairo. In what is described as the worst rail disaster in Egypt's history, a fire sweeps through an overcrowded train en route from Cairo to Luxor; the blaze engulfs seven cars before conductors are able to detach them from the rest of the train; initial reports that an electrical short circuit started the fire are later refuted by investigators' conclusions that flames from a small stove sparked the blaze; 363 persons perish.

21 Feb Near Arkhangelsk, Russia. A military cargo plane crashes while attempting to make an emergency landing; 17 persons die, most of them Russian naval officers.

25 Feb Damietta, Egypt. An aging residential building collapses, claiming the lives of 22 persons.

March 2002

3 Mar Northern Afghanistan. A magnitude 7.2 earthquake shears off a cliff in the Hindu Kush mountains north of Kabul; the ensuing avalanche buries a village and claims the lives of at least 100 persons.

6 Mar Andhra Pradesh, India. An explosion at a warehouse kills some 20 persons. The blast reportedly occurs as explosives are being unloaded at the warehouse.

7 Mar Off the coast of the island of Lampedusa, Italy. An overcrowded wooden boat capsizes about 105 km (65 mi) south of Lampedusa, between Tunisia and Sicily; the boat had been packed with passengers reportedly from North Africa and intent on entering Italy illegally; at least 50 persons perish.

11 Mar Mecca, Saudi Arabia. A fire breaks out in a four-story building that houses a girls' school; 15 students die, most of them as they stampede to escape the blaze. Reports that Saudi religious police, or *mutaween,* had prevented some girls from leaving the school because they were not wearing proper Islamic dress provoke harsh public criticism of the *mutaween.*

11 Mar Near Chongqing, China. An explosion on a bus claims the lives of 21 persons; the bus is believed to have been illegally transporting fireworks.

13 Mar Chincha, Peru. A bus runs off a rain-slickened highway, crashes into a gas station, and explodes in flames; at least 35 persons die.

14 Mar Baez, Cuba. A single-engine charter plane crashes into a pond, reportedly after one of the plane's wings breaks off; at least 16 persons are killed.

14 Mar Lucknow, India. Thousands of people are standing in line at a job recruitment center when a sewer drain collapses and the ground gives way beneath about 100 of them; at least 23 persons die.

25-26 Mar Northern Afghanistan. An earthquake of magnitude 6.1 and as many as six aftershocks jolt the region; the city of Nahrin and numerous mountain villages are destroyed; 2,000 persons die, and some 4,000 are injured.

27 Mar Dubai, UAE. Gates collapse at a dry dock, allowing sea water to flood the dock and submerge a number of ships under repair; 22 persons are killed, and 7 are missing and feared dead.

April 2002

Early Apr Gulf of Aden. A boat en route from Somalia to Yemen sinks in rough seas; more than 90 persons die.

Early Apr Jiangxi province, China. An explosion occurs while maintenance is performed at a coal mine; 16 miners die.

2 Apr Morobe province, Papua New Guinea. A landslide hits two villages in the province, killing 36 persons; another 28 are missing and feared dead.

6-7 Apr Off the coast of southern Nigeria. A boat loaded with passengers and goods sinks between Port Harcourt and Nember, apparently after a leak develops and the boat's water pump fails; some 40 persons are feared dead.

9 Apr Heilongjiang province, China. Two explosions occur at different mines in the same city, Jixi, on the same day. In the largest blast, 24 miners are killed and 40 injured at a coal mine. In the second incident, also at a coal mine, 7 miners die and 4 are missing.

11 Apr Central Philippines. A fire breaks out on a ferry traveling between the island of Mascate and the port city of Lucena, forcing passengers to jump overboard; 23 persons are confirmed dead, and 32 are missing.

11 Apr Central Tanzania. A ferry, possibly overloaded, capsizes on the Kilombero River near the town of Mahenge; at least 38 persons die.

12 Apr Northern Afghanistan. A magnitude-5.8 earthquake strikes the mountainous Hindu Kush region; two villages, Doabi and Khoja Khesir, are devastated; at least 30 persons die and some 100 others are injured.

12 Apr West Bengal state, India. A high-speed collision between a truck and a bus claims the lives of 21 persons and injures 15.

15 Apr Near Busan, South Korea. An Air China Boeing 767 en route from Beijing to Busan slams into a hill while making its approach to land in rainy and foggy conditions; 39 of the reported 166 passengers and crew members aboard the plane survive the crash.

22 & 24 Apr Southwest China. A total of 11 miners are confirmed dead and 4 are missing in a gas explosion at a mine in Chongqing province on April 22. Two days later a gas explosion at a coal mine in Sichuan province kills 23 miners.

23 Apr Central Russia. A steamroller falls from a truck onto a bus that the truck is passing; at least 15 persons on the bus are killed.

26 Apr KwaZulu-Natal province, South Africa. After one of its tires bursts, a bus overturns and rolls down a cliff; at least 22 persons die, and more than 45 are injured.

May 2002

3 May Southeastern Bangladesh. A ferry sinks during a rainstorm on the Meghna River, killing at least 271 persons.

4 May Near Kano, Nigeria. An airliner en route from Kano to Lagos crashes in a heavily populated suburb shortly after takeoff; at least 148 persons die, including 76 persons aboard the plane.

7 May Near Dalian, China. A China Northern Airlines

MD-82 jet goes down in the Bo Hai Sea, apparently after a fire had broken out in the plane's cabin; all 112 persons aboard the aircraft perish.

7 May Near Tunis, Tunisia. An EgyptAir Boeing 737-500 flying through fog, rain, and sandy wind blowing from the Sahara Desert crashes on a hillside while attempting to land; 18 persons are killed, and 25 are injured.

9–15 May Andhra Pradesh state, India. An unusually intense heat wave claims the lives of at least 1,030 persons in the southern Indian state.

12 May Off the coast of Birilan island, Philippines. A ferry overturns and sinks after passengers, seeking shade, gather on one side of the vessel; 19 persons perish.

20 May Lake Victoria. A boat returning to the mainland of Uganda from Kalangala Island experiences engine failure, then capsizes and sinks; 27 persons are feared dead.

24 May Northern India. An electrical short-circuit ignites a fire that sweeps through a shoe factory in Agra, leaving at least 40 persons dead.

25 May Southern Mozambique. Two passenger cars of a train are entirely destroyed when they slam into freight cars parked at a rail station near the town of Moamba; 196 persons are killed, and hundreds more are injured. It is Mozambique's worst-ever rail disaster.

26 May Near Tacna, Peru. A truck loaded with passengers and farm produce experiences brake failure before crashing into a house and overturning; at least 21 persons perish.

26 May Near Webbers Falls OK. An interstate highway bridge over the Arkansas River collapses after a barge being pushed by a towboat slams into one of the bridge's supports; at least 10 vehicles crossing the bridge plummet into the river. There are 14 confirmed deaths. The pilot of the towboat apparently blacked out just prior to the accident.

26 May Off the coast of Taiwan. A China Airlines Boeing 747 bound for Hong Kong from Taipei with 225 persons aboard splits into four pieces over the Taiwan Strait; there are no survivors.

June 2002

Jun Southern Russia. Floods wreak havoc in the regions of Stavropol and Krasnodar and in the republics of Karachayevo-Cherkessia, North Ossetia, Ingushetia, and Chechnya. By June 24 some 70 villages are under water. At least 53 persons are confirmed dead, and 75,000 others are homeless.

Early Jun Northeastern Nigeria. A heat wave claims the lives of more than 60 persons in the city of Maiduguri in Borno state.

Early Jun Saudi Arabia. At least 19 persons die from methanol poisoning after drinking cologne as a substitute for alcohol; 11 of the deaths occur in Mecca, the others in Jizan province.

2 Jun Near Ndalatando, Angola. A military helicopter crashes in bad weather; 20 persons die, including Lt.-Gen. José Domingues Ngueto, commander of the Kwanza-Bengo region.

4 Jun Uttar Pradesh state, India. An express train en route from Kanpur to Kasganj strikes a bus at a railroad crossing, throwing the bus into a canal; 34 persons die; a gatekeeper at the crossing reportedly failed to lower a gate as the train approached.

4–5 Jun Northwestern Syria. The Zeyzoun Dam, near the town of Hamah, collapses after weeks of heavy rains in the area; several villages are flooded, and at least 28 persons are killed.

Early to mid-Jun Northwestern China. Torrential rains produce widespread flooding in the region; more than 200 persons die, including at least 152 in the worst-hit province, Shaanxi.

10 Jun Near Masvingo, Zimbabwe. A collision between a bus and a truck claims the lives of at least 36 persons, most of them students.

11 Jun Riau province, Indonesia. A passenger boat sinks in bad weather on the Kampar River on the island of Sumatra; 2 persons die, and 20 others are missing and feared dead.

11 Jun Rutana province, Burundi. A UN-chartered truck transporting Burundian refugees home from Tanzania crashes after running off a road; 41 persons die, and 40 are injured.

Mid-Jun Northern Egypt. Two trucks collide on a highway between Cairo and Alexandria; 19 persons—all of them farm workers on their way to pick apricots—lose their lives, and 49 others are injured.

16 Jun Beijing, China. A late-night fire engulfs an unlicensed Internet cafe in the city's university district; 24 persons are killed, and 13 are injured.

20 Jun Heilongjiang province, China. A massive gas explosion at a coal mine claims the lives of at least 111 miners.

20 Jun Mererani, Tanzania. An oxygen pump fails at a tanzanite mine, causing the deaths of 42 miners working some 125 m (410 ft) underground.

22 Jun Northwestern Iran. An earthquake of magnitude 6.0 strikes an area between the cities of Qazvin and Hamadan and is followed by more than 20 aftershocks. At least 220 persons are killed, and 1,300 are injured. As many as 100 villages may be flattened.

24 Jun Central Tanzania. A passenger train experiences mechanical failure and careens backward down a hill until it slams into an oncoming cargo train; at least 230 persons die, and as many as 800 are injured.

Personalities

Celebrities & Newsmakers

These mini-biographies are intended to provide backgound information about people in the news. See also the Obituaries (below) for recently deceased persons as well as the presidential biographies and the special Britannica lists: Most Influential Leaders of All Time, All-Time Greatest Authors, and Top Figures in Sports History elsewhere in the Britannica Almanac.

Claudio Abbado (26 Jun 1933, Milan, Italy) Italian orchestra conductor; principal conductor and artistic director of the Berlin Philharmonic, 1990/91–2001/02.

King Abdullah II (Abdallah ibn al-Hussein al-Hashimi; 30 Jan 1962, Amman, Jordan) Jordanian royal; king of Jordan from 1999.

Spencer Abraham (12 Jun 1952, East Lansing MI) American government official; US Secretary of Energy from January 2001.

'Abu Nidal (Sabri I-Banna; May 1937, Jaffa, British Palestine [now Tel Aviv Yafo, Israel]—found dead 19 Aug 2002, Baghdad, Iraq), Palestinian militant leader of the Fatah Revolutionary Council, more commonly known as the Abu Nidal Organization (ANO), or Abu Nidal Group, which engaged in numerous acts of terrorism beginning in the mid-1970s.

Nasr Hamid Abu Zayd (7 Oct 1943, Tanta, Egypt) Egyptian scholar and religious reformer.

Abdulsalam Abubakar (13 Jun 1942, Minna, Nigeria) Nigerian military officer and president of Nigeria, 1998–99.

Salvatore Accardo (26 Sep 1941, Torin, Italy) Italian violinist and conductor.

Josef ("Joe") Ackermann (7 Feb 1948, Mels, St. Gallen, Switzerland) Swiss corporate executive; CEO of Deutsche Bank AG from 1997.

Eddie Fennech Adami (7 Feb 1934, Birkirkara, Malta) Maltese politician and prime minister of Malta, 1987–96 and again from 1998.

Valdas V. Adamkus (Valdas V. Adamkevicius; 3 Nov 1926, Kaunas, Lithuania) Lithuanian politician and president of Lithuania from 1998.

Bryan (Guy) Adams (5 Nov 1959, Kingston, ON, Canada) Canadian rock musician.

Gerry Adams (Gerard Adams; 6 Oct 1948, Belfast, Northern Ireland) Northern Irish resistance leader; president of Sinn Féin, the political wing of the Irish Republican Army.

John Coolidge Adams (15 Feb 1947, Worcester MA) American composer who works in a wide range of genres and is noted for the operas Nixon in China (1987) and The Death of Klinghoffer (1991).

Scott Adams (8 Jun 1957, Windham NY) American cartoonist, creator of Dilbert.

Victoria (Caroline) Adams (7 Apr 1975, Hertfordshire, England) British pop singer ("Posh Spice" of Spice Girls), also known for her marriage to footballer David Beckham.

Thomas Adès (1971, London, England) English composer, pianist, and conductor.

Ben Affleck (Benjamin Geza Affleck; 15 Aug 1972, Berkeley CA) American actor, director, and writer known for commercially successful films.

Isaias Afwerki (2 Feb 1946, Asmara, Ethiopia [now Eritrea]) Eritrean Independence leader, secretary-general of the Provisional Government and first president of Eritrea (from 1993).

Andre (Kirk) Agassi (29 Apr 1970, Las Vegas NV) American tennis player who holds the record for career Grand Slam wins: Wimbledon (1992), US Open (1994, 1999), Australian Open (1995, 2000, 2001), and French Open (1999), and won an Olympic gold medal (1996).

Mehmet Ali Agca (9 Jan 1958, Guzelyurt, Turkey) Turkish assassin; in 2002 Agca was serving time in jail in Turkey for a murder committed before Agca attempted to assassinate Pope John Paul II (13 May 1981).

Christina Aguilera (18 Dec 1980, Staten Island NY) American pop singer.

Bartholomew Patrick ("Bertie") Ahern (12 Sep 1951, Dublin, Ireland) Irish politician; prime minister (taoiseach) of Ireland from 1997.

Martti Ahtisaari (23 Jun 1937, Viipuri, Finland [now Vyborg, Russia]) Finnish statesman and diplomat; president of Finland, 1994–2000.

Askar Akayev (10 Nov 1944, Kyzyl-Bairak village, Kemin district, Kirghiz SSR, USSR [now Kyrgyzstan]) Kyrgyz politician; president of Kyrgyzstan from 1990.

Akebono (Chadwick Haheo Rowan; 8 May 1969, near Honolulu HI) American sumo wrestler, first non-Japanese yokozuna (grand champion), 1993.

George A. Akerlof (17 Jun 1940, New Haven CT) American economist; co-winner of the Nobel Prize in Economic Sciences, 2001, for work in the theory of markets with asymmetrical information.

Emperor Akihito (original name Tsugu Akihito; era name Heisei; 23 Dec 1933, Tokyo, Japan) Japanese royal; emperor of Japan from 1989.

Akil Akilov (1944, Tajikistan?) Tajik politician; prime minister of Tajikistan from 1999.

Vasily Pavlovich Aksyonov (20 Aug 1932, Kazan, Russia, USSR) Russian novelist and short-story writer.

Azzedine Alaïa (1940, Tunis, Tunisia) Tunisian-born French fashion designer known for using unusual fabrics to create body-hugging dresses.

Eddie Albert (Edward Albert Heimberger; 22 Apr 1908, Rock Island IL) American theater, film, and TV actor, best known as star of TV's Green Acres.

Prince Albert (Albert Alexandre Louis Pierre, Hereditary Prince of Monaco, Marquis of Baux; 14 Mar 1958, Monaco) Monegasque royal; heir to the throne of Monaco.

Albert II (6 Jun 1934, Brussels, Belgium) Belgian royal; king of Belgium from 1993.

Bruce Alberts (1938, Chicago IL) American biochemist and microbiologist; president of the US National Academy of Sciences from 1993.

Theo Albrecht (28 Mar 1922, Germany) German business executive; founder (with brother Karl) and CEO of the Aldi supermarket chain; among the richest men in the world.

Alan Alda (Alphonso Joseph D'Abruzzo; 28 Jan 1936, New York NY) American film and TV actor, best

known for playing Hawkeye Pierce in the TV version of *M*A*S*H**.

Edwin Eugene ("Buzz") Aldrin, Jr. (20 Jan 1930, Montclair NJ) American astronaut, the second man to set foot on the Moon.

Jane Alexander (28 Oct 1939, Boston MA) American film actress and administrator.

Jason Alexander (Jay Scott Greenspan; 23 Sep 1959, Newark NJ) American film, TV, and theater actor, best known for playing George on *Seinfeld*.

Monty Alexander (Montgomery Bernard Alexander; 6 Jun 1944, Kingston, Jamaica) Jamaican jazz pianist.

Princess Alexandra (25 Dec 1936, London, England) British royal.

Sherman J. Alexie, Jr. (7 Oct 1966, Wellpinit, Spokane Indian reservation, Washington) American poet and novelist who writes of his Native American upbringing.

Alexis II (23 Feb 1929, Tallinn, Estonia) Russian religious leader; Orthodox Patriarch of Moscow and All Russia from 1990.

Zhores Alferov (Zhores Ivanovich Alfyorov; 15 Mar 1930, Vitebsk, Belorussia, USSR [now Belarus]) Russian physicist; Nobel Prize for Physics, 2000, for work in developing electronic components made from semiconductor heterostructures.

Princess Alice (Lady Alice Christabel Montagu Douglas Scott; 25 Dec 1901, Montagu House, London, England) British royal; Duchess of Gloucester; widow of the Duke of Gloucester.

Heydar Aliyev (Geidar Ali Reza ogly Aliev; 10 May 1923, Nakhichevan, Khanate of Nakhichevan) Azerbaijani politician; first president of independent Azerbaijan, from 1993.

Mari Alkatiri (26 Nov 1946, Dili, East Timor) Timorese politician; first prime minister of independent East Timor (from 20 May 2002).

Paul G. Allan (21 Jan 1953, Mercer Island WA) American businessman; co-founder of Microsoft Corp. (1975) and founder and CEO of Vulcan Ventures (1986).

Debbie Allen (16 Jan 1950, Houston TX) American dancer, choreographer, singer, and TV actress.

Joan Allen (20 Aug 1956, Rochelle IL) American film and theater actress known for substantive roles.

Tim Allen (Timothy Allen Dick; 13 Jun 1953, Denver CO) American TV and film actor and comedian, best known as Tim "The Toolman" Taylor on TV's *Home Improvement*.

Woody Allen (Allen Stewart Konigsberg; 1 Dec 1935, New York NY) American filmmaker, actor, and comedian best known for absurdly comic but sympathetic works.

Isabel Allende (2 Aug 1942, Lima, Peru) Chilean writer in the magic realist tradition who is considered one of the first successful women novelists in Latin America.

Mose Allison (Mose John Allison, Jr.; 11 Nov 1927, Tippo MS) American jazz pianist, singer, and composer.

June Allyson (Ella Geisman; 7 Oct 1917, Bronx NY) American film, stage, and TV actress famous for cheerful, wholesome roles.

Pedro Almodóvar (24 Sep 1949, Calzada de Calatrava, Spain) Spanish film director specializing in film noir; his first success was *Women on the Verge of a Nervous Breakdown* (1988).

Lincoln Almond (16 Jun 1936, Central Falls RI) American Republican politician; governor of Rhode Island from January 1995.

Alicia Alonso (Alicia Ernestina de la Caridad del Cobre Martínez Hoyo; 21 Dec 1921, Havana, Cuba) Cuban ballerina and ballet mistress; director of the National Ballet of Cuba.

Carol Alt (1 Dec 1960, New York NY) American fashion model who appeared on hundreds of magazine covers, then became an actress in Italy.

Robert Altman (20 Feb 1925, Kansas City MO) American filmmaker noted for his unconventional and independent style.

Christiane Amanpour (1958, London, England) American TV news reporter.

Jacques d' Amboise (28 Jul 1934, Dedham MA) American dancer and choreographer of the New York City Ballet (1949–84), admired for his energetic, virile interpretations of both character and classical roles.

Stephen E. Ambrose (10 Jan 1936, Decatur IL) American historian and author of best-selling books.

Martin (Louis) Amis (25 Aug 1949, Oxford, England) English satirist known for his virtuoso storytelling technique and his dark views of 20th-century English society.

Tori Amos (Myra Ellen Amos; 22 Aug 1963, Newton NC) American pop and rock singer.

David Amram (17 Nov 1930, Philadelphia PA) American composer and instrumentalist.

Viswanathan Anand ("Vishy"; 11 Dec 1969, Madras [now Chennai], India) Indian chess grandmaster, won the FIDE world championship in December 2000.

Gillian Anderson (9 Aug 1968, Chicago IL) American TV and film actress, best known as Agent Dana Scully on TV's *The X-Files*.

Jack Anderson (19 Oct 1922, Long Beach CA) American journalist, columnist, and author.

Pamela (Denise) Anderson (1 Jul 1967, Ladysmith, BC, Canada) Canadian-born model, actress.

Rocky Anderson (1951, Logan UT) American politician; mayor of Salt Lake City UT from 2000.

Tadao Ando (1941, Osaka, Japan) Japanese architect; winner of the Pritzker Prize in 1995.

Maurice André (21 May 1933, Alès, near Nîmes, France) French trumpet player.

Marc Andreeson (1972?, New Lisbon WI?) American computer innovator, co-founder (1994) of Mosaic Communications Corp., and developer of Netscape.

Prince Andrew (19 Feb 1960, Buckingham Palace, London, England) British royal; Duke of York; second son of Queen Elizabeth II and Prince Philip, Duke of Edinburgh.

Julie Andrews (Julia Elizabeth Wells; 1 Oct 1935, Walton-on-Thames, England) British stage and screen actress and singer, best known for *Mary Poppins* (1964) and *The Sound of Music* (1965).

Maya Angelou (Marguerite Johnson; 4 Apr 1928, St. Louis MO) American poet whose several volumes of autobiography explore the themes of economic, racial, and sexual oppression.

Jennifer Aniston (Jennifer Linn Anistassakis; 11 Feb 1969, Sherman Oaks CA) American TV and film actress who stars as Rachel in TV's *Friends*.

Paul Anka (30 Jul 1941, Ottawa, ON, Canada) Canadian pop singer and composer.

Ann-Margret (Ann-Margret Olsson; 28 Apr 1941, Stockholm, Sweden) Swedish-born American film actress and dancer.

Princess Anne (15 Aug 1950, Clarence House, London, England) British royal; the Princess Royal; daughter of Queen Elizabeth II and Prince Philip, Duke of Edinburgh.

Walter H. Annenberg (13 Mar 1908, Milwaukee WI) American publisher, philanthropist, and art collector; US ambassador to Britain 1969–74.

Kenny D. Anthony (8 Jan 1951, Saint Lucia) West Indian politician; prime minister of Saint Lucia from 1997.

Marc Anthony (Marco Antonio Muñiz; 16 Sep 1968, Spanish Harlem, New York NY) American salsa singer.

Severino Antinori (c. 1945, Rome, Italy) Italian gynecologist and specialist in human fertility; leader of a project to clone humans.

Michelangelo Antonioni (29 Sep 1912, Ferrara, Italy) Italian film director, cinematographer, and producer.

Fiona Apple (Fiona Apple Maggart; 13 Sep 1977, New York NY) American singer and pianist noted for her introspective lyrics.

(Maria) Corazon Aquino (25 Jan 1933, Manila, Philippines) Philippine political leader and president of the Philippines, 1986–92.

Yasir 'Arafat (Muhammad 'Abd ar-Ra'uf al-Qudwah al-Husayni 'Arafat; 24? Aug 1929, Cairo, Egypt?) Palestinian statesman; president (from 1996) of the Palestinian Authority [see also Most Influential Leaders of All Time].

Jeffrey (Howard) Archer (15 Apr 1940, London, England) British Conservative Party leader and novelist.

Vladislav Ardzinba (1945, Abkhazia?, Georgian SSR, USSR) Georgian politician; chairman of parliament of Georgia's secessionist republic of Abkhazia from 1990.

Martha Argerich (5 Jun 1941, Buenos Aires, Argentina) Argentine concert pianist.

Oscar Arias Sánchez (13 Sep 1941, Heredia, Costa Rica) Costa Rican politician and president of Costa Rica (1986–90); Nobel Peace Prize, 1987.

Jean-Bertrand Aristide (15 Jul 1953, Port Salut, Haiti) Haitian politician; president of Haiti 1991, 1993–94 (in exile) 1994–96, and from 2001.

Alan Arkin (26 Mar 1934, New York NY) American wry, deadpan actor; breakthrough role in The Russians Are Coming, The Russians Are Coming (1966).

Roone Arledge (8 Jul 1931, Forest Hills NY) American TV executive.

Giorgio Armani (11 Jul 1934, Piacenza, Italy) Italian fashion designer whose signature style is relaxed yet luxurious ready-to-wear and elegant evening wear.

Joan Armatrading (9 Dec 1950, Basseterre, Saint Kitts, West Indies) West Indian singer and songwriter.

Richard K. Armey (7 Jul 1940, Cando ND) American politician and congressman; House majority leader.

C. Michael Armstrong (18 Oct 1938, Detroit MI) American corporate executive; CEO of AT&T from 1997.

Lance Armstrong (18 Sep 1971, Plano TX) American cyclist, won the Tour de France four times (1999, 2000, 2001, 2002) after recovering from cancer in the mid-1990s.

Neil (Alden) Armstrong (5 Aug 1930, Wapakoneta OH) American astronaut, the first man to set foot on the Moon.

Tom Arnold (6 Mar 1959, Ottumwa IA) American TV actor and producer, best known for supporting comic roles.

Gerald Arpino (14 Jan 1928, Staten Island NY) American ballet choreographer, a leader of the Joffrey Ballet from its founding in 1956.

Courteney Cox Arquette (15 Jun 1964, Birmingham AL) American TV and film actress, currently featured on TV's Friends.

Beatrice Arthur (Bernice Frankel; 13 May 1926, New York NY) American film and TV actress, known especially for the TV sitcoms Maude and The Golden Girls.

Owen Seymour Arthur (17 Oct 1949, Barbados) Barbadan politician; prime minister of Barbados from 1994.

Ashanti (Ashanti S. Douglas; 1980, Glen Cove NY) American hip-hop singer.

John (Lawrence) Ashbery (28 Jul 1927, Rochester NY) American poet.

John (David) Ashcroft (9 May 1942, Chicago IL) American government official; US attorney general from 2001.

Vladimir (Davidovich) Ashkenazy (6 Jul 1937, Gorky, Russia, USSR [now Nizhny Novgorod, Russia]) Russian-born Icelandic pianist and conductor.

Merrill Ashley (Linda Michelle Merrill; 2 Dec 1950, St. Paul MN) American ballerina.

Hanan Ashrawi (8 Oct 1946, Ram Allah, Palestine) Palestinian academic and spokeswoman for Palestine.

Ed Asner (Yitzak Edward Asner; 15 Nov 1929, Kansas City KS) American TV actor, best known for his role on The Mary Tyler Moore Show.

Bashar al-Assad (11 Sep 1965, Damascus, Syria) Syrian statesman; president of Syria from 2000.

Azali Assoumani (1959, Grand Comoro island, Comoros) Comoran politician; president of Comoros, 1999–January 2002 and again from 26 May 2002.

Rowan (Sebastian) Atkinson (6 Jan 1955, Consett, Durham, England) British comedian and personality popularly known as "Mr. Bean."

Sir Richard (Samuel) Attenborough (29 Aug 1923, Cambridge, England) British motion-picture director who won an Academy Award for Gandhi (1982).

Abdul Rahman ibn Hamad al-Attiyah (1950, Qatar) Qatari international official; secretary-general of the Gulf Cooperation Council from 2001.

Margaret (Eleanor) Atwood (18 Nov 1939, Ottawa, ON, Canada) Canadian poet, novelist, and critic, noted for her Canadian nationalism and her feminism.

Jacques Audiard (30 Apr 1952, Paris, France) French film director, best known for Un Héros très discret (A Self-Made Hero; 1996).

Jean M. Auel (née Jean Marie Untinen; 18 Feb 1936, Chicago IL) American author of books for children, notably her Earth's Children series.

Brian Auger (18 Jul 1939, London, England) British jazz-rock organist and keyboardist.

Daw Aung San Suu Kyi (19 Jun 1945, Rangoon, Burma [now Yangon, Myanmar]) Myanmar (Burmese) opposition leader; winner of the Nobel Peace Prize, 1991.

Frankie Avalon (18 Sep 1940, Philadelphia PA) American singer and film actor.

Emanuel Ax (8 Jun 1949, Lvov, Ukrainian SSR, USSR [now Lviv, Ukraine]) Ukrainian concert pianist.

Francisco Ayala (16 Mar 1906, Granada, Spain) Spanish novelist and sociologist; winner of the Cervantes Prize in 1991.

Alan Ayckbourn (12 Apr 1939, London, England) English playwright, whose works—mostly farces and comedies—deal with marital and class conflicts and point up the fears and weaknesses of the English lower-middle class.

Dan Aykroyd (1 Jul 1952, Ottawa, ON, Canada) Canadian-born comic actor, best known for TV's *Saturday Night Live* and the film *The Blues Brothers* (1980).

Chingiz Aytmatov (12 Dec 1928, Sheker, Kirgiz ASSR, USSR [now Kyrgyzstan]) Kyrgyz author, translator, and journalist, who writes mainly in Kyrgyz; his major themes are love and friendship, the trials and heroism of wartime, and the emancipation of Kyrgyz youth from restrictive custom and tradition.

Hank Azaria (25 Apr 1964, Forest Hills NY) American actor, best known for comic film roles and for providing voices for TV's *The Simpsons*.

José María Aznar López (25 Feb 1953, Madrid, Spain) Spanish politician; prime minister of Spain from 1996.

Charles Aznavour (Chanour Varenagh Aznavourian) (22 May 1924, Paris, France) French singer, songwriter, and film actor of Armenian heritage and world renown, famous for his sad love songs.

'Abd al-Qadir al-Ba Jamal (1946, Yemen?) Yemeni politician; prime minister of Yemen from 2001.

Juan N. Babauta (7 Sep 1953, Tanapag, Saipan, Northern Mariana Islands) American Republican politician; governor of the Northern Mariana Islands from January 2002.

Lauren Bacall (Betty Joan Perske; 16 Sep 1924, New York NY) American film and stage actress and model; best known for playing provocative, hard-edged characters.

Burt Bacharach (12 May 1929, Kansas City MO) American composer and film score writer.

Kevin Bacon (8 Jul 1958, Philadelphia PA) American film and theater actor, best known for his breakthrough role in *Footloose* (1984).

Mark Badgley (12 Jan 1961, East Saint Louis IL) American fashion designer who, with James Mischka, produces the Badgley Mischka line of beaded evening gowns.

Erykah Badu (Erykah Wright; 26 Feb 1972, Dallas TX) American singer-songwriter, appreciated for the phrasing and emotive qualities of her smooth, jazz-inflected vocals.

Joan Baez (9 Jan 1941, Staten Island NY) American folk singer and political activist.

Bob Baffert (13 Jan 1952, Sierra Madre CA) American trainer of Thoroughbred horses, including winners of the Preakness Stakes four times, the Kentucky Derby three times, and the Belmont Stakes once.

Natsagiyn Bagabandi (22 Apr 1950, Yaruu Soum, Zavkhan province, Mongolia) Mongolian politician; president of Mongolia from 1997.

Roberto Baggio (18 Feb 1967, Caldogno, near Vicenza, Italy) Italian association football (soccer) player, a top scorer and member of three World Cup teams (1990, 1994, 1998).

F. Lee Bailey (10 Jun 1933, Waltham MA) American defense lawyer.

Jerry D. Bailey (29 Aug 1957, Dallas TX) American jockey, twice winner of the Kentucky Derby (1993, 1996) and twice the Preakness Stakes (1991, 2000); five times North America's leading jockey, including 2001.

Oksana Baiul (16 Feb 1977, Dnepropetrovsk, Ukrainian SSR, USSR [now Dnipropetrovsk, Ukraine]) Ukrainian figure skater, among the youngest Olympic skating champions (gold medal in 1994, at age 16).

Dame Janet (Abbott) Baker (21 Aug 1933, Hatfield, Yorkshire, England) English operatic mezzo-soprano, known for her vocal expression, stage presence, and effective diction.

Russell Baker (14 Aug 1925, Loudoun county, Virginia) American journalist, newspaper columnist, and Pulitzer Prize winning author.

Alec Baldwin (Alexander Baldwin III; 3 Apr 1958, Massapequa NY) American film and TV actor, noted for both dramatic and comic roles.

Jan Peter Balkenende (7 May 1956, Kapelle, The Netherlands) Dutch Christian-Democratic politician; prime minister of The Netherlands from July 2002.

Robert Duane Ballard (30 Jun 1942, Wichita KS) American oceanographer, underwater explorer, and educator best known for discovering several of history's most famous shipwrecks, including the *Titanic* in 1985, the *Bismarck* in 1989, and John F. Kennedy's *P.T. 109* in 2002.

Severiano ("Seve") Ballesteros (9 Apr 1957, Pedreña, Spain) Spanish golfer who dominated the European PGA in the 1980s.

Steven A. Ballmer (24 Mar 1956) American corporate executive; CEO of Microsoft Corp. from 2000.

Shigeru Ban (5 Aug 1957, Tokyo, Japan) Japanese architect known for his practical solutions and assistance with the reconstruction of Kobe, Japan, following the 1995 earthquake.

Anne Bancroft (Anna Maria Louisa Italiano; 17 Sep 1931, New York NY) American film actress, best known for her portrayal of Annie Sullivan in *The Miracle Worker* (1962).

Enric Banda (1948, Girona, Spain) Spanish Catalan geophysicist; secretary general of the European Science Foundation.

Antonio Banderas (José António Domínguez Banderas; 10 Oct 1960, Málaga, Spain) Spanish actor and director who successfully crossed over to American films in the 1990s.

John Bennett Bani (1940, Pentecost Island, New Hebrides [now Vanuatu]) Vanuatu Anglican priest; president of Vanuatu from 1999.

Russell Banks (28 Mar 1940, Newton MA) American novelist known for his portrayals of the interior lives of characters at odds with economic and social forces.

Tyra Banks (4 Dec 1973, Los Angeles CA) American model and actress, best known for Victoria's Secret ads.

Jill E. Barad (Jill Elikann; 23 May 1951, New York NY) American corporate executive; CEO of Mattel, Inc. from 1997.

Ehud Barak (Ehud Brog; 12 Feb 1942, Mishmar Ha-Sharon kibbutz, Palestine [now northern Israel]) Israeli politician; prime minister of Israel, 1999–2001.

Imamu Amiri Baraka (LeRoi Jones; 7 Oct 1934, Newark NJ) American playwright, poet, novelist, essayist, and black nationalist.

Patricia Barber (8 Nov 1955, Lisle IL) American jazz singer and pianist.

Gato Barbieri (Leandro J. Barbieri; 28 Nov 1934, Rosario, Argentina) Argentine jazz saxophonist and composer.

Ian Graeme Barbour (5 Oct 1923, Beijing, China) American theologian and physicist; Templeton Prize winner, 1999.

Brigitte Bardot (Camille Javal; 28 Sep 1934, Paris, France) French motion-picture actress who became an international sex symbol in the 1950s and '60s and later an activist for animal rights.

Daniel Barenboim (15 Nov 1942, Buenos Aires, Argentina) Israeli pianist and conductor; music director of the Chicago Symphony Orchestra from 1989.

Bob Barker (12 Dec 1923, Darrington WA) American TV personality, host of the game show *The Price is Right*.

Ellen Barkin (16 Apr 1954, New York NY) American film actress, best known for her role in *The Big Easy* (1987).

Charles Barkley (20 Feb 1963, Leeds AL) American basketball player; the fourth player ever to amass 20,000 points, 10,000 rebounds, and 4,000 assists; NBA MVP, 1993.

Roy Barnes (11 Mar 1948, Mableton GA) American Democratic politician; governor of Georgia from January 1999.

Hector V. Barreto, Jr. (Kansas City MO) American government official; head of the US Small Business Administration from 2001.

Craig R. Barrett (29 Aug 1939, San Francisco CA) American materials scientist and corporate executive; CEO of Intel Corp. from 1997.

Kenny Barron (9 Jun 1943, Philadelphia PA) American jazz pianist and composer.

Dave Barry (3 Jul 1947, Armonk NY) American humorist, newspaper columnist, and author.

Drew Barrymore (22 Feb 1975, Culver City CA) American film actress successful both as a child star and as an adult.

Rudolf Barshai (Rudolf Borisovich Barshay; 28 Sep 1924, Labinskaya, Krasnodar kray, USSR) Russian violist and conductor.

John Barth (John Simmons Barth, Jr.; 27 May 1930, Cambridge MD) American writer.

Cecilia Bartoli (4 Jun 1966, Rome, Italy) Italian operatic mezzo-soprano.

Mikhail (Nikolayevich) Baryshnikov (28 Jan 1948, Riga, Latvian SSR, USSR [now in Latvia]) Soviet-born American ballet dancer who was the preeminent male classical dancer of the 1970s and '80s. He subsequently became a noted dance director.

Jacques (Martin) Barzun (30 Nov 1907, Créteil, France) French-born American teacher, historian, and author.

Omar Hassan Ahmad al-Bashir (1944, Hosh Bannaga, Anglo-Egyptian Sudan [now The Sudan]) Sudanese military leader; president of The Sudan from 1989.

Kim Basinger (8 Dec 1953, Athens GA) American motion-picture actress most acclaimed for *L.A. Confidential* (1997).

Angela Bassett (16 Aug 1958, New York NY) American film actress noted for strong characters, including Tina Turner in *What's Love Got to Do with It* (1993).

Shirley (Veronica) Bassey (8 Jan 1937, Cardiff, Wales) British pop singer.

Kathy Bates (28 Jun 1948, Memphis TN) American dynamic film actress most famous for *Misery* (1990).

Jorge Batlle Ibáñez (25 Oct 1927, Uruguay?) Uruguayan politician; president of Uruguay from 2000.

Kathleen Battle (Kathleen Deanne Battle; 13 Aug 1948, Portsmouth OH) American operatic coloratura soprano.

Gary Bauer (1956, Covington KY) American political activist, former presidential candidate.

Beatrice Elizabeth Mary, Princess of York (8 Aug 1988, London, England) British royal; daughter of Prince Andrew and Sarah Ferguson.

Queen Beatrix (31 Jan 1938, Soestdijk, The Netherlands) Dutch royal; queen of The Netherlands from 1980.

(Henry) Warren Beatty (30 Mar 1937, Richmond VA) American film actor and director best known for politically charged portrayals.

Kim Christian Beazley (1948, Australia?) Australian politician; opposition leader.

Jeff Beck (24 Jun 1944, Wallington, Surrey, England) British rock guitarist.

David Beckham (2 May 1975, Leytonstone, East London, England) British association football (soccer) player, star midfielder for Manchester United, and captain of England's national team in the 2002 World Cup; he was also known for his celebrity marriage to Victoria Adams (of the Spice Girls).

Kate Beckinsale (26 Jul 1973, London, England) British star of British and American films, both popular and period pieces.

Maurice Béjart (Maurice-Jean de Berger; 1 Jan 1927, Marseille, France) French-born dancer, choreographer, and opera director known for combining classic ballet and modern dance with jazz, acrobatics, and *musique concrète* (composition by tape recordings).

Harry Belafonte (Harold George Belafonte, Jr; 1 Mar 1927, New York NY) American pop singer and actor who was a key figure in the 1950s popularity of folk music.

Abdelwahed Belkeziz (5 Jul 1939, Marakech, Morocco) Moroccan international official; secretary-general of the Organization of the Islamic Conference from 2001.

Derrick Albert Bell, Jr. (6 Nov 1930, Pittsburgh PA) American legal scholar; civil rights activist.

S. Jocelyn Bell Burnell (15 Jul 1943, Belfast, Northern Ireland) Irish astronomer and astrophysicist; discoverer of the first pulsars.

Jean-Paul Belmondo (9 Apr 1933, Neuilly-sur-Seine, near Paris, France) French motion-picture actor noted for his portrayals of charismatic antiheroes.

Zine al-Abidine Ben Ali (3 Sep 1936, Hammam-Sousse, Tunisia) Tunisian politician; president of Tunisia from 1987.

Pat Benatar (Patricia Andrzejewski; 10 Jan 1953, Brooklyn NY) American singer and influential rock musician of the 1980s.

Francis Bebey (15 Jul 1929, Douala, Cameroon) Cameroonian writer, guitarist, and composer.

Sister Wendy Beckett (1930, South Africa) British TV art critic.

Carlos German Belli (15 Sep 1927, Lima, Peru) Peruvian poet.

Luciano Benetton (13 May 1935, Treviso, Italy) Italian retailer and co-founder (1965) of the Benetton company noted for sportswear and provocative advertisements.

Ali Benflis (8 Sep 1944, Algeria) Algerian politician; prime minister of Algeria from 2000.

Roberto Benigni (27 Oct 1952, Misericordia, Arezzo, Italy) Italian energetic actor, comic, and screenwriter, best known in America for *La vida e bella* (*Life Is Beautiful*; 1998).

Annette Bening (29 May 1958, Topeka KS) American enduring film actress, won critical acclaim for *American Beauty* (1999).

Tony Bennett (Anthony Dominick Benedetto; 3 Aug 1926, Astoria, Queens NY) American pop and jazz singer, one of the most enduring of the crooners.

George Benson (22 Mar 1943, Pittsburgh PA) American jazz and pop guitarist and vocalist.

Yelena Berezhnaya (11 Oct 1971, Nevinnomyssk, Northern Caucasus, USSR) Russian pairs skater (with Anton Sakhuralidze); shared the 2002

Olympic gold medal with Canadians Salé and Pelletier.

Boris (Abramovich) Berezovsky (23 Jan 1946, Moscow, USSR [now Russia]) Russian businessman and "oligarch"; former owner of Russian Public Television (ORT) and Aeroflot, the Russian airline, among other holdings.

Teresa Berganza (Teresa Berganza Vargas; 16 Mar 1935, Madrid, Spain) Spanish operatic mezzo-soprano.

Candice Bergen (9 May 1946, Beverly Hills CA) American film and TV actress best known for the TV series *Murphy Brown.*

(Ernst) Ingmar Bergman (14 Jul 1918, Uppsala, Sweden) Swedish film writer-director noted for his versatile camera work and fragmented narrative style.

Luciano Berio (24 Oct 1925, Oneglia, Italy) Italian music theorist, conductor, composer, and teacher who represented the musical avant-garde.

David Berkowitz (1 Jun 1953) American serial killer convicted as "The Son of Sam."

Milton Berle (Mendel Berlinger; 12 Jul 1908, New York NY—27 Mar 2002, Los Angeles CA), American film, TV, and stage comedian, known as "Mr. Television."

Silvio Berlusconi (29 Sep 1936, Milan, Italy) Italian businessman and politician; prime minister of Italy, 1994–95 and again from 2001.

Tim Berners-Lee (8 Jun 1955, London, England) British inventor of the World Wide Web and director, from 1994, of the World Wide Web Consortium (W3C) at the MIT Laboratory for Computer Science.

Prince Bernhard (29 Jun 1911, Jena, Germany) Dutch royal; prince of Lippe-Biesterfeld.

Sandra Bernhard (6 Jun 1955, Flint MI) American actress and comedian known for her brash and outspoken style.

Carl Bernstein (14 Feb 1944, Washington DC) American journalist and author.

Yogi Berra (Lawrence Peter Berra; 12 May 1925, St. Louis MO) American baseball player and manager; with the NY Yankees (1946–63), established numerous catchers' records.

Chuck Berry (Charles Edward Anderson Berry; 18 Oct 1926, St. Louis MO) American singer, songwriter, and guitarist who was one of the most popular and influential performers in rhythm-and-blues and rock-and-roll music in the 1950s, '60s, and '70s.

Halle (Maria) Berry (14 Aug 1968, Cleveland OH) American actress and model who received an Academy Award in 2001 for her role in *Monster's Ball.*

Bernardo Bertolucci (16 Mar 1940, Parma, Italy) Italian film director, whose erotically charged *Last Tango in Paris* (1972) created an international sensation.

Andris Berzins (4 Aug 1951, Riga, Latvian SSR, USSR [now Latvia]) Latvian politician; prime minister of Latvia from 2000.

Natalya (Igorevna) Bessmertnova (19 Jul 1941, Moscow, USSR) Russian ballet dancer.

Jeff Bezos (12 Jan 1964, Albuquerque NM) American corporate executive; founder and CEO of Amazon.com from 1995.

King Bhumibol Adulyadej (Rama IX; 5 Dec 1927, Cambridge MA) Thai royal; king of Thailand, ninth of the Chakkri dynasty.

Benazir Bhutto (21 Jun 1953, Karachi, Pakistan) Pakistani politician, prime minister 1988–90 and 1993–96, and the first woman leader of a predominantly Muslim nation in modern history.

Acker Bilk (Bernard Stanley Bilk; 28 Jan 1929, Pensford, Somerset, England) British bandleader.

James Hadley Billington (1 Jun 1929, Bryn Mawr PA) American cultural historian; librarian of Congress from 1987.

Osama bin Laden (also spelled Usamah ibn Ladin; 1957?, Riyadh, Saudi Arabia) Saudi Arabian-born terrorist leader, alleged mastermind of the 1993 bombing of the World Trade Center and the 11 Sep 2001 attacks on the World Trade Center and the Pentagon.

Pat Binns (8 Oct 1948, Weyburn, SK, Canada) Canadian politician; premier of Prince Edward Island from 1996.

Juliette Binoche (9 Mar 1964, Paris, France) French film actress famous for complex characterizations; breakthrough performance in *The English Patient* (1996).

Lester Bryant Bird (21 Feb 1938, Antigua) West Indian politician; prime minister of Antigua and Barbuda from 1994.

King Birendra Bir Bikram Shah Dev (28 Dec 1945, Kathmandu, Nepal—1 Jun 2001, Kathmandu, Nepal), Nepalese royal; king of Nepal, 1972–2001.

Harrison Birtwistle (15 Jul 1934, Accrington, Lancashire, England) British composer of operas, chamber music, and orchestral music in a contemporary, avant-garde style.

Jacqueline Bisset (13 Sep 1944, Weybridge, England) British international film actress.

Paul Biya (13 Feb 1933, Mvomeka'a, Cameroon) Cameroonian politician; president of Cameroon from 1982.

Björk (Björk Gudmundsdottir; 21 Nov 1965, Reykjavík, Iceland) Icelandic singer and actress.

Ole Einar Bjørndalen (27 Jan 1974, Drammen, Norway) Norwegian biathlete and cross-country skier; in 2002 was the first ever to sweep Olympic biathlon (4 golds).

Clint Black (1962, Long Branch NJ) American country and western singer.

Conrad (Moffat) Black (25 Aug 1944, Montreal, QC, Canada) Canadian financier and press baron.

Jack Black (7 Apr 1969, Hermosa Beach CA) American comic actor known for his portrayal of offbeat characters.

Shirley Temple Black (23 Apr 1928, Santa Monica CA) American child film actress, internationally beloved for her sentimental musicals.

Rubén Blades, Jr. (16 Jul 1948, Panama City, Panama) Panamanian salsa singer and songwriter, actor, and politician.

Manolo Blahnik (27 Nov 1942, Santa Cruz, Canary Islands, Spain) Spanish shoe designer and maker whose elegant, stylish creations are characterized by high stiletto heels.

Tony Blair (Anthony Charles Lynton Blair; 6 May 1953, Edinburgh, Scotland) British Labour leader and prime minister from 1997.

Marie-Claire Blais (5 Oct 1939, Quebec, QC, Canada) Canadian novelist and poet.

Robert Blake (Michael James Vijencio Gubitosi; 18 Sep 1933, Nutley NJ) American film and TV actor best known for the 1970s cop show *Baretta.*

Cate Blanchett (Catherine Elise Blanchett; 14 May 1969, Melbourne, Australia) Australian film actress known for serious roles, including *Elizabeth* (1998).

Bobby "Blue" Bland (Robert Calvin Bland; 27 Jan 1930, Rosemark TN) American rhythm-and-blues singer noted for his rich baritone voice, sophisticated style, and sensual delivery.

Mary J. Blige (11 Jan 1971, New York NY) American hip-hop soul singer.

Günter Blobel (21 May 1936, Waltersdorf, Silesia, Germany [now Niegoslawice, Poland]) German-born American cell biologist; won the Nobel Prize for Physiology or Medicine in 1999 for his discoveries in the area of protein processing.

Torbjörn Blomdahl (26 Oct 1962, Sweden) Swedish carom (three-cushion) billiards champion who dominated the sport in late 1980s and 1990s.

Harold Irving Bloom (11 Jul 1930, New York NY) American literary critic known for his innovative interpretations of literary history and of the creation of literature and his unconventional approach to writing as in, for example, The Western Canon (1994).

Michael R. Bloomberg (14 Feb 1942, Medford MA) American businessman and Republican politician; mayor of New York City from 1 Jan 2002.

Judy Blume (12 Feb 1938, Elizabeth NJ) American author of popular books for children and adolescents.

David Blunkett (6 Jun 1947, Sheffield, England) British politician, blind from birth; British home secretary from 2001.

Andrea Bocelli (22 Sep 1958, Lajatico, Italy) Italian operatic tenor, blind from the age of 12.

Steven Bochco (16 Dec 1943, New York NY) American creator of TV series, including Hill Street Blues and NYPD Blue.

Eric Bogle (1944, Peebles, Scotland) Australian folk singer and songwriter.

David Boies (1941?, Sycamore IL) American lawyer; deposed Bill Gates for the US Department of Justice in its antitrust case against Microsoft Corp.; represented presidential candidate Al Gore, Jr., in Gore v. Bush (2000); and represented Napster in its survival bid.

Enrique Bolaños Geyer (13 May 1928, Masaya, Nicaragua) Nicaraguan politician; president of Nicaragua from 10 Jan 2002.

William Bolcom (26 May 1938, Seattle WA) American composer, pianist, and teacher.

Sir Haji Hassanal Bolkiah Mu'izzadin Waddaulah (15 Jul 1946, Brunei Town [now Bandar Seri Begawan], Brunei) Bruneian royal; 29th sultan of Brunei, from 1967.

Jon Bon Jovi (John Bongiovi; 2 Mar 1962, Perth Amboy NJ) American singer, musician, and songwriter.

Julian Bond (14 Jan 1940, Nashville TN) American civil rights leader.

Kjell Magne Bondevik (3 Sep 1947, Molde, Norway) Norwegian politician; prime minister of Norway, 1997–2000 and from 2001.

Barry (Lamar) Bonds (24 Jul 1964, Riverside CA) American baseball player who hit a record 73 home runs and 177 walks in 2001; only four-time National League MVP (1990, 1992, 1993, 2001) and the only player with more than 400 home runs and more than 400 stolen bases.

Omar Bongo (Albert-Bernard Bongo; 30 Dec 1935, Lewai, Gabon) Gabonese politican; president of Gabon from 1967.

Helena Bonham Carter (26 May 1966, Golders Green, London, England) British actress known for serious dramatic and period pieces.

Bono (Paul David Hewson; also known as Bono Vox; 10 May 1960, Dublin, Ireland) Irish rock guitarist and vocalist (of U2); activist and mediator.

Booker T. (Booker T. Jones; 12 Nov 1944, Memphis TN) American pop singer and organist.

Pat Boone (Charles Eugene Patrick Boone; 1 Jun 1935, Jacksonville FL) American pop singer and actor.

Cherie Booth (23 Sep 1954, Bury, Lancashire, England) British barrister; wife of prime minister Tony Blair.

Allan Robert Border (27 Jul 1955, Cremorne, Sydney, NSW, Australia) Australian cricketer, all-time leading run-scorer in Test (international) matches.

Ernest Borgnine (Ermes Effron Borgnino; 24 Jan 1917, Hamden CT) American stage, film, and TV actor who achieved success in a wide range of lead and supporting roles.

Frank Borman (14 Mar 1928, Gary IN) American astronaut who, with James A. Lovell and William A. Anders, made the first manned flight, in Apollo 8, around the Moon in December 1968.

Umberto Bossi (19 Sep 1941, Cassano Magnano, Varese, Italy) Italian politician and leader of the separatist Northern League.

Lucien Bouchard (22 Dec 1938, Saint-Coeur-de-Marie, QC, Canada) Canadian (French) Quebec separatist.

Pierre Boulez (26 Mar 1925, Montbrison, France) French composer, conductor, and music theorist whose complex, serialist music is marked by a sensitivity to the nuances of instrumental texture and color.

Louise Bourgeois (25 Dec 1911, Paris, France) French-born sculptor known for her monumental abstract and often biomorphic works that deal with the relationships of men and women.

Matthew Bourne (13 Jan 1950, Hackney, London, England) British choreographer.

Ray Bourque (28 Dec 1960, Montreal, QC, Canada) American ice hockey defenseman; five-time James Norris Trophy winner.

Abdelaziz Bouteflika (2 Mar 1937, Tlemcen, Algeria) Algerian politician; president of Algeria from 1999.

David Bowie (David Robert Jones; 8 Jan 1947, Brixton, London, England) British rock singer and actor.

Boy George (George Alan O'Dowd; 14 Jun 1961, Bexleyheath, England) British pop singer (of Culture Club).

Mame Madior Boye (1940, French West Africa [Senegal]?) Senegalese politician; prime minister of Senegal from 2001.

Lara Flynn Boyle (24 Mar 1970, Davenport IA) American TV and film actress, currently stars in TV's The Practice.

Kenny Brack (31 Mar 1966, Arvika, Sweden) Swedish race-car driver; in 1999 won the Indianapolis 500, Indy Racing League Champion; 2001 CART All Star.

Ray (Douglas) Bradbury (22 Aug 1920, Waukegan IL) American author of science-fiction short stories and novels, nostalgic tales, poetry, radio drama, and television and motion-picture screenplays.

Benjamin (Crowninshield) Bradlee (26 Aug 1921, Boston MA) American journalist and editor of the Washington Post newspaper.

Bill Bradley (William Warren Bradley; 28 Jul 1943, Crystal City MO) American professional basketball player and US senator; Democratic presidential candidate, 2000.

Ed Bradley (22 Jun 1941, Philadelphia PA) American TV journalist.

James Brady (17 Sep 1944, Grand Rapids MI) American former presidential press secretary; gun-control advocate.

Kenneth (Charles) Branagh (10 Dec 1960, Belfast, Northern Ireland) British theater and film actor, di-

rector, and writer, best known for screen adaptations of Shakespearean plays.

Marlon Brando (Jr.) (3 Apr 1924, Omaha NE) American motion-picture and stage actor known for visceral, brooding characterizations.

Brandy (Brandy Norwood; 11 Feb 1979, McComb MS) American R&B singer and actress.

Richard (Charles Nicholas) Branson (18 Jul 1950, Blackheath, South London, England) British entrepreneur; founder of the "Virgin" empire in 1973.

Benjamin Bratt (16 Dec 1963, San Francisco CA) American TV and motion-picture actor; first gained fame on TV's *Law & Order*.

Anthony Braxton (4 Jun 1945, Chicago IL) American jazz saxophonist.

Algirdas Mykolas Brazauskas (22 Sep 1932, Rokiskis, Lithuanian SSR, USSR [now Lithuania]) Lithuanian politician; president of Lithuania, 1992–98, and prime minister from 2001.

Jimmy Breslin (17 Oct 1930, Jamaica NY) American newspaper columnist and author.

Stephen Breyer (15 Aug 1938, San Francisco CA) American jurist; associate justice of the US Supreme Court from 1994.

Beau Bridges (Lloyd Vernet Bridges III; 9 Dec 1941, Los Angeles CA) American likeable and versatile film and TV actor.

Jeff Bridges (4 Dec 1949, Los Angeles CA) American actor whose breakthrough performance came in *The Last Picture Show* (1971).

Dee Dee Bridgewater (Denise Bridgewater; 27 May 1950, Memphis TN) American jazz singer.

David Brinkley (10 Jul 1920, Wilmington NC) American TV journalist.

Jim Broadbent (24 May 1949, Lincoln, Lincolnshire, England) British motion-picture character actor; gained critical acclaim for *Iris* (2001).

David S. Broder (11 Sep 1929, Chicago Heights IL) American journalist and national political correspondent.

Matthew Broderick (21 Mar 1962, New York NY) American comic actor of stage and screen who gained widespread fame following the film *Ferris Bueller's Day Off* (1986).

Tom Brokaw (Thomas John Brokaw; 6 Feb 1940, Webster SD) American TV news anchorman.

James Brolin (James Bruderlin; 18 Jul 1940, Los Angeles CA) American actor best known for his role in TV's *Marcus Welby, MD.*

Charles Bronson (Charles Buchinsky; 3 Nov 1922, Ehrenfeld PA) American motion-picture and TV actor known for tough guy roles.

Albert Brooks (Albert Einstein; 22 Jul 1947, Los Angeles CA) American comedian and film actor, director, and writer.

Garth Brooks (7 Feb 1962, Tulsa OK) American country and western singer.

James L. Brooks (9 May 1940, Brooklyn NY) American motion-picture and TV director, writer, and producer.

Mel Brooks (Melvin Kaminsky; 28 Jun 1926, Brooklyn NY) American comedian, actor, producer, and director; an offbeat comic genius.

Pierce Brendan Brosnan (16 May 1953, County Meath, Ireland) Irish actor known for portrayal of handsome, suave leading men, including Remington Steele and James Bond.

Joyce Brothers (Joyce Diane Bauer; 20 Sep 1928, New York NY) American TV psychologist and medical adviser.

Leo Brouwer (1 Mar 1939, Havana, Cuba) Cuban composer and guitarist whose work moved from nationalist to avant-garde.

Clarence "Gatemouth" Brown (18 Apr 1924, Vinton LA) American blues singer and guitarist.

Edmund G. ("Jerry") Brown, Jr. (7 Apr 1938, San Francisco CA) American politician, governor of California, 1975–83; mayor of Oakland CA from 1998; and presidential candidate.

Gordon Brown (20 Feb 1951, Glasgow, Scotland) British politician and chancellor of the Exchequer.

James Brown (3 May 1933, Barnwell SC) American singer, songwriter, arranger, and dancer.

Ruth Brown (Ruth Weston; 30 Jan 1928, Portsmouth VA) American singer and actress who dominated the rhythm-and-blues charts throughout the 1950s.

Tina Brown (21 Nov 1953, Maidenhead, England) American magazine editor and publisher.

Sir John Browne (Edmund John Phillip Browne; Lord Browne of Maddingly; 20 Feb 1948, Hamburg, Germany) British corporate executive; group CEO of British Petroleum/Amoco from 1998.

Dave Brubeck (David Warren Brubeck; 6 Dec 1920, Concord CA) American pianist-composer who brought elements of classical music into jazz.

Gro Harlem Brundtland (20 Apr 1939, Oslo, Norway) Norwegian politician and international official; prime minister of Norway, 1981, 1986–89, and 1990–96; director-general of the World Health Organization from 1998.

Kobe Bryant (23 Aug 1978, Philadelphia PA) American basketball player who won three straight NBA titles (2000–02) with the Los Angeles Lakers; four-time NBA all star.

Phyllis Bryn-Julson (5 Feb 1945, Bowdon ND) American soprano.

Peabo Bryson (13 Apr 1951, Greenville SC) American soul singer.

Patrick J. Buchanan (2 Nov 1938, Washington DC) American journalist and newspaper columnist; presidential candidate.

Art Buchwald (20 Oct 1925, Mount Vernon NY) American newspaper columnist and author.

William F. Buckley, Jr. (24 Nov 1925, New York NY) American magazine editor and columnist, author, and noted conservative.

Jimmy Buffett (25 Dec 1946, Pascagoula MS) American rock singer and songwriter.

Warren (Edward) Buffett (30 Aug 1930, Omaha NE) American investor; CEO of Berkshire Hathaway Inc. since 1965 and chairman of the board of Solomon Brothers Inc. from 1991.

Fernando Bujones (9 Mar 1955, Miami FL) American ballet dancer.

Sandra (Annette) Bullock (26 Jul 1964, Arlington VA) American film actress who has become a top box-office draw.

Grace Bumbry (Grace Melzia Ann Bumbry; 4 Jan 1937, St. Louis MO) American operatic mezzo-soprano.

Gisele Bündchen (Gisele Caroline Nonnenmacher Bündchen; 20 Jul 1980, Horizontina, Rio Grande do Sul, Brazil) Brazilian fashion model.

Eric Burdon (11 May 1941, Newcastle upon Tyne, England) British rock singer and songwriter (of the Animals).

Solomon Burke (21 Mar 1936, Philadelphia PA) American gospel singer who helped to usher in the soul music era.

Carol (Creighton) Burnett (26 Apr 1936, San Antonio TX) American comedian, actress, and musician;

starred in the popular variety series *The Carol Burnett Show* (1967–79)

Edward J. Burns (Jr.) (29 Jan 1968, Woodside, Queens NY) American motion-picture actor, director, writer, and producer known for down-to-earth characterizations.

Ken Burns (Kenneth Lauren Burns; 29 Jul 1953, Brooklyn NY) American documentary film maker who directed and co-wrote the TV miniseries *The Civil War*, *Baseball*, and *Jazz*, among others.

Kenny Burrell (31 Jul 1931, Detroit MI) American jazz guitarist and composer.

Ellen Burstyn (Edna Rae Gillooley; 7 Dec 1932, Detroit MI) American motion-picture and stage actress of great depth.

Gary Burton (23 Jan 1943, Anderson IN) American jazz vibraphonist and composer.

Tim Burton (Timothy William Burton; 25 Aug 1958, Burbank CA) American director and writer known for offbeat, imaginative films.

Leo Buscaglia (31 Mar 1925, Los Angeles CA) American educator, author, and motivational speaker.

Steve Buscemi (13 Dec 1957, Brooklyn NY) American motion-picture actor known for off-center characters; breakthrough role in *Fargo* (1996).

Barbara Bush (25 Nov 1981, Dallas TX) American personality; daughter of Pres. George W. Bush.

Barbara Pierce Bush (8 Jun 1925, Rye NY) American first lady; wife of Pres. George H.W. Bush.

George Herbert Walker Bush (12 Jun 1924, Milton MA) American statesman; vice president of the U.S., 1981–89 and 41st president of the US, 1989–93 [see full biography at Presidents].

George Walker Bush (6 Jul 1946, New Haven CT) American statesman; 43rd president of the US from 2001 [see full biography at Presidents].

Jeb Bush (John Ellis Bush; 11 Feb 1953, Midland TX) American Republican politician; governor of Florida from January 1999.

Jenna Bush (25 Nov 1981, Dallas TX) American personality; daughter of Pres. George W. Bush.

Kate Bush (30 Jul 1958, Bexleyheath, England) British singer and songwriter.

Laura Bush (née Laura Lane Welch; 4 Nov 1946, Midland TX) American first lady; wife of Pres. George W. Bush (married 5 Nov 1977).

Edwin Bustillos (16 May 1964, [Sierra Madre Occidental], Mexico) Mexican human rights activist and environmentalist.

Chief Mangosuthu Gatsha Buthelezi (27 Aug 1928, Mahlabatini, Natal, South Africa) South African Zulu royal; chief, head (1972–94) of the nonindependent black state of KwaZulu, and leader of the Inkatha Freedom Party.

Jerry "the Iceman" Butler (8 Dec 1939, Sunflower county MS) American soul singer and politician.

Pierre Buyoya (14 Nov 1949, Rutovu, Belgian Rwanda-Urundi [now Burundi]) Burundian Tutsi politician, president of Burundi 1987–93, and from 1996.

Donald Byrd (Donaldson Toussaint L'Ouverture II; 9 Dec 1932, Detroit MI) American jazz trumpeter and flügelhornist.

Gabriel Byrne (12 May 1950, Dublin, Ireland) Irish film actor, writer, and director known for serious dramatic and light comic roles.

James Caan (26 Mar 1939, New York NY) American actor best remembered as Sonny Corleone in *The Godfather* films (1972; 1974; 1990).

Montserrat Caballé (12 Apr 1933, Barcelona, Spain) Spanish operatic soprano.

Sid Caesar (8 Sep 1922, Yonkers NY) American comedian and TV actor, a pioneer of TV comedy with *Your Show of Shows*.

Nicolas Cage (Nicholas Coppola; 7 Jan 1964, Long Beach CA) American versatile film star who garnered critical acclaim for his performance in *Leaving Las Vegas* (1995).

Sir Michael Caine (Maurice Micklewhite, Jr.; 14 Mar 1933, London, England) British film star from the mid-1950s through the late '80s, he reemerged with *The Cider House Rules* (1999).

Sila María Calderón (23 Sep 1942, San Juan PR) Puerto Rican politician; governor of Puerto Rico from 2001.

Lorne Calvert (24 Dec 1952, Moose Jaw, SK, Canada) Canadian politician; premier of Saskatchewan from 8 Feb 2001.

Michel Camdessus (1 May 1933, Bayonne, France) French international executive; managing director of the International Monetary Fund, 1987–2000.

James Cameron (16 Aug 1954, Kapuskasing, ON, Canada) Canadian director and producer whose credits include some of the top-grossing movies of all time, including *Titanic* (1997).

Louis C. Camilleri (1955, Alexandria, Egypt) American corporate executive; president and CEO of Philip Morris Companies Inc. from 2002.

Glen Campbell (22 Apr 1936, near Delight AR) American pop and country singer and guitarist.

Gordon Campbell (12 Jan 1948, Vancouver, BC, Canada) Canadian politician; premier of British Columbia from 5 Jun 2001.

Naomi Campbell (22 May 1970, London, England) British runway and photographic model.

Jane Campion (30 Apr 1954, Wellington, New Zealand) New Zealand pioneering film director, best known for *The Piano* (1993).

Dyan Cannon (Samile Diane Friesen; 4 Jan 1937, Tacoma WA) American film and TV actress.

Jennifer Capriati (29 Mar 1976, New York NY) American tennis player; youngest US player to turn professional (1989, at age 13); winner of the Australian Open in 2001 and 2002.

Julia Carabias Lillo (1954, Mexico City, Mexico) Mexican conservationist and government official; 2001 Getty Prize winner.

Andrew H. Card (10 May 1947, Brockton MA) American government official; White House chief of staff from 2001.

Pierre Cardin (7 Jul 1922, Venice, Italy) French fashion designer of elegantly cut clothes for women and a pioneer in the design of high fashion for men.

Fernando Henrique Cardoso (18 Jun 1931, Rio de Janeiro, Brazil) Brazilian politician; president of Brazil from 1995.

Drew (Allison) Carey (23 May 1958, Cleveland OH) American comic TV actor known for his everyman portrayal in TV's *The Drew Carey Show*.

Mariah Carey (27 Mar 1970, Greenlawn, Long Island NY) American pop singer.

Peter (Philip) Carey (7 May 1943, Bacchus Marsh, Victoria, Australia) Australian author; winner of the Booker Prize in 1988 (*Oscar and Lucinda*) and 2001 (*True History of the Kelly Gang*).

King Carl XVI Gustaf (Carl Gustaf Folke Hubertus; 30 Apr 1946, Stockholm, Sweden) Swedish royal; king of Sweden from 1973.

George Carlin (12 May 1937, New York NY) American comedian and TV actor famous for off-color material.

Wendy Carlos (Walter Carlos; 14 Nov 1939, Pawtucket RI) American synthesizer player and composer.

Arvid Carlsson (25 Jan 1923, Uppsala, Sweden) Swedish pharmacologist; co-winner of the Nobel Prize for Physiology or Medicine, 2000, for studies of brain-cell function.

Richard H. Carmona (22 Nov 1949, Harlem NY) American physician; surgeon general of the US from 23 Jul 2002.

Art Carney (Arthur William Matthew Carney; 4 Nov 1918, Mount Vernon NY) American TV and motion-picture actor beloved as Ed Norton on *The Honeymooners*.

Princess Caroline (Caroline Louise Margaret Grimaldi; 23 Jan 1957, Monte Carlo, Monaco) Monegasque royal; daughter of Prince Rainier III and Princess Grace (Kelly).

M(alcolm) Scott Carpenter (1 May 1925, Boulder CO) American astronaut, the second to make an orbital spaceflight.

José Carreras (5 Dec 1946, Barcelona, Spain) Spanish operatic tenor, one of the popular "Three Tenors" (with Luciano Pavarotti and Plácido Domingo).

Jim Carrey (James Eugene Carrey; 17 Jan 1962, Newmarket, ON, Canada) Canadian actor originally known for his rubber-faced visual comedy, he graduated to more serious roles.

Edwin W. Carrington (Trinidad) Trinidadian international civil servant; secretary-general of the Caribbean Community (CARICOM) from 1992.

Diahann Carroll (Carol Diahann Johnson; 17 Jul 1935, New York NY) American TV and motion-picture actress.

Johnny Carson (John William Carson; 23 Oct 1925, Corning IA) American TV talk-show host noted for his many years on *The Tonight Show*.

Chris Carter (13 Oct 1957, Bellflower CA) American writer and TV producer, creator of *The X-Files*.

E(dward) Graydon Carter (14 Jul 1949, Canada) Canadian magazine and newspaper publisher (*Spy, Observer, Vanity Fair*).

Elliott Carter (Elliott Cook Carter, Jr.; 11 Dec 1908, New York NY) American composer whose erudite style and novel principles of polyrhythm, called metrical modulation, won worldwide attention.

Jimmy Carter (James Earl Carter, Jr.) (1 Oct 1924, Plains GA) American statesman; 39th president of the US, 1977–81 [see full biography at Presidents].

Lynda Carter (Linda Jean Cordova; 24 Jul 1951, Phoenix AZ) American TV actress and singer remembered for her role in the *Wonder Woman* series.

Ron Carter (4 May 1937, Ferndale MI) American jazz bassist.

Rosalynn Carter (née Eleanor Rosalynn Smith; 18 Aug 1927, Plains GA) American first lady (1977–81), the wife of Pres. Jimmy Carter, and mental health advocate.

Stephen L. Carter (26 Oct 1954, Washington DC) American law professor and political commentator.

Henri Cartier-Bresson (22 Aug 1908, Chanteloup, France) French photographer whose humane, spontaneous photographs helped establish photojournalism as an art form.

Dame Silvia Cartwright (1943, Dunedin, New Zealand) New Zealand governor-general from 2001.

Dana (Thomas) Carvey (2 Apr 1955, Missoula MT) American comedian and actor best known for his roles on *Saturday Night Live*.

James Carville, Jr. (25 Oct 1944, Fort Benning GA) American political consultant and commentator; guided Bill Clinton's presidential campaign in 1992.

Stephen McDonnell ("Steve") Case (21 Aug 1958, Honolulu HI) American businessman; founder and CEO of America Online (1991) and chairman of AOL Time Warner from 2001.

Johnny Cash (John R. Cash; 26 Feb 1932, Kingsland AR) American singer and songwriter whose work sparked a revival of American country and western music.

Rosanne Cash (24 May 1955, Memphis TN) American country and western singer.

David Cassidy (12 Apr 1950, New York NY) American pop and rock singer and TV actor.

Shaun Cassidy (27 Sep 1958, Los Angeles CA) American singer and TV actor.

Oleg Cassini (Oleg Loiewski; 11 Apr 1913, Paris, France) French-born American fashion designer who created clothing for Jacqueline Kennedy when she was first lady.

Laetitia (Marie Laure) Casta (11 May 1978, Pont-Audemer, Normandy, France) French fashion model known for advertisements for GUESS? clothing.

Helio Castroneves (10 May 1975, São Paulo, Brazil) Brazilian Formula 1 race-car driver; won the Indy 500 in 2001 and 2002.

Philip Catherine (27 Oct 1942, London, England) British jazz guitarist.

Elizabeth Catlett (15 Apr 1919, Washington DC) American sculptor and printmaker, an expatriate renowned for her intensely political art.

Kim Cattrall (21 Aug 1956, Liverpool, England) British film actress of the 1980s who made a comeback as Samantha Jones on TV's *Sex and the City*.

Dick Cavett (19 Nov 1936, Gibbon NE) American TV talk-show host and actor.

Benjamin J. Cayetano (14 Nov 1939, Honolulu HI) American Democratic politician; governor of Hawaii from 1994.

Raymond Ceulemans (12 July 1937, Rijmenan, Belgium) Belgian carom billiards champion who won 48 European championships from 1962 and 35 world championship titles from 1963.

Ch'en Shui-bian (18 Feb 1951, Tainan county, Taiwan) Taiwanese politician; president of Taiwan from 2000.

Claude Chabrol (24 Jun 1930, Paris, France) French motion-picture director, scenarist, and producer who was France's master of the mystery thriller.

Riccardo Chailly (20 Feb 1953, Milan, Italy) Italian orchestra conductor.

Hussein Chalayan (Huseyin Chaglayan; 12 Aug 1970, Nicosia, Cyprus) Cypriot-born British fashion designer whose experimental creations display an intellectual and artistic flavor.

John T. Chambers (23 Aug 1949, Cleveland OH) American corporate executive; president and CEO of Cisco Systems, Inc. from 1997.

Marge Champion (2 Sep 1923, Los Angeles CA) American dancer and film and TV actress who formed a successful dancing partnership.

Jackie Chan (Kong-sang Chan; 7 Apr 1954, Hong Kong) Chinese actor and director whose martial arts and acrobatic skills have made him an international movie star.

Carol Channing (31 Jan 1921, Seattle WA) American comedienne, actress, and singer, she is best remembered for her Broadway performance in *Hello, Dolly!*

Stockard Channing (Susan Antonia Williams Stockard; 13 Feb 1944, New York NY) American motion-picture and TV actress; currently stars as the first lady on *The West Wing*.

Elaine Chao (26 Mar 1953, Taipei, Taiwan) American government official; US Secretary of Labor from 2001.

Tracy Chapman (20 Mar 1964, Cleveland OH) American folk-rock singer and songwriter.

Jean Charest (John James Charest; 24 Jun 1958, Sherbrooke, QC, Canada) French Canadian politician; leader of the Quebec Liberal Party from 1998.

Cyd Charisse (Tula Ellice Finklea; 8 Mar 1923, Amarillo TX) American dancer and actress who attained fame in some of the leading film musicals of the 1950s.

Charles, Prince of Wales (14 Nov 1948, Buckingham Palace, London, England) British royal; heir apparent to the British throne; eldest son of Queen Elizabeth II and Prince Philip, Duke of Edinburgh.

Pierre Charles (1954, Dominica) West Indian politician; prime minister of Dominica from 2000.

Ray Charles (Ray Charles Robinson; 23 Sep 1930, Albany GA) American blues and pop singer, pianist, and composer.

Chevy Chase (Cornelius Crane Chase; 8 Oct 1943, Woodstock NY) American comic actor on TV and in motion pictures.

Hugo Chávez Frías (28 Jul 1954, Sabaneta, Venezuela) military leader and politician; president of Venezuela from 1999.

Chen Kaige (12 Aug 1952, Beijing, China) Chinese film director known in the West for his *Farewell, My Concubine* (1993).

Lynne Cheney (14 Aug 1941, Casper WY) American political commentator; wife of Vice President Dick Cheney.

Richard Bruce ("Dick") Cheney (30 Jan 1941, Lincoln NE) American politician; US Secretary of Defense, 1989-93; vice president of the US from 2001.

Cher (Cherilyn Sarkaoian LaPier; 20 May 1946, El Centro CA) American pop singer and motion-picture actress; won an Academy Award for best actress in 1987 (*Moonstruck*).

Julia Child (Julia McWilliams; 15 Aug 1912, Pasadena CA) American cooking expert, author, and TV personality noted for her promotion of traditional French cuisine.

Frederick Jacob Titus Chiluba (30 Apr 1943, Kitwe, British Northern Rhodesia [now Zambia]) Zambian statesman; president of Zambia, 1991-2002.

Tadao Chino (1934, Shizuoka prefecture, Japan) Japanese banker; president of the Asian Development Bank from 1999.

Jacques (Rene) Chirac (29 Nov 1932, Paris, France) French politician; prime minister of France, 1974-76 and 1986-88, and president from 1995.

Joaquim (Alberto) Chissanó (22 Oct 1939, Malchice, Mozambique) Mozambican politician; president of Mozambique from 1986.

Chiyotaikai (Yuji Hiroshima; 29 Apr 1976, Chitose, Hokkaido, Japan) Japanese sumo wrestler with the rank of *ozeki* [champion] and winner of the July 2002 Nagoya Basho.

Fujio Cho (1937, Tokyo, Japan) Japanese corporate executive; president of Toyota Motor Corp. from 1999.

Margaret Cho (Moran Cho; 5 Dec 1968, San Francisco CA) Korean-American actress, comedienne known for autobiographical material.

A. Noam Chomsky (7 Dec 1928, Philadelphia PA) American linguist, writer, educator, and political activist, one of the founders of transformational, or generative, grammar.

Chow Yun-Fat (Zhou Runfa; 18 May 1955, Lamma Island, Hong Kong) Hong Kong actor wildly popular in Hong Kong; famous in the West for films such as *Crouching Tiger, Hidden Dragon* (2000).

Jean Chrétien (11 Jan 1934, Shawinigan, QC, Canada) Canadian lawyer, Liberal Party politician, and prime minister from 1993.

Helena Christensen (25 Dec 1968, Copenhagen, Denmark) Danish fashion model.

Julie (Frances) Christie (14 Apr 1941, Chuka, Assam, India) British film actress renowned for a wide range of roles in the 1960s and '70s.

Perry (Gladstone) Christie (1943, The Bahamas?) Bahamian politician; prime minister of The Bahamas from 3 May 2002.

Christo (Khristo Yavachev; 13 Jun 1935, Gabrovo, Bulgaria) Bulgarian conceptual artist and "environmental sculptor."

Connie Chung (20 Aug 1946, Washington DC) American TV journalist and anchorwoman.

Kyung-Wha Chung (26 Mar 1948, Seoul, Korea) Korean violinist.

Myung-Whun Chung (22 Jan 1953, Seoul, Korea) Korean pianist and conductor.

Chung Mong Joon (17 Oct 1951, Seoul, Korea) Korean businessman, sports promoter, and chairman of the Hyundai Group.

Carlo Azeglio Ciampi (9 Dec 1920, Livorno, Italy) Italian politician; prime minister of Italy, 1993-94, and president from 1999.

Liz Claiborne (Elisabeth Claiborne Ortenberg; 31 Mar 1929, Brussels, Belgium) Belgian-born American fashion designer and executive who creates women's casual and career apparel and accessories.

Tom Clancy (Thomas L. Clancy, Jr.; 12 Apr 1947, Baltimore MD) American best-selling novelist.

Eric Clapton (Eric Patrick Clapp; 30 Mar 1945, Ripley, Surrey, England) British guitarist, singer, and songwriter.

Dick Clark (Richard Wagstaff Clark; 30 Nov 1929, Mount Vernon NY) American TV host and producer whose shows have included *American Bandstand* and *The $10,000 Pyramid*.

Helen Clark (1950, Hamilton, New Zealand) New Zealand Labour politician; prime minister of New Zealand from 1999.

Petula Clark (15 Nov 1932, Epsom, England) British pop singer and actress.

Roy (Linwood) Clark (15 Apr 1933, Meherrin VA) American country and western artist.

Adrienne Clarkson (10 Feb 1939, Hong Kong) Canadian journalist, publisher, and governor-general of Canada from 1999.

John (Marwood) Cleese (27 Oct 1939, Weston-super-Mare, England) British comic actor best known for his TV work on *Monty Python's Flying Circus* and *Fawlty Towers*.

(William) Roger Clemens (4 Aug 1962, Dayton OH) American professional baseball pitcher; six-time Cy Young winner (1986, 1987, 1991, 1997, 1998, 2001).

Vassar Clements (25 Apr 1928, Kinard SC) American country fiddle player.

Glafkos (Ioannou) Clerides (24 Apr 1919, Nicosia, Cyprus) Cypriot politician; president of Cyprus in 1974 and again from 1993.

Van Cliburn (Harvey Lavan Cliburn, Jr.; 12 Jul 1934, Shreveport LA) American pianist.

Kim Clijsters (8 Jun 1983, Bilzen, Belgium) Belgian tennis player.

Bill Clinton (William Jefferson Blythe III) (19 Aug 1946, Hope AR) American statesman; 42nd president of the US, 1992–2000 [see full biography at Presidents].

Chelsea Victoria Clinton (27 Feb 1980, Little Rock AR) American personality; daughter of Pres. Bill Clinton and Hillary Rodham Clinton.

Hillary Rodham Clinton (Hillary Diane Rodham; 26 Oct 1947, Chicago IL) American politician; wife of Pres. Bill Clinton; Democratic senator from New York from 2000.

George Clooney (6 May 1961, Lexington KY) American film and TV actor, achieved widespread fame with his TV role on *ER*.

Chuck (Thomas) Close (Charles Thomas Close; 5 Jul 1940, Monroe WA) American painter noted for his highly inventive techniques used to paint the human face. He is best known for his large-scale, Photo-Realist portraits.

Glenn Close (19 Mar 1947, Greenwich CT) American actress who gained fame for *The Big Chill* (1983) and *Fatal Attraction* (1987).

Billy Cobham (16 May 1944, Panama) Panamanian jazz drummer and composer.

James Coburn (31 Aug 1928, Laurel NE) American film actor remembered as super-spy Derek Flint.

Imogene Coca (Imogene Fernandez de Coca; 18 Nov 1908, Philadelphia PA–2 Jun 2001, Westport CT), American actress, best remembered as the comedic partner of Sid Caesar.

Johnnie L. Cochran, Jr. (2 Oct 1937, Shreveport LA) American attorney; known for his successful defense of O.J. Simpson in his 1995 murder trial.

Alexander Cockburn (1941, Ardgay, Scotland) British-born American radical journalist and author.

Joe Cocker (John Robert Cocker; 20 May 1944, Sheffield, England) British rock singer.

Paulo Coelho (August 1947, Rio de Janeiro, Brazil) Brazilian author of best-selling novels, including *The Alchemist* (1988).

Ethan Coen (21 Sep 1958, St. Louis Park MN) American filmmaker, with brother Joel, known for eccentric movies.

Joel Coen (29 Nov 1955, St. Louis Park MN) American filmmaker, with brother Ethan, known for eccentric movies.

Leonard Cohen (21 Sep 1934, Montreal, QC, Canada) Canadian singer and songwriter.

Kenneth Cole (New York NY) American fashion designer of shoes, accessories, and apparel who is known for socially-conscious advertisements.

Natalie Maria Cole (6 Feb 1950, Los Angeles CA) American pop singer.

Dabney Coleman (3 Jan 1932, Austin TX) American film and TV actor.

Eoin Colfer (1965, Wexford, Ireland) Irish best-selling author of novels for children and adults.

Billy Collins (1941, New York NY) American poet; 11th poet laureate of the US, from 2001.

Eileen Collins (19 Nov 1956, Elmira NY) American astronaut, the first woman to pilot and, later, to command a US space shuttle.

Francis Sellers Collins (14 April 1950, Staunton VA) American geneticist, one of the leaders in the project to sequence the human genome.

Judy Collins (Judy Marjorie Collins; 1 May 1939, Seattle WA) American pop and folk singer.

Michael Collins (31 Oct 1930, Rome, Italy) American astronaut, co-pilot of the Gemini 10 flight and Command Module pilot of Apollo 11.

Phil Collins (31 Jan 1951, Chiswick, England) British rock vocalist and percussionist (of Genesis, etc.).

Alice Coltrane (27 Aug 1937, Detroit MI) American jazz pianist and composer.

Rita Rossi Colwell (1934, Beverly MA) American marine microbiologist and epidemiologist; director of the National Science Foundation from 1998.

Sean Combs (Puffy; Puff Daddy; P. Diddy; 4 Nov 1970, New York City NY) American rap artist and impresario.

Blaise Compaoré (1951, Ziniane, French Upper Volta [now Burkina Faso]) Burkinabe politician; president of Burkina Faso from 1987.

Philip M. Condit (2 Aug 1941, Berkeley CA) American aerospace engineer and corporate executive; chairman and CEO of the Boeing Co. from 1996.

Ward Connerty (15 Jun 1939, Leesville LA) American anti-affirmative action activist.

Sir Sean Connery (Thomas Connery; 25 Aug 1930, Edinburgh, Scotland) Scottish film actor of enduring attraction, known for rugged portrayals of leading men, including James Bond; also active in Scottish nationalist politics.

Alain Connes (1 Apr 1947, Darguignan, France) French mathematician; Fields medalist, 1983; winner of the Craoford Prize in 2001 "for penetrating work on the theory of operator algebras and for having been a founder of non-commutative geometry."

Harry Connick, Jr. (11 Sep 1967, New Orleans LA) American singer and film actor.

King Constantine II (2 Jun 1940, Psikhiko, near Athens, Greece) Greek royal; king of Greece, 1964–74.

Lansana Conté (1934, Moussayah Loumbaya, French West Africa [now Guinea]) Guinean military leader; president of Guinea from 1984.

Ry Cooder (Ryland Peter Cooder; 15 Mar 1947, Los Angeles CA) American musician and musicologist.

Alistair Cooke (20 Nov 1908, Manchester, England) British-born American TV host best known for his lively and insightful interpretations of US history and culture.

Coolio (Artis Ivey, Jr.; Aug 1963, Compton CA) American rap performer.

Alice Cooper (Vincent Furnier; 4 Feb 1948, Detroit MI) American singer and songwriter.

Cynthia Cooper (14 Apr 1963, Chicago IL) American collegiate, Olympic, and professional basketball player and coach.

L(eroy) Gordon Cooper, Jr. (6 Mar 1927, Shawnee OK) American astronaut, one of the original team of seven.

Stephen F. Cooper (23 Oct 1946) American corporate executive and turnaround specialist; CEO of Enron from 2002.

Jack Cope (3 Jun 1913, Mooi River, Natal, South Africa) South African writer best known for his short stories and novels about South African life.

Francis Ford Coppola (7 Apr 1939, Detroit MI) American film director, writer, and producer whose works range from sweeping epics to small-scale character studies.

John Corbett (9 May 1961, Wheeling WV) American actor who attracted attention for the TV series *Northern Exposure* and *Sex and the City*.

Chick Corea (Armando Anthony Corea; 12 Jun 1941, Chelsea MA) American jazz pianist and composer.

John Corigliano (16 Feb 1938, New York NY) American composer of lyrical, tonal, expressive works in orchestral music, opera, chamber music, and film scores.

Roger (William) Corman (5 Apr 1926, Detroit MI) American motion-picture director, producer, and distributor known for highly successful low-budget exploitation films.

Eric A. Cornell (19 Dec 1961, Palo Alto CA) American physicist; co-winner of the Nobel Prize for Physics, 2001, for work in the creation of the Bose-Einstein condensate.

Mairead Corrigan-Maguire (27 Jan 1944, Belfast, Northern Ireland) British pacifist and social worker; co-winner of the Nobel Peace Prize, 1976.

Larry Coryell (2 Apr 1943, Galveston TX) American jazz and rock guitarist and singer.

Bill Cosby (William Henry Cosby, Jr.; 12 Jul 1937, Philadelphia PA) American comedian and actor beloved for the groundbreaking 1980s TV series *The Cosby Show*.

Albert Costa (25 Jun 1975, Lérida, Spain) Spanish tennis player; winner of the 2002 French Open.

Gabriel Costa (11 Dec 1954) São Tomé and Priíncipe politician; prime minister of São Tomé and Principe from 26 Mar 2002.

Renato Cláudio Costa Pereira (30 Nov 1936, Brazil) Brazilian international official; secretary general of the International Civil Aviation Organization (ICAO) from 1997.

Costa-Gavras (Konstantin Gavras; 12 Feb 1933, Loutra-Iraias, Greece) Greek-born French motion-picture director known for political filmmaking.

Bob Costas (22 Mar 1952, New York NY) American TV sports journalist.

Elvis Costello (Declan Partick McManus; 25 Aug 1954, Liverpool, England) British songwriter and performer.

Kevin Costner (18 Jan 1955, Compton CA) American motion-picture actor and director most acclaimed for *Dances with Wolves* (1990).

Ileana Cotrubas (9 Jun 1939, Galati, Romania) Romanian soprano.

David Coulthard (27 Mar 1971, Twynholm, Dumfries and Galloway, Scotland) Scottish Formula 1 race-car driver; winner of the Monte Carlo Grand Prix, 2002.

Katie Couric (7 Jan 1957, Arlington VA) American TV talk-show host (*Today*).

Russell Coutts (1 Mar 1962, New Zealand) New Zealand yachtsman; first New Zealander and second non-American to win America's Cup (1995); he successfully defended it in 2000.

Wes Craven (Wesley Earl Craven; 2 Aug 1939, Cleveland OH) American creator of 1980s slash horror films and the *Scream* trilogy.

Cindy Crawford (20 Feb 1966, De Kalb IL) American fashion model.

Michael Crawford (Michael Patrick Dumble Smith, 19 Jan 1942, Wiltshire, England) British actor and singer, star of the stage musical *Phantom of the Opera*.

Robert (White) Creeley (21 May 1926, Arlington MA) American poet and founder of the Black Mountain movement.

(John) Michael Crichton (28 Oct 1942, Chicago IL) American best-selling writer and director specializing in novels on scientific themes.

Robert Laurel Crippen (11 Sep 1937, Beaumont TX) American astronaut who served as pilot on the first US space shuttle orbital flight.

Walter (Leland) Cronkite, Jr. (4 Nov 1916, St. Joseph MO) American broadcast journalist, commentator, and TV news anchor.

Hume Cronyn (Hume Blake; 18 Jul 1911, London, ON, Canada) Canadian-born American stage and screen actor, often with wife Jessica Tandy.

David Crosby (David Van Cortland; 14 Aug 1941, Los Angeles CA) American singer and songwriter with Crosby, Stills & Nash and The Byrds.

Sheryl Crow (11 Feb 1962, Kennett MO) American pop singer-songwriter.

Cameron B. Crowe (13 Jul 1957, Palm Springs CA) American motion-picture director and writer acclaimed for the autobiographical *Almost Famous* (2000).

J.D. Crowe (27 Aug 1937, Lexington KY) American country and western performer.

Russell (Ira) Crowe (7 Apr 1964, Wellington, New Zealand) New Zealand-Australian motion-picture actor famous for *Gladiator* (2000) and *A Beautiful Mind* (2001).

Rodney Crowell (7 Aug 1950, Houston TX) American country and rock singer and songwriter.

Tom Cruise (Thomas Cruise Mapother IV; 3 Jul 1962, Syracuse NY) American film icon since his breakthrough performance in *Risky Business* (1983).

George (Henry) Crumb (24 Oct 1929, Charleston WV) American composer.

Celia Cruz (21 Oct c. 1929, Havana, Cuba) American (Cuban-born) singer, called the "Queen of Salsa Music."

Penélope Cruz (Sánchez) (28 Apr 1974, Madrid, Spain) Spanish actress who achieved international fame in the late 1990s.

Billy Crystal (14 Mar 1947, Long Beach NY) American comedic actor popular for light dramatic comedies.

Macaulay (Carson) Culkin (26 Aug 1980, New York NY) American child star of the early 1990s.

Merce Cunningham (16 Apr 1919, Centralia WA) American modern dancer and choreographer who developed new forms of abstract dance movement.

Tim Curry (19 Apr 1946, Cheshire, England) British film and theater actor and rock performer.

Jane (Therese) Curtin (6 Sep 1947, Cambridge MA) American TV actress and comedienne most famous for *Saturday Night Live* and *Third Rock from the Sun*.

Christopher Paul Curtis (10 May 1954, Flint MI) American author of children's books.

Jamie Lee Curtis (22 Nov 1958, Los Angeles CA) American film and TV actress.

Tony Curtis (Bernard Schwartz; 3 Jun 1925, Bronx NY) American comic and dramatic film actor whose long and illustrious career includes well over 100 films.

Joan Cusack (11 Oct 1962, New York NY) American film actress best known for humorous supporting roles.

John (Paul) Cusack (28 Jun 1966, Evanston IL) American actor first famous for 1980s teen films.

D.M.C. (Darryl McDaniels; 31 May 1964, Hollis, Queens NY) American hip-hop pioneer (of Run-D.M.C.).

Jacques d'Amboise (28 Jul 1934, Dedham MA) American dancer and choreographer of the New York City Ballet (1949–84), admired for his energetic, virile interpretations of both character and classical roles.

Willem Dafoe (William Dafoe, Jr.; 22 Jul 1955, Appleton WI) American dramatic star known for complex, passionate portrayals.

Douglas N. Daft (Australia) American corporate executive; chairman and CEO of the Coca-Cola Co. from 2000.

Richard M. Daley (24 Apr 1942, Chicago IL) American Democratic politician; mayor of Chicago from 1989.

Roger (Harry) Daltrey (1 Mar 1944, London, England) British rock singer (of the Who).

Matt(hew Paige) Damon (8 Oct 1970, Cambridge MA) American actor, screenwriter; breakthrough performance in *Good Will Hunting* (1997) made him a top box-office draw.

Rodney Dangerfield (Jacob Cohen; 22 Nov 1921, Babylon NY) American comedian and film actor.

Charlie Daniels (28 Oct 1936, Wilmington NC) American country fiddler and singer.

Erich von Däniken (14 Apr 1935, Zofingen, Switzerland) Swiss author of several books—notably *Chariots of the Gods* (1968)—about his theories that the Earth was visited by extraterrestrial astronauts in ancient times.

Ted Danson (Edward Bridge Danson III; 29 Dec 1947, San Diego CA) American film and TV actor best known for playing Sam on the TV series *Cheers*.

Edwidge Danticat (19 Jan 1969, Port-au-Prince, Haiti) Haitian-born American author whose works focus on the lives of women and their relationships. She also addressed issues of power, injustice, and poverty.

Mahmoud Darwish (1942, Birwa, Palestine) Palestinian nationalist poet.

Thomas Andrew Daschle (9 Dec 1947, Aberdeen SD) American politician; Senate majority leader; South Dakota Democratic senator from 1987.

Lindsay Davenport (8 Jun 1976, Palos Verdes CA) American tennis player; won an Olympic gold medal (1996), the US Open (1998), Wimbledon (1999), and the Australian Open (2000).

Craig David (5 May 1981, Southampton, Hampshire, England) British R&B and rap performer.

Bella Davidovich (16 Jul 1928, Baku, Azerbaijan, USSR) Azerbaijani pianist.

Mario Davidovsky (4 Mar 1934, Buenos Aires, Argentina) Argentine-born American composer.

Paul Charles William Davies (1946, London, England) Australian mathematical physicist; Templeton Prize winner, 1995.

Angela (Yvonne) Davis (26 Jan 1944, Birmingham AL) American militant black activist of the 1970s and '80s.

Sir Colin (Rex) Davis (25 Sep 1927, Weybridge, Surrey, England) English conductor; principal conductor of the London Symphony Orchestra from 1995.

Geena Davis (Virginia Elizabeth Davis; 21 Jan 1956, Wareham MA) American film and TV actress best known for her role in *Thelma and Louise* (1991).

Gray Davis (26 Dec 1942, New York NY) American Democratic politician; governor of California from 1999.

Mac Davis (21 Jan 1942, Lubbock TX) American pop singer.

(Clinton) Richard Dawkins (26 Mar 1941, Nairobi, Kenya) British zoologist, popularizer of science.

Patrick Day (13 Oct 1953, Brush CO) American jockey; all-time top North American moneywinner with more than 7,000 career victories.

Stockwell Day (16 Aug 1950, Barrie, ON, Canada) Canadian politician; leader of the opposition.

Daniel Day-Lewis (29 Apr 1957, London, England) British motion-picture actor usually in serious and compelling roles.

Inge De Bruijn (24 Aug 1973, Barendrecht, The Netherlands) Dutch swimmer; set numerous world records after returning from retirement in mid-1990s; won three Olympic golds (and set three world records) and one silver in 2000.

Oscar De La Hoya (4 Feb 1973, East Los Angeles CA) American boxer; held professional titles in five weight classes: junior lightweight, 1994; lightweight, 1995; super lightweight, 1996; welterweight, 1997 (lost 1999, recovered 2000); and super welterweight, 2001.

Oscar de la Renta (22 Jul 1932, Santo Domingo, Dominican Republic) Dominican-born American fashion designer who blended European luxury with American ease to define standards of elegant dressing.

Robert De Niro (17 Aug 1943, New York NY) American film actor known for his uncompromising portrayals of violent and abrasive characters.

Brian (Russell) De Palma (11 Sep 1940, Newark NJ) American motion-picture director and screenwriter.

Edo De Waart (1 Jun 1941, Amsterdam, The Netherlands) Dutch conductor.

Howard Dean (17 Nov 1948, New York NY) American physician and Democratic politician; governor of Vermont from 1991.

Idriss Déby (1952, Fada, Chad) Chadian politician; president of Chad from 1990.

Roy DeCarava (9 Dec 1919, Harlem, New York NY) American photographer whose images of African Americans chronicle subjects such as daily life in Harlem, the civil rights movement, and jazz musicians.

Sandra Dee (Alexandra Zuck; 23 Apr 1942, Bayonne NJ) American actress famous for playing the ingenue.

Ellen DeGeneres (26 Jan 1958, Metairie LA) American comedienne and TV personality best known for her TV series *Ellen*.

Jack DeJohnette (9 Aug 1942, Chicago IL) American jazz drummer and composer.

Benicio Del Toro (19 Feb 1967, San Turce, Puerto Rico) American motion-picture actor who won an Academy Award for best supporting actor in 2000 for *Traffic*.

David Del Tredici (16 Mar 1937, Cloverdale CA) American composer.

Kim Delaney (29 Nov 1961, Philadelphia PA) American TV actress, star of *NYPD Blue* and *Philly*.

Bertrand Delanoë (30 May 1950, Tunis, Tunisia) French politician; mayor of Paris from 2001.

Dino DeLaurentis (8 Aug 1919, Torre, Annunziata, Italy) Italian international motion-picture producer.

Michael S. Dell (23 Feb 1965, Houston TX) American businessman; founder and CEO of Dell Computer Corp. from 1984; believed to receive the highest compensation of any US executive.

Ann Demeulemeester (1959, Kortrijk, Belgium) Belgian fashion designer noted for her modernist long coats and unusual fabrics.

John Demjanjuk (3 Apr 1920, Ukriane) Ukrainian-born auto worker; alleged Nazi death-camp guard, expelled from the US and whose US citizenship was revoked for a second time in February 2002.

Jonathan Demme (22 Feb 1944, Baldwin, Long Island NY) American film director noted for *The Silence of the Lambs* (1991) and *Philadelphia* (1993).

Dame Judi Dench (Judith Olivia Dench; 9 Dec 1934, York, England) British actress known for her powerful stage, TV, and screen roles.

Catherine Deneuve (Catherine Dorléac; 22 Oct 1943, Paris, France) French film actress, model, and beauty icon.

Rauf Denktash (1924, Baf [Paphos], Cyprus) Turkish Cypriot politician; president of Turkish Cyprus from 1975.

Brian Dennehy (9 Jul 1938, Bridgeport CT) American TV, film, and stage actor known for serious dramatic roles.

Eumir de Almeida Deodato (22 Jun 1942, Rio de Janeiro, Brazil) Brazilian jazz pianist and composer.

Gérard Depardieu (27 Dec 1948, Châteauroux, France) motion-picture actor of international renown.

Johnny Depp (John Christopher Depp III; 9 Jun 1963, Owensboro KY) American film and TV actor known for eccentric, brooding roles.

Laura Dern (10 Feb 1967, Los Angeles CA) American screen actress who has enjoyed commercial and critical success.

Jacques Derrida (15 Jul 1930, El Biar, Algeria) French deconstructionist philosopher, whose critique of Western philosophy encompasses literature, linguistics, and psychoanalysis.

Alan Dershowitz (1 Sep 1938, Brooklyn NY) American attorney and legal commentator.

Thierry Desmarest (1945) French corporate executive, CEO of TotalFinaElf SA from 1995.

Sir Frankie Dettori (Lanfranco Dettori; 15 Dec 1970, Italy) Italian-born English jockey; winner of more than 2,000 flat races in England and Europe since the mid-1980s.

Danny DeVito (Daniel Michaeli; 17 Nov 1944, Neptune NJ) American actor, director, and producer specializing in supporting comic roles.

Ani Di Franco (23 Sep 1970, Buffalo NY) American singer and songwriter.

Neil Diamond (24 Jan 1941, Brooklyn NY) American pop singer and songwriter.

Diana, Princess of Wales (1 Jul 1961, Sandringham, Norfolk, England—31 Aug 1997, Paris, France), British consort (from 1981) of Charles, Prince of Wales, and mother of the heir second in line to the British throne, Prince William of Wales (born 1982).

Cameron M. Diaz (30 Aug 1972, San Diego CA) American model and actress whose roles range from comic to intense.

Leonardo Wilhelm DiCaprio (11 Nov 1974, Los Angeles CA) American actor and heartthrob who achieved box-office success with Titanic (1997).

Angie Dickinson (Angeline Brown; 30 Sep 1931, Kulm ND) American film and TV actress whose career has spanned five decades.

Bo Diddley (Ellas Bates; 30 Dec 1928, McComb MS) American singer, songwriter, and musician.

Dido (Florian Cloude De Bourneville Armstrong; 25 Dec 1971, London, England) British pop singer.

Barry Diller (2 Feb 1942, San Francisco CA) American executive; CEO of USA Interactive and Vivendi Universal Entertainment.

Matt Dillon (18 Feb 1964, New Rochelle NY) American actor first known as a teen heartthrob, he often plays alienated, dark characters.

Dion (Dion DiMucci; 18 Jul 1939, Bronx NY) American rock-and-roll singer.

Céline Dion (30 Mar 1968, Charlemagne, QC, Caanda) French Canadian pop singer.

Jacques Diouf (1 Aug 1938, Saint-Louis, French West Africa [now Senegal]) Senegalese international civil servant; director-general of the Food and Agriculture Organization from 1994.

King Dipendra Bir Bikram Shah Dev (27 Jun 1971, Kathmandu, Nepal—4 Jun 2001, Kathmandu, Nepal), Nepalese royal; king of Nepal for four days

in 2001 after he murdered his parents and seven other members of the royal family.

Waris Dirie (196?, Somalia) Somali fashion model and women's rights activist.

Zoran Djindjic (1 Aug 1952, Bosanski Samac, Bosnia, Yugoslavia) Yugoslav politician; prime minister of Serbia from 2001.

Milo Djukanovic (15 Feb 1962, Niksic, Montenegro, Yugoslavia) Yugoslavian politician; president of the Yugoslav Republic of Montenegro from 1998.

E.L. Doctorow (Edgar Laurence Doctorow; 6 Jan 1931, New York NY) American novelist known for his skillful manipulation of traditional genres.

Eugène Dodeigne (27 Jul 1923, Rouvreux, near Liège, Belgium) Belgian-born French sculptor best known for his monumental stone figures, usually placed outdoors.

Gary Doer (31 Mar 1948, Winnipeg, MB, Canada) Canadian politician; premier of Manitoba from 1999.

Christoph von Dohnányi (8 Sep 1929, Berlin, Germany) German conductor.

Domenico Dolce (13 Aug 1958, Polizzi Generosa, near Palermo, Italy) Italian fashion designer, along with partner Stefano Gabbana, whose designs are inspired by the Mediterranean region.

Plácido Domingo (21 Jan 1941, Madrid, Spain) Spanish-born Mexican operatic tenor, one of the most popular tenors of the second half of the 20th century.

Fats Domino (Antoine Domino, Jr.; 26 Feb 1928, New Orleans LA) American R&B musician who became one of the first rock-and-roll stars.

Phil Donahue (21 Dec 1935, Cleveland OH) American TV talk-show host, a pioneer of the genre.

Sam Donaldson (11 Mar 1934, El Paso TX) American TV news correspondent.

Donovan (Donovan P. Leitch; 10 May 1946, Glasgow, Scotland) British pop singer and songwriter.

José Eduardo dos Santos (28 Aug 1942, Luanda, Angola) Angolan statesman; president of Angola from 1979.

Manuel dos Santos Lima (28 Jan 1935, Silva Porto, Angola) Angolan poet, dramatist, and novelist.

Abdul Rashid Dostum (1954, Juzjian province, Afghanistan) Afghani Uzbek military leader who worked with the Northern Alliance against the Taliban.

Michael Doucet (14 Feb 1951, Scott LA) American Cajun musician.

Denzil L. Douglas (14 Jan 1953, St. Paul's, St. Kitts and Nevis) West Indian politician; prime minister of Saint Kitts and Nevis from 1995.

Kirk Douglas (Issur Danielovitch Demsky; 9 Dec 1916, Amsterdam NY) American actor known for resolute, emotionally charged roles, including the title character in the film Spartacus (1960).

Michael Douglas (25 Sep 1944, New Brunswick NJ) American film actor and producer who is best known for his intense portrayals of flawed heroes.

Mike Douglas (11 Aug 1925, Chicago IL) American TV show host.

Rita (Frances) Dove (28 Aug 1962, Akron OH) American writer and teacher who was poet laureate of the US in 1993–95.

Robert Downey, Jr. (4 Apr 1965, New York NY) American troubled film and TV actor of substance and intelligence; achieved critical success for the film Chaplin (1992).

Hugh Downs (14 Feb 1921, Akron OH) American TV broadcaster.

Roddy Doyle (1958, Dublin, Ireland) Irish author, who won the Booker Prize in 1993 for his *Paddy Clarke Ha Ha Ha*.

Dr. Dre (Andre Young; 18 Feb 1965, Los Angeles CA) American rap musician and impresario.

Stacy Dragila (25 Mar 1971, Auburn CA) American pole vaulter; won the gold medal in the first-ever Olympic women's pole vault, 2000.

E. Linn Draper, Jr., American energy engineer and corporate executive; chairman, president, and CEO of American Electric Power, Inc. from 1992.

Heike Drechsler (16 Dec 1964, Gera, Thuringia, [East] Germany) German long jumper; world-record holder who won a gold medal at the 1983 world championships and made a big comeback to win again at the 1993 worlds and at the 1992 and 2000 Olympics.

Elizabeth Drew (16 Nov 1935, Cincinnati OH) American journalist.

Richard (Stephan) Dreyfus (29 Oct 1947, Brooklyn NY) American film actor known for portrayals of ordinary men driven to emotional extremes.

Minnie Driver (31 Jan 1970, London, England) British articulate actress who first achieved fame for the film *Circle of Friends* (1995).

Janez Drnovsek (17 May 1950, Celje, Yugoslavia [now Slovenia]) Slovene politician; prime minister of Slovenia from 1992–2000 and again from 2000.

Matt Drudge (27 Oct 1967 Maryland) American Internet journalist.

Andres Duany (7 Sep 1949, New York NY) American urban planner who collabrates with his wife, Elizabeth Plater-Zyberg.

David Duchovny (David William Ducovny; 7 Aug 1960, New York NY) American TV and film actor, best known as Fox Mulder on *The X-Files*.

Eduardo Duhalde (5 Oct 1941, Lomas de Zamora, Argentina) Argentine politican; president of Argentina from 2 Jan 2002.

Wim Duisenberg (Willem Frederik Duisenberg; 9 Jul 1935, Heerenveen, The Netherlands) Dutch banker and first president of the European Central Bank from 1998.

Olympia Dukakis (20 Jun 1931, Lowell MA) American film actress and theatrical director.

Patty Duke (Anna Marie Duke; 14 Dec 1946, New York NY) American TV and film actress best remembered for playing Helen Keller in *The Miracle Worker* (1962).

Faye Dunaway (Dorothy Faye; 14 Jan 1941, Bascom FL) American film actress known for tense, absorbing performances.

Pat Duncan (8 Apr 1960, Edmondton, AB, Canada) Canadian politician; premier of Yukon Territory from 6 May 2000.

Ian Duncan Smith (9 Apr 1954, Edinburgh, Scotland) British politician; leader of the Conservative Party.

Katherine Dunham (22 Jun 1910, Joliet IL) American dancer, choreographer, and anthropologist.

José Manuel Durão Barroso (1956, Portugal?) Portuguese politician; prime minister of Portugal from 6 Apr 2001.

David Duval (9 Nov 1971, Jacksonville FL) American golfer who won the 2001 British Open.

Jean-Claude Duvalier (3 Jul 1951, Port-au-Prince, Haiti) Haitian politician; president of Haiti, 1971–86.

Robert Duvall (5 Jan 1931, San Diego CA) American actor, producer, and screenwriter noted for portrayals of average working people.

Andrea Dworkin (26 Sep 1946, Camden NJ) American feminist; developed theory of pornography as harmful to women.

Ronald Dworkin (1931, Worcester MA) American legal theorist; best known for *Law's Empire*.

Greg Dyke (20 May 1947, London, England) British TV executive and head of the BBC from 1999.

Bob Dylan (Robert Allen Zimmerman; 24 May 1941, Duluth MN) American singer and songwriter.

Esther Dyson (14 Jul 1951, Zürich, Switzerland) American economist and journalist specializing in computer and cyberspace issues.

Freeman (John) Dyson (15 Dec 1923, Crowthorne, Berkshire, England) British-born American physicist and educator best known for his speculative work on extraterrestrial civilizations; Templeton Prize winner, 2001.

Michael Eric Dyson (23 Oct 1958, Detroit MI) American scholar, newspaper columnist, and author.

Mikulas Dzurinda (4 Feb 1955, Spissky Stvrtok, Czechoslovakia [now Slovakia]) Slovak politician; prime minister of Slovakia from 1998.

Michael F. Easley (23 Mar 1950, Nash county NC) American Democratic politician; governor of North Carolina from January 2001.

Clint Eastwood (31 May 1930, San Francisco CA) American enduring film actor and moviemaker, originally famous for tough guy roles such as *Dirty Harry*.

Roger Ebert (18 Jun 1942, Urbana IL) American film critic in newspapers and on TV.

Buddy Ebsen (Christian Rudolf Ebsen, Jr.; 2 Apr 1908, Belleville IL) American actor who starred in the TV series *The Beverly Hillbillies* and *Barnaby Jones*.

Bülent Ecevit (28 May 1925, Constantinople [now Istanbul], Turkey) Turkish politician; prime minister of Turkey 1974, 1977, 1978–79, and from 1999.

Rolf Eckrodt (25 Jun 1942, Gronau, Westphalia, Germany) German business executive; CEO of Mitsubishi Motors Corp. from 2001.

Umberto Eco (5 Jan 1932, Alessandria, Italy) Italian literary critic, novelist, and semiotician.

Duane Eddy (26 Apr 1938, Corning NY) American rock and pop guitarist responsible for twang.

Marian Wright Edelman (6 Jun 1939, Bennettsville SC) American attorney and civil rights advocate; founder of the Children's Defense Fund.

The Edge (Dave Evans; 8 Aug 1961, Barking, Essex [now greater London], England) British rock musician (with U2).

Prince Edward (Edward Anthony Richard Louis, Earl of Wessex; 10 Mar 1964, Buckingham Palace, London, England) British royal; third son of Queen Elizabeth II.

Anthony Edwards (19 Jul 1962, Santa Barbara CA) American TV and film actor; played Dr. Mark Greene on the TV series *ER*.

Blake Edwards (26 Jul 1922, Tulsa OK) American film producer, writer, and director most famous for the *Pink Panther* films.

Jonathan Edwards (10 May 1966, London, England) British track-and-field athlete, the first to triple-jump more than 18 meters, setting three world records.

Jorge Edwards (29 Jul 1931, Santiago, Chile) Chilean writer, literary critic, and diplomat who gained notoriety with the publication of *Persona non grata* (1973), a memoir of his experiences as the Chilean ambassador to Cuba in the early 1970s.

Edward Egan (2 Apr 1932, Oak Park IL) American church leader; Roman Catholic cardinal archbishop of New York.

Atom Egoyan (19 Jul 1960, Cairo, Egypt) Armenian Canadian film director, producer, and writer.

Paul R(alph) Ehrlich (29 May 1932, Philadelphia PA) American biologist and population expert who in 1990 shared the Crafoord Prize.

Julie Nixon Eisenhower (5 Jul 1948, Washington DC) American personality; daughter of Pres. Richard M Nixon and wife of David Eisenhower, the grandson of Pres. Dwight D. Eisenhower.

Michael D. Eisner (7 Mar 1942, Mount Kisco NY) American corporate executive; CEO of the Walt Disney Co. from 1984.

Cyprian (Odiatu Duaka) Ekwensi (26 Sep 1921, Minna, Nigeria) Nigerian Ibo novelist, short-story writer, and children's author.

Hicham El Guerrouj (14 Sep 1974, Berkane, Morocco) Moroccan runner who set world records in the 1,500-m, 2,000-m, and mile races.

Elizabeth II, Queen of the United Kingdom of Great Britain and Northern Ireland (21 Apr 1926, London, England) British royal; queen from 1952.

Ramblin' Jack Elliott (Elliott Charles Adnopoz; 1931, Brooklyn NY) American folk songwriter and singer.

Lawrence J. Ellison (17 Aug 1944, Chicago IL) American corporate executive; founder and CEO of Oracle Corp. from 1977.

James Ellroy (Lee Earle Ellroy; 4 Mar 1948, Los Angeles CA) American mystery writer.

Ernie Els (Theodore Ernest Els; 17 Oct 1969, Johannesburg, South Africa) South African golfer who won the US Open (1994, 1997), the British Open (2002), and numerous other tournaments.

John Elway (28 Jun 1960, Port Angeles WA) American football player, quarterback who led the Denver Broncos to victory in Super Bowl XXXII in 1998.

John Hart Ely, American legal scholar whose book Democracy and Distrust is among the most-cited sources in American law.

Eminem (Marshall Bruce Mathers III; 17 Oct 1973, St. Joseph MO) American entertainer, hip-hop artist.

Emme (New York NY) American fashion model and TV host.

John Engler (12 Oct 1948, Mount Pleasant MI) American Republican politician; governor of Michigan from 1991.

Nambaryn Enhbayar (1 Jun 1958, Ulaanbaatar, Mongolia) Mongolian politician; prime minister of Mongolia from 2000.

Philippe Entremont (6 Jun 1934, Reims, France) French pianist and conductor.

Enya (Eithne Ní Bhraonáin; 17 May 1961, Gweedore, Donegal, Ireland) Irish Celtic singer.

Nora Ephron (19 May 1941, New York NY) American novelist, screenwriter, and director, known for romantic comedies.

Christoph Eschenbach (20 Feb 1040, Wrocław, Poland) Polish-born pianist and conductor; named music director of the Philadelphia Orchestra beginning in 2003.

Amara Essy (20 Dec 1944, Bouake, French West Africa [now Côte d'Ivoire]) Ivoirien diplomat; secretary general of the Organization of African Unity from 2001.

Gloria Estefan (Gloria Fajardo; 1 Sep 1957, Havana, Cuba) Cuban born American salsa singer and lyricist.

Simon Estes (2 Mar 1938, Centerville IA) American operatic bass.

Joseph Estrada (Joseph Ejercito; 19 Apr 1937, Manila, Philippines) Philippine actor and politician; president of the Philippines, 1998–2001.

Melissa Etheridge (29 May 1961, Leavenworth KS) American rock singer and songwriter.

Linda Evangelista (10 May 1965, Saint Catherines, ON, Canada) Canadian fashion model.

Don Evans (27 Jul 1946, Houston TX) American government official; US Secretary of Commerce from January 2001.

Faith Evans (10 Jun 1973, Lakeland FL) American soul singer.

Rupert Everett (29 May 1959, Norfolk, England) English actor in intellectual roles.

Everly Brothers: Don (Isaac Donald Everly; 1 Feb 1937, Brownie KY) and Phil (19 Jan 1939, Brownie KY) American pop singers, songwriters, and guitarists.

Myrlie Evers-Williams (17 Mar 1933, Vicksburg MS) American civil rights activist; chairman of the National Association for the Advancement of Colored People, 1995–98.

Ernie Eves (1946, Windsor, ON, Canada) Canadian politician; premier of Ontario from 15 Apr 2002.

Cesaria Evora (1941, Mindelo, Cape Verde) Cape Verdean singer of mornas.

Eyadema (26 Dec 1937, Pya village, Kabyé region, Togoland [now Togo]) Togolese soldier; president of Togo from 1967.

Fabio (Lanzoni) (15 Mar 1961, Milan, Italy) Italian model and actor known for romance novel covers, television commercials, and brief movie appearances.

Fahd ibn 'Abd al-'Aziz al-Sa'ud (1923, Riyadh, Arabia) Saudi Arabian royal; king of Saudi Arabia from 1982.

Richard D. Fairbank (18 Sep 1950, Menlo Park CA) American corporate executive; founder, chairman, and CEO of Capital One Financial Corp. from 1988.

Morgan Fairchild (Patsy Ann McClenny; 3 Feb 1950, Dallas TX) American TV actress known for her role on Falcon Crest.

Marianne Faithfull (29 Dec 1946, Hampstead, London, England) British singer and actress.

Leo Amy Falcam (20 Nov 1935, Pohnpei Island) Micronesian politician; president of the Federated States of Micronesia from 1999.

Peter Falk (16 Sep 1927, New York NY) American film and TV actor who played detective Columbo on the series of the same name.

Oriana Fallaci (29 Jun 1930, Florence, Italy) Italian journalist and interviewer.

Jerry Falwell (11 Aug 1933, Lynchburg VA) American TV evangelist and religious educator.

Nuruddin Farah (24 Nov 1945, Baidoa, Italian Somaliland [now in Somalia]) Somali writer in English.

Art Farmer (Arthur Stewart Farmer; 21 Aug 1928, Council Bluffs IA) American jazz trumpeter and flügelhornist.

Louis (Abdul) Farrakhan (Louis Eugene Walcott; 11 May 1933, Bronx NY) American leader of the Nation of Islam (Black Muslims) from 1978.

Joe Farrell (Joseph Carl Firrantello; 16 Dec 1937, Chicago Heights IL) American jazz saxophonist and reed man.

Suzanne Farrell (Roberta Sue Ficker; 16 Aug 1945, Cincinnati OH) American dancer especially known for her performances with the New York City Ballet.

Mia Farrow (Maria de Lourdes Villiers Farrow; 9 Feb 1945, Los Angeles CA) American film actress first famous for *Rosemary's Baby* (1968), her stormy relations with director Woody Allen, and as UNICEF special representative from 2000.

Fatboy Slim (Quentin Norman Cook; 13 Jul 1963, Bromley, England) British pop musician.

Farrah Fawcett (Mary Farrah Leni Fawcett; also known as Farrah Fawcett Majors; 2 Feb 1947, Corpus Christi TX) American film and TV actress and model most popular for her role on TV's *Charlie's Angels.*

Mohamed al-Fayed (27 Jan 1933, Alexandria, Egypt) Egyptian businessman; owner of Harrods department store in London from 1985.

Sverre Fehn (14 Aug 1924, Kongsberg, Norway) Norwegian architect; Pritzker Prize winner, 1997.

Dianne (Goldman Berman) Feinstein (22 Jun 1933, San Francisco CA) American Democratic politician; mayor of San Francisco, 1978–88; US senator from 1992.

Eliot Feld (5 Jul 1942, New York NY) American dancer, choreographer, and director who formed the Eliot Feld Ballet in 1973.

José Feliciano (10 Sep 1945, Lares PR) Puerto Rican-born folk-rock and pop guitarist and singer.

Prince Felipe (Felipe de Borbón y Grecia; 30 Jan 1968, Madrid, Spain) Spanish royal; prince of Asturias; heir to the throne of Spain.

Freddy Fender (Baldemar Huerta; 1937, San Benito TX) American country/Tex-Mex rock singer.

Svetlana Feofanova (16 Jul 1980, Moscow) Russian pole vaulter; European champion and worldwide leader, set several European records in succession in 2002.

Maynard Ferguson (4 May 1928, Verdun, QC, Canada) Canadian-born jazz trumpeter and leader.

Sarah (Margaret) Ferguson (15 Oct 1959, London, England) British royal; formerly Duchess of York.

Lawrence Ferlinghetti (24 Mar 1919, Yonkers NY) American poet, one of the founders of the Beat movement.

Gil de Ferran (11 Nov 1967, Paris, France) French-born Brazilian race-car driver; CART (Indy Car) champion, 2000 and 2001.

Gianfranco Ferré (15 Aug 1944, Legnano, Italy) Italian fashion designer noted for his white dress shirts.

Bryan Ferry (26 Sep 1945, Washington, Durham, England) British rock singer and songwriter.

Sally Field (Sally Mahoney; 6 Nov 1946, Pasadena CA) American endearing comic and dramatic actress known for her versatility.

Joseph Fiennes (27 May 1970, Salisbury, England) British classically trained stage actor who gained international attention after playing the bard in *Shakespeare in Love* (1998).

Ralph (Nathaniel) Fiennes (22 Dec 1962, Suffolk, England) British dramatic actor known for intense roles.

Harvey (Forbes) Fierstein (6 Jun 1954, Brooklyn NY) American playwright (*La Cage aux Folles, Torch Song Trilogy*) and performer.

Luis Figo (4 Nov 1972, Lisbon, Portugal) Portuguese association football (soccer) player; FIFA player of the year, 2001.

Harvey V. Fineberg (15 Sep 1945, Pittsburgh PA) American public health physician and medical administrator; president of the Institute of Medicine from 2002.

Albert Finney (9 May 1936, Salford, England) British stage, TV, and film actor best known for his portrayal of Tom Jones in the film of that name (1963).

Carly Fiorina (Cara Carleton S. Fiorina; 6 Sep 1954, Austin TX) American corporate executive; chairman and CEO of Hewlett-Packard Co. and Compaq Computer (which merged in 2002).

Colin Firth (10 Sep 1960, Grayshott, Hampshire, England) British film, stage, and TV actor famous for reserved but likeable characters.

Bobby Fischer (Robert James Fischer; 9 Mar 1943, Chicago IL) American chess grandmaster and world champion, 1972–75.

Joschka Fischer (Joseph Martin Fischer; 12 Apr 1948, Gerabronn, Baden-Würtemberg, Germany) German politician and Green/Alliance 90 leader; foreign minister of Germany from 1998.

Laurence Fishburne (30 Jul 1961, Augusta GA) American powerful stage and screen actor.

Allison Fisher (24 Feb 1968, Cheshunt, Hertfordshire, England) British snooker and pocket billiards champion; won the WPA nine-ball world championships in 1996, 1997, 1998, and 2001.

Eddie Fisher (Edwin Fisher; 10 Aug 1928, Philadelphia PA) American pop singer.

Sarah Fitz-Gerald (1 Dec 1968, Melbourne, Australia) Australian squash rackets champion; World Open champion, 1996–98, 2001; won the British Open in 2001 and 2002; and the Commonwealth Games gold medal, 2002.

Roberta Flack (10 Feb 1940, Black Mountain NC) American pop and jazz singer and pianist.

Michael Flatley (16 Jul 1958, Chicago IL) American dancer and popularizer of Celtic folk dancing.

Mick Fleetwood (24 Jun 1947, Redruth, Cornwall, England) British rock percussionist (of Fleetwood Mac).

(Lawrence) Ari Fleischer (1960, Pound Ridge NY) American government official; White House press secretary from 2001.

Renée Fleming (14 Feb 1959, Indiana PA) American operatic soprano.

Rhonda Fleming (10 Aug 1923, Los Angeles CA) American actress and singer known for roles that showcased her red hair and fiery temperament.

Louise Fletcher (22 Jul 1934, Birmingham AL) American TV and film actress most famous for the film *One Flew Over the Cuckoo's Nest* (1975).

Calista (Kay) Flockhart (11 Nov 1964, Freeport IL) American actress, star of TV's *Ally McBeal.*

Francisco Flores Pérez (19 Oct 1959) Salvadorian politician; president of El Salvador from 1999.

Gaston Flosse (24 Jun 1931, Rikitea, Gambier Islands, French Polynesia) French Polynesian politician; president of French Polynesia, 1984–87 and from 1991.

Larry (Claxton) Flynt (1 Nov 1942, Magoffin county, Kentucky) American publisher of *Hustler Magazine* and freedom of the press advocate.

Dario Fo (24 Mar 1926, Leggiuno-Sangiano, Italy) Italian actor and playwright; won the Nobel Prize for Literature (1997).

Eugene Fodor (5 Mar 1950, Turkey Creek CO) American violinist.

John Fogerty (28 May 1945, Berkeley CA) American rock vocalist (of Creedence Clearwater Revival).

Jane Fonda (21 Dec 1937, New York NY) American motion-picture actress also known for her political activism and her popular exercise program.

Peter Fonda (23 Feb 1939, New York NY) American motion-picture writer, producer, and actor; most famous for *Easy Rider* (1969).

Joan Fontaine (Joan De Beauvoir De Havilland; 22 Oct 1917, Tokyo, Japan) British screen actress known for portraying innocent, victimized women.

Shelby Foote (17 Nov 1916, Greenville MS) American historian and novelist.

Malcolm "Steve" Forbes, Jr. (18 Jul 1947, Morristown NJ) American publisher of *Fortune* magazine and presidential contender.

Carolyn Forché (28 Apr 1950, Detroit MI) American poet noted for her concern for human rights.

Betty Ford (Elizabeth Anne Betty Bloomer Warren; 8 Apr 1918, Chicago IL) American first lady; wife of Pres. Gerald R. Ford.

Eileen Ford (25 Mar 1922, New York NY) American model agency executive who standardized the industry's business practices and excelled at finding new talent.

Gerald R. Ford (Leslie Lynch King, Jr.) (14 Jul 1913, Omaha NE) American statesman; 38th president of the US, 1974–77 [see full biography at Presidents].

Glenn Ford (Gwyllyn Samuel Newton Ford; 1 May 1916, Sainte-Christine, QC, Canada) Canadian-born American film and TV actor.

Harrison J. Ford (13 Jul 1942, Chicago IL) American film actor, a strong leading man, especially in action films.

Tom Ford (27 Aug 1961, Austin TX) American fashion designer who revamped the image of the house of Gucci in the 1990s.

William Clay Ford, Jr. (3 May 1957, Detroit MI) American business executive; chairman and CEO of Ford Motor Co. from 2001.

George Foreman (22 Jan 1948, Marshall TX) American heavyweight boxing champion, 1973–74 and 1994–95.

Milos Forman (Jan Tomaš Forman; 18 Feb 1932, Čáslav, Czechoslovakia) Czech-American film director renowned for *One Flew Over the Cuckoo's Nest* (1975) and *Amadeus* (1984).

Marc Forné Molné (1946) Andorran politician; head of government of Andorra from 1994.

Maureen Forrester (25 Jul 1930, Montreal, QC, Canada) Canadian contralto.

Lukas Foss (Lukas Fuchs; 15 Aug 1922, Berlin, Germany) German-born American composer, pianist, and conductor, widely recognized for his experiments with improvisation and aleatoric (chance) music.

Steve Fossett (22 Apr 1944, Jackson TN) American commodities trader and adventurer; the first to circle the globe solo in a hot-air balloon (2002).

Jodie Foster (Alicia Christian Foster; 19 Nov 1962, Los Angeles CA) American widely respected actress; breakthrough performance in the film *Taxi Driver* (1976).

M.J. "Mike" Foster, Jr. (11 Jul 1930, Shreveport LA) American Republican politician; governor of Louisiana from 1996.

Sir Norman Robert Foster (1 Jun 1935, near Manchester, England) British architect; Pritzker Prize winner in 1999.

Michael J. Fox (Michael Andrew Fox; 9 Jun 1961, Edmondton, AB, Canada) Canadian film and TV actor and lobbyist for funding for Parkinson's disease research.

Vicente Fox Quesada (2 Jul 1942, Mexico City, Mexico) Mexican politician and businessman; president of Mexico from 2000.

Don Francisco (Mario Kreutzberger; 28 Dec 1940, Talca, Chile) Chilean-born American TV personality; host of the popular show *Sábado gigante*, which celebrated its 40th anniversary on the air in 2002, by far the longest-running TV show with the same host.

Helen Frankenthaler (12 Dec 1928, New York NY) American Abstract Expressionist painter whose brilliantly colored canvases have been much admired for their lyric qualities.

Aretha Franklin (25 Mar 1942, Memphis TN) American gospel and blues singer-composer.

John Hope Franklin (2 Jan 1915, Rentiesville OK) American historian and educator.

Dennis Franz (Dennis Schlachta; 28 Oct 1944, Maywood IL) American TV actor famous for police dramas, notably *NYPD Blue*.

Jonathan Franzen (1959, Western Springs IL) American author whose *The Corrections* won a National Book Award in 2001.

Louis Joseph Freeh (6 Jan 1950, Jersey City NJ) American government official; director of the FBI, 1993–2001.

Cathy Freeman (16 Feb 1973, Mackay, Queensland, Australia) Australian Aboriginal sprinter; won the Olympic gold medal in the 400-m race in 2000.

Morgan Freeman (1 Jun 1937, Memphis TN) American prolific theater and film actor most famous for the film *The Shawshank Redemption* (1994).

Mirella Freni (Mirella Fregni; 27 Feb 1935, Modena, Italy) Italian operatic soprano.

Lucien Freud (8 Dec 1922, Berlin, Germany) German-born British painter renowned for his portraits and nudes, often rendered in extreme closeup; he is the grandson of Sigmund Freud.

Betty Friedan (Betty Naomi Goldstein; 4 Feb 1921, Peoria IL) American feminist best known for her book *The Feminine Mystique* (1963).

Milton Friedman (31 Jul 1912, Brooklyn NY) American laissez-faire economist; Nobel Prize for Economic Science, 1976.

Thomas L. Friedman (20 Jul 1953, Minneapolis MN) American newspaper columnist and author.

Pierre Frogier (16 Nov 1950, Nouméa, New Caledonia) New Caledonian politician; president of New Caledonia from 2001.

David Frost (7 Apr 1939, Tenterden, England) British entertainer, media personality, and interviewer.

Rafael Frühbeck de Burgos (15 Sep 1933, Burgos, Spain) Spanish conductor.

Christopher Fry (Christopher Harris; 18 Dec 1907, Bristol, Gloucestershire, England) British writer of verse plays who gained fame with *The Lady's Not for Burning* (1948).

Fu Mingxia (16 Aug 1978, Wuhan?, Hubei province, China) Chinese diver; became youngest world champion diver (1991, at 12) and Olympic champion (1992, at 13, for 10-m platform); gold medalist in 1996 and 2000 Olympics.

Carlos Fuentes (11 Nov 1928, Mexico City, Mexico) Mexican novelist, short-story writer, playwright, critic, and diplomat.

Alberto Fujimori (28 Jul 1938, Lima, Peru) Peruvian politician; president of Peru, 1990–2000.

Francis Fukuyama (27 Oct 1952, Chicago IL) American historian, newspaper columnist, and author, most notably of *The End of History and the Last Man* (1992).

Richard S. Fuld, Jr. (26 Apr 1946) American corporate executive; CEO of Lehman Brothers Holdings from 1993.

Nelly (Kim) Furtado (2 Dec 1978, Victoria, BC, Canada) Canadian singer and songwriter.

Jostein Gaarder (8 Aug 1952, Oslo, Norway) Norwegian teacher, philosopher, and author of the international best-seller *Sophie's World* (English version, 1996).

Stefano Gabbana (14 Nov 1962, Milan, Italy) Italian fashion designer, along with partner Domenico Dolce, whose designs are inspired by the Mediterranean region.

Zsa Zsa Gabor (Sari Gabor; 6 Feb 1917, Budapest, Hungary) Hungarian-born American best known as a much-married celebrity, she also starred in light comic films.

Peter Gabriel (13 Feb 1950, Woking, Surrey, England) British rock and pop singer.

John Kenneth Galbraith (15 Oct 1908, Iona Station, ON, Canada) American Keynesian and post-Keynesian economist and government official.

John (Charles) Galliano (28 Nov 1960, Gibraltar) British fashion designer and designer-in-chief at Christian Dior.

Christopher B. Galvin (21 Mar 1950, Chicago IL) American corporate executive; CEO of the Motorola Corp. from 1997.

James Galway (8 Dec 1939, Belfast, Northern Ireland) Irish classical flutist.

Sonia Gandhi (née Sonia Maino; 9 Dec 1947, Turin, Italy) Italian-born widow of Rajiv Ganhdi and political force in India.

James Gandolfini (18 Sep 1961, Westwood NJ) American TV and film actor, star of TV series The Sopranos.

Jan Garbarek (4 Mar 1947, Mysen, Norway) Norwegian jazz saxophonist and flutist.

Andy Garcia (Andrés Arturo García-Menéndez; 12 Apr 1956, Havana, Cuba) Cuban-born American motion-picture actor often cast in meaty supporting roles.

John Eliot Gardiner (20 Apr 1943, Fontwell Magna, Dorset, England) British conductor.

Rulon Gardner (16 Aug 1971, Afton WY) American Greco-Roman wrestler who won the Olympic gold medal in 2000.

Arthur ("Art") Garfunkel (5 Nov 1941, Forest Hills NY) American singer and film actor.

James Garner (James Scott Bumgarner; 7 Apr 1928, Norman OK) American TV and film actor famous for the series The Rockford Files.

Jean-Pierre Garnier (31 Oct 1947, France) Swiss corporate executive; head of Glaxo SmithKline plc from 2000.

Henry Louis Gates, Jr. (16 Sep 1950, Keyser VA) American scholar of African American studies.

Larry Gatlin (2 May 1949, Odessa TX) American country and western singer and songwriter.

Jean-Paul Gaultier (24 Apr 1952, Arcueil, near Paris, France) French fashion designer known for his unusual and extravagant creations.

Sunil Manohar Gavaskar (10 Jul 1949, Bombay [now Mumbai], India) Indian cricket batsman; scored India's highest individual Test score (236, 1983–84).

Mitzi Gaynor (Francesca Mitzi Marlene de Czanyi von Gerber; 4 Sep 1931, Chicago IL) American singer, dancer, and film actress.

Maumoon Abdul Gayoom (29 Dec 1937, Malé, Maldives) Maldive politician; president of Maldives from 1978.

Laurent Gbagbo (31 May 1945, Gagnoa, French West Africa [now Côte d'Ivoire]) Ivoirien politician; president of Côte d'Ivoire from 2000.

Haile Gebrselassie (18 Apr 1973, Assela, Ethiopia) Ethiopian runner; world record holder in the 5,000-m and 10,000-m distances.

Frank Owen Gehry (28 Feb 1929, Toronto, ON, Canada) Canadian-born American architect and designer whose original, sculptural, often audacious work won him worldwide renown.

Sir Bob Geldof (5 Oct 1954, Dublin, Ireland) Irish musician (of The Boomtown Rats) who was knighted for his humanitarian work.

Sarah Michelle Gellar (14 April 1977, New York NY) American TV actress, star of Buffy the Vampire Slayer.

Ljubco Georgievski (17 Jan 1966, Shtip, Macedonia, Yugoslavia [now Macedonia]) Macedonian politician; prime minister of Macedonia from 1998.

Richard Gephardt (31 Jan 1941, St. Louis MO) American politician; House minority leader and Democratic senator from Missouri from 1977.

Richard (Tiffany) Gere (31 Aug 1949, Philadelphia PA) American film actor and humanitarian known for popular motion pictures.

Jim Geringer (24 Apr 1944, Wheatland WY) American Republican politician; governor of Wyoming from 1995.

Louis Gerstner (1 Mar 1942, Mineola NY) American corporate executive; president of the IBM Corp. from 1993.

Mohamed Ghannouchi (1941) Tunisian politician; prime minister of Tunisia from 1999.

Angela Gheorghiu (7 Sep 1965, Adjud, Romania) Romanian operatic soprano.

Nicolai Ghiaurov (13 Sep 1929, Velingrad, Bulgaria) Bulgarian operatic bass.

Mossimo Giannulli (4 June 1963, California) American fashion designer known for his Mossimo line of sportswear and casual clothing for Target stores.

Mel Gibson (3 Jan 1956, Peekskill NY) Australian-American actor, producer, director; one of Hollywood's biggest box-office draws.

Kathie Lee Gifford (Kathryn Lee Epstein; 16 Aug 1953, Paris, France) American TV talk-show host.

Romeo Gigli (1950, Faenza, Italy) Italian fashion designer whose soft, fluid creations exhibit rich fabrics and detailing.

Melissa Gilbert (8 May 1964, Los Angeles CA) American film and TV actress beloved for her role as Laura on TV's Little House on the Prairie; president of the Screen Actors Guild from 2002.

Astrud Gilberto (Astrud Weinert; 29 Mar 1940, Salvador do Bahia, Brazil) Brazilian bossa nova singer; wife of João Gilberto.

João Gilberto (do Prado Pereira de Oliveira) (10 Jun 1931, Juazeiro, Bahia, Brazil) Brazilian bossa nova songwriter, guitarist, and pianist.

Terry (Vance) Gilliam (22 Nov 1940, Minneapolis MN) American film actor, writer, and director, a member of the Monty Python troupe.

Raymond V. Gilmartin (Sayville NY) American corporate executive; CEO of Merck & Co. from 1994.

Ruth Bader Ginsburg (15 Mar 1933, Brooklyn NY) American jurist; associate justice of the US Supreme Court from 1993.

Nikki Giovanni (Yolande Cornelia Giovanni, Jr.; 7 Jun 1943, Knoxville TN) American poet whose writings range from calls for violent revolution to poems for children and intimate personal statements.

Rudy Giuliani (Rudolph William Giuliani; 28 May 1944, Brooklyn NY) American Republican politician; mayor of New York City, 1994–2002.

Hubert de Givenchy (21 Feb 1927, Beauvais, France) French fashion designer noted for his elegant, classic designs for separates (blouses, skirts, and pants).

Philip Glass (31 Jan 1937, Baltimore MD) American composer of innovative minimalist instrumental, vocal, and operatic music.

Parris N. Glendening (11 Jun 1942, Bronx NY) American Democratic politician; governor of Maryland from 1995.

John H(erschel) Glenn, Jr. (18 Jul 1921, Cambridge OH) American astronaut, the first American to orbit the Earth; later a US senator from Ohio.

Duchess of Gloucester (née Birgitte Eva van Deurs; Odense, Denmark) British royal; wife of the Duke of Gloucester.

Duke of Gloucester (Prince Richard; 1944) British royal.

Danny (Lebern) Glover (22 Jul 1947, San Francisco CA) American talented film and TV actor mostly cast in supporting roles.

Savion Glover (19 Nov 1973, Newark NJ) American dancer and choreographer known for a style of dance called "hitting," a combination of the rhythms of hip-hop music and the pounding of tap dancing.

Louise (Elisabeth) Glück (22 Apr 1943, New York NY) American poet whose willingness to confront the horrible, the difficult, and the painful has resulted in a body of work characterized by insightfulness and a severe lyricism.

Goh Chok Tong (20 May 1941, Singapore) Singaporean politician; prime minister of Singapore from 1990.

Whoopi Goldberg (Caryn Elaine Johnson; 13 Nov 1955, New York NY) American comedienne and established film actress.

Ralph Gonsalves (1946) West Indian politician; prime minister of Saint Vincent and the Grenadines from 2001.

Luis Ángel González Macchi (13 Dec 1947, Asunción, Paraguay) Paraguayan politician; president of Paraguay from 1999.

Jane Goodall (3 Apr 1934, London, England) British ethologist, known for her exceptionally detailed and long-term research on chimpanzees.

Cuba Gooding, Jr. (2 Jan 1968, Bronx NY) American film actor made famous for his supporting role in Jerry Maguire (1996).

Ellen Goodman (11 Apr 1941, Newton MA) American political columnist.

Doris Kearns Goodwin (4 Jan 1943, Rockville Centre NY) American historian, biographer, and TV commentator.

Googoosh (Faegheh Atashin; 1950, Tehran, Iran) Iranian popular singer.

Jeff Gordon (4 Aug 1971, Vallejo CA) American race-car driver; NASCAR Winston Cup champion, 1995, 1997, 1998, 2001.

Berry Gordy, Jr. (28 Nov 1929, Detroit MI) American record and film executive who founded Motown Corp. in 1959.

Albert A. Gore, Jr. (31 Mar 1948, Washington DC) American Democratic politician; vice president of the US, 1993–2001; presidential candidate, 2000.

Lesley Gore (2 May 1946, Tenafly NJ) American singer and songwriter.

Tipper Gore (19 Aug 1948, Washington DC) American personality; wife of Al Gore.

Henryk (Mikolaj) Gorecki (6 Dec 1933, Czernica, near Rybnik, Poland) Polish composer whose often atonal early compositions gave way to works characterized by folk songs, medieval music, and Roman Catholicism.

Eydie Gormé (Edith Gormezano, 16 Aug 1931, Bronx NY) American pop singer.

Louis Gossett, Jr. (27 May 1936, Brooklyn NY) American film, stage, and TV actor.

Robert (Gerard) Goulet (26 Nov 1933, Lawrence MA) American pop singer.

Memo Gracida (Guillermo Gracida, Jr.; 25 Jul 1956, Mexico City, Mexico) Mexican polo player, leader of the Isla Carroll team, who held a 10-goal handicap for 20 years.

Billy Graham (7 Nov 1918, Charlotte NC) American evangelist whose large-scale preaching tours, known as crusades, and friendship with numerous US presidents brought him to international prominence.

Jorie Graham (9 May, 1951, New York NY) American poet whose abstract, intellectual verse is known for its visual imagery, complex metaphors, and philosophical content.

(Allen) Kelsey Grammer (21 Feb 1955, St. Thomas, Virgin Islands) American TV actor, writer, and producer especially known for the TV series Frasier.

Hugh Grant (9 Sep 1960, London, England) British-born versatile film actor whose characters range from awkward to sexy.

Günter (Wilhelm) Grass (16 Oct 1927, Danzig, now Gdansk, Poland) German poet, novelist, playwright, sculptor, and printmaker who became a literary spokesman for the German generation that grew up in the Nazi era and survived the war; he won the Nobel Prize for Literature in 1999.

Bill Graves (9 Jan 1953, Salina KS) American Republican politician; governor of Kansas from 1995.

Michael Graves (9 July 1934, Indianapolis IN) American architect and housewares designer in the Postmodernist style, known for his signature creations for Target stores.

John Gray (1951, Houston TX) American counselor and writer, notably of Men Are from Mars, Women Are from Venus (1992).

Spalding Gray (5 Jun 1941, Barrington RI) American performance artist, actor, and writer.

Andrew M. Greeley (5 Feb 1928, Oak Park IL) American priest, sociologist, author, and commentator.

Al Green (13 Apr 1946, Forrest City AR) American soul singer.

Maurice R. Greenberg (4 May 1925, New York NY) American corporate executive; CEO of American International Group from 1967.

Bob Greene (10 Mar 1947, Columbus OH) American journalist and syndicated columnist.

Maurice ("Mo") Greene (23 Jul 1974, Kansas City KS) American sprinter who won the 100-m world championship 1997, 1999, and 2001; set the 100-m world record, 1999; and won Olympic gold medals in the 100 m and the 4 x 100-m relay, 2000.

Jeff Greenfield (10 Jun 1943, New York NY) American TV journalist.

Paul Greengard (11 Dec 1925, New York NY) American pharmacologist; co-winner of the Nobel Prize for Physiology or Medicine, 2000, for studies of brain-cell function.

Alan Greenspan (6 Mar 1926, New York NY) American monetary policymaker; chairman of the US Federal Reserve Bank from 1987.

Cynthia Gregory (8 Jul 1946, Los Angeles CA) American ballerina.

Joel Grey (11 Apr 1932, Cleveland OH) American energetic musical performer and character actor.

Ken Griffey (George Kenneth Griffey, Jr.; 21 Nov 1969, Donora PA) American baseball player; led the American League in home runs, 1994 and 1997–99.

Merv Griffin (6 Jul 1925, San Mateo CA) American TV host and business executive.

Andy Griffith (1 Jun 1926, Mount Airy NC) American film and TV actor known for wise, folksy leads in *The Andy Griffith Show* and *Matlock*.

Melanie Griffith (9 Aug 1957, New York NY) American film actress often cast in free-spirited roles.

Yury (Nikolayevich) Grigorovich (2 Jan 1927, Leningrad [St. Petersburg], USSR) Russian dancer, choreographer, and ballet director.

Roger Grimes (1950, Grand Falls-Windsor, NL, Canada) Canadian politician; premier of Newfoundland and Labrador from 13 Feb 2001.

Ólafur Ragnar Grímsson (14 May 1943, Ísafjördur, Iceland) Icelandic politician; president of Iceland from 1996.

John Grisham (8 Feb 1955, Jonesboro AR) American lawyer and best-selling novelist.

Matt Groening (15 Feb 1954, Portland OR) American cartoonist, creator of TV's *The Simpsons*.

Andrew S. Grove (Andras Grof; 2 Sep 1936, Budapest, Hungary) American corporate executive; CEO of Intel Corp. from 1997.

Edita Gruberová (23 Dec 1946, Bratislava, Czechoslovakia [now Slovakia]) Slovak operatic soprano.

Sofia (Asgatovna) Gubaidulina (24 Oct 1931, Chistopol, Tatar ASSR, USSR [now Tatarstan, Russia]) Russian Tatar composer whose works are polytonal and characterized by dualities and strongly accented rhythms but also employ traditional genres.

Ismail Omar Guelleh (27 Nov 1947, Diré-Dawa, Ethiopia) Djibouti politician; president of Djibouti from 1999.

Gilbert Guillaume (4 Dec 1930, Bois-Colombes, France) French jurist; president of the International Court of Justice from 2000.

Sylvie Guillem (25 Feb 1965, Paris, France) French ballerina; principal dancer with the Royal Ballet.

Lani Guinier (1950, Queens NY) American legal scholar known for complex race-sensitive civil rights advocacy.

Kenny C. Guinn (24 Aug 1936, Garland AK) American Republican politician; governor of Nevada from 1999.

Bryant Gumbel (29 Sep 1948, New Orleans LA) American TV host and sportscaster.

Vladimir A. Gusinsky (1952, Moscow, USSR [now Russia]) Russian businessman and media tycoon; head of MOST Bank.

José Alexandre ("Xanana") Gusmão (20 Jun 1946, Laleia, Manatuto, Portuguese East Timor) Timorese independence leader; co-winner of the Nobel Peace Prize, 1996; first president of independent East Timor from 20 May 2002.

Alan H. Guth (27 Feb 1947, New Brunswick NJ) American physicist; developed the theory of "inflationary cosmology."

Arlo Guthrie (10 Jul 1947, Coney Island, Brooklyn NY) American folk singer and songwriter.

Carl T.C. Gutierrez (15 Oct 1941, Agana Heights, Guam) American Democratic politician; governor of Guam from 1995.

King Gyanendra Bir Bikram Shah Deva (7 Jul 1947, Kathmandu, Nepal) Nepalese royal; king of Nepal, 1950–51, and from 2001.

Crown Prince Haakon (Haakon Magnus; 20 Jul 1973, Oslo, Norway) Norwegian crown prince.

Jürgen Habermas (1929, Düsseldorf, Germany) German sociologist and originator of the theory of communication ethics.

Grant Hackett (9 May 1980, Gold Coast, Queensland, Australia) Australian swimmer who won the world championship in 1,500-m freestyle, 1997, 1998, and 1999, and an Olympic gold medal in 2000 in the 1,500-m freestyle.

Georg Hackl (9 Sep 1966, Berchtesgaden, Germany) German luger; only singles luger to win three consecutive Olympic golds (1992, 1994, 1998).

Gene Hackman (30 Jan 1930, San Bernardino CA) American motion-picture actor known for emotionally honest and natural performances.

Håkan Hagegard (25 Nov 1945, Karlstad, Sweden) Swedish operatic baritone.

Merle Haggard (6 Apr 1937, Bakersfield CA) American country and western singer and songwriter.

James K. Hahn (3 Jul 1950, Los Angeles CA) American Democratic politician; mayor of Los Angeles from 1 Jul 2001.

Jörg Haider (26 Jan 1950, Bad Giosern, Austria) Austrian ultra-right-wing politician.

Bernard (Johann Herman) Haitink (4 Mar 1929, Amsterdam, The Netherlands) Dutch conductor best known for his interpretations of Gustav Mahler, Anton Bruckner, Ludwig van Beethoven, and Franz Liszt.

Mika (Pauli) Häkkinen (28 Sep 1968, Martinlaakso, Vantaa, Finland) Finnish Formula 1 race-car driver; Grand Prix world champion in 1998 and 1999.

David Halberstam (10 Apr 1934, New York NY) American journalist, author of political works, including *The Best and the Brightest* (1972), and novelist.

Bridget Hall (12 Dec 1977, Springdale AR) American fashion model.

Tom T. Hall (25 May 1936, Olive Hill KY) American singer and songwriter.

Johnny Halliday (Jean-Phillippe Smet; 15 Jun 1943, Paris, France) French rock singer.

Tarja (Kaarina) Halonen (24 Dec 1943, Helsinki, Finland) Finnish politician; president of Finland from 2000.

Pete Hamill (24 Jun 1935, Brooklyn NY) American journalist and author.

Marvin Hamlisch (2 Jun 1944, New York NY) American composer and songwriter.

John Hamm (8 Apr 1938, New Glasgow, NS, Canada) Canadian politician; premier of Nova Scotia from 16 Aug 1999.

Mia Hamm (Mariel Margaret Hamm; 17 Mar 1972, Selma AL) American association football (soccer) player who led the US women's team to an Olympic gold medal in 1996; the world championship in 1991; and the Women's World Cup in 1999.

Hammer (Stanley Kirk Burrell; also known as M.C. Hammer; 30 Mar 1963, Oakland CA) American rap musician.

John Hammond (13 Nov 1942, New York NY) American blues guitarist and singer.

Herbie Hancock (Herbert Jeffrey Hancock; later Mwandishi; 12 Apr 1940, Chicago IL) American jazz keyboardist and composer.

Daniel Handler (nom de plume Lemony Snicket; 28 Feb 1970, San Francisco CA) American children's book author.

Tom Hanks (9 Jul 1956, Concord CA) American film actor and director who won an Academy Award for best actor in 1993 (*Philadelphia*) and 1994 (*Forrest Gump*).

Sir Roland P. Hanna (10 Feb 1932, Detroit MI) American jazz pianist and composer.

Prince Hans Adam II (14 Feb 1945, Vaduz, Liechtenstein) Liechtenstein royal; prince of Liechtenstein since 1989.

Pauline Lee Hanson (27 May 1954, Brisbane, Queensland, Australia) Australian politician, leader of the One Nation party, and independent member of Parliament.

Masahiko ("Happy") Harada (9 May 1968, Kamikawa, Japan) Japanese ski-jumper.

King Harald V (21 Feb 1937, Skaugum, Norway) Norwegian royal; king of Norway from 1991.

John Harbison (20 Dec 1938, Orange NJ) American composer of expressive music in a wide range of forms; he won the Pulitzer Prize in 1987 for his cantata *The Flight into Egypt*.

Marcia Gay Harden (14 Aug 1959, La Jolla CA) American motion-picture actress; gained acclaim for *Pollock* (2000).

David Hare (5 Jun 1947, St. Leonards, Sussex, England) British playwright and director.

Roy Hargrove (16 Oct 1969, Waco TX) American jazz trumpeter.

Rafiq al-Hariri (November 1944, Sidon, Lebanon) Lebanese politician; prime minister of Lebanon, 1992–98 and from 2000.

Katie Marie Harman (1981?, Gresham OR) American beauty, Miss America, 2002.

Nikolaus Harnoncourt (6 Dec 1929, Berlin, Germany) German conductor and viola da gamba player.

Ofra Harnoy (31 Jan 1965, Hadera, Israel) Israeli-born Canadian cellist.

Lynn Harrell (30 Jan 1944, New York NY) American cellist.

Tom Harrell (16 Jun 1946, Urbana IL) American jazz trumpeter.

Woody Harrelson (Woodrow Tracy Harrelson; 23 Jul 1961, Midland TX) American actor, first noticed for his role as Woody on TV's *Cheers*.

Ed Harris (28 Nov 1950, Englewood NJ) American film actor known for the range and depth of his work, especially in *Pollock* (2000).

Emmylou Harris (2 Apr 1947, Birmingham AL) American folk and country singer.

Julie Harris (2 Dec 1925, Grosse Pointe Park MI) American gifted stage, film, and TV actress.

Lou Harris (Louis Harris; 8 Jan 1921, New Haven CT) American pollster and public opinion analyst.

René Harris (1948) Nauruan politician; president of Nauru, 1999–2000 and from 2001.

William B. Harrison, Jr. (1943, Rocky Mount NC) American corporate executive; CEO of J.P. Morgan Chase & Co. (from merger, 2001).

Deborah (Ann) Harry (1 Jul 1945, Miami FL) American vocalist; lead singer of Blondie.

Prince Harry of Wales (15 Sep 1984, London, England) British royal; son of Prince Charles and Princess Diana, third in line to the British throne.

Melissa Joan Hart (18 Apr 1976, Long Island NY) American TV and film actress, star of TV's *Sabrina the Teenage Witch*.

Josh Hartnett (21 Jun 1978, San Francisco CA) American rising young film star who has recently moved into leading roles.

Leland H. Hartwell (30 Oct 1939, Los Angeles CA) American biologist; co-recipient of the Nobel Prize for Physiology or Medicine, 2001, for studies of cell growth cycles.

Paul Harvey (4 Sep 1918, Tulsa OK) American radio news broadcaster and commentator.

Dominik Hasek (29 Jan 1965, Pardubice, Czechoslovakia [now the Czech Republic]) Czech ice hockey goalie; two-time NHL MVP and five-time all star; he led the NHL in saves for six seasons and won the 2002 Stanley Cup with the Detroit Red Wings.

Robert Hass (1 Mar 1941, San Francisco CA) American poet and translator with a deep conviction that poetry, as one critic put it, "is what defines the self"; poet laureate consultant in poetry, 1995–97.

Abdiqasim Salad Hassan (1942, Somaliland?) Somali politician; head of the Transitional National Government of Somalia.

King Hassan II (9 Jul 1929, Rabat, Morocco—23 Jul 1999, Rabat, Morocco), Moroccan royal; king of Morocco from 1961.

David Hasselhoff (17 Jul 1952, Baltimore MD) American TV actor recognized internationally for his roles on *Knight Rider* and *Baywatch*.

Lene Vestergaard Hau (13 Nov 1959, Vejle, Denmark) American physicist whose team reportedly slowed down a beam of light, stopped it, and stored it for a fraction of a second.

Vaclav Havel (5 Oct 1936, Prague, Czechoslovakia [now in Czech Republic]) Czech playwright, poet, and political dissident (president of Czechoslovakia from December 1989 to July 1992 and president of the Czech Republic from January 1993).

Ethan Hawke (6 Nov 1970, Austin TX) American film actor who first gained recognition for *Dead Poets Society* (1989).

Stephen W. Hawking (8 Jan 1942, Oxford, Oxfordshire, England) British theoretical physicist and popularizer of science.

Goldie Hawn (21 Nov 1945, Washington DC) American TV and film actress known for free-spirited, feisty performances.

Melissa Hayden (Mildred Herman; 25 Apr 1923, Toronto, ON, Canada) Canadian ballet dancer renowned for her technical and dramatic skills and her many performances with the New York City Ballet.

Isaac Hayes (20 Aug 1942, Covington TN) American musician, singer, and songwriter.

Bernadine Patricia Healy (2 Aug 1944, New York NY) American cardiologist; director of the National Institutes of Health, 1991–93; president of the American Red Cross to 2001.

Jimmy Heath (25 Oct 1926, Philadelphia PA) American jazz saxophonist.

James J. Heckman (19 April 1944, Chicago IL) American economist; Nobel Prize in Economic Science, 2000, for work in solving problems of analysis of microdata.

Tippi Hedren (Nathalie Hedren; 19 Jan 1935, New Ulm MN) American actress, a favorite of Alfred Hitchcock and star of *The Birds* (1963).

Alan J. Heeger (22 Jan 1936, Sioux City IA) American chemist; co-winner of the Nobel Prize in Chemistry, 2000, for work in electrically conductive polymers.

Hugh M. Hefner (9 Apr 1926, Chicago IL) American founder of *Playboy* magazine in 1953.

André Heller (22 Mar 1947, Vienna, Austria) Austrian-born pop producer and performer.

Leona Helmsley (4 Jul 1920, Brooklyn NY) American hotel and real estate executive.

Heloise (Ponce Kiah Marchelle Heloise Cruse; 15 Apr 1951, Waco TX) American advice columnist.

Robert Helps (23 Sep 1928, Passaic NJ) American composer and pianist.

Carlos ("Slim") Helu (c. 1940, Mexico?) Mexican investor; head of Grupo Carso and reportedly the richest man in Mexico.

Florence Henderson (14 Feb 1934, Dale IN) American singer and actress.

Rickey (Henley) Henderson (25 Dec 1958, Chicago IL) American baseball player who during the 2001 season beat Ty Cobb's longstanding record of

2,246 career runs and Babe Ruth's record of 2,062 bases-on-balls; all-time leader in stolen bases (1,395 [through the 2001 season]).

Stephen Hendry (13 Jan 1969, Edinburgh, Scotland) Scottish billiards player, ranked number one in the world for eight consecutive seasons (1989–97).

Grand Duke Henri (16 Apr 1955, Château de Betzdorf, Luxembourg) Luxembourgian royal; grand duke of Luxembourg from 2000.

Nat Hentoff (10 Jun 1925, Boston MA) American music critic and journalist.

Hans Werner Henze (1 Jul 1926, Gütersloh, Germany) German composer whose operas, ballets, symphonies, and other works are marked by an individual and advanced style within traditional forms.

Katharine Hepburn (12 May 1907, Hartford CT) American indomitable stage and screen actress.

Jerry (Gerald) Herman (10 Jul 1933, New York NY) American musical comedy composer and lyricist (*Hello, Dolly!*).

Orlando Hernández (byname El Duque; 11 Oct 1969, Havana, Cuba) Cuban baseball player; pitcher for the Cuban national team who later won three World Series titles with the New York Yankees, 1999–2001.

Carolina Herrera (María Carolina Josefina Pacanins y Niño; 8 Jan 1939, Caracas, Venezuela) Venezuelan fashion designer and perfume creator whose designs exhibit simple elegance.

Jacques Herzog (19 Apr 1950, Basel, Switzerland) Swiss architect; co-winner, with Pierre de Meuron, of the Pritzker Prize in 2001.

Charlton Heston (John Charlton Carter; 4 Oct 1924, Evanston IL) American enduring film actor known for historical and literary roles.

Lleyton Hewitt (24 Feb 1981, Adelaide, Australia) Australian tennis player who won the 2001 US Open and Wimbledon in 2002; he was the top-ranked men's player in mid-2002.

Oscar Hijuelos (24 Aug 1951, New York NY) American novelist whose writing chronicles the pre-Castro Cuban immigrant experience in the US.

Tommy Hilfiger (Thomas Jacob Hilfiger; 24 Mar 1951, Elmira NY) American fashion designer whose sportswear and jeans collections express an all-American theme.

Faith Hill (Audrey Faith Perry; 21 Sep 1967, Jackson MS) American country singer.

Julia "Butterfly" Hill (18 Feb 1974, Mount Vernon MO) American environmental activist.

Lauryn Hill (26 May 1975, South Orange NJ) American hip-hop singer and actress.

Sir Edmund (Percival) Hillary (20 Jul 1919, Auckland, New Zealand) New Zealand mountain climber and Antarctic explorer who, with Tenzing Norgay, was the first person to set foot on the summit of Mt. Everest.

Gertrude Himmelfarb (8 Aug 1922, New York NY) American historian and biographer.

Sam Hinds (1943) Guyanan politician; president of Guyana in 1997, prime minister 1992–97, 1997–99, and again from 1999.

Gregory Hines (14 Feb 1946, New York NY) American dancer who came to prominence as a child performer and later became a successful film and television actor.

Martina Hingis (30 Sep 1980, Kosice, Czechoslovakia [now Slovakia]) Czech-born Swiss tennis player who won the Australian Open, 1997–99; the French Open, 1997–99; Wimbledon, 1997; and the US Open, 1997.

Ludwig Hirsch (28 Feb 1948, Weinberg, Steiermark, Austria) Austrian songwriter and singer.

Damien Hirst (1965, Bristol, England) British artist.

Christopher Hitchens (13 Apr 1949, Portsmouth, England) American cultural and political critic and journalist.

Don Ho (13 Aug 1930, Honolulu HI) American Hawaiian singer.

David Hockney (9 Jul 1937, Bradford, Yorkshire, England) British painter, draftsman, printmaker, photographer, and stage designer.

Jim Hodges (19 Nov 1956, Lancaster SC) American Democratic politician; governor of South Carolina from 1999.

John Hoeven (13 Mar 1957, Bismarck ND) American Republican politician; governor of North Dakota from 2001.

James P. Hoffa (19 May 1941, Detroit MI) American labor leader; head of the International Brotherhood of Teamsters from 1999.

Dustin Hoffman (8 Aug 1937, Los Angeles CA) American actor acclaimed for versatile portrayals of antiheroes and vulnerable types.

Christopher (Jarvis Haley) Hogwood (10 Sep 1941, Nottingham, England) British harpsichordist.

Richard Charles Albert Holbrooke (24 Apr 1941, New York NY) American diplomat.

Bob Holden (24 Aug 1949, Kansas City MO) American Democratic politician; governor of Missouri from 2001.

Chamique Holdsclaw (9 Aug 1977, Flushing NY) American basketball player; 1999 WNBA Rookie of the Year; three-time WNBA All Star; twice national player of the year; she led the University of Tennessee to three NCAA titles, 1996–98.

Dave Holland (1 Oct 1946, Wolverhampton, England) English-born American jazz bassist.

Evander Holyfield (19 Oct 1962, Atmore AL) American boxer; four-time heavyweight champion, 1990–92 (WBA, WBC, IBF), 1993–94 (WBA, IBF), 1996–99, (WBA, IBF from 1997) 2000–01 (WBA).

Gerardus 't Hooft (5 Jul 1946, Den Helder, The Netherlands) Dutch physicist; shared the Nobel Prize for Physics, 1999, for developing a way to predict mathematically the properties both of subatomic particles and the forces that hold them together.

bell hooks (Gloria Jean Watkins; 25 Sep 1952, Hopkinsville KY) American feminist scholar.

Bob Hope (Leslie Townes Hope; 29 May 1903, Eltham, England) British-born American comedian and film actor, most noted for his Road films and for entertaining US troops abroad.

Sir Anthony Hopkins (31 Dec 1937, Port Talbot, West Glamorgan, Wales) British intense, gifted film and stage actor.

Bernard Hopkins (15 Jan 1965, Philadelphia PA) American middleweight boxer who won the unified title in 2001 by defeating favored Félix Trinidad.

Lena (Calhoun) Horne (30 Jun 1917, Brooklyn NY) American singer and film actress.

Marilyn Horne (16 Jan 1934, Bradford PA) American operatic mezzo-soprano.

Whitney (Elizabeth) Houston (9 Aug 1963, Newark NJ) American pop singer and film actress.

John Winston Howard (26 Jul 1939, Sydney, Australia) Australian politician, Liberal Party chairman, prime minister of Australia from 1996.

Ron Howard (1 Mar 1954, Duncan OK) American TV and film actor famous for his role on TV's *Happy Days* and as an acclaimed movie director.

Freddie Hubbard (Frederick Dewayne Hubbard; 7 Apr 1938, Indianapolis IN) American jazz trumpeter, flügelhornist, and composer.

Mike Huckabee (24 Aug 1955, Hope AR) American Republican politician; governor of Arkansas from 1996.

Kate Hudson (19 Apr 1979, Los Angeles CA) American hardworking young film actress who starred in Almost Famous (2000).

Karen Hughes (27 Dec 1956, Paris, France) American government official; communications director for Pres. George W. Bush until 2002.

Robert (Studley Forrest) Hughes (28 Jul 1938, Sydney, Australia) Australian art critic.

Sarah Hughes (2 May 1985, Great Neck NY) American figure skater; gold medalist at the 2002 Winter Olympic Games.

Jane Dee Hull (8 Aug 1935, Kansas City MO) American Republican politician; governor of Arizona from 1997.

John Hume (18 Jan 1937, Londonderry, Northern Ireland) Northern Ireland politician; Nobel Peace Prize in 1998 and Gandhi Peace Prize in 2002.

Engelbert Humperdinck (Arnold George Dorsey; 3 May 1936, Madras, India) British-born American country and western and pop singer.

(John) Barry Humphries (17 Feb 1934, Melbourne, Australia) Australian comedian whose characters include Dame Edna Everage.

Hun Sen (4 Apr 1951, Kompong Chom province, Cambodia) Cambodian politician and leader of the government beginning in 1985.

Helen Hunt (15 Jun 1963, Culver City CA) American film and TV actress made popular by the series Mad About You.

(Nelson) Bunker Hunt (22 Feb 1926, El Dorado TX) American business executive, oil heir, and speculator.

R. Timothy Hunt (19 Feb 1943, UK) British biologist; co-recipient of the Nobel Prize for Physiology or Medicine, 2001, for studies of cell growth cycles.

Sam Hunt (1946, Castor Bay, Auckland, New Zealand) New Zealand itinerant performance poet.

Rachel Hunter (9 Sep 1969, Auckland, New Zealand) New Zealand-born fashion model famous for her 1990s marriage to rock star Rod Stewart.

Charlayne Hunter-Gault (27 Feb 1942, Due West SC) American TV journalist especially noted for her work with The MacNeil/Lehrer Report.

Elizabeth Hurley (10 Jun 1965, Hampshire, England) British actress and model known for glamorous leading roles.

William Hurt (20 Mar 1950, Washington DC) American actor known for his cerebral, diverse characters.

Maqbul Fida Husain (17 Sep 1915, Pandharpur, Maharashtra, India) Indian painter, printmaker, photographer, and filmmaker whose work evolved from portraits and landscapes to a detached Expressionist style.

Saddam Hussein (in full Saddam Hussein At Tikriti; 28 Apr 1937, Tikrit district, Iraq) Iraqi military leader and politician; president of Iraq from 1979 [see also Most Influential Leaders of All Time].

Anjelica Huston (8 Jul 1951, Santa Monica CA) American original film actress whose work has spanned many decades.

Lauren Hutton (Mary Laurence Hutton; 17 Nov 1944, Charleston SC) American fashion model and actress, one of the first 1970s "supermodels" and

reprising in 21st-century glamorous, mature-woman modeling roles.

Lee A. Iacocca (Lido Anthony Iacocca; 15 Oct 1924, Allentown PA) American industrial engineer and automobile executive (Chrysler Corporation).

Kumba Ialá (1952) Guinea-Bissau politician; president of Guinea-Bissau from 2000.

Janis Ian (Janis Eddy Fink; 7 Apr 1951, New York NY) American pop singer and songwriter.

Sa'd ad-din Ibrahim (3 Dec 1938, near Mansurah, Egypt) Egyptian political sociologist and government critic.

Ice Cube (O'Shea Jackson; 15 Jun 1969) American rap singer, songwriter; actor.

Nobuyuki Idei (22 Nov 1937, Tokyo, Japan) Japanese corporate executive; chairman and CEO of Sony Corp. from 1998.

Enrique Iglesias (8 May 1975, Madrid, Spain) Spanish pop singer.

Enrique Iglesias (1931, Spain) Uruguayan international banker; president of the Inter-American Development Bank from 1988.

Julio Iglesias (Iulio José Iglesia de la Cueva; 23 Sep 1943, Madrid, Spain) Spanish pop singer.

Ion Iliescu (3 Mar 1930, Oltenita, Romania) Romanian politician; president of Romania, 1989–96 and from 2000.

Ratu Josefa Iloilo (1920) Fijian politician; president of Fiji from 2000.

Iman (Abdulmajid) (25 Jul 1955, Mogadishu, Somalia) Somali fashion model of the 1970s and '80s and creator of a signature cosmetics line.

Natalie Imbruglia (4 Feb 1975, Sydney, Australia) Australian pop singer.

Jeffrey R. Immelt (19 Feb 1956, Cincinnati OH) American corporate executive; CEO of the General Electric Co. from 2001.

Don Imus (23 Jul 1940, Riverside CA) American radio talk-show host.

Robert Indiana (13 Sep 1928, New Castle IA) American artist.

Juli Inkster (Juli Simpson; 24 Jun 1960, Santa Cruz CA) American golfer who won the US Women's Open, 1999 and 2002 and the LPGA championship, 1999 and 2000.

Kathy Ireland (8 Mar 1963, Glendale CA) American fashion model, designer, and actress whose clothing and home-furnishings collections are noted for affordability.

Patricia Ireland (19 Oct 1945, Oak Park IL) American feminist, social activist, and the president of the National Organization for Women, 1991–2001.

Jeremy Irons (19 Sep 1948, Cowes, Isle of Wight, England) British stage and film actor famous for dark portrayals.

John (Winslow) Irving (2 Mar 1942, Exeter NH) American novelist and short-story writer who established his reputation with the novel The World According to Garp (1978).

Walter Isaacson (20 May 1952, New Orleans LA) American corporate executive; chairman and CEO of the Cable News Network (CNN) from 2001.

Eugene M. Isenberg (Chelsea MA) American corporate executive; CEO of Nabors Industries, Inc. from 1987.

Yusuf Islam (Steven Georgiou; Cat Stevens; 21 Jul 1947, London, England) British pop singer, songwriter, and pianist.

Goran Ivanisevic (13 Sep 1971, Split, Croatia, Yugoslavia) Croatian tennis player; won Wimbledon

singles in 2001, the first wild-card choice to win the title in history of the tournament.

Allen Iverson (7 Jun 1975, Hampton VA) American basketball player; 2001 all-star and NBA MVP; he led the NBA in points/game and steals/game in 2001–02.

Molly Ivins (30 Aug 1944, Monterey CA) American political commentator and columnist.

James (Francis) Ivory (7 Jun 1928, Berkeley CA) American film director famous for his collaboration with producer Ismail Merchant on many period pieces, including *A Room with a View* (1986), *Howards End* (1992), and *The Remains of the Day* (1993).

B.K.S. Iyengar (14 Dec 1918, Bellur, Karnataka state, India) Indian yoga guru.

Ja Rule (Jeff Atkins; 29 Feb 1976, Queens NY) American rap performer.

Sheikh Jabir al-Ahmad al-Jabir as-Sabah (29 Jun 1928, Kuwait) Kuwaiti royal; emir of Kuwait from 1977.

Janet Jackson (16 May 1966, Gary IN) American singer and film and TV actress.

Jermaine Jackson (11 Dec 1954, Gary IN) American singer and musician.

Jesse Jackson (8 Oct 1941, Greenville SC) American civil-rights leader, Baptist minister, and politician, the first black man to make a serious bid for the US presidency (in the Democratic Party's nomination races in 1983–84 and 1987–88).

Joe Jackson (11 Aug 1955, Burton-upon-Trent, England) British musician and songwriter.

Michael (Joseph) Jackson (29 Aug 1958, Gary IN) American singer, songwriter, and dancer who was the most popular entertainer in the world in the early and mid-1980s.

Phil(ip Douglas) Jackson (17 Sep 1945, Deer Lodge MT) American basketball player and coach; as coach, won nine NBA titles with Chicago Bulls (1991–93, 1996–98) and the Los Angeles Lakers (2000–02); he holds the record for most NBA playoff coaching wins (156).

Samuel L. Jackson (21 Dec 1948, Washington DC) American film actor whose breakthrough performance in *Jungle Fever* (1991) launched a successful career.

Marc Jacobs (9 Apr 1963, New York NY) American fashion designer, creator of his own signature lines and artistic director for Louis Vuitton.

Dan Jacobson (7 Mar 1929, Johannesburg, South Africa) South African-born novelist and short-story writer.

Christian Jacq (1947, Paris, France) French Egyptologist and author.

Susan Jaffe (1962?, Washington DC) American ballerina, retired from American Ballet Theatre in 2002.

Janet Rosenberg Jagan (20 Oct 1920, Chicago IL) American-born Guyanan statesman and president of Guyana, 1997–99.

Bharrat Jagdeo (23 Jan 1964, Unity village, Demarara, Guyana) Guyanan politician and president of Guyana from 1999.

Mick Jagger (Michael Philip Jagger; 26 Jul 1943, Dartford, Kent, England) British rock musician and lead singer of the Rolling Stones.

Jaromír Jágr (15 Feb 1972, Kladno, Czechoslovakia) Czech hockey player; NHL MVP in 1999; won the Art Ross Trophy (leading scorer) 1995, 1998–2001.

Helmut Jahn (4 Jan 1940, Nürnberg, Germany) German-born architect known especially for his use of light and color.

Ahmad Jamal (2 Jul 1930, Pittsburgh PA) American jazz pianist and composer.

Bob James (25 Dec 1939, Marshall MO) American jazz and pop pianist and composer.

Etta James (Jamesetta Hawkins; 25 Jan 1938, Los Angeles CA) American rhythm-and-blues entertainer who later became a successful ballad singer.

P.D. James (3 Aug 1920, Oxford, Oxfordshire, England) British mystery novelist.

Rick James (James Johnson; 1 Feb 1948, Buffalo NY) American pop songwriter and singer.

Judith Jamison (10 May 1944, Philadelphia PA) American dancer and choreographer who became artistic director of the Alvin Ailey Dance Theatre in 1989.

Yahya (Alphonse Jamus Jebulai) Jammeh (25 May 1965, Kanilai village, The Gambia) Gambian politician; president of The Gambia from 1994.

Abduragak Abubakar Janjalani (died December 1998, Lamitan, Basilan Island, Philippines) Philippine revolutionary; founder and leader of the Abu Sayyaf.

William J. Janklow (13 Sep 1939, Chicago IL) American Republican politician; governor of South Dakota from 1995.

Allison Janney (19 Nov 1960, Dayton OH) American TV actress, currently starring as C.J. Cregg on *The West Wing.*

Bert Jansch (3 Nov 1943, Glasgow, Scotland) British folk and pop guitarist and singer.

Mariss Jansons (1943, Riga, Latvia, USSR) Latvian-born American conductor; music director of the Pittsburgh Symphony Orchestra from 1997.

Jim Jarmusch (22 Jan 1953, Akron OH) American avant-garde filmmaker.

Maurice Jarre (13 Sep 1924, Lyons, France) French composer best known for his film scores, including *Lawrence of Arabia* (1962) and *Doctor Zhivago* (1965).

Keith Jarrett (8 May 1945, Allentown PA) American jazz pianist, composer, and saxophonist considered to be one of the most original and prolific jazz musicians of the late 20th century.

Tom Jarriel (Thomas Edwin Jarriel; 29 Dec 1934, LaGrange GA) American broadcast journalist.

Neeme Järvi (7 Jun 1937, Tallinn, Estonia) Estonian conductor; music director of the Detroit Symphony Orchestra from 1990.

Jay-Z (Shawn Carter; 4 Dec 1970, Brooklyn NY) American rap performer.

James M. Jeffords (11 May 1934, Rutland VT) American politician; senator from Vermont who, in 2001, left the Republican Party and declared himself an Independent caucusing with the Democrats, breaking a 50-50 split in the Senate.

Tahar Ben Jelloun (21 Dec 1944, Fès, Morocco) Moroccan poet, novelist, and dramatist.

Mae C. Jemison (17 Oct 1956, Decatur AL) American physician and the first African American woman to become an astronaut (1992).

Peter Jennings (29 Jul 1938, Toronto, ON, Canada) Canadian-born journalist and TV news anchor.

Siegfried Jerusalem (17 Apr 1940, Oberhausen, Germany) German operatic tenor.

Derek Jeter (26 Jun 1974, Pequannock NJ) American baseball player; shortstop for the New York Yankees (from 1995) during four World Series-winning seasons (1996, 1998–2000).

Jewel (Jewel Kilcher; 23 May 1974, Payson UT) American pop singer and songwriter.

Jiang Zemin (17 Aug 1926, Yangzhou, Jiangsu province, China) Chinese politician; general secretary of the Communist Party, and president of China from 1993.

Ha Jin (Xuefei Jin; 21 Feb 1956, Jinzhou, Liaoning province, China) Chinese American writer whose novel Waiting won the 1999 National Book Award and the PEN/Faulkner Award for fiction in 2000.

Sumi Jo (1962, Seoul, South Korea) Korean operatic soprano.

Steven Paul Jobs (24 Feb 1955, San Francisco CA) American corporate executive; co-founder of Apple Computer and CEO of Apple Computer, Inc. from 1997.

Billy Joel (William Martin Joel; 9 May 1949, Hicksville NY) American pop singer, pianist, and songwriter.

Mike Johanns (18 Jun 1950, Osage IA) American Republican politician; governor of Nebraska from 1999.

Thomas Johansson (24 Mar 1975, Linkoping, Sweden) Swedish tennis player, winner of the 2002 Australian Open.

Elton John (Reginald Kenneth Dwight; 25 Mar 1947, Pinner, Middlesex, England) British singer, composer, and pianist who was one of the most popular entertainers of the late 20th century.

John Paul II (Latin Johannes Paulus, original name Karol Jozef Wojtyla) (18 May 1920, Wadowice, Poland) Polish-born pope (from 1978); the first non-Italian pope in 455 years and the first ever from a Slavic country. By 2002 he had made almost 100 trips abroad and traveled greater distances than all other popes combined in his efforts at global bridge-building.

Jasper Johns (15 May 1930, Augusta GA) American painter and graphic artist who is generally associated with the Pop art movement.

Betsey Johnson (10 Aug 1942, Wethersfield CT) American fashion designer whose rock-star personality is exhibited in whimsical creations meant to make fashion fun.

Beverly Johnson (13 Oct 1952, Buffalo NY) American fashion model of the 1970s who became the first African American cover model for Vogue.

Boris Johnson (1964, New York NY) American-born British journalist, editor of The Spectator, and member of Parliament.

Gary E. Johnson (1 Jan 1953, Minot ND) American Republican politician; governor of New Mexico from 1995.

John H(arold) Johnson (19 Jan 1918, Arkansas City AR) American magazine and book publisher; creator of Ebony (1945), Jet, and other periodicals.

Lady Bird Johnson (née Claudia Alta Taylor; 22 Dec 1912, Karnack TX) American first lady; wife of Pres. Lyndon B. Johnson.

Paul Johnson (1928, Barton, Lancashire, England) British historian, author, and editor of The New Statesman.

Randy Johnson (10 Sep 1963, Walnut Creek CA) American baseball player; four-time Cy Young Award winner; league strikeout leader, 1993–94, 1998–2001.

Angelina Jolie (Angelina Jolie Voight; 4 Jun 1975, Los Angeles CA) American motion-picture actress known for her daring personality.

Brian Jones (27 Mar 1947, Bristol, England) British balloonist who, with Bertrand Piccard, became the first to travel nonstop around the world (1999).

Elvin (Ray) Jones (9 Sep 1927, Pontiac MI) American jazz drummer and bandleader.

Etta Jones (25 Nov 1928, Aiken SC) American jazz singer.

George Jones (12 Sep 1931, Saratoga TX) American honky tonk performer and balladeer considered to be one of the greatest country singers of all time.

James Earl Jones (17 Jan 1931, Arkabutla MS) American actor famous both for his work on stage and screen and as the voice of Darth Vader in the Star Wars films.

Marion Jones (12 Oct 1975, Los Angeles CA) American track and field athlete; Olympic gold medalist (2000) in three running events, and won bronzes in two other events, the most medals ever won by a woman in one Olympic Games.

Norah Jones (30 Mar 1979, New York NY) American jazz vocalist and pianist.

Quincy Jones (Quincy Delight Jones, Jr; 14 Mar 1933, Chicago IL) American arranger, composer, and producer.

Rickie Lee Jones (8 Nov 1954, Chicago IL) American pop singer.

Shirley (Mae) Jones (31 Mar 1934, Charleroi PA) American actress, known for lead roles in Rodgers and Hammerstein musicals and for TV's The Partridge Family.

Tom Jones (Thomas Jones Woodward; 7 Jun 1940, Pontypridd, Wales) British pop singer.

Tommy Lee Jones (15 Sep 1946, San Saba TX) American film actor with a long career playing intelligent roles.

Michael (Jeffrey) Jordan (17 Feb 1963, Brooklyn NY) American basketball player; playing for the Chicago Bulls, he led NBA in scoring, 1987–93, 1996–98; MVP, 1988, 1991–92, 1996, 1998; voted ESPN's Athlete of the Century and is believed by many to be the best basketball player in the history of the sport.

Vernon E. Jordan, Jr. (15 Aug 1935, Atlanta GA) American attorney, former presidential adviser, civil rights leader.

Lionel (Robert) Jospin (12 Jul 1937, Meudon, France) French politician; prime minister of France, 1997–2002.

Milla Jovovich (17 Dec 1975, Kiev, Ukrainian SSR, USSR [now Ukraine]) Ukrainian-born American motion-picture actress, model, and singer.

King Juan Carlos I (Juan Carlos Alfonso Victor María de Borbón y Borbón; 5 Jan 1938, Rome, Italy) Spanish royal; king of Spain from 1975.

Ashley Judd (Ashley Tyler Ciminella; 19 Apr 1968, Granada Hills CA) American film actress and star of popular motion pictures.

Naomi Judd (Diana Ellen Judd; 11 Jan 1946, Ashland KY) American country and western singer.

Wynonna Judd (Christina Claire Ciminella; 30 May 1964, Ashland KY) American country and western singer.

Sir Anerood Jugnauth (29 Mar 1930) Mauritian politician; prime minister of Mauritius, 1982–95 and again from 2000.

Jean-Claude Juncker (9 Dec 1954, Rédange-sur-Attert, Luxembourg) Luxembourgian politician; prime minister of Luxembourg from 1995.

Andrea Jung (1959, Toronto, ON, Canada) Canadian-born American business executive; CEO of Avon Products, Inc. from 1999.

Udo Jürgens (Udo Jürgen Bockelmann; 30 Sep 1934, Klagenfurt, Austria) German pop singer, pianist, and songwriter.

Ahmad Tejan Kabbah (16 Feb 1932, Pendembu, Kailahun dstrict, Sierra Leone) Sierra Leonian politician; president of Sierra Leone, 1996–97 and from 1998.

Joseph Kabila (4 Jun 1971, Sud-Kivu province, [Dem. Rep. of the Congo]) Congolese politician; president of the Democratic Republic of the Congo from 17 Jan 2001.

Yevgeny Kafelnikov (18 Feb 1974, Sochi, Russia, USSR) Russian tennis player; won the 1996 French Open and the 1999 Australian Open.

Paul Kagame (c. 1957, Gitarama, Ruanda-Urundi [now Rwanda]) Rwandan politician; president of Rwanda from 2000.

Mauricio Kagel (24 Dec 1931, Buenos Aires, Argentina) Argentine composer and filmmaker.

Dahir Riyale Kahin (1952) Somali politician; president of the secessionist Republic of Somaliland from 3 May 2002.

Stephen Kakfwi (1950, near Fort Good Hope, NWT, Canada) Canadian politician; premier of Northwest Territories from 17 Jan 2000.

A.P.J. Abdul Kalam (Avul Pakir Jainulabdeen Abdul Kalam; 15 Oct 1931, Rameswaram, Tamil Nadu state, India) Indian politician; president of India from 25 Jul 2002.

Siim Kallas (2 Oct 1948, Tallinn, Estonian SSR, USSR [now Estonia]) Estonian politician; prime minister of Estonia from 2002.

Anfinn Kallsberg (1947) Faroese politician; prime minister of Faroe Islands from 1998.

Eric R. Kandel (7 Nov 1929, Vienna, Austria) American (Austrian-born) neurobiologist; co-winner of the Nobel Prize for Physiology or Medicine, 2000, for studies of brain-cell function.

Sheikh Hamidou Kane (3 Apr 1928, Matam, River Region, Senegal) Senegalese writer.

Radovan Karadzic (19 Jun 1945, Montenegro, Yugoslavia) Bosnian (Serb) politician; president of Republika Srpska (Bosnia and Herzegovina), 1992–96; wanted as a war criminal and at large in 2002.

Donna Karan (Donna Faske; 2 Oct 1948, Forest Hills NY) American fashion designer known for the simplicity of her predominately black and neutral-colored designs.

Islam Karimov (30 Jan 1938, Samarkand, Uzbek SSR, USSR [now Uzbekistan]) Uzbek politician; president of Uzbekistan from 1990.

Hamid Karzai (24 Dec 1957, Karz, Afghanistan) Afghani statesman; head of the interim administration of Afghanistan following the ousting of the Taliban; president of Afghanistan from 22 Dec 2001.

Garry Kasparov (Garri Kimovich Kasparov, original name Garri Weinstein or Harry Weinstein; 13 Apr 1963, Baku, Azerbaijan, USSR) Azerbaijani-born Russian chess champion of the world from 1985 to 2000.

Mikhail Mikhaylovich Kasyanov (8 Dec 1957, Solntsevo, Moscow oblast, USSR [now Russia]) Russian politician; prime minister of Russia from 2000.

Moshe Katsav (1945, Iran) Israeli politician; president of Israel from 2000.

Jorma Kaukonen (23 Dec 1940, Washington DC) American rock guitarist (of Jefferson Airplane, Hot Tuna, etc.).

Yoriko Kawaguchi (14 Jan 1941, Tokyo, Japan) Japanese politician; foreign minister of Japan from 2002.

Nobuhiko Kawamoto (3 Mar 1936, Tokyo, Japan) Japanese business executive; president of Honda Motor Co, Ltd. from 1990.

Frank Keating (10 Feb 1944, St. Louis MO) American Republican politician; governor of Oklahoma from 1995.

Diane Keaton (Diane Hall; 5 Jan 1946, Los Angeles CA) American actress and director who achieved fame in quirky comic roles and became a respected dramatic actress.

Michael Keaton (Michael John Douglas; 9 Sep 1951, Coraopolis PA) American film actor known for comic roles and for playing *Batman* (1989; 1992).

Garrison Keillor (Gary Edward Keillor; 7 Aug 1942, Anoka MN) American humorist and writer, best known for his long-running radio variety show, *A Prairie Home Companion.*

Salif Keita (1949, Djoliba, French West Africa [now Mali]) Malian folk and pop musician.

Harvey Keitel (13 May 1939, Brooklyn NY) American film actor known for gritty roles.

Jakob Kellenberger (1944, Heiden, Switzerland) Swiss international official; president of the International Committee of the Red Cross from 2000.

David E. Kelley (4 Apr 1956, Waterville ME) American screenwriter who created the hit TV series *The Practice* and *Ally McBeal.*

Ellsworth Kelly (31 May 1923, Newburgh NY) American painter and sculptor, a leading exponent of the hard-edge style, in which abstract contours are sharply and precisely defined.

Jim Kelly (14 Feb 1960, Pittsburgh PA) American football player; passed for more than 3,000 yd in 8 of 11 seasons as quarterback for the Buffalo Bills.

R. Kelly (Robert S. Kelly; 8 Jan 1969, Chicago IL) American R&B performer.

Sir Allan Kemakeza (1951, Panueli village, Savo Island, Solomon Islands) Solomon Islands politician; prime minister of the Solomon Islands from 2001.

Dirk Kempthorne (29 Oct 1951, San Diego CA) American Republican politician; governor of Idaho from 1999.

Anthony Kennedy (23 Jul 1936, Sacramento CA) American jurist; associate justice of the US Supreme Court from 1988.

Charles Kennedy (25 Nov 1959, Inverness, Scotland) British politician, leader of the Liberal Democratic Party from 1999.

Edward M(oore) Kennedy (22 Feb 1932, Brookline MA) American Democratic politician; senator from Massachusetts from 1963.

Caroline Kennedy Schlossberg (27 Nov 1957, New York NY) American author; daughter of Pres. John F. Kennedy.

Duchess of Kent (Katharine Worsley) British royal; wife of the Duke of Kent.

Duke of Kent (1935) British royal.

Prince Michael of Kent (Michael George Charles Franklin; 4 Jul 1942, Iver, Buckinghamshire, England) British royal.

Mathieu Kérékou (2 Sep 1933, Kouarfa, French West Africa [now Benin]) Benin politician; president of Benin, 1972–91 and from 1996.

Deborah Kerr (Deborah Jane Kerr-Trimmer; 30 Sep 1921, Helensburgh, Scotland) British film star known for poise and complexity of characters.

Joseph Robert ("Bob") Kerrey (27 Aug 1943, Lincoln NE) American businessman and politician; Democratic governor of Nebraska, 1983–87, and senator from Nebraska, 1989–2001.

John Kerry (11 Dec 1943, Denver CO) American Democratic politician; senator from Massachusetts from 1985.

Doug Kershaw (24 Jan 1936, Tiel Ridge LA) American Cajun and pop fiddler and singer.

Wolfgang Ketterle (21 Oct 1957, Heidelberg, Germany) German physicist; co-winner of the Nobel

Prize for Physics, 2001, for work in the creation of the Bose-Einstein condensate.

Jack Kevorkian (26 May 1928, Pontiac MI) American physician, assisted-suicide activist.

Alicia Keys (Alicia Augello Cook; 25 Jan 1981, New York NY) American R&B singer; winner of five Grammy Awards in 2002.

Euphrase Kezilahabi (13 Apr 1944, Ukerewe, Tanganyika [now in Tanzania]) Tanzanian novelist, poet, and scholar writing in Swahili.

Keorapetse Kgositsile (19 Sep 1938, Johannesburg, South Africa) South African poet and essayist.

Cheb Khaled (Khaled Hadj Brahim; 29 Feb 1960, Sidi-El-Houri, near Oran, Algeria) Algerian rai performer.

Sheikh Hamad ibn Isa al-Khalifah (28 Jan 1950, Bahrain) Bahraini royal and chief of state; proclaimed himself king in 2002.

Ayatollah Sayyed Ali Khamenei (1939, Mashad, Iran) Iranian religious leader; supreme political and religious authority in Iran from 1989.

Khamtai Siphandon (8 Feb 1924, Champassak province, Laos) Laotian politician; general secretary of the Lao People's Revolutionary Party from 1992 and president of Laos from 1998.

Ali Akbar Khan (14 Apr 1922, Shibpur, Bengal, India) Indian composer and virtuoso sarod player.

Ismail Khan (1946, Farah province, Afghanistan) Afghani military leader.

Hojatoleslam Mohammad Khatami (1943, Ardakan, Iran) Iranian politician and president of Iran from 1997.

Cheikh El Afia Ould Mohamed Khouna (1956) Mauritanian politician; prime minister of Mauritania, 1996–97, and again from 1998.

Michael Kidd (Milton Greenwald; 12 Aug 1919, Brooklyn NY) American choreographer who earned five Tony Awards for his work on Broadway and who attained even greater fame for the dances he created for several classic film musicals.

Nicole Kidman (20 Jun 1967, Honolulu HI) Australian actress who in recent years has risen to become one of Hollywood's most popular stars.

Anselm Kiefer (8 Mar 1945, Donaueschingen, Germany) German painter in the Neo-Expressionist movement, known for works that deal ironically with 20th-century German history.

Jack S. Kilby (8 Nov 1923, Jefferson City MO) American electrical engineer; Nobel Prize for Physics, 2000, for his role in inventing the integrated circuit, or microchip.

James Jackson Kilpatrick (1 Nov 1920, Oklahoma City OK) American journalist and political commentator.

Kwame M. Kilpatrick (8 Jun 1970, Detroit MI) American Democratic politician; mayor of Detroit from 4 Jan 2002.

Kim Dae Jung (3 Dec 1925, Mokp'o, Korea [now in South Korea]) Korean politician; opposition leader; and president of South Korea from 1998; Nobel Peace Prize, 2000.

Kim Jong Il (16 Feb 1941, Siberia, Russia, USSR) Korean (North) politician; general secretary of the Central Committee of the Worker's party of Korea (i.e., North Korea); successor to his father, Kim Il-Sung.

Kim Soon Kwon (1 May 1945, Ulsan, South Kyongsang province, South Korea) Korean agricultural scientist specializing in developing high-yield, disease-resistant strains of corn, prominent also for his work in aiding Korean reunification.

Kim Woo Choong (19 Dec 1936, Taegu, Korea) Korean businessman; founder and chairman of the Daewoo Group; chairman of the Federation of Korean Industries from 1998.

Kim Young Sam (20 Dec 1927, Koje Island, off Pusan, Korea [now in South Korea]) Korean politician; president of South Korea, 1993–97.

Anatoly Kinakh (4 Aug 1954, Bratushany, Moldavian SSR, USSR [now Moldova]) Ukrainian politician; prime minister of Ukraine from 2001.

Angus S. King, Jr. (31 Mar 1944, Alexandria VA) American politician; Independent governor of Maine from 1995.

B.B. King (Riley B. King; 16 Sep 1925, Itta Bena, near Indianola MS) American guitarist and singer, a principal figure in the development of blues and from whose style leading popular musicians have drawn inspiration.

Coretta Scott King (27 Apr 1927, Marion AL) American lecturer, writer, and widow of Martin Luther King, Jr.

Stephen King (21 Sep 1947, Portland ME) American novelist and short story writer.

Ben Kingsley (Krishna Bhanji; 31 Dec 1943, Scarborough, England) British remarkably talented actor who gained fame for playing the title role in *Gandhi* (1982).

Greg Kinnear (17 Jun 1963, Logansport IN) American actor, gained fame as the first host of TV's *Talk Soup*.

Thomas Kinsella (4 May 1928, Dublin, Ireland) Irish poet.

Michael Kinsley (9 Mar 1951, Detroit MI) American political commentator and editor; originator of the on-line magazine *Slate*.

Ron Kirk (27 Jun 1954, Austin TX) American lawyer; secretary of state of Texas; mayor of Dallas, 1995–2001.

Gelsey Kirkland (29 Dec 1952, Bethlehem PA) American ballerina; principal dancer for George Balanchine at the New York City Ballet and later joined the American Ballet Theatre.

Yevgeny Kissin (1971, Moscow, USSR [now Russia]) Russian concert pianist.

Ewald Kist, Dutch corporate executive; chairman of ING Group from 2000.

R(onald) B(rooks) Kitaj (29 Oct 1932, Chagrin Falls OH) American-born Pop art painter.

Kitaro (Masanori Takahashi; 1953, Japan) Japanese New Age electronic musician.

Eartha (Mae) Kitt (26 Jan 1927, North SC) American singer, dancer, and actress.

John A. Kitzhaber (5 Mar 1947, Colfax WA) American physician and Democratic politician; governor of Oregon from 1995.

Lasse Kjus (14 Jan 1971, Oslo, Norway) Norwegian Alpine skier, the first Olympic skier to win two medals in a single day (1994); twice World Cup winner (1996, 1999).

Calvin (Richard) Klein (19 Nov 1942, Bronx NY) American fashion designer noted for his classic, elegant, and easy-to-wear clothing.

Ralph Klein (1 Nov 1942, Calgary, AB, Canada) Canadian politician; premier of Alberta from 1992.

Thomas Klestil (4 Nov 1932, Erdberg, Vienna, Austria) Austrian politician; president of Austria from 1992.

Kevin Kline (24 Oct 1947, St. Louis MO) American comic and dramatic actor; first film performance in *Sophie's Choice* (1982).

Yana Klochkova (7 Aug 1982, Simferopol, Crimea, Ukraine, USSR [now Ukraine]) Ukrainian swimmer who broke the world record in 400-m individual medley in 2002.

Bob Knight (Robert Montgomery Knight; 25 Oct 1940, Orville OH) American collegiate basketball coach who led Indiana University to NCAA titles in 1976, 1981, and 1987 and the US Olympic team to a gold medal in 1984.

Gladys Knight (28 May 1944, Atlanta GA) American R&B singer (of Gladys Knight and the Pips).

Mark Knopfler (12 Aug 1949, Glasgow, Scotland) British rock vocalist/guitarist (of Dire Straits).

Beyoncé Knowles (4 Sep 1981, Houston TX) American pop singer (of Destiny's Child).

Tony Knowles (1 Jan 1943, Tulsa OK) American Democratic politician; governor of Alaska from 1994.

William S. Knowles (1 Jun 1917, Taunton MA) American chemist; co-winner of the Nobel Prize for Chemistry, 2001, for development of chiral catalysts.

Robert (Sedraki) Kocharyan (31 Aug 1954, Stepanakert, Nagorno-Karabakh, Azerbaijan SSR, USSR [now Azerbaijan]) Armenian politician; president of Armenia from 1998.

Helmut Michael Kohl (3 Apr 1930, Ludwigshafen am Rhein, Germany) German politician; chancellor of (West) Germany, 1982–98.

Horst Köhler (22 Feb 1943, Skierbieszow, Poland) German banker; managing director of the International Monetary Fund from 2000.

Junichiro Koizumi (8 Jan 1942, Yokosuka, Kanagawa prefecture, Japan) Japanese politician; prime minister of Japan from 2001.

Willem ("Wim") Kok (29 Sep 1938, Bergambacht, The Netherlands) Dutch politician; prime minister of The Netherlands, 1994–2002.

Lee Konitz (13 Oct 1927, Chicago IL) American jazz alto saxophonist.

Tim Koogle (1951?, Alexandria VA) American corporate executive; CEO of Yahoo! Inc. from 1995.

Rem Koolhaas (1944, Rotterdam, The Netherlands) Dutch architect known especially for his concepts of large-scale structures; Pritzker Prize winner in 2000.

Jeff Koons (21 Jan 1955, York PA) American Pop-art painter and sculptor.

Al Kooper (5 Feb 1944, Brooklyn NY) American pop singer and pianist.

Ted Koppel (Edward James Koppel; 8 Feb 1940, Lancashire, England) British-born American TV news broadcaster and anchor of the news analysis show *Nightline* from 1980.

Michael Kors (Karl Anderson, Jr.; Michael David Kors; 1959, Merrick, Long Island NY) American fashion designer, creator of his own signature lines and artistic director for Céline.

Johann Olav Koss (29 Oct 1968, Drammen, Norway) Norwegian speed skater who was the dominant long-distance skater of the 1990s; at the 1994 Winter Olympics, Koss set three world records on his way to winning three gold medals.

Janica Kostelic (1 May 1982, Zagreb, Croatia, Yugoslavia [now Croatia]) Croatian Alpine skier who won three gold medals and one silver at the 2002 Winter Olympic Games.

Vojislav Kostunica (24 Mar 1944, Belgrade, Yugoslavia) Yugoslavian politician and president of Yugoslavia from 2000.

Diana Krall (16 Nov 1964, Nanaimo, BC, Canada) Canadian jazz pianist and singer.

Larry Kramer (25 Jun 1935, Bridgeport CT) American writer and AIDS activist.

Vladimir Kramnik (25 Jun 1975, Tuapse, Russia, USSR) Russian chess grandmaster who defeated Garry Kasparov to become world chess champion in 2000.

Alison Krauss (23 Jul 1971, Decatur IL) American bluegrass fiddle player and singer.

Lenny Kravitz (26 May 1964, Brooklyn NY) American rock performer.

Gidon Kremer (1947, Riga, Latvia, USSR) Latvian-born violinist and conductor.

Kris Kristofferson (22 Jun 1936, Brownsville TX) American country-rock singer and songwriter and actor.

Irving Kristol (Irving Horenstein; 1920, New York NY) American essayist and columnist; editor of *The Public Interest* from 1965.

William Kristol (23 Dec 1952, New York NY) American editor and columnist.

Herbert Kroemer (25 Aug 1928, Weimar, Germany) American (German-born) electrical engineer; Nobel Prize for Physics, 2000, for studies of heterostructure transistors.

Milan Kucan (14 Jan 1941, Krizevci, Yugoslavia [now in Slovenia]) Slovene politician; president of Slovenia from 1990.

Leonid Danylovych Kuchma (9 Aug 1938, Chaykyne, Ukrainian SSR, USSR [now Ukraine]) Ukrainian engineer, politician; prime minister of Ukraine, 1992–93, and president from 1994.

Gustavo Kuerten (10 Sep 1976, Florianópolis, Santa Catarina state, Brazil) Brazilian tennis player, three-time winner of the French Open (1997, 2001, 2002).

John (Kofi Agyekum) Kufuor (8 Dec 1938, Kumisi, Gold Coast Colony [now Ghana]) Ghanaian politician; president of Ghana from 2001.

Chandrika (Bandaranaike) Kumaratunga (29 Jun 1945, Colombo, Ceylon [now Sri Lanka]) Sri Lankan politician; president of Sri Lanka from 1994.

Hans Küng (19 Mar 1928, Sursee, Switzerland) Swiss Roman Catholic theologian whose controversial liberal views led to his censorship by the Vatican in 1979.

Stanley (Jasspon) Kunitz (29 Jul 1906, Worcester MA) American poet noted for his subtle craftsmanship and his treatment of complex themes; from 1974 to 1976 and 2000–01 he was consultant in poetry to the Library of Congress (now poet laureate consultant in poetry).

Irv Kupcinet (31 Jul 1912, Chicago IL) American talk-show host and columnist.

Raymond Kurzweil (12 Feb 1948, Queens NY) American computer scientist and visionary, a specialist in pattern recognition, whose work resulted in inventions of flatbed scanners, speech-recognition devices, and reading machines for the blind.

Tony Kushner (July 1956, New York NY) American author of a series of unconventional but highly regarded plays, including *Millennium, Angels in America,* and *Perestroika*.

Michelle Kwan (Kwan Shan Wing; 7 Jul 1980, Torrance CA) American (Chinese-American) figure skater; US (1996, 1998–2001), world (1996, 1998, 2000, 2001), and Olympic medalist (silver medal in 1998 and bronze in 2002).

Aleksander Kwasniewski (15 Nov 1954, Dojlidy, near Bialystok, Poland) Polish politician; president of Poland from 1995.

Patti LaBelle (Patricia Louise Holt; 4 Oct 1944, Philadelphia PA) American soul and rock singer.

Bobby Labonte (8 May 1964, Corpus Christi TX) American race-car driver; NASCAR Winston Cup champion, 2000.

Christian Lacroix (17 May 1951, Arles, France) French fashion designer known for his ostentatious, extravagant, and colorful creations.

Carmen Laforet (Díaz) (6 Sep 1921, Barcelona, Spain) Spanish novelist and short-story writer.

Emeril (John) Lagasse (15 Oct 1959, Fall River MA) American chef, restaurateur, and media personality, known for his energetic TV cooking shows.

Karl Lagerfeld (10 Sep 1938, Hamburg, Germany) German-born French fashion designer known for his highly feminine creations for the houses of Chloé and Chanel.

Ricardo Lagos Escobar (2 Mar 1938, Santiago, Chile) Chilean economist and political leader; president of Chile from 2000.

Émile Jamil Lahoud (12 Jan 1936, Baabdat, Lebanon) Lebanese politician; president of Lebanon from 1998.

Cleo Laine (Clementina Dinah Campbell; 27 Oct 1927, Southall, Middlesex, England) British jazz singer.

Lorenzo Lamas (20 Jan 1958, Los Angeles CA) American TV actor who was featured in the series *Falcon Crest* (1981–90) and *Renegade* (1992–97).

Brian Lamb (9 Oct 1941, Lafayette IN) American cable TV executive, journalist.

Rachael Lampa (8 Jan 1985, Ann Arbor MI) American pop singer.

Martin Landau (20 Jun 1931, Brooklyn NY) American film and TV actor best known for the *Mission: Impossible* TV series.

Bernard Landry (9 Mar 1937, Saint-Jacques-de-Montcalm, QC, Canada) Canadian politician; premier of Quebec from 8 Mar 2001.

Nathan Lane (Joseph Lane; 3 Feb 1956, Jersey City NJ) American comedic actor of stage and screen; recently starred with Matthew Broderick in *The Producers* on Broadway.

Helmut Lang (10 Mar 1956, Vienna, Austria) Austrian fashion designer whose simple creations are changed very little from season to season.

K.D. Lang (Kathryn Dawn Lang; 2 Nov 1961, Consort, AB, Canada) Canadian country-rock singer, songwriter.

Jessica Lange (20 Apr 1949, Cloquet MN) American intense and gifted film actress.

Angela Lansbury (16 Oct 1925, London, England) British character actress; best known to TV audiences as Jessica Fletcher on *Murder, She Wrote.*

Lewis H. Lapham (8 Jan 1935, San Francisco CA) American political commentator and author.

Brian Lara (2 May 1969, Cantaro, Trinidad) West Indian left-handed cricket batsman who in 1994 scored a record 375 not out and a few months later made the highest individual score in first-class cricket with an unbeaten innings of 501.

Jaime Eduardo Laredo (7 Jun 1941, Cochabamba, Bolivia) Bolivian violinist.

Ruth Laredo (née Ruth Meckler; 20 Nov 1937, Detroit MI) American concert pianist.

Alicia de Larrocha (Alicia de Larrocha y de las Calles; 23 May 1923, Barcelona, Spain) Spanish pianist.

Matt(hew Todd) Lauer (30 Dec 1957, New York NY) American TV journalist; host of the *Today* show from 1994.

Cyndi Lauper (Cynthia Anne Stephanie Lauper; 22 Jun 1953, Queens NY) American pop singer.

Ralph Lauren (Ralph Lipschitz; 14 Oct 1939, New York NY) American fashion designer known for his ready-to-wear collections and his use of unconventional materials.

Jude Law (29 Dec 1972, Blackheath, South London, England) British stage and screen star who rose to prominence after appearing in the film *The Talented Mr. Ripley* (1999).

Lucy Lawless (Lucille Frances Ryan; 28 Mar 1968, Mount Albert, New Zealand) New Zealand TV and motion-picture actress best known as the title character on the series *Xena: Warrior Princess.*

Steve Lawrence (Sidney Liebowitz; 8 Jul 1935, Brooklyn NY) American pop singer.

Hubert Laws (10 Nov 1939, Houston TX) American jazz flutist and composer.

Jean-Marie Le Pen (20 Jun 1928, La Trinité-sur-Mer, Brittany, France) French politician, right-wing extremist.

Richard (Erskine Frere) Leakey (19 Dec 1944, Nairobi, Kenya) Kenyan physical anthropologist, paleontologist, conservationist, and politician.

Evelyn Lear (Evelyn Shulman; 8 Jan 1928/31, Brooklyn NY) American soprano.

Norman Lear (27 Jul 1922, New Haven CT) American TV scriptwriter and producer.

Michael O. Leavitt (11 Feb 1951, Cedar City UT) American Republican politician; governor of Utah from 1993.

Joshua Lederberg (23 May 1925, Montclair NJ) American bacterial geneticist; Nobel Prize for Physiology or Medicine, 1958.

Ang Lee (23 Oct 1954, P'ing-Tung county, Taiwan) Taiwanese-born film director of extraordinary versatility most famous for *Crouching Tiger, Hidden Dragon* (2000).

Brenda Lee (Brenda Mae Tarpley; 11 Dec 1944, Lithonia GA) American pop singer.

Jeanette Lee (9 Jul 1971, Brooklyn NY) American billiards player; top-ranked nine-ball player in the WPBA, 1994–96.

(Nelle) Harper Lee (28 Apr 1926, Monroeville AL) American writer nationally acclaimed for her one novel, *To Kill a Mockingbird* (1960).

Spike Lee (20 Mar 1957, Atlanta GA) American filmmaker known for his uncompromising, provocative approach to controversial subject matter.

Lee Kun Hee (9 Jan 1942, Uiryung, Kyongnam province, Korea) Korean corporate executive; chairman of the Samsung Group from 1987.

Michel Legrand (24 Feb 1932, Paris, France) French composer, pianist, and arranger, noted for his Oscar-winning song, "The Windmills Of Your Mind" from *The Thomas Crown Affair* and "I Will Wait For You," from *Les parapluies de Cherbourg.*

James ("Jim") Lehrer (19 May 1934, Wichita KS) American TV journalist and author, co-host with Robert MacNeil of *The MacNeil/Lehrer Report* from 1975.

Tom Lehrer (9 Apr 1928, New York NY) American satirical songwriter, pianist, and mathematician.

Jennifer Jason Leigh (Jennifer Lee Morrow; 5 Feb 1962, Los Angeles CA) American film actress acclaimed for her performance in *Rush* (1991).

Vivien Leigh (Vivian Mary Hartley; 5 Nov 1913, Darjeeling, India) British stage and screen actress immortalized by the films *Gone with the Wind* (1939) and *A Streetcar Named Desire* (1951).

Jean Lemierre (6 Jun 1950, Sainte Adresse, France) French international banking executive; president of the European Bank for Reconstruction and Development from 2000.

Mario Lemieux (5 Oct 1965, Montreal, QC, Canada) American ice hockey player; was the NHL's leading scorer in six seasons and was voted MVP in 1988, 1993, and 1996.

Ute Lemper (4 Jul 1963, Münster, Germany) German cabaret singer.

Julian Lennon (8 Apr 1963, Liverpool, England) British pop musician, singer, and son of John Lennon.

Annie Lennox (25 Dec 1954, Aberdeen, Scotland) British pop singer (of the Eurythmics).

Jay Leno (James Douglas Muir Leno; 28 Apr 1950, Short Hills NJ) American comedian; host of *The Tonight Show* from 1992.

Elmore Leonard (Elmore John Leonard, Jr.; 11 Oct 1925, New Orleans LA) American author of popular crime novels known for his use of local color and his uncanny ear for realistic dialogue.

Aleksey Arkhipovich Leonov (30 May 1934, near Kemerovo, Russian SFSR, USSR [now Russia]) Soviet Russian cosmonaut, the first man to climb out of a spacecraft in space.

Lisa Leslie (7 Jul 1972) American professional basketball player; in 2001 she was named MVP for the regular season, the WNBA championship, and the All-Star Game—the first player to win all three awards in a single year.

Doris (May) Lessing (22 Oct 1919, Kermanshah, Iran) British writer.

King (David Mohato) Letsie III (17 Jul 1963, Morija, Lesotho) Lesotho royal; king of Lesotho from 1996.

David (Michael) Letterman (12 Apr 1947, Indianapolis IN) American TV personality, host of the *Late Show with David Letterman* from 1993.

Rita Levi-Montalcini (22 Apr 1909, Turin, Italy) Italian neurologist; co-winner of the Nobel Prize for Physiology or Medicine, 1986.

Claude Levi-Strauss (28 Nov 1908, Brussels, Belgium) French social anthropologist.

Milcho Leviev (19 Dec 1937, Plovdiv, Bulgaria) Bulgarian jazz pianist.

James Levine (23 Jun 1943, Cincinnati OH) American conductor and pianist, especially noted for his work with the Metropolitan Opera of New York City.

Barry Levinson (6 Apr 1942, Baltimore MD) American writer and director whose standout films include *Diner* (1982) and *Rain Man* (1988).

Monica Lewinsky (23 Jul 1973, San Francisco CA) American personality; former White House intern, key figure in the Clinton presidential scandal.

Jerry Lewis (Jerome Levitch; 16 Mar 1926, Newark NJ) American comedian, actor, and humanitarian often partnered with crooner Dean Martin.

Jerry Lee Lewis (29 Sep 1935, Ferriday LA) American singer and pianist whose virtuosity, ecstatic performances, and colorful personality made him a legendary rock music pioneer.

Kenneth D. Lewis (9 Apr 1947, Meridian MS) American corporate executive; CEO of the Bank of America Corp. from 1999.

Lennox (Claudius) Lewis (2 Sep 1965, West Ham, London, England) British boxer, WBC and IBF world heavyweight champion from 1997.

Ramsey Lewis (27 May 1935, Chicago IL) American jazz pianist, composer, and songwriter.

Ray Lewis (15 May 1975, Bartow FL) American football player; linebacker for the Baltimore Ravens; voted MVP in Superbowl XXXV.

Sol LeWitt (9 Sep 1928, Hartford CT) American sculptor, printmaker, and draftsman of the Minimalist school, noted for his constructions and drawings featuring basic geometric forms.

Li Hongzhi (7 Jul 1952, Jilin province, China) Chinese religious leader who developed the Falun Dafa system, a cultivation of five meditation exercises (known as Falun Gong) that were based on ancient Chinese methods of spiritual healing and enlightenment.

Li Ka-shing (13 Jun 1928, Chaozhou, Guangdong province, China) Chinese (Hong Kong) corporate executive; chairman of Hutchison Whampoa Ltd. and Cheung Kong Holdings.

Daniel Libeskind (1946, Lodz, Poland) Polish-born American architect noted for his design of the Jewish Museum in Berlin.

Joseph I. Lieberman (24 Feb 1942, Stamford CT) American Democratic politician; US senator from Connecticut; vice-presidential candidate in 2000.

Gordon Lightfoot (17 Nov 1938, Orilla, ON, Canada) Canadian singer and songwriter.

Candy Lightner (30 May 1946, Pasadena CA) American social activist; founder of Mothers Against Drunk Driving (MADD).

Rush Limbaugh (12 Jan 1951, Cape Girardeau MO) American radio talk-show host and conservative commentator.

Abbey Lincoln (later Aminata Moseka; 6 Aug 1930, Chicago IL) American jazz singer.

Udo Lindenberg (17 May 1946, Gronau, Westphalia, Germany) German pop singer.

Laura Linney (5 Feb 1964, New York NY) American actress known for powerful lead and supporting roles.

Romulus Linney (21 Sep 1930, Philadelphia PA) American playwright; won the Sidney Kingsley award, 2001.

Tara (Kristen) Lipinski (10 Jun 1982, Philadelphia PA) American figure skater, the youngest ever to win US and world championships (1997); won a gold medal in the 1998 Winter Olympics.

Paavo (Tapio) Lipponen (23 Apr 1941, Turtola [now Pello], Finland) Finnish politician; prime minister of Finland from 1995.

John Lithgow (19 Oct 1945, Rochester NY) American film and TV actor known for his skill at comic and dramatic roles.

Little Richard (Richard Wayne Penniman; 5 Dec 1935, Macon GA) American singer and pianist.

Lucy (Alexis) Liu (2 Dec 1968, Jackson Heights, Queens NY) American emerging TV and film actress who gained fame for playing Ling on TV's *Ally McBeal*.

Kenneth Livingstone (17 Jun 1945, Lambeth, London, England) British politician; mayor of London from 2000.

LL Cool J (James Todd Smith; 16 Aug 1969, Queens NY) American hip-hop artist and actor.

Charles Lloyd (15 Mar 1938, Memphis TN) American jazz saxophonist.

Christopher Lloyd (22 Oct 1938, Stamford CT) American film and TV actor and producer.

Sir Andrew Lloyd Webber (22 Mar 1948, London, England) British composer whose eclectic rock-based works helped revitalize musical theater.

Gary Locke (21 Jan 1950, Seattle WA) American Democratic politician; governor of Washington from 1997.

Anthony Howard ("Tony") Lockett ("Plugger"; 9 Mar 1966, Ballarat, Victoria, Australia) Australian football player; full forward in the Australian Football League who, when he retired in 1999, held the record for goals kicked (1,357).

Keith Alan Lockhart (7 Nov 1959, Poughkeepsie NY) American conductor of the Boston Pops from 1993.

Heather Locklear (25 Sep 1961, Westwood CA) American TV actress best known for her work on *Melrose Place* and *Spin City*.

Jonah Tali Lomu (12 May 1975, Auckland, New Zealand) New Zealand rugby winger of Tongan heritage; perhaps the most famous rugby player in the world.

Shelley Long (23 Aug 1949, Fort Wayne IN) American film and TV actress; played Diane on TV's *Cheers*.

Jeannie Longo (Jeannie Longo-Ciprelli; 31 Oct 1958, Saint-Gervais, France) French cyclist who was world champion 12 times and broke the women's record for distance traveled in one hour (44.767 km) in 2000.

Jennifer Lopez (24 Jul 1970, Bronx NY) American pop singer and actress.

Nancy Lopez (6 Jan 1957, Torrance CA) American golfer; four-time LPGA player of the year and three-time LPGA champion.

Trini Lopez (Trinidad Lopez III; 15 May 1937, Dallas TX) American film actor and pop singer.

Bernard Lord (27 Sep 1965, Moncton?, NB, Canada) Canadian politician; premier of New Brunswick from 21 Jun 1999.

Sophia Loren (Sofia Villani Scicolone; 20 Sep 1934, Pozzuoli, Italy) Italian film actress of many light comedies; she won an Academy Award for *Two Women* in 1961, and in 1991 she won an honorary Oscar for her movie career.

Trent Lott (9 Oct 1941, Grenada MS) American Republican politician; senator from Mississippi from 1989; Senate minority leader.

Julia Louis-Dreyfus (13 Jan 1961, New York NY) American TV actress popularly known as Elaine on *Seinfeld*.

Dame (Calliopa) Pearlette Louisy (1946, Laborie, Saint Lucia) West Indian government official; governor-general of Saint Lucia from 1997.

Courtney Love (Love Michelle Harrison; 9 Jul 1964, San Francisco CA) American pop-punk singer, actress.

Davis Love III (13 Apr 1964, Charlotte NC) American professional golfer.

James A(rthur) Lovell, Jr. (25 Mar 1928, Cleveland OH) American astronaut, commander of the nearly disastrous Apollo 13 flight to the Moon in 1970.

Lyle Lovett (1 Nov 1957, Klein TX) American country music singer.

Rob Lowe (17 Mar 1964, Charlottesville VA) American 1980s heartthrob whose career was revitalized by his role on TV's *The West Wing*.

Henri Loyrette (31 May 1952, Neuilly-sur-Seine, France) French director of the Louvre museum in Paris from 2001.

Ruud Lubbers (Rudolphus Franciscus Marie Lubbers; 7 May 1939, Rotterdam, The Netherlands) Dutch politician; prime minister of The Netherlands from 2001; UN High Commissioner for Refugees from 2001.

Jane Lubchenco (1947, Denver CO) American marine ecologist and science administrator; president of the International Council of Scientific Unions from 2002.

Chiara Lubich (22 Jan 1920, Trento, Italy) Italian humanitarian leader and founder of the Focolare Movement; Templeton Prize winner, 1977.

George Lucas (George Walton Lucas, Jr.; 14 May 1944, Modesto CA) American motion-picture producer and director best known for the *Star Wars* blockbusters; he was the founder of Lucasfilm (1971) which became five companies involved in film production; he is thought to be the richest man in Hollywood.

Susan Lucci (23 Dec 1949, Scarsdale NY) American TV soap opera star, she has played Erica Kane on *All My Children* since its premiere in 1970.

Paco de Lucia (Francisco Sánchez Gómez; 21 Dec 1947, Algeciras, Spain) Spanish flamenco guitarist.

Shannon W. Lucid (14 Jan 1943, Shanghai, China) American astronaut who set the record for the longest space flight by an American (1996).

D(arrell) Wayne Lukas (2 Sep 1935, Antigo WI) American Thoroughbred trainer, whose horses have dominated Triple Crown and other high-stakes racing in the US since the 1980s and made him a top moneywinning trainer.

Alyaksandr Lukashenka (30 Aug 1954, Kopys, Orsha district, Belorussian SSR, USSR [now Belarus]) Belarusian politician; president of Belarus from 1994.

Joan Lunden (19 Sep 1951, Sacramento CA) American broadcast journalist; co-host of *Good Morning America*, 1980–97.

Luo Xuejuan (26 Jan 1984, Hangzhou, Zhejiang province, China) Chinese swimmer who broke the world record in the 50-m breaststroke in 2002.

Yury Mikhaylovich Luzhkov (21 Sep 1936, Moscow, USSR [now Russia]) Russian politician; mayor of Moscow.

David Lynch (20 Jan 1946, Missoula MT) American avant-garde TV and motion-picture director famous for the TV series *Twin Peaks* and the film *Mulholland Dr.* (2001).

Loretta Lynn (Loretta Webb; 14 Apr 1935, Butcher Hollow KY) American country and western singer.

Yo-Yo Ma (7 Oct 1955, Paris, France) American cellist.

Lorin Maazel (6 Mar 1930, Neuilly, France) American conductor and violinist; music director of the Cleveland Orchestra, 1972–82.

Gloria (Macaraeg) Macapagal-Arroyo (5 Apr 1947, San Juan, near Manila, Philippines) Philippine politician; president of the Philippines from 20 Jan 2001.

Alan G. MacDiarmid (14 April 1927, Masterton, New Zealand) American chemist; co-winner of the Nobel Prize in Chemistry, 2000, for work in electrically conductive polymers.

Bob Mackie (Robert Gordon Mackie; 24 Mar 1940, Monterey Park CA) American fashion and costume designer noted for his glamorous and daring evening dresses.

Catharine A(lice) MacKinnon (7 Oct 1946, Minneapolis MN) American legal scholar; helped develop legal theory for hostile work environment and sexual harassment.

Shirley MacLaine (Shirley MacLean Beaty; 24 Apr 1934, Richmond VA) American actress and dancer known for her deft portrayal of charmingly eccentric characters.

Alistair MacLeod (1936, North Battleford, SK, Canada) Canadian writer, won the Dublin IMPAC award in 2001 for his novel *No Great Mischief*.

Robert MacNeil (19 Jan 1931, Montreal, QC, Canada) Canadian TV journalist and author, co-host with Jim Lehrer of *The MacNeil/Lehrer Report* from 1975 to 1995.

Elle Macpherson (Eleanor Gow; 29 Mar 1964, Cronulla, Sydney, New South Wales, Australia) Australian fashion model, actress, and lingerie designer.

Ferenc Madl (29 Jan 1931) Hungarian politician; president of Hungary from 2000.

Madonna (Madonna Louise Veronica Ciccone; 16 Aug 1958, Bay City MI) American singer, songwriter, and actress.

Ricardo Maduro (20 Apr 1946, Panama) Honduran politician; president of Honduras from 27 Jan 2002.

Peter Maffay (Peter Alexander Makkay; 30 Aug 1949, Brasov, Romania) Romanian-born German rock singer.

Tobey Maguire (27 Jun 1975, Santa Monica CA) American talented young film star known for playing unconventional leads.

Taj Mahal (Henry Saint Clair Fredericks; 17 May 1942, New York NY) American blues musician.

Datuk Seri Mahatir bin Mohamad (20 Dec 1925, Alor Setar, Kedah state, Malaya [now Malaysia]) Malaysian politician; prime minister of Malaysia from 1981.

Bill Maher (20 Jan 1956, New York NY) American TV comedian and personality who hosted TV's *Politically Incorrect*, 1993–2002.

Hermann Maier (7 Dec 1972, Flachau, Austria) Austrian Alpine skier who dominated the sport in the late 1980s and may be Austria's greatest downhill racer ever.

John Roy Major (29 Mar 1943, London, England) British politician; prime minister of the United Kingdom 1990–97.

Natalya (Romanovna) Makarova (21 Oct 1940, Leningrad, USSR [now St. Petersburg, Russia]) Russian-born ballerina considered to be one of the greatest classical dancers.

Miriam Makeba (4 Mar 1932, Prospect Township, near Johannesburg, South Africa) South African-born singer.

Tommi Mäkinen (26 Jul 1964, Puuppola, Finland) Finnish rally race-car driver.

Sheik Mohammed bin Rashid al-Maktoum (1949, Dubai?, [now United Arab Emirates]) royal; crown prince of Dubai from 1990; prime minister of the UAE 1971–79 and again from 1990; he is also a noted horse breeder and owner of Godolphin Stables.

Tuilaepa Sailele Malielegaoi (14 Apr 1945, Lepa, Samoa) Samoan politician; prime minister of Samoa from 1998.

Karl Malone (24 Jul 1963, Summerfield LA) American basketball player, forward for the Utah Jazz; was NBA MVP in 1997 and 1999 and all-star 11 times.

David (Alan) Mamet (30 Nov 1947, Chicago IL) American playwright, director, and screenwriter noted for his often desperate working-class characters and for his distinctive and colloquial dialogue that is frequently profane.

Cheb Mami (11 Jul 1956, Saida, Algeria) Algerian rai singer.

Winnie Madikizela Mandela (original name Nomzamo Winifred, original Xhosa name Nkosikazi Nobandle Nomzamo Madikizela; 26 Sep 1934/36, Pondoland district, Transkei, South Africa) South African social worker and black nationalist leader; second wife of Nelson Mandela.

Barbara Ann Mandrell (25 Dec 1948, Houston TX) American country and western singer.

Chuck Mangione (Charles Frank Mangione; 29 Nov 1940, Rochester NY) American jazz and pop flügelhornist.

Barry Manilow (Barry Alan Pincus; 17 Jun 1946, Brooklyn NY) American pop singer and songwriter.

Herbie Mann (Herbert Jay Solomon; 16 Apr 1930, Brooklyn NY) American jazz flutist and composer.

Patrick (Augustus Merving) Manning (17 Aug 1946, San Fernando, Trinidad) West Indian politician; prime minister of Trinidad and Tobago, 1991–95 and from 2001.

Preston Manning (10 Jun 1942, Edmondton, AB, Canada) Canadian politician and leader of the Reform Party.

Charles (Milles) Manson (11 Nov 1934, Cincinnati OH) American cult leader and multiple murderer.

Marilyn Manson (Brian Warner; 5 Jan 1969, Canton OH) American rock singer.

Thomas Mapfumo (2 Jul 1945, near Marondera, Rhodesia [now Zimbabwe]) Zimbabwean singer, songwriter, and bandleader.

John H. Marburger III (Staten Island NY) American physicist; presidential science adviser and head of the Office of Science and Technology Policy from 2001.

Sophie Marceau (Sophie Maupu; 17 Nov 1966, Paris, France) French international film actress.

Subcommandante Marcos (Rafael Sebastián Guillén Vicente; c. 1958, Mexico) Mexican rebel leader; head of the Zapatista National Liberation Army.

Geoffrey W. Marcy (29 Sep 1954, St. Clair Shores MI) American astronomer; discoverer of planetary systems outside the solar system.

Brice Marden (15 Oct 1938, Bronxville NY) American painter and printmaker who combined the techniques of Abstract Expressionism with the philosophies of Minimalism.

Cindy Margolis (1 Oct 1968, Los Angeles CA) American model and actress whose Internet image has reached cult status.

Queen Margrethe II (Margrethe Alexandrine Thorhildur Ingrid; 16 Apr 1940, Copenhagen, Denmark) Danish royal; queen of Denmark from 1972.

Lynn Margulis (5 Mar 1938, Chicago IL) American microbiologist specializing in symbiosis, and science educator.

Dan Marino (Daniel Constantine Marino, Jr.; 15 Sep 1961, Pittsburgh PA) American professional football quarterback who holds the NFL record for passing (5,084 yd and 48 touchdowns).

(Escobar) Marisol (22 May 1930, Paris, France) American sculptor of boxlike figurative works combining wood and other materials and often grouped as tableaux.

Dame Alicia Markova (Lilian Alicia Marks; 1 Dec 1910, London, England) English ballerina noted for the ethereal lightness and poetic delicacy of her dancing.

Ziggy Marley (David Marley; 17 Oct 1968, Kingston, Jamaica) Jamaican reggae performer.

Branford Marsalis (26 Aug 1960, Breaux Bridge LA) American jazz saxophonist and bandleader.

Wynton Marsalis (18 Oct 1961, New Orleans LA) American jazz trumpeter.

Penny Marshall (Carole Penelope Masciarelli; 15 Oct 1942, Bronx NY) American film and TV director, actress, and producer first famous for the TV series *Laverne & Shirley*.

Ricky Martin (Enrique Martin Morales; 24 Dec 1971, San Juan, Puerto Rico) American Latin music singer.

Steve Martin (14 Aug 1945, Waco TX) American comedic actor and author known for many popular films.

Mel Martinez (23 Oct 1946, Sagua la Grande, Cuba) American government official; US Secretary of Housing and Urban Development from January 2001.

Pat Martino (Pat Azzara; 25 Aug 1944, Philadelphia PA) American jazz guitarist and composer.

Peter Martins (27 Oct 1946, Copenhagen, Denmark) Danish dancer and choreographer.

Antônio Martins de la Cruz (1946, Portugal) Portuguese chairman-in-office of the Organization for Security and Cooperation in Europe from 2002.

Martin E(mil) Marty (5 Feb 1928, West Point NE) American cleric and religious educator.

Judy Martz (28 Jul 1943, Big Timber MT) American Republican politician; governor of Montana from 2001.

Princess Masako (Masako Owada; 9 Dec 1963, Tokyo, Japan) Japanese royal; consort of Crown Prince Naruhito.

Hugh (Ramopolo) Masekela (4 Apr 1939, Johannesburg, South Africa) South African pop/jazz trumpet player.

Aslan Maskhadov (1951, Kazakh SSR, USSR [now Kazakhstan]) Chechen politician; president of the Russian Republic of Chechnya from 1997.

Janet Maslin (12 Aug 1949, New York NY) American film critic, author.

Master P (Percy Miller; 29 Apr 1970, New Orleans LA) American gangsta rap performer and producer.

Kurt Masur (18 Jul 1927, Brieg, Germany [now Brzeg, Poland]) German-born conductor; music director of the New York Philharmonic, 1991–2002.

Mary Matalin (19 Aug 1953, Chicago IL) American political commentator.

Mireille Mathieu (24 Jul 1946, Avignon, France) French pop singer.

Mathilde (Mathilde d'Udekem d'Acoz; 21 Jan 1973, Uccle, Belgium) princess of Belgium, consort of Prince Philippe, the heir to the Belgian throne.

Edith Mathis (1 Feb 1938, Lucerne, Switzerland) Swiss operatic soprano.

Johnny Mathis (John Royce Mathis; 30 Sep 1935, Gilmer TX) American pop singer.

Marlee Matlin (24 Aug 1965, Morton Grove IL) American film and TV actress best known for the film *Children of a Lesser God* (1986).

Koichiro Matsuura (1937, Tokyo, Japan) Japanese international official; director-general of UNESCO from 1999.

Chris Matthews (1945, Philadelphia PA) American TV and newspaper journalist, host of cable TV's *Hardball*.

Dave Matthews (9 Jan 1967, Johannesburg, South Africa) South African-born American rock musician, songwriter.

Peter Max (19 Oct 1937, Berlin, Germany) German artist and designer.

Maxwell (23 May 1973, Brooklyn NY) American R&B and soul singer.

Thabo (Mvuyelwa) Mbeki (18 Jun 1942, Idutywa, Queenstown, South Africa) South African politician; president of South Africa from 1999.

Mary Patricia McAleese (27 Jun 1951, Belfast, Northern Ireland) Irish politician; president of Ireland from 1997.

Martina McBride (Martina Marica Schiff; 29 Jul 1966, Sharon KS) American country singer.

Patricia McBride (23 Aug 1942, Teaneck NJ) American ballerina.

John McCain (John Sidney McCain III; 29 Aug 1936, Panama Canal Zone) American Republican politician; senator from Arizona; presidential contender, 2000.

Scott McCallum (2 May 1950, Fond du Lac WI) American Republican politician; governor of Wisconsin from 2001.

Chris McCarron (1955, Dorchester MA) American jockey who has won the Kentucky Derby, Preakness Stakes, and Belmont Stakes each two times and who has been the leading jockey in earnings in four seasons.

Cormac McCarthy (Charles McCarthy, Jr.; 20 Jul 1933, Providence RI) American writer in the Southern gothic tradition whose novels about wayward characters in the rural American South and Southwest are noted for their dark violence.

Sir Paul McCartney (James Paul McCartney; 18 Jun 1942, Liverpool, England) British singer, songwriter; member of the Beatles.

Stella (Nina) McCartney (13 Sep 1971, London, England) British fashion designer who gained fame at a young age as a designer for Chloé and for her own signature line.

Delbert McClinton (4 Nov 1940, Lubbock TX) American country and western singer.

Matthew McConaughey (4 Nov 1969, Uvalde TX) American box-office star made famous by *A Time to Kill* (1996).

Eric McCormack (18 Apr 1963, Toronto, ON, Canada) American TV actor, currently plays Will on *Will & Grace*.

David McCullough (1933, Pittsburgh PA) American biographer and historian, author of best-selling books such as *Truman* (1992) and *John Adams* (2001).

Dylan McDermott (26 Oct 1961, Waterbury CT) American TV and film actor, currently plays Bobby McDonnell on *The Practice*.

Country Joe McDonald (1 Jan 1942, El Monte CA) American rock vocalist and guitarist.

Frances McDormand (23 Jun 1957 IL) American versatile film actress first famous for *Fargo* (1996).

Reba McEntire (28 Mar 1954, McAlester OK) American country singer and TV and film actress.

Rod McEuen (29 Apr 1933, Oakland CA) American songwriter and singer.

Daniel L. McFadden (29 Jul 1937, Raleigh NC) American economist; Nobel Prize in Economic Science, 2000, for work in solving problems of analysis of microdata.

Bobby McFerrin (11 Mar 1950, New York NY) American jazz and pop vocalist.

Maureen McGovern (27 Jul 1949, Youngstown OH) American singer and actress.

Tim McGraw (Samuel Timothy McGraw; 1 May 1967, Delhi LA) American country music singer.

James E. McGreevey (6 Aug 1957, Jersey City NJ) American Democratic politician; governor of New Jersey from 2002.

Roger McGuinn (James Joseph McGuinn; 13 Jul 1942, Chicago IL) American rock vocalist and guitarist (of the Byrds).

Sir Ian (Murray) McKellen (25 May 1939, Burnley, Lancashire, England) British intellectual stage and film actor famous for Shakespearian characterizations.

Dan Peter McKenzie (1942, UK) British geophysicist; winner of the Crafoord Prize in 2002 "for fundamental contributions to the understanding of the dynamics of the lithosphere, particularly plate tectonics, sedimentary basin formation and mantle melting."

Donald Charles ("Don") McKinnon (27 Feb 1939, Greenwich, England) New Zealand international civil servant; secretary-general of the Commonwealth from 2000.

Sarah McLachlan (28 Jan 1968, Halifax, NS, Canada) Canadian singer and songwriter.

Beverley McLachlin (7 Sep 1943, Pincher Creek, AB, Canada) Canadian Supreme Court justice from 1989; chief justice from 2000.

John McLaughlin (29 Mar 1927, Providence RI) American TV journalist.

Ed McMahon (Edward Leo McMahon; 6 Mar 1923, Detroit MI) American TV personality famous as Johnny Carson's sidekick on *The Tonight Show*.

Vince McMahon (Vincent Kennedy McMahon, Jr.; 24 Aug 1945, Pinehurst NC) American wrestling promoter, owner of the World Wrestling Federation from 1982.

Larry McMurtry (3 Jun 1936, Wichita Falls TX) American writer noted for his novels set on the frontier, in contemporary small towns, and in increasingly urbanized and industrial areas of Texas.

Marian McPartland (20 Mar 1918, Windsor, England) British-born jazz pianist and composer.

Alexander McQueen (Lee McQueen; 1969, London, England) British fashion designer known for his rebellious style and his bizarre, extravagant runway shows.

Janet McTeer (8 May 1961, Newcastle upon Tyne, England) British stage actress who achieved fame for the 1990s revival of *A Doll's House*.

Russell Charles Means (10 Nov 1940, Pine Ridge SD) American Native American rights activist.

Meat Loaf (Marvin Lee Aday; 27 Sep 1947, Dallas TX) American rock performer and actor.

Peter Medgyessy (1942, Budapest, Hungary) Hungarian politician; prime minister of Hungary from 27 May 2002.

Zubin Mehta (29 Apr 1936, Bombay [now Mumbai], India) Indian-born orchestral conductor; music director of the Los Angeles Philharmonic, 1962–78, the New York Philharmonic, 1978–91, and the Israel Philharmonic from 1968.

Rafael Hipólito Mejía Dominguez (22 Feb 1941, Gurabo, Santiago, Dominican Republic) Dominican politician; president of Dominican Republic from 2000.

John Mellencamp (also known as John Cougar; 7 Oct 1951, Seymour IN) American rock singer and songwriter.

Rigoberta Menchú (Tum) (9 Jan 1959, Laj Chimel, Guatemala) Guatemalan social activist; winner of the Nobel Peace Prize, 1992.

Samuel Alexander ("Sam") Mendes (1 Aug 1965, Reading, England) British theater and film director who received critical acclaim for *American Beauty* (1999).

Sergio Mendes (11 Feb 1941, Niteroi, Brazil) Brazilian-born musician and band leader.

Carlos Saúl Menem (2 Jul 1930, Anillaco, Argentina) Argentine politician; president of Argentina, 1989–99.

Fradique de Menezes (1942) São Tomé and Príncipe politician; president of São Tomé and Príncipe from 2001.

Gian Carlo Menotti (7 Jul 1911, Cadegliano, Italy) Italian composer of operas of wider popularity than any others of their time.

Ismail (Noormohamed) Merchant (25 Dec 1936, Bombay [now Mumbai], India) Indian-born British film producer famous for his collaboration with James Ivory on many period pieces.

Angela Merkel (Angela Dorothea Kasner; 17 Jul 1954, Hamburg, West Germany) German politician; leader of the Christian Democratic Union and parliament leader.

Stjepan ("Stipe") Mesic (24 Dec 1934, Orahovica, Croatia, Kingdom of Yugoslavia [now Croatia]) Croatian politician; president of Croatia from 18 Feb 2000.

Jean-Marie Messier (13 Dec 1956, Grenoble, France) French corporate executive; chairman of Vivendi Universal.

Debra Messing (15 Aug 1968, Brooklyn NY) American TV actress, currently plays Grace on *Will & Grace*.

Jorge Mester (10 Apr 1935, Mexico City, Mexico) Mexican conductor.

Pat Metheny (12 Aug 1954, Lee's Summit MO) American jazz guitarist.

Princess Mette-Marit (Mette-Marit Tjessem Høiby; 19 Aug 1973, Kristiansand, Norway) Norwegian royal; wife of Crown Prince Haakon of Norway.

Pierre de Meuron (8 May 1950, Basel, Switzerland) Swiss architect; co-winner, with Jacques Herzog, of the Pritzker Prize in 2001.

Kweisi Mfume (Frizzell Gray; Frizzell Gerard Tate; 24 Oct 1948, Baltimore MD) American civil rights leader, former US congressman; chairman of the National Association for the Advancement of Colored People (NAACP) from 1996.

George Michael (Georgios Kyriakos Panayiotou; 25 Jun 1963, London, England) British pop singer.

King Michael (Michael Hohenzollern-Sigmaringen; ruled as Mihai I; 25 Oct 1921, Sinaia, Romania) Romanian royal; king of Romania, 1927–30 and 1940–47.

Kate Michelman (4 Aug 1942 New Jersey) American activist; president of the National Abortion and Reproductive Rights Action League.

Empress Michiko (Michiko Shoda; 20 Oct 1934, Tokyo, Japan) Japanese royal; wife of Emperor Akihito of Japan.

Thomas Middelhoff (11 May 1953, Düsseldorf, Germany) German corporate executive; chairman and CEO of Bertelsmann AG from 1998.

Bette Midler (1 Dec 1945, Honolulu HI) American comedienne, singer, and actress known as "The Divine Miss M."

Midori (1971, Osaka, Japan) American violinist.

Alyssa Milano (19 Dec 1972, Brooklyn NY) American TV actress made famous by the 1980s sitcom *Who's the Boss?*

Ann Miller (Johnnie Lucille Collier; 12 Apr 1923, Cherino TX) American tap dancer who attained fame in Hollywood musicals of the 1940s and '50s.

Leszek Miller (3 Jul 1946, Zyrardow, near Warsaw, Poland) Polish politician; prime minister of Poland from 2001.

Steve Miller (5 Oct 1943, Milwaukee WI) American rock guitarist and vocalist (of the Steve Miller Band).

Kate Millett (née Kathryn Murray; 14 Sep 1934, St. Paul MN) American feminist of the 1970s, author, and sculptor.

Sherrill (Eustace) Milnes (10 Jan 1935, Downers Grove IL) American operatic baritone.

Slobodan Milosevic (29 Aug 1941, Pozarevac, Yugoslavia) Serbian nationalist leader, president of Serbia, 1989-97, and of Yugoslavia, 1997–2000.

Ronnie Milsap (16 Jan 1944, Robbinsville NC) American country and western singer.

Ilhan (Kemaleddin) Mimaroglu (11 Mar 1926, Istanbul, Turkey) Turkish composer.

Norman (Yoshio) Mineta (12 Nov 1931, San Jose CA) American government official; former US Secretary of Commerce 2000-01; US Secretary of Transportation from 2001.

Anthony Minghella (6 Jan 1954, Ryde, Isle of Wight, England) British motion picture director best known for *The English Patient* (1996).

Liza Minnelli (12 Mar 1946, Los Angeles CA) American energetic singer and actress best known for the film musical *Cabaret* (1972).

Ruth Ann Minner (17 Jan 1935, Milford DE) American Democratic politician; governor of Delaware from 2001.

Kylie Minogue (28 May 1968, Melbourne, Australia) Australian pop singer.

Helen Mirren (Ilyena Lydia Mironoff; 26 Jul 1945, Chiswick, London, England) British respected stage and film actress best known for the TV series *Prime Suspect*.

James Mischka (23 Dec 1960, Burlington WI) American fashion designer who, with Mark Badgley, produces the Badgley Mischka line of beaded evening gowns.

Arthur Mitchell (27 Mar 1934, New York NY) American dancer, choreographer, and director of the Dance Theatre of Harlem.

Joni Mitchell (Roberta Joan Anderson; 7 Nov 1943, Fort MacLeod, AB, Canada) Canadian pop singer and songwriter.

Keith Claudius Mitchell (12 Nov 1946, Grenada) Grenadan politician; prime minister of Grenada from 1995.

Issey Miyake (22 Apr 1938, Hiroshima, Japan) Japanese fashion designer whose creations are a blend of Eastern and Western themes.

Jun'ichiro Miyazu, Japanese corporate executive; CEO of Nippon Telephone & Telegraph.

Isaac Mizrahi (14 Oct 1961, Brooklyn NY) American fashion designer and TV personality who was the subject of a 1995 documentary film, *Unzipped*.

Benjamin (William) Mkapa (12 Nov 1938, Masasi, Tanganyika [now Tanzania]) Tanzanian politician; president of Tanzania from 1995.

Moby (Richard Melville Hall; 11 Sep 1965, Darien CT) American techno musician.

Domenico Modugno (9 Jan 1928, Polignano a Mare, Italy) Italian pop songwriter and singer.

Anna Moffo (27 Jun 1932, Wayne PA) American operatic soprano.

Festus Gontebanye Mogae (23 Jul 1939, Kanye, Botswana) Botswanan politician; president of Botswana from 1998.

Igor (Aleksandrovich) Moiseyev (21 Jan [8 Jan Old Style] 1906, Kiev, Ukraine, Russian Empire) Russian choreographer and founder of the State Academic Folk Dance Ensemble of the USSR.

Alfred Moisiu (1 Dec 1929, Shkodër, Albania) Albanian politician; president of Albania from 24 Jul 2002.

N. Scott Momaday (27 Feb 1934, Lawton OK) American author of many works centered on his Kiowa (Native American) heritage.

Meredith (Jane) Monk (20 Nov 1942, Lima, Peru) American performance artist, a pioneer in the avant-garde, whose work skillfully integrated diverse disciplines and media, including singing, filmmaking, choreography, and acting.

Fernanda Montenegro (Arlette Pinheiro Esteves da Silva; 16 Oct 1929, Rio de Janeiro, Brazil) Brazilian actress made famous to US audiences after appearing in *Central do Brasil* (*Central Station*; 1998).

Juan Pablo Montoya (20 Sep 1975, Bogotá, Colombia) Colombian Formula 1 race-car driver and Indy-Car Champion in 1999.

Sir Mark Moody-Stuart (1941, Antigua, West Indies) British corporate executive; CEO of the Royal Dutch/Shell Group (UK).

Robert Moog (23 May 1934, Flushing NY) American inventor of first commercially viable keyboard synthesizer.

Demi Moore (Demetria Gene Guynes; 11 Nov 1962, Roswell NM) American actress and star of commercially successful films.

Julianne Moore (Julie Smith; 3 Dec 1960, Fayetteville NC) American film actress known for powerful, nuanced performances.

Mandy Moore (Amanda Leigh Moore; 10 Apr 1984, Nashua NH) American pop singer.

Mary Tyler Moore (29 Dec 1936, Brooklyn NY) American film and TV actress known for her work on *The Dick Van Dyke Show* and *The Mary Tyler Moore Show* series.

Melba Moore (Beatrice Moore; Melba Hill; 27 Oct 1945, New York NY) American singer and actress.

Jeanne Moreau (23 Jan 1928, Paris, France) French actress known for her multifaceted performances in French New Wave films of the 1950s and '60s.

Airto Moreira (5 Aug 1941, Itaiopolis, Brazil) Brazilian jazz percussionist.

Rita Moreno (Rosita Dolores Alverio; 11 Dec 1931, Humacao, Puerto Rico) Puerto Rican-born film actress, singer, and dancer remembered for her role in *West Side Story* (1961).

Yoshiro Mori (14 Jul 1937, Neagari, Ishikawa prefecture, Japan) Japanese politician; prime minister, 2000–01.

Yasumasa Morimura (1951, Osaka, Japan) Japanese photographer especially known for his large-scale self-portraits.

Alanis Morissette (1 Jun 1974, Ottawa, ON, Canada) Canadian pop singer and songwriter.

Giorgio Moroder (26 Apr 1940, Ortisei, Italy) Italian-born German pop music producer and songwriter.

Mark Morris (29 Aug 1956, Seattle WA) American dancer and leading choreographer for several international dance companies; he founded the Mark Morris Dance Group in 1980.

Robert Morris (9 Feb 1931, Kansas City MO) American artist of minimalist sculptures and personalized performance works.

Van Morrison (George Ivan Morrison; 31 Aug 1945, Belfast, Northern Ireland) British rock singer and songwriter.

Morrissey (Steven Patrick Morrissey; 22 May 1959, Manchester, England) British rock singer and songwriter.

Mireya Elisa Moscoso (de Gruber) (1 Jul 1946, Pedasí, Panama) Panamanian politician; president of Panama from 1999.

Edda Ell Moser (27 Oct 1941, Berlin, Germany) German soprano.

Kate Moss (16 Jan 1974, Croydon, Surrey, England) British fashion model known for her work for Calvin Klein and for introducing the "waif" look to fashion.

Jonathan Motzfeldt (1938) Greenland politician; prime minister of Greenland, 1979–91 and again from 1997.

Mohammed Mourhit (10 Oct 1970, Morocco) Moroccan-born Belgian cross-country runner; world champion in 2000–01.

Nana Mouskouri (13 Oct 1934, Chanos, Crete, Greece) Greek-born French pop singer.

Amr Mohammed Moussa (3 Oct 1936, Cairo, Egypt) Egyptian international diplomat; secretary general of the Arab League from 2001.

Georges Moustaki (3 May 1934, Alexandria, Egypt) French pop singer.

Bill Moyers (6 Jun 1934, Hugo OK) American TV journalist; government official, and author.

Ezekiel Mphahlele (17 Dec 1919, Marabastad, South Africa) South African novelist, essayist, short-story writer, and teacher.

George Mraz (Jiri Mraz; 9 Sep 1944, Písek, Czechoslovakia) Czech jazz bassist.

King Mswati III (19 Apr 1968, Swaziland) Swazi royal; king of Swaziland from 1986.

Cándido Muatetema Rivas (1961) Equatorial Guinean politician; prime minister of Equatorial Guinea from 2001.

Muhammed Hosni Mubarak (4 May 1928, Al-Minufiyah governorate, Egypt) Egyptian politician; president of Egypt from 1981.

Lisel Mueller (née Lisel Neumann; 8 Feb 1924, Hamburg, Germany) German-born American poet who won the 1997 Pulitzer Prize for Poetry for her collection *Alive Together: New and Selected Poems.*

Robert S. Mueller III (7 Aug 1944, New York NY) American government official; FBI director from 2001.

Robert (Gabriel) Mugabe (21 Feb 1924, Kutama, Southern Rhodesia [now Zimbabwe]) Zimbabwean politician; first prime minister (1980–87) of the reconstituted state of Zimbabwe, and president from 1987.

Thierry Mugler (1948, Strasbourg, France) French fashion designer known for his varied, innovative style and theatrical fashion shows.

King Muhammad VI (Muhammad ibn al-Hassan; 21 Aug 1963, Rabat, Morocco) Moroccan royal; king of Morocco from 1999.

Martin Mull (18 Aug 1943, Chicago IL) American comedian and musician.

Brian Mulroney (20 Mar 1939, Baie-Comeau, QC, Canada) Canadian politician, leader of the Progressive Conservative Party of Canada, and prime minister (1984–93).

Bakili Muluzi (17 Mar 1943, Machinga, British Nyasaland [now Malawi]) Malawi politician; president of Malawi from 1994.

Alice Munro (10 Jul 1931, Wingham, ON, Canada) Canadian short-story writer.

Glenn Murcutt (25 Jul 1936, London, England) Australian modernist architect noted for his devotion to ecological designs; winner of the Pritzker Prize in 2002.

(Keith) Rupert Murdoch (11 Mar 1931, Melbourne, Australia) Australian-born British corporate executive and media mogul.

Eddie Murphy (3 Apr 1961, Brooklyn NY) American enduring comedian and film actor from the *Saturday Night Live* cast and later in a string of highly successful film comedies.

Cormac Murphy-O'Connor (24 Aug 1932, Reading, Berkshire, England) British church leader; archbishop of Westminster and head of the Roman Catholic church in the UK.

Anne Murray (20 Jun 1945, Springhill, NS, Canada) Canadian country singer.

Bill Murray (21 Sep 1950, Wilmette IL) American comedian and film actor known for eccentric characterizations.

Ty Murray (11 Oct 1969, Phoenix AZ) American rodeo cowboy who won the title of all-around world champion seven times (1989–94, 1998) and who is the greatest rodeo moneywinner in history.

Said Wilbert Musa (19 Mar 1944, San Ignacio, British Honduras [now Belize]) Belizean politician; prime minister of Belize from 1998.

Musashimaru (Fiamalu [Fia] Penitani; 2 May 1971, Samoa) Samoan-born sumo wrestler, *yokozuna* (grand champion) from 1999; winner of the Spring and Summer bashos, 2002.

Yoweri Kaguta Museveni (1944, Mbarra district, Uganda) Ugandan politician; president of Uganda from 1986.

Ronnie Musgrove (29 Jul 1956, Tocowa MS) American Democratic politician; governor of Mississippi from 2000.

Pervez Musharraf (11 Aug 1943, New Delhi, India) Pakistani military leader and politician; head of Pakistan's government from 1999 and president from 2001.

Musiq Soulchild (Taalib Johnson; Philadelphia PA) American soul singer and songwriter.

Riccardo Muti (28 Jul 1941, Naples, Italy) Italian conductor of both opera and the symphonic repertory; music director of the Philadelphia Orchestra, 1980–92.

Halil Mutlu (Huben Hubenov; "Little Dynamo"; 14 Jul 1973, Postnik, Bulgaria) Bulgarian-born Turkish weightlifter in the 54-kg class who set more than 20 world records during his career, was named Turkey's Best Sportsman of the Year in 1999; gold medalist at the 1999 world championships, the 2000 European championships, and the 2000 Olympic Games.

Anne-Sophie Mutter (29 Jun 1963, Rheinfelden, Baden, Germany) German violinist.

Levy Mwanawasa (3 Sep 1948, Mufulira, Zambia) Zambian politician; president of Zambia from 2 Jan 2002.

Mike Myers (25 May 1963, Scarborough, ON, Canada) Canadian comedian and actor famous for offbeat comedy; best known for the Austin Powers film series.

Richard B. Myers (1 Mar 1942, Kansas City MO) American government official; chairman of the Joint Chiefs of Staff from 2001.

Youssou N'Dour (1959, Dakar, Senegal) Senegalese singer and songwriter.

Joseph P. Nacchio (c. 1950, Brooklyn NY) American corporate executive; CEO of Qwest Communications International Inc. to June 2002.

Ralph Nader (27 Feb 1934, Winsted CT) American social activist and politician; presidential candidate in 2000.

Chandrababu Naidu (20 Apr 1950, Chittoor district, Andhra Pradesh state, India) Indian politician; chief minister of Andhra Pradesh from 1995.

Mira Nair (15 Oct 1957, Bhubaneshwar, Orissa state, India) Indian film director and screenwriter known for controversial documentary and feature films.

Michie Nakamura (24 Jul 1960, Shimodate, Ibaraki prefecture, Japan) Japanese operatic soprano.

Gianna Nannini (14 Jun 1956, Siena, Italy) Italian rock singer.

Fatos Nano (September 1952, Tirana, Albania) Albanian politician; prime minister of Albania in 1991, 1997–98, and again from 31 Jul 2002.

Robert Louis Nardelli (17 May 1948, Old Forge PA) American corporate executive; CEO of The Home Depot, Inc. from 2000.

Crown Prince Naruhito (23 Feb 1960, Tokyo, Japan) Japanese royal, crown prince of Japan.

Milton Nascimiento (1942, Rio de Janeiro, Brazil) Brazilian pop singer and songwriter.

Graham Nash (2 Feb 1942, Blackpool, England) British rock guitarist, vocalist, and keyboardist.

John F. Nash (13 Jun 1928, Bluefield VA) American mathematician, specialist on game theory; shared the Nobel Prize for Economics, 1994.

Johnny Nash (19 Aug 1940, Houston TX) American reggae singer and songwriter.

Taslima Nasrin (25 Aug 1962, Mymensigh, Bangladesh) Bangladeshi Islamic feminist writer.

Adrian Nastase (22 Jun 1950, Bucharest, Romania) Romanian politician; prime minister of Romania from 2000.

Edward Natapei (1954) Vanuatu politician; acting president of Vanuatu, 1999, and prime minister from 2001.

Nursultan Nazarbayev (6 Jul 1940, Chemolgan, Kazakh SSR, USSR [now Kazakhstan]) Kazakh statesman; president of Kazakhstan from 1990.

Catherine Ndereba (c. 1970, Kenya) Kenyan runner who twice in 2001 set record times for the marathon, in Boston and Chicago.

Patricia Neal (Patsy Louise Neal; 20 Jan 1926, Packard KY) American film actress known for her deeply intelligent performances; won an Academy Award for best actress in 1963 (Hud).

Liam Neeson (William Neeson; 7 Jun 1952, Ballymena, Northern Ireland) British film actor respected for his lead role in Schindler's List (1993).

John D. Negroponte (21 Jul 1939, London, England) American diplomat; US representative to United Nations from 2001.

Sam Neill (Nigel Neill; 14 Sep 1947, Omagh, Northern Ireland) Northern Ireland-born New Zealand international film actor best known for Jurassic Park (1993).

Nelly (Cornell Haynes, Jr.; 2 Nov 1980, Austin TX) American rap artist.

Willie Nelson (30 Apr 1933, Fort Worth TX) American country and western music singer and film actor.

Michael Nesmith (30 Dec 1942, Houston TX) American rock and pop singer and songwriter.

Benjamin Netanyahu (21 Oct 1949, Tel Aviv, Israel) Israeli politician (head of Likud); prime minister of Israel, 1996-99.

José Maria Neves (1960) Cape Verdean politician; prime minister of Cape Verde from 2001.

Paul Newman (26 Jan 1925, Cleveland OH) American film actor and director with a long career of critical and box-office successes.

Randy Newman (Randall Stuart Newman; 28 Nov 1943, Los Angeles CA) American singer, songwriter, and composer.

(Carson) Wayne Newton (3 Apr 1942, Roanoke VA) American pop singer.

Helmut Newton (31 Oct 1920, Berlin, Germany) German-born American photographer whose themes were often sex and power.

Juice Newton (Judy Kay Newton; 18 Feb 1952, Lakehurst NJ) American country-pop singer.

Teodoro Obiang Nguema Mbasogo (1942, Acoacan, Río Muni [now Equatorial Guinea]) Equatorial Guinean politician; president of Equatorial Guinea from 1979.

Alamara Nhassé (1950?) Guinea-Bissau politician; prime minister of Guinea-Bissau from 9 Dec 2001.

Fayard Nicholas (20 Oct 1914, Mobile AL) American dancer, who appeared with his brother Harold Lloyd Nicholas as the Nicholas Brothers dance team and attained fame on stage and in films for an energetic blend of jazz, tap, ballet, and acrobatics.

Mike Nichols (Michael Igor Peschowsky; 6 Nov 1931, Berlin, Germany) American motion-picture and stage director whose productions focus on the absurdities and horrors of modern life as revealed in personal relationships.

Jack Nicholson (John Joseph Nicholson; 22 Apr 1937, Neptune NJ) American respected film actor famous for versatile portrayals of unconventional outsiders.

Stevie Nicks (Stephanie Lynn Nicks; 26 May 1948, Phoenix AZ) American singer and songwriter (Fleetwood Mac).

Leslie Nielsen (11 Feb 1926, Regina, SK, Canada) Canadian actor best known for absurd comic roles, including the Naked Gun films.

Gunda Niemann-Stirnemann (Gunda Kleeman; 7 Sep 1966, Sponderhausen, East Germany) German speed skater, dominated the sport in the 1990s, with nine overall world championships and eight Olympic medals.

Leonard Nimoy (26 Mar 1931, Boston MA) American film and TV actor best known as Mr. Spock in the Star Trek series and films.

Uichiro Niwa (c. 1941, Aichi prefecture, Japan) Japanese corporate executive; CEO and president of Itochu Corp. from 1998.

Saparmurad Niyazov (19 Feb 1940, Askhabad, Turkmen SSR, USSR [now Ashgabat, Turkmenistan]) Turkmenistani politician; president of Turkmenistan from 1990.

Ronald K(enneth) Noble (1957? New Jersey?) American secretary general of the International Criminal Police Organization (Interpol) from 2000.

Gustavo Noboa Bejarano (21 Aug 1937, Guayaquil, Ecuador) Ecuadorian politician; president of Ecuador from 2000.

Peggy Noonan (7 Sep 1950, New York NY) American columnist, political writer.

Jessye Norman (15 Sep 1945, Augusta GA) American operatic and concert soprano.

Norodom Sihanouk (Preah Baht Samdach Preah Norodom Sihanuk Varman; 31 Oct 1922, Phnom Penh, Cambodia) Cambodian royal, king of Cambodia from 1941 to 1955 and again from 1993 and head of state, 1960-70 and 1991-93.

Oliver (Laurence) North (7 Oct 1943, San Antonio TX) American Marine colonel; central figure in the Iran-Contra scandal.

Edward Norton (18 Aug 1969, Columbia MD) American talented and versatile young actor made famous by the film Primal Fear (1996).

Gale Norton (11 Mar 1954, Wichita KS) American government official; US Secretary of the Interior from 2001.

Kessai H. Note (1950, Ailinglaplap atoll, Marshall Islands) Marshallese politician; president of the Marshall Islands from 2000.

Dries van Noten (1958, Antwerp, Belgium) Belgian fashion designer who mixes opposing elements, such as classic and contemporary, within a single creation.

Chris Noth (13 Nov 1954, Madison WI) American film and TV actor most recognized for his roles on Law & Order and Sex and the City.

Kim Novak (Marilyn Pauline Novak; 13 Feb 1933, Chicago IL) American classical Hollywood actress best known for Vertigo (1958).

Michael Novak (1933, Johnstown PA) American scholar, journalist, and capitalist theologian; Templeton Prize winner, 1994.

Robert Novak (26 Feb 1931, Joliet IL) American newspaper and TV journalist.

Ryoji Noyori (3 Sep 1938, Kobe, Japan) Japanese chemist; co-winner of the Nobel Prize for Chemistry, 2001, for development of chiral catalysts.

Jean-François Ntoutoume-Emane (1939, Gabon?) Gabonese politician; prime minister of Gabon from 1999.

Sam Nujoma (Samuel Daniel Shafiishuna Nujoma; 12 May 1929, Owambo, South West Africa [now Namibia]) Namibian independence leader and president of Namibia from 1990.

Sir Paul M. Nurse (25 Jan 1949, Norwich, England) British biologist; co-recipient of the Nobel Prize for Physiology or Medicine, 2001, for studies of cell growth cycles.

Frank O'Bannon (30 Jan 1930, Louisville KY) American Democratic politician; governor of Indiana from 1997.

Conan O'Brien (18 Apr 1963, Brookline MA) American TV personality, host of Late Night with Conan O'Brien.

Edna O'Brien (15 Dec 1932, Twamgraney, County Clare, Ireland) Irish novelist, short-story writer, and screenwriter.

Carroll O'Connor (2 Aug 1924, New York NY—21 Jun 2001, Culver City CA), American TV actor most famous as the star of the controversial series All in the Family.

Donald O'Connor (Donald David Dixon Ronald O'Connor; 28 Aug 1925, Chicago IL) American entertainer best known for his comedic and dancing skills and especially for his roles in Hollywood musicals of the 1940s and '50s.

Sandra Day O'Connor (26 Mar 1930, El Paso TX) American jurist; associate justice of the US Supreme Court from 1981 and the first woman appointed to the Court.

Sinead O'Connor (8 Dec 1966, Dublin, Ireland) Irish singer and songwriter.

Roseanne ("Rosie") O'Donnell (21 Mar 1962, Commack NY) American TV talk-show host.

Maureen O'Hara (Maureen FitzSimons; 17 Aug 1920, Dublin, Ireland) Irish-born American film actress from Hollywood's Golden era and known for her stunning beauty.

Shaquille (Rashaun) O'Neal (6 Mar 1972, Newark NJ) American professional basketball center who led the Los Angeles Lakers to NBA titles in 2000, 2001, and 2002; he was only the third player in history to be named MVP of the regular season, the all-star game, and the finals in the same season (2000).

Tatum O'Neal (5 Nov 1963, Los Angeles CA) American child actress made famous by Paper Moon (1973).

Paul H. O'Neill (4 Dec 1935, St. Louis MO) American corporate executive; chairman of Alcoa, Inc., 1987–2000; secretary of the Treasury in the cabinet of Pres. George W. Bush.

David J. O'Reilly (January 1947, Dublin, Ireland) Irish-born American corporate executive; chairman and CEO of ChevronTexaco Corp. (from merger, 2001).

P.J. O'Rourke (Patrick Jake O'Rourke; 14 Nov 1947, Toledo OH) American political satirist.

John O'Sullivan (1942, England) British journalist, commentator, and political adviser; editor-in-chief of United Press International from 1998.

Peter O'Toole (2 Aug 1932, Connemara, County Galway, Ireland) British stage and film actor of great range famous for Shakespearean roles and the film Lawrence of Arabia (1962).

Joyce Carol Oates (16 Jun 1938, Lockport NY) American novelist, short-story writer, and essayist noted for her depictions of violence and evil in modern society.

Thoraya Obaid (2 Mar 1945, Baghdad, Iraq) Iraq-born Saudi Arabian civil servant; executive director of the UN Population Fund.

Olusegun Obasanjo (5 Mar 1937, Abeokuta, Nigeria) Nigerian military leader and politician; president of Nigeria from 1999.

Keizo Obuchi (25 Jun 1937, Nakanojo, Japan) Japanese politician; prime minister of Japan, 1998–2000.

Abdullah Ocalan (1948?, Omerli, Turkey) Turkish Kurdish independence leader; in prison in 2002.

David Oddson (17 Jan 1948, Reykjavík, Iceland) Icelandic politician; prime minister of Iceland from 1991.

Odetta (Holmes) (31 Dec 1930, Birmingham AL) American folk and blues singer and actress.

Nelson O. Oduber (1947) West Indian politician; prime minister of Aruba, 1989–94 and from 2001.

Karl Aguste Offman (1940) Mauritian politician; president of Mauritius from 25 Feb 2002.

Norio Oga (29 Jan 1930, Shizuoka, Japan) Japanese president, chairman, and CEO of Sony Corp. from 1995.

Grace Ogot (15 May 1930, Butere, near Kisumu, central Nyanza Region, Kenya) Kenyan author of widely anthologized short stories and novels.

Cody Ohl (21 Sep 1973, Rosenburg TX) American rodeo cowboy; 2001 all-around world champion.

Garrick Ohlsson (3 Apr 1948, Bronxville NY) American concert pianist.

Motoyuki Oka, Japanese corporate executive; CEO of the Sumitomo Group.

Paul Okalik (26 May 1964, Pangnirtung, NWT [now Nunavut], Canada) Canadian politician; premier of Nunavut from 1 Apr 1999.

Marvin Olasky (Texas?) American academic and commentator, known as the father of "compassionate conservatism."

Claes (Thure) Oldenburg (28 Jan 1929, Stockholm, Sweden) Swedish-born Pop-art sculptor, best known for his giant soft sculptures of everyday objects.

Mike Oldfield (15 May 1953, Reading, England) British pop instrumentalist.

Todd Oldham (1960, Corpus Christi TX) American fashion designer known for his bright and bold colors and patterns.

Gary Oldman (21 Mar 1958, South London, England) British actor of amazing versatility.

Sharon Olds (19 Nov 1942, San Francisco CA) American poet best known for her powerful, often erotic, imagery of the body and her examination of the family.

Pat Oliphant (24 Jul 1935, Adelaide, Australia) Australian-born political cartoonist.

Pauline Oliveros (20 May 1932, Houston TX) American composer.

Kole Omotoso (21 Apr 1943, Akure, Western State, Nigeria) Nigerian Yoruba novelist, playwright, and critic.

(Philip) Michael Ondaatje (12 Sep 1943, Colombo, Ceylon [now Sri Lanka]) Canadian novelist and poet whose musical prose and poetry are created from a blend of myth, history, jazz, memoirs, and other forms.

Yoko Ono (18 Feb 1933, Tokyo, Japan) Japanese-born artist and musician; widow of Beatle John Lennon.

Tony Orlando (Michael Anthony Orlando Cassavitis; 3 Apr 1944, New York NY) American pop singer (Dawn).

Suze Orman (5 Jun 1951, Chicago IL) American financial adviser and best-selling author.

Stacie Orrico (1986?, Seattle WA) American gospel singer.

Amancio Ortega (March 1936, León, Spain) Spanish fashion and textile tycoon; reportedly one of Europe's richest men.

Ozzy Osbourne (John Michael Osbourne; 3 Dec 1948, Birmingham, England) British singer and songwriter (originally the lead singer of Black Sabbath).

Yury (Sergeyevich) Osipov (7 Jul 1936, Tobolsk, USSR [now Russia]) Russian mathematician and computer scientist; president of the Russian Academy of Sciences from 1991.

Yambo Ouologuem (22 Aug 1940, Bandiagary, Mopti region, French Sudan [now The Sudan]) Sudanese writer.

Michael Ovitz (14 Dec 1946, Encino CA) American entertainment executive, co-founder of the Creative Artists Agency (1975).

Bill Owens (22 Oct 1950, Fort Worth TX) American Republican politician; governor of Colorado from 1999.

Amos Oz (4 May 1939, Jerusalem) Israeli novelist, short-story writer, and essayist.

Seiji Ozawa (1 Sep 1935, Hoten, Manchukuo [now in China]) Japanese-born American conductor, notably of the Boston Symphony Orchestra.

Jack Paar (1 May 1918, Canton OH) American TV personality most famous for hosting *The Tonight Show*, 1957–62.

Rajendra K. Pachauri (20 Aug 1940, Nainital, India) Indian businessman; head of the Intergovernmental Panel on Climate Change from 2002.

José Emilio Pacheco (30 Jun 1939, Mexico City, Mexico) Mexican critic, novelist, short-story writer, translator, and poet.

Abel Pacheco de la Espriella (22 Dec 1933, San José, Costa Rica) Costa Rican politician; president of Costa Rica from 8 May 2002.

Al Pacino (25 Apr 1940, East Harlem, New York NY) American film actor known for intense, explosive roles; he won an Academy Award for best actor in 1992 (*Scent of a Woman*).

Clarence Page (2 Jun 1947, Dayton OH) American syndicated columnist and author.

Jimmy Page (James Patrick Page; 9 Jan 1944, Heston, England) British rock guitarist (of Led Zeppelin).

Camille Paglia (2 Apr 1947, Endicott NY) American scholar, author, controversial feminist.

Rod Paige (17 Jun 1933, Monticello MS) American government official; US Secretary of Education from 2001.

Nam June Paik (20 Jul 1932, Seoul, Korea) Korean-born German sculptor and performance artist, called the father of video art.

Jean-François Paillard (12 Apr 1928, Vitry-le-François, France) French conductor.

Pak Se Ri (28 Sep 1977, Daejon, South Korea) Korean golfer who, in her first year on the LPGA circuit (1998), won two major tournaments, became the second highest moneywinner on the tour, and carded the lowest 18- and 72-hole scores in LPGA history.

Jack Palance (Walter Palaniuk; 18 Feb 1919, Lattimer Mines PA) American motion-picture actor known for menacing roles; won an Academy Award for best supporting actor in 1991 (*City Slickers*).

Dan M. Palmer, American corporate executive; founder and CEO of Concord EFS, Inc. from 1982.

Felicity (Joan) Palmer (6 Apr 1944, Cheltenham, England) British soprano.

Robert Palmer (Alan Palmer; 19 Jan 1949, Batley, Yorkshire, England) British soul and R&B vocalist.

Samuel J. Palmisano, American corporate executive; president and CEO of the International Business Machines (IBM) Corp. from 2002.

Gwyneth Paltrow (28 Sep 1972, Los Angeles CA) American motion-picture and stage actress; gained acclaim for the film *Shakespeare in Love* (1998).

Anna Paquin (24 Jul 1982, Winnipeg, MB, Canada) New Zealand motion-picture actress made famous as a girl in *The Piano* (1993—Academy Award).

Sarah Jessica Parker (25 Mar 1965, Nelsonville OH) American TV and film actress popular since the 1980s, she reestablished her reputation as star of TV's *Sex and the City*.

Camilla Parker Bowles (née Camilla Shand; 17 Jul 1947, London, England) English personality, friend of Prince Charles.

Rosa Parks (4 Feb 1913, Tuskegee AL) American civil rights activist.

Van Dyke Parks (3 Jan 1941, Hattiesburg MS) American pop songwriter.

Derek Parra (15 Mar 1970, San Bernardino CA) American speed skater; 2002 Olympic gold medalist in the 1,500-m race in world-record time.

Nicanor Parra (5 Sep 1914, San Fabian, Chile) Chilean poet, the originator of so-called antipoetry.

Richard D. Parsons (4 Apr 1949, Brooklyn NY) American corporate executive; CEO of AOL Time Warner from 2002.

Timothy (Richard) Parsons (1 Nov 1932, Colombo, Ceylon [now Sri Lanka]) Canadian oceanographer; winner of 2001 Japan Prize for his work in fisheries management.

Arvo Pärt (11 Sep 1935, Paide, Estonia) Estonian composer whose works display a simplicity and medieval liturgical sound.

Dolly (Rebecca) Parton (19 Jan 1946, Locust Ridge TN) American country singer, songwriter, and actress.

André Pastrana Arango (17 Aug 1954, Bogotá, Colombia) Colombian politician and president, 1998–2002.

George E. Pataki (24 Jun 1945, Peekskill NY) American Republican politician; governor of New York from 1995.

Ange-Félix Patassé (1937, Paoua, Ubangi-Shari [now Central African Republic]) Central African Republic politician; president of the Central African Republic from 1993.

Ann Patchett (1963, Los Angeles CA) American novelist; her *Bel Canto* won the 2002 PEN/Faulkner Award and the Orange Prize.

Joseph Vincent ("Joe") Paterno (21 Dec 1926, Brooklyn NY) American football coach for Pennsylvania State University, winningest coach in history (327 wins at the end of the 2001 season).

Mandy Patinkin (30 Nov 1952, Chicago IL) American film, stage, and TV actor most recognized for his role on the TV series *Chicago Hope*.

Christopher Francis Patten (12 May 1944, Lancashire, England) British diplomat; last governor general of Hong Kong, 1992–97.

Percival Noel James Patterson (10 Apr 1935, Goodwill, St. James, Jamaica) Jamaican politician; prime minister of Jamaica from 1992.

Paul E. Patton (26 May 1937, Fallsburg KY) American Democratic politician; governor of Kentucky from 1995.

(Margaret) Jane Pauley (31 Oct 1950, Indianapolis IN) American TV personality, co-anchor of the *Today* show, 1976–89.

Luciano Pavarotti (12 Oct 1935, Modena, Italy) Italian operatic lyric tenor, noted for his mastery of the highest notes of a tenor's range.

Tom Paxton (31 Oct 1937, Chicago IL) American folk singer and songwriter.

Johnny Paycheck (Donald Eugene Lytle; 31 May 1938, Greenfield OH) American country singer and songwriter.

Arthur Peacocke (1924, Watford, England) British biophysical chemist and Anglican priest; Templeton Prize, 2001.

Claudia Pechstein (22 Feb 1972, East Berlin, German Democratic Republic [now Berlin, Germany]) German speed skater; 2002 Olympic gold medalist in the 3,000-m and 5,000-m races, and winner of the latter race in the two previous Olympics as well the bronze in 1991.

(Eldred) Gregory Peck (5 Apr 1916, La Jolla CA) American film actor known for playing characters of integrity, as in *To Kill a Mockingbird* (1962).

Niels-Henning Ørsted Pedersen (27 May 1946, Osted, Denmark) Danish jazz bassist.

Viktor (Olegovich) Pelevin (22 Nov 1962, Moscow, USSR) Russian novelist especially popular among young Russians.

David Pelletier (22 Nov 1974, Sayabec, QC, Canada) Canadian pairs skater (with Jamie Salé); shared the 2002 Olympic gold medal with Russians Berezhnaya and Sikharulidze.

Krzysztof Penderecki (23 Nov 1933, Debica, Poland) Polish composer, a leader of the European avant-garde whose works exhibit a novel and masterful treatment of orchestration.

Irving Penn (16 Jun 1917, Plainfield NJ) American photographer noted for his sophisticated fashion images and incisive portraits.

Sean Penn (17 Aug 1960, Santa Monica CA) American actor known for intense, brooding roles.

Murray Perahia (19 Apr 1947, New York NY) American concert pianist.

Angela Perez Baraquio (1 Jun 1976, Oahu HI) American beauty, chosen Miss America, 2001.

Kieran Perkins (14 Aug 1973, Brisbane, Australia) Australian swimmer who held 12 world records in distance freestyle events.

Itzhak Perlman (31 Aug 1945, Tel Aviv, Palestine [now Tel Aviv-Yafo, Israel]) Israeli-born American violinist.

Rhea Perlman (31 Mar 1948, Brooklyn NY) American film and TV actress, best remembered as Carla on the TV series *Cheers*.

Joe Perry (10 Sep 1950, Boston MA) American rock guitarist (of Aerosmith).

Rick Perry (4 Mar 1950, West Texas TX) American Republican politician; governor of Texas from 2000.

Göran Persson (20 Jan 1949, Vingaker, Sweden) Swedish politician; prime minister of Sweden from 1996.

Joe Pesci (9 Feb 1943, Newark NJ) American motion-picture actor, best known for roles in gangster movies and comedies.

Dragisa Pesic (8 Aug 1954, Danilovgrad, Montenegro, Yugoslavia) Yugoslavian politician; prime minister of Yugoslavia from 2001.

Daniela Pestova (14 Oct 1970, Teplice, Czechoslovakia [now Czech Republic]) Czech fashion model.

Bernadette Peters (28 Feb 1948, Queens NY) American singer and actress.

Roberta Peters (4 May 1930, Bronx NY) American operatic soprano.

Oscar (Emanuel) Peterson (15 Aug 1925, Montreal, QC, Canada) Canadian jazz pianist.

Roland Petit (13 Jan 1924, Villemomble, France) French dancer and choreographer whose dramatic ballets combined fantasy with elements of contemporary realism.

Tom Petty (20 Oct 1953, Gainesville FL) American rock singer and songwriter.

Michelle Pfeiffer (29 Apr 1958, Santa Ana CA) American leading actress of great talent and beauty.

Phan Van Khai (25 Dec 1933, Tan Thong Hoi village, near Saigon, French Indochina [now Ho Chi Minh City, Vietnam]) Vietnamese politician; prime minister of Vietnam from 1997.

Regis (Francis Xavier) Philbin (25 Aug 1934, New York NY) American TV personality, host of *Live with Regis and Kelly* and *Who Wants To Be a Millionaire?*

Prince Philip, Duke of Edinburgh (10 Jun 1921, Corfu, Greece) British royal; husband of Queen Elizabeth II.

Philippe Leopold Louis Marie (15 Apr 1960, Brussels, Belgium) Belgian duke of Brabant and prince of Belgium (crown prince).

Mark Philippoussis (7 Nov 1976, Melbourne, Australia) Australian tennis player.

Joaquin Phoenix (28 Oct 1974, San Juan, Puerto Rico) American actor known for intense, dark portrayals.

Renzo Piano (14 Sep 1937, Genoa, Italy) Italian architect; Pritzker Prize winner in 1998.

Bertrand Piccard (1 Mar 1958, Lausanne, Switzerland) Swiss balloonist who, with Brian Jones, became the first to travel nonstop around the world (1999).

Joseph A. Pichler, American corporate executive; chairman and CEO of the Kroger Co. from 1990.

Wilson Pickett (18 Mar 1941, Prattville AL) American R&B singer and songwriter.

Mary Pierce (15 Jan 1975, Montreal, QC, Canada) French tennis player; winner of the Australian Open in 1995 and the French Open in 2000.

Heinrich von Pierer (26 Jan 1941, Erlangen, Germany) German corporate executive; CEO of Siemens AG from 1992.

Pink (Alecia Moore; 8 Sep 1979, Doylestown PA) American pop vocalist.

Steven Pinker (18 Sep 1954, Montreal, QC, Canada) Canadian-born American experimental psychologist and author of scholarly and popular books of language.

Trevor Pinnock (16 Dec 1946, Canterbury, England) English harpsichordist and conductor.

Augusto Pinochet Ugarte (25 Nov 1915, Valparaíso, Chile) Chilean leader of the military junta that overthrew Pres. Salvador Allende of Chile and head of Chile's military government (1974–90).

Robert Pinsky (20 Oct 1940, Long Branch NJ) American poet and critic whose poems searched for the significance underlying everyday acts; poet laureate of the US, 1997–99.

Billie Piper (22 Sep 1982, Swindon, England) British pop singer.

Scottie Pippen (25 Sep 1965, Hamburg AR) American basketball player with the winning Chicago Bulls teams of the 1990s.

Pedro Verona Rodrigues Pires (April 1934, Ilha do Fogo, Cape Verde) Cape Verdean politician; president of Cape Verde from 2001.

Bernd Pischetsrieder (15 Feb 1948, Munich, Germany) German corporate executive; CEO of Volkswagen AG from September 2001.

Brad Pitt (William Bradley Pitt; 18 Dec 1963, Shawnee OK) American film actor, one of the biggest box-office draws.

Bucky Pizzarelli (John Pizzarelli; 9 Jan 1926, Paterson NJ) American jazz guitarist.

Robert Plant (20 Aug 1948, West Bromwich, England) British singer and songwriter.

Elizabeth Plater-Zyberg (20 Dec 1950, Bryn Mawr PA) American urban planner who collabrates with her husband, Andres Duany.

Mikhail Pletnev (14 Apr 1975, Arkhangelsk, USSR [now Russia]) Russian pianist and conductor.

George Plimpton (18 Mar 1927, New York NY) American author, TV host, and editor.

Maya (Mikhaylovna) Plisetskaya (20 Nov 1925, Moscow, USSR [now Russia]) Russian prima ballerina of the Bolshoi Ballet of Moscow, admired particularly for her technical virtuosity, expressive use of her arms, and ability to integrate acting with dancing.

Paul Plishka (28 Aug 1941, Old Forge PA) American operatic bass.

Joan (Anne) Plowright (28 Oct 1929, Brigg, Lincolnshire, England) English theater and film actress who won special acclaim for her roles in two plays by Eugène Ionesco.

Norman Podhoretz (1930, Brooklyn NY) American political commentator and editor of the journal Commentary (1960–95).

Sylvia Poggioli (Providence RI) American foreign correspondent for National Public Radio.

Sidney Poitier (20 Feb 1927?, Miami FL) Bahamian-American motion-picture actor and director; won an Academy Award for best actor in 1963 (Lilies of the Field).

Judit Polgar (23 Jul 1976, Budapest, Hungary) Hungarian chess player; achieved the rank among male chess players of grandmaster in December 1991 at the age of 15.

Sofia Polgar (2 Nov 1974, Budapest, Hungary) Hungarian chess master.

Zsuzsa Polgar (19 Apr 1969, Budapest, Hungary) Hungarian chess master; women's chess champion of the world, 1996–99.

Sigmar Polke (13 Feb 1941, Oels, Lower Silesia, Germany [now Olesnica, Poland]) German painter who was one of the founders of Capitalist Realism, a movement that depicted popular and mundane cultural artifacts with ironic seriousness.

John (Charlton) Polkinghorne (16 Oct 1930, Weston-super-Mare, England) British Anglican priest and particle physicist; winner of the Templeton Prize, 2002.

Sydney Pollack (1 Jul 1934, Lafayette IN) American intelligent actor, director, and producer acclaimed for Out of Africa (1985) and many other films.

Ruslan Ponomaryov (11 Oct 1983, Gorlovka, Ukrainian SSR, USSR [now Horlivka, Ukraine]) Ukrainian chess master; winner of the FIDE world chess championship, 2002.

Jean-Luc Ponty (29 Sep 1942, Avranches, France) French jazz violinist.

Iggy Pop (James Jewel Osterberg; 21 Apr 1947, Ypsilanti MI) American singer.

Paulina Porizkova (9 Apr 1965, Prostejov, Czechoslovakia [now Czech Republic]) Czech fashion model.

Peter (Nevill Frederick) Porter (16 Feb 1929, Brisbane, Queensland, Australia) Australian-born British poet.

Alfonso Portillo Cabrera (1951) Guatemalan politician; president of Guatemala from 2000.

Natalie Portman (Natalie Hershlag; 9 Jun 1981, Jerusalem, Israel) Israeli-born motion-picture actress who appeared in Star Wars episodes II (2002) and III (2005).

Franka Potente (22 Jul 1974, Dülmen, Germany) German motion-picture actress, star of Run Lola Run (1999).

John Potter, American corporate executive; CEO and postmaster general of the US Postal Service from 2001.

Colin (Luther) Powell (5 Apr 1937, New York NY) American military officer and government official; chairman of the Joint Chiefs of Staff, 1989–93; National Security Adviser; and US Secretary of State from 2001.

Velupillai Prabhakaran (26 Nov 1954, Inuvil, Jaffna, Sri Lanka) Sri Lankan secessionist; founder and leader of Liberation Tigers of Tamil Eelam (Tamil Tigers).

Miuccia Prada (1949, Milan, Italy) Italian fashion designer whose clothing, footwear, and accessories designs are characterized by casual luxury.

Azim Hasham Premji (24 Jul 1945, Bombay [now Mumbai], India) Indian corporate executive; chairman of the Wipro Corp. of Bangalore, India.

André (George) Previn (6 Apr 1929, Berlin, Germany) German-born American pianist, composer, and conductor; music director of the Los Angeles Philharmonic, 1985–89.

Leontyne Price (Mary Violet Leontyne Price; 10 Feb 1927, Laurel MS) American lyric soprano.

Charley Pride (18 Mar 1938, Sledge MS) American country and western singer.

Prince (Prince Rogers Nelson; 7 Jun 1958, Minneapolis MN) American singer and songwriter who was among the most talented American musicians of his generation.

Anthony Principi (16 Apr 1944, Bronx NY) American government official; US Secretary of Veterans Affairs from 2001.

John Prine (10 Oct 1946, Maywood IL) American pop singer and songwriter.

Richard B. Priory (15 May 1946, Lakehurst NJ) American energy engineer and corporate executive; CEO of Duke Energy from 1997.

Romano Prodi (9 Aug 1939, Scandiano, Italy) Italian politician; prime minister of Italy, 1996–98 and president of the European Commission from 1999.

E(dna) Annie Proulx (22 Aug 1935, Norwich CT) American writer whose darkly comic yet sad fiction is peopled with quirky, memorable individuals and unconventional families.

Paul Prudhomme (13 Jul 1940, near Opelousas LA) American chef and restaurateur who popularized Louisiana Cajun cooking through his TV appearances and cookbooks.

Stanley Ben Prusiner (28 May 1942, Des Moines IA) American biochemist who discovered the prion; Nobel Prize for Physiology or Medicine, 1997.

Richard Pryor (1 Dec 1940, Peoria IL) American groundbreaking stand-up comedian and film actor most popular in the 1980s.

Gary Puckett (17 Oct 1942, Hibbing MN) American rock vocalist.

Alla Pugacheva (Alla Borisovna Pugachyova; 15 Apr 1949, Moscow, USSR) Russian pop singer.

Philip Pullman (19 Oct 1946, Norwich, England) British author whose *The Amber Spyglass* won the Whitbread Book Award in 2001.

Flora Purim (6 Mar 1942, Rio de Janeiro, Brazil) Brazilian jazz singer.

Georgi Purvanov (28 Jun 1957, Kovachevtsi, near Sofia, Bulgaria) Bulgarian politician; president of Bulgaria from 22 Jan 2002.

Vladimir Vladimirovich Putin (7 Oct 1952, Leningrad, USSR [now St. Petersburg, Russia]) Russian intelligence officer and politician; president of Russia from 2000.

Andrée Putman (André Christine Aynard; 23 Dec 1925, Paris, France) French furniture designer.

Thomas Pynchon (8 May 1937, Glen Cove, Long Island NY) American novelist and short-story writer.

Muammar al-Qaddafi (also spelled Muammar Khadafy, Moammar Gadhafi, or Mu'ammar al-Qadhdhafi; 1942, near Surt, Libya) Libyan military leader; de facto chief of state of Libya from 1969; controversial Arab statesman.

Laisenia Qarase (1941) Fijian politician; prime minister of Fiji, 2000–01 and again from 2001.

Mary Quant (11 Feb 1934, London, England) British fashion designer of youth-inspired 1960s creations such as "hot pants" and the still-popular miniskirt.

Anna Quindlen (8 Jul 1953, Philadelphia PA) American political commentator and author.

Anthony Quinn (Anthony Quinones; 21 Apr 1915, Chihuahaha, Mexico—3 Jun 2001, Boston MA), Mexican-born American character actor known for playing colorful personalities such as Emiliano Zapata (*Viva Zapata!*, 1952) and *Zorba the Greek* (1964).

David (William) Rabe (10 Mar 1940, Dubuque IA) American playwright whose experiences as a draftee assigned to a hospital-support unit in Vietnam were the basis for several acclaimed dramas.

Ivica Racan (24 Feb 1944, Ebersbach, Germany) Croatian politician; prime minister of Croatia from 27 Jan 2000.

Princess Lee Radziwill (Caroline Lee Bouvier; 3 Mar 1933, New York NY) American personality; sister of the late Jackie Kennedy Onassis.

Jean-Pierre Raffarin (3 Aug 1948, Poitiers, France) French politician; prime minister of France from 6 May 2002.

Patrick Rafter (28 Dec 1972, Mount Isa, Australia) Australian tennis player; winner of the US Open in 1997 and 1998.

Ruggero Raimondi (3 Oct 1941, Bologna, Italy) Italian operatic bass.

Franklin D. Raines (14 Jan 1949, Seattle WA) American corporate executive; CEO of Fannie Mae from 1999.

Prince Rainier III (Rainier-Louis-Henri-Maxence-Bertrand de Grimaldi; 31 May 1933, Monaco) Monegasque royal; prince of Monaco from 1949.

Bonnie Raitt (8 Nov 1949, Burbank CA) American blues and rock singer and guitarist.

Imomali Rakhmonov (5 Oct 1952, Dangara, Tadzhik SSR, USSR [now Tajikistan]) Tajik politician; president of Tajikistan from 1992.

Joseph W. Ralston (Hopkinville KY) American general, USAF; head of the US European Command from 2000.

Eros Ramazzotti (28 Oct 1963, near Rome, Italy) Italian pop singer.

Samuel Ramey (28 Mar 1942, Colby KS) American operatic bass.

Fidel Valdez Ramos (18 Mar 1928, Lingayen, Philippines) Philippine military leader and politician, president of the Philippines, 1992–98.

José Ramos-Horta (26 Dec 1949, Dili, Portuguese East Timor) Timorese independence advocate; co-winner of the Nobel Peace Prize, 1996.

Charlotte Rampling (5 Feb 1946, Sturmer, England) British film actress known for psychologically intense roles.

Tony Randall (26 Feb 1920, Tulsa OK) American film and TV actor most famous for playing Felix Unger on the TV series *The Odd Couple.*

Raphael I Bidawid (1922, Mosul, Iraq) Iraqi religious leader; patriarch of the Chaldean Catholic Church from 1989.

Anders Fogh Rasmussen (26 Jan 1953, Ginnerup, Denmark) Danish politician; prime minister of Denmark from 2001.

Poul Nyrup Rasmussen (15 Jun 1943, Esbjerg, Denmark) Danish politician; prime minister of Denmark, 1993–2001.

Dan Rather (31 Oct 1931, Wharton TX) American TV journalist.

Sir Simon (Denis) Rattle (19 Jan 1955, Liverpool, England) British orchestra conductor; principal conductor and artistic director of the Berlin Philharmonic from 2002/03.

Irina (Georgiyevna) Ratushinskaya (4 Mar 1954, Odessa, Ukraine, USSR) Russian lyric poet, essayist, and political dissident.

Johannes Rau (16 Jan 1931, Wuppertal-Barmen, Germany) German politician; president of Germany from 1999.

Robert Rauschenberg (22 Oct 1925, Port Arthur TX) American painter and graphic artist whose early works anticipated the Pop-art movement.

Marc Ravalomanana (1949, Madagascar) Malagasy politician; president of Madagascar from 22 Feb 2002.

Peter H. Raven (13 Jun 1936, Shanghai, China) American botanist and environmentalist specializing in tropical plants.

Lou Rawls (1 Dec 1935, Chicago IL) American soul and R&B singer and actor.

Lee R. Raymond (1938, Waterstown SD) American corporate executive; chairman and CEO of Exxon Mobil Corp. from 1994.

Chris Rea (4 Mar 1951, Middlesborough, England) British pop singer.

Nancy Davis Reagan (née Anne Frances Robbins; 6 Jul 1921, New York NY) American first lady; second wife of Pres. Ronald Reagan.

Ronald (Wilson) Reagan (6 Feb 1911, Tampico IL) American film actor and statesman; 40th president of the US, 1981–89 [see full biography at Presidents].

Helen Reddy (25 Oct 1942, Melbourne, Australia) Australian pop singer and songwriter.

Robert Redford (18 Aug 1937, Santa Monica CA) American film actor and director of great distinction and founder of Sundance Institute and Film Festival.

Lynn Redgrave (8 Mar 1943, London, England) British stage, screen, and TV actress whose breakthrough came in the film *Georgy Girl* (1966).

Vanessa Redgrave (30 Jan 1937, London, England) British stage and screen actress and political activist.

Joshua Redman (1 Feb 1969, Berkeley CA) American jazz saxophone player.

Sumner M. Redstone (27 May 1923, Boston MA) American corporate executive; chairman of the board (from 1987) and CEO (from 1996) of Viacom Inc.

Gabrielle Reece (6 Jan 1970, La Jolla CA) American model and professional beach volleyball player.

Lou Reed (2 Mar 1942, Brooklyn NY) American rock singer and songwriter.

Ralph Eugene Reed, Jr. (24 Jun 1961, Portsmouth VA) American activist; executive director of the Christian Coalition.

Rex Reed (2 Oct 1938, Fort Worth TX) American film critic.

Christopher Reeve (25 Sep 1952, New York NY) American film actor best known for playing Superman, now a crusader for spinal cord injury research.

Keanu Reeves (2 Sep 1964, Beirut, Lebanon) American actor known for many popular films.

Martha Reeves (18 Jul 1941, Eufala AL) American musician, lead singer of Martha and The Vandellas.

William Hubbs Rehnquist (1 Oct 1924, Milwaukee WI) American jurist; associate justice of the US Supreme Court from 1972 and chief justice from 1986.

Robert S. Reich (24 Jun 1946, Scranton PA) American economist, former US labor secretary, academic, and commentator.

Steve Reich (Stephen Michael Reich; 3 Oct 1936, New York NY) American minimalist composer.

Marcel Reich-Ranicki (2 Jun 1920, Wroclawek, Poland) Polish-born German literary critic, author, and TV host.

Carl Reiner (20 Mar 1922, Bronx NY) American writer, director, and actor.

Rob Reiner (6 Mar 1947, Bronx NY) American actor, director, writer, producer of critical and commercially successful films; son of Carl Reiner.

Ann Reinking (10 Nov 1949, Seattle WA) American dancer and film actress and later a noted Broadway choreographer.

Thomas Esang Remengesau, Jr. (1956) Palau politician; president of Palau from 2001.

John Renbourn (1944, Marleybone, London, England) British folk and pop guitarist and singer (of Pentangle).

France-Albert René (16 Nov 1935, Mahé, Seychelles) Seychelles politician; president of Seychelles from 1977.

Janet Reno (21 Jul 1938, Miami FL) American government official; attorney general in the administrations of Pres. Bill Clinton.

Mary Lou Retton (24 Jan 1968, Fairmont WV) American gymnast; first US woman gymnast to win an individual Olympic gold medal (1984).

Burt Reynolds (11 Feb 1936, Waycross GA) American popular star of 1970s and 1980s films.

Debbie Reynolds (1 Apr 1932, El Paso TX) American film and stage actress in highly popular light comedies.

Yasmina Reza (1 May 1959, Paris, France) French playwright of international background and international acclaim, best known for her play *Art*.

Manon Rheaume (24 Feb 1972, Lac Beauport, QC, Canada) Canadian ice hockey goalie; the only woman to play in the National Hockey League.

Lawrence Rhodes (24 Nov 1939, Mount Hope WV) American dancer and ballet director.

Busta Rhymes (Trevor Smith, Jr.; 20 May 1972, Brooklyn NY) American rap performer.

Christina Ricci (12 Feb 1980, Santa Monica CA) American motion-picture starlet and actress.

Katia Ricciarelli (16 Jan 1946, Rovigo, Italy) Italian operatic soprano.

Anne Rice (Howard Allen O'Brien; noms de plume A.N. Roquelaure and Anne Rampling; 4 Oct 1941, New Orleans LA) American gothic novelist known especially for her six-volume *Vampire Chronicles*.

Condoleezza Rice (14 Nov 1954, Birmingham AL) American academic and government official; national security adviser from 2001.

Jerry (Lee) Rice (13 Oct 1962, Starkville MS) American football player; one of greatest wide receivers in NFL history.

Tim Rice (10 Nov 1944, Amersham, Buckinghamshire, England) British lyricist.

Cliff Richard (Harry Roger Webb; 14 Oct 1940, Lucknow, India) British pop singer.

Keith Richards (18 Dec 1943, Dartford, Kent, England) British guitarist and singer with the Rolling Stones.

Dorothy ("Dot") Richardson (22 Sep 1961, Orlando FL) American softball player who led the US team to Olympic gold medals in 1996 and 2000.

Lionel B. Richie, Jr. (20 Jun 1949, Tuskegee AL) American R&B songwriter and singer.

Gerhard Richter (9 Feb 1932, Dresden, Germany) German artist and co-founder of the movement known as Capitalist Realism, in which ordinary objects such as furniture and food, and sometimes the artists themselves, were depicted as art.

Sally K(risten) Ride (26 May 1951, Encino CA) American astronaut and astrophysicist who was the first American woman in space (1983).

Thomas Joseph Ridge (26 Aug 1945, Munhall PA) American government official; designated in 2002 to be director of the Department of Homeland Security.

Leni Riefenstahl (22 Aug 1902, Berlin, Germany) German filmmaker both praised and reviled for documentary films of the 1930s dramatizing the Nazi movement.

Joshua Rifkin (22 Apr 1944, New York NY) American pianist and conductor.

Leonard S. Riggio (28 Feb 1941, Bronx NY) American corporate executive; founder and chairman of Barnes & Noble, Inc.

Bridget Riley (24 Apr 1931, London, England) English Op art painter.

Terry Riley (24 Jun 1935, Colfax CA) American minimalist composer and performer.

LeAnn Rimes (28 Aug 1982, Jackson MS) American country music singer.

Faith Ringgold (8 Oct 1930, New York NY) American artist and author who became famous for innovative, quilted narrations that communicate her political beliefs.

Kelly Ripa (2 Oct 1970, Stratford NJ) American talk-show host and actress on daytime TV.

Pipilotti Rist (Charlotte Rist; 21 Jun 1962, Grabs, Switzerland) Swiss video installation artist.

Rivaldo (Vitor Borba Ferreira; 19 April 1972, Recife, Brazil) Brazilian association football (soccer) player; European footballer of the Year in 1999 and a key player on the Brazilian national team in the 1998 and 2002 World Cup competitions.

Geraldo Rivera (4 Jul 1943, New York NY) American TV journalist and talk-show host.

Joan Rivers (Joan Sandra Molinsky; 8 Jun 1937, New York NY) American comedienne, talk-show host, and fashion commentator.

Johnny Rivers (John Henry Ramistella; 7 Nov 1942, New York NY) American rock singer.

Larry Rivers (Yitzroch Loiza Grossberg; 17 Aug 1923, New York NY) American painter whose works frequently combined the vigorous, painterly brushstrokes of Abstract Expressionism with the commercial images of the Pop art movement.

Tim Robbins (16 Oct 1958, West Covina CA) American actor whose films include *Bull Durham, The Player*, and *The Shawshank Redemption*.

Cecil E(dward) Roberts, Jr. (31 Oct 1946, Kanawha county WV) American labor leader; president of the United Mine Workers of America from 1995.

Cokie Roberts (née Mary Martha Corinne Morrison Claiborne Boggs; 27 Dec 1943, New Orleans LA) American TV journalist.

Julia Roberts (28 Oct 1967, Smyrna GA) American actress, one of the biggest names in Hollywood since her performance in the film *Pretty Woman* (1990).

Oral Roberts (24 Jan 1918, Pontohoc county OK) American TV evangelist and educator.

George (Islay MacNeill) Robertson (Baron Robertson of Port Ellen; 1946, Port Ellen, Isle of Islay, Scotland) British military leader; secretary-general of NATO from 1999.

Pat Robertson (22 Mar 1930, Lexington VA) American TV evangelist and broadcasting executive, one-time presidential contender and president of the Christian Coalition (to 2001).

Robbie Robertson (Jaime Roberts; 5 Jul 1944, Toronto, ON, Canada) Canadian rock musician (guitarist with the Band).

(Michael) Duke Robillard (4 Oct 1948, Woonsocket RI) American blues guitarist, singer, and songwriter.

David Maurice Robinson (6 Aug 1965, Key West FL) American basketball player; center who led the San Antonio Spurs to an NBA championship in 1999.

Mary Robinson (21 May 1944, Ballina, County Mayo, Ireland) Irish statesman; president of Ireland, 1990–97; United Nations High Commissioner for Human Rights from 1997.

Smokey Robinson (William Robinson, Jr.; 19 Feb 1940, Detroit MI) American R&B singer and songwriter.

Chris Rock (7 Feb 1966, Georgetown SC) American stand-up performer and actor known for his brash style.

Kid Rock (Robert James Ritchie; 17 Jan 1971, Romeo MI) American rap-rock artist.

The Rock (Dwayne Douglas Johnson; 2 May 1972 California) American wrestler turned actor.

Anita Roddick (23 Oct 1942, Littlehampton, England) British businesswoman; co-founder of The Body Shop in 1976.

Dennis (Keith) Rodman (13 May 1961, Trenton NJ) American basketball forward who led NBA in rebounding 1991–98 and who was known for his eccentric behavior on and off the court.

Alex Rodriguez (27 Jul 1975, New York NY) American baseball player; shortstop known as a fine all-around player who signed the largest salary deal in history ($252 million over 10 years) in 1998.

Narciso Rodríguez (1961, New Jersey) American fashion designer who rose quickly to fame when he designed Caroline Bissette's dress for her 1996 wedding to John F. Kennedy, Jr.

Fred Rogers (20 Mar 1928, Latrobe PA) American children's TV personality, longtime star of *Mr. Rogers' Neighborhood*.

Kenny Rogers (Kenneth Donald Rogers; 21 Aug 1938, Houston TX) American country and western and pop singer.

Jacques Rogge (2 May 1942, Ghent, Belgium) Belgian Olympic yachtsman, surgeon, and sports executive; president of the International Olympic Committee from 2001.

Sonny Rollins (Theodore Walter Rollins; 7 Sep 1930, Harlem, New York NY) American jazz tenor and soprano saxophonist.

Ray Romano (21 Dec 1957, Queens NY) American comic actor, best known for the prizewinning TV series *Everybody Loves Raymond*.

Romário (de Souza Faria) (29 Jan 1966, Villa Pena, Brazil) Brazilian association football (soccer) player, a brilliant striker who excelled on Brazil's World Cup team and was awarded the Golden Ball in 1994.

Pepe Romero (8 Mar 1944, Málaga, Spain) Spanish classical guitarist, of the Romero Family.

Ronaldo (Ronaldo Luiz Nazario da Lima; 22 Sep 1976, Bento Ribero, Brazil) Brazilian association football (soccer) player; FIFA Player of the Year in 1996 and 1997 and star of Brazil's national team in the 2002 World Cup.

Linda (Marie) Ronstadt (15 Jul 1946, Tucson AZ) American rock and pop singer.

Andy Rooney (14 Jan 1919, Albany NY) American TV commentator.

Mickey Rooney (Joe Yule, Jr.; 23 Sep 1920, Brooklyn NY) American energetic film, stage, and musical star; best known for his portrayal of Andy Hardy in a series of films.

Ned Rorem (23 Oct 1923, Richmond IN) American composer, pianist, and author noted for his French-influenced songs.

Axl Rose (William Bailey; 6 Feb 1962, Lafayette IN) American rock vocalist (of Guns N' Roses).

Charlie Rose (5 Jan 1942, Henderson NC) American TV journalist and interviewer.

Roseanne (also known as Roseanne Barr and Roseanne Arnold; 3 Nov 1953, Salt Lake City UT) American TV and night club personality, best known for her TV series *Roseanne*.

A.M. Rosenthal (Abraham Michael Rosenthal; 3 May 1922, Sault Ste. Marie, ON, Canada) Canadian-born American journalist, longtime political columnist for the *New York Times*.

Annie Ross (Annabelle Short Lynch; 25 Jul 1930, Mitcham, Surrey, England) British jazz singer.

Diana Ross (Diane Earle; 26 Mar 1944, Detroit MI) American R&B singer and actress.

Mstislav (Leopoldovich) Rostropovich (27 Mar 1927, Baku, Azerbaijan SSR, USSR) Russian-born cellist, conductor, and pianist; music director of the National Symphony Orchestra, 1977–94.

Philip (Milton) Roth (19 Mar 1933, Newark NJ) American novelist and short-story writer whose works are characterized by an acute ear for dialogue, a concern with Jewish middle-class life, and the painful entanglements of sexual and familial love.

Johnny Rotten (John Lydon; 31 Jan 1956, London, England) British punk rock singer.

Sister Elaine Roulet (1930, Maspath NY) American "Prison Angel," who has been active in the protection and care of the children of women in prison.

Karl Rove (25 Dec 1950, Denver CO) American politician; chief political strategist for Pres. George W. Bush.

John G. Rowland (24 May 1957, Waterbury CT) American Republican politician; governor of Connecticut from 1995.

Landon H. Rowland, American corporate executive; chairman and CEO of Stilwell Financial Inc.

J.K. Rowling (Joanne Kathleen Rowling; 31 Jul 1965, Chipping Sodbury, near Bristol, England) British author, creator of the popular and critically acclaimed *Harry Potter* series about a young sorcerer in training.

Arundhati Roy (24 Nov 1961, Shillong, Bengal state, India) Indian novelist who won the Booker Prize in 1998 for *The God of Small Things*.

Patrick Roy (5 Oct 1965, Quebec City, QC, Canada) American ice hockey goalie; only three-time NHL playoffs MVP, winning the Conn-Smythe Trophy in 1986, 1993, and 2001.

Gennady (Nikolayevich) Rozhdestvensky (4 May 1931, Moscow, USSR [now Russia]) Russian conductor.

Ibragim Rugova (1944 Kosovo? Serbia, Yugoslavia) Kosovar (Albanian) nationalist leader and officer in the opposition government of Kosovo.

Louis Rukeyser (30 Jan 1933, New York NY) American TV journalist and financial analyst.

Donald H. Rumsfeld (9 Jul 1932, Chicago IL) American government official; US Secretary of Defense, 1975–77 and from 2001.

Geoffrey Rush (6 Jul 1951, Toowoomba, Queensland, Australia) American film actor whose popularity soared following *Shine* (1996).

(Ahmed) Salman Rushdie (19 Jun 1947, Bombay [now Mumbai], India) Anglo-Indian novelist who was condemned to death by leading Iranian Muslim clerics in 1989 for allegedly having blasphemed Islam in his novel *The Satanic Verses*.

Keri Russell (23 Mar 1976, Fountain Valley CA) American TV actress and model.

Kurt Russell (17 Mar 1951, Springfield MA) American actor whose films include *Swing Shift*, *Backdraft*, and *Tombstone*.

Leon Russell (Claude Russell Bridges; 2 Apr 1941, Lawton OK) American rock pianist, instrumentalist, and singer.

Patricia F. Russo (Trenton NJ) American business executive; CEO of Lucent Technologies from 2002.

Rene Russo (17 Feb 1954, Burbank CA) American talented actress in both lead and supporting roles.

Edward B. Rust, Jr. (Illinois) American corporate executive; president and CEO of State Farm Insurance from 1985.

John Rutter (24 Sep 1945, London, England) British composer and conductor; leader of the Cambridge Singers.

Arnold Rüütel (10 May 1928, Saaremaa, Estonia) Estonian politician; chairman of the Supreme Council of Estonia, 1990–92, and president from 2001.

George H. Ryan (24 Feb 1934, Maquoketa IA) American Republican politician; governor of Illinois from 1999.

Meg Ryan (Margaret Mary Emily Anne Hyra; 19 Nov 1961, Fairfield CT) American film star of immense popularity known mostly for upbeat romantic comedies.

Winona Ryder (Winona Laura Horowitz; 29 Oct 1971, Winona MN) American film actress especially noticed for her roles in *The Age of Innocence* (1993) and *Little Women* (1994).

Sade (Helen Folasade Adu; 16 Jan 1950, Ibadan, Nigeria) Nigerian singer and songwriter.

Morley Safer (8 Nov 1931, Toronto, ON, Canada) Canadian TV journalist.

Marat Safin (27 Jan 1980, Moscow, USSR [now Russia]) Russian tennis player who beat Pete Sampras in 2000 for the US Open championship.

William Safire (17 Dec 1929, New York NY) American journalist, political writer, and columnist.

Carole Bayer Sager (8 Mar 1946, New York NY) American singer and songwriter.

Edward Said (1 Nov 1935, Jerusalem, Palestine) Palestinian-born American scholar, postcolonial cultural and literary critic.

Sayyid Qaboos Ibn Said Al Saidi Saidi (18 Nov 1940, Salalah, Dhofar, Oman) Omani royal; sultan of Oman from 1970.

Yves Saint Laurent (Yves-Henri-Donat-Mathieu Saint Laurent; 1 Aug 1936, Oran, Algeria) French fashion designer noted for his popularization of women's trousers for all occasions.

Buffy Sainte-Marie (Beverly Sainte-Marie; 20 Feb 1941, Craven, Piapot Reserve, SK, Canada) Canadian-American folk and pop singer and songwriter and Native American activist.

Ryuichi Sakamoto (17 Jan 1952, Tokyo, Japan) Japanese composer of electronic music.

Jamie Salé (21 Apr 1977, Red Deer, AB, Canada) Canadian pairs skater (with David Pelletier); shared the 2002 Olympic gold medal with Russians Berezhnaya and Sikharulidze.

Sebastião Salgado (8 Feb 1944, Aimorés, Brazil) Brazilian photographer whose work powerfully expresses the suffering of the homeless and downtrodden.

'Ali 'Abdullah Salih (1942) Yemeni politician; president of the unified Yemen from 1990.

Salim Ahmed Salim (23 Jan 1942, Zanzibar, British East Africa [now Tanzania]) Tanzanian diplomat; secretary general of the Organization of African Unity, 1989–2001.

J(erome) D(avid) Salinger (1 Jan 1919, New York NY) American writer whose novel *The Catcher in the Rye* (1951) won critical acclaim and devoted admirers, especially among the post-World War II generation of college students.

Esa-Pekka Salonen (30 Jun 1958, Helsinki, Finland) Finnish conductor; musical director of the Los Angeles Philharmonic from 1992.

Juan Antónlo Samaranch (17 Jul 1920, Barcelona, Spain) Spanish Catalan businessman and sports official; president of the International Olympic Committee, 1980–2000.

Jorge (Fernando Branco de) Sampaio (18 Sep 1939, Lisbon, Portugal) Portuguese politician; president of Portugal from 1996.

Pete Sampras (12 Aug 1971, Washington DC) American tennis player who holds the record for most career Grand Slam wins (14).

Sonia (Benita) Sanchez (9 Sep 1934, Birmingham AL) American poet, playwright, and educator, noted for her black activism.

Gonzalo Sánchez de Lozada Bustamante (1 Jul 1930, La Paz, Bolivia) Bolivian politician; president of Bolivia, 1993–97 and from 6 August 2002.

Jil Sander (Heidemarie Jiline Sander; 27 Nov 1943, Wesselburen, Germany) German fashion designer known for simple, sophisticated, classic creations.

Pharoah Sanders (Farrell Sanders; 13 Oct 1940, Little Rock AR) American jazz tenor and soprano saxophonist and composer.

Adam Sandler (9 Sep 1966, Brooklyn NY) American comic actor and former *Saturday Night Live* star known for playing flawed but endearing comic characters.

Carlos Santana (20 Jul 1947, Autlán de Navarro, Mexico) Mexican-born American guitarist and bandleader.

Cristina Saralegui (29 Jan 1948, Havana, Cuba) Cuban-born American Spanish-language TV talk host.

José Saramago (16 Nov 1922, Azinhaga, Ribatejo province, Portugal) Portuguese novelist and man of letters who was awarded the Nobel Prize for Literature in 1998.

Susan Sarandon (4 Oct 1946, New York NY) American film actress known for her powerful characterizations.

Mikio Sasaki, Japanese corporate executive; president and CEO of Mitsubishi Motors Corp. from 1998.

Vidal Sassoon (17 Jan 1928, London, England) British hairstylist who pioneered the idea of simple haircuts that require little styling and who created his own hair product line.

Denis Sassou-Nguesso (1943, Edou, French Equatorial Africa [now Republic of the Congo]) Congolese politician; president of the Republic of Congo, 1979–92, and again from 1997.

David Satcher (2 Mar 1941, near Anniston AL) American physician; US surgeon general, 1998–2002.

Felix Savon (Félix Savón Fabré; 22 April 1967, San Vicente, Cuba) Cuban heavyweight boxer, three-time Olympic gold medalist.

Diane K. Sawyer (22 Dec 1945, Glasgow KY) American TV reporter.

Antonin Scalia (11 Mar 1936, Trenton NJ) American jurist; associate justice of the US Supreme Court from 1986.

Maximilian Schell (8 Dec 1930, Vienna, Austria) Austrian intelligent film actor, writer, director, and producer.

Peter Schickele (17 Jul 1935, Ames IA) American composer, radio personality, and creator and impersonator of P.D.Q. Bach.

Claudia Schiffer (25 Aug 1970, Düsseldorf, Germany) German fashion model who appeared in hundreds of magazine covers and in advertisements.

Lalo Schifrin (Boris Schifrin; 21 Jun 1932, Buenos Aires, Argentina) Argentine jazz pianist and composer.

Wally Schirra (Walter Marty Schirra, Jr.; 12 Mar 1923, Hackensack NJ) American astronaut who manned the Mercury "Sigma 7" (1962) and was command pilot of Gemini 6 (1965).

Phyllis Stewart Schlafly (15 Aug 1924, St. Louis MO) American antiabortion activist, commentator, and author.

John Schlesinger (16 Feb 1926, London, England) English director known for sensitively told stories.

Daniel Schorr (31 Aug 1916, New York NY) American TV and radio journalist and political commentator.

Jürgen Schrempp (14 Sep 1944, Freiburg im Breisgau, Germany) German executive; chairman of DaimlerChrysler (from merger, 1998).

Gerhard Schröder (7 Apr 1944, Mossenberg, Lower Saxony, Germany) German socialist politician and chancellor from 1998.

Gunther Schuller (11 Nov 1925, Jackson Heights, Queens NY) American classical and jazz composer and conductor.

Dieter Schulte (13 Jan 1940, Duisberg, Germany) German labor leader and head of the German Trade Union Federation from 1994.

Henning Schulte-Noelle (26 Aug 1942, Essen, Germany) German corporate executive; CEO of Allianz AG from 1991.

Michael Schumacher (3 Jan 1969, Hürth-Hermülheim, Germany) German Formula 1 race-car driver who dominated Grand Prix racing in the early 2000s and whose sports winnings, approaching $1 billion, were reportedly the highest of any athlete.

Wolfgang Schüssel (7 Jun 1945, Vienna, Austria) Austrian politician; chancellor of Austria from 2000.

Rudolf Schuster (4 Jan 1934, Kosice, Czechoslovakia [now Slovakia]) Slovakian politician; president of Slovakia from 1999.

Arnold Schwarzenegger (30 Jul 1947, Graz, Austria) Austrian-born American bodybuilder and film actor known for tough-guy leading roles as in the *Terminator* films and *True Lies* (1994).

Mark S. Schweiker (31 Jan 1953, Levittown PA) American Republican politician; governor of Pennsylvania from 2001.

David Schwimmer (12 Nov 1966, Astoria NY) American TV actor, currently plays Ross on *Friends*.

Walter Schwimmer (16 Jun 1942, Vienna, Austria) Austrian international executive; secretary-general of the Council of Europe from 1999.

Martin Scorsese (17 Nov 1942, Flushing, Long Island NY) American motion-picture director, writer, and producer known for harsh, violent depictions.

H. Lee Scott, Jr., American corporate executive; CEO of Wal-Mart Stores from 2000.

Jill Scott (Philadelphia PA) American soul singer and songwriter.

Ridley Scott (30 Nov 1937, South Shields, England) British acclaimed film director known for visual style and rich details.

Kristen Scott Thomas (24 May 1960, Redruth, Cornwall, England) British actress.

Gil Scott-Heron (1 Apr 1949, Chicago IL) American pop singer and songwriter.

Earl (Eugene) Scruggs (6 Jan 1924, Flint Hill NC) American bluegrass banjoist, the developer of a unique instrumental style that helped to popularize the five-string banjo.

Son Seals (13 Aug 1942, Osceola AR) American blues singer.

Don(ald J.) Sebesky (10 Dec 1937, Perth Amboy NJ) American jazz composer.

Neil Sedaka (13 Mar 1939, Brooklyn NY) American singer and songwriter.

Pete Seeger (3 May 1919, New York NY) American singer who sustained the folk music tradition and who was the principal inspiration for younger performers in the folk revival of the 1960s

Bob Seger (6 May 1945, Ann Arbor MI) American musician and singer.

Ivan G. Seidenberg (New York NY) American corporate executive; CEO of Verizon Communications from 2002.

Jerry Seinfeld (29 Apr 1954, Brooklyn NY) American comic and TV personality made famous by his hit series *Seinfeld*.

Monica Seles (2 Dec 1973, Novi Sad, Yugoslavia) Yugoslav-born tennis player who holds nine Grand Slam titles.

Allan H. ("Bud") Selig (30 Jul 1934, Milwaukee WI) American sports executive; Major League Baseball commissioner from 1998.

Tom Selleck (29 Jan 1945, Detroit MI) American film and TV actor best remembered as star of the TV series *Magnum, P.I.*

Amartya Sen (3 Nov 1933, Santiniketan, Bengal state, India) Indian economist; winner of the Nobel Prize for Economics, 1998, for his contributions to welfare economics and social choice and his interest in the problems of society's poorest members.

Paul Sereno (11 Oct 1957, Aurora IL) American paleontologist credited with a number of significant dinosaur finds.

Richard Serra (2 Nov 1939, San Francisco CA) American sculptor known for large, powerful, outdoor works.

Vikram Seth (20 Jun 1952, Calcutta [now Kolkata], India) Indian poet, novelist, and travel writer known for his verse novel *The Golden Gate* (1986) and his epic novel *A Suitable Boy* (1993).

Rodolfo C. Severino (1936, Philippines) Philippine international official; secretary-general of the Association of Southeast Asian Nations (ASEAN) from 1998.

Doc Severinson (Carl Hilding Severinson; 7 Jul 1927, Arlington OR) American jazz trumpeter and band leader.

Jane Seymour (15 Feb 1951, Hillingdon, England) British film and TV actress who recently played *Dr. Quinn, Medicine Woman.*

Stephanie Seymour (23 Jul 1968, San Diego CA) American fashion model.

Ahmed Necdet Sezer (13 Sep 1941, Ayfon, Turkey) Turkish politician; president of Turkey from 2000.

(Levin) Peter Shaffer (15 May 1926, London, England) British playwright.

Paul Shaffer (28 Nov 1949, Thunder Bay, ON, Canada) Canadian-born bandleader.

Shaggy (Orville Richard Burrell; 22 Oct 1968, St. Andrews, Jamaica) Jamaican reggae artist.

Gil Shaham (19 Feb 1971, Champaign-Urbana IL) American violinist.

Jeanne Shaheen (28 Jan 1947, St. Charles MO) American Democratic politician; governor of New Hampshire from 1997.

Shakira (Shakira Isabel Meberak Ripoll; 2 Feb 1977, Barranquilla, Colombia) Colombian-born pop singer.

Garry Shandling (29 Nov 1949, Chicago IL) American actor and talk-show host, star of *The Garry Shandling Show.*

Ravi Shankar (7 Apr 1920, Benares [now Varanasi], India) Indian sitar player, composer, and founder of the National Orchestra of India.

Omar Sharif (Michael Shalhoub; 10 Apr 1932, Alexandria, Egypt) Egyptian-born American film star famous for exotic leading roles; his credits include *Lawrence of Arabia* (1962), *Doctor Zhivago* (1965), and *Funny Girl* (1968); he is also a contract-bridge expert.

Ariel Sharon (Ariel Sheinerman; 26 Feb? 1928, Kefar Malal, Palestine [now Israel]) Israeli politician; prime minister of Israel from 2001.

K. Barry Sharpless (28 Apr 1941, Philadelphia PA) American chemist; co-winner of the Nobel Prize for Chemistry, 2001, for development of chiral catalysts.

Al Sharpton (3 Oct 1954, New York NY) American political activist and civil rights leader.

William Shatner (22 Mar 1931, Montreal, QC, Canada) Canadian TV actor, author, and personality famous as Captain Kirk in the *Star Trek* series and films.

Bernard Shaw (22 May 1940, Chicago IL) American TV journalist and newsman.

Vernon Shaw (13 May 1930, Dominica) West Indian politician; president of Dominica from 1998.

Martin Sheen (Ramon Estevez; 3 Aug 1940, Dayton OH) American stage, film, and TV actor.

Judith Sheindlin (21 Oct 1942, Brooklyn NY) American TV judge (*Judge Judy*).

Sam Shepard (Samuel Shepard Rogers; 5 Nov 1943, Fort Sheridan IL) American playwright and actor whose plays adroitly blend images of the American West, Pop motifs, science fiction, and other elements of popular and youth culture.

Cynthia Morris ("Cindy") Sherman (19 Jan 1954, Glen Ridge NJ) American photographer who is known for her elaborately "disguised" self-portraits that comment on social role-playing and sexual stereotypes.

Eduard Shevardnadze (25 Jan 1928, Mamati, Lanchkhuti region, Georgia) Georgian politician; first president of independent Georgia, from 1992.

Brooke (Christa) Shields (31 May 1965, New York NY) American fashion model and motion-picture and TV actress.

Shinjiro Shimizu, Japanese corporate executive; CEO of Mitsui & Co. from 2000.

Jennifer Mary ("Jenny") Shipley (4 Feb 1952, Gore, New Zealand) New Zealand politician; leader of National Party and prime minister of New Zealand, 1997–99.

Hideki Shirakawa (20 Aug 1936, Tokyo, Japan) Japanese chemist; co-winner of the Nobel Prize in Chemistry, 2000, for work in electrically conductive polymers.

Vandana Shiva (1952, Dehra Dun, India) Indian biologist and social activist; director of the Research Foundation on Science, Technology, and Ecology in India.

Eugene Shoemaker (28 Apr 1928, Los Angeles CA) American astrogeologist; with Carolyn Shoemaker and David Levy, discovered Shoemaker-Levy 9 comet.

Bobby Short (Robert Waltrip Short; 15 Sep 1926, Danville IL) American jazz singer and pianist.

Martin Short (26 Mar 1950, Hamilton ON) American actor and comedian famous for impersonations.

Wayne Shorter (25 Aug 1933, Newark NJ) American jazz saxophonist and composer.

Elaine Showalter (21 Jan 1941, Cambridge MA) American feminist literary critic and teacher.

Etsuhiko Shoyama (c. 1937) Japanese corporate executive; CEO of Hitachi, Ltd. from 1999.

Eunice Mary Kennedy Shriver (10 Jul 1921, Brookline MA) American founder of the Special Olympics.

Elisabeth Shue (6 Oct 1963, South Orange NJ) American actress who successfully transitioned from teen films; she won critical acclaim for *Leaving Las Vegas* (1995).

Than Shwe (1933, Kyaukse, Burma [now Myanmar]) Myanmar (Burmese) military leader; head of state and government of Myanmar from 23 Apr 1992.

M. Night Shyamalan (6 Aug 1970, Pondicherry, India) American film director and screenwriter made famous by *The Sixth Sense* (1999).

John W. Sidgmore (c. 1950) American corporate executive; CEO of WorldCom, Inc. from 2002.

Thomas M. Siebel (February 1953, Chicago IL) American corporate executive; founder and CEO of Siebel Systems from 1993.

Don Siegelman (24 Feb 1946, Mobile AL) American Democratic politician; governor of Alabama from 1999.

Anton Sikharulidze (21 Oct 1976, Leningrad, USSR [now St. Petersburg, Russia]) Russian pairs skater (with Yelena Berezhnaya); shared the 2002 Olympic gold medal with Canadians Salé and Pelletier.

Beverly Sills (Belle Miriam Silverman; 25 May 1929, New York City NY) American operatic soprano.

Álvaro Silva Calderón (9 Jun 1929, Teresén, Monagas state, Venezuela) Venezuelan international official; secretary-general of the Organization of Petroleum Exporting Countries from 2002.

Horace Silver (Horace Ward Martin Tavares Silver; 2 Sep 1928, Norwalk CT) American jazz pianist, composer, and bandleader.

Queen Silvia (Silvia Renate Sommerlath; 23 Dec 1943, Heidelberg, Germany) Swedish royal and social activist, queen consort of King Carl XVI Gustaf of Sweden.

Simeon II (16 Jun 1937, Sofia, Bulgaria) Bulgarian royal; the last king of Bulgaria (1943–46) and prime minister from 2001.

Charles Simic (9 May 1938, Belgarde, Yugoslavia) Yugoslav-born American poet noted for his poetic commentaries on the dearth of spirituality in contemporary life.

Konstantinos Georgiou ("Kostas") Simitis (23 Jun 1936, Athens, Greece) Greek politician and prime minister of Greece from 1996.

Carly Simon (25 Jun 1945, New York NY) American singer and songwriter.

(Marvin) Neil Simon (4 Jul 1927, New York NY) American playwright, screenwriter, television writer, and librettist who was one of the most popular playwrights in the history of the American theater.

Paul Simon (13 Oct 1941, Newark NJ) American singer and songwriter.

Nina Simone (Eunice Kathleen Waymon; 21 Feb 1933, Tryon NC) American blues, R&B, and jazz singer and arranger.

Jessica Simpson (10 Jul 1980, Dallas TX) American dance-pop singer.

Sirhan Bishara Sirhan (19 Mar 1944, Jerusalem, Palestine) Palestinian assassin; convicted of the killing of Sen. Robert F. Kennedy.

Ricky Skaggs (18 Jul 1954, Cordell KY) American bluegrass and country musician.

Antonio Skármeta (7 Nov 1940, Antofagasta, Chile) Chilean novelist and screenwriter.

Slash (Saul Hudson; 23 Jul 1965, Stoke-on-Trent, Staffordshire, England) British rock guitarist (of Guns N' Roses).

Leonard Slatkin (Los Angeles CA) American conductor; music director of the National Symphony Orchestra from 1995.

Grace Slick (Grace Barnett Wing; 30 Oct 1939, Evanston IL) American rock singer (of Jefferson Airplane, etc.).

Dame Maggie Smith (28 Dec 1934, Ilford, Essex, England) British stage and motion-picture actress, noted for her poignancy and wit in comic roles.

Dean Edwards Smith (28 Feb 1931, Emporia KS) American basketball coach (University of North Carolina) with the most wins in collegiate basketball history (879).

Gregg Smith (21 Aug 1931, Chicago IL) American choral conductor.

Jennifer Smith (1947) Bermudan politician; premier of Bermuda from 1998.

Jimmy Smith (James Oscar Smith; 8 Dec 1925, Norristown PA) American jazz organist.

Patti Smith (30 Dec 1946, Chicago IL) American musician; poet; visual artist.

Will Smith (Willard Christopher Smith, Jr.; 25 Sep 1968, Philadelphia PA) American rap singer and actor on TV (The Fresh Prince of Bel Air) and in films, such as Men in Black I (1997) and II (2002).

Phoebe Snow (Phoebe Laub; 17 Jul 1952, Teaneck NJ) American jazz singer and composer.

Gary (Sherman) Snyder (8 May 1930, San Francisco CA) American poet early identified with the Beat movement and, from the late 1960s, an important spokesman for the concerns of communal living and ecological activism.

Tom Snyder (12 May 1936, Milwaukee WI) American broadcast journalist and TV personality.

Angelo Cardinal Sodano (23 Nov 1927, Isola d'Asto, Italy) Italian secretary of state of the Vatican from 1990.

Steven Soderbergh (14 Jan 1963, Atlanta GA) American motion-picture director commercially and critically acclaimed; won an Academy Award for directing Traffic in 2000.

Queen Sofia (Princess Sophie of Greece; Sofia de Grecia y Hannover; 5 Jan 1938, Athens, Greece) Spanish royal; queen consort of King Juan Carlos of Spain.

Javier Solana Madariaga (14 Jul 1942, Madrid, Spain) Spanish politician and NATO secretary-general, 1995–99; president of the Western European Union from 1999.

Howard Solomon (12 Aug 1927, New York NY) American corporate executive; CEO of Forest Laboratories, Inc. from 1977.

Aleksandr (Isayevich) Solzhenitsyn (11 Dec 1918, Kislovodsk, Russia, USSR) Russian novelist and historian who was awarded the Nobel Prize for Literature in 1970.

Sir Michael Somare (9 Apr 1936, Rabaul, East New Britain) Papua-New Guinean politician; the first prime minister of independent Papua New Guinea, 1975–80, a second time in 1982–85, and again from 5 Aug 2002.

Juan Octavio Somavia (21 Apr 1941, Chile) Chilean international civil servant; director-general of the International Labour Organization from 1999.

Stephen (Joshua) Sondheim (22 Mar 1930, New York NY) American composer and lyricist for Broadway musical theatre.

Queen Sonja (Sonja Haraldsen; 4 Jul 1937, Oslo, Norway) Norwegian royal; queen consort of King Harald V of Norway.

Susan Sontag (16 Jan 1933, New York NY) American intellectual and writer best known for her essays on modern culture; 2001 Jerusalem Prize winner.

Saufatu Sopoanga (Tuvalu) Tuvalu politician; prime minister of Tuvalu from 2 Aug 2002.

Kevin Sorbo (24 Sep 1958, Mound MN) American actor best known as Hercules on television.

Annika Sörenstam (9 Oct 1970, Stockholm, Sweden) Swedish golfer; holds the LPGA 18- and 72-hole records.

George Soros (12 Aug 1930, Budapest, Hungary) Hungarian-born American financier and philanthropist.

Mira Sorvino (28 Sep 1967, Tenafly NJ) American motion-picture actress who gained fame from starring in Mighty Aphrodite (1995).

Sammy Sosa (Samuel Peralta Sosa; 12 Nov 1968, San Pedro de Macoris, Dominican Republic) Dominican baseball outfielder for the Chicago Cubs and home-run hitter; the only player to hit more than 60 homers three times (1998, 1999, 2001).

David H(ackett) Souter (17 Sep 1939, Melrose MA) American jurist; associate justice of the US Supreme Court from 1990.

Sissy Spacek (Mary Elizabeth Spacek; 25 Dec 1949, Quitman TX) American film actress in powerful character roles who won an Academy Award for best actress in 1980 (Coal Miner's Daughter).

Kevin Spacey (Kevin Matthew Fowler; 26 Jul 1959, South Orange NJ) American stage and film actor who became a popular leading man in *American Beauty* (1999).

David Spade (22 Jul 1964, Birmingham MI) American comedian, actor; current star of series *Just Shoot Me*.

Otis Spann (21 Mar 1930, Jackson MS) American blues pianist and singer.

Britney (Jean) Spears (2 Dec 1981, Kentwood LA) American pop singer.

Phil Spector (26 Dec 1940, New York NY) American music producer.

George Speight (Naivicula, Fiji) Fijian businessman and coup leader.

Aaron Spelling (22 Apr 1923, Dallas TX) American TV producer.

A. Michael Spence (1943, Montclair NJ) American economist; co-winner of the Nobel Prize in Economic Sciences, 2001, for work in the theory of markets with asymmetrical Information.

Vladimir Spidla (22 Apr 1951, Prague, Czechoslovakia) Czech politician; prime minister of the Czech Republic from 12 Jul 2002.

Steven Spielberg (18 Dec 1947, Cincinnati OH) American film director, widely regarded as one of the greatest of all time.

Gayatri Chakravorty Spivak (24 Feb 1942, Calcutta, [now Kolcata] India) Indian postcolonial literary theorist and professor of comparative literature.

Jerry Springer (13 Feb 1944, London, England) British-born American TV personality, host of a controversial, highly physical talk show.

Bruce Springsteen (23 Sep 1949, Freehold NJ) American rock singer and songwriter who became the arohctypal rock performer of the 1970s and '80s and who enjoyed a new surge of popularity in 2002 with a new album, *The Rising*, that treated the aftermath of 11 September, and a concert tour.

Sylvester Stallone (6 Jul 1946, New York NY) American motion-picture actor and director; best known for macho roles such as Rocky and Rambo.

Ralph (Edmond) Stanley (25 Feb 1927, Stratton VA) American bluegrass songwriter, singer, and banjo player.

Maureen Stapleton (21 Jun 1925, Troy NY) American character actress who won an Academy Award in 1981 for portraying Emma Goldman in *Reds*.

Bart Starr (9 Jan 1934, Montgomery AL) American football player; legendary quarterback for the Green Bay Packers who led the team to two Super Bowl victories.

Kenneth W. Starr (21 Jul 1946, Vernon TX) American lawyer; independent counsel in the Clinton-era Whitewater investigation.

Ringo Starr (Richard Starkey, Jr.; 7 Jul 1940, Liverpool, Merseyside, England) British singer and musician (drummer with the Beatles).

Danielle Steele (14 Aug 1947, New York NY) American author of best-selling novels.

Shelby Steele (1 Jan 1946, Chicago IL) American critic and scholar of race issues who has opposed quota-based affirmative action.

Mary Steenburgen (8 Feb 1953, Newport AK) American talented film and TV actress and producer often cast in supporting roles.

Konstantinos Dimitriou ("Kostis") Stefanopoulos (15 Aug 1926, Patras, Greece) Greek politician; president of Greece from 1995.

Rod Steiger (Rodney Steven Steiger; 14 Apr 1925, Westhampton NY—9 Jul 2002, Los Angeles CA),

American film actor of great intensity whose works include *On the Waterfront* (1954), *Oklahoma!* (1955), *The Pawnbroker* (1964), and *In the Heat of the Night* (1967).

George Michael Steinbrenner III (4 Jul 1930, Rocky River OH) American baseball executive famous for his authoritarian rule of the New York Yankees from 1973.

Gloria Steinem (25 Mar 1934, Toledo OH) American feminist, political activist, and editor.

Frank Stella (12 May 1936, Malden MA) American painter, a leading figure in the Minimal art movement.

George Stephanopoulos (10 Feb 1961, Fall River MA) American journalist, former presidential adviser.

Howard Stern (12 Jan 1954, Roosevelt NY) American radio and TV "shock jock," actor and author.

Sir Sigmund Sternberg (2 Jun 1921, Budapest, Hungary) Hungarian-born British philanthropist and businessman; Templeton Prize winner, 1998.

John Paul Stevens (20 Apr 1920, Chicago IL) American jurist; associate justice of the US Supreme Court from 1975.

Dave Stewart (9 Sep 1952, Sunderland, England) British rock songwriter and guitarist (of the Eurythmics).

Jon Stewart (28 Nov 1962, New York NY) American actor, writer, and comedian; host of *The Daily Show* on TV.

Martha Stewart (Martha Helen Kostyra; 3 Aug 1941, Nutley NJ) American homemaking adviser, TV personality, and entrepreneur.

Rod Stewart (Roderick David Stewart; 10 Jan 1945, London, England) British singer whose soulful, raspy voice has graced rock and pop hits since the late 1960s.

Sir Jackie Stewart (John Young Stewart; 11 Jun 1939, Dumbartonshire, Scotland) Scottish Formula 1 race-car driver who scored 27 Grand Prix wins, 1965–73.

Joseph E. Stiglitz (9 Feb 1943, Gary IN) American economist; co-winner of the Nobel Prize in Economic Sciences, 2001, for work in the theory of markets with asymmetrical information.

Stephen Stills (3 Jan 1945, Dallas TX) American rock and pop singer and guitarist.

R.L. Stine (Robert Lawrence Stine; 8 Oct 1943, Columbus OH) American author of children's books.

Sting (Gordon Matthew Sumner; 2 Oct 1951, Newcastle upon Tyne, England) British musician, singer, songwriter, and actor.

(John) Michael Stipe (4 Jan 1960, Decatur GA) American rock singer (of REM).

Karlheinz Stockhausen (22 Aug 1928, Mödrath, near Cologne, Germany) German composer, an important creator and theoretician of electronic and serial music who strongly influenced avant-garde composers.

Edmund Stoiber (29 Sep 1941, Oberaudorf, Bavaria, Germany) German politician and Christian Socialist Union party leader; premier of Bavaria.

Elvis Stojko (22 Mar 1972, Newmarket, ON, Canada) Canadian figure skater known for his athleticism; he was the first to achieve a quadruple/double combination (1991) and a quadruple/triple (1997).

Oliver Stone (15 Sep 1946, New York NY) American director, writer, and producer of films with often controversial content; he won Academy Awards for directing in 1986 (*Platoon*) and 1989 (*Born on the Fourth of July*).

Sharon Stone (10 Mar 1958, Meadville PA) American actress and model made famous by the film *Basic Instinct* (1992).

Sly Stone (Sylvester Stewart; 15 Mar 1944, Denton TX) American soul singer and musician.

Noel Paul Stookey (30 Nov 1937, Baltimore MD) American singer and songwriter (of Peter Paul & Mary).

George Strait (18 May 1952, Pearsall TX) American country singer.

Mark Strand (11 Apr 1934, Summerside, PE, Canada) Canadian writer whose poetry, noted for its surreal quality, explores the boundaries of the self and the external world.

Jozef Straus (1946, Velke Kapusany, Czechoslovakia) Czechoslovakian-born American corporate executive; CEO of JDS Uniphase, Inc. (from merger, 1999).

Jack Straw (3 Aug 1946, Essex, England) British politician.

Meryl Streep (Mary Louise Streep; 22 Jun 1949, Summit NJ) American film actress in serious roles who won Academy Awards for best supporting actress in 1979 (*Kramer vs. Kramer*) and best actress in 1982 (*Sophie's Choice*).

Picabo Street (3 Apr 1971, Triumph ID) American Alpine skier; two-time Olympic medalist and World Cup winner.

Barbra Streisand (Barbara Joan Streisand; 24 Apr 1942, Brooklyn NY) American singer, actress, and film director.

Susan Stroman (17 Oct 1954, Wilmington DE) American theater director, famous for the recent run of *The Producers*.

William Styron (11 Jun 1925, Newport News VA) American novelist noted for his treatment of tragic themes and his use of a rich, classical prose style.

Juan Manuel Suárez del Toro Rivero (1952?, Spain) Spanish international official; president of the International Federation of Red Cross and Red Crescent Societies from 2001.

Ariano Suassuna (16 Jun 1927, João Pessoa, Brazil) Brazilian dramatist and fiction writer.

Morton Subotnick (14 Apr 1933, Los Angeles CA) American composer of electronic music.

Suharto (8 Jun 1921, Kemusu Argamaulja, Java, Dutch East Indies [now Indonesia]) Indonesian army officer and political leader who was president of Indonesia, 1967–98.

Anna Sui (1955, Dearborn MI) American fashion designer whose clothing and cosmetics reflect a rock-music style mixed with vintage-inspired designs.

Megawati Sukarnoputri (23 Jan 1947, Jakarta, Indonesia) Indonesian politician; president of Indonesia from 23 Jul 2001; she is the daughter of Sukarno, the founder of independent Indonesia.

Andrew Sullivan (10 Aug 1963, South Godstone, England) English-born American journalist, political commentator, and editor of *The New Republic* (1991–96).

Arthur Ochs Sulzberger (5 Feb 1926, New York NY) American newspaper executive, publisher of the *New York Times* from 1963.

Frederick Sumaye (29 May 1950, Hanang district, Arusha region, Tanganyika [now Tanzania]) Tanzanian politician; prime minister of Tanzania from 1995.

Donna Summer (LaDonna Andrea Gaines; 31 Dec 1948, Boston MA) American singer.

Patricia Head Summitt (14 Jun 1952, Henrietta TN) American basketball coach, longtime coach of the winning University of Tennessee Lady Volunteers teams.

Sun Myung Moon (6 Jan 1920, Kwangju Sangsa Ri, P'yongan-puk province, Korea [now in North Korea]) Korean evangelist and founder of the Unification Church.

Per Olof Sundman (4 Sep 1922, Vaxholm, Sweden) Swedish novelist.

Don Sundquist (15 Mar 1936, Moline IL) American Republican politician; governor of Tennessee from 1995.

Tauese P.F. Sunia (29 Aug 1941, Fagatogo, American Samoa) American Democratic politician; governor of American Samoa from 1997.

Cass R. Sunstein (1954) American constitutional scholar and law professor.

Masayuki Suo (29 Oct 1956, Tokyo, Japan) Japanese film director who made his US professional debut in *Shall We Dansu?* (1996; *Shall We Dance?*).

(Lucia Francisca) Susi Susanti (11 Feb 1971, Tasikmalaya, Indonesia) Indonesian badminton player.

Ichiro Suzuki (22 Oct 1973, Aichi, Japan) Japanese baseball player, right fielder for the Orix BlueWave of Japan's Pacific League, who moved to the US to play with the Seattle Mariners, named American League MVP and Rookie of the Year in 2001.

Hilary Swank (30 Jul 1974, Lincoln NE) American motion-picture actress most noted for her performance in *Boys Don't Cry* (1999).

John J. Sweeney (5 May 1934, New York NY) American labor leader; president of the AFL-CIO from 1995.

Jane Swift (24 Feb 1965, North Adams MA) American Republican politician; governor of Massachusetts from 2001.

Tuanku Syed Sirajuddin ibni al-Marhum Syed Putra Jamalullail (16 May 1943, Arau, Perlis, British Malaya [now Malaysia]) Malaysian royal; yang di-pertuan agong (paramount ruler) of Malaysia from 13 Dec 2001.

Wislawa Symborska (2 Jul 1923, Bnin [now Kornik], Poland) Polish poet known for her strong humanism; she received the Nobel Prize for Literature, 1996.

Gabor Szabo (8 Mar 1936, Budapest, Hungary) Hungarian jazz guitarist and composer.

Lew(is Barry) Tabackin (26 Mar 1940, Philadelphia PA) American jazz tenor saxophonist.

Bob Taft (8 Jan 1942, Boston MA) American Republican politician; governor of Ohio from 1999.

Paul Tagliabue (24 Nov 1940, Jersey City NJ) American sports executive; commissioner of the National Football League from 1989.

Maria Tallchief (24 Jan 1925, Fairfax OK) American ballerina.

Vivienne Tam (Guangzhou, China) Chinese fashion designer who combines Eastern and Western style and traditional and contemporary style in her work.

Amy Tan (19 Feb 1952, Oakland CA) American author of novels about Chinese-American women and the immigrant experience.

Makiko Tanaka (14 Jan 1944, Niigata prefecture, Japan) Japanese politician; foreign minister of Japan, 2001–02.

Mamadou Tandja (1938) Nigerois politician; president of Niger from 1999.

Yoshio Taniguchi (17 Oct 1937, Tokyo, Japan) Japanese architect who became internationally prominent in 1997 when his design for the planned expansion of the Museum of Modern Art in New York City was selected in a competition.

Malietoa Tanumafili II (4 Jan 1913, Apia, Western Samoa) Samoan royal; O le Ao o le Malo of Samoa from 1963.

Quentin Tarantino (27 Mar 1973, Knoxville TN) American film director who gained widespread recognition for *Pulp Fiction* (1994).

Vasile Tarlev (9 Oct 1963, Bascalia, Moldovan SSR, USSR [now Moldova]) Moldovan politician; prime minister of Moldova from 2001.

Brandon Tartikoff (13 Jan 1949, Long Island NY) American TV executive

Grady Tate (14 Jan 1932, Durham NC) American jazz drummer and singer.

King Taufa'ahau Tupou IV (4 Jul 1918, Nuku'alofa, Tonga) Tongan royal; king of Tonga from 1965.

Sir John Tavener (28 Jan 1944, London, England) British composer whose works were inspired by sacred and spiritual texts and drew from Russian, Byzantine, and Greek influences.

Maaouya Ould Sidi Ahmed Taya (1941, Atar, French West Africa [now Mauritania]) Mauritanian politician; president of Mauritania from 1992.

Cecil (Percival) Taylor (15 Mar 1933, New York NY) American jazz pianist and composer, the leading free-jazz pianist.

Charles (Ghankay) Taylor (27 Jan 1948, Liberia) Liberian coup leader and president from 1997.

Elizabeth Taylor (27 Feb 1932, London, England) American famous film actress of great distinction noted for emotionally volatile characters.

James (Vernon) Taylor (12 Mar 1948, Boston MA) American pop singer and songwriter

Niki Taylor (5 Mar 1975, Fort Lauderdale FL) American fashion model.

Paul (Belville) Taylor (29 Jul 1930, Wilkinsburg PA) American modern dancer and choreographer.

Dame Kiri (Janette) Te Kanawa (6 Mar 1944, Gisborne, North Island, New Zealand) New Zealand operatic soprano.

Te Ata-i Rangi-Kahu Koroki Te Rata Mahuta Tawhiao Potatau Te Wherowhero (1931) New Zealand queen of the Maori community from 1966.

Edward Teller (Ede Teller; 15 Jan 1908, Budapest, Hungary, Austria-Hungary) Hungarian-born American nuclear physicist who participated in the production of the first atomic bomb (1945) and who led the development of the world's first thermonuclear weapon, the hydrogen bomb.

Sachin Ramesh Tendulkar (24 Apr 1973, Bombay [now Mumbai], India) Indian cricket batsman.

George John Tenet (5 Jan 1953, Queens NY) American government official; Director of Central Intelligence and CIA director from 1997.

Valentina (Vladimirovna) Tereshkova (married name Nikolayeva; 6 Mar 1937, Maslennikovo, Russia, USSR) Soviet cosmonaut, the first woman to travel into space (1963).

Bryn Terfel (Jones; 9 Nov 1965, near Pant Glas, North Wales) Welsh operatic bass-baritone.

Louis ("Studs") Terkel (16 May 1912, New York NY) American author, radio host, and oral historian.

Clark Terry (14 Dec 1920, St. Louis MO) American jazz trumpeter and flügelhornist.

Thaksin Shinawatra (26 Jul 1949, Chiangmai, Thailand) Thai politician; prime minister of Thailand from 2001.

Sheikh Hamad ibn Khalifah ath-Thani (1950, Doha, Qatar) royal; emir of Qatar from 1995.

Twyla Tharp (1 Jul 1941, Portland IN) American dancer, director, and choreographer noted for her innovation and for the humor she brought to much of her work.

Dame Margaret Thatcher (Margaret Hilda Roberts; 13 Oct 1925, Grantham, Lincolnshire, England) British Conservative politician and prime minister (1979–90), Europe's first woman prime minister.

Mikis Theodorakis (29 July 1925, Chios, Greece) Greek composer and political activist whose film scores and dramatic music often deal with Greek themes.

Charlize Theron (7 Aug 1975, Benoni, South Africa) South African actress just gaining fame for playing emotional, strong women.

Thich Nhat Hanh (1926, central Vietnam) Vietnamese Buddhist monk, pacifist, and teacher.

Clarence Thomas (23 Jun 1948, Pinpoint community, near Savannah GA) American jurist; associate justice of the US Supreme Court from 1991.

Michael Tilson Thomas (21 Dec 1944, Hollywood CA) American conductor and composer; music director of the San Francisco Symphony from 1995.

Emma Thompson (15 Apr 1959, London, England) American intellectual motion-picture actress known for heavy dramatic roles and period pieces.

Hunter S(tockton) Thompson (18 Jul 1937/39, Louisville KY) American "gonzo" journalist.

Jonny Thompson (26 Feb 1973, Dover NH) American swimmer; 10-time Olympic medalist (5 gold) in the 1992, 1996, and 2000 Games.

Tommy Thompson (19 Nov 1941, Elroy WI) American government official; former Wisconsin governor; US Secretary of Health and Human Services from 2001.

James Thomson (20 Dec 1958, Chicago IL) American cell biologist; stem cell researcher and the first person to isolate stem cells from human embryos.

Richard Lewis (Dick) Thornburgh, American government official; served as attorney general in the cabinets of presidents Ronald Reagan and George H.W. Bush.

Billy Bob Thornton (4 Aug 1955, Hot Springs AR) American director and actor whose work includes *Sling Blade* (1996), *Monster's Ball* (2001), and *Daddis* (2001).

Ian Thorpe ("The Thorpedo"; 13 Oct 1982, Sydney, Australia) Australian swimmer; won three gold and two silver medals in the 2000 Games, then won six gold medals and set four world records in the 2001 world championships.

Uma Thurman (29 Apr 1970, Boston MA) American film actress in lead and supporting roles.

J. Strom Thurmond (5 Dec 1902, Edgefield SC) American Republican politician; senator from South Carolina from 1954, the longest-serving senator in US history.

Cheryl Tiegs (25 Sep 1947, Breckenridge MN) American fashion model.

Tiffany (Tiffany Darwisch; 2 Oct 1971, Norwalk CA) American pop singer.

Mel Tillis (Lonnie Melvin Tillis; 8 Aug 1932, Tampa FL) American singer and songwriter.

Pam(ela Yvonne) Tillis (1957, Plant City FL) American county singer.

Charles Tilly (20 May 1929, Lombard IL) American social scientist and historian.

Teburoro Tito (25 Aug 1953) Kiribati politician; president of Kiribati from 1994.

Pramoedya Ananta Toer (20 Feb 1925, Blora, Java, Dutch East Indies [now in Indonesia]) Indonesian novelist and short-story writer, the preeminent prose writer of postindependence Indonesia.

Alejandro Toledo (Manrique) (28 Mar 1946, Cabana, Ancash department, Peru) Peruvian politician; president of Peru from 2001.

Marisa Tomei (4 Dec 1964, Brooklyn NY) American motion-picture actress whose breakthrough performance came in *My Cousin Vinny* (1992).

David Toms (4 Jan 1967, Monroe LA) American professional golfer.

Linus (Benedict) Torvalds (28 Dec 1969, Helsinki, Finland) Finnish-born computer scientist who developed the Linux operating system.

Princess Toshi (Toshi no miya Aiko Naishinno; 1 Dec 2001, Tokyo, Japan) Japanese royal; daughter of Crown Prince Naruhito and Crown Princess Masako.

Amadou Toumani Touré (1948, Mpoti, French West Africa [now Mali]) Malian politician; president of Mali, 1991–92 and from 8 Jun 2002.

Emanuel Tov (1941, Amsterdam, The Netherlands) Dutch classical scholar; director of the Dead Sea Scrolls project.

James Anthony Traficant, Jr. (8 May 1941, Youngstown OH) American Republican politician; US representative from Ohio; indicted on several charges in May 2002, including bribery, and expelled from the House of Representatives.

Boris Trajkovski (25 Jun 1956, Strumica, Macedonia, Yugoslavia) Macedonian politician; president of Macedonia from 1999.

Tran Duc Luong (5 May 1937, Quang Ngai province, French Indochina [now Vietnam]) Vietnamese politician; president of Vietnam from 1997.

Tomas Tranströmer (15 Apr 1931, Stockholm, Sweden) Swedish lyrical poet noted for his resonant and strangely suggestive imagery.

Mary Travers (7 Nov 1937, Louisville KY) American folk singer and guitarist (of Peter Paul & Mary).

Randy Travis (Randy Traywick; 4 May 1959, Marshville NC) American country and western singer, songwriter, and actor.

John Travolta (18 Feb 1955, Englewood NJ) American actor known for TV roles and trendsetting films; he later began a career revival with *Pulp Fiction* (1994).

Calvin Trillin (5 Dec 1935, Kansas City MO) American author, commentator, and occasional poet.

David Trimble (15 Oct 1944, Belfast, Northern Ireland) British (Northern Ireland) politician and first minister of Northern Ireland from 1998; Nobel Peace Prize, 1998.

Donald (John) Trump (14 Jun 1946, New York NY) American real estate executive.

Tohru Tsuji, Japanese corporate executive; president and CEO of Marubeni Corp.

Chris Tucker (31 Aug 1972, Decatur GA) American comedian and actor known for *Rush Hour* films with Jackie Chan.

Tanya (Denise) Tucker (10 Oct 1958, Seminole TX) American country and western singer.

Barry (Emmanuel) Tuckwell (5 Mar 1931, Melbourne, Australia) Australian-born British French horn player.

Tommy Tune (28 Feb 1939, Wichita Falls TX) American musical comedy dancer and actor noted especially for his work on Broadway.

Tung Chee-Hwa (29 May 1937, Shanghai, China) Chinese businessman and chief executive of Hong Kong (now the Hong Kong Special Administrative Region of China) from 1997.

Christy Turlington (2 Jan 1969, Oakland CA) American fashion model.

Charles Wesley Turnbull (5 Feb 1935, St. Thomas, Virgin Islands) American Democratic politician; governor of the Virgin Islands from 1999.

Ike Turner (Izear Luster Turner, Jr.; 5 Nov 1931, Brownsville MS) American rock performer.

Kathleen Turner (19 Jun 1954, Springfield MO) American film star known for her distinctive husky voice.

Ted Turner (Robert Edward Turner III; 19 Nov 1938, Cincinnati OH) American TV executive, sports club owner, sportsman, and philanthropist.

Tina Turner (Anna Mae Bullock; 26 Nov 1939, Nutbush TN) American rock performer.

Scott Turow (12 Apr 1949, Chicago IL) American best-selling novelist, the creator of a genre of crime and suspense novels dealing with law and the legal profession.

Shania Twain (Eileen Regina Edwards; 28 Aug 1965, Windsor, ON, Canada) Canadian country music singer.

Anne Tyler (25 Oct 1941, Minneapolis MN) American novelist and short-story writer whose comedies of manners are marked by compassionate wit and precise details of domestic life.

Liv Tyler (Liv Rundgren; 1 Jul 1977, Portland ME) American actress and model; she emerged after starring in *Stealing Beauty* (1996).

Richard Tyler (22 Sep 1950, Melbourne, Australia) Australian fashion designer noted for his evening gowns.

Steven Tyler (Steven Tallarico; 26 Mar 1948, New York NY) American rock vocalist (of Aerosmith).

(Alfred) McCoy Tyner (later Sulaimon Saud; 11 Dec 1938, Philadelphia PA) American jazz pianist and composer.

Mike Tyson (Michael Gerard Tyson; 30 Jun 1966, New York NY) American boxer; undisputed heavyweight champion, 1987–90.

Shigeji Ueshima (25 Aug 1931) Japanese corporate executive; CEO of Mitsui & Co. Ltd. from 1996.

Robert J. Ulrich (Minneapolis MN) American corporate executive; CEO of Target Corp. from 1994.

Emanuel Ungaro (13 Feb 1933, Aix-en-Provence, France) French fashion designer whose creations are characterized by mixtures of bold patterns.

John (Hoyer) Updike (18 Mar 1932, Shillington PA) American writer of novels, short stories, and poetry.

Dawn Upshaw (17 Jul 1960, Nashville TN) American concert soprano.

Michal Urbaniak (22 Jan 1943, Warsaw, Poland) Polish jazz violinist.

Álvaro Uribe Vélez (4 Jul 1952, Medellin, Colombia) Colombian politician; president of Colombia from August 2002.

Leon (Marcus) Uris (3 Aug 1924, Baltimore MD) American novelist.

Usher (Usher Raymond IV; 14 Oct 1978, Chattanooga TN) American R&B singer.

Yoshio Utsumi (14 Aug 1942, Shikoku island, Japan) Japanese director-general of the International Telecommunications Union from 1999.

Jochem Uytdehaage (9 Jul 1976, Utrecht, The Netherlands) Dutch speed skater; Olympic gold medalist in the 5,000-m race, 2002.

Brenda Vaccaro (18 Nov 1939, Brooklyn NY) American Broadway and Hollywood star.

Atal Bihari Vajpayee (25 Dec 1924, Gwalior, Madhya Pradesh state, India) Indian politician; prime minister of India in 1996 and from 1998.

Valentino (Garavani) (11 May 1932, Voghera, Italy) Italian fashion designer known for his elegant and classic evening gowns.

Amber Valletta (9 Feb 1974, Tucson AZ) American fashion model and TV host.

Abigail Van Buren (Pauline Ester Friedman; 4 Jul 1918, Sioux City IA) American advice columnist.

José Van Dam (Joseph Van Damme; 25 Aug 1940, Brussels, Belgium) Belgian operatic bass.

Dick Van Dyke (13 Dec 1925, West Plains MO) American actor and comedian best remembered as the star of The Dick Van Dyke Show and, more recently, for the Diagnosis Murder series on TV.

Eddie Van Halen (Edward van Halen; 26 Jan 1957, Nijmegen, The Netherlands) American rock guitarist (of Van Halen).

Martine Van Hamel (16 Nov 1945, Brussels, Belgium) Belgian dancer and leading choreographer for the American Ballet Theatre.

Gloria Vanderbilt (Gloria Morgan Vanderbilt; 20 Feb 1924, New York NY) American fashion designer, artist, author, and heiress whose fashion career is notable for introducing designer jeans.

Luther Vandross (20 Apr 1951, New York NY) American R&B singer and songwriter.

(Jorge) Mario (Pedro) Vargas Llosa (28 Mar 1936, Arequipa, Peru) Peruvian novelist and presidential candidate; winner of the Cervantes Prize in 1994.

Harold (Eliot) Varmus (18 Dec 1939, Oceanside NY) American virologist; co-winner of Nobel Prize for Physiology or Medicine, 1989; director of the National Institutes of Health, 1993–99.

Naná Vasconcelos (2 Aug 1944, Recife, Brazil) Brazilian jazz percussionist and virtuoso player of the berimbau.

Daniel Lucius Vasella (1953, Fribourg?, Switzerland) Swiss corporate executive and CEO of the Novartis Group (from merger, 1996).

Jeroen van der Veer (1947, Utrecht, The Netherlands) Dutch corporate executive; CFO of Royal Dutch Shell Group (Netherlands).

Suzanne Vega (11 Jul 1959, Santa Monica CA) American pop songwriter and singer.

Martinius J.G. Veltman (27 Jun 1931, Waalwijk, The Netherlands) Dutch physicist; shared the Nobel Prize for Physics 1999, for developing a way to predict mathematically the properties both of subatomic particles and the forces that hold them together.

Helen (Hennessy) Vendler (1933, Boston MA) American poetry critic and university professor.

Ann Veneman (29 Jun 1949, Modesto CA) American government official; US Secretary of Agriculture from 2001.

(Runaldo) Ronald Venetiaan (18 Jun 1936, Paramaribo, Dutch Guiana [now Suriname]) Surinamese politician; president of Suriname, 1991–96 and from 2000.

Maxim Vengerov (20 Aug 1974, Novosibirsk, USSR [now in Russia]) Russian-born violinist.

J. Craig Venter (14 Oct 1946, Salt Lake City UT) American geneticist and researcher into the human genome, founder of Celera Genomics.

Jesse Ventura (Jesse George Janos; "The Body"; 15 Jul 1951, Minneapolis MN) American professional wrestler and independent politician; governor of Minnesota from 1999.

Guy Verhofstadt (11 Apr 1953, Dendermonde, Belgium) Belgian politician; prime minister of Belgium from 1999.

Donatella Versace (1955, Reggio di Calabria, Italy) Italian fashion designer who took over as creative director at her brother Gianni Versace's design house after he was murdered in 1997.

Angela Vía (29 Dec 1981, Raymondville TX) American pop singer.

Princess Victoria (Victoria Ingrid Alice Desiree; 14 Jul 1977, Stockholm, Sweden) Swedish royal; heiress to the throne of Sweden.

Vaira Vike-Freiberga (1 Dec 1937, Riga, Latvia) Canadian-Latvian folklorist and politician; president of Latvia from 1999.

Bob Vila (20 Jun 1946, Miami FL) American host of TV shows about house restoration and repair, This Old House, 1979-89, and Home Again with Bob Vila, from 1990.

Edward Villella (1 Oct 1936, New York NY) American ballet dancer and choreographer.

Kaspar Villiger (5 Feb 1941, Sins, Switzerland) Swiss politician; president of Switzerland, 1995 and 2002.

Tom Vilsack (13 Dec 1950, Pittsburgh PA) American Democratic politician; governor of Iowa from January 1999.

Miroslav Ladislav Vitous (6 Dec 1947, Prague, Czechoslovakia [now Czech Rep.]) Czech jazz bassist.

Jon Voight (29 Dec 1938, Yonkers NY) American character actor remembered for his breakthrough role in Midnight Cowboy (1969).

Diane von Furstenberg (Diane Simone Michelle Halfin; 31 Dec 1946, Brussels, Belgium) Belgian-born American fashion designer who made her name in the 1970s with the wrap dress and successfully relaunched it in the '90s.

Frederica Von Stade (1 Jun 1945, Somerville NJ) American mezzo-soprano.

Vladimir Voronin (25 May 1941, Corjova, near Chisinau, [Moldova]) Moldovan politician, president of Moldova from 2001.

Linda Wachner (3 Feb 1946, New York NY) American apparel industry executive; chairwoman and CEO of Warnaco Group, Inc. and Authentic Fitness Corp.; the first woman to lead a Fortune 500 company.

Norio Wada, Japanese corporate executive; CEO of Nippon Telegraph & Telephone from 2002.

Abdoulaye Wade (29 May 1926, Kébémer, French West Africa [now Senegal]) Senegalese politician; president of Senegal from 2000.

G. Richard Wagoner, Jr. (9 Feb 1953, Wilmington DE) American corporate executive; CEO of General Motors Corp. from 2000.

Tom Waits (Thomas Alan Waits; 7 Dec 1949, Pomona CA) American singer, songwriter, and film actor.

Jan-Ove Waldner (3 Oct 1965, Sweden) Swedish table tennis player.

Lech Walesa (29 Sep 1943, Popowo, near Wloclawek, Poland) Polish politician; president of Poland, 1990–95; Nobel Peace Prize, 1983.

Alice (Malsenior) Walker (9 Feb 1944, Eatonton GA) American writer whose novels, short stories, and poems are noted for their insightful treatment of African American culture; her novels, most notably The Color Purple (1982), focus on women.

Mike Wallace (Myron Leon Wallace; 9 May 1918, Brookline MA) American TV journalist.

Immanuel Wallerstein (28 Sep 1930, New York NY) American sociologist of systems theory.

Courtney (Andrew) Walsh (30 Oct 1962, Kingston, Jamaica) Jamaican cricket bowler who in 2000 became the highest wicket-taker in Test history.

Robert D. Walter (Columbus OH) American corporate executive; founder and CEO of Cardinal Health, Inc. from 1971.

Barbara Walters (25 Sep 1931, Boston MA) American TV journalist, interviewer, and anchorwoman.

Jim C. Walton, American business executive; No. 6 on Forbes magazine's 2002 list of the world's richest persons; chairman and CEO of the Arvest Group.

Vera Wang (27 June 1949, New York NY) American fashion designer known for her elegant and luxurious wedding gowns.

Wang Liqin (18 Jun 1978, Harbin, China) Chinese table tennis player, the top-ranked man in mid-2002.

Wang Nan (23 Oct 1978, Liaoning, China) Chinese table tennis player, the top-ranked woman in mid-2002.

Jigme Singye Wangchuk (11 Nov 1955, Dechchench-holing Palace, Thimphu, Bhutan) Bhutanese royal; king of Bhutan from 1972.

Lloyd Ward (1949, Romulus MI) American corporate executive; CEO of Maytag Co. from 1999; CEO of the US Olympic Commission from 2001.

Shane Keith Warne (13 Sep 1969, Ferntree Gully, Australia) Australian cricketer, a spin bowler named one of Wisden's Five Cricketers of the Century.

Kurt Warner (22 Jun 1971, Burlington IA) American professional football player; quarterback of the St. Louis Rams in Super Bowl XXXVI.

Mark R. Warner (15 Dec 1954, Indianapolis IN) American Democratic politician; governor of Virginia from 2002.

Dionne Warwick (Marie Dionne Warrick; 12 Dec 1941, East Orange NJ) American pop singer, especially associated with the songs of Bert Bacharach.

Denzel Washington (28 Dec 1954, Mount Vernon NY) American motion-picture and TV actor who won Academy Awards for best supporting actor in 1989 (*Glory*) and best actor in 2001 (*Training Day*).

(Chaudhry) Wasim Akram (3 Jun 1966, Lahore, Pakistan) Pakistani cricketer, called the greatest left-handed fast bowler, pioneer of "reverse swing" bowling.

John Waters (22 Apr 1946, Baltimore MD) American underground filmmaker.

Sam Waterston (15 Nov 1940, Cambridge MA) American film and TV actor currently starring on TV's *Law & Order*.

Doc Watson (Arthel L. Watson; 2 Mar 1923, Deep Gap NC) American country guitarist, singer, and songwriter.

James Watson (6 Apr 1928, Chicago IL) American geneticist and biophysicist; co-recipient of the Nobel Prize for Physiology or Medicine, 1962, for determination of the molecular structure of deoxyribonucleic acid (DNA).

Faye Wattleton (8 Jul 1943, St. Louis MO) American Planned Parenthood Federation president.

André Watts (20 Jun 1946, Nuremburg, Germany) American pianist.

Philip B. Watts, American corporate executive; director of Royal Dutch/Shell Group from 1997.

Stephen Rodger Waugh (2 Jun 1965, Canterbury, Sydney, Australia) Australian cricketer.

George Oppong Weah (1 Oct 1966, Monrovia, Liberia) Liberian association football (soccer) player; European, African, and FIFA World Footballer of the Year in 1995.

Sigourney Weaver (8 Oct 1949, New York NY) American strong leading lady most recognized for the *Alien* films.

Jimmy Webb (15 Aug 1946, Elk City OK) American songwriter.

Karrie Webb (21 Dec 1974, Ayr, Queensland, Australia) Australian golfer who won the Women's British Open in 2002, completing a round of wins in the top six major women's tournaments.

Andrew (Thomas) Weil (8 Jun 1942, Philadelphia PA) American physician and champion of alternative medicine.

Sanford I. ("Sandy") Weill (16 Mar 1933, Brooklyn NY) American corporate executive; CEO of Travelers Group and, after its merger in 1998 with Citicorp, CEO of Citigroup.

Alexis Weissenberg (28 Jul 1929, Sofia, Bulgaria) Bulgarian-born French pianist.

Raquel Welch (Raquel Tejada; 5 Sep 1940, Chicago IL) American actress, model, and famed sex symbol.

Jann S. Wenner (7 Jan 1946, New York NY) American journalist and originator (1967) and publisher of *Rolling Stone* magazine and other periodicals.

Sophie, Countess of Wessex (Sophie Helen Rhys-Jones; 20 Jan 1965, Oxford, England) British royal.

Cornel West (23 Jun 1953, Tulsa OK) American scholar, critic, and African American intellectual.

Ruth Westheimer (née Karola Ruth Siegel; 4 Jun 1928, Frankfurt, Germany) American sex therapist and TV personality.

Randy Weston (Randolph Edward Weston; 6 Apr 1926, Brooklyn NY) American jazz pianist and composer.

Vivienne Westwood (Vivienne Swire; 8 Apr 1941, Tintwistle, Derbyshire, England) British fashion designer whose radical, antiestablishment creations started the 1970s punk fashion trend.

Christopher Wheeldon (22 Mar 1973, Yeovil, Somerset, England) British dancer and choreographer with the New York City Ballet.

Margaret C. ("Meg") Whitman (4 Aug 1956, Cold Spring Harbor? NY) American corporate executive; president and CEO of eBay, the Internet auction house, from 1998.

Ranil Wickremesinghe (24 Mar 1949) Sri Lankan politician; prime minister of Sri Lanka, 1993–94 and from 2001.

Carl E. Wieman (26 Mar 1951, Corvallis OR) American physicist; co-winner of the Nobel Prize for Physics, 2001, for work in the creation of the Bose-Einstein condensate.

Simon Wiesenthal (31 Dec 1908, Buczacz, Austria-Hungary) Austrian founder and head (since 1961) of the Jewish Documentation Center in Vienna, which documents the Holocaust and locates war criminals.

Dianne Wiest (28 Mar 1948, Kansas City MO) American stage and screen actress often cast in supportive, maternal roles; currently stars on TV's *Law & Order*.

Jeffrey Wigand (1943?, New York NY) American "whistle-blower" on tobacco company practices.

Richard (Purdy) Wilbur (1 Mar 1921, New York NY) American poet associated with the New Formalist movement and poet laureate of the US, 1987–88.

Billy Wilder (22 Jun 1906, Sucha, Austria [now in Poland]—27 Mar 2002, Beverly Hills CA), Austrian-born film scenarist, director, and producer known for works that humorously treat subjects of controversy and hypocrisy.

Gene Wilder (Jerome Silberman; 11 Jun 1939, Milwaukee WI) American comic actor best known for his portrayals of high-strung neurotic characters, particularly in *Blazing Saddles* and *Young Frankenstein*.

Andrew John Wiles (11 Apr 1953, Cambridge, England) British mathematician who proved Fermat's last theorem.

Bruce Wilkinson (New Jersey) American author of best-selling Christian books, including *The Prayer of Jabez* (2001).

Tom Wilkinson (12 Dec 1948, Leeds, England) British character actor and recent star of *In the Bedroom* (2001).

George F. Will (4 May 1941, Champaign IL) American political commentator and columnist.

Crown Prince Willem-Alexander (27 Apr 1967, Utrecht, The Netherlands) Dutch royal; heir to the throne of The Netherlands.

Prince William of Wales (21 Jun 1982, London, England) British royal; son of Prince Charles and Princess Diana.

Andy Williams (Andrew Williams; 3 Dec 1930, Wall Lake IA) American pop singer.

Hank Williams, Jr. (Randall Hank Williams, Jr.; 26 May 1949, Shreveport LA) American country and western singer.

Jody Williams (9 Oct 1950, Brattleboro VT) American anti-landmine activist; co-winner of the Nobel Peace Prize, 1997.

John Williams (24 Apr 1941, Melbourne, Australia) Australian-born classical guitarist.

John Williams (8 Feb 1932, New York NY) American conductor and composer, especially of film scores; director of the Boston Pops orchestra, 1980–93.

Lucinda Williams (26 Jan 1953, Lake Charles LA) American singer and songwriter.

Robin Williams (21 Jul 1952, Chicago IL) American comedian of an eccentric, energetic bent who has also starred in endearing roles in motion pictures and TV series.

Serena Williams (26 Sep 1981, Saginaw MI) American tennis player and sister of Venus Williams; Olympic and Grand Slam champion; Serena won the French Open and Wimbledon in 2002 and was the top-ranked women's player in mid-2002.

Venus Williams (17 Jun 1980, Lynwood CA) American tennis player, sister of Serena Williams; Venus won both the US Open and Wimbledon in 2000 and 2001.

Walter Ray Williams, Jr. (6 Oct 1959, San Jose CA) American bowler; bowled four perfect games in one tournament and was five-time PBA Bowler of the Year.

Bruce Willis (Walter Willison; 19 Mar 1955, Idar-Oberstein, Germany) American actor first famous as the star of TV's Moonlighting; popular for the Die Hard movies and The Sixth Sense (1999).

Brian Wilson (20 Jun 1942, Inglewood CA) American rock vocalist and bassist (of the Beach Boys).

Cassandra Wilson (4 Dec 1955, Jackson MS) American jazz singer who applies her wide-ranging "smoky contralto" voice to jazz standards, folk songs, Delta blues, and pop classics as well as many original numbers that defy categorization.

Edward O(sborne) Wilson (10 Jun 1929, Birmingham AL) American biologist recognized as the world's leading authority on ants; co-winner of the Crafoord Prize in 1990.

Lanford Wilson (13 Apr 1937, Lebanon MO) American playwright, a pioneer of the Off-Off-Broadway and regional theater movements.

Nancy Wilson (20 Feb 1937, Chillicothe OH) American pop and jazz singer.

Robert Wilson (4 Oct 1941, Waco TX) American avant-garde theater director.

William Julius Wilson (20 Dec 1935, Derry township, Westmoreland county PA) American sociologist of race and urban society, and government adviser.

Oprah Winfrey (29 Jan 1954, Kosciusko MS) American TV host and producer.

Kate Winslet (5 Oct 1975, Reading, England) British intellectual young actress made famous by her performance in Titanic (1997).

Paul (Theodore) Winter, Jr. (31 Aug 1939, Altoona PA) American jazz and pop saxophonist and composer; formed the Paul Winter Consort in 1967.

Anna Wintour (3 Nov 1949, London, England) British-born fashion magazine editor, editor in chief of American Vogue from 1988.

Steve Winwood (Stephen Lawrence Winwood; 12 May 1948, Birmingham, England) British R&B and pop performer.

Jacques Wirtz (1924, Antwerp, Belgium) Belgian landscape designer.

Bob Wise (6 Jan 1948, Washington DC) American Democratic politician; governor of West Virginia from 2001.

Girma Wolde-Giorgis (December 1924, Addis Ababa, Ethiopia) Ethiopian military officer; president of Ethiopia from 2001.

Christa Wolf (née Christa Ihlenfeld; 18 Mar 1929, Landsberg an der Warthe, Germany [now Gorzow Wielkopolski, Poland]) German novelist, essayist, and screenwriter most often associated with East Germany.

Tom Wolfe (Thomas Kennerly Wolfe, Jr.; 2 Mar 1930, Richmond VA) American novelist, journalist, and social commentator who is a leading critic of contemporary life and a proponent of New Journalism (the application of fiction-writing techniques to journalism).

James D. Wolfensohn (1 Dec 1933, Sydney, Australia) Australian-born American banker; president of the World Bank from 1995.

Paul Wolfowitz (22 Dec 1943, New York NY) American scholar and government official; US deputy secretary of defense from March 2001.

Bobby Womack (4 Mar 1944, Cleveland OH) American R&B and pop singer-songwriter.

Lee Ann Womack (19 Aug 1966, Jacksonville TX) American country singer.

Stevie Wonder (Steveland Judkins, later Steveland Morris; 13 May 1950, Saginaw MI) American pop composer, singer, and pianist.

Eldrick ("Tiger") Woods (30 Dec 1975, Cypress CA) American golfer, perhaps the greatest of all time; among his many honors, in 2001 he was the first to hold all four major golf championships at the same time.

James Woods (18 Apr 1947, Vernal UT) American film actor noted for intelligent, intense portrayals.

Phil(ip Wells) Woods (2 Nov 1931, Springfield MA) American jazz alto saxophonist and composer.

Bob Woodward (26 Mar 1943, Geneva IL) American journalist, author.

Joanne Woodward (27 Feb 1930, Thomasville GA) American film actress often paired with husband Paul Newman; best known for The Three Faces of Eve (1957).

Stephen Wozniak (11 Aug 1950, San Jose CA) American electrical engineer and cofounder of Apple Computer Corp.; youth leader.

William A. Wulf (8 Dec 1939, Chicago IL) American computer scientist; president of the National Academy of Engineering from 1997.

Charles Wuorinen (9 Jun 1938, New York NY) American composer whose contemporary, serialist works were created using his own "time-point system."

Andrew (Newell) Wyeth (12 Jul 1917, Chadds Ford PA) American watercolorist and worker in tempera noted primarily for his realistic depictions of the buildings, fields, hills, and people of his private world.

Bill Wyman (William Perks; 24 Oct 1936, London, England) British rock bassist (of the Rolling Stones).

Jane Wyman (Sarah Jane Mayfield, also known as Sarah Jane Fulks; 4 Jan 1914, St. Joseph MO) American film and TV actress best known for the films *The Yearling* (1946), *Johnny Belinda* (1948), and the TV series *Falcon Crest* (1981–90); she was the first wife of Ronald Reagan.

Xie Jun (30 Oct 1970, Baoding, China) Chinese women's chess champion of the world, 1991–96 and 1999–2001.

Yohji Yamamoto (3 Oct 1943, Tokyo, Japan) Japanese fashion designer.

Ryuzo Yanagimachi (27 Aug 1928, Sapporo, Japan) Japanese reproductive biologist, first to clone an adult male mammal (a mouse in 1999).

Yang Yang (A) (24 Aug 1976, Heilongjiang province, China) Chinese short-track speed skater; five-time world champion.

Alfred ("Weird Al") Yankovic (23 Oct 1959, Lynwood CA) American satirical singer and songwriter.

Yanni (Yannis Khrisomalis; 14 Nov 1954, Kalamata, Greece) Greek-born New Age orchestra leader and arranger.

Yury Yarov (1942, Belorussian SSR, USSR [now Belarus]) Russian international civil servant; executive secretary of the Commonwealth of Independent States from 1999.

Peter Yarrow (31 May 1938, New York NY) American folk singer and composer (of Peter Paul & Mary).

Shayk Ahmed Yassin (1936-38?, al-Jura, Palestine) Palestinian founder and spiritual leader of Hamas.

Trisha Yearwood (Patricia Lynn Yearwood; 19 Sep 1964, Monticello GA) American country singer.

Lyubov Yegorova (5 May 1966, Tomsk, Russia) Russian cross-country skier; nine-time Olympic medalist.

Boris Nikolayevich Yeltsin (1 Feb 1931, Sverdlovsk, USSR [now Yekaterinburg, Russia]) Russian politician; president of Russia, 1991–99.

Gloria Yerkovich (1942) American founder of ChildFind, a nationwide organization that helps locate missing children.

Yevgeny (Aleksandrovich) Yevtushenko (18 Jul 1933, Zima, Irkutsk oblast, Russian SFSR, USSR) Russian poet and spokesman for the younger post-Stalin generation of Russian poets.

Frances Yip (Lai Yee) (1948, Hong Kong) Hong Kong popular singer.

Dwight (David) Yoakam (23 Oct 1956, Pikesville KY) American country and western singer, songwriter, and actor.

Michael York (27 Mar 1942, Fulmer, England) British actor most famous for Franco Zeffirelli films.

Banana Yoshimoto (24 Jul 1964, Tokyo, Japan) Japanese bestselling fiction writer.

Hiroyuki Yoshino (1939, Fukui, Japan) Japanese corporate executive; president and CEO of Honda Motor Co., Ltd.

Neil Young (12 Nov 1945, Toronto, ON, Canada) Canadian rock and pop singer and songwriter.

Étienne Ys, Netherlands Antilles politician; prime minister of the Netherlands Antilles from 3 Jun 2002.

Yu Miri (22 Jun 1968, Yokohama, Japan) Japanese writer of Korean ancestry who won the Akutagawa Prize in 1997 for her novel *Kazoku shinema* (1996; "Family Cinema").

Yu Shyi-kun (25 Apr 1948, Taiho village, Ilan county, Taiwan) Taiwanese politician; prime minister of Taiwan from 1 Feb 2002.

Mohammad Zahir Shah (15 Oct 1914, Kabul, Afghanistan) Afghani royal; king of Afghanistan, 1933–73.

Paula Zahn (24 Feb 1956, Omaha NE) American TV anchorwoman and journalist.

Sheikh Zaid ibn Sultan an-Nahayan (1918) ruler of Abu Dhabi from 1966 and president of the United Arab Emirates from 1971.

Joe Zawinul (7 Jul 1932, Vienna, Austria) Austrian-born jazz pianist and composer.

Ernesto Zedillo Ponce de León (27 Dec 1951, Mexico City, Mexico) Mexican politician; president of Mexico, 1994–2000.

Franco Zeffirelli (12 Feb 1923, Florence, Italy) Italian director, designer, and producer of opera, theater, motion pictures, and television.

Renée Zellweger (25 Apr 1969, Katy TX) American actress first famous for her role in the film *Jerry Maguire* (1996).

Robert Zemeckis (14 May 1952) American director, producer of popular mainstream films, including *Forrest Gump* (1994).

Meles Zenawi (8 May 1955, Adoua, Ethiopia) Ethiopian politician; prime minister of Ethiopia from 1995.

Elias (Adam) Zerhouni (1951, Nedroma, Algeria) Algerian-born American radiologist and medical administrator; director of the National Institutes of Health from 2002.

Liamine Zéroual (3 Jul 1941, Batna, Algeria) Algerian politician and head of state of Algeria from 1995.

Catherine Zeta-Jones (25 Sep 1969, Swansea, Wales) British-born American motion-picture actress of great beauty and talent.

Ahmed H. Zewail (26 Feb 1946, Damanhur, Egypt) Egyptian-born American chemist who won the Nobel Prize for Chemistry in 1999 for developing a technique that allows scientists to study chemical reactions in "slow motion."

Zhu Chen (16 Mar 1976, China) Chinese chess grandmaster; women's world champion from 2001.

Zhu Rongji (1 Oct 1928, Changsha, Hunan province, China) Chinese politician; premier of China from 1998.

Khaleda Zia (née Khaleda Majumdar; 15 Aug 1945, Dinajpur, British India [now Bangladesh]) Bangladeshi politician; prime minister of Bangladesh, 1991–96 and from 2001.

Zinedine Zidane (23 Jun 1972, Marseille, France) French association football (soccer) player, star of the French team that won the FIFA World Cup in 1998; named FIFA world footballer of the year, 1999.

Krystian Zimerman (1956, Zabrze, Silesia, Poland) Polish concert pianist.

Anthony C. Zinni (17 Sep 1943, Conshohocken PA) American military leader and diplomat.

Armin Zöggler (4 Jan 1974, Merano, South Tyrol, Italy) Italian luger and World Cup champion.

Máxima Zorreguieta (17 May 1971, Buenos Aires, Argentina) Argentine investment banker; married Crown Prince Willem-Alexander of The Netherlands (2 Feb 2002).

Mortimer B. Zuckerman (4 Jun 1937, Montreal, QC, Canada) American publisher, columnist; editor in chief of *U.S. News & World Report*.

Pinchas Zukerman (16 Jul 1948, Tel Aviv, Israel) Israeli-born American violinist, violist, and conductor.

Ellen Taaffe Zwilich (30 Apr 1939, Miami FL) American composer whose works display both technical expertise and wide audience appeal.

Obituaries

Deaths of notable people, 1 Jul 2001–30 Jun 2002.

Aaliyah (Aaliyah Dana Haughton; 16 Jan 1979, Brooklyn NY–25 Aug 2001, Abaco Islands, The Bahamas), American rhythm-and-blues singer and actress considered on the verge of superstardom after the success of her first two albums, her Grammy nominations for her singles "Are You That Somebody?" (1998) and "Try Again" (2000), and her starring role in the movie *Romeo Must Die* (2000).

Abu Ali Mustafa (Mustafa az-Zibri; 1938, Arabeh, Palestine–27 Aug 2001, Ram Allah, West Bank, Palestine), Palestinian nationalist, a cofounder and, from July 2000, secretary-general of the Popular Front for the Liberation of Palestine (PFLP), a radical faction of the Palestine Liberation Organization (PLO).

Larry Adler (Lawrence Cecil Adler; 10 Feb 1914, Baltimore MD–7 Aug 2001, London, England), American harmonica player generally considered to be responsible for the elevation of the mouth organ to concert status in the world of classical music.

John Agar (31 Jan 1921, Chicago IL–7 Apr 2002, Burbank CA), American actor who first achieved fame when he married (1945) actress Shirley Temple but then became an actor and appeared with her in two films.

Jorge Amado (10 Aug 1912, Ferradas, near Ilhéus, Brazil–6 Aug 2001, Salvador, Brazil), Brazilian novelist, the literary patriarch of his country. In all, he published 32 books, which were translated into some 50 languages and sold 20 million copies.

Maceo Anderson (3 Sep 1910, Charleston SC–4 Jul 2001, Los Angeles CA), American dancer; a founding member of the Four Step Brothers, a widely popular tap-dance act.

Poul William Anderson (25 Nov 1926, Bristol PA–31 Jul 2001, Orinda CA), American science-fiction writer; the prolific author of more than 100 books of science fiction and fantasy.

(William) Kenneth Armitage (18 Jul 1916, Leeds, England–22 Jan 2002, London, England), British sculptor whose semiabstract bronzes, many of which displayed quirky humor, put him at the forefront of post-World War II British art.

Mary Kay Ash (Mary Kathlyn Wagner; 12 May 1918, Hot Wells TX–22 Nov 2001, Dallas TX), American entrepreneur; founder of cosmetics giant Mary Kay Inc. and one of the most famous businesswomen in the world.

Viktor Petrovich Astafyev (1 May 1924, Ovsyanka, Krasnoyarsk *kray*, Russia–29 Nov 2001, Krasnoyarsk, Russia), Soviet Russian novelist; penned novels that chronicled the bleakness and despair of life in Siberia and the madness and horror of war.

Kenneth George Aston (1 Sep 1915, Colchester, Essex, England–23 Oct 2001, Ilford, Essex, England), British association football (soccer) referee; invented the yellow (caution) and red (ejection) disciplinary cards, which were first employed during play at the 1970 World Cup finals and were quickly introduced around the world.

Francis David Langhorne Astor (5 Mar 1912, London, England–7 Dec 2001, London, England), British newspaperman; editor of *The Observer* from 1948 to 1975 and was largely responsible for turning the paper's viewpoint from a conservative, establishment-supporting one to espousal of a number of liberal causes, including anticolonialism, human rights, and prison reform.

Muhammad Atef (Sobhi Abu Sitta; 1944?, Egypt–14/15 Nov 2001, near Kabul, Afghanistan), Egyptian-born Islamist militant; believed to have been a close associate of Osama bin Laden and chief military strategist for the Islamic terrorist organization al-Qaeda.

Kaifi Azmi (Syed At'har Husain Rizvi; 1918, Mijwan, Azamgarh district, Uttar Pradesh, India–10 May 2002, Mumbai, India), Indian poet, screenwriter, and activist; he was associated with the progressive writers movement of the 1930s in Urdu and his protest poetry was informed by his revolutionary political views.

Hugo Bánzer Suárez (10 May 1926, Concepción, Bolivia–5 May 2002, Santa Cruz, Bolivia), Bolivian politician who headed a military regime in Bolivia in the 1970s and a democratically elected government in the late 1990s. Defenders credited him with helping to move Bolivia toward democratic government, but detractors saw him as a dictator.

Christiaan Neethling Barnard (8 Nov 1922, Beaufort West, South Africa–2 Sep 2001, Paphos, Cyprus), South African surgeon; performed the first transplant of a heart from one human to another (1967), the first "piggyback" heart transplant, in which a second heart was inserted in order to aid the patient's own weak one (1974), the first transplantation of an animal's heart into a human, again to assist the patient's heart and give it time to heal (1977), and the first heart-lung transplant (1981).

Nikolay Gennadiyevich Basov (14 Dec 1922, Usman, near Voronezh, Russia–1 Jul 2001, Moscow, Russia), Soviet physicist; was corecipient of the Nobel Prize for Physics in 1964 for fundamental research in quantum electronics that led to the development of the maser and the laser, which produce parallel monochromatic coherent beams of microwaves and light, respectively.

Peter Bauer (6 Nov 1915, Budapest, Hungary–2 May 2002, London, England), Hungarian-born British economist who argued that the key to economic growth in underdeveloped countries lay not simply in foreign aid, but in also cultivating a workforce capable of generating private profit.

Gilbert Bécaud (François Gilbert Silly; 24 Oct 1927, Toulon, France–18 Dec 2001, Paris, France), French singer-songwriter; composed "chansons françaises," romantic melodies that became pop hits for him as well as for many other French- and English-language performers.

Fernando Belaúnde Terry (7 Oct 1912, Lima, Peru–4 Jun 2002, Lima, Peru), Peruvian politician who served two terms as president of Peru, from 1963 to 1968 and from 1980 to 1985. A reformer, he was often called the "father of democracy" in Peru, but his attempts to modernize the economy were not considered successful.

Mildred (Augustine Wirt) Benson (10 Jul 1905, Ladora IA–28 May 2002, Toledo OH), American writer, the original author of the Nancy Drew mysteries.

David Berg (12 Jun 1920, Brooklyn NY—17 May 2002), American comic book artist and writer; he wrote and illustrated the Lighter Side feature in *Mad* magazine for over 40 years.

Milton Berle (Mendel Berlinger; 12 Jul 1908, New York NY—27 Mar 2002, Los Angeles CA), American comedian, actor, and songwriter; came to be known as "Mr. Television" after he pioneered the TV variety show in 1948 and his flamboyant antics inspired hundreds of thousands of Americans to purchase their first TV sets so they could watch his show, *Texaco Star Theater*.

Mongo Beti (Alexandre Biyidi; 30 Jun 1932, Mbalmayo, Cameroon—8 Oct 2001, Douala, Cameroon), Cameroonian novelist and political writer; a critic of colonialism, which he believed destroyed traditional African society, and of the authoritarian regime that ruled Cameroon after independence in 1960.

Michael Anthony Bilandic (13 Feb 1923, Chicago IL—15 Jan 2002, Chicago IL), American politician and judge; succeeded Richard J. Daley as mayor of Chicago and later served as chief justice of the Illinois Supreme Court.

Otis Blackwell (16 Feb 1932, New York NY—6 May 2002, Nashville TN), American singer and songwriter; he began as a singer but saw that career overshadowed by his writing of more than 1,000 songs, which hugely influenced the development of the sound of rock and roll. Among his hits were Elvis Presley's "Don't Be Cruel" and "All Shook Up" and Jerry Lee Lewis's "Great Balls of Fire" and "Breathless," and he collaborated with Peggy Lee on her signature song, "Fever."

James Blackwood (4 Aug 1919, Choctaw county MS—3 Feb 2002, Memphis TN), American gospel singer; a founding member of the Blackwood Brothers Quartet, the first gospel group to sell one million records.

Sir Peter James Blake (1 Oct 1948, Auckland, New Zealand—6 Dec 2001, off Macapá, Brazil), New Zealand yachtsman and explorer; the winner of the two most important yachting competitions—the Whitbread Round the World Race (1989–90) and the America's Cup (1995 and 2000)—and in 1994 in the *ENZA New Zealand* won the Jules Verne Trophy when he set a nonstop circumnavigation world record of 74 days 22 hours 17 minutes 22 seconds.

Bill Blass (William Ralph Blass; 22 Jun 1922, Fort Wayne IN—12 Jun 2002, Washington CT), American fashion designer who launched a multimillion-dollar designer label featuring low-key but classy fashions that greatly influenced the casual-chic sensibility in American fashion.

Budd Boetticher (Oscar Boetticher, Jr.; 29 Jul 1916, Chicago IL—29 Nov 2001, Ramona CA), American film director and screenwriter; he was a professional matador in Mexico before becoming a leading director of classic western movies.

Joseph Bonanno (18 Jan 1905, Castellammare del Golfo, Sicily, Italy—11 May 2002, Tucson AZ), Italian-born American organized crime figure who headed one of New York City's five original crime families from the 1930s to the '60s.

Juan Bosch Gaviño (30 Jun 1909, La Vega, Dominican Republic—1 Nov 2001, Santo Domingo, Dominican Republic), Dominican writer and politician; the country's first democratically elected president. Serving only seven months in 1963 before being deposed, he nonetheless remained a power in Dominican politics.

Louis ("Lou") Boudreau (17 Jul 1917, Harvey IL—10 Aug 2001, Olympia Fields IL), American baseball player and manager; began his professional career as a dazzling defensive shortstop, became the second youngest manager in major league history, and went on to lead the American League in batting and manage the Cleveland Indians to their last world championship; he then managed three more teams and broadcast major league games for nearly three decades.

Roy Boulting (21 Nov 1913, Bray, Berkshire, England—5 Nov 2001, Eynsham, Oxfordshire, England), British filmmaker; created, in partnership with his twin brother, John, some of Great Britain's most popular motion pictures of the 1940s and '50s.

Pierre Bourdieu (1 Aug 1930, Denguin, France—23 Jan 2002, Paris, France), French sociologist; he was a public intellectual in the tradition of Émile Zola and Jean-Paul Sartre. Bourdieu's concept of habitus (socially acquired dispositions) was influential in recent postmodernist humanities and social sciences.

Claude Brown (23 Feb 1937, New York NY—2 Feb 2002, New York NY), American author who wrote a landmark work in African American literature, *Manchild in the Promised Land* (1965), which chronicled his poverty-stricken childhood in the Harlem district of New York City.

J(ohn) Carter Brown (8 Oct 1934, Providence RI—17 Jun 2002, Boston MA), American museum director who transformed the National Gallery of Art in Washington DC into one of the world's major museums.

James Richard ("Buster") Brown (17 Mar 1913, Baltimore MD—7 May 2002, New York NY), American dancer and teacher who performed on stage, on television, and in film alongside the likes of Cab Calloway, Count Basie, Duke Ellington, and Dizzy Gillespie; he was one of the last of the legendary tap dancers known as the Copasetics.

Robert Hanbury Brown (31 Aug 1916, Aravankadu, India—16 Jan 2002, Andover, Hampshire, England), British astronomer; overcame scientific hurdles and the skepticism of his colleagues in the 1950s to invent the optical intensity interferometer.

John Francis ("Jack") Buck (21 Aug 1924, Holyoke MA—18 Jun 2002, St. Louis MO), American broadcaster who worked as an announcer for the St. Louis Cardinals baseball team from 1954 to 2001.

Dean Bumpus (11 May 1912, Newburyport MA—14 Mar 2002, Woods Hole MA), American oceanographer who conducted one of the most comprehensive studies of ocean currents ever undertaken.

Ely Reeves Callaway (3 Jun 1919, La Grange GA—5 Jul 2001, Rancho Santa Fe CA), American golf-equipment manufacturer; founded the Callaway Golf Co. in 1982; under his leadership the company became the world's leading manufacturer of golf equipment.

Pauline Eblé Campanelli (25 Jan 1943, Bronx NY—29 Nov 2001, Pohatcong township NJ), American artist; painted superrealist still lifes that, while never of much interest to prestigious, expensive galleries and art museums, sold by the thousands through catalogs, furniture stores, and print and poster shops, rivaling only Andrew Wyeth in sales by a living artist.

Richard Michael Power Carver, Baron Carver (24 Apr 1915, Bletchingley, Surrey, England—9 Dec 2001, Fareham, Hampshire, England), British field marshal who held a series of prominent military posts, notably chief of staff (1955) in Kenya during the Mau Mau uprising, head (1964) of the UN peacekeeping forces on Cyprus, and commander (1967–69) of all British troops in the Far East.

Barbara Castle (Baroness Castle of Blackburn; 6 Oct 1910, Yorkshire?, England–3 May 2002, Buckinghamshire, England), British politician who served as a parliamentarian from the 1940s to the 1970s, and later became a cabinet minister under Prime Minister Harold Wilson. A major figure in the Labour Party, she was considered a pioneer of women holding political office in Britain.

Régine Cavagnoud (27 Jun 1970, La Clusaz, France–31 Oct 2001, Vienna, Austria), French skier, one of France's finest young Alpine skiers and a top prospect for the 2002 Winter Olympic Games; she died from severe brain injuries she sustained when she collided with a German ski coach during a high-speed training run.

Camilo José Cela (Trulock) (11 May 1916, Iria Flavia, Spain–17 Jan 2002, Madrid, Spain), Spanish writer; won the Nobel Prize for Literature in 1989 "for a rich and intensive prose, which with ro strained compassion forms a challenging vision of man's vulnerability." Cela's literary output included novels, short stories, essays, and travel diaries and was characterized by caustic wit and experimentation in both form and content.

Chang Hsüeh-liang (3 Jun 1901, Haicheng, China–14 Oct 2001, Honolulu HI), Chinese warlord who kidnapped Nationalist leader Chiang Kai-shek in 1936 in an attempt to force him to fight the Japanese rather than the Communists. His action had a decisive effect on subsequent Chinese history.

Robert Lundquist Chapman (28 Dec 1920, Huntington WV–2 Feb 2002, Morristown NJ), American editor who was responsible for updating English-language phraseology as the editor of the *New Dictionary of American Slang* (1986), the *Thesaurus of American Slang* (1989), and *Roget's International Thesaurus* (fourth edition, 1977, and fifth edition, 1992).

(Morton) Jay Chiat (25 Oct 1931, Bronx NY–23 Apr 2002, Marina del Rey CA), American advertising executive; his was the creative mind behind the "1984" television commercial for Apple's Macintosh personal computer, which pioneered the showcasing of commercials during the Super Bowl broadcast.

Choi Hong Hi (9 Nov 1918, Hwa Dae, Myong Chun district, Korea [now North Korea]–15 Jun 2002, P'yongyang, North Korea), Korean military officer who was considered to be the founder of tae kwon do.

Willam (Farr) Christensen (27 Aug 1902, Brigham City UT–14 Oct 2001, Salt Lake City UT), American ballet company director; founded the Utah Ballet.

Grigory Naumovich Chukhrai (23 May 1921, Melitopol, Ukraine, Soviet Russia–28 Oct 2001, Moscow, Russia), Soviet motion picture director who broke away from the restrictions of Socialist Realism to create poignant films about simple people in wartime. His finest work included *The Forty-First* (1956), *Ballad of a Soldier* (1959), and *Clear Skies* (1961).

J(ohn) Desmond Clark (10 Apr 1916, London, England–14 Feb 2002, Oakland CA), British archaeologist and anthropologist, a world-renowned authority on ancient Africa and the leader of archaeological expeditions that opened dramatic new windows on human prehistory.

Rosemary Clooney (23 May 1928, Maysville KY–29 Jun 2002, Beverly Hills CA), American singer and actress; gained popularity in the 1950s with the hit songs "Come-on-a-My House" and "Hey There." She starred in the classic film *White Christmas* (1954) alongside Bing Crosby and Danny Kaye.

Dorothy Love Coates (Dorothy McGriff; 30 Jan 1928, Birmingham AL–9 Apr 2002, Birmingham AL), American gospel singer with a dynamic delivery and an enthusiasm that made her one of the most inspirational performers in her genre.

Francisco da Costa Gomes (30 Jun 1914, Chaves, Portugal–31 Jul 2001, Lisbon, Portugal), Portuguese military leader; president of Portugal's ruling military junta from 1974 to 1976.

Ira Wilmer ("Will") Counts, Jr. (24 Aug 1931, Little Rock AR–6 Oct 2001, Bloomington IN), American photographer of the turmoil that attended the integration of Little Rock (AR) Central High School in 1957.

Frank Cooper Craighead, Jr. (14 Aug 1916, Washington DC–21 Oct 2001, Jackson WY), American naturalist; with his identical twin, John, spent 12 years studying grizzly bears in the Yellowstone National Park area and helped prevent the extinction of grizzlies.

W(allie) A(mos) Criswell (19 Dec 1909, Eldorado OK–9 Jan 2002, Dallas TX), American clergyman and pastor of the First Baptist Church of Dallas from 1944 to 1991; under his leadership, the church grew to become the largest Southern Baptist congregation in the US, with some 26,000 members.

Hansie Cronje (Wessel Johannes Cronje; 25 Sep 1969, Bloemfontein, Orange Free State, South Africa–1 Jun 2002, in a plane crash near George, South Africa), South African cricketer who led the South African team to victory in 27 of the 53 Tests in which he served as captain.

Pablo Antonio Cuadra (4 Nov 1912, Managua, Nicaragua–2 Jan 2002, Managua, Nicaragua), Nicaraguan poet, a leading exponent of the *vanguardia*, a literary movement that emerged in the early 1930s and sought to foster the native literary traditions of Nicaragua while at the same time incorporating them into the international literary vanguard.

(Thomas) Allen Monro Curnow (17 Jun 1911, Timaru, New Zealand–23 Sep 2001, Auckland, New Zealand), New Zealand poet and writer who gained an international reputation for his verse. He was also known as the editor of two anthologies of New Zealand poetry.

Sir (Arthur) Roden Cutler (14 May 1916, Manly, NSW, Australia–21 Feb 2002, Sydney, Australia), Australian diplomat and public servant; he was a distinguished war hero, ambassador, and New South Wales's longest-serving governor (1966–81).

Dagmar (Virginia Ruth Egnor; 29 Nov 1921, Logan WV–9 Oct 2001, Ceredo WV), American comic actress; portrayed a stereotypical sexy dumb blonde in early 1950s television, most notably on the late night talk show *Broadway Open House*, the prototype for *The Tonight Show* and similar programs.

Willie Davenport (8 Jun 1943, Troy AL–17 Jun 2002, Chicago IL), American athlete; won the gold medal in the 110-m hurdles at the 1968 Olympic Games in Mexico City, and won a bronze medal for hurdles at the 1976 Olympic Games.

Arthur Davidsen (26 May 1944, Freeport NY–19 Jul 2001, Baltimore MD), American astrophysicist; a leading researcher in the fields of high-energy astrophysics and ultraviolet space astronomy.

Norman Ralph Davidson (5 Apr 1916, Chicago IL—14 Feb 2002, Pasadena CA), American biochemist who conducted groundbreaking research in molecular biology that contributed to a fuller understanding of the genetic blueprint of human life.

John Myrick Dawson (30 Sep 1930, Champaign IL—17 Nov 2001, Los Angeles CA), American physicist, one of the world's foremost authorities on plasma physics. Dawson was known for his development of the so-called particle-in-cell computer model, a technique for simulating plasmas on computers; he was also the first to suggest using plasma in particle accelerators in order to make them more powerful without increasing their size.

Ramiro de León Carpio (12 Jan 1942, Guatemala City, Guatemala—found dead 16 Apr 2002, Miami FL), Guatemalan politician; as a longtime opponent of racial oppression, helped draft his country's constitution in 1984, served as president of Guatemala, 1993–96, and in 1989 was elected human rights ombudsman.

Alonzo Galloway Decker, Jr. (18 Jan 1908, Orangeville MD—18 Mar 2002, Earleville MD), American business executive who transformed Black & Decker, a power-tool company founded by his father, into a corporate giant.

Dorothy DeLay (31 Mar 1917, Medicine Lodge KS—24 Mar 2002, Upper Nyack NY), American violin teacher who trained some of the world's leading violinists, including Itzhak Perlman, Sarah Chang, Midori, and Nigel Kennedy.

Edward ("Ted") Demme (26 Oct 1963, New York NY—13 Jan 2002, Santa Monica CA), American film director; counted among his credits such films as *Beautiful Girls* (1996), *Life* (1999), and *Blow* (2001), as well as episodes of the television series *Homicide: Life on the Street* and *Action.*

Michael Leonidas Dertouzos (5 Nov 1936, Athens, Greece—27 Aug 2001, Boston MA), Greek-born computer scientist who, as director of the Massachusetts Institute of Technology's computer science laboratory from 1974, provided valuable support that helped enable the World Wide Web Consortium to develop the standards that made the Internet accessible to individual users throughout the world.

Ardito Desio (18 Apr 1897, Palmanova, Italy—12 Dec 2001, Rome, Italy), Italian geologist and explorer; led the first successful expedition to scale K2, the world's second tallest mountain; he did not make the final assault to the peak, however, owing to his age.

Phoolan Devi (10 Aug 1963, Uttar Pradesh state, India—25 Jul 2001, New Delhi, India), Indian bandit and politician; she was the notorious "Bandit Queen" who became legendary for both her acts of revenge on those who had abused her and her Robin Hood-like activities to aid the lower castes.

Daniel John ("Dan") Devine (23 Dec 1924, Augusta WI—9 May 2002, Tempe AZ), American football coach who served three universities as head coach—Arizona State (1955–57), Missouri (1958–70), and Notre Dame (1975–80)—and was head coach and general manager of the Green Bay Packers (1971–74).

Jésus Díaz (10 Oct/Jul 1941, Havana, Cuba—2 May 2002, Madrid, Spain), Cuban writer and filmmaker who supported the Cuban Revolution with his creative efforts, editing the magazines *Pensamiento crítico* and *El caimán barbudo,* publishing the short-story collection *Los años duros* (1966), and making such films about the revolution as *Polvo rojo* (1980).

William T. Dillard, Sr. (2 Sep 1914, Mineral Springs AR—8 Feb 2002, Little Rock AR), American businessman; the founder in 1938 of the first Dillard's store (T.J. Dillard's; now Dillard's Inc.), which became the third largest department-store chain in the US.

Troy Donahue (Merle Johnson, Jr.; 27 Jan 1936, New York NY—2 Sep 2001, Santa Monica CA), American actor; a teen heartthrob in the late 1950s and early '60s, with starring roles in movies, including *A Summer Place* (1959), *Parrish* (1961), *Rome Adventure* (1962), and *Palm Springs Weekend* (1963), and the TV series *Surfside Six* (1960–62) and *Hawaiian Eye* (1962).

Marion Dönhoff (Marion Hedda Ilse Gräfin [Countess] Dönhoff; 2 Dec 1909, Castle Friedrichstein, near Königsberg East Prussia [now Kaliningrad, Russia]—11 Mar 2002, Berlin, Germany), German journalist known as the doyenne of German journalism for her nearly 60-year association with the liberal weekly *Die Zeit,* as a founding staff member (1946–55), political editor (1955–68), editor in chief (1968–72), and copublisher (1972–2002).

Isaias Duarte Cancino (15 Feb 1939, San Gil, Colombia—16 Mar 2002, Cali, Colombia), Colombian cleric, archbishop of Cali from 1995 and an outspoken critic of Colombian guerrillas and drug traffickers. Duarte was slain by two gunmen outside a church where he had just presided over a wedding ceremony.

Jane Dudley (3 Apr 1912, New York NY—19 Sep 2001, London, England), American dancer, choreographer, and teacher; influential in the development of modern dance in the US, Israel, and England.

Duong Van Minh (16 Feb 1916, Long An province, French Indochina—6 Aug 2001, Pasadena CA), South Vietnamese general, a key member of the military coup that overthrew South Vietnamese Pres. Ngo Dinh Diem in November 1963; in April 1975 he succeeded Nguyen Van Thieu as president just days before North Vietnamese forces captured Saigon.

Muhammed Haji Ibrahim Egal (15 Aug 1928?, Odweine, British Somaliland Protectorate [now Somalia]—3 May 2002, Pretoria, South Africa), Somali politician; prime minister of Somalia, 1960 and 1967–69, and president of the secessionist Republic of Somaliland, 1993–2002.

Elizabeth the Queen Mother (Lady Elizabeth Angela Marguerite Bowes-Lyon; "Queen Mum"; 4 Aug 1900, St. Paul's Waldenbury, Hitchin, Hertfordshire, England—30 Mar 2002, Windsor, Berkshire, England), British royal; in a life that spanned three centuries, she was the daughter of a Scottish nobleman, the queen consort of King George VI, the mother of Queen Elizabeth II and Princess Margaret, countess of Snowden, and an almost universally beloved symbol of British tradition and fortitude.

Lhamsurenglyn Enebish (1947, Mogod Sum, Mongolia—29 Sep 2001, Ulaanbaatar, Mongolia), Mongolian politician; secretary-general (from 1996) of the Mongolian People's Revolutionary Party (MPRP) and speaker (from 19 Jul 2000) of the country's Great Hural (parliament).

John Alec Entwistle (9 Oct 1944, London, England—found dead 27 Jun 2002, Las Vegas NV), British bass guitarist whose steady demeanor and superb musicianship anchored the talented but volatile rock band the Who.

John Erickson (17 Apr 1929, Newcastle, England—10 Feb 2002, Edinburgh, Scotland), British military historian widely regarded as the West's foremost authority on the Soviet Union's military development, in particular the role the Red Army played in World War II.

Esquivel (Juan García Esquivel; 20 Jan 1918, Tampico, Mexico—3 Jan 2002, Jiutepec, Mexico), Mexican composer and bandleader who won international fame with eccentric instrumental pop recordings in the 1950s and '60s.

Martin Julius Esslin (Julius Pereszlenyi; 8 Jun 1918, Budapest, Austria-Hungary—24 Feb 2002, London, England), Hungarian-born British broadcaster, critic, and scholar; coined the term "Theatre of the Absurd" (in his 1962 book of that title) to describe post-World War II drama by playwrights he felt reflected existential philosophy and who used poetic metaphor "to convey their sense of bewilderment, anxiety, and wonder in the face of an inexplicable universe."

Willard Z(ebedee) Estey (10 Oct 1919, Saskatoon, SK, Canada—25 Jan 2002, Toronto, ON, Canada), Canadian attorney and judge who served as a justice on the Supreme Court of Canada from 1977 to 1988.

Moss Evans (Arthur Mostyn Evans; 13 Jul 1925, Cefn Coed, Glamorgan, Wales—12 Jan 2002, Heacham, Norfolk, England), British trade unionist; was elected general secretary of the Transport and General Workers' Union in 1978, just before the "winter of discontent," a period of strikes and other labor troubles that disrupted Britain and led to the fall of Prime Minister James Callaghan's Labour Party government in May 1979.

(William) Paterson Ewen (7 Apr 1925, Montreal, QC, Canada—17 Feb 2002, London, ON, Canada), Canadian artist, a relentlessly innovative painter whose expressionistic works of the 1970s and '80s attracted widespread interest.

Annaloo Whitmore Fadiman (27 May 1916, Price UT—5 Feb 2002, Captiva FL), American screenwriter and journalist; cowrote *Andy Hardy Meets Debutante* (1940), a vehicle for Judy Garland and Mickey Rooney, went to China and wrote speeches for Madame Chiang Kai-shek, and landed a job as a reporter with *Liberty* magazine.

Mimi Fariña (Mimi Margharita Baez; 30 Apr 1945, Stanford CA—18 Jul 2001, Mill Valley CA), American folk singer and social activist, the younger sister of folk singer Joan Baez and wife of Richard Fariña, but also a well-known performer in her own right.

Eileen Farrell (13 Feb 1920, Willimantic CT—16 Mar 2002, Park Ridge NJ), American singer; was considered one of the world's outstanding dramatic sopranos.

Jacques Fauvet (9 Jun 1914, Paris, France—1 Jun 2002, Paris, France), French journalist who served as editor of the French newspaper *Le Monde* and as codirector of the Le Monde publishing company from 1969 to 1982.

María Félix (María de los Ángeles Félix Güereña; 4 May 1914, Álamos, Sonora, Mexico—8 Apr 2002, Mexico City, Mexico), Mexican actress; used her extraordinary looks and fiery personality to propel herself from unknown to overnight star to icon of beauty in Spanish-speaking countries.

Timothy (Irving Frederick) Findley (30 Oct 1930, Toronto, ON, Canada—20 Jun 2002, south of France), Canadian writer best known for his novels, although he also wrote a number of dramatic works.

The Rev. Howard Finster (2 Dec 1916, Valley Head AL—22 Oct 2001, Rome GA), American artist and preacher; with his simple colorful works that combined his evangelistic messages with pop culture icons, he became one of the most noted folk artists of the 20th century.

Sir Raymond William Firth (25 Mar 1901, Auckland, New Zealand—22 Feb 2002, London, England), New Zealand-born anthropologist whose most extensive and lasting field work was on the tiny Polynesian island of Tikopia, an atoll in the Solomon Islands, about which he wrote nine books.

Tommy Lee Flanagan (16 Mar 1930, Detroit MI—16 Nov 2001, New York NY), American jazz pianist who improvised fluent melodies with swing, harmonic ingenuity, and a light touch.

Pim Fortuyn (Wilhelmus Simon Petrus Fortuyn; 19 Feb 1948, Velsen, The Netherlands—6 May 2002, Hilversum, The Netherlands), Dutch politician known for his far right-wing, anti-immigration stance; he was assassinated several days before the May 2002 elections in which he was running for office.

Kathleen Freeman (17 Feb 1919, Chicago IL—23 Aug 2001, New York NY), American character actress; who appeared in some 100 films, including nearly a dozen Jerry Lewis movies and, most memorably, in the role of vocal coach Phoebe Dinsmore in *Singin' in the Rain* (1952).

Edward ("Eddie") Futch (9 Aug 1911, Hillsboro MS—10 Oct 2001, Las Vegas NV), American boxing trainer dubbed "the professor of pugilism" for the sharp observation, compassion, and determination that he used to coach more than 20 world champions, including heavyweights Joe Frazier, Ken Norton, Trevor Berbick, Larry Holmes, Michael Spinks, and Riddick Bowe.

Francis S(tanley) Gabreski (28 Jan 1919, Oil City PA—31 Jan 2002, Huntington NY), American fighter pilot; shot down more than three dozen enemy planes as an ace fighter pilot in both World War II and the Korean War.

Hans-Georg Gadamer (11 Feb 1900, Marburg, Germany—14 Mar 2002, Heidelberg, Germany), German philosopher, a principal figure in 20th-century philosophical hermeneutics. His conception of language as a historical phenomenon had great influence in postmodernist and poststructuralist thought.

Sivaji Ganesan (Villupuram Chiniah Pillai Ganesan; 1 Oct 1927, Tamil Nadu, India—21 Jul 2001, Chennai [Madras], India), Indian actor, a legendary star in southern India's Tamil film industry, employing his expressive face and eloquent voice in some 300 motion pictures over nearly 50 years.

Gen. Joseph Garba (17 July 1943, Langtang, Jos Plateau, Nigeria—1 Jun 2002, Abuja, Nigeria), Nigerian military officer and diplomat; participated in the organization of a bloodless military coup in 1975 that briefly restored civilian rule to Nigeria.

John William Gardner (8 Oct 1912, Los Angeles CA—16 Feb 2002, Palo Alto CA), American social and political activist who had a long career of public service including presidency of the philanthropic Carnegie Corporation of New York and several years as secretary of health, education, and welfare.

David Emery Gascoyne (10 Oct 1916, Harrow, Middlesex, England—25 Nov 2001, Newport, Isle of Wight, England), British poet; introduced French Surrealism to Great Britain and became a noted translator and critic.

Gunther Gebel-Williams (12 Sep 1934, Schweidnitz, Germany [now Swidnica, Poland]—19 Jul 2001, Venice FL), German-born American circus animal trainer; was one of the most celebrated circus entertainers in history. As animal trainer for the Ringling Brothers and Barnum & Bailey Circus, he was particularly known for his work with big cats.

Edward Gierek (6 Jan 1913, Porabka, Poland, Austria-Hungary—29 Jul 2001, Cieszyn, Poland), Polish politician; as the first secretary of the Polish Communist Party for almost a decade (1970–80) sought to modernize Poland's economy and introduce social reforms, but his attempts ultimately led to financial insolvency and political unrest.

Sir Ernst Hans Josef Gombrich (30 Mar 1909, Vienna, Austria-Hungary—3 Nov 2001, London, England), Austrian-born art historian who introduced millions of people to art through his best-known book, The Story of Art (1950; 16th rev. ed. 1995) a clearly written, accessible work that was originally intended for young people but eventually sold millions of copies in more than 20 languages.

Carlos Hank González (28 Aug 1927, Santiago Tianguistenco, Mexico—11 Aug 2001, Santiago Tianguistenco, Mexico), Mexican politician; a highly influential member of Mexico's long-ruling Institutional Revolutionary Party and held public office almost continuously from 1955 to 1994.

John Gotti (27 Oct 1940, New York NY—10 Jun 2002, Springfield MO), American organized crime figure and one of America's best-known gangsters; he headed the notorious Gambino crime family before his incarceration in 1992.

Stephen Jay Gould (10 Sep 1941, New York NY—20 May 2002, New York NY), American paleontologist, evolutionary biologist, and writer; was the prolific author of over a dozen books in addition to 300 consecutive monthly "This View of Life" essays in Natural History magazine (1974–2001) in which he made scientific discussion accessible and entertaining to the common reader without diluting its content. He was best known for a theory of evolution he and his colleague Niles Eldredge developed in 1972, known as punctuated equilibria, that contradicted conventional thinking on the subject.

Katharine Meyer Graham (16 Jun 1917, New York NY—17 Jul 2001, Boise ID), American newspaper executive; took over the leadership position at the Washington Post following the death of her publisher husband and guided it to a position of new success, influence, and respect. Among her most important actions were the decisions to publish the Pentagon Papers—secret government documents concerning decisions about the conduct of the Vietnam War—and to allow two of the paper's reporters, Bob Woodward and Carl Bernstein, to investigate what became known as the Watergate scandal and led to the resignation of Pres. Richard M. Nixon. She was the first woman to serve as the head of a Fortune 500 company and was considered the most powerful woman in the US.

Norman Granz (6 Aug 1918, Los Angeles CA—22 Nov 2001, Geneva, Switzerland), American concert and record producer; he presented top musicians in Jazz at the Philharmonic (JATP) concerts around the world and documented them on records for over four decades. At JATP shows, soloists won wild applause for frantic honking-horn "battles," but they also created music of lasting merit.

Dolores Gray (7 Jun 1924, Chicago IL—26 Jun 2002, New York NY), American singer and actress, a star of film and Broadway during the 1940s and '50s.

Jane Greer (Bettejane Greer; 9 Sep 1924, Washington DC—24 Aug 2001, Los Angeles CA), American actress; secured her image as a femme fatale with her portrayal of Kathie Moffat, the quintessential film noir temptress, in the classic Out of the Past (1947).

Peter Gzowski (13 Jul 1934, Toronto, ON, Canada—24 Jan 2002, Toronto, ON, Canada), Canadian broadcaster; was the inimitable gravelly voiced host of the national radio show This Country in the Morning (1971–74) and the three-hour radio program Morningside (1982–97); he infused warmth, intimacy, and passion into his programs, which featured an eclectic blend of interviews and commentary.

Quintin McGarel Hogg, Baron Hailsham of St. Marylebone (9 Oct 1907, London, England—12 Oct 2001, London, England), British politician who between 1938 and 1987 served six Conservative governments in a variety of posts, most notably 12 years (1970–74, 1979–87) as lord high chancellor (head of the British judiciary).

Virginia Hamilton (12 Mar 1936, Yellow Springs OH—19 Feb 2002, Dayton OH), American children's author, a master storyteller who preserved black oral tradition following intensive research that uncovered long-forgotten riddles, stories, and traditions, many of which she resurrected in such books as The People Could Fly (1985) and Many Thousands Gone: African Americans from Slavery to Freedom (1993).

Ruth Mosko Handler (4 Nov 1916, Denver CO—27 Apr 2002, Los Angeles CA), American entrepreneur and businesswoman; was a cofounder of Mattel and created the Barbie doll, which in 1959 became the first mass-produced toy doll in the US with adult features.

Alex Hannum (19 Jul 1923, Los Angeles CA—18 Jan 2002, San Diego CA), American basketball coach, the first to win championships in both the National Basketball Association (NBA) and the American Basketball Association (ABA); he was also one of only two coaches ever to win NBA titles with two different teams.

Abdul Haq (Humayoun Arsala; 1957/58, Nangarhar province, Afghanistan—26 Oct 2001, Kabul, Afghanistan), Afghan resistance leader, an audacious guerrilla commander in Afghanistan's war against the Soviet Union and later became an internationally known English-language spokesman for the anti-Taliban resistance.

Warren Harding (1924, Downieville CA—27 Feb 2002, Happy Valley CA), American rock climber, the first to scale El Capitan, the 1,098-m (3,604-ft) granite monolith in Yosemite National Park.

R(ichard) M(ervyn) Hare (21 Mar 1919, Backwell, Somerset, England—29 Jan 2002, Ewelme, Oxfordshire, England), British moral philosopher who attempted to provide a rational understanding of moral beliefs; his moral theory, called prescriptivism, was first presented in The Language of Morals (1952).

Benjamin Harkarvy (16 Dec 1930, New York NY—30 Mar 2002, New York NY), American dance teacher, choreographer, and artistic director.

Marvin Harris (18 Aug 1927, New York NY—25 Oct 2001, Gainesville FL), American anthropologist and theoretician known for his research on cultural materialism, which led him to pose a number of controversial theories, including that warfare was a means of reducing population numbers when protein became scarce and that cannibalism among the Aztecs arose from a need for protein sufficiency.

George Harrison (25 Feb 1943, Liverpool, England—29 Nov 2001, Los Angeles CA), British musician, singer, and songwriter; he was the lead guitarist of the Beatles, who infused rock and roll with new depth and sophistication and became one of the most important and influential bands in the history of rock music; he later also achieved singular success as a songwriter and performer. Harrison was the youngest of the "Fab Four" and was known as the "quiet Beatle," and though he had wanted to be successful, he never became comfortable with fame.

Signe Hasso (Signe Larsson; 15 Aug 1910, Stockholm, Sweden—8 Jun 2002, Los Angeles CA), Swedish and American actress; appeared in almost two dozen Hollywood films, including Heaven Can Wait (1943).

Sir Nigel Barnard Hawthorne (5 Apr 1929, Coventry, England—26 Dec 2001, Baldock, Hertfordshire, England), British actor who displayed his versatility in roles both comic and classic during a half-century-long career; he costarred as the quintessential civil servant Sir Humphrey Appleby in the satiric BBC series Yes, Minister (1980–83, 1985–86) and its sequel, Yes, Prime Minister (1986–87).

(Anna) Eileen Heckart (29 Mar 1919, Columbus OH—31 Dec 2001, Norwalk CT), American actress who took advantage of her lanky stature, smoky voice, and winning smile to enjoy a long career on the stage, in film, and on television, often playing eccentric characters.

Alfred Henry Heineken (4 Nov 1923, Amsterdam, The Netherlands—3 Jan 2002, Noordwijk, The Netherlands), Dutch brewer; during a lifetime at the brewery founded by his grandfather in 1873, he used aggressive and innovative marketing to build Heineken N.V. into the world's third largest beer company.

Herblock (Herbert Lawrence Block; 13 Oct 1909, Chicago IL—7 Oct 2001, Washington DC), American political cartoonist who enjoyed a 72-year-long career, through the terms of 13 presidents, during which his drawings, syndicated in hundreds of newspapers throughout the US and in several other countries, simply and clearly spotlighted his support of civil liberties and civil rights and his view of the political issues of the day.

Dick Hern (The Major; 20 Jan 1921, Holford, Somerset, England 22 May 2002, England), British racehorse trainer who served as royal trainer under Queen Elizabeth II for more than 20 years and had over a dozen British Classic victories during his career.

Thor Heyerdahl (6 Oct 1914, Larvik, Norway—18 Apr 2002, near Colla Michari, Italy), Norwegian anthropologist, explorer, and writer who attempted to prove his unconventional ideas about prehistoric exploration and migration by re-creating those voyages himself. Although his theories about parallels between ancient cultures far from each other and the possibility that they may have had common origins did not gain acceptance in the scientific community, his exploits and his books about them captured the imagination of the general public.

Stefan Heym (Helmut Flieg; 10 Apr 1913, Chemnitz, Germany—16 Dec 2001, Jerusalem, Israel), German writer and political activist; as the author of over a dozen novels, including The Crusaders (1948), he provoked controversy with his dissident writings.

Elie Hobeika (Elias Joseph Hobeika; 1956, Kleiat, Lebanon—24 Jan 2002, Hazmiyeh, Lebanon), Lebanese militia leader; he was the ruthless head of the Maronite Christian Lebanese militia (Phalangist) military intelligence and was reportedly commander of the forces who in September 1982 slaughtered hundreds of Palestinian men, women, and children in Beirut's Sabra and Shatila refugee camps.

Frances Rappaport Horwich (16 Jul 1908, Ottawa OH—25 Jul 2001, Scottsdale AZ), American educator and host of the popular children's educational television show Ding Dong School from 1952 to 1907.

Harlan Perry Howard (8 Sep 1927/29, Lexington KY—3 Mar 2002, Nashville TN), American country songwriter who wrote more than 4,000 songs during his six-decade-long career and saw over 100 of them—including "Heartaches by the Number" (1959), "I Fall to Pieces" (1961; co-written with Hank Cochran), and "Busted"—reach the top 10.

Sir Fred Hoyle (24 Jun 1915, Bingley, Yorkshire, England—20 Aug 2001, Bournemouth, Dorset, England), British astrophysicist; Hoyle was the foremost promoter of the "steady-state theory," which holds that the universe is always expanding and that new matter is being continuously created to maintain a constant mean density in space. To his great consternation, however, Hoyle was forever associated with the term big bang, which he coined in the early 1950s as a term of derision to denigrate the opposing cosmological theory that the universe began in a sudden explosive expansion of matter and energy from a highly compressed primordial state.

Faith Elliott Hubley (16 Sep 1924, New York NY—7 Dec 2001, New Haven CT), American film animator; made films that combined music, magic, and myth in their celebration of life and humanity.

Roy Huggins (18 Jul 1914, Litelle WA 3 Apr 2002, Santa Monica CA), American writer, producer, and director; counted such innovative hit television series as Maverick (1957–62), 77 Sunset Strip (1958–64), The Fugitive (1963–67), and The Rockford Files (1974–80) among the many successes he was associated with.

Paul Chandler Hume (13 Dec 1915, Chicago IL—26 Nov 2001, Baltimore MD), American music critic who wrote highly esteemed reviews for the Washington Post for 35 years (from 1947), taught music history at Georgetown University, Washington DC (1950–77), and served as a visiting professor at Yale University (1975–83).

Maxwell White Hunter (11 Mar 1922, Hollidaysburg PA—10 Nov 2001, Los Angeles CA), American aeronautical engineer; a leading rocket scientist who was influential in the development of the US space program.

Nasir Hussain (1931, Bhopal, Madhya Pradesh, India—12 Mar 2002, Mumbai [Bombay], India), Indian motion-picture writer, director, and producer; made a score of light-hearted Bollywood films.

Yuji Hyakutake (1951, Japan—10 Apr 2002, Kokubu, Japan), Japanese amateur astronomer who discovered the comet that came to be named after him, Comet Hyakutake, almost by accident.

George Ireland (15 Jun 1913, Madison WI—14 Sep 2001, Addison IL), American basketball coach; served at Loyola University (Chicago) for 24 seasons beginning in 1951 and retired with a 321–255 record.

John Jackson (25 Feb 1924, Woodville VA—20 Jan 2002, Fairfax VA), American blues guitarist who was considered a master of the Piedmont blues tradition.

Elizabeth Joan Jennings (18 Jul 1926, Boston, Lincolnshire, England—26 Oct 2001, Bampton, Oxfordshire, England), British poet who wrote traditional verse that was both intensely personal and universal. Her poetry was direct and understated, and it reflected her devout Roman Catholicism.

Waylon Jennings (15 Jun 1937, Littlefield TX—13 Feb 2002, Chandler AZ), American country music singer and songwriter who recorded some 60 albums and 16 number one country hits and sold more than 40 million records worldwide; in the 1970s he spearheaded, with Willie Nelson, a movement known as "outlaw music," which blended folk lyrics, rock rhythms, and honky tonk-style instrumentation.

Jia Lanpo (25 Nov 1908, Hebei province, China—8 Jul 2001, Beijing, China), Chinese archaeologist who was internationally known for his work as director of the Peking man excavation at the Zhoukoudian cave complex near Beijing.

Charles Martin ("Chuck") Jones (21 Sep 1912, Spokane WA—22 Feb 2002, Corona del Mar CA), American animator; spent 70 years drawing cartoons and during that time created some of the world's most famous and most loved cartoon characters, including Bugs Bunny, Daffy Duck, Porky Pig, Elmer Fudd, Pepe Le Pew, Marvin Martian, Road Runner, and Wile E. Coyote.

June Jordan (9 Jul 1936, New York NY—14 Jun 2002, Berkeley CA), American poet, writer, teacher, and activist; she was one of the most widely published and well-respected African American writers.

William Jovanovich (Vladimir Jovanovich; 6 Feb 1920, Louisville CO—4 Dec 2001, San Diego CA), American publisher who joined the Harcourt Brace and Co. publishing company as a college textbook salesman in 1947 and by 1954 was president. Under his leadership the company—renamed Harcourt Brace Jovanovich in 1970—incorporated such innovations as the use of colorful illustrations and detailed teachers' guides and grew to be one of the largest textbook publishers.

Traudl Junge (Gertraud Humps Junge; 16 Mar 1920, Munich, Germany—11 Feb 2002, Munich, Germany), German secretary; Junge was Adolf Hitler's private secretary from December 1942 until April 1945.

Pauline Kael (19 Jun 1919, Petaluma CA—3 Sep 2001, Great Barrington MA), American film critic, an outspoken reviewer for *The New Yorker* magazine from 1968 to 1979 and 1980 to 1991, wielding untold influence among film fans and perhaps even moviemakers themselves. Celebrated as much for the provocative style of her writing as for the content, she honed a swordlike sharpness that would eviscerate a faulty work as deftly as it would crown a new piece of art.

Shizue Hirota Kato (2 Mar 1897, Tokyo, Japan—22 Dec 2001, Tokyo, Japan), Japanese feminist and political leader; she began in the 1920s to campaign for women's rights and was the first woman to promote family planning in Japan.

Genichi Kawakami (30 Jan 1912, Hamakita, Hamamatsu, Shizuoka prefecture, Japan—25 May 2002, near Hamamatsu, Japan), Japanese businessman, the visionary president of the Yamaha Corp. for three decades (1950–77 and 1980–83).

Stelios Kazantzidis (29 Aug 1931, Athens, Greece—14 Sep 2001, Athens, Greece), Greek folk singer who used his expressive vocal interpretations to capture the joys as well as the melancholy longings of Greeks everywhere, especially those in the working class and emigrants in the Greek diaspora.

John B. Keane (1928, Listowel, Ireland—30 May 2002, Listowel, Ireland), Irish writer and playwright, the author of 32 works of prose and poetry, and almost a score of plays focusing on life in rural Ireland.

Seydou Keïta (1921/23?, French Sudan—21 Nov 2001, Paris, France), Malian photographer who fashioned insightful studio portraits of ordinary Malian people, usually posed with intriguing combinations of African and Western clothing and props that he provided.

Thomas Joseph Kelly (14 Jun 1929, New York NY—23 Mar 2002, Cutchogue NY), American aerospace engineer who led the team of engineers that designed the lunar excursion module *Eagle*, in which Apollo 11 astronauts Neil Armstrong and Edwin Aldrin, Jr., landed on the Moon on 20 Jul 1969.

Gyorgy Kepes (4 Oct 1906, Selyp, Hungary—29 Dec 2001, Cambridge MA), Hungarian-born American artist and theorist who experimented with new technologies for art through design, photography, and painting.

Ken Elton Kesey (17 Sep 1935, La Junta CO—10 Nov 2001, Eugene OR), American writer; became an icon of the counterculture with both his first book, *One Flew over the Cuckoo's Nest* (1962) and his hippie lifestyle as he and a group of friends—the Merry Pranksters—made a cross-country school-bus trip, along the way staging LSD-inspired "happenings."

Leo Kharibian (27 Apr 1927, Boston MA—23 Aug 2001, Leicestershire, England?), American-born dancer, choreographer, and director; he helped change the face of musical theater choreography in Great Britain by incorporating American jazz dance movement in works for the stage, film, and television.

Josef Klaus (15 Aug 1910, Mauthen, Austria, Austria-Hungary—26 Jul 2001, Vienna, Austria), Austrian politician; chairman of the center-right People's Party (ÖVP), was Austria's chancellor in an uneasy coalition with the Socialist Party for two years (1964–66) and served at the head of the country's first post-World War II noncoalition, single-party government (1966–70).

(Geoffrey Goodman) James ("Jimmy") Knapp (29 Sep 1940, Hurlford, Ayrshire, Scotland—13 Aug 2001), British labor leader, from 1983 general secretary of the UK's largest railway workers' federation, the National Union of Railwaymen (NUR) and its successor, the Rail, Maritime and Transport Union (RMT).

Hildegard (Frieda Albertina) Knef (also known as Hildegard Neff) (28 Dec 1925, Ulm, Germany—1 Feb 2002, Berlin, Germany), German actress and singer in Europe and in the US, where she triumphed as the Soviet commissar Ninotchka in Cole

Porter's Broadway musical *Silk Stockings* (1955) and appeared in numerous Hollywood films.

Damon Francis Knight (19 Sep 1922, Baker City OR—15 Apr 2002, Eugene OR), American science-fiction writer, editor, and critic; wrote more than a dozen novels and over 100 short stories—the best known of which, "To Serve Man" (1950), was adapted for the television series *The Twilight Zone* and became a classic—but made a greater impact on the genre as an editor and critic.

John Knowles (16 Sep 1926, Fairmont WV—29 Nov 2001, near Fort Lauderdale FL), American writer; Knowles won instant acclaim for his first novel, *A Separate Peace* (1959) which sold more than eight million copies. The enduring classic became a part of the syllabus of high-school English classes throughout the US.

Hannelore Renner Kohl (7 Mar 1933, Berlin, Germany—5 Jul 2001, Ludwigshafen, Germany), German political wife; as the wife of Helmut Kohl (from 1960) was the de facto first lady during his 16 years as chancellor of West Germany (1982–90) and reunified Germany (1990–98). In 1993 she was stricken with photodermatitis, a rare allergy to sunlight, and the escalating isolation and physical pain she experienced eventually led her to take her own life.

Ashok Kumar (Kumadlal Kunjilal Ganguly; 13 Oct 1911, Bhagalpur, Bihar, India—10 Dec 2001, Mumbai [Bombay], India), Indian actor; became one of the most popular, best-loved, and longest-lasting stars of India's Bollywood motion picture industry in a career that spanned more than 60 years and some 300 films. He had a natural style of acting that allowed him to be effective and believable in a variety of characters, and he set a style—especially for cigarette smoking—that was copied by young men all across the country.

Spyros Kyprianou (28 Oct 1932, Limassol, Cyprus—12 Mar 2002, Nicosia, Cyprus), Greek Cypriot nationalist leader and politician who succeeded independent Cypruo's founder, Archbishop Makarios, as president in 1977.

Jaggernath Lachmon (21 Sep 1916, Nieuw Nickerie, Dutch Guiana [now Suriname]—19 Oct 2001, Amsterdam, The Netherlands), Surinamese politician; a prominent figure in Surinamese politics for over half a century.

R(afael) A(loysius) Lafferty (7 Nov 1914, Neola IA—18 Mar 2002, Broken Arrow OK), American writer, a prolific, award-winning author of science fiction and historical novels; he also published more than 200 short stories.

Robert Joseph Lamphere (14 Feb 1918, Wardner ID—7 Jan 2002, Tucson AZ), American government agent; as a counterintelligence specialist for the FBI, Lamphere supervised several major Soviet espionage cases from the end of World War II to the mid 1950s.

Ann Landers (Esther "Eppie" Lederer; 4 Jul 1918, Sioux City IA—22 Jun 2002, Chicago IL), American advice columnist who wrote one of the most widely syndicated columns in the world for more than 40 years. She was known for her often blunt yet compassionate advice on questions of etiquette, relationships, and social issues.

Dick "Night Train" Lane (16 Apr 1928, Austin TX—29 Jan 2002, Austin TX), American professional football player, one of the leading defensive backs of the NFL in the 1950s and '60s.

Aleksandr Ivanovich Lebed (20 Apr 1950, Novocherkassk, Russia, USSR—28 Apr 2002, Abakan, Russia), Soviet general and politician; was a decorated military hero who made headlines in 1991 when he refused to lead troops against Russian Pres. Boris Yeltsin in the aborted coup against Soviet Pres. Mikhail Gorbachev; in 1996 he unsuccessfully ran against Yeltsin in the Russian Federation's presidential election.

Juan Lechín Oquendo (19 May 1914, Corocoro, Bolivia—27 Aug 2001, La Paz, Bolivia), Bolivian trade union leader and revolutionary politician; he was the key founder (1946) and longtime leader of the Trade Union Confederation, and as such was commander of a workers' uprising that, with its triumph in 1952 and the reforms it brought, began what became known as a "golden decade."

Peggy Lee (Norma Delores Egstrom; 26 May 1920, Jamestown ND—21 Jan 2002, Los Angeles CA), American vocalist who sang in a quiet, intimate voice, with swing and subtle accenting that conveyed intelligence as well as sex appeal. She also won success as an actress and songwriter, most notably in the Walt Disney film *Lady and the Tramp* (1955), for which she co-wrote songs and created the voices for several animated animals.

Francis Lemarque (Nathan Korb; 25 Nov 1917, Paris, France—20 Apr 2002, La Varenne-Saint-Hilaire, France), French singer and songwriter; during a nearly 70-year career, he wrote some 1,000 chansons, notably *"A Paris," "Marjolaine," "Bal petit bal,"* and the ardent pacifist anthem *"Quand un soldat."* He also composed for radio, television, and motion pictures and formed a music publishing company.

Giovanni Leone (3 Nov 1908, Pomigliano d'Arco, Italy—9 Nov 2001, Rome, Italy), Italian politician, a respected member of the Christian Democratic Party, a practicing attorney and professor of criminal law (from 1933), a longtime member of the Italian parliament (1948–67), a life senator (from 1967), and twice interim prime minister (1963 and 1968).

(Ange-)Philippe Léotard (28 Aug 1940, Nice, France—25 Aug 2001, Paris, France), French actor, poet, and chansonnier; appeared in more than 70 French- and English-language films, including *French Connection II* (1975), *Les Misérables* (1995), and *La Balance* (1982; *The Nark*), for which he won a César, France's highest cinema award, as best actor.

David Kellogg Lewis (28 Sep 1941, Oberlin OH—14 Oct 2001, Princeton NJ), American philosopher who created the theory of "modal realism," which considered possible worlds—that is, all conceivable states of affairs that do not involve logical contradictions—as actually existing rather than as mere heuristic devices.

Flora Lewis (29 Jul 1922, Los Angeles CA—2 Jun 2002, Paris, France), American journalist, a top-notch reporter and columnist who specialized in international affairs. From 1980 to 1990 she was the foreign affairs columnist for the *New York Times* and from 1990 to 1994 its senior columnist; beginning in 1994 and continuing until her death, she worked as a syndicated columnist.

R(ichard) W(arrington) B(aldwin) Lewis (1 Nov 1917—13 Jun 2002, Bethany CT), American critic and biographer who explored themes in the history of American culture; he won the Pulitzer Prize for his book *Edith Wharton: A Biography* (1975).

Astrid Lindgren (Astrid Anna Emilia Ericsson; 14 Nov 1907, Vimmerby, Sweden—28 Jan 2002, Stockholm, Sweden), Swedish children's writer; delighted youngsters around the world with more than 70 books, but her greatest creation was the indomitable Pippi Longstocking, a freckle-faced, red-haired nine-year-old character Lindgren had conceived in 1941 to entertain her sick daughter. The anarchic Pippilottta Delicatessa Windowshade Mackrelmint Efraim's Daughter Longstocking first appeared in print in *Pippi Långstrump* (1945; *Pippi Longstocking,* 1950); the novel and its sequels sold millions of copies and inspired both Swedish- and English-language films.

Jay Harold Livingston (28 Mar 1915, McDonald PA—17 Oct 2001, Los Angeles CA), American songwriter; in collaboration with Ray Evans, created songs for some 80 motion pictures, including three songs that won Academy Awards—"Buttons and Bows" from the Bob Hope western comedy *The Paleface* (1948); "Mona Lisa" from *Captain Carey, USA* (1950) and later made famous by Nat ("King") Cole; and "Que Sera, Sera," sung by Doris Day in *The Man Who Knew Too Much* (1956).

Valery Lobanovsky (1 Jun 1939, Kiev, USSR—13 May 2002, Zaporizhya, Ukraine), Soviet Russian athlete and trainer who served as head coach for the Ukraine association football (soccer) team Dynamo Kiev, which under his leadership won several league titles and two European Cup Winners' Cup titles; he also led the Soviet team to second place in the 1988 European Championships.

Francis Aungier Pakenham, 7th earl of Longford (5 Dec 1905, London, England—3 Aug 2001, London, England), British politician admired as an active social reformer in a long political career as a government minister in the 1940s and '50s and later as an outspoken member of the House of Lords, of which he was leader 1964-68.

Lisa Nicole Lopes (27 May 1971, Philadelphia PA—25 Apr 2002, near La Ceiba, Honduras), American rap singer and songwriter; was a member of the ultrasuccessful female rhythm-and-blues group TLC, which had sales in the multimillions and whose albums *CrazySexyCool* (1994) and *Fanmail* (1999) each won two Grammy Awards.

(John) Walter Lord, Jr. (8 Oct 1917, Baltimore MD—19 May 2002, New York NY), American writer who reignited public interest in the 1912 sinking of the *Titanic* with his riveting minute-by-minute account of the ship's final night in the best-seller *A Night to Remember* (1955).

Lord Pretender (Aldric Farrell; 8 Sep 1917, Tobago island, British colony of Trinidad and Tobago—22 Jan 2002, Port of Spain, Trinidad and Tobago), Trinidadian calypso singer; during a 72-year career, he was a master of "extempo" calypso in which the performer spontaneously devises songs filled with intricate lyrics and rhymes, usually in response to suggested subjects shouted from the audience.

Linda Lovelace (Linda Boreman; 10 Jan 1949, Bronx NY—22 Apr 2002, Denver CO), American actress who starred in the classic feature-length pornography movie *Deep Throat* (1972), which ended up being shown in mainstream theaters and earned some $600 million; she later became an antipornography activist.

Peter Maas (27 Jun 1929, New York NY—23 Aug 2001, New York NY), American writer who enjoyed a half-century-long career during which he published over a dozen books as well as numerous magazine articles.

Paul Magloire (19 Jul 1907, Cap-Haitien, Haiti—12 Jul 2001, Port-au-Prince, Haiti), military ruler of Haiti from 1950 to 1956.

Michael Joseph ("Mike") Mansfield (16 Mar 1903, New York NY—5 Oct 2001, Washington DC), American politician and diplomat; served as majority leader of the US Senate from 1961 to 1977 under four presidents—the longest anyone had held that post. In 1978 Mansfield was appointed ambassador to Japan, and upon his return to the US in 1988, he became a senior adviser at the investment banking firm Goldman Sachs.

(Harold) Stanley Marcus (20 Apr 1905, Dallas TX—22 Jan 2002, Dallas TX), American businessman who worked his way up to president (1950-72) and chairman of the board (1972-75) of the family department store, Neiman Marcus, and turned it into a retailing giant, with more than 30 stores across the US.

Princess Margaret (Princess Margaret Rose Windsor, Countess of Snowden; 21 Aug 1930, Glamis Castle, Scotland—9 Feb 2002, London, England), British royal, the second daughter of King George VI and Queen Elizabeth (from 1952 Queen Elizabeth, The Queen Mother; *q.v.*) and the younger sister of Queen Elizabeth II, Margaret was a glamorous beauty who struggled throughout her life to balance an independent spirit and artistic temperament with her duties as a member of Britain's royal family.

James Slattin Martin, Jr. (21 Jun 1920, Washington DC—14 Apr 2002, Rising Sun MD), American aeronautical engineer who served as project manager for NASA's Viking 1 and 2 missions, which in 1976 sent the two unmanned orbiter-lander pairs to Mars, from which the first close-up pictures and detailed maps of that planet were relayed back to Earth.

Ahmad Shah Masoud (1953, Bazarak, Afghanistan—death reported on 15 Sep 2001, Takhar, Afghanistan), Afghan resistance leader and politician; he was a military leader in the Afghan *mujahideen,* first against the Soviets and the Soviet-backed Afghan government (1978-89) and then against the Taliban (from 1992).

Gordon Matthews (26 Jul 1936, Tulsa OK—23 Feb 2002, Dallas TX), American inventor and businessman; Matthews was the inventor in the 1970s of voice mail, the electronic system for recording and accessing spoken messages; the invention revolutionized business communications.

Govan Archibald Mvuyelwa Mbeki (9 Jul 1910, Nqamakwe, South Africa—30 Aug 2001, Port Elizabeth, South Africa), South African nationalist; as a teacher, writer, labor organizer, and editor of the leftist newspaper *New Age,* he was in the vanguard of the antiapartheid struggle against the South African government; father of South African Pres. Thabo Mbeki.

Staley Thomas McBrayer (22 Jun 1909, Saltillo TX—14 Apr 2002, Fort Worth TX), American newspaper publisher who led a team of colleagues in adapting the offset printing press for use in newspaper printing, a cost-saving innovation that revolutionized the industry.

Dorothy Hackett McGuire (14 Jun 1918, Omaha NE—14 Sep 2001, Santa Monica CA), American actress who had a long stage and screen career in which she specialized in portraying gentle, warm, and intelligent women. The qualities she projected—

kindness, integrity, and inner strength—did not rely on glamour, and she was thus able to make a smooth transition into motherly roles in her later years.

Carl Curtis McIntire (17 May 1906, Ypsilanti MI—19 Mar 2002, Voorhees NJ), American evangelist and radio broadcaster; was a firebrand fundamentalist preacher whose radio show, *20th Century Reformation Hour*, was broadcast daily on more than 600 radio stations during the 1960s.

(George Cadogan) Gardner McKay (10 Jun 1932, New York NY—21 Nov 2001, Honolulu HI), American collegiate and professional football coach who guided the University of Southern California football team to four national titles—in 1962, 1967, 1972, and 1974; from 1976 to 1984 he coached the NFL Tampa Bay Buccaneers.

Harry Martin Meyer, Jr. (25 Nov 1928, Palestine TX—19 Aug 2001, Kenmore WA), American pediatric virologist who was co-developer of the first vaccine against rubella (German measles), refinement of which resulted in the MMR (measles, mumps, and rubella) vaccine.

Neal Elgar Miller (3 Aug 1909, Milwaukee WI—23 Mar 2002, Hamden CT), American psychologist who conducted pioneering research on biofeedback—a technique by which unconscious or involuntary bodily processes may be manipulated by conscious mental control.

Spike Milligan (Terence Alan Patrick Sean Milligan; 16 Apr 1918, Poona, India—27 Feb 2002, Rye, England), Irish writer and comedian, the leader and the last surviving member of the zany band of comedians who created and presented the 1950s BBC radio hit *The Goon Show*. His anarchic sense of absurdity and unique comic genius made him a model for succeeding generations of comedians and paved the way for the Monty Python brand of alternative comedy.

César Milstein (8 Oct 1927, Bahía Blanca, Argentina—24 Mar 2002, Cambridge, England), Argentine-born British immunologist who shared the Nobel Prize for Physiology or Medicine in 1984 for his work in the development of a technique for producing monoclonal antibodies.

Vasily Pavlovich Mishin (18 Jan 1917, Orekhovo-Zuyevo, Russia—10 Oct 2001, Moscow, Russia), Soviet rocket scientist who was named the chief designer of the Soviet lunar program when Sergey P. Korolyov died in 1966.

Francis Daniels Moore (17 Apr 1913, Evanston IL—24 Nov 2001, Westwood MA), American surgeon; he was the chief surgeon at Peter Bent Brigham Hospital in Boston when in 1954 a team under his direction performed the first successful human organ transplant—a kidney transplant between identical twins.

Lord Moyola (James Chichester-Clark; 12 Feb 1923, Moyola Park, Castledawson, Co. Londonderry, Northern Ireland—17 May 2002, Moyola Park, Castledawson, Co. Londonderry, Northern Ireland), Irish politician, prime minister of Northern Ireland, 1969–71.

Louis Muhlstock (23 Apr 1904, Narajow, Poland—26 Aug 2001, Montreal, PQ, Canada), Polish-born Canadian painter celebrated for his artistic depictions of the Great Depression.

Juan Muñoz (17 Jun 1953, Madrid, Spain—28 Aug 2001, Ibiza, Spain), Spanish sculptor; created moody and challenging installation artworks, most of which featured monochromatic human figures placed amid unnerving architectural spaces and often incorporating animatronics and sound.

Kazuo Nakamura (13 Oct 1926, Vancouver, BC, Canada—9 Apr 2002, Toronto ON), Canadian artist; was a prominent member of Painters Eleven, a group of Toronto-based avant-garde artists who championed Abstract Expressionism in the 1950s and '60s; Nakamura was highly regarded for geometric paintings that were among the most distinctive abstract works in 20th-century Canadian art.

Nguyen Van Thieu (5 Apr 1923, Tri Thuy, French Indochina [now in Vietnam]—29 Sep 2001, Boston MA), Vietnamese military leader and politician; president of the Republic of Vietnam (South Vietnam) from 1967 to 1975. Although he had US support, he eventually blamed American policies for the collapse of South Vietnam.

Duke of Norfolk (Miles Francis Stapleton Fitzalan-Howard; 21 Jul 1915—24 Jun 2002, Henley-on-Thames, Oxfordshire, United Kingdom), British peer who was regarded as Britain's most senior Catholic layman.

Robert Nozick (16 Nov 1938, New York NY—23 Jan 2002, Cambridge MA), American political philosopher, a highly influential champion of libertarianism (although he later renounced it); in his first and best-known book, *Anarchy, State, and Utopia* (1974), he advocated the "minimal state"—a government whose role is limited to protecting citizens from violence, theft, and breach of contract.

Jens Nygaard (26 Oct 1931, Stephens AR—24 Sep 2001, New York NY), American pianist and conductor, the maverick founder and director of the Jupiter Symphony, which for more than two decades offered concerts of rare and unusual classical music in New York City.

Mohan Singh Oberoi (15 Aug 1899, Bhaun, Punjab [now in Pakistan], India—3 May 2002, New Delhi, India), Indian hotelier who owned numerous luxury hotels in India and abroad, and headed the Oberoi Group, a well-known hospitality company.

Esther Afua Ocloo (18 Apr 1919, Peki-Dzake, Ghana—8 Feb 2002, Accra, Ghana), Ghanaian entrepreneur; as cofounder (1979) and head of Women's World Banking, she pioneered the practice of microlending, providing tiny loans (often as little as $50) to small, home-based businesses, usually those run by women in less-developed countries.

Carl ("Bobo") Olson (11 Jul 1928, Honolulu HI—16 Jan 2002, Honolulu HI), American boxer; he was middleweight champion of the world from 1953 to 1955, but his most notable fights were four losses to the legendary Sugar Ray Robinson.

José Ortega Spottorno (13 Nov 1916, Madrid, Spain—18 Feb 2002, Madrid, Spain), Spanish journalist and publisher who founded Alianza Editorial (1966), Spain's major publisher of affordable, quality paperback books, and *El País* (1976), which was the country's best-selling newspaper.

Jean Patchett (16 Feb 1926, Preston MD—22 Jan 2002, La Quinta CA), American model who became a photographic icon during the 1950s and appeared on over 40 magazine covers.

Daniel Pearl (10 Oct 1963, Princeton NJ—late January [?] 2002, Pakistan), American journalist and South Asia bureau chief for *The Wall Street Journal*. On 23 Jan 2002, thinking he was being taken to interview a radical Islamic leader, he was kidnapped; his murder was announced by Pakistani and US officials in late February.

Bill Peet (William Bartlett Peed; 29 Jan 1915, Grandview IN—11 May 2002, Studio City CA), American animator, screenwriter, and author-illustrator; he worked for Walt Disney for 27 years, during which he earned a reputation as a storyteller second only to Disney himself.

Marcos Pérez Jiménez (25 Apr 1914, Michelena, Venezuela—20 Sep 2001, Madrid, Spain), Venezuelan military dictator who headed a regime (1952–58) that was defined by its brutal suppression of dissent, ambitious public-works schemes, and widespread corruption.

Max Ferdinand Perutz (19 May 1914, Vienna, Austria—6 Feb 2002, Cambridge, England), Austrian-born British chemist; shared the 1962 Nobel Prize for Chemistry with colleague John C. Kendrew and helped launch the field of molecular biology.

James Frederick Phillips (20 Nov 1930, Aurora IL—3 Oct 2001, Aurora IL), American environmentalist who employed a number of creative means of demonstrating his displeasure with pollution, especially that caused by corporations, and he acknowledged his efforts by leaving a note signed "the Fox," with a fox's face drawn in the o.

Julia Miller Phillips (7 Apr 1944, New York NY—1 Jan 2002, West Hollywood CA), American producer and writer; in the 1970s she became one of the very few women to have attained a position of power in the world of Hollywood filmmaking, was a coproducer of several of the decade's most successful motion pictures, and for one of those movies—*The Sting*—became the first woman to win a best-picture Academy Award.

Ogden Phipps (26 Nov 1908, New York NY—22 Apr 2002, West Palm Beach FL), American racehorse owner and breeder; was one of the dominant figures in thoroughbred horse racing in the 20th century.

John Robinson Pierce (27 Mar 1910, Des Moines IA—2 Apr 2002, Sunnyvale CA), American engineer recognized as the father of satellite communications.

Sir John Harold Plumb (20 Aug 1911, Leicester, England—21 Oct 2001, Cambridge, England), British historian and academic, a prolific author and a noted expert on the social and political history of 18th-century England, but he was almost as well-known for his sumptuous epicurean lifestyle, acerbic tongue, and reputation as a cantankerous eccentric.

Roy Sydney Porter (31 Dec 1946, London, England—3 Mar 2002, St. Leonards, East Sussex, England), British historian; who wrote scores of scholarly books and papers on a vast array of subjects, most notably British social history and the history of medicine.

Nathan Marsh Pusey (4 Apr 1907, Council Bluffs IA—14 Nov 2001, New York NY), American educator and president of Harvard University from 1953 to 1971. Despite his success in revitalizing the university, he left the post embittered by confrontations with antiwar protesters in the late 1960s.

Francisco ("Paco") Rabal Valera (8 Mar 1925, Aguilas, Spain—29 Aug 2001, Bordeaux, France), Spanish actor; during his nearly 60-year stage and screen career, he evolved from a handsome leading man into an impressive character actor, notably in films directed by Luis Buñuel—including *Nazarín* (1958), *Viridiana* (1961), and *Belle de jour* (1967)—and in Pedro Almodóvar's *¡Átame!* (1990; *Tie Me Up! Tie Me Down!*).

Alvin Radkowsky (30 Jun 1915, Elizabeth NJ—17 Feb 2002, Tel Aviv, Israel), American-born Israeli nuclear physicist; helped build the world's first nuclear-powered submarine, the USS *Nautilus*, in the early 1950s and, later in his career, worked on developing a nuclear reactor fuel that would produce less dangerous radioactive waste.

Dee Dee Ramone (Douglas Glenn Colvin; 18 Sep 1952, Fort Lee VA—5 Jun 2002, Los Angeles CA), American musician, bassist and one of the founding members of the influential punk rock band the Ramones, which was inducted into the Rock and Roll Hall of Fame in 2002.

Maureen Reagan (4 Jan 1941, Los Angeles CA—8 Aug 2001, Granite Bay CA), American political activist, the daughter of former president Ronald Reagan and his first wife, Jane Wyman; a lifelong Republican, she was nevertheless an outspoken advocate of feminism and abortion rights—positions that clashed with her father's conservative views.

Peter John Reynolds (11 Jun 1939, Shifnal, Shropshire, England—26 Sep 2001, Kemer, Turkey), British archaeologist; was one of the world's experts on the Iron Age and a pioneer in the field of experimental archaeology.

Antoine Riboud (24 Dec 1918, Lyons, France—5 May 2002, Paris, France), French businessman who founded Danone, the global food company known for its yogurt, Evian bottled water, and other products.

Mordecai Richler (27 Jan 1931, Montreal, PQ, Canada—3 Jul 2001, Montreal, PQ, Canada), Canadian writer; was celebrated for his vivid, boldly satiric portraits of the haves and have-nots of his native Quebec. His wickedly acerbic novels and essays often garnered outrage from offended parties (of which there were many) while consistently earning him critical acclaim.

Anne Barbara Bradby Ridler (30 Jul 1912, Rugby, Warwickshire, England—15 Oct 2001, Oxford, England), British poet who wrote verse that was devotional and meditative, reflecting her Christian faith, and that dealt with domestic concerns such as marriage and motherhood. Her Elizabethan sense of form and her use of complex metaphors led critics to compare her to the 17th-century Metaphysical poets, particularly George Herbert and Thomas Traherne.

Gerhart Moritz Riegner (12 Sep 1911, Berlin, Germany—3 Dec 2001, Geneva, Switzerland), German-born lawyer and human rights activist; Riegner was the first to warn government officials in London and Washington DC (in August 1942, in what came to be known as the "Riegner telegram") that the Nazis had made the decision to exterminate the Jews in Europe and had begun putting their plans in motion.

David Riesman, Jr. (22 Sep 1909, Philadelphia PA—10 May 2002, Binghamton NY), American sociologist, the coauthor of the international best-seller *The Lonely Crowd: A Study of the Changing American Character* (1951), which analyzed American life, by dividing people into "other-directed," "tradition-directed," and "inner-directed" character types.

Luise Rinser (30 Apr 1911, Pitzling, Bavaria, Germany—24 Mar 2002, Unterhaching, Germany), German writer, a political activist and a prolific author of best-selling novels, essays, short stories, diaries, plays, travel journals, and children's books.

Jean-Paul Riopelle (7 Oct 1923, Montreal, QC, Canada—12 Mar 2002, Ile-aux-Grues, QC, Canada), Canadian artist; was widely regarded as Canada's most important modern artist; his work, much of which was done in the Abstract Expressionist style, was often compared to that of American artist Jackson Pollock.

Reginald Rose (10 Dec 1920, New York NY—19 Apr 2002, Norwalk CT), American television screenwriter who was known for exploring complex social and political issues in screenplays for many of early television's best dramatic series, including Studio One, for which he wrote "Twelve Angry Men" (1954; film version 1957).

Herbert David Ross (13 May 1927, Brooklyn NY—9 Oct 2001, New York NY), American dancer, choreographer, and film director; had a career as a dancer on Broadway and choreographed for ballet companies, the stage, and motion pictures before turning to film directing. Among his numerous popular movies were five Neil Simon comedies and a drama, The Turning Point (1977), that tapped his knowledge of the dance world.

Paul Runyan (12 Jul 1908, Hot Springs AR—17 Mar 2002, Palm Springs CA), American golfer; was one of most accomplished golfers ever at irons play and putting, Runyan won more than 50 tournaments, including the Professional Golfers' Association of America (PGA) Championship in 1934 and 1938.

Harold John Russell (14 Jan 1914, New Sydney, NS, Canada—29 Jan 2002, Needham MA), Canadian-born American actor; was the only actor ever to win two Academy Awards for the same role; for his sensitive portrayal in The Best Years of Our Lives (1946) of World War II veteran Homer Parrish, a sailor who had lost both hands and had them replaced with hooks, he received both the best supporting actor Oscar and a special award for "bringing aid and comfort to disabled veterans through the medium of motion pictures."

Joseph ("Sandy") Saddler (23 Jun 1926, Boston MA—18 Sep 2001, Bronx NY), American boxer who won 144 of his 162 professional fights, was world junior lightweight champion in 1949–51, and was world featherweight champion in 1948–49 and 1950–57.

Niki de Saint Phalle (Catherine Marie-Agnès Fal de Saint Phalle; 29 Oct 1930, Neuilly-sur-Seine, France—21 May 2002, La Jolla CA), French-born American artist who first gained public attention with her artworks at which darts were thrown or guns fired. Her best-known works, however, were her "Nanas"—large, colorful papier-mâché sculptures of the female form—and her 22-piece Tarot Garden in Tuscany, Italy.

Salahuddin Abdul Aziz Shah (Tuanku Salahuddin Abdul Aziz Shah ibni al-Marhum Sultan Hisamuddin Alam Shah; 8 Mar 1926, Klang, Malaya—21 Nov 2001, Kuala Lumpur, Malaysia), Malaysian monarch, the ceremonial head of state, or yang di-pertuan agong (paramount ruler) of Malaysia from 26 Apr 1999.

Jonas Malheiro Savimbi (3 Aug 1934, Munhango, Portuguese Angola 22 Feb 2002, near Lucuse, Angola), Angolan nationalist guerrilla leader, the charismatic and fiercely ambitious leader of the National Union for the Total Independence of Angola (UNITA). Savimbi originally fought alongside the Marxist-oriented Popular Movement for the Liberation of Angola (MPLA) and the US-backed National Front for the Liberation of Angola (FNLA) in the war for liberation from Portugal, but he later turned against his erstwhile allies and waged war on the MPLA-led postindependence government.

Kin'ichi Sawaki (6 Oct 1919, Toyama, Japan—5 Nov 2001, Tokyo, Japan), Japanese haiku poet, one of the preeminent Japanese haijin during the second half of the 20th century; he served as president of the Haiku Poets Association from 1987 to 1993.

Richard Jay ("Dick") Schaap (27 Sep 1934, Brooklyn NY—21 Dec 2001, New York NY), American journalist, biographer, and talk-show host who zestfully documented the inner workings of public figures, notably sports heroes.

Rabbi Eliezer Menachem Schach (1896?, Wabolnick [now Vabalninkas], Lithuania, Russian Empire—2 Nov 2001, Tel Aviv, Israel), Lithuanian-born Israeli Orthodox Jewish scholar and political leader; as the spiritual leader of Israel's non-Zionist ultra-Orthodox political parties—Agudat Yisrael, Shas, and Degel Hatorah—wielded great influence on Israeli government policies.

Emilie Pelzl Schindler (22 Oct 1907, Alt Moletein, Sudetenland, Austria-Hungary [now Czech Republic]—5 Oct 2001, Strausberg, Germany), German-born industrialist and the wife of Oskar Schindler, whom she helped in saving some 1,300 Jews during World War II.

William Howard Scholl (24 Sep 1920, London, England—15 Mar 2002, Douglas, Isle of Man, UK), British businessman and shoe designer who developed an orthopedic wooden sandal in the late 1950s, but young women, charmed by the shoe's deceptively simple looks and the distinctive clip-clip sound it made when they walked, turned the Dr. Scholl sandal into a fashion rage in the 1960s and '70s.

Madhavrao Scindia (10 Mar 1945, Bombay [now Mumbai], India–30 Sep 2001, Mainpur, India), Indian Hindu prince and politician who succeeded (1961) his father as maharaja of the ancient princely state of Gwalior (which was absorbed by independent India in 1948 and incorporated into the modern state of Madhya Pradesh in 1956); after the government abolished Indian royalty, he went into national politics.

Winifred Georg Sebald (18 May 1944, Wertach im Allgäu, Germany—14 Dec 2001, Norwich, England), German-born novelist and scholar who entranced casual readers and critics alike with his haunting, richly imaginative, nonchronologically constructed stories.

Léopold Sédar Senghor (9 Oct 1906, Joal, Senegal, French West Africa—20 Dec 2001, Verson, Normandy, France), Senegalese poet, philosopher, politician, and statesman; straddled the literary and political spheres in his dual roles—as Senegal's first president from 1960 until he voluntarily stepped down 20 years later and as one of Africa's most distinguished French-language poets and the leading figure of the "Négritude" movement, which reassessed African culture in the 1930s and '40s and affirmed the literary and artistic expression of the black African experience.

Anthony Joshua Shaffer (15 May 1926, Liverpool, England—6 Nov 2001, London, England), British playwright and screenwriter who delighted audiences with his ingenious comic thriller Sleuth, which played 2,359 performances in London's West End and more than 2,000 performances on Broadway, where it won the Tony Award for best play of 1970.

Eileen Shanahan (29 Feb 1924, Washington DC—2 Nov 2001, Washington DC), American journalist; a pioneering writer at the *New York Times* and, from 1977 to 1979, a spokeswoman for the administration of US Pres. Jimmy Carter.

Ralph Shapey (12 Mar 1921, Philadelphia PA—13 Jun 2002, Chicago IL), American composer and teacher who combined atonality with lyricism in his works. He composed some 200 pieces in a number of forms, including works for the voice and for orchestra and various combinations of instruments.

John Amos ("Jack") Shea (10 Sep 1910, Lake Placid NY—22 Jan 2002, Saranac Lake NY), American speed skater who became the first double gold medalist in the Winter Olympics when he won the 500- and 1,500-m speed-skating races at the 1932 Games in Lake Placid; he was also the patriarch of the first US family with three generations of Olympians.

Dame Sheila Patricia Violet Sherlock (18 Mar 1918, Dublin, Ireland—30 Dec 2001, London, England), British hepatologist; Sherlock was one of the world's leading authorities on diseases of the liver and served as professor of medicine (1959–83) at London's Royal Free Hospital School of Medicine.

Frank Shuster (5 Sep 1916, Toronto, ON, Canada—13 Jan 2002, Toronto, ON, Canada), Canadian comedian and writer who, along with his high-school friend Johnny Wayne, formed the Wayne and Shuster comedy team and performed together for some 50 years, first on Canadian Broadcasting Corp. radio and then on television.

George Sidney (4 Oct 1916, New York NY—5 May 2002, Las Vegas NV), American film director who directed a number of the most popular movie musicals of the 1940s and '50s, including *Anchors Aweigh* (1945), *Annie Get Your Gun* (1950), *Show Boat* (1951), and *Kiss Me Kate* (1953).

Howard Kingsbury Smith, Jr. (12 May 1914, Ferriday LA—15 Feb 2002, Bethesda MD), American journalist and broadcaster; Smith was a longtime radio and television newscaster who remained true to his convictions and was willing to take a stand on important issues despite the fact that news reporters were traditionally neutral and despite the difficulties his outspokenness caused him in his career.

Sam Snead (Samuel Jackson Snead; "Slammin' Sammy"; 27 May 1912, near Hot Springs VA—23 May 2002, Hot Springs VA), American golfer who won 81 PGA tournaments and, except for the US Open in which he placed second four times, every major championship for which he was eligible.

Villy Sørensen (13 Jan 1929, Copenhagen, Denmark—16 Dec 2001, Copenhagen, Denmark), writer and philosopher who became one of the most influential Danish intellectuals of his generation. A prominent literary critic after World War II, he began his career writing modernist short stories whose subjects often drew upon the rich allegorical traditions of myth and religion.

Layne Thomas Staley (22 Aug 1967, Kirkland WA—found dead 19 Apr 2002, Seattle WA), American singer and songwriter, the lead singer and guitarist for the grunge band Alice in Chains.

Kim Stanley (Patricia Beth Reid; 11 Feb 1925, Tularosa NM—20 Aug 2001, Santa Fe NM), American actress who achieved renown on the Broadway stage in roles that ranged from the tomboyish Millie in *Picnic* (1953) to the nightclub singer Cherie in *Bus Stop* (1955) and to Masha in *The Three Sisters* (1964), attracting both critical and popular acclaim.

Isaac Stern (21 Jul 1920, Kremenets, Ukraine—22 Sep 2001, New York NY), American violinist; was one of the 20th century's best-known musicians and an influential teacher and advocate for the arts.

Zena Sutherland (1915, Winthrop MA—12 Jun 2002, Chicago IL), American editor, writer, and book reviewer; she revised *Children and Books*, considered a classic textbook on children's literature in America, several times between 1969 and 1996.

Yevgeny Svetlanov (6 Sep 1928, Moscow, USSR—3 May 2002, Moscow, Russia), Russian conductor and composer; served as artistic director and chief conductor of the Soviet State Symphony Orchestra, 1965–2000.

Josef Svoboda (10 May 1920, Cáslav, Czechoslovakia—8 Apr 2002, Prague, Czech Republic), Czech stage scenographer who enhanced more than 700 theater, ballet, and opera productions in Europe and the US with his unique vision and technical ingenuity; his innovative designs ranged from massive pieces of relatively traditional scenery to delicately placed strings, mirrors, projected slides, video screens, and lasers.

Richard Sylbert (16 Apr 1928, New York NY—23 Mar 2002, Woodland Hills CA), American motion-picture set designer who won two Academy Awards for his design work on *Who's Afraid of Virginia Woolf?* (1966) and *Dick Tracy* (1990) and received Academy Award nominations for his work on four other films.

Fabio Taglioni (10 Sep 1920, Lugo di Romagna, Italy—18 Jul 2001, Bologna, Italy), Italian engineer and motorcycle designer; during his 35-year career as the chief engineer for the state-owned Ducati (1954–89) he transformed that company's motorcycles from cheap, low-powered scooters that were little more than motorized bicycles into high-priced, high-performance road-racing cycles.

Herman Eugene Talmadge (9 Aug 1913, McRae GA—21 Mar 2002, Hampton GA), American politician; as governor of Georgia from 1948 to 1955 and US senator from 1957 to 1981, Talmadge evolved from an ardent foe of desegregation to a politician whose policies drew strong support from rural African Americans in his home state.

Fred Taylor (3 Dec 1924, Zanesville OH—16 Jan 2002, Hilliard OH), American basketball coach, the longtime head coach at Ohio State University, Columbus; during his tenure, 1958–76, OSU won the NCAA championship in 1960 and reached the title game the following two seasons.

John Thaw (3 Jan 1942, Manchester, England—21 Feb 2002, Luckington, Wiltshire, England), British actor who starred in several TV series and achieved international recognition as the crusty, cerebral Chief Inspector Morse in a series of 33 two-part detective dramas based on the novels of Colin Dexter.

(Rex) David ("Dave") Thomas (2 Jul 1932, Atlantic City NJ—8 Jan 2002, Fort Lauderdale FL), American businessman who founded (1969) the Wendy's fast-food restaurants and built the company into the world's third largest hamburger chain, with more than 6,000 locations.

Hans Heinrich, Baron Thyssen-Bornemisza de Kaszon (13 Apr 1921, Scheveningen, The Netherlands—27 Apr 2002, Sant Feliu de Guixols, Spain), Dutch-born Swiss industrialist and art collector who amassed one of the world's most extensive and valuable private art collections while expanding his family's World War II-ravaged business conglomerate into a multibillion-dollar global empire.

Clifford Possum Tjapaltjarri (1932?, Napperby Station, near Alice Springs, Australia—21 Jun 2002, Alice Springs, Australia), Australian painter, the first Aboriginal artist to achieve international recognition.

Joe Hin Tjio (2 Nov 1919, Java, Indonesia—27 Nov 2001, Gaithersburg MD), Indonesian-born American geneticist who dispelled a 50-year-held belief that the number of chromosomes in the human cell was 48 when he established that the majority of human cells contain 46 chromosomes, arranged in 23 pairs.

James Tobin (5 Mar 1918, Champaign IL—11 Mar 2002, New Haven CT), American economist; who was awarded the Nobel Prize for Economics in 1981 for his portfolio selection theory—a theoretical formulation of investment behavior that offered valuable insight into financial markets.

Barry Took (19 Jun 1928, London, England—31 Mar 2002, London, England), British stand-up comic and comedy writer; wrote zany, anarchic comedy shows for BBC radio and television, including *Monty Python's Flying Circus.*

Pauline Trigère (1908, Paris, France—13 Feb 2002, New York NY), French-born American fashion designer prominent for some half a century and had a celebrity-laden list of clients. She was noted both for her elegant designs and for her outspokenness, and she was the first major designer to employ an African American model.

Stephen Vukile Tshwete (12 Nov 1938, Springs, South Africa—26 Apr 2002, Pretoria, South Africa), South African activist and politician who was political commissioner of Umkhonto we Sizwe ("Spear of the Nation"), the military wing of the antiapartheid African National Congress (ANC), and a member of the ANC national executive committee; he later held cabinet posts.

Dame Dorothy Tutin (8 Apr 1931, London, England—6 Aug 2001, London, England), British actress whose varied repertoire included most of the leading female characters in Shakespeare, Chekhov, and Ibsen, as well as Sally Bowles in the original 1954 London production of *I Am a Camera* and modern plays by John Osborne, Tom Stoppard, and Harold Pinter.

William Tutte (14 May 1917, Newmarket, Suffolk, England—2 May 2002, Waterloo?, ON, Canada), British-born mathematician; broke the German secret code known as Fish during World War II.

Beate Uhse (Beate Köstlin Rotermund-Uhse; 25 Oct 1919, Wargenau, German East Prussia [now in Poland]—16 Jul 2001, Switzerland), German entrepreneur who revolutionized sexual attitudes in post-war Germany as the founder of Beate Uhse AG, Europe's largest chain of shops selling erotic products.

Robert Urich (19 Dec 1946, Toronto OH—16 Apr 2002, Thousand Oaks CA), American actor best remembered as the engaging star of a number of television series, including *S.W.A.T.* (1975–76), *Soap* (1977), and the two for which he was best known, *Vega$* (1978–81); and *Spenser: For Hire* (1985–88).

Ichimura Uzaemon XVII (Bando Mamoru; 1916, Tokyo, Japan—8 Jul 2001, Tokyo), Japanese actor; was one of the greatest *tachiyaku* (male-role actors) in the traditional kabuki theater of Japan.

Dave Van Ronk (30 Jun 1936, New York NY—10 Feb 2002, New York NY), American folk singer and musician, an influential figure in the American folk music revival of the 1950s and '60s who helped

launch the careers of musicians such as Bob Dylan, Tom Paxton, and Suzanne Vega.

Van Tien Dung (1 May 1917, Co Nhue, French Indochina—17 Mar 2002, Hanoi, Vietnam), North Vietnamese general and one of North Vietnam's greatest war heroes—a peasant soldier who rose to become commander in chief of the North Vietnamese army and lead the final Ho Chi Minh Campaign that captured and occupied Saigon, South Vietnam, in 1975.

Cyrus Roberts Vance (27 Mar 1917, Clarksburg WV—12 Jan 2002, New York NY), American lawyer and statesman; Vance served as US secretary of state from 1977 to 1980 during the administration of Pres. Jimmy Carter; in part to protest ill-fated plans to rescue American hostages in Iran, Vance resigned his post, becoming only the third US secretary of state to do so.

Vavá (Edvaldo Izidio Neto; 12 Nov 1934, Recife, Brazil—19 Jan 2002, Rio de Janeiro, Brazil), Brazilian footballer; he was a powerful center-forward, a pivotal member of Brazil's national team.

Peter Voulkos (29 Jan 1924, Bozeman MT—16 Feb 2002, Bowling Green OH), American ceramic artist who helped the craft of pottery gain acceptance as an art form through his creation of ceramic works that were highly esteemed for their originality.

Fritz Walter (31 Oct 1920, Kaiserslautern, Germany—17 Jun 2002, Alsenborn, Germany), German association football (soccer) player; led West Germany's national football team to its first World Cup victory in 1954.

Vernon Anthony Walters (3 Jan 1917, New York NY—10 Feb 2002, West Palm Beach FL), American diplomat and military officer; Walters served as US ambassador to the UN from 1985 to 1988 and as US ambassador to West Germany from 1989 to 1991; fluent in numerous languages, he also served as an interpreter to five US presidents.

Günter Wand (7 Jan 1912, Elberfeld, Germany—14 Feb 2002, Ulmitz, Switzerland), German conductor notable for his rigorous rehearsals and his strong interpretations of the Austro-German Romantic repertory.

Cornelius Anthony ("Dutch") Warmerdam (22 Jun 1915, Long Beach CA—13 Nov 2001, Fresno CA), American pole-vaulter, the first to clear 4.57 m (15 ft), which he attained with a bamboo pole; he went on to break the outdoor record another six times.

Lew Wasserman (15 Mar 1913, Cleveland OH—3 Jun 2002, Beverly Hills CA), American movie mogul, a longtime chairman and CEO of MCA Inc., the company that once owned Universal Studios.

Sylvester Laflin ("Pat") Weaver, Jr. (21 Dec 1908, Los Angeles CA—15 Mar 2002, Santa Barbara CA), American television executive who revolutionized television programming by shifting the production of shows from the sponsors to the networks, with commercial time then sold to sponsors.

Victor Frederick Weisskopf (19 Sep 1908, Vienna, Austria—21 Apr 2002, Newton MA), Austrian-born American physicist who worked on the Manhattan Project to develop the atomic bomb during World War II and later campaigned against the proliferation of nuclear weapons.

Eudora Alice Welty (13 Apr 1909, Jackson MS—23 Jul 2001, Jackson MS), American short-story writer and novelist; she was known for the lyricism, perception, wit, and humanity that infused her works. Although she wrote primarily about the inhabitants

of her native Deep South and their everyday lives, her characters and stories had an appealing universality in their depictions of human emotions and relationships, and her stories were included in numerous anthologies.

Pierre Werner (29 Dec 1913, Lille, France—24 Jun 2002), Luxembourgeois politician who served as Luxembourg's prime minister from 1959 to 1974 and from 1979 to 1984. Many credit him with having been the first politician to suggest a single European currency.

Garry Weston (Garfield Howard Weston; 28 Apr 1927, Canada—15 Feb 2002, London, England), Canadian-born entrepreneur and philanthropist; who took control of the family's multinational business, Associated British Foods plc (ABF), when his father retired in 1967 and turned it into a vast international conglomerate.

Byron Raymond ("Whizzer") White (8 Jun 1917, Fort Collins CO—15 Apr 2002, Denver CO), American jurist and professional football player; White served as associate justice of the United States Supreme Court from 1962 to 1993. White achieved early fame on the gridiron—and his nickname "Whizzer"—as a speedy halfback on the University of Colorado, Boulder, football team.

Robert Whitehead (3 Mar 1916, Montreal, PQ, Canada—15 Jun 2002, Pound Ridge NY), American theater producer who brought quality productions of the works of such well-regarded American playwrights as Arthur Miller, Eugene O'Neill, and Tennessee Williams to Broadway.

Mary Hutcheson Whitehouse (13 Jun 1910, Nuneaton, Warwickshire, England—23 Nov 2001, Colchester, England), British schoolteacher and campaigner, a founder (1964) and president of the Clean Up TV Campaign (later [1965] the National Viewers' and Listeners' Association and then [1994] Mediawatch) for some three decades pursued her goal of removing sexual and violent content from television, stage, and film.

Daniel Leopold Wildenstein (11 Sep 1917, Verrières-le-Buisson, France—23 Oct 2001, Paris, France), French-born art historian, art dealer, and Thoroughbred race horse owner; he was the head of Wildenstein & Co., a secretive and tightly controlled billion-dollar art dynasty that was founded in the 1870s by his grandfather.

Billy Wilder (Samuel Wilder; 22 Jun 1906, Sucha, Austria [now in Poland]—27 Mar 2002, Beverly Hills CA), Austrian-born American film director and screenwriter who brought his wit and his cynical, satiric sensibility to more than 50 motion pictures in a number of genres, including film noir, drama, melodrama, slapstick, and black comedy. He counted six Academy Awards—three of them for one film, *The Apartment* (1960), a unique achievement—among his numerous honors, and a number of his films came to be considered classics.

Gordon Randolph Willey (7 Mar 1913, Chariton IA—28 Apr 2002, Cambridge MA), American archaeologist and writer who expanded the study of ancient societies to include not only excavations of the tombs of the pre-Columbian elite but also the artifacts of the households of ordinary people.

Harrison Arlington Williams, Jr. (10 Dec 1919, Plainfield NJ—17 Nov 2001, Denville NJ), American politician, a prominent Democrat who later served time in federal prison after being convicted of bribery and conspiracy in the Abscam scandal.

Gösta Winbergh (30 Dec 1943, Stockholm, Sweden—18 Mar 2002, Vienna, Austria), Swedish opera singer; abandoned a career in structural engineering for one in music and was, for almost 30 years, a leading tenor in most of the major opera houses across Europe and the US.

Thomas Winship (1 Jul 1920, Cambridge MA—14 Mar 2002, Boston MA), American newspaper editor; he took over the post of *The Boston Globe* editor from his father, Laurence Winship, in 1965 and served until 1984, raising the paper to the highest ranks and guiding it to 12 Pulitzer Prizes.

Sir Walter Winterbottom (31 Mar 1913, Oldham, Lancashire, England—16 Feb 2002, Guildford, Surrey, England), British association football (soccer) manager; who was, from 1946 to 1962, the first and longest-serving full-time manager of England's national football team as well as the Football Association's director of coaching.

(Elizabeth) Audrey Withers (28 Mar 1905, Hale, Cheshire, England—26 Oct 2001), British journalist; she was appointed editor of *Vogue* in 1940 and over the following two decades increased both the magazine's size and its subscription base through her transformation and modernization of its content.

Mamo Wolde (Degaga Wolde; 12 Jun 1932, Dirre Jille, Ethiopia—26 May 2002, Addis Ababa, Ethiopia), Ethiopian distance runner who won the gold medal in the marathon competition at the 1968 Olympic Games in Mexico City, and the bronze at the 1972 Games in Munich.

Kenneth Wolstenholme (17 Jul 1920, Worsley, Lancashire, England—25 Mar 2002, Torquay, Devon, England), British sports commentator who covered more than 2,000 association football (soccer) matches, 23 FA Cup finals, and five World Cups between 1948 and 1970.

Donald Woods (15 Dec 1933, Elliotdale, South Africa—19 Aug 2001, Sutton, Surrey, England), South African journalist and antiapartheid campaigner who captured the attention of the world in 1977 with an exposé on the death while in police custody of his friend Steve Biko, a prominent young black activist and founder of the Black Consciousness Movement.

Irene Worth (Harriet Elizabeth Abrams; 23 Jun 1915/16, Lincoln NE—10 Mar 2002, New York NY), American actress who enjoyed a distinguished half-century-long international career, especially on the New York City and London stages. She shone in both classical and modern works and counted three Tony Awards among her numerous honors.

Mariana Yampolsky (6 Sep 1925, Chicago IL—3 May 2002, Mexico City, Mexico), American-born Mexican photographer who captured idyllic, elegiac images of that country, its people, and its daily life.

Michael Dunlop Young, Baron Young of Dartington (9 Aug 1915, Manchester, England—14 Jan 2002, London, England), British lawyer, sociologist, and social reformer who was best known for writing the Labour Party's 1945 social-welfare manifesto and for coining the pejorative term "meritocracy."

Rechavam Ze'evi (20 Aug 1926, Jerusalem, Palestine—17 Oct 2001, Jerusalem, Israel), Israeli soldier and politician who pursued hard-line ultranationalist policies, most notably in support of his outspoken belief that all Palestinians should be removed from the Israel-occupied territories in Gaza and the West Bank and transferred to Arab countries and his claim that the kingdom of Jordan should belong to Israel.

Awards

The Alfred B. Nobel Prizes

The Nobel Prizes are widely regarded as the most prestigious awards given for intellectual achievement in the world. They are awarded annually from a fund bequeathed for that purpose by the Swedish inventor and industrialist Alfred Bernhard Nobel and administered by the Nobel Foundation. Nobel's 1895 will established five of the six prizes: those for physics, chemistry, literature, physiology or medicine, and peace. The prize for economic sciences was added in 1969.

Physics

YEAR	WINNER(S)	NATIONALITY*	ACHIEVEMENT
1901	Wilhelm Conrad Röntgen	Germany	discovery of X rays
1902	Hendrik Antoon Lorentz	Neth.	investigation of the influence of magnetism on radiation
	Pieter Zeeman	Neth.	investigation of the influence of magnetism on radiation
1903	Henri Becquerel	France	discovery of spontaneous radioactivity
	Marie Curie	France	investigations of radiation phenomena discovered by Becquerel
	Pierre Curie	France	investigations of radiation phenomena discovered by Becquerel
1904	John William Strutt, 3rd Baron Rayleigh (of Terling Place)	UK	discovery of argon
1905	Philipp Lenard	Germany	research on cathode rays
1906	Sir J.J. Thomson	UK	researches into electrical conductivity of gases
1907	A.A. Michelson	US	spectroscopic and metrological investigations
1908	Gabriel Lippmann	France	photographic reproduction of colors
1909	Ferdinand Braun	Germany	development of wireless telegraphy
	Guglielmo Marconi	Italy	development of wireless telegraphy
1910	Johannes Diederik van der Waals	Neth.	research concerning the equation of state of gases and liquids
1911	Wilhelm Wien	Germany	discoveries regarding laws governing heat radiation
1912	Nils Dalén	Sweden	invention of automatic regulators for lighting coastal beacons and light buoys
1913	Heike Kamerlingh Onnes	Neth.	investigation into the properties of matter at low temperatures; production of liquid helium
1914	Max von Laue	Germany	discovery of diffraction of X rays by crystals
1915	Sir Lawrence Bragg	UK	analysis of crystal structure by means of X rays
	Sir William Bragg	UK	analysis of crystal structure by means of X rays
1917	Charles Glover Barkla	UK	discovery of characteristic X-radiation of elements
1918	Max Planck	Germany	discovery of the elemental quanta
1919	Johannes Stark	Germany	discovery of Doppler effect in positive ion rays and division of spectral lines in electric field
1920	Charles Édouard Guillaume	Switz.	discovery of anomalies in alloys
1921	Albert Einstein	Switz.	work in theoretical physics
1922	Niels Bohr	Denmark	investigation of atomic structure and radiation
1923	Robert Andrews Millikan	US	work on elementary electric charge and the photoelectric effect
1924	Karl Manne Georg Siegbahn	Sweden	work in X-ray spectroscopy
1925	James Franck	Germany	discovery of the laws governing the impact of an electron upon an atom
	Gustav Hertz	Germany	discovery of the laws governing the impact of an electron upon an atom
1926	Jean Perrin	France	work on discontinuous structure of matter
1927	Arthur Holly Compton	US	discovery of wavelength change in diffused X rays
	C.T.R. Wilson	UK	method of making visible the paths of electrically charged particles
1928	Sir Owen Willans Richardson	UK	work on electron emission by hot metals
1929	Louis-Victor, 7° duc (duke) de Broglie	France	discovery of the wave nature of electrons

Physics (continued)

YEAR	WINNER(S)	NATIONALITY*	ACHIEVEMENT
1930	Sir Chandrasekhara Venkata Raman	India	work on light diffusion; discovery of Raman effect
1932	Werner Heisenberg	Germany	creation of quantum mechanics
1933	P.A.M. Dirac	UK	introduction of wave equations in quantum mechanics
	Erwin Schrödinger	Austria	introduction of wave equations in quantum mechanics
1935	Sir James Chadwick	UK	discovery of the neutron
1936	Carl David Anderson	US	discovery of the positron
	Victor Francis Hess	Austria	discovery of cosmic radiation
1937	Clinton Joseph Davisson	US	experimental demonstration of the interference phenomenon in crystals irradiated by electrons
	Sir George Paget Thomson	UK	experimental demonstration of the interference phenomenon in crystals irradiated by electrons
1938	Enrico Fermi	Italy	disclosure of artificial radioactive elements produced by neutron irradiation
1939	Ernest Orlando Lawrence	US	invention of the cyclotron
1943	Otto Stern	US	discovery of the magnetic moment of the proton
1944	Isidor Isaac Rabi	US	resonance method for registration of various properties of atomic nuclei
1945	Wolfgang Pauli	Austria	discovery of the exclusion principle of electrons
1946	Percy Williams Bridgman	US	discoveries in the domain of high-pressure physics
1947	Sir Edward Victor Appleton	UK	discovery of Appleton layer in upper atmosphere
1948	Patrick M.S. Blackett	UK	discoveries in the domain of nuclear physics and cosmic radiation
1949	Yukawa Hideki	Japan	prediction of the existence of mesons
1950	Cecil Frank Powell	UK	photographic method of studying nuclear processes; discoveries concerning mesons
1951	Sir John Douglas Cockcroft	UK	work on transmutation of atomic nuclei by accelerated particles
	Ernest Thomas Sinton Walton	Ireland	work on transmutation of atomic nuclei by accelerated particles
1952	Felix Bloch	US	discovery of nuclear magnetic resonance in solids
	E.M. Purcell	US	discovery of nuclear magnetic resonance in solids
1953	Frits Zernike	Neth.	method of phase-contrast microscopy
1954	Max Born	UK	statistical studies of atomic wave functions
	Walther Bothe	W.Ger.	invention of coincidence method
1955	Polykarp Kusch	US	measurement of magnetic moment of electron
	Willis Eugene Lamb, Jr.	US	discoveries in the hydrogen spectrum
1956	John Bardeen	US	investigations on semiconductors and invention of the transistor
	Walter H. Brattain	US	investigations on semiconductors and invention of the transistor
	William B. Shockley	US	investigations on semiconductors and invention of the transistor
1957	Tsung-Dao Lee	China	discovery of violations of the principle of parity
	Chen Ning Yang	China	discovery of violations of the principle of parity
1958	Pavel Alekseyevich Cherenkov	USSR	discovery and interpretation of the Cherenkov effect
	Ilya Mikhaylovich Frank	USSR	discovery and interpretation of the Cherenkov effect
	Igor Yevgenyevich Tamm	USSR	discovery and interpretation of the Cherenkov effect
1959	Owen Chamberlain	US	confirmation of the existence of the antiproton
	Emilio Segrè	US	confirmation of the existence of the antiproton
1960	Donald A. Glaser	US	development of the bubble chamber
1961	Robert Hofstadter	US	determination of shape and size of atomic nucleons
	Rudolf Ludwig Mössbauer	W.Ger.	discovery of the Mössbauer effect
1962	Lev Davidovich Landau	USSR	contributions to the understanding of condensed states of matter
1963	J. Hans D. Jensen	W.Ger.	development of shell model theory of the structure of the atomic nuclei
	Maria Goeppert Mayer	US	development of shell model theory of the structure of the atomic nuclei
	Eugene Paul Wigner	US	principles governing interaction of protons and neutrons in the nucleus

Physics (continued)

YEAR	WINNER(S)	NATIONALITY*	ACHIEVEMENT
1964	Nikolay Gennadiyevich Basov	USSR	work in quantum electronics leading to construction of instruments based on maser-laser principles
	Aleksandr Mikhaylovich Prokhorov	USSR	work in quantum electronics leading to construction of instruments based on maser-laser principles
	Charles Hard Townes	US	work in quantum electronics leading to construction of instruments based on maser-laser principles
1965	Richard P. Feynman	US	basic principles of quantum electrodynamics
	Julian Seymour Schwinger	US	basic principles of quantum electrodynamics
	Tomonaga Shin'ichiro	Japan	basic principles of quantum electrodynamics
1966	Alfred Kastler	France	discovery of optical methods for studying Hertzian resonances in atoms
1967	Hans Albrecht Bethe	US	discoveries concerning the energy production of stars
1968	Luis W. Alvarez	US	work with elementary particles, discovery of resonance states
1969	Murray Gell-Mann	US	classification of elementary particles and their interactions
1970	Hannes Alfvén	Sweden	work in magnetohydrodynamics and in antiferromagnetism and ferrimagnetism
	Louis-Eugène-Félix Néel	France	work in magnetohydrodynamics and in antiferromagnetism and ferrimagnetism
1971	Dennis Gabor	UK	invention of holography
1972	John Bardeen	US	development of the theory of superconductivity
	Leon N. Cooper	US	development of the theory of superconductivity
	John Robert Schrieffer	US	development of the theory of superconductivity
1973	Leo Esaki	Japan	tunneling in semiconductors and superconductors
	Ivar Giaever	US	tunneling in semiconductors and superconductors
	Brian D. Josephson	UK	tunneling in semiconductors and superconductors
1974	Antony Hewish	UK	work in radio astronomy
	Sir Martin Ryle	UK	work in radio astronomy
1975	Aage N. Bohr	Denmark	work on the atomic nucleus that paved the way for nuclear fusion
	Ben R. Mottelson	Denmark	work on the atomic nucleus that paved the way for nuclear fusion
	James Rainwater	US	work on the atomic nucleus that paved the way for nuclear fusion
1976	Burton Richter	US	discovery of new class of elementary particles (psi, or J)
	Samuel C.C. Ting	US	discovery of new class of elementary particles (psi, or J)
1977	Philip W. Anderson	US	contributions to understanding the behavior of electrons in magnetic, noncrystalline solids
	Sir Nevill F. Mott	UK	contributions to understanding the behavior of electrons in magnetic, noncrystalline solids
	John H. Van Vleck	US	contributions to understanding the behavior of electrons in magnetic, noncrystalline solids
1978	Pyotr Leonidovich Kapitsa	USSR	invention and application of helium liquefier
	Arno Penzias	US	discovery of cosmic microwave background radiation, providing support for the big-bang theory
	Robert Woodrow Wilson	US	discovery of cosmic microwave background radiation, providing support for the big-bang theory
1979	Sheldon Lee Glashow	US	unification of electromagnetism and the weak interactions of subatomic particles
	Abdus Salam	Pakistan	unification of electromagnetism and the weak interactions of subatomic particles
	Steven Weinberg	US	unification of electromagnetism and the weak interactions of subatomic particles
1980	James Watson Cronin	US	demonstration of simultaneous violation of both charge-conjugation and parity-inversion symmetries
	Val Logsdon Fitch	US	demonstration of simultaneous violation of both charge-conjugation and parity-inversion symmetries
1981	Nicolaas Bloembergen	US	applications of lasers in spectroscopy
	Arthur Leonard Schawlow	US	applications of lasers in spectroscopy
	Kai Manne Börje Siegbahn	Sweden	electron spectroscopy for chemical analysis
1982	Kenneth Geddes Wilson	US	analysis of continuous phase transitions

Physics (continued)

YEAR	WINNER(S)	NATIONALITY*	ACHIEVEMENT
1983	Subrahmanyan Chandrasekhar	US	contributions to understanding the evolution and devolution of stars
	William A. Fowler	US	contributions to understanding the evolution and devolution of stars
1984	Simon van der Meer	Neth.	discovery of subatomic particles W and Z, which supports the electroweak theory
	Carlo Rubbia	Italy	discovery of subatomic particles W and Z, which supports the electroweak theory
1985	Klaus von Klitzing	W.Ger.	discovery of the quantized Hall effect, permitting exact measurements of electrical resistance
1986	Gerd Binnig	W.Ger.	development of special electron microscopes
	Heinrich Rohrer	Switz.	development of special electron microscopes
	Ernst Ruska	W.Ger.	development of special electron microscopes
1987	J. Georg Bednorz	W.Ger.	discovery of new superconducting materials
	Karl Alex Müller	Switz.	discovery of new superconducting materials
1988	Leon Max Lederman	US	research in subatomic particles
	Melvin Schwartz	US	research in subatomic particles
	Jack Steinberger	US	research in subatomic particles
1989	Hans Georg Dehmelt	US	development of methods to isolate atoms and subatomic particles for study
	Wolfgang Paul	W.Ger.	development of methods to isolate atoms and subatomic particles for study
	Norman Foster Ramsey	US	development of the atomic clock
1990	Jerome Isaac Friedman	US	discovery of atomic quarks
	Henry Way Kendall	US	discovery of atomic quarks
	Richard E. Taylor	Canada	discovery of atomic quarks
1991	Pierre-Gilles de Gennes	France	discovery of general rules for behavior of molecules
1992	Georges Charpak	France	inventor of detector that traces subatomic particles
1993	Russell Alan Hulse	US	identifying binary pulsars
	Joseph H. Taylor, Jr.	US	identifying binary pulsars
1994	Bertram N. Brockhouse	Canada	development of neutron-scattering techniques
	Clifford G. Shull	US	development of neutron-scattering techniques
1995	Martin Lewis Perl	US	discovery of tau subatomic particle
	Frederick Reines	US	discovery of neutrino subatomic particle
1996	David M. Lee	US	discovery of superfluidity in isotope helium-3
	Douglas D. Osheroff	US	discovery of superfluidity in isotope helium-3
	Robert C. Richardson	US	discovery of superfluidity in isotope helium-3
1997	Steven Chu	US	process of trapping atoms with laser cooling
	Claude Cohen-Tannoudji	France	process of trapping atoms with laser cooling
	William D. Phillips	US	process of trapping atoms with laser cooling
1998	Robert B. Laughlin	US	discovery of fractional quantum Hall effect
	Horst L. Störmer	US	discovery of fractional quantum Hall effect
	Daniel C. Tsui	US	discovery of fractional quantum Hall effect
1999	Gerardus 't Hooft	Neth.	study of quantum structure of electroweak interactions
	Martinus J.G. Veltman	Neth.	study of quantum structure of electroweak interactions
2000	Zhores I. Alferov	Russia	development of fast semiconductors for use in microelectronics
	Jack S. Kilby	US	development of the integrated circuit (microchip)
	Herbert Kroemer	Germany	development of fast semiconductors for use in microelectronics
2001	Eric A. Cornell	US	achievement of Bose-Einstein condensation in dilute gases of alkali atoms, and for early fundamental studies of the properties of the condensates
	Wolfgang Ketterle	Germany	achievement of Bose-Einstein condensation in dilute gases of alkali atoms, and for early fundamental studies of the properties of the condensates
	Carl E. Wieman	US	achievement of Bose-Einstein condensation in dilute gases of alkali atoms, and for early fundamental studies of the properties of the condensates
2002	scheduled to be announced in October		

Nationality given is the citizenship of recipient at the time award was made. Prizes may be withheld or not awarded in years when no worthy recipient can be found or when the world situation (e.g., World Wars I and II) prevents the gathering of information needed to reach a decision.

Chemistry

YEAR	WINNER(S)	NATIONALITY*	ACHIEVEMENT
1901	Jacobus Henricus van 't Hoff	Neth.	laws of chemical dynamics and osmotic pressure
1902	Emil Fischer	Germany	work on sugar and purine syntheses
1903	Svante Arrhenius	Sweden	theory of electrolytic dissociation
1904	Sir William Ramsay	UK	discovery of inert gas elements and their places in the periodic system
1905	Adolf von Baeyer	Germany	work on organic dyes, hydroaromatic compounds
1906	Henri Moissan	France	isolation of fluorine; introduction of Moissan furnace
1907	Eduard Buchner	Germany	discovery of noncellular fermentation
1908	Ernest Rutherford	UK	investigations into the disintegration of elements and the chemistry of radioactive substances
1909	Wilhelm Ostwald	Germany	pioneer work on catalysis, chemical equilibrium, and reaction velocities
1910	Otto Wallach	Germany	pioneer work in alicyclic combinations
1911	Marie Curie	France	discovery of radium and polonium; isolation of radium
1912	Victor Grignard	France	discovery of the Grignard reagents
	Paul Sabatier	France	method of hydrogenating organic compounds
1913	Alfred Werner	Switz.	work on the linkage of atoms in molecules
1914	Theodore William Richards	US	accurate determination of the atomic weights of numerous elements
1915	Richard Willstätter	Germany	pioneer researches in plant pigments, especially chlorophyll
1918	Fritz Haber	Germany	synthesis of ammonia
1920	Walther Hermann Nernst	Germany	work in thermochemistry
1921	Frederick Soddy	UK	chemistry of radioactive substances; occurrence and nature of isotopes
1922	Francis William Aston	UK	work with mass spectrograph; whole-number rule
1923	Fritz Pregl	Austria	method of microanalysis of organic substances
1925	Richard Zsigmondy	Austria	elucidation of the heterogeneous nature of colloidal solutions
1926	Theodor H.E. Svedberg	Sweden	work on disperse systems
1927	Heinrich Otto Wieland	Germany	researches into the constitution of bile acids
1928	Adolf Windaus	Germany	constitution of sterols and their connection with vitamins
1929	Hans von Euler-Chelpin	Sweden	investigations in the fermentation of sugars and the enzyme action involved
	Sir Arthur Harden	UK	investigations in the fermentation of sugars and the enzyme action involved
1930	Hans Fischer	Germany	hemin, chlorophyll research, synthesis of hemin
1931	Friedrich Bergius	Germany	invention and development of chemical high-pressure methods
	Carl Bosch	Germany	invention and development of chemical high-pressure methods
1932	Irving Langmuir	US	discoveries and investigations in surface chemistry
1934	Harold C. Urey	US	discovery of heavy hydrogen
1935	Frédéric and Irène Joliot-Curie	France	synthesis of new radioactive elements
1936	Peter Debye	Neth.	work on dipole moments and diffraction of X rays and electrons in gases
1937	Sir Norman Haworth	UK	research on carbohydrates and vitamin C
	Paul Karrer	Switz.	research on carotenoids, flavins, and vitamins
1938	Richard Kuhn (declined)	Germany	carotenoid and vitamin research
1939	Adolf Butenandt (declined)	Germany	work on sexual hormones
	Leopold Ruzicka	Switz.	work on polymethylenes and higher terpenes
1943	Georg Charles von Hevesy	Hungary	use of isotopes as tracers in chemical research
1944	Otto Hahn	Germany	discovery of the fission of heavy nuclei
1945	Artturi Ilmari Virtanen	Finland	invention of fodder preservation method
1946	John Howard Northrop	US	preparation of enzymes and virus proteins in pure form
	Wendell Meredith Stanley	US	preparation of enzymes and virus proteins in pure form
	James Batcheller Sumner	US	discovery of enzyme crystallization
1947	Sir Robert Robinson	UK	investigation of alkaloids and other plant products
1948	Arne Tiselius	Sweden	researches in electrophoresis and adsorption analysis; serum proteins
1949	William Francis Giauque	US	behavior of substances at extremely low temperatures

Chemistry (continued)

YEAR	WINNER(S)	NATIONALITY*	ACHIEVEMENT
1950	Kurt Alder	W.Ger.	discovery and development of diene synthesis
	Otto Paul Hermann Diels	W.Ger.	discovery and development of diene synthesis
1951	Edwin Mattison McMillan	US	discovery of and research on transuranium elements
	Glenn T. Seaborg	US	discovery of and research on transuranium elements
1952	A.J.P. Martin	UK	development of partition chromatography
	R.L.M. Synge	UK	development of partition chromatography
1953	Hermann Staudinger	W.Ger.	work on macromolecules
1954	Linus Pauling	US	study of the nature of the chemical bond
1955	Vincent du Vigneaud	US	first synthesis of a polypeptide hormone
1956	Sir Cyril Norman Hinshelwood	UK	work on the kinetics of chemical reactions
	Nikolay Nikolayevich Semyonov	USSR	work on the kinetics of chemical reactions
1957	Alexander Robertus Todd, Baron Todd (of Trumpington)	UK	work on nucleotides and nucleotide coenzymes
1958	Frederick Sanger	UK	determination of the structure of the insulin molecule
1959	Jaroslav Heyrovsky	Czecho-slovakia	discovery and development of polarography
1960	Willard Frank Libby	US	development of radiocarbon dating
1961	Melvin Calvin	US	study of chemical steps that take place during photosynthesis
1962	Sir John Cowdery Kendrew	UK	determination of the structure of hemoproteins
	Max Ferdinand Perutz	UK	determination of the structure of hemoproteins
1963	Giulio Natta	Italy	structure and synthesis of polymers in the field of plastics
	Karl Ziegler	W.Ger.	structure and synthesis of polymers in the field of plastics
1964	Dorothy Mary Crowfoot Hodgkin	UK	determining the structure of biochemical compounds essential in combating pernicious anemia
1965	R.B. Woodward	US	synthesis of sterols, chlorophyll, and other substances
1966	Robert Sanderson Mulliken	US	work concerning chemical bonds and the electronic structure of molecules
1967	Manfred Eigen	W.Ger.	studies of extremely fast chemical reactions
	Ronald George Wreyford Norrish	UK	studies of extremely fast chemical reactions
	Sir George Porter	UK	studies of extremely fast chemical reactions
1968	Lars Onsager	US	work on theory of thermodynamics of irreversible processes
1969	Sir Derek H.R. Barton	UK	work in determining actual three-dimensional shape of molecules
	Odd Hassel	Norway	work in determining actual three-dimensional shape of molecules
1970	Luis Federico Leloir	Argentina	discovery of sugar nucleotides and their role in the biosynthesis of carbohydrates
1971	Gerhard Herzberg	Canada	research in the structure of molecules
1972	Christian B. Anfinsen	US	fundamental contributions to enzyme chemistry
	Stanford Moore	US	fundamental contributions to enzyme chemistry
	William H. Stein	US	fundamental contributions to enzyme chemistry
1973	Ernst Otto Fischer	W.Ger.	organometallic chemistry
	Sir Geoffrey Wilkinson	UK	organometallic chemistry
1974	Paul J. Flory	US	studies of long-chain molecules
1975	Sir John Warcup Cornforth	UK	work in stereochemistry
	Vladimir Prelog	Switz.	work in stereochemistry
1976	William Nunn Lipscomb, Jr.	US	structure of boranes
1977	Ilya Prigogine	Belgium	widening the scope of thermodynamics
1978	Peter Dennis Mitchell	UK	formulation of a theory of energy transfer processes in biological systems
1979	Herbert Charles Brown	US	introduction of compounds of boron and phosphorus in the synthesis of organic substances
	Georg Wittig	W.Ger.	introduction of compounds of boron and phosphorus in the synthesis of organic substances
1980	Paul Berg	US	first preparation of a hybrid DNA
	Walter Gilbert	US	development of chemical and biological analyses of DNA structure
	Frederick Sanger	UK	development of chemical and biological analyses of DNA structure

Chemistry (continued)

YEAR	WINNER(S)	NATIONALITY*	ACHIEVEMENT
1981	Fukui Kenichi	Japan	orbital symmetry interpretation of chemical reactions
	Roald Hoffmann	US	orbital symmetry interpretation of chemical reactions
1982	Aaron Klug	UK	determination of structure of biological substances
1983	Henry Taube	US	study of electron transfer reactions
1984	Bruce Merrifield	US	development of a method of polypeptide synthesis
1985	Herbert A. Hauptman	US	development of a way to map the chemical structures of small molecules
	Jerome Karle	US	development of a way to map the chemical structure of small molecules
1986	Dudley R. Herschbach	US	development of methods for analyzing basic chemical reactions
	Yuan T. Lee	US	development of methods for analyzing basic chemical reactions
	John C. Polanyi	Canada	development of methods for analyzing basic chemical reactions
1987	Donald J. Cram	US	development of molecules that can link with other molecules
	Jean-Marie Lehn	France	development of molecules that can link with other molecules
	Charles J. Pedersen	US	development of molecules that can link with other molecules
1988	Johann Deisenhofer	W.Ger.	discovery of structure of proteins needed in photosynthesis
	Robert Huber	W.Ger.	discovery of structure of proteins needed in photosynthesis
	Hartmut Michel	W.Ger.	discovery of structure of proteins needed in photosynthesis
1989	Sidney Altman	US	discovery of certain basic properties of RNA
	Thomas Robert Cech	US	discovery of certain basic properties of RNA
1990	Elias James Corey	US	development of retrosynthetic analysis for synthesis of complex molecules
1991	Richard R. Ernst	Switz.	improvements in nuclear magnetic resonance spectroscopy
1992	Rudolph A. Marcus	US	explanation of how electrons transfer between molecules
1993	Kary B. Mullis	US	inventors of techniques for gene study and manipulation
	Michael Smith	Canada	inventors of techniques for gene study and manipulation
1994	George A. Olah	US	development of techniques to study hydrocarbon molecules
1995	Paul Crutzen	Neth.	explanation of processes that deplete Earth's ozone layer
	Mario Molina	US	explanation of processes that deplete Earth's ozone layer
	F. Sherwood Rowland	US	explanation of processes that deplete Earth's ozone layer
1996	Robert F. Curl, Jr.	US	discovery of new carbon compounds called fullerenes
	Sir Harold W. Kroto	UK	discovery of new carbon compounds called fullerenes
	Richard E. Smalley	US	discovery of new carbon compounds called fullerenes
1997	Paul D. Boyer	US	explanation of the enzymatic conversion of adenosine triphosphate
	Jens C. Skou	Denmark	discovery of sodium-potassium-activated adenosine triphosphatase
	John E. Walker	UK	explanation of the enzymatic conversion of adenosine triphosphate
1998	Walter Kohn	US	development of the density-functional theory
	John A. Pople	UK	development of computational methods in quantum chemistry
1999	Ahmed H. Zewail	Egypt/US	study of the transition states of chemical reactions using femtosecond spectroscopy
2000	Alan J. Heeger	US	discovery of plastics that conduct electricity
	Alan G. MacDiarmid	US	discovery of plastics that conduct electricity
	Shirakawa Hideki	Japan	discovery of plastics that conduct electricity
2001	William S. Knowles	US	work on chirally catalyzed hydrogenation reactions
	Ryoji Noyori	Japan	work on chirally catalyzed hydrogenation reactions
	K. Barry Sharpless	US	work on chirally catalyzed oxidation reactions
2002	scheduled to be announced in October		

Nationality given is the citizenship of recipient at the time award was made. Prizes may be withheld or not awarded in years when no worthy recipient can be found or when the world situation (e.g., World Wars I and II) prevents the gathering of information needed to reach a decision.

Literature

YEAR	WINNER(S)	NATIONALITY*	ACHIEVEMENT
1901	Sully Prudhomme	France	poet
1902	Theodor Mommsen	Germany	historian
1903	Bjørnstjerne Martinus Bjørnson	Norway	novelist, poet, dramatist
1904	José Echegaray y Eizaguirre	Spain	dramatist
	Frédéric Mistral	France	poet
1905	Henryk Sienkiewicz	Poland	novelist

Literature (continued)

YEAR	WINNER(S)	NATIONALITY*	ACHIEVEMENT
1906	Giosuè Carducci	Italy	poet
1907	Rudyard Kipling	UK	poet, novelist
1908	Rudolf Christoph Eucken	Germany	philosopher
1909	Selma Lagerlöf	Sweden	novelist
1910	Paul Johann Ludwig von Heyse	Germany	poet, novelist, dramatist
1911	Maurice Maeterlinck	Belgium	dramatist
1912	Gerhart Hauptmann	Germany	dramatist
1913	Rabindranath Tagore	India	poet
1915	Romain Rolland	France	novelist
1916	Verner von Heidenstam	Sweden	poet
1917	Karl Gjellerup	Denmark	novelist
	Henrik Pontoppidan	Denmark	novelist
1918	Erik Axel Karlfeldt (declined)	Sweden	poet
1919	Carl Spitteler	Switz.	poet, novelist
1920	Knut Hamsun	Norway	novelist
1921	Anatole France	France	novelist
1922	Jacinto Benavente y Martínez	Spain	dramatist
1923	William Butler Yeats	Ireland	poet
1924	Wladyslaw Stanislaw Reymont	Poland	novelist
1925	George Bernard Shaw	Ireland	dramatist
1926	Grazia Deledda	Italy	novelist
1927	Henri Bergson	France	philosopher
1928	Sigrid Undset	Norway	novelist
1929	Thomas Mann	Germany	novelist
1930	Sinclair Lewis	US	novelist
1931	Erik Axel Karlfeldt (posthumous award)	Sweden	poet
1932	John Galsworthy	UK	novelist
1933	Ivan Alekseyevich Bunin	USSR	poet, novelist
1934	Luigi Pirandello	Italy	dramatist
1936	Eugene O'Neill	US	dramatist
1937	Roger Martin du Gard	France	novelist
1938	Pearl Buck	US	novelist
1939	Frans Eemil Sillanpää	Finland	novelist
1944	Johannes V. Jensen	Denmark	novelist
1945	Gabriela Mistral	Chile	poet
1946	Hermann Hesse	Switz.	novelist
1947	André Gide	France	novelist, essayist
1948	T.S. Eliot	UK	poet, critic
1949	William Faulkner	US	novelist
1950	Bertrand Russell	UK	philosopher
1951	Pär Lagerkvist	Sweden	novelist
1952	François Mauriac	France	poet, novelist, dramatist
1953	Sir Winston Churchill	UK	historian, orator
1954	Ernest Hemingway	US	novelist
1955	Halldór Laxness	Iceland	novelist
1956	Juan Ramón Jiménez	Spain	poet
1957	Albert Camus	France	novelist, dramatist
1958	Boris Leonidovich Pasternak (declined)	USSR	novelist, poet
1959	Salvatore Quasimodo	Italy	poet
1960	Saint-John Perse	France	poet
1961	Ivo Andric	Yugoslavia	novelist
1962	John Steinbeck	US	novelist
1963	George Seferis	Greece	poet
1964	Jean-Paul Sartre (declined)	France	philosopher, dramatist
1965	Mikhail Aleksandrovich Sholokhov	USSR	novelist
1966	S.Y. Agnon	Israel	novelist
	Nelly Sachs	Sweden	poet
1967	Miguel Ángel Asturias	Guatemala	novelist
1968	Kawabata Yasunari	Japan	novelist
1969	Samuel Beckett	Ireland	novelist, dramatist
1970	Aleksandr Isayevich Solzhenitsyn	USSR	novelist
1971	Pablo Neruda	Chile	poet
1972	Heinrich Böll	W.Ger.	novelist
1973	Patrick White	Australia	novelist

Literature (continued)

YEAR	WINNER(S)	NATIONALITY*	ACHIEVEMENT
1974	Eyvind Johnson	Sweden	novelist
	Harry Martinson	Sweden	novelist, poet
1975	Eugenio Montale	Italy	poet
1976	Saul Bellow	US	novelist
1977	Vicente Aleixandre	Spain	poet
1978	Isaac Bashevis Singer	US	novelist
1979	Odysseus Elytis	Greece	poet
1980	Czeslaw Milosz	US	poet
1981	Elias Canetti	Bulgaria	novelist, essayist
1982	Gabriel García Márquez	Colombia	novelist, journalist, social critic
1983	Sir William Golding	UK	novelist
1984	Jaroslav Seifert	Czechoslovakia	poet
1985	Claude Simon	France	novelist
1986	Wole Soyinka	Nigeria	playwright, poet
1987	Joseph Brodsky	US	poet, essayist
1988	Naguib Mahfouz	Egypt	novelist
1989	Camilo José Cela	Spain	novelist
1990	Octavio Paz	Mexico	poet, essayist
1991	Nadine Gordimer	South Africa	novelist
1992	Derek Walcott	St. Lucia	poet
1993	Toni Morrison	US	novelist
1994	Oe Kenzaburo	Japan	novelist
1995	Seamus Heaney	Ireland	poet
1996	Wislawa Szymborska	Poland	poet
1997	Dario Fo	Italy	playwright, actor
1998	José Saramago	Portugal	novelist
1999	Günter Grass	Germany	novelist
2000	Gao Xingjian	France	novelist, playwright
2001	Sir V.S. Naipaul	UK	novelist
2002	scheduled to be announced in October		

Nationality given is the citizenship of recipient at the time award was made. Prizes may be withheld or not awarded in years when no worthy recipient can be found or when the world situation (e.g., World Wars I and II) prevents the gathering of information needed to reach a decision.

Physiology or Medicine

YEAR	WINNER(S)	NATIONALITY*	ACHIEVEMENT
1901	Emil von Behring	Germany	work on serum therapy
1902	Sir Ronald Ross	UK	discovery of how malaria enters an organism
1903	Niels Ryberg Finsen	Denmark	treatment of skin diseases with light
1904	Ivan Petrovich Pavlov	Russia	work on the physiology of digestion
1905	Robert Koch	Germany	tuberculosis research
1906	Camillo Golgi	Italy	work on the structure of the nervous system
1906	Santiago Ramón y Cajal	Spain	work on the structure of the nervous system
1907	Alphonse Laveran	France	discovery of the role of protozoa in diseases
1908	Paul Ehrlich	Germany	work on immunity
1908	Élie Metchnikoff	Russia	work on immunity
1909	Emil Theodor Kocher	Switz.	physiology, pathology, and surgery of the thyroid gland
1910	Albrecht Kossel	Germany	researches in cellular chemistry
1911	Allvar Gullstrand	Sweden	work on dioptrics of the eye
1912	Alexis Carrel	France	work on vascular suture; transplantation of organs
1913	Charles Richet	France	work on anaphylaxis
1914	Robert Bárány	Austria-Hungary	work on vestibular apparatus
1919	Jules Bordet	Belgium	work on immunity factors in blood serum
1920	August Krogh	Denmark	discovery of capillary motor-regulating mechanism
1922	A.V. Hill	UK	discoveries concerning heat production in muscles
	Otto Meyerhof	Germany	work on metabolism of lactic acid in muscles
1923	Sir Frederick Grant Banting	Canada	discovery of insulin
	J.J.R. Macleod	UK	discovery of insulin
1924	Willem Einthoven	Neth.	discovery of electrocardiogram mechanism
1926	Johannes Fibiger	Denmark	contributions to cancer research
1927	Julius Wagner-Jauregg	Austria	work on malaria inoculation in dementia paralytica

Physiology or Medicine (continued)

YEAR	WINNER(S)	NATIONALITY*	ACHIEVEMENT
1928	Charles-Jules-Henri Nicolle	France	work on typhus
1929	Christiaan Eijkman	Neth.	discovery of antineuritic vitamin
	Sir Frederick Gowland Hopkins	UK	discovery of growth-stimulating vitamins
1930	Karl Landsteiner	US	grouping of human blood
1931	Otto Warburg	Germany	discovery of nature and action of respiratory enzyme
1932	Edgar Douglas Adrian, 1st Baron Adrian (of Cambridge)	UK	discoveries regarding function of neurons
	Sir Charles Scott Sherrington	UK	discoveries regarding function of neurons
1933	Thomas Hunt Morgan	US	heredity transmission functions of chromosomes
1934	George Richards Minot	US	discoveries concerning liver treatment for anemia
	William P. Murphy	US	discoveries concerning liver treatment for anemia
	George H. Whipple	US	discoveries concerning liver treatment for anemia
1935	Hans Spemann	Germany	organizer effect in embryo
1936	Sir Henry Dale	UK	work on chemical transmission of nerve impulses
	Otto Loewi	Germany	work on chemical transmission of nerve impulses
1937	Albert Szent-Gyorgyi	Hungary	work on biological combustion
1938	Corneille Heymans	Belgium	discovery of role of sinus and aortic mechanisms in respiration regulation
1939	Gerhard Domagk (declined)	Germany	antibacterial effect of Prontosil
1943	Henrik Dam	Denmark	discovery of vitamin K
	Edward Adelbert Doisy	US	discovery of chemical nature of vitamin K
1944	Joseph Erlanger	US	researches on differentiated functions of nerve fibers
	Herbert Spencer Gasser	US	researches on differentiated functions of nerve fibers
1945	Sir Ernst Boris Chain	UK	discovery of penicillin and its curative value
	Sir Alexander Fleming	UK	discovery of penicillin and its curative value
	Howard Walter Florey, Baron Florey	Australia	discovery of penicillin and its curative value
1946	Hermann Joseph Muller	US	production of mutations by X-ray irradiation
1947	Carl and Gerty Cori	US	discovery of how glycogen is catalytically converted
	Bernardo Alberto Houssay	Argentina	pituitary hormone function in sugar metabolism
1948	Paul Hermann Müller	Switz.	properties of DDT
1949	António Egas Moniz	Portugal	therapeutic value of leucotomy in psychoses
	Walter Rudolf Hess	Switz.	discovery of function of interbrain
1950	Philip Showalter Hench	US	research on adrenal cortex hormones, their structure and biological effects
	Edward Calvin Kendall	US	research on adrenal cortex hormones, their structure and biological effects
	Tadeus Reichstein	Switz.	research on adrenal cortex hormones, their structure and biological effects
1951	Max Theiler	South Africa	yellow fever discoveries
1952	Selman Abraham Waksman	US	discovery of streptomycin
1953	Sir Hans Adolf Krebs	UK	discovery of coenzyme A citric acid cycle in metabolism of carbohydrates
	Fritz Albert Lipmann	US	discovery of coenzyme A citric acid cycle in metabolism of carbohydrates
1954	John Franklin Enders	US	cultivation of the poliomyelitis virus in tissue cultures
	Frederick Chapman Robbins	US	cultivation of the poliomyelitis virus in tissue cultures
	Thomas H. Weller	US	cultivation of the poliomyelitis virus in tissue cultures
1955	Axel Hugo Teodor Theorell	Sweden	nature and mode of action of oxidation enzymes
1956	André F. Cournand	US	discoveries concerning heart catheterization and circulatory changes
	Werner Forssmann	W.Ger.	discoveries concerning heart catheterization and circulatory changes
	Dickinson Woodruff Richards	US	discoveries concerning heart catheterization and circulatory changes
1957	Daniel Bovet	Italy	production of synthetic curare

Physiology or Medicine (continued)

YEAR	WINNER(S)	NATIONALITY*	ACHIEVEMENT
1958	George Wells Beadle	US	genetic regulation of chemical processes
	Joshua Lederberg	US	genetic recombination
	Edward L. Tatum	US	genetic regulation of chemical processes
1959	Arthur Kornberg	US	work on producing nucleic acids artificially
	Severo Ochoa	US	work on producing nucleic acids artificially
1960	Sir Macfarlane Burnet	Australia	acquired immunity to tissue transplants
	Sir Peter B. Medawar	UK	acquired immunity to tissue transplants
1961	Georg von Békésy	US	functions of the inner ear
1962	Francis Harry Compton Crick	UK	discoveries concerning the molecular structure of DNA
	James Dewey Watson	US	discoveries concerning the molecular structure of DNA
	Maurice Wilkins	UK	discoveries concerning the molecular structure of DNA
1963	Sir John Carew Eccles	Australia	study of the transmission of impulses along a nerve fiber
	Sir Alan Hodgkin	UK	study of the transmission of impulses along a nerve fiber
	Sir Andrew Fielding Huxley	UK	study of the transmission of impulses along a nerve fiber
1964	Konrad Bloch	US	discoveries concerning cholesterol and fatty-acid metabolism
	Feodor Lynen	W.Ger.	discoveries concerning cholesterol and fatty-acid metabolism
1965	François Jacob	France	discoveries concerning regulatory activities of the body cells
	André Lwoff	France	discoveries concerning regulatory activities of the body cells
	Jacques Monod	France	discoveries concerning regulatory activities of the body cells
1966	Charles B. Huggins	US	research on causes and treatment of cancer
	Peyton Rous	US	research on causes and treatment of cancer
1967	Ragnar Arthur Granit	Sweden	discoveries about chemical and physiological visual processes in the eye
	Haldan Keffer Hartline	US	discoveries about chemical and physiological visual processes in the eye
	George Wald	US	discoveries about chemical and physiological visual processes in the eye
1968	Robert William Holley	US	deciphering of the genetic code
	Har Gobind Khorana	U.S	deciphering of the genetic code
	Marshall Warren Nirenberg	U.S	deciphering of the genetic code
1969	Max Delbrück	US	research and discoveries concerning viruses and viral diseases
	A.D. Hershey	US	research and discoveries concerning viruses and viral diseases
	Salvador Luria	US	research and discoveries concerning viruses and viral diseases
1970	Julius Axelrod	US	discoveries concerning the chemistry of nerve transmission
	Ulf von Euler	Sweden	discoveries concerning the chemistry of nerve transmission
	Sir Bernard Katz	UK	discoveries concerning the chemistry of nerve transmission
1971	Earl W. Sutherland, Jr.	US	action of hormones
1972	Gerald Maurice Edelman	US	research on the chemical structure of antibodies
	Rodney Robert Porter	UK	research on the chemical structure of antibodies
1973	Karl von Frisch	Austria	discoveries in animal behavior patterns
	Konrad Lorenz	Austria	discoveries in animal behavior patterns
	Nikolaas Tinbergen	UK	discoveries in animal behavior patterns
1974	Albert Claude	US	research on structural and functional organization of cells
	Christian René de Duve	Belgium	research on structural and functional organization of cells
	George E. Palade	US	research on structural and functional organization of cells
1975	David Baltimore	US	interaction between tumor viruses and the genetic material of the cell
	Renato Dulbecco	US	interaction between tumor viruses and the genetic material of the cell
	Howard Martin Temin	US	interaction between tumor viruses and the genetic material of the cell
1976	Baruch S. Blumberg	US	studies of origin and spread of infectious diseases
	D. Carleton Gajdusek	US	studies of origin and spread of infectious diseases
1977	Roger Charles Louis Guillemin	US	research on pituitary hormones
	Andrew Victor Schally	US	research on pituitary hormones
	Rosalyn S. Yalow	US	development of radioimmunoassay

Physiology or Medicine (continued)

YEAR	WINNER(S)	NATIONALITY*	ACHIEVEMENT
1978	Werner Arber	Switz.	discovery and application of enzymes that fragment DNA
	Daniel Nathans	US	discovery and application of enzymes that fragment DNA
	Hamilton Othanel Smith	US	discovery and application of enzymes that fragment DNA
1979	Allan MacLeod Cormack	US	development of the CAT scan
	Sir Godfrey Newbold Hounsfield	UK	development of the CAT scan
1980	Baruj Benacerraf	US	investigations of genetic control of the response of the immune system to foreign substances
	Jean-Baptiste-Gabriel-Joachim Dausset	France	investigations of genetic control of the response of the immune system to foreign substances
	George Davis Snell	US	investigations of genetic control of the response of the immune system to foreign substances
1981	David Hunter Hubel	US	processing of visual information by the brain
	Roger Wolcott Sperry	US	functions of the cerebral hemispheres
	Torsten Nils Wiesel	Sweden	processing of visual information by the brain
1982	Sune K. Bergström	Sweden	biochemistry and physiology of prostaglandins
	Bengt Ingemar Samuelsson	Sweden	biochemistry and physiology of prostaglandins
	John Robert Vane	UK	biochemistry and physiology of prostaglandins
1983	Barbara McClintock	US	discovery of mobile plant genes that affect heredity
1984	Niels K. Jerne	UK-Denmark	theory and development of a technique for producing mono-clonal antibodies
	Georges J.F. Köhler	W.Ger.	theory and development of a technique for producing mono-clonal antibodies
	César Milstein	Argentina	theory and development of a technique for producing mono-clonal antibodies
1985	Michael S. Brown	US	discovery of cell receptors relating to cholesterol metabolism
	Joseph L. Goldstein	US	discovery of cell receptors relating to cholesterol metabolism
1986	Stanley Cohen	US	discovery of chemical agents that help regulate the growth of cells
	Rita Levi-Montalcini	Italy	discovery of chemical agents that help regulate the growth of cells
1987	Tonegawa Susumu	Japan	study of genetic aspects of antibodies
1988	Sir James Black	UK	development of new classes of drugs for combating disease
	Gertrude Belle Elion	US	development of new classes of drugs for combating disease
	George Herbert Hitchings	US	development of new classes of drugs for combating disease
1989	J. Michael Bishop	US	study of cancer-causing genes called oncogenes
	Harold Varmus	US	study of cancer-causing genes called oncogenes
1990	Joseph E. Murray	US	development of kidney and bone-marrow transplants
	E. Donnall Thomas	US	development of kidney and bone-marrow transplants
1991	Erwin Neher	Germany	discovery of how cells communicate, as related to diseases
	Bert Sakmann	Germany	discovery of how cells communicate, as related to diseases
1992	Edmond H. Fischer	US	discovery of class of enzymes called protein kinases
	Edwin Gerhard Krebs	US	discovery of class of enzymes called protein kinases
1993	Richard J. Roberts	UK	discovery of "split," or interrupted, genetic structure
	Phillip A. Sharp	US	discovery of "split," or interrupted, genetic structure
1994	Alfred G. Gilman	US	discovery of cell signalers called G-proteins
	Martin Rodbell	US	discovery of cell signalers called G-proteins
1995	Edward B. Lewis	US	identification of genes that control the body's early structural development
	Christiane Nüsslein-Volhard	Germany	identification of genes that control the body's early structural development
	Eric F. Wieschaus	US	identification of genes that control the body's early structural development
1996	Peter C. Doherty	Australia	discovery of how the immune system recognizes virus-infected cells
	Rolf M. Zinkernagel	Switz.	discovery of how the immune system recognizes virus-infected cells
1997	Stanley B. Prusiner	US	discovery of the prion, a type of disease-causing protein
1998	Robert F. Furchgott	US	discovery that nitric oxide (NO) acts as a signaling molecule in the cardiovascular system
	Louis J. Ignarro	US	discovery that nitric oxide (NO) acts as a signaling molecule in the cardiovascular system
	Ferid Murad	US	discovery that nitric oxide (NO) acts as a signaling molecule in the cardiovascular system

Physiology or Medicine (continued)

YEAR	WINNER(S)	NATIONALITY*	ACHIEVEMENT
1999	Günter Blobel	US	discovery that proteins have signals governing cellular organization
2000	Arvid Carlsson	Sweden	discovery of how signals are transmitted between nerve cells in the brain
	Paul Greengard	US	discovery of how signals are transmitted between nerve cells in the brain
	Eric Kandel	US	discovery of how signals are transmitted between nerve cells in the brain
2001	Leland H. Hartwell	US	discovery of key regulators of the cell cycle
	R. Timothy Hunt	UK	discovery of key regulators of the cell cycle
	Sir Paul M. Nurse	UK	discovery of key regulators of the cell cycle
2002	scheduled to be announced in October		

*Nationality given is the citizenship of recipient at the time award was made. Prizes may be withheld or not awarded in years when no worthy recipient can be found or when the world situation (e.g., World Wars I and II) prevents the gathering of information needed to reach a decision.

Peace

YEAR	WINNER(S)	NATIONALITY*
1901	Henri Dunant	Switz.
	Frédéric Passy	France
1902	Élie Ducommun	Switz.
	Charles-Albert Gobat	Switz.
1903	Sir Randal Cremer	UK
1904	Institute of International Law	(founded 1873)
1905	Bertha, Freifrau von Suttner	Austria-Hungary
1906	Theodore Roosevelt	US
1907	Ernesto Teodoro Moneta	Italy
	Louis Renault	France
1908	Klas Pontus Arnoldson	Sweden
	Fredrik Bajer	Denmark
1909	Auguste-Marie-François Beernaert	Belgium
	Paul-H.-B. d'Estournelles de Constant	France
1910	International Peace Bureau	(founded 1891)
1911	Tobias Michael Carel Asser	Neth.
	Alfred Hermann Fried	Austria-Hungary
1912	Elihu Root	US
1913	Henri-Marie Lafontaine	Belgium
1917	International Committee of the Red Cross	(founded 1863)
1919	Woodrow Wilson	US
1920	Léon Bourgeois	France
1921	Karl Hjalmar Branting	Sweden
	Christian Lous Lange	Norway
1922	Fridtjof Nansen	Norway
1925	Sir Austen Chamberlain	UK
	Charles G. Dawes	US
1926	Aristide Briand	France
	Gustav Stresemann	Germany
1927	Ferdinand Édouard Buisson	France
	Ludwig Quidde	Germany
1929	Frank B. Kellogg	US
1930	Nathan Söderblom	Sweden
1931	Jane Addams	US
	Nicholas Murray Butler	US
1933	Sir Norman Angell	UK
1934	Arthur Henderson	UK
1935	Carl von Ossietzky	Germany
1936	Carlos Saavedra Lamas	Argentina
1937	Robert Gascoyne-Cecil, 1st Viscount Cecil (of Chelwood)	UK

YEAR	WINNER(S)	NATIONALITY*
1938	Nansen International Office for Refugees	(founded 1931)
1944	International Committee of the Red Cross	(founded 1863)
1945	Cordell Hull	US
1946	Emily Greene Balch	US
	John R. Mott	US
1947	American Friends Service Committee	US
	Friends Service Council (FSC)	UK
1949	John Boyd Orr, Baron Boyd-Orr of Brechin Mearns	UK
1950	Ralph Bunche	US
1951	Léon Jouhaux	France
1952	Albert Schweitzer	Alsace
1953	George C. Marshall	US
1954	Office of the United Nations High Commissioner for Refugees	(founded 1951)
1957	Lester B. Pearson	Canada
1958	Dominique Pire	Belgium
1959	Philip John Noel-Baker, Baron Noel-Baker (of the City of Derby)	UK
1960	Albert John Luthuli	South Africa
1961	Dag Hammarskjöld	Sweden
1962	Linus Pauling	US
1963	International Committee of the Red Cross	(founded 1863)
	League of Red Cross Societies	
1964	Martin Luther King, Jr.	US
1965	United Nations Children's Fund	(founded 1946)
1968	René Cassin	France
1969	International Labour Organisation	(founded 1919)
1970	Norman Ernest Borlaug	US
1971	Willy Brandt	W.Ger.
1973	Henry Kissinger	US
	Le Duc Tho (declined)	North Vietnam
1974	Seán MacBride	Ireland
	Sato Eisaku	Japan
1975	Andrey Dmitriyevich Sakharov	USSR

Peace (continued)

YEAR	WINNER(S)	NATIONALITY*	YEAR	WINNER(S)	NATIONALITY*
1976	Mairéad Corrigan	Northern Ireland	1990	Mikhail Gorbachev	USSR
	Betty Williams	Northern Ireland	1991	Aung San Suu Kyi	Myanmar
1977	Amnesty International	(founded 1961)	1992	Rigoberta Menchú	Guatemala
1978	Menachem Begin	Israel	1993	F.W. de Klerk	South Africa
	Anwar el-Sadat	Egypt		Nelson Mandela	South Africa
1979	Mother Teresa	India	1994	Yasir 'Arafat	Palestinian
1980	Adolfo Pérez Esquivel	Argentina		Shimon Peres	Israel
1981	Office of the United Nations High Commissioner for Refugees	(founded 1951)		Yitzhak Rabin	Israel
			1995	Pugwash Conferences	(founded 1957)
				Joseph Rotblat	UK
1982	Alfonso García Robles	Mexico	1996	Carlos Filipe Ximenes Belo	Timorese
	Alva Myrdal	Sweden		José Ramos-Horta	Timorese
1983	Lech Walesa	Poland	1997	International Campaign to Ban Landmines	(founded 1992)
1984	Desmond Tutu	South Africa		Jody Williams	US
1985	International Physicians for the Prevention of Nuclear War	(founded 1980)	1998	John Hume	Northern Ireland
				David Trimble	Northern Ireland
1986	Elie Wiesel	US	1999	Doctors Without Borders	(founded 1971)
1987	Oscar Arias Sánchez	Costa Rica	2000	Kim Dae Jung	South Korea
1988	United Nations Peace-keeping Forces		2001	Kofi Annan	Ghana
1989	Dalai Lama	Tibet	2002	scheduled to be announced in October	

Nationality given is the citizenship of recipient at the time award was made. Prizes may be withheld or not awarded in years when no worthy recipient can be found or when the world situation (e.g., World Wars I and II) prevents the gathering of information needed to reach a decision.

Economics

YEAR	WINNER(S)	NATIONALITY*	ACHIEVEMENT
1969	Ragnar Frisch	Norway	work in econometrics
	Jan Tinbergen	Neth.	work in econometrics
1970	Paul Samuelson	US	work in scientific analysis of economic theory
1971	Simon Kuznets	US	extensive research on the economic growth of nations
1972	Kenneth J. Arrow	US	contributions to general economic equilibrium theory and welfare theory
	Sir John R. Hicks	UK	contributions to general economic equilibrium theory and welfare theory
1973	Wassily Leontief	US	input-output analysis
1974	Friedrich von Hayek	UK	pioneering analysis of the interdependence of economic, social, and institutional phenomena
	Gunnar Myrdal	Sweden	pioneering analysis of the interdependence of economic, social, and institutional phenomena
1975	Leonid Vitalyevich Kantorovich	USSR	contributions to the theory of optimum allocation of resources
	Tjalling C. Koopmans	US	contributions to the theory of optimum allocation of resources
1976	Milton Friedman	US	consumption analysis, monetary theory, and economic stabilization
1977	James Edward Meade	UK	contributions to theory of international trade
	Bertil Ohlin	Sweden	contributions to theory of international trade
1978	Herbert Alexander Simon	US	decision-making processes in economic organizations
1979	Sir Arthur Lewis	UK	analyses of economic processes in developing nations
	Theodore William Schultz	US	analyses of economic processes in developing nations
1980	Lawrence Robert Klein	US	development and analysis of empirical models of business fluctuations
1981	James Tobin	US	portfolio selection theory of investment
1982	George J. Stigler	US	economic effects of governmental regulation
1983	Gerard Debreu	US	mathematical proof of supply and demand theory
1984	Sir Richard Stone	UK	development of national income accounting system
1985	Franco Modigliani	US	analyses of household savings and financial markets
1986	James M. Buchanan	US	public-choice theory bridging economics and political science
1987	Robert Merton Solow	US	contributions to the theory of economic growth

Economics (continued)

YEAR	WINNER(S)	NATIONALITY*	ACHIEVEMENT
1988	Maurice Allais	France	contributions to the theory of markets and efficient use of resources
1989	Trygve Haavelmo	Norway	development of statistical techniques for economic forecasting
1990	Harry M. Markowitz	US	study of financial markets and investment decision making
	Merton H. Miller	US	study of financial markets and investment decision making
	William F. Sharpe	US	study of financial markets and investment decision making
1991	Ronald Coase	US	application of economic principles to the study of law
1992	Gary S. Becker	US	application of economic theory to social sciences
1993	Robert William Fogel	US	contributions to economic history
	Douglass C. North	US	contributions to economic history
1994	John C. Harsanyi	US	development of game theory
	John F. Nash	US	development of game theory
	Reinhard Selten	Germany	development of game theory
1995	Robert E. Lucas, Jr.	US	incorporation of rational expectations in macroeconomic theory
1996	James A. Mirrlees	UK	contributions to theory of incentives under conditions of asymmetric information
	William Vickrey	US	contributions to theory of incentives under conditions of asymmetric information
1997	Robert C. Merton	US	method for determining the value of stock options and other derivatives
	Myron S. Scholes	US	method for determining the value of stock options and other derivatives
1998	Amartya Sen	India	contribution to welfare economics
1999	Robert A. Mundell	Canada	analysis of optimum currency areas and of policy under different exchange rate regimes
2000	James J. Heckman	US	development of methods of statistical analysis of individual and household behavior
	Daniel L. McFadden	US	development of methods of statistical analysis of individual and household behavior
2001	George A. Akerlof	US	analyses of markets with asymmetric information
	A. Michael Spence	US	analyses of markets with asymmetric information
	Joseph E. Stiglitz	US	analyses of markets with asymmetric information
2002	scheduled to be announced in October		

*Nationality given is the citizenship of recipient at the time award was made. Prizes may be withheld or not awarded in years when no worthy recipient can be found or when the world situation (e.g., World Wars I and II) prevents the gathering of information needed to reach a decision.

Entertainment Awards

Academy Awards (Oscars), 2001

The Academy of Motion Picture Arts and Sciences was formed in 1927 and first awarded the Academy Awards of Merit in May 1929. The honored categories have varied over the years, but best picture, actor, actress, and director have been awarded since the beginning. Awards for supporting actor and actress were added for the films of 1936 and best foreign language film for 1947. The ceremony is generally held in the early spring of the year following the release of films under consideration; the latest Oscars were awarded 24 Mar 2002 in Los Angeles. Award: gold-plated statuette of a man with a sword. Academy of Motion Picture Arts and Sciences Web site: <www.oscars.org>

CATEGORY	WINNER
Motion picture of the year	A Beautiful Mind (US; Ron Howard, dir.)
Director	Ron Howard (A Beautiful Mind, US)
Actor	Denzel Washington (Training Day, US)
Actress	Halle Berry (Monster's Ball, US)
Supporting actor	Jim Broadbent (Iris, UK/US)
Supporting actress	Jennifer Connelly (A Beautiful Mind, US)
Foreign-language film	No Man's Land (Belgium/Bosnia and Herzegovina/France/Italy/Slovenia/UK; Danis Tanovic, dir.)
Animated feature	Shrek (US; Andrew Adamson, Vicky Jenson, dirs.)
Animated short	For the Birds (US; Ralph Eggleston, dir.)
Live-action short	The Accountant (US; Ray McKinnon, dir.)
Documentary feature	Un coupable idéal (Murder on a Sunday Morning) (France; Jean-Xavier de Lestrade, dir.)
Documentary short	Thoth (US; Sarah Kernochan, dir.)

Academy Awards (Oscars), 2001 (continued)

CATEGORY	WINNER
Art direction	Catherine Martin, art dir., Brigitte Broch, set decor. (*Moulin Rouge*, Australia/US)
Cinematography	Andrew Lesnie (*The Lord of the Rings: The Fellowship of the Ring*, New Zealand/US)
Costume design	Catherine Martin, Angus Strathie (*Moulin Rouge*, Australia/US)
Film editing	Pietro Scalia (*Black Hawk Down*, US)
Makeup	Peter Owen, Richard Taylor (*The Lord of the Rings: The Fellowship of the Ring*, New Zealand/US)
Original score	Howard Shore (*The Lord of the Rings: The Fellowship of the Ring*, New Zealand/US)
Original song	"If I Didn't Have You," Randy Newman (*Monsters, Inc.*, US)
Sound	Mike Minkler, Myron Nettinga, Chris Munro (*Black Hawk Down*, US)
Sound editing	George Watters II, Christopher Boyes (*Pearl Harbor*, US)
Visual effects	Jim Rygiel, Randall William Cook, Richard Taylor, Mark Stetson (*The Lord of the Rings: The Fellowship of the Ring*, New Zealand/US)
Screenplay, adaptation	Akiva Goldsman (*A Beautiful Mind*, US)
Screenplay, original	Julian Fellowes (*Gosford Park*, Italy/UK/US/Germany)

Academy Awards (Oscars), 1928–2001

2002 awards ceremony scheduled to be held 23 Mar 2003 in Los Angeles.

BEST PICTURE
1928 *Wings*
1929 *The Broadway Melody*
1930 *All Quiet on the Western Front*
1931 *Cimarron*
1932 *Grand Hotel*
1933 *Cavalcade*
1934 *It Happened One Night*
1935 *Mutiny on the Bounty*
1936 *The Great Ziegfeld*
1937 *The Life of Emile Zola*
1938 *You Can't Take It with You*
1939 *Gone with the Wind*
1940 *Rebecca*
1941 *How Green Was My Valley*
1942 *Mrs. Miniver*
1943 *Casablanca*
1944 *Going My Way*
1945 *The Lost Weekend*
1946 *Best Years of Our Lives*
1947 *Gentleman's Agreement*
1948 *Hamlet*
1949 *All the King's Men*
1950 *All About Eve*
1951 *An American in Paris*
1952 *The Greatest Show on Earth*

BEST PICTURE (CONTINUED)
1953 *From Here to Eternity*
1954 *On the Waterfront*
1955 *Marty*
1956 *Around the World in 80 Days*
1957 *The Bridge on the River Kwai*
1958 *Gigi*
1959 *Ben-Hur*
1960 *The Apartment*
1961 *West Side Story*
1962 *Lawrence of Arabia*
1963 *Tom Jones*
1964 *My Fair Lady*
1965 *The Sound of Music*
1966 *A Man for All Seasons*
1967 *In the Heat of the Night*
1968 *Oliver!*
1969 *Midnight Cowboy*
1970 *Patton*
1971 *The French Connection*
1972 *The Godfather*
1973 *The Sting*
1974 *The Godfather Part II*
1975 *One Flew Over the Cuckoo's Nest*
1976 *Rocky*

BEST PICTURE (CONTINUED)
1977 *Annie Hall*
1978 *The Deer Hunter*
1979 *Kramer vs. Kramer*
1980 *Ordinary People*
1981 *Chariots of Fire*
1982 *Gandhi*
1983 *Terms of Endearment*
1984 *Amadeus*
1985 *Out of Africa*
1986 *Platoon*
1987 *The Last Emperor*
1988 *Rain Man*
1989 *Driving Miss Daisy*
1990 *Dances with Wolves*
1991 *The Silence of the Lambs*
1992 *Unforgiven*
1993 *Schindler's List*
1994 *Forrest Gump*
1995 *Braveheart*
1996 *The English Patient*
1997 *Titanic*
1998 *Shakespeare in Love*
1999 *American Beauty*
2000 *Gladiator*
2001 *A Beautiful Mind*

BEST ACTOR
1928 Emil Jannings (*The Last Command; The Way of All Flesh*)
1929 Warner Baxter (*In Old Arizona*)
1930 George Arliss (*Disraeli*)
1931 Lionel Barrymore (*A Free Soul*)
1932 Wallace Beery (*The Champ*), Fredric March (*Dr. Jekyll and Mr. Hyde*)
1933 Charles Laughton (*The Private Life of Henry VIII*)
1934 Clark Gable (*It Happened One Night*)
1935 Victor McLaglen (*The Informer*)
1936 Paul Muni (*The Story of Louis Pasteur*)
1937 Spencer Tracy (*Captains Courageous*)
1938 Spencer Tracy (*Boys Town*)
1939 Robert Donat (*Goodbye, Mr. Chips*)
1940 James Stewart (*The Philadelphia Story*)

BEST ACTOR (CONTINUED)
1941 Gary Cooper (*Sergeant York*)
1942 James Cagney (*Yankee Doodle Dandy*)
1943 Paul Lukas (*Watch on the Rhine*)
1944 Bing Crosby (*Going My Way*)
1945 Ray Milland (*The Lost Weekend*)
1946 Fredric March (*The Best Years of Our Lives*)
1947 Ronald Colman (*A Double Life*)
1948 Laurence Olivier (*Hamlet*)
1949 Broderick Crawford (*All the King's Men*)
1950 Jose Ferrer (*Cyrano de Bergerac*)
1951 Humphrey Bogart (*The African Queen*)
1952 Gary Cooper (*High Noon*)
1953 William Holden (*Stalag 17*)
1954 Marlon Brando (*On the Waterfront*)
1955 Ernest Borgnine (*Marty*)
1956 Yul Brynner (*The King and I*)

Academy Awards (Oscars), 1928–2001 (continued)

BEST ACTOR (CONTINUED)

1957 Alec Guinness (The Bridge on the River Kwai)
1958 David Niven (Separate Tables)
1959 Charlton Heston (Ben-Hur)
1960 Burt Lancaster (Elmer Gantry)
1961 Maximilian Schell (Judgment at Nuremberg)
1962 Gregory Peck (To Kill a Mockingbird)
1963 Sidney Poitier (Lilies of the Field)
1964 Rex Harrison (My Fair Lady)
1965 Lee Marvin (Cat Ballou)
1966 Paul Scofield (A Man for All Seasons)
1967 Rod Steiger (In the Heat of the Night)
1968 Cliff Robertson (Charly)
1969 John Wayne (True Grit)
1970 George C. Scott (Patton) (refused)
1971 Gene Hackman (The French Connection)
1972 Marlon Brando (The Godfather)
1973 Jack Lemmon (Save the Tiger)
1974 Art Carney (Harry and Tonto)
1975 Jack Nicholson (One Flew Over the Cuckoo's Nest)
1976 Peter Finch (Network) (posthumous)
1977 Richard Dreyfuss (The Goodbye Girl)
1978 Jon Voight (Coming Home)
1979 Dustin Hoffman (Kramer vs. Kramer)
1980 Robert De Niro (Raging Bull)
1981 Henry Fonda (On Golden Pond)
1982 Ben Kingsley (Gandhi)
1983 Robert Duvall (Tender Mercies)
1984 F. Murray Abraham (Amadeus)
1985 William Hurt (Kiss of the Spider Woman)
1986 Paul Newman (The Color of Money)
1987 Michael Douglas (Wall Street)
1988 Dustin Hoffman (Rain Man)
1989 Daniel Day Lewis (My Left Foot)
1990 Jeremy Irons (Reversal of Fortune)
1991 Anthony Hopkins (The Silence of the Lambs)
1992 Al Pacino (Scent of a Woman)
1993 Tom Hanks (Philadelphia)
1994 Tom Hanks (Forrest Gump)
1995 Nicholas Cage (Leaving Las Vegas)
1996 Geoffrey Rush (Shine)
1997 Jack Nicholson (As Good as It Gets)
1998 Roberto Benigni (Life Is Beautiful)
1999 Kevin Spacey (American Beauty)
2000 Russell Crowe (Gladiator)
2001 Denzel Washington (Training Day)

BEST ACTRESS

1928 Janet Gaynor (7th Heaven; Street Angel; Sunrise)
1929 Mary Pickford (Coquette)
1930 Norma Shearer (The Divorcee)
1931 Marie Dressler (Min and Bill)
1932 Helen Hayes (The Sin of Madelon Claudet)
1933 Katharine Hepburn (Morning Glory)
1934 Claudette Colbert (It Happened One Night)
1935 Bette Davis (Dangerous)
1936 Luise Rainer (The Great Ziegfeld)
1937 Luise Rainer (The Good Earth)
1938 Bette Davis (Jezebel)
1939 Vivien Leigh (Gone with the Wind)
1940 Ginger Rogers (Kitty Foyle)
1941 Joan Fontaine (Suspicion)
1942 Greer Garson (Mrs. Miniver)
1943 Jennifer Jones (The Song of Bernadette)
1944 Ingrid Bergman (Gaslight)
1945 Joan Crawford (Mildred Pierce)
1946 Olivia de Havilland (To Each His Own)

BEST ACTRESS (CONTINUED)

1947 Loretta Young (The Farmer's Daughter)
1948 Jane Wyman (Johnny Belinda)
1949 Olivia de Havilland (The Heiress)
1950 Judy Holliday (Born Yesterday)
1951 Vivien Leigh (A Streetcar Named Desire)
1952 Shirley Booth (Come Back, Little Sheba)
1953 Audrey Hepburn (Roman Holiday)
1954 Grace Kelly (The Country Girl)
1955 Anna Magnani (The Rose Tattoo)
1956 Ingrid Bergman (Anastasia)
1957 Joanne Woodward (The Three Faces of Eve)
1958 Susan Hayward (I Want to Live!)
1959 Simone Signoret (Room at the Top)
1960 Elizabeth Taylor (Butterfield 8)
1961 Sophia Loren (Two Women)
1962 Anne Bancroft (The Miracle Worker)
1963 Patricia Neal (Hud)
1964 Julie Andrews (Mary Poppins)
1965 Julie Christie (Darling)
1966 Elizabeth Taylor (Who's Afraid of Virginia Woolf?)
1967 Katharine Hepburn (Guess Who's Coming to Dinner)
1968 Katharine Hepburn (The Lion in Winter), Barbra Streisand (Funny Girl)
1969 Maggie Smith (The Prime of Miss Jean Brodie)
1970 Glenda Jackson (Women in Love)
1971 Jane Fonda (Klute)
1972 Liza Minnelli (Cabaret)
1973 Glenda Jackson (A Touch of Class)
1974 Ellen Burstyn (Alice Doesn't Live Here Anymore)
1975 Louise Fletcher (One Flew Over the Cuckoo's Nest)
1976 Faye Dunaway (Network)
1977 Diane Keaton (Annie Hall)
1978 Jane Fonda (Coming Home)
1979 Sally Field (Norma Rae)
1980 Sissy Spacek (Coal Miner's Daughter)
1981 Katharine Hepburn (On Golden Pond)
1982 Meryl Streep (Sophie's Choice)
1983 Shirley MacLaine (Terms of Endearment)
1984 Sally Field (Places in the Heart)
1985 Geraldine Page (The Trip to Bountiful)
1986 Marlee Matlin (Children of a Lesser God)
1987 Cher (Moonstruck)
1988 Jodie Foster (The Accused)
1989 Jessica Tandy (Driving Miss Daisy)
1990 Kathy Bates (Misery)
1991 Jodie Foster (The Silence of the Lambs)
1992 Emma Thompson (Howards End)
1993 Holly Hunter (The Piano)
1994 Jessica Lange (Blue Sky)
1995 Susan Sarandon (Dead Man Walking)
1996 Frances McDormand (Fargo)
1997 Helen Hunt (As Good as It Gets)
1998 Gwyneth Paltrow (Shakespeare in Love)
1999 Hilary Swank (Boys Don't Cry)
2000 Julia Roberts (Erin Brockovich)
2001 Halle Berry (Monster's Ball)

BEST SUPPORTING ACTOR

1936 Walter Brennan (Come and Get It)
1937 Joseph Schildkraut (The Life of Emile Zola)
1938 Walter Brennan (Kentucky)
1939 Thomas Mitchell (Stagecoach)
1940 Walter Brennan (The Westerner)

Academy Awards (Oscars), 1928–2001 (continued)

BEST SUPPORTING ACTOR (CONTINUED)

1941 Donald Crisp (How Green Was My Valley)
1942 Van Heflin (Johnny Eager)
1943 Charles Coburn (The More the Merrier)
1944 Barry Fitzgerald (Going My Way)
1945 James Dunn (A Tree Grows in Brooklyn)
1946 Harold Russell (The Best Years of Our Lives)
1947 Edmund Gwenn (Miracle on 34th Street)
1948 Walter Huston (The Treasure of the Sierra Madre)
1949 Dean Jagger (Twelve O'Clock High)
1950 George Sanders (All About Eve)
1951 Karl Malden (A Streetcar Named Desire)
1952 Anthony Quinn (Viva Zapata!)
1953 Frank Sinatra (From Here to Eternity)
1954 Edmond O'Brien (The Barefoot Contessa)
1955 Jack Lemmon (Mister Roberts)
1956 Anthony Quinn (Lust for Life)
1957 Red Buttons (Sayonara)
1958 Burl Ives (The Big Country)
1959 Hugh Griffith (Ben-Hur)
1960 Peter Ustinov (Spartacus)
1961 George Chakiris (West Side Story)
1962 Ed Begley (Sweet Bird of Youth)
1963 Melvyn Douglas (Hud)
1964 Peter Ustinov (Topkapi)
1965 Martin Balsam (A Thousand Clowns)
1966 Walter Matthau (The Fortune Cookie)
1967 George Kennedy (Cool Hand Luke)
1968 Jack Albertson (The Subject Was Roses)
1969 Gig Young (They Shoot Horses, Don't They?)
1970 John Mills (Ryan's Daughter)
1971 Ben Johnson (The Last Picture Show)
1972 Joel Grey (Cabaret)
1973 John Houseman (The Paper Chase)
1974 Robert De Niro (The Godfather Part II)
1975 George Burns (The Sunshine Boys)
1976 Jason Robards (All the President's Men)
1977 Jason Robards (Julia)
1978 Christopher Walken (The Deer Hunter)
1979 Melvyn Douglas (Being There)
1980 Timothy Hutton (Ordinary People)
1981 John Gielgud (Arthur)
1982 Louis Gossett, Jr. (An Officer and a Gentleman)
1983 Jack Nicholson (Terms of Endearment)
1984 Haing S. Ngor (The Killing Fields)
1985 Don Ameche (Cocoon)
1986 Michael Caine (Hannah and Her Sisters)
1987 Sean Connery (The Untouchables)
1988 Kevin Kline (A Fish Called Wanda)
1989 Denzel Washington (Glory)
1990 Joe Pesci (Goodfellas)
1991 Jack Palance (City Slickers)
1992 Gene Hackman (Unforgiven)
1993 Tommy Lee Jones (The Fugitive)
1994 Martin Landau (Ed Wood)
1995 Kevin Spacey (The Usual Suspects)
1996 Cuba Gooding, Jr. (Jerry Maguire)
1997 Robin Williams (Good Will Hunting)
1998 James Coburn (Affliction)
1999 Michael Caine (The Cider House Rules)
2000 Benicio Del Toro (Traffic)
2001 Jim Broadbent (Iris)

BEST SUPPORTING ACTRESS

1936 Gale Sondergaard (Anthony Adverse)
1937 Alice Brady (In Old Chicago)

BEST SUPPORTING ACTRESS (CONTINUED)

1938 Fay Bainter (Jezebel)
1939 Hattie McDaniel (Gone with the Wind)
1940 Jane Darwell (The Grapes of Wrath)
1941 Mary Astor (The Great Lie)
1942 Teresa Wright (Mrs. Miniver)
1943 Katina Paxinou (For Whom the Bell Tolls)
1944 Ethel Barrymore (None but the Lonely Heart)
1945 Anne Revere (National Velvet)
1946 Anne Baxter (The Razor's Edge)
1947 Celeste Holm (Gentleman's Agreement)
1948 Claire Trevor (Key Largo)
1949 Mercedes McCambridge (All the King's Men)
1950 Josephine Hull (Harvey)
1951 Kim Hunter (A Streetcar Named Desire)
1952 Gloria Grahame (The Bad and the Beautiful)
1953 Donna Reed (From Here to Eternity)
1954 Eva Marie Saint (On the Waterfront)
1955 Jo Van Fleet (East of Eden)
1956 Dorothy Malone (Written on the Wind)
1957 Miyoshi Umeki (Sayonara)
1958 Wendy Hiller (Separate Tables)
1959 Shelley Winters (The Diary of Anne Frank)
1960 Shirley Jones (Elmer Gantry)
1961 Rita Moreno (West Side Story)
1962 Patty Duke (The Miracle Worker)
1963 Margaret Rutherford (The V.I.P.s)
1964 Lila Kedrova (Zorba the Greek)
1965 Shelley Winters (A Patch of Blue)
1966 Sandy Dennis (Who's Afraid of Virginia Woolf?)
1967 Estelle Parsons (Bonnie and Clyde)
1968 Ruth Gordon (Rosemary's Baby)
1969 Goldie Hawn (Cactus Flower)
1970 Helen Hayes (Airport)
1971 Cloris Leachman (The Last Picture Show)
1972 Eileen Heckart (Butterflies Are Free)
1973 Tatum O'Neal (Paper Moon)
1974 Ingrid Bergman (Murder on the Orient Express)
1975 Lee Grant (Shampoo)
1976 Beatrice Straight (Network)
1977 Vanessa Redgrave (Julia)
1978 Maggie Smith (California Suite)
1979 Meryl Streep (Kramer vs. Kramer)
1980 Mary Steenburgen (Melvin and Howard)
1981 Maureen Stapleton (Reds)
1982 Jessica Lange (Tootsie)
1983 Linda Hunt (The Year of Living Dangerously)
1984 Peggy Ashcroft (A Passage to India)
1985 Anjelica Huston (Prizzi's Honor)
1986 Dianne Wiest (Hannah and Her Sisters)
1987 Olympia Dukakis (Moonstruck)
1988 Geena Davis (The Accidental Tourist)
1989 Brenda Fricker (My Left Foot)
1990 Whoopi Goldberg (Ghost)
1991 Mercedes Ruehl (The Fisher King)
1992 Marisa Tomei (My Cousin Vinny)
1993 Anna Paquin (The Piano)
1994 Dianne Wiest (Bullets over Broadway)
1995 Mira Sorvino (Mighty Aphrodite)
1996 Juliette Binoche (The English Patient)
1997 Kim Basinger (L.A. Confidential)
1998 Judi Dench (Shakespeare in Love)
1999 Angelina Jolie (Girl, Interrupted)
2000 Marcia Gay-Harden (Pollack)
2001 Jennifer Connelly (A Beautiful Mind)

Academy Awards (Oscars), 1928–2001 (continued)

FOREIGN LANGUAGE FILM

1947 Shoe-Shine (Italy)
1948 Monsieur Vincent (France)
1949 The Bicycle Thief (Italy)
1950 The Walls of Malapaga (France/Italy)
1951 Rashomon (Japan)
1952 Forbidden Games (France)
1953 not awarded
1954 Gate of Hell (Japan)
1955 Samurai, the Legend of Musashi (Japan)
1956 La Strada (Italy)
1957 The Nights of Cabiria (Italy)
1958 My Uncle (France)
1959 Black Orpheus (France)
1960 The Virgin Spring (Sweden)
1961 Through a Glass Darkly (Sweden)
1962 Sundays and Cybele (France)
1963 8½ (Italy)
1964 Yesterday, Today and Tomorrow (Italy)
1965 The Shop on Main Street (Czechoslovakia)
1966 A Man and a Woman (France)
1967 Closely Watched Trains (Czechoslovakia)
1968 War and Peace (USSR)
1969 Z (Algeria)
1970 Investigation of a Citizen Above Suspicion (Italy)
1971 The Garden of the Finzi Continis (Italy)
1972 The Discreet Charm of the Bourgeoisie (France)
1973 Day for Night (France)
1974 Amarcord (Italy)
1975 Dersu Uzala (USSR)
1976 Black and White in Color (Ivory Coast)
1977 Madame Rosa (France)
1978 Get Out Your Handkerchiefs (France)
1979 The Tin Drum (West Germany)
1980 Moscow Does Not Believe in Tears (USSR)
1981 Mephisto (Hungary)
1982 To Begin Again (Spain)
1983 Fanny & Alexander (Sweden)
1984 Dangerous Moves (Switzerland)
1985 The Official Story (Argentina)
1986 The Assault (The Netherlands)
1987 Babette's Feast (Denmark)
1988 Pelle the Conqueror (Denmark)
1989 Cinema Paradiso (Italy)
1990 Journey of Hope (Switzerland)
1991 Mediterraneo (Italy)
1992 Indochine (France)
1993 Belle Epoque (Spain)
1994 Burnt by the Sun (Russia)
1995 Antonia's Line (The Netherlands)
1996 Kolya (Czech Republic)
1997 Character (The Netherlands)
1998 Life Is Beautiful (Italy)
1999 All About My Mother (Spain)
2000 Crouching Tiger, Hidden Dragon (Taiwan)
2001 No Man's Land (Belgium/Bosnia and Herzegovina/France/Italy/Slovenia/UK)

DIRECTING

1928 Lewis Milestone (Two Arabian Knights), Frank Borzage (7th Heaven)
1929 Frank Lloyd (The Divine Lady)
1930 Lewis Milestone (All Quiet on the Western Front)
1931 Norman Taurog (Skippy)
1932 Frank Borzage (Bad Girl)
1933 Frank Lloyd (Cavalcade)

DIRECTING (CONTINUED)

1934 Frank Capra (It Happened One Night)
1935 John Ford (The Informer)
1936 Frank Capra (Mr. Deeds Goes to Town)
1937 Leo McCarey (The Awful Truth)
1938 Frank Capra (You Can't Take It with You)
1939 Victor Fleming (Gone with the Wind)
1940 John Ford (The Grapes of Wrath)
1941 John Ford (How Green Was My Valley)
1942 William Wyler (Mrs. Miniver)
1943 Michael Curtiz (Casablanca)
1944 Leo McCarey (Going My Way)
1945 Billy Wilder (The Lost Weekend)
1946 William Wyler (The Best Years of Our Lives)
1947 Elia Kazan (Gentleman's Agreement)
1948 John Huston (The Treasure of the Sierra Madre)
1949 Joseph L. Mankiewicz (A Letter to Three Wives)
1950 Joseph L. Mankiewicz (All About Eve)
1951 George Stevens (A Place in the Sun)
1952 John Ford (The Quiet Man)
1953 Fred Zinnemann (From Here to Eternity)
1954 Elia Kazan (On the Waterfront)
1955 Delbert Mann (Marty)
1956 George Stevens (Giant)
1957 David Lean (The Bridge on the River Kwai)
1958 Vincente Minnelli (Gigi)
1959 William Wyler (Ben-Hur)
1960 Billy Wilder (The Apartment)
1961 Robert Wise, Jerome Robbins (West Side Story)
1962 David Lean (Lawrence of Arabia)
1963 Tony Richardson (Tom Jones)
1964 George Cukor (My Fair Lady)
1965 Robert Wise (The Sound of Music)
1966 Fred Zinnemann (A Man for All Seasons)
1967 Mike Nichols (The Graduate)
1968 Carol Reed (Oliver!)
1969 John Schlesinger (Midnight Cowboy)
1970 Franklin J. Schaffner (Patton)
1971 William Friedkin (The French Connection)
1972 Bob Fosse (Cabaret)
1973 George Roy Hill (The Sting)
1974 Francis Ford Coppola (The Godfather Part II)
1975 Milos Forman (One Flew Over the Cuckoo's Nest)
1976 John G. Avildsen (Rocky)
1977 Woody Allen (Annie Hall)
1978 Michael Cimino (The Deer Hunter)
1979 Robert Benton (Kramer vs. Kramer)
1980 Robert Redford (Ordinary People)
1981 Warren Beatty (Reds)
1982 Richard Attenborough (Gandhi)
1983 James L. Brooks (Terms of Endearment)
1984 Milos Forman (Amadeus)
1985 Sydney Pollack (Out of Africa)
1986 Oliver Stone (Platoon)
1987 Bernardo Bertolucci (The Last Emperor)
1988 Barry Levinson (Rain Man)
1989 Oliver Stone (Born on the Fourth of July)
1990 Kevin Costner (Dances with Wolves)
1991 Jonathan Demme (The Silence of the Lambs)
1992 Clint Eastwood (Unforgiven)
1993 Steven Spielberg (Schindler's List)
1994 Robert Zemeckis (Forrest Gump)
1995 Mel Gibson (Braveheart)
1996 Anthony Minghella (The English Patient)
1997 James Cameron (Titanic)

Academy Awards (Oscars), 1928–2001 (continued)

DIRECTING (CONTINUED)

1998 Steven Spielberg *(Saving Private Ryan)*
1999 Sam Mendes *(American Beauty)*
2000 Steven Soderbergh *(Traffic)*
2001 Ron Howard *(A Beautiful Mind)*

SCREENPLAY, ADAPTATION[1]

1928 Benjamin Glazer *(7th Heaven)*
1931 Howard Estabrook *(Cimarron)*
1932 Edwin Burke *(Bad Girl)*
1933 Victor Heerman, Sarah Y. Mason *(Little Women)*
1934 Robert Riskin *(It Happened One Night)*
1935 Dudley Nichols *(The Informer)*[2]
1936 Pierre Collings, Sheridan Gibney *(The Story of Louis Pasteur)*[2]
1937 Norman Reilly Raine, Heinz Herald, Geza Herczeg *(The Life of Emile Zola)*[2]
1938 George Bernard Shaw, W.P. Lipscomb, Cecil Lewis, Ian Dalrymple *(Pygmalion)*[2]
1939 Sidney Howard *(Gone with the Wind)*[2]
1940 Donald Ogden Stewart *(The Philadelphia Story)*[2]
1941 Sidney Buchman, Seton I. Miller *(Here Comes Mr. Jordan)*[2]
1942 George Froeschel, James Hilton, Claudine West, Arthur Wimperis *(Mrs. Miniver)*[2]
1943 Julius J. Epstein, Philip G. Epstein, Howard Koch *(Casablanca)*[2]
1944 Frank Butler, Frank Cavett *(Going My Way)*[2]
1945 Charles Brackett, Billy Wilder *(The Lost Weekend)*[2]
1946 Robert E. Sherwood *(The Best Years of Our Lives)*[2]
1947 George Seaton *(Miracle on 34th Street)*[2]
1948 John Huston *(The Treasure of the Sierra Madre)*[2]
1949 Joseph L. Mankiewicz *(A Letter to Three Wives)*[2]
1950 Joseph L. Mankiewicz *(All About Eve)*[2]
1951 Michael Wilson, Harry Brown *(A Place in the Sun)*[2]
1952 Charles Schnee *(The Bad and the Beautiful)*[2]
1953 Daniel Taradash *(From Here to Eternity)*[2]
1954 George Seaton *(The Country Girl)*[2]
1955 Paddy Chayefsky *(Marty)*[2]
1956 James Poe, John Farrow, S.J. Perelman *(Around the World in 80 Days)*
1957 Pierre Boulle, Michael Wilson, Carl Foreman *(The Bridge on the River Kwai)*
1958 Alan Jay Lerner *(Gigi)*
1959 Neil Paterson *(Room at the Top)*
1960 Richard Brooks *(Elmer Gantry)*
1961 Abby Mann *(Judgment at Nuremberg)*
1962 Horton Foote *(To Kill a Mockingbird)*
1963 John Osborne *(Tom Jones)*
1964 Edward Anhalt *(Becket)*
1965 Robert Bolt *(Doctor Zhivago)*
1966 Robert Bolt *(A Man for All Seasons)*
1967 Stirling Silliphant *(In the Heat of the Night)*
1968 James Goldman *(The Lion in Winter)*
1969 Waldo Salt *(Midnight Cowboy)*
1970 Ring Lardner, Jr. *(M*A*S*H)*
1971 Ernest Tidyman *(The French Connection)*
1972 Mario Puzo, Francis Ford Coppola *(The Godfather)*
1973 William Peter Blatty *(The Exorcist)*
1974 Francis Ford Coppola, Mario Puzo *(The Godfather Part II)*

SCREENPLAY, ADAPTATION[1] (CONTINUED)

1975 Lawrence Hauben, Bo Goldman *(One Flew Over the Cuckoo's Nest)*
1976 William Goldman *(All the President's Men)*
1977 Alvin Sargent *(Julia)*
1978 Oliver Stone *(Midnight Express)*
1979 Robert Benton *(Kramer vs. Kramer)*
1980 Alvin Sargent *(Ordinary People)*
1981 Ernest Thompson *(On Golden Pond)*
1982 Costa-Gavras, Donald Stewart *(Missing)*
1983 James L. Brooks *(Terms of Endearment)*
1984 Peter Shaffer *(Amadeus)*
1985 Kurt Luedtke *(Out of Africa)*
1986 Ruth Prawer Jhabvala *(A Room with a View)*
1987 Mark Peploe, Bernardo Bertolucci *(The Last Emperor)*
1988 Christopher Hampton *(Dangerous Liaisons)*
1989 Alfred Uhry *(Driving Miss Daisy)*
1990 Michael Blake *(Dances with Wolves)*
1991 Ted Tally *(The Silence of the Lambs)*
1992 Ruth Prawer Jhabvala *(Howards End)*
1993 Steven Zaillian *(Schindler's List)*
1994 Eric Roth *(Forrest Gump)*
1995 Emma Thompson *(Sense and Sensibility)*
1996 Billy Bob Thornton *(Sling Blade)*
1997 Brian Helgeland, Curtis Hanson *(L.A. Confidential)*
1998 Bill Condon *(Gods and Monsters)*
1999 John Irving *(The Cider House Rules)*
2000 Stephen Gaghan *(Traffic)*
2001 Akiva Goldsman *(A Beautiful Mind)*

SCREENPLAY, ORIGINAL[1]

1928 Ben Hecht *(Underworld)*[4], Joseph Farnham *(The Fair Co-Ed; Laugh, Clown, Laugh; Telling the World* [titles])
1929 Hans Kraly *(The Patriot)*
1930 Frances Marion *(The Big House)*
1931 John Monk Saunders *(The Dawn Patrol)*[4]
1932 Frances Marion *(The Champ)*[4]
1933 Robert Lord *(One Way Passage)*[4]
1934 Arthur Caesar *(Manhattan Melodrama)*[4]
1935 Ben Hecht, Charles MacArthur *(The Scoundrel)*[4]
1936 Pierre Collings, Sheridan Gibney *(The Story of Louis Pasteur)*[4]
1937 William A. Wellman, Robert Carson *(A Star Is Born)*[4]
1938 Eleanore Griffin, Dore Schary *(Boys Town)*[4]
1939 Lewis R. Foster *(Mr. Smith Goes to Washington)*[4]
1940 Preston Sturges *(The Great McGinty)*[3], Benjamin Glazer, John S. Toldy *(Arise, My Love)*[4]
1941 Herman J. Mankiewicz, Orson Welles *(Citizen Kane)*[3], Harry Segall *(Here Comes Mr. Jordan)*[4]
1942 Michael Kanin, Ring Lardner, Jr. *(Woman of the Year)*[3], Emeric Pressburger *(Forty-Ninth Parallel)*[4]
1943 Norman Krasna *(Princess O'Rourke)*[3], William Saroyan *(The Human Comedy)*[4]
1944 Lamar Trotti *(Wilson)*[3], Leo McCarey *(Going My Way)*[4]
1945 Richard Schweizer *(Marie-Louise)*[3], Charles G. Booth *(The House on 92nd Street)*[4]
1946 Muriel Box, Sydney Box *(The Seventh Veil)*[3], Clemence Dane *(Vacation from Marriage)*[4]

Academy Awards (Oscars), 1928–2001 (continued)

SCREENPLAY, ORIGINAL[1] (CONTINUED)

1947 Sidney Sheldon (The Bachelor and the Bobby-Soxer)[3], Valentine Davies (Miracle on 34th Street)[4]

1948 Richard Schweizer, David Wechsler (The Search)[4]

1949 Robert Pirosh (Battleground)[3], Douglas Morrow (The Stratton Story)[4]

1950 Charles Brackett, Billy Wilder, D.M. Marshman, Jr. (Sunset Boulevard)[3], Edna Anhalt, Edward Anhalt (Panic in the Streets)[4]

1951 Alan Jay Lerner (An American in Paris)[3], Paul Dehn, James Bernard (Seven Days to Noon)[4]

1952 T.E.B. Clarke (The Lavender Hill Mob)[3], Fredric M. Frank, Theodore St. John, Frank Cavett (The Greatest Show on Earth)[4]

1953 Charles Brackett, Walter Reisch, Richard L. Breen (Titanic)[3], Dalton Trumbo[5] (as Ian McLellan Hunter, Roman Holiday)[4]

1954 Budd Schulberg (On the Waterfront)[3], Philip Yordan (Broken Lance)[4],

1955 William Ludwig, Sonya Levien (Interrupted Melody)[3], Daniel Fuchs (Love Me or Leave Me)[4]

1956 Albert Lamorisse (The Red Balloon)[3], Dalton Trumbo[5] (as Robert Rich, The Brave One)[4]

1957 George Wells (Designing Woman)

1958 Nedrick Young[5] (as Nathan E. Douglas), Harold Jacob Smith (The Defiant Ones)

1959 Russell Rouse, Clarence Greene, Stanley Shapiro, Maurice Richlin (Pillow Talk)

1960 Billy Wilder, I.A.L. Diamond (The Apartment)

1961 William Inge (Splendor in the Grass)

1962 Ennio de Concini, Alfredo Giannetti, Pietro Germi (Divorce—Italian Style)

1963 James R. Webb (How the West Was Won)

1964 S.H. Barnett, Peter Stone, Frank Tarloff (Father Goose)

1965 Frederic Raphael (Darling)

1966 Claude Lelouch, Pierre Uytterhoeven (A Man and a Woman)

1967 William Rose (Guess Who's Coming to Dinner)

1968 Mel Brooks (The Producers)

1969 William Goldman (Butch Cassidy and the Sundance Kid)

1970 Francis Ford Coppola, Edmund H. North (Patton)

1971 Paddy Chayefsky (The Hospital)

1972 Jeremy Larner (The Candidate)

1973 David S. Ward (The Sting)

1974 Robert Towne (Chinatown)

1975 Frank Pierson (Dog Day Afternoon)

1976 Paddy Chayefsky (Network)

1977 Woody Allen, Marshall Brickman (Annie Hall)

1978 Nancy Dowd, Waldo Salt, Robert C. Jones (Coming Home)

1979 Steve Tesich (Breaking Away)

1980 Bo Goldman (Melvin and Howard)

1981 Colin Welland (Chariots of Fire)

1982 John Briley (Gandhi)

1983 Horton Foote (Tender Mercies)

1984 Robert Benton (Places in the Heart)

1985 Earl W. Wallace, William Kelley, Pamela Wallace (Witness)

1986 Woody Allen (Hannah and Her Sisters)

1987 John Patrick Shanley (Moonstruck)

1988 Ronald Bass, Barry Morrow (Rain Man)

SCREENPLAY, ORIGINAL[1] (CONTINUED)

1989 Tom Schulman (Dead Poets Society)

1990 Bruce Joel Rubin (Ghost)

1991 Callie Khouri (Thelma & Louise)

1992 Neil Jordan (The Crying Game)

1993 Jane Campion (The Piano)

1994 Quentin Tarantino, Roger Avary (Pulp Fiction)

1995 Christopher McQuarrie (The Usual Suspects)

1996 Joel Coen, Ethan Coen (Fargo)

1997 Ben Affleck, Matt Damon (Good Will Hunting)

1998 Marc Norman, Tom Stoppard (Shakespeare in Love)

1999 Alan Ball (American Beauty)

2000 Cameron Crowe (Almost Famous)

2001 Julian Fellowes (Gosford Park)

CINEMATOGRAPHY

1928 Charles Rosher, Karl Struss (Sunrise)

1929 Clyde De Vinna (White Shadows in the South Seas)

1930 Joseph T. Rucker, Willard Van Der Veer (With Byrd at the South Pole)

1931 Floyd Crosby (Tabu)

1932 Lee Garmes (Shanghai Express)

1933 Charles Bryant Lang, Jr. (A Farewell to Arms)

1934 Victor Milner (Cleopatra)

1935 Hal Mohr (A Midsummer Night's Dream)

1936 Gaetano Gaudio (Anthony Adverse)

1937 Karl Freund (The Good Earth)

1938 Joseph Ruttenberg (The Great Waltz)

1939 Gregg Toland (Wuthering Heights)[6], Ernest Haller, Ray Rennahan (Gone with the Wind)[7]

1940 George Barnes (Rebecca)[6], Georges Perinal (The Thief of Bagdad)[7]

1941 Arthur Miller (How Green Was My Valley)[6], Ernest Palmer, Ray Rennahan (Blood and Sand)[7]

1942 Joseph Ruttenberg (Mrs. Miniver)[6], Leon Shamroy (The Black Swan)[7]

1943 Arthur Miller (The Song of Bernadette)[6], Hal Mohr, W. Howard Greene (The Phantom of the Opera)[7]

1944 Joseph LaShelle (Laura)[6], Leon Shamroy (Wilson)[7]

1945 Harry Stradling (The Picture of Dorian Gray)[6], Leon Shamroy (Leave Her to Heaven)[7]

1946 Arthur Miller (Anna and the King of Siam)[6], Charles Rosher, Leonard Smith, Arthur Arling (The Yearling)[7]

1947 Guy Green (Great Expectations)[6], Jack Cardiff (Black Narcissus)[7]

1948 William Daniels (The Naked City)[6], Joseph Valentine, William V. Skall, Winton Hoch (Joan of Arc)[7]

1949 Paul C. Vogel (Battleground)[6], Winton Hoch (She Wore a Yellow Ribbon)[7]

1950 Robert Krasker (The Third Man)[6], Robert Surtees (King Solomon's Mines)[7]

1951 William C. Mellor (A Place in the Sun)[6], Alfred Gilks, John Alton (An American in Paris)[7]

1952 Robert Surtees (The Bad and the Beautiful)[6], Winton C. Hoch, Archie Stout (The Quiet Man)[7]

1953 Burnett Guffey (From Here to Eternity)[6], Loyal Griggs (Shane)[7]

1954 Boris Kaufman (On the Waterfront)[6], Milton Krasner (Three Coins in the Fountain)[7]

1955 James Wong Howe (The Rose Tattoo)[6], Robert Burks (To Catch a Thief)[7]

Academy Awards (Oscars), 1928–2001 (continued)

CINEMATOGRAPHY (CONTINUED)

1956 Joseph Ruttenberg (Somebody Up There Likes Me)[6], Lionel Lindon (Around the World in 80 Days)[7]
1957 Jack Hildyard (The Bridge on the River Kwai)
1958 Sam Leavitt (The Defiant Ones)[6], Joseph Ruttenberg (Gigi)[7]
1959 William C. Mellor (The Diary of Anne Frank)[6], Robert L. Surtees (Ben-Hur)[7]
1960 Freddie Francis (Sons and Lovers)[6], Russell Metty (Spartacus)[7]
1961 Eugen Shuftan (The Hustler)[6], Daniel L. Fapp (West Side Story)[7]
1962 Jean Bourgoin, Walter Wottitz (The Longest Day)[6], Fred A. Young (Lawrence of Arabia)[7]
1963 James Wong Howe (Hud)[6], Leon Shamroy (Cleopatra)[7]
1964 Walter Lassally (Zorba the Greek)[6], Harry Stradling (My Fair Lady)[7]
1965 Ernest Laszlo (Ship of Fools)[6], Freddie Young (Doctor Zhivago)[7]
1966 Haskell Wexler (Who's Afraid of Virginia Woolf?)[6], Ted Moore (A Man for All Seasons)[7]
1967 Burnett Guffey (Bonnie and Clyde)
1968 Pasqualino De Santis (Romeo and Juliet)
1969 Conrad Hall (Butch Cassidy and the Sundance Kid)
1970 Freddie Young (Ryan's Daughter)
1971 Oswald Morris (Fiddler on the Roof)
1972 Geoffrey Unsworth (Cabaret)
1973 Sven Nykvist (Cries and Whispers)
1974 Fred Koenekamp, Joseph Biroc (The Towering Inferno)
1975 John Alcott (Barry Lyndon)
1976 Haskell Wexler (Bound for Glory)
1977 Vilmos Zsigmond (Close Encounters of the Third Kind)
1978 Nestor Almendros (Days of Heaven)
1979 Vittorio Storaro (Apocalypse Now)
1980 Geoffrey Unsworth, Ghislain Cloquet (Tess)
1981 Vittorio Storaro (Reds)
1982 Billy Williams, Ronnie Taylor (Gandhi)
1983 Sven Nykvist (Fanny & Alexander)
1984 Chris Menges (The Killing Fields)
1985 David Watkin (Out of Africa)
1986 Chris Menges (The Mission)
1987 Vittorio Storaro (The Last Emperor)
1988 Peter Biziou (Mississippi Burning)
1989 Freddie Francis (Glory)
1990 Dean Semler (Dances with Wolves)
1991 Robert Richardson (JFK)
1992 Philippe Rousselot (A River Runs Through It)
1993 Janusz Kaminski (Schindler's List)
1994 John Toll (Legends of the Fall)
1995 John Toll (Braveheart)
1996 John Seale (The English Patient)
1997 Russell Carpenter (Titanic)
1998 Janusz Kaminski (Saving Private Ryan)
1999 Conrad L. Hall (American Beauty)
2000 Peter Pau (Crouching Tiger, Hidden Dragon)
2001 Andrew Lesnie (The Lord of the Rings: The Fellowship of the Ring)

VISUAL EFFECTS[8]

1939 E.H. Hansen (The Rains Came)
1940 Lawrence Butler (The Thief of Bagdad)
1941 Farciot Edouart, Gordon Jennings (I Wanted Wings)

VISUAL EFFECTS[8] (CONTINUED)

1942 Farciot Edouart, Gordon Jennings, William L. Pereira (Reap the Wild Wind)
1943 Fred Sersen (Crash Dive)
1944 A. Arnold Gillespie, Donald Jahraus, Warren Newcombe (Thirty Seconds Over Tokyo)
1945 John P. Fulton (Wonder Man)
1946 Thomas Howard (Blithe Spirit)
1947 A. Arnold Gillespie, Warren Newcombe (Green Dolphin Street)
1948 Paul Eagler, J. McMillan Johnson, Russell Shearman, Clarence Slifer (Portrait of Jennie)
1949 Mighty Joe Young
1950 Destination Moon
1951 When Worlds Collide
1952 Plymouth Adventure
1953 The War of the Worlds
1954 20,000 Leagues Under the Sea
1955 The Bridges at Toko-Ri
1956 John Fulton (The Ten Commandments)
1958 Tom Howard (tom thumb)
1959 A. Arnold Gillespie, Robert MacDonald (Ben-Hur)
1960 Gene Warren, Tim Baar (The Time Machine)
1961 Bill Warrington (The Guns of Navarone)
1962 Robert MacDonald (The Longest Day)
1963 Emil Kosa, Jr. (Cleopatra)
1964 Peter Ellenshaw, Hamilton Luske, Eustace Lycett (Mary Poppins)
1965 John Stears (Thunderball)
1966 Art Cruickshank (Fantastic Voyage)
1967 L.B. Abbott (Doctor Dolittle)
1968 Stanley Kubrick (2001: A Space Odyssey)
1969 Robbie Robertson (Marooned)
1970 A.D. Flowers, L.B. Abbott (Tora! Tora! Tora!)
1971 Alan Maley, Eustace Lycett, Danny Lee (Bedknobs and Broomsticks)
1972 L.B. Abbott, A.D. Flowers (The Poseidon Adventure)
1974 Frank Brendel, Glen Robinson, Albert Whitlock (Earthquake)
1975 Albert Whitlock, Glen Robinson (The Hindenburg)
1976 Carlo Rambaldi, Glen Robinson, Frank Van der Veer (King Kong), L.B. Abbott, Glen Robinson, Matthew Yuricich (Logan's Run)
1977 John Stears, John Dykstra, Richard Edlund, Grant McCune, Robert Blalack (Star Wars)
1978 Les Bowie, Colin Chilvers, Denys Coop, Roy Field, Derek Meddings, Zoran Perisic (Superman)
1979 H.R. Giger, Carlo Rambaldi, Brian Johnson, Nick Allder, Denys Ayling (Alien)
1980 Brian Johnson, Richard Edlund, Dennis Muren, Bruce Nicholson (The Empire Strikes Back)
1981 Richard Edlund, Kit West, Bruce Nicholson, Joe Johnston (Raiders of the Lost Ark)
1982 Carlo Rambaldi, Dennis Muren, Kenneth F. Smith (E.T. the Extra-Terrestrial)
1983 Richard Edlund, Dennis Muren, Ken Ralston, Phil Tippet (Return of the Jedi)
1984 Dennis Muren, Michael McAlister, Lorne Peterson, George Gibbs (Indiana Jones and the Temple of Doom)
1985 Ken Ralston, Ralph McQuarrie, Scott Farrar, David Berry (Cocoon)

Academy Awards (Oscars), 1928–2001 (continued)

VISUAL EFFECTS[8] (CONTINUED)

1986 Robert Skotak, Stan Winston, John Richardson, Suzanne Benson (Aliens)

1987 Dennis Muren, William George, Harley Jessup, Kenneth Smith (Innerspace)

1988 Ken Ralston, Richard Williams, Edward Jones, George Gibbs (Who Framed Roger Rabbit)

1989 John Bruno, Dennis Muren, Hoyt Yeatman, Dennis Skotak (The Abyss)

1990 Eric Brevig, Rob Bottin, Tim McGovern, Alex Funke (Total Recall)

1991 Robert Skotak (Terminator 2: Judgment Day)

1992 Ken Ralston, Doug Chiang, Doug Smythe, Tom Woodruff, Jr. (Death Becomes Her)

1993 Dennis Muren, Stan Winston, Phil Tippett, Michael Lantieri (Jurassic Park)

1994 Ken Ralston, George Murphy, Stephen Rosenbaum, Allen Hall (Forrest Gump)

1995 Scott E. Anderson, Charles Gibson, Neal Scanlan, John Cox (Babe)

1996 Volker Engel, Douglas Smith, Clay Pinney, Joseph Viskocil (Independence Day)

1997 Robert Legato, Mark Lasoff, Thomas L. Fisher, Michael Kanfer (Titanic)

1998 Joel Hynek, Nicholas Brooks, Stuart Robertson, Kevin Mack (What Dreams May Come)

1999 John Gaeta, Janek Sirrs, Steve Courtley, Jon Thum (The Matrix)

2000 John Nelson, Neil Corbould, Tim Burke, Rob Harvey (Gladiator)

2001 Jim Rygiel, Randall William Cook, Richard Taylor, Mark Stetson (The Lord of the Rings: The Fellowship of the Ring)

MAKEUP

1981 Rick Baker (An American Werewolf in London)

1982 Sarah Monzani, Michele Burke (Quest for Fire)

1984 Paul LeBlanc, Dick Smith (Amadeus)

1985 Michael Westmore, Zoltan Elek (Mask)

1986 Chris Walas, Stephan Dupuis (The Fly)

1987 Rick Baker (Harry and the Hendersons)

1988 Ve Neill, Steve La Porte, Robert Short (Beetlejuice)

1989 Manlio Rocchetti, Lynn Barber, Kevin Haney (Driving Miss Daisy)

1990 John Caglione, Jr., Doug Drexler (Dick Tracy)

1991 Stan Winston, Jeff Dawn (Terminator 2: Judgment Day)

1992 Greg Cannom, Michele Burke, Matthew W. Mungle (Bram Stoker's Dracula)

1993 Greg Cannom, Ve Neill, Yolanda Toussieng (Mrs. Doubtfire)

1994 Rick Baker, Ve Neill, Yolanda Toussieng (Ed Wood)

1995 Peter Frampton, Paul Pattison, Lois Burwell (Braveheart)

1996 Rick Baker, David LeRoy Anderson (The Nutty Professor)

1997 Rick Baker, David LeRoy Anderson (Men in Black)

1998 Jenny Shircore (Elizabeth)

1999 Christine Blundell, Trefor Proud (Topsy-Turvy)

2000 Rick Baker, Gail Ryan (Dr. Seuss' How the Grinch Stole Christmas)

2001 Peter Owen, Richard Taylor (The Lord of the Rings: The Fellowship of the Ring)

[1]The current screenplay categories were adopted for the 1957 awards. Until then various separate writing awards were given for silent film title writing, screenplay, story and screenplay, and motion picture story. [2]Screenplay (for script only). [3]Story and screenplay (for narrative and script; also called original screenplay). [4]Motion picture story (for narrative only; also called original story). [5]Actual winner was blacklisted at the time of the award and the honored work was attributed to another name or person; pseudonym or nominal winner listed in parentheses. [6]Black and white. [7]Color. [8]Until 1963, both visual and sound effects were honored as special effects. Only those awards for visual effects are listed here.

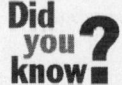

Did you know■ Wings (1927) was the first film to receive an Academy Award for best picture. It is also the only silent film to win the award.

Golden Globes, 2002

The Hollywood Foreign Press Association, a group of non-US film critics working in Hollywood, began awarding prizes for outstanding American motion pictures and acting in 1944, and created the Golden Globe Award in 1945. Over the years the prizes have expanded from recognizing only motion pictures and actors and actresses to include direction (1946), screenwriting and film music (1947), foreign language film (1950), and television (1955) as well as a number of other categories of achievement. Prize: globe encircled by a strip of motion picture film, in gold. Golden Globes/Hollywood Foreign Press Association Web site: <www.hfpa.org>

Film

Drama	A Beautiful Mind (US; director, Ron Howard)
Musical/comedy	Moulin Rouge (Australia/US; director, Baz Luhrmann)
Director	Robert Altman (Gosford Park, Italy/UK/US/Germany)
Actress, drama	Sissy Spacek (In the Bedroom, US)
Actor, drama	Russell Crowe (A Beautiful Mind, US)
Actress, musical/comedy	Nicole Kidman (Moulin Rouge, Australia/US)

Golden Globes, 2002 (continued)

Film (continued)

Actor, musical/comedy	Gene Hackman (*The Royal Tenenbaums,* US)
Foreign-language film	*No Man's Land* (Belgium/Bosnia and Herzegovina/France/Italy/Slovenia/UK; director, Danis Tanovic)
Supporting actress	Jennifer Connelly (*A Beautiful Mind*)
Supporting actor	Jim Broadbent (*Iris*)
Screenplay	Akiva Goldsman (*A Beautiful Mind*)
Original score	Craig Armstrong (*Moulin Rouge*)
Original song	"Until" (*Kate & Leopold*) Sting, music and lyrics

Television

Drama series	*Six Feet Under,* HBO
Actress, drama series	Jennifer Garner (*Alias*)
Actor, drama series	Kiefer Sutherland (*24*)
Musical/comedy series	*Sex and the City,* HBO
Actress, musical/comedy series	Sarah Jessica Parker (*Sex and the City*)
Actor, musical/comedy series	Charlie Sheen (*Spin City*)
Miniseries/movie for TV	*Band of Brothers,* HBO
Actress, miniseries/movie	Judy Davis (*Life with Judy Garland: Me and My Shadows*)
Actor, miniseries/movie	James Franco (*James Dean*)
Supporting actress, series/miniseries/movie	Rachel Griffiths (*Six Feet Under*)
Supporting actor, series/miniseries/movie	Stanley Tucci (*Conspiracy*)

Sundance Film Festival, 2002

Founded as the Utah/US Film Festival in Salt Lake City in 1978, the exhibition has traditionally focused on documentary and dramatic works from outside the Hollywood mainstream. It came under the auspices of actor Robert Redford's Sundance Institute in 1985 and is held every January in Park City UT. Sundance Institute Web site: <www.sundance.org>

Grand Jury Prize, drama	*Personal Velocity* (US; dir. Rebecca Miller)
Grand Jury Prize, documentary	*Daughter from Danang* (US; dirs. Gail Dolgin and Vicente Franco)
Audience Award, drama	*Real Women Have Curves* (US; dir. Patricia Cardoso)
Audience Award, documentary	*Amandla! A Revolution in Four Part Harmony* (US/South Africa; dir. Lee Hirsch)
Audience Award, world cinema	*Bloody Sunday* (Ireland/UK; dir. Paul Greengrass); *L'Ultimo bacio (The Last Kiss)* (Italy; dir. Gabriele Muccino)
Best director, drama	Gary Winick (*Tadpole,* US)
Best director, documentary	Rob Fruchtman and Rebecca Cammisa (*Sister Helen,* US)
Cinematography, drama	Ellen Kuras (*Personal Velocity,* US)
Cinematography, documentary	Daniel B. Gold (*Blue Vinyl,* US)
Freedom of Expression Award	*Amandla! A Revolution in Four Part Harmony* (US/South Africa; dir. Lee Hirsch)
Waldo Scott Screenwriting Award	Gordy Hoffman (*Love Liza,* US)
Special Jury Prize, documentary	*How to Draw a Bunny* (US; dir. John Walter); *Señorita extraviada (Missing Young Woman)* (US/Mexico; dir. Lourdes Portillo)
Special Jury Prize, originality, drama	*Secretary* (US; dir. Steven Shainberg)
Special Jury Prize, ensemble cast, drama	Franky G., Leo Minaya, Manuel Cabral, Hector González, Julissa López, Jessica Morales, and Panchito Gómez (*Manito,* US)
Special Jury Prize, acting, drama	América Ferrera, Lupe Ontiveros (*Real Women Have Curves,* US)
Jury prize, Latin American cinema	*O Invasor (The Trespasser)* (Brazil; dir. Beto Brant)
Jury prize, short filmmaking	*Gasline* (US; dir. Dave Silver)
Sundance/NHK International Filmmakers Award	*The Bleating of Sheep* (Europe; dir. Gjergj Xhuvani); *Crónicas* (Latin America; dir. Sebastian Cordero); *The Sleep Dealer* (US; dir. Alex Rivera); *The Man Who Wipes Mirrors* (Japan; dir. Seisoku Kajita)

Did you know? *Big* (1988) was the first film by a female director (Penny Marshall) to earn more than 100 million dollars at the box office.

Cannes International Film Festival, 2002

Established in 1946, the Cannes International Film Festival is among the best known and most influential film exhibitions in the world. Some 50 feature films and 30 short films are chosen for several categories of the Official Selection each year, with a majority of those competing for the festival's various prizes. A nine-member feature film jury and a four-member short film and Cinéfondation jury give awards to the best film (Palme d'Or) and other outstanding films (special jury prizes) in their respective categories. The Grand Prix goes to the feature film judged the most original, and the feature jury also chooses the winners of the performance, direction, and screenplay awards. The Caméra d'Or, for best first film, draws on feature films from the Official Selection and from two parallel exhibitions, the Directors' Fortnight and the International Critics' Week, and is awarded by a jury comprising film industry professionals and members of the moviegoing public. The Cinéfondation awards are for works of one hour or less by film-school students.

Cannes International Film Festival Web site: <www.festival-cannes.com>

feature films
Palme d'Or: *The Pianist* (France/Germany/Poland/UK; dir. Roman Polanski); ▶ **Grand Prix:** *Mies vailla menneisyyttä (The Man Without a Past)* (Finland; dir. Aki Kaurismäki); ▶ **best actress:** Kati Outinen (*Mies vailla menneisyyttä [The Man Without a Past]*, Finland); ▶ **best actor:** Olivier Gourmet (*Le Fils [The Son]*, Belgium); ▶ **best direction:** Im Kwon-Taek (*Chihwaseon*, South Korea) and Paul Thomas Anderson (*Punch-Drunk Love*, US); ▶ **best screenplay:** Paul Laverty (*Sweet Sixteen*, UK/US); ▶ **special jury award:** *Yadon Ilaheyya (Divine Intervention)* (Palestine; dir. Elia Suleiman); ▶ **55th anniversary special award:** *Bowling for Columbine* (US; dir. Michael Moore); ▶ **Caméra d'Or:** *Bord de mer* ("Seaside") (France; dir. Julie Lopes-Curval)

short films
Palme d'Or: *Eso utan (After Rain)* (Hungary; dir. Peter Meszaros); ▶ **special jury awards:** *A Very Very Silent Film* (India; dir. Manish Jha) and *The Stone of Folly* (Canada; dir. Jesse Rosensweet)

Cinéfondation
1st prize: *Um sol alaranjado (Four Days)* (Brazil; dir. Eduardo Valente), ▶ **2nd prize:** *Seule maman a les yeux bleus (Only Mummy's Blue-Eyed)* (France; dir. Eric Forestier) and *K-G i nöd och lust (K-G for Better or for Worse)* (Sweden; Jens Jonsson); ▶ **3rd prize:** *She'elot shel po'el met (Questions of a Dead Worker)* (Israel; Aya Somech)

Berlin International Film Festival, 2002

The Berlin International Film Festival (Internationale Filmfestspiele Berlin), held annually since its founding in West Berlin in 1951, comprises some 20 separate competitions and juries emphasizing aspects of both worldwide and German cinema, each with their own prizes. The International Jury, made up of film-industry figures from across the globe, selects the winners of the Golden and Silver Berlin Bears, the festival's top awards.

Berlin International Film Festival Web site: <www.berlinale.de>

Golden Berlin Bear	*Sen to chihiro no kamikakushi (Spirited Away)* (Japan; dir. Hayao Miyazaki) and *Bloody Sunday* (Ireland/UK; dir. Paul Greengrass)
Jury Grand Prize (Silver Bear)	*Halbe Treppe (Grill Point)* (Germany; dir. Andreas Dresen)
Silver Berlin Bear, director	Otar Iosseliani (*Lundi matin [Monday Morning]*, France)
Silver Berlin Bear, actress	Halle Berry (*Monster's Ball*, US)
Silver Berlin Bear, actor	Jacques Gamblin (*Laissez-passer [Safe Conduct]*, France)
Silver Berlin Bear, individual artistic contribution	Ensemble of actresses (*8 Femmes [8 Women]*, France)
Silver Berlin Bear, film music	Antoine Duhamel (*Laissez-passer [Safe Conduct]*, France)
Premiere First Movie Award	*Beneath Clouds* (Australia; dir. Ivan Sen)
Ecumenical Jury Prize	*Bloody Sunday* (Ireland/UK; dir. Paul Greengrass)
International Film Critics Prize	*Lundi matin (Monday Morning)* (France; dir. Otar Iosseliani)

Toronto International Film Festival, 2001

Founded in 1976, the Toronto International Film Festival is one of North America's best-attended exhibitions and a frequent forum for the premiere of major feature films. The festival, held in September, awards six prizes, three of which are for Canadian films.

Toronto International Film Festival Web site: <www.e.bell.ca/filmfest>

Canadian feature	*Atanarjuat (The Fast Runner)* (dir. Zacharias Kunuk)
Canadian first feature	*Inertia* (dir. Sean Garrity)
Canadian short	*FILM(dzama)* (dir. Deco Dawson)
FIPRESCI Award	*Inch'Allah dimanche (Inch'Allah Sunday)* (France; dir. Yamina Benguigui)
People's Choice Award	*Le Fabuleux destin d'Amélie Poulain (Amelie)* (France; dir. Jean-Pierre Jeunet)
Discovery Award	*Chicken Rice War* (Singapore; dir. "CheeK" [Cheah Chee Kong])

Emmy Award-winning Television Series, 1948–2001

1948
Most popular program: *Pantomime Quiz,* KTLA
TV film: "The Necklace," *Your Show Time*

1949
Live show: *The Ed Wynn Show,* KTTV
Kinescope show: *The Texaco Star Theater,* KNBH (NBC)
TV film: *The Life of Riley,* KNBH
Pub. svc./cultural/educ.: *Crusade in Europe,* KECA-TV/KTTV (ABC)
Children's: *Time for Beany,* KTLA

1950
Variety: *The Alan Young Show,* KTTV (CBS)
Drama: *Pulitzer Prize Playhouse,* KECA-TV (ABC)
Game/audience particip.: *Truth or Consequences,* KTTV (CBS)
Children's: *Time for Beany,* KTLA
Educational: *KFI-TV University,* KFI-TV
Cultural: *Campus Chorus and Orchestra,* KTSL

1951
Variety: *Your Show of Shows* (NBC)
Comedy: *The Red Skelton Show* (NBC)
Drama: *Studio One* (CBS)

1952
Variety: *Your Show of Shows* (NBC)
Comedy: *I Love Lucy* (CBS)
Drama: *Robert Montgomery Presents* (NBC)
Mystery/action/adventure: *Dragnet* (NBC)
Public affairs: *See It Now* (CBS)
Aud. particip./quiz/panel: *What's My Line?* (CBS)
Children's: *Time for Beany* (syndicated)

1953
Variety: *Omnibus* (CBS)
Comedy: *I Love Lucy* (CBS)
Drama: *The U.S. Steel Hour* (ABC)
Mystery/action/adventure: *Dragnet* (NBC)
Public affairs: *Victory at Sea* (NBC)
Aud. particip./quiz/panel: *This Is Your Life* (NBC); *What's My Line?* (CBS)
Children's: *Kukla, Fran and Ollie* (NBC)

1954
Variety: *Disneyland* (ABC)
Comedy: *Make Room for Daddy* (ABC)
Drama: *The United States Steel Hour* (ABC)
Mystery/intrigue: *Dragnet* (NBC)
Western/adventure: *Stories of the Century* (syndicated)
Cultural/relig./educ.: *Omnibus* (CBS)
Aud. particip./quiz/panel: *This Is Your Life* (NBC)
Children's: *Lassie* (CBS)

1955
Variety: *The Ed Sullivan Show* (CBS)
Comedy: *The Phil Silvers Show: You'll Never Get Rich* (CBS)
Drama: *Producers' Showcase* (NBC)
Action/adventure: *Disneyland* (ABC)
Music: *Your Hit Parade* (NBC)
Documentary: *Omnibus* (CBS)
Aud. particip. *The $64,000 Question* (CBS)

1955 (continued)
Children's: *Lassie* (CBS)

1956
Series (½ hr. or less): *The Phil Silvers Show: You'll Never Get Rich* (CBS)
Series (1 hr. or more): *Caesar's Hour* (NBC)
New series: *Playhouse 90* (CBS)

1957
Mus./var./aud.par./quiz: *The Dinah Shore Chevy Show* (NBC)
Comedy: *The Phil Silvers Show: You'll Never Get Rich* (CBS)
Drama, continuing: *Gunsmoke* (CBS)
Drama, anthology: *Playhouse 90* (CBS)
New series: *The Seven Lively Arts* (CBS)
Public service: *Omnibus* (ABC/NBC)

1959*
Musical/variety: *The Dinah Shore Chevy Show* (NBC)
Comedy: *The Jack Benny Show* (CBS)
Drama (<1 hr.): *Alcoa-Goodyear Playhouse* (NBC)
Drama (1 hr.+): *Playhouse 90* (CBS)
Western: *Maverick* (ABC)
News reporting: *The Huntley-Brinkley Report* (NBC)
Public service: *Omnibus* (NBC)
Panel/quiz/aud. particip.: *What's My Line?* (CBS)

1960
Variety: "The Fabulous Fifties" (CBS)
Humor: "Art Carney Special" (NBC)
Drama: *Playhouse 90* (CBS)
News: *The Huntley-Brinkley Report* (NBC)
Public affairs/education: *The Twentieth Century* (CBS)
Children's: *Huckleberry Hound* (syndicated)

1961
Variety: *Astaire Time* (NBC)
Humor: *The Jack Benny Show* (CBS)
Drama: "Macbeth," *Hallmark Hall of Fame* (NBC)
News: *The Huntley-Brinkley Report* (NBC)
Public affairs/education: *The Twentieth Century* (CBS)
Children's: "Aaron Copland's Birthday Party," *Young People's Concert* (CBS)
Program of the year: "Macbeth," *Hallmark Hall of Fame* (NBC)

1962
Variety: *The Garry Moore Show* (CBS)
Humor: *The Bob Newhart Show* (NBC)
Drama: *The Defenders* (CBS)
News: *The Huntley-Brinkley Report* (NBC)
Educational/public affairs: *David Brinkley's Journal* (NBC)
Children's: "New York Philharmonic Young People's Concert with Leonard Bernstein" (CBS)
Program of the year: "Victoria Regina," *Hallmark Hall of Fame* (NBC)

1963
Variety: *The Andy Williams Show* (NBC)
Humor: *The Dick Van Dyke Show* (CBS)
Drama: *The Defenders* (CBS)

*Because of a change in the eligibility period, no awards were given in 1958; the 1959 awards included all of calendar year 1958 and part of 1959.

Emmy Award-winning Television Series, 1948–2001 (continued)

1963 (continued)
News: *The Huntley-Brinkley Report* (NBC)
Commentary/public affairs: *David Brinkley's Journal* (NBC)
Documentary: "The Tunnel" (NBC)
Panel/quiz/aud. particip.: *G-E College Bowl* (CBS)
Children's: *Walt Disney's Wonderful World of Color* (NBC)
Program of the year: "The Tunnel" (NBC)

1964
Variety: *The Danny Kaye Show* (CBS)
Comedy: *The Dick Van Dyke Show* (CBS)
Drama: *The Defenders* (CBS)
News reports: *The Huntley-Brinkley Report* (NBC)
Commentary/public affairs: "Cuba—Part I: The Bay of Pigs," "Cuba—Part II: The Missile Crisis," *NBC White Paper* (NBC)
Documentary: "The Making of the President 1960" (ABC)
Children's: *Discovery '63–'64* (ABC)
Program of the year: "The Making of the President 1960" (ABC)

1965ᴬ
Entertainment: *The Dick Van Dyke Show* (CBS); "The Magnificent Yankee," *Hallmark Hall of Fame* (NBC); "My Name Is Barbra" (CBS); "What Is Sonata Form?," *New York Philharmonic Young People's Concerts with Leonard Bernstein* (CBS)
News/docu./info./sports: "I, Leonardo da Vinci," *Saga of Western Man* (ABC); "The Louvre" (NBC)

1966
Variety: *The Andy Williams Show* (NBC)
Comedy: *The Dick Van Dyke Show* (CBS)
Drama: *The Fugitive* (ABC)

1967
Variety: *The Andy Williams Show* (NBC)
Comedy: *The Monkees* (NBC)
Drama: *Mission: Impossible* (CBS)

1968
Musical/variety: *Rowan and Martin's Laugh-In* (NBC)
Comedy: *Get Smart* (NBC)
Drama: *Mission: Impossible* (CBS)

1969
Musical/variety: *Rowan and Martin's Laugh-In* (NBC)
Comedy: *Get Smart* (NBC)
Drama: *NET Playhouse* (NET)

1970
Variety/musical: *The David Frost Show* (syndicated)
Comedy: *My World and Welcome to It* (NBC)
Drama: *Marcus Welby, M.D.* (ABC)

1971
Comedy: *All in the Family* (CBS)
Drama: *The Senator* (segment), *The Bold Ones* (NBC)
Variety, musical: *The Flip Wilson Show* (NBC)
Variety, talk: *The David Frost Show* (syndicated)
New series: *All in the Family* (CBS)

1972
Comedy: *All in the Family* (CBS)
Drama: "Elizabeth R," *Masterpiece Theatre* (PBS)
Variety, musical: *The Carol Burnett Show* (CBS)
Variety, talk: *The Dick Cavett Show* (ABC)
New series: "Elizabeth R," *Masterpiece Theatre* (PBS)

1973
Comedy: *All in the Family* (CBS)
Drama (continuing): *The Waltons* (CBS)
Drama/comedy (limited): "Tom Brown's Schooldays," *Masterpiece Theatre* (PBS)
Variety, musical: *The Julie Andrews Hour* (ABC)
New series: *America* (NBC)

1974
Comedy: *M*A*S*H* (CBS)
Drama: "Upstairs, Downstairs," *Masterpiece Theatre* (PBS)
Limited series: *Columbo* (NBC)
Music/variety: *The Carol Burnett Show* (CBS)

1975
Comedy: *The Mary Tyler Moore Show* (CBS)
Drama: "Upstairs, Downstairs," *Masterpiece Theatre* (PBS)
Limited series: "Benjamin Franklin" (CBS)
Comedy-variety/music: *The Carol Burnett Show* (CBS)

1976
Comedy: *The Mary Tyler Moore Show* (CBS)
Drama: *Police Story* (NBC)
Limited series: "Upstairs, Downstairs," *Masterpiece Theatre* (PBS)
Comedy-variety/music: *NBC's Saturday Night* (NBC)

1977
Comedy: *The Mary Tyler Moore Show* (CBS)
Drama: "Upstairs, Downstairs," *Masterpiece Theatre* (PBS)
Limited series: *Roots* (ABC)
Comedy-variety/music: *Van Dyke and Company* (NBC)

1978
Comedy: *All in the Family* (CBS)
Drama: *The Rockford Files* (NBC)
Limited series: *Holocaust* (NBC)
Comedy-variety/music: *The Muppet Show* (syndicated)
Informational: *The Body Human* (CBS)

1979
Comedy: *Taxi* (ABC)
Drama: *Lou Grant* (CBS)
Limited series: *Roots: The Next Generation* (ABC)
Comedy-variety/music: "Steve & Eydie Celebrate Irving Berlin" (NBC)

1980
Comedy: *Taxi* (ABC)
Drama: *Lou Grant* (CBS)
Limited series: *Edward & Mrs. Simpson* (syndicated)
Variety/music: *IBM Presents Baryshnikov on Broadway* (ABC)

Programs this year were classified only so far as "Entertainment" and "News, Documentaries, Information and Sports," with several winners in each classification.

Emmy Award-winning Television Series, 1948–2001 (continued)

1981
Comedy: *Taxi* (ABC)
Drama: *Hill Street Blues* (NBC)
Limited series: *Shogun* (NBC)
Informational: *Steve Allen's Meeting of Minds* (PBS)

1982
Comedy: *Barney Miller* (ABC)
Drama: *Hill Street Blues* (NBC)
Limited series: *Marco Polo* (NBC)
Informational: *Creativity with Bill Moyers* (PBS)

1983
Comedy: *Cheers* (NBC)
Drama: *Hill Street Blues* (NBC)
Limited series: *Nicholas Nickleby* (syndicated)
Informational: *The Barbara Walters Specials* (ABC)

1984
Comedy: *Cheers* (NBC)
Drama: *Hill Street Blues* (NBC)
Limited series: "Concealed Enemies," *American Playhouse* (PBS)
Informational: *A Walk Through the 20th Century with Bill Moyers* (PBS)

1985
Comedy: *The Cosby Show* (NBC)
Drama: *Cagney & Lacey* (CBS)
Limited series: "The Jewel in the Crown," *Masterpiece Theatre* (PBS)
Informational: *The Living Planet: A Portrait of the Earth* (PBS)

1986
Comedy: *The Golden Girls* (NBC)
Drama: *Cagney & Lacey* (CBS)
Miniseries: *Peter the Great* (NBC)
Informational: "Laurence Olivier—A Life," *Great Performances* (PBS); *Planet Earth* (PBS)

1987
Comedy: *The Golden Girls* (NBC)
Drama: *L.A. Law* (NBC)
Miniseries: *A Year in the Life* (NBC)
Informational: *Smithsonian World* (PBS); "Unknown Chaplin," *American Masters* (PBS)

1988
Comedy: *The Wonder Years* (ABC)
Drama: *thirtysomething* (ABC)
Miniseries: *The Murder of Mary Phagan* (NBC)
Informational: "Buster Keaton: A Hard Act to Follow," *American Masters* (PBS); *Nature* (PBS)

1989
Comedy: *Cheers* (NBC)
Drama: *L.A. Law* (NBC)
Miniseries: *War and Remembrance* (ABC)
Variety/music/comedy: *The Tracy Ullman Show* (Fox)
Informational: *Nature* (PBS)

1990
Comedy: *Murphy Brown* (CBS)
Drama: *L.A. Law* (NBC)
Miniseries: *Drug Wars: The Camarena Story* (NBC)
Variety/music/comedy: *In Living Color* (Fox)
Informational: *Smithsonian World* (PBS)

1991
Comedy: *Cheers* (NBC)
Drama: *L.A. Law* (NBC)
Miniseries: *Separate But Equal* (ABC)
Informational: *The Civil War* (PBS)

1992
Comedy: *Murphy Brown* (CBS)
Drama: *Northern Exposure* (CBS)
Miniseries: *A Woman Named Jackie* (NBC)
Variety/music/comedy: *The Tonight Show Starring Johnny Carson* (NBC)
Informational: *MGM: When the Lion Roars* (TNT)

1993
Comedy: *Seinfeld* (NBC)
Drama: *Picket Fences* (CBS)
Miniseries: *Prime Suspect 2* (PBS)
Variety/music/comedy: *Saturday Night Live* (NBC)
Informational: *Healing and the Mind with Bill Moyers* (PBS)

1994
Comedy: *Frasier* (NBC)
Drama: *Picket Fences* (CBS)
Miniseries: *Prime Suspect 3* (PBS)
Variety/music/comedy: *Late Show with David Letterman* (CBS)
Informational: *Later with Bob Costas* (NBC)

1995
Comedy: *Frasier* (NBC)
Drama: *NYPD Blue* (ABC)
Miniseries: *Joseph* (TNT)
Variety/music/comedy: *The Tonight Show with Jay Leno* (NBC)
Informational: *Baseball* (PBS); *TV Nation* (NBC)

1996
Comedy: *Frasier* (NBC)
Drama: *ER* (NBC)
Miniseries: *Gulliver's Travels* (NBC)
Variety/music/comedy: *Dennis Miller Live* (HBO)
Informational: *Lost Civilizations* (NBC)

1997
Comedy: *Frasier* (NBC)
Drama: *Law & Order* (NBC)
Miniseries: *Prime Suspect 5: Errors of Judgment* (PBS)
Variety/music/comedy: *Tracey Takes On . . .* (HBO)
Informational: *Biography* (A&E); *The Great War and the Shaping of the 20th Century* (PBS)

1998
Comedy: *Frasier* (NBC)
Drama: *The Practice* (ABC)
Miniseries: *From the Earth to the Moon* (HBO)
Variety/music/comedy: *Late Show with David Letterman* (CBS)
Non-fiction: *The American Experience* (PBS)

1999
Comedy: *Ally McBeal* (Fox)
Drama: *The Practice* (ABC)
Miniseries: *Horatio Hornblower: The Even Chance* (A&E)
Variety/music/comedy: *Late Show with David Letterman* (CBS)

Emmy Award-winning Television Series, 1948–2001 (continued)

1999 (continued)
Non-fiction: *The American Experience* (PBS); *American Masters* (PBS)

2000
Comedy: *Will & Grace* (NBC)
Drama: *The West Wing* (NBC)
Miniseries: *The Corner* (HBO)
Variety/music/comedy: *Late Show with David Letterman* (CBS)
Non-fiction: "Hitchcock, Selznick and the End of Hollywood," *American Masters* (PBS)

2001
Comedy: *Sex and the City* (HBO)
Drama: *The West Wing* (NBC)
Miniseries: *Anne Frank* (ABC)
Variety/music/comedy: *Late Show with David Letterman* (CBS)
Non-fiction: "Lucille Ball: Finding Lucy," *American Masters* (PBS)

Tony Award Winners, 2002

The American Theatre Wing, a philanthropic and educational organization established in 1939, created the Tony Awards in 1947 to recognize distinguished achievement in the theater arts as presented on Broadway. The award is named for Antoinette Perry, a former director of the American Theatre Wing; since 1967 it has been presented in conjunction with the League of American Theatres and Producers, a Broadway trade association. A 15–30 member nominating committee selects nominees each May from among the year's new or newly revived Broadway shows; a body of some 710 current and former theater professionals, critics, and agents votes for the winners. The awards are presented in New York City in early June. Prize: silver medallion, set in a base, depicting on one face the masks of tragedy and comedy and on the other the profile of Antoinette Perry.

Tony Awards Web site: <www.tonys.org>

musical: *Thoroughly Modern Millie* (book, Richard Morris, Dick Scanlan; music, Jeanine Tesori; lyrics, Dick Scanlan); ▸ **play:** *Edward Albee's The Goat or Who Is Sylvia?* (playwright, Edward Albee); ▸ **special theatrical event**[1]: *Elaine Stritch at Liberty* ("constructed" by John Lahr; "reconstructed" by Elaine

Stritch), ▸ **revival of a musical:** *Into the Woods* (book, James Lapine; music and lyrics, Stephen Sondheim); ▸ **revival of a play:** *Private Lives* (playwright, Noël Coward); ▸ **book, musical:** Greg Kotis (*Urinetown: The Musical*); ▸ **score:** Mark Hollmann (music), Mark Hollmann and Greg Kotis (lyrics) (*Urinetown: The Musical*); ▸ **leading actress, musical:** Sutton Foster (*Thoroughly Modern Millie*); ▸ **leading actor, musical:** John Lithgow (*Sweet Smell of Success*); ▸ **leading actress, play:** Lindsay Duncan (*Private Lives*); ▸ **leading actor, play:** Alan Bates (*Fortune's Fool*); ▸ **featured actress, musical:** Harriet Harris (*Thoroughly Modern Millie*); ▸ **featured actor, musical:** Shuler Hensley (*Oklahoma!*); ▸ **featured actress, play:** Katie Finneran (*Noises Off*); ▸ **featured actor, play:** Frank Langella (*Fortune's Fool*); ▸ **direction, musical:** John Rando (*Urinetown: The Musical*); ▸ **direction, play:** Mary Zimmerman (*Metamorphoses*); ▸ **costume design:** Martin Pakledinaz (*Thoroughly Modern Millie*); ▸ **lighting design:** Brian MacDevitt (*Into the Woods*); ▸ **scenic design:** Tim Hatley (*Private Lives*); ▸ **orchestrations:** Doug Besterman, Ralph Burns (*Thoroughly Modern Millie*); ▸ **choreography:** Rob Ashford (*Thoroughly Modern Millie*); ▸ **special awards for lifetime achievement in the theater:** Julie Harris, Robert Whitehead.

[1]*Award for "productions that are considered neither plays nor musicals."*

Tony Awards, 1947–2002

Tony Awards Web site: <www.tonys.org>

YEAR	BEST MUSICAL	BEST PLAY
1947	*not awarded*	*All My Sons* (Arthur Miller)[1]
1948	*not awarded*	*Mister Roberts* (Thomas Heggen, Joshua Logan)
1949	*Kiss Me, Kate* (book, Bella and Samuel Spewack; music and lyrics, Cole Porter)	*Death of a Salesman* (Arthur Miller)
1950	*South Pacific* (book, Oscar Hammerstein II, Joshua Logan; music, Richard Rodgers; lyrics, Oscar Hammerstein II)	*The Cocktail Party* (T.S. Eliot)
1951	*Guys and Dolls* (book, Jo Swerling, Abe Burrows; music and lyrics, Frank Loesser)	*The Rose Tattoo* (Tennessee Williams)
1952	*The King and I* (book and lyrics, Oscar Hammerstein II; music, Richard Rodgers)	*The Fourposter* (Jan de Hartog)
1953	*Wonderful Town* (book, Joseph Fields, Jerome Chodorov; music, Leonard Bernstein; lyrics, Betty Comden, Adolph Green)	*The Crucible* (Arthur Miller)
1954	*Kismet* (book, Charles Lederer, Luther Davis; music, Alexander Borodin; adaptation and lyrics, Robert Wright, George Forrest)	*The Teahouse of the August Moon* (John Patrick)
1955	*The Pajama Game* (book, George Abbott, Richard Bissell; music and lyrics, Richard Adler, Jerry Ross)	*The Desperate Hours* (Joseph Hayes)
1956	*Damn Yankees* (book and lyrics, George Abbott, Douglass Wallop; music, Richard Adler, Jerry Ross)	*The Diary of Anne Frank* (Frances Goodrich, Albert Hackett)

Tony Awards, 1947–2002 (continued)

YEAR	BEST MUSICAL	BEST PLAY
1957	*My Fair Lady* (book and lyrics, Alan Jay Lerner; music, Frederick Loewe)	*Long Day's Journey into Night* (Eugene O'Neill)
1958	*The Music Man* (book, Meredith Willson, Franklin Lacey; music and lyrics, Meredith Willson)	*Sunrise at Campobello* (Dore Schary)
1959	*Redhead* (book, Herbert and Dorothy Fields, Sidney Sheldon, David Shaw; music, Albert Hague; lyrics, Dorothy Fields)	*J.B.* (Archibald MacLeish)
1960 (tie)	*The Sound of Music* (book, Howard Lindsay, Russel Crouse; music, Richard Rodgers; lyrics, Oscar Hammerstein II); *Fiorello!* (book, Jerome Weidman, George Abbott; music, Jerry Brock; lyrics, Sheldon Harnick)	*The Miracle Worker* (William Gibson)
1961	*Bye, Bye Birdie* (book, Michael Stewart; music, Charles Strouse; lyrics, Lee Adams)	*Beckett* (Jean Anouilh, translated by Lucienne Hill)
1962	*How to Succeed in Business Without Really Trying* (book, Abe Burrows, Jack Weinstock, Willie Gilbert; music and lyrics, Frank Loesser)	*A Man for All Seasons* (Robert Bolt)
1963	*A Funny Thing Happened on the Way to the Forum* (book, Burt Shevelove, Larry Gelbart; music and lyrics, Stephen Sondheim)	*Who's Afraid of Virginia Woolf?* (Edward Albee)
1964	*Hello, Dolly!* (book, Michael Stewart; music and lyrics, Jerry Herman)	*Luther* (John Osborne)
1965	*Fiddler on the Roof* (book, Joseph Stein; music, Jerry Bock; lyrics, Sheldon Harnick)	*The Subject Was Roses* (Frank Gilroy)
1966	*Man of La Mancha* (book, Dale Wasserman; music, Mitch Leigh; lyrics, Joe Darion)	*Marat/Sade* (Peter Weiss, translated by Geoffrey Skelton)
1967	*Cabaret* (book, Joe Masteroff; music, John Kander; lyrics, Fred Ebb)	*The Homecoming* (Harold Pinter)
1968	*Hallelujah, Baby!* (book, Arthur Laurents; music, Jule Styne; lyrics, Betty Comden, Adolph Green)	*Rosencrantz and Guildenstern Are Dead* (Tom Stoppard)
1969	*1776* (book, Peter Stone; music and lyrics, Sherman Edwards)	*The Great White Hope* (Howard Sackler)
1970	*Applause* (book, Betty Comden, Adolph Greene; music, Charles Strouse; lyrics, Lee Adams)	*Borstal Boy* (Frank McMahon)
1971	*Company* (book, George Furth; music and lyrics, Stephen Sondheim)	*Sleuth* (Anthony Shaffer)
1972	*Two Gentlemen of Verona* (book, John Guare, Mel Shapiro; music, Galt MacDermot; lyrics, John Guare)	*Sticks and Bones* (David Rabe)
1973	*A Little Night Music* (book, Hugh Wheeler; music and lyrics, Stephen Sondheim)	*That Championship Season* (Jason Miller)
1974	*Raisin* (book, Robert Nemiroff, Charlotte Zaltzberg; music, Judd Woldin; lyrics, Robert Brittan)	*The River Niger* (Joseph A. Walker)
1975	*The Wiz* (book, William F. Brown; music and lyrics, Charlie Smalls)	*Equus* (Peter Shaffer)
1976	*A Chorus Line* (book, James Kirkwood, Nicholas Dante; music, Marvin Hamlisch; lyrics, Edward Kleban)	*Travesties* (Tom Stoppard)
1977	*Annie* (book, Thomas Meehan; music, Charles Strouse; lyrics, Martin Charnin)	*The Shadow Box* (Michael Christofer)
1978	*Ain't Misbehavin'* (book, Murray Horwitz, Richard Maltby, Jr.; music, Fats Waller; lyrics, Fats Waller and many others)	*Da* (Hugh Leonard)
1979	*Sweeney Todd* (book, Hugh Wheeler; music and lyrics, Stephen Sondheim)	*The Elephant Man* (Bernard Pomerance)
1980	*Evita* (book and lyrics, Tim Rice; music, Andrew Lloyd Webber)	*Children of a Lesser God* (Mark Medoff)
1981	*42nd Street* (book, Michael Stewart, Mark Bramble; music, Harry Warren; lyrics, Al Dubin)	*Amadeus* (Peter Shaffer)
1982	*Nine* (book, Arthur Kopit; music and lyrics, Maury Yeston)	*The Life and Adventures of Nicholas Nickleby* (David Edgar)
1983	*Cats* (book and lyrics, T.S. Eliot; music, Andrew Lloyd Webber)	*Torch Song Trilogy* (Harvey Fierstein)
1984	*La Cage aux Folles* (book, Harvey Fierstein; music and lyrics, Jerry Herman)	*The Real Thing* (Tom Stoppard)
1985	*Big River* (book, William Hauptman; music and lyrics, Roger Miller)	*Biloxi Blues* (Neil Simon)
1986	*The Mystery of Edwin Drood* (book, music, lyrics, Rupert Holmes)	*I'm Not Rappaport* (Herb Gardner)
1987	*Les Misérables* (book, Alain Boublil, Claude-Michel Schönberg; music, Claude-Michel Schönberg; lyrics, Herbert Kretzmer, Alain Boublil)	*Fences* (August Wilson)
1988	*The Phantom of the Opera* (book, Richard Stilgoe, Andrew Lloyd Webber; music, Andrew Lloyd Webber; lyrics, Charles Hart, Richard Stilgoe)	*M. Butterfly* (David Henry Hwang)

Tony Awards, 1947–2002 (continued)

YEAR	BEST MUSICAL	BEST PLAY
1989	*Jerome Robbins' Broadway* (compilation)	*The Heidi Chronicles* (Wendy Wasserstein)
1990	*City of Angels* (book, Larry Gelbart; music, Cy Coleman; lyrics, David Zippel)	*The Grapes of Wrath* (Frank Galati)
1991	*The Will Rogers Follies* (book, Peter Stone; music, Cy Coleman; lyrics, Betty Comden, Adolph Green)	*Lost in Yonkers* (Neil Simon)
1992	*Crazy for You* (book, Ken Ludwig; music and lyrics, George and Ira Gershwin)	*Dancing at Lughnasa* (Brian Friel)
1993	*Kiss of the Spider Woman—The Musical* (book, Terrence McNally; music, John Kander; lyrics, Fred Ebb)	*Angels in America: Millennium Approaches* (Tony Kushner)
1994	*Passion* (book, James Lapine; music and lyrics, Stephen Sondheim)	*Angels in America: Perestroika* (Tony Kushner)
1995	*Sunset Boulevard* (book and lyrics, Don Black, Christopher Hampton; music, Andrew Lloyd Webber)	*Love! Valour! Compassion!* (Terrence McNally)
1996	*Rent* (book, music, lyrics, Jonathan Larson)	*Master Class* (Terrence McNally)
1997	*Titanic* (book, Peter Stone; music and lyrics, Maury Yeston)	*The Last Night of Ballyhoo* (Alfred Uhry)
1998	*The Lion King* (book, Roger Allers, Irene Mecchi; music and lyrics, Elton John, Tim Rice, and others)	*Art* (Yasmina Reza)
1999	*Fosse* (compilation)	*Side Man* (Warren Leight)
2000	*Contact* (book, John Weidman; music and lyrics, various artists)	*Copenhagen* (Michael Frayn)
2001	*The Producers, the New Mel Brooks Musical* (book, Mel Brooks, Thomas Meehan; music and lyrics, Mel Brooks)	*Proof* (David Auburn)
2002	*Thoroughly Modern Millie* (book, Richard Morris, Dick Scanlan; music, Jeanine Tesori; lyrics, Dick Scanlan)	*Edward Albee's the Goat or Who Is Sylvia?* (Edward Albee)

¹Awarded to author.

Grammy Awards

The National Academy of Recording Arts and Sciences was established in 1957 as a professional organization for musicians, producers, technicians, and executives in the US recording industry. The Grammys, first awarded in 1958, recognize excellence in the recording industry without regard to record sales or chart position. Nominees and winners are selected by the Academy's individual members according to the members' areas of expertise. In addition to the four general categories (record, album, and song of the year and best new artist) for which all members are eligible to vote, for 2001 there were 97 categories in 27 fields, of which Academy members were permitted to vote in no more than 8 fields. Prizes for works released 1 Oct 2000–30 Sep 2001 were awarded in Los Angeles on 27 Feb 2002; the ceremony for 2001–02 works is scheduled for 23 Feb 2003 in New York City. Prize: gold miniature phonograph.

Grammy Award Web site: <www.grammy.com>.

category: winner (performer in parentheses for songwriting/production awards)

record (single) of the year: "Walk On," U2; ▸ album of the year: *O Brother, Where Art Thou?*, various artists; ▸ song of the year: "Fallin'," Alicia Keyes, songwriter (Alicia Keyes); ▸ new artist: Alicia Keyes; ▸ pop vocal performance, female: "I'm Like a Bird," Nelly Furtado; ▸ pop vocal performance, male: "Don't Let Me Be Lonely Tonight," James Taylor; ▸ pop vocal performance, duo/group: "Stuck in a Moment You Can't Get Out Of," U2; ▸ pop vocal album: *Lovers Rock*, Sade; ▸ pop vocal album, traditional: *Songs I Heard*, Harry Connick, Jr.; ▸ rock vocal performance, female: "Get Right with God," Lu- cinda Williams; ▸ rock vocal performance, male: "Dig In," Lenny Kravitz; ▸ rock vocal performance, duo/group: "Elevation," U2; ▸ hard rock performance: "Crawling," Linkin Park; ▸ metal performance: "Schism," Tool; ▸ rock song: "Drops of Jupiter," Charlie Colin, Rob Hotchkiss, Pat Monahan, Jimmy Stafford, and Scott Underwood, songwriters (Train); ▸ rock album: *All That You Can't Leave Behind*, U2; ▸ alternative album: *Parachutes*, Coldplay; ▸ R&B vocal performance, female: "Fallin'," Alicia Keyes; ▸ R&B vocal performance, male: "U Remind Me," Usher; ▸ R&B vocal performance, duo/group: "Survivor," Destiny's Child; ▸ R&B song: "Fallin'," Alicia Keyes; ▸ R&B album: *Songs in A Minor*, Alicia Keyes; ▸ R&B vocal album, traditional: *At Last*, Gladys Knight; ▸ rap performance, solo: "Get Ur Freak On," Missy "Misdemeanor" Elliott; ▸ rap performance, duo/group: "Ms. Jackson," Outkast; ▸ rap album: *Stankonia*, Outkast; ▸ country vocal performance, female: "Shine," Dolly Parton; ▸ country vocal performance, male: "O Death," Ralph Stanley, ▸ country vocal performance, duo/group: "The Lucky One," Alison Krauss & Union Station; ▸ country song: "The Lucky One," Robert Lee Castleman, songwriter (Alison Krauss & Union Station); ▸ country album: *Timeless—Hank Williams Tribute*, various artists; ▸ bluegrass album: *New Favorite*, Alison Krauss & Union Station; ▸ new age album: *A Day Without Rain*, Enya; ▸ jazz album, contemporary: *M²*, Marcus Miller; ▸ jazz album, vocal: *The Calling*, Diane Reeves; ▸ jazz album, instrumental: *This Is What I Do*, Sonny Rollins; ▸ jazz album, large ensemble: *Homage to Count Basie*, Bob Mintzer Big Band; ▸ gospel album, rock: *Solo*, DC Talk; ▸ gospel album, pop/contemporary: CeCe Winans, CeCe Winans; ▸ gospel album, southern/country/bluegrass: *A Billy Graham Music Home-*

coming, Bill & Gloria Gaither and the Homecoming Friends; ▶ gospel album, soul, traditional: *Spirit of the Century,* The Blind Boys of Alabama; ▶ gospel album, soul, contemporary: *The Experience,* Yolanda Adams; ▶ gospel album, choir/chorus: *Love Is Live!,* Hezekiah Walker & LFT Church Choir; ▶ Latin album, pop: *La Musica de Baldemar Huerta,* Freddy Fender; ▶ Latin album, rock/alternative: *Embrace the Chaos,* Ozomatli; ▶ Latin album, traditional tropical: *Dejame Entrar,* Carlos Vives; ▶ salsa album: *Encore,* Robert Blades; ▶ merengue album: *Yo por Tí,* Olga Tañón; ▶ Mexican/Mexican-American album: *En Vivo . . . El Hombre y Su Musica,* Ramón Ayala y Sus Bravos del Norte; ▶ Tejano album: *Nadie Como Tu,* Solido; ▶ blues album, traditional: *Do You Get the Blues?,* Jimmie Vaughan; ▶ blues album, contemporary: *Nothing Personal,* Delbert McClinton; ▶ folk album, traditional: *Down from the Mountain,* various artists; ▶ folk album, contemporary: *Love and Theft,* Bob Dylan; ▶ Native American album: *Bless the People—Harmonized Peyote Songs,* Verdell Primeax & Johnny Mike; ▶ reggae album: *Halfway Tree,* Damian Marley; ▶ world music album: *Full Circle: Carnegie Hall 2000,* Ravi Shankar; ▶ polka album: *Gone Polka,* Jimmy Sturr; ▶ spoken word album: *Q: The Autobiography of Quincy Jones,* Quincy Jones; ▶ spoken comedy album: *Napalm & Silly Putty,* George Carlin; ▶ producer, non-classical: T. Bone Burnett; ▶ producer, classical: Manfred Eicher; ▶ classical album: *Berlioz: Les Troyens,* Sir Colin Davis cond. De Young, Heppner, et al., w/ London Sym. Orch.; ▶ orchestral performance: *Boulez Conducts Varèse,* Pierre Boulez cond. Chicago Sym. Orch.; ▶ opera recording: *Berlioz: Les Troyens,* Sir Colin Davis cond. De Young, Heppner, et al., w/ London Sym. Orch.; ▶ chamber music performance: *Haydn: Complete String Quartets,* The Angeles String Quartet; ▶ classical vocal performance: *Dreams & Fables—Gluck Italian Arias,* Cecilia Bartoli, mezzo soprano; ▶ contemporary classical composition: *Concert de Gaudí,* Christopher Rouse; ▶ music video, short form: "Weapon of Choice," Spike Jonze, dir., Vincent Landay & Deannie O'Neil, prod. (Fatboy Slim w/ Bootsy Collins).

Grammy Awards Top Winners, 1958–2001

The year denotes the period for which the winning work or artist was recognized; the prizes were generally awarded during the following year.

YEAR	RECORD (SINGLE) OF THE YEAR	ALBUM OF THE YEAR	BEST NEW ARTIST
1958	"Nel Blu Dipinto Di Blu (Volare)," Domenico Modugno	*The Music from Peter Gunn,* Henry Mancini	not awarded
1959	"Mack the Knife," Bobby Darin	*Come Dance with Me,* Frank Sinatra	Bobby Darin
1960	"Theme from a Summer Place," Percy Faith	*The Button-down Mind of Bob Newhart,* Bob Newhart	Bob Newhart
1961	"Moon River," Henry Mancini	*Judy at Carnegie Hall,* Judy Garland	Peter Nero
1962	"I Left My Heart in San Francisco," Tony Bennett	*The First Family,* Vaughn Meader	Robert Goulet
1963	"The Days of Wine and Roses," Henry Mancini	*The Barbra Streisand Album,* Barbra Streisand	Ward Swingle (The Swingle Singers)
1964	"The Girl from Ipanema," Stan Getz & Astrud Gilberto	*Getz/Gilberto,* Stan Getz & João Gilberto	The Beatles
1965	"A Taste of Honey," Herb Alpert	*September of My Years,* Frank Sinatra	Tom Jones
1966	"Strangers in the Night," Frank Sinatra	*A Man and His Music,* Frank Sinatra	not awarded
1967	"Up, Up and Away," The 5th Dimension	*Sgt. Pepper's Lonely Hearts Club Band,* The Beatles	Bobbie Gentry
1968	"Mrs. Robinson," Simon & Garfunkel	*By the Time I Get to Phoenix,* Glen Campbell	José Feliciano
1969	"Aquarius/Let the Sunshine In," The 5th Dimension	*Blood, Sweat & Tears,* Blood, Sweat & Tears	Crosby, Stills & Nash
1970	"Bridge over Troubled Water," Simon & Garfunkel	*Bridge over Troubled Water,* Simon & Garfunkel	Carpenters
1971	"It's Too Late," Carole King	*Tapestry,* Carole King	Carly Simon
1972	"The First Time Ever I Saw Your Face," Roberta Flack	*The Concert for Bangla Desh,* George Harrison & Friends	America
1973	"Killing Me Softly with His Song," Roberta Flack	*Innervisions,* Stevie Wonder	Bette Midler
1974	"I Honestly Love You," Olivia Newton-John	*Fulfillingness' First Finale,* Stevie Wonder	Marvin Hamlisch
1975	"Love Will Keep Us Together," Captain & Tennille	*Still Crazy After All These Years,* Paul Simon	Natalie Cole
1976	"This Masquerade," George Benson	*Songs in the Key of Life,* Stevie Wonder	Starland Vocal Band
1977	"Hotel California," The Eagles	*Rumours,* Fleetwood Mac	Debby Boone
1978	"Just the Way You Are," Billy Joel	*Saturday Night Fever,* The Bee Gees	A Taste of Honey
1979	"What a Fool Believes," The Doobie Brothers	*52nd Steet,* Billy Joel	Rickie Lee Jones

Grammy Awards Top Winners, 1958–2001 (continued)

YEAR	RECORD (SINGLE) OF THE YEAR	ALBUM OF THE YEAR	BEST NEW ARTIST
1980	"Sailing," Christopher Cross	*Christopher Cross*, Christopher Cross	Christopher Cross
1981	"Bette Davis Eyes," Kim Carnes	*Double Fantasy*, John Lennon & Yoko Ono	Sheena Easton
1982	"Rosanna," Toto	*Toto IV*, Toto	Men at Work
1983	"Beat It," Michael Jackson	*Thriller*, Michael Jackson	Culture Club
1984	"What's Love Got to Do with It," Tina Turner	*Can't Slow Down*, Lionel Richie	Cyndi Lauper
1985	"We Are the World," USA for Africa	*No Jacket Required*, Phil Collins	Sade
1986	"Higher Love," Steve Winwood	*Graceland*, Paul Simon	Bruce Hornsby and the Range
1987	"Graceland," Paul Simon	*The Joshua Tree*, U2	Jody Watley
1988	"Don't Worry, Be Happy," Bobby McFerrin	*Faith*, George Michael	Tracy Chapman
1989	"Wind Beneath My Wings," Bette Midler	*Nick of Time*, Bonnie Raitt	Milli Vanilli (revoked)
1990	"Another Day in Paradise," Phil Collins	*Back on the Block*, Quincy Jones	Mariah Carey
1991	"Unforgettable," Natalie Cole w/ Nat "King" Cole	*Unforgettable*, Natalie Cole w/ Nat "King" Cole	Marc Cohn
1992	"Tears in Heaven," Eric Clapton	*Unplugged*, Eric Clapton	Arrested Development
1993	"I Will Always Love You," Whitney Houston	*The Bodyguard*, Whitney Houston	Toni Braxton
1994	"All I Wanna Do," Sheryl Crow	*MTV Unplugged*, Tony Bennett	Sheryl Crow
1995	"Kiss from a Rose," Seal	*Jagged Little Pill*, Alanis Morissette	Hootie and the Blowfish
1996	"Change the World," Eric Clapton	*Falling into You*, Celine Dion	LeAnn Rimes
1997	"Sunny Came Home," Shawn Colvin	*Time Out of Mind*, Bob Dylan	Paula Cole
1998	"My Heart Will Go On," Celine Dion	*The Miseducation of Lauryn Hill*, Lauryn Hill	Lauryn Hill
1999	"Smooth," Santana feat. Rob Thomas	*Supernatural*, Santana	Christina Aguilera
2000	"Beautiful Day," U2	*Two Against Nature*, Steely Dan	Shelby Lynne
2001	"Walk On," U2	*O Brother, Where Art Thou?*, various artists	Alicia Keys
2002	scheduled to be held 23 February 2003, New York City		

Eurovision Song Contest, 1956–2002

The European Broadcasting Union (EBU), an association of national television and radio companies from Europe and the Mediterranean, began the Eurovision Song Contest in 1956 to promote European pop-music composers and performers. Each EBU member country, along with several provisional participants, can nominate one original song per year, in any language, with a maximum length of three minutes. The overall winner is selected through a point scheme based on call-in votes from viewers and juries in each participating country. Eurovision Song Contest Web site: <www.eurosong.tv>

YEAR	SONG, SONGWRITER(S) (PERFORMER, COUNTRY)
1956	"Refrain," Emile Gardaz, Géo Voumard (Lys Assia, Switzerland)
1957	"Net als toen," Willy van Hemert, Guus Jansen (Corry Brokken, The Netherlands)
1958	"Dors mon amour," Pierre Delanoe, Hubert Giraud (André Claveau, France)
1959	"Een beetje," Willy van Hemert, Dick Schallies (Teddy Scholten, The Netherlands)
1960	"Tom Pillibi," Pierre Cour, André Popp (Jacqueline Boyer, France)
1961	"Nous les amoureux," Jacques Datin, Maurice Vidalin (Jean-Claude Pascal, Luxembourg)
1962	"Un Premier amour," Rolande Valade, Claude Henri Vic (Isabelle Aubret, France)
1963	"Dansevise," Sejr Volmer Sorensen, Otto Francker (Grethe and Jorgen Ingmann, Denmark)
1964	"Non ho l'étà," Nicola Salerno (Gigliola Cinquetti, Italy)
1965	"Poupée de cire, poupée de son," Serge Gainsbourg (France Gall, Luxembourg)
1966	"Merci chérie," Udo Jürgens, Thomas Horbiger (Udo Jürgens, Austria)
1967	"Puppet on a String," Bill Martin, Phil Coulter (Sandie Shaw, United Kingdom)
1968	"La, la, la . . ." Ramon Arcusa, Manuel de la Calva (Massiel, Spain)
1969	"Vivo cantando," A. Alcaide, Maria José de Cerato (Salomé, Spain); "Boom Bang-a-Bang," Peter Warne, Alan Moorhouse (Lulu, United Kingdom); "De Troubadour," Lennie Kuhr, David Hartsena (Lennie Kuhr, The Netherlands); "Un Jour, un enfant," Eddy Marnay, Emile Stern (Frida Boccara, France) (four-way tie)

Eurovision Song Contest, 1956–2002 (continued)

YEAR	SONG, SONGWRITER(S) (PERFORMER, COUNTRY)
1970	"All Kinds of Everything," Derry Lindsay, Jackie Smith (Dana, Ireland)
1971	"Un Banc, un arbre, une rue," Yves Dessca, Jean-Pierre Bourtayre (Séverine, Monaco)
1972	"Après toi," Klaus Munro, Yves Dessca, Mario Panas (Vicky Leandros, Luxembourg)
1973	"Tu te reconnaîtras," Vline Buggy, Claude Morgan (Anne-Marie David, Luxembourg)
1974	"Waterloo," Stikkan Anderson, Benny Andersson, Björn Ulvaeus (Abba, Sweden)
1975	"Ding dinge dong," Wil Luikinga, Eddy Owens, Dick Bakker (Teach-In, The Netherlands)
1976	"Save Your Kisses for Me," Tony Hiller, Lee Sheriden, Martin Lee (Brotherhood of Man, United Kingdom)
1977	"L'Oiseau et l'enfant," José Gracy, Jean-Paul Cara (Marie Myriam, France)
1978	"A-Ba-Ni-Bi," Ehud Manor, Nurit Hirsh (Izhar Cohen and the Alphabeta, Israel)
1979	"Hallelujah," Shimrit Orr, Kobi Oshrat (Gali Atari and Milk and Honey, Israel)
1980	"What's Another Year," Shay Healy (Johnny Logan, Ireland)
1981	"Making Your Mind Up," Andy Hill, John Danter (Bucks Fizz, United Kingdom)
1982	"Ein bisschen Frieden," Bernd Meinunger, Ralph Siegel (Nicole, West Germany)
1983	"Si la vie est cadeau," Alain Garcia, Jean-Pierre Millers (Corinne Hermes, Luxembourg)
1984	"Diggi-loo-diggi-ley," Britt Lindeborg, Torgny Soederberg (Herrey's, Sweden)
1985	"La det swinge," Rolg Loevland (Bobbysocks, Norway)
1986	"J'aime la vie," Marino Atria, J.P. Furnemont, A. Crisci (Sandra Kim, Belgium)
1987	"Hold Me Now," Sean Sherrard (Johnny Logan, Ireland)
1988	"Ne partez pas sans moi," Nella Martinetti, Atilla Sereftug (Céline Dion, Switzerland)
1989	"Rock Me," Stevo Cvikich, Rajko Dujmich (Riva, Yugoslavia)
1990	"Insieme: 1992," Toto Cutugno (Toto Cutugno, Italy)
1991	"Fångad av en stormvind," Stephan Berg (Carola, Sweden)
1992	"Why Me," Sean Sherrard (Linda Martin, Ireland)
1993	"In Your Eyes," Jimmy Walsh (Niamh Kavanagh, Ireland)
1994	"Rock'n Roll Kids," Brendan Graham (Paul Harrington and Charlie McGettigan, Ireland)
1995	"Nocturne," Petter Skavlan, Rolf Lovland (Secret Garden, Norway)
1996	"The Voice," Brendan Graham (Eimear Quinn, Ireland)
1997	"Love Shine a Light," Kimberley Rew (Katrina and the Waves, United Kingdom)
1998	"Diva," Yoav Ginay (Dana International, Israel)
1999	"Take Me to Your Heaven," Gert Lengstrand (Charlotte Nilsson, Sweden)
2000	"Fly on the Wings of Love," Jørgen Olsen (Olsen Brothers, Denmark)
2001	"Everybody," Maian-Anna Käarmas, Ivar Must (Tanel Padar, Dave Benton, and 2XL, Estonia)
2002	"I Wanna," Marija Naumova, Marats Samauskis (Marie N, Latvia)

Brit Awards, 2002

The British Phonographic Industry, a trade association of British record companies, established the Brit Awards in 1977 to recognize pop acts from Great Britain and abroad. Prize: silver statuette. Brit Awards Web site: <www.brits.co.uk>

BRITISH CATEGORIES
Male solo artist: Robbie Williams
Female solo artist: Dido
Group: Travis
Album: *No Angel,* Dido
Newcomer: Blue
Single: "Don't Stop Movin'," S Club 7
Video: "21 Seconds," So Solid Crew
Dance act: Basement Jaxx

INTERNATIONAL CATEGORIES
Male solo artist: Shaggy
Female solo artist: Kylie Minogue
Group: Destiny's Child
Album: *Fever,* Kylie Minogue
Newcomer: The Strokes

ADDITIONAL CATEGORIES
Pop act: Westlife
Outstanding contribution: Sting

Country Music Association Awards, 2001

The Country Music Association, founded in 1958 as a trade organization for the country and western music industry, began its annual awards ceremony in 1967 and made it the first nationally televised music awards show the following year. Ceremonies are held in November. Prize: hand-blown crystal statuette. Country Music Association Web site: <www.cmaworld.com>

▶ **entertainer of the year:** Tim McGraw; ▶ **female vocalist of the year:** Lee Ann Womack; ▶ **male vocalist of the year:** Toby Keith; ▶ **Horizon Award of the year:** Keith Urban; ▶ **vocal duo of the year:** Brooks & Dunn; ▶ **vocal group of the year:** Lonestar; ▶ **album of the year:** *O Brother, Where Art Thou?,* various artists, T. Bone Burnett, prod.; ▶ **song of the year:** "Murder on Music Row," Larry Cordle, Larry Shell, songwriters; ▶ **single of the year:** "I Am a Man of Constant Sorrow," The Soggy Bottom Boys, T. Bone Burnett, prod.; ▶ **music video of the year:** "Born to Fly," Peter Zavadil, dir. (Sara Evans) ; ▶ **vocal event of the year:** "Too Country," Brad Paisley w/George Jones, Bill Anderson, and Buck Owens; ▶ **musician of the year:** Dann Huff

Miss America Winners, 1921–2002

The Miss America Pageant was founded in 1921 as an Atlantic City tourist attraction. Purely a beauty contest in its early years, the competition added a talent category in 1935 and began awarding scholarships a decade later. After 1989 the pageant required evidence of community service, and by 2001 contestants were judged on the basis of talent, community service, leadership, knowledge and understanding, and appearance in swimsuits and eveningwear. Prize: $50,000 college scholarship. Miss America Contest Web site: <www.missamerica.org>

YEAR	WINNER (HOMETOWN)
1921	Margaret Gorman (Washington DC)
1922	Mary Katherine Campbell (Columbus OH)
1923	Mary Katherine Campbell (Columbus OH)
1924	Ruth Malcomson (Philadelphia PA)
1925	Fay Lanphier (Oakland CA)
1926	Norma Smallwood (Tulsa OK)
1927	Lois Delander (Joliet IL)
1928–32	not held
1933	Marian Bergeron (West Haven CT)
1934	not held
1935	Henrietta Leaver (Pittsburgh PA)
1936	Rose Coyle (Philadelphia PA)
1937	Bette Cooper (Bertrand Island NJ)
1938	Marilyn Meseke (Marion OH)
1939	Patricia Donnelly (Detroit MI)
1940	Frances Burke (Philadelphia PA)
1941	Rosemary LaPlanche (Los Angeles CA)
1942	Jo-Carroll Dennison (Tyler TX)
1943	Jean Bartel (Los Angeles CA)
1944	Venus Ramey (Washington DC)
1945	Bess Myerson (New York NY)
1946	Marilyn Buferd (Los Angeles CA)
1947	Barbara Walker (Memphis TN)
1948	BeBe Shopp (Hopkins MN)
1949	Jacque Mercer (Litchfield AZ)
1950	Until the 1950 competition, winners were given the title for the year in which they won; thereafter, they were given the title for the following year, during which most of their reign took place. As a result no Miss America 1950 was named.
1951	Yolande Betbeze (Mobile AL)
1952	Colleen Hutchins (Salt Lake City UT)
1953	Neva Langley (Macon GA)
1954	Evelyn Ay (Ephrata PA)
1955	Lee Meriwether (San Francisco CA)
1956	Sharon Ritchie (Denver CO)
1957	Marian McKnight (Manning SC)
1958	Marilyn Van Derbur (Denver CO)
1959	Mary Ann Mobley (Brandon MS)
1960	Lynda Mead (Natchez MS)

YEAR	WINNER (HOMETOWN)
1961	Nancy Fleming (Montague MI)
1962	Maria Fletcher (Asheville NC)
1963	Jacquelyn Mayer (Sandusky OH)
1964	Donna Axum (El Dorado AR)
1965	Vonda Van Dyke (Phoenix AZ)
1966	Deborah Bryant (Overland Park KS)
1967	Jane Jayroe (Laverne OK)
1968	Debra Barnes (Pittsburg KS)
1969	Judith Ford (Belvidere IL)
1970	Pam Eldred (Bloomfield MI)
1971	Phyllis George (Denton TX)
1972	Laurel Schaefer (Bexley OH)
1973	Terry Meeuwsen (De Pere WI)
1974	Rebecca King (Denver CO)
1975	Shirley Cothran (Denton TX)
1976	Tawny Godin (Saratoga Springs NY)
1977	Dorothy Benham (Edina MN)
1978	Susan Perkins (Columbus OH)
1979	Kylene Barker (Roanoke VA)
1980	Cheryl Prewitt (Ackerman MS)
1981	Susan Powell (Elk City OK)
1982	Elizabeth Ward (Russellville AR)
1983	Debra Maffett (Anaheim CA)
1984	Suzette Charles (Mays Landing NJ)*
1985	Sharlene Wells (Salt Lake City UT)
1986	Susan Akin (Meridian MS)
1987	Kellye Cash (Memphis TN)
1988	Kaye Lani Rae Rafko (Monroe MI)
1989	Gretchen Carlson (Anoka MN)
1990	Debbye Turner (Columbia MO)
1991	Marjorie Vincent (Oak Park IL)
1992	Carolyn Sapp (Honolulu HI)
1993	Leanza Cornett (Jacksonville FL)
1994	Kimberly Aiken (Columbia SC)
1995	Heather Whitestone (Birmingham AL)
1996	Shawntel Smith (Muldrow OK)
1997	Tara Dawn Holland (Overland Park KS)
1998	Kate Shindle (Evanston IL)
1999	Nicole Johnson (Virginia Beach VA)
2000	Heather French (Maysville KY)
2001	Angela Perez Baraquio (Honolulu HI)
2002	Katie Harman (Gresham OR)

*Runner-up, crowned after resignation of Vanessa Williams (Millwood NY).

Miss Universe Winners, 1952–2002

The Miss Universe contest originated in 1952 as a swimwear competition in Long Beach CA in conjunction with the Miss USA pageant. The two pageants were held concurrently until 1965. Women ages 18–27 from some 80 countries and dependencies participate in the competetion annually, and the contest is broadcast across the globe. Judging is based on an interview and appearances in swimwear and evening wear. Though it remains primarily a beauty contest, the competition's organizers emphasize a message of cross-cultural harmony and opportunity for women, and winners work with the United Nations and other organizations to promote HIV/AIDS awareness and women's health and reproductive initiatives. Prize: one-year employment contract, cash, products, and services. Miss Universe Contest Web site: <www.missuniverse.com>

YEAR	WINNER (COUNTRY)
1952	Armi Kuusela (Finland)
1953	Christiane Martel (France)

YEAR	WINNER (COUNTRY)
1954	Miriam Stevenson (US)
1955	Hillevi Rombin (Sweden)

Miss Universe Winners (continued)

YEAR	WINNER (COUNTRY)	YEAR	WINNER (COUNTRY)
1956	Carol Morris (US)	1980	Shawn Nichols Weatherly (US)
1957	Gladys Zender (Peru)	1981	Mona Irene Lailan Sáez Conde (Venezuela)
1958	Luz Marina Zuluaga (Colombia)	1982	Karen Diane Baldwin (Canada)
1959	Akiko Kojima (Japan)	1983	Lorraine Downes (New Zealand)
1960	Linda Bement (US)	1984	Yvonne Ryding (Sweden)
1961	Marlene Schmidt (West Germany)	1985	Deborah Carthy-Deu (Puerto Rico)
1962	Norma Nolan (Argentina)	1986	Bárbara Palacios Teyde (Venezuela)
1963	Ieda Maria Vargas (Brazil)	1987	Cecilia Carolina Bolocco Fonck (Chile)
1964	Kiriaki Corinna Tsopei (Greece)	1988	Porntip Nakhirunkanok (Thailand)
1965	Apasra Hongsakula (Thailand)	1989	Angela Visser (The Netherlands)
1966	Margareta Arvidsson (Sweden)	1990	Mona Grudt (Norway)
1967	Sylvia Louise Hitchcock (US)	1991	Lupita Jones (Mexico)
1968	Martha Vasconcellos (Brazil)	1992	Michelle McLean (Namibia)
1969	Gloria Diaz (Philippines)	1993	Dayanara Torres (Puerto Rico)
1970	Marisol Malaret (Puerto Rico)	1994	Sushmita Sen (India)
1971	Georgina Rizk (Lebanon)	1995	Chelsi Smith (US)
1972	Kerry Anne Wells (Australia)	1996	Joseph Alicia Machado Fajardo (Venezuela)
1973	Margarita Moran (Philippines)	1997	Brook Antoinette Mahealani Lee (US)
1974	Amparo Muñoz (Spain)	1998	Wendy Fitzwilliam (Trinidad and Tobago)
1975	Anne Marie Pohtamo (Finland)	1999	Mpule Kwelagobe (Botswana)
1976	Rina Messinger (Israel)	2000	Lara Dutta (India)
1977	Janelle Commissiong (Trinidad and Tobago)	2001	Denise M. Quiñones August (Puerto Rico)
1978	Margaret Gardiner (South Africa)	2002	Oxana Fedorova (Russia)
1979	Maritza Sayalero (Venezuela)		

Arts and Letters Awards

Pulitzer Prizes, 2002

The Pulitzer Prizes are awarded annually by Columbia University, New York City, based on recommendations from the Pulitzer Prize Board. The prizes, originally endowed by newspaper editor Joseph Pulitzer, were first awarded in 1917. Over the years categories have been added, and 21 prizes are now presented. All prizes include a $7,500 cash award; the exception is the prize for public service in journalism, which is a gold medal.

Pulitzer Prize Web site: <www.pulitzer.org>.

Journalism

CATEGORY AND DESCRIPTION	WINNER	PUBLICATION	SUBJECT
Public Service: awarded to a newspaper for notable public service.		New York Times	"A Nation Challenged," section published regularly after the terrorist attacks of 11 Sep 2001, covering events, victims, and the developing story
Breaking News Reporting: awarded for local reporting of breaking news.	staff	The Wall Street Journal	coverage of the terrorist attacks on New York City on 11 Sep 2001
Investigative Reporting: awarded to an individual or team for an investigative article or series.	Sari Horwitz, Scott Higham, Sarah Cohen	Washington Post	series uncovering the District of Columbia's part in the neglect and death of more than 200 children under protective care in the 1990s, stimulating major changes in its welfare system
Explanatory Reporting: awarded for clarification of a difficult subject through clear communication of in-depth knowledge.	staff	New York Times	in-depth profiling of worldwide network of terrorism and its threats
Beat Reporting: awarded for consistent, intelligent coverage of a particular topic.	Gretchen Morgenson	New York Times	Wall Street coverage
National Reporting: awarded for coverage of national news.	staff	Washington Post	coverage and analysis of the United States's war against terrorism

Journalism (continued)

CATEGORY AND DESCRIPTION	WINNER	PUBLICATION	SUBJECT
International Reporting: awarded for coverage of international news.	Barry Bearak	*New York Times*	reporting on ordinary day-to-day life in Afghanistan
Feature Writing: awarded for a highly . original feature of literary quality	Barry Siegel	*Los Angeles Times*	profiles of a man on trial for negligence in his son's death and of the trial judge
Commentary	Thomas Friedman	*New York Times*	the global effects of terrorism
Criticism	Justin Davidson	*Newsday*, Long Island NY	coverage of classical music
Editorial Writing: awarded for ability to sway public opinion through solid reasoning, clear style, and "moral purpose."	Alex Raksin, Bob Sipchen	*Los Angeles Times*	discussion of issues surrounding the homeless mentally ill
Editorial Cartooning: awarded for a cartoon or group of cartoons displaying creativity, superior drawing, and editorial effectiveness.	Clay Bennett	*The Christian Science Monitor*	
Breaking News Photography: awarded for color or black-and-white photographs of breaking news, individually or as a group.	staff	*New York Times*	coverage of the terrorist attacks on New York City on 11 Sep 2001
Feature Photography: awarded for color or black-and-white feature photographs, individually or as a group	staff	*New York Times*	record of suffering during war in Pakistan and Afghanistan

Letters, Drama, and Music

Fiction
Awarded for a work of fiction, preferably about American life, by an American author.

YEAR	TITLE	AUTHOR	YEAR	TITLE	AUTHOR
1917	no award		1940	*The Grapes of Wrath*	John Steinbeck
1918	*His Family*	Ernest Poole	1941	no award	
1919	*The Magnificent Ambersons*	Booth Tarkington	1942	*In This Our Life*	Ellen Glasgow
			1943	*Dragon's Teeth*	Upton Sinclair
1920	no award		1944	*Journey in the Dark*	Martin Flavin
1921	*The Age of Innocence*	Edith Wharton	1945	*A Bell for Adano*	John Hersey
1922	*Alice Adams*	Booth Tarkington	1946	no award	
1923	*One of Ours*	Willa Cather	1947	*All the King's Men*	Robert Penn Warren
1924	*The Able McLaughlins*	Margaret Wilson			
1925	*So Big*	Edna Ferber	1948	*Tales of the South Pacific*	James A. Michener
1926	*Arrowsmith*	Sinclair Lewis			
1927	*Early Autumn*	Louis Bromfield	1949	*Guard of Honor*	James Gould Cozzens
1928	*The Bridge of San Luis Rey*	Thornton Wilder			
			1950	*The Way West*	A B. Guthrie, Jr.
1929	*Scarlet Sister Mary*	Julia Peterkin	1951	*The Town*	Conrad Richter
1930	*Laughing Boy*	Oliver Lafarge	1952	*The Caine Mutiny*	Herman Wouk
1931	*Years of Grace*	Margaret Ayer Barnes	1953	*The Old Man and the Sea*	Ernest Hemingway
1932	*The Good Earth*	Pearl S. Buck	1954	no award	
1933	*The Store*	T.S. Stribling	1955	*A Fable*	William Faulkner
1934	*Lamb in His Bosom*	Caroline Miller	1956	*Andersonville*	MacKinlay Kantor
1935	*Now in November*	Josephine Winslow Johnson	1957	no award	
			1958	*A Death In The Family**	James Agee
1936	*Honey in the Horn*	Harold L. Davis	1959	*The Travels of Jaimie McPheeters*	Robert Lewis Taylor
1937	*Gone With the Wind*	Margaret Mitchell			
1938	*The Late George Apley*	John Phillips Marquand	1960	*Advise and Consent*	Allen Drury
			1961	*To Kill A Mockingbird*	Harper Lee
1939	*The Yearling*	Marjorie Kinnan Rawlings	1962	*The Edge of Sadness*	Edwin O'Connor
			1963	*The Reivers*	William Faulkner

Letters, Drama, and Music (continued)

Fiction (continued)

YEAR	TITLE	AUTHOR	YEAR	TITLE	AUTHOR
1964	no award		1984	*Ironweed*	William Kennedy
1965	*The Keepers Of The House*	Shirley Ann Grau	1985	*Foreign Affairs*	Alison Lurie
			1986	*Lonesome Dove*	Larry McMurtry
1966	*Collected Stories*	Katherine Anne Porter	1987	*A Summons to Memphis*	Peter Taylor
1967	*The Fixer*	Bernard Malamud	1988	*Beloved*	Toni Morrison
1968	*The Confessions of Nat Turner*	William Styron	1989	*Breathing Lessons*	Anne Tyler
			1990	*The Mambo Kings Play Songs of Love*	Oscar Hijuelos
1969	*House Made of Dawn*	N. Scott Momaday			
1970	*Collected Stories*	Jean Stafford	1991	*Rabbit At Rest*	John Updike
1971	no award		1992	*A Thousand Acres*	Jane Smiley
1972	*Angle of Repose*	Wallace Stegner	1993	*A Good Scent from a Strange Mountain*	Robert Olen Butler
1973	*The Optimist's Daughter*	Eudora Welty			
1974	no award		1994	*The Shipping News*	E. Annie Proulx
1975	*The Killer Angels*	Michael Shaara	1995	*The Stone Diaries*	Carol Shields
1976	*Humboldt's Gift*	Saul Bellow	1996	*Independence Day*	Richard Ford
1977	no award		1997	*Martin Dressler: The Tale of an American Dreamer*	Steven Millhauser
1978	*Elbow Room*	James Alan McPherson			
1979	*The Stories of John Cheever*	John Cheever	1998	*American Pastoral*	Philip Roth
			1999	*The Hours*	Michael Cunningham
1980	*The Executioner's Song*	Norman Mailer			
1981	*A Confederacy of Dunces**	John Kennedy Toole	2000	*Interpreter of Maladies*	Jhumpa Lahiri
			2001	*The Amazing Adventures of Kavalier and Clay*	Michael Chabon
1982	*Rabbit Is Rich*	John Updike			
1983	*The Color Purple*	Alice Walker	2002	*Empire Falls*	Richard Russo

Work published and prize awarded posthumously.

Drama
Awarded for a play, preferably about American life, by an American author.

YEAR	TITLE	AUTHOR	YEAR	TITLE	AUTHOR
1917	no award		1941	*There Shall Be No Night*	Robert E. Sherwood
1918	*Why Marry?*	Jesse Lynch Williams			
			1942	no award	
1919	no award		1943	*The Skin of Our Teeth*	Thornton Wilder
1920	*Beyond the Horizon*	Eugene O'Neill	1944	no award	
1921	*Miss Lulu Bett*	Zona Gale	1945	*Harvey*	Mary Chase
1922	*Anna Christie*	Eugene O'Neill	1946	*State of the Union*	Russel Crouse, Howard Lindsay
1923	*Icebound*	Owen Davis			
1924	*Hell-Bent Fer Heaven*	Hatcher Hughes	1947	no award	
1925	*They Knew What They Wanted*	Sidney Howard	1948	*A Streetcar Named Desire*	Tennessee Williams
1926	*Craig's Wife*	George Kelly	1949	*Death of a Salesman*	Arthur Miller
1927	*In Abraham's Bosom*	Paul Green	1950	*South Pacific*	Richard Rodgers, Oscar Hammerstein II, Joshua Logan
1928	*Strange Interlude*	Eugene O'Neill			
1929	*Street Scene*	Elmer L. Rice			
1930	*The Green Pastures*	Marc Connelly			
1931	*Alison's House*	Susan Glaspell	1951	no award	
1932	*Of Thee I Sing*	George S. Kaufman, Morrie Ryskind, Ira Gershwin	1952	*The Shrike*	Joseph Kramm
			1953	*Picnic*	William Inge
			1954	*The Teahouse of the August Moon*	John Patrick
1933	*Both Your Houses*	Maxwell Anderson	1955	*Cat on a Hot Tin Roof*	Tennessee Williams
1934	*Men in White*	Sidney Kingsley			
1935	*The Old Maid*	Zoe Akins	1956	*Diary of Anne Frank*	Albert Hackett, Frances Goodrich
1936	*Idiots Delight*	Robert E. Sherwood			
1937	*You Can't Take It With You*	Moss Hart, George S. Kaufman	1957	*Long Day's Journey Into Night*	Eugene O'Neill
1938	*Our Town*	Thornton Wilder	1958	*Look Homeward, Angel*	Ketti Frings
1939	*Abe Lincoln in Illinois*	Robert E. Sherwood	1959	*J.B.*	Archibald MacLeish
1940	*The Time of Your Life*	William Saroyan			

Letters, Drama, and Music (continued)

Drama (continued)

YEAR	TITLE	AUTHOR	YEAR	TITLE	AUTHOR
1960	Fiorello!	Jerome Weidman, George Abbott, Jerry Bock, Sheldon Harnick	1978	The Gin Game	Donald L. Coburn
			1979	Buried Child	Sam Shepard
			1980	Talley's Folly	Lanford Wilson
			1981	Crimes of the Heart	Beth Henley
1961	All The Way Home	Tad Mosel	1982	A Soldier's Play	Charles Fuller
1962	How To Succeed In Business Without Really Trying	Frank Loesser, Abe Burrows	1983	'Night, Mother	Marsha Norman
			1984	Glengarry Glen Ross	David Mamet
			1985	Sunday in the Park With George	Stephen Sondheim, James Lapine
1963	no award				
1964	no award				
1965	The Subject Was Roses	Frank D. Gilroy	1986	no award	
1966	no award		1987	Fences	August Wilson
1967	A Delicate Balance	Edward Albee	1988	Driving Miss Daisy	Alfred Uhry
1968	no award		1989	The Heidi Chronicles	Wendy Wasserstein
1969	The Great White Hope	Howard Sackler			
1970	No Place To Be Somebody	Charles Gordone	1990	The Piano Lesson	August Wilson
			1991	Lost in Yonkers	Neil Simon
1971	The Effect of Gamma Rays on Man-in-the-Moon Marigolds	Paul Zindel	1992	The Kentucky Cycle	Robert Schenkkan
			1993	Angels in America: Millennium Approaches	Tony Kushner
1972	no award		1994	Three Tall Women	Edward Albee
1973	That Championship Season	Jason Miller	1995	The Young Man From Atlanta	Horton Foote
1974	no award		1996	Rent	Jonathan Larson*
1975	Seascape	Edward Albee	1997	no award	
1976	A Chorus Line	Michael Bennett, James Kirkwood, Nicholas Dante, Marvin Hamlisch, Edward Kleban	1998	How I Learned to Drive	Paula Vogel
			1999	Wit	Margaret Edson
			2000	Dinner With Friends	Donald Margulies
			2001	Proof	David Auburn
			2002	Topdog/Underdog	Suzan-Lori Parks
1977	The Shadow Box	Michael Cristofer			

*Awarded posthumously.

History
Awarded for a work on the subject of United States history.

YEAR	TITLE	AUTHOR	YEAR	TITLE	AUTHOR
1917	With Americans of Past and Present Days	J.J. Jusserand	1929	The Organization and Administration of the Union Army, 1861–1865	Fred Albert Shannon
1918	A History of the Civil War, 1861–1865	James Ford Rhodes			
1919	no award		1930	The War of Independence	Claude H. Van Tyne
1920	The War with Mexico, 2 vols.	Justin H. Smith	1931	The Coming of the War, 1914	Bernadotte E. Schmitt
1921	The Victory at Sea	William Sowden Sims, Burton Jesse Hendrick	1932	My Experiences in the World War	John J. Pershing
1922	The Founding of New England	James Truslow Adams	1933	The Significance of Sections in American History	Frederick J. Turner
1923	The Supreme Court in United States History	Charles Warren	1934	The People's Choice	Herbert Agar
1924	The American Revolution: A Constitutional Interpretation	Charles Howard McIlwain	1935	The Colonial Period of American History	Charles McLean Andrews
			1936	A Constitutional History of the United States	Andrew C. McLaughlin
1925	History of the American Frontier	Frederic L. Paxson	1937	The Flowering of New England, 1815–1865	Van Wyck Brooks
1926	A History of the United States	Edward Channing	1938	The Road to Reunion, 1865–1900	Paul Herman Buck
1927	Pinckney's Treaty	Samuel Flagg Bemis	1939	A History of American Magazines	Frank Luther Mott
1928	Main Currents in American Thought, 2 vols.	Vernon Louis Parrington	1940	Abraham Lincoln: The War Years	Carl Sandburg
			1941	The Atlantic Migration, 1607–1860	Marcus Lee Hansen

Letters, Drama, and Music (continued)

History (continued)

YEAR	TITLE	AUTHOR
1942	Reveille in Washington, 1860–1865	Margaret Leech
1943	Paul Revere and the World He Lived In	Esther Forbes
1944	The Growth of American Thought	Merle Curti
1945	Unfinished Business	Stephen Bonsal
1946	The Age of Jackson	Arthur M. Schlesinger, Jr.
1947	Scientists Against Time	James Phinney Baxter III
1948	Across the Wide Missouri	Bernard De Voto
1949	The Disruption of American Democracy	Roy Franklin Nichols
1950	Art and Life in America	Oliver W. Larkin
1951	The Old Northwest: Pioneer Period, 1815–1840	R. Carlyle Buley
1952	The Uprooted	Oscar Handlin
1953	The Era of Good Feelings	George Dangerfield
1954	A Stillness at Appomattox	Bruce Catton
1955	Great River: The Rio Grande in North American History	Paul Horgan
1956	The Age of Reform	Richard Hofstadter
1957	Russia Leaves the War: Soviet-American Relations, 1917–1920	George F. Kennan
1958	Banks and Politics in America	Bray Hammond
1959	The Republican Era: 1869–1901	Leonard D. White, Jean Schneider
1960	In the Days of McKinley	Margaret Leech
1961	Between War and Peace: The Potsdam Conference	Herbert Feis
1962	The Triumphant Empire: Thunder-Clouds Gather in the West, 1763–1766	Lawrence H. Gipson
1963	Washington, Village and Capital, 1800–1878	Constance McLaughlin Green
1964	Puritan Village: The Formation of a New England Town	Sumner Chilton Powell
1965	The Greenback Era	Irwin Unger
1966	The Life of the Mind in America	Perry Miller*
1967	Exploration and Empire: The Explorer and the Scientist in the Winning of the American West	William H. Goetzmann
1968	The Ideological Origins of the American Revolution	Bernard Bailyn
1969	Origins of the Fifth Amendment	Leonard W. Levy
1970	Present At The Creation: My Years In The State Department	Dean Acheson
1971	Roosevelt: The Soldier Of Freedom	James MacGregor Burns

YEAR	TITLE	AUTHOR
1972	Neither Black Nor White	Carl N. Degler
1973	People of Paradox: An Inquiry Concerning the Origins of American Civilization	Michael Kammen
1974	The Americans: The Democratic Experience	Daniel J. Boorstin
1975	Jefferson and His Time, Vols. I–V	Dumas Malone
1976	Lamy of Santa Fe	Paul Horgan
1977	The Impending Crisis, 1841–1867	David M. Potter, Don E. Fehrenbacher†
1978	The Visible Hand: The Managerial Revolution in American Business	Alfred D. Chandler, Jr.
1979	The Dred Scott Case	Don E. Fehrenbacher
1980	Been in the Storm So Long	Leon F. Litwack
1981	American Education: The National Experience, 1783–1876	Lawrence A. Cremin
1982	Mary Chesnut's Civil War	C. Vann Woodward‡
1983	The Transformation of Virginia, 1740–1790	Rhys L. Isaac
1984	no award	
1985	Prophets of Regulation	Thomas K. McCraw
1986	...the Heavens and the Earth: A Political History of the Space Age	Walter A. McDougall
1987	Voyagers to the West: A Passage in the Peopling of America on the Eve of the Revolution	Bernard Bailyn
1988	The Launching of Modern American Science, 1846–1876	Robert V. Bruce
1989	Battle Cry of Freedom: The Civil War Era	James M. McPherson
1989	Parting the Waters: America in the King Years, 1954–1963	Taylor Branch
1990	In Our Image: America's Empire in the Philippines	Stanley Karnow
1991	A Midwife's Tale	Laurel Thatcher Ulrich
1992	The Fate of Liberty: Abraham Lincoln and Civil Liberties	Mark E. Neely, Jr.
1993	The Radicalism of the American Revolution	Gordon S. Wood
1994	no award	
1995	No Ordinary Time: Franklin and Eleanor Roosevelt: The Home Front in World War II	Doris Kearns Goodwin
1996	William Cooper's Town: Power and Persuasion on the Frontier of the Early American Republic	Alan Taylor

Letters, Drama, and Music (continued)

History (continued)

YEAR	TITLE	AUTHOR	YEAR	TITLE	AUTHOR
1997	Original Meanings: Politics and Ideas in the Making of the Constitution	Jack N. Rakove	2000	Freedom From Fear: The American People in Depression and War, 1929–1945	David M. Kennedy
1998	Summer for the Gods: The Scopes Trial and America's Continuing Debate Over Science and Religion	Edward J. Larson	2001	Founding Brothers: The Revolutionary Generation	Joseph J. Ellis
1999	Gotham: A History of New York City to 1898	Edwin G. Burrows, Mike Wallace	2002	The Metaphysical Club: A Story of Ideas in America	Louis Menand

*Awarded posthumously.   †Potter died before completing the work; Fehrenbacher wrote the final chapters and edited it.   ‡Edited by Woodward.

Biography or Autobiography
Awarded for a biography or autobiography by an American author.

YEAR	TITLE	AUTHOR	YEAR	TITLE	AUTHOR
1917	Julia Ward Howe	Laura Elizabeth Howe Richards, Maude Howe Elliott; assisted by Florence Howe Hall	1940	Woodrow Wilson, Life and Letters, Vols. VII and VIII	Ray Stannard Baker
1918	Benjamin Franklin, Self-Revealed	William Cabell Bruce	1941	Jonathan Edward	Ola Elizabeth Winslow
1919	The Education of Henry Adams	Henry Adams	1942	Crusader in Crinoline	Forrest Wilson
1920	The Life of John Marshall, 4 vols.	Albert J. Beveridge	1943	Admiral of the Ocean Sea	Samuel Eliot Morison
1921	The Americanization of Edward Bok	Edward Bok	1944	The American Leonardo: The Life of Samuel F.B. Morse	Carleton Mabee
1922	A Daughter of the Middle Border	Hamlin Garland	1945	George Bancroft: Brahmin Rebel	Russell Blaine Nye
1923	The Life and Letters of Walter H. Page	Burton J. Hendrick	1946	Son of the Wilderness	Linnie Marsh Wolfe
1924	From Immigrant to Inventor	Michael Idvorsky Pupin	1947	The Autobiography of William Allen White	William Allen White
1925	Barrett Wendell and His Letters	M.A. De Wolfe Howe	1948	Forgotten First Citizen: John Bigelow	Margaret Clapp
1926	The Life of Sir William Osler, 2 vols.	Harvey Cushing	1949	Roosevelt and Hopkins	Robert E. Sherwood
1927	Whitman	Emory Holloway	1950	John Quincy Adams and the Foundations of American Foreign Policy	Samuel Flagg Bemis
1928	The American Orchestra and Theodore Thomas	Charles Edward Russell			
1929	The Training of an American: The Earlier Life and Letters of Walter H. Page	Burton J. Hendrick	1951	John C. Calhoun: American Portrait	Margaret Louise Coit
			1952	Charles Evans Hughes	Merlo J. Pusey
			1953	Edmund Pendleton, 1721–1803	David J. Mays
			1954	The Spirit of St. Louis	Charles A. Lindbergh
1930	The Raven	Marquis James	1955	The Taft Story	William S. White
1931	Charles W. Eliot	Henry James	1956	Benjamin Henry Latrobe	Talbot Faulkner Hamlin
1932	Theodore Roosevelt	Henry F. Pringle			
1933	Grover Cleveland	Allan Nevins	1957	Profiles in Courage	John F. Kennedy
1934	John Hay	Tyler Dennett	1958	George Washington, Volumes I–VI and Volume VII	Douglas Southall Freeman, John Alexander Carroll, Mary Wells Ashworth*
1935	R.E. Lee	Douglas S. Freeman			
1936	The Thought and Character of William James	Ralph Barton Perry			
			1959	Woodrow Wilson, American Prophet	Arthur Walworth
1937	Hamilton Fish	Allan Nevins			
1938	Andrew Jackson, 2 vols.	Marquis James	1960	John Paul Jones	Samuel Eliot Morison
1938	Pedlar's Progress	Odell Shepard			
1939	Benjamin Franklin	Carl Van Doren	1961	Charles Sumner and the Coming of the Civil War	David Donald

Letters, Drama, and Music (continued)

Biography and Autobiography (continued)

YEAR	TITLE	AUTHOR
1962	no award	
1963	Henry James	Leon Edel
1964	John Keats	Walter Jackson Bate
1965	Henry Adams, three volumes	Ernest Samuels
1966	A Thousand Days	Arthur M. Schlesinger, Jr.
1967	Mr. Clemens and Mark Twain	Justin Kaplan
1968	Memoirs	George E. Kennan
1969	The Man From New York: John Quinn and His Friends	Benjamin Lawrence Reid
1970	Huey Long	T. Harry Williams
1971	Robert Frost: The Years of Triumph, 1915–1938	Lawrance Thompson
1972	Eleanor and Franklin	Joseph P. Lash
1973	Luce and His Empire	W.A. Swanberg
1974	O'Neill, Son and Artist	Louis Sheaffer
1975	The Power Broker: Robert Moses and the Fall of New York	Robert Caro
1976	Edith Wharton: A Biography	R.W.B. Lewis
1977	A Prince of Our Disorder: The Life of T.E. Lawrence	John E. Mack
1978	Samuel Johnson	Walter Jackson Bate
1979	Days of Sorrow and Pain: Leo Baeck and the Berlin Jews	Leonard Baker
1980	The Rise of Theodore Roosevelt	Edmund Morris
1981	Peter the Great: His Life and World	Robert K. Massie
1982	Grant: A Biography	William McFeely
1983	Growing Up	Russell Baker

YEAR	TITLE	AUTHOR
1984	Booker T. Washington: The Wizard of Tuskegee, 1901–1915	Louis R. Harlan
1985	The Life and Times of Cotton Mather	Kenneth Silverman
1986	Louise Bogan: A Portrait	Elizabeth Frank
1987	Bearing the Cross: Martin Luther King Jr. and the Southern Christian Leadership Conference	David J. Garrow
1988	Look Homeward: A Life of Thomas Wolfe	David Herbert Donald
1989	Oscar Wilde	Richard Ellmann†
1990	Machiavelli in Hell	Sebastian de Grazia
1991	Jackson Pollock	Steven Naifeh, Gregory White Smith
1992	Fortunate Son: The Healing of a Vietnam Vet	Lewis B. Puller, Jr.
1993	Truman	David McCullough
1994	W.E.B. Du Bois: Biography of a Race 1868–1919	David Levering Lewis
1995	Harriet Beecher Stowe: A Life	Joan D. Hedrick
1996	God: A Biography	Jack Miles
1997	Angela's Ashes: A Memoir	Frank McCourt
1998	Personal History	Katharine Graham
1999	Lindbergh	A. Scott Berg
2000	Vera (Mrs. Vladimir Nabokov)	Stacy Schiff
2001	W.E.B. Du Bois: The Fight for Equality and the American Century, 1919–1963	David Levering Lewis
2002	John Adams	David McCullough

*Freeman died in 1953 after completing Volumes I–VI; Carroll and Ashworth continued his work with Volume VII. †Awarded posthumously.

Poetry
Awarded for a collection of original verse by an American author.

YEAR	TITLE	AUTHOR
1922	Collected Poems	Edwin Arlington Robinson
1923	The Ballad of the Harp-Weaver: A Few Figs from Thistles: Eight Sonnets in American Poetry, 1922. A Miscellany	Edna St. Vincent Millay
1924	New Hampshire: A Poem with Notes and Grace Notes	Robert Frost
1925	The Man Who Died Twice	Edwin Arlington Robinson
1926	What's O'Clock	Amy Lowell*
1927	Fiddler's Farewell	Leonora Speyer
1928	Tristram	Edwin Arlington Robinson

YEAR	TITLE	AUTHOR
1929	John Brown's Body	Stephen Vincent Benét
1930	Selected Poems	Conrad Aiken
1931	Collected Poems	Robert Frost
1932	The Flowering Stone	George Dillon
1933	Conquistador	Archibald MacLeish
1934	Collected Verse	Robert Hillyer
1935	Bright Ambush	Audrey Wurdemann
1936	Strange Holiness	Robert P. Tristram Coffin
1937	A Further Range	Robert Frost
1938	Cold Morning Sky	Marya Zaturenska
1939	Selected Poems	John Gould Fletcher
1940	Collected Poems	Mark Van Doren

Letters, Drama, and Music (continued)

Poetry (continued)

YEAR	TITLE	AUTHOR	YEAR	TITLE	AUTHOR
1941	Sunderland Capture	Leonard Bacon	1971	The Carrier of Ladders	William S. Merwin
1942	The Dust Which Is God	William Rose Benét	1972	Collected Poems	James Wright
			1973	Up Country	Maxine Kumin
1943	A Witness Tree	Robert Frost	1974	The Dolphin	Robert Lowell
1944	Western Star	Stephen Vincent Benét*	1975	Turtle Island	Gary Snyder
			1976	Self-Portrait in a Convex Mirror	John Ashbery
1945	V-Letter and Other Poems	Karl Shapiro			
			1977	Divine Comedies	James Merrill
1946	no award		1978	Collected Poems	Howard Nemerov
1947	Lord Weary's Castle	Robert Lowell	1979	Now and Then	Robert Penn Warren
1948	The Age of Anxiety	W.H. Auden			
1949	Terror and Decorum	Peter Viereck	1980	Selected Poems	Donald Justice
1950	Annie Allen	Gwendolyn Brooks	1981	The Morning of the Poem	James Schuyler
1951	Complete Poems	Carl Sandburg			
1952	Collected Poems	Marianne Moore	1982	The Collected Poems	Sylvia Plath†
1953	Collected Poems, 1917–1952	Archibald MacLeish	1983	Selected Poems	Galway Kinnell
			1984	American Primitive	Mary Oliver
1954	The Waking	Theodore Roethke	1985	Yin	Carolyn Kizer
1955	Collected Poems	Wallace Stevens	1986	The Flying Change	Henry Taylor
1956	Poems: North & South	Elizabeth Bishop	1987	Thomas and Beulah	Rita Dove
1957	Things of This World	Richard Wilbur	1988	Partial Accounts: New and Selected Poems	William Meredith
1958	Promises: Poems 1954–1956	Robert Penn Warren	1989	New and Collected Poems	Richard Wilbur
1959	Selected Poems 1928–1958	Stanley Kunitz			
			1990	The World Doesn't End	Charles Simic
1960	Heart's Needle	W.D. Snodgrass	1991	Near Changes	Mona Van Duyn
1961	Times Three: Selected Verse From Three Decades	Phyllis McGinley	1992	Selected Poems	James Tate
			1993	The Wild Iris	Louise Gluck
			1994	Neon Vernacular: New and Selected Poems	Yusef Komunyakaa
1962	Poems	Alan Dugan			
1963	Pictures from Breughel	William Carlos Williams*	1995	The Simple Truth	Philip Levine
			1996	The Dream of the Unified Field	Jorie Graham
1964	At The End Of The Open Road	Louis Simpson			
			1997	Alive Together: New and Selected Poems	Lisel Mueller
1965	77 Dream Songs	John Berryman			
1966	Selected Poems	Richard Eberhart	1998	Black Zodiac	Charles Wright
1967	Live or Die	Anne Sexton	1999	Blizzard of One	Mark Strand
1968	The Hard Hours	Anthony Hecht	2000	Repair	C.K. Williams
1969	Of Being Numerous	George Oppen	2001	Different Hours	Stephen Dunn
1970	Untitled Subjects	Richard Howard	2002	Practical Gods	Carl Dennis

*Awarded posthumously.   †Work published and prize awarded posthumously.

General Nonfiction
Awarded for a work of nonfiction, ineligible for any other category, by an American author.

YEAR	TITLE	AUTHOR	YEAR	TITLE	AUTHOR
1962	The Making of the President, 1960	Theodore H. White	1969	The Armies Of The Night	Norman Mailer
1963	The Guns of August	Barbara W. Tuchman	1969	So Human An Animal	Rene Jules Dubos
			1970	Gandhi's Truth	Erik H. Frikson
1964	Anti-Intellectualism in American Life	Richard Hofstadter	1971	The Rising Sun	John Toland
			1972	Stilwell and the American Experience in China, 1911–1945	Barbara W. Tuchman
1965	O Strange New World	Howard Mumford Jones			
1966	Wandering Through Winter	Edwin Way Teale	1973	Fire in the Lake: The Vietnamese and the Americans in Vietnam	Frances Fitzgerald
1967	The Problem of Slavery in Western Culture	David Brion Davis	1973	Children of Crisis, Vols. II and III	Robert Coles
1968	Rousseau and Revolution: A History of Civilization in France, England, and Germany from 1756, and in the Remainder of Europe from 1715 to 1789	Will and Ariel Durant	1974	The Denial of Death	Ernest Becker*
			1975	Pilgrim at Tinker Creek	Annie Dillard
			1976	Why Survive? Being Old In America	Robert N. Butler
			1977	Beautiful Swimmers	William W. Warner
			1978	The Dragons of Eden	Carl Sagan

Letters, Drama, and Music (continued)

General Nonfiction (continued)

YEAR	TITLE	AUTHOR	YEAR	TITLE	AUTHOR
1979	On Human Nature	Edward O. Wilson	1992	The Prize: The Epic Quest For Oil, Money, and Power	Daniel Yergin
1980	Gödel, Escher, Bach: An Eternal Golden Braid	Douglas R. Hofstadter	1993	Lincoln at Gettysburg: The Words That Remade America	Garry Wills
1981	Fin-de-Siècle Vienna: Politics and Culture	Carl E. Schorske	1994	Lenin's Tomb: The Last Days Of The Soviet Empire	David Remnick
1982	The Soul of a New Machine	Tracy Kidder			
1983	Is There No Place On Earth For Me?	Susan Sheehan	1995	The Beak Of The Finch: A Story Of Evolution In Our Time	Jonathan Weiner
1984	The Social Transformation Of American Medicine	Paul Starr	1996	The Haunted Land: Facing Europe's Ghosts After Communism	Tina Rosenberg
1985	The Good War: An Oral History of World War Two	Studs Terkel	1997	Ashes to Ashes: America's Hundred-Year Cigarette War, the Public Health, and the Unabashed Triumph of Philip Morris	Richard Kluger
1986	Common Ground: A Turbulent Decade in the Lives of Three American Families	J. Anthony Lukas			
1986	Move Your Shadow: South Africa, Black and White	Joseph Lelyveld	1998	Guns, Germs and Steel: The Fates of Human Societies	Jared Diamond
1987	Arab and Jew: Wounded Spirits in a Promised Land	David K. Shipler	1999	Annals of the Former World	John McPhee
1988	The Making of the Atomic Bomb	Richard Rhodes	2000	Embracing Defeat: Japan in the Wake of World War II	John W. Dower
1989	A Bright Shining Lie: John Paul Vann and America in Vietnam	Neil Sheehan	2001	Hirohito and the Making of Modern Japan	Herbert P. Bix
1990	And Their Children After Them	Dale Maharidge, Michael Williamson	2002	Carry Me Home: Birmingham, Alabama, the Climactic Battle of the Civil Rights Revolution	Diane McWhorter
1991	The Ants	Bert Holldobler, Edward O. Wilson			

*Awarded posthumously.

Music
Awarded for a musical piece of "significant dimension" composed by an American and first performed in the United States during the year.

YEAR	TITLE	COMPOSER	YEAR	TITLE	COMPOSER
1943	Secular Cantata No. 2. A Free Song	William Schuman	1959	Concerto for Piano and Orchestra	John LaMontaine
1944	Symphony No. 4. Opus 34	Howard Hanson	1960	Second String Quartet	Elliott Carter
			1961	Symphony No. 7	Walter Piston
1945	Appalachian Spring	Aaron Copland	1962	The Crucible	Robert Ward
1946	The Canticle of the Sun	Leo Sowerby	1963	Piano Concerto No. 1	Samuel Barber
1947	Symphony No. 3	Charles Ives	1964	no award	
1948	Symphony No. 3	Walter Piston	1965	no award	
1949	Music for the film Louisiana Story	Virgil Thomson	1966	Variations for Orchestra	Leslie Bassett
			1967	Quartet No. 3	Leon Kirchner
1950	The Consul	Gian Carlo Menotti	1968	Echoes of Time and the River	George Crumb
1951	Giants in the Earth	Douglas S. Moore			
1952	Symphony Concertante	Gail Kubik	1969	String Quartet No. 3	Karel Husa
1953	no award		1970	Time's Encomium	Charles Wuorinen
1954	Concerto For Two Pianos and Orchestra	Quincy Porter	1971	Synchronisms No. 6 for Piano and Electronic Sound (1970)	Mario Davidovsky
1955	The Saint of Bleecker Street	Gian Carlo Menotti	1972	Windows	Jacob Druckman
1956	Symphony No. 3	Ernst Toch	1973	String Quartet No. 3	Elliott Carter
1957	Meditation on Ecclesiastics	Norman Dello Joio	1974	Notturno	Donald Martino
1958	Vanessa	Samuel Barber	1975	From the Diary of Virginia Woolf	Dominick Argento

Letters, Drama, and Music (continued)

Music (continued)

YEAR	TITLE	COMPOSER
1976	Air Music	Ned Rorem
1977	Visions of Terror and Wonder	Richard Wernick
1978	Deja Vu for Percussion Quartet and Orchestra	Michael Colgrass
1979	Aftertones of Infinity	Joseph Schwantner
1980	In Memory of a Summer Day	David Del Tredici
1981	no award	
1982	Concerto for Orchestra	Roger Sessions
1983	Symphony No. 1 (Three Movements for Orchestra)	Ellen Taaffe Zwilich
1984	"Canti del Sole" for Tenor and Orchestra	Bernard Rands
1985	Symphony, RiverRun	Stephen Albert
1986	Wind Quintet IV	George Perle
1987	The Flight Into Egypt	John Harbison
1988	12 New Etudes for Piano	William Bolcom
1989	Whispers Out of Time	Roger Reynolds
1990	"Duplicates": A Concerto for Two Pianos and Orchestra	Mel Powell

YEAR	TITLE	COMPOSER
1991	Symphony	Shulamit Ran
1992	The Face of the Night, The Heart of the Dark	Wayne Peterson
1993	Trombone Concerto	Christopher Rouse
1994	Of Reminiscences and Reflections	Gunther Schuller
1995	Stringmusic	Morton Gould
1996	Lilacs, for voice and orchestra	George Walker
1997	Blood on the Fields	Wynton Marsalis
1998	String Quartet #2 (musica instrumentalis)	Aaron Jay Kernis
1999	Concerto for Flute, Strings and Percussion	Melinda Wagner
2000	Life is a Dream, Opera in Three Acts: Act II, Concert Version	Lewis Spratlan
2001	Symphony No. 2 for String Orchestra	John Corigliano
2002	Ice Field	Henry Brant

Special Awards

YEAR	RECIPIENT	FOR
1944	Richard Rodgers, Oscar Hammerstein II	theatrical musical Oklahoma!
1957	Kenneth Roberts	historical novels
1960	Garrett Mattingly	nonfiction work The Armada
1961	American Heritage Picture History of the Civil War	"a distinguished example of American book publishing"
1973	James Thomas Flexner	nonfiction work George Washington, Vols. I-IV
1974	Roger Sessions	life's work in music
1976	Scott Joplin*	contributions to American music
1977	Alex Haley	novel Roots

YEAR	RECIPIENT	FOR
1978	E.B. White	full body of his work
1982	Milton Babbitt	life's work in music
1984	Theodor Seuss Geisel	Dr. Seuss children's books
1985	William Schuman	life's work in composition and music education
1992	Art Spiegelman	graphic novel Maus
1998	George Gershwin*	centennial commemoration of his birth, celebrating his life's work in music
1999	Duke Ellington*	centennial commemoration of his birth, celebrating his life's work in music

*Awarded posthumously.

National Book Awards

In 1950 a consortium of publishing groups established the National Book Awards. The goal was to bring exceptional books written by Americans to the public's attention, and to encourage reading in general. Award categories have varied from the inaugural 3 to as many as 28 in 1980. Today, the awards recognize achievements in 4 genres: fiction, nonfiction, poetry, and young people's literature. A five-member, independent judging panel chooses a winner for each genre. Award: $10,000 cash and a crystal sculpture.

fiction

YEAR	TITLE	AUTHOR
1950	The Man with the Golden Arm	Nelson Algren
1951	The Collected Stories of William Faulkner	William Faulkner
1952	From Here to Eternity	James Jones
1953	Invisible Man	Ralph Ellison
1954	The Adventures of Augie March	Saul Bellow

fiction (continued)

YEAR	TITLE	AUTHOR
1955	A Fable	William Faulkner
1956	Ten North Frederick	John O'Hara
1957	The Field of Vision	Wright Morris
1958	The Wapshot Chronicle	John Cheever
1959	The Magic Barrel	Bernard Malamud
1960	Goodbye, Columbus	Philip Roth
1961	The Waters of Kronos	Conrad Richter

National Book Awards (continued)

fiction (continued)

YEAR	TITLE	AUTHOR
1962	The Moviegoer	Walker Percy
1963	Morte d'Urban	J.F. Powers
1964	The Centaur	John Updike
1965	Herzog	Saul Bellow
1966	The Collected Stories of Katherine Anne Porter	Katherine Anne Porter
1967	The Fixer	Bernard Malamud
1968	The Eighth Day	Thornton Wilder
1969	Steps	Jerzy Kosinski
1970	Them	Joyce Carol Oates
1971	Mr. Sammler's Planet	Saul Bellow
1972	The Complete Stories	Flannery O'Connor
1973	Augustus	John Williams
1973	Chimera	John Barth
1974	A Crown of Feathers and Other Stories	Isaac Bashevis Singer
1974	Gravity's Rainbow	Thomas Pynchon
1975	Dog Soldiers: A Novel	Robert Stone
1975	The Hair of Harold Roux	Thomas Williams
1976	J.R.	William Gaddis
1977	The Spectator Bird	Wallace Stegner
1978	Blood Tie	Mary Lee Settle

fiction (continued)

YEAR	TITLE	AUTHOR
1979	Going After Cacciato	Tim O'Brien
1980	Sophie's Choice[1]	William Styron
1981	Plains Song[1]	Wright Morris
1982	Rabbit Is Rich[1]	John Updike
1983	The Color Purple[1]	Alice Walker
1984	Victory over Japan: A Book of Stories	Ellen Gilchrist
1985	White Noise	Don DeLillo
1986	World's Fair	E.L. Doctorow
1987	Paco's Story	Larry Heinemann
1988	Paris Trout	Pete Dexter
1989	Spartina	John Casey
1990	Middle Passage	Charles Johnson
1991	Mating	Norman Rush
1992	All the Pretty Horses	Cormac McCarthy
1993	The Shipping News	E. Annie Proulx
1994	A Frolic of His Own	William Gaddis
1995	Sabbath's Theater	Philip Roth
1996	Ship Fever	Andrea Barrett
1997	Cold Mountain	Charles Frazier
1998	Charming Billy	Alice McDermott
1999	Waiting	Ha Jin
2000	In America	Susan Sontag
2001	The Corrections	Jonathan Franzen

nonfiction

YEAR	TITLE	AUTHOR
1950	The Life of Ralph Waldo Emerson	Ralph L. Rusk
1951	Herman Melville	Newton Arvin
1952	The Sea Around Us	Rachel Carson
1953	The Course of Empire	Bernard A. De Voto
1954	A Stillness at Appomattox	Bruce Catton
1955	The Measure of Man: On Freedom, Human Values, Survival, and the Modern Temper	Joseph Wood Krutch
1956	American in Italy	Herbert Kubly
1957	Russia Leaves the War	George F. Kennan
1958	The Lion and the Throne: The Life and Times of Sir Edward Coke (1552–1634)	Catherine Drinker Bowen
1959	Mistress to an Age: A Life of Madame de Staël	J. Christopher Herold
1960	James Joyce	Richard Ellmann
1961	The Rise and Fall of the Third Reich: A History of Nazi Germany	William L. Shirer
1962	The City in History: Its Origins, Its Transformations, and Its Prospects	Lewis Mumford
1963	Henry James, Vol. II: The Conquest of London (1870–1881); Vol. III: The Middle Years (1882–1895)	Leon Edel
1964	The Rise of the West: A History of the Human Community[2]	William H. McNeill
1965	The Life of Lenin[2]	Louis Fischer
1966	A Thousand Days: John F. Kennedy in the White House[2]	Arthur M. Schlesinger, Jr.
1967	The Enlightenment: An Interpretation, Vol. I[2]	Peter Gay
1968	Memoirs: 1925–1950[2]	George F. Kennan
1969	White over Black: American Attitudes Toward the Negro, 1550–1812[2]	Winthrop D. Jordan
1970	Huey Long[2]	T. Harry Williams
1971	Roosevelt: The Soldier of Freedom[2]	James MacGregor Burns
1972	Eleanor and Franklin: The Story of Their Relationship, Based on Eleanor Roosevelt's Private Papers[3]	Joseph P. Lash
1973	George Washington, Vol. IV: Anguish and Farewell, 1793–1799[3]	James Thomas Flexner
1974	Macaulay: The Shaping of the Historian[4]	John Clive
1975	The Life of Emily Dickinson[3]	Richard B. Sewall
1976	The Problem of Slavery in the Age of Revolution, 1770–1823[2]	David Brion Davis
1977	Norman Thomas: The Last Idealist[5]	W.A. Swanberg
1978	Samuel Johnson[5]	W. Jackson Bate
1979	Robert Kennedy and His Times[5]	Arthur M. Schlesinger, Jr.
1980	The Right Stuff[6]	Tom Wolfe
1981	China Men[6]	Maxine Hong Kingston
1982	The Soul of a New Machine[6]	Tracy Kidder
1983	China: Alive in the Bitter Sea[6]	Fox Butterfield
1984	Andrew Jackson and the Course of American Democracy, 1833–1845	Robert V. Remini

National Book Awards (continued)

nonfiction (continued)

YEAR	TITLE	AUTHOR
1985	Common Ground: A Turbulent Decade in the Lives of Three American Families	J. Anthony Lukas
1986	Arctic Dreams	Barry Lopez
1987	The Making of the Atomic Bomb	Richard Rhodes
1988	A Bright Shining Lie: John Paul Vann and America in Vietnam	Neil Sheehan
1989	From Beirut to Jerusalem	Thomas L. Friedman
1990	The House of Morgan: An American Banking Dynasty and the Rise of Modern Finance	Ron Chernow
1991	Freedom	Orlando Patterson
1992	Becoming a Man: Half a Life Story	Paul Monette
1993	United States: Essays, 1952–1992	Gore Vidal
1994	How We Die: Reflections on Life's Final Chapter	Sherwin B. Nuland
1995	The Haunted Land: Facing Europe's Ghosts After Communism	Tina Rosenberg
1996	An American Requiem: God, My Father, and the War That Came Between Us	James Carroll
1997	American Sphinx: The Character of Thomas Jefferson	Joseph J. Ellis
1998	Slaves in the Family	Edward Ball
1999	Embracing Defeat: Japan in the Wake of World War II	John W. Dower
2000	In the Heart of the Sea: The Tragedy of the Whaleship Essex	Nathaniel Philbrick
2001	The Noonday Demon: An Atlas of Depression	Andrew Solomon

poetry

YEAR	TITLE	AUTHOR
1950	Paterson: Book III and Selected Poems	William Carlos Williams
1951	The Auroras of Autumn	Wallace Stevens
1952	Collected Poems	Marianne Moore
1953	Collected Poems, 1917–1952	Archibald MacLeish
1954	Collected Poems	Conrad Aiken
1955	The Collected Poems of Wallace Stevens	Wallace Stevens
1956	The Shield of Achilles	W.H. Auden
1957	Things of This World: Poems	Richard Wilbur
1958	Promises: Poems, 1954–1956	Robert Penn Warren
1959	Words for the Wind: The Collected Verse of Theodore Roethke	Theodore Roethke
1960	Life Studies	Robert Lowell
1961	The Woman at the Washington Zoo	Randall Jarrell
1962	Poems	Alan Dugan
1963	Traveling Through the Dark	William Stafford
1964	Selected Poems	John Crowe Ransom
1965	The Far Field	Theodore Roethke
1966	Buckdancer's Choice: Poems	James Dickey
1967	Nights and Days	James Merrill
1968	The Light Around the Body: Poems	Robert Bly
1969	His Toy, His Dream, His Rest: 308 Dream Songs	John Berryman
1970	The Complete Poems	Elizabeth Bishop
1971	To See, To Take: Poems	Mona Van Duyn
1972	The Collected Poems of Frank O'Hara	Frank O'Hara
1972	Selected Poems	Howard Moss
1973	Collected Poems, 1951–1971	A.R. Ammons
1974	Diving into the Wreck: Poems, 1971–1972	Adrienne Rich
1974	The Fall of America: Poems of These States	Allen Ginsberg
1975	Presentation Piece	Marilyn Hacker
1976	Self-Portrait in a Convex Mirror: Poems	John Ashbery
1977	Collected Poems, 1930–1976	Richard Eberhart
1978	The Collected Poems of Howard Nemerov	Howard Nemerov
1979	Mirabell: Books of Number	James Merrill
1980	Ashes: Poems New & Old	Philip Levine
1981	The Need to Hold Still	Lisel Mueller
1982	Life Supports: New and Collected Poems	William Bronk
1983	Country Music: Selected Early Poems	Charles Wright
1983	Selected Poems	Galway Kinnell
1991	What Work Is: Poems	Philip Levine
1992	New and Selected Poems	Mary Oliver
1993	Garbage	A.R. Ammons
1994	Worshipful Company of Fletchers: Poems	James Tate
1995	Passing Through: The Later Poems, New and Selected	Stanley Kunitz
1996	Scrambled Eggs & Whiskey: Poems, 1991–1995	Hayden Carruth
1997	Effort at Speech: New and Selected Poems	William Meredith
1998	This Time: New and Selected Poems	Gerald Stern
1999	Vice: New and Selected Poems	Ai

National Book Awards (continued)

poetry (continued)

YEAR	TITLE	AUTHOR
2000	Blessing the Boats: New and Selected Poems, 1988–2000	Lucille Clifton
2001	Poems Seven: New and Complete Poetry	Alan Dugan

children's literature

YEAR	TITLE	AUTHOR
1969	Journey from Peppermint Street	Meindert De Jong
1970	A Day of Pleasure: Stories of a Boy Growing Up in Warsaw[7]	Isaac Bashevis Singer
1971	The Marvelous Misadventures of Sebastian[7]	Lloyd Alexander
1972	The Slightly Irregular Fire Engine; or, The Hithering Thithering Djinn[7]	Donald Barthelme
1973	The Farthest Shore[7]	Ursula Le Guin
1974	The Court of the Stone Children[7]	Eleanor Cameron
1975	M.C. Higgins, the Great[7]	Virginia Hamilton
1976	Bert Breen's Barn	Walter D. Edmonds
1977	The Master Puppeteer	Katherine Paterson
1978	The View from the Oak: The Private Worlds of Other Creatures	Judith Kohl & Herbert Kohl
1979	The Great Gilly Hopkins	Katherine Paterson
1980	A Gathering of Days: A New England Girl's Journal, 1830–32[8]	Joan Blos
1981	The Night Swimmers[9]	Betsy Byars
1982	Westmark[9]	Lloyd Alexander
1983	Homesick: My Own Story[9]	Jean Fritz
1996	Parrot in the Oven: Mi Vida[10]	Victor Martinez
1997	Dancing on the Edge[10]	Han Nolan
1998	Holes[10]	Louis Sachar
1999	When Zachary Beaver Came to Town[10]	Kimberly Willis Holt
2000	Homeless Bird[10]	Gloria Whelan
2001	True Believer[10]	Virginia Euwer Wolff

[1]Fiction (Hardcover)　[2]History and Biography (Nonfiction)　[3]Biography　[4]History　[5]Biography and Autobiography　[6]General Nonfiction (Hardcover)　[7]Children's Books　[8]Children's Books (Hardcover)　[9]Children's Books, Fiction (Hardcover)　[10]Young People's Literature

The PEN/Faulkner Award for Fiction

Named for William Faulkner and affiliated with the international writers' organization Poets, Playwrights, Editors, Essayists and Novelists (PEN), the PEN/Faulkner Award was founded by writers in 1980 to honor their peers. A panel of fiction writers selects a winning novel or short-story collection and four runners-up. The winning author receives $15,000, and each of the others receives $5,000. PEN/Faulkner Web site: <www.folger.edu/public/pfaulk/>

YEAR	TITLE	AUTHOR	YEAR	TITLE	AUTHOR
1981	How German Is It?	Walter Abish	1991	Philadelphia Fire	John Edgar Wideman
1982	The Chaneysville Incident	David Bradley	1992	Mao II	Don Delillo
			1993	Postcards	E. Annie Proulx
1983	Seaview	Toby Olson	1994	Operation Shylock	Philip Roth
1984	Sent for You Yesterday	John Edgar Wideman	1995	Snow Falling on Cedars	David Guterson
1985	The Barracks Thief	Tobias Wolff	1996	Independence Day	Richard Ford
1986	The Old Forest and Other Stories	Peter Taylor	1997	Women in Their Beds	Gina Berriault
			1998	The Bear Comes Home	Rafi Zabor
1987	Soldiers in Hiding	Richard Wiley	1999	The Hours	Michael Cunningham
1988	World's End	T. Coraghessan Boyle	2000	Waiting	Ha Jin
1989	Dusk and Other Stories	James Salter	2001	The Human Stain	Philip Roth
1990	Billy Bathgate	E. L. Doctorow	2002	Bel Canto	Ann Patchett

Coretta Scott King Award

Established in 1970, the Coretta Scott King Award honors outstanding African American authors and illustrators of books for young people. The books, which may be fiction or nonfiction, must be original works that portray some aspect of the black experience. In 1982 the award came under the aegis of the American Library Association. Prize: Citation, honorarium, and encyclopedia set. Coretta Scott King Award Web site: <www.ala.org/srrt/csking>

2001
author: Jacqueline Woodson, Miracle's Boys
illustrator: Bryan Collier, Uptown

2002
author: Mildred D. Taylor, The Land
illustrator: Jerry Pinkney, Goin' Someplace Special
2003 prizes scheduled to be awarded in January 2003

Newbery Medal Winners, 1922–2002

The American Library Association (ALA) began awarding the John Newbery Medal in 1922 to the author of the most distinguished American children's book of the previous year, as judged by the ALA's Children's Librarians' Section (now called the Association for Library Service to Children). Established at the suggestion of Frederic G. Melcher of the R.R. Bowker Publishing Company, the award is named for John Newbery, the 18th-century English publisher who was among the first to publish books exclusively for children. Prize: inscribed bronze medal. ALA Newbery Medal Web site: <www.ala.org/alsc/newbery.html>.

YEAR	TITLE	AUTHOR
1922	The Story of Mankind	Hendrik Willem van Loon
1923	The Voyages of Doctor Dolittle	Hugh Lofting
1924	The Dark Frigate	Charles Hawes
1925	Tales from Silver Lands	Charles Finger
1926	Shen of the Sea	Arthur Bowie Chrisman
1927	Smoky, the Cowhorse	Will James
1928	Gay Neck, the Story of a Pigeon	Dhan Gopal Mukerji
1929	The Trumpeter of Krakow	Eric P. Kelly
1930	Hitty, Her First Hundred Years	Rachel Field
1931	The Cat Who Went to Heaven	Elizabeth Coatsworth
1932	Waterless Mountain	Laura Adams Armer
1933	Young Fu of the Upper Yangtze	Elizabeth Lewis
1934	Invincible Louisa: The Story of the Author of Little Women	Cornelia Meigs
1935	Dobry	Monica Shannon
1936	Caddie Woodlawn	Carol Ryrie Brink
1937	Roller Skates	Ruth Sawyer
1938	The White Stag	Kate Seredy
1939	Thimble Summer	Elizabeth Enright
1940	Daniel Boone	James Daugherty
1941	Call It Courage	Armstrong Sperry
1942	The Matchlock Gun	Walter Edmonds
1943	Adam of the Road	Elizabeth Janet Gray
1944	Johnny Tremain	Esther Forbes
1945	Rabbit Hill	Robert Lawson
1946	Strawberry Girl	Lois Lenski
1947	Miss Hickory	Carolyn Sherwin Bailey
1948	The Twenty-One Balloons	William Pène du Bois
1949	King of the Wind	Marguerite Henry
1950	The Door in the Wall	Marguerite de Angeli
1951	Amos Fortune, Free Man	Elizabeth Yates
1952	Ginger Pye	Eleanor Estes
1953	Secret of the Andes	Ann Nolan Clark
1954	...And Now Miguel	Joseph Krumgold
1955	The Wheel on the School	Meindert DeJong
1956	Carry On, Mr. Bowditch	Jean Lee Latham
1957	Miracles on Maple Hill	Virginia Sorenson
1958	Rifles for Watie	Harold Keith
1959	The Witch of Blackbird Pond	Elizabeth George Speare
1960	Onion John	Joseph Krumgold
1961	Island of the Blue Dolphins	Scott O'Dell
1962	The Bronze Bow	Elizabeth George Speare
1963	A Wrinkle in Time	Madeleine L'Engle

YEAR	TITLE	AUTHOR
1964	It's Like This, Cat	Emily Neville
1965	Shadow of a Bull	Maia Wojciechowska
1966	I, Juan de Pareja	Elizabeth Borton de Trevino
1967	Up a Road Slowly	Irene Hunt
1968	From the Mixed-Up Files of Mrs. Basil E. Frankweiler	E.L. Konigsburg
1969	The High King	Lloyd Alexander
1970	Sounder	William H. Armstrong
1971	Summer of the Swans	Betsy Byars
1972	Mrs. Frisby and the Rats of NIMH	Robert C. O'Brien
1973	Julie of the Wolves	Jean Craighead George
1974	The Slave Dancer	Paula Fox
1975	M. C. Higgins, the Great	Virginia Hamilton
1976	The Grey King	Susan Cooper
1977	Roll of Thunder, Hear My Cry	Mildred D. Taylor
1978	Bridge to Terabithia	Katherine Paterson
1979	The Westing Game	Ellen Raskin
1980	A Gathering of Days: A New England Girl's Journal, 1830-1832	Joan W. Blos
1981	Jacob Have I Loved	Katherine Paterson
1982	A Visit to William Blake's Inn: Poems for Innocent and Experienced Travelers	Nancy Willard
1983	Dicey's Song	Cynthia Voigt
1984	Dear Mr. Henshaw	Beverly Cleary
1985	The Hero and the Crown	Robin McKinley
1986	Sarah, Plain and Tall	Patricia MacLachlan
1987	The Whipping Boy	Sid Fleischman
1988	Lincoln: A Photobiography	Russell Freedman
1989	Joyful Noise: Poems for Two Voices	Paul Fleischman
1990	Number the Stars	Lois Lowry
1991	Maniac Magee	Jerry Spinelli
1992	Shiloh	Phyllis Reynolds Naylor
1993	Missing May	Cynthia Rylant
1994	The Giver	Lois Lowry
1995	Walk Two Moons	Sharon Creech
1996	The Midwife's Apprentice	Karen Cushman
1997	The View from Saturday	E.L. Konigsburg
1998	Out of the Dust	Karen Hesse
1999	Holes	Louis Sachar
2000	Bud, Not Buddy	Christopher Paul Curtis
2001	A Year Down Yonder	Richard Peck
2002	A Single Shard	Linda Sue Park

Caldecott Medal Winners, 1938–2002

The American Library Association (ALA) awards the Caldecott Medal annually to "the artist of the most distinguished American picture book for children." It was established by the ALA in 1938 on the suggestion of Frederic G. Melcher, chairman of the board of the R.R. Bowker Publishing Company, and named for the 19th-century English illustrator Randolph Caldecott. If the author/reteller/translator/editor is other than the illustrator, that person's name appears in parentheses after the illustrator. Prize: inscribed bronze medal. ALA Caldecott Medal Web site: <www.ala.org/alsc/caldecott.html>.

YEAR	TITLE	ILLUSTRATOR
1938	*Animals of the Bible: A Picture Book*	Dorothy P. Lathrop (Helen Dean Fish)
1939	*Mei Li*	Thomas Handforth
1940	*Abraham Lincoln*	Ingri and Edgar Parin d'Aulaire
1941	*They Were Strong and Good*	Robert Lawson
1942	*Make Way for Ducklings*	Robert McCloskey
1943	*The Little House*	Virginia Lee Burton
1944	*Many Moons*	Louis Slobodkin (James Thurber)
1945	*Prayer for a Child*	Elizabeth Orton Jones (Rachel Field)
1946	*The Rooster Crows*	Maude and Miska Petersham
1947	*The Little Island*	Leonard Weisgard (Golden MacDonald, pseud. [Margaret Wise Brown])
1948	*White Snow, Bright Snow*	Roger Duvoisin (Alvin Tresselt)
1949	*The Big Snow*	Berta and Elmer Hader
1950	*Song of the Swallows*	Leo Politi
1951	*The Egg Tree*	Katherine Milhous
1952	*Finders Keepers*	Nicolas, pseud.; Nicholas Mordvinoff (Will, pseud. [William Lipkind])
1953	*The Biggest Bear*	Lynd Ward
1954	*Madeline's Rescue*	Ludwig Bemelmans
1955	*Cinderella, or the Little Glass Slipper*	Marcia Brown (translated from Charles Perrault by Marcia Brown)
1956	*Frog Went A-Courtin'*	Feodor Rojankovsky (John Langstaff)
1957	*A Tree Is Nice*	Marc Simont (Janice Udry)
1958	*Time of Wonder*	Robert McCloskey
1959	*Chanticleer and the Fox*	Barbara Cooney (adapted from Chaucer's *Canterbury Tales* by Barbara Cooney)
1960	*Nine Days to Christmas*	Marie Hall Ets (Marie Hall Ets and Aurora Labastida)
1961	*Baboushka and the Three Kings*	Nicolas Sidjakov (Ruth Robbins)
1962	*Once a Mouse*	Marcia Brown
1963	*The Snowy Day*	Ezra Jack Keats
1964	*Where the Wild Things Are*	Maurice Sendak
1965	*May I Bring a Friend?*	Beni Montresor (Beatrice Schenk de Regniers)
1966	*Always Room for One More*	Nonny Hogrogian (Sorche Nic Leodhas, pseud. [Leclair Alger])
1967	*Sam, Bangs & Moonshine*	Evaline Ness
1968	*Drummer Hoff*	Ed Emberley (Barbara Emberley)
1969	*The Fool of the World and the Flying Ship*	Uri Shulevitz (Arthur Ransome)
1970	*Sylvester and the Magic Pebble*	William Steig
1971	*A Story A Story*	Gail E. Haley
1972	*One Fine Day*	Nonny Hogrogian
1973	*The Funny Little Woman*	Blair Lent (Arlene Mosel)
1974	*Duffy and the Devil*	Margot Zemach (Harve Zemach)
1975	*Arrow to the Sun*	Gerald McDermott
1976	*Why Mosquitoes Buzz in People's Ears*	Leo and Diane Dillon (Verna Aardema)
1977	*Ashanti to Zulu: African Traditions*	Leo and Diane Dillon (Margaret Musgrove)
1978	*Noah's Ark*	Peter Spier
1979	*The Girl Who Loved Wild Horses*	Paul Goble
1980	*Ox-Cart Man*	Barbara Cooney (Donald Hall)
1981	*Fables*	Arnold Lobel
1982	*Jumanji*	Chris Van Allsburg
1983	*Shadow*	Marcia Brown (also translator of original French text by Blaise Cendrars)
1984	*The Glorious Flight: Across the Channel with Louis Bleriot*	Alice and Martin Provensen
1985	*Saint George and the Dragon*	Trina Schart Hyman (Margaret Hodges)
1986	*The Polar Express*	Chris Van Allsburg
1987	*Hey, Al*	Richard Egielski (Arthur Yorinks)
1988	*Owl Moon*	John Schoenherr (Jane Yolen)
1989	*Song and Dance Man*	Stephen Gammell (Karen Ackerman)
1990	*Lon Po Po: A Red-Riding Hood Story from China*	Ed Young

Caldecott Medal Winners, 1938–2002 (continued)

YEAR	TITLE	ILLUSTRATOR
1991	Black and White	David Macaulay
1992	Tuesday	David Wiesner
1993	Mirette on the High Wire	Emily Arnold McCully
1994	Grandfather's Journey	Allen Say (Walter Lorraine)
1995	Smoky Night	David Diaz (Eve Bunting)
1996	Officer Buckle and Gloria	Peggy Rathmann
1997	Golem	David Wisniewski
1998	Rapunzel	Paul O. Zelinsky
1999	Snowflake Bentley	Mary Azarian (Jacqueline Briggs Martin)
2000	Joseph Had a Little Overcoat	Simms Taback
2001	So You Want to Be President?	David Small (Judith St. George)
2002	The Three Pigs	David Wiesner

The Booker Prize

Awarded to the best full-length novel of the year written by a citizen of the Commonwealth or the Republic of Ireland and published in the UK between 1 October and 30 September. Prize: £20,000 (about $28,000); each shortlisted author receives £1000 (about $1,400). In 1993, Salman Rushdie was awarded the Booker of Bookers, a special award to mark 25 years of the Booker Prize, for Midnight's Children. Booker Prize Web site: <www.thebookerprize.com>.

YEAR	TITLE	AUTHOR	YEAR	TITLE	AUTHOR
1969	Something to Answer For	P. H. Newby	1985	The Bone People	Keri Hulme
			1986	The Old Devils	Kingsley Amis
1970	The Elected Member	Bernice Rubens	1987	Moon Tiger	Penelope Lively
1971	In a Free State	V. S. Naipaul	1988	Oscar and Lucinda	Peter Carey
1972	G.	John Berger	1989	The Remains of the Day	Kazuo Ishiguro
1973	The Siege of Krishnapur	J. G. Farrell	1990	Possession	A. S. Byatt
			1991	The Famished Road	Ben Okri
1974	The Conservationist	Nadine Gordimer	1992	The English Patient	Michael Ondaatje
1974	Holiday	Stanley Middleton	1992	Sacred Hunger	Barry Unsworth
1975	Heat and Dust	Ruth Prawer Jhabvala	1993	Paddy Clarke Ha Ha Ha	Roddy Doyle
1976	Saville	David Storey	1994	How Late It Was, How Late	James Kelman
1977	Staying On	Paul Scott			
1978	The Sea, The Sea	Iris Murdoch	1995	The Ghost Road	Pat Barker
1979	Offshore	Penelope Fitzgerald	1996	Last Orders	Graham Swift
1980	Rites of Passage	William Golding	1997	The God of Small Things	Arundhati Roy
1981	Midnight's Children	Salman Rushdie	1998	Amsterdam	Ian McEwan
1982	Schindler's Ark	Thomas Keneally	1999	Disgrace	J. M. Coetzee
1983	Life and Times of Michael K	J. M. Coetzee	2000	The Blind Assassin	Margaret Atwood
			2001	True History of the Kelly Gang	Peter Carey
1984	Hotel du Lac	Anita Brookner			

The Whitbread Book Awards

The Whitbread Book Awards were inaugurated in 1971. Since 1985, Whitbread Book Awards have been awarded in five categories: Novel, First Novel, Biography, Poetry, and Children's. From these a panel of judges chooses one overall winner–the Whitbread Book of the Year. The total prize fund is £50,000 (about $71,000): each of the category award winners receives £5,000 (about $7,100), and the Book of the Year winner receives an additional £25,000 (about $35,000). This list includes Novel award winners from 1971 to 1984 and Book of the Year winners from 1985 to 2001. Whitbread Book Awards Web site: <www.whitbread-bookawards.co.uk>.

YEAR	TITLE	AUTHOR	YEAR	TITLE	AUTHOR
1971	The Destiny Waltz	Gerda Charles	1981	Silver's City	Maurice Leitch
1972	The Bird of Night	Susan Hill	1982	Young Shoulders	John Wain
1973	The Chip-Chip Gatherers	Shiva Naipaul	1983	Fools of Fortune	William Trevor
1974	The Sacred and Profane Love Machine	Iris Murdoch	1984	Kruger's Alp	Christopher Hope
			1985	Elegies	Douglas Dunn
1975	Docherty	William McIlvanney	1986	An Artist of the Floating World	Kazuo Ishiguro
1976	The Children of Dynmouth	William Trevor	1987	Under the Eye of the Clock	Christopher Nolan
1977	Injury Time	Beryl Bainbridge			
1978	Picture Palace	Paul Theroux	1988	The Comforts of Madness	Paul Sayer
1979	The Old Jest	Jennifer Johnston			
1980	How Far Can You Go?	David Lodge	1989	Coleridge: Early Visions	Richard Holmes

The Whitbread Book Awards (continued)

YEAR	TITLE	AUTHOR	YEAR	TITLE	AUTHOR
1990	Hopeful Monsters	Nicholas Mosley	1996	The Spirit Level	Seamus Heaney
1991	A Life of Picasso	John Richardson	1997	Tales from Ovid	Ted Hughes
1992	Swing Hammer Swing!	Jeff Torrington	1998	Birthday Letters	Ted Hughes
1993	Theory of War	Joan Brady	1999	Beowulf	Seamus Heaney
1994	Felicia's Journey	William Trevor	2000	English Passengers	Matthew Kneale
1995	Behind the Scenes at the Museum	Kate Atkinson	2001	The Amber Spyglass	Philip Pullman

The Orange Prize

Awarded to a work of published fiction written in English by a woman and published in the United Kingdom between 1 April and 31 March. Prize: £30,000 (about $42,500) and a bronze figurine called "The Bessie." Orange Prize Web site: <www.booktrust.org. uk/ Orange/orange.htm>.

YEAR	TITLE	AUTHOR	YEAR	TITLE	AUTHOR
1996	A Spell of Winter	Helen Dunmore	2000	When I Lived in Modern Times	Linda Grant
1997	Fugitive Pieces	Anne Michaels			
1998	Larry's Party	Carol Shields	2001	The Idea of Perfection	Kate Grenville
1999	A Crime in the Neighborhood	Suzanne Berne	2002	Bel Canto	Ann Patchett

Prix Goncourt

The Prix de l'Académie Goncourt was first awarded in 1903 from the estate of the brothers and French literary figures Edmond Huot de Goncourt (1822–1896) and Jules Huot de Goncourt (1830–1870) for a work of contemporary prose in French. Prize: FF50 (about $6.75). An additional prize is awarded for the best work of new fiction.

YEAR	TITLE	AUTHOR	YEAR	TITLE	AUTHOR
1903	Force ennemie	John Antoine Nau	1930	Malaisie	Henri Fauconnier
1904	La Maternelle	Léon Frapié	1931	Mal d'amour	Jean Fayard
1905	Les Civilisés	Claude Farrère	1932	Les Loups	Guy Mazeline
1906	Dingley, l'illustre écrivain	Jérôme & Jean Tharaud	1933	La Condition humaine	André Malraux
1907	Le Rouet d'ivoire	Emile Moselly	1934	Capitaine Conan	Roger Vercel
1908	Ecrit sur l'eau	Francis de Miomandre	1935	Sang et lumières	Joseph Peyré
			1936	L'Empreinte de Dieu	Maxence Van Der Meersch
1909	En France	Marius & Ary Leblond	1937	Faux passeports	Charles Plisnier
			1938	L'Araignée	Henri Troyat
1910	De Goupil à Margot	Louis Pergaud	1939	Les Enfants gâtés	Philippe Hériat
1911	Monsieur des Lourdines	Alphonse de Chateaubriant	1940	Les Grandes Vacances	Francis Ambrière
			1941	Le Vent de mars	Henri Pourrat
1912	Les Filles de la pluie	André Savignon	1942	Pareil à des enfants	Bernard Marc
1913	Le Peuple de la mer	Marc Elder	1943	Passage de l'homme	Marius Grout
1914	L'Appel du sol	Adrien Bertrand	1944	Le Premier accroc coûte 200 Francs	Elsa Triolet
1915	Gaspard	René Benjamin			
1916	Le Feu	Henri Barbusse	1945	Mon village à l'heure allemande	Jean-Louis Bory
1917	La Flamme au poing	Henri Malherbe			
1918	Civilisation	Georges Duhamel	1946	Histoire d'un fait divers	Jean-Jacques Gautier
1919	A l'ombre des jeunes filles en fleur	Marcel Proust			
			1947	Les Forêts de la nuit	Jean-Louis Curtis
1920	Nene	Ernest Perochon	1948	Les Grandes Familles	Maurice Druon
1921	Batouala	René Maran	1949	Week-end à Zuydcoote	Robert Merle
1922	Le Vitriol de la lune	Henry Béraud	1950	Les Jeux Sauvages	Paul Colin
1922	Le Martyre de l'obèse	Henry Béraud	1951	Le Rivage des Syrtes	Julien Gracq
1923	Rabevel; ou, le mal des ardents	Lucien Fabré	1952	Léon Morin, prêtre	Béatrice Beck
			1953	Les Bêtes	Pierre Gascar
1924	Le Chèvrefeuille, le Purgatoire, le Chapitre XIII	Thierry Sandre	1954	Mandarins	Simone de Beauvoir
			1955	Les Eaux mêlées	Roger Ikor
			1956	Les Racines du ciel	Romain Gary
1925	Raboliot	Maurice Genevoix	1957	La Loi	Roger Vailland
1926	Le Supplice de Phèdre	Henry Deberly	1958	Saint Germain; ou, la négociation	Francis Walder
1927	Latitude nord	Maurice Bedel			
1928	Un Homme se penche sur son passé	Maurice Constantin Weyer	1959	Le Dernier des justes	André Schwartz-Bart
			1960	Dieu est né en exil	Vintila Horia
1929	L'Ordre	Marcel Arland	1961	La Pitié de Dieu	Jean Cau

Prix Goncourt (continued)

YEAR	TITLE	AUTHOR	YEAR	TITLE	AUTHOR
1962	Les Bagages de sable	Anna Langfus	1983	Les Égarés	Frédérick Tristan
1963	Quand la mer se retire	Armand Lanoux	1984	L'Amant	Marguerite Duras
1964	L'État sauvage	Georges Conchon	1985	Les Noces barbares	Yann Queffélec
1965	L'Adoration	Jacques Borel	1986	Valet de nuit	Michel Host
1966	Oublier Palerme	Edmonde Charles-Roux	1987	La Nuit sacrée	Tahar Ben Jelloun
			1988	L'Exposition coloniale	Erik Orsenna
1967	La Marge	André-Pierre de Mandiargues	1989	Un Grand Pas vers le Bon Dieu	Jean Vautrin
1968	Les Fruits de l'hiver	Bernard Clavel	1990	Les Champs d'honneur	Jean Rouaud
1969	Creezy	Félicien Marceau			
1970	Le Roi des Aulnes	Michel Tournier	1991	Les Filles du calvaire	Pierre Combescot
1971	Les Bêtises	Jacques Laurent	1992	Texaco	Patrick Chamoiseau
1972	L'Éporvier de Maheux	Jean Carrière	1993	La Rocher de Tanios	Amin Maalouf
1973	L'Ogre	Jacques Chessex	1994	Un Aller simple	Didier Van Cauwelaert
1974	La Dentellière	Pascal Lainé			
1975	La Vie devant soi	Emile Ajar	1995	Le Testament français	Andreï Makine
1976	Les Flamboyants	Patrick Grainville	1996	Le Chasseur Zéro	Pascale Roze
1977	John l'enfer	Didier Decoin	1997	La Bataille	Patrick Rambaud
1978	Rue des boutiques obscures	Patrick Modiano	1998	Confidence pour confidence	Paule Constant
1979	Pélagie la charrette	Antonine Maillet	1999	Je m'en vais	Jean Echenoz
1980	Le Jardin d'acclimatation	Yves Navarre	2000	Ingrid Caven	Jean-Jacques Schuhl
			2001	Rouge Brésil	Jean-Christophe Rufin
1981	Anne Marie	Lucien Bodard	2002	scheduled to be awarded November 2002	
1982	Dans la main de l'ange	Dominique Fernandez			

The Cervantes Prize (Premio Cervantes) for Hispanic Literature

The Spanish Ministry of Education, Culture and Sport sponsors the annual prize, which carries an award of €100,000 (about $100,000).

YEAR	AUTHOR	YEAR	AUTHOR
1976	Jorge Guillén	1990	Adolfo Bioy Casares
1977	Alejo Carpentier	1991	Francisco Ayala
1978	Dámaso Alonso	1992	Dulce María Loynaz
1979	Jorge Luis Borges and Gerardo Diego	1993	Miguel Delibes
1980	Juan Carlos Onetti	1994	Mario Vargas Llosa
1981	Octavio Paz	1995	Camilo José Cela
1982	Luis Rosales	1996	José García Nieto
1983	Rafael Alberti	1997	Guillermo Cabrera Infante
1984	Ernesto Sábato	1998	José Hierro
1985	Juan Rulfo	1999	Jorge Edwards
1986	Antonio Buero Vallejo	2000	Francisco Umbral
1987	Carlos Fuentes	2001	Álvaro Mutis
1988	María Zambrano	2002	scheduled to be announced in December 2002 and awarded in April 2003
1989	Augusto Roa Bastos		

The Jerusalem Prize

The municipality of Jerusalem awards this prize at the biennial Jerusalem International Book Fair to a writer whose work explores the freedom of the individual in society. Prize: $10,000. Jerusalem Prize Web site: <www.jerusalembookfair.com>.

YEAR	AUTHOR	NATIONALITY	YEAR	AUTHOR	NATIONALITY
1963	Bertrand Russell	UK	1983	V.S. Naipaul	UK
1965	Max Frisch	Switzerland	1985	Milan Kundera	France
1967	André Schwarz-Bart	France	1987	J.M. Coetzee	South Africa
1969	Ignazio Silone	Italy	1989	Ernesto Sábato	Argentina
1971	Jorge Luis Borges	Argentina	1991	Zbigniew Herbert	France
1973	Eugène Ionesco	France	1993	Stefan Heym	Germany
1975	Simone de Beauvoir	France	1995	Mario Vargas Llosa	Peru
1977	Octavio Paz	Mexico	1997	Jorge Semprun	Spain
1979	Sir Isaiah Berlin	UK	1999	Don Delillo	America
1981	Graham Greene	UK	2001	Susan Sontag	America

T.S. Eliot Prize

Great Britain's Poetry Book Society awards the T.S. Eliot Prize to the best new collection of poetry published in the UK or the Republic of Ireland during the preceding year. The prize is £10,000 (about $15,000).

YEAR	WORK	AUTHOR	COUNTRY
1993	*First Language*	Ciaran Carson	Ireland
1994	*The Annals of Chile*	Paul Muldoon	Northern Ireland
1995	*My Alexandria*	Mark Doty	United States
1996	*Sub-Human Redneck Poems*	Les Murray	Australia
1997	*God's Gift to Women*	Don Paterson	United Kingdom
1998	*Birthday Letters*	Ted Hughes	United Kingdom
1999	*Billy's Rain*	Hugo Williams	United Kingdom
2000	*The Weather in Japan*	Michael Longley	Northern Ireland
2001	*The Beauty of the Husband*	Anne Carson	Canada
2002	scheduled to be awarded January 2003		

The Bollingen Prize in Poetry

The Bollingen Prize in Poetry is awarded biennially to "the American poet whose work, in the opinion of the Committee of Award, represents the highest achievement in the field of American poetry during the preceding two year period." The Commitee considers published work, particularly work published during the preceding two year period, although the Committee may consider prior achievement. Former winners of the prize are not eligible. Award amount: $50,000.

YEAR	POET	YEAR	POET
1949	Wallace Stevens	1969	John Berryman and Karl Shapiro
1950	John Crowe Ransom	1971	Richard Wilbur and Mona Van Duyn
1951	Marianne Moore	1973	James Merrill
1952	Archibald MacLeish and William Carlos Williams	1975	A.R. Ammons
		1977	David Ignatow
1953	W.H. Auden	1979	W.S. Merwin
1954	Léonie Adams and Louise Bogan	1981	May Swenson and Howard Nemerov
1955	Conrad Aiken	1983	Anthony Hecht and John Hollander
1956	Allen Tate	1985	John Ashbery and Fred Chappell
1957	E.E. Cummings	1987	Stanley Kunitz
1958	Theodore Roethke	1989	Edgar Bowers
1959	Delmore Schwartz	1991	Laura (Riding) Jackson and Donald Justice
1960	Yvor Winters	1993	Mark Strand
1961	Richard Eberhart and John Hall Wheelock	1995	Kenneth Koch
1963	Robert Frost	1997	Gary Snyder
1965	Horace Gregory	1999	Robert Creeley
1967	Robert Penn Warren	2001	Louise Glück

Encyclopædia Britannica's All-Time Greatest Authors

The list represents the selection by Britannica editors of the world's 250 best or most influential authors of poetry, fiction, and drama.

Chinua Achebe (Albert Chinualumogu Achebe; 16 Nov 1930, Ogidi, Nigeria), Nigerian novelist acclaimed for his unsentimental depictions of the social and psychological disorientation accompanying the imposition of Western customs and values upon traditional African society.

Aeschylus (525/524 BCE–456/455 BCE, Gela, Sicily), Greek dramatist, the first of classical Athens's great tragic playwrights who raised that emerging art to great heights of poetry and theatrical power.

S(hmuel) Y(osef) Agnon (Shmuel Yosef Halevi Czaczkes; 17 Jul 1888, Buczacz, Galicia, Austria-Hungary [now Buchach, Ukraine]–17 Feb 1970, Rehovot, Israel), Israeli novelist and short-story writer known for the denseness and archaic structure of his prose; corecipient of the Nobel Prize for Literature, 1966.

Anna Akhmatova (Anna Andreyevna Gorenko; 23 Jun [11 Jun, Old Style] 1889, Bolshoy Fontan, near Odessa, Ukraine, Russian Empire–5 Mar 1966, Domodedovo, near Moscow, USSR), Russian poet of the Acmeist school recognized as the greatest woman writer in Russian literature.

Edward Albee (12 Mar 1928, Washington DC) American dramatist and three-time Pulitzer Prize winner; his best-known works include *The Zoo Story* (1959) and *Who's Afraid of Virginia Woolf?* (1962).

Jorge Amado (10 Aug 1912, Ferradas, near Ilhéus, Brazil–6 Aug 2001, Salvador), Brazilian novelist whose stories of life in the northeast of his country won international acclaim.

Sherwood Anderson (13 Sep 1876, Camden OH–8 Mar 1941, Colón, Panama), American short-story writer and novelist who was a strong influence on American writing between World Wars. His prose style was based on everyday speech and derived from the experimental writing of Gertrude Stein.

Archilochus (c. 675 BCE, Paros, Greece–c. 635 BCE, Greece), Greek poet and soldier, the earliest Greek writer of elegiac and personal lyric poetry whose works have survived to any considerable extent.

Aristophanes (c. 450 BCE–c. 388 BCE), Greek dramatist regarded as the foremost representative of ancient Greek comedy.

Matthew Arnold (24 Dec 1822, Laleham, Middlesex, England–15 Apr 1888, Liverpool), English Victorian literary figure noted especially for his classical attacks on the contemporary tastes and manners of all classes of society.

Sholem Asch (1 Nov 1880, Kunto, Poland–10 Jul 1957, London, England), Polish-born novelist and playwright, the most controversial and one of the most widely known writers in modern Yiddish literature.

Farid od-Din Attar (Farid od-Din Mohammad ebn Ebrahim 'Attar; c. 1142, Nishapur, Iran–c. 1220, Mecca, Arabia [now in Saudi Arabia]), Persian poet and Muslim mystical writer and thinker who composed at least 45,000 distichs (couplets) and many brilliant prose works.

W(ystan) H(ugh) Auden (21 Feb 1907, York, Yorkshire, England–29 Sep 1973, Vienna, Austria), English-born poet who achieved fame as a hero of the left during the Great Depression. Regarded as the successor to T.S. Eliot as the foremost English-language poet, Auden's poetry examined contemporary social and political realities and often addressed the inner world of dreams and fantasies.

Jane Austen (16 Dec 1775, Steventon, Hampshire, England–18 Jul 1817, Winchester), English writer who first gave the novel its distinctly modern character through her treatment of ordinary people in everyday life.

Honoré de Balzac (Honoré Balssa; 20 May 1799, Tours, France–18 Aug 1850, Paris), French literary artist who helped establish the orthodox classical novel and who produced a vast number of novels and short stories collectively called La Comédie humaine (The Human Comedy).

Basho (Matsuo Basho; Matsuo Munefusa; 15 Sep? 1644, Ueno, Iga Province, Japan–28 Nov 1694, Osaka), Japanese poet who perfected the renga (linked-verse) and haiku and made them accepted mediums of artistic expression.

Charles(-Pierre) Baudelaire (9 Apr 1821, Paris, France–31 Aug 1867, Paris), French poet, translator, and literary and art critic whose reputation rests primarily on Les Fleurs du mal (1857; The Flowers of Evil), perhaps the most important and influential poetry collection published in Europe in the 19th century.

Samuel (Barclay) Beckett (13 Apr 1906, Foxrock, County Dublin, Ireland–22 Dec 1989, Paris), Irish-French author, critic, and playwright, winner of the Nobel Prize for Literature in 1969. He wrote in both French and English and is perhaps best known for his philosophical and absurdist plays, especially En attendant Godot (1952; Waiting for Godot).

Saul Bellow (10 Jun 1915, Lachnine, near Montreal, Quebec) Canadian-born American novelist renowned for his characterizations of modern urban man, disaffected by society but not destroyed in spirit; Nobel Prize for Literature, 1976.

Willem Bilderdijk (7 Sep 1756, Amsterdam, Netherlands–18 Dec 1831, Haarlem), Dutch poet who had considerable influence not only on the poetry but also on the intellectual and social life of The Netherlands.

Elizabeth Bishop (8 Feb 1911, Worcester MA–6 Oct 1979, Boston MA), American short-story writer and poet recognized for her polished, witty, and descriptive prose and verse, which offer spare, powerful meditations on the need for self-exploration, on the value of art (especially poetry) in human life, and on human responsibility in a chaotic world.

William Blake (28 Nov 1757, London, England–12 Aug 1827, London), English poet, one of the earliest of the major Romantics. An original and visionary mystic, Blake was also renowned for his paintings and engravings, many of which illustrated his lyrical and epic poems.

Aleksandr Aleksandrovich Blok (28 Nov [16 Nov, Old Style] 1880, St. Petersburg, Russia–7 Aug 1921, Petrograd [St. Petersburg], Soviet Russia), Russian poet and dramatist, the principal representative of Russian Symbolism, a modernist literary movement that was influenced by its European counterpart but was strongly imbued with indigenous Eastern Orthodox religious and mystical elements.

Giovanni Boccaccio (1313, Paris, France–21 Dec 1375, Certaldo, Tuscany, Italy), Italian poet and scholar best remembered as the author of the earthy tales in the Decameron. With Petrarch he laid the foundations for the humanism of the Renaissance and raised vernacular literature to the level and status of the classics of antiquity.

Heinrich (Theodor) Böll (21 Dec 1917, Cologne, Germany–16 Jul 1985, near Bonn, West Germany), German novelist; winner of the Nobel Prize for Literature in 1972. Böll's ironic novels on the travails of German life during and after World War II capture the changing psychology of the German nation.

Jorge Luis Borges (24 Aug 1899, Buenos Aires, Argentina–14 Jun 1986, Geneva, Switzerland), Argentine poet and essayist credited with establishing the modernist Ultraist movement in South America; his unique, nightmarish works have become classics of 20th century world literature.

Bertolt Brecht (10 Feb 1898, Augsburg, Germany–14 Aug 1956, East Berlin, East Germany), German playwright and theatrical reformer whose "epic theater" departed from the conventions of theatrical illusion and developed the drama as a social and ideological forum for leftist causes.

Joseph Brodsky (Iosip Aleksandrovich Brodsky; 24 May 1940, Leningrad, USSR [now St. Petersburg, Russia]–28 Jan 1996, New York NY), Russian poet who was awarded the Nobel Prize for Literature in 1987 for his lyric and elegiac poems.

Charlotte Brontë (pseudonym Currer Bell; 21 Apr 1816, Thornton, Yorkshire, England–31 Mar 1855, Haworth, Yorkshire), English novelist noted especially for Jane Eyre (1847), a strong narrative of a woman in conflict with her natural desires and social condition, and a novel that gave new truthfulness to Victorian fiction.

Emily Brontë (pseudonym Ellis Bell; 30 Jul 1818, Thornton, Yorkshire, England–10 Dec 1848, Haworth, Yorkshire), English novelist regarded as the greatest of the three Brontë sisters, although she produced but one work, Wuthering Heights (1847), a masterpiece of passion and hate set on the Yorkshire moors.

Gwendolyn (Elizabeth) Brooks (7 Jun 1917, Topeka KS–3 Dec 2000, Chicago IL), American poet whose works deal mostly with the everyday life of urban blacks; she was the first African American poet to win the Pulitzer Prize.

Elizabeth Browning (née Elizabeth Barrett; 6 Mar 1806, near Durham, Durham, England–29 Jun 1861, Florence, Italy), English poet known primarily for the collection of love poems, Sonnets from the Portuguese; she was the wife of Robert Browning.

Robert Browning (7 May 1812, London, England—12 Dec 1889, Venice, Italy), English poet, a major figure of the Victorian age, noted for his mastery of the dramatic monologue and psychological portraiture; he was the husband of Elizabeth Browning.

Anthony Burgess (original name John Anthony Burgess Wilson; also called Joseph Kell; 25 Feb 1917, Manchester, England—22 Nov 1993, London), English novelist known for fictional explorations of modern dilemmas that combine wit, moral earnestness, and a note of the bizarre.

Robert Burns (25 Jan 1759, Alloway, Ayrshire, Scotland—21 Jul 1796, Dumfries, Dumfriesshire), the national poet of Scotland, who wrote lyrics and songs in the Scottish dialect of English. He was also famous for his amours and his rebellion against orthodox religion and morality.

Lord Byron (George Gordon Noel Byron, 6th Baron Byron; 22 Jan 1788, London, England—19 Apr 1824, Missolonghi, Greece), English poet who was perhaps the most autobiographic of the Romantics, known for the satiric realism of his unfinished masterpiece *Don Juan,* the melancholy cynicism of *Childe Harold's Pilgrimage,* and for his own flamboyant personality.

Albert Camus (7 Nov 1913, Mondovi, Algeria—4 Jan 1960, near Sens, France), French novelist, a leading literary figure of the 20th century, known for his existentialist works of alienation; Nobel Prize for Literature, 1957.

Elias Canetti (25 Jul 1905, Ruse, Bulgaria—14 Aug 1994, Zürich, Switzerland), Bulgarian novelist and playwright whose works explore the emotions of crowds, the psychopathology of power, and the position of the individual at odds with the society around him; Nobel Prize for Literature, 1981.

Karel Capek (9 Jan 1890, Male Svatonovice, Bohemia, Austria-Hungary [now in Czech Republic]—25 Dec 1938, Prague, Czechoslovakia), Czech novelist, short-story writer, playwright, and essayist known for works of philosophical inquiry, as in his most successful play, *R.U.R.* (1920), which introduced the word "robot."

Truman Capote (Truman Streckfus Persons; 30 Sep 1924, New Orleans LA—25 Aug 1984, Los Angeles CA), American novelist and short-story writer known for early writings that extended the Southern Gothic tradition, as well as later works that employed a more journalistic approach, as in his best-known work, *In Cold Blood* (1965).

Willa (Sibert) Cather (7 Dec 1873, near Winchester VA—24 Apr 1947, New York NY), American novelist noted for her portrayals of the settlers and frontier life on the American plains.

Jacob Cats (10 Nov 1577, Brouwershaven, Zeeland, Spanish Netherlands [now in The Netherlands]—12 Sep 1660, Zorgh-vliet, near The Hague, Netherlands), Dutch writer of emblem books and didactic verse whose place in the affections of his countrymen is shown by his nickname, "Father Cats."

Gaius Valerius Catullus (c. 84 BCE, Verona, Cisalpine Gaul—c. 54 BCE, Rome), Roman poet generally considered to have produced the finest lyric poetry of ancient Rome.

Constantine Cavafy (Konstantinos Petrou Kavafis; 17 Apr 1863, Alexandria, Egypt—29 Apr 1933, Alexandria), Greek poet known for developing his own consciously individual style, thus becoming one of the most important figures not only in Greek poetry but in Western poetry as well.

Camilo José Cela (Camilo José Cela Trulock; 11 May 1916, Iria Flavia, Spain—17 Jan 2002, Madrid), Spanish novelist perhaps best known for *La familia de Pascual Duarte* (1942; *The Family of Pascual Duarte*). His literary production—primarily novels, short narratives, and travel diaries—is characterized by experimentation and innovation in form and content; Nobel Prize for Literature, 1989.

Miguel de Cervantes (29? Sep 1547, Alcalá de Henares, Spain—22 Apr 1616, Madrid), Spanish novelist, the most important and celebrated figure in Spanish literature; creator of *Don Quixote* (1605, 1615).

Geoffrey Chaucer (c. 1342/43, London?, England—25 Oct 1400, London), English poet and the author of *The Canterbury Tales;* recognized as the outstanding English poet before Shakespeare.

Anton (Pavlovich) Chekhov (29 Jan [17 Jan, Old Style] 1860, Taganrog, Russia—14/15 Jul [1/2 July, Old Style] 1904, Badenweiler, Germany), Russian playwright and short-story writer of the late 19th-century Russian realist school. He is equally esteemed for his plays and stories.

G(ilbert) K(eith) Chesterton (29 May 1874, London, England—14 Jun 1936, Beaconsfield, Buckinghamshire), English critic and author of verse, essays, novels, and short stories, known also for his exuberant personality and rotund figure.

Samuel Taylor Coleridge (21 Oct 1772, Ottery St. Mary, Devonshire, England—25 Jul 1834, Highgate, near London), English poet whose *Biographia Literaria* is the most significant work of English literary criticism produced during the Romantic era; his best-known poems are *The Rime of the Ancient Mariner* and *Kubla Khan.*

Colette (Sidonie-Gabrielle Colette; 28 Jan 1873, Saint-Sauveur-en-Puisaye, France—3 Aug 1954, Paris), French novelist renowned for her command of sensual description and sensory evocation.

Joseph Conrad (Jozef Teodor Konrad Korzeniowski; 3 Dec 1857, Berdichev, Poland, Russian Empire [now Berdychiv, Ukraine]—3 Aug 1924, Canterbury, Kent, England), Polish-born English novelist and short-story writer of complex skill and striking insight, with an intensely personal vision; his works include *Lord Jim* (1900) and *Heart of Darkness* (1902).

(Harold) Hart Crane (21 Jul 1899, Garrettsville OH—27 Apr 1932, at sea in the Caribbean), American poet of visionary intensity who celebrated the richness of life, including the life of the industrial age.

Stephen Crane (1 Nov 1871, Newark NJ—5 Jun 1900, Badenweiler, Baden, Germany), American novelist and short-story writer best known for his novels *Maggie: A Girl of the Streets* (1893) and *The Red Badge of Courage* (1895) and the stories "The Open Boat," "The Bride Comes to Yellow Sky," and "The Blue Hotel."

Sor Juana Inés de la Cruz (Juana Inés de Asbaje; 12 Nov 1651, San Miguel Nepantla, Viceroyalty of New Spain [now in Mexico]—17 Apr 1695, Mexico City, Mexico), Mexican poet, scholar, and nun who was an intellectual prodigy and an outstanding literary representative of Mexico's colonial period.

E(dward) E(stlin) Cummings (14 Oct 1894, Cambridge MA—3 Sep 1962, North Conway NH), American poet known for his experiments with eccentric punctuation and phrasing, and for his use of urbanized colloquial language.

Dante (Dante Alighieri; c. May 21–20 Jun 1265, Florence, Italy—13/14 Sep 1321, Ravenna), Italian poet, prose writer, literary theorist, moral philosopher, and political thinker He is best known for the monumental epic poem *La divina commedia* (*The Divine Comedy*).

Michael Madhusudan Datta (also spelled Dutt; 25 Jan 1824, Sagardari, Bengal, India [now in Bangladesh]—29 Jun 1873, Calcutta), Bengali poet regarded as a dynamic, erratic, and original genius of the highest order, considered a seminal figure of modern Bengali literature.

Daniel Defoe (1660, London, England—24 Apr 1731, London), English novelist called the "Father of the English Novel" and best known for *Robinson Crusoe* (1719–22) and *Moll Flanders* (1722).

Philip K(indred) Dick (16 Dec 1928, Chicago IL—2 Mar 1982, Santa Ana CA), American science-fiction writer whose works often depict the psychological struggles of characters trapped in illusory environments.

Charles Dickens (7 Feb 1812, Portsmouth, Hampshire, England—9 Jun 1870, Gad's Hill, near Chatham, Kent), English novelist, perhaps the greatest of the Victorian era. His many works include *David Copperfield*, *A Tale of Two Cities*, *Oliver Twist*, *Great Expectations*, and *A Christmas Carol*.

Emily Dickinson (10 Dec 1830, Amherst MA—15 May 1886, Amherst), American poet called the "New England Mystic" and heralded for experimentation with poetic rhythms and rhymes; almost all of her poetry was published posthumously.

John Donne (1572, London, England—31 Mar 1631, London), English poet who was regarded as the leading figure of the Metaphysical school and the greatest love poet in the English language.

Fyodor Mikhaylovich Dostoyevsky (11 Nov [30 Oct, Old Style] 1821, Moscow, Russia—9 Feb [28 Jan, Old Style] 1881, St. Petersburg), Russian novelist who was an enormous influence on 20th-century fiction. Literary modernism, existentialism, and various schools of psychology, theology, and literary criticism have been profoundly shaped by his ideas.

Sir Arthur Conan Doyle (22 May 1859, Edinburgh, Scotland—7 Jul 1930, Crowborough, Sussex, England), Scottish novelist and short-story writer best known for his creation of the detective Sherlock Holmes—one of the most vivid and enduring characters in English fiction.

Theodore Dreiser (27 Aug 1871, Terre Haute IN—28 Dec 1945, Hollywood CA), American novelist who was the outstanding American practitioner of Naturalism and the leading figure in a national literary movement that replaced the observance of Victorian notions of propriety with the unflinching presentation of real-life subject matter; best known for *Sister Carrie* (1900).

John Dryden (19 Aug [9 Aug, Old Style] 1631, Aldwinkle, Northamptonshire, England—12 May [1 May, Old Style] 1700, London), English poet, dramatist, and literary critic who so dominated the literary scene of his day that it came to be known as the Age of Dryden.

George Eliot (Mary Ann or Marian Cross; née Evans; 22 Nov 1819, Chilvers Coton, Warwickshire, England—22 Dec 1880, London), English novelist known for developing the psychological analysis characteristic of modern fiction. Major works include *Adam Bede* (1859), *The Mill on the Floss* (1860), *Silas Marner* (1861), and *Middlemarch* (1871–72).

T(homas) S(tearns) Eliot (26 Sep 1888, St. Louis MO—4 Jan 1965, London, England), American-English poet and playwright, a leader in the mod-

ernist movement in poetry in such works as *The Waste Land* (1922) and *Four Quartets* (1943). Eliot had an enormous influence on 20th-century Anglo-American culture; he was awarded the Order of Merit and the Nobel Prize for Literature in 1948.

Shusaku Endo (27 Mar 1923, Tokyo, Japan—29 Sep 1996, Tokyo), Japanese novelist noted for his examination of the relationship between East and West through a unique Christian perspective.

Euripides (c. 484 BCE, Athens, Greece—406 BCE, Macedonia), Greek playwright who was the last of the three great tragedians of Athens, following Aeschylus and Sophocles.

William (Cuthbert) Faulkner (25 Sep 1897, New Albany MS—6 Jul 1962, Byhalia MS), American novelist unmatched for his stylistic and structural resourcefulness, for the range and depth of his characters, and for exploring fundamental human issues; Nobel Prize for Literature, 1949.

Henry Fielding (22 Apr 1707, Sharpham Park, Somerset, England—8 Oct 1754, Lisbon, Portugal), English novelist considered one of the founders of the English novel; major works include *Joseph Andrews* (1742) and *Tom Jones* (1749).

F(rancis) Scott (Key) Fitzgerald (24 Sep 1896, St. Paul MN—21 Dec 1940, Hollywood CA), American novelist and short-story writer famous for his depictions of the Jazz Age (the 1920s). Major works include *The Great Gatsby* (1925) and *Tender Is the Night* (1934).

Gustave Flaubert (12 Dec 1821, Rouen, France—8 May 1880, Croisset), French novelist regarded as the prime mover behind the realist school of French literature and best known for his masterpiece *Madame Bovary* (1857), a realistic portrayal of bourgeois life.

E(dward) M(organ) Forster (1 Jan 1879, London, England—7 Jun 1970, Coventry, Warwickshire), English novelist and critic, best known for *Howards End* (1910) and *A Passage to India* (1924), and for a large body of criticism.

Robert Frost (26 Mar 1874, San Francisco CA—29 Jan 1963, Boston MA), American poet best known for his use of colloquial language, familiar rhythms, and symbols taken from common life to express the quiet values of New England.

Joseph Furphy (Tom Collins; 26 Sep 1843, Yering, near Yarra Glen, Victoria, Australia—13 Sep 1912, Claremont, Western Australia), Australian novelist who combined an acute sense of local Australian life and color with the eclectic philosophy and literary ideas of a self-taught workingman.

Gao Xingjian (Kao Hsing-chien, 4 Jan 1940, Ganzhou, Jiangxi province, China) Chinese-born French novelist, playwright, critic, stage director, and artist awarded the 2000 Nobel Prize for Literature for "an oeuvre of universal validity, bitter insights, and linguistic ingenuity."

Federico García Lorca (5 Jun 1898, Fuente Vaqueros, Granada province, Spain—18 or 19 Aug 1936, between Víznar and Alfacar, Granada province), Spanish poet and playwright who, in a career that spanned just 19 years, resurrected and revitalized the most basic strains of Spanish poetry and theater.

Gabriel García Márquez (6 Mar 1928, Aracataca, Columbia) Colombian novelist and short-story writer, a central figure in the so-called magic realism movement in Latin-American literature; Nobel Prize for Literature, 1982.

Jean Genet (19 Dec 1910, Paris, France—15 Apr 1986, Paris), French novelist and playwright, a social outcast turned writer who transformed erotic and often obscene subject matter into a poetic vision of the universe and became a leading figure in the avant-garde theater, especially the Theater of the Absurd.

André Gide (22 Nov 1869, Paris, France—19 Feb 1951, Paris), French novelist known for early works that explored man's search for individual values, as well as later works concerned with psychological problems and moral ambiguity; Nobel Prize for Literature, 1947.

(Irwin) Allen Ginsberg (3 Jun 1926, Newark NJ—5 Apr 1997, New York NY), American poet best known for his epic poem *Howl* (1956), one of the most significant products of the Beat movement.

(Hyppolyte-)Jean Giraudoux (29 Oct 1882, Bellac, France—31 Jan 1944, Paris), French playwright who created an impressionistic form of drama that emphasized dialogue and style rather than realism.

Johann Wolfgang von Goethe (28 Aug 1749, Frankfurt am Main [Germany]—22 Mar 1832, Weimar, Saxe-Weimar [Germany]), German poet, novelist, playwright, and natural philosopher; considered the greatest figure of German literature.

Nikolay (Vasilyevich) Gogol (31 Mar [19 Mar, Old Style] 1809, Sorochintsy near Poltava, Ukraine, Russian Empire [now in Ukraine]—4 Mar [21 Feb, Old Style] 1852, Moscow, Russia), Russian novelist and short-story writer known for the novel *Myortvye dushi* (*Dead Souls*) and the story "Shinel" ("The Overcoat"), which are considered the foundations of the great 19th-century tradition of Russian realism.

Nadine Gordimer (20 Nov 1923, Springs, Transvaal, South Africa) South African novelist and short-story writer whose works explore the common theme of exile and alienation; Nobel Prize for Literature, 1991.

Günter (Wilhelm) Grass (16 Oct 1927, Danzig [now Gdansk, Poland]) German poet, novelist, playwright, sculptor, and printmaker who became a literary spokesman for the German generation that grew up in the Nazi era and survived the war; Nobel Prize for Literature, 1999.

(Henry) Graham Greene (2 Oct 1904, Berkhamsted, Hertfordshire, England—3 Apr 1991, Vevey, Switzerland), English novelist, one of the most widely read of the 20th century, whose novels treat life's moral ambiguities in the context of contemporary political settings.

Hafez (Mohammad Shams Od-din Hafez; c. 1325–26, Shiraz, Iran—c. 1389–90, Shiraz), Persian lyric poet known for his perfection of the ghazal, a lyric poem of 6 to 15 couplets linked by unity of subject and symbolism rather than by a logical sequence of ideas.

Sakutaro Hagiwara (1 Nov 1886, Maebashi, Japan—11 May 1942, Tokyo), Japanese poet whose attempt to express his perceptions directly in concrete, often unpretty images, rather than in amorphous descriptions, represented a revolutionary trend in Japanese literature.

(Samuel) Dashiell Hammett (27 May 1894, St. Mary's county MD—10 Jan 1961, New York NY), American novelist and short-story writer credited as the creator of the "hard-boiled" school of detective fiction. Best known for *The Glass Key* (1931), *The Thin Man* (1932), and *The Maltese Falcon* (1930), which introduced the detective Sam Spade.

Thomas Hardy (2 Jun 1840, Higher Brockhampton, Dorset, England—11 Jan 1928, Dorchester, Dorset), English novelist and poet whose works are known for a richly varied, accessible style and for their nostalgic evocation of a vanished rural world.

Nathaniel Hawthorne (4 Jul 1804, Salem MA—19 May 1864, Plymouth NH), American novelist and short-story writer, a master of the allegorical and symbolic tale; best known for *The Scarlet Letter* (1850) and *The House of the Seven Gables* (1851).

Seamus (Justin) Heaney (13 Apr 1939, near Castledawson, County Londonderry, Northern Ireland) Irish poet whose works evoke events in Irish history and allude to Irish myths; Nobel Prize for Literature, 1995.

Anne Hébert (1 Aug 1916, Sainte-Catherine-de-Fossambault, Quebec, Canada—22 Jan 2000, Montreal), Canadian novelist noted as an original stylist and for works that are psychological examinations of violence, rebellion, and the quest for personal freedom.

Ernest (Miller) Hemingway (21 Jul 1899, Oak Park IL—2 Jul 1961, Ketchum ID), American novelist and short-story writer noted for both the intense masculinity of his writing and for his succinct and lucid prose style; Nobel Prize for Literature, 1954.

O. Henry (William Sydney Porter; 11 Sep 1862, Greensboro NC—5 Jun 1910, New York NY), American short-story writer known for tales that romanticized the commonplace—in particular the life of ordinary people in New York City. His stories expressed the effect of coincidence on character through humor, grim or ironic, and often had surprise endings, a device that became identified with his name.

Herman Hesse (2 Jul 1877, Calw, Germany—9 Aug 1962, Montagnola, Switzerland), German novelist, winner of the Nobel Prize for Literature in 1946. His main theme deals with man's breaking out of the established modes of civilization to find his essential spirit.

Homer (flourished 8th or 9th century BCE, Ionia? [now in Turkey]), ancient Greek writer, presumed author of the *Iliad* and the *Odyssey*, the most important poems of the classical European tradition.

Gerard Manley Hopkins (28 Jul 1844, Stratford, Essex, England—8 Jun 1889, Dublin, Ireland), English Victorian poet known for the unique "sprung rhythm" of his poetry. Nearly all of his works were unpublished during his lifetime; they were later recognized as among the most original, powerful, and influential literary accomplishments of the century.

Horace (Quintus Horatius Flaccus; December 65 BCE, Venusia, Italy—27 Nov 8 BCE, Rome), Roman poet considered the outstanding Latin lyric poet and satirist under the emperor Augustus. The most frequent themes of his odes and verse epistles are love, friendship, philosophy, and the art of poetry.

(James Mercer) Langston Hughes (1 Feb 1902, Joplin MO—22 May 1967, New York NY), American poet and writer, one of the foremost interpreters of the black experience in the US.

Victor(-Marie) Hugo (26 Feb 1802, Besançon, France—22 May 1885, Paris), French Romantic poet and novelist. Though regarded in France as one of that country's greatest poets, he is better known internationally for such novels as *Notre-Dame de Paris* (*The Hunchback of Notre Dame*, 1831) and *Les Misérables* (1862).

Zora Neale Hurston (7 Jan 1903, Eatonville FL—28 Jan 1960, Fort Pierce FL), American folklorist and writer, a prominent figure of the Harlem Renaissance who celebrated African-American culture of the rural South.

Aldous (Leonard) Huxley (26 Jul 1894, Godalming, Surrey, England—22 Nov 1963, Los Angeles CA), English novelist and critic renowned for his acute and far-ranging intelligence. His works were notable for their elegance, wit, and pessimistic satire.

Henrik (Johan) Ibsen (20 Mar 1828, Skien, Norway—23 May 1906, Kristiania [now Oslo]), Norwegian playwright who introduced to the European stage a new order of moral analysis that was placed against a severely realistic middle-class background and developed with economy of action, penetrating dialogue, and rigorous thought.

Imru' al-Qays (Imru' Al qays Ibn Hujr) (d. c. 550), Arab poet, acknowledged as the most distinguished poet of pre-Islamic times by the Prophet Muhammad, by 'Ali, the fourth caliph, and by Arab critics of the ancient Basra school. He is author of one of the seven odes in the famed collection of pre-Islamic poetry *Al-Mu'allaqat*.

Eugène Ionesco (Eugen Ionescu; 26 Nov 1909, Slatina, Romania—28 Mar 1994, Paris), Romanian-born playwright, perhaps the most important figure of the Theater of the Absurd who popularized a wide variety of nonrepresentational and surrealistic techniques and made them acceptable to audiences conditioned to a naturalistic convention in the theater. Best-known works include *The Bald Soprano* (1949) and *Rhinoceros* (1959).

Washington Irving (3 Apr 1783, New York NY—28 Nov 1859, Tarrytown NY), American short-story writer called the "first American man of letters," and best known for "The Legend of Sleepy Hollow" and "Rip Van Winkle."

Christopher Isherwood (Christopher William Bradshaw-Isherwood; 26 Aug 1904, High Lane, Cheshire, England—4 Jan 1986, Santa Monica CA), Anglo-American novelist best known for his examination of life in Berlin during the early 1930s; most of his novels demonstrated his personal style of "fictional autobiography."

Takuboku Ishikawa (Hajime Ishikawa; 28 Oct 1886, Hinoto, Iwate Prefecture, Japan—13 Apr 1912, Tokyo), Japanese tanka poet whose works enjoyed immediate popularity for their freshness and startling imagery.

al-Jahiz (Abu 'Uthman 'Amr ibn Bahr ibn Mahbub Al-Jahiz; c. 776, Basra, Iraq—c. 868–69, Basra), Arab Islamic theologian, intellectual, and litterateur known for his individual and masterful Arabic prose.

Henry James (15 Apr 1843, New York NY—28 Feb 1916, London, England), American novelist who was a major figure in the transatlantic culture and whose fundamental theme was the innocence and exuberance of the New World in clash with the corruption and wisdom of the Old World.

(Theodora) Sarah Orne Jewett (3 Sep 1849, South Berwick ME—24 Jun 1909, South Berwick), American writer of regional fiction that centered on her life in Maine. Her works were admired for their precision, compactness, and use of naturalism.

Samuel Johnson (Dr. Johnson; 18 Sep 1709, Lichfield, Staffordshire, England—13 Dec 1784, London), English critic, biographer, essayist, poet, and lexicographer regarded as one of the seminal figures of 18th-century life and letters.

James Joyce (2 Feb 1882, Dublin, Ireland—13 Jan 1941, Zürich, Switzerland), Irish novelist noted for his experimental use of language and new literary methods in such large works of fiction as *Ulysses* (1922) and *Finnegans Wake* (1939).

Ismail Kadare (28 Jan 1938, Gjirokastër, Albania) Albanian novelist and poet, renowned in Albania for his poetry and internationally for his prose fiction.

Franz Kafka (3 Jul 1883, Prague, Bohemia, Austria-Hungary [now in Czech Republic]—3 Jun 1924, Kierling, near Vienna, Austria), Czech-born German-language novelist known for his visionary fiction and posthumously published novels such as *Der Prozess* (*The Trial*, 1925) and *Das Schloss* (*The Castle*, 1926), which express the anxieties and alienation of 20th-century man.

Yasunari Kawabata (11 Jun 1899, Osaka, Japan—16 Apr 1972, Zushi), Japanese novelist noted for a melancholic lyricism that echoes an ancient Japanese literary tradition in the modern idiom; Nobel Prize for Literature, 1968.

John Keats (31 Oct 1795, London, England—23 Feb 1821, Rome, Papal States, Italy), English Romantic poet who devoted his short life to the perfection of a poetry marked by vivid imagery, great sensuous appeal, and an attempt to express a philosophy through classical legend.

Yashar Kemal (Kemal Sadik Gogceli; 1922, Hemite, Turkey) Turkish novelist of Kurdish descent best known for his stories of village life and for his outspoken advocacy on behalf of the dispossessed.

Jack Kerouac (Jean-Louis Kerouac; 12 Mar 1922, Lowell MA—21 Oct 1969, St. Petersburg FL), American poet and novelist, the leader of the Beat movement who celebrated its code of poverty and freedom in a series of novels of which the first and best known is *On the Road* (1957).

Rudyard Kipling (30 Dec 1865, Bombay [now Mumbai], India—18 Jan 1936, London, England), English short-story writer, poet, and novelist chiefly remembered for his celebration of British imperialism, his tales and poems of British soldiers in India, and his tales for children; Nobel Prize for Literature, 1907.

Milan Kundera (1 Apr 1929, Brno, Czechoslovakia) Czech novelist, short-story writer, playwright, and poet who wrote various works combining erotic comedy with political criticism.

Selma (Ottiliana Lovisa) Lagerlöf (20 Nov 1858, Mårbacka, Sweden—16 Mar 1940, Mårbacka), Swedish novelist who became the first woman, as well as the first Swedish writer to be awarded the Nobel Prize for Literature in 1909.

D(avid) H(erbert) Lawrence (11 Sep 1885, Eastwood, Nottinghamshire, England—2 Mar 1930, Vence, France), English author of novels, short stories, poems, plays, essays, travel books, and letters; his novels *Sons and Lovers* (1913), *The Rainbow* (1915), and *Women in Love* (1920) made him one of the most influential English writers of the 20th century.

John Le Carré (David John Moore Cornwell; 19 Oct 1931, Poole, Dorset, England) English novelist who created suspenseful, realistic spy novels based on a wide knowledge of international espionage.

(Harry) Sinclair Lewis (7 Feb 1885, Sauk Centre MN—10 Jan 1951, near Rome, Italy), American novelist and social critic who punctured American complacency with his broadly drawn, widely popular satirical works. He won the Nobel Prize for Literature in 1930, the first given to an American.

Li Po (Li Bo; Li T'ai-po; 701, Szechwan province, China—762, Tang-t'u, Anhwei province), Chinese poet, a romantic in his view of life and in his verse who frequently celebrated the joy of drinking; he also wrote of friendship, solitude, the passage of time, and the joys of nature. Popularly referred to as a "banished Immortal," he wrote with brilliance and great freshness of imagination.

Clarice Lispector (10 Dec 1925, Chechelnyk, Ukraine, USSR—9 Dec 1977, Rio de Janeiro, Brazil), Brazilian novelist and short-story writer whose works depict a highly personal, almost existentialist view of the human dilemma and are written in a prose style characterized by a simple vocabulary and an elliptical sentence structure.

Jack London (John Griffith Chaney; 12 Jan 1876, San Francisco CA—22 Nov 1916, Glen Ellen CA), American novelist whose works deal romantically with elemental struggles for survival. He is one of the most extensively translated of American authors.

Robert Lowell (Robert Traill Spence Lowell, Jr.; 1 Mar 1917, Boston MA—12 Sep 1977, New York NY), American poet noted for his complex, autobiographical works and for expressing the major tensions—both public and private—of his time with technical mastery and haunting authenticity.

Lu Hsün (Chou Shu-jen; 25 Sep 1881, Shao-hsing, Chekiang province, China—19 Oct 1936, Shanghai), Chinese short-story writer commonly considered the most important Chinese literary figure of the 20th century. He is credited with introducing the Western-style short story into Chinese literature.

Leopoldo Lugones (13 Jun 1874, Villa María del Río Seco, Argentina—19 Feb 1938, Buenos Aires), Argentine poet, literary and social critic, and cultural ambassador, considered by many the outstanding figure of his age in the cultural life of his country, and whose works reflected his own change from radical socialism to an intense conservative nationalism.

Joaquim Maria Machado de Assis (21 Jun 1839, Rio de Janeiro, Brazil—29 Sep 1908, Rio de Janeiro), Brazilian poet, novelist, and short-story writer whose art is rooted in the traditions of European culture and transcends the influence of Brazilian literary schools.

Naguib Mahfouz (11 Dec 1911, Cairo, Egypt) Egyptian novelist and screenplay writer noted for works dealing with social issues involving women and political prisoners; awarded the Nobel Prize for Literature in 1988, the first Arabic writer to be so honored.

Norman Mailer (31 Jan 1923, Long Branch NJ) American novelist and journalist whose fiction and nonfiction made a radical critique of the totalitarianism he believed inherent in the centralized power structure of 20th-century America.

Stéphane Mallarmé (18 Mar 1842, Paris, France—9 Sep 1898, Valvins, near Fontainebleau), French poet who was an originator (with Paul Verlaine) and a leader of the Symbolist movement.

André(-Georges) Malraux (3 Nov 1901, Paris, France—23 Nov 1976, Paris), French novelist who explored the tragic ambiguities of political idealism and revolutionary struggle. He also served for 10 years as France's minister of cultural affairs.

Thomas Mann (6 Jun 1875, Lübeck, Germany—12 Aug 1955, near Zürich, Switzerland), German novelist whose works explore the nature of Western bourgeois culture; Nobel Prize for Literature, 1929.

Sandor Marai (11 Apr 1900, Kaschau, Hungary—21 Feb 1989, San Diego CA), Hungarian novelist, a survivor of Nazi occupation whose long-neglected works were rediscovered in the 1990s and subsequently translated and published in more than 20 languages.

Christopher Marlowe (baptized 26 Feb 1564, Canterbury, Kent, England—30 May 1593, Deptford, near London), English playwright who was Shakespeare's most important predecessor in English drama, noted especially for his establishment of dramatic blank verse.

Andrew Marvell (31 Mar 1621, Winestead, Yorkshire, England—18 Aug 1678, London), English metaphysical poet whose political reputation overshadowed his poetry until the 20th century.

Guy de Maupassant (Henry-René-Albert-Guy de Maupassant; 5 Aug 1850, Château de Miromesnil?, near Dieppe, France—6 Jul 1893, Paris), French short-story writer whose thoroughly realistic work was marked by characters that inhabit a world of material desires and sensual appetites in which lust, greed, and ambition are the driving forces, and any higher feelings are either absent or doomed to cruel disappointment.

Herman Melville (1 Aug 1819, New York NY—28 Sep 1891, New York City), American novelist, short-story writer, and poet best known for his masterful use of allegory and symbolism, as in Billy Budd (1891, published 1924) and his masterpiece, Moby Dick (1850), regarded by many as the greatest American novel of all time.

Adam (Bernard) Mickiewicz (24 Dec 1798, Zaos'ye, near Novogrudek, Russian Empire [now in Belarus]—26 Nov 1855, Constantinople), Polish poet who was a lifelong apostle of Polish national freedom.

Arthur Miller (17 Oct 1915, New York NY) American playwright, one of the leading figures of post-World War II drama, whose works combine social awareness with a searching concern for his characters' inner lives; best known for Death of a Salesman (1949) and The Crucible (1953).

Czeslaw Milosz (30 Jun 1911, Sateiniai, Lithuania, Russian Empire) Polish-American author, translator, and critic noted for his classical style and preoccupation with philosophical and political issues; Nobel Prize for Literature, 1980.

John Milton (9 Dec 1608, London, England—8 Nov 1674, Chalfont St. Giles, Buckinghamshire), English poet often ranked second only to Shakespeare; best known for Paradise Lost.

Frédéric Mistral (8 Sep 1830, Maillane, France—25 Mar 1914, Maillane), Provençal poet who led the 19th-century revival of Occitan (Provençal) language and literature; he shared the Nobel Prize for Literature in 1904 for his contributions in literature and philology.

Molière (Jean-Baptiste Poquelin) (baptized 15 Jan 1622, Paris, France—17 Feb 1673, Paris), French playwright who was considered the greatest writer of French comedy; his classic farces include The School for Wives (1663), Tartuffe (1664–69), The Misanthrope (1666), and The Imaginary Invalid (1674).

Michel de Montaigne (28 Feb 1533, Château de Montaigne, near Bordeaux, France—23 Sep 1592, Château de Montaigne), French writer whose Essais (Essays) established a new literary form and in which he offered one of the most captivating and intimate self-portraits ever written.

Marianne (Craig) Moore (15 Nov 1887, St. Louis MO—5 Feb 1972, New York NY), American poet whose works distilled moral and intellectual insights from the close and accurate observation of objective detail.

Alberto Moravia (Alberto Pincherle; 28 Nov 1907, Rome, Italy—26 Sep 1990, Rome), Italian novelist, short-story writer, and journalist known for his fictional portrayals of social alienation and loveless sexuality.

Toni Morrison (Chloe Anthony Wofford; 18 Feb 1931, Lorain OH) American novelist noted for her examination of black experience (particularly black female experience) within the African American community; Nobel Prize for Literature, 1993.

Murasaki Shikibu (Lady; c. 978, Kyoto, Japan—c. 1014, Kyoto), Japanese court lady who was the author of *Genji monogatari* (*The Tale of Genji*), generally considered the greatest work of Japanese literature and thought to be the world's oldest full novel.

Dame (Jean) Iris Murdoch (15 Jul 1919, Dublin, Ireland—8 Feb 1999, Oxford, Oxfordshire, England), British novelist known for her psychological novels that contain philosophical and comic elements. Her novels typically have convoluted plots in which innumerable characters representing different philosophical positions undergo kaleidoscopic changes in their relations with each other.

V.S. Naipaul (Vidiadhar Surajprasad Naipaul; 17 Aug 1932, Chaguanas, Trinidad) Trinidadian-born British writer known for his pessimistic novels set in the Third World nations; Nobel Prize for Literature, 2001.

Pablo Neruda (Neftali Ricardo Reyes Basoalto; 12 Jul 1904, Parral, Chile—23 Sep 1973, Santiago), Chilean poet, a major figure in 20th-century Latin-American literature; Nobel Prize for Literature, 1971.

(Mary) Flannery O'Connor (25 Mar 1925, Savannah GA—3 Aug 1964, Milledgeville GA), American novelist and short-story writer whose works, usually set in the rural South and often treating of human alienation, are concerned with the relationship between the individual and God.

Kenzaburo Oe (31 Jan 1935, Ehime prefecture, Shikoku, Japan) Japanese novelist whose works express the disillusionment and rebellion of his post-World War II generation; Nobel Prize for Literature, 1994.

Eugene (Gladstone) O'Neill (16 Oct 1888, New York NY—27 Nov 1953, Boston MA), American playwright considered the foremost American dramatist; winner of the Nobel Prize for Literature, 1936; major works include *Mourning Becomes Electra* (1931), *Ah! Wilderness* (1933), *The Iceman Cometh* (1946), and *Long Day's Journey into Night* (published posthumously, 1956).

Alan Paton (11 Jan 1903, Pietermaritzburg, Natal, South Africa—12 Apr 1988, near Durban), South African novelist best known for *Cry, the Beloved Country* (1948), a passionate tale of racial injustice that brought international attention to the problem of apartheid in South Africa.

Octavio Paz (31 Mar 1914, Mexico City, Mexico—19 Apr 1998, Mexico City), Mexican poet, writer, and diplomat recognized as one of the major Latin American writers of the 20th century; winner of the Cervantes Prize in 1981 and the Nobel Prize for Literature, 1990.

Sandor Petofi (1 Jan 1823, Kiskoros, Hungary—probably 1856, Siberia, Russia), Hungarian poet and revolutionary who symbolized the Hungarian desire for freedom.

Petrarch (20 Jul 1304, Arezzo, Tuscany, Italy—18 Jul 1374, Arquà, near Padua, Carrara), Italian scholar, poet, and Humanist whose poems addressed to Laura, an idealized beloved, contributed to the Renaissance flowering of lyric poetry.

Harold Pinter (10 Oct 1930, London, England) English playwright regarded as one of the most complex and challenging post-World War II dramatists. His plays are noted for their use of understatement, small talk, reticence, and even silence to convey the substance of their characters.

Luigi Pirandello (28 Jun 1867, Agrigento, Sicily, Italy—10 Dec 1936, Rome), Italian playwright, an important innovator in modern drama; Nobel Prize for Literature, 1934.

Edgar Allan Poe (19 Jan 1809, Boston MA—7 Oct 1849, Baltimore MD), American short-story writer and poet, a major influence on the short-story form and the father of the modern detective story. Poe's best-known works are renowned for their atmosphere of mystery and the macabre.

Alexander Pope (21 May 1688, London, England—30 May 1744, Twickenham, near London), English poet, one of the most quotable of English authors and a major figure of the English Augustan period, best known for *An Essay on Criticism* (1711), *The Rape of the Lock* (1712–14), *The Dunciad* (1728), and *An Essay on Man* (1733–34).

Katherine Anne Porter (15 May 1890, Indian Creek IX—18 Sep 1980, Silver Spring MD), American short-story writer, a master stylist whose long stories have a richness of texture and complexity of character delineation usually achieved only in the novel.

Ezra (Loomis) Pound (30 Oct 1885, Hailey ID—1 Nov 1972, Venice, Italy), American poet and critic, a supremely discerning and energetic entrepreneur of the arts who did more than any other single figure to advance a "modern" movement in English and American literature.

Marcel Proust (10 Jul 1871, Auteuil, near Paris, France—18 Nov 1922, Paris), French novelist, author of *À la recherche du temps perdu* (*Remembrance of Things Past*, 1913–27), a seven-volume autobiographical novel told psychologically and allegorically, and regarded as one of the supreme achievements of modern fiction.

Aleksandr Sergeyevich Pushkin (6 Jun 1799 [26 May, Old Style], Moscow, Russia—10 Feb [29 Jan, Old Style] 1837, St. Petersburg), Russian poet, novelist, dramatist, and short-story writer; considered his country's greatest poet and the founder of modern Russian literature.

François Rabelais (Alcofribas Nasier; c. 1494, Poitou, France—9? Apr 1553, Paris), French novelist who was also an eminent priest, physician, and humanist. Author of the comic masterpiece *Gargantua and Pantagruel*, which is composed of four novels outstanding in their rich use of Renaissance French and for their comedy that ranges from gross burlesque to profound satire.

Raja Rao (21 Nov 1909, Hassan, Mysore [now Karnataka], India) Indian English-language novelist and short-story writer known for allegorical and philosophical works, such as the novel *The Serpent and the Rope* (1960), regarded as his masterpiece.

Adrienne (Cecile) Rich (16 May 1929, Baltimore MD) American poet, scholar, teacher, and critic whose many volumes of poetry trace a stylistic transformation from formal, well-crafted but imitative poetry to a more personal and powerful style.

Samuel Richardson (baptized 19 Aug 1689, Mackworth, near Derby, Derbyshire, England—4 Jul 1761, Parson's Green, near London), English novelist who expanded the dramatic possibilities of the novel by his invention and use of the letter form ("epistolary novel"). His major novels were *Pamela* (1740) and *Clarissa* (1747–48).

Rainer Maria Rilke (René Maria Rilke; 4 Dec 1875, Prague, Bohemia, Austria-Hungary [now in Czech Republic]—29 Dec 1926, Valmont, Switzerland), Austro-German poet internationally renowned for such works as *Duino Elegies* and *Sonnets to Orpheus*.

Christina (Georgina) Rossetti (Ellen Alleyne; 5 Dec 1830, London, England—29 Dec 1894, London), English poet who excelled in works of fantasy, in poems for children, and in religious poetry.

Jalal ad-Din ar-Rumi (Mawlana; c. 30 Sep 1207, Balkh, Ghurid empire [now in Afghanistan]—17 Dec 1273), Persian poet and Sufi mystic famous for his lyrics and for his didactic epic *Masnavi-ye Ma'navi* ("Spiritual Couplets"), which widely influenced Muslim mystical thought and literature.

Shota Rustaveli (c. 1172–c. 1216), Georgian poet, author of the Georgian national epic, *The Knight in the Panther's Skin*.

Sa'di (Musharrif Od-din Muslih Od-din; c. 1213, Shiraz, Iran—9 Dec 1291, Shiraz), Persian poet, one of the greatest figures in classical Persian literature.

Saki (H(ector) H(ugh) Munro; 18 Dec 1870, Akyab, Burma [Myanmar]—14 Nov 1916, near Beaumont-Hamel, France), Scottish short-story writer and journalist whose stories depict the Edwardian social scene with a flippant wit and power of fantastic invention used both to satirize social pretension, unkindness, and stupidity and to create an atmosphere of horror.

George Sand (Amandine-Aaurore-Lucile (Lucie) Dudevant, née Dupin; 1 Jul 1804, Paris, France—8 Jun 1876, Nohant), French Romantic writer known for her rustic novels with the common theme of love transcending the obstacles of convention and class.

Carl Sandburg (6 Jan 1878, Galesburg IL—22 Jul 1967, Flat Rock NC), American poet, historian, novelist, and folklorist who celebrated American cities, industries, and workers in Whitmanesque free verse. Also renowned for his multivolume biography of Abraham Lincoln.

Sappho (Psappho) (flourished c. 610–c. 580 BCE, Lesbos, Asia Minor), Greek poet celebrated for her vernacular dialect and her concise, direct, and picturesque phrasing. Considered the most important of Greek poets next to Archilochus and Alcaeus.

Jean-Paul Sartre (21 Jun 1905, Paris, France—15 Apr 1980, Paris), French novelist, playwright, and exponent of Existentialism—a philosophy acclaiming the freedom of the individual human being. He was awarded the Nobel Prize for Literature in 1964, but he declined it.

(Johann Christoph) Friedrich von Schiller (10 Nov 1759, Marbach, Württemberg, Germany—9 May 1805, Weimar, Saxe-Weimar), German dramatist, poet, and literary theorist, best remembered for such dramas as *Die Räuber* (1781; *The Robbers*), the *Wallenstein* trilogy (1800–01), *Maria Stuart* (1801), and *Wilhelm Tell* (1804).

Sir Walter, 1st Baronet Scott (15 Aug 1771, Edinburgh, Scotland—21 Sep 1832, Abbotsford, Rox-burgh), Scottish novelist considered both the inventor and the greatest practitioner of the historical novel.

Jaroslav Seifert (23 Sep 1901, Prague, Bohemia, Austria-Hungary [now in Czech Republic]—10 Jan 1986, Prague, Czechoslovakia), Czech poet and journalist, the first from his country to win the Nobel Prize for Literature, in 1984; the history and other aspects of Czechoslovakia were the most common subjects of his poetry.

William Shakespeare ("The Bard of Avon"; 23? Apr 1564, Stratford-upon-Avon, Warwickshire, England—23 Apr 1616, Stratford-upon-Avon), English playwright and poet, often called the English national poet and widely considered to be the greatest dramatist of all time.

George Bernard Shaw (26 Jul 1856, Dublin, Ireland—2 Nov 1950, Ayot St. Lawrence, Hertfordshire, England), Irish dramatist, literary critic, and Socialist propagandist regarded as the second-greatest dramatist in the English language next to Shakespeare (though he would have bristled at being ranked so low). Known for his great wit and formidable intellect; winner of the Nobel Prize (which he refused) in 1925.

Mary Wollstonecraft Shelley (30 Aug 1797, London, England—1 Feb 1851, London), English Romantic novelist best known as the author of *Frankenstein*; she was the wife of Percy Bysshe Shelley.

Percy Bysshe Shelley (4 Aug 1792, Field Place, near Horsham, Sussex, England—8 Jul 1822, at sea, off Livorno, Tuscany, Italy), English Romantic poet whose poems reflect a passionate search for personal love and social justice; he was the husband of Mary Wollstonecraft Shelley.

Richard Brinsley (Butler) Sheridan (baptized 4 Nov 1751, Dublin, Ireland—7 Jul 1816, London, England), English playwright, also prominent as an impresario, orator, and Whig politician. Sheridan's plays, notably *The School for Scandal* (1777) form a link in the history of the comedy of manners between the 17th century and Oscar Wilde in the 19th century.

Shiki Masaoka (Tsunenori Masaoka; 14 Oct 1867, Matsuyama, Japan—19 Sep 1902, Tokyo), Japanese poet, a major figure in the revival of the haiku and tanka, traditional Japanese poetic forms.

Henryk Sienkiewicz (Henryk Adam Alexander Pius Sienkiewicz; pseudonym Litwos; 5 May 1846, Wola Okrzejska, Poland—15 Nov 1916, Vevey, Switzerland), Polish author of popular historical and heroic novels; Nobel Prize for Literature, 1905.

Georges(-Joseph-Christian) Simenon (13 Feb 1903, Liège, Belgium—4 Sep 1989, Lausanne, Switzerland), Belgian-French novelist who created Inspector Maigret, one of the best-known characters in detective fiction. Enormously prolific, he was perhaps the most widely published author of the 20th century.

Claude(-Eugene-Henri) Simon (10 Oct 1913, Tananarive, Madagascar) French novelist who created some of the most authentic representatives of the French *nouveau roman* ("new novel") that emerged in the 1950s; Nobel Prize for Literature, 1985.

Isaac Bashevis Singer (Yiddish Yitskhek Bashyevis Zinger; 14? Jul 1904, Radzymin, Poland, Russian Empire—24 Jul 1991, Surfside FL), Polish-American novelist, short-story writer, and essayist; Nobel Prize for Literature, 1978. His fiction, depicting Jewish life in Poland and the United States, blends irony, wit, and wisdom, flavored distinctively with the occult and the grotesque.

Dame Edith Sitwell (7 Sep 1887, Scarborough, Yorkshire, England–9 Dec 1964, London), English poet famed during her early career for her stylistic artifices and in later years for emotional depth and profoundly human concerns. She was equally renowned for her formidable personality, Elizabethan dress, and eccentric opinions.

Sophocles (c. 496 BCE, Colonus, near Athens, Greece–406 BCE, Athens), Greek playwright, one of classical Athens's three great tragic dramatists; his best-known works are *Oedipus Rex* and *Antigone*.

Wole Soyinka (13 Jul 1934, Abeokuta, Nigeria) Nigerian playwright, poet, novelist, and critic who received the Nobel Prize for Literature for 1986; he wrote of modern West Africa in a satirical style and with a tragic sense of the obstacles to human progress.

Edmund Spenser (1552/53, London, England–13 Jan 1599, London), English poet best known for his long allegorical poem, *The Faerie Queen,* considered one of the greatest in the English language.

John Steinbeck (27 Feb 1902, Salinas CA–20 Dec 1968, New York NY), American novelist, short-story writer, and playwright known for works that explore the bitterness of the Great Depression and for his humorous and tragic characters that populated California's Salinas Valley, the setting of most of his novels. Best-known works include *Of Mice and Men* (1937) and *The Grapes of Wrath* (1939).

Stendhal (Marie-Henri Beyle; 23 Jan 1783, Grenoble, France–23 Mar 1842, Paris), French writer, one of the most original and complex of the first half of the 19th century, chiefly known for his works of fiction, which include the novels *Le Rouge et la noir* (*The Red and the Black,* 1830) and *La Chartreuse de Parme* (*The Charterhouse of Parma,* 1839).

Laurence Sterne (24 Nov 1713, Clonmel, County Tipperary, Ireland–18 Mar 1768, London, England), English novelist and humorist, author of *Tristam Shandy* (1759–67), an early novel in which story is subordinate to the free associations and digressions of its narrator; also known for the novel *A Sentimental Journey* (1768).

Wallace Stevens (2 Oct 1879, Reading PA–2 Aug 1955, Hartford CT), American poet and insurance-firm vice president who was not recognized as a major poet until late in life. Stevens's best work explores the interaction of reality and what man can make of reality in his mind.

Sir Tom Stoppard (Tomas Straussler; 3 Jul 1937, Zlin, Czechoslovakia [now in Czech Republic]) Czech-born British playwright and screenplay writer whose work is marked by verbal brilliance, ingenious action, and structural dexterity.

Alfonsina Storni (29 May 1892, Sala Capriasca, Switzerland–25 Oct 1938, Mar del Plata, Argentina), Swiss-born Argentine poet known mainly for her simple, sensual, erotic poetry.

Harriet Beecher Stowe (née Harriet Elizabeth Beecher; 14 Jun 1811, Litchfield CT–1 Jul 1896, Hartford CT), American novelist who wrote *Uncle Tom's Cabin,* which contributed so much to popular feeling against slavery that it is cited among the causes of the American Civil War.

(Johan) August Strindberg (22 Jan 1849, Stockholm, Sweden–14 May 1912, Stockholm), Swedish playwright celebrated for combining psychology and Naturalism in a new kind of European drama that evolved into expressionist drama.

Jonathan Swift (Isaac Bickerstaff; 30 Nov 1667, Dublin, Ireland–19 Oct 1745, Dublin), Anglo-Irish novelist and journalist considered the foremost prose satirist in the English language and the author of *Gulliver's Travels* (1726) and the shorter works *A Tale of a Tub* (1704) and *A Modest Proposal* (1729).

Wislawa Szymborska (2 Jul 1923, Bnin [now in Kornik], near Poznan, Poland) Polish poet known for works that explore the philosophical, moral, and ethical issues with intelligence and empathy. In 1996 she received the Nobel Prize for Literature.

Rabindranath Tagore (Rabindranath Thakur; 7 May 1861, Calcutta, India–7 Aug 1941, Calcutta), Bengali poet, short-story writer, song composer, playwright, essayist, and painter regarded as the outstanding creative artist of modern India. Tagore introduced new prose and verse forms and the use of colloquial language into Bengali literature, thereby freeing it from traditional models based on classical Sanskrit; Nobel Prize for Literature, 1913.

Jun'ichiro Tanizaki (24 Jul 1886, Tokyo, Japan–30 Jul 1965, Yugawara), Japanese novelist, whose writing is characterized by eroticism and ironic wit and is often written in the manner of the Japanese classics, in particular the *Genji monogatari* (*Tales of Genji*), which he translated; Tanizaki's work has been characterized as a literary quest for "the eternal female."

Alfred, Lord Tennyson (Alfred, 1st Baron Tennyson of Aldworth and Freshwater; 6 Aug 1809, Somersby, Lincolnshire, England–6 Oct 1892, Aldworth, Surrey), English poet considered the chief representative of the Victorian age in poetry.

Dylan Thomas (27 Oct 1914, Swansea, Glamorgan, Wales–9 Nov 1953, New York NY), Welsh poet celebrated for both the comic exuberance, rhapsodic lilt, and pathos of his writing, as well as his somewhat reckless personal life.

James Thurber (8 Dec 1894, Columbus OH–2 Nov 1961, New York NY), American short-story writer, cartoonist, and playwright who humorously depicted the urban man as one who escapes into fantasy because he is befuddled and beset by a world he neither created nor understands.

J(ohn) R(onald) R(euel) Tolkien (3 Jan 1892, Bloemfontein, South Africa–2 Sep 1973, Bournemouth, Hampshire, England), English novelist renowned for his elaborate fantasy tales *The Hobbit* (1937) and the epic trilogy *The Lord of the Rings* (1954–55).

Leo Tolstoy (Lev Nikolayevich, Count [Graf] Tolstoy; 9 Sep [28 Aug, Old Style] 1828, Yasnaya Polyana, Tula province, Russia–20 Nov [7 Nov, Old Style] 1910, Astapovo, Ryazan province), Russian author, a master of realistic fiction widely regarded as one of history's most important novelists; his best-known works include *War and Peace* and *Anna Karenina.*

Anthony Trollope (24 Apr 1815, London, England–6 Dec 1882, London), English novelist best known for a series of books set in the imaginary English county of Barsetshire; he also wrote convincing novels of political life as well as studies that show great psychological penetration.

Tu Fu (Du Fu; 712, Hsiang-yang, now in Honan province, China–770, Hunan), Chinese poet considered by many to be the greatest poet of all time. His early poetry celebrated the beauties of the natural world and bemoaned the passage of time, and as he matured his verse began to sound a note of profound compassion for humanity caught in the toils of senseless war.

Mark Twain (Samuel L. Clemens; 30 Nov 1835, Florida MO—21 Apr 1910, Redding CT), American writer, humorist, and lecturer renowned for his use of colloquial language. *The Adventures of Huckleberry Finn* is regarded as perhaps the best and most influential novel in American literature.

Lope de Vega (25 Nov 1562, Madrid, Spain—27 Aug 1637, Madrid), Spanish playwright of the Golden Age, author of as many as 1,800 plays and several hundred shorter dramatic pieces.

Paul(-Marie) Verlaine (30 Mar 1844, Metz, France—8 Jan 1896, Paris), French lyric poet first associated with the Parnassians and later known as a leader of the Symbolists. With Stéphane Mallarmé and Charles Baudelaire he formed the so-called Decadents.

Jules Verne (8 Feb 1828, Nantes, France—24 Mar 1905, Amiens), French novelist who was a pioneer of modern science fiction. His works are marked by deft depictions of fantastic but nonetheless carefully conceived imaginary scientific wonders.

Gore Vidal (Eugene Luther Vidal; 3 Oct 1925, West Point NY) American novelist, playwright, and essayist known for his irreverent and intellectually adroit works, some of which vividly recreate prominent figures and events in American history.

Virgil (Vergil; 15 Oct 70 BCE, Andes, near Mantua, Italy—21 Sep 19 BCE, Brundisium), Roman poet best known for his unfinished national epic, the *Aeneid*.

Voltaire (François-Marie Arouet; 21 Nov 1694, Paris, France—30 May 1778, Paris), French writer who was an enormous influence on European civilization from the last years of classicism to the eve of the revolutionary era. A courageous crusader against bigotry, tyranny, and cruelty, known for his critical capactiy, wit, and satire.

Kurt Vonnegut, Jr. (11 Nov 1922, Indianapolis IN) American novelist and short-story writer noted for his pessimistic and satirical works that use fantasy and science fiction to highlight the horrors and ironies of 20th-century civilization.

Derek (Alton) Walcott (23 Jan 1930, Castries, Saint Lucia) West Indian poet and playwright noted for works that explore the Caribbean cultural experience; Nobel Prize for Literature, 1992.

H(erbert) G(eorge) Wells (21 Sep 1866, Bromley, Kent, England—13 Aug 1946, London), English novelist, journalist, sociologist, and historian known for classic science fiction and comic novels, many of which reflect the liberal optimism of the pre-World War I era.

Eudora Welty (13 Apr 1909, Jackson MS—23 Jul 2001, Jackson), American short-story writer and novelist known for her regional works of the Deep South and for her common themes that explore the subjectivity and ambiguity of people's perception of character and the presence of virtue hidden beneath an obscuring surface of convention, insensitivity, and social prejudice.

Edith Wharton (née Edith Newbold Jones; 24 Jan 1862, New York NY—11 Aug 1937, St.-Brice-sous-Forêt, near Paris, France), American short-story writer and novelist best known for her works about the upper-class society into which she was born.

E(lwyn) B(rooks) White (11 Jul 1899, Mount Vernon NY—1 Oct 1985, North Brooklin MN), American writer who was primarily an essayist and literary stylist, although he remains best remembered for his classic children's books *Stuart Little* (1945), *Charlotte's Web* (1952), and *The Trumpet of the Swan* (1970).

Walt Whitman (31 May 1819, West Hills, Long Island NY—26 Mar 1892, Camden NJ), American poet, journalist, and essayist known for his verse collection, *Leaves of Grass*, a landmark in American literature, which reflected Whitman's belief that a poet's chief function is to express his own personality.

Oscar Wilde (Oscar Fingal O'Flahertie Wills Wilde; 16 Oct 1854, Dublin, Ireland—30 Nov 1900, Paris), Irish dramatist, poet, and wit best known for the comic masterpieces *Lady Windermere's Fan* (1892) and *The Importance of Being Earnest* (1895). A spokesman for the late-19th century Aesthetic movement in England, and the object of celebrated criminal and civil suits involving homosexuality and ending in imprisonment (1895–97).

Tennessee Williams (Thomas Lanier Williams; 26 Mar 1911, Columbus MS—25 Feb 1983, New York NY), American playwright, perhaps the most prominent dramatist of the post-World War II era. His plays reveal a world of human frustration in which sex and violence underlie an atmosphere of romantic gentility.

William Carlos Williams (17 Sep 1883, Rutherford NJ—4 Mar 1963, Rutherford), American poet known for poems that reflected his direct impressions of the sensuous world, as well as his skill in making the ordinary appear extraordinary through the clarity and discreteness of his imagery.

August Wilson (27 Apr 1945, Pittsburgh PA) American playwright who created a cycle of plays, each set in a different decade of the 20th century, about black American life. He won Pulitzer Prizes for *Fences* (1986) and for *The Piano Lesson* (1990).

(Adeline) Virginia Woolf (25 Jan 1882, London, England—28 Mar 1941, near Rodmell, Sussex), British novelist who made an original contribution to the form of the novel and was one of the most distinguished critics of her time.

William Wordsworth (7 Apr 1770, Cockermouth, Cumberland, England—23 Apr 1850, Rydal Mount, Westmorland), English poet who was poet laureate of England, 1843–50. One of the major Romantics, known for highly personal poetry that broke the decorum of Neoclassical verse.

Richard Wright (4 Sep 1908, near Natchez MS—28 Nov 1960, Paris, France), American novelist and short-story writer who was among the first African American writers to protest white treatment of blacks, notably in his novel *Native Son* (1940) and his autobiography, *Black Boy* (1945). He inaugurated the tradition of protest explored by other African American writers after World War II.

William Butler Yeats (13 Jun 1865, Sandymount, Dublin, Ireland—28 Jan 1939, Roquebrune-Cap-Martin, France), Irish poet, dramatist, and prose writer whose early works were marked by a dreamlike atmosphere and their use of Irish folklore and legend, and whose later, highly complex poems explored the relation between history, imagination, mythology, and the occult. Recipient of the Nobel Prize in 1923.

Akiko Yosano (Ho Sho; 7 Dec 1878, near Osaka, Japan—29 May 1942, Tokyo), Japanese poet dubbed the "Poetess of Passion," celebrated for her unique tanka poetry; she was also an influential political and social reformer.

Émile Zola (2 Apr 1840, Paris, France—28 Sep 1902, Paris), French novelist, the most prominent French writer of the late 19th century, noted for his theories of naturalism that underlie his monumental 20-novel series *Les Rougon-Macquart*.

The Kennedy Center Honors

The Kennedy Center Honors are bestowed annually by the John F. Kennedy Center for the Performing Arts in Washington DC. First conferred in 1978, the honors salute five artists each year for lifetime achievement in the performing arts and are celebrated by a televised gala in December. Web site. <www.kennedy-center.org/programs/specialevents/honors/>.

YEAR	NAME	FIELD
1978	Marian Anderson	opera singer
	Fred Astaire	dancer, actor
	George Balanchine	choreographer
	Richard Rodgers	composer
	Arthur Rubenstein	pianist
1979	Aaron Copland	composer
	Ella Fitzgerald	singer
	Henry Fonda	actor
	Martha Graham	dancer, choreographer
	Tennessee Williams	playwright
1980	Leonard Bernstein	conductor
	James Cagney	actor
	Agnes de Mille	dancer, choreographer
	Lynn Fontanne	actress
	Leontyne Price	opera singer
1981	Count Basie	jazz pianist
	Cary Grant	actor
	Helen Hayes	actress
	Jerome Robbins	dancer, choreographer
	Rudolf Serkin	pianist
1982	George Abbott	theater producer, director, writer
	Lillian Gish	actress
	Benny Goodman	swing musician
	Gene Kelly	dancer, actor
	Eugene Ormandy	conductor
1983	Katherine Dunham	dancer, choreographer
	Elia Kazan	theater and film director
	Frank Sinatra	singer, actor
	James Stewart	actor
	Virgil Thomson	composer, music critic
1984	Lena Horne	singer, actress
	Danny Kaye	actor, comedian
	Gian Carlo Menotti	composer
	Arthur Miller	playwright
	Isaac Stern	violinist
1985	Merce Cunningham	dancer, choreographer
	Irene Dunne	actress
	Bob Hope	entertainer, actor
	Alan Jay Lerner	playwright, lyricist
	Frederick Loewe	composer
	Beverly Sills	opera singer
1986	Lucille Ball	actress
	Ray Charles	soul musician
	Hume Cronyn	actor
	Jessica Tandy	actress
	Yehudi Menuhin	violinist
	Antony Tudor	choreographer
1987	Perry Como	singer
	Bette Davis	actress
	Sammy Davis, Jr.	singer, dancer, entertainer
	Nathan Milstein	violinist
	Alwin Nikolais	choreographer
1988	Alvin Ailey	dancer, choreographer
	George Burns	actor, comedian

YEAR	NAME	FIELD
	Myrna Loy	actress
	Alexander Schneider	violinist, conductor
	Roger L. Stevens	arts administrator
1989	Harry Belafonte	folk singer, actor
	Claudette Colbert	actress
	Alexandra Danilova	ballet dancer
	Mary Martin	actress, singer
	William Schuman	composer
1990	Dizzy Gillespie	jazz musician
	Katharine Hepburn	actress
	Risë Stevens	opera singer
	Jule Styne	composer
	Billy Wilder	film director
1991	Roy Acuff	country musician
	Betty Comden	theater and film writer
	Adolph Green	theater and film writer
	Fayard Nicholas	dancer
	Harold Nicholas	dancer
	Gregory Peck	actor
	Robert Shaw	choral and orchestral conductor
1992	Lionel Hampton	swing musician
	Paul Newman	actor
	Joanne Woodward	actress
	Ginger Rogers	dancer, actress
	Mstislav Rostropovich	musician, conductor
	Paul Taylor	dancer, choreographer
1993	Johnny Carson	television entertainer
	Arthur Mitchell	dancer, choreographer
	George Solti	conductor
	Stephen Sondheim	composer, lyricist
	Marion Williams	gospel singer
1994	Kirk Douglas	actor
	Aretha Franklin	soul singer
	Morton Gould	composer
	Harold Prince	theater director, producer
	Pete Seeger	folk musician
1995	Jacques d'Amboise	dancer, choreographer
	Marilyn Horne	opera singer
	B.B. King	blues musician
	Sidney Poitier	actor
	Neil Simon	playwright
1996	Edward Albee	playwright
	Benny Carter	jazz musician
	Johnny Cash	country musician
	Jack Lemmon	actor
	Maria Tallchief	ballet dancer
1997	Lauren Bacall	actress
	Bob Dylan	singer, songwriter
	Charlton Heston	actor
	Jessye Norman	opera singer
	Edward Villella	dancer, choreographer
1998	Bill Cosby	actor, comedian
	Fred Ebb and John Kander	lyricist and composer

The Kennedy Center Honors (continued)

YEAR	NAME	FIELD
	Willie Nelson	country musician
	André Previn	pianist, composer, conductor
	Shirley Temple Black	actress
1999	Victor Borge	pianist, comedian
	Sean Connery	actor
	Judith Jamison	dancer, choreographer
	Jason Robards	actor
	Stevie Wonder	musician
2000	Mikhail Baryshnikov	dancer

YEAR	NAME	FIELD
	Chuck Berry	musician
	Plácido Domingo	opera singer
	Clint Eastwood	actor, director
	Angela Lansbury	actress
2001	Julie Andrews	actress
	Van Cliburn	pianist
	Quincy Jones	music producer, composer
	Jack Nicholson	actor
	Luciano Pavarotti	opera singer

The National Medal of Arts

The National Medal of Arts, awarded annually since 1985 by the National Endowment for the Arts (NEA) and the president of the United States, honors artists and art patrons for remarkable contributions to American arts. As many as 12 medals may be given out each year. Both the NEA and the president choose candidates for the award, and the winners are selected by the president. Web sites: <www.arts.gov/guide/allmedalists.html> and <www.arts.endow.gov/endownews/news00/MedalsFacts.html>.

YEAR	NAME	FIELD
1985	Elliott Carter, Jr.	composer
	Ralph Ellison	writer
	José Ferrer	actor
	Martha Graham	dancer, choreographer
	Louise Nevelson	sculptor
	Georgia O'Keeffe	painter
	Leontyne Price	opera singer
	Dorothy Buffum Chandler	patron
	Lincoln Kirstein	patron
	Paul Mellon	patron
	Alice Tully	patron
	Hallmark Cards, Inc.	patron
1986	Marian Anderson	opera singer
	Frank Capra	film director
	Aaron Copland	composer
	Willem de Kooning	painter
	Agnes de Mille	dancer, choreographer
	Eva Le Gallienne	actress, theater producer
	Alan Lomax	ethnomusicologist
	Lewis Mumford	architectural critic, historian
	Eudora Welty	writer
	Dominique de Menil	patron
	Exxon Corporation	patron
	Seymour H. Knox	patron
1987	Romare Bearden	painter
	Ella Fitzgerald	singer
	Howard Nemerov	writer, scholar
	Alwin Nikolais	choreographer
	Isamu Noguchi	sculptor
	William Schuman	composer
	Robert Penn Warren	writer
	J.W. Fisher	patron
	Armand Hammer	patron
	Sydney and Frances Lewis	patrons
1988	Saul Bellow	writer
	Helen Hayes	actress
	Gordon Parks	photographer, writer
	I.M. Pei	architect
	Jerome Robbins	dancer, choreographer
	Rudolf Serkin	pianist
	Virgil Thomson	composer, music critic

YEAR	NAME	FIELD
	Sydney J. Freedberg	art historian, museum curator
	Roger L. Stevens	arts administrator
	Brooke Astor	patron
	Francis Goelet	patron
	Obert C. Tanner	patron
1989	Leopold Adler	historic preservationist, civic leader
	Katherine Dunham	dancer, choreographer
	Alfred Eisenstaedt	photojournalist
	Martin Friedman	museum director
	Leigh Gerdine	civic leader, patron
	Dizzy Gillespie	jazz musician
	Walker Kirtland Hancock	sculptor
	Vladimir Horowitz*	pianist
	Czelaw Milosz	writer
	Robert Motherwell	painter
	John Updike	writer
	Dayton Hudson Corporation	patron
1990	George Abbott	theater producer, director, writer
	Hume Cronyn	actor, director
	Jessica Tandy	actress
	Merce Cunningham	dancer, choreographer
	Jasper Johns	painter, sculptor
	Jacob Lawrence	painter
	B.B. King	blues musician
	Beverly Sills	opera singer
	Ian McHarg	landscape architect
	Harris & Carroll Sterling Masterson	patrons
	David Lloyd Kreeger	patron
	Southeastern Bell Corporation	patron
1991	Maurice Abravanel	conductor, music director
	Roy Acuff	country musician
	Pietro Belluschi	architect
	J. Carter Brown	museum director
	Charles "Honi" Coles	tap dancer
	John O. Crosby	opera director, conductor
	Richard Diebenkorn	painter

The National Medal of Arts (continued)

YEAR	NAME	FIELD	YEAR	NAME	FIELD
	Isaac Stern	violinist		Sarah Caldwell	opera conductor, producer
	Kitty Carlisle Hart	actress, singer, arts administrator		Harry Callahan	photographer
	Pearl Primus	choreographer, anthropologist		Zelda Fichandler	theater founder, director
	R. Philip Hanes, Jr.	patron		Eduardo "Lalo" Guerrero	Chicano musician
	Texaco Inc.	patron		Lionel Hampton	swing musician
1992	Marilyn Horne	opera singer		Bella Lewitzky	dancer, choreographer
	James Earl Jones	actor		Robert Redford	actor, film director
	Allan Houser	sculptor		Maurice Sendak	illustrator, writer
	Minnie Pearl	Grand Ole Opry performer		Stephen Sondheim	composer, lyricist
				Boys Choir of Harlem	youth performance group
	Robert Saudek	television producer, museum director		Vera List	patron
	Earl Scruggs	banjo player	1997	Louise Bourgeois	sculptor
	Robert Shaw	choral and orchestral conductor		Betty Carter	jazz singer
	Billy Taylor	jazz pianist		Daniel Urban Kiley	landscape architect
	Robert Venturi and Denise Scott Brown	architects		Angela Lansbury	actress
				James Levine	opera conductor, pianist
	Robert Wise	film director			
	AT&T	patron		Tito Puente	jazz and mambo musician
	Lila Wallace-Reader's Digest Fund	patron		Jason Robards	actor
1993	Cabell "Cab" Calloway	jazz musician		Edward Villella	dancer, choreographer
				Doc Watson	folk and country musician
	Ray Charles	soul musician			
	Bess Lomax Hawes	folklorist, musician		MacDowell Colony	artists' colony
	Stanley Kunitz	poet		Agnes Gund	patron
	Robert Merrill	opera singer	1998	Jacques d'Amboise	dancer, choreographer
	Arthur Miller	playwright		Antoine "Fats" Domino	rock-and-roll musician
	Robert Rauschenberg	painter		Ramblin' Jack Elliott	folk musician
	Lloyd Richards	theater director		Frank O. Gehry	architect
	William Styron	writer		Agnes Martin	painter
	Paul Taylor	dancer, choreographer		Gregory Peck	actor
	Billy Wilder	film director, producer, writer		Roberta Peters	opera singer
				Philip Roth	writer
	Walter and Leonore Annenberg	patrons		Gwen Verdon	actress, dancer
1994	Harry Belafonte	folk singer, actor		Steppenwolf Theatre Company	arts organization
	Dave Brubeck	jazz musician		Sara Lee Corporation	patron
	Celia Cruz	salsa singer		Barbara Handman	patron
	Dorothy DeLay	violin instructor	1999	Aretha Franklin	soul singer
	Julie Harris	actress		Michael Graves	architect, designer
	Erick Hawkins	dancer, choreographer		Odetta	folk singer
	Gene Kelly	dancer, actor		Norman Lear	television producer, writer
	Pete Seeger	folk musician			
	Wayne Thiebaud	painter		Rosetta LeNoire	actress, theater founder
	Richard Wilbur	poet			
	Young Audiences	arts organization		Harvey Lichtenstein	arts administrator
	Catherine Filene Shouse	patron		Lydia Mendoza	Tejano musician
				George Segal	sculptor
1995	Licia Albanese	opera singer		Maria Tallchief	ballet dancer
	Gwendolyn Brooks	poet		The Juilliard School	performing arts school
	Ossie Davis and Ruby Dee	actors		Irene Diamond	patron
	David Diamond	composer	2000	Maya Angelou	poet, writer
	James Ingo Freed	architect		Eddy Arnold	country musician
	Bob Hope	entertainer		Mikhail Baryshnikov	dancer, dance company director
	Roy Lichtenstein	painter			
	Arthur Mitchell	dancer, choreographer		Benny Carter	jazz musician
	William S. Monroe	bluegrass musician		Chuck Close	painter
	Urban Gateways	arts education organization		Horton Foote	dramatist
				Claes Oldenburg	sculptor
	B. Gerald and Iris Cantor	patrons		Itzhak Perlman	violinist
1996	Edward Albee	playwright		Harold Prince	theater director, producer

The National Medal of Arts (continued)

YEAR	NAME	FIELD	YEAR	NAME	FIELD
	Barbra Streisand	singer, actress, film director		Rudolfo Anaya	writer
	National Public Radio, Cultural Programming Division	broadcaster		Johnny Cash	country musician
				Kirk Douglas	actor
				Helen Frankenthaler	painter
	Lewis Manilow	patron		Judith Jamison	dancer, choreographer
2001	Alvin Ailey Dance Foundation	modern dance company and school		Yo-Yo Ma	cellist
				Mike Nichols	theater and film director

Awarded posthumously.

Pritzker Architecture Prize

The Pritzker Prize, awarded by the Hyatt Foundation since 1979, is given to an outstanding living architect for built work. Prize amount: $100,000. Web site: <www.pritzkerprize.com>.

YEAR	NAME	COUNTRY	YEAR	NAME	COUNTRY
1979	Philip Johnson	United States	1992	Alvaro Siza	Portugal
1980	Luis Barragan	Mexico	1993	Fumihiko Maki	Japan
1981	James Stirling	Great Britain	1994	Christian de Portzamparc	France
1982	Kevin Roche	United States			
1983	Ieoh Ming Pei	United States	1995	Tadao Ando	Japan
1984	Richard Meier	United States	1996	Rafael Moneo	Spain
1985	Hans Hollein	Austria	1997	Sverre Fehn	Norway
1986	Gottfried Boehm	West Germany	1998	Renzo Piano	Italy
1987	Kenzo Tange	Japan	1999	Sir Norman Foster	Great Britain
1988	Gordon Bunshaft	United States	2000	Rem Koolhaas	The Netherlands
	Oscar Niemeyer	Brazil	2001	Jacques Herzog	Switzerland
1989	Frank O. Gehry	United States		Pierre de Meuron	Switzerland
1990	Aldo Rossi	Italy	2002	Glenn Murcutt	Australia
1991	Robert Venturi	United States			

AIA Gold Medal

The American Institute of Architects awards the gold medal for an outstanding body of work.

YEAR	NAME	YEAR	NAME	YEAR	NAME
1907	Sir Aston Webb	1953	William Adams Delano	1977	Richard Joseph Neutra*
1909	Charles Follen McKim	1955	Willem Marinus Dudok	1978	Philip C. Johnson
1911	George Browne Post	1956	Clarence S. Stein	1979	Ieoh Ming Pei
1914	Jean Louis Pascal	1957	Ralph Walker	1981	José Luis Sert
1922	Victor Laloux		Louis Skidmore	1982	Romaldo Giurgola
1923	Henry Bacon	1958	John Wellborn Root*	1983	Nathaniel A. Owings
1925	Sir Edwin Landseer Lutyens	1959	Walter Gropius	1985	William Wayne Caudill*
		1960	Ludwig Mies van der Rohe	1986	Arthur Erickson
	Bertram Grosvenor Goodhue*	1961	Le Corbusier (Charles-Édouard Jeanneret)	1989	Joseph Esherick
				1990	E. Fay Jones
1927	Howard Van Doren Shaw	1962	Eero Saarinen*	1991	Charles W. Moore
1929	Milton Bennett Medary	1963	Alvar Aalto	1992	Benjamin Thompson
1933	Ragnar Ostberg	1964	Pier Luigi Nervi	1993	Thomas Jefferson*
1938	Paul Philippe Cret	1966	Kenzo Tange		Kevin Roche
1944	Louis Henry Sullivan*	1967	Wallace K. Harrison	1994	Sir Norman Foster
1947	Eliel Saarinen	1968	Marcel Breuer	1995	César Pelli
1948	Charles Donagh Maginnis	1969	William Wilson Wurster	1997	Richard Meier
1949	Frank Lloyd Wright	1970	Richard Buckminster Fuller	1999	Frank O. Gehry
1950	Sir Patrick Abercrombie			2000	Ricardo Legorreta
1951	Bernard Ralph Maybeck	1971	Louis I. Kahn	2001	Michael Graves
1952	Auguste Perret	1972	Pietro Belluschi	2002	Tadao Ando

Awarded posthumously.

American Academy of Arts and Letters Awards, 2002

Each year the American Academy of Arts and Letters, a 250-member organization founded in 1898, confers some two dozen awards for excellence in the fields of art, music, literature, and architecture. Of the prizes, the Academy Awards in each field are the most prestigious. Winners receive $7,500; music winners receive an additional $7,500 to be used for the recording of a musical piece. The recipients for 2002 were as follows: ▶ **Art**, Polly Apfelbaum, Mel Kendrick, Lucas Samaras, Peter Saul, and Stephen Westfall; ▶ **Architecture**, Rick Joy and Office dA (Monica Ponce de Leon and Nader Tehrani); ▶ **Literature**, Benson Bobrick, Christopher Durang, Linda Gregerson, Tony Hoagland, Charles Johnson, Stanley Plumly, James Richardson, and Alan Shapiro; ▶ **Music**, Claude Baker, Daniel Docker, David Liptak, and Cindy McTee.

Science Awards

Fields Medal

The Fields Medal, officially known as the International Medal for Outstanding Discoveries in Mathematics, is granted every four years to between two and four mathematicians for outstanding or groundbreaking research. It is traditionally given to mathematicians under the age of 40. Prize; $1,500.

YEAR	NAME	BIRTHPLACE	PRIMARY RESEARCH
1936	Lars Ahlfors	Helsinki, Finland	Riemann surfaces
1936	Jesse Douglas	New York NY	Plateau problem
1950	Laurent Schwartz	Paris, France	functional analysis
1950	Atle Selberg	Langesund, Norway	number theory
1954	Kunihiko Kodaira	Tokyo, Japan	algebraic geometry
1954	Jean-Pierre Serre	Bages, France	algebraic topology
1958	Klaus Roth	Breslau, Germany	number theory
1958	René Thom	Montbéliard, France	topology
1962	Lars Hörmander	Mjällby, Sweden	partial differential equations
1962	John Milnor	Orange NJ	differential topology
1966	Michael Atiyah	London, England	topology
1966	Paul Cohen	Long Branch NJ	set theory
1966	Alexandre Grothendieck	Berlin, Germany	algebraic geometry
1966	Stephen Smale	Flint MI	topology
1970	Alan Baker	London, England	number theory
1970	Heisuke Hironaka	Yamaguchi prefecture, Japan	algebraic geometry
1970	Sergey Novikov	Gorky, Russia	topology
1970	John Thompson	Ottawa KS	group theory
1974	Enrico Bombieri	Milan, Italy	number theory
1974	David Mumford	Worth, Sussex, UK	algebraic geometry
1978	Pierre Deligne	Brussels, Belgium	algebraic geometry
1978	Charles Fefferman	Washington DC	classical analysis
1978	Gregory Margulis	Moscow, Russia	Lie groups
1978	Daniel Quillen	Orange NJ	algebraic K-theory
1983	Alain Connes	Darguignan, France	operator theory
1983	William Thurston	Washington DC	topology
1983	Ching-Tung Yau	Swatow, China	differential geometry
1986	Simon Donaldson	Cambridge, UK	topology
1986	Gerd Faltings	Gelsenkirchen, West Germany	Mordell conjecture
1986	Michael Freedman	Los Angeles CA	Poincaré conjecture
1990	Vladimir Drinfeld	Kharkov, Ukraine	algebraic geometry
1990	Vaughan Jones	Gisborne, New Zealand	knot theory
1990	Shigefumi Mori	Nagoya, Japan	algebraic geometry
1990	Edward Witten	Baltimore MD	superstring theory
1994	Jean Bourgain	Ostend, Belgium	analysis
1994	Pierre-Louis Lions	Grasse, France	partial differential equations
1994	Jean-Christophe Yoccoz	France	dynamical systems
1994	Yefim Zelmanov	Khabarovsk, Russia	group theory
1998	Richard Borcherds	Cape Town, South Africa	mathematical physics
1998	William Gowers	Marlborough, Wiltshire, UK	functional analysis
1998	Maksim Kontsevich	Khimki, Russia	mathematical physics
1998	Curt McMullen	Berkeley CA	chaos theory
2002	Laurent Lafforgue	Antony, France	number theory and analysis
	Vladimir Voevodsky	Russia	algebraic geometry

National Medal of Science

The National Medal of Science was established by Congress in 1959. Awarded annually since 1962 by the National Science Foundation and the president of the United States, it recognizes notable achievements in mathematics, engineering, and the physical, natural, and social sciences. A presidentially-appointed committee selects the winners from a pool of nominees. For more information, see the National Science Foundation Web site at <www.nsf.gov/nsb/awards/nms/start.htm>

YEAR	NAME	FIELD
1962	Theodore von Karman	aerospace engineering
1963	Luis W. Alvarez	physics
	Vannevar Bush	electrical engineering
	John Robinson Pierce	communications engineering
	Cornelius Barnardus van Niel	biology
	Norbert Wiener	mathematics
1964	Roger Adams	chemistry
	Othmar Herman Ammann	bridge design engineering
	Theodosius Dobzhansky	genetics
	Charles Stark Draper	aerospace engineering
	Solomon Lefschetz	mathematics
	Neal Elgar Miller	psychology
	H. Marston Morse	mathematics
	Marshall Warren Nirenberg	biochemistry
	Julian Seymour Schwinger	physics
	Harold C. Urey	chemistry
	Robert Burns Woodward	chemistry
1965	John Bardeen	physics
	Peter J.W. Debye	physical chemistry
	Hugh L. Dryden	physics
	Clarence L. Johnson	aerospace engineering
	Leon M. Lederman	physics
	Warren K. Lewis	chemical engineering
	Francis Peyton Rous	pathology
	William W. Rubey	geology
	George Gaylord Simpson	paleontology
	Donald D. Van Slyke	chemistry
	Oscar Zariski	mathematics
1966	Jacob A.B. Bjerknes	meteorology
	Subrahmanyan Chandrasekhar	astrophysics
	Henry Eyring	chemistry
	Edward F. Knipling	entomology
	Fritz Albert Lipmann	biochemistry
	John Willard Milnor	mathematics
	William C. Rose	biochemistry
	Claude E. Shannon	mathematics, electrical engineering
	John H. Van Vleck	physics
	Sewall Wright	genetics
	Vladimir Kosma Zworykin	electrical engineering
1967	Jesse W. Beams	physics
	Francis Birch	geophysics
	Gregory Breit	physics
	Paul Joseph Cohen	mathematics
	Kenneth S. Cole	biophysics
	Louis P. Hammett	chemistry
	Harry F. Harlow	psychology
	Michael Heidelberger	immunology

YEAR	NAME	FIELD
	George B. Kistiakowsky	chemistry
	Edwin Herbert Land	physics
	Igor I. Sikorsky	aircraft design
	Alfred H. Sturtevant	genetics
1968	Horace A. Barker	biochemistry
	Paul D. Bartlett	chemistry
	Bernard B. Brodie	pharmacology
	Detlev W. Bronk	biophysics
	J. Presper Eckert, Jr.	engineering, computer science
	Herbert Friedman	astrophysics
	Jay L. Lush	livestock genetics
	Nathan M. Newmark	civil engineering
	Jerzy Neyman	mathematics, statistics
	Lars Onsager	chemistry
	B.F. Skinner	psychology
	Eugene Paul Wigner	mathematical physics
1969	Herbert C. Brown	chemistry
	William Feller	mathematics
	Robert J. Huebner	virology
	Jack Kilby	electrical engineering
	Ernst Mayr	biology
	Wolfgang K.H. Panofsky	physics
1970	Richard Dagobert Brauer	mathematics
	Robert H. Dicke	physics
	Barbara McClintock	genetics
	George E. Mueller	physics
	Albert Bruce Sabin	medicine, vaccine development
	Allan R. Sandage	astronomy
	John C. Slater	physics
	John Archibald Wheeler	physics
	Saul Winstein	chemistry
1971	no awards given	
1972	no awards given	
1973	Daniel I. Arnon	biochemistry
	Carl Djerassi	chemistry
	Harold E. Edgerton	electrical engineering, photography
	Maurice Ewing	geophysics
	Arie Jan Haagen-Smit	biochemistry
	Vladimir Haensel	chemical engineering
	Frederick Seitz	physics
	Earl W. Sutherland, Jr.	biochemistry
	John Wilder Tukey	statistics
	Richard T. Whitcomb	aerospace engineering
	Robert Rathbun Wilson	particle physics
1974	Nicolaas Bloembergen	physics
	Britton Chance	biophysics
	Erwin Chargaff	biochemistry
	Paul J. Flory	physical chemistry
	William A. Fowler	nuclear astrophysics
	Kurt Gödel	mathematics

National Medal of Science (continued)

YEAR	NAME	FIELD
	Rudolf Kompfner	physics
	James Van Gundia Neel	genetics
	Linus Pauling	chemistry
	Ralph Brazelton Peck	geotechnical engineering
	Kenneth Sanborn Pitzer	physical chemistry
	James Augustine Shannon	physiology
	Abel Wolman	sanitary engineering
1975	John W. Backus	computer science
	Manson Benedict	nuclear engineering
	Hans Albrecht Bethe	theoretical physics
	Shiing-shen Chern	mathematics
	George B. Dantzig	mathematics
	Hallowell Davis	physiology
	Paul Gyorgy	medicine, vitamin research
	Sterling Brown Hendricks	chemistry
	Joseph O. Hirschfelder	chemistry
	William Hayward Pickering	physics
	Lewis H. Sarett	chemistry
	Frederick Emmons Terman	electrical engineering
	Orville Alvin Vogel	research agronomy
	Wernher von Braun	aerospace engineering
	E. Bright Wilson, Jr.	chemistry
	Chien-Shiung Wu	physics
1970	Morris Cohen	materials science
	Kurt Otto Friedrichs	mathematics
	Peter C. Goldmark	communications engineering
	Samuel Abraham Goudsmit	physics
	Roger Charles Louis Guillemin	physiology
	Herbert S. Gutowsky	chemistry
	Erwin W. Mueller	physics
	Keith Roberts Porter	cell biology
	Efraim Racker	biochemistry
	Frederick D. Rossini	chemistry
	Verner E. Suomi	meteorology
	Henry Taube	chemistry
	George Eugene Uhlenbeck	physics
	Hassler Whitney	mathematics
	Edward O. Wilson	biology
1977	no awards given	
1978	no awards given	
1979	Robert H. Burris	biochemistry
	Elizabeth C. Crosby	neuroanatomy
	Joseph L. Doob	mathematics
	Richard P. Feynman	theoretical physics
	Donald E. Knuth	computer science
	Arthur Kornberg	biochemistry
	Emmett N. Leith	electrical engineering
	Herman F. Mark	chemistry
	Raymond D. Mindlin	mechanical engineering
	Robert N. Noyce	computer science
	Severo Ochoa	biochemistry
	Earl R. Parker	materials science
	Edward M. Purcell	physics
	Simon Ramo	electrical engineering

YEAR	NAME	FIELD
	John H. Sinfelt	chemical engineering
	Lyman Spitzer, Jr.	astrophysics
	Earl Reece Stadtman	biochemistry
	George Ledyard Stebbins	botany, genetics
	Victor F. Weisskopf	physics
	Paul Alfred Weiss	biology
1980	no awards given	
1981	Philip Handler	biochemistry
1982	Philip W. Anderson	physics
	Seymour Benzer	molecular biology
	Glenn W. Burton	genetics
	Mildred Cohn	biochemistry
	F. Albert Cotton	chemistry
	Edward H. Heinemann	aerospace engineering
	Donald L. Katz	chemical engineering
	Yoichiro Nambu	theoretical physics
	Marshall H. Stone	mathematics
	Gilbert Stork	organic chemistry
	Edward Teller	nuclear physics
	Charles Hard Townes	physics
1983	Howard L. Bachrach	biochemistry
	Paul Berg	biochemistry
	E. Margaret Burbidge	astronomy
	Maurice Goldhaber	physics
	Herman H. Goldstine	computer science
	William R. Hewlett	electrical engineering
	Roald Hoffmann	chemistry
	Helmut E. Landsberg	climatology
	George M. Low	aerospace engineering
	Walter H. Munk	oceanography
	George C. Pimentel	chemistry
	Frederick Reines	physics
	Wendell L. Roelofs	chemistry, entomology
	Bruno B. Rossi	astrophysics
	Berta V. Scharrer	neuroscience
	John Robert Schrieffer	physics
	Isadore M. Singer	mathematics
	John G. Trump	electrical engineering
	Richard N. Zare	chemistry
1984	no awards given	
1985	no awards given	
1986	Solomon J. Buchsbaum	physics
	Stanley Cohen	biochemistry
	Horace R. Crane	physics
	Herman Feshbach	physics
	Harry Gray	chemistry
	Donald A. Henderson	medicine, public health
	Robert Hofstadter	physics
	Peter D. Lax	mathematics
	Yuan Tseh Lee	chemistry
	Hans Wolfgang Liepmann	aerospace engineering
	T.Y. Lin	civil engineering
	Carl S. Marvel	chemistry
	Vernon B. Mountcastle	neurophysiology
	Bernard M. Oliver	electrical engineering
	George Emil Palade	cell biology
	Herbert A. Simon	social science
	Joan A. Steitz	molecular biology
	Frank H. Westheimer	chemistry
	Chen Ning Yang	theoretical physics

National Medal of Science (continued)

YEAR	NAME	FIELD
	Antoni Zygmund	mathematics
1987	Philip Hauge Abelson	physical chemistry
	Anne Anastasi	psychology
	Robert Byron Bird	chemical engineering
	Raoul Bott	mathematics
	Michael E. DeBakey	heart surgery
	Theodor O. Diener	plant pathology
	Harry Eagle	cell biology
	Walter M. Elsasser	physics
	Michael H. Freedman	mathematics
	William S. Johnson	chemistry
	Har Gobind Khorana	biochemistry
	Paul C. Lauterbur	chemistry
	Rita Levi-Montalcini	neurology
	George E. Pake	research, physics
	H. Bolton Seed	civil engineering
	George J. Stigler	economics
	Walter H. Stockmayer	chemistry
	Max Tishler	chemistry
	James Alfred Van Allen	physics
	Ernst Weber	electrical engineering
1988	William O. Baker	chemistry
	Konrad E. Bloch	biochemistry
	David Allan Bromley	physics
	Michael S. Brown	molecular genetics
	Paul C.W. Chu	physics
	Stanley N. Cohen	genetics
	Elias James Corey	chemistry
	Daniel C. Drucker	engineering education
	Milton Friedman	economics
	Joseph L. Goldstein	molecular genetics
	Ralph E. Gomory	mathematics, research
	Willis M. Hawkins	aerospace engineering
	Maurice R. Hilleman	vaccine research
	George W. Housner	earthquake engineering
	Eric Kandel	neurobiology
	Joseph B. Keller	mathematics
	Walter Kohn	physics
	Norman Foster Ramsey	physics
	Jack Steinberger	physics
	Rosalyn S. Yalow	medical physics
1989	Arnold O. Beckman	chemistry
	Richard B. Bernstein	chemistry
	Melvin Calvin	biochemistry
	Harry G. Drickamer	chemistry, physics
	Katherine Esau	botany
	Herbert E. Grier	aerospace engineering
	Viktor Hamburger	biology
	Samuel Karlin	mathematics
	Philip Leder	genetics
	Joshua Lederberg	genetics
	Saunders Mac Lane	mathematics
	Rudolph A. Marcus	chemistry
	Harden M. McConnell	chemistry
	Eugene N. Parker	theoretical astrophysics
	Robert P. Sharp	geology
	Donald C. Spencer	mathematics
	Roger Wolcott Sperry	neurobiology
	Henry M. Stommel	oceanography
	Harland G. Wood	biochemistry

YEAR	NAME	FIELD
1990	Baruj Benacerraf	pathology, immunology
	Elkan R. Blout	chemistry
	Herbert W. Boyer	biochemistry, genetics
	George F. Carrier	mathematics
	Allan MacLeod Cormack	physics
	Mildred S. Dresselhaus	physics
	Karl August Folkers	chemistry
	Nick Holonyak, Jr.	electrical engineering
	Leonid Hurwicz	economics
	Stephen Cole Kleene	mathematics
	Daniel E. Koshland, Jr.	biochemistry
	Edward B. Lewis	developmental genetics
	John McCarthy	computer science
	Edwin Mattison McMillan	nuclear physics
	David G. Nathan	pediatrics
	Robert V. Pound	physics
	Roger R.D. Revelle	oceanography
	John D. Roberts	chemistry
	Patrick Suppes	philosophy and statistics education
	E. Donnall Thomas	medicine
1991	Mary Ellen Avery	pediatrics
	Ronald Breslow	chemistry
	Alberto P. Calderon	mathematics
	Gertrude B. Elion	pharmacology
	George H. Heilmeier	electrical engineering
	Dudley R. Herschbach	chemistry
	G. Evelyn Hutchinson	zoology
	Elvin A. Kabat	immunology
	Robert W. Kates	geography
	Luna B. Leopold	hydrology, geology
	Salvador Luria	biology
	Paul A. Marks	hematology, cancer research
	George A. Miller	psychology
	Arthur L. Schawlow	physics
	Glenn T. Seaborg	nuclear chemistry
	Folke K. Skoog	botany
	H. Guyford Stever	aerospace engineering
	Edward C. Stone	physics
	Steven Weinberg	nuclear physics
	Paul C. Zamecnik	molecular biology
1992	Eleanor J. Gibson	psychology
	Allen Newell	computer science
	Calvin F. Quate	electrical engineering
	Eugene M. Shoemaker	planetary geology
	Howard E. Simmons, Jr.	chemistry
	Maxine F. Singer	biochemistry, administration
	Howard Martin Temin	virology
	John Roy Whinnery	electrical engineering
1993	Alfred Y. Cho	electrical engineering
	Donald J. Cram	chemistry
	Val Logsdon Fitch	particle physics
	Norman Hackerman	chemistry
	Martin D. Kruskal	mathematics
	Daniel Nathans	microbiology

National Medal of Science (continued)

YEAR	NAME	FIELD	YEAR	NAME	FIELD
	Vera C. Rubin	astronomy		George M. Whitesides	chemistry
	Salome G. Waelsch	molecular genetics		William Julius Wilson	sociology
1994	Ray W. Clough	civil engineering	1999	David Baltimore	virology, administra-
	John Cocke	computer science			tion
	Thomas Eisner	chemical ecology		Felix E. Browder	mathematics
	George S. Hammond	chemistry		Ronald R. Coifman	mathematics
	Robert K. Merton	sociology		James Watson Cronin	particle physics
	Elizabeth F. Neufeld	biochemistry		Jared Diamond	physiology
	Albert W. Overhauser	physics		Leo P. Kadanoff	theoretical physics
	Frank Press	geophysics, adminis-		Lynn Margulis	microbiology
		tration		Stuart A. Rice	chemistry
1995	Thomas Robert Cech	biochemistry		John Ross	chemistry
	Hans Georg Dehmelt	physics		Susan Solomon	atmospheric science
	Peter M. Goldreich	astrophysics		Robert M. Solow	economics
	Hermann A. Haus	electrical engineering		Kenneth N. Stevens	electrical engineer-
	Isabella L. Karle	chemistry			ing, speech
	Louis Nirenberg	mathematics	2000	Nancy C. Andreasen	psychiatry
	Alexander Rich	molecular biology		John D. Baldeschwieler	chemistry
	Roger N. Shepard	psychology		wieler	
1996	Wallace S. Broecker	geochemistry		Gary S. Becker	economics
	Norman Davidson	chemistry, molecular		Yuan-Cheng B. Fung	bioengineering
		biology		Ralph F. Hirschmann	chemistry
	James L. Flanagan	electrical engineering		Willis Eugene Lamb,	physics
	Richard M. Karp	computer science		Jr.	
	C. Kumar N. Patel	electrical engineering		Jeremiah P. Ostriker	astrophysics
	Ruth Patrick	limnology		Peter H. Raven	botany
	Paul Samuelson	economics		John Griggs Thomp-	mathematics
	Stephen Smale	mathematics		son	
1997	William K. Estes	psychology		Karen K. Uhlenbeck	mathematics
	Darleane C. Hoffman	chemistry		Gilbert F. White	geography
	Harold S. Johnston	chemistry		Carl R. Woese	microbiology
	Marshall N. Rosen-	theoretical plasma	2001	Andreas Acrivos	chemical engineering
	bluth	physics		Francisco J. Ayala	molecular biology
	Martin Schwarzschild	astrophysics		George F. Bass	nautical archaeology
	James Dewey Watson	genetics, biophysics		Mario R. Capecchi	genetics
	Robert A. Weinberg	biology, cancer		Marvin I. Cohen	materials science
		research		Ernest R. Davidson	chemistry
	George W. Wetherill	planetary science		Raymond Davis, Jr.	chemistry, astro-
	Shing-Tung Yau	mathematics			physics
1998	Bruce N. Ames	biochemistry, cancer		Ann M. Graybiel	neuroscience
		research		Charles D. Keeling	oceanography
	Don L. Anderson	geophysics		Gene E. Likens	ecology
	John N. Bahcall	astrophysics		Victor A. McKusick	medical genetics
	John W. Cahn	materials science		Calyampudi R. Rao	mathematics, statis-
	Cathleen Synge	mathematics			tics
	Morawetz			Gabor A. Somorjai	chemistry
	Janet D. Rowley	medicine, cancer		Elias M. Stein	mathematics
		research		Harold Varmus	virology, administra-
	Eli Ruckenstein	chemical engineering			tion

The National Inventor of the Year Award

The National Inventor of the Year Award is given by the Intellectual Property Owners Association, a trade organization established in 1972. Patented American inventions from the preceding four years are eligible for nomination annually; runners-up receive recognition as Distinguished Inventors. The winners for 2002 were 10 scientists from Eli Lilly and Co. who invented Xigris, a drug that combats severe sepsis. The winners were: Robert J. Beckmann, Nils U. Bang, Brian W. Grinnell, Daniel L. Hartman, Richard Jaskunas, Mei-Hui T. Lai, Sheila Little, George L. Long, Robert F. Santerre, and Sau-Chi Betty Yan. Award amount: $5,000. Web site: <www.ipo.org/IOY.html>

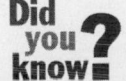

Did you know? Among the inventions attributed to women are bulletproof vests, windshield wipers, fire escapes, and laser printers.

Intel Science Talent Search

The Intel Science Talent Search encourages American high school seniors to pursue careers in the sciences by awarding scholarships for outstanding science projects. Created in 1942 by Science Service, a nonprofit organization devoted to public appreciation of science, and Westinghouse Electric Corporation, the contest brings 40 finalists each year to exhibit their projects at the Science Talent Institute in Washington DC, and compete for the top prizes. Since 1998 the talent search has been sponsored by Intel Corporation. The highest-place winners for 2002 were **Ryan Patterson** of Grand Junction CO (first prize, $100,000), **Jacob Licht** of West Hartford CT (second prize, $75,000), and **Emily Riehl** of Bloomington IL (third prize, $50,000). For more information see <www.sciserv.org/sts>.

Patterson invented a glove to translate American Sign Language into text on a portable screen. Sensors in the glove record the person's hand movements, and a transmitter relays them to a receiver that converts the movements into letters. Licht studied "rainbow" Ramsey theory, a variant of a branch of mathematics that states that patterns must exist even within disorder. When a set of integers is printed in two different colors, there is always an arithmetic progression of one of the colors; the rainbow variant uses sets printed in three different colors and attempts to find arithmetic progressions using integers in each of the colors. Riehl studied Coxeter groups, a type of mathematical set. She assigned a graph to each group and showed that the graph never contains a triangle.

Templeton Prize Winners

Formerly the Templeton Prize for Progress in Religion, the Templeton Prize for Progress Toward Research or Discoveries about Spiritual Realities was established in 1972 by American-born British businessman and philanthropist Sir John Templeton. It recognizes the diversity of and rewards advancement in the ideas and perceptions of divinity. Each year a group of international, interfaith judges chooses a winner from any of the world's religions. Award amount: £700,000 (about $1 million). Templeton Prize Web site: <www.templetonprize.org>

YEAR	NAME	FIELD
1973	Mother Teresa	founder, Missionaries of Charity
1974	Brother Roger	founder, Taizé Community
1975	Sir Sarvepalli Radhakrishnan	president of India, 1962–67
1976	Leon Joseph Cardinal Suenens	pioneer, Charismatic Renewal Movement
1977	Chiara Lubich	founder, Focolare Movement
1978	Thomas F. Torrance	educator, writer on religion and science
1979	Nikkyo Niwano	founder, Rissho Kosei-Kai
1980	Ralph Wendell Burhoe	founder and editor, *Zygon, Journal of Religion and Science*
1981	Dame Cicely Saunders	founder, Hospice and Palliative Care Movement
1982	Billy Graham	Christian evangelist
1983	Aleksandr Solzhenitsyn	writer, dissident
1984	Michael Bourdeaux	scholar, religious freedom activist
1985	Sir Alister Hardy	scientist, educator
1986	James McCord	chancellor, Center of Theological Inquiry; president, Princeton Theological Seminary
1987	Stanley L. Jaki	Benedictine monk, professor of astrophysics
1988	Inamullah Khan	interfaith peace activist; founder, Modern World Muslim Congress
1989	Lord George MacLeod	founder, Iona Community
	Carl Friedrich von Weizsäcker	physics and theology scholar
1990	Baba Amte	social activist, philanthropist
	L. Charles Birch	natural scientist
1991	Lord Immanuel Jakobovits	Chief Rabbi of Great Britain and the Commonwealth, 1967–91
1992	Kyung-Chik Han	founder, Young Nak Presbyterian Church
1993	Charles W. Colson	prison ministry founder
1994	Michael Novak	theologian, writer on theology and economics
1995	Paul Charles William Davies	mathematical physicist
1996	William R. Bright	founder, Campus Crusade for Christ
1997	Pandurang Shastri Athavale	founder, *swadhyaya* self-study
1998	Sir Sigmund Sternberg	philanthropist, businessman
1999	Ian Graeme Barbour	technology ethicist
2000	Freeman J. Dyson	physicist, social activist
2001	Arthur Peacocke	founder, Society of Ordained Scientists
2002	John C. Polkinghorne	Anglican priest, mathematical physicist

Did you know?  The rosary, a sequence of devotions in the Roman Catholic church, has been traced to the 9th century Irish church, where it originated as a type of prayer in monasteries.

13 Feb 2002, Mazar-i-Sharif, Afghanistan: a teacher takes a break from her newly resumed duties.
Claro Cortes IV/Reuters

PLATE 2   TRAGEDIES

24 Jun 2002, Show Low AZ: *(above)* a bus carries fire-fighters through evacuated streets as the massive Chediski/Rodeo Fire, the largest wildfire in Arizona history, closes in.
David McNew/Getty Images

2 Jul 2002, Über-lingen, Germany: *(right)* the tail section of a Russian airliner sits on the ground after a mid-air collision with a DHL cargo plane. All aboard were killed, includ-ing 52 children.
AP/Wide World Photos

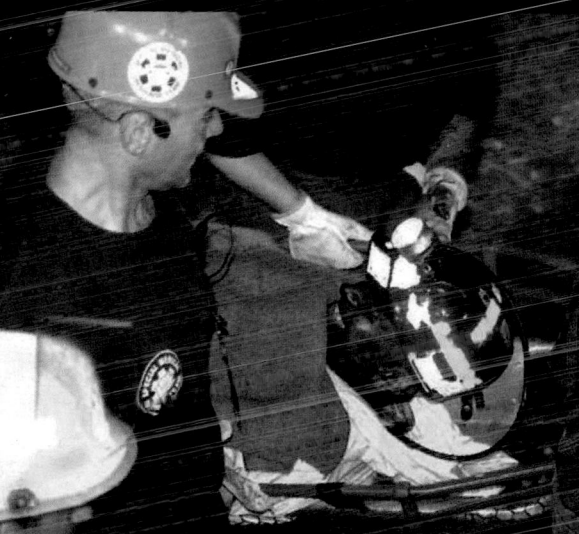

20 Jan 2002, Goma, Dem. Rep. of the Congo: *(top left)* a woman carries her child and belongings across lava following the eruption of Nyiragongo Volcano on 17 January. Dozens died and thousands were left homeless.

Jacky Naegelen/Reuters

3 Dec 2001, Houston TX: *(top right)* Enron employees sit with their belongings after layoffs by the bankrupt energy-trading company left thousands out of work.

AP/Wide World Photos

28 Jul 2002, Somerset PA: *(left)* Mark Popernack is the last of nine miners pulled from a flooded, 240-ft-deep shaft 77 hours after millions of gallons of water inundated the Quecreek mine.

Reuters

PLATE 4   REMEMBERING SEPTEMBER 11

11 Sep 2001, Sarasota FL: *(above)* an aide notifies Pres. George W. Bush of the attacks on the World Trade Center.
AP/Wide World Photo

11 Mar–13 Apr 2002, New York NY: *(right)* two beams of light illumine the sky from near the site of the World Trade Center, part of a temporary memorial.
AP/Wide World Photo

11 Sep 2001, New York NY: *(below)* New Yorkers witness the destruction.
Patrick Witty

9 May 2002, Rotterdam, The Netherlands: *(above)* tens of thousands of Dutch demonstrate outside the funeral of radical nationalist Pim Fortuyn, who was murdered just days before elections in which his party was expected to win 17% of the vote.

Jerry Lampen/Reuters

8 May 2002, Manila, Philippines: *(left)* a young girl holds a candle as she marches with other street children to protest child labor.   AP/Wide World Photos

5 Apr 2002, Weston MA: *(below)* Cardinal Bernard Law, leader of the Boston Archdiocese, comes under intense pressure to resign in the wake of evidence that he and archdiocese officials protected a priest accused of child sexual abuse.

AP/Wide World Photos

PLATE 6   **SPORTS**

15 Apr 2002, Boston MA: *(left)* Kenyan Margaret Okayo beats countrywoman Catherine Ndereba in the Boston Marathon, setting a course record of 2:20:43.   Brian J. Myers@Photo Run

17 Feb 2002, Salt Lake City UT: *(above)* Canadians Jamie Salé and David Pelletier and Russians Yelena Berezhnaya and Anton Sikharulidze pose with their shared gold medals. AP/Wide World Photo

30 Jun 2002, Seoul, South Korea: *(below)* Brazilian forward Ronaldo (second from left) scores his second goal in spite of the efforts of Germans Christoph Metzelder (right) and Thomas Linke (center), leading Brazil to its fifth FIFA title with a 2–0 victory.
© AFP 2002, by Pedro Ugarte

26 Jun 2002: *(left)* China's 7'5" Yao
Ming, the No. 1 NBA draft pick, goes
to the Houston Rockets (file photo).
AP/Wide World Photos

20 Feb 2002, Salt Lake City UT: *(top)*
American Jim Shea, third generation
Olympian, holds aloft a photo of his
grandfather as he celebrates winning
the gold medal in the men's skeleton
event.   © AFP 2002, by Kazuhiro Nogi

29 Sep 2001, Tokyo, Japan: *(above)*
Hawaiian-born sumo wrestler
Akebono sheds a tear as his stable
master chops off his topknot during
a retirement ceremony.
AP/Wide World Photos

PLATE 8   **PERSONALITIES**

8 Dec 2001, Tokyo, Japan: *(right)* Crown Prince Naruhito and Crown Princess Masako beam as they leave the palace hospital with their newborn daughter Princess Aiko.

AP/Wide World Photos

19 Feb 2002, Tokyo, Japan: *(above)* Ozzy Osbourne, surrounded by wife Sharon, son Jack, and daughter Kelly, pose during a promotional tour for the MTV documentary about their home life, "The Osbournes."

Tom Wagner/Corbis SABA

17 Mar 2002, New York NY: *(right)* Nathan Lane (left) and Matthew Broderick take a curtain call after their last performance in the smash hit *The Producers*.

AP/Wide World Photos

22 Apr 2002, Washington DC: *(above)* cellist Yo-Yo Ma performs with Condoleezza Rice, the US National Security Advisor, during the National Endowment for the Arts National Medal of Arts Awards ceremony.
AP/Wide World Photos

24 Mar 2002, Hollywood CA: *(above)* American screen stars Denzel Washington and Halle Berry celebrate their Oscar wins for *Training Day* and *Monster's Ball*, respectively. Washington is the first African American man to win the Academy Award for best actor since Sidney Poitier won in 1963, and Berry is the first African American woman ever to win in the best actress category.
© AFP 2002, by Lee Celano

10 Jun 2002, Glasslough, Ireland: *(above right)* Sir Paul McCartney kisses his fiancée Heather Mills shortly before their wedding. Paul McErlane/Reuters

3 May 2002, Los Angeles CA: *(right)* Tobey Maguire (left) and Kirsten Dunst star in *Spider-Man.*

PLATE 10   **PERSONALITIES**

22 Jun 2002, Chicago IL: *(right)* advice columnist Ann Landers passes away at the age of 83.
AP/Wide World Photos

25 Jul 2001, New Delhi, India: *(far right)* Phoolan Devi, India's "Bandit Queen," is shot dead outside her home by unknown assailants.
Getty Images

9 Feb 2002 and 30 Mar 2002, London, England: *(right)* Princess Margaret (left) dies of a stroke at age 71, and the Queen Mother (center) dies in her sleep at 101.
AP/Wide World Photos

18 Apr 2002, near Laigueglia, Italy: *(right)* Norwegian explorer Thor Heyerdahl dies of cancer. Heyerdahl is pictured here in Morocco with a reed raft on which he crossed the Atlantic Ocean.
AP/Wide World Photos

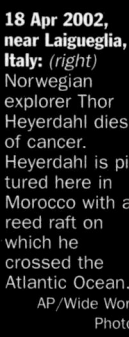

12 Jun 2002, Washington CT: *(above)* legendary American fashion
designer Bill Blass dies of cancer at home at the age of 79.

© AFP 1999, by Stan Honda

25 Aug 2001, The Bahamas:
(above) R&B singer and actress
Aaliyah dies when the small
plane carrying her and eight others crashes after takeoff.

AP/Wide World Photos

27 Mar 2002, Plainfield NJ: *(left)*
English comic actor Dudley
Moore dies at the age of 66.

The Kobal Collection

22 Feb 2002, Angola: *(above)*
Angolan rebel UNITA leader Jonas
Savimbi is killed by the Angolan
army.   AP/Wide World Photos

12 Jun 2002, Bogotá, Colombia: *(above)* Colombians bury themselves up to their necks to protest rate hikes on public services.
Eliana Aponte/ Reuters

22 Apr 2002, Lyon, France: *(right)* a student holds a page torn from the French newspaper *Liberation* to protest right-wing presidential candidate Jean-Marie Le Pen.
AP/Wide World Photos

29 May 2002, Kampala, Uganda: *(left)* U2 frontman Bono dances with an AIDS orphan while on a debt-study tour of Africa with US Treasury Secretary Paul O'Neill.

Patrick Olum/Reuters

27 Feb 2002, Godhra, India: *(below)* a brawl between Muslims and Hindus leads to the setting on fire of a train, which left 58 Hindus dead and set off more violence that left more than 500 dead, mostly Muslims.

AP/Wide World Photos

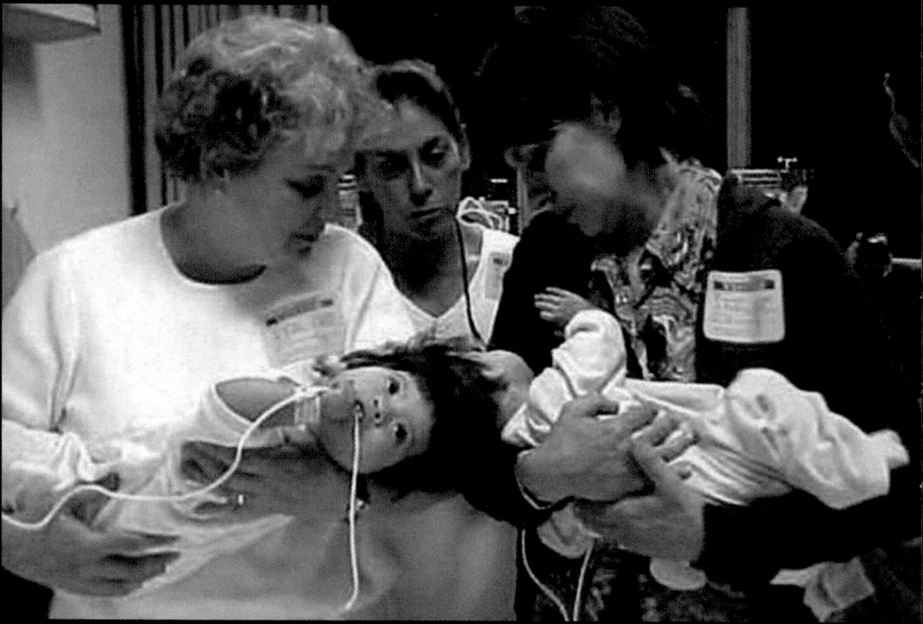

PLATE 14

SCIENCE

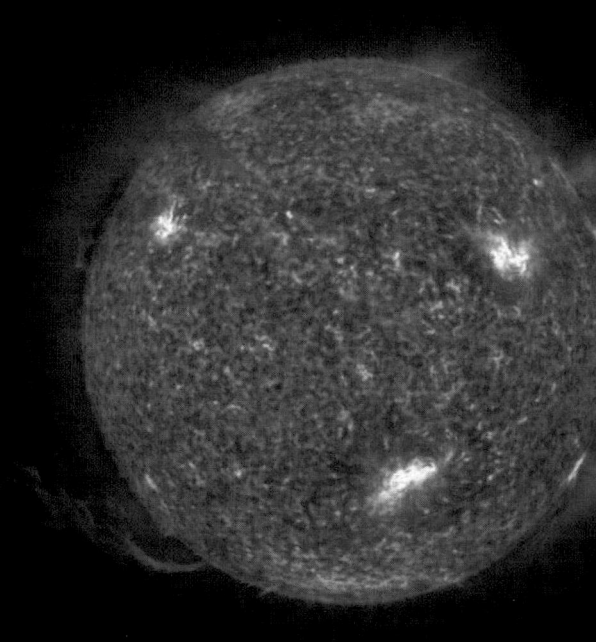

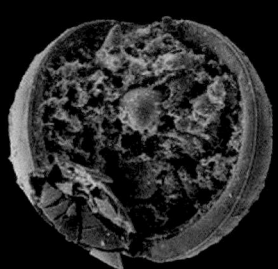

5 Aug 2002, Los Angeles CA: *(top)*
UCLA Medical Center staff members hold year-old sisters María
Teresa and María de Jesús Quiej-
Álvarez, twins born with their
heads fused, prior to the 22-hour
operation that separated them.
UCLA/Getty Images

19 Jul 2001, UK: *(above)* an electron microscope photograph
shows the fossilized remains of a
1/2-mm-long, 511-million-year-old
crustacean, an ancient relative of
lobsters, crabs, and crayfish,
found in English limestone
deposits.   Reuters

1 July 2002: *(right)* The Solar and
Heliospheric Observatory (SOHO)
satellite reveals a massive solar
eruption more than 30 times the
Earth's diameter. The eruption
formed when a loop of magnetic
fields over the surface of the
Sun trapped hot gas.   NASA

2 May 2002, London: *(top left)* this pungent-smolling specimen of the world's largest flower, the Titan arum *(Amorphophallus titanum)*, from Sumatra's rainforests, is one of the few cultivated specimens known to exist.

Dan Chung/Reuters

22 May 2002, Rehovot, Israel: *(above)* a genetically engineered "naked chicken" has less fat and matures earlier than its feathered counterparts.

Moshe Milner/GPO/Getty Images

10 Jul 2002, Djurab Desert, Chad: *(left)* Archeologists publish findings about a recently discovered 7 million-year-old hominid skull, thought to be modern humans' most ancient family member.

© Corbis/Sygma

PLATE 16   CONFLICT

3 Aug 2001, Jerusalem, Israel: *(top)* an Israeli policeman struggles with a Palestinian who was denied entry to Al-Aqsa Mosque in Jerusalem's Old City.
Mahfouz Abu Turk/Reuters

23 Jan 2002, Pakistan: *(above)* reporter Daniel Pearl is abducted; on 21 February his murder is confirmed.   Reuters

6 Jan 2002, Kabul, Afghanistan: *(right)* interim leader Hamid Karzai speaks to a group of children.   AP/Wide World Photos

National Humanities Medal

The National Humanities Medal (originally known as the Charles Frankel Prize, 1988–96) is awarded by the National Endowment for the Humanities for notable contributions to Americans' understanding of and involvement with the humanities. As many as 12 medals may be conferred each year. The recipients for 2001 were illustrator José Cisneros, child psychologist Robert Coles, literacy advocate Sharon Darling, historian William Manchester, author Richard Peck, musicologist Eileen Jackson Southern, author Tom Wolfe, and the National Trust for Historic Preservation. <www.neh.gov/whowecare/awards.html>

Special Achievement Awards

Congressional Gold Medal

Individuals, institutions, or events of distinguished achievement are honored by the Congressional Gold Medal. First awarded in 1776, 125 medals have since been given out. Early medals went primarily to military figures; beginning in the mid-19th century, they were given to a wide variety of people. Past recipients include George Washington, Andrew Jackson, railroad magnate Cornelius Vanderbilt, the Wright Brothers, Richard E. Byrd's Antarctic expedition, composer Irving Berlin, physician Jonas Salk, cartoon producer Walt Disney, the American Red Cross, Gen. Colin Powell, Mother Teresa, civil-rights activist Rosa Parks, and the Navajo Code Talkers of World War II. In January 2002 an additional gold medal recipient was chosen: Gen. Henry H. Shelton, former chairman (1997–2001) of the Joint Chiefs of Staff.

The Spingarn Medal

The National Association for the Advancement of Colored People (NAACP) presents the medal for distinguished achievement among African Americans.

YEAR	NAME	FIELD
1915	Ernest Everett Just	zoologist, marine biologist
1916	Charles Young	army officer
1917	Harry Thacker Burleigh	singer, composer
1918	William Stanley Braithwaite	poet, literary critic
1919	Archibald Henry Grimké	lawyer, diplomat, social activist
1920	W.E.B. Du Bois (William Edward Burghardt Du Bois)	sociologist, social activist
1921	Charles S. Gilpin	actor
1922	Mary Burnett Talbert	civil rights activist
1923	George Washington Carver	agricultural chemist
1924	Roland Hayes	singer, composer
1925	James Weldon Johnson	writer, diplomat, anthologist
1926	Carter G. Woodson	historian
1927	Anthony Overton	businessman
1928	Charles W. Chesnutt	writer
1929	Mordecai W. Johnson	minister, university president
1930	Henry Alexander Hunt	educator, government official
1931	Richard B. Harrison	actor
1932	Robert Russa Moton	educator, civil rights leader
1933	Max Yergan	civil rights leader
1934	William T.B. Williams	educator
1935	Mary McLeod Bethune	educator, social activist
1936	John Hope	educator
1937	Walter White	civil rights leader
1938	no medal awarded	
1939	Marian Anderson	opera singer
1940	Louis T. Wright	surgeon, civil rights leader
1941	Richard Wright	writer

YEAR	NAME	FIELD
1942	A. Philip Randolph	labor and civil rights leader
1943	William H. Hastie	lawyer, judge
1944	Charles Richard Drew	surgeon, research scientist
1945	Paul Robeson	actor, singer, social activist
1946	Thurgood Marshall	lawyer, US Supreme Court justice
1947	Percy L. Julian	chemist
1948	Channing H. Tobias	civil rights leader
1949	Ralph Bunche	diplomat, scholar
1950	Charles Hamilton Houston	lawyer
1951	Mabel Keaton Staupers	nurse, social activist
1952	Harry T. Moore	civil rights activist, educator
1953	Paul R. Williams	architect
1954	Theodore K. Lawless	dermatologist, philanthropist
1955	Carl Murphy	journalist, civil rights activist
1956	Jackie Robinson (Jack Roosevelt Robinson)	baseball player
1957	Martin Luther King, Jr.	civil rights leader
1958	Daisy Bates and the Little Rock Nine	school integration activists
1959	Duke Ellington (Edward Kennedy Ellington)	jazz musician
1960	Langston Hughes	writer
1961	Kenneth Bancroft Clark	educator
1962	Robert C. Weaver	economist, government official
1963	Medgar Evers	civil rights activist
1964	Roy Wilkins	civil rights leader
1965	Leontyne Price	opera singer
1966	John H. Johnson	publisher
1967	Edward W. Brooke III	lawyer, US senator

The Spingarn Medal (continued)

YEAR	NAME	FIELD	YEAR	NAME	FIELD
1968	Sammy Davis, Jr.	singer, dancer, entertainer	1987	Percy Ellis Sutton	civil rights activist, politician
1969	Clarence M. Mitchell, Jr.	civil rights lobbyist	1988	Frederick Douglass Patterson	educator
1970	Jacob Lawrence	painter			
1971	Leon H. Sullivan	minister, civil rights activist	1989	Jesse Jackson	minister, politician, civil rights leader
1972	Gordon Parks	photographer, writer	1990	L. Douglas Wilder	politician
1973	Wilson C. Riles	educator	1991	Colin Powell	army general, government official
1974	Damon Keith	lawyer, judge			
1975	Hank Aaron	baseball player	1992	Barbara Jordan	lawyer, politician
1976	Alvin Ailey	dancer, choreographer	1993	Dorothy I. Height	social activist
			1994	Maya Angelou	poet
1977	Alex Haley	writer	1995	John Hope Franklin	historian, educator
1978	Andrew Young	politician, civil rights leader	1996	A. Leon Higginbotham	lawyer, judge, scholar
1979	Rosa Parks	civil rights activist	1997	Carl T. Rowan	journalist, commentator
1980	Rayford W. Logan	educator, writer			
1981	Coleman A. Young	labor activist, politician	1998	Myrlie Evers-Williams	civil rights activist
			1999	Earl G. Graves	publisher
1982	Benjamin E. Mays	educator, minister	2000	Oprah Winfrey	television host, media personality
1983	Lena Horne	singer, actress			
1984	Thomas Bradley	politician	2001	Vernon E. Jordan, Jr.	lawyer, civil rights activist
1985	Bill Cosby	actor, comedian			
1986	Benjamin L. Hooks	civil rights leader, government official	2002	John Lewis	politician, civil rights activist

Hasty Pudding Theatricals Woman of the Year and Man of the Year

The Hasty Pudding Theatricals of Harvard University, an organization of undergraduates, has presented the Woman of the Year award since 1951 and the Man of the Year award since 1967 to performers who have made a "lasting and impressive contribution to the world of entertainment."

1951	Gertrude Lawrence	1977	Elizabeth Taylor and Johnny Carson
1952	Barbara Bel Geddes	1978	Beverly Sills and Richard Dreyfuss
1953	Mamie Eisenhower	1979	Candice Bergen and Robert De Niro
1954	Shirley Booth	1980	Meryl Streep and Alan Alda
1955	Debbie Reynolds	1981	Mary Tyler Moore and John Travolta
1956	Peggy Ann Garner	1982	Ella Fitzgerald and James Cagney
1957	Carroll Baker	1983	Julie Andrews and Steven Spielberg
1958	Katharine Hepburn	1984	Joan Rivers and Sean Connery
1959	Joanne Woodward	1985	Cher and Bill Murray
1960	Carol Lawrence	1986	Sally Field and Sylvester Stallone
1961	Jane Fonda	1987	Bernadette Peters and Mikhail Baryshnikov
1962	Piper Laurie	1988	Lucille Ball and Steve Martin
1963	Shirley MacLaine	1989	Kathleen Turner and Robin Williams
1964	Rosalind Russell	1990	Glenn Close and Kevin Costner
1965	Lee Remick	1991	Diane Keaton and Clint Eastwood
1966	Ethel Merman	1992	Jodie Foster and Michael Douglas
1967	Lauren Bacall and Bob Hope	1993	Whoopi Goldberg and Chevy Chase
1968	Angela Lansbury and Paul Newman	1994	Meg Ryan and Tom Cruise
1969	Carol Burnett and Bill Cosby	1995	Michelle Pfeiffer and Tom Hanks
1970	Dionne Warwick and Robert Redford	1996	Susan Sarandon and Harrison Ford
1971	Carol Channing and James Stewart	1997	Julia Roberts and Mel Gibson
1972	Ruby Keeler and Dustin Hoffman	1998	Sigourney Weaver and Kevin Kline
1973	Liza Minnelli and Jack Lemmon	1999	Goldie Hawn and Samuel L. Jackson
1974	Faye Dunaway and Peter Falk	2000	Jamie Lee Curtis and Billy Crystal
1975	Valerie Harper and Warren Beatty	2001	Drew Barrymore and Anthony Hopkins
1976	Bette Midler and Robert Blake	2002	Sarah Jessica Parker and Bruce Willis

Did you know? The symbol "#," often referred to as the "pound key" on a telephone, is called an octothorp.

Nature, Science, Medicine & Technology

Time

Measuring Time

The measurement of time is an ancient science, though many of its discoveries are relatively recent. The **Cro-Magnons** recorded the phases of the Moon some 30,000 years ago—but the first minutes were counted accurately only 400 years ago, and the atomic clocks that allow us to track time to the billionth of a second are less than 50 years old. Timekeeping has been both a lens through which humanity has observed the heavens and a mirror reflecting the progress of science and civilization.

Our millennia-long struggle to **define and calibrate** time through calendars and clocks has meant trying to bring the register of human affairs in line with natural cycles—of the Earth, Sun, Moon, and stars, of the physics of matter—but always, cycles. What vary are the cultural values and goals that dictate which cycles are significant.

With a religious culture dominated by gods of the Sun and sky, and a civilization dependent on the annual cycle of a river, the **ancient Egyptians** were expert astronomers who studied the Sun's recurrent movements and their effects on the Earth very closely. By plotting the beginning of the Nile's flood each year, a reliable harbinger of seasonal change, they measured a cycle 365 days long—a reasonable approximation of the duration of the tropical solar year. Observations of the star Sirius eventually allowed Egyptian astronomers to adjust the solar year to 365.25 days.

About 127 BC the **Greek astronomer Hipparchus** further refined the year. His adjustments centered on the equinoxes—which he discovered to be shifting to the west at the barely perceptible rate of two degrees in 150 years. Because of this discovery Hipparchus realized that the solar year was slightly shorter than the accepted 365.25 days. His calculation of 365.242 days was remarkably close to the present calculation of 365.242199 days.

Unfortunately for civic and religious leaders of the next 1,600 years, Hipparchus's discoveries were virtually ignored by calendar makers. **Julius Caesar's** calendrical reforms in 46 BC left the calendar year at 365.25 days—more than 11 minutes too long. By the 1500s the Julian calendar was 10 days behind the solar year. The shortfall alarmed Christian religious leaders because it meant that holy days, including Easter, were being observed at the wrong times. In 1582, **Pope Gregory XIII** officially revised the accepted length of the year to 365.2422 days, adjusted the leap-year rule, and lopped off the 10 extra days, creating in the process the calendar in most widespread use today.

Meanwhile, the quest to measure time accurately on a much smaller scale was still in its early phases. The invention of the **weight-driven mechanical clock** some 200 years earlier had revolutionized timekeeping, making it possible to count equal units of time.

This leap forward in precision radically changed the way people thought about time and the best ways to measure it.

Calendars are deemed accurate according to how well they accommodate the variations in larger celestial cycles. Clocks, on the other hand, have historically been judged accurate in relation to the average duration of the Earth's rotation around the Sun—that is, by how well they keep **"mean time."** While calendrical standards have remained fairly stable, however, the clock's units of measure have gradually shifted away from using the Earth-Sun relationship as a norm. With the introduction of mechanical clocks in the late 13th or early 14th century, clock time became increasingly removed from cyclical events in the sky, for the cycles on which mechanical clocks base their measures are independent of Earth and Sun. A pendulum clock, for example, measures only the beat of its pendulum, not any part of a "real" day.

The **pendulum clock** kicked off the modern search for the perfect clock, a timepiece governed by a naturally cycling period—like a pendulum's—that operated free from mechanical friction and fatigue. Another 300 years would pass before any clock came close. In 1927 W.A. Marrison invented a clock that operated via a tiny **quartz crystal.** The crystal vibrated at an ultrasonic frequency when exposed to an electric field. These vibrations were constant and delivered a virtually frictionless beat to the counting mechanism of the clock. Accurate to thousandths of a second, quartz clocks led scientists to make the belated discovery that the Earth was not a reliable clock to begin with. Disparities between the measurements of quartz clocks and the rotation of the Earth revealed unpredictable irregularities in the rotation, which had to that point defined the duration of a second (1/86,400 of the mean solar day).

In 1967, the **definition of a second** was officially divorced from the Earth's rotation. That year, the 13th General Conference of Weights and Measures redefined the second as "9,192,631,770 periods of the radiation corresponding to the transition between the two hyperfine levels of the ground state of the cesium-133 atom." **Cesium atoms** are superior to quartz crystals because they do not wear out. These atoms have cycles that comprise oscillations between precisely defined energy states; these cycles can oscillate forever without any distortion whatsoever. Furthermore, each atom of cesium oscillates at exactly the same frequency as all others, making each one a perfect timekeeper—too perfect, even. To keep solar time and atomic time from drifting too far apart, the two were combined in 1964 to form **Coordinated Universal Time,** which is based on the atomic second and kept within 0.9 second of solar time by adding a leap second as needed.

Time Zone Map

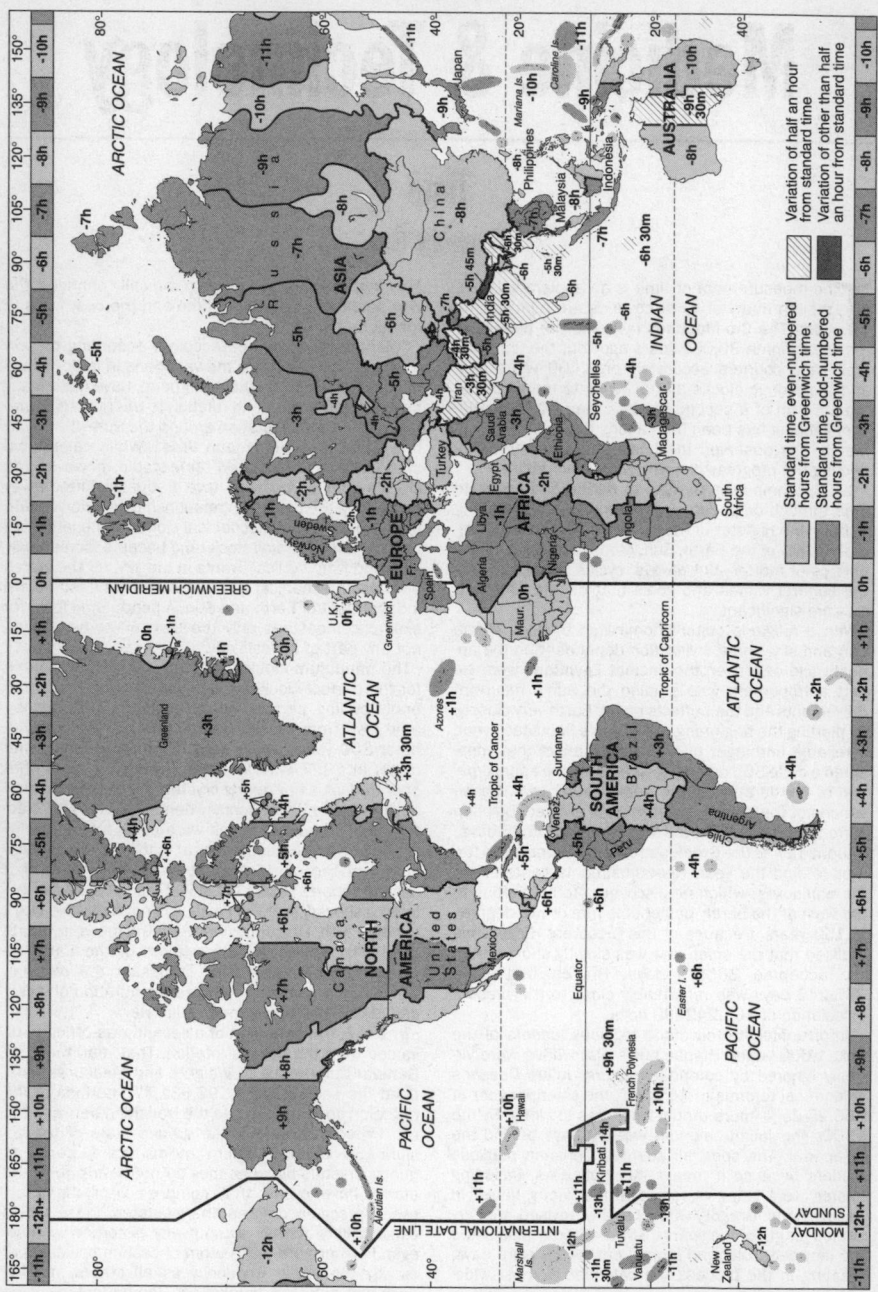

Julian and Gregorian Calendars

The Julian calendar, also called the Old Style calendar, is a dating system established by Julius Caesar as a reform of the Roman republican calendar. Caesar, advised by the Alexandrian astronomer Sosigenes, made the new calendar solar, not lunar, and he took the length of the solar year as 365¼ days. The year was divided into 12 months, all of which had either 30 or 31 days except February, which contained 28 days in common (365-day) years and 29 in every fourth year (a leap year, of 366 days). Because of misunderstandings, the calendar was not established in smooth operation until AD 8. Further, Sosigenes had overestimated the length of the year by 11 minutes 14 seconds, and by the mid-1500s, the cumulative effect of this error had shifted the dates of the seasons by about 10 days from Caesar's time.

This inaccuracy led Pope Gregory XIII to reform the Julian calendar. His Gregorian calendar, also called the New Style calendar, is still in general use. Gregory's proclamation in 1582 restored the calendar to the seasonal dates of AD 325, an adjustment of 10 days. Although the amount of regression was some

14 days by Pope Gregory's time, Gregory based his reform on restoration of the vernal equinox, then falling on 11 March, to the date (21 March) it had in AD 325, the time of the Council of Nicaea. Advancing the calendar 10 days after 4 Oct 1582, the day following being reckoned as 15 October, effected the change.

The Gregorian calendar differs from the Julian only in that no century year is a leap year unless it is exactly divisible by 400 (e.g., 1600, 2000). A further refinement, the designation of years evenly divisible by 4,000 as common (not leap) years, will keep the Gregorian calendar accurate to within one day in 20,000 years.

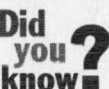

Did you know? The traditional Gregorian calendar is somewhat imperfect. A day is more accurately measured at 23 hours, 56 minutes, and 4 seconds; whereas a year is 365.25 days long.

Daylight Saving Time

Also called **summer time, daylight saving time** is a system for uniformly advancing clocks, especially in summer, so as to extend daylight hours during conventional waking time. In the Northern Hemisphere, clocks are usually set ahead one hour in late March or in April and are set back one hour in late September or in October.

The practice was first suggested in a whimsical essay by **Benjamin Franklin** in 1784. In 1907 an Englishman, William Willett, campaigned for setting the clock ahead by 80 minutes in four moves of 20 minutes each during the spring and summer months. In 1908 the House of Commons rejected a bill to advance the clock by one hour in the spring and return to Greenwich Mean (standard) Time in the autumn. Several countries, including Australia, Great Britain, Germany, and the United States, adopted **summer daylight saving time** during World War I to conserve

fuel by reducing the need for artificial light. During World War II, clocks were kept continuously advanced by an hour in some nations—e.g., in the United States from 9 Feb 1942 to 30 Sep 1945; and England used "double summer time" during part of the year, advancing clocks two hours from the standard time during the summer and one hour during the winter months.

In the US, daylight saving time formerly began on the last Sunday in April and ended on the last Sunday in October. In 1986 the US Congress passed a law moving up the start of daylight saving time to the first Sunday in April, while keeping its end date the same. In most of the countries of Western Europe, daylight saving time starts on the last Sunday in March and ends on the last Sunday in September. In Britain and many other countries worldwide, it lasts from 30 March to 26 October.

Perpetual Calendar

The perpetual calendar is a type of dating system that makes it possible to find the correct day of the week for any date over a wide range of years. Aspects of the perpetual calendar can be found in the Jewish religious and the Julian calendars, and some form of it has appeared in many proposed calendar reforms.

To find the day of the week for any Gregorian or Julian date in the perpetual calendar provided in this table,

first find the proper dominical letter (one of the letters A through G) for the year in the upper table. Leap years have two dominical letters, the first applicable to dates in January and February, the second to dates in the remaining months. Then find the same dominical letter in the lower table, in whichever column it appears opposite the month in question. The days then fall as given in the lowest section of the column.

YEAR				CENTURY										
					JULIAN CALENDAR						GREGORIAN CALENDAR			
				0	100	200	300	400	500	600	1500**	1600	1700	1800	1900
				700	800	900	1000	1100	1200	1300		2000	2100	2200	2300
				1400	1500*										
0				DC	ED	FF	GF	AG	BA	CB	...	BA	C	E	G
1	29	57	85	B	C	D	E	F	G	A	F	G	B	D	F
2	30	58	86	A	B	C	D	E	F	G	E	F	A	C	E
3	31	59	87	G	A	B	C	D	E	F	D	E	G	B	D
4	32	60	88	FE	GF	AG	BA	CB	DC	ED	CB	DC	FE	AG	CB
5	33	61	89	D	E	F	G	A	B	C	A	B	D	F	A

Perpetual Calendar (continued)

YEAR				JULIAN CALENDAR							GREGORIAN CALENDAR				
				0 700 1400	100 800 1500*	200 900	300 1000	400 1100	500 1200	600 1300	1500**	1600 2000	1700 2100	1800 2200	1900 2300
6	34	62	90	C	D	E	F	G	A	B	G	A	C	E	G
7	35	63	91	B	C	D	E	F	G	A	F	G	B	D	F
8	36	64	92	AG	BA	CB	DC	ED	FE	GF	ED	FE	AG	CB	ED
9	37	65	93	F	G	A	B	C	D	E	C	D	F	A	C
10	38	66	94	E	F	G	A	B	C	D	B	C	E	G	B
11	39	67	95	D	E	F	G	A	B	C	A	B	D	F	A
12	40	68	96	CB	DC	ED	FE	GF	AG	BA	GF	AG	CB	ED	GF
13	41	69	97	A	B	C	D	E	F	G	E	F	A	C	E
14	42	70	98	G	A	B	C	D	E	F	D	E	G	B	D
15	43	71	99	F	G	A	B	C	D	E	C	D	F	A	C
16	44	72		ED	FE	GF	AG	BA	CB	DC	...	CB	ED	GF	BA
17	45	73		C	D	E	F	G	A	B	...	A	C	E	G
18	46	74		B	C	D	E	F	G	A	...	G	B	D	F
19	47	75		A	B	C	D	E	F	G	...	F	A	C	E
20	48	76		GF	AG	BA	CB	DC	ED	FE	...	ED	GF	BA	DC
21	49	77		E	F	G	A	B	C	D	...	C	E	G	B
22	50	78		D	E	F	G	A	B	C	...	B	D	F	A
23	51	79		C	D	E	F	G	A	B	...	A	C	E	G
24	52	80		BA	CB	DC	ED	FE	GF	AG	...	GF	BA	DC	FE
25	53	81		G	A	B	C	D	E	F	...	E	G	B	D
26	54	82		F	G	A	B	C	D	E	C	D	F	A	C
27	55	83		E	F	G	A	B	C	D	B	C	E	G	B
28	56	84		DC	ED	FE	GF	AG	BA	CB	AG	BA	DC	FE	AG

MONTH	DOMINICAL LETTER						
January, October	A	B	C	D	E	F	G
February, March, November	D	E	F	G	A	B	C
April, July	G	A	B	C	D	E	F
May	B	C	D	E	F	G	A
June	E	F	G	A	B	C	D
August	C	D	E	F	G	A	B
September, December	F	G	A	B	C	D	E

1	8	15	22	29	Sunday	Saturday	Friday	Thursday	Wednesday	Tuesday	Monday
2	9	16	23	30	Monday	Sunday	Saturday	Friday	Thursday	Wednesday	Tuesday
3	10	17	24	31	Tuesday	Monday	Sunday	Saturday	Friday	Thursday	Wednesday
4	11	18	25		Wednesday	Tuesday	Monday	Sunday	Saturday	Friday	Thursday
5	12	19	26		Thursday	Wednesday	Tuesday	Monday	Sunday	Saturday	Friday
6	13	20	27		Friday	Thursday	Wednesday	Tuesday	Monday	Sunday	Saturday
7	14	21	28		Saturday	Friday	Thursday	Wednesday	Tuesday	Monday	Sunday

*On and before 1582, October 4 only.   **On and after 1582, October 15 only.
Source: Smithsonian Physical Tables, 9th edition, rev. 1956.

Chinese Calendar

The Chinese calendar is a dating system used concurrently with the Gregorian (Western) calendar in China and Taiwan and in neighboring countries (e.g., Japan). The calendar consists of 12 months of alternately 29 and 30 days, equal to 354 or 355 days, or approximately 12 full lunar cycles. Intercalary months have been inserted to keep the calendar year in step with the solar year of about 365 days. Months have no name but are instead referred to by number within a year and sometimes also by a series of 12 animal names that from ancient times have been attached to years and to hours of the day.

The calendar also incorporates a meteorological cycle that contains 24 points, each beginning one of the periods named. The establishment of this cycle required a fair amount of astronomical understanding of the Earth as a celestial body. Modern scholars acknowledge the superiority of pre-Sung Chinese astronomy (at least until about the 13th century AD) over that of other, contemporary nations.

The 24 points within the meteorological cycle coincide with points 15° apart on the ecliptic (the plane of the Earth's yearly journey around the Sun or, if it is thought that the Sun turns around the Earth, the apparent journey of the Sun against the stars). It takes about 15.2 days for the Sun to travel from one of these points to another (because the ecliptic is a complete circle of 360°), and the Sun needs 365¼ days to finish its journey in this cycle. Supposedly, each of the 12 months of the year contains two points, but, because a lunar month has only 29½ days and the two points share about 30.4 days, there is always the chance that a lunar month will fail to contain both points, though the distance between any two given points is only 15°. If such an occasion occurs, the intercalation of an extra month takes place. For instance, one may find a year with two "Julys" or with two "Augusts" in the Chinese calendar. In fact, the exact length of the month in the Chinese calendar is either 30 days or 29 days—a phenomenon that reflects its lunar origin.

SOLAR MONTHS—CHINESE (ENGLISH EQUIVALENTS)	GREGORIAN DATE (APPROXIMATE)	LUNAR MONTH (CORRESPONDENCE OF LUNAR AND SOLAR MONTHS APPROXIMATE)
Lichun (spring begins)	5 February	1—tiger
Yushui (rain water)	19 February	
Jingzhe (excited insects)	5 March	2—rabbit/hare
Chunfen (vernal equinox)	20 March	
Qingming (clear and bright)	5 April	3—dragon
Guyu (grain rains)	20 April	
Lixia (summer begins)	5 May	4—snake
Xiaoman (grain fills)	21 May	
Mangzhong (grain in ear)	6 June	5—horse
Xiazhi (summer solstice)	21 June	
Xiaoshu (slight heat)	7 July	6—sheep/ram
Dashu (great heat)	23 July	
Liqiu (autumn begins)	7 August	7—monkey
Chushu (limit of heat)	23 August	
Bailu (white dew)	8 September	8—chicken/rooster
Qiufen (autumn equinox)	23 September	
Hanlu (cold dew)	8 October	9—dog
Shuangjiang (hoar frost descends)	24 October	
Lidong (winter begins)	8 November	10—pig/boar
Xiaoxue (little snow)	22 November	
Daxue (heavy snow)	7 December	11—rat
Dongzhi (winter solstice)	22 December	
Xiaohan (little cold)	6 January	12—cow/ox
Dahan (severe cold)	20 January	

CHINESE NEW YEAR	GREGORIAN DATE	ANIMAL	CHINESE NEW YEAR	GREGORIAN DATE	ANIMAL
4696	28 Jan 1998	tiger	4703	9 Feb 2005	chicken/rooster
4697	16 Feb 1999	rabbit/hare	4704	29 Jan 2006	dog
4698	5 Feb 2000	dragon	4705	18 Feb 2007	pig/boar
4699	24 Jan 2001	snake	4706	7 Feb 2008	rat
4700	12 Feb 2002	horse	4707	26 Jan 2009	cow/ox
4701	1 Feb 2003	sheep/ram	4708	14 Feb 2010	tiger
4702	22 Jan 2004	monkey			

Jewish Calendar

The Jewish calendar is lunisolar—i.e., regulated by the positions of both the Moon and the Sun. It consists usually of 12 alternating lunar months of 29 and 30 days each (except for Heshvan and Kislev, which sometimes have either 29 or 30 days), and totals 353, 354, or 355 days per year. The average lunar year (354 days) is adjusted to the solar year (365¼ days) by the periodic introduction of leap years in order to assure that the major festivals fall in their proper season. The leap year consists of an additional 30-day month called First Adar, which always precedes the month of (Second) Adar. (During leap year, the Adar holidays are postponed to Second

Adar.) A leap year consists of either 383, 384, or 385 days and occurs seven times during every 19 year period (the so-called Metonic cycle). Among the consequences of the lunisolar structure are these: (1) The number of days in a year may vary considerably, from 353 to 385 days. (2) The first day of a month can fall on any day of the week, that day varying from year to year. Consequently, the days of the week upon which an annual Jewish festival falls vary from year to year despite the festival's fixed position in the Jewish month. The months of the Jewish calendar and their Gregorian equivalents are as follows:

JEWISH MONTH	GREGORIAN MONTH(S)	JEWISH MONTH	GREGORIAN MONTH(S)
Tishri	September–October	Nisan	March–April
Heshvan, or Marheshvan	October–November	Iyyar	April–May
Kislev	November–December	Sivan	May–June
Tevet	December–January	Tammuz	June–July
Shevat	January–February	Av	July–August
Adar	February–March	Elul	August–September

Muslim Calendar

The Muslim calendar (also called the Islamic calendar, or Hijrah) is a dating system used in the Muslim world that is based on a year of 12 months. Each month begins approximately at the time of the New Moon. The months of the Muslim calendar are: Muharram, Safar, Rabi I, Rabi II, Jumada I, Jumada II, Rajab, Sha'ban, Ramadan, Shawwal, Dhu al-Qa'dah, and Dhu al-Hijjah.

In the standard Muslim calendar the months are alternately 30 and 29 days long except for the 12th month, Dhu al-Hijjah, the length of which is varied in a 30-year cycle intended to keep the calendar in step with the true phases of the Moon. In 11 years of this cycle, Dhu al-Hijjah has 30 days, and in the other 19 years it has 29. Thus the year has either 354 or 355 days. No months are intercalated, so that the named months do not remain in the same seasons but retrogress through the entire solar, or seasonal, year (of about 365.25 days) every 32.5 solar years.

There are some exceptions to this calendar in the Muslim world. Turkey uses the Gregorian calendar, while the Iranian Muslim calendar is based on a solar year. The Iranian calendar still begins from the same dating point as other Muslim calendars (that is, some 10 years prior to the death of Muhammad in AD 632). Thus, the Gregorian year AD 2000 corresponded to the Hijrah year of AH 1420/1421.

Religious and Traditional Holidays

The word holiday comes from "holy day," and it was originally a day of dedication to religious observance; in modern times a holiday may be of either religious or secular commemoration. All dates in this article are Gregorian.

Jewish holidays—The major holidays are the Pilgrim Festivals: **Pesach** (Passover), **Shavuot** (Feast of Weeks, or Pentecost), and **Sukkot** (Tabernacles); and the High Holidays: **Rosh Hashana** (New Year) and **Yom Kippur** (Day of Atonement).

Pesach commemorates the Exodus from Egypt and the servitude that preceded it. As such it is the most significant of the commemorative holidays, for it celebrates the very inception of the Jewish people—i.e., the event that provided the basis for the covenant between God and Israel. The term Pesach refers originally to the paschal (Passover) lamb sacrificed on the eve of the Exodus, the blood of which marked the Jewish homes to be spared from God's plague. Leaven (se'or) and foods containing leaven (hametz) are neither to be owned nor consumed during Pesach. Aside from meats, fresh fruits, and vegetables, it is customary to consume only those foods prepared under rabbinic supervision and labeled "kosher for Passover." The unleavened bread (matzo) consists entirely of flour and water. On the eve of Pesach families partake of the Seder, an elaborate festival meal. The table is bedecked with an assortment of foods symbolizing the passage from slavery (e.g., bitter herbs) into freedom (e.g., wine). Pesach will begin on 17 April and end on 24 April in 2003. (All Jewish holidays begin at sundown.)

The most distinctive **Rosh Hashana** observance is the sounding of the ram's horn (shofar) at the synagogue service. Symbolic ceremonies, such as eating bread and apples dipped in honey, accompanied by prayers for a "sweet" and propitious year, are performed at the festive meals. Rosh Hashana will begin at sundown on 27 September and will end on 28 September of 2003. **Yom Kippur** is a day when sins are confessed and expiated and man and God are reconciled. It is the holiest and most solemn day of the Jewish year. It is marked by fasting, penitence, and prayer. Working, eating, drinking, washing, anointing one's body, engaging in sexual intercourse, and donning leather shoes are all forbidden. Yom Kippur begins on 6 Oct 2003.

Though not as important theologically, the feast of **Hanukka** has become socially significant, especially in western cultures. Hanukka commemorates the rededication (164 BCE) of the Second Temple of Jerusalem after its desecration three years earlier. Though modern Israel tends to emphasize the military victory of the general Judas Maccabeus, the distinctive rite of lighting the menorah also recalls the Talmud story of how the small supply of nondesecrated oil—enough for one day—miraculously burned in the Temple for eight full days until new oil could be obtained. During Hanukka, in addition to the lighting of the ceremonial candles, gifts are exchanged and children play holiday games. The festival spans 30 November through 7 December in 2002 and 20 through 27 December in 2003.

Christian holidays—The major holidays celebrated by nearly all Christians are **Easter** and **Christmas**.

Easter celebrates the resurrection of Jesus on the third day after his crucifixion. In the Christian liturgical year, Easter is preceded by the period of **Lent**, the 40 days (not counting Sundays) before Easter, which traditionally were observed as a period of penance and fasting. Lent begins on **Ash Wednesday**; a day devoted to penitence. Holy Week precedes **Easter Sunday** and includes **Maundy Thursday**, the commemoration of Jesus' last supper with his disciples; **Good Friday**, the day of his crucifixion; and **Holy Saturday**, the transition between crucifixion and resurrection. Easter shares with Christmas the presence of numerous customs, some of which have little to do with the Christian celebration of the resurrection but clearly derive from folk customs. In 2003 the Western churches (nearly all Christian denominations) will observe Ash Wednesday on 5 March and Easter on 20 April. For the Eastern Orthodox Christians, Lent begins on 10 March and Easter will be observed on 27 Apr 2003.

Christmas commemorates the birth of Jesus Christ. Since the early part of the 20th century, Christmas has also become a secular family holiday, observed by non-Christians, devoid of Christian elements, and marked by an increasingly elaborate exchange of gifts. In this secular Christmas celebration, a mythical figure named Santa Claus plays the pivotal role. Christmas is held on 25 December in most Christian cultures, but will occur on 7 Jan 2003 for the Eastern Orthodox faith.

Islamic holidays—**Ramadan** for Muslims is the holy month of fasting. The Islamic ordinance prescribes abstention from evil thoughts and deeds as well as from food, drink, and sexual intercourse from dawn until dusk throughout the month. The beginning and end of Ramadan are announced when one trustworthy witness testifies before the authorities that the new moon has been sighted; a cloudy sky may, therefore, delay or prolong the fast. The end of the fast is celebrated as the feast of 'Id al-Fitr. Ramadan begins on 26 October in 2003 and 'Id al-Fitr falls on 25 November of that year (all Islamic holidays begin at sundown). The Muslim New Year, **Hijra,** is on 5 Mar 2003.

After 'Id al-Fitr, the second major Islamic festival is **'Id al-Adha.** Throughout the Muslim world, all who can sacrifice sheep, goats, camels, or cattle and then divide the flesh equally among themselves, the poor, and friends and neighbors, to commemorate the ransom of Ishmael with a ram. This festival falls at the end of the hajj, the pilgrimage to the holy city of Mecca in Saudi Arabia, which every adult Muslim of either sex must make at least once in his or her lifetime. 'Id al-Adha will be observed on 11 February in 2003.

Ashura was originally designated in AD 622 by Muhammad as a day of fasting from sunset to sunset, probably patterned on the Jewish Day of Atonement, Yom Kippur. Among the Shi'ites, Ashura is a major festival that commemorates the death of Husayn (Hussein), son of Ali and grandson of Muhammad. It is a period of expressions of grief and of pilgrimage to Karbala (the site of Husayn's death, now in present-day Iraq). Ashura is on 13 March in 2003.

Buddhist holidays—Holidays practiced by a large number of Buddhists are *uposatha* days and days that commemorate events in the life of the Buddha.

The four monthly holy days of ancient Buddhism continue to be observed in the Theravada countries of Southeast Asia. These *uposatha* days—the new moon and full moon days of each lunar month and the eighth day following the new and full moons—have their origin, according to some scholars, in the fast days that preceded the Vedic soma sacrifices.

The three major events of the Buddha's life—his birth, Enlightenment, and entrance into final nirvana—are commemorated in all Buddhist countries but not everywhere on the same day. In the Theravada countries the three events are all observed together on **Vesak,** the full moon day of the sixth lunar month, which usually occurs in May. In Japan and other Mahayana countries, the three anniversaries of the Buddha are observed on separate days (in some countries the birth date is 8 April, the Enlightenment date is 8 December, and the death date is 15 February).

Chinese holidays—The **Chinese New Year** is celebrated with a big family meal and presents of cash are given to children in red envelopes. In 2003 the Chinese New Year will be on 1 February.

During the **Chinese Moon Festival,** on the 15th day of the 8th month of the lunar calendar, people return to their homes to visit with their family. The traditional food is moon cakes, round pastries stuffed with food such as red bean paste. The Moon Festival will occur on 11 Sep 2003.

Japanese holidays—The Japanese celebrate **3-5-7 day** (Shichigosan no hi) in which parents bring children of those ages to the Shinto shrine to pray for their continued health. This day is held on 15 November.

In mid-July (or mid-August, in some areas) the Japanese celebrate **Obon** (also known as Bon Matsuri, or Urabon). The festival honors the spirits of deceased householders and of the dead generally. Memorial stones are cleaned, community dances are performed, and paper lanterns and fires are lit to welcome the dead and to bid them farewell at the end of their visit. The Shinto New Year, **Gantan-sai,** is celebrated on 31 December-1 January.

Hindu holidays—**Dussehra** celebrates the victory of Rama over Ravana, the symbol of evil on earth. In 2003 Dussehra falls on 5 October. **Diwali** is a festival of lights devoted to Laksmi, the goddess of wealth. During the festival, small earthenware lamps filled with oil are lighted and placed in rows along the parapets of temples and houses and set adrift on rivers and streams. Diwali is on 25 Oct 2003. **Sivaratri,** the most important sectarian festival of the year for devotees of the Hindu god Shiva, occurs on 1 Mar 2003. **Holi** is a spring festival, probably of ancient origin. Participants throw colored waters and powders on one another, and, on this day, the usual restrictions of caste, sex, status, and age are disregarded. It will be on 18 Mar 2003.

Sikh holidays—Sikhs observe all festivals celebrated by the Hindus of northern India. In addition, they celebrate the birthdays of the first and the last Gurus and the martyrdom of the fifth (Arjun) and the ninth (Tegh Bahadur). In 2003 the observance of **Guru Nanak Dev Sahib's birthday** falls on 8 November and that of **Guru Gobind Singh Sahib** on 5 January. On 16 June **Arjun's martyrdom** will be observed. *Kachi lassi* (sweetened milk) is offered to passersby to commemorate his death. On 24 November the **martyrdom of Tegh Bahadur** is observed.

Baha'i holidays—The Bahai New Year (**Naw Ruz**) in 2003 will fall on 21 March. Other important observances include the **declaration of the Bab** on 23 May, the **Baha 'Ullah's birth** (12 November), and **Ascension** (29 May).

Zoroastrian holidays—**Noruz** (New Day) is on 21 March for 2003 and the 26th of that month is **Khordad Sal,** the birth of the prophet Zarathustra.

Finally, the **African American holiday** of **Kwanzaa** (Swahili for "First Fruits") is celebrated each year from 26 December to 1 January and is patterned after various African harvest festivals. Maulana Karenga, a black-studies professor, created Kwanzaa in 1966 as a nonreligious celebration of family and social values. Each day of Kwanzaa is dedicated to one of seven principles: unity (*umoja*), self-determination (*kuji chagulia*), collective responsibility (*ujima*), cooperative economics (*ujamaa*), purpose (*nia*), creativity (*kuumba*), and faith (*imani*).

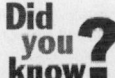
Did you know? Gravitation, a universal force of attraction acting between all matter, is by far the weakest known force in nature. Because of its long reach and universality, however, gravity shapes the structure and evolution of stars, galaxies, and the entire universe.

Civil Holidays

DAY	EVENT
1 January	New Year's Day, the first day of the modern calendar (various countries)
20 January	Inauguration Day, for quadrennial inauguration of US president
3rd Monday in January	Martin Luther King Day, for birth of US civil-rights leader
2nd new moon after winter solstice (at the earliest 21 January and at the latest 19 February)	New Year, for Chinese lunar year, inaugurating a 15-day celebration
Shevat 15	Tu Bishevat, for Jewish arbor day
6 February	Waitangi Day, for Treaty of Waitangi, granting British sovereignty (New Zealand)
6 February	National Foundation Day, for founding by first emperor (Japan)
14 February	St. Valentine's Day, celebrating the exchange of love messages and named for either of two 3rd-century Christian martyrs (various)
3rd Monday in February	Presidents' Day, Washington-Lincoln Day, or Washington's Birthday, for birthdays of US Presidents George Washington and Abraham Lincoln
8 March	International Women's Day, celebration of the women's liberation movement
17 March	St. Patrick's Day, for patron saint of Ireland (Ireland and various)
21 or 22 March	Vernal Equinox Day, for beginning of spring (Japan)
25 March	Independence Day, for proclamation of independence from the Ottoman Empire (Greece)
4th Sunday in Lent	Mothering Day (UK)
1 April	April Fools' Day, or All Fools' Day, day for playing jokes, falling one week after the old New Year's Day of 25 March (various)
5 April	Ching Ming (Qingming), for sweeping tombs and honoring the dead (China)
7 April	World Health Day, for founding of World Health Organization
21/22 April	Earth Day, for conservation and reclaiming of the natural environment (various)
25 April	ANZAC Day, for landing at Gallipoli (Australia/New Zealand/Samoa/Tonga)
30 April	Queen's Birthday, for Queen Beatrix's investiture and former queen Juliana's birthday (The Netherlands)
1 May	May Day, celebrated as labor day or as festival of flowers (various)
3 May	Constitution Memorial Day, for establishment of democratic government (Japan)
5 May	Children's Day, for honoring children (Japan/South Korea)
8/9 May	V-E Day, or Liberation Day, for end of World War II in Europe (various)
2nd Sunday in May	Mother's Day, honoring mothers (US)
30 or last Monday in May	Memorial Day, or Decoration Day, in honor of the deceased, especially the war dead (US)
2 June	Anniversary of the Republic, for referendum establishing republic (Italy)
5 June	Constitution Day (Denmark)
6 June	National Day, for Gustav I Vasa's ascension to the throne and adoption of Constitution (Sweden)
10 June	Portugal's Day, or Camões Memorial Day, for anniversary of Luis de Camões's death
14 June	Flag Day, for honoring flag (US)
3rd Saturday in June	Queen's Official Birthday, for Queen Elizabeth II (UK)
3rd Sunday in June	Father's Day, honoring fathers (US)
23 June	National Day, for Grand Duke Jean's official birthday (Luxembourg)
23–24 June	Midsummer Eve and Midsummer Day, for celebrating the return of summer (various European)
last Sunday in June	Gay and Lesbian Pride Day, final day of week-long advocacy of rights of homosexuals (international)
1 July	Canada Day (formerly Dominion Day) for establishment of dominion
4 July	Independence Day, for Declaration of Independence from Britain (US)
12 July	Orangemen's Day, or Orange Day, anniversary of the Battle of the Boyne (Northern Ireland)
14 July	Bastille Day, for fall of the Bastille and onset of French Revolution
21 July	National Day, for separation from The Netherlands (Belgium)
1 August	National Day, for anniversary of the founding of the Swiss Confederation (Switzerland)
6 August	Hiroshima Day, for dropping of atomic bomb (Japan)
full-moon day of 8th lunar month	Chusok, harvest festival (Korea)
1st Monday in September	Labor Day, tribute to workers (US, Canada)
15 September	Respect-for-the-Aged Day, for the elderly (Japan)
23 or 24 September	Autumnal Equinox Day, for beginning of autumn; in honor of ancestors (Japan)
two weeks ending on 1st Sunday in October	Oktoberfest, festival of food and drink, formerly commemorating marriage of King Louis (Ludwig) I (Germany)
3 October	Day of German Unity, for reunification of Germany
5 October	Republic Day, for founding of the republic (Portugal)

Civil Holidays (continued)

DAY	EVENT
12 or 2nd Monday in October	Hispanic Day, Columbus Day, Discovery Day, or Day of the Race, for Christopher Columbus's discovery of the New World on behalf of Spain (Spain, various)
2nd Monday in October	Thanksgiving Day, harvest festival (Canada)
24 October	United Nations Day, for effective date of UN Charter (international)
26 October	National Day, for end of postwar occupation and return of sovereignty (Austria)
31 October	Halloween, or All Hallows' Eve, festive celebration of ghosts and spirits, on eve of All Saints' Day (various)
5 November	Guy Fawkes Day, anniversary of the Gunpowder Plot to blow up the king and Parliament (UK)
1st Tuesday after 1st Monday in November	Election Day, for general and presidential elections (US)
11 November	Armistice Day, Remembrance Day, or Veterans' Day, honoring participants in past wars and recalling the Armistice of World War I (various)
23 November	Labor Thanksgiving Day, honoring workers (Japan)
4th Thursday in November	Thanksgiving Day, harvest festival (US)
23 December	Emperor's Birthday, for birthday of Emperor Akihito (Japan)
26 December	Boxing Day, second day of Christmas, for giving presents to service people (various)
31 December	New Year's Eve, celebration ushering out the old year and in the new year (various)

The Universe

Cosmogony (Theories of the Origin of the Universe)

Three great ages of scientific thinking about the universe can be distinguished. The first began in Greece in the 6th century BC when the **Pythagoreans** introduced the concept of a **spherical Earth** and postulated a universe in which the motions of heavenly bodies were governed by natural laws. The **infinite atomist universe** of Leucippus and Democritus followed, wherein countless worlds, teeming with life, were the result of chance aggregations of atoms. The **geocentric Aristotelian universe** arose in the 4th century BC. It consisted of a central Earth surrounded by revolving, translucent spheres to which were attached the Sun and the planets; the outermost sphere supported the fixed stars.

The **Copernican revolution** ushered in the second great age. In the 16th century, Nicolaus Copernicus revived ancient ideas and proposed a heliocentric universe, which during the following century was transformed into the mechanistic, infinite **Newtonian universe** that flourished until the early 1900s. In the mid-18th century, Thomas Wright proposed the influential notion of a universe composed of numerous **galaxies**, and William Herschel, followed by many other astronomers, made rapid strides in the study of stars and of the Milky Way Galaxy, of which the Earth is a component.

The third great age began in the early years of the 20th century, with the discovery of special relativity and its development into general relativity by **Albert Einstein**. These years also saw momentous developments in astronomy: extragalactic redshifts were detected by Vesto Slipher; extragalactic nebulae were shown to be galaxies comparable with the Milky Way; and **Edwin Hubble** began to estimate the distances of these galactic systems. Such discoveries and the application of general relativity to cosmology eventually gave rise to the view that the **universe is expanding**. The basic premise of modern thinking on the universe is the principle that asserts that the universe is homogeneous in space (on the average all places are alike at any time) and that the laws of physics are everywhere the same.

Two theories of the origin of the universe have been the most influential during the last century—the steady state theory and the big bang theory. The **steady state theory** posits that the universe is always expanding but maintains a constant average density, matter being continuously created to form new stars and galaxies at the same rate that old ones become unobservable as a consequence of their increasing distance and velocity of recession. A steady-state universe has no beginning or end in time; and from any point within it the view on the grand scale—i.e., the average density and arrangement of galaxies—is the same. Galaxies of all possible ages are intermingled. Observations since the 1950s have produced much evidence contradictory to the steady-state picture and supportive of the big-bang model.

The essential feature of the widely-held **big bang theory** is the emergence of the universe from a state of extremely high temperature and density—the so-called big bang that occurred at least 10,000,000,000 years ago. Although this type of universe was proposed by Alexander Friedmann and Abbé Georges Lemaître in the 1920s, the modern version was developed by George Gamow and colleagues in the 1940s.

One current problem that scientists are studying is the **amount of matter in the universe**. Based upon such things as the rate of the motion of galaxies, scientists realized that there is some 90% more matter in the universe than can be seen. Scientists refer to the matter that can be observed as "**bright matter**" and this other 90% is called "**dark matter**." Whether dark matter is of a different and exotic nature from the matter with which we are familiar, or whether dark matter is just like luminous matter (and for some reason we cannot detect it), is something a large number of scientists are studying.

Astronomical Constants

QUANTITY	SYMBOL	VALUE	WHAT IT QUANTIFIES
astronomical unit	AU	length of the semi-major axis of the Earth to the Sun— 149,597,870 km (92,955,808 mi).	Large distances in space—AU is the average distance from the Earth to the Sun.
parsec	pc	One parsec equals 3.26 light years	Measure that represents the distance at which the radius of the Earth's orbit subtends an angle of one second of arc.
light year	ly	9.46089×10^{12} km (5.8787×10^{12} mi)	The distance traveled by light moving in a vacuum in the course of one year.
solar parallax		8.79414″	The angular difference in direction of the Sun as measured from two points on the Earth's orbit.
lunar parallax		57′ 02.608″	The angular difference in direction of the Moon as measured from two points on the Earth's orbit.
general precession		50.29 arc seconds per year	A cyclic wobbling in the orientation of the Earth's axis of rotation with a period of almost 26,000 years.
constant of aberration		about 20.49″ of arc	The maximum amount of the apparent yearly aberrational displacement of a star or other celestial body, resulting from the Earth's orbital motion around the Sun.
constant of nutation		9.202″	A small irregularity in the precession of the equinoxes that occurs over a period of 18.6 years.
speed of light (in a vacuum)	c	$2.99792458 \times 10^{10}$ cm per sec (186,282 mi per sec)	
radius of the Sun	Sun R	6.96×10^{8} m (109 times the radius of Earth)	
mass of the Sun	Sun M	1.989×10^{30} kg (330,000 times the mass of the Earth)	
Earth's mean radius		6,378 km (3,963 mi)	
sidereal day (on Earth)		23 h 56 min 4.10 sec of mean solar time.	Defined by the period between two passages of a star across the meridian.
mean solar day on Earth		24 h 3 min 56.55 sec duration	The interval between two passages of the Sun across the meridian is a solar day. In practice, since the rate of the Sun's motion varies with the seasons, use is made of a fictitious Sun that always moves across the sky at an even rate.
tropical year (on Earth)		365.242190 days (for 2003)	The rotation period it takes for the Earth to return the Sun to the Spring equinoctial point.
sidereal year (on Earth)		365.256363 days (for 2003)	The rotation period it takes for the Earth to return to the longitude of a fixed star.
synodic month (on Earth)		29.530589 days (for 2003)	Rotation period between two successive full moons.
sidereal month (on Earth)		27.321662 days (for 2003)	Rotation period it takes the Moon to return to a set place in relation to the stars.

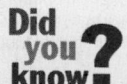

Did you know? The seven brightest stars in the constellation of Ursa Major, or Great Bear (also called the Big Dipper), constitute one of the most characteristic figures in the northern sky. Five of these stars form an associated group with common proper motion, but Dubhe (the upper pointer) and Alcaid (the last star of the tail) have no connection with the others.

Definitions of Astronomical Positions

A conjunction is an apparent meeting or passing of two or more celestial bodies. For example, the Moon is in conjunction with the Sun at the phase of new Moon, when it moves between the Earth and Sun and the side turned toward the Earth is dark. Inferior planets—those with orbits smaller than the Earth's (namely, Venus and Mercury)—have two kinds of conjunctions with the Sun. An **inferior conjunction** occurs when the planet passes approximately between Earth and Sun; if it passes exactly between them, moving across the Sun's face as seen from Earth, it is said to be in transit (see below). A **superior conjunction** occurs when Earth and the other planet are on opposite sides of the Sun, but all three bodies are again nearly in a straight line. Superior planets, those having orbits larger than the Earth's can have only superior conjunctions with the Sun.

When celestial bodies appear in opposite directions in the sky they are said to be in **opposition**. The Moon, when full, is said to be in opposition to the Sun (the Earth is then approximately between them). A superior planet (one with an orbit farther from the Sun than Earth's) is in opposition when Earth passes between it and the Sun. The opposition of a planet is a good time to observe it, because the planet is then at its nearest point to the Earth and in its full phase. The inferior planets, Venus and Mercury, can never be in opposition to the Sun.

When a celestial body as seen from the Earth makes a right angle with the direction of the Sun it is said to be in **quadrature**. The Moon at first or last quarter is said to be at east or west quadrature, respectively. A superior planet is at west quadrature when its position is 90° west of the Sun.

The east–west coordinate by which the position of a celestial body is ordinarily measured is known as **right ascension**. Right ascension in combination with **declination** defines the position of a celestial object. Declination is the angular distance of a body north or south of the celestial equator. North declination is considered positive and south, negative. Thus, +90° declination marks the north celestial pole, 0° the celestial equator, and −90° the south celestial pole. The symbol for right ascension is the Greek letter α (alpha) and for declination the lowercase Greek letter Δ (delta).

The angular distance in celestial longitude separating the Moon or a planet from the Sun is known as **elongation**. The greatest elongation possible for the two inferior planets is about 48° in the case of Venus and about 28° in that of Mercury. Elongation may also refer to the angular distance of any celestial body from another around which it revolves or from a particular point in the sky; e.g., the extreme east or west position of a star with reference to the north celestial pole.

The point at which a planet is closest to the Sun is called the **perihelion**, and the most distant point in that planet's orbit is the **aphelion**. The term helion refers specifically to the Sun as the primary body about which the planet is orbiting.

Occultation refers to the obscuring of the light of an astronomical body, most commonly a star, by another astronomical body, such as a planet or a satellite. Hence, a solar eclipse is the occultation of the Sun by the Moon. From occultations of stars by planets, asteroids, and satellites, astronomers are able to determine the precise sizes and shapes of the latter bodies in addition to the temperatures of planetary atmospheres. For example, astronomers unexpectedly discovered the rings of Uranus during a stellar occultation on 10 Mar 1977.

A complete or partial obscuring of a celestial body by another is an **eclipse**; these occur when three celestial objects become aligned. The Sun is eclipsed when the Moon comes between it and the Earth; the Moon is eclipsed when it moves into the shadow of the Earth cast by the Sun. Eclipses of natural or artificial satellites of a planet occur as the satellites move into the planet's shadow. When the apparent size of the eclipsed body is much smaller than that of the eclipsing body, the phenomenon is known as an **occultation** (see above). Examples are the disappearance of a star, nebula, or planet behind the Moon, or the vanishing of a natural satellite or space probe behind some body of the solar system. A **transit** (see above) occurs when, as viewed from the Earth, a relatively small body passes across the disk of a larger body, usually the Sun or a planet, eclipsing only a very small area: Mercury and Venus periodically transit the Sun, and a satellite may transit its planet.

When an object orbiting the Earth is at the point in its orbit that is the greatest distance from the center of the Earth, this point is known as **apogee**; the term is also used to describe the point farthest from a planet or a satellite (as the Moon) reached by an object orbiting it. **Perigee** is the opposite of apogee.

The difference in direction of a celestial object as seen by an observer from two widely separated points is termed **parallax**. The measurement of parallax is used directly to find the distance of the body from the Earth (geocentric parallax) and from the Sun (heliocentric parallax). The two positions of the observer and the position of the object form a triangle; if the base line between the two observing points is known and the direction of the object as seen from each has been measured, the apex angle (the parallax) and the distance of the object from the observer can be determined.

An **hour angle** is the angle between an observer's meridian (a great circle passing over his head and through the celestial poles) and the hour circle (any other great circle passing through the poles) on which some celestial body lies. This angle, when expressed in hours and minutes, is the time elapsed since the celestial body's last transit of the observer's meridian. The hour angle can also be expressed in degrees, 15° of arc being equal to one hour.

Constellations

Constellations are certain groupings of stars that were imagined—at least by those who named them—to form conspicuous configurations of objects or creatures in the sky. Constellations are useful in tracking artificial satellites and in assisting astronomers and navigators to locate certain stars.

From the earliest times the star groups known as constellations, the smaller groups (parts of constellations) known as **asterisms**, and, also, **individual stars** have received names connoting some meteorological phenomena or symbolizing religious or mythological beliefs. At one time it was held that the constellation

Constellations (continued)

names and myths were of Greek origin; this view has now been disproved. It is now thought that the Greek constellation system and the cognate legends are primarily of Semitic or even pre-Semitic origin and that they came to the Greeks through the Phoenicians.

The Alexandrian astronomer **Ptolemy** lists the names and orientation of the 48 constellations in his *Almagest*, and, with but few exceptions, they are iden-

tical with those used at the present time. The majority of the remaining 40 constellations that are now accepted were added by European astronomers in the 17th and 18th centuries. In the 20th century the delineation of precise boundaries for all the 88 constellations was undertaken by a committee of the International Astronomical Union. By 1930 it was possible to assign any star to a constellation.

NAME	GENITIVE	MEANING	NOTES
Constellations described by Ptolemy: the zodiac			(First-magnitude stars are given in italics in this column)
Aries	Arietis	Ram	
Taurus	Tauri	Bull	*Aldebaran* is the constellation's brightest star. Taurus also contains the Pleiades star cluster and the Crab Nebula.
Gemini	Geminorum	Twins	The brightest stars in Gemini are Castor and *Pollux*.
Cancer	Cancri	Crab	Cancer contains the well-known star cluster Praesepe.
Leo	Leonis	Lion	*Regulus* is the brightest star in Leo.
Virgo	Virginis	Virgin	*Spica* is the brightest star in Virgo.
Libra	Librae	Balance	
Scorpius	Scorpii	Scorpion	*Antares* is the brightest star of Scorpius, which also contains many star clusters.
Sagittarius	Sagittarii	Archer	The center of the Milky Way Galaxy lies in Sagittarius, with the densest star clouds of the galaxy.
Capricornus	Capricorni	Sea-goat	
Aquarius	Aquarii	Water-bearer	
Pisces	Piscium	Fishes	

Other Ptolemaic constellations

NAME	GENITIVE	MEANING	NOTES
Andromeda	Andromedae	Andromeda (an Ethiopian princess of Greek legend, daughter of Cepheus and Cassiopeia)	The constellation's most notable feature is the great spiral galaxy Andromeda (also called M31).
Aquila	Aquilae	Eagle	The brightest star in Aquila is *Altair*.
Ara	Arae	Altar	
Argo Navis	Argus Navis	the ship *Argo*	Argo Navis is now divided into smaller constellations that include Carina, Puppis, Pyxis, and Vela.
Auriga	Aurigae	Charioteer	The brightest star in Auriga is *Capella*. The constellation also contains open star clusters M36, M37, and M38.
Boötes	Boötis	Herdsman	*Arcturus* is the brightest star in Boötes.
Canis Major	Canis Majoris	Greater Dog	*Sirius* is the brightest star in Canis Major.
Canis Minor	Canis Minoris	Smaller Dog	*Procyon* is the brightest star in Canis Minor.
Cassiopeia	Cassiopeiae	Cassiopeia was a legendary queen of Ethiopia	Tycho's nova, one of the few recorded supernovae in the Galaxy, appeared in Cassiopeia in 1572.
Centaurus	Centauri	Centaur (possibly represents Chiron)	*Alpha Centauri* in Centaurus contains Proxima, the nearest star to the Sun.
Cepheus	Cephei	Cepheus (legendary king of Ethiopia)	Delta Cephei was the prototype for cepheid variables (a class of variable stars).
Cetus	Ceti	Whale	Mira Ceti was the first recognized variable star.
Corona Austrina	Coronae Austrinae	Southern Crown	
Corona Borealis	Coronae Borealis	Northern Crown	
Corvus	Corvi	Raven	
Crater	Crateris	Cup	
Cygnus	Cygni	Swan	Cygnus contains the asterism (grouping of stars) known as the Northern Cross; the constellation's brightest star is *Deneb*.
Delphinus	Delphini	Dolphin	Delphinus contains the asterism known as Job's Coffin.
Draco	Draconis	Dragon	Drac contains the star Thuban, which was the polestar in 3000 BC.

Constellations (continued)

NAME	GENITIVE	MEANING	NOTES
Other Ptolemaic constellations (continued)			
Equuleus	Equulei	Little Horse	
Eridanus	Eridani	River Eridanus or river god	*Achernar* is the brightest star in Eridanus.
Hercules	Herculis	Hercules (Greek hero)	Hercules contains the great globular star cluster M13.
Hydra	Hydrae	Water Snake	
Lepus	Leporis	Hare	
Lupus	Lupi	Wolf	
Lyra	Lyrae	Lyre	The brightest star in Lyra is *Vega*. In some 10,000 years, *Vega* will become the polestar. Lyra also contains the Ring Nebula (M57).
Ophiuchus	Ophiuchi	Serpent-bearer	When the Zodiac was conceived of, Ophiuchus was not in the Sun's path, but the Sun does now pass through Ophiuchus each December.
Orion	Orionis	Hunter	*Rigel* is the brightest star in Orion, followed closely by *Betelgeuse;* M42 (the Great Nebula) resides in Orion.
Pegasus	Pegasi	Pegasus (winged horse)	The constellation contains stars of the Great Square of Pegasus.
Perseus	Persei	Perseus (legendary Greek hero)	
Piscis Austrinus	Piscis Austrini	Southern Fish	The brightest star in Piscis Austrinus is *Fomalhaut.*
Sagitta	Sagittae	Arrow	
Serpens	Serpentis	Serpent	
Triangulum	Trianguli	Triangle	The constellation contains M33, a nearby spiral galaxy.
Ursa Major	Ursae Majoris	Great Bear	The seven brightest stars of this constellation are the Big Dipper (also called the Plough).
Ursa Minor	Ursae Minoris	Lesser Bear	Ursa Minor contains Polaris (the north polestar).
Southern constellations, added c. 1600			
Apus	Apodis	Bird of Paradise	
Chamaeleon	Chamaeleontis	Chameleon	
Dorado	Doradus	Swordfish	The most notable object in Dorado is the Large Magellanic Cloud.
Grus	Gruis	Crane	
Hydrus	Hydri	Water Snake	
Indus	Indi	Indian	
Musca	Muscae	Fly	
Pavo	Pavonis	Peacock	
Phoenix	Phoenicis	Phoenix (mythical bird)	
Triangulum Australe	Trianguli Australis	Southern Triangle	
Tucana	Tucanae	Toucan	The most notable object in Tucana is the Small Magellanic Cloud.
Volans	Volantis	Flying Fish	
Constellations of Bartsch, 1624			
Camelopardalis	Camelopardalis	Giraffe	
Columba	Columbae	Dove	This constellation was formed by Petrus Plancius in the early 1600s.
Monoceros	Monocerotis	Unicorn	
Constellations of Hevelius, 1687			
Canes Venatici	Canum Venaticorum	Hunting Dogs	The constellation contains M51 (the Whirlpool Galaxy).
Lacerta	Lacertae	Lizard	
Leo Minor	Leonis Minoris	Lesser Lion	
Lynx	Lyncis	Lynx	
Scutum	Scuti	Shield	Scutum contains the Scutim star cloud in the Milky Way.
Sextans	Sextantis	Sextant	
Vulpecula	Vulpeculae	Fox	Vulpecula contains M27 (the Dumbbell Nebula).

Constellations (continued)

NAME	GENITIVE	MEANING	NOTES
Ancient asterisms that are now separate constellations			
Carina	Carinae	Keel [of the legendary ship the *Argo*]	The brightest star in Carina is *Canopus*.
Coma Berenices	Comae Berenices	Berenice's Hair	The constellation contains both a coma (star cluster) and the north galactic pole (a point that lies perpendicular to the Milky Way).
Crux	Crucis	[Southern] Cross	
Puppis	Puppis	Stern [of the *Argo*]	
Pyxis	Pyxidis	Compass [of the *Argo*]	
Vela	Velorum	Sails [of the *Argo*]	
Southern constellations of Lacaille, c. 1750			
Antlia	Antliae	Pump	
Caelum	Caeli	[Sculptor's] Chisel	
Circinus	Circini	Drawing Compasses	
Fornax	Fornacis	[Chemical] Furnace	
Horologium	Horologii	Clock	
Mensa	Mensae	Table [Mountain]	
Microscopium	Microscopii	Microscope	
Norma	Normae	Square	
Octans	Octantis	Octant	Octans contains the south celestial pole.
Pictor	Pictoris	Painter's [Easel]	
Reticulum	Reticuli	Reticle	
Sculptor	Sculptoris	Sculptor's [Workshop]	Sculptor contains the south galactic pole.
Telescopium	Telescopii	Telescope	

Astrology: The Zodiac

NAME	SYMBOL	DATES	SEX/NATURE	TRIPLICITY	HOUSE	EXALTATION
Aries the Ram	♈	21 Mar–19 Apr	masculine/moving	fire	Mars	Sun (19°)
Taurus the Bull	♉	20 Apr–20 May	feminine/fixed	earth	Venus	Moon (3°)
Gemini the Twins	♊	21 May–21 Jun	masculine/common	air	Mercury	
Cancer the Crab	♋	22 Jun–22 Jul	feminine/moving	water	Moon	Jupiter (15°)
Leo the Lion	♌	23 Jul–22 Aug	masculine/fixed	fire	Sun	
Virgo the Virgin	♍	23 Aug–22 Sep	feminine/common	earth	Mercury	Mercury (15°)
Libra the Balance	♎	23 Sep–23 Oct	masculine/moving	air	Venus	Saturn (21°)
Scorpius the Scorpion	♏	24 Oct–21 Nov	feminine/fixed	water	Mars	
Sagittarius the Archer	♐	22 Nov–21 Dec	masculine/common	fire	Jupiter	
Capricorn the Goat	♑	22 Dec–19 Jan	feminine/moving	earth	Saturn	Mars (28°)
Aquarius the Water Bearer	♒	20 Jan–18 Feb	masculine/fixed	air	Saturn	
Pisces the Fish	♓	19 Feb–20 Mar	feminine/common	water	Jupiter	Venus (27°)

Classification of Stars

The spectral sequence O–M represents stars of essentially the same chemical composition but of different temperatures and atmospheric pressures. Stars belonging to other, more rare types of spectral classifications differ in chemical composition from O–M stars.

Each spectral class is additionally subdivided into 10 spectral types. For example, spectral class A is subdivided into spectral types A0–A9 with 0 being the hottest and 9 the coolest. (Spectral class O is unusual in that it is subdivided into O4–O9.)

Between two stars of the same spectral type, the more luminous star will also be largest in diameter. Thus the Yerkes system of luminosity also tells something of a star's radius, with Ia being the largest and V the smallest. Approximately 90% of all stars are main sequence, or type V, stars.

Based upon these systems, the Sun would be a G2 V star (a yellow, relatively hot dwarf star).

SPECTRAL CLASS	COLOR	APPROXIMATE SURFACE TEMP (°C)	EXAMPLES
O	blue	30,000 or greater	These stars are relatively rare
B	blue-white	20,000 to 30,000	Rigel, Alpha Crucis, Beta Crucis
A	white	10,000 to 20,000	Sirius, Vega, Fomalhaut
F	yellow-white	7,000 to 10,000	Canopus, Procyon

Classification of Stars (continued)

SPECTRAL CLASS	COLOR	APPROXIMATE SURFACE TEMP (°C)	EXAMPLES
G	yellow	6,000 to 7,000	Sun
K	orange	4,500 to 6,000	Arcturus, Aldebaran
M	red	3,000 to 4,500	Betelgeuse, Antares

LUMINOSITY CLASSES (BASED UPON THE YERKES SYSTEM)

Ia	most luminous supergiants
Ib	luminous supergiants
II	bright giants
III	normal giants
IV	subgiants
V	main sequence stars (dwarfs)

The 20 Brightest Stars in the Night Sky

This table lists the stars in descending order from brightest to least bright, based on apparent visual magnitude. Formal names of stars, such as Alpha Carinae, refer to the constellation in which the star appears (Carina) and to which star appears the brightest in that constellation; the second highest would be designated as Beta. Some anomalies exist within the naming convention, such as Betelgeuse being the Alpha star of Orion, though Rigel appears brighter.

Negative magnitudes on the scale of brightness are brightest, and one magnitude difference corresponds to a difference in brightness of 2.5 times; e.g., a star of magnitude −1 is 10 times brighter than one of magnitude +1.5.

Apparent magnitude is a measure of how bright a star appears to a viewer on Earth. Absolute magnitude is the brightness one would perceive if all stars were at the same distance from Earth. The distance from Earth that scientists assume to compute absolute magnitude is 10 parsecs (around 32.6 light-years; one light-year equals about 9.46×10^{12} km). With absolute magnitude a comparison can be made between a star such as Rigel, which is very bright but very distant, and a star such as Sirius, which is not that bright but is fairly close to Earth. The Sun, for purposes of comparison with the stars in the table, has an apparent magnitude of −26.8 and an actual magnitude of +4.8, and is a yellow dwarf star that is 8.3 light-minutes from Earth.

NAME	APPARENT VISUAL MAGNITUDE*	ABSOLUTE VISUAL MAGNITUDE	DISTANCE FROM THE SOLAR SYSTEM (LIGHT-YEARS)	TYPE OF STAR	CONSTELLATION	NOTES
Sirius (Alpha Canis Majoris, or Dog Star)	−1.46	+1.43	8.6	binary star, blue white dwarf with a white dwarf companion	Canis Major	Among the ancient Romans, the hottest part of the year was associated with the time in which the Dog Star rose just before dawn; this connection survives in the expression "dog days."
Canopus (Alpha Carinae)	−0.72	around −3.1 (reported values vary)	74 (reported values vary)	yellow-white supergiant	Carina	Canopus is sometimes used as a guide in the attitude control of spacecraft because of its angular distance from the Sun and the contrast of its brightness among nearby celestial objects.
Alpha Centauri (Rigel Kentaurus)	−0.01	+4.5	4.3	triple star, a binary yellow dwarf circled by a red dwarf with a much smaller red dwarf	Centaurus	The faintest of Alpha Centauri's three stars, Proxima, is the closest star to the Sun.
Arcturus (Alpha Boötis)	−0.04	−0.3	34	orange-colored giant	Boötes	Arcturus lies in an almost direct line with the tail of Ursa Major (the Great Bear); hence its name, derived from the Greek words for "bear guard."
Vega (Alpha Lyrae)	+0.03	+0.58	25.3	blue dwarf	Lyra	Vega will become the northern polestar by about AD 14,000 because of the precession of the equinoxes.

The 20 Brightest Stars in the Night Sky (continued)

NAME	APPAR-ENT VISU-AL MAG-NITUDE*	ABSOLUTE VISUAL MAGNI-TUDE	DISTANCE FROM THE SOLAR SYSTEM (LIGHT-YEARS)	TYPE OF STAR	CONSTELLA-TION	NOTES
Capella (Alpha Aurigae)	+0.08	−0.48	41	Capella is actually four stars, two yellow giants and two red-dwarf companion stars	Auriga	Scientists are studying Capella with interest to determine why it emits more X rays than other stars of its type.
Rigel (Beta Orionis)	+0.12 (variable)	−6.4	815	blue-white supergiant with two smaller companion stars	Orion	The name Rigel derives from an Arabic term meaning "the left leg of the giant," referring to the figure of Orion.
Procyon (Alpha Canis Minoris)	+0.38	+2.7	11.4	yellow-white subgiant with a faint, white dwarf companion	Canis Minor	The name Procyon apparently derives from Greek words for "before the dog," as in northern latitudes the star rises just before Sirius, the "Dog Star."
Achernar (Alpha Eridani)	+0.46	−2.6	69	blue dwarf	Eridanus	The name Achernar probably derives from an Arabic phrase meaning "the end of the river," in which the river referred to is the constellation.
Betelgeuse (Alpha Orionis)	+0.50 (variable)	−5.1	650	red supergiant	Orion	Betelgeuse is huge. Its diameter varies between 430 and 625 times the diameter of the Sun over a period of 5.8 years.
Beta Centauri (Hadar)	+0.61	−3.1	320	blue-white supergiant with two smaller companion stars	Centaurus	The constellation Centaurus most likely is meant to represent the centaur Chiron. In Greek myth Chiron was renowned for his wisdom and knowledge of medicine. He renounced his immortality to escape a painful wound and Zeus placed him in the Southern sky.
Altair (Alpha Aquilae)	+0.77	+2.2	16.8	blue dwarf	Aquila	Altair spins nearly 470,000 miles per hour, as opposed to Earth, which spins some 1,000 miles per hour. This rapid spinning flattens Altair from a spherical shape.
Aldebaran (Alpha Tauri)	+0.85	−0.63	60	red giant	Taurus	Aldebaran, derived from the Arabic for "the follower," was perhaps so named because it rises after the Pleiades cluster of stars.
Antares (Alpha Scorpii)	+0.96	−5.28	425	red supergiant	Scorpio	The name Antares seems to come from a Greek phrase meaning "rival of Ares" (i.e., rival of the planet Mars) and was probably given because of the star's color and brightness.
Spica (Alpha Virginis)	+0.98	−3.55	220	binary blue-white dwarf with a non-visible companion	Virgo	Spica is derived from the Latin for "ear of wheat," and the star is said to represent the wheat being held by the Virgin.
Pollux (Beta Geminorum)	+1.14	+1.09	40	red giant	Gemini	The stars Castor and Pollux are named for the mythological twins of ancient Greece.

The 20 Brightest Stars in the Night Sky (continued)

NAME	APPARENT VISUAL MAGNITUDE*	ABSOLUTE VISUAL MAGNITUDE	DISTANCE FROM THE SOLAR SYSTEM (LIGHT-YEARS)	TYPE OF STAR	CONSTELLATION	NOTES
Fomalhaut (Alpha Piscis Austrini)	+1 16	1.74	22	blue-white dwarf	Piscis Austrinus	The name is derived from the Arabic for "mouth of the fish."
Deneb (Alpha Cygni)	+1.25	−8.73	1,630	blue-white supergiant	Cygnus	Deneb is from an Arabic word meaning "tail," as it is considered the tail of the swan Cygnus.
Becrux (Beta Crucis, or Mimosa)	+1.25	−3.92	460	blue-white giant	Crux (The Southern Cross)	Becrux forms the eastern tip of The Southern Cross.
Regulus (Alpha Leo)	+1.35	−0.3	69	blue-white main sequence star	Leo	Regulus is the diminutive form of the Latin "rex" (king).

*Data for apparent visual magnitudes taken from The Astronomical Almanac for 2003, issued jointly by the Nautical Almanac Office of the United States Naval Observatory and Her Majesty's Nautical Almanac Office of the United Kingdom.

Astronomical Phenomena for 2003

HOUR (IN GREENWICH MEAN TIME)	DAY	MONTH	EVENT
10	2	January	Mercury stationary
20	2		new Moon
23	3		Mercury 5° north of Moon
05	4		Earth at perihelion
19	4		Neptune 5° north of Moon
01	6		Uranus 5° north of Moon
13	10		Moon in first quarter
01	11		Moon at apogee
03	11		Venus greatest elongation west (47°)
20	11		Mercury in inferior conjunction
20	15		Saturn 3° south of Moon
22	15		Venus 8° north of Antares
11	18		full Moon
15	19		Jupiter 4° south of Moon
23	22		Mercury stationary
22	23		Moon at perigee
09	25		Moon in last quarter
15	27		Mars 0.4° north of Moon (occultation)
19	28		Venus 4° north of Moon
10	30		Mercury 5° north of Moon
00	31		Neptune in conjunction with Sun
05	31		Mars 5° north of Antares
11	1	February	new Moon
09	2		Jupiter at opposition
01	4		Mercury greatest elongation west (25°)
22	7		Moon at apogee

HOUR (IN GREENWICH MEAN TIME)	DAY	MONTH	EVENT
11	9	February	Moon in first quarter
03	12		Saturn 3° south of Moon
18	15		Jupiter 4° south of Moon
06	16		Vesta stationary
00	17		full Moon
22	17		Uranus in conjunction with Sun
16	19		Moon at perigee
00	21		Mercury 1.6° south of Neptune
10	22		Saturn stationary
17	23		Moon in last quarter
05	25		Mars 1.9° north of Moon
11	27		Venus 5° north of Moon
15	28		Neptune 5° north of Moon
15	1	March	Mercury 3° north of Moon
03	3		new Moon
13	4		Mercury 1.5° south of Uranus
23	6		Pallas in conjunction with Sun
17	7		Moon at apogee
07	11		Moon in first quarter
12	11		Saturn 3° south of Moon
10	12		Juno stationary
20	12		Venus 0.2° north of Neptune
00	15		Jupiter 4° south of Moon
11	18		full Moon
19	19		Moon at perigee
01	21		Equinox

Astronomical Phenomena for 2003 (continued)

HOUR (IN GREENWICH MEAN TIME)	DAY	MONTH	EVENT
00	22	March	Mercury in superior conjunction
17	23		Pluto stationary
02	25		Moon in last quarter
18	25		Mars 3° north of Moon
23	26		Vesta at opposition
22	27		Neptune 5° north of Moon
13	28		Venus 0.05° north of Uranus
08	29		Uranus 5° north of Moon
10	29		Venus 5° north of Moon
19	1	April	new Moon
04	4		Moon at apogee
05	4		Jupiter stationary
22	7		Saturn 3° south of Moon
00	10		Moon in first quarter
08	11		Jupiter 4° south of Moon
15	16		Mercury greatest elongation east (20°)
20	16		full Moon
05	17		Moon at perigee
07	23		Mars 3° north of Moon
12	23		Moon in last quarter
04	24		Neptune 5° north of Moon
16	25		Uranus 5° north of Moon
22	26		Mercury stationary
17	28		Venus 3° north of Moon
08	1	May	Moon at apogee
12	1		new Moon
11	3		Juno at opposition
09	5		Saturn 3° south of Moon
07	7		Mercury in inferior conjunction, transit over Sun
18	8		Jupiter 4° south of Moon
12	9		Moon in first quarter
14	13		Mars 2° south of Neptune
04	15		Vesta stationary
16	15		Moon at perigee
03	16		Neptune stationary
04	16		full Moon (eclipse)
23	16		Ceres in conjunction with Sun
14	19		Mercury stationary
12	21		Neptune 5° north of Moon
20	21		Mars 3° north of Moon
00	23		Uranus 5° north of Moon
01	23		Moon in last quarter
00	28		Mercury 2° south of Venus
13	28		Moon at apogee
03	29		Mercury 2° south of Moon
04	29		Venus 0.1° south of Moon (occultation)
04	31		new Moon (eclipse)
21	1	June	Saturn 4° south of Moon
06	3		Mercury greatest elongation west (24°)

HOUR (IN GREENWICH MEAN TIME)	DAY	MONTH	EVENT
06	5	June	Jupiter 4° south of Moon
15	7		Uranus stationary
20	7		Moon in first quarter
21	9		Pluto at opposition
23	12		Moon at perigee
11	14		full Moon
21	17		Neptune 5° north of Moon
19	18		Venus 5° north of Aldebaran
06	19		Mars 1.7° north of Moon
08	19		Uranus 5° north of Moon
12	19		Mercury 4° north of Aldebaran
23	20		Mars 3° south of Uranus
02	21		Mercury 0.4° south of Venus
15	21		Moon in last quarter
19	21		Solstice
14	24		Saturn in conjunction with Sun
02	25		Moon at apogee
19	29		new Moon
16	2	July	Juno stationary
21	2		Jupiter 4° south of Moon
06	4		Earth at aphelion
10	5		Mercury in superior conjunction
03	7		Moon in first quarter
08	8		Venus 0.8° north of Saturn
22	10		Moon at perigee
19	13		full Moon
05	15		Neptune 5° north of Moon
16	16		Uranus 5° north of Moon
08	17		Mars 0.3° south of Moon (occultation)
07	21		Moon in last quarter
20	22		Moon at apogee
01	26		Mercury at 0.4° north of Jupiter
00	27		Saturn 4° south of Moon
07	29		new Moon
11	30		Mercury 0.2° north of Regulus
13	30		Jupiter 4° south of Moon
22	30		Mars stationary
01	31		Mercury 5° south of Moon
14	4	August	Neptune at opposition
07	5		Moon in first quarter
14	6		Moon at perigee
13	11		Neptune 5° north of Moon
05	12		full Moon
00	13		Uranus 5° north of Moon
17	13		Mars 1.9° south of Moon
21	14		Mercury greatest elongation east (27°)
18	18		Venus in superior conjunction
14	19		Moon at apogee
01	20		Moon in last quarter

Astronomical Phenomena for 2003 (continued)

HOUR (IN GREENWICH MEAN TIME)	DAY	MONTH	EVENT	HOUR (IN GREENWICH MEAN TIME)	DAY	MONTH	EVENT
10	22	August	Jupiter in conjunction with Sun	20	26	October	Venus 0.08° north of Moon (occultation)
14	23		Saturn 4° south of Moon				
10	24		Uranus at opposition	04	1	November	Moon in first quarter
10	27		Mars closest at approach	06	1		Neptune 5° north of Moon
17	27		new Moon	15	2		Uranus 5° north of Moon
00	28		Mercury stationary	09	3		Mars 3° north of Moon
18	28		Mars at opposition				
01	29		Mercury 9° south of Moon	19	8		Uranus stationary
06	30		Pluto stationary	01	9		full Moon (eclipse)
19	31		Moon at perigee	07	10		Venus 4° north of Antares
				12	10		Moon at apogee
13	3	September	Moon in first quarter	19	13		Saturn 5° south of Moon
21	5		Pallas stationary				
19	7		Neptune 5° north of Moon	04	17		Moon in last quarter
06	9		Uranus 5° north of Moon	12	18		Mercury 3° north of Antares
13	9		Mars 1.2° south of Moon (occultation)	16	18		Jupiter 4° south of Moon
17	10		full Moon	23	23		Moon at perigee
02	11		Mercury in inferior conjunction	23	23		new Moon (eclipse)
09	16		Moon at apogee	03	25		Mercury 0.3° north of Moon (occultation)
19	18		Moon in last quarter	18	25		Venus 2° north of Moon
13	19		Mercury stationary	09	26		Ceres stationary
03	20		Saturn 5° south of Moon	14	28		Neptune 5° north of Moon
11	23		Equinox	22	29		Uranus 5° north of Moon
04	24		Jupiter 4° south of Moon	17	30		Moon in first quarter
17	24		Mercury 5° south of Moon	16	1	December	Mars 4° north of Moon
03	26		new Moon				
00	27		Mercury greatest elongation west (18°)	19	5		Juno in conjunction with Sun
06	28		Moon at perigee	12	7		Moon at apogee
14	29		Mars stationary	19	8		Pallas stationary
				21	8		full Moon
19	2	October	Moon in first quarter	06	9		Mercury greatest elongation east (21°)
22	3		Venus 3° north of Spica	22	10		Saturn 5° south of Moon
00	5		Neptune 5° north of Moon	01	12		Ceres 1.1° north of Moon (occultation)
10	6		Uranus 5° north of Moon	05	12		Pluto in conjunction with Sun
15	6		Mars 1.1° north of Moon (occultation)	04	16		Jupiter 4° south of Moon
07	10		full Moon	18	16		Moon in last quarter
15	13		Pallas at opposition	13	17		Mercury stationary
02	14		Moon at apogee	07	22		Solstice
13	17		Saturn 5° south of Moon	12	22		Moon at perigee
13	18		Moon in last quarter	10	23		new Moon
23	21		Jupiter 4° south of Moon	10	24		Vesta in conjunction with Sun
00	23		Neptune stationary	16	25		Venus 3° north of Moon
10	25		Mercury in superior conjunction	01	26		Neptune 5° north of Moon
13	25		new Moon	01	27		Mercury in inferior conjunction
00	26		Saturn stationary				
12	26		Moon at perigee				

Astronomical Phenomena for 2003 (continued)

HOUR (IN GREENWICH MEAN TIME)	DAY	MONTH	EVENT	HOUR (IN GREENWICH MEAN TIME)	DAY	MONTH	EVENT
08	27	December	Uranus 5° north of Moon	07	30	December	Venus 1.9° south of Neptune
07	30		Mars 4° north of Moon	10	30		Moon in first quarter
				21	31		Saturn at opposition

Morning and Evening Stars

This table gives the morning and evening stars for autumn 2002 and for 2003. The morning and evening stars are actually planets that are visible during the early morning and at evening twilight.

PLANET	MORNING STAR	EVENING STAR
Mercury	October through mid-November 2002	mid-November 2002 through first week of January 2003
	mid-January through mid-March 2003	31 March through the end of April 2003
	mid-May through 28 Jun 2003	mid-July to the first week in September 2003
	mid-September through mid-October 2003	10 Nov–21 Dec 2003
Venus	31 Oct 2002 through mid-July 2003	ending 31 Oct 2002; 25 Sep–31 Dec 2003
Mars	October 2002–28 Aug 2003	28 Aug–31 Dec 2003
Jupiter	October 2002–2 Feb 2003	2 Feb–9 Aug 2003
	5 Sep—31 Dec 2003	
Saturn	October through 17 Dec 2002	17 Dec 2002 through 6 Jun 2003
	13 Jul–31 Dec 2003	beginning 31 Dec 2003
Uranus	mid-March through late November 2003	October 2002 through 2003

Did you know The association of meteorites with the miraculous and the religious made 18th-century scientists suspicious of their reality. A shower of stones that fell in 1803 at L'Aigle, France, finally convinced the scientific world that meteorites existed.

Meteors, Meteorites, and Meteor Showers

A meteor (also called a **shooting star** or **falling star**) is a streak of light in the sky that results when a particle or small chunk of stony or metallic matter enters the Earth's atmosphere and vaporizes. The term is sometimes applied to the falling object itself, but the latter is properly called a **meteoroid**. The vast majority of meteoroids burn up in the upper atmosphere, but occasionally one of relatively large mass survives its fiery plunge and reaches the surface as a solid body. Such an object is known as a **meteorite**.

On any clear night in the countryside beyond the bright lights of cities, one can observe with the naked eye several meteors per hour as they streak through the sky. Quite often they vary in brightness along the path of their flight, appear to emit "sparks" or flares, and sometimes leave a luminous train that lingers after their flight has ended. These meteors are the result of the high-velocity collision of meteoroids with the Earth's atmosphere. Nearly all such interplanetary bodies are small fragments derived from comets or asteroids.

The brightest meteor (possibly of cometary origin) for which historical documentation exists—called the **Tunguska event**—struck on 30 Jun 1908, in central Siberia and rivaled the Sun in brightness. The energy delivered to the atmosphere by this impact was roughly equivalent to that of a 10-megaton thermonuclear explosion and caused the destruction of forest over an area of about 2,000 sq km (772.2 sq mi). The geologic record of cratering attests to the impact of much more massive meteoroids. Fortunately, impacts of this magnitude occur only once or twice every 100 million years. It is hypothesized that large impacts of this kind may have played a major role in determining the course of biological evolution by causing simultaneous **mass extinctions** of many species of organisms, possibly including the dinosaurs some 65 million years ago. If so, the replacement of reptiles by mammals as the dominant land animals, the eventual consequence of which was the rise of the human species, would be the result of a grand example of a phenomenon observable every clear night.

The **visibility of meteors** is a consequence of the high velocity of meteoroids in interplanetary space. Before entering the region of the Earth's gravitational influence, their **velocities** range from a few kilometers per second up to as high as 72 km (44.7 mi) per second. As they approach the Earth, the Earth's gravitational field accelerates them to even higher velocities. This great release of energy destroys meteoroids of small mass—particularly those with relatively high velocities—very quickly. Numerous meteors end their observed flight at altitudes above 80 km (49.7 mi), and penetration to as low as 50 km (31 mi) is unusual.

"**Showers**" of meteors have been known since ancient times. On rare occasions, these showers are very dramatic, with thousands of meteors falling per hour. More often, the background hourly rate of roughly 6 observed meteors increases up to about 10–50. Some of the best-known meteor showers are listed below, with their average date of maximum strength and associated comet, if known:

Quadrantid (3 January); **Lyrid** (22 April; 1861 I [Thatcher]); **Eta Aquarid** (3 May; Halley); **S. Delta Aquarid** (29 July); **Capricornid** (30 July); **Perseid** (12 August; Swift-Tuttle); **Andromedid** (3 October; Biela); **Draconid** (9 October; Giacobini-Zinner); **Orionid** (21 October; Halley); **Taurid** (8 November; Encke); **Leonid** (17 November; Temple-Tuttle); **Germinid** (14 December; 3200 Phaeton [this body exhibits no cometary activity and may be of asteroidal rather than cometary origin]).

Auroras

Auroras are **luminous phenomena** of the upper atmosphere that occur primarily in high latitudes of both hemispheres; auroras in the Northern Hemisphere are called **aurora borealis**, or **northern lights**; in the Southern Hemisphere, **aurora australis**, or **southern lights**.

Auroras are caused by the interaction of energetic particles (electrons and protons) from outside the atmosphere with atoms of the upper atmosphere. Such interaction occurs in zones surrounding the Earth's magnetic poles. During periods of intense solar activity, auroras occasionally extend to the middle latitudes; for example, the aurora borealis has been seen at latitudes as far south as 40° in the US.

Auroras take many **forms**, including luminous curtains, arcs, bands, and patches. The uniform arc is the most stable form of aurora, sometimes persisting for hours without noticeable variation. In a great display, however, other forms appear, commonly under

going dramatic variation. The lower edges of the arcs and folds are usually much more sharply defined than the upper parts. Greenish rays may cover most of the sky polewards of the magnetic zenith, ending in an arc that is usually folded and sometimes edged with a lower red border that may ripple like drapery. The display ends with a poleward retreat of the auroral forms, the rays gradually degenerating into diffuse areas of white light.

The **mechanisms** that produce auroral displays are not completely understood. It is known, however, that charged particles arriving in the vicinity of Earth as part of the solar wind are captured by the Earth's magnetic field and conducted downward toward the magnetic poles. They collide with oxygen and nitrogen atoms, knocking away electrons to leave ions in excited states. These ions emit radiation at various wavelengths, creating the characteristic colors (red or greenish blue) of the aurora.

Eclipses

An **eclipse** is a complete or partial obscuring of one celestial body by another; this event occurs when three celestial objects become aligned.

The Sun is eclipsed when the Moon comes between it and the Earth. (Hence, a **solar eclipse** can only occur during a new Moon.) The moon's shadow sweeps across the Earth, darkening the sky, while the Moon blocks out some portion of the view of the Sun. During a total eclipse of the Sun, the Moon's elliptical orbit brings the satellite closer to Earth and causes it to appear larger than the Sun. When the Moon's orbit places it at its farthest distance from Earth, the Moon appears smaller than the Sun and the eclipse will appear as a ring or "annulus" of bright sunlight around the Moon.

The **Moon is eclipsed** when it moves into the shadow of the Earth cast by the Sun. A lunar eclipse can only occur during a full moon. Lunar eclipses can be penumbral, partial, or total. The first type is of interest to astronomers but is difficult to detect. With the next two types either a portion of the Moon or the entire Moon passes through Earth's umbral shadow.

It is safe to watch a lunar eclipse, but solar eclipses must be viewed via a projection onto another surface or through protective filters designed specially for eclipses.

The eclipses for 2003 are given in the table below.

	DATE	TYPE	VISIBLE IN:	ANNULAR OR TOTAL ECLIPSE AREA
Solar eclipses	31 May	Annular eclipse	Europe, Asia, northern regions of North America	Iceland, Greenland
	23–24 November	Total eclipse	Australia, New Zealand, Antarctica, southern South America	Antarctica
Lunar eclipses	16 May	Total eclipse	central Pacific, Americas, Europe, Asia	
	8–9 November	Total eclipse	Americas, Europe, Africa, central Asia	

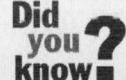

Did you know? The first scientific discovery made with instruments orbiting in space was the existence of the Van Allen radiation belts, by Explorer 1—the first successful US satellite—and other spacecraft in 1958.

Characteristics of Celestial Bodies

Mean orbital velocity indicates the speed with which a planet orbits the Sun unless otherwise specified. *Inclination of orbit to ecliptic* indicates the angle of tilt between a planet's orbit and the plane at which the solar system lies (in degrees). *Orbital period* indicates the planet's year (in Earth days except where noted). *Rotation period* indicates the planet's day (in Earth days except where noted). *Inclination of equator to orbit* indicates the angle of tilt between a planet's orbit and its equator (in degrees). *Gravitational acceleration* measures the body's effect on other objects. *Escape velocity* measures the speed needed at the surface to escape the planet's gravitational pull.

Sun
diameter (at equator): 1,390,000 km (863,705 mi)
mass (in 10^{20} kg): 19.8 billion
density (mass/volume, in kg/m³): 1,408
eccentricity of orbit*: near 0
mean orbital velocity: the Sun orbits the galactic center at around 220 km/sec (136.7 mi/sec)
orbital period: the Sun takes approximately 250 million Earth years to complete its orbit around the Milky Way's galactic center
rotation period: 25–36 Earth days
inclination of equator to orbit: 7.25°
gravitational acceleration: 275 m/sec² (902.2 ft/sec²)
escape velocity: 618.02 km/sec (384.01 mi/sec)
mean temperature at surface**: 5527 °C (9980 °F)
satellites: all planets in solar system
probes and space missions: (US) NASA–Pioneer 5-9, launched 1959–1987; Skylab, launched 1973; Ulysses, 1990. European Space Agency (ESA)–SOHO, 1995.

Mercury
average distance from Sun: 58 million km (36 million mi)
diameter (at equator): 4,879 km (3,032 mi)
mass (in 10^{20} kg): 3,300
density (mass/volume, in kg/m³): 5,427
eccentricity of orbit*: 0.205
mean orbital velocity: 47.9 km/sec (29.7 mi/sec)
inclination of orbit to ecliptic: 7.0°
orbital period: 88 Earth days
rotation period: 176 Earth days
inclination of equator to orbit: .001°
gravitational acceleration: 3.7 m/sec² (12.1 ft/sec²)
escape velocity: 4.3 km/sec (2.7 mi/sec)
mean temperature at surface**: 167 °C (333 °F)
satellites: none
probes and space missions: NASA–Mariner 10, 1973; Messenger, 2004.

Venus
average distance from Sun: 108.2 million km (67.2 million mi)
diameter (at equator): 12,104 km (7,521 mi)
mass (in 10^{20} kg): 48,700
density (mass/volume, in kg/m³): 5,243
eccentricity of orbit*: 0.007
mean orbital velocity: 35.0 km/sec (21.8 mi/sec)
inclination of orbit to ecliptic: 3.4°
orbital period: 224.7 Earth days
rotation period: 243.0 (retrograde)
inclination of equator to orbit: 177.4°
gravitational acceleration: 8.9 m/sec² (29.1 ft/sec²)
escape velocity: 10.4 km/sec (6.4 mi/sec)
mean temperature at surface**: 464 °C (867 °F)
satellites: none
probes and space missions: USSR–Venera 1–10, 1961–1975; Vega 1 and 2, 1984; NASA–Mariner 2, 5, and 10, 1962, 1967, and 1973; Galileo, 1989; Magellan, 1989.

Earth
average distance from Sun: 149.6 million km (93 million mi)
diameter (at equator): 12,756 km (7,926 mi)
mass (in 10^{20} kg): 59,700
density (mass/volume, in kg/m³): 5,515
eccentricity of orbit*: 0.017
mean orbital velocity: 29.8 km/sec (18.5 mi/sec)
inclination of orbit to ecliptic: 0.00°
orbital period: 365.25 mean solar days
rotation period: 23 hours, 56 minutes, and 4 seconds
inclination of equator to orbit: 23.5°
gravitational acceleration: 9.8 m/sec² (32.1 ft/sec²)
escape velocity: 11.2 km/sec (7.0 mi/sec)
mean temperature at surface**: 15 °C (59 °F)
satellites: 1–the Moon.

Moon (of Earth)
average distance from Earth: 384,401 km (238,855.7 mi)
diameter (at equator): 3,475 km (2,159 mi)
mass (in 10^{20} kg): 730
density (mass/volume, in kg/m³): 3,340
eccentricity of orbit*: orbital eccentricity of Moon around Earth is 0.055
mean orbital velocity: the Moon orbits Earth at 1.0 km/sec (0.64 mi/sec)
inclination of orbit to ecliptic: 5.1°
orbital period: the Moon revolves around the Earth in 27.3 Earth days
rotation period: the Moon rotates on its axis every 27.32 Earth days
inclination of equator to orbit: 6.7°
gravitational acceleration: 1.6 m/sec² (5.3 ft/sec²)
escape velocity: 2.4 km/sec (1.5 mi/sec)
mean temperature at surface**: daytime: 107 °C (224.6 °F); nighttime: –153 °C (–243.4 °F)
probes and space missions: On July 20, 1969, the first men stepped foot on the Moon, from NASA's Apollo 11. NASA–Pioneer 0-4, 1958–59; USSR Luna 1–24 1959–76.

Mars
average distance from Sun: 227.9 million km (141.6 million mi)
diameter (at equator): 6,794 km (4,222 mi)
mass (in 10^{20} kg): 6,420
density (mass/volume, in kg/m³): 3,933
eccentricity of orbit*: 0.094
mean orbital velocity: 24.1 km/sec (15 mi/sec)
inclination of orbit to ecliptic: 1.9°
orbital period: 687 Earth days (1.88 Earth years)
rotation period: 24.6 hours
inclination of equator to orbit: 25.2°
gravitational acceleration: 3.7 m/sec² (12.1 ft/sec²)
escape velocity: 5.0 km/sec (3.1 mi/sec)
mean temperature at surface**: –65 °C (–85 °F)
satellites: 2–Phobos and Deimos
probes and space missions: NASA–Mariner 3-8, 1964–71; Viking 1 and 2, 1975; Mars Pathfinder,

1996; 2001 Mars Odyssey, 2001. USSR Phobos 1 and 2, 1988.

Jupiter
average distance from Sun: 778.6 million km (483.8 million mi)
diameter (at equator): 142,984 km (88,846 mi)
mass (in 10^{20} kg): 18,990,000
density (mass/volume, in kg/m³): 1,326
eccentricity of orbit*: 0.049
mean orbital velocity: 13.1 km/sec (8.1 mi/sec)
inclination of orbit to ecliptic: 1.3°
orbital period: 11.86 Earth years
rotation period: 9.9 hours
inclination of equator to orbit: 3.1°
gravitational acceleration: 23.1 m/sec² (75.9 ft/sec²)
escape velocity: 59.5 km/sec (37.0 mi/sec)
mean temperature at surface**:–110 °C (–166 °F)
satellites: 39 moons—including Callisto, Ganymede, Europa, and Io, plus rings
probes and space missions: NASA–Pioneer 10 and 11, 1972–73; Voyager 1 and 2, 1977; Ulysses, 1990; Galileo, 1989.

Saturn
average distance from Sun: 1.433 billion km (890.8 million mi)
diameter (at equator): 120,536 km (74,897 mi)
mass (in 10^{20} kg): 5,680,000
density (mass/volume, in kg/m³): 687
eccentricity of orbit*: 0.057
mean orbital velocity: 9.7 km/sec (6 mi/sec)
inclination of orbit to ecliptic: 2.5°
orbital period: 29.43 Earth years
rotation period: 10.7 hours
inclination of equator to orbit: 26.7°
gravitational acceleration: 9.0 m/sec² (29.4 ft/sec²)
escape velocity: 35.5 km/sec (22.1 mi/sec)
mean temperature at surface**: –140 °C (–220 °F)
satellites: 30 moons, plus rings
probes and space missions: NASA–Pioneer 11, 1973; Voyager 1 and 2, 1977. NASA and ESA–Cassini/Huygens, 1997.

Uranus
average distance from Sun: 2.872 billion km (1.784 billion miles)
diameter (at equator): 51,118 km (31,763 mi)
mass (in 10^{20} kg): 868,000
density (mass/volume, in kg/m³): 1,270
eccentricity of orbit*: 0.046
mean orbital velocity: 6.8 km/sec (4.2 mi/sec)
inclination of orbit to ecliptic: 0.8°
orbital period: 83.76 Earth years
rotation period: 17.2 hours (retrograde)
inclination of equator to orbit: 97.8°
gravitational acceleration: 8.7 m/sec² (28.5 ft/sec²)
escape velocity: 21.3 km/sec (13.2 mi/sec)
mean temperature at surface**: –105 °C (–320 °F)
satellites: 20 moons, plus rings
probes and space missions: NASA–Voyager 2, 1986.

Neptune
average distance from Sun: 4.495 billion km (2.793 billion mi)
diameter (at equator): 49,528 km (30,775 mi)
mass (in 10^{20} kg): 1,020,000
density (mass/volume, in kg/m³): 1,638
eccentricity of orbit*: 0.011
mean orbital velocity: 5.4 km/sec (3.4 mi/sec)
inclination of orbit to ecliptic: 1.8°

orbital period: 163.75 Earth years
rotation period: 16.1 hours
inclination of equator to orbit: 28.3°
gravitational acceleration: 11.0 m/sec² (36.0 ft/sec²)
escape velocity: 23.5 km/sec (14.6 mi/sec)
mean temperature at surface**: –200 °C (–330 °F)
satellites: 8 moons, plus rings
probes and space missions: NASA–Voyager 2, 1989.

Pluto
average distance from Sun: 5.870 billion km (3.647 billion mi)
diameter (at equator): 2,390 km (1,485 mi)
mass (in 10^{20} kg): 125
density (mass/volume, in kg/m³): 1,750
eccentricity of orbit*: 0.244
mean orbital velocity: 4.72 km/sec (2.93 mi/sec)
inclination of orbit to ecliptic: 17.2°
orbital period: 248 Earth years
rotation period: 6.38 Earth days (retrograde)
inclination of equator to orbit: 122.5°
gravitational acceleration: 0.6 m/sec² (1.9 ft/sec²)
escape velocity: 1.1 km/sec (0.7 mi/sec)
mean temperature at surface**: –225 °C (–375 °F)
satellites: 1–Charon.

Charon (moon of Pluto)
average distance from Pluto: 19,600 km (12,178.8 mi)
diameter (at equator): 1,186 km (736.9 mi)
mass (in 10^{20} kg): 19
density (mass/volume, in kg/m³): 2,000
eccentricity of orbit*: 0
mean orbital velocity: Charon orbits Pluto at 0.23 km/sec (0.142 mi/min)
inclination of orbit to ecliptic: 98.8°
orbital period: 6.38725 Earth days
rotation period: 6.38725 Earth days
inclination of equator to orbit: 98.9°
gravitational acceleration: 0.21 m/s² (0.69 ft/s²)
escape velocity: 0.58 km/sec (0.36 mi/sec)
mean temperature at surface**: as low as –240 °C (–400 °F).

Comet 1P Halley
average distance from Sun at closest point is 87.8 million km (54 million mi). Farthest distance from the Sun is 5.2 billion km (3.2 billion mi).
diameter (at equator): 16 x 8 x 8 km (9.9 x 4.9 x 4.9 mi)
mass (in 10^{20} kg): unknown
density (mass/volume, in kg/m³): 1
eccentricity of orbit*: 0.967
inclination of orbit to ecliptic: 18°
orbital period: 76.1 to 79.3 years. The next appearance will be 2061. The comet's orbit is retrograde.
rotation period: 52 hours
probes and space missions: ESA–Giotto, 1985; USSR Vega, 1985.

Comet 2P Encke
average distance from Sun at closest point is 50 million km (31 million mi). Farthest distance from the Sun is 658 million km (408 million mi).
eccentricity of orbit*: 0.847
orbital period: 3.3 years, Encke will be visible on Earth 28 Dec 2003.

Comet 81P Wild 2
average distance from Sun at closest point is 236.8 million km (147.1 million mi). Farthest distance from the Sun is 10 billion km (6.2 billion mi).

eccentricity of orbit*: 0.54
orbital period: 6.39 years, thus Wild 2 will be visible from Earth on 25 Sep 2003.

Comet Hale-Bopp
average distance from Sun at closest point is 136 million km (84.5 million mi). Farthest distance from the Sun is 74.7 billion km (46.4 billion mi).
eccentricity of orbit*: 0.995
orbital period: 4,000 years, last appearance from Earth was 31 Mar 1997.

Comet Hyakutake
average distance from Sun at closest point is 34 million km (0.230 AU). Farthest distance from the Sun is 344 billion km (2300 AU).
eccentricity of orbit*: 0.9998
orbital period: ~40,000 years, last appearance from Earth was 1 May 1996.

Kuiper Belt
(a huge belt located beyond Neptune containing residual material left over from the formation of the planets)
average distance from Sun: 4.742 billion km (2.946 billion mi) to 7.120 billion km (4.424 billion mi)
diameter (at equator): asteroids in the Kuiper Belt have a general range from between 100–1200 km (62.1 mi–745.6 mi)
mass (in 10^{20} kg): Scientists estimate there may be as many as 70,000 asteroids of a size greater than 100 km in the Kuiper Belt, the belt is theorized to have a mass of 6000 x 10^{20} kg.
density: not known
eccentricity of orbit*: not known
mean orbital velocity: not known for the majority of objects
inclination of orbit to ecliptic: varies
orbital period: typically these objects have orbital periods of less than 200 years
rotation period: not known
inclination of equator to orbit: not known
gravitational acceleration: not known
escape velocity: not known

Oort cloud
(information about the Oort cloud is based on inference, as scientists cannot observe this phenomenon)
average distance from Sun: 30 trillion km (18.6 trillion mi)
diameter (at equator): spherical cloud of comets that extends some 3 light-years out at the edge of the solar system.
mass (in 10^{20} kg): some 1 to 6 trillion icy objects have an estimated density of not more than 2.4 million and not less than 700,000 x 10^{20} kg?

Milky Way Galaxy
diameter (at equator): 100,000 light-years in diameter by 2,000 light-years in width
mass (in 10^{20} kg): The Milky Way is thought to contain enough mass to equal the mass of one trillion of the earth's Sun. Most of this mass cannot be accounted for and is thought to reside in dark matter.
mean orbital velocity: Galaxies do not travel; however, because space is expanding in all directions, the galaxy is moving along with the space containing it at a rate of around 300 km per second.

Visible universe
diameter (at equator): 30 billion light-years in diameter
mass (in 10^{20} kg): difficult to know; approximately 10^{52} kg
density: The density of the universe has not been ascertained. However, whether the universe will continue to expand forever, will instead begin to contract at a certain point, or whether it is balanced and stop expanding but never contract, depends on its density.
mean orbital velocity: Somewhere around 40 to 90 km/sec/megaparsec (3.26 million light-years). Thus, for every 3.26 million light-years between two galaxies, they're moving away at between 40 and 90 km/sec. (The rate at which the universe is expanding is known as the Hubble constant.)
mean temperature at surface**: The temperature of the cosmic background radiation is 2.735° above absolute zero (–273 °C and –459 °F).

*eccentricity of orbit measures circularity or elongation of an orbit; 0 indicates circular orbits, and closer to 1 more elliptical ones
**for planets with no surface, temperature given is at a level in the atmosphere = to 1 bar of pressure.

Solar System Superlatives

Largest planet in solar system: Jupiter (142,984 km [88,846 mi] diameter); all of the other planets in the solar system could fit inside Jupiter.
Largest moon in the solar system: Jupiter's moon Ganymede, which also is likely to have an ocean beneath its icy crust.
Smallest planet in solar system: Pluto (2,390 km [1,485 mi] diameter).
Smallest moon in the solar system: Saturn and Jupiter both have numerous satellites that are smaller than 10 km (6 mi) in diameter.
Planet closest to the Sun: Mercury (average distance from the Sun of 58,000,000 km [36,000,000 mi]).
Planet farthest from the Sun: usually Pluto; occasionally Neptune crosses Pluto's orbit and so becomes the planet farthest from the Sun.
Planet with the most eccentric (least circular) orbit: Pluto (eccentricity of 0.248).

Moon with the most eccentric orbit: Neptune's moon Nereid (eccentricity of 0.75).
Planet with the least eccentric orbit: Venus (eccentricity of 0.007).
Moon with the least eccentric orbit: Plato's moon, Charon (eccentricity of 0.0).
Planet most tilted on its axis: Uranus (axial tilt of 98°).
Planet with the most moons: Jupiter (39).
Planet with the fewest moons: Mercury and Venus (no moons).
Planet with the longest day: Mercury (1 day on Mercury equals 176 Earth days).
Planet with the shortest day: Jupiter (1 day on Jupiter equals 9.9 Earth hours).
Planet with the longest year: Pluto (1 year on Pluto takes 248 Earth years).
Planet with the shortest year: Mercury (1 year on Mercury takes 88 Earth days).

Fastest orbiting planet in the solar system: Mercury (47.87 km per second [29.75 mi per second] average orbital speed).

Slowest orbiting planet in the solar system: Pluto (4.72 km per second [2.93 mi per second] average orbital speed).

Hottest planet in solar system: Venus (464 °C [867 °F] average temperature); although Mercury is closer to the Sun, Venus is hotter because Mercury has no atmosphere, whereas the atmosphere of Venus traps heat and causes higher temperatures.

Coldest planet in the solar system: Pluto (-223 °C [-369 °F] average temperature).

Brightest visible star in the night sky: Sirius (-1.46 apparent visual magnitude).

Brightest planet in solar system: Venus (apparent visual magnitude -4.5 to -3.77).

Densest planet: Earth (density of 5,515 kg/m³).

Least dense planet: Saturn (density of 687 kg/m³).

Planet with most gravity: Jupiter (more than twice the gravitational force of Earth).

Planet with least gravity: Pluto (about 1/17 the gravitational force of Earth).

Planet with the largest mountain: Mars (Olympus Mons, an extinct volcano, is some 27 km [17 mi] tall and 520 km [320 mi] across).

Planet with deepest valley: Mars (Valles Marineris, a system of canyons is some 4,000 km [2,500 mi] long and from about 2 to 7 km [1 to 5 mi] deep).

Largest known impact crater: Valhalla, a crater on Jupiter's moon Callisto, has a bright central area that is about 600 km (370 mi) across with sets of concentric ridges extending about 1,500 km (900 mi) from the center. For contrast, the largest known impact crater on Earth is the Barringer Crater in Arizona, which is about 1.2 km (0.8 mi) wide.

The Sun

The Sun is the star around which the Earth and the other components of the solar system revolve. It is the dominant body of the system, constituting more than 99% of the system's entire mass. The Sun is the source of an enormous amount of energy, a portion of which provides the Earth with the light and heat necessary to support life. The geologic record of the Earth and Moon reveals that the Sun was formed about 4.5 billion years ago. The energy radiated by the Sun is produced during the conversion of hydrogen atoms to helium. The Sun is at least 90% hydrogen by number of atoms, so the fuel is readily available.

The Sun is classified as a G2 V star, where G2 stands for the second hottest stars of the yellow G class—of surface temperature about 5,500 °C (10,000 °F)—and V represents a main sequence, or dwarf, star, the typical star for this temperature class (see also "Classification of Stars"). The Sun exists in the outer part of the Milky Way Galaxy and was formed from material that had been processed inside a supernova.

The mass of the Sun is 743 times the total mass of all the planets in the solar system and 330,000 times that of the Earth. All the interesting planetary and interplanetary gravitational phenomena are negligible effects in comparison to the force exerted by the Sun. Under the force of gravity, the great mass of the Sun presses inward, and to keep the star from collapsing, the central pressure outward must be great enough to support its weight. The Sun's core, which occupies approximately 25% of the star's radius, has a density about 100 times that of water (roughly 6 times that at the center of the Earth), but the temperature at the core is at least 15,000,000 °C (27,000,000 °F), so the central pressure is at least 10,000 times greater than that at the center of the Earth. In this environ-

ment the nuclei of atoms are completely stripped of their electrons, and at this high temperature they collide to produce the nuclear reactions that are responsible for generating the energy vital to life on Earth.

The temperature of the Sun's surface is so high that no solid or liquid can exist; the constituent materials are predominantly gaseous atoms, with a very small number of molecules. As a result, there is no fixed surface. The surface viewed from Earth, the photosphere, is approximately 400 km (250 mi) thick and is the layer from which most of the radiation reaches us; the radiation from below the photosphere is absorbed and reradiated, while the emission from overlying layers drops sharply, by about a factor of six every 200 km (124 mi).

While the temperature of the Sun drops from 15,000,000 °C at the core to around 5,500 °C (10,000 °F) at the photosphere, a surprising reversal occurs above that point; the temperature begins to rise in the chromosphere, a layer several thousand kilometers thick. Temperatures there range from 4,200 °C (7,600 °F) to 100,000 °C (180,000 °F). Above the chromosphere is a dim, extended halo called the corona, which has a temperature of 1,000,000 °C (1,800,000 °F) and reaches far past the planets. Beyond a distance of around 3,500,000 km (2,200,000 mi) from the Sun, the corona flows outward at a speed (near the Earth) of 400 km/sec (250 mi/sec); this flow of charged particles is called the solar wind.

The Sun is a very stable source of energy. Superposed on this stable star, however, is an interesting 11-year cycle of magnetic activity manifested by regions of transient strong magnetic fields called sunspots. Sunspots, the largest of which can be seen even without a telescope, are regions of extremely strong magnetic field found on the Sun's surface.

Mercury

Mercury is the planet closest to the Sun, revolving around it at an average distance of 58 million km (36 million mi). In Sumerian times it was already known to be a planet, some 5,000 years ago. In classical Greece the planet was called Apollo when it appeared as a morning star and Hermes, for the Greek equivalent of the Roman god Mercury, when it appeared as an evening star.

Mercury's orbit lies inside the orbit of the Earth and is more elliptical than those of most of the other planets. At its closest approach (perihelion), Mercury is only 46 million km (28.5 million mi) from the Sun, while its greatest distance (aphelion) approaches 70 million km (43.5 million mi). Mercury orbits the Sun in 88 Earth days at an average speed of 48 km per second (29.8 mi per sec), allowing it to overtake and pass Earth every 116 Earth days (synodic period).

Because of its proximity to the Sun, the surface of Mercury can become extremely hot. High temperatures at "noon" may reach 400 °C (755 °F) while the "predawn" lowest temperatures –173 °C (–280 °F). Mercury's equator is almost exactly in its orbital plane (its spin axis inclination is nearly zero), and thus Mercury does not have seasons as does the Earth. Because of its elliptical orbit and a peculiarity of its rotational period (see below), however, certain longitudes experience cyclical variations in temperatures on a "yearly" as well as on a "diurnal" basis.

Mercury is about 4,878 km (3031 mi) in diameter, smaller than any other planet with the exception of Pluto. Mercury is only a bit larger than the Moon. Its mass, measured by the gravitational perturbation of the path of the Mariner 10 spacecraft during close flybys in 1974 and 1975 is about one-eighteenth of the mass of the Earth. Escape velocity, the speed needed to escape from a planet's gravitational field, is about 4.25 km per second (2.64 mi per second)—compared with 11.2 km per sec (7 mi per sec) for the Earth.

The mean density of Mercury, calculated from its mass and radius, is about 5.44 grams per cubic cm

(0.48 ounce per inch), nearly the same as that of the Earth (5.5 grams per cubic cm, or 0.49 ounce per inch).

Photographs relayed by the Mariner 10 spacecraft showed that Mercury spins on its axis (rotates) once every 58.646 Earth days, exactly two-thirds of the orbital period of 87.9694 Earth days. This observation confirmed that Mercury is in a 3:2 spin-orbit tidal resonance—i.e., that tides raised on Mercury by the Sun have forced it into a condition that causes it to rotate three times on its axis in the same time it takes to revolve around the Sun twice.

The 3:2 spin-orbit coupling combines with Mercury's eccentric orbit to create very unusual temperature effects. Although it rotates on its axis once every 59 Earth days, one rotation does not bring the Sun back to the same part of the sky, because during that time Mercury has moved partway around the Sun. A solar day on Mercury (for example, from one sunrise to another, or one noon to another) is 176 Earth days (exactly two Mercurian years).

Mercury's low escape velocity and high surface temperatures do not permit it to retain a significant atmosphere.

Venus

Venus is the second planet from the Sun and the planet whose orbit is closest to that of the Earth. When visible, Venus is the brightest planet in the sky. Viewed through a telescope, it presents a brilliant, yellow-white, essentially featureless face to the observer. The obscured appearance results because the surface of the planet is hidden from sight by a continuous and permanent cover of clouds.

Venus' orbit is the most nearly circular of that of any planet, with a deviation from perfect circularity of only about 1 part in 150. The period of the orbit—that is, the length of the Venusian year—is 224.7 Earth days. The rotation of Venus is unusual in both its direction and speed. Most of the planets in the solar system rotate in a counterclockwise direction when viewed from above their north poles; Venus, however, rotates in the opposite, or retrograde, direction. Were it not for the planet's clouds, an observer on Venus' surface would see the Sun rise in the west and set in the east.

Venus spins on its axis very slowly, taking 243 Earth days to complete one rotation. Venus' spin and orbital periods are synchronized with the Earth's orbit such that Venus always presents the same face toward the Earth when the two planets are at their closest approach.

Venus is nearly the Earth's twin in terms of size and mass. Venus' diameter is about 95% of the Earth's diameter at the Equator, while its mass is 81.5% that of the Earth. The similarities to the Earth in size and mass also produce a similarity in density; Venus' density is 5.24 grams per cubic centimeter, as compared with 5.52 for the Earth. (See Table.)

In terms of its shape, Venus is more nearly a perfect sphere than are most planets. A planet's rotation generally causes a slight flattening at the poles and bulging at the equator, but Venus' very slow rotation rate allows it to maintain its highly spherical shape.

Venus has the most massive atmosphere of all the terrestrial planets. Its atmosphere is composed of 96.5% carbon dioxide and 3.5% nitrogen. The atmospheric pressure at the planet's surface varies with the surface elevation but averages about 90 bars, or 90 times the atmospheric pressure at the Earth's surface. This is the same pressure found at a depth of about one kilometer in the Earth's oceans. Temperatures range between a minimum temperature of –45 °C (–49 °F) and a maximum temperature of 500 °C (932 °F); the average temperature is 464 °C (867.2 °F).

Earth

The Earth is the third planet in distance outward from the Sun. It is the only planetary body in the solar system that has conditions suitable for life, at least as known to modern science.

The average distance of the Earth from the Sun— 149.9 million km (93 million mi)—was designated as the distance of the unit of measurement known as the AU (astronomical unit). The Earth orbits the Sun at a speed of 29.8 km (18.5 mi) per second, making one complete revolution in 365.25 days. As it revolves around the Sun, the Earth spins on its axis and rotates completely once every 23 h 56 min 4 sec. The Earth has a single natural satellite, the Moon.

The fifth largest planet of the solar system, the Earth has a total surface area of roughly 509,600,000 sq km (197,000,000 sq mi), of which about 29%, or 148,000,000 square km (57,000,000 square mi), is land. Oceans and smaller seas cover the balance of the surface. The Earth is the only planet known to have liquid water. Together with ice, the liquid water constitutes the hydrosphere. Seawater makes up more than 98% of the total mass of the hydrosphere and covers about 71% of the Earth's surface. Significantly, seawater constituted the environment of the earliest terrestrial life forms. The Earth's surface is subdivided into continental masses, of which there are seven: Europe, Asia, Africa, Australia, North America, South America, and Antarctica. These continents are surrounded by the so-called World Ocean, which is commonly broken down into three major bodies—namely, the Atlantic, Pacific, and Indian oceans.

The centrifugal force of the Earth's rotation makes the planet bulge at the Equator. Because of this, the Earth has the shape of an oblate spheroid, being flatter near the poles than near the Equator. The gravitational field, or gravity, of the Earth is manifested as the force acting upon a free, unsupported body causing it to move in the general direction of the center of the planet. The Earth's gravity is not fixed, but rather varies from place to place on the surface, with the main variation occurring with latitude. It averages approximately 983.22 cm (32.26 ft) per second per second at the poles, which is somewhat higher than at the Equator, where it is only about 973.03 cm (31.92 ft) per second per second.

The Earth's atmosphere consists of a mixture of gases, chiefly nitrogen (78%) and oxygen (21%). Argon makes up much of the remainder of the gaseous envelope, with trace amounts of water vapor, carbon dioxide, and various other gases also present.

The Earth is surrounded by a magnetosphere, a region of strong magnetic forces that extends upward from about 140 km (90 mi) in the upper atmosphere. In the magnetosphere, the magnetic field of the Earth traps rapidly moving charged particles (e.g., electrons and high-energy protons), the majority of which appear to be emitted by the Sun during periods of intense activity. If it were not for this shielding effect, such particles would bombard the terrestrial surface and destroy life. High concentrations of the trapped particles make up two doughnut-shaped zones called the Van Allen radiation belts. These belts play a key role in several geophysical phenomena, as, for example, auroras.

The Moon

The Moon is the sole natural satellite of the Earth. It revolves around the planet from west to east at a mean distance of about 384,400 km (239,900 mi). The Moon is less than one-third the size of the Earth, having a diameter of only about 3,476 km (2,160 mi) at its equator. The Moon shines by reflected sunlight, but its albedo—i.e., the fraction of light received that is reflected—is only 0.073.

The Moon rotates about its own axis in about 29½ days, which is virtually identical to the time it takes to complete its orbit around the Earth. As a result, the Moon always presents nearly the same face to the Earth. The rate of actual rotation is uniform, but the arc through which the Moon moves from day to day varies somewhat, causing the lunar globe (as seen by a terrestrial observer) to oscillate slightly over a period nearly equal to that of revolution.

The surface of the Moon has been a subject of continuous telescopic study from the time of Galileo's first observation in 1609. The Italian Jesuit astronomer Giovanni B. Riccioli designated the dark areas on the Moon as seas, with such fanciful names as Mare Imbrium ("Sea of Showers") and Mare Nectaris ("Sea of Nectar"). This nomenclature continues to be used even though it is now known that the Moon is completely devoid of surface water. During the centuries that followed the publication of these early works, more detailed maps and eventually photographs were produced. A Soviet space probe photographed the side of the Moon facing away from the Earth in 1959. By the late 1960s the US Lunar Orbiter missions had yielded close-up photographs of the entire lunar surface, including both the visible and far sides. On 20 Jul 1969, Apollo 11 astronauts Neil Armstrong and Edwin ("Buzz") Aldrin set foot on the Moon.

The most striking formations on the Moon are its craters. These features, which measure up to about 200 km (320 mi) or more in diameter, are scattered over the surface in great profusion and often overlap one another. Meteorites hitting the lunar surface at high velocity produced most of the large craters. Many of the smaller ones—those measuring less than 1 km (0.6 mi) across—could have been formed by explosive volcanic activity, however. The darker areas of the Moon, known as maria, have relatively few craters. They are thought to be huge lava flows that spread over an area after most of the craters had already been formed.

Various theories for the Moon's origin have been proposed. At the end of the 19th century the English astronomer Sir George II. Darwin advanced a hypothesis the Moon had been originally part of the Earth but was broken away by tidal action and receded from the planet. This was proved unlikely in the 1930s. Another theory that arose during the 1950s postulated that the Moon formed elsewhere in the solar system and was then later captured by the Earth. This idea was also proved to be physically implausible and was dismissed. Today, most investigators favor an explanation known as the giant-impact hypothesis, which postulates that a Mars-sized body struck the proto-Earth early in the history of the solar system. As a result, a cloud of fragments was ejected into orbit around the Earth, and these later accreted into the Moon.

Moon's Perigee and Apogee, 2003

The distance between the centers of mass of the Earth and the Moon varies rather widely due to the combined gravity of the Earth, the Sun, and the planets. For example, during the period 1969–2000, apogee (when the Moon is at the greatest distance from Earth) varied from 404,063 to 406,711 km, while perigee (when the Moon is closest to Earth) varied from 356,517 to 370,354 km. Tidal interactions have braked the Moon's spin so that presently the same side always faces the Earth.

MOON AT APOGEE	
DATE	FARTHEST PHASE OF MOON
11 January	first quarter
7 February	first quarter
7 March	between new moon and first quarter
4 April	new moon

MOON AT PERIGEE	
DATE	CLOSEST PHASE OF MOON
23 January	last quarter
19 February	full moon
19 March	between first quarter and full moon
17 April	full moon

Moon's Perigee and Apogee, 2003 (continued)

	MOON AT APOGEE		MOON AT PERIGEE
	FARTHEST PHASE		CLOSEST PHASE
DATE	OF MOON	DATE	OF MOON
1 May	new moon	15 May	full moon
28 May	new moon	12 June	between first quarter and full moon
25 June	between last quarter and new moon	10 July	between first quarter and full moon
22 July	last quarter	6 August	first quarter
19 August	last quarter	31 August	between new moon and first quarter
16 September	last quarter	28 September	new moon
14 October	between full moon and last quarter	26 October	new moon
10 November	full moon	23 November	new moon
7 December	full moon	22 December	new moon

Moon Phases, 2003

As the Moon orbits the Earth, more or less of the half of the Moon illuminated by the Sun is visible on Earth. During the lunar month the Moon's appearance changes from dark (the new moon) to being illuminated more and more on the right side (waxing crescent, first quarter, and waxing gibbous) to the full disc being illuminated (the full moon). The phases of the moon are completed by the Moon being illuminated less and less on the left side (waning gibbous, last quarter, and waning crescent) and ends with another new moon. The cycle of the moon takes place over a period of around 29 days; the time from new moon to new moon is referred to as a lunation.

The phases of the moon are caused by the positions of the Sun in relationship to the Moon. Thus, when the Sun and Moon are close in the sky a dark new moon is the result (the Sun is lighting the half of the Moon not visible to Earth). When the Sun and Moon are at opposition (in opposite parts of the sky) the full moon occurs (the Sun illuminates fully the half of the Moon seen on Earth). When the Sun and Moon are at about a 90-degree angle, one sees either a first quarter or last quarter moon.

The dates for the new moon, first quarter, full moon, and last quarter for July 2002–December 2003 are given in the table below.

	NEW MOON	FIRST QUARTER	FULL MOON	LAST QUARTER
July 2002	10	17	24	2
August 2002	8	15	22	1, 31
September 2002	7	13	21	29
October 2002	6	13	21	29
November 2002	4	11	20	27
December 2002	4	11	19	27
January 2003	2	10	18	25
February 2003	1	9	16	23
March 2003	3	11	18	25
April 2003	1	9	16	23
May 2003	1, 31	9	16	23
June 2003	(May 31)	7	14	21
July 2003	(June 29)	7	13	21
August 2003	(July 29)	5	12	20
September 2003	(August 27)	3	10	18
October 2003	(September 26)	2	10	18
November 2003	(October 25)	1	9	17
December 2003	(November 23)	(November 30)	8	16
	(December 23)	(December 30)		

Mars

Mars is the fourth planet in order of distance from the Sun and the seventh in order of diminishing size and mass. It orbits the Sun once in 687 Earth days and spins on its axis once every 24 h and 37 min.

Owing to its blood-red color, Mars has often been associated with the gods of war. It is named for the Roman god of war; as far back as 3,000 years ago, Babylonian astronomer-astrologers called the planet Nergal for their god of death and pestilence. The Greeks called it Ares for their god of battle: the planet's two satellites, Phobos (Fear) and Deimos (Terror), were named for the two sons of Ares and Aphrodite.

Mars moves around the Sun at a mean distance of approximately 1.52 times that of the Earth from the

Sun. Because the orbit of Mars is highly elliptical, the distance between Mars and the Sun varies from 206.6 to 249.2 million km (128.4 to 154.8 million mi). Mars completes a single orbit in roughly the time in which the Earth completes two. At its closest approach, Mars is less than 56 million km (34.8 million mi) from the Earth, but it recedes to almost 400 million km (248.5 million mi). Mars is a small planet. Its equatorial radius is about half that of Earth, and its mass is only one-tenth the terrestrial value.

The axis of rotation is inclined to the orbital plane at an angle of 24.935°, and, as for the Earth, the tilt gives rise to the seasons on Mars. The Martian year consists of 668.6 Martian solar days (called sols). The orientation and eccentricity of the orbit (eccentricity denotes how circular or elliptical the orbit is, the more elliptical the more oeocentric) leads to seasons that are quite uneven in length.

The Martian atmosphere is composed mainly of carbon dioxide. It is very thin (less than 1% of the Earth's atmospheric pressure). Evidence suggests that the atmosphere was much denser in the remote past and that water was once much more abundant at the surface. Only small amounts of water are found in the lower atmosphere today, occasionally forming thin ice clouds at high altitudes and, in several localities, morning ice fogs.

The characteristic temperature in the lower atmosphere is about -73.15 °C (-99.67 °F). Unlike that of Earth, the total mass (and pressure) of the atmosphere experiences large seasonal variations, as carbon dioxide "snows out" at the winter pole.

The two satellites of Mars, Phobos and Deimos, were discovered in 1877 by Asaph Hall of the United States Naval Observatory. Little was known about these bodies until observations were sent from orbiting spacecraft a century later.

The orbit of Phobos is exceptionally close to Mars. At a mean distance of 2.8 planetary radii from the center of Mars, it is so close that, without internal strength, it would have been torn apart by gravitational (tidal) forces. These gravitational forces also slow the motion of Phobos and may ultimately cause the satellite to fall onto the surface of Mars, possibly in less than 100 million years. The orbit of Deimos suffers an opposite fate, for it moves in a more distant orbit, and tidal forces cause it to recede from the planet. The orbital period of Phobos around Mars is 7 hours and 39 minutes. This short period means that an observer at a suitable point on the planet would see Phobos rise and set twice in a sol. The moons of Mars cannot be seen from all locations on the planet because of their small size, proximity to the planet, and near-equatorial orbits.

Did you know The largest known volcano in the solar system is Olympus Mons, a shield volcano on Mars. It is 590 km (370 mi) in diameter and 24 km (15 mi) high. In comparison, the largest volcano on Earth, Mauna Loa, Hawaii, is 118 km (74 mi) across and extends 8.8 km (5.5 mi) above the ocean floor.

Small Celestial Bodies

Small bodies are defined as all the natural objects in the solar system other than the major planets and their satellites. The solar system is populated by vast numbers of these small bodies, which can be grouped as asteroids, comets, and meteoroids (at times, however, the distinctions between these groupings can be somewhat blurred).

Small bodies are found in several regions of the solar system. Most asteroids reside in the belt between Mars and Jupiter at approximately 330–508 million km (204–316 million mi). For example, the Trojan asteroids are found between Mars and Jupiter.

The trans-Neptunian objects (considered comets) are located outside the orbit of Neptune, located from around 4.4 billion km (2.7 billion mi) to 7.4 billion km (4.6 billion mi) in the area known as the Kuiper belt. A spherical cloud known as the Oort cloud also contains comets at a distance of some 3–15 trillion km (1.8–9 trillion mi).

Other small bodies travel in unstable paths which cross planetary orbits. These include: 1) all observable comets, 2) near-Earth objects, including asteroids classed as Atens, Apollos, and Amors, and 3) other planet-crossing objects (a mixture of both asteroids and comets). All objects on planet-crossing orbits will eventually collide with the Sun (or a planet) or be permanently ejected from the solar system, although many of these objects do survive for long periods of time due to stabilizing orbital resonances.

Comets originated, and most are still located, in the Kuiper belt and Oort cloud. Even though comets are brief visitors to the inner solar system, their population is constantly replenished through perturbations of the comets in these areas.

There are several characteristics that distinguish asteroids, comets, and meteoroids. These are based upon origin, orbital, and physical differences. An object is classified as a comet when it displays a coma or tail (or any evidence of gas or dust coming from it). In addition, objects found in the Kuiper belt (and the Oort cloud, though none of these are observable) are also considered to be comets. They are defined as comets even though they may not have originated in their present location and they do not display cometary activity (because of their great distance from the Sun). Nevertheless, they are believed to be made up of low-volatility material—primarily water and carbon dioxide—and it is the presence of these volatiles on the surface that is responsible for cometary activity. Finally, objects on parabolic or hyperbolic orbits are generally considered to be comets.

Meteoroids are defined as any object that moves in space and is larger than a molecule but smaller than around 1 km (the light that emanates from this phenomena is a meteor). Should any part of a meteoroid enter Earth's atmosphere without being completely vaporized, that object is termed a meteorite. Asteroids are objects usually larger than 1 km and are frequently made of the same materials that formed the planets.

Asteroids and the Asteroid Belt

Asteroids are any of a host of small rocky bodies, about 1,000 km (620 mi) or less in diameter, that orbit the Sun. About 95% of the known asteroids move in orbits between those of Mars and Jupiter in an area known as the asteroid belt. The orbits of the asteroids, however, are not uniformly distributed within the asteroid belt, but exhibit "gaps." Known as Kirkwood gaps, these asteroid-less areas were created by the gravitational force exerted by Jupiter upon asteroids in certain orbits.

The vast majority of asteroids have orbital periods between three years and six years—i.e., between one-fourth and one-half of Jupiter's orbital period. These asteroids are said to be main-belt asteroids. Within the main belt are asteroids that share certain traits. Known as families, about 40% of all known asteroids belong to such groupings. Families are usually assigned the name of the lowest numbered asteroid in the family. The three largest families (Eos, Koronis, and Themis) have been determined to be compositionally homogeneous.

Besides the few asteroids in highly unusual orbits, there are a number of groups that fall outside the main belt. Those that have orbital periods greater than one-half that of Jupiter are called **outer-belt asteroids**. There are four such groups: the Cybeles, Hildas, and Thule, as well as the Trojan group, so called because all its members are named after characters from Homer's epic work about the Trojan War, the *Iliad*.

There is only one known group of **inner-belt asteroids**—namely, the Hungarias. The Hungaria asteroids have orbital periods that are less than one-fourth that of Jupiter. Finally, Asteroids that can pass inside the orbit of Mars are said to be near-Earth asteroids. There are two groups of **near-Earth asteroids** that deeply cross the Earth's orbit on an almost continuous basis. The first of these to be discovered were the

Apollo asteroids. The other group of Earth-crossing asteroids is named Atens.

Asteroids are thought to have been created from the same **material** that formed the planets. Scientists believe that at the time the planets were forming from the low-velocity collisions among asteroid-size planetesimals (small celestial bodies thought to have existed at an early stage in the development of the solar system), one of them grew at a high rate and to a size larger than the others. This large planetesimal became Jupiter. The gravity of Jupiter scattered other large planetesimals, some of which may have been as massive as the Earth is today. These planetesimals were eventually either captured by Jupiter or another of the trans-Jovian planets (Saturn, Uranus, and Neptune) or ejected from the solar system. While they were passing through the inner solar system, however, such large planetesimals strongly perturbed the orbits of the planetesimals in the region of the asteroid belt, raising their mutual velocities to the average 5 km per second (3.1 mi per second) they exhibit today.

Jupiter

Jupiter is the most massive of the planets, and is fifth in distance from the Sun. When ancient astronomers named the planet Jupiter for the ruler of the gods in the Greco-Roman pantheon, they had no idea of the planet's true dimensions, but the name is appropriate, for Jupiter is larger than all the other planets combined. It has a narrow ring system and 39 known satellites, 3 larger than the Earth's Moon. Jupiter also has an internal heat source—i.e., it emits more energy than it receives from the Sun. This giant has the strongest magnetic field of any planet, with a magnetosphere so large that, if it could be seen from Earth, its apparent diameter would exceed that of the Moon. Jupiter's system is the source of intense bursts of radio noise, at some frequencies occasionally radiating more energy than the Sun.

Of special interest concerning Jupiter's physical properties is the low mean density of 1.33 grams per cubic cm—in contrast with Earth's 5.52 grams/cm³—coupled with the large dimensions and mass and the short rotational period. The low density and large mass indicate that Jupiter's composition and structure are quite unlike those of the Earth and the other inner planets, a deduction that is supported by detailed investigations of the giant planet's atmosphere and interior.

Jupiter has no solid surface; the transition from the atmosphere to the core occurs gradually at great depths. The close-up views of Jupiter from the Voyager spacecraft revealed a variety of cloud forms, with a predominance of elliptical features reminiscent of cyclonic and anticyclonic storm systems on the Earth. All these systems are in motion, appearing and disappearing on time scales dependent on their sizes and locations. Also observed to vary are the

pastel shades of various colors present in the cloud layers—from the tawny yellow that seems to characterize the main layer, through browns and blue-grays, to the well-known salmon-colored Great Red Spot, Jupiter's largest, most prominent, and longest-lived feature.

Because Jupiter has no solid surface it has no topographic features, and latitudinal currents dominate the planet's large-scale circulation. The lack of a solid surface with physical boundaries and regions with different heat capacities makes the persistence of these currents and their associated cloud patterns all the more remarkable. The Great Red Spot, for example, moves in longitude with respect to all three of the rotation systems, yet it does not move in latitude.

The first Voyager spacecraft verified the existence of a ring system surrounding Jupiter when it crossed the planet's equatorial plane. The ring system is comprised of large numbers of micrometer-sized particles that produce strong forward scattering of incident sunlight. Submicrometric dust is also present. The presence of such small particles requires a source. Indeed, the finest material extends all the way into the planet itself. It seems likely that the source of this material is large boulders, or small moonlets, within the ring. Visible examples of what are presumably among the largest of such objects are satellites Thebe and Metis. The ring particles are generated by impacts of micrometeoroids, cometary debris, and possibly volcanically produced material from Io. It seems plausible that the orbit of one of these moonlets defines the inner edge of Jupiter's ring, even as the outer edge appears to be defined by the satellite Thebe.

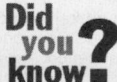**Did you know?** The Great Red Spot, the most conspicuous feature on the planet Jupiter, is an enormous storm system that has been raging for more than 300 years. It is about 26,000 km long and 14,000 km (16,200 by 8,700 miles) wide—large enough to engulf two Earth-sized planets side by side.

Jovian Moons

The satellites orbiting Jupiter are numerous; there are 39 known Jovian moons and may be more as yet undiscovered.

The first objects in the solar system discovered by means of a telescope were the four brightest satellites of Jupiter. Galileo, who first observed them in 1610, proposed that the satellites be named the Medicean stars, in honor of his patron, Cosimo II de' Medici, but they soon came to be known as the Galilean satellites in honor of their discoverer. Galileo regarded their existence as a fundamental argument in favor of the Copernican model of the solar system in which the planets orbit the Sun. In order of increasing distance from the planet, these satellites are called Io, Europa, Ganymede, and Callisto, for legendary figures closely associated with Jupiter (Zeus) in Greek mythology. The names were assigned by the German astronomer Simon Marius, Galileo's contemporary and rival. Those more recent satellites that have names, as opposed to numeric designations, are also named for mythological figures associated with Zeus.

Jovian satellite data is summarized below. The orbits of the inner eight satellites have low inclinations (they are not tilted relative to the planet's equator) and low eccentricities (their orbits are relatively circular). The orbits of the outer satellites have much higher inclinations and eccentricities. The innermost satellites seem to be intimately associated with Jupiter's ring and may in fact be the sources of the fine particles within the ring itself.

In May 2002 researchers from the University of Hawaii's Institute for Astronomy announced that 11 more moons had been discovered, bringing the total count to 39 moons. These new moons ranged in size from 1.9 km to 3.8 km (1.2 to 2.4 mi). With this latest find, Scott Sheppard, David Jewitt, Yan Fernandez, and Gene Magnier had found the last 22 known moons of Jupiter. The satellites will be designated S/2001 J 1 through J 11. All of the satellites are beyond the orbit of S/1999 J 1.

"Syn" denotes that the orbital period and rotational period are the same, or synchronous.

NAME (DESIGNATION)	DISCOVERY	MEAN DISTANCE FROM JUPITER	DIAMETER	MASS (10²⁰ KG)	ORBITAL PERIOD/ ROTATIONAL PERIOD (EARTH DAYS)
Metis (JXVI)	S. Synnott in 1979	128,000 km (79,500 mi)	40 km (25 mi)	0.0009	0.29/N/A
Adrastea (JXV)	D. Jewitt and E. Danielson in 1979	129,000 km (80,000 mi)	20 km (12 mi)	0.0002	0.298/N/A
Amalthea (JV)	E.E. Barnard in 1892	181,000 km (112,500 mi)	189 km (117 mi)	0.072	0.498/Syn
Thebe (JXIV)	S. Synnott in 1979	221,000 km (137,000 mi)	100 km (62 mi)	0.008	0.6745/Syn
Io (JI)[1]	Galileo in 1610	422,000 km (262,000 mi)	3,630 km (2,256 mi)	893.16	1.769/Syn
Europa (JII)[1]	Galileo in 1610	671,000 km (417,000 mi)	3,138 km (1,949 mi)	479.982	3.55/Syn
Ganymede (JIII)[1]	Galileo in 1610	1,070,000 km (665,000 mi)	5,268 km (3,273 mi)	1,481.86	7.15/Syn
Callisto (JIV)[1]	Galileo in 1610	1,883,000 km (1,170,000 mi)	4,806 km (2,986 mi)	1,075.93	16.689/Syn
S/1975 J1[2]	C. Kowal in 1975, S. Sheppard, et al, in 2000	7,411,000 km (4,605,000 mi)	8 km (5 mi)	N/A	130.02/N/A
Leda (JXIII)	C. Kowal in 1974	11,110,000 km (6,903,400 mi)	10 km (6 mi)	0.00006	238.72/N/A
Himalia (JVI)	C.D. Perrine in 1904	11,480,000 km (7,133,000 mi)	170 km (106 mi)	0.095	250.566/0.4
Lysithea (JX)	S.B. Nicholson in 1938	11,720,000 km (7,282,500 mi)	24 km (15 mi)	0.0008	259.2/N/A
Elara (JVII)	C.D. Perrine in 1905	11,737,000 km (7,293,000 mi)	80 km (50 mi)	0.008	259.6/0.5
S/2000 J 11	S. Sheppard, et al., in 2000	12,657,000 km (7,865,000 mi)	4 km (2.5 mi)	N/A	287.0/N/A
S/2000 J 3	S. Sheppard, et al., in 2000	20,478,000 km (12,724,400 mi)	5.2 km (3.2 mi)	N/A	595.2[3]/N/A
S/2000 J 5	S. Sheppard, et al., in 2000	20,892,000 km (12,982,000 mi)	4.4 km (2.73 mi)	N/A	624.6[3]/N/A
Ananke (JXII)	S.B. Nicholson in 1951	21,200,000 km (13,173,000 mi)	28 km (17.3 mi)	0.0004	610.5[3]/N/A
S/2000 J 7	S. Sheppard, et al., in 2000	21,399,000 km (13,297,000 mi)	7 km (4.3 mi)	N/A	617.2[3]/N/A
S/2000 J 9	S. Sheppard, et al., in 2000	22,409,000 km (13,303,000 mi)	5 km (3.1 mi)	N/A	730.0[3]/N/A
S/2000 J 10	S. Sheppard, et al., in 2000	22,512,000 km (13,988,000 mi)	4 km (2.4 mi)	N/A	733.7[3]/N/A
S/2000 J 2	S. Sheppard, et al., in 2000	22,684,000 km (14,095,000 mi)	5.2 km (3.23 mi)	N/A	750.8[3]/N/A

Jovian Moons (continued)

NAME (DESIGNATION)	DISCOVERY	MEAN DISTANCE FROM JUPITER	DIAMETER	MASS (10^{20} KG)	ORBITAL PERIOD/ ROTATIONAL PERIOD (EARTH DAYS)
Carme (JXI)	S.B. Nicholson in 1938	22,600,000 km (14,043,000 mi)	30 km (18.6 mi)	0.0009	694[3]/N/A
S/2000 J 8	S. Sheppard, et al., in 2000	23,527,000 km (14,619,000 mi)	5.4 km (3.3 mi)	N/A	758.1[3]/N/A
Pasiphae (JVIII)	P. Mellote in 1908	23,500,000 km (14,602,000 mi)	36 km (22.3 mi)	0.002	708[3]/N/A
S/2000 J 6	S. Sheppard, et al., in 2000	23,851,000 km (14,820,000 mi)	3.8 km (2.36 mi)	N/A	718.7[3]/N/A
Sinope (JIX)	S.B. Nicholson in 1914	23,700,000 km (14,726,500 mi)	28 km (17.3 mi)	0.0008	724.5[3]/N/A
S/2000 J 4	S. Sheppard, et al., in 2000	24,127,000 km (14,992,000 mi)	3.2 km (1.9 mi)	N/A	723.0[3]/N/A
S/1999 J 1	Spacewatch 1999	24,241,000 km (15,062,600 mi)	5 km (3 mi)	N/A	767[3]/N/A

[1]Densities are known for these moons. They are: Io (3.55 grams/cm3); Europa (3.04 grams/cm3); Ganymede (1.93 grams/cm3); Callisto (1.83 grams/cm3).   [2]This satellite was observed in 1975 but then lost and was not rediscovered until 2000, thus it is also called S/2000 J 1.   [3]Retrograde.

Jovian Rings

One of the tasks of the Pioneer 11 mission of 1974 was to monitor the charged particles around Jupiter. As the spacecraft sped toward its closest approach a sudden decrease in the density of charged particles was detected that led to the suggestion that a moon or a ring of material might be orbiting the planet at this distance. The existence of these rings was verified by the first Voyager spacecraft In 1979. Jupiter's rings consist of the Main ring and the Halo, which are both composed of dark particles. The third ring, known as the Gossamer ring, is actually two rings composed of debris formed from dust raised during collisions between meteoroids and the three small Jovian moons Amalthea, Thebe, and Adrastea.

RING	RADIUS[1]	THICKNESS
Jupiter (for comparison purposes)	71,492 km (44,423 mi)	N/A
Halo	100,000–122,000 km (62,137–75,807 mi)	20,000 km (12,427 mi)
Main	122,000–129,000 km (75,807–80,156 mi)	<30 km (18.6 mi)
Gossamer	129,200–224,900 km (80,281–139,746 mi)	N/A

[1]The radius for rings is measured from the center of the planet to the start of the ring.

Saturn

Saturn is the sixth planet in order of distance from the Sun and the second largest of the planets in mass and size. Its dimensions are almost equal to those of Jupiter, while its mass is about three times smaller; it has the lowest mean density of any object in the solar system.

Both Saturn and Jupiter resemble stellar bodies in that the light gas hydrogen dominates their bulk chemical composition. Saturn's atmosphere is 91% hydrogen by mass and is thus the most hydrogen-rich atmosphere in the solar system. Saturn's structure and evolutionary history, however, differ significantly from those of its larger counterpart. Like the other giant planets Jupiter, Uranus, and Neptune, Saturn has an extensive satellite and ring system, which may provide clues to its origin and evolution. Saturn's satellites have, with the exception of the outermost moons, prograde, low-inclination, and low-eccentricity orbits with respect to the planet. Saturn's dense and extended rings, which lie in its equatorial plane, are currently the most impressive in the solar system.

Saturn has no single rotation period. Cloud motions in its massive upper atmosphere can be used to trace out a variety of rotation periods, with periods as short as about 10 hours, 10 minutes near the equator and increasing with some oscillation to about 30 minutes longer at latitudes higher than 40°. The rotation period of Saturn's deep interior can be determined from the rotation period of the magnetic field, which is presumed to be rooted in a metallic outer core. The "surface" of Saturn that is seen through telescopes and in spacecraft images is actually a complex layer of clouds.

The atmosphere of Saturn shows many smaller-scale time-variable features similar to those found in Jupiter, such as red, brown, and white spots, bands, eddies, and vortices. The atmosphere generally has a much blander appearance than Jupiter's, however, and is less active on a small scale. A spectacular exception occurred during September–November 1990, when a large white spot appeared near the equator, expanded to a size exceeding 20,000 km (12,400 mi), and eventually spread around the equator before fading.

Saturnian Moons

Thirty natural satellites have been discovered circling the planet Saturn. The orbital and rotational dynamics of Saturn's satellites show complexities unique to this system. Saturnian satellite data are summarized in the table below. As with many planets, those satellites closest to Saturn are mostly regular, meaning their orbits are not greatly inclined (tilted) with respect to the planet's equator and ring plane and the orbits are fairly circular. The outer satellites tend to belong to the "irregular" class, meaning that their orbits are highly inclined and elliptical.

Titan is the largest moon of Saturn and the only satellite in the solar system known to have clouds and a dense atmosphere. As a deep-frozen repository of the types of organic molecules that led to the origin of life on Earth four billion years ago, and as the most probable locale in the solar system for a liquid hydrocarbon ocean, Titan represents an extraordinary objective for future spacecraft exploration.

The second largest moon of Saturn is Rhea. This moon's surface is the most heavily cratered in the Saturn system. Next in order of size are Iapetus and Dione.

An unusual Saturnian satellite is Hyperion. Although tidal friction ordinarily forces satellites into a state of synchronous rotation, Hyperion appears to be a spectacular exception to this rule. Because of its large orbital eccentricity and highly unspherical shape, there is a complicated interaction between Hyperion's spin and orbital angular momentum leading to a chaotic feedback process. Although Hyperion was observed from the Voyager spacecraft to be rotating with a nonsynchronous period of about 13 days, chaos theory shows that it is actually tumbling in an essentially unpredictable manner. Hyperion is the only object known to be in chaotic rotation.

In the table, Syn denotes that the orbital period and rotational period are the same, or synchronous.

NAME	DESIG-NATION	DISCOVERY	MEAN DISTANCE FROM SATURN	DIAMETER	MASS (10²⁰ KG)	DENSITY (KG/M³)	ORBITAL PERIOD/ ROTATIONAL PERIOD (EARTH DAYS)
Pan	SXVIII	M. Showalter in 1990	133,580 km (83,000 mi)	20 km (12 mi)	0.00003	630	0.5750/N/A
Atlas	SXV	R. Terrile in 1980	137,670 km (85,540 mi)	28 km (17 mi)	0.0001	630	0.6019/N/A
Prometheus	SXVI	S.A. Collins and D. Carlson in 1980	139,350 km (86,590 mi)	92 km (57 mi)	0.0033	630	0.6130/N/A
Pandora	SXVII	S.A. Collins and D. Carlson in 1980	141,700 km (88,050 mi)	92 km (57 mi)	0.002	630	0.6285/N/A
Epimetheus	SXI	R. Walker in 1966; J. Fountain and S. Larson in 1978	151,420 km (94,090 mi)	114 km (71 mi)	0.0054	600	0.6942/Syn
Janus	SX	A. Dollfus in 1966	151,470 km (94,120 mi)	178 km (111 mi)	0.0192	650	0.6945/Syn
Mimas	SI	W. Herschel in 1789	185,520 km (115,280 mi)	392 km (244 mi)	0.375	1,140	0.94/Syn
Enceladus	SII	W. Herschel in 1789	238,020 km (147,900 mi)	520 km (323 mi)	0.7	1,000	1.37/Syn
Tethys	SIII	G.D. Cassini in 1684	294,660 km (183,090 mi)	1,060 km (659 mi)	6.27	1,000	1.88/Syn
Telesto	SXIII	B. Smith, H. Reitsema, S. Larson, and J. Fountain in 1980	294,660 km (183,090 mi— in the same orbit as Tethys but about 60° ahead)	30 km (19 mi)	0.00007	1,000	1.88/N/A
Calypso	SXIV	D. Pascu, P.K. Seidelmann, W. Baum, and D. Currie in 1980	294,660 km (183,090 mi— in the same orbit as Tethys but about 60° behind)	26 km (16 mi)	0.00004	1,000	1.88/N/A
Dione	SIV	G.D. Cassini in 1684	377,400 km (234,510 mi)	1,120 km (696 mi)	11	1,500	2.73/Syn
Helene	SXII	P. Laques and J. Lecacheus in 1980	377,400 km (234,510 mi— in the same orbit as Dione but about 60° ahead)	32 km (20 mi)	0.0003	1,500	2.73/N/A
Rhea	SV	G.D. Cassini in 1672	527,040 km (327,490 mi)	1,530 km (951 mi)	23.1	1,240	4.51/Syn

Saturnian Moons (continued)

NAME	DESIG-NATION	DISCOVERY	MEAN DISTANCE FROM SATURN	DIAMETER	MASS (10²⁰ KG)	DENSITY (KG/M³)	ORBITAL PERIOD/ ROTATIONAL PERIOD (EARTH DAYS)
Titan	SVI	C. Huygens in 1655	1,221,830 km (759,210 mi)	5,150 km (3,200 mi)	1,350	1,881	15.94/Syn
Hyperion	SVII	W. and G. Bond and (independently by) W. Lassell in 1848	1,481,100 km (920,310 mi)	286 km (178 mi)	0.2	1,500	21.27/ Chaotic
Iapetus	SVIII	G.D. Cassini in 1671	3,561,300 km (2,212,890 mi)	1,460 km (907 mi)	16	1,020	79.3/Syn
S/2000 S 5[1]			11,365,000 km (7,061,880 mi)	~14 km (~9 mi)	N/A	N/A	N/A
S/2000 S 6[1]			11,440,000 km (7,108,490 mi)	~10 km (~6 mi)	N/A	N/A	N/A
Phoebe	SIX	W. Pickering in 1898	12,952,000 km (8,048,000 mi)	220 km (137 mi)	0.004	1,300	550.48 (retrograde)/0.4
S/2000 S 2[1]			15,199,000 km (9,444,220 mi)	~20 km (~12 mi)	N/A	N/A	N/A
S/2000 S 8[1]			15,645,000 km (9,721,350 mi)	~6 km (~4 mi)	N/A	N/A	N/A
S/2000 S 11[1]			16,392,000 km (10,185,520 mi)	~26 km (~16 mi)	N/A	N/A	N/A
S/2000 S 10[1]			17,611,000 km (10,942,970 mi)	~8 km (~5 mi)	N/A	N/A	N/A
S/2000 S 3[1]			18,160,000 km (11,284,100 mi)	~32 km (~20 mi)	N/A	N/A	N/A
S/2000 S 4[1]			18,239,000 km (11,333,190 mi)	~14 km (~9 mi)	N/A	N/A	N/A
S/2000 S 9[1]			18,709,000 km (11,625,230 mi)	~6 km (~4 mi)	N/A	N/A	N/A
S/2000 S 12[1]			19,470,000 km (12,098,100 mi)	~6 km (~4 mi)	N/A	N/A	N/A
S/2000 S 7[1]			20,470,000 km (12,719,470 mi)	~6 km (~4 mi)	N/A	N/A	N/A
S/2000 S 1[1]			23,096,000 km (14,351,190 mi)	~16 km (~10 mi)	N/A	N/A	N/A

[1]B. Gladman, J. Kavelaars, J.-M. Petit, H. Scholl, M. Holman, B.G. Marsden, P. Nicholson, and J.A. Burns discovered S/2000 S 1 through S/2000 S 12 in 2000.

Saturnian Rings

Saturn's ring system ranks among the most spectacular phenomena in the solar system. Like the rings of the other giant planets Jupiter, Uranus, and Neptune, those of Saturn lie for the most part within the classical Roche limit. This limit is the minimum distance to which a large satellite can approach its primary body without being torn apart by tidal forces. If satellite and primary are of similar composition, the theoretical limit is about 2½ times the radius of the larger body. (For Saturn, with a radius of 60,268 km, the Roche limit is about 150,000 km.) The limit applies only to objects held together by gravitational attraction and thus does not restrict the stability of relatively small bodies for which molecular cohesion is important. Thus, small moons with sizes in the range of tens of kilometers or less can persist indefinitely within the Roche limit.

The Saturnian ring system shows structures on many scales, ranging from the broad divisions into the classical A, B, and C rings down to a myriad of individual ringlets with radial scales on the order of kilometers (1 km = 0.621 mile).

Numerous gaps are seen in the major ring regions. Some of the major gaps have been named after famous astronomers who were associated with studies of Saturn. In addition to the Cassini division, they include the Maxwell gap, the Huygens gap, and the Encke gap.

	RADIUS[1]	WIDTH	MASS (IN 10²⁰ KG)
Saturn	60,268 km (37,449 mi)	not applicable	5,680,000
D ring (Guerin division lies between D & C)	66,900 (41,569 mi)	7,500 km (4,660 mi)	unknown

Saturnian Rings (continued)

	RADIUS[1]	WIDTH	MASS (IN 10^{20} KG)
C ring (Maxwell gap lies between C & B)	74,500 km (46,292 mi)	17,500 km (10,874 mi)	0.011
B ring (Cassini division and Huygens gap lie between B & A)	92,000 km (57,166 mi)	25,500 km (15,845 mi)	0.28
A ring (Encke gap lies between inner & outer edge of A ring)	122,200 km (75,932 mi)	14,600 km (9,072 mi)	0.062
F ring	140,210 km (87,122 mi)	30-500 km (19-311 mi)	unknown
G ring	165,800 km (103,023 mi)	8,000 km (4,971 mi)	unknown
E ring	180,000 km (111,847 mi)	300,000 km (186,411 mi)	unknown

[1]The radius for a ring is measured from the center of the planet to the start of the ring.

Uranus

Uranus is the seventh planet in order of distance from the Sun. Its low density and large size place it among the four giant planets, all of which are composed primarily of hydrogen, helium, water, and other volatile compounds and which thus are without solid surfaces. Absorption of red light by methane gas gives the planet a blue-green color. The planet has more than 20 known satellites, ranging up to 789 km (490 mi) in radius, and 11 narrow rings.

Uranus spins on its side; its rotation axis is tipped at an angle of 98° relative to its orbit axis. The 98° tilt is thought to have arisen during the final stages of planetary accretion when bodies comparable in size to the present planets collided in a series of violent events that knocked Uranus onto its side.

Although Uranus is nearly featureless, extreme contrast enhancement of the Voyager images reveals faint bands oriented parallel to circles of constant latitude. Apparently the rotation of the planet and not the distribution of absorbed sunlight controls the cloud patterns.

Wind is the motion of the atmosphere relative to the rotating planet. At high latitudes on Uranus, as on the Earth, this relative motion is in the direction of the planet's rotation. At low (that is, equatorial) latitudes, the relative motion is in the opposite direction. On the Earth these directions are called east and west, respectively, but the more general terms are prograde and retrograde. The winds that exist on Uranus are several times stronger than are those of the Earth. The wind is 200 m (656 ft) per second (prograde) at a latitude of –55° and 110 m (360.8 ft) per second (retrograde) at the equator. Neptune's equatorial winds are also retrograde, although those of Jupiter and Saturn are prograde. No satisfactory theory exists to explain these differences.

Uranus has no large spots like the Great Red Spot of Jupiter or the Great Dark Spot of Neptune. Since the giant planets have no solid surfaces, the spots repre-

sent atmospheric storms. For reasons that are not clear, Uranus seems to have the smallest number of storms of any of the giant planets.

Uranus was discovered in 1781 by the English astronomer William Herschel, who had undertaken a survey of all stars down to eighth magnitude—i.e., those about five times fainter than stars visible to the naked eye. Herschel suggested naming the new planet the Georgian Planet after his patron, King George III of England, but the planet was eventually named according to the tradition of naming planets for the gods of Greek and Roman mythology; Uranus is the father of Saturn, who is in turn the father of Jupiter.

After the discovery, Herschel continued to observe the planet with larger and better telescopes and eventually discovered the outer two satellites, Titania and Oberon, in 1787. Two more satellites, Ariel and Umbriel, were discovered by the British astronomer William Lassell in 1851. The names of the four satellites come from English literature, three taken from Shakespeare, and were proposed by Herschel's son, John Herschel. A fifth satellite, Miranda, was discovered by Gerard P. Kuiper in 1948. The tradition of naming the satellites after characters in Shakespeare's plays continues to the present.

Did you know? Uranus was the first planet to be discovered with a telescope. The German-born astronomer William Herschel accidentally discovered the planet in 1781 during a routine sky survey at his observatory in Bath, England. At first he thought it was a comet. When astronomers concluded that the object was really a planet, the German astronomer J.E. Bode suggested that it be called Uranus, in honor of the ancient sky god who was the father of Saturn in Greco-Roman mythology.

Uranian Moons

Uranus has some 20 satellites and 11 narrow rings. With the exception of the very outer satellites (which are known as irregulars) all the satellites and rings are in nearly circular orbits with low inclinations relative to the equatorial plane of the planet. In general, the rings orbit closest to the planet, the smaller satellites orbit just outside the rings, and the larger satellites orbit farthest from the planet.

The four largest satellites, Ariel, Umbriel, Titania, and Oberon, have densities that range from 1.2 to 1.7 grams per cubic centimeter (.693 to .98 ounces per cubic inch), which is slightly greater than the density of a hypothetical satellite that is 60% ice and 40% rock. Oberon and Umbriel display a dense population of large impact craters, similar to the lunar highlands and many of the oldest terrains in the solar system.

Uranian Moons (continued)

In contrast, Titania and Ariel have far fewer craters in the large size range (50 to 100 km, or 31 to 62 miles, in diameter) but have comparable numbers in the smaller size ranges.

The former craters are thought to date back more than four billion years to the early history of the solar system, while the latter are thought to reflect more recent events including, perhaps, secondary objects knocked loose from other satellites in the Uranian system. Thus the surfaces of Titania and Ariel are younger than those of Oberon and Umbriel.

Three new moons, S 2001 U 1, S 2001 U 2, and S 2001 U 3, were discovered by J.J. Kavelaars, M. Holman, J.-M. Petit, B. Gladman, and D. Milisavljevic in 2001.

NAME	DESIGNATION	DISCOVERY	MEAN DISTANCE FROM URANUS	DIAMETER	MASS (10^{20} KG)	DENSITY (KG PER CUBIC METER)	ORBITAL PERIOD/ ROTATIONAL PERIOD (BOTH IN EARTH DAYS)
Cordelia	U VI	R. Terrile/ Voyager 2 in 1986	49,770 km (30,930 mi)	40 km (25 mi)	unknown	unknown	0.335/ unknown
Ophelia	U VII	R. Terrile/ Voyager 2 in 1986	53,790 km (33,420 mi)	42 km (26 mi)	unknown	unknown	0.376/ unknown
Bianca	U VIII	Voyager 2 in 1986	59,170 km (36,770 mi)	54 km (34 mi)	unknown	unknown	0.434/ unknown
Cressida	U IX	S. Synnott/ Voyager 2 in 1986	61,780 km (38,390 mi)	80 km (50 mi)	unknown	unknown	0.463/ unknown
Desdemona	U X	S. Synnott/ Voyager 2 in 1986	62,680 km (38,950 mi)	64 km (40 mi)	unknown	unknown	0.473/ unknown
Juliet	U XI	S. Synnott/ Voyager 2 in 1986	64,350 km (39,990 mi)	94 km (58 mi)	unknown	unknown	0.493/ unknown
Portia	U XII	S. Synnott/ Voyager 2 in 1986	66,090 km (41,070 mi)	136 km (85 mi)	unknown	unknown	0.513/ unknown
Rosalind	U XIII	S. Synnott/ Voyager 2 in 1986	69,940 km (43,460 mi)	72 km (45 mi)	unknown	unknown	0.558/ unknown
Belinda	U XIV	S. Synnott/ Voyager 2 in 1986	75,260 km (46,760 mi)	80 km (50 mi)	unknown	unknown	0.623/ unknown
1986 U 10[1]	XVIII	E. Karkoschka in 1999	75,000 km (46,600 mi)	40 km (25 mi)	unknown	unknown	0.62/ unknown
Puck	XV	S. Synnott/ Voyager 2 in 1986	86,010 km (53,440 mi)	162 km (101 mi)	unknown	unknown	0.761/ unknown
Miranda	V	G. Kuiper in 1948	129,390 km (80,400 mi)	472 km (293 mi)	0.66	1,200	1.413/syn[2]
Ariel	I	W. Lassell in 1851	191,020 km (118,690 mi)	1,158 km (720 mi)	13.5	1,670	2.52/syn[2]
Umbriel	II	W. Lassell in 1851	266,300 km (165,470 mi)	1,169 km (726 mi)	11.7	1,400	4.14/syn[2]
Titania	III	W. Herschel in 1787	435,910 km (270,860 mi)	1,578 km (981 mi)	35.2	1,710	8.70/syn[2]
Oberon	IV	W. Herschel in 1787	583,520 km (362,580 mi)	1,523 km (946 mi)	30.1	1,630	13.46/syn[2]
Caliban	XVI	B. Gladman, P. Nicholson, J. Burns, and J.J. Kavelaars in 1997	7,230,000 km (4,492,510 mi)	96 km (60 mi)	unknown	unknown	579.5 retrograde/ unknown
Stephano	XX	B. Gladman, M. Holman, J.J. Kavelaars, J.-M. Petit, H. Scholl in 1999	8,002,000 km (4,972,210 mi)	20 km (12 mi)	unknown	unknown	676.5 retrograde/ unknown

Uranian Moons (continued)

NAME	DESIGNATION	DISCOVERY	MEAN DISTANCE FROM URANUS	DIAMETER	MASS $(10^{20}$ KG)	DENSITY (KG PER CUBIC METER)	ORBITAL PERIOD/ ROTATIONAL PERIOD (BOTH IN EARTH DAYS)
Sycorax	XVII	B. Gladman, P. Nicholson, J. Burns, and J.J. Kavelaars in 1997	12,179,000 km (7,567,680 mi)	190 km (118 mi)	unknown	unknown	1283.4 retrograde/ unknown
Prospero	XVIII	B. Gladman, M. Holman, J.J. Kavelaars, J.-M. Petit, H. Scholl in 1999	16,418,000 km (10,201,670 mi)	30 km (19 mi)	unknown	unknown	1992.8 retrograde/ unknown
Setebos	XIX	B. Gladman, M. Holman, J.J. Kavelaars, J.-M. Petit, H. Scholl in 1999	17,459,000 km (10,848,520 mi)	30 km (19 mi)	unknown	unknown	2202.3 retrograde/ unknown

[1]The status of this satellite is unoffical. In December of 2001 the International Astronomical Union (IAU) concluded there was not as yet enough information to confirm that S/1986 U 10 is in fact a natural satellite of Uranus.   [2]syn denotes that the orbital period and rotational period are the same, or synchronous.

Uranian Rings

The rings of Uranus were discovered from the Earth during stellar occultations—i.e., when the planet passed between a star and the Earth, thereby momentarily blocking the star's light. The rings are narrow and fairly opaque. Observed widths are simply the radial distances between the beginning and end of the occultation. Equivalent widths are the product (more precisely, the integral) of the radial distance and the fraction of starlight removed. The fact that the equivalent widths are generally less than the observed widths indicates that the rings are not completely opaque. 1 km = 0.6214 miles.

RING	RADIUS[1]	WIDTH	RING	RADIUS[1]	WIDTH
Uranus	25,559 km	N/A	Beta	45,670 km	7–12 km
1986 U2 R	38,000 km	2,500 km	Eta	47,190 km	0–2 km
6	41,840 km	1–3 km	Gamma	47,630 km	1–4 km
5	42,230 km	2–3 km	Delta	48,290 km	3–9 km
4	42,580 km	2–3 km	1986 U1 R	50,020 km	1–2 km
Alpha	44,720 km	7–12 km	Epsilon	51,140 km	20–100 km

[1]The radius for rings is measured from the center of the planet to the start of the ring.

Neptune

Neptune is the eighth planet in average distance from the Sun. It was named for the Roman god of the sea. The sea-god's three-pronged trident serves as the planet's astronomical symbol.

Neptune's distance from the Sun varies between 29.8 and 30.4 astronomical units (AUs). Its diameter is nearly four times that of the Earth, but because of its great distance Neptune cannot be seen from the Earth without the aid of a telescope. Neptune's deep blue color is due to the absorption of red light by methane gas in its atmosphere. It receives less than half as much sunlight as Uranus, but heat escaping from its interior makes Neptune slightly warmer than the latter. The heat released may also be responsible for Neptune's stormier atmosphere, which exhibits the fastest winds seen on any planet in the solar system.

Neptune's orbital period is 163.7 Earth years. It has not completely circled the Sun since its discovery in 1846, so some refinements in its orbital size and shape are still expected. The planet's orbital eccentricity of 0.009 means that its orbit is very nearly circular; among the nine planets in the solar system, only Venus has a smaller eccentricity. Neptune's seasons (and the seasons of its moons) are therefore nearly equal length, each more than 41 Earth years in duration. The length of Neptune's day, as determined by Voyager 2, is 16.11 hr.

As with the other giant planets of the outer solar system, Neptune's atmosphere is composed predominantly of hydrogen and helium. The temperature of Neptune's atmosphere varies with altitude. A minimum temperature of about -223.15 °C (-369.67 °F) occurs at pressure near 0.1 bar. The temperature increases with altitude to about 476.85 °C (890.33 °F) at 2,000 km (1,240 mi, which corresponds to a pressure of 10–11 bars) and remains uniform above that altitude.

As with the other giant planets of the outer solar system, the winds on Neptune are constrained to blow generally along lines of constant latitude and are relatively invariable with time. Winds on Neptune vary from about 100 m/sec (328 ft/sec) in an easterly (prograde) direction near latitude 70° S to as high as 700 m/sec (2,300 ft/sec) in a westerly (retrograde) direction near latitude 20° S.

The high winds and relatively large contribution of escaping internal heat may be responsible for the observed turbulence in Neptune's visible atmosphere. Two large dark ovals are clearly visible in images of Neptune's southern hemisphere taken by Voyager 2. The largest, called the "Great Dark Spot" because of its similarity in latitude and shape to Jupiter's Great Red Spot, is comparable to the entire Earth in size. It is near this Great Dark Spot that the highest wind speeds were measured. A somewhat smaller "Small Dark Spot" circles the planet near latitude 55° S. These two atmospheric storms may be centers where strong upwelling of gases from the interior takes place.

Neptune's mean density is slightly less than 30% that of the Earth; nevertheless, it is the densest of the giant planets. Neptune's greater density implies that a larger percentage of its interior is composed of melted ices and molten rocky materials than is the case for the other gas giants.

Neptunian Moons

Neptune has 8 moons, but only 2 of them were discovered before Voyager 2 traveled to Neptune in 1989. Neptune's largest moon, Triton, was discovered by William Lassell in Liverpool, England, less than one month after the discovery of Neptune, on 23 Sep 1846, although it was not confirmed until July 1847. Triton is the only large satellite in the solar system to have a retrograde orbit around its planet (that is, Triton circles Neptune in the direction opposite the planet's rotation).

Nereid was discovered in 1949 when Gerard P. Kuiper detected it in photographs he obtained at the McDonald Observatory in Texas. The chance occultation of a star by Larissa revealed the presence of a third satellite of Neptune in 1981, but verification of Larissa's existence and its orbit were not achieved until the Voyager 2 encounter with Neptune in 1989. Naiad, Thalassa, Despina, Galatea, and Proteus were also discovered by Voyager. The first 7 moons, Naiad through Triton, have very regular (circular) orbits. Only Nereid has a highly irregular (eccentric, or noncircular) orbit.

NAME	DESIGNATION	DISCOVERY	MEAN DISTANCE FROM NEPTUNE	DIAMETER	ORBITAL PERIOD (IN EARTH DAYS)
Naiad	III	Voyager 2 in 1989	48,230 km (29,970 mi)	58 km (36 mi)	0.294
Thalassa	IV	R. Terrile/Voyager 2 in 1989	50,070 km (31,110 mi)	80 km (50 mi)	0.311
Despina	V	S. Synnott/Voyager 2 in 1989	52,530 km (32,640 mi)	148 km (92 mi)	0.335
Galatea	VI	S. Synnott/Voyager 2 in 1989	61,950 km (38,490 mi)	158 km (98 mi)	0.429
Larissa	VII	H. Reitsema, W. Hubbard, L. Lebofsky, and D. Tholen in 1981	73,550 km (45,700 mi)	192 km (119 mi)	0.555
Proteus	VIII	S. Synnott/Voyager 2 in 1989	117,640 km (73,100 mi)	416 km (258 mi)	1.122
Triton	I	W. Lassell in 1846	354,800 km (220,460 mi)	2,700 km (1,678 mi)	5.877 (retrograde)
Nereid	II	G. Kuiper in 1949	5,509,100 km (3,423,200 mi)	340 km (211 mi)	359.632

Neptunian Rings

Neptune's system of narrow rings, which may be a relatively new addition to the planet's family, displays a quite unusual feature. Although narrow rings have been seen around each of the other three gas giants (Jupiter, Saturn, and Uranus), none have displayed the striking nonuniformity of particle density of Neptune's outermost ring, called Adams (1989N1R). Material is clumped in at least five brighter regions, called arcs, that are found within a 45° segment of the ring. The arcs—called Courage, Liberté, Egalité 1, Egalité 2, and Fraternité—range in length from about 1,000 km (621.4 mi) to more than 10,000 km (6,213.7 mi). Although the moon Galatea may gravitationally interact with the Adams ring to temporarily trap ring particles in such arclike regions, collisions between ring particles should eventually spread the constituent material relatively uniformly around the circumference of the ring. The Adams ring's enigmatic arcs may be the result of the breakup of a small satellite within the past few thousand years. The inner rings of Neptune. (LeVerrier, Galle, Lassell, and Arago) lack the unusual nonuniformity exhibited by the Adams ring.

Neptunian Rings (continued)

RING	RADIUS[1]	WIDTH	RING	RADIUS[1]	WIDTH
Neptune	24,766 km (15,388.9 mi)	N/A	Lassell[2]	53,200 km (33,057 mi)	4,000 km (2485.4 mi)
Galle (formerly 1989N3R)	41,900 km (26,035 mi)	2000 km (1,242.7 mi)	Arago[2]	57,200 km (35,542 mi)	c. 100 km (62.1 mi)
			Unnamed	61,950 km (38,494 mi)	unknown (indistinct)
LeVerrier (formerly 1989N2R)	53,200 km (33,057 mi)	110 km (68.3 mi)	Adams	62,933 km (39,105 mi)	50 km (31 mi)

[1]The radius for a ring is measured from the center of the planet to the inner edge of the ring.   [2]Lassell and Arago were originally thought to be one ring, which was identified as 1989N4R.

Pluto

Pluto is the planet normally farthest from the Sun. It is named for the god of the underworld in Roman mythology (Greek: Hades). Pluto has a single natural satellite, Charon. Because their dimensions are sufficiently similar and they orbit around a common center of gravity, it has become common to speak of the Pluto-Charon system as a double planet.

Pluto was the third planet to be discovered, as opposed to the six planets that had been visible in the sky to the naked eye since ancient times. Pluto is so distant that sunlight traveling at 299,792 km/sec (186,282.1 mi/sec) takes more than five hours to reach the planet. An observer standing on the planet's surface would see the Sun as an extremely bright star in the dark sky, providing Pluto with only 1/1600 the amount of sunlight reaching the Earth.

Pluto's average distance from the Sun (39.6 astronomical units, or AU—an AU is equal to 149,597,871 km or 92,955,807 mi), as well as its orbital eccentricity (0.244) and inclination (17.2°), are the greatest of any of the planets in the solar system. In traveling in its highly eccentric orbit, Pluto varies in distance from the Sun from 29.7 AU at perihelion to 49.5 AU at aphelion. Therefore, Pluto at times is actually closer to the Sun than Neptune, which has a nearly circular orbit at approximately 30 AU. A 3:2 resonance between the orbital periods of Neptune and Pluto prevents the two planets from ever passing closer than about 17 AU to one another. The most recent perihelion of Pluto occurred on 5 Sep 1989, so that Neptune was the most distant planet from the Sun from 1979 through 1999.

Pluto is by far the smallest planet, having a diameter less than half that of Mercury; it is about two-thirds the size of the Moon. Pluto's physical characteristics are unlike those of any other planet. Pluto resembles most closely Neptune's icy satellite Triton, which implies a similar origin for these two bodies.

Observations of Pluto show that its color is slightly reddish, although not as red as Mars or Io. Thus, the surface of Pluto cannot be composed simply of pure ices. Its overall reflectivity, or albedo, ranges from 0.3 to 0.5, as compared with 0.1 for the Moon and 0.8 for Triton.

The surface temperature of Pluto has proved very difficult to measure. Observations made from the Infrared Astronomical Satellite suggest values in the range of −228.1 to −215.1 °C (−378.5 to −355.1 °F), whereas measurements at radio wavelengths imply a range of −238.1 to −223.1 °C (−396.5 to −369.5 °F). The temperature certainly must vary over the surface, depending on the local reflectivity and solar zenith angle. There is also expected to be a seasonal decrease in incident solar energy by a factor of roughly three as Pluto moves from perihelion to aphelion.

The detection of methane ice on the planet's surface made scientists confident that Pluto had an atmosphere before one was actually discovered. The atmosphere was finally detected in 1988 when Pluto passed in front of a star as observed from the Earth. The light of the star was dimmed before disappearing entirely behind the planet during the occultation. This proved that a thin, greatly distended atmosphere was present. Because Pluto's atmosphere must consist of vapors in equilibrium with their ices, small changes in temperature will have a large effect on the amount of gas in the atmosphere.

Pluto's only known satellite was discovered as a small bump on images of the planet that were recorded photographically at the U.S. Naval Observatory in Flagstaff AZ less than six km from the site of Pluto's discovery nearly 50 years earlier. The new satellite was named Charon, after the boatman who ferries dead souls across the River Styx to the underworld in Greek mythology. Subsequent observations showed that Charon's period of revolution around Pluto is exactly equal to the period of rotation of the planet itself. In other words, Pluto is the only planet in the solar system with a natural satellite in a synchronous orbit. As a result, Charon is only visible from one hemisphere of Pluto. In addition, as with most planetary satellites, Charon is in a state of synchronous rotation—i.e., it always presents the same face to its primary planet.

Comets

Comets are a class of small celestial objects orbiting the Sun and developing diffuse gaseous envelopes. They also often form long luminous tails when near the Sun. The comet makes a transient appearance in the sky and is often said to have a "hairy" tail. In fact, the word comes from the Greek kometes, meaning "hairy one," a description that fits the bright comets noticed by the ancients.

Despite their name, many comets do not develop tails. Moreover, a comet is not surrounded by nebulosity during most of its lifetime. The only permanent feature of a comet is its nucleus, which is a small body that may be seen as a stellar image in large telescopes when tail and nebulosity do not exist, particularly when the comet is still far away from the Sun. Two characteristics differentiate the cometary nucleus from a very small asteroid—its orbit and its chemical nature. A comet's orbit is more eccentric (less circular); therefore, its distance to the Sun varies considerably. Its material is more volatile. When far from the Sun, however, a comet remains in its pristine state for eons without losing any volatile components because of the deep cold of space. For this reason, astronomers believe that pristine cometary nuclei may represent the oldest and best-preserved material in the solar system.

During a close passage near the Sun, the nucleus of a comet loses water vapor and other more volatile compounds, as well as dust dragged away by the sublimating gases. It is then surrounded by a transient dusty "atmosphere" that is steadily lost to space. This feature is the coma, which gives a comet its nebulous appearance.

The astronomer Edmond Halley, a friend of Isaac Newton, endeavored to compute the orbits of 24 comets for which he had found fairly accurate historical documents. Applying a method Newton had developed, Halley predicted that the comet that now bears his name would return to Earth in 1758, and that proved correct. Since its prediction by astronomers and its appearance in 1758/59, Comet Halley has reappeared three more times—in 1835, 1910, and 1986.

Each century, a score of comets brighter than Comet Halley have been discovered. Many are periodic comets like Comet Halley, but their periods are extremely long (millennia or even scores or hundreds of millennia), and they have not left any identifiable trace in prehistory. Bright Comet Bennett 1970 II will return in 17 centuries, whereas the spectacular Comet West 1976 VI will reappear in about 500,000 years. Among the comets that can easily be seen with the unaided eye, Comet Halley is the only one that returns in a single lifetime. Approximately 100 comets whose periods are between 3 and 200 years are known, however. Unfortunately, they are or have become too faint to be readily seen without the aid of telescopes.

For faraway objects that contain volatile ices, the distinction between asteroids and comets becomes a matter of semantics because many orbits are unstable; an asteroid that comes closer to the Sun than usual may become a comet by producing a transient atmosphere that gives it a fuzzy appearance and that may develop into a tail. Some objects have been reclassified as a result of such occurrences. For example, asteroid 1990 UL3, which crosses the orbit of Jupiter, was reclassified as Comet P/Shoemaker-Levy 2 late in 1990. Conversely, it is suspected that some of the Earth-approaching asteroids (Amors, Apollos, and Atens) could be the extinct nuclei of comets that have now lost most of their volatile ices.

Did you know? Pluto is the farthest planet from the Sun. It is so distant that sunlight traveling at roughly 300,000 kilometers per second takes more than five hours to reach the planet. The Sun provides Pluto with only 1/1600 as much sunlight as reaches the Earth. Pluto's surface temperature is therefore expected to be only 35° to 50° above absolute zero, suggesting that its surface may consist largely of ices of nitrogen, methane, and carbon monoxide.

Measurements and Numbers

The International System of Units (SI)

Rapid advances in science and technology in the 19th and 20th centuries fostered the development of several overlapping systems of units of measurements as scientists improvised to meet the practical needs of their disciplines. The General Conference on Weights and Measures was chartered by international convention in 1875 to produce standards of physical measurement based upon an earlier international standard, the meter-kilogram-second (MKS) system. The convention calls for regular General Conference meetings to consider improvements or modifications in standards, an International Committee of Weights and Measures elected by the Conference (meets annually), and several consultative committees. The International Bureau of Weights and Measures (Bureau International des Poids et Mesures) at Sèvres, France, serves as a depository for the primary international standards and as a laboratory for certification and intercomparison of national standard copies.

The 1960 International System (universally abbreviated as SI, from *système international*) builds upon the MKS system. Its seven basic units, from which other units are derived, are currently defined as follows: the meter, defined as the distance traveled by light in a vacuum in 1/299,792,458 second; the kilogram (about 2.2 pounds avoirdupois), which equals 1,000 grams as defined by the international prototype kilogram of platinum-iridium in the keeping of the International Bureau of Weights and Measures; the second, the duration of 9,192,631,770 periods of radiation associated with a specified transition of the cesium-133 atom; the ampere, which is the current that, if maintained in two wires placed one meter apart in a vacuum, would produce a force of 2×10^{-7} newton per meter of length; the candela, defined as the intensity in a given direction of a source emitting radiation of frequency 540×10^{12} hertz and that has a radiant intensity in that direction of 1/683 watt per steradian; the mole, defined as containing as many elementary entities of a substance as there are atoms in 0.012 kilogram of carbon-12; and the kelvin, which is 1/273.16 of the thermodynamic temperature of the triple point (equilibrium among the solid, liquid, and gaseous phases) of pure water. International Bureau of Weights and Measures Web site: <www.bipm.fr>.

Elemental and Derived SI Units and Symbols

Quantity	SI Units		
	UNIT	FORMULA/EXPRESSION IN BASE UNITS	SYMBOL
elemental units			
length	meter	—	m
mass	kilogram	—	kg
time	second	—	s
electric current	ampere	—	A
luminous intensity	candela	—	cd
amount of substance	mole	—	mol
thermodynamic temperature	kelvin	—	K
derived units			
acceleration	meter/second squared	m/s^2	
area	square meter	m^2	
capacitance	farad	$A \times s/V$	F
charge	coulomb	$A \times s$	C
Celsius temperature	degree Celsius	K	°C
density	kilogram/cubic meter	kg/m^3	
electric field strength	volt/meter	V/m	
electrical potential	volt	W/A	V
energy	joule	$N \times m$	J
force	newton	$kg \times m/s^2$	N
frequency	hertz	s^{-1}	Hz
illumination	lux	lm/m^2	lx
inductance	henry	$V \times s/A$	H
kinematic viscosity	square meter/second	m^2/s	
luminance	candela/square meter	cd/m^2	
luminous flux	lumen	$cd \times sr$	lm
magnetic field strength	ampere/meter	A/m	
magnetic flux	weber	$V \times s$	Wb
magnetic flux density	tesla	Wb/m^2	T
plane angle	radian	$m \times m^{-1} = 1$	rad
power	watt	J/s	W
pressure	pascal (newton/square meter)	N/m^2	Pa
resistance	ohm	V/A	Ω
solid angle	steradian	$m^2 \times m^{-2} = 1$	sr
stress	pascal (newton/square meter)	N/m^2	Pa
velocity	meter/second	m/s	
viscosity	newton second/square meter	$N \times s/m^2$	
volume	cubic meter	m^3	

Conversion of Metric Weights and Measures

The International System of Units (SI) is a decimal system of weights and measures derived from and extending the metric system of units. Adopted by the 11th General Conference on Weights and Measures in 1960, it is abbreviated "SI" in all languages.

Rapid advances in science and technology in the 19th and 20th centuries fostered the development of several overlapping systems of units of measurements as scientists improvised to meet the practical needs of their disciplines. The early international system devised to rectify this situation was called the meter-kilogram-second (MKS) system. The 1960 International System builds upon the MKS system. Below are common equivalents and conversion factors for US customary and SI Systems.

approximate common equivalents

1 inch	= 25 millimeters
1 foot	= 0.3 meter
1 yard	= 0.9 meter
1 mile	= 1.6 kilometers
1 square inch	= 6.5 sq. centimeters
1 square foot	= 0.09 square meter
1 square yard	= 0.8 square meter
1 acre	= 0.4 hectare[2]
1 cubic inch	= 16 cubic centimeters
1 cubic foot	= 0.03 cubic meter
1 cubic yard	= 0.8 cubic meter
1 quart (liq)	= 1 liter[2]
1 gallon	= 0.004 cubic meter

conversions accurate within 10 parts per million

inches × 25.4[1]	= millimeters
feet × 0.3048[1]	= meters
yards × 0.9144[1]	= meters
miles × 1.60934	= kilometers
square inches × 6.4516[1]	= square centimeters
square feet × 0.0929030	= square meters
square yards × 0.836127	= square meters
acres × 0.404686	= hectares
cubic inches × 16.3871	= cubic centimeters
cubic feet × 0.0283168	= cubic meters
cubic yards × 0.764555	= cubic meters
quarts (liq) × 0.946353	= liters
gallons × 0.00378541	= cubic meters

Conversion of Metric Weights and Measures (continued)

approximate common equivalents		conversions accurate within 10 parts per million	
1 ounce (avdp)[3]	= 28 grams	ounces (avdp)[3] × 28.3495	= grams
1 pound (avdp)[3]	= 0.45 kilogram	pounds (avdp)[3] × 0.453592	= kilograms
1 horsepower	= 0.75 kilowatt	horsepower × 0.745700	= kilowatts
1 millimeter	= 0.04 inch	millimeters × 0.0393701	= inches
1 meter	= 3.3 feet	meters × 3.28084	= feet
1 meter	= 1.1 yards	meters × 1.09361	= yards
1 kilometer	= 0.6 mile (statute)	kilometers × 0.621371	= miles (statute)
1 square centimeter	= 0.16 square inch	square centimeters × 0.155000	= square inches
1 square meter	= 11 square feet	square meters × 10.7639	= square feet
1 square meter	= 1.2 square yards	square meters × 1.19599	= square yards
1 hectare[2]	= 2.5 acres	hectares × 2.47105	= acres
1 cubic centimeter	= 0.06 cubic inch	cubic centimeters × 0.0610237	= cubic inches
1 cubic meter	= 35 cubic feet	cubic meters × 35.3147	= cubic feet
1 cubic meter	= 1.3 cubic yards	cubic meters × 1.30795	= cubic yards
1 liter[2]	= 1 quart (liq)	liters × 1.05669	= quarts (liq)
1 cubic meter	= 264 gallons	cubic meters × 264.172	= gallons
1 gram	= 0.035 ounce (avdp)[3]	grams × 0.0352740	= ounces (avdp)[3]
1 kilogram	= 2.2 pounds (avdp)[3]	kilograms × 2.20462	= pounds (avdp)[3]
1 kilowatt	= 1.3 horsepower	kilowatts × 1.34102	= horsepower

[1]Exact.   [2]Common term not used in SI.   [3]avdp = avoirdupois.
Source: National Institute of Standards and Technology

British/US System (ft-lb-second, fps)

length

1 statute mi	= 5,280 ft	= 1,760 yd	= 320 rods	= 8 furlongs
1 nautical mi	= 6,076 ft	= 1.151 mi		
1 furlong	= 660 ft	= 220 yd	= 40 rods	= 1/8 mi
1 chain (Gunter's)	= 66 ft	= 22 yd	= 100 links	= 4 rods
1 rod	= 16.5 ft	= 5.5 yd	= 25 links	
1 fathom	= 6 ft	= 72 in		
1 yd	= 3 ft	= 36 in		
1 ft	= 12 in			
1 link (Gunter's)	= 0.66 ft	= 7.92 in		
1 hand	= 4 in			
1 mil	= 0.001 in			

area

1 sq mi	= 640 acres	= 102,400 sq rods	= 3,097,600 sq yd	= 27,878,400 sq ft
1 acre	= 10 sq chains	= 160 sq rods	= 4,840 sq yd	= 43,560 sq ft
1 sq ft	= 144 sq in			

volume

1 cu ft	= 1/27 cu yd	= 12 board ft	= 1,728 cu in
1 cu in	= 1/46,656 cu yd	= 1/1,728 cu ft	
1 acre-ft	= 43,560 cu ft	= 1,613 cu yd	
1 board ft	= 144 cu in	= 1/12 cu ft	= 1 super ft (lumber)
1 cord (US)	= 128 cu ft		

capacity

1 cu ft	= 7.481 gal (US)	= 6.229 gal (British)

liquid measure (US)

1 barrel, oil	= 42 gal (US)	= 34.97 gal (British)		
1 gal	= 0.833 gal (British)	= 4 quarts	= 231.00 cu in	= 128 fl oz
1 quart	= 1/4 gal	= 2 pints	= 57.75 cu in	= 32 fl oz
1 pint	= 1/8 gal	= 1/2 quart	= 28.88 cu in	= 16 fl oz
1 gill	= 1/32 gal	= 1/4 pint	= 7.22 cu in	= 4 fl oz
1 fl oz	= 1/128 gal	= 1/16 pint	= 1.80 cu in	

dry measure (US)

1 bushel = 1.24 cu ft	= 0.97 bushel (British)	= 4 pecks	= 2,150.4 cu in

British/US system (ft-lb-second, fps) (continued)

dry measure (US) (continued)

1 quart	= 1/32 bushel	= 2 pints	= 67.2 cu in	= 1/8 peck
1 pint	= 1/64 bushel	= 1/2 quart	= 33.6 cu in	

liquid and dry measure (British)

1 bushel	= 1.03 bushels (US)	= 8 gal	= 4 pecks	= 2,219.36 cu in	= 1.284 cu ft
1 peck	= 0.25 bushel	= 2 gal	= 8 quarts	= 554.84 cu in
1 gal	= 1.20 gal (US)	= 4 quarts		= 277.42 cu in
1 quart	= 0.30 gal	= 2 pints	= 1/8 peck	= 69.36 cu in
1 pint	= 4.80 gills (US)	= 4 gills		= 34.68 cu in	= 20 fl oz
1 gill	= 1.20 gills (US)			= 8.67 cu in	= 5 fl oz
1 fl oz	= 0.96 fl oz (US)			= 1.73 cu in

weight

1 short ton (US)	= 0.89 long ton	= 2,000 lbs	= 20 short cwt*
1 long ton (British)	= 1.12 short tons	= 2,240 lbs	= 22.4 short cwt*
1 short cwt* (US)	= 0.05 short ton	= 100 lbs
1 long cwt* (British)	= 0.05 long ton	= 112 lbs
1 stone (person)	= 0.14 short cwt*	= 14 lbs
1 lb	= 0.07 stone (British)
1 oz avdp†	= 437.50 grains	= 1/16 lb	= 0.911 oz troy
1 oz troy	= 480.00 grains	= 1/12 lb	= 1.097 oz
1 grain		= 0.0023 oz	= 0.0021 oz troy

cwt = hundredweight.   †avdp = avoirdupois.

Tables of Equivalents: Metric System Units and Prefixes

base unit*

QUANTITY	NAME OF UNIT	SYMBOL
length	meter	m
area	square meter	square m, or m^2
	are (100 square meters)	a
volume	cubic meter	cubic m, or m^3
	stere (1 cubic meter)	s
mass	gram	g
	metric ton (1,000,000 grams)	t
capacity	liter	l
temperature	degree Celsius	°C

prefixes designating multiples and submultiples

PREFIX	SYMBOL	FACTOR BY WHICH UNIT IS MULTIPLIED		EXAMPLES
exa-	E	10^{18}	= 1,000,000,000,000,000,000	
peta-	P	10^{15}	= 1,000,000,000,000,000	
tera-	T	10^{12}	= 1,000,000,000,000	
giga-	G	10^9	= 1,000,000,000	
mega-	M	10^6	= 1,000,000	megaton (Mt)
kilo-	k	10^3	= 1,000	kilometer (km)
hecto-, hect-	h	10^2	= 100	hectare (ha)
deca- dec-	da	10	= 10	decastere (das)
			1	
deci-	d	10^{-1}	= 0.1	decigram (dg)
centi-, cent-	c	10^{-2}	= 0.01	centimeter (cm)
milli-	m	10^{-3}	= 0.001	milliliter (ml)
micro-, micr-	μ	10^{-6}	= 0.000001	microgram (μg)
nano-	n	10^{-9}	= 0.000000001	
pico-	p	10^{-12}	= 0.000000000001	
femto-	f	10^{-15}	= 0.000000000000001	
atto-	a	10^{-18}	= 0.000000000000000001	

The metric system of bases and prefixes has been applied to many other units, such as decibel (0.1 bel), kilowatt (1,000 watts), and microhm (one-millionth of an ohm).

Electrical Units

UNIT	SYMBOL	ATTRIBUTE MEASURED	EXPRESSION IN OTHER UNITS
ampere	A	current	C/s or V/Ω

the basic electrical unit of the International System of Units (SI), since 1948 defined by the International Bureau of Weights and Measures as the constant current which, if maintained in two straight parallel conductors of infinite length, of negligible circular cross section, and placed one meter apart in a vacuum, would produce between these conductors a force equal to 2 × 10^{-7} newton per meter of length. One ampere is equal to a flow of one coulomb of electricity per second; or, the flow produced in a conductor with a resistance of one ohm by a potential difference of one volt.

farad	F	capacitance (ability to hold a charge)	A × s/V or C/V

the ability of two parallel, oppositely charged plates (a capacitor) to hold an electric charge equals one farad when one coulomb of electricity changes the potential between the plates by one volt.

coulomb	C	charge	A × s

the quantity of electricity transported in one second by a current of one ampere. Approximately equal to 6.24 × 10^{18} electrons.

watt	W	power	J/s or V × A

one joule of work performed per second; or, the power dissipated in an electrical conductor carrying one ampere current between points at one volt potential difference.

ohm	Ω	resistance	V/A or W/A^2

resistance of a circuit in which a potential difference of one volt produces a current of one ampere; or, the resistance in which one watt of power is dissipated when one ampere flows through it.

volt	V	potential	W/A or A × Ω

the difference in potential between two points in a conductor carrying one ampere current when the power dissipated between the points is one watt; or, the difference in potential between two points in a conductor across a resistance of one ohm when one ampere is flowing through it.

Temperature Equivalents

Instructions for converting °F into °C or K*, and °C into °F: Find the figure you wish to convert in the second column. If this figure is in °F, the corresponding temperature in °C and K will be found in the third and fourth columns; if the figure is in °C, the corresponding temperature in °F will be found in the first column. To convert a temperature range between two scales, rather than finding equivalent temperatures, see the temperature conversion instructions, below.

°FAHRENHEIT (°F)	FIGURE TO BE CONVERTED	°CELSIUS (°CENTIGRADE) (°C)	KELVIN (K)	°FAHRENHEIT (°F)	FIGURE TO BE CONVERTED	°CELSIUS (°CENTIGRADE) (°C)	KELVIN (K)
...	−459.67	−273.15	0	+46.4	+8	−13.33	+259.82
				+48.2	+9	−12.78	+260.37
...	−400	−240.00	+33.15				
...	−300	−184.44	+88.71	+50.0	+10	−12.22	+260.93
−459.67	−273.15	−169.53	+103.62	+68.0	+20	−6.67	+266.48
				+86.0	+30	−1.11	+272.04
−328.0	−200	−128.89	+144.26	+89.6	+32	0.00	+273.15
−148.0	−100	−73.33	+199.82	+104.0	+40	+4.44	+277.59
				+122.0	+50	+10.00	+283.15
−130.0	−90	−67.78	+205.37	+140.0	+60	+15.56	+288.71
−112.0	−80	−62.22	+210.93	+158.0	+70	+21.11	+294.26
−94.0	−70	−56.67	+216.48	+176.0	+80	+26.67	+299.82
−76.9	−60	−51.11	+222.04	+194.0	+90	+32.22	+305.37
−58.0	−50	−45.56	+227.59				
−40.0	−40	−40.00	+233.15	+212.0	+100	+37.78	+310.93
−22.0	−30	−34.44	+238.71	+392.0	+200	+93.33	+366.48
−4.0	−20	−28.89	+244.26	+572.0	+300	+148.89	+422.04
+14.0	−10	−23.33	+249.82	+752.0	+400	+204.44	+477.59
				+932.0	+500	+260.00	+533.15
+32.0	0	−17.78	+255.37	+1112.0	+600	+315.56	+588.71
+33.8	+1	−17.22	+255.93	+1292.0	+700	+371.11	+644.26
+35.6	+2	−16.67	+256.48	+1472.0	+800	+426.67	+699.82
+37.4	+3	−16.11	+257.04	+1652.0	+900	+482.22	+755.37
+39.2	+4	−15.56	+257.59				
+41.0	+5	−15.00	+258.15	+1832.0	+1000	+537.78	+810.93
+42.8	+6	−14.44	+258.71	+3632.0	+2000	+1093.33	+1366.45
+44.6	+7	−13.89	+259.26	+5432.0	+3000	+1648.89	+1922.05

Temperature Equivalents (continued)

All systems of measuring temperature in degrees or units (kelvins) on a scale are based on the interval between the freezing and boiling points of water and differ only in the number of degrees or units into which this interval is divided.

Fahrenheit: interval is divided into 180 degrees (32° to 212°); 0° is at 32° below the freezing point of water.

Rankine: degree is the same as the Fahrenheit degree; 0° is at absolute zero (the theoretical point at which a thermodynamic system has the lowest energy, −459.67 °F). Once common in engineering applications in the US, the Rankine scale is now rarely used.

Celsius: interval is divided into 100 degrees; 0° is at the freezing point of water.

Kelvin: interval is the same as the Celsius degree; 0 K is at absolute zero (the theoretical point at which a thermodynamic system has the lowest energy, −273.15 °C).

Réaumur: interval is divided into 80 degrees; 0° is at the freezing point of water. One of the earliest (1730) temperature scales in widespread use, the Réaumur scale had been supplanted by other scales by the late 19th century.

*temperature conversion instructions:***
°Fahrenheit	into	°Celsius	subtract 32, divide by 1.8**
°Celsius	into	°Fahrenheit	multiply by 1.8, add 32**
°Celsius	into	kelvin	add 273.15

Because a kelvin is itself a unit of measurement, it is incorrect to use "degree" or the ° symbol with it, as is necessary with the units of the Rankine, Fahrenheit, Celsius, and Réaumur scales. One kelvin is equal to one degree Celsius.
**Instructions are for finding equivalent temperatures; to find the equivalent number of degrees in a temperature range (e.g., tomorrow's temperature will be 11.0 °F, or 6.1 °C, warmer than today's temperature), omit the step of adding or subtracting 32.*

Did you know? 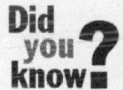 Daily minimum temperature readings at related urban and rural sites frequently show that the urban site is 10 to 20 °F warmer than the rural site. During summer, urban masonry and asphalt absorb, store, and reradiate more solar energy per unit area than do the vegetation and soil of rural areas. Furthermore, less of this energy can be used for evaporation in cities, which characteristically exhibit greater precipitation runoff from streets and buildings.

Melting and Boiling Points of Selected Substances

Note: values are in °C at a pressure of 1 atmosphere (atm.; 101.325 kPa), except when a substance has a triple point pressure greater than 1 atm.; in those cases the triple point temperature and sublimation temperature are given and noted accordingly (see footnotes 1 and 2); figures are given only for those temperatures for which measurements or reliable estimates are available.

SUBSTANCE	MELTING POINT (°C)	BOILING POINT (°C)	SUBSTANCE	MELTING POINT (°C)	BOILING POINT (°C)
common compounds			**selected elements** (continued)		
ammonia (H_3N)	−77.74	−33.34	calcium (Ca)	842	1,484
carbon dioxide (CO_2)	−56.57[1]	−78.5[2]	carbon (C)	4,492[1]	3,642[2]
ethyl alcohol (C_2H_5OH)	−114.1	78.5	chlorine (Cl)	−101.5	−34.04
heavy water (D_2O)	3.82	101.42	cobalt (Co)	1,495	2,927
hydrogen chloride (HCl)	−114	85	copper (Cu)	1,084.62	2,562
hydrogen peroxide (H_2O_2)	−0.43	150.2	fluorine (F)	−219.62	−188.12
methane (CH_4)	−182.5	−162	gold (Au)	1,064.18	2,856
ozone (O_3)	−251.4	−112	helium (He)		−268.93
propane (C_3H_8)	−187.6	−42.1	hydrogen (H)	259.34	−252.87
sulfuric acid (H_2SO_4)	10.37	338	iodine (I)	113.7	184.4
water (H_2O)	0.00	100.00	iron (Fe)	1,538	2,861
			lead (Pb)	327.46	1,749
selected elements			lithium (Li)	180.5	1,342
aluminum (Al)	660.32	2,519	magnesium (Mg)	650	1,090
argon (Ar)	189.35	−185.85	manganese (Mn)	1,246	2,061
arsenic (As)	817[1]	614[2]	mercury (Hg)	−38.83	356.73
bromine (Br)	−7.2	58.8	molybdenum (Mo)	2,623	4,639
cadmium (Cd)	321.07	767	neon (Ne)	−248.59	−246.08

Melting and Boiling Points of Selected Substances (continued)

SUBSTANCE	MELTING POINT (°C)	BOILING POINT (°C)	SUBSTANCE	MELTING POINT (°C)	BOILING POINT (°C)
selected elements (continued)			selected elements		
nickel (Ni)	1,455	2,913	silver (Ag)	691.78	2,162
nitrogen (N)	-210	-195.79	sodium (Na)	97.80	883
oxygen (O)	-218.79	-182.95	sulfur (S)	115.21	444.6
phosphorus (P)	44.15	280.5	tin (Sn)	231.93	2,602
platinum (Pt)	1,768.4	3,825	titanium (Ti)	1,668	3,287
plutonium (Pu)	640	3,228	uranium (U)	1,135	4,131
potassium (K)	63.38	759	xenon (Xe)	-111.75	-108.04
radon (Rn)	-71	-61.7	zinc (Zn)	419.53	907
silicon (Si)	1,414	3,265			

[1]triple point temperature (equilibrium among the solid, liquid, and gaseous phases); [2]sublimation temperature at 1 atm. (substance passes directly from solid to gaseous phase at a pressure of 1 atm.)

Selected Physical Properties of Water

molar mass	18.0151 g/mol
melting point	0.00 °C
boiling point	100.00 °C
density	
freshwater	
ice	0.92 g/cm³
0 °C	0.99987 g/cm³
3.98 °C	1.0000 g/cm³ (maximum density)
20 °C	0.99823 g/cm³
25 °C	0.99701 g/cm³
100 °C	0.95841 g/cm³

seawater (salinity 35 parts/thousand, at 0 °C)

DEPTH (M)	PRESSURE (DECIBARS)	DENSITY (G/CM³)
0	0	1.02813
1,000	1,000	1.03285
2,000	2,000	1.03747
4,000	4,000	1.04640
6,000	6,000	1.05495
8,000	8,000	1.06315
10,000	10,000	1.07104

vapor pressure (25 °C)	23.75 torr
heat of fusion (0 °C)	6.010 kJ/mol
heat of vaporization (100 °C)	40.65 kJ/mol
heat of formation (25 °C)	-285.85 kJ/mol
entropy of vaporization (25 °C)	118.8 J/°C mol
viscosity	0.8903 centipoise
surface tension (25 °C)	71.97 dynes/cm

Playing Cards and Dice Chances

Blackjack

Number of two-card combinations in a 52-card deck (where aces equal 11 and face cards equal 10) for each number between 13 and 21

TOTAL WITH TWO CARDS	POSSIBLE COMBINATIONS FROM 52 CARDS
21	64
20	136
19	80
18	86
17	96
16	86
15	96
14	102
13	118

Playing Cards and Dice Chances (continued)

Blackjack (continued)

Approximate chances of various hands reaching or exceeding 21

TOTAL IN HAND BEFORE DEAL (TWO OR MORE CARDS)	CHANCE OF REACHING A COUNT OF 17 TO 21	CHANCE OF EXCEEDING 21	
		ONE CARD	ANY NUMBER OF CARDS
(%)	(%)	(%)	(%)
16	38	62	62
15	42	54	58
14	44	46	56
13	48	38	52

Poker

Number of ways to reach and odds of reaching various five-card combinations on a single deal (52-card deck, no wild cards)

HAND	NUMBER OF COMBINATIONS	ODDS OF RECEIVING ON A SINGLE DEAL
royal flush	4	1 in 649,740
straight flush	36	1 in 72,193
four of a kind	624	1 in 4,165
full house	3,744	1 in 694
flush	5,108	1 in 509
straight	10,200	1 in 255
three of a kind	54,912	1 in 47
two pairs	123,552	1 in 21
one pair	1,098,240	1 in 2

Dice

Probabilities of two-die totals

TWO-DIE TOTAL	NUMBER OF COMBINATIONS	PROBABILITY (%)
2	1	2.78
3	2	5.56
4	3	8.33
5	4	11.11
6	5	13.89
7	6	16.67
8	5	13.89
9	4	11.11
10	3	8.33
11	2	5.56
12	1	2.78
total	36	100[1]

[1] Detail does not add to total because of rounding.

Spirits Measure

From smallest to largest. Many specific volumes have varied over time and from place to place, but the proportional relationships within the various families of measures have generally remained the same.

MEASURE	CONVENTIONAL EQUIVALENTS*	METRIC EQUIVALENT†
pony	0.75 oz = ¾ shot= ½ jigger	22.17 ml
shot/ounce/finger	1 oz = 1⅓ ponies = ⅔ jigger	29.57 ml
jigger	1.5 oz = 2 ponies = 1½ shots	44.36 ml
double	2 oz = 2 shots	59.15 ml
triple	3 oz = 3 shots	88.72 ml
noggin/imperial gill/drink (whiskey)	4.8 oz	142.1 ml
pint	16 oz = ⅝ fifth = ½ quart	473.2 ml
quarter yard	20 oz = 1¼ pints	591.5 ml
bottle (champagne or other wine)	about 25.5 oz or ⅙ imperial gallon	about 750 ml†
fifth	25.6 oz = ⅘ quart = ⅕ gallon	757.1 ml
quart	32 oz = ½ magnum = ¼ gallon	946.3 ml
half yard	40 oz = 2½ pints	1.182 l
magnum	2 bottles (champagne or other wine)	1.5 l
magnum	64 oz = 2 quarts = ½ gallon	1.893 l
yard	80 oz = 5 pints	2.365 l

Spirits Measure (continued)

MEASURE	CONVENTIONAL EQUIVALENTS*	METRIC EQUIVALENT†
jeroboam	4 bottles (champagne or other wine)	3 l
gallon/double magnum	128 oz = 4 quarts = 5 fifths = 2 magnums	3.785 l
rehoboam	6 bottles (champagne or other wine)	4 l
imperial gallon	1.20 gallons = ⅖ barn gallon = ¹⁄₁₀ anker	4.546 l
ale/beer gallon	1.22 gallons	4.620 l
methuselah	8 bottles (champagne or other wine)	6 l
salmanazar	12 bottles (champagne or other wine)	9 l
barn gallon	2½ imperial gallons = ¼ anker	11.37 l
balthazar	16 bottles (champagne or other wine)	12 l
half keg	5 gallons (type varies)	varies
nebuchadnezzar	20 bottles (champagne or other wine)	15 l
firkin	9 gallons	34.07 l
keg	10 gallons (type varies)	varies
anker	60 bottles = 10 imperial gallons = 4 barn gallons	45.46 l
runlet/rundlet/rudlet	144 pints = 72 quarts = 18 gallons = 2 firkins	68.14 l
octave	15.75 imperial gallons = ⅛ butt (wine)	71.60 l
British bottle	126 bottles = 21 imperial gallons	95.47 l
aum	120 quarts = 30 gallons	113.6 l
barrel (wine)	126 quarts = 31½ gallons = ¾ tierce	119.2 l
barrel (ale/beer)	144 quarts = 36 gallons = ½ puncheon (ale/beer)	136.3 l
tierce	168 quarts = 42 gallons = ½ tun (wine)	159.0 l
British hogshead (ale/beer)	54 imperial gallons = ½ butt (ale/beer) = ¼ tun (ale/beer)	245.5 l
puncheon (ale/beer)	72 gallons = 2 barrels (ale/beer)	272.5 l
British hogshead (wine)	63 imperial gallons = ½ butt (wine) = ¼ tun (wine)	286.4 l
puncheon (wine)	84 gallons = 2 tierces	318.0 l
butt/pipe (ale/beer)	108 imperial gallons = ½ tun (ale/beer)	491.0 l
butt/pipe (wine)	126 imperial gallons = ½ tun (wine)	572.8 l
tun (ale/beer)	216 imperial gallons = 4 British hogsheads (ale/beer) = 2 butts (ale/beer)	982.0 l
tun (wine)	252 imperial gallons = 12 British bottles = 2 butts (wine)	1,146 l

*All ounce measures are in US fluid ounces.   †Wine bottle sizes have varied from 700 to 800 ml in various countries; industry standard is 750 ml.

Cooking Measurements

MEASURE	CONVENTIONAL EQUIVALENTS*	METRIC EQUIVALENT
drop	1/60 teaspoon	0.08 ml
dash	1/8 teaspoon	0.62 ml
teaspoon	8 dashes; 1/3 tablespoon; 1/6 fluid ounce	4.93 ml
tablespoon	3 teaspoons; 1/2 fluid ounce	14.79 ml
ounce (weight)	1/16 pound	28.35 g
fluid ounce (volume)	2 tablespoons	29.57 ml
cup	8 fluid ounces; 16 tablespoons; 1/2 pint	236.59 ml
pound	16 ounces	453.6 g
pint	16 fluid ounces; 2 cups; 1/2 quart	473.18 ml
quart	32 fluid ounces; 4 cups; 2 pints; 1/4 gallon	946.36 ml
gallon	128 fluid ounces; 16 cups; 8 pints; 4 quarts	3.785 l
peck	2 gallons	7.57 l
bushel	8 gallons; 4 pecks	30.28 l

*All ounce measurements are in US ounces or fluid ounces.

		OVEN TEMPERATURE EQUIVALENTS		
		AMERICAN OVEN TEMPERATURE	FRENCH OVEN TEMPERATURE TERMS AND THERMOSTAT	BRITISH "GAS MARK" OVEN THERMOSTAT
°F	°C	TERMS	SETTINGS	SETTINGS
160	71		#1	
170	77			
200	93		très doux; étuve	
212	100			
221	105		#2	
225	107	very slow	doux	
230	110		#3	#1/4 (241 °F)
250	121			

Cooking Measurements (continued)

OVEN TEMPERATURE EQUIVALENTS (CONTINUED)

°F	°C	AMERICAN OVEN TEMPERATURE TERMS	FRENCH OVEN TEMPERATURE TERMS AND THERMOSTAT SETTINGS	BRITISH "GAS MARK" OVEN THERMOSTAT SETTINGS
275	135			#1/2 (266 °F)
284	140	slow	moyen; modéré	#1 (291 °F)
300	149			
302	150		#4	
320	160			#2 (313 °F)
325	163			
350	177	moderate	assez chaud; bon four	#3 (336 °F)
356	180			#4 (358 °F)
375	190		#5	
390	200			#5 (379 °F)
400	205			#6 (403 °F)
410	210	hot	chaud	
425	218		#6	#7 (424 °F)
428	220			
437	225			
450	232			#8 (446 °F)
475	246	very hot	très chaud; vif	#9 (469 °F)
500	260		#7	
525	274		#8	
550	288		#9	

Large Numbers

The American system of numeration for denominations above one million was modeled on the French system, but more recently the French system has been changed to correspond to the German and British systems. In the American system each of the denominations above 1,000 millions (the American billion) is 1,000 times the preceding one (one trillion = 1,000 billions; one quadrillion = 1,000 trillions). In the British system the first denomination above 1,000 millions (the British milliard) is 1,000 times the preceding one, but each of the denominations above 1,000 milliards (the British billion) is 1,000,000 times the preceding one (one trillion = 1,000,000 billions; one quadrillion = 1,000,000 trillions).

Source: Merriam-Webster's Collegiate Dictionary, Tenth Edition, Merriam-Webster, Inc., 1993.

AMERICAN NAME	VALUE IN POWERS OF TEN	NUMBER OF ZEROS	BRITISH NAME	VALUE IN POWERS OF TEN	NUMBER OF ZEROS
billion	10^9	9	milliard	10^9	9
trillion	10^{12}	12	billion	10^{12}	12
quadrillion	10^{15}	15	trillion	10^{18}	18
quintillion	10^{18}	18	quadrillion	10^{24}	24
sextillion	10^{21}	21	quintillion	10^{30}	30
septillion	10^{24}	24	sextillion	10^{36}	36
octillion	10^{27}	27	septillion	10^{42}	42
nonillion	10^{30}	30	octillion	10^{48}	48
decillion	10^{33}	33	nonillion	10^{54}	54
undecillion	10^{36}	36	decillion	10^{60}	60
duodecillion	10^{39}	39	undecillion	10^{66}	66
tredecillion	10^{42}	42	duodecillion	10^{72}	72
quattuordecillion	10^{45}	45	tredecillion	10^{78}	78
quindecillion	10^{48}	48	quattuordecillion	10^{84}	84
sexdecillion	10^{51}	51	quindecillion	10^{90}	90
septendecillion	10^{54}	54	sexdecillion	10^{96}	96
octodecillion	10^{57}	57	septendecillion	10^{102}	102
novemdecillion	10^{60}	60	octodecillion	10^{108}	108
vigintillion	10^{63}	63	novemdecillion	10^{114}	114
centillion	10^{303}	303	vigintillion	10^{120}	120
			centillion	10^{600}	600

Roman Numerals

Seven numeral-characters compose the Roman numeral system. When a numeral appears with a line above it, it represents the base value multiplied by 1,000. However, because Roman numerals are now seldom utilized for values beyond 4,999, this convention is no longer in use.

Roman Numerals (continued)

ARABIC	ROMAN	ARABIC	ROMAN	ARABIC	ROMAN	ARABIC	ROMAN
1	I	15	XV	70	LXX	1,000	M
2	II	16	XVI	80	LXXX	1,001	MI
3	III	17	XVII	90	XC	1,002	MII
4	IV	18	XVIII	100	C	1,003	MIII
5	V	19	XIX	101	CI	1,900	MCM
6	VI	20	XX	102	CII	2,000	MM
7	VII	21	XXI	200	CC	2,001	MMI
8	VIII	22	XXII	300	CCC	2,002	MMII
9	IX	23	XXIII	400	CD	2,100	MMC
10	X	24	XXIV	500	D	3,000	MMM
11	XI	30	XXX	600	DC	4,000	MMMM or $M\bar{V}$
12	XII	40	XL	700	DCC	5,000	$\bar{V}$
13	XIII	50	L	800	DCCC		
14	XIV	60	LX	900	CM		

Ancient Measures

The standard unit of measure is listed first, with a rough modern equivalent in parentheses. Often, standard units varied over time, so a range is sometimes given. The subdivisions below relate to the standard unit of measure given first.

CULTURE	LENGTH	WEIGHT	LIQUID
Egyptian	cubit (524 mm; 20.62 in)	kite (4.5–29.9 g; 0.16–1.05 oz)	cubic cubit (0.14 cubic m; 37 gal)[1]
	digit (1/28 of a cubit)	deben (10 kites)	khar
	palm (4 digits)	sep (10 debens)	hekat
	hand (5 digits)		hin
	small span (12 digits, or 3 palms)		ro
	large span (14 digits, or 1/2 cubit)		
	t'ser (16 digits, or 4 palms)		
	small cubit (24 digits, or 6 palms)		
Babylonian	kus[2] (530 mm; 20.9 in)	mina (640–978 g; 23–34 oz)	ka (99–102 cubic mm; 3.9–4.0 cubic in)
	foot (2/3 kus)	shekel	gur (300 ka)
	shusi (1/30 kus)		
Hebrew[3]		sacred mina (60 shekels)	bat[4]
		sacred talent (3,000 shekels, or 50 sacred minas)	hin
		Talmudic mina (25 shekels)	log
		Talmudic talent (1,500 shekels, or 60 Talmudic minas)	
Greek	finger (19.3 mm; 0.76 in)	talent (25.8 kg; 56.9 lb)	metretes (39.4 l; 10.4 gal)
	foot (16 fingers)		
	Olympic cubit (24 fingers)		
Roman	foot (subdivided into the uncia [plural unciae; 1/12 ft])	libra (327.45 g; 11.55 oz)	sextarius (0.53 l; 0.14 gal)
	pace, or double step (5 ft)	uncia (1/12 lb)	amphora (48 sextarii)
	mille passus (1,000 paces)		
Chinese[5]	chih (25 cm; 9.8 in)	shih, or tan (60 kg; 132 lb)	
	chang (3 m; 9.8 ft)		

[1]Measures given below the cubic cubit run from small to large.   [2]Also called the Babylonian cubit.   [3]The Hittites, Assyrians, Phoenicians, and Hebrews derived their systems from the Babylonians and Egyptians. Hebrew standards were based on the relationship between the mina, the talent (the basic unit), and the shekel.   [4]Volumes are not definitely known but are listed from largest to smallest.   [5]The Chinese system of measurement exhibited all the principal characteristics of the Western. It was, however, fundamentally chaotic in that there was no relationship between different types of units, such as those of length and those of volume. It also fluctuated from region to region and according to use. The first emperor of China, Shi Huangdi (221–210/09 BC), fixed the basic units given here.

Prime Numbers

A prime number is a positive integer greater than 1 that is divisible only by itself and 1. Every positive integer greater than 1 can be expressed as the product of only a single set of prime numbers. Primes have been recognized since at least 300 BC, when they were studied by the Greek mathematicians Euclid and Eratosthenes. They have always fascinated mathematicians, and even today there remain certain open questions regarding them. The first 100 prime numbers are: 2, 3, 5, 7, 11, 13,

17, 19, 23, 29, 31, 37, 41, 43, 47, 53, 59, 61, 67, 71, 73, 79, 83, 89, 97, 101, 103, 107, 109, 113, 127, 131, 137, 139, 149, 151, 157, 163, 167, 173, 179, 181, 191, 193, 197, 199, 211, 223, 227, 229, 233, 239, 241, 251, 257, 263, 269, 271, 277, 281, 283, 293, 307, 311, 313, 317, 331, 337, 347, 349, 353, 359, 367, 373, 379, 383, 389, 397, 401, 409, 419, 421, 431, 433, 439, 443, 449, 457, 461, 463, 467, 479, 487, 491, 499, 503, 509, 521, 523, and 541. For more information, see <www.utm.edu/research/primes>

Decimal Equivalents of Common Fractions

4THS	8THS	16THS	32NDS	DECIMAL		3RDS	6THS	12THS	DECIMAL
				0.015625				1	0.833334
			1	0.03125			1	2	0.166667
		1	2	0.0625				3	0.25
			3	0.09375		1	2	4	0.333334
	1	2	4	0.125				5	0.416667
			5	0.15625			3	6	0.5
		3	6	0.1875				7	0.583333
			7	0.21875		2	4	8	0.666667
1	2	4	8	0.25				9	0.75
			9	0.28125			5	10	0.833333
		5	10	0.3125				11	0.916667
			11	0.34375			6	12	1
	3	6	12	0.375					
			13	0.40625					
		7	14	0.4375				5THS	DECIMAL
			15	0.46875				1	0.2
2	4	8	16	0.5				2	0.4
			17	0.53125				3	0.6
		9	18	0.5625				4	0.8
			19	0.59375				5	1
	5	10	20	0.625					
			21	0.65625					
		11	22	0.6875				7THS	DECIMAL
			23	0.71875				1	0.142857
3	6	12	24	0.75				2	0.285714
			25	0.78125				3	0.428571
		13	26	0.8125				4	0.571428
			27	0.84375				5	0.714285
	7	14	28	0.875				6	0.857142
			29	0.90625				7	1
		15	30	0.9375					
			31	0.96875					
4	8	16	32	1					

Mathematical Formulas

The ratio of the circumference of a circle to its diameter is π (3.14159265358979323846264338327..., generally rounded to 22/7 or 3.1416). It occurs in various mathematical problems involving the lengths of arcs or other curves, the areas of surfaces, and the volumes of many solids.

	ACTION	FORMULA
circumference		
circle	multiply diameter by π	πd
area		
circle	multiply radius squared by π	πr^2
rectangle	multiply height by length	hl
sphere surface	multiply radius squared by π by 4	$4\pi r^2$
square	length of one side squared	s^2
trapezoid	parallel side length A + parallel side length B multiplied by height and divided by 2	$(A+B)h/2$
triangle	multiply base by height and divide by 2	$hb/2$
volume		
cone	multiply base radius squared by π by height and divide by 3	$br^2\pi h/3$
cube	length of one edge cubed	$a3$
cylinder	multiply base radius squared by π by height	$br^2\pi h$
pyramid	multiply base area by height and divide by 3	$hb/3$
sphere	multiply radius cubed by π by 4 and divide by 3	$4\pi r^3/3$

Encyclopædia Britannica's Great Inventions

INVENTION	YEAR	INVENTOR	COUNTRY
aerosol can	1926	Erik Rotheim	Norway
air conditioning	1902	Willis Haviland Carrier	US
airbag, automotive	1952	John Hetrick	US
airplane, engine-powered	1903	Wilbur & Orville Wright	US
airship	1852	Henri Giffard	France
alphabet	c. 1700–1500 BC	Semitic-speaking peoples	eastern coast of Mediterranean Sea
American Sign Language	1817	Thomas H. Gallaudet	US
animation, motion-picture	1906	J. Stuart Blackton	US
answering machine, telephone	1898	Valdemar Poulsen	Denmark
aspartame	1965	James Schlatter	US
aspirin	1897	Felix Hoffmann (Bayer)	Germany
assembly line	1913	Henry Ford	US
astrolabe	c. 2nd century	—	—
AstroTurf	1965	James M. Faria, Robert T. Wright	US
audiotape	1928	Fritz Pfleumer	Germany
automated teller machine (ATM)	1968	Don Wetzel	US
automobile	1889	Gottlieb Daimler	Germany
baby food, prepared	1927	Dorothy Gerber	US
bag, flat-bottomed paper	1870	Margaret Knight	US
Bakelite	1907	Leo Hendrik Baekeland	US
ball bearing	1794	Philip Vaughan	England
balloon, hot-air	1783	Joseph & Étienne Montgolfier	France
bandage, adhesive	1921	Earle Dickson	US
bar code	1952	Joseph Woodland	US
barbed wire	1874	Joseph Glidden	US
barometer	1643	Evangelista Torricelli	Italy
battery, electric storage	1800	Alessandro Volta	Italy
beer	before 6000 BC	Sumerians, Babylonians	Mesopotamia
bicycle	1818	Baron Karl de Drais de Sauerbrun	Germany
bifocal lens	1784	Benjamin Franklin	US
bikini	1946	Louis Réard	France
blood bank	late 1930s	Charles Richard Drew	US
blow-dryer	1920	Racine Universal Motor Co., Hamilton Beach Manufacturing Co.	US
bomb, atomic	1945	J. Robert Oppenheimer, et al.	US
bomb, thermonuclear (hydrogen)	1952	Edward Teller, et al.	US
boomerang	c. 15,000 years ago	Aboriginal peoples	Australia
Braille system	1824	Louis Braille	France
brassiere (bra)	1913	Mary Phelps Jacob	US
bread, sliced (bread-slicing machine)	1928	Otto Frederick Rohwedder	US
button	c. 700 BC	Greeks, Etruscans	Greece, Italy
buttonhole	13th century	—	Europe
calculator, electronic hand-held	1967	Jack S. Kilby	US
calculus	1680s	Sir Isaac Newton and Gottfried Wilhelm Leibniz (invented separately)	England and Germany (respectively)
calendar, modern (Gregorian)	1582	Pope Gregory XIII	Italy
camcorder	1982	Sony Corp.	Japan
camera, motion picture	1891	Thomas Alva Edison, William K.L. Dickson	US
camera, portable photographic	1888	George Eastman	US
can, metal beverage	1933	American Can Co.	US
can opener	1858	Ezra J. Warner	US
candle	c. 3000 BC	—	Egypt, Crete
canning, food	1809	Nicolas Appert	France
carbon-14 dating	1946	Willard F. Libby	US
cardboard, corrugated	1871	Albert Jones	US
cards, playing	c. 10th century	—	China
cash register	1879	James Ritty	US
cat litter	1947	Edward Lowe	US
catalog, mail-order	1872	Aaron Montgomery Ward	US

Encyclopædia Britannica's Great Inventions (continued)

INVENTION	YEAR	INVENTOR	COUNTRY
cellophane	1911	Jacques E. Brandenberger	Switzerland
celluloid	1869	John Wesley Hyatt	US
cement, portland	1824	Joseph Aspdin	England
cereal flakes, breakfast	1894	John Harvey Kellogg	US
chewing gum (modern)	c. 1870	Thomas Adams	US
chocolate	c. 3rd–10th century	Maya, Aztecs	Central America, Mexico
chronometer	1762	John Harrison	England
clock, pendulum	1656	Christiaan Huygens	The Netherlands
clock, quartz	1927	Warren A. Marrison	Canada/US
cloning, animal	1970	John B. Gurdon	UK
coffee, drip	1908	Melitta Bentz	Germany
coffee, decaffeinated	1905	Ludwig Roselius	Germany
coins	c. 650 BC	Lydians	Turkey
compact disc (CD)	1980	Philips Electronics, Sony Corp.	The Netherlands, Japan
compass, magnetic	c. 12th century	—	China, Europe
computed tomography (CT scan, CAT scan)	1972	Godfrey Hounsfield, Allan Cormack	UK, US
computer, electronic digital	1939	John V. Atanasoff, Clifford E. Berry	US
computer, laptop	1983	Radio Shack Corp.	US
computer, personal	1974	MITS (Micro Instrumentation Telemetry Systems)	US
concrete, reinforced	1867	Joseph Monier	France
condom, latex	c. 1930	—	—
contact lenses	1887	Adolf Fick	Germany
contraceptives, oral	early 1950s	Gregory Pincus, John Rock, Min Chueh Chang	US
corn, hybrid	1917	Donald F. Jones	US
correction fluid, white	1951	Bette Nesmith	US
cotton gin	1793	Eli Whitney	US
coupon, grocery	1894	Asa Candler	US
crayons, children's wax	1903	Edwin Binney, C. Harold Smith	US
cream separator (dairy processing)	1878	Carl Gustaf Patrik de Laval	Sweden
credit card	1950	Frank McNamara, Ralph Schneider (Diners' Club)	US
crossword puzzles	1913	Arthur Wynne	US
DDT	1874	Othmar Zeidler	Germany
defibrillator	1952	Paul M. Zoll	US
dentures	c. 700 BC	Etruscans	Italy
detector, metal	late 1920s	Gerhard Fisher	Germany/US
detector, home smoke	1969	Randolph Smith, Kenneth House	US
diamond, artificial	1955	General Electric Co.	US
diapers, disposable	1950	Marion Donovan	US
digital videodisc (DVD)	1995	consortium of international electronics companies	Japan, US, The Netherlands
dishwasher	1886	Josephine Cochrane	US
DNA fingerprinting	1984	Alec Jeffreys	UK
doughnut, ring-shaped	1847	Hanson Crockett Gregory	US
door, revolving	1888	Theophilus von Kannel	US
drinking fountain	c. 1905–1912	Luther Haws, Halsey W. Taylor (invented separately)	US
dry cleaning	1855	Jean Baptiste Jolly	France
dynamite	1867	Alfred Nobel	Sweden
elastic, fabric	c. 1830	Thomas Hancock	UK
electric chair	1888	Harold P. Brown, Arthur E. Kennelly	US
electrocardiogram (ECG, EKG)	1903	Willem Finthoven	The Netherlands
electroencephalogram (EEG)	1929	Hans Berger	Germany
electronic mail (e-mail)	1971	Ray Tomlinson	US
elevator, passenger	1852	Elisha Graves Otis	US

Encyclopædia Britannica's Great Inventions (continued)

INVENTION	YEAR	INVENTOR	COUNTRY
encyclopedia	c. 4th century BC or 77 AD	Speusippus (compliation of Plato's teachings) or Pliny the Elder (comprehensive work)	Greece or Rome
engine, internal-combustion	1859	Étienne Lenoir	France
engine, jet	1930	Sir Frank Whittle	UK
engine, liquid-fueled rocket	1926	Robert H. Goddard	US
engine, steam	1698	Thomas Savery	England
escalator	1891	Jesse W. Reno	US
eyeglasses	1280s	Salvino degli Armati or Alessandro di Spina	Italy
facsimile (fax)	1842	Alexander Bain	Scotland
fiber optics	1955	Narinder S. Kapany	India
fiberglass	1938	Owens Corning (corp.)	US
film, photographic	1884	George Eastman	US
flashlight, battery-operated portable	1899	Conrad Hubert	Russia/US
flask, vacuum (Thermos)	1892	Sir James Dewar	Scotland
food processor	1971	Pierre Verdon	France
foods, freeze-dried	1946	Earl W. Flosdorf	US
foods, frozen	c. 1924	Clarence Birdseye	US
Fresnel lens	1820	Augustin-Jean Fresnel	France
fuel cell	1839	William R. Grove	UK
genetic engineering	1973	Stanley N. Cohen, Herbert W. Boyer	US
Geiger counter	1908	Hans Geiger	Germany
glass	c. 2500 BC	Egyptians or Phoenicians	Egypt or Lebanon
glass, safety	1909	Édouard Bénédictus	France
greeting card, Christmas	1843	John Callcott Horsley	England
guillotine	1792	Joseph-Ignace Guillotin	France
guitar, electric	1941	Les Paul	US
gunpowder	c. 10th century	–	China or Arabia
hanger, wire coat	1903	Albert J. Parkhouse	US
helicopter	1939	Igor Sikorsky	Russia/US
holography	1948	Dennis Gabor	Hungary
hypodermic syringe	1853	Charles Gabriel Pravaz	France
in vitro fertilization (IVF), human	1978	Patrick Steptoe, Robert Edwards	UK
ink	c. 2500 BC	–	Egypt, China
insulin, extraction and preparation of	1921	Sir Frederick Grant Banting, Charles H. Best	Canada
integrated circuit	1958	Jack S. Kilby	US
Internet	1969	Advanced Research Projects Agency (ARPA) at the Dept. of Defense	US
iron, electric	1882	Henry W. Seely	US
irradiation, food	1905	–	US/UK
jeans	1873	Levi Strauss, Jacob Davis	US
JELL-O (gelatin dessert)	1897	Pearle B. Wait	US
jukebox	1889	Louis Glass	US
Kevlar	1965	Stephanie Kwolek	US
Kool-Aid (fruit drink mix)	1927	Edwin E. Perkins	US
laser	1958	Gordon Gould and Charles Hard Townes, Arthur L. Schawlow (invented separately)	US
laundromat	1934	J.F. Cantrell	US
lawn mower, gasoline-powered	c. 1940	Leonard Goodall	US
Lego	late 1940s	Ole Kirk Christiansen	Denmark
light bulb, incandescent	1879	Thomas Alva Edison	US
light bulb, fluorescent	1934	Arthur Compton	US
light-emitting diode (LED)	1962	Nick Holonyak, Jr.	US
linoleum	1860	Frederick Walton	UK
lipstick, tube	1915	Maurice Levy	US
liquid crystal display (LCD)	1963	George Heilmeier	US
lock and key	c. 2000 BC	Assyrians	Mesopotamia

Encyclopædia Britannica's Great Inventions (continued)

INVENTION	YEAR	INVENTOR	COUNTRY
locomotive	1829	George Stephenson	England
longbow	c. 1000	—	Wales
loudspeaker	1924	Chester W. Rice, Edward W. Kellogg	US
magnetic resonance imaging (MRI)	early 1970s	Raymond Damadian, Paul Lauterbur	US
margarine	1869	Hippolyte Mège-Mouriès	France
matches, friction	1827	John Walker	England
metric system of measurement	1795	French Academy of Sciences	France
microphone	1878	David E. Hughes	UK/US
microscope, compound optical	c. 1600	Hans & Zacharias Jansen	The Netherlands
microscope, electron	1933	Ernst Ruska	Germany
microwave oven	1945	Percy L. Spencer	US
miniature golf	c. 1930	Garnet Carter	US
mirror, glass	c. 1200	Venetians	Italy
missile, guided	1942	Wernher von Braun	Germany
mobile home	1919	Glenn H. Curtiss	US
money, paper	late 900s	—	China
Monopoly (board game)	1934	Charles B. Darrow	US
Morse code	1838	Samuel F.B. Morse	US
motor, electric	1834	Thomas Davenport	US
motor, outboard	1907	Ole Evinrude	Norway/US
motorcycle	1885	Gottlieb Daimler, Wilhelm Maybach	Germany
mouse, computer	1963–64	Douglas Engelbart	US
Muzak	1922	George Owen Squier	US
nail, construction	c. 3300 BC	Sumerians	Mesopotamia
necktie	17th century	—	Croatia
neon lighting	1910	Georges Claude	France
nuclear reactor	1942	Enrico Fermi	US
nylon	1937	Wallace H. Carothers	US
oil lamp	1784	Aimé Argand	Switzerland
oil well	1859	Edwin Laurentine Drake	US
pacemaker, cardiac	1952	Paul M. Zoll	US
paper	c. 105	Ts'ai Lun	China
paper clip	1899	Johan Vaaler	Norway
paper towel	1931	Arthur Scott	US
parachute, modern	1797	André-Jacques Garnerin	France
parking meter	1932	Carl C. Magee	US
particle accelerator	1929	Sir John Douglas Cockcroft, Ernest Thomas Sinton Walton	Ireland/UK
pasteurization	1864	Louis Pasteur	France
pen, ballpoint	1938	Lazlo Biro	Hungary
pencil	1565	Conrad Gesner	Switzerland
periodic table	1871	Dmitry Ivanovich Mendeleyev	Russia
personal watercraft, motorized	1968	Bombardier, Inc.	Canada
petroleum jelly	1870s	Robert Chesebrough	US
phonograph	1877	Thomas Alva Edison	US
photocopying (xerography)	1937	Chester F. Carlson	US
photography	1837	Louis-Jacques-Mandé Daguerre	France
photography, instant	1947	Edwin Herbert Land	US
Play-Doh	1950	Noah W. & Joseph S. McVicker	US
plow, steel	1836	John Deere	US
pocket watch	c. 1500	Peter Henlein	Germany
polyethylene	1935	Eric Fawcett, Reginald Gibson	UK
polygraph (lie detector)	1921	John A. Larson	US
polyvinyl chloride (PVC)	1872	Eugen Baumann	Germany
Post-it Notes	mid-1970s	Arthur Fry (3M)	US
potato chips	1853	George Crum	US
printing press, movable type	c. 1450	Johannes Gutenberg	Germany
Prozac	1972	Ray W. Fuller, Bryan B. Molloy, David T. Wong	US

Encyclopædia Britannica's Great Inventions (continued)

INVENTION	YEAR	INVENTOR	COUNTRY
radar	c. 1904	Christian Hülsmeyer	Germany
radio	1896	Guglielmo Marconi	Italy
radio, car	early 1920s	William P. Lear	US
rayon	1884	Louis-Marie-Hilaire Bernigaud, count of Chardonnet	France
razor, electric	1928	Jacob Schick	US
razor, safety	c. 1900	King Camp Gillette	US
reaper, mechanical	1831	Cyrus Hall McCormick	US
record, long-playing (LP)	1948	Peter Carl Goldmark	US
refrigerator	1842	John Gorrie	US
remote control, television	1950	Robert Adler	US
respirator	c. 1955	Forrest M. Bird	US
revolver	1835–36	Samuel Colt	US
Richter scale	1935	Charles Francis Richter, Beno Gutenberg	US
rifle, assault	1944	Hugo Schmeisser	Germany
roller coaster	1884	LeMarcus A. Thompson	US
rubber, vulcanized	1839	Charles Goodyear	US
rubber band	1845	Stephen Perry	UK
saccharin	1879	Ira Remsen, Constantin Fahlberg	US, Germany
saddle	c. 200 BC	–	China
safety pin	1849	Walter Hunt	US
satellite, successful artificial earth	1957	Sergey Korolyov, et al.	USSR
satellite, communications	1960	John Robinson Pierce	US
saxophone	1846	Antoine-Joseph Sax	Belgium
Scotch tape	1930	Richard Drew (3M)	US
scuba gear	1943	Jacques Cousteau, Émile Gagnan	France
seat belt, automotive shoulder	1959	Nils Bohlin (Volvo)	Sweden
sewing machine	1841	Barthélemy Thimonnier	France
shoelaces	1790	–	England
silicone	1904	Frederic Stanley Kipping	UK
skateboard	1958	Bill & Mark Richards	US
skates, ice	1000 BC	–	Scandinavia
skates, roller	1760s	Joseph Merlin	Belgium
ski, snow	c. 2000–3000 BC	–	Sweden, Finland, Norway
skyscraper, steel-frame	1884	William Le Baron Jenney	US
slot machine	1890s	Charles Fey	US
snowmobile	1922	Joseph-Armand Bombardier	Canada
soap	600 BC	Phoenicians	Lebanon
soft drinks, carbonated	1772	Joseph Priestley	UK
sonar	1915	Paul Langevin	France
stamps, postage	1840	Sir Rowland Hill	UK
stapler	1866	George W. McGill	US
steamboat, successful	1807	Robert Fulton	US
steel, mass-production	1856	Henry Bessemer	UK
steel, stainless	1914	Harry Brearley	UK
stereo, personal	1979	Sony Corp.	Japan
stereophonic sound recording	1931	Alan Dower Blumlein	UK
stethoscope	1819	René-Théophile-Hyacinthe Laënnec	France
stock ticker	1867	Edward A. Calahan	US
stove, electric	1896	William Hadaway	US
stove, gas	1826	James Sharp	UK
straw, drinking	1888	Marvin Stone	US
submarine	1620	Cornelis Drebbel	The Netherlands
sunglasses	1752	James Ayscough	UK
sunscreen	1944	Benjamin Green	US
supermarket	1930	Michael Cullen	US
synthesizer, music	1955	Harry Olson, Herbert Belar	US
synthetic skin	1981	Ioannis V. Yannas, John F. Burke	US
tampon, cotton	1931	Earle Cleveland Haas	US

Encyclopædia Britannica's Great Inventions (continued)

INVENTION	YEAR	INVENTOR	COUNTRY
tank, military	1915	Admiralty Landships Committee	UK
tea bag	early 1900s	Thomas Sullivan	US
teddy bear	1902	Morris Michtom	US
Teflon	1938	Roy Plunkett	US
telegraph	1832–35	Samuel F.B. Morse	US
telephone, wired-line	1876	Alexander Graham Bell	Scotland/US
telephone, mobile	1946	Bell Laboratories	US
telescope, optical	1608	Hans Lippershey	The Netherlands
television	1923, 1927	Vladimir Kosma Zworykin, Philo Taylor Farnsworth	Russia/US, US
thermometer	1592	Galileo	Italy
thermostat	1830	Andrew Ure	UK
threshing machine	1778	Andrew Meikle	Scotland
tire, pneumatic	1888	John Boyd Dunlop	UK
tissue, disposable facial	1924	Kimberly-Clark Co.	US
tissue, toilet	1857	Joseph Gayetty	US
toaster, electric	1893	Crompton Co.	UK
toilet, flush	c. 1591	Sir John Harington	England
toothbrush	1498	—	China
tractor	1892	John Froehlich	US
traffic lights, automatic	1923	Garrett A. Morgan	US
transistor	1947	John Bardeen, Walter H. Brattain, William B. Shockley	US
typewriter	1868	Christopher Latham Sholes	US
ultrasound imaging, obstetric	1958	Ian Donald	UK
vaccination	1796	Edward Jenner	England
vacuum cleaner, electric	1901	Herbert Cecil Booth	UK
Velcro	1948	George de Mestral	Switzerland
vending machine	c. 100–200 BC	—	Egypt
Viagra	1997	Pfizer Inc.	US
video games	1972	Nolan Bushnell	US
videocassette recorder	1969	Sony Corp.	Japan
videotape	1950s	Charles Ginsburg	US
virtual reality	1989	Jaron Lanier	US
vision correction, laser	1987	Stephen Trokel	US
washing machine, electric	1907	Alva J. Fisher	US
wheel	about 3500 BC	proto-Aryan people or Sumerians	Russia/Kazakhstan or Mesopotamia
wheelbarrow	1st century BC	—	China
wheelchair	1590s	—	Spain
windmill	644	—	Persia
wine	before 4000 BC	—	Middle East
World Wide Web	1989	Tim Berners-Lee	UK
wristwatch, digital	1970	John M. Bergey	US
X-ray imaging	1895	Wilhelm Conrad Röntgen	Germany
Zamboni (ice resurfacing machine)	1949	Frank J. Zamboni	US
zipper	1893	Whitcomb L. Judson	US

Applied Science

Chemistry

Chemistry is the science that deals with the properties, composition, and structure of substances (defined as elements and compounds), the transformations that they undergo, and the energy that is released or absorbed during these processes. Every substance, whether naturally occurring or artificially produced, consists of one or more of the hundred-odd species of atoms that have been identified as elements. Although these atoms, in turn, are composed of more elementary particles, they are the basic building blocks of chemical substances; there is no quantity of oxygen, mercury, or gold, for example, smaller than an atom of that substance. Chemistry, therefore, is concerned not with the subatomic domain but with the properties of atoms and the laws governing their combinations and with how the knowledge of these properties can be used to achieve specific purposes.

Periodic Table of the Elements

The periodic table arranges the elements into groups (vertically) of elements sharing common physical and chemical characteristics, and into periods (horizontally) of sequentially increasing atomic number and electron-shell configuration. Elements 110, 111, 112, and 114 have been created experimentally and have temporary names. The claim that elements 116 and 118 were prepared has been retracted.

IA	IIA	IIIB	IVB	VB	VIB	VIIB	VIII			IB	IIB	IIIA	IVA	VA	VIA	VIIA	Zero
1 H																	2 He
3 Li	4 Be											5 B	6 C	7 N	8 O	9 F	10 Ne
11 Na	12 Mg											13 Al	14 Si	15 P	16 S	17 Cl	18 Ar
19 K	20 Ca	21 Sc	22 Ti	23 V	24 Cr	25 Mn	26 Fe	27 Co	28 Ni	29 Cu	30 Zn	31 Ga	32 Ge	33 As	34 Se	35 Br	36 Kr
37 Rb	38 Sr	39 Y	40 Zr	41 Nb	42 Mo	43 Tc	44 Ru	45 Rh	46 Pd	47 Ag	48 Cd	49 In	50 Sn	51 Sb	52 Te	53 I	54 Xe
55 Cs	56 Ba	57 La	72 Hf	73 Ta	74 W	75 Re	76 Os	77 Ir	78 Pt	79 Au	80 Hg	81 Tl	82 Pb	83 Bi	84 Po	85 At	86 Rn
87 Fr	88 Ra	89 Ac	104 Rf	105 Db	106 Sg	107 Bh	108 Hs	109 Mt	110 Uun	111 Uuu	112 Uub		114 Uuq				

Lanthanide Series

58 Ce	59 Pr	60 Nd	61 Pm	62 Sm	63 Eu	64 Gd	65 Tb	66 Dy	67 Ho	68 Er	69 Tm	70 Yb	71 Lu

Actinide Series

90 Th	91 Pa	92 U	93 Np	94 Pu	95 Am	96 Cm	97 Bk	98 Cf	99 Es	100 Fm	101 Md	102 No	103 Lr

Element	Symbol	Atomic no.	Atomic weight*	Element	Symbol	Atomic no.	Atomic weight*
Actinium	Ac	89	227.028	Molybdenum	Mo	42	95.94
Aluminum	Al	13	26.9815	Neodymium	Nd	60	144.24
Americium	Am	95	(243)	Neon	Ne	10	20.180
Antimony	Sb	51	121.75	Neptunium	Np	93	(237.0482)
Argon	Ar	18	39.948	Nickel	Ni	28	58.69
Arsenic	As	33	74.9216	Niobium	Nb	41	92.9064
Astatine	At	85	(210)	Nitrogen	N	7	14.0067
Barium	Ba	56	137.33	Nobelium	No	102	(259)
Berkelium	Bk	97	(247)	Osmium	Os	76	190.2
Beryllium	Be	4	9.01218	Oxygen	O	8	15.9994
Bismuth	Bi	83	208.9804	Palladium	Pd	46	106.42
Bohrium	Bh	107	(264)	Phosphorus	P	15	30.97376
Boron	B	5	10.81	Platinum	Pt	78	195.08
Bromine	Br	35	79.904	Plutonium	Pu	94	(244)
Cadmium	Cd	48	112.41	Polonium	Po	84	(209)
Calcium	Ca	20	40.08	Potassium	K	19	39.0983
Californium	Cf	98	(251)	Praseodymium	Pr	59	140.9077
Carbon	C	6	12.011	Promethium	Pm	61	(145)
Cerium	Ce	58	140.12	Protactinium	Pa	91	231.0359
Cesium	Cs	55	132.9054	Radium	Ra	88	(226.0254)
Chlorine	Cl	17	35.453	Radon	Rn	86	(222)
Chromium	Cr	24	51.996	Rhenium	Re	75	186.207
Cobalt	Co	27	58.9332	Rhodium	Rh	45	102.9055
Copper	Cu	29	63.546	Rubidium	Rb	37	85.4678
Curium	Cm	96	(247)	Ruthenium	Ru	44	101.07
Dubnium	Db	105	(262)	Rutherfordium	Rf	104	(261)
Dysprosium	Dy	66	162.50	Samarium	Sm	62	150.36
Einsteinium	Es	99	(252)	Scandium	Sc	21	44.9559
Erbium	Er	68	167.26	Seaborgium	Sg	106	(266)
Europium	Eu	63	151.96	Selenium	Se	34	78.96
Fermium	Fm	100	(257)	Silicon	Si	14	28.0855
Fluorine	F	9	18.9984	Silver	Ag	47	107.868
Francium	Fr	87	(223)	Sodium	Na	11	22.98977
Gadolinium	Gd	64	157.25	Strontium	Sr	38	87.62
Gallium	Ga	31	69.72	Sulfur	S	16	32.07
Germanium	Ge	32	72.61	Tantalum	Ta	73	180.9479
Gold	Au	79	196.9665	Technetium	Tc	43	(98)
Hafnium	Hf	72	178.49	Tellurium	Te	52	127.60
Hassium	Hs	108	(277)	Terbium	Tb	65	158.9254
Helium	He	2	4.00260	Thallium	Tl	81	204.383
Holmium	Ho	67	164.930	Thorium	Th	90	232.0381
Hydrogen	H	1	1.0079	Thulium	Tm	69	168.9342
Indium	In	49	114.82	Tin	Sn	50	118.71
Iodine	I	53	126.9045	Titanium	Ti	22	47.867
Iridium	Ir	77	192.22	Tungsten (wolfram)	W	74	183.85
Iron	Fe	26	55.845	Ununbium	Uub	112	(285)
Krypton	Kr	36	83.80	Ununnilium	Uun	110	(281)
Lanthanum	La	57	138.9055	Ununquadium	Uuq	114	(289)
Lawrencium	Lr	103	(262)	Unununium	Uuu	111	(272)
Lead	Pb	82	207.2	Uranium	U	92	238.029
Lithium	Li	3	6.941	Vanadium	V	23	50.9415
Lutetium	Lu	71	174.967	Xenon	Xe	54	131.29
Magnesium	Mg	12	24.305	Ytterbium	Yb	70	173.04
Manganese	Mn	25	54.9380	Yttrium	Y	39	88.9059
Meitnerium	Mt	109	(268)	Zinc	Zn	30	65.39
Mendelevium	Md	101	(258)	Zirconium	Zr	40	91.224
Mercury	Hg	80	200.59				

*Parentheses indicate the mass number of the most stable isotope of a radioactive element.

Common Alloys

ALLOY	COMPOSITION	ALLOY	COMPOSITION
brass	55% copper, 45% zinc	pewter	tin, antimony, copper
bronze	copper, tin	solder	tin, lead
cast Iron	iron, carbon, silicon, manganese, trace impurities	stainless steel	iron, carbon, chromium, nickel
cupronickel	copper, nickel	steel	iron, carbon
		sterling silver	silver, copper

Physics

Physics is the science that deals with the structure of matter and the interactions between the fundamental constituents of the observable universe. The basic physical science, its aim is the discovery and formulation of the fundamental laws of nature. In the broadest sense, physics (from the Greek *physikos*) is concerned with all aspects of nature on both the macroscopic and submicroscopic levels. Its scope of study encompasses not only the behavior of objects under the action of given forces but also the nature and origin of gravitational, electromagnetic, and nuclear force fields. Its ultimate objective is the formulation of a few comprehensive principles that bring together and explain all such disparate phenomena. Physics can, at base, be defined as the science of matter, motion, and energy. Its laws are typically expressed with economy and precision in the language of mathematics.

A person standing near a mountaintop when the sun is low may see his or her apparently enormously magnified shadow on the upper surfaces of clouds below the level where the observer is standing. This optical illusion is called the Brocken bow, for the Brocken peak in Germany.

Weight, Mass, and Density

Mass, strictly defined, is the quantitative measure of inertia, the resistance a body offers to a change in its speed or position when force is applied to it. The greater the mass of a body, the smaller the change produced by an applied force. In more practical terms, it is the measure of the amount of material in an object, and in common usage is often expressed as weight. However, the mass of an object is constant regardless of its position, while weight varies according to gravitational pull.

In the International System of Units (SI, the metric system), the kilogram is the standard unit of mass, defined as equaling the mass of the international prototype of the kilogram, currently a platinum-iridium cylinder kept at Sèvres, near Paris, France; it is roughly equal to the mass of 1,000 cubic centimeters of pure water at the temperature of its maximum density. In the US customary system, the unit is the slug, defined as the mass which a one pound force can accelerate at a rate of one foot per second per second, which is the same as the mass of an object weighing 32.17 pounds on the earth's surface.

Weight is the gravitational force of attraction on an object, caused by the presence of a massive second object, such as the Earth or Moon. Weight is the product of an object's mass and the acceleration of gravity at the point where the object is located. A given object will have the same mass on the Earth's surface, on the Moon, or in the absence of gravity, while its weight on the Moon would be about one sixth of its weight on the Earth's surface, because of the Moon's smaller gravitational pull (due in turn to the Moon's smaller mass and radius), and in the absence of gravity the object would have no weight at all.

Weight is measured in units of force, not mass, though in practice units of mass (such as the kilogram) are often substituted because of mass's relatively constant relation to weight on the Earth's surface. The weight of a body can be obtained by multiplying the mass by the acceleration of gravity. In SI, weight is expressed in newtons, or the force required to impart an acceleration of one meter per second per second to a mass of one kilogram. In the US customary system, it is expressed in pounds.

Density is the mass per unit volume of a material substance. It offers a convenient means of obtaining the mass of a body from its volume, or vice versa; the mass is equal to the volume multiplied by the density, while the volume is equal to the mass divided by the density. In SI, density is expressed in kilograms per cubic meter.

Electronics

Introduction to the Internet

The Internet is a dynamic collection of computer networks that has revolutionized communications and methods of commerce by enabling those networks around the world to interact with each other. Sometimes referred to as a "network of networks," the Internet was developed in the United States in the 1970s but was not widely used by the general public until the early 1990s. By the beginning of the 21st century approximately 360 million people, or roughly 6% of the world's population, were estimated to have access to the Internet. It is widely assumed that at least half of the world's population will have some form of Internet access by 2010 and that wireless access will play a growing role.

The Internet is so powerful and general that it can be used for almost any purpose that depends on the processing of information, and it is accessible by every individual who connects to one of its constituent networks. It supports human communication via **electronic mail** (e-mail), as well as real-time "chat rooms," newsgroups, and audio and video transmission and allows people to work collaboratively at many different locations. It supports access to information by many applications, including the **World Wide Web**, which uses text and graphical presentations. Publishing has been revolutionized, as whole novels and reference works are available on the Web, and periodicals, including data prepared daily for an individual subscriber (such as stock market reports or news summaries), are also common. The Internet has attracted a large and growing number of "e-businesses" (including subsidiaries of traditional "brick-and-mortar" companies) that carry out most of their sales and services over the Internet. (See electronic commerce.) Many experts believe that the Internet will dramatically transform business as well as society.

Most Visited Web Sites in the US
As of April 2002

RANK	PARENT WEB SITE	UNIQUE VISITORS	RANK	PARENT WEB SITE	UNIQUE VISITORS
1	AOL Time Warner	92,950	11	Walt Disney	23,477
2	MSN-Microsoft	83,792	12	Classmates.com	22,428
3	Yahoo!	80,165	13	Viacom	21,711
4	Terra Lycos	40,320	14	AT&T	20,068
5	About/Primedia	36,574	15	Ask Jeeves	17,906
6	Google	34,236	16	Real.com	17,759
7	Amazon	29,474	17	Vivendi-Universal	17,742
8	eBay	29,456	18	Excite	17,535
9	CNET	23,986	19	Ticketmaster	17,121
10	InfoSpace	23,784	20	eUniverse	17,111

Source: Jupiter Media Metrix

Estimated Number of Internet Users, 1991–2002

YEAR	UNITED STATES	WORLD	YEAR	UNITED STATES	WORLD
1991	3,000,000	11,100,000	1997	45,000,000	101,000,000
1992	4,500,000	12,300,000	1998	73,000,000	160,000,000
1993	5,500,000	15,000,000	1999	102,000,000	270,000,000
1994	8,500,000	17,500,000	2000	124,000,000	385,000,000
1995	20,000,000	23,700,000	2001	143,000,000	499,000,000
1996	30,000,000	55,000,000	2002	164,000,000	544,000,000

Source: International Telecommunications Union Yearbook of Statistics

Personal Computers (PCs)

Computers small and inexpensive enough to be purchased by individuals for use in their homes first became feasible when large-scale integration made it possible to construct a sufficiently powerful microprocessor on a single semiconductor chip. The personal computer industry truly began in 1977, when Apple Computer introduced the **Apple II**, one of the first pre-assembled, mass-produced personal computers. Radio Shack and Commodore Business Machines also introduced personal computers that year. These machines all used 8-bit microprocessors and possessed limited memory.

The IBM Corporation entered the new market in 1981, when it introduced the **IBM PC**. The IBM PC was only slightly faster than rival machines, but it had about 10 times their memory capacity. It became the world's most popular personal computer, and both its microprocessor, the Intel 8088, and its operating system, which was adapted from the Microsoft Corporation's MS-DOS system, became industry standards. In 1983 Apple introduced **Lisa**, a personal computer with a **graphical user interface** (GUI), which allowed the user to perform routine operations using a mouse. The Lisa's GUI became the basis of Apple's **Macintosh** personal computer, which was introduced in 1984 and proved extremely successful. In 1985 the Microsoft Corporation introduced **Microsoft Windows**, a GUI that gave MS-DOS–based computers many of the same capabilities of the Macintosh. Windows became the dominant operating environment for personal computers.

These advances in software and operating systems were matched by the development of microprocessors containing ever-greater numbers of circuits, with resulting increases in the processing speed and power of personal computers, in part through the developments of chip manufacturers Intel and Motorola. The memory capacity of personal computers had increased from 64 kilobytes (64,000 characters) in the late 1970s to 100 megabytes (100 million characters) by the early 1990s.

Laptop computers, notebook computers, and palm pilots became increasingly common in the early 1990s, and by the middle of the decade the **Internet** had revolutionized computer use. By 1997 about 40% of all households in the US owned a personal computer; by 2001 there were 178,000,000 personal computers in the US and 495,366,000 worldwide.

Worldwide Cellular Mobile Telephone Subscribers, 2001

COUNTRY	SUBSCRIBERS	COUNTRY	SUBSCRIBERS	COUNTRY	SUBSCRIBERS
China	144,812,000	France	35,922,300	Turkey	20,000,000
United States	127,000,000	South Korea	29,045,600	Netherlands	11,900,000
Japan	72,795,900	Brazil	28,745,800	Australia	11,169,000
Germany	56,245,000	Spain	26,494,200	Phillipines	10,568,000
Italy	48,698,000	Taiwan	21,633,000	Poland	10,050,000
United Kingdom	47,026,000	Mexico	20,136,000		

Source: International Telecommunications Union Yearbook of Statistics.

Growth of Cell Phone Use in the US

Estimated number of cellular mobile telephone subscribers in the US, 1990–2001.

YEAR	SUBSCRIBERS	YEAR	SUBSCRIBERS	YEAR	SUBSCRIBERS	YEAR	SUBSCRIBERS
1990	5,283,000	1993	16,009,000	1996	44,043,000	1999	86,047,000
1991	7,557,000	1994	24,134,000	1997	55,312,000	2000	109,478,000
1992	11,033,000	1995	33,786,000	1998	69,209,000	2001	127,000,000

Source: International Telecommunications Union Yearbook of Statistics.

Encyclopædia Britannica's Great Web Sites

This table lists the Web sites most frequently used by Britannica editors, whether informative and relevant or simply amusing.

SITE	SUBJECT	URL
general		
Nobel e-Museum	Nobel Prizes	<www.nobel.se>
The Internet Archive Wayback Machine	Internet search	<http://web.archive.org/collections/web.html>
Blogger	Web site creation	<www.blogger.com>
Google	Internet search	<www.google.com>
Amazon.com	e-commerce	<www.amazon.com>
eBay	e-commerce	<www.ebay.com>
Encyclopædia Britannica	encyclopedia	<www.britannica.com>
periodicals		
The New York Times	news and features	<www.nytimes.com>
The Economist	news and features	<www.economist.com>
BBC	news and features	<http://news.bbc.co.uk>
Hoover's	business news	<www.hoovers.com>
education		
Big Chalk	education for children	<www.bigchalk.com>
Britannica Online: School Edition	education for children	<http://school.eb.com>
world		
United Nations	international organization	<www.un.org>
World Heritage Center: UNESCO	distinguished global places	<http://whc.unesco.org/nwhc/pages/home/pages/homepage.htm>
Lonely Planet	travel destinations	<www.lonelyplanet.com>
Rulers.org	country leaders	<http://rulers.org>
Ethnologue	languages of the world	<www.ethnologue.com>
Governments on the WWW	governments	<www.gksoft.com/govt/en>
Tourism Offices Worldwide Directory	tourism	<www.towd.com>
Background Notes: US Department of State	countries of the world	<www.state.gov/r/pa/ei/bgn>
Global IDP Project	internally displaced persons	<www.idpproject.org>
International Rescue Committee	refugees	<www.theirc.org>
UN Refugee Agency	refugees	<www.unhcr.ch/cgi-bin/texis/vtx/home>

Encyclopædia Britannica's Great Web Sites (continued)

SITE	SUBJECT	URL
politics		
Electionworld.org	world election data	<www.electionworld.org>
Political Science Resources	politics	<www.psr.keele.ac.uk>
Political Resources	politics	<www.politicalresources.net>
Inter-Parliamentary Union	world politics	<www.ipu.org>
The International Institute for Democracy and Electoral Assistance	voter participation	<www.idea.int>
National Parks Worldwide	global nature reserves	<http://hum.amu.edu.pl/~zbzw/ph/pnp/swiat.htm>
US Census Bureau	US people	<www.census.gov>
Thomas–US Library of Congress	US politics and legislation	<http://thomas.loc.gov>
Political Money Line	US political campaign donations	<www.fecinfo.com>
science		
Mammal Species of the World: Smithsonian	mammals	<www.nmnh.si.edu/msw>
Plants Database: US Department of Agriculture	plants	<http://plants.usda.gov>
FishBase	fish	<www.fishbase.org/home.htm>
EMBL Reptile Database	reptiles	<www1.embl-heidelberg.de/~uetz/LivingReptiles.html>
IUCN Red List of Threatened Species	endangered species of the world	<www.redlist.org>
BIOSIS	taxonomy	<www.biosis.org/zrdocs/zoolinfo/vernac.htm>
arts and entertainment		
The Grove Dictionary of Art	art	<www.groveart.com>
OCLC FirstSearch	library database	<http://newfirstsearch.oclc.org>
The Internet Movie Database	motion pictures	<www.imdb.com>
Oscar.com: Academy Awards	motion pictures	<www.oscar.com>
The British Film Institute	motion pictures	<www.bfi.org.uk>
The Olympic Movement	Olympic sports	<www.olympic.org>
Rock's Backpages	rock and pop music	<www.rocksbackpages.com>
This Week in Chess: London Chess Centre	chess	<www.chesscenter.com/twic/twic.html>
GardenWeb	gardening	<www.gardenweb.com>
The Onion	humor magazine	<www.onion.com>
ESPN	sports	<www.espn.com>
society and history		
Cyndi's List	genealogy	<www.cyndislist.com>
US GenWeb Project	genealogy	<www.usgenweb.com>
Encyclopedia of Greek Mythology	mythology	<www.mythweb.com/encyc/index.html>
The Religious Movements Homepage: University of Virginia	new religious movements	<http://religiousmovements.lib.virginia.edu/home.html>
Internet Medieval Sourcebook	medieval studies	<www.fordham.edu/halsall/sbook.html>
Skyscrapers.com	world's tallest buildings	<www.skyscrapers.com>
StarChefs	cuisine	<www.starchefs.com>
health		
Medline Plus: National Library of Medicine	health and medicine	<www.nlm.nih.gov/medlineplus>
eMedicine World Medical Library	health and medicine	<www.emedicine.com>
The National Women's Health Information Center (US)	women's health	<www.4woman.gov>
National Institute on Aging (US)	geriatrics	<www.nih.gov/nia>
American Cancer Society	cancer	<www.cancer.org>

Encyclopædia Britannica's Great Web Sites (continued)

SITE	SUBJECT	URL
health (continued)		
UNAIDS/WHO Global Surveillance fact sheets	STDs by country	<www.unaids.org/hivaidsinfo/statistics/fact_sheets/all_countries_en.html>
Human Genome Project Information	genetics	<www.ornl.gov/hgmis>
National Human Genome Research Institute	genetics	<www.genome.gov>
The Council for Responsible Genetics	genetics; ethics	<www.gene-watch.org>
University of St. Andrews School of Mathematics and Statistics	mathematics	<www-groups.cs.st-and.ac.uk/~history/Indexes/HistoryTopics.html>
philosophy		
Stanford Encyclopedia of Philosophy	philosophy	<http://plato.stanford.edu>
Lexicon of Linguistics	linguistics	<http://tristram.let.uu.nl/UiL-OTS/Lexicon>
Guide to Philosophy on the Internet	philosophy	<www.earlham.edu/~peters/gpi/index.htm>
Dictionary of Philosophy of Mind	philosophy	<www.artsci.wustl.edu/~philos/MindDict>
astronomy and space		
The Nine Planets	solar system	<http://seds.lpl.arizona.edu/nineplanets/nineplanets/nineplanets.html>
NASA Jet Propulsion Laboratory	astronomy	<www.jpl.nasa.gov/index.html>
European Space Agency	outer space	<www.esa.int/export/esaCP/index.html>
NASA Human Space Flight	space exploration	<http://spaceflight.nasa.gov>
Space Science: NASA	outer space	<http://spacescience.nasa.gov>
Encyclopedia Astronautica	outer space	<www.astronautix.com>
Space.com	outer space	<www.space.com>
technology		
Association for Computing Machinery	computers	<www.acm.org>
Computer History Museum	computers	<www.computerhistory.org>
Tom's Hardware Guide	computers	<www6.tomshardware.com>

Aerospace Technology

Space Exploration

Three men were the first scientists to conceive pragmatically of space flight: the Russian Konstantin Tsiolkovsky, the American Robert Goddard, and the German Hermann Oberth. Technology in the early 20th century, however, was a long way from the level required for rocket-powered flight. Nonetheless, the theory and dynamics of such flights were rigorously studied. By the end of World War II, the German development of rocket propulsion for aircraft and guided missiles (notably the V-2) had reached a high level. With the German surrender in 1945, the US and its Allies fell heir to the technical knowledge of rocket power developed by the Germans. The technical director of the German missile effort, Wernher von Braun, and some 150 of his top aides surrendered to US troops. Most emigrated to the US, where they assembled and launched V-2 missiles that had been captured and shipped there. The USSR carried out an unpublicized but extensive program that must have been very similar; Britain and France conducted smaller programs.

In both the US and the USSR the development of military missile technology was essential to the achievement of satellite flight. Preparations for the International Geophysical Year (IGY, 1957–58) stimulated discussion of the possibility of launching artificial Earth satellites for scientific investigations. Both the US and the USSR became determined to prepare scientific satellites for launching during the IGY. While the US was still developing a satellite launch vehicle, the USSR startled the world by placing Sputnik 1 in orbit on 4 Oct 1957. This was followed a month later by Sputnik 2 carrying a live dog. The failure by the US to launch its small payload on 6 Dec 1957 heightened that nation's political discomfiture in view of its supposed advanced status in science. Following debates on the necessity of achieving parity, the US government established the National Aeronautics and Space Administration (NASA) in 1958. Since that time, NASA has conducted virtually all major aspects of the US space program.

The first successful US satellite, Explorer 1, was launched about four months after Sputnik 1. During the next decades the two nations participated in a space race, with more than 5,000 successful launches of satellites and space probes of all varieties: scientific research, communications, meteorological, photographic reconnaissance, and navigation satellites, lunar and planetary probes, and manned space flights. The USSR launched the first man into orbit around the Earth on 12 Apr 1961. On 20 July 1969, the US landed two men on the surface of the Moon. On 12 Apr 1981, the 20th anniversary of manned space flight, the US launched the first reusable manned vehicle, the Space Shuttle. The European nations, Japan, and India have formed their own agencies for space exploration. Private corporations, too, offer space launches for communications satellites. The European Space Agency, or ESA, consists of 15 member nations.

Significant space programs:

Sputnik (Russian for "fellow traveler")
Years launched: 1957–58. **Country or space agency:** USSR. **Designation:** 1 through 3 (the first time Sputnik 3 was launched it exploded, so four Sputniks in total were launched). **Not Manned. Events of note:** Sputnik 1 was the first satellite to be successfully launched into space; Sputnik 2 carried a small dog named Laika ("Barker").

Vanguard
Years launched: 1957–58. **Country or space agency:** US. **Designation:** 1 through 7. **Not Manned. Events of note:** Seven Vanguards were launched; only Vanguard 1 (the third launch) was successful.

Explorer
Years launched: 1958. **Country or space agency:** US. **Designation:** 1 through 5. **Not Manned. Events of note:** First successful launch for Americans; Explorer 1 discovered Earth's radiation belt.

Pioneer
Years launched: 1958–78. **Country or space agency:** US. **Designation:** 1 through 13. **Not Manned. Events of note:** Pioneer 10 became the first man-made object to travel through the asteroid belt. In September 1995 Pioneer 11 stopped transmitting data to Earth as its power source was depleted.

Mercury
Years launched: 1959–63. **Country or space agency:** US. **Designation:** Each spacecraft was given a name. The manned spacecraft were called names, such as "Freedom," followed by "7" to honor the seven original NASA astronauts. **Manned. Events of note:** There were some 20 unmanned Mercury missions between 1959 and 1961. Of the manned Mercury missions, Freedom 7 was launched with Alan Shepherd aboard in 1961; Liberty Bell 7 with Virgil "Gus" Grissom in 1961; Friendship 7 in 1962 with John Glenn; Aurora 7 with Scott Carpenter in 1962; Sigma 7 with Walter Schirra in 1962; and Faith 7 with Gordon Cooper in 1963.

Luna (Russian for "Moon")
Years launched: 1959–76. **Country or space agency:** USSR. **Designation:** 1 through 24. **Not Manned.**

Vostok (Russian for "east")
Years launched: 1961–63. **Country or space agency:** USSR. **Designation:** 1 through 6. **Manned. Events of note:** The first man in space was Soviet cosmonaut Yury Gagarin in Vostok 1, launched on 12 April 1961. Vostok 2 was launched with Gherman Titov in 1961,

Vostok 3 with Andriyan Nikolayev in 1962, Vostok 4 with Pavel Popovich in 1962, Vostok 5 with Valery Bykovsky in 1963, and Vostok 6 with Valentina Tereshkova, the first woman in space, in 1963.

Venera (Russian for "Venus")
Years launched: 1961–83. **Country or space agency:** USSR. **Designation:** 1 through 16. **Not Manned. Events of note:** First Venus flyby was performed by Venera 1. Venera 3 was the first spacecraft to land on another planet.

Ranger
Years launched: 1961–65. **Country or space agency:** US. **Designation:** 1 through 9. **Not Manned. Events of note:** Lunar landers put down on the Moon's surface.

Mariner
Years launched: 1962–75. **Country or space agency:** US. **Designation:** 1 through 10. **Not Manned. Events of note:** Venus flyby, Mars flybys, Mars orbiter; in 1971 Mariner 9 was the first spacecraft to orbit another planet.

Voskhod (Russian for "sunrise" or "ascent")
Years launched: 1964–65. **Country or space agency:** USSR. **Designation:** 1 and 2. **Manned. Events of note:** First multi-manned spacecraft; Aleksey Leonov of Voskhod 2 performed the first space walk on 18 Mar 1965.

Gemini
Years launched: 1965–66. **Country or space agency:** US. **Designation:** 1 through 12. **Manned:** 10 manned and two unmanned missions. **Events of note:** Gemini VIII was the first spacecraft to dock with another craft.

Lunar Orbiter
Years launched: 1966–67. **Country or space agency:** US. **Designation:** 1 through 5. **Not Manned. Events of note:** Probes photographed the far side of the Moon, then landed on the lunar surface on command.

Apollo
Years launched: 1967–72. **Country or space agency:** US. **Designation:** 1 through 17 (but there were no Apollos 2 or 3). **Manned. Events of note:** Apollo 1 astronauts Gus Grissom, Edward White, and Roger Chaffee died when the spacecraft caught fire while still on the ground. Apollo 8 was the first to take astronauts to the Moon and back as a prelude to landing on the Moon. Apollo 11 was crewed by Neil Armstrong, Michael Collins, and Buzz Aldrin and was the first manned mission to land on the Moon, on 20 Jul 1969. Apollo 13 had an onboard explosion while en route to the Moon and had great difficulties returning to Earth, but Apollo 13 astronauts James Lovell, John Swigert, and Fred Haise did return to Earth safely.

Soyuz (Russian for "union")
Years launched: 1967–76. **Country or space agency:** USSR. **Designation:** 1 through 40. **Manned. Events of note:** On 24 Apr 1967 cosmonaut Vladimir Komarov was the first spaceflight fatality as Soyuz 1 crashed the day after it is launched.

Salyut (Russian for "salute")
Years launched: 1971–82. **Country or space agency:** USSR. **Designation:** 1 through 7. **Manned. Events of note:** Salyut 1 was the first space station; it orbited the Earth until 1973. The first crew to visit it on Soyuz

10 returned home after being unable to open the hatch after docking. The second crew to visit on Soyuz 11 reached Salyut 1 and spent 24 days onboard the station. Their craft depressurized on the return journey and cosmonauts Georgy Dobrovolsky, Vladislav Volkov and Viktor Patsayev all died. Salyut 7 was last staffed in 1986.

Skylab
Years launched: 1973. Country or space agency: US. Manned. Events of note: Solar astronomy was a key point of study. Skylab's debris entered the Earth's atmosphere in 1979 and fell over Australia and the Indian Ocean.

Apollo Soyuz
Years launched: 1975. Country or space agency: USSR/US. Manned. Events of note: Apollo 18 docked with Soyuz 19 in space and cosmonauts and astronauts performed a series of joint experiments in the first internationally manned mission.

Viking
Years launched: 1975. Country or space agency: US. Designation: 1 and 2. Not Manned. Events of note: Viking 2 landed on Mars on 3 Sep 1976 and discovered water frost.

Voyager
Years launched: 1977. Country or space agency: US. Designation: 1 and 2. Not Manned. Events of note: Voyager 1 arrived on Jupiter in 1979 and Voyager 2 arrived on Saturn in 1981. Voyager 2 went on to fly by Uranus in 1986 and Neptune in 1989.

STS (Space Transportation System, or space shuttle)
Years launched: 1981–present. Country or space agency: US. Designation: 1 through 111. Manned. Events of note: The first launch of a manned space shuttle was Columbia, on 12 Apr 1981. Other shuttles include Challenger, Discovery, Atlantis, and Endeavour. Another shuttle, Enterprise, did not fly in space but did perform test landings. On shuttle mission 51-L the Challenger exploded after liftoff on 28 Jan 1986, killing all of the crew, including civilian astronaut Christa McAuliffe. NASA did not launch another shuttle for more than 2½ years after the disaster. STS-31 (Discovery) deployed the Edwin P. Hubble Space Telescope observatory in 1990. In 1994 the US and the USSR had their first joint mission when cosmonaut Sergey Krikalyov flew aboard STS-60 (Discovery). On 23 Jul 1999 STS-93 deployed the Chandra X-Ray Observatory.

Giotto (named for the Italian artist)
Years launched: 1985. Country or space agency: US and ESA. Not Manned. Events of note: Giotto collected data on Halley's Comet.

Mir (Russian for "peace" and "world")
Years launched: 1986. Country or space agency: USSR. Manned. Events of note: The core of the Mir space station launched on 20 Feb 1986. Designed to be used for 5 years, the Mir station was actually decommissioned on 23 Mar 2001. Retro-rockets were used to guide Mir during its re-entry into Earth's atmosphere.

Magellan
Years launched: 1989. Country or space agency: US. Not Manned. Events of note: Magellan arrived at Venus in 1990 and entered and burned up in the Venusian atmosphere in 1994 at the end of its mission, having mapped some 98% of the surface of Venus.

Phobos
Years launched: 1988. Country or space agency: USSR. Designation: 1 and 2. Not Manned. Events of note: Probe studies Mars and its moon Phobos.

Galileo
Years launched: 1989. Country or space agency: US. Not Manned. Events of note: In 1995 Galileo arrived at Jupiter and released its probe and satellite. Galileo then proceeded to moons Io and Europa.

Ulysses
Years launched: 1990. Country or space agency: US and ESA. Not Manned. Events of note: In 1992 Ulysses flew by Jupiter on its way to the Sun; the probe was designed to explore interplanetary space at high solar latitudes.

International Space Station
Years launched: 1998. Country or space agency: US, Canada, Japan, Russia, the ESA, and Brazil. Manned. Events of note: The first mission on the ISS was launched on 31 Oct 2000, and the crew returned to Earth on 18 Mar 2001.

Air Travel

Flight History

Humanity has been fascinated with the possibility of flight for millennia; a myriad of myths and stories feature humans with the ability to fly. Indeed, an important characteristic of the history of flight is the pervasive human interest in the subject; inventors from many countries took up the challenge over the years, achieving varying degrees of success. The history of flight began at least as early as about AD 400 with historical references to a Chinese kite that used a rotary wing as a source of lift. Other toys using the principle of the helicopter—in this case a rotary blade turned by the pull of a string—were known during the Middle Ages. During the latter part of the 15th century, Leonardo da Vinci made drawings pertaining to flight. In the 1700s experiments were made with the ornithopter, a machine with flapping wings.

The history of successful flight begins with the hot air balloon. In southwestern France, two brothers, Joseph and Étienne Montgolfier, normally papermakers, experimented with a large cell contrived of paper in which they could collect heated air. On 19 Sep 1783 the Montgolfiers sent aloft a balloon with a rooster, a duck, and a sheep, and on 21 November the first manned flight was made. Balloons gained importance as their flights increased into hundreds of miles, but they were essentially unsteerable.

During the American Civil War, a volunteer officer in the Union army, the former German cavalryman

Count Ferdinand von Zeppelin, observed a free balloon ascent. He spent much of the remainder of his life working with balloons, particularly on the steering problem. As his experimentation on what would come to be known as dirigibles continued, hydrogen and illuminating gas were substituted for hot air, and a motor was mounted on a bag filled with gas that had been fitted with propellers and rudders. It was Zeppelin who first saw clearly that maintaining a steerable shape was essential, so he created a rigid but light frame. On 2 Jul 1900 Zeppelin undertook the first experimental flight of what he called an airship. All went well with the development of the dirigible until the docking procedure at Lakehurst NJ, on 6 May 1937, when the Hindenburg burst into flames and exploded with a loss of 36 lives. Public feeling about the craft made further development futile.

It should be remembered, however, that neither balloons or dirigibles had produced true flight: what they had done was to harness the dynamics of the atmosphere to lift a craft off the ground, using what power (if any) they supplied primarily to steer. The first scientific exposition of the principles that ultimately led to the successful flight with a heavier-than-air device came in 1843 from Sir George Cayley, who is also regarded by many as the father of fixed-wing flight. It was Cayley who built the successful man-carrying glider that came closest to permitting real flight. Cayley's work was built upon in the experiments and writings on gliders from the late 1800s by aviation pioneers Otto Lilienthal of Germany and Octave Chanute of the United States. The works of Cayley, Lilienthal, and Chanute would eventually inspire and form the base work of the Wright brothers.

The Americans Wilbur and Orville Wright by 1902 had developed a fully practical biplane (double-winged) glider that could be controlled in every direction. Fitting a small engine and two propellers to another biplane, the Wrights on 17 Dec 1903 made the world's first successful man-carrying, engine-powered, heavier-than-air flight at a site near Kitty Hawk, on the coast of North Carolina.

The Wright brothers' success soon inspired successful aircraft designs and flights by others, and World War I (1914–18) further accelerated the expansion of aviation. Though initially used for aerial reconnaissance, aircraft were soon fitted with machine guns to shoot at other aircraft and with bombs to drop on ground targets; military aircraft with these types of missions and armaments became known, respectively, as fighters and bombers.

By the 1920s the first small commercial airlines had begun to carry mail, and the increased speed and range of aircraft made possible the first nonstop flights over the world's oceans, poles, and continents. In the 1930s more efficient monoplane (single-wing) aircraft with an all-metal fuselage (body) and a retractable undercarriage became standard. Aircraft played a vitally important role in World War II (1939–45), developing in size, weight, speed, power, range, and armament. The war marked the high point of piston-engined propeller craft while also introducing the first aircraft with jet engines, which could fly at higher speeds. Jet-engined craft became the norm for fighters in the late 1940s and proved their superiority as commercial transports beginning in the '50s. The high speeds and low operating costs of jet airliners led to a massive expansion of commercial air travel in the second half of the 20th century.

The next great aviation innovation after the jet engine was aircraft able to fly at supersonic speeds. The first was a Bell XS-1 rocket-powered research plane piloted by Maj. Charles E. Yeager of the US Air Force on 14 Oct 1947. The XS-1 broke the sound barrier at 1,066 km/hr (662 mph) and attained a top speed of 1,126 km/hr (700 mph). Thereafter many military aircraft capable of supersonic flight were built. The first supersonic, passenger-carrying, commercial airplane, the Concorde, was built jointly by aircraft manufacturers in Great Britain and France and entered regular service in 1976.

Scheduling: US Airline Industry On-Time Arrivals of Selected US Airlines

September 1987–April 2002. Source: US Department of Transportation.

	AIRLINE	% OF ALL FLIGHTS		AIRLINE	% OF ALL FLIGHTS
1	Southwest	82.4	6	US Airways	78.2
2	Northwest	79.7	7	Delta	77.5
3	American	78.8	8	Alaska	75.7
4	Continental	78.6	9	United	75.3
5	America West	78.4	10	American Eagle	72.9

US Aviation Safety, 1982–2001

Source: US National Transportation Safety Board.

	US AIRLINES[1]				US GENERAL AVIATION			
YEAR	NO. OF ACCIDENTS	NO. OF ACCIDENTS WITH FATALITIES	TOTAL NO. OF DEATHS	HOURS FLOWN	ALL ACCIDENTS	FATAL ACCIDENTS	TOTAL FATALITIES	HOURS FLOWN
1982	18	5	235	7,040,325	3,233	591	1,187	29,640,000
1983	23	4	15	7,298,799	3,076	555	1,068	28,673,000
1984	16	1	4	8,165,124	3,017	545	1,042	29,099,000
1985	21	7	526	8,709,894	2,739	498	956	28,322,000
1986	24	3	8	9,976,104	2,581	474	967	27,073,000
1987	34	5	232	10,645,192	2,494	446	837	26,972,000
1988	30	3	285	11,140,548	2,387	460	797	27,446,000
1989	28	11	278	11,274,543	2,242	431	768	27,920,000
1990	24	6	39	12,150,116	2,241	443	767	28,510,000

US Aviation Safety, 1982–2001 (continued)

	US AIRLINES[1]				US GENERAL AVIATION			
YEAR	NO. OF ACCIDENTS	NO. OF ACCIDENTS WITH FATALITIES	TOTAL NO. OF DEATHS	HOURS FLOWN	ALL ACCIDENTS	FATAL ACCIDENTS	TOTAL FATALITIES	HOURS FLOWN
1991	26	4	62	11,780,610	2,197	438	799	27,678,000
1992	18	4	33	12,359,715	2,111	451	867	24,780,000
1993	23	1	1	12,706,206	2,063	400	740	22,796,000
1994	23	4	239	13,124,315	2,022	404	730	22,235,000
1995	36	3	168	13,505,257	2,056	413	735	24,906,000
1996	37	5	380	13,746,112	1,908	361	636	24,881,000
1997	49	4	8	15,838,109	1,845	350	631	25,591,000
1998	50	1	1	16,813,435	1,904	364	624	25,518,000
1999	52	2	12	17,555,208	1,906	340	619	29,713,000
2000	57	3	92	18,295,143	1,838	343	594	29,057,000
2001	40	6	531	16,730,700	1,721	321	553	26,220,000

[1]Scheduled and nonscheduled service.

World's Busiest Airports

Ranked by total aircraft movement, 2001. Source: Airports Council International (preliminary statistics).

RANK	AIRPORT	LOCATION	AIRPORT CODE	TOTAL MOVEMENTS (TAKEOFFS AND LANDINGS)
1	O'Hare International Airport	Chicago IL	ORD	909,535
2	Hartsfield Atlanta International Airport	Atlanta GA	ATL	890,320
3	Dallas/Fort Worth International Airport	Dallas/Ft. Worth TX	DFW	783,546
4	Los Angeles International Airport	Los Angeles CA	LAX	738,114
5	Phoenix Sky Harbor International Airport	Phoenix AZ	PHX	560,827
6	Paris Charles de Gaulle International Airport	Paris, France	CDG	522,557
7	Detroit Metropolitan Airport	Detroit MI	DTW	522,132
8	Minneapolis/St. Paul International Airport	Minneapolis/St. Paul MN	MSP	499,939
9	McCarran International Airport	Las Vegas NV	LAS	493,722
10	Denver International Airport	Denver CO	DEN	484,479
11	Lambert St. Louis International Airport	St. Louis MO	STL	474,161
12	Miami International Airport	Miami FL	MIA	471,008
13	George Bush Intercontinental Airport	Houston TX	IAH	470,916
14	Philadelphia International Airport	Philadelphia PA	PHL	466,985
15	London Heathrow Airport	London, England	LHR	463,568
16	Charlotte/Douglas International Airport	Charlotte NC	CLT	461,264
17	Frankfurt Airport	Frankfurt, Germany	FRA	456,452
18	Logan International Airport	Boston MA	BOS	454,625
19	Pittsburgh International Airport	Pittsburgh PA	PIT	451,739
20	Newark International Airport	Newark NJ	EWR	436,000
21	Amsterdam Airport Schiphol	Amsterdam, The Netherlands	AMS	431,961
22	Lester B. Pearson International Airport	Toronto ON	YYZ	406,360
23	Seattle-Tacoma International Airport	Seattle/Tacoma WA	SEA	399,285
24	Orlando Sanford International Airport	Sanford FL	SFB	397,557
25	Cincinnati/Northern Kentucky International Airport	Cincinnati OH	CVG	397,000
26	Washington/Dulles International Airport	Washington DC	IAD	396,843
27	Oakland International Airport	Oakland CA	OAK	395,653
28	Memphis International Airport	Memphis TN	MEM	394,826
29	San Francisco International Airport	San Francisco CA	SFO	387,594
30	John Wayne Airport	Santa Ana CA	SNA	379,300

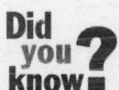

Did you know? Palm trees are of special interest because of their long fossil record, structural diversity, and economic importance. They have, however, been difficult to study. Their large size and extreme hardness deterred early collectors and led Liberty Hyde Bailey, an eminent American horticulturist of the early 20th century, to call them the big game of the plant world. Few studies of palms were conducted until air travel to remote tropical areas became feasible.

Meteorology

Global Temperatures and Precipitation

Listed in alphabetical order of countries. For more information see <www.weatherbase.com>.

CITY	AVERAGE TEMPERATURE (°F)				AVERAGE ANNUAL RAIN LEVELS IN INCHES
	JAN	APR	JUL	OCT	
Kandahar, Afghanistan	44	68	89	64	7.4
South Pole, Antarctica	−16	−69	−74	−58	0.1
Buenos Aires, Argentina	75	62	50	61	38.5
Sydney, Australia	72	65	53	64	44.5
São Paulo, Brazil	74	70	63	69	53.2
Toronto, ON, Canada	21	44	70	48	30.1
Pala, Chad	77	87	77	78	40.4
Santiago, Chile	70	59	47	58	13.4
Beijing, China	26	57	79	57	25.1
Havana, Cuba	71	76	82	78	N/A
Cairo, Egypt	57	71	83	75	1
Nice, France	48	55	74	62	32.4
Nuuk, Greenland	17	25	45	31	23.9
Reykjavík, Iceland	31	37	52	40	32.2
Jerusalem, Israel	46	59	73	66	23
Tokyo, Japan	42	57	77	64	60.2
Vilnius, Lithuania	23	41	62	42	26.3
Casablanca, Morocco	55	60	73	66	16.1
Rotterdam, The Netherlands	38	47	63	52	N/A
Christchurch, New Zealand	63	54	44	53	25.5
Lima, Peru	74	71	64	65	0.3
Lisbon, Portugal	51	58	73	64	N/A
Doha, Qatar	63	80	96	85	3.2
Moscow, Russia	16	42	63	39	23.6
Johannesburg, South Africa	69	61	52	64	28.7
Colombo, Sri Lanka	81	84	83	82	87.8
Ankara, Turkey	27	49	69	52	N/A
Mbarara, Uganda	69	69	68	69	35.3
London, UK	39	46	62	51	29.7
Hanoi, Vietnam	62	76	86	78	N/A

N/A: not available

Did you know? Many insects are sensitive to small variations in temperature. Insects placed on a surface that is warmer at one end and cooler at the other often congregate in a narrow band of temperature. Mosquitoes fly readily to a warm, odorless, inanimate surface as if it were that of a warm-blooded creature. Bees, in the brood season, accurately regulate temperature in the hive between 95 and 97 °F by behavior such as beating their wings to circulate air.

World Temperature Extremes

REGION	highest recorded air temperature			lowest recorded air temperature		
	PLACE (ELEVATION)	°C	°F	PLACE (ELEVATION)	°C	°F
Africa	Al-'Aziziyah, Libya (112 m [367 ft])	57.7	136	Ifrane, Morocco (1,635 m [5,363 ft])	−23.9	−11
Antarctica	Lake Vanda, 77° 32′ S, 161° 40′ E (99 m [325 ft])	15	59	Vostok, 78° 27′ S, 106° 52′ E (3,420 m [11,218 ft])	−89.2	−128.6
Asia	Tirat Zevi, Israel (−300 m [−984 ft])	53.9	129	Oymyakon, Russia (806 m [2,625 ft])	−67.7	−89.9
Australia	Cloncurry, Queensland (193 m [633 ft])	53.1	127.5	Charlotte Pass, New South Wales (1,780 m [5,840 ft])	−22.2	−8
Europe	Seville, Spain (39 m [128 ft])	50	122	Ust-Shchuger, Russia (85 m [279 ft])	−55	−67
North America	Greenland Ranch, Death Valley, California (−54 m [−177 ft])	56.7	134.5	Snag, Yukon (646 m [2,119 ft])	−62.8	−81
South America	Rivadavia, Argentina (205 m [672 ft])	48.9	120	Colonia, Sarmiento, Argentina (268 m [879 ft])	−33	−27
Tropical Pacific	Echague, Luzon, Philippines (78 m [257 ft])	40.5	105	Haleakala, Hawaii (2,972 m [9,748 ft])	−7.8	18

Normal Temperatures and Precipitation for Selected US Cities

Statistics from city airports, 1971–2000. Alphabetical by state.
Source: National Oceanic and Atmospheric Administration, National Climatic Data Center, Asheville NC.

CITY	MEAN TEMPERATURE (°F)				ANNUAL PRE-CIPITATION (IN)
	JAN	APR	JUL	OCT	
Montgomery AL	46.6	64.3	81.8	65.4	54.77
Anchorage AK	15.8	36.3	58.4	34.1	16.08
Phoenix AZ	54.2	70.2	92.8	74.6	8.29
Little Rock AR	40.1	61.4	82.4	63.3	50.93
Los Angeles CA	57.1	60.8	69.3	66.9	13.15
San Francisco CA	49.4	56.2	62.8	61.0	20.11
Denver CO	29.2	47.6	73.4	51.0	15.81
Hartford CT	25.7	48.9	73.7	51.9	46.16
Wilmington DE	31.5	52.4	76.6	55.8	42.81
Miami FL	68.1	75.7	83.7	78.8	58.53
Atlanta GA	42.7	61.6	80.0	62.8	50.20
Honolulu HI	73.0	75.6	80.8	80.2	18.29
Boise ID	30.2	50.6	74.7	52.8	12.19
Chicago IL[1]	22.0	47.8	73.3	52.1	36.27
Indianapolis IN	26.5	52.0	75.4	54.6	40.95
Des Moines IA	20.4	50.6	76.1	52.8	34.72
Topeka KS	27.2	54.5	78.4	56.6	35.64
Louisville KY	33.0	56.4	78.4	58.5	44.54
New Orleans LA	52.6	68.2	82.7	70.0	64.16
Portland ME	21.7	43.7	68.7	47.7	45.83
Baltimore MD	32.3	53.2	76.5	55.4	41.94
Boston MA	29.3	48.3	73.9	54.1	42.53
Detroit MI	24.5	48.1	73.5	51.9	32.89
Minneapolis MN	13.1	46.6	73.2	48.7	29.41
Jackson MS	45.0	63.4	81.4	64.4	55.95
St. Louis MO	29.6	56.6	80.2	58.3	38.75
Missoula MT	23.5	45.2	66.9	44.4	13.82
Lincoln NE	23.2	51.0	77.3	54.1	28.37
Las Vegas NV	47.0	66.0	91.2	68.7	4.49
Concord NH	20.1	44.6	70.0	47.8	37.60
Newark NJ	31.3	52.3	77.2	56.4	46.25
Albuquerque NM	35.7	55.6	78.5	57.3	9.47
New York NY[2]	31.8	50.1	74.8	56.5	42.46
Charlotte NC	41.7	60.9	80.3	61.7	43.51
Fargo ND	6.8	43.5	70.6	45.3	21.19
Cleveland OH	25.7	47.6	71.9	52.2	38.71
Tulsa OK	36.4	60.8	83.5	62.6	42.42
Portland OR	39.9	51.2	68.1	54.3	37.07
Philadelphia PA	32.3	53.1	77.6	57.2	42.05
Providence RI	28.7	48.6	73.3	53.0	46.45
Charleston SC	47.9	64.2	81.7	66.2	51.53
Rapid City SD	22.4	44.7	71.7	48.2	16.64
Memphis TN	39.9	62.1	82.5	63.8	54.65
Dallas TX[3]	44.1	65.0	85.0	67.2	34.73
Salt Lake City UT	29.2	50.0	77.0	52.5	16.50
Burlington VT	18.0	43.5	70.6	47.7	36.05
Richmond VA	36.4	57.1	77.9	58.3	43.91
Seattle WA	40.9	50.2	65.3	52.7	37.07
Charleston WV	33.4	54.3	73.9	55.1	44.05
Milwaukee WI	20.7	45.2	72.0	51.4	34.81
Casper WY	22.3	42.7	70.0	45.7	13.03

[1]Data from O'Hare International Airport. [2]Data from John F. Kennedy International Airport. [3]Data from Dallas/Fort Worth International Airport.

Hurricane and Tornado Classifications

Hurricane classifications.
Category 1. *barometric pressure:* 28.94 in or more; *wind speed:* 74–95 mph; *storm surge:* 4–5 ft; *damage:* minimal.
Category 2. *barometric pressure:* 28.50–28.93 in; *wind speed:* 96–110 mph; *storm surge:* 6–8 ft; *damage:* moderate.

Category 3. *barometric pressure:* 27.91–28.49 in; *wind speed:* 111–130 mph; *storm surge:* 9–12 ft; *damage:* extensive.
Category 4. *barometric pressure:* 27.17–27.90 in; *wind speed:* 131–155 mph; *storm surge:* 13–18 ft; *damage:* extreme.

Category 5. *barometric pressure:* less than 27.17 in; *wind speed:* 155 mph or more; *storm surge:* 18 ft or more; *damage:* catastrophic.

Tornado classifications.
Tornado intensity is commonly estimated after the fact by analyzing damaged structures and then correlating the damage with the wind speeds known to produce various degrees of damage. Tornadoes are assigned specific values on the Fujita Scale, or F-Scale, of tornado intensity established by meteorologist T. Theodore Fujita.

Categories are:
F0. *wind speed:* 40–72 mph; *damage:* light.
F1. *wind speed:* 73–112 mph; *damage:* moderate.
F2. *wind speed:* 113–157 mph; *damage:* considerable.
F3. *wind speed:* 158–206 mph; *damage:* severe.
F4. *wind speed:* 207–260 mph; *damage:* devastating.
F5. *wind speed:* 261–318 mph; *damage:* incredible.

Indices

Wind Chill Table

The wind chill index is based upon a formula that determines how cold the atmosphere feels by combining the temperature and wind speed and applying other factors. For more information, see <www.nws.noaa.gov/om/windchill/index.shtml>.

							TEMPERATURE (°F)								
CALM	**40**	**35**	**30**	**25**	**20**	**15**	**10**	**5**	**0**	**-5**	**-10**	**-15**	**-20**	**-25**	**-30**
5	36	31	25	19	13	7	1	-5	-11	-16	-22	-28	-34	-40	-46
10	34	27	21	15	9	3	-4	-10	-16	-22	-28	-35	-41	-47	-53
15	32	25	19	13	6	0	-7	-13	-19	-26	-32	-39	-45	-51	-58
20	30	24	17	11	4	-2	-9	-15	-22	-29	-35	-42	-48	-55	-61
25	29	23	16	9	3	-4	-11	-17	-24	-31	-37	-44	-51	-58	-64
30	28	22	15	8	1	-5	-12	-19	-26	-33	-39	-46	-53	-60	-67
35	28	21	14	7	0	-7	-14	-21	-27	-34	-41	-48	-55	-62	-69
40	27	20	13	6	-1	-8	-15	-22	-29	-36	-43	-50	-57	-64	-71
45	26	19	12	5	-2	-9	-16	-23	-30	-37	-44	-51	-58	-65	-72
50	26	19	12	4	-3	-10	-17	-24	-31	-38	-45	-52	-60	-67	-74
55	25	18	11	4	-3	-11	-18	-25	-32	-39	-46	-54	-61	-69	-75
60	25	17	10	3	-4	-11	-19	-26	-33	-40	-48	-55	-62	-69	-76

WIND SPEED (MPH)

Heat Index

The Heat Index shows the effects of the combination of heat and humidity. Apparent temperature is the temperature as it feels to your body. For more information see <www.jeonet.com/heat.htm>.

relative humidity	70	75	80	85	90	95	100	105	110	115	120
						apparent temperature					
0%	64	69	73	78	83	87	91	95	99	103	107
10%	65	70	75	80	85	90	95	100	105	111	116
20%	66	72	77	82	87	93	99	105	112	120	130
30%	67	73	78	84	90	96	104	113	123	135	148
40%	68	74	79	86	93	101	110	123	137	151	
50%	69	75	81	88	96	107	120	135	150		
60%	70	76	82	90	100	114	132	149			
70%	70	77	85	93	106	124	144				
80%	71	78	86	97	113	136	157				
90%	71	79	88	102	122	150	170				
100%	72	80	91	108	133	166					

AIR TEMPERATURE (°F)

HEAT INDEX/HEAT DISORDERS

Heat Index	Possible heat disorders for people in higher risk groups*
130°F or higher	Heatstroke/sunstroke highly likely with continued exposure.
105°–130°F	Sunstroke, heat cramps, or heat exhaustion likely, and heatstroke possible with prolonged exposure and/or physical activity.
90°–105°F	Sunstroke, heat cramps, and heat exhaustion possible with prolonged exposure and/or physical activity.
80°–90°F	Fatigue possible with prolonged exposure and/or physical activity.

Small children, the elderly, the chronically ill, those on certain medications or drugs (especially tranquilizers and anticholinergics), and persons with weight and alcohol problems are particularly susceptible to heat reactions, especially during heat waves in areas where moderate climate usually prevails.

Ultraviolet (UV) Index

The Ultraviolet (UV) Index predicts the intensity of the sun's ultraviolet rays. It was developed by the National Weather Service and the US Environmental Protection Agency to provide a daily forecast of the expected risk of overexposure to the sun. The Index is calculated on a next day basis for dozens of cities across the US. Other local conditions, such as cloud cover, are taken into account in determining the UV Index number. UV Index numbers are: 0–2 (minimal exposure); 3–4 (low exposure); 5–6 (moderate exposure); 7–9 (high exposure); and 10 and over (very high exposure).

Some simple precautions can be taken to reduce the risk of sun-related illness: limit time in the sun between 10 AM and 4 PM, when rays are generally the strongest; seek shade whenever possible; use a broad spectrum sunscreen with an SPF of at least 15; wear a wide-brimmed hat and, if possible, tightly woven, full-length clothing; wear UV-protective sunglasses; avoid sunlamps and tanning salons; and watch for the UV Index daily.

The UV Index should not be used by seriously sun-sensitive individuals, who should consult their doctors and take additional precautions regardless of the exposure level.

National Weather Service Watches, Warnings, and Advisories

For more information, see *National Weather Service Web site*: <www.crh.noaa.gov>

Blizzard warning. Winter storms with sustained winds or frequent gusts of 35 mph (56 km/hr) or greater and considerable falling and/or blowing snow; visibility reduced to less than ¼ mile. Conditions expected to last at least three hours.

Excessive heat warning. Heat index is expected to equal or exceed 115 °F (46 °C) for three hours or more. In these cases, the heat becomes dangerous for a large portion of the population.

Flash flood. *Watch:* Flash flooding is possible in and close to the watch area. Those in the affected area are urged to be ready to take quick action if a flash flood warning is issued or flooding is observed. *Warning:* Rapid flooding of small rivers, streams, creeks, or urban areas is imminent or already occurring.

Flood. *Watch:* Widespread flooding is possible in and close to the watch area. Those in the affected area are urged to be ready to take quick action if a flood warning is issued or flooding is observed. Issued for general flooding that is expected to occur during or within 12 hours after heavy rain has ended. *Warning:* Issued for life- or property-threatening general flooding that occurs during or within 12 hours after heavy rainfall has ended. Can be issued for rural or urban areas as well as for areas along small streams and creeks. **Coastal flood.** *Watch:* Alerts coastal residents to the possibility of flooding. *Warning:* Flooding is imminent or occurring. Coastal waters extend out 100 nautical miles (100 mi; 185 km). **River flood.** *Warning:* Alerts residents of long-term flooding (more than 12 hours) along major streams and rivers that is a threat to life and/or property. Usually contains river stage forecast, crest information, and the history and impact of the flood.

Gale warning. Sustained winds of 34 to 47 knots (39 to 54 mph; 63 to 87 km/hr) are expected or occurring (not directly associated with tropical cyclones).

Health warning. Ground level ozone readings are expected to be in the unhealthful range. The elderly and persons with heart or respiratory problems should stay indoors near a fan or circulating air and reduce physical activity. Motorists are asked to reduce unnecessary driving by carpooling or using public transportation.

Heavy snow warning. Snowfall amounts of four inches or more in 12 hours or six inches or more in 24 hours are expected.

Heavy surf advisory. Describes all tropical cyclone watches and warnings in effect along with details concerning locations, intensity, movement, and precautions. Also issued to describe tropical cyclones and subtropical cyclones prior to the issuance of watches and warnings. High surf may pose a threat to life or property. May be issued alone or in conjunction with coastal flood watches or warnings.

High wind warning. Sustained winds of 40 mph (64 km/hr) or more are expected to last for at least one hour, or for nonthunderstorm winds of 58 mph (93 km/hr) or greater for any duration.

Hurricane. *Local statement:* A public release in or near the threatened area giving specific details on weather conditions, evacuation decisions made by local officials, and other necessary precautions to protect life and property. *Watch:* An announcement for specific locations that a hurricane poses a possible threat, generally within 36 hours. *Warning:* A warning that sustained surface winds of 64 knots (74 mph; 119 km/hr) or higher are expected in specified coastal areas within 24 hours or less. A hurricane warning can remain in effect when dangerously high water and/or exceptionally high waves continue even though winds may be less than hurricane force. **Inland hurricane force wind.** *Watch:* Issued for inland locations when hurricane force winds are anticipated beyond the coastal areas, though the actual occurrence, timing, and location are still uncertain.

Ice storm warning. Damaging ice accumulations are expected during freezing rain situations; walking and driving becomes extremely dangerous. Ice accumulations are usually ¼ inch or greater.

Severe thunderstorm. *Watch:* Conditions are favorable for the development of severe thunderstorms in and close to the watch area. Usually in effect for several hours. *Warning:* Issued when a thunderstorm produces hail ¾ of an inch or larger in diameter and/or winds of 58 mph (93 km/hr) or more.

Sleet warning. Accumulations of sleet covering the ground to a depth of ½ inch or more are expected.

Special tropical disturbance statement. Issued to furnish information on strong formative, nondepression systems. Focuses on major threats of the disturbance, such as the potential for torrential rains on island or inland areas.

Storm warning (coastal, oceanic, or marine). Sustained winds of 48 knots (55 mph; 89 km/hr) or greater are expected or occurring and are not directly associated with tropical cyclones.

Strike probability forecast of tropical cyclone conditions. The probability that the cyclone center will pass within 50 miles (80 km) to the right or 75 miles (121 km) to the left of the listed locations within the indicated time period when looking at the coast in the direction of the cyclone's movement.

Tornado. *Watch:* Conditions are favorable for the development of tornadoes in and close to the watch area. Usually in effect for several hours. *Warning:* A tornado is indicated by radar or sighted by storm spotters. The warning will include where the tornado is and what towns will be in its path.

Tropical storm. *Watch:* An announcement that a tropical storm or tropical storm conditions pose a threat to coastal areas, generally within 36 hours. A tropical storm watch is not usually issued if a tropical cyclone is expected to attain hurricane strength. *Warning:* Sustained winds of 34 to 63 knots (39 to 73 mph; 63 to 118 km/hr) inclusive are expected in specified coastal areas within 24 hours.

Wind chill warning. Wind chill temperatures are expected to reach −35 °F (−37 °C) or colder, with a minimum wind speed of about 10 mph (16 km/hr).

Winter storm. *Watch:* Conditions are favorable for the development of hazardous weather elements, such as heavy snow or sleet, blizzard conditions, significant accumulations of freezing rain or drizzle, or any combination thereof. Usually issued 12 to 48 hours in advance of an event. *Warning:* Hazardous winter weather conditions are imminent or very likely, including any occurrence or combination of heavy snow, wind-driven snow, sleet, or freezing rain or drizzle. Usually issued for up to 12 hours, but can be extended to 24 hours. The term "near-blizzard" may be incorporated into the winter storm warning for serious situations which fall just short of official blizzard conditions.

Meteorological Phenomena

Tides

"Tides" refer to any of the cyclic deformations of one astronomical body caused by the gravitational forces exerted by others. The most familiar are the **periodic variations in sea level** on the Earth that correspond to changes in the relative positions of the Moon and the Sun.

At the surface of the Earth the gravitational force of the Moon is about 2.2 times greater than that of the Sun. The tide-producing action of the Moon arises from the variations in its gravitational field over the surface of the Earth as compared with its strength at the Earth's center. The effect is that the water tends to accumulate on the parts of the Earth's surface directly toward and directly opposite the Moon and to be depleted elsewhere. The regions of accumulation move over the surface as the position of the Moon varies relative to the Earth, mainly because of the Earth's rotation but also because of the Moon's orbital motion around the Earth. There are approximately two high and two low tides per day at any given place, but they occur at times that change from day to day; the average interval between consecutive high tides is 12 hours 25 minutes. The effect of the Sun is similar and additive to that of the Moon. Consequently, the tides of largest range or amplitude (**spring tides**) occur at New Moon, when the Moon and the Sun are in the same direction, and at Full Moon, when they are in opposite directions; the tides of smallest range (**neap tides**) occur at intermediate phases of the Moon.

Although the observed tides possess the broad features discussed above, this pattern does not correspond to a pair of bulges that move around the Earth. The inertia of the water, the existence of continents, and effects associated with the water depth result in much more complicated behavior. For the main oceans, a combination of theory and observation indicates the existence of **amphidromic points**, at which the tidal rise and fall is zero: patterns of high and low tides rotate around these points (either clockwise or counterclockwise). Amplitudes are typically less than a meter.

Tides are most easily observed—and of greatest practical importance—along **seacoasts**, where the amplitudes are exaggerated. When tidal motions run into the shallow waters of the continental shelf, their rate of advance is reduced, energy accumulates in a smaller volume, and the rise and fall is amplified. The details of tidal motions in coastal waters, particularly in channels, gulfs, and estuaries, depend on the details of coastal geometry and water-depth variation. Tidal amplitudes, the contrast between spring and neap tides, and the variation of times of high and low tide all vary widely from place to place.

Monsoons

A **monsoon** is a type of major wind system that seasonally reverses its direction—e.g., one that blows for approximately six months from the northeast and six months from the southwest. The most prominent examples of such seasonal winds occur in southern Asia and in Africa. Monsoonal tendencies also are apparent along the Gulf Coast of the United States and in central Europe, as well as in various other areas. The **primary cause** of monsoons lies in the difference of the annual temperature trends over land and sea. Seasonal changes in temperature are large over land but small over ocean waters. A monsoon blows from cold toward warm regions: from sea toward land in summer and from land toward sea in winter. Atmospheric pressure is high in cold regions and low in warm ones, permitting the movement of air to occur. Most **summer monsoons** have a dominant westerly component and a strong tendency to ascend and produce copious amounts of rain (because of the condensation of water vapor in the rising air). The intensity and duration, however, are not uniform from year to year. **Winter monsoons**, by contrast, have a dominant easterly component and a strong tendency to diverge, subside, and cause drought.

El Niño

In oceanography and climatology, El Niño ("The Christ Child" in Spanish) is the anomalous appearance, every few years, of unusually warm ocean conditions along the tropical west coast of South America. This event is associated with adverse effects on fishing, agriculture, and local weather from Ecuador to Chile and with far-field climatic anomalies in the equatorial Pacific and occasionally in Asia and North America as well.

The name El Niño was originally used during the 19th century by the fishermen of northern Peru in reference to the annual flow of warm equatorial waters southward around Christmastime. Peruvian scientists later noted that more intense changes occurred at intervals of several years and were associated with catastrophic seasonal flooding along the normally arid coast, while the thermal anomalies lasted for a year or more. The more unusual episodes gained world attention during the 20th century, and the original annual connotation of the name was replaced by that of the anomalous occurrence.

The timing and intensity of El Niño events vary widely. The first recorded occurrence of unusual desert rainfall was in 1525, when the Spanish conquistador Francisco Pizarro landed in northern Peru.

Historians suggest that the desert rains and vegetation encountered by the Spaniards may have facilitated their conquest of the Inca empire. The intensity of El Niño episodes varies from weak thermal anomalies (2–3 °C [about 4–5 °F]) with only moderate local effects to very strong anomalies (8–10 °C [14–18 °F]) associated with worldwide climatic perturbations. El Niño events typically occur at three- to four-year intervals, with the strong events being less common. The intermittency varies widely, however, and the phenomenon is neither periodic nor predictable in the sense that ocean tides are.

The warm ocean conditions in the equatorial Pacific induce large-scale anomalies in the atmosphere. Rainfall increases manyfold in Ecuador and northern Peru, causing coastal flooding and erosion and consequent hardships in transportation and agriculture. Additionally, strong El Niño events are associated with droughts in Indonesia, Australia, and northeastern South America and with altered patterns of tropical storms in the tropical belt. During the stronger El Niño episodes, the atmospheric "teleconnections" are extensive enough to cause unusually severe winter weather at the higher latitudes of North and South America.

Environmental Change

Pollution

Pollution is the addition of any substance or form of energy to the environment at a rate faster than the environment can accommodate it by dispersion, breakdown, recycling, or storage in some harmless form. All living things exert some pressure on the natural environment, but modern efforts to improve the standard of living for humans—through the control of nature and the development of new consumer products—have partially contaminated much of the world's air, water, and land with chemical wastes. As a result, governments have passed laws to limit or reverse the threat of environmental pollution.

The branch of science that deals with how living things, including humans, are related to their surroundings is called ecology. The Earth supports some five million species of plants, animals, and microorganisms that form a vast network of interrelated environmental systems called ecosystems. The arctic tundra is an ecosystem and so is a Brazilian rain forest.

If left undisturbed, natural environmental systems tend to achieve balance or stability among the various species of plants and animals. Sudden changes in the relative population of a particular species can begin a kind of chain reaction among other elements of the ecosystem. For example, eliminating a species of insect through the use of a chemical pesticide also may eliminate a bird species that depends upon the insect as a source of food. As another example, overhunting by humans caused the extinction of the passenger pigeon in 1914.

Environmental pollution has existed since people began to congregate in towns and cities; ancient Athenians and Romans stored garbage outside city walls, a practice that may have contributed to outbreaks of viral diseases. The adverse effects of pollution became more noticeable as cities grew during the Middle Ages, as the human population grew steadily after 1650, and with the advent of the Industrial Revolution in the 19th century. The reduction of the Earth's resources has been closely linked to the rise in human population.

In 1997 representatives from 160 nations signed the Kyoto Protocol, an international agreement that called for the gradual reduction of greenhouse-gas emissions. These are emissions that increase atmospheric carbon dioxide and contribute to the greenhouse effect, an overwarming of the Earth's surface and lower atmosphere. Originally a supporter of the Protocol, the US, shortly after George W. Bush became president, in 2001, opted not to participate.

The various kinds of pollution are most conveniently considered under three headings: air, ground, and water.

Air Pollution

Air pollution is the release into the atmosphere of gases, finely divided solids, or finely dispersed liquid aerosols at rates that exceed the capacity of the atmosphere to dissipate them or to dispose of them through incorporation into the biosphere.

Dust storms in desert areas and smoke from forest and grass fires contribute to particulate and chemical air pollution. Volcanic activity is the major natural source of air pollution, pouring huge amounts of ash and toxic fumes into the atmosphere.

Air pollution may affect humans directly, causing irritation of the eyes or coughing. More indirectly, its effects can be measured far from the source, as, for example, the fallout of tetraethyl lead from automobile exhausts, which has been observed in the oceans and on the Greenland ice sheet. Still less direct are possible effects on global climates.

Though not generally categorized as air pollution, **noise pollution**, or excessively loud noises, is another form of airborne contamination that has deleterious effects on the environment.

Ground Pollution

Ground pollution occurs when the land is unable to accommodate in a natural manner the addition of substances to the soil, such as solid wastes that can't be broken down quickly, or, in some instances, at all. It can also refer to the unintended removal of needed components from the earth, such as topsoil. In many areas, the overuse of croplands in the quest to maximize yields results in the erosion of topsoil, which, in turn, causes the over-silting or sedimentation of rivers and streams.

One of the most hazardous forms of pollution comes from **agricultural pesticides**. These chemicals are designed to deter or kill insects, weeds, fungi, or rodents that pose a threat to crops. When airborne pesticides drift with the wind or become absorbed into the fruits and vegetables they are meant to protect, they can become a source of many illnesses, including cancer and birth defects. Pesticides are often designed to withstand rain, which means they are not always water-soluble, and therefore they may persist in the environment for long periods of time. In addition, some pests have developed a genetic resistance to these chemicals, forcing farmers to increase the amounts or types of pesticide.

Some urban areas are experiencing serious problems regarding the disposal of **garbage and hazardous wastes**, such as solvents and industrial dyes and inks. In many areas landfill sites have reached full capacity, forcing municipalities to consider alternative disposal methods, including incineration. Giant high-temperature incinerators have become another source of air pollution, however, because incineration ashes sometimes contain very high concentrations of metals as well as dioxins, a dangerous family of chemical poisons.

One step toward solving the garbage problem is **recycling**. Some towns have passed ordinances that encourage or require residents to separate glass and aluminum cans and bottles from other refuse so that these substances can be melted down and reused. Although lightweight steel, cardboard, and paper are also economically recyclable, most industries and cities still burn or bury large amounts of scrap metal and paper products.

Water Pollution

Water pollution occurs when substances are released into a body of water, where they become dissolved or suspended or deposited on the bottom, accumulating to the extent that they overwhelm the body of water's capacity to absorb, break down, or recycle them, and thus interfere with the functioning of aquatic ecosystems.

Contributions to water pollution include substances drawn from the air (such as **acid rain**), silt from **soil erosion**, chemical **fertilizers** and **pesticides**, runoff from **septic tanks**, outflow from **livestock feedlots**, **chemical wastes** from industries, and **sewage** and other urban wastes. A community far upstream in a watershed may thus receive relatively clean water, whereas one farther downstream receives a partly diluted mixture of urban, industrial, and rural wastes.

When organic matter exceeds the capacity of microorganisms in the water to break it down and recycle it, the excess of nutrients in such matter encourages **algal water blooms**. When these algae die, their remains add further to the organic wastes already in the water, and eventually the water becomes deficient in oxygen. Organisms that do not require oxygen then attack the organic wastes, releasing gases such as methane and hydrogen sulfide, which are harmful to the oxygen-requiring forms of life. The result is a foul-smelling, waste-filled body of water.

Natural Disasters

Geologic Disasters

Major Historical Earthquakes

Magnitudes given for pre-20th-century events are generally estimations from intensity data. When no magnitude was available, the maximum intensity, written as a Roman numeral from I to XII, is given.

YEAR (AD)	AFFECTED AREA	MAGNITUDE OR INTENSITY	DEATHS	YEAR (AD)	AFFECTED AREA	MAGNITUDE OR INTENSITY	DEATHS
365	Knossos, Crete (Greece)	XI	50,000	856	Qumis, Damghan, Iran	unknown	200,000
526	Antioch, Syria	unknown	250,000	893	Caucasus	unknown	82,000
844	Damascus, Syria	VIII	50,000	893	Daipur, India	unknown	180,000
847	Mosul, Iraq	unknown	50,000	893	Ardabil, Iran	unknown	150,000
847	Damascus, Syria	X	70,000	1042	Palmyra, Baalbek, Syria	X	50,000

Major Historical Earthquakes (continued)

YEAR (AD)	AFFECTED AREA	MAGNITUDE OR INTENSITY	DEATHS	YEAR (AD)	AFFECTED AREA	MAGNITUDE OR INTENSITY	DEATHS
1138	Ganzah, Aleppo, Syria	XI	230,000	1963	Skopje, Yugoslavia	6.0	1,070
1201	Upper Egypt or Syria	IX	1,100,000	1964	Prince William Sound AK	8.3	131
1268	Cilicia, Anatolia (Turkey)	unknown	60,000	1970	southern Yunnan province, China	7.7	10,000
1290	China	6.7	100,000	1970	northern Peru	7.8	66,794
1556	Shaanxi province, China	IX	830,000	1972	Managua, Nicaragua	6.2	5,000
1667	Shemakha, Azerbaijan	6.9	80,000	1976	Guatemala City, Guatemala	7.5	22,778
1668	Shandong province, China	XII	50,000	1976	northeastern Italy	6.5	929
1693	Sicily, Catania (Italy)	XI	100,000	1976	Tangshan, China	7.8	240,000
1703	Jeddo, Japan	unknown	200,000	1977	Bucharest, Romania	7.2	1,581
1727	Tabriz, Iran	VIII	77,000	1978	Khorasan, Iran	7.4	25,000
1730	Hokkaido, Japan	unknown	137,000	1979	Colombia; Ecuador	7.9	579
1731	Beijing, China	unknown	100,000	1980	El-Asnam (Ech-Cheliff), Algeria	7.7	5,000
1737	Kolkata (Calcutta), India	unknown	300,000	1980	southern Italy	6.9	3,114
1739	China	X	50,000	1983	eastern Turkey	6.9	1,400
1755	Lisbon, Portugal; Spain; Morocco	XI	62,000	1985	Mexico City, Mexico	8.1	9,500
1780	Tabriz, Iran	unknown	100,000	1986	San Salvador, El Salvador	5.4	1,000
1811	New Madrid MO	8.6	unknown	1988	Leninakan (Kumayri), Armenia	6.8	25,000
1835	northern Japan	7.6	28,300	1989	northern California	7.1	62
1857	Tejon Pass (Palmdale) CA	8.3	unknown	1990	Rasht, Iran	7.6	50,000
1868	Ecuador; Colombia	7.7	70,000	1990	Luzon, Philippines	7.7	1,600
1883	Java, Indonesia	unknown	100,000	1991	northern India	7.1	2,000
1905	Jammu and Kashmir, India	8.6	19,000	1992	Flores Island, Indonesia	7.5	2,500
1906	San Francisco CA	8.3	700	1993	southern India	6.4	30,000
1906	Valparaíso, Chile	8.6	1,500	1995	Kobe, Japan	7.2	5,000
1908	Calabria, Messina, Italy	7.5	58,000	1995	Sakhalin Island, Russia	7.1	2,000
1915	Abruzzi, Italy	7.5	32,600	1997	northwestern Iran	5.5	1,000
1920	Gansu province, China	8.5	200,000	1997	eastern Iran	7.1	1,560
1923	Tokyo; Yokohama, Japan	8.3	142,800	1998	Takhar province, Afghanistan	6.1	4,000
1927	Nan Ling, China	8.0	40,900	1999	Colombia	6.2	1,185
1932	Gansu province, China	7.6	70,000	1999	Turkey	7.6	17,000
1935	Quetta, India	7.5	30,000	1999	Taiwan	7.7	2,400
1939	Chillán, Chile	8.3	28,000	2000	Sulawesi, Indonesia	7.6	46
1939	Erzincan, Turkey	8.0	32,700	2000	southern Sumatra, Indonesia	7.9	103
1948	Ashkhabad, Turkmenistan	7.3	19,800	2001	El Salvador	7.7	844
1950	Assam, India	8.7	574	2001	India	7.7	20,085
1960	Agadir, Morocco	5.9	12,000	2001	El Salvador	6.6	315
1960	Puerto Montt, Valdivia, Chile	8.5	5,700	2001	southern Peru; northern Chile	8.4	75
				2002	Turkey	6.5	44
				2002	Hindu Kush region, Afghanistan	7.4	150
				2002	Hindu Kush region, Afghanistan	6.1	1,000

Measuring Earthquakes

The seismologists Beno Gutenberg and Charles Francis Richter introduced measurement of the seismic energy released by earthquakes on a magnitude scale in 1935. Each increase of one unit on the scale represents a 10-fold increase in the magnitude of an earthquake. Seismographs are designed to measure different components of seismic waves, such as wave type, intensity, and duration. This table shows the typical effects of earthquakes in various magnitude ranges. For further information, please see <www.seismo.unr.edu/ftp/pub/louie/class/100/magnitude.html>.

MAGNITUDE	EARTHQUAKE EFFECTS
Less than 3.5	Generally not felt, but recorded.
3.5–5.4	Often felt, but rarely causes damage.

Measuring Earthquakes (continued)

MAGNITUDE	EARTHQUAKE EFFECTS
Less than 6.0	At most slight damage to well-designed buildings. Can cause major damage to poorly constructed buildings over small regions.
6.1–6.9	Can be destructive in areas up to about 100 km across where people live.
7.0–7.9	Major earthquake. Can cause serious damage over larger areas.
8 or greater	Great earthquake. Can cause serious damage in areas several hundred km across.

Tsunamis

A tsunami is a **catastrophic ocean wave**, usually caused by a submarine earthquake occurring less than 30 mi (50 km) beneath the seafloor, with a magnitude greater than 6.5. Underwater or coastal landslides or volcanic eruptions also may cause a tsunami. The often-used term **tidal wave** is a misnomer: the wave has no connection with the tides. After the earthquake or other generating impulse, a train of simple, progressive oscillatory waves is propagated great distances at the ocean surface in ever-widening circles, much like the waves produced by a pebble falling into a shallow pool. In deep water, the wavelengths are enormous, about 60 to 125 mi (100 to 200 km), and the wave heights are very small, only 1 to 2 ft (0.3 to 0.6 m). The resulting wave steepness is extremely low; coupled with the waves' long periods that vary from five minutes to an hour, this enables normal wind waves and swell to completely obscure the waves in deep water. Thus, a ship in the open ocean experiences the passage of a tsunami as an insignificant rise and fall. As the waves approach the continental coasts, friction with the increasingly shallow bottom reduces the velocity of the waves. The period must remain constant; consequently, as the velocity lessens, the wavelengths become shortened and the wave amplitudes increase, coastal waters rising as high as **100 feet (30 m)** in 10 to 15 minutes. By a poorly understood process, the continental shelf waters begin to oscillate after the rise in sea level. Between three and five major oscillations generate most of the damage; the oscillations cease, however, only several days after they begin. Occasionally, the first arrival of a tsunami at a coast may be a trough, the water receding and exposing the shallow seafloor.

Avalanches

An **avalanche** is a large mass of rock debris or snow that moves rapidly down a mountain slope, sweeping and grinding everything in its path. An avalanche begins when a mass of material overcomes frictional resistance of the sloping surface, often after its foundation is loosened by spring rains or is rapidly melted by a warm, dry wind. Vibrations caused by loud noises, such as artillery fire, thunder, or blasting, can start the mass in motion. **Rock avalanches** (rockfalls) are commonly composed of bedrock fragments a few centimeters (an inch or so) in diameter and include much soil and dust; they are thought to ride on a cushion of compressed air that allows them to travel long distances. A **debris avalanche** usually occurs in unconsolidated earth materials when weakened by moisture. **Snow avalanches** may develop during heavy snowstorms and slide while the snow is still falling, but more often they occur after the snow has accumulated at a given site. One of the causes of snow avalanches is the slow formation of depth hoar (hexagonal cuplike ice crystals that begin to form at ground level) under the snowpack. Depth-hoar crystals develop in loose array from the evaporation of the original snow particles and the simultaneous vapor deposition of larger, denser ice crystals near the ground; thus a zone of weakness occurs within the snowpack near the ground, the particles of which act as a lubricant when the upper layers of the snow start sliding down the mountain. The **wet snow avalanche** is perhaps the most dangerous because of its great weight, heavy texture, and tendency to solidify as soon as it stops moving. The dry type is also dangerous because its entraining of great amounts of air makes it act like a fluid; this kind of avalanche may flow up the opposite side of a narrow valley. Avalanches can carry a considerable amount of rock debris with the snow.

Deadly Volcano Eruptions

Casualty figures are approximate.

VOLCANO (LOCATION)	YEAR	CASUALTIES	VOLCANO (LOCATION)	YEAR	CASUALTIES
Tambora (Indonesia)	1815	92,000[1]	Raung (Indonesia)	1730	3,000
Krakatoa (Indonesia)	1883	36,000[1]	Lamington (Papua New Guinea)	1951	3,000
Pelée (Martinique)	1902	30,000	Awu (Indonesia)	1856	2,800
Ruiz (Colombia)	1985	25,000[2]	Taal, Luzon (Philippines)	1906	1,500
Etna (Italy)	1669	20,000	Taal, Luzon (Philippines)	1911	1,300
Unzen (Japan)	1792	15,000	Etna (Italy)	1536	1,000
Kelud (Indonesia)	1586	10,000	Paricutín (Mexico)	1949	1,000
Laki (Iceland)	1783	9,000	Purace (Colombia)	1949	1,000
Kelud (Indonesia)	1919	5,000	Pinatubo (Philippines)	1991	350
Vesuvius (Italy)	79	3,360	El Chichón (Mexico)	1982	100
Awu (Indonesia)	1711	3,200	St. Helens (Washington, US)	1980	66[3]
Raung (Indonesia)	1638	3,000			

[1]*Includes tidal wave triggered by eruption.*   [2]*Includes mudflow triggered by eruption.*   [3]*Includes persons missing.*

Weather-Related Disasters

Storms

A storm is simply a disturbed state of the atmosphere. The term strongly implies destructive or unpleasant weather conditions characterized by strong winds, heavy rain, snow, sleet, hail, lightning, or a combination of these occurrences. Each type of storm—thunderstorms, cyclonic storms and tornadoes, hurricanes and typhoons—follows a particular cycle and occurs in specific seasons when atmospheric conditions are right for its creation.

Thunderstorms arise when layers of warm, moist air rise in a large, swift updraft to cooler regions of the atmosphere. There the moisture contained in the updraft condenses to form towering cumulonimbus clouds and, eventually, precipitation. Columns of cooled air then sink earthward, striking the ground with strong downdrafts and horizontal winds. At the same time, electrical charges accumulate on cloud particles (water droplets and ice). Lightning discharges occur when the accumulated electric charge becomes sufficiently large. Lightning heats the air it passes through so intensely and quickly that shock waves are produced; these shock waves are heard as claps and rolls of thunder. On occasion, severe thunderstorms are accompanied by swirling vortices of air that become concentrated and powerful enough to form tornadoes. The temperate and tropical regions of the world are the most prone to thunderstorms.

A tornado is a small-diameter column of violently rotating air developed within a convective cloud and in contact with the ground. Tornadoes occur most often in association with thunderstorms during the spring and summer in the mid-latitudes of both the Northern and Southern Hemispheres. These whirling atmospheric vortices can generate the strongest winds known on Earth: wind speeds in the range of 500 km/h (300 mph) have been estimated. When winds of this magnitude strike a populated area, they can cause fantastic destruction and great loss of life, mainly through injuries from flying debris and collapsing structures. Most tornadoes, however, are comparatively weak events that occur in sparsely populated areas and cause minor damage.

A cyclone is any large system of winds that rotates about a center of low atmospheric pressure in a counterclockwise direction north of the Equator and in a clockwise direction to the south. Cyclonic winds move across nearly all regions of the Earth except the equatorial belt and are generally associated with rain or snow. In the Atlantic and Caribbean regions, tropical cyclones are commonly called hurricanes, while in the western Pacific and China Sea the term typhoon is applied.

Hurricanes are characterized by very strong winds and torrential rains; severe thunderstorms and waterspouts are embedded in the storm's cloud system. Storm surge, similar to a tidal wave, is sometimes created by the storm's high winds and by variations in air pressure. When a storm surge slams into a coastline, it usually inflicts severe damage.

Typhoons in the western Pacific are generally much stronger and more deadly than their Atlantic hurricane counterparts. This is because the Pacific Ocean is much larger than the Atlantic, and the typhoons have more time to develop before striking land.

A blizzard is a severe weather condition that is distinguished by low temperatures, strong winds, and large quantities of snow. The US Weather Service defines a blizzard as a storm with winds of more than 51 km/h (32 mph) and enough snow to limit visibility to 150 m (500 ft) or less. A severe blizzard has winds of over 72 km/h (about 45 mph), visibility near zero, and temperatures of −12 °C (10 °F) or lower. The name originated in the central US, where blizzards are brought by northwesterly winds following winter depressions, or low-pressure systems. In the US and in England, the term is commonly used for any strong, heavy snowstorm. In Antarctica, blizzards are associated with winds spilling over the edge of the ice plateau at an average velocity of 160 km/h (about 100 mph).

Floods

A flood occurs when water overflows its natural or artificial banks onto normally dry land. The effects of floods on human well-being range from unqualified blessings to catastrophes. The regular seasonal spring floods of the Nile River prior to construction of the Aswan High Dam, for example, were depended upon to provide moisture and soil enrichment for the fertile floodplains of its delta. The uncontrolled floods of the Yangtze River and the Huang Ho (Yellow River) in China, however, have repeatedly wrought disaster when these rivers habitually rechart their courses. Uncontrollable floods likely to cause considerable damage commonly result from excessive rainfall over brief periods of time, as, for example, the floods of Paris (1658 and 1910), of Warsaw (1861 and 1964), and of Rome (1530 and 1557). Potentially disastrous floods may also result from ice jams during the spring rise, as with the Danube River (1342, 1402, 1501, and 1830); from storm tides such as those of 1099 and 1953 that flooded the coasts of England, Belgium, and The Netherlands; and from tsunamis, the mountainous sea waves caused by earthquakes, as in Lisbon (1755) and Hawaii (Hilo, 1946).

Floods can be measured for height, peak discharge, area inundated, and volume of flow. These factors are important to judicious land use, construction of bridges and dams, and prediction and control of floods. Common measures of flood control include the improvement of channels, the construction of protective levees and storage reservoirs, and, indirectly, the implementation of programs of soil and forest conservation to retard and absorb runoff from storms.

The discharge volume of an individual stream is often highly variable from month to month and year to year. A particularly striking example of this variability is the flash flood, a sudden, unexpected torrent of muddy and turbulent water rushing down a canyon or a gulch. It is uncommon, of relatively brief duration, and generally the result of summer thunderstorms in mountains. A flash flood can take place in a single tributary while the rest of the drainage basin remains dry. The suddenness of its occurrence makes a flash flood extremely dangerous.

Wildfires

Fire danger in a wildland setting varies with weather conditions: drought, heat, and wind participate in drying out the timber or other fuel, making it easier to ignite. Once a fire is burning, these factors all increase its intensity. Topography also affects wildland fire, which spreads quickly uphill and slowly downhill.

In the past, a combination of high summer temperatures, strong winds, late summer drought, and accumulations of dead vegetation set the stage for many naturally caused **prairie fires**, which prevented trees from becoming abundant in prairie vegetation. Now the fertile prairie soils are cultivated or grazed.

Peat bogs, which cover vast areas in the tundra and boreal forest regions of Canada, northern Europe, Russia, and Britain, are also prone to potentially dangerous fires. Although usually moist, peat may dry out and then burns easily. Peat bog fires are especially hazardous, as they emit carbon monoxide and carbon dioxide and burn deep underground. They may smolder for years, nearly impossible to extinguish.

Dried grass, leaves, and light branches are considered **flash fuels**; they ignite readily, and fire spreads quickly in them, often generating enough heat to ignite heavier fuels such as tree stumps, heavy limbs, and the matted duff of the forest floor. Such fuels, ordinarily slow to kindle, are difficult to extinguish. **Green fuels**—growing vegetation—are not considered flammable, but an intense fire can dry out leaves and needles quickly enough to allow ready ignition. Green fuels sometimes carry a special danger: evergreens, such as pine, cedar, fir, and spruce, contain flammable oils that burst into flames when heated sufficiently by the searing drafts of a forest fire.

Tools for fighting wildland fires range from the standard equipment of urban fire departments to portable pumps, tank trucks, and earth-moving equipment. **Firefighting forces** specially trained to deal with wildland fires are maintained by public and private owners of forestlands. Such a force may attack a fire directly by spraying water, beating out flames, and removing vegetation at the edge of the fire to contain it behind a **fire line**. When the very edge is too hot to approach, a fire line is built at a safe distance, sometimes using **strip burning** or **backfire** to eliminate fuel in the path of the uncontrolled fire or to change the fire's direction or slow its progress. Backfiring is used only as a last resort.

Aircraft were first used in fighting wildland fires in California in 1919. Airplanes and helicopters are primarily used for dumping water, for observation, and occasionally for assisting in communication and transporting personnel, supplies, and equipment.

Humans cause most of the nation's wildfires, either intentionally or through negligence. In the summer of 2002 enormous wildfires spread through much of the western US, including Arizona, Colorado, Utah, and Oregon. The wildfire in Arizona, the largest in that state's history, was started in part by a lost woman trying to attract attention by lighting a signal fire.

Did you know? Dalmatians were originally bred as guard dogs for stagecoaches. Because they were used to running long distances and being around horses, and because their bright white coats with black spots were easily visible, they were chosen by fire departments to run ahead of horse-drawn fire engines, barking a warning and clearing the path of onlookers.

Deadliest Hurricanes in the US

Listed below, in order of number of deaths, are the 30 deadliest hurricanes to hit the US mainland 1900–2001. Hurricane names are given in parentheses after the location, when applicable. The list includes Atlantic/Gulf Coast hurricanes only. Source: National Hurricane Center. National Hurricane Center Web site: <www.nhc.noaa.gov/pastdead.html>

	HURRICANE LOCATION	YEAR	CATEGORY	DEATHS
1	Galveston TX	1900	4	8,000[1]
2	Lake Okeechobee FL	1928	4	1,836
3	south TX; FL Keys	1919	4	600[2]
4	New England	1938	3	600
5	FL Keys	1935	5	408
6	southwest LA/ north TX (Audrey)	1957	4	390
7	northeast US	1944	3	390[3]
8	Grand Isle LA	1909	4	350
9	New Orleans LA	1915	4	275
10	Galveston TX	1915	4	275
11	MS; LA (Camille)	1969	5	256
12	FL; LA; MS; AL	1926	4	243
13	northeast US (Diane)	1955	1	184
14	southeast Florida	1906	2	164
15	FL; MS; AL	1906	3	134
16	northeast US (Agnes)	1972	1	122
17	SC; NC (Hazel)	1954	4	95
18	southeast FL; southeast LA (Betsy)	1965	3	75
19	northeast US (Carol)	1954	3	60
20	eastern US (Floyd)	1999	2	57
21	southeast FL; LA; MS	1947	4	51
22	FL; eastern US (Donna)	1960	4	50
23	GA; SC; NC	1940	2	50
24	TX (Carla)	1961	4	46
25	Velasco TX	1909	3	41
26	Freeport TX	1932	4	40
27	south TX	1933	3	40
28	LA (Hilda)	1964	3	38
29	southwest LA	1918	3	34
30	southwest FL	1910	3	30

[1]*Death toll may actually have been as high as 10,000–12,000.*   [2]*More than 500 of these lost on ships at sea; 600–900 estimated deaths.*   [3]344 of these lost on ships at sea.

The Costliest Hurricanes in the US

*Thirty Atlantic cyclones that caused the most damage on the US mainland. For more information see
<www.nhc.noaa.gov/pastcost.html>.
Note: ranking numbers 8, 16, 22, and 27 on the main list are doubled due to the equal
damage amount in dollars of two separate hurricanes.*

RANKING	HURRICANE (LOCATION)	YEAR	CATEGORY	DAMAGE ($)
1	Andrew (southeastern FL/southeastern LA)	1992	4	26,500,000,000
2	Hugo (SC)	1989	4	7,000,000,000
3	Fran (NC)	1996	3	3,200,000,000
4	Opal (northwestern FL/AL)	1995	3	3,000,000,000
5	Frederic (AL/MS)	1979	3	2,300,000,000
6	Agnes (northeastern US)	1972	1	2,100,000,000
7	Alicia (northern TX)	1983	3	2,000,000,000
8	Bob (NC and northeastern US)	1991	2	1,500,000,000
8	Juan (LA)	1985	1	1,500,000,000
10	Camille (MS/AL)	1969	5	1,420,700,000
11	Betsy (FL/LA)	1965	3	1,420,500,000
12	Elena (MS/AL/northwestern FL)	1985	3	1,250,000,000
13	Gloria (eastern US)	1985	3[1]	900,000,000
14	Diane (northeastern US)	1955	1	831,700,000
15	Erin (central & northwestern FL/AL)	1995	2	700,000,000
16	Allison (northern TX)	1989	T.S.[2]	500,000,000
16	Alberto (northwestern FL/GA/AL)	1994	T.S.[2]	500,000,000
18	Eloise (northwestern FL)	1975	3	490,000,000
19	Carol (northeastern US)	1954	3[1]	461,000,000
20	Celia (southern TX)	1970	3	453,000,000
21	Carla (TX)	1961	4	408,000,000
22	Claudette (northern TX)	1979	T.S.[2]	400,000,000
22	Gordon (southern & central FL/NC)	1994	T.S.[2]	400,000,000
24	Donna (FL/eastern US)	1960	4	387,000,000
25	David (FL/eastern US)	1979	2	320,000,000
26	New England	1938	3[1]	306,000,000
27	Kate (FL Keys/northwestern FL)	1985	2	300,000,000
27	Allen (southern TX)	1980	3	300,000,000
29	Hazel (SC/NC)	1954	4[1]	281,000,000
30	Bertha (NC)	1996	2	270,000,000
	non-Atlantic or non-Gulf coast systems			
8	Iniki (Kauai, HI)	1992	unknown[3]	1,800,000,000
8	Marilyn (US Virgin Islands/eastern Puerto Rico)	1995	2	1,500,000,000
13	Hugo (US Virgin Islands/Puerto Rico)	1989	4	1,000,000,000
15	Hortense (Puerto Rico)	1996	4	500,000,000
24	Olivia (CA)	1982	T.D.[4]	325,000,000
25	Iwa (Kauai, HI)	1982	unknown[3]	312,000,000
26	Norman (CA)	1978	T.D.[4]	300,000,000

[1]*Moving more than 30 mph.*   [2]*Of tropical storm intensity but included because of high damage.*   [3]*Intensity not sufficiently known to establish category.*   [4]*Tropical depression.*

Hurricane Names

Source: National Hurricane Center.

In 1953, the National Hurricane Center developed a list of given names for Atlantic tropical storms. This list is now maintained by the World Meteorological Organization (WMO). Until 1979, only women's names were used, but since then men's and women's names have alternated. There are six lists currently in rotation, so names are reused every six years. Any country affected by a hurricane, however, can request its name be retired for ten years. Also, if a storm has been particularly destructive, the WMO can remove it from the list and replace it with a different name.

Did you know? Tropical cyclones are classified as tropical storms and given names when wind speeds reach 39 mph. Tropical storms become hurricanes when wind speeds reach 74 mph.

Civil Engineering

History of Civil Engineering

Civil engineering describes the design and construction of public structures. The term first came into use in the 18th century, though the discipline has been in practice since antiquity. Civil engineering is generally distinguished from military engineering and often times from architecture. It is the oldest of the four traditional disciplines of engineering: civil, mechanical, electrical, and chemical.

The first engineer known by name and achievement is **Imhotep**, builder of the **Step Pyramid** at Saqqarah, Egypt, (c. 2550 BC). Imhotep's successors—Egyptian, Persian, Greek, and Roman—carried civil engineering to remarkable heights on the basis of empirical methods aided by arithmetic, geometry, and a smattering of physical science. The lighthouse **Pharos** of Alexandria, **Solomon's Temple** in Jerusalem, the **Colosseum** in Rome, the **Persian Royal Road** and **Roman road systems**, the **Pont du Gard** aqueduct in France, and many other large structures testify to their skill, imagination, and daring. Of many treatises written by them, one in particular survives to provide a picture of engineering education and practice in classical times: *De architectura* by Vitruvius of Rome, published in the 1st century AD.

In construction, medieval European engineers carried technique, in the form of the **Gothic arch** and the **flying buttress**, to a height unknown to the Romans. The sketchbook of the 13th-century French engineer **Villard de Honnecourt** reveals a wide knowledge of mathematics, geometry, natural and physical science, and draftsmanship.

In Asia, engineering had a separate but very similar development, with more and more sophisticated techniques of construction, hydraulics, and metallurgy helping to create advanced civilizations such as the **Mongol empire**, whose large, beautiful cities impressed Marco Polo in the 13th century.

The appearance of civil engineering as a distinct discipline began in France in 1747 with the establishment of the **École Nationale des Ponts et Chaussées** ("National School of Bridges and Highways"), whose faculty and students helped to define the emerging field. Soon, craftsmen, stonemasons, and toolmakers from France and England became civil engineers. In Britain, **James Brindley** began as a millwright and became the foremost canal builder of the century; **John Rennie** was a millwright's apprentice who eventually built the new London Bridge; **Thomas Telford**, a stonemason, became Britain's leading road builder; and **John Smeaton**, an instrument maker, built the Eddystone Lighthouse (1756–59), before founding the Society of Civil Engineers (1771; now known as the **Smeatonian Society**). Other institutions included the **École Polytechnique** in Paris (1794), the **Bauakademie** in Berlin (1799) and the **Institution of Civil Engineers** in London (1818).

Today civil engineering is taught in universities across the world and national organizations of civil engineers have been formed widely.

The Seven Wonders of the Ancient World

The seven wonders of the ancient world were considered to be the preeminent architectural and sculptural achievements of the Mediterranean and Middle East. The best known are those of the 2nd-century-BC writer Antipater of Sidon. Some early lists included the Walls of Babylon or the Palace of King Cyrus of Persia, but the established list usually contained the following:

Pyramids of Giza. The oldest of the wonders and the only one substantially in existence today, the pyramids of Giza were erected c. 2575–c. 2465 BC on the west bank of the Nile River near Al-Jizah in northern Egypt. The designations of the pyramids—Khufu, Khafre, and Menkaure—correspond to the kings for whom they were built. Khufu (also called the Great Pyramid) is the largest of the three, the length of each side at the base averaging 230 m (755 ¾ ft). Its original height was 147 m (481.4 ft); none of the pyramids reach their original heights because they have been almost entirely stripped of their outer casings of smooth white limestone. According to Herodotus, the Great Pyramid took 20 years to construct and demanded the labor of 100,000 men.

Hanging Gardens of Babylon. A series of landscaped terraces ascribed to either Queen Sammuramat (810–783 BC) or King Nebuchadrezzar II (c. 605–c. 561 BC), the gardens were built within the walls of the royal palace at Babylon (in present-day southern Iraq). They did not actually "hang" but were instead "up in the air"—that is, they were roof gardens laid out on a series of ziggurat terraces that were irrigated by pumps from the Euphrates River. Although no traces of the Hanging Gardens have been found, classical authors related that the terraces were roofed with stone balconies on which were layered various materials, such as reeds, bitumen, and lead, so that the irrigation water would not seep through them.

Statue of Zeus. A large, ornate figure of Zeus on his throne, this wonder was made around 430 BC by Phidias of Athens. It was placed in the huge Temple of Zeus at Olympia in western Greece. The statue, almost 12 m (40 ft) high and plated with gold and ivory, represented the god sitting on an elaborate cedarwood throne ornamented with ebony, ivory, gold, and precious stones. On his outstretched right hand was a statue of Nike (Victory), and in the god's left hand was a scepter on which an eagle was perched. The statue, which took eight years to construct, may have been destroyed along with the temple in AD 426, or in a fire at Constantinople (Istanbul) about 50 years later.

Temple of Artemis. The great temple was built by Croesus, king of Lydia, in about 550 BC and was rebuilt after being burned by a madman named Herostratus in 356 BC. The artemesium was famous not only for its great size (over 110 by 55 m [350 by 80 ft]) but also for the magnificent works of art that adorned it. It was destroyed by invading Goths in AD 262 and was never rebuilt. Little remains of the temple, but excavation has revealed traces of it, and copies survive of the famous statue of Artemis. A mummylike figure, this early representation of the goddess stands stiffly straight, with her hands extended outward. The original statue was made of gold, ebony, silver, and black stone, the legs and hips covered by a garment decorated with reliefs of animals and bees and the head adorned with a high-pillared headdress.

Mausoleum of Halicarnassus. Monumental tomb of Mausolus, the tyrant of Caria in southwestern Asia Minor, the mausoleum was built between about 353 and 351 BC by Mausolus' sister and widow, Artemisia. The architect was Pythius (Pytheos), and the sculptures that adorned the building were the work of four leading Greek artists. According to the description of Pliny the Elder, the monument was almost square, with a total periphery of 125 m (411 ft). It was bounded by 36 columns, and the top formed a 24-step pyramid surmounted by a four-horse marble chariot. Fragments of the mausoleum's sculpture are preserved in the British Museum. The mausoleum was probably destroyed by an earthquake between the 11th and 15th century AD, and the stones were reused in local buildings.

Colossus of Rhodes. This huge bronze statue was built at the harbor of Rhodes in ancient Greece in commemoration of the raising of the siege of Rhodes (305–304 BC). The sculptor was Chares of Lyndus, and the statue was made of bronze, reinforced with iron, and weighted with stones. The Colossus was said to be 70 cubits (32 m [105 ft]) high and stood beside Mandrákion harbor. It is technically impossible that the statue could have straddled the harbor entrance, and the popular belief that it did so dates only from the Middle Ages. The Colossus took 12 years to build (c, 294–282 BC) and was toppled by an earthquake about 225 BC. The fallen Colossus was left in place until AD 654, when Arabian forces raided Rhodes and had the statue broken up and the bronze sold for scrap.

Pharos of Alexandria. The most famous lighthouse of the ancient world, it was built by Sostratus of Cnidus, perhaps for Ptolemy I Soter, but was finished during the reign of his son, Ptolemy II of Egypt, about 280 BC. The lighthouse stood on the island of Pharos off Alexandria and is said to have been more than 100 m (350 ft) high; the only taller man-made structures at the time would have been the pyramids of Giza. It was a technological triumph and is the archetype of all lighthouses since. According to ancient sources, a broad spiral ramp led to the top, where a fire burned at night. The lighthouse was destroyed by an earthquake in the 1300s. In 1994 a large amount of masonry blocks and statuary was found in the waters off Pharos.

25 Tallest Buildings in the World

Until their destruction in the terrorist attacks of 11 Sep 2001, One World Trade Center and Two World Trade Center in New York City were numbers 5 and 6, respectively.

RANK	BUILDING	CITY	YEAR COMPLETED	HEIGHT IN FT/M	STORIES
1	Petronas Tower 1	Kuala Lumpur, Malaysia	1996	1483/452	88
2	Petronas Tower 2	Kuala Lumpur, Malaysia	1996	1483/452	88
3	Sears Tower	Chicago IL	1974	1450/442	110
4	Jin Mao Building	Shanghai, China	1998	1379/420	88
5	Empire State Building	New York NY	1931	1250/381	102
6	Central Plaza	Hong Kong, China	1992	1227/374	78
7	Bank of China	Hong Kong, China	1989	1209/369	70
8	Tuntex Building	Kaoshiung, Taiwan	1997	1140/347	85
9	Amoco	Chicago IL	1973	1136/346	80
10	John Hancock Center	Chicago IL	1969	1127/344	100
11	Shun Hing Square	Shenzen, China	1996	1066/325	81
12	Sky Central Plaza	Guangzhou, China	1996	1056/322	80
13	Chicago Beach Hotel	Dubai, UAE	1998	1053/321	60
14	Baiyoke Tower II	Bangkok, Thailand	1997	1050/320	90
15	Chrysler Building	New York NY	1930	1046/319	77
16	NationsBank Plaza	Atlanta GA	1992	1023/312	55
17	Library Tower	Los Angeles CA	1990	1018/310	73
18	Malaysia Telecom HQ	Kuala Lumpur, Malaysia	1998	1017/310	77
19	AT&T Corporate Centre	Chicago IL	1989	1007/307	61
20	Chase Tower	Chicago IL	1982	1002/305	75
21	Two Prudential Plaza	Chicago IL	1990	995/303	65
22	Ryugyong Hotel	Pyongyang, N. Korea	1995	984/300	105
23	Commerzbank	Frankfurt, Germany	1997	981/299	63
24	First Interstate Plaza	Houston TX	1983	972/296	71
25	Landmark Tower	Yokohama, Japan	1993	971/296	70

Notable Towers

A tower is any structure that is relatively tall in proportion to the dimensions of its base. It may be either freestanding or attached to a building or wall. Modifiers frequently denote a tower's function (e.g., watchtower, water tower, church tower, and so on).

Historically, there are several types of structures particularly implied by the name. **Defensive towers** served as platforms from which a defending force could rain missiles down upon an attacking force. The Romans, Byzantines, and medieval Europeans built such towers along their city walls and adjoining important gates. The Romans and other peoples also used offensive, or **siege**, towers as raised platforms for attacking troops to overrun high city walls. **Military towers** often gave their name to an entire fortress;

the **Tower of London**, for example, includes the entire complex of buildings contiguous with the **White Tower** of William I the Conqueror.

Towers were an important feature of the **churches and cathedrals** built during the Romanesque and Gothic periods. Some Gothic church towers were designed to carry a spire, while others had flat roofs. Many church towers were used as belfries, though the most famous **campanile**, or bell tower, the **Leaning Tower of Pisa** (1174), is a freestanding structure. In civic architecture, towers were often used to hold clocks, as in town halls in France and Germany. The use of towers declined somewhat during the Renaissance but reappeared in the more flamboyant Baroque architecture of the 17th and 18th centuries.

The use of **steel frames** enabled buildings to reach unprecedented heights in the late 19th and 20th centuries; the **Eiffel Tower** (1889) in Paris was the first structure to reveal the true vertical potential of steel construction. The ubiquity of modern skyscrapers has robbed the word *tower* of most of its meaning, though the **Petronas Twin Towers** in Kuala Lumpur, Malaysia, the **Sears Tower** in Chicago, and other skyscrapers still bear the term in their official names.

The world's **tallest freestanding structure** is the CN Tower (1976), an observation and broadcasting tower in Toronto that rises to more than 553 m (1,815 ft). **The tallest supported structure** is a 629-m (2,063-ft) stayed television broadcasting tower, completed in 1963 and located between Fargo and Blanchard ND.

Bridges

A bridge is a structure that spans horizontally between supports to allow pedestrians and vehicles to cross a void, such as a river or a valley. The bridge supports must be strong enough to hold the structure up, and the span between the supports must be strong enough to carry the vertical loads. Spans are generally made as short as possible; long spans are justified where good foundations are limited—for example, over estuaries with deep water.

The loads that bridges transfer to their vertical supports are of various kinds. Dead load is the weight of the bridge, live load is the weight of the traffic on it, and wind load is the pressure of the wind against the bridge. Major bridges are usually built with public money, and bridge-building can achieve a high level of prominence. Civil engineers often design a bridge to be elegant, as well as efficient and economical.

Beam bridge

The simplest bridge is the beam (or girder) bridge, consisting of straight, rigid beams placed across a span (e.g., a tree trunk laid across a stream). A more complex example is a plate girder bridge over a highway; a plate girder is a built-up beam consisting of a steel plate to which angles are riveted or welded. Because a simple beam tends to bend down at its middle, particularly over a long chasm, the beam may rest on more than one support to form a continuous beam.

Another beam bridge is the **truss bridge**, made up of members forming rigid triangles. Trusses are popular because they use a relatively small amount of material to carry relatively large loads. A variation of the beam principle is used in the **cantilever bridge**. A cantilever is a beam that extends beyond its support. Sometimes two cantilever arms meet at mid-span or are connected by a light suspended span.

Arch bridge

Based on a different principle than the beam is the arch bridge. In the beam bridge the load is transmitted vertically to the supports, whereas the arch bridge pushes outward against its supports, which must be heavy to resist the horizontal thrust of the arch. The arch may be fixed, with each end rigid; two-hinged, with a hinge at each support; or three-hinged, with a third hinge at its crown. The hinges permit movement because of loads or temperature changes.

Suspension bridge

In the suspension bridge huge cables are hung over two high towers. The cable ends are fastened to heavy concrete or masonry anchorages. Suspender cables hanging from the main cables support the roadway. As in the arch, the thrust on the suspension bridge is horizontal. Instead of horizontal compression, or push, however, there is horizontal tension, or pull, upon the anchorages.

Cable-stayed bridge

Cable-stayed bridges carry the vertical main-span loads by nearly straight diagonal cables in tension. The towers transfer the cable forces to the foundations through vertical compression. The tensile forces in the cables also put the deck into horizontal compression.

Other bridges

A **drawbridge** over the moat of a medieval castle is an example of a movable bridge. The **bascule bridge**, in either single-leaf or double-leaf, is the modern-day version. Bascule in French means "a seesaw;" a counterweight balances the span in every open position.

The **swing span** bridge turns about a vertical axis to allow ships to pass. It is balanced on a pivot pier, usually in its center. Its span is measured by including the length of both arms. The vertical lift bridge has a tower at each end of its span. Cables attached to ends of the span pass over pulleys at the top of the towers and are fastened to counterweights that equal the weight of the span. The span moves up and down like an elevator.

In the **floating bridge**, boats or pontoons support the road. The bridge retracts or swings aside to allow ships to pass. The **transporter bridge** has two towers supporting a fixed span from which a moving platform or car is hung.

Early history of bridgebuilding

The earliest bridges were made from materials at hand. The Swiss lake dwellers built their timber houses by driving piles into the lake bed. From this evolved the timber pile and trestle railroad bridge. In warmer parts of the world bridgebuilders erected suspension bridges. In one Chinese type the traveler sat in a basket or saddle suspended from a cable and slid to the opposite bank. Bridgemakers in the Himalayas threw ropes across a chasm and from these hung thinner ropes to carry the road. This was the origin of the modern suspension bridge. The cantilever bridge also originated in Asia, in India; wooden planks, weighted down by abutment stones, were projected from the two banks until they met in the center.

Basic Types of Bridges

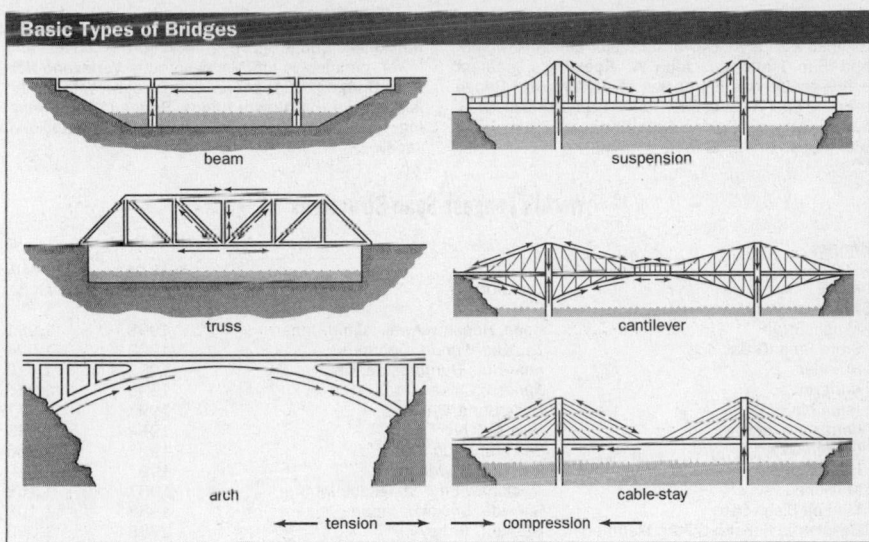

beam

suspension

truss

cantilever

arch

cable-stay

← tension → → compression ←

The ancient **Romans** were notable bridgebuilders. Six of their masonry arch bridges over the Tiber River still stand in Rome. The most beautiful of the existing Roman bridges is the **Ponte di Augusto**, built at Rimini about 5 bc. The greatest Roman aqueduct is the **Pont du Gard** at Nîmes, France. It has three tiers of arches, which rise 155 feet (47 meters) above the Gard River.

Medieval bridges
During the Middle Ages the church became the chief builder of bridges. Churchmen formed the **Brotherhood of Bridgebuilders** in Italy and France at the end of the 12th century. St. Bénézet built a beautiful stone bridge over the Rhone at Avignon, in southern France. Four arches still remain.

Monks also built the old **London Bridge** (1209) over the River Thames, in London. By the 16th century more than a hundred shops and dwellings had been erected on it. Another covered bridge with shops along the sides was the **Ponte Vecchio** (1345), which still stands over the Arno River, at Florence, Italy.

A major contribution of the Renaissance was the theory of the truss. **Andrea Palladio** of Italy wrote about truss design in *The Four Books of Architecture* (1570). Typical of the bridgebuilding of this period is the stone arch **Rialto Bridge** over the Grand Canal, in Venice. Two Renaissance stone bridges remain over the Seine in Paris—the **Pont Notre Dame** (1505) and the **Pont Neuf** (1606).

The 18th century
In the 18th century, bridge design came to be considered a science. **Hubert Gautier**, a French engineer, wrote a treatise on bridgebuilding. The first engineering school was founded in Paris. Its director, **Jean Perronet**, is called the father of modern bridgebuilding. He perfected the masonry arch, using a flat arch and slender piers. One of his finest bridges is the Pont de la Concorde, in Paris.

Also in the 1700s the **wooden truss bridge** was rediscovered, and the covered wooden bridge began to appear in Switzerland. The **Grubenmann brothers**,

Swiss carpenters, built a 200-foot span at Wettingen. The picturesque covered bridge was highly developed in the American Colonies. **Col. Enoch Hale** built the first framed **timber bridge** in the United States, over the Connecticut River at Bellows Falls VT, in 1785.

The invention of the steam locomotive changed bridgebuilding, for stronger spans were needed. Iron was first used for chain cables of a suspension over the Tees River, in England, in 1741. Abraham Darby and John Wilkinson built the first **iron bridge** over the Severn River at Coalbrookdale, England, in 1779.

Modern bridges
Thomas Telford built the first modern iron arch bridge in 1813—Craig Ellachie Bridge over the River Spey at Banffshire, Scotland. In the 1820s Telford built the forerunner of the modern suspension bridge—the 570-foot span over **Menai Strait**, in Wales. It had wrought-iron chains for cables. The first to design railroad bridges was George Stephenson, who with his son Robert invented the Rocket, the first practical locomotive. Many truss designs were patented in the 1850s for railroad bridges. After numerous failures of cast-iron bridges, wrought iron was used, then steel.

The first bridge to use steel extensively was the triple-arched **Eads Bridge** over the Mississippi at St. Louis MO, in 1874. The first major use of pneumatic caissons for large piers was made in this bridge. It was an important link in the transcontinental railroad and made St. Louis a crossroads.

At the turn of the 20th century, the construction of **masonry arch bridges** reached its peak. Then the more economical and easier to use concrete became common for arch bridges. Later, reinforced concrete and then prestressed concrete were used.

The first **modern cantilever bridge** was built in 1867 by **Heinrich Gerber** over the Main River at Hassfurt, Germany. The first major example of the cantilever, however, was the **Firth of Forth Bridge**, in Scotland. It was built in 1882–90 with two 1,700-foot spans and steel truss members that are tubular in shape.

As the suspension bridge replaced the cantilever, the United States became the world leader in this type of long-span bridgebuilding. One reason was the peninsula sites of two of its major cities—New York and San Francisco. **John A. Roebling**'s greatest achievement was his design of the Brooklyn Bridge over the East River in New York City in 1883. In 1937 San Francisco's **Golden Gate Bridge** was completed with a span of 4,200 feet.

After World War II, bridges of note included the **Mackinac Bridge** (1957), linking the upper and lower peninsulas of Michigan; the **Verrazano-Narrows Bridge** (1964) connecting Brooklyn with Staten Island; and the **Akashi Kaikyo Bridge** (1998), bringing together the islands of Honshu and Shikoku, Japan.

World's Longest-Span Structures

Bridges

BRIDGE	LOCATION	YEAR OF COMPLETION	MAIN SPAN (M)
Steel suspension			
Akashi Strait	Kobe, Honshu–Awaji Island, Japan	1998	1,991
Store Bælt (Great Belt)	Zealand–Funen, Denmark	1998	1,624
Humber	near Hull, Humberside, UK	1981	1,410
Jiangyin	Jiangsu, China	1999	1,385
Tsing Ma	Hong Kong, China	1997	1,377
Verrazano-Narrows	New York NY	1964	1,298
Golden Gate	San Francisco CA	1937	1,280
Höga Kusten	Kramfors, Sweden	1997	1,210
Mackinac	Mackinaw City–St. Ignace MI	1957	1,158
Minami Bisan-Seto	Sakaide, Shikoku, Japan	1988	1,100
Bosphorus II (Fatih Sultan Mehmet)	Istanbul, Turkey	1988	1,090
Bosphorus I	Istanbul, Turkey	1973	1,074
George Washington	New York NY	1931	1,067
Kurushima-3	Onomichi–Imabari, Japan	1999	1,030
Kurushima-2	Onomichi–Imabari, Japan	1999	1,020
Ponte 25 de Abril (Salazar)	Lisbon, Portugal	1966	1,013
Forth Road	Queensferry, Scotland	1964	1,006
Kita Bisan-Seto	Kojima–Sakaide, Japan	1988	990
Severn	Bristol, UK	1966	988
Yicang	Hubei, China	2001	960
Cable-stayed			
Tatara Great	southern route Shikok–Honshu, Japan	1999	890
Normandie	near Le Havre, France	1995	856
Nancha	Nanjing, China	2001	628
Wuhan Baishazhou	Hubei, China	2000	618
Qingzhou Minjiang	Fuzhou, China	2001	605
Yangpu	Shanghai, China	1993	602
Xupu	Shanghai, China	1997	590
Meikouchuou (Meiko Central)	Nagoya, Japan	1998	590
Skarnsundet	near Trondheim, Norway	1991	530
Jueshi	Shantou, China	1998	518
Steel cantilever (steel truss)			
Pont de Québec	Quebec City, QC, Canada	1917	549
Forth (rail)	Queensferry, Scotland	1890	2 spans, each 521
Nanko (Minato)	Osaka–Amagasaki, Japan	1974	510
Commodore John J. Barry	Bridgeport NJ–Chester PA	1974	501
Greater New Orleans-1	New Orleans LA	1958	480
Steel arch			
New River Gorgec	Fayetteville WV	1977	518
Bayonne (Kill Van Kull)	Bayonne NJ–New York NY	1931	504
Sydney Harbour	Sydney, Australia	1932	503
Fremont	Portland OR	1973	383
Port Mann	Vancouver, BC, Canada	1964	366
Prestressed concrete cable-stayed			
Barrios de Luna	Cordillera, Spain	1983	440
Helgeland	Alsten Island, Norway	1991	425
Vasco da Gama	Lisbon, Portugal	1998	420
Clark	Alton IL	1994	415
Broward (Dame Point)	Jacksonville FL	1988	396
Reinforced concrete arch			
Wanxian	Sichuan, China	1997	425
Krk I	Krk Island, Croatia	1980	390
Jiangjiehe	Guizhou, China	1995	330
Yongning	Guangxi, China	1998	312
Gladesville	Sydney, Australia	1964	305

World's Longest-Span Structures (continued)

BRIDGE	LOCATION	YEAR OF COMPLETION	MAIN SPAN (M)
Steel span truss			
Ikitsuki Ohashi	Nagasaki Prefecture, Japan	1991	400
Astoria	Columbia River OR	1966	376
Francis Scott Key	Baltimore MD	1977	366
Oshima	Yanai City–Oshima, Japan	1976	325
Tenmon	Kumamoto, Japan	1966	984
Steel plate and box girder			
Presidente Costa e Silva	Rio de Janeiro–Niterói, Brazil	1974	300
Neckartalbrücke-1	Weitingen, Germany	1978	263
Sava I	Belgrade, Yugoslavia	1956	261
Ponte de Vitoria-3	Espírito Santo, Brazil	1989	260
Zoobrücke	Cologne, Germany	1966	259
Prestressed concrete cantilever (girder)			
Stolmasundet	Austevoll, Norway	1998	301
Raftsundet	Lofoten, Norway	1998	298
Sundoy	Nordland, Norway	2000	298
Boca Tigris-2	Humen, China	1997	270
Gateway	Brisbane, Australia	1986	260
Vertical lift (movable)[1]			
Arthur Kill	Elizabeth NJ	1959	170
Cape Cod Canal	Cape Cod MA	1935	166
Delair	Delair NJ	1960	165
Marine Parkway	New York NY	1937	165
Swing span (movable)			
Al-Firdan	Suez Canal, Egypt	2001	340
Mississippi River	Fort Madison IA	1927	160
Willamette River	Portland OR	1908	159
Missouri River	East Omaha NE	1903	158
Bascule (movable)			
South Capitol Street	Washington DC	1949	118
Sault Sainte Marie	Sault Sainte Marie MI–Ontario, Canada	1941	102
Erie Avenue	Lorain OH	1940	101
Tennessee River	Chattanooga TN	1917	94

Causeways[2]

CAUSEWAY	LOCATION	YEAR COMPLETED	LENGTH OF BRIDGE (M)	LENGTH OF BRIDGE (MI)	TYPE
Lake Pontchartrain-2	Metairie–Mandeville LA	1969	38,422	23.9	precast prestressed concrete
Lake Pontchartrain-1	Metairie–Mandeville LA	1956	38,352	23.8	precast prestressed concrete
Chesapeake Bay Bridge-Tunnel[3]	Virginia Beach–Northhampton VA	1964, 1999	28,324	17.6	steel trestle
King Fahd Causeway	Bahrain–Saudi Arabia	1986	24,950	15.5	precast prestressed concrete
Sunshine Skyway	St. Petersburg–Bradenton FL	1987	24,500	15.2	prestressed concrete cable-stayed
Vasco da Gama	Lisbon, Portugal	1998	17,190	10.7	prestressed concrete cable-stayed
Øresund Link	Øresund, Sweden–Copenhagen, Denmark	2000	16,400	10.0	cable-stayed
Presidente Costa e Silva	Rio de Janeiro–Niterói, Brazil	1974	13,900	8.6	steel plate and box girder
Pinang	Pinang Island–Perai, Malaysia	1985	13,800	8.6	cable-stayed concrete girder
Chesapeake Bay[3]	Sandy Point–Stevensville MD	1952, 1973	12,900	8.0	steel trestle
Confederation Bridge	Borden-Carleton, PE–Cape Jourimain, NB, Canada	1997	12,900	8.0	precast concrete box girder

[1]Excludes railway bridges.   [2]In possible conjunction with any combination of bridges, tunnels, viaducts, and trestles. Bridges listed here may also be listed elsewhere.   [3]Two bridges.

Roads

A road is the traveled way on which people, animals, or wheeled vehicles move. The term street implies an urban roadway, boulevard denotes a broad landscaped road, and highway suggests a high-speed or heavily traveled route, with controlled points of entrance and exit. Thruway, expressway, motorway, tollway, and freeway are variations of highway.

The earliest roads developed from paths and trails and appeared with the invention of wheeled vehicles, around 3000 BC. Road systems developed to facilitate trade in early civilizations. The Persian Royal Road, the first major road, extended 1,775 miles (2,857 km) from the Persian Gulf to the Aegean Sea and was used c. 3500–300 BC.

The Romans used roads to maintain control of their empire, with over 53,000 miles (85,000 km) of roadways extending across its lands. Their roads were often several feet thick, characteristically straight, and composed of layers of flintlike lava, gravel mixed with lime, flat stones, and sand or mortar—all stacked on a graded soil foundation. Roman construction techniques and design remained the most advanced until the late 1700s.

In the 19th century, invention of macadam road construction provided a quick and durable method for building roads, and asphalt and concrete also began to be used. The widespread use of bicycles created a demand for roads with smoother surfaces. New types of pavement were developed, in both flexible and rigid varieties.

Motorized traffic in the 20th century led to the limited-access highway, the first of which was the Bronx River Parkway in New York City (1925). In the 1930s superhighways also appeared in Italy, as the autostrada, and in Germany, as the autobahn. Military use was an important design feature of these highways, which could accommodate heavy traffic at high speeds. In the 1950s the US interstate highway system was inaugurated to link the country's major cities. It included toll roads, for which users pay in increments while traveling on them.

In industrialized nations, roadway planners must account for existing traffic congestion, future traffic needs, and the effects of urban sprawl, in addition to the measures of affordability, quality, and project duration. Engineers must consider material durability, local climatic conditions, drainage patterns, and safety improvements, such as reflective markings, rumble strips, guardrails, and crash cushions.

Notable Tunnels

A tunnel is a horizontal underground or underwater passageway, generally produced by excavation. Tunnels are used for mining, as passageways for trains and motor vehicles, for diverting rivers around damsites, for housing underground installations such as power plants and military bases, and for conducting water.

When natural obstacles—such as mountains, hills, or rivers—block the path proposed for a railway, highway, or pipeline, engineers bore tunnels through or under the obstacles. Structures built as trenches and later covered are also often called tunnels. A tunnel that carries water from reservoirs to cities for drinking and irrigation is an aqueduct, while those transporting water-borne freight through hillsides are canals. Mass-transit railway tunnels constructed under cities to relieve crowded streets are known as subways.

Excavation of a drift, or horizontal shaft, can begin from a hill or mountain slope, in which case the entrance is called a portal. Work can also begin from a vertical shaft, in which workers and equipment are raised and lowered and out of which rubble or muck is removed. All tunnels need some form of ventilation to supply air to workers and, later, to traffic. Ventilation also draws out potentially dangerous fumes from blasting or from gas deposits and prevents temperatures from getting too high. Tunnels can be divided into four general categories, depending on the material through which they pass: soft ground, solid rock, soft rock, and under water.

Tunneling in soft ground

Soft-ground tunnels are generally shallow and are often built for use as subways, water-supply systems, and sewers. Excavation in soft ground is much easier than it is in solid rock, but the stand-up time—that is, the time an excavated section will safely stand up without support—is very short. To prevent the tunnel from collapsing, a support structure is continuously built around the heading, or excavation face. A circular or arch-shaped design has been found to be the best at bearing the ground load from above. Brick and stone were used for support in early tunnels, but in modern tunneling steel is generally used to provide temporary support until a concrete lining can be installed.

Soft-soil excavation can be accomplished by a number of methods, from simple hand mining with shovel and pickax to full-face boring with sophisticated machinery. One such device, the tunneling mole, utilizes a rotating wheel set with teeth that continuously excavates material and loads it onto a conveyor belt. When the ground being excavated is extremely soft or a tunnel of large diameter is being constructed, it is sometimes necessary to use what is called the multiple-drift method: a number of small, parallel drifts are bored and connected to create the sides and crown, or top, of the tunnel; the core can then be safely excavated.

Soft-ground tunnels can be built under rivers or in water-bearing strata by using a tunneling shield. The problem of tunneling under a river had defied the engineering imagination for centuries because of the difficulty of preventing mud and water from seeping in and causing the tunnel to collapse. In 1818 Marc Isambard Brunel, a former French naval officer who had immigrated to England, observed the action of a tiny marine borer, the shipworm. The animal's shell plates permitted it to bore through timber and push the sawdust out behind it. Brunel built a giant iron casing, or shield, that could be pushed forward through soft ground by means of screw jacks, while miners dug through shutter openings in the face.

Brunel's rectangular shield was used successfully in driving the world's first underwater tunnel beneath the River Thames in London in 1825–42. Later improvements on Brunel's shield included that of Peter Barlow in 1865, perfected by James Henry Greathead to burrow under the Thames. In the 1880s Greathead used compressed air behind a shield in a

London subway tunnel to prevent flooding while the lining was being installed. Modern tunneling shields are essentially the same as the Greathead design—that is, strong steel cylinders shoved forward by hydraulic jacks.

Tunneling through rock

Although tunnels through solid rock can be excavated at only about half the rate of tunnels through soft earth, rock bores have much longer stand-up times. If a tunnel is pushed through unfractured blocks, it may need little or no additional support. Tunnelers, however, must be able to change their method of tunneling quickly to suit the conditions. Jointed rock exists in much larger sections and may not settle or shift for several days. Rock bolts, which are rods driven into the joints and kept under tension with nuts, provide extra support.

The introduction of gunpowder blasting in the 17th century marked a great advance in solid-rock excavation. Railroad and, later, motor-vehicle transportation in the 19th–20th centuries led to a tremendous expansion in the number and length of tunnels. Brick and stone were used for support in early tunnels, but in modern tunneling steel is generally used until a concrete lining can be installed. A common method of lining involves spraying a cement mixture called shotcrete onto the tunnel crown immediately after excavation. A permanent shield can then be built by thickening the concrete lining; steel ribs can be used for additional support.

The problem of water inflow can occur in any type of tunneling operation; it is a constant danger during the construction of underwater tunnels. An early solution involved using a pressurized excavation chamber that held back incoming water. Alternative methods include the construction of drainage tunnels and the use of prefabricated sections that can be floated into position, sunk, and attached to other sections.

History

Ancient civilizations used tunnels to divert water for consumption and farming, and cave dwellers cut short passageways through clay or soft rock to connect adjacent caves or burrow into the sides of hills. In about 2180–60 BC the Babylonians built a tunnel for pedestrian traffic under the Euphrates River. An early Greek tunnel was completed in 687 BC on the island of Samos as part of an aqueduct system.

Initial tunnel-building techniques varied. The Egyptians used copper saws that were capable of cutting soft rock, while the Babylonians constructed masonry tunnels. The Romans built aqueduct tunnels through mountains by heating the rock face with fire and rapidly cooling it with water, causing the rock to crack.

Their greatest feat was a 3.5-mile (5.6-kilometer) tunnel to drain Lake Fucino in Italy to create Fucino Basin.

The first tunnel that can rightly be called modern was built near Malpas, France, as part of the Canal du Midi, or Languedoc Canal. More than 500 feet (150 meters) long, the tunnel was completed in the late 1600s. The Union Canal Tunnel in Pennsylvania, several hundred miles long and completed in 1826, is the oldest existing transportation tunnel in the US. The Hoosac Tunnel, drilled for a railroad through the Berkshire Mountains in Massachusetts in 1851–75, contributed advances in tunneling, including the first use of nitroglycerin as a blasting agent, the first use of electric firing of explosives, and the introduction of power drills—initially steam and later air, from which there ultimately developed a compressed-air industry.

Simultaneously, more spectacular railroad tunnels were being started through the Alps, beginning with the Mont Cenis Tunnel (1857–71). Its engineer, Germain Sommeiller, introduced pioneering techniques such as rail-mounted drill carriages, hydraulic ram air compressors, and construction camps for workers. Subsequent Alpine railroad tunnels were the 9-mile St. Gotthard (1872–82), the 12-mile Simplon (1898–1906), and the 9-mile Lötschberg (1906–11). Nearly 7,000 feet below the mountain crest, Simplon encountered major problems from highly stressed rock bursting off the walls; from high pressure in weak schists and gypsum, requiring 10-foot-thick masonry lining to resist swelling; and from high-temperature water (130 °F [54 °C]), which was partly treated by spraying from cold springs. Driving Simplon as two parallel tunnels with frequent crosscut connections considerably aided ventilation and drainage. The Mont Blanc Tunnel, which links France and Italy through the Alps, was at its opening in 1965 the world's longest vehicular tunnel.

Other tunnels of note include the Cascade Tunnel (1925–29) in Washington, at 7.8 miles (12.5 km) in length, and the Kanmon Tunnel (1936–44), connecting the Japanese islands of Honshu and Kyushu—the first tunnel built under an ocean. The Seikan Tunnel (1964–88) links Honshu to Hokkaido and is the longest tunnel in the world, with a length of 33.5 miles (53.9 km). A series of passageways, extending the Italian high-speed railway system through the Apennine Range between Bologna and Florence, Italy, is projected to top Seikan as the world's longest, with 41 miles (66 km) of tunnel scheduled to be driven by 2006. One of the most famous tunnels, opened in 1994, is the Eurotunnel, or Channel Tunnel (or Chunnel), a 31-mile (50-kilometer) route beneath the English Channel, connecting Folkstone, England, with Calais, France.

World's Longest Tunnels

TUNNEL	LOCATION	COMPLETED	KM	MI	USE
Seikan	Japan	1988	53.9	33.5	railway
Channel Tunnel	United Kingdom–France	1994	50.0	31.1	railway
Laerdal	Norway	2000	24.5	15.3	highway
Daishimizu	Japan	1982	22.2	13.8	railway
Simplon II	Italy–Switzerland	1922	19.8	12.3	railway
Simplon I	Italy–Switzerland	1906	19.8	12.3	railway
Shin-Kanmon	Japan	1975	18.7	11.6	railway
Apennine	Italy	1934	18.5	11.5	railway
Qinling	China	2001	18.7	11.5	railway
Saint Gotthard	Switzerland	1980	16.3	10.1	highway
Rokko	Japan	1971	16.3	10.1	railway

World's Longest Tunnels (continued)

TUNNEL	LOCATION	COMPLETED	KM	MI	USE
Henderson	Colorado	1975	15.8	9.8	railway
Haruna	Japan	1982	15.4	9.6	railway
Furka	Switzerland	1981	15.3	9.5	railway
Saint Gotthard	Switzerland	1882	15.0	9.3	railway
Nakayama	Japan	1982	14.9	9.2	railway
Lötschberg	Switzerland	1913	14.6	9.1	railway
Mount MacDonald	British Columbia	1988	14.6	9.1	railway
Ta-yao Shan	China	1988	14.3	8.9	railway
Arlberg	Austria	1978	14.0	8.7	highway
Hokuriku	Japan	1962	13.9	8.6	railway
Mont Cenis	France–Italy	1871	13.7	8.5	railway
Shin-Shimizu	Japan	1967	13.5	8.4	railway
Aki	Japan	1973	13.0	8.1	railway
Fréjus	France–Italy	1980	12.9	8.0	highway
Cascade	Washington	1929	12.5	7.8	railway
Flathead	Montana	1970	12.5	7.8	railway
Kita-Kyushu	Japan	1975	11.7	7.3	railway
Mont Blanc	France–Italy	1965	11.7	7.3	highway

World's Largest Dams

Source: International Water Power and Dam Construction Handbook (1992).

NAME	TYPE*	DATE OF COMPLETION	RIVER	COUNTRY	
by height					**height (m)**
Rogun	ER	N/A	Vakhsh	Tajikistan	335
Ching-p'ing	EG	N/A	Ya-Lung	China	314
Nurek	E	1980	Vakhsh	Tajikistan	300
Hsiao-wang	ER	N/A	Mekong	China	296
Grand Dixence	G	1961	Dixence	Switzerland	285
Lung-t'an	RCC	N/A	Hung-shui	China	285
Inguri	A	1980	Inguri	Georgia	272
Boruca	ER	N/A	Terraba	Costa Rica	267
Vaiont[2]	A	1961	Vaiont	Italy	262
Pancheswor	G	N/A	Kali	Nepal	262
Chicoasen	ER	1980	Grijalva	Mexico	261
Tehri	ER	1995[1]	Bhagirathi	India	261
					volume ('000 cubic m)
by volume					
Syncrude Tailings	E	N/A	...[3]	Canada	540,000
Chapeton	EG	N/A	Parana	Argentina	296,200
Pati	EG	N/A	Parana	Argentina	238,180
New Cornelia Tailings	E	1973	Ten Mile Wash	US	209,500
Kambaratinsk	ER	N/A	Naryn	Kyrgyzstan	112,200
Tarbela	ER	1976	Indus	Pakistan	106,000
Fort Peck	E	1937	Missouri	US	96,050
Lower Usuma	E	1990	Usuma	Nigeria	93,000
Cipasang	ER	N/A	Cimanuk	Indonesia	90,000
Ataturk	ER	1990	Euphrates	Turkey	84,500
Guri	EGR	1986	Caroni	Venezuela	77,971
Rogun	ER	N/A	Vakhsh	Tajikistan	71,000
					reservoir capacity ('000 cubic m)
by size of reservoir					
Owen Falls	G	1954	Victoria Nile	Uganda	2,700,000,000[4]
Kakhovsk	EG	1955	Dnieper	Ukraine	182,000,000
Kariba	A	1959	Zambezi	Zimbabwe-Zambia	180,600,000
Bratsk	EG	1964	Angara	Russia	169,270,000
Aswan High	ER	1970	Nile	Egypt	168,900,000
Akosombo	ER	1965	Volta	Ghana	148,000,000
Daniel Johnson	M	1968	Manicouagan	Canada	141,852,000
Guri	EGR	1986	Caroni	Venezuela	138,000,000
Krasnoyarsk	G	1967	Yenisey	Russia	73,300,000
Bennett, W.A.C.	E	1967	Peace	Canada	70,309,000
Zeya	B	1978	Zeya	Russia	68,400,000
Cabora Bassa	A	1974	Zambezi	Mozambique	63,000,000

World's Largest Dams (continued)

NAME by power capacity	TYPE*	DATE OF COMPLETION	RIVER	COUNTRY	planned power capacity (megawatts)
Turukhansk	EG	N/A	Lower Tunguska	Russia	20,000
Three Gorges	G	N/A	Yangtze	China	17,680
Itaipu	EGR	1982	Parana	Brazil-Paraguay	12,600
Grand Coulee	G	1941	Columbia	US	10,830
Gurl	EGR	1986	Caroni	Venezuela	10,300
Tucurui	EGR	1984	Tocantins	Brazil	7,960
Corpus Christi	EG	N/A	Parana	Argentina-Paraguay	6,900
Sayano-Shushensk	GA	1989	Yenisey	Russia	6,400[5]
Krasnoyarsk	G	1967	Yenisey	Russia	6,000[5]
Churchill Falls	E	1971	Churchill	Canada	5,428
La Grande 2	R	1978	LaGrande	Canada	5,328
Xingo	ER	1994[1]	Sao Francisco	Brazil	5,020

*Key: A, arch; B, buttress; E, earth fill; G, gravity; M, multi-arch; R, rock fill; RCC, roller-compacted-concrete. [1]Estimated year of completion.   [2]Valont Dam was severely damaged by a massive landslide in 1963 and no longer operates.   [3]Near Fort McMurray AB.   [4]Most of this reservoir is a natural lake.   [5]Planned and actual power capacity.

Lighthouses: Illuminating Facts

A lighthouse is a structure, usually with a tower, built onshore or on the seabed to signal danger or to help those on ships determine location. Lighthouses have been built for centuries in areas where naval or commercial vessels sail. They have guided marine navigators through busy and often tortuous coastal waters and harbor approaches. Lighthouses were intially manned by lighthouse keepers, who lived in or nearby the structure in order to keep the light shining. Most modern lighthouses, however, have automatic lights that need little tending.

History

The first known lighthouse was built on the island of Pharos, near Alexandria, Egypt, about 280 BC. It was regarded as one of the seven wonders of the ancient world. The modern lighthouse dates only from the early 18th century. Initially made of wood, these towers were often washed away in severe storms.

The first lighthouse made of interlocking masonry blocks was built on the treacherous Eddystone Rocks reef, off Plymouth, England. Celebrated in ballad and folklore, it endured four successive constructions: in timber (1696–99), until it was swept out to sea in 1703; in oak and iron (1708), until it was destroyed by fire in 1755; in interlocking stone (1756–59), until its foundation deteriorated; and again in stone (1882). Interlocking masonry blocks remained the principal material of construction until they were replaced by concrete and steel in the 20th century.

Lighthouse construction

Modern construction techniques have facilitated the building of lighthouses in the open sea. On soft ground, the submerged caisson method is used, a system applied first in the late 19th century in Germany and the United States. With this method a large steel caisson is sunk deep into the seabed, then pumped dry and filled with concrete to form a solid base on which the lighthouse proper is built. Where the seabed is suitable, it is possible to build a float-out lighthouse, consisting of a cylindrical tower—constructed on shore, towed out to sea, and sunk into position—with a broad concrete base that is fillled with sand. This design was pioneered largely in Sweden.

Another design, which is more independent of seabed conditions, is the conventional steel-piled structure used for offshore oil and gas rigs. Piles may be driven as deep as 46 m (150 ft) into the seabed, depending on the underlying strata. Helicopters are widely employed in the servicing and maintenance of offshore towers, so that modern designs normally include a helipad.

Lighthouse illumination

Historically illuminants included wood fires, discontinued c. 1800, and coal, begun c. 1550. In 1782 Swiss scientist Aimé Argand invented an oil lamp with a steady smokeless flame. It had a circular wick with a glass chimney that ensured an adequate current of air up the center and the outside of the wick for even combustion of the oil. These lamps originally burned fish oil, later vegetable oil, and by 1860 mineral oil. The Argand lamp became the principal lighthouse illuminant for more than 100 years. In 1901 the Briton Arthur Kitson invented the vaporized oil burner, which was subsequently improved by David Hood of Trinity House and others. This burner utilized kerosene vaporized under pressure, mixed with air, and burned to heat an incandescent mantle.

Early proposals to use coal gas at lighthouses did not meet with great success. However, acetylene gas, generated in situ from calcium carbide and water and safe to compress for storage, was pioneered by Gustaf Dalén of Sweden between 1900 and 1910. Its great advantage was that it could be readily controlled; thus, for the first time automatic unattended lights were possible. Its main use today is in buoys, which inherently have to operate unattended. Floating lights (i.e., lightships and buoys) have an important function in coastal waters, guiding both passing ships and those making for or leaving harbor.

Liquefied petroleum gas, such as propane, has also found use as an illuminant, although both oil and gas lamps have largely been superseded by electricity. Electric illumination in the form of carbon arc lamps was first employed at Dungeness, England, in 1862, even while oil lamps were still in vogue. The electric-filament lamp, which came into general use in the 1920s, is now the standard illuminant. Most lamps are of the **tungsten-halogen** type for better efficiency and longer life.

Optical equipment

With the advent of the **Argand lamp**, a reliable and steady illuminant, it became possible to develop effective optical apparatuses for increasing the intensity of the light. In the first equipment of this type, known as the **catoptric system**, paraboloidal reflectors concentrated the light into a beam. In 1777 William Hutchinson of Liverpool, England, produced the first practical mirrors for lighthouses. The first revolving-beam lighthouse was at Carlsten, near Marstrand, Sweden, in 1781.

In 1828 Augustin Fresnel of France produced the first apparatus using the refracting properties of glass, now known as the **dioptric system**. On a lens panel he surrounded a central bull's-eye lens with a series of concentric glass prismatic rings. The panel collected light emitted by the lamp over a wide horizontal angle and also the light that would otherwise escape to the sky or to the sea, concentrating

it into a narrow, horizontal pencil beam, which he later expanded to be several revolving beams and then a fixed all-around light. Thus emerged the full **Fresnel catadioptric system**, the basis of all lighthouse lens systems today, although many have been converted to electric lamps with electric-motor drives.

Other innovations

The limitations of purely visual navigation very early led to the idea of supplementary audible warning in lighthouses. Early **sound signals** included cannonfire and bells, but at the beginning of the 20th century, **compressed-air** fog signals, which sounded a series of blasts, were developed. The most widely used were the siren and the diaphone. A later compressed-air signal was the tyfon, employing a metal diaphragm vibrated by differential air pressure. Modern fog signals are almost invariably electric.

Radio and **satellite-based** navigation systems have greatly reduced the need for large lighthouses in sighting land.

Notable Civil Engineering Projects (in progress or completed, as of December 2001)

1 sq m = 1.196 sq ft; 1 m = 3.28 ft; 1 km = 0.62 mi; 1 ha = 2.47 ac

NAME	LOCATION	YEAR OF COMPLETION	NOTES
airports		Terminal Area (sq m)	
Incheon International (new airport)	Incheon (Inchon), South Korea	369,000 / 2001	landfill between islands; opened 22 Mar 2001
Guangzhou International	Guangzhou (Canton), China	300,000 / 2002	new replacement airport
Pearson International	Toronto ON	332,000 / 2003	new horseshoe-shaped terminal at Canada's busiest airport
Athens International	Spata, Greece	209,000 / 2001	Europe's biggest airport project; opened 28 Mar 2001
JFK International	Queens NY	139,000 / 2001	new Terminal 4; opened 24 May 2001
Nong Ngu Hao	Bangkok, Thailand	? / 2004	new international airport; construction began December 2001
aqueduct		Length (m)	
Great Man-Made River (phase 2)	Libyan interior to Tripoli area	1,650,000 / 2001	phase 1 to Benghazi area (1983–93); phase 2 begun 1990
bridges		Length (main span; m)	
Carquinez (#3)	Crockett CA–Vallejo CA	728 / 2003	begun 2000; first major US suspension bridge since 1965
Rion Antirion	Patrai, Greece (across Gulf of Corinth)	560 / 2004	multicable-stayed; complex deepwater foundations
San Francisco–Oakland Bay (East Span)	Yerba Buena Island CA–Oakland CA	385 / 2006	2-km causeway plus world's largest suspension bridge hung from single tower
William Natcher	Owensboro KY–near Rockport IN	366 / 2002	to be longest cable-stayed bridge over US inland waterway
Rosario–Victoria	Rosario to Victoria, Argentina	350 / 2002	bridges/viaducts across 59-km-wide Paraná wetlands
Millau Viaduct	Tarn Gorge, west of Millau, France	342 / 2004	8 cable-stayed spans; world's highest (285 m) road viaduct

Notable Civil Engineering Projects (in progress or completed, as of December 2001) (continued)

NAME	LOCATION		YEAR OF COMPLETION	NOTES
bridges (continued)		Length (main span; m)		
Leonard P. Zakim Bunker Hill	Boston MA	227	2002	widest (56 m) cable-stayed bridge in world
Maria Valeria (cross-Danube link)	Esztergom, Hungary–Sturovo, Slovakia	119	2001	replication of 106-year-old bridge destroyed in 1944; opened 11 Oct 2001
Kizuna	Mekong River, near Kampong Cham, Cambodia	?	2001	first bridge across Mekong in Cambodia; opened 4 Dec 2001
buildings		Height (m)		
Lotte World Tower	Busan (Pusan), South Korea	464.5	2005	begun December 2000; will be world's tallest
Taipei Financial Center	Taipei, Taiwan	448	2003	begun 1999; will be world's 2nd tallest to rooftop (with spire, 508 m)
Two International Finance Centre	Hong Kong, China	412	2003	begun 2000; to be world's 4th tallest building
Plaza Rakyat	Kuala Lumpur, Malaysia	382	2002	will be tallest reinforced–concrete complex; 7th tallest overall
Migdal (Tower) Egged	Tel Aviv, Israel	326	2006	begun 2001
Trump World Tower	New York NY	262	2001	tallest residential development in the world
Torre Generali	Panama City, Panama	250	2003	begun mid-2000; will be Latin America's tallest building
City Tower	Birmingham, England	245	2004	will be tallest building in the UK
Torre Mayor	Mexico City, Mexico	225	2003	will be tallest building in Mexico
canal		Length (m)		
Sheikh Zayed	into bedrock of Lake Nasser, Egypt	72,000	2002	feeds irrigation system for central Egypt oases
dams		Crest length (m)		
Birecik Dam	Euphrates River, Turkey	2,507	2001	first major hydroelectric plant in Turkey
Three Gorges	west of Yichang, China	1,983	2009	world's largest hydroelectric project; begun 1993
San Roque Multipurpose	Agno River, Luzon, Philippines	1,100	2003	irrigation and flood control; tallest earth-and-rock fill dam in Asia
Mohale (Lesotho Highlands Water Project, phase 1B)	Senqunyane River, 100 km east of Maseru	700	2002	first transfer of water to South Africa in 1998, second transfer in 2003
Sardar Sarovar Project	Narmada River, Madhya Pradesh, India	?	?	construction halted 1995, resumed 2000
Alqueva Dam	Guadiana River, 180 km SE of Lisbon, Portugal	?	2002	will create Europe's largest (250 sq km) reservoir; extends into Spain
Bakun Dam	Balui River, Sarawak, Borneo, Malaysia	?	2006	hydroelectricity to peninsular Malaysia via world's longest submarine cable
highways		Length (km)		
Indus Highway	Karachi–Peshawar, Pakistan	1,265	?	59% complete as of September 2001
Beijing–Shanghai Expressway or "Jinghu"	Beijing–Shanghai, China	1,262	2000	opened late December 2001
Egnatia Motorway	Ignoumenitsa–Thessaloniki, Greece	687	2006	first Greek highway at modern international standards; 70 tunnels
railways (Heavy)		Length (km)		
Qinghai–Tibet	Golmud, Qinghai, China–Lhasa, Tibet, China	1,118	2007	highest world rail (5,072 m at summit); half built across permafrost

Notable Civil Engineering Projects (in progress or completed, as of December 2001) (continued)

NAME	LOCATION	YEAR OF COMPLETION	NOTES
railways (Heavy) (continued)		**Length (km)**	
Guangdong–Hainan	Zhangjiang, China, to northern tip of Hainan	568	2001	rail with container terminal
Panama Canal	Cristóbal–Balboa, Panama	89	2001	rebuilt railroad for transcontinental container traffic
Kyongui (51-year-old reconnection)	Munsan, South Korea– Kaesong, North Korea	24	2002?	6.8 km South Korean part complete as of September 2001
railways (High Speed)		**Length (km)**	
Spanish High Speed (second line)	Madrid–Barcelona, Spain	760	2004	Madrid–Lleida to be completed by 2002
Kyongbu	Seoul–Busan (Pusan), South Korea	323	2003	connects largest and 3rd largest cities
TGV Méditerranée	Valence–Marseille, France (branch to Montpellier)	249	2001	completes high-speed rail across France ("Calais to Marseille")
German High Speed (third line)	Frankfurt–Cologne, Germany	226	2002	connects Ruhr to Frankfurt International Airport
Italian High Speed (second line)	Rome–Naples, Italy	222	2004	begun 1994; part of planned 1,300-km high-speed network
Shanghai maglev ("magnetic levitation")	Pudong International airport–metro line 2, Shanghai, China	29.9	2003	world's first maglev train for public use; will travel at 430 km/h
subways/Metros/ Light Rails		**Length (km)**	
Oporto Light Rail	Oporto, Portugal	70	2003	Europe's largest total rail system project; first line opened in 2001
Hong Kong Railway (West Rail, phase 1)	Western New Territories to Kowloon, Hong Kong	30.3	2003	5,500-m tunnel and viaduct
Los Angeles Metro (Blue Line ext.)	L.A. Union Station to Pasadena CA	22	2003	
Copenhagen Metro	Copenhagen, Denmark	21	2002–05	first line to open in 2002; most extensive driverless system in world
Tren Urbano (phase 1)	San Juan PR	17.2	2003	Bayamón (western suburbs) to north San Juan; 60% elevated
Istanbul Metro (phase 2)	Istanbul, Turkey	5.4	2001	bridge link across Golden Horn; extends under historic city center
tunnels		**Length (m)**	
Apennine Range tunnels (9)	Bologna–Florence, Italy (high-speed railway)	66,000	2006	begun 1996; longest tunnel is 18.6 km; tunnels to cover 90% of railway
Qinling	between Xi'an and Ankang, China	18,457	2001	world's 9th largest railway tunnel
A86 Ring Road	around Paris, France	17,700	2008	two tunnels (to east [10,100 m], to west [7,600 m])
Södra Länken	part of Stockholm, Sweden, ring road	16,600	2004	complex underground interchanges
Pinglin Highway	near Taipei, Taiwan	12,900	2003	twin tunnels under Sheuhshan Range; Taipei-I-lan expressway link
Westerschelde	Terneuzen to Ellewoutsdijk, Netherlands	6,600	2003	World's longest tunnel in "bored weak soil"
Vestmannasund Subsea Tunnel	Streym (Streymoy) and Vágar Islands, Faroe Islands	4,700	2002	first subsea tunnel in the Faroe Islands

Notable Civil Engineering Projects (in progress or completed, as of December 2001) (continued)

NAME	LOCATION	YEAR OF COMPLETION	NOTES
Urban Developments		Area (ha)	
Putrajaya	25 km south of Kuala Lumpur, Malaysia	4,581	planned national capital begun 1996; first staff moved in June 1999
Central Artery/Tunnel	Boston MA	N/A	2004	complex highway/tunnel/ bridge project begun in 1991

Life on Earth

Animals

Notable Venomous Animals

REPRESENTATIVE VENOMOUS ANIMALS THAT INFLICT A STING

Marine animals

cone shell (*Conus* species; tropical Indo-Pacific region): quaternary ammonium compounds and others (blanching at site of injection, cyanosis of surrounding area, numbness, stinging or burning sensation, blurred vision, loss of speech, difficulty swallowing, nausea, extreme weakness, coma, death in some cases; no specific antidote)

crown-of-thorns starfish (*Acanthaster planci*; Indo-Pacific): unknown (penetration of spines produces a painful wound, redness, swelling, vomiting, numbness, and paralysis)

long-spined sea urchin (*Diadema setosum*; Indo-Pacific): unknown (penetration of spines produces an immediate and intense burning sensation, redness, swelling, numbness, muscular paralysis)

Portuguese man-of-war (*Physalia* species; tropical seas): tetramine, 5-hydroxytryptamine (immediate stinging, throbbing, or burning sensation; inflammatory rash; blistering; shock; collapse; death in very rare cases)

scorpion fish (*Scorpaena* species; temperate and tropical seas): unknown (fin spines can inflict painful stings and intense, immediate pain, followed by redness, swelling, loss of consciousness, ulceration of the wound, paralysis, cardiac failure, delirium, convulsions, nausea, prostration, and respiratory distress, but rarely death; no known antidote)

sea anemone (*Actinia equina*; Mediterranean, Black Sea, etc.): unknown (burning or stinging sensation, itching, swelling, redness, ulceration, nausea, vomiting, prostration; no specific antidote)

sea urchin (*Toxopneustes pileolus*; Indo-Pacific): unknown (bites from stinging jaws or small pincerlike organs produce an immediate, intense, radiating pain, faintness, numbness, muscular paralysis, respiratory distress, and occasionally death)

sea wasp (*Chironex fleckeri*; northern and northeast Australia): cardiotoxin (immediate and extremely painful stinging sensation, seared reddened lines wherever tentacles touched the skin, large in diameter lesions, prostration, dizziness, circulatory failure, respiratory distress, rapid death in a high percentage of cases)

spotted octopus (*Octopus maculosus*; Indo-Pacific, Indian Ocean): cephalotoxin, a neuromuscular poison (sharp stinging pain, numbness of mouth and tongue, blurred vision, loss of tactile sensation, difficulty in speech and swallowing, paralysis of legs, nausea, prostration, coma, death in a high percentage of cases)

stingray (*Dasyatis* species; warm temperate and tropical seas): cardiotoxin (penetration of tail spines inflicts jagged wounds that produce sharp, shooting, throbbing pain, fall in blood pressure, nausea, vomiting, cardiac failure, muscular paralysis, and rarely death; no known antidote; stingrays are among the most common causes of envenomizations in the marine environment)

stonefish (*Synanceja* species; Indo-Pacific region): unknown (produces an extremely painful sting by means of the dorsal fin spines; symptoms similar to other scorpion fish stings but more serious)

weever fish (*Trachinus draco*; Mediterranean Sea): unknown (penetration of opercular and dorsal fin spines can produce instant pain, burning, stabbing, or crushing sensation; pain spreads and becomes progressively more intense, causing victim to lose consciousness; numbness around the wound, swelling, redness, nausea, delirium, difficulty breathing, convulsions, and death; no known antidote)

Arthropods

kissing bug (*Triatoma* species; Latin America, US): unknown (bite usually painless; later itching, edema around the bite, nausea, palpitation, redness; the bite is of minor importance but spreads Chagas disease caused by a trypanosome)

puss caterpillar (*Megalopyge* species; US, Latin America): unknown (contact with hairs produces an intense burning pain, itching, pustules, redness, nausea, fever, numbness, swelling, and paralysis; recovery usually within six days)

honeybee (*Apis* species; worldwide): neurotoxin, hemolytic, melittin, hyaluronidase, phospholipase A, histamine, and others (acute local pain or burning sensation, blanching at site of sting surrounded by redness, and itching; local symptoms usually die away after 24 hours; severe cases may develop massive swelling, shock, prostration, vomiting, rapid heartbeat, respiratory distress, trembling, coma, and death; estimated that 500 stings in a short period of time can produce a lethal dose; bee stings kill more people in the US than do venomous reptiles)

bumblebee (*Bombus* species; temperate regions): similar to (*Apis*) honeybee venom (stings are similar to honeybee stings; bumblebees are not as vicious as honeybees)

yellow jacket, hornet (*Vespula* species; temperate regions): similar to bee venom; also acetylcholine (yellow jackets are quite aggressive and can both bite and sting; the sting is similar to a honeybee's but more painful and may be fatal)

wasp (*Polistes* and *Vespa* species; worldwide): similar to bee venom; also acetylcholine (wasps are less aggressive than hornets, and their stings are similar to the honeybee's but generally less painful than the hornet's; stings may be fatal)

harvester ant (*Pogonomyrmex* species; US): bradykinin, formic acid, hyaluronidase, hemolytic, phospholipase A, and others (immediate intense burning, pain, blanched area at site of sting surrounded by redness, ulceration, fever, blistering, itching, hemorrhaging into the skin, eczematoid dermatitis, pustules, respiratory distress, prostration, coma, and death in some instances)

fire ant (*Solenopsis* species; US, Latin America): similar to harvester ant venom (similar to harvester ant)

millipede (*Apheloria* species [and others]; temperate areas): hydrogen cyanide and benzaldehyde (toxic liquid or gas from lateral glands causes inflammation, swelling, and blindness in contact with eyes; brown stain, swelling, redness, and vesicle formation in contact with skin)

centipede (*Scolopendra* species; temperate and tropical regions): hemolytic phospholipase and serotonin (local pain, swelling, and redness at bite site)

brown spider (*Loxosceles* species; US, South America, Europe, Asia): cytotoxic, hyaluronidase, hemolytic, and others (bite causes stinging or burning, blanching at site of bite surrounded by redness, blistering, hemorrhaging into the skin and internal organs, ulceration, vomiting, fever, cardiovascular collapse, convulsions, and sometimes death)

black widow (*Latrodectus* species; tropical and temperate regions): neurotoxin (bite may be painful; two tiny red dots at site, localized swelling after a few minutes; intense cramping pain of abdomen, legs, chest, back; rigidity of muscles lasting 12–48 hours, nausea, sweating, respiratory distress, abnormal and painful erection of the penis, chills, skin rash, restlessness, fever, numbness, tingling; about 4% are fatal; antiserum is available)

tarantula (*Dugesiella* and *Lycosa* species; temperate and tropical regions): venom varies, usually mild (most of the large tarantulas found in the US, Mexico, and Central America are harmless to humans; some of the large tropical species may be more poisonous, but their effects are largely localized)

scorpion (species of *Centruroides, Tityus,* and *Leiurus*; warm temperate and tropical regions): neurotoxin, cardiotoxin, hemolytic, lecithinase, hyaluronidase, and others (symptoms vary depending upon species; sting from the tail causes a sharp burning sensation, swelling, sweating, restlessness, salivation, confusion, vomiting, abdominal pain, chest pain, numbness, muscular twitching, respiratory distress, convulsions, and often death; the mortality rate from certain species of scorpions is very high; antiserum is available)

Reptiles

Gila monster (*Heloderma suspectum*; southwestern US): heloderma venom, primarily a neurotoxin (all of the teeth are venomous; bite causes local pain, swelling, weakness, ringing of the ears, nausea, respiratory distress, and cardiac failure; may cause death; no antiserum available)

REPRESENTATIVE CRINOTOXIC ANIMALS (THOSE THAT RELEASE POISON THROUGH A PORE)

Sponges

red moss (*Microciona prolifera*; eastern US coastal waters): unknown (contact produces chemical irritation of the skin, redness, stiffness of finger joints, swelling, blisters, and pustules)

Flatworms

flatworm (*Leptoplana tremellaris*; European coastal waters): unknown (poison is produced by epidermal skin glands; no human intoxications recorded, but extracts from the skin injected into laboratory animals produces cardiac arrest)

Arthropods

blister beetles (*Cantharis vesicatorea*; US): cantharidin (toxic substance is found throughout the body of the beetle; no discomfort from initial contact; after about 8–10 hours large blisters on the skin accompanied by slight burning or tingling; swallowing of the beetles may cause kidney damage; cantharidin is used as an aphrodisiac known as Spanish Fly, a very dangerous substance; ingestion can cause severe gastroenteritis, kidney damage, blood in the urine, abnormal and painful erection of the penis, profound collapse, and death)

millipedes (species of *Orthoporus, Rhinocrichus, Julus,* and *Spirobolus*; temperate and tropical regions): unknown (a fluid distasteful to enemies may be exuded or forcefully squirted from body pores a distance of 76 cm [30 in] or more; contact with the skin induces mild to moderately intense burning pain, redness, and pigmentation of the skin; toxic fluid squirted in the eyes may cause temporary blindness, inflammation, and pain)

venomous ticks (species of *Ixodes* and *Ornithodoros*; temperate and tropical regions): unknown (bites result in swelling, redness, intense pain, headache, muscle cramps, loss of memory)

Fishes

sea lamprey (*Petromyzon marinus*; Atlantic Ocean): unknown (slime is toxic; ingestion may cause diarrhea)

soapfish (*Rypticus saponaceus*; tropical and subtropical Atlantic): neurotoxin (slime is toxic; produces irritation of the mucous membrane)

Amphibians

European earth salamander (*Salamandra maculosa*; Europe): skin glands are poisonous; contain the alkaloids samandarine, samandenone, samandine, samanine, samandarone, samandaridine, and others (effects on humans not known; affects the heart and nervous system; in animals causes convulsions, cardiac irregularity, paralysis, and death)

toads (*Bufo* species; temperate and tropical regions): bufotoxin, bufogenins, and 5-hydroxytryplanime; poison includes a complex of many substances (produces a poisonous secretion in parotid glands and skin; handling of some toads may cause skin irritation; ingestion causes nausea, vomiting, numbness of mouth and tongue, and tightness of chest; the poison has a digitalis-like action)

frogs (some species of *Dendrobates, Physalaemus,* and *Rana*; northern South America and Central

America): skin secretions are poisonous; hista-mine, bufotenine, physalaemin, serotonin, and other substances; composition varies with the species (secretions produce a burning sensation; used by indigenous peoples as an arrow poison)

tree frogs (some species of *Hyla* and *Phyllobates*; northern South American and Central America): skin secretions are poisonous; batrachotoxin, steroidal alkaloids, serotonin, histamine, and other sub-stances; bufotenine varies with the species (burning sensation and skin rash; skin secretions in the eye may produce a severe inflammatory reaction; if in-gested, poison causes vomiting and abdominal pain; batrachotoxin is extremely toxic if injected; used by indigenous peoples as an arrow poison)

SELECTED HIGHLY VENOMOUS SNAKES

inland taipan (*Oxyuranus microlepidotus*): Australia
eastern brown snake (*Pseudonaja textilis*): Australia
Malayan krait (*Bungarus candidus*): Southeast Asia and Indonesia
coastal taipan (*Oxyuranus scutellatus*): Australia
tiger snake (*Notechis scutatus*): Australia
beaked sea snake (*Enhydrina schistosa*): South Asian waters
saw-scaled viper (*Echis carinatus*): Middle East, Asia
eastern coral snake (*Micrurus fulvius*): North America
boomslang (*Dispholidus typus*): Africa
death adder (*Acanthophis antarcticus*): Australia and New Guinea

Period of Gestation and Longevity of Selected Mammals

ANIMAL	AVERAGE GESTATION (DAYS)	AVERAGE LONGEVITY (YEARS)	ANIMAL	AVERAGE GESTATION (DAYS)	AVERAGE LONGEVITY (YEARS)
bear (black)	219	18	horse	330	20
bear (grizzly)	225	25	human (worldwide)	266–70	Men: 64.7;
bear (polar)	240	20			Women: 68.9
cat (domestic)	63	12	monkey (rhesus)	164	15
dog (domestic)	61	12	mouse (domestic white)	19	3
elephant (Asian)	645	40	pig (domestic)	112	10
fox (red)	52	7	rabbit (domestic)	31	5
guinea pig	68	4	sheep (domestic)	154	12
hippopotamus	238	25–30	squirrel (gray)	44	9–10

Names of the Male, Female, Young, and Group of Animals

ANIMAL	MALE	FEMALE	YOUNG	GROUP
ape	male	female	baby	shrewdness
bear	boar	sow	cub	sleuth, sloth
camel	bull	cow	calf	flock
cattle	bull	cow	calf	drift, drove, herd, mob
chicken	rooster	hen	chick, pullet (hen), cockrell (rooster)	flock, brood (hens), clutch & peep (chicks)
deer	buck, stag	doe	fawn	herd
donkey	jack, jackass	jennet, jenny	colt, foal	drove, herd
elephant	bull	cow	calf	herd, parade
ferret	hob	jill	kit	business, fesynes
fox	reynard	vixen	kit, cub, pup	skulk, leash
giraffe	bull	doe	calf	herd, corps, tower, group
goat	buck, billy	doe, nanny	kid, billy	herd, tribe, trip
gorilla	male	female	infant	band
hamster	buck	doe	pup	horde
hippopotamus	bull	cow	calf	herd, bloat
horse	stallion, stud	mare, dam	foal, colt (male), filly (female)	stable, harras, herd, team (working) string or field (racing)
human	man	woman	baby, infant, toddler	clan (related), crowd, family (closely related), community, gang, mob, tribe, etc.
lion	lion	lioness	cub	pride
louse	male	female	nymph	lice, colony, infestation
mouse	buck	doe	pup, pinkie, kitten	horde, mischief
ostrich	cock	hen	chick	flock
pig	boar	sow	piglet, shoat, farrow	drove, herd, litter (of pups), sounder
quail	cock	hen	chick	bevy, covey, drift
rhinoceros	bull	cow	calf	crash
seal	bull	cow	pup	herd, pod, rookery, harem
sheep	buck, ram	ewe, dam	lamb, lambkin, cosset	drift, drove, flock, herd, mob, trip
turkey	tom	hen	poult	rafter
turtle	male	female	hatchling	bale
whale	bull	cow	calf	gam, grind, herd, pod, school
wolf	dog	bitch	pup, whelp	pack, rout
zebra	stallion	mare	colt, foal	herd, crossing

Plants

Notable Medicinal Plants

Source: <http://world.std.com/~krahe/html1.html>; <www.hort.purdue.edu/newcrop/med-aro/toc.html>

PLANT	NATIVE REGION	MAIN PROPERTIES (USES)
angelica	Europe	antispasmodic, promotes menstrual flow
basil (holy basil)	India	antispasmodic, analgesic, fungicidal, lowers blood pressure, lowers blood sugar, reduces fever, anti-inflammatory
chamomile	Europe, Western Asia, North America, Africa	anti-inflammatory, antispasmodic, relaxant, carminative, bitter, nervine
chicory	Europe	digestive, liver tonic, anti-rheumatic, mild laxative
cinnamon	Sri Lanka	warming stimulant, carminative, antispasmodic, antiseptic, anti-viral
coriander	Europe, Mediterranean	digestive, antispasmodic, anti-rheumatic
cymbopogon (lemon grass)	Sri Lanka, south India	digestive, antispasmodic, analgesic
dandelion	Asia	diuretic, digestive, antibiotic, bitter
eucalyptus	Australia	antiseptic, expectorant, stimulates local blood flow, anti-fungal
fennel	Mediterranean	digestive, antispasmodic, anti-inflammatory
garlic	Central Asia	antibiotic, expectorant, diaphoretic, hypotensive, antispasmodic, expels worms
ginger	Southeast Asia	diaphoretic, carminative, circulatory stimulant, anti-inflammatory, antiseptic, inhibits coughing
ginkgo	China	anti-asthmatic, antispasmodic, anti-allergenic, anti-inflammatory, circulatory stimulant and tonic
ginseng	northeastern China, eastern Russia, Korea	tonic, stimulant, physical and mental revitalizer
gumplant	Southwestern US, Mexico	antispasmodic, expectorant, hypotensive
hamamelis (witch hazel)	eastern North America	astringent, anti-inflammatory, stops external and internal bleeding
hyssop	Mediterranean	antispasmodic, expectorant, diaphoretic, anti-inflammatory, hepatic
jasmine	Iran	aromatic, antispasmodic, expectorant
lavender	Mediterranean	carminative, antidepressant, antiseptic, antibacterial, stimulates blood flow, relieves muscle spasms
marjoram (wild marjoram)	Asia	antiseptic, antispasmodic, digestive
melissa (lemon balm)	Mediterranean	relaxant, antispasmodic, carminative, anti-viral, nerve tonic, increases sweating
myrrh	northeast Africa	stimulant, antiseptic, anti-inflammatory, astringent, expectorant, antispasmodic, carminative
nettle	Eurasia	diuretic, tonic, astringent, anti-allergenic, prevents hemorrhaging, reduces prostate enlargement (root)
parsley	North & Central Europe, Western Asia	digestive, diuretic
passiflora (passion flower)	North America	anti-inflammatory, antispasmodic, hypotensive, sedative, tranquilizing
peppermint	unknown	carminative, antiseptic, relieves muscle spasms, increases sweating, stimulates secretion of bile
rosemary	Mediterranean	tonic, stimulant, astringent, nervine, anti-inflammatory, carminative
rue	southern Europe	antispasmodic, increases peripheral blood circulation, relieves eye tension
sesame	Africa	digestive, aromatic, antispasmodic
St. John's wort	Europe	antidepressant, antispasmodic, astringent, sedative, anti-viral, relieves pain
thyme	western Mediterranean, southwest Italy	antiseptic, expectorant, tonic, relieves muscle spasm
turmeric	India, southern Asia	anti-inflammatory, antioxidant, antibacterial, eases stomach pain, stimulates secretion of bile
valerian	Europe, Western Asia	sedative, relaxant, relieves muscle spasm, relieves anxiety, lowers blood pressure
verbena	Europe	nervine, tonic, mild sedative, stimulates bile secretion, mild bitter

Notable Medicinal Plants (continued)

PLANT	NATIVE REGION	MAIN PROPERTIES (USES)
wormwood	Europe	aromatic bitter, anti-inflammatory, mild antidepressant, stimulates bile secretion, eliminates worms, eases stomach pains
yarrow	Europe	antispasmodic, astringent, bitter tonic, mild diuretic, urinary antiseptic, increases sweating, lowers blood pressure, reduces fever

World's Oldest Trees and Flowering Plants

	MAXIMUM AGE IN YEARS		
	ESTIMATED	VERIFIED	LOCATION
trees			
bristlecone pine		4,900	Wheeler Peak, Humboldt National Forest, Nevada
Sierra redwood	4,000	2,200–2,300	northern California
Swiss stone pine	1,200	750	Riffel Alp, Switzerland
common juniper	2,000	544	Kola Peninsula, northeastern Russia
European larch	700	417	Riffel Alp, Switzerland
Norway spruce	1,200	350–400	Eichstätt, Bavaria, Germany
flowering plants			
bo tree	2,000–3,000		Buddh Gaya, India; Anuradhapura, Ceylon
English oak	2,000	1,500	Hasbruch Forest, Lower Saxony, Germany
linden		815	Lithuania
European beech	900	250	Montigny, Normandy, France
English ivy	440		Ginac, near Montpellier, France
dragon tree	200		Tenerife, Canary Islands
dwarf birch		80	eastern Greenland

Endangerment

Selected Endangered Species: Flora

For a complete list of endangered and threatened flora, see
<http://endangered.fws.gov/wildlife.html#Species>.

Flowering plants
Akoko, Ewa Plains
Alani (*Melicope reflexa*)
Arrowhead, bunched
Avens, spreading
Ayenia, Texas
Barberry, Truckee
Bird's-beak, salt marsh
Bittercress, small-anthered
Bladderpod, Missouri
Bluegrass, Hawaiian
Bluet, Roan Mountain
Doxwood, Vahl's
Buckwheat, steamboat
Bulrush, Northeastern
Cactus, Key tree
Cactus, Knowlton
Cactus, Pima pineapple
Cactus, Sneed pincushion
Cactus, star
Campion, fringed
Chaffseed, American
Checker-mallow, pedate
Clarkia, Pismo
Clover, running buffalo
Clover, showy Indian
Coneflower, smooth
Desert-parsley, Bradshaw's
Dropwort, Canby's
Flannelbush, Mexican
Frankenia, Johnston's

Flowering plants (continued)
Geranium, Hawaiian red-flowered
Gerardia, sandplain
Grass, Tennessee yellow-eyed
Ha'iwale (*Cyrtandra munroi*)
Haha (*Cyanea superba*)
Harperella
Hau kuahiwi (*Hibiscadelphus giffardianus*)
Iagu, Hayun
Ipomopsis, Holy Ghost
Jewelflower, California
Kamakahala (*Labordia lanaiensis*)
Koki'o, Cooke's
Larkspur, San Clemente Island
Lau'ehu
Lily, Western
Liveforever, Santa Barbara Island
Loosestrife, rough-leaved
Lo'ulu (*Pritchardia munroi*)
Lousewort, Furbish
Love grass, Fosberg's
Lupine, scrub
Manioc, Walker's
Mesa-mint, Otay
Milk-vetch, Jesup's
Milk-vetch, Mancos
Mint, longspurred
Monardella, willowy

Flowering plants (continued)
Na'ena'e (*Dubautia herbstobatae*)
Nehe (*Lipochaeta lobata*)
Niterwort, Amargosa
Oha wai (*Clermontia mauiensis*)
Orcutt grass, California
Penstemon, blowout
Phacelia, clay
Pinkroot, gentian
Pitcher-plant, green
Pitcher-plant, mountain sweet
Pondberry
Prairie-clover, leafy
Prickly-ash, St. Thomas
Rock-cress, Hoffmann's
Rock-cress, McDonald's
Rock-cress, shale barren
Rosemary, short-leaved
Sandwort, Cumberland
Sandwort, Marsh
Spineflower, slender-horned
Sumac, Michaux's
Sunflower, Schweinitz's
Thistle, Chorro Creek bog
Trillium, persistent
Trillium, relict
Wallflower, Contra Costa
Walnut, West Indian or nogal
Water-umbel, Huachuca

Selected Endangered Species: Flora (continued)

Conifers and cycads
Cypress, Santa Cruz
Torreya, Florida

Ferns and allies
Diellia, asplenium-leaved
Fern, Aleutian shield

Ferns and allies (continued)
Fern, Elfin tree
Fern, pendant kihi
  Ihi'ihi
Pauoa
Quillwort, black spored
Quillwort, Louisiana

Ferns and allies (continued)
Quillwort, mat-forming
Wawae'iole (*Huperzia mannii*)
Wawae'iole (*Lycopodium nutans*)

Lichens
Lichen, rock gnome

Selected Endangered Species: Fauna

For a complete list of endangered and threatened fauna, see
<http://endangered.fws.gov/wildlife.html#Species>.

Vertebrate animals
Mammals
Bat, gray
Bat, Indiana
Caribou, woodland
Deer, Columbian white-tailed
Deer, Key
Ferret, black-footed
Fox, San Joaquin kit
Jaguar
Manatee, West Indian
Mouse, Perdido Key beach
Ocelot
Panther, Florida
Pronghorn, Sonoran
Puma (cougar), eastern
Rabbit, Lower Keys marsh
Rabbit, pygmy
Rat, rice
Seal, Caribbean monk
Seal, Hawaiian monk
Sea-lion, Steller
Sheep, bighorn (two varieties)
Shrew, Buena Vista Lake ornate
Squirrel, Carolina northern flying
Squirrel, Delmarva Peninsula fox
Vole, Amargosa
Vole, Hualapai Mexican
Whale, blue
Whale, humpback
Whale, sperm
Wolf, gray
Wolf, red
Woodrat, Key Largo
Woodrat, riparian (San Joaquin Valley)

Birds
Albatross, short-tailed
Blackbird, yellow-shouldered
Bobwhite, masked (quail)
Broadbill, Guam
Condor, California
Coot, Hawaiian
Crane, whooping
Creeper, Molokai
Crow, Mariana
Crow, white-necked
Curlew, Eskimo
Duck, Hawaiian
Duck, Laysan
Elepaio, Oahu
Falcon, northern aplomado
Finch, Laysan
Finch, Nihoa
Flycatcher, southwestern willow

Birds (continued)
Goose, Hawaiian
Hawk, Hawaiian
Hawk, Puerto Rican broad-winged
Honeycreeper, crested
Kingfisher, Guam Micronesian
Kite, Everglade snail
Mallard, Mariana
Megapode, Micronesian
Millerbird, Nihoa (Old World warbler)
Parrot, Puerto Rican
Pelican, brown
Pigeon, Puerto Rican plain
Plover, piping
Pygmy-owl, cactus ferruginous
Rail, Yumma clapper
Sparrow, Cape Sable seaside
Stilt, Hawaiian
Stork, wood
Swiftlet, Mariana gray
Tern, least
Thrush, large Kauai
Thrush, small Kauai
Vireo, black-capped
Vireo, least Bell's
Warbler (wood), Bachman's
Warbler (wood), golden-cheeked
Warbler (wood), Kirtland's
White-eye, bridled
Woodpecker, ivory-billed
Woodpecker, red-cockaded

Reptiles
Anole, Culebra Island giant
Boa, Puerto Rican
Boa, Virgin Islands tree
Crocodile, American
Gecko, Monito
Lizard, blunt-nosed leopard
Lizard, St. Croix ground
Sea turtle, green
Sea turtle, hawksbill
Sea turtle, Kemp's ridley
Sea turtle, leatherback
Snake, San Francisco garter
Turtle, Alabama red-belly
Turtle, Plymouth redbelly

Amphibians
Frog, Mississippi gopher
Salamander, California tiger
Salamander, desert slender
Salamander, Santa Cruz long-toed
Salamander, Shenandoah

Amphibians (continued)
Salamander, Sonoran tiger
Salamander, Texas blind
Toad, arroyo (arroyo southwestern)
Toad, Houston
Toad, Wyoming

Fish
Chub, bonytail
Chub, humpback
Dace, Moapa
Darter, amber
Darter, boulder
Darter, Maryland
Gambusia, Pecos
Gambusia, San Marcos
Goby, tidewater
Logperch, Conasauga
Madtom, Scioto
Minnow, Rio Grande silvery
Pikeminnow (squawfish), Colorado
Pupfish, desert
Salmon, Atlantic
Salmon, sockeye
Shiner, palezone
Shiner, Topeka
Sturgeon, pallid
Sturgeon, shortnose
Sucker, Lost River
Sucker, razorback
Topminnow, Gila (incl. Yaqui)
Trout, Gila
Woundfin

Invertebrate animals
Clams
Acornshell, southern
Bean, Cumberland (pearlymussel)
Bean, purple
Blossom, tubercled (pearlymussel)
Blossom, turgid (pearlymussel)
Catspaw (purple cat's paw pearlymussel)
Catspaw, white (pearlymussel)
Clubshell
Clubshell, southern
Combshell, Cumberlandian
Combshell, upland
Elktoe, Appalachian
Elktoe, Cumberland
Fanshell
Heelsplitter, Carolina
Higgins eye (pearlymussel)

Selected Endangered Species: Fauna (continued)

Invertebrate Animals (continued)
Clams (continued)
Kidneyshell, triangular
Lampmussel, Alabama
Lilliput, pale (pearlymussel)
Mapleleaf, winged (mussel)
Moccasinshell, Coosa
Moccasinshell, Gulf
Monkeyface, Appalachian (pearly-
  mussel)
Monkeyface, Cumberland (pearly-
  mussel)
Mussel, oyster
Mussel, scaleshell
Pearlymussel, cracking
Pearlymussel, littlewing
Pigtoe, finerayed
Pigtoe, rough
Pimpleback, orangefoot (pearly-
  mussel)
Pocketbook, fat
Pocketbook, shinyrayed
Rabbitsfoot, rough
Riffleshell, northern
Riffleshell, tan
Ring pink (mussel)
Spinymussel, James
Stirrupshell
Three-ridge, fat (mussel)
Wartyback, white (pearlymussel)
Wedgemussel, dwarf

Snails
Ambersnail, Kanab
Riversnail, Anthony's
Snail, Iowa Pleistocene
Snail, Utah valvata
Springsnail, Idaho

Insects
Beetle, American burying
Beetle, Hungerford's crawling
  water
Butterfly, Karner blue
Butterfly, Mitchell's satyr
Dragonfly, Hine's emerald
Fly, Delhi Sands flower-loving
Grasshopper, Zayante band-
  winged
Ground beetle (unnamed,
  Rhadine exilis)
Ground beetle (unnamed,
  Rhadine infernalis)
Mold beetle, Helotes
Moth, Blackburn's sphinx
Skipper, Carson wandering
Tiger beetle, Ohlone

Arachnids
Harvestman, Bee Creek Cave
Harvestman, Bone Cave
Pseudoscorpion, Tooth Cave
Spider, Government Canyon cave

Arachnids (continued)
Spider, Kauai cave wolf (pe'e pe'e
  maka 'ole)
Spider, Madla's cave
Spider, Robber Baron Cave
Spider, spruce-fir moss
Spider, Tooth Cave
Spider, Vesper Cave

Crustaceans
Amphipod, Hay's Spring
Amphipod, Illinois cave
Amphipod, Kauai cave
Amphipod, Peck's cave
Crayfish, cave (*Cambarus
  aculabrum*)
Crayfish, cave (*Cambarus
  zophonastes*)
Crayfish, Nashville
Crayfish, Shasta
Fairy shrimp, Conservancy
Fairy shrimp, Riverside
Isopod, Lee County cave
Isopod, Socorro
Shrimp, Alabama cave
Shrimp, California freshwater
Shrimp, Kentucky cave
Tadpole shrimp, vernal pool

Geology

The Continents

Figures given are approximate. Area and population as of 2001. Lowest points listed are all below sea level.

CONTINENT	POPULATION	AREA	% OF TOTAL LAND AREA[1]	HIGHEST/LOWEST POINT
Asia	3,714,141,000	12,312,740 sq mi 31,889,660 sq km	29.9	Mount Everest (China, Nepal): 29,035 ft (8,850 m) Dead Sea (Israel, Jordan): 1,312 ft (400 m)
Africa	816,524,000	11,717,370 sq mi 30,348,110 sq km	20.6	Mt. Kilimanjaro (Tanzania): 19,340 ft (5,895 m) Lake Assal (Djibouti): 515 ft (157 m)
North America	1,015,255,000	16,247,180 sq mi 42,080,010 sq km	14.8	Mt. McKinley (Alaska): 20,320 ft (6,194 m) Death Valley (California): 282 ft (86 m)
South America	424,569,000	6,895,210 sq mi 17,858,520 sq km	12.0	Mt. Aconcagua (Argentina): 22,831 ft (7,959 m) Valdón Peninsula (Argentina): 131 ft (40 m)
Antarctica	N/A	5,500,000 sq mi 14,200,000 sq km	10.5	Vinson Massif: 16,066 ft (4,897 m) N/A
Europe	726,833,000	8,868,680 sq mi 22,969,900 sq km	7.0	Mt. Elbrus (Russia): 18,510 ft (5,595 m) Caspian Sea (Russia): 90 ft (27 m)
Australia	31,377,000	3,287,600 sq mi 8,514,830 sq km	5.2	Mt. Kosciusko: 7,310 ft (2,228 m) Lake Eyre: 50 ft (15 m)

[1]*Together, the continents make up about 29.2% of the Earth's surface.*

Geologic Time Scale

* Millions of years before the present.
** International ages have not been established. These are regional (Laurentian) only.

Cenozoic Era

period	epoch	age	boundaries*
Quaternary	Holocene		0.01
Quaternary	Pleistocene	Calabrian	1.8
Tertiary — Neogene	Pliocene L	Piacenzian	3.6
	Pliocene E	Zanclean	5.3
	Miocene L	Messinian	7.1
	Miocene L	Tortonian	11.2
	Miocene M	Serravallian	14.8
	Miocene M	Langhian	16.4
	Miocene E	Burdigalian	20.5
	Miocene E	Aquitanian	23.8
Tertiary — Paleogene	Oligocene L	Chattian	28.5
	Oligocene E	Rupelian	33.7
	Eocene L	Priabonian	37.0
	Eocene M	Bartonian	41.3
	Eocene M	Lutetian	49.0
	Eocene E	Ypresian	54.8
	Paleocene L	Thanetian	57.9
	Paleocene	Selandian	61.0
	Paleocene E	Danian	65.0

Mesozoic Era

period	epoch	age	boundaries*
Cretaceous	L	Maastrichtian	65.0
		Campanian	71.3
		Santonian	83.5
		Coniacian	85.8
		Turonian	89.0
		Cenomanian	93.5
	E (Neocomian)	Albian	99.0
		Aptian	112
		Barremian	121
		Hauterivian	127
		Valanginian	132
		Berriasian	137
Jurassic	L	Tithonian	144
		Kimmeridgian	151
		Oxfordian	154
	M	Callovian	159
		Bathonian	164
		Bajocian	169
		Aalenian	176
	E	Toarcian	180
		Pliensbachian	190
		Sinemurian	195
		Hettangian	202
Triassic	L	Rhaetian	206
		Norian	210
		Carnian	221
	M	Ladinian	227
		Anisian	234
	E	Olenekian	242 / 245
		Induan	248

Paleozoic Era

period	epoch	age	boundaries*
Permian	L	Tatarian	248
		Ufimian-Kazanian	252
		Kungurian	256
	E	Artinskian	260
		Sakmarian	269
		Asselian	282
Carboniferous — Pennsylvanian	L	Gzhelian	290
		Kasimovian	296
		Moscovian	303
	E	Bashkirian	311
Carboniferous — Mississippian	L	Serpukhovian	323
	E	Visean	327
		Tournaisian	342
Devonian	L	Famennian	354
		Frasnian	364
	M	Givetian	370
		Eifelian	380
	E	Emsian	391
		Pragian	400
		Lochkovian	412
Silurian	L	Pridoli	417
		Ludlow	419
	M	Wenlock	423
	E	Llandovery	428
Ordovician	L	Ashgillian	443
		Caradocian	449
	M	Llandeilian	458
		Llanvirnian	464
	E	Arenigian	470
		Tremadocian	485
Cambrian**	D	Sunwaptan**	490
		Steptoean**	495
	C	Marjuman**	500
		Delamaran**	506
	B	Dyeran**	512
	A	Montezuman**	516 / 520 / 543

Precambrian time

eon	era	boundaries*
Proterozoic	L	543
		900
	M	1,600
	E	2,500
Archean	L	3,000
	M	3,400
	E	3,800?

Published with permission of the Geological Society of America.

50 Largest Islands of the World

NAME AND LOCATION	CONTINENT	AREA* SQ MI	AREA* SQ KM
Greenland	North America	822,700	2,130,800
New Guinea, Papua New Guinea-Indonesia	Oceania	309,000	800,000
Borneo, Indonesia-Malaysia-Brunei	Asia	283,400	734,000
Madagascar	Africa	226,658	587,041
Baffin, Nunavut, Canada	North America	195,928	507,451
Sumatra, Indonesia	Asia	167,600	434,000
Honshu, Japan	Asia	87,805	227,414
Victoria, Northwest Territories-Nunavut, Canada	North America	83,897	217,291
Great Britain	Europe	83,698	216,777
Ellesmere, Nunavut, Canada	North America	75,767	196,236
Celebes, Indonesia	Asia	69,100	179,000
South Island, New Zealand	Oceania	58,676	151,971
Java, Indonesia	Asia	49,000	126,900
North Island, New Zealand	Oceania	44,204	114,489
Newfoundland, Canada	North America	42,031	108,860
Cuba	North America	40,519	104,945
Luzon, Philippines	Asia	40,420	104,688
Iceland	Europe	39,699	102,819
Mindanao, Philippines	Asia	36,537	94,630
Ireland, Ireland-UK	Europe	32,589	84,406
Hokkaido, Japan	Asia	30,144	78,073
Sakhalin, Russia	Asia	29,500	76,400
Hispaniola, Haiti-Dominican Republic	North America	29,418	76,192
Banks, Northwest Territories, Canada	North America	27,038	70,028
Sri Lanka (Ceylon)	Asia	25,332	65,610
Tasmania, Australia	Oceania	24,868	64,409
Devon, Nunavut, Canada	North America	21,331	55,247
Severny, Novaya Zemlya, Russia	Europe	18,882	48,904
Tierra del Fuego, Argentina-Chile	South America	18,530	47,992
Alexander I	Antarctica	16,700	43,200
Axel Heiberg, Nunavut, Canada	North America	16,671	43,178
Melville, Northwest Territories-Nunavut, Canada	North America	16,274	42,149
Southampton, Nunavut, Canada	North America	15,913	41,214
Marajó, Pará, Brazil	South America	15,500	40,100
Spitsbergen, Svalbard, Norway	Europe	15,075	39,044
Kyushu, Japan	Asia	14,114	30,554
New Britain, Papua New Guinea	Oceania	14,100	36,500
Taiwan (Formosa)	Asia	13,851	35,873
Hainan, China	Asia	12,962	33,572
Prince of Wales, Nunavut, Canada	North America	12,872	33,339
Yuzhny, Novaya Zemlya, Russia	Europe	12,848	33,275
Vancouver, British Columbia, Canada	North America	12,079	31,285
Timor, Indonesia-East Timor	Asia	11,883	30,777
Sicily, Italy	Europe	9,830	25,460
Somerset, Nunavut, Canada	North America	9,570	24,786
Sardinia, Italy	Europe	9,194	23,813
Bananal, Tocantins, Brazil	South America	7,700	20,000
Shikoku, Japan	Asia	7,049	18,256
Halmahera, Indonesia	Asia	6,865	17,780
Seram, Indonesia	Asia	6,621	17,148

*Area given may include small adjoining islands. Conversions for rounded figures are rounded to nearest hundred.

Highest Mountains of the World

"I" in the name of a peak refers to the highest in a group of numbered peaks of the same name.

NAME AND LOCATION	HEIGHT IN M	HEIGHT IN FT	YEAR FIRST CLIMBED
Africa			
Kilimanjaro (Kibo peak) (Tanzania)	5,895	19,340	1889
Mt. Kenya (Batian peak) (Kenya)	5,199	17,058	1899
Margherita, Ruwenzori Range (Zaire–Uganda)	5,119	16,795	1906
Ras Dashen, Simen Mtns. (Ethiopia)	4,620	15,157	1841
Meru (Tanzania)	4,565	14,978	N/A
Lageda (Ethiopia)	4,532	14,869	N/A

Highest Mountains of the World (continued)

NAME AND LOCATION	HEIGHT IN M	HEIGHT IN FT	YEAR FIRST CLIMBED
Africa (continued)			
Karisimbi, Virunga Mtns. (Zaire–Rwanda)	4,507	14,787	1903
Analu (Ethiopia)	4,480	14,698	N/A
Weynober (Ethiopia)	4,472	14,672	N/A
Mikeno, Virunga Mtns. (Zaire–Rwanda)	4,437	14,557	1927
Antarctica			
Vinson Massif, Sentinel Range, Ellsworth Mtns.	4,897	16,066	1966
Tyree, Sentinel Range, Ellsworth Mtns.	4,852	15,919	1967
Shinn, Sentinel Range, Ellsworth Mtns.	4,801	15,751	1966
Kirkpatrick, Queen Alexandra Range	4,528	14,856	N/A
Markham, Queen Elizabeth Range	4,350	14,272	N/A
Asia			
Everest (Chomolungma), Himalayas (Nepal–Tibet, China)	8,848	29,028	1953
K2 (Godwin Austen) (Chogori), Karakoram Range (Pakistan–Sinkiang, China)	8,611	28,251	1954
Kanchenjunga I (Gangchhendzonga), Himalayas (Nepal–India)	8,586	28,169	1955
Lhotse I, Himalayas (Nepal–Tibet, China)	8,516	27,940	1956
Makalu I, Himalayas (Nepal–Tibet, China)	8,463	27,766	1955
Cho Oyu, Himalayas (Nepal–Tibet, China)	8,201	26,906	1954
Dhaulagiri I, Himalayas (Nepal)	8,167	26,795	1960
Manaslu I, Himalayas (Nepal)	8,163	26,781	1956
Nanga Parbat I, Himalayas (Pakistan)	8,126	26,660	1953
Annapurna I, Himalayas (Nepal)	8,091	26,545	1950
Caucasus			
Elbrus (Russia)	5,642	18,510	1874
Dykh–Tau (Russia)	5,204	17,073	1888
Koshtan–Tau (Russia)	5,151	16,900	1889
Shkhara (Russia–Georgia)	5,068	16,627	1888
Dzhangi–Tau (Russia–Georgia)	5,058	16,594	1903
Kazbek (Georgia)	5,033	16,512	1868
Shota Rustaveli (Russia–Georgia)	4,960	16,273	N/A
Dzhimara (Georgia)	4,780	15,682	N/A
Ushba (Georgia)	4,700	15,420	1888
Uilpata (Russia)	4,649	15,253	N/A
Europe			
Mont Blanc, Alps (France–Italy)	4,807	15,771	1786
Dufourspitze (Monte Rosa), Alps (Switzerland–Italy)	4,634	15,203	1855
Dom (Mischabel), Alps (Switzerland)	4,545	14,911	1858
Weisshorn, Alps (Switzerland)	4,505	14,780	1861
Matterhorn, Alps (Switzerland–Italy)	4,478	14,692	1865
Mont Maudit, Alps (France–Italy)	4,471	14,669	N/A
Dent Blanche, Alps (Switzerland)	4,357	14,295	1862
Grand Combin, Alps (Switzerland)	4,314	14,154	1859
Dôme du Goûter, Alps (France)	4,304	14,121	1784
Finsteraarhorn, Alps (Switzerland)	4,274	14,022	1812
North America			
McKinley, Alaska Range (Alaska, US)	6,194	20,320	1913
Logan, St. Elias Mtns. (Yukon, Canada)	5,951	19,524	1925
Citlaltépetl (Orizaba), Cordillera Neo–Volcánica (Mexico)	5,610	18,406	1848
St. Elias, St. Elias Mtns. (Alaska, (US–Canada)	5,489	18,009	1897
Popocatépetl, Cordillera Neo–Volcánica (Mexico)	5,465	17,930	1519
Foraker, Alaska Range (Alaska, US)	5,304	17,400	1934
Iztaccíhuatl (Ixtacihuatl), Cordillera Neo–Volcánica (Mexico)	5,230	17,159	1889
Lucania, St. Elias Mtns. (Yukon, Canada)	5,226	17,146	1937
King, St. Elias Mtns. (Yukon, Canada)	5,173	16,972	1952
Steele, St. Elias Mtns. (Yukon, Canada)	5,073	16,644	1935

Highest Mountains of the World (continued)

NAME AND LOCATION	HEIGHT IN M	HEIGHT IN FT	YEAR FIRST CLIMBED
Oceania			
Jaya (Sukarno, Carstensz), Sudirman Range (Indonesia)	5,030	16,500[1]	1962
Pilimsit (Idenburg), Sudirman Range (Indonesia)	4,800	15,750[1]	1962
Trikora (Wilhelmina), Jayawijaya Mtns. (Indonesia)	4,750	15,580[1]	1912
Mandala (Juliana), Jayawijaya Mtns. (Indonesia)	4,700	15,420[1]	1959
Wisnumurti (Jan Pieterszoon Coen), Jayawijaya, Mtns. (Indonesia)	4,595	15,080[1]	N/A
Wilhelm, Bismarck Range (Papua New Guinea)	4,509	14,793	N/A
Giluwe, Hagen Range (Papua New Guinea)	4,368	14,331	N/A
Kubor, Kubor Range (Papua New Guinea)	4,359	14,301	N/A
Herbert, Bismarck Range (Papua New Guinea)	4,267	13,999	N/A
Mauna Kea (Hawaii, US)	4,205	13,796	N/A
South America			
Aconcagua, Andes (Argentina-Chile)	6,959	22,831	1897
Ojos del Salado, Andes (Argentina-Chile)	6,893	22,615	1937
Bonete, Andes (Argentina)	6,872	22,546	1913
Tupungato, Andes (Argentina-Chile)	6,800	22,310	1897
Pissis, Andes (Argentina)	6,779	22,241	1937
Mercedario, Andes (Argentina)	6,770	22,211	1934
Huascarán, Cordillera Blanca, Andes (Peru)	6,768	22,205	1908
Tres Cruces, Andes (Argentina-Chile)	6,753	22,156	1937
Llullaillaco, Cordillera Occidental, Andes (Argentina-Chile)	6,723	22,057	1952
Cachi (El Libertador), Sierra de Pastos Grandes, Andes (Argentina)	6,720	22,047	1904

[1]Conversions rounded to the nearest 10 ft.

Did you know?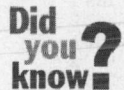
Dogs were tamed and domesticated many thousands of years before cats. Ancient drawings in caves depict dogs side by side with their human masters, whom they assisted as hunters, trackers, and protectors. In some early civilizations, such as Egypt, dogs became objects of worship; an entire Egyptian city was once built in honor of a dog. Cats were first tamed by the Egyptians about 3,000 BCE to control the population of grain-eating rats and mice in the Egyptian granaries. Cats, like dogs, soon became objects of worship.

Major Caves and Cave Systems of the World

NAME AND LOCATION	DEPTH[1]		LENGTH[2]	
	FEET	M	MILES	KM
Africa				
Achra Lemoun, Algeria	1,060	323	N/A	N/A
Ambatoanjahana, Madagascar	N/A	N/A	6.7	10.8
Ambatoharanana, Madagascar	N/A	N/A	11.2	18.1
Andrafiabe, Madagascar	N/A	N/A	7.5	12
Antsatrabonko, Madagascar	N/A	N/A	6.5	10.5
Apocalypse Pothole, South Africa	279	85	7.5	12.1
Bou Hadjar, Algeria	896	273	N/A	N/A
Boussouil, Algeria	2,641	805	2	3.2
Friouato, Morocco	889	271	N/A	N/A
Ifflis, Algeria	3,802	1,159	1	1.6
Jabal As-Sarj, Tunisia	876	267	1.1	1.7
Leviathani, Kenya	1,526	465	7	11.2
Sof 'Umar, Ethiopia	N/A	N/A	9.4	15.1
Tafna (Bou Ma'za), Algeria	N/A	N/A	11.4	18.4
Tikhoubaï, Morocco	1,017	310	N/A	N/A
Toghobeït, Morocco	2,339	713	2.3	3.7

Antarctica: no significant caves

Asia				
Air Jernih, Malaysia	1,165	355	32.1	51.6
Bilremos, South Korea	N/A	N/A	7.3	11.7
Byakuren, Japan	1,476	450	0.7	1.1

Major Caves and Cave Systems of the World (continued)

NAME AND LOCATION	DEPTH[1]		LENGTH[2]	
	FEET	M	MILES	KM
Asia (continued)				
Faouar Dara, Lebanon	2,041	622	1.5	2.5
Jaran, Indonesia	518	158	6.9	11.1
Kap-Kutan/Promezhutochnaya, Uzbekistan	N/A	N/A	31.3	50.3
Kiev, Uzbekistan	3,248	990	1.1	1.8
Manjung, South Korea	N/A	N/A	8.3	13.3
Nasib Bagus, Malaysia	1,388	423	1.8	2.9
Omi-senri, Japan	1,198	365	N/A	N/A
Oreshnaya, Russia	623	190	25.5	41
Parau, Iran	2,464	751	0.9	1.4
Sallukan Kallang, Indonesia	673	205	7.6	12.3
Sarang Laba-Laba, Malaysia	381	116	9.4	15.2
Ural, Uzbekistan	1,854	565	1.5	2.5
Wu-chia, China	1,430	436	N/A	N/A
Europe				
Arañonera, Spain	3,888	1,185	4	6.5
Badalona, Spain	3,770	1,149	N/A	N/A
Berger, France	4,072	1,241	12.9	20.7
Bracas de Thurugne 6, France	3,825	1,166	4.2	6.7
56 de Andara, Spain	3,835	1,169	3.5	5.7
Coumo d'Hyouernèdo, France	3,294	1,004	56.2	90.5
Dachstein-Mammut, Austria	3,871	1,180	23.9	38.5
Dent de Crolles, France	1,978	603	33.6	54.1
Ease Gill, United Kingdom	N/A	N/A	32.6	52.5
Eisriesenwelt, Austria	1,335	407	26.1	42
Ffynnon Ddu, United Kingdom	1,010	308	26.7	43
Fighiera-Farolfi-Antro del Corchia, Italy	3,986	1,215	28	45
Hirlatz, Austria	2,008	612	35.4	57
Hölloch, Switzerland	2,844	867	82.7	133.1
Jean Bernard, France	5,036	1,535	11.1	17.9
Jubiläums, Austria	3,848	1,173	N/A	N/A
Kuybyshevskaya, Georgia	3,642	1,110	1.2	2
L'Alpe, France	2,014	614	28.7	46.2
Laminako Ateak (Illamina), Spain	4,619	1,408	7.4	11.9
Mirolda, France	3,973	1,211	5.6	9
Ojo Guareña, Spain	N/A	N/A	55.4	89.1
Optimisticheskaya, Ukraine	N/A	N/A	102.5	165
Ozernaya, Ukraine	N/A	N/A	66.5	107
Pierre Saint-Martin, France-Spain	4,403	1,342	32.3	52
Raucherkar, Austria	2,379	725	29.8	48
Red del Río Silencio, Spain	1,614	492	32.9	53
Schwer, Austria	3,999	1,219	3.8	6.1
Siebenhengste-Hohgant-Höhlen, Switzerland	3,346	1,020	68.4	110
Snezhnoye-Mezhonnogo, Georgia	4,495	1,370	11.8	19
Soaso, Spain	3,871	1,180	N/A	N/A
Trave, Spain	4,528	1,380	1.8	2.9
V.V. Iliyukhina, Georgia	4,068	1,240	3.1	5
Vyacheslav Pantyukhina, Georgia	4,948	1,508	N/A	N/A
Xitu, Spain	3,766	1,148	4.7	7.5
Zolushka, Moldova	N/A	N/A	51	82
Oceania				
Atea, Papua New Guinea	1,148	350	21.4	34.5
Bibima, Papua New Guinea	1,621	494	N/A	N/A
Bulmer, New Zealand	2,388	728	6.8	11
Cora-Lynn, Australia	N/A	N/A	8.3	13.3
Gambo, Papua New Guinea	1,568	478	3.7	6
Gardners Gut, New Zealand	N/A	N/A	7.4	11.9
H.H. Hole, New Zealand	2,044	623	N/A	N/A
Honeycomb, New Zealand	N/A	N/A	8.1	13.1
Ipaku-Kukumbu, Papua New Guinea	1,273	388	6.8	11
Kavakuna II, Papua New Guinea	1,499	457	2.2	3.5
Mamo, Papua New Guinea	1,732	528	34.1	54.8
Mini-Martin-Exit, Australia	722	220	9.9	16
Minye, Papua New Guinea	1,535	468	3.4	5.4
Muruk, Papua New Guinea	2,090	637	2.9	4.6

Major Caves and Cave Systems of the World (continued)

NAME AND LOCATION	DEPTH[1]		LENGTH[2]	
	FEET	M	MILES	KM
Oceania (continued)				
Nettlebed, New Zealand	2,917	889	15.2	24.4
Selminum, Papua New Guinea	N/A	N/A	12.7	20.5
North America				
Agua de Carrizo, Mexico	2,743	836	2.3	3.7
Akemati, Mexico	3,707	1,130	N/A	N/A
Aztotempa, Mexico	2,297	700	2.5	4
Binkley's, Indiana	N/A	N/A	19.1	30.7
Blue Spring, Tennessee	N/A	N/A	20.1	32.3
Butler-Sinking Creek, Virginia	623	190	20	32.2
Carlsbad Caverns, New Mexico	1,027	313	20.8	33.5
Crevice, Missouri	N/A	N/A	28.2	45.4
Cuicateca, Mexico	4,035	1,230	5.8	9.3
Culverson Creek, West Virginia	341	104	20.8	33.5
Cumberland Caverns, Tennessee	N/A	N/A	27.6	44.4
Fisher Ridge, Kentucky	N/A	N/A	44.4	71.5
Friars Hole, West Virginia	617	188	42.8	68.8
Guixani Ndia Guinjao, Mexico	3,084	940	1.2	2
Hidden River, Kentucky	N/A	N/A	19.8	31.8
Hole, The, West Virginia	N/A	N/A	22.9	36.8
Huautla, Mexico	4,439	1,353	32.4	52.1
Jewel, South Dakota	443	135	76.9	123.8
Lechuguilla, New Mexico	1,503	458	32.9	53
Mammoth-Flint Ridge, Kentucky	360	110	329.3	530
Ocotempa, Mexico	3,488	1,063	N/A	N/A
Organ, West Virginia	N/A	N/A	37.6	60.5
Planos, Mexico	2,277	694	N/A	N/A
Purificación, Mexico	2,936	895	44.5	71.6
Sloan's Valley, Kentucky	N/A	N/A	24.6	39.6
Sonyance, Mexico	2,444	745	1.1	1.8
Tilaco, Mexico	2,129	649	N/A	N/A
Trinidad, Mexico	2,736	834	N/A	N/A
Whigpistle, Kentucky	N/A	N/A	22.5	36.2
Wind, South Dakota	564	172	51	82.1
Windymouth, West Virginia	N/A	N/A	18	29
Xanadu, Tennessee	N/A	N/A	24	38.6
Xonga, Mexico	2,428	740	1	1.6
South America				
Angélica, Brazil	N/A	N/A	4	6.4
Aonda, Venezuela	1,188	362	N/A	N/A
Aonda Este 2, Venezuela	968	295	N/A	N/A
Aonda Sur 1, Venezuela	951	290	N/A	N/A
Auyantepuy Norte, Venezuela	1,050	320	N/A	N/A
Brejões, Brazil	N/A	N/A	4.8	7.8
Canabrava, Brazil	N/A	N/A	3.4	5.5
Convento, Brazil	N/A	N/A	3.5	5.7
Guácharo, Venezuela	164	50	6.3	10.2
Guarataro, Venezuela	1,001	305	N/A	N/A
Kaukiran, Peru	1,335	407	1.3	2.1
Major de Sarisarinama, Venezuela	1,030	314	N/A	N/A
Ölhos d'Água, Brazil	N/A	N/A	3.9	6.3
San Andrés, Peru	1,096	334	N/A	N/A
Sant'Anna, Brazil	N/A	N/A	3.2	5.2
São Mateus-Imbira, Brazil	N/A	N/A	12.7	20.5

[1]Below highest entrance.   [2]Explored portion of cave.
Source: Paul Courbon et al., Atlas of the Great Caves of the World (1989).

Did you know? The discovery in 1856 of bones in a cave above the Neander Valley in Germany, not far from Düsseldorf, immediately caused a lively controversy as to whether they were remains of ancient humans or merely bones of modern humans distorted by disease. From that discovery derives the name Neanderthal for an early form of Homo sapiens that inhabited much of Europe and the Mediterranean lands about 100,000 to 35,000 years ago.

Major Deserts of the World

DESERT (LOCATION)	AREA SQ KM	AREA SQ MI	DESERT (LOCATION)	AREA SQ KM	AREA SQ MI
Africa			**Australia**		
Sahara (northern Africa)	8,600,000	3,320,000	Great Victoria (western and south Australia)	647,000	250,000
Libyan (Libya, Egypt, and Sudan)	N/A	N/A	Great Sandy (northern Western Australia)	400,000	150,000
Kalahari (southwestern Africa)	930,000	360,000	Gibson (western Australia)	N/A	N/A
Namib (southwestern Africa)	135,000	52,000	Simpson (northern Territory)	145,000	56,000
			North America		
Asia			Great Basin (southwestern US)	492,000	190,000
Arabia (southwestern Asia)	2,330,000	900,000			
Rub'al-Khali (southern Arabian Peninsula)	650,000	250,000	Chihuahuan (northern Mexico)	450,000	175,000
Gobi (Mongolia and northeastern China)	1,300,000	500,000	Sonoran (southwestern US and Baja California)	310,000	120,000
Kyzylkum (Kazakhstan-Uzbekistan)	300,000	115,000	Colorado (California, US, and northern Mexico)	N/A	N/A
Takla Makan (northern China)	270,000	105,000	Yuma (Arizona, US, and Sonora, Mexico)	N/A	N/A
Karakum (Turkmenistan)	350,000	135,000	Mojave (southwestern US)	65,000	25,000
Kavir (central Iran)	260,000	100,000			
Syrian (Saudi Arabia, Jordan, Syria, and Iraq)	260,000	100,000	**South America**		
Thar (India and Pakistan)	200,000	77,000	Patagonian (southern Argentina)	673,000	260,000
Lut (eastern Iran)	52,000	20,000	Atacama (northern Chile)	140,000	54,000

Major Volcanoes of the World

VOLCANO, LOCATION	ELEVATION M	ELEVATION FT	FIRST RECORDED ERUPTION	MOST RECENT ERUPTION
Africa				
Kilimanjaro, Tanzania[1]	5,895	19,340	N/A	N/A[2]
Cameroon, Cameroon	4,100	13,451	1650	2000
Teide (Tenerife), Canary Islands	3,718	12,198	N/A	1909
Nyiragongo, Dem. Rep. of the Congo	3,475	11,400	1884	2002
Nyamuragira, Dem. Rep. of the Congo	3,055	10,023	1882	2001
Fogo, Cape Verde	2,829	9,281	1500	1995
Karthala, Comoros	2,361	7,745	1828	1991
Fournaise, Reunion Islands	1,823	5,981	1640	2001
Antarctica				
Erebus, Ross Island	3,743	12,280	1841	1991
Darnley, Sandwich Islands	1,100	3,608	1823	N/A
Asia–Oceania–Pacific				
Klyuchevskaya, Kamchatka, Russia[3]	4,750	15,584	1697	2002
Mauna Kea, Hawaii[4]	4,205	13,796	N/A	dormant[4]
Mauna Loa, Hawaii	4,169	13,678	1750	1984
Kerinci, Sumatra, Indonesia	3,800	12,467	1838	1970
Fuji, Honshu, Japan	3,776	12,388	1050 BC	1708
Rinjani, Lombok, Indonesia	3,726	12,224	1847	1994
Tolbachik, Kamchatka, Russia	3,682	12,080	1740	1976
Semeru, Java, Indonesia	3,676	12,060	1818	2002
Ichinskaya, Kamchatka, Russia	3,621	11,880	N/A	N/A
Kronotskaya, Kamchatka, Russia	3,528	11,575	1922	1922
Koryakskaya, Kamchatka, Russia	3,456	11,339	1895	1956
Slamet, Java, Indonesia	3,428	11,247	1772	1988
Raung, Java, Indonesia	3,332	10,932	1586	2000
Shiveluch, Kamchatka, Russia	3,283	10,771	1793	2002
Dempo, Sumatra, Indonesia	3,159	10,364	1817	1974
Sundoro, Java, Indonesia	3,151	10,338	1818	1971
Cereme, Java, Indonesia	3,078	10,098	1698	1951
Ontake, Honshu, Japan	3,063	10,049	1979	1979
Papandayan, Java, Indonesia	2,987	9,802	1772	1998
Gede, Java, Indonesia	2,958	9,705	1747	1957

Major Volcanoes of the World (continued)

VOLCANO, LOCATION	ELEVATION M	FT	FIRST RECORDED ERUPTION	MOST RECENT ERUPTION
Asia-Oceania-Pacific (continued)				
Zhupanovsky, Kamchatka, Russia	2,958	9,705	1770	1959
Apo, Mindanao, Philippines	2,954	9,692	N/A	N/A
Merapi, Java, Indonesia	2,911	9,551	1006	2002
Bezymianny, Kamchatka, Russia	2,900	9,514	1055	2001
Marapi, Sumatra, Indonesia	2,891	9,485	1770	1994
Tambora, Sumbawa, Indonesia	2,850	9,350	1812	1815
Ruapehu, North Island, New Zealand	2,797	9,177	1861	1999
Peuet Sague, Sumatra, Indonesia	2,780	9,121	1918	1998
Avachinskaya, Kamchatka, Russia	2,751	9,026	1737	1991
Balbi, Bougainville, Papua New Guinea	2,743	8,999	N/A	N/A[2]
Mayon, Luzon, Philippines	2,421	7,943	1616	2001
Alaid, Kuril Islands, Russia	2,335	7,662	1790	1981
Ulawun, New Britain, Papua New Guinea	2,296	7,532	1700	2002
Lamington, New Guinea, Papua New Guinea	1,780	5,840	1951	1951
Kelud, Java, Indonesia	1,731	5,679	1000	2001
Pinatubo, Luzon, Philippines	1,460	4,800	1380	1991
Lopevi, Vanuatu	1,364	4,755	1864	2001
Unzen, Kyushu, Japan	1,360	4,462	860	1991
Awu, Pulau Sangihe, Indonesia	1,320	4,331	1640	1966
Kilauea, Hawaii	1,243	4,077	1750	2002
Krakatoa, Krakatau, Indonesia	813	2,667	1680	2001
Suwanose-jima, Ryukyu Islands, Japan	799	2,621	1813	1996
Taal, Luzon, Philippines	400	1,312	1572	1999
Europe and the Atlantic				
Etna, Italy	3,323	10,899	N/A	2002
Beerenberg, Norway	2,277	7,470	1558	N/A
Tristan da Cunha, South Atlantic	2,060	6,760	1700	N/A
Kverkfjöll, Iceland	1,920	6,298	1477	N/A
Askja, Iceland	1,570	5,149	1875	1961
Hekla, Iceland	1,491	4,890	1104	2000
Katla, Iceland	1,363	4,470	1177	1918
Vesuvius, Italy	1,280	4,198	N/A	1944
Stromboli, Italy	926	3,038	N/A	2002
Krafla, Iceland	818	2,683	1300	1984
North America				
Citlaltépetl, Mexico	5,610	18,406	N/A	N/A
Popocatépetl, Mexico	5,465	17,930	1347	2002
Rainier, Washington	4,392	14,410	N/A	c. 200 BC
Shasta, California	4,317	14,160	N/A	1786 (?)
Colima, Mexico	4,240	13,911	1576	2002
Tajumulco, Guatemala	4,220	13,845	1821	N/A
Acatenango, Guatemala	3,976	13,041	1924	1972
Fuego, Guatemala	3,763	12,342	1524	2002
Hood, Oregon	3,424	11,235	1800	c. 1800
Spurr, Alaska	3,374	11,067	1953	1992
Baker, Washington	3,285	10,775	1820	1880
Lassen, California	3,187	10,457	1650	1921
Redoubt, Alaska	3,108	10,194	1778	1990
Iliamna, Alaska	3,053	10,016	1708	1953
Shishaldin, Alaska	2,857	9,371	1775	2000
Parícutin, Mexico	2,807	9,210	1943	1952
Pavlof, Alaska	2,714	8,902	1790	1997
Poas, Costa Rica	2,704	8,869	1834	N/A
Pacaya, Guatemala	2,552	8,371	1565	2001
St. Helens, Washington	2,549	8,360	1500	1998
Veniaminof, Alaska	2,507	8,223	c. 1750	1993
El Chichón, Mexico	2,225	7,300	N/A	1982
San Miguel, El Salvador	2,180	7,150	1586	1976
Chiginagak, Alaska	2,126	6,973	1852	1997
Katmai, Alaska	2,047	6,714	1912	1912
Makushin, Alaska	2,035	6,674	1786	1987
Izalco, El Salvador	1,965	6,445	1770	1966
San Cristóbal, Nicaragua	1,745	5,724	1522	2001

Major Volcanoes of the World (continued)

VOLCANO, LOCATION	ELEVATION		FIRST RECORDED ERUPTION	MOST RECENT ERUPTION
	M	FT		
North America (continued)				
Great Sitkin, Alaska	1,737	5,697	1760	1974
Arenal, Costa Rica	1,633	5,356	1968	2001
Concepción, Nicaragua	1,610	5,281	1750	1986
Pelée, Martinique	1,397	4,582	1792	1932
Momotombo, Nicaragua	1,280	4,198	1550	1996
Kiska, Alaska	1,220	4,001	1907	1969
Telica, Nicaragua	1,060	3,477	1527	1999
South America				
Guallatiri, Chile	6,060	19,876	1825	1985
Cotopaxi, Ecuador[5]	5,897	19,347	1532	1904
El Misti, Peru	5,823	19,101	1542	1870
Tupungatito, Chile	5,640	18,499	1829	1986
Lascar, Chile	5,592	18,342	1848	2000
Ruiz, Colombia	5,400	17,716	1595	1985
Sangay, Ecuador	5,230	17,154	1628	1983
Tolima, Colombia	5,215	17,105	c. 1600 BC	1822
Tungurahua, Ecuador	5,033	16,512	1534	2002
Purace, Colombia	4,800	15,744	1827	1977
Guagua Pichincha, Ecuador	4,794	15,724	1533	2000
Lautaro, Chile	3,380	11,115	1878	N/A
Llaima, Chile	3,125	10,250	1640	1995
Villarrica, Chile	2,840	9,318	1558	2000
Hudson, Chile	2,615	8,580	1971	1991

[1]Includes three dormant volcanoes (Kibo, Mawensi, and Shira) that have not erupted in historic times.   [2]Has not erupted in historic times.   [3]Highest of the 22 active volcanoes on the Kamchatka Peninsula.   [4]Usually snowcapped dormant volcano.   [5]The world's highest continuously active volcano.

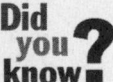

Did you know? One of the youngest volcanoes on Earth is Parícutin in west-central Mexico. On 20 Feb 1943, it began to erupt in an open field. Within a year the volcano's cone had risen 1,475 feet above its base and had buried the village of Parícutin. Its peak reached an elevation of 9,210 feet in 1952, when the eruption finally ended.

Oceans & Seas

	AREA		VOLUME	
	SQ KM	SQ MI	CU KM	CU MI
Pacific Ocean				
without marginal seas	165,250,000	63,800,000	707,600,000	169,900,000
with marginal seas	179,680,000	69,370,000	723,700,000	173,700,000
Atlantic Ocean				
without marginal seas	82,440,000	31,830,000	324,600,000	77,900,000
with marginal seas	106,460,000	41,100,000	354,700,000	85,200,000
Indian Ocean				
without marginal seas	73,440,000	28,360,000	291,000,000	69,900,000
with marginal seas	74,920,000	28,930,000	291,900,000	70,100,000
Arctic Ocean	14,090,000	5,440,000	17,000,000	4,100,000
Australasian Central Sea	8,140,000	3,140,000	9,900,000	2,400,000
Gulf of Mexico and Caribbean Sea	4,320,000	1,670,000	9,600,000	2,300,000
Mediterranean and Black Seas	2,970,000	1,150,000	4,200,000	100,000
Bering Sea	2,304,000	890,000	3,330,000	80,000
Sea of Okhotsk	1,583,000	611,000	1,300,000	30,000
Hudson Bay	1,230,000	47,000	160,000	40,000
North Sea	570,000	22,000	50,000	10,000
Baltic Sea	420,000	16,000	20,000	5,000
Irish Sea	100,000	40,000	6,000	1,000
English Channel	75,000	2,900	4,000	1,000

Oceans & Seas (continued)

	AVERAGE DEPTH		
	M	FT	DEEPEST POINT
Pacific Ocean			
without marginal seas	4,280	14,040	Mariana Trench
with marginal seas	4,030	13,220	(11,034 m; 36,201 ft)
Atlantic Ocean			
without marginal seas	3,930	12,890	Puerto Rico Trench
with marginal seas	3,330	10,920	(8,380 m; 27,493 ft)
Indian Ocean			
without marginal seas	3,960	10,040	Sunda Deep of the Java
with marginal seas	3,900	12,790	Trench (7,450 m; 24,442 ft)
Arctic Ocean	1,205	3,950	(5,502 m; 18,050 ft)
Australasian Central Sea	1,210	3,970	NA
Gulf of Mexico and	2,220	7,280	Cayman Trench
Caribbean Sea			(7,686 m; 25,216 ft)
Mediterranean and	1,430	4,690	Ionian Basin
Black Seas			(4,900 m; 16,000 ft)
Bering Sea	1,440	4,720	Bowers Basin (4,097 m; 13,442 ft)
Sea of Okhotsk	838	2,750	Kuril Basin (2,499 m; 8,200 ft)
Hudson Bay	128	420	(867 m; 2,846 ft)
North Sea	94	310	Skagerrak (700 m; 2,300 ft)
Baltic Sea	55	180	Landsort Deep (459 m; 1,506 ft)
Irish Sea	60	200	Mull of Galloway (175 m; 576 ft)
English Channel	54	180	Hurd Deep (172 m; 565 ft)

Major Natural Lakes of the World

Conversions for figures have been rounded, thousands to the nearest hundred and hundreds to the nearest ten.

NAME	LOCATION	AREA		NAME	LOCATION	AREA	
		SQ MI	SQ KM			SQ MI	SQ KM
Caspian Sea	central Asia	149,200	386,400	Nyasa (Malawi)	eastern Africa	11,430	29,604
Superior	Canada-US	31,700	82,100	Great Slave	Northwest	11,031	28,570
Victoria	eastern Africa	26,828	69,485		Territories,		
Huron	Canada-US	23,000	59,600		Canada		
Michigan	US	22,300	57,800	Erie	Canada-US	9,910	25,667
Aral Sea[1]	central Asia	13,000	33,800	Winnipeg	Manitoba,	9,417	24,390
Tanganyika	eastern Africa	12,700	32,900		Canada		
Great Bear	Northwest	12,028	31,153	Ontario	Canada-US	7,340	19,010
	Territories,						
	Canada						

[1]*Salt lake.*

Longest Rivers of the World

This list includes both rivers and river systems. Conversions of rounded figures are rounded to nearest 10 or 100 miles or kilometers.

NAME	OUTFLOW	LENGTH	
		MI	KM
Africa			
Nile	Mediterranean Sea	4,132	6,650
Congo	South Atlantic Ocean	2,900	4,700
Niger	Bight of Biafra	2,600	4,200
Zambezi	Mozambique Channel	2,200	3,500
Kasai	Congo River	1,338	2,153
Orange	South Atlantic Ocean	1,300	2,100
White Nile (al-Bahr al-Abyad)	Nile River	1,295	2,084
Lualaba	Congo River	1,100	1,800
Limpopo	Mozambique Channel	1,100	1,800
Jubba (Juba)	Indian Ocean	1,030	1,658
Asia			
Yangtze	East China Sea	3,915	6,300
Yenisey-Baikal-Selenga	Kara Sea	3,442	5,540
Huang Ho (Yellow)	Gulf of Chihli	3,395	5,464

Longest Rivers of the World (continued)

NAME	OUTFLOW	LENGTH MI	LENGTH KM
Asia (continued)			
Ob-Irtysh	Gulf of Ob	3,362	5,410
Amur-Argun	Sea of Okhotsk	2,761	4,444
Lena	Laptev Sea	2,734	4,400
Mekong	South China Sea	2,700	4,350
Ob-Katun	Gulf of Ob	2,696	4,338
Irtysh-Chorny Irtysh	Ob River	2,640	4,248
Yenisey	Kara Sea	2,549	4,102
Europe			
Volga	Caspian Sea	2,193	3,530
Danube	Black Sea	1,770	2,850
Ural	Caspian Sea	1,509	2,428
Dnieper	Black Sea	1,367	2,200
Don	Sea of Azov	1,162	1,870
Pechora	Barents Sea	1,124	1,809
Kama	Volga River	1,122	1,805
Oka	Volga River	932	1,500
Belaya	Kama River	889	1,430
Dniester	Black Sea	840	1,352
North America			
Mississippi-Missouri-Red Rock	Gulf of Mexico	3,710	5,971
Mackenzie-Slave-Peace	Beaufort Sea	2,635	4,241
Missouri-Red Rock	Mississippi River	2,540	4,090
St. Lawrence-Great Lakes	Gulf of St. Lawrence	2,500	4,000
Mississippi	Gulf of Mexico	2,340	3,770
Missouri	Mississippi River	2,315	3,726
Yukon-McNeil	Bering Sea	1,980	3,190
Rio Grande	Gulf of Mexico	1,900	3,060
Yukon	Bering Sea	1,875	3,018
Nelson-Saskatchewan	Hudson Bay	1,600	2,575
Oceania			
Darling	Murray River	1,702	2,739
Murray	Great Australian Bight	1,609	2,589
Murrumbidgee	Murray River	981	1,579
Lachlan	Murrumbidgee River	922	1,484
Cooper Creek	Lake Eyre	882	1,420
South America			
Amazon-Ucayali-Apurimac	South Atlantic Ocean	4,000	6,400
Paraná	Río de la Plata	3,032	4,880
Madeira-Mamoré-Guaporé	Amazon River	2,082	3,350
Jurua	Amazon River	2,040	3,283
Purus	Amazon River	1,995	3,211
São Francisco	South Atlantic Ocean	1,811	2,914
Japurá (Caquetá)	Amazon River	1,750	2,816
Ucayali-Apurimac	Amazon River	1,701	2,738
Orinoco	South Atlantic Ocean	1,700	2,736
Tocantins	Pará River	1,677	2,699

Glaciers

A glacier is a large mass of perennial ice that originates on land by the recrystallization of snow or other forms of solid precipitation and that shows evidence of past or present flow. The term **ice sheet** is commonly applied to a glacier that occupies an extensive tract of relatively level land and that flows from the center outward. Exact limits for glaciers cannot be set. Except in size, a small snow patch that persists for more than one season is hydrologically indistinguishable from a true glacier.

Glaciers occur where snowfall in winter exceeds melting in summer, conditions that prevail only in high mountain areas and polar regions. Glaciers occupy about 11% of the earth's land surface but hold roughly three-fourths of its fresh water; 99% of glacier ice lies in Antarctica and Greenland. At the end of the 20th century, scientists became increasingly concerned with **glacial melting**, which is often linked to **global warming** trends and may lead to changes in sea level and weather patterns.

Preserving Nature

National Parks, US

For more information, see <www.nps.gov/parks.html>.

Note: *The names of parks have sometimes been changed. Dates in parentheses indicate when the area was first designated a park.*

PARK	LOCATION	DESIGNATION DATE	SQ MI	SQ KM
Acadia	Bar Harbor ME	1929 (1916)	74	192
Arches	Moab UT	1971 (1929)	120	311
Badlands	southwestern South Dakota	1978 (1939)	379	982
Big Bend	curve of the Rio Grande river, Texas	1944	1,252	3,243
Biscayne	near Miami FL	1980 (1968)	270	699
Black Canyon of the Gunnison	near Montrose CO	1999 (1933)	43	112
Bryce Canyon	Bryce Canyon, Utah	1928 (1923)	56	145
Canyonlands	near Moab UT	1964	527	1,366
Capitol Reef	near Torrey UT	1971 (1937)	379	982
Carlsbad Caverns	near Carlsbad NM	1930 (1923)	73	189
Channel Islands	Ventura CA	1980 (1938)	75	194
Crater Lake	Crater Lake OR	1902	286	741
Cuyahoga Valley	near Cleveland and Akron OH	2000 (1974)	51	133
Death Valley	Death Valley, California	1994 (1933)	5,219	13,518
Dry Tortugas	Key West FL	1992 (1935)	101	262
Everglades	southern Florida	1947	2,358	6,107
Gates of the Arctic	Bettles AK	1980 (1978)	13,238	34,287
Glacier	northwest Montana	1910	1,584	4,102
Glacier Bay	Gustavus AK	1980 (1925)	5,130	13,287
Grand Canyon	Grand Canyon, Arizona	1919 (1908)	1,902	4,927
Grand Teton	Moose WY	1950 (1929)	484	1,255
Great Basin	near Baker NV	1986 (1922)	121	313
Great Smoky Mountains	Tennessee and North Carolina	1934	815	2,110
Guadalupe Mountains	Salt Flat TX	1972	135	350
Haleakala	Kula, Maui HI	1960 (1916)	47	121
Hawaii Volcanoes	near Hilo HI	1961 (1916)	328	849
Hot Springs	Hot Springs AR	1921 (1832)	9	22
Isle Royale	Houghton MI	1940 (1931)	893	2,314
Joshua Tree	near Palm Springs CA	1994 (1936)	1,501	4,120
Katmai	near King Salmon AK	1980 (1918)	7,385	19,128
Kenai Fjords	Seward AK	1980 (1978)	1,047	2,711
Kobuk Valley	Kotzebue AK	1980 (1978)	2,672	6,920
Lake Clark	Port Alsworth AK	1980 (1978)	6,297	16,309
Lassen Volcanic	Mineral CA	1916 (1907)	166	430
Mammoth Cave	Mammoth Cave, Kentucky	1941	83	214
Mesa Verde	near Cortez and Mancos CO	1906	81	211
Mount Rainier	near Ashford WA	1899	368	954
North Cascades	near Marblemount WA	1968	1,069	2,769
Olympic	near Port Angeles WA	1938	1,442	3,734
Petrified Forest	Arizona	1962 (1906)	146	379
Rocky Mountain	near Estes Park and Grand Lake CO	1915	415	1,076
Saguaro	Tucson AZ	1994 (1933)	143	370
Sequoia & Kings Canyon	near Three Rivers CA	1940 (1890)	1,351	3,498
Shenandoah	near Luray VA	1935	311	805
Theodore Roosevelt	Medora ND (south unit); near Watford City ND (north unit)	1978 (1947)	110	285
Virgin Islands	St. John, US Virgin Islands	1956	23	59
Voyageurs	International Falls MN	1975	341	883
Wind Cave	near Hot Springs SD	1903	44	115
Yellowstone	Idaho, Montana, and Wyoming	1872	3,468	8,983
Yosemite	in the Sierra Nevada, California	1890 (1864)	1,189	3,081
Zion	Springdale UT	1919 (1909)	229	593

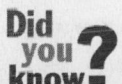 **Did you know?** The largest living things in the world are the giant redwood trees of California.

Major World Zoos

Numbers given for species and animals are approximate.

ZOO (LOCATION)	FOUNDED	NUMBER OF SPECIES	NUMBER OF ANIMALS	FEATURES OF INTEREST
Antwerp Zoo (Belgium)	1843	1,160	6,000	Père David's deer, white rhinoceroses, okapi, Congo peafowl
Bronx Zoo (New York)	1899	700	6,000	largest US metropolitan zoo, Wildlife Conservation Society headquarters, snow leopards, Congo Gorilla forest
Cincinnati Zoo (Ohio)	1875	750	17,000	red pandas, Reptile House, Vanishing Giants exhibit
Columbus Zoo (Ohio)	1927	700	6,000	first lowland gorilla born in captivity, bonobos, koalas
Denver Zoo (Colorado)	1896	700	4,000	conservation center, Primate Panorama, Dragons of Komodo exhibit
Hagenbeck Zoo (Hamburg, Germany)	1907	300	2,000	first zoo with natural animal habitats
Indianapolis Zoo (Indiana)	1964	320	3,800	incorporates zoo, aquarium, and botanical garden; five biomes
Lincoln Park Zoo (Chicago IL)	1868	210	1,330	Great Ape House, wildlife conservation department
Leningrad Zoo (Russia)	1865	410	2,000	polar bears, ornithological exhibit, 130 threatened species
London Zoo (England)	1828	650	N/A	largest zoological library of any zoo, apes and monkeys, giant pandas
National Zoological Gardens of South Africa (Pretoria)	1899	640	5,500	antelope, cheetah-breeding area
Philadelphia Zoo (Pennsylvania)	1874	400	1,800	first white lions and blue-eyed lemurs exhibited in the US
Phoenix Zoo (Arizona)	1962	N/A	N/A	wildlife relief program, reptile exhibit
San Diego Zoo (California)	1916	800	4,000	international conservation program, koalas, white rhinoceroses
Scottish National Zoo (Edinburgh)	1913	150	1,500	largest penguin colony in Europe
National Zoological Park (Washington DC)	1889	500	5,800	giant pandas, Sumatran tigers
Sri Lanka Zoo (Dehiwala)	1936	330	3,890	elephant orphanage
Taronga Zoological Park (Sydney, Australia)	1884	730	4,000	native Australian wildlife, mountain pygmy possum, bird collection
Toronto Zoo (Ontario, Canada)	1974	450	5,000	gorillas, Siberian tigers, African bush elephants
Ueno Zoological Garden (Japan)	1882	960	8,860	insectarium, giant salamander, rare pheasants and wallabies, giant pandas

Major World Botanical Gardens

Most botanical gardens are concerned primarily with exhibiting ornamental plants, insofar as possible in a scheme that emphasizes natural relationships. A major contemporary objective of botanical gardens is to maintain extensive collections of plants, labeled with common and scientific names and regions of origin. Numbers given for species are approximate.

GARDEN (LOCATION)	FOUNDED	NUMBER OF SPECIES	FEATURES OF INTEREST
Atlanta Botanical Garden (Georgia)	1976	N/A	plant conservation
Australian National Botanic Gardens (Canberra)	1970	5,500	Australian flora
The Botanical Garden of the University of Vienna (Austria)	1754	9,000	woody tropical plants, teaching and research
The Botanic Garden of Padova (Italy)	1545	N/A	oldest university garden, medicinal plants
Brooklyn Botanic Garden (New York)	1911	12,000	rose, cactus, and orchid collections; garden for the blind
Cheyenne Botanic Gardens (Wyoming)	1977	N/A	solar heated conservatory, solar energy research
Chicago Botanic Garden (Illinois)	1890	8,819 taxa	23 gardens, ornamentals, Midwest plant conservation
Denver Botanic Gardens (Colorado)	1951	15,000	Rocky Mountain region plants
Fort Worth Botanic Garden (Texas)	N/A	2,500	21 specialty gardens

Major World Botanical Gardens (continued)

GARDEN (LOCATION)	FOUNDED	NUMBER OF SPECIES	FEATURES OF INTEREST
National Botanic Gardens, Glasnevin (Dublin, Ireland)	1795	20,000	palms, native strawberry trees, Atlantic cedar
National Botanic Garden of Belgium (Meise)	1829	N/A	classical herbarium studies
The New York Botanical Garden (Bronx NY)	N/A	18,000	48 gardens and plant collections, 50 acre forest, International Plant Science Center
Peradeniya Botanic Gardens (Sri Lanka)	1821	4,000	orchids, gymnosperms, flowering trees
Royal Botanic Garden Edinburgh (Scotland)	1670	17,000	botanical library, among largest collections of living plants
Royal Botanic Gardens, Kew (London, England)	1759	N/A	alpines, junipers, seed conservation
Santa Barbara Botanic Garden (California)	N/A	1,000 taxa	native California vegetation
Singapore Botanic Gardens	1859	2,700	orchids, bromeliads, palms
Tower Hill Botanic Garden (Boylston MA)	1986	N/A	apples, flowering bulbs
University of Copenhagen Botanic Garden (Denmark)	1872	13,000	Palm House, research and education
United States Botanic Garden (Washington DC)	1820	N/A	conservatory, large greenhouse

Health

Worldwide Health Indicators

Column data as follows: **Life expectancy** *in 2002;* **Infant mortality** *per 1,000 births in 2000;* **Food** *= percentage (%) of the FAO recommended minimum (1999)[1].* **N/A** *= not available.* **Water** *= percentage (%) of population with access to safe drinking water (1989–98);* **Doctors** *= persons per doctor, latest data[2].*

REGION/BLOC	LIFE EXPECTANCY MALE	LIFE EXPECTANCY FEMALE	INFANT MORTALITY	FOOD	WATER	DOCTORS
Africa	**51.1**	**53.2**	**86.9**	**104**	**57**	**2,560**
Central Africa	46.9	50.4	107.8	83	44	12,890
East Africa	45.0	46.5	95.4	84	44	13,620
North Africa	63.2	66.8	57.7	125	82	890
Southern Africa	49.6	50.8	63.0	116	70	1,610
West Africa	50.3	51.5	86.6	113	52	6,260
Americas	**68.8**	**75.2**	**25.4**	**128**	**83**	**520**
Anglo-America[3]	74.4	80.2	6.7	140	91	370
Canada	76.0	83.0	5.1	119	100	540
United States	74.2	79.9	6.8	142	90	360
Latin America	65.2	72.2	32.6	119	78	690
Caribbean	67.6	72.4	43.5	102	77	380
Central America	66.9	72.2	35.8	105	76	950
Mexico	68.5	74.7	26.2	135	85	810
South America	63.8	71.5	33.0	117	76	710
Andean Group	67.9	74.3	31.3	106	79	830
Brazil	58.5	67.6	38.0	122	76	770
Other South America	71.4	78.1	20.7	129	71	410
Asia	**65.8**	**69.0**	**50.9**	**117**	**75**	**970**
Eastern Asia	70.3	74.6	26.5	125	71	610
China	69.6	73.3	28.9	126	67	620
Japan	77.5	84.1	3.9	123	97	530
South Korea	70.8	78.5	7.9	131	93	740
Other Eastern Asia	71.2	76.9	18.4	107	96	500
South Asia	61.3	62.4	70.3	108	80	2,100
India	61.9	63.1	64.9	112	81	1,920
Pakistan	60.3	61.9	82.5	106	79	1,840
Other South Asia	59.1	59.1	84.6	89	78	5,080
Southeast Asia	64.5	69.5	40.3	120	70	3,120
Southwest Asia	65.8	70.3	610	52.3	79	116
Central Asia	59.2	67.7	330	77.1	85	98

Worldwide Health Indicators (continued)

REGION/BLOC	LIFE EXPECTANCY MALE	LIFE EXPECTANCY FEMALE	INFANT MORTALITY	FOOD	WATER	DOCTORS
Asia (continued)						
Gulf Cooperation Council	67.7	71.1	620	46.2	95	122
Iran	68.3	71.1	1,200	30.0	95	117
Other Southwest Asia	66.6	70.9	690	51.8	65	122
Europe	**70.0**	**77.9**	**300**	**10.8**	**99**	**125**
Eastern Europe	64.1	73.9	290	18.1	95	116
Russia	62.0	72.7	240	20.3	N/A	111
Ukraine	60.4	71.9	330	21.7	97	112
Other Eastern Europe	67.5	75.9	370	15.1	94	122
Western Europe	75.0	81.5	300	5.1	100	134
European Union (EU)	74.9	81.5	290	5.1	100	134
France	74.9	82.9	330	4.5	100	141
Germany	74.3	80.8	290	4.8	100	128
Italy	75.9	82.4	180	5.9	100	143
Spain	75.3	82.5	240	5.0	99	136
United Kingdom	75.0	80.5	720	5.6	100	129
Other EU	74.8	80.9	320	4.9	100	132
Non-EU	76.3	82.3	480	4.4	100	123
Oceania	**73.2**	**78.8**	**480**	**24.0**	**86**	**117**
Australia	76.9	82.7	400	5.0	95	120
Pacific Ocean Islands	67.0	72.2	770	40.3	68	111
World	**64.7**	**68.9**	**730**	**53.6**	**76**	**118**

[1]The Food and Agriculture Organization of the United Nations (FAO) calculates this percentage by dividing the caloric equivalent to the known average daily supply of foodstuffs for human consumption in a given country by its population, thus arriving at a minimum daily per capita caloric intake. The higher the percentage, the more calories consumed.   [2]Latest data available for individual countries.   [3]Includes Canada, the US, Greenland, Bermuda, and St. Pierre and Miquelon.

Causes of Death, Worldwide, by Sex and Region

Global estimates for 2000 as published in the *World Health Report 2001*, unless otherwise noted. Top causes listed for All Categories; top 20 causes listed for males/females; top 15 causes listed for countries. Regions are as defined by the World Health Organization. Gaps in the information below often reflect the difficulty of collecting accurate data. Data are percentages of total deaths in each category.

LEADING CAUSES OF DEATH	ALL CATEGORIES	MALES	FEMALES	COUNTRIES[2] HIGH-INCOME	COUNTRIES[2] MID-/LOW-INCOME
1. Ischemic heart disease	12.4	12.2	12.6	17.9	11.5
2. Cerebrovascular disease	9.2	8.1	10.4	10.7	8.9
3. Lower respiratory infections	6.9	7.0	6.9	4.7	7.3
4. HIV disease	5.3	5.0	5.6	—	6.1
5. COPD[1]	4.5	4.6	4.4	3.5	4.7
6. Perinatal conditions	4.4	4.4	4.4	—	5.1
7. Diarrheal diseases	3.8	4.0	3.6	—	4.4
8. Tuberculosis	3.0	3.5	2.4	—	3.4
9. Road traffic accidents	2.3	3.1	1.3	1.6	2.4
10. Trachea, bronchus, lung cancers	2.2	3.0	1.2	5.6	1.6
11. Malaria	1.9	1.8	2.1	—	2.3
12. Hypertensive heart disease	1.7	1.5	1.9	1.6	1.7
13. Self-inflicted injuries	1.5	1.7	1.2	1.5	1.5
14. Diabetes mellitus	1.5	1.2	1.8	2.3	—
15. Cirrhosis of the liver	1.4	1.8	—	1.5	1.4
16. Measles	1.4	1.3	1.5	—	1.6
17. Stomach cancer	1.3	1.6	1.1	2.0	—
18. Congenital anomalies	1.2	1.1	1.2	—	—
19. Liver cancer	1.1	1.5	—	—	—
20. Nephritis and nephrosis	1.1	—	1.1	—	—

Causes of Death, Worldwide, by Sex and Region (continued)

LEADING CAUSES OF DEATH	ALL CATEGORIES	MALES	FEMALES	COUNTRIES[2] HIGH-INCOME	MID-/LOW-INCOME
21. Colon and rectum cancers	1.0	—	—	3.2	—
22. Violence	0.9	1.4	—	—	—
23. Breast cancer	0.8	—	1.8	2.0	—
24. Drowning	0.8	—	—	—	—
25. Esophagus cancer	0.7	—	—	—	—
26. War	0.6	—	—	—	—
27. Tetanus	0.6	—	—	—	—
28. Poisoning	0.6	—	—	—	—
29. Mouth and oropharynx cancers	0.6	—	—	—	—
30. Cervix uteri cancer	0.5	—	1.1	—	—
31. Whooping cough	0.5	—	—	—	—
32. Prostate cancer	0.5	—	—	1.5	—
33. Alzheimer's and other dementias	0.5	—	—	1.8	—

LEADING CAUSES OF DEATH	ALL CATEGORIES	AMERICAN	AFRICAN	EASTERN MEDITERRANEAN	EUROPEAN	SOUTHEAST ASIAN	WESTERN PACIFIC
1. Ischemic heart disease	12.4	15.6	3.1	10.5	24.3	13.7	8.2
2. Cerebrovascular disease	9.2	7.7	2.9	5.3	15.4	5.7	16.2
3. Lower respiratory infections	6.9	4.4	10.1	9.1	3.0	9.5	4.7
4. HIV disease	5.3	—	22.6	—	—	2.6	—
5. COPD[1]	4.5	3.5	1.1	1.4	2.8	2.2	13.8
6. Perinatal conditions	4.4	2.6	5.5	7.5	—	7.1	2.8
7. Diarrheal diseases	3.8	1.3	6.7	7.1	—	6.7	—
8. Tuberculosis	3.0	—	3.6	3.4	—	4.8	3.0
9. Road traffic accidents	2.3	2.4	1.6	2.3	1.3	3.1	2.7
10. Trachea, bronchus, lung cancers	2.2	3.9	—	—	3.9	—	3.5
11. Malaria	1.9	—	9.1	—	—	—	—
12. Hypertensive heart disease	1.7	2.3	—	1.8	1.6	1.5	2.7
13. Self-inflicted injuries	1.5	—	—	—	1.9	—	3.0
14. Diabetes mellitus	1.5	3.7	—	1.6	1.4	1.4	—
15. Cirrhosis of the liver	1.4	1.8	—	—	1.8	1.6	1.7
16. Measles	1.4	—	4.3	2.0	—	1.4	—
17. Stomach cancer	1.3	—	—	—	1.0	—	3.2
18. Congenital anomalies	1.2	—	—	2.2	—	1.9	—
19. Liver cancer	1.1	—	—	—	—	—	3.5
20. Nephritis and nephrosis	1.1	1.4	—	1.7	—	—	—
21. Colon and rectum cancers	1.0	1.8	—	—	2.5	—	—
22. Violence	0.9	2.7	1.1	—	—	—	—
23. Breast cancer	0.8	1.5	—	—	1.6	—	—
24. Drowning	0.8	—	—	—	—	—	1.5
25. Esophagus cancer	0.7	—	—	—	—	—	1.9
26. War	0.6	—	1.6	—	—	—	—
27. Tetanus	0.6	—	1.1	1.4	1.1	—	—
28. Poisoning	0.6	—	—	—	1.1	—	—
29. Mouth and oropharynx cancers	0.6	—	—	—	—	1.2	—
30. Cervix uteri cancer	0.5	—	—	—	—	—	—
31. Whooping cough	0.5	—	1.6	1.4	—	—	—
32. Prostate cancer	0.5	—	—	—	1.0	—	—
33. Alzheimer's and other	0.5	—	—	—	—	—	—

[1]Chronic obstructive pulmonary disease.   [2]As defined in the World Health Report 1999.

Did you know? With the exception of snakes and bees, scorpions cause more deaths than any other nonparasitic group of animals. More than 5,000 people are thought to die each year from scorpion stings. Scorpions often play the role of evildoers in fables and legends. A long curved tail with a venomous stinger and grasping, fingerlike first appendages are typical scorpion features.

Ten Leading Causes of Death in the US, by Age

Data for 1999. Numbers in thousands. Rates per 100,000 population.

CAUSE	NUMBER	%	RATE
1–4 years			
1. Accidents	1,898	36.2	12.6
2. Congenital malformations, deformations, and chromosomal abnormalities	549	10.5	3.6
3. Malignant neoplasms	418	8.0	2.8
4. Assault (homicide)	376	7.2	2.5
5. Diseases of the heart	183	3.5	1.2
6. Influenza and pneumonia	130	2.5	0.9
7. Perinatal conditions	92	1.8	0.6
8. Septicemia	87	1.7	0.6
9. Nonmalignant/unknown neoplasms	63	1.2	0.4
10. Chronic lower respiratory diseases	54	1.0	0.4
All other causes	1,399	26.7	9.3
All causes, 1–4 years	**5,249**	**100.0**	**34.7**
5–9 years			
1. Accidents	1,459	42.0	7.3
2. Malignant neoplasms	509	14.7	2.6
3. Congenital malformations, deformations, and chromosomal abnormalities	207	6.0	1.0
4. Assault (homicide)	186	5.4	0.9
5. Diseases of the heart	116	3.3	0.6
6. Nonmalignant/unknown neoplasms	64	1.8	0.3
7. Chronic lower respiratory diseases	49	1.4	0.2
8. Septicemia	47	1.4	0.2
9. Influenza and pneumonia	46	1.3	0.2
10. HIV disease	38	1.1	0.2
All other causes	753	21.7	3.8
All causes, 5–9 years	**3,474**	**100.0**	**17.4**
10–14 years			
1. Accidents	1,632	39.6	8.3
2. Malignant neoplasms	503	12.2	2.6
3. Assault (homicide)	246	6.0	1.3
4. Intentional self-harm (suicide)	242	5.9	1.2
5. Congenital malformations, deformations, and chromosomal abnormalities	221	5.4	1.1
6. Diseases of the heart	161	3.9	0.8
7. Chronic lower respiratory diseases	90	2.2	0.5
8. Influenza and pneumonia	47	1.1	0.2
9. Cerebrovascular diseases	39	0.9	0.2
10. Nonmalignant/unknown neoplasms	37	0.9	0.2
All other causes	903	21.9	4.6
All causes, 10–14 years	**4,121**	**100.0**	**21.1**
15–19 years			
1. Accidents	6,688	48.5	33.9
2. Assault (homicide)	2,093	15.2	10.6
3. Intentional self-harm (suicide)	1,615	11.7	8.2
4. Malignant neoplasms	745	5.4	3.8
5. Diseases of the heart	463	3.4	2.3
6. Congenital malformations, deformations, and chromosomal abnormalities	222	1.6	1.1
7. Chronic lower respiratory diseases	107	0.8	0.5

CAUSE	NUMBER	%	RATE
15–19 years (continued)			
8. Influenza and pneumonia	73	0.5	0.4
9. Cerebrovascular diseases	67	0.5	0.3
10. Nonmalignant/unknown neoplasms	52	0.4	0.3
All other causes	1,653	12.0	8.4
All causes, 15–19 years	**13,778**	**100.0**	**69.8**
20–24 years			
1. Accidents	6,968	41.3	38.7
2. Assault (homicide)	2,905	17.2	16.1
3. Intentional self-harm (suicide)	2,286	13.5	12.7
4. Malignant neoplasms	979	5.8	5.4
5. Diseases of the heart	606	3.6	3.4
6. Congenital malformations, deformations, and chromosomal abnormalities	212	1.3	1.2
7. HIV disease	167	1.0	0.9
8. Cerebrovascular diseases	115	0.7	0.6
9. Influenza and pneumonia	106	0.6	0.6
10. Diabetes mellitus	104	0.6	0.6
All other causes	2,430	14.4	13.5
All causes, 20–24 years	**16,878**	**100.0**	**93.6**
25–34 years			
1. Accidents	11,890	29.0	31.3
2. Intentional self-harm (suicide)	5,106	12.4	13.5
3. Assault (homicide)	4,231	10.3	11.2
4. Malignant neoplasms	4,005	9.8	10.6
5. Diseases of the heart	3,066	7.5	8.1
6. HIV disease	2,729	6.6	7.2
7. Diabetes mellitus	582	1.4	1.5
8. Cerebrovascular diseases	580	1.4	1.5
9. Congenital malformations, deformations, and chromosomal abnormalities	465	1.1	1.2
10. Chronic liver disease and cirrhosis	407	1.0	1.1
All other causes	8,005	19.5	21.1
All causes, 25–34 years	**41,066**	**100.0**	**108.3**
35–44 years			
1. Malignant neoplasms	16,732	18.7	37.3
2. Accidents	15,231	17.1	34.0
3. Diseases of the heart	13,600	15.2	30.3
4. Intentional self-harm (suicide)	6,466	7.2	14.4
5. HIV disease	6,232	7.0	13.9
6. Chronic liver disease and cirrhosis	3,302	3.7	7.4
7. Assault (homicide)	3,206	3.6	7.2
8. Cerebrovascular diseases	2,574	2.9	5.7
9. Diabetes mellitus	1,942	2.2	4.3
10. Influenza and pneumonia	1,063	1.2	2.4
All other causes	18,908	21.2	42.2
All causes, 35–44 years	**89,256**	**100.0**	**199.2**
45–54 years			
1. Malignant neoplasms	46,681	30.5	130.4
2. Diseases of the heart	34,994	22.9	97.7
3. Accidents	11,639	7.6	32.5
4. Chronic liver disease and cirrhosis	6,368	4.2	17.8
5. Cerebrovascular diseases	5,563	3.6	15.5

Ten Leading Causes of Death in the US, by Age (continued)

CAUSE	NUMBER	%	RATE
45–54 years (continued)			
6. Intentional self-harm (suicide)	5,081	3.3	14.2
7. Diabetes mellitus	4,735	3.1	13.2
8. HIV disease	3,907	2.6	10.9
9. Chronic lower respiratory diseases	3,110	2.0	8.7
10. Influenza and pneumonia	1,697	1.1	4.7
All other causes	29,199	19.1	81.6
All causes, 45–54 years	**152,974**	**100.0**	**427.3**
55–64 years			
1. Malignant neoplasms	89,067	37.3	380.8
2. Diseases of the heart	64,167	26.9	274.3
3. Chronic lower respiratory diseases	11,297	4.7	48.3
4. Cerebrovascular diseases	9,652	4.0	41.3
5. Diabetes mellitus	9,097	3.8	38.9
6. Accidents	7,285	3.0	31.1
7. Chronic liver disease and cirrhosis	5,637	2.4	24.1
8. Intentional self-harm (suicide)	2,896	1.2	12.4
9. Nephritis, nephrotic syndrome, and nephrosis	2,864	1.2	12.2
10. Septicemia	2,714	1.1	11.6
All other causes	34,303	14.4	146.7
All causes, 55–64 years	**238,979**	**100.0**	**1,021.8**
65–74 years			
1. Malignant neoplasms	152,338	33.7	836.2
2. Diseases of the heart	129,253	28.6	709.5
3. Chronic lower respiratory diseases	32,644	7.2	179.2
4. Cerebrovascular diseases	24,092	5.3	132.2
5. Diabetes mellitus	16,908	3.7	92.8
6. Accidents	8,208	1.8	45.1
7. Influenza and pneumonia	6,861	1.5	37.7
8. Nephritis, nephrotic syndrome, and nephrosis	6,841	1.5	37.6
9. Septicemia	5,750	1.3	31.6
10. Chronic liver disease and cirrhosis	5,642	1.2	31.0
All other causes	64,063	14.2	351.6
All causes, 65–74 years	**452,600**	**100.0**	**2,484.3**
75–84 years			
1. Diseases of the heart	226,152	32.4	1,861.8
2. Malignant neoplasms	162,770	23.3	1,340.0

CAUSE	NUMBER	%	RATE
75–84 years (continued)			
3. Cerebrovascular diseases	57,427	8.2	472.8
4. Chronic lower respiratory diseases	48,635	7.0	400.4
5. Diabetes mellitus	21,757	3.1	179.1
6. Influenza and pneumonia	19,192	2.7	158.0
7. Alzheimer's disease	15,836	2.3	130.4
8. Accidents	12,282	1.8	101.1
9. Nephritis, nephrotic syndrome, and nephrosis	11,927	1.7	98.2
10. Septicemia	9,710	1.4	79.9
All other causes	112,902	16.2	929.5
All causes, 75–84 years	**698,590**	**100.0**	**5,751.3**
85 years and over			
1. Diseases of the heart	251,860	39.0	6,032.5
2. Malignant neoplasms	75,014	11.6	1,796.7
3. Cerebrovascular diseases	67,080	10.4	1,606.7
4. Influenza and pneumonia	31,229	4.8	748.0
5. Chronic lower respiratory diseases	26,833	4.2	642.7
6. Alzheimer's disease	24,980	3.9	598.3
7. Diabetes mellitus	13,178	2.0	315.6
8. Accidents	11,729	1.8	280.9
9. Nephritis, nephrotic syndrome, and nephrosis	11,170	1.7	267.5
10. Septicemia	9,166	1.4	219.5
All other causes	123,902	19.2	2,967.7
All causes, 85 years and over	**646,141**	**100.0**	**15,476.1**
All ages[1]			
1. Diseases of the heart	725,192	30.3	265.9
2. Malignant neoplasms	549,838	23.0	201.6
3. Cerebrovascular diseases	167,366	7.0	61.4
4. Chronic lower respiratory diseases	124,181	5.2	45.5
5. Accidents	97,860	4.1	35.9
6. Diabetes mellitus	68,399	2.9	25.1
7. Influenza and pneumonia	63,730	2.7	23.4
8. Alzheimer's disease	44,536	1.9	16.3
9. Nephritis, nephrotic syndrome, and nephrosis	35,525	1.5	13.0
10. Septicemia	30,680	1.3	11.3
All other causes	484,092	20.2	177.5
All causes, all ages	**2,391,399**	**100.0**	**877.0**

[1]Includes under 1 year.

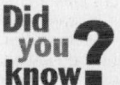

Did you know? Sharks never get sick. They are apparently the only animal immune to every known disease.

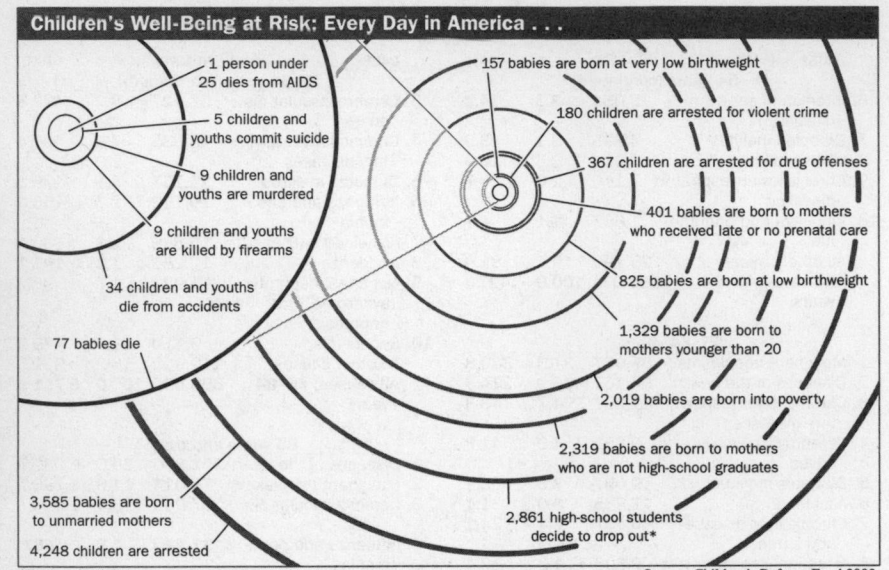

Children's Well-Being at Risk: Every Day in America . . .

1 person under 25 dies from AIDS

5 children and youths commit suicide

9 children and youths are murdered

9 children and youths are killed by firearms

34 children and youths die from accidents

77 babies die

3,585 babies are born to unmarried mothers

4,248 children are arrested

157 babies are born at very low birthweight

180 children are arrested for violent crime

367 children are arrested for drug offenses

401 babies are born to mothers who received late or no prenatal care

825 babies are born at low birthweight

1,329 babies are born to mothers younger than 20

2,019 babies are born into poverty

2,319 babies are born to mothers who are not high-school graduates

2,861 high-school students decide to drop out*

*Every school day   Source: Children's Defense Fund 2002.

Infectious Diseases

Infectious diseases are caused by microscopic organisms, including viruses, bacteria, fungi, and animal parasites, that invade the body and multiply. Some infections, such as measles and malaria, affect the entire body; other infections affect only one body organ or system. **Infectious agents** may enter the body in a variety of ways, including inhalation of airborne microbes, skin-to-skin or sexual contact, ingestion of contaminated food or water, insect bites, and transmission from women to their unborn children. The outcome of any infection depends on the number and virulence of infectious agents, as well as on the response of the immune system.

Although progress has been made in the **eradication** of many infectious diseases, new diseases are emerging and many previously controlled diseases are making a resurgence. Unprecedented population growth, an increase in international travel, worldwide transport of animals and food products, and human encroachment on wilderness habitats all play a role in the spread of infectious diseases. In addition, microbial evolution has led to new strains of disease that are resistant to the antibiotics available to treat them. This has led to a call for a decrease in the use of antibiotics by health professionals, as the more often these drugs are administered, the more likely it is that antibiotic-resistant strains of microorganisms will emerge. **Immunization**, increased public health measures, and the development of new treatments are all crucial to controlling infectious diseases.

Autoimmune Diseases

In autoimmune diseases, the immune system mistakenly attacks the cells, tissues, or organs of a person's own body. The cells that normally work to defend against infection effectively misrecognize parts of one's own body as alien. Autoimmune diseases are not contagious; genetic makeup increases one's chances of developing an autoimmune disease, but other environmental triggers may also play a role in disease onset. Many autoimmune diseases are rare, but as a group they afflict millions of Americans. For 2001 it was estimated that 50 million Americans (or one in five people) suffered from one or more than 80 autoimmune diseases. Women of childbearing age are most often afflicted.

Each autoimmune disease affects the body in a different way. Some of the most common diseases are listed by main target organs in the table below. All involve a collection of immune system cells and molecules at a target site, broadly referred to as **inflammation.** For example, in multiple sclerosis the autoimmune reaction is directed against the brain, and in inflammatory bowel diseases (Crohn's disease and ulcerative colitis) the immune system attacks the gut. In autoimmune diseases such as lupus, affected tissues and organs vary among individuals.

Autoimmune diseases are often difficult to **diagnose,** particularly in the early stages. Laboratory tests and close supervision are necessary for proper diagnosis and treatment. The majority of autoimmune diseases are **chronic;** health professionals seek to manage the inflammation caused by the disease rather than to cure it. Research into the intricate workings of the immune system and pathways of inflammation is being conducted in the hopes of future disease prevention.

Autoimmune Diseases

For information on specific autoimmune diseases, see <www.nlaid.nih.gov>.

Blood
Autoimmune hemolytic anemia
Autoimmune thrombocytopenia
Pernicious anemia

Blood vessels
Anti-phospholipid syndrome
Behcet's disease
Temporal artertis
Vasculitides (such as Wegener's granulomatosis)

Endocrine glands
Autoimmune disease of the adrenal gland
Autoimmune oophoritis and orchitis
Diabetes mellitus (type I or immune mediated)
Graves' disease
Hashimoto's thyroiditis

Gastrointestinal system
Autoimmune hepatitis
Crohn's disease
Primary biliary cirrhosis
Ulcerative colitis

Multiple organs (including the musculoskeletal systems)
Polymyositis, dermatomyositis
Rheumatoid arthritis
Scleroderma
Sjogren's syndrome
Spondyloarthropathies (such as ankylosing spondylitis)
Systemic lupus erythematosus

Nervous systems
Autoimmune neuropathies (such as Guillain-Barré)
Autoimmune ureitis
Multiple sclerosis
Myasthenia gravis

Skin
Dermatitis herpetiformis
Pemphigus vulgaris
Psoriasis
Vitiligo

Cardiovascular Diseases

Cardiovascular diseases are the leading cause of death in the US, accounting for more than 40% of fatalities each year. There are many different diseases that can lead to congestive **heart failure**, a condition in which the heart muscle is less able to pump blood. Some of the common cardiovascular diseases are:

Ischemic Heart Disease (coronary heart disease)—the effect of an inadequate supply of oxygen-rich blood to the heart muscle because of narrowing or blocking of a coronary artery by fatty and fibrous tissue (arteriosclerosis). If the oxygen depletion is extreme, the effect may be the death of a section of heart muscle (myocardial infarction); if the deprivation is insufficient to cause infarction, the effect may be angina pectoris. Both conditions can be fatal because they can cause left ventricular failure or ventricular fibrillation—an uncontrolled and uncoordinated twitching of the ventricle muscle that induces sudden cardiac death. Coronary bypass surgery or balloon angioplasty are indicated if medication and diet do not control progressive coronary heart disease and if the myocardial damage is not too extensive.

Pulmonary Heart Disease—enlargement and eventual failure of the right ventricle of the heart because of disorders of the lungs, disorders of the blood vessels of the lungs, or abnormalities of the chest wall. The most common causes are chronic bronchitis and emphysema. The condition is such that the network of capillaries in the lungs is progressively destroyed, causing pressure in the pulmonary artery to be increased. The resultant back pressure on the right ventricle increases the work and the size of the chamber, leading to heart enlargement and eventually, if uncorrected, heart failure. The disease is characterized by a chronic cough, difficulty in breathing after exertion, wheezing, and weakness and fatigue. Treatment of the acute form of the disease is often by removal of the pulmonary blockage. Other treatment may include the use of antibiotics to combat respiratory infection; the use of a respirator to ease breathing; the restriction of sodium intake; and the administration of diuretics and digitalis.

Heart Malformation (congenital heart disease)—any deformity of the heart that develops within the first two months of fetal life. After birth, some of these deformities impair the supply of oxygen to the tissues and may cause disability or death. Approximately 40,000 children are born with a heart defect each year. These malformations can be repaired by modern surgical procedures with varying degrees of success.

Other cardiovascular-related conditions that may increase one's likelihood of heart disease include arrhythmias and blood pressure irregularities:

Arrhythmias are disorders of the rhythmic beating of the heart and are fairly common. Although often relatively harmless, they may indicate a more serious heart problem.

Blood pressure is the force originating in the pumping action of the heart, exerted by the blood against the walls of the blood vessels. It is usually measured indirectly over the brachial or femoral artery. The highest (systolic) pressure, normally about 120, occurs during contraction of the ventricles; the lowest (diastolic) pressure, normally about 80, occurs during ventricular relaxation. **Hypertension**, or high blood pressure, occurs when the blood vessels lose their flexibility or the muscles surrounding them force them to contract. As a result, the heart must pump more forcefully to move the same amount of blood through the narrowed vessels into the capillaries, thereby increasing blood pressure. The increased risk of death from congestive heart failure, kidney failure, or stroke is the chief danger of hypertension. **Hypotension**, or low blood pressure, is a condition in which the blood pressure is abnormally low, either because of reduced blood volume or because of increased blood-vessel capacity. Although not in itself an indication of ill health, it often accompanies disease conditions. Some causes are extensive bleeding or burns and exposure to cold.

To help prevent heart disease, the American Heart Association recommends maintaining a healthy diet, exercising, keeping cholesterol low, and managing stress.

Internet resources: <www.americanheart.org>

Stroke

A stroke is a sudden impairment of brain function resulting either from a substantial reduction in blood flow to some part of the brain or from intracranial bleeding. The consequences may include transient or lasting paralysis on one or both sides of the body, difficulties in using words or in eating, and a loss in muscular coordination. A stroke may cause cerebral infarctions (dead sections of brain tissue).

Stroke occurs in conjunction with at least one of the following four events:

A blood clot forms within a blood vessel of the brain (thrombosis). This is the most common cause.

A blood clot lodges in an artery supplying brain tissue after originating in another portion of the body (embolism). A heart attack, damage to a valve, and an irregular heartbeat can cause blood clots that may reach the brain.

An intermittent insufficiency in the flow of blood results temporarily from a spasm of the arteries or the sludging of the blood as it passes through segments of vessels that have been narrowed by arteriosclerosis.

Hemorrhage occurs after an artery ruptures, usually as a result of a weakening of the arterial wall because of arteriosclerosis or because of a thinning of the wall along with bulging (an aneurysm), which may be congenital or develop later in life. The walls of arteries in the brain can become weakened by the assault of **high blood pressure**.

So-called "little strokes" result when long, thin arteries penetrating deep into the brain become blocked by arteriosclerosis, causing areas of surrounding tissue to lose their blood supply. Whereas the initial onset of stroke may be massive in its effects, producing widespread paralysis within several hours, the onset may also be manifested by a series of transient little strokes during which the patient may experience weakness and numbness of an arm, a leg, or a side of the face.

Precise history and physical examination are essential to differentiate stroke from a tumor and from brain injury resulting from other causes. Examination of spinal fluid for evidence of blood and diagnostic imaging may clarify the **diagnosis**. Surgery may be attempted to remove the obstruction or to insert a graft or synthetic bypass. Physical and speech therapy may also help prevent deformity. Many victims of stroke may live for a further 10 to 20 years or longer after the occurrence.

Smoking, high cholesterol, aging, diabetes, and heritable defects are among the major **risk factors** for stroke. Statistically, men and African Americans also have a higher stroke risk.

The National Stroke Association recommends maintaining a healthy diet that is low in sodium and fat, exercising, keeping cholestorol and alcohol consumption low, and not smoking.

Internet resources: <www.stroke.org>

Diabetes

D iabetes mellitus is a disease in which the body does not produce or properly use insulin, a hormone that is needed to convert sugar, starches, and other food into energy. Two common problems thus caused by diabetes are hyperglycemia (high blood sugar) and hypoglycemia (low blood sugar). There are two types of diabetes: type I, insulin-dependent diabetes (formerly referred to as juvenile-onset diabetes as it usually arises in childhood; and type II, non-insulin-dependent diabetes (formerly referred to as adult-onset diabetes, as it usually occurs after 40 years of age). Despite their former classifications, either type of diabetes can occur at any age. Type II diabetes is by far the most common type of the disease, accounting for about 90% of all cases.

Type I diabetes is an **autoimmune disorder** in which the diabetic's immune system produces antibodies that destroy insulin-producing beta cells. People with type I diabetes require insulin injections to stay alive. Meal planning and exercise also help keep blood sugar levels regular.

Type II diabetes arises from either sluggish pancreatic secretion of insulin or reduced responsiveness in target cells of the body to secreted insulin, or both. It is linked to genetics and obesity. Some cases of type II diabetes can be controlled through diet and exercise, but often medication or insulin shots are needed as well.

It is estimated that 17 million Americans have diabetes, and one in three does not know it. Often diabetes goes undiagnosed because its symptoms seem harmless at first. Diabetes is also more common in African Americans, Latinos, Native Americans, Asian Americans, and Pacific Islanders. Some of the early **warning signs** of diabetes are: frequent urination, excessive thirst, extreme hunger, unusual weight loss, increased fatigue, irritability, and blurry vision.

Diabetes is the sixth leading cause of death by disease in the United States. Each year, at least 190,000 people die as a result of complications associated with diabetes. Possible complications include:

Blindness. Each year, 12,000 to 24,000 people lose their sight due to diabetes. It is the leading cause of new blindness in people 20–74 years of age.

Kidney disease. Diabetic nephropathy, the most common cause of end-stage renal disease, requires dialysis or a kidney transplant to prevent death; 10–21% of all people with diabetes develop kidney disease.

Heart disease and stroke. People with diabetes are two to four times more likely to have heart disease, to die from heart disease, or to suffer a stroke.

Nerve disease and amputations. Approximately 70% of people with diabetes have mild to severe forms of diabetic nerve damage, which can lead to lower limb amputation. Diabetes is the most frequent cause of non-traumatic lower limb amputations in the US.

Impotence. Approximately 13% of men with Type I diabetes and 8% of men with Type II report problems with impotence.

Diabetes is a serious condition, but with proper treatment patients can lead productive lives. To avoid complications, people with diabetes should keep blood-sugar levels close to normal, control their weight, eat a healthy diet, exercise, see a doctor regularly, check their feet carefully for abnormalities, and refrain from smoking.

Internet resources: <www.diabetes.org>

Cancer

Cancer is any of a group of related diseases characterized by uncontrolled multiplication and disorganized growth of the affected cells; it may arise in any of the body's tissues. If left untreated, cancer cells infiltrate and destroy adjacent tissues, eventually gain access to the circulatory system, are transported to distant parts of the body, and ultimately destroy the host. Not all abnormal growths are **malignant**, however; those that are not are referred to as **benign** tumors.

Cancer was known as far back as antiquity, and malignant tumors have been found in mummies 5,000 years old. It is estimated that nearly 1.3 million new cases will arise in the US in 2002. The disease can be caused by a variety of factors, including chemical substances, ionizing radiation, and viruses. Although much is known about how cancer is caused, the precise mechanism involved continues to elude researchers. Certain cancers have the ability to spread from their sites of origin, rendering their treatment and eradication difficult; this results either from direct extension from the primary site as a consequence of growth and tumor cell movement or from the cancer cells entering the vascular system by invading lymphatics or blood vessels (**metastasis**). The more the cancer spreads, the more difficult it is to treat, making early diagnosis of utmost importance.

Some of the major types of cancer are listed below, along with cancer-detection guidelines from the American Cancer Society.

Breast cancer. Breast cancer is the leading cause of death from cancer in women, afflicting approximately 192,200 US women in 2001. *Treatment:* Most patients will require some type of surgery to treat the tumor, possibly in combination with chemotherapy, hormone therapy, or radiation therapy. *Prevention:* Women age 20 and over should perform monthly breast self-exams. Women between the ages of 20 and 39 should have a clinical breast exam every 3 years; women over 40 should have one annually. Women 40 and over should also have a mammogram each year.

Colorectal cancer. Colorectal cancer is very common in the Western world, with an equal incidence in men and women. Generally, the tumors metastasize to the liver, lungs, and other distant sites. *Treatment:* Surgery is the most favored treatment, although chemotherapy and radiation may also be used. *Prevention:* There are five tests to detect colorectal cancer. Individuals 50 and over should choose one of the following options, even if they have no symptoms of the disease:

Fecal occult blood test (every year)
Flexible sigmoidoscopy (every 5 years)
Fecal occult blood test every year plus sigmoidoscopy every 5 years (preferred to either of the above treatments alone)
Double-contrast barium enema (every 5 years)
Colonoscopy (every 10 years)

Leukemias. Leukemias are a heterogeneous group of malignancies of the blood-forming tissues, which include the bone marrow, lymph nodes, and spleen. The acute form of the disease in adults is rapidly fatal, with infiltration of bone marrow and other blood-forming tissues by the malignant cells, while the acute form in children has yielded to treatment and a number of cures are documented. The best established cause involves chronic exposure to ionizing radiation. Other factors, including congenital disorders such as Down syndrome, viruses, and certain chemicals and drugs, have also been implicated. Patients afflicted with leukemia are rendered anemic and are susceptible to infection. *Treatment:* Treatment involves attempts to correct leukemia-related complications by transfusion of normal blood, as well as antibiotics to combat infection and chemotherapy to destroy malignant cells. *Prevention:* There are no special tests that can detect any form of leukemia and no known way to prevent most cases, as the disease is not linked to lifestyle risk factors.

Lung cancer. The most common forms of lung cancer are squamous-cell carcinomas, which arise in bronchial glandular epithelium that has been altered by long exposure to cigarette smoke. Cancers of the lung tend to metastasize widely; the average survival of persons with untreated lung cancer is about 9 months after diagnosis, and the spreading to regional or distant lymph nodes has already occurred in the majority of cases. *Treatment:* Removal of the tumor may prolong life for a number of months. *Prevention:* Do not smoke and avoid second-hand smoke as well as cancer-causing chemicals such as radon gas.

Ovarian cancer. Very common in the industrialized Western world, ovarian cancer may be linked to environmental factors. Many different types of ovarian cancer have been identified, arising either in the epithelium or in connective tissue components. *Treatment:* Tumors may be treated successfully through surgery if diagnosed early. Extension of the disease may require radiation or chemotherapy. *Prevention:* Only 25% of ovarian cancers are found at an early stage, as they often manifest no symptoms early on. Therefore, women 18 and over should have a yearly pelvic exam. If symptoms do present, imaging studies or biopsy may be used to properly diagnose the disease.

Prostate cancer. A common form of cancer in men, prostate cancer commonly metastasizes to the bones and, together with involvement of nerves in the pelvis, creates considerable pain and discomfort. Fortunately, prostate cancer differs from other cancers in its slow rate of growth; if the cancer does not spread, the 5-year survival rate is nearly 100%, even if it remains untreated. *Treatment:* Surgery, radiation, and chemotherapy are the most-frequently used treatments. PSA blood tests and digital rectal exams can help diagnose the disease. *Prevention:* The exact cause of prostate cancer is not known, but a diet low in animal fat and high in vegetables, fruits, and grains is recommended for overall health.

Skin cancer. Approximately 82% of skin cancer arises from basal cells in the deepest layer of the skin, resulting in basal-cell carcinoma. This type of cancer grows slowly and rarely metastasizes, but does invade locally and can cause considerable destruction of adjacent tissues, which can result in disfigurement. Sqamous-cell carcinoma arises from the platelike flat cells that constitute the major cellular component of skin, and these cells may metastasize to regional lymph nodes. *Treatment*: Surgical excision or radiation therapy is often successful. *Prevention*:

The best way to lower one's risk of skin cancer is to avoid UV light. A sunscreen with an SPF of 15 or above is recommended, even on cloudy days. A self-exam each month should reveal any new or changing spots or blemishes on the skin; anything unusual should be reported to a health care provider.

Internet resources: <www.cancer.org>

Alzheimer's Disease

Alzheimer's disease is the most common form of dementia—it is estimated that up to 4 million Americans are currently afflicted. An irreversible, progressive brain disorder that involves the death of brain cells and the breakdown of the connections between them, Alzheimer's usually begins gradually, with symptoms increasing as the disease progresses. On average, patients live for 8 to 10 years after diagnosis, but some have been known to survive for as long as 20.

Scientists are still trying to understand the underlying mechanisms of Alzheimer's; the disease develops differently among individuals, and this suggests that more than one pathological process may lead to the same outcome. One key element is the presence in the brain of two abnormalities—amyloid plaques and neurofibrillary tangles. Unfortunately, these growths can be detected only during an autopsy, and it is not known whether the plaques and tangles are a cause or a consequence of the disease. The majority of cases of Alzheimer's occur after age 60, but about 10% of those who develop the disease are younger. These cases, referred to as early-onset familial Alzheimer's disease, result from an inherited genetic mutation.

The Alzheimer's Association recognizes 10 **warning signs** of disease onset: memory loss; difficulty performing familiar tasks; problems with language; disorientation to time and place; poor or decreased judgment; problems with abstract thinking; misplacing things; changes in mood or behavior; changes in personality; and loss of initiative. These symptoms become progressively more severe, and eventually people with Alzheimer's lose all memory, thinking, and reasoning abilities and become dependent on others for their daily needs.

No single diagnostic test can detect if a person has Alzheimer's. Standard clinical methods of **diagnosis** involve a complete medical history, various medical and neuropsychological tests, a mental status evaluation, a neurological examination, and a psychiatric evauulation. These procedures help rule out other diseases and enable physicians to make a positive clinical diagnosis of Alzheimer's with approximately 90% accuracy.

There is currently no **treatment** to prevent or reverse the effects of Alzheimer's disease; however, four FDA-approved drugs may help prevent worsening of some symptoms for a limited time. Other medications may help control the behavioral symptoms of the disease and make patients more comfortable and easier to care for.

Internet resources: <www.alz.org>

Arthritis

There are more than 100 different medical conditions that fall under the category "arthritis," a blanket term for inflammation of the joints. Arthritis is the number one cause of disability in the US; nearly 43 million (one in six) Americans are affected by it, including almost 300,000 children. Arthritis is generally a chronic condition that requires ongoing treatment. Many forms of arthritis are initially difficult to diagnose; health professionals will generally perform a physical exam, conduct various medical tests, and order X-rays to confirm a **diagnosis.**

Osteoarthritis, the most common joint disease, is characterized by progressive deterioration of the articular cartilage and afflicts more than 80% of those who reach the age of 70. It often affects the hands and the weight-bearing joints, such as the knees, hips, feet, and back, resulting in stiffness, pain, and a limitation in movement as the disease progresses. The genesis of this disorder is not completely understood, but biomechanical forces that place stress on the joints are thought to interact with biochemical and genetic factors to contribute to the degenerative process. Obesity, joint injury owing to sports, and work-related activities may place individuals at increased risk for developing osteoarthritis. Corticosteroids and NSAIDS are commonly prescribed for **treatment**; glucocorticoids may be injected into the affected joints; and surgery may be needed to relieve chronic pain and improve joint function. In addition, joint protection, weight control, and non-weight-bearing exercise are recommended.

Rheumatoid arthritis is an **autoimmune** disease that typically affects many different joints and may also affect other internal organs. Inflammation and thickening of the synovial membranes can result in irreversible damage to the joint, as the inflamed joint lining invades and damages bone and cartilage. In addition to joint swelling, redness, warmth, stiffness, and pain, symptoms may include loss of appetite or energy, fever, anemia, and the development of rheumatoid nodules. Rheumatoid arthritis is about three times as common in women as in men and afflicts about 1% of the adult population in developed nations. Although the exact cause of the disease remains unknown, approximately 80% of individuals with rheumatoid arthritis have characteristic autoantibodies in their blood that are collectively called rheumatoid factor, and there is evidence that such individuals have a genetic susceptibility to some environment agent related to disease onset. Rheumatoid arthritis is generally chronic, often with periods of disease flare-up and remission. There are a variety of drugs available for **treatment.** Symptomatic medications such as NSAIDS, analgesics, and glucocorticoids help reduce joint pain, stiffness, and swelling, while disease-modifying anti-rheumatic medications, including methotrexate, antimalarials, and biologic agents, may actually help stop disease progression.

Fibromyalgia is an arthritis-related syndrome that is characterized by widespread musculoskeletal pain, fatigue, and tenderness in precise areas of the body. It affects approximately 2% of Americans, primarily women of childbearing age. It was not until 1990 that fibromyalgia was officially recognized as a distinct syndrome. **Treatment** often includes a combination of exercise, medication (including antidepressants), physical therapy, and relaxation.

Other conditions related to arthritis include lupus, ankylosing spondylitis, gout, and psoriatic arthritis.

Internet resources: <www.arthritis.org>

Allergies

An allergy is a hypersensitive reaction by the body to foreign substances that in similar amounts and circumstances are harmless within the bodies of other people.

Antigens that provoke allergic reactions are called **allergens**. Typical allergens include pollens, drugs, lints, bacteria, foods, and dyes or chemicals. Allergies tend to run in families and are common among children. Skin testing is often used to determine the source of the allergen.

Allergic reactions can be the result of inhaled allergens, such as weed, tree, and grass pollen, mold spores, animal dander, or house dust. These generally result in runny nose, sneezing, and watery and itchy eyes (allergic rhinitis). Eczema and contact dermatitis are common skin allergies that may result in a variety of problems, including rashes, hives, and itching. Certain foods, most frequently milk, fish, eggs, nuts, and wheat, tend to produce allergic reactions that result in intestinal disturbances.

Anaphylactic shock is the most severe allergic reaction and often occurs in individuals sensitive to stinging insects, penicillin, nuts, or shellfish. Anaphylaxis causes swelling of body tissues, vomiting, cramps, and a drop in blood pressure.

The most effective **treatment** is avoidance of the allergen. Additionally, allergy shots allow patients to build an immunity to the allergen. Antihistamines, decongestants, bronchodilators, and anti-inflammatory agents may also be used.

Internet resources: <www.aaaai.org>

Asthma

Asthma is a chronic lung disorder affecting 12–17 million Americans, including approximately 5 million children. During an **asthmatic episode**, the airways become inflamed and may constrict, causing episodes of breathlessness, wheezing, coughing, and chest tightness that range in severity from mild to life-threatening. Although the mechanisms underlying an asthmatic episode are not fully understood, in general it is known that exposure to an inciting factor stimulates the release of chemicals from the immune system that cause spasmodic contraction of the smooth muscle surrounding the bronchi, swelling and inflammation of the bronchial tubes, and excessive secretion of mucus. The inflamed, mucus-clogged airways act as a one-way valve, preventing air from being expired.

Asthma is classified into four categories depending on severity and frequency: mild intermittent, mild persistent, moderate persistent, and severe persistent. Childhood asthma is often associated with an inherited susceptibility to **allergens**, substances such as pollen or dust mites. In adults, asthma also may develop in response to allergens, but viral infections, aspirin, exercise, and exposure to certain materials in the workplace may cause the disease as well.

Asthma sufferers are encouraged to minimize their exposure to substances that may trigger an attack. A number of **medications** are available to prevent and control the symptoms of asthma, including long-term and quick-relief prescriptions. A prolonged asthma attack that does not respond to medication may require hospitalization and administration of oxygen. Individuals can also monitor their level of airflow obstruction by using a pocket-size device called a **peak-flow meter**.

Internet resources: <www.aaaai.org>

HIV/AIDS

Acquired Immunodeficiency Syndrome, or AIDS, is a fatal transmissable disorder of the immune system that is caused by the human immunodeficiency virus (HIV). HIV was first isolated in 1983. In most cases, HIV slowly attacks and destroys the **immune system**, leaving the infected individual vulnerable to malignancies and infections that eventually cause death. AIDS is the last stage of HIV infection, during which time these diseases arise. An average interval of 10 years exists between infection with HIV and development of the conditions typical of AIDS. **Pneumonia** and **Kaposi's sarcoma** are two of the most common diseases seen in AIDS patients.

HIV is contracted through semen, vaginal fluid, breast milk, blood, or other body fluids containing blood. Health care workers may come into contact with other body fluids that may transmit the HIV virus, including amniotic and synovial fluids. Although it is a transmissable virus, it is not contagious and it cannot be spread through coughing, sneezing, or casual physical contact. Other **STDs**, such as genital herpes, may increase the risk of contracting AIDS through sexual contact.

The main **cellular target** of HIV is a special class of white blood cells critical to the immune system known as T4 helper cells. Once HIV has entered a helper T cell, it can cause the cell to function poorly or it can destroy the cell. A hallmark of the onset of AIDS is a drastic reduction in the number of helper T cells in the body. Two predominant strains of the virus, designated HIV-1 and HIV-2, are known. Worldwide the most common strain is HIV-1, with HIV-2 more common primarily in western Africa; the two strains act in a similar manner, but the latter causes a form of AIDS that progresses much more slowly.

Diagnosis is made on the basis of blood tests approved by the CDC that may be administered by a doctor or at a local health department. Alternately, a home collection kit may be purchased at many pharmacies. No vaccine or cure has yet been developed that can prevent HIV infection. Several **drugs** are now used to slow the development of AIDS, including azidothymidine (AZT). **Protease inhibitors**, such as ritonavir and indinavir, have been shown to block the development of AIDS, at least temporarily. Protease inhibitors are most effective when used in conjunction with two different reverse transcriptase inhibitors—the so-called "triple-drug therapy."

HIV/AIDS is a major problem in developing countries, particularly sub-Saharan Africa. At the end of 2001, 40 million people were estimated to have contracted HIV, with 95% of those living in the developing world.

For information on **prevention**, see "Safer Sex Defined."

For confidential information on HIV/AIDS, call 1-800-342-AIDS.

Internet resources: <www.cdc.gov/hiv>

Sexually Transmitted Diseases (STDs)

A sexually transmitted disease (STD) is usually passed from person to person by direct sexual contact. It may also be transmitted from a mother to her child before or at birth or, less frequently, may be passed from person to person in nonsexual contact. STDs usually initially affect the genitals, the reproductive tract, the urinary tract, the oral cavity, the anus, or the rectum but may mature in the body to attack various organs and systems. Some of the major STDs are:

Syphilis was first widely reported by European writers in the 16th century, and a virtual epidemic swept Europe around the year 1500. Syphilis is spread through direct contact with a syphilis sore (chancre); development of this sore is the first stage of the disease. The second stage manifests itself as a rash on the palms and the bottoms of the feet. In the last stage, symptoms disappear, but the disease remains in the body and may damage internal organs and lead to paralysis, blindness, dementia, and even death. For individuals infected less than a year, a single dose of penicillin will cure the disease. Larger doses are needed for those who have had it for a longer period of time.

Gonorrhea, a form of urethritis (an infection and inflammation of the urethra), gonorrhea is one of the most common STDs. Although spread through sexual contact, the gonorrhea infection can also be spread to other parts of the body after touching the infected area. Men manifest symptoms, which include discharge and a burning sensation when urinating, more often than women. If left untreated, women may develop pelvic inflammatory disease (PID) and men may become infertile. The disease can also spread to the blood or joints and is potentially life-threatening.

Many available antibiotics can cure gonorrhea.

Chlamydia, another form of urethritis, chlamydia can be transmitted during vaginal, anal, or oral sex. Since there are frequently no warning symptoms, most infected individuals do not know they have the disease until complications develop. Untreated chlamydia can cause urethral infection in men and PID in women. Antibiotics can successfully cure the disease.

Genital herpes, disease that became especially widespread in the 1960s and 1970s, genital herpes often presents minimal symptoms upon infection. The most common sign, however, is blistering in the genital area; outbreaks can occur over many years, but generally decrease in severity and number. Genital herpes is caused by the herpes simplex viruses type 1 (HSV-1) and type 2 (HSV-2). The former causes infections on and around the mouth but may be spread through the saliva to the genitals; the latter is transmitted during sexual contact with someone who has a genital infection. The HSV-2 infection can cause problems for people with suppressed immune systems and for infants who contract the disease upon delivery. Herpes can also leave individuals more susceptible to HIV infection and make those carrying the disease more infectious. A variety of treatments, including antiviral medications, have been used to help manage genital herpes, but currently there is no cure for the disease.

Almost all STDs have reasonably effective drug cures. For information on STD **prevention**, see "Safer Sex Defined." For information on **HIV disease**, see individual entry.

Internet resources: <www.cdc.gov/nchstp/od/nchstp.html>

Safer Sex Defined

D efining risky sexual behavior. Any activity involving the exchange of body fluids—vaginal secretions, semen, or blood—could result in the transmission of HIV and other STDs. Unprotected vaginal and anal intercourse present the highest risks for contraction of STDs. Women are at greater risk than men of developing an infection as a result of heterosexual intercourse, and many STDs present fewer symptoms in women than in men. However, men and women of all sexual orientations should practice safer sex to reduce their risk of contracting an STD.

HIV testing. It can take years to develop symptoms of HIV disease, so it is important to be tested for HIV after any behavior that might have resulted in infection. The CDC recommends undergoing two separate HIV-antibody tests, six months apart. If the second test is negative, there is a reasonable certainty that HIV is not present.

STD testing. It is important to get checked for other STDs at least once a year. Do not assume that STD testing is part of a routine checkup.

Abstinence. Refraining from any sexual activity that would allow the exchange of body fluids is by far the most effective method of birth control and disease prevention.

Monogamous intercourse. Sexual intercourse with only one partner can be as effective as abstinence in preventing disease transmission, if both partners have been properly tested for HIV and other STDs. Most health professionals, however, recommend continuing to practice safer sex, even in monogamous relationships, as there is no way to be sure a partner is being faithful.

Condoms. Using a latex or female condom correctly and consistently significantly reduces the chance of unplanned pregnancy. Condoms also reduce the risk of transmission of HIV, vaginitis, chlamydia, honeymoon cystitis, syphilis, pelvic inflammatory disease, chancroid, and gonorrhea. Condoms may be less ef-

fective in preventing genital warts, herpes, cervical cancer, and hepatitis B. Male and female condoms should not be worn simultaneously.

Birth control. There are many methods of birth control for women that can help prevent unwanted pregnancy, including birth control pills, Norplant, Depo-Provera, condoms, diaphragms, and cervical caps. However, of these, only condoms protect against STDs. Emergency contraception, including the "morning-after" pill, should be used only when necessary and not relied upon as a regular method of birth control. Withdrawal and family planning are not recommended forms of birth control.

Contraceptive Use by US Women

Percent distribution by age. Totals may not add to 100% due to rounding. "..." indicates less than 0.05. Data are for 1995.

	AGE 15–44	AGE 15–19	20–24	25–29	30–34	35–39	40–44
Using contraception							
Pill	17.3	13.0	33.1	27.0	20.7	8.1	4.2
Condom	13.1	10.9	16.7	16.8	13.4	12.3	8.8
Female sterilization	17.8	0.1	2.5	11.8	21.4	29.8	35.6
Male sterilization	7.0	0.0	0.7	3.1	7.6	13.6	14.5
Implant	0.9	0.8	2.4	1.4	0.5	0.2	0.1
Injectable	1.9	2.9	3.9	2.9	1.3	0.8	0.2
Intrauterine device (IUD)	0.5	0.0	0.2	0.5	0.6	0.7	0.9
Diaphragm	1.2	...	0.4	0.6	1.7	2.2	1.9
Female condom	...	0.0	0.1	0.0	0.0	0.0	0.0
Periodic abstinence	1.5	0.4	0.6	1.2	2.3	2.1	1.8
—Natural family planning	0.2	0.0	0.1	0.2	0.3	0.4	0.2
Withdrawal	2.0	1.2	2.1	2.6	2.1	2.3	1.4
Other[1]	1.0	0.3	0.9	1.2	1.3	0.9	1.8
Total using contraception	**64.2**	**29.8**	**63.4**	**69.3**	**72.7**	**72.9**	**71.5**
Not using contraception							
Surgically sterile female	3.0	0.1	0.1	0.6	1.7	5.1	9.6
Nonsurgically sterile female	1.3	0.7	0.5	0.7	1.2	2.3	1.9
Pregnant or postpartum	4.6	4.5	7.3	8.4	5.6	2.1	0.4
Seeking pregnancy	4.0	0.9	3.4	6.1	6.2	4.6	2.2
Other							
—Never had intercourse	10.9	49.8	12.1	4.2	2.7	1.4	1.4
—No intercourse in last 3 months	6.2	7.1	6.8	5.7	4.9	6.2	6.8
—Had intercourse in last 3 months	5.2	7.1	6.0	4.7	4.4	4.3	5.1
Total not using contraception[2]	**35.8**	**70.2**	**36.6**	**30.7**	**27.3**	**27.1**	**28.5**

[1]*Includes morning-after pill, cervical cap, Today™ sponge, suppository, and other methods.*   [2]*Includes other categories not listed.*

Complementary and Alternative Medicine and Treatment

In the past decade, the use of **alternative therapy** has doubled in North America and Europe, where conventional Western medicine generally had been the only accepted form of treatment. Alternative therapy encompasses both remedies and practices, including the use of herbs, homeopathy, therapeutic massage, acupuncture, hypnotism, and traditional Oriental medicine. Also called **complementary medicine** (as it may be used in conjunction with conventional practices), alternative medicine approaches are often **holistic**, or focused on the whole person, including physical, mental, emotional, and spiritual aspects. Related to alternative therapies in their treatment of the body as whole, **osteopathy** and **chiropractic** have also enjoyed greater acceptance in recent years, particularly in the US.

In 1998 Congress established the National Center

for Complementary and Alternative Medicine as a division of the NIH to develop and support research on alternative medicine. In May 2002 WHO announced the development of a **global strategy** for researching and regulating alternative treatments; it is currently compiling reports on more than 100 medicinal plants. At issue is the safety and usefulness of alternative medicine, which remain largely unregulated. Often patients pursue treatment without the advice of a health care professional; as with conventional medicines, if used incorrectly alternative treatments can cause injury or even death. WHO is urging member states to adopt regulations to license providers and determine the authenticity and safety of alternative products. Only China, Vietnam, North Korea, and South Korea have integrated traditional medicines into their official health care systems.

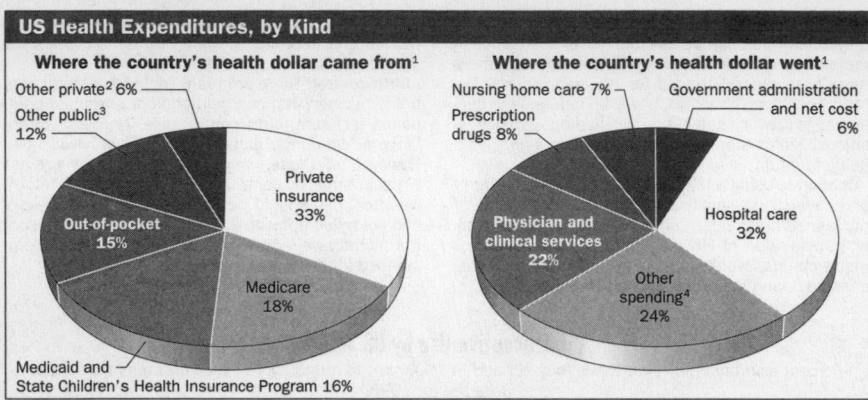

US Health Expenditures, by Kind

Where the country's health dollar came from[1]

- Other private[2] 6%
- Other public[3] 12%
- Out-of-pocket 15%
- Private insurance 33%
- Medicare 18%
- Medicaid and State Children's Health Insurance Program 16%

Where the country's health dollar went[1]

- Nursing home care 7%
- Prescription drugs 8%
- Government administration and net cost 6%
- Physician and clinical services 22%
- Hospital care 32%
- Other spending[4] 24%

[1] Calendar year 1999.
[2] Other private includes industrial in-plant, privately funded construction, and non-patient revenues, including philanthropy.
[3] Other public includes programs such as workers' compensation, public health activity, US Department of Defense, US Department of Veterans Affairs, Indian Health Service, state and local hospital subsidies, and school health.
[4] Other spending includes dentist and other professional services, home health care, durable medical equipment, other nondurable medical products, government public health activities, and research and construction.

Source: Centers for Medicare & Medicaid Services, Office of the Actuary, National Health Statistics Group.

The Centers for Disease Control and Prevention (CDC) and the National Institutes of Health (NIH)

Both the CDC and the NIH are part of the US Department of Health and Human Services.
CDC Web site: <www.cdc.gov>
NIH Web site: <www.nih.gov>

CDC. *Mission:* To promote health and quality of life by preventing and controlling disease, injury, and disability. *Location:* Atlanta, GA. *Acting Director:* David W. Fleming. *Budget:* $4.3 billion for FY 2002 (excludes bioterrorism-related activities). *Functions:* Monitors health problems and infectious diseases worldwide; conducts research to enhance disease prevention; develops public health policy; provides leadership and training; assists state and local health departments.

NIH. *Mission:* To uncover new knowledge that will lead to better health for everyone. *Location:* Bethes-

da, MD. *Director:* Harold Varmus. *Budget:* FY 2002 $23.5 million (est.). *Functions:* Supports and conducts biomedical research, both in its own laboratories and through research grants to universities, medical schools, hospitals, and research institutes. Future research will center on disease treatment and prevention in a variety of areas, including mental illness, cancer, AIDS, arthritis, and other unconquered diseases; improving the health of children, women, and minorities; and better understanding the aging process.

Mental Health

Diagnostic and Statistical Manual of Mental Disorders (DSM)

The *Diagnostic and Statistical Manual of Mental Disorders* (DSM) is the standard reference for mental health professionals in the US (worldwide, the World Health Organization's *International Classification of Diseases* is used). Published by the American Psychiatric Association (APA), the *DSM* sets forth diagnostic criteria, descriptions, and other information to help classify and diagnose mental disorders.

There are three main components of the *DSM*. The **diagnostic classification** is a list of mental disorders that are officially recognized by the APA. These labels include diagnostic codes, which are used by institutions for data collection and billing. For each of these disorders, **diagnostic criteria** indicate what symptoms must be present and what others must not be present in order to make a particular diagnosis. A **descriptive text** also follows each disorder and includes information on subtypes, specific age and gender fea-

tures, prevalence, and familial patterns, among other categories.

The *DSM-I* was published in 1952, at a time when little empirical data existed for the evaluation of mental illness; its primary purpose was to standardize this data collection and establish a consensus among clinicians. Today the *DSM* is used mainly as a diagnostic, rather than a statistical, tool, but it is still an evolving entity, and changes are made with every new edition. One example of the way the *DSM* has evolved involves the classification of homosexuality as a mental disorder. Facing mounting empirical data, changing social norms, and pressure from the gay community, the board of trustees of the APA removed homosexuality from the *DSM* in 1973; it was subsequently replaced with a more refined diagnosis, ego-dystonic homosexuality, which was marked by a lack of heterosexual arousal despite the desire for such and by unwanted homosexual impulses. This disorder was in turn criticized, and homosexuality was entirely removed from the *DSM* in 1987.

The most recent edition, *DSM-IV*, was completed in 1994; a text revision, *DSM-IV-TR*, was made available in July 2000 (changes to the diagnostic criteria for Tourette disorder and Alzheimer disease were among the revisions). The *DSM-V* is slated for publication in 2010.

Anxiety Disorders

Anxiety is defined as a feeling of fear, dread, or apprehension that arises without a clear or appropriate real-life justification. Generally, intense, persistent, or chronic anxiety that is not justified and that interferes with daily functioning is classified as a manifestation of a mental disorder. The most common anxiety disorders are:

Panic disorder. Panic disorder is characterized by recurrent panic attacks, with at least one of the attacks followed by persistent fear of having another attack, worry about the implications or consequences of the attack, or a change in behavior related to the attack; these feelings last for one month or more. A **panic attack** is the sudden onset of intense apprehension, fear, or terror and at least four of the following conditions: shortness of breath or a smothering sensation; palpitations or accelerated heart rate; chest pain or discomfort; choking; dizziness or faintness; trembling or shaking; sweating; nausea or abdominal distress; a feeling of unreality; numbness or tingling; hot flashes or chills; fear of dying; and fear of "going crazy" or losing control. A panic attack is unexpected and does not immediately precede or follow a stressful situation, although the person who experiences the attack usually is in a period of increased stress. It is easy to mistake the attack for other problems such as heart disease, as somatic symptoms play a prominent role. There is a close association between panic disorder and **depression**, and a large percentage of persons suffering from panic disorder go on to experience a major depression within the next few years. *Treatment:* Short-term individual psychotherapy is usually helpful, during which relaxation and imagery techniques may be taught. For more severe cases, benzodiazepines or selective serotonin reuptake inhibitor antidepressants may be prescribed.

Generalized anxiety disorder. Generalized anxiety disorder is characterized as the unrealistic or excessive worry about two or more life circumstances that is experienced more days than not for a period of six months or longer. Examples are excessive worry about finances or danger to one's child when there is no reason for this concern. The anxious behavior indicative of this disorder includes symptoms such as trembling, muscle soreness, restlessness, shortness of breath, palpitations, dizziness, difficulty concentrating, and an exaggerated startle response. *Treatment:* The first stage of treatment should be a full medical exam to rule out a biological or environmental cause. If the anxiety is found to be a psychological disorder, there are a number of treatment options, including cognitive-behavioral therapy, which often teaches relaxation techniques; hypnotherapy and self-help treatments can also be useful. Medication is often used in treatment as well. Traditionally, benzodiazepines were used, but they are often habit-forming and sedating; Buspar (buspirone) does not have these side effects and is now often prescribed. Some antidepressant medications may also relieve the symptoms of anxiety.

Post-traumatic stress disorder. The result of exposure to a very distressing event that elicits feelings of intense terror, fear, or helplessness, post-traumatic stress disorder often results in frequent flashbacks, nightmares, or an exaggerated startle response. Events that may cause this disorder include witnessing a murder, participating in a military battle, or being raped. *Treatment:* Three main psychotherapy treatments are used: stress inoculation, in which the patients learn coping skills to conquer their fears; prolonged exposure, in which the event is talked about repeatedly and thus rendered less threatening; and cognitive processing, in which memories of the event are written about and discussed with the therapist in order to reevaluate the emotions affected by the trauma. Medication is not generally used to treat this disorder except when specific symptoms, such as anxiety or depression, are also present. Self-help and a good support network are also valuable in the healing process.

Phobias. A phobic disorder involves the persistent and irrational fear of a specific object, activity, or situation that results in avoidance. Individuals with phobias recognize that their fear is excessive or unreasonable but cannot control the anxiety associated with it. **Specific phobias** usually develop in adolescence or adulthood and affect more than 1 in 10 people. Examples include fear of dogs, water, or flying; some of the most severe types are **agoraphobia** (characterized by a fear of being in open or public places) and **claustrophobia** (fear of confined spaces). The immediate response often resembles a panic attack. *Treatment:* Behavioral approaches are used, including desensitization, in which the patient is gradually exposed to a phobic object or situation, and emotive imagery, in which relaxation techniques help guide the patient through an imagined phobic encounter. **Social phobia** is the fear of social situations in which the individual dreads being criticized or humiliated. *Treatment:* Cognitive-behavioral therapy is widely used; tricyclic antidepressants can be useful in combatting panic attacks.

Obsessive-compulsive disorder. This disorder is marked by recurrent obsessions or compulsions that cause extreme distress and interfere with the normal activities of daily life. **Obsessions** are persistent ideas, thoughts, impulses, or images that are experienced as intrusive, senseless, and generally repugnant but which cannot be ignored or suppressed. Common obsessions include thoughts about committing violent acts, worries about contamination, and doubt (as in wondering whether one had turned off the stove before leaving the house). **Compulsions** are repetitive, intentional behaviors performed in a ritualized manner in an attempt to neutralize the obsession and control the anxiety associated with it. Persistent hand washing, counting, or touching are common compulsive behaviors. *Treatment:* Behavioral therapy, including systematic desensitization and flooding techniques, is common. The antidepressant drugs clomipramine (Anafranil), fluoxetine (Prozac), and fluvoxamine (Luvox) are helpful in relieving symptoms for the majority of sufferers.

Internet resources: <www.nimh.nih.gov/anxiety/anxietymenu.cfm>

Autism

Autism is a neurobiological disorder that affects physical, social, and language skills. The term was first used by the psychiatrist Leo Kanner in the 1940s to describe children who appeared to be excessively withdrawn and self-preoccupied. The syndrome usually appears before 2½ years of age. According to the Autism Society of America, the following areas may be affected by autism:

Social Interaction. Autistic infants generally appear indifferent or averse to affection and physical contact, though attachment to caregivers often develops later. Children are less responsive to eye contact or other social cues. Inappropriate attachment to objects may occur.

Communication. Speech develops slowly and abnormally or not at all. It may be characterized by meaningless repetition or strange mechanical sounds.

Sensory impairment. There may be underemphasized reaction to sound, no reaction to pain, or no recognition of genuine danger, as well as sensitivities in the areas of sight, touch, hearing, smell, and taste.

Play. Autistic children do not play spontaneously, imitate the play of others, or imagine their own games.

Behaviors. Usually the syndrome is accompanied by an obsessive desire to prevent environmental change, and frequently, rhythmic body movements such as rocking or hand-clapping. The behavior of children with autism varies greatly, from overactivity to passivity.

About 25% of autistic children develop **seizures** by late adolesence. Some individuals with autism also have other disorders of the brain, including epilepsy, Down syndrome, or mental retardation, or genetic disorders such as Tourette's syndrome, thus making the disease very difficult to diagnose. There are no medical tests for the **diagnosis** of autism, but tests may help rule out other diseases. Initial diagnosis may include a number of different health care professionals, including a psychologist, neurologist, developmental pediatrician, speech and language therapist, learning consultant, or other autism specialist.

The **cause** of autism remains unknown and the disease is incompletely understood. Recent research has revealed abnormalities in the brain structure of autistic individuals, abnormalities likely to have occurred during early brain development. Researchers also have noted a deficiency of large nerve cells called Purkinje cells and an excess of serotonin. There appears to be a complex genetic component as well. Since the early 1990s the global rate of autism has increased greatly; researchers speculate that over-vaccination has contributed to this disturbing rise.

Treatment of autism centers around helping the patient, as well as caregivers, understand and cope with the disorder. Whereas most sufferers were previously institutionalized, children and adults with autism are now living more independently and becoming integrated into mainstream society. Some autistic individuals display remarkable talents, such as enhanced musical or mathmatical prowess. Currently, there is no prescribed medical regime for autistic individuals.

Depression

Clinical depression usually involves one or more of the following symptoms consistently for at least a two-week period: feelings of sadness, hopelessness, or pessimism; lowered self-esteem and heightened self-depreciation; a decrease or loss of ability to enjoy daily life; reduced energy and vitality; slowness of thought or action; loss of appetite; suicidal ideation; and disturbed sleep or insomnia. Depression differs from simple grief or mourning, which are appropriate emotional responses to the loss of loved persons or objects. Where there are clear grounds for a person's unhappiness, depression is considered to be present if the depressed mood is disproportionately long or severe.

Depression is probably the most common psychiatric complaint; the rate of incidence increases with age in men, while the peak for women is between the ages of 35 and 45 (women in general suffer from depression more often than men). Most professionals now agree that biological, social, and psychological factors all contribute to depression. The chief biochemical cause seems to be the defective regulation of the release of one or more naturally occurring monoamines in the brain, particularly norepinephrine and serotonin. Reduced quantities or reduced activity of these chemicals is linked to depression.

Treatment of depression has been a controversial topic in recent years as new drugs have been approved by the Food and Drug Administration. Many types of psychotherapy, both individual and group, are used to treat depressed patients; the medications most often prescribed are selective serotonin reuptake inhibitors (SSRIs), which regulate serotonin. A combination of psychotherapy and medication is generally the preferred choice for treatment. Hospitalization may be necessary if a patient is contemplating **suicide.** Although most depressed individuals are only mildly suicidal, poorly monitored administration of medications may actually increase the risk of suicide. The energizing effects of an anti-depressant can empower patients to act on suicidal thoughts, whereas they previously lacked the energy or will to do so; an inadequate or incomplete trial of a medication has also been correlated with increased suicide rates. An alternate or complementary approach to the treatment of depression involves the use of self-help techniques, including depression-oriented support groups.

Internet resources: <www.nimh.nih.gov/publicat/depressionmenu.cfm>

Bipolar Disorder

Bipolar disorder, or manic-depression, is characterized by alternating periods of extreme moods, from excessive irritability or elation (manic state) to despondency or severe tension (depressed state), often with periods of normal mood in between. The frequency and duration of this cycling of moods varies between individuals but usually begins in adolescence or early adulthood. Bipolar disorder may also feature such psychotic symptoms as delusions and hallucinations. **Depression** is the more common symptom, and many patients never develop a genuine manic phase, although they may experience a brief period of overoptimism and mild euphoria while recovering from a depression. Patients in a manic state are highly sociable, gregarious, and optimistic and have grandiose notions and an inflated sense of self-esteem.

At any given time, at least two million Americans suffer from bipolar disorder. The first manic episode may be caused by some external stress the patient has experienced, but ensuing cycles are beyond control. Statistical studies have suggested a hereditary predisposition to the disorder, and this has now been linked to a defect on a dominant gene located on chromosome 11. In a physiological sense, it is believed that bipolar disorder is caused by the faulty regulation of one or more amines at sites in the brain where the transmission of nerve impulses takes place; a deficiency of the amines results in depression, and an excess of them causes mania. However, there is no single known cause for the disorder, and the best **treatment** involves individual or group therapy and medication. The two complement one another, as follow-up care can help ensure medical compliance, often an issue for manic-depressive patients: one of the main causes of a return of the disorder is the patient's discontinuance of medication. **Lithium** is the drug of choice and is generally prescribed long-term. However, if a patient first presents in a depressive state, appropriate antidepressants may be used initially. If left untreated, the disease worsens and the patient eventually experiences full-fledged mania and clinical depression. With proper treatment, people with bipolar disorder can lead productive, functional lives.

Eating Disorders

Eating disorders are characterized by an unhealthy relationship with food in which normal eating habits are disrupted or polarized. They most often afflict women in adolescence or early adulthood and are linked to low self-esteem and poor body image rather than any biomedical cause. The main eating disorders are:

Anorexia nervosa. The most defining feature of anorexia is starvation, accompanied by the patients' misperception that they are actually overweight. Emotional manifestations may range from a neurotic overreaction to a weight-reduction diet to full-blown schizophrenic delusions resulting in the abhorrence of food. As with bulimia, **binging** (extreme overindulgence in food) may be part of this destructive eating cycle. These patterns are related to a preoccupation with self-control through starvation, and loss of that control leads to shame and self-loathing. Sufferers are often able to maintain their strength and daily activities at approximately normal levels; they appear characteristically unconcerned with their undernourished state. Associated symptoms include vomiting and, in women, failure to menstruate. *Treatment:* A complete medical examination is needed to assess any possible physical damage done during the course of the disease. In severe cases hospitalization may be necessary. Since people suffering from anorexia often rationalize their behavior, they may be unwilling to seek help. A trusting relationship with a therapist is key, though patients may relapse during the course of treatment. Group therapy may also prove useful. Often, specific childhood trauma triggers the patient's negative self-image; exploring these issues may help reach the goal of an improved self-evaluation. Medications, particularly anti depressants, may be prescribed.

Bulimia nervosa. Bulimia is characterized by periods of **binging** followed by **purging** via one or more of the following: self-induced vomiting, unnecessary ingestion of laxatives, or exercising too much. Binging is often done in secret and is followed by a shame and self-loathing similar to that experienced by anorexic individuals, which results in the subsequent purging. Although sufferers are also obsessed with body image, unlike anorexic patients the majority are close to their proper weight. If left untreated, bulimia can result in serious medical complications, such as dental decay, stomach rupture, and dehydration, and can also be fatal. *Treatment:* Like anorexia, a prominent feature of bulimia is a negative self-image, and treatment options are the same. Since bulimic patients may purge medication, careful monitoring is necessary.

A new diagnostic category, **binge-eating disorder**, was recently classified as a medical condition. Patients with this disorder also overindulge in food but do not follow the cycle of purging.

Personality Disorders

Personality disorders are marked by deeply ingrained and lasting patterns of inflexible, maladaptive, or antisocial behavior. A personality disorder is an accentuation of one or more personality traits. It need not disrupt a person's daily functioning, but in times of extreme stress symptoms increase and may interfere with psychological and emotional functioning. Individuals with personality disorders generally have difficulty with interpersonal relationships, range of emotion, self-perception, and impulse control. There are many different types of personality disorders, classified below according to the **DSM-IV**. All manifest themselves by early adulthood.

Antisocial personality disorder. Individuals follow a pattern of behavior that disregards and often violates the rights of others, including at least three of the following symptoms: failure to conform to social norms and the law (frequent arrests are common); deceitfulness, including lying, using aliases, and deceiving others for profit; impulsivity (failure to plan ahead); irritability and aggressiveness (physical fights); reckless disregard for individual's own safety or the safety of others; consistent irresponsibility, including failure to sustain work or be financially responsible; and a lack of remorse concerning mistreatment of others. *Treatment:* Psychotherapy is the usual treatment, with medication being used to help with mood swings or other specific problems. Many individuals will be mandated to therapy by the court, though not all people who commit crimes can be classified as having antisocial personality disorder, and thorough psychological testing is needed. Proper therapy may help individuals realize greater emotional depth. Group therapy centered around the disorder may also be useful in exploring these issues and establishing relationships.

Avoidant personality disorder. This disorder involves extreme social inhibition, hypersensitivity, and feelings of inadequacy. Four or more of the following symptoms must be present: avoidance of occupational activities involving significant interpersonal contact; unwillingness to become involved with people socially unless certain of being accepted; restraint within intimate relationships; preoccupation with social criticism or rejection; inhibition in new interpersonal situations; negative self-perception (views self as inferior and unappealing to others); and a reluctance to take risks or participate in new activities due to fear of embarrassment. *Treatment:* Short-term individual psychotherapy is the preferred treatment, though some patients may attend group therapy later in the process. Medication is not useful unless there is a concurrent disorder that requires it.

Borderline personality disorder. Individuals with this disorder experience unstable interpersonal relationships, self-image, and emotions and display impulsive behaviors. These problems are present in social, familial, and occupational settings. Five or more of the following are necessary for diagnosis: frantic efforts to avoid real or imagined abandonment; a pattern of unstable but intense interpersonal relationships characterized by alternating idealization and devaluation (a person is either "good" or "bad"); identity disturbance (unstable self-image); impulsivity in at least two areas that are potentially self-damaging (including spending, substance abuse, reckless driving, binge eating, and sexual activity); recurrent suicidal behavior or threats, or self-mutilation; emotional instability owing to a marked reactivity of mood (intense episodic irritability or anxiety usually lasting a few hours); long-term feelings of emptiness; inappropriate, intense anger and lack of control over this emotion; and transient, stress-related paranoia or severe dissociative symptoms. *Treatment:* People with this disorder are notoriously difficult to treat, as they place a considerable emotional burden on a therapist. Fairly long-term psychotherapy is the preferred treatment, and the use of medication is controversial. Suicidal feelings may require hospitalization and should always be evaulated by the therapist. A popular new treatment called dialectical behavior therapy teaches patients how to better control their emotions and lives through regulation and self-knowledge.

Dependent personality disorder. This disorder is characterized by a fear of separation or abandonment and manifests itself in submissive and clinging behavior. Five or more of the following symptoms are present: difficulty making everyday decisions; the need for others to assume responsibility over the patient's life; difficulty expressing disagreement; difficulty initiating projects or doing things alone; going to excessive lengths to garner other's support; discomfort or helplessness when left alone; need to seek a new relationship as soon as a close relationship ends; and fears of being left to care for oneself. *Treatment:* Psychotherapy is preferred, though the relationship between therapist and patient is often a delicate one given the latter's need for constant reassurance and support. Long-term therapy is generally not recommended, and ending therapy may be

an indication of how well the patient has progressed. Assertiveness training and group therapy later in treatment may also be useful. Medication is generally avoided, as drug abuse and overdose are common in individuals with this disorder.

Histrionic personality disorder. Individuals exhibit excessive emotionality and seek attention. Five or more of the following symptoms are present: discomfort in situations in which the individual is not the center of attention; interaction with others that is often characterized by sexually seductive behavior; rapidly shifting emotions that appear shallow; use of physical appearance to draw attention; excessively impressionistic speech that lacks detail; self-dramatization, theatricality, and exaggerated emotional expression; suggestibility (easily influenced by criticism); and relationships that the individual deems more intimate than they actually are. *Treatment:* Individual psychotherapy is preferred, as group therapy may exacerbate the patients' needs to dramatize and draw attention to themselves. Boundary issues between therapist and client are key, and solution-focused treatment dedicated to helping the individual view social interactions objectively is usually helpful. Medication is generally prescribed with great caution, as suicidal behavior is common.

Narcissistic personality disorder. This disorder is characterized by a pattern of grandiosity, the need for admiration, and a lack of empathy; patients manifest five or more of the following symptoms: grandiose sense of self-importance; preoccupation with fantasies of unlimited success, power, brilliance, beauty, or ideal love; belief that they are unique and can only associate with or be understood by others who are equally special; need for excessive admiration; sense of entitlement (unreasonable expectations of favorable treatment or compliance with wishes); exploitation of interpersonal relationships; difficulty identifying with others' needs and a lack of empathy; envy of others or the belief that others envy them; and arrogance or haughtiness. *Treatment:* Frequently, patients with narcissistic personality disorder are hospitalized. Individual therapists will often be devalued by clients in an attempt to gain dominance and maintain their fragile sense of grandeur. In extreme cases, treatment may be symptom-oriented; less-resistant patients often are taught how to acknowledge the needs and ideas of others while maintaining a healthier sense of self (this goal may be aided by group therapy).

Obsessive-compulsive personality disorder. Defined as a pervasive preoccupation with orderliness, perfectionism, and mental and interpersonal control, individuals with this disorder engage in behaviors even when they impair flexibility, openness, and efficiency. Four or more of the following symptoms are present: preoccupation with details, rules, lists, order, organization, or schedules; perfectionism that interferes with task completion; excessive devotion to work and productivity (to the exclusion of leisure activities); inflexibility about morals, ethics, or values to the point of being overly scrupulous or conscientious; inability to discard worn-out objects; reluctance to delegate authority or to work with others; hoarding of money; and rigidity and stubbornness. *Treatment:* Psychotherapy is often focused on short-term symptom relief and coping mechanisms, as well as helping the patient identify and realize more complex emotions. Patients are usually resistent to long-term therapy with the goal of personality change. Group therapy and medication are not often used, though newer medications such as Prozac may provide some relief.

Paranoid personality disorder. Persons with this disorder are distrustful and suspicious of others and interpret others' motives as malevolent. Four or more of the following symptoms are present: suspicion that others are exploiting, harming, or deceiving them (without sufficient cause); preoccupation with the trustworthiness or loyalty of friends or associates; reluctance to confide in others (with the fear that this information will be used against them); misinterpretation of benign remarks or events; persistence in bearing a grudge; perception of character attacks that do not exist; and suspicions regarding the fidelity of a sexual partner. *Treatment:* Paranoid personality disorder is very difficult to treat, as individuals with this disorder rarely seek help and usually suffer from it their whole lives. There has been no substantive work done to determine a course of treatment, but a straightforward, trusting relationship with a therapist may prove promising. Clients often view medication with suspicion, and there is no specific drug used to treat this condition.

Schizoid personality disorder. A pervasive detachment from social relationships and a restricted range of emotions in interpersonal settings characterize this disorder, which may manifest itself in four or more of the following symptoms: lack of desire to form close relationships; limitation to solitary activities; little interest in sexual experiences; little plea-sure in most activities; no close friends other than immediate relatives; indifference to praise or criticism; and emotional coldness and detachment. *Treatment:* Psychotherapy is usually best kept short-term, with clear and simple goals in mind. Individuals may attempt group therapy following initial treatment. No medication has proven effective for this disorder.

Schizotypal personality disorder. Individuals with this disorder exhibit acute discomfort with close relationships as well as cognitive or perceptual distortions and eccentricities of behavior. Five or more of the following symptoms are present: ideas of reference; odd beliefs or magical thinking that influences behavior; unusual perceptual experiences, including bodily illusions; odd thinking and speech; suspiciousness or paranoid ideation; inappropriate or constricted emotions; behavior or appearance that is eccentric; lack of close friends other than immediate relatives; and excessive social anxiety that does not diminish with familiarity and tends to be associated with paranoia. *Treatment:* Psychotherapy usually focuses on developing a supportive, non threatening relationship with the client as well as social skills training and other behavioral approaches. Group therapy may be appropriate after the initial treatment. Antipsychotic medications may be useful for treating the more acute phases of this disorder.

Schizophrenia

Schizophrenia refers to any of a group of severe mental disorders that have in common such symptoms as hallucinations, delusions, blunted emotions, disordered thinking, and a withdrawal from reality. The most common psychotic disorder, schizophrenia affects approximately 1% of the world's population; it is estimated that between one third and one half of all homeless Americans have schizophrenia. There is no known cause, but scientists are currently researching possible genetic and hereditary factors (the disorder tends to run in families). There are four main types of this disorder:

Paranoid type. This type of schizophrenia usually arises later in life than others and is characterized primarily by delusions of persecution and grandeur combined with unrealistic, illogical thinking, often accompanied by hallucinations.

Catatonic type. Characterized by striking motor behavior, patients with this form may remain in a state of almost complete immobility, often assuming statuesque positions. Mutism (the inability to talk), extreme incompliance, and absence of almost all voluntary actions are also common. This state of inactivity is at times preceded or interrupted by episodes of excessive motor activity and excitement, generally of an impulsive, unpredictable nature.

Disorganized (hebephrenic) type. Patients display shallow and inappropriate emotional responses, fool-ish or bizarre behavior, disorganized speech, delusions, and hallucinations.

Undifferentiated type. The simplest form of schizophrenia, it manifests as an insidious and gradual reduction in external relations and interests. A lack of emotional depth, a simplicity of ideation, a relative absence of mental activity, a progressive lessening in the use of inner resources, and a retreat to simpler or stereotyped behavior is common.

These types are not mutually exclusive, and schizophrenic patients may display a combination of symptoms that defy convenient classification. There may also be a mixture of schizophrenic symptoms with those of other psychoses, notably those of **bipolar disorder.**

Treatment always focuses on medication. Unfortunately, patients often relapse after failing to take their medications; therapy, including family therapy, may aid in support and help prevent such a relapse. A combination of antipsychotic, antianxiety, and antidepressant medications are often combined. Newer antipsychotics, which block both serotonin and dopamine receptors, prove promising, as they effectively treat a fuller range of symptoms with fewer side effects.

Internet resources: <www.nimh.nih.gov/publicat/schizmenu.cfm>

Alcohol and Substance Abuse

Alcoholism. Simply defined, alcoholism is the excessive and repeated use of alcoholic beverages that causes harm to the drinker; this harm may be physical, mental, social, or economic. It has recently been accepted that alcoholism is a disease, a compulsive behavior out of the user's control akin to other substance abuse problems. Unlike other ad-dictions, however, alcoholics do not need increased doses to produce the desired effect. Although consciousness of the disease is high, the nature and causes of alcoholism remain marginally understood.

Many theories of the **cause** of alcoholism rest on the limited perspectives of specialists in particular disciplines or professions, most of which have their own definitions of the disease. The most comprehensive conceptions recognize that alcoholism may have a genetic or constitutional underlying factor—not a fateful heredity but a predisposition that renders some people more disposed to alcoholism than others. Other factors, such as childhood trauma, may also make a person more vulnerable to addiction. Some evidence links alcoholism to other mental illness and hypothesizes that alcohol intake is a form of self-medicating behavior that masks a different condition, such as depression or anxiety.

Because of the lack of a precise definition, it is difficult to rely on statistics regarding alcoholism. However, in the US rates are generally higher in urban and industrialized areas and among men, and alcoholism is certainly in the front rank of public-health problems. Suicide rates are 2.5 times higher; accidental death rates are seven times higher; and there is an enormously higher rate of general morbidity among alcoholics.

Treatment may be physiological (with drugs that cause vomiting and a feeling of panic when alcohol is consumed); psychological (with therapy and rehabilitation); or social (group therapy). These may take place in or out of an institutional setting, though there is a growing trend in the US toward detoxification centers. Suddenly stopping heavy drinking can lead to **withdrawal** symptoms, including delirium tremens. Many professionals recommend a variety of treatments pursued simultaneously, and even clients in individual therapy are encouraged to attend Alcoholics Anonymous (AA) meetings. AA was founded in 1935 and is based on Twelve Steps, a nonsectarian spiritual program the central points of which are reliance on God or a higher power as each individual understands that concept and the value of help to other alcoholics. AA is thought by many to be the single most successful method yet devised for coping with alcoholism.

Substance abuse. Abused substances include anabolic steroids, which are used by some athletes to enhance performance, and psychotropic agents, substances that affect the user's mental state and are mood- and perception-altering. The latter category, which has a much longer history of abuse, includes opium (and the derivative heroin), hallucinogens, barbiturates, cocaine, amphetamines, tranquilizers, and cannabis (alcohol is also often included in this group). Dependence on prescribed drugs is increasingly common, particularly with tranquilizers and hypnotics. Ecstasy abuse and solvent abuse became increasingly popular among young people in the late 1990s.

Like alcoholics, individuals addicted to drugs are compelled to use them despite the deterioration in health, work, or social activities they may cause. This dependence varies from drug to drug in its extent and effect; it can be physical or psychological or both. Physical dependence becomes apparent only when the drug intake is decreased or stopped and **withdrawal** occurs. Psychological dependence is indicated when the user relies on a drug to produce a feeling of well-being. Another related phenomenon is **tolerance**, a gradual decrease in the effect of a certain dose as the drug is repeatedly taken, causing the user to consume larger doses to produce the desired effect (most marked with habitual opiate users). **Treatment** is similar to that for alcoholism and involves an initial process of detoxification, which should be medically supervised.

Internet resources:
<www.niaaa.nih.gov> (alcohol abuse)
<www.samhsa.gov> (substance abuse)

Suicide

Suicide prevention hotline: 1-800-SUICIDE; Suicide prevention online: <www.samaritans.org>;
Other Internet resources: <www.nimh.nih.gov/publicat/depsuicidemenu.cfm>

Every year approximately 30,000 Americans commit suicide, making it the 11th leading cause of death in 1999. Suicide has historically been condoned by some groups, including the Brahmans of India and the samurai of Japan. In some countries suicide attempts are punishable by law, but in many there is now a greater readiness to sympathize with rather than condemn suicide, though a tendency to conceal suicidal acts still persists.

Although not classified as a distinct mental disorder, suicide is closely linked to **depression** and **bipolar disorder**. It is estimated that approximately 60% of people who commit suicide have had some form of mood disorder. In younger people, substance abuse often plays a role as well. Early recognition and treatment of mental disorders is thus an important deterrent.

Over half of all suicides occur in men aged 25–65; men are often more deliberate in their suicide intentions, are less likely to confide in someone about their plans, and often use more lethal measures.

Among the **warning signs** of suicide are: suicidal talk, including threats of self-harm; previous suicide attempts; preoccupation with death; signs of depression, including social withdrawal, agitation, and behavioral changes; a recent life crisis, such as divorce or the loss of a loved one; and disposal of possessions. Friends and relatives who suspect a person of suicidal ideation are encouraged to get help from agencies specializing in suicide prevention and to always take seriously the threat of suicide.

Assisted suicide, or euthanasia, is currently illegal in the US. The exception is Oregon, where physician-assisted suicide is permitted under tightly controlled conditions. Those in favor of assisted suicide argue that the terminally ill have a right to die with dignity and on their own terms. Many in the medical profession oppose physician-assisted suicide on ethical grounds, as health care workers are bound to prevent injury, even if it is self-induced. Others note that depression, and thus suicidal ideation, is a natural response to a debilitating disease.

Incidence of Suicide in the US, 1900–98

Age-adjusted rates per 100,000 population. Figures based on death registration data.
Courtesy of National Center for Injury Prevention and Control.

YEAR	MALE	FEMALE	TOTAL	YEAR	MALE	FEMALE	TOTAL
1900	17.7	5.0	11.3	1954	16.3	4.1	10.1
1906	22.0	6.2	14.3	1960	16.5	4.9	10.6
1912	26.0	7.9	17.3	1966	16.1	5.9	10.9
1918	20.0	6.9	13.6	1972	17.4	6.7	11.9
1924	20.2	6.2	13.4	1978	18.7	6.2	12.3
1930	26.2	7.4	17.0	1984	18.6	5.2	11.6
1936	22.4	7.0	14.8	1990	19.0	4.5	11.5
1942	18.0	5.8	11.8	1996	18.0	4.1	10.8
1948	16.7	5.1	10.8	1998	17.2	4.0	10.4

Diet and Exercise

The Food and Drug Administration (FDA)

The FDA is a division of the US Department of Health and Human Services. FDA Web site: <www.fda.gov>.

Mission: To promote and protect the public health by helping safe and effective products reach the market in a timely way and monitoring products for continued safety after they are in use. **Location:** Rockville, MD. **Deputy Commissioner:** Lester M. Crawford, Jr. **Budget:** Approximately $1.4 billion for FY 2002. **Functions:** The FDA is the agency of the US federal government authorized by Congress to inspect, test, approve, and set safety standards for foods and food additives, drugs, chemicals, cosmetics, and household and medical devices. Generally, the FDA is empowered to prevent untested products from being sold and to take legal action to halt sale of undoubtedly harmful products or of products which involve a health or safety risk. Through court procedure, the FDA can seize products and prosecute the persons or firms responsible for legal violation. FDA authority is limited to interstate commerce. The agency cannot control prices nor directly regulate advertising except of prescription drugs and medical devices.

Vitamins, with Daily Recommendations

Vitamins are organic substances that are usually divided into two types: water-soluble and fat-soluble. Small quantities are necessary for normal health and growth in higher forms of animal life, as they work to regulate reactions that occur in metabolism (in contrast to macronutrients such as fats, carbohydrates, and proteins, which are the compounds utilized in the reactions regulated by vitamins). Absence of a vitamin blocks one or more specific metabolic reactions in a cell; thus, vitamin deficiency may result in specific diseases. As they generally cannot be synthesized by humans, vitamins must be obtained from the diet or from a synthetic source.

mg: milligram; mcg: microgram; RE: retinol equivalent; IU: international unit

The name of each vitamin is followed by its alternative name and usual pharmaceutical preparation, respectively.

Water-soluble vitamins
Thiamin (vitamin B₁; thiamine hydrochloride)
   Purpose: energy metabolism and initiation of nerve impulses; **Dietary sources:** cereal grains, pork, nuts; **Men over 14:** 1.2 mg; **Women over 18:** 1.1 mg; **Pregnant women:** 1.4 mg; **Lactating women:** 1.5 mg

Riboflavin (vitamin B₂; riboflavin)
   Purpose: release of energy from carbohydrates, fats, and proteins; maintaining integrity of red blood cells; **Dietary sources:** milk, eggs, kidney, liver, leafy vegetables; **Men over 14:** 1.3 mg; **Women over 18:** 1.0 mg; **Pregnant women:** 1.4 mg; **Lactating women:** 1.6 mg

Niacin (nicotonic acid; nicotinamide; nicotinamide)
   Purpose: release of energy from carbohydrates and fats; red blood cell formation; metabolism of proteins; **Dietary sources:** liver, kidney; **Men over 14:** 16.0 mg; **Women over 18:** 14.0 mg; **Pregnant women:** 18.0 mg; **Lactating women:** 17.0 mg

Vitamin B₆ (pyroxidine; pyroxidine hydrochloride)
   Purpose: amino acid, carbohydrate, and fat metabolism; **Dietary sources:** cereal grains, liver, fish, nuts; **Men 14–50:** 1.3 mg; **Men over 50:** 1.7 mg; **Women 19–50:** 1.3 mg; **Women over 50:** 1.5 mg; **Pregnant women:** 1.9 mg; **Lactating women:** 2.0 mg

Pantothenic acid (vitamin B₅; calcium pantothenate)
   Purpose: metabolism of carbohydrates; synthesis and degradation of fats; synthesis of sterols and other compounds; **Dietary sources:** liver, kidney, eggs, yeast; **All adults:** 4.0–7.0 mg

Vitamins, with Daily Recommendations (continued)

Water-soluble vitamins (continued)

Biotin (N/A; biotin)
   Purpose: carbohydrate and fat metabolism; **Dietary sources:** beef liver, eggs, yeast; **All adults:** 0.3 mg

Folate (folacin; vitamin B₉; folic acid)
   Purpose: cellular metabolism, including synthesis of DNA components; normal red blood cell formation; **Dietary sources:** liver, green leafy vegetables, wheat bran and germ, citrus fruits, cereals, beans, poultry, egg yolks; **Adults over 13:** 400 mcg; **Pregnant women:** 600 mcg; **Lactating women:** 500 mcg

Vitamin B₁₂ (cobalamin; cyanocobalamin; hydroxocobalamin)
   Purpose: proper functioning of many enzymes involved in carbohydrate, fat, and protein metabolism; synthesis of the insulating sheath around nerve cells; cell reproduction and normal growth; red blood cell formation; **Dietary sources:** eggs, meat, milk; **Adults:** 2.4 mcg; **Pregnant women:** 2.6 mcg; **Lactating women:** 2.8 mcg

Vitamin C (ascorbic acid; ascorbic acid)
   Purpose: prevention of oxidative damage to DNA, membrane lipids, and proteins; synthesis of collagen, hormones, transmitters of the nervous sytem, lipids, and proteins; proper immune function; **Dietary sources:** citrus fruits, green peppers, broccoli, cantaloupe, green leafy vegetables; **Adults over 14:** 60 mg; **Pregnant women:** 70 mg; **Lactating women** (first 6 months): 95 mg; (second 6 months): 90 mg

Fat-soluble vitamins

Vitamin A (retinol; retinol)
   Purpose: functioning of the retina; growth and maturation of epithelial cells; growth of bone; reproduction and embryonic development; **Dietary sources:** fish and fish-liver oils, liver, butter, orange vegetables and fruits, dark green leafy vegetables; tomatoes; **Men over 10:** 1000 RE; **Women over 10:** 800 RE; **Pregnant women:** 800 RE; **Lactating women** (first 6 months): 1300 RE; (second 6 months): 1200 RE

Vitamin D (vitamins D₂ and D₃; [ergo] calciferol)
   Purpose: promotes formation of bone by increasing the blood levels of calcium and phosphorus; **Dietary sources:** fish-liver oils, eggs, milk enriched with Vitamin D; **All adults:** 400 IU

Vitamin E (N/A; tocopherol)
   Purpose: protection of cell membranes and prevention of damage to membrane-associated enzymes; **Dietary sources:** vegetable oils, margarine, cereal grains; **Men over 10:** 15 IU; **Women over 10:** 12 IU; **Pregnant women:** 15 IU; **Lactating women** (first 6 months): 18 IU; (second 6 months): 16.5 IU

Vitamin K (N/A; vitamin K₁)
   Purpose: formation of several blood blotting factors; **Dietary sources:** green leafy vegetables, vegetable oils; *no recommended daily allowance*

Food Guide Pyramid

The USDA recommends following the food guide pyramid as a way of maintaining a healthful diet. It is designed to help you get the proper nutrients while at the same time consuming the amount of calories necessary to maintain a healthy weight. It is important to choose a diet that is low in saturated fat and cholesterol and moderate in total fat. You should eat at least the lower number of servings from the five food groups and pick the lowest fat choices from each.

Serving amounts given are for a single day. Typical serving sizes are:
Bread, Cereal, Rice, and Pasta Group: 1 slice bread; 1 oz cereal; ½ cup rice or pasta.
Vegetable Group: 1 cup raw leafy vegetables; ½ cup other vegetables; ¾ cup vegetable juice.
Fruit Group: 1 medium apple, banana, or orange; ½ cup chopped, cooked, or canned fruit; ¾ cup fruit juice.
Milk, Yogurt, and Cheese Group: 1 cup milk or yogurt; 1 ½ oz natural cheese; 2 oz processed cheese.
Fish, Meat, Poultry, Dry Beans, Eggs, and Nuts Group: 2–3 oz cooked lean meat, poultry, or fish; ½ cup cooked dry beans; 1 egg; 2 tablespoons peanut butter.

No specific serving is recommended for the Fats, Oils, and Sweets Group, but you should use these only sparingly. Remember to count a larger portion as more than one serving—a typical restaurant serving of pasta, for example, would count as 2–3 servings on the pyramid.

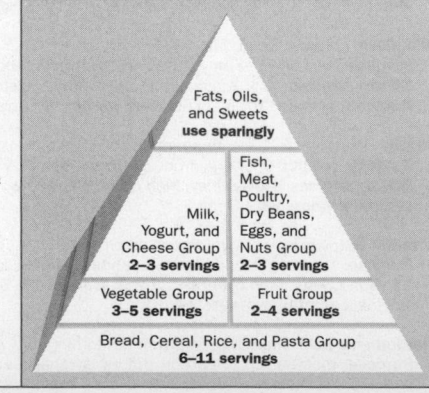

Fats, Oils, and Sweets
use sparingly

Fish, Meat, Poultry, Dry Beans, Eggs, and Nuts Group
2–3 servings

Milk, Yogurt, and Cheese Group
2–3 servings

Vegetable Group
3–5 servings

Fruit Group
2–4 servings

Bread, Cereal, Rice, and Pasta Group
6–11 servings

Source: USDA.

Fat Intake in US Diet

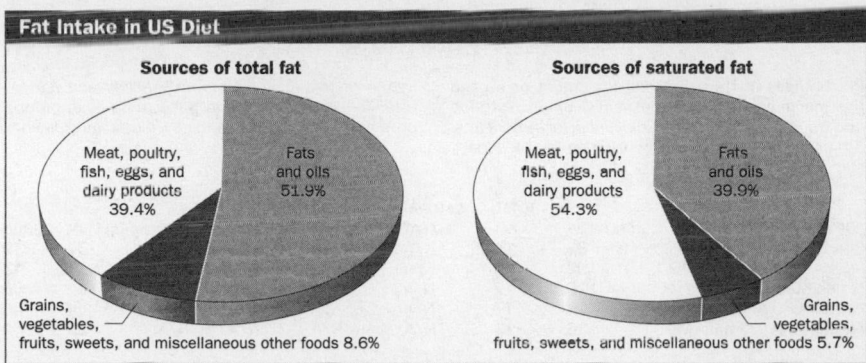

Sources of total fat
Fats and oils 51.9%
Meat, poultry, fish, eggs, and dairy products 39.4%
Grains, vegetables, fruits, sweets, and miscellaneous other foods 8.6%
Sources of saturated fat
Fats and oils 39.9%
Meat, poultry, fish, eggs, and dairy products 54.3%
Grains, vegetables, fruits, sweets, and miscellaneous other foods 5.7%

US, Annual Per Capita Food Consumption (in pounds)

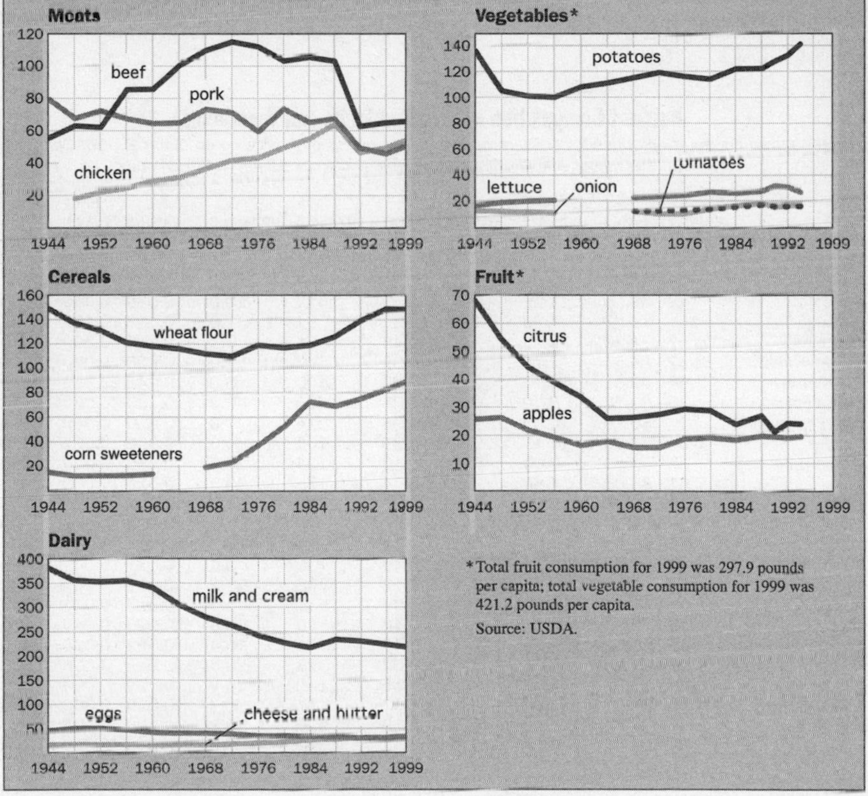

Meats
beef
pork
chicken
120
100
80
60
40
20
1944 1952 1960 1968 1976 1984 1992 1999
Vegetables*
potatoes
lettuce
onion
tomatoes
140
120
100
80
60
40
20
1944 1952 1960 1968 1976 1984 1992 1999
Cereals
wheat flour
corn sweeteners
160
140
120
100
80
60
40
20
1944 1952 1960 1968 1976 1984 1992 1999
Fruit*
citrus
apples
70
60
50
40
30
20
10
1944 1952 1960 1968 1976 1984 1992 1999
Dairy
milk and cream
eggs
cheese and butter
400
350
300
250
200
150
100
50
1944 1952 1960 1968 1976 1984 1992 1999

*Total fruit consumption for 1999 was 297.9 pounds per capita; total vegetable consumption for 1999 was 421.2 pounds per capita.

Source: USDA.

Individuals Meeting Dietary Guidelines
1977-78 and 1994-96.

Percentages of US population that meet or exceed the minimum dietary guidelines given in *Nutrition and Your Health: Dietary Guidelines for Americans, 5th edition* (2000), a joint publication of the department of Health and Human Services and Agriculture. To view the complete publication or to order a print copy, visit <www.health.gov/dietaryguidelines>.

AGE AND GENDER	CALORIES	TOTAL FAT	SATURA-TED FAT	CHOL-ESTEROL	SODIUM	FIBER	CALCIUM	IRON
				1977-78				
Children (2–17)	33	14	N/A	N/A	N/A	N/A	37	39
Adults (18 and over)	23	13	N/A	N/A	N/A	N/A	15	43
Males 60 and over	29	12	N/A	N/A	N/A	N/A	11	66
Females 60 and over	18	17	N/A	N/A	N/A	N/A	4	40
All individuals 2 and over	**26**	**13**	**N/A**	**N/A**	**N/A**	**N/A**	**22**	**42**
				1994-96				
AGE AND GENDER								
Children (2–17)	38	37	31	77	39	39	37	59
Adults (18 and over)	27	37	43	69	34	20	21	60
Males 60 and over	28	36	43	65	30	26	16	77
Females 60 and over	18	41	49	79	54	35	6	56
All individuals 2 and over	**30**	**37**	**40**	**71**	**35**	**25**	**25**	**59**

N/A: Not available

Nutrient Composition of Selected Fruits and Vegetables
Values shown are approximations for 100 grams. Foods raw unless otherwise noted. Source: USDA Nutrient Data Laboratory. kcal: kilocalorie; g: gram; mg: milligram; IU: international unit.

	ENERGY (KCAL)	WATER (G)	CARBO-HYDRATE (G)	PROTEIN (G)	FAT (G)	VITAMIN A (IU)	VITAMIN C (MG)	THIAMINE (MG)	RIBO-FLAVIN (MG)	NIACIN (MG)
Fruits:										
Apple	59	83.93	15.25	0.19	0.36	53	5.7	0.017	0.014	0.077
Apricot	48	86.35	11.12	1.40	0.39	2,612	10.0	0.030	0.040	0.600
Avocado	161	74.27	7.39	1.98	15.32	61	7.9	0.108	0.122	1.921
Banana	92	74.26	23.43	1.03	0.48	81	9.1	0.045	0.100	0.540
Blackberries	52	85.64	12.76	0.72	0.39	165	21.0	0.030	0.040	0.400
Blueberries	56	84.61	14.13	0.67	0.38	100	13.0	0.048	0.050	0.359
Cantaloupe	35	89.78	8.36	0.88	0.28	3,224	42.2	0.036	0.021	0.574
Cherries (sweet)	72	80.76	16.55	1.20	0.96	214	7.0	0.050	0.060	0.400
Grapes	67	81.30	17.15	0.63	0.35	100	4.0	0.092	0.057	0.300
Grapefruit	32	90.89	8.08	0.63	0.10	124	34.4	0.036	0.020	0.250
Kiwi	61	83.05	14.88	0.99	0.44	175	98.0	0.020	0.050	0.500
Lemon	29	88.98	9.32	1.10	0.30	29	53.0	0.040	0.020	0.100
Lime	30	88.26	10.54	0.70	0.20	10	29.1	0.030	0.020	0.200
Mango	65	81.71	17.00	0.51	0.27	3,894	27.7	0.058	0.057	0.584
Nectarine	49	86.28	11.78	0.94	0.46	736	5.4	0.017	0.041	0.990
Orange	47	86.75	11.75	0.94	0.12	205	53.2	0.087	0.040	0.282
Peach	43	87.66	11.10	0.70	0.09	535	6.6	0.017	0.041	0.990
Pear	59	83.81	15.11	0.39	0.40	20	4.0	0.020	0.040	0.100
Pineapple	49	86.50	12.39	0.39	0.43	23	15.4	0.092	0.036	0.420
Plum	55	85.20	13.01	0.79	0.62	323	9.5	0.043	0.096	0.500
Raspberries	49	86.57	11.57	0.91	0.55	130	25.0	0.030	0.090	0.900
Strawberries	30	91.57	7.02	0.61	0.37	27	56.7	0.020	0.066	0.230
Tangerine	44	87.60	11.19	0.63	0.19	920	30.8	0.105	0.022	0.160
Watermelon	32	91.51	7.18	0.62	0.43	366	9.6	0.080	0.020	0.200
Vegetables:										
Artichokes[1]	50	83.97	11.18	3.48	0.16	177	10.0	0.065	0.066	1.001
Asparagus[1]	24	92.20	4.23	2.59	0.31	539	10.8	0.123	0.126	1.082
Beans (snap, green)	31	90.27	7.14	1.82	0.12	668	16.3	0.084	0.105	0.752
Beets	43	87.58	9.56	1.61	0.17	38	4.9	0.031	0.040	0.334
Broccoli	28	90.69	5.24	2.98	0.35	1,542	93.2	0.065	0.119	0.638
Brussels sprouts	43	86.00	8.96	3.38	0.30	883	85.0	0.139	0.090	0.745
Cabbage	25	92.15	5.43	1.44	0.27	133	32.2	0.050	0.040	0.300
Carrots	43	87.79	10.14	1.03	0.19	28,129	9.3	0.097	0.059	0.928
Cauliflower	25	91.91	5.20	1.98	0.21	19	46.4	0.057	0.063	0.526

Nutrient Composition of Selected Fruits and Vegetables (continued)

	ENERGY (KCAL)	WATER (G)	CARBO-HYDRATE (G)	PROTEIN (G)	FAT (G)	VITAMIN A (IU)	VITAMIN C (MG)	THIAMINE (MG)	RIBO-FLAVIN (MG)	NIACIN (MG)
Vegetables: (continued)										
Celery	16	94.64	3.65	0.75	0.14	134	7.0	0.046	0.045	0.323
Collards[1]	26	91.86	4.90	2.11	0.36	3,129	18.2	0.040	0.106	0.575
Corn (sweet, yellow)[1]	108	69.57	25.11	3.32	1.28	217	6.2	0.215	0.072	1.614
Cucumber	13	96.01	2.76	0.69	0.13	215	5.3	0.024	0.022	0.221
Eggplant[1]	28	91.77	6.64	0.83	0.23	64	1.3	0.076	0.020	0.600
Lettuce (iceberg)	12	95.89	2.09	1.01	0.19	330	3.9	0.046	0.030	0.187
Mushrooms[1]	27	91.08	5.14	2.17	0.47	0	4.0	0.073	0.300	4.460
Okra[1]	32	89.91	7.21	1.87	0.17	575	16.3	0.132	0.055	0.871
Onions[1]	44	87.86	10.15	1.36	0.19	0	5.2	0.042	0.023	0.165
Peppers (sweet, green)	27	92.19	6.43	0.89	0.19	632	89.3	0.066	0.030	0.509
Peppers (sweet, red)	27	92.19	6.43	0.89	0.19	5,700	190.0	0.066	0.030	0.509
Potatoes[2]	93	75.42	21.56	1.96	0.10	0	12.8	0.105	0.021	1.395
Spinach	22	91.58	3.50	2.86	0.35	6,715	28.1	0.078	0.189	0.724
Sweet potato[2]	103	72.85	24.27	1.72	0.11	21,822	24.6	0.073	0.127	0.604
Tomatoes (red)	21	93.76	4.64	0.85	0.33	623	19.1	0.059	0.048	0.628

[1]Boiled   [2]Baked

Nutritional Value of Selected Foods

Values shown are approximations. Source: Home and Garden Bulletin No. 72, USDA. kcal: kilocalorie; g: gram; mg: milligram; oz: ounce; fl oz: fluid ounce.

FOOD	AMOUNT	GRAMS	ENERGY (KCAL)	CARBO-HYDRATE (G)	PROTEIN (G)	TOTAL FAT (G)	SATU-RATED FAT (G)	CALCIUM (MG)	IRON (MG)	SODIUM (MG)
Beverages										
Beer	12 fl oz	360	150	13	1	0	0	14	0.1	18
Cola, regular	12 fl oz	369	160	41	0	0	0	11	0.2	18
Cola, diet (w/aspartame and saccharine)	12 fl oz	355	0	0	0	0	0	14	0.2	32
Coffee, brewed	6 fl oz	180	0	0	0	0	0	4	0	2
Orange juice, canned	8 fl oz	249	105	25	1	0	0	20	1.1	5
Tea, instant, prepared, unsweetened	8 fl oz	241	0	1	0	0	0	1	0	1
Wine, table, red	3.5 fl oz	102	75	3	0	0	0	8	0.4	5
Dairy										
Butter, salted	4 oz	113	810	0	1	92	57.1	27	0.2	933
Cheese, American (pasteurized, processed)	1 oz	28.35	105	0	6	9	5.6	174	0.1	406
Cheese, cheddar	1 oz	28.35	115	0	7	9	6	204	0.2	176
Cheese, mozzarella (whole milk)	1 oz	28.35	80	1	6	6	3.7	147	0.1	106
Cheese, swiss	1 oz	28.35	105	1	8	8	5	272	0	74
Cottage cheese, small curd	8 oz	210	215	6	26	9	6	126	0.3	850
Cream cheese	1 oz	28.35	100	1	2	10	6.2	23	0.3	84
Cream, half and half	0.5 oz	15	20	1	0	2	1.1	16	0	6
Cream, sour	8 oz	230	495	10	7	48	30	268	0.1	123
Eggs, cooked, fried	1 egg	46	90	1	6	7	1.9	25	0.7	162
Eggs, cooked, hard-cooked	1 egg	50	75	1	6	5	1.6	25	0.6	62
Eggs, cooked, scrambled	1 egg	61	100	1	7	7	2.2	44	0.7	171
Ice cream, vanilla, 11% fat	8 oz	133	270	32	5	14	8.9	176	0.1	116
Milk, whole, 3.3% fat	8 oz	244	150	11	8	8	5.1	291	0.1	120
Milk, low fat, 2% fat	8 oz	244	120	12	8	5	2.9	297	0.1	122
Milk, skim	8 oz	245	85	12	8	0	0.3	302	0.1	126
Milk, chocolate	8 oz	250	210	26	8	8	5.3	280	0.6	149
Yogurt, plain, low fat	8 oz	227	145	16	12	4	2.3	415	0.2	159
Fats, oils										
Lard	0.5 oz	13	115	0	0	13	5.1	0	0	0
Margarine, hard, 80% fat	0.5 oz	14	100	0	0	11	2.2	4	0	132

Nutritional Value of Selected Foods (continued)

FOOD	AMOUNT	GRAMS	ENERGY (KCAL)	CARBO-HYDRATE (G)	PROTEIN (G)	TOTAL FAT (G)	SATU-RATED FAT (G)	CALCIUM (MG)	IRON (MG)	SODIUM (MG)
Fats, oils (continued)										
Olive oil	0.5 oz	14	125	0	0	14	1.9	0	0	0
Vegetable shortening	0.5 oz	13	115	0	0	13	3.3	0	0	0
Fish										
Crabmeat, canned	8 oz	135	135	1	23	3	0.5	61	1.1	1350
Fish sticks, frozen	1 piece	28	70	4	6	3	0.8	11	0.3	53
Ocean perch, breaded, fried	1 piece	85	185	7	16	11	2.6	31	1.2	138
Oysters, raw	8 oz	240	160	8	20	4	1.4	226	15.6	175
Salmon, baked, red	3 oz	85	140	0	21	5	1.2	26	0.5	55
Shrimp, fried	3 oz	85	200	11	16	10	2.5	61	2	384
Trout, broiled, w/butter and lemon juice	3 oz	85	175	0	21	9	4.1	26	1	122
Tuna, canned, white, in water	3 oz	85	135	0	30	1	0.3	17	0.6	468
Fruits, fruit products										
Apples, peeled, sliced	8 oz	110	65	16	0	0	0.1	4	0.1	0
Applesauce, canned, sweetened	8 oz	255	195	51	0	0	0.1	10	0.9	8
Apricots	3 apricots	106	50	12	1	0	0	15	0.6	1
Bananas	1 banana	114	105	27	1	1	0.2	7	0.4	1
Blackberries	8 oz	144	75	18	1	1	0.2	46	0.8	0
Blueberries	8 oz	145	80	20	1	1	0	9	0.2	9
Grapefruit, pink	½ grapefruit	120	40	10	1	0	0	14	0.1	0
Grapes, European, Thompson	10 grapes	50	35	9	0	0	0.1	6	0.1	1
Oranges	1 orange	131	60	15	1	0	0	52	0.1	0
Peaches	1 peach	87	35	10	1	0	0	4	0.1	0
Pears, Bartlett	1 pear	166	100	25	1	1	0	18	0.4	0
Pineapple, canned, heavy syrup	8 oz	255	200	52	1	0	0	36	1	3
Plums, 2⅛-in. diam.	1 plum	66	35	9	1	0	0	3	0.1	0
Prunes, dried, large	5 prunes	49	115	31	1	0	0	25	1.2	2
Raisins	8 oz	145	435	115	5	1	0.2	71	3	17
Strawberries	8 oz	149	45	10	1	1	0	21	0.6	1
Watermelon	1 piece	482	155	35	3	2	0.3	39	0.8	10
Grains										
Bagels, plain	1 bagel	68	200	38	7	2	0.3	29	1.8	245
Bread, rye, light	1 slice	25	65	12	2	1	0.2	20	0.7	175
Bread, wheat	1 slice	25	65	12	2	1	0.2	32	0.9	138
Bread, white	1 slice	25	65	12	2	1	0.3	32	0.7	129
Bread, whole wheat	1 slice	28	70	13	3	1	0.4	20	1	180
Cereal, Cheerios	1 oz	28.35	110	20	4	2	0.3	48	4.5	307
Cereal, Kellogg's Corn Flakes	1 oz	28.35	110	24	2	0	0	1	1.8	351
Cereal, Lucky Charms	1 oz	28.35	110	23	3	1	0.2	32	4.5	201
Cereal, Post Raisin Bran	1 oz	28.35	85	21	3	1	0.1	13	4.5	185
Cake, white, w/white frost., commercial	1 piece	71	260	42	3	9	2.1	33	1	176
Cheesecake	1 piece	92	280	26	5	18	9.9	52	0.4	204
Chocolate chip cookies, commercial	4 cookies	42	180	28	2	9	2.9	13	0.8	140
Cornmeal, whole-ground, dry	8 oz	122	435	90	11	5	0.5	24	2.2	1
Doughnuts, cake, plain	1 doughnut	50	210	24	3	12	2.8	22	1	192
English muffins, plain	1 muffin	57	140	27	5	1	0.3	96	1.7	378
Oatmeal, instant, cooked, w/salt	8 oz	234	145	25	6	2	0.4	19	1.6	374
Macaroni, cooked, firm	8 oz	130	190	39	7	1	0.1	14	2.1	1
Muffins, blueberry, commercial mix	1 muffin	45	140	22	3	5	1.4	15	0.9	225
Pancakes, plain, commercial mix	1 pancake	27	60	8	2	2	0.5	36	0.7	160
Pie, apple	1 piece	158	405	60	3	18	4.6	13	1.6	476

Nutritional Value of Selected Foods (continued)

FOOD	AMOUNT	GRAMS	ENERGY (KCAL)	CARBO-HYDRATE (G)	PROTEIN (G)	TOTAL FAT (G)	SATU-RATED FAT (G)	CALCIUM (MG)	IRON (MG)	SODIUM (MG)
Grains (continued)										
Popcorn, air-popped, un-salted	8 oz	8	30	6	1	0	0	1	0.2	0
Pretzels, stick	10 pieces	3	10	2	0	0	0	1	0.1	48
Rice, brown, cooked	8 oz	195	230	50	5	1	0.3	23	1	0
Rice, white, instant, cooked	8 oz	165	180	40	4	0	0.1	5	1.3	0
Saltines	4 pieces	12	50	9	1	1	0.5	3	0.5	165
Spaghetti, cooked, tender	8 oz	140	155	32	5	1	0.1	11	1.7	1
Waffles, from commercial mix	1 waffle	75	205	27	7	8	2.7	179	1.2	515
Meat, poultry										
Bacon, regular, cooked	3 slices	19	110	0	6	9	3.3	2	0.3	303
Beef, chuck, lean, cooked	2.2 oz	62	170	0	19	9	3.9	8	2.3	44
Chicken, breast, roasted	3 oz	86	140	0	27	3	0.9	13	0.9	64
Chicken, drumstick, floured, fried	1.7 oz	49	120	1	13	7	1.8	0	0.7	44
Ground beef, broiled	3 oz	85	245	0	20	18	6.9	9	2.1	70
Ham, roasted, lean and fat	3 oz	85	205	0	18	14	5.1	6	0.7	1009
Hamburger	4 oz patty	174	445	38	25	21	7.1	75	4.8	763
Lamb chops, braised, lean	1.7 oz	48	135	0	17	7	2.9	12	1.3	36
Turkey, roasted, light and dark	8 oz	140	240	0	41	7	2.3	35	2.5	98
Veal cutlet, med. fat, braised or broiled	3 oz	85	185	0	23	9	4.1	9	0.8	56
Nuts, legumes, seeds										
Mixed nuts w/peanuts, dry, salted	1 oz	28.35	170	7	5	15	2	20	1	190
Peanuts, oil-roasted, unsalted	8 oz	145	840	27	39	71	9.9	125	2.8	22
Peanut butter	0.5 oz	16	95	3	5	8	1.4	5	0.3	75
Pinto beans, dry, cooked	8 oz	180	265	49	15	1	0.1	86	5.4	3
Sunflower seeds	1 oz	28.35	160	5	6	14	1.5	33	1.9	1
Tofu	1 piece	120	85	3	9	5	0.7	108	2.3	8
Sauces, dressings, condiments										
Catsup	0.5 oz	15	15	4	0	0	0	3	0.1	156
Cheese sauce w/milk, from mix	8 fl oz	279	305	23	16	17	9.3	569	0.3	1565
Honey	0.5 oz	21	65	17	0	0	0	1	0.1	1
Jams/preserves	0.5 oz	20	55	14	0	0	0	4	0.2	2
Mayonnaise	0.5 oz	14	100	0	0	11	1.7	3	0.1	80
Mustard, yellow	0.17 oz	5	5	0	0	0	0	4	0.1	63
Salad dressing, French	0.5 oz	16	85	1	0	9	1.4	2	0	188
Salad dressing, Italian, low calorie	0.5 oz	15	5	2	0	0	0	1	0	136
Syrup, table	1 oz	42	122	32	0	0	0	1	0	19
Sugars, sweets, miscellaneous snacks										
Caramels, plain or chocolate	1 oz	28.35	115	22	1	3	2.2	42	0.4	64
Chocolate, milk, candy, w/ almonds	1 oz	28.35	150	15	3	10	4.8	65	0.5	23
Chocolate, dark, sweet	1 oz	28.35	150	16	1	10	5.9	7	0.6	5
Gelatin dessert, prepared	4 oz	120	70	17	2	0	0	2	0	55
Hard candy	1 oz	28.35	110	28	0	0	0	0	0.1	7
Popsicle	1 popsicle	95	70	18	0	0	0	0	0	11
Potato chips	10 chips	20	105	10	1	7	1.8	5	0.2	94
Pudding, chocolate, instant	4 oz	130	155	27	4	4	2.3	130	0.3	440
Sugar, brown	8 oz	220	820	212	0	0	0	187	4.8	97
Sugar, white, granulated	8 oz	200	770	199	0	0	0	3	0.1	5
Vegetables										
Beans, snap, yellow, canned, no salt	8 oz	135	25	6	2	0	0	35	1.2	3
Broccoli	1 spear	151	40	8	4	1	0.1	72	1.3	41

Nutritional Value of Selected Foods (continued)

FOOD	AMOUNT	GRAMS	ENERGY (KCAL)	CARBO-HYDRATE (G)	PROTEIN (G)	TOTAL FAT (G)	SATU-RATED FAT (G)	CALCIUM (MG)	IRON (MG)	SODIUM (MG)
Vegetables (continued)										
Carrots, cooked from frozen	8 oz	146	55	12	2	0	0	41	0.7	86
Cauliflower, cooked from raw	8 oz	125	30	6	2	0	0	34	0.5	8
Celery, Pascal, raw	1 stalk	40	5	1	0	0	0	14	0.2	35
Corn, yellow, cooked from frozen	8 oz	165	135	34	5	0	0	3	0.5	8
Cucumber, w/peel	6 slices	28	5	1	0	0	0	4	0.1	1
Lettuce, crisphead	1 wedge	135	20	3	1	0	0	26	0.7	12
Mushrooms	8 oz	70	20	3	1	0	0	4	0.9	3
Onions, sliced	8 oz	115	40	8	1	0	0.1	29	0.4	2
Peas, green, cooked from frozen	8 oz	160	125	23	8	0	0.1	38	2.5	139
Potatos, boiled, peeled after	1 potato	136	120	27	3	0	0	7	0.4	5
Tomatoes, raw	1 tomato	123	25	5	1	0	0	9	0.6	10

Reading Food Labels

The FDA requires most food manufacturers to provide standardized nutritional information about certain nutrients. The nutritional labels are designed to aid the consumer in making informed dietary decisions, as well as to regulate claims made by manufacturers about their products.

The percent daily value is based on a 2,000-calorie-per-day diet. Some larger packages will have listings for both 2,000-calorie and 2,500-calorie diets. For products that require additional preparation before eating, such as dry cake mixes, manufacturers often provide two columns of nutritional information, one with the values of the food as purchased, the other with the value of the food as prepared.

The use of certain key terms is also regulated by the FDA. They include the following amounts, per serving:

Low fat: 3 g or less
Low saturated fat: 1 g or less
Low sodium: 140 mg or less
Low cholesterol: 20 mg or less and 2 g or less of saturated fat
Low calorie: 40 calories or less

Did you know? Azerbaijan is renowned for the longevity of its people, which is attributed to the healthful foods they eat, especially fresh vegetables and fruit, yogurt, fish, and green tea.

Nutrition Facts

Serving Size ½ cup (114g)
Servings Per Container 4

Amount Per Serving

Calories 90   Calories from Fat 30

                      %Daily Value*

Total Fat 3g   **5%**

    Saturated Fat 0g   **0%**

Cholesterol 0mg   **0%**

Sodium 300mg   **13%**

Total Carbohydrate 13g   **4%**

    Dietary Fiber 3g   **12%**

    Sugars 3g

Protein 3g

Vitamin A 80% • Vitamin C 60%

Calcium 4% • Iron 4%

* Percent Daily Values are based on a 2,000 calorie diet. Your daily values may be higher or lower depending on your calorie needs:

	Calories	2,000	2,500
Total Fat	Less than	65g	80g
Sat. Fat	Less than	20g	25g
Cholesterol	Less than	300mg	300mg
Sodium	Less than	2,400mg	2,400mg
Total Carbohydrate		300g	375g
Dietary Fiber		25g	30g

Calories per gram:
Fat 9 • Carbohydrate 4 • Protein 4

Americans and Physical Activity

Data from the National Health Interview Survey, 1991. Percentage of participants who reported taking part in specific activities during the two weeks preceding the interview. Percentages do not total 100, as only the most popular activities are listed and participants may have taken part in more than one activity.

males / ACTIVITY	ALL AGES/SEXES (%)	18-29 (%)	30-44 (%)	45-64 (%)	65-74 (%)	75+ (%)	ALL (%)
1 Walking	44.1	32.8	37.6	43.3	50.1	47.1	39.4
2 Gardening/yard work	29.4	22.2	36.0	39.8	42.6	38.4	34.2
3 Stretching	25.5	32.1	27.2	20.0	15.5	15.7	25.0
4 Cycling¹	15.4	18.7	18.5	14.0	10.8	8.4	16.2
5 Weight lifting/ muscle strengthening	14.1	33.6	21.2	12.2	6.4	4.7	20.0
6 Stair climbing	10.8	10.5	11.4	9.6	6.0	4.0	9.9
7 Jogging/running	9.1	22.6	14.1	7.7	1.4	0.5	12.8
8 Aerobics	7.1	3.4	3.3	2.1	1.6	1.0	2.8
9 Swimming	6.5	10.1	7.6	5.3	3.1	1.4	6.9
10 Basketball	5.8	24.2	10.5	2.4	0.1	0.1	10.5
11 Golf	4.9	7.9	8.6	7.9	9.7	4.9	8.2

females / ACTIVITY	ALL AGES/SEXES (%)	18-29 (%)	30-44 (%)	45-64 (%)	65-74 (%)	75+ (%)	ALL (%)
1 Walking	44.1	47.4	49.1	49.4	50.1	40.5	48.3
2 Gardening/yard work	29.4	15.4	28.6	29.6	28.2	21.5	25.1
3 Stretching	25.5	32.5	27.7	21.4	21.9	17.9	26.0
4 Cycling¹	15.4	17.4	16.9	12.6	11.4	6.0	14.6
5 Weight lifting/ muscle strengthening	14.1	14.5	10.6	5.1	2.8	1.1	8.8
6 Stair climbing	10.8	14.6	12.8	10.3	7.3	5.6	11.6
7 Jogging/running	9.1	11.6	6.5	2.5	0.8	0.4	5.7
8 Aerobics	7.1	19.3	12.3	6.6	4.2	1.6	11.1
9 Swimming	6.5	8.0	7.5	4.6	4.2	1.5	6.2
10 Basketball	5.8	3.1	1.7	0.4	0.0	0.2	1.5
11 Golf	4.9	1.4	1.7	2.2	3.3	0.7	1.8

¹Riding a bicycle or stationary bike.

Target Heart Rate Training Zones

Measuring **target heart rate** involves monitoring your pulse periodically as you exercise. To use the Target Heart Rate chart:

1. Calculate your maximum heart rate by subtracting your age from 220.
2. Determine your target heart rate zone (50–70% of your maximum heart rate).
3. While exercising, monitor your pulse regularly. Count the number of beats for 10 seconds, then multiply by 6 to determine in what zone you are working.

The American Heart Association recommends using the target heart rate scale when participating in more vigorous athletic activity, such as jogging or aerobics. If your activity is moderate or taking your pulse is too bothersome, a "talk test" can be used as a substitute. If you can converse with someone with minimal effort, you are not working too hard. Alternately, if you can sing without difficulty, you are not working hard enough.

Note: For optimal cardiovascular fitness, you should work toward the middle of your 50 and 70% zones. Always check with your physician before starting any fitness routine, especially if you have heart or respiratory concerns.

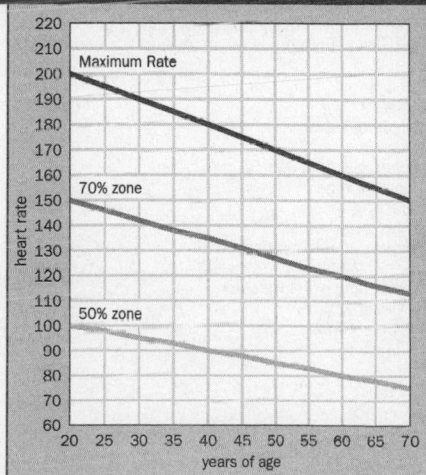

Body Mass Index (BMI)

The BMI is a measure expressing the relationship of weight to height determined by dividing body weight in kilograms by the square of height in meters (for convenience, the information has been converted to standard US measurements in the table below). It is more highly correlated with body fat than any other indicator of height and weight. The National Institutes of Health recommend using the BMI scale to help assess the risk of diseases and disabilities associated with an unhealthy weight. Individuals with a BMI below 18.5 are considered underweight; those with a BMI from 18.5 to 24.9 are considered normal; those with a BMI between 25.0 and 29.9 are considered overweight; and those with a BMI of 30.0 or more are considered obese. The BMI may overestimate body fat in athletes and others who have a muscular build, and it may underestimate body fat in older persons and others who have lost muscle mass. Source: <www.nhlbi.nih.gov>.

HEIGHT (INCHES)							BODY WEIGHT (POUNDS)																	
58	91	96	100	105	110	115	119	124	129	134	138	143	148	153	158	162	167	172	177	181	186
59	94	99	104	109	114	119	124	128	133	138	143	148	153	158	163	168	173	178	183	188	193
60	97	102	107	112	118	123	128	133	138	143	148	153	158	163	168	174	179	184	189	194	199
61	100	106	111	116	122	127	132	137	143	148	153	158	164	169	174	180	185	190	195	201	206
62	104	109	115	120	126	131	136	142	147	153	158	164	169	175	180	186	191	196	202	207	213
63	107	113	118	124	130	135	141	146	152	158	163	169	175	180	186	191	197	203	208	214	220
64	110	116	122	128	134	140	145	151	157	163	169	174	180	186	192	197	204	209	215	221	227
65	114	120	126	132	138	144	150	156	162	168	174	180	186	192	198	204	210	216	222	228	234
66	118	124	130	136	142	148	155	161	167	173	179	186	192	198	204	210	216	223	229	235	241
67	121	127	134	140	146	153	159	166	172	178	185	191	198	204	211	217	223	230	236	242	249
68	125	131	138	144	151	158	164	171	177	184	190	197	203	210	216	223	230	236	243	249	256
69	128	135	142	149	155	162	169	176	182	189	196	203	209	216	223	230	236	243	250	257	263
70	132	139	146	153	160	167	174	181	188	195	202	209	216	222	229	236	243	250	257	264	271
71	136	143	150	157	165	172	179	186	193	200	208	215	222	229	236	243	250	257	265	272	279
72	140	147	154	162	169	177	184	191	199	206	213	221	228	235	242	250	258	265	272	279	287
73	144	151	159	166	174	182	189	197	204	212	219	227	235	242	250	257	265	272	280	288	295
74	148	155	163	171	179	186	194	202	210	218	225	233	241	249	256	264	272	280	287	295	303
75	152	160	168	176	184	192	200	208	216	224	232	240	248	256	264	272	279	287	295	303	311
76	156	164	172	180	189	197	205	213	221	230	238	246	254	263	271	279	287	295	304	312	320
BMI	19	20	21	22	23	24	25	26	27	28	29	30	31	32	33	34	35	36	37	38	39
			NORMAL					OVERWEIGHT							OBESE						

Ways to Burn 150 Calories

Values shown are approximations. Activities are listed from more to less vigorous—the more vigorous an activity, the less time it takes to burn a calorie. When specific distances are given, the activity must be performed in the time shown (for example, one must run 1.5 miles in 15 minutes to burn 150 calories).

ACTIVITY	DURATION (MINUTES)
Climbing stairs	15
Shoveling snow	15
Running 1.5 miles	15
Jumping rope	15
Bicycling 4 miles	15
Playing basketball	15–20
Playing wheelchair basketball	20
Swimming laps	20
Performing water aerobics	30
Walking 2 miles	30
Raking leaves	30

ACTIVITY	DURATION (MINUTES)
Pushing a stroller 1.5 miles	30
Dancing fast	30
Bicycling 5 miles	30
Shooting baskets	30
Walking 1.75 miles	35
Wheeling oneself in a wheelchair	30–40
Gardening	30–45
Playing touch football	30–45
Playing volleyball	45
Washing windows or floors	45–60
Washing and waxing a car	45–60

Comparative Timelines

Introduction to Timelines

The timelines on the following pages, drawn from the *Encyclopædia Britannica* Deluxe Edition CD-ROM, encapsulate historical events from 14 areas of human experience from the dawn of history to the present day. Some events of crucial consequence appear, and some more whimsical events show up, too. Each pair of pages shows a span of time, indicated in the upper left corner of the left-hand page, and time progresses with each page turned. Because the Timelines cover many traditions outside the Western Christian one, the abbreviations BCE ("before the common era") and CE ("common era") appear instead of BC and AD.

Readers may compare what was going on, say, in architecture during the 12th century with what was happening at the same time in religion or science or art, or what events in the history of medicine in the 19th century coincided with events in the history of technology. Readers may also track developments in each area of endeavor across time.

Events of 1903 and 1503

These are snapshots of what was going on one hundred and five hundred years ago:

One hundred years ago . . .
Orville Wright began the first successful controlled flight in history, at Kill Devil Hill, North Carolina.
King Camp Gillette began selling the first safety razor and blade, which soon made the straight-edge **razor** obsolete.
Albert Peter Low commanded *Neptune* on the first Canadian **Arctic exploring mission**, employing science to bolster Canadian claims to sovereignty.
Russian playwright **Anton Chekhov** wrote his final play, *The Cherry Orchard*, which was performed the following year in Moscow.
Marie and Pierre Curie shared the Nobel Prize for Physics with Henri Becquerel for the discovery of radioactivity.
In baseball's first **World Series**, the Boston Pilgrims (later Red Sox) of the American League beat the Pittsburgh Pirates of the National League.
W.E.B. Du Bois published *The Souls of Black Folk*, asserting that agitation and protest are necessary to accomplish social change.
The French literary award **Prix Goncourt** was created by a bequest of Edmond de Goncourt.

Five hundred years ago . . .
The **Renaissance** was in full swing (though the period would end in 1527 with the fall of Rome and would not be called Renaissance for another couple centuries).
Nostradamus, astrologer and physician and the most widely read seer of the Renaissance, was born in Saint-Rémy, France. He went on the compose a book titled *Centuries*, which contained prophecies many believe foretold actual historical events.
Margaret Tudor, daughter of Henry VII, married James IV of Scotland. When James died fighting the English in 1513, Margaret ruled for her infant son and played a key role in the conflict between pro-French and pro-English factions in Scotland.
Mapmaking was becoming increasingly widespread in Europe, with printers and dealers specializing in this popular market.
Leonardo da Vinci began painting the psychologically intriguing *Mona Lisa*, building atmosphere and texture through multiple layers of paint.
Scholar **Desiderius Erasmus** published his *Handbook of a Christian Knight*, which advocated humanist learning and ecclesiastical reform.
Ottoman sultan **Bayezid II** concluded a war with the Venetian empire in the Levant and in the Balkans. Due in part to advanced naval construction, the Ottomans conquered Venetian strongholds on the Peloponnesus and Adriatic shores and further consolidated Ottoman rule in the area.
Court tennis enjoyed widespread popularity in France.

Did you know? In the 17th century, Archbishop James Ussher of Ireland added up the ages of men mentioned in the Old Testament and concluded that the creation had occurred on Sunday 23 October 4004 BCE. The English divine John Lightfoot additionally observed that the exact time was 9:00 am.

The Beginning – 2500 BCE

Architecture

Art

c. **30,000** BCE: The Panaramittee rock-art style appears in parts of Australia and Tasmania. It is characterized by circles, crescents, and radiating lines, as well as footprints and animal tracks.

Childhood

Daily Life

Ecology

c. **20,000** BCE: First known stone-tipped spear, a weapon that makes people far more dangerous to other large mammals and probably plays a role in the numerous extinctions of the late Pleistocene Epoch.

Exploration

Literature

Medicine

c. **10,000** BCE: Neolithic skeletons show evidence of arthritis, tumors, and spina bifida. Trephined skulls may be associated with healing or ritual practices.

Music

Religion

The Beginning: Various religions have creation myths describing the origins of the universe and, through them, the meaning of life, the underlying order of nature, and destiny of humans and the cosmos.

c. **70,000** BCE: Some Neanderthal peoples bury their dead with food, artifacts, and red ochre, suggesting belief in an afterlife.

Science

Sports

Technology

2.6 million BCE: First appearance of deliberately shaped tools produced by ancestors of human beings.

c. **35,000** BCE: Cro-Magnon man begins to produce rope, sewing needles, blades with attached handles, and other relatively complex tools.

Women

c. **7000** BCE: Work begins on the Cuicuilco pyramid in Mexico. It is the oldest man-made structure in North America.

c. **3100** BCE: Work begins on the circular monument at Stonehenge, England. Dismantled and rebuilt several times during the next 2,000 years, the purpose of the large rings of standing stones is not known.

c. **15,000** BCE: Paintings in a cave near Lascaux, France, reveal the human capacity for representation. Expertly fitted to cave surfaces, the painted animals may have served a ritual function.

c. **2900** BCE: The "Palette of Narmer" depicts Egyptian King Narmer in battle. The best-known work from the Early Dynastic Kingdom, this carved slate piece displays the mature ancient Egyptian style.

c. **2600** BCE: Word lists found at Ur and tablets of text found at Abu Salabikh suggest the existence of formal scribal education in Mesopotamia.

c. **9000** BCE: Cow's milk becomes a part of the human diet in the West.

6500 BCE: The Stone Age comes to an end as craftsmen in Anatolia (modern-day Turkey) begin to fashion objects of copper.

c. **2990** BCE: Rice cultivation begins in India. Both wetland and dry-land varieties will be developed, enabling it to grow in many climates. The grain becomes a staple in the Asian world.

c. **12,000** BCE: The dog is domesticated, starting a long history of human-canine relations and setting a precedent for domestication of many other animals.

c. **5000** BCE: First agriculture in sub-Saharan Africa, in the Lake Chad basin.

c. **2500** BCE: Agriculture begins in Japan, with attendant clearance of forests and faster population growth.

2900 BCE: Egyptians perhaps begin maritime exploration of the Indian Ocean, reaching the "land of Punt" on the Somali coast.

c. **3000** BCE: A Babylonian temple in Nippur features rooms of clay tablets, suggesting an early form of library.

c. **2700** BCE: Legendary Chinese emperor Shen Nung invents acupuncture, a healing practice based on the insertion of needles to influence the balance of the *qi*, or life force.

c. **6000** BCE: People in Moravia, Central Europe, fashion a drum. Drums are apparently among the oldest musical instruments and are played around the world.

c. **3000** BCE: Sumerian musicians play the lyre, an instrument that would diffuse throughout the Old World.

c. **8000** BCE: Development of desert cultures in southwestern North America, in which religion is associated with food plant gathering and some shamanism.

c. **5000** BCE: Development of agriculture in Central America leads to established settlements and ritual centers that involve sacred rulers and plant spirits.

c. **5200** BCE: The tomb of an Egyptian child contains nine stone pins, which were probably used in an ancient variation of bowling.

c. **2500** BCE: Swimming is practiced in Egypt for recreation, according to archaeological evidence.

c. **9000** BCE: Pottery production, agriculture, and domestication of animals appear, first in the region of Iraq and Syria, then through the valleys of the Indus and Nile rivers.

c. **3500** BCE: The wheel comes into use in Mesopotamia.

c. **2500** BCE: Silkworm cultivation begins in China, which dominates production of the fabric for millennia; global demand for silk leads to creation of the "Silk Road."

c. **3500** BCE: Egyptian women begin brewing beer.

2400 BCE – 1200 BCE

Architecture	**c. 2000 BCE:** Work begins on the Palace at Knossos. The rambling structure was expanded over the centuries, and at its largest contained dwellings, storerooms, and a theater.		
Art			**c. 1700 BCE:** Early developments are made in Chinese calligraphy, one of the oldest and most fundamental forms of Chinese art.
Childhood	**c. 2100 BCE:** The first Mesopotamian schools are established by King Shulgi at Nippur and Ur. The Sumerian name for scribal academy is *edubba*, "tablet house."		**c. 1700 BCE:** The Code of Hammurabi provides the first written rules for apprenticeships.
Daily Life	**2000 BCE:** The horse, domesticated since about 4000 BCE, is widely ridden by the nomadic peoples of Central Asia. One group, the Scythians, later invents the stirrup.		
Ecology	**c. 2400 BCE:** Salt buildup in irrigated areas of Mesopotamia begins to reduce wheat yields, causing a shift to barley and abandonment of some croplands.		
Exploration			**1750 BCE:** Goods and ideas are being traded between Mesopotamian civilizations and the Shang dynasty of China.
Literature	**c. 2400 BCE:** Ptahhotep becomes widely regarded for his wisdom literature, which includes proverbial sayings that stress humanity and loyalty.		
Medicine			**c. 1790 BCE:** The Code of Hammurabi includes laws regulating fees for medical practice and punishments for malpractice in the Babylonian Empire.
Music	**c. 2000 BCE:** The earliest trumpet, sounding one or two notes and used in martial events, appears in Egypt. The instrument would later be adopted by Greek and Roman armies; it is still used in military ceremonies.		
Religion	**c. 2000 BCE:** According to traditional sources, Abraham (the first Hebrew patriarch) leads his people out of Mesopotamia into Canaan, between modern-day Syria and Egypt.	**c. 1800 BCE:** Gathering of traditions regarding *Gilgamesh*, a 3rd-millennium Sumerian king. His epic journey weaves together themes of immortality, the Flood, and divine retribution.	
Science			
Sports	**c. 2000 BCE:** A rock carving in Norway near the Arctic Circle shows two men on skis.		
Technology	**c. 2000 BCE:** Improvements to the wheel include independent axles and spokes, which allow more efficient transport of heavier loads.	**c. 1750 BCE:** Babylonians under King Hammurabi (1792–1750 BCE) embark on canal-building and artificial irrigation, improving water-diversion and irrigation techniques dating to 5000 BCE.	
Women	**c. 2300 BCE:** In Akkad, theologian and writer Enheduanna, daughter of Sargon, is made chief priestess of the gods at Ur and Uruk.	**c. 1850 BCE:** Egyptian texts describe contraceptive suppositories, mixed out of honey and crocodile dung. This is the first known reference to contraceptives.	**c. 1750 BCE:** Hammurabi's code protects a woman's right to hold and inherit property.

c. 1300 BCE: "Treasury of Atreus" built. Actually a large beehive tomb, this structure was misnamed by its discoverer, Heinrich Schliemann, who thought it was a storehouse.

c. 1550 BCE: The so-called "Toreador Fresco" from the Palace at Knossos, Crete, depicts a ritual game involving athletes and a bull.

c. 1350 BCE: Egyptian pharaoh Akhenaton established monotheistic worship of Aton. Under his reign artistic works, which had previously depicted pharaohs in timeless settings, take on a new narrative specificity.

c. 1600 BCE: Children's swings are used for recreation on the island of Crete.

c. 1290 BCE: 10-year-old Egyptian Prince Ramses becomes a captain in his father's army. He would later achieve historical renown as pharaoh Ramses II.

1500 BCE: Indigo, one of the most important and popular dyes, is in use in Asia, Egypt, and the Mediterranean.

1200 BCE: Advances in mining and metallurgy usher in the Iron Age.

c. 1500 BCE: The first mechanical device for lifting water, a counterpoise-lift commonly known as a shadur, is invented. It expands the scope for irrigation by making water more easily available.

1600 BCE: Seafaring skill of the Mycenaean civilization promotes long-distance trade networks within the Aegean Sea and elsewhere in the Mediterranean and Middle East.

c. 1460 BCE: During her reign, Egyptian Queen Hatshepsut dispatches the first recorded maritime expedition down the Red Sea to open direct trade with coastal Africa for myrrh, ebony, animal skins, and gold.

c. 1500 BCE: Composition begins on the collection of sacred Hindu hymns and verses known as the Vedas.

c. 1600 BCE: The Edwin Smith papyrus gives a written account of Egyptian medical practices from diagnosis to therapeutic measures, including surgery.

c. 1500 BCE: Beginning of early Vedic period in medicine in India. Vedic practices include expulsion of demons believed to cause disease.

c. 1200 BCE: The Vedic chant, a three-tone system for reciting the Hindu Vedas, is developed. It is the world's oldest continuous vocal tradition.

c. 1500 BCE: In Mesoamerica, Olmec urban culture grows along with the importance of sacred rulers, powerful deities, and shamanic practices.

c. 1290 BCE: Under the leadership of Moses, Hebrew slaves escape from Egyptian captivity and travel to Canaan. At Mount Sinai they receive the Ten Commandments, sealing a covenant with God.

c. 1250 BCE: The sport of hurling, a game like field hockey, appears, according to old Irish manuscripts.

c. 1200 BCE: According to Sophocles, Palamedes invents dice during the siege of Troy. Later archaeological finds prove that dice had existed much earlier.

c. 1500 BCE: Simple water clocks, or clepsydras, are used throughout the ancient world and take a variety of forms.

1200 BCE: Paved roads come into use in Near Eastern cities.

c. 1500 BCE: The Egyptian medical school at Heliopolis enrolls women students.

1150 BCE – 480 BCE

Architecture		**706 BCE:** Sargon II's palace at Khorsabad, now in Iraq, is dedicated. Built in monumental dimensions, it covers more than 9 ha (23 ac).
Art	**c. 1150 BCE:** The Olmec people of Mexico begin carving tremendous "colossal heads." The stone monuments are characterized by flat faces and helmetlike headgear.	**c. 700 BCE:** Greek potters at Corinth develop black-figure pottery, in which images are drawn on a vase's clay surface in black pigment. Animals are the most popular early subjects.
Childhood		**c. 700 BCE:** Sparta, the military center of Greek culture in the Archaic era, flourishes. Beginning at age seven, Spartan boys are taught the art of war through games and exercises.
Daily Life	**1000 BCE:** Chinese calligraphers are the first to use the pen.	**c. 710 BCE:** The ancient Egyptians invent the sundial as a means of telling time.
Ecology	**c. 1150 BCE:** In China, the empress Tanki establishes one of the first known zoological gardens. For thousands of years royalty around the world would found zoos, botanical gardens, and game reserves.	**c. 800 BCE:** The Arabian camel is domesticated in the Middle East. A hardy traveler and valuable source of wool and meat, it is later adopted by traders and nomads in North Africa, Central Asia, and India.
Exploration	**1000 BCE:** Malay navigators and sailors spread out across the Pacific and Indian oceans, settling thousands of islands.	
Literature	**c. 900 BCE:** Homer, the father of Greek literature, composes (probably relying on oral traditions) his two masterpieces: the *Iliad* and the *Odyssey*.	
Medicine		
Music	**c. 957 BCE:** Israelite king Solomon the Great builds the Temple of Jerusalem, which supports a large musical establishment.	**c. 647 BCE:** Terpander, lyric poet of Lesbos, flourishes. The *kithara*, a seven-stringed instrument that he invents, becomes one of the most popular instruments in ancient Greek music.
Religion	**c. 1000 BCE:** Probable period of Zoroaster, an eastern Iranian thinker who breaks from Indo-Iranian religious traditions in advocating monotheism and ethical dualism.	**c. 950 BCE:** The First Jewish Temple in Jerusalem is built by King Solomon, son of David, to house the Ark of the Covenant.
Science		
Sports		**776 BCE:** The ancient Olympic Games are held for the first time, in Olympia, Greece. The games are outlawed by Emperor Theodosius I in 393 CE.
Technology	**c. 1100 BCE:** Phoenician dominance of Mediterranean seas begins, continuing until about 800 BCE. The efficient Phoenician ships replace traditional paddles with oars.	
Women	**c. 1000 BCE:** Most Chinese shamans are women. They are particularly important for performing rites to bring rain.	**c. 600 BCE :** In Sparta, girls are trained in athletics, including running, javelin, and discus, so that they will become strong and healthy mothers.

c. 530 BCE: Development of the red-figure painting technique, in which details are painted, not incised, on clay. It permits greater expressiveness, flexibility, and a fuller use of foreshortening.

c. 490 BCE: Confucianism elaborates the concept of *xiao*, or filial piety, which requires that the duty of elders be placed above duty to children.

610 BCE: Phoenician ships under orders of the Egyptian pharaoh Necho II purportedly circumnavigate Africa.

c. 484 BCE: Birth of Herodotus, a Greek explorer and writer whose geography and world map are based on personal observations made during many years of travel.

c. 600 BCE: One of the only known female poets of the ancient world, classical poet Sappho of Lesbos composes and performs (with a lyre) her sensual poetry.

c. 525 BCE: Greek philosopher and mathematician Pythagoras recognizes intervals in music as consonant and invariant.

528 BCE: One of the dates—which vary according to tradition—for the enlightenment of Siddhartha Gautama and his attainment of the title "Buddha" ("Awakened One").

c. 500 BCE: K'ung-fu-tzu (Confucius) attempts ethical reforms in China to restore the social balance according to the Tao ("Way") as willed by Heaven.

c. 600 BCE: Ionian school of philosophy seeks to explain phenomena in terms of matter and physical forces rather than the actions of gods.

c. 525 BCE: Flourishing of Pythagoreanism, a school of philosophy that believes that reality has a mathematical nature and ascribes a mystical power to certain numbers.

c. 600 BCE: Remains of tlachtli, courts for the ritual ball game of *ollama*, suggest that the game developed among the Olmecs during the La Venta culture period.

c. 500 BCE: Cockfighting makes its way from China and other eastern countries into Greece.

480 BCE: Artemisia I, queen of Halicarnassus, commands five ships in the Battle of Salamis.

470 BCE – 200 BCE

Architecture	**c. 460 BCE:** Temple of Hera II (or Temple of Neptune), built at Paestum. With its massive columns closely spaced, this provincial temple shows the Doric style at its most powerful.	**447 BCE:** Ictinus and Callicrates begin work on the Parthenon. Built by the city of Athens, this complex includes the temple of Athena Nike.
Art		**c. 400 BCE:** Scythian artisans produce the oldest surviving examples of embroidery.
Childhood		
Daily Life		**400 BCE:** Knotted Oriental carpets are being produced in Persia. Some of their design motifs will remain popular to the 21st century.
Ecology	**460 BCE:** A Chinese book offers the earliest-known documentation of fish farming. By the end of the 20th century, aquaculture is one of the fastest-growing sectors in world food production.	
Exploration	**c. 470 BCE:** Beginning of a dispersal of Bantu-speaking people across Africa that by 1000 CE results in development of Pan-African traditions and practices.	
Literature	**468 BCE:** Beginning of Sophocles' 62-year career as a successful Athenian dramatist, during which he writes over 120 plays.	**411 BCE:** Aristophanes, the foremost comic playwright in ancient Greece whose works survive, produces his masterpiece *Lysistrata*.
Medicine	**c. 431 BCE:** Greek medical writings are assembled into the Hippocratic corpus, which establishes ethical standards of practice.	**c. 400 BCE:** Brahmanic hospitals are established in Sri Lanka.
Music		
Religion		**c. 400 BCE:** Composition of early versions of the Dharmasutra and Dharmashastra texts, which define Hindu behavior in ritual, society, politics, and law.
Science	**c. 460 BCE:** Greek philosopher Zeno advances his famous paradoxes intended to show that motion is illusory. He is described by Aristotle as the inventor of dialectic.	
Sports		**c. 400 BCE:** Flourishing of Greek Pythagorean Archytas of Tarentum, who is the first documented kite flier.
Technology		**400 BCE:** Greek engineers invent the catapult, exploiting gravity and expanding their arsenal of battering rams and wheeled vehicles.
Women	**c. 450 BCE:** In Athens, Aspasia opens a school for upper-class women. She teaches rhetoric and philosophy.	

c. 200 BCE: Construction begins on the Ellora Caves in central India. Eventually 34 in number, these rock-cut temples are highlighted by the Kailasa cave complex, which was excavated downward to receive sunlight.

c. 280 BCE: Chares of Lindos completes the immense bronze "Colossus of Rhodes," a monument commemorating the lifting of the siege of 305–304. Contrary to popular belief, it did not straddle the harbor entrance.

c. 340 BCE: Children's recreational objects in Greek culture often take the form of horse-shaped figures with wheels, one type of which is equipped with jars for playing "going to the market."

c. 220 BCE: Chinese reformer Shang Yang puts new taxes on households, forcing the breakup of extended families.

200 BCE: The Chinese learn to prepare tofu, a cheap, versatile, and nutritious protein source from soybeans.

c. 300 BCE: Greek naturalist Theophrastus, a student of Aristotle, writes *Inquiry into Plants*, an ecologically perceptive treatise.

c. 250 BCE: In northern India, Mauryan emperor Ashoka, a recent convert to Buddhism, issues edicts on nature conservation. These are inspired in part by his new religious beliefs.

300 BCE: Arawak voyagers from northeastern South America reach and gradually move up the islands of the Lesser Antilles into the Greater Antilles (Cuba, Hispaniola, Jamaica, and Puerto Rico).

c. 300 BCE: *Ramayana*, an epic poem of India, is completed. The classical narrative of the Hindu deity Rama stresses love and harmony.

c. 285 BCE: A library is established in Alexandria, Egypt, staffed by notable Greek writers and scholars. It becomes the greatest in antiquity, featuring copies of Aristotle's library.

c. 290 BCE: Alexandrian physician Herophilus of Chalcedon performs dissection on human cadavers and gives the first accurate anatomical descriptions of the eyes, brain, and body vessels.

c. 325 BCE: In his *Politics*, Aristotle divides music into two categories: ritual music (the music of ecstasy) and music of diversion (for relaxation and daily life).

c. 250 BCE: The expansion of Roman power in the Mediterranean leads to the diffusion of Roman musical forms, such as the seven-note diatonic scale.

c. 200 BCE: The transverse flute, which is held sideways to the player's right, is used in Greece.

c. 300 BCE: Development of Mayan civilization in south-central Mesoamerica. Prominent in religious life are ceremonial centers, which later develop into cities.

247 BCE: The Third Buddhist Council is called by emperor Ashoka at Pataliputra. By now divided into various schools, this council may have included only members of the Theravada school of Buddhism.

c. 300 BCE: Greek mathematician Euclid of Alexandria produces his *Elements*, a work that dominates elementary mathematics for more than 2,000 years.

c. 250 BCE: Greek mathematician and astronomer Eratosthenes, director of the great library at Alexandria, calculates the circumference of the Earth.

c. 270 BCE: Iberians Celts engage in an early form of bullfighting as they hunt bulls for sport.

c. 206 BCE: The Chinese play a kickball game called *tsu-chu*, the ancestor of modern soccer.

c. 280 BCE: The Pharos of Alexandria is built and becomes an archetype for all later lighthouses.

c. 214 BCE: The Great Wall of China is completed when existing defensive structures are united and extended. It reaches a height of 9 m (30 ft) and extends 6,400 km (4,000 mi).

c. 200 BCE: Alexander the Great sponsors the development of iron armor, a more durable alternative to bronze.

380 BCE: Greek women have no independent status in society and may not make transactions worth more than one *medimnos* of barley, although they may own their own slaves.

195 BCE – 100 CE

Architecture	**175 BCE:** Altar of Zeus, a masterpiece of Hellenistic design, completed at Pergamun, in Asia Minor.	**c. 37 BCE:** The Temple of Hathor is completed in Egypt, featuring an elaborately designed hall.
Art	**c. 150 BCE:** The "Venus de Milo" is carved by a Hellenist sculptor in Antioch. Endowed with great grace and nobility, it remains one of the most famous ancient sculptures.	**c. 40 BCE:** Greek sculptors Polydorus, Agesander, and Athenodorus create the "Laocoön" group, showing Laocoön and his sons attacked by sea serpents.
Childhood	**c. 190 BCE:** The Romans consider the family as the natural milieu in which the child should grow and be educated. The role of the mother as educator extends beyond the early years and often has lifelong influence.	**c. 6 BCE** Jesus Christ is born. The figure of the infant Jesus is one of the more compelling in all religion.
Daily Life	**c. 190 BCE:** Temple reliefs portray the *sari* and *dhoti* as standard Indian costume. The styles persist to the present day.	**100 BCE:** The Syrians invent glassblowing, enabling the creation of hollow objects such as drinking vessels, bottles, and vases.
Ecology	**c. 150 BCE:** The peach is introduced into the Mediterranean world from China.	**c. 100 BCE:** The invention of the horse collar in China allows efficient use of horses for pulling heavy loads, such as plows, and increases the area that a farmer can till.
Exploration	**150 BCE:** The Silk Road, connecting China and the Middle East across Central Asia, becomes an important conduit for exchanging agricultural goods, manufactured products, ideas, and people.	
Literature	**c. 190 BCE:** Parchment is invented in Pergamum. Made from animal skins, it is processed so that both sides can be used for writing.	**c. 39 BCE:** Gaius Asinius Pollio uses war booty to build the first public library in Rome.
Medicine	**c. 100 BCE:** Romans establish institutions called *valetudinaria* for the care of sick and injured soldiers.	
Music	**c. 65 BCE:** Greek Epicurean philosopher Philodemus writes his treatise *On Music*, of which extensive fragments remain.	
Religion	**136 BCE:** Chinese emperor Wudi (Wu-ti) declares Confucianism the imperial ideology and state cult. Confucianism flourishes and eventually spreads to Korea, Japan, and Vietnam.	
Science	**c. 130 BCE:** Greek astronomer Hipparchus of Rhodes makes relatively accurate predictions of the precession of the equinoxes and a very accurate determination of the tropical year.	
Sports	**c. 150 BCE:** Venationes, or animal hunts, are staged in Rome for the amusement of nobles and the general public. The events are more slaughters than hunts.	**c. 60 BCE:** Rome's Circus Maximus, one of the largest sporting arenas in the world, is expanded under Julius Caesar's direction. The facility can hold about 150,000 spectators.
Technology	**c. 110 BCE:** Roman use of nailed horseshoes gives horses' hooves protection against hard ground.	**c. 85 BCE:** Vertical undershot waterwheels appear in the eastern Mediterranean. Waterwheels will be an important source of mechanical power in the West until the 19th century.
Women	**c. 195 BCE:** Kao-hou seizes power from her son Hui-ti to become the first woman ruler of China.	**51 BCE:** Cleopatra becomes queen of Egypt.

70: Work begins on the Colosseum in Rome. The site of ancient spectacles, the Colosseum is designed for gladiatorial games, and can be flooded to re-create naval battles.

c. 100: North African city of Thamugadi, a stunning example of Roman city planning, with its clear and geometrical organization, is founded by Emperor Trajan.

c. 80: A bronze equestrian statue of Emperor Marcus Aurelius is cast during a late period of Imperial stability.

c. 100: The Portland Vase, the finest example of Roman cameo glass (made from two pieces of glass blown together and then etched), is produced by an unknown artist.

c. 70: Quintilian argues that children have individual needs and should be educated and allowed to develop in ways appropriate to their age.

99: The Roman Emperor Trajan instigates the first official large-scale welfare program to make public funds available for the support of children.

1: In the 6th century, Dionysius Exiguus centers the Western Christian calendar on this, the supposed year of Jesus' birth, dividing time into "AD" and "BC".

100: Soap, previously considered to be medicinal, comes into common use as a cleaning agent.

c. 50 BCE: Lions are driven extinct in ancient Greece. Wildlife depletion and extinctions are routine in the ancient Mediterranean.

c. 75: Pliny the Elder publishes his *Natural History*. This encyclopedic survey of the natural world is a major reference work in the Western world until the Renaissance.

40: The apostle Paul, a Jew from the Greek city Tarsus, converts to Christianity and travels on Roman roads from Syria-Palestine through Greece to convert Gentiles and establish Christian communities.

8: Roman poet Ovid completes *The Metamorphoses*, a 15-book poetic retelling of Greek and Roman myths and legends.

c. 70: A collection of Jewish psalms, manuals, and commentaries that later will be called the Dead Sea Scrolls, is composed.

c. 30: Roman nobleman Aulus Celsus writes *De medicina*. It describes Greek medical practices, including surgery, and is influential in the Renaissance.

c. 77: Greek physician Pedanius Dioscorides begins work on his *De materia medica*, a study of the effects of 1,000 drugs and herbal remedies. This work, too, is used into the Renaissance.

70: The Second Temple of Jerusalem is destroyed, ending Jewish use of musical instruments in worship.

c. 32: Following a three-year ministry in Judea, Samaria, and Galilee, Jesus is crucified by Jewish and Roman leaders and, according to tradition, resurrected.

c. 70: Construction begins on the Colosseum in Rome. One of the most remarkable architectural achievements of the Roman era, it seats about 50,000 and can even be flooded for mock naval combats.

c. 30: Chinese sources describe horizontal waterwheels being used to operate bellows of iron-smelting furnaces. Horizontal waterwheels are popular in Asia, India, and the Near East.

c. 98: Work begins on the Segovia, Spain, aqueduct, which carries water for 16 km (10 mi).

39: Two Vietnamese sisters, Trung Trac and Trung Nhi, lead the first revolt in Southeast Asia against Chinese domination. Despite early successes, the revolt eventually fails.

100 – 400

Architecture	**c. 122:** Work begins on Hadrian's Wall. Built across the width of northern Britain to guard against barbarians, the divider covers 118 km (73 mi) and features forts and towers.	
Art		**c. 150:** First appearance of Christian art, decorating Roman catacombs. Early Christian art appropriated and adapted local or classical styles but did not flourish until the conversion of Constantine I in 313.
Childhood	**c. 130:** Greek physician Soranus of Ephesus writes about the care of infants and diseases of later childhood. His writings set medical opinion concerning pregnancy and infant care for nearly 1,500 years.	**c. 150:** Jewish records mention 13 as the age of religious manhood.
Daily Life		
Ecology	**107:** To celebrate Trajan's conquest of Dacia, 11,000 captured wild animals are slaughtered in Rome.	**165:** Beginning of 15 years of epidemic in the Roman world. The plague, brought from Mesopotamia by Roman soldiers, reduces Mediterranean populations by about a quarter.
Exploration	**127:** Ptolemy writes his *Guide to Geography*, an influential work that assembles geographic knowledge, confirms the spherical nature of Earth, and establishes the latitude-longitude grid.	**161:** Silk merchant-travelers sent by Emperor Marcus Aurelius Antoninus arrive at the court of the Chinese emperor Huan-ti. They are the first Roman delegates to reach Han China.
Literature	**c. 105:** Ts'ai Lun develops paper using tree bark, hemp waste, old rags, and fishnets. His apprentice perfects the process, and paper spreads throughout the world, reaching Baghdad in 893. It arrives in Europe in the 1300s, transforming writing, book production, and the cultures that adopt it.	
Medicine		**c. 160:** Galen of Pergamum begins his synthesis of Greek and Roman practical and theoretical work on medicine and physiology. His doctrines dominate medical thinking for the next 13 centuries.
Music		**c. 150:** Alexandrian geographer, astronomer, and mathematician Ptolemy writes a three-volume treatise on *Harmonics*.
Religion	**c. 120:** Emergence of Gnosticism. A syncretic faith drawing on Iranian religion, Platonic philosophy, and Jewish mysticism, it has a strong impact on early Christianity.	**c. 150:** Canonization of the 27 books of the New Testament begins. Previously a more fluid body of writings, the Scriptures are defined more precisely in part to counter emergent heretical writings.
Science	**c. 130:** Alexandrian astronomer and geographer Ptolemy produces the *Almagest*. His geocentric model of the universe dominates astronomical thought for the next 1,400 years.	
Sports		**c. 150:** Greek writer Julius Pollux describes the game *apodidraskinda*, later commonly known as hide-and-seek.
Technology		
Women	**115:** Chinese poet and historian Pan Chao dies after a long and renowned career.	

c. 200: The "Treasury" is built at Petra. This massive structure, cut into solid rock, shows the experimentation with classical form in which later Roman architecture delighted.

c. 326: Work begins on Old Saint Peter's Basilica in Rome. One of the most influential buildings ever, its design has influenced the form for churches up until the present day.

c. 200: Development of Coptic art, which combines Egyptian artistic style with Christian subjects.

178: Roman law recognizes the right of children to succeed their mother if she should die without a will.

c. 320: Agnes, the future patron saint of girls, grows up in Rome. According to tradition, she refuses marriage at age 13, declaring that she can have no spouse but Jesus Christ.

216: The Baths of Caracalla are completed in Rome; 1,600 bathers can be accommodated at the 11-ha (28-ac) site's therapeutic and hygienic facilities.

c. 200: Roman road network reaches 53,000 miles of major highways and many more miles of smaller roads. The roads mark the land for centuries to come and unite inland ecosystems as never before.

c. 260: Neoplatonist philosopher Plotinus develops the concept of the Great Chain of Being. Elaborated over the centuries, it has a significant impact on biological thought in the West.

c. 400: Easter Island, 3,520 km (2,200 mi) off the coast of South America, is inhabited by Polynesians from the Marquesas Islands.

397: St. Augustine, the Roman bishop of Hippo, begins his Confessions, thought to be the first authentic autobiography.

c. 370: St. Basil establishes a hospital outside Caesarea, with special housing for those suffering from leprosy. His work helps make the hospital a common institution throughout Byzantium and the Levant.

330: The establishment of the Byzantine Empire, and separation of western and eastern churches, gives rise to Byzantine chant, which draws on Hellenistic and Middle Eastern sources.

379: St. Ambrose, bishop of Milan, is credited with bringing the practice of alternation in hymnody from the East to the West and with writing some of the most popular Latin hymns.

337: Constantine the Great abolishes crucifixion, a method of execution practiced in the Roman world since the 6th century BCE.

c. 400: The Palestinian Talmud ("study"), a commentary on the Mishna, is completed after nearly 300 years' work. The Babylonian Talmud is completed 100 years later.

c. 360: Byzantine philosopher Themistius writes the first Eastern commentaries on works of Aristotle.

c. 200: Circle-and-cross board games resembling nyout are played throughout Korea.

c. 350: As Christianity gains prominence in Greece, the Isthmian Games, an ancient athletic and musical festival in honor of Poseidon, come to an end.

239: Queen Himiko of Yamatai, the first known ruler of Japan, establishes diplomatic relations with China.

c. 385: Roman St. Paulina founds a pilgrims' hospice and communal houses in Bethlehem. Her daughter Eustochium becomes head of the women's community on her death in 404.

400 – 900

Architecture	**537:** The Hagia Sophia, Constantinople, is completed. Originally a church, this vast building was converted after the Ottoman conquest in 1453 to a mosque, when the minarets were added.	**c. 600:** The Puuc architectural style begins to flourish in Mexico. Characterized by limestone construction with plaster finishes, it is fully realized at Uxmal.
Art	**c. 550:** Byzantine art begins to develop a highly sophisticated and formal style, mainly concerned with religious subjects, and most fully expressed in church design and mosaics.	**c. 680:** Manuscript illumination develops as an artistic form in England, particularly in Canterbury and Northumbria. The centers draw upon Roman and Irish styles, respectively.
Childhood	**529:** The prototype of Western monasticism is founded by Benedict of Nursia at Monte Cassino. The presence of young boys to be educated is fundamental to the institution's mission.	**c. 670:** In Ostrogothic Italy and Carthage, schools and private instructors teach ancient grammar and rhetoric, maintaining the pedagogical tradition of classical culture.
Daily Life		**c. 600:** Windmills come into use in Iran. These extend the possibilities of irrigation by allowing farmers to tap deeper groundwater.
Ecology		**610:** The newly-opened Grand Canal links China's north and south in a single economy. Expansion of southern rice farming follows, as farmers are now able to transport their crops more quickly and reliably.
Exploration	**c. 500:** Indian and Sri Lankan merchants develop an all-sea trade route via the Strait of Malacca between China and the Mediterranean, replacing the lengthy overland trek across the Malay peninsula.	**c. 740:** Trans-Saharan trade involves the exchange of gold dust for salt needed by sub-Saharan Africans.
Literature	**c. 529:** European monasteries emerge as important book centers as monks copy manuscripts and later lend them to libraries and other monasteries.	**c. 700** *Beowulf*, the oldest of the great heroic epics written in English, is believed to have been composed.
Medicine	**c. 512:** The making of a Byzantine copy of Dioscorides' *De materia medica* illustrates the great importance of practical medical treatments, such as the use of herbals, in the ancient world.	
Music		**590:** St. Gregory the Great is elected Pope. His reform of the Mass, intended to make liturgy more widely accessible, leads to the development of the Gregorian chant, which is named in his honor.
Religion	**402:** The Chinese monk Fa-hsien begins a long pilgrimage through Buddhist centers in India and Sri Lanka, returning with a large body of sacred texts previously unknown to the Chinese.	**622:** Muhammad flees persecution and escapes to Medina, where he establishes the Muslim community (umma). The first year of the Muslim lunar calendar dates from this *hijrah* (emigration).
Science	**c. 550:** Alexandrian philosopher John Philoponus writes commentaries on Aristotle.	**c. 600:** Isidore of Seville, author of the *Etymologies*, an influential medieval encyclopedia and source of information about ancient geography, becomes archbishop of Seville.
Sports	**c. 570:** Chess is invented in northwest India.	
Technology	**c. 500:** Teutonic tribes bring heavy iron plowshares into Western Europe, inaugurating extensive agriculture-based settlement in this region.	**c. 700:** The stirrup is adopted by European horsemen, stabilizing the rider and eventually transforming mounted warfare by giving attacking riders greater stability in combat.
Women	**431:** The council of Ephesus recognizes Mary as the Mother of God, resulting in the spread westward from Byzantium of the cult of the Virgin.	**600:** Women in England may be publicly punished as "scolds," a practice that continues for 1,000 years.

c. 715: Great Mosque of Damascus is built. Its marble grilles are the earliest examples of geometric interlace in Islamic architecture.

c. 850: Borobuur is constructed in central Java. Enclosing a small hill, the massive Buddhist temple is shaped like a stepped pyramid and is topped by more than 70 bell-shaped stupas.

c. 700: Large stone statues begin to be constructed on Easter Island; the early busts are characterized by rounded heads and short bodies.

c. 800: *The Book of Kells*, teeming with Celtic knot-work and animal designs, is finished at the monastery of Kells. Its elaborate calligraphy and decoration represent the height of the Hiberno-Saxon style.

c. 800: In the Islamic world, the *maktab* emerges as an institution for teaching the Qur'an to young boys.

868: In China, the first printed book, a copy of the Buddhist *Diamond Sutra*, is produced using carved wooden blocks to print the text on paper.

821: The Japanese emperor issues regulations on peasant woodcutting to protect farmland. The order shows an understanding of vegetation, soil, and hydrologic dynamics.

c. 820: Founding of the coastal city of Seylac, Somalia. For a millennium, the city is a center of African-Arabian trade, exporting ivory and slaves and importing cloth and metals.

c. 900: Vikings begin three centuries of exploration throughout the Arctic region. During their travels they colonize Iceland, settle Greenland, and visit North America.

712: One of the first written records of Japan, the *Kojiki* ("Records of Ancient Matters"), offers discussions on the islands' history, topography, and literature.

c. 900: The Vercelli book, containing *The Dream of the Rood*, the finest example of an Old English religious poem, is produced in Italy. It was discovered in 1822.

c. 840: Translation of Western medical writings reaches its peak in Baghdad under Hunayn ibn Ishaq (al-Ibadi), allowing a later assimilation of Western medical theory into Islamic medicine.

c. 740: St. John of Damascus organizes the hymnody of the Byzantine Church, creating the *Octoechos* ("Book of Eight Tones").

900: The system of *te'amim*, which provides guidance for the cantillation (intoned recitation) of the Torah, is created at Tiberias in Palestine. The system is influenced by early Byzantine chant.

c. 890: Khmer rulers begin construction of Hindu temples at Angkor. The most famous of these, the Angkor Wat temple complex (completed c. 1150), is the world's largest religious structure.

c. 800: Arab scholars begin to translate Greek and Roman scientific works into Arabic and Syriac. This preserves them against loss during the Middle Ages in the West.

860: Arab mathematician Thabit ibn Qurrah becomes court astronomer in Baghdad and translates a number of Greek mathematical texts.

c. 800: Chinese blend charcoal, sulfur, and saltpeter to create incendiary mixtures, leading to the development of gunpowder. Gunpowder reaches Europe in the 14th century.

787: The Second Council of Nicaea is called by Byzantine Empress Irene to settle the question of worshiping icons. The bishops rule in favor of icon worship.

c. 900: The practice of foot binding becomes popular in the Chinese Court.

900 – 1200

Architecture	c. 1000: Wooden stave churches begin to appear in Norway.	
Art	c. 1000: Muslim artists develop the arabesque style of decoration into a highly sophisticated form of nonrepresentational art, based on botanical and abstract motifs.	c. 1075: The Bayeux Tapestry is completed. The embroidered linen band depicts William the Conqueror's invasion of England.
Childhood	983: Otto III becomes Holy Roman emperor at age three. During his reign he makes plans to recreate the glory and power of the ancient Roman empire in a universal Christian state governed from Rome.	
Daily Life	c. 900: Archaeological evidence suggests Mayan smokers have invented an early version of the modern cigar.	
Ecology	c. 1000: Polynesians arrive in New Zealand, beginning human settlement of the world's last sizeable unoccupied landmass.	
Exploration	907: The collapse of the Tang dynasty in China disrupts the eastern end of the Silk Road. The trade route remains severed until the 13th century, when it is restored by Mongol rulers.	c. 1050: Founding of the port city of Mombasa in eastern Africa.
Literature		1066: Norman duke William conquers the British Isles, sparking a radical shift in the English language and fueling a revitalization of literature in England.
Medicine	918: The earliest known mental hospitals are established in Baghdad and Cairo.	c. 1010: Iranian physician Avicenna (Ibn Sina) compiles Arab medical knowledge in *Al-Qanun fi at-tibb* (The Canon of Medicine), a classic text that influences both Islamic and medieval Western medicine.
Music	988: St. Volodymyr (Vladimir) of Kiev converts to Christianity and imports Greek musicians into Kievan Rus.	
Religion	c. 900: The Toltec empire develops in Mesoamerica. Its iconography suggests it is a militaristic culture, whose members are followers of warrior cults.	1054: The Schism of 1054 over theological and political differences and the mutual excommunication of the pope and the patriarch, mark the break between Greek and Latin churches.
Science	967: Gerbert of Aurillac begins study of mathematical sciences. As Pope Sylvester II (999–1003), he helps revive the study of mathematics in cathedral schools.	
Sports	c. 980: A game very much like modern handball is developed in Ireland.	
Technology	c. 1000: The gearless "Norse" or "Greek" mill emerges in Europe, employing waterpower to drive a pair of grindstones.	
Women	c. 950: An anonymous Norwegian woman writes *Wise Women's Prophesy*, a history of the world, including prophecies for the future.	1004: Japanese author Murasaki Shikibu finishes the *Genji monogatari* (*The Tale of Genji*), the world's first novel.

1088: A second, smaller dome is added to the Great Mosque of Esfahan. A structural masterpiece, it is known for its proportion and size.

c. 1163: Work begins on the cathedral of Notre-Dame, Paris, and continues until about 1350. This early Gothic building still has some Romanesque elements, notably the bay system.

c. 1130: English Romanesque illustrations in the Bible of the Abbey of St. Edmund at Bury distill color and gesture for narrative effect, producing one of the great medieval illuminated manuscripts.

c. 1190: Eleazar ben Judah's *Sefer ha-Roqeah*, "Book of the Perfumer," provides the earliest account of Talmudic education.

1200: The chimney is adopted in Europe as a means of carrying off smoke and heat from the fireplace.

c. 1100: A surge of metallurgical production in Sung China drives a wave of deforestation and atmospheric pollution. The latter is still detectable in samples of Greenland's glaciers.

1154: Arab geographer ash-Sharif al-Idrisi issues the first of many warnings that the Sahara desert is advancing southward. He is right: eight centuries of relatively high rainfall ends around 1100 in West Africa.

c. 1090: First naval application of the magnetic compass occurs when Chinese traders reach the Middle East, the Philippines, and possibly more distant points.

c. 1200: First appearance of the wind rose on Italian and Spanish maps. Its eight points show the direction of principal winds at different locations.

c. 1180: Marie de France, the first female French poet, completes her *lai* (a narrative of a magical event) *Elduc* (also titled *Guildelüec and Guilliadun*)

c. 1200: Faculties of medicine and philosophy are formed at the University of Bologna.

1152: German abbess and visionary mystic St. Hildegard collects her music and verse in *Symphonia harmoniae*.

c. 1200: The lute, a stringed instrument developed in Muslim Spain and based on the Arab oud, appears in Europe. The Arab oud, in turn, came from 7th-century Persia and probably had Asian antecedents.

1098: Establishment of the Cistercian monastic order, led by St. Robert of Molesme. The Cistercians observed strict rules requiring manual labor and poverty.

1198: Spanish Muslim Averroës (Ibn Rushd) dies. His work challenged the antiphilosophical arguments of al-Ghazali and established him as the foremost commentator on Aristotle.

c. 1125: Adelard of Bath produces a translation of Euclid's *Elements*. Elsewhere he advocates philosophical naturalism, arguing against the importance of supernatural forces in everyday life.

c. 1170: The University of Oxford is founded after English students are barred from the University of Paris.

c. 1100: The modern board game of draughts, or checkers, is invented in the south of France.

c. 1150: Dominoes is played in China. The numbers probably represent the throws of two dice, as there are no blank faces.

c. 1100: Padded horse collars improve use of horses for agricultural and other transportation purposes in Europe.

c. 1120: Windmills, first invented in Persia in the 7th century, come into use in Europe, bringing mechanical power to areas lacking in reliable sources of flowing water.

1118: Héloïse is made prioress of Argenteuil, where she fled after the discovery of her secret marriage to Peter Abelard.

1147: Eleanor of Aquitaine accompanies her husband, French King Louis VII, on the Second Crusade. After their marriage collapses in 1152, she marries the future English King Henry II.

1200 – 1400

Architecture	**c. 1220:** Founding of Salisbury Cathedral. A typical example of English Gothic, its plan influenced the design of Winchester Cathedral. Its notable façade places a distinct emphasis on the horizontal.	**c. 1297:** Work begins on Siena's Palazzo Pubblico. The palace includes many great works of art, and the surrounding town square is an example of early Renaissance city planning.
Art		**c. 1279:** Mu-ch'i, a leading Chinese Ch'an (Zen) Buddhist painter, paints the triptych "Six Persimmons."
Childhood	**1212:** In a religious movement known as the "Children's Crusade," thousands of children set out to conquer the Holy Land from the Muslims by love instead of by force. The crusade fails.	
Daily Life		**c. 1250:** The buttonhole is adopted in Europe from Moorish tailors as a means of fastening garments; previously, buttons had been fastened to loops of fabric.
Ecology	**1209:** Francis of Assisi founds the Franciscan order, which preaches the importance of humans' kinship with nature. According to legend, Francis himself delivered sermons to animals.	**1273:** In Castile, King Alfonso X charters the sheep owners association (the Mesta) and delineates land use rights of pastoralists and farmers.
Exploration	**1206:** The rise to power of Genghis Khan revitalizes the Silk Road. Mongol policies facilitate rapid movement of people and ideas from one end of Eurasia to the other.	**c. 1250:** Pilots learn to use winter monsoons to sail to Africa and summer monsoons to return to India. Trade expands along the East African coast, giving rise to city-states such as Great Zimbabwe.
Literature	**1222:** The *Prose Edda*, part of Iceland's ancient literature, includes tales of Norse myth, told with humor and charm.	
Medicine		**c. 1300:** Under the leadership of Jacob ben Machir ibn Tibbon, France's University of Montpellier develops into the most important medical school in Europe.
Music	**c. 1200:** Pérotin, a composer associated with the Cathedral of Notre-Dame in Paris, introduces four-part polyphony into Western music.	**1280:** The Cantigas de Santa Maria, a set of Galician folk hymns, are collected under the direction of King Alfonso the Wise of Castile.
Religion	**c. 1200:** Inca rule expands from the Andes and will reach from Argentina to Ecuador, using an imperial religion of the Sun to unify the state.	**1231:** Pope Gregory IX initiates the Catholic Inquisition in an effort to discover and try heretics. At first using only verbal interrogation, from 1252 it was authorized to use physical torture.
Science	**1209:** The University of Cambridge is founded by faculty and students escaping the riotous atmosphere of Oxford.	**1270:** Étienne Tempier, bishop of Paris, issues condemnations of philosophical doctrine that reinforce subordinating science to theology. A second round of condemnations is promulgated in 1277.
Sports	**c. 1250:** The game of *paille-maille*, croquet's precursor, is regularly played in France.	**c. 1300:** In China, Chang San-Feng incorporates gentler elements of more aggressive martial arts into kung fu. He is probably the founder of the discipline of t'ai chi chuan.
Technology		**c. 1275:** Spinning wheel, known earlier in India, appears in Europe. It is probably the first machine with a belt transmission and parts that move at different rates.
Women	**1220:** At the University of Paris, women are banned from practicing medicine.	

1358: Completion of the Alhambra, the last Muslim stronghold in Spain. The complex, finished after 80 years' work, contains a citadel and palace.

c. 1300: Giotto di Bondone probably paints the remarkable frescoes at the Church of San Francesco, Assisi. This and his later work establish Giotto as a master, one of the first in Italy.

c. 1400: Tempera painting, which combines pigment powder with an emulsion (usually egg yolks and water), is the preferred medium for early Renaissance painters. It is later displaced by oils.

1391: Geoffrey Chaucer writes the *Treatise on the Astrolabe* for his son "little Lewis."

1340: The kimono, derived from Chinese court costume, is adapted as an outer garment for women in Japan.

1346: Start of the Black Death. Reaching from India to Iceland, it reduces population in Asia and Europe by a fourth or a third. It is the last time global population declines.

c. 1400: The Dutch use windmills to accelerate the drainage and reclamation of the Netherlands. Over the centuries they create the world's largest reclaimed landscape.

1324: On a pilgrimage to Mecca, the ruler of the West African empire of Mali tells of a transatlantic voyage attempted by his predecessor Mansa Muhammad.

1396: Bavarian crusader Johann Schiltberger is captured by Turks and spends 31 years as a slave of the Ottoman sultan and the Tartar Timur. He writes a fanciful but valuable account of his life.

1321: The most revered poem of the Middle Ages, *La divina commedia* (*The Divine Comedy*), is completed shortly before the death of Italian poet Dante Alighieri.

1387: *The Canterbury Tales*, Geoffrey Chaucer's most enduring literary work and the project he devotes himself to until his death, is begun in London.

1316: Italian scholar Mondino de' Luzzi writes his *Anatomy*. It becomes a standard text for medical schools as practice in dissections is incorporated into the curriculum.

c. 1320: Philippe de Vitry writes *Ars nova*, a treatise outlining changes in French music caused by the adoption of new notational techniques, such as mensural notation and colored notes.

1377: The return of the papacy from Avignon to Rome leads to the Great, or Western, Schism, which divides the papacy between two and then three rival popes. The schism ends in 1417.

1328: Jean Buridan, famous for his work in logic, optics, and mechanics, becomes rector of the University of Paris. His theory of "impetus" becomes important in late medieval physics.

c. 1370: Nicholas Oresme presents arguments for the possibility of a heliocentric universe. His advocacy of geometrical analysis of motion advanced kinematics.

c. 1390: Violent, large-scale games of lacrosse, with as many as a thousand players per side, are played by the Iroquois nation. The game is also popular among the Cherokee and other Native Americans.

c. 1305: The English develop standardized shoe sizes, making it possible to produce well-fitting shoes in large numbers, rather than make each pair based on individual measurements.

c. 1350: Blast furnaces are used in iron-ore smelting, encouraging large-scale production of cast-iron building and machine components.

1350: There are more than 3,000 nuns in England, reflecting the flourishing of convents and religious orders for women in the Middle Ages.

1390: At the University of Bologna, Dorotea Bocchi takes the chair of medicine and moral philosophy, formerly held by her father.

1400 – 1500

Architecture		**1438:** Work begins on the Porta della Carta, Doges' Palace, Venice. Rebuilt several times, the palace's exotic appearance testifies to both its maritime wealth and connections with the Orient.
Art	**c. 1410:** Florentine architect Filippo Brunelleschi conducts experiments that lead to his rediscovery of linear perspective, one of the fundamental advances in Renaissance art.	**c. 1425:** Donatello casts the bronze statue of a youthful "David," reintroducing the free-standing male nude of antiquity into the sculptural language of the Renaissance.
Childhood		**1427:** According to the *Catasto* of 1427, 41.5% of male servants and 34% of female servants in Florentine households are between 8 and 17 years old.
Daily Life	**1403:** King Htai Tjong of Korea orders the production of 100,000 bronze characters, the first metal movable type.	
Ecology		**c. 1430:** Coffee is introduced into cultivation in Arabia from its native East Africa.
Exploration	**1405:** First of seven voyages led by Zheng He to lands on the China Sea and Indian Ocean. After 1433, Chinese interest in exploration dissipates.	**1419:** Venetian merchant Niccolò dei Conti travels through Arabia and India to Java. He speculates that European merchants could reach the Spice Islands directly by circumnavigating Africa.
Literature		**1425:** The best existing example of a medieval mystery play, the *Second Shepherds' Play*, is performed for the first time.
Medicine		
Music		**1430:** Flemish composer Gilles Binchois enters the service of Philip III the Good of Burgundy, where he composes some of the finest religious and secular music of the period.
Religion	**1415:** Czech reformer Jan Hus, an opponent of the practice of selling indulgences and one of many pre-Reformation critics of the Catholic church, is burned at the stake for heresy.	
Science		
Sports		**c. 1420:** Fox hunting develops in England.
Technology	**c. 1400:** The carpenter's brace, the first complete crank, is used by Flemish carpenters. It leads to the use of connecting rods and flywheels and, ultimately, to machine designs using rotary motion.	**1420:** Italian architect Filippo Brunelleschi begins construction of the octagonal ribbed dome of the Florence Cathedral.
Women	**1406:** In Korea plans are made for training women doctors to serve female patients who refuse to be treated by male doctors.	**1429:** Joan of Arc, supported by Queen Yolande, begins her military and religious campaign against the English. At the Battle of Orléans she leads the French army to victory.

1452: Pope Nicholas orders Bernardo Rossellino to begin work on St. Peter's Basilica. The most important church in Roman Catholicism, it will absorb the attention of numerous architects, including Michelangelo.

1493: Benedikt Ried begins work on Vladislav Hall, Prague. With its interweaving and truncating ribs, this unique late-Gothic-style building was later an inspiration for the Czech Baroque.

c. 1455: Paolo Uccello paints the three-panel *Rout of San Romano.* It combines Gothic colors and decorative motifs with Renaissance foreshortening and forms to create an electrifying battle scene.

1495: Leonardo da Vinci begins work on his mural, the *Last Supper,* at Sta. Maria delle Grazie. The fresco, created with an unknown technique, marks the beginning of the High Renaissance in Italy.

1453: Under Ottoman rule, Christian boys from the Balkans are conscripted by Muslims through the system of *devsirme.* They are converted to Islam, educated, and employed in a variety of posts.

c. 1455: Johannes Gutenberg publishes his *Forty-two-Line Bible* on a printing press with movable type.

1477: In France, King Louis XI sets up a national mail-delivery system, the Royal Postal Service.

c. 1490: Newsbooks are being issued at the rate of 20 per year in England and on the Continent. They provide information on major events and public issues.

c. 1450: King Nezahualcóyotl of Texcoco (Mexico) enacts strict forest preservation laws. This is an attempt to slow the progressive deforestation of Central Mexico in the 15th century.

1492: Christopher Columbus's first transatlantic voyage between Europe and the Americas inaugurates a vast biological exchange of animals, plants, and diseases between Afro-Eurasia and the New World.

1445: Portuguese navigator and explorer Dinís Dias reaches the mouth of the Sénégal River and later rounds Cape Verde, the western tip of Africa.

1499: Merchant-explorer Amerigo Vespucci, who calculated the most accurate estimate of the Earth's circumference to date, explores the South American coast for the Spanish government.

1470: In prison, English writer Sir Thomas Malory finishes *Le Morte Darthur,* the first English prose account of King Arthur and the fellowship of the Round Table.

c. 1450: Simple single-lens microscopes are in use in Europe. The compound microscope will be invented in The Netherlands after 1590.

1494: Syphilis appears among soldiers at the siege of Naples in Italy, then spreads rapidly throughout Europe. French and Italian writers blame each other's armies for introducing the disease.

1473: Two decades after the invention of the printing press by Johannes Gutenberg, the first mechanically printed music, the *Constance Gradual,* is published in southern Germany.

1489: Jakob Obrecht is made choir master at St. Donatian, Brugge, where he writes the *Missa Salve diva parens,* a masterpiece of contrapuntal Franco-Flemish music.

1453: The Gutenberg Bible is published on the newly invented printing press. It foreshadows the mass production and distribution of texts, which contribute to the Protestant Reformation.

1492: Spanish Christians conquer Granada, ending the Muslim Nasrid dynasty, which ruled southern Spain from 1238. They expel those Jews and Moors (Muslims) who refuse to convert to Catholicism.

1463: Regiomontanus completes his translation of Ptolemy's *Almagest.* His translation, published in 1496 as the *Epitome,* would be a major source for Renaissance astronomers.

1457: The Scottish parliament warns that golf is distracting the populace from the more essential military skill of archery.

c. 1480: The Italian card game baccarat is introduced into French circles. The game would later become popular in European casinos in the 19th century.

c. 1480: French manufacturers begin to make silk, in part on the basis of knowledge of Asian techniques.

1455: Female English silk manufacturers petition the Crown to stop competition from silk made in Lombardy.

1492: Queen Isabella I of Spain finances Christopher Columbus's voyage of exploration to the East Indies. Columbus instead finds the West Indies.

1500 – 1560

Architecture	**1502:** Donato Bramante designs the Tempietto, Rome. Supposedly marking the site of St. Peter's crucifixion, this high Renaissance "Little Temple" appears to be an oversized shrine.	**c. 1525:** Giulio Romano begins work for Duke Federigo Gonzaga II on the Palazzo del Te, Mantua. An example of Mannerist architecture, the building, which breaks all classical rules, is interestingly confusing and confounding.
Art	**c. 1500:** Sixteenth-century Venetian painters create the modern method of oil painting, exploring the artistic possibilities of the medium and replacing wood with canvas as the preferred support.	**c. 1530:** The nude reappears in northern European art, in the work of Lucas Cranach the Elder. Inspired in part by Italian painters, he paints a series of studies of Venus, including "Venus and Cupid" in 1530.
Childhood	**1509:** Children of the Chapel emerges as one of the most important children's acting companies in England. Often the first to stage works by Ben Jonson, the troupe continues to perform until 1615.	**c. 1525:** Martin Luther argues that the primary purpose of a humanist education should be to promote piety through reading Scripture and that all children must be permitted to attend school.
Daily Life	**1501:** Portuguese traders open an ocean route from India to Europe, bringing spices from the East much more quickly by ship than by the tedious overland route.	**1519:** Spanish explorer Hernán Cortés is served a chocolate drink at the court of Montezuma in Mexico. Until about 1850 most chocolate will be consumed as a beverage.
Ecology	**c. 1500:** Extinction of the moa, a giant flightless bird of New Zealand, after about 500 years of pressure from Maori hunters.	**c. 1520:** Corn (maize) is established in the Mediterranean world. It is the first important crop from the Americas to succeed in Afro-Eurasia and becomes a staple in many parts of the Old World.
Exploration	**1502:** Christopher Columbus departs on his fourth voyage in which he still does not discover that Cuba is an island. He dies in 1506 believing that he had explored the eastern coast of Asia.	**1522:** After Magellan's death in the Philippines, Juan Sebastián de Elcano is honored by the Spanish emperor for completing the first circumnavigation of the Earth.

Literature	**1507:** Nicolas de la Chesnaye composes the most famous of the French morality plays, *Condemnation des banquets*.	**1516:** English Humanist poet Sir Thomas More publishes his masterpiece (written in Latin), *Utopia*.	**1528:** Italian courtier Baldassare Castiglione publishes his idealization of the court of Urbino, *Il libro del cortegiano* (The Book of the Courtier).

Medicine	**1503:** Relying on close observation and dissection, Italian artist Leonardo da Vinci undertakes detailed anatomical drawings.	**1518:** English physician Thomas Linacre, a late advocate of Galenic physiology, founds the Royal College of Physicians to regulate medical practice in England.
Music	**c. 1500:** After 1700 years' development, the pipe organ reaches its mature form in northern Germany, leading to the growth of a body of music tailored to exploit its grand and complex capabilities.	**c. 1520:** Spanish instrument-makers invent the guitar, a six-stringed instrument based on the vihuela.
Religion	**1503:** Renaissance scholar Desiderius Erasmus publishes his *Handbook of a Christian Knight* in 1503 and 1504, which advocates humanist learning and ecclesiastical reform.	**1516:** Rajput princess Mira Bai refuses to consummate her marriage, claiming to having already married the god Krishna, and begins her life as a model of Hindu loving-devotion.
Science		**1524:** German-Swiss physician Paracelsus begins lecturing at the University of Basel. His wide-ranging and influential works include studies of alchemy, chemistry, medicine, and fossils.
Sports		**c. 1525:** Henry VIII of England is presented a gift of jewel-encrusted darts by Anne Boleyn. Darts become a popular diversion for Tudor monarchs.
Technology	**c. 1500:** Leonardo da Vinci designs a screw-cutting machine.	
Women		**1528:** In the Gulf of Mexico, 10 Spanish women accompany their husbands on a voyage of discovery. After the men are lost, the women search for them a year, then settle in Veracruz.

1538: Michelangelo begins work on the Capitoline Square. The design shows his brilliance not only as an architect but as an urban planner.

1554: Work begins on Saint Basil the Blessed Cathedral. The ornate Russian building is topped by magnificent onion-shaped domes.

1534: Death of Parma-based painter Correggio, whose sensuous mythological paintings–"Danäe," "The Rape of Ganymede," and "Jupiter and Io"–strongly influence a later generation of Baroque artists.

1541: Michelangelo completes the "Last Judgment" in the Sistine Chapel. The fresco's writhing forms convey a darker vision than his ceiling frescoes, completed in 1512.

1535: The Ursulines, a Roman Catholic religious order named for St. Ursula, is founded by Angela Merici at Brescia, Italy. It is the first institute for women dedicated exclusively to the education of girls.

1560: Queen Elizabeth I reestablishes the Westminster School in London. It becomes one of the best-known public schools in England.

1538: The first university in the Western Hemisphere is founded, at Santo Domingo (on Hispaniola), by the Spanish.

c. 1550: The potato is introduced into Europe from South America. Although initially suspected of being poisonous, by the end of the 17th century it will be a major food crop.

1535: The Galápagos Islands are discovered. Their unusual flora and fauna are of special interest to naturalists and contribute to Charles Darwin's studies on natural selection in the 19th century.

c. 1550: Escaped Spanish horses reestablish wild horse populations in North America. They quickly change the way of life of Plains Indians, who adopt the horse for transport and hunting.

1535: Gugielmo de Lorena designs a diving bell for exploring sunken ships in Italy's Lake Nemi.

1541: Spanish soldier-explorer Francisco de Orellana follows the Amazon River from the Peruvian Andes to the Atlantic Ocean, becoming the river's first European explorer.

c. 1530: England achieves a 60% literacy rate owing in part to the introduction (by English printer William Caxton) of the German printing press late in the 15th century.

1558: Queen Elizabeth I's ascension to the throne of England marks the beginning of the prolific literary period named in her honor.

1543: Flemish anatomist Andreas Vesalius writes *De humani corporis fabrica* ("On the Fabric of the Human Body"), a revolutionary anatomy text that ends the dominance of Galen's doctrines.

1552: French surgeon Ambroise Paré, famous for his humanizing reforms of surgical practice, serves King Henry II of France.

1536: John Calvin orders the removal of organs from churches in the city of Geneva.

1550: John Marbeck publishes The *Booke of Common Praier Noted*, which provides the first music in English for the Anglican liturgy.

1539: The death of Indian guru ("religious teacher") Nanak is followed by a lineage of nine other gurus, each of whom helps further establish the Sikh tradition.

c. 1550: Unitarianism develops in central Europe. A non-Trinitarian Christian movement, it is roundly attacked by both Catholics and Calvinists in its early years.

1543: Polish astronomer Nicolaus Copernicus' *De revolutionibus orbium coelestium* advances a heliocentric model of the solar system.

1545: Italian physician and mathematician Gerolamo Cardano publishes his *Ars magna* ("Great Art"), a landmark in the history of algebra.

1530: In Florence, La Lotto di Firenze is believed to be the first lottery to award cash prizes. Lotteries are used by Renaissance cities and states to raise money for public welfare, works, and defense.

c. 1550: Railroads first appear in European mines.

1556: German engineer Georgius Agricola's widely influential *De re metallica* is published posthumously. The treatise describes mining and engineering techniques, including shaft and pump design.

1553: Mary Tudor becomes queen of England and has Lady Jane Grey, who was queen for nine days in July, beheaded. Mary's persecution of Protestants earns her the name Bloody Mary.

1560 – 1625

Architecture	**1563:** Juan de Herrera begins work on the monumental Escorial, near Madrid. Under his direction (from 1572), the Escorial becomes one of the greatest expressions of Spanish imperial culture and wealth.	**c. 1600:** Emergence of the Baroque style in Western art and architecture.
Art	**c. 1568:** The Flemish artist Pieter Bruegel the Elder paints *Peasant Dance*, depicting village life with movement and lively characterization.	**1577:** Greek-born, Italian-trained El Greco paints an intensely spiritual *Assumption of the Virgin* after his arrival in Spain, using a personal vocabulary of figures, space and color.
Childhood	**1567:** Thirteen-month-old Prince James becomes king of Scotland after his mother, Mary, abdicates the throne. At 16 he is kidnapped by one of his earls and spends a year in captivity.	**c. 1590:** Hornbooks become popular as aids to literacy. They consist of a piece of wood with a printed alphabet on parchment pasted on and enclosed behind a transparent sliver of horn.
Daily Life	**c. 1560:** The first cafés are operating in Constantinople (Istanbul). Cafés appear in France, Italy, Germany, and England in the 1600s.	**1582:** The Gregorian calendar is introduced into use in the Western world. It replaces the Julian calendar, which had been in use since Roman times.
Ecology	**1570:** A century of accelerated deforestation begins in Japan, leaving the islands south of Hokkaido substantially stripped. Population growth and vast construction projects drive this forest clearance.	
Exploration	**1569:** Gerardus Mercator transforms mapmaking for the secular world through his projection that allows sailors to lay out courses on flat charts that account for the true shape of the Earth.	**1577:** Francis Drake's voyage around the world, the first English circumnavigation, demonstrates the open route to the Pacific south of the tip of South America.
Literature	**1573:** English writer George Gascoigne completes what is considered by some to be the first novel in the English language, *The Adventures of Master F.J.*	**1588:** French essayist Michel de Montaigne, pioneer of the personal essay form, publishes all three books of his *Essays* in a single volume.
Medicine	**1561:** Italian anatomist Gabriel Fallopius gives detailed descriptions of the female reproductive system, including the tubes that connect the ovaries to the uterus, in *Observationes anatomicae*.	**1574:** Italian scholar Ulisse Aldrovandi publishes an official pharmacopeia describing the proper mixtures of plant remedies.
Music	**1567:** Orlando di Lasso publishes three complete cycles of the *Magnificat* in eight tones, showing remarkable compositional dexterity and variety.	**c. 1580:** Italian instrument-makers create the violin, based on the medieval fiddle.
Religion	**1572:** In the Saint Bartholomew's Day Massacre, French Catholics murder some 3,000 Huguenots (Protestants) in Paris. The massacre was plotted by Catherine de Médicis.	**1589:** The metropolitan of Moscow is elevated to the position of patriarch in the Eastern Orthodox Church, thus granting the Russian Orthodox Church self-governance.
Science		**1576:** Danish astronomer Tycho Brahe founds his observatory in Uraniborg. His observations of stellar motion possess unprecedented accuracy and contribute to the rejection of Aristotelian cosmology.
Sports		**c. 1580:** The Spanish Riding School of Vienna is founded. The school is famous for its Lipizzaner horses, which receive an extraordinary classical training.
Technology	**1565:** German-Swiss naturalist Conrad Gesner provides the first description of the lead pencil. Pencils gain popularity in Europe from the late 1500s.	**1590:** Coal mining is established in Germany's Ruhr valley, laying an early foundation for extensive industrial development in the region.
Women		**1587:** Mary Queen of Scots is beheaded by order of Queen Elizabeth I.

1609: Mehmed Aga begins work on his masterpiece, the Sultan Ahmed Cami, Istanbul. Perfectly symmetrical in design, it is known as the Blue Mosque because of its colored tiles.

1619: Inigo Jones designs the great Banqueting House at Whitehall, England. Strongly influenced by Palladio and using familiar motifs, it is nonetheless a highly distinctive composition.

1601: Roguish, brilliant painter Caravaggio brings dramatic lighting and visceral force to *The Conversion of St. Paul*, introducing elements that will characterize the Baroque era.

c. 1625: Roman artist Artemisia Gentileschi creates an oeuvre depicting heroic women. Most dramatic are her several paintings of Judith's killing of the Roman general Holofernes, painted between 1610 and 1625.

c. 1610: The hook-nosed character Pulcinella appears on puppet stages in Italy. An international star, he becomes Polichinelle in France, Petrushka in Russia, and Punch (of Punch and Judy fame) in England.

1620: The first book on deaf education, by Juan Pablo Bonet, is published, inaugurating the field of special education.

1609: Johann Carolus of Strassbourg issues the *Relation*, considered to be the first modern newspaper. A German paper is also issued.

1611: The King James Bible is published in England. The translation has a marked influence on English style and is generally accepted as the standard English Bible for more than three centuries.

c. 1610: Cassava reaches Kongo from the Americas. It spreads rapidly in equatorial Africa and becomes the staple crop in many societies.

1620: Francis Bacon publishes *Novum organum*, one of his several works advocating systematic use of natural philosophy to further human dominion over nature.

1600: The East India Company, the first of several European companies that compete for the rich Indian Ocean trade in spices and luxury goods, is founded.

1616: In search of the Northwest Passage, William Baffin pilots the ship *Discovery* farther into Baffin Bay than English navigator John Davis had earlier but concludes that it did not lead to India.

1600: William Shakespeare completes *Hamlet*, one of his four greatest tragedies. The others, *Othello*, *King Lear*, and *Macbeth*, are written between 1600 and 1606.

1604: Spanish novelist Miguel de Cervantes obtains official license for the publication of Part I of his adventure novel *Don Quixote*.

1624: *The General History of Virginia*, one of the first texts to be published in the New World, is completed by John Smith.

1610: The first documented case of a cesarean section performed on a living woman is published.

1611: Mikolaj Zielenski publishes his *Offertoria* in Gniezno, Poland, bringing the Polish Renaissance to its height.

1617: Heinrich Schütz is appointed Kapellmeister to the court of Saxony. He brings Italian musical style to Germany and writes the first German opera.

1612: Thomas Helwys founds the General Baptist church, the first Baptist church in England. He argues that Christ's atonement applied to all persons, not only a chosen few.

1620: English separatists, or Pilgrims, lead the founding of Plymouth Colony in what is now Massachusetts.

1600: English physician William Gilbert's *De magnete*, the first broad discussion of magnetism since the 13th century, postulates that the Earth is a giant lodestone and has magnetic properties.

1614: Scottish mathematician John Napier's *Mirifici logarithmorum canonis descriptio*, based on work begun about 1590, describes the nature and use of logarithms.

c. 1608: King James I of England introduces the game of golf to London from Scotland.

1608: Dutch opticians develop the refracting telescope. It is soon copied elsewhere in Europe, most famously by Galileo, who uses it to discover the moons of Jupiter.

1623: England's Statute of Monopolies, the first modern patent law, is passed by Parliament.

1603: A Japanese dancer of the Izumo shrine invents kabuki theater.

1619: A proposal to give women an equal portion in colonial lands is rejected by the Virginia House of Burgesses.

1625 – 1700

Architecture	**1634:** Francesco Borromini is commissioned to design San Carlo alle Quattro Fontane, Rome. Its deeply sculptured facade and unusual, fluid floor plan set an example of Baroque design.		**1656:** Work begins on Gian Lorenzo Bernini's design for St. Peter's Square. The square is united with St. Peter's through Bernini's colonnade, which mimics a human embrace.
Art	**1633:** Pietro da Cortona's ceiling fresco in the Barberini Palace, Rome, imagines a sculptural canopy with multitudes of foreshortened heavenly figures coursing through it.		**1656:** Diego Velázquez paints his masterwork, *Las Meninas*, which apparently captures a moment with the Spanish royal family.
Childhood	**1635:** The Boston Public Latin School is founded. It is the oldest secondary school in the US.		**1658:** Publication of *Orbis Sensualium Pictus* (*The Visible World in Pictures*) by Moravian educator John Amos Comenius. It is the first known picture book for children.
Daily Life			**c. 1650:** The mass production of glass bottles and the development of cork stoppers begins to make possible the controlled aging of wine.
Ecology		**1641:** The first ban on animal cruelty is enacted by the Massachusetts Bay Colony.	**1652:** Dutch settlers establish a permanent European colony at the Cape of Good Hope. They bring new crops, plants, animals, and diseases to southern Africa.
Exploration	**1634:** French explorer Jean Nicolet seeks the Northwest Passage by crossing Lake Huron and passing through the Straits of Mackinac. He discovers Lake Michigan and sails to Green Bay.		**1642:** Dutch navigator Abel Janszoon Tasman explores the southern coast of Australia and discovers the island of Tasmania, opening up the South Indian Ocean and the Southwest Pacific Ocean for trade.
Literature	**1633:** *Poems*, the complete collection of John Donne's poetry, is published for the first time; it is revised by the author in 1635.		**1651:** British philosopher Thomas Hobbes, Francis Bacon's pupil, publishes *Leviathan*, one of the great works of political philosophy.
Medicine	**c. 1630:** Jesuit missionaries bring cinchona bark from Peru to Europe. The bark, which contains trace amounts of naturally occurring quinine, is used to treat malaria.		**1648:** Chemist and alchemist Jan Baptista van Helmont, known for applying chemical principles to physiology, describes digestion as a kind of fermentation in *Ortus medicinae*.
Music		**1637:** The Ancient Society of College Youths is formed in England to promote "change ringing" of church bells.	
Religion	**1630:** John Winthrop sets forth his vision of the colony of Massachusetts as "a Citty upon a Hill" in his sermon "A Modell of Christian Charity."		**1645:** The Congregation for the Propagation of the Faith condemns Confucian rites as incompatible with Catholicism. Jesuits had urged tolerance of the rites.
Science	**1627:** German astronomer Johannes Kepler's *Tabulae rudolphinae* gives far more accurate planetary positions than those of earlier observers.	**1637:** French philosopher René Descartes publishes *Discourse on Method*, a highly influential attempt to reduce all of nature to mathematical law.	
Sports			**1653:** English author Izaak Walton publishes his book *The Compleat Angler*. More than 300 editions of the classic fishing treatise are published over the next 300 years.
Technology			**1656:** Dutch mathematician, astronomer, and physicist Christiaan Huygens invents the pendulum clock.
Women	**1629:** Tokugawa shogun Iemitsu bans women from kabuki theater because it is considered immoral for women to dance in public.		**1650:** The first poetry collection written in the New World, Anne Bradstreet's *The Tenth Muse Lately Sprung Up in America*, is published in London.

1666: Great Fire of London. Christopher Wren, in charge of reconstruction (with others), designs 53 churches in the rebuilt city. Most notable is St. Paul's Cathedral, which takes 35 years to complete.

1660: Jacob van Ruisdael paints *Jewish Cemetery.* The painting's glowering scene exemplifies the trend toward turbulence in Dutch landscape at mid-century.

1671: The first printed reference to an alphabet rhyme, a ditty composed to help children learn their letters, appears.

1697: Charles Perrault writes *The Tales of Mother Goose.* Reprinted and retold over the centuries, the tales are among the most famous children's stories.

c. 1667: In France, during the reign of King Louis XIV, the fork begins to achieve popularity as an eating implement. Formerly, only knives and spoons had been used.

c. 1690: Life insurance policies begin to come into use in Europe.

1681: First sighted in about 1507, the dodo, a flightless bird of Mauritius, becomes extinct.

1698: The first small steam engine is built by Thomas Savery, leading to increased coal use by industry.

1670: Founding of the Hudson's Bay Company, whose trappers and fur traders collect information about the people, geography, and flora and fauna of North America.

1698: English astronomer and Royal Society fellow Edmond Halley commands a scientific voyage through the Atlantic to study terrestrial magnetism.

1667: The greatest writer of French comedy, Molière, performs his comic masterpiece, *Le Misanthrope.*

1694: Matsuo Basho, the greatest of the Japanese haiku masters, publishes his travel journal of northern Japan, *Oku no hosomichi (The Narrow Road to the Deep North).*

1665: The Great Plague kills about 75,000 of the 460,000 residents of London.

1680: Italian physiologist Giovanni Borelli publishes *De Motu animalium,* an account of iatromechanics, the application of mechanical principles to the study of locomotion and physiology.

1669: The Paris Opéra is founded as La Académie Royale de Musique (the Royal Academy of Music).

1684: Italian violin-maker Antonio Stradivari begins to experiment with varnishes, wood thicknesses, and designs for his violins, producing some of the finest instruments ever made.

c. 1700: Invention of the balalaika, a Russian mandolin-like instrument.

1670: William Penn, founder of the Commonwealth of Pennsylvania, publishes his defense of religious toleration, *The Great Case of Liberty of Conscience Once More Debated & Defended.*

c. 1697: A schism among Mennonites leads to the rise of the Amish, a conservative Christian group headed by Jakob Ammann.

1674: Dutch microscopist and biologist Antonie van Leeuwenhoek concludes that the moving objects he sees through his microscope are little animals, or microorganisms.

1687: A professor at Cambridge since 1669, Isaac Newton publishes his *Philosophiae naturalis principia mathematica,* which announces the three laws of universal motion.

1669: The manufacture of weapons, including even ceremonial swords, is outlawed on the island of Okinawa, Japan. This leads to the development of karate.

1697: The first documented 11-a-side cricket match is played in Sussex, England.

1679: The pressure cooker is invented by French-born British engineer and physicist Denis Papin.

c. 1700: Agriculture in England begins to employ technological improvements, including crop rotation and the mechanical sower.

1660: Mary Dyer is executed in Boston for her Quaker proselytizing.

1682: Mary Rowlandson publishes *A Narrative of the Captivity and Restoration of Mrs. Mary Rowlandson,* describing her capture by Narragansett warriors and 12 weeks' captivity.

1700 – 1775

Architecture	**1705:** Architect and dramatist John Vanbrugh begins work on Blenheim Palace, Oxfordshire. The palace is a highly theatrical complex and the finest example of English Baroque.	**1743:** German architect Balthasar Neumann designs the pilgrimage church at Vierzehnheiligen, near Bamberg. A fine southern German Baroque church, its complex plan uses no straight lines.
Art	**1713:** Antoine Watteau depicts the nobility of love and leisure in *La Partie quarree* (completed in 1714), a work that contributes to the development of French Rococo.	**1743:** William Hogarth executes his moralizing series of paintings and engravings *Marriage à la Mode*, which satirize English upper-class life (the engravings were printed in 1745.).
Childhood	**1724:** Russian Emperor Peter I the Great founds an Academy of Sciences, which includes a secondary school. Its secular and scientific characteristics set the tone for Russian education.	**1745:** The first specialized children's hospitals, such as the London Foundling Hospital, are opened. These facilities later become major centers for training in pediatrics.
Daily Life	**c. 1700:** The Old English sheepdog, bred to herd and protect sheep, is developed in England.	**c. 1740:** The Industrial Revolution promotes the growth of cities, the factory system, and a myriad of other changes to everyday life in Europe.
Ecology	**1712:** The Newcomen steam engine is installed in a coal mine. It is used especially for pumping water out of shafts and tunnels, which allows deeper mining and increased coal production.	**1752:** One of the first modern zoological gardens in Europe, the Schönbrunn Tiergarten (Imperial Menagerie), opens on the grounds of Schloss Schönbrunn, in Vienna.
Exploration	**1722:** On a circumnavigation of the globe and search for the southern continent, Dutch admiral Jacob Roggeveen lands on Easter Island and sights Samoa.	**1753:** Scottish naval surgeon James Lind demonstrates the efficacy of citrus fruits in preventing and curing scurvy, long a major health hazard in long-distance sea travel.
Literature	**1700:** English Poet John Dryden publishes *Fables Ancient and Modern*, a collection of translations of works by Ovid, Boccaccio, and Chaucer containing one of his most astute critical essays.	**1729:** Jonathan Swift publishes *A Modest Proposal*, one of the most successful satires in the English language.
Medicine	**c. 1700:** Dutch physician Hermann Boerhaave founds the influential tradition of medical education at the University of Leiden. His training emphasizes chemistry, physiology, and bedside observation of patients.	**1733:** In his *Haemastaticks*, English physiologist and chemist Stephen Hales describes the process for measuring blood pressure quantitatively.
Music	**c. 1709:** Italian instrument-maker Bartolomeo Cristofori invents the piano. He continues refining his instrument until 1726, when he produces the instrument on which the modern piano is modeled.	**c. 1750:** The string quartet, consisting of two violins, viola, and cello, emerges as the most popular type of group in chamber music.
Religion	**c. 1720:** Start of the First Great Awakening, a religious revival that sweeps the American colonies. Its leading figures were Anglican George Whitefield and Congregationalist Jonathan Edwards.	**1745:** Muslim reformer Muhammad 'Abd al-Wahhab meets political leader Muhammad ibn Sa'ud, with whom he will form an alliance promoting Wahhabism in Arabia.
Science	**1705:** In his *Synopsis of the Astronomy of Comets*, Oxford astronomer Edmond Halley argues that comets seen in 1531, 1607, and 1682 are actually the same comet with a period of 75 or 76 years.	**1735:** Swedish naturalist Carolus Linnaeus publishes his *Systema naturae*, the first of his works on botanical classification.
Sports	**1719:** English pugilist James Figg wins the first world heavyweight boxing championship. The bare-knuckle fighter is also known for his skills at fencing and wrestling.	**1742:** Edmond Hoyle publishes *A Short Treatise on the Game of Whist*. He becomes the first recognized authority on card and board games and the inspiration for the phrase "according to Hoyle."
Technology	**c. 1710:** Precision lathes are developed in Europe for the production of clocks and scientific instruments. They also provide an important foundation for industrial machine tools.	**1733:** English inventor John Kay patents the flying shuttle loom, mechanizing a cumbersome feature of loom operation.
Women	**1718:** Lady Mary Wortley Montagu advocates smallpox inoculation, which she has seen in Constantinople.	**1741:** Elizabeth Lucas Pinckney introduces indigo cultivation in South Carolina; by 1742 she has a successful crop.

1768: Thomas Jefferson begins work on his estate, Monticello. Jefferson tears down his half-completed original structure and redesigns it in 1793, after visiting Paris.

1766: Jean-Honoré Fragonard brings erotic wit and deft use of light to *The Swing*, painted in the style of François Boucher's outdoor party scenes.

1771: An American born painter working in England, Benjamin West paints the first contemporary "history" scene, *The Death of General Wolfe*.

1761: Five-year-old Wolfgang Amadeus Mozart begins composing short musical pieces. The child prodigy develops into one of the West's great musical talents.

1767: Johann Friedrich Oberlin, an Alsatian Lutheran pastor, founds the first *salle d'asile*, or infant school, for the care and instruction of very small children while their parents work in the fields.

1761: The first steel scissors are produced by English industrialist Robert Hinchliffe. Scissors in various forms had been in use in Asia and Europe since ancient times.

1770: English chemist Joseph Priestly gives the name "rubber" to caoutchouc resin because it can rub out marks.

1769: James Watt patents a more efficient steam engine, one of the key components of the Industrial Revolution and the fossil-fuel age.

1761: A chronometer built by Englishman John Harrison keeps time during a 9-week voyage, winning a prize offered by Parliament for the invention of a practical way of finding longitude at sea.

1769: James Cook begins the first of three expeditions to the South Pacific. He surveys the islands of New Zealand, discovers the Great Barrier Reef, and charts over 4,000 miles of coastline.

1759: French writer Voltaire publishes his best-known work, *Candide*, a satirical novel denouncing metaphysical optimism.

1771: Scottish natural historian William Smellie completes publication of the first edition of the *Encyclopædia Britannica* in three volumes in Edinburgh.

1769: American doctor Benjamin Rush begins practicing medicine in Philadelphia. An advocate of heroic intervention in treating disease, he is best known for his advocacy of humane treatment of the insane.

1761: Austrian composer Franz Joseph Haydn enters the service of Prince Pal Antal Esterhazy. One of the most important figures in classical music, Haydn helps establish both the string quartet and symphony.

1770: William Billings publishes *The New-England Psalm-Singer*, the first collection of music composed entirely in America.

c. 1770: Beginning of *Haskala* ("Jewish Enlightenment"), during which reformers seek to introduce Central and Eastern European Jews to European secular education and culture.

1766: British chemist Henry Cavendish demonstrates the existence of inflammable air (hydrogen) as a distinct substance.

1772: Captain Robert Jones's *A Treatise of Skating* provides the first account of figure skating.

c. 1750: The sextant replaces the octant as European mariners' favorite instrument for making celestial measurements on land and water.

1769: English inventor Richard Arkwright patents a steam powered rotary engine spinning machine, which, by the 1790s, leads to the extensive employment of steam power in cotton mills.

1762: In Russia, Sophie Auguste von Anhalt-Zerbst, widow of Peter III, ascends to the throne as Catherine II. She rules as an "enlightened despot" until 1796.

1774: In Edenton NC 51 women sign a petition endorsing the Nonimportation Association resolves, joining many other colonial women boycotting British goods.

1775 – 1850

Architecture	**1775:** Claude-Nicolas Ledoux designs the Arc-et-Senans, Salines de Chaux. The stark, geometric plan represents a significant evolution in Ledoux's architectural vision.	**1809:** Thomas Jefferson begins work on his architectural masterpiece, the University of Virginia (opened in 1825). The Neoclassical campus was organized around a graceful lawn, capped by the elegant Rotunda.
Art	**1784:** Shortly before the French Revolution, Jacques-Louis David's *Oath of the Horatii* helps define Neoclassical style in France, drawing on the theme of liberty.	**1798:** German Alois Senefelder invents lithographic process, which allows a variety of graphic effects and inexpensive reproduction.
Childhood	**1779:** Young Napoleon Bonaparte arrives at the military school of Brienne in France and is subjected to hazing and humiliation. He later conquers much of Europe.	**1802:** The Health and Morals of Apprentices Act is passed in Britain. It marks the beginning of government efforts to improve the lot of factory workers and regulate child labor.
Daily Life	**1781:** Thomas Jefferson raises tomatoes at Monticello VA. Native to South America, the fruit is introduced to North America from Europe.	**1809:** Frenchman Nicolas Appert develops a process for canning food by sealing it in airtight containers and sterilizing it with heat.
Ecology	**1788:** Anglo-Irish settlement of Australia begins; this involves the introduction of numerous new plants and animals and some extinctions of indigenous flora and fauna.	
Exploration	**1776:** Spanish missionary Silvestre Vélez de Escalante explores western Colorado and journeys north into Utah, almost reaching the Great Salt Lake.	**1792:** George Vancouver surveys the coast of North America from San Francisco to British Columbia. While he proves that no northwest passage exists, his work stimulates development of North Pacific trade.
Literature	**1776:** "Common Sense," the first pamphlet in America strongly supporting independence from England, is published anonymously by Thomas Paine.	**1794:** Early Romantic British poet William Blake publishes his poetry collection *Songs of Innocence and Experience.*
Medicine	**1784:** American statesman and inventor Benjamin Franklin invents bifocal lenses.	**1796:** Edward Jenner inoculates an eight-year-old boy with smallpox matter, resulting in the development of a vaccine against the disease.
Music	**1776:** La Scala, one of the world's major operatic venues, is built in Milan.	**c. 1800:** Philadelphia instrument-maker John Isaac Hawkins invents the upright piano. Smaller and cheaper than the grand piano, it becomes a fixture of middle-class homes in the 19th century.
Religion	**1787:** The United States Constitution is drafted in Philadelphia. It embodies the ideal of secular government with deliberate separation of "church and state."	
Science	**1776:** Adam Smith publishes his *Inquiry into the Nature and Causes of the Wealth of Nations,* a founding document of modern economics with its discussion of market behavior and the "invisible hand."	**1800:** Italian physicist Alessandro Volta invents the voltaic pile, the first battery, using zinc and copper disks.
Sports	**1777:** During his third expedition to the South Pacific, English explorer James Cook and his crew observe Tahitians surfing.	**1795:** The Duddingston Curling Society is founded in Edinburgh, Scotland. The club frames the first set of curling rules.
Technology	**1783:** French brothers Joseph-Michel and Jacques-Étienne Montgolfier stage the first manned untethered balloon flight, using a large linen bag inflated with hot air.	**1793:** American inventor Eli Whitney designs a cotton gin that mechanically separates the fibers and seeds of short-staple cotton.
Women	**1778:** Laura Bassi, author of *De problemate quodam mechanico* and *De problemate quodam hydrometrico* and the first woman professor of physics (at the University of Bologna), dies.	**1803:** Parliament passes the first British abortion law, prohibiting abortion after quickening.

1822: Karl Friedrich Schinkel begins work on the Altes Museum, Berlin. Completed in 1830, its Greek design gives expression to Prussian political and cultural ambitions.

1836: Charles Barry and A.W.N. Pugin begin work on the Houses of Parliament, London. The buildings, finished in 1867, became a major monument of English Neo-Gothic and established Pugin as its greatest talent.

1814: Responding to the Napoleonic occupation of Spain, Francisco de Goya highlights atrocities in *The Third of May, 1808*.

1848: British painters Dante Gabriel Rossetti, William Holman Hunt, and John Everett Millais form the short-lived but influential Pre-Raphaelite Brotherhood.

1817: The kaleidoscope is patented and soon begins to be sold as a children's toy.

1840: In one of the first formal studies of child psychology, Charles Darwin begins a record of the growth and development of one of his own children.

1825: The Stockton & Darlington Railway begins carrying passengers as well as freight. Henceforth, most transportation will rely on mechanical rather than animal power.

1850: In an effort to give women freedom of movement, Amelia Jenks Bloomer invents a "rational dress," which includes a jacket, skirt, and the now-famous bloomers.

1819: A decades-long cholera pandemic begins with transmission from endemic centers in Indonesia to China. In 1832 cholera attacks Egypt, Europe, and America, and it reappears in 1842 and 1848.

1845: Beginning of the Irish Potato Famine, the last great famine in the Western world. It kills more than one million of Ireland's eight million people and forces many others to emigrate.

1831: Charles Darwin leaves England aboard the *Beagle* to spend five years exploring South America, the Galápagos Islands, and the Pacific. The voyage establishes Darwin as a promising young naturalist.

1821–1829: German writer Johann Wolfgang von Goethe publishes *Wilhelm Meisters Wanderjahre* (*Wilhelm Meister's Travels*).

1847: English novelist Charlotte Brontë publishes the powerful narrative *Jane Eyre*.

c. 1820: French pharmacists Pierre Pelletier and Joseph Caventou isolate several physiologically active alkaloids from plants, including caffeine, strychnine, and quinine.

1846: At Massachusetts General Hospital in Boston, American physician William Thomas Morton demonstrates the use of ether as a general anesthetic.

1816: The first Southern "shape-note" tune book, *Kentucky Harmony*, is published for use in song-schools.

c. 1830: The cancan becomes popular in the music halls of Paris.

1846: Antoine-Joseph Sax patents the first saxophone.

1816: The African Methodist Episcopal church is established. One of the most important African-American churches, it expands after the Civil War through missionary work in the South.

1844: Mirza 'Ali Mohammad claims to be the Bab (gateway) to the hidden imam (the perfect embodiment of Islamic faith). He founds the Babi religion, which breaks with Islam in 1848.

1820: Danish physicist Hans Christian Ørsted discovers the relationship between electricity and magnetism. His discovery becomes one of the foundations of electromagnetic theory.

1846: German astronomers Johann Gottfried Galle and Heinrich Louis d'Arrest observe Neptune, confirming earlier predictions of the planet's existence.

1823: During a soccer match at the Rugby School in Rugby, Warwickshire, England, a player carries the ball instead of kicking it. According to rugby legend, this violation paved the way for the new sport; the first rules of rugby were later published at the same school.

c. 1850: The game of mah jongg originates in China.

1820: Charles Babbage, an English mathematician, develops plans for a mechanical "analytical engine," predecessor to computers of later eras.

1839: The daguerreotype, the first successful form of photography, is publicly unveiled.

1821: In Colombia, women gain the right to attend university.

1848: The first women's rights convention occurs at Seneca Falls, NY. The resulting Declaration of Sentiments, modeled on the Declaration of Independence, advocates women's rights.

1850 – 1900

Architecture	**1851:** Joseph Paxton's Crystal Palace opens to the public in London. The first modern exhibition building, it is a spectacular construction of cast iron and glass and is a symbol of Victorian ingenuity.	**1867:** The use of concrete in architecture increases with the development of reinforced concrete. Embedded with metal, it displays great tensile strength.
Art	**c. 1850:** Jean-François Millet monumentalizes farmwork in *The Sower*, in which an anonymous and timeless figure sweeps across the canvas.	**1865:** Mathew Brady, Timothy O'Sullivan, and Alexander Gardner record the horrors of the American Civil War in photographs such as "Ruins of the Gallego Flour Mill."
Childhood	**1852:** *Butter's Tangible Arithmetic and Geometry for Children*, a box of 144 oak blocks and an accompanying book of instructions and diagrams, goes on sale in England.	**1870:** F.A.O. Schwarz opens a modest toy shop in New York City. By 1908 it becomes a mammoth store offering 16,000 items.
Daily Life	**1850:** Levi Strauss begins selling dry goods to California miners and develops denim jeans for them. **c. 1855:** The screwdriver comes into popular use after advances in precision machining make the manufacture of screws easier.	**1859:** Ebenezer Butterick develops paper patterns to be used for the home sewing of clothing.
Ecology	**c. 1850:** Great Britain becomes the first sizeable country in the world in which more than half of the population lives in cities.	**1859:** Successful hard-rock drilling for oil in Titusville PA inaugurates the age of intensive oil use.
Exploration	**1853:** Missionary-doctor David Livingstone embarks on a series of treks through southern and central Africa, tracing the course of the Zambezi River and naming Victoria Falls.	**1867:** Geologist John Wesley Powell begins his series of scientific explorations of the Green and Colorado rivers and the Rocky Mountains.
Literature	**1850:** The most prolific and talented of all the British Victorian novelists, Charles Dickens, publishes *David Copperfield*. He quickly follows with *Bleak House* (1853) and *Hard Times* (1854).	**1863:** Russian novelist Leo Tolstoy publishes his epic historical novel, *War and Peace*.
Medicine	**1851:** German scientist Hermann von Helmholtz invents the ophthalmoscope, to study the structure and function of the eye and the condition of retinal blood vessels.	**1865:** Scottish physician Joseph Lister begins developing techniques for antiseptic surgery, including sterilization of instruments, which vastly reduce surgical mortality rates.
Music	**1853:** Italian composer Giuseppe Verdi writes his classic *La traviata* (*The Fallen Woman*). He is the leading figure in 19th-century opera, writing such great works as *Aïda* (1871) and *Otello* (1887).	**1869:** Nationalist composer Aleksandr Borodin, whose music draws on Russian folk melodies, begins work on his opera *Prince Igor*.
Religion	**1853:** Antoinette Brown is the first female ordained by a recognized denomination in the US, the Congregationalists.	**1863:** Mirza Hoseyn 'Ali Nuri (Baha' Ullah) diverges from Babism and founds the Baha'i religion in Iran.
Science	**1851:** French physicist Jean-Bernard-Léon Foucault's pendulum demonstrations illustrate the diurnal rotation of the Earth.	**1859:** Charles Darwin publishes his *Origin of Species*, advancing the theory of evolution by natural selection, profoundly upsetting a literalist interpretation of the Bible.
Sports	**c. 1855:** The racket sport of squash is developed at the English public school Harrow.	**1863:** The Football Association is established in England, and a uniform set of soccer rules is set down.
Technology	**1851:** American Isaac Singer founds I.M. Singer & Company, which by 1860 is the world's largest sewing machine manufacturer. It also pioneers the installment credit plan.	**1859:** Belgian inventor Jean-Joseph-Étienne Lenoir designs the first internal-combustion engine, based on the horizontal steam engine and using gas as fuel.
Women	**1853:** Queen Victoria delivers her eighth child under chloroform. Her approval and recommendation of it popularizes use of the anesthetic.	**1860:** Although the mountain is supposed to be forbidden to women, 16 women make a pilgrimage up Mount Fuji.

1880: The Chicago School of architecture emerges. The members of this influential group developed the modern skyscraper and contributed to the development of Modernism.

1900: Antonio Gaudí designs the Villa Bell Esguard, Barcelona, Spain. The idiosyncratic architect designed buildings that featured undulating lines and complex textured surfaces.

1874: A journalist reviewing a show by Monet, Renoir, Pisarro, and others dismisses them as "Impressionists," drawing on an 1872 painting by Monet. The group adopts the epithet as their name.

1892: American Mary Cassatt paints *The Bath*. Influenced by Japanese prints, it evokes the intimacy of mother and child in a flat, bold style.

1885: The safety bicycle is popularized by the Rover Safety model, manufactured by John K. Starley, a significant advance over earlier, more dangerous models of bicycle.

1900: English author Beatrix Potter publishes the *Tale of Peter Rabbit*. Potter's charming and well-illustrated stories establish her as one of the most beloved children's writers of the 20th century.

1874: The ice-cream soda is invented in Philadelphia, the center of ice-cream making in the US.

1884: A plan formulated by Canadian Sandford Fleming for defining 24 time zones is adopted. It creates a standard framework for worldwide timekeeping.

1896: Colgate Ribbon Dental Cream, the first toothpaste in a tube, is marketed.

1878: The Indian Forest Act appropriates 100,000 sq mi of forest to the state in the British colony of India in the name of conservation.

1896: Swedish scientist Svante Arrhenius describes the physics of the atmosphere's greenhouse effect, whereby solar energy is trapped on Earth and predicts global warming.

1872: The British *Challenger* begins its nearly 4-year expedition surveying deep-sea life.

1889: German geographer Hans Meyer ascends to the summit of Kibo, the central cone of Kilimanjaro and the highest point in Africa.

1898: Norwegian Otto Sverdrup leads an Arctic expedition that spends an unprecedented four winters in the north, claiming much land for Norway and accomplishing important scientific work.

1876: American writer and critic Mark Twain finishes his enduring classic *Tom Sawyer*. He begins *The Adventures of Huckleberry Finn* the same year.

1890: Norwegian playwright Henrik Ibsen produces his puzzling, uniquely satirical play *Hedda Gabler*.

1900: American novelist Theodore Dreiser completes his resonant first novel, *Sister Carrie*.

1881: Theodor Billroth, head of a surgical clinic in Vienna and the founder of modern abdominal surgery, performs the first successful operation to remove part of the stomach to treat cancer.

1897: Japanese bacteriologist Shiga Kiyoshi, a student of Kitasato Shibasaburo and Paul Ehrlich, discovers the dysentery bacillus.

c. 1870: Portuguese visitors introduce the machada to Hawaii. It is adapted by the Hawaiians and renamed the ukulele, Hawaiian for "flea."

1889: The Moulin Rouge, one of the earliest and most famous cabarets, opens in Paris.

1899: African-American composer Scott Joplin publishes his *Maple Leaf Rag*, which quickly sells one million copies.

1882: The resurgence of Zionism (Jewish nationalism) leads to the first European Jewish immigration to Israel and the revival of Hebrew as a vernacular language.

1900: An alliance of secret religious societies and Qing dynasty officials initiate the Boxer Rebellion, which spreads antiforeign sentiment throughout north China.

1871: British physicist John William Strutt (later Lord Rayleigh) argues that the scattering of blue light out of the direct beam of sunlight as it passes through the atmosphere causes the sky to appear blue.

1895: German physicist Wilhelm Conrad Röntgen discovers X rays. The discovery soon revolutionizes physics, medical diagnosis, and engineering.

c. 1873: The Indian court game of *poona* is introduced to England at the country estate of Badminton. The game's name is soon changed to that of the estate.

c. 1890: Euchre becomes popular as a family card game in the US.

1896: Due largely to the efforts of Pierre, baron de Coubertin, the first modern Olympic Games are held, in Athens.

1876: American inventor Alexander Graham Bell patents the telephone.

1883: The Brooklyn Bridge, designed by John and Washington Roebling. The bridge is hailed as one of the masterworks of 19th-century engineering.

1897: The *Argonaut*, designed by Simon Lake, is the first submarine to operate extensively in open water.

1872: Susan B. Anthony leads 15 women to vote in Rochester NY. Anthony is arrested two weeks later for the demonstration.

1884: Wimbledon holds its first women's singles championship; Maud Watson is the first winner.

1899: Korean women organize *Yo-u-hoe*, the Association of Women Friends, to fight against concubinage.

1900 – 1950

Architecture	**1906:** Frank Lloyd Wright designs the Unity Temple, Oak Park IL. The church displays a masterful use of concrete and a simple but powerful arrangement of space.		**1927:** Alvar Aalto designs the Viipuri Library, Finland, a building that blends into the wooded landscape and is an important regional adaptation of the International style.
Art	**1905:** Henri Matisse begins his *Joy of Life*. The modernist touchstone features a radical flattening of picture plane, pure color, and simplified shapes.		**1913:** The Armory Show, an exhibition of avant-garde and other modern European and American art in New York City, shocks critics and the public but inspires a generation of American artists.
Childhood	**1907:** Maria Montessori opens her Casa dei Bambini (Children's House). The educational philosophy of the Montessori school movement stresses individual student interests and self-directed learning.		**1926:** A.A. Milne publishes *Winnie-the-Pooh*. The chronicles of Christopher Robin and his toy animals, including Pooh, Tigger, and Eeyore, become children's classics.
Daily Life	**1902:** American inventor Willis Haviland Carrier develops the air conditioner to control indoor levels of temperature and humidity.	**1908:** Henry Ford's Detroit MI factory begins manufacturing the Model T, the first automobile priced within the range of the middle class.	**1928:** Cartoonist Walt Disney introduces Mickey Mouse in the animated cartoon *Steamboat Willie*.
Ecology	**1900:** Chicago authorities reverse the flow of the Chicago River, sending the untreated sewage of Chicago away from the city's water supply (Lake Michigan) and to the Mississippi River instead.		**1921:** Thomas Midgley, Jr., recommends the use of tetraethyl lead in gasoline to permit higher compression engines. Automobile exhausts begin to disperse lead into the atmosphere and biosphere.
Exploration	**1903:** Norwegian Roald Amundsen on the small sloop *Gjöa* becomes the first to navigate the Northwest Passage.		**1912:** British polar explorer Robert Falcon Scott arrives at the South Pole, only to find that Amundsen beat him by a month. He and his party perish during their return trek.
Literature	**1902:** British writer Joseph Conrad publishes his novella *Heart of Darkness*, which recounts his experiences on the Congo River.		**1915:** Czech novelist Franz Kafka publishes *The Metamorphosis*, the story of a man who wakes up one morning to find himself transformed into a beetle.
Medicine	**1901:** Austrian immunologist and pathologist Karl Landsteiner identifies type A, B, and O blood groups on the basis of the antigens on the surface of the red blood cells.		**1918:** The most destructive influenza epidemic in history kills approximately 20 million people worldwide.
Music	**1906:** Bela Bartok and Zoltan Kodaly publish their first volume of *Hungarian Folk Songs*, sparking a new interest in the ethnomusicology of Central Europe.		**1913:** The opening-night performance of Igor Stravinsky's modern ballet *The Rite of Spring*, at the Théâtre des Champs Élysées, causes a riot.
Religion	**1902:** American philosopher and psychologist William James applies psychology to the analysis of religion in *The Varieties of Religious Experience*.	**c. 1920:** In rural Jamaica, the Rastafarian movement develops, which identifies Ethiopian emperor Haile Selassie I as the Messiah.	**1929:** Hasan al-Banna' founds the Muslim Brotherhood in Egypt.
Science	**1900:** German physicist Max Planck formulates quantum theory, sparking a revolution in modern physics continued by Albert Einstein and other physicists.		**1924:** South African physical anthropologist and paleontologist Raymond Dart discovers the first *Australopithecus* fossil, in a limestone quarry near Taung, South Africa.
Sports	**1904:** The Fédération Internationale de Football Association (FIFA) organized as the global governing body of amateur soccer.		**1920:** Negro league baseball begins in the US, with the formation of the Negro National League. Negro league play is rendered obsolete in the 1940s, when the major leagues are integrated.
Technology	**1906:** Canadian American engineer Reginald Fessenden broadcasts the first radio program featuring voice and music.	**1914:** The 80-km (50-mi) Panama Canal opens. Work began by the French in 1879.	**1929:** American pilot Jimmy Doolittle completes a flight using only instruments.
Women	**1902:** Ida Tarbell begins publishing her "History of the Standard Oil Company" in *McClure's Magazine*. Her exposé will contribute to the breakup of the company by Supreme Court order in 1911.		**1920:** The 19th Amendment to the Constitution is signed into law, giving women in the United States the right to vote.

1943: Frank Lloyd Wright begins work on the Guggenheim Museum, New York City. Completed in 1959, its massive spiral form breaks out of the typical urban streetscape.

1949: Philip Johnson designs his Glass House, New Canaan CT. One of Johnson's first works, this building derives from the work of Mies van der Rohe.

1937: After the German Luftwaffe bombs the Basque village, Pablo Picasso paints *Guernica*, revealing Cubism's power to express horror and tragedy.

1950: American Jackson Pollock creates nonrepresentational *Autumn Rhythm* by dripping and pouring paint on the canvas.

1932: Melanie Klein publishes *The Psychoanalysis of Children*. Influenced by Freudian theory, it presents her object-relations theory of child analysis.

1946: Benjamin Spock publishes *Common Sense Book of Baby and Child Care*. The book, which encourages parents to trust their instincts over expert advice, shapes the childhoods of millions of baby boomers.

1935: The US Social Security Act establishes federal pensions in an effort to alleviate the effects of poverty on retired workers, dependent children, the blind, and the disabled.

1945: John H. Johnson founds *Ebony*, the first US mass-market magazine aimed at a black audience.

c. 1930: World's population surpasses two billion.

1942: Enrico Fermi oversees the first sustained nuclear chain reaction. This leads directly to atomic bombs and the development of civilian nuclear energy.

1948: Al-Ghawar, the world's largest oilfield, is discovered. Middle East oil strikes lower energy prices and drive a great burst of energy intensification in the Western world.

1943: Jacques-Yves Cousteau and Émile Gagnan perfect the first practical, automatically-regulated underwater breathing apparatus.

1947: American pilot Chuck Yeager breaks the sound barrier, flying an experimental X-1 rocket craft. He sets a world speed record of 2,655 k/hr (1,650 mph) in 1953.

1930: American Dashiell Hammett publishes his masterpiece of "hard-boiled" fiction, *The Maltese Falcon*.

1940: American writer Richard Wright completes his ground-breaking novel, *Native Son*.

1948: Senegalese poet Léopold Sédar Senghor edits and publishes *Anthology of the New Negro and Madagascan Poetry*, which includes some of the major works of the Negritude movement.

1932: German researcher Gerhard Domagk announces the discovery of the antibacterial effects of the sulfonamide Prontosil, the first synthetic compound to cure general bacterial infections in humans.

1948: The UN founds the World Health Organization to further international cooperation in medicine and public health.

1931: American composer Hoagy Carmichael records his hit song "Stardust" with Isham Jones. The song had been popular since its publication in 1927 and remains a classic.

1944: Dizzy Gillespie founds the first "bop" orchestra.

1948: Bluegrass is invented by mandolin player Bill Monroe, leader of the Blue Grass Boys, and banjo player Earl Scruggs.

1938: Nazis harness European anti-Jewish sentiment in the Holocaust (*Shoah*). By the end of World War II, six million Jews and many others considered socially or religiously deviant have been annihilated.

1947: The first of the Dead Sea Scrolls are discovered in a cave near the Dead Sea. The scrolls provide detailed insights into the history of Palestine, Judaism, and early Christianity.

1930: American astronomer Clyde Tombaugh discovers the planet Pluto.

1940: American physicists Edwin McMillan and Philip Abelson, artificially create a transuranium element (neptunium).

1948: George Gamow and Ralph Alpher elaborate the modern version of the "big-bang" model of the origins of the universe.

1930: The first modern pinball machines begin to appear.

1941: Willie Mosconi wins the first of 15 pocket billiards championships. Known for his accuracy and fancy shots, he elevates the game to respectability in the US.

1948: The design for the Frisbee flying disc is patented by Fred Morrison.

1936: Boulder Dam, harnessing the Colorado River for electricity production, is completed after six years' work. It is renamed the Hoover Dam in 1947.

1942: American research on nuclear fission is organized into the Manhattan Project. The project develops and builds the atomic bombs dropped on Hiroshima and Nagasaki in 1945.

1933: Portugal's new constitution specifically denies women's equal rights.

1941: In the Soviet Union, three regiments of all female pilots are created. The most highly decorated is the 586th Women's Fighter Regiment.

1949: French writer Simone de Beauvoir publishes *The Second Sex*, a key text for the mid-20th-century women's liberation movement.

1950 – 2000

Architecture	**1956:** Mies van der Rohe begins work on the Seagram Building, New York City, which features a restrained but sophisticated use of materials.	**1967:** The 1967 Montreal Expo is dominated by the US Pavilion, a massive geodesic dome designed by Buckminster Fuller.	**1974:** At a height of 443 m (1,454 ft), the Sears Tower in Chicago is the world's tallest building until the late 1990s.
Art	**1951:** American painter Helen Frankenthaler stages her first one-woman show. Her work is noted for its brilliant color and lyric style.	**1963:** Isolating and radically enlarging frames from comic strips, Roy Lichtenstein adopts the stylized violence of popular images in *Whaam!*	
Childhood	**c. 1950:** Jean Piaget develops his theory of cognition in children, which features four stages of development. Piaget's work in child psychology made him one of the central figures in the discipline.	**1968:** The first Special Olympics are held in Chicago's Soldier Field. In 1977 the first winter Special Olympics are held in Steamboat Springs CO.	
Daily Life	**1954:** The US Supreme Court unanimously rules in *Brown v. Board of Education* that racial segregation in public schools violates the 14th Amendment, overturning the doctrine of "separate but equal."	**1969:** Patrons of the Stonewall Inn in New York City riot after a police raid. The event is often considered the start of the gay rights movement in the US.	
Ecology	**1951:** Australian authorities intentionally introduce a Brazilian rabbit disease, myxomatosis, in an effort to control the rabbit population. It works.	**1962:** Rachel Carson's *Silent Spring*, an exposé of the biological costs of chemical pesticides in wide use in the US, is published and helps foment a new environmental consciousness.	
Exploration	**1953:** New Zealand mountaineer Edmund Hillary and his Sherpa partner, Tenzing Norgay, reach the summit of Mount Everest. They are the first humans to reach the summit and return.	**1969:** Americans Neil A. Armstrong and Edwin E. "Buzz" Aldrin, Jr., become the first humans to walk on the Moon.	
Literature	**1952:** Irish playwright Samuel Beckett produces his postmodernist, experimental play *Waiting for Godot*, during which nothing happens.	**1958:** Nigerian author Chinua Achebe completes his novel *Things Fall Apart.*	**1970:** Japanese novelist Yukio Mishima completes his *Hojo no umi* (Sea of Fertility) series. He then commits ritual suicide.
Medicine	**1955:** A vaccine against polio developed by American medical researcher Jonas Salk is released to the public.	**1967:** South African surgeon Christiaan Barnard carries out the first human heart transplant.	**c. 1970:** British and American researchers develop the CAT scan, which integrates thousands of X-ray images into a detailed picture.
Music	**1956:** Elvis Presley releases "Heartbreak Hotel" and helps popularize rock and roll among white audiences.	**1965:** The Beatles tour the US for the first time. Their "The Ed Sullivan Show" appearance draws 73 million viewers.	**1971:** Duke Ellington becomes the first jazz musician elected to the Royal Music Academy of Stockholm.
Religion	**1955:** The Rev. Martin Luther King, Jr., leads the Montgomery AL bus boycott to protest racial inequality, basing his tactics of nonviolent resistance on those of Mahatma Gandhi.	**1967:** Following the Six-Day War, Israel occupies the West Bank and East Jerusalem, allowing Jewish devotions at the Western Wall of the Second Temple of Jerusalem.	
Science	**1953:** British biophysicist Francis Crick and American biologist James Watson announce the double-helix structure of DNA.	**1958:** American physicist James Van Allen announces discovery of the Van Allen radiation belts surrounding the Earth.	**1974:** The X-ray source Cygnus X-1 emerges as a strong candidate for being a black hole.
Sports	**1954:** England's Roger Bannister is the first person to run the mile in under four minutes.	**1958:** Seventeen-year-old soccer sensation Pelé leads Brazil to a 5–2 victory over Sweden in the World Cup final.	**1973:** The Iditarod Trail Sled Dog Race is contested for the first time at its traditional distance of 1,770 km (1,100 mi).
Technology	**1956:** Transatlantic telephone service begins.	**1961:** Soviet cosmonaut Yury Gagarin orbits the Earth in the first manned spaceflight.	**1970:** The US establishes the Environmental Protection Agency (EPA) to monitor and regulate pollution.
Women	**1955:** Rosa Parks's arrest for refusing to give up her seat on a bus to a white man sparks the Montgomery bus boycott. African American women, the system's main users, support the boycott.	**1973:** Tennis champion Billie Jean King defeats champion player Bobby Riggs in a "Battle of the Sexes" match.	

1981: I.M. Pei begins designing his glass pyramid addition to the Grand Louvre, Paris. Originally a source of much controversy, the pyramid has become as beloved as the surrounding building.

1997: Frank Gehry's Guggenheim Museum in Bilbao, Spain, opens. The much-discussed building features curved exterior surfaces sheathed in gleaming titanium and cavernous interior spaces.

1977: In her *Untitled Film Stills* series (completed in 1980), American photographer Cindy Sherman, serving as her own model, creates film-noir-style images that question stereotypes and identity.

1995: Bulgarian-born environmental sculptor Christo (famous for wrapping large objects, including islands) and his wife, Jeanne-Claude, wrap the Berlin Reichstag in silver fabric.

1977: George Lucas's *Star Wars* debuts. The movie creates a set of characters that become a sort of 20th-century mythology.

c. 1985: Brazilian street children organize the National Movement for Street Boys and Girls, an advocacy group that helps craft new child protection laws.

1999: The US Supreme Court declares that schools may be liable for failing to stop student-on-student sexual harassment.

c. 1978: The Citicorp bank builds a network of automated teller machines, which become popular for conducting basic transactions.

1983: The Internet is established to link computer users worldwide and enable them to share data; E-mail is a primary use.

1999: As the world population passes the 6 billion mark, a study is issued that projects a crisis in 2100 if the current rate of growth is not slowed.

1975: Eighteen nations adopt the Mediterranean Action Plan, an agreement designed to limit pollution of the Mediterranean Sea.

1983: The Green Party enters the West German parliament with 27 members. It is the first new party in the Bundestag (Federal Diet) in three decades.

1998: The Brazilian government announces that it will set aside 25 million ha (62 million ac) of the Amazon rain forest for conservation.

1976: Two unmanned US spacecraft land on Mars and begin investigating its atmosphere and soil. No evidence of life is detected.

1985: The wreckage of the *Titanic* is discovered at a depth of about (3,963 m (13,000 ft) by a team of oceanographers led by Robert Ballard. The ship sank in 1912.

1999: The American unmanned satellite Chandra X-ray Observatory is launched. It transmits highly detailed images of the universe.

1980: South African writer Nadine Gordimer publishes her short-story collection *A Soldier's Embrace*. She wins the Nobel Prize for Literature in 1991.

1988: Anglo-Indian novelist Salman Rushdie publishes his controversial novel *The Satanic Verses*. After being condemned to death by Iranian Muslim clerics, he retreats into hiding.

1976: The first known outbreak of the Ebola virus, in Zaire, causes hundreds of deaths through severe hemorrhaging.

1981: The Centers for Disease Control recognizes AIDS as a new disease.

2000: The first-ever analysis of the world's health care systems is conducted, with France's being found the best in the world.

c. 1980: The compact disc begins to appear in record stores. Within a decade the small, digital discs all but replace phonograph records and radically improve the quality of music recording.

1995: The death of guitarist Jerry Garcia marks the end of an era for the Grateful Dead, one of the most long lived and iconoclastic groups in rock music.

1976: The Aboriginal Land Rights Act recognizes Australian Aborigine land rights, especially over territory with particular religious significance.

1984: South African Anglican archbishop Desmond Tutu is awarded the Nobel Prize for Peace for his work in opposition to apartheid.

1998: Millions of Hindus make pilgrimages to the holy city of Haridwar, India, to bathe in the Ganges River in celebration of the Kumbh Mela.

1975: Polish-born mathematician Benoit Mandelbrot discovers fractals.

1984: DNA fingerprinting, based on scientific analysis of individuals' genetic makeup, is developed by British geneticist Alec Jeffreys.

2000: The rise of genetically modified plants draws heated debates over possible dangers.

1976: At the Summer Olympics in Montreal, Romanian gymnast Nadia Comaneci is the first to achieve a perfect score of 10 in an Olympic gymnastic event, receiving seven such scores during the competition.

1989: Wayne Gretzky breaks Gordie Howe's National Hockey League all-time scoring record (1,850 points). He finishes his career in 1999 with 2,857 points.

1976: Steven Jobs and Steve Wozniak found Apple Computer Inc., the first company devoted to selling personal computers. The Apple II goes on sale in 1977.

1986: Explosions at the nuclear power plant at Chernobyl, Ukraine, bring about the worst nuclear reactor accident in history.

1999: The Dow Jones industrial average stock index tops the 10,000 mark, partially on the strength of Internet stocks.

1977: In Argentina, mothers of "disappeared" political prisoners begin a series of vigils.

1990: In Saudi Arabia, women drive cars in Riyadh to protest laws preventing them from operating motor vehicles. They are imprisoned and fired from their jobs.

2000 – The Present

Architecture	**2000:** Green Architecture, a movement to construct buildings that are environmentally friendly, gains in popularity around the world, especially in Europe.	**2001:** New York's World Trade Center towers collapse following the September 11 terrorist attacks.
Art	**2000:** The Tate Modern art museum opens in a converted power station on the South Bank of the Thames.	**2001:** The Art Institute of Chicago and the Van Gogh Museum, Amsterdam, organize *Van Gogh and Gauguin: The Studio of the South*, a show that explores the impact Vincent van Gogh and Paul Gauguin had on each other.
Childhood	**2000:** At the World Education Forum, it is reported that some 113 million children, most of whom are girls, do not have access to primary education.	**2001:** The film *Harry Potter and the Sorcerer's Stone* ("*Philosopher's Stone*" in the international release) translates J.K. Rowling's best-selling 1997 story to the screen.
Daily Life	**2000:** Anxiety over computer system problems associated with the rollover to the year 2000—the so-called "Y2K Bug"—proves unfounded.	**2001:** George W. Bush is sworn in as the 43rd president of the US after defeating Al Gore in one of the country's most heated and controversial elections.
Ecology	**2000:** In an effort to protect the Amazonian forest and its wildlife, Peru doubles the size of the Bahuaja-Sonene National Park. Much of the added area had been previously marked for oil drilling.	**2002:** Eugene Odum, the father of modern ecology, dies. His *Fundamentals of Ecology* (1953) made "ecosystems" a household word.
Exploration	**2000:** NASA's Mars Global Surveyor spacecraft finds evidence suggesting water flowed on Mars in the relatively recent past.	**2001:** The Near Earth Asteroid Rendezvous probe becomes the first spacecraft to land on an asteroid.
Literature	**2000:** Peruvian Mario Vargas Llosa produces *La fiesta del chivo* (*The Feast of the Goat*); many scholars consider it Latin America's finest novel to date.	**2002:** Russian writer Vladimir Sorokin faces pornography charges for scenes in his 1999 satiric novel *Goluboe salo* (*Blue Lard*).
Medicine		**2001:** Anonymous letters carrying spores of anthrax arrive at print and broadcast media offices on the US East Coast. More than 20 confirmed cases and several deaths occur as a result.
Music	**2000:** The Experience Music Project, a rock and roll museum, opens in Seattle WA to much fanfare.	**2001:** Conductor Daniel Barenboim sets off a furor in Jerusalem by presenting the Prelude to Richard Wagner's *Tristan und Isolde* as a concert encore. Wagner's works have been traditionally banned in Israel.
Religion	**2000:** Many denominations struggle with ordination for women and homosexuals as well as recognition of same-sex unions.	**2002:** Sexual abuse of children and teens by Roman Catholic clergy surfaces as a global scandal.
Science	**2000:** The 10-year Human Genome Project finishes early as researchers begin to publish details of human genes.	**2001:** Scientists report findings that suggest the Earth was struck by an asteroid some 250 million years ago, triggering volcanic eruptions that caused the worst extinction in the planet's history.
Sports	**2000:** With his win at the British Open, American golfer Tiger Woods becomes the youngest player to win the sport's four major championships.	**2001:** NASCAR driver Dale Earnhardt dies after crashing during the final lap of the Daytona 500.
Technology	**2000:** An e-mail virus, known as the Love Bug, sweeps through much of the world, causing many businesses to shut down their e-mail systems.	**2002:** After 77 hours in a flooded mineshaft in Pennsylvania, 9 miners emerge safely through a drilled passage.
Women	**2000:** Sirimavo Bandaranaike of Sri Lanka, the world's first female prime minister, retires in August.	**2001:** Hillary Clinton is sworn in as a New York senator, becoming the first American first lady to win elected office.

The World

The information about the countries of the world that follows has been assembled and analyzed by Encyclopædia Britannica editors from hundreds of private, national, and international sources. Included are all the sovereign states of the world as well as the major dependent, or nonsovereign, areas. The historical background sketches have been adapted, augmented, and updated from *Britannica Concise Encyclopedia* (2002), the statistical sections from *Britannica World Data,* which is published annually as part of *Britannica Book of the Year.* The section called "Recent Developments" also has been adapted from material appearing in recent issues of the yearbook, as well as from other sources inside and outside Britannica. The locator maps have been prepared by Britannica's Cartography Department, and the recommended Web sites are from Britannica Online.

All information is the latest available to Britannica, although it must be understood that in many cases it takes several years for the various countries or agencies to gather and process data, such that the most current data available will normally be dated several years earlier.

A few definitions of terms used in the articles may be useful. **Gross domestic product** (GDP) is the total value of goods and services produced in a country during a given accounting period, usually a year. Unless otherwise noted, the value is given in current prices of the year indicated. **Gross national product** (GNP) is essentially GDP plus income from foreign transactions minus payments made outside the country. **Balance of payments** is a financial statement for a given period showing the balance among: (1) transactions in goods, services, and income between that country and the rest of the world, (2) changes in ownership or valuation of that country's monetary gold, special drawing rights (a unit of account utilized by the International Monetary Fund to denominate monetary reserves available under a quota system to IMF members to maintain the value of their national currency unit in international transactions), and claims on and liabilities to the rest of the world, and (3) unrequited transfers and counterpart entries needed (in an accounting sense) to balance transactions and changes among any of the foregoing types of exchange that are not mutually offsetting. There are slight differences in accounting methods among various countries so balance of payments figures may not be completely comparable from one country to another.

The symbol $ indicates US dollars unless otherwise indicated. A few helpful **conversions** for the statistical section are given at the foot of the left-hand pages.

Afghanistan

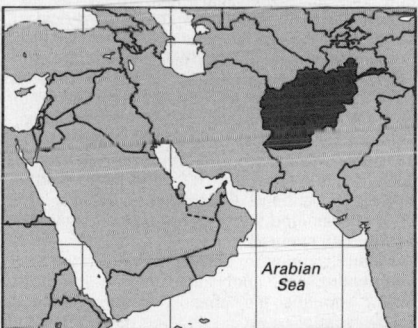

Arabian
Sea

Official name: Islamic State of Afghanistan. **Form of government:** interim regime. **Head of state and government:** President Hamid Karzai (from 13 Jun 2002). **Capital:** Kabul. **Official languages:** Dari (Persian); Pashto. **Official religion:** Islam. **Monetary unit:** 1 afghani (Af) = 100 puls (puli); valuation (28 Jun 2002) $1 = Af 4,750 (black market rate in April 2000. $1 = Af 64,000; most currency transactions are conducted with the Pakistan rupee or US dollar).

Demography

Area. 251,825 sq mi, 652,225 sq km. **Population** (2001): 26,813,000 (includes Afghan refugees [estimated to number about 2.0 million in Pakistan and about 2.0 million in Iran in August 2001]). **Density** (2001): persons per sq mi 106.5, persons per sq km 41.1. **Urban** (1999): 21.5%. **Sex distribution** (2000): male 51.31%; female 48.69%. **Age breakdown**

(2000): under 15, 43.8%; 15–29, 25.4%; 30–44, 16.8%; 45–59, 9.1%; 60–74, 4.2%; 75 and over, 0.7%. **Ethnolinguistic composition** (early 1990s): Pashtun 52.4%; Tajik 20.4%; Hazara 8.8%; Uzbek 8.8%; Chahar Aimak 2.8%; Turkmen 1.9%; other 4.9%. **Religious affiliation** (2000): Sunni Muslim 89.2%; Shi'i Muslim 8.9%; Zoroastrian 1.4%; Hindu 0.4%; other 0.1%. **Major cities** (1988): Kabul 2,454,000 (1999 estimate for urban agglomeration); Kandahar (Qandahar) 225,500; Herat 177,300; Mazar-e Sharif 130,600; Jalalabad 55,000. **Location:** southern Asia, bordering Uzbekistan, Tajikistan, China, Pakistan, Iran, and Turkmenistan.

Vital statistics

Birth rate per 1,000 population (2000): 41.8 (world avg. 22.5). **Death rate** per 1,000 population (2000): 18.0 (world avg. 9.0). **Natural increase rate** per 1,000 population (2000): 23.8 (world avg. 13.5). **Total fertility rate** (avg. births per childbearing woman; 2000): 5.9. **Life expectancy** at birth (2000): male 46.6 years; female 45.1 years.

National economy

Budget (1997–98). *Revenue*: primarily from narcotics trade. *Expenditures*: more than 90% of revenue used to finance war effort. **Gross national product** (1998): $6,738,000,000 ($280 per capita). **Public debt** (external, outstanding; 1993): $5,381,000,000. **Production** (metric tons except as noted). *Agriculture, forestry, fishing* (1999): wheat 2,834,000, rice 450,000, grapes 330,000, barley 300,000, corn (maize) 240,000, potatoes 235,000; livestock (number of live animals) 14,300,000 sheep, 2,200,000 goats, 1,500,000 cattle; roundwood (1998) 8,091,000 cu m; fish catch (1997)

1,250. *Mining and quarrying* (1997): salt 13,000; copper (metal content) 5,000. *Manufacturing* (by production value in Af '000,000; 1988–89): food products 4,019; leather and fur products 2,678; textiles 1,760; printing and publishing 1,070; industrial chemicals (including fertilizers) 1,053. *Energy production (consumption):* electricity (kW-hr; 1996) 593,000,000 (703,000,000); coal (metric tons; 1996) 4,000 (4,000); petroleum products (metric tons; 1996) none (254,000); natural gas (cu m; 1996) 160,169,000 (160,169,000). **Population economically active** (1994): total 5,557,000; activity rate of total population 29.4% (participation rates: female 9.0%; unemployed [1995] c. 8%). **Tourism:** receipts (1997) $1,000,000; expenditures (1997) $1,000,000. **Land use** (1994): forested 2.9%; meadows and pastures 46.0%; agricultural and under permanent cultivation 12.4%; other 38.7%.

Foreign trade

Imports (1997-c.i.f.): $525,000,000 (1995; food 18.8%, machinery and transport equipment 15.2%, unspecified commodities 46.5%). *Major import sources* (1997): Singapore 19.2%; Japan 18.5%; China 6.9%; India 4.8%; Russia 4.0%. **Exports** (1997-f.o.b.): $149,000,000 (1995; carpets and rugs 54.3%, dried fruits and nuts 15.6%). *Major export destinations* (1997): Pakistan 20.1%; Belgium-Luxembourg 8.7%; France 7.4%; United States 6.7%; Japan 6.0%.

Transport and communications

Transport. *Railroads* (1997): length 16 mi (25 km). *Roads* (1996): total length 21,000 km (paved 13%). *Vehicles* (1996): passenger cars 31,000; trucks and buses 25,000. *Air transport* (Ariana Afghan Airlines only): passenger-km (1995) 276,000,000; metric ton-km cargo 38,000,000; airports (1996) 3. **Communications.** Daily newspaper circulation (1996): 113,000 (5 units per 1,000 persons); Radio receivers (1997): 2,750,000 (116 units per 1,000 persons); Television receivers (1997): 270,000 (11 units per 1,000 persons) (officially outlawed between 1998 and 2001); Telephone main lines (1999): 29,000 (1.2 units per 1,000 persons).

Education and health

Educational attainment (1980). Population age 25 and over having: no formal schooling 88.5%; some primary education 6.8%; complete primary 0.3%; some secondary 1.2%; postsecondary 3.2%. **Literacy** (1995): Total population age 15 and over literate 31.5%; males 47.2%; females 15.1%. **Health:** physicians (1997) 2.555 (1 per 9,091 persons); hospital beds, n.a.; infant mortality rate (2000) 149.3. **Food** (1999): daily per capita caloric intake 1,755 (vegetable products 79%, animal products 21%); 72% of FAO recommended minimum requirement.

Military

Total active duty personnel (1999): no national military from 1992 until April 2002; UN International Security and Assistance Force (March 2002) 4,900.

Did you know? The Khyber Pass near Afghanistan's eastern frontier with Pakistan has historically served as the prinicipal gateway between Central Asia and the Indian subcontinent.

Background

The area was part of the Persian empire in the 6th century BC and was conquered by Alexander the Great in the 4th century BC. Hindu influence entered with the Hephthalites and Sasanians; Islam became entrenched during the rule of the Saffarids, c. AD 870. Afghanistan was divided between the Mughal empire of India and the Safavid empire of Persia until the 18th century, when other Persians under Nadir Shah took control. Great Britain and Russia fought several wars in the area in the 19th century. From the 1930s the country had a stable monarchy; it was overthrown in the 1970s. The rebels' intention was to institute Marxist reforms, but the reforms sparked rebellion, and troops from the USSR invaded to establish order. Afghan guerrillas prevailed, and the Soviet Union withdrew in 1988–89. In 1992 rebel factions overthrew the government and established an Islamic republic, but fighting among factions continued. In 1996 the government was taken over by the Taliban faction.

Recent Developments

The terrorist attacks in the United States on 11 Sep 2001 set off a chain reaction that reversed fortunes and produced Afghanistan's first orderly change of government in decades. A year that saw the rigid control of the Taliban on the verge of total victory also witnessed its military defeat and political marginalization.

Blaming Saudi-born militant Osama Bin Laden for the 11 September attacks, the US turned its military wrath against the Taliban for protecting Bin Laden. A bombing campaign begun by US and British forces on 7 October was aimed at Taliban military targets and coordinated to support an offensive by the Northern Alliance, an anti-Taliban coalition of Uzbeks, Tajiks, and Hazaras—the three largest ethnic minorities of northern Afghanistan.

Taliban fighters were pushed out of Mazar-e Sharif and Kunduz in the north with significant losses, and on 12 November they abandoned Kabul. Soon the Taliban seat of power in Kandahar had been surrendered, and many Taliban had disappeared into the countryside, fled to Pakistan, or shifted their allegiance. US bombing continued in the mountainous Tora Bora area near the border with Pakistan, where Bin Laden and many of his al-Qaeda fighters were thought to have fled.

International moves to solve the resulting political crisis focused on avoiding the chaos and destruction that had followed the mujahideen takeover from the communist government of Mohammad Najibullah in 1992. On 27 Nov 2001, a UN-sponsored conference in Bonn, Germany, convened to settle on an interim government to replace the Taliban. The largest share of delegates represented the Northern Alliance, whose political leader, Burhanuddin Rabbani, had retained international recognition even after being driven from Kabul in 1996. Supporters of former king

---

1 metric ton = about 1.1 short tons;   1 kilometer = 0.6 mi (statute);   1 metric ton-km cargo = about 0.68 short ton-mi cargo;   c.i.f.: cost, insurance, and freight;   f.o.b.: free on board

Zahir Shah also participated. The result was an agreement that Hamid Karzai, a Pashtun tribal leader and supporter of the former king, would lead an interim administration for six months, when a *loya jirga*, a traditional Afghan assembly of notables, would choose a new government. Karzai and a cabinet that included two women were installed in a peaceful ceremony joined by outgoing President Rabbani and most of the country's ethnic and political factions. On 13 Jun 2002 Karzai was elected president.

Internet resources: <www.afghan-web.com/politics>

Albania

Official name: Republika e Shqipërisë (Republic of Albania). **Form of government:** unitary multiparty republic with one legislative house (Assembly [140]). **Chief of state:** President Rexhep Meidani (from 1997). **Head of government:** Prime Minister Pandeli Majko (from 22 Feb 2002). **Capital:** Tirana (Tiranë). **Official language:** Albanian. **Official religion:** none. **Monetary unit:** 1 lek = 100 qindars; valuation (28 Jun 2002) $1 = 140 leks.

Demography

Area: 11,082 sq mi, 28,703 sq km. **Population** (2001): 3,091,000. **Density** (2001): persons per sq mi 278.9, persons per sq km 107.7. **Urban** (1999): 41.0%. **Sex distribution** (2000): male 48.90%; female 51.10%. **Age breakdown** (2000): under 15, 30.2%; 15–29, 26.6%; 30–44, 19.8%; 45–59, 13.2%; 60–74, 7.9%; 75 and over, 2.3%. **Ethnic composition** (1989): Albanian 98.0%; Greek 1.8%; Macedonian 0.2%. **Religious affiliation** (2000): Muslim 38.8%; Roman Catholic 16.7%; nonreligious 16.6%; Albanian Orthodox 10.4%; other Orthodox 5.7%; other 11.8%. **Major cities** (1991): Tirana (1999) 279,000; Durrës 86,900; Shkodër 83,700; Elbasan 83,200. **Location:** southeastern Europe, bordering Yugoslavia, Macedonia, Greece, and the Mediterranean Sea.

Vital statistics

Birth rate per 1,000 (2000): 19.5 (world avg. 22.5). **Death rate** per 1,000 (2000): 6.0 (world avg. 9.0). **Natural increase rate** per 1,000 (2000): 13.5 (world avg. 13.5). **Total fertility rate** (avg. births per childbearing woman; 2000): 2.4. **Marriage rate** per 1,000 (1990): 8.9. **Divorce rate** per 1,000 (1990): 0.8. **Life expectancy** at birth (2000): male 68.8 years; female 74.9 years.

National economy

Budget (2000). *Revenue*: 120,588,000,000 leks (taxes 86.3%, of which value-added tax 31.6%, import duties and export taxes 18.8%, income tax 11.9%, social security contributions 11.2%, other 12.8%; nontax revenue 13.7%). *Expenditures*: 169,423,000,000 leks (current expenditure 79.3%, of which social security 22.1%, interest on debt 17.5%, wages 15.2%, government operations 11.4%, other 13.1%; capital expenditure 20.7%). **Public debt** (1999): $849,100,000. **Production** (metric tons except as noted). *Agriculture, forestry, fishing* (2000): cereals 580,000; vegetables 444,000 (mainly beans, peas, onions, tomatoes, cabbage, eggplants, and carrots), potatoes 180,000; livestock (number of live animals) 1,941,000 sheep, 1,120,000 goats, 720,000 cattle; roundwood (2000) 409,000 cu m; fish catch (1999) 3,055. *Mining and quarrying* (1999): chromium ore 79,000; copper ore 34,000. *Manufacturing* (1999): cement 106,000; bread 67,000; rolled steel 20,000; cheese 7,000; beer 91,000 hectolitres; wine 10,000 hectolitres. *Energy production (consumption)*: electricity (kW-hr; 1999) 5,396,000,000 (5,396,000,000); coal (metric tons; 1996) 111,000 (91,000); crude petroleum (barrels; 1999) 2,368,000 (3,257,000 [1996]); petroleum products (metric tons; 1996) 282,000 (363,000); natural gas (cu m; 1996) 22,911,000 (22,911,000). **Gross national product** (1999): $3,146,000,000 ($930 per capita). **Population economically active** (2000): total 1,940,000; activity rate of total population 57.0% (participation rates [1998]: ages 15–64, 69.9%; female 49.9%; unemployed 16.8%). **Household income and expenditure.** Average household size (1998): 3.9; annual income per rural household (1989) 80,835 leks; sources of income: wages 53.0%, transfers from relatives abroad 21.5%, social insurance 11.4%. **Tourism** (1999): receipts $211,000,000; expenditures $12,000,000.

Foreign trade

Imports (2000): $1,070,000,000 (manufactured goods 23.8%; machinery and transport equipment 21.6%; food and beverages 19.8%; mineral fuels 9.0%; chemicals 7.0%; crude materials 1.4%). *Major import sources*: Italy 36.2%; Greece 28.0%; Germany 5.5%; Turkey 5.5%. **Exports** (2000): $256,000,000 (miscellaneous manufactured articles 68.0%; manufactured goods 12.1%; crude materials 8.7%; food and beverages 6.6%). *Major export destinations*: Italy 70.3%; Greece 12.9%; Germany 6.6%.

Transport and communications

Transport. *Railroads* (1998): length 416 mi (670 km); passenger-km 116,000,000; metric ton-km cargo 25,000. *Roads* (1998): total length 18,000 km (paved 30%). *Vehicles* (1998): passenger cars 90,766; trucks and buses 34,378. *Air transport* (1997): passenger-km 3,519,000; short ton-mi 223,000, metric ton-km 325,000; airports (1999) with scheduled flights 1. **Communications** Total units (units per 1,000 persons) Daily newspaper circulation (1996): 116,000 (37); Radio receivers (1997): 810,000 (259); Television receivers (1998): 430,000 (137); Telephone main lines (1999): 140,392 (45); Cellular telephone subscribers (1998): 11,008 (3.5); Internet users (1999): 2,500 (0.8).

Education and health

Educational attainment (1989). Percentage of pop. age 10 and over having: primary education 65.3%; secondary 29.1%; higher 5.6%. **Literacy** (1989): total pop. age 10 and over literate 91.8%; males 95.5%; females 88.0%. **Health** (1995): physicians 4,848 (1 per 657 persons); hospital beds (1994) 10,200 (1 per 333 persons); infant mortality rate per 1,000 live births (2000) 41.3. **Food** (1999): daily per capita caloric intake 2,717 (vegetable products 73%, animal products 27%); 113% of FAO recommended minimum requirement.

Military

Total active duty personnel (2000): 47,000 (army 85.1%, navy 5.3%, air force 9.6%). **Military expenditure as percentage of GNP** (1997): 1.4% (world 2.6%); per capita expenditure $19.

Background

The Albanians are descended from the Illyrians, an ancient Indo-European people who lived in central Europe and migrated south by the beginning of the Iron Age. Of the two major Illyrian migrating groups, the Ghegs settled in the north and the Tosks in the south, along with Greek colonizers. The area was under Roman rule by the 1st century BC; after AD 395 it was connected administratively to Constantinople. Turkish invasion began in the 14th century and continued into the 15th century; though the national hero, Skanderbeg, was able to resist them for a time, after his death (1468) the Turks consolidated their rule. The country achieved independence in 1912 and was admitted into the League of Nations in 1920. It was briefly a republic 1925–28, then became a monarchy under Zog I, whose initial alliance with Benito Mussolini led to Italy's invasion of Albania in 1939. After the war a socialist government under Enver Hoxha was installed, and gradually Albania cut itself off from the nonsocialist international community, and eventually from all nations, including China, its last political ally. By 1990 economic hardship had produced antigovernment demonstrations, and in 1992 a non-Communist government was elected and Albania's international isolation ended. In 1997 it plunged into chaos, brought on with the collapse of pyramid investment schemes. In 1999 it was overwhelmed by ethnic Albanians seeking refuge from Yugoslavia.

Recent Developments

The fourth democratic general elections in Albania's history were held in June–July 2001. The Socialist Party (PS—the former Communists), with a reform-oriented program, gained an absolute majority in the parliament with 73 of the 140 seats. The opposition coalition Union for Victory (BpF), dominated by the Democratic Party (PD) of former president Sali Berisha, received only 46 seats. The opposition had been split since 2000, when the New Democrat Party split off from the PD.

Internet resources: <www.albania.co.uk>

Algeria

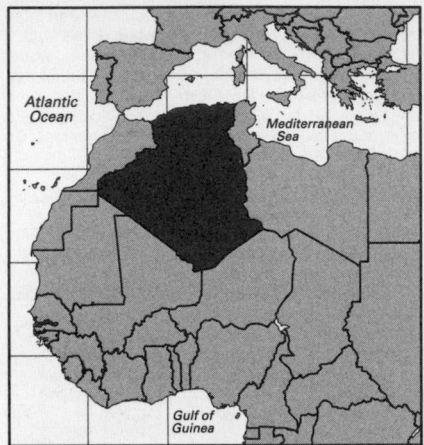

Official name: Al-Jumhuriyah al-Jaza'iriyah ad-Dimuqratiyah ash-Sha'biyah (Arabic) (People's Democratic Republic of Algeria). **Form of government:** multiparty republic with two legislative bodies (Council of the Nation [144] [includes 48 nonelected seats appointed by the president]; National People's Assembly [380]). **Chief of state:** President Abdelaziz Bouteflika (from 1999). **Head of government:** Prime Minister Ali Benflis (from 2000). **Capital:** Algiers. **Official language:** Arabic. **Official religion:** Islam. **Monetary unit:** 1 Algerian dinar (DA) = 100 centimes; valuation (28 Jun 2002) $1 = DA 121.99.

Demography

Area: 919,595 sq mi, 2,381,741 sq km. **Population** (2001): 30,821,000. **Density** (2001): persons per sq mi 33.5, persons per sq km 12.9. **Urban** (1998): 80.8%. **Sex distribution** (1998): male 50.56%; female 49.44%. **Age breakdown** (1998): under 15, 36.2%; 15–29, 30.6%; 30–44, 17.7%; 45–59, 8.9%; 60–74, 5.1%; 75 and over, 1.5%. **Ethnic composition** (2000): Algerian Arab 59.1%; Berber 26.2%, of which Arabized Berber 3.0%; Bedouin Arab 14.5%; other 0.2%. **Religious affiliation** (2000): Muslim 99.7%, of which Sunni 99.1%, Ibadiyah 0.6%; Christian 0.3%. **Major cities** (1998): Algiers 1,519,570; Oran 692,516; Constantine 462,187; Annaba 348,554; Batna 242,514. **Location:** northern Africa, bordering the Mediterranean Sea, Tunisia, Libya, Niger, Mali, Mauritania, Western Sahara, and Morocco.

Vital statistics

Birth rate per 1,000 pop. (2000): 19.8 (world avg. 22.5). **Death rate** per 1,000 pop. (2000): 5.5 (world avg. 9.0). **Natural increase rate** per 1,000 pop. (2000): 14.3 (world avg. 13.5). **Total fertility rate** (avg. births per childbearing woman; 2000): 2.8. **Marriage rate** per 1,000 pop. (2000): 5.8. **Life expectancy** at birth (2000): male 68.3 years; female 71.0 years.

1 metric ton = about 1.1 short tons;   1 kilometer = 0.6 mi (statute);   1 metric ton-km cargo = about 0.68 short ton-mi cargo;   c.i.f.: cost, insurance, and freight;   f.o.b.: free on board

National economy

Budget (1997). *Revenue*: DA 926,600,000,000 (taxes on hydrocarbons 63.9%, value-added taxes 16.0%). *Expenditures*: DA 845,100,000,000 (current expenditure 69.4%, development expenditure 30.6%). **Land use** (1994): forested 1.6%; meadows and pastures 13.3%; agricultural and under permanent cultivation 3.4%; other (mostly desert) 81.7%. **Production** (metric tons except as noted). *Agriculture, forestry, fishing* (1999): wheat 1,503,000, potatoes 1,100,000, tomatoes 790,000; livestock (number of live animals) 18,000,000 sheep, 3,200,000 goats; roundwood (1997) 2,735,000 cu m; fish catch (1997) 99,332. *Mining and quarrying* (1999): iron ore (gross weight) 2,330,000; mercury 12,000 flasks. *Manufacturing* (value added in US$'000,000; 1995): iron and steel 634; food products 622; fabricated metal products 518. *Energy production (consumption)*: electricity (kW-hr; 1996) 20,654,000,000 (20,378,000,000); coal (metric tons; 1996) 22,000 (1,202,000); crude petroleum (barrels; 2000) 307,091,000 ([1996] 165,220,000); petroleum products (metric tons; 1996) 39,628,000 (7,510,000); natural gas (cu m; 2000) 89,300,000,000 (25,981,000,000). **Household income and expenditure.** Average household size (1998) 7.1; sources of income (1997): wages and salaries 43.2%, self-employment 39.1%, transfers 17.7%; expenditure (1995): food and beverages 58.5%, transportation and communications 9.5%, clothing and footwear 13.9%, health 4.4%, other 13.7%. **Gross national product** (1999): $46,548,000,000 ($1,550 per capita). **Population economically active** (1994): total 6,814,000; activity rate of pop. 24.8% (participation rates [1987] ages 15–64, 44.3%; female 9.2%; unemployed ([February 2000] 29.8%). **Public debt** (external, outstanding; 1999): $25,913,000,000. **Tourism**: receipts from visitors (1998) $24,000,000; expenditures by nationals abroad (1997) $64,000,000.

Foreign trade

Imports (1996-c.i.f.): $9,102,000,000 (food 27.5%, machinery and apparatus 15.8%, transport equipment 7.0%). *Major import sources* (1997): France 28.3%; Italy 8.7%; US 8.6%; Spain 7.4%; Brazil 5.3%. **Exports** (1996-f.o.b.): $13,586,000,000 (crude and refined petroleum 61.7%, natural gas 31.7%, dates 0.5%). *Major export destinations* (1997): Italy 19.5%; US 17.3%; France 14.2%; Spain 10.2%; The Netherlands 5.6%.

Transport and communications

Transport. *Railroads* (1997): route length 2,451 mi, 3,945 km; (1996) passenger-km 1,820,000,000; metric ton-km cargo 2,139,000,000. *Roads* (1995): total length 63,643 mi, 102,424 km (paved 69%). *Vehicles* (1996): passenger cars 725,000; trucks and buses 780,000. *Air transport* (1998-Air Algérie): passenger-km 2,901,000,000; metric ton-km cargo 18,285,000; airports (1996) 28. **Communications** Total units (units per 1,000 population). Daily newspaper circulation (1996): 1,080,000 (38); Radio receivers (1997): 7,100,000 (253); Television receivers (1999): 3,300,000 (110); Telephone main lines (1999): 1,600,000 (53); Cellular telephone subscribers (1999): 72,000 (2); Personal computers (1999): 180,000 (6); Internet users (1999): 20,000 (0.7).

Education and health

Educational attainment (1998). Percentage of economically active pop. age 6 and over having: no formal schooling 30.1%; primary education 29.9%; lower secondary 20.7%; upper secondary 13.4%; higher 4.3%; other 1.6%. **Literacy** (1998): total pop. age 10 and over literate 15,314,109 (68.1%); males literate 8,650,719 (76.3%); females literate 6,663,392 (59.7%). **Health** (1996): physicians 27,650 (1 per 1,015 persons); hospital beds 34,544 (1 per 812 persons); infant mortality rate per 1,000 live births (2000) 51.1. **Food** (1999): daily per capita caloric intake 2,965 (vegetable products 90%, animal products 10%); 124% of FAO recommended minimum requirement.

Military

Total active duty personnel (1999): 122,000 (army 86.1%, navy 5.7%, air force 8.2%). **Military expenditure as percentage of GNP** (1997): 3.9% (world 2.6%); per capita expenditure $61.

Did you know? Algeria is Africa's only producer of mercury and produces about one-tenth of the world's supply.

Background

Phoenician traders settled the area early in the 1st millennium BC; several centuries later the Romans invaded, and by AD 40 they had control of the Mediterranean coast. The fall of Rome in the 5th century led to invasion by the Vandals, and later by Byzantium. The Islamic invasion began in the 7th century; by 711 all of northern Africa was under the control of the Umayyad caliphate. Several Islamic Berber empires followed, most prominently the Almoravid (c. 1054–1130), which extended its domain to Spain, and the Almohad (c. 1130–1269). The Barbary Coast pirates, operating in the area, had menaced Mediterranean trade for centuries, and France seized this pretext to enter Algeria in 1830. By 1847 France had established control in the region, and by the late 19th century had instituted civil rule. Popular movements resulted in the bloody Algerian War (1954–62); independence was achieved following a referendum in 1962. In the 1990s Islamic fundamentalists opposing the military brought Algeria to a state of virtual civil war.

Recent Developments

Algeria has continued to suffer from the chronic and endemic violence of the past decade. Though official sources claimed that 3,000 people had died from terrorism in 2000, private military sources admitted that the number of dead was three times as high; the killing continued into 2001 with the Armed Islamic Group and the Salafist Group for Preaching and Combat attacking civilians and military targets. Following the 11 September attacks in the US, Algiers offered to hand over details of the Algerian nationals involved in the al-Qaeda movement.

Internet resources: <www.algeria.com>

American Samoa

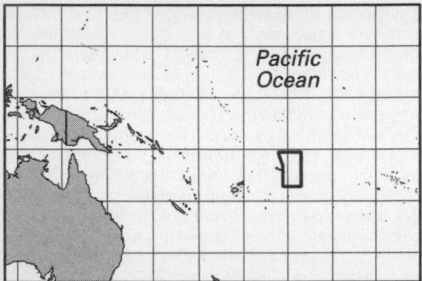

Pacific
Ocean

Official name: American Samoa (English); Amerika Samoa (Samoan). **Political status:** unincorporated and unorganized territory of the United States with two legislative houses (Senate [18]; House of Representatives [20; excluding a nonvoting representative from Swains Island]). **Chief of state:** President of the United States George W. Bush (from 2001). **Head of government:** Governor Tauese P.F. Sunia (from 1997). **Capital:** Fagatogo (legislative and judicial) and Utulei (executive), both within the Pago Pago urban agglomeration. **Official languages:** English; Samoan. **Official religion:** none. **Monetary unit:** US dollar ($) = 100 cents.

Demography

Area: 84.4 sq mi, 218.6 sq km. **Population** (2001): 58,000. **Density** (2000): persons per sq mi 769.3, persons per sq km 297.1. **Urban** (1998): 51.5%. **Sex distribution** (2000): male 50.51%; female 49.49%. **Age breakdown** (2000): under 15, 38.8%; 15–29, 24.1%; 30–44, 17.8%; 45–59, 11.7%; 60–74, 6.3%; 75 and over, 1.3%. **Ethnic composition** (1990): Samoan 88.6%; Tongan 3.7%; Caucasian 1.9%; Asian 1.8%; other 4.0%. **Religious affiliation** (1995): 4 major Protestant groups 60.1%; Roman Catholic 19.4%; Mormon 12.5%; other 8.0%. **Major villages** (1990): Tafuna 5,174; Nu'uuli 3,893; Pago Pago 3,519 (urban agglomeration [1999] 14,000); Leone 3,013; Fagatogo 2,323 (within Pago Pago urban agglomeration). **Location:** group of islands in the south Pacific Ocean.

Vital statistics

Birth rate per 1,000 pop. (2000): 25.8 (world avg. 22.5). **Death rate** per 1,000 pop. (2000): 4.3 (world avg. 9.0). **Natural increase rate** per 1,000 pop. (2000): 21.5 (world avg. 13.5). **Total fertility rate** (avg. births per childbearing woman; 2000): 3.6. **Marriage rate** per 1,000 pop. (1993): 6.1. **Divorce rate** per 1,000 pop. (1993): 0.5. **Life expectancy** at birth (2000): male 70.7 years; female 79.8 years.

National economy

Budget (1992). *Revenue:* $146,905,000 (US government grants 73.5%; taxes 16.4%; insurance claims 3.5%; other 6.6%). *Expenditures:* $165,950,000 (general government 45.7%; education and culture 21.0%; health and welfare 16.0%; economic development 5.6%; public works and parks 5.1%; other 6.6%). **Gross national product** (at current market prices; 1997): $253,000,000 ($4,300 per capita). **Production** (metric tons except as noted). *Agriculture, forestry, fishing* (1999): coconuts 4,700, taros 1,500, fruits (excluding melons) 1,200; livestock (number of live animals; 1999) 10,700 pigs, 37,000 chickens; fish catch (1998) 910, of which tunas, bonitos, and billfish 865. *Manufacturing* (1994): canned tuna shipped to US 211,600,000. *Energy production (consumption):* electricity (kW-hr; 1996) 130,000,000 (130,000,000); petroleum products (metric tons; 1996) none (92,000). **Population economically active** (1994): total 16,822; activity rate of total pop. 30.5% (participation rates: ages 16–64, 51.2%; female 39.5%; unemployed [1995] 16.7%). **Household income and expenditure.** Average household size (1995) 6.3; income per household (1995): US$15,715; expenditure (1988): food and beverages 44.3%, housing and furnishings 23.4%, transportation and communications 14.9%, clothing and footwear 5.8%, other 11.6%. **Tourism:** receipts from visitors (1997) US$10,000,000; expenditures by nationals abroad (1996) US$2,000,000. **Land use** (1993): forested 70%; agricultural and under permanent cultivation 15%; other 15%.

Foreign trade

Imports (1999-c.i.f.): $452,600,000 (fish and cannery related products 57.4%, petroleum and petroleum products 10.8%, food 10.5%, manufactured goods 9.9%, transport equipment 4.3%, building materials 3.4%). *Major import sources* (1999): US 66.5%; New Zealand 9.2%; Australia 8.6%; Fiji 5.6%; Western Samoa 2.9%; Japan 1.9%; South Korea 1.4%; Taiwan 1.1%; China 0.7%. **Exports** (1999-f.o.b.): $345,100,000 (tuna in airtight containers 96.8%, finished garments 1.3%, pet food 1.2%, fish meal 0.6%). *Major export destinations:* US 100.0%.

Transport and communications

Transport. *Roads* (1991): total length 217 mi, 350 km (paved, 43%). *Vehicles* (1994): passenger cars 5,300; buses (1994) 199; motorcycles (1994) 27. *Air transport* (1990): incoming flights 4,426; incoming passengers 66,580; incoming cargo 706 metric tons; airports (1994) with scheduled flights 3. **Communications** Total units (units per 1,000 persons). Daily newspaper circulation (1996): 5,000 (85); Radio receivers (1997): 57,000 (929); Television receivers (1997): 14,000 (221); Telephone main lines (1999): 13,900 (248); Cellular telephone subscribers (1999) 2,377 (42).

Education and health

Educational attainment (1995). Percentage of pop. age 25 and over having: no formal schooling to some secondary education 32.7%; completed secondary 61.3%; higher 6.0%. **Literacy** (1990): total pop. age 10 and over literate 33,993 (99.4%); males literate 17,704 (99.4%); females literate 16,589 (99.5%). **Health** (1991): physicians 26 (1 per 1,888 persons); hospital beds (1995) 140 (1 per 4.7 persons); infant mortality rate per 1,000 live births (2000) 10.6.

1 metric ton = about 1.1 short tons;   1 kilometer = 0.6 mi (statute);   1 metric ton-km cargo = about 0.68 short ton-mi cargo;   c.i.f.: cost, insurance, and freight;   f.o.b.: free on board

Military

Military defense is the responsibility of the United States.

Background

The Samoan islands were probably inhabited by Polynesians 2,500 years ago. Dutch explorers first arrived in 1722. A haven for runaway sailors and escaped convicts, the islands were ruled by native chiefs until c. 1860. The US gained the right to establish a naval station at Pago Pago in 1878, and the US, Britain, and Germany administered a tripartite protectorate in 1889–99. The islands were ceded to the US in 1904 and 1925. The first constitution was approved in 1960, and in 1977 the territory's first elected governor took office.

Recent Developments

In 2001 the government attempted to tighten immigration controls by deporting those who were discovered to have overstayed their visas and proposing to hold the passports of visitors. It also adjusted employment laws to facilitate employment in the fish-canning and garment-manufacturing industries.

Internet resources: <http://amerikasamoa.info>

Andorra

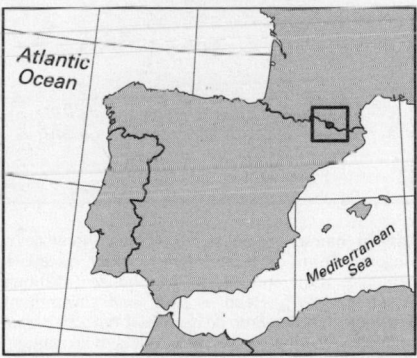

Atlantic
Ocean

Mediterranean
Sea

Official name: Principat d'Andorra (Principality of Andorra). **Form of government:** parliamentary coprincipality with one legislative house (General Council [28]). **Chiefs of state:** President of France Jacques Chirac (from 1995); Bishop of Urgell, Spain Joan Martí Alanís (from 1971). **Head of government:** Head of Government Marc Forné Molné (from 1994). **Capital:** Andorra la Vella. **Official language:** Catalan. **Official religion:** none (Roman Catholicism enjoys special recognition in accordance with Andorran tradition). **Monetary unit:** 1 euro (€) = 100 cents; valuation (28 Jun 2002) $1 = €1.01 (at conversion on 1 Jan 2002; 1€ = 166.386 Spanish pesetas [Ptas]).

Demography

Area: 181 sq mi, 468 sq km. **Population** (2001): 66,900. **Density** (2001): persons per sq mi 369.7, persons per sq km 143.0. **Urban** (1999): 93%. **Sex** distribution (2000): male 52.19%; female 47.81%. **Age breakdown** (2000): under 15, 15.4%; 15–29, 20.9%; 30–44, 29.3%; 45–59, 18.6%; 60–74, 10.5%; 75 and over, 5.3%. **Ethnic composition** (by nationality; 2000): Spanish 41.8%; Andorran 34.5%; Portuguese 10.5%; French 6.6%; British 1.4%; Moroccan 0.7%; German 0.5%; other 4.0%. **Religious affiliation** (2000): Roman Catholic 89.1%; other Christian 4.3%; Muslim 0.6%; Hindu 0.5%; nonreligious 5.0%; other 0.5%. **Major urban areas** (2000): Andorra la Vella 21,189; Les Escaldes–Engordany 15,299; Encamp 10,595. **Location:** southwestern Europe, between France and Spain.

Vital statistics

Birth rate per 1,000 population (1999): 12.6 (world avg. 22.5). **Death rate** per 1,000 population (1999): 3.1 (world avg. 9.0). **Natural increase rate** per 1,000 population (1999): 9.5 (world avg. 13.5). **Total fertility rate** (avg. births per childbearing woman; 2000): 1.2. **Marriage rate** per 1,000 population (1998): 3.2. **Life expectancy** at birth (2000): male 80.6 years; female 86.6 years.

National economy

Budget (1997). *Revenue*: Ptas 50,720,000,000 (extraordinary income 45.9%, indirect taxes 41.1%, property income 7.3%). *Expenditures*: Ptas 50,720,000,000 (extraordinary expenditures 43.0%, current expenditures 30.8%, development expenditures 26.2%). **Production.** *Agriculture* (1997): tobacco 1,047 metric tons; other traditional crops include hay, potatoes, and grapes; livestock (number of live animals; 1997) 2,021 sheep (but large herds of sheep and goats from Spain and France feed in Andorra in the summer), 1,187 cattle, 738 horses. *Quarrying*: small amounts of marble are quarried. *Manufacturing* (value of recorded exports in Ptas '000; 1997): electrical machinery and apparatus 1,397,000; motor vehicles and parts 947,000; newspapers and periodicals 743,000; clothing 632,000; toys and games 459,000. *Energy production (consumption)*: electricity (kW-hr; 1997) 116,000,000 ([1999] 393,000,000). **Tourism** (1999): 9,422,000 visitors; number of hotels 271. **Population economically active** (1997): total 29,088; activity rate of total population 44.5% (participation rates: ages 15–64, 60.9%; female, n.a.; unemployed [1998] unofficially, none [the restricted size of the indigenous labor force has in the near past necessitated immigration to serve the tourist trade]). **Gross national product** (1998): $1,110,000,000 ($16,930 per capita). **Land use** (1994): forested 22.0%; meadows and pastures 56.0%; agricultural and under permanent cultivation 2.0%; other 20.0%. **Household expenditure** (1997): food, beverages, and tobacco 25.5%, housing and energy 19.4%, transportation 17.7%, clothing and footwear 9.2%.

Foreign trade

Imports (1997): Ptas 157,054,000,000 (food, beverages, and tobacco 30.2%; machinery and apparatus 14.0%; chemicals and chemical products 8.7%; transport equipment 7.7%; textiles and wearing apparel 7.6%; photographic and optical goods and watches and clocks 4.5%). *Major import sources*: Spain 40.2%; France 29.2%; United Kingdom 5.7%; United States 4.9%; Germany 4.6%. **Exports** (1997):

Ptas 7,041,000,000 (electrical machinery and apparatus 19.8%; motor vehicles and parts 13.4%; newspapers, books, and periodicals 10.6%; clothing 9.0%; toys and games 6.5%). *Major export destinations*: Spain 47.4%; France 41.6%; Belgium 3.4%; The Netherlands 2.6%.

Transport and communications

Transport. Railroads: none; however, both French and Spanish railways stop near the border. *Roads* (1994): total length 167 mi, 269 km (paved 74%). *Vehicles* (1996): passenger cars 35,358; trucks and buses 4,238. *Airports* (1997) with scheduled flights: none. **Communications.** Daily newspaper circulation (1996): 4,000 (62 units per 1,000 persons); Radio receivers (1997): 16,000 (247 units per 1,000 persons); Television receivers (1998): 30,000 (457 units per 1,000 persons); Telephone main lines (1999): 33,607 (510 units per 1,000 persons); Cellular telephone subscribers (1999): 20,600 (312 units per 1,000 persons); Internet users (1999): 5,000 (76 per 1,000 persons).

Education and health

Educational attainment (mid-1980s). Percentage of population age 15 and over having: no formal schooling 5.5%; primary education 47.3%; secondary education 21.6%; postsecondary education 24.9%; unknown 0.7%. **Literacy:** resident population is virtually 100% literate. **Health** (1998): physicians 190 (1 per 345 persons); hospital beds 203 (1 per 323 persons); infant mortality rate per 1,000 live births (1998–2000 avg.) 4.1.

Military

Total active duty personnel (1996): none. France and Spain are responsible for Andorra's external security; the police force is assisted in alternate years by either French gendarmerie or Barcelona police.

Did you know? Andorra has the longest cable-car route in the world, which climbs the 8,208 ft (2,502 m) Collada de Enradort; it is used by outdoor enthusiasts, particularly skiers and snowboarders, who flock to resorts in the country in the Pyrenees and represent a key source of national income.

Background

Andorra's independence is traditionally ascribed to Charlemagne, who recovered the region from the Muslims in 803. It was placed under the joint suzerainty of the French counts of Foix and the Spanish bishops of the See of Urgell in 1278, and it was subsequently governed jointly by the Spanish bishop of Urgell and the French head of state. This feudal system of government, the last in Europe, lasted until 1993, when a constitution was adopted that transferred most of the coprinces' powers to the Andorran General Council, a body elected by universal suffrage. Andorra has long had a strong affinity

with Catalonia; its institutions are based in Catalonian law, and it is part of the diocese of the See of Urgell (Spain). The traditional economy was based on sheep raising, but tourism has been very important since the 1950s.

Recent Developments

Led by Chief Executive Marc Forné Molné, the ruling Liberal Party of Andorra (PLA) swept to victory in parliamentary elections held on 4 Mar 2001. With a turnout of 81.6% of the electorate, the PLA won an absolute majority—15 of the 28 seats; the Social Democratic Party garnered 6 seats, the Democratic Party 5, and the Lauredian Union 2.

Internet resources: <www.turisme.ad>

Angola

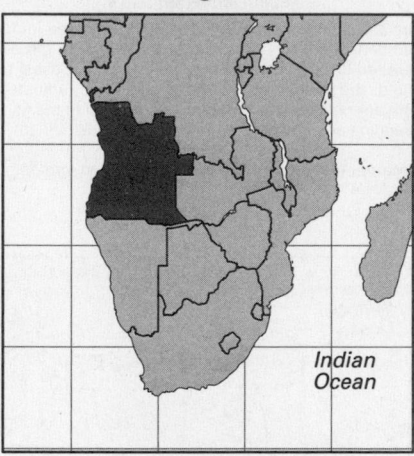

Indian Ocean

Official name: República de Angola (Republic of Angola). **Form of government:** unitary multiparty republic with one legislative house (National Assembly [220]). **Head of state and government:** President José Eduardo dos Santos (from 1992: president annulled post of prime minister in January 1999). **Capital:** Luanda. **Official language:** Portuguese. **Official religion:** none. **Monetary unit:** 1 refloated kwanza (NKz) = 100 lwei; valuation (28 Sep 2001) $1 = refloated kwanza 24.08.

Demography

Area: 481,354 sq mi, 1,246,700 sq km. **Population** (2001): 10,366,000. **Density** (2001): 21.5 persons per sq mi, 8.3 persons per sq km. **Urban** (1999): 43.2%. **Sex distribution** (2000): male 50.59%; female 49.41%. **Age breakdown** (2000): under 15, 43.2%; 15–29, 26.5%; 30–44, 16.9%; 45–59, 8.7%; 60 and over, 4.7%. **Ethnolinguistic composition** (1983): Ovimbundu 37.2%; Mbundu 21.6%; Kongo 13.2%; Luimbe-Nganguela 5.4%; Nyaneka-Humbe 5.4%; others 17.2%. **Religious affiliation** (2001): Christian

---

1 metric ton = about 1.1 short tons;   1 kilometer = 0.6 mi (statute);   1 metric ton-km cargo = about 0.68 short ton-mi cargo;   c.i.f.: cost, insurance, and freight;   f.o.b.: free on board

94.1%, of which Roman Catholic 62.1%, Protestant 15.0%; traditional beliefs 5.0%, other 0.9%. **Major cities** (1999): Luanda 2,555,000; Huambo 400,000 (1995); Benguela 155,000 (1983); Lobito 150,000 (1983); Lubango 105,000 (1984). **Location:** southern Africa, bordering Democratic Republic of the Congo, Zambia, Namibia, and the Atlantic Ocean.

Vital statistics

Birth rate per 1,000 pop. (2000): 46.9 (world avg. 22.5). **Death rate** per 1,000 pop. (2000): 25.0 (world avg. 9.0). **Natural increase rate** per 1,000 pop. (2000): 21.9 (world avg. 13.5). **Total fertility rate** (avg. births per childbearing woman; 2000): 6.5. **Life expectancy** at birth (2000): male 37.1 years; female 39.6 years.

National economy

Budget (1999). *Revenue:* NKz 7,540,000,000 (tax revenue 99.4%, of which petroleum corporate taxes 71.1%, tax on goods 20.5%, import duties 3.0%; nontax revenue 0.6%). *Expenditures:* NKz 8,940,000,000; defense and internal security 41%; administration 16.1%; interest 10.7%; economic services 10.3%; education 4.8%; health 2.8%; other 14.3%. **Public debt** (external, outstanding; 1999): $9,428,000,000. **Tourism:** receipts (1999) $13,000,000; expenditures (1997) $70,000,000. **Household income and expenditure.** Average household size (1998) 5.0. **Production** (metric tons except as noted). *Agriculture, forestry, fishing* (2000): cassava 3,129,734, corn (maize) 428,045, sugarcane 330,000, livestock (number of live animals) 4,042,000 cattle, 2,150,000 goats, 800,000 pigs; roundwood (2000) 6,676,000 cu m; fish catch (1999) 177,497. *Mining and quarrying* (1999): diamonds 1,080,000 carats. *Manufacturing* (1999): bread 87,500; frozen fish 57,700; wheat flour 57,500. *Energy production (consumption):* electricity (kW-hr; 1998) 1,885,000,000 (1,885,000,000); crude petroleum (barrels; 1999) 278,900,000 (14,100,000); petroleum products (metric tons; 1999) 1,956,000 (1,124,000). **Gross national product** (at current market prices; 1999): $3,276,000,000 ($270 per capita). **Population economically active** (1999): total 5,729,000; activity rate of total pop. 57.7% (participation rates over age 10 [1991] 60.1%; female 38.4%). **Land use** (1995): forested 18.5%; meadows and pastures 43.3%; agricultural and under permanent cultivation 2.8%; other 35.4%.

Foreign trade

Imports (1999): $3,267,000,000 (1991; current consumption goods 50.2%, capital goods 20.2%, intermediate consumption goods 18.9%, transport equipment 6.8%). *Major import sources* (1999): Portugal 18.8%; US 14.6%; South Africa 11.9%; France 8.2%; UK 6.2%; Spain 5.9%; Brazil 5.1%. **Exports** (1999): $5,344,000,000 (mineral fuels 87.8%, diamonds 11.8%). *Major export destinations* (1999): US 59.5%; China 8.2%; Taiwan 7.7%; Germany 2.4%; France 2.1%.

Transport and communications

Transport. *Railroads* (1998): route length 1,834 mi, 2,952 km; passenger-mi 203,000,000 (1988), passenger-km 326,000,000 (1988); short ton-mi cargo 1,178,000,000 (1988), metric ton-km cargo 1,720,000,000 (1988). *Roads* (1988): total length 45,128 mi, 72,626 km (paved 25%). *Vehicles* (1997): passenger cars 207,000; trucks and buses 25,000. *Air transport* (1997): passenger-mi 385,000,000, passenger-km 620,000,000; short ton-mi cargo 60,300,000, metric ton-km cargo 97,000,000; airports (1999) with scheduled flights 17. **Communications** Total units (units per 1,000 persons). Daily newspaper circulation (1996): 128,000 (14); Television receivers (1999): 190,000 (19); Telephone main lines (1999): 96,350 (9.7); Cellular telephone subscribers (1999): 24,000 (2.4); Personal computers (1999): 12,000 (1.2); Internet users (1999) 10,000 (1).

Education and health

Literacy (1998): percentage of pop. age 15 and over literate 41.7%; males literate 55.6%; females literate 28.5%. **Health** (1997): physicians 736 (1 per 12,985 persons); hospital beds (1990) 11,857 (1 per 845 persons); infant mortality rate per 1,000 live births (2000) 195.8. **Food** (1999): daily per capita caloric intake 1,873 (vegetable products 92%, animal products 8%); 82% of FAO recommended minimum requirement.

Military

Total active duty personnel (2000): 107,500 (army 93.0%, navy 1.4%, air force 5.6%). **Military expenditure as percentage of GNP** (1997): 20.5% (world 2.6%); per capita expenditure $147.

Background

An influx of Bantu-speaking peoples in the 1st millennium an led to their dominance in the area by c. 1500. The most important Bantu kingdom was the Kongo; south of the Kongo was the Ndongo kingdom of the Mbundu people. Portuguese explorers arrived in 1483 and over time gradually extended their rule. Angola's frontiers were largely determined with other European nations in the 19th century, but not without severe resistance by the indigenous peoples. Its status as a Portuguese colony was changed to that of an overseas province in 1951. Resistance to colonial rule led to the outbreak of fighting in 1961, which led ultimately to independence in 1975. Rival factions continued fighting after independence; although a peace accord was reached in 1994, forces led by Jonas M. Savimbi continued to resist government control.

Recent Developments

By 2002, despite ample resources of oil and minerals, Angola continued to suffer from widespread poverty and high inflation. International donors and aid agencies complained of corruption in government circles and of the diversion of money to military activities in the Democratic Republic of the Congo, as well as to the continuing struggle against the National Union for the Total Independence of Angola (UNITA) rebels at home. The killing of UNITA leader Savimbi in February 2002 was expected to alter the virtual political and military stalemate.

Internet resources: <www.angola.org>

Antigua and Barbuda

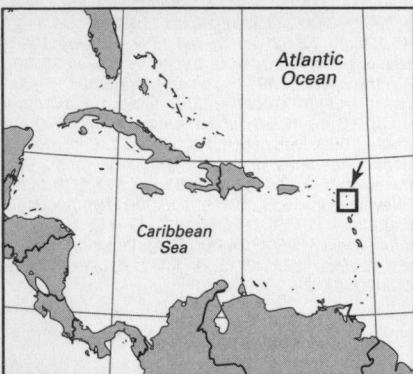

Official name: Antigua and Barbuda. **Form of government:** constitutional monarchy with two legislative houses (Senate [17]; House of Representatives [17] [directly elected seats only; attorney general and speaker may serve ex officio if they are not elected to House of Representatives]). **Chief of state:** British Monarch Queen Elizabeth II (from 1952) represented by Governor-General Sir James Carlisle (from 1993). **Head of government:** Prime Minister Lester Bird (from 1994). **Capital:** Saint John's. **Official language:** English. **Official religion:** none. **Monetary unit:** 1 Eastern Caribbean dollar (EC$) = 100 cents; valuation (28 Jun 2002) US$1 = EC$2.70.

Demography

Area: 170.5 sq mi, 441.6 sq. km. **Population** (2001): 71,500 (includes evacuees from Montserrat). **Density** (2001): persons per sq mi 419.4, persons per sq km 161.9. **Urban** (1995): 36.5%. **Sex distribution** (1991): male 48.20%; female 51.80%. **Age breakdown** (1991): under 15, 30.4%; 15–29, 27.8%; 30–44, 20.5%; 45–59, 10.2%; 60–74, 7.7%; 75 and over, 3.4%. **Ethnic composition** (1994): black 91.3%; mixed 3.7%; white 2.4%; Syrian/Lebanese 0.6%; Indo-Pakistani 0.4%; Amerindian 0.3%; other 1.3%. **Religious affiliation** (1991): Protestant 73.7%, of which Anglican 32.1%, Moravian 12.0%, Methodist 9.1%, Seventh-day Adventist 8.8%; Roman Catholic 10.8%; Jehovah's Witness 1.2%; Rastafarian 0.8%; other religion/no religion/not stated 13.5%. **Major city** (1991): Saint John's 22,342. **Location:** eastern Caribbean Sea.

Vital statistics

Birth rate per 1,000 pop. (2000): 20.2 (world avg. 22.5); (1988) legitimate 23.4%; illegitimate 76.6%. **Death rate** per 1,000 pop. (2000): 6.0 (world avg. 9.0). **Natural increase rate** per 1,000 pop. (2000): 14.2 (world avg. 13.5). **Total fertility rate** (avg. births per childbearing woman; 2000): 2.3. **Marriage rate** per 1,000 pop. 1995): 22.1. **Divorce rate** per 1,000 pop. 1988): 0.2. **Life expectancy** at birth (2000): male 68.2 years; female 72.8 years.

National economy

Budget (1998). *Revenue:* EC$362,300,000 (taxes on international transactions 35.6%, of which import duties 15.8%; consumption taxes 24.9%; nontax revenue 12.5%; corporate income taxes 7.1%). *Expenditures:* EC$427,300,000 (current expenditures 90.1%; development expenditures 9.9%). **Public debt** (external, outstanding; end of 1998): US$406,400,000. **Production** (metric tons except as noted). *Agriculture, forestry, fishing* (1999): tropical fruit 6,500, mangoes 1,300, eggplants 250; livestock (number of live animals) 15,700 cattle, 12,200 sheep; fish catch (1997) 500. *Mining and quarrying:* crushed stone for local use. *Manufacturing* (1994): beer and malt 166,000 cases; T-shirts 179,000 units; *Energy production (consumption):* electricity (kW-hr; 1997) 153,700,000 (115,300,000); petroleum products (metric tons; 1996) negligible (105,000). **Population economically active** (1991): total 26,753; activity rate of total pop. 45.1% (participation rates: ages 15–64, 69.7%; female 45.6%; unemployed [end of 1999] c. 5%). **Household size.** Average household size (1991) 3.2. **Gross national product** (1999): US$606,000,000 (US$8,990 per capita). **Land use** (1994): forested 11.0%; meadows and pastures 9.0%; agricultural and under permanent cultivation 18.0%; other 62.0%. **Tourism:** receipts from visitors (1999) US$291,000,000; expenditures by nationals abroad (1997) US$26,000,000.

Foreign trade

Imports (1998): US$357,500,000 (agricultural products 11.0%, other [including petroleum products for reexport] 89%). *Major import sources* (1997): United States 26.3%; United Kingdom 10.0%; Caricom 7.8%. **Exports** (1998): US$36,200,000 (reexports [significantly, petroleum products reexported to neighboring islands] 59.1%, domestic exports 40.9%). *Major export destinations* (1994): United States 40.0%; others include the United Kingdom, Canada, and Caricom.

Transport and communications

Transport. *Railroad,* mostly nonoperative privately owned tracks. *Roads* (1996): total length 155 mi, 250 km. *Vehicles* (1995): passenger cars 13,588; trucks and buses 1,342. *Air transport* (1995): passenger-mi 157,000,000, passenger-km 252,000,000; (1991) short ton-mi cargo 137,000, metric ton-km cargo 200,000; airports (1996) with scheduled flights 2. **Communications** Total units (units per 1,000 persons). Daily newspaper circulation (1996): 6,000 (87); Radio receivers (1997): 36,000 (523); Television receivers (1997): 31,000 (451); Telephone main lines (1999): 36,500 (518); Cellular telephone subscribers (1999): 8,500 (121).

Education and health

Educational attainment (1991). Percentage of pop. age 25 and over having: no formal schooling 1.1%; primary education 50.5%; secondary 33.4%; higher (not university) 5.4%; university 6.2%; other/unknown 3.4%. **Literacy** (1995): percentage of total pop. age

---

1 metric ton = about 1.1 short tons;   *1 kilometer = 0.6 mi (statute);*   *1 metric ton-km cargo = about 0.68 short ton-mi cargo;*   *c.i.f.: cost, insurance, and freight;*   *f.o.b.: free on board*

15 and over literate, 90.0%. **Health** (1996): physicians 75 (1 per 915 persons); hospital beds 255 (1 per 269 persons); infant mortality rate per 1,000 live births (2000) 23.0. **Food** (1999): daily per capita caloric intake 2,396 (vegetable products 68%, animal products 32%); 102% of FAO recommended minimum requirement.

Military

Total active duty personnel (2000): a 170-member defense force (army 73.5%, navy 26.5%) is part of the Eastern Caribbean regional security system. Military expenditure as percentage of GNP (1998): 0.7%.

Background

Christopher Columbus visited Antigua in 1493 and named it after a church in Seville, Spain. It was colonized in 1632 by English settlers, who imported African slaves to grow tobacco and sugarcane. Barbuda was colonized by the English in 1678. In 1834 its slaves were emancipated. Antigua (with Barbuda) was part of the British colony of the Leeward Islands from 1871 until that colony was defederated in 1956. The islands achieved full independence in 1981.

Recent Developments

In July 2001 the UK lifted its two-year-old financial advisory against Antigua and Barbuda, whose government—led by Prime Minister Lester Bird—had been dogged by accusations of a lax attitude toward money laundering. The US followed in August.

Internet resources: <www.antigua-barbuda.org>

Argentina

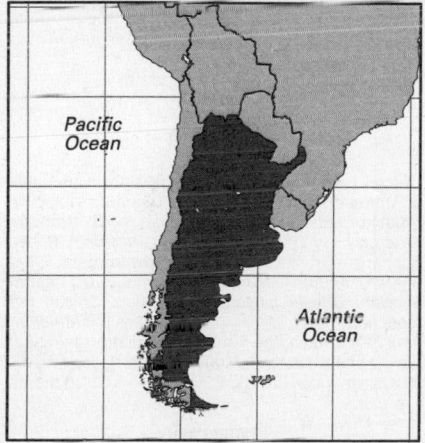

Pacific Ocean

Atlantic Ocean

Official name: República Argentina (Argentina Republic). **Form of government:** federal republic with two legislative houses (Senate [72]; Chamber of Deputies [257]). **Head of state and government:** President Eduardo Duhalde (from 2 Jan 2002) assisted by Cabinet Chief Jorge Capitanich (from 3 Jan 2002). **Capital:** Buenos Aires. **Official language:**

Spanish. **Official religion:** Roman Catholicism. **Monetary unit:** 1 peso (pl. pesos) (Arg$) = 100 centavos; valuation (28 Jun 2002) $1 = Arg$3.87.

Demography

Area: 1,073,400 sq mi, 2,780,092 sq km. **Population** (2001): 37,487,000. **Density** (2001): persons per sq mi 34.9, persons per sq km 13.5. **Urban** (2000): 89.6%. **Sex distribution** (2000): male 49.05%; female 50.95%. **Age breakdown** (2000): under 15, 27.7%; 15–29, 25.6%; 30–44, 18.8%; 45–59, 14.6%; 60–74, 9.6%; 75 and over, 3.7%. **Ethnic composition** (2000): European extraction 86.4%; mestizo 6.5%; Amerindian 3.4%; Arab 3.3%; other 0.4%. **Religious affiliation** (2000): Roman Catholic 79.8%; Protestant 5.4%; Muslim 1.9%; Jewish 1.3%; other 11.6%. **Major cities** (1999): Buenos Aires 2,904,192 (urban agglomeration 12,423,000); Córdoba 1,275,585; Rosario 1,000,000; Mar del Plata 579,483; La Plata 556,308. **Location:** southern South America, bordering Bolivia, Paraguay, Brazil, Uruguay, the South Atlantic Ocean, and Chile.

Vital statistics

Birth rate per 1,000 pop. (2000): 18.6 (world avg. 22.5). **Death rate** per 1,000 pop. (2000): 7.6 (world avg. 9.0). **Natural increase rate** per 1,000 pop. (2000): 11.0 (world avg. 13.5). **Total fertility rate** (avg. births per childbearing woman, 2000): 2.5. **Life expectancy** at birth (2000): male 71.7 years; female 78.6 years.

National economy

Budget (1999). *Revenue:* Arg$56,621,300,000 (current revenue 98.2%, of which tax revenue 90.4%, nontax revenue 7.8%; capital revenue 1.8%). *Expenditure:* Arg$63,662,000,000 (social security 35.3%, debt service 13.6%; general public services 8.4%; education 5.0%; health 5.0%; economic services 3.9%; defense 3.3%). **Public debt** (external, outstanding; 1999): US$84,568,000,000. **Tourism** (1999): receipts US$2,812,000,000; expenditures US$4,107,000,000. **Gross national product** (1999): US$276,097,000,000 (US$7,550 per capita). **Production** (metric tons except as noted). *Agriculture, forestry, fishing* (1999): soybeans 19,500,000, sugarcane 16,700,000, wheat 14,200,000; livestock (number of live animals) 55,000,000 cattle, 14,000,000 sheep; roundwood (1998) 11,428,000 cu m; fish catch 1,012,804. *Mining and quarrying* (1999): silver 1,149,970 troy oz; gold 655,870 troy oz. *Manufacturing* (1999): cement 7,187,000; vegetable oil 5,658,000; wheat flour 3,563,000. *Energy production (consumption):* electricity (kW-hr; 1996) 69,746,000,000 (73,100,000,000); coal (metric tons; 1996) 311,000 (1,396,000); crude petroleum (barrels; 1996) 275,000,000 (175,000,000); petroleum products (metric tons; 1996) 20,782,000 (19,152,000); natural gas (cu m; 1996) 29,693,000,000 (31,883,000,000). **Population economically active** (1995): total 14,345,171; activity rate of total pop. 41.5% (participation rates: ages 15–64, 64.5%; female 36.9%; unemployed [1996] 17.0%). **Household size and expenditure.** Average household size (1991) 3.8; expenditure (1985–86): food 38.2%, transportation 11.6%, housing 9.3%, energy 9.0%, clothing 8.0%, health 7.9%, recreation 7.5%, other 8.5%.

Foreign trade

Imports (1999-c.i.f.): US$25,508,000,000 (machinery and transport equipment 46.5%, chemical products 19.4%, manufactured products 15.0%, food products and live animals 4.4%). *Major import sources:* Brazil 21.9%; US 19.6%; France 5.9%; Germany 5.5%; Italy 5.3%; Japan 4.2%; Spain 3.9%. **Exports** (1999-c.i.f.): US$23,333,000,000 (food products and live animals 35.1%, petroleum and petroleum products 12.1%, machinery and transport equipment 12.0%, manufactured products 10.8%, vegetable and animal oils 9.9%, crude materials 8.0%, chemical products 7.7%). *Major export destinations:* Brazil 24.4%; US 11.4%; Chile 8.0%; The Netherlands 4.3%; Spain 4.1%; Uruguay 3.5%; Italy 3.0%.

Transport and communications

Transport. *Railroads* (1999): route length 33,958 km; passenger-km 9,102,000,000; metric ton-km cargo 9,101,852,000. *Roads* (1996): total length 135,630 mi, 218,276 km (paved 29%). *Vehicles* (1997): passenger cars 4,901,608; commercial vehicles and buses 1,379,044. *Air transport* (1999): passenger-km 11,735,034,000; metric ton-km cargo 1,306,500; airports (1997) 39. **Communications.** Total units (units per 1,000 persons). Daily newspaper circulation (1996): 4,320,000 (123); Radio receivers (1998): 21,500,000 (595); Television receivers (1998): 10,600,000 (293); Telephone main lines (1999) 7,223,168 (197); Cellular telephone subscribers (1999): 4,434,000 (121); Personal computers (1999): 1,800,000 (49); Internet users (1999): 900,000 (25).

Education and health

Educational attainment (1991). Percentage of pop. age 25 and over having: no formal schooling 5.7%; less than primary education 22.3%; primary 34.6%; incomplete secondary 12.5%; complete secondary 12.8%; higher 12.0%. **Literacy** (1995): percentage of total pop. age 15 and over literate 96.2%; males literate 96.2%; females literate 96.2%. **Health:** physicians (1992) 88,800 (1 per 376 persons); hospital beds (1996) 115,803 (1 per 304 persons); infant mortality rate (2000) 18.3. **Food** (1999): daily per capita caloric intake 3,176 (vegetable products 68%, animal products 32%); 135% of FAO recommended minimum requirement.

Military

Total active duty personnel (2000): 71,100 (army 57.8%, navy 24.2%, air force 17.6%). **Military expenditure as percentage of GNP** (1997): 1.2% (world 2.6%); per capita expenditure US$104.

Did you know? Beef is the national dish of Argentina.

Background

Little is known of the indigenous population before the Europeans' arrival. The area was explored for Spain by Sebastian Cabot in 1526–30; by 1580, Asunción, Santa Fe, and Buenos Aires had been settled. At first attached to the viceroyalty of Peru (1620), it was later included with regions of modern Uruguay, Paraguay, and Bolivia in the viceroyalty of La Plata, or Buenos Aires (1776). With the establishment of the United Provinces of the Plate River in 1816, Argentina achieved its independence from Spain, but its boundaries were not set until the early 20th century. In 1943 the government was overthrown by the military; Col. Juan Perón took control in 1946. He in turn was overthrown in 1955. He returned in 1973 after two decades of turmoil. His second wife, Isabel, became president on his death in 1974 but lost power after a military coup in 1976. The military government tried to take the Falkland Islands (Islas Malvinas) in 1982 but was defeated by the British, with the result that the government returned to civilian rule in 1983. The government of Raúl Alfonsín worked to end the human-rights abuses that characterized the former regimes. Hyperinflation led to public riots and Alfonsín's electoral defeat in 1989; his Peronist successor, Carlos Menem, instituted laissez-faire economic policies. In 1999 Fernando de la Rúa of the Alliance coalition was elected president, and his administration struggled with rising unemployment, foreign debt, and government corruption.

Recent Developments

Months of economic decline sparked a political crisis in Argentina at the end of 2001. Antigovernment protesters rioted in the capital, prompting the resignations of Minister of Economy Domingo Cavallo and President de la Rúa. On 23 December Adolfo Rodríguez Saá was installed as interim president, and that same day he suspended payment on the country's $132 billion debt. The rioting continued, however, and Saá was forced to resign on 30 December after he was unable to secure political support from his party. On 1 Jan 2002 Eduardo Duhalde, a populist senator from Buenos Aires province, was elected president by Congress.

Internet resources: <www.sectur.gov.ar>

Armenia

Official name: Hayastani Hanrape-tut'yun (Republic of Armenia). **Form of government:** unitary multiparty republic with a single legislative body (National Assembly [131]). **Head of state:** President Robert Kocharyan (from 1998). **Head of government:** Prime Minister Andranik Markaryan (from 2000). **Capital:** Yerevan. **Official language:** Armenian. **Official religion:** none (but a 1991 law establishes the Armenian Apostolic Church [the Armenian Orthodox Church] as having special status). **Monetary unit:** 1 dram = 100 lumas; valuation (28 Jun 2002), $1 = 582.36 drams.

Demography

Area: 11,484 sq mi, 29,743 sq km; in addition, nearly 20% of neighboring Azerbaijan (including the 1,700-sq mi [4,400-sq km] geographic region of Nagorno-Karabakh [Armenian: Artsakh]) has been occupied by Armenian forces since 1993. **Population**

---

1 metric ton = about 1.1 short tons;   1 kilometer = 0.6 mi (statute);   1 metric ton-km cargo = about 0.68 short ton-mi cargo;   c.i.f.: cost, insurance, and freight;   f.o.b.: free on board

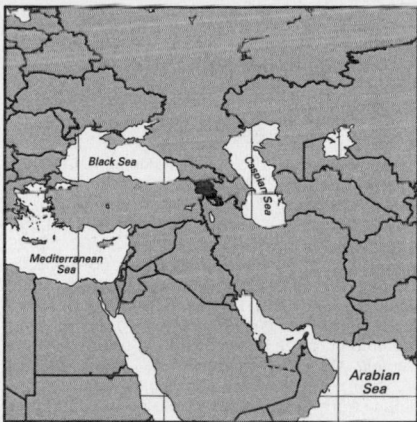

(2001): 3,807,000; c. (de facto; 2000) 3,000,000 (about 20% of the pop. has left the country since 1993 because of an energy crisis). Density (2001): persons per sq mi 331.5, persons per sq km 128.0. Urban (1998): 69.4%. Sex distribution (2000): male 48.73%; female 51.27%. Age breakdown (2000): under 15, 24.3%; 15–29, 24.0%; 30–44, 23.6%; 45–59, 13.9%; 60–74, 11.6%; 75 and over, 2.6%. Ethnic composition (1989): Armenian 93.3%; Azerbaijani 2.6%; other 4.1%. Religious affiliation (1995): Armenian Apostolic 64.5%; other Christian 1.3%; other (mostly nonreligious) 34.2%. Major cities (1999): Yerevan 1,248,700; Gyumri 211,700; Vanadzor 172,700. Location: southwestern Asia, bordering Georgia, Azerbaijan, Iran, and Turkey.

Vital statistics

Birth rate per 1,000 pop. (2000): 11.0 (world avg. 22.5); (1993) legitimate 86.0%; illegitimate 14.0%. Death rate per 1,000 pop. (2000): 9.5 (world avg. 9.0). Natural increase rate per 1,000 pop. (2000): 1.5 (world avg. 13.5). Total fertility rate (avg. births per childbearing woman; 2000): 1.5. Marriage rate per 1,000 pop. (1999): 3.3. Divorce rate per 1,000 pop. (1999): 0.3. Life expectancy at birth (2000): male 62.0 years; female 71.0 years.

National economy

Budget (2000). Revenue: 202,005,000,000 drams (tax revenue 96.7%, of which value-added tax 33.4%, excise tax 12.5%, payroll tax 11.6%, enterprise profit tax 10.1%, income tax 7.3%; grants 3.3%). Expenditures: 267,411,000,000 drams (current expenditures 79.1%; capital expenditure and net lending 20.9%). Public debt (external, outstanding; 1999): $681,900,000. Tourism (1998): receipts from visitors $6,000,000; expenditures by nationals abroad $45,000,000. Land use (1994): forest 13.4%; pasture 23.1%; agriculture 20.1%; other 43.4%. Gross national product (1999): $1,878,000,000 ($490 per capita). Production (metric tons except as noted) Agriculture, forestry, fishing (2000): potatoes 320,000, wheat 142,000, grapes 110,000; livestock (number of live animals) 540,000 sheep and goats, 478,730 cattle, 4,100,000 poultry; roundwood (1998) 35,700 cu m; fish catch (1998) 1,135. Mining and quarrying (1998): copper concentrate 9,200; gold (metal content) 400 kg. Manufacturing (value in

'000,000 drams; 1994): machine-building and metalworking equipment 18,436; food products 13,842; chemicals 5,330. Energy production (consumption): electricity (kW-hr; 2000) 5,958,000,000 (5,958,000,000); coal (metric tons; 2000) none (5,000); crude petroleum (barrels; 1996) none (1,026,000); petroleum products (metric tons; 1996) none (358,000); natural gas (cu m; 1996) none (1,050,700). Population economically active (2000): total 1,436,900; activity rate of total pop. 37.8% (participation rates [1996] ages 16–60, 75.1%; unemployed [2000] 10.7%). Household income and expenditure. Average household size (1997) 4.5; income per household (1994) 47,352 drams; sources of income (1994): wages and salaries 52.3%, agricultural income 7.7%, other 40.0%; expenditure (1994): goods and services 78.0%, taxes and payments to government 22.0%.

Foreign trade

Imports (2000): $899,000,000 (minerals and chemicals 29.4%, food 16.6%, jewelry 12.6%, machinery and equipment 2.7%). Major import sources: EU countries 33.6%; former Soviet Union 18.7%, of which Russia 14.7%; US 11.5%; Iran 9.3%. Exports (2000): $307,000,000 (jewelry 39.4%, machinery and equipment 14.3%, mineral products 12.4%, agricultural products 9.8%). Major export destinations: Belgium 24.5%; Russia 14.7%; US 12.4%; Iran 9.1%; Georgia 4.9%.

Transport and communications

Transport. Railroads (1999): length 516 mi, 830 km; passenger-mi 28,832,000, passenger-km 46,400,000; ton-mi cargo 201,262,000, metric ton-km cargo 323,900,000. Roads (1997): length 5,238 mi, 8,431 km (paved 100%). Vehicles (1996): passenger cars 1,300; trucks and buses 4,460. Air transport (2000): passenger-mi 355,672,000, passenger-km 572,400,000; short ton-mi cargo 5,931,000, metric ton-km cargo 9,545,000; airports (1999) 1. Communications. Total units (units per 1,000 persons). Daily newspaper circulation (1995): 80,000 (23); Television receivers (1998): 840,000 (221); Telephone main lines (1999): 547,000 (144); Cellular telephone subscribers (1999): 8,148 (2.1); Personal computers (1999): 20,000 (5.3); Internet users (1999): 30,000 (7.9).

Education and health

Educational attainment (1989). Percentage of pop. age 25 and over having: primary education or no formal schooling 7.4%; some secondary 18.6%; completed secondary and some postsecondary 57.7%; higher 13.5%. Literacy (1989): total pop. age 15 and over literate 98.8%; males literate 99.4%; females literate 98.1%. Health (1994): physicians 13,000 (1 per 288 persons); hospital beds 30,000 (1 per 125 persons); infant mortality rate (2000) 41.5. Food (1999): daily per capita caloric intake 2,167 (vegetable products 86%, animal products 14%); 85% of FAO recommended minimum requirement.

Military

Total active duty personnel (2000): 41,300 (army 100%). Military expenditure as percentage of GNP (1997): 3.5% (world 2.6%); per capita expenditure $100.

Background

Armenia is a successor state to a historical region in southwestern Asia. Historical Armenia's boundaries have varied considerably, but the region extended over what is now northeastern Turkey and the Republic of Armenia. The area was later conquered by the Medes and Macedonia, and still later allied with the Roman empire. Armenia adopted Christianity as its national religion in AD 303. It came under the rule of the Ottoman Turks in 1514. Over the next centuries, as parts were ceded to other rulers, nationalism arose among the scattered Armenians; by the late 19th century it was causing widespread disruption. Fighting between Turks and Russians escalated when part of Armenia was ceded to Russia in 1878, and it continued through World War I, leading to Armenian deaths on a genocidal scale. With the Turkish defeat, the Russian-controlled part of Armenia was set up as a Soviet republic in 1921. Armenia became a constituent republic of the USSR in 1936. With the latter's dissolution in the late 1980s, Armenia declared its independence in 1990. It fought Azerbaijan for control over Nagorno-Karabakh until a cease-fire in 1994. About one-fifth of the population has left the country since 1993 because of an energy crisis. Political tension escalated, and in 1999 the prime minister and some legislators were killed in a terrorist attack on the legislature.

Recent Developments

Armenia was accepted into full membership of the Council of Europe in January 2001. Pres. Robert Kocharyan and Russian Pres. Vladimir Putin earlier signed a declaration on cooperation in the 21st century.

Internet resources: <www.armeniaemb.org>

Aruba

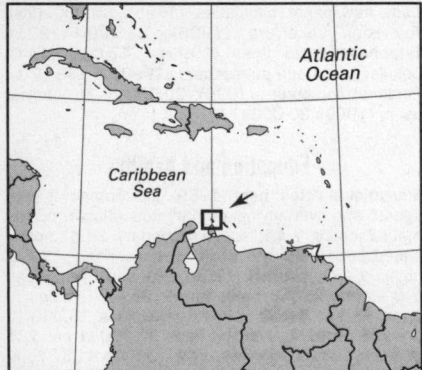

Atlantic Ocean

Caribbean Sea

Official name: Aruba. **Political status:** nonmetropolitan territory of The Netherlands with one legislative house (States of Aruba [21]). **Chief of state:** Dutch Monarch Queen Beatrix (from 1980) represented by Governor. **Head of government:** Prime Minister Nelson O. Oduber (from 30 Oct 2001). **Capital:**

Oranjestad. **Official language:** Dutch. **Official religion:** none. **Monetary unit:** 1 Aruban florin; the Aruban florin (Af.) is pegged to the US dollar at a fixed rate of Af. 1.79 = 1 $).

Demography

Area: 75 sq mi, 193 sq km. **Population.** (2001): 97,200. **Density** (2000): persons per sq mi 1,296.0, persons per sq km 503.6. **Urban** (2000): 67.0%. **Sex distribution** (1999): male 49.41%; female 50.59%. **Age breakdown** (1999): under 15, 22.3%; 15–29, 21.0%; 30–44, 27.8%; 45–59, 18.2%; 60–74, 8.1%; 75 and over, 2.6%. **Linguistic composition** (1991): Papiamento 76.6%; English 8.9%; Spanish 7.4%; Dutch 5.4%; Portuguese 0.3%; other 1.4%. **Religious affiliation** (2000): Christian 96.2%, of which Roman Catholic 81.9%, Protestant 7.3%, other Christian (Jehovah's Witnesses) 1.3%; Spiritist 1.0%; nonreligious 1.4%; other 1.4%. **Major urban areas:** Oranjestad (1998) 28,000; San Nicolas (1991) 13,510. **Location:** southern Caribbean, north of Venezuela.

Vital statistics

Birth rate per 1,000 pop. (2000): 13.1 (world avg. 22.5); (1998) legitimate 57.5%; illegitimate 42.5%. **Death rate** per 1,000 pop. (2000): 6.1 (world avg. 9.0). **Natural increase rate** per 1,000 pop. (2000): 7.0 (world avg. 13.5). **Total fertility rate** (avg. births per childbearing woman; 2000): 1.8. **Marriage rate** per 1,000 pop. (1998): 6.1. **Divorce rate** per 1,000 pop. (1998): 3.6. **Life expectancy** at birth (2000): male 75.0 years; female 81.9 years.

National economy

Budget (1999). *Revenue*: Af. 712,900,000 (tax revenue 85.4%, of which taxes on wages and income 32.1%, import duties 13.7%, taxes on profits 11.2%, excise taxes on gasoline 8.4%; nontax revenue 14.4%). *Expenditures*: Af. 736,900,000. **Production** (metric tons except as noted). *Agriculture, forestry, fishing*: aloes are cultivated for export; tomatoes, beans, cucumbers; (livestock; number of live animals) Aruba has very little livestock; fish catch (1997) 205. *Mining and quarrying*: excavation of sand for local use. *Manufacturing*: rum, cigarettes, aloe products. *Energy production (consumption)*: electricity (kW-hr; 1999) 738,000,000 ([2000] 644,000,000); crude petroleum (barrels; 1996) none (2,287,000); petroleum products (metric tons; 1996) none (238,000). **Gross domestic product** (2000): $1,970,000,000 ($21,760 per capita). **Population economically active** (1997): total 44,840; activity rate of total pop. 48.9% (participation rates: ages 15–64, 68.3%; female 43.8%; unemployed 7.4%). **Public debt** (external, outstanding; December 2000): $209,800,000. **Household income and expenditure** (1999): average household size 3.6; average annual income per household: Af. 39,000; expenditure (1994) weights of consumer price index components): transportation and communications 20.7%, food and beverages 18.4%, clothing and footwear 11.3%, household furnishings 10.4%, housing 9.8%. **Tourism:** receipts from visitors (2000) $837,300,-000; expenditures by nationals abroad (1999)

---

1 metric ton = about 1.1 short tons;   1 kilometer = 0.6 mi (statute);   1 metric ton-km cargo = about 0.68 short ton-mi cargo;   c.i.f.: cost, insurance, and freight;   f.o.b.: free on board

$122,000,000. **Land use** (1998): forest, negligible; meadows and pastures, negligible; agricultural and under permanent cultivation 11.0%; other (dry savanna and built-up) 89.0%.

Foreign trade

Imports (1999): $2,003,000,000 (petroleum [all forms] and free-zone imports 61.0%, electrical and nonelectrical machinery 8.0%, base and fabricated metals 4.3%). *Major import sources* (1999; excludes petroleum [all forms] and free-zone trade): United States 63.3%; The Netherlands 11.1%; Venezuela 3.0%; Netherlands Antilles 2.8%. **Exports** (1999): $1,420,000,000 (petroleum [all forms] and free-zone exports 97.9%). *Major export destinations* (excludes petroleum [all forms] and free-zone trade): United States 41.4%; Colombia 20.3%; The Netherlands 12.1%; Netherlands Antilles 8.4%.

Transport and communications

Transport. *Railroads*: none. *Roads* (1984): total length 236 mi, 380 km (paved 100%). *Vehicles* (1999): passenger cars 38,834; trucks and buses 990. *Air transport* (1998; Air Aruba only): passenger-mi 318,000,000, passenger-km 511,000,000; airports (1998) with scheduled flights 1. **Communications** Total units (units per 1,000 persons). Daily newspaper circulation (1996): 73,000 (851); Radio receivers (1997): 50,000 (558); Television receivers (1997): 20,000 (223); Telephone main lines (1999): 36,557 (388); Cellular telephone subscribers (2000): 24,313 (251).

Education and health

Educational attainment (1991). Percentage of pop. age 25 and over having: no formal schooling or incomplete primary education 15.0%; completed primary 37.3%; completed lower secondary/vocational 28.1%; completed upper secondary/vocational 4.0%; higher vocational 5.5%; undergraduate 5.3%; graduate 1.7%; other 3.1%. **Literacy** (1990): percentage of total pop. age 15 and over literate 95.0%. **Health** (1999): physicians (1997) 103 (1 per 870 persons); hospital beds 308 (1 per 306 persons); infant mortality rate per 1,000 live births (2000) 6.5.

Military

Total active duty personnel (1999): a 45-member Dutch naval/air force contingent is stationed in Aruba and the Netherlands Antilles.

Background

Aruba's earliest inhabitants were Arawak Indians, whose cave drawings can still be seen. Though the Dutch took possession of Aruba in 1636, they did not begin to develop it aggressively until 1816. In 1986 Aruba seceded from the Federation of the Netherlands Antilles in an initial step toward independence.

Recent Developments

In 2001 Aruba was commended by the International Monetary Fund for having improved surveillance and detection procedures relating to its growing offshore-banking sector. The opposition People's Electoral Movement emerged victorious in the September election.

Internet resources: <www.aruba.com>

Australia

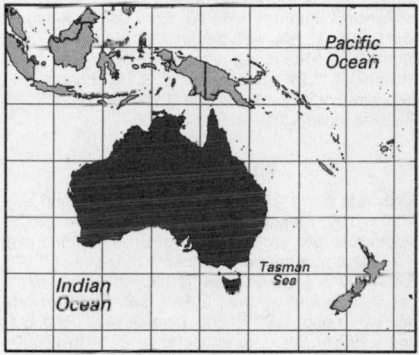

Official name: Commonwealth of Australia. **Form of government:** federal parliamentary state (formally a constitutional monarchy) with two legislative houses (Senate [76]; House of Representatives [150]). **Chief of state:** British Monarch Queen Elizabeth II (from 1952) represented by Governor-General Peter Hollingworth (from 2001). **Head of government:** Prime Minister John Howard (from 1996). **Capital:** Canberra. **Official language:** English. **Official religion:** none. **Monetary unit:** 1 Australian dollar ($A) = 100 cents; valuation (28 Jun 2002) US$1 = $A1.78.

Demography

Area: 2,969,910 sq mi, 7,692,030 sq km. **Population** (2001): 19,358,000. **Density** (2001): persons per sq mi 6.5, persons per sq km 2.5. **Urban** (2000): 85.0%. **Sex distribution** (1999): male 49.77%; female 50.23%. **Age breakdown** (1999): under 15, 20.7%; 15–24, 14.2%; 25–44, 30.7%; 45–64, 22.2%; 65 and over, 12.2%. **Ethnic composition** (1999): white 91.4%; Asian 6.4%; aboriginal 1.5%; other 0.7%. **Religious affiliation** (1996): Christian 70.9%, of which Roman Catholic 27.0%, Anglican Church of Australia 22.0%, other Protestant 21.9% (Uniting Church and Methodist 7.5%, Presbyterian 3.8%), Orthodox 2.8%, other Christian 2.4%; Muslim 1.1%; Buddhist 1.1%; Jewish 0.4%; Hindu 0.4%; no religion 16.6%; other 9.5%. **Metropolitan areas** (1999): Sydney 4,041,400; Melbourne 3,417,200; Brisbane 1,601,400; Perth 1,364,200; Adelaide 1,092,000; Newcastle 479,300; Gold Coast Tweed 391,200; Canberra-Queanbeyan 348,600; Wollongong 262,600; Hobart 194,200. **Location:** Oceania; continent between the Indian Ocean and the South Pacific Ocean. **Dependent territories:** Christmas Island, Cocos (Keeling) Islands, and Norfolk Island. **Place of birth** (1999): 76.4% native-born; 23.6% foreign-born, of which Europe 10.8% (United Kingdom 6.5% [includes both Northern Ireland and Republic of Ireland], Italy 1.3%, Greece 0.7%, Germany 0.7%, The Netherlands 0.5%, other Europe 1.1%), Asia and Middle East 2.7%, New Zealand 1.9%, Africa, the Americas, and other 8.2%. **Mobility** (1995–96). Pop. age 15 and over living in the same residence as in 1994: 81.6%; different residence between states, regions, and neighborhoods 18.4%. **Households** (1996). Total number of households 7,100,000. Average household size 2.6; couples only 34.1%, couples with dependent children only 40.6%, couples with nondependent children 9.0%, single parent with children 9.9%, other 6.4%. **Immigration** (1996): permanent immigrants admitted 96,970, from United Kingdom and Ireland 12.8%, New Zealand 11.8%, China 7.6%, Vietnam 4.8%, Hong Kong 4.6%, India 4.4%, Philippines 3.9%, South Africa 3.2%, Bosnia and Herzegovina 3.2%, Yugoslavia 3.1%, Sri Lanka 2.2%. Refugee arrivals (1998–99): 8,790.

Vital statistics

Birth rate per 1,000 pop. (2000): 13.0 (world avg. 22.5); (1997) legitimate 72.0%; illegitimate 28.0%. **Death rate** per 1,000 pop. (2000): 7.6 (world avg. 9.0). **Natural increase rate** per 1,000 pop. (2000): 5.4 (world avg. 13.5). **Total fertility rate** (avg. births per childbearing woman; 2000): 1.8. **Marriage rate** per 1,000 pop. (1999): 6.0. **Divorce rate** per 1,000 pop. (1999): 2.8. **Life expectancy** at birth (2000): male 76.0 years; female 81.0 years.

Social indicators

Quality of working life (1999–2000). Average workweek: 35.7 hours (1994: 16.8% overtime). Annual rate per 100,000 workers for: accidental injury and industrial disease, 3,200 (1992–93); Proportion of employed persons insured for damages or income loss resulting from: injury 100% (1992–93); permanent disability 100% (1992–93); death 100% (1992–93). Working days lost to industrial disputes per 1,000 employees (1999): 87. Means of transportation to work (1986): private automobile 69.4%; public transportation 10.1%; motorcycle and bicycle 3.2%; foot 6.6%; other 10.7%. Discouraged job seekers (considered by employers to be too young or too old, having language or training limitations, or no vacancies in line of work; 1999): 1.1% of labor force. **Social participation**. Eligible voters participating in last national election (1996): 95.8%; voting is compulsory. Trade union membership in total workforce (1996): 31%. **Social deviance** (1999). Offense rate per 100,000 pop. for: murder 1.8; sexual assault 74.2; assault 704.5; auto theft 684.8; burglary and housebreaking 2,191.6; armed robbery 49.8. Incidence per 100,000 in general pop. of (1996): prisoners with drug offenses 539.5; suicide 13.1. **Material wellbeing** (1995). Households possessing: automobile 85%; telephone 95%; refrigerator 99.7%; personal computers 54.0% (1994); washing machine 90.0%.

National economy

Gross national product (1999): US$397,345,-000,000 (US$20,950 per capita). **Budget** (1998–99). *Revenue*: $A146,444,000,000 (income tax 70.3%, of which individual 52.4%, corporate 14.2%; excise duties and sales tax 22.1%). *Expenditures*: $A140,814,000,000 (social security and welfare 37.5%; health 16.6%; economic and public services 11.2%; defense 8.0%; education 6.9%; interest on public debt 5.3%). **Public debt** (1999–2000):

$A72,358,000,000. **Tourism** (1999): receipts from visitors US$7,525,000,000; expenditures by nationals abroad US$5,792,000,000. **Production** (gross value in $A '000 except as noted). *Agriculture, forestry, fishing* (1998–99): livestock slaughtered 7,401,400 (cattle 4,476,600, sheep and lambs 1,045,500, poultry 1,174,300, pigs 689,700); wheat 3,860,000, wool 2,139,100, seed cotton 1,353,000, grapes 1,115,600, sugarcane 1,044,000; livestock (number of live animals; 1999) 115,456,000 sheep and lamb, 26,578,000 cattle, 2,626,000 pigs, 93,578,000 poultry; roundwood (1999) 22,938,000 cu m; fish catch (1998) 201,216 metric tons. *Mining and quarrying* (metric tons [tons of contained metal]; 1997–98): iron ore 169,568,000; bauxite 50,418,000; zinc 2,029,000; copper 1,665,000; lead 943,000; uranium oxide 5,797. *Manufacturing* (value added in US$'000,000 except as noted; 1995): food products 12,239; transport equipment 5,745; printing and publishing 5,252; metal products 4,840; nonferrous metals 4,766; nonelectrical machinery 4,054. *Energy production (consumption)*: electricity (kW-hr; 1994) 167,151,000,000 (167,-151,000,000); coal (metric tons; 1994) 176,078,-000 (52,678,000); crude petroleum (barrels; 1994) 159,160,000 (202,490,000); petroleum products (metric tons; 1994) 33,086,000 (33,707,000); natural gas (cu m; 1994) 25,185,000,000 (17,438,-000,000). **Population economically active** (1999–2000): total 9,577,900; activity rate of total pop. 50.5% (participation rates: over age 15, 63.4%; female 43.6%; unemployed 6.9%. **Household income and expenditure** (1998–99). Average household size (1996) 2.6; average annual income per household $A45,708; sources of income: wages and salaries 39.9%, self-employment 32.1%, transfer payments 10.1%, other 17.9%; expenditure: food and nonbeverages 18.2%, transportation and communications 16.9%, housing 13.9%, recreation 12.7%, household durable goods 6.0%, household services and operation 5.9%, clothing and footwear 4.6%, health 4.6%, alcoholic beverages 2.9%, energy 2.6%, other 11.7%. **Land use** (1998): agricultural and under permanent cultivation 7.0%; other 93.0% (of which, meadows and pastures 54.0%).

Foreign trade

Imports (1999–2000): $A110,083,000,000 (machinery and transport equipment 46.6%, of which road motor vehicles 11.6%, office machines and automatic data-processing equipment 6.9%, telecommunications equipment 6.2%; basic manufactures 12.4%, of which textile yarn and fabrics 2.4%, paper and paperboard products 2.1%; chemicals and related products 11.4%; mineral fuels and lubricants 7.0%; food and live animals 3.6%). *Major import sources*: US 20.9%; Japan 12.8%; China 6.8%; UK 5.8%; Germany 5.3%; New Zealand 4.0%; Singapore 4.0%. **Exports** (1999–2000): $A97,255,000,000 (crude materials excluding fuels 18.9%, of which metalliferous ores and metal scrap 11.6%, textile fibres and their waste 4.4%; mineral fuels and lubricants 18.6%, of which coal, coke, and briquettes 8.6%, petroleum, petroleum products, and natural gas 7.3%; food and live animals 17.3%, of which cereals and cereal preparations 5.1%, meat and meat preparations 4.6%, dairy products 2.4%; basic manufac-

---

1 metric ton = about 1.1 short tons;   1 kilometer = 0.6 mi (statute);   1 metric ton-km cargo = about 0.68 short ton-mi cargo;   c.i.f.: cost, insurance, and freight;   f.o.b.: free on board

tures 12.7%). *Major export destinations:* Japan 19.3%; US 9.8%; South Korea 7.8%; New Zealand 6.9%; China 5.1%; Singapore 5.0%; Taiwan 4.8%.

Transport and communications

Transport. *Railroads* (1998–99; government railways only): route length 22,233 mi, 35,780 km; passengers carried 595,200,000; short ton-mi cargo 87,262,000,000, metric ton-km cargo 127,400,-000,000. *Roads* (2000): total length 502,356 mi, 808,465 km (paved 40%). *Vehicles* (1999): passenger cars 9,719,900; trucks and buses 2,214,900. *Air transport* (1999; includes Qantas and Ansett Australia): passenger-mi 46,646,591,000, passenger-km 75,070,556,000; short ton-mi cargo 1,156,331,000, metric ton-km cargo 1,688,-215,000; *airports* (1996) with scheduled flights 400. **Communication** Total units (units per 1,000 persons). Daily newspaper circulation (1996): 5,370,000 (296); Radio receivers (1997): 25,500,000 (1,391); Television receivers (1999): 13,400,000 (706); Telephone main lines (1999): 9,857,000 (519); Cellular telephone subscribers (1999): 6,501,000 (343); Personal computers (1999): 8,900,000 (469); Internet users (1999): 6,000,000 (316 per 1,000 persons).

Education and health

Educational attainment (1999). Percentage of pop. age 15 to 64 having: no formal schooling and incomplete secondary education 38.0%; completed secondary 18.3%; postsecondary, technical, or other certificate/diploma 28.3%; university 15.4%. **Literacy** (1996): total pop. literate, virtually 100%. **Health:** physicians (1999–2000) 55,200 (1 per 345 persons); hospital beds (1998–99) 77,631 (1 per 243 persons); infant mortality rate (2000) 6.0. **Food** (1999): daily per capita caloric intake 3,150 (vegetable products 69%, animal products 31%); (1997) 118% of FAO recommended minimum requirement.

Military

Total active duty personnel (2000): 50,600 (army 47.7%, navy 24.7%, air force 27.6%). **Military expenditure as percentage of GNP** (1997): 2.2% (world 2.6%); per capita expenditure US$460.

Background

Australia has long been inhabited by Aborigines, who arrived on the continent 40,000–60,000 years ago. Estimates of the population at the time of European settlement in 1788 range from 300,000 to more than 1,000,000. Widespread European knowledge of Australia began with 17th-century explorations. The Dutch landed in 1616 and the British in 1688, but the first large-scale expedition was that of James Cook in 1770, which established Britain's claim to Australia. The first English settlement, at Port Jackson (1788), consisted mainly of convicts and seamen; convicts were to make up a large proportion of the incoming settlers. By 1859 the colonial nuclei of all Australia's states had been formed, but with devastating effects on the Aborigines, whose population declined sharply with the introduction of European diseases and weaponry. Britain granted its colonies limited self-government in the mid 19th century, and Australia achieved federation in 1901. Australia fought along-

side the British in World War I, notably at Gallipoli, and again in World War II, preventing Australian occupation by the Japanese. It joined the US in the Korean and Vietnam wars. Since the 1960s the government has sought to deal more fairly with the Aborigines, and a loosening of immigration restrictions has led to a more heterogeneous population. Constitutional links allowing British interference in government were formally abolished in 1968, and Australia has assumed a leading role in Asian and Pacific affairs. During the 1990s, it experienced several debates about giving up its British ties and becoming a republic.

Recent Developments

In 2000 Australia staged its second Olympic Games of the modern era (and its first since Melbourne played host in 1956) in Sydney. Nearly 11,000 athletes participated. The Games featured a spectacular opening ceremony, during which Aboriginal runner Cathy Freeman lit the Olympic flame. Sydney's festivities were pronounced "the best Olympic Games ever" by International Olympic Committee Pres. Juan António Samaranch.

Australians had another reason to celebrate in 2001: the country marked its centenary of federation. Amid a year of festivities, a grand meeting of all the elected members of the state and commonwealth parliaments took place on 9 May. The gala event was held in the Royal Exhibition Building in Melbourne, where 100 years earlier the Australian states had formally convened the first federal Parliament.

In national elections held on 10 Nov 2001, the ruling coalition of the Liberal and National parties came out on top, with the Liberals garnering 37.4% of the vote and the National Party 5.4%; the victory handed Prime Minister John Howard a historic third term in office. The Labor Party claimed 38.2%, the Democrats 5.3%. The Greens' national vote (4.7%) was a record for the party, while Pauline Hanson's One Nation party lost support, collecting only 4.3%. Howard announced his new cabinet on 23 November.

Australia has tried to improve relations with Indonesia. As part of the process, Indonesian Pres. Abdurrahman Wahid traveled to Australia in 2001; it was the first visit by an Indonesian leader to the country in more than a quarter of a century. Howard hoped that the two countries could overcome Indonesian resentment of Australia's leadership role in peacekeeping during the East Timor crisis in 1999, and Wahid reassured Australia that Indonesia would find political stability in a short time. When Wahid was replaced by Megawati Sukarnoputri, however, relations took a step backward. The newly installed Indonesian president refused to accept any responsibility for an incident in which more than 430 refugees—mostly Afghan asylum seekers—had sailed from Indonesia toward Australia. In his biggest crisis in office, Howard had declared that none of the refugees would be allowed to set foot on Australian soil; the refugees were forcibly transported to Nauru and New Zealand.

Australia and Thailand began a new era in their relationship by exploring a free-trade deal in return for help from Thailand in overcoming Australia's exclusion from such key regional bodies as the Association of Southeast Asian Nations. Singapore and Australia improved economic cooperation when Canberra gave Singapore's government-controlled company SingTel permission to buy Australia's second largest telecommunications carrier, Cable & Wireless Optus.

Australia also reinforced good relations with the US. Defense Secretary Donald Rumsfeld and Secretary of State Colin Powell were leaders of a distinguished team sent to Australia in August 2001 to thank the Howard government for its support of US policy on missile defense and the Kyoto Protocol on global warming. After the 11 September terrorist attacks in the US, both Howard and opposition leader Kim Beazley of the Labor Party affirmed their support for the US and sought to reassure Indonesia, a predominantly Muslim country, that the US and its allies were waging a fight against terrorism and not against Islam.

Internet resources: <www.australia.com>

Austria

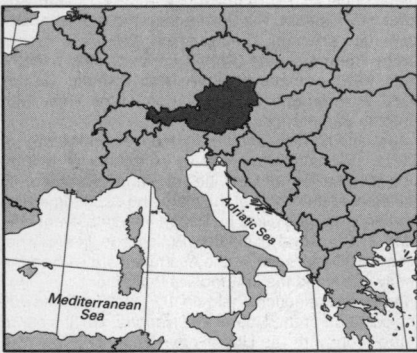

Official name: Republik Österreich (Republic of Austria). Form of government: federal state with two legislative houses (Federal Council [64]; National Council [183]). Chief of state: President Thomas Klestil (from 1992). Head of government: Chancellor Wolfgang Schüssel (from 2000). Capital: Vienna. Official language: German. Official religion: none. Monetary unit: 1 euro (€) = 100 cents; $1 = €1.01 (28 Jun 2002); at conversion on 1 Jan 2002, €1 = 13.76 Austrian schilling (S).

Demography

Area: 32,378 sq mi, 83,858 sq km. Population (2001): 8,069,000. Density (2001): persons per sq mi 249.2, persons per sq km 96.2. Urban (1999): 64.6%. Sex distribution (2000): male 48.61%; female 51.39%. Age breakdown (2000): under 15, 16.7%; 15–29, 18.8%; 30–44, 25.1%; 45–59, 18.7%; 60–74, 13.5%; 75 and over, 7.2%. Ethnic composition (national origin; 1998): Austrian 91.2%; citizens of former Yugoslavia 4.0%; Turkish 1.6%; other 3.2%. Religious affiliation (1995): Roman Catholic 75.1%; nonreligious and atheist 8.6%; Protestant (mostly Lutheran) 5.4%; Muslim 2.1%; Eastern Orthodox 0.7%; Jewish 0.1%; other 1.9%; unknown 6.1%. Major cities (2000): Vienna 1,608,144; Graz 240,967; Linz 188,022; Salzburg 144,247; Innsbruck 111,752. Location: central Europe, bordering the Czech Republic, Slovakia, Hungary, Slovenia, Italy, Switzerland, Liechtenstein, and Germany.

Vital statistics

Birth rate per 1,000 pop. (1999): 9.5 (world avg. 22.5); legitimate 69.5%; illegitimate 30.5%. Death rate per 1,000 pop. (1999): 9.4 (world avg. 9.0). Natural increase rate per 1,000 pop. (1999): 0.1 (world avg. 13.5). Total fertility rate (avg. births per childbearing woman; 1999): 1.3. Marriage rate per 1,000 pop. (1999): 4.9. Divorce rate per 1,000 pop. (1999): 2.3. Life expectancy at birth (1999): male 75.1 years; female 80.9 years.

National economy

Budget (1997). Revenue: S 950,820,000,000 (tax revenue 92.0%, of which social security contributions 37.7%, individual income taxes 17.3%, value-added taxes 16.2%). Expenditures: S 1,017,870,000 (social security and welfare 42.0%; health 14.4%; education 9.2%; interest 9.2%; defense 2.0%). National debt (end of year 1998): $133,897,000,000. Production (metric tons except as noted). Agriculture, forestry, fishing (2000): sugar beets 2,600,000; corn (maize) 1,800,000; wheat 1,313,000; livestock (number of live animals) 3,790,000 pigs, 2,150,000 cattle, 13,540,000 chickens; roundwood (1999) 14,083,000 cu m; fish catch (1997) 3,486. Mining and quarrying (1999): iron ore 1,747,000; magnesite 748,600. Manufacturing (value added in S '000,000; 1997): nonelectrical machinery and apparatus 46.1; food and beverages 44.1; electrical machinery and apparatus 42.9. Energy production (consumption): electricity (kW-hr; 1999) 60,348,000,000 ([1996] 55,787,000,000); hard coal (metric tons; 1999) negligible ([1996] 3,795,000); lignite (metric tons; 1999) 1,137,000 ([1996] 1,659,000); crude petroleum (barrels; 1999) 7,054,000 ([1996] 63,566,000); petroleum products (metric tons; 1996) 8,227,000 (10,503,000); natural gas (cu m; 1999) 1,833,000,000 ([1996] 8,042,000,000). Tourism ($'000,000; 1999): receipts $12,533; expenditures $9,803. Population economically active (1999): total 3,909,000; activity rate of total pop. 48.3% (participation rates: ages 15–64 [1998] 70.7%; female 43.2%; unemployed [October 1999–September 2000] 6.0%). Gross national product (at current market prices; 1999): $205,743,000,000 ($25,430 per capita). Household income and expenditure. Average household size (1999) 2.5; sources of income (1995): wages and salaries 54.8%, transfer payments 25.9%; expenditure (1995): transportation and communications 15.4%, housing 15.4%, food and beverages 15.3%, cafe and hotel expenditures 12.6%. Land use (1994): forested 39.2%; meadows and pastures 24.3%; agricultural and under permanent cultivation 18.3%; other 18.2%.

Foreign trade

Imports (1999-c.i.f.): S 898,800,000,000 (machinery and transport equipment 41.3%, of which road vehicles 12.1%, electrical machinery and apparatus 7.5%; chemicals and related products 10.3%; food products 5.2%; clothing 4.4%). Major import sources: Germany 41.9%; Italy 7.6%; United States 5.3%; France 5.0%; Switzerland 3.4%; Hungary 3.3%. Exports (1999-f.o.b.): S 829,300,000,000 (machinery and transport equipment 43.1%, of which road vehicles 10.0%, elec-

1 metric ton = about 1.1 short tons;   1 kilometer = 0.6 mi (statute);   1 metric ton-km cargo = about 0.68 short ton-mi cargo;   c.i.f.: cost, insurance, and freight;   f.o.b.: free on board

trical machinery and apparatus 8.1%; chemical products 9.4%; fabricated metals 4.9%); paper and paper products 4.7%. *Major export destinations*: Germany 34.9%; Italy 8.4%; Switzerland 6.0%; Hungary 4.9%; United States 4.6%; France 4.4%.

Transport and communications

Transport. *Railroads* (federal railways only): (1999) length 5,643 km; (1998) passenger-km 7,971,-000,000; (1998) metric ton-km cargo 15,348,000,-000. *Roads* (1997): total length 200,000 km (paved 100%). *Vehicles* (1999): passenger cars 4,009,604; trucks and buses 328,591. *Air transport* (Austrian Airlines and Lauda Air; 1999): passenger-km 12,460,000,000; metric ton-km cargo 361,348,000; airports (1999) with scheduled flights 6. **Communications** Total units (units per 1,000 persons). Daily newspaper circulation (1996): 2,382,000 (296); Radio receivers (1996): 6,000,000 (744); Television receivers (1998): 4,200,000 (520); Telephone main lines (1999): 3,863,000 (477); Cellular telephone subscribers (1999): 4,206,000 (520); Personal computers (1999): 2,100,000 (260); Internet users (1999): 1,840,000 (227).

Education and health

Educational attainment (1993). Percentage of pop. age 25 and over having: lower-secondary education 37.5%; vocational education ending at secondary level 44.6%; completed upper secondary 6.1%; high or vocational 5.5%; higher 6.3%. **Literacy:** virtually 100%. **Health:** physicians (2000) 24,223 (1 per 335 persons); hospital beds (1998) 68,918 (1 per 117 persons); infant mortality rate per 1,000 live births (1999) 4.4. **Food** (1998): daily per capita caloric intake 3,531 (vegetable products 65%, animal products 35%); 134% of FAO recommended minimum requirement.

Military

Total active duty personnel (2000): 35,500 (army 100%). **Military expenditure as percentage of GNP** (1997): 0.9% (world 2.6%); per capita expenditure $222.

Did you know? The modern waltz, based on a German country dance, the Ländler, emerged in rural 18th-century Vienna. With its turning, embracing couples, the waltz at first shocked polite society but soon gained international popularity as the ballroom dance par excellence.

Background

Settlement in Austria goes back some 3,000 years, when Illyrians were probably the main inhabitants. The Celts invaded c. 400 BC and established Noricum. The Romans arrived after 200 BC and established the provinces of Raetia, Noricum, and Pannonia; prosperity followed and the population became Romanized. With the fall of Rome in the 5th century AD, many tribes invaded, including the Slavs; they were eventually subdued by Charlemagne, and the area became ethnically Germanic. The distinct political entity that would become Austria emerged in 976 with Leopold I of Babenberg as margrave. In

1278 Rudolf I of the Holy Roman Empire (formerly Rudolf IV of Habsburg) conquered the area; Habsburg rule lasted until 1918. While in power, the Habsburgs created a kingdom centered on Austria, Bohemia, and Hungary. The Napoleonic Wars brought about the creation of the Austrian empire (1804) and the end of the Holy Roman Empire (1806). Count von Metternich tried to assure Austrian supremacy among Germanic states, but war with Prussia led Austria to divide the empire into the Dual Monarchy of Austria-Hungary. Nationalist sentiment plagued the kingdom, and the assassination of Francis Ferdinand by a Serbian nationalist in 1914 triggered World War I, which destroyed the Austrian empire. In the postwar carving up of Austria-Hungary, Austria became an independent republic. It was annexed by Nazi Germany in 1938 and joined the Axis powers in World War II. The republic was restored in 1955 after 10 years of Allied occupation. Austria became a member of the European Union in 1995.

Recent Developments

Negotiations between Austria's center-left and center-right coalition partners broke down in January 2000, and the conservative Austrian People's Party (ÖVP) quickly agreed to enter into coalition with the populist right-wing Freedom Party of Austria (FPÖ). The ÖVP's former coalition partner, the Social Democratic Party of Austria (SPÖ), reacted angrily to the inclusion in government of the FPÖ, which had been considered too extremist to participate. The new coalition's policies and actions remained on a moderate and for the most part uncontroversial course, however, largely because the ÖVP continued to dominate the arrangement, remaining in almost complete control of the political and policy agenda.

Internet resources: <www.austria.org>

Azerbaijan

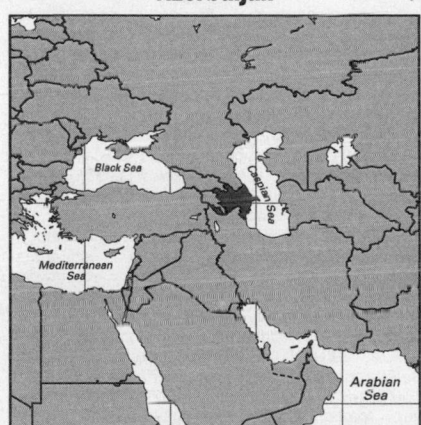

Official name: Azerbaycan Cumhuriyeti (Azerbaijani Republic). **Form of government:** unitary multiparty republic with a single legislative body (National Assembly [124 seats, excluding one vacancy reserved for a Nagorno-Karabakh representative]). **Head of state and government:** President Heydar Aliyev (from 1993) assisted by Prime Minister Artur

Rasizade (from 1996). **Capital:** Baku. **Official language:** Azerbaijani. **Official religion:** none. **Monetary unit:** 1 manat (A.M.) = 100 gopik; valuation (28 Jun 2002) free rate, $1 = A.M. 4,857.

Demography

Area: 33,400 sq mi, 86,600 sq km. **Population** (2001): 8,105,000. **Density** (2001): persons per sq mi 242.7, persons per sq km 93.6. **Urban** (1998): 56.6%. **Sex distribution** (1999): male 49.1%; female 50.9%. **Age breakdown** (1999): under 15, 32.8%; 15–29, 25.9%; 30–44, 22.3%; 45–59, 10.0%; 60–69, 5.9%; 70 and over, 3.1%. **Ethnic composition** (1995): Azerbaijani 89.0%; Russian 3.0%; Lezgian 2.2%; Armenian 2.0%; other 3.8%. **Religious affiliation** (1995): Muslim 93.4% of which Shi'i 65.4%, Sunni 28.0%; Russian Orthodox 1.1%; Armenian Apostolic (Orthodox) 1.1%; other 4.4%. **Major cities** (1997): Baku 1,727,200; Ganca (formerly Kirovabad) 291,900; Sumqayit (Sumgait) 248,500; Mingacevir (Mingechaur) 97,200. **Location:** eastern Transcaucasia, bordering Russia, the Caspian Sea, Iran, Turkey, Armenia, and Georgia.

Vital statistics

Birth rate per 1,000 population (2001): 13.7 (world avg. 22.5); (1994) legitimate 94.8%; illegitimate 5.2%. **Death rate** per 1,000 population (2001): 6.2 (world avg. 9.0). **Natural increase rate** per 1,000 population (2001): 7.5 (world avg. 13.5). **Total fertility rate** (avg. births per childbearing woman; 2001): 1.6. **Marriage rate** per 1,000 population (1994): 6.3. **Divorce rate** per 1,000 population (1994): 0.8. **Life expectancy** at birth (2001): male 68.0 years; female 75.0 years.

National economy

Budget (1998). *Revenue:* A.M. 2,318,400,000,000 (tax revenue 93.7%, of which value-added tax 30.0%, individual income tax 17.8%, enterprise profits tax 14.1%, tax on international trade 12.6%, property tax 7.4%, excise tax 4.1%, other taxes 7.7%; nontax revenue 6.3%). *Expenditures:* A.M. 2,642,200,000,000 (social protection 23.3%; education 21.4%; national economy 8.6%; health 5.8%; culture 3.5%; other 37.4%). **Public debt** (external, outstanding; 1999): $493,300,000. **Production** (metric tons except as noted). *Agriculture, forestry, fishing* (1999): cereals 932,111, fruit 482,846, vegetables (except potatoes) 369,000, potatoes 334,000, cotton lint 39,000, tobacco leaves 9,000; livestock (number of live animals) 5,502,800 sheep and goats, 1,909,800 cattle, 13,300,000 poultry; roundwood (1993) 17,000 cu m; fish catch (1998) 4,678. *Mining and quarrying* (1996): iron ore 1,000,000; alunite 600,000. *Manufacturing* (value of production in A.M. '000,000,000; 1998): oil refinery products 2,980; electricity and gas 2,005; food products 1,972; textiles 468; chemicals 320. *Energy production (consumption):* electricity (kW-hr; 1997) 16,800,000,000 (16,800,000,000); coal (metric tons; 1994) none (8,000); crude petroleum (barrels; 1997) 66,703,000 (76,672,000); petroleum products (metric tons; 1998) 7,800,000 (6,200,000); natural gas (cu m; 1998) 6,000,000,000 (6,000,-

000,000). **Household income and expenditure.** Average household size (1997) 5.2; sources of income (1993): wages and salaries 50.9%, agricultural income 24.0%, social benefits 10.2%; expenditure: food 61.2%, clothing 11.1%, services 3.0%. **Tourism** (1999): receipts from visitors $81,000,000; expenditures by nationals abroad $139,000,000. **Gross national product** (at current market prices; 1999): $3,705,000,000 ($460 per capita). **Population economically active** (1998): total 3,743,800, activity rate of total population 47.1% (participation rates: ages 15–59 [male], 15–54 [female] 85.9%; female 82.1%; unemployed 1.3%). **Land use** (1994): forest 11.0%; pasture 25.4%; agriculture 48.5%; other 15.1%.

Foreign trade

Imports (1998-c.i.f.): $1,077,169,100 (machinery and equipment 40.4%, food 16.4%, metals 12.4%, chemical products 7.4%). *Major import sources:* Turkey 20.4%; Russia 18.0%; Ukraine 8.6%; UK 6.4%; Germany 4.3%; United Arab Emirates 4.2%; Iran 4.0%; US 3.7%. **Exports** (1998-f.o.b.): $606,150,-500,000 (petroleum products 69.1%, textile 9.2%, food 7.7%, machinery and equipment 6.0%, metals 2.2%). *Major export destinations:* Turkey 22.4%; Russia 17.4%; Georgia 12.7%; Italy 7.4%.

Transport and communications

Transport. *Railroads* (1998): length 2,120 km; passenger-km (1996) 550,000,000; metric ton-km cargo 4,613,000,000. *Roads* (1998): total length 45,870 km (paved 93.8%). *Vehicles* (1998): passenger cars 281,100; trucks and buses 104,300. *Air transport* (1995): passenger-km 1,650,000,000; metric ton-km cargo 183,000,000; airports (1998) 3. **Communications.** Daily newspaper circulation (1995): 210,000 (28 units per 1,000 persons); Radio receivers (1997): 175,000 (23 units per 1,000 persons); Television receivers (1998): 1,950,000 (253 units per 1,000 persons); Telephone main lines (1999): 730,000 (95 units per 1,000 persons); Cellular telephone subscribers (1999): 180,000 (23 units per 1,000 persons); Internet users (1999): 8,000 (1 per 1,000 persons).

Education and health

Educational attainment (1995). Percentage of population age 15 and over having: primary education or no formal schooling 12.1%, some secondary 9.1%; completed secondary and some postsecondary 27.5%; higher 7.6%. **Literacy** (1989): percentage of total population 15 and over literate 97.3%; males literate 98.9%; females 95.9%. **Health** (1998): physicians 28,850 (1 per 276 persons); hospital beds 71,100 (1 per 110 persons); infant mortality rate per 1,000 live births (2001) 30.0. **Food** (1999): daily per capita caloric intake 2,224 (vegetable product 84%, animal products 16%); (1997) 87% of FAO recommended minimum.

Military

Total active duty personnel (2000): 72,100 (army 85.7%, navy 3.1%, air force 11.2%). **Military expendi-**

1 metric ton = about 1.1 short tons;   1 kilometer = 0.6 mi (statute);   1 metric ton-km cargo = about 0.68 short ton-mi cargo;   c.i.f.: cost, insurance, and freight;   f.o.b.: free on board

ture as percentage of GNP (1997): 1.9% (world 2.6%); per capita expenditure (1997) $29.

Background

Azerbaijan adjoins the Iranian region of the same name, and the origin of their respective inhabitants is the same. By the 9th century AD it had come under Turkish influence, and in ensuing centuries it was fought over by Arabs, Mongols, Turks, and Iranians. Russia acquired the territory of what is now Independent Azerbaijan in the early 19th century. After the Russian Revolution of 1917, Azerbaijan declared its independence; it was subdued by the Red Army in 1920 and became a Soviet Socialist Republic. It declared independence from the collapsing Soviet Union in 1991. Azerbaijan has two geographic peculiarities. The exclave Nakhichevan is separated from the rest of Azerbaijan by Armenian territory. Nagorno-Karabakh, which lies within Azerbaijan and is administered by it, has a Christian Armenian majority. Azerbaijan and Armenia went to war over both territories in the 1990s, causing great economic disruption. Though a ceasefire was declared in 1994, the political situation remained unresolved.

Recent Developments

Azerbaijan was admitted to full membership of the Council of Europe in January 2001. Talks between Pres. Heydar Aliyev and his Armenian counterpart, Robert Kocharyan, in Paris later in the year were billed as heralding a formal agreement ending the conflict over Nagorno-Karabakh, but Aliyev subsequently denied that any agreement in principle had been reached.

Internet resources: <www.president.az>

Bahamas, The

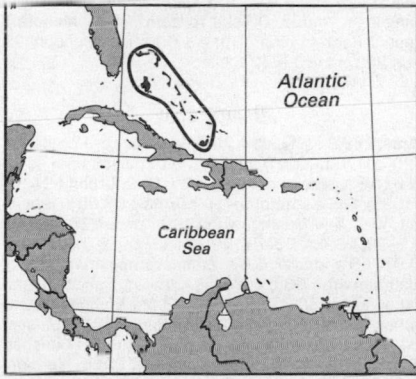

Atlantic Ocean

Caribbean Sea

Official name: The Commonwealth of The Bahamas. Form of government: constitutional monarchy with two legislative houses (Senate [16]; House of Assembly [40]). Chief of state: Queen Elizabeth II represented by Governor-General Dame Ivy Dumont (from 13 Nov 2001). Head of government: Prime Minister Hubert Ingraham (from 1992). Capital: Nassau. Official language: English. Official religion: none. Monetary unit: 1 Bahamian dollar (B$) = 100 cents; valuation (28 Jun 2002) US$1 = B$1.00.

Demography

Area: 5,382 sq mi, 13,939 sq km. Population (2001): 298,000. Density (2001; based on land area only): persons per sq mi 76.6, persons per sq km 29.6. Urban (2000): 88.3%. Sex distribution (1995): male 48.91%; female 51.09%. Age breakdown (1995): under 15, 31.4%; 15–29, 27.9%; 30–44, 22.5%; 45–59, 11.4%; 60–74, 5.0%; 75 and over, 1.8%. Ethnic composition (1990): black 86.0%; white 6.0%; mixed/other 8.0%. Religious affiliation (1995): non-Anglican Protestant 45.4% of which Baptist 17.5%; Roman Catholic 16.8%; Anglican 10.8%; non-religious 5.3%; Spiritist 1.5%; other (mostly independent and unaffiliated Christian) 20.2%. Major cities (1990): Nassau 172,196 (pop. of New Providence Island); Freeport/Lucaya 26,574. Location: chain of islands in the Caribbean Sea, southeast of Florida.

Vital statistics

Birth rate per 1,000 pop. (2000): 19.5 (world avg. 22.5); (1995) legitimate 45.7%; illegitimate 54.3%. Death rate per 1,000 pop. (2000): 6.8 (world avg. 9.0). Natural increase rate per 1,000 pop. (2000): 12.7 (world avg. 13.5). Total fertility rate (avg. births per childbearing woman; 2000): 2.3. Marriage rate per 1,000 pop. (1996): 9.3. Life expectancy at birth (2000): male 68.3 years; female 73.9 years.

National economy

Budget (1998–99). Revenue: B$730,102,000 (import taxes 45.1%, stamp taxes from imports 11.0%, business and professional licenses 7.4%, departure taxes 6.6%, fines and forfeits 6.1%). Expenditures: B$748,150,000 (education 19.7%, health 15.5%, interest on public debt 13.2%, general administration 12.8%, public order 11.1%, tourism 6.0%, defense 3.7%). National debt (December 2000): US$1,521,000,000. Production (value of production in B$'000 except as noted). Agriculture, forestry, fishing (1998): crayfish 54,100, poultry products 28,300, citrus and other fruit 21,300, fish 6,600, ornamental plants and flowers 6,000; roundwood (1998) 117,000 cu m. Mining and quarrying (value of export production; 1996): salt 18,100, aragonite 4,900. Manufacturing (value of export production; 1996): pharmaceuticals and other chemical products (1995) 74,200, rum 5,200. Energy production (consumption): electricity (kW-hr; 1996) 1,340,000,000 (1,340,000,000); petroleum products (metric tons; 1996) none (555,000). Tourism: receipts (2000) US$1,814,000,000; expenditures (1999) US$309,000,000. Household income and expenditure. Average household size (1996) 3.9; income per household (1996) B$27,252; expenditure (1995): housing 32.8%, transportation and communications 14.8% food and beverages 13.8%, household furnishings 8.9%. Gross national product (1998): US$3,432,000,000 (US$11,890 per capita). Population economically active (1996): total 146,635; activity rate of total pop. 51.6% (participation rates: [1994] ages 15–64, 77.8%; female 47.5%; unemployed [1998] 9.5%). Land use (1994): forest 32.4%; pasture 0.2%; agriculture 1.0%; other 66.4%.

Foreign trade

Imports (1999-c.i.f.): B$1,907,000,000 (machinery and transport equipment 30.8%; food products

13.7%; chemicals and chemical products 11.7%; petroleum for domestic use 8.7%). *Major import sources* (1998; excludes all petroleum): US 91.5%; EC 1.6%. **Exports** (1999-f.o.b.): B$486,300,000 (domestic exports 48.3%, of which crayfish 14.9%, rum 6.4%; reexports 44.2%; petroleum exports 7.5%). *Major export destinations* (1998; excludes all petroleum): US 56.5%; EC 31.4%; Canada 2.1%.

Transport and communications

Transport. *Railroads*: none. *Roads* (1995): total length 1,522 mi, 2,450 km (paved 57%). Vehicles (1996): passenger cars 89,263; trucks and buses 17,228. *Air transport* (1997; Bahamasair scheduled traffic only): passenger-mi 87,000,000, passenger-km 140,000,000; short ton-mi cargo 312,000, metric ton-km cargo 455,000; airports (1997) with scheduled flights 22. **Communications.** Total units (units per 1,000 persons). Daily newspaper circulation (1996): 28,000 (99); Radio receivers (1997): 215,000 (744); Television receivers (1997): 67,000 (232); Telephone main lines (1999): 111,184 (381); Cellular telephone subscribers (1999): 15,911 (55).

Education and health

Educational attainment (1990). Percentage of pop. age 25 and over having: no formal schooling 3.5%; incomplete primary education 25.4%; complete primary/incomplete secondary 57.6%; complete secondary/higher 13.5%. **Literacy** (1995): total percentage age 15 and over literate 98.2%. **Health:** physicians (1996) 419 (1 per 678 persons); hospital beds (1997) 1,119 (1 per 258 persons); infant mortality rate per 1,000 live births (2000) 17.0. **Food** (1999): daily per capita caloric intake 2,500 (vegetable products 71%, animal products 29%); 103% of FAO recommended minimum requirement.

Military

Total active duty personnel (2000): 860 (paramilitary coast guard 100%). **Military expenditure as percentage of GNP** (1997): 0.9% (world 2.6%); per capita expenditure US$100.

Background

The islands were inhabited by Lucayan Indians when Christopher Columbus sighted them on 12 Oct 1492. He is thought to have landed on San Salvador (Watling) Island. The Spaniards made no attempt to settle but carried out slave raids that depopulated the islands; when English settlers arrived in 1648 from Bermuda, the islands were uninhabited. They became a haunt of pirates, and few of the ensuing settlements prospered. The islands enjoyed some prosperity following the American Revolution, when Loyalists fled the US and established cotton plantations there. The islands were a center for blockade runners during the American Civil War. Not until the development of tourism after World War II did permanent economic prosperity arrive. The Bahamas was granted internal self-government in 1964 and became independent in 1973.

Recent Developments

The highly successful offshore financial sector of The Bahamas was rocked to its foundations in 2000, when the Paris-based Financial Action Task Force included it on a list of countries that had not been taking sufficient action against money launderers. After several subsequent government initiatives, including the banning of anonymous ownership of the more than 100,000 international business companies registered in The Bahamas, the task force removed the country from its list in 2001.

Internet resources: <www.bahamas.com>

Bahrain

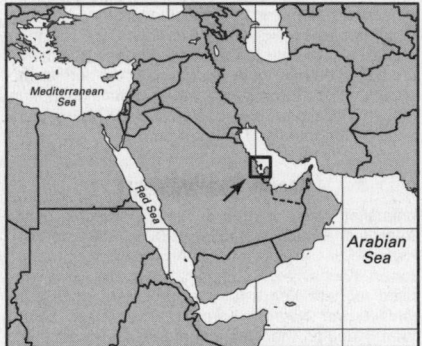

Official name: Mamlakat al-Bahrayn (Kingdom of Bahrain). **Form of government:** constitutional monarchy (declared 14 Feb 2002). **Chief of state:** Sheikh Hamad ibn 'Isa al-Khalifah (from 6 Mar 1999). **Head of Government:** Prime Minister Khalifah ibn Sulman al-Khalifah (from 1970). **Capital:** Manama. **Official language:** Arabic. **Official religion:** Islam. **Monetary unit:** 1 Bahrain dinar (BD) = 1,000 fils; valuation (28 Jun 2002) 1 BD = $2.63.

Demography

Area: 268.0 sq mi, 694.2 (rounded) sq km. **Population** (2001): 701,000. **Density** (2001): persons per sq mi 2,616.8, persons per sq km 1,010.2. **Urban** : 90.3% (1995). **Sex distribution** (1999): male 58.60%; female 41.40%. **Age breakdown** (1999): under 15, 30.9%; 15–29, 28.4%; 30–44, 29.1%; 45–59, 8.0%; 60–74, 3.0%; 75 and over, 0.6%. **Ethnic composition** (1991): Bahraini Arab 63.6%; Persian, Indian, Pakistani, and other Asians 30.3%; other Arab 3.5%; European 1.2%; other 1.4%. **Religious affiliation** (1991): Muslim 81.8%, of which Shi'i 61.3%, Sunni 20.5%; Christian 8.5%; other 9.7%. **Major cities** (1991): Manama (1992) 140,401; Ar-Rifa' 45,956; Al-Muharraq 45,337; Madinat 'Isa 34,509. **Location:** Middle East, archipelago in the Persian Gulf, east of Saudi Arabia.

Vital statistics

Birth rate per 1,000 pop. (2000): 20.6 (world avg. 22.5). **Death rate** per 1,000 pop. (2000): 3.9 (world

1 metric ton = about 1.1 short tons;   1 kilometer = 0.6 mi (statute);   1 metric ton-km cargo = about 0.68 short ton-mi cargo;   c.i.f.: cost, insurance, and freight;   f.o.b.: free on board

avg. 9.0). **Natural increase rate** per 1,000 pop. (2000): 16.7 (world avg. 13.5). **Total fertility rate** (avg. births per childbearing woman; 2000): 2.8. **Life expectancy at birth** (2000): male 70.6 years; female 75.5 years.

National economy

Budget (1999). *Revenue*: BD 566,000,000 ([1995] entrepreneurial and property income 57.7%, import duties 8.4%, foreign grants 6.7%). *Expenditures*: BD 726,000,000 ([1995] general administration and public order 33.2%, defense 17.3%, education 13.4%, fuel and energy 9.6%, health 9.3%, transportation and communications 9.0%). **Population economically active** (1991): total 226,448; activity rate of total pop. 44.6% (participation rates: ages 15–64, 66.1%; female 17.5%; unemployed [1997] c. 30%). **Production** (metric tons except as noted). *Agriculture, forestry, fishing* (1999): fruit (excluding melons) 21,800, dates 16,800, cow's milk 14,000, livestock (number of live animals) 17,100 sheep, 16,000 goats, 13,000 cattle; fish catch (1998) 9,849. *Manufacturing* (barrels; 1994): gas oil 28,900,000; fuel oil 20,900,000; kerosene 10,400,000. *Energy production (consumption)*: electricity (kW-hr; 1998) 5,773,000,000 (5,226,000,000); crude petroleum (barrels; 1998) 13,751,000 ([1996] 82,723,000); petroleum products (metric tons; 1996) 13,100,000 (538,000). **Gross national product** (1998): $4,909,000,000 ($7,640 per capita). **Public debt** (1999): BD 589,800,000 ($1,568,632,000). **Household income and expenditure**. Average household size (1991) 5.8; expenditure (1984): food and tobacco 33.3%, housing 21.2%, household durable goods 9.8%, transportation and communications 8.5%, recreation 6.4%, clothing and footwear 5.9%, education 2.7%, health 2.3%, energy and water 2.2%. **Tourism** (1999): receipts from visitors $408,000,000; expenditures by nationals abroad $159,000,000. **Land use** (1994): meadows and pastures 5.8%; agricultural and under permanent cultivation 2.9%; built on and wasteland 91.3%.

Foreign trade

Imports (1998-c.i.f.): BD 1,340,900,000 (machinery and transport equipment 27.6%, crude petroleum products 20.4%, food and live animals 12.8%, chemicals 11.2%). *Major import sources*: Japan 11.5%; United States 10.4%; Australia 9.7%; United Kingdom 7.4%; Saudi Arabia 7.2%; Italy 5.8%; Germany 5.7%. **Exports** (1998-f.o.b.): BD 1,229,600,000 (petroleum products 51.8%, metal and metal products 29.5%). *Major export destinations*: Saudi Arabia 8.2%; United States 6.0%; Japan 4.4%; India 2.8%; Taiwan 2.6%.

Transport and communications

Transport. *Roads* (1998): total length 3,164 km (paved 77%). *Vehicles* (1997): passenger cars 149,636; trucks and buses 32,213. *Air transport* (1999 one-fourth apportionment of international flights of Gulf Air): passenger-km 2,835,900,000; metric ton-km cargo 118,681,000; airports (1997) with scheduled flights 1. **Communications** Total units (units per 1,000 persons). Daily newspaper circulation (1996): 67,000 (117); Radio receivers (1997): 338,000 (580); Television receivers (1999): 270,000 (405); Telephones main lines (1999): 165,369 (248); Cellular telephone subscribers (1999): 133,468

(200); Personal computers (1999): 93,000 (139); Internet users (1999): 30,000 (45).

Education and health

Educational attainment (1991). Percentage of pop. age 25 and over having: no formal education 38.4%; primary education 26.2%; secondary 25.1%; higher 10.3%. **Literacy** (1995): percentage of pop. age 15 and over literate 85.2%; males literate 89.1%; females literate 79.4%. **Health** (1998): physicians 709 (1 per 907 persons); hospital beds 1,832 (1 per 351 persons); infant mortality rate per 1,000 live births (2000) 20.5.

Military

Total active duty personnel (2000): 11,000 (army 77.3%, navy 9.1%, air force 13.6%). **Military expenditure as percentage of GNP** (1997): 10.3% (world 2.6%); per capita expenditure $883.

Background

The area has long been an important trading center and is mentioned in Persian, Greek, and Roman references. It was ruled by Arabs from the 7th century AD, but then occupied by the Portuguese 1521–1602. Since 1783 it has been ruled by the Khalifah family, though through a series of treaties its defense remained a British responsibility from 1820 to 1971. After Britain withdrew its forces from the Persian Gulf (1968), Bahrain declared its independence in 1971. It served as a center for the allies in the Persian Gulf War. Since 1994 it has experienced bouts of political unrest, mainly by Shi'ites, who have attempted to get the government to restore the parliament (abolished in 1975).

Recent Developments

In February 2001 Bahrainis approved by referendum the National Action Charter by an overwhelming majority—98.4%. The charter, proposed by the government, promised democratic reforms, including parliamentary elections and a separation of powers.

Internet resources: <www.bahraintourism.com>

Bangladesh

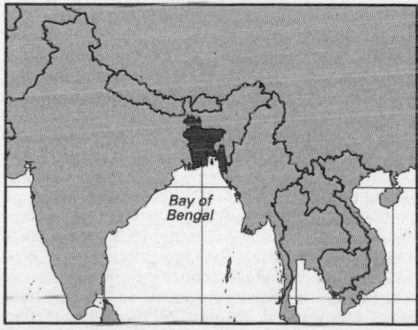

Official name: People's Republic of Bangladesh. **Form of government**: unitary multiparty republic with one legislative house (Parliament [330 seats, includes 30 reserved for women]). **Chief of state:** President A.Q.M. Badruddoza Chowdhury (from 14 Nov 2001). **Head of government:** Prime Minister Khaleda Zia (from 10 Oct 2001). **Capital:** Dhaka. **Official language:** Bengali. **Official religion:** Islam. **Monetary unit:** 1 Bangladesh taka (Tk) = 100 paisa; valuation (28 Jun 2002) $1 = Tk 57.45.

Demography

Area: 56,977sq mi, 147,570 sq km. **Population** (2001): 131,270,000. **Density** (2001): persons per sq mi 2,303.9, persons per sq km 889.5. **Urban** (2000): 25%. **Sex distribution** (1996): male 51.72%; female 48.28%. **Age breakdown** (1996): under 15, 42.0%; 15–29, 26.4%; 30–44, 17.8%; 45–59, 8.9%; 60–74, 3.8%; 75 and over, 1.1%. **Ethnic composition** (1997): Bengali 97.7%; tribal 1.9%. **Religious affiliation** (2000): Muslim 85.8%; Hindu 12.4%; Christian 0.7%; Buddhist 0.6%; other 0.5%. **Major cities** (1991-metropolitan population): Dhaka 6,105,160; Chittagong 2,040,663; Khulna 877,388; Rajshahi 517,136; Mymensingh 185,517 (municipal population). **Location:** South Asia, bordering India, Burma, and Bay of Bengal.

Vital statistics

Birth rate per 1,000 pop. (2000): 27.0 (world avg. 22.5). **Death rate** per 1,000 pop. (2000): 9.1 (world avg. 9.0). **Natural increase rate** per 1,000 pop. (2000): 17.9 (world avg. 13.5). **Total fertility rate** (avg. births per childbearing woman; 2000): 3.0. **Marriage rate** per 1,000 pop. (1996): 10.1. **Divorce rate** per 1,000 pop. (1981): 3.6. **Life expectancy** at birth (2000): male 59.0 years; female 60.0 years.

National economy

Budget (1998-99). *Revenue:* Tk 210,000,000,000 (value-added tax 37.4%; customs duties 24.0%; income taxes 11.7%; service charges 5.0%; public telephone enterprises 4.3%; interest receipts 2.8%). *Expenditures:* Tk 157,500,000,000 (goods and services 52.4%; transfer payments 28.4%; interest payments 16.3%). **Production** (metric tons except as noted). *Agriculture, forestry, fishing* (2000): paddy rice 35,821,000, sugarcane 6,951,000, wheat 1,900,000; livestock (number of live animals) 33,800,000 goats, 23,652,000 cattle, 139,300,000 chickens; roundwood 33,629,000 cu m; fish catch (1998) 839,141. *Mining and quarrying* (1997-98): marine salt 350,000; industrial limestone 26,000. *Manufacturing* (value added in $'000,000; 1995): textiles 651; industrial chemicals 441; food products 331. *Energy production (consumption):* electricity (kW-hr; 1996) 12,404,000,000 (12,404,000,000); coal (metric tons; 1996) none (negligible); crude petroleum (barrels; 1996) 52,000 (10,423,000); petroleum products (metric tons; 1996) 688,000 (2,049,000); natural gas (cu m; 1996) 8,278,000,000 (8,278,000,000). **Household income.** Average household size (1995-96) 5.3; average annual income per household Tk 52,389; sources of income: self-employment 56.9%, wages and salaries 28.1%, transfer pay-

ments 9.1%, other 5.9%; expenditure: food and drink 57.7%, housing and rent 11.1%, clothing and footwear 6.5%, energy 5.6%, other 19.1%. **Population economically active** (1995-96): total 56,014,000; activity rate of total pop. 46.0% (participation rates: over age 10, 64.8%; female 38.1%; unemployed 2.5% [excluding underemployment]). **Public debt** (external, outstanding; 1998): $15,804,-000,000. **Gross national product** (1998): $44,244,-000,000 ($350 per capita). **Land use** (1998): pasture 4.6%; agriculture 68.6%; forest and other 26.8%. **Tourism** (1999): receipts $50,000,000; expenditures $212,000,000.

Foreign trade

Imports (1997-98): Tk 341,850,000,000 (textile yarn, fabrics, and made-up articles 24.6%; machinery and transport equipment 12.5%; petroleum and products 5.8%; iron and steel 5.2%; cereals and cereal preparations 3.9%). *Major import sources:* India 15.0%; Western Europe 13.0%; China 10.0%; Japan 9.0%; South Korea 7.0%; Hong Kong 6.0%; Singapore 5.0%; US 5.0%. **Exports** (1997-98): Tk 203,970,000,000 (ready-made garments 61.9%; fish and prawns 7.3%; jute manufactures 6.5%; hides, skins, and leather 4.0%; raw jute 2.4%; tea 1.0%). *Major export destinations:* Western Europe 49.0%; US 32.0%; Hong Kong 3.0%; Japan 2.7%; Canada 2.0%; Pakistan 1.2%.

Transport and communications

Transport. *Railroads* (1998-99): route length 1,699 mi, 2,734 km; passenger-mi 3,094,000,000, passenger-km 4,980,000,000; short ton-mi cargo 567,000,000, metric ton-km cargo 828,000,000. *Roads* (1996): total length 126,773 mi, 204,022 km (paved 12%). *Vehicles* (1998): passenger cars 54,784; trucks and buses 69,394. *Air transport* (1999—Bangladesh Biman only): passenger-mi 2,153,757,000, passenger-km 3,466,143,000; short ton-mi cargo 94,885,000, metric ton-km cargo 138,530,000; airports with scheduled flights (1997) 8. **Communications.** Total units (units per 1,000 persons). Daily newspaper circulation (1996): 1,117,-000 (9); Radio receivers (1998): 8,000,000 (64); Television receivers (1999): 940,000 (7.4); Telephone main lines (1999): 432,968 (3.4); Cellular telephone subscribers (1999): 149,000 (1.2); Personal computers (1999): 130,000 (1); Internet users (1999): 50,000 (0.4).

Education and health

Educational attainment (1991). Percentage of pop. age 25 and over having: no formal schooling 65.4%; primary education 17.1%; secondary 13.8%; post-secondary 3.7%. **Literacy** (1995): total pop. age 15 and over literate 38.1%; males literate 49.4%; females literate 26.1%. **Health** (1997): physicians 26,608 (1 per 4,627 persons); hospital beds 39,900 (1 per 3,086 persons); infant mortality rate (2000) 73.0. **Food** (1999): daily per capita caloric intake 2,201 (vegetable products 97%, animal products 3%); (1997) 95% of FAO recommended minimum requirement.

---

1 metric ton = about 1.1 short tons; 1 kilometer = 0.6 mi (statute); 1 metric ton-km cargo = about 0.68 short ton-mi cargo; c.i.f.: cost, insurance, and freight; f.o.b.: free on board

Military

Total active duty personnel (2000): 137,000 (army 87.6%, navy 7.7%, air force 4.7%). **Military expenditure as percentage of GNP** (1997): 1.4% (world 2.6%); per capita expenditure $5.

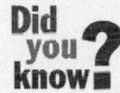

Bangladesh is the location of the Sundarbans, a large forest and swampy area in the delta of the Ganges River, one of the last preserves of the endangered Bengal tiger.

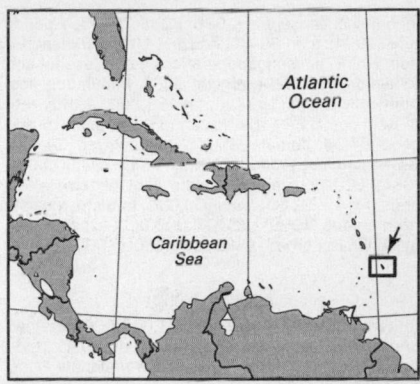

Atlantic Ocean

Caribbean Sea

Background

In its early years Bangladesh was known as Bengal. When the British left the subcontinent in 1947, the area that was East Bengal became the part of Pakistan called East Pakistan. Bengali nationalist sentiment increased after the creation of an independent Pakistan. In 1971 violence erupted; some one million Bengalis were killed, and millions more fled to India, which finally entered the war on the side of the Bengalis, ensuring West Pakistan's defeat. East Pakistan became the independent nation of Bangladesh. Little of the devastation caused by the war has been repaired, and political instability, including the assassination of two presidents, has continued. In addition, the low-lying country has been repeatedly battered by natural disasters, notably tropical storms and flooding.

Recent Developments

In a stunning upset in the parliamentary elections held on 1 Oct 2001, the four-party opposition alliance headed by the Bangladesh Nationalist Party (BNP) won a two-thirds majority, taking 214 of the 300 seats. The Awami League, which had run the country since 1996, suffered its worst-ever defeat, securing only 62 seats. The BNP itself claimed 191 seats. Just two days before the presidential elections were to be held on 13 November, independent candidate Mohammad Raushan Ali withdrew from the race; running unopposed, Foreign Minister A.Q.M. Badruddoza Chowdhury was named president by the Election Commission.

Internet resources: <www.bangladeshgov.org>

Barbados

Official name: Barbados. **Form of government:** constitutional monarchy with two legislative houses (Senate [21]; House of Assembly [28]). **Chief of state:** Queen Elizabeth II represented by Governor-General Sir Clifford Husbands (from 1996). **Head of government:** Prime Minister Owen Arthur (from 1994). **Capital:** Bridgetown. **Official language:** English. **Official religion:** none. **Monetary unit:** 1 Barbados dollar (BDS$) = 100 cents; valuation (28 Jun 2002) US$1 = BDS$1.99.

Demography

Area: 166 sq mi, 430 sq km. **Population** (2001): 269,000. **Density** (2001): persons per sq mi 1,618, persons per sq km 624. **Urban** (1998): 48.9%. **Sex distribution** (2000): male 48.07%; female 51.93%. **Age breakdown** (2000): under 15, 22.0%; 15–29, 24.2%; 30–44, 26.1%; 45–59, 15.7%; 60–74, 7.9%; 75 and over, 4.1%. **Ethnic composition** (1990): black 92.5%; white 3.2%; mixed 2.8%; other 1.5%. **Religious affiliation** (1995): Protestant 63.0%, of which Anglican 26.3%, Pentecostal 10.6%, Methodist 5.7%; Roman Catholic 4.8%; other Christian 2.0%; nonreligious/other 30.2%. **Major cities** (1990): Bridgetown 6,070 (urban agglomeration [1999] 133,000); Speightstown, c. 3,500. **Location:** northeast of Venezuela at the eastern edge of the Caribbean Sea where it adjoins the North Atlantic Ocean.

Vital statistics

Birth rate per 1,000 pop. (2000): 13.6 (world avg. 22.5). **Death rate** per 1,000 pop. (2000): 8.7 (world avg. 9.0). **Natural increase rate** per 1,000 pop. (2000): 4.9 (world avg. 13.5). **Total fertility rate** (avg. births per childbearing woman; 2000): 1.6. **Marriage rate** per 1,000 pop. (1995): 13.5. **Divorce rate** per 1,000 pop. (1995): 1.5. **Life expectancy** at birth (2000): male 70.4 years; female 75.6 years.

National economy

Budget (1997–98). Revenue: BDS$1,458,274,000 (tax revenue 94.7%, of which goods and services taxes 49.5%, personal income and company taxes 29.5%, import duties 8.8%; nontax revenue 5.3%). Expenditures: BDS$1,508,869,000 (current expenditure 83.2%, of which education 18.8%, economic services 11.5%, health 10.9%, social security and welfare 8.3%). **Production** (metric tons except as noted). Agriculture, forestry, fishing (1998): raw sugar 48,000, sweet potatoes 5,100, cucumbers 1,400; livestock (number of live animals) 41,000 sheep, 33,000 pigs, 23,000 cattle; fish catch (1997) 2,764. Manufacturing (value added in BDS$'000; 1995): food, beverages, and tobacco (mostly sugar, molasses, rum, beer, and cigarettes) 108,000; paper products, printing, and publishing 33,400; metal products and assembly-type goods (mostly electronic components) 28,000. Energy production (consumption): electricity (kW-hr; 1996) 650,000,000 (571,000,000); crude petroleum (barrels; 1996) 364,000 (1,552,000); petroleum products (metric tons; 1996) 255,000 (288,000); natural gas (cu m; 1996) 29,112,000 (29,112,000). **Household income and expenditure.** Average household size (1990) 3.5;

income per household (1988) BDS$13,455; expenditure (1994): food 39.4%, housing 16.8%, transportation 10.5%, household operations 8.1%, alcohol and tobacco 6.4%, fuel and light 5.2%. **Population economically active** (1997): total 135,800; activity rate of total pop. 51.3% (participation rates: ages 15 and over, 67.5%, female 62.1%, unemployed 14.5%). **Gross national product** (1999): US$2,294,000,000 (US$8,600 per capita). **Public debt** (external, outstanding; 1999): US$359,100,000. **Tourism:** receipts from visitors (1999) US$677,000,000; expenditures by nationals abroad (1998) US$82,000,000.

Foreign trade

Imports (1997-c.i.f.): BDS$1,991,001,000 (retained imports 92.7%, of which capital goods 20.4%, food and beverages 15.0%, construction materials 8.2%, chemicals 5.6%, fuels 3.7%; reexported imports 7.3%). *Major import sources* (1997): US 45.4%; Trinidad and Tobago 9.2%; U.K. 8.1%; Canada 3.9%. **Exports** (1997-f.o.b.): BDS$565,887,000 (domestic exports 74.4%, of which sugar 12.7%, chemicals 10.0%, electrical components 9.2%, rum 4.9%, margarine and lard 2.0%, clothing 1.2%; reexports 25.6%). *Major export destinations* (1997): UK 17.1%; US 14.7%; Jamaica 6.6%; Trinidad and Tobago 5.5%; St. Lucia 3.7%.

Transport and communications

Transport. *Railroads*: none. *Roads* (1996): total length 1,025 mi, 1,650 km (paved 96%). *Vehicles* (1995): passenger cars 43,711; trucks and buses 10,583. *Air transport* (1995): passenger arrivals 699,000, passenger departures 707,400; cargo unloaded 8,382 metric tons, cargo loaded 4,717 metric tons; airports (1997) with scheduled flights 1. **Communications** Total units (units per 1,000 persons). Daily newspaper circulation (1996): 53,000 (199); Radio receivers (1997): 237,000 (888); Television receivers (1999): 78,000 (292); Telephone main lines (1999): 115,000 (430); Cellular telephone subscribers (1999): 30,000 (112); Personal computers (1999): 21,000 (79); Internet users (1999): 6,000 (22).

Education and health

Educational attainment (1990). Percentage of pop. age 25 and over having: no formal schooling 0.4%; primary education 23.7%; secondary 60.3%; higher 11.2%; other 4.4%. **Literacy** (1995): total pop. age 15 and over literate 97.4%; males literate 98.0%; females literate 96.8%. **Health** (1992): physicians 312 (1 per 842 persons); hospital beds 1,966 (1 per 134 persons); infant mortality rate per 1,000 live births (2000) 12.4. **Food** (1999): daily per capita caloric intake 3,203 (vegetable products 74%, animal products 26%); 132% of FAO recommended minimum requirement.

Military

Total active duty personnel (2000): 610 (army 82.0%, navy 18.0%). **Military expenditure as percentage of GNP** (1996): 0.8% (world 2.6%); per capita expenditure US$54.

Background

The island was probably inhabited by Arawaks who originally came from South America. Spaniards may have landed by 1518, and by 1536 they had apparently wiped out the Indian population. Barbados was settled by the English in the 1620s. Slaves were brought in to work the sugar plantations, which were especially prosperous in the 17th—18th century. The British empire abolished slavery in 1834, and all the Barbados slaves were freed by 1838. In 1958 Barbados joined the West Indies Federation. When the latter dissolved in 1962, Barbados sought independence from Britain; it achieved Commonwealth status in 1966.

Recent Developments

The House of Assembly took an important step toward modernizing Barbados's constitution when in May 2000 it considered recommendations made by a Constitution Review Commission. The panel recommended that the country adopt a republican form of government—similar to the one in Trinidad and Tobago—with a nonexecutive president elected by the House of Assembly and the Senate.

Internet resources: <www.barbados.org>

Belarus

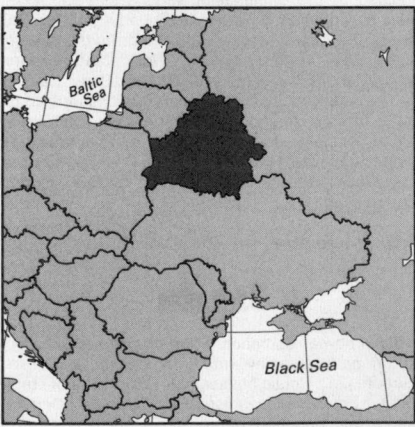

Official name: Respublika Belarus (Republic of Belarus). **Form of government:** republic with two legislative bodies (Council of the Republic [64]; House of Representatives [110]); legal status of government is controversial. **Head of state and government:** President Alyaksandr Lukashenka (from 1994)

---

1 metric ton = about 1.1 short tons;   1 kilometer = 0.6 mi (statute);   1 metric ton-km cargo = about 0.68 short ton-mi cargo;   c.i.f.: cost, insurance, and freight;   f.o.b.: free on board

assisted by a prime minister. **Capital:** Minsk. **Official languages:** Belarusian; Russian. **Official religion:** none. **Monetary unit:** rubel (Rbl; plural rubli) valuation (28 Jun 2002) $1= (new) Rbl 1,804; rubel re-denominated 1 Jan 2000; as of this date 1,000 old rubli = 1 (new) rubel.

Demography

Area: 80,153 sq mi, 207,595 sq km. **Population** (2001): 9,986,000. **Density** (2001): persons per sq mi 124.5, persons per sq km 48.1. **Urban** (2000): 69.7%. **Sex distribution** (2000): male 46.94%; female 53.06%. **Age breakdown** (2000): under 15, 18.9%; 15–29, 22.2%; 30–44, 23.4%; 45–59, 16.5%; 60–69, 10.4%; 70 and over, 8.6%. **Ethnic composition** (1999): Belarusian 81.2%; Russian 11.4%; Polish 3.9%; Ukrainian 2.4%; other 1.1%. **Religious affiliation** (1995): Belarusian Orthodox 31.6%; Roman Catholic 17.7%; other (mostly nonreligious) 50.7%. **Major cities** (2000): Minsk 1,688,000; Homel 487,000; Mahilyou 358,000. **Location:** Eastern Europe, bordering Latvia, Russia, Ukraine, Poland, and Lithuania.

Vital statistics

Birth rate per 1,000 pop. (1999): 9.3 (world avg. 22.5); legitimate 82.2%; illegitimate 17.8%. **Death rate** per 1,000 pop. (1999): 14.2 (world avg. 9.0). **Natural increase rate** per 1,000 pop. (1999): –4.9 (world avg. 13.5). **Total fertility rate** (avg births per childbearing woman; 1998): 1.3. **Marriage rate** per 1,000 pop. (1999): 7.3. **Divorce rate** per 1,000 pop.(1999): 4.7. **Life expectancy** at birth (1999): male 62.2 years; female 73.9 years.

National economy

Budget (1997). *Revenue:* (old) Rbl 111,736,000,000,000 (value-added tax 30.0%, taxes on profits 14.8%, taxes on income 10.2%, excise taxes 13.1%, taxes on international trade 8.3%, other 23.6%). *Expenditures:* (old) Rbl 115,875,000,000,000 (education 20.1%, health 15.8%, subsidies 11.1%, capital expenditure 8.6%, Chernobyl expenditures 6.5%, transfers 5.8%, other 32.1%). **Public debt** (external, outstanding; 1999): $851,000,000. **Household income and expenditure.** Average household size (1998) 3.6; sources of income (1997): wages and salaries 55.5%, business activities 20.5%, transfers 15.5%; expenditure (1997): retail goods 74.9%, savings 18.6%. **Production** (metric tons except as noted). *Agriculture, forestry, fishing* (1999): potatoes 8,000,000, cereal 3,353,000, sugar beets 1,000,000; livestock (number of live animals) 4,515,000 cattle, 3,608,000 pigs, 233,200 horses; roundwood (1998) 17,745,000 cu m; fish catch (1998) 457. *Mining and quarrying* (1997): potash 3,400,000; peat 3,000,000. *Manufacturing* (value of production in [old] Rbl '000,000; 1994): machine-building equipment 1,086,650; chemical products 659,438; food products 562,438. *Energy production (consumption):* electricity (kW-hr; 1997) 26,057,000,000 (33,677,000,000); coal (1994) none (1,199,000); crude petroleum (barrels; 1997) 13,355,000 (86,406,000); petroleum products (1997) 9,589,000 (10,473,000); natural gas (cu m; 1997) 242,000,000 (16,402,000,000). **Population economically active** (1997): 4,369,900; activity rate of total pop. 42.7% (participation rate: n.a.; female 53.6%; unem-

ployed [1998] 2.6%). **Gross national product** (1999): $26,299,000,000 ($2,620 per capita). **Tourism** (1999): receipts $13,000,000; expenditures $116,000,000. **Land use** (1994): forested 33.7%; meadows and pastures 14.1%; agricultural and under permanent cultivation 30.5%; other 21.7%; 25% of territory is severely affected by radioactive fallout from Chernobyl accident.

Foreign trade

Imports (1997-c.i.f.): $8,689,000,000 (industrial products 96.3%, of which petroleum and gas 24.0%, machinery and metalworking 21.7%, chemical and petroleum products 16.8%, iron and steel 10.1%, food and beverages 9.6%; agricultural products 3.7%). *Major import sources:* Russia 53.8%; Ukraine 11.1%; Germany 8.0%; Poland 2.9%; Italy 1.8%. **Exports** (1997-f.o.b.): $7,301,000,000 (industrial products 98.3%, of which machinery and metalworking 32.9%, chemical and petroleum products 20.9%, light industry 9.5%, petroleum and gas 8.2%, iron and steel 8.1%; agricultural products 1.7%). *Major export destinations:* Russia 64.8%; Ukraine 5.8%; Poland 3.4%; Germany 3.0%.

Transport and communications

Transport. *Railroads* (1998): length 5,488 km; (1997) passenger-km 12,909,000,000; metric ton-km cargo 30,636,000,000. *Roads* (1998): total length 53,407 km (paved 98.6%). *Vehicles* (1998): passenger cars 1,132,843; trucks and buses 8,867. *Air transport* (1997): passenger-km 910,000,000; metric ton-km cargo 84,000,000; airports 1. **Communications** Total units (units per 1,000 persons). Daily newspaper circulation (1997): 1,437,000 (140); Radio receivers (1998): 3,021,000 (296); Television receivers (1999): 3,300,000 (327); Telephone main lines (2000): 2,638,000 (263); Cellular telephone subscribers (2000): 22,230 (2.2); Internet users (2000): 50,000 (5).

Education and health

Educational attainment (1999). Percentage of pop. age 15 and over having: no formal schooling 14.8%; primary and secondary education 71.2%; higher 14.0%. **Literacy** (1989): total pop. age 15 and over literate 7,690,000 (97.9%); males literate 3,661,000 (99.4%); females literate 4,029,000 (96.6%). **Health** (1995): physicians 46,000 (1 per 224 persons); hospital beds 127,000 (1 per 81 persons); infant mortality rate per 1,000 live births (1999) 11.5. **Food** (1999): daily per capita caloric intake 3,171 (vegetable products 72%, animal products 28%); 124% of FAO recommended minimum requirement.

Military

Total active duty personnel (2000): 83,100 (army 52.3%, air force and air defense 27.1%, other 20.6%). **Military expenditure as percentage of GNP** (1997): 1.7% (world 2.6%); per capita expenditure $81.

Background

While Belarusians share a distinct identity and language, they did not enjoy political sovereignty until the late 20th century. The territory that is now

Belarus underwent partition and changed hands often; as a result its history is entwined with its neighbors'. In medieval times the region was ruled by Lithuanians and Poles. Following the Third Partition of Poland it was ruled by Russia. After World War I the western part was assigned to Poland and the eastern part became USSR territory. After World War II the Soviets expanded what had been the Belorussian SSR by annexing more of Poland. Much of the area suffered contamination from the Chernobyl accident in 1986, forcing many to evacuate. Belarus declared its independence in 1991 and later joined the Commonwealth of Independent States. Amid increasing political turmoil in the 1990s, it proposed a union with Russia in 1997, which was still in debate at the start of the 21st century.

Recent Developments

In the presidential election held on 9 Sep 2001, incumbent Pres. Alyaksandr Lukashenka emerged wiith a controversial victory. Despite promises made to European election monitors, the government did not allow a democratic vote. During the campaign, Lukashenka threatened to expel the chief observer and placed restrictions on opposition rallies. About 15% of the electorate voted early, and government workers were threatened with dismissal unless they voted for the president. The results were predictable. With a reported turnout of 83.9%, 75.6% voted for Lukashenka, while opposition candidate Uladzimir Hancharyk was second with 15.6%.

Internet resources: <www.belarusembassy.org>

Belgium

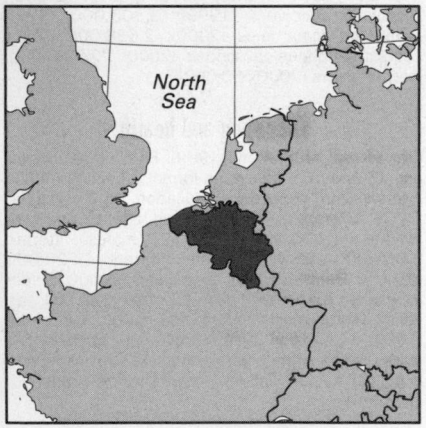

North Sea

Official name: Koninkrijk België (Dutch); Royaume de Belgique (French) (Kingdom of Belgium). Form of government: federal constitutional monarchy with a Parliament composed of two legislative chambers (Senate [71; excludes children of the monarch serving ex officio from age 18]; House of Representatives [150]). Chief of state: King Albert II (from 1993). Head of government: Prime Minister Guy Verhofstadt

(from 1999). Capital: Brussels. Official languages: Dutch; French; German. Official religion: none. Monetary unit: 1 euro (€) = 100 cents; $1 = €1.01 (28 Jun 2002); at conversion on 1 Jan 2002, €1 = BF40.3399.

Demography

Area: 11,7874 sq mi, 30,528 sq km. Population (2001): 10,268,000. Density (2000): persons per sq mi 871.2, persons per sq km 336.4. Urban (1996): 96.8% (includes Luxembourg). Sex distribution (2000): male 48.89%; female 51.11%. Age breakdown (2000): under 15, 17.5%; 15–29, 18.8%; 30–44, 22.9%; 45–59, 18.8%; 60–74, 14.8%; 75 and over, 7.2%. Nationality (1992): Belgian 91.0%; Italian 2.4%; Moroccan 1.4%; French 0.9%; Turkish 0.8%; Dutch 0.6%; other 2.9%. Religious affiliation (1995): Roman Catholic 87.9%; Muslim 2.5%; other Christian 2.4%, of which Protestant 1.0%; Jewish 0.3%; other 6.9%. Major cities (1 Jan 2000): Brussels 959,318 (capital region); Antwerp 446,525; Ghent 224,180; Charleroi 200,827; Liège 185,639. Location: Western Europe, bordering The Netherlands, Germany, Luxembourg, France, and the North Sea.

Vital statistics

Birth rate per 1,000 pop. (2000): 10.9 (world avg. 22.5). Death rate per 1,000 pop. (2000): 10.1 (world avg. 9.0). Natural increase rate per 1,000 pop. (2000): 0.8 (world avg. 13.5). Total fertility rate (avg. births per childbearing woman; 2000): 1.5. Marriage rate per 1,000 pop. (1999): 4.3. Divorce rate per 1,000 pop. (1994): 2.2. Life expectancy at birth (2000): male 74.5 years; female 81.3 years.

National economy

Budget (1999). Revenue: €107,764,000,000 (social security contributions 29.6%, taxes on goods and services 26.9%, income tax 26.7%). Expenditures: C 109,772,000,000 (transfer payments 49.4%, interest on debt 15.1%, other 35.5%). Public debt (1999): $250,459,000,000. Production (metric tons except as noted). Agriculture, forestry, fishing (2000; includes Luxembourg): sugar beets 6,200,000, potatoes 3,000,000, wheat 1,634,000; livestock (number of live animals) 7,671,000 pigs, 3,085,000 cattle, 152,000 sheep; roundwood (2000; includes Luxembourg) 4,400,000 cu m; fish catch (1999) 29,900. Mining and quarrying (1997): limestone 30,000,000; granite (Belgium bluestone) 2,115,000 cu m; marble 400 cu m. Manufacturing (value added in BF '000,000; 1996): metal products 468,894; food 263,382; chemicals 243,787. Energy production (consumption): electricity (kW-hr; 1998) 83,244,000,000 ([1996] 80,241,000,000); coal (metric tons; 1996) negligible (11,556,000); crude petroleum (barrels; 1996) none (231,305,000); petroleum products (metric tons; 1996) 28,400,000 (17,684,000); natural gas (cu m; 1996) 2,514,000 (14,086,000,000). Household income and expenditure. Avg. household size (1999) 2.5; sources of income (1992): wages 49.6%, transfer payments 20.7%, property income 18.8%, self-employment 10.9%; expenditure (1992): food 18.0%, housing 17.0%, transp. 13.3%, health 11.8%, durable goods

10.7%, clothing 7.7%. **Land use** (1994; includes Luxembourg): forest 21.3%; pasture 21.0%; agriculture 24.2%; other 33.5%. **Population economically active** (1999): total 3,905,500; activity rate 38.2% (participation rates: ages 15–64, 58.0%; female 42.7%; unemployed 9.6%). **Gross national product** (1999): $252,051,000,000 ($24,650 per capita). **Tourism** (1999): receipts $7,039,000,000; expenditures $10,057,000,000.

Foreign trade

Imports (1999; includes Luxembourg): BF6,237,963,000,000 (machinery and transport equipment 31.9%; basic manufactures 20.8%; chemicals 16.4%; food 7.8%; mineral fuels 5.7%; diamonds 3.9%). *Major import sources:* Germany 17.4%; The Netherlands 16.7%; France 13.7%; UK 8.6%; US 7.5%. **Exports** (1999; includes Luxembourg): BF6,780,785,000,000 (machinery and transport equipment 30.0%; chemicals 20.3%, of which plastics 4.4%; food 8.7%; iron and steel 4.0%; textiles 3.7%; petroleum products 2.5%). *Major export destinations:* Germany 17.9%; France 17.7%; The Netherlands 12.8%; UK 10.0%; US 5.2%.

Transport and communications

Transport. *Railroads* (1999): route length 3,380 km; passenger-km 7,354,000,000; metric ton-km cargo 7,392,000,000. *Roads* (1997): total length 143,800 km (paved 97%). *Vehicles* (1998): passenger cars 4,491,734; trucks and buses 453,122. *Air transport* (2000): Sabena airlines only): passenger-km 19,378,689,000; metric ton-km cargo 568,244,000; airports (1999) 2. **Communications** Total units (units per 1,000 persons). Daily newspaper circulation (1996): 1,625,000 (161); Radio receivers (1997): 8,075,000 (795); Television receivers (1999): 5,300,000 (518); Telephones main lines (1999): 5,100,000 (502); Cellular telephone subscribers (1999 3,193,000) 315); Personal computers (1999): 3,200,000 (313); Internet users (1999): 1,400,000 (137).

Education and health

Educational attainment (1981). Percentage of pop. age 15 and over having: less than secondary education 44.4%; lower secondary 26.5%; upper secondary 17.0%; vocational 2.9%; teacher's college 0.6%; university 3.5%. **Literacy** (1995): virtually 99% literate. **Health:** physicians (1998) 40,300 (1 per 253 persons); hospital beds (1994) 77,181 (1 per 131 persons); infant mortality rate (2000) 4.8. **Food** (1999; includes Luxembourg): daily per capita caloric intake 3,625 (vegetable products 68%, animal products 32%); 137% of FAO recommended minimum requirement.

Military

Total active duty personnel (2000): 39,250 (army 68.3%, navy 6.6%, air force 21.9%, medical service 3.6%). **Military expenditure as percentage of GNP** (1997): 1.5% (world 2.6%); per capita expenditure $362.

Background

Inhabited in ancient times by the Belgae, a Celtic people, the area was conquered by Caesar in 57 BC;

under Augustus it became the Roman province of Belgica. Conquered by the Franks, it later broke up into semi-independent territories, including Brabant and Luxembourg. By the late 15th century the territories of the Netherlands, of which the future Belgium was a part, gradually united and passed to the Habsburgs. In the 16th century it was a center for European commerce. The basis of modern Belgium was laid in the southern Catholic provinces that split from the northern provinces after the Union of Utrecht in 1579. Overrun by the French and incorporated into France in 1801, it was reunited to Holland and with it became the independent Kingdom of The Netherlands in 1815. After the revolt of its citizens in 1830, it became the independent Kingdom of Belgium. Under Leopold II it acquired vast lands in Africa. Overrun by the Germans in World Wars I and II, it was the scene of the Battle of the Bulge. Internal discord led to legislation in the 1970s and 1980s that created three nearly autonomous regions in accordance with language distribution: Flemish Flanders, French Wallonia, and bilingual Brussels. In 1993 it became a federation comprising the three regions. It is a member of the European Union.

Recent Developments

The Belgian Parliament approved a further decentralization of power to the country's three regions during 2001. After six months of intense negotiations between the major political parties, it was agreed in July that responsibility for agricultural policy, foreign trade, development cooperation, and control over communal and provincial councils would pass from the national to the regional level at the beginning of 2002.

Internet resources: <www.belgium-tourism.com>

Belize

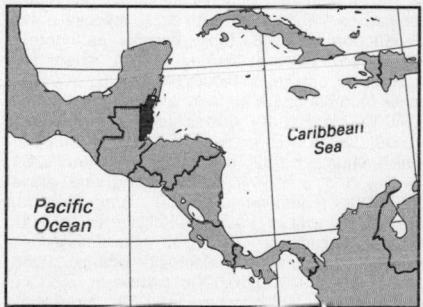

Official name: Belize. **Form of government:** constitutional monarchy with two legislative houses (Senate [8—excludes president of the Senate]; House of Representatives [29—excludes speaker of the House of Representatives]). **Chief of state:** Queen Elizabeth II represented by Governor-General Sir Colville Young (from 1993). **Head of government:** Prime Minister Said Musa (from 1998). **Capital:** Belmopan. **Official language:** English. **Official religion:** none. **Monetary unit:** 1 Belize dollar (BZ$) = 100 cents; valuation (28 Jun 2002) US$1 = BZ$1.97 (pegged to the US dollar).

Demography

Area: 8,867 sq mi, 22,965 sq km (includes offshore cays totaling 266 sq mi (689 sq km). **Population** (2001): 247,000. **Density** (2001): persons per sq mi 27.9, persons per sq km 10.8. **Urban** (2000): 48%. **Sex distribution** (2000): male 50.49%; female 49.51%. **Age breakdown** (1998): under 15, 41.2%; 15–29, 26.5%; 30–44, 16.7%; 45–59, 8.8%; 60–74, 5.0%; 75 and over, 1.8%. **Ethnic composition** (1991): mestizo (Spanish-Indian) 43.6%; Creole (predominantly black) 29.8%; Mayan Indian 11.0%; Garifuna (black-Carib Indian) 6.7%; white 3.9%; East Indian 3.5%; other or not stated 1.5%. **Religious affiliation** (1991): Roman Catholic 57.7%; Protestant 34.3%, of which Anglican 7.0%, Pentecostal 6.3%, Methodist 4.2%, Seventh-day Adventist 4.1%, Mennonite 4.0%; other Christian 1.7%; nonreligious/other 6.3%. **Major cities** (2000): Belize City 49,050; Orange Walk 13,483; San Ignacio/Santa Elena 13,260; Dangriga 8,814; Belmopan 8,130. **Location:** Central America, bordering Mexico, Caribbean Sea, and Guatemala.

Vital statistics

Birth rate per 1,000 pop. (2000): 32.3 (world avg. 22.5); (1997) legitimate 40.3%; illegitimate 59.7%. **Death rate** per 1,000 pop. (2000): 4.8 (world avg. 9.0). **Natural increase rate** per 1,000 pop. (2000): 27.5 (world avg. 13.5). **Total fertility rate** (avg. births per childbearing woman; 2000): 4.1. **Marriage rate** per 1,000 pop. (1997): 6.6. **Divorce rate** per 1,000 pop. (1997): 0.2. **Life expectancy** at birth (2000): male 68.7 years; female 73.3 years.

National economy

Budget (1997). *Revenue:* BZ$324,600,000 (tax revenue 77.4%, of which import duties 25.7%, general sales taxes 23.6%; grants 12.7%; nontax revenue 9.2%). *Expenditures:* BZ$362,300,000 (education 20.5%; transportation and communication 16.7%; general admin. 11.4%; health 8.2%; defense 5.4%). **Production** (metric tons except as noted). *Agriculture, forestry, fishing* (1998): sugarcane 1,208,000, oranges 170,000, bananas 81,000; livestock (number of live animals; 1999) 58,000 cattle, 23,000 pigs, 1,400,000 chickens; roundwood (1998) 187,600 cu m; fish catch (1998) 2,620, of which shrimp 1,682, conchs 253, lobsters 251. *Mining and quarrying* (1997): sand and gravel 350,000; limestone 310,000. *Manufacturing* (1996): sugar (1997) 123,800; cigarettes 80,000,-000 units; garments 2,100,000 units. *Energy production (consumption):* electricity (kW-hr; 1996) 152,000,000 (177,000,000); petroleum products (metric tons; 1996) none (116,000). **Household income and expenditure.** Average household size (2000) 4.5; average annual income of employed head of household (1993, based on a sample of 33,000 employed heads of household) BZ$6,450 (US$3,225); expenditure (1990): food, beverages, and tobacco 34.0%, transportation 13.7%, energy and water 9.1%, housing 9.0%, clothing and footwear 8.8%, household furnishings 8.0%. **Tourism** (1999): receipts from visitors US$112,000,000; expenditures by nationals abroad US$24,000,000.

Land use (1994): forested 92.1%; meadows and pastures 2.2%; agricultural and under permanent cultivation 3.6%; other 2.1%. **Population economically active** (1998, based on April survey): total 85,595; activity rate of total pop. 36.2% (participation rates: ages 14–64, 64.1%; female 34.5%; unemployed 14.3%). **Gross national product** (1999): US$673,-000,000 (US$2,730 per capita). **Public debt** (external, outstanding; 1999): US$294,600,000.

Foreign trade

Imports (1998-c.i.f.): BZ$594,100,000 (machinery and transport equipment 25.6%; food and beverages 16.7%; mineral fuels and lubricants 11.1%; chemicals and chemical products 10.7%). *Major import sources:* US 53.6%; Mexico 11.7%; UK 4.7%; Caricom 3.6%; other EU 5.3%. **Exports** (1998-f.o.b.): BZ$336,700,000 (domestic exports 90.9%, of which raw sugar 26.4%, bananas 14.6%, marine products 12.9%, citrus concentrate 12.8%, garments 11.7%; reexports 9.1%). *Major export destinations* (domestic exports only): US 42.6%; UK 33.3%; Caricom 7.5%; other EU 11.9%.

Transport and communications

Transport. *Roads* (1995): total length 2,250 km (paved 18%). *Vehicles* (1997): passenger cars 9,695; trucks and buses 11,698. *Air transport* (1998, Belize international airport only): passenger arrivals 199,475, passenger departures 193,620; cargo loaded 166 metric tons, cargo unloaded 1,082 metric tons. Airports (1997) with scheduled flights 9. **Communications.** Total units (units per 1,000 persons): Radio receivers (1997): 133,000 (571); Television receivers (1998): 42,000 (183); Telephone main lines (1999): 36,632 (156); Cellular telephone subscribers (1999): 6,193 (26); Personal computers (1999): 25,000 (106); Internet users (1999): 12,000 (51).

Education and health

Educational attainment (1991). Percentage of pop. age 25 and over having: no formal schooling 13.0%; primary education 64.3%; secondary 14.9%; higher 6.6%; other 1.2%. **Literacy** (1991): total pop. age 14 and over literate 75,500 (70.3%). **Health** (1998): physicians 155 (1 per 1,558 persons); hospital beds 554 (1 per 435 persons); infant mortality rate per 1,000 live births (2000) 26.0. **Food** (1999): daily per capita caloric intake 2,889 (vegetable products 79%, animal products 21%); 128% of FAO recommended minimum requirement.

Military

Total active duty personnel (2000): 1,050 (army 100%). **Military expenditure as percentage of GNP** (1998): 1.4% (world, n.a.); per capita expenditure US$35.

Background

The area was inhabited by the Maya c. 300 BC—AD 900; the ruins of their ceremonial centers, including Caracol and Xunantunich, can still be seen. The

---

1 metric ton = about 1.1 short tons;   1 kilometer = 0.6 mi (statute);   1 metric ton-km cargo = about 0.68 short ton-mi cargo;   c.i.f.: cost, insurance, and freight;   f.o.b.: free on board

Spanish claimed sovereignty from the 16th century but never tried to settle Belize, though they regarded as interlopers the British who did, British logwood cutters arrived in the mid—17th century; Spanish opposition was finally overcome in 1798. When settlers began to penetrate the interior they met with Indian resistance. In 1871 British Honduras became a crown colony, but an unfulfilled provision of a 1859 British—Guatemalan treaty led Guatemala to claim the territory. The situation had not been resolved when Belize was granted its independence in 1981. A British force, stationed there to ensure the new nation's security, was withdrawn after Guatemala officially recognized the territory's independence in 1991.

Recent Developments

Belize celebrated its 20th anniversary of independence in 2001. In his state of the nation address, Prime Minister Said Musa highlighted the accomplishments of the ruling People's United Party. These included a booming tourist industry and increased cocoa production, which showed promise of one day rivaling the citrus, banana, and sugar industries in terms of foreign-exchange earnings for the country.

Internet resources: <www.belize.gov.bz>

Benin

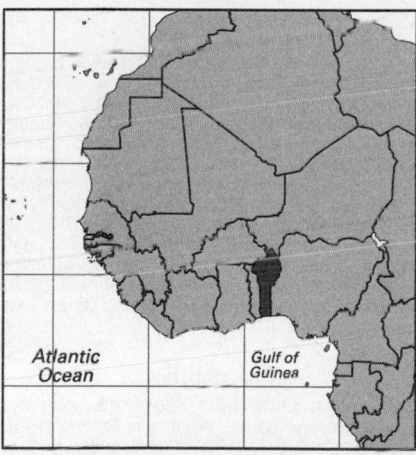

Atlantic Ocean

Gulf of Guinea

Official name: République du Bénin (Republic of Benin). **Form of government:** multiparty republic with one legislative house (National Assembly [83]), **Head of state and government:** President Mathelu Kérékou (from 1996). **Capital** : Porto-Novo (legislative capital; administrative capital in Cotonou). **Official language:** French. **Official religion:** none. **Monetary unit:** 1 CFA franc (CFAF) = 100 centimes; valuation (28 Jun 2002) $1 = CFAF 664.20.

Demography

Area: 44,300 sq mi, 114,760 sq km. **Population** (2001): 6,591,000. **Density** (2001): persons per sq mi 148.8, persons per sq km 57.4. **Urban** (1999): urban 41.5%. **Sex distribution** (2000): male 49.21%; female 50.79%. **Age breakdown** (2000): under 15, 47.5%; 15–29, 27.7%; 30–44, 13.9%; 45–59, 7.1%; 60–74, 3.1%; 75 and over, 0.7%. **Ethnic composition** (1992): Fon 39.7%; Yoruba (Nago) 12.1%; Adjara 11.1%; Dariba 8.6%; Aizo 8.6%; Somba (Otomary) 6.6%; Fulani 5.6%; other 7.7%. **Religious affiliation** (1992): Christian 35.4%, of which Roman Catholic 25.9%, Protestant 9.5%; traditional beliefs, including voodoo 35.0%; Muslim 20.6%; other 9.0%. **Major cities** (1994): Cotonou 750,000; Porto-Novo 200,000; Djougou 132,000; Abomey-Calavi 125,565 (1992); Parakou 120,000. **Location:** western Africa, bordering Burkina Faso, Niger, Nigeria, the Atlantic Ocean, and Togo.

Vital statistics

Birth rate per 1,000 (2000): 44.8 (world avg. 22.5). **Death rate** per 1,000 (2000): 14.5 (world avg. 9.0). **Natural increase rate** per 1,000 (2000): 30.3 (world avg. 13.5). **Total fertility rate** (avg. births per childbearing woman; 2000): 6.3. **Life expectancy** at birth (2000): male 49.2 years; female 51.2 years.

National economy

Budget (1998). *Revenue:* CFAF 255,100,000,000 (tax revenue 71.5%; grants 17.3%; nonfiscal receipts 11.2%). *Expenditures:* CFAF 233,400,000,000 (current expenditures 64.5%, of which debt service 12.7%; development expenditure 34.3%). **Production** (metric tons except as noted). *Agriculture, forestry, fishing* (1999): cassava 2,377,339, yams 1,770,973, corn (maize) 822,739, seed cotton 436,240; livestock (number of live animals; 1999) 1,345,000 cattle, 1,087,000 goats, 634,000 sheep; roundwood (1998) 5,994,000 cu m; fish catch (1997) 43,771. *Manufacturing* (1998): cement 380,000 (1996); cotton fiber 175,000; meat 70,000. *Energy production (consumption):* electricity (kW-hr; 1996) 6,000,000 (269,432,000); coal, none (none); crude petroleum (barrels; 1996) 652,000 (negligible); petroleum products (metric tons; 1996) none (149,000). **Public debt** (external, outstanding; 1999): $1,472,000,000. **Gross national product** (1999): $2,320,000,000 ($380 per capita). **Population economically active** (1997): total 2,608,000; activity rate of total population 44.2% (participation rates: ages 15–64, 84.3%; female 48.3%; unemployed, n.a.). **Household income and expenditure.** Average household size (1992) 5.9; income per household (1983) $240; sources of income; self-employement 73.7%, wages and salaries 26.3%. **Land use** (1995): agricultural and under permanent cultivation 17.0%; other 83.0% (of which [1994] forested 30.7%, meadows and pastures 4.0%). **Tourism** (1998): receipts from visitors $33,000,000; expenditures by nationals abroad $7,000,000.

Foreign trade

Imports (1997-c.i.f.): CFAF 300,800,000,000 (cotton yarn and fabric 20.2%; machinery and transport equipment 16.2%; rice 7.4%; iron and steel 4.5%). *Major import sources* (1995): France 27.1%; United Kingdom 9.6%; China 9.3%; Thailand 9.1%; Hong Kong 8.8%; The Netherlands 5.6%; United States 4.8%; Germany 4.3%. **Exports** (1997-f.o.b.): CFAF 231,100,000,000 (cotton yarn 51.6%, reexport 38.5%, cotton seed 2.8%, crude petroleum 2.2%). *Major export destinations* (1997): Brazil 18.0%; Portugal 11.0%; Morocco 10.0%; India 6.5%; Libya 6.0%; Italy 4.5%; United States 4.5%.

Transport and communications

Transport. *Railroads* (1997): length 578 km; passenger-km 121,800,000; metric ton-km cargo 311,400,000. *Roads* (1996): total length 6,787 km (paved 20.0%). *Vehicles* (1996): passenger cars 37,772; trucks and buses 8,058. *Air transport* (1998-about 10% of West Africa's Air Afrique): passenger-mi 160,477,000, passenger-km 258,263,000; metric ton-km cargo 13,524,000; airports (1998) with scheduled flights 1. **Communications** Total units (units per 1,000 persons). Daily newspaper circulation (1996): 12,000 (2); Radio receivers (1996): 620,000 (110); Television receivers (1998): 65,000 (10.8); Telephone main lines (1998): 38,354 (6.1); Cellular telephone subscribers (1998): 6,286 (1); Internet users (1999): 10,000 (1.6).

Education and health

Educational attainment (1992). Percentage of pop. age 25 and over having: no formal schooling 78.5%; primary education 10.8%; some secondary 8.2%; secondary 1.2%; postsecondary 1.3%. **Literacy** (1995): total percentage of pop. age 15 and over literate 37.0%; males literate 48.7%; females literate 25.8%. **Health:** physicians (1993) 363 (1 per 14,216 persons); hospital beds (1993) 1,235 (1 per 4,182 persons); infant mortality rate (2000) 90.8. **Food** (1999): daily per capita caloric intake 2,489 (vegetable products 96%, animal products 4%); 108% of FAO recommended minimum requirement.

Military

Total active duty personnel (2000): 4,750 (army 94.7%, navy 2.1%, air force 3.2%). **Military expenditure as percentage of GNP** (1997): 1.3% (world 2.6%); per capita expenditure $5.

Background

In southern Benin, the Dahomey, or Fon, established the Abomey kingdom in 1625. In the 18th century the kingdom expanded to include Allada and Ouidah, where French forts had been established in the 17th century. In 1857 the French reestablished themselves in the area, and eventually fighting ensued. In 1894 Dahomey became a French protectorate; it was incorporated into the federation of French West Africa in 1904. It achieved independence in 1960. Dahomey was renamed Benin in 1975. At the end of the 20th century, its chronically weak economy produced tension between laborers and the government.

Recent Developments

Amid widespread criticism of the handling of Benin's presidential elections in March 2001, incumbent Pres. Mathieu Kérékou triumphed again at the polls. The victory ensured that Kérékou would maintain his grip upon a nation that he had ruled for all but five years since 1972.

Internet resources:
<www.siftthru.com/benintrav.htm>

Bermuda

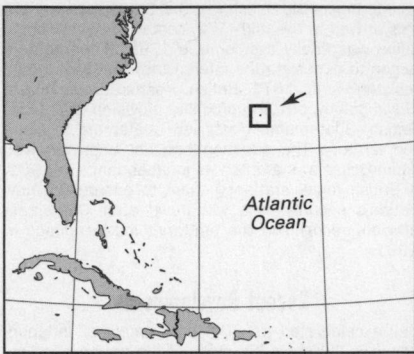

Atlantic Ocean

Official name: Bermuda. **Political status:** colony (United Kingdom) with two legislative houses (Senate [11]; House of Assembly [40]). **Chief of state:** Queen Elizabeth II, represented by Governor John Vereker (from 2002). **Head of government:** Premier Jennifer Smith (from 1998). **Capital:** Hamilton. **Official language:** English. **Official religion:** none. **Monetary unit:** 1 Bermuda dollar (Bd$) = 100 cents; valuation (28 Jun 2002) US$1 = Bd$1.00.

Demography

Area: 20.5 sq mi, 53.1 sq km. **Population** (2001): 63,500. **Density** (2001): persons per sq mi 3,098, persons per sq km 1,196. **Urban** (2000): 100.0%. **Sex distribution** (1999): male 48.57%; female 51.43%. **Age breakdown** (1999): under 15, 19.8%; 15–29, 18.3%; 30–44, 27.5%; 45–59, 19.4%; 60–74, 11.2%; 75 and over, 3.8%. **Ethnic composition** (1991): black 57.8%; white 36.2%; other 6.0%. **Religious affiliation** (2000): Protestant 67.2%, of which Anglican 37.2%; Roman Catholic 16.0%; unaffiliated Christian 7.0%; nonreligious 4.0%; other 5.8%. **Major cities** (1991): St. George 1,648; Hamilton 1,100. **Location:** North Atlantic Ocean, east of North Carolina (US).

Vital statistics

Birth rate per 1,000 pop. (1999): 13.2 (world avg. 22.5); legitimate 61.7%; illegitimate 38.3%. **Death rate** per 1,000 pop. (1999): 7.1 (world avg. 9.0). **Natural increase rate** per 1,000 pop. (1999): 6.1 (world avg. 13.5). **Total fertility rate** (avg. births per childbearing woman; 2000): 1.8. **Marriage rate** per 1,000 pop. (1999): 17.5. **Divorce rate** per 1,000 pop. (1996): 3.7. **Life expectancy** at birth (2000): male 74.9 years; female 78.9 years.

National economy

Budget (1999). *Revenue:* Bd$562,200,000 (customs duty 31.3%; payroll tax 27.0%; fees, sales, recoveries, and other miscellaneous receipts 15.0%; tax on international companies 6.3%). *Expenditures:* Bd$545,700,000 (current expendi-

---

1 metric ton = about 1.1 short tons;　1 kilometer = 0.6 mi (statute);　1 metric ton-km cargo = about 0.68 short ton-mi cargo;　c.i.f.: cost, insurance, and freight;　f.o.b.: free on board

ture 91.4%, of which public debt 2.3%; development expenditure 8.6%). **Production** (value in Bd$'000 except as noted). *Agriculture, forestry, fishing* (1996): vegetables 3,000, milk 2,060, fruits 800; livestock (number of live animals; 1999) 900 horses, 600 cattle, 45,000 chickens; fish catch (metric tons; 1998) 457. *Mining and quarrying*: crushed stone for local use. *Manufacturing*: industries include pharmaceuticals, cosmetics, electronics. *Energy production (consumption)*: electricity (kW-hr; 1996) 525,000,000 (525,000,000); petroleum products (metric tons; 1996) none (151,000). **Land use** (1988): forested 20.0%; meadows and pastures 0.9%; agricultural and under permanent cultivation 3.1%; built-on, wasteland, and other 76.0%. **Tourism**: receipts from visitors (1998) US$487,000,000; expenditures by nationals abroad (1997) US$148,000,000. **Population economically active** (1991): total 35,222; activity rate of total pop. 60.2% (participation rates: ages 15–64, 80.9%; female 47.1%; unemployed [1995] 1.5%). **Gross national product** (1997): US$2,128,000,000 (US$34,470 per capita). **Household income and expenditure** (1993). Average household size 2.5; average annual income per household Bd$65,676 (US$65,676); sources of income: wages and salaries 65.3%, imputed income from owner occupancy 10.6%, self-employment 9.0%, net rental income 4.8%, pensions 3.3%, interest 3.3%; expenditure: housing 27.7%, household furnishings 16.6%, food and nonalcoholic beverages 14.6%, health care 7.6%, transportation 7.3%.

Foreign trade

Imports (1999): Bd$720,000,000 (machinery 20.4%; food, beverages, and tobacco 18.7%; chemicals and chemical products 9.4%; transport equipment 9.0%; clothing 5.3%). *Major import sources*: United States 74.1%; Canada 6.6%; United Kingdom 4.6%. **Exports** (1993): Bd$35,272,000 (reexports 99.99%, of which drugs and medicine 71.12%; Bermuda-originated exports 0.01%). *Major export destinations* (1995): United States 49.8%; United Kingdom 6.2%; nonspecified 44.0%.

Transport and communications

Transport. *Roads* (1997): total length 225 km (paved 100%) (222 km of private roads are also paved). *Vehicles* (1996): passenger cars 21,220; trucks and buses 4,007. *Air transport* (1996): passenger arrivals 519,772, passenger departures 516,759; cargo unloaded 5,909 metric tons, cargo loaded 727 metric tons; airports (1998) with scheduled flights 1. **Communications** Total units (units per 1,000 persons). Daily newspaper circulation (1996): 17,000 (277); Radio receivers (1997): 82,000 (1,328); Television receivers (1997): 66,000 (1,069); Telephone main lines (1999): 54,933 (879); Cellular telephone subscribers (1998): 12,572 (202).

Education and health

Educational attainment (1991). Percentage of total pop. age 25 and over having: no formal schooling 0.5%; incomplete or complete primary 18.2%; incomplete or complete secondary 62.9%; higher 18.4%. **Literacy** (1997): total pop. age 15 and over literate

98%. **Health** (1996): physicians 96 (1 per 639 persons); hospital beds (excluding beds in geriatric, rehabilitaton, and hospice units) 251 (1 per 244 persons); infant mortality rate per 1,000 live births (1997–99 avg.) 3.2. **Food** (1999): daily per capita caloric intake 2,883 (vegetable products 73%, animal products 27%); 114% of FAO recommended minimum requirement.

Military

Total active duty personnel (1997): 700; part-time defense force assists police and is drawn from Bermudian conscripts.

Background

The archipelago was named for Juan de Bermúdez, who may have visited the islands in 1503. Colonized by the English in 1612, Bermuda became a crown colony in 1684. Its economy is based on tourism and international finance; its per-capita gross national product is among the world's highest.

Recent Developments

Attracted by favorable tax and corporate residency laws, some American companies have opted recently to establish their headquarters in Bermuda.

Internet resources: <bermudatourism.org>

Bhutan

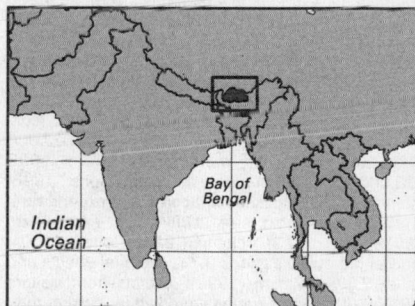

Official name: Druk-Yul (Kingdom of Bhutan). **Form of government:** de facto constitutional monarchy with one legislative house (National Assembly [150 seats, including 45 nonelective seats representing the King and religious groups]). **Chief of state:** King Jigme Singye Wangchuk (from 1972). **Head of government:** Chairman of Council of Ministers Sangay Ngedup (from 1999). **Capital:** Thimphu. **Official language:** Dzongkha (a Tibetan dialect). **Official religion:** Mahayana Buddhism. **Monetary unit:** 1 ngultrum (Nu) = 100 chetrum; valuation (28 Jun 2002) $1 = Nu 48.86; Indian rupee also accepted legal tender.

Demography

Area: 18,150 sq mi, 47,000 sq km. **Population** (2001): 692,000 (excludes nearly 100,000 Bhutanese of Nepalese origin). **Density** (2001): persons per sq mi 38.1, persons per sq km 14.7. **Urban**

(1999): 7%. **Sex distribution** (1988): male 50.97%; female 49.03%. **Age breakdown** (1988): under 15, 40.3%; 15–29, 26.4%; 30–44, 16.5%; 45–59, 10.5%; 60–74, 5.2%; 75 and over, 1.1%. **Ethnic composition** (1993): Bhutia (Ngalops) 50.0%; Nepalese (Gurung) 35.0%; Sharchops 15.0%. **Religious affiliation** (2000): Buddhist 74.0%; Hindu 20.5%; other 5.5%. **Major cities** (1997 est.): Thimphu 45,000; Phuntsholing 45,000. **Location:** southern Asia, bordering China and India.

Vital statistics

Birth rate per 1,000 pop. (2001): 35.2 (world avg. 22.5). **Death rate** per 1,000 pop. (2001): 9.0 (world avg. 9.0). **Natural increase rate** per 1,000 pop. (2001): 26.2 (world avg. 13.5). **Total fertility rate** (avg. births per childbearing woman; 2001): 5.2. **Marital status** of pop. 15 years and over (1985): married 71.2%; single 19.7%; widowed 7.5%; divorced 1.6%. **Life expectancy** at birth (1999): male 61.0 years; female 64.0 years.

National economy

Budget (1998–99). *Revenue:* Nu 6,844,000,000 (internal revenue 45.2%, grants from government of India 33.2%, grants from UN and other international agencies 21.6%). *Expenditures:* Nu 6,999,000,000 (capital expenditures 59.3%, current expenditures 40.7%). **Public debt** (external, outstanding; 1999): $181,800,000. **Production** (metric tons except as noted). *Agriculture, forestry, fishing* (1999): oranges 58,000, rice 50,000, corn (maize) 39,000; livestock (number of live animals) 435,000 cattle, 74,900 pigs, 58,500 sheep; roundwood (1998) 1,702,000 cu m; fish catch (1997) 330. *Mining and quarrying* (1997): limestone 270,000; dolomite 250,000; gypsum 50,000. *Manufacturing* (value in Nu '000,000; 1994): chemical products 419.0; cement 255.1; wood board products 230.6. *Energy production (consumption):* electricity (kW-hr; 1996) 1,737,000,000 (261,000,000); coal (metric tons; 1996) 2,000 (23,000); petroleum products (metric tons; 1996) none (39,000). **Household income and expenditure.** Average household size (1980) 5.4; expenditure (1979): food 72.3%, clothing 21.2%, energy 3.7%, household durable goods 0.7%, personal effects and other 2.1%. **Tourism** (1999): receipts from visitors $9,000,000. **Gross national product** (at current market prices; 1999): $399,000,000 ($510 per capita). **Population economically active** (1984): total 348,000; activity rate of total pop. 53.4% (participation rates: ages 15–64, 94.8%; female 55.0%; unemployed 6.5%). **Land use** (1994): forested 66.0%; meadows and pastures 5.8%; agricultural and under permanent cultivation 2.8%; other 25.4%.

Foreign trade

Imports (1997-c.i.f.): Nu 4,978,000,000 (petroleum products [1996] 4.6%, rice 4.6%, vegetable fats and oils 3.0%, steel products 2.4%, wheat 2.0%, industrial machinery 1.7%). *Major import source* (1997–98): India 70.5%. **Exports** (1997): Nu 4,274,100,000 (electricity [1996] 21.0%, calcium carbide 15.0%, particle board 8.0%, cement 7.1%). *Major export destination* (1997–98): India 94.5%.

Transport and communications

Transport. *Roads* (1996): total length 1,998 mi, 3,285 km (paved 61%). *Vehicles* (1988): passenger cars 2,590; trucks and buses 1,367. *Air transport* (1996): passenger-mi 29,000,000, passenger-km 46,000,000; airports (1997) with scheduled flights 1. **Communications** Total units (units per 1,000 persons). Radio receivers (1997): 37,000 (19); Television receivers (1999): 13,000 (20); Telephone main lines (1999): 11,800 (18); Personal computers (1999): 3,000 (4.6); Internet users (1999): 500 (0.8).

Education and health

Literacy (1995 est.): total pop. age 15 and over literate 42.2%; males literate 56.2%; females literate 28.1%. **Health:** physicians (1994) 100 (1 per 8,000 persons); hospital beds 970 (1 per 825 persons); infant mortality rate per 1,000 live births (2001) 56.0. **Food** (1975–77): daily per capita caloric intake 2,058 (vegetable products 98%, animal products 2%); 89% of FAO recommended minimum requirement.

Military

Total active duty personnel (1993): about 7,000 (army 100%).

 **Did you know?** Archery is the national sport in Bhutan, where it is a team event, rather than an Olympic-style contest between individuals. Tournaments, often held during holidays, are festive occasions at which entire villages enjoy, food, drink, and merrymaking.

Background

Bhutan's mountains and forests long made it inaccessible to the outside world, and its feudal rulers banned foreigners until well into the 20th century. It nevertheless became the object of foreign invasions; in 1865 it came under British influence, and in 1910 it agreed to be guided by Britain in its foreign affairs. It later became oriented toward British-ruled India, though much of its trade continued to be with Tibet. India took over Britain's role in 1949, and Communist China's 1950 occupation of neighboring Tibet further strengthened Bhutan's ties with India. The apparent Chinese threat made Bhutan's rulers aware of the need to modernize, and it has embarked on a program to build roads and hospitals and to create a system of secular education.

Recent Developments

A Civil and Criminal Procedure Code, under which the powers of the country's judiciary were expanded and the judicial process defined, was passed by the National Assembly in 2001. Bhutan's economy continued to flourish, owing primarily to the expansion of hydropower resources.

Internet resources:
<lcweb2.loc.gov/frd/cs/bttoc.html>

---

1 metric ton = about 1.1 short tons; 1 kilometer = 0.6 mi (statute); 1 metric ton-km cargo = about 0.68 short ton-mi cargo; c.i.f.: cost, insurance, and freight; f.o.b.: free on board

Bolivia

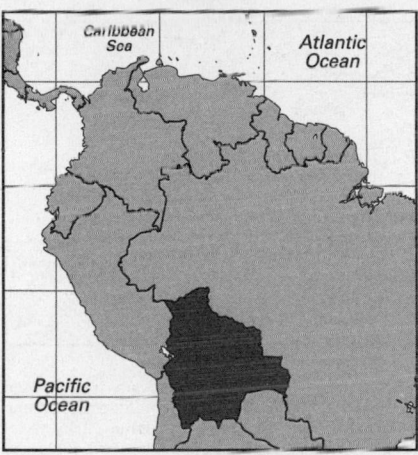

Official name: República de Bolivia (Republic of Bolivia). **Form of government:** unitary multiparty republic with two legislative houses (Chamber of Senators [27]; Chamber of Deputies [130]). **Head of state and government:** President Gonzalo Sánchez de Lozada (from 6 Aug 2002). **Capitals:** La Paz (administrative); Sucre (judicial). **Official languages:** Spanish, Aymara, Quechua. **Official religion:** Roman Catholicism. **Monetary unit:** 1 boliviano (Bs) = 100 centavos; valuation (28 Jun 2002) $1 = Bs 7.17.

Demography

Area: 424,164 sq mi, 1,098,581 sq km. **Population** (2001): 8,516,000. **Density** (2001): persons per sq mi 20.1, persons per sq km 7.8. **Urban** (2000): 63.7%. **Sex distribution** (2000): male 49.99%; female 50.01%. **Age breakdown** (2000): under 15, 39.1%; 15–29, 28.1%; 30–44, 16.6%; 45–59, 9.9%; 60–74, 4.5%; 75 and over, 1.8%. **Ethnic composition** (1996): Indian 55.0%; mestizo 30.0%; white 15.0%. **Religious affiliation** (1995): Roman Catholic 88.5%; Protestant 9.0%; other 2.5%. **Major cities** (2000): Santa Cruz 1,016,137; La Paz 1,000,899; Cochabamba 607,129; El Alto 568,919; Oruro 232,311; Sucre 192,238. **Location:** central South America, bordering Brazil, Paraguay, Argentina, Chile, and Peru.

Vital statistics

Birth rate per 1,000 pop. (2000): 31.9 (world avg. 22.5). **Death rate** per 1,000 pop. (2000): 8.6 (world avg. 9.0). **Natural increase rate** per 1,000 pop. (2000): 23.3 (world avg. 13.5). **Total fertility rate** (avg. births per childbearing woman; 2000): 3.7. **Life expectancy** at birth (2000): male 61.2 years; female 66.3 years.

National economy

Budget (1998). *Revenue:* Bs 11,698,500,000 (tax revenue 78.9%, of which indirect taxes 49.0%, taxes on petroleum and petroleum products 18.8%; nontax revenue 8.9%). *Expenditures:* Bs 13,681,300,-000 (current expenditure 78.8%, of which wages and salaries 31.3%, transfers 21.9%; capital expenditure 21.2%). **Production** (metric tons except as noted). *Agriculture, forestry, fishing* (1999): sugarcane 4,160,000, soybeans 762,000; livestock (number of live animals) 8,575,000 sheep, 6,556,-000 cattle, 2,715,000 pigs; roundwood (1998) 1,989,000 cu m; fish catch (1998) 6,055. *Mining and quarrying* (metric tons of pure metal; 1998): zinc 150,709; lead 13,848; tin 10,542. *Manufacturing* (value added in $'000; 1994): petroleum products 375; food products 169; beverages 99. *Energy production (consumption):* electricity (kW-hr; 1998) 3,771,000,000 (3,252,000,000); crude petroleum (barrels; 1998) 12,628,000 (10,382,-000); petroleum products (metric tons; 1996) 1,325,000 (1,480,000); natural gas (cu m; 1998) 3,106,000,000 (1,511,000,000). **Population economically active** (1997): total 3,645,165; activity rate of total pop. 46.6% (participation rates: ages 15–64, 72.1%; female 43.7%; unemployed 2.1%). **Tourism** (1999): receipts $179,000,000; expenditures $165,000,000. **Gross national product** (at current market prices; 1999): $8,092,000,000 ($990 per capita). **Public debt** (external, outstanding; 1999): $3,864,000,000. **Household income and expenditure.** Average household size (1997): 4.4; expenditure (1988): food 35.5%, transportation and communications 17.7%, housing 14.8%, household durable goods 7.3%, clothing and footwear 5.1%, beverages and tobacco 4.5%, recreation 2.7%, health 2.1%, education 0.3%. **Land use** (1994): forested 53.5%; meadows and pastures 24.4%; agricultural and under permanent cultivation 2.2%; other 19.9%.

Foreign trade

Imports (1998-c.i.f.): $1,983,000,000 (raw materials 42.2%, of which raw materials for industry 32.8%; capital goods 40.0%, of which transportation equipment 23.1%, capital goods for industry 15.9%; consumer goods 18.2%, of which nondurable consumer goods 9.3%, durable consumer goods 8.9%; other 0.4%). *Major import sources:* US 26.3%; Japan 20.0%; Brazil 10.3%; Argentina 10.0%; Chile 6.0%. **Exports** (1998-f.o.b.): $1,104,900,000 (zinc 14.1%; soybeans 13.6%; gold 10.1%; silver 6.6%; oils 5.8%; natural gas 5.1%; tin 5.1%; timber 4.6%). *Major export destinations:* US 18.4%; UK 17.8%; Peru 11.9%; Argentina 10.9%; Chile 2.9%.

Transport and communications

Transport. *Railroads* (1997): route length 3,519 km; passenger-km 136,700,000; metric ton-km cargo 524,200,000. *Roads* (1996): total length, 49,400 km (paved 6% in 1995). *Vehicles* (1996): passenger cars 223,820; trucks and buses 138,536. *Air transport* (1998; LAB airlines only): passenger-mi 1,222,606,000, passenger-km 1,967,597,000; metric ton-km cargo 41,964,000; airports (1997) with scheduled flights 14. **Communications.** Total units (units per 1,000 persons). Daily newspaper circulation (1996): 420,000 (55); Radio receivers (1997): 5,250,000 (675); Television receivers (1999): 960,000 (118); Telephone main lines (1999): 502,000 (62); Cellular telephone subscribers (1999): 420,344 (52); Personal computers (1999): 100,000 (12.3); Internet users (1999): 78,000 (9.6).

Education and health

Educational attainment (1992). Percentage of pop. age 25 and over having: no formal schooling 23.3%; some primary 20.3%; primary education 21.7%; some secondary 9.0%; secondary 6.5%; some higher 5.0%; higher 4.8%; not specified 9.4%. Literacy (1995): total pop. age 15 and over literate 82.3%; males literate 92.1%; females literate 79.4%. Health (1996): physicians 4,346 (1 per 1,747 persons); hospital beds (1998) 11,548 (1 per 689 persons); infant mortality rate (2000) 60.4. Food (1999): daily per capita caloric intake 2,237 (vegetable products 82%, animal products 18%); 94% of FAO recommended minimum requirement.

Military

Total active duty personnel (2000): 32,500 (army 76.9%, navy 13.8%, air force 9.2%). Military expenditure as percentage of GNP (1997): 1.9% (world 2.6%); per capita expenditure $20.

Background

The Bolivian highlands were the location of the advanced Tiwanaku culture in the 7th—11th centuries, and, with its passing, became the home of the Aymara, an Indian group conquered by the Incas in the 15th century. The Incas were overrun in the invading Spanish under Francisco Pizarro in the 1530s. By 1600 Spain had established the cities of Charcas (now Sucre), La Paz, Santa Cruz, and what would become Cochabamba, and had begun to exploit the silver wealth of Potosí. Bolivia flourished in the 17th century, and for a time Potosí was the largest city in the Americas. By the end of the century, the mineral wealth had dried up. Talk of independence began as early as 1809, but not until 1825 were Spanish forces finally defeated. Bolivia shrank in size when it lost Atacama province to Chile in 1884 at the end of the War of the Pacific, and again in 1939 when it lost most of Gran Chaco to Paraguay. One of South America's poorest countries, it was plagued by governmental instability for much of the 20th century. By the 1990s Bolivia had become one of the world's largest producers of coca, from which cocaine is derived. The government subsequently instituted a largely successful program to eradicate the crop, although such efforts were resisted by the many poor farmers who depended on coca.

Recent Developments

Pres. Hugo Bánzer Suárez, a major political figure in Bolivian public life for 30 years, resigned for health reasons on 6 Aug 2001. Vice Pres. Jorge Quiroga Ramírez was sworn in as president the next day. Presidential balloting in August 2002 resulted in the election of Gonzalo Sánchez de Lozada, a millionaire mining executive who grew up in the US and speaks Spanish with an accent, to the top post in the country. Sánchez, who had served as president in 1993–97, was viewed as a centrist.

Internet resources: <www.boliviabiz.com>

Bosnia and Herzegovina

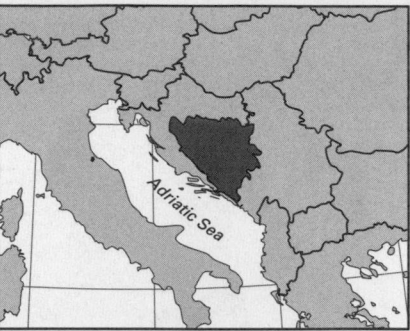

Official name: Bosna i Hercegovina (Bosnia and Herzegovina). Form of government: federal multiparty republic with bicameral legislature (House of Peoples [15—all seats are nonelective]; House of Representatives [42]). Chiefs of state: Tripartite presidency with 8-month-long rotating presidency. Head of government: Prime minister with rotating chairmanship. Capital: Sarajevo. Official language: Bosnian (Serbo-Croatian). Official religion: none. Monetary unit: 1 marka (KM) = 100 pfenning; valuation (28 Jun 2002) $1 = KM 2.26.

Demography

Area: 19,741 sq mi, 51,129 sq km. Population (2001): 3,922,000 (excludes nearly 300,000 refugees in adjacent countries and Western Europe). Density (2001): persons per sq mi 198.7, persons per sq km 76.7. Urban (1999): 42.5%. Sex distribution (2000): male 50.66%; female 49.34%. Age breakdown (2000): under 15, 20.4%; 15–29, 22.3%; 30–44, 26.2%; 45–59, 17.2%; 60–74, 11.9%; 75 and over, 2.0%. Ethnic composition (1999): Bosniac (Bosnian Muslim) 44.0%; Serb 31.0%; Croat 17.0%; other 8.0%. Religious affiliation (1999): Sunni Muslim 43.0%; Serbian Orthodox 30.0%; Roman Catholic 18.0%; other (mostly nonreligious) 9.0%. Major cities (1991): Sarajevo (1997) 360,000; Banja Luka (1997) 160,000; Zenica 96,027; Tuzla 83,770; Mostar 75,865. Location: southeastern Europe, bordered by Croatia, Serbia and Montenegro, and the Adriatic Sea.

Vital statistics

Birth rate per 1,000 pop. (2000): 12.9 (world avg. 22.5); (1993) legitimate 92.6%; illegitimate 7.4%. Death rate per 1,000 pop. (2000): 7.9 (world avg. 9.0). Natural increase rate per 1,000 pop. (2000): 5.0 (world avg. 13.5). Total fertility rate (avg. births per childbearing woman; 2000): 1.7. Marriage rate per 1,000 pop. (1991): 6.0. Divorce rate per 1,000 pop. (1991): 0.3. Life expectancy at birth (2000): male 68.8 years; female 74.4 years.

National economy

Budget (1998). Revenue: KM 3,148,000,000 (tax revenue 64.6%, of which taxes on goods and services

1 metric ton = about 1.1 short tons; 1 kilometer = 0.6 mi (statute); 1 metric ton-km cargo = about 0.68 short ton-mi cargo; c.i.f.: cost, insurance, and freight; f.o.b.: free on board

37.8%, customs duties 12.9%; nontax revenue 35.4%). *Expenditures*: KM 3,657,000,000 (social funds 24.9%; district, canton, or municipal expenditures 22.7%; disability benefits 10.2%; defense 10.1%). **Public debt** (external, outstanding; 1999): $1,826,000,000. **Gross national product** (1999): $4,706,000,000 ($1,210 per capita). **Production** (metric tons except as noted). *Agriculture, forestry, fishing* (1999): potatoes 380,000, wheat 188,000, corn (maize) 160,000; livestock (number of live animals) 350,000 cattle, 285,000 sheep; roundwood (1998) 40,000 cu m; fish catch (1997) 2,550. *Mining* (1996): iron ore (gross weight) 100,000; bauxite 75,000. *Manufacturing* (1996): cement 150,000; crude steel 115,000; pig iron 100,000. *Energy production (consumption)*: electricity (kW-hr; 1996) 2,203,000,000 (2,408,000,000); coal (metric tons; 1996) 1,640,000 (1,640,000); petroleum products (metric tons; 1996) none (516,000); natural gas (cu m; 1996) none (252,000,000). **Population economically active** (1991): total 992,000; activity rate of total pop. 22.7% (participation rates: ages 15–64, 35.6%; female [1990] 37.7%; unemployed [December 2000] c. 40%). **Household income and expenditure.** Average household size (1991) 3.4; sources of income (1990): wages 53.2%, transfers 18.2%, self-employment 12.0%, other 16.6%; expenditure (1988): food 41.3%, clothing 8.3%, fuel and lighting 7.8%, housing 7.8%, transportation 6.0%, beverages and tobacco 5.7%. **Tourism** (1999): receipts from visitors $21,000,000; expenditures by nationals abroad, n.a. **Land use** (1994): forested 53.1%; meadows and pastures 23.5%; agricultural and under permanent cultivation 15.7%; other 7.7%.

Foreign trade

Imports (2000): $2,629,000,000. *Major import sources*: Croatia 20.6%; Italy 15.9%; Slovenia 14.2%; Germany 10.7%; Yugoslavia 5.7%. **Exports** (2000): $968,000,000. *Major export destinations*: Italy 23.4%; Yugoslavia 21.6%; Switzerland 11.9%; Germany 9.2%; Croatia 7.9%.

Transport and communications

Transport. *Railroads* (1999): length 1,031 km; passenger-km 31,100,000; metric ton-km cargo 92,800,000. *Roads* (1996): total length 21,846 km (paved 52%). *Vehicles* (1996): passenger cars 96,182; trucks and buses 10,919. *Air transport* (1998; Air Bosna only): passenger-km 40,390,000; metric ton-km 430,000. Airports (1997) with scheduled flights 1. **Communications** Total units (units per 1,000 persons). Daily newspaper circulation (1995): 520,000 (155); Radio receivers (1997): 940,000 (282); Telephone main lines (1999): 368,000 (100); Cellular telephone subscribers (1999): 52,607 (14).

Education and health

Health. physicians (1998) 5,000 (estimated figure; 1 per 700 persons); hospital beds (1996) 15,586 (1 per 208 persons); infant mortality rate (2000) 25.2. **Food** (1999): daily per capita caloric intake 2,960 (vegetable products 86%, animal products 14%); 117% of FAO recommended minimum requirement.

Military

Total active duty personnel (2000): n.a.; about 20,000 troops of the NATO-commanded Stabilization Force are stationed in Bosnia and Herzegovina to assure implementation of the Dayton accords. **Military expenditure as percentage of GNP** (1997): 5.9% (world 2.6%); per capita expenditure $78.

Background

Habitation long predates the era of Roman rule, when much of the country was included in the province of Dalmatia. Slav settlement began in the 6th century AD. For the next several centuries, parts of the region fell under the rule of Serbs, Croats, Hungarians, Venetians, and Byzantines. The Ottoman Turks invaded Bosnia in the 14th century, and after many battles it became a Turkish province in 1463. Herzegovina, then known as Hum, was taken in 1482. In the 16th–17th century the area was an important Turkish outpost, constantly at war with the Habsburgs and Venice. During this period much of the native population converted to Islam. At the Congress of Berlin after the Russo-Turkish War of 1877–78, Bosnia and Herzegovina was assigned to Austria-Hungary and annexed in 1908. Growing Serb nationalism resulted in the 1914 assassination of the Austrian Archduke Francis Ferdinand at Sarajevo by a Bosnian Serb, an event that precipitated World War I. After the war the area was annexed to Serbia. Following World War II the twin territory became a republic of communist Yugoslavia. With the collapse of communist regimes in Eastern Europe, Bosnia and Herzegovina declared its independence in 1992, its Serb population objected, and conflict ensued among Serbs, Croats, and Muslims. The 1995 peace accord established a loosely federated government roughly divided between a Muslim Croat federation and a Serb Republic (Republika Srpska). In 1996 a NATO peacekeeping force was installed there.

Recent Developments

In 2001 Bosnia and Herzegovina began to stand on its own administratively without extensive international supervision. Moderate parties took over the leadership of the Muslim-Croat Federation and won considerable influence in the Serb Republic. The return of Bosnian refugees to their former homes continued to move slowly. By 2000, according to estimates, only about 5% of all the refugees and displaced persons created by the war had returned to their prewar places of residence.

Internet resources: <www.bosnet.org>

Botswana

Official name. Republic of Botswana. **Form of government:** multiparty republic with one legislative body (National Assembly [47]) and House of Chiefs (15-member advisory board). **Head of state and government:** President Festus Mogae (from 1998). **Capital:** Gaborone. **Official language:** English (Tswana is the national language) **Official religion:** none. **Monetary unit:** 1 pula (P) = 100 thebe; valuation (28 Jun 2002) $1 = P 6.18.

Demography

Area: 224,607 (rounded) sq mi, 581,730 sq km. **Population** (2001): 1,586,000. **Density** (2001): persons per sq mi 7.1, persons per sq km 2.7. **Urban**

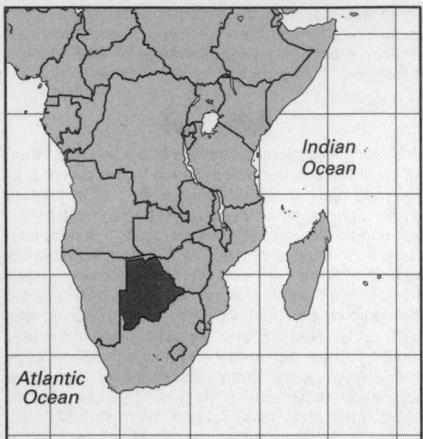

Indian Ocean

Atlantic Ocean

(1999): 29.4%. **Sex distribution** (2000): male 48.58%; female 51.42%. **Age breakdown** (2000): under 15, 40.6%; 15–29, 30.8%; 30–44, 15.0%; 45–59, 7.7%; 60–74, 4.3%; 75 and over, 1.6%. **Ethnic composition** (2000): Tswana 66.8%; Kalanga 14.8%; Ndebele 1.7%; Herero 1.4%; San (Bushman) 1.3%; Afrikaner 1.3%. **Religious affiliation** (2000): traditional beliefs 38.8%; African Christian 30.7%; Protestant 10.9%; Roman Catholic 3.7%. **Major cities** (1997): Gaborone 183,487; Francistown 88,195; Selebi-Pikwe 45,651; Molepolole 36,931; Kanye 31,354. **Location**: southern Africa, bordering Zambia, Zimbabwe, South Africa, and Namibia.

Vital statistics

Birth rate per 1,000 pop. (2001): 28.8 (world avg. 22.5); (1986- registered births only) legitimate 28.8%; illegitimate 71.2%. **Death rate** per 1,000 pop. (2001): 24.8 (world avg. 9.0). **Natural increase rate** per 1,000 pop. (2001): 4.0 (world avg. 13.5). **Total fertility rate** (avg. births per childbearing woman; 2001): 3.7. **Marriage rate** per 1,000 pop. (1987): 1.6. **Life expectancy** at birth (2001): male 36.8 years; female 37.5 years.

National economy

Budget (1997–98). *Revenue*: P 8,468,900,000 (mineral royalties 57.7%, customs and excise taxes 14.0%, property income 13.2%, non-mineral income tax 6.4%). *Expenditures*: P 7,616,400,000 (education 24.2%, defense 8.4%, health 5.1%, interest 1.3%). **Population economically active** (1995): total 439,933; activity rate of total pop. 29.9% (participation rates: ages 15–64, 59.6% (1991), female 35.5%, unemployed 21.5%). **Public debt** (external, outstanding; 1999): $442,300,000. **Tourism** (1999): receipts $234,000,000; expenditures $143,000,000. **Production** (metric tons except as noted). *Agriculture, forestry, fishing* (1999): cereals 19,800, pulses 16,000, vegetables and melons 15,000; livestock (number of live animals) 2,380,000 cattle, 1,835,000 goats, 250,000 sheep; roundwood (1998) 1,066,000 cu m; fish catch (1998) 2,000. *Mining and quarrying* (1998): nickel 19,432; copper 15,593; dia-

monds 19,773,000 carats. *Manufacturing* (value added in P '000,000; 1994): food products 164.3; wearing apparel 78.9; paper and paper products 28.0. *Energy production (consumption):* electricity (kW-hr; 1993) 970,000,000 (970,000,000); coal (metric tons; 1992) 901,452 (not available). **Gross national product** (1999): $5,139,000,000 ($3,240 per capita). **Household income and expenditure** (1991). Average household size 4.8; average annual income per household (1985–86) P 3,910; sources of income (1987): wages and salaries 73.3%, self-employment 15.9%, transfers 10.8%; expenditure: food 39.4%, household durable goods 14.0%, rent and services 13.3%, transportation 13.1%, clothing 5.6%, health 2.3%. **Land use** (1994): forest 46.8%; pasture 45.2%; agriculture 0.7%; other 7.3%.

Foreign trade

Imports (1997-c.i.f.): P 8,255,800,000 (machinery and transport equipment 37.6%, of which transport equipment 20.0%; food, beverages, and tobacco 13.1%; metal and metal products 10.7%; chemical and rubber products 9.1%). *Major import sources*: Customs Union of Southern Africa (CUSA) 72.4%; South Korea 9.5%; Zimbabwe 4.5%; UK 2.0%; US 1.1%. **Exports** (1997-f.o.b.): P 10,390,700,000 (diamonds 73.8%; vehicles and parts 11.4%; copper-nickel matte 4.6%; textiles 2.4%; meat products 2.2%). *Major export destinations*: UK 56.2%; CUSA 14.3%; Zimbabwe 3.7%; US 1.0%.

Transport and communications

Transport. *Railroads* (1996–97): 1,135 km; passenger-km 96,000,000; metric ton-km cargo 795,000. *Roads* (1996): total length 18,327 km (paved 25%). *Vehicles* (1996): passenger cars 30,517; trucks and buses 59,710. *Air transport* (1998–Air Botswana only): passenger-km 56,835,000; metric ton-km cargo 211,000; airports (1998) 7. **Communications** Total units (units per 1,000 persons). Daily newspaper circulation (1996): 40,000 (27); Radio receivers (1997): 237,000 (154); Television receivers (1999) 33,000 (21); Telephone main lines (1999): 123,819 (79); Cellular telephone subscribers (1999): 120,000 (77); Personal computers (1999): 50,000 (32); Internet users (1999): 12,000 (7.7).

Education and health

Educational attainment (1993). Percentage of pop. age 25 and over having: no formal schooling 34.7%; primary education 44.1%; some secondary 19.8%; postsecondary 1.4%. **Literacy** (2000): total pop. over age 15 literate 934,200 (77.2%); males literate 449,200 (74.4%); females literate 485,000 (79.8%). **Health** (1994): physicians 339 (1 per 4,395 persons); hospital beds (1993) 3,299 (1 per 434 persons); infant mortality rate (2001) 63.2. **Food** (1998): daily per capita caloric intake 2,159 (vegetable products 82%, animal products 18%); 93% of FAO recommended minimum requirement.

Military

Total active duty personnel (2000): 9,000 (army 94.4%, navy, air force 5.6%). **Military expenditure as**

---

1 metric ton = about 1.1 short tons;   1 kilometer = 0.6 mi (statute);   1 metric ton-km cargo = about 0.68 short ton-mi cargo;   c.i.f.: cost, insurance, and freight;   f.o.b.: free on board

percentage of GNP (1997): 5.1% (world 2.6%); per capita expenditure $168.

Background

The region's earliest inhabitants were the Khoikhoi and San (Bushmen). Sites were settled as early as AD 190 during the southerly migration of Bantu-speaking farmers. Tswana dynasties, which developed in the western Transvaal in the 13th–14th century, moved into Botswana in the 18th century and established several powerful states. European missionaries arrived in the early 19th century, but it was the discovery of gold in 1867 that excited European interest. In 1885 the area became the British Bechuanaland Protectorate. The next year, the region south of the Molopo River became a crown colony, and it was annexed by the Cape Colony 10 years later. Bechuanaland itself continued as a British protectorate until the 1960s. In 1966 the Republic of Bechuanaland (later, Botswana) was proclaimed an independent member of the British Commonwealth. Independent Botswana tried to maintain a delicate balance between its economic dependence on South Africa and its relations with the surrounding black countries; the independence of Namibia in 1990 and South Africa's rejection of apartheid eased tensions.

Recent Developments

Botswana enjoys a remarkably stable liberal democracy with solid growth, a by-product of the October 1999 elections that confirmed the mandate of the Botswana Democratic Party under Pres. Festus Mogae. In the Transparency International 2001 survey, Botswana was ranked the least-corrupt state in Africa (and 26th in the world). On the health front, however, the country faces a growing crisis; nearly 36% of adults in Botswana are believed to have HIV, the virus that causes AIDS.

Internet resources: <www.gov.bw/tourism>

Brazil

Official name: República Federativa do Brasil (Federative Republic of Brazil). Form of government:

multiparty federal republic with 2 legislative houses (Federal Senate [81]; Chamber of Deputies [513]). Chief of state and government: President Fernando Henrique Cardoso (from 1995). Capital: Brasília. Official language: Portuguese. Official religion: none. Monetary unit: real (R$) = 100 centavos; valuation (28 Jun 2002) $1 = 2.85 reais.

Demography

Area: 3,300,171 sq mi, 8,547,404 sq km (land area excluding inland water is 3,265,076 sq mi [8,456,508 sq km]). Population (2001): 172,118,000. Density (2001): persons per sq mi 52.2, persons per sq km 20.1. Urban (1997): 79.6%. Sex distribution (2000): male 49.26%; female 50.74%. Age breakdown (2000): under 15, 29.0%; 15–29, 28.4%; 30–44, 22.2%; 45–59, 12.5%; 60–74, 6.3%; 75 and over, 1.6%. Racial composition (1997: excludes rural pop. of Acre, Amapá, Amazonas, Pará, Rondônia, and Roraima states): white 54.4%; mulatto and mestizo 39.9%; black and black/Amerindian 5.2%; Asian 0.4%; Amerindian 0.1%. Religious affiliation (1995; Christian data include nominal Christians): Catholic 74.3% (includes syncretic Afro-Catholic cults having Spiritist beliefs and rituals), of which Roman Catholic 72.3%; Protestant 23.2%, of which Pentecostal 19.1%; other Christian 0.9%; New-Religionist 0.3%; Buddhist 0.3%; Jewish 0.2%; Muslim 0.1%; other 0.7%. Major cities and metropolitan areas (2000; preliminary populations are for municípios, which may include adjacent urban or rural districts): São Paulo 9,785,640 (17,833,757); Rio de Janeiro 5,850,544 (10,871,960); Salvador 2,439,881 (3,018,326); Belo Horizonte 2,229,697 (4,208,508); Fortaleza 2,138,-234 (2,843,304); Brasília 2,043,169 (2,043,169). Location: eastern South America, bordering French Guiana, the Atlantic Ocean, Uruguay, Argentina, Paraguay, Bolivia, Peru, Colombia, Venezuela, Guyana, and Suriname. Families (1996): Average family size 3.9; 1–2 persons 25.2%, 3 persons 20.3%, 4 persons 22.2%, 5–6 persons 23.3%, 7 or more persons 9.0%. Domestic migration. Percent of pop. moving to different município between 1991 and 1996: 7.6%. Number of emigrants/immigrants (1986–96): 2,355,057/169,303. Emigrants' most popular destinations in order of preference are the United States, Japan, and the United Kingdom.

Vital statistics

Birth rate per 1,000 pop. (2000): 18.8 (world avg. 22.5). Death rate per 1,000 pop. (2000): 9.4 (world avg. 9.0). Natural increase rate per 1,000 pop. (2000): 9.4 (world avg. 13.5). Total fertility rate (avg. births per childbearing woman; 2000): 2.1. Marriage rate per 1,000 pop. (1995): 4.7. Divorce rate per 1,000 pop. (1995): 0.6. Life expectancy at birth (2000): male 58.5 years; female 67.6 years.

Social indicators

Quality of working life. Annual estimated rate per 100,000 insured workers (1990) for: on-the-job injury 2,032; industrial illness 17; death 4. Proportion of labor force participating in national social insurance system (1990): 50.1%. Proportion of formally employed pop. receiving minimum wage (1993): 25.0%. Access to services (1997; excludes rural pop. of Acre, Amapá, Amazonas, Pará, Rondônia, and Roraima states): Proportion of households having access to: electricity 93.3%, of which urban households having access 99.0%, rural households having access 68.8%; safe public (piped) water supply 73.8%, of which urban households having access 87.4%, rural households having access 14.9%; public (piped) sewage system 40.8%, of which urban household having access 49.4%, rural households having access 3.5%; no sewage disposal 10.0%, of which urban households having no disposal 3.7%, rural households having no disposal 37.2%. **Social participation.** Voting is mandatory for national elections; abstention is punishable by a fine. Trade union membership in total workforce (1991): 16,748,155. Practicing Roman Catholic pop. in total affiliated Roman Catholic pop. (2000): large cities 10–15%; towns and rural areas 60–70%. **Social deviance.** Annual murder rate per 100,000 pop. (1996): Brazil 23, Rio de Janeiro alone 69, São Paulo 55. **Leisure.** Favorite leisure activities include: soccer, water sports, volleyball, basketball, dancing (rehearsing all year in neighborhood samba "schools" for celebrations of Carnival). **Material well-being** (1997; excludes rural pop. of Acre, Amapá, Amazonas, Pará, Rondônia, and Roraima). Households possessing: telephone lines 27.9%, of which urban 33.2%, rural 4.9%; television receiver 86.2%, of which urban 92.7%, rural 58.4%; refrigerator 80.3%, of which urban 88.1%, rural 46.6%; washing machine 31.7%, of which urban 36.9%, rural 9.3%.

National economy

Gross national product (at current market prices; 1999): US$730,424,000,000 (US$4,350 per capita). **Budget.** *Revenue* (1995): R$320,178,000,000 (development receipts 62.6%, of which credits 58.4%; current receipts 37.4%, of which social contributions 19.3% [including social security 9.2%], taxes 13.3%). *Expenditures:* R$320,178,000,000 (administration and planning 59.5%; social welfare 13.9%; regional development 6.0%; health and sanitation 4.9%; agriculture 3.1%; education 2.7%; defense and public order 2.6%). **Public debt** (external, outstanding; 1999): US$95,233,000,000. **Production** ('000 metric tons except as noted). *Agriculture, forestry, fishing* (2000): sugarcane 324,668, soybeans 32,687, corn (maize) 32,038; livestock (number of live animals) 167,471,000 cattle, 27,320,000 pigs, 18,300,000 sheep; roundwood (1999) 197,897,000 cu m, of which fuelwood 90,210,000 cu m, sawlogs and veneer logs 46,779,000 cu m, pulpwood 30,701,000 cu m; fish catch (1997) 820, of which freshwater fishes 267. *Mining and quarrying* (value of export production in US$'000,000; 1998): iron ore 3,066; ferroniobium 242. *Manufacturing* (value added in R$'000,000; 1995): industrial chemicals 21,937; transport equipment 20,434; food products 18,117. **Land use** (1994): forested 57.7%; meadows and pastures 21.9%; agricultural and under permanent cultivation 6.0%; other 14.4%. **Population economically active** (1998; excludes rural pop. of Acre, Amapá, Amazonas, Pará, Rondônia, and Roraima states and members of armed forces in barracks): total 76,885,700; activity rate of total pop. 47.4% (participation rates: ages 15–59 [1997] 72.0%; female 40.7%; unemployed [May 1999] officially 8%). **Tourism** (1999): receipts from visitors US$3,994,-

000,000; expenditures by nationals abroad US$3,059,000,000. **Households.** Average household size (1997) 3.8. **Family income and expenditure.** Average family size (1997; excludes rural pop. of Acre, Amapá, Amazonas, Pará, Rondônia, and Roraima) 3.5; annual income per family (1993) R$608,364 (excludes rural pop. of Acre, Amapá, Amazonas, Pará, Rondônia, and Roraima and is based on a year-end exchange rate); sources of income (1987–88; based on 10,408,833 families in Brazil's nine largest metropolitan regions); wages and salaries 62.4%, self-employed 14.7%, transfers 10.9%, other 12.0%; expenditure (1995–96; based on survey of 11 metropolitan areas only): housing, energy, and household furnishings 28.8%, food and beverages 23.4%, transportation and communications 13.8%, health care 9.2%, education and recreation 8.4%. **Energy production** (consumption): electricity (kW-hr; 1998) 288,996,000,000 (287,864,-000,000); coal (metric tons; 1999) 4,284,000 ([1996] 17,294,000); crude petroleum (barrels; 1999) 398,228,000 ([1996] 485,343,000); petroleum products (metric tons; 1996) 57,378,000 (66,388,000); natural gas (cu m; 1999) 11,854,-000,000 ([1996] 4,936,000,000); carburant alcohol (barrels; 1997) 76,650,000 (76,650,000).

Foreign trade

Imports (1998-c.i.f.): US$60,793,000,000 (nonelectrical machinery and apparatus 19.7%; chemicals and chemical products 16.2%; electrical machinery and apparatus 12.8%; motor vehicles 9.5%; mineral fuels 9.3%). *Major import sources:* United States 23.6%; Argentina 13.9%; Germany 9.0%; Japan 5.6%; Italy 5.5%; France 3.4%; United Kingdom 2.6%; Canada 2.4%; Spain 2.1%; China 1.9%. **Exports** (1998-f.o.b.): US$51,120,000,000 (food products 20.3%, of which coffee 4.6%, sugar [all forms] 4.0%, vegetables and fruit 3.3%; road vehicles 9.4%; nonelectrical machinery and apparatus 8.5%; iron and steel 7.2%; iron ore 6.4%; chemicals and chemical products 6.2%; soybeans 4.3%). *Major export destinations:* United States 19.3%; Argentina 13.2%; Germany 5.9%; The Netherlands 5.4%; Japan 4.3%; Belgium–Luxembourg 4.3%; Italy 3.8%; United Kingdom 2.6%; France 2.5%; Paraguay 2.4%.

Transport and communications

Transport. *Railroads* (1998; includes suburban services): route length (1997) 29,706 km; passenger-km 12,667,000,000; metric ton-km cargo 141,239,-000,000. *Roads* (1997): total length 1,658,677 km (paved 9%). *Vehicles* (1998): passenger cars 21,313,351; trucks and buses 3,743,836. *Air transport* (1999; TAM Regional, TAM Meridional, VARIG, and VASP airlines only): passenger-km 35,028,000,-000; metric ton-km cargo 1,301,000,000; airports (1995) with scheduled flights 139. **Communications** Total units (units per 1,000 persons). Daily newspaper circulation (1996): 6,472,000 (41); Radio receivers (1997): 71,000,000 (446); Television receivers (1999): 56,000,000 (336); Telephone main lines (1999): 24,985,000 (150); Cellular telephone subscribers (1999): 15,033,000 (90); Personal computers units (1999): 6,100,000 (37); Internet users (1999): 3,500,000 (21).

---

1 metric ton = about 1.1 short tons;   1 kilometer = 0.6 mi (statute);   1 metric ton-km cargo = about 0.68 short ton-mi cargo;   c.i.f.: cost, insurance, and freight;   f.o.b.: free on board

Education and health

Educational attainment (1996). Percentage of pop. age 25 and over having: no formal schooling or less than one year of primary education 17.7%; lower primary only 19.1%; upper primary 30.7%; complete primary to some secondary 11.6%; complete secondary to some higher 13.9%; complete higher 6.2%; unknown 0.8%. Literacy (2000): total pop. age 15 and over literate 103,500,000 (86.3%); males literate 50,300,000 (85.1%); females literate 53,200,000 (85.4%). Health (1997): physicians 205,828 (1 per 774 persons); hospital beds 496,740 (1 per 321 persons); infant mortality rate per 1,000 live births (2000) 38.0. Food (1997): daily per capita caloric intake 2,974 (vegetable products 80%, animal products 20%); 124% of FAO recommended minimum requirement.

Military

Total active duty personnel (2000): 287,600 (army 65.7%, navy 16.9%, air force 17.4%). Military expenditure as percentage of GNP (1997): 1.8% (world 2.6%); per capita expenditure US$89.

Background

Little is known about Brazil's early indigenous inhabitants. Though the area was theoretically allotted to Portugal by the 1494 Treaty of Tordesillas, it was not formally claimed by discovery until Pedro Alvares Cabral accidentally touched land in 1500. It was first settled by the Portuguese in the early 1530s on the southeastern coast and at São Vicente (near modern São Paulo); the French and Dutch created small settlements over the next century. A viceroyalty was established in 1640 and Rio de Janeiro became the capital in 1763. In 1808 Brazil became the refuge and seat of the government of John VI of Portugal when Napoleon invaded Portugal; ultimately the Kingdom of Portugal, Brazil, and the Algarves was proclaimed, and John ruled from Brazil in 1815–21. On John's return to Portugal, his son Pedro I proclaimed Brazilian independence. In 1889 his successor, Pedro II, was deposed, and a constitution mandating a federal republic was adopted. The 20th century saw increased immigration and growth in manufacturing along with frequent military coups and suspensions of civil liberties. Construction of a new capital at Brasília, intended to spur development of the country's interior, worsened the inflation rate. After 1979 the military government began a gradual return to democratic practices, and in 1989 the first popular presidential election in 29 years was held.

Recent Developments

Policies enacted during Pres. Fernando Henrique Cardoso's first term (1995–99) permitted strong economic growth while lowering the annual inflation rate dramatically—from nearly 1,000% in 1994 to less than 20% within a year and nearly zero by 1998. The political parties backing Cardoso's policies won a majority of the 1996 municipal elections.

Cardoso pushed through a law in 1997 that permitted presidents and governors to be reelected. His Brazilian Social Democratic Party formed a coalition with the Liberal Front Party, the Party of the Brazilian Democratic Movement, the Progressive Renewal Party, and several smaller entities to enact major fiscal and administrative reforms, notably the decision to privatize such government-owned enterprises as the Rio Doce Valley Company. Brazil's economy slowed as a result of financial crises in Asia and Russia in 1998, but Cardoso retained his popularity, won reelection to the presidency, and saw his coalition retain a decisive congressional majority.

The government subsequently attained support from the International Monetary Fund, carried out additional fiscal and administrative reforms, and devalued Brazil's currency by allowing its exchange rate to float rather than continue its near parity with the US dollar. Inflation remained under control, in spite of fears to the contrary, and the military seemed unlikely to intervene in civil affairs in the near future. Cardoso appointed a civilian-led minister of defense, whose duties replaced those of the separate military service ministers. The governing coalition fragmented, however, as parties and politicians maneuvered for advantage in the October 2000 municipal elections. Still, a record harvest and robust economic growth allowed Cardoso to move forward with his priority programs.

Major demographic shifts continued to affect Brazil at the turn of the 21st century, including a growing population that was increasingly concentrated in cities. The nation's cities were, however, ill-prepared to serve the needs of their growing multitudes, and, in spite of increased regional growth, Brazil's economic opportunities and population remained heavily concentrated in the Southeast and South. At the same time, the frontiers of agricultural and mining operations persistently expanded, and Brazil remained embroiled in domestic and international controversies regarding threats to the Amazon rainforest and to forest-dwelling Indian groups such as the Yanomami. In addition, landless groups continued to clamor for agrarian reform. Notwithstanding Brazil's problems, foreign investors and major trading partners showed renewed interest in the nation.

Internet resources: <www.embratur.gov.br>

Brunei

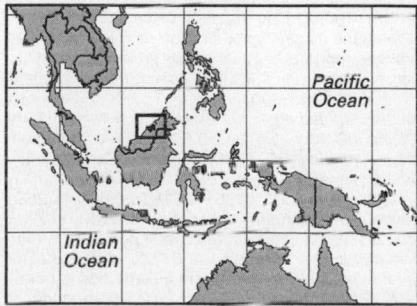

Official name: Negara Brunei Darussalam, State of Brunei, Abode of Peace. Form of government: monarchy (advised by a 21-member appointed body on legislative matters). Head of state and government: Sultan Haji Hassanal Bolkiah Mu'izzadin Waddaulah (from 1967). Capital: Bandar Seri Begawan. Official language: Malay. Official religion: Islam. Monetary unit: 1 Brunei dollar (B$) = 100 cents; valuation (28 Jun 2002) US$1 = B$1.77.

Demography

Area: 2,226 sq mi, 5,765 sq km. **Population** (2001): 344,000. **Density** (2001): persons per sq mi 154.5, persons per sq km 59.7. **Urban** (1999): 72%. **Sex distribution** (1998): male 53.06%; female 46.94%. **Age breakdown** (1996): under 15, 32.9%; 15–29, 27.5%; 30–44, 25.5%; 45–59, 9.4%; 60 and over, 4.7%. **Ethnic composition** (1999): Malay 67.6%; Chinese 14.9%; other indigenous 5.9%; Indian and other 11.6%. **Religious affiliation** (2000): Muslim 64.4%; traditional beliefs 11.2%; Buddhist 9.1%; Christian 7.7%; other religions and nonreligious 7.6%. **Major cities** (1991): Bandar Seri Begawan (1999) 85,000 (urban agglomeration); Kuala Belait 21,163; Seria 21,082; Tutong 13,049. **Location:** southeastern Asia, bordering the South China Sea and Malaysia.

Vital statistics

Birth rate per 1,000 pop. (1999): 22.3 (world avg. 22.5); (1982) legitimate 99.6%; illegitimate 0.4%. **Death rate** per 1,000 pop. (1999): 2.8 (world avg. 9.0). **Natural increase rate** per 1,000 pop. (1999): 19.5 (world avg. 13.5). **Total fertility rate** (avg. births per childbearing woman; 1999): 2.7. **Marriage rate** per 1,000 pop. (1995): 6.1. **Divorce rate** per 1,000 pop. (1992): 1.1. **Life expectancy** at birth (1999): male 74.0 years; female 76.0 years.

National economy

Budget (1998). *Revenue:* B$2,775,000,000 (tax revenue 54.6%, of which corporate income tax 47.3%, import duty 7.2%; nontax revenue 45.4%, of which property income 33.8%, commercial receipts 10.9%). *Expenditures:* B$4,295,000,000 (current expenditure 65.5%; capital expenditure 34.5%). **Tourism** (1995): receipts from visitors US$40,000,000; expenditures by nationals abroad US$1,000,000. **Production** (metric tons except as noted). *Agriculture, forestry, fishing* (1999): vegetables and melons 8,700, fruits (excluding melons) 5,225, cassava 1,500; livestock (number of live animals) 6,000 buffalo, 4,500 pigs, 4,929,000 chickens; roundwood (1998) 296,000 cu m; fish catch (1997) 4,677. *Mining and quarrying:* other than petroleum and natural gas, none except sand and gravel for construction. *Manufacturing* (1998): gasoline 187,600; distillate fuel oils 147,800; kerosene 76,500. *Energy production (consumption):* electricity (kW-hr; 1996) 1,575,000,000 (1,575,000,000); crude petroleum (barrels; 1996) 60,000,000 (900,000); petroleum products (metric tons; 1996) 851,000 (909,000); natural gas (cu m; 1996) 9,218,000,000 (1,269,-000,000). **Population economically active** (1991): total 111,955; activity rate of total pop. 43.0% (participation rates: ages 15–64, 67.6%; female 32.9%; unemployed 4.7%). **Household income and expenditure.** Average household size (1991) 5.8; expenditure (1990): food 38.7%, transportation and communications 19.9%, housing 18.6%, clothing 6.4%, other 16.4%. **Gross national product** (at current market prices; 1998): US$7,209,000,000 (US$22,278 per capita). **Land use** (1994): forested 85.4%; meadows

and pastures 1.1%; agricultural and under permanent cultivation 1.3%; other 12.2%.

Foreign trade

Imports (1997): B$3,154,000,000 (machinery and transport equipment 39.0%, manufactured goods 25.5%, miscellaneous manufactured articles 11.6%, food and live animals 11.1%, chemicals 6.4%, crude materials 3.4%, beverages and tobacco 1.9%). *Major import sources:* ASEAN 45.5%, of which Singapore 25.6%, Malaysia 13.6%; EEC 17.9%; Japan 11.2%; United States 10.0%. **Exports** (1997): B$3,973,000,-000 (natural gas 46.8%, crude petroleum 41.5%, petroleum products 2.8%). *Major export destinations:* Japan 53.1%; ASEAN 20.9%, of which Thailand 11.2%, Singapore 6.6%; South Korea 18.1%; Taiwan 2.7%.

Transport and communications

Transport. *Railroads* (privately owned): length 12 mi, 19 km. *Roads* (1996): total length 1,064 mi, 1,712 km (paved 75%). *Vehicles* (1997): passenger cars 91,047; trucks and buses 15,918. *Marine transport* (1998): cargo loaded 25,900,000 metric tons, cargo unloaded 1,195,200 metric tons. *Air transport* (1998): passenger-mi 1,742,000,000, passenger-km 2,803,000,000; short ton-mi cargo 75,020,000, metric ton-km cargo 109,527,000; airports (1996) with scheduled flights 1. **Communications** Total units (units per 1,000 persons). Daily newspaper circulation (1996): 21,000 (69); Radio receivers (1997): 93,000 (302); Television receivers (1999): 205,000 (637); Telephone main lines (1999): 79,086 (246); Cellular telephone subscribers (1999): 66,000 (205); Personal computers (1999): 20,000 (62); Internet users (1999): 25,000 (78).

Education and health

Educational attainment (1991). Percentage of pop. age 25 and over having: no formal schooling 17.0%; primary education 43.3%; secondary 26.3%; postsecondary and higher 12.9%; not stated 0.5%. **Literacy** (1995): percentage of total pop. age 15 and over literate 89.1%; males literate 93.2%; females literate 84.6%. **Health** (1996): physicians 281 (1 per 1,086 persons); hospital beds 961 (1 per 317 persons); infant mortality rate per 1,000 live births (1999) 6.0. **Food** (1999): daily per capita caloric intake 2,793 (vegetable products 82%, animal products 18%); (1997) 125% of FAO recommended minimum requirement.

Military

Total active duty personnel (2000): 5,000 (army 78.0%, navy 14.0%, air force 8.0% [all services form part of the army]). British troops (a Gurkha batallion; 2000): 1,050. **Military expenditure as percentage of GNP** (1997): 4.6% (world 2.6%); per capita expenditure US$1,190.

Background

Brunei traded with China in the 6th century AD. Through allegiance to the Javanese Majapahit king-

---

1 metric ton = about 1.1 short tons;   1 kilometer = 0.6 mi (statute);   1 metric ton-km cargo = about 0.68 short ton-mi cargo;   c.i.f.: cost, insurance, and freight;   f.o.b.: free on board

dom (13th—15th century), it came under Hindu influence. In the early 15th century, with the decline of the Majapahit kingdom, many converted to Islam, and Brunei became an independent sultanate. When Ferdinand Magellan's ships visited in 1521, the sultan of Brunei controlled almost all of Borneo and its neighboring islands. Beginning in the late 16th century, Brunei lost power because of the Portuguese, Dutch, and, later, British activities in the region. By the 19th century, the sultanate of Brunei included Sarawak (present-day Brunei) and part of North Borneo (now part of Sabah). In 1841 a revolt took place against the sultan, and a British soldier, James Brooke, helped put it down; he was later proclaimed governor. In 1847 the sultanate entered into a treaty with Great Britain, and by 1906 had yielded all administration to a British Resident. Brunei rejected membership in the Federation of Malaysia in 1963, negotiated a new treaty with Britain in 1979, and achieved independence in 1984, with membership in the Commonwealth. Today Brunei is considering ways to diversify the economy and to encourage tourism.

Recent Developments

The Asian financial crisis of 1997–98 exacted a heavy toll on the government's stock portfolio and other investments. In addition, Brunei's royal family found itself increasingly under scrutiny. The sultan's once much-favored youngest brother, former finance minister Prince Jefri Bolkiah, returned from exile in 2000 and reached an out-of-court settlement after having been sued by the state for the misuse of more than $15 billion in the government coffers.

Internet resources: <www.brunet.bn>

Bulgaria

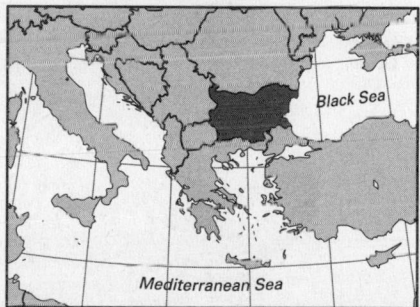

Black Sea

Mediterranean Sea

Official name: Republika Bulgaria (Republic of Bulgaria) Form of government: unitary multiparty republic with one legislative body (National Assembly [240]). Chief of state: President Georgi Parvanov (from 22 Jan 2002). Head of government: Prime Minister Simeon Saxecoburggotski (from 2001). Capital: Sofia. Official language: Bulgarian. Official religion: none. Monetary unit: 1 lev (Lw; leva) = 100 stotinki; valuation (28 Jun 2002) $1 = 1.98 (new) leva (re-denominated in 1000 to 1 new leva = 1,000 old leva).

Demography

Area: 110,971.4 sq mi, 8,190,876 sq km. Population (2001): 7,953,000. Density (2001): persons per sq mi 185.6, persons per sq km 71.7. Urban (1999): 68%. Sex distribution (2000): male 48.48%; female 51.52%. Age breakdown (2000): under 15, 15.6%; 15–29, 21.8%; 30–44, 20.0%; 45–59, 20.5%; 60–74, 16.3%; 75 and over, 5.8%. Ethnic composition (1992): Bulgarian 83.2%; Turkish 9.4%; Gypsy 3.6%; other 1.3%. Religious affiliation (1995): Bulgarian Orthodox 36.5%, Protestant 1.4%, Roman Catholic 0.8%; Sunni Muslim 13.1%; other/nonreligious 47.8%. Major cities (2000): Sofia 1,133,183; Plovdiv 344,976; Varna 296,204. Location: southeastern Europe, bordering Romania, the Black Sea, Turkey, Greece, Macedonia, and Serbia and Montenegro.

Vital statistics

Birth rate per 1,000 pop. (1999): 8.8 (world avg. 22.5). Death rate per 1,000 pop. (1999): 13.6 (world avg. 9.0). Natural increase rate per 1,000 pop. (1999): −4.8 (world avg. 13.5). Total fertility rate (avg. births per childbearing woman; 1999): 1.2. Life expectancy at birth (2000): male 67.5 years; female 74.6 years.

National economy

Budget (1998). Revenue: 8,913,064,200,000 (old) leva (tax revenue 79.4%, of which social insurance 22.9%, value-added tax 20.6%, income tax 11.5%, profit tax 9.6%, excises 7.6%, customs and duties 5.0%, other 2.2%; nontax revenue 20.0%; other 0.6%). Expenditures: 8,689,188,600,000 (old) leva (social insurance 27.1%; administration 16.3%; wages 12.9%; interest on debt 11.0%; capital expenditure 10.9%; defense 10.8%; education 10.2%). Public debt (external, outstanding; 1999): $7,602,-000,000. Gross national product (1999): $11,572,-000,000 ($1,410 per capita). Production (metric tons except as noted). Agriculture, forestry, fishing (1999): wheat 3,000,000, corn (maize) 1,100,000, sunflower seeds 700,000; livestock (number of live animals) 2,774,000 sheep, 1,721,000 pigs, 1,048,000 goats; roundwood (1998) 3,041,000 cu m; fish catch (1998) 10,756. Mining and quarrying (1997): iron ore 895,000; lead 72,975; zinc 72,755. Manufacturing (value of production in '000,000 (old) leva; 1997): food, beverages, and tobacco 2,834,-413; chemical and oil processing 1,633,583; machine and metalworking 1,460,220. Energy production (consumption): electricity (kW-hr; 1998) 42,803,000,000 (42,803,000,000); coal (metric tons; 1998) 31,248,000 (34,200,000); crude petroleum (barrels; 1998) 232,360 (50,979,000); petroleum products (metric tons; 1996) 5,810,000 (4,361,000); natural gas (cu m; 1996) 44,000,000 (6,197,000,000). Household income and expenditure. Average household size (1998) 3.0; income per household (1999) 4,179 (new) leva; sources of income (1999): wages and salaries 39.6%, transfer payments 16.8%, self-employment in agriculture 16.7%; expenditure (1999): food 41.8%, housing and energy 11.3%, transportation 5.4%, clothing 5.0%, household durable goods 3.1%, education and culture 3.1%, health 2.7%, other 27.6%. Population economically active (1997): total 3,581,800; activity rate of total pop. 51.9% (participation rates: age 16–59 [male], 16–54 [female] 57.3%; female 47.6%; unemployed 13.7%). Tourism (1999): receipts $932,000,000; expenditures by nationals abroad $524,000,000.

Foreign trade

Imports (1997): 8,268,462,200 (new) leva (petroleum and natural gas 28.7%; machine-building and metalworking equipment 13.9%; chemical products 9.9%; electrical and electronic equipment 6.6%; food, beverages, and tobacco 6.3%; textiles and knitwear 4.5%). *Major import sources*: Russia 28.0%; Germany 11.8%; Italy 7.2%; Greece 4.2%; US 3.7%; Ukraine 3.7%. **Exports** (1997): 8,281,386,500 (new) leva (chemicals and plastics 22.3%; food, beverages, and tobacco 13.5%; machine-building and metalworking equipment 9.6%; clothing and footwear 7.1%). *Major export destinations*: Italy 11.7%; Germany 9.5%; Turkey 9.0%; Greece 8.2%; Russia 7.9%.

Transport and communications

Transport. *Railroads* (1998): track length 6,470 km; (1997) passenger-km 5,866,000,000; metric ton-km cargo 7,444,000,000. *Roads* (1998): length 37,320 km (paved 92%). *Vehicles* (1998): cars 1,730,506; trucks and buses 251,382. *Air transport* (1997): passenger-km 2,025,752,000; metric ton-km cargo 30,371,000; airports (1997) with scheduled flights 3. **Communications** Total units (units per 1,000 persons). Daily newspaper circulation (1998): 2,145,000 (254); Television receivers (1998): 3,400,000 (418); Telephone main lines (1999): 2,933,000 (363); Cellular telephone subscribers (1999): 350,000 (43); Personal computers (1999) 220,000 (27); Internet users (1999): 235,000 (29).

Education and health

Educational attainment (1992). Percentage of pop. age 25 and over having: no formal schooling 4.7%; incomplete primary education 12.5%; primary 31.9%; secondary 35.7%; higher 15.0%. **Literacy** (1995): total pop. age 15 and over literate 98.0%; males 98.8%; females 97.4%. **Health** (1998): physicians 28,823 (1 per 285 persons); hospital beds 85,408 (1 per 97 persons); infant mortality rate per 1,000 live births (1999) 14.6. **Food** (1999): daily per capita caloric intake 2,847 (vegetable products 76%, animal products 24%); 114% of FAO recommended minimum requirement.

Military

Total active duty personnel (2000): 79,760 (army 53.2%, navy 6.6%, air force 22.9%, other 17.3%). **Military expenditure as percentage of GNP** (1997): 3.0% (world 2.6%); per capita expenditure $114.

Background

Evidence of human habitation in Bulgaria dates from prehistoric times. Thracians were its first recorded inhabitants, dating from c. 3500 BC, and their first state dates from about the 5th century BC; the area was subdued by the Romans, who divided it into the provinces of Moesia and Thrace. In the 7th century AD the Bulgars took the region to the south of the Danube. The Byzantine empire in 681 formally recognized Bulgar control over the area between the Balkans and the Danube. In the second half of the 14th century, Bulgaria fell to the Turks and ultimately lost its independence. At the end of the Russo–Turkish War (1877–78), Bulgaria rebelled. The ensuing Treaty of San Stefano was unacceptable to the Great Powers, and the Congress of Berlin (1878) resulted. In 1908 the Bulgarian ruler, Ferdinand, declared Bulgaria's independence. After its involvement in the Balkan Wars (1912–13), Bulgaria lost territory. It sided with the Central Powers in World War I and with Germany in World War II. A communist coalition seized power in 1944, and in 1946 a people's republic was declared. With other Eastern European countries in the late 1980s, Bulgaria experienced political unrest; its communist leader resigned in 1989. A new constitution proclaiming a republic was implemented in 1991. The rest of the decade brought economic turmoil.

Recent Developments

In the spring of 2001, the government of Ivan Kostov became the first postcommunist administration in Bulgaria to run its full four-year course. It was not returned to power. Early in the year rumors had circulated that the former king, Simeon II, would return to Bulgaria and contest the presidential elections to be held in the fall. The constitution forbade this, however, and Simeon decided to compete in the parliamentary campaign instead. In the elections of 17 June, his National Movement for Simeon II secured 120 of the 240 seats. In July Simeon agreed to take the post of prime minister; Bulgaria thereby became the first country ever to elect its exiled king as head of government.

Internet resources: <www.bulgaria2net.com>

Burkina Faso

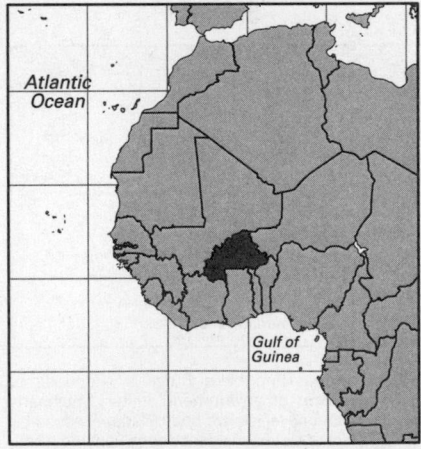

Official name: Burkina Faso (Burkina Faso). **Form of government:** multiparty republic with one advisory body (Chamber of Representatives [178 appointed or indirectly elected]) and one legislative body (National Assembly [111]). **Chief of state:** President Blaise Compaoré (from 1987). **Head of government:** Prime Minister Ernest Paramanga Yonli (from 2000).

---

1 metric ton = about 1.1 short tons;   1 kilometer = 0.6 mi (statute);   1 metric ton-km cargo = about 0.68 short ton-mi cargo;   c.i.f.: cost, insurance, and freight;   f.o.b.: free on board

Capital: Ouagadougou. Official language: French. Official religion: none. Monetary unit: 1 CFA franc (CFAF) = 100 centimes; valuation (28 Jun 2002) $1 = CFAF 664.20 (formerly pegged to the French franc and since 1 Jan 2002 to the euro at €1 = CFAF 655.96.

Demography

Area: 105,946 sq mi, 274,400 sq km. Population (2001): 12,272,000. Density (2001): persons per sq mi 115.8, persons per sq km 44.7. Urban (1999): 17.0%. Sex distribution (2000): male 48.76%; female 51.24%. Age breakdown (2000): under 15, 47.6%; 15–29, 27.5%; 30–44, 13.0%; 45–59, 7.3%; 60–74, 3.8%; 75 and over, 0.8%. Ethnic composition (1983): Mossi 47.9%; Mande 8.8%; Fulani 8.3%; Lobi 6.9%; Bobo 6.8%; Senufo 5.3%; Grosi 5.1%; Gurma 4.8%; Tuareg 3.3%. Religious affiliation (2000): Muslim 48.6%; traditional beliefs 34.1%; Christian 16.7%, of which Roman Catholic 9.5%. Major cities (1993): Ouagadougou 690,000; Bobo-Dioulasso 300,000; Koudougou 105,000; Ouahigouya 38,902 (1985); Banfora 35,319 (1985). Location: western Africa, bordering Mali, Niger, Benin, Togo, Ghana, and Côte d'Ivoire.

Vital statistics

Birth rate per 1,000 pop. (2000): 45.3 (world avg. 22.5). Death rate per 1,000 pop. (2000): 17.0 (world avg. 9.0). Natural increase rate per 1,000 pop. (2000): 28.3 (world avg. 13.6). Total fertility rate (avg. births per childbearing woman; 2000): 6.4. Life expectancy at birth (2000): male 46.3 years; female 47.2 years.

National economy

Budget (1999) Revenue: CFAF 238,100,000,000 (tax revenue 93.4%, of which sales tax 43.3%, import duties 25.3%, personal income taxes 22.6%, other 2.2%; nontax revenue 6.6%). Expenditures: CFAF 246,900,000,000 (wages and salaries 27.5%; investment 27.3%; health and education 22.4%; transfers 17.3%; debt service 5.5%). Public debt (external, outstanding; 1999): $1,295,000,000. Household income and expenditure. Average household size (1985) 6.2; average annual income per household CFAF 303,000; expenditure (1985; Ouagadougou only): food 38.7%, transportation 18.6%, electricity and fuel 13.7%, beverages 9.0%, health 5.2%, housing 5.1%. Tourism: receipts (1998) $42,000,000; expenditures (1994) $23,000,000. Production (metric tons except as noted). Agriculture, forestry, fishing (1999): sorghum 1,178,400, millet 945,000, corn (maize) 468,900; livestock (number of live animals) 7,950,000 goats, 6,350,000 sheep, 4,550,000 cattle; roundwood (1998) 10,794,000 cu m; fish catch (1998) 8,335. Mining and quarrying (1999): gold 869 kg (does not include substantial illegal production); silver 120 kg. Manufacturing (1999): sugar 29,905; flour 21,454; edible oils 11,850; Energy production (consumption): electricity (kW-hr; 1998) 267,000,000 (267,000,000); petroleum products (metric tons; 1996) none (315,000). Gross national product (1999): $2,602,000,000 ($240 per capita). Population economically active (1991): total 4,679,193; activity rate 50.9% (participation rates: over age [1988] 10, 78.1%; female 48.7%; unemployed 1.1%). Land use (1994): forest 50.5%; pasture 21.9%; agriculture 13.0%; other 14.6%.

Foreign trade

Imports (1999): CFAF 368,700,000,000 (capital equipment 36.8%, petroleum products 16.9%, food products 12.3%, raw materials 9.5%). Major import sources (1998): France 29.8%; Côte d'Ivoire 17.4%; Japan 5.4%; United States 3.6%; Italy 3.3%; The Netherlands 3.0%; Germany 2.9%. Exports (1999): CFAF 156,600,000,000 (raw cotton 53.4%, live animals 10.1%, hides and skins 7.5%, gold 5.9%). Major export destinations (1998): France 23.1%; Belgium 10.8%; Côte d'Ivoire 9.8%; Singapore 3.6%; Mali 1.7%.

Transport and communications

Transport. Railroads (1995; Passenger-km and metric ton-km are based on traffic between Abidjan, Côte d'Ivoire, and Ouagadougou): route length, 622 km; passenger-km 202,000,000; metric ton-km cargo 45,000,000. Roads (1996): total length, 12,100 km (paved 16%). Vehicles (1996): passenger cars 38,220; trucks and buses 17,980. Air transport (1993): passenger-km 217,154,000; metric ton-km cargo 34,204,000; airports (1998) 2. Communications Total units (units per 1,000 persons). Daily newspaper circulation (1996): 14,000 (1.3). Radio receivers (1997): 370,000 (34); Television receivers (1998): 120,000 (10.6); Telephone main lines (1999): 47,338 (4.1); Cellular telephone subscribers (1999): 5,036 (0.4); Personal computers (1999): 12,000 (1); Internet users (1999): 4,000 (0.3).

Education and health

Educational attainment (1985). Percentage of pop. age 10 and over having: no formal schooling 86.1%; some primary 7.3%; general secondary 2.2%; specialized secondary and postsecondary 3.8%; other 0.6%. Literacy (1995): percentage of total pop. age 15 and over literate 23.0%; males literate 31.2%; females literate 13.1%. Health (1991): physicians 341 (1 per 27,158 persons); hospital beds 5,041 (1 per 1,837 persons); infant mortality rate (2000) 108.5. Food (1999): daily per capita caloric intake 2,376 (vegetable products 95%, animal products 5%); 100% of FAO recommended minimum requirement.

Military

Total active duty personnel (2000): 5,800 (army 96.6%, air force 3.4%). Military expenditure as percentage of GNP (1997): 2.8% (world 2.6%); per capita expenditure $6.

Did you know? Burkina Faso hosts Africa's largest film festival, the Panafrican Film and Television Festival of Ouagadougou (FESPACO). The event has been held every other year since 1969.

Background

Probably in the 14th century, the Mossi and Gurma peoples established themselves in eastern and central areas of what is now Burkina Faso. The Mossi kingdoms of Yatenga and Ouagadougou existed into the early 20th century. A French protectorate was established over the region (1895–97), and its southern boundary was demarcated through an Anglo–French agreement. It was part of the Upper Senegal–Niger colony, then became a separate colony in 1919. Named Upper Volta, it was constituted an overseas territory within the French Union in 1947, became an autonomous republic within the French Community in 1958, and achieved total independence in 1960. Since then, the country has been ruled primarily by the military and has experienced several coups; following one in 1983, the country received its present name. A new constitution, adopted in 1991, restored multiparty rule.

Recent Developments

A severe meningitis epidemic struck Burkina Faso in 2001, with more than 7,000 cases reported by the beginning of April. There remained a crippling shortage of vaccine. In August grants for poverty alleviation totaling $45 million were approved by the World Bank and the International Monetary Fund. A $70 million water project for Ouagadougou was to be undertaken with further World Bank funding.

Internet resources: <www.ouaganet.com>

Burundi

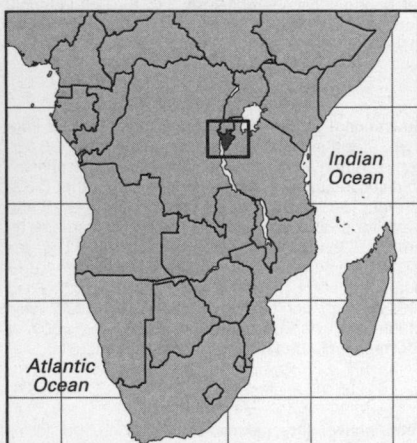

Indian Ocean

Atlantic Ocean

Official name: Republika y'u Burundi (Rundi); République du Burundi (French) (Republic of Burundi). **Form of government:** transitional regime. **Head of state and government:** President Pierre Buyoya (from 1996) assisted by a vice president. **Capital:** Bujumbura. **Official languages:** Rundi; French. **Official religion:** none. **Monetary unit:** 1 Burundi franc (FBu) = 100 centimes; valuation (28 Jun 2002) $1 = FBu 866.44.

Demography

Area: 10,740 sq mi, 27,816 sq km. **Population** (2001): 6,224,000. **Density** (2001 [excluding Burundian part of Lake Tanganyika]): persons per sq mi 621.2, persons per sq km 239.9. **Urban** (1999): 8.6%. **Sex distribution** (2000): male 49.54%; female 50.46%. **Age breakdown** (2000): under 15, 47.1%; 15–29, 26.6%; 30–44, 14.8%; 45–59, 7.2%; 60–74, 3.2%; 75 and over, 1.0%. **Ethnic composition** (1995): Rundi 98.0%, of which Hutu 82.5%, Tutsi 14.5%; Twa Pygmy 1.0%; other 2.0%. **Religious affiliation** (1990): Roman Catholic 65.1%; Protestant 13.8%; Muslim 1.6%; nonreligious 18.6%; traditional beliefs 0.3%; other 0.6%. **Major cities** (1990): Bujumbura (1994) 300,000; Gitega 101,827; Bururi 15,816; Ngozi 14,511; Cibitoke 8,280. **Location:** central Africa, bordering Rwanda, Tanzania, Lake Tanganyika, and the Dem. Rep. of the Congo.

Vital statistics

Birth rate per 1,000 pop. (2000): 40.5 (world avg. 22.5). **Death rate** per 1,000 pop. (2000): 16.4 (world avg. 9.0). **Natural increase rate** per 1,000 pop. (2000): 24.1 (world avg. 13.5). **Total fertility rate** (avg. births per childbearing woman; 2000): 6.3. **Life expectancy** at birth (2000): male 45.2 years; female 47.2 years.

National economy

Budget (1999). *Revenue:* FBu 70,400,000,000 (tax revenue 92.9%, of which taxes on goods and services 39.3%, taxes on international trade 23.3%, income tax 13.8%, corporate tax 13.1%, administrative receipts 3.4%; nontax revenue 7.1%). *Expenditures:* FBu 99,000,000,000 (wages and salaries 29.1%, goods and services 28.0%, subsidies and transfers 8.5%, public debt 6.1%). **Public debt** (external, outstanding; 1999): $1,050,000,000. **Production** (metric tons except as noted). *Agriculture, forestry, fishing* (1999): bananas 1,511,270, sweet potatoes 734,172, cassava 617,483; livestock (number of live animals) 593,657 goats, 329,000 cattle, 4,400,000 chickens; roundwood (1998) 1,799,000 cu m; fish catch (1998) 32,039. *Mining and quarrying* (1995): peat 8,000; kaolin clay 5,000. *Manufacturing* (1998): beer 1,036,321 hectoliters; cottonseed oil 133,600 liters; cigarettes 316,820,000 units. *Energy production (consumption):* electricity (kW-hr; 1998): 107,081,000 (112,209,000); petroleum products (metric tons; 1998) none (60,667); peat (metric tons; 1995) 8,000 (8,000). **Household income and expenditure.** Average household size (1998) 5.0; expenditure: (1990) food 59.6%, clothing and footwear 11.1%, furniture and household goods 6.0%, energy and water 5.8%, housing 4.4%. **Land use** (1994): forested 12.7%; meadows and pastures 38.6%; agricultural and under permanent cultivation 45.9%; other 2.8%. **Gross national product** (at current market prices; 1999): $823,000,000 ($120 per capita). **Population economically active** (1997): total 3,475,000; activity rate of total pop. 63.1% (participation rates (1991): ages 15–64, 91.4%; female 48.9%; unemployed, n.a.). **Tourism** (1999): receipts from visitors $1,000,000; expenditures by nationals abroad $8,000,000.

Foreign trade

Imports (1998): FBu 55,300,000,000 (1994; machinery and transport equipment 21.3%, food and

1 metric ton = about 1.1 short tons; 1 kilometer = 0.6 mi (statute); 1 metric ton-km cargo = about 0.68 short ton-mi cargo; c.i.f.: cost, insurance, and freight; f.o.b.: free on board

food products 17.9%, petroleum products 8.2%, pharmaceutical products 6.4%). *Major import sources* (1997): Belgium-Luxembourg 23.2%; France 21.0%; Zambia 8.2%; The Netherlands 7.5%; Germany 6.4%; Japan 5.2%. **Exports** (1998): FBu 28,600,000,000 (coffee 79.7%, tea 17.1%, animal hides and skins 0.2%). *Major export destinations* (1997): UK 25.2%; Germany 21.4%; Belgium-Luxembourg 10.0%; France 8.1%.

Transport and communications

Transport. *Roads* (1996): total length 14,480 km (paved 7%). *Vehicles* (1996): passenger cars 19,200; trucks and other vehicles 18,240. *Air transport* (1998; Bujumbura airport only): passenger arrivals 12,113, departures 11,725; cargo loaded 1,490 metric tons, unloaded 9,329 metric tons; airports (1998) 1. **Communications** Total units (units per 1,000 persons). Daily newspaper circulation (1996): 20,000 (3.2); Radio receivers (1997): 440,000 (69); Television receivers (1999): 100,000 (15.2); Telephone main lines (1999): 18,003 (2.9); Cellular telephone subscribers (1999): 800 (0.1); Internet users (1999): 2,000 (0.3).

Education and health

Educational attainment: n.a. **Literacy** (1995): percentage of total pop. age 15 and over literate 35.3%; males literate 49.7%; females literate 22.5%. **Health** (1996): physicians 329 (1 per 16,507 persons); hospital beds 3,560 (1 per 1,526 persons); infant mortality rate per 1,000 live births (2000) 71.5. **Food** (1999): daily per capita caloric intake 1,628 (vegetable products 97%, animal products 3%); 70% of FAO recommended minimum requirement.

Military

Total active duty personnel (2000): 40,000 (army 100%). **Military expenditure as percentage of GNP** (1997): 6.1% (world 2.6%); per capita expenditure $11.

Background

Original settlement by the Twa people was followed by Hutu settlement, which occurred gradually and was completed by the 11th century. The Tutsi arrived 300–400 years later; though a minority, they established the kingdom of Burundi in the 16th century. In the 19th century the area came within the German sphere of influence, but the Tutsi remained in power. Following World War I the Belgians took control of the area, which became a UN trusteeship after World War II. Colonial-period conditions had intensified Hutu–Tutsi ethnic animosities, and as independence neared, hostilities flared. Independence was granted in 1962 in the form of a kingdom ruled by the Tutsi. In 1965 the Hutu rebelled but were brutally repressed. The rest of the 20th century saw violent clashes between the two groups, leading to charges of genocide in the 1990s. The very unstable government that existed in these surroundings was overthrown by the military in 1996.

Recent Developments

Years of war between the Tutsi-dominated army and Hutu rebels have devastated Burundi. The fighting

has claimed the lives of an estimated 200,000 people. In February 2000 peace talks were held in Arusha, Tanz., with former South African president Nelson Mandela serving as mediator. The peace process foundered, however, when the parties failed to agree on the composition of a transitional government, and widespread fighting between army and rebel groups resumed.

Internet resources: <www.burundi.gov.bi>

Cambodia

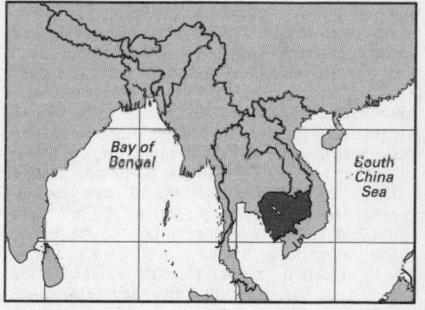

Official name: Preah Reach Ana Pak Kampuchea (Kingdom of Cambodia). **Form of government:** constitutional monarchy with two legislative houses (Senate [61; all seats appointed in 1999; all seats to be elected in future]; National Assembly [122]). **Chief of state:** King Norodom Sihanouk (from 1993). **Head of government:** Prime Minister Hun Sen (from 1998). **Capital:** Phnom Penh. **Official language:** Khmer. **Official religion:** Buddhism. **Monetary unit:** 1 riel = 100 sen; valuation (28 Jun 2002) $1 = 3,835 riels.

Demography

Area: 69,898 sq mi, 181,035 sq km. **Population** (2001): 12,720,000. **Density** (2001; based on land area): persons per sq mi 185.0, persons per sq km 71.4. **Urban** (1998): 20.9%. **Sex distribution** (1998): male 48.19%; female 51.81%. **Age breakdown** (1998): under 15, 42.8%; 15–29, 26.1%; 30–44, 17.3%; 45–59, 8.6%; 60–74, 4.2%; 75 and over, 1.0%. **Ethnic composition** (1994): Khmer 88.6%; Vietnamese 5.5%; Chinese 3.1%; Cham 2.3%; other (Thai, Lao, and Kola) 0.5%. **Religious affiliation** (2000): Buddhist 84.7%; Chinese folk religionist 4.7%; traditional beliefs 4.3%; Muslim 2.3%; Christian 1.1%; other 2.9%. **Major cities** (1998): Phnom Penh 999,804; Preah Sihanouk 155,690; Kaeb 28,660; Pailin 22,906. **Location:** southeastern Asia, bordering Thailand, Laos, Vietnam, and the Gulf of Thailand.

Vital statistics

Birth rate per 1,000 pop. (2001): 35.9 (world avg. 22.5). **Death rate** per 1,000 pop. (2001): 10.7 (world avg. 9.0). **Natural increase rate** per 1,000 pop. (2001): 25.2 (world avg. 13.5). **Total fertility rate** (avg. births per childbearing woman; 2001): 5.0. **Life expectancy** at birth (2001): male 54.0 years; female 59.0 years.

National economy

Budget (1999). *Revenue:* 1,224,000,000,000 riels (taxes on international trade 36.0%; indirect taxes 27.1%, of which value-added taxes 13.7%; nontax revenue 28.2%). *Expenditures:* 1,485,000,000,000 riels (current expenditure 74.4%, of which civil administration 36.1%, defense and security 30.7%; development expenditure 25.6%). **Public debt** (external, outstanding; 1999): $2,136,000,000. **Production** (metric tons except as noted). *Agriculture, forestry, fishing* (1999): rice 3,800,000, bananas 145,000, sugarcane 138,000; livestock (number of live animals; 1999) 2,821,000 cattle, 2,438,000 pigs, 694,000 buffalo; roundwood (1998) 8,008,000 cu m; fish catch (1997) 114,600. *Manufacturing* (value added in '000,000 riels; 1995): glass and glass products 42,659; cigarettes 1,064.5; wearing apparel 37,567. *Energy production (consumption):* electricity (kW-hr; 1996) 201,000,000 (201,000,000); petroleum products (metric tons; 1996) none (163,000). **Household income and expenditure.** Average household size (1998) 5.2. **Gross domestic product** (1999): $3,023,000,000 ($260 per capita). **Population economically active** (1996): total 4,904,294; activity rate of total pop. 47.4% (participation rates: ages 15 and over, 78.9%; female 52.7%). **Tourism** (1999): receipts $190,000,000; expenditures $18,000,000. **Land use** (1994): forested 69.1%; meadows and pastures 8.5%; agricultural and under permanent cultivation 21.7%; other 0.7%.

Foreign trade

Imports (1998): $1,334,000,000 (cigarettes 11.2%; petroleum products 10.4%; motorcycles 2.8%; clothing 1.6%). *Major import sources* (1996): Singapore 34.2%; Thailand 23.9%; Vietnam 7.3%. **Exports** (1998): $999,000,000 (reexports 39.6%; garments 39.0%; sawed timber and logs 17.8%; rubber 2.5%). *Major export destinations* (1996): Thailand 13.0%; Singapore 13.0%; India 9.3%.

Transport and communications

Transport. *Railroads* (1995): length (1999) 649 km; passenger-km 38,443,600; metric ton-km 7,797,600. *Roads* (1997): total length 35,769 km (paved 8%). *Vehicles* (1997): passenger cars 52,919; trucks and buses 13,574. *Air transport* (1977): passenger-km 42,000,000; metric ton-km cargo 400,000; airports (1997) with scheduled flights 8. **Communications** Total units (units per 1,000 persons). Daily newspaper circulation (1996): 17,000 (1.7); Radio receivers (1997): 1,340,000 (128); Television receivers (1999): 98,000 (9); Telephone main lines (1999): 27,704 (2.5); Cellular telephone subscribers (1999): 89,117 (8.1); Personal computers (1999): 13,000 (1.2); Internet users (1999): 4,000 (0.4).

Education and health

Educational attainment (1998). Percentage of pop. age 25 and over having: no formal schooling 2.1%; some primary education 56.6%; primary 24.7%; some secondary 11.8%; secondary and above 4.8%. **Literacy** (1998): percentage of total pop. age 15 and over literate 67.3%; males literate 79.5%; females literate 57.0%. **Health:** physicians (1994) 1,200 (1 per 7,900 persons); hospital beds (1994) 12,098 (1 per 791 persons; public hospitals only); infant mortality rate (2001) 76.0. **Food** (1999): daily per capita caloric intake 2,000 (vegetable products 93%, animal products 7%); (1997) 90% of FAO recommended minimum requirement.

Military

Total active duty personnel (2000; figures include provincial and exclude paramilitary forces): 140,000 (army 64.3%, navy 2.1%, air force 1.4%, provincial 32.2%). **Military expenditure as percentage of GNP** (1997): 4.1% (world 2.6%); per capita expenditure $11.

Background

In the early Christian era, the area was under Hindu and to a lesser extent Buddhist influence. The Khmer state gradually spread in the early 7th century and reached its height under Jayavarman II and his successors in the 9th–12th centuries, when it ruled the Mekong Valley and the tributary Shan states and built Angkor. Widespread adoption of Buddhism occurred in the 13th century, resulting in a script change from Sanskrit to Pali. From the 13th century Cambodia was attacked by Annam and Siamese city-states and was alternately a province of one or the other. The area became a French protectorate in 1863. It was occupied by the Japanese in World War II and became independent in 1954. Cambodia's borders were the scene of fighting in the Vietnam War from 1961, and in 1970 its northeastern and eastern areas were occupied by the North Vietnamese and penetrated by US and South Vietnamese forces. An indiscriminate US bombing campaign alienated much of the population, enabling the communist Khmer Rouge under Pol Pot to seize power in 1975. Their regime of terror resulted in the deaths of at least 1 million Cambodians. Vietnam invaded in 1979 and drove the Khmer Rouge into the western hinterlands, but it was unable to effect reconstruction of the country, and Cambodian infighting continued. A peace accord was reached by most Cambodian factions under UN auspices in 1991, and elections were held in 1993. Civil and military unrest continued. In 1997 King Norodom Sihanouk left the country, which was on the verge of civil war.

Recent Developments

On 6 Jul 1997, a coup d'état was staged against the government by army troops loyal to Hun Sen. Following the coup, Hun Sen established himself as the leader of Cambodia. Widespread fighting in northern Cambodia between troops loyal to both sides of the struggle sparked a refugee crisis that forced as many as 35,000 Cambodians to seek asylum in Thailand. Following the announcement in April 1998 of the death of Pol Pot—who earlier had been taken into custody—representatives from the Cambodian government stated that they would continue to consider the possibility of seizing other Khmer Rouge leaders for trial by an international war crimes tribunal.

Internet resources: <www.cambodia.org>

1 metric ton = about 1.1 short tons;   1 kilometer = 0.6 mi (statute);   1 metric ton-km cargo = about 0.68 short ton-mi cargo;   c.i.f.: cost, insurance, and freight;   f.o.b.: free on board

Cameroon

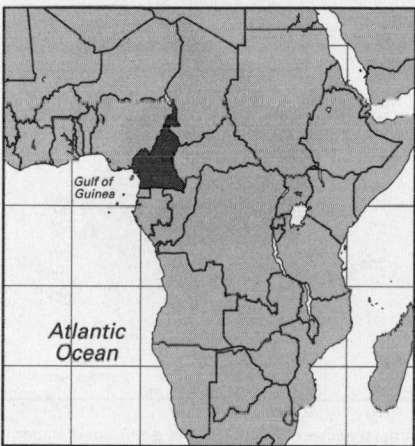

Gulf of Guinea

Atlantic Ocean

Official name: République du Cameroun (French); Republic of Cameroon (English). **Form of government:** unitary multiparty republic with one legislative house (National Assembly [180]). **Chief of state:** President Paul Biya (from 1982). **Head of government:** Prime Minister Peter Mafany Musonge (from 1996). **Capital:** Yaoundé. **Official languages:** French; English. **Official religion:** none. **Monetary unit:** 1 CFA franc (CFAF) = 100 centimes; valuation (28 Jun 2002) $1 = CFAF 664.20. Earlier pegged to the French franc, after 1 Jan 2002 the CFAF was pegged at 655.96 to the euro.

Demography

Area (rounded): 183,569 sq mi, 475,442 sq km. **Population** (2001): 15,803,000. **Density** (2001; land area only): persons per sq mi 88.0; persons per sq km 34.0. **Urban** (1999): 48.1%. **Sex distribution** (2000): male 50.21%; female 49.79%. **Age breakdown** (2000): under 15, 42.7%; 15–29, 27.9%; 30–44, 15.6%; 45–59, 8.7%; 60–74, 4.1%; 75 and over, 1.0%. **Ethnic composition** (1983): Fang 19.6%; Bamileke and Bamum 18.5%; Duala, Luanda, and Basa 14.7%; Fulani 9.6%; Tikar 7.4%; Mandara 5.7%; Maka 4.9%; Chamba 2.4%; Mbum 1.3%; Hausa 1.2%; French 0.2%; other 14.5%. **Religious affiliation** (2000): Roman Catholic 26.4%; traditional beliefs 23.7%; Muslim 21.2%; Protestant 20.7%. **Major cities** (1992): Douala 1,200,000; Yaoundé 800,000; Garoua 160,000; Maroua 140,000; Bafoussam 120,000. **Location:** western Africa, bordering Chad, Central African Republic, Republic of the Congo, Equatorial Guinea, Gabon, the Bight of Biafra and Nigeria.

Vital statistics

Birth rate per 1,000 pop. (2000): 36.6 (world avg. 22.5). **Death rate** per 1,000 pop. (2000): 11.9 (world avg. 9.0). **Natural increase rate** per 1,000 pop. (2000): 24.7 (world avg. 13.5). **Total fertility rate** (avg. births per childbearing woman; 2000): 4.9. **Life expectancy** at birth (2001): male 54.0 years; female 55.6 years.

National economy

Budget (1998–99). *Revenue:* CFAF 838,000,000,000 (taxes on goods and services 40.5%; income tax 20.8%; customs duties 16.5%; oil revenue 15.9%). *Expenditures:* CFAF 1,023,000,000,000 (current expenditure 80.9%, of which debt services 27.6%, wages and salaries 26.9%, goods and services 16.3%, transfers 9.8%; capital expenditure 19.1%). **Public debt** (external, outstanding; 1999): $7,614,000,000. **Gross national product** (1999): $8,798,000,000 ($600 per capita). **Household income and expenditure.** Average household size (1998) 5.7; average annual income per household (1983); expenditure (1993): food 49.1%, housing 18.0%, transportation and communications 13.0%, health 8.6%, clothing 7.6%, recreation 2.4%. **Population economically active** (1991): total 4,740,000; activity rate of total pop. 40.0% (participation rates [1985]: ages 15–69, 66.3%; female 38.5%). **Production** (metric tons except as noted). *Agriculture, forestry, fishing* (1999): cassava 1,500,000, sugarcane 1,350,000, plantains 1,000,000; livestock (number of live animals) 5,900,000 cattle, 3,880,000 sheep, 3,850,000 goats, 1,430,000 pigs; roundwood (1998) 15,172,000 cu m; fish catch (1998) 97,000. *Mining and quarrying* (1996): pozzolana 100,000; aluminum 82,000; limestone 50,000. *Manufacturing* (value added in CFAF '000,000; 1994): beverages 49,314; wood and wood products 42,756; rubber and plastic products 38,928. *Energy production (consumption):* electricity (kW-hr; 1996) 2,753,000,000 (2,753,000,-000); coal (metric tons; 1996) 1,000 (1,000); crude petroleum (barrels; 1996) 42,770,000 (6,856,000). **Land use** (1994): forested 77.1%; meadows and pastures 4.3%; agricultural and under permanent cultivation 15.1%; other 3.5%. **Tourism** (1995): receipts $36,000,000; expenditures $105,000,000.

Foreign trade

Imports (1998–99): CFAF 881,500,000,000 (semi-finished goods 15.9%; industrial equipment 13.3%; food and beverages 11.3%; minerals 10.6%; transport equipment 10.3%; unrecorded trade 6.1%). *Major import sources:* France 25.6%; Germany 6.4%; US 5.7%; Japan 5.0%; Belgium-Luxembourg 4.8%. **Exports** (1998–99): CFAF 993,900,000,000 (crude petroleum 31.6%; lumber 12.1%; coffee 7.5%; cocoa 7.4%; aluminum 5.0%; cotton 4.7%). *Major export destinations:* Italy 22.4%; France 12.6%; Spain 9.4%; The Netherlands 9.4%; Portugal 3.3%; Germany 1.9%.

Transport and communications

Transport. *Railroads* (1997): route length 625 mi, 1,006 km; (1995) passenger-mi 197,000,000, passenger-km 317,000,000; short ton-mi cargo 556,000,000, metric ton-km cargo 812,000,000. *Roads* (1997): total length 30,074 mi, 48,400 km (paved 8%). *Vehicles* (1997): passenger cars 98,000; trucks and buses 64,350. *Air transport* (1996): passenger-mi 347,970,000, passenger-km 560,000,000; short ton-mi cargo 56,540,000, metric ton-km cargo 91,000,000; airports (1998) with scheduled flights 5. **Communications.** Total units (units per 1,000 persons). Daily newspaper circulation (1996): 91,000 (6.7); Radio receivers (1997): 2,270,000 (163); Television receivers (1998): 480,000 (33.5); Telephone main lines (1999): 94,599 (6.4); Cellular telephone subscribers

(1997): 4,200 (0.3); Personal computers units (1999): 40,000 (2.7); Internet users (1999): 20,000 (1.4).

Education and health

Educational attainment (1976). Percentage of pop. age 15 and over having: no schooling 51.1%; primary education 41.7%; some postprimary 0.2%; secondary 5.7%; some postsecondary 0.3%; higher 0.2%; other 0.8%. **Literacy** (1995): percentage of total pop. age 15 and over literate 63.4%; males literate 75.0%; females literate 52.1%. **Health:** physicians (1996) 1,031 (1 per 13,510 persons); hospital beds (1988) 29,285 (1 per 371 persons); infant mortality rate (2000) 70.9. **Food** (1999): daily per capita caloric intake 2,260 (vegetable products 94%, animal products 6%); 97% of FAO recommended minimum requirement.

Military

Total active duty personnel (2000): 13,100 (army 87.8%, navy 9.9%, air force 2.3%). **Military expenditure as percentage of GNP** (1997): 3.0% (world 2.6%); per capita expenditure $16.

 **Did you know?** Cameroon is home to the world's largest frog. The Goliath frog can grow to have a body length of one foot or more.

Background

The area had long been inhabited before European colonization. Bantu speakers from equatorial Africa settled in the south, followed by Muslim Fulani from the Niger River basin, who settled in the north. Portuguese explorers visited in the late 15th century and established a foothold, but they lost control to the Dutch in the 17th century. In 1884 the Germans took control and extended their protectorate over Cameroon. In World War I joint French—British action forced the Germans to retreat, and after the war the region was divided into French and British administrative zones. After World War II the two areas became UN trusteeships. In 1960 the French trust territory became an independent republic. In 1961 the southern part of the British trust territory voted for union with the new republic of Cameroon, and the northern part for union with Nigeria. In recent decades economic problems have produced unrest in the country.

Recent Developments

Fears that a military coup might be under way created near panic in Cameroon in 2001. On 26 July, in an effort to defuse reports of growing discontent within the military, Pres. Paul Biya ordered a total reorganization of the nation's armed forces. The government also took vigorous action to reduce its internal debt, and full payment of all outstanding salary arrears was made to civil servants.

Internet resources: <www.cameroon.net>

Canada

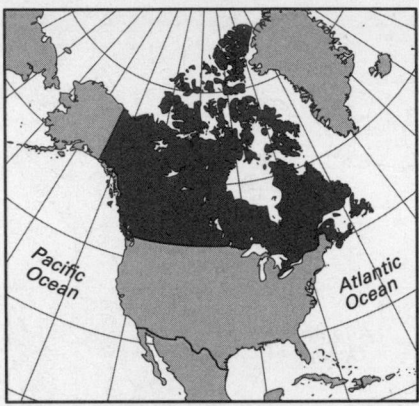

Official name: Canada. **Form of government:** federal multiparty parliamentary state with two legislative houses (Senate [105]; House of Commons [301]). **Chief of state:** Queen Elizabeth II. **Representative of chief of state:** Governor-General Adrienne Clarkson (from 1999). **Head of government:** Prime Minister Jean Chrétien (from 1993). **Capital:** Ottawa. **Official languages:** English; French. **Official religion:** none. **Monetary unit:** 1 Canadian dollar (Can$) = 100 cents; valuation (28 Jun 2002) US$1 = Can$1.52.

Demography

Area: 3,849,674 sq mi, 9,970,610 sq km. **Population** (2001): 31,081,900. **Density** (2001; based on land area of 3,558,096 sq mi [9,215,430 sq km]): persons per sq mi 8.7, persons per sq km 3.4. **Urban** (1996): 77.9%. **Sex distribution** (2001): male 49.51%; female 50.49%. **Age breakdown** (2001): under 15, 18.8%; 15–29, 20.3%; 30–44, 24.4%; 45–59, 19.7%; 60–74, 11.1%; 75 and over, 5.7%. **Ethnic origin** (1996): British 11.5%; French 9.4%; other European 13.1%, of which Southern European 4.8%, Western European 3.9%, Eastern European 3.0%; Asian origin 7.0%; Amerindian and Inuit (Eskimo) 1.7%; Latin American origin 1.4%; Arab origin 0.6%; African origin 0.5%; multiple origin and other 54.8%. **Religious affiliation** (2000): Roman Catholic 41.8%; Protestant 39.7%; Eastern Orthodox 1.9%; Jewish 1.3%; Muslim 1.0%; Hindu 1.0%; Buddhist 0.8%; nonreligious 10.9%; other 1.6%. **Major metropolitan areas** (1999): Toronto 4,680,300; Montreal 3,438,500; Vancouver 2,016,-600; Ottawa-Hull 1,065,000; Calgary 933,700; Edmonton 929,100; Quebec 688,100; Winnipeg 677,600; Hamilton 665,200; London 418,700. **Location:** northern North America, bordering the Arctic Ocean, the North Atlantic Ocean, the United States, and the North Pacific Ocean. **Place of birth** (1996): 83.4% native-born; 16.6% foreign-born, of which U.K. 2.2%, other European 4.2%, Asian countries 5.2%, U.S. 0.8%, other 4.2%. **Mobility** (1996). Population living in the same residence as in 1991: 56.7%; different residence, same municipality 23.0%; same province, different municipality 3.3%;

---

1 metric ton = about 1.1 short tons;   1 kilometer = 0.6 mi (statute);   1 metric ton-km cargo = about 0.68 short ton-mi cargo;   c.i.f.: cost, insurance, and freight;   f.o.b.: free on board

different province 13.4%; different country 3.5%. **Households** (1999). Total number of households 11,563,000. Average household size 2.5; (1997) 1 person 25.2%, 2 persons 33.0%, 3 persons 16.7%, 4 persons 16.3%, 5 or more persons 8.8%. Family households (1999): 8,139,700 (70.6%), nonfamily 3,413,300 (29.4%, of which 1 person 83.6%). **Immigration** (1999–2000): permanent immigrants admitted 252,088; from Asia 62.1%, of which India 11.6%, Philippines 5.6%, Vietnam 0.7%, Hong Kong 0.3%; United States 2.4%; United Kingdom 2.1%; refugee arrivals 22,899.

Vital statistics

Birth rate per 1,000 pop. (2000): 11.3 (world avg. 22.5); (1997) legitimate 72.3%; illegitimate 27.7%. **Death rate** per 1,000 pop. (2000): 7.4 (world avg. 9.0). **Natural increase rate** per 1,000 pop. (2000): 3.9 (world avg. 13.5). **Total fertility rate** (avg. births per childbearing woman; 2000): 1.6. **Marriage rate** per 1,000 pop. (2000): 5.0. **Divorce rate** per 1,000 pop. (2000): 2.2. **Life expectancy** at birth (2000): male 76.0 years; female 83.0 years.

Social indicators

Quality of working life. Average workweek (1997): 31.3 hours. Annual rate per 100,000 workers for (1997): injury, accident, or industrial illness 1,330; death 2.7. Average days lost to labor stoppages per 1,000 employee-workdays (1997): 0.9. Average duration of journey to work (1996): n.a.; mode of transportation: automobile 80.6%, public transportation 10.1%, other 9.3%. **Access to services.** Proportion of households having access to: electricity (1999) 100.0%; public water supply (1990) 99.8%; public sewage collection (1990) 99.3%. **Social participation.** Eligible voters participating in last national election (November 2000): 61.2%. Pop. over 18 years of age participating in voluntary work (2000): 26.7%. Union membership in total workforce (1999): 32.9%. Practicing religious pop. in total affiliated pop. (1996): 92.5%. **Social deviance** (2000). Offense rate per 100,000 population for: violent crime 981, of which assault 758.9, sexual assault 78.2, homicide 1.6; property crime 4,067, of which auto theft 521, burglary 954. **Leisure** (1998). Favorite leisure activities (hours weekly): television 15.4; social time 13.3; reading 2.8; sports and entertainment 1.4. **Material well-being** (1998). Households possessing: automobile 78.8%, of which two or more 34.5%; telephone 98.2%; color television 98.8%; refrigerator 99.8%; central air conditioner 33.1%; cable television 66.5%; video recorder 88.1%; microwave oven 88.7%; home computers 45.1%.

National economy

Gross national product (1999): US$614,003,000,000 (US$20,140 per capita). **Budget** (1999–2000). *Revenue:* Can$172,532,000,000 (individual income taxes 47.8%, value-added tax 20.3%, corporate income tax 13.0%, contributions to social security 10.8%, import duties 1.3%). *Expenditures:* Can$169,966,000,000 (social services 29.6%, public debt interest 24.5%, defense and social protection 10.8%, education 2.6%, health 1.0%). **National debt** (1997): Can$619,710,000,000. **Tourism** (1999): receipts US$10,171,000,000; expenditures US$11,345,000,000. **Production** (metric tons except as noted).

Agriculture, forestry, fishing (2001): wheat 20,695,300, barley 11,103,300, rapeseed 7,778,000, corn (maize) 7,550,000, potatoes 4,568,500, oats 2,838,300, soybeans 2,040,100; livestock (number of live animals) 12,860,000 cattle, 12,600,000 pigs, 694,800 sheep; roundwood (2000) 148,871,000 cu m; fish catch (1999) 1,135,516. *Mining and quarrying* (1999): iron ore 33,004,000; zinc (metal content) 960,099; copper (metal content) 580,036; nickel (metal content) 177,029; lead (primary metal content) 156,102; gold 157,790 kg. *Manufacturing* (value of shipments in Can$'000,000; 1999): transportation equipment 125,034; food 52,353; electrical machinery 36,761; paper products 33,150; wood industries 30,601; metal products 26,884. *Energy production (consumption):* electricity (kW-hr; 1999) 541,900,000,000 (545,460,300,000); coal (metric tons; 2000) 69,164,000 (60,761,000); crude petroleum (barrels; 1997) 719,729,000 (608,411,000); petroleum products (metric tons; 1997) 95,026,000 (81,240,000); natural gas (cu m; 1999) 163,384,000,000 ([1998]; 89,163,000,000). **Population economically active** (2000): total 15,999,200; activity rate of total pop. 52.0% (participation rates: ages 15 and over 65.9%; female 45.9%; unemployed [2001] 7.3%). **Household income and expenditure** (1999). Average household size 2.6; average annual income per family (1999) Can$63,818; sources of income (1995): wages and salaries 57.0%, transfer payments 20.7%, property and entrepreneurial income 13.7%, profits 8.6%; expenditure (1999): housing 27.2%, food, alcohol, and tobacco 19.3%, transportation and communications 18.2%, recreation 7.9%, utilities 6.4%, clothing 6.2%, household durable goods 3.9%, health 3.3%, education 2.0%. **Land use** (1994): forested 53.6%; meadows and pastures 3.0%; agricultural and under permanent cultivation 4.9%; built-on, wasteland, and other 38.5%.

Foreign trade

Imports (2000): Can$363,281,300,000 (1999; machinery and transport equipment 56.3%, of which motor vehicles 23.2%; chemical products 6.9%; food 5.4%; petroleum and energy products 3.3%; forestry products 0.8%). *Major import sources* (1999): U.S. 67.2%; Japan 4.7%; Mexico 3.0%; China 2.8%; U.K. 2.5%; Germany 2.2%; France 1.7%; Taiwan 1.4%; Italy 1.1%; South Korea 1.1%. **Exports** (2000): Can$422,558,700,000 (1999; machinery and transport equipment 50.3%, of which motor vehicles 26.5%; mineral fuels 8.2%, of which crude petroleum 3.1%; food 7.1%; lumber 5.5%; newsprint and paper products 3.5%; wood pulp 1.9%). *Major export destinations* (1999): U.S. 86.8%; Japan 2.5%; U.K. 1.3%; South Korea 0.6%.

Transport and communications

Transport. Railroads (1998): length 65,403 km; passenger-km 1,458,000,000; metric ton-km cargo 299,508,000,000. Roads (1999): total length 901,903 km (paved 35%). Vehicles (1998): passenger cars 13,887,270; trucks and buses 3,694,125. Air transport (2000): passenger-km 68,202,000,000; metric ton-km cargo 1,786,600,000; airports (1997) with scheduled flights 269. **Communications.** Total units (units per 1,000 persons). Daily newspaper circulation (1996): 4,718,000 (159); Radio receivers (1997): 32,300,000 (1,077); Television receivers (1998): 21,450,000 (715); Telephone main lines (1999): 19,957,000 (655); Cellular telephone subscribers (1999): 6,876,000 (256); Personal computers (1999): 11,000,000 (361); Internet users (1999): 11,000,000 (361).

Education and health

Educational attainment (1996). Percentage of pop. age 15 and over having: no formal schooling or not known 4.2%; at least primary education 12.3%; some secondary 19.6%; completed secondary 19.8%; postsecondary 30.5%; university graduates 13.6%. **Literacy** (1996): total pop. age 15 and over literate virtually 100%. **Health:** physicians (2000) 60,559 (1 per 508 persons); hospital beds (1997) 161,867 (1 per 185 persons); infant mortality rate (2000) 5.1. **Food** (1999): daily per capita caloric intake 3,161 (vegetable products 71%, animal products 29%); 119% of FAO recommended minimum requirement.

Military

Total active duty personnel (2001): 56,800 (army 32.7%, navy 15.8%, air force 23.7%, not identified by service 27.8%). **Military expenditure as percentage of GNP** (1997): 1.3% (world 2.6%); per capita expenditure US$257.

Background

Originally inhabited by American Indians and Inuit, Canada was visited c. AD 1000 by Scandinavian explorers, whose discovery is confirmed by archaeological evidence from Newfoundland. Fishing expeditions off Newfoundland by the English, French, Spanish, and Portuguese began as early as 1500. The French claim to Canada was made in 1534 when Jacques Cartier entered the Gulf of St. Lawrence. A small settlement was made in Nova Scotia (Acadia) in 1605, and in 1608 Samuel de Champlain founded Quebec. Fur trading was the impetus behind the early colonizing efforts. In response to French activity, the English in 1670 formed the Hudson's Bay Company.

The British—French rivalry for the interior of upper North America lasted almost a century. The first French loss occurred in 1713 at the conclusion of Queen Anne's War (War of the Spanish Succession) when Nova Scotia and Newfoundland were ceded to the British. The Seven Years' War (French and Indian War) resulted in France's expulsion from continental North America in 1763. After the American Revolution the population was augmented by Loyalists fleeing the US, and the increasing number arriving in Quebec led the British to divide the colony into Upper and Lower Canada in 1791. The British reunited the two provinces in 1841. Canadian expansionism resulted in the confederation movement of the mid-19th century, and in 1867 the Dominion of Canada, comprising Nova Scotia, New Brunswick, Quebec, and Ontario, came into existence. After confederation, Canada entered a period of westward expansion.

The prosperity that accompanied Canada into the 20th century was marred by continuing conflict between the English and French communities. Through the Statute of Westminster (1931), Canada was recognized as an equal partner of Great Britain.

With the Constitution Act of 1982, the British gave Canada total control over its constitution and severed the remaining legal connections between the two countries. French—Canadian unrest continued to be a major concern, with a movement growing for Quebec separatism in the late 20th century. Referendums for more political autonomy for Quebec were rejected in 1992 and 1995, but the issue remained unresolved. In 1999 Canada formed the new territory of Nunavut, and on 6 Dec 2001 Newfoundland was renamed Newfoundland and Labrador.

Recent Developments

The Liberal Party government under Prime Minister Jean Chrétien, who was reelected to a third term in 2000, has dominated Canadian politics for a decade. Chrétien's grasp on power came from his long experience and unrivaled political skills. It was also helped by the fragmented nature of his opposition.

In 2001, with the Liberals holding 172 of 301 seats in the House of Commons, this opposition seemed the weakest ever. During the previous year a determined effort had been made to unite the right around a Western protest movement, the Reform Party. The new grouping, the Canadian Alliance, had turned away from Reform's founder, Preston Manning, and chosen Stockwell Day as its leader. Day had served successfully as provincial treasurer and Acting Premier of Alberta, but he was inexperienced in national politics. He led the Alliance to 66 seats in the November 2000 election and became official leader of the opposition.

Criticism of Day came forward soon after Parliament resumed sitting in 2001. Statements and actions by the Alliance leader raised questions about his political judgment. He was accused of disregarding the views of his caucus and being out of touch with the party membership. By July, amid rancorous quarreling, 12 Alliance MPs had left the caucus, threatening to set up a new party. The divisions within the Alliance damaged it seriously in the eyes of the public. Support dropped everywhere in Canada to a 6% approval rating in late June. By contrast, Liberal support rose to 60%. Some Alliance members talked of cooperating electorally with the rival Progressive Conservative Party (PCP), which had formed the government before Chrétien came to power in 1993.

Day eventually delivered an ultimatum to the dissident Alliance members: return to the party caucus and accept his leadership by 10 September, or be expelled. Four of the dissidents returned, while the other eight entered into a working coalition with the PCP, acknowledging PCP leader Joe Clark as head of the new grouping. It was the first opposition coalition in Canadian history.

The steadily rising costs of public health care brought about labor unrest in several provinces during 2001. The federal government, eager to investigate possible changes to the system that would bring about greater efficiency, appointed Roy Romanow, a former premier of Saskatchewan, to oversee a study of the system.

Canada cautiously considered new directions in US foreign policy. The administration of US Pres. George W. Bush made it clear that it considered relations with Mexico a top priority. Within a decade, it was surmised, Mexico might become the US's largest trading partner. To Canada, which had occupied this position for many years, this was a sobering reassessment. Chrétien wasted no time in traveling to Washington DC to meet with Bush on 5 Feb 2001, only 11 days before Bush visited his Mexican counterpart. Canadian spokesmen pointed out that Canada possessed a more substantial bilateral relationship with the US than did Mexico. It was also a long standing partner with the US in important international organizations, including NATO.

In the wake of the 11 September attacks in the US, Canada was among the countries that pledged troops to participate in the US led war on terrorism. Canada sent more than 2,000 military personnel—the country's largest combat force abroad since the Korean War. Safety along the Canadian–US border was also a major concern. A "smart border" declaration was signed between the two countries that increased cooperation on intelligence matters and provided for the deployment of additional troops at some 43 border crossings.

Internet resources: <www.travelcanada.ca>

Cape Verde

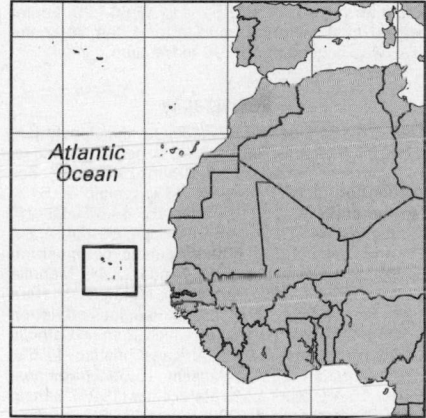

Atlantic Ocean

Official name: República de Cabo Verde (Republic of Cape Verde). **Form of government:** multiparty republic with one legislative house (National Assembly [72]). **Chief of state:** President Pedro Pires (from 2001). **Head of government:** Prime Minister José Maria Neves (from 2001). **Capital:** Praia. **Official language:** Portuguese. **Official religion:** none. **Monetary unit:** 1 escudo (C.V.Esc.) = 100 centavos; valuation (28 Jun 2002) $1 = C.V.Esc. 119.80 (fixed par value rate of the C.V.Esc. relative to the Portuguese escudo, and, since 1 Jan 2002, a fixed rate of 110.27 to the euro).

Demography

Area: 1,557 sq mi, 4,033 sq km. **Population** (2001): 446,000. **Density** (2001): persons per sq mi 286.2, persons per sq km 110.5. **Urban** (1990): 30%. **Sex distribution** (2000): male 48.17%; female 51.83%. **Age breakdown** (2000): under 15, 43.6%; 15–29, 24.8%; 30–44, 17.1%; 45–59, 5.8%; 60–74, 6.3%; 75 and over, 2.4%. **Ethnic composition** (1986): mixed

71.0%; black 28.0%; white 1.0%. **Religious affiliation** (2000): Roman Catholic 91.4%; Muslim 2.8%; other 5.8%. **Major cities** (2000): Praia 94,757; Mindelo 62,970; São Filipe 7,894. **Location:** off the coast of western Africa; consists of 10 islands in the North Atlantic Ocean.

Vital statistics

Birth rate per 1,000 pop. (2000): 29.7 (world avg. 22.5); (1989) legitimate 28.9%; illegitimate 71.1%. **Death rate** per 1,000 pop. (2000): 7.4 (world avg. 9.0). **Natural increase rate** per 1,000 pop. (2000): 22.3 (world avg. 13.5). **Total fertility rate** (avg. births per childbearing woman; 2000): 4.2. **Marriage rate** per 1,000 pop. (1990): 4.5. **Life expectancy** at birth (2000): male 65.6 years; female 72.3 years.

National economy

Budget (1998). *Revenue:* C.V.Esc. 11,656,000,000 (tax revenue 72.1%, of which taxes on international trade 42.1%, income taxes 26.3%, other taxes 3.7%; nontax revenue 27.9%). *Expenditures:* C.V.Esc. 19,037,000,000 (current expenditure 56.3%, of which wages and salaries 25.7%, transfers 14.0%, public debt 9.9%, goods and services 1.8%; capital expenditure 43.7%). **Public debt** (external, outstanding; 1999): $265,100,000. **Production** (metric tons except as noted). *Agriculture, forestry, fishing* (1999): sugarcane 12,500, corn (maize) 10,000, bananas 6,000; livestock (number of live animals) 636,000 pigs, 112,000 goats, 22,000 cattle; fish catch (1998) 9,999. *Mining and quarrying* (1992): salt 4,000. *Manufacturing* (1998): flour 25,916; bread (1995) 5,628; paint (1996) 628. *Energy production (consumption):* electricity (kW-hr; 1998) 100,764,000,000 (80,039,000,000); petroleum products (metric tons; 1998) none (98,392). **Tourism:** receipts from visitors (1999) $23,000,000; expenditures by nationals abroad (1998) $24,000,000. **Land use** (1994): forest 0.2%; pasture 6.2%; agriculture 11.2%; other 82.4%. **Gross national product** (1999): $569,000,000 ($1,330 per capita). **Population economically active** (1997): total 160,000; activity rate of total pop. 41.2% (participation rates [1990]: ages 15–64, 64.3%; female 39.0%; unemployed [1990] 25.8%). **Household income and expenditure.** Average household size (1990) 5.1; expenditure (1988): food 51.1%, housing, fuel, and power 13.5%, beverages and tobacco 11.8%, transportation and communications 8.8%, household durable goods 6.9%, other 7.9%.

Foreign trade

Imports (1998): C.V.Esc. 19,999,000,000 (food 39.0%, machinery and apparatus 19.4%, nonmetallic mineral products 9.7%, metal products 8.2%, transport equipment 7.8%). *Major import sources* (1998): Portugal 49.9%; The Netherlands 11.8%; US 3.1%; Spain 2.7%. **Exports** (1998): C.V.Esc. 2,702,000,000 (shoes 22.5%; clothing 7.1%; fish and fish preparations 6.7%; reexports 62.1%). *Major export destinations* (1998): Portugal 89.3%; Spain 7.9%.

Transport and communications

Transport. *Roads* (1996): total length 1,095 km (paved 78%). *Vehicles* (1996): passenger cars 3,280; trucks and buses 820. *Air transport* (1994, TACV air-

line only): passenger-km 171,000,000; metric ton-km cargo 19,207,000; *airports* (1997) with scheduled flights 9. **Communications** Total units (units per 1,000 persons). Radio receivers (1997): 71,000 (179); Television receivers (1999): 2,000 (4.7); Telephone main lines (1999): 46,865 (110); Cellular telephone subscribers (1999): 8,068 (19); Internet users (1999): 5,000 (12).

Education and health

Educational attainment (1990). Percentage of pop. age 25 and over having: no formal schooling 47.9%; primary 40.9%; incomplete secondary 3.9%; complete secondary 1.4%; higher 1.5%; unknown 4.4%. **Literacy** (1995): total pop. age 15 and over literate 71.6%; males 81.4%; females 63.8%. **Health** (1996): physicians 66 (1 per 5,818 persons); hospital beds (1987) 625 (1 per 550 persons); infant mortality rate per 1,000 live births (2000) 54.6. **Food** (1999): daily per capita caloric intake 3,166 (vegetable products 84%, animal products 16%); 135% of FAO recommended minimum requirement.

Military

Total active duty personnel (2000): 1,100 (army 90.9%, air force 9.1%). **Military expenditure as percentage of GNP** (1997): 0.9% (world 2.6%); per capita expenditure $10.

Background

When visited by the Portuguese in 1456–60, the islands were uninhabited. In 1460 Diogo Gomes sighted and named Maio and São Tiago, and in 1462 the first settlers landed on São Tiago, founding the city of Ribeira Grande. The city's importance grew with the development of the slave trade, and its wealth attracted pirates so often that it was abandoned after 1712. The prosperity of the Portuguese-controlled islands vanished with the decline of the slave trade in the 19th century, but later improved because of their position on the great trade routes between Europe, South America, and South Africa. In 1951 the colony became an overseas province of Portugal. Many islanders preferred outright independence, and it was finally granted in 1975. Once associated politically with Guinea-Bissau, Cape Verde split from it in 1981.

Recent Developments

The year 2001 marked the end of 10 years of rule by the Movement for Democracy and the return to power of the African Party for the Independence of Cape Verde (PAICV). In legislative elections held in January, the PAICV won the majority of seats, and its leader, José Maria Neves, became the new prime minister.

Internet resources: <www.ine.cv>

Central African Republic

Official name: République Centrafricaine (Central African Republic). **Form of government:** multiparty republic with one legislative body (National Assembly

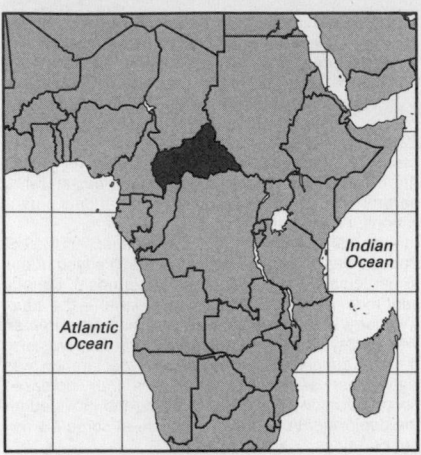

[109]). **Chief of state:** President Ange-Félix Patassé (from 1993). **Head of government:** Prime Minister Martin Ziguélé (from 2001). **Capital:** Bangui. **Official languages:** French; Sango. **Official religion:** none. **Monetary unit:** 1 CFA franc (CFAF) = 100 centimes; valuation (28 Jun 2002) $1 = CFAF 664.20. Earlier pegged to the French franc, after 1 Jan 2002 the CFAF was pegged at 655.96 to the euro.

Demography

Area: 240,324 sq mi, 622,436 sq km. **Population:** (2001): 3,577,000. **Density** (2001): persons per sq mi 14.9, persons per sq km 5.7. **Urban** (1999): 41%. **Sex distribution** (2001): male 49.43%; female 50.57%. **Age breakdown** (2001): under 15, 43.5%; 15–29, 28.0%; 30–44, 14.9%; 45–59, 8.1%; 60–74, 4.2%; 75 and over, 1.3%. **Ethnolinguistic composition** (1988): Baya (Gbaya) 23.7%; Banda 23.4%; Mandjia 14.7%; Ngbaka 7.6%; Sara 6.5%; Mbum 6.3%; Kare 2.4%; French 0.1%; other 15.3%. **Religious affiliation** (2000): Christian 67.8%, of which Roman Catholic 18.4%, Protestant 14.4%, African Christian 11.6%, other Christian 23.4%; Muslim 15.6%; traditional beliefs 15.4%; other 1.2%. **Major cities** (1994): Bangui 524,000; Berbérati 47,000; Bouar 43,000; Bambari 41,000; Carnot 41,000. **Location:** central Africa, bordering Chad, The Sudan, Democratic Republic of the Congo, Republic of the Congo, and Cameroon.

Vital statistics

Birth rate per 1,000 pop. (2000): 37.5 (world avg. 22.5). **Death rate** per 1,000 pop. (2000): 18.4 (world avg. 9.0). **Natural increase rate** per 1,000 pop. (2000): 19.1 (world avg. 13.5). **Total fertility rate** (avg. births per childbearing woman; 2000): 5.0. **Life expectancy** at birth (2000): male 42.3 years; female 45.8 years.

National economy

Budget (1997). *Revenue:* CFAF 45,000,000,000 (taxes 94.2%, of which international trade tax 38.0%, indirect domestic tax 36.7%, other 19.5%; nontax receipts 5.8%). *Expenditures:* CFAF 82,900,000,000

1 metric ton = about 1.1 short tons;   1 kilometer = 0.6 mi (statute);   1 metric ton-km cargo = about 0.68 short ton-mi cargo;   c.i.f.: cost, insurance, and freight;   f.o.b.: free on board

(current expenditure 63.0%, of which wages 32.1%; capital expenditure 37.0%). **Public debt** (external, outstanding; 1999): $830,100,000. **Production** (metric tons except as noted). *Agriculture, forestry, fishing* (1999): cassava 559,000, yams 360,000, bananas 115,000; livestock (number of live animals) 2,992,100 cattle, 2,350,000 goats, 622,000 pigs; roundwood (1998) 3,518,000 cu m; fish catch (1998) 13,000. *Mining and quarrying* (1997): gold 29 kg, diamonds 486,800 carats (an unknown but substantial amount is believed to be smuggled out of the country annually). *Manufacturing* (value added in $'000; 1994): food, beverages, and tobacco 19,000; chemical products 3,000; wood products 2,000. *Energy production (consumption):* electricity (kW-hr; 1996) 104,000,000 (104,000,000); petroleum products (metric tons; 1996) none (92,000). **Household income and expenditure.** Average household size (1998) 5.9; average annual income per household (1988) CFAF 91,985; expenditure (1991; weights of consumer price index components): food 70.5%, clothing 8.5%, other manufactured products 7.6%, energy 7.3%, services (including transportation and communications, recreation, and health) 6.1%. **Gross national product** (1999): $1,035,000,000 ($290 per capita). **Population economically active** (1988): total 1,186,972; activity rate of total pop. 48.2% (participation rates: ages 15–64, 78.3%; female 46.8%; unemployed 7.5%). **Land use** (1994): forest 75.0%; meadows 4.8%; agriculture 3.2%; other 17.0%. **Tourism** (1997): receipts $5,000,000; expenditures $39,000,000.

Foreign trade

Imports (1997): CFAF 84,400,000,000 (1992; food products 22.2%, transportation equipment 16.6%, chemical products 13.7%, energy products 11.0%). *Major import sources:* France 30.5%; Côte d'Ivoire 18.0%; Cameroon 10.8%; Germany 3.6%; Belgium-Luxembourg 3.6%; United States 2.4%. **Exports** (1997): CFAF 89,700,000,000 (diamonds 38.7%, wood 25.4%, cotton 16.1%, coffee 10.3%). *Major export destinations:* Belgium-Luxembourg 36.2%; Côte d'Ivoire 5.2%; Spain 4.4%; France 3.0%; Democratic Republic of the Congo 1.8%; Republic of the Congo 1.1%.

Transport and communications

Transport. *Railroads:* none. Roads (1996): total length 14,900 mi, 24,000 km (paved 2%). *Vehicles* (1995): passenger cars 9,500; trucks and buses 7,000. *Air transport* (1996; Represents ¹⁄₁₁ of the traffic of Air Afrique, which is operated by 11 West African states): passenger-mi 139,644,000, passenger-km 224,736,000; short ton-mi cargo 11,247,000, metric ton-km cargo 16,420,000; *airports* (1998; international air service only) 1. **Communications** Total units (units per 1,000 persons). Daily newspaper circulation (1996): 6,000 (1.8); Radio receivers (1997): 283,000 (83); Television receivers (1999): 20,000 (5.6); Telephone main lines (1999): 9,860 (2.8); Cellular telephone subscribers (1999): 4,162 (1.2); Personal computers (1999): 5,000 (1.4); Internet users (1999): 1,000 (0.3).

Education and health

Educational attainment (1988). Percentage of pop. age 10 and over having: no formal schooling 59.3%;

primary education 29.6%; lower secondary 7.5%; upper secondary 2.3%; higher 1.3%. **Literacy** (1995): total pop. age 15 and over literate 60.0%; males literate 68.5%; females literate 52.4%. **Health** (1992): physicians 157 (1 per 18,660 persons); hospital beds (1991) 4,258 (1 per 672 persons); infant mortality rate (2000) 106.7. **Food** (1999): daily per capita caloric intake 1,978 (vegetable products 91%, animal products 9%); 88% of FAO recommended minimum requirement.

Military

Total active duty personnel (2000): 3,150 (excludes 1,000 gendarmerie, who are part of the armed forces; army 95.2%; navy, none; air force 4.8%). **Military expenditure as percentage of GNP** (1997): 3.9% (world 2.6%); per capita expenditure $12.

Background

For several centuries before the arrival of Europeans, the territory was subjected to slave traders. The French explored and claimed central Africa and in 1889 established a post at Bangui. In 1898 they partitioned the colony among commercial concessionaires. United with Chad in 1906 to form the French colony of Ubangi-Shari, it later became part of French Equatorial Africa. It was separated from Chad in 1920 and became an overseas territory in 1946. An autonomous republic within the French Community in 1958, the country achieved independence in 1960. In 1966 the military overthrew a civilian government and installed Jean-Bédel Bokassa, who in 1976 declared himself Emperor Bokassa I and renamed the country the Central African Empire. He was overthrown in 1979, but the military again seized power in the 1980s. Elections in 1993 led to installation of a civilian government.

Recent Developments

Army rebels loyal to former president André Kolingba attempted to overthrow the government on 28 May 2001. The mutineers attacked the presidential palace. Fighting ensued for more than a week, and unofficial estimates put the number of persons killed at between 250 and 300. The coup was suppressed by government forces on 7 June, though Kolingba and other suspected coup leaders remained at large.

Internet resources: <www.sas.upenn.edu/African_Studies/Country_Specific/CAR.html>

Chad

Official name: Jumhuriyah Tshad (Arabic); République du Tchad (French) (Republic of Chad). **Form of government:** unitary republic with one legislative body (National Assembly [125]). **Chief of state:** President Idriss Déby (from 1990). **Head of government:** Prime Minister Nagoum Yamassoum (from 1999). **Capital:** N'Djamena. **Official languages:** Arabic; French. **Official religion:** none. **Monetary unit:** 1 CFA franc (CFAF) = 100 centimes; valuation (28 Jun 2002) $1 = CFAF 664.20. Earlier pegged to the French franc, after 1 Jan 2002 the CFAF was pegged at 655.96 to the euro.

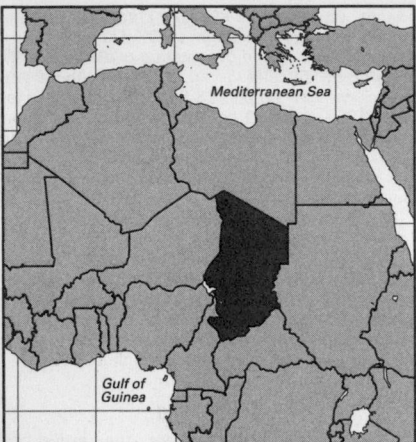

Demography

Area: 495,755 sq mi, 1,284,000 sq km. **Population** (2001): 8,707,000. **Density** (2001): persons per sq mi 17.6, persons per sq km 6.8. **Urban** (1999): 23.4%. **Sex distribution** (2000): male 48.50%; female 51.50%. **Age breakdown** (2000): under 15, 47.7%; 15–29, 26.1%; 30–44, 14.1%; 45–59, 7.6%; 60–74, 3.7%; 75 and over, 0.8%. **Ethnolinguistic composition** (1993): Sara 27.7%; Sudanic Arab 12.3%; Mayo-Kebbi peoples 11.5%; Kanem-Bornu peoples 9.0%; Ouaddaï peoples 8.7%; Hadjeray (Hadjaraï) 6.7%; Tangale (Tandjilé) peoples 6.5%; Gorane peoples 6.3%; Fitri-Batha peoples 4.7%; Fulani (Peul) 2.4%; other 4.2%. **Religious affiliation** (1993): Muslim 53.9%; Christian 34.7%, of which Roman Catholic 20.3%, Protestant 14.4%; traditional beliefs 7.4%; other 4.0%. **Major cities** (1993): N'Djamena 530,965; Moundou 282,103; Bongor 196,713; Sarh 193,753; Abéché 187,936. **Location:** central Africa, bordered by Libya, The Sudan, Central African Republic, Cameroon, Nigeria, and Niger.

Vital statistics

Birth rate per 1,000 pop. (2000): 48.8 (world avg. 22.5). **Death rate** per 1,000 pop. (2000): 15.7 (world avg. 9.0). **Natural increase rate** per 1,000 pop. (2000): 33.1 (world avg. 13.5). **Total fertility rate** (avg. births per childbearing woman; 2000): 6.6. **Life expectancy** at birth (2000): male 48.5 years; female 52.6 years.

National economy

Budget (1998). *Revenue:* CFAF 127,100,000,000 (tax revenue 54.9%, of which taxes on international trade 21.6%, income tax 18.3%, taxes on goods and services 11.3%, other taxes 3.7%; nontax revenue 5.1%; grants 40.0%). *Expenditures:* CFAF 153,800,-000,000 (current expenditure 49.0%, of which government salaries 20.5%, materials and supply 10.7%, defense 6.2%, debt service 5.8%, transfer payments 5.6%, other 2.0%; capital expenditure 51.0%). **Public debt** (external, outstanding; 1999): $1,045,000,000. **Tourism** (1994): receipts from visi-

tors $12,000,000; expenditures by nationals abroad $26,000,000. **Production** (metric tons except as noted). *Agriculture, forestry, fishing* (1999): sorghum 636,900, peanuts (groundnuts) 471,150, millet 365,600; livestock (number of live animals) 5,582,092 cattle, 4,968,256 goats, 2,431,555 sheep; roundwood (1998) 1,919,000 cu m; fish catch (1998) 84,000. *Mining and quarrying* (1997): aggregate (gravel) 170,000; limited commercial production of natron (10,000). *Manufacturing:* cotton fibre (1996) 61,700; woven cotton fabrics (1998) 1,100,000 metres; edible oil (1998) 160,000 hecto-liters. *Energy production (consumption):* electricity (kW-hr; 1998) 74,878,000 (56,489,000); petroleum products (metric tons; 1998) none (47,057). **Household income and expenditure** (1993). Average household size 5.0; average annual income per household CFAF 96,806; sources of income (1995–96; urban) informal-sector employment and entrepreneurship 36.7%, transfers 24.8%, wages 23.6%, ownership of real estate 8.6%; expenditure (1983; N'Djamena only): food 45.3%, health 11.9%, energy 5.8%, clothing 3.3%. **Population economically active** (1997): total 3,433,000; activity rate of total pop. 47.9% (participation rates: over age 15, 72.3%; female 44.5%; unemployed [1993] 0.6%). **Gross national product** (1999): $1,555,000,000 ($210 per capita). **Land use** (1994): forested 25.7%; meadows and pastures 35.7%; agricultural and under permanent cultivation 2.6%; other 36.0%.

Foreign trade

Imports (1998): CFAF 175,000,000,000 (1995; petroleum products 17.9%; machinery 15.5%; road vehicles 8.3%; raw and refined sugar 7.9%; cereal products 7.4%; pharmaceuticals and other chemical products 7.2%). *Major import sources* (1997; estimated data): France 41%; Nigeria 10%; Cameroon 7%; India 6%; Belgium-Luxembourg 5%. **Exports** (1998): CFAF 145,300,000,000 (cotton lint 59.3%; other 40.7%). *Major export destinations* (1997; estimated data): Portugal 30%; Germany 14%; Thailand 7%; Costa Rica 6%; Hong Kong 5%; Taiwan 5%.

Transport and communications

Transport. *Railroads:* none. Roads (1996): total length 33,400 km (paved 1%). Vehicles (1996): passenger cars 10,560; trucks and buses 14,550. *Air transport* (1996; 1/11th portion of Air Afrique traffic): passenger-km 233,000,000; metric ton-km cargo 37,000,000; airports (1998) with scheduled flights 1. **Communications** Total units (units per 1,000 persons). Daily newspaper circulation (1997): 2,000 (0.2); Radio receivers (1997): 1,310,000 (206); Television receivers (1999): 10,300 (1.4); Telephone main lines (2000): 9,700 (1.3); Internet users (2000): 1,000 (0.1).

Education and health

Educational attainment (1993). Percentage of economically active pop. age 15 and over having: no formal schooling 81.1%; Qur'anic education 4.2%; primary education 11.2%; secondary education 2.7%; higher education 0.3%; professional education 0.5%. **Literacy** (1995): percentage of total pop. age 15 and

1 metric ton = about 1.1 short tons; 1 kilometer = 0.6 mi (statute); 1 metric ton-km cargo = about 0.68 short ton-mi cargo; c.i.f.: cost, insurance, and freight; f.o.b.: free on board

over literate 48.1%; males literate 62.1%; females literate 34.7%. **Health** (1993): physicians 217 (1 per 27,765 persons); hospital beds 3,962 (1 per 1,521 persons); infant mortality rate per 1,000 live births (2000) 96.7. **Food** (1999): daily per capita caloric intake 2,206 (vegetable products 93%, animal products 7%); 93% of FAO recommended minimum requirement.

Military

Total active duty personnel (2000): 30,350 (army 82.4%; air force 1.2%; paramilitary 16.4%); 990 French troops were based in Chad in mid-2001. **Military expenditure as percentage of GNP** (1997): 2.7% (world 2.6%); per capita expenditure $6.

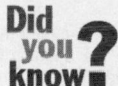

Did you know? Chad is a country of more than 200 ethnic groups and more than 100 different spoken languages and dialects. The Tibesti Mountains in the northern, Saharan (arid) part of Chad are the location of fine cliff and cave paintings depicting large animals formerly native to the area. Hunters of these animals painted them 4,000 to 7,000 years ago when the climate was evidently more conducive to large game. The sites at Zouar and Gonoa are particularly noteworthy.

Background

Around AD 800 the kingdom of Kanem was founded, and by the early 1200s its borders had expanded to form a new kingdom, Kanem–Bornu, in the northern regions of the area. Its power peaked in the 16th century with its command of the southern terminus of the trans–Sahara trade route to Tripoli. Around this time the rival kingdoms of Baguirmi and Wadai evolved in the south. In the years 1883–93 all three kingdoms fell to the Sudanese adventurer Rabih az–Zubayr, who was in turn pushed out by the French in 1891. Extending their power, the French in 1910 made Chad a part of French Equatorial Africa. Chad became a separate colony in 1920 and was made an overseas territory in 1946. The country achieved independence in 1960. This was followed by decades of civil war, and frequent intervention by France and Libya.

Recent Developments

Chadian Pres. Idriss Déby won 63% of the vote in the May 2001 presidential election, securing for himself another five-year term. Citing many irregular electoral practices, opposition parties refused to accept the results, but their appeal to the constitutional court failed.

Internet resources: <www.chadembassy.org>

Chile

Official name: República de Chile (Republic of Chile). **Form of government:** multiparty republic with two legislative houses (Senate [49; includes 11 nonelective seats]; Chamber of Deputies [120]). **Head of state and government:** President Ricardo Lagos Escobar

(from 2000). **Capital:** Santiago (legislative bodies meet in Valparaíso). **Official language:** Spanish. **Official religion:** none. **Monetary unit:** 1 peso (Ch$) = 100 centavos; valuation (28 Jun 2002) US$1 = Ch$688.75.

Demography

Area: 292,135 sq mi, 756,626 sq km (includes 205 sq mi [530 sq km] of waters, known as Laguna del Desierto, lost in a border dispute with Argentina, resolved on 21 Oct 1994). **Population** (2001): 15,402,000. **Density** (2001): persons per sq mi 52.7, persons per sq km 20.4. **Urban** (1999): 85.4%. **Sex distribution** (2000): male 49.51%; female 50.49%. **Age breakdown** (2000): under 15, 28.5%; 15–29, 24.2%; 30–44, 22.9%; 45–59, 14.3%; 60–74, 7.5%; 75 and over, 2.6%. **Ethnic composition** (1992): European and mestizo 89.7%; Araucanian (Mapuche) 9.6%; Aymara 0.5%; Rapa Nui Polynesian 0.2%. **Religious affiliation** (1992): Roman Catholic 76.7%; Protestant 13.2%; atheist and nonreligious 5.8%; other 4.3%. **Major cities** (1999): Greater Santiago 4,640,635; Concepción 362,589; Viña del Mar 330,736; Valparaíso 283,489; Talcahuano 269,265; Temuco 253,451. **Location:** southern South America, bordering Peru, Bolivia, Argentina, South Atlantic Ocean, and the South Pacific Ocean.

Vital statistics

Birth rate per 1,000 pop. (2000): 17.2 (world avg. 22.5). **Death rate** per 1,000 pop. (2000): 5.5 (world avg. 9.0). **Natural increase rate** per 1,000 pop. (2000): 11.7 (world avg. 13.5). **Total fertility rate** (avg. births per childbearing woman, 2000): 2.2. **Life expectancy** at birth (2000): male 72.4 years; female 79.2 years.

National economy

Budget (1999). *Revenue:* Ch$7,580,300,000,000 (income from taxes 85.3%, nontax revenue 14.7%). *Expenditures:* Ch$8,392,800,000,000 (social security and welfare 29.1%, transfers 24.3%, wages 19.6%, capital expenditure 16.6%, economic affairs and services 8.3%). **Public debt** (external, outstanding; 1999): US$5,655,000,000. **Population economically active** (1999): total 5,822,700; activity rate of total pop. 38.6% (participation rates [1995]: ages 15–64, 58.6%; female 32.4%; unemployed [1999] 9.7%). **Production** (metric tons except as noted). *Agriculture, forestry, fishing* (1999): sugar beets 3,100,000, grapes 1,575,000, tomatoes 1,243,000; livestock (number of live animals) 4,134,000 cattle, 4,116,000 sheep, 2,221,000 pigs; roundwood (1998) 31,670,000 cu m; fish catch (1998) 3,265,300. *Mining* (1998): iron 8,277,000; copper 3,843,000; zinc 26,000. *Manufacturing* (value added in Ch$'000,000; 1997): food products 3,810,200; metal and metal products 2,631,900; petroleum and petroleum products 1,100,200; paper and paper products 964,900; beverages 807,400; nonmetallic mineral products 593,000. *Energy production (consumption):* electricity (kW-hr; 1999) 38,389,000,000 (31,204,000,000); coal (metric tons; 1996) 1,119,000 (3,558,000); crude petroleum (barrels; 1996) 3,364,000 (61,498,000); petroleum products (metric tons; 1996) 8,608,000 (10,373,000); natural gas (cu m; 1996) 2,056,000,000 (1,983,000,000). **Gross national product** (1999): US$69,602,000,000 (US$4,630 per capita). **Household income and expenditure.** Average household size (1998) 4.6; average annual income per household (1994) Ch$5,981,706 at November prices; sources of income (1990): wages and salaries 75.1%, transfer payments 12.0%, other 12.9%; expenditure (1989): food 27.9%, clothing 22.5%, housing 15.2%, transportation 6.4%. **Tourism** (1999): receipts US$894,000,000; expenditures US$806,000,000.

Foreign trade

Imports (1999): US$15,137,000,000 (intermediate goods 59.5%; capital goods 21.8%; consumer goods 18.7%). *Major import sources:* US 20.8%; Argentina 13.9%; Brazil 6.7%; Japan 4.4%; Germany 4.3%; France 2.9%. **Exports** (1999): US$15,616,000,000 (mining products 44.4%, of which copper 37.7%; industrial products 38.5%; foodstuffs 17.1%). *Major export destinations:* US 19.4%; Japan 14.3%; United Kingdom 6.8%; Argentina 4.6%; Brazil 4.3%; Germany 3.5%; Taiwan 3.2%.

Transport and communications

Transport. *Railroads* (1999): route length 5,410 mi, 8,707 km; passenger-km 605,900,000; metric ton-km cargo (1994) 2,329,246,000. *Roads* (1996): total length 49,590 mi, 79,800 km (paved 14%). *Vehicles* (1999): passenger cars 1,323,800; trucks and buses 687,500. *Air transport* (1999): passenger-km 10,650,500,000; metric ton-km cargo 2,107,000,000; airports (1998) with scheduled flights 23. **Communications** Total units (unit per 1,000 persons). Daily newspaper circulation (1996): 1,410,000 (98); Radio receivers (1997): 5,180,000 (354); Television receivers (1999): 3,600,000 (240); Telephone main lines (1999): 3,109,000 (207); Cellular telephone subscribers (1999): 2,260,687 (150); Personal computers units (1999): 1,000,000 (66.6); Internet users (1999): 700,000 (46.6).

Education and health

Educational attainment (1992). Percentage of pop. age 25 and over having: no formal schooling 5.7%;

primary education 44.2%; secondary 42.2%; higher 7.9%. **Literacy** (1995): total pop. age 15 and over literate 95.2%; males 95.4%; females 95.0%. **Health** (1999): physicians 17,853 (1 per 841 persons); hospital beds (1998) 41,706 (1 per 355 persons); infant mortality rate (2000) 9.6. **Food** (1999): daily per capita caloric intake 2,858 (vegetable products 79%, animal products 21%); 117% of FAO recommended minimum requirement.

Military

Total active duty personnel (2000): 87,000 (army 58.6%, navy 27.6%, air force 12.8%). **Military expenditure as percentage of GNP** (1997): 3.9% (world 2.6%); per capita expenditure US$196.

Background

Originally inhabited by native peoples, including the Mapuche, the area was invaded by the Spanish in 1536. A settlement begun at Santiago in 1541 was governed under the viceroyalty of Peru but became a separate captaincy general in 1778. It revolted against Spanish rule in 1810; its independence was finally assured by the victory of José de San Martín in 1818, and the area was then governed by Bernardo O'Higgins to 1823. In the War of the Pacific against Peru and Bolivia, it won the rich nitrate fields on the coast of Bolivia, effectively forcing that country into a landlocked position. Chile remained neutral in World War I and in World War II, but severed diplomatic ties with the Axis in 1943. In 1970 Salvador Allende was elected president, becoming the first avowed Marxist to be elected chief of state in Latin America. Following economic upheaval, he was ousted in 1973 in a coup led by Gen. Augusto Pinochet, whose military junta for many years harshly suppressed all internal opposition. A national referendum in 1988 rejected Pinochet, and elections held in 1989 returned the country to civilian rule.

Recent Developments

Ricardo Lagos Escobar won a five-year term as president of Chile after narrowly defeating Joaquín Lavín Infante in the 2000 elections. Lagos was the third consecutive Concertación coalition candidate elected to the post. Much attention in the country has also focused on the case of Pinochet. Although the former ruler had been charged with more than 250 cases of human rights abuses, he was deemed by the Chilean Appeals courts not fit to stand trial after undergoing a series of medical exams in 2001. Judicial proceedings continued against him elsewhere, including France, where Pinochet was indicted on human rights charges along with six other senior Chilean military officers.

Internet resources: <www.visit-chile.org>

China

Official name: Zhonghua Renmin Gongheguo (People's Republic of China). **Form of government:** single-party people's republic with one legislative house (National People's Congress [2,989]). **Chief of state:** President Jiang Zemin (from 1993). **Head of**

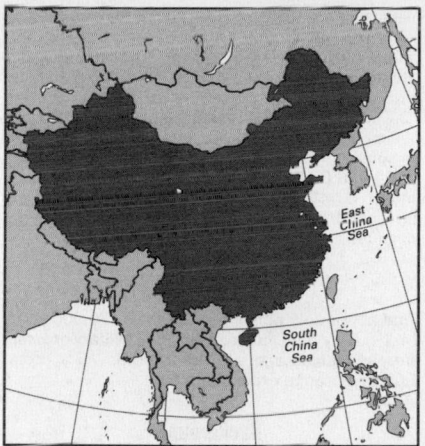

government: Premier Zhu Rongji (from 1998). Capital: Beijing (Peking). Official language: Mandarin Chinese. Official religion: none. Monetary unit: 1 Renminbi (yuan) (Y) = 10 jiao = 100 fen; valuation (28 Jun 2002) $1 = Y 8.28.

Demography

Area (includes 4,600 sq mi [11,900 sq km] not shown separately): 3,600,100 sq mi, 9,572,900 sq km. **Population** (2001): 1,274,915,000. **Density** (2001): persons per sq mi 344.9, persons per sq km 133.2. **Urban** (2000): 36.1%. **Sex distribution** (2000): male 51.63%; female 48.37%. **Age breakdown** (1998): under 15, 24.3%; 15–29, 24.6%; 30–44, 24.8%; 45–59, 15.2%; 60–74, 8.8%; 75 and over, 2.3%. **Ethnic composition** (1990): Han (Chinese) 91.96%; Zhuang 1.37%; Manchu 0.87%; Hui 0.76%; Miao 0.65%; Uighur 0.04%; Yi 0.58%; Tujia 0.50%; Mongolian 0.42%; Tibetan 0.41%; Buyi 0.23%; Dong 0.22%; Yao 0.18%; Korean 0.17%; Bai 0.14%; Hani 0.11%; Kazakh 0.10%; Dai 0.09%; Li 0.09%; other 0.51%. **Religious affiliation** (2000): nonreligious 42.1%; Chinese folk-religionist 28.5%; Buddhist 8.4%; atheist 8.1%; Christian 7.1%; traditional beliefs 4.3%; Muslim 1.5%. **Major cities** (1998): Shanghai 8,937,175; Beijing 6,633,929; Tianjin 4,835,327; Wuhan 3,911,824; Shenyang 3,876,289; Guangzhou (Canton) 3,306,277; Chongqing 3,193,889; Harbin 2,586,978; Nanjing 2,388,915; Xian 2,294,790. **Households.** Average rural household size (1996) 4.4; urban household size (1998) 3.2. Family households (1990): 277,390,000 (99.4%); collective 1,671,000 (0.6%) **Location:** eastern Asia, bordering Mongolia, Russia, North Korea, the Yellow Sea, the East China Sea, the South China Sea, Vietnam, Laos, Myanmar (Burma), Bhutan, Nepal, India, Pakistan, Afghanistan, Tajikistan, Kyrgyzstan, and Kazakhstan.

Vital statistics

Birth rate per 1,000 pop. (2001): 14.9 (world avg. 22.5). **Death rate** per 1,000 pop. (2001): 7.0 (world avg. 9.0). **Natural increase rate** per 1,000 pop. (2001): 7.9 (world avg. 13.5). **Total fertility rate** (avg. births per childbearing woman; 2001):

1.8. **Marriage rate** per 1,000 pop. (1996): 7.6. **Divorce rate** per 1,000 pop. (1996): 0.9. **Life expectancy** at birth (2001): male 69.0 years; female 73.0 years.

Social indicators

Quality of working life (1991). Average workweek: 48 hours. Funds for pensions and social welfare relief (1996): Y 181,780,000,000. **Access to services.** Percentage of urban pop. with: safe public water supply (1996) 95.0%. **Social deviance.** Annual reported arrest rate per 100,000 pop. (1986) for: property violation 20.7; infringing personal rights 7.2; disruption of social administration 3.3; endangering public security 1.0 (excludes arrests for anti-Communist activities). **Material well-being.** Urban families possessing (number per family; 1996): bicycles 1.9; televisions 1.2; washing machines 0.9; refrigerators 0.7; sewing machines 0.6; cameras 0.3. Rural families possessing (number per family; 1998): bicycles 1.4; televisions 1.3; sewing machines 0.7; washing machines 0.2.

National economy

Gross national product (at current market prices; 1998): $923,560,000,000 ($750 per capita). **Budget** (1997). *Revenue:* Y 492,650,000,000 (taxes on goods and services 66.6%; grants 12.3%; income taxes 8.2%; import duties 6.5%; nontax revenue 2.3%). *Expenditures:* Y 601,720,000,000 (defense 13.6%; general public services 7.5%; agriculture 6.0%; industry 2.9%; public order 2.6%; education 2.0%; utilities 1.8%; other economic affair expenditures 5.9%; nonfunctional expenditures 56.3%). **Public debt** (external, outstanding; 1999): $108,163,000,000. **Tourism:** receipts from visitors (1999) $14,098,000,000; expenditures by nationals abroad (1999) $10,864,000,000. **Production** (metric tons except as noted). *Agriculture, forestry, fishing* (2000): grains—rice 190,168,000, corn (maize) 105,231,000, wheat 99,370,000; livestock (number of live animals) 437,551,000 pigs, 148,401,000 goats, 131,095,000 sheep, 104,582,000 cattle; roundwood (1999) 291,330,000 cu m; fish catch (1998) 17,229,957. *Mining and quarrying* (1998): metal concentrates—zinc 1,540,000, copper 1,150,000; metal ores—iron ore 210,000,000, bauxite 8,500,000, manganese ore 6,100,000. *Manufacturing* (1998): cement 536,000,000; rolled steel 105,180,000; chemical fertilizer 30,100,000; sulfuric acid 21,710,000; paper and paperboard 21,260,000; sugar 8,260,000; cotton yarn 5,420,000; cotton fabrics 24,100,000,000 m; color television sets 34,970,000 units; bicycles 23,125,000 units; household washing machines 12,073,000 units; household refrigerators 10,000,000 units; motor vehicles 1,630,000 units. *Energy production (consumption):* electricity (kW-hr; 1996) 1,081,310,000,000 (1,078,910,000,000); coal (metric tons; 1996) 1,397,000,000 (1,383,170,000,000); crude petroleum (barrels; 1996) 1,152,000,000 (1,157,000,000); petroleum products (metric tons; 1996) 121,858,000 (130,506,000); natural gas (cu m; 1996) 20,067,000,000 (20,067,000,000). **Household income and expenditure** (1996). Average household size (2000) 3.4; rural household 4.4, urban household (1998) 3.2. Average annual income per household Y 13,459; rural household Y 12,406, urban household (1998) Y 17,248.

Sources of income: rural household—income from household businesses 79.6%, wages 16.1%, other 4.3%; urban household—wages 80.5%, business income 5.9%, other 13.6%. Expenditure: rural household—food 56.3%, housing 13.9%, cultural activities 8.4%, clothing 7.2%, household materials 5.4%, health 3.7%, transportation 3.0%; urban household (1998)—food 44.5%, clothing 11.1%, housing 9.4%, household materials 8.2%, education 6.3%, transportation and communications 5.9%, health 4.7%. **Population economically active** (1998): total 699,570,000; activity rate of total pop. 55.7% (participation rates: over age 15 [1996] 75.9%; female [1987] 49.7%; unemployed 3.1%). Urban workforce by sector 1978 (1998): state enterprises 74,500,000 (90,580,000); collectives 20,000,000 (19,630,000); self-employment or privately run enterprises 150,000 (96,570,000). **Land use** (1999): meadows and pastures 42.9%; agricultural and under permanent cultivation 14.5%; forested and other 42.6%.

Foreign trade

Imports (1998-c.i.f.): $140,166,000,000 (machinery and transport equipment 40.5%; products of textile industries, rubber and metal products 22.2%; chemical and related products 14.4%; inedible raw materials 7.6%; mineral fuel and lubricants 4.8%; food and live animals 2.7%). *Major import sources:* Japan 20.1%; United States 12.1%; Taiwan 11.9%; South Korea 10.7%; Germany 5.0%; Hong Kong 4.8%. **Exports** (1998-f.o.b.): $183,757,000,000 (machinery and transport equipment 27.3%; products of textile industries, rubber and metal products 17.6%; food and live animals 5.8%; chemicals and allied products 5.6%; mineral fuels and lubricants 2.8%; inedible raw materials 1.9%). *Major export destinations:* Hong Kong 21.1%; United States 20.7%; Japan 16.2%; Germany 4.0%; South Korea 3.4%.

Transport and communications

Transport. *Railroads* (1998): length 35,781 mi, 57,584 km; passenger-mi 229,657,000,000, passenger-km 369,598,000,000; short ton-mi cargo 843,302,000,000, metric ton-km cargo 1,231,200,-000,000. *Roads* (1998): total length 794,405 mi, 1,278,474 km (paved 93%). *Vehicles* (1998): passenger cars 6,548,300; trucks and buses 6,278,-900. *Air transport* (1998): passenger-mi 49,725,-000,000, passenger-km 80,024,000,000; short ton-mi cargo 2,291,000,000, metric ton-km cargo 3,345,000,000; airports (1996) with scheduled flights 113. **Communications** Total units (units per 1,000 persons). Daily newspaper circulation (1994): 27,790,000 (23); Radio receivers (1997): 417,000,-000 (335); Television receivers (1999): 370,000,000 (292); Telephone main lines (1999): 108,716,000 (86) Cellular telephone subscribers (1999): 43,296,-000 (34); Personal computers (1999): 15,500,000 (12); Internet users (1999): 8,900,000 (7).

Education and health

Educational attainment (1997). Percentage of pop. age 15 and over having: no schooling and incom-

plete primary 20.7%; completed primary 37.6%; some secondary and complete secondary 39.2%; college and postsecondary education 2.5%. **Literacy** (1995): total pop. age 15 and over literate 81.5%; males literate 89.9%; females literate 72.7%. **Health** (1998): physicians 1,999,500 (1 per 629 persons); hospital beds 2,913,700 (1 per 431 persons); infant mortality rate per 1,000 live births (2001) 38.0. **Food** (1999): daily per capita caloric intake 3,042 (vegetable products 81%, animal products 19%); (1997) 129% of FAO recommended minimum.

Military

Total active duty personnel (2000): 2,470,000 (army 74.1%, navy 8.9%, air force 17.0%). **Military expenditure as percentage of GNP** (1997): 2.2% (world 2.6%); per capita expenditure $61.

Background

The discovery of Peking man in 1927 dates the advent of early hominids to the Paleolithic period. Chinese civilization probably spread from the Huang He (Yellow River) valley, where it existed c. 3000 BC. The first dynasty for which there is definite historical material is the Shang (c. 16th century BC), which had a writing system and a calendar. The Zhou, a subject state of the Shang, overthrew its Shang rulers in the 11th century BC and ruled until the 3rd century BC. Taoism and Confucianism were founded in this era.

A time of conflict, called the Warring States Period, lasted from the 5th century BC until the Qin (Ch'in) dynasty (from whose name China is derived) was established after its rulers had conquered rival states and created a unified empire. The Han dynasty was established in 206 BC and ruled until AD 220. A time of turbulence followed, and Chinese reunification was not achieved until the Sui dynasty was established in 581.

After the founding of the Song dynasty in 960, the capital was moved to the south because of northern invasions. In 1279 this dynasty was overthrown and Mongol (Yuan) domination began. During this time, Marco Polo visited Kublai Khan. The Ming dynasty followed the period of Mongol rule and lasted from 1368 to 1644, cultivating antiforeign feelings to the point that China closed itself off from the rest of the world.

Peoples from Manchuria overran China in 1644 and established the Qing (Manchu) dynasty. Ever-increasing incursions by Western and Japanese interests led in the 19th century to the Opium Wars, the Taiping Rebellion, and the Sino-Japanese War, all of which weakened the Manchus.

The dynasty fell in 1911 and a republic was proclaimed in 1912 by Sun Yat-sen. The power struggles of warlords weakened the republic. Under Sun's successor, Chiang Kai-shek, some national unification was achieved in the 1920s, but Chiang soon broke with the Communists, who then formed their own armies. Japan invaded northern China in 1937; its occupation lasted until 1945. The Communists gained support after the Long March (1934–35), in which Mao Zedong emerged as their leader.

1 metric ton = about 1.1 short tons;   1 kilometer = 0.6 mi (statute);   1 metric ton-km cargo = about 0.68 short ton-mi cargo;   c.i.f.: cost, insurance, and freight;   f.o.b.: free on board

Upon Japan's surrender at the end of World War II, a fierce civil war began; in 1949 the Nationalists fled to Taiwan and the Communists proclaimed the People's Republic of China. The Communists undertook extensive reforms, but pragmatic policies alternated with periods of revolutionary upheaval, most notably in the Great Leap Forward and the Cultural Revolution. The chaos of the latter led, after Mao's death in 1976, to a turn to moderation under Deng Xiaoping, who undertook economic reforms and renewed China's ties to the West. The government established diplomatic ties with the US in 1979. It suppressed the Tiananmen Square student demonstration in 1989. The economy has been in transition since the late 1970s, moving from central planning and state-run industries to a mixture of state-owned and private enterprises in manufacturing and services. The death of Deng in 1997 marked the end of a political era, but power passed peacefully to Jiang Zemin. In 1997 Hong Kong reverted to Chinese rule, as did Macao in 1999.

Recent Developments

In 1999 Pres. Jiang Zemin and leaders of the Communist Party of China (CPC) celebrated the 50th anniversary of communist rule. The country over which Jiang presided was vastly more wealthy and powerful than the China of 50 years before, but it still faced a daunting set of problems. In just two decades China had witnessed a dramatic growth in its population, rapid urbanization, the transition from planning to market, and integration into the global economy. There was also continuing international pressure on China over the issue of human rights abuses.

As China's population—growing by 10 million annually—approached the 1.3 billion mark, authorities reaffirmed the one-child policy, which they claimed had prevented at least 250 million births over the past 20 years. Widespread evasion of this policy persisted in rural areas, although not in the cities. The country's huge population had pressed against the limits of natural resources, particularly water. Beijing addressed the severe water shortage affecting all of northern China by encouraging less-water-intensive agricultural practices, shutting factories that polluted groundwater and surface water, and constructing new sewage-treatment plants.

The determination of officials to improve Beijing's environment was motivated in part by the desire to show the city's best face to the world. The long-hoped-for payoff came in July 2001 when the International Olympic Committee awarded the 2008 Summer Olympics to Beijing. In this connection Beijing planned to invest $34 billion in new stadiums, parks, transportation systems, housing, and pollution-abatement measures.

Also in 2001, the World Trade Organization finally certified China for membership following 15 years of difficult multilateral negotiations. On the human rights front, however, doubts persisted regarding China's announced intention to bring its practices into conformity with international norms. In February Amnesty International issued a report alleging that China was stepping up its use of torture in police interrogations of dissidents, Tibetan nationalists, migrants, and other criminal defendants.

Internet resources: <www.chinaonline.com>

Colombia

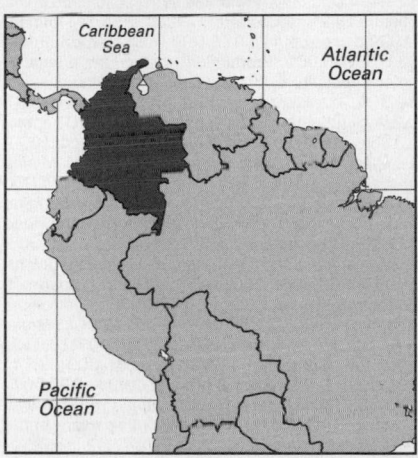

Official name: República de Colombia (Republic of Colombia). **Form of government:** unitary, multiparty republic with two legislative houses (Senate [102]; House of Representatives [103, including two representatives from indigenous communities]). **Head of state and government:** President Álvaro Uribe Vélez (from 7 Aug 2002). **Capital:** Santafé de Bogotá, D.C. **Official language:** Spanish. **Official religion:** none. **Monetary unit:** 1 peso (Col$) = 100 centavos; valuation (28 Jun 2002) US$1 = Col$2,399.

Demography

Area: 440,762 sq mi, 1,141,568 sq km. **Population** (2001): 43,071,000 (de jure). **Density** (2001); persons per sq mi 97.7, persons per sq km 37.7. **Urban** (1999): 74%. **Sex distribution** (2000): male 49.14%; female 50.86%. **Age breakdown** (2000): under 15, 32.2%; 15–29, 26.6%; 30–44, 22.6%; 45–59, 11.6%; 60–74, 5.6%; 75 and over, 1.4%. **Ethnic composition** (2000): mestizo 47.3%; mulatto 23.0%; white 20.0%; black 6.0%; black-Amerindian 1.0%; Amerindian/other 2.7%. **Religious affiliation** (1995): Roman Catholic 91.9%; other 8.1%. **Major cities** (1999): Santafé de Bogotá, D.C., 6,276,428; Cali 2,110,571; Medellín 1,957,928; Barranquilla 1,226,292; Bucaramanga 520,874. **Location:** northern South America, bordering the Caribbean Sea, Venezuela, Brazil, Peru, Ecuador, the Pacific Ocean, and Panama.

Vital statistics

Birth rate per 1,000 pop. (2000): 22.0 (world avg. 22.5). **Death rate** per 1,000 pop. (2000): 5.7 (world avg. 9.0). **Natural increase rate** per 1,000 pop. (2000): 17.2 (world avg. 13.5). **Total fertility rate** (avg. births per childbearing woman; 2000): 2.7. **Life expectancy** at birth (2000): male 66.4 years; female 74.3 years.

National economy

Budget (1998). *Revenue:* Col$16,706,000,000,000 (tax revenue 70.8%, nontax revenue 25.6%, transfers 3.6%). *Expenditures:* Col$21,526,000,000,000 (current expenditure 77.0%, of which wages 23.9%, interest 12.2%, goods and services 10.9%; capital expenditure

23.0%). **Public debt** (external, outstanding; 1999): $19,434,000,000. **Land use** (1994): forest 22.0%; pasture 18.2%; agriculture 5.7%; other 54.1%. **Tourism** (1999): receipts $938,000,000; expenditures $1,078,000,000. **Production** (metric tons except as noted). *Agriculture, forestry, fishing* (1999): sugarcane 36,900,000, plantains 2,789,000; coffee 648,000; livestock (number of live animals) 25,614,200 cattle, 2,195,600 sheep, 2,764,000 pigs; roundwood (1998) 18,618,000 cu m; fish catch (1998) 167,464. *Mining and quarrying* (1997): iron ore 631,500; gold 521,800 troy oz; silver 109,500 troy oz. *Manufacturing* (value added in Col$'000,000; 1996): processed food 9,362,300; beverages 2,485,900; textiles 2,107,300. *Energy production (consumption)*: electricity (kW-hr; 1996) 44,605,000,000 (44,769,000,000); coal (metric tons; 1996) 30,065,000 (4,919,000); petroleum (barrels; 1996) 237,395,000 (113,211,000); petroleum products (metric tons; 1996) 13,310,000 (10,913,000); natural gas (cu m; 1996) 5,674,035,000 (5,674,035,000). **Gross national product** (1999): $90,007,000,000 ($2,170 per capita). **Population economically active** (1998): total 6,550,679 (data relate to the seven largest cities only); activity rate 47.4% (participation rates: ages 15–69, 67.7%; female 45.1%; unemployed 19.7%). **Household income and expenditure.** Average household size (1998) 5.3; sources of income (1992): wages 45.1%, self-employment 35.4%, transfer payments 14.2%; expenditure (1992): food 34.2%, transportation 18.5%, housing 7.8%, health care 6.4%, household durable goods 5.7%, clothing 4.5%.

Foreign trade

Imports (1998): $14,634,000,000 (1997; machinery and transport equipment 41.2%, chemicals 21.0%, vegetable products 7.7%, metals 5.1%, food and tobacco 4.4%, paper and paper products 3.4%). *Major import sources* (1997): US 41.5%; Venezuela 10.0%; Germany 5.0%; Japan 4.3%. **Exports** (1998): $11,362,000,000 (1997; petroleum products 23.5%, coffee 19.6%, chemicals 9.4%, coal 7.7%, food and tobacco 5.9%, textiles and apparel 5.5%). *Major export destinations* (1997): US 37.8%; Venezuela 8.9%; Germany 6.3%; Ecuador 4.7%; Peru 4.7%; Japan 3.1%.

Transport and communications

Transport. *Railroads* (1997): route length 3,230 km; passenger-km (1992) 15,524,000; metric ton-km cargo 736,247,000. *Roads* (1997): total length 115,564 km (paved 12%). *Vehicles* (1996): cars 762,000; trucks 672,000. *Air transport* (1997): passenger-km 5,991,000,000; metric ton-km cargo 836,000,000; *airports* (1998) 43. **Communications** Total units (units per 1,000 persons). Daily newspaper circulation (1996, 26 newspapers only): 1,800,000 (46); Radio receivers (1997): 21,000,000 (524); Television receivers (1999): 8,273,000 (199); Telephone main lines (1999): 6,665,000 (160); Cellular telephone subscribers (1999): 3,134,000 (75); Personal computers (1999): 1,400,000 (34); Internet users (1999): 664,000 (16).

Education and health

Educational attainment (1985). Percentage of pop. age 25 and over having: no schooling 15.3%; primary education 50.1%; secondary 25.4%; higher 6.8%; not stated 2.4%. **Literacy** (1995): pop. age 15 and over literate 91.3%; males literate 91.2%; females literate 91.4%. **Health:** physicians (1997) 40,355 (1 per 1,102 persons); hospital beds 40,043 (1 per 1,000 persons); infant mortality rate (1999) 25.6. **Food** (1999): daily per capita caloric intake 2,567 (vegetable products 83%, animal products 17%); 111% of FAO recommended minimum requirement.

Military

Total active duty personnel (2000): 153,000 (army 85.0%, navy 9.8%, air force 5.2%). **Military expenditure as percentage of GNP** (1997): 3.7% (world 2.6%); per capita expenditure $91.

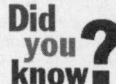

Colombia is a bird watchers' paradise. There are more than 1,550 species of birds recorded, more than in North America and Europe combined. They range from the huge Andean condor to the tiny hummingbird.

Background

The Spanish arrived in what is now Colombia c. 1500 and by 1538 had defeated the area's Chibchan-speaking Indians and made the area subject to the viceroyalty of Peru. After 1740 authority was transferred to the newly created viceroyalty of New Granada. Parts of Colombia threw off Spanish jurisdiction in 1810, and full independence came after Spain's defeat by Simón Bolívar in 1819. Civil war in 1840 checked development. Conflict between the Liberal and Conservative parties led to the War of a Thousand Days (1899–1903). Years of relative peace followed, but hostility erupted again in 1948; the two parties agreed in 1958 to a scheme for alternating governments. A new constitution was adopted in 1991, but democratic power remained threatened by civil unrest. In the early 21st century, many leftist rebels and right-wing paramilitary groups funded their activities through kidnappings and narcotics trafficking.

Recent Developments

Economic uncertainties and the specter of political violence remained major issues in Colombia at the beginning of the 21st century. In February 2002 presidential candidate Ingrid Betancourt was abducted at a roadblock by the Revolutionary Armed Forces of Colombia (FARC), one of the leading guerrilla groups that exercised de facto control over much of the country. The following month the outspoken Roman Catholic archbishop Isaias Duarte Cancino was gunned down outside his church in the city of Cali. In elections in May 2002, Álvaro Uribe Vélez, who campaigned on a strong anticrime platform and vowed to get tough on the guerrillas who have waged war with the government for almost four decades, was convincingly elected president. Uribe, a lawyer educated at Harvard and Oxford, took office in August.

Internet resources: <www.dane.gov.co>

---

1 metric ton = about 1.1 short tons;   1 kilometer = 0.6 mi (statute);   1 metric ton-km cargo = about 0.68 short ton-mi cargo;   c.i.f.: cost, insurance, and freight;   f.o.b.: free on board

Comoros

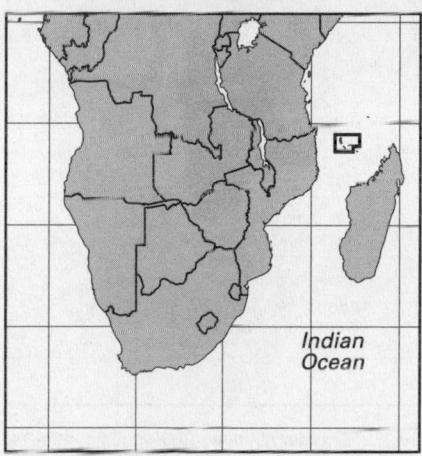

Indian
Ocean

Official name: Federal Islamic Republic of the Comoros (name change to Union of Comoro Islands is pending). **Form of government:** transitional government. **Head of state and government:** Interim President Hamada Madi Bolero (since 2000). **Capital:** Moroni. **Official languages:** Comorian; Arabic; French. **Official religion:** Islam. **Monetary unit:** 1 Comorian franc (CF) = 100 centimes; valuation (28 Jun 2002) $1 = CF 495.41.

Demography

Area: 719 sq mi, 1,862 sq km. **Population** (2001): 566,000 (at least 100,000 Comorians live abroad). **Density** (2001): persons per sq mi 787.5, persons per sq km 304.1. **Urban** (1995): 24.1%. **Sex distribution** (2000): male 49.62%; female 50.38%. **Age breakdown** (2000): under 15, 42.7%; 15–29, 28.6%; 30–44, 15.9%; 45–59, 8.1%; 60–74, 3.9%; 75 and over, 0.8%. **Ethnic composition** (1995): nearly all Comorian (a mixture of Bantu, Arab, Malay, and Malagasy peoples). **Religious affiliation** (2000): Sunni Muslim 98.0%; Christian 1.2%; other 0.8%. **Major cities** (1995): Moroni 34,168; Mutsamudu (1991) 20,000; Domoni (1990) 8,000; Fomboni (1990) 5,600. **Location:** western Indian Ocean, lying between Madagascar and Mozambique.

Vital statistics

Birth rate per 1,000 pop. (2000): 40.0 (world avg. 22.5). **Death rate** per 1,000 pop. (2000): 9.6 (world avg. 9.0). **Natural increase rate** per 1,000 pop. (2000) 30.4 (world avg. 13.5). **Total fertility rate** (avg. births per childbearing woman; 2000): 5.4. **Life expectancy** at birth (2000): male 57.8 years; female 62.2 years.

National economy

Budget (1998). *Revenue:* CF 14,066,000,000 (tax revenue 64.0%, grants 29.4%, nontax revenue 6.6%). *Expenditures:* CF 16,307,000,000 (current expenditures 85.4%, development expenditures 14.6%). **Production** (metric tons except as noted). *Agriculture, forestry, fishing* (1997): coconuts 60,000 (includes Mayotte), bananas 60,000 (1998), cassava 50,700, taro 8,500, corn (maize) 3,800; livestock (number of live animals; 1998) 40,000 goats, 40,000 cattle; fish catch (1997) 12,500. *Mining and quarrying:* sand, gravel, and crushed stone from coral mining for local construction. *Manufacturing:* products of small-scale industries include processed vanilla and ylang-ylang, cement, handicrafts, soaps, soft drinks, woodwork, and clothing. *Energy production (consumption):* electricity (kW-hr; 1999) 34,900,000 (22,000,000); petroleum products (metric tons; 1996) none (22,000). **Population economically active** (1991): total 215,000; activity rate of total pop. 44.4% (participation rates: ages 10 years and over, 57.8%; female 40.0%; unemployed [2000] 20%). **Tourism:** receipts from visitors (1999) $24,700,000; expenditures by nationals abroad (1998) $3,000,000. **Public debt** (external, outstanding; 1999): $179,900,000. **Household income and expenditure.** Average household size (1995) 6.3 (sample data); average annual income per household (1995) CF 188,985; expenditure (1993): food and beverages 67.3%, clothing and footwear 11.6%, tobacco and cigarettes 4.1%, energy 3.8%. **Gross national product** (at current market prices; 1999): U.S.$189,000,000 (U.S.$350 per capita). **Land use** (1994; includes Mayotte): forested 17.9%; meadows and pastures 6.7%; agricultural and under permanent cultivation 44.9%; other 30.5%.

Foreign trade

Imports (1999-c.i.f.): CF 24,929,000,000 (iron and steel 28.5%, rice 18.9%, cement 13.4%, meat and fish 6.1%, petroleum products 5.5%). *Major import sources:* France 32%; South Africa 8%; Réunion 8%; United Arab Emirates 6%; Kenya 6%. **Exports** (1999-f.o.b.): CF 4,248,000,000 (vanilla 43.2%, cloves 27.7%, ylang-ylang 13.3%). *Major export destinations:* United States 26.8%; France 25.4%; Germany 12.2%; Singapore 8.0%.

Transport and communications

Transport. *Railroads:* none. *Roads* (1996): total length 900 km (paved [1995] 76%). *Vehicles* (1996): passenger cars 9,100; trucks and buses 4,950. *Air transport* (1996): passenger-mi 1,900,000, passenger-km 3,000,000; short ton-mi cargo, n.a., metric ton-mi cargo, n.a.; airports (1997) with scheduled flights 2. **Communications** Total units (units per 1,000 persons). Radio receivers (1997): 90,000 (170); television receivers (1997): 1,000 (1.8); Telephone main lines (1999): 6,521 (12).

Education and health

Educational attainment (1980). Percentage of pop. age 25 and over having: no formal schooling 56.7%; Qur'anic school education 8.3%; primary 3.6%; secondary 2.0%; higher 0.2%; not specified 29.2%. **Literacy** (1995; includes Mayotte): total pop. age 15 and over literate 192,000 (57.0%); males literate 108,000 (64.0%); females literate 84,000 (50.0%). **Health** (1995): physicians 64 (1 per 7,800 persons); hospital beds 1,450 (1 per 342 persons); infant mortality rate per 1,000 live births (2000) 86.3. **Food** (1997; includes Mayotte): daily per capita caloric intake 1,800 (vegetable products 94%, animal products 6%); 77% of FAO recommended minimum requirement.

Military

Total active duty personnel (1997): 1,500.

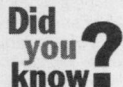

Did you know? The coelacanth, a fish long thought to have been extinct for 65 million years, was discovered in 1938. It is believed that the largest—perhaps the only—population of the fish, which is older than the dinosaurs, exists off the coast of the Comoros.

Background

The islands were known to European navigators from the 16th century. In 1843 France officially took possession of Mayotte and in 1886 placed the other three islands under protection. Subordinated to Madagascar in 1912, the Comoros became an overseas territory of France in 1947. In 1961 they were granted autonomy. In 1974 majorities on three of the islands voted for independence, which was granted in 1975. The following decade saw several coup attempts, culminating in the assassination of the president in 1989. French intervention permitted multiparty elections in 1990, but the country remained in a state of chronic instability. Anjouan seceded from the Comoros federation in 1997. The army took control of the government in 1999.

Recent Developments

Ending the crisis brought about by Anjouan's secession has been a major priority. In 2001 Organization of African Unity envoy José Francisco Madeira Caetano led intensive talks that produced a reconciliation agreement tentatively accepted by federal and Anjouan government officials. The agreement provided greater autonomy for individual island governments but reserved defense and foreign policy for the national government. Disputes ensued, however, over how to implement the agreement provisions.

Internet resources: <travel.state.gov/comoros>

Democratic Republic of the Congo

Official name: République Democratique du Congo (Democratic Republic of the Congo). Form of government: transitional military regime (civil war began in the Dem. Rep. of the Congo in 1998; peace talks were under way from Feb 2002). Chief of state: President Joseph Kabila (from 2001). Capitals: Kinshasa (executive and judicial); Lubumbashi (legislative). Official languages: French; English. Official religion: none. Monetary unit: Congolese franc (FC); valuation (28 Jun 2002) $1 = FC 346.00.

Demography

Area: 905,354 sq mi, 2,344,858 sq km. Population (2001): 53,625,000 (figure includes 1998–2001 war deaths approaching 3 million in the eastern part of the Dem. Rep. of the Congo and an unknown figure in the western part). Density (2001): persons per sq mi 59.2, persons per sq km 22.9. Urban (1999):

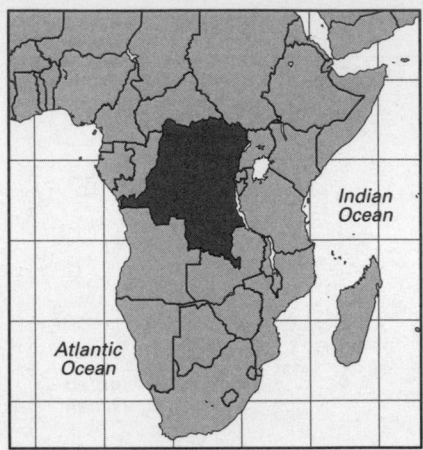

Indian Ocean

Atlantic Ocean

29.9%. **Sex distribution** (2000): male 49.40%; female 50.60%. **Age breakdown** (2000): under 15, 48.3%; 15–29, 26.9%; 30–44, 13.8%; 45–59, 7.0%; 60–74, 3.3%; 75 and over, 0.7%. **Ethnic composition** (1983): Luba 18.0%; Kongo 16.1%; Mongo 13.5%; Rwanda 10.3%; Azande 6.1%; Bangi and Ngale 5.8%; Rundi 3.8%; Teke 2.7%; Boa 2.3%; Chokwe 1.8%; Lugbara 1.6%; Banda 1.4%; other 16.6%. **Religious affiliation** (1995): Roman Catholic 41.0%; Protestant 32.0%; indigenous Christian 13.4%, of which Kimbanguist 13.0%; other Christian 0.8%; Muslim 1.4%; traditional beliefs and other 11.4%. **Major cities** (1994): Kinshasa 4,655,313; Lubumbashi 851,381; Mbuji-Mayi 806,475; Kolwezi 417,800; Kisangani 417,517. **Location:** central Africa, bordering the Central African Republic, The Sudan, Uganda, Rwanda, Burundi, Tanzania, Zambia, Angola, the South Atlantic Ocean, and the Republic of the Congo.

Vital statistics

Birth rate per 1,000 pop. (2000): 46.4 (world avg. 22.5). **Death rate** per 1,000 pop. (2000): 15.4 (world avg. 9.0). **Natural increase rate** per 1,000 pop. (2000): 31.0 (world avg. 13.5). **Total fertility rate** (avg. births per childbearing woman; 2000): 6.9. **Life expectancy** at birth (2000): male 47.6 years; female 50.8 years.

National economy

Budget (1999). *Revenue:* FC 2,328,600,000 (tax revenue 76.9%, of which taxes on international trade 18.5%, taxes on goods and services 13.8%, income tax 12.6%; nontax revenue 12.8%. *Expenditures:* FC 4,113,800,000; wages and salaries 50.5%; defense 14.6%; investment 13.5%; interest on debt 7.2%). **Public debt** (external, outstanding; 1999): $8,188,-000,000. **Tourism** (1997): receipts $9,000,000; expenditures $7,000,000. **Production** (metric tons except as noted). *Agriculture, forestry, fishing* (2000): cassava 15,959,000, plantains 1,800,000, corn (maize) 1,184,000; livestock (number of live animals) 4,131,321 goats, 1,048,710 pigs, 21,559,-000 chickens; roundwood (2000) 50,754,000 cu m;

1 metric ton = about 1.1 short tons;   1 kilometer = 0.6 mi (statute);   1 metric ton-km cargo = about 0.68 short ton-mi cargo;   c.i.f.: cost, insurance, and freight;   f.o.b.: free on board

fish catch (1999) 208,862. *Mining and quarrying* (1000): copper (metal content) 29,600; cobalt (metal content) 1,600; gold 207 kg; diamonds 20,100,000 carats. *Manufacturing* (1999): iron and steel 965,000; cement 172,900; printed fabrics 13,615,000 sq m. *Energy production (consumption):* electricity (kW-hr; 1999) 5,087,000,000 (5,087,- 000,000); coal (metric tons; 1996) 95,000 (140,- 000); crude petroleum (barrels; 1996) 8,403,000 (505,000); petroleum products (metric tons; 1996) 48,000 (459,000). **Household income and expenditure.** Average household size (1998) 2.3; expenditure (1985): food 61.7%, housing and energy 11.5%, clothing and footwear 9.7%, transportation 5.9%, furniture and utensils 4.9%. **Gross national product** (2000): $4,417,000,000 ($85 per capita). **Population economically active** (1997): total 19,618,000; activity rate 42.0% (participation rates [1987]: over age 10, 57.4%; female 43.5%). **Land use** (1994): forested 76.7%; meadows and pastures 6.6%; agricultural and under permanent cultivation 3.5%; other 13.2%.

Foreign trade

Imports (1999): $1,108,000,000 (nonpetroleum 95.0%; petroleum 5.0%). *Major import sources* (1999 est.): South Africa 22%; Belgium 16%; Nigeria 10%; Zambia 5%; France 5%. **Exports** (1999): $933,000,- 000 (diamonds 61.3%, crude petroleum 12.4%, coffee 9.8%, cobalt 8.6%, copper 5.1%). *Major export destinations* (1999): Belgium-Luxembourg 63.8%, US 19.0%; Finland 4.1%; Italy 3.0%.

Transport and communications

Transport. *Railroads:* (1996) length 5,138 km; (1994) passenger-km 29,000,000; (1994) metric ton-km cargo 176,000,000. *Roads* (1996): total length 154,027 km (paved 2%). *Vehicles* (1996): passenger cars 787,000; trucks and buses 60,000. *Air transport* (1996): passenger-km 279,000,000; metric ton-km cargo 42,000,000; airports (1997) with scheduled flights 22. **Communications** Total units (units per 1,000 persons). Daily newspaper circulation (1996): 124,000 (2.7); Radio receivers (1997): 18,030,000 (376); Television receivers (1997): 6,478,000 (135); Telephone main lines (1999): 20,000 (0.4); Cellular telephone subscribers (1999): 10,000 (0.2).

Education and health

Educational attainment: n.a. **Literacy** (1995): percentage of total pop. age 15 and over literate 77.3%; males literate 86.6%; females literate 67.7%. **Health:** physicians (1990) 2,469 (1 per 15,584 persons); hospital beds (1986) 68,508 (1 per 487 persons); infant mortality rate (2000) 101.6. **Food** (1999): daily per capita caloric intake 1,637 (vegetable products 97%, animal products 3%); 72% of FAO recommended minimum requirement.

Military

Total active duty personnel (2001 est.): 79,000 (army 97.1%, navy 1.1%; air force 1.8%); national opposition forces 41,000; assorted foreign forces support both the government and opposition. **Military expenditure as percentage of GNP** (1997): 5.0% (world 2.6%); per capita expenditure $5.

Background

Prior to European colonization, several native kingdoms had emerged in the Congo region, including the 16th-century Luba kingdom and the Kuba federation, which reached its peak in the 18th century. European development began late in the 19th century when King Léopold II of Belgium financed Henry Morton Stanley's exploration of the Congo River. The 1884– 85 Berlin West Africa Conference recognized the Congo Free State with Léopold as its sovereign. The growing demand for rubber helped finance the exploitation of the Congo, but abuses against native peoples outraged Western nations and forced Léopold to grant the Free State a colonial charter as the Belgian Congo (1908). Independence was granted in 1960, and the country's name was changed to Zaire. The post-independence period was marked by unrest, culminating in a military coup that brought Gen. Mobutu Sese Seko to power in 1965. Mismanagement, corruption, and increasing violence devastated the infrastructure and economy. Mobutu was deposed in 1997 by Laurent Kabila, who restored the country's name to Congo. Instability in neighboring countries and desire for Congo's mineral wealth led to military involvement by numerous African countries. Kabila was assassinated in 2001 and succeeded by his son.

Recent Developments

Joseph Kabila's first actions as president impressed Western observers. After undertaking a round of visits to Brussels, Paris, Berlin, London, and Washington DC, he returned to the DRC and replaced corrupt cabinet members with men who appeared better qualified to direct the country's affairs. Kabila also promised free elections and expressed his willingness to negotiate directly with rebel groups.

Internet resources: <www.un.int/drcongo>

Republic of the Congo

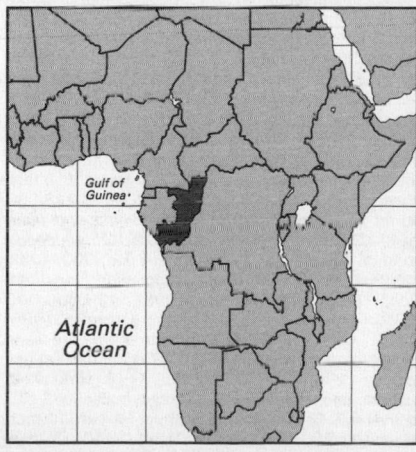

Gulf of Guinea

Atlantic Ocean

Official name: République du Congo (Republic of the Congo). **Form of government:** transitional regime (from Feb 1998 through early 2002) with one legislative house (National Transitional Council [75]). **Chief of state and government:** President Denis Sassou-Nguesso (from 1997). **Capital:** Brazzaville. **Official language:** French (Lingala and Monokutuba are national languages). **Official religion:** none. **Monetary unit:** 1 CFA franc (CFAF) = 100 centimes; valuation (28 Jun 2002) $1 = CFAF 664.20; the CFAF is pegged to the euro (€) at €1 = CFAF 655.96 from 1 Jan 2002.

Demography

Area: 132,047 sq mi, 342,000 sq km. **Population** (2001): 2,894,000. **Density** (2001): persons per sq mi 21.9, persons per sq km 8.5. **Urban** (1999): 61.8%. **Sex distribution** (2000): male 49.17%; female 50.83%. **Age breakdown** (2000): under 15, 42.5%; 15–29, 28.7%; 30–44, 16.1%; 45–59, 7.7%; 60–74, 4.1%; 75 and over, 0.9%. **Ethnic composition** (1983): Kongo 51.5%; Teke 17.3%; Mboshi 11.5%; Mbete 4.9%; Punu 3.0%; Sango 2.7%; Maka 1.8%; Pygmy 1.5%; other 5.8%. **Religious affiliation** (2000): Roman Catholic 49.3%; Protestant 17.0%; African Christian 12.6%; unaffiliated Christian 11.9%; traditional beliefs 4.8%; other 4.4%. **Major cities** (1992): Brazzaville 937,579; Pointe-Noire 576,206; Loubomo 83,605; Nkayi 42,465; Mossendjo 16,405. **Location:** west-central Africa, bordering Cameroon, the Central African Republic, the Dem. Rep. of the Congo, Angola, the South Atlantic Ocean, and Gabon.

Vital statistics

Birth rate per 1,000 pop. (2000): 38.6 (world avg. 22.5). **Death rate** per 1,000 pop. (2000): 16.4 (world avg. 9.0). **Natural increase rate** per 1,000 pop. (2000): 22.2 (world avg. 13.5). **Total fertility rate** (avg. births per childbearing woman; 2000): 5.1. **Life expectancy** at birth (2000): male 44.5 years; female 50.5 years.

National economy

Budget (1999). *Revenue:* CFAF 390,600,000,000 (petroleum revenue 70.6%; nonpetroleum receipts 27.8%; grants 1.6%). *Expenditures:* CFAF 475,400,-000,000 (current expenditure 81.3%, of which debt service 35.4%; salaries 21.2%; transfers and subsidies 5.5%; capital expenditure 18.7%). **Public debt** (external, outstanding; 1999): $3,932,000,000. **Production** (metric tons except as noted). *Agriculture, forestry, fishing* (2000): cassava 790,000, sugarcane 450,000, oil palm fruit 90,000; livestock (number of live animals) 285,000 goats, 116,000 sheep, 77,000 cattle; roundwood (2000) 3,243,000 cu m; fish catch (1999) 43,886. *Mining and quarrying* (1998): gold 10 kg. *Manufacturing* (1998): residual fuel oil 240,000; cement 110,000; distillate fuel oils 85,000. *Energy production (consumption):* electricity (kW-hr; 1998) 408,000,000 (535,000,000); crude petroleum (barrels; 1996) 77,837,000 (11,882,000); petroleum products (metric tons; 1996) 534,000 (507,000); natural gas (cu m; 1996) 3,357,000 (3,357,000). **Household income and expenditure.** Average household size (1984) 5.2. **Gross national product** (at current market prices; 1999): $1,571,000,000 ($550 per capita). **Population economically active** (1997): total 1,110,000; activity rate of total pop. 42.0% (participation rates [1984]: ages 15–64, 54.0%; female [1997] 43.4%). **Land use** (1994): forested 58.3%; meadows and pastures 29.3%; agricultural and under permanent cultivation 0.5%; other 11.9%. **Tourism** (1999): receipts $12,000,000; expenditures $60,000,000.

Foreign trade

Imports (1999): CFAF 378,100,000,000 (machinery and transport equipment 20.8%, basic manufactures 20.1%, food and live animals 20.0%, chemicals and chemical products 14.2%, mineral fuels 12.1%). *Major import sources:* France 23.2%; US 7.8%; Italy 7.8%; Hong Kong 4.9%; Belgium 3.8%. **Exports** (1999): CFAF 1,022,200,000,000 (petroleum and petroleum products 91.9%, wood and wood products 4.3%, other 3.8%). *Major export destinations:* Taiwan 31.5%; US 22.8%; South Korea 15.3%; Germany 6.7%; France 2.6%.

Transport and communications

Transport. *Railroads:* (1998) length 894 km; passenger-km 242,000,000; metric ton-km cargo 135,000,000. *Roads* (1997): total length 12,800 km (paved 10%). *Vehicles* (1997): passenger cars 37,240; trucks and buses 15,500. *Air transport* (1998; 1/11th of Air Afrique traffic): passenger-km 258,272,000; metric ton-km cargo 13,524,000; airports (1998) with scheduled flights 10. **Communications** Total units (units per 1,000 persons). Daily newspaper circulation (1995): 20,000 (7.8); Radio receivers (1997): 341,000 (126); Television receivers (1997): 33,000 (12); Telephone main lines (1999): 22,000 (7.7); Cellular telephone subscribers (1998): 3,390 (1.2).

Education and health

Educational attainment (1984). Percentage of pop. age 25 and over having: no formal schooling 58.7%; primary education 21.4%; secondary education 16.9%; postsecondary 3.0%. **Literacy** (1995): total pop. age 15 and over literate 80.7%; males literate 87.5%; females literate 74.4%. **Health:** physicians (1995) 632 (1 per 4,083 persons); hospital beds (1989) 4,817 (1 per 446 persons); infant mortality rate per 1,000 live births (2000) 101.6. **Food** (1999): daily per capita caloric intake 2,212 (vegetable products 94%, animal products 6%); 100% of FAO recommended minimum requirement.

Military

Total active duty personnel (2000): 8,000 (army 75.0%, navy 10.0%, air force 15.0%). **Military expenditure as percentage of GNP** (1997): 4.1% (world 2.6%); per capita expenditure $28.

Background

In precolonial days the Congo area was home to several thriving kingdoms, including the Kongo, which had its beginnings in the 1st millennium AD. The slave trade began in the 15th century with the arrival of the Portuguese; it supported the local kingdoms

---

1 metric ton = about 1.1 short tons; 1 kilometer = 0.6 mi (statute); 1 metric ton-km cargo = about 0.68 short ton-mi cargo; c.i.f.: cost, insurance, and freight; f.o.b.: free on board

and dominated the area until its suppression in the 19th century. The French arrived in the mid-19th century and established treaties with two of the kingdoms, placing them under French protection prior to becoming part of the colony of French Congo. In 1910 it was renamed French Equatorial Africa and the area of the Congo became known as Middle (Moyen) Congo. In 1946 Middle Congo became a French overseas territory and in 1958 voted to become an autonomous republic within the French Community. Full independence came two years later. The area has suffered from political instability since independence. Congo's first president was ousted in 1963. A Marxist party, the Congolese Labor Party, gained strength, and in 1968 another coup, led by Maj. Marien Ngouabi, created the People's Republic of the Congo. Ngouabi was assassinated in 1977. A series of military rulers followed, at first militantly socialist but later oriented toward social democracy. Fighting between local militias in 1997 badly disrupted the economy; a peace process was under way in 2000.

Recent Developments

The search for national reconciliation seemed threatened in 2002 as fighting erupted between government troops loyal to Pres. Denis Sassou-Nguesso and dissident factions of the rebel force led by Frederic Bintsangou. Sassou-Nguesso had been overwhelmingly confirmed in the March presidential election, though most opposition parties, citing irregularities, had pulled out of the contest.

Internet resources:
<www.cia.gov/cia/publications/factbook/geos/cf.html>

Costa Rica

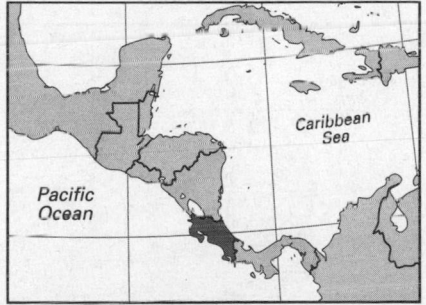

Caribbean Sea

Pacific Ocean

Official name: República de Costa Rica (Republic of Costa Rica). Form of government: unitary multiparty republic with one legislative house (Legislative Assembly [57]). Head of state and government: President Miguel Ángel Rodríguez Echeverría (from 1998). Capital: San José. Official language: Spanish. Official religion: Roman Catholicism. Monetary unit: 1 Costa Rican colón (¢) = 100 céntimos; valuation (28 Jun 2002) $1 = ¢359.24.

Demography

Area: 19,730 sq mi, 51,100 sq km. Population (2001): 3,936,000. Density (2001): persons per sq mi 199.5, persons per sq km 77.0. Urban (1999):

48%. Sex distribution (2000): male 50.04%; female 49.96%. Age breakdown (2000): under 15, 32.1%; 15–29, 27.1%; 30–44, 21.6%; 45–59, 11.7%; 60–74, 5.6%; 75 and over, 1.9%. Ethnic composition (2000): white 77.0%; mestizo 17.0%; black/mulatto 3.0%; East Asian (mostly Chinese) 2.0%; Amerindian 1.0%. Religious affiliation (1995): Roman Catholic 86.0%; Protestant 9.3%, of which Pentecostal 4.9%; other Christian 2.4%; other 2.3%. Major cities/metropolitan areas (1 Jan 2000 est.): San José canton 344,349 (1,082,269); Limón district 61,494; Alajuela district 53,430 (209,098); San Isidro de El General district 45,145; Liberia district 36,407; Cartago (pop. of two districts) 33,539 (303,010); Heredia district 30,968 (258,815). Location: Central America, bordering Nicaragua, the Caribbean Sea, Panama, and the North Pacific Ocean.

Vital statistics

Birth rate per 1,000 pop. (1999): 21.7 (world avg. 22.5); legitimate 51.0%; illegitimate 49.0%. Death rate per 1,000 pop. (1999): 4.2 (world avg. 9.0). Natural increase rate per 1,000 pop. (1999): 17.5 (world avg. 13.5). Total fertility rate (avg. births per childbearing woman; 1999): 2.6. Marriage rate per 1,000 pop. (1999): 7.3. Divorce rate per 1,000 pop. (1995): 1.4. Life expectancy at birth (1999): male 74.2 years; female 79.9 years.

National economy

Budget (1998). Revenue: ¢459,700,000,000 (general sales tax 38.3%, selective taxes on goods and services 21.6%, income and profit taxes 19.3%, import duties 11.0%). Expenditures: ¢562,300,000,000 (current expenditures 91.3%, development expenditures 8.7%). Public debt (external, outstanding; 1999): $3,186,000,000. Gross national product (1999): $12,828,000,000 ($3,570 per capita). Production (metric tons except as noted). Agriculture, forestry, fishing (1999): sugarcane 3,950,000, bananas 2,101,000, oil palm fruit 440,000; livestock (number of live animals) 1,617,000 cattle, 290,000 pigs, 17,000,000 chickens; roundwood (1998) 5,311,000 cu m; fish catch (1997) 33,613, of which shrimp 5,717. Mining and quarrying (1997): limestone 1,500,000; gold 17,700 troy oz. Manufacturing (value added in ¢'000,000; 1996): food products 90,498; beverages 43,101; fertilizers and pesticides 18,360. Energy production (consumption): electricity (kW-hr; 1996) 4,853,000,000 (4,997,000,000); crude petroleum (barrels; 1996) none (4,523,000); petroleum products (metric tons; 1996) 597,000 (1,387,000). Population economically active (1998): total 1,376,540; activity rate of total pop. 41.2% (participation rates: ages 12–59, 59.3%; female 32.6%; unemployed [1999] 6.0%). Tourism (1999): receipts $1,002,000,000; expenditures $428,000,000. Household income and expenditure. Average household size (1997) 4.1; average annual household income (1997) ¢1,468,597; sources of income (1987–88): wages and salaries 61.0%, self-employment 22.6%, transfers 9.6%; expenditure (1987–88): food and beverages 39.1%, housing and energy 12.1%, transportation 11.6%, household furnishings 10.9%. Land use (1994): forested 30.8%; meadows and pastures 45.8%; agricultural and under permanent cultivation 10.4%; other 13.0%.

Foreign trade

Imports (1998-c.i.f., includes goods for reassembly): $6,255,000,000 (raw materials for industry 50.6%, capital goods for industry 14.9%, nondurable consumer goods 11.9%, durable consumer goods 8.6%). *Major import sources* (excludes goods for reassembly): US 38.8%; Japan 7.6%; Mexico 6.9%; Venezuela 3.8%; Guatemala 3.1%. **Exports** (1998-f.o.b.): $3,047,000,000 (bananas 21.8%, coffee 13.3%, processed food and tobacco products 9.3%, fish and shrimp 7.6%, machinery and metal products 6.0%, tropical fruit 5.5%). *Major export destinations* (estimated figures): US 42%; United Kingdom 7%; Germany 7%; The Netherlands 6%; Guatemala 5%.

Transport and communications

Transport. *Roads* (1997): total length 35,597 km (paved 17%). *Vehicles* (1997): passenger cars 294,083; trucks and buses 163,428. *Air transport* (1998, Costa Rican Airlines only): passenger-km 3,487,000,000; metric ton-km cargo 90,378,000; airports (1996) 14. **Communications** Total units (units per 1,000 persons). Daily newspaper circulation (1996): 320,000 (94); Radio receivers (1997): 980,000 (283); Television receivers (1999): 900,000 (242); Telephone main lines (1999): 802,597 (216); Cellular telephone subscribers (1999): 138,727 (37); Personal computers (1999): 400,000 (108); Internet users (1999): 150,000 (40).

Education and health

Educational attainment (1996). Percentage of pop. age 5 and over having: no formal schooling 11.7%; incomplete primary education 28.5%; complete primary 25.8%; incomplete secondary 16.0%; complete secondary 9.0%; higher 8.5%; other/unknown 0.5%. **Literacy** (1995): total pop. age 15 and over literate 2,118,000 (94.8%); males literate 1,054,000 (94.7%); females literate 1,064,000 (95.0%). **Health** (1997): physicians 5,500 (1 per 630 persons); hospital beds 5,953 (1 per 582 persons); infant mortality rate per 1,000 live births (1999) 11.8. **Food** (1999): daily per capita caloric intake 2,761 (vegetable products 82%, animal products 18%); 123% of FAO recommended minimum requirement.

Military

Paramilitary expenditure as percentage of GNP (1997): 0.6% (world 2.6%); per capita expenditure $17. The army was officially abolished in 1948. Paramilitary (police) forces had 8,400 members in 2000.

Did you know? To protect its wildlife and ecosystems, Costa Rica has set aside 21% of its area as national parks and sanctuaries, a greater proportion than any other country in the world. This makes it a favorite destination for birdwatchers and ecotourists.

Background

Christopher Columbus landed in Costa Rica in 1502 in an area inhabited by a number of small, independent Indian tribes. These peoples were not easily dominated, and it took almost 60 years for the Spaniards to establish a permanent settlement. Ignored by the Spanish crown because of its lack of mineral wealth, the colony grew slowly. Coffee exports and the construction of a rail line improved its economy in the 19th century. It joined the short-lived Mexican empire in 1821, was a member of the United Provinces of Central America 1823–38, and adopted a constitution in 1871. In 1890 Costa Ricans held what is considered to be the first free and honest election in Central America, beginning a tradition of democracy for which Costa Rica is renowned. In 1987 then president Oscar Arias Sanchez was awarded the Nobel Peace Prize. During the 1990s Costa Rica struggled with its economic policies. It suffered severe damage from a hurricane in 1996.

Recent Developments

Abel Pacheco of Costa Rica's ruling Social Christian Unity Party continued his party's grip on the presidency by defeating Rolando Araya of the opposition National Liberation Party in a runoff election held in April 2002. Pacheco's victory broke a long tradition of alternation in power between the country's two leading parties. His administration was expected to focus on reversing a sharp decline in economic growth and taming a 10% inflation rate that ranked among the highest in Latin America.

Internet resources: <www.casapres.go.cr>

Côte d'Ivoire

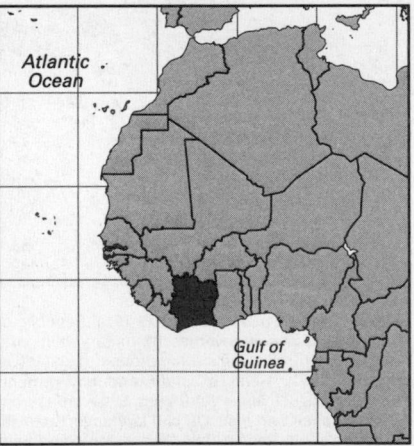

Official name: République de Côte d'Ivoire (Republic of Côte d'Ivoire). **Form of government:** republic with one legislative house (National Assembly [225, including unoccupied seats]); constitutional referen-

---

1 metric ton = about 1.1 short tons;   1 kilometer = 0.6 mi (statute);   1 metric ton-km cargo = about 0.68 short ton-mi cargo;   c.i.f.: cost, insurance, and freight;   f.o.b.: free on board

dum approved Jul 2000, but status of new constitution unclear as of Apr 2002. **Chief of state and government:** President Laurent Gbagbo (from Oct 2000) assisted by a prime minister. **Capital:** Abidjan (de facto; legislative). **Capital designate:** Yamoussoukro (de jure; administrative). **Official language:** French. **Official religion:** none. **Monetary unit:** 1 CFA franc (CFAF) = 100 centimes; valuation (28 Jun 2002) $1 = CFAF 664.20; the CFAF is pegged to the euro (€) at €1 = CFAF 655.96 from 1 Jan 2002.

Demography

Area: 124,504 sq mi, 322,463 sq km. **Population** (2001): 16,393,000. **Density** (2001): persons per sq mi 131.7, persons per sq km 50.8. **Urban** (1998): 45.3%. **Sex distribution** (2000): male 50.84%; female 49.16%. **Age breakdown** (2000): under 15, 46.5%; 15–29, 27.8%; 30–44, 14.5%; 45–59, 7.6%; 60–74, 3.0%; 75 and over, 0.6%. **Ethnolinguistic composition** (1988; data are for Ivoirian nationals only [in 1999 Ivoirian nationals accounted for only c. 60% of de facto population]): Akan 41.8%; Voltaic 16.3%; Malinke 15.9%; Kru 14.6%; Southern Mande 10.7%; other 0.7%. **Religious affiliation** (1988): Muslim 38.7%; Catholic 20.8%; animist 17.0%; nonreligious/atheist 13.4%; Protestant 5.3%, excluding Harrism (1.4%); other 3.4%. **Major cities** (1995): Abidjan (1996) 2,500,000; Bouaké 330,000; Daloa 123,000; Yamoussoukro 110,000. **Location:** western Africa, bordering Mali, Burkina Faso, Ghana, the Atlantic Ocean, Liberia, and Guinea.

Vital statistics

Birth rate per 1,000 pop. (2000): 40.8 (world avg. 22.5). **Death rate** per 1,000 pop. (2000): 16.6 (world avg. 9.0). **Natural increase rate** per 1,000 pop. (2000): 24.2 (world avg. 13.5). **Total fertility rate** (avg. births per childbearing woman; 2000): 5.8. **Life expectancy** at birth (2000): male 43.7 years; female 46.6 years.

National economy

Budget (1997). *Revenue:* CFAF 1,372,100,000,000 (tax revenue 81.1%, of which import taxes and duties 22.7%, export taxes 12.6%, taxes on profits 10.7%, income tax 7.1%; nontax revenue 15.7%; grants 3.2%). *Expenditures:* CFAF 1,191,300,000,000 (wages and salaries 34.3%, capital expenditure 31.3%, debt service 25.5%; other 8.9%). **Production** (metric tons except as noted). *Agriculture, forestry, fishing* (1999): yams 2,923,175, paddy rice 1,161,518, cacao beans 1,153,000; livestock (number of live animals) 1,370,000 sheep, 1,330,000 cattle, 1,070,000 goats; roundwood (1998) 13,283,000 cu m; fish catch (1997) 67,617. *Mining and quarrying* (1997): gold 4,000 kg; diamonds 84,300 carats. *Manufacturing* (value added in CFAF '000,000,000; 1993): meat products 717, chemicals and chemical products 357, cocoa and chocolate 275. *Energy production (consumption):* electricity (kW·hr; 1996) 3,221,000,000 (2,309,000,000); crude petroleum (barrels; 1996) 9,258,000 (31,446,000); petroleum products (metric tons; 1996) 2,192,000 (2,161,000). **Household income and expenditure.** Average household size (1998) 8.0; expenditure (1992–93; for worker's family in Abidjan): food 48.0%, transportation 12.2%, clothing 10.1%, energy and water 8.5%, housing 7.8%, house-

hold equipment 3.4%. **Population economically active** (1997): total 5,684,000; activity rate of total pop. 37.7% (participation rates: [1994] over ages 10, 64.3%; female 33.0%). **Gross national product** (1999): $10,387,000,000 ($670 per capita). **Public debt** (external, outstanding; 1999): $9,699,000,000. **Tourism** (1998): receipts $108,000,000; expenditures $237,000,000.

Foreign trade

Imports (1997): CFAF 1,602,000,000,000 (food and food products 19.4%, machinery and transport equipment 18.6%, crude and refined petroleum 18.5%, plastics 4.6%, iron and steel products 4.4%). *Major import sources* (1995): France 32.0%; Nigeria 19.6%; U.S. 5.9%; Ghana 4.0%; Germany 3.9%. **Exports** (1997): CFAF 2,379,000,000,000 (cocoa beans and products 33.5%, petroleum products 16.8%, coffee and coffee products 7.3%, wood and wood products 7.0%, fish products 5.3%). *Major export destinations:* France 17.3%; The Netherlands 13.2%; United States 7.6%; Italy 5.3%; Mali 4.9%; Germany 4.8%.

Transport and communications

Transport. *Railroads* (1995): route length 639 km; passenger-km 129,000,000; metric ton-km cargo 58,000,000. *Roads* (1996): total length 50,400 km (paved 9.7%). *Vehicles* (1996): passenger cars 293,000; trucks and buses 163,000. *Air transport* (1990): passenger-km 307,000,000; metric ton-km cargo 44,000,000; airports (1998) 5. **Communications** Total units (units per 1,000 persons). Daily newspaper circulation (1996): 231,000 (17); Radio receivers (1998): 1,600,000 (97); Television receivers (1998): 1,000,000 (65); Telephone main lines (1999): 219,283 (14); Cellular telephone subscribers (1999): 257,134 (16); Personal computers (1999): 80,000 (5.1); Internet users (1999): 20,000 (1.3).

Education and health

Educational attainment (1988). Percentage of pop. age 6 and over having: no formal schooling 60.0%; Koranic school 3.6%; primary education 24.8%; secondary 10.7%; higher 0.9%. **Literacy** (1995): percentage of pop. age 15 and over literate 40.1%; males 49.9%; females 30.0%. **Health:** physicians (1996) 1,318 (1 per 11,111 persons); hospital beds (1993) 7,928 (1 per 1,698 persons); infant mortality rate (2000) 95.1. **Food** (1999): daily per capita caloric intake 2,582 (vegetable products 97%, animal products 3%); 112% of FAO recommended minimum requirement.

Military

Total active duty personnel (2000): 8,400 (army 81.0%, navy 10.7%, air force 8.3%); French troops (2001) 680. **Military expenditure as percentage of GNP** (1997): 1.1% (world avg. 2.6%); per capita expenditure $7.

Background

Europeans came to the area to trade in ivory and slaves beginning in the 15th century, and local kingdoms gave way to French influence in the 19th century. The French colony of Côte d'Ivoire was founded in 1893, and full occupation took place 1908–18. In 1946 it became a territory in the French Union. Côte d'Ivoire achieved independence in 1960, when Félix Houphouët-Boigny was elected president. The country's first multiparty presidential elections were held in 1990.

Recent Developments

Pres. Henri Konan Bédié was ousted in a bloodless military coup by Brig. Gen. Robert Gueï in December 1999. Tensions remained high through 2000, and the year's presidential elections resulted in violence when Gueï lost to opponent Laurent Gbagbo but attempted to remain in office by halting the vote count. Gueï went into hiding, and Gbagbo assumed office. Violent demonstrations also accompanied the parliamentary elections and continued throughout 2001. Traffickers were arrested in neighboring countries for selling thousands of children into slavery on Ivorian cocoa farms. The government accused multinational chocolate companies of keeping cocoa prices low, leading impoverished farmers to use slave labor.

Internet resources: <www.tourisme.ci>

Croatia

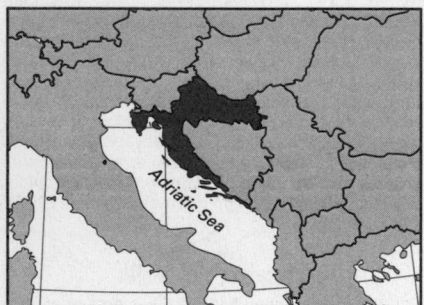

Official name: Republika Hrvatska (Republic of Croatia). **Form of government:** multiparty republic with one legislative house (House of Representatives [151—six seats represent Croatians living abroad]). **Head of state:** President Stipe Mesic (from 2000). **Head of government:** Prime Minister Ivica Racan (from 2000). **Capital:** Zagreb. **Official language:** Croatian (Serbo-Croatian). **Official religion:** none. **Monetary unit:** 1 kuna (HrK; plural kune) = 100 lipa; valuation (28 Jun 2002) $1 = HrK 7.42.

Demography

Area: 56,542 sq km. **Population** (2001): 4,393,000. **Density** (2001): persons per sq mi 201.3, persons per sq km 77.7. **Urban** (2000): 57.7%. **Sex distribution** (2000): male 48.58%; female 51.42%. **Age breakdown** (2000): under 15, 18.0%; 15–29, 20.1%; 30–44, 21.6%; 45–59, 19.6%; 60–74, 15.4%; 75 and over, 5.3%. **Ethnic composition** (2000): Croat 82.0%; Serb 5.9%; other 12.1%. **Religious affiliation** (2000): Christian 95.2%, of which Roman Catholic 88.5%, Eastern Orthodox 5.6%, Protestant 0.6%; Sunni Muslim 2.3%; nonreligious/atheist 2.5%. **Major cities** (1991): Zagreb (2000) 770,058; Split 200,459; Rijeka 167,964; Osijek 129,792; Zadar 76,343. **Location:** southeastern Europe, bordering Slovenia, Hungary, Yugoslavia, Bosnia and Herzegovina, and the Adriatic Sea.

Vital statistics

Birth rate per 1,000 pop. (1999): 9.9 (world avg. 22.5); legitimate 91.8%; illegitimate 8.2%. **Death rate** per 1,000 pop. (1999): 11.4 (world avg. 9.0). **Natural increase rate** per 1,000 pop. (1999): –1.5 (world avg. 13.5). **Total fertility rate** (avg. births per childbearing woman; 2000): 1.9. **Marriage rate** per 1,000 population (1999): 5.2. **Divorce rate** per 1,000 population (1999): 0.8. **Life expectancy** at birth (2000): male 70.0 years; female 77.5 years.

National economy

Budget (1999). *Revenue:* HrK 67,907,000,000 (sales tax 34.1%, social security 32.2%, excise taxes 9.5%). *Expenditures:* HrK 70,358,000,000 (social security and welfare 37.8%, health 14.0%, defense 7.7%, education 7.4%). **Population economically active** (1991): total 2,040,000; activity rate 42.6% (participation rates: ages 15–64, 61.1%; female 42.8%; unemployed [March 1998] 17.4%). **Production** (metric tons except as noted). *Agriculture, forestry, fishing* (1999): corn (maize) 2,135,000, sugar beets 1,114,000, potatoes 729,000, wheat 558,000, grapes 394,000; livestock (number of live animals) 1,362,000 pigs, 489,000 sheep, 439,000 cattle; roundwood (1998) 3,398,000 cu m; fish catch (1997) 19,885. *Mining and quarrying* (1998): gypsum 100,000; ferrochromium 15,000. *Manufacturing* (value added in $'000,000; 1996): food products 895; transport equipment 425; electrical machinery 362; textiles 285; wearing apparel 260. *Energy production (consumption):* electricity (kW-hr; 1998) 10,356,000,000 ([1996] 12,878,000,000); hard coal (metric tons; 1998) 48,000 ([1996] 117,000); lignite (metric tons; 1996) 2,000 (149,000); crude petroleum (barrels; 1998) 8,532,000 ([1996] 38,248,000); petroleum products (metric tons; 1996) 4,500,000 (3,393,000); natural gas (cu m; 1998) 1,566,000,000 ([1996] 2,584,000,000). **Gross national product** (1999): $20,222,000,000 ($4,530 per capita). **Public debt** (external, outstanding; 1999): $5,433,000,000. **Household income and expenditure.** Average household size (1991) 3.1; income per household (1990) Din 165,813; sources (1990): self-employment 40.8%, wages 40.2%, transfers 12.1%, other 6.9%; expenditure (1988): food 34.2%, transportation 9.3%, clothing 8.6%, housing 8.3%, energy 7.6%, drink and tobacco 5.1%, durable goods 4.5%, health care 4.3%. **Tourism** (1999): receipts from visitors $2,493,000,000; expenditures by nationals abroad $751,000,000. **Land use** (1994): forest 37.1%; pasture 19.3%; agriculture 21.6%; other 22.0%.

Foreign trade

Imports (1998-c.i.f.): $8,383,000,000 (machinery and transport equipment 35.2%; chemicals and

---

1 metric ton = about 1.1 short tons;   1 kilometer = 0.6 mi (statute);   1 metric ton-km cargo = about 0.68 short ton-mi cargo;   c.i.f.: cost, insurance, and freight;   f.o.b.: free on board

chemical products 11.7%; food and live animals 8.1%; mineral fuels and lubricants 7.1%). *Major import sources:* Germany 19.2%; Italy 17.9%; Slovenia 8.6%; Austria 7.3%; France 4.8%. **Exports** (1998-f.o.b.): $4,541,000,000 (machinery and transport equipment 30.4%; clothing 12.2%; chemical and chemical products 12.7%; food 8.4%; mineral fuels and lubricants 5.8%). *Major export destinations:* Italy 17.7%; Germany 16.9%; Bosnia and Herzegovina 14.4%; Slovenia 9.5%; Austria 5.4%.

Transport and communications

Transport. *Railroads* (1997): length 2,726 km; passenger-km 981,000,000; metric ton-km cargo 1,876,000,000. *Roads* (1997): total length 27,840 km (paved 82%). *Vehicles* (1997): passenger cars 932,278; trucks and buses 114,505. *Air transport* (1997): passenger-km 546,000,000; metric ton-km cargo 2,997,000; airports (1997) 4. **Communications** Total units (units per 1,000 persons). Daily newspaper circulation (1996): 515,000 (118); Radio receivers (1997): 1,510,000 (350); Television receivers (1998): 1,250,000 (293); Telephone main lines (1999): 1,634,000 (384); Cellular telephone subscribers (1999): 295,000 (69); Personal computers (1999): 300,000 (71); Internet users (1999): 200,000 (47).

Education and health

Educational attainment (1991). Percentage of pop. age 15 and over having: no schooling or unknown 10.1%; less than full primary education 21.2%; primary 23.4%; secondary 36.0%; postsecondary and higher 9.3%. **Literacy** (1995): pop. age 15 and over literate 98.3%; males 99.4%; females 97.3%. **Health** (1997): physicians 9,315 (1 per 501 persons); hospital beds 27,472 (1 per 170 persons); infant mortality rate per 1,000 live births (2000) 7.4. **Food** (1999): daily per capita caloric intake 2,617 (vegetable products 81%, animal products 19%); 103% of FAO recommended minimum requirement.

Military

Total active duty personnel (2000): 61,000 (army 86.9%, navy 4.9%, air force and air defense 8.2%). **Military expenditure as percentage of GNP** (1997): 6.3% (world 2.6%); per capita expenditure $345.

Background

The Croats, a southern Slavic people, arrived in the area in the 7th century AD, and in the 8th century came under Charlemagne. They converted to Christianity soon afterward and formed a kingdom in the 10th century. Most of Croatia was taken by the Turks in 1526; the rest voted to accept Austrian rule. In 1867 it became part of the Austro-Hungarian empire, with Dalmatia and Istria ruled by Vienna and Croatia-Slavonia a Hungarian crown land. In 1918, after the defeat of Austria-Hungary in World War I, it joined other south Slav territories to form the Kingdom of Serbs, Croats, and Slovenes, renamed Yugoslavia in 1929. In World War II, an independent state of Croatia was established by Germany and Italy, embracing Croatia-Slavonia, part of Dalmatia, and Bosnia and Herzegovina; after the war Croatia was rejoined to Yugoslavia as a people's republic. It declared its independence in 1991, sparking insur-

rections by Croatian Serbs, who carved out autonomous regions with Serbian-led Yugoslav army help; Croatia had taken back most of these regions by 1995. With some stability returning, Croatia's economy began to revive in the late 1990s.

Recent Developments

In 2000 the defeat of the ruling Croatian Democratic Union, which had firmly governed the former Yugoslav republic since independence in 1991, was a watershed in the country's relations with the international community and signaled the beginning of real, if difficult, domestic reforms. A coalition of six opposition political parties led by the center-left Social Democratic Party of Croatia and the center-right Croatian Social-Liberal Party swept the parliamentary elections, taking 71 of 151 seats. In October 2001 former Yugoslav president Slobodan Milosevic was indicted by the UN International Criminal Tribunal for Former Yugoslavia for war crimes in Croatia in 1991–92.

Internet resources: <www.mint.hr>

Cuba

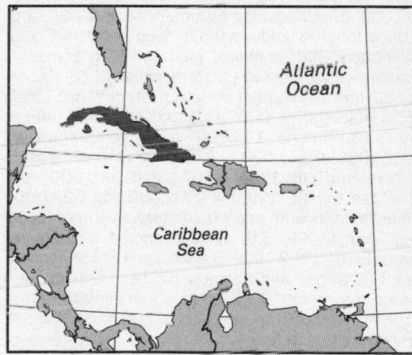

Official name: República de Cuba (Republic of Cuba). **Form of government:** unitary socialist republic with one legislative house (National Assembly of the People's Power [601]). **Head of state and government:** President Fidel Castro (from 1976). **Capital:** Havana. **Official language:** Spanish. **Official religion:** none. **Monetary unit:** 1 Cuban peso (CUP) = 100 centavos; valuation (28 Jun 2002) $1 = 21.00 CUP.

Demography

Area: 42,804 sq mi, 110,861 sq km. **Population** (2001): 11,190,000. **Density** (2001): persons per sq mi 261.4, persons per sq km 100.9. **Urban** (1999): 75.2%. **Sex distribution** (2000): male 50.00%; female 50.00%. **Age breakdown** (2000): under 15, 21.4%; 15–29, 22.7%; 30–44, 26.2%; 45–59, 16.1%; 60–74, 9.2%; 75 and over, 4.4%. **Ethnic composition** (1994): mixed 51.0%; white 37.0%; black 11.0%; other 1.0%. **Religious affiliation** (1995): Roman Catholic 39.5%; Protestant 2.4%; other Christian 0.2%; other (mostly Santería) 57.9%. **Major cities** (1993): Havana 2,175,995; Santiago de Cuba 440,084; Camagüey 293,961; Holguín 242,085; Guantánamo 207,796. **Location:** island southeast of Florida, US, between the North Atlantic and the Caribbean Sea.

Vital statistics

Birth rate per 1,000 pop. (2000): 12.7 (world avg. 22.5). **Death rate** per 1,000 pop. (2000): 7.3 (world avg. 9.0). **Natural increase rate** per 1,000 pop. (2000): 5.4 (world avg. 13.5). **Total fertility rate** (avg. births per childbearing woman; 2000): 1.6. **Marriage rate** per 1,000 pop. (1999): 5.1. **Divorce rate** per 1,000 pop. (1993): 6.0. **Life expectancy** at birth (2000): male 73.8 years; female 78.3 years.

National economy

Budget (1999). *Revenue:* CUP 13,575,000,000. *Expenditures:* CUP 14,270,000,000 (education and health 26.5%; investment 11.9%; other 61.6%). **Public debt** (external, outstanding; 1999): $11,078,-000,000. **Production** (metric tons except as noted). *Agriculture, forestry, fishing* (2000): sugarcane 36,000,000, rice 368,770, oranges and tangerines 447,000, potatoes 344,215, plantains 329,000; livestock (number of live animals) 4,700,000 cattle, 2,800,000 pigs, 15,000,000 chickens; roundwood (2000) 1,593,000 cu m; fish catch (1999) 122,425. *Mining and quarrying* (1998): nickel 67,700; chromite 30,000. *Manufacturing* (value added in $'000,000; 1990): tobacco products 2,629; food products 1,033; beverages 358; chemical products 354; transport equipment 225; nonelectrical machinery 176. *Energy production (consumption):* electricity (kW-hr; 1996) 13,236,000,000 (13,236,000,000); coal (metric tons; 1996) none (163,000); crude petroleum (barrels; 1996) 9,377,000 (9,899,000); petroleum products (metric tons; 1996) 4,767,000 (8,240,000); natural gas (cu m; 1996) 43,002,000 (43,002,000). **Household income and expenditure.** Average household size (1999) 3.6; average annual income per household (1982) CUP 3,680; sources of income (1982): wages and salaries 57.3%, bonuses and other payments 42.7%; personal consumption (1989): food 26.7%, other retail purchases 60.5%, transportation services 5.4%, energy 2.7%, value of self-produced and consumed food 1.5%, household repairs 1.3%, other 1.9%. **Population economically active** (1988): total 4,570,236; activity rate of total pop. 43.7% (participation rates: over age 15, 56.9%; female [1998] 37.0%; unemployed [1998] 6.0%). **Gross domestic product** (1999): $18,600,000,000 ($1,700 per capita). **Tourism:** receipts from visitors (1999) $1,714,000,000; expenditures by nationals abroad (1990) $48,000,000. **Land use** (1994): forested 23.7%; meadows and pastures 27.0%; agricultural and under permanent cultivation 30.7%; other 18.6%.

Foreign trade

Imports (1999-c.i.f.): $3,200,000,000 (1996; mineral fuels and lubricants 27.9%, food and live animals 19.8%, machinery and transport equipment 16.1%, basic manufactures 14.9%, chemicals 8.7%, inedible crude materials 2.8%). *Major import sources* (1999): Spain 19.5%; France 8.2%; Canada 8.1%; China 7.7%; Italy 7.0%; Russia 3.8%. **Exports** (1999-f.o.b.): $1,400,000,000 (1996; sugar 52.8%, minerals and

concentrates 23.7%, fish products 6.8%, raw tobacco and tobacco products 5.9%, citrus and other agricultural products 2.1%). *Major export destinations* (1999): Russia 23.3%; Canada 14.5%; The Netherlands 12.9%; Spain 8.0%; China 3.6%.

Transport and communications

Transport. *Railroads* (1999): length 4,807 km; (1997) passenger-km 1,962,200; metric ton-km cargo 1,074,800,000. *Roads* (1997): total length 60,858 km (paved 49%). *Vehicles* (1998): passenger cars 172,574; trucks and buses 185,495. *Air transport* (1997): passenger-km 3,543,176,000; metric ton-km cargo 56,239,000; airports with scheduled flights (1999) 14. **Communications** Total units (units per 1,000 persons). Daily newspaper circulation (1996): 1,300,000 (118); Radio receivers (1997): 3,900,000 (352); Television receivers (1999): 2,750,000 (246); Telephone main lines (1999): 434,000 (39); Cellular telephone subscribers (1999): 5,136 (0.5); Personal computers (1999): 110,000 (9.9); Internet users (1999): 34,800 (3.1).

Education and health

Educational attainment (1981). Percentage of pop. age 25 and over having: no formal schooling or some primary education 39.6%; completed primary 26.6%; secondary 29.6%; higher 4.2%. **Literacy** (1995): total pop. age 15 and over literate 95.7%; males 96.2%; females 95.3%. **Health** (1998): physicians 63,554 (1 per 175 persons); hospital beds 80,684 (1 per 123 persons); infant mortality rate per 1,000 live births (2000) 7.5. **Food** (1999): daily per capita caloric intake 2,490 (vegetable products 86%, animal products 14%); 108% of FAO recommended minimum requirement.

Military

Total active duty personnel (2000): 58,000 (army 77.6%, navy 5.2%, air force 17.2%). **Military expenditure as percentage of GDP** (1997): 2.3% (world 2.6%); per capita expenditure: $65.

Did you know? Cuba has developed a health care system that is well-respected throughout the world. Its infant mortality rate is the lowest in Latin America.

Background

Several Indian groups, including the Ciboney, the Taino, and the Arawak, inhabited Cuba at the time of the first Spanish contact. Christopher Columbus claimed the island for Spain in 1492, and the Spanish conquest began in 1511, when the settlement of Baracoa was founded. The native Indians were eradicated over the succeeding centuries, and African slaves, from the 18th century until slavery was abolished in 1886, were imported to work the sugar plantations. Cuba revolted unsuccessfully against Spain in the Ten Years' War (1868–78); a second war of independence began in 1895. In 1898

---

1 metric ton = about 1.1 short tons;   1 kilometer = 0.6 mi (statute);   1 metric ton-km cargo = about 0.68 short ton-mi cargo;   c.i.f.: cost, insurance, and freight;   f.o.b.: free on board

the US entered the war; Spain relinquished its claim to Cuba, which was occupied by the US for three years before gaining its independence in 1902. The US invested heavily in the Cuban sugar industry in the first half of the 20th century, and this, combined with tourism and gambling, caused the economy to prosper. Inequalities in the distribution of wealth persisted, however, as did political corruption. In 1958–59 the communist revolutionary Fidel Castro overthrew its longtime dictator Fulgencio Batista and established a socialist state aligned with the Soviet Union, abolishing capitalism and nationalizing foreign-owned enterprises. Relations with the US deteriorated, reaching a low point with the 1961 Bay of Pigs invasion and the 1962 Cuban missile crisis. In 1980 about 125,000 Cubans, including many officially labeled "undesirables" were shipped to the US in the so-called Mariel Boat Lift. When communism collapsed in the USSR, Cuba lost important financial backing and its economy suffered greatly. The latter gradually improved in the 1990s with the encouragement of tourism, though diplomatic relations with the US were not resumed.

Recent Developments

Owing to its internal politics, Cuba often remains isolated from important international events. It was the only country in the Americas not invited to the third Summit of the Americas in Quebec City in 2001. International human rights groups as well as press-freedom organizations continue to condemn Cuba's record on free speech and harassment of dissidents. Despite tension in Cuban-American relations in recent years, there have been a few hopeful signs. In July 2001 the Bush administration oversaw new regulations that would allow limited agricultural sales to Cuba for the first time in the 40-year-long embargo, and in 2002 former US president Jimmy Carter led a delegation to Cuba for the purpose of fostering an exchange of ideas between the two countries. Carter was the first former US president to visit the island since the US broke off relations with the Caribbean nation in 1961.

Internet resources: <www.cubatravel.cu>

Cyprus

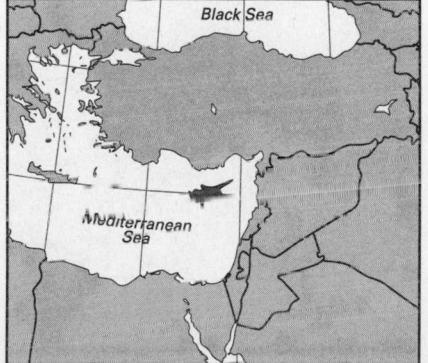

Two de facto states currently exist on the island of Cyprus: the Republic of Cyprus (ROC), predominantly Greek in character, occupying the southern two-thirds of the island, which is the original and still the internationally recognized de jure government of the whole island; and the Turkish Republic of Northern Cyprus (TRNC), proclaimed unilaterally 15 Nov 1983, on territory originally secured for the Turkish Cypriot population by the 20 Jul 1974 intervention of Turkey. Only Turkey recognizes the TRNC. The two ethnic communities have failed to reestablish a single state. Provision of separate data below does not imply recognition of either state's claims, but unified data is not collected for the whole island.

Area: 3,572 sq mi, 9,251 sq km. **Population** (2001): 873,000 (includes 75,000 "settlers" from Turkey and 31,000 Turkish military in the TRNC; excludes 3,200 British military in the Sovereign Base Areas (SBA) in the ROC and 1,300 UN peacekeeping forces). **Location:** Middle East, island in the Mediterranean Sea, south of Turkey.

Republic of Cyprus

Background

Cyprus was inhabited by the early Neolithic Age; by the late Bronze Age it had been visited and settled by Mycenaeans and Achaeans, who introduced Greek culture and language, and it became a trading center. By 800 BC Phoenicians had begun to settle there. Ruled over the centuries by the Assyrian, Persian, and Ptolemaic empires, it was annexed by Rome in 58 BC. It was part of the Byzantine empire in the 4th–12th centuries AD. It was conquered by Richard I in 1191. A part of the Venetian empire from 1489, it was taken by Ottoman Turks in 1571. In 1878 the British assumed control, and Cyprus became a British crown colony in 1925. It gained independence in 1960. Conflict between Greek and Turkish Cypriots led to the establishment of a UN peacekeeping mission in 1964. In 1974, fearing a movement to unite Cyprus with Greece, Turkish soldiers occupied the northern third of the country and Turkish Cypriots established a functioning government, which obtained recognition only from Turkey. Conflict has continued to the present, and the UN peacekeeping mission has remained in place. Reunification talks have remained deadlocked.

Recent Developments

Greek Cyprus reported in 2001 that it had provisionally completed two-thirds of the accession requirements for European Union membership. Completion of the requirements was expected in 2002, with full membership in 2003. In May 2001 the European Court of Human Rights found Turkey guilty of human rights violations when it invaded northern Cyprus in 1974, a finding rejected by both Turkey and Turkish Cyprus.

Official name: Kipriakí Dhimokratía (Greek); Kibris Cumhuriyeti (Turkish) (Republic of Cyprus). **Form of government:** unitary multiparty republic with a unicameral legislature (House of Representatives [80]; 24 seats reserved for Turkey Cypriots are not occupied). **Head of state and government:** President Glafcos Clerides (from 1993). **Capital:** Lefkosa (Nicosia). **Official languages:** Greek; Turkish. **Monetary unit:** 1 Cyprus pound (£C) = 100 cents; valuation (28 Jun 2002) 1 £C = $1.69.

Demography

Area (includes 99 sq mi [256 sq km] of British military SBA and c. 107 sq mi [c. 278 sq km] of the UN Buffer Zone): 2,276 sq mi, 5,896 sq km. **Population** (2001): 675,000. **Urban** (1999): 68.9%. **Age breakdown** (1999): under 15, 23.8%; 15–29, 21.5%; 30–44, 22.3%; 45–59, 17.2%; 60–74, 10.6%; 75 and over, 4.6%. **Ethnic composition** (2000): Greek Cypriot 91.8%; Armenian 3.3%; Arab 2.9%, of which Lebanese 2.5%; British 1.4%; other 0.6%. **Religious affiliation** (1995): Greek Orthodox 93.4%; Armenian Apostolic 2.9%; Roman Catholic 1.5%; Muslim 1.0%; other 1.2%. **Urban areas** (1999): Lefkosia 195,000; Limassol 154,400; Larnaca 68,500.

Vital statistics

Birth rate per 1,000 pop. (1999): 12.8 (world avg. 22.5). **Death rate** per 1,000 pop. (1999): 7.6 (world avg. 9.0). **Natural increase rate** per 1,000 pop. (1999): 5.2 (world avg. 13.5). **Life expectancy** at birth (1998–99): male 75.3 years; female 80.1 years.

National economy

Budget (1998). *Revenue:* £C 1,473,900,000 (income taxes 19.7%, value-added taxes 15.3%, social security contributions 14.9%). *Expenditures:* £C 1,731,500,000 (current expenditures 89.7%, development expenditures 10.3%). **Tourism** (1999): receipts $1,885,000,000; expenditures $289,000,-000. **Household expenditure** (1994): food and beverages 23.0%, transportation and communications 14.5%, expenditures in cafés and hotels 14.5%. **Gross national product** (at current market prices; 1999): $9,086,000,000 ($11,950 per capita). **Production.** *Agriculture* (in '000 metric tons; 1997): grapes 101.0, potatoes 81.5, oranges 50.5. *Manufacturing* (value added in £C '000,000; 1996): food 84.7; cement, bricks, and tiles 48.2. *Energy production:* electricity (kW-hr; 1998) 2,954,000,000.

Foreign trade

Imports (1998-c.i.f.): £C 1,904,700,000 (consumer goods 34.2%; transport equipment 12.9%; capital goods 11.2%; mineral fuels 6.6%). *Major import sources:* US 12.5%; UK 11.3%; Italy 9.4%; Germany 8.5%; Greece 8.2%. **Exports** (1998-f.o.b.): £C 551,134,000 (reexports 55.6%; domestic exports 38.7%, of which clothing 5.3%, chemicals 5.2%; ships' stores 5.7%). *Major export destinations:* UK 14.6%; Russia 10.3%, Greece 9.8%; Lebanon 5.5%; United Arab Emirates 4.9%.

Transport and communications

Transport. *Roads* (1997): total length 10,654 km (paved 58%). *Vehicles* (1997): cars 234,976; trucks and buses 108,452. *Air transport* (1998; Cyprus Airways): passenger-km 2,711,000,000; metric ton-km cargo 38,158,000; airports (1996) 2. **Communications** Total units (units per 1,000 persons). Daily newspapers circulation (1996; Island of Cyprus): 84,000 (111); Radio receivers (1997; Island of Cyprus): 310,000 (406); Television receivers (1999):

120,000 (180); Telephone main lines (1999): 421,600 (634); Cellular telephone subscribers (1999): 151,649 (228); Personal computers (1999): 130,000 (195); Internet users (1999): 88,000 (132).

Education and health

Educational attainment (1997). Percentage of pop. age 20 and over having: no formal schooling 4%; higher education 17%. **Health** (1997): physicians 1,725 (1 per 379 persons); hospital beds 3,113 (1 per 210 persons); infant mortality rate per 1,000 live births (2000) 8.1.

Turkish Republic of Northern Cyprus

Official name: Kuzey Kibris Türk Cumhuriyeti (Turkish) (Turkish Republic of Northern Cyprus). **Capital:** Lefkosa (Nicosia). **Official language:** Turkish. **Monetary unit:** 1 Turkish lira (LT) = 100 kurush; valuation (28 Jun 2002) $1 = LT 1,585,500. **Population** (2001): 198,000 (1996 census Lefkosa 36,834; Gazimagusa 23,295). **Ethnic composition** (1996): Turkish Cypriot/Turkish 96.4%; other 3.6%. **Budget** (1998). *Revenue:* $406,200,000 (aid from Turkey 33.3%, direct taxes 25.2%, indirect taxes 19.8%, loans 7.3%). *Expenditures:* $406,200,000 (investments 13.6%, defense 10.4%, other 76.0%). **Imports** (1998): $390,100,000 (transport equipment 18.6%, prepared foodstuffs 12.3%). *Major import sources:* Turkey 59.3%; UK 12.8%. **Exports** (1998): $53,400,000 (ready-made garments 40.2%, citrus fruits 24.0%). *Major export destinations:* Turkey 50.7%; UK 30.9%. **Health** (1998): physicians 451 (1 per 416 persons); hospital beds 1,002 (1 per 187 persons); infant mortality rate per 1,000 live births 5.8.

Internet resources:
<www.cyprustourism.org> (Republic of Cyprus); <www.trncwashdc.org> (Turkish Republic of Northern Cyprus)

Czech Republic

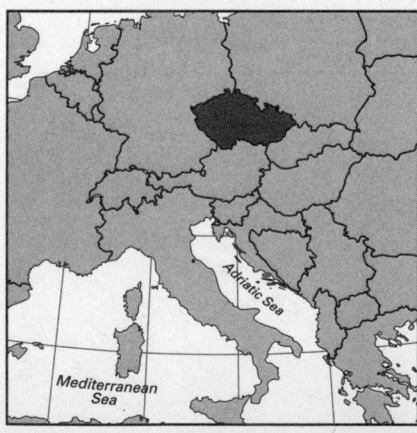

Official name: Ceska Republika. Form of government: unitary multiparty republic with two legislative houses (Senate [81]; Chamber of Deputies [200]). Chief of state: President Vaclav Havel (from 1993). Head of government: Prime Minister Vladimir Spidla (from 12 Jul 2002). Capital: Prague. Official language: Czech. Official religion: none. Monetary unit: 1 koruna (Kc) = 100 halura; valuation (28 Jun 2002) $1 = 29.58 Kc.

Demography

Area: 78,866 sq mi, 10,272,939 sq km. Population (2001): 10,269,000. Density (2001): persons per sq mi 337.2, persons per sq km 130.2. Urban (1999): 74.6%. Sex distribution (2000): male 48.66%; female 51.34%. Age breakdown (2000): under 15, 16.6%; 15–29, 23.5%; 30–44, 20.2%; 45–59, 21.5%; 60–74, 12.8%; 75 and over, 5.4%. Ethnic composition (1991): Czech 81.2%; Moravian 13.2%; Slovak 3.1%; Polish 0.6%; German 0.5%; Silesian 0.4%; Gypsy 0.3%; Hungarian 0.2%; Ukrainian 0.1%; other 0.4%. Religious affiliation (1991): Catholic 40.9%, of which Roman Catholic 39.0%, Hussite Church of the Czech Republic 1.7%; Protestant 2.5%, of which Evangelical Church of Czech Brethren 2.0%; not stated 16.2%; nonreligious/other 40.4%. Major cities (2000): Prague 1,186,855; Brno 383,569; Ostrava 321,263; Plzen 167,534; Olomouc 103,015. Location: central Europe, bordering Germany, Poland, Slovakia, and Austria.

Vital statistics

Birth rate per 1,000 pop. (1999): 8.7 (world avg. 22.5); legitimate 79.4%; illegitimate 20.6%. Death rate per 1,000 pop. (1999): 10.7 (world avg. 9.0). Natural increase rate per 1,000 pop. (1999): −2.0 (world avg. 13.5). Total fertility rate (avg. births per childbearing woman; 1999): 1.1. Marriage rate per 1,000 pop. (1999): 5.2 Divorce rate per 1,000 pop. (1999): 2.3. Life expectancy at birth (2000): male 71.1 years; female 78.2 years.

National economy

Budget (1998). Revenue: Kc 596,193,000,000 (social security contributions 45.1%, of which from employers 30.8%; value-added tax 20.0%; excise tax 11.4%; corporate tax 8.6%; personal income tax 6.1%). Expenditures: Kc 638,019,000,000 (social security and welfare 36.4%; health 17.9%; education 9.6%; defense 4.8%; police 4.5%). Public debt (external, outstanding; 1998): $12,901,000,000. Production (metric tons except as noted) Agriculture, forestry, fishing (2000): cereals 6,507,000 (of which wheat 4,117,000), sugar beets 2,686,-000, potatoes 1,417,000; livestock (number of live animals) 3,680,000 pigs, 1,574,000 cattle, 29,500,000 chickens; roundwood (1999) 14,203,-000 cu m; fish catch (1997) 20,881. Mining and quarrying (1998): kaolin 3,720,000; feldspar 360,000. Manufacturing (value added in Kc '000,000,000; 1997): nonelectrical machinery and apparatus 45.8; food products 38.0; fabricated metals 36.3. Energy production (consumption): electricity (kW-hr; 1999) 64,692,000,000 (61,417,000,-000); hard coal (metric tons; 1999) 14,342,000 ([1996] 13,035,000); lignite (metric tons; 1999) 44,790,000 ([1996] 54,181,000). Tourism (1999):

receipts from visitors $3,035,000,000; expenditures by nationals abroad $1,474,000,000. Household income and expenditure. Average household size (1998) 2.8; disposable income per household (1998) Kc 289,851; sources of income (1996): wages and salaries 56.2%, transfer payments 20.3%, rent 6.0%; expenditure (1999): food and beverages 26.6%, transportation and communications 13.8%, recreation 11.3%, energy 9.9%. Population economically active (1998): total 5,232,500; activity rate of total pop. 50.9% (participation rates: ages 15–64, 72.5%; female 44.3%; unemployed [July 1999–June 2000] 9.2%). Gross national product (1999): $51,623,000,000 ($5,020 per capita). Land use (1994): forested 33.3%; meadows and pastures 11.3%; agricultural and under permanent cultivation 43.0%; other 12.4%.

Foreign trade

Imports (1998): Kc 985,355,000,000 (machinery and apparatus 31.0%, chemicals and chemical products 11.0%, transport equipment 9.0%, mineral fuels 6.2%). Major import sources (1999): Germany 33.9%; Slovakia 6.1%; Austria 5.6%; France 5.3%; Italy 5.3%; Russia 4.8%. Exports (1998): Kc 913,740,000,000 (machinery and apparatus 32.7%, transport equipment 9.8%, chemicals and chemical products 6.9%, iron and steel 6.2%, fabricated metals 5.5%). Major export destinations (1999): Germany 42.1%; Slovakia 8.2%; Austria 6.4%; Poland 5.5%; France 3.9%.

Transport and communications

Transport. Railroads (1999): length 9,444 km; passenger-km 6,957,000,000; metric ton-km cargo 16,713,000,000. Roads (1997): total length 125,905 km. Vehicles (1999): passenger cars 3,695,792; trucks and buses 426,684. Air transport (1999): passenger-km 4,353,602,000; metric ton-km 30,326,000; airports (1997) with scheduled flights 2. Communications Total units (units per 1,000 persons). Daily newspaper circulation (1996): 2,620,-000 (254); Television receivers (1999): 5,000,000 (486); Telephone main lines (1999): 3,694,000 (359); Cellular telephone subscribers (1999): 1,944,-553 (189); Personal computers (1999): 1,100,000 (107); Internet users (1999): 700,000 (68).

Education and health

Educational attainment (1991). Percentage of adult pop. having: no schooling through complete primary education 31.7%; secondary 58.6% higher 8.5%; unknown 1.2%. Literacy (1998): 99%. Health (2000): physicians 39,245 (1 per 262 persons); hospital beds 103,280 (1 per 100 persons [excludes long-term care facilities; includes 20,687 beds in therapeutic baths]); infant mortality rate per 1,000 live births (1999) 4.6. Food (1998): daily per capita caloric intake 3,292 (vegetable products 75%, animal products 25%); 133% of FAO recommended minimum requirement.

Military

Total active duty personnel (2000): 57,500 (army 43.5%, air force 23.2%, ministry of defense 33.3%). Military expenditure as percentage of GNP (1997): 1.9% (world 2.6%); per capita expenditure: $193.

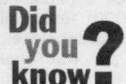

Did you know? The Czech Republic consumes more beer per capita than any other country. The Czech cities of Plzen and Ceske Budejovice, respectively, are the origins of the names "pilsner" and "Budweiser."

Background

Until 1918, the history of what is now the Czech Republic was largely that of Bohemia. In that year the independent republic of Czechoslovakia was born through the union of Bohemia and Moravia with Slovakia. Czechoslovakia came under the domination of the Soviet Union after World War II, and from 1948 to 1989 it was ruled by a communist government. Its growing political liberalization was suppressed by a Soviet invasion in 1968. After communist rule collapsed in 1989–90, separatist sentiments emerged among the Slovaks, and in 1992 the Czechs and Slovaks agreed to break up their federated state. On 1 Jan 1993, the Czechoslovakian republic was peacefully dissolved and replaced by two new countries, the Czech Republic and Slovakia, with the region of Moravia remaining in the former. In the late 1990s the Czech Republic started membership talks with the European Union, and in 1999 it entered NATO.

Recent Developments

General elections in the Czech Republic in mid-June 2002 resulted in a victory for the center-left Social Democratic Party (CSSD) over the center-right coalition that had been in power since 1998. CSSD leader Vladimir Spidla was asked to form a government. The coalition cabinet, which included the participation of the centrist Twin-Coalition of the Christian Democrats and the Freedom Union, was announced on 15 July. Devastating flooding of the Vltava and other Central European rivers in August necessitated the evacuation of more than 200,000 persons from their homes.

Internet resources: <www.visitczech.cz>

Denmark

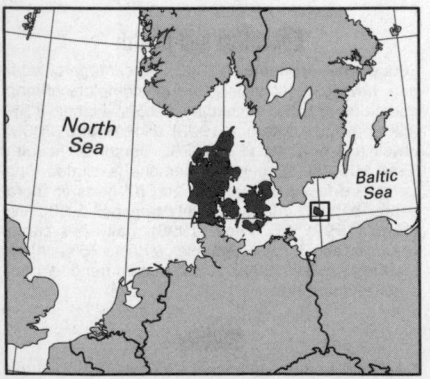

Official name: Kongeriget Danmark (Kingdom of Denmark). **Form of government:** parliamentary state and constitutional monarchy with one legislative house (Folketing [179]). **Chief of state:** Queen Margrethe II (from 1972). **Head of government:** Prime Minister Anders Fogh Rasmussen (from 27 Nov 2001). **Capital:** Copenhagen. **Official language:** Danish. **Official religion:** Evangelical Lutheran. **Monetary unit:** 1 Danish krone (Dkr; plural kroner) = 100 øre; valuation (28 Jun 2002) $1 = Dkr 7.52.

Demography

Area: 16,639 sq mi, 43,096 sq km (excludes the Faroe Islands and Greenland). **Population** (2001): 5,358,000. **Density** (2001): persons per sq mi 322.0, persons per sq km 124.3. **Urban** (2001): 85.1%. **Sex distribution** (2001): male 49.43%; female 50.57%. **Age breakdown** (2001): under 15, 18.6%; 15–29, 18.5%; 30–44, 22.3%; 45–59, 20.8%; 60–74, 12.7%; 75 and over, 7.1%. **Ethnic composition** (2001; based on nationality): Danish 95.2%; Asian 1.7%, of which Turkish 0.7%; residents of former Yugoslavia 0.7%; African 0.5%; German 0.2%; English 0.2%; other 1.5%. **Religious affiliation** (1998): Christian 87.5%, of which Evangelical Lutheran 85.8%; Muslim 2.2%; other/nonreligious 10.3%. **Major urban areas** (2001): Greater Copenhagen 1,081,673; Århus 286,688; Odense 144,849; Ålborg 119,996; Frederiksberg 91,076. **Location:** northern Europe, bordering the North Sea, the Baltic Sea, and Germany. **Dependent territories:** Faroe Islands and Greenland.

Vital statistics

Birth rate per 1,000 pop. (2000): 12.6 (world avg. 22.5); (1995) legitimate 53.5%; illegitimate 46.5%. **Death rate** per 1,000 pop. (2000): 10.9 (world avg. 9.0). **Natural increase rate** per 1,000 pop. (2000): 1.7 (world avg. 13.5). **Total fertility rate** (avg. births per childbearing woman; 2000): 1.7. **Marriage rate** per 1,000 pop. (2000): 7.2. **Divorce rate** per 1,000 pop. (2000): 2.7. **Life expectancy** at birth (2001): male 74.3 years; female 79.1 years.

National economy

Budget (1997; includes both central and local governments). *Revenue:* Dkr 612,077,000,000 (direct taxes 52.2%, indirect taxes 30.7%). *Expenditures:* Dkr 626,536,000,000 (social security assistance 31.8%, education 12.2%, welfare services 10.1%, health 8.4%, defense 2.8%). **National debt** (end of year; 1996): Dkr 664,128,000,000. **Tourism** (1999): receipts $3,682,000,000; expenditures $5,084,-000,000. **Population economically active** (2000): total 2,877,000; activity rate of total pop. 54.0% (participation rates: ages 16–66 77.5%; female 46.5%; unemployed [May 2000–April 2001 avg.] 5.3%). **Household income and expenditure.** Average household size (2001) 2.2; income per household (1988) Dkr 199,354; expenditure (1993): housing 22.9%, food and beverages 17.9%, transportation and communications 15.5%, recreation 8.3%, household furnishings 6.1%, energy 6.1%. **Production** (in Dkr '000,000 except as noted). *Agriculture, forestry, fishing* (value added; 2000):

1 metric ton = about 1.1 short tons; 1 kilometer = 0.6 mi (statute); 1 metric ton-km cargo = about 0.68 short ton-mi cargo; c.i.f.: cost, insurance, and freight; f.o.b.: free on board

meat 21,059; milk 11,254; cereals 7,458; livestock (number of live animals) 11,921,573 pigs, 1,867,-937 cattle; roundwood (2000) 3,086,000 cu m; fish catch (1999) 1,447,664 metric tons. *Mining and quarrying* (1994): sand and gravel 24,829,000 cu m; chalk 3,522,000 cu m. *Manufacturing* (value added in Dkr '000,000; 1994): food products 38,325; nonelectrical machinery and apparatus 23,331; chemicals and chemical products 18,504. *Energy production (consumption)*: electricity (kW-hr; 1999) 38,604,000,000 ([1996] 39,582,000,000); coal (metric tons; 1996) none (10,948,000); crude petroleum (barrels; 2000) 136,095,000 ([1996] 80,374,000); petroleum products (metric tons; 1996) 10,426,000 (7,730,000); natural gas (cu m; 2000) 8,168,000,000 ([1996] 4,185,000,000). **Gross national product** (1999): $170,685,000,000 ($32,050 per capita). **Land use** (1994): forested 10.5%; meadows and pastures 7.5%; agricultural and under permanent cultivation 55.9%; other 26.1%.

Foreign trade

Imports (2000-c.i.f.): Dkr 360,790,000,000 (machinery and apparatus 14.2%, chemicals and chemical products 12.3%, food and live animals 8.2%, transport equipment and parts 7.8%, fuels 5.4%). *Major import sources:* Germany 21.0%; Sweden 12.2%; The Netherlands 8.6%; U.K. 7.6%; Norway 5.1%; France 5.1%. **Exports** (2000-f.o.b.): Dkr 403,285,000,000 (machinery and apparatus 23.5%, food and live animals 18.4%, pharmaceuticals 5.1%, mineral fuels and lubricants 4.8%, furniture 3.8%). *Major export destinations:* Germany 18.9%; Sweden 13.0%; U.K. 9.8%; Norway 5.5%; France 4.9%.

Transport and communications

Transport. *Railroads* (2001): route length 2,743 km; passenger-km 5,318,000,000; metric ton-km cargo 2,025,000,000. *Roads* (2001): total length 71,663 km (paved 100%). *Vehicles* (2001): passenger cars 1,854,060; trucks and buses 335,690. *Air transport* (1996; Danish share of Scandinavian Airlines System (scheduled air service only) and Maersk Air): passenger-km 5,376,000,000; metric ton-km cargo 170,768,000; *airports* (1996) with scheduled flights 13. **Communications** Total units (units per 1,000 persons). Daily newspaper circulation (1998): 1,613,000 (284); Radio receivers (1997): 6,020,-000 (1,145); Television receivers (1999): 3,300,000 (621); Telephone main lines (1999): 3,638,000 (684); Cellular telephone subscribers (1999): 2,629,000 (495); Personal computers (1999): 2,200,000 (414); Internet users (1999): 1,500,000 (282).

Education and health

Educational attainment (2000). Percentage of pop. age 25–69 having: completed lower secondary or not stated 34.6%; completed upper secondary or vocational 42.3%; undergraduate 17.6%; graduate 5.5%. **Literacy:** 100%. **Health:** physicians (1994) 14,497 (1 per 358 persons); hospital beds (1999) 23,052 (1 per 228 persons); infant mortality rate per 1,000 live births (2001) 5.0. **Food** (1999): daily per capita caloric intake 3,317 (vegetable products 63%, animal products 37%); 123% of FAO recommended minimum requirement.

Military

Total active duty personnel (2000): 21,810 (army 58.9%, navy 18.6%, air force 22.5%). **Military expenditure as percentage of GNP** (1997): 1.8% (world 2.6%); per capita expenditure $529.

 Denmark was the first European country to legalize same-sex marriages and to offer gay couples the same rights as heterosexual couples.

Background

The Danes, a Scandinavian branch of the Teutons, settled the area in c. 6th century AD. During the Viking period the Danes expanded their territory, and by the 11th century the united Danish kingdom included parts of what are now Germany, Sweden, England, and Norway. Scandinavia was united under Danish rule from 1397 until 1523, when Sweden became independent; a series of debilitating wars with Sweden in the 17th century resulted in the Treaty of Copenhagen (1660), which established the modern Scandinavian frontiers. Denmark gained and lost various other territories, including Norway, in the 19th and 20th centuries; it went through three constitutions between 1849 and 1915 and was occupied by Nazi Germany in 1940–45. A founding member of NATO (1949), Denmark adopted its current constitution in 1953. It became a member of the European Community in 1973 and modified its membership during the 1990s. The island of Zealand, on which Copenhagen stands, was connected to the central island of Funen by a rail tunnel and bridge in 1997. This ended more than 100 years of ferry service and cut the crossing time to under 10 minutes.

Recent Developments

The Liberal Party of Anders Fogh Rasmussen won a landslide victory in Denmark's national elections held on 20 Nov 2001. The Liberals, with the support of the Conservatives and centrist and rightist groups, won 98 seats in Folketing (parliament); the Social Democrats and the center-left bloc garnered 77 seats, down from the 89 held in the previous parliament. Rasmussen announced that he would head a Liberal-Conservative minority-rightist coalition government, which called for a major tightening of immigration laws, cuts in overseas development aid, an income-tax freeze, improvements in hospital services and social welfare, tougher law-and-order provisions, and a reduction by half of Denmark's $70 billion gross public debt by 2002.

Internet resources. <www.visitdenmark.com>

Djibouti

Official name: Jumhuriyah Jibuti (Arabic); République de Djibouti (French) (Republic of Djibouti). **Form of government:** multiparty republic with one legislative house (National Assembly [65]). **Head of state and government:** President Ismail Omar Guelleh (from 1999) assisted by a prime minister. **Capital:** Djibouti. **Official languages:** Arabic; French. **Official religion:**

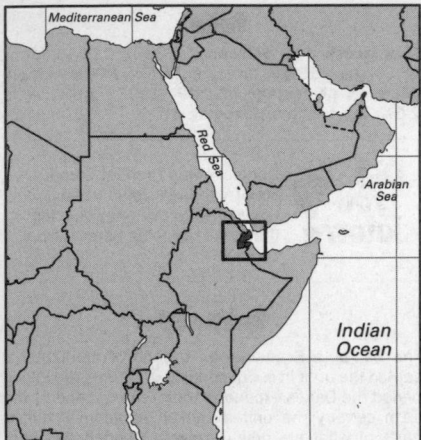

none. **Monetary unit:** 1 Djibouti franc (DF) = 100 centimes; valuation (28 Jun 2002) $1 = DF 164.90.

Demography

Area: 8,950 sq mi, 23,200 sq km. **Population** (2001): 461,000. **Density** (2001): persons per sq mi 51.5, persons per sq km 19.9. **Urban** (1999): 83.1%. **Sex distribution** (1999): male 51.66%; female 48.34%. **Age breakdown** (1999): under 15, 47.5%; 15–29, 28.9%; 30–44, 13.1%; 45–59, 5.2%; 60–74, 4.7%; 75 and over, 0.6%. **Ethnic composition** (2000): Somali 46.0%; Afar 35.4%; Arab 11.0%; mixed African and European 3.0%; French 1.6%; other/unspecified 3.0%. **Religious affiliation** (1995): Sunni Muslim 97.2%; Christian 2.8%, of which Roman Catholic 2.2%, Orthodox 0.5%, Protestant 0.1%. **Major city and towns** (1991): Djibouti (1995) 383,000; 'Ali Sabih 8,000; Tadjoura 7,500; Dikhil 6,500. **Location:** eastern Africa, bordering Eritrea, the Red Sea, the Gulf of Aden, Somalia, and Ethiopia.

Vital statistics

Birth rate per 1,000 pop. (2000): 41.0 (world avg. 22.5). **Death rate** per 1,000 pop. (2000): 14.9 (world avg. 9.0). **Natural increase rate** per 1,000 pop. (2000): 26.1 (world avg. 13.5). **Total fertility rate** (avg. births per childbearing woman; 2000): 5.8. **Life expectancy** at birth (2000): male 49.0 years; female 52.7 years.

National economy

Budget (1998). *Revenue:* DF 23,154,000,000 (tax revenue 87.5%, of which domestic consumption taxes 27.1%, wages and salary tax 13.7%, surcharge on khat 8.9%, income and profit tax 6.1%; nontax revenue 12.5%). *Expenditures:* DF 30,427,000,000 (current expenditures 80.0%, of which general administration 26.7%, defense and mobilization 20.0%, education 8.7%, health 5.4%; capital expenditures 20.0%). **Tourism** (1995): receipts from visitors $4,000,000; expenditures by nationals abroad $4,000,000. **Production** (metric tons except as noted). *Agriculture,*

forestry, fishing (1999): vegetables and melons 22,390, of which tomatoes 1,000, eggplant 45; livestock (number of live animals) 511,000 goats, 463,000 sheep, 269,000 cattle; fish catch (1998) 350. *Mining and quarrying:* mineral production limited to locally used construction materials and evaporated salt. *Manufacturing* (1999): structural detail, n.a.; main products include furniture, nonalcoholic beverages, and meat and hides. *Energy production (consumption):* electricity (kW-hr; 1996) 185,000,000 (185,000,000); petroleum products (metric tons; 1996) none (119,000). **Population economically active** (1991): total 282,000; activity rate of total pop. 61.5% (participation rates: over age 10, 70.4%; female 40.8%;). **Household income and expenditure.** Average household size (1985; city of Djibouti only) 7.2; expenditure (expatriate households; 1984): food 50.3%, energy 13.1%, recreation 10.4%, housing 6.4%, clothing 1.7%. **Public debt** (external, outstanding; 1999): $252,700,000. **Gross national product** (1999): $511,000,000 ($790 per capita). **Land use** (1994): forested 0.9%; meadows and pastures 56.1%; agricultural and under permanent cultivation, negligible; built-on, wasteland, and other 43.0%.

Foreign trade

Imports (1998): $238,800,000 (food, beverages, khat, and tobacco 53.2%; petroleum products 12.4%; machinery and electric appliances 10.9%; base metals and base metal products 4.9%; chemical products 4.6%). *Major import sources:* France 12.5%; Ethiopia 12.0%; Italy 9.2%; U.K. 6.2%; Saudi Arabia 5.7%; Japan 4.2%. **Exports** (1998): $59,100,000 (1992: unspecified special transactions 60.0%; live animals [including camels] 21.3%; basic manufactures 5.2%; crude materials 4.5%). *Major export destinations:* Somalia 53.0%; Yemen 22.5%; Ethiopia 5.0%; Saudi Arabia 0.7%.

Transport and communications

Transport. *Railroads* (1997): length (1989) 106 km; passenger-km 762,000,000; metric ton-km cargo 232,000,000. *Roads* (1996): total length 2,890 km (paved 13%). *Vehicles* (1996): passenger cars 9,200; trucks and buses 2,040. *Air transport* (1997): passengers handled 107,369; metric tons of freight handled 7,290; airports (1998) with scheduled flights 1. **Communications** Total units (units per 1,000 persons). Daily newspaper circulation (1995): 500 (0.8); Radio receivers (1997): 52,000 (84); Television receivers (1999): 30,000 (67); Telephone main lines (1999): 8,831 (20); Cellular telephone subscribers (1999): 280 (0.6); Internet users (1999): 750 (1.7).

Education and health

Educational attainment: n.a. **Literacy** (1995): percentage of pop. age 15 and over literate 46.2%; males literate 60.3%; females literate 32.7%. **Health** (1996): physicians 60 (1 per 7,100 persons); hospital beds (1989; public health facilites only) 1,383 (1 per 369 persons); infant mortality rate per 1,000 live births (2000) 103.3. **Food** (1999): daily per capita caloric intake 2,129 (vegetable products 90%, animal products 10%); 92% of FAO recommended minimum requirement.

1 metric ton = about 1.1 short tons;   1 kilometer = 0.6 mi (statute);   1 metric ton-km cargo = about 0.68 short ton-mi cargo;   c.i.f.: cost, insurance, and freight;   f.o.b.: free on board

Military

Total active duty personnel (2000): 11,400 (army 70.2%, navy 1.8%, air force 1.8%, paramilitary 26.2%); French troops (2000) 3,200. **Military expenditure as percentage of GNP** (1997): 4.1% (world 2.6%); per capita expenditure $47.

Background

Settled around the 3rd century BC by the Arab ancestors of the Afars, Djibouti was later populated by Somali Issas. In AD 825 Islam was brought to the area by missionaries. Arabs controlled the trade in this region until the 16th century; it became the French protectorate of French Somaliland in 1888. In 1946 it became a French overseas territory, and in 1977 gained its independence. In the late 20th century, the country received refugees from the Ethiopian–Somali war, and from civil conflicts in Eritrea. In the 1990s it suffered from political unrest.

Recent Developments

In February 2001 Prime Minister Barkat Gourad Hamadou, who had served in the post since 1978, resigned for health reasons. Pres. Ismael Omar Guelleh named Dileita Muhammad Dileita, a senior civil servant and Djibouti's ambassador to Ethiopia, as the new prime minister. Later in the year the government concluded a peace agreement with the radical wing of the rebel Front for the Restoration of Unity and Democracy, though details of the agreement were not announced.

Internet resources: <www.republique-djibouti.com>

Dominica

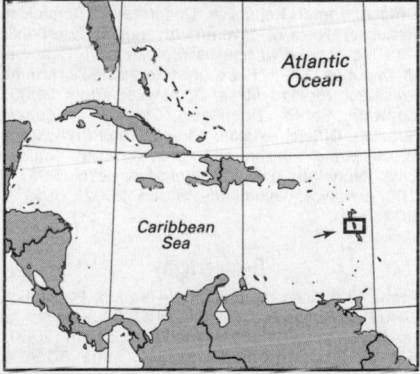

Atlantic Ocean

Caribbean Sea

Official name: Commonwealth of Dominica. **Form of government:** multiparty republic with one legislative house (House of Assembly [32; includes 22 seats that are elective [including speaker if elected from outside of the House of Assembly] and 10 seats that are nonelective [including 9 appointees of the president and the attorney general serving ex officio]]). **Chief of state:** President Vernon Shaw (from 1998). **Head of government:** Prime Minister Pierre Charles (from 2000). **Capital:** Roseau. **Official language:** English. **Official religion:** none. **Monetary unit:** 1 East Caribbean dollar (EC$) = 100 cents; valuation (28 Jun 2002) US$1 = EC$2.70.

Demography

Area: 285.3 sq mi, 739.0 sq km (total area of Dominica per more recent survey is 290 sq mi [750 sq km]). **Population** (2001): 71,700. **Density** (2001): persons per sq mi 247.2; persons per sq km 95.6. **Urban** (2000): 70%. **Sex distribution** (2001): male 51%; female 49%. **Age breakdown** (2000): under 15, 29.1%; 15–29, 27.2%; 30–44, 23.7%; 45–59, 9.6%; 60–74, 7.0%; 75 and over, 3.4%. **Ethnic composition** (1991): black 89.1%; mixed race 7.2%; Amerindian/Carib 2.4%; white 0.4%; other 0.7%; not stated 0.2%. **Religious affiliation** (1991): Roman Catholic 70.1%; six largest Protestant groups 17.2%, of which Seventh-day Adventist 4.6%, Pentecostal 4.3%, Methodist 4.2%; other 8.9%; nonreligious 2.9%; unknown 0.9%. **Major towns** (1991): Roseau 15,853; Portsmouth 3,621. **Location:** southern Caribbean Sea, south of Guadeloupe and north of Martinique.

Vital statistics

Birth rate per 1,000 pop. (2000): 18.3 (world avg. 22.5); (1991) legitimate 24.1%; illegitimate 75.9%. **Death rate** per 1,000 pop. (2000): 7.3 (world avg. 9.0). **Natural increase rate** per 1,000 pop. (2000): 11.0 (world avg. 13.5). **Total fertility rate** (avg. births per childbearing woman; 2000): 2.0. **Marriage rate** per 1,000 pop. (1996): 3.1. **Divorce rate** per 1,000 pop. (1996): 0.7. **Life expectancy** at birth (2000): male 70.5 years; female 76.3 years.

National economy

Budget (1998–99). *Revenue:* EC$232,700,000 (tax revenue 73.9%, of which consumption taxes on imports 26.9%, income taxes 20.9%; nontax revenue 14.7%; grants 9.2%). *Expenditures:* EC$260,300,000 (current expenditures 77.1%; development expenditures 22.9%). **Public debt** (external, outstanding; 1999): US$89,000,000. **Land use** (1994): forested 66.0%; meadows and pastures 3.0%; agricultural and under permanent cultivation 23.0%; other 8.0%. **Tourism:** receipts from visitors (1999) US$47,300,000; expenditures by nationals abroad (1998) US$8,000,000. **Gross national product** (at current market prices; 1999): US$238,000,000 (US$3,260 per capita). **Population economically active** (1991): total 26,364; activity rate of total pop. 38.0% (participation rates: ages 15–64, 62.4%; female 34.5%; unemployed [1994] 23%). **Household income and expenditure.** Average household size (1991) 3.6; expenditure (1984; weights of consumer price index components): food and nonalcoholic beverages 43.1%, housing and utilities 16.1%, transportation 11.6%, clothing and footwear 6.5%, household furnishings 6.0%. **Production** (metric tons except as noted). *Agriculture, forestry, fishing* (1998): bananas 28,640 (export production only), root crops 23,168 (of which dasheens 11,903, yams 7,560, tanias 3,534), plantains 22,236; livestock (number of live animals; 1999) 13,400 cattle, 9,700 goats, 7,600 sheep; fish catch (1997) 855 metric tons. *Mining and quarrying:* pumice, limestone, and sand and gravel are quarried primarily for local consumption. *Manufacturing* (value of production in EC$'000; 1998): toilet soap 21,816; laundry soap 16,467; crude coconut oil 1,848; toothpaste 1,662 metric tons; other products include fruit juices, beer, garments, bottled spring water, and cardboard boxes. *Energy production* (consumption): electricity (kW-hr; 1996) 37,000,000 (37,000,000); petroleum products (metric tons; 1996) none (26,000).

Foreign trade

Imports (1999-c.i.f.): EC$343,400,000 (food and beverages 20.8%; machinery 16.4%; transport equipment 9.3%; mineral fuels 6.4%). *Major import sources:* US 30.7%; Caricom 27.0%; UK 8.8%; Japan 7.8%; France 5.0%. **Exports** (1999-f.o.b.): EC$147,-400,000 (manufactured exports 61.7%, of which coconut-based laundry and toilet soaps 26.7%; agricultural exports 38.3%, of which bananas 27.1%). *Major export destinations:* Caricom 55.3%; UK 27.5%; Guadeloupe 4.9%; US 4.0%.

Transport and communications

Transport. *Railroads:* none. *Roads* (1996): total length 485 mi, 780 km (paved 50%). *Vehicles* (1994): passenger cars 6,581; trucks and buses 2,825. *Air transport:* (1991) passenger arrivals 43,312, passenger departures, n.a.; (1997) cargo unloaded 575 metric tons, cargo loaded 363 metric tons; airports (1996) with scheduled flights 2. **Communications** Total units (units per 1,000 persons). Radio receivers (1997): 46,000 (608); Television receivers (1997): 6,000 (79); Telephone main lines (1999): 21,332 (296); Cellular telephone subscribers (1998): 650 (8.9).

Education and health

Educational attainment (1991). Percentage of pop. age 25 and over having: no formal schooling 4.2%; primary education 78.4%; secondary 11.0%; higher vocational 2.3%; university 2.8%; other/unknown 1.3%. **Literacy** (1994): total pop. age 15 and over literate, c. 44,000 (90.0%). **Health** (1998): physicians 38 (1 per 2,007 persons); hospital beds 262 (1 per 291 persons); infant mortality rate per 1,000 live births (2000) 17.1. **Food** (1999): daily per capita caloric intake 2,947 (vegetable products 79%, animal products 21%); 122% of FAO recommended minimum requirement.

Military

Total active duty personnel (1999): A 300-member police force includes a coast guard unit.

Background

At the time of the arrival of Christopher Columbus in 1493, Dominica was inhabited by the Caribs. With its steep coastal cliffs and inaccessible mountains, it was one of the last islands to be explored by Europeans, and the Caribs remained in possession until the 18th century; it was then settled by the French and ultimately taken by Britain in 1783. Subsequent hostilities between the settlers and the native inhabitants resulted in the Caribs' near extinction. Incorporated with the Leeward Islands in 1883 and with the Windward Islands in 1940, it became a member of the West Indies Federation in 1958. Dominica became independent in 1978.

Recent Developments

Although the Dominica Labour Party (DLP) fell short of capturing an overall majority in the country's 2000 general election, winning 10 of the 21 seats in the House of Assembly, it was able to form a government by persuading the Dominica Freedom Party, which obtained two seats, to join forces. DLP leader Roosevelt ("Rosie") Douglas became the new prime minister but suffered a fatal heart attack later that year. Communications and Works Minister Pierre Charles succeeded Douglas as prime minister.

Internet resources: <www.ndcdominica.dm>

Dominican Republic

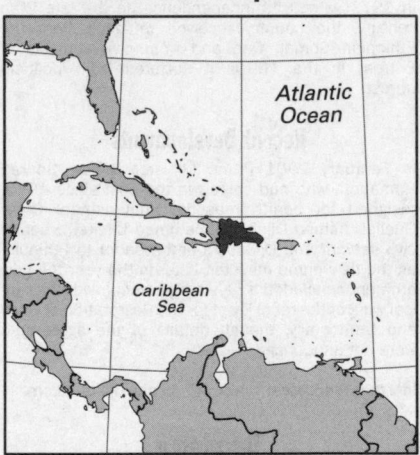

Official name: República Dominicana (Dominican Republic). **Form of government:** multiparty republic with two legislative houses (Senate [30]; Chamber of Deputies [149]). **Head of state and government:** President Hipólito Mejía Dominguez (from 2000). **Capital:** Santo Domingo. **Official language:** Spanish. **Official religion:** none (Roman Catholicism is the state religion per concordat with Vatican City). **Monetary unit:** 1 Dominican peso (RD$) = 100 centavos; valuation (28 Jun 2002) US$1 = RD$17.20.

Demography

Area: 48,671 sq mi, 8,553,744 sq km. **Population** (2001): 8,693,000. **Density** (2001): persons per sq mi 462.6, persons per sq km 178.6. **Urban** (2000): 65.2%. **Sex distribution** (2000): male 50.80%; female 49.20%. **Age breakdown** (2000): under 15, 34.5%; 15–29, 27.3%; 30–44, 20.3%; 45–59, 10.8%; 60–74, 5.7%; 75 and over, 1.4%. **Ethnic composition** (2000): mulatto 69.5%; white 17.0%; local black 9.4%; Haitian black 2.4%; other/unknown 1.7%. **Religious affiliation** (1995): Roman Catholic 81.8%; Protestant 6.4%; other Christian 0.6%; other 11.2%. **Major urban centres** (1993): Santo Domingo ([urban population of nation-

1 metric ton = about 1.1 short tons;   1 kilometer = 0.6 mi (statute);   1 metric ton-km cargo = about 0.68 short ton-mi cargo;   c.i.f.: cost, insurance, and freight;   f.o.b.: free on board

al district] 1,609,966, [urban agglomeration (1999)] 3,523,000); Santiago 365,463; La Romana 140,204; San Pedro de Macorís 124,735; San Francisco de Macorís 108,485. **Location:** eastern two-thirds of the island of Hispaniola, bordered by the North Atlantic Ocean, the Caribbean Sea, and Haiti.

Vital statistics

Birth rate per 1,000 pop. (2000): 25.2 (world avg. 22.5). **Death rate** per 1,000 pop. (2000): 4.7 (world avg. 9.0). **Natural increase rate** per 1,000 pop. (2000): 20.5 (world avg. 13.5). **Total fertility rate** (avg. births per childbearing woman; 2000): 3.0. **Marriage rate** per 1,000 pop. (1994): 2.0. **Life expectancy** at birth (2000): male 71.1 years; female 75.4 years.

National economy

Budget (1998). *Revenue:* RD$38,566,000,000 (tax revenue 93.8%, of which taxes on goods and services 47.7%, import duties 27.0%, income taxes 17.9%; nontax revenue 5.3%). *Expenditures:* RD$41,179,-000,000 (current expenditure 72.2%; development expenditure 27.8%). **Public debt** (external, outstanding; 1999): US$3,665,000,000. **Gross national product** (1999): US$16,130,000,000 (US$1,920 per capita). **Production** (metric tons except as noted). *Agriculture, forestry, fishing* (1998): sugarcane 5,097,000, rice 475,000, bananas 359,000; live stock (number of live animals) 2,528,000 cattle, 960,000 pigs, 38,000,000 chickens; roundwood (1997) 982,300 cu m; fish catch (1997) 14,536. *Mining* (1998): nickel (metal content) 25,200; gold 40,700 troy oz. *Manufacturing* (1998; excludes free-zone sector for reexport [mostly ready-made garments]): cement 1,872,000; refined sugar 105,000; rum 420,000 hectolitres. *Energy production (consumption):* electricity (kW-hr; 2000) 9,788,000,000 (5,777,000,000); coal (metric tons; 1996) none (128,000); crude petroleum (barrels; 1996) none (17,035,000); petroleum products (metric tons; 1996) 2,147,000 (3,671,000); natural gas, none (none). **Tourism** (1999): receipts US$2,524,000,000; expenditures US$282,000,000. **Population economically active** (1993): total 2,556,225; activity rate of total pop. 35.0% (participation rates: ages 15–64, 54.3%; female 24.9%; unemployed [2000] 13.9%). **Household income and expenditure.** Average household size (1993) 3.9; expenditure (1980–85): food and beverages 46.0%, housing 10.0%, household goods 8.0%. **Land use** (1994): forested 12.4%; meadows and pastures 43.4%; agricultural and under permanent cultivation 30.6%; other 13.6%.

Foreign trade

Imports (1998). US$4,897,000,000 (capital goods 22.1%; consumer durables 13.2%; crude petroleum and petroleum products 11.0%); imports total and commodities breakdown exclude imports of free zones = US$2,701,000,000. *Major import sources* (1997; estimated figures): US 56%; Venezuela 23%; Mexico 9%; Japan 4%. **Exports** (1998): US$889,000,000 (ships' stores 15.8%; ferronickel 15.0%; cacao and cocoa 13.6%; raw sugar 13.2%; raw coffee 7.2%); exports total and commodities breakdown exclude exports of free zones = US$4,100,000,000. *Major export destinations*

(1997): US 53.9%; Belgium 11.9%; Puerto Rico 7.0%.

Transport and communications

Transport. *Railroads* (1997): route length 1,743 km (most track is privately owned and serves the sugar industry). *Roads* (1996): total length 12,600 km (paved 49%). *Vehicles* (1996): passenger cars 224,000; trucks and buses 151,550. *Air transport* (1997; Aerochago and Dominair airlines only): passenger-km, 15,808,000; metric ton-km cargo 11,624,000; airports (1997) 7. **Communications** Total units (units per 1,000 persons). Daily newspaper circulation (1996): 416,000 (53); Radio receivers (1997): 1,440,000 (179); Television receivers (1997): 770,000 (96); Telephone main lines (1999): 820,926 (99); Cellular telephone subscribers (1999): 420,080 (51).

Education and health

Literacy (1995): total pop. age 15 and over literate, c. 4,164,000 (82.1%); males literate, c. 2,118,000 (82.0%); females literate, c. 2,046,000 (82.2%). **Health:** physicians (1997) 17,460 (1 per 460 persons); hospital beds (1996) 11,921 (1 per 662 persons); infant mortality rate per 1,000 live births (2000) 35.9. **Food** (1999): daily per capita caloric intake 2,333 (vegetable products 85%, animal products 15%); 103% of FAO recommended minimum.

Military

Total active duty personnel (2000): 24,500 (army 61.2%, navy 16.3%, air force 22.5%). **Military expenditure as percentage of GNP** (1997): 1.1% (world 2.6%); per capita expenditure US$21.

Background

The Dominican Republic was originally part of the Spanish colony of Hispaniola. In 1697 the western third of the island, which later became Haiti, was ceded to France; the remainder of the island passed to France in 1795. The eastern two-thirds of the island were returned to Spain in 1809, and the colony declared its independence in 1821. Within a matter of weeks it was overrun by Haitian troops and occupied until 1844. Since then the country has been under the rule of a succession of dictators, except for short interludes of democratic government, and the US has frequently been involved in its affairs. The termination of the dictatorship of Rafael Trujillo in 1961 led to civil war in 1965 and US military intervention. The country suffered from severe hurricanes in 1979 and 1998.

Recent Developments

Hipólito Mejía Dominguez was elected to the presidency on 16 May 2000. The election, perhaps the cleanest in the Dominican Republic's history, brought to office the Dominican Revolutionary Party, which had last been in power in 1986 and was deprived of office in 1994 owing to election irregularities. Recognizing that poverty and environmental degradation required Hispaniola-wide solutions, Mejía gave priority to improving relations with Haiti and asked international donors to examine the challenge through this lens.

Internet resources: <www.dominicana.com.do>

East Timor

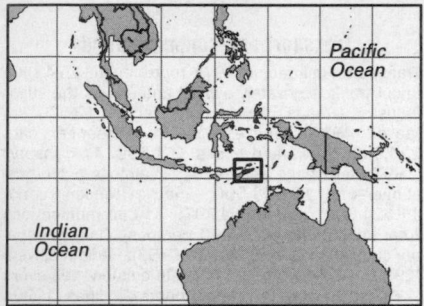

Pacific Ocean

Indian Ocean

Official name: Republika Democratika Timor-Leste (Tetum); República Democrática de Timor-Leste (Portuguese); (Democratic Republic of East Timor). **Form of government:** multiparty republic. **Chief of state and head of government:** President Xanana Gusmão (from 20 May 2002). **Capital:** Dili. **Official languages:** Tetum and Portuguese. **Official religion:** none. **Monetary unit:** US dollar.

Demography

Area: 5,641 sq mi, 14,609 sq km. **Population** (2001): 897,000. **Density:** persons per sq mi 159.1; per sq km 61.4. **Urban** (1990): 7.8%. **Sex distribution** (1990): male: 51.7%; female: 48.3% **Religious affiliation** (2000): Christian 92.2%; Muslim: 3.3 %; other 4.4%. **Major urban areas** (2002): Dili 49,900; Dare 17,800; Baucau 14,700; Maliana 12,300; Ermera 12,400. **Location:** southeast Asia, eastern end of the island of Timor plus an exclave on the western end, bordering the Timor Sea and Indonesia. **Gross domestic product** (1998): $113,000,000 ($130 per capita).

Did you know? The East Timorese Constitution, a model of aspirational governance, guarantees equal rights between men and women and asserts its citizens' rights to work in a safe environment, to unionize and strike, and to gain access to all personal data.

Background

The Portuguese first settled on the island of Timor in 1520 and were granted rule over Timor's eastern half in 1860. The Timor political party Fretilin declared East Timor independent in 1975 after Portugal withdrew its troops. It was invaded by Indonesian forces and was incorporated as a province of Indonesia in 1976. The takeover, which resulted in thousands of East Timorese deaths during the next two decades, was disputed by the United Nations. In 1999 an independence referendum won overwhelmingly; civilian militias, armed by the military and led by local supporters of integration, then rampaged through the province, killing 1,000–2,000 people. The Indonesian parliament rescinded Indonesia's annexation of the territory, and East Timor was returned to its preannexation status as a non-self-governing territory, though this time under UN supervision. Preparation for independence got under way in 2001, with East Timorese voting by universal suffrage in August for a Constituent Assembly of 88 members; by the end of the year, the assembly had drafted a constitution for the new state.

Recent Developments

On 14 Apr 2002 former guerrilla leader Xanana Gusmão easily won the country's first-ever presidential election. East Timor officially declared its independence on 20 May, with UN Secretary-General Kofi Annan attending ceremonies in Taci Tolu, outside of the capital, Dili, where he formally ended the world body's authority over the territory. The declaration of independence was followed by the swearing in of Gusmão and the raising of the flag of the world's newest country.

Internet resources: <www.gov.east-timor.org>

Ecuador

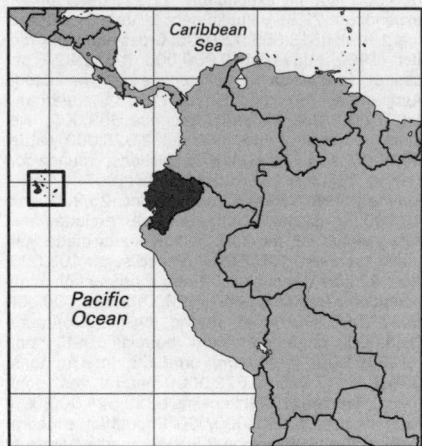

Caribbean Sea

Pacific Ocean

Official name: República del Ecuador (Republic of Ecuador). **Form of government:** unitary multiparty republic with one legislative house (National Congress [121]). **Head of state and government:** President Gustavo Noboa Bejarano (from 2000). **Capital:** Quito. **Official language:** Spanish (Quechua and Shuar are also official languages for the indigenous peoples). **Official religion:** none. **Monetary unit:** dollar ($) (28 Jun 2002; the US dollar became the principal national currency from March 2000 and was formally adopted as the national currency on 9 Sep 2000; the pegged value of the sucre [S/.], the former national currency from March 2000 was $1 = S/. 25,000).

Demography

Area: 105,037 sq mi, 272,045 sq km (includes 884 sq mi [2,289 sq km] in nondelimited areas). **Population** (2001): 12,879,000. **Density** (2001): persons per sq mi 122.6, persons per sq km 47.3. **Urban** (1998): 61.0%. **Sex distribution** (1998): male 50.23%; female 49.77%. **Age breakdown** (1997): under 15, 35.4%; 15–29, 29.1%; 30–59, 28.9%; 60 and over, 6.6%. **Ethnic composition** (1989): Amerindian 40.0%; mestizo 40.0%; white 15.0%; black 5.0%. **Religious affiliation** (1995): Roman Catholic 93.4%; other 6.6%. **Major cities** (2000): Guayaquil 2,118,000; Quito 1,616,000; Cuenca 278,000; Machala 217,000; Portoviejo 181,000. **Location:** northwestern South America, bordering Colombia, Peru, and the Pacific Ocean.

Vital statistics

Birth rate per 1,000 pop. (2000; excluding nomadic Indian tribes): 26.5 (world avg. 22.5). **Death rate** per 1,000 pop. (2000; excluding nomadic Indian tribes): 5.5 (world avg. 9.0). **Natural increase rate** per 1,000 pop. (2000; excluding nomadic Indian tribes): 21.0 (world avg. 13.5). **Total fertility rate** (avg. births per childbearing woman; 2000): 3.2. **Marriage rate** per 1,000 pop. (1997): 5.6 (total includes 73,000 persons in nondelimited areas). **Life expectancy** at birth (2000): male 68.3 years; female 74.0 years.

National economy

Budget (1996). *Revenue:* S/. 10,233,300,000,000 (petroleum revenue 45.9%, indirect taxes 30.9%, direct taxes 11.1%). *Expenditures:* S/. 11,836,700,-000,000 (administration 40.8%, debt service 20.7%, subsidies 7.4%). **Public debt** (external, outstanding; 1999): $12,756,000,000. **Production** (metric tons except as noted). *Agriculture, forestry, fishing* (1999): sugarcane 6,800,000, bananas 4,563,000, rice 1,043,000; livestock (live animals) 5,534,000 cattle, 2,892,000 pigs, 2,182,000 sheep; roundwood (1998) 11,340,000 cu m; fish catch (1997) 688,297. *Mining and quarrying* (1994): limestone 1,900,000; gold 7,000 kg. *Manufacturing* (value added in S/. '000,000; 1996): chemical products 2,364,091; food products 1,779,894; nonmetallic mineral products 453,148. *Energy production (consumption):* electricity (kW-hr; 1996) 9,260,000,000 (9,260,000,000); crude petroleum (barrels; 1996) 137,203,000 (58,373,000); petroleum products (metric tons; 1996) 7,130,000 (5,726,000); natural gas (cu m; 1996) 534,000,000 (534,000,000). **Household income and expenditure.** Average household size (1990) 4.1; average annual income per household (1995) S/. 9,825,610; sources of income (1995): self-employment 70.9%, wages 16.0%, transfer payments 6.7%, other 6.4%; expenditure (1995): food and tobacco 37.9%, transportation and communications 15.0%, clothing 9.2%, household furnishings 6.5%. **Population economically active** (1997): total 3,373,810; activity rate of total pop. 44.9% (participation rates: ages 15 and over, 64.2%; female 39.1%. **Gross national product** (1999): $16,841,000,000 ($1,360 per capita). **Tourism** (1999): receipts $343,000,000; expenditures $271,000,000.

Foreign trade

Imports (1997-c.i.f.): $4,510,600,000 (machines and transport equipment 35.6%; industrial supplies 34.9%; consumer goods 14.1%; food and live animals 7.6%; mineral fuels 7.6%). *Major import sources:* US 30.5%; Colombia 10.6%; Venezuela 6.7%; Japan

5.8%; Germany 4.2%; Spain 3.6%. **Exports** (1997-f.o.b.): $5,214,100,000 (food and live animals 56.6%, of which bananas 25.4%, crustaceans 16.8%; crude petroleum 26.9%). *Major export destinations:* US 38.2%; Colombia 6.8%; Italy 5.2%; Chile 4.6%.

Transport and communications

Transport. *Railroads* (1995): route length 966 km; passenger-km 47,000,000; metric ton-km cargo 2,592,000. *Roads* (1997): total length 43,197 km (paved 19%). *Vehicles* (1996): passenger cars 464,902; trucks and buses 52,630. *Air transport* (1998): passenger-km 923,822,000; metric ton-km cargo 116,378,000. **Communications** Total units (units per 1,000 persons). Daily newspaper circulation (1996): 820,000 (70); Radio receivers (1997): 4,150,000 (348); Television receivers (1998): 2,500,000 (205); Telephone main lines (1999): 1,129,528 (91); Cellular telephone subscribers (1999): 383,185 (31); Personal computers (1999): 250,000 (20); Internet users (1999): 35,000 (2.8).

Education and health

Educational attainment (1990). Percentage of pop. age 25 and over having: no formal schooling 2.2%; incomplete primary 54.3%; primary 28.0%; postsecondary 15.5%. **Literacy** (1995): total pop. age 15 and over literate 90.1%; males 92.0%; females 88.2%. **Health** (1997): physicians 20,243 (1 per 600 persons); hospital beds 18,510 (1 per 645 persons); infant mortality rate (2000) 35.1. **Food** (1999): daily per capita caloric intake 2,679 (vegetable products 84%, animal products 16%); (1997) 117% of FAO recommended minimum requirement.

Military

Total active duty personnel (2000): 57,500 (army 87.0%, navy 7.8%, air force 5.2%). **Military expenditure as percentage of GNP** (1997): 4.0% (world 2.6%); per capita expenditure $62.

Background

Ecuador was conquered by the Incas in AD 1450 and came under Spanish control in 1534. Under the Spaniards it was a part of the viceroyalty of Peru until 1740, when it became a part of the viceroyalty of New Granada. It gained its independence from Spain in 1822 as part of the republic of Gran Colombia, and in 1830 became a sovereign state. A succession of authoritarian governments ruled into the mid-20th century, and economic hardship and social unrest prompted the military to take a strong role. Border disputes led to war between Peru and Ecuador in 1941; the two fought periodically until agreeing to a final demarcation in 1998. The economy, booming in the 1970s with petroleum profits, was depressed in the 1980s by reduced oil prices and earthquake damage. A new constitution was adopted in 1979. In the 1990s social unrest caused political instability and several changes of heads of state. In a controversial move to help stabilize the economy, the US dollar replaced the sucre as the national currency in 2000.

Recent Developments

On 21 Jan 2000 Indian protesters aided by middle-ranking military officers stormed the National

Congress building in Quito and proclaimed a new government, led by a junta composed of Indian leader Antonio Vargas, army Col. Lucio Gutiérrez, and former Supreme Court president Carlos Solórzano. Troops escorted Pres. Jamil Mahuad Witt from the presidential palace, but the military high command moved immediately to block a full-scale insurrection. Gen. Carlos Mendoza, the armed forces chief of staff, replaced Gutiérrez in the junta, but within hours he announced that it would be scrapped and that Vice Pres. Gustavo Noboa Bejarano would assume the presidency. In 2001 Noboa proposed a number of political reforms, including a new electoral system and a second legislative chamber.

Internet resources: <www.ecuador.com>

Egypt

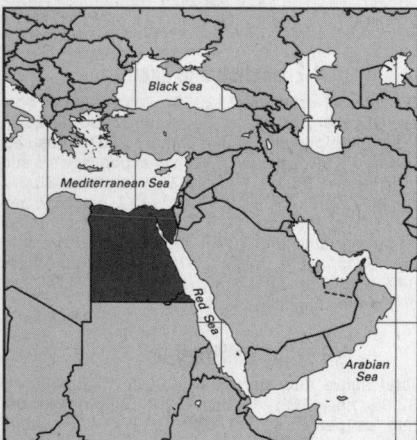

Black Sea

Mediterranean Sea

Red Sea

Arabian Sea

Official name: Jumhuriyah Misr al-'Arabiyah (Arab Republic of Egypt). **Form of government:** republic with one legislative house (People's Assembly [454; including 10 nonelective seats]). **Chief of state:** President Hosni Mubarak (from 1981). **Head of government:** Prime Minister Atef Obeid (from 1999). **Capital:** Cairo. **Official language:** Arabic. **Official religion:** Islam. **Monetary unit:** 1 Egyptian pound (£E) = 100 piastres; valuation (28 Jun 2002) $1 = £E 4.64.

Demography

Area: 385,210 sq mi, 997,690 sq km. **Population** (2001): 65,239,000. **Density** (2000): persons per sq mi 169.4; persons per sq km 65.4. **Urban** (1996): 43.0%. **Sex distribution** (2000): male 50.50%; female 49.50%. **Age breakdown** (2000): under 15, 35.1%; 15–29, 28.5%; 30–44, 19.0%; 45–59, 11.3%; 60–74, 5.0%; 75 and over, 1.0%. **Ethnic composition** (2000): Egyptian Arab 84.1%; Sudanese Arab 5.5%; Arabized Berber 2.0%; Bedouin 2.0%; Rom (Gypsy) 1.6%; other 4.8%. **Religious affiliation** (1997; based on unofficial estimates): Sunni Muslim

89%; Christian 11%. **Major cities** (1996): Cairo 6,789,000 (urban agglomeration [1999] 10,345,000); Alexandria 3,328,000; Al-Jizah 2,222,000; Shubra al-Khaymah 871,000; Port Said 470,000. **Location:** northern Africa, bordering the Mediterranean Sea, the Gaza Strip, Israel, the Red Sea, The Sudan, and Libya.

Vital statistics

Birth rate per 1,000 pop. (2000): 25.4 (world avg. 22.5). **Death rate** per 1,000 pop. (2000): 7.8 (world avg. 9.0). **Natural increase rate** per 1,000 pop. (2000): 17.6 (world avg. 13.5). **Total fertility rate** (avg. births per childbearing woman; 2000): 3.2. **Life expectancy** at birth (2000): male 61.3 years; female 65.5 years.

National economy

Budget (1998–99). *Revenue:* £E 71,295,000,000 (income and profits taxes 21.9%, sales taxes 20.1%, customs duties 14.2%, Suez Canal fees 4.1%, oil revenue 3.1%). *Expenditures:* £E 75,285,000,000 (current expenditure 79.1%, of which wages and pensions 31.7%, public debt interest 20.8%, defense 11.0%, capital expenditure 20.9%). **Public debt** (external, outstanding; 1999): $25,998,000,000. **Population economically active** (1999–2000): total 18,818,000; activity rate 29.7% (participation rates (1995): ages 15–64, 49.8%; female 22.0%; unemployed 7.4%). **Production** (metric tons except as noted). *Agriculture, forestry, fishing* (2000): sugarcane 15,668,000, wheat 6,564,000, corn (maize) 6,395,000; livestock (number of live animals) 4,450,000 sheep, 3,300,000 goats, 3,200,000 water buffalo; roundwood (2000) 2,883,000 cu m; fish catch (1999) 606,780. *Mining and quarrying* (1998–99): iron ore 3,002,000; gypsum 2,666,000. *Manufacturing* (1999–2000): cement 26,000,000; nitrate fertilizers 1,550,000; sugar 1,285,000. *Energy production (consumption):* electricity (kW-hr; 1997) 54,924,000,000 (54,924,000,000); coal (metric tons; 1997) none (1,880,000); crude petroleum (barrels; 1999) 303,576,000 (210,243,000); petroleum products (metric tons; 1999) 28,538,000 (23,761,000); natural gas (cu m; 1997) 14,897,000,000 (14,897,000,000). **Gross national product** (1999): $86,544,000,000 ($1,380 per capita). **Household income and expenditure.** Average household size (1986) 4.9; expenditure (1986–87; urban households only): food 55.7%, clothing 10.9%, housing 10.5%. **Tourism** (1999): receipts $3,903,000,000; expenditures $1,078,000,000.

Foreign trade

Imports (1999): $15,165,000,000 (machinery and transport equipment 32.7%; foodstuffs 21.2%; iron and steel products 7.7%; wood and paper 6.2%; chemical products 5.1%). *Major import sources:* US 14.3%; Germany 8.6%; Italy 6.6%; France 4.9%; Saudi Arabia 4.4%. **Exports** (1999): $5,327,000,000 (petroleum and petroleum products 22.9%; cotton yarn, textiles, and clothing 9.7%; basic metals and manufactures 9.4%). *Major export destinations:* US 12.4%; Italy 10.1%; The Netherlands 7.1%; Israel 5.3%; bunkers & ships' stores 10.3%.

1 metric ton = about 1.1 short tons;   1 kilometer = 0.6 mi (statute);   1 metric ton-km cargo = about 0.68 short ton-mi cargo;   c.i.f.: cost, insurance, and freight;   f.o.b.: free on board

Transport and communications

Transport. *Railroads* (1999): length 4,810 km; passenger-km (1998) 56,667,000,000; metric ton-km cargo (1996) 4,117,000,000. *Roads* (1998): length 64,000 km (paved 78%). *Vehicles* (1998): passenger cars 1,154,753; trucks and buses 510,766. *Inland water* (1999): Suez Canal, number of transits 13,490; metric ton cargo 384,994,000. *Air transport* (1999): passenger-km 9,074,000,000; metric ton-km cargo 269,520,000; airports (1998) 11. **Communications** Total units (units per 1,000 persons). Daily newspaper circulation (1996): 2,400,000 (38); Radio receivers (1997): 20,500,000 (330); Television receivers (1999): 11,400,000 (183); Telephone main lines (1999): 4,666,000 (75); Cellular telephone subscribers (1999): 480,974 (77); Personal computers (1999): 750,000 (12); Internet users (1999): 200,000 (3.2).

Education and health

Literacy (1995): total pop. age 15 and over literate 51.4%; males 63.6%; females 38.8%. **Health:** physicians (1996) 129,000 (1 per 472 persons); hospital beds (1994) 113,020 (1 per 515 persons); infant mortality rate (2000) 62.3. **Food** (1999): daily per capita caloric intake 3,323 (vegetable products 93%, animal products 7%); 120% of FAO recommended minimum requirement.

Military

Total active duty personnel (2000): 448,500 (army 71.3%, navy 4.1%, air force [including air defense] 24.6%). **Military expenditure as percentage of GNP** (1997): 2.8% (world 2.6%); per capita expenditure $34.

Background

Egypt is home to one of the world's oldest continuous civilizations. Upper and Lower Egypt were united c. 3000 BC, beginning a period of cultural achievement and a line of native rulers that lasted nearly 3,000 years. Egypt's ancient history is divided into the Old, Middle, and New Kingdoms, spanning 31 dynasties and lasting to 332 BC. The Pyramids date from the Old Kingdom; the cult of Osiris and the refinement of sculpture from the Middle Kingdom; the era of empire and the Exodus of the Jews from the New Kingdom. An Assyrian invasion occurred in the 7th century BC, and the Persian Achaemenids established a dynasty in 525 BC. The invasion by Alexander the Great in 332 BC inaugurated the Macedonian Ptolemaic period and the ascendancy of Alexandria. The Romans held Egypt from 30 BC to AD 395; later it was placed under the control of Constantinople. Constantine's granting of tolerance in 313 to the Christians began the development of a formal Egyptian (Coptic) church. Egypt came under Arab control in 642 and ultimately was transformed into an Arabic-speaking state, with Islam as the dominant religion. Held by the Umayyad and Abbasid dynasties, in 969 it became the center of the Fatimid dynasty. In 1250 the Mamluks established a dynasty that lasted until 1517, when Egypt fell to the Ottoman Turks. An economic decline ensued, and with it a decline in Egyptian culture. Egypt became a British protectorate in 1914 and received nominal independence in 1922, when a constitutional monarchy was established. A coup overthrew the monarchy in 1952, with Gamal Abdel Nasser taking power. Following three wars with Israel, Egypt, under Nasser's successor, Anwar al-Sadat, ultimately played a leading role in Middle East peace talks. Sadat was succeeded by Hosni Mubarak, who followed Sadat's peace initiatives and in 1982 regained Egyptian sovereignty (lost in 1967) over the Sinai peninsula. Although Egypt took part in the coalition against Iraq during the Persian Gulf War (1991), it later began peace overtures with countries in the region, including Iraq.

Recent Developments

The Egyptian government held parliamentary elections in 2000. Amid charges that the voting was rigged and notwithstanding several violent clashes between protesters and the police, Pres. Hosni Mubarak's National Democratic Party won a large majority (388 of the 444 seats) in the new People's Assembly. After the elections, the government's attention was mostly focused on foreign affairs. In April 2001 Mubarak visited the US to discuss the deadlocked Middle East peace process and economic relations between the two countries. Egypt and the European Union signed an association agreement the following June to establish a free-trade area for manufactured goods. In the wake of the terrorist attacks on 11 September, Mubarak expressed his support for the US but advised against extending military actions beyond Afghanistan.

Internet resources: <www.touregypt.net>

El Salvador

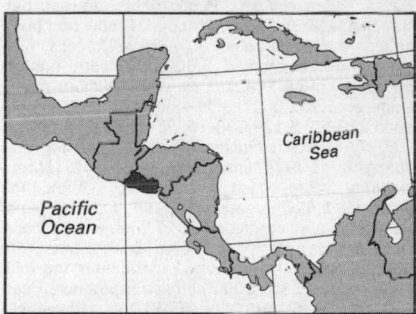

Official name: República de El Salvador (Republic of El Salvador). **Form of government:** republic with one legislative house (Legislative Assembly [84]). **Chief of state and government:** President Francisco Flores Pérez (from 1999). **Capital:** San Salvador. **Official language:** Spanish. **Official religion:** none (Roman Catholicism, although not official, enjoys special recognition in the constitution). **Monetary units:** 1 colón (¢) = 100 centavos; valuation (28 Jun 2002; pegged rate) $1 = ¢8.75 (the US dollar is also legal tender from 1 Jan 2001).

Demography

Area: 8,124 sq mi, 21,041 sq km. **Population** (2001): 6,238,000. **Density** (2001): persons per sq mi 767.8, persons per sq km 296.5. **Urban** (2000): 46.6%. **Sex distribution** (2000): male 48.65%;

female 51.35%. **Age breakdown** (2000): under 15, 38.0%; 15–29, 28.7%; 30–44, 16.6%; 45–59, 9.5%; 60–74, 5.3%; 75 and over 1.9%. **Ethnic composition** (2000): mestizo 88.3%; Amerindian 9.1%, of which Pipil 4.0%; white 1.6%; other/unknown 1.0%. **Religious affiliation** (1995): Roman Catholic 78.2%; Protestant 17.1%, of which Pentecostal 13.3%; other Christian 1.9%; other 2.8%. **Major urban areas** (1992): San Salvador 415,346 (metro area 1,522,126); Soyapango (within San Salvador metro area) 261,122; Santa Ana 139,389; Mejicanos (within San Salvador metro area) 131,972; San Miguel 127,696. **Location:** Central America, bordering Guatemala, Honduras, and the North Pacific Ocean.

Vital statistics

Birth rate per 1,000 pop. (2000): 29.0 (world avg. 22.5); (1998) legitimate 27.2%; illegitimate 72.8%. **Death rate** per 1,000 pop. (2000): 6.3 (world avg. 9.0). **Natural increase rate** per 1,000 pop. (2000): 22.7 (world avg. 13.5). **Total fertility rate** (avg. births per childbearing woman; 2000): 3.4. **Marriage rate** per 1,000 pop. (1998): 4.4. **Divorce rate** per 1,000 pop. (1998): 0.5. **Life expectancy** at birth (2000): male 66.1 years; female 73.5 years.

National economy

Budget. *Revenue* (1997): ¢11,345,000,000 (sales taxes 50.2%, corporate taxes 14.7%, individual income taxes 11.7%, import duties 11.2%). *Expenditures:* ¢12,027,000,000 (education 19.6%, police 16.3%, general public services 13.6%, transportation and communications 12.4%, health 10.3%, defense 7.1%). **Public debt** (external, outstanding; 1999): $2,649,000,000. **Production** (metric tons except as noted). *Agriculture, forestry, fishing* (1999): sugarcane 5,500,000, corn (maize) 683,500, coffee 143,800; livestock (number of live animals) 1,141,000 cattle, 335,000 pigs; roundwood (1998) 5,129,000 cu m; fish catch (1997) 10,987, of which crustaceans 3,920. *Mining and quarrying* (1997): limestone 3,000,000. *Manufacturing* (value added in ¢'000,000; 1996): food products 1,426; wearing apparel 1,009; soaps, cleansers, and cosmetics 932. *Energy production (consumption):* electricity (kW-hr; 1998) 3,868,000,000 (3,906,000,000); crude petroleum (barrels; 1996) none (5,358,000); petroleum products (metric tons; 1996) 698,000 (1,348,000). **Household income and expenditure.** Average household size (1992–93): 4.8; average income per household (1992–93): ¢22,930; expenditure (1990–91; 537,000 urban households only): food and beverages 37.0%, housing 12.1%, transportation and communications 10.2%, clothing and footwear 6.7%. **Land use** (1994): forested 5.0%; meadows and pastures 29.5%; agricultural and under permanent cultivation 35.2%; other 30.3%. **Population economically active** (1995): total 2,136,400; activity rate of total pop. 39.1% (participation rates: ages 15–64, 62.9%; female 37.1%; unemployed [1998] 7.5%). **Gross national product** (at current market prices; 1999): $11,806,000,000 ($1,920 per capita). **Tourism** (1999): receipts $211,000,000; expenditures $80,000,000.

Foreign trade

Imports (1997-c.i.f.): $2,961,500,000 (chemicals and chemical products 17.0%, food and beverages 13.6%, nonelectrical machinery and equipment 12.8%, mineral fuels 11.4%). *Major import sources:* US 41.4%; Guatemala 10.9%; Mexico 7.9%; Costa Rica 3.9%; Germany 3.2%. **Exports** (1997-f.o.b.): $1,353,900,000 (coffee 38.1%, paper and paper products 4.8%, pharmaceuticals 3.9%, raw sugar 3.9%, refined petroleum products 3.3%). *Major export destinations:* Guatemala 19.5%; US 19.2%; Germany 17.5%; Honduras 10.0%; Costa Rica 8.2%.

Transport and communications

Transport. *Railroads* (1997): route length 562 km (operational, 283 km); (1996) passenger-km 4,800,000; (1996) metric ton-km cargo 17,300,000. *Roads* (1997): total length 10,029 km (paved 20%). *Vehicles* (1997): passenger cars 177,488; trucks and buses 184,859. *Air transport:* (1996) passenger-km 2,181,000,000; (1995) metric ton-km cargo 16,006,000; airports (1997) with scheduled flights 1. **Communications** Total units (units per 1,000 persons). Daily newspaper circulation (1996): 278,000 (46); Radio receivers (1997): 2,750,000 (475); Television receivers (1999): 1,777,000 (196); Telephone main lines (1999): 468,068 (78); Cellular telephone subscribers (1999): 382,610 (64); Personal computers (1999): 100,000 (17); Internet users (1999) 40,000 (6.7).

Education and health

Educational attainment (1992). Percentage of pop. over age 25 having: no formal schooling 34.7%; incomplete primary education 37.6%; complete primary ("through ninth grade") 10.8%; secondary 9.4%; higher technical 2.4%; incomplete undergraduate 1.1%; complete undergraduate 2.9%; other/unknown 1.1%. **Literacy** (1992): total pop. age 15 and over literate 2,326,800 (74.1%); males literate 1,141,007 (77.4%); females literate 1,185,793 (71.3%). **Health:** physicians (1997) 6,177 (1 per 936 persons); hospital beds (1996) 9,571 (1 per 593 persons); infant mortality rate per 1,000 live births (2000) 29.2. **Food** (1997): daily per capita caloric intake 2,562 (vegetable products 88%, animal products 12%); 112% of FAO recommended minimum requirement.

Military

Total active duty personnel (2000): 16,800 (army 89.3%, navy 4.2%, air force 6.5%). **Military expenditure as percentage of GNP** (1997): 0.9% (world 2.6%); per capita expenditure $17.

Background

The Spanish arrived in the area in 1524 and subjugated the Pipil Indian kingdom of Cuzcatlán by 1539. The country was divided into two districts, San Salvador and Sonsonate, both attached to Guatemala. When independence came in 1821, San Salvador was incorporated into the Mexican empire; upon its collapse in 1823, Sonsonate and San Salvador combined to form the new state of El

1 metric ton = about 1.1 short tons;   1 kilometer = 0.6 mi (statute);   1 metric ton-km cargo = about 0.68 short ton-mi cargo;   c.i.f.: cost, insurance, and freight;   f.o.b.: free on board

Salvador within the United Provinces of Central America. From its founding, El Salvador experienced a high degree of political turmoil and was under military rule from 1931 to 1979, when the government was ousted in a coup. Elections held in 1982 set up a new government, and in 1983 a new constitution was adopted, but civil war continued through the 1980s. An accord in 1992 brought an uneasy truce.

Recent Developments

Although after taking office in 1999 Pres. Francisco Flores Pérez promised to improve the standard of living, create jobs, and arrest the high crime rate in El Salvador, little progress was made toward these goals. About 50% of the population continued to live in extreme poverty, and violent crime and kidnapping rose along with popular criticism of the new National Civilian Police force. A United Nations Development Programme report for 2001 ranked El Salvador 95th among 162 countries for human development on the basis of its poverty, low rate of tax collection, and meager spending on social programs.

Internet resources: <www.elsalvadorturismo.gob.sv>

Equatorial Guinea

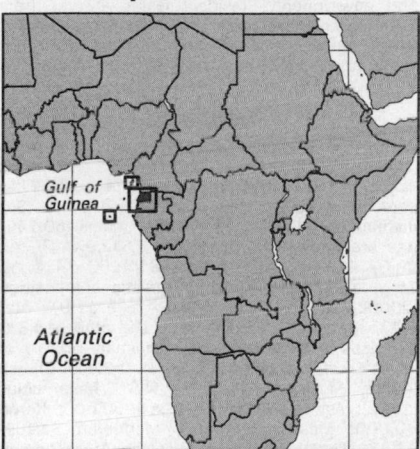

Gulf of Guinea

Atlantic Ocean

Official name: República de Guinea Ecuatorial (Spanish); République du Guinée Équatoriale (French) (Republic of Equatorial Guinea). Form of government: republic with one legislative house (House of Representatives of the People [80]). Chief of state: President Teodoro Obiang Nguema Mbasogo (from 1979). Head of government: Prime Minister Cándido Muatetema Rivas (from 2001). Capital: Malabo. Official languages: Spanish; French. Official religion: none. Monetary unit: 1 CFA franc (CFAF) = 100 centimes; valuation (28 Jun 2002) $1 = CFAF 664.20; the CFAF is pegged to the euro (€) at €1 = CFAF 655.96 from 1 Jan 2002.

Demography

Area: 10,831 sq mi, 28,051 sq km. Population (2001): 486,000. Density (2001): persons per sq mi 44.9, persons per sq km 17.3. Urban (1998): urban 45.7%. Sex distribution (2000): male 48.71%; female 51.29%. Age breakdown (2000): under 15, 42.7%; 15–29, 26.8%; 30–44, 15.9%; 45–59, 8.6%; 60–74, 4.9%; 75 and over, 1.1%. Ethnic composition (1995): Fang 82.9%; Bubi 9.6%; other 7.5%. Religious affiliation (2000): Roman Catholic 80.1%; Muslim 4.0%; African Christian 3.7%; Protestant 3.1%; other 9.1%. Major cities (1983): Malabo (1995) 47,500; Bata (1995) 37,000; Ela-Nguema 6,179; Campo Yaunde 5,199; Los Angeles 4,079. Location: western Africa, the mainland portion bordering Cameroon, Gabon, and the Bight of Biafra (inlet of the Atlantic Ocean).

Vital statistics

Birth rate per 1,000 pop. (2000): 38.1 (world avg. 22.5). Death rate per 1,000 pop. (2000): 13.4 (world avg. 9.0). Natural increase rate per 1,000 pop. (2000): 24.7 (world avg. 13.5). Total fertility rate (avg. births per childbearing woman; 2000): 4.9. Life expectancy at birth (2000): male 51.5 years; female 55.7 years.

National economy

Budget (1996). Revenue: CFAF 24,637,000,000 (domestic revenue 95.1%, of which oil revenue 46.9%, tax revenue 36.8%, nontax revenue 11.4%; foreign grants 4.9%). Expenditures: CFAF 32,955,000,000 (current expenditure 60.6%, of which goods and services 23.8%, salaries 17.3%, interest on debt 15.6%, transfers 3.9%; capital expenditure 9.7%). Public debt (external, outstanding; 1999): $207,900,000. Gross national product (at current market prices; 1999): $516,000,000 ($1,170 per capita). Production (metric tons except as noted). Agriculture, forestry, fishing (1999): roots and tubers 84,000, bananas 15,000, coconuts 8,000; livestock (number of live animals) 36,000 sheep, 8,100 goats, 5,300 pigs; roundwood (1998) 811,000 cu m; fish catch (1997) 6,090. Manufacturing (1998): sawed timber 21,500 cu m; processed timber 3,900 cu m. Energy production (consumption): electricity (kW-hr; 1996) 20,000,000 (20,000,000); crude petroleum (barrels; 1999) 39,487,000 ([1996] 37,000); petroleum products (metric tons; 1996) none (42,000). Population economically active (1997): total 177,000; activity rate of total pop. 40.0% (participation rates: ages 15–64, 74.7%; female 35.4%; unemployed [1983] 24.2%). Household income and expenditure. Average household size (1980) 4.5; sources of income (1988): wages and salaries 57.0%, business income 42.0%, other 1.0%; expenditure (1988): food and beverages 62.0%, clothing and footwear 10.0%; medical care 6.0%. Tourism: tourism is a government priority but remains undeveloped. Land use (1994): forested 65.2%; meadows and pastures 3.7%; agricultural and under permanent cultivation 8.2%; built-on, wasteland, and other 22.9%.

Foreign trade

Imports (1998 c.i.f.): CFAF 256,200,000,000 (petroleum sector 83.1%; other 16.9%). Major import sources: US 35.4%; France 15.0%; Spain 9.9%; Cameroon 9.9%; UK 6.2%; The Netherlands 5.7%. Exports (1998-f.o.b.): CFAF 271,800,000,000 (petroleum 87.6%; wood 9.2%; cocoa 1.5%). Major export destinations: US 62.0%; Spain 17.3%; China 8.9%; Japan 3.4%; France 3.4%.

Transport and communications

Transport. *Roads* (1996): total length 2,800 km (paved 13%). *Vehicles* (1994): passenger cars 6,500; trucks and buses 4,000. *Air transport* (1996): passenger-km 7,000,000; metric ton-km cargo 1,000,000; airports (1998) with scheduled flights 1. **Communications** Total units (units per 1,000 persons). Daily newspaper circulation (1996): 2,000 (4.9); Radio receivers (1997): 180,000 (428); Television receivers (1997): 4,000 (9.8); Telephone main lines (1999): 5,580 (12.9); Cellular telephones (1999): 297 (0.7).

Education and health

Educational attainment (1983). Percentage of pop. age 15 and over having: no schooling 35.4%; some primary education 46.6%; primary 13.0%; secondary 2.3%; postsecondary 1.1%; not specified 1.6%. **Literacy** (1995): percentage of total pop. age 15 and over literate 77.8%; males literate 89.3%; females literate 67.4%. **Health:** physicians (1996) 106 (1 per 4,065 persons); hospital beds (1990) 992 (1 per 350 persons); infant mortality rate per 1,000 live births (2000) 94.8.

Military

Total active duty personnel (2000): 1,320 (army 83.3%, navy 9.1%, air force 7.6%). **Military expenditure as percentage of GNP** (1996): 1.5% (world 2.6%); per capita expenditure $6.

Background

The first inhabitants of the mainland region appear to have been Pygmies. The now-prominent Fang and Bubi reached the mainland region in the 17th-century Bantu migrations. Equatorial Guinea was ceded by the Portuguese to the Spanish in the late 18th century; it was frequented by slave traders, as well as by British, German, Dutch, and French merchants. Bioko was administered by British authorities (1827–58) before the official takeover by the Spanish. The mainland (Río Muni) was not effectively occupied by the Spanish until 1926. Independence was declared in 1968, followed by a reign of terror and economic chaos under the dictatorial president Macías Nguema, who was overthrown by a military coup in 1979 and later executed. A new constitution was adopted in 1982, but political unrest persisted.

Recent Developments

At the end of February 2001, the government of Prime Minister Ángel Serafín Seriche Dougan, which had been accused by the ruling Democratic Party of Equatorial Guinea of corruption and mismanagement, resigned. Pres. Teodoro Obiang Nguema Mbasogo then appointed a new prime minister, Cándido Muatetema Rivas, and cabinet. With oil production at almost 200,000 bbl a day, Equatorial Guinea had the world's fastest-growing economy in 2001.

Internet resources:
<www.cia.gov/cia/publications/factbook/geos/ek.html>

Eritrea

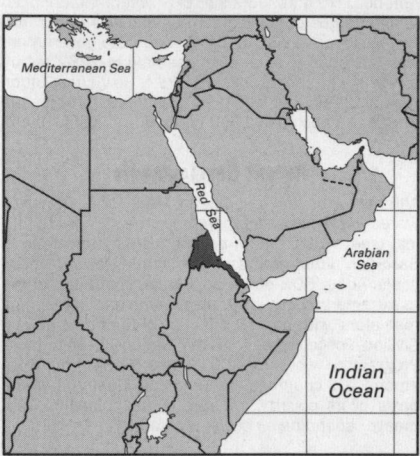

Official name: State of Eritrea. **Form of government:** transitional regime with one interim legislative body (Transitional National Assembly [150]). **Head of state and government:** President Isaias Afwerki (from 1993). **Capital:** Asmara. **Official language:** none. **Official religion:** none. **Monetary unit:** nakfa = 100 cents; valuation (20 Aug 2002) $1 = Nfa 13.55.

Demography

Area: 46,770 sq mi, 121,100 sq km. **Population** (2001; US Bureau of the Census estimate): 4,298,000. **Density** (2001): persons per sq mi 91.9, persons per sq km 35.5. **Urban** (1992): 16.3%. **Sex distribution** (2000): male 49.86%; female 50.14%. **Age breakdown** (2000): under 15, 42.9%; 15–29, 29.0%; 30–44, 14.1%; 45–59, 8.9%; 60–74, 4.1%; 75 and over, 1.0%. **Ethnolinguistic composition** (2000): Tigrinya (Tigray) 51.8%; Tigré 17.9%; Afar 8.1%; Saho 4.3%; Kunama 4.1%; other 13.8%. **Religious affiliation** (2000): Christian 50.5%, of which Eritrean diocese of Ethiopian Orthodox Church j46.1%; Muslim 44.7%; other 4.8%. **Major cities** (1992): Asmara 400,000; Asseb 50,000; Keren 40,000; Massawa 40,000; Mendefera (1989) 14,833. **Location:** the Horn of eastern Africa, bordering The Sudan, the Red Sea, Djibouti, and Ethiopia.

Vital statistics

Birth rate per 1,000 pop. (2000): 42.7 (world avg. 22.5). **Death rate** per 1,000 pop. (2000): 12.3 (world avg. 9.0). **Natural increase rate** per 1,000 pop. (2000): 30.4 (world avg. 13.5). **Total fertility rate** (avg. births per childbearing woman; 2000): 5.9. **Marriage rate** per 1,000 pop. (1992): 6.8. **Life expectancy** at birth (2000): male 53.4 years; female 58.3 years.

National economy

Budget (1997). *Revenue:* Nfa 1,967,400,000 (taxes 48.8%, of which direct taxes 22.8%, import duties 15.2%, indirect taxes 10.8%; nontax revenue

1 metric ton = about 1.1 short tons;   1 kilometer = 0.6 mi (statute);   1 metric ton-km cargo = about 0.68 short ton-mi cargo;   c.i.f.: cost, insurance, and freight;   f.o.b.: free on board

51.2%). *Expenditures:* Nfa 2,588,800,000 (current expenditure 55.8%, of which wages and salaries 27.3%; capital expenditure 44.2%). **Public debt** (external, outstanding; 1999): $253,800,000. **Production** (metric tons except as noted). *Agriculture, forestry, fishing* (1999): sorghum 150,000, roots and tubers 125,000, barley 40,000; livestock (number of live animals) 1,530,000 sheep, 1,400,- 000 goats, 1,320,000 cattle; fish catch (1996) 3,272. *Mining and quarrying* (1995): salt 305,120; small amounts of marble and granite; *Manufacturing* (gross value in Nfa '000; 1997). food production 203,700; beverages 159,600; leather products and shoes 69,400. *Energy production:* commercial electricity production for 1997 was 179,192,000 kW-hr. **Tourism** (1999): receipts from visitors $28,000,000. **Household income and expenditure.** Average household size (1998) 4.7. **Gross national product** (at current market prices; 1999): $779,000,000 ($200 per capita). **Land use** (1994): forested 7.3%; agricultural and under permanent cultivation 5.1%; meadows and pastures 69.0%; other (predominantly barren land) 18.6%.

Foreign trade

Imports (1998-c.i.f.): $526,800,000 (machinery and transport equipment 38.3%, manufactured goods 23.9%, food products 17.1%, chemical products 5.7%, animal and vegetable oil 2.6%). *Major import sources:* Italy 17.4%; United Arab Emirates 16.2%; Germany 5.7%; United Kingdom 4.5%; United States 4.2%. **Exports** (1998-f.o.b.): $27,900,000 (raw materials 46.5%, food products 29.6%, manufactured goods 13.2%, machinery and transport equipment 2.4%, chemical products 2.1%). *Major export destinations:* The Sudan 27.2%; Ethiopia 26.5%; Japan 13.2%; United Arab Emirates 7.3%; Italy 5.3%.

Transport and communications

Transport. *Railroads* (2002): a 306-km rail line that formerly connected Massawa and Agordat is currently under reconstruction. *Roads* (1996): total length 4,010 km (paved 22%). *Vehicles* (1996): automobiles 5,940, trucks and buses, n.a. *Air transport* (1993; Asmara airport only): passenger arrivals (first 6 months; 47,645), passenger departures (first 6 months; 42,548); metric ton cargo handled (1987–88) 28,557; airports (1997) with scheduled flights 2. **Communications** Total units (units per 1,000 persons). Radio receivers (1995): 310,000 (90); Television receivers (1999): 60,000 (15); Telephone main lines (1999): 27,375 (6.9); Internet users (1999): 900 (0.2).

Education and health

Literacy (1993): total pop. literate c. 20%. **Health** (1993): physicians 69 (1 per 36,000 persons); hospital beds (1986–87): 2,449 (1 per 1,100 persons); infant mortality rate per 1,000 live births (2000) 76.7. **Food** (1999): daily per capita caloric intake 1,646 (vegetable 93.6%, animal products 6.4%); 71% of FAO recommended minimum requirement.

Military

Total active duty personnel (2000): estimated strength of Eritrean armed forces (predominantly former guerrillas) is between 200,000 and 250,000. UN peacekeeping force along Eritrean-Ethiopian border (October 2001): 3,900.

Background

As the site of the main ports of the Aksumite empire, Eritrea was linked to the beginnings of the Ethiopian kingdom, but it retained much of its independence until it came under Ottoman rule in the 16th century. In the 17th-19th centuries, control of the territory was disputed among Ethiopia, the Ottomans, the kingdom of Tigray, Egypt, and Italy; it became an Italian colony in 1890. Eritrea was used as the main base for the Italian invasions of Ethiopia (1896 and 1935–36) and in 1936 became part of Italian East Africa. It was captured by the British in 1941, federated to Ethiopia in 1952, and made a province of Ethiopia in 1962. Thirty years of guerrilla warfare by Eritrean secessionist groups ensued. A provisional Eritrean government was established in 1991 after the overthrow of the Ethiopian government, and independence came in 1993. A new constitution was ratified in 1997.

Recent Developments

On 24 May 2001 Eritrea celebrated the 10th anniversary of its effective independence from Ethiopia. This followed significant steps toward the resolution of the two countries' border dispute, which had erupted in mid-1998. In July 2000 the United Nations Mission in Ethiopia and Eritrea (UNMEE) was established and authorized to deploy 4,200 peacekeeping forces. By December of that year UNMEE personnel had opened up secure corridors between the two countries, and a formal comprehensive peace accord was signed in Algiers.

Internet resources: <www.eriemb.se>

Estonia

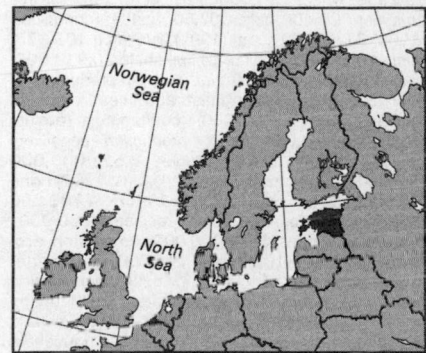

Official name: Eesti Vabariik (Republic of Estonia). **Form of government:** unitary multiparty republic with a single legislative body (Riigikogu [101]). **Chief of state:** President Arnold Ruutel (from 8 Oct 2001). **Head of government:** Prime Minister Siim Kallas (from 28 Jan 2002). **Capital:** Tallinn. **Official language:** Estonian. **Official religion:** none. **Monetary unit:** 1 kroon (EEK) = 100 sents; valuation (28 Jun 2002) $1 = EEK 15.85.

Demography

Area: 16,769 sq mi, 43,431 sq km. **Population** (2001): 1,363,000. **Density** (2001): persons per sq mi 81.3, persons per sq km 31.4. **Urban** (1999): 69.1%. **Sex distribution** (2000): male 46.52%; female 53.48%. **Age breakdown** (2000): under 15, 18.0%; 15–29, 21.9%; 30–44, 21.5%; 45–59, 18.3%; 60–74, 15.0%; 75 and over, 5.3%. **Ethnic composition** (2000): Estonian 65.3%; Russian 28.1%; Ukrainian 2.5%; Belarusian 1.5%; Finnish 0.9%; other 1.7%. **Religious affiliation** (1995): Christian 38.1%, of which Orthodox 20.4%, Evangelical Lutheran 13.7%; other (mostly nonreligious) 61.9%. **Major cities** (2001): Tallinn 399,850; Tartu 101,240; Narva 68,538; Kohtla-Jarve 47,484. **Location:** Eastern Europe, bordering the Gulf of Finland, Russia, Latvia, the Gulf of Riga, and the Baltic Sea.

Vital statistics

Birth rate per 1,000 pop. (2000): 9.6 (world avg. 22.5); legitimate 45.5%; illegitimate 54.5%. **Death rate** per 1,000 pop. (2000): 13.5 (world avg. 9.0). **Natural increase rate** per 1,000 pop. (2000): –3.9 (world avg. 13.5). **Total fertility rate** (avg. births per childbearing woman; 1999): 1.2. **Marriage rate** per 1,000 pop. (1998): 3.7. **Divorce rate** per 1,000 pop. (1998): 3.1. **Life expectancy** at birth (1999): male 65.4 years; female 76.1 years.

National economy

Budget (1998). *Revenue:* EEK 24,130,000,000 (social security contributions 32.9%, value-added taxes 26.6%, excise taxes 11.6%, personal income taxes 11.4%). *Expenditures:* EEK 24,103,000,000 (social security and welfare 30.6%, health 16.4%, education 8.6%, police 7.3%, defense 4.0%). **Public debt** (external, outstanding; 1999): $205,500,000. **Production** (metric tons except as noted). *Agriculture, forestry, fishing* (1999): potatoes 340,000, barley 198,000, wheat 135,000; livestock (number of live animals) 326,400 pigs, 307,500 cattle; roundwood (1998) 6,061,000 cu m; (1997) fish catch 123,873. *Mining and quarrying* (1998): oil shale 10,913,000; peat 333,500. *Manufacturing* (value of production in EEK '000,000; 1996): meat and meat products 2,888; dairy products 2,260; wood products (excluding furniture) 2,054. *Energy production (consumption):* electricity (kW-hr; 1998) 8,521,000,000 (5,579,000,000); hard coal (metric tons; 1996) none (97,000); lignite (metric tons; 1996) 14,700,000 (16,000,000). **Tourism** (1999): receipts $560,000,000; expenditures $217,000,000. **Population economically active** (1997): total 707,800 (first quarter avg.); activity rate of total pop. 48.4% (participation rates: ages 15–64, 71.3%; female 47.9%; unemployed [July 2000–June 2001] 13.4%). **Household income and expenditure** (1998). Average household size 2.3; average disposable income per household EEK 53,049; sources of income: wages and salaries 63.8%, transfers 24.1%, self-employment 6.2%, other 5.9%; expenditure: food and beverages 35.5%, housing 14.6%, transportation 10.7%, clothing and footwear 9.0%. **Gross national product** (1999): $4,906,000,000 ($3,400 per capita). **Land use**

(1994): forest 44.7%; pasture 7.2%; agriculture 32.2%; other 15.9%.

Foreign trade

Imports (2000-c.i.f.): EEK 72,246,000,000 (electrical and nonelectrical machinery 38.5%, fabricated and base metals 8.1%, textiles and apparel 7.5%). *Major import sources:* Finland 27.4%; Sweden 9.8%; Germany 9.5%; Russia 6.1%; Japan 6.1%. **Exports** (2000-f.o.b.): EEK 53,877,000,000 (electrical and nonelectrical machinery 37.5%, wood and wood products 13.4%, textiles and clothing 11.3%). *Major export destinations:* Finland 32.3%; Sweden 20.5%; Germany 8.5%; Latvia 7.0%; United Kingdom 4.4%.

Transport and communications

Transport. *Railroads* (1998): route length 1,018 km; passenger-km 236,000,000; metric ton-km cargo 6,079,000,000. *Roads* (1998): total length 16,430 km (paved 51%). *Vehicles* (1998): passenger cars 451,000; trucks and buses 86,900. *Air transport* (1998 [Estonia Air]): passenger-km 166,742,000; metric ton-km cargo 901,000; airports (1997) 1. **Communications** Total units (units per 1,000 persons). Daily newspaper circulation (1996): 255,000 (174); Radio receivers (1997): 1,010,000 (693); Television receivers (1999): 800,000 (568); Telephone main lines (1999): 515,486 (366); Cellular telephone subscribers (1999): 387,000 (275); Personal computers (1999): 195,000 (138); Internet users (1999): 200,000 (142).

Education and health

Educational attainment (1989). Percentage of persons age 25 and over having: no formal schooling 2.2%; primary education 39.0%; secondary 45.1%; higher 13.7%. **Health** (1998): physicians 4,471 (1 per 324 persons); hospital beds 10,509 (1 per 138 persons); infant mortality rate per 1,000 live births (2000) 8.4. **Food** (1999): daily per capita caloric intake 3,154 (vegetable products 74%, animal products 26%); 123% of FAO recommended minimum requirement.

Military

Total active duty personnel (2000): 4,710 (army 91.7%, navy 5.3%, air force 3.0%). **Military expenditure as a percentage of GNP** (1997): 1.5% (world 2.6%); per capita expenditure $76.

Did you know? Old Town Centre, located in Tallinn, is one of the few surviving city fortresses in the world. Dating back to the 13th century, Old Town, in its heyday, consisted of 8 gates and 48 towers enclosed by a wall. Today, more than 20 towers still stand despite several fires and wars.

Background

The lands on the eastern shores of the Baltic Sea were invaded by Vikings in the 9th century AD and later by Danes, Swedes, and Russians, but the

1 metric ton = about 1.1 short tons;   1 kilometer = 0.6 mi (statute);   1 metric ton-km cargo = about 0.68 short ton-mi cargo;   c.i.f.: cost, insurance, and freight;   f.o.b.: free on board

Estonians were able to withstand the assaults until the Danes took control in 1219. In 1346 the Danes sold their sovereignty to the Teutonic Order, which was then in possession of Livonia (southern Estonia and Latvia). In the mid-16th century Estonia was once again divided, with northern Estonia capitulating to Sweden and Poland gaining Livonia, which it surrendered to Sweden in 1629. Russia acquired Livonia and Estonia in 1721. Nearly a century later, serfdom was abolished, and from 1881 Estonia underwent intensive Russification. In 1918 Estonia obtained independence from Russia, which lasted until the Soviet Union occupied the country in 1940 and forcibly incorporated it into the USSR. Germany held the region (1941–44) during World War II, but the Soviet regime was restored in 1944, after which Estonia's economy was collectivized and integrated into that of the Soviet Union. In 1991, along with other parts of the former USSR, it proclaimed its independence and subsequently held elections. Estonia continued negotiations with Russia to settle their common border.

Recent Developments

On 21 Sep 2001 Arnold Rüütel, a leading former communist and candidate of the rural-oriented People's Union, was elected Estonia's second post-communist president for a five-year term by gaining a bare majority (186 votes) in the 367-member electoral college. By year's end Rüütel had begun negotiations with chairmen of the coalition Reform and Center Party Siim Kallas and Edgar Savisaar to form a new government. Ruutel's election did not signify any change in Estonia's strongly Western-oriented foreign policy.

Internet resources: <www.ee/welcome.html>

Ethiopia

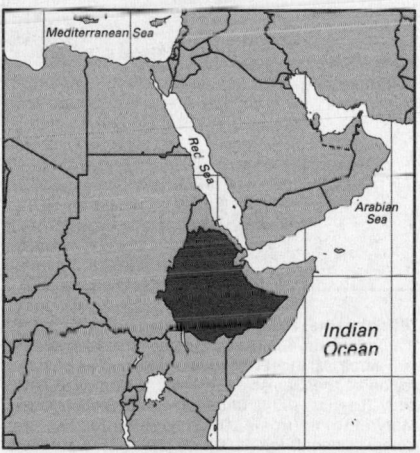

Official name: Federal Democratic Republic of Ethiopia. **Form of government:** federal republic with two legislative houses (Federal Council [108]; Council of People's Representatives [546]). **Chief of state:** President Negasso Gidada (from 1995). **Head of government:** Prime Minister Meles Zenawi (from 1995).

Capital: Addis Ababa. **Official language:** none (Amharic is the "working" language). **Official religion:** none. **Monetary unit:** 1 birr (Br) = 100 cents; valuation (28 Jun 2002) $1 = Br 8.30.

Demography

Area: 437,794 sq mi, 1,133,882 sq km. **Population** (2001): 65,892,000. **Density** (2001): persons per sq mi 150.5, persons per sq km 58.1. **Urban** (1999): 17.2%. **Sex distribution** (2000): male 50.19%; female 49.81%. **Age breakdown** (2000): under 15, 47.0%; 15–29, 26.4%; 30–44, 14.2%; 45–59, 7.9%; 60–74, 3.7%; 75 and over, 0.8%. **Ethnolinguistic composition** (1994): Galla (Oromo) 31.8%; Amharic 29.3%; Somali 6.2%; Tigrinya 5.9%; Walaita 4.6%; Gurage 4.2%; Sidamo 3.4%; Afar 1.9%; Hadya-Libide 1.7%; other 11.0%. **Religious affiliation** (1994): Ethiopian Orthodox 50.3%; Muslim 32.9%; Protestant 10.1%; traditional beliefs 4.8%; Roman Catholic 0.6%; other 1.3%. **Major cities** (1994): Addis Ababa 2,112,737; Dire Dawa 164,851; Harer 131,139; Nazret 127,842; Gonder 112,249. **Location:** the Horn of eastern Africa, bordering Eritrea, Djibouti, Somalia, Kenya, and The Sudan.

Vital statistics

Birth rate per 1,000 pop. (2000): 45.1 (world avg. 22.5). **Death rate** per 1,000 pop. (2000): 17.6 (world avg. 9.0). **Natural increase rate** per 1,000 pop. (2000): 27.5 (world avg. 13.5). **Total fertility rate** (avg. births per childbearing woman; 2001): 7.1. **Life expectancy** at birth (2000): male 44.4 years; female 45.9 years.

National economy

Budget (1997–98). *Revenue:* Br 9,686,000,000 (taxes 54.4%, of which import duties 21.0%, income and profit tax 17.1%, sales tax 12.2%, export duties 1.9%; nontax revenue 29.2%; grants 13.1%; privatization receipts 3.3%). *Expenditures:* Br 7,140,000,-000 (general services 45.2%, of which defense 29.3%; social services 24.1%, of which education 15.8%, public health 5.6%; debt payment 12.3%). **Public debt** (external, outstanding; 1999): $5,360,-000,000. **Tourism** (1999): receipts $16,000,000; expenditures $55,000,000. **Gross national product** (1999): $6,524,000,000 ($100 per capita). **Production** (metric tons except as noted). *Agriculture, forestry, fishing* (1999): corn (maize) 2,840,000, sugarcane 2,200,000, sorghum 1,340,000, wheat 1,150,000; livestock (number of live animals) 35,095,230 cattle, 22,000,000 sheep, 16,950,000 goats; roundwood (1998) 50,148,000 cu m; fish catch (1998) 14,000. *Mining and quarrying* (1995): cement 400,000; limestone 200,000; salt 105,000. *Manufacturing* (gross value in Br '000; 1997): food 1,351,200; beverages 876,408; textiles 593,341. *Energy production (consumption)* [includes Eritrea]: electricity (kW-hr; 1996) 1,675,000,000 (1,675,-000,000); crude petroleum (barrels; 1996) n.a. (5,549,000); petroleum products (metric tons; 1996) 612,000 (861,000). **Land use** (1994): forest 13.3%; pasture 20.0%; agriculture 11.0%; other 55.7%. **Population economically active** (1997): total 26,408,000; activity rate of total pop. 44.8% (participation rates [1995]: ages 15–64, 72.2%; female [1997] 41.0%; unemployed [1994] 62.9%). **Household income and expenditure.** Average household size (1998) 5.0; income per household (1981–82; includes Eritrea) Br 1,728; sources of income (1981–82): self-employment 79.5%, wages and salaries 0.2%, other 20.3%; expenditure (1988; includes Eritrea): food 66.7%, fuel and power 15.9%, clothing and footwear 6.8%, health care 3.1%, education 2.5%, household goods 2.1%.

Foreign trade

Imports (1997–98): Br 7,615,100,000 (consumer goods 24.9%, semifinished goods 17.2%, petroleum products 16.2%, transport equipment 13.2%, food and live animals 13.9%, machinery 13.1%, raw materials 2.1%). *Major import sources:* Japan 10.5%; Germany 9.8%; Saudi Arabia 9.7%; Italy 9.5%; UK 6.0%. Exports (1997–98): Br 3,966,000,000 (coffee 69.8%, hides 8.4%, pulses 2.5%, petroleum products 0.2%). *Major export destinations:* Germany 24.8%; Japan 12.2%; Saudi Arabia 9.9%; Italy 6.8%; US 6.8%.

Transport and communications

Transport. *Railroads* (1996–97; includes 100 km of the Chemin de Fer Djibouti-Ethiopiën in Djibouti): length 782 km; passenger-km 157,000,000; metric ton-km cargo 106,000,000. *Roads* (1996): total length 19,500 km (paved 15%). *Vehicles* (1997): passenger cars 52,012; trucks and buses 39,936. *Air transport* (1997; Ethiopian Airlines only): passenger-km 1,915,000,000; metric ton-km cargo 328,000,-000; airports (1997) 31. Communications Total units (units per 1,000 persons). Daily newspaper circulation (1996): 86,000 (1.5); Radio receivers (1997): 11,750,000 (202); Television receivers (1999): 350,000 (6.1); Telephone main lines (1999): 194,490 (3.2); Personal computers (1999): 45,000 (0.7); Internet users (1999): 8,000 (0.1).

Education and health

Literacy (1995): total pop. age 15 and over literate 35.5%; males 45.5%; females 25.3%. Health: physicians (1988; includes Eritrea) 1,466 (1 per 30,195 persons); hospital beds (1986–87; includes Eritrea) 11,745 (1 per 3,873 persons); infant mortality rate (2000) 101.3. Food (1998): daily per capita caloric intake 1,805 (vegetable products 94%, animal products 6%); 77% of FAO recommended minimum.

Military

Total active duty personnel (2000): 352,500 (army 99.3%, air force 0.7%); UN peacekeeping troops along Ethiopian-Eritrean border (October 2001): 3,900. Military expenditure as percentage of GNP (1997): 1.9% (world 2.6%); per capita expenditure $2.

Background

Ethiopia, the Biblical land of Cush, was inhabited from earliest antiquity and was once under ancient Egyptian rule. Geez-speaking agriculturalists established the kingdom of Daamat in the 2nd millennium BC. After 300 BC they were superseded by the kingdom of Aksum, whose king Menilek I, according to legend, was the son of King Solomon and the Queen of Sheba. Christianity was introduced in the 4th century AD and

became widespread. Ethiopia's prosperous Mediterranean trade was cut off by the Muslim Arabs in the 7th–8th centuries and the area's interests were directed eastward. Contact with Europe resumed in the late 15th century with the arrival of the Portuguese. Modern Ethiopia began with the reign of Tewodros II, who began the consolidation of the country. In the wake of European encroachment, the coastal region was made an Italian colony in 1890, but under Emperor Menilek II, the Italians were defeated and ousted in 1896. Ethiopia prospered under his rule, and his modernization programs were continued by emperor Haile Selassie in the 1930s. In 1936 Italy again gained control of the country and held it as part of Italian Africa until 1941, when it was liberated by the British. Ethiopia incorporated Eritrea in 1952. In 1974 Haile Selassie was deposed and a Marxist government, plagued by civil wars and famine, controlled the country until 1991. In 1993 Eritrea gained its independence, but border conflicts with it and neighboring Somalia continued in the 1990s.

Recent Developments

Local elections were held across Ethiopia in early 2001. Local elections in February resulted in the overwhelming victory of the ruling Ethiopian People's Revolutionary Democratic Front (EPRDF) coalition. Criticisms that the elections were not free and fair led to an opposition boycott of the March township elections, which the EPRDF also won handily. In economic affairs, Ethiopia benefited from a canceling of 67% of its $430 million debt to Paris Club countries under the World Bank's Heavily Indebted Poor Countries program.

Internet resources: <www.ethiopians.com>

Faroe Islands

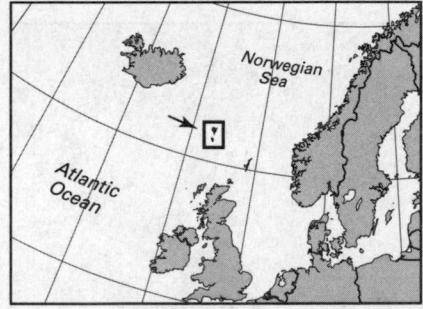

Official name: Føroyar (Faroese); Færøerne (Danish) (Faroe Islands; English-language alternative spelling is Faeroe Islands). Political status: self-governing region of the Danish realm with a single legislative body (Lagting [32]). Chief of state: Danish Queen Margrethe II (from 1972) represented by High Commissioner Birgit Kleis (from 1 Nov 2001). Head of home government: Prime Minister Anfinn Kallsberg (from 1998). Capital: Tórshavn (Thorshavn). Official languages: Faroese; Danish. Official religion: Evangelical Lutheran. Monetary unit: 1 Danish krone

1 metric ton = about 1.1 short tons;   1 kilometer = 0.6 mi (statute);   1 metric ton-km cargo = about 0.68 short ton-mi cargo;   c.i.f.: cost, insurance, and freight;   f.o.b.: free on board

(Dkr) = 100 øre; valuation (28 Jun 2002) $1 = Dkr 7.52 (the local currency, the Faroese króna (Fkr), is equivalent to the Danish krone. Banknotes used are Faroese or Danish; coins are Danish).

Demography

Area: 540 sq mi, 1,399 sq km. **Population** (2001): 46,600. **Density** (2001): persons per sq mi 86.3; persons per sq km 33.3. **Urban** (2000): 36.3% (Tórshavn only). **Sex distribution** (2000): male 51.76%; female 48.24%. **Age breakdown** (2000): under 15, 23.0%; 15–29, 21.1%; 30–44, 19.5%; 45–59, 18.4%; 60–74, 11.5%; 75 and over, 6.5%. **Ethnic composition** (2000): Faroese 97.0%; Danish 2.5%; other Scandinavian 0.4%; other 0.1%. **Religious affiliation** (1995): Evangelical Lutheran Church of Denmark 80.8%; Plymouth Brethren 10.1%; Roman Catholic 0.2%; other (mostly nonreligious) 8.9%. **Major towns** (2000): Tórshavn 16,673; Klaksvík 4,762; Runavík 2,461; Tvøroyri 1,822. **Location:** island group north of the British Isles between the Norwegian Sea and the North Atlantic Ocean.

Vital statistics

Birth rate per 1,000 pop. (2000): 15.2 (world avg. 22.5); (1998) legitimate 62.0%; illegitimate 38.0%. **Death rate** per 1,000 pop. (2000): 7.8 (world avg. 9.0). **Natural increase rate** per 1,000 pop. (2000): 7.4 (world avg. 13.5). **Total fertility rate** (avg. births per childbearing woman; 2000): 2.3. **Marriage rate** per 1,000 pop. (1998): 4.7. **Divorce rate** per 1,000 pop. (1994): 0.8. **Life expectancy** at birth (2000): male 75.0 years; female 81.9 years.

National economy

Budget (1999). *Revenue:* Dkr 3,104,530,000 (income taxes 33.8%; customs and excise duties 32.4%; transfers from the Danish government 30.4%). *Expenditures:* Dkr 3,105,530,000 (health and social welfare 43.3%; education 16.6%; debt service 7.7%; agriculture, fishing, and commerce 7.5%; administration 6.0%). **Gross national product** (2000): $1,029,000,000 ($22,460 per capita). **Production** (metric tons except as noted). *Agriculture, forestry, fishing* (2000): potatoes 1,500, other vegetables, grass, hay, and silage are produced; livestock (number of live animals) 68,100 sheep, 2,000 cattle; fish catch (1999) 358,013 (of which blue whiting 105,106, mackerel 56,476, saithe 34,423). *Manufacturing* (value added in Dkr '000,000; 1999): processed fish 393; all other manufacturing 351; important products include handicrafts and woolen textiles and clothing. *Energy production (consumption):* electricity (kW-hr; 1999) 201,000,000 ([1997] 181,000,000); petroleum products (metric tons; 1998) none (206,000). **Population economically active** (1997): total 26,500; activity rate of total pop. c. 60% (participation rates: female c. 46%; unemployed c. 10%). **Public debt** (to Denmark; end of 1999): $653,000,000. **Household income and expenditure.** Average household size (1977) 3.7; sources of income: self-employment 11.7%, wages and salaries 88.3% (percentages refer to principal sources of income of economically active pop); expenditure (1980): food and beverages 40.9%, fuel and energy 18.9%, housing 17.5%, clothing and footwear 11.3%, other 11.4%. **Tourism** (1987): receipts from visitors $10,000,000; expenditures by

nationals abroad $42,600,000. **Land use** (1994): agricultural and under permanent cultivation 2.1%; other 97.9%.

Foreign trade

Imports (1999): Dkr 3,276,000,000 (goods for household consumption 25.7%; machinery and transport equipment 16.1%; petroleum products 8.1%). *Major import sources:* Denmark 27.8%; Norway 26.1%; Germany 7.2%; United Kingdom 5.9%; Sweden 4.5%. **Exports** (1999): Dkr 3,252,154,000 (fish for human consumption 90.3%, of which frozen fish 29.9%, fresh chilled fish 15.3%, dried, salted, and smoked fish 13.8%; ships 4.3%). *Major export destinations:* Denmark 32.1%; United Kingdom 21.2%; France 9.4%; Spain 6.7%; Germany 6.7%; United States 4.6%.

Transport and communications

Transport. *Railroads:* none. *Roads* (1998): total length 285 mi, 458 km (paved, n.a.). *Vehicles* (2000): passenger cars 14,608; trucks and buses 3,455. *Air transport* (1998): airports with scheduled flights 1. **Communications** Total units (units per 1,000 persons). Daily newspaper circulation (1996): 6,000 (136); Radio receivers (1997): 26,000 (582); Television receivers (1997): 15,000 (333); Telephone main lines (1999): 25,000 (556); Cellular telephone subscribers (1999): 11,000 (244); Internet users (1999): 5,000 (113).

Education and health

Health (1998): physicians 83 (1 per 537 persons); hospital beds 277 (1 per 161 persons); infant mortality rate per 1,000 live births (2000) 6.9. **Food** (1979–81): daily per capita caloric intake 3,195 (vegetable products 68%, animal products 32%); 120% of FAO recommended minimum requirement.

Military

Defense responsibility lies with Denmark.

Background

First settled by Irish monks (c. 700), the islands were colonized by the Vikings (c. 800) and were ruled by Norway from the 11th century until 1380, when they passed to Denmark. They unsuccessfully sought independence in 1946 but received self-government in 1948.

Recent Developments

Relations between the Faroe Islands and Denmark remained strained following the postponement of a local referendum on the issue of independence that had been scheduled for May 2001. Danish Prime Minister Poul Nyrup Rasmussen had threatened to cut off Copenhagen's annual $120 million grant to the Islands, about one-third of Faroese public expenditure. Undeterred by this development and the inconclusive results from the first test drillings for oil off the islands, the Faroese home-rule government announced plans to phase out Danish aid and influence gradually, starting in 2002.

Internet resources: <www.tourist.fo>

Fiji

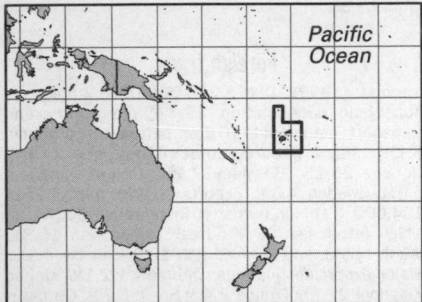

Pacific Ocean

Official name: Republic of the Fiji Islands. **Form of government:** multiparty republic with two legislative houses (Senate [32 [all seats are nonelected]]; House of Representatives [71]). **Chief of state:** President Ratu Josefa Iloilo (from 2000). **Head of government:** Prime Minister Laisenia Qarase (from 15 Mar 2001). **Capital:** Suva. **Official languages:** English, Fijian, and Hindustani have equal status per constitution; the English version of a document prevails, however, if meanings differ. **Official religion:** none. **Monetary unit:** 1 Fiji dollar (F$) = 100 cents; valuation (28 Jun 2002) US$1 = F$2.11.

Demography

Area: 7,055 sq mi, 18,272 sq km. **Population** (2001): 827,000. **Density** (2001): persons per sq mi 117.3, persons per sq km 45.3. **Urban** (1996): 46.4%. **Sex distribution** (2000): male 50.25%; female 49.75%. **Age breakdown** (2000): under 15, 33.4%; 15–29, 28.3%; 30–44, 20.3%; 45–59, 12.1%; 60–74, 5.2%; 75 and over, 0.7%. **Ethnic composition** (1996): Fijian 50.8%; Indian 43.7%; other 5.5%. **Religious affiliation** (2000): Christian 56.8%, of which Protestant 37.1%, independent Christian 8.5%, Roman Catholic 8.4%; Hindu 33.3%; Muslim 6.9%; nonreligious 1.3%; Sikh 0.7%; other 1.0%. **Major cities** (1996; "urban centers"): Suva 167,421; Lautoka 42,917; Nadi 30,791; Labasa 24,187; Nausori 21,645. **Location:** South Pacific Ocean, between Hawaii (US) and New Zealand.

Vital statistics

Birth rate per 1,000 pop. (2000): 23.5 (world avg. 22.5). **Death rate** per 1,000 pop. (2000): 5.8 (world avg. 9.0). **Natural increase rate** per 1,000 pop. (2000): 17.7 (world avg. 13.5). **Total fertility rate** (avg. births per childbearing woman; 2000): 2.9. **Life expectancy** at birth (2000): male 65.5 years; female 70.5 years.

National economy

Budget (1998). *Revenue:* F$848,646,000 (income taxes, estate taxes, and gift duties 58.4%; customs duties and port dues 27.0%; fees, royalties, and sales 5.5%). *Expenditures:* F$1,029,456,000 (departmental expenditure 61.1%; public-debt charges 35.8%; pensions and gratuities 3.1%). **Production** (metric

tons except as noted). *Agriculture, forestry, fishing* (1999): sugarcane 4,398,000, coconuts 209,000, cassava 27,000; livestock (number of live animals) 345,000 cattle, 235,000 goats, 112,000 pigs; roundwood (1998) 594,000 cu m; fish catch (1998) 28,212. *Mining and quarrying* (1995): gold 3,477 kg; silver 1,572 kg. *Manufacturing* (US$'000,000; 1994): food products 84; wearing apparel 28; wood and wood products 16. *Energy production (consumption):* electricity (kW-hr; 1996) 545,000,000 (545,000,000); coal (metric tons; 1996) none (22,000); petroleum products (metric tons; 1996) none (219,000). **Tourism** (1999): receipts from visitors US$275,000,000; expenditures by nationals abroad US$66,000,000. **Land use** (1994): forested 64.9%; agricultural and under permanent cultivation 14.2%; meadows and pastures 9.5%; other 11.4%. **Population economically active** (1986): total 241,160; activity rate of total pop. 33.7% (participation rates: ages 15–64, 56.0%; female 21.2%; unemployed [1990] 6.4%). **Gross national product** (1999): US$1,848,000,000 (US$2,310 per capita). **Public debt** (external, outstanding; 1999): US$120,700,000. **Household income and expenditure.** Average household size (1999) 6.1; expenditure (1991; 3,000 urban households only): food, beverages, and tobacco 41.5%, housing and energy 21.4%, transportation and communications 12.9%, household durable goods 6.5%.

Foreign trade

Imports (1997): F$1,392,664,000 (durable manufactures 27.6%; machinery and transport equipment 20.6%; food, beverages, and tobacco 14.8%; petroleum products 14.1%; chemicals and chemical products 7.8%). *Major import sources:* Australia 45.2%; New Zealand 15.4%; Japan 6.9%; US 5.2%; Singapore 4.2%. **Exports** (1997; excludes reexports = F$138,906,000): F$714,621,000 (sugar 24.4%; clothing 23.5%; gold 8.7%; fish 5.3%; timber 3.5%). *Major export destinations:* Australia 40.5%; UK 21.4%; Japan 13.4%; US 10.2%; New Zealand 6.3%.

Transport and communications

Transport. *Railroads* (1995; owned by the Fiji Sugar Corporation): length 595 km. *Roads* (1995): total length 5,100 km (paved 20%). *Vehicles* (1995): passenger cars 49,712; trucks and buses 33,928. *Air transport* (1996; Air Pacific only): passenger-km 1,194,652,000; metric ton-km cargo 75,367,000; airports (1997) with scheduled flights 13. **Communications** Total units (units per 1,000 persons). Daily newspaper circulation (1996): 40,000 (51); Radio receivers (1997): 500,000 (636); Television receivers (1999): 88,908 (111); Telephone main lines (1999): 81,518 (101); Cellular telephone subscribers (1999): 23,380 (29); Personal computers (1999): 40,000 (50); Internet users (1999): 7,500 (9.3).

Education and health

Educational attainment (1986). Percentage of pop. age 25 and over having: no formal schooling 28.3%; primary only 19.1%; some secondary 44.1%; secondary 4.1%; postsecondary 3.3%; other 1.1%. **Literacy** (1995): total pop. age 15 and over literate

---

1 metric ton = about 1.1 short tons;　1 kilometer = 0.6 mi (statute);　1 metric ton-km cargo = about 0.68 short ton-mi cargo;　c.i.f.: cost, insurance, and freight;　f.o.b.: free on board

91.6%; males 93.8%; females 89.3%. **Health** (1998): physicians 252 (1 per 3,147 persons); hospital beds 1,797 (1 per 441 persons); infant mortality rate per 1,000 live births (2000) 14.5. **Food** (1999): daily per capita caloric intake 2,934 (vegetable products 81%, animals products 19%); 129% of FAO recommended minimum requirement.

Military

Total active duty personnel (2000): 3,500 (army 91.4%, navy 8.6%). **Military expenditure as percentage of GNP** (1997): 2.4% (world 2.6%); per capita expenditure US$61.

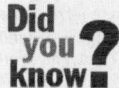

Did you know? Prior to the early 1800s the islands of Fiji were usually avoided by seafarers because of their reputation for tough, man-eating warriors (thus the unofficial name "the Cannibal Isles"). The Fiji Museum in Suva, the capital, does not avoid mention of this history and in addition includes a special display of war canoes.

Background

Archaeological evidence shows that the islands of Fiji were occupied in the late 2nd millennium BC and the inhabitants had developed pottery by c. 1300 BC. The first European sighting was by the Dutch in the 17th century; in 1774 the islands were visited by Capt. James Cook, who found a mixed Melanesian-Polynesian population with a complex society. Traders and the first missionaries arrived in 1835. In 1857 a British consul was appointed, and in 1874 Fiji was proclaimed a crown colony. It became independent as a member of the Commonwealth in 1970, and was declared a republic in 1987 following a military coup. Elections in 1992 restored civilian rule. A new constitution was approved in 1997.

Recent Developments

On 1 Oct 2001—after more than a year of political instability stemming from a coup in May 2000, when Fiji's Parliament was stormed by ethnic-Fijian armed nationalists—newly elected lawmakers were sworn in amid tight security. Coup leader George Speight remained in prison on treason and firearms charges. In recognition of Fiji's return to democracy, the country was readmitted as a full member of the Commonwealth in December.

Internet resources: <www.fiji.org.nz>

Finland

Official names: Suomen Tasavalta (Finnish); Republiken Finland (Swedish) (Republic of Finland). **Form of government:** multiparty republic with one legislative house (Parliament [200; includes one representative from Åland not taking part in the 1999 general elections]). **Chief of state:** President Tarja Halonen (from 2000). **Head of government:** Prime Minister Paavo Lipponen (from 1995). **Capital:** Helsinki. **Official languages:** none (Finnish and Swedish were official languages until mid-1995 and

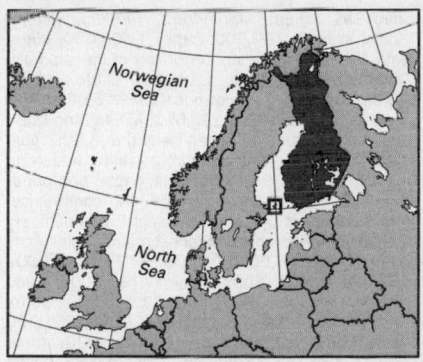

national languages thereafter). **Official religion:** none. **Monetary unit:** 1 euro (€) = 100 cents; $1 = €1.01 (28 Jun 2002); at conversion on 1 Jan 2002, €1 = 5.95 Finnish markka (Fmk).

Demography

Area: 130,559 sq mi, 338,145 sq km (total includes land area of 117,580 sq mi [304,530 sq km] and inland water area of 12,979 sq mi [33,615 sq km]). **Population** (2001): 5,185,000. **Density** (2000; based on land area only): persons per sq mi 44.1, persons per sq km 17.0. **Urban** (2000): 60.4%. **Sex distribution** (2000): male 48.79%; female 51.21%. **Age breakdown** (2000): under 15, 18.2%; 15–29, 18.7%; 30–44, 21.8%; 45–59, 21.5%; 60–74, 13.4%; 75 and over, 6.4%. **Ethnolinguistic composition** (by place of birth; 2000): Finland 97.5%; Russia 0.6%; Sweden 0.5%; Africa 0.2%. **Religious affiliation** (2000): Evangelical Lutheran 85.2%; Finnish (Greek) Orthodox 1.1%; nonreligious 12.6%; other 1.1%. **Major cities** (2000): Helsinki 551,123 (metro area 945,725); Espoo 209,667 (within Helsinki metro area); Tampere 193,174; Vantaa 176,386 (within Helsinki metro area); Turku 172,107; Oulu 117,670. **Location:** northern Europe, bordering Norway, Russia, the Gulf of Finland, the Baltic Sea, the Gulf of Bothnia, and Sweden.

Vital statistics

Birth rate per 1,000 pop. (1999): 11.2 (world avg. 22.5); legitimate 61.3%; illegitimate 38.7%. **Death rate** per 1,000 pop. (1999): 9.5 (world avg. 9.0). **Natural increase rate** per 1,000 pop. (1999): 1.7 (world avg. 13.5). **Total fertility rate** (avg. births per childbearing woman; 1999): 1.7. **Marriage rate** per 1,000 pop. (1999): 4.7. **Divorce rate** per 1,000 pop. (1999): 2.7. **Life expectancy** at birth (1999): male 73.7 years; female 81.0 years.

National economy

Budget (2000). *Revenue:* Fmk 199,579,000,000 (income and property taxes 33.7%, value-added taxes 27.7%, excise duties 13.8%). *Expenditures:* Fmk 199,575,000,000 (social security and health 21.8%, education 14.0%, interest on state debt 13.4%, agriculture and forestry 6.6%, defense 4.9%). **National debt** (December 1998): $82,690,-000,000. **Tourism** (in $'000,000; 1999): receipts 1,517; expenditures 2,021. **Production** (metric tons except as noted). *Agriculture, forestry, fishing* (1999): silage 6,799,000, barley 1,568,000, sugar beets 1,172,000; livestock (number of live animals; 2000) 1,541,000 pigs, 1,101,000 cattle, (1999) 195,000 reindeer; roundwood (1999) 53,851,000 cu m; fish catch (1997) 196,513. *Mining and quarrying* (1998): chromite (gross weight) 498,000; gold 5,000 kilograms. *Manufacturing* (value added in Fmk '000,000; 1998): wood pulp, paper, and paper products 24,304; radio, television, and communications equipment 21,271; nonelectrical machinery 17,398. *Energy production (consumption):* electricity (kW-hr; 1999) 66,655,000,000 (77,779,000,000); coal (metric tons; 1996) none (7,704,000); crude petroleum (barrels; 1996) none (71,746,000); petroleum products (metric tons; 1996) 11,861,000 (10,355,000); natural gas (cu m; 1996) none (3,582,000,000). **Population economically active** (1999): total 2,557,000; activity rate of total pop. 49.5% (participation rates: ages 15–64, 73.6%; female 47.8%; unemployed [October 1999–September 2000] 10.0%). **Household income and expenditure** (1998). Average household size 2.2; disposable income per household Fmk 146,400; sources of gross income: wages and salaries 55.4%, transfer payments 27.4%, other 17.2%; expenditure: housing and energy 27.3%, transportation and communications 18.9%, food, beverages, and tobacco 16.5%. **Gross national product** (1999): $127,764,-000,000 ($24,730 per capita). **Land use** (1994): forested 76.1%; meadows and pastures 0.4%; agricultural and under permanent cultivation 8.5%; other 15.0%.

Foreign trade

Imports (1999-c.i.f.): Fmk 176,536,000,000 (electrical machinery and apparatus 16.7%; nonelectrical machinery and apparatus 15.4%; mineral fuels 8.5%; automobiles 8.4%). *Major import sources:* Germany 15.3%; Sweden 11.2%; US 7.9%; Russia 7.2%; UK 6.6%; Japan 6.2%; France 4.3%. **Exports** (1999-f.o.b.): Fmk 233,343,000,000 (electrical machinery and apparatus 23.7%; paper and paper products 20.5%; nonelectrical machinery and apparatus 11.8%; wood products and furniture 7.2%). *Major export destinations:* Germany 13.1%; Sweden 9.9%; UK 9.1%; US 7.9%; France 5.3%; The Netherlands 4.3%; Russia 4.1%.

Transport and communications

Transport. *Railroads:* route length (1999) 5,836 km; passenger-km 3,415,000,000; metric ton-km cargo 9,753,000,000. *Roads* (2000; excludes Åland Islands): total length 77,900 km (paved 65%). *Vehicles* (2000): passenger cars 2,069,055; trucks and buses 300,048. *Air transport* (1999): passenger-km 12,916,000,000; metric ton-km cargo 315,883,-000; airports (1999) 27. **Communications** Total units (units per 1,000 persons). Daily newspaper circulation (1996): 2,332,000 (455); Radio receivers (1997): 7,700,000 (1,498); Television receivers (1997): 3,200,000 (623); Telephone main lines (1999): 2,850,000 (552); Cellular telephone subscribers (1999): 3,364,000 (651); Personal computers (1999): 1,860,000 (360); Internet users (1999): 2,143,000 (415).

Education and health

Educational attainment (end of 1998). Percentage of pop. age 25 and over having: incomplete upper-secondary education 40.7%; complete upper secondary or vocational 33.6%; higher 25.7%. **Literacy:** virtually 100%. **Health** (1999): physicians 15,794 (1 per 327 persons; registered professionals of working age); hospital beds (1998) 39,718 (1 per 130 persons); infant mortality rate per 1,000 live births 4.2. **Food** (1998): daily per capita caloric intake 3,180 (vegetable products 61%, animal products 39%); 117% of FAO recommended minimum requirement.

Military

Total active duty personnel (2000): 31,700 (army 75.7%, navy 15.8%, air force 8.5%). **Military expenditure as percentage of GNP** (1997): 1.7% (world 2.6%); per capita expenditure $381.

Background

Recent archaeological discoveries have led some to suggest that human habitation in Finland dates back at least 100,000 years. Ancestors of the Sami apparently were present in Finland by about 7000 BC. The ancestors of the present-day Finns came from the southern shore of the Gulf of Finland in the 1st millennium BC. The area was gradually Christianized from the 11th century. From the 12th century Sweden and Russia contested for supremacy in Finland, until in 1323 Sweden ruled most of the country. Russia was ceded part of Finnish territory in 1721; in 1808 Alexander I of Russia invaded Finland, which in 1809 was formally ceded to Russia. The subsequent period saw the growth of Finnish nationalism. Russia's losses in World War I and the Russian Revolution of 1917 set the stage for Finland's independence in 1917. It was defeated by the Soviet Union in the Russo-Finnish War (1939–40) but then sided with Nazi Germany against the Soviets during World War II and regained the territory it had lost. Facing defeat again by the advancing Soviets in 1944, it reached a peace agreement with the USSR, ceding territory and paying reparations. Finland's economy recovered after World War II. It joined the European Union in 1995.

Recent Developments

Tarja Halonen of the left-wing Social Democratic Party was elected Finland's first woman president in February 2000. Though other countries in the region made plans in 2001 to join NATO, Finland maintained its nonalliance stance but welcomed NATO's open-door policy and pledged to cooperate closely within NATO's Partnership for Peace.

Internet resources: <www.finland-tourism.com>

France

Official name: République Française (French Republic). **Form of government:** republic with two legislative houses (Parliament; Senate [321], National Assembly [577]). **Chief of state:** President Jacques

---

1 metric ton = about 1.1 short tons;   1 kilometer = 0.6 mi (statute);   1 metric ton-km cargo = about 0.68 short ton-mi cargo;   c.i.f.: cost, insurance, and freight;   f.o.b.: free on board

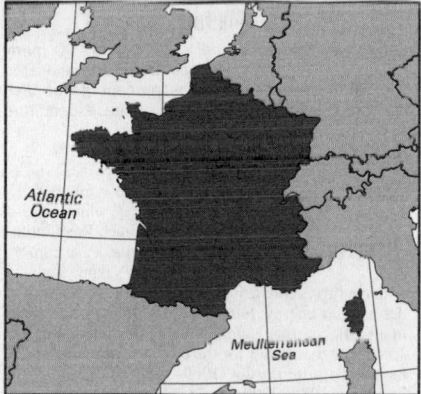

Chirac (from 1995). **Head of government:** Prime Minister Lionel Jospin (from 1997). **Capital:** Paris. **Official language:** French. **Official religion:** none. **Monetary unit:** 1 euro (€) = 100 cents; $1 = €1.01 (28 Jun 2002); at conversion on 1 Jan 2002, €1 = 6.56 French francs (F).

Demography

Area: 210,026 sq mi, 543,965 sq km. **Population** (2001): 59,090,000. **Density** (2001): persons per sq mi 281.3, persons per sq km 108.6. **Urban** (1999): 75.5%. **Sex distribution** (1999): male 48.56%; female 51.44%. **Age breakdown** (1999): under 15, 17.9%; 15–29, 20.2%; 30–44, 21.9%; 45–59, 18.7%; 60–74, 13.6%; 75 and over, 7.7%. **Ethnic composition** (2000): French 76.9%; Algerian & Moroccan Berber 2.2%; Italian 1.9%; Portuguese 1.5%; Moroccan Arab 1.5%; Fleming 1.4%; Algerian Arab 1.3%; Basque 1.3%; Jewish 1.2%; German 1.2%; Vietnamese 1.0%; Catalan 0.5%; other 9.3%. **Religious affiliation** (2000): Roman Catholic 82.3%; Muslim 7.1%; atheist 4.4%; Protestant 3.7%; Orthodox 1.1%; Jewish 1.0%; other 0.4%. **Major cities** (1999): Paris 2,125,246 (metropolitan area 9,644,507); Marseille 798,430 (1,349,772); Lyon 445,452 (1,348,832); Toulouse 390,350 (761,090); Nice 342,738 (888,784); Nantes 270,251 (544,932); Strasbourg 264,115 (427,245); Montpellier 225,392 (287,981); Bordeaux 215,363 (753,931). **National origin** (1990): French 93.6%, of which Martiniquais 0.2%, Guadeloupian 0.2%, Réunionese 0.2%; Portuguese 1.1%; Algerian 1.1%; Moroccan 1.0%; Italian 0.4%; Spanish 0.4%; Turkish 0.3%; other 2.1%. **Mobility** (1990). Population living in same residence as in 1982: 51.4%; same region 89.0%; different region 8.8%; different country 2.2%. **Households** (1993). Average household size 2.6; 1 person 27.7%, 2 persons 32.0%, 3 persons 17.4%, 4 persons 14.7%, 5 persons or more 8.2%. Family households (1990): 14,118,940 (72.1%); nonfamily 5,471,460 (27.9%, of which 1-person 24.6%). **Immigration** (1998): immigrants admitted 100,014 (Algeria 15.3%, Turkey 6.0%, Tunisia 4.9%, Sri Lanka 1.7%, Vietnam 1.0%). **Location:** western Europe, bordering the North Atlantic Ocean, Belgium, Luxembourg, Germany, Switzerland, Italy, the Mediterranean Sea, Spain, and Andorra. **Dependent territories:** French Guiana, French Polynesia, Guadeloupe, Martinique, Mayotte, New Caledonia,

Réunion, Saint Pierre and Miquelon, and Wallis and Futuna.

Vital statistics

Birth rate per 1,000 pop. (1998): 12.7 (world avg. 22.5); (1997) legitimate 59.9%; illegitimate 40.1%. **Death rate** per 1,000 pop. (1998): 9.0 (world avg. 9.0). **Natural increase rate** per 1,000 population (1998): 3.7 (world avg. 13.5). **Total fertility rate** (avg. births per childbearing woman; 2000): 1.7. **Marriage rate** per 1,000 pop. (1998): 4.6. **Divorce rate** per 1,000 pop. (1998): 2.0. **Life expectancy** at birth (2000); male 74.8 years; female 82.9 years.

Social indicators

Quality of working life. Average workweek (1994): 38.9 hours. Annual rate per 100,000 workers for: injury or accident 5,322 (deaths 0.8%); accidents in transit to work 708 (deaths 68.3); industrial illness (1989) 16.6; death (1989) 4.8. Average days lost to labor stoppages per 1,000 workers (1994): 21.0. Average length of journey to work (1990): 8.7 mi (14 km). **Access to services** (1992). Proportion of dwellings having: central heating 86.0%; piped water 97.0%; indoor plumbing 95.8%. **Social participation.** Eligible voters participating in last (May and June 1997) national election: c. 78%. Pop. over 15 years of age participating in voluntary associations: 28.0%. **Social deviance.** Offense rate per 100,000 pop. (1998) for: murder 1.6, rape 13.4, other assault 583.8; theft (including burglary and housebreaking) 6,107.6. Incidence per 100,000 in general pop. of: alcoholism, n.a. (deaths related to alcoholism; 1991) 5.0; suicide (1993) 21.1. **Leisure** (1987–88). Participation rate for favorite leisure activities: watching television 82%; reading magazines 79%; listening to radio 75%; entertaining relatives 64%; visiting relatives 61%; attending fairs/expositions 56%. **Material well-being** (1994). Households possessing: automobile 79.5%; color television 92.4%; VCR 52.8%; refrigerator 99.0%; washing machine 89.4%.

National economy

Gross national product (1999): $1,453,211,000,-000 ($24,170 per capita). **Budget** (1998). *Revenue:* F 1,331,838,000,000 (value-added taxes 58.3%, personal income tax 22.2%, corporate income tax 16.5%). *Expenditure:* F 1,585,307,000,000 (education 21.1%, defense 15.0%, health and social services 4.6%, research and development 2.5%). **Production** (metric tons except as noted). *Agriculture, forestry, fishing* (2000): wheat 37,559,000, sugar beets 31,454,000, corn (maize) 16,469,000, barley 9,927,000, grapes 7,627,000, rapeseed 3,569,000; livestock (number of live animals) 20,527,000 cattle, 14,635,000 pigs, 10,004,000 sheep, 1,190,000 goats; roundwood 50,170,000 cu m; fish catch (1999) 845,649. *Mining and quarrying* (1999): potash 345,000; bauxite 160,000; gold 114,778 troy oz; iron ore production ceased at the end of 1998. *Manufacturing* (1996): cement (1995) 19,896,000; crude steel 17,633,000; pig iron 12,132,000; paper products 8,556,000; tires (1995) 59,268,000 units; automobiles (1995) 3,200,000 units. *Energy production (consumption):* electricity (kW-hr; 1997) 515,468,000,000 (450,072,000,-000); coal (metric tons; 1997) 7,298,000

(21,527,000); crude petroleum (barrels; 1997) 13,048,000 (651,981,000); petroleum products (metric tons; 1997) 79,634,000 (70,965,000); natural gas (cu m; 1997) 1,437,900,000 (37,102,600,000). **Population economically active** (1998): total 25,459,200; activity rate of total population 43.4% (participation rates: ages 15–64 (1994), 67.6%; female 45.8%; unemployed 11.9%). **Household income and expenditure** (1995). Average household size 2.6; average annual income per household F 302,560; sources of income: wages and salaries 70.0%, self-employment 24.4%, social security 5.6%, expenditure (1997): housing 22.5%, food 17.9%, transportation 16.3%, health 10.3%, recreation and education 7.4%, clothing 5.2%. **Tourism** (1999): receipts $31,507,000,000; expenditures $18,631,000,000. **Public debt** (1998): F 5,030,000,000,000 ($853,000,000,000). **Land use** (1994): forest 27.3%; pasture 19.3%; agriculture 35.4%; other 18.0%.

Foreign trade

Imports (1998): F 1,687,500,000,000 (machinery and transport equipment 39.1%; chemicals and chemical products 12.2%; agricultural products 7.9%; fuels 5.9%). *Major import sources:* Germany 17.2%; Italy 9.9%, UK 8.4%; US 8.2%; Belg.-Lux. 7.7%; Spain 7.1%. **Exports** (1998): F 1,773,200,000,000 (machinery and apparatus 26.1%; transport equipment 17.7%; chemicals and chemical products 12.7%; agricultural products 12.0%). *Major export destinations:* Germany 16.1%; UK 10.0%; Italy 9.2%; Spain 8.7%; Belg.-Lux. 7.7%; US 7.4%.

Transport and communications

Transport. *Railroads:* route length (1997) 31,821 km; (1999) passenger-km 66,590,000,000; (1999) metric ton-km cargo 52,110,000,000. *Roads* (1999): total length 893,300 km (paved 100%). *Vehicles* (1998): passenger cars 26,800,000; trucks and buses 5,500,000. *Air transport* (1999): passenger-km 89,066,600,000; metric ton-km cargo 4,774,900,000; airports (1996) 61. **Communications** Total units (units per 1,000 persons). Daily newspaper circulation (1996): 12,725,000 (218); Radio receivers (1997): 55,300,000 (946); Television receivers (1999): 36,500,000 (623); Telephone main lines (1999): 34,100,000 (582); Cellular telephone subscribers (1999): 21,434,000 (366); Personal computers (1999): 13,000,000 (222); Internet users (1999): 5,370,000 (92).

Education and health

Educational attainment (1990). Percentage of pop. age 25 and over having: primary education 22.1%; lower secondary 7.8%; higher secondary and vocational 29.4%; postsecondary 11.6%; undeclared attainment 29.1%. **Health:** physicians (1996) 171,704 (1 per 346 persons); hospital beds (1998) 651,208 (1 per 91 persons); infant mortality rate (2000) 4.5. **Food** (1999): daily per capita caloric intake 3,575 (vegetable products 62%, animal products 38%); 141% of FAO recommended minimum requirement.

Military

Total active duty personnel (2000): 294,430 (army 57.5%, navy 16.8%, air force 20.5%, unallocated 5.2%). **Military expenditure as percentage of GNP** (1997): 3.0% (world 2.6%); per capita expenditure $708.

Did you know? The modern mythical symbol of France is "Marianne," which originated during the French Revolution (1789–1792); "Marianne," a common French woman's name in the 18th century, represented the proud female leader defying her enemy. Now busts of "Marianne" appear in all village, town, and city halls. Recent women serving as the model for the bust of "Marianne" include Brigitte Bardot (1969–1985), Catherine Deneuve (1985–2000), and Laetitia Casta (2000–).

Background

Archaeological excavations in France indicate continuous settlement from Paleolithic times. In c. 1200 BC the Gauls migrated into the area and in 600 BC Ionian Greeks established several settlements, including one at Marseille. Julius Caesar completed the Roman conquest of Gaul in 50 BC. During the 6th century AD, the Salian Franks ruled; by the 8th century power had passed to the Carolingians, the greatest of whom was Charlemagne. The Hundred Years' War (1337–1453) resulted in the return to France of land that had been held by the British; by the end of the 15th century, France approximated its modern boundaries. The 16th century was marked by the Wars of Religion between Protestants (Huguenots) and Roman Catholics. Henry IV's Edict of Nantes (1598) granted substantial religious toleration, but this was revoked in 1685 by Louis XIV, who helped to raise monarchical absolutism to new heights. In 1789 the French Revolution proclaimed the rights of the individual and destroyed the ancient regime. Napoleon ruled from 1799 to 1814, after which a limited monarchy was restored until 1871, when the Third Republic was created. World War I (1914–18) ravaged the northern part of France. After Nazi Germany's invasion during World War II, the collaborationist Vichy regime governed. Liberated by Allied and Free French forces in 1944, France restored parliamentary democracy under the Fourth Republic. A costly war in Indochina and rising nationalism in French colonies during the 1950s overwhelmed the Fourth Republic. The Fifth Republic was established in 1958 under Charles de Gaulle, who presided over the dissolution of most of France's overseas colonies. In 1981 Francois Mitterrand became France's first elected Socialist president. During the 1990s the French government, balancing right- and left-wing forces, moved toward solidifying European unity.

Recent Developments

On 5 May 2002 French Pres. Jacques Chirac won reelection by a margin of 82%–18% over challenger Jean-Marie Le Pen. The founder of the far-right

1 metric ton = about 1.1 short tons;   1 kilometer = 0.6 mi (statute);   1 metric ton-km cargo = about 0.68 short ton-mi cargo;   c.i.f.: cost, insurance, and freight;   f.o.b.: free on board

National Front, Le Pen had earned the right to challenge Chirac with a surprise second-place finish in the election's preliminary round. Prime Minister Lionel Jospin, who was among the candidates bested by Le Pen, resigned his post after the results of the first round were announced. Those results had ignited mass protests against Le Pen and raised concerns about the growth of the far right in France and throughout Europe. Chirac's margin of victory over Le Pen in the final round was the widest ever in a French presidential election, though it was largely the result of a short-lived alliance of the country's left- and right-wing groups that had been forged specifically with the aim of denying Le Pen the presidency.

Two elements of French statehood were recently phased out—the franc, which gave way to the euro in January 2002, and military conscription, which was abandoned in December 2001 in favor of a smaller volunteer army. Both changes could be seen in the context of a France far more willing to cooperate—at least with its European neighbors—than it had been under de Gaulle. The integration was obvious in the case of the euro, to be shared with 11 other countries in the European Union, but it was also an element in France's acceptance that defense of its territory was better ensured by a smaller professional army working in close cooperation with allies than by a mass army maintained on its own.

Internet resources: <www.franceguide.com>

French Guiana

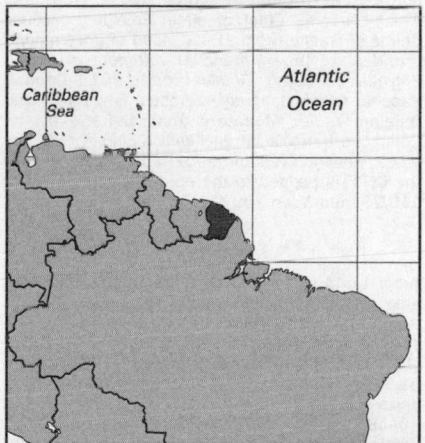

Caribbean Sea

Atlantic Ocean

Official name: Département de la Guyane française (Department of French Guiana). **Political status:** overseas department of France with two legislative houses (General Council [19]; Regional Council [31]). **Chief of state:** President Jacques Chirac of France (from 1995). **Heads of government:** Prefect (for France); President of the General Council Andre Lecante (from 1998); President of the Regional Council Antoine Karam (from 1992). **Capital:** Cayenne. **Official language:** French. **Official religion:** none. **Monetary unit:** 1 euro (€) = 100 cents; $1 = €1.01 (28 Jun 2002); at conversion on 1 Jan 2002, €1 = 6.56 French francs (F).

Demography

Area: 33,399 sq mi, 86,504 sq km. **Population** (2001): 168,000. **Density** (2001): persons per sq mi 5.0, persons per sq km 1.9. **Urban** (2000): 78.2%. **Sex distribution** (1999): male 50.36%; female 49.64%. **Age breakdown** (1999): under 15, 34.0%; 15–29, 24.2%; 30–44, 23.3%; 45–59, 12.5%; 60–74, 4.3%; 75 and over, 1.7%. **Ethnic composition** (2000): Guianese Mulatto 37.9%; French 8.0%; Haitian 8.0%; Surinamese 6.0%; Antillean 5.0%; Chinese 5.0%; Brazilian 4.9%; East Indian 4.0%; other (other West Indian, Hmong, other South Americans) 21.2%. **Religious affiliation** (1995): Roman Catholic 82.1%; other 17.9%. **Major cities** (1999 [commune pop.]): Cayenne 50,594 (urban agglomeration 84,181); Saint-Laurent-du-Maroni 19,211; Kourou 19,107; Matoury 18,032; Rémire-Montjoly 15,555. **Location:** northern South America, bordering the Atlantic Ocean, Brazil, and Suriname.

Vital statistics

Birth rate per 1,000 pop. (2000): 22.4 (world avg. 22.5); (1993) legitimate 20.0%; illegitimate 80.0%. **Death rate** per 1,000 pop. (2000): 4.7 (world avg. 9.0). **Natural increase rate** per 1,000 pop. (2000): 17.7 (world avg. 13.2). **Total fertility rate** (avg. births per childbearing woman; 2000): 3.2. **Marriage rate** per 1,000 pop. (1993): 5.0. **Divorce rate** per 1,000 pop. (1993): 0.4. **Life expectancy** at birth (2000): male 75.0 years; female 81.9 years.

National economy

Budget (1995). *Revenue:* F 945,000,000 (current receipts 78.2%, of which taxes 50.8%, revenue from French central government 22.5%; development receipts 21.8%). *Expenditures:* F 945,000,000 (current expenditures 78.2%; capital expenditures 21.8%). **Production** (metric tons except as noted). *Agriculture, forestry, fishing* (2000): rice 31,000, cassava 10,400, sugarcane 5,300, cabbages 4,800, taro 4,100; livestock (number of live animals) 10,500 pigs, 9,000 cattle; roundwood (1998) 118,000 cu m; fish catch (1998) 7,709. *Mining and quarrying:* gold (2000) 90,000 troy oz.; stone, sand, and gravel (1994) 1,034 metric tons. *Manufacturing* (1998): pork 1,245; chicken meat 461; finished wood products 3,172 cu m (1996); *Energy production (consumption):* electricity (kW-hr; 1998) 566,000,000 ([1996] 455,000,000). **Household income and expenditure.** Average household size (1999) 3.3; income per household (1980) F 75,762; sources of income (1989): wages and salaries 64.4%, industrial and commercial profits 15.4%, pensions and rents 18.0%, other 2.2%; expenditure (1994): food and beverages 28.7%, housing 11.7%, energy 9.0%, clothing and footwear 6.4%, health 2.7%, other 41.5%. **Land use** (1994): forested 90.6%; meadows and pastures 0.1%; agricultural and under permanent cultivation 0.2%; other 9.1%. **Gross national product** (at current market prices; 1997): $1,430,000,000 ($9,410 per capita). **Population economically active** (1998): total 61,100; activity rate of total pop. 39.0% (participation rates (1990): ages 15–64, 67.3%; female 38.2%; unemployed [1998] 21.4%). **Tourism** (1999): receipts $50,000,000.

Foreign trade

Imports (1998): F 3,449,000,000 (food products 21.3%; unspecified 78.7%). *Major import sources* (1997): France 51.6%; United States 14.3%; Trinidad and Tobago 6.0%. **Exports** (1996): F 856,000,000 (gold 21.5%; shrimp 20.5%; parts for air and space vehicles 14.6%; rice 7.0%). *Major export destinations* (1997): France 61.5%; Switzerland 6.6%; United States 2.2%.

Transport and communications

Transport. *Roads* (1996): total length 774 mi, 1,245 km. *Vehicles* (1993): passenger cars 29,100; trucks and buses 10,600. *Air transport* (1998): passenger arrivals 204,078, passenger departures 199,637; cargo unloaded 4,083 metric tons, cargo loaded 2,483 metric tons; airports (1998) with scheduled flights 1. **Communications** Total units (units per 1,000 persons). Daily newspaper circulation (1996): 2,000 (7.0); Radio receivers (1997): 104,000 (650); Television receivers (1997): 30,000 (172); Telephone main lines (1999): 49,000 (282); Cellular telephone subscribers (1999): 18,000 (103).

Education and health

Educational attainment (1990). Percentage of pop. age 25 and over having: incomplete primary education or no declaration 61.7%; completed primary 5.3%; some secondary 15.9%; completed secondary 8.2%; some higher 4.9%; completed higher 4.0%. **Literacy** (1982): total pop. age 16 and over literate 38,964 (82.0%); males literate 21,021 (82.5%); females literate 17,943 (81.3%). **Health:** physicians (1998) 223 (1 per 684 persons); hospital beds (1996) 730 (1 per 196 persons); infant mortality rate per 1,000 live births (2000) 14.0. **Food** (1992): daily per capita caloric intake 2,900 (vegetable products 70%, animal products 30%); 128% of FAO recommended minimum requirement.

Military

Total active duty personnel (1999): 2,200 (includes French Foreign Legion troops assigned to guard the Kourou Space Center).

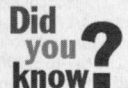

Did you know? Less than one percent of the land area of French Guiana is cultivated, and a good part of the area that is developed includes the spaceport for the European Space Agency and the infamous Devil's Island (former prison for hardened criminals).

Background

Originally settled by the Spanish, French, and Dutch, the territory of French Guiana was awarded to France in 1667, and the inhabitants were made French citizens after 1877. By 1852 the French began using the territory as a penal colony with one, on Devil's Island, especially notorious. It became a *département* of France in 1946; the penal colonies were closed by 1939.

Recent Developments

The European Space Agency has regularly launched communication satellites from French Guiana since the completion of a space center near Kourou in 1968. A high-profile launch took place in French Guiana on 1 Mar 2002 when Envisat, a $2.2 billion, climate-monitoring satellite, was successfully put into orbit for a five-year mission.

Internet resources:
<www.emulateme.com/french.htm>

French Polynesia

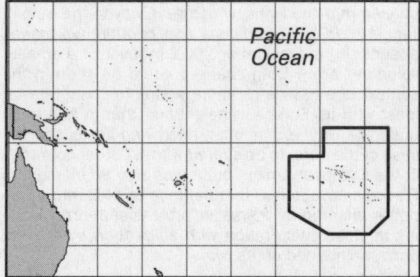

Official name: Territoire de la Polynésie française (French); Polynesia Farani (Tahitian) (Territory of French Polynesia). **Political status:** overseas territory (France) with one legislative house (Territorial Assembly [49]). **Chief of state:** President Jacques Chirac of France (from 1995). **Head of government:** President of the Territorial Government of French Polynesia, Gaston Flosse (from 1991). **Capital:** Papeete. **Official languages:** French; Tahitian. **Official religion:** none. **Monetary unit:** 1 franc of the Comptoirs français du Pacifique (CFPF) = 100 centimes; valuation (28 Jun 2002) $1 = CFPF 120.44; the CFPF is pegged to the euro (€) at €1 = CFPF 119.25 from 1 Jan 2002.

Demography

Area: 1,544 sq mi, 4,000 sq km (approximate total area including inland water). **Population** (2001): 238,000. **Density** (2001; based on land area): persons per sq mi 175.1, persons per sq km 67.6. **Urban** (1999): 57.0%. **Sex distribution** (1996): male 51.92%; female 48.08%. **Age breakdown** (1996): under 15, 33.7%; 15–29, 27.3%; 30–44, 21.6%; 45–59, 11.4%; 60–74, 5.0%; 75 and over, 1.0%. **Ethnic composition** (1996): Polynesian and part-Polynesian 82.8%; European (mostly French) 11.9%; Asian (mostly Chinese) 4.7%; other 0.6%. **Religious affiliation** (1995): Protestant 50.2%, of which Evangelical Church of French Polynesia (Presbyterian) 46.1%; Roman Catholic 39.5%; other Christian 9.9%, of which Mormon 5.9%; other 0.4%. **Major cities** (1996): Faaa 25,888; Papeete 25,553 (urban agglomeration [1999] 121,000); Punaauia 19,524; Pirae 13,974; Mahina 11,640. **Location:** Oceania, archipelago in the South Pacific Ocean, about halfway between South America and Australia.

---

1 metric ton = about 1.1 short tons;   1 kilometer = 0.6 mi (statute);   1 metric ton-km cargo = about 0.68 short ton-mi cargo;   c.i.f.: cost, insurance, and freight;   f.o.b.: free on board

Vital statistics

Birth rate per 1,000 pop. (2001): 20.7 (world avg. 22.5); (1996) legitimate 35.4%; illegitimate 64.6%. Death rate per 1,000 pop. (2001): 4.8 (world avg. 9.0). Natural increase rate per 1,000 pop. (2001): 15.9 (world avg. 13.5). Total fertility rate (avg. births per childbearing woman; 2001): 2.5. Marriage rate per 1,000 pop. (1996): 5.7. Life expectancy at birth (2001): male 70.0 years; female 75.0 years.

National economy

Budget (1998). Revenue: CFPF 85,671,000,000 (indirect taxes 60.3%, direct taxes and nontax revenue 39.7%). Expenditures: CFPF 114,143,000,000 (current expenditure 72.5%; capital expenses 27.5%). Public debt (external, outstanding; 1995): $863,000,-000. Production (metric tons except as noted). Agriculture, fishing (1999): coconuts 85,000, copra (1998) 11,000, cassava 5,500; livestock (number of live animals) 33,000 pigs, 6,500 cattle, 16,000 goats; fish catch (1998) 11,406; export production of black pearls (1998) 6,050 kg. Mining and quarrying: estimated annual production of phosphates range from 1,000,000 to 1,200,000 tons. Manufacturing (1999): coconut oil 6,386; other manufactures include monoï oil (primarily refined coconut and sandalwood oils), beer. Energy production (consumption): electricity (kW-hr; 1996) 360,000,000 (360,000,000). Tourism (1998): number of visitors 189,000; receipts from visitors $354,000,000; number of hotel rooms 3,021; occupancy percentage 59.0%. Household income and expenditure (1986). Average household size (1996) 4.3; average annual income per household CFPF 2,153,112; sources of income (1993): salaries 61.9%, self-employment 21.5%, transfer payments 16.6%; expenditure: food and beverages 32.1%, household furnishings 12.3%, transportation 12.2%, energy 8.1%, recreation and education 6.9%, clothing 6.3%. Gross domestic product (at current market prices; 1999): $3,908,000,000 ($16,930 per capita). Population economically active (1996): total 87,121; activity rate of total pop. 39.7% (participation rates: ages 14 and over, 68.3%; female 38.7%; unemployed 13.2%). Land use (1998): forested and other 81.4%; meadows and pastures 5.5%; agricultural and under permanent cultivation 13.1%.

Foreign trade

Imports (1997-c.i.f.) CFPF 99,300,000,000 (machinery and appliances 16.3%, food products 6.8%, pharmaceutical products 3.1%, metal manufactures 2.6%). Major import sources (1996): France 43.9%; United States 13.7%; Australia 7.0%; New Zealand 6.6%. Exports (1997-f.o.b.): CFPF 16,481,000,000 (black cultured pearls 61.6%, coconut oil 1.6%, mother-of-pearl 1.4%, vanilla 0.5%). Major export destinations (1996): Japan 40.6%; France 28.7%; United States 8.7%; New Caledonia 2.9%.

Transport and communications

Transport. Roads (1996): total length 549 mi, 884 km (paved 44%). Motor vehicles (1993): passenger cars 37,000; trucks and buses 15,300. Air transport (1998): passengers carried 1,219,907; freight handled 9,542 metric tons; airports (1994) with scheduled flights 17. Communications Total units (units per 1,000 persons). Daily newspaper circulation (1996); 24,000 (110); Radio receivers (1997): 128,000 (574); Television receivers (1999): 43,000 (186); Telephone main lines (1999): 52,272 (226); Cellular telephone subscribers (1999); 21,929 (95); Personal computers (1995): 20,000 (1.2); Internet users (1999): 5,000 (22).

Education and health

Educational attainment (1996). Percentage of pop. age 15 and over having: no formal schooling 4.9%; primary education 37.4%; secondary 49.0%; higher 8.7%. Literacy (1983): total pop. age 15 and over literate 98,314 (95.0%); males literate 51,910 (94.9%); females literate 46,404 (95.0%). Health (1996): physicians 384 (1 per 175 persons); hospital beds 981 (1 per 447 persons); infant mortality rate per 1,000 live births (2001) 9.0. Food (1999): daily per capita caloric intake 2,969 (vegetable products 72%, animal products 28%); (1997) 130% of FAO recommended minimum.

Military

Total active duty personnel (2000): 3,100 French military personnel.

Background

European contact with the islands of French Polynesia was gradual. Portuguese navigator Ferdinand Magellan sighted Pukapuka in the Tuamotu group in 1521. The southern Marquesas Islands were discovered in 1595. Dutch explorer Jacob Roggeveen in 1722 discovered Makatea, Bora-Bora, and Maupiti. Captain Samuel Wallis in 1767 discovered Tahiti, Moorea, and Maiao Iti. The Society Islands were named after the Royal Society, which had sponsored the expedition under Captain James Cook that observed from Tahiti the 1769 transit of the planet Venus. Tubuai was discovered on Cook's last voyage, in 1777. The islands became French protectorates in the 1840s, and in the 1880s the French colony of Oceania was established. French Polynesia became an overseas territory of France after World War II and was granted partial autonomy in 1977.

Recent Developments

In French Polynesian elections of May 2001, the pro-autonomy Tahoeraa Huiaatira (TH) party was successful, winning 28 of 49 seats; the leading pro-independence party secured 13 seats. Gaston Flosse of the TH was returned as territorial president by the assembly, which for the first time was chaired by a woman, Lucette Taero, a former minister of employment with responsibility for women's affairs. The new government placed a high priority on economic development. Flosse advocated an expansion of local responsibilities under the constitutional arrangements with France, as well as increased formal representation in the French government through the Senate.

Internet resources: <www.polynesianislands.com/fp>

Gabon

Official name: République Gabonaise (Gabonese Republic). Form of government: unitary multiparty republic with a Parliament comprising two legislative

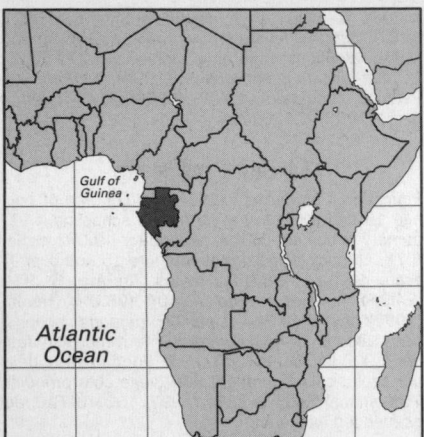

houses (Senate [91]; National Assembly [120]). **Chief of state:** President El Hadj Omar Bongo (from 1967). **Head of government:** Prime Minister Jean-François Ntoutoume-Emane (from 1999). **Capital:** Libreville. **Official language:** French. **Official religion:** none. **Monetary unit:** 1 CFA franc (CFAF) = 100 centimes; valuation (28 Jun 2002) $1 = CFAF 664.20; the CFAF is pegged to the euro (€) at €1 = 655.96 from 1 Jan 2002.

Demography

Area: 103,347 sq mi, 267,667 sq km. **Population** (2001): 1,221,000. **Density** (2001): persons per sq mi 11.8, persons per sq km 4.6. **Urban** (1998): 46.9%. **Sex distribution** (2001): male 49.77%; female 50.23%. **Age breakdown** (1999): under 15, 33.3%; 15–29, 25.7%; 30–44, 15.3%; 45–59, 16.2%; 60–74, 8.0%; 75 and over, 1.4%. **Ethnic composition** (1983): Fang 35.5%; Punu, Sira, and Nzebi 16.9%; Mpongwe 15.1%; Mbete 14.2%; other 18.3%. **Religious affiliation** (2000): Christian 90.6%, of which Roman Catholic 56.6%, Protestant 17.7%; Muslim 3.1%; traditional beliefs 1.7%. **Major cities** (1993); Libreville 362,386; Port-Gentil 80,841; Franceville 30,246; Oyem 22,669; Moanda 21,921. **Location:** western Africa, bordering Cameroon, Rep. of the Congo, the South Atlantic Ocean, and Equatorial Guinea.

Vital statistics

Birth rate per 1,000 pop. (2001): 27.4 (world avg. 22.5). **Death rate** per 1,000 pop. (2001): 17.2 (world avg. 9.0). **Natural increase rate** per 1,000 pop. (2001): 10.2 (world avg. 13.5). **Total fertility rate** (avg. births per childbearing woman; 2001): 3.7. **Life expectancy** at birth (2001): male 48.5 years; females 50.8 years.

National economy

Budget (1997). *Revenue:* CFAF 914,700,000,000 (oil revenues 62.4%; taxes on international trade 18.8%; customs duties 10.7%; other revenues

8.1%). *Expenditures:* CFAF 756,100,000,000 (current expenditure 71.5%, of which wages and salaries 25.0%, service on public debt 23.5%; capital expenditure 28.5%). **Public debt** (external, outstanding; 1999): $3,290,000,000. **Tourism** (1999): receipts from visitors $11,000,000; expenditures by nationals abroad $183,000,000. **Production** (metric tons except as noted). *Agriculture, forestry, fishing* (1999): roots and tubers 436,300, plantains 280,000, sugarcane 175,000; livestock (number of live animals) 212,000 pigs, 195,000 sheep, 90,000 goats; roundwood (1998) 5,332,000 cu m; fish catch (1997) 44,772. *Mining and quarrying* (1997): manganese ore 1,995,500; uranium ore 516,000. *Manufacturing* (1995): fuel oil 295,000; diesel and gas oil 274,000; cement 130,000. *Energy production (consumption):* electricity (kW-hr) 1,076,000,000 (917,000,000); crude petroleum (barrels; 1997) 135,873,000 ([1996] 6,120,000); petroleum products (metric tons; 1997) 676,300 (549,500). **Household income and expenditure.** Average household size (1998) 6.1; sources of income (1983): private sector 73.4%, public sector 26.6%; expenditure (1969; Libreville only): food and tobacco 54.7%, clothing and footwear 17.5%, housing 13.0%, recreation 6.6%, transportation and communications 6.3%, health care 1.9%. **Population economically active** (1997): total 542,000; activity rate of total pop. 45.5% (participation rates [1985]: ages 15–64, 68.2%; female 44.5%; unemployed [1996] 20%). **Gross national product** (1999): $3,987,000,000 ($3,300 per capita). **Land use** (1994): forested 77.2%; meadows and pastures 18.2%; agricultural and under permanent cultivation 1.8%; other 2.8%.

Foreign trade

Imports (1997): CFAF 578,100,000,000 (machinery and mechanical equipment 26.4%, food and agricultural products 23.1%, consumer products 15.5%, transport equipment 11.5%, metals 6.2%). *Major import sources:* France 39.1%; Belgium 9.7%; US 8.1%; UK 4.3%; Japan 4.0%. **Exports** (1997): CFAF 1,776,300,000,000 (crude petroleum and petroleum products 77.1%, wood 14.5%, manganese ore and concentrate 5.0%, uranium ore and concentrate 0.7%). *Major export destinations:* US 68.2%; France 8.1%; other EU 4.4%; Japan 3.2%; Africa 1.6%.

Transport and communications

Transport. *Railroads* (1998): route length 814 km; passenger-km 85,000,000 (1996); metric ton-km cargo carried 503,000,000 (1995). *Roads* (1996): total length 7,670 km (paved 8.2%). *Vehicles* (1997): passenger cars 24,750; trucks and buses 16,490. *Air transport* (1996): passenger-km 728,000,000; metric ton-km cargo 100,000,000; airports (1997) 17. **Communications** Total units (units per 1,000 persons). *Daily newspaper* circulation (1997): 33,000 (30.0); *Radio* receivers (1997): 195,000 (16.1); *Television* receivers (1999): 300,000 (251); *Telephone* main lines (1999): 37,978 (31.7); *Cellular telephone* subscribers (1999): 8,891 (7.4); *Personal computers* (1999): 10,000 (8.4); *Internet* users (1999): 3,000 (2.5).

1 metric ton = about 1.1 short tons; 1 kilometer = 0.6 mi (statute); 1 metric ton-km cargo = about 0.68 short ton-mi cargo; c.i.f.: cost, insurance, and freight; f.o.b.: free on board

Education and health

Educational attainment of economically active pop. (1993): none, or incomplete primary 37.7%; complete primary 32.1%; complete secondary 16.4%; postsecondary certificate or degree 13.8%. **Literacy** (1995): total pop. age 15 and over literate 63.2%; males literate 73.7%; females literate 53.3%. **Health:** physicians (1989) 448 (1 per 2,377 persons); hospital beds (1988) 5,329 (1 per 199 persons); infant mortality rate per 1,000 live births (1998) 83.1. **Food** (1998): daily per capita caloric intake 2,560 (vegetable products 87%, animal products 13%), 109% of FAO recommended minimum requirement.

Military

Total active duty personnel (2000): 4,700 (army 68.1%, navy 10.6%, air force 21.3%), excluding 700 French troops. **Military expenditure as percentage of GNP** (1997): 2.0% (world 2.6%); per capita expenditure $76.

Background

Artifacts dating from late Paleolithic and early Neolithic times have been found in Gabon, but it is not known when the Bantu speakers who established Gabon's ethnic composition arrived. Pygmies were probably the original inhabitants. The Fang arrived in the late 18th century and were followed by the Portuguese and by French, Dutch, and English traders. The slave trade dominated commerce in the 18th and much of the 19th century. The French then took control, and Gabon was administered (1843–86) with French West Africa. In 1886 the colony of French Congo was established to include both Gabon and the Congo; in 1910 Gabon became a separate colony within French Equatorial Africa. An overseas territory of France from 1946, it became an autonomous republic within the French Community in 1958 and declared its independence in 1960. Rule by a sole political party was established in the 1960s, but discontent with it led to riots in Libreville in 1990. Legalization of opposition parties led to new elections in 1990. Peace negotiations with neighboring Chad rebels and with the Republic of the Congo were ongoing in the 1990s.

Recent Developments

Eight African nations conducted French-sponsored military exercises in Gabon in January 2000. This was designed as a preliminary step toward creating a rapid-reaction peace force to be deployed to rescue and protect refugees in the case of ethnic conflict of the severity of that experienced in Rwanda in 1999. In the legislative elections held in December 2001, the ruling Gabonese Democratic Party won 84 of the 120 seats in the legislature.

Internet resources: <www.gabonnews.com>

The Gambia

Official name: The Republic of the Gambia. **Form of government:** multiparty republic with one legislative house (National Assembly [53, including 5 nonelected seats]). **Head of state and government:** President Yahya A.J.J. Jammeh (from 1994). **Capital:** Banjul. **Official language:** English. **Official religion:** none.

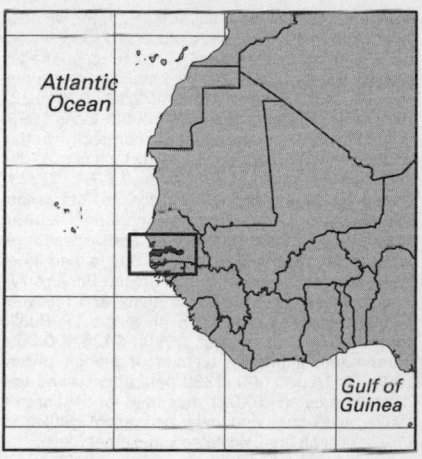

Monetary unit: 1 dalasi (D) = 100 butut; valuation (28 Jun 2002) $1 = D 18.83.

Demography

Area: 4,127 sq mi, 10,689 sq km. **Population** (2001): 1,411,000. **Density** (2001; based on land area of 3,325 sq mi [8,612 sq km]): persons per sq mi 424.4, persons per sq km 158.7. **Urban** (1999): 36.8%. **Sex distribution** (2000): male 49.97%; female 50.03%. **Age breakdown** (2000): under 15, 45.3%; 15–29, 26.1%; 30–44, 15.6%; 45–59, 8.7%; 60–74, 3.5%; 75 and over, 0.8%. **Ethnic composition** (1993): Malinke 34.1%; Fulani 16.2%; Wolof 12.6%; Diola 9.2%; other 7.7%. **Religious affiliation** (1993): Muslim 95.0%; Christian 4.1%; traditional beliefs and other 0.9%. **Major cities/urban areas** (1993): Serekunda (within Greater Banjul) 151,450; Brikama 42,480; Banjul 42,326 (Greater Banjul 270,540); Bakau (within Greater Banjul) 38,062; Farafenni 21,142. **Location:** western Africa, bordering Senegal on three sides and the North Atlantic Ocean.

Vital statistics

Birth rate per 1,000 pop. (2000): 42.3 (world avg. 22.5). **Death rate** per 1,000 pop. (2000): 13.2 (world avg. 9.0). **Natural increase rate** per 1,000 pop. (2000): 29.1 (world avg. 13.5). **Total fertility rate** (avg. births per childbearing woman; 2000): 5.8. **Life expectancy** at birth (2000): male 51.3 years; female 55.2 years.

National economy

Budget (1999). *Revenue:* D 944,500,000 (tax revenue 81.9%, of which import duties and excises 29.0%, income taxes 19.4%, sales tax 6.9%; nontax revenue 11.1%; grants 7.0%). *Expenditures:* D 1,118,200,000 (wages and salaries 26.9%; interest payments 22.2%; goods and services 16.9%; education and culture 13.1%; health 7.9%; defense 3.6%). **Production** (metric tons except as noted). *Agriculture, forestry, fishing* (1999): peanuts (groundnuts) 123,000, millet 83,000, paddy rice 31,700; livestock (number of live animals) 360,000 cattle, 265,000 goats, 190,000 sheep; roundwood (1998) 661,000 cu m; fish catch (1998) 29,002. *Mining and quarrying:* sand and gravel are excavated for local use. *Manufacturing* (value of production in D '000; 1982): processed food, including peanut and palm-kernel oil 62,878; beverages 10,546; textiles 3,253. *Energy production (consumption):* electricity (kW-hr; 1998) 122,187,000 (122,187,000); petroleum products (metric tons; 1998) none (44,000). **Population economically active** (1998): total 575,140; activity rate of total pop. 47.3% (participation rates: [1983] ages 15–64, 78.2%; female 46.3%). **Tourism** (1997): receipts from visitors $32,000,000; expenditures by nationals abroad $16,000,000. **Household income and expenditure.** Average household size (1998) 9.4; expenditure (1991; low-income population in Greater Banjul only): food and beverages 58.0%, clothing and footwear 17.5%, energy and water 5.4%, housing 5.1%. **Public debt** (external, outstanding; 1999): $425,400,000. **Gross national product** (at current market prices; 1999): $415,000,000 ($330 per capita). **Land use** (1994): forested 10.0%; meadows and pastures 19.0%; agricultural and under permanent cultivation 17.2%; built-on area, wasteland, and other 53.8%.

Foreign trade

Imports (1999-f.o.b.): D 2,186,820,000 (food 32.9%; basic manufactures 23.9%; machinery and transport equipment 20.7%; mineral fuels and lubricants 7.2%; chemicals and related products 7.3%). *Major import sources:* China 17.2%; Hong Kong 10.6%; UK 8.7%; The Netherlands 7.3%; Senegal 5.2%; France 4.7%. **Exports** (1999): D 80,600,000 (domestic exports 13.3%, of which groundnuts 8.3%, fish products 2.2%; reexports 86.7%). *Major export destinations:* Belgium-Luxembourg 61.0%; Japan 19.4%; UK 6.8%; Spain 1.8%.

Transport and communications

Transport. *Roads* (1996): total length 2,700 km (paved 35%). *Vehicles* (1996): passenger cars 8,640; trucks and buses 9,000. *Air transport* (1994): passenger-km 50,000,000; metric ton-km cargo 5,000,000; airports (1997) with scheduled flights 1. **Communications** Total units (units per 1,000 persons). Daily newspaper circulation (1996): 2,000 (1.7); Radio receivers (1997): 196,000 (165); Television receivers (1999): 4,000 (3.1); Telephone main lines (1999): 29,216 (23); Cellular telephone subscribers (1999): 5,307 (4.2); Internet users (1999): 3,000 (2.4).

Education and health

Educational attainment: n.a. **Literacy** (1995): total pop. age 15 and over literate 38.6%; males literate 52.8%; females literate 24.9%. **Health:** physicians (1997) 43 (1 per 28,791 persons); hospital beds (1994) 780 (1 per 1,428 persons); infant mortality rate per 1,000 live births (2000) 79.3. **Food** (1999): daily per capita caloric intake 2,598 (vegetable products 95%, animal products 5%); 109% of FAO recommended minimum requirement.

Military

Total active duty personnel (2000): 800 (army 100%). **Military expenditure as percentage of GNP** (1997): 3.7% (world 2.6%); per capita expenditure $12.

Background

Beginning around the 13th century AD, the Wolof, Malinke, and Fulani peoples settled in different parts of what is now Gambia and established villages and then kingdoms in the region. European exploration began when the Portuguese sighted the Gambia River in 1455. In the 17th century, when Britain and France both settled in the area, the British Fort James, on an island about 20 mi (32 km) from the river's mouth, was an important collection point for the slave trade. In 1783 the Treaty of Versailles reserved the Gambia River for Britain. After the British abolished slavery in 1807, they built a fort at the mouth of the river to block the continuing slave trade. In 1889 Gambia's boundaries were agreed upon by Britain and France; the British declared a protectorate over the area in 1894. Independence was proclaimed in 1965, and Gambia became a republic within the Commonwealth in 1970. It formed a limited confederation with Senegal in 1982, which was dissolved in 1989. During the 1990s, the government was in turmoil.

Recent Developments

In the presidential election held on 18 Oct 2001, incumbent Pres. Yahya Jammeh captured 53% of the vote, compared with opposition candidate Ousainou Darboe's 32%. Though the opposition claimed that a number of irregularities had occurred, it accepted the election results, which was a significant victory for Jammeh, whose win in the 1996 election had been tainted by allegations of fraud.

Internet resources: <www.gambiatourism.info>

Georgia

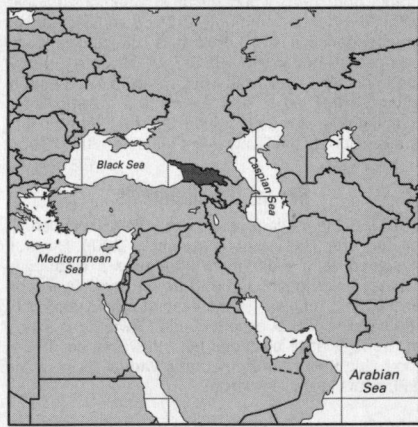

Official name: Sak'art'velo (Georgia). **Form of government:** unitary multiparty republic with a single legislative body (Parliament [235]). **Head of state and government:** President Eduard Shevardnadze (from 1992), assisted by Minister of State. **Capital:** T'bilisi. **Official language:** Georgian. **Official religion:**

1 metric ton = about 1.1 short tons;   1 kilometer = 0.6 mi (statute);   1 metric ton-km cargo = about 0.68 short ton-mi cargo;   c.i.f.: cost, insurance, and freight;   f.o.b.: free on board

none; but special recognition is given to the Georgian Orthodox Church. **Monetary unit:** 1 Georgian lari = 100 tetri; valuation (28 Jun 2002) $1 = 2.23 lari.

Demography

Area: 26,911 sq mi, 69,700 sq km. **Population** (2001): 4,989,000. **Density** (2001): persons per sq mi 185.4, persons per sq km 71.6. **Urban** (2000): 60.7%. **Sex distribution** (2000): male 47.55%; female 52.45%. **Age breakdown** (2000): under 15, 20.2%; 15–29, 23.8%; 30–44, 22.3%; 45–59, 15.5%; 60–74, 14.4%; 75 and over, 3.8%. **Ethnic composition** (1989): Georgian 70.1%; Armenian 8.1%; Russian 6.3%; Azerbaijani 5.7%; Ossetian 3.0%; Greek 1.9%; Abkhazian 1.8%; other 3.1%. **Religious affiliation** (1995): Christian 46.2%, of which Georgian Orthodox 36.7%, Armenian Apostolic 5.6%, Russian Orthodox 2.7%, other Christian 1.2%; Sunni Muslim 11.0%; other (mostly nonreligious) 42.8%. **Major cities** (1997): T'bilisi (1998) 1,398,968; K'ut'aisi 240,000; Rust'avi 158,000; Bat'umi 137,100; Zugdidi 105,000. **Location:** Caucasus region of southwestern Asia, bordering Russia, Azerbaijan, Armenia, Turkey, and the Black Sea.

Vital statistics

Birth rate per 1,000 pop. (2000): 10.9 (world avg. 22.5). **Death rate** per 1,000 pop. (2000): 14.5 (world avg. 9.0). **Natural increase rate** per 1,000 pop (2000): −3.6 (world avg. 13.5). **Total fertility rate** (avg. births per childbearing woman; 2000): 1.4. **Marriage rate** per 1,000 pop. (1996): 3.7. **Life expectancy** at birth (2000): male 60.9 years; female 68.2 years.

National economy

Budget (1998). *Revenue:* 726,200,000 lari (tax revenue 65.6%, of which value added tax 34.9%, excise tax 14.9%; extrabudgetary revenue 21.7%; nontax revenue 8.0%; grants 4.7%). *Expenditures:* 938,800,-000 lari (current expenditure 89.5%; development expenditure 5.9%; net lending 4.6%). **Public debt** (external, outstanding; 1999): $1,308,000,000. **Population economically active** (1993): total 1,920,000 (excluding informal sector); activity rate of total pop. 35.7% (participation rates: ages 16–59 [male], 16–54 [female] 58.1%; female [1996] 46.0%; urban unemployed [April–June 2000] 24.7%). **Production** (metric tons except as noted). *Agriculture, forestry, fishing* (1999): corn (maize) 486,000, wheat 243,500, grapes 230,000; livestock (number of live animals) 1,051,000 cattle, 550,000 sheep; fish catch (1997) 6,933. *Mining and quarrying* (1996): manganese ore 97,000. *Manufacturing* (1995; excluding Abkhazia and South Ossetia): steel 88,000; cigarettes 1,900,000,000 units; wine 412,000 hectoliters. *Energy production (consumption):* electricity (kW-hr; 1996) 7,195,000,000 (7,315,000,000); coal (metric tons; 1996) 20,000 (230,000); crude petroleum (barrels; 1996) 938,000 (938,000); petroleum products (metric tons; 1996) 22,000 (104,000); natural gas (cu m; 1996) 2,896,000 (917,831,000). **Tourism** (in $'000,000; 1999): receipts 400; expenditures 270. **Gross national product** (at current market prices; 1999): $3,362,000,000 ($620 per capita). **Household income and expenditure** (1993). Average household size 4.0; sources of income: wages and salaries 34.5%, benefits 21.9%, agricultural income 21.6%, other 22.0%; expenditure: taxes 42.5%, retail goods 32.3%, savings 16.4%, transportation 4.2%.

Foreign trade

Imports (2000 c.i.f.): $700,200,000 (mineral fuels 16.7%; wheat and flour 7.6%; medicines 6.5%; tobacco products 4.2%; unspecified 54.4%). *Major import sources:* Turkey 15.5%; Russia 12.9%; US 10.1%; Azerbaijan 8.1%; Germany 8.0%. **Exports** (2000 f.o.b.): $329,900,000 (scrap metals 11.5%; wine 8.6%; nuts 6.8%; fertilizers 4.7%; precious metallic ores 4.5%). *Major export destinations:* Turkey 22.3%; Russia 20.6%; Germany 9.4%; Azerbaijan 6.4%; Ukraine 5.9%.

Transport and communications

Transport. *Railroads* (1997): 1,546 km; (1995) passenger-km 371,000,000; (1993) metric ton-km cargo 1,750,000,000. *Roads* (1996): 20,700 km (paved 93%). *Vehicles* (1996): passenger cars 427,000; trucks and buses 41,510. *Air transport* (1997; Orbi Georgian Airways only): passenger-km 127,077,000; metric ton-km cargo 840,000; airports (1997) with scheduled flights 1. **Communications** Total units (units per 1,000 persons). Radio receivers (1997): 3,020,000 (586); Television receivers (1998): 2,580,000 (506); Telephone main lines (1999): 671,511 (133); Cellular telephone subscribers (2000): 185,000 (37); Internet users (1999): 20,000 (4.0).

Education and health

Food (1999): daily per capita caloric intake 2,347 (vegetable products 84%, animal products 16%); 92% of FAO recommended minimum requirement. **Health** (1997): physicians 21,846 (1 per 236 persons); hospital beds 24,500 (1 per 210 persons); infant mortality rate per 1,000 live births (2000) 52.9.

Military

Total active duty personnel (2000): 26,900 (army 88.5%, air force 6.9%, navy 3.0%, centrally controlled units/other 1.6%). About 4,000 Russian troops remained in Georgia in mid-2001. **Military expenditure as percentage of GNP** (1997): 1.4% (world 2.6%); per capita expenditure $31.

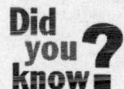 **Did you know?** The Georgian national epic, *The Knight in the Panther's Skin*, was written in about 1200 by Shota Rustaveli. On the basis of this poem, some scholars credit Rustaveli with the creation of the Georgian literary language.

Background

Ancient Georgia was the site of the kingdoms of Iberia and Colchis, whose fabled wealth was known to the ancient Greeks. The area was part of the Roman empire by 65 BC and became Christian in AD 337. For the next three centuries it was involved in the conflicts between the Byzantine and Persian empires; after 654 it was controlled by Arab caliphs, who established an emirate in Tbilisi. It was controlled by the Armenian Bagratids from the 8th to the 12th century, and the zenith of Georgia's power was reached in the reign of Queen Tamara, whose realm stretched from Azerbaijan to Circassia, forming a pan-Caucasian empire. Invasions by Mongols and Turks in the 13th–14th centuries disintegrated the kingdom, and the fall of Constantinople (now Istanbul) to the Ottoman Turks in 1453 isolated it from western Christendom. The next three centuries saw repeated invasions by the Armenians, Turks, and Persians. Georgia sought Russian protection in 1783, and in 1801 was annexed to Russia. After the Russian Revolution of 1917, the area was briefly independent; in 1921 a Soviet regime was installed, and in 1936 Georgia became the Georgian SSR, a full member of the Soviet Union. In 1990 a noncommunist coalition came to power in the first free elections ever held in Soviet Georgia, and in 1991 Georgia declared independence. In the 1990s, while Pres. Eduard Shevardnadze tried to steer a middle course, internal dissension resulted in conflicts with the northwestern republic of Abkhazia, and external distrust of Russian motives in the area grew.

Recent Developments

In 1992 Abkhazia reinstated its 1925 constitution and declared independence, which Georgia refused to recognize. By the mid-1990s tentative cease-fires were in effect, but hostilities—which forced thousands of ethnic Georgians to flee their homes in Abkhazia—continued during the late 1990s. In May 2002 a contingent of US troops arrived in Georgia to help train Georgian forces in antiterrorism warfare.

Internet resources:
<www.parliament.ge/gotoGeorgia.htm>

Germany

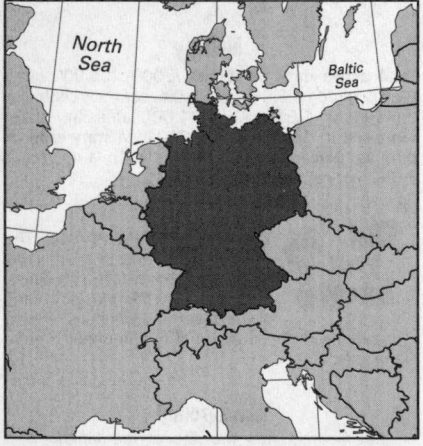

Official name: Bundesrepublik Deutschland (Federal Republic of Germany). **Form of government:** federal multiparty republic with two legislative houses

(Federal Council [69]; Federal Diet [672—expected to be reduced to 598 seats as of September 2002 elections]). **Chief of state:** President Johannes Rau (from 1999). **Head of government:** Chancellor Gerhard Schröder (from 1998). **Capital:** Berlin, some ministries remain in Bonn. **Official language:** German. **Official religion:** none. **Monetary unit:** 1 euro (€) = 100 cents; valuation (28 Jun 2002) $1 = €1.01; at conversion on 1 Jan 2002, €1= 1.96 deutsche mark (DM).

Demography

Area: 137,846 sq mi, 357,021 sq km. **Population** (2001): 82,386,000. **Density** (2001): persons per sq mi 597.7, persons per sq km 230.8. **Urban** (1997): 82.4%. **Sex distribution** (2000): male 48.79%; female 51.21%. **Age breakdown** (2000): under 15, 15.7%; 15–29, 17.6%; 30–44, 24.7%; 45–59, 19.1%; 60–74, 15.9%; 75 and over, 7.0%. **Ethnic composition** (by nationality; 2000): German 88.2%; Turkish 3.4%, of which Kurdish 0.7%; Italian 1.0%; Greek 0.7%; Serb 0.6%; Russian 0.6%; Polish 0.4%; other 5.1%. **Religious affiliation:** (2000) Christian 75.8%, of which Protestant 35.6% (including Lutheran 33.9%), Roman Catholic 33.5%, Orthodox 0.9%, independent Christian 0.9%, other Christian 4.9%; Muslim 4.4%; Jewish 0.1%; nonreligious 17.2%; atheist 2.2%; other 0.3%. **Households** (2000). Number of households 38,124,000; average household size 2.2; 1 person 36.0%, 2 persons 33.4%, 3 persons 14.7%, 4 persons 11.5%, 5 or more persons 4.4%. **Major cities** (1999): Berlin 3,392,900; Hamburg 1,701,800; Munich 1,193,-600; Cologne 963,200; Frankfurt am Main 644,700; Essen 600,700; Dortmund 590,300; Stuttgart 581,200; Düsseldorf 568,500; Bremen 542,300; Duisburg 521,300; Hannover 515,200; Leipzig 490,000; Nürnberg 486,400. **Location:** central Europe, bordering Denmark, the Baltic Sea, Poland, the Czech Republic, Austria, Switzerland, France, Luxembourg, Belgium, The Netherlands, and the North Sea.

Vital statistics

Birth rate per 1,000 pop. (1999): 9.4 (world avg. 22.5); legitimate 77.8%; illegitimate 22.2%. **Death rate** per 1,000 pop. (1999): 10.3 (world avg. 9.0). **Natural increase rate** per 1,000 pop. (1999): –0.9 (world avg. 13.5). **Total fertility rate** (avg. births per childbearing woman; 1999): 1.4. **Marriage rate** per 1,000 pop. (1999): 5.2. **Divorce rate** per 1,000 pop. (1999): 2.3. **Life expectancy** at birth (1997–99): male 74.4 years; female 80.6 years.

Social indicators

Quality of working life. Average workweek (1998): 39.8 hours. Annual rate per 100,000 workers (1993) for: injuries or accidents at work 4,808; deaths, including commuting accidents, 6.7. Proportion of labor force insured for damages of income loss resulting from: injury, virtually 100%; permanent disability, virtually 100%; death, virtually 100%. Average days lost to labor stoppages per 1,000 workers (1996): 4.1. **Access to services.** Proportion of dwellings (1996) having: electricity, virtually 100%;

1 metric ton = about 1.1 short tons; 1 kilometer = 0.6 mi (statute); 1 metric ton-km cargo = about 0.68 short ton-mi cargo; c.i.f.: cost, insurance, and freight; f.o.b.: free on board

piped water supply, virtually 100%; flush sewage disposal (1993) 98.4%; public fire protection, virtually 100%. **Social participation.** Eligible voters participating in last (September 1998) national election c. 81%. Trade union membership in total workforce (1994): c. 27%. Practicing religious population (1994): 5% of Protestants and 25% of Roman Catholics "regularly" attend religious services. **Social deviance** (1996), Offense rate per 100,000 pop. for: murder and manslaughter 3.3; sexual abuse 46.0, of which rape and forcible sexual assault 13.4, child molestation 7.3; assault and battery 116.9; theft 688.9. Incidence per 100,000 in general pop. of suicide (1996) 14.9. **Material well-being** (2000). Households possessing: automobile 75.4%; telephone 96.7%; color television receiver 95.5%; refrigerator 79.3%; washing machine 97.9%; home freezer 73.8%; personal computer 48.2%; video recorder 83.8%.

National economy

Budget (2000). *Revenue:* DM 1,910,161,000,000 (taxes 84.7%, interest 7.7%). *Expenditures:* DM 1,873,837,000,000 (pensions and other social security payments 34.4%, purchase of current goods and services 21.9%, personnel costs 18.4%). **Total national debt** (1998): DM 718,440,000,000. **Production** (value of production in DM except as noted; 1999–2000). *Agriculture, forestry, fishing:* cereal grains 7,007,000,000, flowers and ornamental plants 3,010,000,000, sugar beets 2,541,000,000, grapes for wine 2,289,000,000, fruits 2,095,000,000, potatoes 2,024,000,000; livestock (number of live animals; 2000) 27,049,000 pigs, 14,658,000 cattle, 2,100,000 sheep, 110,000,000 chickens; roundwood (2000) 37,634,000 cu m; fish catch (metric tons; 1999) 312,492. *Mining and quarrying* (metric tons; 1998): potash 37,100,000. *Manufacturing* (value added at factor cost in DM '000,000; 1996): capital equipment 252,226, of which machinery 90,213, transport equipment 80,418; electrical equipment 57,269; chemicals (including pharmaceuticals) 60,842; food and beverages 39,184; plastics and other synthetic products 27,853; glass and ceramic products 22,730. *Energy production (consumption):* electricity (kW-hr; 1997) 546,412,000,000 (544,063,000,000); hard coal (metric tons; 1997) 51,212,000 (72,236,000); lignite (metric tons; 1997) 177,159,000 (179,403,000); crude petroleum (barrels; 1997) 20,553,000 (745,355,000); petroleum products (metric tons; 1997) 93,230,000 (113,289,000); natural gas (cu m; 1997) 23,925,000,000 (108,390,000,000). **Gross national product** (at current market prices; 1999): $2,103,804,000,000 ($25,620 per capita). **Population economically active** (2000): total 40,326,000; activity rate of total pop. 49.0% (participation rates [1998]; ages 15–64, 70.7%; female 43.1%; unemployed 10.7%). **Household income and expenditure.** Average annual income per household (1998) DM 75,144; sources of take-home income: wages 77.6%, self-employment 12.0%, transfer payments 10.4%; expenditure: rent 24.7%, food and beverages 13.9%, transportation 13.7%, entertainment, education, and leisure 11.8%, household operations, durables, and maintenance 7.0%, clothing and footwear 5.5%. **Tourism** (1999): receipts $16,730,000,000; expenditures $48,495,000,000. **Land use** (1994): forest 30.6%; pasture 15.1%; agriculture 19.9%; other 34.4%.

Foreign trade

Imports (2000): DM 1,064,308,800,000 (machinery and transport equipment 37.0%, of which road transport equipment 8.3%, electrical machinery other than office equipment 7.9%; chemicals and chemical products 8.9%, of which organic chemical products 2.5%; mineral fuels 8.7%, of which crude petroleum and petroleum products 6.5%; food and beverages 6.1%; iron and steel 2.2%). *Major import sources:* France 9.6%; The Netherlands 8.8%; US 8.5%; UK 7.0%; Italy 6.6%; Japan 4.9%; Belgium 4.8%. **Exports** (2000): DM 1,167,343,300,000 (machinery and transport equipment 51.2%, of which road transport equipment 17.4%, electrical machinery other than office equipment 8.4%; chemicals and chemical products 12.7%, of which organic chemical products 2.4%, unfabricated plastics 2.2%). *Major export destinations:* France 11.4%; US 10.2%; UK 8.3%; Italy 7.6%; The Netherlands 6.4%; Austria 5.3%; Belgium 5.1%.

Transport and communications

Transport. *Railroads:* length (1998) 82,413 km; (1999) passenger-km 73,587,000,000; (1999) metric ton-km cargo 71,356,000,000. *Roads* (1999): total length 230,735 km (paved 99%). *Vehicles* (2000): passenger cars 42,423,300; trucks and buses 2,576,000. *Air transport* (1999): passenger-km 88,867,173,000; metric ton-km cargo 6,598,776,000; airports (1997) 35. **Communications** Total units (units per 1,000 persons). Daily newspaper circulation (1996): 25,500,000 (311); Radio receivers (1997): 77,800,000 (948); Television receivers (1999): 47,600,000 (580); Telephone main lines (1999): 48,500,000 (590); Cellular telephone subscribers (1999): 23,470,000 (286); Personal computers (1999): 24,400,000 (297); Internet users (1999): 14,400,000 (175).

Education and health

Educational attainment (2000). Percentage of pop. age 25 and over having: primary and lower secondary 50.6%; intermediate secondary 17.9%; vocational secondary 8.7%; post-secondary and higher (all levels) 22.8%. **Health** (1999): physicians (2000) 294,676 (1 per 279 persons); hospital beds 565,268 (1 per 145 persons); infant mortality rate per 1,000 live births 4.5. **Food** (1999): daily per capita caloric intake 3,411 (vegetable products 69%, animal products 31%); 128% of FAO recommended minimum requirement.

Military

Total active duty personnel (2000): 321,000 (army 68.9%, navy 8.3%, air force 22.8%). **Military expenditure as percentage of GNP** (1997): 1.6% (world 2.6%); per capita expenditure $401.

Background

Germanic tribes entered Germany in about the 2nd century BC, displacing the Celts. The Romans failed to conquer the region, which only became a political entity with the division of the Carolingian empire in the 9th century AD. The monarchy's control was weak, and power increasingly devolved upon the nobility, organized in feudal states. The monarchy was restored under Saxon rule in the 10th century, and the Holy Roman Empire, centering on Germany and northern Italy, was revived. Continuing conflict between the Holy Roman emperors and the Roman Catholic popes undermined the empire, and its dissolution was accelerated by Martin Luther's revolt in 1517, which divided Germany, and ultimately Europe, into Protestant and Catholic camps, culminating in the Thirty Years' War (1618–48). Germany's population and borders were greatly reduced, and its numerous feudal princes gained virtually full sovereignty. In 1862 Otto von Bismarck came to power in Prussia and over the next decade reunited Germany in the German empire. It was dissolved in 1918 after the German defeat in World War I. Germany was stripped of much of its territory and all of its colonies. In 1933 Adolf Hitler became chancellor and established a totalitarian state, the Third Reich, dominated by the Nazi Party. Hitler's invasion of Poland in 1939 plunged the world into World War II. Following its defeat in 1945, Germany was divided by the Allied Powers into four zones of occupation. Disagreement with the Soviet Union over their reunification led to the creation in 1949 of the Federal Republic of Germany (West Germany) and the German Democratic Republic (East Germany). Berlin, the former capital, remained divided. West Germany became a prosperous parliamentary democracy, East Germany a one-party state under Soviet control. The East German communist government was overthrown peacefully in 1989, and Germany was reunited in 1990. After the initial euphoria over unity, the former West Germany sought to incorporate the former East Germany both politically and economically, resulting in heavy financial burdens for the wealthier western Germans. The country continued to move toward deeper political and economic integration with Western Europe through its membership in the European Union.

Recent Developments

By 2002 Germany had witnessed a slowdown in the pace of economic growth and reform, though the country's involvement in world affairs was increasing. Despite diminished personal approval ratings, Chancellor Gerhard Schröder had gained in stature as a statesman as Germany embarked on a more active and assertive foreign policy course after more than half a century of restraint. Throughout 2001 Germany assumed a greater leadership role in European affairs and grew more active in other international trouble spots such as Macedonia and the Middle East. In the wake of the terrorist attacks in the US in September, Germany announced that it would support the American response with both diplomatic and military means if necessary. In the past the country had avoided military intervention, especially outside Europe.

Internet resources: <www.germany-tourism.de>

Ghana

Official name: Republic of Ghana. **Form of government:** unitary multiparty republic with one legislative house (House of Parliament [200]). **Head of state and government:** President John Agyekum Kufuor

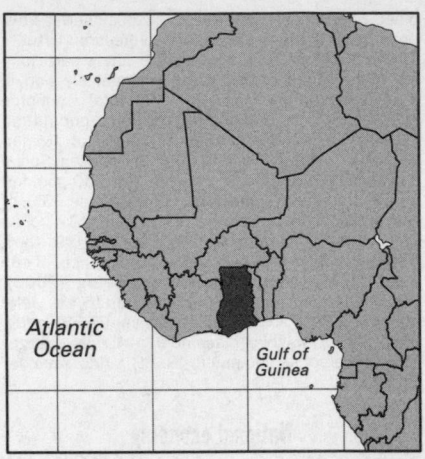

(from 7 Jan 2001). **Capital:** Accra. **Official language:** English. **Official religion:** none. **Monetary unit:** 1 cedi = 100 pesewas; valuation (28 Jun 2002) $1 = 7,922.50 cedi.

Demography

Area: 92,098 sq mi, 238,533 sq km. **Population** (2001): 19,894,000. **Density** (2001): persons per sq mi 216.0, persons per sq km 83.4. **Urban** (1999): 37.8%. **Sex distribution** (1999): male 49.77%; female 50.23%. **Age breakdown** (2000): under 15, 41.9%; 15–29, 27.7%; 30–44, 17.4%; 45–59, 7.8%; 60–74, 4.2%; 75 and over, 1.0%. **Ethnolinguistic composition** (1983): Akan 52.4%; Mossi 15.8%; Ewe 11.9%; Ga-Adangme 7.8%; Gurma 3.3%; Yoruba 1.3%; other 7.5%. **Religious affiliation** (2000): Christian 55.4%, of which Protestant 16.6%, African Christian 14.4%, Roman Catholic 9.5%; traditional beliefs 24.4%; Muslim 19.7%; other 0.5%. **Major cities** (2001): Accra 1,551,200; Kumasi 610,600; Tamale 259,200; Tema 225,900; Obuasi 118,000. **Location:** western Africa, bordering Burkina Faso, Togo, the Atlantic Ocean, and Côte d'Ivoire.

Vital statistics

Birth rate per 1,000 pop. (2001): 29.0 (world avg. 22.5). **Death rate** per 1,000 pop. (2001): 10.3 (world avg. 9.0). **Natural increase rate** per 1,000 pop. (2001): 18.7 (world avg. 13.5). **Total fertility rate** (avg. births per childbearing woman; 2001): 3.8. **Life expectancy** at birth (2001): male 55.9 years; females 58.7 years.

National economy

Budget (1996). *Revenue:* 1,997,600,000,000 cedi (excise and value-added taxes 36.7%, of which petroleum tax 14.5%; import-export duties 27.3%; income taxes 21.7%; nontax revenue 14.4%). *Expenditures* (1995): 1,697,893,000,000 cedi (1994: education 22.3%; debt service 20.1%; health 6.9%; transportation and communications 5.3%; social security and welfare 3.6%; defense 2.9%). **Public debt** (external,

---

1 metric ton = about 1.1 short tons;   1 kilometer = 0.6 mi (statute);   1 metric ton-km cargo = about 0.68 short ton-mi cargo;   c.i.f.: cost, insurance, and freight;   f.o.b.: free on board

outstanding; 1999): $5,647,000,000. **Production** (metric tons except as noted). *Agriculture, forestry, fishing* (2000): cassava 7,845,000, yams 3,249,-000, bananas and plantains 2,061,000; livestock (number of live animals) 2,739,000 goats, 2,516,000 sheep, 1,273,000 cattle; roundwood (1998) 21,905,000 cu m; fish catch (1998) 442,692. *Mining and quarrying* (1998): manganese ore 384,173; bauxite 341,121; gold 113,064 kg. *Manufacturing* (value added in cedi; 1993): tobacco 71,474,700,000; footwear 60,350,600,000; chemical products 40,347,600,000. *Energy production (consumption)*: electricity (kW-hr; 1996) 6,631,000,-000 (6,405,000,000); coal (metric tons; 1998) none (3,000); crude petroleum (barrels; 1998) none (7,315,000); petroleum products (metric tons; 1998) 926,000 (1,077,000); natural gas, none (n.a.). **Tourism** (1999): receipts $304,000,000; expenditures $36,000,000. **Household income and expenditure.** Average household size (1984) 4.9; average annual income per household (1978) 9,600 cedi; expenditure (1978): food 57.4%, clothing 14.3%, housing 11.5%, transportation and communications 3.3%, health care 1.3%. **Gross national product** (1999): $7,451,000,000 ($400 per capita). **Population economically active** (1984): total 5,580,104; activity rate of total pop. 45.4% (participation rates: over age 15, 82.5%; female 51.2%; unemployed 2.8%). **Land use** (1994): forest 42.2%; pasture 36.9%; agriculture 19.0%; other 1.9%.

Foreign trade

Imports (1998): $2,896,900,000 (petroleum [all forms] 7.4%; unspecified 92.6%). *Major import sources* (1999): Nigeria 14.9%; UK 9.5%; Côte d'Ivoire 9.0%; US 8.1%; France 7.7%. **Exports** (1998): $2,091,400,000 (gold 32.9%; cacao 25.9%; wood products 8.2%; cocoa products 3.8%). *Major export destinations* (1999): Togo 12.6%; UK 11.6%; US 9.4%; Italy 8.9%; The Netherlands 7.5%.

Transport and communications

Transport. *Railroads* (1993): route length 953 km; passenger-km 1,177,000,000; metric ton-km cargo 137,100,000. *Roads* (1996): total length 38,700 km (paved 40%). *Vehicles* (1996): passenger cars 90,000; trucks and buses 45,000. *Air transport* (1996 [Ghana Airways only]): passenger-km 655,122,000; metric ton-km cargo 29,549,000; airports (1996) with scheduled flights 1. **Communications** Total units (units per 1,000 persons). Daily newspaper circulation (1996): 250,000 (14); Radio receivers (1997): 4,400,000 (236); Television receivers (1999): 2,266,000 (118); Telephone main lines (1999): 158,555 (8.3); Cellular telephone subscribers (1999): 70,026 (3.7); Personal computers (1999): 50,000 (2.6); Internet users (1999): 20,000 (1.0).

Education and health

Educational attainment (1984). Percentage of pop. age 25 and over having: no formal schooling 60.4%; primary education 7.1%; middle school 25.4%; secondary 3.5%; vocational and other postsecondary 2.9%; higher 0.6%. **Literacy** (2000): total pop. age 15 and over literate 8,070,000 (70.2%); males literate 4,520,000 (79.8%); females literate 3,550,000 (61.2%). **Health:** physicians (1994) 735 (1 per 22,970 persons); hospital beds (1994) 26,455 (1

per 638 persons); infant mortality rate per 1,000 live births (2001) 56.5. **Food** (1998): daily per capita caloric intake 2,568 (vegetable products 97%, animal products 3%): 112% of FAO recommended minimum.

Military

Total active duty personnel (2000): 7,000 (army 71.4%, navy 14.3%, air force 14.3%). **Military expenditure as percentage of GNP** (1997): 0.7% (world 2.8%); per capita expenditure $3.

Background

The modern state of Ghana is named after the ancient Ghana empire that flourished until the 13th century AD in the western Sudan, about 500 mi (800 km) northwest of the modern state. The Akan peoples then founded their first states in modern Ghana. Gold-seeking Mande traders arrived by the 14th century and Hausa merchants by the 16th century. During the 15th century the Mande founded the states of Dagomba and Mamprussi in the northern half of the region. The Ashanti, an Akan people, originated in the central forest region and formed a strongly centralized empire that was at its height in the 18th–19th centuries. European exploration of the region began early in the 15th century, when the Portuguese landed on the Gold Coast; they later established a settlement at Elmina as headquarters for the slave trade. By the mid-18th century the Gold Coast was dominated by numerous forts controlled by Dutch, British, and Danish merchants. Britain made the Gold Coast a crown colony in 1874, and British protectorates over the Ashanti and the northern territories were established in 1901. In 1957 the Gold Coast became the independent state of Ghana. Since independence, numerous political coups have occurred, but that of 1981 produced a government that lasted into the 1990s.

Recent Developments

The year 2001 witnessed the first peaceful transfer of power between democratically elected governments in Ghana's 44-year history. On 7 January, John Agyekum Kufuor commenced his first term as president. His New Patriotic Party also gained a majority in Parliament.

Internet resources: <www.ghanatourism.com>

Greece

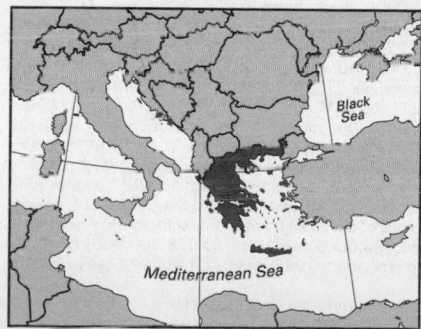

Black Sea

Mediterranean Sea

Official name: Elliniki Dhimokratia (Hellenic Republic). **Form of government:** unitary multiparty republic with one legislative house (Greek Chamber of Deputies [300]). **Chief of state:** President Kostis Stephanopoulos (from 1995). **Head of government:** Prime Minister Konstandinos Simitis (from 1996). **Capital:** Athens. **Official language:** Greek. **Official religion:** Eastern Orthodox. **Monetary unit:** 1 euro (€) = 100 cents; valuation (28 Jun 2002) $1 = €1.01; at conversion on 1 Jan 2002, €1= 340.75 Greek drachma (Dr).

Demography

Area: 50,949 sq mi, 131,957 sq km. **Population** (2001): 10,975,000. **Density** (2001): persons per sq mi 215.4, persons per sq km 83.2. **Urban** (2000): 60.1%. **Sex distribution** (1998): male 49.29%; female 50.71%. **Age breakdown** (1998): under 15, 15.6%; 15–29, 22.1%; 30–44, 21.5%; 45–59, 18.1%; 60–74, 16.3%; 75 and over, 6.5%. **Ethnic composition** (1995): Greek 98.5%; Turkish 0.9%; other 0.6%. **Religious affiliation** (1995): Christian 95.2%, of which Eastern Orthodox 94.0%, Roman Catholic 0.5%; Muslim 1.3%; other 3.5%. **Major cities** (1991): Athens 772,072 (urban agglomeration [1999]; 3,112,000); Thessaloniki 383,967; Piraeus 182,671; Patrai 152,570; Peristerion 137,288. **Location:** southern Europe, bordering Albania, Macedonia, Bulgaria, Turkey, and the Mediterranean Sea.

Vital statistics

Birth rate per 1,000 pop. (2000): 11.7 (world avg. 22.5); (1998) legitimate 96.2%; illegitimate 3.8%. **Death rate** per 1,000 pop. (2000): 10.5 (world avg. 9.0). **Natural increase rate** per 1,000 pop. (2000): 1.2 (world avg. 13.5). **Total fertility rate** (avg. births per childbearing woman; 2000): 1.3. **Marriage rate** per 1,000 pop. (1998): 5.3. **Divorce rate** per 1,000 pop. (1997): 0.8. **Life expectancy** at birth (2000): male 75.9 years; female 81.2 years.

National economy

Budget (1999). *Revenue:* Dr 12,409,000,000,000 (indirect taxes 47.2%, direct taxes 32.6%, nontax revenue 20.2%). *Expenditures:* Dr 17,737,000,000,000 (debt service 36.8%, health and social insurance 12.4%, education and culture 7.9%, agriculture 7.1%, defense 5.9%). **Public debt** (1997): $18,331,000,-000. **Tourism** (1999): receipts $8,783,000,000; expenditures $3,989,000,000. **Production** (metric tons except as noted). *Agriculture, forestry, fishing* (2000): sugar beets 2,906,000, olives 2,000,000, tomatoes 1,960,000, corn (maize) 1,850,000, wheat 1,770,000; livestock (number of live animals) 9,041,000 sheep, 5,293,000 goats, 906,000 pigs; roundwood (1999) 2,215,260 cu m; fish catch (1997) 214,228. *Mining and quarrying:* bauxite (1999) 1,813,000; nickel (1998) 18,000 [metal content]. *Manufacturing* (value added in Dr '000,000,000; 1999): food 573; paints, soaps, varnishes, drugs, and medicines 371; electrical machinery 287; textiles 259; cement, bricks, and tiles 227; beverages 214. *Energy production (consumption):* electricity (kW-hr; 1999) 44,724,000,000 ([1997] 36,528,000,000); hard coal (metric tons; 1996) none (1,484,000); lignite (metric tons; 1999) 61,464,000 ([1996] 61,410,000); crude petroleum (barrels; 1996) 3,144,000 (128,379,000); petroleum products (metric tons; 1996) 18,572,000 (15,174,000); natural gas (cu m; 1996) 53,868,000 (57,430,000). **Household income and expenditure.** Average household size (1993–94) 2.9; income per household Dr 3,900,000; sources of income (1995): wages and salaries 36.6%, transfer payments 19.0%, other 44.4%; expenditure: food and beverages 32.7%, transportation and communications 13.5%, housing 11.5%, café/hotel expenditures 7.6%, household furnishings 7.4%. **Gross national product** (1999): $127,648,000,000 ($12,110 per capita). **Population economically active** (1998): total 4,445,700; activity rate of total pop. 42.3% (participation rates: ages 15 and over, 50.1%; female 39.4%; unemployed 10.8%). **Land use** (1994): forest 20.3%; pasture 40.7%; agriculture 27.2%; other 11.8%.

Foreign trade

Imports (1998-c.i.f.): Dr 8,933,500,000,000 (machinery and transport equipment 34.7%; chemicals and chemical products 12.3%; food products 10.9%; mineral fuels 7.3%). *Major import sources:* Italy 15.9%; Germany 14.9%; France 8.6%; UK 6.4%; The Netherlands 6.2%; US 4.6%. **Exports** (1998-f.o.b.): Dr 3,203,000,000,000 (food 18.4%, of which fruits and nuts 7.7%; clothing and apparel 16.8%; petroleum 6.4%; aluminum 4.2%; tobacco products 4.1%). *Major export destinations:* Germany 18.3%; Italy 11.9%; UK 7.0%; US 4.7%; France 4.6%; Bulgaria 4.1%.

Transport and communications

Transport. *Railroads* (1997): route length 2,503 km; passenger-km 1,783,000,000; metric ton-km cargo 330,000,000. *Roads* (1996): total length 117,000 km (paved 92%). *Vehicles* (1998): passenger cars 2,675,676; trucks and buses 1,013,677. *Air transport* (1999; Olympic Airways only): passenger-km 8,305,451,000; metric ton-km cargo 103,243,000; airports (1997) 36. **Communications** Total units (units per 1,000 persons). Daily newspaper circulation (1996): 1,600,000 (150); Radio receivers (1997): 5,020,000 (470); Television receivers (1999): 5,100,000 (471); Telephone main lines (1999): 5,611,000 (518); Cellular telephone subscribers (1999): 3,904,000 (360); Personal computers (1999): 640,000 (59); Internet users (1999): 750,000 (69).

Education and health

Educational attainment (1991). Percentage of pop. age 25 and over having: no formal schooling (illiterate) 6.8%; some primary education 10.6%; completed primary 39.7%; lower secondary 10.8%; higher secondary 20.6%; some postsecondary 4.9%; completed higher 6.6%. **Literacy** (2000): total pop. age 15 and over literate 9,080,000 (97.2%); males literate 4,570,000 (98.6%); females literate 4,510,000 (96.0%). **Health** (1997): physicians 43,030 (1 per 248 persons); hospital beds 52,474 (1 per 204 persons); infant mortality rate per 1,000 live births (1999) 6.7. **Food** (1999): daily per capita caloric intake 3,689 (vegetable products 78%, animal products 22%); 148% of FAO recommended minimum requirement.

---

1 metric ton = about 1.1 short tons;   1 kilometer = 0.6 mi (statute);   1 metric ton-km cargo = about 0.68 short ton-mi cargo;   c.i.f.: cost, insurance, and freight;   f.o.b.: free on board

Military

Total active duty personnel (2000): 159,200 (army 69.1%, navy 11.9%, air force 19.0%). Military expenditure as percentage of GNP (1997): 4.6% (world 2.6%); per capita expenditure $527.

Background

The earliest urban society in Greece was the palace-centered Minoan civilization, which reached its height on Crete c. 2000 BC. It was succeeded by the mainland Mycenaean civilization, which arose c. 1600 BC following a wave of Indo-European invasions. In c. 1200 BC a second wave of invasions destroyed the Bronze Age cultures, and a dark age followed, known mostly through the epics of Homer. At the end of this time, classical Greece began to emerge (c. 750 BC) as a collection of independent city-states, including Sparta in the Peloponnese and Athens in Attica. The civilization reached its zenith after repelling the Persians at the beginning of the 5th century BC and began to decline after the civil strife of the Peloponnesian War at the century's end. In 338 BC the Greek city-states were taken over by Philip II of Macedon, and Greek culture was spread by Philip's son Alexander the Great throughout his empire. The Romans, themselves heavily influenced by Greek culture, conquered the Greek states in the 2nd century BC. After the fall of Rome, Greece remained part of the Byzantine empire until the mid 15th century, when it became part of the expanding Ottoman empire; it gained its independence in 1832. It was occupied by Nazi Germany during World War II. Civil war followed and lasted until 1949, when communist forces were defeated. In 1952 Greece joined NATO. A military junta ruled the country from 1967 to 1974, when democracy was restored and a referendum declared an end to the Greek monarchy. In 1981 Greece joined the European Community, the first Eastern European country to do so. Upheavals in the Balkans in the 1990s strained Greece's relations with some neighboring states, notably the former Yugoslav entity that took the name the Republic of Macedonia.

Recent Developments

On 6 Apr 2001 the Greek Parliament adopted a thorough constitutional revision, which changed 78 articles of the country's basic law. Many amendments were passed jointly by the two biggest political parties, the ruling Panhellenic Socialist Movement and the center-right New Democracy. Changes to the constitution included better protection of citizens' private data, the constitutional guarantee of alternative service for conscientious objectors, and the abolition of the death penalty in times of peace. Another key amendment stipulated that changes to the electoral legislation would affect the next elections only if passed by a two thirds majority. Previously, the ruling party had often changed the election law in order to bolster its majority or limit its defeat in upcoming elections.

Internet resources: <www.gnto.gr>

Greenland

Official name: Kalaallit Nunaat (Greenlandic); Grønland (Danish) (Greenland). Political status: integral part of the Danish realm with one legislative

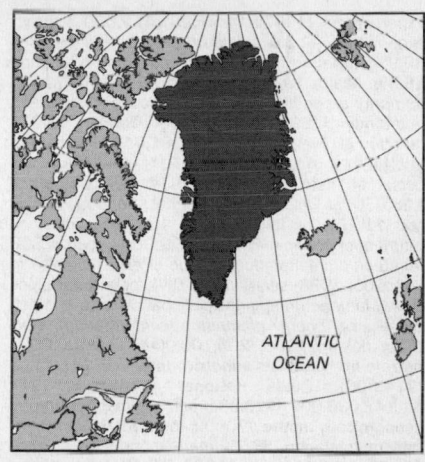

house (Parliament [31]). Chief of state: Danish monarch Queen Margrethe II (from 1972). Heads of government: High Commissioner (for Denmark) Gunnar Martens (from 1995); Prime Minister (for Greenland) Jonathan Motzfeldt (from 1997). Capital: Nuuk (Godthåb). Official languages: Greenlandic; Danish. Official religion: Evangelical Lutheran (Lutheran Church of Greenland). Monetary unit: 1 Danish krone (Dkr) = 100 øre; valuation (28 Jun 2002) $1 = Dkr 7.52.

Demography

Area: 840,000 sq mi, 2,175,600 sq km. Population (2001): 56,300. Density (2001 [ice-free area only]): persons per sq mi 0.43, persons per sq km 0.16. Urban (2001): 84.3%. Sex distribution (2000): male 53.43%; female 46.57%. Age breakdown (2000): under 15, 27.1%; 15–29, 19.2%; 30–44, 29.3%; 45–59, 16.4%; 60–69, 5.3%; 70 and over, 2.7%. Ethnic composition (2000): Greenland Eskimo 79.1%; Danish 13.6%; other 7.3%. Religious affiliation (2000): Protestant 69.2%, of which Evangelical Lutheran 64.2%, Pentecostal 2.8%; other Christian 27.4%; other/nonreligious 3.4%. Major towns (2001): Nuuk (Godthåb) 13,650; Sisimiut (Holsteinsborg) 5,165; Ilulissat (Jakobshavn) 4,165. Location: northern Atlantic Ocean (northeast of Canada).

Vital statistics

Birth rate per 1,000 pop. (2000): 16.8 (world avg. 22.5); (1993) legitimate 29.2%; illegitimate 70.8%. Death rate per 1,000 pop. (2000): 7.6 (world avg. 9.0). Natural increase rate per 1,000 pop. (2000): 9.2 (world avg. 13.5). Total fertility rate (avg. births per childbearing woman; 2000): 2.5. Marriage rate per 1,000 pop. (1993): 7.1. Divorce rate per 1,000 pop. (1993): 2.7. Life expectancy at birth (2000): male 64.5 years; female 71.7 years.

National economy

Budget (1998). Revenue: Dkr 4,304,000,000 (block grant from Danish government 59.8%; taxes and royalties for Greenland treasury 13.5%; import duties 11.3%; EEC fishery license fees 6.4%; other 6.6%).

Expenditures (1997): Dkr 5,987,442,000 (current expenditure 93.3%, of which wages and salaries 35.9%, social welfare 22.3%, culture and education 15.3%, health 10.7%, defense 5.5%; capital [development] expenditure 6.7%). **Public debt** (external, outstanding; 1995): $243,000,000. **Tourism** (1997): number of overnight visitors 181,043. **Production** (metric tons except as noted). *Fishing, animal products: fish catch* (1998) 372,974 (by local boats 128,630, of which shrimp 73,581, halibut 29,965, cod 11,776; by foreign boats 123,748); livestock (number of live animals; 1999) 22,000 sheep, 4,800 reindeer; animal products (value of external sales in Dkr '000; 1998) sealskins 31,044, polar bear skins 579. *Manufacturing:* principally handicrafts and fish processing. *Energy production (consumption):* electricity (kW-hr; 1998) 205,700,000 (158,300,000); petroleum products (metric tons; 1991) none (214,000). **Gross national product** (1997): $1,142,000,000 ($20,381 per capita). **Population economically active** (2000): total 31,518; activity rate of total pop. 56.2% (participation rates: ages 15–60, 86.6%; female [1987] 43.4%; unemployed [1999] 10.0%). **Household income and expenditure.** Average household size (1998): 2.6; income per person (1997): Dkr 144,700; expenditure (1994): food, beverages, and tobacco 41.6%, housing and energy 22.4%, transportation and communications 10.2%, recreation 6.4%. **Land use** (1994): forested 0.03%; meadows and pastures 0.69%; other (principally ice cap) 99.28%.

Foreign trade

Imports (1999): Dkr 2,789,000,000 (1998; machinery and transport equipment 26.1%; manufactured goods 14.9%; food and live animals 12.1%; miscellaneous manufactured articles 11.4%; petroleum and petroleum products 9.3%; beverages and tobacco 4.0%). *Major import sources* (1998): Denmark 65.2%; Norway 12.0%; US 3.0%; Japan 2.9%; Germany 2.3%; Sweden 1.8%. **Exports** (1999): Dkr 1,930,000,000 (1998; fish and fish products 91.7%, of which shrimp 69.0%). *Major export destinations* (1998): Denmark 84.3%; UK 3.5%; Japan 3.4%; US 2.1%; Norway 1.6%.

Transport and communications

Transport. *Railroads:* none. *Roads* (1998): total length 150 km (paved 60%). *Vehicles* (1998): passenger cars 2,242; trucks and buses 1,474. *Air transport* (1998; Greenlandair only): passenger-km 167,000,000; metric ton-km cargo 339,000; airports (1998) with scheduled flights 18. **Communications** Total units (units per 1,000 persons). Daily newspaper circulation (1996): 1,000 (18); Radio receivers (1997): 27,000 (482); Television receivers (1997): 22,000 (393); Telephone main lines (1999): 26,000 (464); Cellular telephone subscribers (1999): 14,000 (250).

Education and health

Literacy (1999): total pop. age 15 and over literate: virtually 100%. **Health** (1998): physicians 84 (1 per 668 persons); hospital beds (1993) 465 (1 per 125 persons); infant mortality rate per 1,000 live births (2000) 18.3.

Military

Total active duty personnel. Denmark is responsible for Greenland's defense. Greenlanders are not liable for military service.

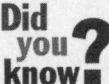 **Did you know?** Approximately 10% of the Earth's fresh water is found in Greenland, most of it trapped in the island's extensive ice sheets. These ice sheets also provide scientists with a long-range history of climate change. The development of technology that allows boring thousands of meters into the ice enables examination of annual changes in climate and pollution revealed in the ice layers.

Background

The Inuit probably crossed to northwestern Greenland from North America, along the islands of the Canadian Arctic, from 4000 BC to AD 1000. The Norwegian Erik the Red visited Greenland in 982; his son, Leif Eriksson, introduced Christianity in the 11th century. Greenland came under joint Danish-Norwegian rule in the late 14th century. The original Norse settlements became extinct in the 15th century, but Greenland was recolonized by Denmark in 1721. In 1776 Denmark closed the Greenland coast to foreign trade; it was not reopened until 1950. Greenland became part of the kingdom of Denmark in 1953, and home rule was established in 1979.

Recent Developments

In the 1999 elections to Greenland's 31-seat home-rule parliament, the main government party, Siumut, remained the largest party despite having dropped from 14 to 11 seats. In July 2000 National Aeronautics and Space Administration scientists reported that Greenland's ice cap was shrinking at a net rate of 51 cu km (12.2 cu mi) of ice per year.

Internet resources: <www.greenland-guide.gl>

Grenada

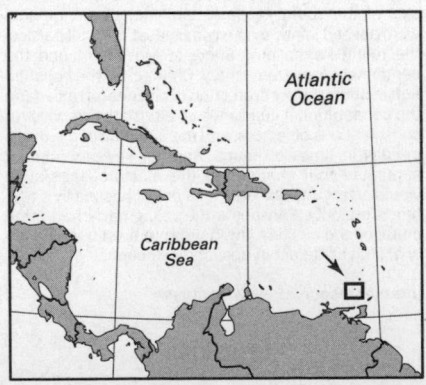

Atlantic Ocean

Caribbean Sea

---

1 metric ton = about 1.1 short tons;   1 kilometer = 0.6 mi (statute);   1 metric ton-km cargo = about 0.68 short ton-mi cargo;   c.i.f.: cost, insurance, and freight;   f.o.b.: free on board

Official name: Grenada. Form of government: constitutional monarchy with two legislative houses (Senate [13]; House of Representatives [15 (excludes the speaker)]). Chief of state: Queen Elizabeth II (from 1952) Represented by Governor-General Daniel Williams (from 1996). Head of government: Prime Minister Keith Mitchell (from 1995). Capital: St. George's. Official language: English. Official religion: none. Monetary unit: 1 East Caribbean dollar (EC$) = 100 cents; valuation (28 Jun 2002) US$1 = EC$2.70.

Demography

Area: 133 sq mi, 344 sq km. Population (2001): 102,000. Density (2001): persons per sq mi 766.9, persons per sq km 296.5. Urban (2000): 38.3%. Sex distribution (2000): male 51.70%; female 48.30%. Age breakdown (2000): under 15, 38.1%; 15–29, 33.3%; 30–44, 17.7%; 45–59, 4.9%; 60–74, 4.7%; 75 and over, 1.3%. Ethnic composition (2000): black 51.7%; mixed 40.0%; Indo-Pakistani 4.0%; white 0.9%; other 3.4%. Religious affiliation (1995): Roman Catholic 57.8%; Protestant 37.6%, of which Anglican 14.4%, Pentecostal 8.3%, Seventh-day Adventist 7.0%; other 4.6%, of which Rastafarian c. 3.0%. Major localities (1991): St. George's 4,621 (urban agglomeration [1999] 35,000); Gouyave 3,100; Grenville 2,300; Victoria 2,100. Location: island between the Caribbean Sea and the Atlantic Ocean, north of Trinidad and Tobago.

Vital statistics

Birth rate per 1,000 pop. (2000): 23.2 (world avg. 22.5); (1987) legitimate 18.1%; illegitimate 81.9%. Death rate per 1,000 pop. (2000): 8.0 (world avg. 9.0). Natural increase rate per 1,000 pop. (2000): 15.2 (world avg. 13.5). Total fertility rate (avg. births per childbearing woman; 2000): 2.6. Marriage rate per 1,000 pop. (1991): 4.3. Divorce rate per 1,000 pop. (1991): 0.8. Life expectancy at birth (2000): male 62.7 years; female 66.3 years.

National economy

Budget (1998). Revenue: EC$229,000,000 (current revenue 90.0%, of which tax on international trade 52.3%, general sales taxes 17.8%, income taxes 9.6%; grants from abroad 10.0%). Expenditures: EC$281,700,000 (current expenditure 73.7%, of which wages 37.2%, transfers 16.1%, debt 11.6%; capital expenditure 26.3%). Public debt (external, outstanding; 1999): US$122,000,000. Tourism (1999): receipts from visitors US$63,000,000; expenditures by nationals abroad US$5,000,000. Gross national product (at current market prices; 1999): US$334,000,000 (US$3,440 per capita). Production (metric tons except as noted). Agriculture, forestry, fishing (1999): coconuts 6,800, sugarcane 6,600, bananas 4,400, nutmeg 2,500; livestock (number of live animals) 13,000 sheep, 7,000 goats, 5,300 pigs; fish catch (1998) 1,713. Mining and quarrying: excavation of gravel for local use. Manufacturing (value of production in EC$'000; 1997): wheat flour 13,390; soft drinks 9,798; beer 7,072. Energy production (consumption): electricity (kW-hr; 1996) 95,000,000 (95,000,000). Household income and expenditure. Average household size (1991) 3.7; income per household (1988) EC$7,097; expenditure (1987): food, beverages, and tobacco 40.7%, household furnishings and operations 13.7%, housing 11.9%, transportation 9.1%, personal effects and medical care 8.6%. Population economically active (1988): total 38,920; activity rate of total pop. 39.9% (participation rate: ages 15–65, 72.7%; female 48.6%; unemployed [1997] 17.0%). Land use (1994): forested 9.0%; meadows and pastures 3.0%; agricultural and under permanent cultivation 35.0%; other 53.0%.

Foreign trade

Imports (1997-c.i.f.): US$166,600,000 (machinery and transport equipment 25.8%; food 21.6%; basic manufactures 18.6%; chemicals and chemical products 7.4%). Major import sources: Trinidad and Tobago 40.4%; United States 24.6%; United Kingdom 7.1%; Barbados 3.8%; Japan 3.8%; St. Vincent and the Grenadines 1.6%. Exports (1997-f.o.b.): US$25,900,000 (domestic exports 91.5%, of which nutmeg 26.3%, fish 14.3%, cocoa beans 7.3%, clothing 4.6%; reexports 8.5%). Major export destinations: Germany 46.9%; United States 12.2%; St. Lucia 6.1%; Trinidad and Tobago 6.1%.

Transport and communications

Transport. Roads (1996): total length 646 mi, 1,040 km (paved 61%). Vehicles (1991): passenger cars 4,739; trucks and buses 3,068. Air transport (1997; Point Salines airport): passengers 322,000; cargo 2,300 metric tons; airports (1998) with scheduled flights 2. Communications Total units (units per 1,000 persons). Radio receivers (1997): 57,000 (615); Television receivers (1997): 33,000 (353); Telephone main lines (1999): 27,484 (298); Cellular telephone subscribers (1999): 1,410 (15).

Education and health

Educational attainment (1991). Percentage of pop. age 25 and over having: no formal schooling 1.8%; primary education 74.9%; secondary 15.5%; higher 4.7%, of which university 2.8%; other/unknown 3.1%. Literacy (1995): total pop. age 15 and over literate 50,000 (85.0%). Health (1997): physicians 80 (1 per 1,236 persons); hospital beds 340 (1 per 290 persons); infant mortality rate per 1,000 live births (2000) 14.6. Food (1999): daily per capita caloric intake 2,685 (vegetable products 80%, animal products 20%); 111% of FAO recommended minimum requirement.

Background

The warlike Carib Indians dominated Grenada when Christopher Columbus sighted the island in 1498 and named it Concepcion, they ruled it for the next 150 years. In 1674 it became subject to the French crown and remained so until 1762, when British forces captured it. In 1833 the island's black slaves were freed. Grenada was the headquarters of the government of the British Windward Islands 1885–1958 and a member of the West Indies Federation 1958–62. It became a self-governing state in association with Britain in 1967 and gained its independence in 1974. In 1979 a left-wing government took control in a bloodless coup. Relations with its US-oriented Latin-American neighbors became strained as Grenada leaned toward Cuba and the Soviet bloc. In order to counteract this trend, the US invaded the island in

1983; democratic self-government was reestablished in 1984. Its relations with Cuba, once suspended, were restored in 1997.

Recent Developments

Grenada has been as active as any other Caribbean state against undesirable offshore banks in recent years, closing down 17 in one day in March 2001. They were all linked to the First International Bank of Grenada, which collapsed in October 2000, taking $150 million worth of mainly American depositors' money along with it. Despite its actions against offshore banks, Grenada was added to the list of countries deemed by the Paris-based Financial Action Task Force to have failed in cooperating with international efforts to stop money laundering.

Internet resources: <www.grenada.org>

Guadeloupe

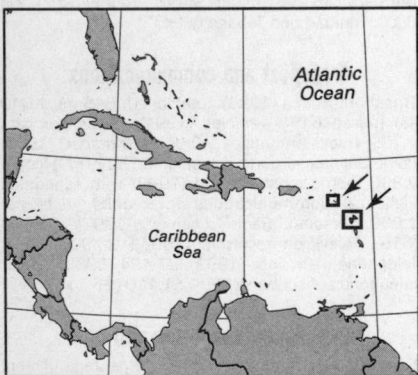

Atlantic Ocean

Caribbean Sea

Official name: Département de la Guadeloupe (Department of Guadeloupe). Political status: overseas department (France) with two legislative houses (General Council [42]; Regional Council [43]). Chief of state: President Jacques Chirac of France (from 1995). Heads of government: President of the General Council Marcellin Lubeth (from 1998); President of the Regional Council Lucette Michaux-Chevry (from 1992). Capital: Basse-Terre. Official language: French. Official religion: none. Monetary unit: 1 euro (€) = 100 cents; $1 = €1.01 (28 Jun 2002); at conversion on 1 Jan 2002, €1 = 6.56 French francs (F).

Demography

Area: 687 sq mi, 1,780 sq km. Population (2001): 432,000. Density (2001): persons per sq mi 628.8, persons per sq km 242.7. Urban (1999): 99.6%. Sex distribution (1999): male 48.11%; female 51.89%. Age breakdown (1999): under 15, 23.6%; 15–29, 22.4%; 30–44, 24.3%; 45–59, 15.7%; 60–74, 9.3%; 75 and over, 4.7%. Ethnic composition (2000): Creole (mulatto) 76.7%; black 10.0%; Guadeloupe mestizo (French-East Asian) 10.0%; white 2.0%; other 1.3%. Religious affiliation (1995):

Roman Catholic 81.1%; Jehovah's Witness 4.8%; Protestant 4.7%; other 9.4%. Major communes (1999): Les Abymes 63,054; Saint-Martin 29,078; Le Gosier 25,360; Baie-Mahault 23,389; Pointe-à-Pitre 20,948; Le Moule 20,827. Location: islands in the eastern Caribbean Sea, southeast of Puerto Rico.

Vital statistics

Birth rate per 1,000 pop. (2000): 17.2 (world avg. 22.5); (1997) legitimate 37.0%; illegitimate 63.0%. Death rate per 1,000 pop. (2000): 6.0 (world avg. 9.0). Natural increase rate per 1,000 pop. (2000): 11.2 (world avg. 13.5). Total fertility rate (avg. births per childbearing woman; 2000): 1.9. Marriage rate per 1,000 pop. (1997): 4.7. Divorce rate per 1,000 pop. (1997): 1.3. Life expectancy at birth (2000): male 73.8 years; female 80.3 years.

National economy

Budget (1998). Revenue: F 4,227,000,000 (tax revenues 69.0%, of which direct taxes 42.5%, value-added taxes 25.1%; advances, loans, and transfers 26.8%). Expenditures: F 7,874,000,000 (current expenditures 70.6%, capital [development] expenditures 10.6%; advances and loans 18.8%). Public debt (external, outstanding; 1990): $58,000,000. Tourism (1999): receipts from visitors $375,000,-000. Production (metric tons except as noted). Agriculture, forestry, fishing (1999): sugarcane 499,980, bananas 141,140, yams 9,030; livestock (number of live animals) 80,410 cattle, 63,000 goats, 15,000 pigs; roundwood (1998) 15,000 cu m; fish catch (1998) 9,084. Mining and quarrying (1993): pumice 210,000. Manufacturing (1996): cement 282,571; raw sugar 48,896; rum 66,483 hectolitres. Energy production (consumption): electricity (kW-hr; 1996) 1,098,000,000 (987,600,000). Population economically active (1998): total 182,200; activity rate of total pop. 41.8% (participation rates: ages [1995] 15–64, 73.2%; female 46.8%; unemployed 30.7%). Gross national product (1995): $3,877,000,000 ($9,145 per capita). Household income and expenditure. Average household size (1990) 3.4; income per household (1988) F 105,400; sources of income (1988): wages and salaries 78.9%, self-employment 12.7%, transfer payments 8.4%; expenditure (1994–95): housing 26.2%, food and beverages 21.4%, transportation and communications 14.1%, household durables 6.0%, culture and leisure 4.2%. Land use (1994): forest 39.1%; pasture 14.2%; agriculture 16.0%; other 30.7%.

Foreign trade

Imports (1998): F 10,663,000,000 (consumer goods 23.7%, food and agriculture products 21.1%, machinery and equipment 19.7%, transport vehicles and parts 12.3%). Major import sources: France 63.4%; Germany 4.4%; Italy 3.5%; Martinique 3.4%; US 2.9%; Japan 1.9%. Exports (1998): F 667,000,000 (1995: bananas 25.4%, sugar 11.4%, rum 4.4%, melons 2.9%). Major export destinations: France 68.5%; Martinique 9.4%; Italy 4.8%; Belgium-Luxembourg 3.3%; French Guiana 3.0%.

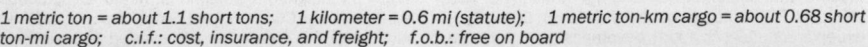
1 metric ton = about 1.1 short tons;   1 kilometer = 0.6 mi (statute);   1 metric ton-km cargo = about 0.68 short ton-mi cargo;   c.i.f.: cost, insurance, and freight;   f.o.b.: free on board

Transport and communications

Transport. *Roads* (1998): total length 1,988 mi, 3,415 km (paved [1986] 80%). *Vehicles* (1993): passenger cars 101,600; trucks and buses 37,500. *Air transport* (1998): passenger arrivals and departures 1,807,100; cargo handled 16,496 metric tons, cargo unloaded 5,493 metric tons; airports (1997) with scheduled flights 7. **Communications** total units (units per 1,000 persons). Daily newspaper circulation (1995): 35,000 (81); Radio receivers (1997): 113,000 (258); Television receivers (1999): 118,000 (262); Telephone main lines (1999): 201,000 (447); Cellular telephone subscribers (1999): 88,000 (196).

Education and health

Educational attainment (1990). Percentage of pop. age 25 and over having: incomplete primary, or no declaration 59.8%; primary education 14.5%; secondary 19.0%; higher 6.7%. **Literacy** (1982): total pop. age 15 and over literate 225,400 (90.1%); males literate 108,700 (89.7%); females literate 116,700 (90.5%). **Health** (1998): physicians 760 (1 per 550 persons); hospital beds 2,796 (1 per 149 persons); infant mortality rate per 1,000 live births (2000) 9.8. **Food** (1995): daily per capita caloric intake 2,732 (vegetable products 75%, animal products 25%); 129% of FAO recommended minimum requirement.

Military

Total active duty personnel (1994): 535 French troops.

Background

The Carib Indians held off the Spanish and French for a number of years before the islands of Guadeloupe became part of France in 1674. The British occupied Guadeloupe for short periods in the 18th and 19th centuries; the islands became officially French in 1816. In 1946 Guadeloupe was made a department of France. Tourism has benefited the economy in recent decades.

Recent Developments

French Pres. Jacques Chirac gave a clear hint in March 2000 that the hitherto highly centralized relationship between Paris and French overseas departments (DOMs) might be relaxed in favor of a looser arrangement. He said that the era of "uniform status" was over and that DOMs such as Guadeloupe might enjoy more local control in the future. The introduction of the euro in Guadeloupe in 2002 was expected to help attract more European tourists to the islands.

Internet resources: <www.exploreguadeloupe.com>

Guam

Official name: Teritorion Guam (Chamorro); Territory of Guam (English). **Political status:** self-governing, organized, unincorporated territory of the United States with one legislative house (Guam Legislature [15]). **Chief of state:** President of the United States George W. Bush (from 2001). **Head of government:** Governor Carl T.C. Gutierrez (from 1994). **Capital:**

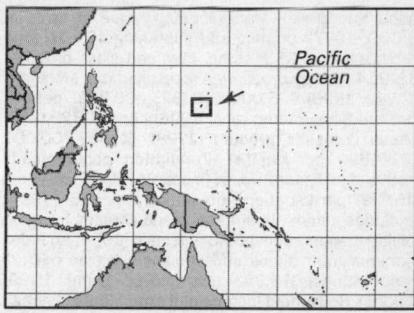

Agana. **Official languages:** Chamorro; English. **Official religion:** none. **Monetary unit:** 1 United States dollar ($1) = 100 cents.

Demography

Area: 209 sq mi, 541 sq km (total area per most recent survey including area designated as inland water equals 217 sq mi [561 sq km]). **Population** (2001): 158,000. **Density** (2001): persons per sq mi 728.1, persons per sq km 281.6. **Urban** (1999): 39.0%. **Sex distribution** (1990): male 53.99%; female 46.01%. **Age breakdown** (1990): under 15, 29.8%; 15–29, 29.9%; 30–44, 22.4%; 45–59, 11.2%; 60–74, 5.2%; 75 and over, 1.5%. **Ethnic composition** (1990): Pacific Islander 42.4%, of which Chamorro 37.5%; Asian 29.5%, of which Filipino 22.6%, Korean 3.0%; white 14.4%; mixed 9.7%; black 2.4%; other 1.6%. **Religious affiliation** (1995): Roman Catholic 74.7%; Protestant 12.8%; other Christian 2.4%; other 10.1%. **Major populated places** (1990): Tamuning 9,534; Apra Harbor 7,956; Mangilao 5,608; Andersen Air Force Base 5,531; Agana 1,139. **Location:** Oceania, island in the North Pacific Ocean, south of the Northern Mariana Islands.

Vital statistics

Birth rate per 1,000 pop. (2001): 27.0 (world avg. 22.5); (1997) legitimate 50.1%; illegitimate 49.9%. **Death rate** per 1,000 pop. (2001): 4.8 (world avg. 9.0). **Natural increase rate** per 1,000 pop. (2001): 22.2 (world avg. 13.5). **Total fertility rate** (avg. births per childbearing woman; 2001): 4.0. **Marriage rate** per 1,000 pop. (1997): 9.5. **Divorce rate** per 1,000 pop. (1995): 4.3. **Life expectancy** at birth (2001): male 72.0 years; female 77.0 years.

National economy

Budget (1997–98). Revenue: $738,100,000 (local taxes 68.7%, federal contributions 25.5%, interest 2.2%, licenses, fees, and permits 1.7%). Expenditures: $501,900,000 (current expenditures 80.2%, debt service 10.6%, capital expenditures 8.6%). **Tourism** (1999): receipts from visitors $1,908,000,000. **Land use** (1998): forested 14.6%; meadows and pastures 14.5%; agricultural and under permanent cultivation 21.8%; other 49.1%. **Production.** *Agriculture, forestry, fishing* (value of production in $'000; 1996): eggplant 625, long beans 592, bananas 418; livestock (number of live animals) 205,000 poultry, 4,000 pigs, 610 goats; fish catch (metric tons; 1998) 253, value of aquaculture production (1996) $1,442,000. *Mining and quarrying:*

sand and gravel. *Manufacturing* (value of sales in $'000; 1997): printing and publishing 40,307; food processing 24,333; stone, clay, and glass products 16,914. *Energy production (consumption)*: electricity (kW-hr; 1996) 825,000,000 (825,000,000); petroleum products (metric tons; 1996) none (1,329,000). **Gross domestic product** (1998): $3,302,700,000 ($20,660 per capita). **Population economically active** (1997): total 71,400; activity rate of total pop. 45.7% (participation rates: over age 16 [1994; excludes nonimmigrant aliens and civilians living on military reservations] 69.3%; female [1994; excludes nonimmigrant aliens and civilians living on military reservations] 43.3%; unemployed [June 1999] 15.2%). **Household income and expenditure.** Average household size (1998) 3.9 (excludes US military and dependents); average annual income per household (1998) $47,374 (excludes US military and dependents); expenditure (1978): housing 28.6%, food 24.1%, transportation 18.0%, clothing 10.6%, entertainment 5.1%, medical care 4.7%.

Foreign trade

Imports (fiscal year November 1998–October 1999): $205,800,000 (food products 34.2%; leather products including footwear 15.8%; motor vehicles and parts 14.3%; construction materials 6.4%; clothing 5.0%). **Exports** (1999): $75,700,000 (food products 54.7%, of which fish 53.8%; petroleum and natural gas products 20.0%; tobacco products 6.7%). *Major export destinations:* Japan 53.9%; Federated States of Micronesia 18.6%; Palau 6.3%; Hong Kong 2.0%.

Transport and communications

Transport. *Railroads:* none. *Roads* (1999): total length 550 mi, 885 km (paved 76%). *Vehicles* (1995): passenger cars 79,800; trucks and buses 34,700. *Air transport* (1998): passenger arrivals 1,375,000; passenger departures 1,378,000; cargo loaded and unloaded (1997) 35,295 metric tons; airports (1999) with scheduled flights 1. **Communications** Total units (units per 1,000 persons). Daily newspaper circulation (1996): 28,000 (178); Radio receivers (1997): 221,000 (1,400); Television receivers (1997): 106,000 (668); Telephone main lines (1999): 77,609 (472); Cellular telephone subscribers (1999): 20,000 (122).

Education and health

Educational attainment (1995). Percentage of pop. age 25 and over having: no formal schooling to some secondary education 26.9%; completed secondary 55.4%; completed higher 17.7%. **Literacy** (1990): total pop. age 15 and over literate 99.0%; males literate 99.0%; females literate 99.0%. **Health** (1999): physicians 130 (1 per 1,169 persons; members of Guam Medical Society only); hospital beds 192 (1 per 792 persons; Guam Memorial Hospital only); infant mortality rate per 1,000 live births (2001) 10.0.

Military

Total active duty US personnel (2000): 3,740 (army, 1.0%; navy 49.5%; air force 49.5%).

Did you know? About one-third of all the land on Guam is owned by the US armed forces, all branches of which are present on the island.

Background

Possibly visited by Ferdinand Magellan in 1521, Guam was formally claimed by Spain in 1565. It remained Spanish until it was ceded to the US after the Spanish-American War in 1898. During World War II the Japanese occupied the island (1941–44). It subsequently became a major US air and naval base. In 1950 it was made a US territory.

Recent Developments

Following the 11 Sep 2001 terrorist attacks, Andersen Air Force Base in Guam assumed greater importance for both staging and training exercises.

Internet resources: <http://ns.gov.gu>

Guatemala

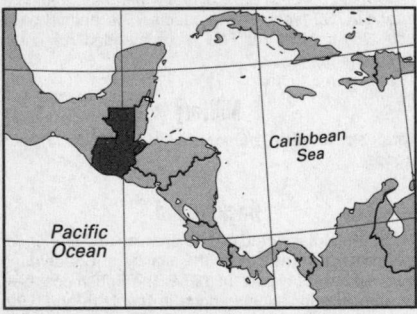

Caribbean Sea

Pacific Ocean

Official name: República de Guatemala (Republic of Guatemala). **Form of government:** republic with one legislative house (Congress of the Republic [113]). **Head of state and government:** President Alfonso Antonio Portillo Cabrera (from 2000). **Capital:** Guatemala City. **Official language:** Spanish. **Official religion:** none. **Monetary unit:** 1 quetzal (Q) = 100 centavos; valuation (28 Jun 2002) $1 = Q 7.89.

Demography

Area: 42,042 (rounded) sq mi, 108,889 sq km. **Population** (2001): 11,687,000. **Density** (2001): persons per sq mi 278.0, persons per sq km 107.3. **Urban** (2000): 39.4%. **Sex distribution** (1998): male 50.44%; female 49.56%. **Age breakdown** (1998): under 15, 44.2%; 15–29, 28.0%; 30–44, 14.6%; 45–59, 7.9%; 60–74, 4.3%; 75 and over, 1.0%. **Ethnic composition** (1994): Amerindian 42.8%; non-Amerindian 57.2%. **Religious affiliation** (1995): Roman Catholic 75.9%, of which Catholic/traditional syncretist 25.0%; Protestant 21.8%; other Christian 1.3%; other 1.0%. **Major cities** (1995): Guatemala City 1,167,495; Mixco 436,668; Villa Nueva 165,567; Chinautla 61,335; Amatitlan 40,229.

1 metric ton = about 1.1 short tons; 1 kilometer = 0.6 mi (statute); 1 metric ton-km cargo = about 0.68 short ton-mi cargo; c.i.f.: cost, insurance, and freight; f.o.b.: free on board

Location: Central America, bordering Mexico, Belize, the Caribbean Sea, Honduras, El Salvador, and the Pacific Ocean.

Vital statistics

Birth rate per 1,000 pop. (2000): 35.1 (world avg. 22.5). **Death rate** per 1,000 pop. (2000): 6.9 (world avg. 9.0). **Natural increase rate** per 1,000 pop. (2000): 28.2 (world avg. 13.5). **Total fertility rate** (avg. births per childbearing woman; 2000): 4.7. **Marriage rate** per 1,000 pop. (1995): 4.6. **Divorce rate** per 1,000 pop. (1995): 0.05. **Life expectancy** at birth (2000): male 63.5 years; female 69.0 years.

National economy

Budget (1998). *Revenue:* Q 11,997,000,000 (tax revenue 90.3%, nontax revenue 8.9%). *Expenditures:* Q 14,828,000,000 (current expenditures 61.7%, of which disbursements for wages and salaries 25.3%, transfer payments 18.0%; capital expenditures 38.3%). **Public debt** (external, outstanding; 1999): $3,129,000,000. **Tourism** (1999): receipts $570,000,000; expenditures $183,000,000. **Production** (metric tons except as noted). *Agriculture, forestry, fishing* (1999): sugarcane 15,459,000, corn (maize) 1,109,000 bananas 733,000; livestock (number of live animals) 2,300,000 cattle, 825,000 pigs, 24,000,000 chickens; roundwood (1998) 12,995,000 cu m; fish catch (1998) 10,847. *Mining and quarrying* (1997): gypsum 30,000; iron ore 3,300; antimony ore 880. *Manufacturing* (value added in Q '000,000; 1998 [1958]): food and beverage products 298; clothing and textiles 119; machinery and metal products 55. *Energy production (consumption):* electricity (kW-hr; 1996) 3,500,000,000 (3,500,000,000); crude petroleum (barrels; 1996) 5,256,000 (5,198,000); petroleum products (metric tons; 1996) 687,000 (1,990,000). **Household income and expenditure.** Average household size (1994) 5.2; income per household (1989) Q 4,306; expenditure (1981): food 64.4%, housing and energy 16.0%, transportation and communications 7.0%, household furnishings 5.0%, clothing 3.1%. **Gross national product** (1999): $18,625,000,000 ($1,680 per capita). **Population economically active** (1999): total 3,183,173; activity rate of total pop. 29.1% (participation rates [1994] ages 15–64, 51.0%; female 19.5%; unemployed [1995] 1.4%). **Land use** (1998): forested and nonarable land 58.4%; meadows and pastures 24.0%; agricultural and under permanent cultivation 17.6%.

Foreign trade

Imports (1998-c.i.f.): $4,650,900,000 (intermediate goods 34.9%, consumer goods 29.5%, capital goods 26.3%, lubricants and fuels 0.1%, construction materials 3.2%). *Major import sources:* United States 41.5%; Mexico 10.4%; Japan 4.5%; Venezuela 3.3%; Germany 2.8%. **Exports** (1998-f.o.b.): $2,846,700,000 (coffee 20.4%, sugar 11.0%, bananas 6.2%, petroleum 2.0%). *Major export destinations:* United States 32.2%; Germany 4.3%; Mexico 4.1%; Japan 2.2%.

Transport and communications

Transport. *Railroads* (1996): route length 884 km; passenger-km (1995) 16,580,000; metric ton-km cargo 85,615,000. *Roads* (1996): total length 13,100 km (paved 28%). *Vehicles* (1996): passenger cars 102,000; trucks and buses 97,000. *Air transport* (1995; Aviateca Airlines): passenger-km 500,000,000; metric ton-km cargo 70,000,000; airports (1996) 2. **Communications** Total units (units per 1,000 persons). Daily newspaper circulation (1996): 338,000 (33); Radio receivers (1997): 835,000 (79); Television receivers (1998): 660,000 (61); Telephone main lines (1999): 610,701 (55); Cellular telephone subscribers (1999): 337,800 (30); Personal computers (1999): 110,000 (9.9); Internet users (1999): 65,000 (5.9).

Education and health

Educational attainment (1994). Percentage of pop. age 25 and over having: no formal schooling 45.2%; incomplete primary education 20.8%; complete primary 18.0%; some secondary 4.8%; secondary 7.2%; higher 4.0%. **Literacy** (1995): total pop. age 15 and over literate 55.6%; males literate 62.5%; females literate 48.6%. **Health** (1988): physicians (1997) 9,812 (1 per 1,072 persons); hospital beds (1995) 10,974 (1 per 909 persons); infant mortality rate (2000) 47.0. **Food** (1999): daily per capita caloric intake 2,331 (vegetable products 92%, animal products 8%); (1997) 106% of FAO recommended minimum.

Military

Total active duty personnel (2000): 31,400 (army 93.0%, navy 4.8%, air force 2.2%). **Military expenditure as percentage of GNP** (1996): 1.4% (world 2.6%); per capita expenditure $23.

Background

From simple farming villages dating to 2500 BC, the Maya of Guatemala and the Yucatán developed an impressive civilization. Mayan civilization declined after AD 900, and the Spanish began the subjugation of their descendants in 1523. Independence from Spain was declared by the Central American colonies in Guatemala City in 1821, and Guatemala was incorporated into the Mexican empire until its collapse in 1823. In 1839 Guatemala became an independent republic under the first of a series of dictators who held power almost continuously for the next century. In 1945 a liberal-democratic coalition came to power and instituted sweeping reforms. Attempts to expropriate land belonging to US business interests prompted the US government in 1954 to sponsor an invasion. In the following years Guatemala's social revolution came to an end and most of the reforms were reversed. Chronic political instability and violence henceforth marked Guatemalan politics; most of the 200,000 deaths that resulted were blamed on government forces. In 1991 it abandoned its long-standing claims of sovereignty over Belize and the two countries established diplomatic relations. It continued to experience violence as guerrillas sought to seize power. A peace treaty was signed in 1996, and the country started slowly to recover from its civil war.

Recent Developments

On 15 March 2001 Guatemala entered into a limited free-trade agreement with Mexico and other Central American states, but it excluded Guatemalan coffee and sugar. The United Nation's 2001 Human Development Index, based on life expectancy, educational attainment, and per capita gross domestic product, ranked Guatemala lower than any other country in the Americas except Haiti.

Internet resources: <www.guatemalatravel.com.gt>

Guernsey

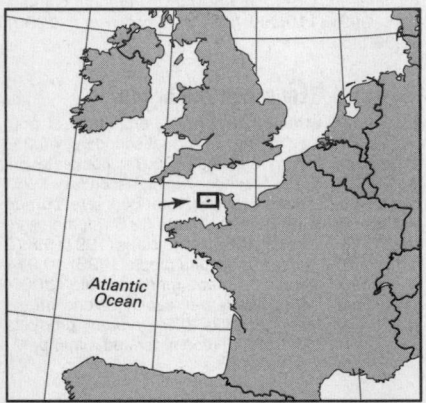

Atlantic
Ocean

Data in this table exclude Guernsey dependencies (particularly Alderney and Sark) unless otherwise indicated. **Official name:** Bailiwick of Guernsey. **Political status:** crown dependency (United Kingdom) with one legislative house (States of Deliberation [57; elected seats only]); Alderney and Sark are dependencies of Guernsey having their own parliaments. **Chief of state:** Queen Elizabeth II represented by Lieutenant Governor Sir John Foley (from 2000). **Head of government:** The government of Guernsey is conducted by committees appointed by the States of Deliberation. **Capital:** St. Peter Port. **Official language:** English. **Official religion:** n.a. **Monetary unit:** 1 Guernsey pound (equivalent to pound sterling) = 100 pence; valuation (28 Jun 2002) 1 Guernsey pound = $1.47.

Demography

Area: 30.2 sq mi, 78.1 sq km (including areas of Guernsey dependencies, of which Alderney 3.1 sq mi [7.9 sq km], Sark 1.6 sq mi [4.2 sq km] , others 1.2 sq mi [3.0 sq km]. **Population** (2001): 64,300 (including pops. of Guernsey dependencies, of which Alderney [1996] 2,100, Sark [1996] 550, others [1996] 100). **Density** (2001; including dependencies): persons per sq mi 2,129.1, persons per sq km 823.3. **Sex distribution** (1996): male 48.13%; female 51.87%. **Age breakdown** (1996): under 15, 17.6%; 15–29, 20.6%; 30–44, 22.3%; 45–59, 19.0%; 60–74, 13.2%; 75 and over, 7.3%. **Population by place of birth** (1996): Guernsey 65.5%, United Kingdom 27.2%, Portugal 1.9%, Jersey 0.7%, Ireland 0.7%, Alderney 0.3%, Sark 0.1%, other 3.6%. **Religious affiliation** (c. 1990): Anglican 65.2%; other 34.8%. **Major cities** (1996; pop. of parish): St. Peter

Port 16,194; Vale 9,504; Castel 8,922; St. Sampson 8,540; St. Martin 6,082. **Location:** western Europe, island in the English Channel, northwest of France.

Vital statistics

Birth rate per 1,000 pop. (2000): 10.5 (world avg. 22.5). **Death rate** per 1,000 pop. (2000): 9.3 (world avg. 9.0). **Natural increase rate** per 1,000 pop. (2000): 1.2 (world avg. 13.5). **Total fertility rate** (avg. births per childbearing woman; 2000): 1.3. **Marriage rate** per 1,000 pop. (1995): 6.0. **Divorce rate** per 1,000 pop. (1993): 2.5. **Life expectancy** at birth (2000): male 76.7 years; female 82.8 years.

National economy

Budget (1999). *Revenue:* £306,991,000 (income tax 79.7%; custom duties and excise taxes 5.7%; document duties 2.7%; corporation taxes 2.1%; automobile taxes 1.9%). *Expenditures:* £244,418,000 (welfare 31.1%; health 26.2%; education 15.9%; administrative services 6.7%; law and order 4.9%; community services 4.1%). **Gross national product** (at current market prices; 2000): $1,883,550,000 ($30,840 per capita). **Production** (metric tons except as noted). *Agriculture, forestry, fishing* (1999): tomatoes (1998) 2,449, flowers 1,153,857 boxes, of which roses 287,915 boxes; livestock (number of live animals) 3,262 cattle; fish catch (1997; including Jersey): 4,368, of which crustaceans 2,934. *Manufacturing:* milk 98,830 hectolitres. *Energy production (consumption):* electricity (kW-hr; 1999–2000), n.a. (273,013,000). **Household income and expenditure** (1999). Average household size (1996) 2.6; expenditure: housing 21.6%, food 12.7%, household goods and services 11.2%, recreation services 9.2%, transportation 8.5%, clothing and footwear 5.6%. **Population economically active** (1999): total 31,153; activity rate of total pop. 48.8%. **Tourism** (1996): receipts $275,000,000.

Foreign trade

Imports (1997): principal imports, n.a. *Major import sources* (1997): mostly United Kingdom. **Exports** (1999): £525,718,000 (mostly flowers and tomatoes). *Major export destinations* (1999): mostly United Kingdom.

Transport and communications

Transport. *Vehicles* (2000): passenger cars 37,598; trucks and buses 7,338. *Air transport:* (2000) passenger arrivals 884,284; (1996) freight loaded and unloaded 7,616 metric tons; airports (1999) with scheduled flights 2 (including an airport on Alderney). **Communications** Total units (units per 1,000 persons). Daily newspaper circulation (1998): 15,784 (260); Telephone main lines (1999): 50,739 (834); Cellular telephone subscribers (1999): 15,320 (251).

Education and health

Educational attainment: n.a. **Literacy** (1993): percentage of total pop. age 15 and over literate 100.0%. **Health** (1999): physicians 93 (1 per 654 persons); infant mortality rate per 1,000 live births

1 metric ton = about 1.1 short tons;   1 kilometer = 0.6 mi (statute);   1 metric ton-km cargo = about 0.68 short ton-mi cargo;   c.i.f.: cost, insurance, and freight;   f.o.b.: free on board

(2000) 5.1. **Food** (1999; data are for the UK): daily per capita caloric intake 3,318 (vegetable products 68%, animal products 32%); 132% of FAO recommended minimum requirement.

Military

Total active duty personnel: n.a.; the United Kingdom is responsible for defense.

 **Did you know?** Victor Hugo, the famous 19th century French Romantic writer, lived in Guernsey (1855–70) during most of his years in exile. While there he completed his most famous work, *Les Misérables*, and produced some of his other better known works. *Les Travailleurs de la mer* (*The Toilers of the Sea*, published in 1866) was dedicated to Guernsey and its sailors.

Internet resources: <www.guernseymap.com>

Guinea

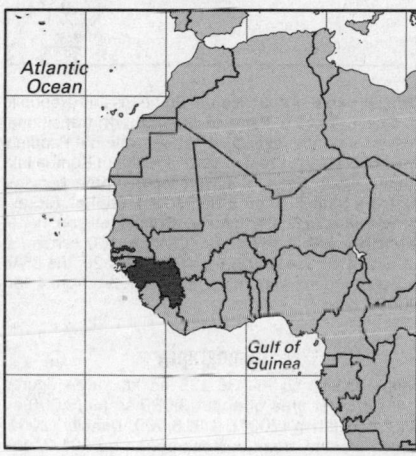

Atlantic Ocean

Gulf of Guinea

Official name: République de Guinée (Republic of Guinea). **Form of government:** unitary multiparty republic with one legislative house (National Assembly [114 seats]). **Head of state and government:** President Lansana Conté (from 1984) assisted by extraconstitutional Prime Minister Lamine Sidimé (from 1999). **Capital:** Conakry. **Official language:** French. **Official religion:** none. **Monetary unit:** 1 Guinean franc (GF) = 100 cauris; valuation (28 Jun 2002) $1 = GF 1,976.50.

Demography

Area: 94,926 sq mi, 245,857 sq km. **Population** (2001): 7,614,000. **Density** (2001): persons per sq mi 80.2, persons per sq km 31.0. **Urban** (1998): 31%. **Sex distribution** (1998): male 50.28%; female 49.72%. **Age breakdown** (1999): under 15, 43.6%; 15–29, 26.9%; 30–44, 16.0%; 45–59, 9.0%; 60–74, 3.9%; 75 and over, 0.6%. **Ethnic composition** (1996): Fulani 38.6%; Malinke 23.2%; Susu 11.0%;

Kissi 6.0%; Kpelle 4.6%; other 16.6%. **Religious affiliation** (1996): Muslim 85.0%; Christian 10.0%; other 5.0%. **Major cities** (2001): Conakry 1,565,200; Kankan 88,800; Labé 64,500; Kindia 56,000; Nzérékoré 55,000. **Location:** western Africa, bordering Guinea-Bissau, Senegal, Mali, Côte d'Ivoire, Liberia, Sierra Leone, and the North Atlantic Ocean.

Vital statistics

Birth rate per 1,000 pop. (2001): 39.8 (world avg. 22.5). **Death rate** per 1,000 pop. (2001): 17.5 (world avg. 9.0). **Natural increase rate** per 1,000 pop. (2001): 22.3 (world avg. 13.5). **Total fertility rate** (avg. births per childbearing woman; 2001): 5.4. **Life expectancy** at birth (2001): male 43.5 years; female 48.4 years.

National economy

Budget (1998). *Revenue:* GF 624,500,000,000 (current revenues 79.5%, of which indirect taxes 34.8%, mining sector 20.2%, tax on trade 11.5%, direct taxes 7.7%, nontax revenue 5.3%; foreign aid 20.5%). *Expenditures:* GF 655,600,000,000 (wages and salaries 27.6%, goods and services 13.6%, interest 9.8%, transfers 8.1%; capital spending 38.2%). **Production** (metric tons except as noted). *Agriculture, forestry, fishing* (1999): roots and tubers 1,064,888, fruits 996,078, paddy rice 750,000; livestock (number of live animals) 2,368,000 cattle, 864,000 goats, 8,900,000 chickens; roundwood (1998) 8,650,000 cu m; fish catch (1997) 102,589. *Mining and quarrying* (1996): bauxite 15,888,600; alumina 564,237; gold (1995) 7,863 kg. *Manufacturing* (value of production in GF '000; 1985): corrugated and sheet iron 571,081; plastics 462,242; tobacco products 375,154. *Energy production (consumption):* electricity (kW-hr; 1996) 541,000,000 (541,000,000); petroleum products (metric tons; 1996) none (356,000). **Gross national product** (1999): $3,556,000,000 ($490 per capita). **Public debt** (external, outstanding; 1999): $3,057,000,000. **Population economically active** (1997): total 3,321,000; activity rate of total pop. 44.8% (participation rates [1983]: ages 15–64, 63.5%; female 47.3%; unemployed, n.a.). **Household income and expenditure.** Average household size (1997): 4.1; average annual income per capita (1984) GS 7,660; expenditure (1985): food 61.5%, health 11.2%, clothing 7.9%, housing 7.3%. **Tourism** (1999): receipts $7,000,000; expenditures $31,000,000. **Land use** (1994): forest 27.3%; pasture 43.5%; agriculture 3.3%; other 25.9%.

Foreign trade

Imports (1997): $571,800,000 (capital goods 52.4%, consumer products 18.0%, food 17.1%, petroleum 12.5%). *Major import sources:* France 24.8%; US 9.8%; Belgium 7.9%; Côte d'Ivoire 6.6%; China 5.6%. **Exports** (1998): $709,200,000 (bauxite 45.7%, gold 17.7%, alumina 14.1%, diamonds 7.2%, fish 5.4%, coffee 3.3%). *Major export destinations:* US 16.4%; Hong Kong 14.7%; Belgium 13.7%; Spain 12.4%; Ireland 12.2%.

Transport and communications

Transport. *Railroads* (1998): route length 662 km; (latest) passenger-km 41,500,000; metric ton-km cargo 7,300,000. *Roads* (1997): total length 30,500 km (paved 16.5%). *Vehicles* (1996): passenger cars 14,100; trucks and buses 21,000. *Air transport* (1995): passenger-km 52,000,000; metric ton-km cargo 5,000,000; airports (1998) 1. **Communications** Total units (units per 1,000 persons). Daily newspaper circulation (1988): 13,000 (2.0); Radio receivers (1998): 325,000 (43); Television receivers (1999): 343,000 (44); Telephone main lines (1999): 46,246 (6.0); Cellular telephone subscribers (1999): 25,182 (3.2); Personal computers (1998): 26,720 (3.5); Internet users (1999): 5,000 (0.6).

Education and health

Educational attainment of those age 6 and over having attended school (1983): primary 55.2%; secondary 32.7%; vocational 3.4%; higher 8.7%. **Literacy** (1995): percentage of total pop. age 15 and over literate 35.9%; males 49.9%; females 21.9%. **Health:** physicians (1991) 920 (1 per 6,840 persons); hospital beds (1988) 3,382 (1 per 1,652 persons); infant mortality rate (2001) 120.0. **Food** (1999): daily per capita caloric intake 2,133 (vegetable products 97%, animal products 3%); 92% of FAO recommended minimum requirement.

Military

Total active duty personnel (2000): 9,700 (army 87.6%, navy 4.1%, air force 8.2%). **Military expenditure as percentage of GNP** (1997): 1.5% (world 2.6%); per capita expenditure $7.

Background

In c. AD 900 successive migrations of the Susu swept down from the desert and pushed the original inhabitants of Guinea, the Baga, to the Atlantic coast. Small kingdoms of the Susu rose in importance in the 13th century and later extended their rule to the coast. In the mid-15th century the Portuguese visited the coast and developed a slave trade. In the 16th century the Fulani established domination over the Fouta Djallon region; they ruled into the 19th century. In the early 19th century the French arrived, and in 1849 proclaimed the coastal region a French protectorate. In 1895 French Guinea became part of the federation of French West Africa. In 1946 it was made an overseas territory of France, and in 1958 achieved independence. Following a military coup in 1984, Guinea began implementing Westernized government systems. A new constitution was adopted in 1991, and the first multiparty elections were held in 1993. During the 1990s Guinea accommodated several hundred thousand war refugees from neighboring Liberia and Sierra Leone.

Recent Developments

Conflicts along Guinea's borders with Liberia and Sierra Leone have hampered economic growth in the country. On 7 May 2001 the International Monetary Fund underwrote a three-year, $82 million aid package designed to finance antipoverty measures and accelerate economic development. Later that year the World Bank approved $120 million in credits for education reforms and the alleviation of poverty, and the African Development Fund announced that it would loan Guinea nearly $16 million for a new structural-adjustment program.

Internet resources: <www.guinee.net>

Guinea-Bissau

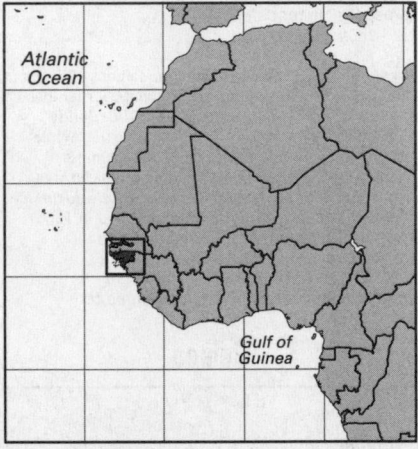

Official name: República da Guiné-Bissau (Republic of Guinea-Bissau). **Form of government:** transitional regime with one legislative house (National People's Assembly [102]). **Chief of state:** President Kumba Ialá (from 2000). **Head of government:** Prime Minister Alamara Nhassé (from 8 Dec 2001). **Capital:** Bissau. **Official language:** Portuguese. **Official religion:** none. **Monetary unit:** 1 CFA franc (CFAF) = 100 centimes; valuation (28 Jun 2002) $1 = CFAF 664.20; the CFAF is pegged to the euro (€) at €1 = 655.96 from 1 Jan 2002.

Demography

Area: 13,948 sq mi, 36,125 sq km; area figures include water area of about 3,089 sq mi (8,000 sq km). **Population** (2001): 1,316,000. **Density** (2001; based on land area): persons per sq mi 121.2, persons per sq km 46.8. **Urban** (1996): 22.0%. **Sex distribution** (1997): male 48.52%; female 51.48%. **Age breakdown** (1997): under 15, 42.7%; 15–29, 28.1%; 30–44, 15.4%; 45–59, 9.2%; 60–74, 3.8%; 75 and over, 0.8%. **Ethnic composition** (1995): Balante 30%; Fulani 20%; Mandyako 14%; Malinke 13%; Pepel 7%; nonindigenous Cape Verdean mulatto 2%; other 14%. **Religious affiliation** (2000): traditional beliefs 45.2%; Muslim 39.9%; Christian 13.2%, of which Roman Catholic 9.9%; other 1.7%. **Major cities** (1997): Bissau 200,000 (urban agglomeration [1999] 274,000); Bafatá 15,000; Cacheu 14,000; Gabú 10,000. **Location:** western Africa, bordering Senegal, Guinea, and the North Atlantic Ocean.

Vital statistics

Birth rate per 1,000 pop. (2000): 39.6 (world avg. 22.5). **Death rate** per 1,000 pop. (2000): 15.6 (world

---

1 metric ton = about 1.1 short tons;   1 kilometer = 0.6 mi (statute);   1 metric ton-km cargo = about 0.68 short ton-mi cargo;   c.i.f.: cost, insurance, and freight;   f.o.b.: free on board

avg. 9.0). **Natural increase rate** per 1,000 pop. (2000): 24.0 (world avg. 13.5). **Total fertility rate** (avg. births per childbearing woman; 2000): 5.3. **Life expectancy** at birth (2000): male 46.8 years; female 51.4 years.

National economy

Budget (1998). *Revenue:* CFAF 10,500,000,000 (foreign grants 37.1%; taxes on international trade 21.6%, of which import duties 12.9%; nontax revenues 19.8%, of which fishing licenses 7.3%; taxes on goods and services 10.7%; income taxes 8.2%). *Expenditures:* CFAF 30,200,000,000 (current expenditures 75.2%, of which scheduled external interest payments 27.0%; capital expenditures 24.8%). **Production** (metric tons except as noted). *Agriculture, forestry, fishing* (1999): rice 130,000, oil palm fruit 80,000, cashew nuts 38,000; livestock (number of live animals) 520,000 cattle, 340,000 pigs, 315,000 goats; roundwood (1998) 589,000 cu m; fish catch (1997) 7,250. *Mining and quarrying:* extraction of construction materials only. *Manufacturing* (1997): processed wood 21,400; fresh pork 0,720; wood products 7,000. *Energy production (consumption):* electricity (kW-hr; 1999) 27,500,000 (10,200,000); petroleum products (metric tons; 1996) none (75,000). **Population economically active** (1992): total 471,000; activity rate of total pop. 46.9% (participation rates [1991]: over age 10, 67.1%; female 40.5%). **Public debt** (external, outstanding; 1999): $831,700,000. **Gross national product** (at current market prices; 1999): $194,000,000 ($160 per capita). **Land use** (1994): forested 38.1%; meadows and pastures 38.4%; agricultural and under permanent cultivation 12.1%; other 11.4%. **Household income.** Average household size (1996) 6.9.

Foreign trade

Imports (1997-c.i.f.): CFAF 51,800,000,000 (foodstuffs 35.1%, of which rice 25.1%; transport equipment 14.1%; fuel and lubricants 10.7%; construction materials 9.6%). *Major import sources* (1999): Portugal 24.0%; Senegal 18.2%; China 12.9%; Japan 8.1%; The Netherlands 6.7%. **Exports** (1997-f.o.b.): CFAF 28,300,000,000 (cashews 94.0%; sawn wood 1.6%; shrimp 0.8%; logs 0.8%). *Major export destinations* (1999): India 85.2%; Spain 1.7%; other/unspecified 13.1%.

Transport and communications

Transport. *Roads* (1996): total length 4,400 km (paved 10%). *Vehicles* (1996): passenger cars 7,120; trucks and buses 5,640. *Air transport* (1996): passenger-km 10,000,000; airports (1997) with scheduled flights 2. **Communications** total units (units per 1,000 persons). Daily newspaper circulation (1996): 6,000 (5.1); Radio receivers (1997): 49,000 (41); Telephone main lines (1998): 8,079 (6.6); Internet users (1999): 1,500 (1.2).

Education and health

Educational attainment (1979). Percentage of pop. age 7 and over having: no formal schooling or knowledge of reading and writing 90.4%; primary education 7.9%; secondary 1.0%; technical 0.5%; higher 0.2%. **Literacy** (1995): total pop. age 15 and over literate 54.9%; males literate 68.0%; females literate 42.5%. **Health:** physicians (1991) 184 (1 per 5,556 persons); hospital beds (1993) 1,300 (1 per 834 persons); infant mortality rate per 1,000 live births (2000) 112.3. **Food** (1999): daily per capita caloric intake 2,245 (vegetable products 93%, animal products 7%); 97% of FAO recommended minimum requirement.

Military

Total active duty personnel (2000): 7,250 (army 93.8%, navy 4.8%, air force 1.4%). **Military expenditure as percentage of GNP** (1997): 3.2% (world 2.6%); per capita expenditure $7.

Background

More than 1,000 years ago the coast of Guinea-Bissau was occupied by iron-using agriculturists. They grew irrigated and dry rice and were also the major suppliers of marine salt to the western Sudan. At about the same time, it came under the influence of the Mali empire and became a tributary kingdom known as Gabú. After 1546 Gabú was virtually autonomous; vestiges of the kingdom lasted until 1867. The earliest overseas contacts came in the 15th century with the Portuguese, who imported slaves from the Guinea area to the offshore Cape Verde Islands. Portuguese control of Guinea-Bissau was marginal despite their claims to sovereignty there. The end of the slave trade forced the Portuguese inland in search of new profits. Their subjugation of the interior was slow and sometimes violent; it was not effectively achieved until 1915, though sporadic resistance continued until 1936. Guerrilla warfare in the 1960s led to the country's independence in 1974, but political turmoil continued and the government was overthrown by a military coup in 1980. A new constitution was adopted in 1984, and the first multiparty elections were held in 1994. A destructive civil war in 1998 was followed by a military coup in 1999.

Recent Developments

Following the 1999 coup, elections brought to power Kumba Ialá, who began a five-year term as president on 17 Feb 2000. His council of ministers included no members of the previously dominant African Party for the Independence of Guinea-Bissau and Cape Verde. According to a report from a UN agency in June 2002, Guinea-Bissau was the poorest country in the world with a −7.5 GDP growth rate in 1997–2000.

Internet resources: <www.izf.net/izf/Index.htm>

Guyana

Official name: Co-operative Republic of Guyana. **Form of government:** unitary multiparty republic with one legislative house (National Assembly [65]). **Head of state and government:** President Bharrat Jagdeo (from 1999) assisted by Prime Minister Sam Hinds. **Capital:** Georgetown. **Official language:** English. **Official religion:** none. **Monetary unit:** 1 Guyana dollar (G$) = 100 cents; valuation (28 Jun 2002) US$1 = G$180.50.

Demography

Area: 83,044 sq mi, 215,083 sq km. **Population** (2001): 776,000. **Density** (2000; land area only): persons per sq mi 10.2, persons per sq km 3.9. **Urban** (1998): 37.1%. **Sex distribution** (1995): male 49.46%; female 50.54%. **Age breakdown** (1995): under 15, 32.2%; 15–29, 30.1%; 30–44, 22.2%; 45–59, 9.5%; 60–74, 4.8%; 75 and over, 1.2%. **Ethnic composition** (1992–93): East Indian 49.4%; black (African Negro and Bush Negro) 35.6%; mixed 7.1%; Amerindian 6.8%; Portuguese 0.7%; Chinese 0.4%. **Religious affiliation** (1995): Christian 40.9%, of which Protestant 27.5% (including Anglican 8.6%), Roman Catholic 11.5%, Ethiopian Orthodox 1.1%; Hindu 34.0%; Muslim 9.0%; other 16.1%. **Major cities** (1997): Georgetown 230,000; Linden 35,000; New Amsterdam 25,000; Corriverton 24,000. **Location:** northern South America, bordering the North Atlantic Ocean, Suriname, Brazil, and Venezuela.

Vital statistics

Birth rate per 1,000 pop. (2000): 17.9 (world avg. 22.5). **Death rate** per 1,000 pop. (2000): 8.4 (world avg. 9.0). **Natural increase** rate per 1,000 pop. (2000): 9.5 (world avg. 13.5). **Total fertility rate** (avg. births per childbearing woman; 2000): 2.1. **Life expectancy** at birth (2000): male 61.1 years; female 67.2 years.

National economy

Budget (1999): *Revenue:* G$36,544,000,000 (tax revenue 91.6%, of which consumption taxes 32.0%, income taxes on companies 22.2%, personal income taxes 15.5%, import duties 11.4%; nontax revenue 8.2%). *Expenditures:* G$41,983,000,000 (current expenditure 71.2%, of which debt charges 13.8%; development expenditure 28.8%). **Production** (metric tons except as noted). *Agriculture, forestry, fishing* (1999): rice 365,469, raw sugar 321,438, coconuts 56,449; livestock (number of live animals) 220,000 cattle, 130,000 sheep, 11,600,000 chickens; roundwood 442,000 cu m; fish catch (1997) 57,409. *Mining and quarrying* (1999): bauxite 2,359,272; gold 414,905 troy oz;

diamonds (1998) 34,385 carats. *Manufacturing* (1999): flour 35,290; rum 137,800 hectoliters; beer and stout 129,200 hectoliters. *Energy production (consumption):* electricity (kW-hr; 2000) 477,900,-000 ([1996] 255,000,000). **Population economically active** (1992–93): total 278,000; activity rate of total pop. 38.8% (participation rates: ages 15–64, 61.8%; female 34.1%; unemployed [1998] c. 12%). **Gross national product** (at current market prices; 1999): US$651,000,000 (US$760 per capita). **Public debt** (external, outstanding; 1999): US$1,238,000,000. **Household income and expenditure.** Average household size (1997) 4.5. **Tourism:** receipts from visitors (1998) US$52,000,000; expenditures by nationals abroad (1997) US$22,-000,000. **Land use** (1994): forested 83.8%; meadows and pastures 6.3%; agricultural and under permanent cultivation 2.5%; other 7.4%.

Foreign trade

Imports (1999-c.i.f.): US$550,200,000 (consumer goods 35.2%; capital goods 29.6%; fuels and lubricants 13.1%). *Major import sources* (1998 est.): US 28%; Trinidad and Tobago 21%; Netherlands Antilles 14%; UK 7%; Japan 3%. **Exports** (1999-f.o.b.): US$525,000,000 (domestic exports 96.1%, of which sugar 25.9%, gold 20.7%; bauxite 14.7%, rice 13.5%, timber 7.1%; reexports 3.9%). *Major export destinations* (1998 est.): US 24%; Canada 23%; UK 19%; Netherlands Antilles 10%.

Transport and communications

Transport. *Roads* (1996): total length 4,952 mi, 7,970 km (paved 7%). *Vehicles* (1995): passenger cars 24,000; trucks and buses 9,000. *Air transport* (1996): passenger-km 248,000,000; metric ton-km cargo 3,300,000; airports (1996; international only) with scheduled flights 1. **Communications** Total units (units per 1,000 persons). Daily newspaper circulation (1996): 42,000 (54); Radio receivers (1997): 420,000 (539); Television receivers (1999): 60,000 (77); Telephone main lines (1999): 64,034 (82); Cellular telephone subscribers (1999): 2,815 (3.6); Personal computers (1999): 21,000 (27); Internet users (1999): 3,000 (3.8).

Education and health

Educational attainment (1980). Percentage of pop. age 25 and over having: no formal schooling 8.1%; primary education 72.8%; secondary 17.3%; higher 1.8%. **Literacy** (1995): total pop. age 15 and over literate, c. 511,000 (98.1%); males literate, c. 254,000 (98.6%); females literate, c. 257,000 (97.5%). **Health:** physicians (1997) 153 (1 per 5,090 persons); hospital beds (1996) 3,242 (1 per 240 persons); infant mortality rate per 1,000 live births (2000) 39.1. **Food** (1999): daily per capita caloric intake 2,569 (vegetable products 84%, animal products 16%); 113% of FAO recommended minimum requirement.

Military

Total active duty personnel (2000): 1,600 (army 87.5%, navy 6.3%, air force 6.2%) **Military expendi-

---

1 metric ton = about 1.1 short tons;   1 kilometer = 0.6 mi (statute);   1 metric ton-km cargo = about 0.68 short ton-mi cargo;   c.i.f.: cost, insurance, and freight;   f.o.b.: free on board

ture as percentage of GNP (1997): 1.1% (world 2.6%); per capita expenditure US$10.

Background

Guyana was colonized by the Dutch in the 17th century; during the Napoleonic Wars the British occupied the territory and afterward purchased the colonies of Demerara, Berbice, and Essequibo, united in 1831 as British Guiana. The slave trade was abolished in 1807, but emancipation of the 100,000 slaves in the colonies was not completed until 1838. From the 1840s East Indian and Chinese indentured servants were brought to work the plantations; by 1917 almost 240,000 East Indians had migrated to British Guiana. It was made a crown colony in 1928 and granted home rule in 1953. Political parties began to emerge, developing on racial lines as the People's Progressive Party (largely East Indian) and the People's National Congress (largely black). The PNC formed a coalition government and led the country into independence as Guyana in 1966. In 1970 Guyana became a republic within the Commonwealth; in 1980 it adopted a new constitution. Venezuela has long claimed land west of the Essequibo River, and the UN has continued to arbitrate the issue.

Recent Developments

Guyana's ruling People's Progressive Party (PPP)/Civic alliance was returned to office in the general election held on 19 Mar 2001. The victory gave the alliance's leader, Bharrat Jagdeo, another five-year term as president and head of state. PPP/Civic, which took 209,031 of the 393,709 votes cast, secured 34 of the nation's 65 parliamentary seats. The opposition People's National Congress (PNC)/Reform Party won 164,074 votes and claimed 27 seats.

Internet resources: <www.guyana.org>

Haiti

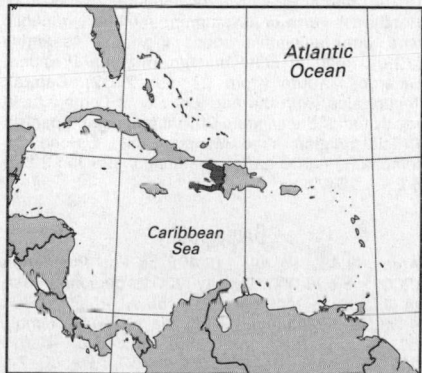

Atlantic Ocean

Caribbean Sea

Official name: Repiblik Dayti (Haitian Creole); République d'Haïti (French) (Republic of Haiti). Form of government: multiparty republic with two legislative houses (Senate [27]; Chamber of Deputies [82]). Chief of state: President Jean-Bertrand Aristide (from 7 Feb 2001). Head of government: Prime Minister Yvon Neptune (from 15 Mar 2002). Capital:

Port-au-Prince. Official languages: Haitian Creole; French. Official religion: none. Monetary unit: 1 gourde (G) = 100 centimes; valuation (28 Jun 2002) $1 = G 27.50.

Demography

Area: 10,695 sq mi, 27,700 sq km. Population (2001): 6,965,000. Density (2001): persons per sq mi 651.2, persons per sq km 251.4. Urban (1999): 35.1%. Sex distribution (2000): male 49.26%; female 50.74%. Age breakdown (2000): under 15, 41.1%; 15–29, 28.7%; 30–44, 15.2%; 45–59, 8.6%; 60–74, 5.0%; 75 and over, 1.4%. Ethnic composition (2000): black 94.2%; mulatto 5.4%; other/unspecified 0.4%. Religious affiliation (1995): Roman Catholic 68.5% (of which 80% practice voodoo); Protestant 24.1%, of which Baptist 5.9%, Pentecostal 5.3%, Seventh-day Adventist 4.6%; other 7.4%. Major cities (1997): Port-au-Prince 917,112 (metropolitan area 1,556,588, including Carrefour 306,074; Delmas 257,247; Pétion-Ville 76,155); Cap-Haïtien 107,026. Location: western third of the island of Hispaniola, between the North Atlantic Ocean and the Caribbean Sea.

Vital statistics

Birth rate per 1,000 pop. (2000): 32.0 (world avg. 22.5). Death rate per 1,000 pop. (2000): 15.1 (world avg. 9.0). Natural increase rate per 1,000 pop. (2000): 16.9 (world avg. 13.5). Total fertility rate (avg. births per childbearing woman; 2000): 4.5. Life expectancy at birth (2000): male 47.5 years; female 51.1 years.

National economy

Budget (1998; excludes G 3,7000,000,000 in foreign grants). *Revenue:* G 5,371,000,000 (general sales tax 26.4%; customs duties 20.1%; excises 15.9%; taxes on income and profits 11.7%). *Expenditures:* G 6,036,000,000 (current expenditure 80.0%, of which interest on public debt 7.2%; development expenditure 20.0%). Production (metric tons except as noted). *Agriculture, forestry, fishing* (1999): sugarcane 1,000,100, cassava (manioc) 325,000, plantains 290,000; livestock (number of live animals) 1,618,000 goats, 1,300,000 cattle, 800,000 pigs; roundwood (1998) 6,397,000 cu m; fish catch (1997) 5,630. *Mining and quarrying:* small amounts of limestone, calcareous clay, salt, and marble. *Manufacturing* (1995–96): cigarettes 837,900,000 units; malt liquor 13,800,000 bottles; beer 4,200,000 bottles. *Energy production (consumption):* electricity (kW-hr; 1996) 633,000,000 (633,000,000). Land use (1994): forested 5.1%; meadows and pastures 18.0%; agricultural and under permanent cultivation 33.0%; other 43.9%. Population economically active (1996): total 3,209,000; activity rate of total pop. 49.3% (participation rates: ages 15–64 [1990] 64.8%; female 43.0%; unemployed unofficially about 60%). Household income and expenditure. Average household size (1982) 4.4; average annual income of urban wage earners (1984): G 1,545; expenditure (1996): food, beverages, and tobacco 49.4%, housing and energy 9.1%, transportation 8.7%, clothing and footwear 8.5%. Public debt (external, outstanding; 1999): $1,049,000,000. Gross national product (1999): $3,584,000,000 ($460 per capita). Tourism

(1998): receipts from visitors $57,000,000; expenditures by nationals abroad $37,000,000.

Foreign trade

Imports (1997–98, c.i.f.): $811,500,000 (est.; food and live animals 27%, machinery and transport equipment 16%, petroleum and derivatives 9%, animal and vegetable oils 7%). *Major import sources* (1998; est.): US 60%; Japan 4%; Dominican Rep. 4%; France 3%; Colombia 3%. **Exports** (1997–98, f.o.b.): $284,300,000 (est.; reexports [mostly clothing] 74%, handicrafts [includes wood carvings, paintings, and woven sisal products] 7%, coffee 7%). *Major export destinations* (1998; est.): US 88%; Belgium 3%; France 3%.

Transport and communications

Transport. *Roads* (1996): total length 4,160 km (paved 24%). *Vehicles* (1996): passenger cars 32,000; trucks and buses 21,000. *Air transport* (1994; Port-au-Prince Airport only): passenger arrivals 167,882, passenger departures 177,072; cargo unloaded 11,967 metric tons, cargo loaded 10,087 metric tons; airports (1997) with scheduled flights 2. **Communications** Total units (units per 1,000 persons). Daily newspaper circulation (1996): 20,000 (3.1); Radio receivers (1997): 415,000 (63); Television receivers (1997): 38,000 (5.8); Telephone main lines (1999): 70,000 (10); Cellular telephone subscribers (1999): 25,000 (3.7).

Education and health

Educational attainment (1986–87). Percentage of pop. age 25 and over having: no formal schooling 59.5%; primary education 30.5%; secondary 8.6%; vocational and teacher training 0.7%; higher 0.7%. **Literacy** (1995): total pop. age 15 and over literate 1,930,000 (45.0%); males literate 992,000 (48.0%); females literate 938,000 (42.2%). **Health:** physicians (1993–94) 641 (public health services only; 1 per 9,846 persons); hospital beds (1996) 5,241 (1 per 1,242 persons); infant mortality rate (2000) 97.1. **Food** (1999): daily per capita caloric intake 1,977 (vegetable products 94%, animal products 6%); 87% of FAO recommended minimum requirement.

Background

Haiti gained its independence when the former slaves of the island, initially led by Toussaint-Louverture, and later by Jean-Jacques Dessalines, rebelled against French rule in 1791–1804. The new republic encompassed the entire island of Hispaniola, but the eastern portion was restored to Spain in 1809. It was reunited under Haitian Pres. Jean-Pierre Boyer (1818–43); after his overthrow the eastern portion revolted and formed the Dominican Republic. Haiti's government was marked by instability, with frequent coups and assassinations. It was occupied by the US in 1915–34. In 1957 the dictator François ("Papa Doc") Duvalier came to power. Despite an economic decline and civil unrest, Duvalier ruled until his death in 1971. He was succeeded by his son, Jean-Claude ("Baby Doc")

Duvalier, who was forced into exile in 1986. Haiti's first free presidential elections, held in 1990, were won by Jean-Bertrand Aristide. He was deposed by a military coup in 1991, after which tens of thousands of Haitians attempted to flee to the US in small boats. The military government stepped down in 1994, and Aristide returned from exile and resumed the presidency.

Recent Developments

Elections in 1995 brought about the first peaceful transfer of power between elected presidents in Haiti's history when René Préval, an associate of President Aristide, was chosen to succeed him. In allegedly fraudulent elections in 2000, Préval's supporters took control of the legislature, and Aristide again claimed the presidency. Amid allegations of corruption Prime Minister Jean-Marie Chérestal left office and was replaced in March 2002 by Yvon Neptune. Haiti's economy showed few signs of improving at the outset of the 21st century.

Internet resources: <www.haiti.org>

Honduras

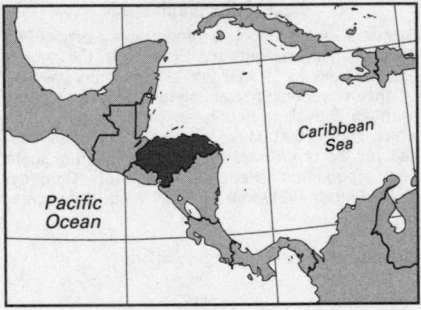

Official name: República de Honduras (Republic of Honduras). **Form of government:** multiparty republic with one legislative house (National Assembly [128]). **Head of state and government:** President Ricardo Maduro (from 27 Jan 2002). **Capital:** Tegucigalpa (with the adjacent city of Comayaguela jointly forms the capital). **Official language:** Spanish. **Official religion:** none. **Monetary unit:** 1 Honduran lempira (L) = 100 centavos; valuation (28 Jun 2002) $1 = L 16.40.

Demography

Area: 43,433 sq mi, 112,492 sq km. **Population** (2001): 6,626,000. **Density** (2001): persons per sq mi 152.6, persons per sq km 58.9. **Urban** (1999): 44%. **Sex distribution** (1999): male 48.94%; female 51.06%. **Age breakdown** (1998): under 15, 42.6%; 15–29, 28.4%; 30–44, 16.2%; 45–59, 7.8%; 60–74, 3.9%; 75 and over, 1.1%. **Ethnic composition** (2000): mestizo 86.6%; Amerindian 5.5%; black (including Black Carib) 4.3%; white 2.3%; other 1.3%. **Religious affiliation** (1995): Roman Catholic 86.7%; Protestant 10.4%, of which Pentecostal 5.7%; other 2.9%. **Major**

1 metric ton = about 1.1 short tons;   1 kilometer = 0.6 mi (statute);   1 metric ton-km cargo = about 0.68 short ton-mi cargo;   c.i.f.: cost, insurance, and freight;   f.o.b.: free on board

cities (1999): Tegucigalpa and Comayaguela 988,400; San Pedro Sula 452,100; El Progreso 104,100, La Ceiba 103,400; Choluteca 92,400. **Location:** Central America, bordering the Caribbean Sea, Nicaragua, North Pacific Ocean, El Salvador, and Guatemala.

Vital statistics

Birth rate per 1,000 pop. (2000): 32.7 (world avg. 22.5). **Death rate** per 1,000 pop. (2000): 5.3 (world avg. 9.0). **Natural Increase rate** per 1,000 pop. (2000): 27.4 (world avg. 13.5). **Total fertility rate** (avg. births per childbearing woman; 2000): 4.3. **Marriage rate** per 1,000 pop. (1983): 4.9. **Divorce rate** per 1,000 pop. (1983): 0.4. **Life expectancy** at birth (2000): male 67.9 years; female 72.1 years.

National economy

Budget (1998). *Revenue:* L 13,197,000,000 (current revenue 99.8%, of which indirect taxes 65.1%, direct taxes 25.6%, nontax revenue 6.9%, transfers 2.2%). *Expenditures:* L 11,387,000,000 (current expenditure 72.6%; capital expenditure 27.4%). **Production** (metric tons except as noted). *Agriculture, forestry, fishing* (1999): sugarcane 4,286,000, bananas 861,000, coffee 164,000; livestock (number of live animals) 2,061,000 cattle, 700,000 pigs, 18,000,000 chickens; roundwood (1998) 7,176,000 cu m; fish catch (1998) 14,881. *Mining and quarrying* (1997): zinc 25,500; lead 3,400, gold 150 kilograms. *Manufacturing* (value added in L '000,000; 1996): food products 1,937.3; wearing apparel 1,266.4; beverages 699.6. *Energy production (consumption):* electricity (kW-hr; 1996) 2,815,000,000 (2,819,000,000); crude petroleum (barrels; 1992) none (3,064,000); petroleum products (metric tons; 1996) none (1,157,000). **Household income and expenditure.** Average household size (1988) 5.4; *sources of income* (1985): wages and salaries 58.8%, transfer payments 1.8%, other 39.4%; *expenditure* (1986): food 44.4%, utilities and housing 22.4%, clothing and footwear 9.0%, household furnishings 8.3%, health care 7.0%, transportation 3.0%, other 5.9%. **Land use** (1998): forested and other 67.9%; meadows and pastures 13.8%; agricultural and under permanent cultivation 18.3%. **Gross national product** (1999): $4,829,000,000 ($760 per capita). **Public debt** (external, outstanding; 1999): $4,231,000,000. **Population economically active** (1999): total 2,131,300; activity rate of total pop. 33.4% (participation rates: over age 15 [1998] 61.2%; female [1998] 34.6%; unemployed [1998] 4.3%). **Tourism** (1999): receipts $195,000,000; expenditures $94,000,000.

Foreign trade

Imports (1999-c.i.f.): $2,727,800,000 (machinery and electrical equipment 20.8%, industrial chemicals 13.0%, transport equipment 12.1%, food products 10.3%, mineral fuels and lubricants 9.4%). *Major import sources.* US 47.1%; Guatemala 7.4%; Mexico 4.8%; Japan 4.7%; Costa Rica 2.5%. **Exports** (1999): $1,303,900,000 (coffee 20.5%, shrimp and lobsters 15.5%, melons 3.7%, lead and zinc 3.4%). *Major export destinations:* US 35.4%; Germany 7.5%; El Salvador 6.4%; Guatemala 5.8%; Nicaragua 4.8%.

Transport and communications

Transport. *Railroads* (1989): length (1999) 988 km; passenger-km 7,700,000; metric ton-km cargo 30,200,000. *Roads* (1999): total length 14,602 km (paved 18%). *Vehicles* (1995): passenger cars 81,439; trucks and buses 170,006. *Air transport* (1995): passenger-km 341,000,000; metric ton-km cargo 33,000,000; airports (1996) with scheduled flights 8. **Communications** Total units (units per 1,000 persons). Daily newspaper circulation (1996): 320,000 (55); Radio receivers (1997): 2,450,000 (410); Television receivers (1999): 600,000 (95); Telephone main lines (1999): 279,197 (44); Cellular telephone subscribers (1999): 78,588 (12); Personal computers (1999): 60,000 (9.5); Internet users (1999): 20,000 (3.2).

Education and health

Educational attainment (1988). Percentage of pop. age 10 and over having: no formal schooling 33.4%; primary education 50.1%; secondary education 13.4%; higher 3.1%. **Literacy** (1995): total pop. age 15 and over literate 72.7%; males literate 72.6%; females literate 72.7%. **Health:** physicians (1993) 3,803 (1 per 1,358 persons); hospital beds (1999) 5,720 (1 per 1,098 persons); infant mortality rate (2000) 31.3. **Food** (1999): daily per capita caloric intake 2,396 (vegetable products 84%, animal products 16%); (1997) 106% of FAO recommended minimum.

Military

Total active duty personnel (2000): 8,300 (army 66.3%, navy 12.0%, air force 21.7%). **Military expenditure as percentage of GNP** (1995): 1.3% (world 2.7%); per capita expenditure $9.

Background

Early residents of Honduras were part of the Maya civilization that flourished in the 1st millennium AD. Christopher Columbus reached Honduras in 1502, and permanent settlement followed. A major war between the Spaniards and the Indians broke out in 1537, culminating in the decimation of the Indian population through disease and enslavement. After 1570 it was part of the captaincy general of Guatemala until Central American independence in 1821. Part of the United Provinces of Central America, Honduras withdrew in 1838 and declared its independence. In the 20th century, under military rule, there was constant civil war and some intervention by the US. A civilian government assumed office in 1982. The military remained in the background, however, as the activity of leftist guerrillas increased. Flooding caused by a hurricane in 1998 devastated the country, killing several thousand people and leaving hundreds of thousands homeless. In 2001 Honduras was hit by a severe drought.

Recent Developments

The national elections held on 25 Nov 2001 were the sixth since 1981, marking an unprecedented two decades of democracy in Honduras. The presidential election was won by Ricardo Maduro of the National Party. The new government took office in January 2002.

Internet resources: <http://ine.online.hn>

Hong Kong

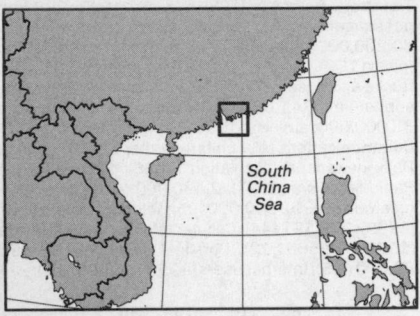

South
China
Sea

Official name: Xianggang Tebie Xingzhengqu (Chinese); Hong Kong Special Administrative Region (English). **Political status:** special administrative region (People's Republic of China) with one legislative house (Legislative Council [60]). **Chief of state:** President Jiang Zemin of China (from 1993). **Head of government:** Chief Executive Tung Chee-hwa (from 1997). **Capital:** None. **Official languages:** Chinese; English. **Official religion:** none. **Monetary unit:** 1 Hong Kong dollar (HK$) = 100 cents; valuation (28 Jun 2002) US$1 = HK$7.80.

Demography

Area: 421.6 sq mi, 1,091.9 sq km. **Population** (2001): 6,732,000. **Density** (2001): persons per sq mi 15,968.0, persons per sq km 6,165.5. **Urban** (2000): 100.0%. **Sex distribution** (2001): male 48.97%; female 51.03%. **Age breakdown** (2001): under 15, 16.5%; 15–29, 21.6%; 30–44, 28.9%; 45–59, 18.0%; 60–74, 10.6%; 75 and over, 4.4%. **Linguistic composition** (1991): Chinese 96.8%, of which Cantonese 88.7%; English 2.2%; other 1.0%. **Religious affiliation** (1994): Buddhist and Taoist 73.8%; Christian 8.4%, of which Protestant 4.3%; Roman Catholic 4.1%; New Religionist 3.2%; Muslim 0.8%; Hindu 0.2%; nonreligious/atheist 13.5%; other 0.1%. **Location:** east Asia, bordering China and the South China Sea.

Vital statistics

Birth rate per 1,000 pop. (2000): 8.1 (world avg. 22.5); (1985) legitimate 94.5%; illegitimate 5.5%. **Death rate** per 1,000 pop. (2000): 5.1 (world avg. 9.0). **Natural increase rate** per 1,000 pop. (2000): 3.0 (world avg. 13.5). **Total fertility rate** (avg. births per childbearing woman; 2000): 1.3. **Marriage rate** per 1,000 pop. (2000): 4.6. **Life expectancy** at birth (2000): male 77.0 years; female 82.2 years.

National economy

Budget (1999–2000). *Revenue:* HK$229,322,000,000 (earning and profit taxes 28.5%; capital revenue 25.0%; indirect taxes 17.8%, of which entertainment and stamp duties 9.8%, duties 3.2%). *Expenditures:* HK$278,416,000,000 (education 18.8%; housing 16.9%; health 11.6%; social welfare

10.2%; law and order 9.8%; transportation and public works 8.7%; culture and recreation 3.5%). **Gross domestic product** (1999): US$158,737,000,000 (US$23,620 per capita). **Tourism** (1999): receipts from visitors US$7,210,000,000. **Production** (metric tons except as noted). *Agriculture, forestry, fishing* (1999): vegetables 48,000, fruits and nuts 3,770, field crops 540; livestock (number of live animals) 415,000 pigs, 36 cattle; roundwood (1996) 206,000 cu m; fish catch 127,880. *Manufacturing* (value added in HK$; 1997): publishing and printed materials 13,398,000,000; textiles 9,316,000,000; wearing apparel 9,089,000,000. *Energy production (consumption):* electricity (kW-hr; 1995) 27,916,000,000 (33,979,000,000); coal (metric tons; 1995) none (9,109,000); petroleum products (metric tons; 1995) none (3,387,000). **Population economically active** (2000): total 3,382,700; activity rate of total pop. 49.3% (participation rates: over age 15, 60.7%; female 49.1%; unemployed 5.0%). **Household income and expenditure.** Average household size (2000) 3.3; monthly income per household (1996) HK$17,500; expenditure (1994–95): food 29.5%, housing 28.8%, transportation and vehicles 7.8%, clothing and footwear 6.7%, durable goods 5.5%. **Land use** (1995): forested 20.1%; agricultural and under permanent cultivation 5.8%; fishponds 1.5%; built-on, scrublands, and other 72.6%.

Foreign trade

Imports (2000-c.i.f.): HK$1,657,962,000,000 (machinery and transport equipment 42.7%, manufactured goods 17.0%, chemicals and other related products 6.3%, food and beverages 4.1%, mineral fuels and lubricants 2.1%). *Major import sources:* China 43.1%; Japan 12.0%; Taiwan 7.5%; US 6.8%; South Korea 4.9%; Singapore 4.5%. **Exports** (2000-f.o.b.): HK$180,967,000,000 (clothing accessories and apparel 42.8%, electrical machinery 15.8%, textile fabrics 5.1%, office and automatic data-processing machines 3.2%, jewelry 3.2%, printed materials 2.5%, telecommunications equipment 2.3%, watches and clocks 1.7%, articles of artificial resins and plastics 0.8%). *Major export destinations:* US 30.1%; China 29.9%; UK 5.9%; Germany 5.1%; Taiwan 3.3%.

Transport and communications

Transport. *Railroads* (1995): route length 21 mi, 34 km; passenger-mi 2,231,000,000, passenger-km 3,591,000,000; short ton-mi cargo 68,000,000 (1994), metric ton-km cargo 99,000,000 (1994). *Roads* (2000): total length 1,183 mi, 1,904 km (paved 100%). *Vehicles* (2000): passenger cars 332,000; trucks and buses 133,000. *Air transport* (2000): passenger arrivals 11,566,000, passenger departures 11,458,000; airports (1997) with scheduled flights 1. **Communications** Total units (units per 1,000 persons). Daily newspaper circulation (1996): 5,000,000 (792); Radio receivers (1998): 3,700,000 (553); Television receivers (1998): 1,749,000 (262); Telephone main lines (2000): 3,946,000 (575); Cellular telephone subscribers (1999): 4,275,000 (647); Personal computers (1999): 2,000,000 (303); Internet users (1999): 2,430,000 (368).

---

1 metric ton = about 1.1 short tons;   1 kilometer = 0.6 mi (statute);   1 metric ton-km cargo = about 0.68 short ton-mi cargo;   c.i.f.: cost, insurance, and freight;   f.o.b.: free on board

Education and health

Educational attainment (1996). Percentage of pop. age 15 and over having: no formal schooling 9.5%; primary education 22.6%; secondary 46.6%; matriculation 6.1%; nondegree higher 4.8%; higher degree 10.4%. Literacy (1995): total pop. age 15 and over literate 92.2%; males literate 96.0%; females literate 88.2%. Health (2000): physicians 10,130 (1 per 658 persons); hospital beds 35,100 (1 per 190 persons); infant mortality rate per 1,000 live births (2000) 2.9. Food (1999): daily per capita caloric intake 3,231 (vegetable products 63%, animal products 37%); 141% of FAO recommended minimum requirement.

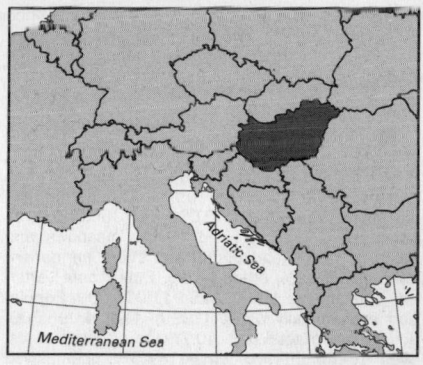

 **Did you know?** *Feng shui* is an important tradition in Hong Kong. Rooted in the belief that success will come to those who are associated with a building that is in alignment with the spiritual and natural world, the system is employed in the planning of most buildings. A *feng shui* master usually gives advice on everything from the site of the building to the furniture used in it.

Background

The island of Hong Kong and adjacent islets were ceded by China to the British in 1842, and the Kowloon Peninsula and the New Territories were leased by the British from China for 99 years (1898–1997). A joint Chinese-British declaration, signed on 19 Dec 1984, paved the way for the entire territory to be returned to China, which occurred on 1 Jul 1997.

Recent Developments

In December 1996 a selection committee approved by the Chinese government chose shipping magnate Tung Chee hwa to become Hong Kong's first chief executive when the British governor stepped down in July 1997. Tung raised concerns in Hong Kong when he announced in April 1997 that certain rights—such as the right of assembly—guaranteed by laws passed by the British government would be repealed or amended once the transfer of power had been completed. During the power-transfer ceremony on 30 Jun 1997, Chinese Pres. Jiang Zemin expressed his commitment to maintaining Hong Kong's continued economic, legislative, and judicial autonomy. In July 2001 Hong Kong's Legislative Council, chosen in elections that favored elite occupational groups over direct popular representation, voted by a 2–1 margin to give Beijing the right to fire the chief executive. This seemingly small action enhanced the power of Chinese central authorities responsible for selecting Tung, who had proved to be a faithful, if locally unpopular, executor of Beijing's wishes.

Internet resources:
<http://hongkong.asiadragons.com>

Hungary

Official name: Magyar Koztarsasag (Republic of Hungary). Form of government: unitary multiparty republic with one legislative house (National Assembly [386, excluding 13 seats set aside for ethnic minorities]). Chief of state: President Ferenc Madl (from 2000). Head of government: Prime Minister Peter Medgyessy (from 27 May 2002). Capital: Budapest. Official language: Hungarian. Official religion: none. Monetary unit: 1 forint (Ft) = 100 filler; valuation (28 Jun 2002) $1 = Ft 247.89.

Demography

Area: 35,919 sq mi, 93,030 sq km. Population (2001): 10,190,000. Density (2001): persons per sq mi 283.7, persons per sq km 109.5. Urban (1999): 63.3%. Sex distribution (2000): male 47.71%; female 52.29%. Age breakdown (2000): under 15, 17.1%; 15–29, 22.6%; 30–44, 20.2%; 45–59, 20.5%; 60–74, 14.0%; 75 and over, 5.6%. Ethnic composition (1998): Hungarian 92%; Roma (Gypsy) 4%; German 2%; Slovak 1%; other 1%. Religious affiliation (1995): Roman Catholic 63.1%; Protestant 25.5% (of which Reformed 19.8%, Lutheran 4.5%); Jewish 0.8%; other 10.6%. Major cities (2000): Budapest 1,811,552; Debrecen 203,648; Miskolc 172,357; Szeged 158,158; Pecs 157,332. Location: central Europe, bordering Slovakia, Ukraine, Romania, Serbia and Montenegro, Croatia, Slovenia, and Austria.

Vital statistics

Birth rate per 1,000 pop. (1999): 9.4 (world avg. 22.5); legitimate 72.0%; illegitimate 28.0%. Death rate per 1,000 pop. (1999): 14.2 (world avg. 9.0). Natural increase rate per 1,000 pop. (1999): –4.8 (world avg. 13.5). Total fertility rate (avg. births per childbearing woman; 1999): 1.3. Marriage rate per 1,000 pop. (1999): 4.5. Life expectancy at birth (1999): male 66.3 years; female 75.1 years.

National economy

Budget (1999). *Revenue:* Ft 4,955,000,000,000 (social security contributions 29.6%, value-added taxes 19.0%, personal income taxes 15.5%, excise taxes 9.4%). *Expenditures:* Ft 5,396,000,000,000 (current expenditures 93.9%, development expenditures 6.1%). Production (metric tons except as noted). *Agriculture, forestry, fishing* (2000): corn (maize) 5,000,000, wheat 3,709,000, sugar beets 2,300,000; livestock (number of live animals) 5,335,000 pigs, 857,000 cattle; roundwood (1999) 4,287,500 cu m; fish catch (1997) 21,916. *Mining and quarrying* (1999): bauxite 935,000. *Manufac-*

turing (value added in Ft '000,000; 1998): refined petroleum products 296,000; food and beverages 278,800; electrical machinery and apparatus 218,000. *Energy production (consumption):* electricity (kW-hr; 1999) 37,154,000,000 (33,348,000,000); hard coal (metric tons; 1999) 732,000 (1,110,000); lignite (metric tons; 1999) 13,704,000 (14,341,000); crude petroleum (barrels; 1999) 8,349,000 (51,633,000); petroleum products (metric tons; 1996) 6,333,000 (6,168,000); natural gas (cu m; 1999) 3,625,000,000 (12,365,000,000). **Land use** (1994): forested 19.1%; meadows and pastures 12.4%; agricultural and under permanent cultivation 53.9%; other 14.6%. **Public debt** (external, outstanding; 1998): $15,941,000,000. **Population economically active** (1999): total 4,096,200; activity rate of total pop. 40.7% (participation rates: ages 15–64, 59.9%; female 44.5%; unemployed 7.0%). **Tourism** ($'000,000; 1999): receipts 3,394; expenditures 1,191. **Gross national product** (1999): $46,751,000,000 ($4,640 per capita). **Household income and expenditure.** Average household size (1998) 2.5; income per household (1998; adjusted disposable income including transfers) Ft 1,828,441; sources of income (1998): wages 49.9%, transfers 17.9%, self-employment 17.2%, other 15.0%; expenditure (1999): food and beverages 33.6%; transportation and communications 14.9%; energy 14.6%; housing 8.0%.

Foreign trade

Imports (1999): Ft 6,645,600,000,000 (nonelectrical machinery 16.3%, electrical machinery 12.4%, road vehicles 8.6%, computers and office machines 6.7%, telecommunications equipment 6.1%). *Major import sources:* Germany 29.2%; Austria 8.9%; Italy 7.7%; Russia 5.9%; France 4.7%. **Exports** (1999): Ft 5,938,500,000,000 (nonelectrical machinery 16.8%, office machines and computers 13.4%, electrical machinery 11.0%, road vehicles 9.0%, telecommunications equipment 7.9%). *Major export destinations:* Germany 38.4%; Austria 9.6%; Italy 5.9%; The Netherlands 5.2%; US 5.2%.

Transport and communications

Transport. *Railroads:* route length (1998) 7,768 km; (1999) passenger-km 9,514,000,000; (1999) metric ton-km cargo 7,733,000,000. *Roads* (1997): total length 188,203 km (paved 43%). *Vehicles* (1999): passenger cars 2,255,526; trucks and buses 321,634. *Air transport* (1999): passenger-km 3,513,000,000; metric ton-km cargo 55,500,000; airports (1997) with scheduled flights 1. **Communications** Total units (units per 1,000 persons). Daily newspaper circulation (1996): 1,895,000 (186); Radio receivers (1997): 7,000,000 (689); Television receivers (1998): 4,500,000 (445); Telephone main lines (1999): 3,609,000 (358); Cellular telephone subscribers (1999): 1,620,000 (161); Personal computers (1998): 600,000 (59); Internet users (1999): 453,000 (45).

Education and health

Educational attainment (1990). Pop. age 25 and over having: no formal schooling 1.3%; primary edu-cation 57.9%; secondary 30.7%; higher 10.1%. **Health** (1999): physicians 32,240 (1 per 312 persons); hospital beds 83,992 (1 per 120 persons); infant mortality rate per 1,000 live births 8.4. **Food** (1998): daily per capita caloric intake 3,408 (vegetable products 69%, animal products 31%); 130% of FAO recommended minimum requirement.

Military

Total active duty personnel (2000): 43,790 (army 53.7%, air force 26.3%, headquarters staff 20.0%). **Military expenditure as percentage of GNP** (1997): 1.9% (world 2.6%); per capita expenditures $129.

Background

The western part of Hungary was incorporated into the Roman empire in 14 BC. The Magyars, a nomadic people, occupied the middle basin of the Danube River in the late 9th century AD. Stephen I, crowned in 1000, Christianized the country and organized it into a strong and independent state. Invasions by the Mongols in the 13th century and by the Ottoman Turks in the 14th century devastated the country, and by 1568 the territory of modern Hungary had been divided into three parts: Royal Hungary fell to the Habsburgs; Transylvania gained autonomy in 1566 under the Turks; and the central plain remained under Turkish control until the late 17th century, when the Austrian Habsburgs took over. Hungary declared its independence from Austria in 1849, and in 1867 the dual monarchy of Austria-Hungary was established. Its defeat in World War I resulted in the dismemberment of Hungary, leaving it only those areas in which Magyars predominated. In an attempt to regain some of this lost territory, Hungary cooperated with the Germans against the Soviet Union during World War II. After the war, a pro-Soviet provisional government was established, and in 1949 the Hungarian People's Republic was formed. Opposition to this Stalinist regime broke out in 1956 but was suppressed. Nevertheless, from 1956 to 1988 communist Hungary grew to become the most tolerant of the Soviet-bloc nations of Eastern Europe. It gained its independence in 1989 and soon attracted the largest amount of direct foreign investment in eastern central Europe. In 1999 it joined NATO.

Recent Developments

Numerous political scandals during 2001 led to a de facto, if not actual, breakup of the coalition that held power in Budapest. A bribery scandal triggered a wave of allegations against the Independent Smallholders' Party (FKGP), the junior coalition partner, although it did not affect the Federation of Young Democrats (Fidesz)–Hungarian Civic Party, the senior governing party. The affair resulted in the ousting of Jozsef Torgyan from both the FKGP presidency and the top position in the Ministry of Agriculture. In 2002 the coalition limped to defeat in Hungary's parliamentary elections. The Socialists, led by Peter Medgyessy, and its ally, the Alliance of Free Democrats, claimed 198 of parliament's 386 seats; Fidesz-Hungarian Civic Party won 188 seats. Medgyessy took office as prime minister on 27 May.

Internet resources: <www.hungarytourism.hu>

1 metric ton = about 1.1 short tons;　1 kilometer = 0.6 mi (statute);　1 metric ton-km cargo = about 0.68 short ton-mi cargo;　c.i.f.: cost, insurance, and freight;　f.o.b.: free on board

Iceland

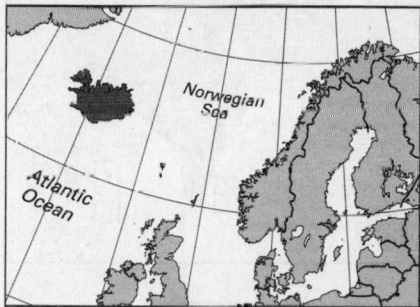

Official name: Lydhveldidh Ísland (Republic of Iceland). **Form of government:** unitary multiparty republic with one legislative house (Althing [63]). **Chief of state:** President Ólafur Ragnar Grímsson (from 1996). **Head of government:** Prime Minister David Oddsson (from 1991). **Capital:** Reykjavík. **Official language:** Icelandic. **Official religion:** Evangelical Lutheran. **Monetary unit:** 1 króna (ISK) = 100 aurar; valuation (28 Jun 2002) $1 = ISK 86.83.

Demography

Area: 39,699 sq mi, 102,819 sq km. **Population** (2001): 284,000. **Density** (2001; calculated with reference to 9,191 sq mi [23,805 sq km] area free of glaciers, lava fields, and lakes): persons per sq mi 30.9, persons per sq km 11.9. **Urban** (1999): urban 93.5%. **Sex distribution** (2000): male 50.07%; female 49.93%. **Age breakdown** (2000): under 15, 23.2%; 15–29, 22.7%; 30–44, 22.2%; 45–59, 16.9%; 60–74, 9.9%; 75 and over, 5.1%. **Ethnic composition** (1999; by country of birth): Icelandic 94.7%; Danish 0.8%; Swedish 0.6%; persons born in the United States 0.5%; Poland 0.5%; German 0.3%; other 2.6%. **Religious affiliation** (2000): Protestant 92.3%, of which Evangelical Lutheran 87.8%, other Lutheran 3.9%; Roman Catholic 1.5%; other and not specified 6.2%. **Major cities** (2000): Reykjavík 111,345 (urban area 174,991); Kópavogur 23,518 (within Reykjavík urban area); Hafnarfjördhur 19,640 (within Reykjavík urban area); Akureyri 15,385; Gardhabær 8,050 (within Reykjavík urban area). **Location:** northern Europe, an island between the Greenland Sea, Norwegian Sea, and the North Atlantic Ocean.

Vital statistics

Birth rate per 1,000 pop. (1999): 14.8 (world avg. 22.5); (1999) legitimate 37.4%; illegitimate 62.6%. **Death rate** per 1,000 pop. (1999): 6.9 (world avg. 9.0). **Natural increase rate** per 1,000 pop. (1999): 7.9 (world avg. 13.5). **Total fertility rate** (avg. births per childbearing woman; 1999): 2.0. **Marriage rate** per 1,000 pop. (1999): 5.6. **Divorce rate** per 1,000 pop. (1999): 1.7. **Life expectancy** at birth (1998–99): male 77.5 years; female 81.4 years.

National economy

Budget (1997). *Revenue:* ISK 193,567,000,000 (indirect taxes 49.1%, of which value-added taxes 26.0%; direct taxes 44.4%; nontax revenue 6.5%). *Expenditures:* ISK 197,804,000,000 (health and welfare 39.6%; education 14.3%; general administration 8.7%; communications 7.5%; cultural affairs 6.2%; agriculture 4.0%). **Public debt** (2000): $2,242,600,000. **Production** (metric tons except as noted). *Agriculture, forestry, fishing* (1999): potatoes 9,000, silage 1,612,500 cu m, hay 722,800 cu m; livestock (number of live animals) 490,500 sheep, 77,300 horses, 74,500 cattle; fish catch (value in ISK '000,000; 1999) cod 21,548, shrimp 7,583, redfish 4,922. *Mining and quarrying* (1998): diatomite 27,100. *Manufacturing* (value added in ISK '000,000; 1993): preserved and processed fish 17,534; printing and publishing 5,020; fabricated metal products 3,996. *Energy production (consumption):* electricity (kW-hr; 1998) 5,131,000,000 ([1996] 5,131,000,000); coal (metric tons; 1996) none (66,000); crude petroleum, none (none); petroleum products (metric tons; 1996) none (623,000). **Land use** (1994): forested 1.2%; meadows and pastures 22.7%; agricultural and under permanent cultivation 0.1%; other 76.0%. **Population economically active** (1998): total 152,100; activity rate of total pop. 55.5% (participation rates: ages 16–74, 79.5%; female 46.8%; unemployed 2.7%). **Tourism** (1999): receipts $227,000,000; expenditures $430,000,000. **Gross national product** (1999): $8,197,000,000 ($29,540 per capita). **Household income and expenditure.** Average household size (1990; based on sample survey) 3.6; annual income per household (1995; based on sample survey) ISK 1,976,066; sources of income (1995): wages and salaries 74.1%, pension 10.5%, self-employment 2.7%, other 12.7%; expenditure (1995): food and beverages 24.0%, transportation and communications 20.8%, recreation and education 13.9%, household furnishings and equipment 8.3%, clothing and footwear 8.0%, energy 4.3%, health 4.0%.

Foreign trade

Imports (1999- c.i.f.): ISK 182,321,500,000 (nonelectrical machinery and apparatus 11.2%; road vehicles 11.0%; food products 8.9%; chemicals 8.0%; electrical machinery and apparatus 6.3%; crude petroleum and petroleum products 5.2%). *Major import sources:* Germany 11.8%; US 10.9%; Norway 10.4%; UK 9.2%; Denmark 8.1%; Sweden 6.2%; Japan 5.5%. **Exports** (1999- f.o.b.): ISK 144,928,100,000 (marine products 61.2%, of which frozen fish 36.3%, salted fish 15.0%; lobster and shrimp 8.3%; aluminum 15.6%; transportation equipment 4.5%). *Major export destinations:* UK 19.6%; US 14.7%; Germany 13.1%; The Netherlands 6.0%; France 5.2%; Spain 5.2%.

Transport and communications

Transport. Roads (1996): total length 7,691 mi, 12,378 km (paved 25%). *Vehicles* (1999): passenger cars 151,409; trucks and buses 19,428. *Air transport* (1999; Icelandair only): passenger-mi 2,272,749,000, passenger-km 3,657,642,000; short ton-mi cargo 50,966,000, metric ton-km cargo 74,409,000; airports (1996) with scheduled flights 24. **Communications.** Total units (units per 1,000 persons). Daily newspaper circulation (1996): 145,000 (535); Radio receivers (1997): 260,000 (950); Television receivers (1999): 145,000 (523); Telephone main lines (1999): 188,800 (681); Cellular telephone subscribers (1999): 172,614 (623); Personal computers (1999): 100,000 (361); Internet users (1999): 150,000 (541).

Education and health

Literacy: virtually 100%. **Health:** physicians (1997) 884 (1 per 307 persons); hospital beds (1993; excludes nursing wards in old-age homes) 2,798 (1 per 95 persons); infant mortality rate (1999) 2.4. **Food** (1999): daily per capita caloric intake 3,313 (vegetable products 59%, animal products 41%); 125% of FAO recommended minimum requirement.

Military

Total active duty personnel (2000): 120 coast guard personnel; NATO-sponsored US-manned Iceland Defense Force: 1,640. **Military expenditure as percentage of GNP** (1997): none (world average 2.6%).

Did you know? Due to its location on the Mid-Atlantic Ridge, Iceland is one of the most active volcanic regions in the world. It has more hot springs and solfataras—volcanic vents that emit hot gases and vapors—than any other country.

Background

Iceland was settled by Norwegian seafarers in the 9th century and was Christianized by 1000. Its legislature, the Althing, was founded in 930, making it one of the oldest legislative assemblies in the world. Iceland united with Norway in 1262. It became an independent state of Denmark in 1918 but severed those ties to become an independent republic in 1944. Vigdís Finnbogadóttir became the world's first female elected president in 1980. Much of Iceland's 1990s economic growth was in the expansion of its aluminum production capacity.

Recent Developments

Elections to the Althing took place on 8 May 1999. The incumbent government, a coalition of the Independence and Progressive parties, was continued in office. By 2001 Iceland's economic growth had slowed to 2% after five years of more than 4.5% growth. Signs of recession emerged, though employment continued to be virtually full.

Internet resources: <www.icetourist.is>

India

Official name: Bharat (Hindi); Republic of India (English). **Form of government:** multiparty federal republic with two legislative houses (Council of States [245], House of the People [545 {includes 2 nonelective seats}]). **Chief of state:** President A.P.J. Abdul Kalam (from 25 Jul 2002). **Head of government:** Prime Minister Atal Bihari Vajpayee (from 1998). **Capital:** New Delhi. **Official languages:** Hindi; English. **Official religion:** none. **Monetary unit:** 1 Indian rupee (Re, plural Rs) = 100 paise; valuation (28 Jun 2002) $1 = Rs 48.86.

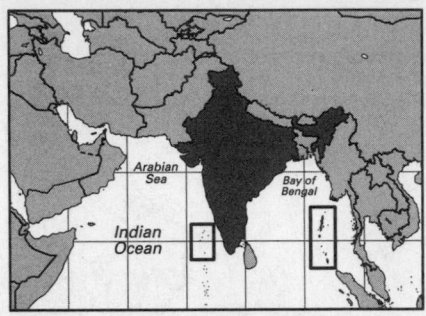

Demography

Area: 1,222,559 sq mi, 3,166,414 sq km (excludes 46,660 sq mi [120,849 sq km] of territory claimed by India as part of Jammu and Kashmir but occupied by Pakistan or China). **Population** (2001): 1,029,991,000. **Density** (2000): persons per sq mi 842.5, persons per sq km 325.3. **Urban** (2000): 28.4%. **Sex distribution** (2001): male 51.73%; female 48.27%. **Age breakdown** (2000): under 15, 33.6%; 15–29, 27.7%; 30–44, 19.8%; 45–59, 11.9%; 60–74, 5.6%; 75 and over, 1.4%. **Major cities** (1991; *urban agglomerations*, 1995): Greater Mumbai (Bombay) 9,925,891 (15,093,000); Delhi 7,206,704 (9,882,000); Kolkata (Calcutta) 4,399,-819 (11,673,000); Chennai (Madras) 3,841,396 (5,906,000); Bangalore 3,302,296 (4,749,000); Hyderabad 3,145,939 (5,343,000); Ahmadabad 2,954,526 (3,688,000); Kanpur 1,879,420 (2,356,-000); Nagpur 1,624,752 (1,847,000); Lucknow 1,619,115 (2,029,000); Pune 1,566,651 (2,940,-000); New Delhi (within Delhi urban agglomeraton) 301,297. **Linguistic composition** (1991): Hindi 27.58% (including associated languages and dialects, 39.85%); Bengali 8.22%; Telugu 7.80%; Marathi 7.38%; Tamil 6.26%; Urdu 5.13%; Gujarati 4.81%; Kannada 3.87%; Malayalam 3.59%; Oriya 3.32%; Punjabi 2.76%; Assamese 1.55%; Bhili/Bhilodi 0.66%; Santhali 0.62%; Kashmiri (1981) 0.47%; Gondi 0.25%; Sindhi 0.25%; Nepali 0.25%; Konkani 0.21%; Tulu 0.18%; Kurukh 0.17%; Manipuri 0.15%; Bodo 0.14%; Khandeshi 0.12%; other 3.26%. Hindi (66.00%) and English (19.00%) are also spoken as lingua francas (second languages). **Religious affiliation** (2000): Hindu 73.72%; Muslim 11.96%, of which Sunni 8.97%, Shi'i 2.99%; Christian 6.08%, of which Independent 2.99%, Protestant 1.47%, Roman Catholic 1.35%, Orthodox 0.27%; traditional beliefs 3.39%; Sikh 2.16%; Buddhist 0.71%; Jain 0.40%; Baha'i 0.12%; Zoroastrian (Parsi) 0.02%; other 1.44%. **Households** (1991 [excludes Jammu and Kashmir]). Total households 151,032,-898. Average household size 5.6; 1–2 persons 12.1%, 3–5 persons 44.4%, 6–8 persons 30.5%, 9 or more persons 13.0%. Average number of rooms per household 2.2; 1 room 40.5%, 2 rooms 30.6%, 3 rooms 13.8%, 4 rooms 7.1%, 5 rooms 3.2%, 6 or more rooms 3.9%, unspecified number of rooms 0.9%. Average number of persons per room 2.6. **Location:** southern Asia, bordering Pakistan, China, Nepal, Bhutan, Myanmar, Bangladesh, and the Indian Ocean.

---

1 metric ton = about 1.1 short tons;   1 kilometer = 0.6 mi (statute);   1 metric ton-km cargo = about 0.68 short ton-mi cargo;   c.i.f.: cost, insurance, and freight;   f.o.b.: free on board

Vital statistics

Birth rate per 1,000 pop. (2000): 24.8 (world avg. 22.5). **Death rate** per 1,000 pop. (2000): 8.9 (world avg. 9.0). **Natural increase rate** per 1,000 pop. (2000): 15.9 (world avg. 13.5). **Total fertility rate** (avg. births per childbearing woman; 2000): 3.1. **Marital status** of male (female) pop. age 6 and over (1992–93): single 48.3% (37.1%); married 47.5% (55.2%); widowed 3.6% (7.2%); divorced or separated 0.6% (0.5%). **Life expectancy** at birth (2000): male 61.9 years; female 63.1 years.

Social indicators

Quality of working life. Average workweek (1989; "organized sector" only): 42 hours. Agricultural workers in servitude to creditors (early 1990s) 10–20%. **Access to services** (1991). Percentage of total (urban, rural) households having access to: electricity for lighting purposes 42.4% (75.8%, 30.5%); attached toilet or nearby latrine 23.7% (63.9%, 0.6%). Source of drinking water: piped water 32.3%, well 32.2%, hand pump or tube well 30.0%, river or canal 2.0%, public tank 1.3%, other 2.2%. **Social participation.** Eligible voters participating in September/October 1999 national election: 59.6%. Trade union membership (1998): c. 16,000,000 (primarily in the public sector). **Social deviance** (1990; crimes reported to National Crime Records Bureau). Offense rate per 100,000 population for: murder 4.1; dacoity (gang robbery) 1.3; theft and housebreaking 56.6; riots 12.0. Rate of suicide per 100,000 population (1991): 9.0. **Material well-being** (1994). Households possessing: black and white television receivers 18.8%, color television receivers 6.3%, videocassette recorders 1.3%, refrigerators 6.9%, washing machines 2.3%.

National economy

Gross national product (1999): $441,834,000,000 ($440 per capita). **Budget** (1999–2000). *Revenue:* Rs 3,288,000,000,000 (tax revenue 48.6%, of which excise taxes 19.4%, customs duties 15.3%, corporation taxes 9.4%; nontax revenue 36.5%, of which economic services 20.7%, interest receipts 10.0%; other sources of revenue 14.9%). *Expenditures:* Rs 3,288,000,000,000 (interest payments and debt servicing 26.8%; transportation 11.0%; defense 10.5%; grants in aid to state governments 9.4%; communications 7.2%; agriculture 5.0%; social services 4.7%). **Public debt** (external, outstanding; 1999): $82,380,000,000. **Production** (in '000 metric tons except as noted). *Agriculture, forestry, fishing* (2000): sugarcane 315,100, cereals 239,814, fruits 49,199, oilseeds (1998) 31,015, pulses (1998) 14,237, seed cotton 6,172; livestock (number of live animals; 2000) 218,800,000 cattle, 123,000,000 goats, 93,772,000 water buffalo, 57,900,000 sheep, 16,500,000 pigs, 1,030,000 camels; roundwood (1999) 302,794,000 cu m; fish catch (metric tons; 1997) 5,378,000. *Mining and quarrying* (1998): limestone 108,920; iron ore (1999; metal content) 44,200; bauxite (1999) 6,658; manganese (metal content) 610; chromium 1,311. *Manufacturing* (value added in Rs '000,000,000; 1999): iron and steel 188.1; industrial chemicals 167.7; paints, soaps, varnishes, drugs, and medicines 164.2; transport equipment

159.7; food products 139.0; textiles 136.8. *Energy production (consumption):* electricity (kW-hr; 1999) 473,214,000,000 ([1996] 433,914,000,000); coal (metric tons; 1999) 292,356,000 ([1996] 319,233,000); crude petroleum (barrels; 1999) 247,426,000 ([1996] 492,646,000); petroleum products (metric tons; 1996) 47,648,000 (67,219,000); natural gas (cu m; 1999) 20,006,000,000 ([1996] 27,113,000,000). **Land use** (1994): forested 23.0%; meadows and pastures 3.8%; agricultural and under permanent cultivation 57.1%; other 16.1%. **Population economically active** (1993–94): total 372,000,000; activity rate of total pop. c. 41% (participation rates: n.a.; female 32.5%). **Household income and expenditure.** Average household size (1991; excludes Jammu and Kashmir) 5.6; sources of income (1984–85): salaries and wages 42.2%, self-employed 39.7%, interest 8.6%, profits and dividends 6.0%, rent 3.5%; expenditure (1995–96): food and beverages 49.2%, transportation and communications 12.3%, clothing and footwear 11.4%, housing 5.2%, household furnishings 5.0%. **Service enterprises** (net value added in Rs '000,000,000; 1995–96): wholesale and retail trade 1,315; finance and insurance 861; transport and storage 632; community, social, and personal services 594; construction 566; real estate and business services 286; electricity, gas, and steam 240. **Tourism** (1999): receipts from visitors $3,036,000,000; expenditures by nationals abroad $2,010,000,000.

Foreign trade

Imports (1999–2000-c.i.f.): Rs 2,006,570,000,000 (crude petroleum and refined petroleum 22.3%; precious and semiprecious stones 11.6%; chemicals 6.0%; nonelectrical machinery 5.8%; electronic goods 5.6%). *Major import sources:* Belgium 7.7%; US 7.5%; UK 5.8%; Switzerland 5.5%; Japan 5.1%; Saudi Arabia 4.8%; United Arab Emirates 4.5%; Malaysia 4.3%. **Exports** (1999–2000-f.o.b.): Rs 1,607,430,000,000 (cut and polished diamonds and jewelry 20.0%; cotton ready-made garments 9.2%; cotton yarn, fabrics, and thread 7.9%; leather and leather manufactures 4.2%; drugs and pharmaceuticals 4.2%; fabricated metals 3.2%). *Major export destinations:* US 22.2%; Hong Kong 6.7%; UK 5.6%; United Arab Emirates 5.6%; Germany 4.6%; Japan 4.5%; Belgium 3.6%; Italy 3.0%.

Transport and communications

Transport. *Railroads* (1998–99): route length 62,809 km; (1999–2000) passenger-km 420,449,000,000; (1999–2000) metric ton-km cargo 305,513,000,000. *Roads* (1996): total length 3,319,644 km (paved 46%). *Vehicles* (1996): passenger cars 4,189,000; trucks and buses 2,234,000. *Air transport* (1999; Air India and Indian Airlines only): passenger-km 18,436,000,000; metric ton-km cargo 480,946,000; airports (1996) with scheduled flights 66. **Communications.** Total units (units per 1,000 persons). Daily newspaper circulation (1993): 18,800,000 (21); Radio receivers (1997): 116,000,000 (120); Television receivers (1999): 75,000,000 (75); Telephone main lines (1999): 26,511,000 (27); Cellular telephone subscribers (1999): 1,884,000 (1.9); Personal computers (1999): 3,300,000 (3.3); Internet users (1999): 2,800,000 (2.8).

Education and health

Educational attainment (1991; excludes Jammu and Kashmir). Percentage of pop. age 25 and over having: no formal schooling 57.5%; incomplete primary education 28.0%; complete primary or some secondary 7.2%; complete secondary or higher 7.3%. Literacy (2001): total pop. age 7 and over literate 566,715,000 (65.4%); males literate 339,969,000 (75.8%); females literate 226,746,000 (54.2%). Health: physicians (1992) 410,875 (1 per 2,173 persons); hospital beds (1993) 659,000 (1 per 1,364 persons); infant mortality rate (2000) 64.9. Food (1999): daily per capita caloric intake 2,417 (vegetable products 92%, animal products 8%); 109% of FAO recommended minimum requirement.

Military

Total active duty personnel (2000): 1,303,000 (army 84.4%, navy 4.1%, air force 11.5%); personnel in paramilitary forces 1,069,000. Military expenditure as percentage of GNP (1997): 2.8% (world 2.6%); per capita expenditure $11.

Background

India has been inhabited for thousands of years. Agriculture dates back to at least the 7th millennium BC, and an urban civilization, that of the Indus valley, was established by 2600 BC. Buddhism and Jainism arose in the 6th century BC in reaction to the caste-based society created by the Vedic religion and its successor, Hinduism. Muslim invasions began c. AD 1000, establishing the long-lived Delhi sultanate in 1206 and the Mughal dynasty in 1526. Vasco da Gama's voyage to India in 1498 initiated several centuries of commercial rivalry among the Portuguese, Dutch, English, and French. British conquests in the 18th and 19th centuries led to the rule of the British East India Co., and direct administration by the British empire began in 1858. After Mohandas K. Gandhi helped end British rule in 1947, Jawaharlal Nehru became India's first prime minister and he, his daughter Indira Gandhi, and grandson Rajiv Gandhi guided the nation's destiny for all but a few years until 1989. The subcontinent was partitioned into two countries—India, with a Hindu majority, and Pakistan, with a Muslim majority, in 1947. A later clash with Pakistan resulted in the creation of Bangladesh in 1971. In the 1980s and '90s, Sikhs sought to establish an independent state in Punjab, and ethnic and religious conflicts took place in other parts of the country as well.

Recent Developments

In 2001 secessionists and raiders from across India's borders had stepped up their activities in Jammu and Kashmir state and in the capital itself. On 13 December five terrorists, armed with automatic weapons and explosives, made a daring bid to enter Parliament House in New Delhi. Security guards prevented their entrance, and in the exchange of fire all five raiders and nine other persons were killed. India held two Pakistan-based organizations, Jaish-e-Mohammad and Lashkar-e-Taiba, responsible. On 1 Oct 2001 a car-bomb attack on the Jammu and Kashmir Assembly had killed 38 persons and injured dozens more. Jaish-e-Mohammad claimed responsibility.

Early in 2001 the government had made a serious attempt at peace by holding talks with militant organizations, especially those that it suspected were encouraged by Pakistan. The talks yielding no results, Prime Minister Atal Bihari Vajpayee made a bold decision to negotiate directly with the chief executive of Pakistan, Gen. Pervez Musharraf, and invited him to New Delhi. The general arrived on 14 July. His discussions with Vajpayee, which were held in Agra over the next two days, remained deadlocked, with Pakistan maintaining that a political solution to the Kashmir issue should be found first and India insisting that cross-border terrorism should be stopped first.

India was deeply shaken by the events of 11 Sep 2001 and hastened to assure the US of its full cooperation, as did Pakistan. Although Pakistan and India found themselves on the same side, there was no abatement in mutual rancor. By mid-2002 about 750,000 Indian troops and some 250,000 Pakistani troops had mobilized along the Line of Control in disputed Kashmir. The threat of war prompted intense efforts by Western diplomats to defuse tensions between the two nuclear neighbors.

Internet resources: <www.tourismofindia.com>

Indonesia

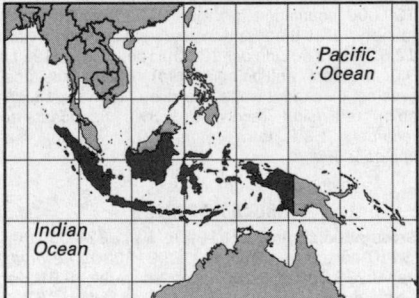

Official name: Republik Indonesia (Republic of Indonesia). Form of government: unitary multiparty republic with two legislative houses (People's Consultative Assembly [700—includes members of the House of People's Representatives and 200 other appointees]; House of People's Representatives [500—includes 38 nonelective seats reserved for the military]). Head of state and government: President Megawati Sukarnoputri (from 23 Jul 2001). Capital: Jakarta. Official language: Indonesian (Bahasa Indonesia). Official religion: monotheism. Monetary unit: 1 Indonesian rupiah (Rp) = 100 sen; valuation (28 Jun 2002) $1 = Rp 8,713.

Demography

Area: 1,922,570 sq km (excludes East Timor). Population (2001): 212,195,000. Density (2001; excludes area and population of East Timor): persons per sq mi 285.9, persons per sq km 110.4. Urban (2001): 42.0%. Sex distribution (1995): male

49.77%: female 50.23%. **Age breakdown** (1995): under 15, 35.6%; 15–29, 27.5%; 30–44, 19.6%; 45–59, 10.8%; 60–74, 5.4%; 75 and over, 1.1%. **Ethnolinguistic composition** (1990): Javanese 39.4%; Sundanese 15.8%; Indonesian (Malay) 12.1%; Madurese 4.3%; Minang 2.4%; other 26.0%. **Religious affiliation** (1990): Muslim 87.2%; Christian 9.6%, of which Roman Catholic 3.6%; Hindu 1.8%; Buddhist 1.0%; other 0.4%. **Major cities** (1996): Jakarta 9,341,000; Surabaya 2,743,000; Bandung 2,429,000; Medan (1995) 1,909,700; Palembang (1995) 1,283,100. **Location**: archipelago in southeast Asia, bordering Malaysia, the Pacific Ocean, Papua New Guinea, and the Indian Ocean.

Vital statistics

Birth rate per 1,000 pop. (2001): 20.8 (world avg. 22.5). **Death rate** per 1,000 pop. (2001): 7.2 (world avg. 9.0). **Natural increase rate** per 1,000 pop. (2001): 13.6 (world avg. 13.5). **Total fertility rate** (avg. births per childbearing woman; 2001): 2.4. **Marriage rate** per 1,000 pop. (1997–98; Muslim population only): 8.1. **Life expectancy** at birth (2001): male 65.0 years; female 69.0 years.

National economy

Budget (1999–2000). *Revenue*: RP 188,428,500,-000,000 (income tax 31.7%, oil and gas revenues 31.0%, value-added tax 17.6%, nontax revenue 9.1%, excise taxes 5.5%). *Expenditures*: RP 204,900,300,-000,000 (development 23.9%, subsidies 22.9%, salaries 15.7%, debt repayment 10.1%, transfers 8.5%). **Production** (metric tons except as noted). *Agriculture, forestry, fishing* (2000): rice 51,000,000, palm fruit oil 34,000,000, sugarcane 21,400,000; livestock (number of live animals) 14,121,000 goats, 12,102,000 cattle, 7,502,000 sheep; roundwood (1999) 190,601,000 cu m; fish catch (1998) 3,600,000. *Mining and quarrying* (1998): copper concentrate 2,640,000; nickel ore 1,642,000; gold 118,246 kg. *Manufacturing* (value added in RP '000,000,000; 1997 [medium and large establishments only]): transport equipment 10,038.6; textiles 9,629.7; food products 9,028.1. *Energy production (consumption)*: electricity (kW-hr; 1996) 73,794,-000,000 (73,794,000,000); coal (metric tons; 1999) 70,704,000 ([1996] 15,796,000); crude petroleum (barrels; 1999) 500,642,000 ([1996] 311,201,000); petroleum products (metric tons; 1996) 43,307,000 (40,759,000); natural gas (cu m; 1998) 84,348,-000,000 ([1996] 38,885,000,000). **Gross national product** (1999): $125,043,000,000 ($600 per capita). **Public debt** (external, outstanding; 1999): $72,554,000,000. **Population economically active** (1999): total 94,800,000; activity rate 46.0% (participation rates: over age 15, 70.7%; unemployed 6.3%). **Household income and expenditure**. Average household size (1998) 4.1. **Tourism** (1999): receipts $4,710,000,000; expenditures $2,353,000,000.

Foreign trade

Imports (1999): $27,336,000,000 (machinery and transport equipment 36.3%, basic manufactures 16.6%, chemicals 15.1%, mineral fuels 9.8%, food and live animals 9.6%). *Major import sources*: Japan 15.7%; US 12.9%; Singapore 9.3%; Germany 8.7%; Australia 6.4%; South Korea 5.6%. **Exports** (1998): $48,847,600,000 (crude petroleum 8.3%, natural

gas 7.8%, garments 5.4%, plywood 4.3%, processed rubber 2.3%). *Major export destinations*: Japan 18.7%; US 14.4%; Singapore 10.6%; Australia 3.1%.

Transport and communications

Transport. *Railroads* (1999): route length 6,458 km; passenger-km 18,585,000,000; metric ton km cargo 5,035,000,000. *Roads* (1997): length 341,467 km (paved 56%). *Vehicles* (1998): passenger cars 2,734,769; trucks and buses 2,189,876. *Air transport* (1999): passenger-km 12,389,000,000; metric ton-km cargo 340,932,000; airports (1996) 81. **Communications** Total units (units per 1,000 persons). Daily newspaper circulation (1996): 4,665,-000 (23); Radio receivers (1998): 26,000,000 (128); Television receivers (1999): 30,000,000 (143); Telephone main lines (1999): 6,080,200 (29); Cellular telephone subscribers (1999): 2,221,000 (11); Personal computers (1999): 1,900,000 (9.1); Internet users (1999): 900,000 (4.3).

Education and health

Educational attainment (1990). Percentage of pop. age 25 and over having: no schooling 34.6%; less than complete primary 28.2%; primary 23.3%; secondary 12.5%; higher 1.4%. **Literacy** (1995 est.): total pop. age 15 and over literate 83.8%; males literate 89.6%; females literate 78.0%. **Health**: physicians (1996) 31,435 (1 per 6,259 persons); hospital beds (1997) 121,996 (1 per 1,638 persons); infant mortality rate (2001) 42.0. **Food** (1999): daily per capita caloric intake 2,931 (vegetable products 95%, animal products 5%); (1997) 136% of FAO recommended minimum.

Military

Total active duty personnel (2000): 297,000 (army 77.4%, navy 13.5%, air force 9.1%). **Military expenditure as percentage of GNP** (1997): 2.3% (world 2.6%); per capita expenditure $24.

Did you know? Indonesia is the largest archipelago in the world and home to the largest living reptile, the Komodo dragon. Indonesia's rich flora includes the *Rafflesia arnoldii*, the world's largest flower.

Background

Proto-Malay peoples migrated to Indonesia from mainland Asia before 1000 BC. Commercial relations were established with China in about the 5th century AD, and Hindu and Buddhist cultural influences from India began to take hold. Arab traders brought Islam to the islands in the 13th century; the religion took hold throughout the islands, except for Bali, which retained its Hindu religion and culture. European influence began in the 16th century, and the Dutch ruled Indonesia from the late 17th century until 1942, when the Japanese invaded. Independence leader Sukarno declared Indonesia's independence in 1945, which the Dutch granted, with nominal union to The Netherlands, in 1949; Indonesia dissolved this union in 1954. The suppression of an alleged coup attempt in 1965 resulted in the deaths of more than

300,000 people the government claimed to be communists, and by 1968 Gen. Suharto had taken power. His government forcibly incorporated East Timor into Indonesia in 1975–76, with much loss of life. In the 1990s the country was beset by political, economic, and environmental problems, and Suharto was deposed in 1998; he was replaced by his vice president, B.J. Habibie.

Recent Developments

Muslim leader Abdurrahman Wahid was elected president in 1999 but was removed from office in 2001 after being implicated in scandals. He was replaced by his vice president, Megawati Sukarnoputri, the eldest daughter of Sukarno. In 1999 the people of East Timor voted for independence from Indonesia, and though afterward civilian militias rampaged through the province, killing 1,000–2,000 people, the Indonesian parliament rescinded Indonesia's annexation of the territory. East Timor became a non-self-governing territory under UN supervision and achieved full independence in 2002.

Internet resources: <www.bps.go.id>

Iran

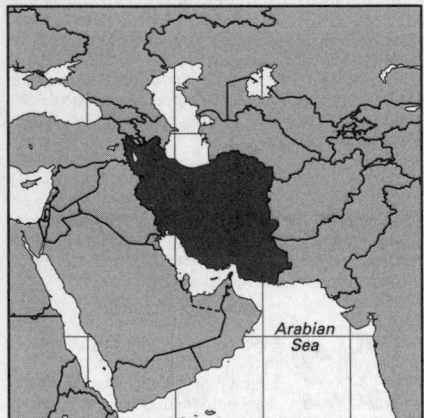

Arabian Sea

Official name: Jomhuri-ye Eslami-ye Iran (Islamic Republic of Iran). **Form of government:** unitary Islamic republic with one legislative house (Islamic Consultative Assembly [290]). **Supreme political/religious authority:** Leader (not required to be a supreme theological authority) Ayatollah Ali Hoseini-Khamenei (from 1989). **Head of state and government:** President Mohammad Khatami-Ardakani (from 1997). **Capital:** Tehran. **Official language:** Farsi (Persian). **Official religion:** Islam. **Monetary unit:** 1 rial (Rls); valuation (28 Jun 2002) $1 = Rls 1,750 (official floating rate).

Demography

Area: 629,315 sq mi, 1,629,918 sq km. **Population** (2001): 63,442,000 (de jure estimate, excludes roughly 2,000,000 Afghan refugees and less than

400,000 Iraqi refugees in mid-2001). **Density** (2001): persons per sq mi 100.8, persons per sq km 38.9. **Urban** (2000): 63.8%. **Sex distribution** (2000): male 50.73%; female 49.27%. **Age breakdown** (2000): under 15, 34.4%; 15–29, 32.0%; 30–44, 17.9%; 45–59, 9.2%; 60–74, 5.1%; 75 and over, 1.4%. **Ethnic composition** (1995): Persian 51%; Azerbaijani 24%; Gilaki/Mazandarani 8%; Kurd 7%; Arab 3%; Luri 2%; Balochi 2%; other 3%. **Religious affiliation** (2000): Muslim 95.6% (Shi'i 90.1%, Sunni 5.5%); Zoroastrian 2.8%; Christian 0.5%; other 1.1%. **Major cities** (1996): Tehran 6,758,845; Mashhad 1,887,405; Esfahan 1,266,072; Tabriz 1,191,043; Shiraz 1,053,025. **Location:** Middle East, bordering the Caspian Sea, Turkmenistan, Afghanistan, Pakistan, the Gulf of Oman, the Persian Gulf, Iraq, Turkey, Azerbaijan, and Armenia.

Vital statistics

Birth rate per 1,000 pop. (2000): 18.3 (world avg. 22.5). **Death rate** per 1,000 pop. (2000): 5.5 (world avg. 9.0). **Natural increase rate** per 1,000 pop. (2000): 12.8 (world avg. 13.5). **Total fertility rate** (avg. births per childbearing woman; 2000): 2.2. **Life expectancy** at birth (2000): male 68.3 years; female 71.5 years.

National economy

Budget (2000–01). *Revenue:* Rls 150,212,000,-000,000 (petroleum and natural gas revenue 55.2%; taxes 22.6%, of which corporate 8.9%; import duties 4.6%; other 17.6%). *Expenditures:* Rls 136,761,-000,000,000 (current expenditure 65.1%; development expenditure 22.0%; other 12.9%). **Public debt** (external, outstanding; 2000): $6,184,000,000. **Tourism** (1999): receipts $662,000,000; expenditures $918,000,000. **Gross national product** (1999): $113,729,000,000 ($1,810 per capita). **Production** (metric tons except as noted). *Agriculture, forestry, fishing* (1998): wheat 8,673,000, sugar beets 5,587,000, potatoes 3,433,000; livestock (number of live animals) 55,000,000 sheep, 8,100,000 cattle; roundwood (2000) 1,151,000 cu m; fish catch (1999) 419,000. *Mining and quarrying* (1998): copper ore 14,500,000; iron ore 12,300,000; gypsum 9,750,000. *Manufacturing* (value added in $'000,-000; 1995): iron and steel 1,393; food products 1,170; textiles 989. *Energy production (consumption):* electricity (kW-hr; 2000–01) 120,611,000,000 (120,611,000,000); coal (metric tons; 1997) 1,750,000 (1,320,000); crude petroleum (barrels; 1999–2000) 1,255,000,000 (496,000,000); petroleum products (metric tons; 1997) 50,135,000 (53,936,000); natural gas (cu m; 1999–2000) 80,000,000,000 (58,700,000,000). **Population economically active** (2000–01): total 18,700,000; activity rate 29.3% (participation rates: over age 15 [1996] 44.0%; female [1996] 12.7%; unemployed 13.9%). **Household income and expenditure.** Average household size (1999): 5.0; income per urban household (1988) Rls 1,339,970; sources of urban income (1988): wages 37.4%, self-employment 30.5%, other 32.1%; expenditure (1990–91): food, beverages, and tobacco (includes café and hotel expenditures) 42.6%, housing and energy 24.9%, clothing 11.8%, household furnishings 6.4%. **Land use**

(1994): forest 7.0%; pasture 26.9%; agriculture 11.1%; other 55.0%.

Foreign trade

Imports (1998–99): $14,286,000,000 (nonelectrical machinery 24.4%, electrical machinery 10.6%, iron and steel 9.0%, transportation equipment 9.3%, grains and derivatives 6.1%). *Major import sources:* Germany 11.6%; Italy 8.3%; Japan 7.0%; Belgium 6.3%; UAE 5.3%; Argentina 4.4%. **Exports** (1998–99): $13,118,000,000 (petroleum and natural gas 75.7%, fruit 4.5%, carpets 4.3%, iron and steel 1.1%). *Major export destinations:* UK 16.8%; Japan 15.7%; Italy 8.6%; UAE 6.7%; South Korea 5.0%; Greece 5.0%; Turkey 3.8%.

Transport and communications

Transport. *Railroads* (1999): route length 6,300 km; (1997) passenger-km 6,103,000,000; (1997) metric ton-km cargo 14,100,000,000. *Roads* (1997): length 165,724 km (paved 50%). *Vehicles* (1996): passenger cars 1,793,000; trucks and buses 692,000. *Air transport* (2000; Iran Air only): passenger-km 6,228,670,000; metric ton-km cargo 72,150,000; airports (1996) with scheduled flights 19. **Communications** Total units (units per 1,000 persons). Daily newspaper circulation (1996): 1,651,000 (28); Radio receivers (1997): 17,000,000 (280); Television receivers (1999): 10,500,000 (157); Telephone main lines (1999): 8,371,000 (125); Cellular telephone subscribers (1999): 490,478 (7.3); Personal computers (1999): 3,500,000 (52); Internet users (1999): 100,000 (1.5).

Education and health

Educational attainment (1986). Percentage of pop. age 25 and over having: no formal schooling 12.8%; secondary education 38.0%; higher 7.8%. **Literacy** (1997): total pop. age 15 and over literate 73.4%; males literate 79.7%; females literate 65.9%. **Health** (1998–99): physicians 60,000 (1 per 1,033 persons); hospital beds 98,669 (1 per 628 persons); infant mortality rate (2000) 30.0. **Food** (1999): daily per capita caloric intake 2,898 (vegetable products 91%, animal products 9%); 120% of FAO recommended minimum requirement.

Military

Total active duty personnel (2000): 513,000 (revolutionary guard corps 24.4%, army 63.4%, navy 3.5%, air force 8.7%). **Military expenditure as percentage of GNP** (1997): 3.0% (world 2.6%); per capita expenditure $78.

Background

Habitation in Iran dates to c. 100,000 BC, but recorded history began with the Elamites c. 3000 BC. The Medes flourished from c. 728 BC but were overthrown (550 BC) by the Persians, who were in turn conquered by Alexander the Great in the 4th century BC. The Parthians created a Greek-speaking empire that lasted from 247 BC to AD 226, when control passed to the Sasanians. Arab Muslims conquered them in 640 and ruled Iran for 850 years. In 1502 the Safavids established a dynasty that lasted until 1736. The Qajars ruled from 1779, but in the 19th century the country was economically controlled by the Russian and British empires. Reza Khan seized power in a coup (1921). His son Mohammad Reza Shah Pahlavi alienated religious leaders with a program of modernization and westernization and was overthrown in 1979; Shi'ite cleric Ruhollah Khomeini then set up a fundamentalist Islamic republic, and Western influence was suppressed. The destructive Iran-Iraq War of the 1980s ended in a stalemate. During the 1990s the government gradually moved to a more liberal conduct of state affairs.

Recent Developments

In Iran's presidential election held on 8 Jun 2001, incumbent Pres. Mohammad Khatami was returned to power with an overwhelming 77% of the votes—an outcome that rebutted the hard-line contention that Khatami and his followers had lost the support of the nation. Khatami's political platform was extremely modest, promising only that he would continue within a formula of extreme moderation to pursue reform and move Iran toward an Islamic democracy. Although the Iranian leadership, notably President Khatami, was quick to condemn the September terrorist attacks in the US, hopes that the campaign against terrorism would offer some degree of rapprochement with the US were dimmed when the Iranian spiritual leader, Ali Khamenei, made a hard-line anti-American speech. In the speech Khamenei explicitly rejected, except under a UN banner, Iranian participation in any actions against the Taliban government in Afghanistan or in a global antiterrorist movement. Meanwhile, Iranian diplomatic relations with Central Asia, the Arabian peninsula, China, and the European Union were generally lukewarm. On 23 Jun 2002 a magnitude-6.0 earthquake in northwestern Iran left some 25,000 families homeless.

Internet resources: <www.irantourism.org>

Iraq

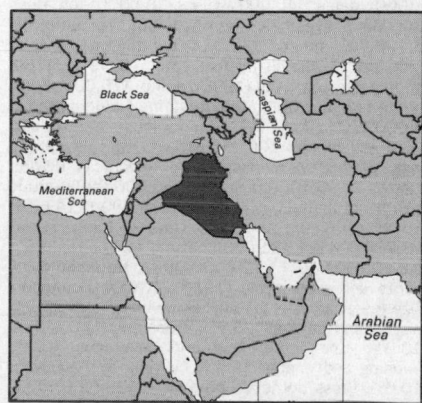

Official name: Al-Jumhuriyah al-'Iraqiyah (Republic of Iraq). **Form of government:** republic with one legislative house (National Assembly [220; 30 additional seats allotted to the Kurdish Autonomous Region filled by presidential appointment]). **Head of state and government:** President Saddam Hussein (from 1979). **Capital:** Baghdad. **Official language:** Arabic

(Kurdish is official in the Kurdish Autonomous Region). **Official religion:** Islam. **Monetary unit:** 1 Iraqi dinar (ID) = 20 dirhams = 1,000 fils; valuation (28 Jun 2002) $1 = ID 3.11.

Demography

Area: 167,975 sq mi, 435,052 sq km. **Population** (2001): 23,332,000. **Density** (2001): persons per sq mi 138.9, persons per sq km 53.6. **Urban** (1999): 76.4%. **Sex distribution** (2001): male 50.57%; female 49.43%. **Age breakdown** (2000): under 15, 42.1%; 15–29, 30.4%; 30–44, 15.6%; 45–59, 7.4%; 60–74, 3.5%; 75 and over, 1.0%. **Ethnic composition** (2000): Arab 64.7%; Kurd 23.0%; Azerbaijani 5.6%; Turkmen 1.2%; Persian 1.1%; other 4.4%. **Religious affiliation** (2000): Shi'i Muslim 62.0%; Sunni Muslim 34.0%; Christian (primarily Chaldean rite and Syrian rite Roman Catholic and Nestorian) 3.2%; other (primarily Yazidi syncretist) 0.8%. **Major cities** (1987): Baghdad (1999; urban agglomeration) 4,689,000; Mosul 664,221; Irbil 485,968; Karkuk (Kirkuk) 418,624; Al-Basrah 406,296. **Location:** Middle East, bordering Turkey, Iran, the Persian Gulf, Kuwait, Saudi Arabia, Jordan, and Syria.

Vital statistics

Birth rate per 1,000 pop. (2001): 34.6 (world avg. 22.5). **Death rate** per 1,000 pop. (2001): 6.2 (world avg. 9.0). **Natural increase rate** per 1,000 pop. (2001): 28.4 (world avg. 13.5). **Total fertility rate** (avg. births per childbearing woman; 2001): 4.8. **Marriage rate** per 1,000 pop. (1992): 7.8. **Life expectancy** at birth (2001): male 65.9 years; female 68.0 years.

National economy

Budget (1992). *Revenue:* ID 13,935,000,000. *Expenditures:* ID 13,935,000,000. Details of more recent budgets are not available. **Production** (metric tons except as noted). *Agriculture, forestry, fishing* (2000): dates 540,000, wheat 384,000, tomatoes 300,000; livestock (number of live animals) 6,100,000 sheep, 1,150,000 cattle; roundwood (2000) 177,000 cu m; fish catch (1999) 26,789. *Mining and quarrying* (1995): sulfur 475,000; phosphate rock 440,000. *Manufacturing* (value added in $'000,000; 1994): refined petroleum 127; bricks, tiles, and cement 100; industrial chemicals 79. *Energy production (consumption):* electricity (kW-hr; 1997) 29,950,000,000 (29,950,000,000); crude petroleum (barrels; 1997) 419,584,000 (214,678,-000); petroleum products (metric tons; 1997) 23,730,000 (21,531,000); natural gas (cu m; 1997) 3,620,000,000 (3,620,000,000). **Household income and expenditure** (1988). Average household size 8.9; sources of income: self-employment 33.9%; wages and salaries 23.9%, transfers 23.0%, rent 18.6%; expenditure: food and beverages 50.2%, housing and energy 19.9%, clothing and footwear 10.6%. **Gross domestic product** (1999): $19,000,-000,000 ($850 per capita). **Public debt** (external, outstanding; 1999): $23,000,000,000. **Population economically active** (1988): total 4,127,294; activity rate of total pop. 24.7% (participation rates: ages 15–64, 45.3%; female 12.0%). **Tourism** (1995): receipts $13,000,000; expenditures, n.a. **Land use** (1994): forest 0.4%; pasture 9.1%; agriculture 13.1%; other 77.4%.

Foreign trade

(UN-imposed trade sanctions in place from August 1990 through early 2002) **Imports** (1995-c.i.f.): $2,500,000,000 est. (agricultural products 42.7%, of which cereals 9.9%; unspecified 57.3%). *Major import sources* (1996): Turkey 36%; Jordan 26%; Malaysia 4%; Australia 3%. **Exports** (1995-f.o.b.): $419,000,000 est. (mostly crude petroleum and petroleum products). *Major export destinations* (1996): Jordan 91%; Turkey 6%.

Transport and communications

Transport. *Railroads* (1997): route length 2,032 km; passenger-km 1,169,000,000; metric ton-km cargo 956,000,000. *Roads* (1999): total length 45,550 km (paved 84%). *Vehicles* (1996): passenger cars 772,986; trucks and buses 323,906. *Air transport:* scheduled domestic and limited international air service resumed in 2000 and 2001, respectively. **Communications** Total units (units per 1,000 persons). Daily newspaper circulation (1996): 407,000 (20); Radio receivers (1997): 4,850,000 (229); Television receivers (1997): 1,750,000 (78); Telephone main lines (1999): 675,000 (30).

Education and health

Educational attainment (1987). Percentage of pop. age 10 and over having: no formal schooling 52.8%; primary education 21.5%; secondary 11.6%; higher 4.1%; unknown 10.0%. **Literacy** (1995): total pop. age 15 and over literate 58.0%; males 70.7%; females 45.0%. **Health** (1993): physicians 8,787 (1 per 2,181 persons); hospital beds 27,202 (1 per 704 persons); infant mortality rate per 1,000 live births (2001) 60.0. **Food** (1999): daily per capita caloric intake 2,446 (vegetable products 96%, animal products 4%); 101% of FAO recommended minimum requirement.

Military

Total active duty personnel (2000): 429,000 (army 91.3%, navy 0.5%, air force 8.2%). **Military expenditure as percentage of GDP** (1997): 4.9% (world 2.6%); per capita expenditure $59.

 **Did you know?** Ziggurats are religious structures associated with the major cities of ancient Mesopotamia (modern Iraq). Built between about 2200 BC and 500 BC, they were stepped, pyramidal towers, possibly with temples on their highest levels. Dedicated to the deity of a city, ziggurats were usually landscaped with trees and shrubs. None of the approximately 25 known ziggurats is preserved to its original height.

Background

Called Mesopotamia in classical times, the region gave rise to the world's earliest civilizations, including

---

1 metric ton = about 1.1 short tons; 1 kilometer = 0.6 mi (statute); 1 metric ton-km cargo = about 0.68 short ton-mi cargo; c.i.f.: cost, insurance, and freight; f.o.b.: free on board

those of Sumer, Akkad, and Babylon. Conquered by Alexander the Great in 330 BC, the area later became a battleground between Romans and Parthians, then between Sasanians and the Byzantines. Arab Muslims conquered it in the 7th century AD and ruled until the Mongols took over in 1258. The Ottomans took control in the 16th century and ruled until 1917. The British occupied the country during World War I and created the kingdom of Iraq in 1921. The British occupied Iraq again during World War II. A king was restored following the war, but a revolution ended the monarchy in 1958. Following a series of military coups, the socialist Baath Party, led by Saddam Hussein, took control and established totalitarian rule in 1968. The Iran-Iraq War of the 1980s and the Persian Gulf War (precipitated by the Iraqi invasion of Kuwait in 1990) brought heavy casualties and disrupted the economy. The 1990s were dominated by economic turmoil.

Recent Developments

In the wake of the terrorist attacks in the US on 11 Sep 2001, Iraq was virtually alone among countries in failing to offer official condolences to the US. In line with his adversarial relationship with the US, Pres. Saddam Hussein publicly opposed the US-led war on terrorism and called on other Islamic countries to help defeat it. He also decried the military action in Afghanistan, calling it a spark that could set "the world on fire." In response, US Secretary of State Colin Powell suggested that once the US had concluded its campaign in Afghanistan, it would deal with Iraq's weapons program as part of its effort against terrorism. Meanwhile, the US focused on persuading Russia to sign off on a "smart sanctions" package that would ease the restrictions on civilian goods imported into Iraq but tighten restrictions on military supplies. The package also included measures to prevent Iraq from smuggling oil to the outside world, as it continued to do. Pending action on new UN measures, the existing "oil-for-food" program was renewed, while the US and its allies dealt with Afghanistan. During the summer of 2002 the US publicly debated the apparent inclinations of Pres. George W. Bush to invade Iraq and remove Hussein from power.

Internet resources: <www.uruklink.net/iraqinfo>

Ireland

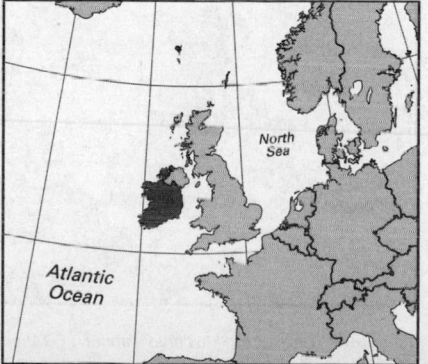

Official name: Éire (Irish); Ireland (English). Form of government: unitary multiparty republic with two legislative houses (Senate [60; includes 11 nonelective seats]; House of Representatives [166]). Chief of state: President Mary McAleese (from 1997). Head of government: Prime Minister Bertie Ahern (from 1997). Capital: Dublin. Official languages: Irish; English. Official religion: none. Monetary unit: 1 euro (€) = 100 cents; valuation (28 Jun 2002) $1 = €1.01; at conversion on 1 Jan 2002, €1 = 0.79 Irish pound (£Ir).

Demography

Area: 27,133 sq mi, 70,273 sq km. Population (2001): 3,823,000. Density (2001): persons per sq mi 140.9, persons per sq km 54.4. Urban (1996): 58.0%. Sex distribution (2000): male 49.59%; female 50.41%. Age breakdown (2000): under 15, 21.9%; 15–29, 24.9%; 30–44, 21.1%; 45–59, 16.9%; 60–74, 10.3%; 75 and over, 4.9%. Ethnic composition (2000): Irish 95.0%; British 1.7%, of which English 1.4%; Ulster Irish 1.0%; US white 0.8%; other 1.5%. Religious affiliation (1991): Roman Catholic 91.6%; Church of Ireland (Anglican) 2.5%; Presbyterian 0.4%; other 5.5%. Major cities (1996; for Ireland's five administrative county boroughs): Dublin 481,854 (urban agglomeration [1999] 977,000); Cork 127,187; Galway 57,241; Limerick 52,039; Waterford 42,540. Location: western Europe, bordering the UK (Northern Ireland), the Irish Sea, the Celtic Sea, and the North Atlantic Ocean.

Vital statistics

Birth rate per 1,000 pop. (2000): 14.5 (world avg. 22.5). Death rate per 1,000 pop. (2000): 8.1 (world avg. 9.0). Natural increase rate per 1,000 pop. (2000): 6.4 (world avg. 13.5). Marriage rate per 1,000 pop. (1999): 4.9. Total fertility rate (avg. births per childbearing woman; 2000): 1.9. Life expectancy at birth (2000): male 74.1 years; female 79.7 years.

National economy

Budget (2000). Revenue: £Ir 21,741,000,000 (income taxes 33.0%, value-added tax 27.0%, excise taxes 15.4%). Expenditures: £Ir 19,297,000,000 (social welfare 27.9%, health 20.9%, education 14.9%, debt service 10.5%). Public debt (1996): $47,876,000,000. Gross national product (1999): $80,559,000,000 ($21,470 per capita). Tourism (1999): receipts $3,392,000,000; expenditures $2,620,000,000. Production (metric tons except as noted). Agriculture, forestry, fishing (2000): sugar beets 1,564,000, barley 1,129,000, wheat 706,000; livestock (number of live animals) 8,393,000 sheep, 6,607,500 cattle, 1,763,000 pigs; roundwood (2000) 2,673,000 cu m; fish catch (1999) 329,777. Mining and quarrying (1999): gypsum 480,000; zinc ore 199,300 (metal content of ores); lead ore 44,100 (metal content of ores). Manufacturing (value added in £Ir '000,000; 1995): office equipment and computers 2,163; basic chemicals 2,112; reproduction of recorded media 1,531. Energy production (consumption): electricity (kW-hr; 1997) 19,856,000,000 (19,856,000,000); coal (metric tons; 1997) none (3,070,000); crude petroleum (barrels, 1997) none (20,800,000); petroleum products (metric tons; 1997) 2,795,000 (5,616,000); natural gas (cu m; 1997) 1,012,000,000 (3,242,000,000). Population economically active (2000): total 1,745,600; activity rate 46.1% (participation rates: ages 15–64, c. 68%; female 40.3%; unemployed 4.3%). **Household income and expenditure.** Average household size (1997) 3.1; income per household (1994–95): £Ir 16,224; expenditure (Nov 1996): food and beverages 35.4%, transportation 13.9%, rent/household goods 11.6%.

Foreign trade

Imports (1999-c.i.f.): £Ir 34,682,100,000 (machinery and transport equipment 51.5%, chemicals 11.2%, manufactured goods 11.0%, food 5.8%, petroleum and petroleum products 2.8%). *Major import sources:* UK 33.1%; US 16.7%; Germany 6.2%; Japan 5.8%; France 4.1%. **Exports** (1999-f.o.b.): £Ir 52,537,200,000 (machinery and transport equipment 38.8%, chemical products 31.6%, manufactured goods 11.1%, food 8.2%). *Major export destinations:* UK 22.0%; US 15.4%; Germany 11.9%; France 8.4%; The Netherlands 6.0%.

Transport and communications

Transport. *Railroads* (1999): route length 1,945 km; passenger-km 1,295,000,000; metric ton-km cargo 570,000,000. *Roads* (1999): length 92,500 km (paved 94%). *Vehicles* (2000): passenger cars 1,269,245; trucks and buses 188,814. *Air transport* (1998; Aer Lingus only): passenger-km 6,466,383,-000; metric ton-km cargo 129,648,000; airports (1996) 9. **Communications** Total units (units per 1,000 persons). Daily newspaper circulation (1996): 543,000 (150); Radio receivers (1998): 2,150,000 (580); Television receivers (1999): 2,144,000 (578); Telephone main lines (1999): 1,770,000 (477); Cellular telephone subscribers (1999): 1,655,000 (446); Personal computers (1999): 1,500,000 (404); Internet users (1999): 679,000 (183).

Education and health

Educational attainment (1991). Percentage of pop. age 15 and over having: primary education or no schooling 33.7%; secondary 42.7%; some postsecondary 12.6%; university or like institution 11.0%. **Health:** physicians (1998) 8,114 (1 per 457 persons); hospital beds (1995) 11,953 (1 per 301 persons; acute-care public hospitals only); infant mortality rate (2000) 5.6. **Food** (1999): daily per capita caloric intake 3,649 (vegetable products 67%, animal products 33%); 145% of FAO recommended minimum requirement.

Military

Total active duty personnel (2000): 11,460 (army 81.2%, navy 9.6%, air force 9.2%). **Military expenditure as percentage of GNP** (1997): 1.2% (world 2.6%); per capita expenditure $203.

Background

Human settlement in Ireland began c. 6000 BC, and Celtic migration dates from c. 300 BC. St. Patrick is credited with Christianizing the country in the 5th century AD. Norse domination began in 795 and ended in 1014, when the Norse were defeated by Brian Boru. Gaelic Ireland's independence ended in 1171 when English king Henry II proclaimed himself overlord of the island. Beginning in the 16th century, Irish Catholic landowners fled religious persecution by the English and were replaced by English and Scottish Protestant migrants. The United Kingdom of Great Britain and Ireland was established in 1801. The Great Famine of the 1840s led over 2 million people to emigrate and built momentum for Irish Home Rule. The Easter Rising (1916) was followed by civil war (1919–21) between the Catholic majority in southern Ireland, who favored complete independence, and the Protestant majority in the north, who preferred continued union with Britain. Southern Ireland was granted dominion status and became the Irish Free State in 1921, and in 1937 it adopted the name Éire and became a sovereign independent nation. It remained neutral during World War II. Britain recognized the status of Ireland in 1949 but declared that cession of the northern six counties could not occur without the consent of the Parliament of Northern Ireland. In 1973 Ireland joined the European Economic Community (later the European Community) and is now a member of the European Union. The late 20th century was dominated by sectarian hostilities between the island's Catholics and Protestants.

Recent Developments

Prime Minister Bertie Ahern's Fianna Fail party triumphed in the May 2002 general election, though it fell a few seats short of an outright majority in the 166-seat parliament. The nationalist Sinn Féin and the environmental Green Party also made notable gains. Meanwhile, the future of the 1998 Good Friday Accords, which envisaged a lasting peace in Northern Ireland, appeared more secure after the illegal Irish Republican Army destroyed or "put beyond use" at least part of its armory. Irish voters rejected a referendum to endorse the Treaty of Nice, which provided for EU expansion, in 2001, though the business community eagerly welcomed the advent of the euro in 2002.

Internet resources: <www.ireland.ie>

Isle of Man

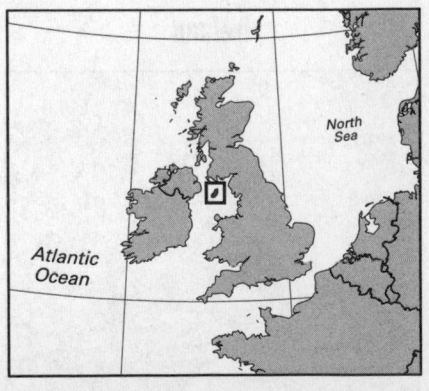

Official name: Isle of Man (Manx Gaelic: Ellan Vannin). **Political status:** crown dependency (UK) with Tynwald comprising two legislative bodies (Legislative Council [11; includes 3 nonelective seats]; House of Keys [24]). **Chief of state:** Queen Elizabeth II represented by Lieutenant Governor Ian David Macfadyen (from 2000). **Head of government:** Chief Minister Richard Corkill (from 4 Dec 2001). **Capital:** Douglas. **Official language:** English. **Official religion:** none. **Monetary unit:** 1 Manx pound (£M) = 100 new pence; valuation (28 Jun 2002) 1 £M = $1.52; the Manx pound is equivalent in value to the pound sterling.

Demography

Area: 227 sq mi, 588.1 km. **Population** (2001): 73,500. **Density** (2001): persons per sq mi 323.6, persons per sq km 125.0. **Urban** (1999): 76.3%. **Sex distribution** (1996): male 48.52%; female 51.48%. **Age breakdown** (1996): under 15, 17.6%; 15–29, 19.0%; 30–44, 20.6%; 45–59, 19.5%; 60–74, 14.4%; 75 and over, 8.9%. **Population by place of birth** (1996): Isle of Man 49.9%; UK 44.1%, of which England 37.5%, Scotland 3.3%, Northern Ireland 2.1%; Ireland 2.4%. **Religious affiliation** (2000): Christian 63.7%, of which Anglican 40.5%, Methodist 9.9%, Roman Catholic 8.2%; other (mostly nonreligious) 36.3%. **Major towns** (1996): Douglas 23,487; Onchan 8,656; Ramsey 6,874; Peel 3,819; Port Erin 3,218. **Location:** Irish Sea, midway between Ireland and Great Britain.

Vital statistics

Birth rate per 1,000 pop. (1999): 12.3 (world avg. 22.5); legitimate 68.1%; illegitimate 31.9%. **Death rate** per 1,000 pop. (1999): 13.5 (world avg. 9.0). **Natural increase rate** per 1,000 pop. (1999): -1.2 (world avg. 13.5). **Total fertility rate** (avg. births per childbearing woman; 1999): 1.6. **Marriage rate** per 1,000 pop. (1999): 5.5. **Divorce rate** per 1,000 pop. (1996): 4.0. **Life expectancy** at birth (1999): male 73.9 years; female 80.8 years.

National economy

Budget (1997–98). *Revenue:* £265,716,000 (customs duties and excise taxes 51.7%; income taxes 43.7%, of which resident 34.6%, nonresident 9.1%; interest on investments 4.2%). *Expenditures:* £240,140,000 (health and social security 42.2%; education 19.2%; transportation 6.4%; home affairs 6.3%; tourism and recreation 5.4%). **Public debt:** n.a. **Production.** *Agriculture, forestry, fishing* (1998): main crops include hay, oats, barley, wheat, and orchard crops; livestock (number of live animals) 173,900 sheep, 34,000 cattle, 6,600 pigs; fish catch (value of catch in £ sterling; 1997) 1,666,000; whitefish 244,000; herring 138,000. *Mining and quarrying:* sand and gravel. *Manufacturing* (value added in $; 1996–97): electrical and nonelectrical machinery/apparatus, textiles, other 103,700,000; food and beverages 18,600,000. *Energy production (consumption):* electricity (kW-hr; 1997–98) n.a. (275,400,000). **Household income and expenditure.** Average household size (1996) 2.4; income per household (1981–82): £7,479; sources of income (1981–82): wages and salaries 64.1%, transfer payments 16.9%, interest and dividends 11.2%, self-employment 6.6%; expenditure (1981–82): food and beverages 31.0%, transportation 14.9%, energy

11.0%, housing 7.9%, clothing and footwear 7.0%. **Gross national product** (at current market prices; 1997–98): $1,282,000,000 ($17,730 per capita). **Population economically active** (1996): total 34,811; activity rate of total pop. 48.5% (participation rates: ages 16 and over 59.8%; female 44.0%; unemployed 3.5%). **Tourism:** receipts from visitors (1997–98) $68,000,000.

Foreign trade

Imports (1998): n.a. *Major import sources:* mostly the UK. **Exports** (1998): traditional exports include scallops, herring, beef, lambs, and tweeds. *Major export destinations:* mostly the UK.

Transport and communications

Transport. *Railroads* (1998): route length (length of 3 tourist railways operating in summer) 52 km. *Roads* (1998): total length, more than 805 km (paved, n.a.). *Vehicles* (1998): passenger cars 40,168; trucks and buses, n.a. *Air transport* (1998; Manx Airlines): passenger-km 846,775,000; metric ton-km cargo 168,000; airports (1999) with scheduled flights 1. **Communications** Daily newspaper circulation (1997): n.a., no daily newspapers are published; Television receivers (1997): 27,000 (375); Telephone main lines (1996): 46,000 (641).

Education and health

Educational attainment: n.a. **Literacy:** n.a. **Health** (1998): physicians 117 (1 per 619 persons); hospital beds 505 (1 per 143 persons); infant mortality rate per 1,000 live births (1997–99 avg.) 3.7. **Food** (1998; data for the UK): daily per capita caloric intake 3,257 (vegetable products 68%, animal products 32%); 129% of FAO recommended minimum requirement.

Military

Total active duty personnel: none; the UK is responsible for defense.

Internet resources: <www.gov.im/tourism>

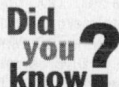

Did you know? The Isle of Man considers itself the motorcycle road racing capital of the world. Road racing events have been held there since 1907, when the Tourist Trophy motorcycle races debuted. Since 1960, the only course used for these races has been the Isle's rugged mountain circuit, a course considered the greatest of all challenges for motorcyclists.

Israel

Official name: Medinat Yisra'el (Hebrew); Isra'il (Arabic) (State of Israel). **Form of government:** multiparty republic with one legislative house (Knesset [120]). **Chief of state:** President Moshe Katzav (from 31 Jul 2000). **Head of government:** Prime Minister Ariel Sharon (from 2 Mar 2001). **Capital:** Jerusalem is the proclaimed capital of Israel and the actual seat of government, but recognition of its status as capital by the international community has largely been withheld pending final settlement of territorial and other

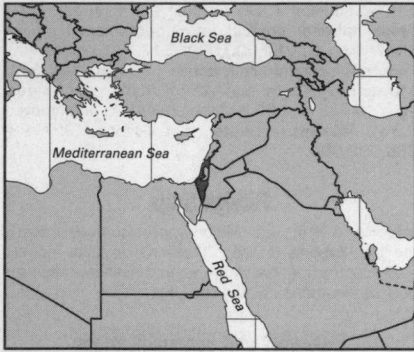

issues through peace talks between Israel and the Arab parties concerned. **Official languages:** Hebrew; Arabic. **Official religion:** none. **Monetary unit:** 1 New (Israeli) shekel (NIS) = 100 agorot; valuation (28 Jun 2002) $1 = NIS 4.76.

Demography

Area: 7,886 sq mi, 20,425 sq km. **Population** (2001): 6,258,000. **Density** (2001): persons per sq mi 793.6, persons per sq km 306.4. **Urban** (2000): 90.6%. **Sex distribution** (2000): male 49.33%; female 50.67%. **Age breakdown** (2000): under 15, 28.6%; 15–29, 25.1%; 30–44, 18.7%; 45–59, 14.5%; 60–74, 8.8%; 75 and over, 4.3%. **Ethnic composition** (2000): Jewish 78.1%; Arab and other 21.9%. **Religious affiliation** (2000): Jewish 78.1%; Muslim (mostly Sunni) 15.1%; Christian 2.1%; Druze 1.6%; other 3.1%. **Major cities** (2001): Jerusalem 657,500; Tel Aviv–Yafo 354,400; Haifa 270,500; Rishon LeZ-iyyon 202,200. **Location:** Middle East, bordering Lebanon, Syria, Jordan, West Bank, Egypt, and the Gaza Strip.

Vital statistics

Birth rate per 1,000 pop. (2000): 21.7 (world avg. 22.5); (1994—Jewish only) legitimate 98.2%; illegitimate 1.8%. **Death rate** per 1,000 pop. (2000): 6.0 (world avg. 9.0). **Natural increase rate** per 1,000 pop. (2000): 15.7 (world avg. 13.5). **Total fertility rate** (avg. births per childbearing woman; 2000): 3.0. **Marriage rate** per 1,000 pop. (1999): 6.6. **Divorce rate** per 1,000 pop. (1999): 1.7. **Life expectancy** at birth (2000): male 76.6 years; female 80.4 years.

National economy

Budget (2000). *Revenue:* NIS 178,037,000,000 (tax revenue 74.6%, of which income tax and property tax 34.7%, value-added tax 26.0%, sales tax and fuel tax 4.7%; nontax revenue 18.5%; grants 6.9%). *Expenditures:* NIS 188,927,000,000 (defense 20.7%; education 14.8%; interest on loans 13.9%; labor and welfare 12.1%; health 8.5%). **Public debt** (external, outstanding; 1999): $27,323,000,000. **Gross national product** (1999): $99,574,000,000 ($16,310 per capita). **Production** (metric tons except as noted). *Agriculture, forestry, fishing* (2000): tomatoes 550,200, grapefruit 370,000, potatoes 348,-

600; livestock (number of live animals) 388,000 cattle, 350,000 sheep; roundwood (2000) 113,000 cu m; fish catch (1999) 24,661. *Mining and quarrying* (1999): phosphate rock 4,100,000, potash 1,750,-000. *Manufacturing* (1996): cement 6,723,000; polyethylene 144,147 (1993); sulfuric acid 130,000 (1993). *Energy production (consumption):* electricity (kW-hr; 2000) 42,916,000 (39,317,000); coal (metric tons; 1996) none (7,808,000); crude petroleum (barrels; 1996) 29,000 (77,000,000). **Population economically active** (2000): total 2,435,000; activity rate 39.9% (participation rates: over ages 15, 54.3%; female 45.6%; unemployed 8.8%). **Household income and expenditure** (1999). Average household size 3.6; monthly income per household (1995) NIS 6,125; sources of income (1993): salaries and wages 63.4%, allowances and assistance 18.9%, self-employment 14.6%; expenditure (1998): housing 23.7%, food, beverages, and tobacco 21.1%, household durable goods 8.2%. **Tourism** (1999): receipts $2,974,000,000; expenditures $2,566,000,000.

Foreign trade

Imports (2000): $35,749,500,000 (investment goods 21.3%; diamonds 17.0%; consumer goods 12.3%; fuel and lubricants 6.0%). *Major import sources:* US 20.7%; Belgium 11.1%; Germany 8.1%; UK 7.6%; Italy 5.3%. **Exports** (2000): $31,403,700,-000 (machinery and transport equipment 39.7%; diamonds 23.7%; chemicals 13.4%; apparel 4.9%; food, beverages, and tobacco 3.1%). *Major export destinations:* US 35.5%; UK 5.5%; Belgium 5.4%; Germany 4.5%; Hong Kong 3.4%.

Transport and communications

Transport. *Railroads* (1999): route length 610 km; passenger-km 529,000,000; metric ton-km cargo 1,128,000,000. *Roads* (1999): total length 15,464 km (paved 100%). *Vehicles* (2000): passenger cars 1,316,765; trucks and buses 319,581. *Air transport* (2000): passenger-km 14,125,067,000; metric ton-km cargo 1,288,345,000; airports (1999) with scheduled flights 7. **Communications** Total units (units per 1,000 persons). Daily newspaper circulation (1997): 1,650,000 (288); Radio receivers (1997): 3,070,000 (524); Television receivers (1999): 1,690,000 (288); Telephone main lines (1999): 2,877,000 (471); Cellular telephone subscribers (1999): 2,880,000 (472); Personal computers (1999): 1,500,000 (221); Internet users (1999): 800,000 (131).

Education and health

Educational attainment (2000). Percentage of pop. age 15 and over having: no formal schooling 3.3%; primary 1.9%; secondary 57.4%; postsecondary, vocational, and higher 37.4%. **Literacy** (2000): total pop. age 15 and over literate 96.7%. **Health** (2000): physicians 21,500 (1 per 284 persons); hospital beds 38,577 (1 per 158 persons); infant mortality rate (2000) 5.1. **Food** (1999): daily per capita caloric intake 3,542 (vegetable products 81%, animal products 19%); 138% of FAO recommended minimum.

1 metric ton = about 1.1 short tons;   1 kilometer = 0.6 mi (statute);   1 metric ton-km cargo = about 0.68 short ton-mi cargo;   c.i.f.: cost, insurance, and freight;   f.o.b.: free on board

Military

Total active duty personnel (2000): 172,500 (army 75.4%, navy 3.8%, air force 20.8%). **Military expenditure as percentage of GNP** (1997): 9.7% (world 2.6%); per capita expenditure $1,698.

Did you know? There are seven kosher McDonald's restaurants in Israel. The menu, which excludes all dairy products, includes meat that uses 100% kosher beef patties. Additionally, these restaurants do not operate on the Sabbath or religious holidays.

Background

The record of human habitation in Israel is at least 100,000 years old. Efforts by Jews to establish a national state there began in the late 19th century. Britain supported Zionism and in 1922 assumed political responsibility for what was Palestine. Migration of Jews there during Nazi persecution led to deteriorating relations with Arabs. In 1947 the UN voted to partition the region into separate Jewish and Arab states, a decision opposed by neighboring Arab countries. The State of Israel was proclaimed in 1948, and Egypt, Transjordan, Syria, Lebanon, and Iraq immediately declared war on it. Israel won this war as well as the 1967 Six-Day War, in which it claimed the West Bank from Jordan and the Gaza Strip from Egypt. Another war with its Arab neighbors followed in 1973, but the Camp David Accords led to the signing of a peace treaty between Israel and Egypt in 1979. Israel invaded Lebanon to quell the Palestine Liberation Organization (PLO) in 1982, and in the late 1980s a Palestinian resistance movement arose in the occupied territories. Peace negotiations between Israel and the Arab states and Palestinians began in 1991. Israel and the PLO agreed in 1993 upon a five-year extension of self-government to the Palestinians of the West Bank and the Gaza Strip. Israel signed a full peace treaty with Jordan in 1994. Israeli soldiers and Lebanon's Hezbollah forces clashed in 1997. Following numerous contentious talks between Israel and Lebanon, Israeli troops abruptly withdrew from Lebanon in 2000.

Recent Developments

Negotiations between Israeli Prime Minister Ehud Barak and PLO leader Yasir Arafat stalled in February 2000, and a July summit at Camp David in Maryland ended with the two sides deadlocked over the future of Jerusalem. While seeking to revive the peace process, Barak saw his political support erode. Hardline Likud party leader Ariel Sharon, in a move perceived by critics as highly provocative, toured the al-Aqsa/Temple Mount complex in Jerusalem the following September. A new round of Israeli-Palestinian clashes ensued. Facing pressure from the opposition over his failure to stop the violence and for his concessions to the Palestinians, Barak resigned as prime minister in December and called for a special election to be held in February 2001. At the end of a campaign marked by continuing violence, Barak was decisively defeated by Sharon.

Following the September terrorist attacks in the US, Arafat declared a cease-fire in the yearlong Palestinian confrontation with Israel, but the violence soon resumed. On 17 October Tourism Minister Rehavam Ze'evi was assassinated in retaliation for the killing in August of Palestinian Popular Front leader Abu Ali Mustafa. The action led Israeli forces to invade Bethlehem and five other West Bank cities. Sharon cut short a visit to the US when 26 Israelis were killed and more than 270 injured in a string of suicide and car bombings in a crowded Jerusalem mall late on the night of 1 December and on a bus in Haifa the following morning. By mid-December, under pressure from the US and other countries, Arafat called for a halt to "terrorist activities," and he ordered the closure of about a dozen Hamas and Islamic Jihad offices.

In April 2002 Israeli forces launched Operation Defensive Shield, a military campaign that the Israeli government maintained was intended to destroy a Palestinian terrorist infrastructure. The forces eventually withdrew from most of the West Bank cities they entered, forming cordons around the cities and Palestinian refugee camps.

Internet Resources: <www.goisrael.com>

Italy

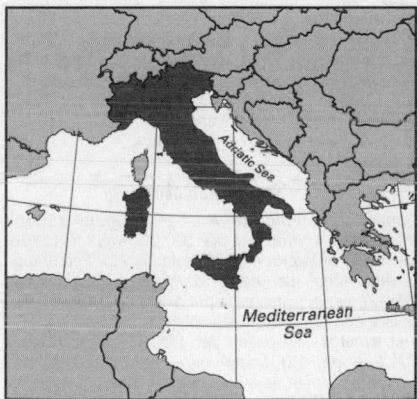

Official name: Repubblica Italiana (Italian Republic). **Form of government:** republic with two legislative houses (Senate [321]; Chamber of Deputies [630]). **Chief of state:** President Carlo Azeglio Ciampi (from 1999). **Head of government:** Prime Minister Silvio Berlusconi (from 11 Jun 2001). **Capital:** Rome. **Official language:** Italian. **Official religion:** none. **Monetary unit:** 1 euro (€) = 100 cents; valuation (28 Jun 2002) $1 = €1.01; at conversion on 1 Jan 2002, €1 = 1,936.27 Italian lire (Lit).

Demography

Area: 116,324 sq mi, 301,277 sq km. **Population** (2001): 57,892,000. **Density** (2001): persons per sq mi 497.8, persons per sq km 192.2. **Urban** (2000): 67.0%. **Sex distribution** (2000): male 48.55%; female 51.45%. **Age breakdown** (2000): under 15, 14.4%; 15–29, 19.5%; 30–44, 23.1%; 45–59, 19.1%; 60–74, 16.1%; 75 and over, 7.8%. **Ethnolinguistic composition** (2000): Italian 96.0%; North African Arab 0.9%; Italo-Albanian 0.8%; Albanian 0.5%; German 0.4%; Austrian 0.4%; other 1.0%. **Religious affiliation** (1996): Roman Catholic 81.7%; nonreligious

13.6%; Muslim 1.2%; other 3.5%. **Major cities** (2000): Rome 2,643,581; Milan 1,300,977; Naples 1,002,619; Turin 903,703; Palermo 683,794; Genoa 636,104; Bologna 381,161; Florence 376,682; Catania 337,862; Bari 331,848; Venice 277,305. **Location**: southern Europe, bordering Switzerland, Austria, Slovenia, the Mediterranean Sea, and France. **National origin** (1991): Italian 99.3%; foreign-born 0.7%, of which European 0.3%, African 0.2%, Asian 0.1%, other 0.1%. **Mobility** (1991). Population living in the same commune as in 1986: 93.3%; another commune, same province 3.4%; different province 2.5%; abroad 0.8%. **Households**. Average household size (1991) 2.7; composition of households: 1 person 19.5%, 2 persons 21.9%, 3 persons 25.2%, 4 persons 21.4%, 5 or more persons 12.0%. Family households (1991): 15,538,335 (73.8%); nonfamily 5,527,105 (26.2%), of which one-person 19.5%. **Immigration** (1997): immigrants 162,857, from Europe 41.1%, of which EU countries 14.2%; Africa 25.5%; Asia 19.0%; Western Hemisphere 14.0%.

Vital statistics

Birth rate per 1,000 pop. (2000): 9.1 (world avg. 22.5); (1998) legitimate 91.0%; illegitimate 8.0%. **Death rate** per 1,000 pop. (2000): 10.1 (world avg. 9.0). **Natural increase rate** per 1,000 pop. (2000): −1.0 (world avg. 13.5). **Total fertility rate** (avg. births per childbearing woman; 2000): 1.2. **Marriage rate** per 1,000 pop. (1998): 4.8. **Divorce rate** per 1,000 pop. (1994): 0.5. **Life expectancy** at birth (2001): male 75.9 years; female 82.5 years.

Social indicators

Quality of working life. Average workweek (1995): 37.0 hours. Annual rate per 100,000 workers (1996) for: injury or accident 3,208; death 7.5. Percentage of labor force insured for damages or income loss (1992) resulting from: injury 100%; permanent disability 100%; death 100%. Number of working days lost to labor stoppages per 1,000 workers (1996): 97. Rate per 1,000 workers of discouraged (unemployed no longer seeking work; 1990): 1.1. **Material well-being.** Rate per 1,000 of pop. possessing (1995): telephone 434; automobile 550; television 436. **Social participation.** Eligible voters participating in last national election (May 13, 2001): 81.2%. Trade union membership in total workforce (1990): c. 28%. **Social deviance** (1999). Offense rate per 100,000 pop. for: murder 1.4; rape 68.3; assault 210.4 (1995); theft, including burglary and housebreaking 2,567; suicide 6.3 (1996). **Access to services** (1999). Nearly 100% of dwellings have access to electricity, a safe water supply, and toilet facilities. **Leisure** (1998). Favorite leisure activities (as percentage of household spending on culture): cinema 21.8%; sporting events 14.6%; theater 13.8%.

National economy

Gross national product (1999): $1,162,910,000,-000 ($20,170 per capita). **Budget** (1999). *Revenue:* Lit 620,534,000,000,000 (income taxes 46.9%, of which individual 37.5%, corporate 9.4%; value-added and excise taxes 30.6%). *Expenditures:* Lit 668,251,-000,000,000 (1995; debt service 27.5%; social se-

curity 18.4%; education 9.1%; transportation 4.7%; defense 2.8%). **Public debt** (1999): $766,000,000,-000. **Tourism** (1999): receipts $28,359,000,000; expenditures $16,913,000,000. **Production** (metric tons except as noted). *Agriculture, forestry, fishing* (2001): sugar beets 12,000,000, corn (maize) 11,300,000, grapes 9,770,000, tomatoes 6,990,-000, wheat 6,500,000; livestock (number of live animals) 10,970,000 sheep, 8,400,000 pigs, 7,180,-000 cattle; roundwood (2000) 9,329,000 cu m; fish catch (1999) 540,523. *Mining and quarrying* (1998): rock salt 3,413,522; feldspar 2,503,541; barite 31,792; lead 10,102; zinc 5,242. *Manufacturing* (1998): cement 33,714,914 (1995); crude steel 25,782,300; pig iron 10,792,700; glass 3,981,104 (1995); textiles 2,340,600 (1997). *Energy production (consumption):* electricity (kW-hr; 1996) 241,413,-000,000 (278,802,000,000); coal (metric tons; 1996) none (16,335,000); crude petroleum (barrels; 1996) 39,802,000 (588,438,000); petroleum products (metric tons; 1996) 80,002,000 (86,550,000); natural gas (cu m; 1996) 19,993,000,000 (56,284,-000,000). **Population economically active** (1999): total 23,135,000; activity rate of total pop. 40.1% (participation rates: ages 15–64, 57.7% (1996) female 38.2%; unemployed 11.4%). **Household income and expenditure** (1995). Average household size 2.7; average annual income per household (1984) Lit 19,692,000 ($11,208); sources of income (1996): salaries and wages 38.8%, property income and self-employment 38.5%, transfer payments 22.0%; expenditure (1997): food and beverages 18.1%, housing 18.0%, transportation and communications 13.3%, recreation and education 8.4%. **Land use** (1994): forest 23.0%; pasture 15.4%; agriculture 37.9%; other 23.7%.

Foreign trade

Imports (1999-c.i.f.): Lit 394,271,000,000,000 (machinery and transport equipment 38.4%, of which transport equipment 15.1%; chemicals 13.6%; metal 9.8%; food 7.5%; textiles 5.2%; plastics 2.3%). *Major import sources:* Germany 19.0%; France 12.6%; The Netherlands 6.3%; UK 6.1%; US 4.9%; Belgium-Luxembourg 4.6%; Spain 4.3%. **Exports** (1999-f.o.b.): Lit 419,124,000,000,000 (machinery and transport equipment 41.7%, of which transport equipment 11.5%, electrical machinery 9.8%; textiles and wearing apparel 10.7%; chemicals 8.9%; plastics 3.7%). *Major export destinations:* Germany 16.5%; France 13.0%; US 9.5%; UK 7.1%; Spain 6.3%.

Transport and communications

Transport. *Railroads* (1998): length 19,527 km (1997); passenger-km 41,392,000,000; metric ton-km cargo 22,386,000,000. *Roads* (1997): total length 308,139 km (paved 100%). *Vehicles* (1998): passenger cars 31,370,000; trucks and buses 5,127,000. *Air transport* (1996): passenger-km 29,471,000,000; metric ton-km cargo 1,219,000,-000; airports (1997) 34. **Communications.** Total units (units per 1,000 persons). Daily newspaper circulation (1997): 5,970,000 (104); Radio receivers (1997): 50,500,000 (880); Television receivers (1998): 28,000,000 (488); Telephone main lines (1999): 26,506,000 (460); Cellular telephone sub-

---

1 metric ton = about 1.1 short tons;   1 kilometer = 0.6 mi (statute);   1 metric ton-km cargo = about 0.68 short ton-mi cargo;   c.i.f.: cost, insurance, and freight;   f.o.b.: free on board

scribers (1999): 30,296,000 (526); Personal computers (1999): 11,000,000 (191); Internet users (1999): 3,300,000 (57).

Education and health

Educational attainment (1995). Percentage of labor force age 15 and over having: basic literacy or primary education 40.4%; secondary 30.5%; postsecondary technical training 5.1%; some college 19.2%; college degree 4.3%. **Literacy** (1995): total pop. age 15 and over literate 48,100,000 (98.1%); males literate 23,800,000 (98.6%); females literate 24,300,000 (97.6%). **Health** (1997): physicians (1993) 207,319 (1 per 193 persons); hospital beds 334,613 (1 per 172 persons); infant mortality rate (2001) 5.8. **Food** (1999): daily per capita caloric intake 3,629 (vegetable products 74%, animal products 26%); 144% of FAO recommended minimum requirement.

Military

Total active duty personnel (2000): 250,000 (army 61.0%, navy 15.2%, air force 23.8%). **Military expenditure as percentage of GNP** (1997): 2.0% (world 2.6%); per capita expenditure $395.

Background

The Etruscan civilization arose in the 9th century BC and was overthrown by the Romans in the 4th-3rd centuries BC. Barbarian invasions of the 4th-5th centuries AD destroyed the western Roman empire. Italy's political fragmentation lasted for centuries but did not diminish its impact on European culture, notably during the Renaissance. From the 15th to the 18th century, Italian lands were ruled by France, the Holy Roman Empire, Spain, and Austria. When Napoleonic rule ended in 1815, Italy was again a grouping of independent states. The Risorgimento successfully united most of Italy, including Sicily and Sardinia by 1861, and the unification of peninsular Italy was completed by 1870. Italy joined the Allies during World War I, but social unrest in the 1920s brought to power the Fascist movement of Benito Mussolini, and Italy allied itself with Nazi Germany in World War II. Defeated by the Allies in 1943, Italy proclaimed itself a republic in 1946. It was a charter member of NATO (1949) and of the European Community. It completed the process of setting up regional legislatures with limited autonomy in the 1970s. Since World War II it has experienced rapid changes of government but has remained socially stable. It has worked with other European countries to establish the European Union.

Recent Developments

In Italy six and a half years of rule by center-left governments came to an end in 2001 when elections swept into power a center-right coalition led by media magnate Silvio Berlusconi, who had already enjoyed seven months of premiership in 1994. Berlusconi's House of Freedoms scooped up 368 seats in the Chamber of Deputies against the center-left Olive Tree's 242, while in the smaller Senate the figures were 177 to 125, respectively. Forza Italia increased its share of the House by 9%, while Umberto Bossi's Northern League—which championed more autonomy for the north of Italy—fared worse than predicted. It took Berlusconi a month to put together a 23-member cabinet, in which Bossi, after much haggling, be-

came minister for devolution, while the foreign minister's post went to a nonpolitician, Renato Ruggiero. The new prime minister's team won a vote of confidence in June by 351-261. Before the vote Berlusconi had promised an unspecified solution to a much-aired issue, that of the "conflict of interest" he faced as a political leader involved in big business.

Following the September terrorist attacks in the US, Berlusconi was among the European leaders who pledged support for the US-led war on terrorism. The prime minister put the country on heightened alert and promised that Italy was "by the side of the United States and all who are committed to the battle against terrorism." Italy offered troops as well as the use of its ports and airports, but many in the country were anxious over possible repercussions from the conflict. Berlusconi hardly helped allay these anxieties with his statement to reporters in late September that the West was "superior" to Islamic civilization because it provided wealth and guaranteed respect for human rights. While the prime minister maintained that his comments had been taken out of context, European Union leaders took pains to distance themselves from his remarks.

Internet resources: <www.italy-daily.com>

Jamaica

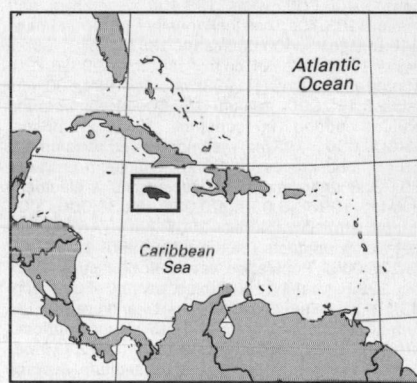

Official name: Jamaica. **Form of government:** constitutional monarchy with two legislative houses (Senate [21]; House of Representatives [60]). **Chief of state:** Queen Elizabeth II (from 1952). **Head of government:** Prime Minister Percival James Patterson (from 1992). **Capital:** Kingston. **Official language:** English. **Monetary unit:** 1 Jamaica dollar (J$) = 100 cents; valuation (28 Jun 2002) US$1 = J$48.25.

Demography

Area: 4,244 sq mi, 10,991 sq km. **Population** (2001): 2,624,000. **Density** (2001): persons per sq mi 618.2, persons per sq km 238.7. **Urban** (1998): 55.1%. **Sex distribution** (1998): male 49.85%; female 50.15%. **Age breakdown** (1998): under 15, 31.5%; 15-29, 27.5%; 30-44, 20.9%; 45-59, 10.4%; 60-74, 6.6%; 75 and over, 3.1%. **Ethnic composition** (2000): local black 77.0%; local mulatto 14.6%; Haitian 2.0%; East Indian 1.7%; black-East Indian 1.6%; other 3.1%. **Religious affiliation** (1995): Protestant 39.0%, of which Pentecostal 10.5%, Seventh-day Adventist 6.1%, Baptist 5.3%; Roman Catholic 10.4%; Anglican 3.7%; other (including non-religious) 46.9%. **Major cities** (1991): Kingston 103,771 (metropolitan area 587,798); Spanish Town 92,383; Portmore 90,138; Montego Bay 83,446; May Pen 46,785. **Location:** island in the Caribbean Sea south of Cuba.

Vital statistics

Birth rate per 1,000 pop. (2000): 20.0 (world avg. 22.5). **Death rate** per 1,000 pop. (2000): 5.1 (world avg. 9.0). **Natural increase rate** per 1,000 pop. (2000): 14.9 (world avg. 13.5). **Total fertility rate** (avg. births per childbearing woman; 1997): 2.8. **Marriage rate** per 1,000 pop. (1996): 7.4. **Life expectancy** at birth (2000): male 73.3 years; female 77.3 years.

National economy

Budget (1998–99). *Revenue:* J$74,096,000,000 (tax revenue 90.4%, of which income taxes 34.9%, consumption taxes 28.3%, custom duties 9.6%; non-tax revenue 9.6%). *Expenditures:* J$93,267,000,000 (current expenditure 91.5%, of which debt interest 37.4%). **Public debt** (external, outstanding; 1999): US$2,905,000,000. Production (metric tons except as noted). *Agriculture, forestry, fishing* (1999): sugarcane 2,400,000, yams 198,400, vegetables and melons 183,701; livestock (number of live animals) 440,000 goats, 400,000 cattle, 180,000 pigs; roundwood (1998) 342,700 cu m; fish catch (1998) 6,720. *Mining and quarrying* (1999): bauxite 4,034,600; alumina 3,440,000; gypsum 154,500. *Manufacturing* (valued added in constant 1991–95 prices, J$'000,000; 1995): machinery and equipment 593.6; food processing 580.3; petroleum products 351.3. *Energy production (consumption):* electricity (kW-hr; 1996) 6,038,000,000 (6,038,000,000); crude petroleum (barrels; 1996) none (7,828,000); petroleum products (metric tons; 1996) 1,055,000 (3,135,000). **Population economically active** (October 1999): total 1,115,600; activity rate of total pop. 43.1% (participation rates: ages 14 and over 64.1%; female 44.7%; unemployed 16.0%). **Gross national product** (1999): US$6,311,000,000 (US$2,430 per capita). **Household income and expenditure.** Average household size (1991) 4.2; average annual income per household (1988) J$8,356; sources of income (1989): wages and salaries 66.1%, self-employment 19.3%, transfers 14.6%; expenditure (1988): food and beverages 55.6%, housing 7.9%, fuel and other household supplies 7.4%, health care 7.0%, transportation 6.4%. **Tourism:** receipts (2000) US$1,332,-600,000; expenditures (1999) US$227,000,000.

Foreign trade

Imports (1999): US$2,892,761,000 (raw materials 50.5%, of which fuels 10.8%; consumer goods 33.2%, of which food 9.4%; capital goods 16.3%, of which machinery and apparatus 7.6%). *Major import sources* (1997): US 48.1%; Trinidad and Tobago 7.8%; Japan 6.9%; France 5.0%; UK 3.7%; Canada 3.0%. **Exports** (1999): US$1,237,982,000 (crude materials 55.7%; food 19.1%; beverages and tobacco 4.8%; chemicals 3.6%; machinery and transport

equipment 2.2%; manufactured goods 0.7%). *Major export destinations:* US 33.4%; Canada 14.1%; UK 13.4%; The Netherlands 10.2%; Norway 5.8%.

Transport and communications

Transport. *Railroads* (1991): route length 129 mi, 208 km; passenger-mi 12,127,000 (1990), passenger-km 19,516,000; short ton-mi cargo 1,700,000, metric ton-km cargo 2,482,000. *Roads* (1996): total length 11,800 mi, 19,000 km (paved 71%). *Vehicles* (1999–00): passenger cars 160,948; trucks and buses 55,596. *Air transport* (1999): passenger-mi 1,037,565,000, passenger-km 1,669,803,000; short ton-mi cargo 20,186,000, metric ton-km cargo 29,471,000; airports (1997) with scheduled flights 4. **Communications** Total units (units per 1,000 persons). Daily newspaper circulation (1996): 158,000 (63); Radio receivers (1997): 1,215,000 (483); Television receivers (1998): 480,000 (187); Telephone main lines (1999): 509,646 (197); Cellular telephone subscribers (1999): 144,388 (56); Personal computers (1999): 110,000 (43); Internet users (1999): 60,000 (23).

Education and health

Educational attainment (1982). Percentage of pop. age 25 and over having: no formal schooling 3.2%; some primary education 79.8%; some secondary 15.0%; complete secondary and higher 2.0%. **Literacy** (2000): total pop. age 15 and over literate 88%; males 83%; females 91%. **Health** (2000): physicians 435 (1 per 5,988 persons); hospital beds 3,511 (1 per 742 persons); infant mortality rate 14.6. **Food** (1999): daily per capita caloric intake 2,708 (vegetable products 83%, animal products 17%); 121% of FAO recommended minimum requirement.

Military

Total active duty personnel (2000): 2,830 (army 88.3%; coast guard 6.7%; air force 5.0%). **Military expenditure as percentage of GNP** (1997): 0.9% (world 2.6%); per capita expenditure US$20.

Background

The island was settled by Arawak Indians c. AD 600. It was sighted by Christopher Columbus in 1494; Spain colonized it in the early 16th century but neglected it because it lacked gold reserves. Britain gained control in 1655, and by the end of the 18th century it had become a prized colonial possession due to the volume of sugar produced by slave laborers. Slavery was abolished in the late 1830s, and the plantation system collapsed. Jamaica gained full internal self-government in 1959 and became an independent country within the British Commonwealth in 1962.

Recent Developments

Tourism was dealt a severe blow in 2001 when four cruise lines dropped Jamaica from their itineraries following complaints about visitor harassment. Jamaica's police service was sharply criticized for its violations of human rights in an Amnesty International report the government described as "one-sided,

---

1 metric ton = about 1.1 short tons;　1 kilometer = 0.6 mi (statute);　1 metric ton-km cargo = about 0.68 short ton-mi cargo;　c.i.f.: cost, insurance, and freight;　f.o.b.: free on board

false, and misleading." After responding to public concern over an increase in crime by establishing a specialized police unit in 2000, the government set up a commission of inquiry in 2001 to recommend measures for dealing with inner-city gang warfare linked with the drug trade and organized crime.

Internet Resources: <www.discoverjamaica.com>

Japan

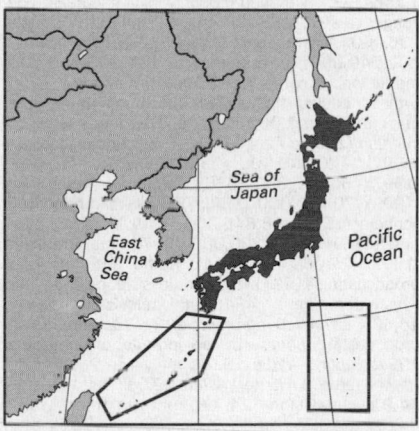

Official name: Nihon (Japan). **Form of government:** constitutional monarchy with a national Diet consisting of two legislative houses (House of Councillors [247]; House of Representatives [480]). **Chief of state:** Emperor Akihito (from 1989). **Head of government.** Prime Minister Junichiro Koizumi (from 2001). **Capital:** Tokyo. **Official language:** Japanese. **Official religion:** none. **Monetary unit:** 1 yen (¥) = 100 sen; valuation (28 Jun 2002) $1 = ¥119.86.

Demography

Area: 145,884 sq mi, 377,837 sq km. **Population** (2001): 127,100,000. **Density** (2001): persons per sq mi 871.2, persons per sq km 336.4. **Urban** (1999): 78.6%. **Sex distribution** (1999): male 48.9%; female 51.1%. **Age breakdown** (1999): under 15, 14.8%; 15–29, 20.9%; 30–44, 19.3%; 45–59, 22.2%; 60–74, 16.0%; 75 and over, 6.8%. **Composition** by nationality (1997): Japanese 99.1%; Korean 0.5%; Chinese 0.2%; other 0.2%. **Place of birth** (1995): 99.3% native-born; 0.7% foreign-born (mainly Korean). **Immigration** (1998): permanent immigrants/registered aliens admitted 1,482,707, from North and South Korea 43.5%, Taiwan, Hong Kong, and China 17.0%, Brazil 15.7%, Philippines 6.3%, US 2.9%, Peru 2.7%, Thailand 1.4%, UK 1.0%, Indonesia 0.8%, Vietnam 0.8%, Canada 0.6%, Iran 0.5%, India 0.5%, other 6.3%. **Major cities** (2000): Tokyo 8,130,000; Yokohama 3,427,000; Osaka 2,599,000; Nagoya 2,171,000; Sapporo 1,822,000; Kobe 1,494,000; Kyoto 1,468,000; Fukuoka 1,341,000; Kawasaki 1,250,000; Hiroshima 1,126,000; Kita-Kyushu 1,011,000; Sendai 1,008,000. **Location:** eastern Asia; island chain between the North Pacific Ocean and the Sea of Japan. **Religious affiliation** (1995): Shinto and related religions 93.1% (many Japanese

practice both Shintoism and Buddhism); Buddhism 69.6%; Christian 1.2%; other 8.1%. **Households** (1995). Total households 43,899,923; average household size 2.8; composition of households 1 person 25.6%, 2 persons 23.0%, 3 persons 18.5%, 4 persons 18.8%, 5 persons 8.0%, 6 or more persons 6.1%. Family households 32,533,000 (74.1%); nonfamily 11,366,900 (25.9%), of which 1 person 11,239,400 (25.6%). **Mobility** (October 1990). Population living in same residence as in October 1985, 74.7%; different residence, same town 9.5%; same prefecture 7.9%; different prefecture 7.6%; different country 0.3%.

Vital statistics

Birth rate per 1,000 pop. (1999): 9.3 (world avg. 22.5); (1985) legitimate 99.0%; illegitimate 1.0%. **Death rate** per 1,000 pop. (1999): 7.8 (world avg. 9.0). **Natural increase rate** per 1,000 pop. (1999): 1.5 (world avg. 13.5). **Total fertility rate** (avg. births per childbearing woman; 1999): 1.4. **Marriage rate** per 1,000 pop. (1998): 6.3; (1996) average age at first marriage men 28.5 years, women 26.4 years. **Divorce rate** per 1,000 pop. (1998): 0.7. **Life expectancy** at birth (2000): male 77.5 years; female 84.0 years.

Social indicators

Quality of working life. Average hours worked per month (1998): 153.5. Annual rate of industrial deaths per 100,000 workers (1998): 1.7. Proportion of labor force insured for damages or income loss resulting from injury, permanent disability, and death (1991): 50.1%. Average man-days lost to labor stoppages per 1,000,000 workdays (1998): 6.8. Average duration of journey to work (1996): 19.0 minutes (1983; 26.7% private automobile. 67.4% public transportation, 5.5% taxi, 0.4% other). Rate per 1,000 workers of discouraged (unemployed no longer seeking work; 1997): 89.4. **Access to services** (1989). Proportion of households having access to: gas supply 64.6%; safe public water supply 94.0%; public sewage collection 89.4%. **Social participation.** Eligible voters participating in last national election (October 1996): 59.6%. Population 15 years and over participating in social-service activities on a voluntary basis (1991): 26.3%. Trade union membership in total workforce (1996): 18.7%. **Social deviance** (1998). Offense rate per 100,000 pop. for: homicide 1.1; rape 1.5; robbery 2.7; larceny and theft 1,415. Rate of suicide per 100,000 pop.: 25.4. **Material well-being** (1994). Households possessing: automobile 79.7%; telephone, virtually 100%; color television receiver 99.3%; refrigerator 98.9%; air conditioner 72.3%; washing machine 99.4%; vacuum cleaner 98.7%; videocassette recorder 82.8%; camera 86.8%; microwave oven 84.3%; compact disc player 53.8%.

National economy

Gross national product (at current market prices; 1999): $4,045,545,000,000 ($32,035 per capita). **Budget** (2000–01). *Revenue:* ¥52,377,000,000,-000 (income tax 35.7%; corporation tax 19.0%; value-added tax 18.8%; liquor and tobacco tax 6.4%; fuel taxes 4.0%; stamp and customs duties 2.9%). *Expenditures:* ¥70,057,000,000,000 (debt service 31.4%; social security 23.9%; public works 14.2%; national defense 7.0%). **Public debt** (1998):

$2,412,200,000,000 (¥278,847,900,000,000). **Population economically active** (1998): total 67,930,000; activity rate of total pop. 53.7% (participation rates: age 15 and over, 63.7% (1997); female 40.7%; unemployed 4.1%). **Household income and expenditure** (1999). Average household size 2.8; average annual income per household ¥6,896,100; sources of income (1994): wages and salaries 59.0%, transfer payments 20.5%, self-employment 12.8%, other 7.3%; expenditure (1999): food 23.7%, transportation and communications 10.6%, recreation 10.3%, fuel, light, and water charges 6.7%, housing 6.5%, clothing and footwear 5.4%, education 4.2%, furniture and household utensils 3.6%, medical care 3.5%. **Tourism** (1999): receipts from visitors $3,428,000,000; expenditures by nationals abroad $32,808,000,000. **Land use** (1994): forested 66.4%; meadows and pastures 1.8%; agricultural and under permanent cultivation 11.7%; other 20.1%. **Production** (metric tons except as noted). *Agriculture, forestry, fishing* (2000): rice 11,863,000, sugar beets 3,800,000, potatoes 2,900,000, cabbages 2,600,000, sugarcane 1,512,000; livestock (number of live animals) 9,879,000 pigs, 4,658,000 cattle, 296,000,000 chickens; roundwood (1999) 19,031,000 cu m; fish catch (1998) 5,315,000, of which mackerel 1,122,000, sardines 739,000, squid 385,000, Alaska pollack 316,000, crabs 44,000. *Mining and quarrying* (1999): limestone 180,193,000; silica stone 18,312,000; dolomite 3,648,000; pyrophyllite 694,000; zinc 64,263. *Manufacturing* (1999): crude steel 94,192,000; steel products 86,335,000 (1996); cement 80,120,000; pig iron 74,520,000; sulfuric acid 6,493,000; 9,639,000 computers (1998), 8,100,000 passenger cars, 3,444,000 color television receivers, 5,975,000 bicycles (1998), 4,851,000 electric refrigerators (1998), 4,468,000 automatic washing machines (1998), 2,959,000 microwave ovens (1998), 2,252,000 motorcycles, 1,903,000 (1996) photocopy machines. *Energy production (consumption):* electricity (kW-hr; 1996) 1,012,145,000,000 (1,012,145,000,000); coal (metric tons; 1996) 6,480,000 (132,582,000); crude petroleum (barrels; 1996) 3,796,000 (1,616,793,000); petroleum products (metric tons; 1996) 185,422,000, of which (by volume) diesel 34.3%, heavy fuel oil 22.0%. Composition of energy supply by source (1998): crude oil and petroleum products 50.9%, coal 17.0%, natural gas 12.8%, nuclear power 14.2%, hydroelectric power 4.1%, other 1.0%. Domestic energy demand by end use (1998): mining and manufacturing 46.3%, residential and commercial 26.3%, transportation 25.2%, other 2.2%.

Foreign trade

Imports (1998): ¥36,654,000,000,000 (machinery and transport equipment 27.6%, food products 13.0%, petroleum and petroleum products 9.5%, chemicals and chemical products 7.4%, textiles 5.2%). *Major import sources:* US 23.9%; China 13.2%; Australia 4.6%; South Korea 4.3%; Indonesia 3.9%. **Exports** (1998): ¥50,645,000,000,000 (electrical machinery 23.2%, motor vehicles 12.9%, chemicals 7.0%, scientific and optical equipment 4.2%, iron and steel products 3.8%, textiles and allied products 2.0%). *Major export destinations:* US

30.5%; Taiwan 6.6%; Hong Kong 6.5%; China 5.2%; Germany 4.9%.

Transport and communications

Transport. *Railroads* (1998): length 27,258 km (1996); rolling stock—locomotives 1,787 (1995), passenger cars 25,973 (1995), freight cars 12,688 (1995); passengers carried 22,013,000,000; passenger-km 388,938,000,000; metric ton-km cargo 22,920,000,000. *Roads* (1998): total length 1,156,000 km (paved 73%). *Vehicles* (1998): passenger cars 51,222,000; trucks 18,425,000; buses 236,000. *Air transport* (1998): passengers carried 102,749,000; passenger-km 157,305,000,000; metric ton-km cargo 7,183,000,000; airports (1996) with scheduled flights 73. **Communications** Total units (units per 1,000 persons). Daily newspaper circulation (1998): 72,410,000 (572); Radio receivers (1997): 120,500,000 (955); Television receivers (1997): 86,500,000 (686); Telephone main lines (1999): 70,530,000 (558); Cellular telephone subscribers (1999): 56,846,000 (449); Personal computers (1999): 36,300,000 (287); Internet users (1999): 27,060,000 (214). **Radio and television broadcasting** (1994): total radio stations 1,340, of which commercial 481; total television stations 14,625, of which commercial 7,736. *Commercial broadcasting hours* (by percentage of programs; 1994): reports—radio 13.0%, television 21.0%; education—radio 3.4%, television 12.0%; culture—radio 14.9%, television 24.7%; entertainment—radio 67.6%, television 40.0%. *Advertisements* (daily average; 1994): radio 148, television 295.

Education and health

Educational attainment (1990). Percentage of pop. age 25 years and over having: primary education 34.3%; secondary 44.5%; postsecondary 21.2%. **Literacy:** total pop. age 15 and over literate, virtually 100%. **Health** (1998): physicians 248,611 (1 per 508 persons); dentists 88,061 (1 per 1,436 persons); nurses 985,821 (1 per 128 persons); pharmacists 205,953 (1 per 614 persons); midwives 24,202 (1 per 5,223 persons); hospital beds 1,656,415 (1 per 76 persons), of which general 76.1%, mental 21.7%, tuberculosis 1.6%, other 0.6%; infant mortality rate per 1,000 live births (1999) 3.4. **Food** (1999): daily per capita caloric intake 2,782 (vegetable products 79%, animal products 21%); 119% of FAO recommended minimum.

Military

Total active duty personnel (2000): 236,700 (army 62.7%, navy 18.0%, air force 18.7%). **Military expenditure as percentage of GNP** (1997): 1.0% (world 2.6%); per capita expenditure $325.

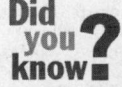 **Did you know?** More than 80% of Japan is covered by mountains. As a result, most of the population is concentrated on the habitable plains and valleys, making these areas some of the most densely populated on Earth.

1 metric ton = about 1.1 short tons;   1 kilometer = 0.6 mi (statute);   1 metric ton-km cargo = about 0.68 short ton-mi cargo;   c.i.f.: cost, insurance, and freight;   f.o.b.: free on board

Background

Japan's history began with the accession of the legendary first emperor, Jimmu, in 660 BC. The Yamato court established the first unified Japanese state in the 4th–5th century AD; during this period, Buddhism arrived in Japan by way of Korea. For centuries Japan borrowed heavily from Chinese culture, but it began to sever its links with the mainland by the 9th century. In 1192 Minamoto Yoritomo established Japan's first *bakufu*, or shogunate. Unification was achieved in the late 1500s under the leadership of Oda Nobunaga, Toyotomi Hideyoshi, and Tokugawa Ieyasu. During the Tokugawa shogunate, beginning in 1603, the government imposed a policy of isolation. Under the leadership of Emperor Meiji (1868–1912), it adopted a constitution (1889) and began a program of modernization and Westernization. Japanese imperialism led to war with China (1894–95) and Russia (1904–05) as well as to the annexation of Korea (1910) and Manchuria (1931). During World War II Japan attacked US forces in Hawaii and the Philippines (December 1941) and occupied European colonial possessions in South Asia. In 1945 the US dropped atomic bombs on Hiroshima and Nagasaki, and Japan surrendered to the Allied powers. US postwar occupation of Japan led to a new democratic constitution in 1947. In rebuilding Japan's ruined industrial plant, new technology was used in every major industry. A tremendous economic recovery followed, and it was able to maintain a favorable balance of trade into the 1990s.

Recent Developments

A recession in 1998 came on the heels of a financial crisis and resulted in dissatisfaction with the ruling Liberal-Democratic Party (LDP). After the party's poor showing in the legislative elections, Prime Minister Ryutaro Hashimoto resigned and was replaced by Keizo Obuchi. Bank failures and a shrinking gross domestic product meant that Japan's expected role as an engine of growth for Asia and the rest of the world remained in doubt. Obuchi's popularity grew during 1999, and the economy underwent a mild recovery mid-year after unemployment rates reached record highs at the end of 1998. In May 2000, however, Obuchi died and was succeeded by Yoshiro Mori.

During 2000 economic recovery measures were put in place after another downturn at the end of 1999. Also in 2000, Tokyo Governor Shintaro Ishihara urged controversial actions such as expanding the Japanese military and outraged the public with remarks doubting the occurrence of the Nanking Massacre and using derogatory terms for immigrants. More positive events included the election of Japan's first two female governors and the holding of the G-8 summit on Okinawa in July. After committing several major and very public blunders during his year in office, Mori garnered the lowest public-approval rating ever for a Japanese prime minister; he resigned in April 2001. Junichiro Koizumi was chosen president of the LDP and prime minister later that month.

The new regime has enjoyed popular support, resulting in party gains in the legislative elections, and its cabinet includes several women and representatives of diverse political factions. Koizumi, however, raised international tensions in August 2001 when he visited a shrine memorializing Japan's dead veterans, including several well-known convicted war criminals. A collision in February 2001 between an American submarine and a Japanese fishing trawler left nine of the trawler's passengers missing. In December the royal family celebrated the birth of the first child—a daughter—to Crown Princess Masako and Crown Prince Naruhito, prompting calls to change a national law prohibiting female successors to the throne. Japan entered another recession in 2001, again encountering some of its highest-ever unemployment rates. Economic problems were exacerbated by the country's declining birthrate and its status as the fastest-aging society among advanced industrial powers. Signs of recovery began to appear in mid-2002. Incidents involving US military personnel based on Okinawa increased controversy in 2001 over the American military presence on the island, and in March 2002 a US sergeant was found guilty of rape by a Japanese court.

Internet Resources: <www.jnto.go.jp>

Jersey

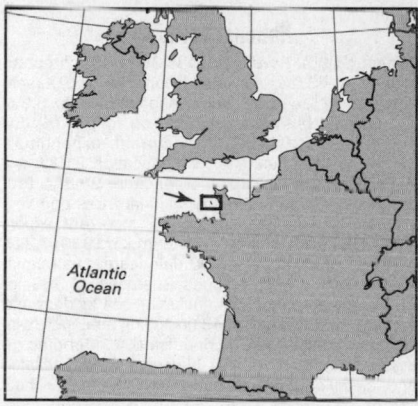

Atlantic Ocean

Official name: Bailiwick of Jersey. **Political status:** Crown dependency (UK) with one legislative house (States of Jersey [57; {53 elected members include 12 senators popularly elected for 6-year terms, 12 constables popularly elected triennially, and 29 deputies also popularly elected triennially; 4 non-elected members include the bailiff, the dean of Jersey, the attorney general, and the solicitor general}]). **Chief of state:** British Monarch Queen Elizabeth II (from 1952) represented by Lieutenant Governor Sir John Cheshire (from 2001). **Head of government:** Executive committees appointed by the States of Jersey (alternately called States Assembly). **Capital:** Saint Helier. **Official language:** English (until the 1960s French was an official language of Jersey and is still used by the court and legal professions; Jerriais, a Norman-French dialect, is spoken by a small number of residents). **Official religion:** none. **Monetary unit:** 1 Jersey pound (£J) = 100 pence; valuation (28 Jun 2002) 1 Jersey pound = $1.52.

Demography

Area: 44.9 sq mi, 116.2 sq km. **Population (2001):** 89,400. **Density (2001):** persons per sq mi 1,991.1, persons per sq km 769.4. **Sex distribution (2000):** male 49.07%; female 50.93%. **Age breakdown**

(2000): under 15, 17.7%; 15–29, 15.8%; 30–44, 27.2%; 45–59, 19.7%; 60–74, 12.9%; 75 and over, 6.7%. **Population by place of birth** (1996): Jersey 52.7%; UK, Guernsey, or Isle of Man 34.5%; Portugal 5.4%; Ireland 2.6%; France 1.1%; other European Union 1.1%; other 2.6%. **Religious affiliation** (2000; includes Guernsey): Christian 86.0%, of which Anglican 44.1%, Roman Catholic 14.6%, other Protestant 6.9%, unaffiliated Christian 20.1%; nonreligious/atheist 13.4%; other 0.6%. **Major cities** (1996; pop. of parishes): St. Helier 27,523; St. Saviour 12,680; St. Brelade 9,560. **Location:** western Europe, island in the English Channel.

Vital statistics

Birth rate per 1,000 pop. (2000): 11.6 (world avg. 22.5). **Death rate** per 1,000 pop. (2000): 9.3 (world avg. 9.0). **Natural increase rate** per 1,000 pop. (2000): 2.3 (world avg. 13.5). **Total fertility rate** (avg. births per childbearing woman; 2000): 1.6. **Life expectancy** at birth (2000): male 76.1 years; female 81.1 years.

National economy

Budget (2000). *Revenue:* £388,389,000 (corporate income tax 43.0%, individual income tax 26.9%, self-employment tax 11.6%, spirits and tobacco tax 6.0%, international business 5.4%, tax on fuel 3.0%). *Expenditures:* £300,030,000 (current expenditure 79.2%, of which health 27.8%, education 21.3%, social security 20.5%; capital expenditure 20.8%). **Production.** *Agriculture, forestry, fishing:* fruits and vegetables; greenhouse flowers are important export crops; livestock (number of live animals; 1999) 7,315 cattle, of which about 4,500 dairy cattle; fish catch (metric tons; 1997; includes Guernsey): 4,368, of which crustaceans 2,934 (including sea spiders and crabs 2,713); mollusks 743 (including abalones, winkles, and conch 438); marine fish 691. *Manufacturing:* light industry, mainly electrical goods, textiles and clothing; dairy products (including 179 hectolitres of milk in 1999). *Energy production (consumption):* electricity (kW-hr; 1995) 266,000,000 (467,000,000). **Gross national product** (at current market prices; 1995): $2,670,000,000 ($30,940 per capita). **Household income and expenditure.** Average household size (1996) 2.4; expenditure (1998–99; weights of retail price index components): housing 20.1%, recreation 16.5%, transportation 12.8%, household furnishings 11.6%, food 11.5%, alcoholic beverages 6.0%, clothing and footwear 5.5%. **Population economically active** (1996): total 46,992; activity rate of total pop. 55.2% (participation rates: ages 15–64, n.a.; female 44.6%; unemployed 3.3%). **Tourism** (1996): receipts $429,000,000; number of visitors for at least one night 670,000. **Land use** (1997): land under cultivation 56.8%, other 43.2%.

Foreign trade

Imports: customs ceased recording imports and exports as of 1980. *Major import sources* (1999): mostly the UK. **Exports:** (customs ceased recording imports and exports as of 1980); agricultural exports (1996): £45,400,000 (potatoes 61.2%, greenhouse tomatoes 17.2%, zucchini 6.4%, greenhouse carnations and narcissus 6.0%). *Major export destinations:* mostly the UK.

Transport and communications

Transport. *Railroads:* none. *Roads* (1995): total length 346 mi, 557 km (paved 100%). *Vehicles* (1995): passenger cars 58,491; trucks and buses 9,109. *Air transport* (1999; Jersey European Airways): passenger-mi 553,291,000, passenger-km 890,438,000; short ton-mi cargo 632,000, metric ton-km cargo 923,000; *airports* (1999) with scheduled flights 1. **Communications** Total units (units per 1,000 persons). Daily newspaper circulation (1997): 25,542 (299); Telephone main lines (1998): 68,721 (781); Cellular telephone subscribers (1998): 18,255 (208); Internet users (1999): 1,000 (12).

Education and health

Literacy (1996): total pop. age 15 and over literate 71,033 (100.0%). **Health** (1995): physicians 95 (1 per 895 persons); hospital beds 651 (1 per 130 persons); infant mortality rate per 1,000 live births (2000) 5.7.

Military

Total active duty personnel (2000): none; defense is the responsibility of the UK.

Internet resources: <www.jersey.com>

Jordan

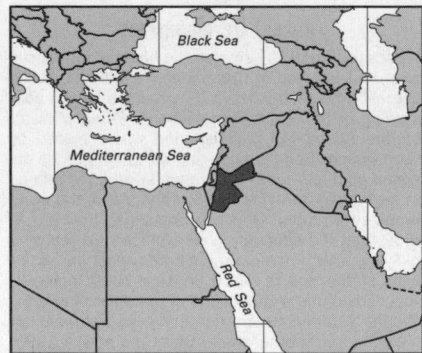

Official name: Al-Mamlakah al-Urdunniyah al-Hashimiyah (Al-Urdun) (Hashemite Kingdom of Jordan). **Form of government:** constitutional monarchy with two legislative houses (Senate [40 (all seats are appointed by king)]; House of Representatives [80]). **Head of state and government:** King Abdullah II (from 1999) assisted by Prime Minister 'Ali Abu ar-Raghib (from 2000). **Capital:** Amman. **Official language:** Arabic. **Official religion:** Islam. **Monetary unit:** 1 Jordan dinar (JD) = 1,000 fils; valuation (28 Jun 2002) JD 1.00 = $0.71.

Demography

Area: 34,495 sq mi, 89,342 sq km. **Population** (2001): 5,132,000. **Density** (2001): persons per sq mi 148.8, persons per sq km 57.4. **Urban** (2000):

---

1 metric ton = about 1.1 short tons;   1 kilometer = 0.6 mi (statute);   1 metric ton-km cargo = about 0.68 short ton-mi cargo;   c.i.f.: cost, insurance, and freight;   f.o.b.: free on board

74.2%. **Sex distribution** (2001): male 52.35%; female 47.65%. **Age breakdown** (2000): under 15, 37.9%; 15–29, 30.9%; 30–44, 18.3%; 45–59, 7.8%; 60–74, 4.2%; 75 and over, 0.9%. **Ethnic composition** (2000): Arab 97.8%, of which Jordanian 32.4%, Palestinian 32.2%, Iraqi 14.0%, Bedouin 12.8%; Circassian 1.2%; Armenian 1.7%. **Religious affiliation** (2000): Shi'i Muslim 59.5%; Sunni Muslim 36.5%; Christian 3.2%. **Major cities** (1994): Amman 969,598; Az-Zarqa' 350,849; Irbid 208,329; Ar-Rusayfah 137,247; Al-'Aqabah 62,773. **Location:** the Middle East, bordering Syria, Iraq, Saudi Arabia, the Gulf of Aqaba, Israel, and parts of the Emerging Palestinian Autonomous Areas.

Vital statistics

Birth rate per 1,000 pop. (2000): 26.2 (world avg. 22.5). **Death rate** per 1,000 pop. (2000): 2.6 (world avg. 9.0). **Natural increase rate** per 1,000 pop. (2000): 23.6 (world avg. 13.5). **Total fertility rate** (avg. births per childbearing woman; 2000): 3.4. **Life expectancy** at birth (2000): male 74.9 years; female 79.9 years.

National economy

Budget (1998 est.). *Revenue:* JD 1,688,000,000 (taxes 50.8%, of which sales tax 20.7%, custom duties 17.1%, income and profits taxes 8.3%; nontax 37.1%, of which licenses and fees 11.4%; external aid 12.0%). *Expenditures:* JD 2,047,000,000 (current expenditure 81.9%, of which defense 24.1%, interest expense 11.7%, wages and salaries 17.2%; development expenditure 18.1%). **Public debt** (external, outstanding; 1999): $7,546,000,000. **Production** (metric tons except as noted). *Agriculture, forestry, fishing* (1999): tomatoes 305,100, watermelons 97,400, potatoes 92,600; livestock (number of live animals) 2,000,000 sheep, 795,000 goats, 65,000 cattle; roundwood (1998) 3,000 cu m; fish catch (1998) 470. *Mining and quarrying* (1998): phosphate ore 5,925,000; potash 1,527,000. *Manufacturing* (value added in JD '000; 1997): chemicals 130,276; nonmetallic mineral products, pottery, and china 114,897; tobacco products 96,380. *Energy production (consumption):* electricity (kW-hr; 1996) 6,058,000,000 (6,058,000,000); crude petroleum (barrels; 1996) 14,400 (23,790,000); petroleum products (metric tons; 1996) 3,102,000 (3,932,000). **Land use** (1994): forest 0.8%; pasture 8.9%; agriculture 4.6%; other 85.7%. **Tourism** (1999): receipts $795,000,000; expenditures $355,000,000. **Population economically active** (1993): total 859,300; activity rate of total pop. 22.2% (participation rates: over age 15, 43.6%; female 14.0%; unemployed [1996] 13.0%). **Gross national product** (1999): $7,717,000,-000 ($1,630 per capita). **Household income and expenditure.** Average household size (1995) 6.1; income per household (1995) JD 4,010; sources of income (1995): wages and salaries 51.4%, rent and property income 23.8%, transfer payments 13.7%, self-employment 11.1%; expenditure (1992): food and beverages 40.6%, housing and energy 26.9%, transportation 11.2%, clothing and footwear 8.2%, education 3.5%, health care 2.2%.

Foreign trade

Imports (1998): JD 2,719,900,000 (machinery and transport equipment 28.5%; food and live animals

19.6%; chemicals and chemical products 12.7%; mineral fuels 9.4%; iron and steel 4.0%). *Major import sources:* Germany 9.8%; US 9.5%; Iraq 8.8%; Japan 5.8%; UK 5.1%; Italy 4.9%. **Exports** (1998): JD 1,275,600,000 (domestic exports 81.9%, of which chemicals and chemical products 25.3%, phosphate fertilizers 11.0%, potash 8.7%, fruits, vegetables, and nuts 8.3%, machinery and transport equipment 3.5%; reexports 18.1%). *Major export destinations* (domestic exports only): India 11.2%; Iraq 10.3%; Saudi Arabia 9.9%; Lebanon 2.9%; Kuwait 2.6%.

Transport and communications

Transport. *Railroads* (1995): route length 677 km; passenger traffic was negligible; metric ton-km cargo (for Aqaba Railway Corporation only) 1,336,000,000. *Roads* (1998): total length 7,133 km (paved 100%). *Vehicles* (1996): passenger cars 213,874; trucks and buses 79,153. *Air transport* (1998; Royal Jordanian airlines only): passenger-km 4,064,737,000; metric ton-km cargo 219,219,000; airports (1997) 2. **Communications.** Total units (units per 1,000 persons). Daily newspaper circulation (1996): 250,000 (57); Radio receivers (1997): 1,660,000 (395); Television receivers (1999): 540,000 (83); Telephone main lines (1999): 565,000 (85); Cellular telephone subscribers (1999): 118,000 (18); Personal computers (1999): 90,000 (14); Internet users (1999): 120,000 (19).

Education and health

Educational attainment (2000). Percentage of pop. age 25 and over having: no formal schooling 16.7%; primary education 49.2%; secondary 16.7%; postsecondary and vocational 9.5%; higher 8.2%. **Literacy** (2000): percentage of pop. age 15 and over literate 88.8%; males literate 94.9%; females literate 84.4%. **Health** (1998): physicians 7,480 (1 per 625 persons); hospital beds 8,565 (1 per 546 persons); infant mortality rate per 1,000 live births (2000) 21.1. **Food** (1999): daily per capita caloric intake 2,834 (vegetable products 89%, animal products 11%); 115% of FAO recommended minimum requirement.

Military

Total active duty personnel (2000): 103,800 (army 86.6%, navy 0.5%, air force 12.9%). **Military expenditure as percentage of GDP** (1997): 9.0% (world 2.6%); per capita expenditure $145.

Background

Jordan shares much of its history with Israel, since both occupied the area known historically as Palestine. Much of present-day eastern Jordan was incorporated into Israel under David and Solomon c. 1000 BC. It fell to the Seleucids in 330 BC and to Muslim Arabs in the 7th century AD. The Crusaders extended the kingdom of Jerusalem east of the Jordan River in 1099. Jordan submitted to Ottoman Turkish rule during the 16th century. In 1920 the area comprising Jordan (then known as the Transjordan) was established within the British mandate of Palestine. Transjordan became an independent state in 1927, although the British mandate did not end until 1948. After hostilities with the new state of Israel ceased in 1949, Jordan annexed the West Bank of the Jordan River, administering the territory until Israel gained control of it in the Six-Day War of 1967. In 1970–71

Jordan was wracked by fighting between the government and guerrillas of the Palestine Liberation Organization (PLO), a struggle that ended in the expulsion of the PLO from Jordan. In 1988 King Hussein renounced all Jordanian claims to the West Bank in favor of the PLO. In 1994 Jordan and Israel signed a full peace agreement.

Recent Developments

Upon the death of King Hussein in 1999, his son Abdullah took over the throne. King Abdullah II pursued an active foreign policy to consolidate Jordan's relationships with other Middle Eastern nations and to advance the Israeli-Palestinian peace process. He was also the first Arab leader to visit the United States after the 11 Sep 2001 terrorist attacks, where he pledged his support against terrorism. The Islamic Action Front, Jordan's most influential political group, opposed the revival of the Middle East peace process, declaring that "the strategic option of peace with Israel is no longer valid."

Internet resources: <www.seejordan.org>

Kazakhstan

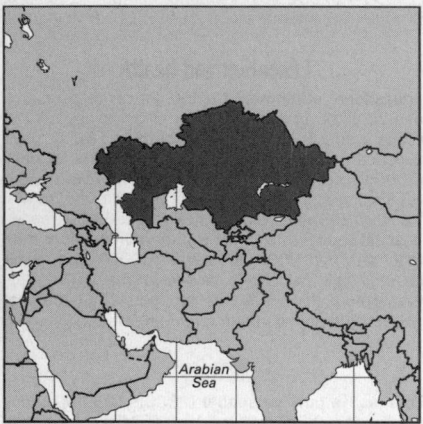

Arabian
Sea

Official name: Qazaqstan Respublikasy (Republic of Kazakhstan). **Form of government:** unitary republic with a Parliament consisting of two chambers (Senate [39, including 7 nonelective seats] and Assembly [77]). **Head of state and government:** President Nursultan Nazarbayev (from 1991) assisted by Prime Minister Imangali Tasmagambetov (from 28 Jan 2002). **Capital:** Astana (new name for the city of Akmola). **Official language:** Kazakh (Russian commands equal status at state-owned organizations and local government bodies). **Official religion:** none. **Monetary unit:** 1 tenge (T) = 100 tiyn; valuation (28 Jun 2002) free rate, $1 = 153.27 tenge.

Demography

Area: 1,052,100 sq mi, 2,724,900 sq km. **Population** (2001): 14,868,000. **Density** (2001): persons per sq mi 14.1, persons per sq km 5.5. **Urban** (1997): 57.0%. **Sex distribution** (1997): male 48.61%; female 51.39%. **Age breakdown** (1997): under 15, 29.3%; 15–29, 25.4%; 30–44, 22.2%; 45–59, 12.9%; 60 and over, 10.2%. **Ethnic composition** (1995): Kazakh 46.0%; Russian 34.7%; Ukrainian 4.9%; German 3.1%; Uzbek 2.3%; Tatar 1.9%; other 7.1%. **Religious affiliation** (1995): Muslim (mostly Sunni) 47.0%; Russian Orthodox 8.2%; Protestant 2.1%; other (mostly nonreligious) 42.7%. **Major cities** (1999): Almaty (Alma-Ata) 1,129,400; Qaraghandy (Karaganda) 436,900; Shymkent (Chimkent) 360,100; Taraz 330,100. **Location:** central Asia, bordering Russia, China, Kyrgyzstan, Uzbekistan, the Aral Sea, Turkmenistan, and the Caspian Sea.

Vital statistics

Birth rate per 1,000 pop. (2001): 16.5 (world avg. 22.5); (1994) legitimate 86.6%; illegitimate 13.4%. **Death rate** per 1,000 pop. (2001): 10.1 (world avg. 9.0). **Natural increase rate** per 1,000 pop. (2001): 6.4 (world avg. 13.5). **Total fertility rate** (avg. births per childbearing woman; 2001): 2.0. **Marriage rate** per 1,000 pop. (1996): 6.4. **Divorce rate** per 1,000 pop. (1996): 2.5. **Life expectancy** at birth (2001): male 59.0 years; female 71.0 years.

National economy

Budget (1998). *Revenue:* 262,916,000,000 tenge (taxes on goods and services 32.6%, social security contributions 23.4%, income, profits, and capital gains taxes 8.5%, taxes on international trade 3.7%, payroll taxes 3.2%). *Expenditures:* 318,252,000,000 tenge (social security and welfare 38.1%, general public services 7.9%, health 7.7%, public order 7.3%, defense 5.1%). **Public debt** (external, outstanding; 1999): $2,995,000,000. **Population economically active** (1995): total 6,976,000; activity rate of total pop. 41.8% (participation rates: ages 16–59 [male], 16–54 [female] 80.1%; female [1994] 48.0%; unemployed 2.3%). **Production** (metric tons except as noted). *Agriculture, forestry, fishing* (1999): wheat 11,242,000, barley 2,265,000, potatoes 1,695,000; livestock (number of live animals) 9,556,000 sheep and goats, 3,958,000 cattle, 986,000 horses; roundwood (1998) 315,000 cu m; fish catch (1997) 41,367. *Mining and quarrying* (1998): titanium 12,000,000; magnesium 9,000,000; iron ore 8,693,000. *Manufacturing* (value of production in '000,000 tenge; 1996): food products 107,397; nonferrous metallurgy 89,052; ferrous metallurgy 81,026. *Energy production (consumption):* electricity (kW-hr; 1996) 58,657,000,000 (65,502,000,000); coal (metric tons; 1996) 76,597,000 (55,852,000); crude petroleum (barrels; 1996) 150,000,000 (63,000,000); petroleum products (metric tons; 1996) 10,894,000 (10,627,000); natural gas (cu m; 1996) 7,107,000,000 (10,609,000,000). **Gross national product** (1999): $18,732,000,000 ($1,250 per capita). **Household income and expenditure.** Average household size (1989) 4.0; sources of income (1994): salaries and wages 67.7%, social benefits 16.9%, agricultural income 5.8%, other 9.6%; expenditure (1994): retail goods 60.6%, taxes 16.8%, services 11.7%, other 10.9%.

1 metric ton = about 1.1 short tons;   1 kilometer = 0.6 mi (statute);   1 metric ton-km cargo = about 0.68 short ton-mi cargo;   c.i.f.: cost, insurance, and freight;   f.o.b.: free on board

Foreign trade

Imports (1998): $6,574,700,000 (electrical equipment and mechanical tools 18.3%, vehicles 5.9%, nonfood consumer goods 5.4%, foodstuffs 3.7%, petroleum products 2.8%). *Major import sources*: Russia 39.4%; Germany 8.6%; US 6.3%; UK 5.0%; Uzbekistan 2.3%. **Exports** (1998): $5,773,800,000 (oil and gas condensate 28.6%, rolled ferrous metal 8.9%, refined copper 8.8%, coal 5.6%, grain 5.1%). *Major export destinations*: Russia 28.9%; UK 9.0%; China 7.2%; Switzerland 6.1%.

Transport and communications

Transport. *Railroads*: (1999) route length 13,500 km; (1998) passenger-km 13,000,000,000; metric ton-km cargo 107,500,000,000. *Roads* (1997): total length 125,796 km (paved 83%). *Vehicles* (1997): passenger cars 973,323; trucks and buses 361,920. *Air transport* (1995): passenger-km 2,429,000,000; metric ton-km cargo 237,000,000; airports (1997) with scheduled flights 20. **Communications** Total units (units per 1,000 persons). Radio receivers (1997): 6,470,000 (395); Television receivers (1998): 3,890,000 (238); Telephone main lines (1999): 1,760,000 (108); Cellular telephone subscribers (1999): 49,500 (3.0); Internet users (1999): 70,000 (4.3).

Education and health

Educational attainment (1989). Pop. age 25 and over having: primary education or no formal schooling 16.2%; some secondary 19.8%; completed secondary and some postsecondary 54.1%; higher 9.9%. **Literacy** (1989): pop. age 15 and over literate 97.5%; males 99.1%; females 96.1%. **Health** (1997): physicians 55,800 (1 per 287 persons); hospital beds 136,000 (1 per 115 persons); infant mortality rate per 1,000 live births (2001) 43.0.

Military

Total active duty personnel (2000): 64,000 (army 70.3%, air force 29.7%). **Military expenditure as percentage of GNP** (1997): 1.3% (world avg. 2.6%); per capita expenditure $41.

Background

Named for its earliest inhabitants, the Kazakhs, the area came under Mongol rule in the 13th century. The Kazakhs consolidated a nomadic empire in the 15th–16th century. Under Russian rule by the mid 19th century, it became part of the Kirgiz Autonomous Republic formed by the Soviets in 1920, and in 1925 its name was changed to the Kazakh Autonomous Soviet Socialist Republic. Kazakhstan obtained its independence from the Soviet Union in 1991, and during the 1990s was attempting to stabilize its economy.

Recent Developments

In 1998 Kazakhstan's capital, formerly at Almaty (Alma Ata), was moved to Astana. Concern grew over the activities of Islamic extremists in the south during 1999; in 2000 the country joined neighboring nations in drafting a program to combat international terrorism and stepped up its military presence along

the southern border. Conflicts also arose over government harassment of the media. In 2001 the government was criticized for its poor human rights record and its intolerance of certain religious groups.

Internet resources:
<www.kazstat.asdc.kz/indexe.htm>

Kenya

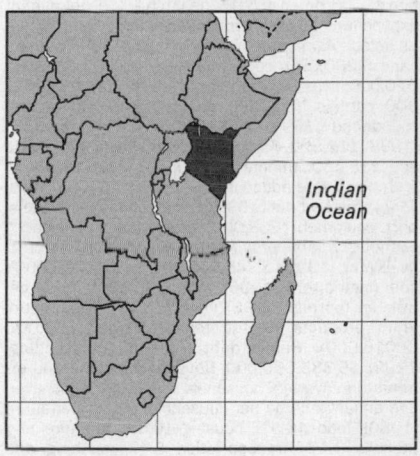

Official name: Jamhuri ya Kenya (Swahili); Republic of Kenya (English). **Form of government:** unitary multiparty republic with one legislative house (National Assembly [224; including 14 nonelective seats]). **Head of state and government:** President Daniel arap Moi (from 1978). **Capital:** Nairobi. **Official languages:** Swahili; English. **Official religion:** none. **Monetary unit:** 1 Kenya shilling (K Sh) = 100 cents; valuation (28 Jun 2002) $1 = K Sh 78.76.

Demography

Area: 224,961 sq mi, 582,646 sq km. **Population** (2001): 30,766,000. **Density** (2001): persons per sq mi 136.8, persons per sq km 52.8. **Urban** (1999): 32.2%. **Sex distribution** (1999): male 49.52%; female 50.48%. **Age breakdown** (1999): under 15, 43.6%; 15–29, 31.2%; 30–44, 14.1%; 45–59, 7.0%; 60–74, 3.3%; 75 and over, 0.8%. **Ethnic composition** (1989): Kikuyu 17.7%; Luhya 12.4%; Luo 10.6%; Kalenjin 9.8%; Kamba 9.8%; other 39.7%. **Religious affiliation** (2000): Christian 79.3%, of which Roman Catholic 22.0%, African Christian 20.8%, Protestant 20.1%; Muslim 7.3%; other 13.4%. **Major cities** (1999): Nairobi 2,143,254; Mombasa 465,000; Nakuru 231,262; Kisumu 185,100; Meru 126,427; Eldoret 104,900. **Location:** eastern Africa, bordering Ethiopia, Somalia, the Indian Ocean, Tanzania, Uganda, and The Sudan.

Vital statistics

Birth rate per 1,000 pop. (2000): 29.4 (world avg. 22.5). **Death rate** per 1,000 pop. (2000): 14.1 (world avg. 9.0). **Natural increase rate** per 1,000 pop. (2000): 15.3 (world avg. 13.5). **Total fertility rate** (avg. births per childbearing woman; 2000): 3.7.

Life expectancy at birth (2000): male 47.0 years; female 49.0 years.

National economy

Budget (1996–97). *Revenue:* K Sh 155,032,000,000 (tax revenue 83.4%, nontax revenue 12.9%, grants 3.7%). *Expenditures:* K Sh 168,403,000,000 (1995–96; recurrent expenditure 80.7%, of which interest on debt 24.3%, administration 21.9%, education 19.3%, defense 5.9%, health 5.8%; development expenditure 19.3%). **Production** (metric tons except as noted). *Agriculture, forestry, fishing* (1999): sugarcane 5,200,000, corn (maize) 2,100,000, cassava 920,000; livestock (number of live animals) 13,392,000 cattle, 7,600,000 goats, 5,800,000 sheep; roundwood (1998) 29,337,000 cu m; fish catch (1998) 172,592. *Mining and quarrying* (1995): soda ash 218,450; fluorite 80,230; salt 71,400. *Manufacturing* (value added in K £ [1 K £ = 20 K Sh] '000; 1994): food products 639,000; machinery and transport equipment 233,000; beverages and tobacco 190,000. *Energy production (consumption):* electricity (kW-hr; 1996) 3,745,000,000 (3,920,000,000); coal (metric tons; 1996) none (100,000); crude petroleum (barrels; 1996) none (13,487,000); petroleum products (metric tons; 1996) 1,722,000 (2,016,000). **Public debt** (external, outstanding; 1999): $5,385,000,000. **Household income and expenditure.** Average household size (1998): 3.4; average annual income per household: n.a.; expenditure (1980): food 46.5%, housing 10.0%, furniture and utensils 9.4%, transportation 8.4%, clothing and footwear 7.7%, energy 2.6%, health 2.2%. **Tourism** (1999): receipts from visitors $304,000,000; expenditures by nationals abroad $115,000,000. **Population economically active** (1997): total 14,592,000; activity rate of total pop. 50.0% (participation rates [1985]: ages 15–64, 76.2%; female [1997] 46.1%; unemployed, n.a.). **Gross national product** (1999): $10,696,000,000 ($360 per capita). **Land use** (1994): forest 29.5%; pasture 37.4%; agriculture 8.0%; other 25.1%.

Foreign trade

Imports (1997-c.i.f.): $3,294,000,000 (machinery and transport equipment 28.9%, manufactured goods 22.0%, mineral fuels 15.6%, chemical products 14.5%, food and beverages 12.4%). *Major import sources:* Middle East 15.8%; UK 10.7%; US 7.9%; Japan 7.4%; India 7.5%; South Africa 7.4%; Germany 6.0%; Italy 5.2%; Saudi Arabia 2.0%. **Exports** (1997-f.o.b.): $2,105,000,000 (tea 20.5%, coffee [not roasted] 14.3%, petroleum products 7.8%, horticulture 7.3%, fruits and vegetables 3.1%, cement 2.1%, soda ash 1.1%, hides and skins 0.6%). *Major export destinations:* Uganda 15.1%; Tanzania 12.9%; UK 11.4%; Germany 6.8%; The Netherlands 4.8%; US 3.0%.

Transport and communications

Transport. *Railroads* (1996): route length 3,034 km; passenger-km 385,000,000; metric ton-km cargo 1,309,000,000. *Roads* (1996): total length 63,800 km (paved 14%). *Vehicles* (1996): passenger cars 278,000; trucks and buses 81,200. *Air transport*

(1996): passenger-km 1,709,000,000; metric ton-km cargo 203,000,000; airports (1997) with scheduled flights 11. **Communications** Total unit (units per 1,000 persons). Daily newspaper circulation (1996): 263,000 (9.4 [for 4 newspapers only]); Radio receivers (1997): 3,070,000 (107); Television receivers (1999): 660,000 (23.0); Telephone main lines (1999): 304,626 (10.6); Cellular telephone subscribers (1999): 23,757 (0.8); Personal computers (1999): 125,000 (4.4); Internet users (1999): 35,000 (1.2).

Education and health

Educational attainment (1979). Percentage of pop. age 25 and over having: no formal schooling 58.6%; primary education 32.2%; some secondary 7.9%; complete secondary and higher 1.3%. **Literacy** (1995): total pop. over age 15 literate 77.3%; males literate 85.6%; females literate 69.1%. **Health** (1994): physicians 4,558 (1 per 5,999 persons); hospital beds 37,271 (1 per 734 persons); infant mortality rate per 1,000 live births (2000): 68.7. **Food** (1999): daily per capita caloric intake 1,887 (vegetable products 88%, animal products 12%); 81% of FAO recommended minimum requirement.

Military

Total active duty personnel (2000): 22,200 (army 82.0%, navy 4.5%, air force 13.5%). **Military expenditure as percentage of GNP** (1997): 7.2% (world 2.6%); per capita expenditure $7.

Background

The coastal region of East Africa was dominated by Arabs until it was seized by the Portuguese in the 16th century. The Masai people held sway in the north and moved into central Kenya in the 18th century, while the Kikuyu expanded from their home region in southern central Kenya. The interior was explored by European missionaries in the 19th century. After the British took control, Kenya was established as a British protectorate (1890) and a crown colony (1920). The Mau Mau rebellion of the 1950s was directed against European colonialism. In 1963 the country became fully independent, and a year later a republican government under Jomo Kenyatta was elected. In 1992 Kenyan president Daniel arap Moi allowed the country's first multiparty elections in three decades, though the balloting was marred by violence and fraud. Political turmoil occurred over the next years.

Recent Developments

In 1998 the bombing of the US embassy in Nairobi resulted in some 260 deaths. Governmental corruption continued to create problems with foreign aid distribution by the International Monetary Fund into 2002, despite efforts at reform during 2000. In 2001 Kenya joined Tanzania and Uganda in launching the East African Economic Community. During 2001 and 2002, a merger was arranged between the National Development Party, the country's major opposition group, and the ruling party, the Kenya African National Union.

Internet resources: <www.kenyatourism.org>

1 metric ton = about 1.1 short tons;   1 kilometer = 0.6 mi (statute);   1 metric ton-km cargo = about 0.68 short ton-mi cargo;   c.i.f.: cost, insurance, and freight;   f.o.b.: free on board

Kiribati

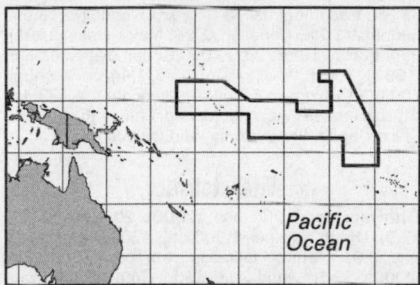

Pacific
Ocean

Official name: Republic of Kiribati. **Form of government:** unitary republic with a unicameral legislature (House of Assembly [42, including two nonelective members]). **Head of state and government:** President Teburoro Tito (from 1994). **Capital:** Bairiki, on Tarawa Atoll. **Official language:** English. **Official religion:** none. **Monetary unit:** 1 Australian dollar ($A) = 100 cents; valuation (28 Jun 2002) US$1 = $A 1.78.

Demography

Area: 313 sq mi, 811 sq km. **Population** (2001): 94,000. **Density** (2001 [for inhabited islands (280 sq mi, 726 sq km)]): persons per sq mi 335.7, persons per sq km 129.5. **Urban** (1998): 37.0%. **Sex distribution** (1995): male 49.55%; female 50.45%. **Age breakdown** (1995): under 15, 41.2%; 15–29, 25.8%; 30–44, 18.3%; 45–59, 9.3%; 60–74, 4.4%; 75 and over, 1.0%. **Ethnic composition** (1995): I-Kiribati 97.7%; mixed (part I-Kiribati and other) 1.5%; Tuvaluan 0.3%; European 0.2%; other 0.3%. **Religious affiliation** (1995): Roman Catholic 54.3%; Kiribati Protestant (Congregational) 37.9%; Baha'i 2.6%; other Protestant 2.5%; other Christian (Mormon) 1.7%; other/nonreligious 1.0%. **Major cities** (1999): Tarawa (urban area) 32,000. **Location:** western Pacific Ocean, south of the Hawaiian Islands.

Vital statistics

Birth rate per 1,000 pop. (2000): 33.1 (world avg. 22.5); legitimate, n.a.; illegitimate, n.a. **Death rate** per 1,000 pop. (2000): 8.4 (world avg. 9.0). **Natural increase rate** per 1,000 pop. (2000): 24.7 (world avg. 13.5). **Total fertility rate** (avg. births per childbearing woman; 1999): 4.4. **Marriage rate** per 1,000 pop. (1988): 5.2. **Life expectancy** at birth (1999): male 56.5 years; female 62.4 years.

National economy

Budget (1997). *Revenue:* $A 79,100,000 (nontax revenue 46.6%, tax revenue 20.4%, grants 33.0%). *Expenditures:* $A 79,100,000 (current expenditure 66.3%, of which wages 25.4%; capital expenditure 33.7%). **Public debt** (external, outstanding; 1993): US$18,000,000. **Tourism** (1999): receipts from visitors US$2,000,000; expenditures by nationals abroad US$2,000,000. **Production** (metric tons except as noted). *Agriculture, forestry, fishing* (1999): coconuts 85,000, roots and tubers 6,500, bananas 4,700; livestock (number of live animals) 9,500 pigs, 300,000 chickens; fish catch (1997) 23,000. *Manufacturing* (1996): processed copra 9,321; other important prod-

ucts are processed fish, baked goods, clothing, and handicrafts. *Energy production (consumption):* electricity (kW-hr; 1996) 7,000,000 (7,000,000); petroleum products (metric tons; 1996) none (7,000). **Gross national product** (1999): US$81,000,000 (US$910 per capita). **Population economically active** (1995): total 38,407; activity rate of total pop. 49.5% (participation rates: over age 15, 84.0%; female 47.8%; unemployed 0.2%). **Household income and expenditure.** Average household size (1995) 6.5; income per household: n.a.; sources of income (1978): wages 69.7%, self-employment 21.4%, transfer payments 6.0%, other 2.9%; expenditure (1982): food 50.0%, tobacco and alcohol 14.0%, clothing 8.0%, transportation 8.0%, housing, energy, and household operation 7.5%. **Land use** (1994): forest 2.7%; agricultural and under permanent cultivation 50.7%; other 46.6%.

Foreign trade

Imports (1996): $A 47,829,000 (food and live animals 33.4%; machinery and transport equipment 18.1%; basic manufactures 14.6%; mineral fuels 10.3%; beverages and tobacco 6.7%; chemicals 6.6%; crude materials 2.1%). *Major import sources:* Australia 46.1%; Fiji 18.7%; Japan 8.6%; New Zealand 8.4%; China 5.9%; US 3.3%. **Exports** (1996): $A 7,447,000 (domestic exports 91.7%, of which copra 62.8%, pet fish 11.6%, fish and fish preparations 4.0%, seaweed 3.6%; reexports 8.3%). *Major export destinations* (1994): Japan 32.9%; US 17.1%; Hong Kong 12.9%; Bangladesh 8.6%; Germany 8.0%; Malaysia 7.1%.

Transport and communications

Transport. *Roads* (1996): total length 670 km (paved 5%). *Vehicles* (1988): passenger cars 222; trucks and buses 115. *Air transport* (1996): passenger-km 7,000,000; metric ton-km cargo 1,000,000; airports 9. **Communications** Total units (units per 1,000 persons). Radio receivers (1997): 17,000 (212); Television receivers (1997): 1,000 (15); Telephone main lines (1999): 3,502 (43); Cellular telephone subscribers (1999): 200 (2.4).

Education and health

Educational attainment (1995). Percentage of pop. age 25 and over having: no schooling 7.8%; primary education 68.5%; secondary or higher 23.7%. **Literacy** (1995): population age 15 and over literate 90%. **Health:** physicians (1998) 26 (1 per 3,378 persons); hospital beds (1990) 283 (1 per 253 persons); infant mortality rate per 1,000 live births (1999) 56.8. **Food** (1999): daily per capita caloric intake 2,982 (vegetable products 89%, animal products 11%); (1997) 131% of FAO recommended minimum.

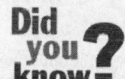

Did you know? Since none of Kiribati lies more than 3 m (10 ft) above sea level, the inhabitants of this tiny country take the prospect of global warming and the possibility of rising ocean levels more seriously than residents of other countries.

Background

The islands were settled by Austronesian-speaking peoples before the 1st century AD. In 1765 the British discovered the island of Nikunau; the first permanent European settlers arrived in 1837. In 1916 the Gilbert and Ellice islands and Banaba became a crown colony of Britain; they were later joined by the Phoenix and Line islands. In 1979 the colony became the nation of Kiribati.

Recent Developments

Kiribati caused controversy among neighboring nations when, in 1995, it moved its calculation of the International Date Line in order to be the first country to reach midnight on 31 Dec 1999. One of its islands was renamed Millennium Island, the first spot in the world to see the new millennium. Also that year, the country joined the United Nations. In 2001 Kiribati opened its first overseas diplomatic mission (in Fiji), while Britain reopened its mission in Kiribati.

Internet Resources: <www.tskl.net.ki/Kiribati>

North Korea

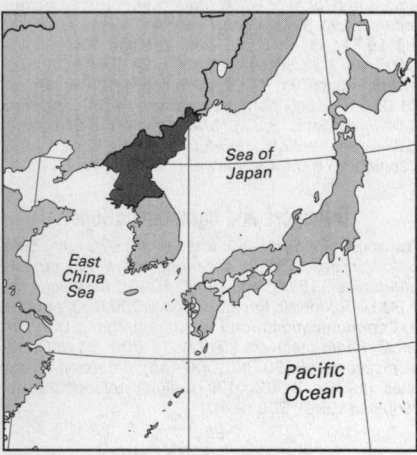

Official name: Choson Minjujuui In'min Konghwaguk (Democratic People's Republic of Korea). Form of government: unitary single-party republic with one legislative house (Supreme People's Assembly [687]). Chief of state: Chairman of the National Defense Commission Kim Jong Il (from 1998) (enhanced military post with revised constitutional powers). Head of state and government: Premier Hong Sang Nam (from 1998). Capital: P'yongyang. Official language: Korean. Official religion: none. Monetary unit: 1 won = 100 chon; valuation (28 Jun 2002) $1 = 2.20 won.

Demography

Area: 47,399 sq mi, 122,762 sq km. Population (2001): 21,968,000. Density (2001): persons per sq mi 463.5, persons per sq km 178.9. Urban (1998): 62.2%. Sex distribution (2000): male 48.48%; female 51.52%. Age breakdown (2000): under 15, 25.6%; 15–29, 24.5%; 30–44, 24.7%; 45–59, 14.4%; 60–74, 9.0%; 75 and over, 1.8%. Ethnic com-

position (1999): Korean 99.8%; Chinese 0.2%. Religious affiliation (1980): atheist or nonreligious 68.3%; traditional beliefs 15.6%; Ch'ondogyo 13.9%; Buddhist 1.7%; Christian 0.5%. Major cities (1993): P'yóngyang (1996) 2,500,000 (urban agglomeration [1999] 3,136,000); Namp'o 731,448; Hamhung 709,000; Ch'ongjin 582,480; Kaesong 334,433. Location: eastern Asia, bordering China, Russia, the Sea of Japan, South Korea, and the Yellow Sea.

Vital statistics

Birth rate per 1,000 pop. (2000): 20.4 (world avg. 22.5). Death rate per 1,000 pop. (2000): 6.9 (world avg. 9.0). Natural increase rate per 1,000 pop. (2000): 13.5 (world avg. 13.5). Total fertility rate (avg. births per childbearing woman; 2000): 2.3. Marriage rate per 1,000 pop. (1987): 9.3. Divorce rate per 1,000 pop. (1987): 0.2. Life expectancy at birth (2000): male 67.8 years; female 73.9 years.

National economy

Budget (1999). *Revenue:* 19,801,000,000 won (turnover tax and profits from state enterprises). *Expenditures:* 20,018,200,000 won (1994; national economy 67.8%, social and cultural affairs 19.0%, defense 11.6%). Population economically active (1997): total 11,898,000; activity rate of total population 55.8% (participation rates [1988–93]: ages 15–64, 49.5%; female 46.0%; unemployed, n.a.). Production (metric tons except as noted). *Agriculture, forestry, fishing* (2000): rice 1,690,000, potatoes 1,402,000, corn (maize) 1,041,000; livestock (number of live animals) 2,970,000 pigs, 2,100,000 goats, 600,000 cattle; roundwood (2000) 4,900,000 cu m; fish catch (1999): 278,500. *Mining and quarrying* (2000): iron ore (metal content) 300,000; zinc (metal content) 190,000; *Manufacturing* (2000): cement 15,000,000; coke 2,000,000; crude steel 1,000,000; *Energy production (consumption):* electricity (kW-hr; 1999) 28,600,000 (28,600,000); coal (metric tons; 1999) 85,500,000 (87,600,000); crude petroleum (barrels; 1999) none (26,000,000); petroleum products (metric tons; 1996) 2,785,000 (4,258,000). Household income and expenditure. Average household size (1987) 4.8; average annual income per household (1980) 3,677 won; expenditure (1984; workers and clerical workers only): food 46.5%, clothing 29.9%, furniture 3.8%, energy 3.3%, housing 0.6%. Public debt (external, outstanding; 1996): $12,000,000,000. Gross national product (1999): $9,912,000,000 ($457 per capita). Land use (1994): forested 61.2%; meadows and pastures 0.4%; agricultural and under permanent cultivation 16.6%; other 21.8%.

Foreign trade

Imports (1999-f.o.b.): $965,000,000 (crude petroleum, coal and coke, industrial machinery and transport equipment [including trucks], industrial chemicals, textile yarn and fabrics, and grain are among the major imports). *Major import sources* (1995): China 30.0%; Japan 15.8%; Austria 9.3%; Ukraine 5.9%. Exports (1999): $515,000,000 (minerals [including lead, magnesite, zinc], metallurgical products [iron and steel, nonferrous metals], cement, agricultural

---

1 metric ton = about 1.1 short tons;   1 kilometer = 0.6 mi (statute);   1 metric ton-km cargo = about 0.68 short ton-mi cargo;   c.i.f.: cost, insurance, and freight;   f.o.b.: free on board

products [including fish, grain, fruit and vegetables, tobacco], and manufactured goods [textile fabrics, clothing] are among the major exports). *Major export destinations* (1995): Japan 31.4%; Austria 17.3%; India 6.9%.

Transport and communications

Transport. *Railroads* (1999): length 8,533 km. *Roads* (1997): total length 23,377 km (paved 8%). *Vehicles* (1990): passenger cars 248,000. *Air transport* (1997): passenger-km 286,000,000; metric ton-km cargo 30,000,000; airports (1999) with scheduled flights 1. **Communications** Total units (units per 1,000 persons). Daily newspaper circulation (1996): 4,500,000 (199); Radio receivers (1997): 3,360,000 (146); Television receivers (1997): 1,200,000 (52); Telephone main lines (1999): 1,100,000 (46).

Education and health

Educational attainment (1987–88). Percentage of pop. age 16 and over having attended or graduated from postsecondary-level school: 13.7%. **Literacy** (1997): 95%. **Health** (1993): physicians 61,200 (1 per 370 persons); hospital beds (1989) 290,590 (1 per 74 persons); infant mortality rate (2000) 24.3. **Food** (1999): daily per capita caloric intake 2,100 (vegetable products 94%, animal products 6%); 90% of FAO recommended minimum requirement.

Military

Total active duty personnel (1999): 1,082,000 (army 87.8%, navy 4.2%, air force 8.0%). **Military expenditure as percentage of GNP** (1997): 27.5% (world 2.6%); per capita expenditure $282.

Background

According to tradition, the ancient kingdom of Choson was established in the northern part of the Korean Peninsula, probably by peoples from northern China, in the 3rd millennium BC and was conquered by China in 108 BC. The kingdom was ruled by the Yi dynasty from 1392 to 1910. That year Korea was formally annexed by Japan. It was freed from Japanese control in 1945, at which time the USSR occupied the area north of latitude 38° N and the US occupied the area south of it. The Democratic People's Republic of Korea was established as a communist state in 1948. North Korea launched an invasion of South Korea in 1950, initiating the Korean War, which ended with an armistice in 1953. Under Kim Il-sung, North Korea became one of the most harshly regimented societies in the world, with a state-owned economy that failed to produce adequate food. In the late 1990s, under Kim Il-sung's successor, Kim Chong Il, the country endured a serious famine; as many as a million Koreans may have died.

Recent Developments

In 2000 a summit between the leaders of North and South Korea raised hopes for an end to North Korea's long isolation. North Korea also began to reestablish relations with Western nations. It was revealed in 2001, however, that health conditions had badly deteriorated within the country during the 1990s. In early 2002, US Pres. George W. Bush named North Korea as a state intent on developing weapons of

mass destruction; his administration later expressed willingness to resume talks with the country about its weapons programs.

Internet resources: <www.kcna.co.jp>

South Korea

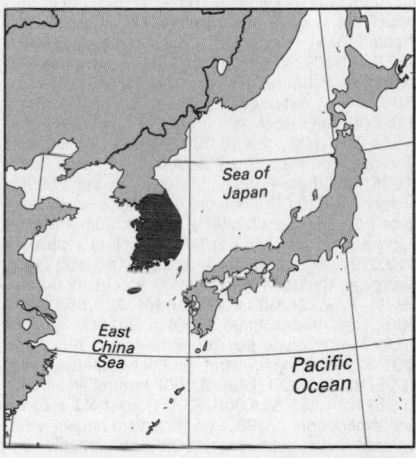

Official name: Taehan Min'guk (Republic of Korea). **Form of government:** unitary multiparty republic with one legislative house (National Assembly [273]). **Head of state and government:** President Kim Dae Jung (from 1998), assisted by Prime Minister Chang Dae Whan (from 0 Aug 2002). **Capital:** Seoul. **Official language:** Korean. **Official religion:** none. **Monetary unit:** 1 won (W) = 100 chon; valuation (28 Jun 2002) $1 = W 1,203.

Demography

Area: 38,402 sq mi, 99,461 sq km. **Population** (2001): 47,676,000. **Density** (2001): persons per sq mi 1,241.5, persons per sq km 479.3. **Urban** (2001): 82.0%. **Sex distribution** (2001): male 50.42%; female 49.58%. **Age breakdown** (1998): under 15, 22.0%; 15–29, 26.8%; 30–44, 26.2%; 45–59, 14.8%; 60–74, 8.1%; 75 and over, 2.1%. **Ethnic composition** (1990): Korean 99.9%; other 0.1%. **Religious affiliation** (1995): religious 50.7%, of which Buddhist 23.2%, Protestant 19.7%, Roman Catholic 6.6%, Confucian 0.5%, Wonbulgyo 0.2%, Ch'ondogyo 0.1%, other 0.4%; nonreligious 49.3%. **Major cities** (2000; preliminary): Seoul 9,891,000; Pusan 3,804,000; Taegu 2,480,000; Inch'on 2,476,000; Taejon 1,367,000. **Location:** northeast Asia, bordering North Korea, the East Sea, and the Yellow Sea.

Vital statistics

Birth rate per 1,000 pop. (1999): 15.3 (world avg. 22.5). **Death rate** per 1,000 pop. (1999): 5.8 (world avg. 9.0). **Natural increase rate** per 1,000 pop. (1999): 9.5 (world avg. 13.5). **Total fertility rate** (avg. births per childbearing woman; 1999): 1.7. **Marriage rate** per 1,000 pop. (1997): 6.8. **Divorce rate** per 1,000 pop. (1997): 1.6. **Life expectancy** at birth (1999): male 70.5 years; female 78.4 years.

National economy

Budget (1998). *Revenue*: W 96,673,000,000,000 (taxes on income and profits 28.9%, taxes on goods and services 28.1%, nontax revenue 18.1%, social security contributions 10.9%, education tax 5.4%). *Expenditures*: W 115,689,000,000,000 (economic services 24.6%, education 15.4%, defense 11.8%, social security and welfare 10.6%, general public services 9.4%, housing and community amenities 6.3%). **Public debt** (external, outstanding; 1999): $57,231,000,000. **Production** (metric tons except as noted). *Agriculture, forestry, fishing* (2000): rice 7,067,000, cabbages 2,755,000, dry onions 936,000; livestock (number of live animals) 7,864,000 pigs, 2,486,000 cattle, 97,000,000 chickens; roundwood 1,722,000 cu m; fish catch (1998) 2,026,934. *Mining and quarrying* (1998): copper ore 226,000; iron ore 133,000; zinc concentrate 10,488. *Manufacturing* (2000): computer peripherals $12,060,000,000; mobile phones $12,019,000,000; motor vehicles 3,115,000 units. *Energy production (consumption)*: electricity (kW-hr; 1999) 239,328,000,000 ([1996] 227,554,000,000); coal (metric tons; 1999) 4,140,000 ([1996] 50,277,000); crude petroleum (barrels; 1996) none (721,829,000); petroleum products (metric tons; 1996) 83,721,000 (74,869,000); natural gas (cu m; 1996) none (12,814,000,000). **Household income and expenditure** (2000; excluding farm households). Average household size (1998) 3.6; income per household W 54,025,000; sources of income: wages 53.0%, other 47.0%; expenditure: food and beverages 27.5%, transportation and communications 16.4%, education and recreation 16.2%, clothing and footwear 5.7%, utilities 5.1%, health care 4.1%, household durable goods 3.7%, housing 3.3%, other 18.0%. **Gross national product** (1999): $397,910,000,000 ($8,490 per capita). **Population economically active** (2000): total 21,950,000; activity rate 46.4% (participation rates: ages 15 and over, 60.7%; female [1998] 38.8%; unemployed 4.1%). **Tourism** (1999): receipts $6,802,000,000; expenditures $3,975,000,000.

Foreign trade

Imports (2000-c.i.f.): $160,481,000,000 (electric and electronic products 27.0%, crude petroleum 15.7%, machinery and transport equipment 13.2%, manufactured consumer goods 10.0%, chemicals 7.4%, iron and steel products 3.7%). *Major import sources*: Japan 19.8%; US 18.2%; China 8.0%; Saudi Arabia 6.0%; Australia 3.7%; Malaysia 3.0%. **Exports** (2000-f.o.b.): $172,267,500,000 (electric and electronic products 36.0%, machinery and transport equipment 18.2%, chemicals 7.0%, crude materials and fuels 6.7%). *Major export destinations*: US 21.8%; Japan 11.9%; China 10.7%; Hong Kong 6.2%; Taiwan 4.7%; Singapore 3.3%; UK 3.1%.

Transport and communications

Transport. *Railroads* (1998): length (2000) 6,706 km; passenger-km 30,072,000,000; metric ton-km cargo 12,708,000,000. *Roads* (2000): total length 88,775 km (paved 76%). *Vehicles* (2000): passenger cars 8,084,000; trucks and buses 3,938,000. *Air*

transport (1998): passenger-km 47,712,000,000; metric ton-km cargo 7,280,640,000; airports (1996) with scheduled flights 14. **Communications** Total units (units per 1,000 persons). Daily newspaper circulation (1995): 17,700,000 (394); Radio receivers (1997): 47,500,000 (1,033); Television receivers (1999): 16,896,000 (361); Telephone main lines (2000): 21,931,000 (464); Cellular telephone subscribers (2000): 26,816,000 (567); Personal computers (1999): 8,519,000 (182); Internet users (2000): 19,040,000 (403).

Education and health

Educational attainment (1995). Percentage of pop. age 25 and over having: no formal schooling 8.5%; primary education or less 17.7%; some secondary and secondary 53.1%; postsecondary 20.6%. **Literacy** (1995): total pop. age 15 and over literate 98.0%; males 99.3%; females 96.7%. **Health** (1999): physicians 69,724 (1 per 672 persons); hospital beds (1997) 220,427 (1 per 209 persons); infant mortality rate per 1,000 live births 10.0. **Food** (1999): daily per capita caloric intake 3,073 (vegetable products 86%, animal products 14%); (1997) 131% of FAO recommended minimum.

Military

Total active duty personnel (2000): 683,000 (army 82.0%, navy 8.8%, air force 9.2%); US military forces (2001): 36,000. **Military expenditure as percentage of GNP** (1997): 3.4% (world 2.6%); per capita expenditure $326.

Did you know? Even though there are more than 47 million people in South Korea, only about 300 surnames are in use.

Background

Civilization in the Korean Peninsula dates to the 3rd millennium BC (see background of Democratic People's Republic of Korea, above). The Republic of Korea was established in 1948 in the southern portion of the Korean peninsula. In 1950 North Korean troops invaded South Korea, precipitating the Korean War. UN forces intervened on the side of South Korea, while Chinese troops backed North Korea in the war, which ended with an armistice in 1953. The devastated country was rebuilt with US aid, and South Korea prospered in the postwar era, developing a strong export-oriented economy. It experienced an economic downturn in the mid-1990s that affected many economies in the area.

Recent Developments

In 2000 the leaders of North and South Korea held a summit that revived hopes for reunification. Good relations between the two nations continued that year when athletes from both countries marched under a single flag in the opening ceremony of the Olympic Games, and families were reunited with relatives on the other side of the border. South Korea's president, Kim Dae Jung, was awarded the Nobel Prize for

1 metric ton = about 1.1 short tons;   1 kilometer = 0.6 mi (statute);   1 metric ton-km cargo = about 0.68 short ton-mi cargo;   c.i.f.: cost, insurance, and freight;   f.o.b.: free on board

Peace in recognition of his efforts toward reconciliation with the North. The economy continued to recover throughout 1999 and 2000. In 2002 corruption scandals within the government and Kim's family negatively affected his popularity. National pride swelled as South Korea cohosted, with Japan, the 2002 World Cup in association football (soccer).

Internet resources: <www.nso.go.kr/eng>

Kuwait

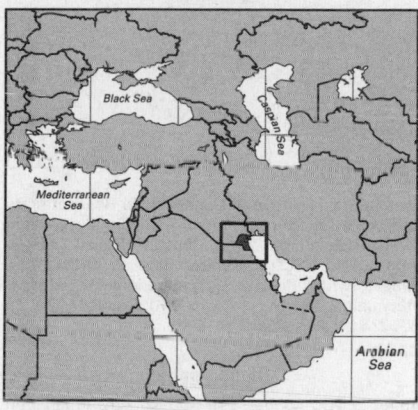

Official name: Dawlat al-Kuwayt (State of Kuwait). Form of government: constitutional monarchy with one legislative body (National Assembly [65; including 50 elected members plus cabinet ministers not elected to National Assembly serving ex offico]). Head of state and government: Emir Sheikh Jabir al-Ahmad al-Jabir al-Sabah (from 1977) assisted by a prime minister. Capital: Kuwait City. Official language: Arabic. Official religion: Islam. Monetary unit: 1 Kuwaiti dinar (KD) = 1,000 fils; valuation (28 Jun 2002) $1 = KD 0.30.

Demography

Area: 6,880 sq mi, 17,818 sq km. Population (2001): 2,275,000. Density (2001): persons per sq mi 330.7, persons per sq km 127.7. Urban (1995): 97.0%. Sex distribution (2000): male 60.04%; female 39.96%. Age breakdown (2000): under 15, 29.4%; 15–29, 28.2%; 30–44, 25.8%; 45–59, 12.6%; 60–74, 3.5%; 75 and over, 0.5%. Ethnic composition (2000): Arab 74%, of which Kuwaiti 30%, Palestinian 17%, Jordanian 10%, Bedouin 9%; Kurd 10%, Indo-Pakistani 8%; Persian 4%; other 4%. Religious affiliation (1995): Muslim 85%, of which Sunni 45%, Shi'i 30%; other Muslim 10%; other (mostly Christian and Hindu) 15.0%. Major cities (1995): Al-Salimiyah 130,215; Qalib al-Shuyukh 102,178; Hawalli 82,238; Kuwait City 28,859 (urban agglomeration [1999] 1,165,000). Location: the Middle East, bordering Iraq, the Persian Gulf, and Saudi Arabia.

Vital statistics

Birth rate per 1,000 pop. (2000): 22.0 (world avg. 22.5). Death rate per 1,000 pop. (2000): 2.4 (world avg. 9.0). Natural increase rate per 1,000 pop.

(2000): 19.6 (world avg. 13.5). Total fertility rate (avg. births per childbearing woman; 2000): 3.3. Marriage rate per 1,000 pop. (1999): 7.0. Divorce rate per 1,000 pop. (1999): 3.9. Life expectancy at birth (2000): male 75.3 years; female 76.9 years.

National economy

Budget (2001–02). Revenue: KD 2,224,000,000 (oil revenue 79.2%). Expenditures: KD 4,295,000,000 (transfers 21.2%, defense 20.9%, education 9.1%, economic development 8.0%, health 6.3%). Tourism (2000): receipts from visitors $243,000,000; expenditures by nationals abroad $2,510,000,000. Gross national product (1998): $42,387,000,000 ($20,910 per capita). Production (metric tons except as noted). Agriculture, forestry, fishing (2000): cucumber and gherkins 33,004, tomatoes 31,788, eggplants 12,002; livestock (number of live animals) 450,000 sheep, 150,000 goats, 8,900 camels; fish catch (1999) 6,535. Mining and quarrying (1997): sulfur 600,000; lime 40,000. Manufacturing (value added in KD '000,000; 1997): refined petroleum products 3,632; industrial chemicals 962; fabricated metal products 68. Energy production (consumption): electricity (kW-hr; 1998) 29,988,000,000 ([1996] 25,925,000,000); crude petroleum (barrels; 1999) 795,000,000 ([1998] 314,515,000); petroleum products (metric tons; 1996) 36,572,000 (6,478,000); natural gas (cu m; 1998) 11,081,000,000 (11,081,000,000). Population economically active (1999): total 1,226,134; activity rate of total pop. 53.9% (participation rates [1995]: ages 15–59, 70.7%; female 26.1%; unemployed 0.7%). Household income and expenditure. Average household size (1995) 3.9; sources of income (1986): wages and salaries 53.8%, self-employment 20.8%, other 25.4%; expenditure (1992): food, beverages, and tobacco 37.0%, housing and energy 18.7%, transportation 15.3%, household appliances and services 11.1%, clothing and footwear 10.0%, education and health 2.5%. Land use (1994): forest 0.1%; pasture 7.7%; agriculture 0.3%; other 91.9%.

Foreign trade

Imports (1999): KD 2,318,305,000 (machinery and transport equipment 39.7%, manufactured goods 16.3%, food and live animals 14.9%, miscellaneous manufactured articles 14.5%, chemicals and chemical products 8.7%). Major import sources: Japan 12.8%; US 12.3%; Germany 7.7%; Saudi Arabia 6.2%; UK 5.8%; Italy 5.8%. Exports (1999): KD 3,696,000,000 (crude petroleum and petroleum products 96.5%, chemicals and chemical products 2.9%). Major export destinations (estimated figures): Japan 27%; US 14%; South Korea 13%; Singapore 10%; The Netherlands 8%; Pakistan 8%.

Transport and communications

Transport. Roads (1997): total length 4,450 km (paved 81%). Vehicles (1998): passenger cars 747,042; trucks and buses 140,480. Air transport (2000): passenger-km 6,137,195,000; metric ton-km cargo 243,204,000; airports (1999) with scheduled flights 1. Communications Total units (units per 1,000 persons). Daily newspaper circulation (1996): 635,000 (377); Radio receivers (1997): 1,175,000 (678); Television receivers (1999): 910,000 (520); Telephone main lines (1999): 456,000 (240); Cellular telephone subscribers (1999): 30,000 (158); Personal computers (1999): 230,000 (120); Internet users (1999): 100,000 (54).

Education and health

Educational attainment (1988). Percentage of pop. age 25 and over having: no formal schooling 44.8%; primary education 8.6%; some secondary 15.1%; complete secondary 15.1%; higher 16.4%. **Literacy** (1995): total pop. age 15 and over literate 79.3%; males literate 82.3%; females literate 76.0%. **Health** (1998): physicians 3,447 (1 per 541 persons); hospital beds (public hospitals) 4,389 (1 per 425 persons); infant mortality rate per 1,000 live births (2000) 11.5. **Food** (1999): daily per capita caloric intake 3,167 (vegetable products 76%, animal products 24%); 131% of FAO recommended minimum requirement.

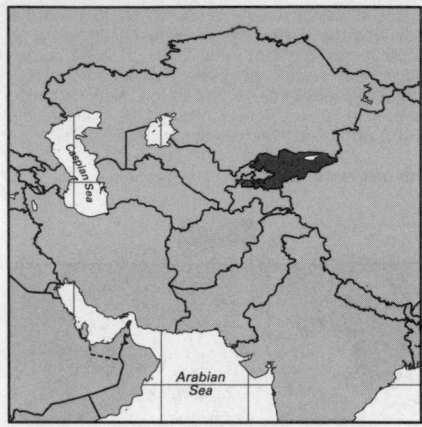

Arabian Sea

Military

Total active duty personnel (2000): 15,300 (army [including central staff] 71.9%, navy 11.8%, air force 16.3%). **Military expenditure as percentage of GNP** (1997): 7.5% (world 2.6%); per capita expenditure $1,525.

Background

Faylakah Island, in Kuwait Bay, had a civilization dating back to the 3rd millennium BC that flourished until 1200 BC. Greek colonists again settled the island in the 4th century BC. Abd Rahim of the Sabah dynasty became sheikh in 1756, the first of a family that continues to rule Kuwait. In 1899, to thwart German and Ottoman influences, Kuwait gave Britain control of its foreign affairs. Following the outbreak of war in 1914, Britain established a protectorate there. In 1961, after Kuwait became independent, Iraq laid claim to it. British troops defended Kuwait, the Arab League recognized its independence, and Iraq dropped its claim. Iraqi forces invaded and occupied Kuwait in 1990, and a US-led military coalition drove them out in 1991. The destruction of many of Kuwait's oil wells complicated reconstruction efforts.

Recent Developments

Iraq remained a threat to Kuwait's independence in the first years of the 21st century. Following the terrorist attacks on the US on 11 Sep 2001, slumping oil demand in Kuwait's principal markets, Asia and Europe, exposed the fragility of the economy. Islamist agitation continued, including fallout from the revelation following the 11 September attacks that a member of the inner circle of the al-Qaeda terrorist organization was a Kuwaiti.

Internet resources: <www.kuwait-info.org>

Kyrgyzstan

Official name: Kyrgyz Respublikasy (Kyrgyz); Respublika Kirgizstan (Russian) (Kyrgyz Republic). **Form of government:** unitary multiparty republic with two legislative houses (Assembly of People's Representa-

tives [45]; Legislative Assembly [60]). **Head of state and government:** President Askar Akayev (from 1990) assisted by Prime Minister Nikolay Tanayev (from 22 May 2002). **Capital:** Bishkek. **Official languages:** Kyrgyz; Russian. **Official religion:** none. **Monetary unit:** 1 som (K.S.) = 100 tyiyn; valuation (28 Jun 2002) $1 = K.S. 46.52.

Demography

Area: 77,200 sq mi, 199,900 sq km. **Population** (2001): 4,934,000. **Density** (2001): persons per sq mi 64.4, persons per sq km 24.9. **Urban** (1999): 40.0%. **Sex distribution** (1997): male 49.37%; female 50.63%. **Age breakdown** (1997): under 15, 37.3%; 15–29, 26.3%; 30–44, 19.5%; 45–59, 8.8%; 60–74, 6.5%; 75 and over, 1.6%. **Ethnic composition** (1999): Kyrgyz 64.9%; Uzbek 13.8%; Russian 12.5%; Hui 1.1%; Ukrainian 1.0%; Uighur 1.0%; other 5.7%. **Religious affiliation** (1997): Muslim (mostly Sunni) 75.0%; Christian 6.7%, of which Russian Orthodox 5.6%; other (mostly nonreligious) 18.3%. **Major cities** (1999 est.): Bishkek (Frunze) 619,000; Osh 220,500; Jalal-Abad (1991) 74,200; Tokmok (1991) 71,200; Kara-Köl (1991) 64,300. **Location:** central Asia, bordering Kazakhstan, China, Tajikistan, and Uzbekistan.

Vital statistics

Birth rate per 1,000 pop. (2001): 20.6 (world avg. 22.5); (1994) legitimate 83.2%; illegitimate 16.8%. **Death rate** per 1,000 pop. (2001): 7.3 (world avg. 9.0). **Natural increase rate** per 1,000 pop. (2001): 13.3 (world avg. 13.5). **Total fertility rate** (avg. births per childbearing woman; 2001): 2.5. **Marriage rate** per 1,000 pop. (1995): 6.0. **Divorce rate** per 1,000 pop. (1995): 1.3. **Life expectancy** at birth (2001): male 64.0 years; female 72.0 years.

National economy

Budget (1998). *Revenue*: K.S. 6,090,700,000 (tax revenue 79.9%, of which taxes on goods and services 54.2%, taxes on income and profits 14.6%, taxes on international trade 6.2%; nontax revenue 18.7%). *Expenditures*: K.S. 7,531,600,000 (education 22.3%;

1 metric ton = about 1.1 short tons;   1 kilometer = 0.6 mi (statute);   1 metric ton-km cargo = about 0.68 short ton-mi cargo;   c.i.f.: cost, insurance, and freight;   f.o.b.: free on board

social security 13.0%; general public services 13.5%; health 12.8%; economic development 11.2%; defense 6.5%). **Public debt** (external, outstanding; 1999): $1,130,400,000. **Land use** (1994): forest 3.7%; pasture 45.4%; agriculture 7.2%; other 43.7%. **Population economically active** (1995): total 1,692,000; activity rate of total pop. 37.2% (1993; participation rates: ages 16–59 [male], 16–54 [female] 81.1%; female 49.0%; (1996) unemployed 4.3%). **Production** (metric tons except as noted). *Agriculture, forestry, fishing* (1999): grain 1,630,000, potatoes 957,000, vegetables (other than potatoes) and melons 485,000; livestock (number of live animals) 3,570,000 sheep and goats, 825,000 cattle, 320,000 horses; roundwood (1998) 42,400 cu m; fish catch (1997) 300. *Mining and quarrying* (1998): antimony 1,297; mercury 630; uranium 450. *Manufacturing* (value of production in '000,000 som; 1994): textiles 1,112; processed foods 729; ferrous and nonferrous metals 678. *Energy production (consumption):* electricity (kW hr; 1996) 13,480,000,000 (11,400,000,000); coal (metric tons; 1996) 410,000 (1,018,000); crude petroleum (barrels; 1996) 600,000 (500,000); petroleum products (metric tons; 1996) 3,000 (566,000); natural gas (cu m; 1996) 26,000,000 (1,053,000,000). **Household income and expenditure.** Average household size (1999) 4.3; income per household (1994) 4,359 som; sources of income (1990): wages and salaries 49.7%, pensions and stipends 11.1%, income from agricultural products 3.5%, other 35.7%; expenditure (1990): food and clothing 48.0%, health care 13.1%, housing 5.9%, cultural affairs 5.2%, appliances 4.4%. **Gross national product** (1999): $1,465,000,000 ($300 per capita). **Tourism** (1998): receipts from visitors, $8,000,000; expenditures by nationals abroad, $3,000,000.

Foreign trade

Imports (1997): $709,300,000 (oil and gas 24.8%, machine-building equipment 21.7%, chemical products 13.5%, food products 11.7%, light industrial products 6.8%). *Major import sources:* Russian Federation 26.9%; Uzbekistan 18.1%; Kazakhstan 9.8%; Turkey 6.2%; US 5.6%. **Exports** (1997): $603,800,000 (metals 36.3%, electricity 13.8%, food products 13.2%, machinery 10.2%, light industrial products 10.0%, construction materials 4.4%). *Major export destinations:* Switzerland 26.9%; Uzbekistan 16.8%; Russian Federation 16.4%; Kazakhstan 14.4%; China 5.2%.

Transport and communications

Transport. *Railroads* (1999): length 424 km; (1995) passenger-km 30,000,000; metric ton-km cargo 403,000,000. *Roads* (1996): total length 18,500 km (paved 91%). *Vehicles* (1996): passenger cars 146,000. *Air transport* (1996): passenger-km 4,408,000,000; metric ton-km cargo 65,199,000; airports (1997) with scheduled flights 2. **Communications** Total units (units per 1,000 persons). Daily newspaper circulation (1996): 67,000 (15); Radio receivers (1997): 520,000 (113); Television receivers (1998): 220,000 (47); Telephone main lines (1999): 356,000 (76); Cellular phone subscribers (1999): 2,574 (0.6); Internet users (1999): 10,000 (2.1).

Education and health

Educational attainment (1989). Percentage of pop. age 19 and over having: primary education 4.7%; some secondary 20.9%; completed secondary 44.4%; some postsecondary 19.3%; higher 10.7%. **Literacy** (1989): total pop. age 15 and over literate 4,130,562 (97.0%); males literate 2,048,536 (98.6%); females literate 2,082,026 (95.5%). **Health** (1997): physicians 15,100 (1 per 307 persons); hospital beds 40,700 (1 per 114 persons); infant mortality rate per 1,000 live births (2001) 39.0. **Food** (1999): daily per capita caloric intake 2,833 (vegetable products 81%, animal products 19%); (1997) 111% of FAO recommended minimum.

Military

Total active duty personnel (2000): 9,000 (army 73.3%, air force 26.7%). **Military expenditure as percentage of GNP** (1997): 1.6% (world 2.6%); per capita expenditure $35.

Background

The Kyrgyz, a nomadic people of Central Asia, settled in the Tian Shan region in ancient times. They were conquered by Genghis Khan's son Jochi in 1207. The area became part of the Qing empire of China in the mid-18th century. The region came under Russian control in the 19th century, and its rebellion against Russia in 1916 resulted in a long period of brutal repression. Kirgiziya became an autonomous province of the USSR in 1924 and was made the Kirgiz Soviet Socialist Republic in 1936. Kyrgyzstan gained independence in 1991. In the 1990s it struggled with its democratization process and with establishing a thriving economy.

Recent Developments

In 1999 and 2000 Kyrgyzstan dealt with violence by Islamic militants in the southern part of the country, and by mid-2000 armed forces were sent to the area. Additional efforts to counter Muslim extremists in the south were made throughout 2001. In December the government allowed the US to use Manas International Airport as a base in the war on terrorism. Violence between police and demonstrators in March 2002 led to the resignation of the government in May.

Internet resources:
<www.bishkek.su/KyrgyzstanTourism>

Laos

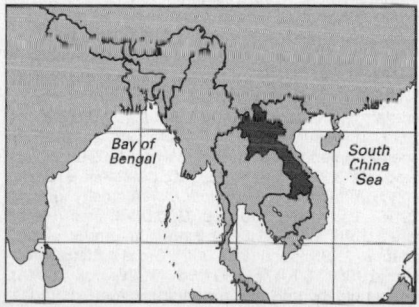

Bay of Bengal

South China Sea

Official name: Sathalanalat Paxathipatai Paxaxôn Lao (Lao People's Democratic Republic). **Form of government:** unitary single-party people's republic with one legislative house (National Assembly [109]). **Chief of state:** President Khamtai Siphandon (from 1998). **Head of government:** Prime Minister Boungnang Vorachith (from 2001). **Capital:** Vientiane (Viangchan). **Official language:** Lao. **Official religion:** none. **Monetary unit:** 1 kip (KN) = 100 at; valuation (28 Jun 2002) managed floating rate, $1 = KN 7,600.

Demography

Area: 91,429 sq mi, 236,800 sq km. **Population** (2001): 5,636,000. **Density** (2001): persons per sq mi 61.6, persons per sq km 23.8. **Urban** (1999): 23.0%. **Sex distribution** (1996): male 49.42%; female 50.58%. **Age breakdown** (1996): under 15, 44.2%; 15–29, 25.4%; 30–44, 16.0%; 45–59, 8.7%; 60–74, 4.5%; 75 and over, 1.2%. **Ethnic composition** (2000): Lao-Lum (Lao) 53.0%; Lao-Theung (Mon-Khmer) 23.0%; Lao-Tai (Tai) 13.0%; Lao-Soung (Miao [Hmong] and Man [Yao]) 10.0%; other (ethnic Chinese or Vietnamese) 1.0%. **Religious affiliation** (2000): Buddhist 48.8%; traditional beliefs 41.7%; nonreligious 4.3%; Christian 2.1%; other 3.1%. **Major cities** (1995): Vientiane (Viangchan) 528,100; Louangphrabang 55,300; Savannakhét 47,500; Salavan 42,500; Pakxe 32,500. **Location:** southeastern Asia, bordering China, Vietnam, Cambodia, Thailand, and Myanmar (Burma).

Vital statistics

Birth rate per 1,000 pop. (2001): 36.5 (world avg. 22.5). **Death rate** per 1,000 pop. (2001): 13.1 (world avg. 9.0). **Natural increase rate** per 1,000 pop. (2001): 23.4 (world avg. 13.5). **Total fertility rate** (avg. births per childbearing woman; 2001): 5.0. **Life expectancy** at birth (2001): male 53.0 years; female 55.0 years.

National economy

Budget (1998–99). *Revenue:* KN 1,312,100,000,-000 (taxes 52.3%, foreign grants 37.0%, nontax revenue 10.7%). *Expenditures:* KN 1,685,100,000,000 (current expenditure 31.8%, capital expenditure 68.2%). **Public debt** (external, outstanding; 1999): $2,471,000,000. **Tourism** (1999): receipts from visitors $97,000,000; expenditures by nationals abroad $12,000,000. **Population economically active** (1989): total 1,888,000; activity rate of total pop. 49.0% (participation rates [1985]: ages 15–64, 84.2%; female 45.3%; unemployed [1994] 2.6%). **Production** (metric tons except as noted). *Agriculture, forestry, fishing* (1999): rice 2,103,000, sugarcane 174,000, corn (maize) 96,000; livestock (number of live animals) 1,937,000 pigs, 1,497,000 cattle, 1,286,000 water; roundwood (1998) 4,591,000 cu m; fish catch (1997) 40,000. *Mining and quarrying* (1997): gypsum 145,000; rock salt 18,000; tin (metal content) 618. *Manufacturing* (1998): plastic products 3,225; tobacco 1,000; detergent 912. *Energy production (consumption):* electricity (kW-hr; 1996) 1,294,000,000 (517,000,000); coal (metric tons; 1996) 1,000 (1,000); petroleum products (metric tons; 1996) none (107,000). **Gross national product** (1999): $1,476,000,000 ($290 per capita). **Household income and expenditure.** Average household size (1995) 6.1%; average annual income per

household KN 3,710. **Land use** (1994): forested 54.4%; meadows and pastures 3.5%; agricultural and under permanent cultivation 3.9%; other 38.2%.

Foreign trade

Imports (1998-c.i.f.): $552,800,000 (consumption goods 42.3%; investment goods 41.0%, of which construction and electrical equipment 14.7%, motor vehicles 7.1%; materials for garment assembly 12.1%). *Major import sources* (1997): Thailand 52.0%; Vietnam 3.9%; Japan 1.6%; Hong Kong 1.5%; China 0.8%. **Exports** (1998): $369,500,000 (wood products 34.3%; garments 20.8%; electricity 18.0%; coffee 14.3%). *Major export destinations* (1997): Vietnam 42.7%; Thailand 22.1%; France 6.3%; Belgium 5.6%; Germany 5.1%.

Transport and communications

Transport. *Roads* (1996): total length 22,321 km (paved [1995] 14%). *Vehicles* (1996): passenger cars 16,320; trucks and buses 4,200. *Air transport* (1995): passenger-km 48,000,000; metric ton-km cargo 5,000,000; airports (1996) with scheduled flights 11. **Communications** Total units (units per 1,000 persons). Daily newspaper circulation (1996): 18,000 (3.7); Radio receivers (1997): 730,000 (145); Television receivers (1999): 51,000 (9.6); Telephone main lines (1999): 34,493 (6.5); Cellular telephone subscribers (1999): 9,048 (1.7); Personal computers (1999): 12,000 (2.3); Internet users (1999): 2,000 (0.4).

Education and health

Educational attainment (1985). Percentage of pop. age 6 and over having: no schooling 49.3%; primary 41.2%; secondary 9.1%; higher 0.4%. **Literacy** (1995): total pop. age 15 and over literate 56.6%; males literate 69.4%; females literate 44.4%. **Health:** physicians (1995) 3,100 (1 per 1,563 persons); hospital beds (1990) 10,364 (1 per 402 persons); infant mortality rate (2001) 91.0. **Food** (1999): daily per capita caloric intake 2,152 (vegetable products 93%, animal products 7%); (1997) 97% of FAO recommended minimum requirement.

Military

Total active duty personnel (2000): 29,100 (army 85.9%, navy 2.1%, air force 12.0%). **Military expenditure as percentage of GNP** (1997): 3.4% (world 2.6%); per capita expenditure $12.

Background

The Lao people migrated into Laos from southern China after the 8th century AD, displacing indigenous tribes. In the 14th century Fa Ngum founded the first Laotian state, Lan Xang. Except for a period of rule by Burma (1574–1637), the Lan Xang kingdom ruled Laos until 1713, when it split into three kingdoms. France gained control of the region in 1893. In 1945 Japan seized it and declared Laos independent. The area reverted to French rule after World War II. The Geneva Conference of 1954 unified and granted independence to Laos. Communist forces took control

1 metric ton = about 1.1 short tons;   1 kilometer = 0.6 mi (statute);   1 metric ton-km cargo = about 0.68 short ton-mi cargo;   c.i.f.: cost, insurance, and freight;   f.o.b.: free on board

in 1975, establishing the Lao People's Democratic Republic. Laos held its first election in 1989 and promulgated a new constitution in 1991. Although its economy was adversely affected by the mid-1990s Asian monetary crises, it realized a longtime goal in 1997 when it joined the Association of Southeast Asian Nations.

Recent Developments

A spate of bombings beginning 30 Mar 2000, at a restaurant in Vientiane and continuing throughout the year caused much puzzled speculation in Laos. The country suffered from record flooding of the Mekong River basin in September. In 2001 human rights groups in the US heavily criticized the continuing forced repatriation of refugees from Thailand.

Internet resources: <http://visit.laos.com>

Latvia

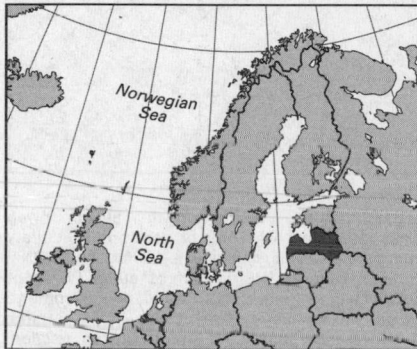

Official name: Latvijas Republika (Republic of Latvia). **Form of government:** unitary multiparty republic with a single legislative body (Parliament, or Saeima [100]). **Chief of state:** President Vaira Vike-Freiberga (from 1999). **Head of government:** Prime Minister Andris Berzins (from 2000). **Capital:** Riga. **Official language:** Latvian. **Official religion:** none. **Monetary unit:** 1 lats (Ls; plural lati) = 100 santimi; valuation (28 Jun 2002) $1 = 0.60 lats.

Demography

Area: 24,938 sq mi, 64,589 sq km. **Population** (2001): 2,358,000. **Density** (2001): persons per sq mi 94.5, persons per sq km 36.5. **Urban** (2000): 68.9%. **Sex distribution** (2000): male 46.03%; female 53.97%. **Age breakdown** (2000): under 15, 17.8%; 15–29, 21.2%; 30–44, 22.1%; 45–59, 18.2%; 60–74, 15.4%; 75 and over, 5.3%. **Ethnic composition** (2000): Latvian 57.6%; Russian 29.6%; Belarusian 4.1%; Ukrainian 2.7%; Polish 2.5%; Lithuanian 1.4%; other 2.1%. **Religious affiliation** (1995): Christian 39.6%, of which Protestant 16.7% (of which Lutheran 14.6%), Roman Catholic 14.9%, Orthodox 8.0%, Jewish 0.6%; other (mostly nonreligious) 59.8%. **Major cities** (2000): Riga (2001) 755,600; Daugavpils 114,829; Liepaja 89,439; Jelgava 63,269; Jurmala 55,671. **Location:** Eastern Europe, bordering Estonia, Russia, Belarus, Lithuania, and the Baltic Sea.

Vital statistics

Birth rate per 1,000 pop. (1999): 8.0 (world avg. 22.5); (1998) legitimate 62.9%; illegitimate 37.1%. **Death rate** per 1,000 pop. (1999): 13.5 (world avg. 9.0). **Natural increase rate** per 1,000 pop. (1999): –5.5 (world avg. 13.5). **Total fertility rate** (avg. births per childbearing woman; 1999): 1.2. **Marriage rate** per 1,000 pop. (1999): 3.9. **Divorce rate** per 1,000 pop. (1999): 2.5. **Life expectancy** at birth (1999): male 64.9 years; female 76.2 years.

National economy

Budget (1998). *Revenue:* Ls 1,577,400,000 (social security contributions 27.1%, value-added taxes 20.1%, personal income taxes 13.9%, excises 10.7%, nontax revenue 10.1%). *Expenditures:* Ls 1,572,-300,000 (social security and welfare 34.4%, education 15.7%, health 9.4%, police 5.8%, defense 2.4%). **Production** (metric tons except as noted). *Agriculture, forestry, fishing* (1999): grasses for forage and silage 13,800,000, hay 1,355,000, potatoes 795,500, livestock (number of live animals) 403,400 pigs, 375,700 cattle; roundwood (1998) 10,030,000 cu m; fish catch (1997) 106,027. *Mining and quarrying* (1998): peat 171,700; gypsum 119,100. *Manufacturing* (value added in Ls '000,000; 1996): alcoholic beverages 58.7; fish processing 32.8. *Energy production (consumption):* electricity (kW-hr; 1998) 5,797,000,000 (5,133,000,000); coal (1996) none (293,000); (1996) none (2,079,000). **Household income and expenditure.** Average household size (1996) 2.7; annual disposable income per household (1996) Ls 1,659; sources of income (1998): wages and salaries 55.8%, pensions and transfers 25.7%, self-employment 9.5%; expenditure (1998): food, beverages, and tobacco 46.4%, housing and energy 16.6%, transportation and communications 9.8%, clothing and footwear 6.9%. **Public debt** (external, outstanding; 1999): $864,800,000. **Gross national product** (1999): $5,913,000,000 ($2,420 per capita). **Population economically active** (1997): total 1,186,100; activity rate of total pop. 48.2% (participation rates: ages 15–64, 70.2%; female 48.1%; unemployed [1998] 7.6%). **Tourism** (in $'000,000; 1999): receipts 118; expenditures 268. **Land use** (1994): forested 44.4%; meadows and pastures 12.4; agricultural and under permanent cultivation 27.0%; other 16.2%.

Foreign trade

Imports (1998-c.i.f.): Ls 1,881,000,000 (machinery and equipment 20.5%, chemicals and chemical products 11.1%, mineral fuels 10.5%, transport vehicles 10.4%, base and fabricated metals 8.4%). *Major import sources:* Germany 16.8%; Russia 11.8%; Finland 9.5%; Sweden 7.2%; Estonia 6.6%. **Exports** (1998-f.o.b.): Ls 1,069,000,000 (wood and paper products 33.5%, textiles and clothing 16.1%, food and beverages 9.8%, base and fabricated metals 9.8%). *Major export destinations:* Germany 15.6%; UK 13.5%; Russia 12.1%; Sweden 10.3%; Lithuania 7.4%.

Transport and communications

Transport. *Railroads* (1998): length 2,413 km; passenger-km (1998) 1,059,000,000; metric-km cargo (1998) 12,995,000,000. *Roads* (1997): total length 55,942 km (paved 38%). Vehicles (1997): passenger

cars 431,816; trucks and buses 95,329. *Air transport* (1998): passenger-km 298,000,000; metric ton-km cargo 9,000,000; airports with scheduled flights (1996) 1. **Communications** Total units (units per 1,000 persons). Daily newspaper circulation (1996): 616,000 (247); Radio receivers (1997): 1,760,000 (713); Television receivers (1999): 1,808,000 (755); Telephone main lines (1999): 731,527 (306); Cellular telephone subscribers (1999): 274,344 (115); Personal computers (1999): 200,000 (84); Internet users (1999): 105,000 (44).

Education and health

Educational attainment (2000). Percentage of pop. age 15 and over having: incomplete primary education 2.4%; complete primary 6.1%; lower secondary 26.5%; upper secondary 51.1%; higher 13.9%. **Literacy** (1995): percentage of total pop. age 15 and over literate 99.6%. **Health** (1998): physicians 6,900 (1 per 355 persons); hospital beds 23,165 (1 per 106 persons); infant mortality rate per 1,000 live births (1999) 11.4. **Food** (1999): daily per capita caloric intake 2,904 (vegetable products 75%, animal products 25%); 113% of FAO recommended minimum requirement.

Military

Total active duty personnel (2000): 5,050 (army 47.5%, navy 16.6%, air force 4.2%, national guard 31.7%); 3,500 paramilitary not included. **Military expenditure as percentage of GNP** (1997): 0.9% (world 2.6%); per capita expenditure $39.

Did you know? Riga, Latvia, is allegedly home of the first decorated Christmas tree, in 1510. The "Riga tree" was burned after being used in ceremonies that combined Christian and pagan customs.

Background

Latvia was settled by the Balts in ancient times. It was conquered by the Vikings in the 9th century and later dominated by its German-speaking neighbors, who Christianized the people in the 12th–13th centuries. By 1230 German rule was established. From the mid-16th to the early 18th century, the region was split between Poland and Sweden, but by the end of the 18th century all of Latvia had been annexed by Russia. Latvia declared its independence after the Russian Revolution of 1917, but in 1940 the Soviet Red Army invaded. Held by Nazi Germany in 1941–44, the country was recaptured by the Soviets and incorporated into the Soviet Union. Latvia gained its independence in 1991 with the breakup of the Soviet Union; throughout the 1990s it sought to privatize the economy and build ties with Western Europe.

Recent Developments

Latvians celebrated the 800th anniversary of the capital, Riga, in 2001. They were also buoyant with optimism as the country neared membership in the

European Union and NATO, a process that continued into 2002. Russia opposed both Latvia's intention to join NATO, claiming that Latvia discriminated against its large Russian-speaking population, and the country's support of the campaign against terrorism, claiming that Latvia was aiding Chechen terrorists.

Internet resources: <www.eunet.lv/VT>

Lebanon

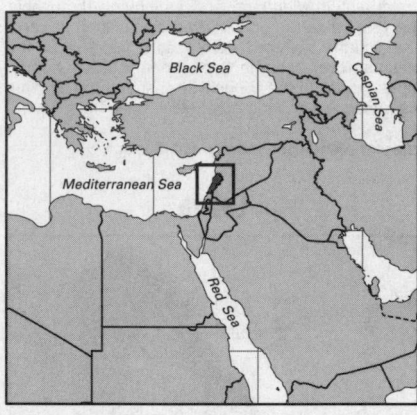

Official name: Al-Jumhuriyah al-Lubnaniyah (Lebanese Republic). **Form of government:** unitary multiparty republic with one legislative house (National Assembly [128]). **Chief of state:** President Émile Lahoud (from 1998). **Head of government:** Prime Minister Rafiq Hariri (from 2000). **Capital:** Beirut. **Official language:** Arabic. **Official religion:** none. **Monetary unit:** 1 Lebanese pound (£L) = 100 piastres; valuation (28 Jun 2002) $1 = £L 1,513.50.

Demography

Area: 4,016 sq mi, 10,400 sq km. **Population** (2001): 3,628,000. **Density** (2001): persons per sq mi 903.3, persons per sq km 348.8. **Urban** (1999): 89.4%. **Sex distribution** (2000): male 48.44%; female 51.56%. **Age breakdown** (2000): under 15, 27.9%; 15–29, 33.5%; 30–44, 19.0%; 45–59, 10.1%; 60–74, 7.2%; 75 and over, 2.3%. **Ethnic composition** (1996): Arab c. 93%, of which Lebanese c. 84%, Palestinian c. 9%; Armenian c. 6%; Kurd and other c. 1%. **Religious affiliation** (1995): Muslim 55.3%, of which Shi'i 34.0%, Sunni 21.3%; Christian 37.6%, of which Catholic 25.1% (Maronite 19.0%, Greek Catholic or Melchite 4.6%), Orthodox 11.7% (Greek Orthodox 6.0%, Armenian Apostolic 5.2%), Protestant 0.5%; Druze 7.1%. **Major cities** (1994): Beirut 1,100,000; Tripoli 240,000; Sidon (Sayda) 150,000; Juniyah 100,000; Zahlah 100,000. **Location:** the Middle East, bordering Syria, Israel, and the Mediterranean Sea.

Vital statistics

Birth rate per 1,000 pop. (2000): 20.3 (world avg. 22.5). **Death rate** per 1,000 pop. (2000): 6.4 (world

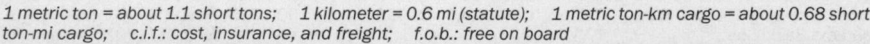

1 metric ton = about 1.1 short tons;   1 kilometer = 0.6 mi (statute);   1 metric ton-km cargo = about 0.68 short ton-mi cargo;   c.i.f.: cost, insurance, and freight;   f.o.b.: free on board

avg. 9.0). **Natural increase rate** per 1,000 pop. (2000): 13.9 (world avg. 13.5). **Total fertility rate** (avg. births per childbearing woman; 2000): 2.1. **Life expectancy** at birth (1999): male 68.9 years; female 73.7 years.

National economy

Budget (2000). *Revenue:* £L 4,091,435,000,000 (1998; tax revenue 74.6%, of which customs revenues 44.1%, income tax 9.0%, taxes on goods and services 8.4%, property tax 8.4%, miscellaneous taxes and fees 2.1%; nontax revenue 25.4%). *Expenditures:* £L 8,190,034,000,000 (current expenditures 81.1%, of which debt service 40.0%, public services 13.3%, defense 9.7%, education 8.3%, social security 6.4%, health 2.6%; capital expenditures 18.9%). **Production** (metric tons except as noted). *Agriculture, forestry, fishing* (2000): tomatoes 335,000, sugar beets 330,000; livestock (number of live animals) 445,000 goats, 380,000 sheep, 77,000 cattle; roundwood (2000) 412,150 cu m; fish catch (1999) 3,860. *Mining and quarrying* (1996): lime 16,000; salt 4,000; gypsum 2,000. *Manufacturing* (1999): cement 2,715,000; flour 411,300; olive oil 6,000. *Energy production (consumption):* electricity (kW-hr; 2000) 9,236,000,000 (1998; 9,010,000,000); crude petroleum (barrels; 1998) none (1,358,000). **Gross national product** (1999): $15,796,000,000 ($3,700 per capita). **Population economically active** (1995): total 1,028,000; activity rate of total pop. 25.4% (participation rates: over age 15 [1988] 44%; female c. 30%). **Public debt** (external, outstanding; 1999): $5,568,000,000. **Household income and expenditure.** Average household size (1998) 4.4; average annual income per household (1994) £L 2,400,000: sources of income (1974): wages 27.9%, transfers 3.0%, other 69.1%; expenditure (1966): food 42.8%, housing 16.8%, clothing 8.0%, health care 7.2%. **Tourism** (1999): receipts from visitors $673,000,000. **Land use** (1994): forested 7.8%; meadows and pastures 1.0%; agricultural and under permanent cultivation 29.9%; wasteland and other areas 61.3%.

Foreign trade

Imports (2000-c.i.f.): £L 6,228,000,000 (1995; machinery and transport equipment 27.0%, metals and metal products 9.8%, mineral products 8.8%, processed food 7.8%, chemicals 6.7%). *Major import sources* (1999): Italy 10.9%; France 9.6%; Germany 8.9%; US 8.1%; Switzerland 7.1%. **Exports** (2000): £L 714,000,000 (1995; pharmaceuticals and detergents 15.2%, food and beverages 15.1%, machinery and transport equipment 10.2%, paper products 8.9%, aluminum products 6.1%, metals and metal products 4.3%, gold products 2.6%). *Major export destinations* (1999): Saudi Arabia 10.5%; UAE 8.0%; France 7.7%; US 6.2%; Syria 4.8%.

Transport and communications

Transport. Railroads (1999): length 222 km. *Roads* (1996): total length 6,350 km (paved 95%). *Vehicles* (1997): passenger cars 1,299,398; trucks and buses 85,242. *Air transport* (1997; MEA-Airliban international flights): passenger-km 2,116,000,000; metric ton-km cargo 319,000,000; airports (1999) 1. **Communications** Total units (units per 1,000 persons). Daily newspaper circulation (1996): 435,000 (141);

Radio receivers (1997): 2,850,000 (907); Television receivers (1998): 1,120,000 (351); Telephone main lines (1999): 650,000 (201); Cellular telephone subscribers (1999): 627,000 (194); Personal computers (1999): 150,000 (42); Internet users (1999): 200,000 (56).

Education and health

Literacy (1995): total pop. age 15 and over literate 1,829,000 (92.4%); males literate 94.7%; females literate 90.3%. **Health** (1997): physicians 7,203 (1 per 476 persons); hospital beds (1995) 11,596 (1 per 319 persons); infant mortality rate per 1,000 live births (2000) 29.3. **Food** (1999): daily per capita caloric intake 3,256 (vegetable products 86%, animal products 14%); 131% of FAO recommended minimum.

Military

Total active duty personnel (2000): Lebanese national armed forces 63,570 (army 95.4%, navy 1.9%, air force 2.7%). External regular military forces include: UN peacekeeping force in Lebanon (August 2001) 4,486; Syrian army 22,000. **Military expenditure as percentage of GDP** (1997): 3.0% (world 2.6%); per capita expenditure: $135.

Background

Much of present-day Lebanon corresponds to ancient Phoenicia, which was settled c. 3000 BC. In the 6th century AD, Christians fleeing Syrian persecution settled in what is now northern Lebanon and founded the Maronite Church. Arab tribesmen settled in southern Lebanon and by the 11th century had founded the Druze faith. Lebanon was later ruled by the Mamluks. In 1516 the Ottoman Turks seized control; the Turks ended the local rule of the Druze Shihab princes in 1842. After the massacre of Maronites by Druze in 1860, France forced the Ottomans to form an autonomous province for the Christian area, known as Mount Lebanon. Following World War I, it was administered by the French military, but by late 1946 it was fully independent. After the Arab-Israeli War of 1948-49, Palestinian refugees settled in southern Lebanon. In 1970 the Palestine Liberation Organization (PLO) moved its headquarters there and began raids into northern Israel. The Christian-dominated Lebanese government tried to curb them, and in response the PLO sided with Lebanon's Muslims in their conflict with Christians, sparking a civil war by 1975. In 1982 Israeli forces invaded in an effort to drive Palestinian forces out of southern Lebanon. Israeli troops withdrew from most of Lebanon in 1985, leaving the conflict unresolved, but later returned. A cease-fire, agreed to in 1996, was broken in 1997 when Israeli soldiers and Lebanon's Hezbollah forces clashed.

Recent Developments

Following numerous contentious talks between Lebanon and Israel, Israeli troops abruptly withdrew from Lebanon in 2000. Pressure to deploy the Lebanese army in the liberated southern areas and thus put an end to any further possible activities by Hezbollah either there or south of the Lebanese border was resisted by the government. In 2001 Hezbollah still refused to consider that the country had regained its full sovereignty, since Israel still controlled the Sheba farms enclave and had not released all Lebanese prisoners of war, and Israeli warplanes patrolled Lebanese skies at will.

Internet resources: <www.presidency.gov.lb>

Lesotho

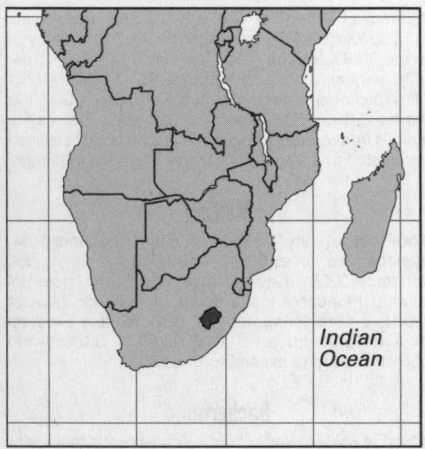

Indian Ocean

Official name: Lesotho (Sotho); Kingdom of Lesotho (English). **Form of government:** transitional regime with 2 legislative houses (Senate [33]; National Assembly [80; will have 120 seats as of 25 May 2002 elections]); traditionally a hereditary monarchy, an interim political authority was mandated in 1998 to make Lesotho more democratic. **Chief of state:** King Letsie III (from 1996). **Head of government:** Prime Minister Pakalitha Mosisili (from 1998). **Capital:** Maseru. **Official languages:** Sotho; English. **Official religion:** Christianity. **Monetary unit:** 1 loti (plural maloti [M]) = 100 lisente; valuation (28 Jun 2002) $1 = M 10.31.

Demography

Area: 11,720 sq mi, 30,355 sq km. **Population** (2001): 2,177,000. **Density** (2001): persons per sq mi 185.8, persons per sq km 71.7. **Urban** (1996): 16.9%. **Sex distribution** (1996): male 49.20%; female 50.80%. **Age breakdown** (1996): under 15, 43.1%; 15–29, 27.6%; 30–44, 15.0%; 45–59, 8.6%; 60–74, 4.8%; 75 and over, 0.9%. **Ethnic composition** (2000): Sotho 80.3%; Zulu 14.4%; other 5.3%. **Religious affiliation** (2000): Christian 91.0%, of which Roman Catholic 37.5%, Protestant (mostly Presbyterian) 13.0%, African Christian 11.8%; other (mostly traditional beliefs) 9.0%. **Major urban centers** (1996): Maseru 137,837; Teyateyaneng 48,869; Maputsoe 27,951; Hlotse 23,122; Mafeteng 20,804. **Location:** southern Africa, surrounded by South Africa.

Vital statistics

Birth rate per 1,000 pop. (2000): 31.7 (world avg. 22.5). **Death rate** per 1,000 pop. (2000): 14.6 (world avg. 9.0). **Natural increase rate** per 1,000 pop.

(2000): 17.1 (world avg. 13.5). **Total fertility rate** (avg. births per childbearing woman; 2000): 4.2. **Life expectancy** at birth (2000): male 49.8 years; female 51.8 years.

National economy

Budget (1999–2000). *Revenue:* M 2,580,700,000 (customs receipts 45.8%, grants and nontax revenue 28.8%, income tax 13.5%, sales tax 10.2%). *Expenditures:* M 2,913,500,000 (personal emoluments 41.9%, capital expenditure 32.4%, subsidies and transfers 13.0%, interest payments 12.7%). **Production** (metric tons except as noted). *Agriculture, forestry, fishing* (1999): corn (maize) 125,000, roots and tubers 85,000, sorghum 33,000; livestock (number of live animals) 720,000 sheep, 560,000 goats, 510,000 cattle; roundwood (1998) 1,594,000 cu m; fish catch (1998) 30. *Mining and quarrying* (1998): diamonds 2,398 carats. *Manufacturing* (value added in $'000,000; 1995): food products 58; beverages 38; textiles 14. *Energy production (consumption):* energy data for Lesotho compiled with South Africa energy data. **Public debt** (external, outstanding; 1999): $661,800,000. **Tourism** (1999): receipts from visitors $19,000,000; expenditures by nationals abroad $12,000,000. **Population economically active** (1993): total 617,871; activity rate of total pop. 45.1% (participation rates: ages 15–64 [1986] 79.8%; female 23.7%; unemployed [1992] 35.0%). **Household income and expenditure.** Average household size (1996) 5.0; average annual income per household (1986–87) M 2,832; sources of income (1986–87): transfer payments 44.7%, self-employment 27.8%, wages and salaries 22.4%, other 5.1%; expenditure (1989): food 48.0%, clothing 16.4%, household durable goods 11.9%, housing and energy 10.1%, transportation 4.7%. **Gross national product** (at current market prices; 1999): $1,158,000,000 ($550 per capita). **Land use** (1998): meadows and pastures 65.9%; agricultural and under permanent cultivation 10.7%; other 23.4%.

Foreign trade

Imports (1998-c.i.f.): M 5,199,800,000 (1990; manufactured goods [excluding chemicals, machinery, and transport equipment] 42.5%; food and live animals 19.1%; machinery and transport equipment 15.3%; petroleum products 8.6%). *Major import sources:* Customs Union of Southern Africa (largely South Africa) 88.7%; Asia 7.2%; the Americas 1.3%. **Exports** (1998): M 1,109,600,000 (manufactured goods 71.6%; machinery and transport equipment 15.1%; food and live animals 4.0%; beverages and tobacco 3.5%; crude materials 1.8%). *Major export destinations:* Customs Union of Southern Africa (largely South Africa) 65.5%; the Americas 33.6%; Europe 0.5%.

Transport and communications

Transport. *Railroads* (1999): length 2.6 km. *Roads* (1996): total length 4,955 km (paved 18%). *Vehicles* (1996): passenger cars 12,610; trucks and buses 25,000. *Air transport* (1996): passenger-km 6,200,000; metric ton-km cargo 577,000; airports

---

1 metric ton = about 1.1 short tons;   1 kilometer = 0.6 mi (statute);   1 metric ton-km cargo = about 0.68 short ton-mi cargo;   c.i.f.: cost, insurance, and freight;   f.o.b.: free on board

(1997) with scheduled flights 1. **Communications** Total units (units per 1,000 persons). Daily newspaper circulation (1996): 15,000 (7.6); Radio receivers (1997): 104,000 (52); Television receivers (1999): 33,000 (16); Telephone main lines (1998): 21,000 (10); Cellular telephone subscribers (1998): 9,831 (4.8); Internet users (1999): 1,000 (0.5).

Education and health

Educational attainment (1986-87). Percentage of pop. age 10 and over having: no formal education 22.9%; primary 52.8%; secondary 23.2%; higher 0.6%. **Literacy** (1995): total pop. age 15 and over literate 849,700 (71.3%); males literate 468,000 (81.1%); females literate 381,700 (62.3%). **Health:** physicians (1995) 105 (1 per 18,527 persons); hospital beds (1992) 2,400 (1 per 765 persons); infant mortality rate per 1,000 live births (2000) 83.0. **Food** (1999): daily per capita caloric intake 2,300 (vegetable products 95%, animal products 5%); (1997) 101% of FAO recommended minimum requirement

Military

Total active duty personnel (2000): 2,000. **Military expenditure as percentage of GNP** (1997): 2.5% (world 2.6%); per capita expenditure $16.

Background

Bantu-speaking farmers began to settle the area in the 16th century, and a number of chiefdoms arose. The most powerful organized the Basotho in 1824, and obtained British protection in 1843, as tension between the Basotho and the South African Boers increased. The area became a British territory in 1868 and was annexed to the Cape Colony in 1871. The colony's effort to disarm the Basotho resulted in revolt in 1880, and four years later it separated from the colony and became a British High Commission Territory. In 1966 it declared its independence. A new constitution (1993) ended seven years of military rule. In the late 20th century, Lesotho suffered from internal political problems and a deteriorating economy.

Recent Developments

Political tensions boiled over after Lesotho's May 1998 elections, resulting in the September arrival of troops from South Africa and Botswana and the looting and destruction of much of Maseru. The troops withdrew in the spring of 1999. Throughout 1999 and 2000 electoral reforms were debated, and a new plan was agreed upon in February 2001. Parliamentary elections were held under the new system in May 2002.

Internet resources: <www.lesotho.gov.ls>

Liberia

Official name: Republic of Liberia. **Form of government:** multiparty republic with two legislative houses (Senate [26]; House of Representatives [64]). **Head of state and government:** President Charles Taylor (from 1997). **Capital:** Monrovia. **Official language:** English. **Official religion:** none. **Monetary unit:** 1 Liberian dollar (L$) = 100 cents; valuation (28 Jun 2002) US$1 = L$1.00 (par value rate to US$ ineffec-

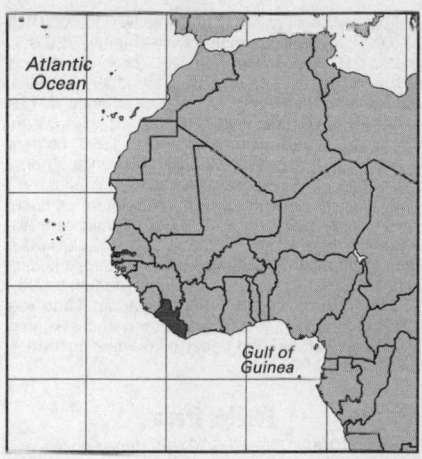

tive from January 1998; the independent free market exchange rate was roughly US$1 = L$60 in August 2001).

Demography

Area: 37,743 sq mi, 97,754 sq km. **Population** (2001): 3,226,000. **Density** (2001): persons per sq mi 85.5, persons per sq km 33.3. **Urban** (1999): 44.2%. **Sex distribution** (2000): male 49.37%; female 50.63%. **Age breakdown** (2000): under 15, 43.0%; 15-29, 26.9%; 30-44, 15.2%; 45-59, 9.5%; 60-74, 4.2%; 75 and over, 1.2%. **Ethnic composition** (1984): Kpelle 19.4%; Bassa 13.9%; Grebo 9.0%; Gio 7.8%; Kru 7.3%; Mano 7.1%; other 35.5%. **Religious affiliation** (1995): traditional beliefs 63.0%; Christian 21.0%, of which Protestant 13.5%, African Christian 5.1%, Roman Catholic 2.4%, Muslim 16.0%. **Major cities:** Monrovia (1999) 479,000; Harbel (1985) 60,000; Gbarnga (1986) 30,000; Buchanan (1985) 25,000; Yekepa (1985) 16,000. **Location:** western Africa, bordering Guinea, Côte d'Ivoire, the Atlantic Ocean, and Sierra Leone.

Vital statistics

Birth rate per 1,000 pop. (2000): 47.2 (world avg. 22.5). **Death rate** per 1,000 pop. (2000): 16.6 (world avg. 9.0). **Natural increase rate** per 1,000 pop. (2000): 30.6 (world avg. 13.5). **Total fertility rate** (avg. births per childbearing woman; 2000): 6.4. **Life expectancy** at birth (2000): male 49.6 years; female 52.5 years.

National economy

Budget (1999). *Revenue:* US$65,500,000,000 (tax revenue 92.2%, of which import duties and consular fees 29.9%, maritime revenue 23.2%, income and profit taxes 22.4%, sales tax 15.9%, property taxes 0.5%). *Expenditures:* US$67,500,000,000 (current expenditure 85.2%, of which goods and services 49.3%, wages 21.0%, subsidies and transfers 8.8%, interest on debt 5.2%; development expenditure 8.3%; other 6.5%). **Population economically active** (1997): total 1,183,000; activity rate 51.4% (participation rates: ages 10-64 [1994] 64.0%; female 39.5%; unemployed [1996] 95%). **Production** (metric tons except as noted). *Agriculture, forestry, fishing*

(1999): cassava 313,000, sugarcane 250,000, rice 210,000; livestock (number of live animals) 220,000 goats, 210,000 sheep, 120,000 pigs; roundwood (1998) 3,021,000 cu m; fish catch (1998) 10,830. *Mining and quarrying* (1998): diamonds 7,719 carats (export figure); gold 72 kg (export figure). *Manufacturing*: (1996) palm oil 45,000; (1993) cement 8,300; (1992) cigarettes 22,000,000 units. *Energy production (consumption):* electricity (kW-hr; 1996) 488,000,000 (488,000,000); petroleum products (metric tons; 1994) none (106,000). **Public debt** (external, outstanding; 1999): US$1,062,000,000. **Household income and expenditure.** Average household size (1983) 4.3. **Gross national product** (1996): US$1,174,000,000 (US$490 per capita). **Land use** (1994): forested 47.8%; meadows and pastures 20.8%; agricultural and under permanent cultivation 3.8%; other 27.6%.

Foreign trade

Imports (1999): US$167,500,000 (food and live animals 31.9%, machinery and transport equipment 21.7%, petroleum and petroleum products 10.4%, basic manufactures 10.2%, chemicals 7.9%, beverages and tobacco 4.2%). *Major import sources* (1998): South Korea 26.8%; Italy 21.7%; Japan 16.9%; France 13.4%; Croatia 5.7%; Singapore 4.8%. **Exports** (1999): US$55,700,000 (rubber 56.9%, logs and timber 39.1%, cocoa 2.0%, coffee 1.8%). *Major export destinations* (1999): United States 54.3%; France 24.3%; Singapore 5.2%; Belgium 4.4%; Italy 3.3%; Malaysia 2.4%.

Transport and communications

Transport. *Railroads* (1998): route length 304 mi, 490 km; short ton-mi cargo 534,000,000, metric ton-km cargo 860,000,000. *Roads* (1996): total length 6,600 mi, 10,600 km (paved 6%). *Vehicles* (1996): passenger cars 9,400; trucks and buses 25,000. *Air transport* (1992): passenger-mi 4,300,000, passenger-km 7,000,000; short ton-mi cargo 68,000, metric ton-km cargo 100,000; airports (1998) with scheduled flights 1. **Communications** Total units (units per 1,000 persons). Daily newspaper circulation (1996): 35,000 (16); Radio receivers (1997): 790,000 (329); Television receivers (1997): 70,000 (29); Telephone main lines (1999): 6,600 (2.2).

Education and health

Literacy (1995): total pop. age 15 and over literate 705,000 (38.3%); males literate 523,000 (53.9%); females literate 182,000 (22.4%). **Health:** physicians (1992) 257 (1 per 8,333 persons); infant mortality rate (2000) 134.6. **Food** (1999): daily per capita caloric intake 2,089 (vegetable products 97%, animal products 3%); 90% of FAO recommended minimum requirement.

Military

Total active duty personnel: About 11,000–15,000 in all armed forces as of 2000. West African (ECOMOG) peacekeepers withdrew in January 1999 and the civil war resumed in remote locales as of April 1999. The fighting continued as of May 2002.

Did you know? Liberia is the only sub-Saharan state in Africa never subjected to colonial rule, and it is the oldest republic on the continent.

Background

Africa's oldest republic, Liberia was established as a home for freed US slaves under the American Colonization Society, which founded a colony at Cape Mesurado in 1821. In 1822 Jehudi Ashmun, a Methodist minister, became the director of the settlement and Liberia's real founder. Joseph Jenkins Roberts, Liberia's first nonwhite governor, proclaimed Liberian independence in 1847 and expanded its boundaries, which were officially established in 1892. In 1980 a coup led by Samuel K. Doe marked the end of the Americo-Liberians' long political dominance over the indigenous Africans. A rebellion in 1989 escalated into a destructive civil war in the 1990s. A peace agreement was reached in 1996, and elections were held in 1997.

Recent Developments

Violence and instability continued into 2002, despite the official end of the civil war. The Liberian government accused neighboring Guinea of supporting antigovernment rebels in northern Liberia. UN sanctions were imposed on Liberia in 2001 due to its support of rebel factions in neighboring Sierra Leone. Several newspapers were closed in 2001, and journalists were arrested after criticizing the government. A state of emergency was declared in February 2002 as rebels approached Monrovia.

Internet resources: <www.liberiaemb.org>

Libya

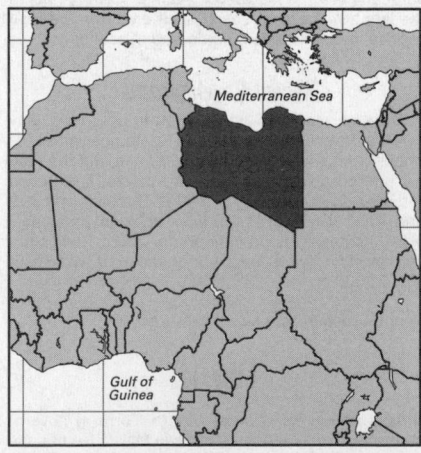

Official name: Al-Jamahiriyah al-'Arabiyah al-Libiyah ash-Sha'biyah al-Ishtirakiyah al-Uzma (Socialist Peo-

1 metric ton = about 1.1 short tons;   1 kilometer = 0.6 mi (statute);   1 metric ton-km cargo = about 0.68 short ton-mi cargo;   c.i.f.: cost, insurance, and freight;   f.o.b.: free on board

ple's Libyan Arab Jamahiriya). **Form of government:** socialist state with one policy-making body (General People's Congress [760]). **Chief of state:** Muammar al-Qaddafi (de facto; from 1969); Secretary of General People's Congress Zentani Muhammad az-Zentani (de jure; from 1992). **Head of government:** Secretary of the General People's Committee (prime minister) Mubarak Abdallah ash-Shamikh (from 2000). **Capital:** Tripoli. **Official language:** Arabic. **Official religion:** Islam. **Monetary unit:** 1 Libyan dinar (LD) = 1,000 dirhams; valuation (28 Jun 2002) $1 = LD 1.26.

Demography

Area: 678,400 sq mi, 1,757,000 sq km. **Population** (2001): 5,241,000. **Density** (2001): persons per sq mi 7.7, persons per sq km 3.0. **Urban** (2000): 87.6%. **Sex distribution** (2000): male 51.44%; female 48.56%. **Age breakdown** (2000): under 15, 35.9%; 15–29, 32.1%; 30–44, 18.4%; 45–59, 7.9%; 60–74, 4.5%; 75 and over, 1.2%. **Ethnic composition** (1995): Libyan Arab 78%; Berber 1%; other 21% (mostly Egyptians, Sudanese, and Chadians). **Religious affiliation** (1995): Sunni Muslim 97.0%; other 3.0%. **Major cities** (1995): Tripoli 1,140,000; Banghazi 650,000; Misratah 280,000; Surt 150,000; Az-Zawiyah (1988) 89,338. **Location:** northern Africa, bordering the Mediterranean Sea, Egypt, The Sudan, Chad, Niger, Algeria, and Tunisia.

Vital statistics

Birth rate per 1,000 pop. (2000): 27.7 (world avg. 22.5). **Death rate** per 1,000 pop. (2000): 3.5 (world avg. 9.0). **Natural increase rate** per 1,000 pop. (2000): 24.2 (world avg. 13.5). **Total fertility rate** (avg. births per childbearing woman; 2000): 3.7. **Marriage rate** per 1,000 pop. (1991; based on civil registry): 5.1. **Divorce rate** per 1,000 pop. (1988; based on civil registrty): 0.6. **Life expectancy** at birth (2000): male 73.3 years; female 77.7 years.

National economy

Budget (1998). *Revenue:* LD 5,311,000,000 (oil revenues 68.4%, other 31.6%). *Expenditures:* LD 5,311,-000,000 (1990–91; current expenditures 55.7%, of which municipalities 39.4%, education and scientific research 4.3%, health 2.7%; capital expenditures 44.3%, of which agriculture and land reclamation 13.6%, industry 5.3%). **Production** (metric tons except as noted). *Agriculture, forestry, fishing* (1998): tomatoes 250,000, potatoes 230,000, olives 200,000; livestock (number of live animals; 1998) 3,700,000 sheep, 1,300,000 goats, 24,000,000 chickens; roundwood (1998) 651,000 cu m; fish catch (1998) 33,594. *Mining and quarrying* (1997): lime 280,000; gypsum 180,000; salt 32,000. *Manufacturing* (value of production in '000,000 LD; 1996): base metals 212, electrical equipment 208, petrochemicals 175. *Energy production (consumption):* electricity (kW-hr; 1996) 18,300,000,000 (18,300,000,000); coal (metric tons; 1996) none (5,000); crude petroleum (barrels; 1999) 481,380,000 ([1996] 112,725,000); petroleum products (metric tons; 1996) 14,070,000 (7,863,000); natural gas (cu m; 1996) 6,392,000,-000 (5,192,000,000). **Land use** (1994): forested 0.5%; meadows and pastures 7.6%; agricultural and under permanent cultivation 1.2%; desert and built-up areas 90.7%. **Population economically active** (1996): total 1,224,000; activity rate of total pop.

26.1% (participation rates [1993]: ages 10 and over, 35.2%; female 9.8%; unemployed [1999] 30.0%). **Gross domestic product** (1998): $32,662,500,000 ($6,700 per capita). **Household income and expenditure.** Average household size (1980) 5.1; expenditure (1977): food 37.2%, housing and energy 32.2%, transportation 9.4%, education and recreation 8.5%, clothing 6.9%, health care 3.3%. **Tourism** (1999): receipts $28,000,000; expenditures $150,000,000.

Foreign trade

Imports (1997): $5,593,000,000 (machinery 25.9%; food products 20.0%; road vehicles 10.1%; chemical products 7.5%). *Major import sources:* Italy 15.8%; Germany 12.8%; Japan 8.1%; UK 7.8%; France 6.2%. **Exports** (1997): $9,029,000,000 (crude petroleum 76.4%; refined petroleum 16.5%; iron and steel 1.5%). *Major export destinations:* Italy 36.2%; Germany 15.0%; Spain 9.1%; Turkey 5.6%; Austria 5.2%.

Transport and communications

Transport. *Roads* (1996): total length 81,600 km (paved 57%). *Vehicles* (1996): passenger cars 809,514; trucks and buses 357,528. *Air transport* (1997): passenger-km 377,000,000; metric ton-km cargo, n.a. **Communications** Total units (units per 1,000 persons). Daily newspaper circulation (1996): 71,000 (14); Radio receivers (1997): 1,350,000 (259); Television receivers (1999): 730,000 (133); Telephone main lines (1999): 550,000 (101); Cellular telephone subscribers (1999): 20,000 (3.6).

Education and health

Educational attainment (1984). Percentage of pop. age 25 and over having: no formal schooling (illiterate) 59.7%; incomplete primary education 15.4%; complete primary 8.5%; some secondary 5.2%; secondary 8.5%, higher 2.7%. **Literacy** (1995): percentage of total pop. age 15 and over literate 76.2%; males literate 87.9%; females literate 63.0%. **Health:** physicians (1997) 6,092 (1 per 781 persons); hospital beds 1998; including beds in clinics) 18,100 (1 per 312 persons); infant mortality rate (2000) 30.1. **Food** (1999): daily per capita caloric intake 3,277 (vegetable products 88%, animal products 12%); 138% of FAO recommended minimum requirement.

Military

Total active duty personnel (2000): 76,000 (army 59.2%, navy 10.5%, air force 30.3%). **Military expenditure as percentage of GNP** (1995): 6.1% (world 2.7%); per capita expenditure $389.

Background

Greeks and Phoenicians settled the area in the 7th century BC. It was conquered by Rome in the 1st century BC and by Arabs in the 7th century AD. In the 16th century the Ottoman Turks combined Libya's three regions under one regency in Tripoli. In 1911 Italy claimed control of Libya, and by the outbreak of World War II 150,000 Italians had immigrated there. The scene of much fighting in the war, it became an independent state in 1951. The discovery of oil in 1959 brought wealth to Libya. A decade later a group of army officers led by Muammar al-Qaddafi deposed the king and made the country an Islamic republic. Under Qaddafi's rule it supported the Palestinian Liberation Organization and terrorist groups, bringing protests from many countries, particularly the US. Intermittent warfare with Chad during the 1970s and '80s ended with Chad's defeat of Libya in 1987. International relations in the 1990s were dominated by the consequences of the 1988 bombing of a US airliner over Lockerbie, Scotland; the US accused Libyan nationalists of the deed and imposed a trade embargo on Libya, endorsed by the UN in 1992.

Recent Developments

Libya handed over the bombing suspects for trial in The Netherlands in 1999, and UN sanctions were suspended the same year. Most US sanctions remained in place pending the outcome of the trial, which began in May 2000. Of the two suspects, one was found guilty and the other not guilty in January 2001. An appeal was heard in early 2002 but was denied, and the convicted man was imprisoned in Scotland. Debate over the lifting of UN and US sanctions continued into 2002.

Internet resources:
<www.arab.net/libya/libya_contents.html>

Liechtenstein

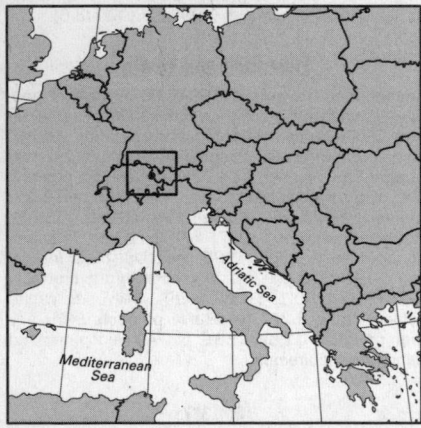

Official name: Fürstentum Liechtenstein (Principality of Liechtenstein). **Form of government:** constitutional monarchy with one legislative house (Diet [25]). **Chief of state:** Prince Hans Adam II (from 1989). **Head of government:** Prime Minister Otmar Hasler (from 5 Apr 2001). **Capital:** Vaduz. **Official language:** German. **Official religion:** none. **Monetary unit:** 1 Swiss franc (Sw F) = 100 centimes; valuation (28 Jun 2002) $1 = Sw F 1.49.

Demography

Area: 61.8 sq mi, 160.0 sq km. **Population** (2001): 33,000. **Density** (2000): persons per sq mi 534.1,

persons per sq km 206.3. **Urban:** n.a. **Sex distribution** (2000): male 48.70%; female 51.30%. **Age breakdown** (2000): under 15, 18.7%; 15–29, 22.3%; 30–44, 25.4%; 45–59, 19.4%; 60–74, 9.7%; 75 and over, 4.5%. **Ethnic composition** (2000): Liechtensteiner 65.5%; Swiss 11.9%; Austrian 6.2%; German 3.4%; Italian 2.8%; other 10.2%. **Religious affiliation** (1998): Roman Catholic 80.0%; Protestant 7.5%; Muslim 3.3%; Eastern Orthodox 0.7%; atheist 0.6%; other 7.9%. **Major cities** (1999): Schaan 5,262; Vaduz 5,106. **Location:** Central Europe, between Austria and Switzerland.

Vital statistics

Birth rate per 1,000 pop. (2000): 11.8 (world avg. 22.5); (1997) legitimate 86.0%; illegitimate 14.0%. **Death rate** per 1,000 pop. (2000): 6.7 (world avg. 9.0). **Natural increase rate** per 1,000 pop. (2000): 5.1 (world avg. 13.5). **Total fertility rate** (avg. births per childbearing woman; 2000): 1.5. **Marriage rate** per 1,000 pop. (1998): 13.2. **Divorce rate** per 1,000 pop. (1994): 1.4. **Life expectancy** at birth (2000): male 75.2 years; female 82.5 years.

National economy

Budget (1999). *Revenue:* Sw F 690,200,000 (taxes and duties 78.2%, investment income 11.3%, charges and fees 8.5%). *Expenditures:* Sw F 537,200,000 (financial affairs 35.8%, social welfare 17.0%, education 15.1%, transportation 9.1%, general administration 9.4%, public safety 4.9%, health 4.7%). **Public debt:** none. **Tourism** (1999): 124,173 tourist overnight stays; receipts from visitors, n.a.; expenditures by nationals abroad, n.a. **Population economically active** (2000): total 16,368; activity rate of total pop. 50.1% (participation rates: ages 15–64, 71.2%; female 40.3%; unemployed 1.8%). **Household income and expenditure.** Average household size (1990) 2.7; sources of earned income (1987): wages and salaries 92.9%, self-employment 7.1%; expenditure (1990; based on sample survey): rent 20.9%, food 17.7%, transportation 11.0%, education and self-improvement 9.7%, clothing 7.0%, health 4.7%. **Production** (metric tons except as noted). *Agriculture, forestry, fishing* (2000): significantly market gardening, other crops include cereals and apples; livestock (number of live animals; 2000) 6,000 cattle, 3,000 pigs, 2,900 sheep; commercial timber (1998) 19,527 cu m. *Manufacturing* (1997): processed milk 13,304; small-scale precision manufacturing includes optical lenses, electron microscopes, and electronic equipment. *Energy production (consumption):* electricity (kW-hr; 1997) 75,842,000 ([2000] 295,031,000); coal (metric tons; 1996) none (24); petroleum products (metric tons; 1995) none (49,291); natural gas (cu m; 1994) none (19,350,000). **Gross domestic product** (1996): $714,000,000 ($23,000 per capita). **Land use** (latest): forested 34.8%; meadows and pastures 15.7%; agricultural and under permanent cultivation 24.3%; other 25.2%.

Foreign trade

Imports (1997): Sw F 1,179,318,000 (machinery and transport equipment 35.2%; other finished goods 23.6%; metal products 12.5%; limestone, cement, and other building materials 12.4%; unrefined and semifabricated metal 5.7%; chemical products 5.2%). *Major import sources:* n.a. **Exports** (1997): Sw F 2,694,357,000 (machinery and transport equipment 49.2%; metal products 15.1%; other finished goods 12.7%; limestone, cement, and other building materials 9.8%; chemical products 7.7%; food and beverages 4.2%). *Major export destinations* (1998): European Economic Community 49.5%; Switzerland 12.7%; other 37.8%.

Transport and communications

Transport. *Railroads* (1998): length 18.5 km. *Roads* (1999): total length 323 km. *Vehicles:* passenger cars (1999) 21,150; trucks and buses (1998) 2,684. *Air transport:* the nearest scheduled airport service is through Zürich, Switzerland. **Communications** Total units (units per 1,000 persons). Daily newspaper circulation (1996): 19,000 (602); Radio receivers (1997): 21,000 (658); Television receivers (1997): 12,000 (364); Telephone main lines (1999): 19,763 (597).

Education and health

Educational attainment (1990). Percentage of pop. not of preschool age or in compulsory education having: no formal schooling 0.3%; primary and lower secondary education 39.3%; higher secondary and vocational 47.6%; some postsecondary 7.4%; university 4.2%; other and unknown 1.1%. **Literacy:** virtually 100%. **Health:** physicians (1997) 41 (1 per 764 persons); hospital beds 108 (1 per 288 persons); infant mortality rate per 1,000 live births (2000) 5.7. **Food** (1999; data for Switzerland): daily per capita caloric intake 3,528 (vegetable products 67%, animal products 33%); 121% of FAO recommended minimum requirement.

Military

Total active duty personnel: none; Liechtenstein has had no standing army since 1868.

Did you know? Opening in November 2000, the ultramodern Liechtenstein Art Museum in Vaduz is a principal cultural attraction of Liechtenstein. At the core of the exhibits are paintings collected by the princes of Liechtenstein since the 17th century, including the works of Flemish artists such as Rubens and Van Dyck as well as Rembrandt.

Background

The Rhine plain was occupied for centuries by two independent lordships of the Holy Roman Empire, Vaduz and Schellenberg. The principality of Liechtenstein, consisting of these two lordships, was founded in 1719 and remained part of the Holy Roman Empire. It was included in the German Confederation (1815–66). In 1866 it became independent, recognizing Vaduz and Schellenberg as unique regions forming separate electoral districts. An almost 60-year ruling coalition dissolved in 1997, and the prince urged adoption of constitutional reforms.

Recent Developments

Allegations that the principality was a haven for money laundering by Latin American drug cartels, Russian gangsters, and the Italian Mafia was a central issue in 2000. Liechtenstein remained the only European nation on an Organisation for Economic Cooperation and Development task force's blacklist of 15 countries accused of failure to cooperate in the international fight against money laundering. In 2001 the prince demanded constitutional changes increasing his power.

Internet resources: <www.news.li>

Lithuania

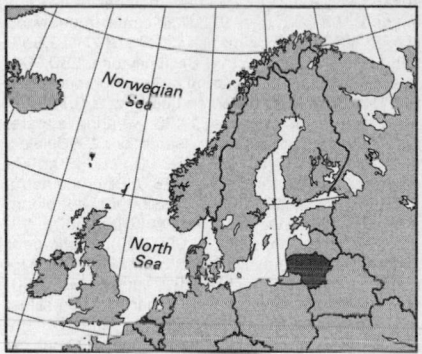

Official name: Lietuvos Respublika (Republic of Lithuania). **Form of government:** unitary multiparty republic with a single legislative body, the Seimas (141). **Head of state:** President Valdas Adamkus (from 1998). **Head of government:** Premier Algirdas Brazauskas (from 3 Jul 2001). **Capital:** Vilnius. **Official language:** Lithuanian. **Official religion:** none. **Monetary unit:** 1 litas (LTL) = 100 centai; valuation (28 Jun 2002) $1 = LTL 3.50.

Demography

Area: 25,212 sq mi, 65,300 sq km. **Population** (2001): 3,691,000. **Density** (2001): persons per sq mi 146.4, persons per sq km 56.5. **Urban** (2001): 68.1%. **Sex distribution** (2001): male 47.14%; female 52.86%. **Age breakdown** (2001): under 15, 19.1%; 15–29, 22.0%; 30–44, 23.0%; 45–59, 17.0%; 60–74, 13.8%; 75 and over, 5.1%. **Ethnic composition** (1997): Lithuanian 81.6%; Russian 8.2%; Polish 6.9%; Belarusian 1.5%; Ukrainian 1.0%; other 0.8%. **Religious affiliation** (1995): Roman Catholic 72.2%; Orthodox 3.3%; Protestant 1.3%; other (mostly nonreligious) 23.2%. **Major cities** (2001): Vilnius 576,400; Kaunas 409,800; Klaipeda 201,800; Siauliai 146,200; Panevezys 133,600. **Location:** Eastern Europe, bordering Latvia, Belarus, Poland, Russia, and the Baltic Sea.

Vital statistics

Birth rate per 1,000 pop. (2000): 9.2 (world avg. 22.5); (1998) legitimate 82.0%; illegitimate 18.0%. **Death rate** per 1,000 pop. (2000): 10.5 (world avg. 9.0). **Natural increase rate** per 1,000 pop. (2000):

−1.3 (world avg. 13.5). **Total fertility rate** (avg. births per childbearing woman; 2000): 1.3. **Marriage rate** per 1,000 pop. (2000): 4.6. **Divorce rate** per 1,000 pop. (2000): 2.9. **Life expectancy** at birth (2000): male 67.6 years; female 77.9 years.

National economy

Budget (1998). *Revenue:* LTL 9,378,000,000 (value-added tax 38.5%, individual income tax 25.8%, excise taxes 14.3%, nontax revenue 7.5%). *Expenditures:* LTL 9,916,000,000 (education 27.7%, police 12.3%, social security and welfare 10.0%, health 6.6%, defense 4.5%). **Gross national product** (1999): $9,751,000,000 ($2,640 per capita). **Production** (metric tons except as noted). *Agriculture, forestry, fishing* (1999): hay 2,621,000, potatoes 1,699,000, sugar beets 890,000; livestock (number of live animals) 1,168,000 pigs, 928,000 cattle; roundwood (1998) 4,879,000 cu m; fish catch (1997) 19,837. Mining and quarrying (1998): limestone 250,000; peat 195,300. *Manufacturing* (value of production in LTL '000,000; 1997): food and beverages 5,785; refined petroleum products 3,488; wearing apparel 1,378. *Energy production (consumption; 1996):* electricity (kW-hr; 2000) 11,388,000,000 (11,630,000,-000); coal (metric tons) none (338,000); crude petroleum (barrels) 1,136,000 (27,583,000); petroleum products (metric tons) 3,974,000 (2,993,000); natural gas (cu m) none (2,327,000,000). **Public debt** (external outstanding; 1999): $1,891,500,000. **Population economically active** (1997): total 1,819,800; activity rate of total pop. 49.1% (participation rates: ages 14–64, 71.1%; female 47.3%; registered unemployed [2000] 11.5%). **Household income and expenditure.** Average household size (1997) 2.9; average annual household disposable income (1997): LTL 12,914; sources of income (1998): wages and salaries 52.7%, transfers 21.3%, self-employment 14.8%, other 11.2%; expenditure (1998): food, beverages, and expenditures in cafés/hotels 54.6%, housing and energy 12.4%, transportation and communications 8.6%, clothing and footwear 8.0%. **Land use** (1994): forested 30.4%; meadows and pastures 7.6%; agricultural and under permanent cultivation 53.9%; other 8.1%. **Tourism** (1999): receipts from visitors $550,000,000; expenditures by nationals abroad $341,000,000.

Foreign trade

Imports (1998-c.i.f.): LTL 23,174,000,000 (machinery/apparatus 18.4%, mineral fuels 14.3%, motor vehicles 11.4%, chemicals and chemical products 9.2%, textiles and clothing 8.8%). *Major import sources:* Russia 21.1%; Germany 18.2%; Poland 5.5%; Italy 4.4%; Denmark 3.8%. **Exports** (1998-f.o.b.): LTL 14,842,000,000 (mineral fuels 18.6%, textiles and clothing 18.6%, food products 12.3%, machinery/apparatus 10.8%, chemicals and chemical products 9.6%). *Major export destinations:* Russia 16.5%; Germany 13.1%; Latvia 11.1%; Belarus 8.9%; Ukraine 7.8%.

Transport and communications

Transport. *Railroads* (1998): route length 1,997 km; passenger-km 715,000,000; metric ton-km cargo 8,265,000,000. *Roads* (1998): total length 71,375 km (paved 91%). *Vehicles* (1998): passenger cars 980,910; trucks and buses 105,022. *Air transport* (1998; Lithuanian and Lietuva airlines): passenger-km 306,585,000; metric ton-km cargo 2,600,000; airports with scheduled flights (1996) 3. **Communications** Total units (units per 1,000 persons). Daily newspaper circulation (1996): 344,000 (93); Radio receivers (1997): 1,900,000 (513); Television receivers (1999): 1,555,000 (420); Telephone main lines (1999): 1,153,000 (312); Cellular telephone subscribers (1999): 332,000 (90); Personal computers (1999): 220,000 (59); Internet users (1999): 103,000 (28).

Education and health

Educational attainment (1989). Percentage of pop. age 25 and over having: no schooling 9.1%; incomplete and complete primary education 21.3%; incomplete and complete secondary 57.0%; postsecondary 12.6%. **Literacy** (1995): total pop. age 15 and over literate 99.2%. **Health** (1998): physicians 14,622 (1 per 253 persons); hospital beds 35,612 (1 per 104 persons); infant mortality rate per 1,000 live births (2000) 8.5. **Food** (1999): daily per capita caloric intake 2,959 (vegetable products 77%, animal products 23%); 116% of FAO recommended minimum requirement.

Military

Total active duty personnel (2000): 12,700 (army 73.5%, navy 4.4%, air force 6.3%, volunteer national defense force 15.8%). **Military expenditure as percentage of GNP** (1997): 0.8% (world 2.6%); per capita expenditure $34.

Background

Lithuanian tribes united in the mid-13th century to oppose the Teutonic knights. Gediminas, one of the grand dukes, expanded Lithuania into an empire that dominated much of Eastern Europe in the 14th–16th centuries. In 1386 the Lithuanian grand duke became the king of Poland, and the two countries remained closely associated until Lithuania was acquired by Russia in the Third Partition of Poland in 1795. Occupied by Germany during World War I, it declared its independence in 1918. In 1940 the Red Army gained control of Lithuania. Germany occupied it again in 1941–44, but the USSR regained control in 1944. With the breakup of the USSR, Lithuania became independent in 1991. During the 1990s it sought economic stability and hoped to join the European Community and NATO. It signed a border treaty with Russia in 1997.

Recent Developments

In 1999 Lithuania saw two prime ministers step down amid growing economic problems. It also participated in NATO actions in the former Yugoslavia. Elections were held in 2000, and the economy improved. Again in 2001, the prime minister resigned. The process of admitting Lithuania into the European Union and NATO continued into 2002.

Internet resources: <www.tourism.lt>

---

1 metric ton = about 1.1 short tons;   1 kilometer = 0.6 mi (statute);   1 metric ton-km cargo = about 0.68 short ton-mi cargo;   c.i.f.: cost, insurance, and freight;   f.o.b.: free on board

Luxembourg

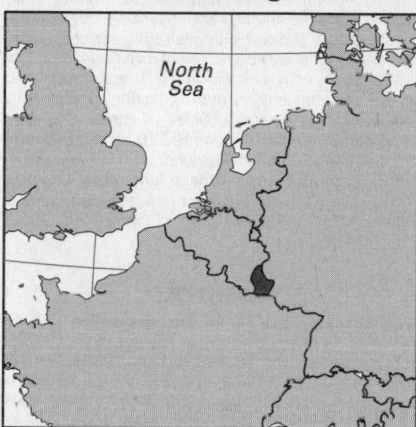

North Sea

Official name: Groussherzogtum Lëtzebuerg (Luxemburgian); Grand-Duché de Luxembourg (French); Grossherzogtum Luxemburg (German) (Grand Duchy of Luxembourg). **Form of government:** constitutional monarchy with two legislative houses (Council of State [21]; Chamber of Deputies [60]). **Chief of state:** Grand Duke Henri (from 2000). **Head of government:** Prime Minister Jean-Claude Juncker (from 1995). **Capital:** Luxembourg. **Official language:** none; Luxemburgian (national); French (used for most official purposes); German (lingua franca). **Official religion:** none. **Monetary unit:** 1 euro (€) = 100 cents; valuation (28 Jun 2002) $1 = €1.01; at conversion on 1 Jan 2002, €1= 40.3 Luxembourg franc (Lux F).

Demography

Area: 999 sq mi, 2,586 sq km. **Population** (2001): 444,000. **Density** (2001): persons per sq mi 444.7, persons per sq km 171.8. **Urban** (1999): 91.1% **Sex distribution** (2000): male 49.16%; female 50.84%. **Age breakdown** (2000): under 15, 18.9%; 15–29, 18.3%; 30–44, 25.3%; 45–59, 18.7%; 60–74, 13.1%; 75 and over, 5.7%. **Ethnic composition** (nationality; 1999): Luxemburger 64.4%; Portuguese 13.0%; Italian 4.7%; French 4.1%; Belgian 3.2%; German 2.4%; English 1.1%; other 7.1%. **Religious affiliation** (1996): Roman Catholic 95.1%; other 4.9%. **Major cities** (2000): Luxembourg 80,700; Esch-sur-Alzette 25,200; Differdange 17,300; Dudelange 17,100; Petange 13,700. **Location:** Western Europe, bordering Belgium, Germany, and France.

Vital statistics

Birth rate per 1,000 pop. (2000): 12.5 (world avg. 22.5); (1998) legitimate 82.5%, illegitimate 17.5%. **Death rate** per 1,000 pop. (2000): 8.9 (world avg. 9.0). **Natural increase rate** per 1,000 pop. (2000): 3.6 (world avg. 13.5). **Total fertility rate** (avg. births per childbearing woman; 2000): 1.7. **Marriage rate** per 1,000 pop. (1999): 4.8. **Divorce rate** per 1,000 pop. (1999): 2.4. **Life expectancy** at birth (2000): male 73.8 years; female 80.6 years.

National economy

Budget (1998). *Revenue:* Lux F 170,310,600,000 (income and excise taxes 58.2%, customs taxes 13.4%). *Expenditures:* Lux F 170,413,400,000 (social security 21.3%, education 11.7%, transportation 8.2%, administration 6.5%, defense 2.7%, debt service 0.9%). **Public debt** (1997): $668,420,000. **Production** (metric tons except as noted). *Agriculture, forestry, fishing* (1999): barley 63,200, wheat 60,100, potatoes 21,100; livestock (number of live animals) 207,862 cattle, 85,830 pigs; roundwood (1997) 315,500 cu m. Mining and quarrying (1999): gypsum and anhydrite 400,000. *Manufacturing* (1999): rolled steel 4,239,000; crude steel 2,600,000. *Energy production (consumption):* electricity (kW-hr; 1998) 382,000,000 (5,856,000,000); coal (metric tons; 1997) none (194,000); petroleum products (metric tons; 1997) none (1,615,000). **Land use** (1992): forested 34.2%; meadows and pastures 25.6%; agricultural and under permanent cultivation 23.2%; other 17.0%. **Gross national product** (1999): $18,545,000,000 ($42,930 per capita). **Population economically active** (1999): total 248,300; activity rate of total pop. 57.9% (participation rates: ages 15–64 [1997] 51.4%; female [1997] 38.2%; unemployed 2.9%). **Household income and expenditure.** Average household size (1991) 2.6; income per household (1992) Lux F 1,438,000; sources of income (1992): wages and salaries 67.1%, transfer payments 28.1%, self-employment 4.8%; expenditure (1994): food, beverages, and tobacco 19.7%, housing 17.3%, transportation and communications 16.2%, household goods and furniture 9.9%, clothing and footwear 8.2%, health 7.9%. **Tourism** (1997): receipts from visitors $297,000,000.

Foreign trade

Imports (1999-c.i.f.): Lux F 409,000,000,000 (machinery and transport equipment 20.2%; transport equipment 18.4%; fabricated metals 10.9%; chemicals and chemical products 9.5%; food products 6.6%). *Major import sources:* Belgium 34.9%; Germany 25.5%; France 11.9%; US 9.1%; The Netherlands 3.7%. **Exports** (1999-f.o.b.): Lux F 299,600,-000,000 (fabricated metals 28.3%; machinery and equipment 20.5%; chemicals and chemical products 6.3%; food products 4.0%). *Major export destinations:* Germany 25.4%; France 21.1%; Belgium 13.0%; UK 8.1%; Italy 5.3%.

Transport and communications

Transport. *Railroads* (1999): route length 274 km; passenger-km 310,000,000; metric ton-km cargo 660,000,000. *Roads* (1999): total length 5,166 km (paved 100%). *Vehicles* (2000): passenger cars 263,683; trucks and buses 20,228. *Air transport* (1999): passengers carried 1,599,000; cargo 448,393 metric tons; airports (1999) with scheduled flights 1. **Communications.** Total units (units per 1,000 persons). Daily newspaper circulation (1996): 135,000 (325); Radio receivers (1997): 285,000 (677); Television receivers (1998): 165,000 (389); Telephone main lines (1999): 310,893 (724); Cellular telephone subscribers (1999): 209,000 (487); Personal computers (1999): 170,000 (396); Internet users (1999): 75,000 (175).

Education and health

Literacy (1995): virtually 100% literate. **Health** (1996): physicians 908 (1 per 454 persons); hospital beds (1995) 4,443 (1 per 92 persons); infant mortality rate per 1,000 live births (2000) 4.8. **Food** (1995): daily per capita caloric intake 3,530 (vegetable products 68%, animal products 32%); 134% of FAO recommended minimum.

Military

Total active duty personnel (2000): 899 (army 100.0%). **Military expenditure as percentage of GNP** (1997): 0.8% (world 2.6%); per capita expenditure $318.

Background

At the time of Roman conquest (57–50 BC), Luxembourg was inhabited by a Belgic tribe. After AD 400, Germanic tribes invaded the region. Made a duchy in 1354, it was ceded to the house of Burgundy in 1443 and to the Habsburgs in 1477. In the mid-16th century it became part of the Spanish Netherlands. It was made a grand duchy in 1815. After an uprising in 1830, its western portion became part of Belgium, while the remainder was held by the Netherlands. In 1867 the European powers guaranteed the neutrality and independence of Luxembourg. In the late 19th century it exploited its extensive iron-ore deposits. It was invaded and occupied by Germany in both world wars. It abandoned its neutrality by joining NATO in 1949; it had joined the Benelux Economic Union in 1944. A member of the European Union, its economy has continued to expand.

Recent Developments

On 7 Oct 2000, Grand Duke Jean abdicated power in favor of his son, Crown Prince Henri, after 36 years on the throne. In the wake of the 11 Sep 2001 terrorist attacks in the US, several Luxembourg banks reported that some of their customers might have ties to Osama bin Laden, and their bank accounts were placed under investigation.

Internet resources: <www.luxembourg.co.uk>

Macau

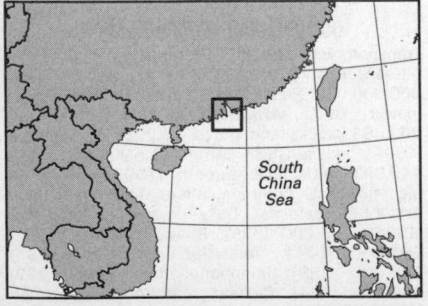

South China Sea

Official name: Aomen Tebie Xingzhengqu (Chinese); Região Administrativa Especial de Macau (Portuguese) (Macau Special Administrative Region). **Political status:** special administrative region (China) with one legislative house (Legislative Council [27; includes 10 directly elected seats, 7 seats appointed by the chief executive, and 10 seats appointed by special-interest groups]). **Chief of state:** President Jiang Zemin of China (from 1993). **Head of government:** Chief Executive Edmund Ho Hau-wah (from 1999). **Capital:** Macau. **Official languages:** Chinese; Portuguese. **Official religion:** none. **Monetary unit:** 1 pataca (MOP) = 100 avos; valuation (28 Jun 2002) $1 = MOP 8.03.

Demography

Area: 9.1 sq mi, 23.6 sq km. **Population** (2001): 445,000. **Density** (2001): persons per sq mi 48,901, persons per sq km 18,856. **Urban** (1999): virtually 100% (about 1% of Macau's pop. live on sampans and other vessels). **Sex distribution** (1998): male 47.55%; female 52.45%. **Age breakdown** (1998): under 15, 24.0%; 15–29, 23.0%; 30–44, 29.4%; 45–59, 13.8%; 60–74, 6.7%; 75 and over, 3.1%. **Nationality** (1991): Chinese 68.2%; Portuguese 27.9%; English 1.8%; other 2.1%. **Religious affiliation** (1998): nonreligious 60.8%; Buddhist 16.7%; other 22.5%. **Major city** (2000 est.): Macau 437,900. **Location:** eastern Asia, bordering China and the South China Sea.

Vital statistics

Birth rate per 1,000 pop. (2001): 9.4 (world avg. 22.5). **Death rate** per 1,000 pop. (2001): 4.5 (world avg. 9.0). **Natural increase rate** per 1,000 pop. (2001): 4.9 (world avg. 13.5). **Total fertility rate** (avg. births per childbearing woman; 2001): 1.1. **Marriage rate** per 1,000 pop. (1998): 3.4. **Divorce rate** per 1,000 pop. (1998): 0.6. **Life expectancy** at birth (2001): male 77.0 years; female 81.0 years.

National economy

Budget (1998). *Revenue:* 14,831,099,000 patacas (recurrent receipts 69.1%, autonomous agency receipts 21.4%, capital receipts 2.2%). *Expenditures:* 14,831,099,000 patacas (recurrent payments 61.1%, autonomous agency expenditures 21.4%, capital payments 17.5%). **Tourism** (1999): receipts from visitors $2,466,000,000; expenditures by nationals abroad $131,000,000. **Land use** (1992): built-on area, wasteland, and other 100.0%. **Gross domestic product** (at current market prices; 1999): $6,161,000,000 ($14,200 per capita). **Production** (metric tons except as noted). *Agriculture, forestry, fishing* (1999): eggs 650; livestock (number of live animals) 500,000 chickens; fish catch (1997) 1,500. *Quarrying* (value added in '000,000 patacas; 1997): 13. *Manufacturing* (value added in '000,000 patacas; 1997): wearing apparel 2,161; textiles 607; electrical appliances 131. *Energy production (consumption):* electricity (kW-hr; 1996) 1,620,000,000 (1,794,000,000); petroleum products (metric tons; 1996) none (459,000). **Public debt** (long-term, external; 1995): $506,000,000. **Population economically active** (1998): total 210,700; activity rate of total pop. 48.9% (participation rates: age 15–64, 70.2%; female 44.8%; unemployed [1999] 6.6%). **Household income and expenditure.** Average household size (1991) 3.5; expenditure (1987–88): food 38.3%, housing 19.7%, education, health, and other services 12.1%, transportation 7.4%, clothing and footwear 6.8%, energy 4.0%, household durable goods 3.7%, other goods 8.0%.

Foreign trade

Imports (1998-c.i.f.): 15,596,446,000 patacas (raw materials 54.1%, capital goods 14.2%, foodstuffs 9.3%, fuels and lubricants 6.3%). *Major import sources:* China 32.7%; Hong Kong 23.7%; European Economic Community 10.5%; Taiwan 9.9%; Japan 7.8%; US 4.7%. **Exports** (1998): 17,083,616,000 patacas (garments 76.4%, textiles 4.5%, machinery and mechanical appliances 3.5%, textile yarn and thread 3.1%, footwear 2.2%). *Major export destinations:* US 47.7%; European Economic Community 30.5%; Hong Kong 7.6%; China 6.8%; Taiwan 1.5%; Japan 0.7%.

Transport and communications

Transport. *Roads* (1996): total length 50 km (paved 100%). *Vehicles* (1998): passenger cars 45,184; trucks and buses 6,578. **Communications** Total units (units per 1,000 persons). Daily newspaper circulation (1996): 200,000 (455); Radio receivers (1997): 160,000 (366); Television receivers (1999): 125,492 (287); Telephone main lines (1999): 178,445 (408); Cellular telephone subscribers (1999): 88,561 (203); Personal computers (1999): 60,000 (137); Internet users (1999): 40,000 (92).

Education and health

Educational attainment (1991). Pop. age 25 and over having: no formal schooling 13.1%; incomplete primary education 16.0%; completed primary 19.9%; some secondary 45.1%; post-secondary 5.9%. **Literacy** (1995): percentage of pop. age 15 and over literate 91.7%; males literate 95.6%; females literate 88.2%. **Health** (1998): physicians 369 (1 per 1,167 persons); hospital beds 1,086 (1 per 396 persons); infant mortality rate per 1,000 live births (2001) 8.0. **Food** (1998): daily per capita caloric intake 2,471 (vegetable products 76%, animal products 24%); 108% of FAO recommended minimum requirement.

Military

Total active duty personnel: The People's Liberation Army is responsible for Macau's defense and security.

Background

Portuguese traders first arrived in Macau in 1513, and it soon became the chief market center for the trade between China and Japan. It was declared a Portuguese colony in 1849 and an overseas territory in 1951. In December 1999 Portugal returned it to Chinese rule.

Recent Developments

In 2002 Macau broke the long-standing monopoly on its important casino industry by awarding three new gaming licenses. Two of the licenses went to Las Vegas–connected enterprises. Plans were underway to boost the struggling economy by bringing flashy Las Vegas glamour to the industry.

Internet resources: <www.macautourism.gov.mo>

Macedonia

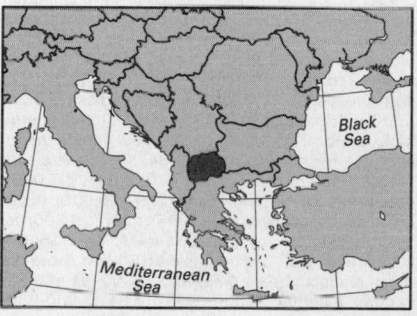

Official name: Republika Makedonija (Republic of Macedonia [member of the UN under the name The Former Yugoslav Republic of Macedonia]). **Form of government:** unitary multiparty republic with a unicameral legislative (Assembly [120]). **Head of state:** President Boris Trajkovski (from 1999). **Head of government:** Prime Minister Ljubco Georgievski (from 1998). **Capital:** Skopje. **Official language:** Macedonian (pending approval of Albanian as second official language at the local level). **Official religion:** none. **Monetary unit:** denar; valuation (28 Jun 2002) $1 = 61.12 denar.

Demography

Area: 25,713 sq km. **Population** (2001): 2,046,000. **Density** (2001): persons per sq mi 206.0, persons per sq km 79.6. **Urban** (2000): 62.0%. **Sex distribution** (2000): male 50.06%; female 49.94%. **Age breakdown** (2000): under 15, 23.4%; 15–29, 24.3%; 30–44, 21.6%; 45–59, 16.5%; 60–64, 11.1%; 65 and over, 3.0%. **Ethnic composition** (2000): Macedonian 53.9%; Albanian 18.0%; Turkish 7.7%; Roma (Gypsy) 5.3%; Aromanian 5.0%; Serbian 2.1%; Croat 2.0%; other 6.0%. **Religious affiliation** (1995): Serbian (Macedonian) Orthodox 54.2%; Sunni Muslim 30.0%; other 15.8%. **Major cities** (1994): Skopje 440,577; Bitola 75,386; Prilep 67,371; Kumanovo 66,237; Tetovo 50,376. **Location:** southeastern Europe, bordering Serbia, Bulgaria, Greece, and Albania.

Vital statistics

Birth rate per 1,000 pop. (2000): 13.7 (world avg. 22.5); (1998) legitimate 90.5%; illegitimate 9.5%. **Death rate** per 1,000 pop. (2000): 7.7 (world avg. 9.0). **Natural increase rate** per 1,000 pop. (2000): 6.0 (world avg. 13.5). **Total fertility rate** (avg. births per childbearing woman; 2000): 1.8. **Marriage rate** per 1,000 pop. (1998): 7.0. **Life expectancy at birth** (2000): male 71.6 years; female 76.2 years.

National economy

Budget (1996). *Revenue:* 64,184,000,000 denar (social security contributions 38.1%, income and profits tax 17.1%, excise taxes 16.3%, sales tax 11.3%, import duties 10.4%). *Expenditure:* 63,970,000,000 denar (1995; pensions 24.1%, wages and salaries 22.7%, health 13.3%). **Production** (metric tons except as noted). *Agriculture, forestry, fishing* (1999): wheat 378,000, grapes 244,000, corn (maize) 200,000; livestock (number of live animals) 1,550,000 sheep, 290,000 cattle, 3,340,000 chickens; roundwood (1998) 720,000 cu m; fish catch (1997) 1,388 (all freshwater). *Mining and quarrying* (1998): lead 17,000; copper 8,000; refined silver 20,000 kg. *Manufacturing* (1998): cement 461,195; steel sheets 276,464; cotton fabric 13,700,000 sq m. *Energy production (consumption)*: electricity (kW-hr; 1996) 6,489,000,000 (6,489,000,000); coal (metric tons; 1996) 7,195,000 (7,330,000); crude petroleum (barrels; 1996) none (6,047,000); petroleum products (metric tons; 1996) 770,000 (1,383,000); natural gas (cu m; 1993) none (269,100,000). **Population economically active** (1998): total 823,800; activity rate 41.1% (participation rates: ages 15–64, 61.2%; female 38.5%; unemployed 34.5%). **Gross national product** (1999): $3,348,000,000 ($1,660 per capita). **External debt** (1999): $1,135,000,000. **Household income and expenditure** (1994). Average household size 3.8; income per household Din 49,635; sources of income: wages and salaries 59.9%, transfer payments 17.0%, transfers from abroad 13.4%, other 9.7%; expenditure: food 42.2%, fuel and lighting 7.5%, clothing and footwear 7.4%, transportation and communications 7.2%, drink and tobacco 7.0%, health care 4.7%, education and entertainment 3.2%. **Tourism** (1998): receipts from visitors $15,000,000; expenditures by nationals abroad $30,000,000. **Land use** (1994): forested 38.9%; meadows and pastures 24.7%; agricultural and under permanent cultivation 25.7%; other 10.7%.

Foreign trade

Imports (1998): $1,310,697,000 (machinery and transport equipment 19.1%, manufactured products 14.5%, food products 13.4%, chemical products 10.6%, petroleum products 8.5%). *Major import sources*: Germany 13.3%; Yugoslavia 12.8%; Slovenia 7.8%; Ukraine 6.2%; Italy 5.7%; US 5.3%. **Exports** (1998): $1,914,663,000 (manufactured products 34.2%, machinery and transport equipment 7.5%, food products 5.0%, chemical products 5.0%, raw materials 4.3%). *Major export destinations*: Germany 21.4%; Yugoslavia 18.3%; US 13.3%; Italy 7.0%; Greece 6.4%.

Transport and communications

Transport. *Railroads* (1998): length 925 km; passenger-km 150,000,000; metric ton-km cargo 408,000,-000. *Roads* (1998): length 11,513 km (paved 63%). *Vehicles* (1998): passenger cars 288,678; trucks and buses 24,745. *Air transport* (1998): passenger-km 890,710,000; metric ton-km cargo 163,840,000; airports (1997) with scheduled flights 2. **Communications** Total units (units per 1,000 persons). Daily newspaper circulation (1996): 41,000 (20); Radio receivers (1997): 410,000 (204); Television receivers (1999): 500,000 (248); Telephone main lines (1999): 471,000 (234); Cellular telephone subscribers (1998): 48,000 (24); Personal computer (1999): 2,000 (1.1); Internet users (1999): 30,000 (15).

Education and health

Educational attainment (1981). Percentage of pop. age 15 and over having: less than full primary education 45.3%; primary 28.1%; secondary 21.2%; postsecondary and higher 5.1%; unknown 0.3%. **Literacy** (1981): total pop. age 10 and over literate 1,365,000 (89.1%); males literate 729,000 (94.2%); females literate 636,000 (83.8%). **Health** (1998): physicians 4,508 (1 per 445 persons); hospital beds 10,333 (1 per 194 persons); infant mortality rate per 1,000 live births (2000) 13.4.

Military

Total active duty personnel (2000): 16,000 (army 95.6%, air force 4.4%). **Military expenditure as percentage of GNP** (1997): 2.5% (world 2.6%); per capita expenditure $42.

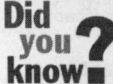 **Did you know?** Skopje, Macedonia's capital, originated as the Illyrian city of Scupi and was an important Roman provincial capital. It was leveled in 518 by an earthquake, burned to the ground in 1689 by the Austrians to eradicate a cholera epidemic, and 80% destroyed, again by an earthquake, in 1963.

Background

Macedonia has been inhabited since before 7000 BC. Part of it was incorporated into a Roman province in AD 29. It was settled by Slavic tribes by the mid-6th century AD. Seized by the Bulgarians in 1185, it was ruled by the Ottoman empire from 1371–1912. The north and center of the region were annexed by Serbia in 1913 and in 1918 became part of what was later known as Yugoslavia. When Yugoslavia was partitioned by the Axis powers in 1941, Yugoslav Macedonia was occupied principally by Bulgaria. Macedonia again became part of Yugoslavia in 1946. After Croatia and Slovenia seceded from Yugoslavia, fear of Serbian dominance drove Macedonia to declare its independence in 1991. Because of Greek objections to the new state using the name of an ancient Greek province, it entered the UN as "the Former Yugoslav Republic of Macedonia."

Recent Developments

During 1999 Macedonia received an influx of ethnic Albanian refugees fleeing the conflict in Kosovo. Its economy was negatively affected as the Kosovo crisis led to the collapse of trade with Yugoslavia. In 2001 ethnic strife endangered national stability as pro-Albanian rebel forces in the north, near the Kosovo border, led guerilla attacks on government forces. A peace agreement was signed in August.

Internet resources: <www.sinf.gov.mk>

Madagascar

Official name: Repoblikan'i Madagasikara (Malagasy); République de Madagascar (French) (Republic

---

1 metric ton = about 1.1 short tons;   1 kilometer = 0.6 mi (statute);   1 metric ton-km cargo = about 0.68 short ton-mi cargo;   c.i.f.: cost, insurance, and freight;   f.o.b.: free on board

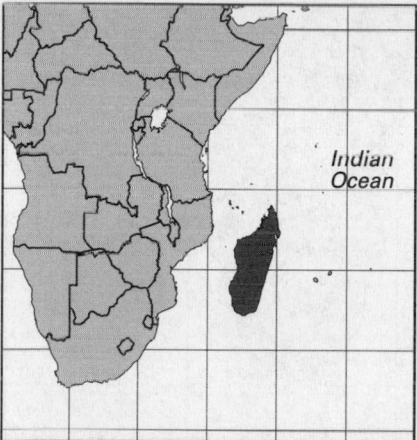

Indian Ocean

of Madagascar). **Form of government:** federal multi-party republic with two legislative houses (Senate [90]; National Assembly [150]). **Heads of state and government:** President Marc Ravalomanana (from 22 Feb 2002 [re-inaugurated 6 May 2002]) assisted by a prime minister. **Capital:** Antananarivo. **Official languages:** none; Malagasy is the national language and French is widely spoken; two versions of the constitution are in Malagasy and French. **Official religion:** none. **Monetary unit:** 1 Malagasy franc (FMG) = 100 centimes; valuation (28 Jun 2002) $1 = FMG 6,030.

Demography

Area: 226,658 sq mi, 587,041 sq km. **Population** (2001): 15,983,000. **Density** (2001): persons per sq mi 70.5, persons per sq km 27.2. **Urban** (1999): 29.0%. **Sex distribution** (2000): male 49.70%; female 50.30%. **Age breakdown** (2000): under 15, 45.0%; 15–29, 26.5%; 30–44, 15.8%; 45–59, 7.9%; 60–74, 3.8%; 75 and over, 1.0%. **Ethnic composition** (1983): Malagasy 98.9%, of which Merina 26.6%, Betsimisaraka 14.9%, Betsileo 11.7%, Tsimihety 7.4%, Sakalava 6.4%; Comorian 0.3%; Indian and Pakistani 0.2%; French 0.2%; other 0.4%. **Religious affiliation** (2000): Christian 49.5%, of which Protestant 22.7%, Roman Catholic 20.3%; traditional beliefs 48.0%; Muslim 1.9%; other 0.6%. **Major cities** (1993): Antananarivo 1,103,304; Toamasina 137,782; Antsirabe 126,062; Fianarantsoa 109,248; Mahajanga 106,780. **Location:** island in the Indian Ocean east of the mainland of southern Africa.

Vital statistics

Birth rate per 1,000 pop. (2000): 42.9 (world avg. 22.5). **Death rate** per 1,000 pop. (2000): 12.7 (world avg. 9.0). **Natural increase rate** per 1,000 pop. (2000): 30.2 (world avg. 13.5). **Total fertility rate** (avg. births per childbearing woman; 2000): 5.8. **Life expectancy** at birth (2000): male 52.7 years; female 57.3 years.

National economy

Budget (1999). *Revenue:* FMG 2,667,000,000,000 (taxes 96.7%, of which duties on trade 55.5%, value-added tax 15.0%, income tax 14.9%; nontax receipts

3.3%). *Expenditures:* FMG 3,791,000,000,000 (current expenditure 57.4%, of which debt service 13.0%, general administration 10.8%, education 10.3%, defense 7.5%, health 4.0%; capital expenditure 42.6%). **Public debt** (external, outstanding; 1999): $4,023,000,000. **Production** (metric tons except as noted). *Agriculture, forestry, fishing* (2000): paddy rice 2,300,000, cassava 2,228,000, coffee 65,000; livestock (number of live animals) 10,364,000 cattle, 1,370,000 goats, 800,000 sheep; roundwood (2000) 10,359,000 cu m; fish catch (1999) 141,057. *Mining and quarrying* (1998): chromite ore 119,000; graphite 14,300; mica 431. *Manufacturing* (1998): refined sugar 79,775 metric tons, cement 44,327 metric tons, beer 207,400 hectolitres. *Energy production (consumption):* electricity (kW-hr; 1998) 642,000,000 (642,000,000); coal (metric tons; 1996) none (14,000); crude petroleum (barrels; 1996) none (1,530,000); petroleum products (metric tons; 1996) 191,000 (358,000). **Population economically active** (1993): total 5,914,000; activity rate of total pop. 48.9% (participation rates [1995]: over age 10, 59.4%; female 38.4%). **Gross national product** (1999): $3,712,000,000 ($250 per capita). **Household income and expenditure.** Average household size (1993) 4.6; expenditure (1983; Antananarivo only): food 60.4%, fuel and light 9.1%, clothing and footwear 8.6%, household goods and utensils 2.4%. **Land use** (1994): forest 39.9%; pasture 41.3%; agriculture 5.3%; other 13.5%. **Tourism** (1999): receipts from visitors $100,000,000; expenditures by nationals abroad $111,000,000.

Foreign trade

Imports (1998): FMG 2,748,989,000,000 (chemical products 14.9%; food 14.1%; minerals 11.2%, of which crude petroleum 7.1%; machinery and equipment 9.3%). *Major import sources* (1999): France 24.1%; Iran 7.1%; Japan 6.2%; South Africa 6.0%; US 4.0%. **Exports** (1998): FMG 1,273,787,000,000 (coffee 17.2%; cotton fabrics 14.1%; minerals 11.3%; shrimp 6.0%; cloves and clove oil 3.9%; vanilla 3.0%). *Major export destinations* (1998): France 39.4%; Mauritius 6.8%; US 5.5%; Germany 4.5%; Italy 3.7%.

Transport and communications

Transport. *Railroads:* route length (1998) 1,095 km; passenger-km 35,000,000; metric ton-km cargo 71,000,000. *Roads* (1996): total length 49,837 km (paved 17%). *Vehicles* (1996): passenger cars 62,000; trucks and buses 16,460. *Air transport* (1998): passenger-km 836,000,000; metric ton-km cargo 29,533,000; airports (1994) with scheduled flights 44. **Communications.** Total units (units per 1,000 persons). Daily newspaper circulation (1996): 66,000 (4.6); Radio receivers (1997): 3,050,000 (209); Television receivers (1998): 340,000 (22); Telephone main lines (1999): 50,226 (3.2); Cellular telephone subscribers (1998): 12,784 (0.9); Personal computer users (1998): 25,000 (1.7); Internet users (1999): 8,000 (0.5).

Education and health

Literacy (1995): percentage of total pop. age 15 and over literate 45.7%; males literate 59.8%; females literate 32.0%. **Health:** physicians (1996) 1,470 (1 per 9,351 persons); hospital beds (1989) 10,900 (1 per 1,029 persons); infant mortality rate (2000) 87.0.

Food (1999): daily per capita caloric intake 1,994 (vegetable products 90%, animal products 10%); 88% of FAO recommended minimum requirement.

Military

Total active duty personnel (1999): 21,000 (army 95.2%, navy 2.4%, air force 2.4%). **Military expenditure as percentage of GNP** (1997): 1.5% (world 2.6%); per capita expenditure $4.

Background

Indonesians migrated to Madagascar about AD 700. The first European to visit the island was Portuguese navigator Diogo Dias in 1500. Trade in arms and slaves allowed the development of Malagasy kingdoms at the beginning of the 17th century. In the 18th century the Merina kingdom became dominant and in 1868 signed a treaty granting France control over the northwestern coast. In 1895 French troops took the island, and Madagascar became a French overseas territory in 1946. As the Malagasy Republic, it gained independence in 1960. It severed ties with France in the 1970s, taking its present name in 1975. A new constitution was adopted in 1992. The country has since been both politically and economically unstable.

Recent Developments

Madagascar suffered through a cholera epidemic, drought, cyclones, and tropical storms in 2000, leaving thousands dead or reduced to poverty on the streets of the capital, Antananarivo. More than twice as much money was spent on debt servicing as on national health and education combined, and the nation's infant mortality rate remained among the highest in the world. The Senate was reinstated in 2001. Disputed presidential elections resulted in violent demonstrations in early 2002. Challenger Marc Ravalomanana declared himself president in February and was named the winner by a court in April, a decision the incumbent president refused to accept.

Internet resources: <www.embassy.org/madagascar>

Malawi

Official name: Republic of Malawi. **Form of government:** multiparty republic with one legislative house (National Assembly [192]). **Head of state and government:** President Bakili Muluzi (from 1994). **Capital:** Lilongwe (ministerial, financial, and legislative government operations) and Blantyre (executive and judicial government operations). **Official language:** none. **Official religion:** none. **Monetary unit:** 1 Malawi kwacha (MK) = 100 tambala; valuation (28 Feb 2001) $1 = MK 76.28.

Demography

Area: 45,747 sq mi, 118,484 sq km. **Population** (2001): 10,491,000. **Density** (2001; land area only): persons per sq mi 288.2, persons per sq km 111.3. **Urban** (1998): 10.7%. **Sex distribution** (1998): male 48.89%; female 51.11%. **Age breakdown** (1987): under 15, 46.0%; 15–29, 25.4%; 30–44, 14.5%;

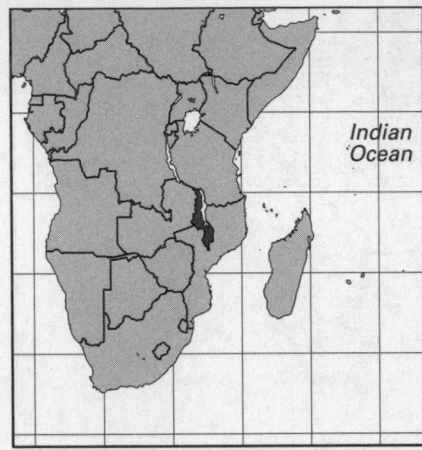

45–59, 8.1%; 60 and over, 6.0%. **Ethnic composition** (2000): Chewa 34.7%; Maravi 12.2%; Ngoni 9.0%; Yao 7.9%; Tumbuka 7.9%; Lomwe 7.7%; Ngonde 3.5%; other 17.1%. **Religious affiliation** (1995): Christian 50.3%, of which Protestant 20.5%, Roman Catholic 18.0%; Muslim 20.0%; traditional beliefs 10.0%; other 19.7%. **Major cities** (1998): Blantyre 478,155; Lilongwe 435,964; Mzuzu 87,030. **Location:** southeastern Africa, bordering Tanzania, Mozambique, and Zambia.

Vital statistics

Birth rate per 1,000 pop. (2000): 38.5 (world avg. 22.5). **Death rate** per 1,000 pop. (2000): 22.4 (world avg. 9.0). **Natural increase rate** per 1,000 pop. (2000): 16.1 (world avg. 13.5). **Total fertility rate** (avg. births per childbearing woman; 2000): 6.3. **Life expectancy** at birth (2000): male 37.2 years; female 38.0 years.

National economy

Budget (1997–98). *Revenue:* MK 8,366,200,000 (tax revenue 96.7%, of which income tax 40.3%, sales tax 35.1%; nontax revenue 3.3%). *Expenditures:* MK 12,785,600,000 (administration 17.3%, education 16.5%, health 7.0%). **Public debt** (external, outstanding; 1999): $2,596,000,000. **Production** (metric tons except as noted). *Agriculture* (1999): corn (maize) 2,480,000, sugarcane 1,900,000, potatoes 385,000; livestock (number of live animals) 1,260,000 goats, 750,000 cattle, 230,000 pigs; roundwood (1998) 9,692,000 cu m; fish catch (1998) 41,111. *Mining and quarrying* (1998): limestone 171,900; gemstone 934 kg. *Manufacturing* (value added in MK '000; 1986): chemicals 30,805; textiles 19,630; food products 11,988. *Energy production (consumption):* electricity (kW-hr; 1996) 874,000,000 (874,000,000); coal (metric tons; 1996) none (17,000); petroleum products (metric tons; 1996) none (199,000). **Land use** (1994): forested 39.3%; meadows and pastures 19.6%; agricultural and under permanent cultivation 18.1%; other 23.0%. **Population economically active** (1987):

1 metric ton = about 1.1 short tons; 1 kilometer = 0.6 mi (statute); 1 metric ton-km cargo = about 0.68 short ton-mi cargo; c.i.f.: cost, insurance, and freight; f.o.b.: free on board

total 3,457,753, activity rate 45.9% (participation rates: age 15–64, 84.6%; female 51.5%; unemployed 5.4%). **Gross national product** (1999): $1,961,000,000 ($180 per capita). **Household income and expenditure.** Average household size (1998) 4.3; income per household n.a.; expenditure (1990): food 55.5%, clothing and footwear 11.7%, housing 9.6%, household goods 8.4%. **Tourism:** receipts (1999) $20,000,000; expenditures (1994) $15,000,000.

Foreign trade

Imports (1995-c.i.f.): MK 7,254,949,000 (1990; transport equipment 9.2%, petroleum products 8.3%, clothing 3.8%, pharmaceutical products 2.2%). *Major import sources:* South Africa 44.4%; Germany 4.5%; UK 4.3%; US 3.7%. **Exports** (1995): MK 6,192,563,-000 (tobacco 63.2%, tea 6.7%, sugar 6.5%, cotton 0.9%). *Major export destinations:* South Africa 16.2%; Germany 14.7%; Japan 11.1%; US 10.9%; Mozambique 7.6%.

Transport and communications

Transport. *Railroads* (1995–96): route length 797 km; passenger-km 18,048,000; metric ton-km cargo 43,431,000. *Roads* (1997): total length 16,451 km (paved 19%). *Vehicles* (1996): passenger cars 27,000; trucks and buses 29,700. *Air transport* (1996; Air Malawi only): passenger-km 110,000,000; metric ton-km cargo 14,000,000; airports (1997) 5. **Communications** Total units (units per 1,000 persons). Daily newspaper circulation (1996; one newspaper only): 22,000 (2.3); Radio receivers (1997): 2,600,000 (258); Television receivers (1999): 27,000 (2.5); Telephone main lines (1999): 41,362 (4.1); Cellular telephone subscribers (1999): 22,500 (2.2); Personal computers (1999): 10,000 (1.0); Internet users (1999): 2,000 (0.2).

Education and health

Educational attainment (1987). Percentage of pop. age 25 and over having: no formal education 55.0%; primary education 39.8%; secondary and higher 5.2%. **Literacy** (1995): total pop. age 15 and over literate 56.4%; males literate 71.9%; females literate 41.8%. **Health:** physicians (1989) 186 (1 per 47,634 persons); hospital beds (1987) 12,617 (1 per 627 persons); infant mortality rate (1999) 123.4. **Food** (1999): daily per capita caloric intake 2,164 (vegetable products 98%, animal products 2%); 91% of FAO recommended minimum requirement.

Military

Total active duty personnel (2000): 5,000 (army 100%). **Military expenditure as percentage of GNP** (1997): 1.0% (world 2.6%); per capita expenditure $3.

Background

Inhabited since 8000 BC, the region was settled by Bantu-speaking peoples between the 1st and 4th century AD. About 1480 they founded the Maravi Confederacy, which encompassed most of central and southern Malawi. In northern Malawi the Ngonde people established a kingdom about 1600. The slave trade flourished during the 18th–19th century. Britain established colonial authority in 1891, and

the area became known as Nyasaland in 1907. The colonies of Northern and Southern Rhodesia and Nyasaland formed a federation (1951–53), which was dissolved in 1963. The next year Malawi achieved independence. In 1966 it became a republic, with Hastings Banda as president. In 1971 he was designated president for life, and he ruled until he was defeated in multiparty elections in 1994. A new constitution was adopted in 1995.

Recent Developments

Banda died in November 1997. Opposition parties sued the government in early 2000, claiming the 1999 presidential and legislative elections had been rigged. Later that year allegations of corruption were leveled at government officials, and several were arrested in early 2001. Malawi suffered severe food shortages in 2002 after two years of poor harvests.

Internet resources:
<http://members.tripod.com/~malawi>

Malaysia

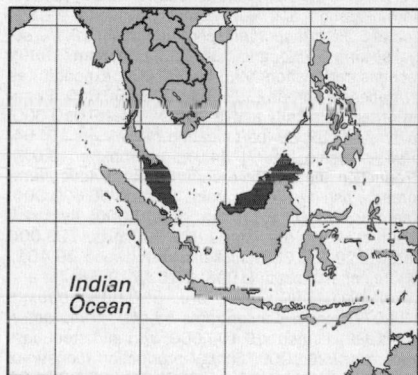

Indian Ocean

Official name: Malaysia. **Form of government:** federal constitutional monarchy with two legislative houses (Senate [70]; House of Representatives [193]). **Chief of state:** Yang di-Pertuan Agong (Paramount Ruler) Tuanku Syed Sirajuddin ibni al-Marhum Tuanku Syed Putra Jamalullail (from 13 Dec 2001). **Head of government:** Prime Minister Datuk Seri Mahathir bin Mohamad (from 1981). **Capital:** transferring from Kuala Lumpur to Putrajaya between 1999 and 2012. **Official language:** Malay. **Official religion:** Islam. **Monetary unit:** 1 ringgit, or Malaysian dollar (RM) = 100 cents; pegged since 8 Oct 2000 to the US dollar at the rate of $1 = RM 3.80.

Demography

Area: 127,354 sq mi, 329,845 sq km. **Population** (2001): 22,602,000. **Density** (2001): persons per sq mi 177.5, persons per sq km 68.5. **Urban** (2001): 58.0%. **Sex distribution** (2000): male 50.45%; female 49.55%. **Age breakdown** (1999): under 15, 33.5%; 15–29, 28.2%; 30–44, 21.0%; 45–59, 11.3%; 60–74, 4.9%, 75 and over, 1.1%. **Ethnic composition** (1999): Malay and other indigenous 57.9%; Chinese 24.7%; Indian 7.0%; other nonindigenous

3.2%; noncitizen 7.2%. **Religious affiliation** (2000): Muslim 47.6%; Chinese folk religionist 24.1%; Christian 8.3%; Hindu 7.3%; Buddhist 6.6%; other 6.1%. **Major cities** (1991): Kuala Lumpur 1,145,342; Ipoh 382,853; Johor Baharu 328,436; Melaka 296,897; Petaling Jaya 254,350. **Location:** southeastern Asia, on the Malay Peninsula and the northern third of the island of Borneo, bordering Thailand, the South China Sea, Brunei, and Indonesia.

Vital statistics

Birth rate per 1,000 pop. (2001): 23.5 (world avg. 22.5). **Death rate** per 1,000 pop. (2001): 4.4 (world avg. 9.0). **Natural increase rate** per 1,000 pop. (2001): 19.1 (world avg. 13.5). **Total fertility rate** (avg. births per childbearing woman; 1999): 3.1. **Life expectancy** at birth (2001): male 70.3 years; female 75.2 years.

National economy

Budget (1999). *Revenue:* RM 59,157,000,000 (income tax 42.5%, taxes on goods and services 24.6%, nontax revenue 19.0%, taxes on international trade 9.1%). *Expenditures:* RM 71,429,000,000 (education 21.5%, defense and internal security 12.9%, general administration 12.7%, interest payments 11.1%, health 6.2%, transport and communications 6.1%, social security 5.7%, agriculture 3.2%). **Tourism** (1999): receipts from visitors $3,540,000,000; expenditures by nationals abroad (1997) $1,973,000,000. **Population economically active** (1999): total 9,010,000; activity rate 39.7% (participation rates: ages 15–64, 60.6%; female [1997] 34.0%; unemployed 3.0%). **Production** (metric tons except as noted). *Agriculture, forestry, fishing* (2000): palm fruit oil 56,600,000, rice 2,037,000, sugarcane 1,600,000; livestock (number of live animals) 1,829,000 pigs, 723,000 cattle, 120,000,000 chickens; roundwood 29,461,-000 cu m; fish catch (1998) 1,153,719. *Mining and quarrying* (1998): iron ore 316,808; bauxite 134,077; copper concentrates 53,001. *Manufacturing* (1999): cement 10,104,000; iron and steel bars and rods 2,261,000. *Energy production (consumption):* electricity (kW-hr; 1996) 53,000,000,000 (52,986,000,000); coal (metric tons; 1996) 83,000 (2,416,000); crude petroleum (barrels; 1996) 258,000,000 (132,000,000); petroleum products (metric tons; 1996) 11,406,000 (17,007,000); natural gas (cu m; 1996) 35,268,000,000 (18,885,-000,000). **Gross national product** (1999): $76,944,-000,000 ($3,390 per capita). **Public debt** (external, outstanding; 1999): $18,929,000,000. **Household income and expenditure.** Average household size (2000) 4.5; annual income per household (1997) RM 31,280; expenditure (1983): food 28.7%, transportation 20.9%, recreation and education 11.0%, housing 10.2%, household durable goods 7.7%.

Foreign trade

Imports (1998): RM 228,309,000,000 (machinery and transport equipment 63.0%, basic manufactures 11.1%, chemicals 7.1%, food 4.6%, mineral fuels 3.1%). *Major import sources:* Japan 20.8%; US 17.4%; Singapore 14.0%; Taiwan 5.3%; South Korea 5.2%; Thailand 3.8%. **Exports** (1998): RM 286,756,-000,000 (machinery and transport equipment

59.2%, basic manufactures 8.3%, animal and vegetable oils 7.5%, mineral fuels 6.2%, chemicals 3.5%, inedible crude materials 3.3%). *Major export destinations:* US 21.9%; Singapore 16.5%; Japan 11.6%; The Netherlands 5.1%; Taiwan 4.5%; Hong Kong 4.2%; UK 3.8%.

Transport and communications

Transport. *Railroads* (1999): route length 2,227 km; passenger-km 1,332,000,000; metric ton-km cargo 912,000,000. *Roads* (1998): total length 66,437 km (paved 76%). *Vehicles* (1998): passenger cars 3,517,484; trucks and buses 644,792. *Air transport* (1999): passenger-km 33,708,000,000; metric ton-km cargo 1,424,556,000; airports (1997) 39. **Communications** Total units (units per 1,000 persons). Daily newspaper circulation (1996): 3,345,000 (163); Radio receivers (1997): 9,100,000 (434); Television receivers (1999): 3,800,000 (174); Telephone main lines (1999): 4,431,000 (203); Cellular telephone subscribers (1999): 2,990,000 (137); Personal computers (1999): 1,500,000 (69); Internet users (1999): 1,500,000 (69).

Education and health

Educational attainment (1996). Percentage of pop. age 25 and over having: no formal schooling 16.7%; primary education 33.7%; secondary 42.8%; higher 6.8%. **Literacy** (1995): total pop. age 15 and over literate 83.5%; males literate 89.1%; females literate 78.1%. **Health** (1998): physicians 15,016 (1 per 1,402 persons); hospital beds 42,398 (1 per 497 persons); infant mortality rate per 1,000 live births (2001) 7.9. **Food** (1999): daily per capita caloric intake 2,946 (vegetable products 81%, animal products 19%); (1997) 132% of FAO recommended minimum.

Military

Total active duty personnel (2000): 96,000 (army 83.4%, navy 8.3%, air force 8.3%). **Military expenditure as percentage of GDP** (1997): 2.2% (world 2.6%); per capita expenditure $102.

Background

Malaya has been inhabited for 6,000–8,000 years, and small kingdoms existed in the 2nd–3rd century AD, when adventurers from India first arrived. Sumatran exiles founded the city-state of Malacca about 1400, and it flourished as a trading and Islamic religious center until its capture by the Portuguese in 1511. Malacca passed to the Dutch in 1641. The British founded a settlement on Singapore Island in 1819, and by 1867 they had established the Straits Settlements, including Malacca, Singapore, and Penang. During the late 19th century the Chinese began to migrate to Malaya, and Japan invaded in 1941. Opposition to British rule led to the creation of the United Malays National Organization (UNMO) in 1946, and in 1948 the peninsula was federated with Penang. Malaya gained independence in 1957, and the federation of Malaysia was established in 1963. Its economy expanded greatly from the late 1970s, but it suffered from the economic slump that struck the area in the mid-1990s.

---

1 metric ton = about 1.1 short tons;   1 kilometer = 0.6 mi (statute);   1 metric ton-km cargo = about 0.68 short ton-mi cargo;   c.i.f.: cost, insurance, and freight;   f.o.b.: free on board

Recent Developments

The September 1998 firing of Anwar Ibrahim from his government posts and his subsequent trial for corruption and sexual misconduct caused tumult in Malaysia for the remainder of the year and throughout 1999. In August 2000 Anwar was found guilty and sentenced to prison; the few protests that followed were swiftly quashed by police. Maintaining his innocence, Anwar claimed that the charges had been fraudulently concocted because of Prime Minister Mahathir's fear of an electoral challenge within the UNMO. Although Mahathir's legitimacy among the nation's majority Malay citizens was threatened in 2001 by various issues, by year's end he had turned the situation around decisively. In the months after the 11 Sep 2001 terrorist attacks in the US, Malaysia arrested dozens of suspected Islamic militants. In June 2002 Mahathir announced he would step down on 25 Oct 2003. He appointed Deputy Prime Minister Abdullah Ahmad Badawi his successor.

Internet resources: <www.geographia.com/malaysia>

Maldives

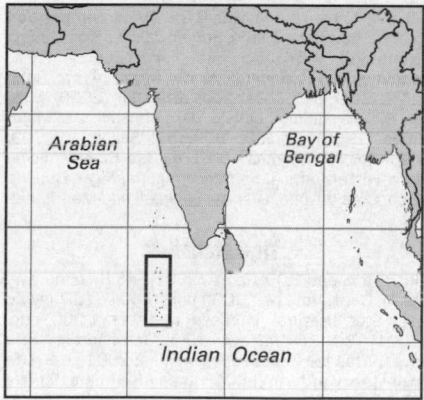

Arabian Sea

Bay of Bengal

Indian Ocean

Official name: Divehi Jumhuriyya (Republic of Maldives). **Form of government:** republic with one legislative house (Majlis [42]). **Head of state and government:** President Maumoon Abdul Gayoom (since 1978). **Capital:** Male. **Official language:** Divehi. **Official religion:** Islam. **Monetary unit:** 1 Maldivian rufiyaa (Rf) = 100 laari; valuation (28 Jun 2002) $1 = Rf 11.77.

Demography

Area: 115 sq mi, 298 sq km. **Population** (2001): 275,000. **Density** (2001): persons per sq mi 2,391, persons per sq km 922.8. **Urban** (1999): 28.0%. **Sex distribution** (2000): male 50.80%; female 49.20%. **Age breakdown** (2000): under 15, 40.7%; 15–29, 28.5%; 30–44, 17.1%; 45–59, 7.7%; 60–74, 5.1%; 75 and over, 0.9%. **Ethnic composition:** the majority is of Sinhalese and Dravidian extraction; Arab, African, and Negrito influences are also present. **Religious affiliation:** virtually 100% Sunni Muslim. **Major city** (2000): Male 74,069. **Location:** Indian Ocean, islands south of India.

Vital statistics

Birth rate per 1,000 pop. (2001): 36.3 (world avg. 22.5). **Death rate** per 1,000 pop. (2001): 6.3 (world avg. 9.0). **Natural increase rate** per 1,000 pop. (2001): 30.0 (world avg. 13.5). **Total fertility rate** (avg. births per childbearing woman; 2001): 5.5. **Marriage rate** per 1,000 pop. (1996): 9.6. **Divorce rate** per 1,000 pop. (1996): 2.8. **Life expectancy** at birth (2001): male 68.0 years; female 66.0 years.

National economy

Budget (1998). *Revenue:* Rf 1,941,400,000 (taxation 45.9%, nontax revenue 45.8%, foreign aid 8.2%). *Expenditures:* Rf 2,216,300,000 (general public services 40.7%, education 19.0%, housing 10.5%, health 10.0%, transportation and communications 9.5%). **Public debt** (external, outstanding; 1999): $192,500,000. **Production** (metric tons except as noted). *Agriculture, forestry, fishing* (1999): vegetables and melons 25,300, coconuts 13,000, fruits (excluding melons) 8,850, roots and tubers (including cassava, sweet potatoes, and yams) 7,010; fish catch (1997) 107,676. *Mining and quarrying:* coral for construction materials. *Manufacturing:* details, n.a.; however, major industries include boat building and repairing, coir yarn and mat weaving, coconut and fish processing, lacquerwork, garment manufacturing, and handicrafts. *Energy production (consumption):* electricity (kW-hr; 1996) 63,000,000 (63,000,000); petroleum products (metric tons; 1996) none (97,000). **Tourism** (1999): receipts from visitors $334,000,000; expenditures by nationals abroad $45,000,000. **Population economically active** (1995): total 67,476; activity rate of total pop. 27.6% (participation rates: ages 15–64, 62.6%; female 27.1%; unemployed [1995] 0.9%). **Household income and expenditure** (1990). Average household size 7.2; annual income per household Rf 2,616, expenditure (1981): food and beverages 61.8%, housing equipment 17.0%, clothing 8.0%, recreation and education 5.9%, transportation 2.6%, health 2.5%, rent 1.6%. **Gross national product** (1999): $322,000,000 ($1,200 per capita). **Land use** (1994): forested 3.3%; meadows and pastures 3.3%; agricultural and under permanent cultivation 10.0%; built-on, wasteland, and other 83.4%.

Foreign trade

Imports (1996-c.i.f.): Rf 3,551,289,000 (machinery and transport equipment 27.9%, basic manufactures 23.7%, food and live animals 21.4%, petroleum products 9.1%). *Major import sources:* Singapore 32.0%; India 12.0%; Malaysia 8.5%; Sri Lanka 7.6%; UK 3.6%; Japan 3.5%. **Exports** (1996-f.o.b.): Rf 699,191,000 (canned fish 28.0%, yellowfin tuna 20.5%, apparel and clothing 17.4%, dried skipjack tuna 11.0%). *Major export destinations:* UK 21.7%; Sri Lanka 18.3%; US 10.2%; Germany 10.8%; Japan 10.6%; Thailand 9.5%.

Transport and communications

Transport. *Vehicles* (1997): passenger cars 1,716; trucks and buses 586. *Air transport* (1995): passengers carried 159,000; passenger-km 71,000,000; airports (1997) with scheduled flights 5. **Communications** Total units (units per 1,000 persons). *Daily newspaper* circulation (1996):5,000 (19); *Radio* receivers (1997): 34,000 (129); *Television receivers*

(1999): 10,650 (38);Telephone main lines (1999): 22,179 (80); Cellular telephone subscribers (1999): 2,926 (11); Personal computers (1999): 5,000 (18); Internet users (1999): 3,000 (11).

Education and health

Educational attainment (1990). Percentage of pop. age 15 and over having: no standard passed 25.6%; primary standard 37.2%; middle standard 25.9%; secondary standard 6.3%; preuniversity 3.4%; higher 0.4%; not stated 1.2%. **Literacy** (1995): total pop. age 15 and over literate 93.2%; males literate 93.0%; females literate 93.3%. **Health** (1996): physicians 99 (1 per 1,995 persons); hospital beds 318 (1 per 806 persons); infant mortality rate per 1,000 live births (2001) 40. **Food** (1999): daily per capita caloric intake 2,298 (vegetable products 81%, animal products 19%); (1997) 104% of FAO recommended minimum requirement.

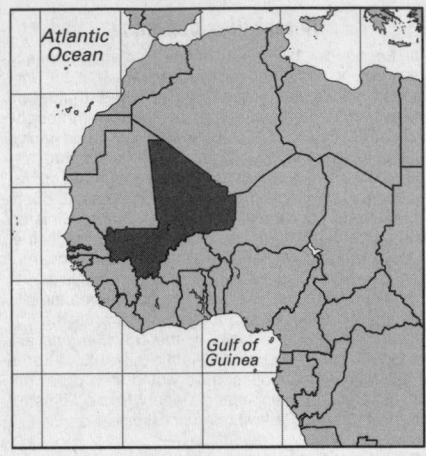

Military

Total active duty personnel: Maldives maintains a single security force numbering about 700–1,000; it performs both army and police functions.

Background

The archipelago was settled in the 5th century BC by Buddhists from Sri Lanka and southern India, and Islam was adopted in 1153. The Portuguese held sway in Male in 1558–73. The islands were a sultanate under the Dutch rulers of Ceylon (now Sri Lanka) during the 17th century. After the British gained control of Ceylon in 1796, the area became a British protectorate, a status formalized in 1887. The islands won full independence from Britain in 1965, and in 1968 a republic was founded. During the 1990s its economy gradually improved.

Recent Developments

In 2001 Maldives asked the US to adopt the Kyoto Protocol, the international agreement to fight global warming. Rising sea levels caused by global warming could submerge the nation.

Internet resources: <www.visitmaldives.com>

Mali

Official name: République du Mali (Republic of Mali). **Form of government:** multiparty republic with one legislative house (National Assembly [147]). **Chief of state:** President Amadou Toumani Touré (from 8 Jun 2002). **Head of government:** Prime Minister Ahmed Mohamed Ag Hamani (from 9 Jun 2002). **Capital:** Bamako. **Official language:** French. **Official religion:** none. **Monetary unit:** 1 CFA franc (CFAF) = 100 centimes; valuation (28 Jun 2002) $1 = CFAF 664.2; the CFAF is pegged to the euro (€) at €1 = 655.96 from 1 Jan 2002.

Demography

Area: 482,077 sq mi, 1,248,574 sq km. **Population** (2001): 11,009,000. **Density** (2001): persons per sq mi 22.8, persons per sq km 8.8. **Urban** (1998): 28.7%. **Sex distribution** (2001): male 48.9%; female 51.1%. **Age breakdown** (2001): under 15, 47.2%; 15–29, 26.8%; 30–44, 13.3%; 45–59, 7.9%; 60–74, 4.0%; 75 and over, 0.8%. **Ethnic composition** (2000): Bambara 30.6%; Senufo 10.5%; Fula Macina (Niafunke) 9.6%; Soninke 7.4%; Tuareg 7.0%; Maninka 6.6%; Songhai 6.3%; Dogon 4.3%; Bobo 3.5%; other 14.2%. **Religious affiliation** (2000): Muslim 82%; traditional beliefs 16%; Christian 2%. **Major cities** (1996): Bamako 809,552; Ségou 106,799; Mopti 86,355; Sikasso 90,174; Gao 62,667. **Location:** western Africa, bordering Algeria, Niger, Burkina Faso, Côte d'Ivoire, Guinea, Senegal, and Mauritania.

Vital statistics

Birth rate per 1,000 pop. (2001): 48.8 (world avg. 22.5). **Death rate** per 1,000 pop. (2001): 18.7 (world avg. 9.0). **Natural increase rate** per 1,000 pop. (2001): 30.1 (world avg. 13.5). **Total fertility rate** (avg. births per childbearing woman; 2001): 6.8. **Life expectancy** at birth (2001): male 45.8 years; female 48.2 years.

National economy

Budget (1999). *Revenue:* CFAF 356,000,000,000 (tax revenue 66.1%, grants 23.4%, nontax revenue 10.5%). *Expenditures:* CFAF 417,400,000,000 (current expenditure 46.3%, of which wages and salaries 15.6%, education 10.3%, defense 8.3%, interest on public debt 3.6%, health 2.8%; capital expenditure 53.7%). **Public debt** (external, outstanding; 1999): $2,798,000,000. **Tourism** (1999): receipts from visitors $50,000,000; expenditures by nationals abroad $29,000,000. **Population economically active** (1997): total 5,042,000; activity rate of total pop. 51.5% (participation rates [1987] ages 15–64, 67.4%; female 46.3%; unemployed 0.8%). **Production** (metric tons except as noted). *Agriculture, forestry, fishing* (2001): millet 802,500, rice 745,100, sorghum 591,700; livestock (number of live animals) 14,550,000 goats and sheep, 6,200,000 cattle, 652,000 asses; roundwood

---

1 metric ton = about 1.1 short tons;   1 kilometer = 0.6 mi (statute);   1 metric ton-km cargo = about 0.68 short ton-mi cargo;   c.i.f.: cost, insurance, and freight;   f.o.b.: free on board

(2000) 6,596,900 cu m; fish catch (1999) 98,776.
Mining and quarrying (1997): limestone 20,000;
phosphate 3,000; iron oxide 708. *Manufacturing*
(1999): sugar 27,000; cement 20,000; soap (1995)
10,097. *Energy production (consumption):* electricity
(kW-hr; 1997) 391,000,000 (391,000,000); petroleum products (metric tons; 1997) none (154,000).
Gross national product (at current market prices;
1999): $2,577,000,000 ($240 per capita). **Household income and expenditure.** Average household
size (1997) 5.0; expenditure (1986–87): food 54.6%,
clothing 14.2%, transportation and communications
11.9%, housing and energy 8.7%, household durable
goods 4.2%. **Land use** (1994): forested 5.7%; meadows and pastures 24.6%; forest 9.7%; agricultural
and under permanent cultivation 2.1%; other 63.6%.

Foreign trade

Imports (1999-c.i.f.): CFAF 490,600,000,000 (machinery, appliances, and transport equipment 31.1%;
petroleum products 14.3%; food products 13.9%;
construction products 10.5%; chemicals 10.2%).
Major import sources: African countries 49.9%, of
which Côte d'Ivoire 18.9%; France 18.7%; China
4.4%; Germany 2.7%; Belgium-Luxembourg 2.4%. **Exports** (1999): CFAF 348,600,000,000 (raw cotton
and cotton products 43.9%; gold 40.8%; live animals
9.4%). *Major export destinations:* Western Europe,
US, and other non-Asian industrial countries 52.7%;
Asian countries 33.9%; African countries 8.4%.

Transport and communications

Transport. *Railroads* (1995): route length 641 km;
passenger-km 929,600,000; metric ton-km cargo
542,800,000. *Roads* (1996): total length 15,100 km
(paved 12%). *Vehicles* (1996): passenger cars 26,190;
trucks and buses 18,240. *Air transport* (1997): passenger-km 242,000,000; metric ton-km cargo
38,000,000; airports (1999) with scheduled flights 9.
Communications Total units (units per 1,000 persons). Daily newspaper circulation (1997): 45,000
(4.0); Radio receivers (1997): 1,600,000 (163); Television receivers (1999): 130,000 (12); Telephone main
lines (1999): 26,758 (2.5); Cellular phone subscribers
(1999): 4,473 (0.4); Personal computers (1999):
11,000 (1.1); Internet users (1999): 1,000 (0.1).

Education and health

Educational attainment (1987). Percentage of pop.
age 6 and over having: no formal schooling 86.0%;
primary education 12.5%; secondary 1.2%; postsecondary and higher 0.3%. **Literacy** (1995): Percentage
of total pop. age 15 and over literate 1,760,000
(31.0%); males literate 1,084,000 (39.4%); females
literate 676,000 (23.1%). **Health:** physicians (1993)
483 (1 per 18,376 persons); hospital beds (1987)
3,430 (1 per 2,253 persons); infant mortality rate per
1,000 live births (2001) 121.4. **Food** (1999): daily
per capita caloric intake 2,314 (vegetable products
91%, animal products 9%); 90% of FAO recommended minimum requirement.

Military

Total active duty personnel (1999): 7,350 (army
93.9%, navy 0.7%, air force 5.4%). **Military expenditure as percentage of GNP** (1997): 1.7% (world
2.6%); per capita expenditure $4.

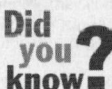

Did you know? Timbuktu, Mali, was once fabled
as the "City of Gold" because of its
trans-Saharan commerce. The
desert terrain and the high temperatures make the area very difficult to
traverse. However, tourists visit Timbuktu to see its
famous mosques and to stroll through markets
where locals sell ornate silverwork.

Background

Inhabited since prehistoric times, the region was situated on a caravan route across the Sahara. In the
12th century the Malinke empire of Mali was founded
on the Upper and Middle Niger. In the 15th century
the Songhai empire in the Timbuktu-Gao region
gained control. In 1591 Morocco invaded the area,
and Timbuktu remained under the Moors for two centuries. In the mid-19th century the French conquered
the area, which became a part of French West Africa
known as the French Sudan. In 1946 it became an
overseas territory of the French Union. It was proclaimed the Sudanese Republic in 1958, briefly
joined with Senegal (1959–60) to form the Mali Federation, and formed the Republic of Mali in 1960. The
government was overthrown by military coups in
1968 and 1991. Elections were held in 1992 and
1997, but political instability continued.

Recent Developments

Presidential elections in May 2002 resulted in a win
for Amadou Toumani Touré, an army general who had
led the 1991 coup and who had led the state for 14
months in 1991–92. Bamako was the site of the
African Nations Cup soccer championship in February
2002.

Internet resources:
<www.oxfam.org.uk/coolplanet/
ontheline/explore/journey/mali/malindex.htm>

Malta

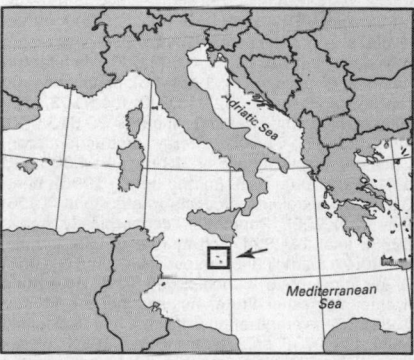

Official name: Repubblikka ta' Malta (Maltese); Republic of Malta (English). **Form of government:** unitary multiparty republic with one legislative house
(House of Representatives [65]). **Chief of state:** President Guido de Marco (from 1999). **Head of government:** Prime Minister Eddie Fenech Adami (from
1998). **Capital:** Valletta. **Official languages:** Maltese;

English. **Official religion:** Roman Catholicism. **Monetary unit:** 1 Maltese lira (Lm) = 100 cents = 1,000 mils; valuation (28 Jun 2002) $1 = Lm 0.42.

Demography

Area: 122 sq mi, 316 sq km (rounded). **Population** (2001): 381,000. **Density** (2001): persons per sq mi 3,123, persons per sq km 1,206. **Urban** (2000): 90.5%. **Sex distribution** (2000): male 49.49%; female 50.51%. **Age breakdown** (2000): under 15, 20.3%; 15–29, 21.6%; 30–44, 20.8%; 45–59, 20.4%; 60–74, 12.0%; 75 and over, 4.9%. **Ethnic composition** (by nationality; 2000): Maltese 93.8%; British 2.1%; Arab 2.0%; other 2.1%. **Religious affiliation** (1996): Roman Catholic 93.4%; other 6.6%. **Major cities** (1999): Birkirkara 21,350; Qormi 17,881; Sliema 12,308; Hamrun 11,014; Valletta 7,100. **Location:** islands in the Mediterranean Sea south of Sicily (Italy).

Vital statistics

Birth rate per 1,000 population (2000): 12.7 (world avg. 22.5); (1998) legitimate 91.8%; illegitimate 8.2%. **Death rate** per 1,000 population (2000): 7.7 (world avg. 9.0). **Natural increase rate** per 1,000 population (2000): 5.0 (world avg. 13.5). **Total fertility rate** (avg. births per childbearing woman; 2000): 1.9. **Marriage rate** per 1,000 population (1998): 6.3. **Divorce rate** per 1,000 population: n.a. **Life expectancy** at birth (2000): male 75.5 years; female 80.6 years.

National economy

Budget (1999). *Revenue:* Lm 637,852,000 (direct taxes 42.7%; indirect taxes 32.6%; nontax revenue 23.1%; foreign grants 1.5%). *Expenditures* (1997): Lm 690,965,000 [2001] (recurrent expenditures 84.6% [2001], of which social security 27.2%, education 10.4%, health 10.0%, debt service 4.9%, defense 4.2%; capital expenditure 15.4% [2001]). **Public debt** (1998): $2,224,400,000. **Production** (metric tons except where noted). *Agriculture, forestry, fishing* (1999): tomatoes 32,800, potatoes 32,000, grapes 10,000, barley 2,000; livestock (number of live animals; 1999) 69,000 pigs, 21,000 cattle, 16,000 sheep; fish catch 979,432. *Quarrying* (value of production in Lm; 1996): 6,898,000. *Manufacturing* (value of sales in Lm; 1994–95): machinery and transport equipment 402,993,000; food 103,733,-000; textiles and wearing apparel 80,813,000; chemicals 35,151,000. *Energy production (consumption):* electricity (kW-hr; 1996) 1,514,000,000 (1,514,000,000); coal (metric tons; 1996) none (310,000); petroleum products (metric tons; 1996) none (342,000). **Population economically active** (1998): total 144,824; activity rate of total population 38.4% (participation rates: ages 15–64 [1985] 45.9%; female 27.6%; unemployed 5.1%). **Household income and expenditure.** Average household size (1985) 3.3; average annual income per household (1982) Lm 4,736; sources of income (1993): wages and salaries 63.8%, professional and unincorporated enterprises 19.3%, rents, dividends, and interest 16.9%; expenditure (1993): food and beverages 27.9%, transportation and communications 15.7%, household furnishings and operations 9.5%, recre-

ation, entertainment, and education 7.2%, clothing and footwear 6.9%, housing 5.5%, health 3.3%, tobacco 2.6%. **Tourism** (1999): receipts from visitors $675,000,000; expenditures by nationals abroad $201,000,000. **Gross domestic product** (1999): $3,492,000,000 ($9,210 per capita). **Land use** (1994): agricultural and under permanent cultivation 40.6%; other (infertile clay soil with underlying limestone) 59.4%.

Foreign trade

Imports (1998-c.i.f., f.o.b.): Lm 1,034,994,000 (machinery and transport equipment 50.3%, manufactured and semimanufactured goods 24.8%, food 9.3%, chemicals 7.7%, mineral fuels 3.8%). *Major import sources:* Italy 19.3%; France 17.8%; UK 12.4%; Germany 10.5%; US 8.9%. **Exports** (1998): Lm 703,442,000 (machinery and transport equipment 64.6%, manufactured 27.7%, food and live animals 2.0%). *Major export destinations:* France 20.5%; US 18.0%; Singapore 14.3%; Germany 12.8%; UK 7.8%.

Transport and communications

Transport. *Roads* (1997): total length 1,219 mi, 1,961 km (paved 94%). Vehicles (1998): passenger cars 185,247; trucks and buses 49,520. *Air transport* (1998): passenger-mi 1,172,982,000, passenger-km 1,887,736,000; short ton-mi cargo 7,689,-800; metric ton-km cargo 11,227,000; airports (1999) with scheduled flights 1. **Communications** Total units (units per 1,000 persons). Daily newspaper circulation (1996): 54,000 (145); Radio receivers (1997): 255,000 (680); Television receivers (1999): 212,000 (549); Telephone main lines (1999): 198,000 (513); Cellular telephone subscribers (1999): 38,000 (98); Personal computers (1998): 100,000 (260); Internet users (1999): 30,000 (77).

Education and health

Educational attainment (1967). Percentage of economically active population having: no formal schooling 10.8%; primary education 60.4%; lower secondary 3.4%; upper secondary 17.6%; technical secondary 3.9%; postsecondary and higher 3.9%. **Literacy** (2000): total population age 15 and over literate 279,000 (92.1%); males literate 138,000 (91.4%); females literate 141,000 (92.8%). **Health** (1996): physicians 925 (1 per 403 persons); hospital beds 2,140 (1 per 174 persons); infant mortality rate per 1,000 live births (2000) 5.9. **Food** (1999): daily per capita caloric intake 3,482 (vegetable products 72%, animal products 28%); 139% of FAO recommended minimum requirement.

Military

Total active duty personnel (2000): 2,140 (army 100%). **Military expenditure as percentage of GNP** (1997): 0.9% (world 2.6%); per capita expenditure $81.

Background

Inhabited as early as 3800 BC, Malta was ruled by the Carthaginians from the 6th century BC until it came

---

1 metric ton = about 1.1 short tons;   1 kilometer = 0.6 mi (statute);   1 metric ton-km cargo = about 0.68 short ton-mi cargo;   c.i.f.: cost, insurance, and freight;   f.o.b.: free on board

under Roman control in 218 BC. In AD 60 the apostle Paul converted the inhabitants to Christianity. It was under Byzantine rule until the Arabs seized control in 870. In 1091 the Normans defeated the Arabs, and it was ruled by feudal lords until it came under the Knights of Malta in 1530. Napoleon seized control in 1798, the British took it in 1800, and it was returned to the Knights in 1802. The Maltese protested and acknowledged the British as sovereign, an arrangement ratified in 1814. It became self-governing in 1921 but reverted to a colonial regime in 1936. Malta was severely bombed by Germany and Italy during World War II, and in 1942 it received the George Cross, Britain's highest civilian decoration. In 1964 it gained independence within the Commonwealth, and in 1974 became a republic. When its alliance with Britain ended in 1979, Malta proclaimed its neutral status.

Recent Developments

Pope John Paul II beatified three Maltese citizens in 2001, the first so honored. Negotiations were under way in 2002 for Malta to join the European Union, a move expected to take place by the end of the year.

Internet resources: <www.mol.net.mt>

Marshall Islands

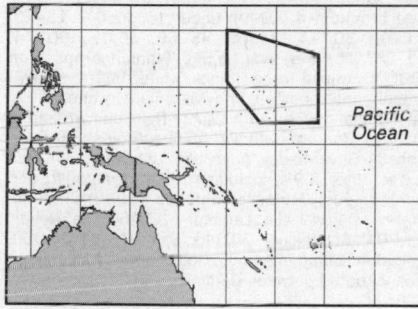

Pacific Ocean

Official name: Majol (Marshallese); Republic of the Marshall Islands (English). **Form of government:** unitary republic with two legislative houses (Council of Iroij [12]; Nitijela [33]). **Head of state and government:** President Kessai Hesa Note (from 2000). **Capital:** Majuro. **Official languages:** Marshallese (Kajin Majol); English. **Official religion:** none. **Monetary unit:** 1 US dollar ($) = 100 cents.

Demography

Area: 70.07 sq mi, 181.48 sq km. **Population** (2001): 52,300. **Density** (2001): persons per sq mi 746.4, persons per sq km 280.2. **Urban** (1999): 71.0%. **Sex distribution** (2000): male 42.45%; female 57.55%. **Age breakdown** (1997): under 15, 50.2%; 15–29, 26.0%; 30–44, 13.9%; 45–59, 6.5%; 60–74, 2.6%; 75 and over, 0.8%. **Ethnic composition** (nationality; 2000). Marshallese 88.5%; US white 6.5%; other Pacific islanders and East Asians 5.0%. **Religious affiliation** (1995): Protestant 62.8%; Roman Catholic 7.1%; Mormon 3.1%; Jehovah's Witness 1.0%. **Major cities:** Majuro (1999) 23,676; Ebeye (1988) 8,324. **Location:**

Oceania, group of atolls and reefs in the North Pacific Ocean, halfway between Hawaii and Papua New Guinea.

Vital statistics

Birth rate per 1,000 pop. (2000): 41.8 (world avg. 22.5). **Death rate** per 1,000 pop. (2000): 4.9 (world avg. 9.0). **Natural increase rate** per 1,000 pop. (2000): 36.9 (world avg. 13.5). **Total fertility rate** (avg. births per childbearing woman; 2000): 6.6. **Life expectancy** at birth (2000): male 63.7 years; female 67.4 years.

National economy

Budget (1997–98). *Revenue:* $61,400,000 (US government grants 59.7%, income tax 12.7%, import tax 10.7%, value-added and excise taxes 4.4%, fishing rights 2.9%, fees and charges 2.1%). *Expenditures:* $50,900,000 (wages and salaries 33.4%, goods and services 32.4%, capital expenditures 14.3%, interest payments 10.8%, subsidies 7.1%). **Production** (metric tons except as noted). *Agriculture, forestry, fishing* (1997): coconuts 140,000, copra 18,000, cassava 12,000; fish catch (1998) 400. *Mining and quarrying:* high-grade phosphate mining on Ailinglaplap Atoll, quarrying of sand and aggregate for local construction only. *Manufacturing* (1995): copra 7,728; coconut oil and processed (chilled or frozen) fish are important products. *Energy production (consumption):* electricity (kW-hr; 1994) 57,891,000 (57,891,000); gasoline, oil, and lubricants (imported barrels; 1988) n.a. (84,588). **Public debt** (external, outstanding; 1996–97): $124,900,000. **Gross national product** (at current market prices; 1999): $99,000,000 ($1,950 per capita). **Land use** (1989): forested 22.5%; meadows and pastures 13.5%; agricultural and under permanent cultivation 33.1%; other 30.9%. **Household income and expenditure.** Average household size (1988) 8.7; income per household (1979) $3,366; expenditure (1982): food 57.7%, housing 15.6%, clothing 12.0%, personal effects and other 14.7%. **Population economically active** (1988): total 11,488; activity rate of total pop. 26.5% (participation rates: over age 14, 54.1%; female 30.1%; unemployed 12.5%). **Tourism** (1999): receipts from visitors $4,000,000.

Foreign trade

Imports (1997-c.i.f.): $60,995,000 (mineral fuels and lubricants 23.4%, food, beverages, and tobacco 22.8%, machinery and transport equipment 9.5%, manufactured goods 7.4%, chemical products 6.6%). *Major import sources:* US 47.2%; Guam 4.8%; Australia 4.0%; Singapore 3.4%; Japan 3.3%. **Exports** (1997): $12,665,000 (chilled fish 78.2%, frozen fish 10.7%, crude coconut oil 9.6%). *Major export destinations:* US c. 80.0%; other c. 20.0%.

Transport and communications

Transport. *Vehicles* (1995): passenger cars 1,374; trucks and buses 262. *Air transport* (1996): passenger-km 28,000,000; metric ton-km cargo 5,000; airports (1997) with scheduled flights 25. **Communications** Total units (units per 1,000 persons). Telephone main lines (1998): 3,744 (62); Cellular telephone subscribers (1998): 345 (5.8).

Education and health

Educational attainment (1988). Percentage of pop. age 25 and over having: no grade completed 5.1%; elementary education 43.2%; secondary 39.7%; higher 11.4%; not stated 0.6%. **Literacy** (latest): total pop. age 15 and over literate 19,377 (91.2%); males literate 9,993 (92.4%); females literate 9,384 (90.0%). **Health** (1997): physicians 34 (1 per 1,785 persons); hospital beds 129 (1 per 470 persons); infant mortality rate per 1,000 live births (2000) 41.0.

Military

Under the 1984 Compact of Free Association, the United States provides for the defense of the Republic of the Marshall Islands.

 **Did you know?** After World War II, the United States used the Enewetak and Bikini atolls of the Marshall Islands as nuclear test sites. The Enewetok atoll was declared safe in 1980, and many of the former residents have since returned. Bikini is still under cleanup, although it has already become a popular destination for scuba divers.

Background

The islands were sighted in 1529 by the Spanish navigator Álvaro Saavedra. Germany purchased them from Spain in 1899, and Japan seized them in 1914. During World War II the US took Kwajalein and Enewetak, and the Marshall Islands were made part of a UN trust territory under US jurisdiction in 1947. Bikini and Enewetak atolls served as testing grounds for US nuclear weapons from 1946 to 1958. The country became an internally self-governing republic in 1979. In 1986 it entered into a compact of free association with the US, some provisions of which were set to expire in 2001, and became fully self-governing.

Recent Developments

A two-year negotiation period (2001–03) was included in the compact, allowing US financial assistance to continue while discussions were ongoing. In 2002 the US proposed a new funding plan for the Marshall Islands, which was to be voted on by Congress by October 2003.

Internet resources: <http://marshall.csu.edu.au>

Martinique

Official name: Département de la Martinique (Department of Martinique). **Political status:** overseas department (France) with two legislative houses (General Council [45]; Regional Council [41]). **Chief of state:** President Jacques Chirac of France (from 1995). **Heads of government:** Prefect (for France) Michel Cadot (from 2000); President of the General Council (for Martinique) Claude Lise (from 1992); President of the Regional Council (for Martinique) Alfred Marie-Jeanne (from 1998). **Capital:** Fort-de-

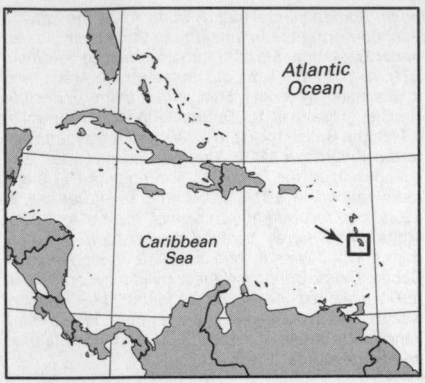

France. **Official language:** French. **Official religion:** none. **Monetary unit:** 1 euro (€) = 100 cents; $1 = €1.01 (28 Jun 2002); at conversion on 1 Jan 2002, €1 = 6.56 French francs (F).

Demography

Area: 436 sq mi, 1,128 sq km. **Population** (2001): 388,000. **Density** (2001): persons per sq mi 889.9, persons per sq km 344.0. **Urban** (1999): 94.6%. **Sex distribution** (1999): male 47.44%; female 52.56%. **Age breakdown** (1999): under 15, 22.0%; 15–29, 21.0%; 30–44, 24.4%; 45–59, 16.0%; 60–74, 11.1%; 75 and over, 5.5%. **Ethnic composition** (2000): mixed race (black/white/Asian) 93.4%; French (metropolitan and Martinique white) 3.0%; East Indian 1.9%; other 1.7%. **Religious affiliation** (1995): Roman Catholic 86.5%; Protestant 8.0% (mostly Seventh-day Adventist); Jehovah's Witness 1.6%; other 3.9%, including Hindu, syncretist, and nonreligious. **Major communes** (1999): Fort-de-France 94,049; Le Lamentin 35,460; Le Robert 21,201; Schoelcher 20,845; Sainte-Marie 20,058. **Location:** island in Atlantic Ocean and the Caribbean Sea, situated between Dominica and Saint Lucia.

Vital statistics

Birth rate per 1,000 pop. (2000): 16.1 (world avg. 22.5); (1992) legitimate 34.1%; illegitimate 65.9%. **Death rate** per 1,000 pop. (2000): 6.4 (world avg. 9.0). **Natural increase rate** per 1,000 pop. (2000): 9.7 (world avg. 13.5). **Total fertility rate** (avg. births per childbearing woman; 2000): 1.8. **Marriage rate** per 1,000 pop. (1997): 4.1. **Divorce rate** per 1,000 pop. (1996): 1.1. **Life expectancy** at birth (2000): male 79.0 years; female 77.5 years.

National economy

Budget (1994). *Revenue:* F 1,816,000,000 (general receipts from French central government and local administrative bodies 45.0%; tax receipts 34.0%, of which indirect taxes 19.5%, direct taxes 14.5%). *Expenditures:* F 1,816,000,000 (health and social assistance 42.0%; wages and salaries 16.7%; other administrative services 7.2%; debt amortization 5.0%). **Public debt** (1994): $186,700,000. **Production** (met-

1 metric ton = about 1.1 short tons;   1 kilometer = 0.6 mi (statute);   1 metric ton-km cargo = about 0.68 short ton-mi cargo;   c.i.f.: cost, insurance, and freight;   f.o.b.: free on board

ric tons except as noted). *Agriculture, forestry, fishing* (1999): bananas 321,454, sugarcane 188,827, pineapples 20,200; livestock (number of live animals) 42,000 sheep, 33,000 pigs, 30,000 cattle; roundwood (1998) 12,000 cu m; fish catch (1998) 5,500. *Mining and quarrying* (1996): pumice 130,000; sand and gravel for local construction. *Manufacturing* (1998): cement 225,000; processed pineapples 20,210; sugar 6,543; rum 68,716 hectolitres; other products include clothing, fabricated metals, and yawls and sails. *Energy production (consumption):* electricity (kW-hr; 1996) 906,000,000 (906,000,000); crude petroleum (barrels; 1996) none (5,827,000); petroleum products (metric tons; 1996) 738,000 (566,000). **Household income and expenditure**. Average household size (1997) 3.0; income per household (1989) F 147,150; sources of income (1989): wages and salaries 80%, other 20%; expenditure (1993): food and beverages 32.1%, transportation and communications 20.7%, housing and energy 10.6%, household durable goods 9.4%, clothing and footwear 8.0%, education and recreation 5.4%, health care 5.2%, other 8.6%. **Tourism** (1999): receipts from visitors $404,000,000; number of visitors 904,000. **Gross national product** (1998): $4,888,000,000 ($12,875 per capita). **Population economically active** (1998): total 165,900; activity rate of total pop. 41.6% (participation rates: ages 15-64, 71.2%; [1997] female 32.6%; unemployed [1998] 28.2%). **Land use** (1994): forested 45.3%; meadows and pastures 13.2%; agricultural and under permanent cultivation 17.0%; other 24.5%.

Foreign trade

Imports (1998-c.i.f.): F 9,997,000,000 (1996; consumer goods 23.9%, goods for intermediate consumption [inputs to the manufacturing process changed or destroyed in the final product] 15.9%, automobiles 15.0%, professional equipment 15.2%, energy products 8.3%). *Major import sources* (1996): France 62.3%; Italy 4.1%; Venezuela 3.8%; Germany 3.3%; United States 3.0%; UK 2.0%; Guadeloupe 0.9%. **Exports** (1998-f.o.b.): F 1,692,000,000 (1996; bananas 36.9%, refined petroleum 19.9%, rum 11.3%, yachts and boats 7.1%). *Major export destinations* (1996): France 51.7%; Guadeloupe 21.0%; UK 7.2%; French Guiana 3.8%.

Transport and communications

Transport. *Roads* (1994): total length 1,299 mi, 2,091 km (paved [1988] 75%). *Vehicles* (1993): passenger cars 108,300; trucks and buses 32,200. *Air transport* (1997): passenger arrivals and departures 1,552,000; cargo handled 14,400 metric tons; airports (1998) with scheduled flights 1. **Communications** Total units (units per 1,000 persons). Daily newspaper circulation (1000): 32,000 (83); Radio receivers (1997): 82,000 (213); Television receivers (1999); 66,000 (168); Telephone main lines (1999): 172,192 (443); Cellular telephone subscribers (1999): 102,000 (206); Personal computers (1999): 36,000 (93).

Education and health

Educational attainment (1990). Percentage of pop. age 25 and over having: incomplete primary, or no declaration 54.3%; primary education 18.0%; secondary 20.0%; higher 7.7%. **Literacy** (1982): total

pop. age 15 and over literate 206,807 (92.5%); males literate 97,538 (91.8%); females literate 109,269 (93.2%). **Health** (1998): physicians 780 (1 per 487 persons); hospital beds 2,907 (1 per 131 persons); infant mortality rate per 1,000 live births (2000) 8.0. **Food** (1998): daily per capita caloric intake 2,865 (vegetable products 75%, animal products 25%); 118% of FAO recommended minimum requirement.

Military

Total active duty personnel (2000): 3,800 French troops.

Background

Carib Indians, who had ousted earlier Arawak inhabitants, resided on the island when Christopher Columbus visited it in 1502. In 1635 the French established a colony there. The British captured and held the island in 1762-63 and again during the Napoleonic Wars, but each time it was returned to France. Made a département of France in 1946, Martinique remains under French rule despite a 1970s independence movement.

Recent Developments

French Pres. Jacques Chirac gave a clear hint in 2000 that the hitherto highly centralized relationship between Paris and French overseas departments might be relaxed and that Martinique might enjoy more local control in the future. As a part of France, Martinique joined in the adoption of the euro in 2002.

Internet resources: <www.martinique.org>

Mauritania

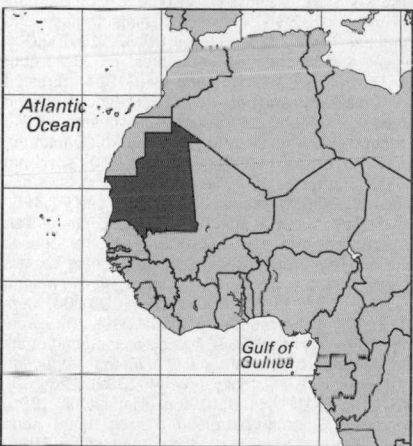

Official name: Al-Jumhuriyah al-Islamiyah al-Muritaniyah (Arabic) (Islamic Republic of Mauritania). **Form of government:** unitary multiparty republic with two legislative houses (Senate [56]; National Assembly [81]). **Head of state and government:** President Maaouya Ould Sidi Ahmad Taya (from 1984) assisted by a prime minister. **Capital:** Nouakchott. **Official language:** Arabic (Arabic, Fulani, Soninke, and Wolof are national languages). **Official religion:** Islam. **Monetary unit:** 1 ouguiya (UM) = 5 khoums; valuation (28 Jun 2002) $1 = UM 276.

Demography

Area: 398,000 sq mi, 1,030,700 sq km. **Population** (2001): 2,591,000. **Density** (2001): persons per sq mi 6.5, persons per sq km 2.5. **Urban** (1999): 56.5%. **Sex distribution** (2000): male 48.68%; female 51.32%. **Age breakdown** (2000): under 15, 46.2%; 15–29, 26.6%; 30–44, 15.6%; 45–59, 7.8%; 60–74, 3.3%; 75 and over, 0.5%. **Ethnic composition** (1993): Moor 70% (of which about 40% "black" Moor [Haratin, or African Sudanic] and about 30% "white" Moor [Bidan, or Arab-Berber]); other black African 30% (mostly Wolof, Tukulor, Soninke, and Fulani). **Religious affiliation** (2000): Sunni Muslim 99.1%; traditional beliefs 0.5%; Christian 0.3%; other 0.1%. **Major cities** (2000): Nouakchott 611,883; Nouadhibou 74,414; Kiffa (1999) 50,800; Kaedi (1992) 35,241; Rosso (1992) 30,000. **Location:** northern Africa, bordering Western Sahara (annexed by Morocco), Algeria, Mali, Senegal, and the North Atlantic Ocean.

Vital statistics

Birth rate per 1,000 pop. (2000): 43.4 (world avg. 22.5). **Death rate** per 1,000 pop. (2000): 14.0 (world avg. 9.0). **Natural increase rate** per 1,000 pop. (2000): 29.4 (world avg. 13.5). **Total fertility rate** (avg. births per childbearing woman; 2000): 6.3. **Life expectancy** at birth (2000): male 48.7 years; female 52.9 years.

National economy

Budget (1997). *Revenue:* UM 44,800,000,000 (tax revenue 58.3%, of which taxes on goods and services 26.5%, import taxes 12.1%, income taxes 9.6%; nontax revenue 39.9%, of which fishing royalties and penalties 32.3%). *Expenditures:* UM 32,110,000,000 (wages and salaries 24.9%; interest on public debt 15.3%; defense 11.4%). **Land use** (1994): forested 4.3%; meadows and pastures 38.3%; agricultural and under permanent cultivation 0.2%; desert 57.2%. **Production** (metric tons except as noted). *Agriculture, forestry, fishing* (1999): rice 101,900, sorghum 74,800, dates 22,000; livestock (number of live animals) 6,200,000 sheep, 4,133,000 goats, 1,395,-000 cattle; roundwood (1998) 15,000 cu m; fish catch (metric tons; 1997) 82,000, of which octopuses 23,500; fish catch including foreign fishing vessels (1996) 564,200. *Mining and quarrying* (gross weight; 1998): iron ore 11,411,000; gypsum 100,000. *Manufacturing* (value added in $'000,000; 1993): cement, tiles, and bricks 5.9; fabricated metal products 5.4; paper and paper products 2.1. *Energy production (consumption):* electricity (kW-hr; 1999) 226,700,-000 ([1996] 153,000,000); coal (metric tons; 1996) none (6,000); crude petroleum (barrels; 1996) none (6,927,000); petroleum products (metric tons; 1996) 840,000 (927,000). **Population economically active** (1994): total 687,000; activity rate of total pop. 31.3% (participation rates: over age 10 [1991] 45.5%; female 22.9%). **Household income and expenditure.** Average household size (1996): 5.3; expenditure (1990): food and beverages 73.1%, cloth-

ing and footwear 8.1%, energy and water 7.7%, transportation and communications 2.0%. **Gross national product** (1999): $1,001,000,000 ($390 per capita). **Public debt** (external, outstanding; 1999): $2,138,-000,000. **Tourism** (1999): receipts $28,000,000; expenditures $55,000,000.

Foreign trade

Imports (1997): $403,400,000 (imports for National Industrial and Mining Company 20.2%; petroleum products 13.6%; investment including food aid 10.0%; equipment and machinery 6.5%). *Major import sources:* France 25.5%; Spain 7.5%; Germany 6.7%; Belgium-Luxembourg 6.4%; Thailand 5.1%. **Exports** (1997): $405,000,000 (iron ore 52.4%; fish 47.6%, of which cephalopods 28.3%). *Major export destinations:* Japan 23.3%; Italy 16.7%; France 13.9%; Spain 8.3%; Belgium-Luxembourg 7.1%.

Transport and communications

Transport. *Railroads* (1998): route length 704 km; passenger-km, negligible; (1997) metric ton-km cargo 2,340,000,000. *Roads* (1996): total length 7,660 km (paved 11%). *Vehicles* (1996): passenger cars 18,810; trucks and buses 10,450. *Air transport* (1998; 1/11th proportion of Air Afrique): passenger-km 258,263,000; metric ton-km cargo 13,524,000; airports (1997) with scheduled flights 9. **Communications** Total units (units per 1,000 persons). Daily newspaper circulation (1996): 1,000 (0.4); Radio receivers (1997): 360,000 (147); Television receivers (1999): 247,000 (100); Telephone main lines (1999): 16,525 (6.7); Personal computers (1999): 70,000 (28); Internet users (1999): 12,500 (5.1).

Education and health

Educational attainment (1988). Percentage of pop. age 25 and over having: no formal schooling 60.8%; primary and incomplete secondary 34.1%; secondary 3.8%; higher 1.3%. **Literacy** (1995): percentage of total pop. age 15 and over literate 37.7%; males literate 49.6%; females literate 26.3%. **Health:** physicians (1994) c. 200 (1 per 11,085 persons); hospital beds (1988) 1,556 (1 per 1,217 persons); infant mortality rate per 1,000 live births (2000) 78.1. **Food** (1999): daily per capita caloric intake 2,702 (vegetable products 85%, animal products 15%); 117% of FAO recommended minimum requirement.

Military

Total active duty personnel (2000): 15,650 (army 95.8%, navy 3.2%, air force 1.0%). **Military expenditure as percentage of GNP** (1997): 2.3% (world 2.6%); per capita expenditure $10.

Background

Inhabited in ancient times by Sanhadja Berbers, in the 11th–12th centuries Mauritania was the center of the Berber Almoravid movement, which imposed Islam. Arab tribes arrived in the 15th century and formed powerful confederations; the Portuguese also arrived then. France gained control of the coast in 1817 and in 1903 made the territory a protectorate.

1 metric ton = about 1.1 short tons;   1 kilometer = 0.6 mi (statute);   1 metric ton-km cargo = about 0.68 short ton-mi cargo;   c.i.f.: cost, insurance, and freight;   f.o.b.: free on board

In 1904 it was added to French West Africa, and later It became a colony. In 1960 Mauritania achieved independence. Its first president was ousted in a 1978 military coup. After a series of military rulers, in 1991 a new constitution was adopted and multiparty elections were held in 1992. During the 1990s, relations between the government and opposition groups deteriorated, even as there was some success in liberalizing the economy.

Recent Developments

On 8 Apr 2001, police arrested Mohamed Lemine Ch'Bih Ould Cheikh Melainine, leader of the opposition Popular Front. Despite widespread criticism by opposition parties and international human rights organizations, he was brought to trial and charged with conspiracy. Though critics condemned the trial as nothing more than a show, Melainine was sentenced to five years' imprisonment.

Internet resources: <www.mauritania.mr/ami>

Mauritius

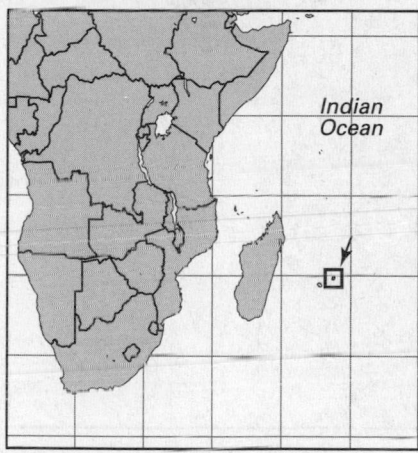

Indian Ocean

Official name: Republic of Mauritius. **Form of government:** republic with one legislative house (National Assembly [70—includes 8 "bonus" seats allocated to minor parties]. **Chief of state:** President Karl Offman (from 25 Feb 2002). **Head of government:** Prime Minister Sir Anerood Jugnaugth (from 2000). **Capital:** Port Louis. **Official language:** English. **Official religion:** none. **Monetary unit:** 1 Mauritian rupee (Mau Re; plural Mau Rs) = 100 cents; valuation (28 Jun 2002) $1 = Mau Rs 30.03.

Demography

Area: 788 sq mi, 2,040 sq km. **Population** (2001): 1,195,000. **Density** (2001): persons per sq mi 1,516.5, persons per sq km 585.8. **Urban** (2000): 41.3%. **Sex distribution** (2000): male 49.47%; female 50.53%. **Age breakdown** (2000): under 15, 25.7%; 15–29, 25.6%; 30–44, 24.7%; 45–59, 15.1%; 60–74, 6.8%; 75 and over, 2.1%. **Ethnic composition** (2000): Indo-Pakistani 67.0%; Creole (mixed Caucasian, Indo-Pakistani, and African) 27.4%; Chi-

nese 3.0%; other 2.0%. **Religious affiliation** (1990): Hindu 50.6%; Roman Catholic 27.2%; Muslim 16.3%; Protestant 5.2%; Buddhist 0.3%; other 0.4%. **Major urban areas** (2000): Port Louis 148,506; Beau Bassin-Rose Hill 102,377; Vacoas-Phoenix 100,490; Curepipe 80,973; Quatre Bornes 78,096. **Location:** island in the Indian Ocean, east of Madagascar.

Vital statistics

Birth rate per 1,000 pop. (2000): 16.7 (world avg. 22.5). **Death rate** per 1,000 pop. (2000): 6.8 (world avg. 9.0). **Natural increase** rate per 1,000 pop. (2000): 9.9 (world avg. 13.5). **Total fertility rate** (avg. births per childbearing woman; 2000): 2.0. **Marriage rate** per 1,000 pop. (1998): 9.4. **Divorce rate** per 1,000 pop. (1997): 0.8. **Life expectancy** at birth (2000): male 67.0 years; female 75.0 years.

National economy

Budget (1997–98). *Revenue:* Mau Rs 18,501,000,-000 (tax revenue 84.8%, of which import duties 33.3%, taxes on goods and services 32.5%, income tax 13.0%; nontax revenue 14.0%; grants 1.2%). *Expenditures:* Mau Rs 21,872,000,000 (social security 19.4%, government services 18.8%, education 16.0%, interest on debt 16.0%, economic services 11.4%, health 8.1%). **Tourism** (1999): receipts from visitors $545,000,000; expenditures by nationals abroad $187,000,000. **Public debt** (external, outstanding; 1999): $1,155,000,000. **Gross national product** (1999): $4,157,000,000 ($3,540 per capita). **Production** (metric tons except as noted). *Agriculture, forestry, fishing* (1999): sugarcane 3,500,000, potatoes 15,000, tomatoes 11,000; livestock (number of live animals) 93,000 goats, 27,000 cattle, 20,000 pigs; roundwood (1998) 14,760 cu m; fish catch (1998) 13,734. *Manufacturing* (value added in Mau Rs '000; 1994): apparel 5,065,000; beverages and tobacco 1,995,800; food products 1,580,400. *Energy production (consumption):* electricity (kW-hr; 1998) 1,364,800 (1,364,800); coal (metric tons; 1998) none (86,300); petroleum products (metric tons; 1998) none (576,000). **Population economically active** (1998): total 507,000; activity rate of total pop. 43.8% (participation rates: ages 12 and over, 55.6%; female 37.1%; unemployed 5.7%). **Household income and expenditure.** Average household size (2000) 4.2; annual income per household (1996–97) Mau Rs 122,148; sources of income (1990): salaries and wages 48.4%, entrepreneurial income 41.2%, transfer payments 10.4%; expenditure (1996–97): food, beverages, and tobacco 45.2%, transportation and communications 14.2%, housing and household furnishings 13.2%, clothing and footwear 7.9%, recreation and education 6.0%, energy 4.4%, health 3.8%. **Land use** (1994): forested 21.7%; meadows and pastures 3.4%; agricultural and under permanent cultivation 52.2%; other 22.7%.

Foreign trade

Imports (1998): Mau Rs 49,811,000,000 (manufactured goods classified chiefly by material 34.6%, machinery and transport equipment 22.8%, food 13.8%, chemicals 7.8%, mineral fuels and lubricants 6.3%, inedible crude materials excluding fuels 3.9%, animal and vegetable oils and fats 1.3%). *Major import sources:* France 11.1%; South Africa 10.5%; India 9.3%; Taiwan 5.2%; United Kingdom 5.2%; Japan

5.1%; Hong Kong 5.0%; Germany 4.1%. **Exports** (1998): Mau Rs 39,634,000,000 (clothing 55.9%, sugar 21.3%, yarn 3.7%, chemicals 0.5%, other 18.6%). *Major export destinations*: United Kingdom 32.3%; France 17.1%; United States 16.3%; Germany 5.3%; Italy 3.5%.

Transport and communications

Transport. *Roads* (1998): total length 1,905 km (paved 93%). *Vehicles* (1998): passenger cars 46,300; trucks and buses 12,100. *Air transport* (1998; Air Mauritius only): passenger-km 3,858,695; metric ton-km cargo 819,432,000; airports (1998) with scheduled flights 1. **Communications** Total units (units per 1,000 persons). Daily newspaper circulation (1996): 85,000 (76); Radio receivers (1997): 420,000 (371); Television receivers (1999): 265,000 (230); Telephone main lines (1999): 257,000 (223); Cellular telephone subscribers (1999): 102,000 (89); Personal computers (1999): 110,000 (96); Internet users (1999): 55,000 (48).

Education and health

Educational attainment (1990). Percentage of pop. age 25 and over having: no formal education 18.3%; incomplete primary 42.6%; primary 6.1%; incomplete secondary 18.0%; secondary 13.1%; higher 1.9%. **Literacy** (1995): percentage of total pop. age 15 and over literate 82.9%; males literate 87.1%; females literate 78.8%. **Health** (1998): physicians 1,033 (1 per 1,123 persons); hospital beds 3,826 (1 per 303 persons); infant mortality rate per 1,000 live births (2000) 17.7. **Food** (1999): daily per capita caloric intake 2,972 (vegetable products 86%, animal products 14%); 131% of FAO recommended minimum requirement.

Military

Total active duty personnel: none; however, a special 1,500-person paramilitary force ensures internal security. **Military expenditure as percentage of GNP** (1997): 0.3% (world 2.6%); per capita expenditure $10.

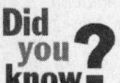

Did you know? The dodo, a large flightless bird, was first seen and named by Portuguese seamen in 1598; the name means "simpleton" in Portuguese and refers to the gentle, trusting nature of the bird. Only 83 years later the dodo was extinct, killed off by humans and the exotic animals, such as dogs and pigs, they introduced to Mauritius.

Background

The island was visited by the Portuguese in the early 16th century. The Dutch took possession in 1598 and attempted to settle it (1638–58, 1664–1710) before abandoning it to pirates. The French East India Company occupied Mauritius in 1721 and administered it until the French government took over in 1767. Sugar production allowed the colony to prosper. The British captured the island in 1810 and were granted formal control in 1814. In the late 19th century competition from beet sugar and the opening of the Suez Canal caused an economic decline. After World War II, Mauritius adopted political and economic reforms, and in 1968 it became an independent state within the Commonwealth. In 1992 it became a republic. It experienced political unrest during the 1990s.

Recent Developments

Mauritius made a concerted effort during 2001 to develop a high-technology economy and offered a variety of tax incentives for Indian businesses to establish export operations on the island. Pres. Cassam Uteem, faced with signing an antiterrorism law that he felt was undemocratic, resigned instead, in February 2002.

Internet resources:
<http://ncb.intnet.mu/cso.htm>

Mayotte

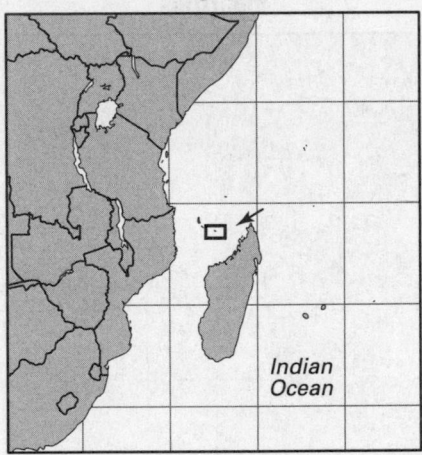

Indian Ocean

Official name: Collectivité Départementale de Mayotte (Departmental Collectivity of Mayotte); known as Mahoré in Comorian Swahili. **Political status:** overseas dependency of France with one legislative house (General Council [19]); claimed by the Comoros since 1975. **Chief of state:** President of France Jacques Chirac (from 1995). **Head of government:** Prefect Philippe de Mester (for France; from 18 Sep 2001); President of the General Council Younoussa Bamana (for Mayotte; from 1976). **Capitals:** Dzaoudzi (French administrative); Mamoudzou (local administrative). **Official language:** French. **Official religion:** none. **Monetary unit:** 1 euro (€) = 100 cents; $1 = €1.01 (28 Jun 2002); at conversion on 1 Jan 2002, €1 = 6.56 French francs (F).

Demography

Area: 144.1 sq mi, 373.2 sq km. **Population** (2001): 159,000. **Density** (2001): persons per sq mi

---

1 metric ton = about 1.1 short tons;   1 kilometer = 0.6 mi (statute);   1 metric ton-km cargo = about 0.68 short ton-mi cargo;   c.i.f.: cost, insurance, and freight;   f.o.b.: free on board

1,103.4, persons per sq km 426.0. **Urban** (1985): 59.7%. **Sex distribution** (2000): male 52.45%; female 47.55%. **Age breakdown** (2000): under 15, 46.6%; 15–29, 25.2%; 30–44, 18.1%; 45–59, 7.2%; 60–74, 2.4%; 75 and over, 0.5%. **Ethnic composition** (2000): Comorian (a mixture of Bantu, Arab, and Malagasy peoples) 92.3%; Swahili 3.2%; white (French) 1.8%; Makua 1.0%; other 1.7%. **Religious affiliation** (2000): Sunni Muslim 96.5%; Christian, principally Roman Catholic, 2.2%; other 1.3%. **Major towns** (1997; commune pop.): Mamoudzou 32,733; Dzaoudzi 10,792; Koungou 10,165. **Location:** island in the Indian Ocean, between the northern tip of Madagascar and the African mainland.

Vital statistics

Birth rate per 1,000 pop. (2000): 45.3 (world avg. 22.5). **Death rate** per 1,000 pop. (2000): 9.1 (world avg. 9.0). **Natural increase rate** per 1,000 pop. (2000): 36.2 (world avg. 13.5). **Total fertility rate** (avg. births per childbearing woman; 2000): 6.3. **Life expectancy** at birth (2000): male 59.9; female 69.2.

National economy

Budget (1993). *Revenue:* F 551,700,000 (current revenue 68.8%, of which subsidies 40.0%, indirect taxes 16.8%, direct taxes 4.9%; development revenue 31.2%, of which loans 11.6%, subsidies 7.9%). *Expenditures:* F 551,700,000 (current expenditure 68.8%, development expenditure 31.2%). **Production** (metric tons except as noted). *Agriculture, forestry, fishing* (1997): bananas 30,200, ylang-ylang 14,300 kg, vanilla 4,417 kg; livestock (number of live animals; 1997) 25,000 goats, 17,000 cattle; fish catch (1998) 1,570. *Mining and quarrying:* negligible. *Manufacturing:* mostly processing of agricultural products and materials used in housing construction (including siding and roofing materials, joinery, and latticework). *Energy production (consumption):* electricity (kW-hr; 1999) 68,387,000 (68,387,000); petroleum products, none (n.a.). **Gross national product** (1998): $486,409,000 ($3,704 per capita). **Household income and expenditure.** Average household size (1997) 4.6; expenditure (1991): food 42.2%, clothing and footwear 31.5%, household furnishings 8.8%, energy and water 6.8%, transportation 5.1%. **Population economically active** (1997): total 42,896; activity rate of total pop. 32.7% (participation rates: ages 15–64, 58.6%; female 43.4%; unemployed 41.5%). **Land use** (1987): meadows 35.0%; agricultural 29.0%; other 36.0%. **Tourism** (number of visitors; 1997): 9,500.

Foreign trade

Imports (1999): F 628,266,000 (1997: food products 23.8%; machinery 20.4%; transport equipment 10.4%; metals and metal products 10.3%; chemical products 7.7%). *Major import sources* (1997): France 66.0%; South Africa 14.0%; Asia 11.0%. **Exports** (1999): F 12,540,000 (1997; domestic exports 37.2%, of which ylang-ylang 27.9%, vanilla 3.5%; re-exports 62.8%). *Major export destinations* (1997): France 80.0%; Comoros 15.0%.

Transport and communications

Transport. *Roads* (1997): total length 233 km (paved 77%). *Vehicles* (1997): 6,553. *Air transport* (1997): passenger arrivals and departures 75,077; cargo un-

loaded and loaded 1,119 metric tons; airports (1998) with scheduled flights 1. **Communications.** Total units (units per 1,000 persons). Daily newspaper circulation (1998): none; Mayotte has one weekly newspaper. Radio receivers (1996): 50,000 (427); Television receivers (1999): 3,500 (30); Telephone main lines (1998): 12,200 (95).

Education and health

Educational attainment (1991). Percentage of pop. age 25 and over having: no formal education 72.8%; primary 14.2%; lower secondary 7.5%; higher secondary 3.2%; higher 2.3%. **Literacy** (1997): total pop. age 15 and over literate 63,053 (86.1%). **Health** (1997): physicians 57 (1 per 2,304 persons); hospital beds 186 (1 per 706 persons); infant mortality rate per 1,000 live births (2000) 71.3.

Military

Total active duty personnel (2000): 4,200 French troops are assigned to Mayotte and Réunion.

Background

Originally inhabited by descendants of Bantu and Malayo-Indonesian peoples, Mayotte was converted to Islam by Arab invaders in the 15th century. Taken by a Malagasy tribe from Madagascar at the end of the 18th century, it came under French control in 1843. Together with the other Comoros islands and Madagascar, it became part of a single French overseas territory in the early 20th century. It has been administered separately since 1975, when the three northernmost islands of the Comoros declared independence.

Recent Developments

In 2000 Mayotte residents voted to change the island's status from that of a "territorial collectivity" to a "departmental collectivity" with closer links to France. In July 2001 the change became official; the full transition would take place over 10 years, with the administrative and political systems adapting to a basically Muslim society.

Internet resources: <www.mayotte-online.com>

Mexico

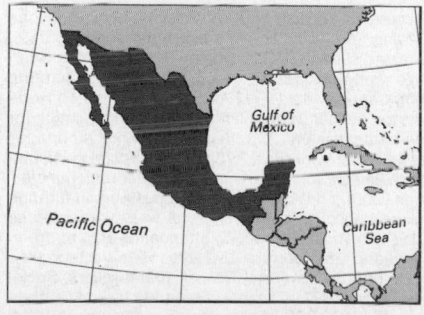

Official name: Estados Unidos Mexicanos (United Mexican States). **Form of government:** federal republic with two legislative houses (Senate [128]; Chamber of Deputies [500]). **Head of state and government:** President Vicente Fox Quesada (from 2000). **Capital:** Mexico City. **Official language:** Spanish. **Official religion:** none. **Monetary unit:** 1 Mexican peso (Mex$) = 100 centavos; valuation (28 Jun 2002) US$1 = Mex$9.95.

Demography

Area: 758,449 sq mi, 1,964,375 sq km. **Population** (2001): 99,969,000. **Density** (2001): persons per sq mi 132.2, persons per sq km 51.1. **Urban** (1990): 71.3%. **Sex distribution** (2000): male 49.28%; female 50.72%. **Age breakdown** (2000): under 15, 33.8%; 15–29, 29.8%; 30–44, 19.1%; 45–59, 10.7%; 60–74, 5.2%; 75 and over, 1.4%. **Ethnic composition** (1990): mestizo 60.0%; Amerindian 30.0%; Caucasian 9.0%; other 1.0%. **Religious affiliation** (1995): Roman Catholic 90.4%; Protestant (including Evangelical) 3.8%; other 5.8%. **Major cities** (2000): Mexico City 8,591,309; Guadalajara 1,647,000; Puebla 1,270,989; Ciudad Netzahualcóyotl 1,224,500; Juárez 1,190,000. **Location:** middle America, bordering the United States, the Gulf of Mexico, the Caribbean Sea, Belize, Guatemala, and the North Pacific Ocean. **Place of birth** (1990): 93.1% native-born; 6.9% foreign-born and unknown. **Mobility** (1990). Pop. 5 years and older living in the same state as in 1985: 94.3%; different state 4.9%; unspecified 0.8%. **Households.** Total households (2000) 21,948,000; distribution by size (1995): 1 person 5.7%, 2 persons 10.9%, 3 persons 15.8%, 4 persons 20.1%, 5 persons 17.7%, 6 persons 11.6%, 7 or more persons 18.2%. Family households (1990): 17,064,507 (98.4%); nonfamily 1,039,738 (1.3%); unspecified 256,554 (0.3%). **Emigration** (1998): 131,600 legal immigrants into the United States.

Vital statistics

Birth rate per 1,000 pop. (2000): 23.2 (world avg. 22.5); (1983) legitimate 72.5%; illegitimate 27.5%. **Death rate** per 1,000 pop. (2000): 5.0 (world avg. 9.0). **Natural increase rate** per 1,000 pop. (2000): 18.2 (world avg. 13.5). **Total fertility rate** (avg. births per childbearing woman; 2000): 2.7. **Marriage rate** per 1,000 pop. (1997): 7.5. **Divorce rate** per 1,000 pop. (1995): 0.4. **Life expectancy** at birth (2000): male 68.5 years; female 74.7 years.

Social indicators

Access to services (1995). Proportion of dwellings having: electricity 93.2%; piped water supply 85.6%; drained sewage 74.7%. **Quality of working life.** Average workweek (1997): 44.8 hours (manufacturing only). Annual rate (1992) per 100,000 insured workers for: temporary disability 6,426; indemnification for permanent injury 239; death 18. Labor stoppages (1997): 39, involving 9,375 workers. **Social participation.** Eligible voters participating in last national election (2000): 64%. Practicing religious pop. in total affiliated pop.: national average of weekly attendance (1993) 11%; (1970) weekly attendance 10% of urban dwellers, 25% of rural dwellers; yearly attendance 55% of urban dwellers, 73% of rural dwellers. **Social deviance** (1991). Criminal cases tried by local authorities per 100,000 pop. for: murder 60.3; rape 22.4;

other assault 301.0; theft 703.8. Suicide (1994) 2.47. **Material well-being** (1985). Households possessing: radio 96%; television 73%; washing machine 33%; automobile 29%; telephone 27%; refrigerator 23%.

National economy

Gross national product (1999): US$428,877,000,-000 (US$4,440 per capita). **Budget** (2000). *Revenue:* Mex$866,231,000,000 (1997; income tax 30.9%, VAT 20.9%, social security contributions 12.3%, excise tax 9.9%, import duties 3.9%). *Expenditures:* Mex$936,738,000,000 (1997; education 22.1%, social security and welfare 18.0%, interest on public debt 13.7%). **Public debt** (external, outstanding; 1999): US$87,531,000,000. **Tourism** (1999): receipts from visitors US$7,223,000,000; expenditures by nationals abroad US$4,541,000,000. **Production** (metric tons except as noted). *Agriculture, forestry, fishing* (2000): sugarcane 49,274,780, corn (maize) 17,988,060, sorghum 5,981,835, oranges 4,059,769, wheat 3,404,576; livestock (number of live animals) 30,540,000 cattle, 14,900,000 pigs, 9,600,000 goats, 8,000,000 ducks, 6,250,000 horses; roundwood (2000) 24,122,000 cu m; fish catch (1999) 1,250,592. *Mining and quarrying* (1999): salt 8,900,000, iron 6,855,219, gypsum 4,100,000, silica 1,700,000, phosphate 950,649, gold 23,476 kg. *Manufacturing* (gross value of production in Mex$'000; 1998): machinery and equipment 423,579,725; food, beverages, and tobacco products 279,104,375; chemical products 212,479,904; metal products 108,951,844; mineral products 55,612,499. *Energy production (consumption):* electricity (kW-hr; 1997) 170,751,000,000 (172,212,000,000); coal (metric tons; 1997) 10,337,000 (11,538,000); crude petroleum (barrels; 1997) 1,099,400,000 (470,400,000); petroleum products (metric tons; 1997) 72,362,000 (83,281,-000); natural gas (cu m; 1997) 29,708,000,000 (30,314,000,000). **Population economically active** (1999): total 39,751,000; activity rate of total pop. 41.2% (participation rates: ages 15–64, 63.4%; female 33.5%; unemployed [2000] 4.0%). **Household income and expenditure.** Average household size (1999) 4.4; income per household (1989) Mex$3,461; sources of income (1992): wages and salaries 61.5%, property and entrepreneurship 29.1%, transfer payments 7.8%, other 1.6%; expenditure (1992): food, beverages, and tobacco 36.9%, housing (includes household furnishings) 25.2%, transportation and communications 10.1%, clothing and footwear 8.5%, recreation and entertainment 5.5%, health and medical services 3.5%. **Land use** (1994): forest 25.5%; pasture 39.0%; agriculture 13.0%; other 22.5%.

Foreign trade

Imports (2000): US$174,458,000,000 (intermediate goods 76.6%; capital goods 13.8%; consumer goods 9.6%). *Major import sources:* US 73.1%; Japan 3.7%; Germany 3.6%; Canada 2.3%; Italy 1.2%; China 1.1%. **Exports** (2000): US$166,455,000,000 (machinery and transport equipment 33.3%; electrical equipment 10.7%; crude petroleum 8.9%; agricultural goods 3.3%). *Major export destinations:* US 88.7%; Europe 3.9%; Canada 2.0%; Japan 0.6%.

---

1 metric ton = about 1.1 short tons;   1 kilometer = 0.6 ml (statute);   1 metric ton-km cargo = about 0.68 short ton-mi cargo;   c.i.f.: cost, insurance, and freight;   f.o.b.: free on board

Transport and communications

Transport. *Railroads* (1998): route length 16,543 mi, 26,623 km; passenger-mi 677,000,000, passenger-km 1,089,000,000; short ton-mi cargo 19,726,000,-000, metric ton-km cargo 31,747,000,000. *Roads* (1999): total length 226,874 mi, 365,119 km (paved 29%). *Vehicles* (1999): passenger cars 9,842,006; trucks and buses 4,749,789. *Air transport* (1997): passenger-mi 14,707,000,000, passenger-km 23,668,000,000; short ton-mi cargo 1,426,000,000, metric ton-km cargo 2,295,000; airports (1997) 83. **Communications** Total units (units per 1,000 persons). Daily newspaper circulation (1996): 9,030,000 (97); Radio receivers (1997): 31,000,000 (329); Television receivers (1999): 26,000,000 (267); Telephone main lines (1999): 10,927,000 (112); Cellular telephone subscribers (1999): 7,732,000 (79); Personal computers (1999): 4,300,000 (44); Internet users (1999): 1,822,000 (19).

Education and health

Educational attainment (1995). Pop. age 15 and over having: no primary education 13.4%; some primary 22.8%; completed primary 19.3%; incomplete secondary 19.9%; complete secondary 16.3%; higher 8.3%. **Literacy** (1995): total pop. age 15 and over literate 89.6%; males literate 91.8%; females literate 87.4%. **Health:** physicians (1994) 146,021 (1 per 613 persons); hospital beds 107,288 (1 per 864 persons); infant mortality rate per 1,000 live births (2000) 26.2. **Food** (1999): daily per capita caloric intake 3,168 (vegetable products 82%, animal products 18%), 136% of FAO recommended minimum requirement.

Military

Total active duty personnel (2000): 192,770 (army 74.7%, navy 19.2%, air force 6.1%). **Military expenditure as percentage of GNP** (1997): 1.1% (world 2.6%); per capita expenditure US$44.

Did you know?  In addition to having the world's largest Spanish speaking population, Mexico has 62 other languages that are indigenous. According to the Mexican census, about 7 million people speak their native tribal language. Nahuatl is the most widely used with more than 2.5 million speakers.

Background

Inhabited for more than 20,000 years, Mexico produced great civilizations in AD 100-900, including the Olmec, Toltec, Mayan, and Aztec. The Aztec were conquered in 1521 by Spanish explorer Hernán Cortés, who established Mexico City on the site of the Aztec capital, Tenochtitlán. Francisco de Montejo conquered the remnants of Maya civilization in the mid-16th century, and Mexico became part of the viceroyalty of New Spain. In 1821 rebels negotiated a status quo independence from Spain, and in 1823 a new congress declared Mexico a republic. In 1845 the US voted to annex Texas, initiating the Mexican War. Under the Treaty of Guadalupe Hidalgo in 1848, Mexico ceded a vast territory in what is now the western

and southwestern US. The Mexican government endured several rebellions and civil wars in the late 19th and early 20th centuries. During World War II it declared war on the Axis powers (1942), and in the postwar era it was a founding member of the United Nations (1945) and the Organization of American States (1948). In 1993 it ratified the North American Free Trade Agreement. The election of Vicente Fox to the presidency in 2000 ended 71 years of rule by the Institutional Revolutionary Party.

Recent Developments

Although economic and political constraints slowed change in some areas, Fox's personal-approval ratings remained in the 60% range throughout 2001. He had promised quick resolution of the long-simmering conflict in Chiapas state, and in his first months in office he devoted substantial political capital to seeking a peaceful resolution of the matter. In July an initiative known as the Law on Indigenous Rights and Culture was ratified by the required number of state legislatures. The rebel Zapatista National Liberation Army (EZLN) and its allies, however, harshly denounced the measure, claiming that it broke with an earlier peace accord by not creating an autonomous territorial base for the exercise of indigenous rights.

The Fox administration's other major legislative initiative concerned fiscal reform. The proposal sought to stabilize the Mexican banking system and expand the country's tax base for future social spending, education, infrastructure development, and the national savings rate. Fox had also promised significant measures to reduce poverty, but during 2001 a sharp downturn in the Mexican economy constrained a number of social-policy initiatives.

It was in the foreign-affairs arena that the Fox administration initially made the most rapid progress. Fox and US Pres. George W. Bush met in February to discuss closer bilateral cooperation, and in the months following there was evidence of more effective collaboration against drug traffickers and immigrant smugglers. Immigration policy was the area in which the most novel developments occurred. Discussions focused primarily on expanded visa quotas for temporary workers and ways to normalize over time the status of the estimated 3.5 million undocumented Mexican migrants in the US. When political opposition in the US threatened to stall negotiations, Fox used his state visit to Washington DC in September to highlight the importance of the issue. The terrorist attacks of 11 September, however, reordered American foreign-policy priorities. American attitudes toward border enforcement shifted dramatically, accompanied by stringent new border and visa controls. The country attracted unfavorable headlines in late November when a National Human Rights Commission released a report that held the Mexican government responsible for the detention and torture of hundreds of those who "disappeared" in the 1970s in the "dirty war" against leftist groups; Fox appointed a special prosecutor to investigate the cases.

In March 2002 the Tijuana drug cartel, the largest drug-trafficking organization in Mexico, was brought down as one of its leaders was arrested and the other killed. Later that month Fox and Bush signed a border security agreement to make legal crossings easier while also improving security.

Internet resources: <www.mexonline.com>

Micronesia

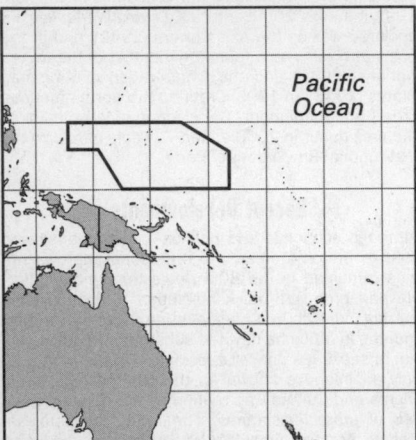

Pacific
Ocean

Official name: Federated States of Micronesia. **Form of government:** federal nonparty republic in free association with the United States with one legislative house (Congress [14]). **Head of state and government:** President Leo A. Falcam (from 1999). **Capital:** Palikir, on Pohnpei. **Official language:** none. **Official religion:** none. **Monetary unit:** 1 US dollar ($) = 100 cents.

Demography

Area (rounded): 270.8 sq mi, 701.4 sq km. **Population** (2001): 118,000. **Density** (2001): persons per sq mi 435.7, persons per sq km 168.2. **Urban** (2000): 28.5%. **Sex distribution** (2000): male 51.26%; female 48.74%. **Age breakdown** (1999): under 15, 40.6%; 15–29, 28.4%; 30–44, 16.5%; 45–59, 9.1%; 60 and over, 5.4%. **Ethnic composition** (2000): Chuukese 28.0%; Pohnpeian 24.9%; Yapese 10.6%; Mortlockese 5.6%; Kosraean 5.2%; white (US) 4.5%; Ulithian 3.3%; Carolinian 2.8%; other 15.1%. **Religious affiliation** (2000): Christianity is the predominant religious tradition; Roman Catholic 53.9%, Protestant 34.0%; the Kosraeans, Pohnpeians, and Chuukese are mostly Protestant and the Yapese mostly Roman Catholic. **Major cities** (1994): Weno (Moen) 16,121; Tol 4,816; Kolonia 6,660. **Location:** Oceania, island group in the North Pacific Ocean, northeast of New Guinea.

Vital statistics

Birth rate per 1,000 pop. (2000): 27.1 (world avg. 22.5). **Death rate** per 1,000 pop. (2000): 6.0 (world avg. 9.0). **Natural increase rate** per 1,000 pop. (2000): 21.1 (world avg. 13.5). **Total fertility rate** (avg. births per childbearing woman; 2000): 3.8. **Life expectancy** at birth (2000): male 66.7 years; female 70.6 years.

National economy

Budget (1997–98). *Revenue:* $152,300,000 (external grants 60.0%; tax revenue 15.1%; fishing rights fees 13.4%). *Expenditures:* $154,700,000 (current expenditures 79.6%, of which government services 71.4%, transfer payments 4.7%, debt services 3.4%; capital expenditure 20.4%). **Public debt** (external, outstanding; 1999): $98,200,000. **Population economically active** (1994): total 27,573; activity rate of total pop. 26.3% (participation rates: ages 15–64, 43.6%; female 33.8%; unemployed 15.3%). **Production** (metric tons except as noted). *Agriculture, forestry, fishing:* n.a.; however, Micronesia's major crops include coconuts (which provide annually more than 4,000 tons of copra), breadfruit, cassava, sweet potatoes; livestock comprises mostly pigs and poultry; fish catch (1998) 15,393, of which skipjack tuna 15,000, yellowfin tuna 5,000. *Mining and quarrying:* quarrying of sand and aggregate for local construction only. *Manufacturing:* n.a.; however, copra and coconut oil, traditionally important products, are being displaced by garment production; the manufacture of handicrafts and personal items (clothing, mats, boats, etc.) by individuals is also important. *Energy production (consumption):* electricity (kW-hr; 1997) 100,333,000 (100,333,000); petroleum products (metric tons; 1992) none (77,000). **Household income and expenditure.** Average household size (1994) 6.8; annual income per household (1994); sources of income (1994): wages and salaries 51.8%, operating surplus 23.0%, social security 2.1%; expenditure (1985): food and beverages 73.5%. **Land use** (1984): forested 22.5%; meadows and pastures 13.5%; agricultural and under permanent cultivation 33.5%; other 30.5%. **Gross national product** (1999): $229,880,000 ($1,980 per capita). **Tourism** (1998): expenditures $4,383,000; number of visitors 16,283.

Foreign trade

Imports (1998): $82,486,915 (1997; food, beverages, and tobacco 41.9%; manufactured goods 32.0%; machinery and transport equipment 28.4%; petroleum products 11.2%; chemicals 4.4%). *Major import sources* (1997): United States (including Guam) 72.5%; Japan 13.5%; Australia 6.6%. **Exports** (1998): $8,037,207 (1997; marine products 89.2%; agricultural products 4.4%, of which bananas 3.2%, copra 1.2%). *Major export destinations* (1992): Japan 80.0%; United States 9.3%; Guam 8.3%; South Pacific Region 2.4%.

Transport and communications

Transport. *Roads* (1990): total length 140 mi, 226 km (paved 17%). *Vehicles* (1998): passenger cars 2,044; trucks and buses 354. *Air transport:* airports (1997) with scheduled flights 4. **Communications** Total units (units per 1,000 persons). Radio receivers (1996): 70,000 (667); Television receivers (1999): 2,400 (21); Telephone main lines (1999): 9,100 (78); Internet users (1999): 2,000 (17).

Education and health

Educational attainment (1998). Percentage of pop. age 25 and over having: no formal schooling 4.4%; primary education 46.0%; some secondary 18.3%; secondary 12.9%; some college 14.7%; bachelor's degree 2.9%; higher 0.8%. **Literacy** (1994): total pop.

1 metric ton = about 1.1 short tons;　1 kilometer = 0.6 mi (statute);　1 metric ton-km cargo = about 0.68 short ton-mi cargo;　c.i.f.: cost, insurance, and freight;　f.o.b.: free on board

age 10 and over literate 69,779 (93.9%), males literate 35,688 (94.7%); females literate 34,091 (93.0%). **Health** (1998): physicians 68 (1 per 1,677 persons); hospital beds (1997) 260 (1 per 447 persons); infant mortality rate per 1,000 live births (2000) 33.5.

Military

External security is provided by the United States.

Background

The islands of Micronesia were probably settled by people from eastern Melanesia some 3,500 years ago. Europeans first landed on the islands in the 16th century. Spain took control of the islands 1886, then sold them to Germany in 1899. The islands came under Japanese rule after World War I. They were captured by US forces during World War II, and in 1947 they were included as a UN trust territory administered by the US. The islands became an internally self-governing federation in 1979. In 1986 Micronesia entered a compact of free association with the US, some provisions of which were set to expire in 2001. In the late 1990s, the republic was struggling to solve its economic difficulties.

Recent Developments

In 2001 voters in Falchuk, a part of Chuuk state, overwhelmingly passed a referendum to declare the district a separate state. A two-year negotiation period (2001–03) included in the compact of free association allowed US financial assistance to continue while discussions were ongoing. In 2002 the US proposed a new funding plan for Micronesia, which was to be voted on by Congress by October 2003.

Internet resources: <www.fm>

Moldova

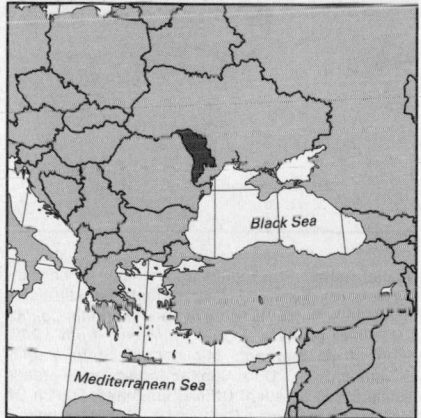

Black Sea

Mediterranean Sea

Official name: Republica Moldova (Republic of Moldova). **Form of government:** unitary parliamentary republic with a single legislative body (Parliament [101]). **Head of state:** President Vladimir Voronin (from 7 Apr 2001). **Head of government:** Prime Min-

ister Vasile Tarlev (from 10 Apr 2001). **Capital:** Chisinau. **Official language:** Romanian (constitutionally designated as Moldovan). **Official religion:** none. **Monetary unit:** 1 Moldovan leu (plural lei) = 100 bani; valuation (28 Jun 2002) free rate, $1 = 13.85 Moldovan lei.

Demography

Area: 13,000 sq mi, 33,700 sq km. **Population** (2001): 4,431,000. **Density** (2001): persons per sq mi 323.5, persons per sq km 124.9. **Urban** (1999): 54.4%. **Sex distribution** (2000): male 47.66%; female 52.34%. **Age breakdown** (2000): under 15, 23.2%; 15–29, 24.9%; 30–44, 21.4%; 45–59, 16.3%; 60–74, 11.0%; 75 and over, 3.2%. **Ethnic composition** (2000): Moldovan 48.2%; Ukrainian 13.8%; Russian 12.9%; Bulgarian 8.2%; Roma (Gypsy) 6.2%; Gagauz 4.2%; other 6.5%. **Religious affiliation** (1995): Orthodox 46.0%, of which Romanian Orthodox 35.0%, Russian Orthodox 9.5%; Muslim 5.5%; Catholic 1.8%, of which Roman Catholic 0.6%; Protestant 1.7%; Jewish 0.9%; other (mostly nonreligious) 44.1%. **Major cities** (1999): Chisinau 655,000; Tiraspol 200,700, Balti 156,600. **Location:** Eastern Europe, bordering Ukraine and Romania.

Vital statistics

Birth rate per 1,000 pop. (2000): 12.9 (world avg. 22.5); (1995) legitimate 87.7%; illegitimate 12.3%. **Death rate** per 1,000 pop. (2000): 12.6 (world avg. 9.0). **Natural increase rate** per 1,000 pop. (2000): 0.3 (world avg. 13.5). **Total fertility rate** (avg. births per childbearing woman; 2000): 1.6. **Marriage rate** per 1,000 pop.(1994): 7.8. **Life expectancy** at birth (2000): male 59.9 years; female 69.2 years.

National economy

Budget (1997). *Revenue:* 3,473,000,000 lei (value-added tax 23.8%, excise taxes 12.4%, personal income tax 7.4%, profits tax 6.2%, duties and customs taxes 3.3%). *Expenditures:* 2,354,000,000 lei (current expenditures 94.5%, of which education 20.4%, health care 12.5%, interest payments 9.1%; capital expenditure 5.5%). **Public debt** (external, outstanding; 1999): $722,000,000. **Land use** (1994): forest 10.6%; pasture 10.9%; agriculture 75.9%; other 2.6%. **Production** (metric tons except as noted). *Agriculture, forestry, fishing* (2000): sugar beets 1,800,000, corn (maize) 900,000, wheat 770,000; livestock (number of live animals) 974,000 sheep, 705,000 pigs, 416,000 cattle; roundwood (1998) 406,000 cu m; fish catch (1998) 491. *Mining and quarrying* (1995): sand and gravel 376,000; gypsum 13,600. *Manufacturing* ('000,000 lei; 1995): food 1,446,824; machinery 383,153; construction materials 164,198. *Energy production (consumption):* electricity (kW-hr; 1997): 5,274,000,000 (7,226,000,-000); coal (metric tons; 1997) none (322,000); petroleum products (metric tons; 1997) none (862,000). **Population economically active** (1994): total (1995) 1,693,000; activity rate of total pop. 44.8% (participation rates: ages 16–59 [male], 16–54 [female] 85.2%; female 53.0%; unemployed 1.4%). **Gross national product** (at current market prices; 1999): $1,481,000,000 ($410 per capita). **Household income and expenditure.** Average household size (1989) 3.4; sources of income (1994): wages and salaries 41.2%, social benefits 15.3%, agricultural income 10.4%, other 33.1%; expenditure (1995): food and drink 49.1%, clothing 9.7%, health 4.1%.

Foreign trade

Imports (1996): 4,967,200,000 lei (mineral products 36.8%, machinery 14.5%, agricultural goods 10.8%, chemical products 6.6%, textiles 5.1%). *Major import sources:* Ukraine 27.5%; Russia 27.3%; Romania 6.7%. **Exports** (1996): 3,691,200,000 lei (food and agricultural goods 72.8%, textile products 6.2%, machinery 5.3%, metals and metal products 1.7%). *Major export destinations:* Russia 53.6%; Romania 9.4%; Ukraine 5.9%.

Transport and communications

Transport. *Railroads* (1997): length 2,710 km; passenger-km 949,300,000; metric ton-km cargo (1995) 3,133,600,000. *Roads* (1995): total length 12,259 km (paved 87.2%). *Vehicles* (1996): passenger cars 166,757; trucks and buses 67,638. *Air transport* (1994): passenger-km 225,000; metric ton-km cargo 1,000,000; airports (1997) 1. **Communications** Total units (units per 1,000 persons). Daily newspaper circulation (1996): 261,000 (59); Radio receivers (1997): 3,220,000 (736); Television receivers (1998): 1,300,000 (297); Telephone main lines (1998): 657,000 (150); Cellular telephone subscribers (1999): 18,000 (4.1); Personal computers (1999): 35,000 (8.0); Internet users (1999): 25,000 (5.7).

Education and health

Educational attainment (1989). Percentage of pop. age 15 and over having: no formal schooling or some primary education 24.5%; some secondary 20.4%; secondary 46.4%; higher 8.7%. **Literacy** (2000): total pop. age 15 and over literate 98.9%; males 99.6%; females 98.3%. **Health** (1995): physicians 17,200 (1 per 250 persons); hospital beds 53,000 (1 per 82 persons); infant mortality rate per 1,000 live births (2000) 43.3. **Food** (1999): daily per capita caloric intake 2,728 (vegetable products 85%, animal products 15%); 106% of FAO recommended minimum requirement.

Military

Total active duty personnel (2000): 9,500 (army 89.5%, air force 10.5%). **Military expenditure as percentage of GNP** (1997): 1.0% (world 2.6%); per capita expenditure $14.

Background

Moldova, once part of the principality of Moldavia, was founded by the Vlachs in the 14th century. In the mid-16th century it was under the Ottoman empire. In 1774 it came under Russian control and lost portions of its territory. In 1859 it joined with the principality of Walachia to form the state of Romania, and in 1918 some of the territory it had ceded earlier also joined Romania. Romania was compelled to cede some of the Moldavian area to Russia in 1940, and that area combined with what Russia already controlled to become the Moldavian SSR. In 1991 Moldavia declared independence from the Soviet Union. It adopted the Romanian spelling of Moldova after having legitimized (1989) the use of the Roman rather than the Cyrillic alphabet. During the 1990s the country struggled to find economic equilibrium.

Recent Developments

In the February 2001 elections Moldova became the first former Soviet republic to return unreformed Communists to power. Playing on widespread dissatisfaction with the post-Communist transition, the Communist Party took 71 of the 101 seats in Parliament. One main goal was to increase the role of the state in the economy. Another was the introduction of Russian as the country's second official language, an issue that evoked protests.

Internet resources: <www.ournet.md>

Monaco

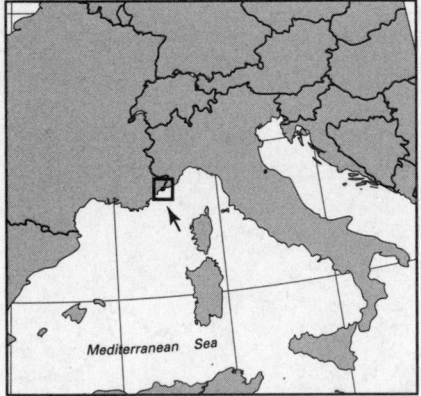

Mediterranean Sea

Official name: Principauté de Monaco (Principality of Monaco) **Form of government:** constitutional monarchy with one legislative body (National Council [18]) **Chief of state:** Prince Rainier III (from 1949) **Head of government:** Minister of State Patrick LeClerque (from 2000) **Capital:** (no separate area is distinguished as such) **Official language:** French **Official religion:** Roman Catholicism **Monetary unit:** 1 euro (€) = 100 cents; $1 = €1.01 (28 Jun 2002); at conversion on 1 Jan 2002, €1 = 6.56 French francs (F).

---

1 metric ton = about 1.1 short tons;   1 kilometer = 0.6 mi (statute);   1 metric ton-km cargo = about 0.68 short ton-mi cargo;   c.i.f.: cost, insurance, and freight;   f.o.b.: free on board

Demography

Area: 0.75 sq mi, 1.95 sq km **Population (2001):** 31,800 **Density (2001):** persons per sq mi 42,400, persons per sq km 16,307 **Urban (2000):** 100% **Sex distribution (2000):** male 47.58%; female 52.42% **Age breakdown (2000):** under 15, 15.1%; 15–29, 14.0%; 30–44, 21.2%; 45–59, 21.3%; 60–74, 17.2%; 75 and over, 11.2% **Ethnic composition (2000):** French 45.8%; Ligurian (Genoan) 17.2%; Moneguasque 16.9%; British 4.5%; Jewish 1.7%; other 13.9% **Religious affiliation (2000):** Christian 93.2%, of which Roman Catholic 89.3%, Jewish 1.7%; nonreligious and other 5.1% **Location:** Western Europe, bordering the Mediterranean Sea and France.

Vital statistics

Birth rate per 1,000 pop (2000): 9.9 (world avg. 22.5) **Death rate** per 1,000 pop (2000): 13.1 (world avg. 9.0) **Natural increase rate** per 1,000 pop (2000): -3.2 (world avg. 13.5) **Total fertility rate** (avg. births per childbearing woman; 2000): 1.8 **Marriage rate** per 1,000 pop (1997): 6.0 **Divorce rate** per 1,000 pop (1997): 2.5 **Life expectancy** at birth (2000): male 74.9 years; female 83.0 years.

National economy

Budget (1997). *Revenue:* F 3,225,658,000 (value-added taxes 50.0%). *Expenditures:* F 3,139,854,000 **Production.** *Manufacturing:* in the 1990s, principal manufactures included chemicals, cosmetics; light electronics; paper and card manufactures. *Energy production (consumption):* electricity (kW-hr; 1997) 403,000,000 (imported from France) **Gross domestic product** (1994): $785,000,000 ($24,460 per capita) **Population economically active** (1990): total 12,574 (42.0%); female participation in labour force 5,002 (39.8%); ages 17–64, 63.6%; unemployed (1996) 3.0% **Household income and expenditure.** Average household size (1998) 2.2 **Tourism** (1999): 2,210 hotel rooms; 278,000 overnight stays **Land use** (2000): forested 0%; meadows and pastures 0%; agricultural and under permanent cultivation 0%; built-up and other 100%.

Foreign trade

Monaco participates in a customs union (since 1963) with France; separate figures are not available.

Transport and communications

Transport. *Railroads* (1997): length 1.1 mi, 1.7 km; passengers 2,171,100; cargo 3,357 tons. *Roads* (1997): total length 31 mi, 50 km (paved 100%). *Vehicles* (1997): passenger cars 21,120, trucks and buses 2,770 **Communications** Total units (units per 1,000 persons). Daily newspaper circulation (1999): 10,000 (300); Radio receivers (1997): 34,000 (1,030); Television receivers (1997): 25,000 (758); Telephone main lines (1999): 33,000 (990); Cellular telephone subscribers (1999): 12,000 (360).

Education and health

Literacy: virtually 100% **Health** (1997): physicians 188 (1 per 170 persons); hospital beds 555 (1 per 58 persons); infant mortality rate per 1,000 live births (2000) 5.9 **Food:** daily per capita caloric intake, assuming consumption patterns similar to France (1999) 3,575 (vegetable products 62%, animal products 38%), 142% of FAO recommended minimum requirement.

Military

Defense responsibility lies with France according to the terms of the Versailles Treaty of 1919.

Background

Inhabited since prehistoric times, Monaco was known to the Phoenicians, Greeks, Carthaginians, and Romans. In 1191 the Genoese took possession of it; in 1297 the reign of the Grimaldi family began. The Grimaldis allied themselves with France except for the period 1524–1641, when they were under the protection of Spain. France annexed Monaco in 1793, and it remained under French control until the fall of Napoleon, when the Grimaldis returned. In 1815 it was put under the protection of Sardinia. A treaty in 1861 called for the sale of the towns of Menton and Roquebrune to France and the establishment of Monaco's independence. Monaco is one of Europe's most luxurious resorts. In 1997 the 700-year rule of the Grimaldis, now under Prince Rainier III, was celebrated.

Recent Developments

A 2000 report from the French parliament called Monaco a money-laundering paradise. It accused the principality of having such lax banking laws that officials could not cooperate in the international fight against money laundering even if they desired to do so. Outraged by the accusations, Monaco threatened to break with France and "endow the principality with full sovereignty." As health problems continued to sideline Prince Rainer III, his son, Prince Albert, took the spotlight in 2001, making a number of official trips abroad.

Internet Resources: <www.monaco.mc>

Mongolia

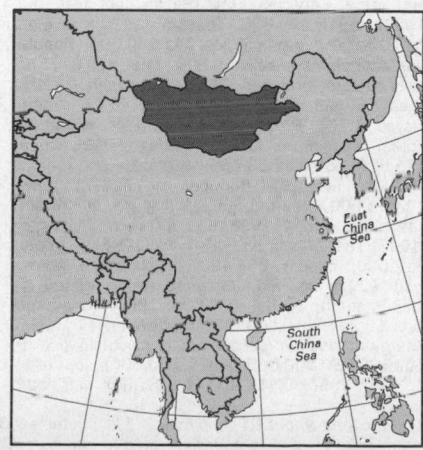

Official name: Mongol Uls (Mongolia). Form of government: unitary multiparty republic with one legislative house (State Great Hural [76]). Chief of state: President Natsagiyn Bagabandi (from 1997). Head of government: Prime Minister Nambaryn Enkhbayar (from 2000). Capital: Ulaanbaatar (Ulan Bator). Official language: Khalkha Mongolian. Official religion: none. Monetary unit: 1 tugrik (Tug) = 100 mongo; valuation (28 Jun 2002) $1 = Tug 1,105.

Demography

Area: 603,930 sq mi, 1,564,160 sq km. Population (2001): 2,435,000. Density (2001): persons per sq mi 4.0, persons per sq km 1.6. Urban (2000): 56.6%. Sex distribution (2000): male 49.63%; female 50.37%. Age breakdown (1999): under 15, 34.6%; 15–29, 30.6%; 30–44, 20.8%; 45–59, 8.3%; 60–69, 3.3%; 70 and over, 2.4%. Ethnic composition (1989): Khalkha Mongol 78.8%; Kazakh 5.9%; Dörbed Mongol 2.7%; Bayad 1.9%; Buryat Mongol 1.7%; Dariganga Mongol 1.4%; other 7.6%. Religious affiliation (1995): Tantric Buddhist (Lamaism) 96.0%; Muslim 4.0%. Major cities (1999): Ulaanbaatar (Ulan Bator) 691,000; Darhan 72,600; Erdenet 65,700; Choybalsan 38,500; Olgiy 23,700. Location: North-central Asia, bordering Russia and China.

Vital statistics

Birth rate per 1,000 pop. (2001): 22.4 (world avg. 22.5). Death rate per 1,000 pop. (2001): 7.5 (world avg. 9.0). Natural increase rate per 1,000 pop. (2001): 14.9 (world avg. 13.5). Total fertility rate (avg. births per childbearing woman; 2001): 2.4. Marriage rate per 1,000 pop. (1999): 9.7. Divorce rate per 1,000 pop. (1999): 0.7. Life expectancy at birth (2001): male 61.0 years; female 65.0 years.

National economy

Budget (1999). Revenue: Tug 243,504,400,000 (taxes 67.9%, of which sales tax 27.0%, social security contributions 15.3%, special taxes 10.2%, income taxes 8.5%, custom duties 3.7%; nontax revenue 19.4%). Expenditures: Tug 334,455,400,000 (transfers to provincial governments 11.2%; capital investment 8.8%; wages 7.5%; defense 5.8%; general social services 5.6%). Public debt (external; 1999): $816,300,000. Tourism (1999): receipts $36,000,000; expenditures $41,000,000. Population economically active (1998): total 840,877; activity rate of total pop. 36.7% (participation rates: ages 15 and over 59.2%; female 48.0%; unemployed 5.7%). Production (metric tons except as noted). Agriculture, forestry, fishing (1999): wheat 171,520, potatoes 63,765, vegetables and melons 46,524; livestock (number of live animals) 14,694,000 sheep, 11,062,000 goats, 3,726,000 cattle; roundwood (1998) 631,000 cu m; fish catch (1997) 181. Mining and quarrying (1998): fluorspar 612,000; copper 358,400; molybdenum 4,240; gold 9,531 kg. Manufacturing (value added by manufacturing in Tug '000,000; 1996): food products 10,261.3; textiles 6,522.8; beverages 3,316.6. Energy production (consumption): electricity (kW-hr; 1996) 2,580,000,000 (2,975,-000,000); coal (metric tons; 1996) 5,111,000 (4,928,000); petroleum

products (metric tons; 1996) none (544,000). Gross national product (1999): $927,000,000 ($390 per capita). Household income and expenditure (1999): Average household size (2000) 4.4; monthly income per household Tug 67,426; sources of income: wages and salaries 36.4%, transfer payments 11.7%, self-employment 41.2% (includes income from agricultural cooperatives), other 10.7%; expenditure: food 41.1%, housing 11.4%, clothing 9.7%, education 7.5%, transportation and communications 7.1%, healthcare 3.6%. Land use (1998): forest and other 24.4%; pasture 74.8%; agriculture 0.8%.

Foreign trade

Imports (1998): $582,400,000 (capital equipment 33.5%, energy 15.7%, food 13.9%, consumer goods 12.6%, raw materials and spare parts 10.8%). Major import sources: Russia 29.9%; Japan 11.8%; China 11.6%; South Korea 7.5%; United States 7.2%; France 5.3%; Germany 5.1%. Exports (1998): $462,300,000 (mineral products 59.0%, textile and cashmere products 13.5%, wool, hides, and leather goods 5.5%). Major export destinations: China 29.3%; Switzerland 20.4%; Russia 11.8%; South Korea 9.6%; United States 8.5%.

Transport and communications

Transport. Railroads (1999): length 1,815 km; passenger-km 559,800,000; metric ton-km cargo 1,942,000. Roads (1996): total length 50,000 km (paved 3%). Vehicles (1999): passenger cars 39,921; trucks and buses 31,061. Air transport (1996): passenger-km 525,000,000; metric ton-km cargo 48,000,000; airports (1997) with scheduled flights 1. Communications Total units (units per 1,000 persons). Daily newspaper circulation (1996): 68,000 (27); Radio receivers (1997): 360,000 (142); Television receivers (1998): 152,000 (58); Telephone main lines (1999): 103,400 (39); Cellular telephone subscribers (1999): 34,562 (13); Personal computers (1999): 24,000 (9.2); Internet users (1999): 6,000 (2.3).

Education and health

Educational attainment (1989). Percentage of pop. age 10 and over having: primary education 33.7%; some secondary 31.9%; complete secondary 16.9%; vocational secondary 9.4%; some higher and complete higher 8.1%. Literacy (2000): percentage of total pop. age 7 and over literate 97.8%; males literate 98.0%; females literate 97.5%. Health (1999): physicians 6,162 (1 per 384 persons) hospital beds 17,877 (1 per 132 persons); infant mortality rate per 1,000 live births (2001) 61.0. Food (1999): daily per capita caloric intake 1,963 (vegetable products 55%, animal products 45%); (1997) 81% of FAO recommended minimum.

Military

Total active duty personnel (2000): 9,100 (army 82.4%, air force 17.6%). Military expenditure as percentage of GNP (1997): 1.9% (world 2.6%); per capita expenditure $8.

1 metric ton = about 1.1 short tons;   1 kilometer = 0.6 mi (statute);   1 metric ton-km cargo = about 0.68 short ton-mi cargo;   c.i.f.: cost, insurance, and freight;   f.o.b.: free on board

Did you know? With a total population of about two and a half million and an area slightly larger than Alaska, Mongolia has one of the lowest population densities of any country in the world.

Background

In Neolithic times Mongolia was inhabited by small groups of nomads. During the 3rd century BC it became the center of the Xiongnu empire. Turkic-speaking peoples held sway in the 4th–10th centuries AD. In the early 13th century Genghis Khan united the Mongol tribes and conquered central Asia. His successor, Ogodei, conquered the Chin dynasty of China in 1234. Kublai Khan established the Yuan, or Mongol, dynasty in China in 1279. After the 14th century, the Ming dynasty of China confined the Mongols to their homeland in the steppes; later they became part of the Chinese Ch'ing dynasty. Inner Mongolia was incorporated into China in 1644. After the fall of the Ch'ing dynasty in 1911, Mongol princes declared Mongolia's independence from China, and in 1921 Russian forces helped drive off the Chinese. The Mongolian People's Republic was established in 1924 and recognized by China in 1946. The nation adopted a new constitution in 1992 and shortened its name to Mongolia.

Recent Developments

Mongolia underwent several leadership changes during the late 1990s. Consolidating its victory in the July 2000 elections to the Great Hural (parliament), the reformed communist Mongolian People's Revolutionary Party won the May 2001 presidential elections.

Internet resources: <www.travelmongolia.com>

Morocco

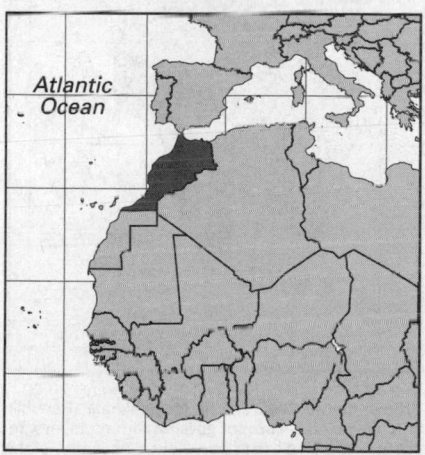

Atlantic Ocean

Official name: Al-Mamlakah al-Maghribiyah (Kingdom of Morocco). **Form of government:** constitutional monarchy with two legislative houses (House of Councillors [270 (indirectly elected seats)]; House of Representatives [325]). **Chief of state and head of gov-**ernment: King Muhammad VI (from 1999) assisted by Prime Minister Abderrahmane El Youssoufi (from 1998). **Capital:** Rabat. **Official language:** Arabic. **Official religion:** Islam. **Monetary unit:** 1 Moroccan dirham (DH) = 100 Moroccan francs; valuation (28 Jun 2002) $1 = DH 10.65.

Demography

Area (includes Western Sahara): 274,461 sq mi, 710,850 sq km. **Population** (2001; includes Western Sahara): 29,237,000. **Density** (2001; includes Western Sahara): persons per sq mi 106.5, persons per sq km 41.1. **Urban** (1999): 52.7%. **Sex distribution** (1999): male 49.89%; female 50.11%. **Age breakdown** (1999): under 15, 35.7%; 15–29, 28.9%; 30–44, 18.9%; 45–59, 9.2%; 60–74, 5.3%; 75 and over, 2.0%. **Ethnolinguistic composition** (1995): Arab 65%; Berber 33%; other 2%. **Religious affiliation** (2000): Muslim (mostly Sunni) 98.3%; Christian 0.6%; other 1.1%. **Major urban areas** (1994): Casablanca 2,940,623; Rabat-Salé 1,385,872; Fès 774,574; Marrakech 745,541; Oujda 678,778. **Location:** Northern Africa, bordering the Mediterranean Sea, Algeria, and the North Atlantic Ocean.

Vital statistics

Birth rate per 1,000 pop. (2001): 24.2 (world avg. 22.5). **Death rate** per 1,000 pop. (2001): 5.9 (world avg. 9.0). **Natural increase rate** per 1,000 pop. (2001): 18.3 (world avg. 13.5). **Total fertility rate** (avg. birth per childbearing woman; 2001): 3.0. **Life expectancy** at birth (2001): male 67.2 years; female 71.7 years.

National economy

Budget. *Revenue* (1997): DH 79,747,000,000 (taxes on income and profits 25.2%; value-added tax 22.7%; excise taxes 17.9%; international trade 15.0%; stamp tax 4.4%). *Expenditures* (1997): DH 86,058,000,000 (current expenditure 78.7%, of which wages 39.7%, debt payment 20.1%; capital expenditure 21.3%). **Public debt** (external, outstanding; 1999): $17,284,000,-000. **Tourism** (1999): receipts $1,880,000,000; expenditures $440,000,000. **Production** (metric tons except as noted). *Agriculture, forestry, fishing* (1999): sugar beets 3,223,400, wheat 2,153,540, barley 1,473,980; livestock (number of live animals) 16,576,400 sheep, 5,114,400 goats, 2,559,800 cattle; roundwood (1998) 1,746,000 cu m; fish catch (1997) 625,000. *Mining and quarrying* (1996): phosphate rock 20,792,000; barite 283,000; zinc 152,000. *Manufacturing* (value added in DH '000,000; 1996): food 39,280; chemical products 13,508; textiles 12,392. *Energy production (consumption):* electricity (kW-hr; 1996) 12,178,000,000 (13,228,000,000); coal (metric tons; 1996) 504,000 (2,649,000); crude petroleum (barrels; 1996) 30,400 (45,600,000); petroleum products (metric tons; 1996) 5,112,000 (5,888,000); natural gas (cu m; 1996) 20,399,000 (20,399,000). **Population economically active** (1998): total 5,137,539; activity rate 34.4% (participation rates: over age 15, 48.1%; female 23.8%; unemployed 19.0%). **Gross national product** (1999): $33,715,000,000 ($1,190 per capita). **Household income and expenditure.** Average household size (1998) 5.7; expenditure (1994; weights of consumer price index components): food 45.2%, housing 12.5%, transportation 7.6%.

Foreign trade

Imports (1999): DH 95,577,000,000 (1996; capital goods 23.5%; food, beverages, and tobacco 17.1%; energy products 17.0%; consumer goods 14.6%). *Major import sources* (1996): France 20.8%; Spain 8.8%; US 7.4%; Germany 6.1%. **Exports** (1999): DH 72,283,000,000 (1996; food 31.6%; consumer goods 23.0%; minerals 11.0%). *Major export destinations* (1996): France 28.3%; Spain 9.9%; Japan 6.9%; India 6.3%; Italy 6.3%.

Transport and communications

Transport. *Railroads* (1996): route length 1,768 km; passenger-km 1,776,000,000; metric ton-km cargo 4,757,000,000. *Roads* (1996): total length 57,810 km (paved 52%). *Vehicles* (1996): passenger cars 1,018,146; trucks and buses 278,075. *Air transport* (1996): passenger-km (Royal Air Maroc only) 4,489,000,000; metric ton-km cargo 380,000,000; airports (1998) with scheduled flights 11. **Communications** Total units (units per 1,000 persons). Daily newspaper circulation (1996): 704,000 (27); Radio receivers (1997): 6,640,000 (247); Television receivers (1997): 3,100,000 (115); Telephone main lines (1999): 1,515,000 (55); Cellular telephone subscribers (1999): 116,645 (4.2); Personal computers (1999): 200,000 (7.1); Internet users (1999): 40,000 (1.4).

Education and health

Educational attainment (1982). Percentage of pop. age 25 and over having: no formal education 47.8%; some primary education 47.8%; some secondary 3.8%; higher 0.6%. **Literacy** (1995): total pop. over age 15 literate 43.7%; males literate 56.6%; females literate 31.0%. **Health** (1994): physicians 8,838 (1 per 2,923 persons); hospital beds 26,407 (1 per 978 persons); infant mortality rate per 1,000 live births (2001) 48.1. **Food** (1999): daily per capita caloric intake 3,010 (vegetable products 94%, animal products 6%); 124% of FAO recommended minimum.

Military

Total active duty personnel (2000): 198,500 (army 88.2%, navy 5.0%, air force 6.8%). **Military expenditure as percentage of GDP** (1997): 4.3% (world 2.6%); per capita expenditure $49.

Did you know? Couscous is Morocco's most famous dish. It is made from half-baked flour and ground into semolina-like grains. It is steamed over a rich lamb, chicken, or fish stock seasoned with saffron, onions, ginger, and peppers.

Background

The Berbers entered Morocco near the end of the 2nd millennium BC. Phoenicians established trading posts along the Mediterranean during the 12th century BC, and Carthage had settlements along the Atlantic in the 5th century BC. After the fall of Carthage, Morocco became a loyal ally of Rome, and in AD 42 it was annexed by Rome as part of the province of Mauretania. It was invaded by Muslims in the 7th century. Beginning in the mid-11th century, the Almoravids, Almohads, and Marinids ruled successively. After the fall of the Marinids in the mid-15th century, the Sa'dis ruled for a century after 1550. The French fought Morocco over the Algerian boundary in the 1840s, and the Spanish seized part of Moroccan territory in 1859. It was a French protectorate from 1912 until its independence in 1956. In the mid-1970s it reasserted claim to the Western Sahara, and in 1976 Spanish troops left. Conflicts with Mauritania and Algeria over the region continued into the 1990s. As the decade wore on, the UN tried to solve the dispute.

Recent Developments

King Hassan II died in July 1999 after 38 years on the throne and was succeeded by his eldest son, Sidi Muhammad, who took the name Muhammad VI. James Baker, the former US secretary of state serving as special envoy for the UN in resolving the territorial dispute over the Western Sahara, put forward a new peace plan in June 2001, just before the UN Security Council granted a five-month extension to the peace-keeping force there. The plan envisioned limited autonomy for the region under Moroccan sovereignty for a five-year period, after which the promised referendum for self-determination could be held. In the first visit of his reign, the king traveled to the Western Sahara in November to underscore Morocco's claim to the disputed area.

Internet resources: <www.mincom.gov.ma>

Mozambique

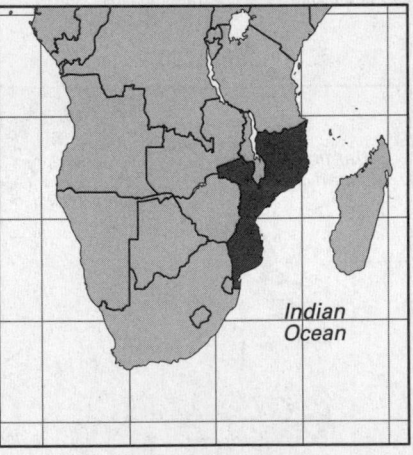

Indian Ocean

Official name: República de Moçambique (Republic of Mozambique). **Form of government:** multiparty republic with a single legislative house (Assembly of the Republic [250]). **Head of state and government:** President Joaquim Chissano (from 1986) assisted by a prime minister. **Capital:** Maputo. **Official language:**

Portuguese. **Official religion:** none. **Monetary unit:** 1 metical (Mt; plural meticais) = 100 centavos; valuation (28 Jun 2002) $1 = Mt 23,223.

Demography

Area: 313,661 sq mi, 812,379 sq km. **Population** (2001): 19,371,000. **Density** (2001): persons per sq mi 61.9, persons per sq km 23.9. **Urban** (2000): 40.2%. **Sex distribution** (2000): male 49.30%; female 50.70%. **Age breakdown** (2000): under 15, 42.9%; 15–29, 29.1%; 30–44, 15.1%; 45–59, 8.5%; 60–74, 3.7%; 75 and over, 0.7%. **Ethnic composition** (2000): Makuana 15.3%; Makua 14.5%; Tsonga 8.6%; Sena 8.0%; Lomwe 7.1%; Tswa 5.7%; Chwabo 5.5%; other 35.3%. **Religious affiliation** (2000): traditional beliefs 50.4%; Christian 38.4%, of which Roman Catholic 15.8%, Protestant 8.9%; Muslim 10.5%. **Major cities** (1997): Maputo 989,386; Matola 440,927; Beira 412,588; Nampula 314,965; Chimoio 177,608. **Location:** Southern Africa, bordering Tanzania, the Indian Ocean, South Africa, Swaziland, Zimbabwe, Zambia, and Malawi.

Vital statistics

Birth rate per 1,000 pop. (2000): 38.0 (world avg. 22.5). **Death rate** per 1,000 pop. (2000): 23.3 (world avg. 9.0). **Natural increase rate** per 1,000 pop. (2000): 14.7 (world avg. 13.5). **Total fertility rate** (avg. births per childbearing woman; 2000): 4.9. **Life expectancy** at birth (2000): male 38.3 years; female 36.7 years.

National economy

Budget (1997). *Revenue:* Mt 4,522,000,000 (1995; sales tax 47.8%, customs taxes 24.0%, individual income tax 16.6%). *Expenditures:* Mt 8,196,000,000 (current expenditure 52.2%, of which goods and services 23.6%, administrative salaries 22.3%, defense and security 19.4%; capital expenditure 47.8%). **Public debt** (external, outstanding; 1999): $4,625,000,000. **Production** (metric tons except as noted). *Agriculture, forestry, fishing* (2000): cassava 4,643,000, corn (maize) 1,109,000, sorghum 252,000; livestock (number of live animals) 1,320,000 cattle, 392,000 goats, 28,000,000 chickens; roundwood (1998) 17,977,000 cu m; fish catch (1998) 36,775. *Mining and quarrying* (2000): bauxite 8,130; semiprecious gemstones (cut stones) 3,400 carats. *Manufacturing* (value in Mt '000,000; 1995): food processing 696,611; beverages and tobacco 395,871; textiles 207,378. *Energy production (consumption):* electricity (kW-hr; 1996) 568,000,000 (1,168,000,000); petroleum products (metric tons; 1997) none (277,000). **Household income and expenditure** (1992 Q3; Maputo only). Average family size 6.7; sources of income: wages and salaries 51.6%, self-employment 12.5%, barter 11.5%, private farming 7.7%; expenditure: food, beverages, and tobacco 74.6%; housing and energy 11.7%; transportation and communications 4.7%; clothing and footwear 3.7%; education and recreation 1.4%; health 0.8%. **Population economically active** (1980): total 5,671,290; activity rate 48.6% (participation rates: over age 15, 87.3%; female 52.4%; unemployed 1.7%). **Gross national product** (1999): $3,804,000,000 ($220 per capita). **Land use** (1994): forested 22.1%; meadows and pastures 56.1%; agricultural 4.0%; other 17.8%.

Foreign trade

Imports (1996-c.i.f.): $782,640,000 (machinery and transport equipment 32.3%, food and beverages 18.3%, basic manufactures 17.4%, petroleum products 9.6%). *Major import sources:* South Africa 34.5%; European Union 27.1%; Portugal 6.3%; US 4.2%; Japan 4.0%; Zimbabwe 3.9%. **Exports** (1996): $226,090,000 (food and beverages 66.4%, of which shellfish 38.1%; machinery and transport equipment 11.5%, cotton 5.7%, sugar and honey 5.7%). *Major export destinations:* European Union 34.7%; South Africa 19.4%; India 11.8%; US 11.4%; Japan 7.6%.

Transport and communications

Transport. *Railroads* (1995): route length 3,123 km; passenger-km 312,000,000; metric ton-km cargo 893,000,000. *Roads* (1996): total length 30,400 km (paved 19%). *Vehicles* (1995): passengers cars 84,000; trucks and buses 26,800. *Air transport* (1996): passenger-km 259,927,000; metric ton-km cargo 5,415,000; airports (1997) with scheduled flights 7. **Communications** Total units (units per 1,000 persons). Daily newspaper circulation (1996): 49,000 (2.7); Radio receivers (1997): 730,000 (40); Television receivers (1999): 95,000 (5.0); Telephone main lines (1999): 78,000 (4.0); Cellular telephone subscribers (1999): 12,000 (0.6); Personal computers (1998): 40,000 (2.1); Internet users (1999): 15,000 (0.8).

Education and health

Literacy (2000): percentage of total pop. age 15 and over literate 43.8%; males literate 59.9%; females literate 28.4%. **Health:** physicians (1996; government personnel only) 120 (1 per 124,697 persons); hospital beds (1997) 12,630 (1 per 1,210 persons); infant mortality rate (2000) 139.9. **Food** (1999): daily per capita caloric intake 1,939 (vegetable products 97%, animal products 3%); 83% of FAO recommended minimum requirement.

Military

Total active duty personnel (2001): c. 11,100 (army 86%, navy 5%, air force 9%). **Military expenditure as percentage of GNP** (1997): 2.8% (world 2.6%); per capita expenditure $4.

Background

Inhabited in prehistoric times, Mozambique was settled by Bantu peoples about the 3rd century AD. Arab traders occupied the coastal region from the 14th century, and the Portuguese controlled the area from the early 16th century. The slave trade later became an important part of the economy. In the late 19th century private trading companies began to administer parts of the inland areas. It became an overseas province of Portugal in 1951. After years of war beginning in the 1960s, the country was granted independence in 1975. It was wracked by civil war in the 1970s and '80s. In 1990 a new constitution was promulgated, and a peace treaty was signed with the rebels in 1992.

Recent Developments

The economy of Mozambique received a serious setback in February 2000, when the worst rains in more than 40 years resulted in flooding in the south. This was compounded almost immediately by a cyclone. Some 600 people were killed, and an estimated one million more were rendered homeless. More serious flooding occurred in the first months of 2001. A train crash in May 2002 killed more than 200 people.

Internet resources: <www.mozambique.mz>

Myanmar (Burma)

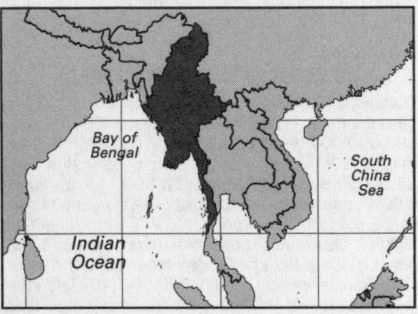

Official name: Pyidaungzu Myanma Naingngandaw (Union of Myanmar). **Form of government:** military regime. **Head of state and government:** Chairman of the State Peace and Development Council and Prime Minister Than Shwe (from 1992). **Capital:** Yangon (Rangoon). **Official language:** Burmese. **Official religion:** none. **Monetary unit:** 1 Myanmar kyat (K) = 100 pyas; valuation (28 Jun 2002) $1 = K 6.51 (pegged rate to the Special Drawing Right of the International Monetary Fund).

Demography

Area: 261,228 sq mi, 676,577 sq km. **Population** (2001): 41,995,000. **Density** (2001): persons per sq mi 160.8, persons per sq km 62.1. **Urban** (1999): 27.0%. **Sex distribution** (1997): male 49.65%; female 50.35%. **Age breakdown** (1997): under 15, 33.3%; 15–29, 27.7%, 30–44, 19.8%; 45–59, 11.5%; 60 and over, 7.7%. **Ethnic composition** (2000): Burman 55.9%; Karen 9.5%; Shan 6.5%; Han Chinese 2.5%; Mon 2.3%; Yangbye 2.2%; Kachin 1.5%; other 19.6%. **Religious affiliation** (1983): Buddhist 89.4%; Christian 4.9%; Muslim 3.8%; traditional beliefs 1.2%; other 0.7%. **Major cities** (1993 est.): Yangon (Rangoon) 3,361,700; Mandalay 885,300; Moulmein (Mawlamyine) 307,600; Pegu (Bago) 190,900; Bassein (Pathein) 183,900. **Location:** southeastern Asia, bordering China, Laos, Thailand, the Andaman Sea, the Bay of Bengal, and India.

Vital statistics

Birth rate per 1,000 pop. (2001): 24.2 (world avg. 22.5). **Death rate** per 1,000 pop. (2001): 11.7 (world avg. 9.0). **Natural increase rate** per 1,000 pop. (2001): 12.5 (world avg. 13.5). **Total fertility rate** (avg. births per childbearing woman; 2001): 3.0. **Life expectancy** at birth (2001): male 60.0 years; female 59.0 years.

National economy

Budget (1998–99). *Revenue:* K 80,400,000,000 (nontax revenue 55.6%; revenue from taxes 43.7%, of which taxes on goods and services 17.4%, taxes on income 15.3%; foreign grants 0.7%). *Expenditures:* K 72,100,000,000 (defense 34.0%; agriculture and forestry 13.3%; interest payments 12.5%; education 11.1%; public works and housing 8.7%; general services 6.8%). **Public debt** (external, outstanding; 1999): $5,333,000,000. **Tourism:** receipts from visitors (1999) $35,000,000; expenditures by nationals abroad $18,000,000. **Production** (metric tons except as noted). *Agriculture, forestry, fishing* (1999): rice 17,075,000, sugarcane 5,429,000, pulses 1,895,000; livestock (number of live animals) 10,740,000 cattle, 6,100,000 ducks, 3,715,000 pigs; roundwood (1998) 22,430,000 cu m; fish catch (1997) 917,666. *Mining and quarrying* (1997–98): gypsum 40,642; copper concentrates 14,634; refined lead 1,585. *Manufacturing* (1996): cement 513,000; fresh meat 116,000; fertilizers 66,000. *Energy production (consumption):* electricity (kW-hr; 1996) 4,256,000,000 (4,256,000,000); coal (metric tons; 1996) 72,000 (78,000); crude petroleum (barrels; 1996) 2,800,000 (5,300,000); petroleum products (metric tons; 1996) 679,000 (1,227,000); natural gas (cu m; 1996) 1,576,000,-000 (1,576,000,000). **Household income and expenditure.** Average household size (1994) 5.6; expenditure (1994; Yangon only): food and beverages 67.1%, fuel and lighting 6.6%, transportation 4.0%, charitable contributions 3.1%, medical care 3.1%. **Gross national product** (1996): $119,334,000,000 ($2,610 per capita). **Population economically active** (1997–98): total 19,743,000; activity rate of total pop. 42.5% (participation rates: ages 15–64 [1983] 64.2%; female [1987–88] 35.3%; unemployed 6.2%). **Land use** (1994): forested 49.3%; meadows and pastures 0.5%; agricultural and under permanent cultivation 15.3%; other 34.9%.

Foreign trade

Imports (1997–98-c.i.f.): K 12,735,900,000 (machinery and transport equipment 28.6%, intermediate raw materials 19.9%, basic manufactures 15.8%, capital construction materials 12.3%, consumer durable goods 4.3%). *Major import sources:* Singapore 31.1%; Japan 15.3%; Thailand 9.8%; China 9.4%; Malaysia 7.0%; South Korea 5.5%; Indonesia 4.8%. **Exports** (1997–98-f.o.b.): K 5,415,800,000 (pulses and beans 22.3%, teak 11.1%, fish and fish products 4.6%, hardwood 2.5%, rubber 2.1%). *Major export destinations:* India 22.6%; Singapore 13.2%; Thailand 11.9%; China 10.6%; Hong Kong 5.8%; Japan 3.8%; United States 3.5%.

Transport and communications

Transport. *Railroads* (1998): route length (1999–2000) 3,955 km; passenger-km 3,948,000,000; metric ton-km cargo 984,000,000. *Roads* (1996): total length 28,200 km (paved 12%). *Vehicles* (1996): passenger cars 27,000; trucks and buses 42,000. *Air transport* (1995–96): passenger-km 438,000,000; metric ton-km cargo 3,212,000; airports (1996) 19. **Communications** Total units (units

---

1 metric ton = about 1.1 short tons;   1 kilometer = 0.6 mi (statute);   1 metric ton-km cargo = about 0.68 short ton-mi cargo;   c.i.f.: cost, insurance, and freight;   f.o.b.: free on board

per 1,000 persons). Daily newspaper circulation (1996): 449,000 (10); Radio receivers (1997): 4,200,000 (96); Television receivers (1999): 323,000 (7.?); Telephone main lines (1999): 249,083 (5.5); Cellular telephone subscribers (1999): 11,389 (0.3); Personal computers (1999): 50,000 (1.1); Internet users (1999): 500 (0.01).

Education and health

Educational attainment (1983). Percentage of pop. age 25 and over having: no formal schooling 55.8%; primary education 39.4%; secondary 4.6%; religious 0.1%; postsecondary 0.1%. **Literacy** (1995): total pop. age 15 and over literate 83.1%; males literate 88.7%; females literate 77.7%. **Health** (1995–96): physicians 12,950 (1 per 3,114 persons); hospital beds 28,732 (1 per 1,404 persons); infant mortality rate per 1,000 live births (2001) 89.0. **Food** (1999): daily per capita caloric intake 2,803 (vegetable products 96%, animal products 4%); (1997) 130% of FAO recommended minimum requirement.

Military

Total active duty personnel (2000): 429,000 (army 95.6%, navy 2.3%, air force 2.1%). **Military expenditure as percentage of GNP** (1996): 7.6% (world 2.6%); per capita expenditure $87.

Background

Myanmar, until 1989 known as Burma, has long been inhabited, with the Mon and Pyu states dominant between the 1st century BC and the 9th century AD. It was united in the 11th century under a Burmese dynasty that was overthrown by the Mongols in the 13th century. The Portuguese, Dutch, and English traded there in the 16th–17th centuries. The modern Burmese state was founded in the 18th century. It fell to the British in 1885 and became a province of India. It was occupied by Japan in World War II and became independent in 1948. A military coup took power in 1962 and nationalized major economic sectors. Civilian unrest in the 1980s led to antigovernment rioting. In 1990 opposition parties won in national elections, but the army remained in control. Trying to negotiate for a freer government amid the unrest, Aung San Suu Kyi was awarded the Nobel Peace Prize in 1991.

Recent Developments

The ruling military regime and the opposition National League for Democracy (NLD) continued their power struggle into 2002. Suu Kyi was confined to her home beginning in September 2000. The government was successful in 2000 in eliminating the threat posed by a rebel group led by 12-year-old twin brothers. Talks between the NLD and the military resumed in late 2000 and resulted in the release of dozens of political prisoners. In May 2002 Suu Kyi was released from house arrest and allowed to move freely about the country.

Internet resources: <www.myanmar-tourism.com>

Namibia

Official name: Republic of Namibia. **Form of government:** republic with two legislative houses (National Council [mostly an advisory body; 26]; National As-

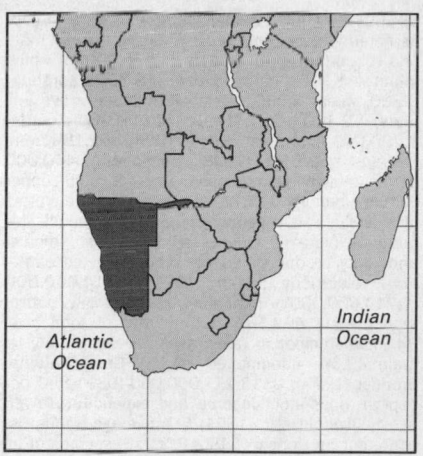

sembly [72]). **Head of state and government:** President Sam Nujoma (from 1990). **Capital:** Windhoek. **Official language:** English. **Official religion:** none. **Monetary unit:** 1 Namibian dollar (N$) = 100 cents; valuation (28 Jun 2002) US$1 = N$10.31.

Demography

Area: 318,580 sq mi, 825,118 sq km. **Population** (2001): 1,798,000. **Density** (2001) persons per sq mi 5.6, persons per sq km 2.2. **Urban** (1999): 39.8%. **Sex distribution** (1999): male 49.85%; female 50.15%. **Age breakdown** (1999): under 15, 43.2%; 15–29, 28.6%; 30–44, 15.1%; 45–59, 7.7%; 60–74, 4.0%; 75 and over, 1.4%. **Ethnic composition** (1991): Ovambo 50.7%; Nama 12.5%; Kavango 9.7%; Herero 8.0%; San (Bushman) 1.9%; Tswana 0.4%; other 16.8%. **Religious affiliation** (2000): Protestant (mostly Lutheran) 47.5%; Roman Catholic 17.7%; African Christian 10.8%; traditional beliefs 6.0%; other 18.0%. **Major cities** (1991 census): Windhoek 147,056; Walvis Bay 22,999; Oshakati 21,603; Rehoboth 21,439; Rundu 19,366. **Location:** southwestern Africa, bordering Angola, Zambia, Botswana, South Africa, and the Atlantic Ocean.

Vital statistics

Birth rate per 1,000 pop. (2001): 34.7 (world avg. 22.5). **Death rate** per 1,000 pop. (2001): 20.9 (world avg. 9.0). **Natural increase rate** per 1,000 pop. (2001): 13.8 (world avg. 13.5). **Total fertility rate** (avg. births per childbearing woman; 2001): 4.8. **Life expectancy** at birth (2001): male 42.5 years; female 38.7 years.

National economy

Budget (1999–2000). *Revenue:* N$7,128,400,000 (customs taxes 31.4%, general sales tax 28.2%, individual income taxes 17.9%, nontax revenues 8.9%, mining taxes 3.1%). *Expenditures:* N$8,009,-400,000 (1996–97; education 23.2%, health and welfare 10.3%, transportation 6.1%, defense 5.8%, social security 5.4%). **Tourism** (1998): receipts from visitors US$288,000,000; expenditures by nationals abroad US$88,000,000. **Public debt** (1997):

US$697,000,000. **Production** (metric tons except as noted). *Agriculture, forestry, fishing* (1999): roots and tubers 260,000, cereals 71,100,000 (of which millet 46,300, corn [maize] 18,300, sorghum 3,300, wheat 3,000); livestock (number of live animals) 2,100,000 sheep, 2,000,000 cattle, 1,700,000 goats; fish catch (1998) 352,188. *Mining and quarrying* (1998): diamonds 1,440,000 carats (mostly gem quality); zinc 78,617; copper 8,014; uranium 3,257. *Manufacturing*: n.a.; products include cut gems (primarily diamonds), fur products (karakul), processed foods (fish, meats, and dairy products). *Energy production (consumption)*: electricity (kW-hr; 1992) 1,714,000,000 (1,714,000,000). **Population economically active**: total (1991) 493,580; activity rate of total pop. 34.9% (participation rates: ages 15–64, 61.3%; female 43.5%; unemployed 20.1%). **Gross national product** (1999): US$3,211,000,000 (US$1,890 per capita). **Household income and expenditure.** Average household size (1991) 5.2; average annual income per household (1980) R 3,223; sources of income (1992): wages and salaries 69.0%, income from property 25.6%, transfer payments 5.4%. **Land use** (1994): forested 15.2%; meadows and pastures 46.2%; agricultural and under permanent cultivation 0.8%; other 37.8%.

Foreign trade

Imports (1994): N$4,467,700,000 (machinery and transport equipment 27.1%, of which transport equipment 16.2%; food and live animals 22.3%; minerals and fuels 11.4%; chemical products 8.1%). *Major import sources* (1993): South Africa 87.0%; Germany 3.0%; France 2.0%; Japan 2.0%. **Exports** (1994): N$4,692,000,000 (minerals 50.1%, of which diamonds 31.4%; food and live animals 47.0%, of which fish and fish products 28.6%, cattle and meat products 12.6%; karakul pelts 0.2%). *Major export destinations* (1993): UK 34.0%; South Africa 27.0%; Japan 10.0%; Spain 6.0%.

Transport and communications

Transport. *Railroads:* length (1995) 2,382 km; passenger-km 34,700,000; metric ton-km 1,077,000,-000. *Roads* (1996): total length 65,220 km (paved 7.7%). *Vehicles* (1996): passenger cars 74,875; trucks and buses 66,500 (1995). *Air transport* (Namib Air only; 1996): passenger-km 756,000,000; metric ton-km cargo 23,000,000; airports (1997) with scheduled flights 11. **Communications** Total units (units per 1,000 persons). Daily newspaper circulation (1996): 30,000 (19); Radio receivers (1997): 232,000 (143); Television receivers (1999): 65,000 (38); Telephone main lines (1999): 108,000 (64); Cellular telephone subscribers (1999): 30,000 (18); Personal computers (1999): 50,000 (29); Internet users (1999): 6,000 (3.5).

Education and health

Educational attainment (1991). Percentage of pop. age 25 and over having: no formal schooling 35.1%; primary education 31.9%; secondary 28.5%; higher 4.5%. **Literacy** (2000): total pop. age 15 and over literate 830,200 (82.1%); males literate 416,000

(82.9%); females literate 414,200 (81.2%). **Health:** physicians (1992) 324 (1 per 4,594 persons); hospital beds (1989) 6,997 (1 per 216 persons); infant mortality rate per 1,000 live births (2001) 71.7. **Food** (1999): daily per capita caloric intake 2,096 (vegetable products 89%, animal products 11%); 92% of FAO recommended minimum requirement.

Military

Total active duty personnel (2000): 9,000 (army 98.9%, navy [Coast Guard for fishery protection; 1.1%). **Military expenditure as percentage of GNP** (1997): 2.7% (world 2.6%); per capita expenditure US$57.

Background

Long inhabited by indigenous peoples, Namibia was explored by the Portuguese in the late 15th century. In 1884 it was annexed by Germany as German South West Africa. It was captured in World War I by South Africa, which received it as a mandate from the League of Nations in 1920 and refused to give it up after World War II. A UN resolution in 1966 ending the mandate was challenged by South Africa in the 1970s and '80s. Through long negotiations involving many factions and interests, Namibia achieved independence in 1990.

Recent Developments

In 2000 Namibia continued its military involvement in the Democratic Republic of the Congo, and the 1999 decision to allow the Angolan armed forces to operate from Namibia meant that it became embroiled in the Angolan civil war. The security situation in northeastern Namibia remained tense in 2001 in the aftermath of Angolan attacks from Namibia on National Union for the Total Independence of Angola (UNITA) rebels and the failed secessionist attempt in the Caprivi Strip. Troops were withdrawn from Congo during the year.

Internet resources: <www.met.gov.na>

Nauru

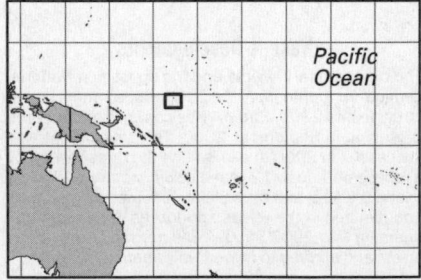

Pacific Ocean

Official name: Naoero (Republic of Nauru). **Form of government:** republic with one legislative house (Parliament [18]). **Head of state and government:** President René Harris (from 30 Mar 2001). **Capital:** Gov-

---

1 metric ton = about 1.1 short tons;   1 kilometer = 0.6 mi (statute);   1 metric ton-km cargo = about 0.68 short ton-mi cargo;   c.i.f.: cost, insurance, and freight;   f.o.b.: free on board

ernment offices are located in Yaren district . **Official language;** none. Official religion: none. **Monetary unit:** 1 Australian dollar ($A) = 100 cents; valuation (28 Jun 2002) US$1 = $A 1.78.

Demography

Area: 8.2 sq mi, 21.2 sq km. **Population** (2001): 12,100. **Density** (2001): persons per sq mi 1,476, persons per sq km 570.8. **Urban** (1999): 100%. **Sex distribution** (1999): male 50.50%, female 49.50%. **Age breakdown** (1999): under 15, 41.6%; 15–29, 25.5%; 30–44, 19.7%; 45–59, 10.0%; 60–74, 2.9%; 75 and over 0.3%. **Ethnic composition** (1992): Nauruan 68.9%; other Pacific Islander 23.7%, of which Kiribati 12.8%, Tuvaluan 8.7%; Asian 5.9%, of which Filipino 2.5%, Chinese 2.3%; other 1.5%. **Religious affiliation** (1995): Protestant 53.5%, of which Congregational 35.3%, Pentecostal 4.8%; Roman Catholic 27.5%; other 19.0%. **Major cities:** none; population of Yaren district (1996) 700. **Location:** Western Pacific Ocean, lying near the equator east of Papua New Guinea.

Vital statistics

Birth rate per 1,000 pop. (2000): 22.9 (world avg. 22.5). **Death rate** per 1,000 pop. (2000): 5.1 (world avg. 9.0). **Natural increase rate** per 1,000 pop. (2000): 17.8 (world avg. 13.5). **Total fertility rate** (avg. births per childbearing woman; 1999): 3.8. **Marriage rate** per 1,000 pop. (1995): 5.3. **Life expectancy** at birth (1999): male 57.0 years; female 64.1 years.

National economy

Budget (1999). *Revenue:* $A 38,700,000. *Expenditures:* $A 37,200,000. **Public debt** (external, outstanding; beginning of 1996): c. US$150,000,000. **Tourism:** receipts from visitors (1999) virtually none; expenditures by nationals abroad, n.a. **Gross national product** (at current market prices; 1997): US$128,000,000 (US$11,538 per capita). **Production** (metric tons except as noted). *Agriculture, forestry, fishing* (1999): coconuts 1,600, vegetables 450, tropical fruit (including mangoes) 275; livestock (number of live animals) 3,000 pigs; fish catch 500. *Mining and quarrying* (1998): phosphate rock (gross weight) 500,000. *Manufacturing:* none; virtually all consumer manufactures are imported. *Energy production (consumption):* electricity (kW-hr; 1996) 32,000,000 (32,000,000); none petroleum products (metric tons; 1996) none (45,000). **Population economically active** (Nauruan only; 1992): 2,453; activity rate of total pop. 35.9% (unemployed, 18.2%). **Household income and expenditure.** Average household size (Nauruan only; 1992) 10.0. **Land use** (1995): forested, nil; meadows and pastures, nil; agricultural and under permanent cultivation c. 10%; other c. 90%.

Foreign trade

Imports (1995): US$20,000,000 (agricultural products 20.5%, of which food 14.5%; remainder 79.5%). *Major import sources:* Australia more than 50%; UK c. 10%; New Zealand c. 10%. **Exports** (1995): US$40,000,000 (phosphate, virtually 100%). *Major export destinations:* New Zealand c. 50%; Australia c. 25%.

Transport and communications

Transport. *Railroads* (1997): length 5 km. *Roads* (1996): total length 30 km (paved 79%). *Vehicles* (1989): passenger cars, trucks, and buses 1,448. *Air transport* (1996): passenger-mi 151,000,000, passenger-km 243,000,000; short ton-mi cargo 15,000,000, metric ton-km cargo 24,000,000; airports (1999) with scheduled flights 1. **Communications** Total units (units per 1,000 persons). Radio receivers (1997): 7,000 (609); Television receivers (1997): 500 (48); Telephone main lines (1998): 1,700 (149); Cellular telephone subscribers (1998): 850 (75).

Education and health

Educational attainment (Nauruan only; 1992). Percentage of pop. age 5 and over having primary education or less 77.4%; secondary education 12.9%; higher 4.1%; not stated 5.6%. **Literacy** (1995): total pop. age 15 and over literate 99%. **Health: physicians** (1995) 17 (1 per 637 persons); hospital beds (1990) 207 (1 per 46 persons); infant mortality rate per 1,000 live births (1999) 11.1. **Food** (1998): daily per capita caloric intake 3,011 (vegetable products 70%, animal products 30%); (1997) 132% of FAO recommended minimum requirement.

Military

Total active duty personnel (2001): Nauru does not have any military establishment. The defense is assured by Australia, but no formal agreement exists.

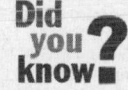

Did you know? The name of an inhabitant of Nauru, a Nauruan, is a palindrome (reads the same backward as forward)—unique among sovereign nations.

Background

Nauru was inhabited by Pacific islanders when British explorers arrived in 1798 and named it Pleasant Island for the friendly welcome they received. Annexed by Germany in 1888, it was occupied by Australia at the start of World War I, and in 1919 it was placed under a joint mandate of Britain, Australia, and New Zealand. During World War II it was occupied by the Japanese. Made a UN trust territory under Australian administration in 1947, it gained independence in 1968. During the mid-1990s it suffered political unrest.

Recent Developments

Pres. Bernard Dowiyogo lost office after a no-confidence vote in April 1999 and was replaced by René Harris. Although reelected in April 2000, Harris was unable to form a government and was quickly replaced by Dowiyogo. Harris returned as president following a vote of no-confidence against Dowiyogo in March 2001; Dowiyogo lost his job over international criticism of Nauru's financial system and in particular over allegations of money laundering for the Russian mafia.

Internet resources:
<www.travelershub.com/destination_guide/pacific/nauru.html>

Nepal

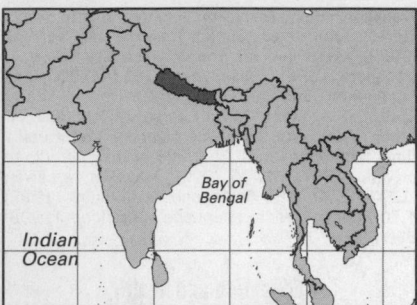

Official name: Nepal Adhirajya (Kingdom of Nepal). **Form of government:** constitutional monarchy with a bicameral parliament consisting of two legislative houses (National Council [60, including 10 members appointed by king]; House of Representatives [205]). **Chief of state:** King Gyanendra Bir Bikram Shah Deva (from 4 Jun 2001). **Head of government:** Prime Minister Sher Bahadur Deuba (from 6 Jul 2001). **Capital:** Kathmandu. **Official language:** Nepali. **Official religion:** Hinduism. **Monetary unit:** 1 Nepalese rupee (NRs) = 100 paisa (pice); valuation (28 Jun 2002) $1 = NRs 77.61.

Demography

Area: 56,827 sq mi, 147,181 sq km. **Population** (2001): 25,284,000. **Density** (2001): persons per sq mi 444.9, persons per sq km 171.8. **Urban** (1999): 11.0%. **Sex distribution** (1997): male 50.20%; female 49.80%. **Age breakdown** (1996): under 15, 43.1%; 15–29, 26.0%; 30–44, 16.0%; 45–59, 9.4%; 60–74, 4.6%; 75 and over, 0.9%. **Ethnic composition** (1991): Nepalese 53.2%; Bihari (including Maithili and Bhojpuri) 18.4%; Tharu 4.8%; Tamang 4.7%; Newar 3.4%; Magar 2.2%; Abadhi 1.7%; other 11.6%. **Religious affiliation** (2000): Hindu 75.9%; traditional beliefs 9.3%; Buddhist 8.1%; Muslim 3.8%; Christian 2.4%; other 0.5%. **Major cities** (2000 est.): Kathmandu 701,499; Pokhara 168,806; Biratnagar 168,544; Lalitpur 157,495; Birganj 103,880. **Location:** southern Central Asia, bordering China and India.

Vital statistics

Birth rate per 1,000 pop. (2001): 34.7 (world avg. 22.5). **Death rate** per 1,000 pop. (2001): 10.3 (world avg. 9.0). **Natural increase rate** per 1,000 pop. (2001): 24.4 (world avg. 13.5). **Total fertility rate** (avg. births per childbearing woman; 2001): 4.6. **Life expectancy** at birth (2001): male 59.0 years; female 59.0 years.

National economy

Budget (1999). *Revenue:* NRs 40,698,000,000 (taxes on goods and services 29.2%, taxes on international trade 23.9%, foreign grants 14.5%, income taxes 14.2%, state property revenues 8.4%, administrative fees 5.5%). *Expenditures:* NRs 58,391,000,000 (education 13.6%, transport and commu-

nications 11.4%, fuel and energy 9.0%, health 6.5%, agriculture 5.5%, housing 4.7%, defense 4.5%, public order 4.3%, general public services 3.7%). **Public debt** (external, outstanding; 1999): $2,910,000,000. **Land use** (1994): forested 42.0%; meadows and pastures 14.6%; agricultural and under permanent cultivation 17.2%; other 26.2%. **Tourism** (1999): receipts from visitors $168,000,000; expenditures by nationals abroad $71,000,000. **Production** (metric tons except as noted). *Agriculture, forestry, fishing* (1999): rice 3,710,000, sugarcane 1,972,000, corn (maize) 1,346,000; livestock (number of live animals) 7,030,698 cattle, 6,204,616 goats, 3,470,600 buffalo; roundwood (1998) 21,474,000 cu m; fish catch (1997) 23,206. *Mining and quarrying* (1997): limestone 369,000; salt 7,000; talc 6,800. *Manufacturing* (value added in $'000,000; 1995): textiles 78; food products 74; wearing apparel 54. *Energy production (consumption):* electricity (kW-hr; 1996) 1,218,000,000 (1,243,000,000); coal (metric tons; 1996) (50,000); petroleum products (metric tons; 1996) (427,000). **Gross national product** (1999): $5,173,000,000 ($220 per capita). **Population economically active** (1991): total 7,339,586; activity rate of total pop. 39.7% (participation rates: ages 10 years and over, 57.0%; female 45.5%; unemployed [1996] 4.9%). **Household income and expenditure** (1984–85). Average household size (1991) 5.6; income per household NRs 14,796; sources of income: self-employment 63.4%, wages and salaries 25.1%, rent 7.5%, other 4.0%; expenditure: food and beverages 61.2%, housing 17.3%, clothing 11.7%, health care 3.7%, education and recreation 2.9%, transp. and commun. 1.2%, other 2.0%.

Foreign trade

Imports (1996–97-c.i.f.): NRs 96,006,000,000 (basic manufactured goods 47.6%; machinery and transport equipment 14.7%; chemicals 8.8%; mineral fuels and lubricants 7.5%; food and live animals, chiefly for food 6.6%; crude materials except fuels 5.5%). *Major import sources:* India 23.3%; Hong Kong 14.3%; Singapore 13.0%; Japan 11.2%; China 6.4%; New Zealand 5.1%. **Exports** (1996–97-f.o.b.): NRs 22,481,000,000 (basic manufactures 48.7%; miscellaneous manufactures 29.2%; food and live animals, chiefly for food 12.6%; chemicals and drugs 5.9%; crude materials except fuels 2.6%). *Major export destinations:* US 34.4%; India 9.5%; Bangladesh 1.4%; China 0.9%.

Transport and communications

Transport. *Railroads* (1995–96): route length (1999) 59 km; passengers carried 1,379,000; freight handled 5,320 metric tons. *Roads* (1997): total length 7,700 km (paved 42%). *Vehicles* (1997–98): passenger cars 47,541; trucks and buses 29,371. *Air transport* (1995): passenger-km 856,000,000; metric ton-km cargo 93,000,000; airports (1996) with scheduled flights 24. **Communications** Total units (units per 1,000 persons). Daily newspaper circulation (1996): 250,000 (11); Radio receivers (1997): 840,000 (38); Television receivers (1999): 150,000 (6.7); Telephone main lines (1999): 253,035 (11);

---

1 metric ton = about 1.1 short tons;   1 kilometer = 0.6 mi (statute);   1 metric ton-km cargo = about 0.68 short ton-mi cargo;   c.i.f.: cost, insurance, and freight;   f.o.b.: free on board

Cellular telephone subscribers (1999): 5,500 (0.2); Personal computers (1999): 60,000 (2.7); Internet users (1999): 35,000 (1.6).

Education and health

Educational attainment (1981). Percentage of pop. age 25 and over having: no formal schooling 41.2%; primary education 29.4%; secondary 22.7%; higher 6.8%. **Literacy** (1995): total pop. age 15 and over literate 27.5%; males literate 40.9%; females literate 14.0%. **Health** (1996): physicians 872 (1 per 25,745 persons); hospital beds 3,604 (1 per 6,229 persons); infant mortality rate per 1,000 live births (2001) 74. **Food** (1999): daily per capita caloric intake 2,264 (vegetable products 93%, animal products 7%); (1997) 103% of FAO recommended minimum.

Military

Total active duty personnel (2000): 46,000 (army 99.5%, air force 0.5%). **Military expenditure as percentage of GNP** (1997): 0.8% (world 2.6%); per capita expenditure $2.

Background

Nepal developed under early Buddhist influence, and dynastic rule dates from about the 4th century AD. It was formed into a single kingdom in 1769 and fought border wars with China, Tibet, and British India in the 18th–19th centuries. Its independence was recognized by Britain in 1923. A new constitution in 1990 restricted royal authority and accepted a democratically elected parliamentary government. Nepal signed trade agreements with India in 1997.

Recent Developments

On 1 Jun 2001, King Birendra was fatally shot by his son Crown Prince Dipendra during a dinner party. Also killed were the queen and seven other members of the royal family. Dipendra then turned the gun on himself. It was believed that he acted under the influence of drugs and alcohol and was despondent because his parents disapproved of his choice of a bride. Birendra was succeeded by his brother, Gyanendra. A state of emergency was declared in November following Maoist rebel attacks on the government and was extended in February 2002 after further attacks; by mid-year the violence was continuing. In May the parliament was dissolved by the king and Prime Minister Sher Bahadur Deuba was suspended by his party; in June the king extended the state of emergency to August.

Internet resources: <www.welcomenepal.com>

The Netherlands

Official name: Koninkrijk der Nederlanden (Kingdom of The Netherlands). **Form of government:** constitutional monarchy with a parliament (States General) comprising two legislative houses (First Chamber [75]; Second Chamber [150]). **Chief of state:** Queen Beatrix (from 1980). **Head of government:** Prime Minister Jan Peter Balkeneude (from 22 Jul 2002). **Seat of government:** The Hague. **Capital:** Amsterdam. **Official language:** Dutch. **Official religion:** none. **Monetary unit:** 1 euro (€) = 100 cents; $1 = €1.01 (28 Jun

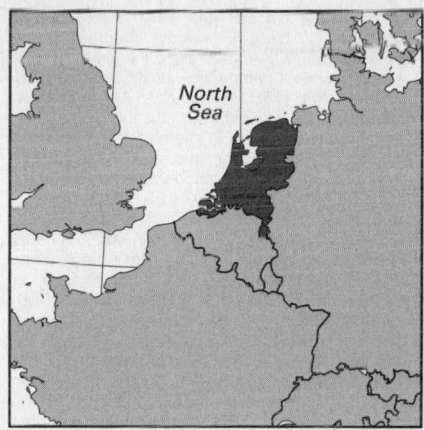

2002); at conversion on 1 Jan 2002, €1 = 2.20 Netherlands guilders (f.).

Demography

Area: 16,033 sq mi, 41,526 sq km (including inland water area totaling 2,955 sq mi [7,653 sq km]). **Population** (2001): 15,968,000. **Density** (2000; land area only): persons per sq mi 1,221.0, persons per sq km 471.4. **Urban** (1999): 89.3%. **Sex distribution** (2000): male 49.46%; female 50.54%. **Age breakdown** (2000): under 15, 18.6%; 15–29, 19.3%; 30–44, 24.2%; 45–59, 19.8%; 60–74, 12.1%; 75 and over, 6.0%. **Ethnic composition** (by place of origin [including 2nd generation]; 2000): Netherlander 82.5%; Indonesian 2.6%; Turkish 1.9%; Surinamese 1.9%; Moroccan 1.7%; Netherlands Antillean/Aruban 0.7%; other 8.7%. **Religious affiliation** (1999): Roman Catholic 31.0%; Reformed (NHK) 14.0%; other Reformed 7.0%; Muslim 4.5%; Hindu 0.5%; nonreligious 41.0%; other 2.0%. **Major urban agglomerations** (2000): Amsterdam 1,002,868; Rotterdam 989,956; The Hague 610,245; Utrecht 366,186; Eindhoven 302,274. **Location:** northwestern Europe, bordering the North Sea, Germany, and Belgium.

Vital statistics

Birth rate per 1,000 pop. (1999): 12.7 (world avg. 22.5); legitimate 77.3%; illegitimate 22.7%. **Death rate** per 1,000 pop. (1999): 8.9 (world avg. 9.0). **Natural increase rate** per 1,000 pop. (1999): 3.8 (world avg. 13.5). **Total fertility rate** (avg. births per childbearing woman; 2000): 1.6. **Marriage rate** per 1,000 population (2000): 5.3. **Life expectancy** at birth (2000): male 75.3 years; female 80.6 years.

National economy

Budget (1997). *Revenue:* f. 324,360,000,000 (social security taxes 41.1%; income and corporate taxes 24.8%; value-added and excise taxes 22.7%; property taxes 3.0%). *Expenditures:* f. 337,620,-000,000 (social security and welfare 37.4%; health 14.8%; education 10.0%; interest payments 9.1%; defense 3.9%; transportation 3.5%). **Public debt** (1999): $251,763,000,000. **Production** (metric tons except as noted). *Agriculture, forestry, fishing*

(2000): potatoes 8,200,000, sugar beets 5,504,-000, wheat 1,183,000; livestock (number of live animals; 2000) 13,140,000 pigs, 4,200,000 cattle, 1,401,000 sheep; roundwood (1999) 1,044,000 cu m; fish catch (1997) 550,009. *Manufacturing* (value added in f. '000,000; 1998): food, beverages, and tobacco 24,323; chemicals and chemical products 15,009; printing and publishing 11,267. *Energy production (consumption):* electricity (kW-hr; 1999) 86,616,000,000 (93,505,000,000); coal (metric tons; 1996) negligible (14,996,000); crude petroleum (barrels; 1999) 10,973,000 ([1996] 424,957,000); petroleum products (metric tons; 1996) 65,755,000 (33,662,000); natural gas (cu m; 1999) 70,777,000,000 ([1996] 54,789,000). **Household income and expenditure.** Average household size (2000) 2.3; spendable income per household (1997) f. 53,597; sources of income (1995): wages 48.2%, transfers 29.0%, property income 11.8%; expenditure (1995): housing 15.2%; food and beverages 13.5%; transportation and communications 13.1%; health care 13.1%; recreation 9.9%. **Gross national product** (1999): $397,384,-000,000 ($25,140 per capita). **Population economically active** (1998): total 7,735,000; activity rate of total pop. 49.3% (participation rates: ages 15–64, 72.9%; female 42.5%; unemployed [October 1999–September 2000] 2.7%). **Tourism** (1999): receipts $7,092,000,000; expenditures $11,366,-000,000. **Land use** (1994): forested 10.3%; meadows and pastures 31.0%; agricultural and under permanent cultivation 28.0%; other 30.7%.

Foreign trade

Imports (1999-c.i.f.): f. 393,845,000,000 (machinery 31.5%, chemicals and chemical products 11.0%, food 8.7%, road vehicles 8.0%). *Major import sources:* Germany 19.3%; Belgium-Luxembourg 10.0%; UK 9.7%; US 9.5%; France 6.5%. **Exports** (1999-f.o.b.): f. 415,618,000,000 (machinery 27.8%, chemicals and chemical products 15.3%, food 13.4%, mineral fuels 5.9%). *Major export destinations:* Germany 26.1%; Belgium-Luxembourg 12.2%; France 10.8%; UK 10.8%; Italy 6.0%.

Transport and communications

Transport. *Railroads* (1999): length 2,808 km; passenger-km 14,330,000,000; metric ton-km cargo 3,521,000,000. *Roads* (1996): total length 124,530 km (paved 91%). *Vehicles* (2000): passenger cars 6,343,000; trucks and buses 826,000. *Air transport* (1999; KLM only): passenger-km 58,112,000,000; metric ton-km cargo 3,910,532,000; airports (1996) 6. **Communications** Total units (units per 1,000 persons). Daily newspaper circulation (1996): 4,753,000 (306); Radio receivers (1998): 12,000,000 (764); Television receivers (1999): 9,500,000 (601); Telephone main lines (1999): 9,610,000 (608); Cellular telephone subscribers (1999): 6,900,000 (436); Personal computers (1999): 5,700,000 (361); Internet users (1999): 3,000,000 (190).

Education and health

Educational attainment (1999). Percentage of pop. ages 15–64 having: primary education 13.4%; lower secondary 10.4%; upper secondary/vocational 53.9%; tertiary vocational 15.5%; university 6.8%. **Health** (1999): physicians 27,090 (1 per 582 persons); hospital beds 81,328 (1 per 194 persons); infant mortality rate per 1,000 live births 5.2. **Food** (1999): daily per capita caloric intake 3,243 (vegetable products 64%, animal products 36%); 121% of FAO recommended minimum requirement.

Military

Total active duty personnel (2000): 51,940 (army 44.5%, navy 23.8%, air force 21.8%, paramilitary 10.0%). **Military expenditure as percentage of GNP** (1997): 1.9% (world 2.6%); per capita expenditure $438.

Background

Celtic and Germanic tribes inhabited The Netherlands at the time of the Roman conquest. Under the Romans trade and industry flourished, but by the mid-3rd century AD Roman power had waned, eroded by resurgent German tribes and the encroachment of the sea. A Germanic invasion (406–07) ended Roman control. The Merovingian dynasty followed the Romans but was supplanted in the 7th century by the Carolingian dynasty, which converted the area to Christianity. After Charlemagne's death in 814, the area was increasingly the target of Viking attacks. It became part of the kingdom of Lotharingia, which established an Imperial Church. In the 12th–14th centuries dike building occurred on a large scale. The dukes of Burgundy gained control in the late 14th century. By the early 16th century the Low Countries were ruled by the Spanish Habsburgs. In 1581 the seven northern provinces, led by Calvinists, declared their independence from Spain, and in 1648, following the Thirty Years' War, Spain recognized Dutch independence. The 17th century was the golden age of Dutch civilization. The Dutch East India Company secured Asian colonies, and the country's standard of living soared. In the 18th century the region was conquered by the French and became the kingdom of Holland under Napoleon (1806). It remained neutral in World War I and declared neutrality in World War II but was occupied by Germany. It joined NATO in 1949, was a founding member of what is now the European Community, and is part of the European Union.

Recent Developments

Two landmark pieces of legislation were passed late in 2000. In November the parliament voted to allow physicians to end the lives of seriously ill patients who have asked to die, making The Netherlands the first country to legalize mercy killing and doctor-assisted suicide. In December the government gave final approval to laws that allow same-sex couples to marry and to adopt children. In 2001 the nation suffered from an outbreak of foot-and-mouth disease. A variety of political shakeups occurred in 2002, beginning with the resignation of the government in April. A report blaming the Dutch military and government for their failure to prevent the 1995 Srebrenica massacre in Bosnia led to the resignation of the prime minister and his cabinet. In May flamboyant nationalist politician Pim Fortuyn was murdered, and later that month the ruling Labor Party was defeated in national elections by the conservative Christian Democrats.

Internet resources: <www.holland.com>

Netherlands Antilles

Official name: Nederlandse Antillen (Netherlands Antilles). **Political status:** nonmetropolitan territory of The Netherlands with one legislative house (States of the Netherlands Antilles [22]). **Chief of state:** Dutch Queen Beatrix represented by Governor-General Jaime M. Saleh (from 1989). **Head of government:** Prime Minister Etienne Ys (from 3 Jun 2002). **Capital:** Willemstad. **Official language:** Dutch. **Official religion:** none. **Monetary unit:** 1 Netherlands Antillean guilder (NA f.) = 100 cents; valuation (28 Jun 2002) $1 = NA f. 1.78.

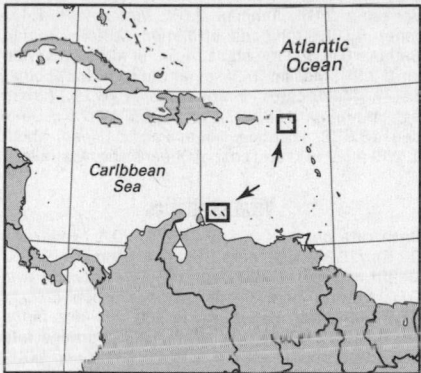

Demography

Area: 308 sq mi, 800 sq km. **Population** (2001): 205,000. **Density** (2001): persons per sq mi 665.6, persons per sq km 256.2. **Urban** (2000): 70.0%. **Sex distribution** (2000): male 47.99%; female 52.01%. **Age breakdown** (2000): under 15, 25.5%; 15–29, 18.2%; 30–44, 26.0%; 45–59, 18.9%; 60–74, 8.6%; 75 and over, 2.8%. **Ethnic composition** (2000): local black-other (Antillean Creole) 81.1%; Dutch 5.3%; Surinamese 2.9%; other (significantly West Indian black) 10.7%. **Religious affiliation** (1992): Roman Catholic 73.9%; Protestant 10.4%, of which Methodist 3.0%, Seventh-day Adventist 2.2%; Jehovah's Witness 1.5%; Jewish 0.3%; Muslim 0.2%; nonreligious 6.3%; other 8.9%. **Major cities:** Willemstad (urban area; 1999) 123,000; Kralendijk (2001) 7,900; Philipsburg (2001) 6,300. **Location:** two separate island groups in the Caribbean Sea, one lying just north of Venezuela, the other east of Puerto Rico.

Vital statistics

Birth rate per 1,000 pop. (1999): 13.7 (world avg. 22.5); (1988) legitimate 51.6%; illegitimate 48.4%. **Death rate** per 1,000 pop. (1999): 6.5 (world avg. 9.0). **Natural increase** rate per 1,000 pop. (1999): 7.2 (world avg. 13.5). **Total fertility rate** (avg. births per childbearing woman; 2000): 2.1. **Marriage rate** per 1,000 population (1999): 4.7. **Divorce rate** per 1,000 population (1999): 2.6. **Life expectancy** at birth (2000): male 72.6 years; female 77.0 years.

National economy

Budget (1999). *Revenue:* NA f. 498,300,000 (tax revenue 83.2%, of which import duties 28.0%, sales tax 20.4%, excise on gasoline 18.8%; nontax revenue 15.3%). *Expenditures:* NA f. 626,200,000 (current expenditures 91.9%; development expenditures 8.1%). **Production** (metric tons except as noted). *Agriculture, forestry, fishing:* tomatoes, beans, cucumbers; livestock (number of live animals; 1999) 13,000 goats, 7,300 sheep, 2,600 asses; fish catch (1997) 1,105. *Mining and quarrying* (1997): salt 432,225, sulfur by-product 27,600. *Manufacturing* (1996): residual fuel oil 5,013,000; gas-diesel oils 2,218,000; other manufactures include electronic parts, cigarettes, textiles, rum, and Curaçao liqueur. *Energy production (consumption):* electricity (kW-hr; 1996) 1,482,000,000 (1,482,000,000); crude petroleum (barrels; 1996) none (93,334,000); petroleum products (metric tons; 1996) 9,952,000 (851,000). **Land use** (1998): forested, negligible; meadows and pastures, negligible; agricultural and under permanent cultivation 10.0%; other (dry savanna) 90.0%. **Tourism** (2000): receipts from visitors $765,000,000; expenditures by nationals abroad $339,000,000. **Household income and expenditure.** Average household size (1999) 3.2; expenditure (1996 [Curaçao only]): housing 26.5%, transportation and communications 19.9%, food 14.7%, household furnishings 8.8%, recreation and education 8.2%, clothing and footwear 7.5%. **Gross national product** (at current market prices; 1997): $2,609,000,000 ($12,490 per capita). **Population economically active** (1992): total 87,756; activity rate of total pop. 46.3% (participation rates: ages 15–64, 68.6%; female 45.1%; unemployed [1998] 16.7%). **Public debt** (external, outstanding; 1999): $294,600,000.

Foreign trade

Imports (1999): NA f. 2,375,000,000 (nonpetroleum domestic imports 71.3%, crude petroleum and petroleum products 14.8%, imports of Curaçao free zone 13.9%). *Major import sources* (1998): Venezuela 37%; US 22%; Mexico 7%; The Netherlands 5%; Italy 5%. **Exports** (1999): NA f. 470,000,000 (reexports of Curaçao free zone 59.1%, nonpetroleum domestic exports 37.5%, petroleum products 3.4%). *Major export destinations* (1998): US 23%; Guatemala 10%; The Bahamas 6%; Guyana 6%; Chile 4%.

Transport and communications

Transport. *Roads* (1992): total length 590 km (paved, 51%). *Vehicles* (1996): passenger cars 75,105; trucks and buses 17,753. *Air transport* (1998 [Curaçao airport only]): passenger arrivals and departures 959,000; freight loaded and unloaded 11,100 metric tons; airports (1995) with scheduled flights 6. **Communications.** Total units (units per 1,000 persons). Daily newspaper circulation (1996): 70,000 (341); Radio receivers (1997): 217,000 (1,039); Television receivers (1997): 69,000 (330); Telephone main lines (1999): 79,000 (386); Cellular telephone subscribers (1998): 16,000 (77).

Education and health

Educational attainment (1992). Percentage of employed pop. having: no formal schooling or some primary education 21.5%; completed primary 50.8%;

completed vocational or secondary 24.3%; completed higher 3.4%. **Literacy** (1995): total population age 15 and over literate 194,900 (96.6%); males literate 93,300 (96.6%); females literate 101,600 (96.6%). **Health** (1997): physicians 339 (1 per 616 persons); hospital beds 1,466 (1 per 142 persons); infant mortality rate per 1,000 live births (2000) 11.7. **Food** (1999): daily per capita caloric intake 2,591 (vegetable products 67%, animal products 33%); 107% of FAO recommended minimum.

Military

Total active duty personnel (1999): a 45-member Dutch naval/air force contingent is stationed in the Netherlands Antilles and Aruba.

Background

The Netherlands Antilles were sighted by Christopher Columbus in 1493 and claimed for Spain. In the 17th century the Dutch gained control, and in 1845 the islands became the Netherlands Antilles. In 1954 they became an integral part of The Netherlands, with full autonomy in domestic affairs. Aruba seceded from the group in 1986.

Recent Developments

In June 2000 the majority of voters in a referendum on Sint Maarten (St. Martin) indicated a preference for the island's becoming a separate entity within The Netherlands rather than remaining part of the Netherlands Antilles federation. The Dutch government promptly quashed the idea.

Internet resources:
<http://netherlandsantilles.com>

New Caledonia

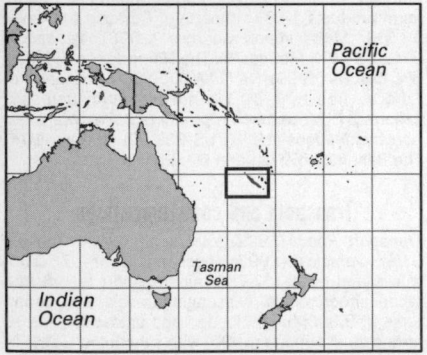

Official name: Nouvelle-Calédonie (New Caledonia). **Political status:** overseas country (France) with one legislative house (Congress [54]; operates in association with 3 provincial assemblies). The Nouméa Accord of 1999 granted New Caledonia limited autonomy with likely independence by 2013. **Chief of state:** President of France Jacques Chirac (from 1995) represented by High Commissioner Thierry Lataste (from 1999). **Head**

of government: President Pierre Frogier (from 5 Apr 2001). **Capital:** Nouméa. **Official language:** none; Kanak languages and French have special recognition per the Nouméa Accord. **Official religion:** none. **Monetary unit:** 1 franc of the Comptoirs français du Pacifique (CFPF) = 100 centimes; valuation (28 Jun 2002) $1 = CFPF 120.44; the CFPF is pegged to the euro (€) at €1 = CFPF 119.25 from 1 Jan 2002.

Demography

Area: 7,172 sq mi, 18,575 sq km. **Population** (2001): 216,000. **Density** (2001): persons per sq mi 30.1, persons per sq km 11.6. **Urban** (1999): 75.7%. **Sex distribution** (1996): male 51.23%; female 48.77%. **Age breakdown** (1996): under 15, 30.7%; 15–29, 27.2%; 30–44, 21.3%; 45–59, 13.3%; 60–74, 5.9%; 75 and over, 1.6%. **Ethnic composition** (1996): Melanesian 45.3%, of which local (Kanak) 44.1%, Vanuatuan 1.2%; European 34.1%; Wallisian or Futunan 9.0%; Indonesian 2.6%; Tahitian 2.6%; Vietnamese 1.4%; other 5.0%. **Religious affiliation** (1995): Roman Catholic 61.3%; Protestant 14.5%, of which Presbyterian 12.3%; Muslim 2.7%; other Christian 2.3%; other 19.2%. **Major cities** (1996): Nouméa 76,293 (urban agglomeration 118,823); Mont-Dore 20,780; Dumbéa 13,888. **Location:** south Pacific Ocean, about 1,100 mi (1,800 km) east of Queensland, Australia.

Vital statistics

Birth rate per 1,000 pop. (2001): 20.1 (world avg. 22.5); (1996) legitimate 36.4%; illegitimate 63.6%. **Death rate** per 1,000 pop. (2001): 4.9 (world avg. 9.0). **Natural increase rate** per 1,000 pop. (2001): 15.2 (world avg. 13.5). **Total fertility rate** (avg. births per childbearing woman; 2001): 2.5. **Marriage rate** per 1,000 pop. (1999): 4.5. **Divorce rate** per 1,000 pop. (1996): 0.8. **Life expectancy** at birth (2001): male 72.0 years; female 77.0 years.

National economy

Budget (1999). *Revenue:* CFPF 77,477,000,000 (indirect taxes 49.7%, direct taxes 30.9%, French government subsidies 8.6%, tobacco excises 6.3%). *Expenditures:* CFPF 74,218,000,000 (current expenditure 93.4%, development expenditure 6.6%). **Production** (metric tons except as noted). *Agriculture, forestry, fishing* (1999): roots and tubers 21,100; coconuts 16,000; vegetables 3,785; livestock (number of live animals) 120,000 cattle, 38,000 pigs, 390,000 chickens; roundwood (1998) 4,800 cu m; fish catch (1997) 3,421. *Mining and quarrying* (metric tons; 1999): nickel ore 6,562,000, of which nickel content (1997) 110,000. *Manufacturing* (metric tons; 1999): cement 92,714; ferronickel (metal content) 45,289; nickel matte (metal content) 11,353. *Energy production (consumption):* electricity (kW-hr; 1996) 1,476,000,000 (1,476,000,000); coal (metric tons; 1996) none (168,000); petroleum products (metric tons; 1996) none (409,000). **Tourism:** receipts from visitors (1998) $110,000,000; expenditures by nationals abroad, n.a. **Population economically active** (1996): total 80,589; activity rate of total pop. 40.9% (participation rates: over age 14, 57.3%; female 39.7%; unemployed 18.6%). **Public debt** (external, outstanding; 1995 [includes long-term private debt not guaranteed by the

---

1 metric ton = about 1.1 short tons; 1 kilometer = 0.6 mi (statute); 1 metric ton-km cargo = about 0.68 short ton-mi cargo; c.i.f.: cost, insurance, and freight; f.o.b.: free on board

government]): $1,033,000,000. **Gross national product** (1999): $3,169,000,000 ($15,160 per capita). **Household income and expenditure** (1991). Average household size (1996) 3.8; average annual income per household CFPF 3,361,233 ; sources of income: wages and salaries 68.2%, transfer payments 13.7%, other 18.1%; expenditure: food and beverages 25.9%, housing 20.4%, transportation and communications 16.1%, recreation 4.8%. **Land use** (1994): forested 38.7%; meadows and pastures 11.8%; agricultural and under permanent cultivation 0.7%; other 48.8%.

Foreign trade

Imports (1999-c.i.f.): CFPF 112,888,000,000 (machinery and apparatus 20.0%, food 16.2%, transportation equipment 15.6%, mineral fuels 9.4%, chemicals and chemical products 7.8%). *Major import sources* (1998): France 52.2%; Australia 13.9%; New Zealand 5.3%; Singapore 4.2%; Japan 3.4%. **Exports** (1999-f.o.b.): CFPF 44,763,000,000 (ferronickel 54.8%, nickel ore 18.8%, nickel matte 13.9%, shrimp 4.2%). *Major export destinations:* Japan 32.2%; France 22.1%; Taiwan 8.4%; South Korea 7.6%; Australia 7.1%.

Transport and communications

Transport. *Roads* (1996): total length 5,764 km (paved [1993] 52%). *Vehicles:* passenger cars (1996) 56,700; trucks and buses (1993) 21,200. *Air transport* (1999; La Tontouta international airport only): passenger arrivals 171,887, passenger departures 170,815; (1998) freight unloaded 3,530 metric tons, freight loaded 1,371 metric tons; airports (1999) with scheduled flights 11. **Communications** Total units (units per 1,000 persons). Daily newspaper circulation (1996): 24,000 (121); Radio receivers (1997): 107,000 (533); Television receivers (1999): 101,000 (480); Telephone main lines (1999): 50,652 (241); Cellular telephone subscribers (1999): 25,450 (121); Internet users (1999): 5,000 (24).

Education and health

Educational attainment (1996). Percentage of pop. age 14 and over having: no formal schooling 5.7%; primary education 28.9%; lower secondary 30.2%; upper secondary 24.6%; higher 10.5%. **Literacy:** n.a. **Health** (1996): physicians 362 (1 per 549 persons); hospital beds 898 (1 per 221 persons); infant mortality rate per 1,000 live births (2001) 7.0. **Food** (1999): daily per capita caloric intake 2,772 (vegetable products 73%, animal products 27%); (1997) 122% of FAO recommended minimum requirement.

Military

Total active duty personnel (2000): 3,100 French troops

Background

Excavations indicate an Austronesian presence in New Caledonia about 2000–1000 BC. The islands were visited by James Cook in 1774 and by various navigators and traders in the 18th–19th centuries. They were occupied by France in 1853 and were a penal colony from 1864 to 1897. During World War II the islands were the site of Allied bases. They became a French overseas territory in 1946. In 1987 residents voted by referendum to remain part of France.

Recent Developments

In 1998 New Caledonia and France signed the Nouméa Accord, allowing New Caledonia to gain autonomy through a gradual transfer of power over a period of several years. In future a vote would be taken to determine whether the islands would become fully independent. Legislation was passed in 1999 defining the powers of various political bodies.

Internet resources:
<www.newcaledoniatourism-south.com>

New Zealand

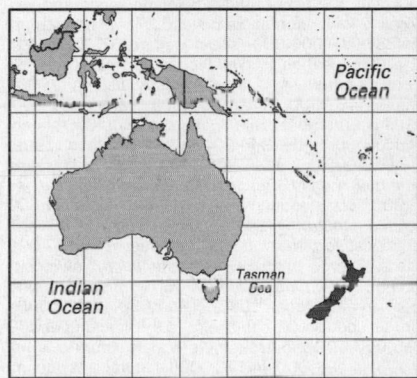

Official name: New Zealand (English); Aotearoa (Maori). **Form of government:** constitutional monarchy with one legislative house (House of Representatives [120—includes six elected seats allocated to Maoris]). **Chief of state:** Queen Elizabeth II (from 1952), represented by Governor-General Dame Silvia Cartwright (from 2001). **Head of government:** Prime Minister Helen Clark (from 1999). **Capital:** Wellington. **Official languages:** English; Maori. **Official religion:** none. **Monetary unit:** 1 New Zealand dollar ($NZ) = 100 cents; valuation (28 Jun 2002) US$1 = $NZ2.06.

Demography

Area: 104,454 sq mi, 270,534 sq km. **Population** (2001): 3,861,000. **Density** (2001): persons per sq mi 37.0, persons per sq km 14.3. **Urban** (2001): 86.0%. **Sex distribution** (2000): male 49.26%; female 50.74%. **Age breakdown** (1998): under 15, 22.7%; 15–29, 21.6%; 30–44, 23.3%; 45–59, 17.0%; 60–74, 10.3%; 75 and over, 5.1%. **Ethnic composition** (2000): Anglo-New Zealander 69.4%; Maori 10.0%; British 9.1%; other Polynesian 3.7%; Anglo-

Australian 1.7%; Chinese 1.4%; other 4.7%. **Religious affiliation** (1996): Christian 60.8%, of which Protestant 39.4% (including Anglican 17.5%), Roman Catholic 13.1%; nonreligious 24.7%; other religions/not specified 14.5%. **Major cities** (1999 est.): Auckland 381,800 (urban agglomeration 1,078,-000); Christchurch 324,200; Manukau 281,800 (part of Auckland urban agglomeration); North Shore 187,700 (part of Auckland urban agglomeration); Waitakere 170,600 (part of Auckland urban agglomeration). **Location**: southeast of Australia in the South Pacific Ocean and Tasman Sea. **Dependent territories**: Cook Islands, Niue, and Tokelau.

Vital statistics

Birth rate per 1,000 pop. (2001): 14.7 (world avg. 22.5); (1996) legitimate 58.0%; illegitimate 42.0%. **Death rate** per 1,000 pop. (2001): 6.9 (world avg. 9.0). **Natural increase rate** per 1,000 pop. (2001): 7.8 (world avg. 13.5). **Total fertility rate** (avg. births per childbearing woman; 2001): 2.0. **Life expectancy** at birth (2000): male 75.7 years; female 80.8 years.

National economy

Budget (2000–2001). *Revenue:* $NZ37,156,000,-000 (income taxes 59.4%, taxes on goods and services 34.4%, nontax revenue 6.2%). *Expenditures:* $NZ37,019,000,000 (social welfare 37.0%, health 19.0%, education 17.6%). **Production** (metric tons except as noted). *Agriculture, forestry, fishing* (2000): apples 482,000, wheat 360,000, barley 281,000; livestock (number of live animals) 45,800,000 sheep, 9,457,000 cattle, 344,000 pigs; roundwood (1999) 17,953,000 cu m; fish catch (1998) 635,711. *Mining and quarrying* (1998): iron ore and sand concentrate 2,000,000; aluminum metal 315,600; silver 31,500 kg. *Manufacturing* (1996–97): wood pulp 1,405,300; chemical fertilizers 1,365,000; beer 343,457,000 liters. *Energy production (consumption)*: electricity (kW-hr; 1996) 35,932,000,000 (35,932,000,000); coal (metric tons; 1996) 3,611,000 (2,438,000); crude petroleum (barrels; 1996) 16,000,000 (35,000,000); petroleum products (metric tons; 1996) 4,481,000 (4,778,000); natural gas (cu m; 1996) 4,781,000,000 (4,780,000,000). **Household income and expenditure**. Average household size (1996) 2.8; annual disposable income per household (1996–97) $NZ59,444; sources of income (1998): wages and salaries 65.8%, transfer payments 15.2%, self-employment 9.8%, other 9.2%; expenditure (1996–97): housing 20.2%, transportation 18.2%, food 16.4%, household goods 13.7%, clothing 3.8%. **Tourism** (1999): receipts US$2,083,000,000; expenditures US$1,493,000,000. **Gross national product** (1999): US$53,299,000,000 (US$13,990 per capita). **Population economically active** (2000): total 1,923,700; activity rate 50.1% (participation rates: over age 15, 66.2%; female 45.3%; unemployed 5.7%). **Land use** (1999): pasture 49.6%; agriculture 12.2%; forest and other 38.2%.

Foreign trade

Imports (1999): $NZ24,248,000,000 (machinery 24.6%; transport equipment 17.2%; mineral fuels 5.7%; textiles and textile products 4.7%; plastics 4.1%). *Major import sources:* Australia 22.1%; US 17.7%; Japan 12.6%; China 5.1%; Germany 4.5%; UK 4.4%. **Exports** (1998–99): $NZ22,600,000,000 (food 47.2%; wood and wood products 10.6%; machinery 7.7%; metals and metal products 7.2%; wool 3.8%). *Major export destinations:* Australia 21.4%; US 13.3%; Japan 12.7%; UK 6.2%; South Korea 3.9%; Germany 2.8%; China 2.7%.

Transport and communications

Transport. *Railroads* (1999): route length 3,912 km; passengers carried (1998) 11,751,000; metric ton-km cargo 3,960,000,000. *Roads* (1999): total length 92,075 km (paved 62%). *Vehicles* (1998–99): passenger cars 1,831,118; trucks and buses (1998) 368,723. *Air transport* (1999; Air New Zealand only): passenger-km 19,879,000,000; metric ton-km cargo 851,744,000; airports (1997) 36. **Communications** Total units (units per 1,000 persons). Daily newspaper circulation (1999): 850,000 (223); Radio receivers (1997): 3,750,000 (997); Television receivers (1999): 1,975,000 (518); Telephone main lines (1999): 1,889,000 (496); Cellular telephone subscribers (1999): 1,395,000 (366); Personal computers (1999): 1,250,000 (328); Internet users (1999): 700,000 (184).

Education and health

Educational attainment (1991). Percentage of pop. age 25 and over having: primary and some secondary education 54.9%; secondary 31.1%; higher 6.9%; not specified 6.1%. **Literacy**: virtually 100.0%. **Health**: physicians (1999) 13,360 (1 per 285 persons); hospital beds (2000) 31,425 (1 per 122 persons); infant mortality rate per 1,000 live births (2001) 5.9. **Food** (1999): daily per capita caloric intake 3,152 (vegetable products 68%, animal products 32%); 119% of FAO recommended minimum.

Military

Total active duty personnel (2000): 9,230 (army 48.2%, air force 30.3%, navy 21.5%). **Military expenditure as percentage of GNP** (1997): 1.3% (world 2.6%); per capita expenditure $204.

Background

Polynesian occupation of New Zealand dates to about AD 1000. First sighted by Dutch explorer Abel Janszoon Tasman in 1642, the main islands were charted by Captain James Cook in 1769. Named a British crown colony in 1840, the area was the scene of warfare between colonists and native Maori through the 1860s. In 1907 the colony became the Dominion of New Zealand. It administered Western Samoa during 1919–62 and participated in both world wars. When Britain joined what is now the European Community in the early 1970s, its influence led New Zealand to expand its export markets and diversify its economy.

Recent Developments

In November 1999 the center-right government of New Zealand's National Party (NP), which had be-

---

1 metric ton = about 1.1 short tons;   1 kilometer = 0.6 mi (statute);   1 metric ton-km cargo = about 0.68 short ton-mi cargo;   c.i.f.: cost, insurance, and freight;   f.o.b.: free on board

come an institution over the years, was voted out of office. An eager center-left Labour Party (LP) was waiting to pounce, assisted by an assortment of smaller parties. For the first time, the leadership battle was contested by two women, with LP leader Helen Clark ultimately prevailing over NP Prime Minister Jennifer Shipley. Clark became New Zealand's first elected woman prime minister. Shipley had been appointed to the post in 1997 after then prime minister Jim Bolger resigned.

Events in the Pacific in 2000 focused attention on New Zealand's long-running debate on defense forces that it might need in the southern oceans. A record fall of the New Zealand dollar also occurred that year. Following the terrorist attacks in the US on 11 Sep 2001, New Zealand offered deployment of its elite Special Air Service to an antiterrorism operation. In May the government had announced plans to scrap all of New Zealand's combat aircraft. A legal challenge to the decision was rejected by a High Court judge in November, and the squadrons were disbanded in December. The government passed initiatives to help Australia place Afghan and other refugees and also to save New Zealand's international airline. Beginning in late August Afghan "boat people" bearing down on northern and western Australia were refused permission to land. New Zealand agreed to accept a quota for settlement, and in late September more than 140 refugees were flown to Auckland from a transshipment center on Nauru. Air New Zealand's crisis was partly attributable to world reaction against flying, as well as to a failed attempt to digest fully the Australian airline Ansett in a many-sided takeover operation. For the New Zealand government, which assumed control in October, it meant returning to the business of running an airline 12 years after privatization. In November New Zealand yachtsman and two-time America's Cup winner Sir Peter Blake was killed by robbers on a river in Brazil.

Internet resources: <www.stats.govt.nz>

Nicaragua

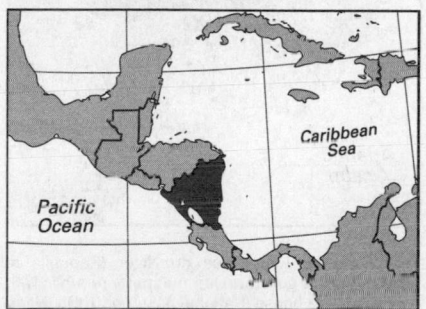

Caribbean Sea

Pacific Ocean

Official name: República de Nicaragua (Republic of Nicaragua). **Form of government:** unitary multiparty republic with one legislative house (National Assembly [93; including three unsuccessful presidential candidates in 2001 elections]). **Head of state and government:** President Enrique Bolaños Geyer (from 10 Jan 2002). **Capital:** Managua. **Official language:** Spanish. **Official religion:** none. **Monetary unit:** 1 córdoba oro (C$) = 100 centavos; valuation (28 Jun 2002) $1 = C$14.19.

Demography

Area: 50,337 sq mi, 130,373 sq km; land area only equals 46,464 sq mi, 120,340 sq km. **Population** (2001): 4,918,000. **Density** (2001; based on land area): persons per sq mi 104.9, persons per sq km 40.5. **Urban** (1998): 56.4%. **Sex distribution** (2000): male 49.96%; female 50.04%. **Age breakdown** (2000): under 15, 39.7%; 15–29, 30.6%; 30–44, 17.0%; 45–59, 8.2%; 60–74, 3.7%; 75 and over, 0.8%. **Ethnic composition** (1997): mestizo (Spanish/Indian) 69.0%; white 17.0%; black 9.0%; Amerindian 5.0%. **Religious affiliation** (1995): Roman Catholic 72.9%; Protestant 16.7%, of which Evangelical 15.1%, Moravian 1.5%; nonreligious 8.5%; other 1.9%. **Major cities** (1995): Managua 864,201; León 123,865; Chinandega 97,387; Masaya 88,971; Granada 71,783; Estelí 71,550. **Location:** Central America, bordering Honduras, the Caribbean Sea, Costa Rica, and the North Pacific Ocean.

Vital statistics

Birth rate per 1,000 pop. (2000): 28.3 (world avg. 22.5). **Death rate** per 1,000 pop. (2000): 4.9 (world avg. 9.0). **Natural increase rate** per 1,000 pop. (2000): 23.4 (world avg. 13.5). **Total fertility rate** (avg. births per childbearing woman; 2000): 3.3. **Life expectancy** at birth (2000): male 66.8 years; female 70.8 years.

National economy

Budget (1998). *Revenue:* C$6,581,000,000 (tax revenue 85.7%, of which import duties 23.0%, excise taxes on petroleum products 16.7%, general sales taxes 14.2%, income taxes 12.3%; grants 10.3%). *Expenditures:* C$7,037,000,000 (current expenditure 67.2%; development expenditure 31.6%). **Public debt** (external, outstanding; 1999): $5,799,000,000. **Production** (metric tons except as noted). *Agriculture, forestry, fishing* (1999): sugarcane 3,748,000, corn (maize) 302,000, coffee 65,000; livestock (number of live animals) 1,693,000 cattle, 400,000 pigs; roundwood (1998) 4,198,000 cu m; fish catch (1997) 16,130, of which shrimp 6,437. *Mining and quarrying* (1997): gold 109,000 troy oz. *Manufacturing* (value added in C$'000,000; 1998 [at prices of 1980]): food 1,816; beverages 1,245; cement, bricks, tiles 381. *Energy production (consumption):* electricity (kW-hr; 1998) 2,084,000,000 (1,392,000,000); crude petroleum (barrels; 1996) none (4,479,000); petroleum products (metric tons; 1996) 593,000 (882,000). **Tourism** (1999): receipts from visitors $107,000,000; expenditures by nationals abroad $74,000,000. **Land use** (1994): forested 26.3%; meadows and pastures 45.3%; agricultural and under permanent cultivation 10.5%; other 17.9%. **Population economically active** (1995): total 1,447,847; activity rate of total pop. 33.2% (participation rates: 15–64, 59.5%; female 29.5%; unemployed [2000] 9.8%). **Gross national product** (1999): $2,012,000,000 ($410 per capita). **Household income and expenditure.** Average household size (1995) 5.8.

Foreign trade

Imports (1999-c.i.f. [commodities and trading partners]; f.o.b. [balance of trade]): $1,845,700,000 (capital goods 32.2%, nondurable consumer goods 23.9%, mineral fuels 8.7%). *Major import sources:* US

34.5%; Costa Rica 11.4%; Guatemala 7.3%; Panama 6.9%. **Exports** (1999): $543,800,000 (coffee 24.9%, manufactured products 19.9%, crustaceans 15.4%, beef 7.7%, raw sugar 5.6%, gold 5.6%). *Major export destinations:* US 37.7%; El Salvador 12.5%; Germany 9.8%; Honduras 6.5%; Costa Rica 5.1%.

Transport and communications

Transport. *Railroads:* no rail service from 1994. *Roads* (1996): total length 18,000 km (paved 10%). *Vehicles* (1996): passenger cars 73,000; trucks and buses 61,650. *Air transport* (1995; Nica only): passenger-km 78,985,000; metric ton-km cargo 8,985,000; airports (1997) with scheduled flights 10. **Communications** Total units (units per 1,000 persons). Daily newspaper circulation (1996): 135,000 (30); Radio receivers (1997): 1,240,000 (265); Television receivers (1999): 340,000 (72); Telephone main lines (1999): 150,258 (32); Cellular telephone subscribers (1999): 44,249 (9.4); Personal computers (1999): 40,000 (8.5); Internet users (1999): 20,000 (4.2).

Education and health

Educational attainment (1995). Percentage of pop. age 25 and over having: no formal schooling 30.6%, no formal schooling (literate) 3.9%, primary education 39.2%, secondary 17.0%, technical 3.1%, incomplete undergraduate 2.2%; complete undergraduate 4.0%. **Literacy** (1995): total pop. age 15 and over literate 1,769,000 (74.0%); males literate 853,000 (74.4%); females literate 916,000 (73.6%). **Health:** physicians (1997) 3,725 (1 per 1,255 persons); hospital beds (1996) 6,666 (1 per 674 persons); infant mortality rate (2000) 34.8. **Food** (1999): daily per capita caloric intake 2,314 (vegetable products 93%, animal products 7%); 103% of FAO recommended minimum requirement.

Military

Total active duty personnel (2000): 16,000 (army 87.5%, navy 5.0%, air force 7.5%). **Military expenditure as percentage of GNP** (1997): 1.5% (world 2.6%); per capita expenditure $6.

Did you know? A Nicaraguan, Rubén Darío, is considered one of the greatest poets in the Spanish language, particularly from the standpoint of technical perfection and artistic resourcefulness. At the end of the 19th century he was a leader of Modernism, a movement that gave new life to poetry in both Latin America and Spain. He attributed his success in revitalizing Spanish poetry to the fact that he started thinking in French and writing in Spanish.

Background

Nicaragua has been inhabited for thousands of years, most notably by the Maya. Christopher Columbus arrived in 1502, and Spanish explorers discovered Lake Nicaragua soon thereafter. Nicaragua was gov-

erned by Spain until 1821, when it declared its independence. It was part of Mexico and then the United Provinces of Central America until 1938 when full independence was achieved. The US intervened in political affairs by maintaining troops there in 1912–33. Ruled by the dictatorial Somoza dynasty from 1936–79, it was taken over by the Sandinistas after a popular revolt. They were opposed by armed insurgents, the US-backed Contras, from 1981. The Sandinista government nationalized several sectors of the economy but lost the national elections in 1990. The new government returned many economic activities to private control, but unrest continued through the 1990s.

Recent Developments

Hurricane Mitch devastated Nicaragua in 1998, leaving thousands dead; recovery continued through 1999. That year archrivals Daniel Ortega and Pres. Arnoldo Alemán offended the public by making a pact to protect their economic and partisan interests. By utilizing a working majority in the legislature, they packed government offices with their supporters and altered electoral laws to make it more difficult for smaller parties to challenge the two major ones. The 2001 elections were won by Liberal Party candidate Enrique Bolaños.

Internet resources: <www.intur.gob.ni>

Niger

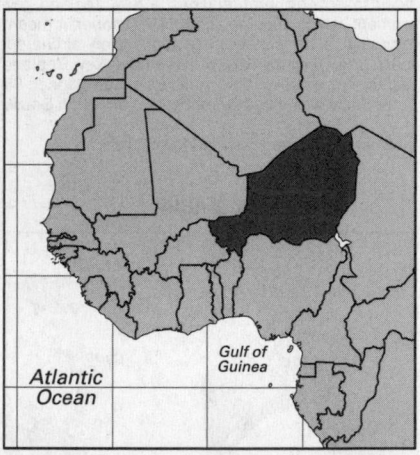

Official name: République du Niger (Republic of Niger). **Form of government:** multiparty republic with one legislative house (National Assembly [83]). **Head of state and government:** President Tandja Mamadou (from 1999), assisted by Prime Minister Hama Amadou (from 2000). **Capital:** Niamey. **Official language:** French. **Official religion:** none. **Monetary unit:** 1 CFA franc (CFAF) = 100 centimes; valuation (28 Jun 2002) $1 = CFAF 662.52 (earlier pegged to the French Franc, after 1 Jan 2002 the CFAF was pegged at 655.96 to the euro).

---

1 metric ton = about 1.1 short tons;   1 kilometer = 0.6 mi (statute);   1 metric ton-km cargo = about 0.68 short ton-mi cargo;   c.i.f.: cost, insurance, and freight;   f.o.b.: free on board

Demography

Area: 458,075 sq mi, 1,186,408 sq km. **Population** (2001): 10,355,000. **Density** (2000): persons per sq mi 21.2, persons per sq km 8.2. **Urban** (1999): 20.1%. **Sex distribution** (2000): male 49.91%; female 50.09%. **Age breakdown** (2000): under 15, 48.0%; 15–29, 26.3%; 30–44, 14.1%; 45–59, 7.8%; 60–74, 3.2%; 75 and over, 0.6%. **Ethnic composition** (1988): Hausa 53.0%; Zerma- (Djerma-) Songhai 21.2%; Tuareg 10.4%; Fulani (Peul) 9.8%; Kanuri-Nanga 4.4%; Teda 0.4%; Arab 0.3%; Gurma 0.3%; other 0.2%. **Religious affiliation** (2000): Sunni Muslim 90.7%; traditional beliefs 8.7%; Christian 0.5%; other 0.1%. **Major cities** (1988): Niamey 391,876 (urban agglomeration [1999] 731,000); Zinder 119,827; Maradi 110,005; Tahoua 49,948; Agadez 32,272. **Location:** western Africa, bordering Algeria, Libya, Chad, Nigeria, Benin, Burkina Faso, and Mali.

Vital statistics

Birth rate per 1,000 pop. (2000): 51.4 (world avg. 22.5). **Death rate** per 1,000 pop. (2000): 23.2 (world avg. 9.0). **Natural increase rate** per 1,000 pop. (2000): 28.2 (world avg. 13.5). **Total fertility rate** (avg. births per childbearing woman; 2000): 7.2. **Life expectancy** at birth (2000): male 41.4 years; female 41.1 years.

National economy

Budget (1998). *Revenue:* CFAF 164,400,000,000 (taxes 59.3%, external aid and gifts 34.1%, nontax revenue 6.6%). *Expenditures:* CFAF 188,000,000,-000 (current expenditures 69.2%, development expenditures 30.8%). **Public debt** (external, outstanding; 1999): $1,424,000,000. **Tourism** (1999): receipts from visitors $24,000,000; expenditures by nationals abroad (1997) $26,000,000. **Gross national product** (1999): $1,974,000,000 ($190 per capita). **Production** (metric tons except as noted). *Agriculture, forestry, fishing* (1999): millet 2,253,000, cowpeas 641,000, sorghum 481,000; livestock (number of live animals) 6,469,000 goats, 4,312,000 sheep, 2,174,000 cattle; roundwood (1998) 6,460,000 cu m; fish catch (1997) 6,341. *Mining and quarrying:* salt (1997) 3,000; uranium (1999) 2,916. *Manufacturing* (value added in CFAF '000,000; 1997): traditional-sector handicrafts 56,200; food 1,320; soaps and other chemical products 1,249; construction materials 836. *Energy production (con sumption):* electricity (kW hr; 1999) 170,200,000 (379,200,000); coal (metric tons; 1996) 173,000 (173,000); petroleum products (metric tons; 1996) (205,000). **Population economically active** (1988; excluding nomadic pop): total 2,315,694; activity rate of total pop. 31.9% (participation rates: ages 15–64, 55.2%; female 20.4%). **Household income and expenditure.** Average household size (1998) 6.3; expenditure (1987): food and beverages 43.1%, housing 22.8%, clothing 10.0%. **Land use** (1994): forested 2.0%; meadows and pastures 8.2%; agricultural and under permanent cultivation 2.9%; other (largely desert) 86.9%.

Foreign trade

Imports (1998): CFAF 196,700,000,000 (consumer goods 74.0%, of which food products 24.1%, petroleum products 7.0%; intermediate and capital goods

26.0%). *Major import sources* (estimated figures): France 17%; Côte d'Ivoire 9%; Belgium 5%; Germany 4%; unspecified countries/special categories 37%. **Exports** (1998): CFAF 175,600,000,000 (uranium 43.6%; livestock [mostly live cattle, sheep, and goats] 13.8%; cowpeas 7.1%). *Major export destinations* (estimated figures): France 52%; South Korea 34%; UK 4%.

Transport and communications

Transport. *Roads* (1996): total length 6,276 mi, 10,100 km (paved 8%). *Vehicles* (1996): passenger cars 38,220, trucks and buses 15,200. *Air transport* (1998; represents $\frac{1}{11}$ of the traffic of Air Afrique, which is operated by 11 West African states): passenger-mi 160,477,000, passenger-km 258,263,-000; short ton-mi cargo 9,263,000, metric ton-km cargo 13,524,000; airports (1996) with scheduled flights 6. **Communications** Total units (units per 1,000 persons). Daily newspaper circulation (1996): 2,000 (0.2); Radio receivers (1997): 680,000 (73); Television receivers (1999): 285,000 (29); Telephone main lines (1998): 18,114 (1.9); Cellular telephone subscribers (1998): 1,349 (0.1); Personal computers (1999): 4,000 (0.4); Internet users (1999): 3,000 (0.3).

Education and health

Educational attainment (1988). Percentage of pop. age 25 and over having: no formal schooling 85.0%; Koranic education 11.2%; primary education 2.5%; secondary 1.1%; higher 0.2%. **Literacy** (1995): total pop. age 15 and over literate 641,000 (13.6%); males literate 482,000 (20.9%); females literate 159,000 (6.6%). **Health:** physicians (1993) 237 (1 per 35,141 persons); hospital beds (1987) c. 3,500 (1 per 2,000 persons); infant mortality rate per 1,000 live births (2000) 124.9. **Food** (1999): daily per capita caloric intake 2,064 (vegetable products 95%, animal products 5%); 88% of FAO recommended minimum requirement.

Military

Total active duty personnel (2000): 5,300 (army 98.1%, air force 1.9%). **Military expenditure as percentage of GNP** (1997): 1.1% (world 2.6%); per capita expenditure $2.

Background

There is evidence of Neolithic culture and several kingdoms existed on the territory of Niger before the colonialists arrived. First explored by Europeans in the late 18th century, it became a French colony in 1922. It became an overseas territory of France in 1946 and gained independence in 1960. The first multiparty elections were held in 1993.

Recent Developments

Pres. Ibrahim Baré Maïnassara, who came to power in the military coup of 1996, was assassinated on 9 Apr 1999. The army assumed control of the country, dissolved the National Assembly and the Supreme Court, and annulled the results of the February local elections but promised a return to civilian rule within the year. The government drew up a new constitution that contained provisions for power sharing between the president and the prime minister; it became law in August. Retired army colonel Mamadou Tandja was elected the new civilian president and reappointed former prime minister Hama Amadou. Foreign aid resumed in 2000 as donors signaled their approval of the return to civil rule. Thousands of University of Niamey students, protesting against government plans to reduce their grants, clashed with security forces in February 2001.

Internet resources:
<www.nigerembassyusa.org/travel.html>

Nigeria

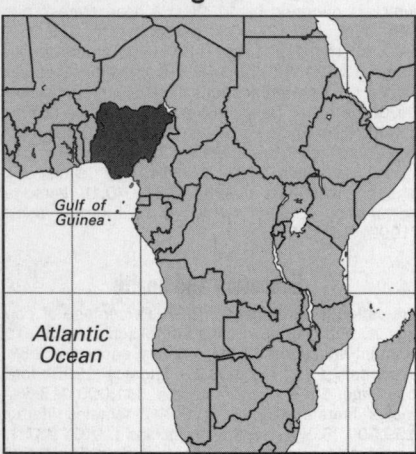

Official name: Federal Republic of Nigeria. **Form of government:** federal republic with two legislative bodies (Senate [109]; House of Representatives [360]). **Head of state and government:** President Olusegun Obasanjo (from 1999). **Capital:** Abuja (statutory transfer from Lagos occurred in 1991; judiciary and some ministries remain in Lagos). **Official language:** English. **Official religion:** none. **Monetary unit:** 1 Nigerian naira (₦) = 100 kobo; valuation (28 Jun 2002) $1 = ₦119.85.

Demography

Area: 923,768 sq km. **Population** (2001): 126,636,-000. **Density** (2001): persons per sq mi 355.1, persons per sq km 137.1. **Urban** (1996): 40.1%. **Sex distribution** (2000): male 50.59%; female 49.41%. **Age breakdown** (2000): under 15, 43.8%; 15–29, 27.7%; 30–44, 15.3%; 45–59, 8.7%; 60–74, 3.8%; 75 and over, 0.7%. **Ethnic composition** (2000): Yoruba 17.5%; Hausa 17.2%; Igbo (Ibo) 13.3%; Fulani 10.7%; Ibibio 4.1%; Kanuri 3.6%; Egba 2.9%; Tiv 2.6%; Igbirra (Ebira) 1.1%%; Nupe 1.0%; Edo 1.0%; other 25.0%. **Religious affiliation** (2000): Christian 45.9%, of which independent Christian c. 15%, Anglican c. 13%; other Protestant c. 9%; Roman Catholic c. 8%; Muslim 43.9%; traditional beliefs 9.8%; other 0.4%. **Major cities** (1991): Lagos 5,197,247 (urban agglomeration [1999] 12,763,000); Kano

2,166,554; Ibadan 1,835,300; Kaduna 993,642; Benin City 762,719. **Location:** western Africa, bordering Niger, Chad, Cameroon, the Gulf of Guinea, and Benin.

Vital statistics

Birth rate per 1,000 pop. (2000): 40.2 (world avg. 22.5). **Death rate** per 1,000 pop. (2000): 13.7 (world avg. 9.0). **Natural increase rate** per 1,000 pop. (2000): 26.5 (world avg. 13.5). **Total fertility rate** (avg. births per childbearing woman; 2000): 5.7. **Life expectancy** at birth (2000): male 51.6 years; female 51.6 years.

National economy

Budget (2000). *Revenue:* ₦1,927,087,000,000 (tax revenue 33.1%, of which petroleum profit tax 17.3%; import duties, excise taxes, and fees 6.0%; nontax revenue 66.9%, of which oil export proceeds 49.1%). *Expenditures:* ₦1,834,305,000,000 (1999; recurrent expenditure 75.6%, of which debt service 18.8%, education 5.2%, defense 4.6%, health 2.0%; capital expenditure 24.4%). **Public debt** (external, outstanding; 1999): $22,423,000,000. **Production** (metric tons except as noted). *Agriculture, forestry, fishing* (2000): cassava 33,854,000, yams 26,201,000, sorghum 7,711,000; livestock (number of live animals) 24,300,000 goats, 20,500,000 sheep, 19,830,000 cattle; roundwood (2000) 100,637,000 cu m; fish catch (1999) 477,365. *Mining and quarrying* (1998): limestone 3,660,000; marble 22,460. *Manufacturing* (value added in ₦'000,000; 1995): food and beverages 25,415; textiles 16,193; chemicals and chemical products 11,181. *Energy production (consumption):* electricity (kW-hr; 1997) 14,830,000,000 (14,830,000,000); coal (metric tons; 1997) 50,000 (50,000); crude petroleum (barrels; 2000) 733,139,000 ([1997] 41,257,000); petroleum products (metric tons; 1997) 5,550,000 (6,175,000); natural gas (cu m; 1997) 5,500,-000,000 (5,500,000,000). **Tourism:** receipts (1998) $142,000,000; expenditures (1999) $620,000,000. **Household income and expenditure.** Avg. household size (1995) 4.7; annual income per household (1992–93) ₦15,000; sources of income (1979): self-employment 49.4%, wages 30.2%, interest 5.4%, rent 4.7%, transfer payments 4.3%; expenditures (1979): food 53.0%, fuel and light 11.4%, clothing 6.0%, transportation 4.7%, household goods 3.8%. **Gross national product** (1999): $31,600,000,000 ($260 per capita). **Population economically active** (1993–94): total 29,000,000; activity rate 31.0% (participation rates: ages 15–59, 64.4%; female 44.0%). **Land use** (1994): forest 15.7%; pasture 43.9%; agriculture 35.9%; other 4.5%.

Foreign trade

Imports (1995): ₦111,728,000,000 (machinery and transport equipment 42.0%; manufactured goods [mostly iron and steel products, textiles, and paper products] 24.0%; chemicals 17.0%; food 8.4%). *Major import sources* (1999): UK 11.0%; Germany 9.9%; US 9.5%; France 8.4%; China 5.8%; Italy 4.9%. **Exports** (1995): ₦220,408,900,000 (crude petroleum 94.8%; cocoa beans 0.7%; rubber 0.3%; other exports include cocoa products, textiles, and cashew

1 metric ton = about 1.1 short tons;　1 kilometer = 0.6 mi (statute);　1 metric ton-km cargo = about 0.68 short ton-mi cargo;　c.i.f.: cost, insurance, and freight;　f.o.b.: free on board

nuts). *Major export destinations* (1999): US 36.2%; India 8.6%; Spain 7.5%; France 5.9%.

Transport and communications

Transport. *Railroads* (1999): length 3,505 km; passenger-km (1995) 161,000,000; metric ton-km cargo (1995) 108,000,000. *Roads* (1996): total length 62,598 km (paved 19%). *Vehicles:* passenger cars (1996) 773,000; trucks and buses (1995) 68,300. *Air transport* (2000; Nigeria Airways only): passenger-km 111,566,000; metric ton-km cargo 2,068,000; airports (1996) 12. **Communications** Total units (units per 1,000 persons). Daily newspaper circulation (1996): 2,500,000 (24); Radio receivers (1996): 20,500,000 (197); Television receivers (1998): 7,200,000 (66); Telephone main lines (1999): 410,000 (3.6); Cellular telephone subscribers (1998): 20,000 (0.2); Personal computers (1999): 700,000 (6.4); Internet users (1999): 100,000 (0.9).

Education and health

Literacy (2000): total pop. age 15 and over literate 40,700,000 (64.1%); males literate 22,600,000 (62.3%); females literate 18,100,000 (56.2%). **Health** (1995): physicians 27,230 (1 per 3,707 persons); hospital beds 68,350 (1 per 1,477 persons); infant mortality rate (2000) 74.2. **Food** (1999): daily per capita caloric intake 2,833 (vegetable products 97%, animal products 3%); 120% of FAO recommended minimum requirement.

Military

Total active duty personnel (2000): 76,500 (army 81.0%, navy 6.6%, air force 12.4%). **Military expenditure as percentage of GNP** (1997): 1.4% (world 2.6%); per capita expenditure $17.

Background

Inhabited for thousands of years, Nigeria was the center of the Nok culture from 500 BC to AD 200 and several precolonial empires, including the state of Kanem-Bornu and the Songhai, Hausa, and Fulani kingdoms. Visited in the 15th century by Europeans, it became a center for the slave trade. The area began to come under British control in 1861; by 1903 British rule was total. Nigeria gained independence in 1960 and became a republic in 1963. Ethnic strife soon led to military coups, and military groups ruled the country from 1966–79 and from 1983–99. Civil war between the central government and the former Eastern Region, which seceded and called itself Biafra, in 1967–70 ended in Biafra's surrender after widespread starvation and civilian deaths. In 1991 the capital was moved from Lagos to Abuja. The government's execution of environmental activist Ken Saro-Wiwa in 1995 led to international sanctions, and civilian rule was finally reestablished in 1999. By far the most populous nation in Africa, Nigeria suffers from rapid population increase, political instability, foreign debt, slow economic growth, a high rate of violent crime, and rampant government corruption.

Recent Developments

In 1999 Nigeria underwent major political change. Gen. Abdulsalam Abubakar, interim leader since the death of Sani Abacha in June 1998, oversaw the transition to a democratically elected government and the establishment of a new constitution. Olusegun Obasanjo, who had ruled Nigeria from 1976 to 1979, was elected president. In June the legislature held session for the first time in 15 years. Nigeria continued to face huge problems of corruption and civil violence. During 2000 Obasanjo took steps to secure Nigeria's transition to democracy. Chief among these were reform of the military and the curbing of government corruption. Ongoing investigations had already located more than $1 billion looted by Abacha and his associates. Relations between Christians and Muslims remained tense as more northern states adopted Shari'ah (Islamic law); although it applied only to Muslims, many Christians opposed its imposition. Riots between supporters and opponents of Shari'ah flared during February and March and again in October. Throughout 2001 Nigeria experienced ethnic and religious violence, and the oil-producing Niger Delta region was again the site of environmental problems and political conflicts. In early 2002 Lagos was rocked by explosions at a weapons depot that resulted in more than 1,000 deaths, as well as continuing ethnic violence.

Internet resources:
<www.nigeriahighcommottawa.com>

Northern Mariana Islands

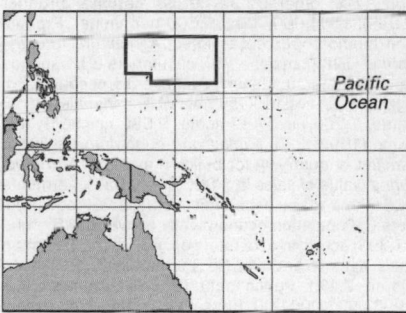

Official name: Commonwealth of the Northern Mariana Islands. **Political status:** self-governing commonwealth in association with the US, having two legislative houses (Senate [9]; House of Representatives [18]; residents elect a nonvoting representative to the US Congress). **Chief of state:** President George W. Bush (from 20 Jan 2001). **Head of government:** Governor Juan N. Babauta (from 14 Jan 2002). **Capital:** Capital Hill, Saipan. **Official languages:** Chamorro, Carolinian, and English. **Official religion:** none. **Monetary unit:** 1 dollar ($) = 100 cents.

Demography

Area: 176.5 sq mi, 457.1 sq km. **Population** (2001): 73,400. **Density** (2001): persons per sq mi 415.9, persons per sq km 160.6. **Urban** (1999): 55.0%. **Sex distribution** (1995): male 49.75%; female 50.25%. **Age breakdown** (1995): under 15, 24.3%; 15–29, 31.7%; 30–44, 31.6%; 45–59, 9.7%; 60–74, 2.2%; 75 and over, 0.5%. **Ethnic composition** (1995; includes aliens): Filipino 33.1%; Chamorro 24.1%; Chinese 11.5%; Carolinian 10.1%; other Asian 7.6%; Micronesian 7.1%; white 3.0%; other 3.5%. **Religious affiliation** (1995 unofficial est.): Roman Catholic 59.6%; Protestant 18.7%; other Christian 1.4%; other 20.3%. **Major villages** (1995): Garapan 6,634; San Antonio 6,256; Chalan Kanoa 6,229; Capital Hill 2,698; San Jose (on Tinian) 1,896. **Location:** Oceania, islands in the North Pacific Ocean between Hawaii and the Phillipines.

Vital statistics

Birth rate per 1,000 pop. (2000): 20.7 (world avg. 22.5); legitimate, 32.4%; illegitimate, 67.6%. **Death rate** per 1,000 pop. (2000): 2.2 (world avg. 9.0). **Natural increase rate** per 1,000 pop. (2000): 18.5 (world avg. 13.5). **Total fertility rate** (avg. births per childbearing woman; 1999 est.): 1.8. **Marriage rate** per 1,000 pop. (1989): 28.5. **Divorce rate** per 1,000 pop. (1986): 2.9. **Life expectancy** at birth (1999 est.): male 72.0 years; female 78.4 years.

National economy

Budget (1994–95). *Revenue:* $217,100,000 (local revenue 87.7%, grants from US Office of Insular Affairs for capital improvements 12.3%). *Expenditures:* $190,400,000 (general government 46.1%, education 19.6%, health and social welfare 18.4%, public safety 6.6%). **Tourism** (1998): receipts from visitors, $394,000,000. **Land use** (1990): meadows and pastures 3.7%; agricultural and under permanent cultivation 4.0%; other 92.3%. **Gross national product** (1999): $664,600,000 ($9,600 per capita). **Production** (metric tons except as noted). *Agriculture, forestry, fishing* (1989): melons 165, cucumbers 83, bananas 46, betelnuts 38, Chinese cabbage 33, coconuts 30, eggplant 23; livestock (number of live animals) 4,513 cattle, 1,260 pigs, 482 goats, 9,580 chickens; fish catch (1998) 235. *Mining and quarrying:* negligible amount of quarrying for building material. *Manufacturing* (value of sales in $'000,000; 1997): garments 700; stone, glass, or ceramic products 21; food products 6. **Population economically active** (1995): total 37,393; activity rate of total pop. 63.5% (participation rates: ages 16 and over, 85.3%; female 48.1%; unemployed 7.1%). **Public debt** (external, outstanding; 1995): $27,000,000. **Household income and expenditure.** Average household size (1995) 4.0.

Foreign trade

Imports (1991): $392,250,000 (machinery and transport equipment 22.2%, petroleum and petroleum products 20.9%, special transactions not elsewhere specified 14.8%, food 13.9%, manufactured goods 11.7%, manufactured articles 8.8%, beverages and tobacco 5.4%). *Major import sources:* US 18.2%, Japan 16.6%, other Asian countries 10.3%, Australia 3.4%, unspecified countries 51.5%. **Exports** (1999): $1,049,000,000 (clothing and accessories 99.9%). *Major export destinations:* nearly all to the US.

Transport and communications

Transport. *Roads* (1998): total length c. 360 km (paved, nearly 100%). *Vehicles* (1993): passenger cars 12,000; trucks and buses 6,300. *Air transport* (1993; Saipan International Airport): aircraft land-

ings 21,555; boarding passengers 590,857; airports (1999) with scheduled flights 2. **Communications** Total units (units per 1,000 persons). Radio receivers (1999): 10,500 (152); Television receivers (1999): 4,100 (59); Telephone main lines (1999): 24,945 (480); Cellular telephone subscribers (1999): 2,905 (56).

Education and health

Educational attainment (1995). Percentage of pop. age 25 and over having: no formal schooling 0.7%; primary education, 5.5%; some secondary 13.5%; completed secondary 38.8%; some postsecondary 23.3%; completed undergraduate 18.2%. **Literacy** (1990): total pop. age 10 and over literate 35,490 (98.8%); males literate 18,790 (99.0%); females literate 16,700 (98.6%). **Health:** physicians (1986): 23 (1 per 1,326 persons); hospital beds (1998): 74 (1 per 899 persons); infant mortality rate per 1,000 live births (1999 est.): 5.9.

Military

The US is responsible for military defense; headquarters of the US Pacific Command are in Hawaii.

Did you know? The deepest known point on Earth can be found at the extreme southwest point of the Mariana Trench, east of the Mariana Islands. Called the Challenger Deep, it plunges 36,201 ft (11,034 m) below the ocean's surface.

Background

The Northern Mariana Islands were discovered by Ferdinand Magellan in 1521 and colonized by Spain in 1668. Sold to Germany in 1899, they were occupied by Japan in 1914 and became a Japanese mandate from the League of Nations after 1919. They were the scene of fierce fighting in World War II; Tinian was the base for US planes that dropped atomic bombs on Hiroshima and Nagasaki. They were granted to the US in 1947 as a UN trust territory, became self-governing in 1978, and became a commonwealth under US sovereignty in 1986, when its residents became US citizens. The UN trusteeship ended in 1986.

Recent Developments

In 1999 the islands' government opposed US proposals to extend federal immigration law, a measure that would seriously affect the viability of the garment industry there. On Saipan the spreading effects of chemical waste dumped in the 1960s brought about a debate on responsibility for clearance. In 2000 major concerns continued regarding the status of the garment industry. Some 90% of the Marianas population comprises foreign migrant labor. Under a 1986 agreement, the garment industry was exempt from US tariffs, minimum wages, and immigration standards; against the protests of local businesses, the US was considering legislation that would apply tighter controls.

Internet resources: <http://visit-marianas.com>

1 metric ton = about 1.1 short tons; 1 kilometer = 0.6 mi (statute); 1 metric ton-km cargo = about 0.68 short ton-mi cargo; c.i.f.: cost, insurance, and freight; f.o.b.: free on board

Norway

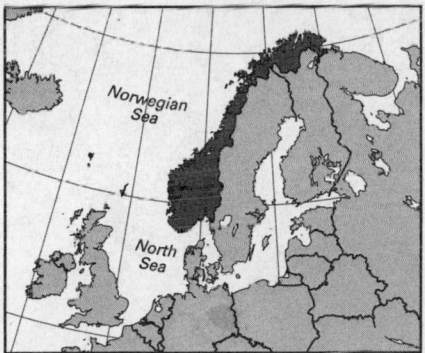

Official name: Kongeriket Norge (Kingdom of Norway). **Form of government:** constitutional monarchy with one legislative house (Parliament [165]). **Chief of state:** King Harald V (from 1991). **Head of government:** Prime Minister Kjell Magne Bondevik (from 17 Oct 2001). **Capital:** Oslo. **Official language:** Norwegian. **Official religion:** Evangelical Lutheran. **Monetary unit:** 1 Norwegian krone (NKr) = 100 øre; valuation (28 Jun 2002) $1 = NKr 7.50.

Demography

Area: 125,004 sq mi, 323,758 sq km. **Population (2001):** 4,516,000. **Density (2001):** persons per sq mi 36.1, persons per sq km 13.9. **Urban (1990):** 75.0%. **Sex distribution (2000):** male 49.51%; female 50.49%. **Age breakdown (2000):** under 15, 20.0%; 15–29, 19.6%; 30–44, 22.3%; 45–59, 18.8%; 60–74, 11.5%; 75 and over, 7.8%. **Ethnic composition** (by country of citizenship; 2000): Norway 96.0%; Sweden 0.6%; Denmark 0.4%; Bosnia and Herzegovina 0.3%; UK 0.3%; Yugoslavia 0.2%; US 0.2%; Pakistan 0.2%; Germany 0.1%; Iraq 0.1%; Somalia 0.1%, Iran 0.1%; other 1.4%. **Major cities (2000):** Oslo 507,467; Bergen 229,496; Trondheim 148,859. **Location:** Northern Europe, bordering the Barents Sea, Russia, Sweden, the North Sea, and the Norwegian Sea.

Vital statistics

Birth rate per 1,000 population (2000): 13.2 (world avg. 22.5); (1999) legitimate 49.1%; illegitimate 50.9%. **Death rate** per 1,000 population (2000): 9.8 (world avg. 9.0). **Natural increase rate** per 1,000 population (2000): 3.4 (world avg. 13.5). **Total fertility rate** (avg. births per childbearing woman; 1999): 1.9. **Marriage rate** per 1,000 population (1998): 5.3. **Divorce rate** per 1,000 population (1998): 2.1. **Life expectancy** at birth (1999): male 75.6 years; female 81.1 years.

National economy

Budget (1999). *Revenue:* NKr 609,315,000,000 (value-added taxes 30.7%, tax on income 28.6%, social security taxes 20.2%). *Expenditures:* NKr 551,803,000,000 (social security and welfare 37.8%, health 15.9%, education 13.0%, debt service 4.6%). **Land use** (1994): forested 27.2%; meadows and pastures 0.4%; agricultural and under permanent cultivation 2.9%; built-up and other 69.5%. **Production** (metric tons except as noted). *Agriculture, forestry, fishing* (2000): barley 649,400, potatoes 446,000, oats 372,400; livestock (number of live animals) 2,400,000 sheep, 1,042,000 cattle, 690,000 pigs; roundwood (1999) 8,424,000 cu m; fish catch (1999) 2,598,733, of which herring 807,635, cod 256,621, saithe 197,857, capelin 86,767. *Mining and quarrying* (1998): iron ore 621,000, ilmenite-titanium 589,500, copper 11,400, zinc 1,800. *Manufacturing* (value added in NKr '000,000; 1997): machinery and transport equipment 27,779; food products 25,646; paper and paper products 18,139. *Energy production (consumption):* electricity (kW-hr; 1996) 104,756,000,000 (103,732,000,000); coal (metric tons; 1996) 230,000 (934,000); crude petroleum (barrels; 1996) 1,193,000,000 (109,000,000). **Household income and expenditure.** Average household size (1996–98) 2.2; consumption expenditure per household (1998) NKr 357,458; expenditure (1996–98): transportation 24.1%, housing 16.6%, food 12.9%, recreation and education 11.3%, household furniture and equipment 8.7%, clothing and footwear 6.1%. **Gross national product** (1999): US$149,280,000,000 (US$33,470 per capita). **Population economically active** (1999): total 2,333,000; activity rate of total population 52.4% (participation rates: ages 16–64 [1996] 79.1%; female 46.0%; unemployed 4.9%). **Public debt** (1997): US$33,763,000,000. **Tourism** (1999): receipts from visitors US$2,229,000,000.

Foreign trade

Imports (1999 c.i.f.): NKr 266,676,500,000 (machinery and transport equipment 51.1%, of which road vehicles 8.6%, ships 3.6%; metals and metal products 8.2%, of which iron and steel 2.8%; food products 5.7%, of which fruits and vegetables 1.4%; petroleum products 2.3%). *Major import sources:* Sweden 15.1%; Germany 12.8%; UK 9.2%; Denmark 6.8%. **Exports** (1999 f.o.b.): NKr 355,171,500,000 (petroleum products 41.6%; machinery and transport equipment 14.3%; metals and metal products 10.3%; food products 8.7%, of which fish 8.0%). *Major export destinations:* UK 18.2%; The Netherlands 10.5%; Germany 10.0%; Sweden 9.4%.

Transport and communications

Transport. *Railroads* (1998): route length 4,006 km; passenger-km 2,589,000,000; metric ton-km cargo 2,142,000,000. *Roads* (2000): total length 90,880 km (paved 74%). *Vehicles* (1999): passenger cars 1,813,642; trucks and buses 447,583. *Air transport* (1999): passenger-km 10,371,135,000; metric ton-km cargo 1,199,090,000; airports (1996) 50. **Communications.** Total units (units per 1,000 persons). Daily newspaper circulation (1999): 2,294,000 (514); Radio receivers (1996): 4,000,000 (913); television receivers (1999): 2,900,000 (650); Telephone main lines (1999): 3,176,000 (711); Cellular telephone subscribers (1999): 2,744,793 (615); Personal computers (1999): 2,000,000 (448); Internet users (1999): 2,000,000 (448).

Education and health

Educational attainment (1998). Percentage of population age 16 and over having: primary and lower secondary education 30.0%; higher secondary 45.9%; higher 20.8%; unknown 3.3%. **Literacy** (1998): virtually 100% literate. **Health:** physicians (1996) 15,368 (1 per 285 persons); hospital beds (1998) 21,287 (1 per 208 persons); infant mortality rate (1999) 3.9. **Food** (1999): daily per capita caloric intake 3,425 (vegetable products 67%, animal products 33%); 128% of FAO recommended minimum requirement.

Military

Total active duty personnel (2000): 25,800 (army 57.0%, navy 23.6%, air force 19.4%). **Military expenditure as percentage of GNP** (1997): 2.1% (world avg. 2.6%); per capita expenditure US$739.

 **Did you know?** The Nobel Prize for Peace is the only one of the six Nobel prizes that is not awarded by a Swedish committee. It is not known why, but Alfred Nobel, the founder of the famed award, gave the task of selecting a recipient to Norway.

Background

Several principalities were united into the kingdom of Norway in the 11th century. From 1380 it had the same king as Denmark until it was ceded to Sweden in 1814. The union with Sweden was dissolved in 1905, and Norway's economy grew rapidly. It remained neutral during World War I, although its shipping industry played a vital role in the conflict. It declared its neutrality in World War II but was invaded and occupied by German troops. Norway is a member of NATO but turned down membership in the European Union in 1994. Its economy grew consistently during the 1990s.

Recent Developments

On 10 Mar 2000, Prime Minister Kjell Magne Bondevik officially resigned from office, one day after his government lost a vote of confidence in Parliament. Bondevik and his supporters wanted to delay the construction of Norway's first natural gas-fired power plants until new technology could be developed that would reduce air pollution. The opposition, however, favored immediate construction. One week later Jens Stoltenberg of the Norwegian Labour Party was named the new prime minister. Norway's long-dominant Labour Party lost much of its grip on power after its worst showing since 1924 in the general election held on 10 Sep 2001. The Labour government chose to resign as a result of the elections. In October a minority government was formed, and Bondevik became prime minister for the second time. The marriage of Crown Prince Haakon to Mette-Marit Tjessem Høiby on August 25 captured the nation's attention; the prince's choice of bride had raised eyebrows because she was a commoner and had a son by a convicted drug dealer. In May 2002 Princess Martha Louise also wed a commoner, author Ari Behn.

Internet resources: <www.norway.org>

Oman

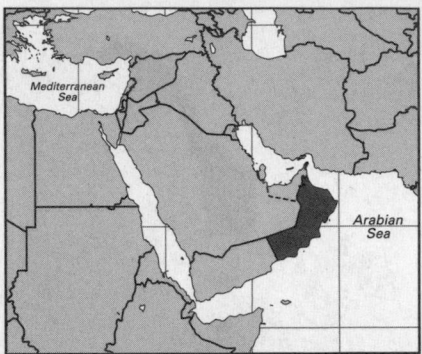

Official name: Saltanat 'Uman (Sultanate of Oman). **Form of government:** monarchy with two advisory bodies (Council of State [41]; Consultative Council [83]). **Head of state and government:** Sultan and Prime Minister Qabus ibn Sa'id (from 1970). **Capital:** Muscat. **Official language:** Arabic. **Official religion:** Islam. **Monetary unit:** 1 rial Omani (RO) = 1,000 baizas; valuation (28 Jun 2002) 1 RO = $0.39.

Demography

Area: 119,500 sq mi, 309,500 sq km. **Population** (2001): 2,497,000. **Density** (2001): persons per sq mi 20.9, persons per sq km 8.1. **Urban** (1999): 82.7%. **Sex distribution** (2000): male 56.8%; female 43.2%. **Age breakdown** (1998): under 15, 36.8%; 15–29, 29.7%; 30–44, 22.1%; 45–59, 7.9%; 60 and over, 3.5%. **Ethnic composition** (1993): Omani Arab 73.5%; Indian 13.3%; Bangladeshi 4.3%; Pakistani (mostly Balochi) 3.1%; Egyptian 1.6%; other 4.2%. **Religious affiliation** (1993): Muslim 87.7%, of which Ibadiyah Muslim c. 75% (principal minorities are Sunni Muslim and Shi'i Muslim); Hindu 7.4%; Christian 3.9%; Buddhist 0.5%; other 0.5%. **Major cities** (1993): As-Sib 155,000; Salalah 116,000; Bawshar 107,500; Suhar 84,300; 'Ibri 76,000; Muscat 40,900 (urban agglomeration [1999] 887,000). **Location:** Middle East, bordering the Gulf of Oman, the Arabian Sea, Yemen, Saudi Arabia, and the United Arab Emirates.

Vital statistics

Birth rate per 1,000 pop. (2000): 38.1 (world avg. 22.5). **Death rate** per 1,000 pop. (2000): 4.2 (world avg. 9.0). **Natural increase rate** per 1,000 pop. (2000): 33.9 (world avg. 13.5). **Total fertility rate** (avg. births per childbearing woman; 2000): 6.1. **Life expectancy** at birth (1999): male 69.7 years; female 74.0 years.

National economy

Budget (2000). *Revenue:* RO 2,284,300,000 (oil revenue 75.3%; other 24.7%). *Expenditures:* RO 2,608,200,000 (current expenditure 78.8%, of which civil ministries 41.0%, defense 30.6%, interest paid on loans 4.1%; capital development projects and subsidies 21.2%). **Public debt** (external, outstanding;

---

1 metric ton = about 1.1 short tons;   1 kilometer = 0.6 mi (statute);   1 metric ton-km cargo = about 0.68 short ton-mi cargo;   c.i.f.: cost, insurance, and freight;   f.o.b.: free on board

1999): $1,768,000,000. **Gross national product** (1998): $13,135,000,000 ($5,950 per capita). **Tourism** (1997): receipts $108,000,000; expenditures $47,000,000. **Household income and expenditure.** Average household size (1999) 6.9; expenditure (1990): housing and utilities 27.8%, food, beverage, and tobacco 26.4%, transportation 19.8%, clothing and shoes 7.8%, household goods and furniture 6.1%, education, health services, entertainment, and other 12.1%. **Production** (metric tons except as noted). *Agriculture, forestry, fishing* (2000): vegetables and melons 165,000 (of which watermelons 32,000), dates 135,000, bananas 28,000; livestock (number of live animals) 729,000 goats, 180,000 sheep, 149,000 cattle; fish catch (1999) 108,819. *Mining and quarrying* (2000): copper 26,000; chromite 15,000; silver 4,692 kg. *Manufacturing* (value of production in RO '000,000; 1993): textiles and apparel 78,200; food and beverages 72,930; chemical products 40,950. *Energy production (consumption):* electricity (kW-hr; 1999) 8,600,000,000 (8,600,000,000); crude petroleum (barrels; 2000) 349,500,000 (22,700,000); petroleum products (metric tons; 1996) 3,770,000 (1,656,000). **Population economically active** (1993): total 704,798; activity rate of total pop. 34.9% (participation rates: over age 15, 60.9%; female 9.7%; unemployed [1996] c. 20%). **Land use** (1994): meadows and pastures 4.7%; agricultural and under permanent cultivation 0.3%; other (mostly desert and developed area) 95.0%.

Foreign trade

Imports (2000-c.i.f.): RO 1,937,700,000 (machinery and transport equipment 43.1%; basic manufactured goods 16.0%; food and live animals 12.2%; beverages and tobacco 8.7%; miscellaneous manufactured articles 6.6%). *Major import sources:* United Arab Emirates 29.5%; Japan 18.1%; UK 5.8%; US 5.4%; Germany 3.7%. **Exports** (2000-f.o.b.): RO 4,352,000,000 (domestic exports 88.5%, of which petroleum 82.8%, manufactured goods 2.4% [of which copper and copper products 0.5%], food and live animals 1.9%, mineral fuels 0.7%; reexports 11.5%, of which machinery and transport equipment 7.8%). *Major export destinations* (non-oil): United Arab Emirates 40.1%; Saudi Arabia 8.4%; Iran 7.8%; Yemen 7.8%; US 5.5%.

Transport and communications

Transport. *Roads* (1999): total length 20,518 mi, 33,020 km (paved 24%). *Vehicles* (1999): passenger cars 229,029; trucks and buses 110,717. *Air transport* (2000-Oman Air): passenger-mi 601,400,000, passenger-km 968,000,000; short ton-mi cargo 11,250,000, metric ton-km cargo 18,106,000; airports (1999) with scheduled flights 6. **Communications** Total units (units per 1,000 persons). Daily newspaper circulation (1996): 63,000 (28); Radio receivers (1997): 1,400,000 (607); Television receivers (1999): 1,415,000 (608); Telephone main lines (1999): 220,373 (90); Cellular telephone subscribers (1999): 120,941 (49); Personal computers (1999): 65,000 (28); Internet users (1999): 50,000 (22).

Education and health

Educational attainment (1993). Percentage of pop. age 15 and over having: no formal schooling (illiterate) 41.2%; no formal schooling (literate) 14.9%; primary 18.9%; secondary 21.1%; higher technical

2.0%; higher undergraduate 1.5%; higher graduate 0.1%; other 0.3%. **Literacy** (1995): percentage of total pop. age 15 and over literate 64.0%; males literate 74.6%; females literate 50.7%. **Health** (1998): physicians 3,061 (1 per 747 persons); hospital beds 5,075 (1 per 444 persons); infant mortality rate per 1,000 live births (2000) 23.3.

Military

Total active duty personnel (2000): 39,800 (army 62.8%, navy 10.8%, air force 10.3%, royal household 16.3%). **Military expenditure as percentage of GDP** (1997): 26.1% (world 2.6%); per capita expenditure $795.

Background

Oman has been inhabited for at least 10,000 years. The Arab migration began in the 9th century BC. Tribal warfare continued until the conversion to Islam in the 7th century AD. It was ruled by Ibadi imams until 1154, when a royal dynasty was established. The Portuguese controlled the coastal areas from about 1507 to 1650, when they were expelled. The Al Bu Sa'id dynasty, founded in the mid-18th century, still rules Oman. Oil was discovered in 1964. In 1970 the sultan was deposed by his son, who began a policy of modernization and joined the Arab League and the UN. In the Persian Gulf War, Oman cooperated with the allied forces against Iraq. In the 1990s it continued to expand its foreign relations.

Recent Developments

In 1997 Sultan Qabus appointed 41 members to a new Council of State (including 4 women), which, in addition to the older Consultative Council, advised the government on matters of public policy. Oman during 2000 held the first-ever direct elections for its parliament. In a first among its fellow Gulf Cooperation Council member nations, two women were elected. The nation also became a member of the World Trade Organization. Oman was supportive of the campaign against terrorism following the 11 Sep 2001 attacks on the US, allowing the deployment of American bombers to its bases and agreeing to serve as a staging area for British and American special forces. Qabus was among the regional leaders who met with US Secretary of Defense Donald Rumsfeld in early October 2001 as Rumsfeld gathered international support.

Internet resources: <www.exploreoman.com>

Pakistan

Official name: Islam-i Jamhuriya-e Pakistan (Islamic Republic of Pakistan). **Form of government:** interim military regime. **Chief of state and government:** President Pervez Musharraf (from 20 Jun 2001; term extended after winning national referendum of 30 Apr 2002). **Capital:** Islamabad. **Official language:** Urdu. **Official religion:** Islam. **Monetary unit:** 1 Pakistan rupee (PRs) = 100 paisa, valuation (28 Jun 2002) $1 = PRs 60.01.

Demography

Area: 307,374 sq mi, 796,095 sq km. **Population** (2001; excludes Afghan refugees): 144,617,000.

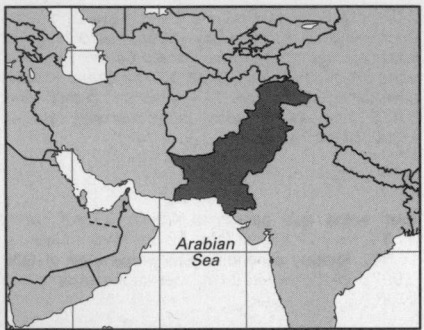

Arabian
Sea

Density (2001): persons per sq mi 470.5, persons per sq km 181.7. **Urban** (2001; excludes Federally administered tribal areas): 38.0%. **Sex distribution** (1999; excludes Federally administered tribal areas): male 51.89%; female 48.11%. **Age breakdown** (1998; excludes Federally administered tribal areas): under 15, 43.2%; 15–29, 26.9%; 30–44, 15.6%; 45–59, 8.8%; 60–74, 4.3%; 75 and over, 1.2%. **Ethnic composition** (2000): Punjabi 52.6%; Pashtun 13.2%; Sindhi 11.7%; Urdu-speaking muhajirs 7.5%; Balochi 4.3%; other 10.7%. **Religious affiliation** (2000): Muslim 96.1% (mostly Sunni); Christian 2.5%; Hindu 1.2%; others (including Ahmadiyah) 0.2%. **Major cities** (1998): Karachi 9,269,000; Lahore 5,063,000; Faisalabad 1,977,000; Rawalpindi 1,406,000; Multan 1,182,000. **Location**: south Asia, bordering China, India, the Arabian Sea, Iran, and Afghanistan.

Vital statistics

Birth rate per 1,000 pop. (2001): 36.8 (world avg. 22.5). **Death rate** per 1,000 pop. (2001): 10.0 (world avg. 9.0). **Natural increase rate** per 1,000 pop. (2001): 26.8 (world avg. 13.5). **Total fertility rate** (avg. births per childbearing woman; 2001): 5.2. **Life expectancy** at birth (2001): male 61.0 years; female 60.0 years.

National economy

Budget (1999–2000). *Revenue:* PRs 505,921,000,-000 (nontax receipts 23.5%, sales tax 23.1%, income taxes 21.3%, customs duties 12.2%, excise taxes 11.0%). *Expenditures:* PRs 573,788,000,000 (public-debt service 42.7%, defense 26.2%, development 11.8%, general administration 8.3%, grants and subsidies 5.9%). **Production** (metric tons except as noted). *Agriculture, forestry, fishing* (2000): sugarcane 46,333,000, wheat 21,079,000, rice 7,000,-000; livestock (number of live animals) 47,400,000 goats, 24,100,000 sheep, 148,000,000 chickens; roundwood (1999) 33,075,000 cu m; fish catch (1998) 596,980. *Mining and quarrying* (1998–99): limestone 9,467,000; rock salt 1,190,000; gypsum 242,000. *Manufacturing* (1998–99): refined sugar 3,568,000; chemical fertilizers 3,543,000; cotton textiles 385,000,000 sq m. *Energy production (consumption):* electricity (kW-hr; 1997–98) 59,088,-000,000 ([1996] 56,946,000,000); coal (metric tons, 1997–98) 3,144,000 ([1996] 4,718,000);

crude petroleum (barrels; 1997–98) 20,520,000 ([1996] 49,609,000); petroleum products (metric tons; 1996) 5,890,000 (15,842,000); natural gas (cu m; 1997–98) 19,809,000,000 ([1996] 17,894,-000). **Household income and expenditure** (1988). Average household size 6.3; income per household PRs 25,572; sources of income: self-employment 56.0%, wages and salaries 22.0%, other 22.0%; expenditure: food 47.0%, housing 12.0%, clothing and footwear 8.0%, other 33.0%. **Population economically active** (1999): total 38,590,000; activity rate of total pop. 28.7% (participation rates: ages 15–64, 43.1%; female [1996–97] 14.4%; unemployed 6.1%). **Gross national product** (1999): $62,915,000,000 ($470 per capita). **Public debt** (external, outstanding; 1999): $28,514,000,000. **Tourism** (1999): receipts $76,000,000; expenditures $180,000,000. **Land use** (1999): pasture 6.5%; agriculture 28.4%; forest and other 65.1%.

Foreign trade

Imports (1999–2000; f.o.b.): $10,361,000,000 (1998–99; petroleum products 14.7%, fixed vegetable oil and fats 8.9%, specialized machinery 6.9%, organic chemicals 5.6%, wheat 4.1%, general industrial machinery 3.7%, road vehicles and parts 3.4%, iron and steel manufactures 3.2%). *Major import sources* (1998–99): Japan 8.3%; US 7.7%; Saudi Arabia 6.8%; United Arab Emirates 6.7%; Malaysia 6.7%; Kuwait 5.9%; UK 4.4%; China 4.2%; Germany 4.2%. **Exports** (1999–2000): $8,569,000,000 (textile fabrics 18.1%, ready-made apparel and made-up articles 14.2%, cotton yarn 12.5%, rice 6.3%, leather goods 6.0%). *Major export destinations* (1998–99): US 21.8%; Hong Kong 7.1%; Germany 6.6%; UK 6.6%; United Arab Emirates 5.4%; Japan 3.5%; France 3.2%; The Netherlands 3.1%; Italy 2.7%.

Transport and communications

Transport. *Railroads* (1998–99): route length 8,774 km; passenger-km 19,164,000,000; metric ton-km cargo 4,020,000,000. *Roads* (1997–98): total length 240,885 km (paved 55%). *Vehicles* (1998): passenger cars 1,167,635; trucks and buses 251,407. *Air transport* (1999): passenger-km 10,466,000,000; metric ton-km cargo 329,832,000; airports (1997) 35. **Communications** Total units (units per 1,000 persons). Daily newspaper circulation (1995): 2,800,000 (21); Radio receivers (1997): 13,500,000 (102); Television receivers (1999): 16,000,000 (119); Telephone main lines (1999): 2,986,000 (22); Cellular telephone subscribers (1999): 278,830 (2.1); Personal computers (1999): 580,000 (4.3); Internet users (1999): 80,000 (0.6).

Education and health

Educational attainment (1990). Percentage of pop. age 25 and over having: no formal schooling 73.8%; some primary education 9.7%; secondary 14.0%; postsecondary 2.5%. **Literacy** (1995): total pop. age 15 and over literate 37.8%; males literate 50.0%; females literate 24.4%. **Health** (1998): physicians 82,682 (1 per 1,638 persons); hospital beds 90,659 (1 per 1,494 persons); infant mortality rate per 1,000 live births (2001) 89.0. **Food** (1999): daily per capita

1 metric ton = about 1.1 short tons;   1 kilometer = 0.6 mi (statute);   1 metric ton-km cargo = about 0.68 short ton-mi cargo;   c.i.f.: cost, insurance, and freight;   f.o.b.: free on board

caloric intake 2,462 (vegetable products 83%, animal products 17%); 107% of FAO recommended minimum.

Military

Total active duty personnel (2000): 587,000 (army 89.9%, navy 3.6%, air force 6.5%). **Military expenditure as percentage of GNP** (1997): 5.7% (world 2.6%); per capita expenditure $26.

Background

Pakistan has been inhabited since about 3500 BC. From the 3rd century BC to the 2nd century AD, it was part of the Mauryan and Kushan kingdoms. The first Muslim conquests were in the 8th century AD. The British East India Company subdued the reigning Mughal dynasty in 1757. During the period of British colonial rule, what is now Pakistan was part of India. The new state of Pakistan came into existence in 1947 by act of the British Parliament. Kashmir remained a disputed territory between Pakistan and India, resulting in military clashes and full-scale war in 1965. Civil war between East Pakistan (now Bangladesh) and West Pakistan in 1971 resulted in independence for Bangladesh in 1971. Many Afghan refugees migrated to Pakistan during the Soviet–Afghan War in the 1980s. Pakistan elected Benazir Bhutto, the first woman to head a modern Islamic state, in 1988. She was ousted in 1990 on charges of corruption and incompetence. During the 1990s conditions were volatile. Border flare-ups with India continued and Pakistan conducted nuclear tests.

Recent Developments

Political conditions in Pakistan worsened and the army carried out a coup in October 1999, deposing Prime Minister Mohammed Nawaz Sharif and placing Gen. Pervez Musharraf in power. Sharif was exiled in 2000. Musharraf found himself walking a political tightrope. After having consolidated his grip on power by declaring himself president in June 2001, he made a risky decision—in the wake of the terrorist attacks in the US on 11 September—to side with the US in its war against the Taliban government in Afghanistan and the al-Qaeda terrorist network. Pakistan had been one of only three countries ever officially to recognize the Taliban, a regime which enjoyed the support of many of Pakistan's Muslims. Islamic militants staged protests in dozens of cities throughout Pakistan, but by the end of the year they had failed to ignite any real threat against Musharraf. Thousands of Pakistanis were thought to have crossed the border into Afghanistan to fight alongside the Taliban against the US-led forces. In return for Pakistan's support, the US ended economic sanctions imposed after Pakistan's 1998 nuclear tests.

Relations between Pakistan and India deteriorated severely after India blamed two Pakistan-based organizations for a terrorist attack on Parliament on 13 Dec 2001 that was prompted by the standoff over the Kashmir region. As 2002 began both nations massed troops along their common border and continued to conduct attacks; international fear of war between the two countries was heightened, especially since both possessed nuclear weapons. The sides exchanged fire along the border in May, where as many as a million soldiers

were stationed; Pakistan also began testing missiles, and India threatened to take more serious action. Early in 2002, *Wall Street Journal* reporter Daniel Pearl was kidnapped and eventually murdered by a militant group; four suspects went on trial in April. A top al-Qaeda official was captured in Pakistan in March.

Internet resources: <www.pak.gov.pk>

Palau

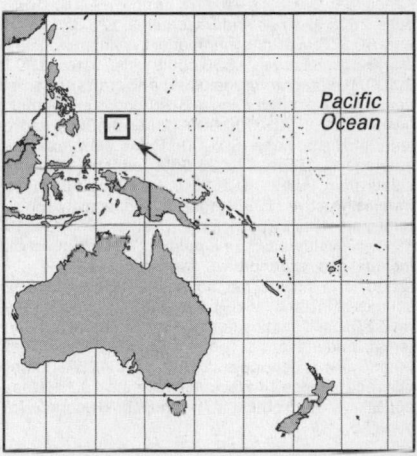

Pacific Ocean

Official name: Belu'u er a Belau (Palauan); Republic of Palau (English). **Form of government:** unitary republic with a national congress composed of two legislative houses (Senate [14]; House of Delegates [16]). **Head of state and government:** President Tommy Remengesau (from 19 Jan 2001). **Capital:** Koror; Melekeok on Babelthuap (the main island of Palau) is to be the eventual permanent capital. **Official languages:** Palauan; English. **Official religion:** none. **Monetary unit:** 1 US dollar ($) = 100 cents.

Demography

Area: 188 sq mi, 488 sq km. **Population** (2001): 19,700. **Density** (2001): persons per sq mi 104.8, persons per sq km 40.4. **Urban** (1990): 59.6%. **Sex distribution** (2000): male 54.63%; female 45.37%. **Age breakdown** (2000): under 15, 23.9%; 15–29, 24.2%; 30–44, 29.9%; 45–59, 14.2%; 60–74, 5.5%; 75 and over 2.3%. **Ethnic composition** (1997): Palauan 74.5%; Filipino 16.0%; Chinese 3.2%; other 6.3%. **Religious affiliation** (1995): Roman Catholic 38.4%; Protestant 24.7%; Modekne (marginal Christian sect) 26.5%; other 10.4%. **Major city** (2000): Koror 13,303. **Location:** island group in the North Pacific Ocean, 500 mi (800 km) east of the Philippines.

Vital statistics

Birth rate per 1,000 pop. (2000): 21.1 (world avg. 22.5). **Death rate** per 1,000 pop. (2000): 7.2 (world avg. 9.0). **Natural increase rate** per 1,000 pop. (2000): 13.9 (world avg. 13.5). **Total fertility rate** (avg. births per childbearing woman; 1999): 2.5. **Life**

expectancy at birth (1999): male 65.2 years; female 71.5 years.

National economy

Budget (1999). *Revenue:* $59,102,000 (grants from the US 40.5%, tax revenue 39.0%, nontax revenue 20.5%). *Expenditures:* $69,900,000 (current expenditure 86.0%, of which wages and salaries 38.9%; capital expenditure 14.0%). **Gross national product** (at current market prices; 1997): $159,800,000 ($8,810 per capita). **Production** (metric tons except as noted). *Agriculture, forestry, fishing* (value of sales in $; 1993): eggs 262,701, fruit and vegetables 126,325, betel nuts 60,376; livestock (number of live animals; 1984) 1,343 pigs, 82 cows, 9,500 poultry; fish catch (1997) 1,500. *Manufacturing:* includes handicrafts and small items. *Energy production (consumption):* electricity (kW-hr; 1996) 208,000,000 (208,000,000); petroleum products, none (80,000). **Pubic debt** (external, outstanding; 1998): $1,433,000. **Tourism** (1999): receipts from visitors $68,200,000. **Population economically active** (1995): total 8,368; activity rate of total pop. 48.6% (participation rates: over age 15, 69.0%; female 39.6%; unemployed 7.0%). **Household income and expenditure.** Average household size (2000) 5.7; income per household (1989) $8,882; sources of income (1989): wages 63.7%, social security 12.0%, self-employment 7.4%, retirement 5.5%, interest, dividend, or net rental 4.3%, remittance 4.1%, other 3.0%; expenditure (1997): food 42.2%, beverages and tobacco 14.8%, entertainment 13.1%, transportation 6.4%, clothing 5.7%, household goods 2.7%, other 15.1%.

Foreign trade

Imports (1997–98): $63,222,000 (1997; machinery and transport equipment 27.8%; food, beverages, and tobacco 27.1%; manufactured articles 27.1%; mineral fuels 13.2%; chemicals and related products 4.5%). *Major import sources* (1997): US 44.1%; Guam 19.3%; Japan 14.8%; Singapore 14.3%; Taiwan 5.4%. **Exports** (1997–98): $11,095,000 (mostly high-grade tuna; also garments and handicrafts). *Major export destinations:* mostly Japan.

Transport and communications

Transport. *Roads* (1993): total length 64 km (paved 59%). *Vehicles* (1994): passenger cars and trucks 4,271. *Air transport* (1993): passenger arrivals 50,366, passenger departures 49,376; airports (1997) with scheduled flights 1. **Communications** Total units (units per 1,000 persons). Radio receivers (1997): 12,000 (663); Television receivers (1997): 11,000 (606); Telephone main lines (1994): 2,615 (160).

Education and health

Educational attainment (1997). Percentage of pop. age 25 and over having: no formal schooling 0.1%; some primary education 4.4%; completed primary 5.7%; some secondary 16.3%; completed secondary 41.0%; some postsecondary 13.0%; higher 19.5%. **Literacy** (1997): total pop. age 15 and over literate 99.9%. **Health** (1990): physicians (government-em-

ployed only) 10 (1 per 1,518 persons); hospital beds 70 (1 per 200 persons); infant mortality rate per 1,000 live births (1999) 17.7.

Military

The US is responsible for the external security of Palau, as specified in the Compact of Free Association of 1 Oct 1994.

Background

The islands of Palau had been under nominal Spanish ownership for more than three centuries when they were sold to Germany in 1899. They were seized by Japan in 1914 and taken by Allied forces in 1944 during World War II. Palau became part of the UN Trust Territory of the Pacific Islands in 1947 and became a sovereign state in 1994; the US provides economic assistance and maintains a military presence in the islands.

Recent Developments

During 1999 and 2000, Palau strengthened relations with Japan, which provided financial assistance, and Taiwan. In a major change at the top, voters in Palau elected a new president, Tommy Remengesau, who began his four-year term in January 2001. He replaced Kuniwo Nakamura, who enthusiastically endorsed his successor. Remengesau moved quickly to strengthen economic relations with Taiwan.

Internet resources: <www.visit-palau.com>

Panama

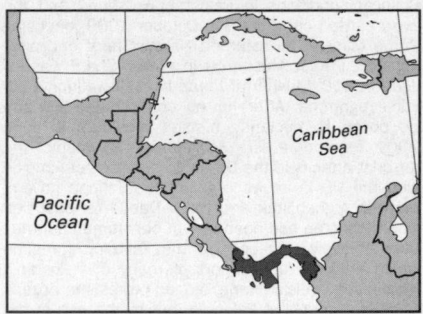

Official name: República de Panamá (Republic of Panama). **Form of government:** multiparty republic with one legislative house (Legislative Assembly [71]). **Head of state and government:** President Mireya Elisa Moscoso Rodríguez (from 1999). **Capital:** Panama City. **Official language:** Spanish. **Official religion:** none. **Monetary unit:** 1 balboa (B) = 100 cents; valuation (28 Jun 2002) $1 = B 1.00.

Demography

Area: 28,950 sq mi, 74,979 sq km. **Population** (2001): 2,903,000. **Density** (2001): persons per sq mi 100.3, persons per sq km 38.7. **Urban** (1999):

---

1 metric ton = about 1.1 short tons;   1 kilometer = 0.6 mi (statute);   1 metric ton-km cargo = about 0.68 short ton-mi cargo;   c.i.f.: cost, insurance, and freight;   f.o.b.: free on board

56.0%. **Sex distribution** (2000): male 50.46%; female 49.54%. **Age breakdown** (1999): under 15, 31.7%; 15–29, 27.4%; 30–44, 20.9%; 45–59, 12.0%; 60–74, 5.9%; 75 and over, 2.1%. **Ethnic composition** (1992): mestizo 64.0%; black and mulatto 14.0%; white 10.0%; Amerindian 8.0%; Asian 4.0%. **Religious affiliation** (1995): Roman Catholic 80.2%; Protestant 15.0%, of which Pentecostal 8.4%; other Christian 1.6%; other 3.2%. **Major cities** (2000): Panama City 415,064 (urban agglomeration [1999] 1,141,000); San Miguelito 293,745; David 77,734; Arraiján 63,753; La Chorrera 55,871. **Location:** Central America, bordering the Caribbean Sea, Colombia, the North Pacific Ocean, and Costa Rica.

Vital statistics

Birth rate per 1,000 pop. (2000): 19.5 (world avg. 22.5). **Death rate** per 1,000 pop. (2000): 5.0 (world avg. 9.0). **Natural increase rate** per 1,000 pop. (2000): 14.5 (world avg. 13.5). **Total fertility rate** (avg. births per childbearing woman; 2000): 2.3. **Marriage rate** per 1,000 pop. (1997; excludes indigenous pop.): 4.1. **Divorce rate** per 1,000 pop. (1997; excludes indigenous pop.): 0.7. **Life expectancy** at birth (2000): male 72.7 years; female 78.3 years.

National economy

Budget (1997). *Revenue:* B 2,266,300,000 (tax revenue 70.3%, of which income taxes 20.2%, social security contributions 19.1%; nontax revenue 26.8%, of which entrepreneurial and property income 15.4%). *Expenditures:* B 2,341,300,000 (social security and welfare 20.5%; health 18.7%; education 18.3%; economic affairs 8.0%; defense 5.0%). **Public debt** (external, outstanding; 1999): $5,678,000,000. **Production** (metric tons except as noted). *Agriculture, forestry, fishing* (1999): sugarcane 2,050,000, bananas 650,000, rice 232,000; livestock (number of live animals; 1999) 1,400,000 cattle, 252,000 pigs, 165,000 horses; roundwood (1998) 1,098,300 cu m; fish catch (value of production in B '000,000; 1998): fish 63, shrimps 40. *Mining and quarrying* (1997): limestone 326,000; gold 38,600 troy oz. *Manufacturing* (value of production in B '000,000; 1998): food products 1,203, of which meat 341, dairy products 144; refined petroleum 299. *Energy production (consumption):* electricity (kW-hr; 1998) 4,183,000,000 (3,416,-000,000); coal (metric tons; 1996) (56,000); crude petroleum (barrels; 1996) (12,615,000); petroleum products (metric tons; 1996) 1,171,000 (1,497,000); natural gas (cu m; 1996) (60,736,000). **Tourism** (1999): receipts from visitors $538,000,000; expenditures by nationals abroad $184,000,000. **Household income and expenditure.** Average household size (2000) 4.2; average annual income per household (1990) B 5,450; expenditure (1983–84; Panama City only): food and beverages 34.9%, transportation and communications 15.1%, housing and energy 12.6%, education and recreation 11.7%. **Population economically active** (1998; excludes indigenous pop): total 1,083,580; activity rate of total pop. 42.2% (est.); (participation rates: ages 15–69 [1997] 64.3%, female [1997] 35.6%, unemployed 13.6%). **Gross national product** (1999): $8,657,000,000 ($3,080 per capita). **Land use** (1994): forested 43.8%; meadows and pastures 19.8%; agricultural and under permanent cultivation 8.9%; other 27.5%.

Foreign trade

Imports (1998-c.i.f.): B 3,398,000,000 (machinery and apparatus 22.9%, transport equipment 15.1%, mineral fuels 10.3%, chemicals and chemical products 9.6%). *Major import sources:* US 39.7%; Colón Free Zone 12.8%; Japan 9.0%; Mexico 4.8%; Ecuador 3.2%. **Exports** (1998-f.o.b.): B 705,000,000 (bananas 19.7%, shrimps 10.4%, fish 7.9%, sugar 3.6%, clothing 3.6%). *Major export destinations:* US 40.0%; Sweden 7.2%; Costa Rica 6.6%; Spain 5.4%; Belgium 4.3% (excludes Colón Free Zone [1998 imports f.o.b. B 5,319,000,000; 1998 reexports f.o.b. B 5,969,-000,000, of which machinery and apparatus 28.4%, textiles and clothing 21.3%]).

Transport and communications

Transport. *Railroads* (1997): route length 354 km. *Roads* (1997): total length 11,301 km (paved 33%). *Vehicles:* passenger cars (1996) 203,760; trucks and buses 74,637. Panama Canal traffic (1997–98): oceangoing transits 13,158; cargo 189,865,000 metric tons. *Air transport* (1998; COPA only): passenger-km 1,373,000,000; metric ton-km cargo 21,778,000; airports (1996) 10. **Communications** Total units (units per 1,000 persons). Daily newspaper circulation (1996): 166,000 (63); Radio receivers (1997): 815,000 (306); Television receivers (1998): 530,000 (195); Telephone main lines (1999): 462,476 (166); Cellular telephone subscribers (1999): 242,000 (87); Personal computers (1999): 90,000 (32); Internet users (1999): 45,000 (16).

Education and health

Educational attainment (1990). Percentage of pop. age 25 and over having: no formal schooling 11.6%; primary 41.6%; secondary 28.7%; undergraduate 12.4%; graduate 0.7%; other/unknown 5.0%. **Literacy** (1995): total pop. age 15 and over literate 1,590,000 (90.8%). **Health** (1998): physicians 3,518 (1 per 772 persons); hospital beds 7,287 (1 per 373 persons); infant mortality rate per 1,000 live births (2000) 20.8. **Food** (1999): daily per capita caloric intake 2,496 (vegetable products 78%, animal products 22%); 108% of FAO recommended minimum.

Did you know? Construction began on the Torre Generali building in Panama City in mid 2000. Upon completion in 2003 it will be the tallest building in Latin America.

Military

Total active duty personnel. Panama has an 11,000-member national police force. **Military expenditure as percentage of GNP** (1997): 1.4% (world avg. 2.6%); per capita expenditure $43.

Background

Panama was inhabited by Native Americans when the Spanish arrived in 1501. The first successful Spanish settlement was founded by Vasco Núñez de Balboa in 1510. Panama was part of the viceroyalty of New Granada until it declared its independence from

Spain in 1821 to join the Gran Colombia union. In 1903 it revolted against Colombia and was recognized by the US, to whom it ceded the Canal Zone. The completed Panama Canal was opened in 1914; its jurisdiction reverted from the US to Panama in 1999. An invasion by US troops in 1989 overthrew the de facto ruler, Gen. Manuel Noriega.

Recent Developments

In conjunction with the 1999 canal handover, the US military left Panama. The same year, Panama elected its first female president, Mireya Moscoso Rodríguez. Mass protests were sparked in 2001 by a 67% transit hike that had been part of a government effort to modernize public transportation. Under pressure, the government formed a negotiating commission and in the end backed away from the hike.

Internet resources: <www.ipat.gob.pa> (Spanish only)

Papua New Guinea

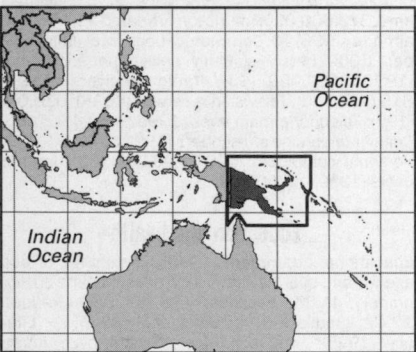

Official name: Independent State of Papua New Guinea. **Form of government:** constitutional monarchy with one legislative house (National Parliament [109]). **Chief of state:** Queen Elizabeth II represented by Governor-General Silas Atopare (from 1997). **Head of government:** Prime Minister Sir Michael Somare (from 5 Aug 2002). **Capital:** Port Moresby. **Official language:** English; English, Motu, and Tok Pisin (English Creole) are national languages. **Official religion:** none. **Monetary unit:** 1 Papua New Guinea kina (K) = 100 toea; valuation (28 Jun 2002) $1 = K 3.98.

Demography

Area: 178,704 sq mi, 462,840 sq km. **Population** (2001): 5,287,000. **Density** (2001): persons per sq mi 29.6, persons per sq km 11.4. **Urban** (2000): 15.0%. **Sex distribution** (2000): male 51.30%; female 48.70%. **Age breakdown** (2000): under 15, 38.8%; 15–29, 28.7%; 30–44, 17.1%; 45–59, 9.7%; 60–74, 4.7%; 75 and over, 1.0%. **Ethnic composition** (1983): New Guinea Papuan 84.0%; New Guinea Melanesian 15.0%; other 1.0%. **Religious affiliation** (1990): non-Anglican Protestant 64.3%, of which Evangelical Lutheran 23.2%, Uniting Church 12.7%, Seventh-day Adventist 8.1%, Pentecostal 7.1%;

Roman Catholic 28.3%; Anglican 3.9%; other (mostly animists) 3.5%. **Major cities** (1997): Port Moresby 271,813; Lae 113,118; Madang 32,117; Wewak 25,143; Goroka 17,269. **Location:** group of islands, including the eastern half of the island of New Guinea in the South Pacific Ocean near the Equator bordering Indonesia and to the north of Australia.

Vital statistics

Birth rate per 1,000 pop. (2000): 32.7 (world avg. 22.5). **Death rate** per 1,000 pop. (2000): 8.0 (world avg. 9.0). **Natural increase rate** per 1,000 pop. (2000): 24.7 (world avg. 13.5). **Total fertility rate** (avg. births per childbearing woman; 2000): 4.4. **Life expectancy** at birth (2000): male 61.1 years; female 65.3 years.

National economy

Budget (2000). *Revenue:* K 2,866,700,000 (tax revenue 72.5%, of which income tax 19.5%, corporate tax 18.3%, VAT 11.8%; foreign grants 18.9%, nontax revenue 8.6%). *Expenditures:* K 3,081,-800,000 (current expenditure 70.8%, of which transfer to provincial governments 16.8%, interest payments 12.4%; development expenditure 29.2%). **Public debt** (external, outstanding; 1999): $1,517,-000,000. **Production** (metric tons except as noted). *Agriculture, forestry, fishing* (2000): coconuts 826,000, bananas 700,000, sweet potatoes 480,000; livestock (number of live animals) 1,500,000 pigs, 87,000 cattle, 3,600,000 chickens; roundwood (2000) 8,597,000 cu m; fish catch (1999) 53,763. *Mining and quarrying* (1999): copper (metal content) 187,900; silver (metal content) 66,500; gold 65,700 kg. *Manufacturing* (1998): palm oil 241,485; copra 124,349; coffee 80,700. *Energy production (consumption):* electricity (kW-hr; 1997) 1,161,900,000 ([1996] 1,790,000,000); coal (metric tons; 1996) (1,000); crude petroleum (barrels; 1996) 546,000 (7,500); natural gas (cu m; 1996) 83,300,000 (83,300,000); petroleum products (metric tons; 1996) 50,000 (727,000). **Land use** (1997): forested 92.3%; agricultural and under permanent cultivation 1.5%; meadows and pastures 0.2%; other 6.0%. **Gross national product** (1999): $3,834,000,000 ($810 per capita). **Population economically active** (1990; persons in "money-raising activities" only): total 1,715,330; activity rate 36.9% (participation rates: over age 10 [1980] 35.2%; female 41.5%; unemployed 7.7%). **Tourism** (1999): receipts $76,000,000; expenditures $53,000,000.

Foreign trade

Imports (2000): K 2,758,100,000 (1998; nonelectrical machinery 18.3%; food and live animals 16.2%; transport equipment 14.8%; chemicals and chemical products 9.6%; fabricated metals 8.6%%). *Major import sources* (1999): Australia 53.5%; Singapore 12.9%; Japan 5.6%; New Zealand 4.1%; US 3.6%. **Exports** (2000): K 4,695,000,000 (gold 35.3%; crude petroleum 19.8%; copper 14.7%; coffee 7.0%; palm oil 5.2%). *Major export destinations* (1999): Australia 38.1%; Japan 16.9%; Germany 9.6%; US 6.6%; South Korea 5.8%.

1 metric ton = about 1.1 short tons;   1 kilometer = 0.6 mi (statute);   1 metric ton-km cargo = about 0.68 short ton-mi cargo;   c.i.f.: cost, insurance, and freight;   f.o.b.: free on board

Transport and communications

Transport. *Roads* (1000): total length 19,736 km (paved 6%). *Vehicles* (1994): passenger cars 13,000; trucks and buses 32,000. *Air transport* (1997): passenger-km 735,000,000; metric ton-km cargo 86,000,000; airports (1999) with scheduled flights 42.

Communications. Total units (units per 1,000 persons). Daily newspapers circulation (1996): 65,000 (15); Radio receivers (1997): 410,000 (91); Television receivers (1999): 60,000 (13); Telephone main lines (1999): 59,773 (13); Cellular telephones (1999): 7,059 (1.5); Internet users (1999): 2,000 (0.7).

Education and health

Educational attainment (1990). Percentage of pop. age 25 and over having: no formal schooling 82.6%; some primary education 8.2%; completed primary 5.0%; some secondary 4.2%. **Literacy** (1995 est.): total pop. age 15 and over literate 72.2%; males literate 81.0%; females literate 62.7%. **Health:** physicians (1998) 342 (1 per 13,708 persons); hospital beds (1989) 15,335 (1 per 234 persons); infant mortality rate (2000) 59.9. **Food** (1999): daily per capita caloric intake 2,186 (vegetable products 89%, animal products 11%); 96% of FAO recommended minimum.

Military

Total active duty personnel (1999): 4,400 (army 86.4%, navy 9.1%, air force 4.5%). **Military expenditure as percentage of GNP** (1997): 1.3% (world 2.6%); per capita expenditure $14.

Background

Papua New Guinea has been inhabited since prehistoric times. The Portuguese sighted the coast in 1512, and in 1545 the Spanish claimed the island. The first colony was founded in 1793 by the British. In 1828 the Dutch claimed the western half as part of the Dutch East Indies. In 1884 Britain annexed the southeastern part and Germany took over the northeastern sector. The British part became the Territory of Papua in 1906 and passed to Australia, which also governed the German sector after World War I. After World War II, Australia governed both sectors as the Territory of Papua and New Guinea. Dutch New Guinea was annexed to Indonesia in 1969. Papua New Guinea achieved independence in 1975 and joined the British Commonwealth. It moved to resolve its war with Bougainville independence fighters in 1997.

Recent Developments

In a dramatic atmosphere of crisis, the National Parliament voted in July 1999 to replace Sir Bill Skate as prime minister. Almost the whole of the government defected to Sir Mekere Morauta. The decade-long war on the island of Bougainville ended when final terms for peace were negotiated on 1 Jun 2001. Under an agreement signed by the minister for Bougainville affairs, Moi Avei, on behalf of the national government, the island was to have statelike autonomy and the option of total independence by 2011–16. Widespread breakdowns in law and order caused by difficult economic conditions and popular hostility to the Papua New Guinea Privatization Commission, the World Bank, and the International Monetary Fund posed serious problems in 2001. In Port Moresby four students died during protests against privatization.

Internet resources: <www.paradiselive.org.pg>

Paraguay

Official name: República del Paraguay (Spanish); Tetã Paraguáype (Guaraní) (Republic of Paraguay). **Form of government:** multiparty republic with two legislative houses (Senate [46; includes 1 nonelective seat]; Chamber of Deputies [80]). **Head of state and government:** President Luis González Macchi (from 1999). **Capital:** Asunción. **Official languages:** Spanish; Guaraní. **Official religion:** none, although Roman Catholicism enjoys special recognition in the 1992 constitution. **Monetary unit:** 1 Paraguayan Guaraní (G) = 100 céntimos; valuation (28 Jun 2002) $1 = G 5,845.00.

Demography

Area: 157,048 sq mi, 406,752 sq km. **Population** (2001): 5,636,000. **Density** (2001): persons per sq mi 35.9, persons per sq km 13.9. **Urban** (1999): 54.0%. **Sex distribution** (1999): male 50.42%; female 49.58%. **Age breakdown** (1999): under 15, 39.3%; 15–29, 26.2%; 30–44, 17.9%; 45–59, 9.9%; 60–74, 5.1%; 75 and over, 1.6%. **Ethnic composition** (2000): mixed (white/Amerindian) 85.6%; white 9.3%, of which German 4.4%, Latin American 3.4%; Amerindian 1.8%; black 1.0%; other 2.3%. **Religious affiliation** (1995): Roman Catholic 88.5%; Protestant 5.0%; other 0.5%. **Major cities** (1992): Asunción 500,938 (urban agglomeration [1999] 1,224,000); Ciudad del Este 133,881; San Lorenzo 133,395; Lambaré 99,572. **Location:** central South America, bordering Brazil, Argentina, and Bolivia.

Vital statistics

Birth rate per 1,000 pop. (2000): 31.3 (world avg. 22.5). **Death rate** per 1,000 pop. (2000): 4.8 (world avg. 9.0). **Natural increase rate** per 1,000 pop. (2000): 26.5 (world avg. 13.5). **Total fertility rate** (avg. births per childbearing woman; 2000): 4.2. **Marriage rate** per 1,000 pop. (1999; civil registry records): 3.6.

Life expectancy at birth (2000): male 71.2 years; female 76.3 years.

National economy

Budget (1999): Revenue: G4,011,200,000,000 (tax revenue 69.4%, of which taxes on goods and services 39.0%, income tax 13.4%, customs duties 10.3%, social security 6.7%; nontax revenue including grants 30.6%). Expenditures: G4,605,800,000,000 (current expenditure 75.6%; capital expenditure 24.4%). Public debt (external, outstanding; 1999): $1,672,000,-000. Population economically active (1996): total 1,747,488; activity rate 35.3% (participation rates [1992]: ages 12 and over, 51.0%; female 23.8%; unemployed [1998] 7.2%). Production (metric tons except as noted). Agriculture, forestry, fishing (1999): cassava 3,500,000, soybeans 3,303,500; livestock (number of live animals) 9,863,000 cattle, 2,500,-000 pigs, 15,000,000 chickens; roundwood (1998) 8,097,000 cu m; fish catch (1998) 26,000. Mining and quarrying (1997): limestone 600,000; kaolin 66,700; gypsum 4,500. Manufacturing (value added in constant prices of 1982, G'000,000; 1998): food products 59,100; wood products and furniture 23,500; handicrafts 10,300; printing and publishing 9,200. Energy production (consumption): electricity (kW-hr; 1996) 48,200,000,000 (7,938,000,000); crude petroleum (barrels; 1996) (1,143,000); petroleum products (metric tons; 1996) 157,000 (1,084,000). Gross national product (1999): $8,374,-000,000 ($1,560 per capita). Household income and expenditure. Average household size (1999) 4.6; sources of income (1989): wages and salaries 33.9%, transfer payments 2.5%. Tourism (1999): receipts $81,000,000; expenditures $109,000,000.

Foreign trade

Imports (1998-f.o.b.): $2,470,800,000 (machinery and transport equipment 30.6%, of which transport equipment 8.1%; food, beverages, and tobacco 23.7%; fuels and lubricants 7.6%; chemicals and pharmaceuticals 5.4%). Major import sources: Brazil 32.2%; US 20.2%; Argentina 15.6%; Hong Kong 6.9%; Japan 2.7%. Exports (1998): $1,014,100,000 (soybean flour 43.4%; cotton fibers 9.1%; timber 6.9%; vegetable oil 7.5%, of which soybean oil 6.0%; processed meats 6.7%; hides and skins 3.8%). Major export destinations: Brazil 28.1%; Argentina 25.7%; The Netherlands 15.3%; Japan 4.8%; Chile 4.7%.

Transport and communications

Transport. Railroads (1998): route length 441 km; passenger-km 3,000,000; metric ton-km cargo 5,500,000. Roads (1997): total length 29,500 km (paved 10%). Vehicles (1996): passenger cars 71,000; trucks 50,000. Air transport (1997): passenger-km 215,000,000; metric ton-km cargo 19,000,000; airports (1998) 5. Communications Total units (units per 1,000 persons). Daily newspaper circulation (1996): 213,000 (43); Radio receivers (1997): 925,000 (182); Television receivers (1999): 1,100,000 (205); Telephone main lines (1999): 297,000 (55); Cellular telephone subscribers (1999): 435,610 (81); Personal computers (1999): 60,000 (11); Internet users (1999): 20,000 (3.7).

Education and health

Educational attainment (1999). Percentage of pop. age 15 and over having: no formal schooling 5.5%; primary education 52.8%; secondary 34.0%; higher 7.6%; not stated 0.1%. Literacy (1999): percentage of total pop. age 15 and over literate 92.3%; males literate 94.1%; female literate 90.6%. Health (1995): physicians 3,730 (1 per 1,294 persons); hospital beds 6,759 (1 per 714 persons); infant mortality rate per 1,000 live births (2000) 30.8. Food (1999): daily per capita caloric intake 2,588 (vegetable products 76%, animal products 24%); 112% of FAO recommended minimum.

Military

Total active duty personnel (2000): 20,200 (army 73.8%, navy 17.8%, air force 8.4%). Military expenditure as percentage of GNP (1997): 1.3% (world 2.6%), per capita expenditure $25.

Background

Seminomadic tribes speaking Guaraní were in Paraguay long before it was settled by Spain in the 16th–17th centuries. Paraguay was part of the viceroyalty of Río de la Plata until it became independent in 1811. It suffered from dictatorial governments in the 19th century and from the 1865 war with Brazil, Argentina, and Uruguay. The Chaco War with Bolivia over disputed territory was settled primarily in Paraguay's favor by the peace treaty of 1938. Military governments, including that of Alfredo Stroessner, predominated in the mid-20th century until the election of a civilian president, Juan Carlos Wasmosy, in 1993. Paraguay suffered a financial crisis in the late 1990s, and democratic government was in jeopardy.

Recent Developments

In 1999 Paraguay faced a political crisis. Pres. Raúl Cubas Grau refused a Supreme Court order to return his political mentor, retired general Lino Oviedo, to prison to serve out his term for an attempted coup in 1996. Vice Pres. Luis María Argaña sought to undermine Cubas so that he could assume office. On 23 March Argaña was assassinated by a group allegedly linked to Oviedo. Protesters filled the streets of Asunción demanding Cubas's resignation and the detention of Oviedo, and Congress began impeachment proceedings. Oviedo followers fired on the demonstrators, claiming at least four lives. By 29 March Cubas had resigned, and both he and Oviedo fled the country. The president of the legislature, Luis Ángel González Macchi, was inaugurated president of the country. In May 2000 rebels said to be loyalists of Oviedo attempted to overthrow the government, prompting González to declare a state of emergency. During 2001 Paraguay faced a series of political and socioeconomic challenges—largely dealing with corruption scandals and ineffective economic policies—that threatened to overwhelm the country's weak democracy and fragile economic system. Opposition parties and striking workers demanded González's removal from office.

Internet resources: <www.onparaguay.com>

1 metric ton = about 1.1 short tons;   1 kilometer = 0.6 mi (statute);   1 metric ton-km cargo = about 0.68 short ton-mi cargo;   c.i.f.: cost, insurance, and freight;   f.o.b.: free on board

Peru

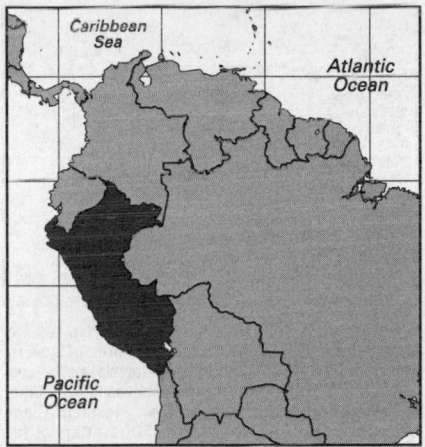

Caribbean Sea

Atlantic Ocean

Pacific Ocean

Official name: República del Perú (Spanish) (Republic of Peru). **Form of government:** unitary multiparty republic with one legislative house (Congress [120]). **Head of state and government:** President Alejandro Toledo (from 28 Jul 2001). **Capital:** Lima. **Official languages:** Spanish; Quechua; Aymara. **Official religion:** Roman Catholicism. **Monetary unit:** 1 nuevo sol (S/.) = 100 céntimos; valuation (28 Jun 2002) $1 = S/. 3.51.

Demography

Area: 496,225 sq mi, 1,285,216 sq km. **Population** (2001): 26,090,000. **Density** (2001): persons per sq mi 52.6, persons per sq km 20.3. **Urban** (2000): 72.3%. **Sex distribution** (2000): male 49.59%; female 50.41%. **Age breakdown** (2000): under 15, 33.4%; 15–29, 29.1%; 30–44, 19.3%; 45–59, 10.9%; 60–74, 5.7%; 75 and over, 1.6%. **Ethnic composition** (2000): Quechua 47.0%; mestizo 31.9%; white 12.0%; Aymara 5.4%; Japanese 0.5%; other 3.2%. **Religious affiliation** (1995): Roman Catholic 88.8%; Protestant 6.7%; other Christian 1.5%; other 3.0%. **Major cities** (1998 est.): metropolitan Lima 7,060,600; Arequipa 710,103; Trujillo 603,657; Chiclayo 469,200; Iquitos 334,013. **Location:** western South America, bordering Ecuador, Colombia, Brazil, Bolivia, Chile, and the South Pacific Ocean.

Vital statistics

Birth rate per 1,000 pop. (2000): 24.5 (world avg. 22.5); (1977) legitimate 57.8%; illegitimate 42.2%. **Death rate** per 1,000 pop. (2000): 5.8 (world avg. 9.0). **Natural increase rate** per 1,000 pop. (2000): 18.7 (world avg. 13.5). **Total fertility rate** (avg. births per childbearing woman; 2000): 3.0. **Life expectancy** at birth (2000): male 67.6 years; female 72.5 years.

National economy

Budget (1998). *Revenue:* S/. 25,980,000,000 (taxes on goods and services 54.3%, income taxes 22.6%, import duties 9.5%, nontax revenue 7.0%, payroll tax 4.9%). *Expenditures:* S/. 27,389,000,000 (current expenditure 69.5%, capital expenditure 19.4%, interest

payments 11.1%). **Public debt** (external, outstanding; 1999): $20,709,000,000. **Tourism** (1999): receipts $890,000,000; expenditures $443,000,000. **Production** (metric tons except as noted). *Agriculture, forestry, fishing* (1999): sugarcane 6,900,000, potatoes 3,050,000, rice 1,947,000; livestock (number of live animals) 13,700,000 sheep, 4,898,000 cattle, 2,784,000 pigs; roundwood (1998) 9,157,000 cu m; fish catch (1998) 4,338,437. *Mining and quarrying* (1998): iron ore 3,224,000; zinc 725,000; copper 356,000. *Manufacturing* (value in S/. '000,000 [1979 prices]; 1996): processed foods 275.1; base metal products 188.6; textiles and leather products 129.5. *Energy production (consumption):* electricity (kW-hr; 1996) 20,038,000,000 (20,038,000,000); coal (metric tons; 1996) 58,000 (302,000); crude petroleum (barrels; 1996) 44,000,000 (52,000,000). **Household income and expenditure.** Average household size (1993) 5.1; Income per household (1988); sources of income (1991): business income 67.1%, wages 23.3%, transfers 7.6%, other 2.0%; expenditure (1990): food 29.4%, recreation and education 13.2%, household durables 10.1%, clothing and footwear 8.5%, transportation 7.5%, health 7.0%. **Gross national product** (at current market prices; 1999): $53,705,000,000 ($2,130 per capita). **Population economically active** (1998): total 7,407,280; activity rate of total pop. 45.7% (participation rates: over age 15, 66.9%; female 43.8%; unemployed 7.7%). **Land use** (1998): forest and other 75.7%; pasture 21.1%; agricultural 3.2%.

Foreign trade

Imports (1998): $8,200,000,000 (raw and intermediate materials 41.3%, machinery 24.9%, consumer goods 23.0%, transport equipment 6.7%). *Major import sources:* US 32.5%; Colombia 7.4%; Germany 5.6%; Venezuela 4.3%. **Exports** (1998): $5,722,900,000 (gold 16.2%, copper and copper products 13.6%, zinc products 7.8%, fish meal fodder 6.8%, coffee 5.0%, petroleum and derivatives 3.9%, lead products 3.7%, silver 2.3%, tin 2.1%). *Major export destinations:* US 32.3%; Japan 8.7%; UK 4.8%; Switzerland 4.2%; Spain 4.1%.

Transport and communications

Transport. *Railroads* (1996): route length 1,992 km; passenger-km 171,091,000; metric ton-km cargo 850,329,000. *Roads* (1996): total length 73,766 km (paved 12%). *Vehicles* (1996): passenger cars 557,042; trucks and buses 359,374. *Air transport* (1996): passenger-km 2,634,000,000; metric ton-km cargo 251,000,000; airports (1996) 27. **Communications** Total units (units per 1,000 persons). Daily newspaper circulation (1996): 2,000,000 (84); Radio receivers (1997): 6,650,000 (270); Television receivers (1999): 3,700,000 (147); Telephone main lines (1999): 1,688,600 (67); Cellular telephone subscribers (1999): 1,013,314 (40); Personal computers (1999): 900,000 (36); Internet users (1999): 400,000 (16).

Education and health

Educational attainment (1993). Percentage of pop. age 15 and over having: no formal schooling 12.3%; less than primary education 0.3%; primary 31.5%; secondary 35.5%; higher 20.4%. **Literacy** (1995): total pop. age 15 and over literate 88.0%; males

93.5%; females 82.7%. **Health:** physicians (1996) 24,708 (1 per 969 persons); hospital beds (1994) 42,979 (1 per 538 persons); infant mortality rate per 1,000 live births (2000) 40.6. **Food** (1999): daily per capita caloric intake 2,621 (vegetable products 87%, animal products 13%); (1997) 112% of FAO recommended minimum.

Military

Total active duty personnel (2000): 115,000 (army 65.2%, navy 21.7%, air force 13.1%). **Military expenditure as percentage of GNP** (1997): 2.1% (world 2.6%); per capita expenditure $55.

Background

Peru was the center of the Inca empire, which was established about 1230 with its capital at Cuzco. In 1533 it was conquered by Francisco Pizarro, and it was dominated by Spain for almost 300 years as the viceroyalty of Peru. It declared its independence in 1821, and freedom was achieved in 1824. Peru was defeated in the War of the Pacific with Chile (1879–83). A boundary dispute with Ecuador erupted into war in 1941 and gave Peru control over a larger part of the Amazon basin; further disputes ensued until the border was demarcated again in 1998. The government was overthrown by a military junta in 1968, and civilian rule was restored in 1980. The government of Alberto Fujimori dissolved the legislature in 1992 and promulgated a new constitution the following year. It later successfully combated the Shining Path and Tupac Amarú rebel movements. Fujimori won a second term in 1995.

Recent Developments

Peru underwent a tumultuous and volatile year in 2000 as a cascade of events threatened the very fabric of its political system. Charges of fraud accompanied Fujimori's election to a third term. When inauguration day arrived on 28 July, widespread demonstrations occurred in Lima, sparked largely by outrage at Fujimori's undemocratic actions. In September two scandals shook the administration to its roots. The first involved an arms-smuggling scheme whereby Peruvian military officers purchased automatic weapons from Jordan and then sold them to Colombian guerrillas for a profit. The second concerned a videotape showing an opposition congressman accepting a bribe to switch his vote to Fujimori. These events persuaded Fujimori to call for new presidential and congressional elections. In November he announced from Japan that he was resigning as president and would not return to Peru. In his absence Valentin Paniagua was named interim president. Paniagua was able to bring a certain calm to Peru, stabilize a chaotic political situation, and shepherd elections through two rounds in mid- 2001. Alejandro Toledo became Peru's first democratically elected president of Quechua ethnicity. A fire in Lima at the end of the year left some 300 dead. In mid-2002 procedures were underway to request the extradition of Fujimori from Japan to face murder charges.

Internet resources: <www.peru.org.pe>

Philippines

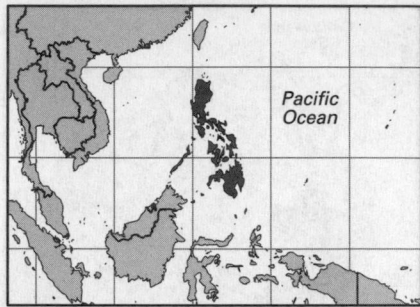

Pacific Ocean

Official name: Republika ng Pilipinas (Pilipino); Republic of the Philippines (English). **Form of government:** unitary republic with two legislative houses (Senate [24]; House of Representatives [260]). **Chief of state and head of government:** President Gloria Macapagal Arroyo (from 20 Jan 2001). **Capital** (region): Quezon City/Manila. **Official languages:** Pilipino; English. **Official religion:** none. **Monetary unit:** 1 Philippine peso (P) = 100 centavos; valuation (28 Jun 2002) $1 = P 50.33.

Demography

Area: 115,860 sq mi, 300,076 sq km. **Population** (2001): 78,609,000. **Density** (2001): persons per sq mi 678.5, persons per sq km 262.0. **Urban** (2001): 59.0%. **Sex distribution** (2000): male 50.37%; female 49.63%. **Age breakdown** (2000): under 15, 36.2%; 15–29, 28.1%; 30–44, 19.0%; 45–59, 10.7%; 60–74, 4.8%; 75 and over, 1.2%. **Ethnolinguistic composition** (by mother tongue of households; 1995): Pilipino (Tagalog) 29.3%; Cebuano 23.3%; Ilocano 9.3%; Hiligaynon Ilongo 9.1%; Bicol 5.7%; Waray 3.8%; Pampango 3.0%; Pangasinan 1.8%; other 14.7%. **Religious affiliation** (1996): Roman Catholic 82.9%; Protestant 5.4%; Muslim 4.6%; Aglipayan (Philippine Independent Church) 2.6%; other 4.5%. **Major cities** (2000): Quezon City 2,173,831; Manila 1,581,082; Caloocan 1,177,604; Davao 1,147,116; Cebu 718,821. **Location:** southeastern Asia, archipelago between the Philippine Sea and the South China Sea, east of Vietnam.

Vital statistics

Birth rate per 1,000 pop. (2001): 26.7 (world avg. 22.5); (1982) legitimate 93.9%; illegitimate 6.1%. **Death rate** per 1,000 pop. (2001): 5.3 (world avg. 9.0). **Natural increase rate** per 1,000 pop. (2001): 21.4 (world avg. 13.5). **Total fertility rate** (avg. births per childbearing woman; 2001): 3.3. **Life expectancy** at birth (2001): male 68.0 years; female 72.0 years.

National economy

Budget (1998). *Revenue:* P 462,515,000,000 (income taxes 39.8%, taxes on goods and services 27.8%, international duties 16.5%, nontax revenues 9.9%). *Expenditures:* P 528,263,000,000 (debt service 20.4%, education 20.1%, transportation and

1 metric ton = about 1.1 short tons; 1 kilometer = 0.6 mi (statute); 1 metric ton km cargo = about 0.68 short ton-mi cargo; c.i.f.: cost, insurance, and freight; f.o.b.: free on board

communications 8.5%, public order and safety 7.3%, general administration 6.8%, defense 5.6%). **Production** (metric tons except as noted). *Agriculture, forestry, fishing* (2000): sugarcane 33,732,000, rice 12,415,000, coconuts 5,761,000; livestock (number of live animals) 10,398,000 pigs, 6,780,000 goats, 3,018,000 buffalo; roundwood (1999) 43,399,000 cu m; fish catch (1998) 1,827,971. *Mining and quarrying* (1999): nickel ore 436,970; copper concentrate 98,857; chrome concentrate 17,562. *Manufacturing* (gross value added in P '000,000; 1998): food products 246,300; electrical machinery 53,000; chemicals 49,100. *Energy production (consumption):* electricity (kW-hr; 1996) 34,775,000,000 (34,775,000,000); coal (metric tons; 1996) 1,109,000 (2,589,000); crude petroleum (barrels; 1996) 3,000,000 (117,000,000). **Household income and expenditure** (2000). Average household size 5.0; income per family P 144,506; sources of income (1997): wages 45.6%, entrepreneurial income 26.2%, rent 10.3%, transfers 6.8%, other 11.1%; expenditure: food, beverage, and tobacco 45.0%, housing 15.1%, transportation 6.8%, fuel and power 6.2%, education 4.2%, personal care 3.6%. **Gross national product** (1999): $77,967,-000,000 ($1,050 per capita). **Public debt** (external, outstanding; 1999): $33,568,000,000. **Population economically active** (2000): total 31,848,000; activity rate 41.5% (participation rates: ages 15–64, 65.0%; female [1995] 37.4%; unemployed 9.3%). **Tourism** (1999): receipts $2,534,000,000; expenditures $1,308,000,000.

Foreign trade

Imports (1999-c.i.f.): $30,723,340,000 (chemicals 8.1%, mineral fuels and lubricants 7.9%, power generating and specialized machinery 7.8%, telecommunications equipment and electrical machinery 7.6%, base metals 4.3%). *Major import sources:* US 20.7%; Japan 19.9%; South Korea 8.9%; Singapore 5.7%; Taiwan 5.3%. **Exports** (1999-f.o.b.): $35,036,560,000 (electronics 56.2%, garments 6.5%, ignition wiring sets 1.5%, woodcraft and furniture 1.4%, coconut oil 1.0%, bananas 0.7%). *Major export destinations:* US 29.6%; Japan 13.0%; Taiwan 8.5%; The Netherlands 8.2%; Singapore 7.0%; Hong Kong 5.6%.

Transport and communications

Transport. *Railroads* (2000): route length 897 km; passenger-km 12,000,000; metric ton-km cargo 660,000,000. *Roads* (1998): total length 199,950 km (paved 39%). *Vehicles* (1998): passenger cars 745,144; trucks and buses 263,037. *Air transport* (1999; Philippines Airlines): passenger-km 10,292,-338,000; metric ton-km cargo 240,918,000; airports (1996) with scheduled flights 21. **Communications** Total Units (units per 1,000 persons). Daily newspaper circulation (1990). 5,700,000 (82); Radio receivers (1997): 11,500,000 (161); Television receivers (1999): 8,200,000 (110); Telephone main lines (1999): 2,892,000 (39); Cellular telephone subscribers (1999): 2,850,000 (38); Personal computers (1999): 1,260,000 (17); Internet users (1999): 500,000 (6.7).

Education and health

Education attainment (1995). Percentage of pop. age 15 and over having: no schooling 3.7%; elemen-

tary education 35.8%; secondary 38.4%; postsecondary 21.9%; not stated 0.2%. **Literacy** (1995): total pop. age 15 and over literate 94.6%; males literate 95.0%; females literate 94.3%. **Health:** physicians (1993) 78,445 (1 per 849 persons); hospital beds (1998) 81,200 (1 per 903 persons); infant mortality rate per 1,000 live births (2001) 31.0. **Food** (1999): daily per capita caloric intake 2,357 (vegetable products 85%, animal products 15%); (1997) 104% of FAO recommended minimum.

Military

Total active duty personnel (2000): 106,000 (army 62.3%, navy 22.6%, air force 15.1%). **Military expenditure as percentage of GNP** (1997): 1.5% (world 2.6%); per capita expenditure $17.

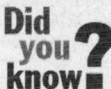

Did you know? The modern-day yo-yo was invented by Pedro Flores from the Philippines. The word is Tagalog, meaning "come-come," and is believed to have been used as a weapon by 16th century hunters in the Philippines.

Background

Ferdinand Magellan first arrived in the Philippines in 1521. The islands were colonized by the Spanish, who retained control until the islands were ceded to the US in 1898 following the Spanish-American War. The Commonwealth of the Philippines was established in 1935 to prepare the country for political and economic independence, which was delayed by World War II and the Japanese invasion. The islands were liberated by US forces during 1944–45, and the Republic of the Philippines was proclaimed in 1946, with a government patterned on that of the US. In 1965 Ferdinand Marcos was elected president. He declared martial law in 1972, which lasted until 1981. After 20 years of dictatorial rule, he was driven from power in 1986. Corazon Aquino became president and instituted a period of democratic rule that continued with the 1992 election of Fidel Ramos. Through the 1990s the government tried to come to terms with independence fighters in the southern islands.

Recent Developments

Pres. Joseph Estrada appointed a preparatory commission to recommend changes in the Philippine constitution in 1999. The Philippines argued with Malaysia and China over rights to some of the Spratly Islands in the South China Sea, and tensions led the Philippine Senate to ratify a Visiting Forces Agreement permitting US military visits and joint exercises. On 13 Nov 2000 Estrada was impeached by the House of Representatives, accused of bribery, corruption, betrayal of public trust, and violation of the constitution. Estrada was driven from office on 20 Jan 2001, and Vice Pres. Gloria Macapagal Arroyo took over.

The southern Philippines was disturbed by guerrilla warfare and kidnapping. Some Muslim rebels fought for independence from the predominantly Roman Catholic nation, while other Muslims seemed to be primarily bandits. In April 2001 the Muslim extremist group Abu Sayyaf, thought to be linked to Osama bin Laden, kidnapped 21 people from a Malaysian resort. As various Abu Sayyaf bands seized more

hostages, the government lost its patience, and in September it sent troops to attack the extremists. A larger Islamic group, the Moro Islamic Liberation Front (MILF), continued its long-running fight for independence. After the army captured the MILF's headquarters on Mindanao in July, the exiled MILF leader called for a holy war against the government.

Estrada went on trial in October. More than 100 people were killed in bloody congressional and local elections in May. On Basilan Island, government troops fought Abu Sayyaf as the group continued its campaign of kidnapping and murder. In November a rebel faction of the Moro National Liberation Front launched its own attacks and kidnappings. In early 2002, US troops and Special Forces began training Philippine forces on Basilan and Mindanao in a program to assist in the fight against Abu Sayyaf, which held two Americans hostage. The training exercise was scheduled to last six months, and US troops were required to stay out of actual combat. In April additional US troops arrived for another joint exercise in the northern part of the country.

Internet resources: <www.philstar.com>

Poland

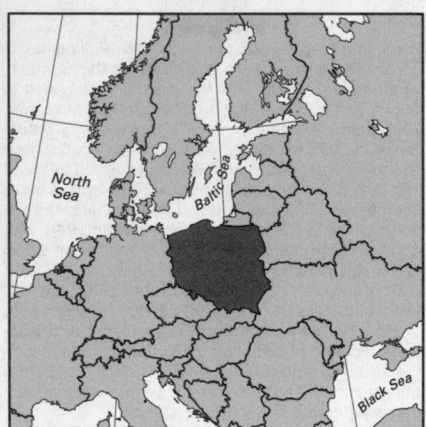

North Sea

Baltic Sea

Black Sea

Official name: Rzeczpospolita Polska (Republic of Poland). **Form of government:** unitary multiparty republic with two legislative houses (Senate [100]; Diet [460]). **Chief of state:** President Aleksander Kwasniewski (from 1995). **Head of government:** Prime Minister Leszek Miller (from 19 Oct 2001). **Capital:** Warsaw. **Official language:** Polish. **Official religion:** none (Roman Catholicism has special recognition per 1997 concordat with the Holy See). **Monetary unit:** 1 zloty (Zl; redenominated at a rate of 10,000 old zloty to 1 new zloty in 1995) = 100 groszy; valuation (28 Jun 2002) $1 = Zl 4.06.

Demography

Area: 120,728 sq mi, 312,685 sq km. **Population** (2001): 38,647,000. **Density** (2001): persons per sq mi 320.1, persons per sq km 123.6. **Urban** (2000):

62.0%. **Sex distribution** (1998): male 48.61%; female 51.39%. **Age breakdown** (1998): under 15, 20.6%; 15–29, 23.3%; 30–44, 22.2%; 45–59, 17.5%; 60–74, 12.2%; 75 and over, 4.2%. **Ethnolinguistic composition** (1997): Polish 94.2%; Ukrainian 3.9%; German 1.3%; Belarusian 0.6%. **Religious affiliation** (1995): Roman Catholic 90.7%; Ukrainian Catholic 1.4%; Polish Orthodox 1.4%; Protestant 0.5%; Jehovah's Witness 0.5%; other (mostly nonreligious) 5.5%. **Major cities** (2000): Warsaw 1,615,369; Lodz 800,110; Krakow 738,150; Wroclaw 636,785; Poznan 576,899. **Location:** Central Europe, bordering the Baltic Sea, Russia (exclave of Kaliningrad), Lithuania, Belarus, Ukraine, Slovakia, Czech Republic, and Germany.

Vital statistics

Birth rate per 1,000 pop. (1999): 9.9 (world avg. 22.5). **Death rate** per 1,000 pop. (1999): 9.9 (world avg. 9.0). **Natural increase rate** per 1,000 pop. (1999): 0.0 (world avg. 13.5). **Total fertility rate** (avg. births per childbearing woman; 2000): 1.4. **Marriage rate** per 1,000 pop. (1999): 5.7. **Divorce rate** per 1,000 pop. (1999): 1.1. **Life expectancy** at birth (2000): male 69.0 years; female 77.6 years.

National economy

Budget (1998). *Revenue:* Zl 126,560,000,000 (income tax 39.1%, value-added tax 33.9%, excise tax 16.6%). *Expenditures:* Zl 139,752,000,000 (social security 18.0%, health 15.0%, education 8.1%, welfare 6.6%, defense 6.0%). **Public debt** (external, outstanding; 1999): $34,528,000,000. **Gross national product** (1999): $157,429,000,000 ($4,070 per capita). **Production** (metric tons except at noted). *Agriculture, forestry, fishing* (1999): (gross value of production in Zl '000,000) potatoes 4,066, wheat 3,747, fruit 3,578; livestock (number of live animals) 18,538,000 pigs, 6,555,000 cattle; roundwood (1999) 24,300,000 cu m; fish catch (1997) 390,586. *Mining and quarrying* (1998): sulfur 1,672,000; copper ore (metal content) 432,243; silver (recoverable metal content) 1,108. *Manufacturing* (value added in Zl '000,000; 1999): food products 13,764; beverages 13,582; transport equipment 10,596. *Energy production (consumption):* electricity ('000,000 kW-hr; 2000) 141,629 ([1996] 136,666); hard coal ('000 metric tons; 2000) 103,173 ([1996] 109,355); lignite ('000 metric tons; 2000) 59,366 ([1996] 63,864); crude petroleum (barrels; 1996) 2,400,000 (107,000,000); petroleum products (metric tons; 1996) 13,691,000 (16,305,000); natural gas (cu m; 2000) 4,970,000,000 ([1996] 14,160,000,000). **Population economically active** (1998): total 17,162,000; activity rate of total pop. 44.4% (participation rates: 15–64, 66.1%; female 45.7%; unemployed [March 2000–February 2001] 14.3%). **Household income and expenditure.** Average household size (1997) 2.9; average annual income (1995) Zl 8,431; sources of income (1996): wages 43.9%, transfers 25.2%, self-employment 21.9%; expenditure (1996): food, beverages, and tobacco 36.3%, housing and energy 19.1%, transportation and communications 11.3%. **Tourism** (1999): receipts $6,100,000,000; expenditures $3,600,000,000. **Land use** (1994): forest 28.8%; meadow 13.3%; agri-

---

1 metric ton = about 1.1 short tons;   1 kilometer – 0.6 mi (statute);   1 metric ton-km cargo = about 0.68 short ton-mi cargo;   c.i.f.: cost, insurance, and freight;   f.o.b.: free on board

cultural and under permanent cultivation 47.0%; other 10.9%.

Foreign trade

Imports (1999): Zl 182,362,000,000 (machinery and transport equipment 38.2%, chemicals and chemical products 14.3%, mineral fuels and lubricants 7.2%, food 5.5%). *Major import sources:* Germany 25.2%; Italy 9.4%; France 6.8%; Russia 5.9%; UK 4.6%. **Exports** (1999): Zl 108,706,000,000 (machinery and transport equipment 30.3%, food 8.5%, chemicals and chemical products 6.2%, mineral fuels and lubricants 5.0%). *Major export destinations:* Germany 36.1%; Italy 6.5%; The Netherlands 5.3%; France 4.8%; UK 4.0%.

Transport and communications

Transport. *Railroads* (2000): length 22,981 km; (1999) passenger-km 26,198,000,000; (1999) metric ton-km cargo 55,471,000,000. *Roads* (1997): total length 377,048 km (paved 66%). *Vehicles* (2000): passenger cars 9,283,000; trucks and buses 1,762,000. *Air transport* (1999; LOT only): passenger-km 4,632,000,000; metric ton-km cargo 80,304,000; airports (1997) 8. **Communications** Total units (units per 1,000 persons). Daily newspaper circulation (1996): 4,351,000 (113); Radio receivers (1997): 20,200,000 (523); Television receivers (1999): 15,000,000 (388); Telephone main lines (2000): 10,076,000 (261); Cellular telephones subscribers (2000): 3,956,000 (102); Personal computers (1999): 2,400,000 (62); Internet users (1999): 2,100,000 (54).

Education and health

Educational attainment (1995). Percentage of pop. age 15 and over having: no formal schooling/incomplete primary education 6.3%; primary 33.7%; secondary/vocational 53.2%; higher 6.8%. **Literacy** (2000): 99.8%. **Health** (1999): physicians 90,080 (1 per 429 persons); hospital beds (2000) 239,341 (1 per 161 persons); infant mortality rate per 1,000 live births 8.9. **Food** (1999): daily per capita caloric intake 3,368 (vegetable products 73%, animal products 27%); 129% of FAO recommended minimum.

Military

Total active duty personnel (2000): 217,290 (army 61.1%, navy 7.7%, air force 21.3%, paramilitary 9.9%). **Military expenditure as percentage of GNP** (1997): 2.3% (world 2.6%); per capita expenditure $145.

Background

Established as a kingdom in 922 under Mieszko I, Poland was united with Lithuania in 1386 under the Jagiellon dynasty (1386–1572) to become the dominant power in east-central Europe. In 1466 it wrested western and eastern Prussia from the Teutonic Order, and its lands eventually stretched to the Black Sea. Wars with Sweden and Russia in the late 17th century led to the loss of considerable territory. In 1697 the electors of Saxony became kings of Poland, virtually ending Polish independence. In the late 18th century Poland was divided among Prussia, Russia, and

Austria and ceased to exist. After 1815 the former Polish lands came under Russian domination, and from 1863 Poland was a Russian province. After World War I an independent Poland was established by the Allies. The invasion of Poland in 1939 by the USSR and Germany precipitated World War II, during which the Nazis sought to purge its culture and its large Jewish population. Reoccupied by Soviet forces in 1945, it was controlled by a Soviet-dominated government from 1947. In the 1980s the Solidarity labor movement achieved major political reforms, and free elections were held in 1989. An economic austerity program instituted in 1990 sped the transition to a market economy.

Recent Developments

Poland experienced considerable political ferment in 2000. The two-party "Solidarity coalition" that had governed since 1997 collapsed in June, leaving a fragile and increasingly ineffectual minority government headed by the Solidarity Electoral Action (AWS). The AWS chairman, Marian Krzaklewski, suffered a stinging defeat in presidential elections in October, finishing third to the popular incumbent, Aleksander Kwasniewski. The focal point during 2001 was the 23 September parliamentary election. The big winner was the Democratic Left Alliance (SLD), led by former communist Leszek Miller. In June the first checks from a German fund set up to reimburse workers from Nazi-occupied countries who had been forced into slave labor were distributed. Poland also continued working toward membership in the European Union.

In mid-August 2002 Pope John Paul II made what seemed likely to be his farewell visit to his Polish homeland. During his 4-day stay the Pontiff said Mass for an unprecedented two million people in Krakow.

Internet resources: <www.stat.gov.pl/english>

Portugal

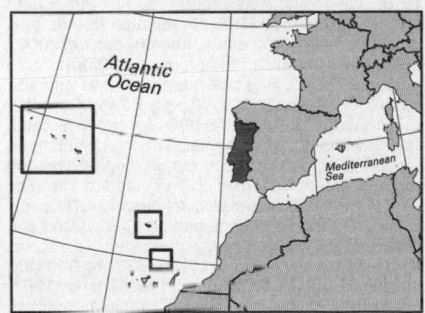

Official name: República Portuguesa (Portuguese Republic). **Form of government:** republic with one legislative house (Assembly of the Republic [230]). **Chief of state:** President Jorge Sampaio (from 1996). **Head of government:** Prime Minister José Manuel Durão Barroso (from 6 Apr 2002). **Capital:** Lisbon. **Official language:** Portuguese. **Official religion:** none. **Monetary unit:** 1 euro (€) = 100 cents; valuation (28 Jun 2002) $1 = €1.01; at conversion on 1 Jan 2002, € 1= 200.482 Portuguese escudos (Esc).

Demography

Area: 35,662 sq mi, 92,365 sq km (includes the 169 sq mi [439 sq km] of water areas comprising the Tagus and Sado estuaries and the Aveiro lagoon). **Population** (2001): 10,328,000 (includes March 2001 preliminary census results totaling 10,318,084). **Density** (2001): persons per sq mi 289.6, persons per sq km 111.8. **Urban** (1996): 36.0%. **Sex distribution** (2001): male 48.34%; female 51.66%. **Age breakdown** (2000): under 15, 17.1%; 15–29, 23.0%; 30–44, 21.5%; 45–59, 17.8%; 60–74, 14.5%; 75 and over, 6.1%. **Ethnic composition** (2000): Portuguese 91.9%; mixed race 1.6% (refugees and descendants of refugees from Angola, Cape Verde, or Mozambique); Brazilian 1.4%; Marrano 1.2%; other European 1.2%; Han Chinese 0.9%; other 1.8%. **Religious affiliation** (1995): Christian 94.8%, of which Roman Catholic 92.2%, Protestant 1.5%, other Christian (Jehovah's Witness 0.7%; Mormon 0.4%) 1.1%; Muslim 0.1%; other and nonreligious 5.1%. **Major cities** (2001): Lisbon 556,797 (urban agglomeration 3,447,173); Porto 262,928; Amadora 174,788; Braga 105,000; Coimbra 103,000. **Location:** southwestern Europe, bordering Spain and the North Atlantic Ocean.

Vital statistics

Birth rate per 1,000 pop. (2000): 11.5 (world avg. 22.5). **Death rate** per 1,000 pop. (2000): 10.2 (world avg. 9.0). **Natural increase rate** per 1,000 pop. (2000): 1.3 (world avg. 13.5). **Total fertility rate** (avg. births per childbearing woman; 2000): 1.5. **Life expectancy** at birth (2000): male 72.2 years; females 79.5 years.

National economy

Budget (1997). *Revenue:* Esc 7,041,700,000,000 (social security contributions 22.5%, general sales tax 19.3%, individual income tax 14.9%, excise tax 11.6%, grants 9.2%, nontax revenue 9.1%). *Expenditures:* Esc 7,242,200,000,000 (current expenditure 87.3%, development expenditure 12.7%). **Public debt** (1996): $40,504,000,000. **Production** (metric tons except as noted). *Agriculture, forestry, fishing* (2000): potatoes 1,250,000, tomatoes 1,000,000, corn (maize) 905,000; livestock (number of live animals) 5,850,000 sheep, 2,330,000 pigs, 1,245,000 cattle; roundwood (2000) 8,978,000 cu m; fish catch (1999) 215,230. *Mining and quarrying* (1999): marble 900,000; copper (mine output, copper content) 99,500. *Manufacturing* (value added in Esc '000,000; 1995): petroleum refining 424,700; machinery and transport equipment 412,300; food and beverages 312,800. *Energy production (consumption):* electricity (kW-hr; 1998) 33,144,000,000 ([1997] 37,086,000,000); coal (metric tons; 1997) negligible (5,758,000); crude petroleum (barrels; 1997) (90,452,000); petroleum products (metric tons; 1997) 11,333,000 (11,100,000); natural gas (cu m; 1997) (103,328,000). **Tourism** (1999): receipts $5,131,000,000; expenditures $2,266,000,000. **Land use** (1994): forest 35.9%; pasture 10.9%; agriculture 31.5%; other 21.7%. **Population economically active** (1999): total 5,046,800; activity rate of total pop. 50.5% (participation rates: ages 15–64

[1997], 68.5%; female 45.4%; unemployed 4.4%). **Gross national product** (at current market prices; 1999): $110,175,000,000 ($11,030 per capita). **Household income and expenditure.** Average household size (1999) 3.1; sources of income (1994–95): wages and salaries 45.8%, property and entrepreneurial income 32.4%, transfer payments 21.5%; expenditure (1994–95): food 23.9%, housing 20.6%, transportation and communications 18.9%, clothing and footwear 6.3%, health 4.6%, other 25.7%.

Foreign trade

Imports (1999-c.i.f.): Esc 7,519,000,000,000 (machinery and transport equipment 37.8%, of which road vehicles and parts 14.5%; basic manufactures 20.1%, of which textiles 5.8%; food products 10.4%; chemicals and chemical products 9.4%; mineral fuels 5.6%). *Major import sources* (1999): Spain 25.3%; Germany 14.7%; France 11.4%; Italy 7.7%; UK 7.7%; The Netherlands 4.8%. **Exports** (1999-f.o.b.): Esc 4,616,000,000,000 (1998; machinery and transport equipment 32.9%, of which transport equipment 15.3%; textiles and wearing apparel 25.5%; footwear 6.6%; chemicals and chemical products 4.7%; food 4.0%; cork and wood products 3.8%). *Major export destinations* (1999): Germany 19.8%; Spain 18.1%; France 13.9%; UK 12.0%; US 5.0%; Belgium 4.7%.

Transport and communications

Transport. *Railroads* (1998): route length 3,259 km; passenger-km 4,602,185; metric ton-km cargo 2,339,895,000. *Roads* (1996): total length 68,732 km (paved 88%). *Vehicles* (1998): passenger cars 3,200,000; trucks and buses 1,097,000. *Air transport* (1998): passenger-km 10,104,000,000; metric ton-km cargo 232,000,000; airports (1998) 16. **Communications** Total units (units per 1,000 persons). Daily newspaper circulation (1996): 744,000 (74); Radio receivers (1997): 3,020,000 (298); Television receivers (1999): 5,600,000 (547); Telephone main lines (1999): 4,230,000 (413); Cellular telephone subscribers (1999): 4,671,000 (456); Personal computers (1999): 930,000 (91); Internet users (1999): 700,000 (68).

Education and health

Educational attainment (1991). Percentage of pop. age 25 and over having: no formal schooling 16.1%; some primary education 61.5%; some secondary 10.6%; postsecondary 3.5%. **Literacy** (2000): total pop. age 15 and over literate 92.2%; males 94.8%; females 90.0%. **Health** (1998): physicians 31,087 (1 per 321 persons); hospital beds 39,870 (1 per 250 persons); infant mortality rate per 1,000 live births (2000) 6.1. **Food** (1999): daily per capita caloric intake 3,768 (vegetable products 72%, animal products 28%); 154% of FAO recommended minimum.

Military

Total active duty personnel (1999): 44,650 (army 57.4%, navy 26.0%, air force 16.6%). **Military expenditure as percentage of GNP** (1997): 2.4% (world 2.6%); per capita expenditure $240.

---

1 metric ton = about 1.1 short tons;   1 kilometer = 0.6 mi (statute);   1 metric ton-km cargo = about 0.68 short ton-mi cargo;   c.i.f.: cost, insurance, and freight;   f.o.b.: free on board

Background

Celtic peoples settled the Iberian peninsula in the 1st millennium BC. They were conquered about 140 BC by the Romans, who ruled until the 5th century AD, when the area was invaded by Germanic tribes. A Muslim invasion in 711 left only the northern part of Portugal in Christian hands. In 1139 it became the kingdom of Portugal and expanded as it reconquered the Muslim-held sectors. The boundaries of modern continental Portugal were completed in 1270 under King Afonso III. In the 15th and 16th centuries the monarchy encouraged exploration that took Portuguese navigators to Africa, India, Indonesia, China, the Middle East, and South America, where colonies were established. António de Oliveira Salazar ruled Portugal as a dictator in the mid-20th century; he died in office in 1970, and his successor was ousted in a coup in 1974. A new constitution was adopted in 1976 (revised 1982), and civilian rule resumed. Portugal was a charter member of NATO and is a member of the European Union.

Recent Developments

In October 1999, Prime Minister António Guterres was elected to a second term. Against a backdrop of slowing growth, rising inflation, and growing public deficits, Portugal's government lost its popular appeal in 2001; opposition parties remained fragmented, however, and were unable to capitalize on the Socialist government's woes. In the December 2001 local and municipal elections, the center-right Social Democratic Party (PSD) won control of 144 councils, compared to the 98 captured by the Portuguese Socialist Party (PSP). Guterres took responsibility for the poor PSP showing and resigned. Pres. Jorge Sampaio dissolved the parliament and called a general election for the following March. In July the parliament voted that drug users would not face jail sentences, a law that effectively decriminalized drugs and replaced prison time with counseling and monitoring of addicts. In the March 2002 elections the Socialist government was ousted by the Social Democrats, and PSD leader José Manuel Durão Barroso became prime minister. Large-scale construction of stadiums and other infrastructure for the Euro 2004 soccer championship was under way.

Internet resources: <www.portugal.org>

Puerto Rico

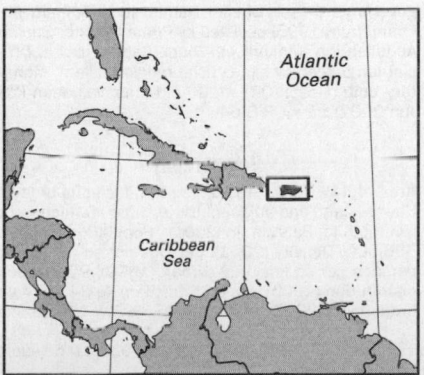

Atlantic Ocean

Caribbean Sea

Official name: Estado Libre Asociado de Puerto Rico; Commonwealth of Puerto Rico. **Political status:** self-governing commonwealth in association with the US, having two legislative houses (Senate [27]; House of Representatives [51]). **Chief of state:** President of the US George W. Bush (from 20 Jan 2001). **Head of government:** Governor Sila Maria Calderón (from 2 Jan 2001). **Capital:** San Juan. **Official languages:** Spanish; English. **Monetary unit:** 1 US dollar ($) = 100 cents.

Demography

Area: 3,515 sq mi, 9,104 sq km. **Population** (2001): 3,829,000. **Density** (2001): persons per sq mi 1,089.4, persons per sq km 420.6. **Urban** (1990): 74.9%. **Sex distribution** (2000): male 48.14%; female 51.86%. **Age breakdown** (2000): under 15, 23.8%; 15–34, 30.1%; 35–54, 25.7%; 55–64, 9.2%; 65 and over, 11.2%. **Linguistic composition** (1990): Spanish 51.3%; Spanish-English 46.9%; English 0.5%; other 1.3%. **Religious affiliation** (1995): Roman Catholic 64.8%; Protestant 28.7%; other 6.5%. **Major urban agglomerations** (1998): San Juan 2,004,054; Ponce 366,273; Caguas 315,921; Mayagüez 258,283; Arecibo 176,814. **Location:** island in the Caribbean Sea, east of Cuba.

Vital statistics

Birth rate per 1,000 pop. (2000): 15.5 (world avg. 22.5). **Death rate** per 1,000 pop. (2000): 7.7 (world avg. 9.0). **Natural increase rate** per 1,000 pop. (2000): 7.8 (world avg. 13.5). **Total fertility rate** (avg. births per childbearing woman; 2000): 1.9. **Marriage rate** per 1,000 pop. (1996): 8.7. **Life expectancy** at birth (2000): male 71.1 years; female 80.3 years.

National economy

Budget. *Revenue* (1997–98): $8,784,000,000 (tax revenue 68.3%, of which income taxes 45.5%, excise taxes 15.5%, intergovernment transfers 31.7%). *Expenditures* (1997–98): $6,263,000,000 (welfare 25.6%; education 20.3%; debt service 9.0%; public safety and protection 8.7%; health 3.5%). **Public debt** (outstanding; 1999): $22,678,200,000. **Tourism** (1999): receipts $2,138,000,000; expenditures $815,000,000. **Production** (in metric tons except as noted). *Agriculture, forestry, fishing* (1999): sugarcane 307,358, plantains 76,140, bananas 38,215; livestock (number of live animals) 388,307 cattle, 174,748 pigs; fish catch (1997) 2,744 metric tons. *Mining* (value of production in $'000; 1993): stone 50. *Manufacturing* (value added in $'000,000; 1997): chemicals, pharmaceuticals, and allied products 21,393; food 3,532; machinery and metal products 2,940. *Energy production (consumption):* electricity (kW-hr; 1996) 19,029,000,000 (19,029,000,000); coal (metric tons; 1996) (170,000); crude petroleum (barrels; 1996) (43,080,000); petroleum products (metric tons; 1996) 5,877,000 (6,743,000). **Gross national product** (1997): $25,380,000,000 ($7,010 per capita). **Population economically active** (1997): total 1,298,000; activity rate 34.1% (participation rates: ages 16 and over, 48.0%; female 39.5%; unemployed 13.1%). **Household income and expenditure** (1999). Average family size (2000) 3.0; income per family $32,892; sources of income: wages and salaries 60.6%, transfers 31.3%, rent 6.5%, self-employment 6.1%; expenditure: food and beverages 18.8%, health care 17.8%, transportation 12.8%, housing 12.1%, household furnishings 11.6%, clothing 7.9%, recreation 7.7%.

Foreign trade

Imports (1997–98): $27,308,700,000 (chemicals [all forms] 26.8%, electrical machinery 11.8%, food 10.2%, transport equipment 9.6%, petroleum and petroleum products 7.2%, nonelectrical machinery 6.8%, professional and scientific instruments 4.2%, clothing and textiles 4.2%). *Major import sources* (1995–96): US 62.5%; Japan 6.4%; Dominican Republic 4.0%; UK 2.9%. **Exports** (1997–98): $33,416,400,000 (chemicals and chemical products 43.6%, nonelectrical machinery 13.2%, food 12.1%, electrical machinery 7.7%). *Major export destinations:* US 88.5%; other 11.5%.

Transport and communications

Transport. *Railroads* (1988 [for sugarcane transport only]): length 96 km. *Roads* (1996): total length 14,400 km (paved 100%). *Vehicles* (1996): passenger cars 878,000; trucks and buses 190,000. *Air transport* (1998): passenger arrivals and departures 9,285,000; cargo loaded and unloaded 275,500 metric tons; airports (1998) with scheduled flights 7. **Communications** Total units (units per 1,000 persons). Daily newspaper circulation (1996): 475,000 (128); Radio receivers (1997): 2,700,000 (724); Television receivers (1998): 1,250,000 (333); Telephone main lines (1999): 1,295,000 (342); Cellular telephone subscribers (1999): 814,000 (215); Internet users (1999): 200,000 (53).

Education and health

Educational attainment (1990). Percentage of pop. age 25 and over having: primary education 26.8%; some secondary 23.5%; complete secondary 21.0%; higher 28.7%. **Literacy** (1995): total pop. age 15 and over literate 92.8%; males literate 92.7%; females literate 92.8%. **Health:** physicians (1992) 6,269 (1 per 575 persons); hospital beds (1993–94) 9,598 (1 per 381 persons); infant mortality rate (2000) 9.7.

Military

Total active duty personnel (2001): 2,840 US personnel.

Did you know? El Morro Fortress, the largest fort in the Caribbean, is one of the most impressive of the many architectural features of Old San Juan.

Background

Puerto Rico was inhabited by Arawak Indians when it was settled by the Spanish in the early 16th century. It remained largely undeveloped economically until the late 18th century. After 1830 it gradually developed a plantation economy based on the export crops of sugarcane, coffee, and tobacco. The independence movement began in the late 19th century, and Spain ceded the island to the US in 1898, after the Spanish-American War. In 1917 Puerto Ricans

were granted US citizenship, and in 1952 the island became a commonwealth with autonomy in internal affairs. The question of Puerto Rican statehood has been a political issue, with commonwealth status approved by voters in 1967, 1993, and 1998.

Recent Developments

Two US military aircraft accidentally bombed a lookout post in Puerto Rico during exercises over the island of Vieques in April 1999, killing one person and injuring four others. Residents of Vieques had been campaigning for years against the use of the island for bombing practice, and Pres. Bill Clinton temporarily granted a request to end weapons training there. News that the bombing might be resumed brought an estimated 85,000 people out into the streets in February 2000 to demonstrate their disapproval; 55 protesters cut their way into Vieques base in May. Environmentalists and other concerned individuals moved to file a restraining order when bombing recommenced in October. Sila María Calderón of the Popular Democratic Party was sworn in as governor on 2 Jan 2001. In June 2001 the US announced it would cease using Vieques for target practice by May 2003; bombing resumed in April 2002.

Internet resources: <www.prtourism.com>

Qatar

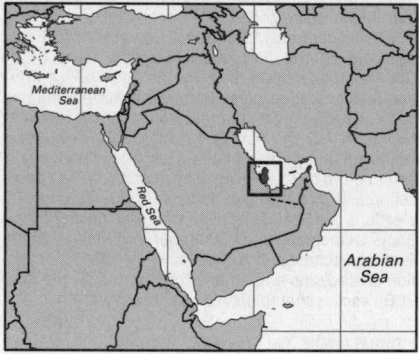

Official name: Dawlat Qatar (State of Qatar). **Form of government:** monarchy (emirate); Islamic law is the basis of legislation in the state. **Heads of state and government:** Emir Sheikh Hamad ibn Khalifah ath-Thani (from 1995) assisted by Prime Minister Sheikh Abdullah ibn Khalifah ath-Thani. **Capital:** Doha. **Official language:** Arabic. **Official religion:** Islam. **Monetary unit:** 1 riyal (QR) = 100 dirhams; valuation (28 Jun 2002) $1 = QR 3.64.

Demography

Area: 4,412 sq mi, 11,427 sq km (includes area of Hawar Island and adjacent islets, most of which were awarded to Bahrain in 2001). **Population** (2001): 596,000. **Density** (2001): persons per sq mi 135.1; persons per sq km 52.2. **Urban** (1999): 92.3%. **Sex distribution** (2000): male 65.9%; female 34.1%. **Age breakdown** (2000): under 15, 26.3%; 15–29, 22.6%;

---

1 metric ton = about 1.1 short tons;   1 kilometer = 0.6 mi (statute);   1 metric ton-km cargo = about 0.68 short ton-mi cargo;   c.i.f.: cost, insurance, and freight;   f.o.b.: free on board

30–44, 27.1%; 45–59, 19.4%; 60–74, 4.1%; 75 and over, 0.5%. **Ethnic composition** (2000): Arab 52.5%, of which Palestinian 13.4%, Qatari 13.3%, Lebanese 10.4%, Syrian 9.4%; Persian 16.5%; Indo-Pakistani 15.2%; black African 9.5%; other 6.3%. **Religious affiliation** (2000): Muslim (mostly Sunni) 82.7%; Christian 10.4%; Hindu 2.5%; other 4.4%. **Major cities** (1997): Ad-Dawhah (Doha) 264,009 (urban agglomeration [1999] 391,000); Ar-Rayyan 161,453; Al-Wakrah 20,205; Umm Salal 15,935. **Location:** the Middle East, bordering the Persian Gulf and Saudi Arabia.

Vital statistics

Birth rate per 1,000 pop. (2000): 16.1 (world avg. 22.5). **Death rate** per 1,000 pop. (2000): 4.2 (world avg. 9.0). **Natural increase rate** per 1,000 pop. (2000): 11.9 (world avg. 13.5). **Total fertility rate** (avg. births per childbearing woman; 2000): 3.3. **Marriage rate** per 1,000 pop. (1994): 2.8. **Divorce rate** per 1,000 pop. (1994): 1.0. **Life expectancy** at birth (2000): male 69.9 years; female 74.9 years.

National economy

Budget (1999–2000). *Revenue:* QR 14,098,000,-000 (crude petroleum c. 90%). *Expenditures:* QR 14,353,000,000 (current expenditure 91.7%, of which wages and salaries 37.5%; capital expenditure 8.3%). **Production** (metric tons except as noted). *Agriculture, forestry, fishing* (2000): dates 16,500, tomatoes 11,000, pumpkin and squash 8,500; livestock (number of live animals; 2000) 215,000 sheep, 179,000 goats, 50,000 camels; fish catch (1999) 4,207. *Mining and quarrying* (1996): limestone 900,000; sulfur 61,000. *Manufacturing* (value added in QR '000,000; 1994): refined petroleum 919; chemical products 887; iron and steel 319. *Energy production (consumption):* electricity (kW-hr; 1996) 6,340,000,000 (6,340,000,000); crude petroleum (barrels; 1999) 224,910,000 ([1996] 22,425,000); petroleum products (metric tons; 1996) 5,430,000 (745,000); natural gas (cu m; 1996) 13,700,000,000 (13,700,000,000). **Tourism** (1994): total number of tourists staying in hotels 241,000. **Population economically active** (1997): total 280,122; activity rate of total pop. 53.7% (participation rates: ages 15–64, 59.7%; female 21.0%). **Gross national product** (1998): $6,473,000,000 ($11,600 per capita). **Household income and expenditure.** Average household size (1998) 7.0; sources of income (1988): wages and salaries 80.8%, rents and royalties 10.6%, self-employment 5.6%, other 3.0%; expenditure (1993): food 28.7%, transportation 19.3%, housing 12.4%, clothing 10.6%, education 7.6%, health 1.2%. **Land use** (1994): meadows and pastures 4.5%; agricultural and under permanent cultivation 0.7%; built-up, desert, and other 94.7%.

Foreign trade

Imports (1999-c.i.f., f.o.b.): QR 9,098,400,000 (machinery and transport equipment 34.6%, manufactured goods 19.0%, food and live animals 13.2%, chemicals and chemical products 8.2%, raw materials 3.1%). *Major import sources* (1999): UK 11.5%; US 11.4%; Japan 10.3%; UAE 8.0%; Saudi Arabia 7.1%; Germany 6.1%. **Exports** (1999): QR 26,258,-000,000 (1994; mineral fuels and lubricants 81.2%,

chemicals and chemical products 10.4%, manufactured goods 5.9%). *Major export destinations* (1999): Japan 51.0%; South Korea 12.9%; Singapore 9.1%; US 4.3%; Thailand 3.4%.

Transport and communications

Transport. *Roads* (1996): total length 1,230 km (paved 90%). *Vehicles* (1996): passenger cars 126,000; trucks and buses 64,000. *Air transport* (1999; Qatar Airways only): passenger-km 2,857,-529,000; metric ton-km cargo 104,947,000; airports (1999) with scheduled flights 1. **Communications** Total units (units per 1,000 persons). Daily newspaper circulation (1995): 90,000 (161); Radio receivers (1997): 250,000 (432); Television receivers (1998): 490,000 (846); Telephone main lines (1999): 154,904 (263); Cellular telephone subscribers (1999): 84,365 (143); Personal computers (1999): 80,000 (136); Internet users (1999): 24,000 (41).

Education and health

Educational attainment (1986). Percentage of pop. age 25 and over having: no formal education 53.3%, of which illiterate 24.3%; primary 9.8%; preparatory (lower secondary) 10.1%; secondary 13.3%; postsecondary 13.3%; other 0.2%. **Literacy** (1995): total pop. age 15 and over literate 460,000 (79.4%); males literate 298,000 (79.2%); females literate 122,000 (79.9%). **Health:** physicians (1996) 703 (1 per 793 persons); hospital beds (1995) 892 (1 per 555 persons); infant mortality rate per 1,000 live births (2000) 22.1.

Military

Total active duty personnel (2000): 12,330 (army 68.9%, navy 14.0%, air force 17.1%). **Military expenditure as percentage of GNP** (1996): 10.5% (world 2.6%); per capita expenditure $1,540.

Did you know? The most influential news service in the Arab World is Al-Jazeera ("The Peninsula") television network based in Doha, Qatar. Al-Jazeera grew rapidly in viewership after its founding in 1996 by a decree of the emir as part of an effort to democratize his country, because of its uncensored, if tendentious, news and lively debate.

Background

Qatar was partly controlled by Bahrain in the 18th–19th century and was nominally part of the Ottoman empire until World War I. In 1916 it became a British protectorate. Oil was discovered in 1939, and the country rapidly modernized. Qatar declared independence in 1971, when the British protectorate ended. In 1991 it served as a base for air strikes against Iraq in the Persian Gulf War.

Recent Developments

In 1999, in what was a first for the Arabian Peninsula countries, women voted and campaigned as candidates in elections for Doha's municipal council. In 2000 the border between Qatar and Saudi Arabia was successfully demarcated, and Qatar became leader of the Organization of the Islamic Conference. In November 2001 the nation hosted a meeting of the World Trade Organization. In the summer of 2002 the US military began quietly building up its forces at Al-Udeid Air Base in Qatar, a facility that would be strategically vital in case of a US attack on Iraq.

Internet resources: <www.mofa.gov.qa>

Réunion

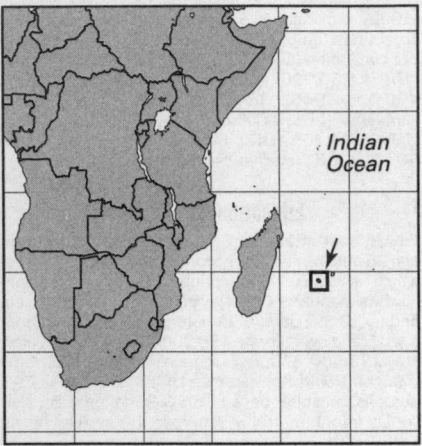

Indian Ocean

Official name: Département de la Réunion (Department of Réunion). **Political status:** overseas department (France) with two legislative houses (General Council [47]; Regional Council [45]). **Chief of state:** President of France Jacques Chirac (from 1995). **Heads of government:** Prefect (for France) Gonthier Friederici (from 2001); President of General Council (for Réunion) Jean-Luc Poudroux (from 1998); President of Regional Council (for Réunion) Paul Vergès (from 1998). **Capital:** Saint-Denis. **Official language:** French. **Official religion:** none. **Monetary unit:** 1 euro (€) = 100 cents; valuation (28 Jun 2002) $1 = €1.01 (1 French franc [F] = 100 centimes; at conversion on 1 Jan 2002, €1 = 6.56 French francs [F]).

Demography

Area: 968 sq mi, 2,507 sq km. **Population** (2001): 733,000. **Density** (2001): persons per sq mi 757.2, persons per sq km 292.4. **Urban** (1999): 71.6%. **Sex distribution** (1999): male 49.15%; female 50.85%. **Age breakdown** (1999): under 15, 27.0%; 15–29, 24.8%; 30–44, 24.4%; 45–59, 13.8%; 60–74, 7.2%; 75 and over, 2.8%. **Ethnic composition** (2000): mixed race (black-white-South Asian) 42.6%; local white 25.6%; South Asian 23.0%, of which Tamil 20.0%; Chinese 3.4%; East African 3.4%; Malagasy 1.4%; other 0.6%. **Religious affiliation** (1995): Roman Catholic 89.4%; Pentecostal 2.7%; other Christian 1.8%; other (mostly Muslim) 6.1%. **Major cities** (1999): Saint-Denis 131,557 (agglomeration 158,139); Saint-Paul 87,712; Saint-Pierre 68,915 (agglomeration 129,238); Le Tampon 60,323 (within Saint-Pierre ag-

glomeration); Saint-Louis 43,519. **Location:** western Indian Ocean, lying east of Madagascar.

Vital statistics

Birth rate per 1,000 pop. (1998): 19.3 (world avg. 22.5); (1997) legitimate 41.5%; illegitimate 58.5%. **Death rate** per 1,000 pop. (1998): 5.4 (world avg. 9.0). **Natural increase rate** per 1,000 pop. (1998): 13.9 (world avg. 13.5). **Total fertility rate** (avg. births per childbearing woman; 1997): 2.2. **Marriage rate** per 1,000 pop. (1998): 4.8. **Divorce rate** per 1,000 pop. (1997): 1.3. **Life expectancy** at birth (1998): male 70.2 years; female 78.5 years.

National economy

Budget (1998). *Revenue:* F 4,624,000,000 (receipts from the French central government and local administrative bodies 52.7%, tax receipts 20.2%, loans 8.9%). *Expenditures:* F 4,300,000,000 (current expenditures 68.7%, development expenditures 31.3%). **Tourism** (1999): receipts $270,000,000. **Gross national product** (at current market prices; 1998): $5,070,000,000 ($7,270 per capita). **Production** (metric tons except as noted). *Agriculture, forestry, fishing* (1999): sugarcane 1,800,000, corn (maize) 17,000, cabbages 14,000; livestock (number of live animals) 89,000 pigs, 38,000 goats, 27,000 cattle; roundwood (1998) 36,100 cu m; fish catch (1998) 6,453. *Mining and quarrying:* gravel and sand for local use. *Manufacturing* (value added in F '000,000; 1997): food and beverages 1,019, of which meat and milk products 268; construction materials (mostly cement) 394. *Energy production (consumption):* electricity (kW-hr; 1998) 1,431,000,000 ([1996] 1,132,000,000); petroleum products (metric tons; 1996) none (509,000). **Household income and expenditure.** Average household size (1999) 3.3; average annual income per household (1997) F 136,800; sources of income (1997): wages and salaries and self-employment 41.8%, transfer payments 41.3%, other 16.9%; expenditure (1994–95): food and beverages 22.0%, transportation and communications 19.0%, housing and energy 10.0%, household furnishings 8.0%, recreation 6.0%. **Population economically active** (1998): total 288,760; activity rate of total pop. 41.2% (participation rates: ages 15–64, 57.5%; female 44.3%; unemployed 41.1%). **Land use** (1994): forested 35.2%; meadows and pastures 4.8%; agricultural and under permanent cultivation 19.6%; other 40.4%.

Foreign trade

Imports (1998): F 15,310,000,000 (food and agricultural products 17.1%, transport equipment 14.7%, machinery and apparatus 13.4%, clothing and footwear 6.8%). *Major import sources:* France 66.0%; EC 14.0%. **Exports** (1998): F 1,215,000,000 (sugar 58.9%, machinery, apparatus, and transport equipment 17.5%, rum 2.5%, lobster 1.7%). *Major export destinations:* France 70.0%; EC 9.0%; Madagascar 4.5%; Mauritius 2.3%.

Transport and communications

Transport. *Roads* (1994): total length 2,754 km (paved [1991] 79%). *Vehicles* (1999): passenger cars

---

1 metric ton = about 1.1 short tons; 1 kilometer = 0.6 mi (statute); 1 metric ton-km cargo = about 0.68 short ton-mi cargo; c.i.f.: cost, insurance, and freight; f.o.b.: free on board

190,300; trucks and buses 44,300. *Air transport* (1998): passenger arrivals 677,487; passenger departures 674,051, cargo unloaded 15,060 metric tons, cargo loaded 7,270 metric tons; airports (1999) with scheduled flights 2. **Communications** Total units (units per 1,000 persons). Daily newspaper circulation (1996): 83,000 (123); Radio receivers (1997): 173,000 (252); Television receivers (1997): 127,000 (185); Telephone main lines (1999): 268,496 (378); Cellular telephone subscribers (1998): 50,300 (72).

Education and health

Educational attainment (1986–87). Percentage of pop. age 25 and over having: no formal schooling 18.8%; primary education 44.3%; lower secondary 21.6%; upper secondary 11.0%; higher 4.3%. **Literacy** (1996): total pop. age 16–66 literate 373,487 (91.3%); males literate 179,154 (89.9%); females literate 194,333 (92.7%). **Health** (1999): physicians 1,346 (1 per 525 persons); hospital beds (1998) 2,734 (1 per 254 persons); infant mortality rate per 1,000 live births (1997) 6.4.

Military

Total active duty personnel (2000): 4,200 French troops (includes troops stationed on Mayotte).

Background

The island of Réunion was settled in the 17th century by the French, who brought slaves from eastern Africa to work on coffee and sugar plantations there. It was a French colony until 1946, when it became an overseas *département* of France. Its economy is based almost entirely on the export of sugar.

Recent Developments

A proposal to split the island into two separate dependencies was rejected by the the voters, as reflected in the victory in March 2001 elections of rightist parties opposed to the split. Social unrest was traced to inequties between the various ethnic groups, a very high rate of unemployment (40%), exploding population, and dependence on welfare and foreign aid.

Internet resources: <www.runweb.com/uk_main.asp>

Romania

Official name: Romania. **Form of government:** unitary republic with two legislative houses (Senate [143]; Assembly of Deputies [346, including 19 non-elective seats]). **Chief of state:** President Ion Iliescu (from 2000). **Head of government:** Prime Minister Adrian Nastase (from 2000). **Capital:** Bucharest. **Official language:** Romanian. **Official religion:** none. **Monetary unit:** 1 Romanian leu (plural lei) = 100 bani; valuation (28 Jun 2002) $1 = 33,457.50 lei.

Demography

Area: 91,699 sq mi, 237,500 sq km. **Population** (2001): 22,413,000. **Density** (2000): persons per sq mi 244.4, persons per sq km 94.4. **Urban** (2000): 56.2%. **Sex distribution** (2000): male 48.84%; female 51.16%. **Age breakdown** (2000): under 15, 18.4%;

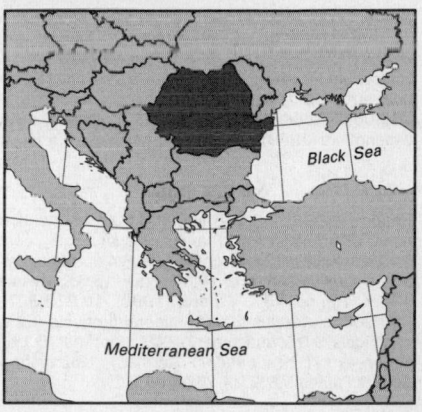

15–29, 24.1%; 30–44, 21.0%; 45–59, 17.7%; 60–74, 14.3%; 75 and over, 4.5%. **Ethnic composition** (1992): Romanian 90.7%; Hungarian 7.2%; other 2.1%. **Religious affiliation** (1992): Romanian Orthodox 86.8%; Protestant 5.5%; Roman Catholic 5.1%; Greek Orthodox 1.0%; Muslim 0.2%; other 1.4%. **Major cities** (1997): Bucharest 2,027,512; Iasi 348,399; Constanta 344,876; Timisoara 334,098; Cluj-Napoca 332,792. **Location:** southeastern Europe, bordering Ukraine, Moldova, the Black Sea, Bulgaria, Serbia and Montenegro, and Hungary.

Vital statistics

Birth rate per 1,000 pop. (2000): 10.8 (world avg. 22.5). **Death rate** per 1,000 pop. (2000): 12.3 (world avg. 9.0). **Natural increase rate** per 1,000 pop. (2000): –1.7 (world avg. 13.5). **Total fertility rate** (avg. births per childbearing woman; 2000): 1.4. **Marriage rate** per 1,000 pop. (1995): 6.8. **Life expectancy** at birth (2000): male 66.1 years; female 74.0 years.

National economy

Budget ('000,000,000,000 lei; 1996). *Revenue:* 76.7 (social security 23.0%, personal income tax 18.2%, value-added tax 15.2%). *Expenditures:* 85.6 (social security 28.2%, debt service 10.0%, education 9.6%, health 7.5%). **Tourism** (1999): receipts $254,000,000; expenditures $395,000,000. **Production** (metric tons). *Agriculture, forestry, fishing* (2000): wheat 4,320,000, corn (maize) 4,200,000, potatoes 3,650,000; livestock (number of live animals) 7,972,000 sheep, 5,951,000 pigs, 3,154,000 cattle; roundwood (1998) 11,515,000 cu m; fish catch (1998) 9,020. *Mining* (1995): iron 184,000; bauxite 174,000; zinc 35,000; copper 24,000. *Manufacturing* (value-added in '000,000,000,000 lei; 1996): food products 5.8; beverages 3.0; iron and steel 1.6. *Energy production (consumption):* electricity (kW-hr; 1996) 61,350,000,000 (62,157,000,000); coal (metric tons; 1996) 41,869,000 (45,477,000,000), crude petroleum (barrels; 1996) 70,558,000 (100,440,000); petroleum products (metric tons; 1996) 10,956,000 (10,933,000); natural gas (cu m; 1996) 14,460,000,000 (20,401,000,000). **Public debt** (external, outstanding; 1999): $5,985,000,000. **Gross national product** (1999): $33,034,000,000 ($2,250 per capita). **Population**

economically active (1998): total 11,577,300; activity rate 51.4% (participation rates: ages 15–64, 67.2% [1992]; female 42.8%; unemployed 6.3%). **Household income and expenditure.** Average household size (1992) 3.1; income per household (1989) 73,500 lei; sources of income (1982): wages 62.6%; expenditure (1989): food 51.1%; housing 16.4%.

Foreign trade

Imports (1996): 10,368,000,000,000 lei (mineral fuels 25.4%, machinery and transport equipment 24.1%, textiles 12.0%, chemicals 8.4%). *Major import sources:* Germany 16.5%; Italy 15.6%; Russia 13.1%; France 4.8%. **Exports** (1996): 10,272,827,-000,000 lei (textiles 20.8%, mineral products 9.2%, chemicals 9.0%, machinery 8.0%, footwear 6.1%). *Major export destinations:* Germany 18.2%; Italy 16.6%; France 5.6%; UK 2.9%; US 2.2%.

Transport and communications

Transport. *Railroads* (1997): length 11,365 km (1994); passenger-km 15,794,000,000; metric ton-km cargo 24,789,000,000. *Roads* (1996): length 153,358 km (paved 51%). *Vehicles* (1997): cars 2,605,565; trucks and buses 427,579. *Air transport* (1998): passenger-km 1,712,300,000; metric ton-km cargo 12,110,000; airports (1997) 8. **Communications** Total units (units per 1,000 persons). Daily newspaper circulation (1996): 6,800,000 (297); Radio receivers (1997): 7,200,000 (319); Television receivers (1999): 7,000,000 (312); Telephone main lines (1999): 3,740,000 (167); Cellular telephone subscribers (1999): 1,356,000 (61); Personal computers (1998): 230,000 (10); Internet users (1999): 600,000 (28).

Education and health

Educational attainment (1992). Percentage of pop. age 25 and over having: no schooling 5.4%; some primary education 24.4%; some secondary 63.2%; postsecondary 6.9%. **Literacy** (2000): total pop. age 15 and over literate 98.2%; males 99.1%; females 97.3%. **Health:** physicians (1994) 47,990 (1 per 474 persons); hospital beds (1992) 174,900 (1 per 130 persons); infant mortality rate (2000) 19.8. **Food** (1999): daily per capita caloric intake 3,254 (vegetable products 77%, animal products 23%); 132% of FAO recommended minimum requirement.

Military

Total active duty personnel (2000): 207,000 (army 51.2%, navy 10.0%, air force 21.0%, other 17.8%). **Military expenditure as percentage of GNP** (1997): 2.4% (world 2.6%); per capita expenditure $102.

Did you know? A theme park called Dracula Land was once planned for Sighisoara, Transylvania, Romania, the birthplace of the 15th-century Prince Vlad, known as Vlad the Impaler. Prince Vlad is the model for the vampire Dracula in the novel of the same name by Bram Stoker.

Background

Romania was formed in 1862 by the unification of the principalities Moldavia and Walachia, which had once been part of the ancient country of Dacia. During World War I, Romania sided with the Allies and doubled its territory in 1918 with the addition of Transylvania, Bukovina, and Bessarabia. Allied with Germany in World War II, it was occupied by Soviet troops in 1944 and became a satellite country of the USSR in 1948. During the 1960s Romania's foreign policy was frequently independent of the Soviet Union's. The communist regime of Nicolae Ceausescu was overthrown in 1989, and free elections were held in 1990. Throughout the 1990s Romania struggled with rampant corruption and organized crime as it tried to stabilize its economy.

Recent Developments

Attempts to reverse decades of Soviet-style government included movement toward a market economy, decentralization, privatization, increased production, removal of bureaucratic impediments, and improved relations with neighboring countries such as Hungary and Moldova. Policies were adopted with the goal of eventual membership in the European Union and NATO. Parliamentary and president elections saw a power shift as new parties arose to challenge the ruling Social Democratic Party. In 2001 King Michael, who had been forced by the communists to abdicate in 1947, returned to Romania to live, and some of the royal family's property was returned to him.

Internet resources: <www.rotravel.com>

Russia

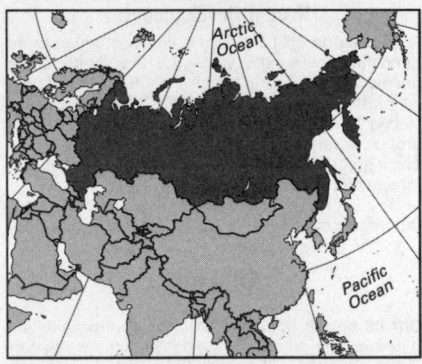

Official name: Rossiyskaya Federatsiya (Russian Federation). **Form of government:** federal multiparty republic with a bicameral legislative body (Federal Assembly comprising a Federation Council [178] and a State Duma [450]). **Head of state:** President Vladimir Putin (from 2000). **Head of government:** Prime Minister Mikhail Kasyanov (from 2000). **Capital:** Moscow. **Official language:** Russian. **Official religion:** none. **Monetary unit:** 1 ruble (Rub) = 100 kopecks; valuation (28 Jun 2002) market rate, $1 = Rub 31.52.

1 metric ton = about 1.1 short tons;   1 kilometer = 0.6 mi (statute);   1 metric ton-km cargo = about 0.68 short ton-mi cargo;   c.i.f.: cost, insurance, and freight;   f.o.b.: free on board

Demography

Area: 6,592,800 sq mi, 17,075,400 sq km. **Population** (2001): 144,417,000. **Density** (2001): persons per sq mi 21.9, persons per sq km 8.5. **Urban** (2000): 73.0%. **Sex distribution** (2000): male 46.78%; female 53.22%. **Age breakdown** (2000): under 15, 18.3%; 15–29, 22.5%; 30–44, 23.3%; 45–59, 17.5%; 60–74, 14.4%; 75 and over, 4.0%. **Ethnic composition** (1997): Russian 86.6%; Tatar 3.2%; Ukrainian 1.3%; Chuvash 0.9%; Bashkir 0.7%; Chechen 0.6%; Mordovian 0.5%; Belorussian 0.3%; other 5.9%. **Religious affiliation** (1997): Russian Orthodox 16.3%; Muslim 7.0%; Protestant 0.9%; Jewish 0.4%; other (mostly nonreligious) 75.4%. **Major cities** (2000): Moscow 8,369,200; St. Petersburg 4,694,000; Novosibirsk 1,398,800; Nizhny Novgorod 1,357,000; Yekaterinburg 1,266,300; Samara 1,156,100; Omsk 1,148,900; Kazan 1,101,000; Ufa 1,091,200; Chelyabinsk 1,083,000; Rostov-na-Donu 1,012,700; Perm 1,009,700. **Location:** Eastern Europe and northern Asia, bordering the Arctic Ocean, the Pacific Ocean, North Korea, China, Mongolia, Kazakhstan, the Caspian Sea, Azerbaijan, Georgia, the Black Sea, Ukraine, Belarus, Latvia, Estonia, Finland, and Norway; the exclave of Kaliningrad on the Baltic Sea borders Lithuania and Poland. **Mobility** (1989). Pop. living in the same residence as in 1988: 78.8%; different residence, same oblast 11.5%; different republic 9.7%. **Households** (1999). Total family households 52,116,000; average household size 2.8; distribution by size (1995): 1 person 19.2%; 2 persons 26.2%; 3 persons 22.6%; 4 persons 20.5%; 5 persons or more 11.5%. Pop. in family households (1989): 128,787,000 (87.0%), nonfamily population 19,254,000 (13.0%).

Vital statistics

Birth rate per 1,000 pop. (2000): 8.3 (world avg. 22.5); legitimate 70.5%; illegitimate 29.5%. **Death rate** per 1,000 pop. (2000): 14.7 (world avg. 9.0). **Natural increase rate** per 1,000 pop. (2000): –6.4 (world avg. 13.5). **Total fertility rate** (avg. births per childbearing woman; 2000): 1.3. **Marriage rate** per 1,000 pop. (1999): 6.3. **Divorce rate** per 1,000 pop. (1999): 3.7. **Life expectancy** at birth (1999): male 59.9 years; female 72.4 years.

Social indicators

Quality of working life (1999). Average workweek: 40 hours. Annual rate per 100,000 workers of: injury or accident 520; industrial illness 17.6; death 14.4. Proportion of labor force insured for damages or income loss resulting from: injury 100%; permanent disability 100%; death 100%. Average days lost to labor stoppages per 1,000 workdays (1992): 1.1. **Access to services** (1990). Proportion of dwellings having access to: electricity, virtually 100%; safe public water supply 94%; public sewage collection 92%; central heating 92%; bathroom 87%; gas 72%; hot water 79%. **Social participation.** Eligible voters participating in last national election (2000): 64.2%. Trade union membership in total workforce (1989): 100%. Practicing religious pop. in total affiliated pop. (1991): 32%. **Social deviance.** Offense rate per 100,000 population (1999) for: murder 21.3; rape 5.6; serious injury 32.6; larceny-theft 952.5. Incidence per 100,000 population (1992) of: alcoholism 1,727.5; substance abuse 25.1; suicide 26.5. **Material well-being** (1999).

Durable goods possessed per 100 family households: automobile 37; radio receiver 100; television receiver 112; refrigerator or freezer 93; washing machine 80; camera 35; motorcycle 22; bicycle 51.

National economy

Budget (1999). Revenue: Rub 615,500,000,000 (tax revenue 82.8%, of which value-added tax 35.9%, profit tax 13.2%, individual income tax 10.9%, excise tax 5.9%; nontax revenue 17.2%). Expenditures: Rub 666,900,000,000 (interest on foreign debt 24.4%; defense 17.4%; social and cultural 12.8%; law enforcement 8.3%; administrative 2.2%). **Public debt** (external, outstanding; 1999): $120,375,000,000. **Gross national product** (1999): $328,995,000,000 ($2,250 per capita.) **Production** (metric tons except as noted). Agriculture, forestry, fishing (2000): wheat 36,000,000, potatoes 32,597,000, vegetables (other than potatoes) 15,600,000, sugar beets 14,040,800, barley 13,266,000, oats 5,500,000; livestock (number of live animals) 27,500,000 cattle, 18,300,000 pigs; 14,000,000 sheep; roundwood (2000) 158,100,000 cu m; fish catch (1999) 4,209,772. Mining and quarrying (1997): nickel 260,000,000; chrome ore 151,000,000; iron ore 70,800,000; tin 7,500,000; molybdenum 8,500,-000; antimony 6,000,000; gold 3,955,000 troy oz. Manufacturing (1999): crude steel 51,500,000; pig iron 41,000,000; rolled steel 40,900,000; cement 28,529,000; mineral fertilizers 11,496,000; sulfuric acid 7,100,000; cellulose 4,225,000; synthetic resins and plastics 2,206,000. Energy production (consumption): electricity (kW-hr; 1999) 846,200,-000,000 (832,100,000,000); hard coal (metric tons; 1999) 166,000,000 (1996; 161,020,000); lignite (metric tons; 1999) 83,500,000 ([1996] 86,091,-000); crude petroleum (barrels; 1999) 2,115,740,-000 ([1996] 1,315,000,000); petroleum products (metric tons; 1996) 157,884,000 (105,168,000); natural gas (cu m; 1999) 564,000,000,000 ([1996] 323,175,000,000); peat (metric tons; 1995) 4,401,-000 (3,683,000); oil shale (metric tons; 1994) 2,000,000 (1993; 3,300,000). **Population economically active** (total): total 72,900,000; activity rate of total pop. 49.9% (participation rates: ages over 15, 78.0%; female 47.6%; unemployed 12.3%). **Household income and expenditure.** Average household size (1999): 2.8; income per household: Rub 37,800; sources of income (1999): wages 64.2% (includes nondeclared income), pensions and stipends 13.3%, income from entrepreneurial activities 14.3%, property income 7.3%, other 0.9%; expenditure (1999): food 52.0%, clothing 13.5%, furniture and household appliances 7.3%, housing 4.7%, transportation 2.4%. **Land use** (1994): forest 44.9%; pasture 5.2%; agriculture 7.7%; other 42.2%. **Tourism** (1999): receipts $7,510,000,000; expenditures $7,434,000,000.

Foreign trade

Imports (1999-c.i.f.): $40,200,000,000 (1998; machinery and transport equipment 23.9%, food 17.5%, chemicals 10.3%, ferrous and nonferrous metals 4.6%, wood and wood products 2.6%, fuels and lubricants 2.5%, textiles and clothing 2.2%). Major import sources (1999): Germany 13.9%; Belarus 10.6%; Ukraine 8.3%; US 7.9%; Kazakhstan 4.5%; Italy 3.8%; France 3.8%; Finland 3.1%; Poland 2.0%. **Exports** (1999-f.o.b.): $75,100,000,000 (fuels and lubricants 43.8%, of which oil and oil products 26.5%; ferrous and nonferrous metals 20.5%; machinery and transport equipment 10.6%; chemicals 8.3%; precious metals 6.4%, forestry products 5.3%). *Major export destinations:* US 8.9%; Germany 8.5%; Ukraine 6.6%; Belarus 5.2%; Italy 5.1%; China 4.9%; The Netherlands 4.8%; Switzerland 4.8%; UK 3.9%; Poland 3.9%; Finland 3.3%; Kazakhstan 1.7%.

Transport and communications

Transport. *Railroads* (1999): length 151,000 km; passenger-km 141,700,000,000; metric ton-km cargo 1,205,000,000. *Roads* (1999): total length 570,719 km (paved 79%). *Vehicles* (1999): passenger cars 19,717,800; trucks and buses 5,021,000. *Air transport* (1999): passenger-km 53,400,000,-000; metric ton-km cargo 2,300,000,000; airports (1998) 75. **Communications** Total units (units per 1,000 persons). Daily newspaper circulation (1996): 15,517,000 (105); Radio receivers (1997): 61,500,000 (417); Television receivers (1999): 62,000,000 (425); Telephone main lines (1999): 30,949,000 (212); Cellular telephone subscribers (1999): 1,370,600 (9.4); Personal computers (1999): 5,500,000 (37.7); Internet users (1999): 2,700,000 (18.5).

Education and health

Educational attainment (1998). Percentage of pop. age 16 and over having: primary or no formal education 11.2%; some secondary 25.3%; secondary and some postsecondary 40.9%; higher and postgraduate 22.6%. **Health** (2000): physicians 682,500 (1 per 214 persons); hospital beds 1,672,400 (1 per 87 persons); infant mortality rate per 1,000 live births (1999) 16.9. **Food** (1999): daily per capita caloric intake 2,879 (vegetable products 77%; animal products 23%); 112% of FAO recommended minimum.

Military

Total active duty personnel (2000): 1,004,100 (army 34.6%, navy 17.1%, air force 18.4%, other 29.9% [includes 300,000 personnel not allocated by service]). **Military expenditure as percentage of GNP** (1997): 5.8% (world 2.6%); per capita expenditure $283.

Did you know? Russia has its own (larger and older) version of America's Liberty Bell. Called the Tsar Bell, the 200-ton bronze bell was cast in 1734 on commission from Tsarina Anna I, but it was cracked in a fire in the Kremlin in 1737 before it could be raised, so it never rang.

Background

The region between the Dniester and the Volga rivers was inhabited from ancient times by various peoples, including the Slavs. The area was overrun from the 8th century BC to the 6th century AD by successive nomadic peoples, including the Sythians, Sarmatians, Goths, Huns, and Avars. Kievan Rus, a confederation of principalities ruled from Kiev, emerged c. 10th century. It lost supremacy in the 11th–12th centuries to independent principalities, including Novgorod and

Vladimir. Novgorod ascended in the north and was the only Russian principality to escape the domination of the Mongol Golden Horde in the 13th century. In the 14th–15th centuries the princes of Moscow gradually overthrew the Mongols. Under Ivan IV, Russia began to expand. The Romanov dynasty arose in 1613. Expansion continued under Peter I (the Great) and Catherine II (the Great). The area was invaded by Napoleon in 1812; after his defeat, Russia received most of the grand duchy of Warsaw (1815). Russia annexed Georgia, Armenia, and Caucasus territories in the 19th century. The Russian southward advance against the Ottoman empire was of key importance to Europe. Russia was defeated in the Crimean War. Russia sold Alaska to the US in 1867. Its defeat in the Russo–Japanese War led to an unsuccessful uprising in 1905. In World War I it fought against the Central Powers.

The Russian Revolution that overthrew the czarist regime in 1917 marked the beginning of a government of soviets ("councils"). The Bolsheviks brought the main part of the former empire under communist control and organized it as the Russian Soviet Federated Socialist Republic (RSFSR; coextensive with present-day Russia). The Russian SFSR joined other soviet republics in 1922 to form the USSR. Although it fought with the Allies in World War II, after the war tensions with the West led to the decades-long Cold War.

Upon the dissolution of the USSR in 1991, the Russian SFSR was renamed and became the leading member of the Commonwealth of Independent States. It adopted a new constitution in 1993. During the 1990s, it struggled on several fronts, beset with economic difficulties, political corruption, and independence movements.

Recent Developments

Vladimir Putin was elected president in 2000, with economic reform, governmental reorganization, cutbacks in the military, and rooting out corruption and favoritism as his chief goals. Putin targeted reforms in government structure and the judicial system in an effort to coordinate federal and local government and eliminate long-standing abuses. In 2001 the Duma passed legislation making it possible to buy land for the first time since the establishment of Soviet power.

Although foreign debt, capital flight, and a balance of payments deficit were a drag on the economy, production improved significantly. Oil production boomed and a significant increase in the GDP led to a welcome budget surplus. A flat income tax of 13% was levied, aimed at wiping out inequities and increasing government income.

After 11 Sep 2001, Putin offered the US help in combating terrorism. Both the US and Russia pledged to reduce the number of nuclear weapons over the ensuing decade. In May 2002 the landmark NATO-Russian Council established an alliance to work toward common security goals. Russia worked to improve foreign relations on many fronts—with surrounding countries, members of the former Soviet Union, China, the US, and Western Europe. Critics still found reason for concern in the treatment of the media and in the unresolved conflict with the breakaway Chechen Republic.

Internet resources: <www.russia-travel.com>

1 metric ton = about 1.1 short tons; 1 kilometer = 0.6 mi (statute); 1 metric ton-km cargo = about 0.68 short ton-mi cargo; c.i.f.: cost, insurance, and freight; f.o.b.: free on board

Rwanda

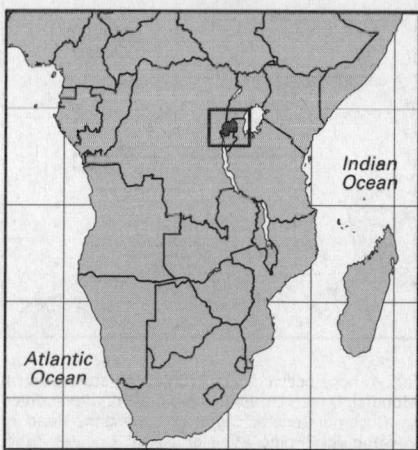

Indian Ocean

Atlantic Ocean

Official name: Repubulika y'u Rwanda (Rwanda); République Rwandaise (French); Republic of Rwanda (English). **Form of government:** transitional regime (until July 2003) with one legislative body (Transitional National Assembly [74]). **Head of state and government:** President Paul Kagame (from 2000) assisted by a prime minister. **Capital:** Kigali. **Official languages:** Rwanda; French; English. **Official religion:** none. **Monetary unit:** 1 Rwanda franc (RF); valuation (28 Jun 2002) $1 = RF 460.80.

Demography

Area: 10,169 sq mi, 26,338 sq km. **Population** (2001): 7,313,000. **Density** (2001 [land area only]): persons per sq mi 749.5, persons per sq km 289.4. **Urban** (1999): 6.0%. **Sex distribution** (2001): male 49.60%; female 50.40%. **Age breakdown** (2001): under 15, 43.0%; 15–29, 30.4%; 30–44, 15.0%; 45–59, 7.3%; 60–74, 3.5%; 75 and over, 0.8%. **Ethnic composition** (1996): Hutu 80.0%; Tutsi 19.0%; Twa 1.0%. **Religious affiliation** (1996): Roman Catholic 65.0%; Protestant 9.0%; Muslim 1.0%; indigenous beliefs and other 25.0%. **Major cities** (1991): Kigali 237,782; Ruhengeri 29,578; Butare 28,645; Gisenyi 21,918. **Location:** eastern central Africa, bordering Uganda, Tanzania, Burundi, and the Dem. Rep. of the Congo.

Vital statistics

Birth rate per 1,000 pop. (2000): 34.8 (world avg. 22.5). **Death rate** per 1,000 pop. (2000): 21.0 (world avg. 9.0). **Natural increase rate** per 1,000 pop. (2000): 13.8 (world avg. 13.5). **Total fertility rate** (avg. births per childbearing woman; 2000): 5.1. **Life expectancy** at birth (2000): male 38.6 years; female 40.1 years.

National economy

Budget (1998). *Revenue:* RF 99,000,000,000 (grants 33.3%, taxes on goods and services 28.9%, import and export duties 16.0%, income tax 3.4%). *Expenditures:* RF 117,400,000,000 (capital expenditures 35.9%, wages 24.6%, goods and services

21.7%, transfers 7.9%, debt payment 4.9%). **Production** (metric tons except as noted). *Agriculture, forestry, fishing* (1999): plantains 2,897,433, sweet potatoes 862,562, cassava 316,934; *livestock* (number of live animals) 725,541 cattle, 634,046 goats, 290,000 sheep; roundwood (1998) 3,000,000 cu m; fish catch (1998) 6,641. *Mining and quarrying* (1997): cassiterite (tin ore) 330; wolframite (tungsten ore) 188; gold 17 kg. *Manufacturing* (1997): cement 58,929; lye soap 6,966; beer 650,000 hectolitres. *Energy production (consumption):* electricity (kW-hr; 1998) 153,630,000 (186,080,000); petroleum products (metric tons; 1998) none (95,500); natural gas (cu m; 1996) 179,389 (179,389). **Population economically active** (1991): total 3,649,000; activity rate of total pop. 50.2% (participation rates: ages 14–74 [1989] 46.3%; female 53.5%; unemployed, n.a.). **Public debt** (external, outstanding; 1999): $1,162,000,000. **Tourism:** receipts (1993) $2,000,000; expenditures (1992) $17,000,000. **Land use** (1994): forested 10.1%; meadows and pastures 28.4%; agricultural and under permanent cultivation 47.4%; other 14.1%. **Gross national product** (1999): $2,041,000,000 ($250 per capita). **Household income and expenditure.** Average household size (1991) 4.7; average annual income per household (1983) RF 122,870; sources of income (1977): self-employment 71.0%, salaries and wages 16.5%, transfers 9.5%; expenditure (1982): food 44.2%, housing 13.2%, clothing and footwear 11.4%, transportation 10.3%, household equipment 8.4%.

Foreign trade

Imports (1999): $224,500,000 (food 16.7%, energy products 16.6%, capital goods 15.8%, intermediate goods 13.1%). *Major import sources* (1998): Kenya 25.8%; US 8.4%; Belgium 5.9%; France 5.2%; Germany 3.8%; The Netherlands 3.1%; Italy 2.8%; UK 1.7%; Democratic Republic of the Congo 1.7%. **Exports** (1999): $61,200,000 (coffee 43.3%, tea 28.6%, cassiterite and tin 1.8%). *Major export destinations* (1998): Belgium 47.6%; Germany 25.4%; US 6.3%; Italy 6.3%.

Transport and communications

Transport. *Roads* (1996): total length 14,900 km (paved 9%). *Vehicles* (1995): passenger cars 13,000; trucks 17,100. *Air transport:* (1994) passenger-mi 1,243,000, passenger-km 2,000,000; (1991) metric ton cargo loaded 2,674, metric ton cargo unloaded 4,794; airports (1998) with scheduled flights 2. **Communications** Total units (units per 1,000 persons). Daily newspaper circulation (1995): 500 (0.1); Radio receivers (1997): 601,000 (101); Telephone main lines (1999): 12,651 (1.8); Cellular telephone subscribers (1999): 11,000 (1.5).

Education and health

Educational attainment (1978). Percentage of pop. age 25 and over having: no formal schooling 76.9%; some primary education 16.8%; complete primary education 4.0%; some secondary and complete secondary education 2.0%; some postsecondary vocational and higher education 0.3%. **Literacy** (1995): percentage of total pop. age 15 and over literate 67.0%; males literate 73.7%; females literate 60.6%. **Health:** physicians (1992) 150 (1 per 50,000 persons); hospital beds (1990) 12,152 (1 per 588 persons); infant mortality rate (2000) 120.1. **Food** (1999): daily per capita caloric intake 2,011 (vegetable products 97%, animal products 3%); 87% of FAO recommended minimum requirement.

Military

Total active duty personnel (2000): 49,000–64,000 (army 100%). **Military expenditure as percentage of GNP** (1997): 4.4% (world 2.6%); per capita expenditure $10.

 **Did you know?** In addition to the dreadful human toll taken in Rwanda's civil war, the remaining mountain gorilla population in the country, made famous by naturalist Dian Fossey, also suffered grievously.

Background

Originally inhabited by the Twa, a Pygmy people, Rwanda became home to the Hutu, who were well established there when the Tutsi appeared in the 14th century. The Tutsi conquered the Hutu and in the 15th century founded a kingdom near Kigali. The Belgians occupied Rwanda in 1916, and the League of Nations created Ruanda-Urundi as a Belgian mandate in 1923. The Tutsi retained their dominance until shortly before Rwanda reached independence in 1962, when the Hutu took control of the government and stripped the Tutsi of much of their land. Many Tutsi fled Rwanda, and the Hutu dominated the country's political system, waging sporadic civil wars until mid-1994, when the death of the country's leader in a plane crash—apparently shot down—led to massive violence. The Tutsi-led Rwandan Patriotic Front (RPF) took over the country by force after the massacre of almost 500,000 Tutsi by Hutu. Two million refugees, mostly Hutu, fled to neighboring countries after the RPF's victory.

Recent Developments

Some 115,000 people suspected of taking part in the genocide of 1994 awaited trial; both international and Rwandan tribunals were trying those involved. Relations with neighboring Uganda and Congo continued to be strained; both countries accused Rwanda of interference in the Congo and Rwanda accused Congo of harboring Rwandan rebels. Extremist Hutu groups began to launch attacks in 2001 after two years' peace. In a reconstruction effort, local elections were held for the first time to choose district representatives and mayors, and a new flag and national anthem were adopted.

Internet resources:
<www.rwandemb.org/tourism.html>

Saint Kitts and Nevis

Official name: Federation of Saint Kitts and Nevis. **Form of government:** constitutional monarchy with one legislative house (National Assembly [15, includ-

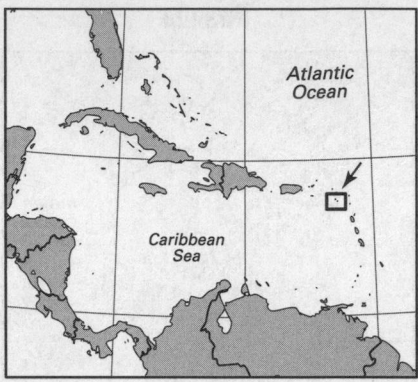

Atlantic Ocean

Caribbean Sea

ing 4 nonelective seats]). **Chief of state:** British Monarch Queen Elizabeth II (from 1952) represented by Governor-General Cuthbert Sebastian. **Head of government:** Prime Minister Denzil Douglas (from 1995). **Capital:** Basseterre. **Official language:** English. **Official religion:** none. **Monetary unit:** 1 Eastern Caribbean dollar (EC$) = 100 cents; valuation (28 Jun 2002) US$1 = EC $2.70.

Demography

Area: 104.0 sq mi, 269.4 sq km. **Population** (2001): 38,800. **Density** (2001): persons per sq mi 373.1, persons per sq km 144.0. **Urban** (2000): 34.2%. **Sex distribution** (2000): male 49.46%; female 50.54%. **Age breakdown** (2000): under 15, 30.3%; 15–29, 24.9%; 30–44, 22.2%; 45–59, 11.2%; 60–74, 7.1%; 75 and over, 4.3%. **Ethnic composition** (2000): black 90.4%; mulatto 5.0%; Indo-Pakistani 3.0%; white 1.0%; other/unspecified 0.6%. **Religious affiliation** (1995): Protestant 84.6%, of which Anglican 25.2%, Methodist 25.2%, Pentecostal 8.4%, Moravian 7.6%; Roman Catholic 6.7%; Hindu 1.5%; other 7.2%. **Major towns** (1994): Basseterre 12,605; Charlestown 1,411. **Location:** island in the Caribbean Sea, between Puerto Rico and Trinidad and Tobago.

Vital statistics

Birth rate per 1,000 pop. (2000): 19.1 (world avg. 22.5); (1983) legitimate 19.2%, illegitimate 80.8%. **Death rate** per 1,000 pop. (2000): 9.4 (world avg. 9.0). **Natural increase rate** per 1,000 pop. (2000): 9.7 (world avg. 13.5). **Total fertility rate** (avg. births per childbearing woman; 2000): 2.4. **Life expectancy** at birth (2000): male 67.9 years; female 73.7 years.

National economy

Budget (1999). *Revenue:* EC$252,400,000 (tax revenue 72.8% of which taxes on income and profits 19.6%, consumption taxes 16.3%, import duties 15.4%, taxes on domestic goods and services 14.9%; nontax revenue 26.1%). *Expenditures:* EC$298,300,000 (current expenditure 88.4%; development expenditure 11.6%). **Production** (metric tons except as noted). *Agriculture, forestry, fishing* (1999): sugarcane 196,784, tropical fruit 1,300, coconuts 1,000;

1 metric ton = about 1.1 short tons;   1 kilometer = 0.6 mi (statute);   1 metric ton-km cargo = about 0.68 short ton-mi cargo;   c.i.f.: cost, insurance, and freight;   f.o.b.: free on board

livestock (number of live animals) 14,500 goats, 8,000 sheep, 3,600 cattle; fish catch (1997) 161. *Mining and quarrying:* excavation of sand for local use. *Manufacturing* (2001): raw sugar 20,193; carbonated beverages 45,000 hectolitres (1995); beer 20,000 hectolitres (1995). *Energy production (consumption):* electricity (kW-hr; 1996) 82,000,000 (82,000,000); petroleum products (metric tons; 1996) none (33,000). **Gross national product** (1999): US$259,000,000 (US$6,330 per capita). **Household income and expenditure.** Average household size (1980) 3.7; average annual income per wage earner (1994) EC$9,940; expenditure (1978): food, beverages, and tobacco 55.6%, household furnishings 9.4%, housing 7.6%, clothing and footwear 7.5%, fuel and light 6.6%, transportation 4.3%, other 9.0%. **Public debt** (external, outstanding; 1999): US$131,700,-000. **Population economically active** (1980): total 17,125; activity rate of total pop. 39.5% (participation rates: ages 15–64, 69.5%; female 41.0%; unemployed [1997] 4.5%). **Land use** (1994): forested 17%; meadows and pastures 3%; agricultural and under permanent cultivation 39%; other 41%. **Tourism:** receipts from visitors (1999) US$307,000,000; expenditures by nationals abroad (1998) US$6,000,000.

Foreign trade

Imports (1997): EC$401,100,000 (machinery and transport equipment 30.3%, basic and miscellaneous manufactures 20.6%, food 16.1%, chemicals and chemical products 8.2%). *Major import sources:* US 45.5%; Caricom countries 13.4%, of which Trinidad and Tobago 9.8%; UK 9.7%. **Exports** (1997): EC$109,900,000 (food 56.0%, machinery and transport equipment [mostly electronic goods] 31.7%). *Major export destinations* (1997): US 55.0%; UK 32.6%; Caricom countries 2.9%.

Transport and communications

Transport. *Railroads* (1995): length 22 mi, 36 km. *Roads* (1996): total length 199 mi, 320 km (paved 43%). *Vehicles* (1995): passenger cars 5,200; trucks and buses 2,300. *Air transport:* passenger arrivals (1992) 123,195 (St. Kitts airports); airports (1998) with scheduled flights 2. **Communications** Total units (units per 1,000 persons). Radio receivers (1997): 28,000 (701); Television receivers (1997): 10,000 (264); Telephone main lines (1999): 20,059 (515); Cellular telephone subscribers (1999): 700 (18).

Education and health

Educational attainment (1980). Percentage of pop. age 25 and over having: no formal schooling 1.1%; primary education 29.6%; secondary 67.2%; higher 2.1%. **Literacy** (1990): total pop. age 15 and over literate 25,500 (90.0%); males literate 13,100 (90.0%); females literate 12,400 (90.0%). **Health** (1998): physicians 50 (1 per 815 persons); hospital beds 244 (1 per 167 persons); infant mortality rate per 1,000 live births (2000): 16.7. **Food** (1998): daily per capita caloric intake 2,766 (vegetable products 75%, animal products 25%); 114% of FAO recommended minimum requirement.

Military

Total active duty personnel: in July 1997 the National Assembly approved a bill creating a 50-member army.

Military expenditure as percentage of GNP (1998): 3.5%; per capita expenditure US$226 (may include expenditure for police).

Background

St. Kitts became the first British colony in the West Indies in 1623. Anglo-French rivalry grew in the 17th century and lasted more than a century. In 1783, by the Treaty of Versailles, the islands became wholly British possessions. They were united with Anguilla from 1882 to 1980 but became an independent federation within the British Commonwealth in 1983. In 1997 Nevis considered becoming independent.

Recent Developments

In elections for the National Assembly in 2000, the St. Kitts–Nevis Labour Party swept all eight seats for St. Kitts, with two opposition parties splitting the three seats for Nevis. The Finance Ministry was under investigation for irregularities during the previous administration. An offshore banking site, St. Kitts and Nevis was attempting to meet international standards set by the Paris-based Financial Action Task Force for combatting money laundering.

Internet resources: <www.stkittsnevis.net>

Saint Lucia

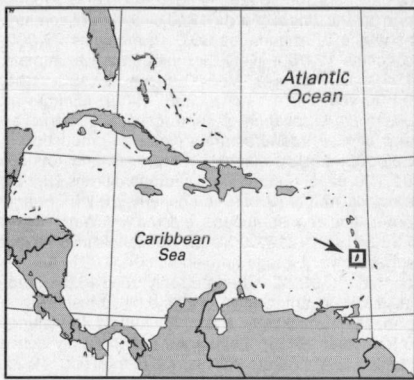

Official name: Saint Lucia. **Form of government:** constitutional monarchy with a Parliament consisting of two legislative chambers (Senate [11]; House of Assembly [17]). **Chief of state:** Queen Elizabeth II (from 1952) represented by Governor General Perlette Louisy (from 1997). **Head of government:** Prime Minister Kenneth Anthony (from 1997). **Capital:** Castries. **Official language:** English. **Official religion:** none. **Monetary unit:** 1 Eastern Caribbean dollar (EC$) = 100 cents; valuation (28 Jun 2002) US$1 = EC$2.70.

Demography

Area: 238 sq mi, 617 sq km. **Population** (2001): 158,000. **Density** (2001): persons per sq mi 663.9, persons per sq km 256.1. **Urban** (1998): 37.3%. **Sex distribution** (1997): male 48.34%; female 51.66%. **Age breakdown** (1999): under 15, 33.5%; 15–29, 30.9%; 30–44, 20.4%; 45–59, 8.0%; 60–74, 4.9%; 75 and over, 2.3%. **Ethnic composition** (2000): black

50%; mulatto 44%; East Indian 3%; white 1%; other 2%. **Religious affiliation** (1995): Roman Catholic 79.2%; Protestant 19.4%, of which Pentecostal 5.4%, Seventh-day Adventist 5.2%; other 1.4%. **Major city** (1997): Castries city proper 2,249 (urban area 16,187). **Location:** island between the Caribbean Sea and North Atlantic Ocean, north of Trinidad and Tobago.

Vital statistics

Birth rate per 1,000 pop. (2000): 22.2 (world avg. 22.5); legitimate (1998) 14.2%; illegitimate 85.8%. **Death rate** per 1,000 pop. (2000): 5.4 (world avg. 9.0). **Natural increase rate** per 1,000 pop. (2000): 16.8 (world avg. 13.5). **Total fertility rate** (avg. births per childbearing woman; 2000): 2.4. **Marriage rate** per 1,000 pop. (1997): 3.1. **Divorce rate** per 1,000 pop. (1997): 0.2. **Life expectancy** at birth (2000): male 68.7 years; female 76.1 years.

National economy

Budget (1998–99). *Revenue:* EC$469,900,000 (current revenue 86.9%, of which consumption duties on imported goods 24.4%; taxes on income and profits 21.9%; import duties 14.7%; nontax revenue 9.2%; grants 3.9%). *Expenditures:* EC$496,600,000 (current expenditures 69.4%; development expenditures and net lending 30.6%). **Public debt** (external, outstanding; 1999): US$125,600,000. **Tourism:** receipts from visitors (1999) US$311,000,000; expenditures by nationals abroad (1997) US$29,000,000. **Production** (metric tons except as noted). *Agriculture, forestry, fishing* (1999): bananas 80,000, mangoes 27,000, coconuts 12,000; livestock (number of live animals; 1999) 14,750 pigs, 12,500 sheep, 12,450 cattle, 9,800 goats; fish catch (1998) 1,462. *Mining and quarrying:* excavation of sand for local construction and pumice. *Manufacturing* (value of production in EC$'000; 1998): alcoholic beverages and tobacco 31,120; paper products and cardboard boxes 28,747; electrical and electronic components 16,245. *Energy production (consumption):* electricity (kW-hr; 1998) 235,881,000 (213,000,000). **Household income and expenditure.** Average household size (1991) 4.0; expenditure (1982-Castries area only): food 46.8%, housing 13.5%, clothing and footwear 6.5%, transportation and communications 6.3%, household furnishings 5.8%, other 21.1%. **Population economically active** (1998): total 73,660; activity rate of total pop. 49.2% (participation rates: ages 15–64, 79.1%; female 44.4%; unemployed 22.2%). **Gross national product** (at current market prices; 1999): US$590,000,000 (US$3,820 per capita). **Land use** (1994): forested 13%; meadows and pastures 5%; agricultural and under permanent cultivation 30%; other 52%.

Foreign trade

Imports (1998): US$279,600,000 (food 21.7%; machinery and transportation equipment 21.1%; manufactured goods 19.0%; chemicals and chemical products 8.6%; crude petroleum and petroleum products 8.5%). *Major import sources:* United States 40.0%; Caricom countries 21.2%, of which Trinidad and Tobago 11.5%; United Kingdom 9.2%; Japan 4.4%. **Exports** (1998): US$78,500,000 (bananas 50.5%; clothing 7.5%; primarily paper and paperboard 5.9%;

beer 5.0%). *Major export destinations:* United Kingdom 60.0%; United States 21.0%; Caricom countries 16.3%.

Transport and communications

Transport. *Roads* (1997): total length 750 mi, 1,210 km (paved 5%). *Vehicles* (1997): passenger cars 14,783; trucks and buses 1,020. *Air transport* (1999-Casties and Vieux Fort airports): passenger arrivals and departures 912,000; cargo unloaded and loaded 4,600 metric tons; airports (1998) with scheduled flights 2. **Communications** Total units (units per 1,000 persons). Radio receivers (1997): 100,000 (668); Television receivers (1997): 40,000 (267); Telephone main lines (1999): 44,465 (289); Cellular telephone subscribers (1998): 1,900 (12.5).

Education and health

Educational attainment (1980). Percentage of pop. age 25 and over having: no formal schooling 17.5%; primary education 74.4%; secondary 6.8%; higher 1.3%. **Literacy** (1995): about 82%. **Health** (1997): physicians 81 (1 per 1,847 persons); hospital beds 527 (1 per 284 persons); infant mortality rate per 1,000 live births (2000) 15.6. **Food** (1999): daily per capita caloric intake 2,812 (vegetable products 77%, animal products 23%); 116% of FAO recommended minimum requirement.

Background

Caribs replaced early Arawak inhabitants c. AD 800–1300. Settled by the French in 1650, it was ceded to Great Britain in 1814 and became one of the Windward Islands in 1871. It became fully independent in 1979. The economy is based on agriculture and tourism.

Recent Developments

In the 2001 elections, the Labour Party maintained its dominance, with 14 of the 17 seats in the National Assembly. Along with other Caribbean offshore banking sites, St. Lucia was under the scrutiny of international regulatory agencies concerned about money laundering and other practices. The tourist industry, an economic mainstay, was already stagnating before the terrorist attacks of 11 Sep 2001 and experienced a severe drop in arrivals and loss of revenue.

Internet resources: <www.slucia.com>

Saint Vincent and the Grenadines

Official name: Saint Vincent and the Grenadines. **Form of government:** constitutional monarchy with one legislative house (House of Assembly [21; includes 6 nonelective seats]). **Chief of state:** British Monarch Queen Elizabeth II (from 1952) represented by Governor-General Monica Dacon (acting from 3 Jun 2002). **Head of government:** Prime Minister Ralph Gonsalves (from 2001). **Capital:** Kingstown. **Official language:** English. **Official religion:** none. **Monetary unit:** 1 Eastern Caribbean dollar (EC$) = 100 cents; valuation (28 Jun 2002) US$1 = EC$2.70.

1 metric ton = about 1.1 short tons;   1 kilometer = 0.6 mi (statute);   1 metric ton-km cargo = about 0.68 short ton-mi cargo;   c.i.f.: cost, insurance, and freight;   f.o.b.: free on board

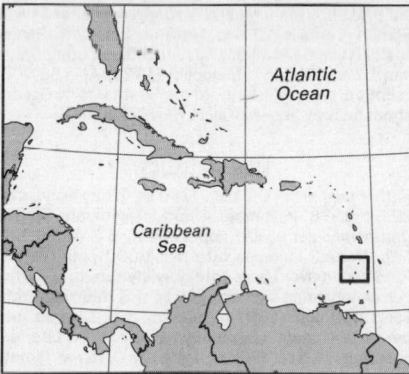

Demography

Area: 150.3 sq mi, 389.3 sq km. **Population** (2001): 113,000. **Density** (2001): persons per sq mi 751.8, persons per sq km 290.3. **Urban** (2000): 54.4%. **Sex distribution** (1999): male 50.50%; female 49.50%. **Age breakdown** (1999): under 15, 31.3%; 15–29, 31.2%; 30–44, 19.6%; 45–59, 9.4%; 60–74, 5.9%; 75 and over, 2.6%. **Ethnic composition** (1999): black 65.5%; mulatto 23.5%; Indo-Pakistani 5.5%; white 3.5%; black-Amerindian 2.0%. **Religious affiliation** (1995): Protestant 57.6%; unaffiliated Christian 20.6%; Roman Catholic 10.7%; Hindu 3.3%; Muslim 1.5%; other/nonreligious 6.3%. **Major city** (1999): Kingstown 16,175. **Location:** islands in the Caribbean Sea, north of Trinidad and Tobago.

Vital statistics

Birth rate per 1,000 pop. (2000): 18.3 (world avg. 22.5). **Death rate** per 1,000 pop. (2000): 6.2 (world avg. 9.0). **Natural increase rate** per 1,000 pop. (2000): 12.1 (world avg. 13.5). **Total fertility rate** (avg. births per childbearing woman; 2000): 2.1. **Marriage rate** per 1,000 pop. (1997): 4.6. **Divorce rate** per 1,000 pop. (1997): 0.8. **Life expectancy** at birth (2000): male 70.6 years; female 74.1 years.

National economy

Budget (1998). *Revenue:* EC$285,200,000 (current revenue 73.8%, of which income tax 25.1%, consumption duties on imports 23.3%, taxes on goods and services 9.3%, import duties 7.9%; grants 14.5%; nontax revenue 9.5%; capital revenue 2.2%). *Expenditures:* EC$303,100,000 (current expenditure 65.9%; development expenditure 34.1%). **Public debt** (external, outstanding; 1999): US$150,800,000. **Production** (metric tons except as noted). *Agriculture, forestry, fishing* (1999): bananas 43,000, coconuts 23,600, roots and tubers 9,000; livestock (number of live animals) 13,000 sheep, 9,400 pigs, 6,200 cattle; fish catch (1998) 835. *Mining and quarrying:* sand and gravel for local use. *Manufacturing* (export value of manufactures in US$'000,000; 1995): packaged flour 8.7; packaged rice 6.4; other goods (mostly garments, sporting goods, and electronic goods) 8.1. *Energy production (consumption):* electricity (kW-hr; 1998) 82,773,000 (82,773,000); petroleum products (metric tons; 1996) none (41,000). **Tourism:** receipts from visitors (1999) US$77,000,000; expendi-

tures by nationals abroad (1998) US$8,000,000. **Gross national product** (1999): US$301,000,000 (US$2,640 per capita). **Population economically active** (1991): total 41,682; activity rate of total pop. 39.1% (participation rates: ages 15–64, 67.5%; female 35.9%; unemployed [1996] more than 30%). **Household income and expenditure.** Average household size (1991) 3.9; income per household (1988) EC$4,579; expenditure (1975–76); food and beverages 59.8%, clothing 7.7%, household furnishings 6.6%, housing 6.3%, energy 6.2%, other 13.4%. **Land use** (1994): forested 36%; meadows and pastures 5%; agricultural and under permanent cultivation 28%; other 31%.

Foreign trade

Imports (1998): US$169,100,000 (basic manufactures 33.7%; food products 23.1%; machinery and transport equipment 22.2%; chemical products 9.7%; fuels 5.6%). *Major import sources:* US 39.4%; Caricom countries 24.5%, of which Trinidad and Tobago 16.8%; UK 12.5%; other 6.8%. **Exports** (1998-c.i.f., f.o.b.): US$49,600,000 (domestic exports 94.1%, of which bananas 41.5%, packaged flour 13.9%, packaged rice 12.9%, eddoes and dasheens 3.8%; reexports 5.9%). *Major export destinations:* Caricom countries 49.1%, of which Trinidad and Tobago 11.0%, St. Lucia 10.4%; UK 42.2%; US 5.2%; other 3.5%.

Transport and communications

Transport. *Roads* (1996): total length 1,040 km (paved 31%). *Vehicles* (1997): passenger cars 6,089; trucks and buses 3,670. *Air transport* (1997): passenger arrivals 125,400; passenger departures 130,166; airports (1998) with scheduled flights 5. **Communications** Total units (units per 1,000 persons). Radio receivers (1995): 65,000 (591); Television receivers (1995): 17,700 (161); Telephone main lines (1999): 23,631 (212); Cellular telephone subscribers (1999): 1,420 (13).

Education and health

Educational attainment (1980). Percentage of pop. age 25 and over having: no formal schooling 2.4%; primary education 88.0%; secondary 8.2%; higher 1.4%. **Literacy** (1991): total pop. age 15 and over literate 64,000 (96.0%). **Health** (1998): physicians 59 (1 per 1,883 persons); hospital beds 209 (1 per 531 persons); infant mortality rate per 1,000 live births (1999) 17.7. **Food** (1999): daily per capita caloric intake 2,540 (vegetable products 83%, animal products 17%); 105% of FAO recommended minimum.

Military

Total active duty personnel (1992): 634-member police force includes a coast guard and paramilitary unit.

Did you know? Saint Vincent's Royal Botanic Gardens are the oldest such facility in the western hemisphere. The 30-acre gardens were founded in 1765 and are located in the place where Captain Bligh (of HMS *Bounty*) brought the breadfruit tree to the islands.

Background

The French and the British contested for control of St. Vincent and the Grenadines until 1763, when it was ceded to England by the Treaty of Paris. The original inhabitants, the Caribs, recognized British sovereignty but revolted in 1795. Most of the Caribs were deported; many who remained were killed in volcanic eruptions in 1812 and 1902. In 1969 St. Vincent and the Grenadines became a self-governing state in association with the United Kingdom, and in 1979 it achieved full independence.

Recent Developments

In the general elections held two years early in March 2001, voters expressed their dissatisfaction with the New Democratic Party, which had held power since 1984, by returning a resounding victory for the Unity Labour Party. Antigovernment protests had prompted the elections. A new package of legislation governing offshore banking activities was promised following a negative assessment by the Paris-based Financial Action Task Force.

Internet resources: <www.svgtourism.com>

Samoa

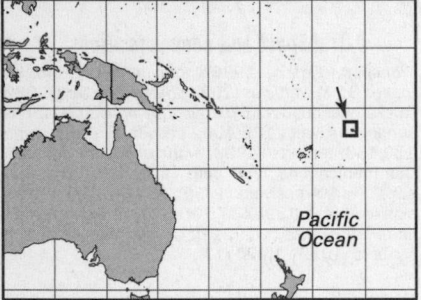

Pacific
Ocean

Official name: Malo Sa'oloto Tuto'atasi o Samoa (Samoan); Independent State of Samoa (English). **Form of government:** constitutional monarchy with one legislative house (Legislative Assembly [49]). **Chief of state:** Chief Tanumafili II Malietoa (from 1962). **Head of government:** Prime Minister Sailele Malielegaoi Tuila'Epa (from 1998). **Capital:** Apia. **Official languages:** Samoan; English. **Official religion:** none. **Monetary unit:** 1 tala (SA$, plural tala) = 100 sene; valuation (28 Jun 2002) US$1 = SA$3.24.

Demography

Area: 1,093 sq mi, 2,831 sq km. **Population** (2001): 179,000. **Density** (2001): persons per sq mi 163.8, persons per sq km 63.2. **Urban** (1999): 21.0%. **Sex distribution** (1991): male 52.45%; female 47.55%. **Age breakdown** (1991): under 15, 40.6%; 15–29, 29.9%; 30–44, 14.6%; 45–59, 8.8%; 60–74, 5.0%; 75 and over, 1.1%. **Ethnic composition** (1997): Samoan (Polynesian) 92.6%; Euronesian (European and Polynesian) 7.0%; European 0.4%. **Religious affil-**

iation (1995): Mormon 25.8%; Congregational 24.6%; Roman Catholic 21.3%; Methodist 12.2%; Pentecostal 8.0%; Seventh-day Adventist 3.9%; other Christian 1.7%; other 2.5%. **Major city** (1999): Apia 38,000. **Location:** group of islands in the South Pacific Ocean, about halfway from Hawaii to New Zealand.

Vital statistics

Birth rate per 1,000 pop. (2001): 28.2 (world avg. 22.5); (1978) legitimate 43.5%; illegitimate 56.5%. **Death rate** per 1,000 pop. (2001): 5.7 (world avg. 9.0). **Natural increase rate** per 1,000 pop. (2001): 22.5 (world avg. 13.5). **Total fertility rate** (avg. births per childbearing woman; 2001): 4.3. **Marriage rate** per 1,000 pop. (1992-registered): 5.0. **Divorce rate** per 1,000 pop. (1989-registered): 0.2. **Life expectancy** at birth (2001): male 67.0 years; female 73.0 years.

National economy

Budget (1998–99). *Revenue:* SA$276,900,000 (tax revenue 56.1%; grants 30.7%; nontax revenue 13.2%). *Expenditures:* SA$279,400,000 (current expenditure 61.9%; development expenditure 32.3%; net lending 5.8%). **Public debt** (external, outstanding; 1999): US$156,500,000. **Production** (metric tons except as noted). *Agriculture, forestry, fishing* (1999): coconuts 130,000, taro 36,900, bananas 10,000; livestock (number of live animals) 178,800 pigs, 26,000 cattle, 350,000 chickens; roundwood (1998) 131,000 cu m; fish catch (1997) 4,590. *Manufacturing* (in WS$'000; 1990): beer 8,708; cigarettes 6,551; coconut cream 5,576. *Energy production (consumption):* electricity (kW-hr; 1996) 65,000,000 (65,000,000); petroleum products (metric tons; 1996) (43,000). **Household income and expenditure.** Average household size (1981) 5.1; income per household (1972) WS$1,518; sources of income (1972): wages 49.4%, self-employment 22.8%, remittances, gifts, and other assistance 18.0%, land rent 8.7%, other 1.1%; expenditure (1987)[6]: food 58.8%, transportation 9.0%, housing and furnishings 5.1%, fuel and lighting 5.0%, clothing 4.2%, other goods and services 1.9%, other 16.0%. **Tourism** (1999): receipts from visitors US$42,000,000; expenditures by nationals abroad US$4,000,000. **Gross national product** (1999): US$181,000,000 (US$1,070 per capita). **Population economically active** (1994): total 47,207; activity rate of total pop. 28.7% (participation rates: ages 15–64 [1981] 48.6%; female [1991] 32.0%). **Land use** (1994): forested 47.3%; meadows and pastures 0.4%; agricultural and under permanent cultivation 43.1%; other 9.2%.

Foreign trade

Imports (1997-c.i.f.): WS$247,377,000 ([1996] food 33.9%, industrial supplies 26.4%, machinery 16.9%, petroleum products 11.8%, consumer goods 11.0%). *Major import sources:* New Zealand 37.9%; Australia 20.7%; US 15.6%; Fiji 15.0%; Japan 4.5%. **Exports** (1997-f.o.b.): WS$38,531,000 (fresh fish 33.0%, copra 21.1%, coconut oil 18.1%, coconut cream 12.8%, beer 4.3%, kava 4.0%, copra meal 1.5%). *Major export destinations:* New Zealand 48.1%; American Samoa 15.3%; Australia 9.2%; US 3.3%; Germany 2.9%.

1 metric ton = about 1.1 short tons;   1 kilometer = 0.6 mi (statute);   1 metric ton-km cargo = about 0.68 short ton-mi cargo;   c.i.f.: cost, insurance, and freight;   f.o.b.: free on board

Transport and communications

Transport. Roads (1996). total length 491 mi, 790 km (paved 42%). Vehicles (1995): passenger cars 1,068; trucks and buses 1,169. Air transport (1996): passenger-km 265,000,000; metric ton-km cargo 26,000,000; airports (1997) with scheduled flights 3. Communications Total units (units per 1,000 persons). Radio receivers (1997): 178,000 (1,035); Television receivers (1998): 9,000 (52); Telephone main lines (1998): 8,480 (49); Cellular telephone subscribers (1999): 3,000 (17); Personal computers (1999): 1,000 (5.6); Internet users (1999): 500 (2.8).

Education and health

Educational attainment (1981). Percentage of pop. age 25 and over having: some primary education 16.5%; complete primary 24.5%; some secondary 52.1%; complete secondary 3.1%; higher 2.0%; unknown 1.8%. Literacy (1981): virtually 100%. Health: physicians (1996) 62 (1 per 2,919 persons); hospital beds (1991) 863 (1 per 255 persons); infant mortality rate per 1,000 live births (2001) 27.0. Food (1992): daily per capita caloric intake 2,828 (vegetable products 74%, animal products 26%); 124% of FAO recommended minimum requirement.

Military

No military forces are maintained; New Zealand is responsible for defense.

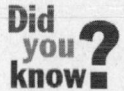

Did you know? Tattooing is a significant rite of passage in Samoa. Males about age 13 are tattooed from waist to knee using bamboo needles. The ability to withstand the pain is considered a sign of manhood.

Background

Polynesians inhabited the islands of the Samoan archipelago for thousands of years before they were visited by Europeans in the 18th century. The islands were contested by the US, Britain, and Germany until 1899, when they were divided between the US and Germany. In 1914, Western Samoa was occupied by New Zealand, which received it as a League of Nations mandate in 1920. After World War II, it became a UN trust territory administered by New Zealand, and it achieved independence in 1962. In 1997, the word Western was dropped from the country's name.

Recent Developments

The Human Rights Protection Party continued its dominance after the March 2001 election, but it relied on the support of independent members of parliament for a ruling majority. Three women took seats in parliament. Samoa broke with other South Pacific nations when it failed to support the establishment of a sanctuary for whales in the face of Japan's planned expansion of whaling in the region.

Internet resources: <www.samoaobserver.ws>

San Marino

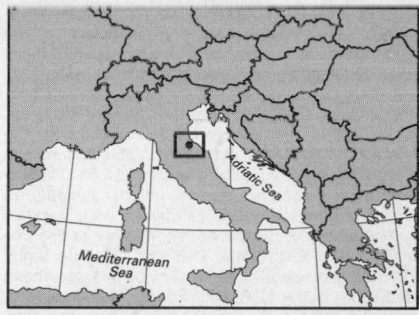

Official name: Serenissima Repubblica di San Marino (Most Serene Republic of San Marino). Form of government: unitary multiparty republic with one legislative house (Great and General Council [60]). Head of state and government: Captains-Regent Antonio Lazzaro Volpinari and Giovanni Francesco Ugolini (from 1 Apr 2002). Capital: San Marino. Official language: Italian. Official religion: none. Monetary unit: 1 euro (€) = 100 cents; valuation (28 Jun 2002) $1 = €1.01; at conversion on 1 Jan 2002, €1= 1,936.27 Italian lire (Lit).

Demography

Area: 23.63 sq mi, 61.19 sq km. Population (2001): 27,200. Density (2001): persons per sq mi 1,152.4, persons per sq km 445.0. Urban (1999): 96.0%. Sex distribution (2000): male 48.34%; female 51.66%. Age breakdown (2000): under 15, 15.7%; 15–29, 18.8%; 30–44, 25.5%; 45–59, 18.8%; 60–74, 14.0%; 75 and over, 7.2%. Ethnic composition (1997): Sammarinesi 83.1%; Italian 12.0%; other 4.8%. Religious affiliation (2000): Roman Catholic 88.7%; Pentecostal 1.8%; other 9.5%. Major cities (1997): Serravalle/Dogano 4,802; Borgo Maggiore 2,394; San Marino 2,294. Location: southern Europe, completely surrounded by Italy.

Vital statistics

Birth rate per 1,000 pop. (2000): 10.9 (world avg. 22.5); (1985) legitimate 95.2%; illegitimate 4.8%. Death rate per 1,000 pop. (2000): 7.6 (world avg. 9.0). Natural increase rate per 1,000 pop. (2000): 3.3 (world avg. 13.5). Total fertility rate (avg. births per childbearing woman; 2000): 1.3. Marriage rate per 1,000 pop. (1992–96): 8.1. Divorce rate per 1,000 pop. (1991–95): 1.0. Life expectancy at birth (2000): male 77.6 years; female 85.0 years.

National economy

Budget (1997). Revenue: Lit 411,000,000,000 (taxes on goods and services 37.2%; taxes on income and profits 31.6%; social security 19.7%). Expenditures: Lit 448,000,000,000 (current expenditures 90.4%, of which social security and subsidies 48.2%, wages and salaries 31.2%; capital expenditures 6.9%; other 2.7%). Tourism: number of tourist arrivals (1999) 3,148,000; receipts from visitors (1994) $252,500,000. Population economically active (1999): total 19,347; activity rate of total pop. 73.2% (participation rates: ages 15–64, 88.4%; female

41.2%; unemployed 4.4%). **Household income and expenditure.** Total number of households (1997) 10,093; average household size 2.5; expenditure (1991; based on the weighting coefficient for the 1991 CPI index for the North-Central region of Italy): food, beverages, and tobacco 22.1%, housing, fuel, and electrical energy 20.9%, transportation and communications 17.6%, clothing and footwear 8.0%, furniture, appliances, and goods and services for the home 7.2%, education 7.1%, health and sanitary services 2.6%, other goods and services 14.5%. **Production** (metric tons except as noted). *Agriculture, forestry, fishing* (early 1980s): wheat c. 4,400, grapes c. 700, barley c. 500; livestock (number of live animals; 1998) 831 cattle, 748 pigs. *Manufacturing* (1998): processed meats 324,073 kg; cheese 61,563 kg; butter 12,658 kg. *Energy production (consumption)*: all electrical power is imported via electrical grid from Italy. **Gross national product** (at current market prices; 1998): $344,000,000 ($13,200 per capita). **Land use** (1985): agricultural and under permanent cultivation 74%; meadows and pastures 22%; forested, built-on, wasteland, and other 4%.

Foreign trade

Imports (1996): $1,719,300,000 (manufactured goods of all kinds, oil, and gold). *Major import source:* Italy. **Exports** (1996): $1,741,900,000 (manufactured goods, traditionally wine, wheat, woolen goods, furniture, wood, ceramics, building stone, dairy products, meat, and postage stamps). *Major export destination:* Italy.

Transport and communications

Transport. *Roads* (1999): total length 252 km. *Vehicles* (1999): passenger cars 26,320; trucks and buses 2,763. *Air transport*: There is a heliport that provides passenger and cargo service between San Marino and Rimini, Italy, during the summer months. **Communications** Total units (units per 1,000 persons). Daily newspaper circulation (1996): 2,000 (72); Radio receivers (1998): 16,000 (610); Television receivers (1998) 9,055 (358); Telephone main lines (1999) 19,970 (769); Cellular telephone subscribers (1999): 10,000 (369).

Education and health

Educational attainment (1997). Percentage of pop. age 14 and over having: basic literacy (includes 0.9% illiterate population) or primary education 35.6%; secondary 30.7%; some postsecondary 27.9%; higher degree 5.8%. **Literacy** (1997): total pop. age 15 and over literate 21,885 (99.1%); males literate 10,546 (99.4%); females literate 11,339 (98.8%). **Health** (1999): physicians 84 (1 per 315 persons); hospital beds 143 (1 per 185 persons); infant mortality rate per 1,000 live births (2000) 6.3. **Food** (1999; figures are for Italy): daily per capita caloric intake 3,269 (vegetable products 82%, animal products 18%); 130% of FAO recommended minimum requirement.

Military

Total active duty personnel: All fit males ages 16-55 constitute the militia that provides national security.

Military expenditure as percentage of national budget (1992): 1.0% (world 3.6%); per capita expenditure (1987) $155.

 San Marino claims to be the oldest republic in the world. It was also the smallest republic in the world until the independence of Nauru in 1968. The sale of postage stamps to foreign collectors is a significant source of revenue for San Marino.

Background

According to tradition, San Marino was founded in the early 4th century AD by St. Marinus. By the 12th century it had developed into a commune and remained independent despite challenges from neighboring rulers, including the Malatesta family in nearby Rimini, Italy. San Marino survived the Renaissance as a relic of the self-governing Italian city-state and remained an independent republic after the unification of Italy in 1861. It is one of the smallest republics in the world, and it may be the oldest one in Europe.

Recent Developments

In parliamentary elections held in June 2001, the ruling Christian Democratic–Socialist coalition remained in power with two-thirds of the seats. The European Union announced plans to close loopholes in tax laws that allowed San Marino to function as a tax haven for investments. San Marino joined neighboring Italy in adopting the euro as currency in 2002.

Internet resources:
<http://emulateme.com/sanmarino.htm>

São Tomé and Príncipe

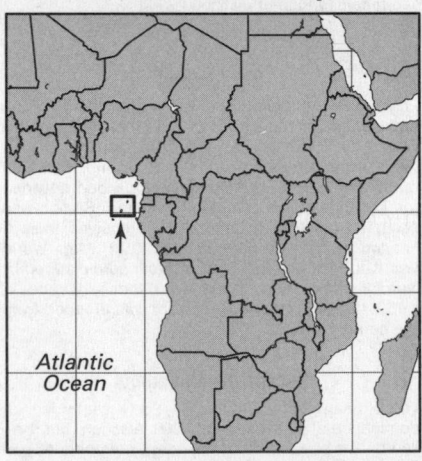

Atlantic
Ocean

Official name: República democrática de São Tomé e Príncipe (Democratic Republic of São Tomé and Príncipe). **Form of government:** Multiparty republic

1 metric ton = about 1.1 short tons;   1 kilometer = 0.6 mi (statute);   1 metric ton-km cargo = about 0.68 short ton-mi cargo;   c.i.f.: cost, insurance, and freight;   f.o.b.: free on board

with one legislative house (National Assembly [55]). **Chief of state:** President Fradique de Menezes (from 3 Sep 2001). **Head of government:** Prime Minister Gabriel de Costa (from 26 Mar 2002). **Capital:** São Tomé. **Official language:** Portuguese. **Official religion:** none. **Monetary unit:** 1 dobra (Db) = 100 cêntimos; valuation (28 Jun 2002) $1 = Db 9,019.70.

Demography

Area: 386 sq mi, 1,001 sq km. **Population** (2001): 147,000. **Density** (2001): persons per sq mi 379.9, persons per sq km 146.5. **Urban** (1999): 46.0%. **Sex distribution** (2000): male 49.26%, female 50.74%. **Age breakdown** (2000): under 15, 47.7%; 15–29, 27.4%; 30–44, 12.6%; 45–59, 6.3%; 60–74, 4.7%; 75 and over, 1.3%. **Ethnic composition** (2000): blackwhite admixture 79.5%; Fang 10.0%; angolares (descendants of former Angolan slaves) 7.6%; Portuguese 1.9%; other 1.0%. **Religious affiliation** (1995): Roman Catholic, about 89.5%; remainder mostly Protestant, predominantly Seventh-Day Adventist and an indigenous Evangelical Church. **Major cities:** São Tomé (1991) 43,420; Trindade (1981) 11,388. **Location:** islands in the Gulf of Guinea, straddling the Equator west of Gabon.

Vital statistics

Birth rate per 1,000 pop. (2000): 43.0 (world avg. 22.5). **Death rate** per 1,000 pop. (2000): 7.8 (world avg. 9.0). **Natural increase rate** per 1,000 pop. (2000): 35.2 (world avg. 13.5). **Total fertility rate** (avg. births per childbearing woman; 2000): 6.1. **Life expectancy** at birth (2000): male 63.8 years; females 66.7 years.

National economy

Budget (1997). *Revenue:* Db 55,528,000,000 (grants 43.7%; taxes 38.2%, of which import taxes 8.5%, sales taxes 7.5%, export taxes 3.4%; nontax revenue 18.1%). *Expenditures:* Db 140,174,000,-000 (capital expenditure 60.3%; recurrent expenditure 39.7%, of which debt service 15.9%, defense 1.2%). **Public debt** (external, outstanding; 1999): $233,200,000. **Tourism** (1997): receipts from visitors $2,000,000; expenditures by nationals abroad $1,000,000. **Production** (metric tons except as noted). *Agriculture, forestry, fishing* (1999): coconuts 28,000, bananas 18,000, cacao 4,197; livestock (number of live animals) 4,750 goats, 4,000 cattle, 2,550 sheep; roundwood (1998) 9,000 cu m; fish catch (1998) 3,305. *Mining and quarrying:* some quarrying to support local construction industry. *Manufacturing* (value in Db; 1995): beer 880,000; clothing 679,000; lumber 369,000. *Energy production (consumption):* electricity (kW-hr; 1996) 15,000,000 (15,000,000); petroleum products (metric tons; 1996) (26,000). **Household income and expenditure.** Average household size (1981): 4.0; expenditure (1995): food 71.9%, housing and energy 10.2%, transportation and communications 6.4%, clothing and other items 5.3%, household durable goods 2.8%, education and health 1.7%. **Population economically active** (1994): total 51,789; activity rate of total population 40.8% (participation rates [1981] ages 15–64, 61.1%; female [1991] 32.4%; unemployed [1994] 29.0%). **Gross national product** (1999): $40,000,000 ($270 per capita). **Land use** (1994): meadows and pastures 1.3%; agricultural and under permanent cultivation 54.0%; forest, built-on, wasteland, and other 44.7%.

Foreign trade

Imports (1997): $19,200,000 (capital goods 29.2%, food and other agricultural products 19.8%, petroleum products 19.8%). *Major import sources:* Portugal 26.3%; France 17.9%; Angola 6.7%; Belgium 5.8%; Japan 3.3%. **Exports** (1997): $5,300,000 (cocoa 86.8%). *Major export destinations:* The Netherlands 50.9%; Germany 5.7%; Portugal 5.7%.

Transport and communications

Transport. *Roads* (1996): total length 320 km (paved 68%). *Vehicles* (1996): passenger cars 4,040; trucks and buses 1,540. *Air transport* (1997): passenger-km 9,000,000; short ton-km cargo 1,000,000; airports (1998) 2. **Communications** Total units (units per 1,000 persons). Radio receivers (1997): 38,000 (272); Television receivers (1997): 23,000 (163); Telephone main lines (1999): 4,526 (32).

Education and health

Educational attainment (1981). Percentage of pop. age 25 and over having: no formal schooling 56.6%; incomplete primary education 18.0%; complete primary 19.2%; incomplete secondary 4.6%; complete secondary 1.3%; postsecondary 0.3%. **Literacy** (1981): total pop. age 15 and over literate 28,114 (54.2%); males literate 17,689 (70.2%); females literate 10,425 (39.1%). **Health:** physicians (1996) 61 (1 per 2,147 persons); hospital beds (1983) 640 (1 per 158 persons); infant mortality rate per 1,000 live births (2000) 50.4. **Food** (1999): daily per capita caloric intake 2,269 (vegetable products 95%, animal products 5%); 97% of FAO recommended minimum requirement.

Military

Total active duty personnel: from 1992, a police force of about 900 men. **Military expenditure as percentage of GNP** (1997): 0.9% (world 2.6%); per capita expenditure $2.

Background

First visited by European navigators in the 1470s, the islands of São Tomé and Príncipe were colonized by the Portuguese in the 16th century and were used in the trade and transshipment of slaves. Sugarcane and cacao were the main cash crops. The islands became an overseas province of Portugal in 1951 and achieved independence in 1975. During recent decades its economy was heavily dependent on international assistance.

Recent Developments

Presidential elections in 2001 brought a change in government, with the victorious Independent Democratic Action candidate dismissing the prime minister, dissolving the cabinet and parliament, and calling for new legislative elections.

Internet resources:
<www.cstome.net/diario/index.htm>

Saudi Arabia

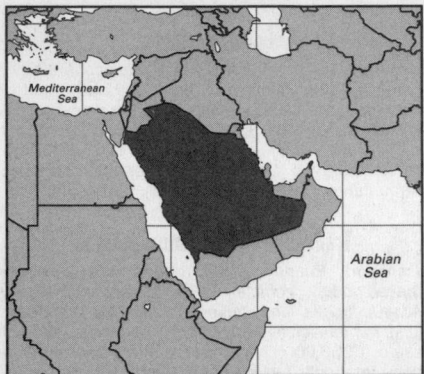

Official name: Al-Mamlakah al-'Arabiyah al-Sa'udiyah (Kingdom of Saudi Arabia). **Form of government:** monarchy (assisted by the Consultative Council consisting of 90 appointed members). **Head of state and government:** Crown Prince Abdullah acting as regent (from 1996). **Capital:** Riyadh. **Official language:** Arabic. **Official religion:** Islam. **Monetary unit:** 1 Saudi riyal (SRIs) = 100 halalah; valuation (28 Jun 2002) $1 = SRIs 3.75.

Demography

Area: 868,000 sq mi, 2,248,000 sq km. **Population** (2001): 22,757,000. **Density** (2001 est.; not adjusted to reflect boundary agreement with Yemen): persons per sq mi 26.2, persons per sq km 10.1. **Urban** (2000): 83.0%. **Sex distribution** (2000): male 55.33%; female 44.67%. **Age breakdown** (2000): under 15, 42.6%; 15–29, 22.8%; 30–44, 17.9%; 45–59, 12.1%; 60–74, 3.9%; 75 and over, 0.7%. **Ethnic composition** (2000): Arab 88.1%, of which Saudi Arab 74.2%, Bedouin 3.9%, Gulf Arab 3.0%; Indo-Pakistani 5.5%; African black 1.5%; Filipino 1.0%; other 3.9%. **Religious affiliation** (1992): Sunni Muslim 93.3%; Shi'i Muslim 3.3%; Christian 3.0%; other 0.4%. **Major cities** (1992): Riyadh (Ar-Riyad) 2,776,096; Jiddah 2,046,251; Mecca (Makkah) 965,697; Medina 608,295; At-Ta'if 416,121. **Location:** the Middle East, bordering Iraq, Kuwait, the Persian Gulf, Qatar, United Arab Emirates, Oman, Yemen, the Red Sea, the Gulf of Aqaba, and Jordan.

Vital statistics

Birth rate per 1,000 pop. (2000): 37.5 (world avg. 22.5). **Death rate** per 1,000 pop. (2000): 6.0 (world avg. 9.0). **Natural increase rate** per 1,000 pop. (2000): 31.5 (world avg. 13.5). **Total fertility rate** (avg. births per childbearing woman; 2000): 6.3. **Life expectancy** at birth (2000): male 66.1 years; female 69.5 years.

National economy

Budget (2000). *Revenue:* SRIs 157,000,000,000 (oil revenues 75.1%). *Expenditures:* SRIs 185,000,000,-000 (defense and security 40.5%, human resource development 26.6%, public administration, municipal transfers, and subsidies 16.5%, health and social development 8.9%). **Production** (metric tons except as noted). *Agriculture, forestry, fishing* (2000): wheat 2,046,000, alfalfa 1,400,000, dates 712,000; livestock (number of live animals) 7,576,000 sheep, 4,305,000 goats, 400,000 camels; fish catch (1999) 51,949. *Mining and quarrying* (1999): gypsum 330,000; silver 20,000 kg; gold 9,000 kg. *Manufacturing* (value added in $'000,000; 1995): industrial chemicals 3,014; cement, glass, and other nonmetal mineral products 943; refined petroleum 830. *Energy production (consumption):* electricity (kW-hr; 1996) 104,118,000,000 (104,118,000,000); crude petroleum (barrels; 2000) 2,939,000,000 ([1996] 635,000,000); petroleum products (metric tons; 1996) 97,311,000 (45,396,000); natural gas (cu m; 1999) 46,200,000,000 ([1996] 41,339,000,000). **Population economically active** (1994): total 5,614,000; activity rate of total pop. 32.2% (participation rates [1988] ages 15–64, 59.1%, female 3.5%; unemployed [1997] c. 25%). **Gross national product** (1999): $139,365,000,000 ($6,900 per capita). **Household income and expenditure.** Average household size (1992) 6.1; expenditure (1994; urban middle-income households only): food and tobacco 38.5%, transportation and communications 16.4%, housing 15.2%, clothing 8.8%, household furnishings 9.7%, education and entertainment 2.3%, other 9.1%. **Tourism** (1997): receipts $1,420,000,000. **Land use** (1994): forested 0.8%; meadows and pastures 55.8%; agricultural and under permanent cultivation 1.8%; built-on, waste, and other 41.6%.

Foreign trade

Imports (1999-c.i.f.): SRIs 104,980,000,000 (machinery and appliances 24.0%, transport equipment 14.5%, chemicals and chemical products 9.0%, base metals and articles 8.4%, vegetables 7.3%, textiles and clothing 6.2%). *Major import sources:* US 18.9%; Japan 9.2%; UK 8.1%; Germany 7.3%; Italy 4.2%. **Exports** (1999-f.o.b.; includes reexports): SRIs 190,100,-000,000 (crude petroleum 72.8%; refined petroleum 15.8%; chemical products 4.8%; plastic products 1.9%). *Major export destinations* (1998): US 16.3%; Japan 14.9%; South Korea 9.6%; Singapore 6.0%; The Netherlands 4.2%.

Transport and communications

Transport. *Railroads* (1997–98): route length 1,390 km; passenger-km 222,000,000 metric ton-km cargo 856,000,000. *Roads* (1996): total length 162,000 km (paved 42.7%). *Vehicles* (1996): passenger cars 1,744,000; trucks and buses 1,192,-000. *Air transport* (1997): passenger-km 18,949,-000,000; metric ton-km cargo 2,650,000,000; airports (1998) with scheduled flights 28. **Communication** Total units (units per 1,000 persons). Daily newspaper circulation (1996): 1,105,000 (59); Radio receivers (1997): 6,250,000 (313); Television receivers (1999): 5,500,000 (256); Telephone main lines (1999): 2,706,000 (129); Cellular telephone subscribers (1999): 837,000 (40); Personal computers (1999): 1,200,000 (56); Internet users (1999): 300,000 (14).

1 metric ton = about 1.1 short tons;   1 kilometer = 0.6 mi (statute);   1 metric ton-km cargo = about 0.68 short ton-mi cargo;   c.i.f.: cost, insurance, and freight;   f.o.b.: free on board

Education and health

Educational attainment (1986). Percentage of pop. age 25 and over having: no formal schooling 31.8%; primary, secondary, or higher education 68.2%. Literacy (1995): percentage of pop. age 15 and over literate 62.8%; males literate 71.5%; females literate 50.2%. Health (1995): physicians 30,306 (1 per 590 persons); hospital beds 41,916 (1 per 427 persons); infant mortality rate per 1,000 live births (2000) 52.9. Food (1999): daily per capita caloric intake 2,953 (vegetable products 85%, animal products 15%); 138% of FAO recommended minimum requirement.

Military

Total active duty personnel (2000): 126,500 (army 59.3%, navy 12.3%, air force 28.4%); US military (2001) 5,200. Military expenditure as percentage of GDP (1997): 14.5% (world 2.6%); per capita expenditure $1,050.

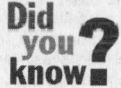

Did you know?

After crude oil, water is the most important resource of this arid kingdom. Saudi Arabia is the leading producer of desalinated water, with some 33 plants turning sea water into drinkable water.

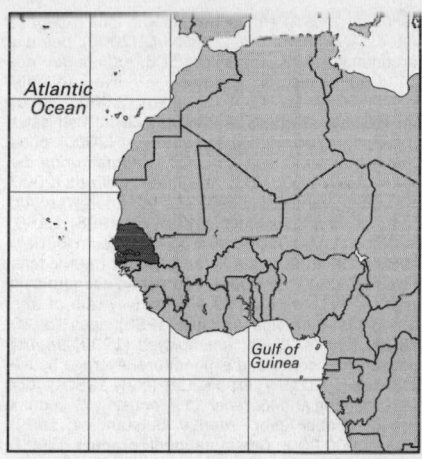

Atlantic Ocean

Gulf of Guinea

Head of state and government: President Abdoulaye Wade (from 2000) assisted by a prime minister. Capital: Dakar. Official language: French. Official religion: none. Monetary unit: 1 CFA franc (CFAF) = 100 centimes; valuation (28 Jun 2002) $1 = CFAF 664.20; the CFAF is pegged to the euro (€) at €1 = CFAF 655.96 from 1 Jan 2002.

Background

Saudi Arabia is the historical home of Islam, founded by Muhammad in Medina in 622. During medieval times, local and foreign rulers fought for control of the Arabian Peninsula; in 1517 the Ottomans prevailed. In the 18th–19th century Islamic leaders supporting religious reform struggled to regain Saudi territory, all of which was restored by 1904. The British held Saudi lands as a protectorate from 1915 to 1927; then they acknowledged the sovereignty of the Kingdom of the Hejaz and Najd. The two kingdoms were unified as the Kingdom of Saudi Arabia in 1932. Since World War II, it has supported the Palestinian cause in the Middle East and maintained close ties with the US.

Recent Developments

In 2000 Saudi Arabia and Yemen settled their long-standing border dispute. Saudi Arabia was deeply affected by the terrorist bombings on 11 Sep 2001, since Osama bin Laden, identified as the mastermind, was a former Saudi citizen. Limited aid was given to US antiterrorist activities and to the war in Afghanistan, but solidarity with the Palestinian cause and with Muslim states was maintained. Economic reforms, including an expanded role for the private sector, aimed at obtaining membership in the World Trade Organization. The aftermath of 11 September adversely affected crude oil prices, which had been experiencing a boom.

Internet resources: <www.saudinf.com>

Senegal

Official name: République du Sénégal (Republic of Senegal). Form of government: multiparty republic with one legislative house (National Assembly [120]).

Demography

Area: 75,951 sq mi, 196,712 sq km. Population (2001): 10,285,000. Density (2001): persons per sq mi 135.4, persons per sq km 52.3. Urban (2000): 47.4%. Sex distribution (2000): male 48.98%; female 50.02%. Age breakdown (2000): under 15, 44.6%; 15–29, 27.5%; 30–44, 15.6%; 45–59, 7.7%; 60–74, 3.7%; 75 and over, 0.9%. Ethnic composition (1988): Wolof 48.1%; Peul (Fulani) and Tukulor 21.7%; Serer 12.6%; Diola 5.0%; Malinke (Mandingo) 3.7%; other 8.9%. Religious affiliation (1988): Sunni Muslim 92.0%; traditional beliefs and other 6.0%; Christian (predominantly Roman Catholic) 2.0%. Major cities (1994): Dakar 785,071 (urban agglomeration 1,869,323 [urbanized area of Pikine [1994 est.; 855,287] is within the Dakar urban agglomeration]); Thiès 216,381; Kaolack 193,115; Ziguinchor 161,680; Rufisque 138,837 (within Dakar urban agglomeration). Location: western Africa, bordering Mauritania, Mali, Guinea, Guinea-Bissau, the North Atlantic Ocean, and The Gambia.

Vital statistics

Birth rate per 1,000 pop. (2000): 37.9 (world avg. 22.5). Death rate per 1,000 pop. (2000): 8.6 (world avg. 9.0). Natural increase rate per 1,000 pop. (2000): 29.3 (world avg. 13.5). Total fertility rate (avg. births per childbearing woman; 2000): 5.2. Life expectancy at birth (2000): male 60.6 years; female 63.8 years.

National economy

Budget (1997). Revenue: CFAF 432,200,000,000 (value-added taxes 30.3%, individual income tax 12.4%, taxes on petroleum products 9.1%, corporate income tax 6.7%). Expenditures: CFAF 432,200,000,-000 (current expenditures 73.5%, of which education 19.0%, defense 9.3%, health 3.7%; development expenditure 26.5%). **Production** (metric tons except as noted). *Agriculture, forestry, fishing* (2000): peanuts (groundnuts) 828,000; millet 506,000; paddy rice 240,000; livestock (number of live animals) 4,300,000 sheep, 3,595,000 goats, 2,960,000 cattle; roundwood (1998) 4,934,000 cu m; fish catch (1998) 425,766. *Mining and quarrying* (2000): phosphate 2,000,000; salt 130,000. *Manufacturing:* cement (2000) 1,000,000; phosphate fertilizers (2000) 160,000; peanut oil (1996) 91,200. *Energy production (consumption):* electricity (kW-hr; 1998) 1,160,-000,000 (1,160,000,000); crude petroleum (barrels; 1998) (6,392,000); petroleum products (metric tons; 1998) 852,000 (895,000). **Population economically active** (1991): total 2,739,476; activity rate of total pop. 36.1% (participation rates [1988]: ages 15–60, 53.1%; female 25.6%; unemployed [1992] 24.4%). **Household income and expenditure.** Average household size (1991) 8.7; expenditure (early 1980s): food 49%, clothing and footwear 11%, housing 7%, education 6%. **Public debt** (external, outstanding; 1999): $3,111,000,000. **Gross national product** (1999): $4,685,000,000 ($500 per capita). **Tourism:** receipts (1999) $166,000,000; expenditures (1997) $53,000,000. **Land use** (1994): forested 39.5%; meadows and pastures 29.6%; agricultural and under permanent cultivation 12.2%; other 18.7%.

Foreign trade

Imports (1999-c.i.f.): CFAF 1,155,300,000,000 (food and live animals 22.5%, of which cereals 14.0%, non-electrical machinery 12.9%; chemicals and chemical products 11.8%; mineral fuels 10.2%). *Major import sources:* France 30.2%; Nigeria 7.1% Italy 5.9%; Thailand 5.2%; Germany 4.2%. **Exports** (1999-f.o.b.): CFAF 339,250,000,000 (chemicals and chemical products 35.9%; refined petroleum 16.7%; machinery and transport equipment 10.9%). *Major export destinations:* India 27.9%; France 14.8%; ships' stores 11.1%; Mali 9.1%; Mauritania 5.2%.

Transport and communications

Transport. *Railroads:* (1995) route length 1,225 km; (1993) passenger-km 206,000,000; metric ton-km cargo 695,000,000. *Roads* (1996): total length 14,700 km (paved 29%). *Vehicles* (1996): passenger cars 85,488, trucks and buses 36,962. *Air transport* (1996; represents 1/11th scheduled traffic of Air Afrique): passenger-km 224,736,000; metric ton-km cargo 16,420,000; airports (1996) with scheduled flights 7. **Communications** Total units (units per 1,000 persons). Daily newspaper circulation (1996): 45,000 (5.3); Radio receivers (1997): 1,240,000 (141); Television receivers (1998): 370,000 (41); Telephone main lines (1999): 166,000 (18); Cellular telephone subscribers (1999): 88,000 (9.5); Personal computers (1999): 140,000 (15); Internet users (1999): 30,000 (3.2).

Education and health

Educational attainment (1988). Percentage of pop. age 6–34 having: no formal schooling 62.6%; primary education 25.7%; secondary 8.4%; higher 0.8%; other 2.5%. **Literacy** (1995): percentage of total pop. age 15 and over literate 1,960,000 (37.3%); males literate

1,220,000 (47.2%); females literate 740,000 (27.6%). **Health** (1992): physicians 520 (1 per 14,825 persons); hospital beds 7,408 (1 per 1,041 persons); infant mortality rate per 1,000 live births (2000): 58.1. **Food** (1999): daily per capita caloric intake 2,307 (vegetable products 91%, animal products 9%); 97% of FAO recommended minimum requirement.

Military

Total active duty personnel (2000): 9,400 (army 85.1%, navy 6.4%, air force 8.5%); French troops (2000) 1,170. **Military expenditure as percentage of GNP** (1997): 1.6% (world 2.6%); per capita expenditure $7.

Background

Links between the peoples of Senegal and North Africa were established in the 10th century AD. Islam was introduced in the 11th century, although animism retained a hold on the country into the 19th century. The Portuguese explored the coast in 1445, and in 1638 the French established a trading post at the mouth of the Senegal River. Throughout the 17th–18th century, Europeans exported slaves, ivory, and gold from Senegal. The French gained control over the coast in the early 19th century and moved inland, checking the expansion of the Tukulor empire; in 1895 Senegal became part of French West Africa. Its inhabitants were made French citizens in 1946, and it became an overseas territory of France. It became an autonomous republic in 1958 and was federated with Mali 1959–60. It became an independent state in 1960. In 1982 it entered a confederation with The Gambia, called Senegambia, which was dissolved in 1989.

Recent Developments

Runoff presidential elections held in March 2000 ushered in a change of government, as Senegalese Democratic Party leader Abdoulaye Wade, representing Sopi ("Change"), an opposition coalition, defeated the incumbent Socialist Abdou Diouf. Sopi went on to sweep the April 2001 parliamentary elections, winning 89 of the 120 seats in the National Assembly. A woman, Mame Madior Boye, was appointed prime minister.

Rebels in the separatist Casamance region continued to stage attacks, clashing with army troops and causing civilian casualties. Efforts to reach a settlement with the rebels were not successful.

Internet resources: <www.senegal-tourism.com>

Seychelles

Official name: Repiblik Sesel (Creole); Republic of Seychelles (English); République des Seychelles (French). **Form of government:** multiparty republic with one legislative house (National Assembly [34]). **Head of state and government:** President France Albert Rene (from 1977). **Capital:** Victoria. **Official languages:** none. **Official religion:** none. **Monetary unit:** 1 Seychelles rupee (SR) = 100 cents; valuation (28 Jun 2002) $1 = SR 5.62.

---

1 metric ton = about 1.1 short tons;   1 kilometer = 0.6 mi (statute);   1 metric ton-km cargo = about 0.68 short ton-mi cargo;   c.i.f.: cost, insurance, and freight;   f.o.b.: free on board

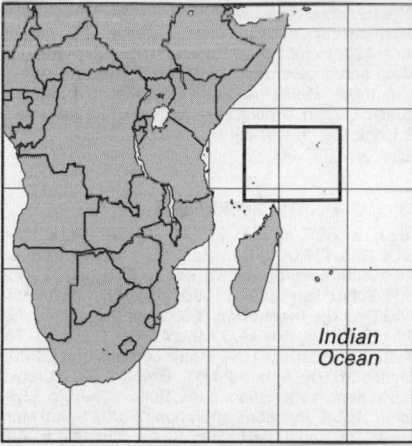

Indian
Ocean

Demography

Area: 176 sq mi, 455 sq km. **Population** (2001): 80,600. **Density** (2001): persons per sq mi 457.8, persons per sq km 177.1. **Urban** (1999): 63.0%. **Sex distribution** (2000): male 48.30%; female 51.70%. **Age breakdown** (2000): under 15, 28.8%; 15–29, 29.6%; 30–44, 24.6%; 45–59, 8.6%; 60–74, 5.8%; 75 and over, 2.6%. **Ethnic composition** (2000): Seychellois Creole (mixture of Asian, African, and European) 93.2%; British 3.0%; French 1.8%; Chinese 0.5%; Indian 0.3%; other unspecified 1.2%. **Religious affiliation** (1996): Roman Catholic 86.6%; other Christian (mostly Anglican) 9.3%; Hindu 1.3%; other 2.8%. **Major city** (1999): Victoria 28,000. **Location:** group of islands in the Indian Ocean, northeast of Madagascar.

Vital statistics

Birth rate per 1,000 pop. (2000): 18.0 (world avg. 22.5); (1998) legitimate 24.7%; illegitimate 75.3%. **Death rate** per 1,000 pop. (2000): 6.7 (world avg. 9.0). **Natural increase rate** per 1,000 pop. (2000): 11.3 (world avg. 13.5). **Total fertility rate** (avg. births per childbearing woman; 2000): 1.9. **Marriage rate** per 1,000 pop. (1998): 4.5. **Divorce rate** per 1,000 pop. (1998): 1.0. **Life expectancy** at birth (2000): male 64.9 years; female 76.1 years.

National economy

Budget (1999). *Revenue:* SR 1,399,600,000 (1997; customs taxes and duties 42.3%, transfers from Social Security Fund 17.4%, administrative fees 11.2%, income tax 10.5%, business taxes 6.1%, fees and fines 1.3%, grants 0.2%). *Expenditures:* SR 1,754,000,000 (1997; wages and salaries 27.4%, capital expenditure 17.5%, transfers 17.2%, debt service 16.5%, defense 3.3%). **Tourism** (1999): receipts from visitors $112,000,000; expenditures by nationals abroad $21,000,000. **Land use** (1994): forested 11.1%; agricultural and under permanent cultivation 15.6%; built-on, wasteland, and other 73.3%. **Gross national product** (1999): $520,000,-000 ($6,500 per capita). **Production** (metric tons except as noted). *Agriculture, forestry, fishing* (1999): coconuts 3,200, bananas 1,950, cinnamon 650; livestock (number of live animals) 18,200 pigs,

5,150 goats, 1,400 cattle; fish catch (1999) 4,418, of which (1998) jack 30.2%, snapper 18.3%, capitaine 8.3%. *Mining and quarrying* (1998): guano 5,000. *Manufacturing* (1999): canned tuna 33,234; soft drinks 105,610 hectolitres; beer and stout 67,680 hectolitres; fruit juices 22,530 hectolitres; cigarettes 60,300,000 units. *Energy production (consumption):* electricity (kW-hr; 1999) 172,400,-000 (172,400,000); petroleum products (metric tons; 1996) (55,000). **Population economically active** (1999): total 30,786; activity rate of total pop. 38.3% (participation rates: ages 15–64 [1989] 74.3%; female [1989] 42.5%; unemployed 11.5%). **Public debt** (external, outstanding; 1999): $132,-200,000. **Household income and expenditure.** Average household size (1997) 4.2; average annual income per household (1978) SR 18,480; sources of income: wages and salaries 77.2%, self-employment 3.8%, transfer payments 3.2%; expenditure (1991–92): food and beverages 47.6%, housing 15.1%, clothing and footwear 8.6%, transportation 8.0%, energy and water 7.4%, recreation 6.7%, household and personal goods 6.6%.

Foreign trade

Imports (1999): SR 2,316,200,000 (manufactured goods 30.8%, machinery and transport equipment 29.5%, food, beverages, and tobacco 22.2%, mineral fuels [including petroleum], lubricants, and related materials 9.9%, chemicals 6.0%). *Major import sources* (1997): South Africa 14.5%; UK 11.8%; Bahrain 11.2%; Singapore 11.2%; France 9.6%. **Exports** (1999): SR 771,900,000 (canned tuna 70.2%, petroleum products 21.9%, other fish, including dried shark fins 1.9%, frozen prawns 1.0%, cinnamon bark 0.3%). *Major export destinations* (1997): France 29.2%; Germany 27.3%; Italy 24.0%; Japan 7.0%; South Africa 4.0%.

Transport and communications

Transport. *Roads* (1999): total length 263 mi, 424 km (paved 87%). *Vehicles* (1997): passenger cars 7,120; trucks and buses 1,980. *Air transport* (1999): passenger arrivals 155,000, passenger departures 156,000; metric ton cargo unloaded 4,526, metric ton cargo loaded 1,960; airports (1998) with scheduled flights 2. **Communications** Total units (units per 1,000 persons). Daily newspaper circulation (1996): 3,000 (46); Radio receivers (1997): 42,000 (560), Television receivers (1998): 12,000 (149); Telephone main lines (1999): 16,635 (207); Cellular telephone subscribers (1999): 16,316 (203); Internet users (1998): 2,000 (25).

Education and health

Educational attainment (1994). Percentage of pop. age 12 and over having: primary education 37.0%; some secondary 16.8%; complete secondary 19.0%; vocational 15.2%; postsecondary 3.0%; not stated 9.0%. **Literacy** (1994): total pop. age 12 and over literate 49,136 (87.5%); males literate 24,086 (86.3%); females literate 25,050 (88.6%). **Health** (1999): physicians 104 (1 per 773 persons); hospital beds 445 (1 per 181 persons); infant mortality rate per 1,000 live births (2000) 17.7. **Food** (1999). daily per capita caloric intake 2,422 (vegetable products 82%, animal products 18%); 104% of FAO recommended minimum requirement.

Military

Total active duty personnel (2000): 450. **Military expenditure as percentage of GNP** (1997): 3.8% (world 2.6%); per capita expenditure $194.

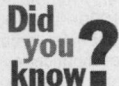

Did you know? Almost half of the land in Seychelles has been made into a national park, nature preserve, or a nationally protected area. As a result Seychelles has one of the most unspoiled habitats in the world.

Background

The first recorded landing on the uninhabited Seychelles was made in 1609 by an expedition of the British East India Co. The archipelago was claimed by the French in 1756 and surrendered to the British in 1810. In 1903 the Seychelles became a British crown colony, and a republic within the Commonwealth in 1976. A one-party socialist state since 1979, the Seychelles began moving toward democracy in the 1990s; it adopted a new constitution in 1993.

Recent Developments

In the September 2001 presidential elections, the incumbent since 1977, France-Albert René, was elected to another five-year term. Economic issues had dominated the contest, as a report by the International Monetary Fund had revealed slow economic growth and falling foreign exchange reserves. In an agreement with the Organisation for Economic Co-operation and Development (OECD), Seychelles undertook to reform its banking sector, increase regulation of offshore accounts, and to cooperate with OECD criminal and tax investigations.

Internet resources: <www.seychelles-online.com.sc>

Sierra Leone

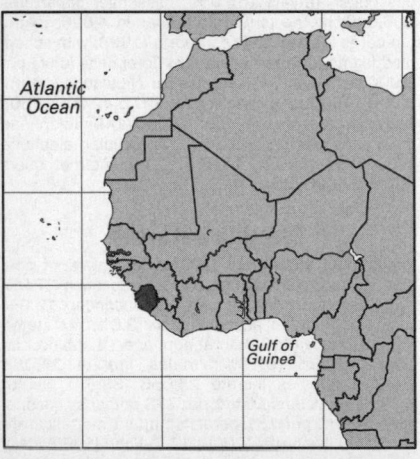

Atlantic Ocean

Gulf of Guinea

Official name: Republic of Sierra Leone. **Form of government:** republic with one legislative body (Parliament [80, including 12 paramount chiefs]). **Head of state and government:** President Ahmad Tejan Kabbah (from 1998). **Capital:** Freetown. **Official language:** English. **Official religion:** none. **Monetary unit:** 1 leone (Le) = 100 cents; valuation (28 Jun 2002) $1 = Le 2,035.00.

Demography

Area: 27,699 sq mi, 71,740 sq km. **Population** (2001): 5,427,000. **Density** (2001): persons per sq mi 195.9, persons per sq km 75.6. **Urban** (2000): 36.6%. **Sex distribution** (2000): male 48.44%; female 51.56%. **Age breakdown** (2000): under 15, 44.7%; 15–29, 26.1%; 30–44, 14.9%; 45–59, 9.2%; 60–74, 4.3%; 75 and over, 0.8%. **Ethnic composition** (2000): Mende 26.0%; Temne 24.6%; Limba 7.1%; Kuranko 5.5%; Kono 4.2%; Fulani 3.8%; Bullom-Sherbro 3.5%; other 25.3%. **Religious affiliation** (2000): Sunni Muslim 45.9%; traditional beliefs 40.4%; Christian 11.4%; other 2.3%. **Major cities** (1985): Freetown 469,776 (urban agglomeration [1999]: 822,000); Koidu–New Sembehun 80,000; Bo 26,000; Kenema 13,000; Makeni 12,000. **Location:** western Africa, bordering Guinea, Liberia, and the North Atlantic Ocean.

Vital statistics

Birth rate per 1,000 pop. (2000): 45.6 (world avg. 22.5). **Death rate** per 1,000 pop. (2000): 19.6 (world avg. 9.0). **Natural increase rate** per 1,000 pop. (2000): 26.0 (world avg. 13.5). **Total fertility rate** (avg. births per childbearing woman; 2000): 6.1. **Life expectancy** at birth (2000): male 42.4 years; female 48.2 years.

National economy

Budget (1996–97). *Revenue:* Le 85,708,000,000 (customs duties 47.4%; excise taxes 25.4%; corporate income tax 9.5%; personal income tax 7.3%). *Expenditures:* Le 143,293,000,000 (recurrent expenditures 75.6%, of which transfers 24.4%, wages and salaries 19.8%, goods and services 18.9%, debt service 12.5%; capital expenditures 24.4%). **Gross national product** (1999): $653,000,000 ($130 per capita). **Production** (metric tons except as noted). Agriculture, forestry, fishing (1999): rice 247,235, cassava 239,597, oil palm fruit 163,000; livestock (number of live animals) 400,000 cattle, 350,000 sheep, 190,000 goats; roundwood (1998) 3,315,000 cu m; fish catch (1998) 52,700. *Mining and quarrying* (2000): diamonds 350,000 carats; gold 965 troy oz. *Manufacturing* (value added in Le '000,000; 1993): food 36,117; chemicals 10,560; earthenware 1,844. *Energy production (consumption):* electricity (kW-hr; 1996) 241,000,000 (241,000,000); crude petroleum (barrels; 1996) (1,657,000); petroleum products (metric tons; 1996) 173,000 (128,000). **Household income and expenditure.** Average household size (1998) 6.3; average annual income per household (1984): $320; sources of income (1984): self-employment 61.6%, wages and salaries 27.9%, other 10.5%; expenditure (1989): food 66.2%, clothing 9.9%, housing 5.8%, transportation 4.4%, household goods 4.0%, recreation and education 3.8%, health 3.5%. **Public debt** (external, outstanding; 1999):

---

1 metric ton = about 1.1 short tons;   *1 kilometer = 0.6 mi (statute);*   *1 metric ton-km cargo = about 0.68 short ton-mi cargo;*   *c.i.f.: cost, insurance, and freight;*   *f.o.b.: free on board*

$938,000,000. **Population economically active** (1998): total 1,610,000; activity rate of total pop. 34.8% (participation rates [1991]: ages 10–64, 53.3%; female 32.4%; unemployed [registered; 1992] 10.6%). **Tourism** (1999): receipts $8,000,000; expenditures $4,000,000. **Land use** (1994): forest 28.5%; pasture 30.7%; agriculture 7.5%; other 33.3%.

Foreign trade

Imports (1999-c.i.f.): Le 153,856,000,000 (1995–96; food and live animals 51.6%; fuels 11.6%; chemicals 10.2%; machinery and transport equipment 8.9%). *Major import sources* (1998): UK 20.0%; US 13.0%; Belgium 7.5%; Italy 6.5%; Nigeria 5.5%. **Exports** (1999-f.o.b.): Le 11,347,000,000 (1995–96; mineral exports 56.4%, of which diamonds 50.6%, rutile [titanium ore] 5.7%; cocoa 5.0%; coffee 3.7%; reexports 4.8%). *Major export destinations* (1999): Belgium 40.8%; US 7.5%; Spain 6.1%; UK 4.1%.

Transport and communications

Transport. *Railroads* (1995): route length 84 km. *Roads* (1996): total length 11,700 km (paved 11%). *Vehicles* (1996): passenger cars 17,640; trucks and buses 10,890. *Air transport* (1996): passenger-km 24,000,000; metric ton-km cargo 2,000,000; airports (1998) with scheduled flights 1. **Communications** Total units (units per 1,000 persons). Daily newspaper circulation (1996): 20,000 (4.7); Radio receivers (1997): 1,121,000 (253); Television receivers (1998): 60,000 (13); Telephone main lines (1998): 17,000 (3.8); Personal computers (1999): 100 (0.02); Internet users (1999): 2,000 (0.4).

Education and health

Educational attainment (1985). Percentage of pop. age 5 and over having: no formal schooling 64.1%; primary education 18.7%; secondary 9.7%; higher 1.5%. **Literacy** (1995): total pop. age 15 and over literate 791,000 (31.4%); males literate 555,000 (45.4%); females 236,000 (18.2%). **Health:** physicians (1996) 339 (1 per 13,696 persons); hospital beds (1988) 4,025 (1 per 980 persons); infant mortality rate per 1,000 live births (2000) 148.7. **Food** (1999): daily per capita caloric intake 2,017 (vegetable products 96%, animal products 4%); 88% of FAO recommended minimum requirement.

Military

Total active duty personnel (2000): 3,000 (army c. 93%, navy c. 7%); UN troops (June 2001) 13,500. **Military expenditure as percentage of GNP** (1997): 5.9% (world 2.6%); per capita expenditure $10.

Background

The earliest inhabitants of Sierra Leone were probably the Buloms; the Mende and Temne peoples arrived in the 15th century. The coastal region was visited by the Portuguese in the 15th century, and by 1495 there was a Portuguese fort on the site of modern Freetown. European ships visited the coast regularly to trade for slaves and ivory, and the English built trading posts on offshore islands in the 17th century. British abolitionists and philanthropists founded Freetown in 1787 as a private venture for freed and runaway slaves. In 1808 the coastal settlement became a British colony.

The region became a British protectorate in 1896. It achieved independence in 1961 and became a republic in 1971. It was marked by political and economic turmoil in the late 20th century as successive military regimes tried to assume power. UN peacekeeping forces were stationed there but were ineffectual in preventing bloodletting and atrocities.

Recent Developments

In July 1999 the Lomé Agreement attempted to bring peace to Sierra Leone after the rebel Revolutionary United Front (RUF) attacked the capital, Freetown. Troops from the Economic Community of West African States Cease-Fire Monitoring Group battled the rebels, with great loss of civilian life, and the Organization of African Unity and the UN helped mediate the cease-fire. Amnesty and participation in government were granted to the RUF, despite protests that the rebels had perpetrated numerous war crimes, including mass killings, amputation of limbs, and rape. After the agreement the situation soon deteriorated, with UN, British, and government troops unable to entirely quash the RUF, which controlled and was funded by the diamond-producing areas of the country. Progress was made in 2001, however, in disarming the rebels. An influx of humanitarian aid from local and international sources was promised to ameliorate the desperate conditions caused by years of warfare.

Internet resources: <www.Sierra-Leone.org>

Singapore

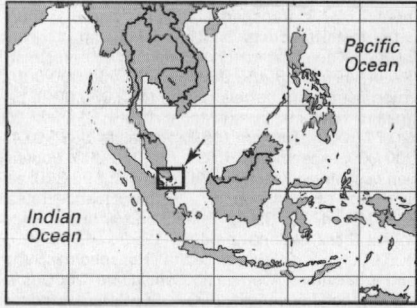

Pacific Ocean

Indian Ocean

Official name: Hsin-chia-p'o Kung-ho-kuo (Mandarin Chinese); Republik Singapura (Malay); Singapore Kudiyarasu (Tamil); Republic of Singapore (English). **Form of government:** unitary multiparty republic with one legislative house (Parliament [93]). **Chief of state:** President Sellapan Rama (S. R.) Nathan (from 1999). **Head of state government:** Prime Minister Chok Tong Goh (from 1990). **Capital:** Singapore. **Official languages:** Chinese; Malay; Tamil; English. **Official religion:** none. **Monetary unit:** 1 Singapore dollar (S$) = 100 cents; valuation (28 Jun 2002) US$1 = S$1.77.

Demography

Area: 263.6 sq mi, 682.7 sq km. **Population** (2001): 3,322,000. **Density** (2001): persons per sq mi 12,602, persons per sq km 4,866. **Urban:** 100.0%. **Sex distribution** (2000): male 49.96%; female 50.04%. **Age breakdown** (2000): under 15, 21.5%; 15–34, 30.1%; 35–54, 33.9%; 55–74, 12.1%; 75 and over, 2.4%. **Ethnic composition** (2000): Chinese 76.8%; Malay 13.9%; Indian 7.9%. **Religious affiliation** (2000): Buddhist 42.5%; Muslim 14.9%; Christian 14.6%; Taoist 8.5%; Hindu 4.0%; traditional beliefs 0.6%; nonreligious 14.9%. **Location:** southeastern Asia, islands between Malaysia and Indonesia.

Vital statistics

Birth rate per 1,000 pop. (2000): 13.6 (world avg. 22.5). **Death rate** per 1,000 pop. (2000): 4.5 (world avg. 9.0). **Natural increase rate** per 1,000 pop. (2000): 9.1 (world avg. 13.5). **Total fertility rate** (avg. births per childbearing woman; 2000): 1.6. **Marriage rate** per 1,000 pop. (1999): 6.7. **Life expectancy** at birth (2000): male 76.0 years; female 80.0 years.

National economy

Budget (2000). *Revenue:* S$33,526,600,000 (income tax 40.0%, nontax revenue 24.6%, goods and services tax 6.7%, motor vehicle taxes 6.5%, customs and excise duties 5.3%). *Expenditures:* S$18,896,900,000 (security 47.0%, education 20.6%, communications 12.8%, health 5.2%, trade and industry 2.1%). **Production** (metric tons except as noted). *Agriculture, forestry, fishing* (2000): vegetables and fruits 4,811; livestock (number of live animals) 2,000,000 chickens; fish catch (1999) 6,489. *Mining and quarrying* (value of output in S$; 1994): granite 75,800,000. *Manufacturing* (value added in S$'000,000; 1996): electronic products 16,982.1; chemical products 3,326.5; machinery and equipment 2,623.3; transport equipment 2,216.1; fabricated metal products 2,121.1; petroleum products 2,038.3. *Energy production (consumption):* electricity (kW-hr; 1996) 23,458,000,000 (23,458,000,000); crude petroleum (barrels; 1996) (432,000,000); petroleum products (metric tons; 1996) 51,025,000 (20,777,000). **Tourism** (1999): receipts US$5,974,000,000; expenditures US$2,749,000,000. **Population economically active** (2000): total 2,192,300; activity rate of total pop. 67.2% (participation rates: ages 15 and over, 85.6%; female 55.5%; unemployed 3.5%). **Gross national product** (1999): US$95,429,000,000 (US$29,660 per capita). **Household income and expenditure.** Average household size (2000) 3.7; income per household (2000) S$59,316; expenditure (1998): food 23.7%, transportation and communications 22.8%, housing costs and furnishings 21.6%, education 6.9%, clothing and footwear 4.1%, health 3.3%, other 17.6%.

Foreign trade

Imports (2000-c.i.f.): S$232,175,000,000 (office machines 12.4%, crude petroleum 6.5%, petroleum products 5.6%, telecommunications apparatus 4.7%, electric power machinery 4.7%, scientific instruments 3.7%, industrial machinery 2.1%). *Major import sources* (1999): US 17.0%; Japan 16.6%; Malaysia 15.6%; China 5.1%; Thailand 4.7%. **Exports** (2000-f.o.b.): S$237,826,000,000 (office machines 22.6%, petroleum products 7.2%, telecommunications apparatus 5.5%, electrical generators 3.4%, optical instru-

ments 2.6%, industrial machinery 1.4%, clothing 1.3%). *Major export destinations* (1999): US 19.2%; Malaysia 16.6%; Hong Kong 7.7%; Japan 7.4%; Taiwan 4.9%.

Transport and communications

Transport. *Railroads* (2000): length 117 km. *Roads* (1997): total length 3,017 km (paved 97%). *Vehicles* (2000): passenger cars 413,545; trucks and buses 147,325. *Air transport* (1999): passenger-km 64,528,800,000; metric ton-km cargo 5,481,708,000; airports (2000) 1. **Communications** Total units (units per 1,000 persons). Daily newspaper circulation (2000): 1,197,301 (367); Radio receivers (1997): 2,550,000 (821); Television receivers (1999): 1,200,000 (373); Telephone main lines (2000): 1,936,000 (593); Cellular telephone subscribers (2000): 2,442,000 (748); Personal computers (1999): 1,700,000 (528); Internet users (2000): 1,940,000 (595).

Education and health

Educational attainment (2000). Percentage of pop. age 15 and over having: no schooling 19.6%; primary education 23.1%; secondary 39.5%; postsecondary 17.8%. **Literacy** (1995): total pop. age 15 and over literate 90.8%; males literate 95.6%; females literate 86.1%. **Health** (2000): physicians 5,577 (1 per 585 persons); hospital beds 11,798 (1 per 277 persons); infant mortality rate per 1,000 live births 2.5. **Food** (1988–90): daily per capita caloric intake 3,121 (vegetable products 76%, animal products 24%); 136% of FAO recommended minimum requirement.

Military

Total active duty personnel (2000): 60,500 (army 82.7%, navy 7.4%, air force 9.9%). **Military expenditure as percentage of GNP** (1997): 5.7% (world 2.6%); per capita expenditure US$1,665.

Did you know? Since 1982, Singapore has held a national songbird competition in which owners showcase the singing talents of their birds. Many locals spend large amounts of time training birds to sing in the competition, which can bring in thousands of dollars.

Background

Long inhabited by fishermen and pirates, Singapore was an outpost of the Sumatran empire of Shrivijaya until the 14th century, when it passed to Java and then Siam. It became part of the Malacca empire in the 15th century. In the 16th century the Portuguese controlled the area; they were followed by the Dutch in the 17th century. In 1819 Singapore was ceded to the British East India Co., becoming part of the Straits Settlements and the center of British colonial activity in Southeast Asia. The Japanese occupied the island 1942–45. In 1946 it became a crown colony. It achieved full internal self-government in 1959, became a part of Malaysia in 1963, and became independent in 1965. It is influential in the affairs of the

---

1 metric ton = about 1.1 short tons;   1 kilometer = 0.6 mi (statute);   1 metric ton-km cargo = about 0.68 short ton-mi cargo;   c.i.f.: cost, insurance, and freight;   f.o.b.: free on board

Association of Southeast Asian Nations. The country's dominant voice in politics for 30 years after independence was Lee Kuan Yew.

Recent Developments

The Asian economic crisis of the late 1990s continued to trouble Singapore in the 21st century. Although Singapore's economy was one of the strongest and most prosperous in the region, two of its main trading partners, Japan and the US, were experiencing prolonged downturns, and Singapore also began to slip into recession when worldwide demand for its products, especially electronics, dropped. In parliamentary elections held in October 2001, the ruling People's Action Party won a landslide victory of 82 of 84 seats, as voters were reluctant to risk a change in leadership. A $6.2 billion package of tax cuts and government spending was launched to stimulate the economy. Also of concern was the country's birthrate, which had declined past the point needed to maintain the population level.

Internet resources: <http://www.sg>

Slovakia

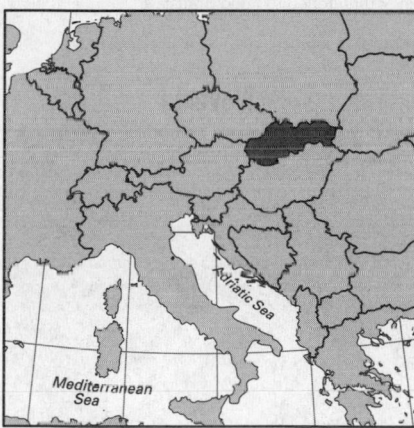

Official name: Slovenska Republika (Slovak Republic). Form of government: unitary multiparty republic with one legislative house (National Council [150]). Chief of state: President Rudolf Schuster (from 1999). Head of government: Prime Minister Mikulas Dzurinda (from 1998). Capital: Bratislava. Official language: Slovak. Official religion: none. Monetary unit: 1 Slovak koruna (Sk) = 100 halura; valuation (28 Jun 2002) $1 = Sk 44.55.

Demography

Area: 18,933 sq mi, 49,035 sq km (de jure). Population (2001): 5,410,000 (de jure estimate not adjusted for May 2001 de jure census results). Density (2001): persons per sq mi 285.7, persons per sq km 110.3. Urban (1998): 60.2%. Sex distribution (2001): male 48.61%; female 51.39%. Age breakdown (2000): under 15, 19.8%; 15–29, 24.9%; 30–44, 21.8%; 45–59, 18.1%; 60–74, 11.0%; 75

and over, 4.4%. Ethnic composition (2000). Slovak 85.6%; Hungarian 10.5%; Rom (Gypsy) 1.7%; Czech 1.1%; Ruthenian and Ukrainian 0.6%; other 0.5%. Religious affiliation (1991): Roman Catholic 60.4%; nonreligious and atheist 9.8%; Protestant 8.0%, of which Slovak Evangelical 6.2%, Reformed Christian 1.6%; Greek Catholic 3.4%; Eastern Orthodox 0.7%; other 17.7%. Major cities (2000): Bratislava 448,292; Kosice 241,874; Presov 93,977; Nitra 87,591; Zilina 86,818. Location: Central Europe, bordering Poland, Ukraine, Hungary, Austria, and the Czech Republic.

Vital statistics

Birth rate per 1,000 pop. (2000): 10.2 (world avg. 22.5); (1999) legitimate 83.1%; illegitimate 16.9%. Death rate per 1,000 pop. (2000): 9.8 (world avg. 9.0). Natural increase rate per 1,000 pop. (2000): 0.4 (world avg. 13.5). Total fertility rate (avg. births per childbearing woman; 2000): 1.3. Marriage rate per 1,000 pop. (1999): 5.1. Divorce rate per 1,000 pop. (1999): 1.8. Life expectancy at birth (2000): male 69.7 years; female 78.0 years.

National economy

Budget (1998). Revenue: Sk 304,100,000,000 (tax revenue 87.5%, of which social security contribution 33.0%, value-added tax 18.2%, income tax 14.0%; nontax revenue 12.5%). Expenditures: Sk 340,200,-000,000 (current expenditure 86.1%, of which social welfare 31.6%, wages 16.6%, health 13.1%, debt service 5.1%; investment 13.9%). Public debt (external, outstanding; 1999): $4,457,000,000. Production (metric tons except as noted). Agriculture, forestry, fishing (1999): sugar beets 1,405,-000, wheat 1,187,000, corn [maize] 779,000; livestock (number of live animals) 1,592,599 pigs, 704,792 cattle, 326,199 sheep; roundwood (1998) 5,532,000 cu m; fish catch (1998) 2,531. Mining and quarrying (1998): iron ore 899,000; gold 10,900 troy oz. Manufacturing (1998): crude steel 3,700,000; pig iron 3,100,000; cement 3,000,000. Energy production (consumption): electricity (kW-hr; 1998) 25,465,000,000 (21,020,000,000); coal (metric tons; 1996) 3,829,000 (7,142,000); crude petroleum (barrels; 1997) 462,800 (38,497,000); petroleum products (metric tons; 1996) 3,930,000 (2,134,000); natural gas (cu m; 1997) 284,000,-000 (5,743,400,000). Population economically active (1999): total 2,662,000; activity rate of total pop. 47.6% (participation rates [1997]: ages 15–64, 76.8%; female 67.3%; unemployed [1999] 17.1%). Household income and expenditure. Average household size (1997) 3.2; income per household (1997) Sk 74,052; sources of income (1999): wages and salaries 62.4%, transfer payments 25.6%; expenditure (1999): food, beverages, and tobacco 31.0%, housing and energy 14.0%, transportation and communications 10.4%, clothing and footwear 8.6%. Gross national product (1999): $20,318,000,000 ($3,770 per capita). Land use (1994): forested 40.6%; meadows and pastures 17.0%; agricultural and under permanent cultivation 32.9%; other 9.5%.

Foreign trade

Imports (1999): $11,321,000,000 (machinery and transport equipment 37.7%; semimanufactured products 18.3%; mineral fuels 12.9%; chemicals and chemical products 11.3%). *Major import sources* (2000): Germany 25.0%; Czech Republic 18.7%; Russia 17.0%; Italy 6.2%; Austria 3.9%. **Exports** (1999): $10,229,000,000 (machinery and transport equipment 39.5%; manufactured goods 27.3%; chemicals and chemical products 7.9%; mineral fuels 4.8%). *Major export destinations* (2000): Germany 26.7%; Czech Republic 20.0%; Italy 9.1%; Austria 8.3%; Poland 5.8%; Hungary 4.8%.

Transport and communications

Transport. *Railroads* (1997): length 3,673 km; passenger-km 3,057,000,000; metric ton-km cargo 12,373,000,000. *Roads* (1997): total length 17,627 km. *Vehicles* (1997): passenger cars 1,135,914; trucks and buses 100,254. *Air transport* (1997): passenger-km 231,396,000; metric ton-km cargo 729,000; airports (1998) with scheduled flights 2. **Communications** Total units (units per 1,000 persons). Daily newspaper circulation (1996): 989,000 (184); Television receivers (1999): 2,250,000 (417); Telephone main lines (1999): 1,655,000 (307); Cellular telephone subscribers (1999): 918,039 (170); Personal computers (1999): 590,000 (109); Internet users (1999): 600,000 (111).

Education and health

Educational attainment (1991). Percentage of adult pop. having: incomplete primary education 0.7%; primary and incomplete secondary 37.9%; complete secondary 50.9%; higher 9.5%; unknown 1.0%. **Literacy** (1997): total pop. age 15 and over literate 4,253,972 (100%). **Health** (1997): physicians 17,940 (1 per 300 persons); hospital beds 61,288 (1 per 88 persons); infant mortality rate per 1,000 live births (2000) 8.3. **Food** (1998): daily per capita caloric intake 2,953 (vegetable products 72%, animal products 28%); 121% of FAO recommended minimum requirement.

Military

Total active duty personnel (2000): 38,600 (army 61.7%, air force 29.8%, headquarters staff 8.5%). **Military expenditure as percentage of GNP** (1997): 2.1% (world 2.6%); per capita expenditure $167.

 **Did you know?** In May 2002 Slovakia's national ice hockey team won its first-ever gold medal at the world championship by beating Russia 4 to 3 in the final game.

Background

Slovakia was inhabited in the first centuries AD by Illyrian, Celtic, and Germanic tribes. Slovaks settled there around the 6th century. It became part of Great Moravia in the 9th century but was conquered by the Magyars c. 907. It remained in the kingdom of Hungary until the end of World War I, when the Slovaks joined the Czechs to form the new state of Czecho-

slovakia in 1918. In 1938 Slovakia was declared an autonomous unit within Czechoslovakia; it was nominally independent under German protection 1939–45. After the expulsion of the Germans, Slovakia joined a reconstituted Czechoslovakia, which came under Soviet domination in 1948. In 1969 a partnership between the Czechs and Slovaks established the Slovak Socialist Republic. The fall of the Communist regime in 1989 led to a revival of interest in autonomy, and Slovakia became an independent nation in 1993.

Recent Developments

Although its coalition government remained subject to factional tensions, Slovakia continued to work toward integration with the international community. It joined the Organisation for Economic Co-operation and Development in 2000 and pushed for early membership in the European Union and NATO. Reforms delegated authority from the central government to the regions and municipalities. The first regional elections, held in December 2001, were disappointing because of low voter turnout.

The economy showed some improvement, but unemployment remained high and there was double-digit inflation. The government declared a state of emergency in August 2002 as the swollen Danube River threatened to flood Bratislava.

Internet resources: <www.slovakiatourism.sk>

Slovenia

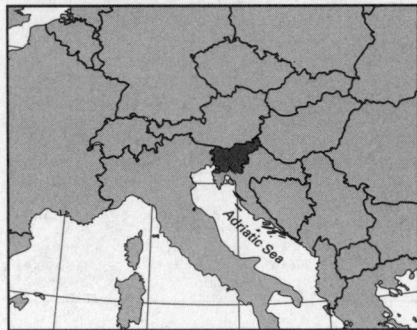

Official name: Republika Slovenija (Republic of Slovenia). **Form of government:** unitary multiparty republic with two legislative houses (National Council [40]; National Assembly [90]). **Head of state:** President Milan Kucan (from 1990). **Head of government:** Prime Minister Janez Drnovsek (from 2000). **Capital:** Ljubljana. **Official language:** Slovene (Hungarian and Italian are official where indigenous). **Official religion:** none. **Monetary unit:** 1 Slovene tolar (SIT; plural tolarji) = 100 stotin; valuation (28 Jun 2002) $1 = 227.14 tolarji.

Demography

Area: 7,827 sq mi, 20,273 sq km. **Population** (2001): 1,991,000. **Density** (2001): persons per sq mi 254.4, persons per sq km 98.2. **Urban** (1999): 50.3%. **Sex distribution** (2000): male 48.84%; female 51.16%. **Age breakdown** (2000): under 15, 16.1%; 15–29, 21.9%; 30–44, 23.4%; 45–59, 19.6%; 60–74, 14.0%; 75 and over, 5.0%. **Ethnic composition** (1991): Slovene 87.8%; Croat 2.8%; Serb 2.4%; Bosnian Muslim 1.4%; Hungarian 0.4%; other 5.2%. **Religious affiliation** (1995): Christian 86.2%, of which Roman Catholic 82.7%, Orthodox 2.0%, Protestant 1.3%; Muslim 1.0%; other 12.8%. **Major cities** (2000; populations of municipalities, which may include nearby small towns and rural areas): Ljubljana 270,986; Maribor 115,532; Kranj 51,923; Celje 49,572; Koper 47,905. **Location:** southeastern Europe, bordering Austria, Hungary, Croatia, the Adriatic Sea, and Italy.

Vital statistics

Birth rate per 1,000 pop. (1999): 8.8 (world avg. 22.5); legitimate 64.4%; illegitimate 35.6%. **Death rate** per 1,000 pop. (1999): 9.5 (world avg. 9.0). **Natural increase rate** per 1,000 pop. (1999): –0.7 (world avg. 13.5). **Total fertility rate** (avg. births per child-bearing woman; 1999): 1.2. **Marriage rate** per 1,000 pop. (1999): 3.9. **Divorce rate** per 1,000 pop. (1999): 1.1. **Life expectancy** at birth (2000): male 71.0 years; female 79.0 years.

National economy

Budget (2000). *Revenue:* SIT 1,725,791,000,000 (taxes on goods and services 34.9%, social security contributions 32.0%, personal income tax 15.0%, nontax revenue 7.3%). *Expenditures:* SIT 1,781,-311,000,000 (current expenditures 90.4%, development expenditures 9.6%). **Public debt** (external, outstanding; 2000): $2,665,000,000. **Production** (metric tons except as noted). *Agriculture, forestry, fishing* (2000): silage 1,900,000, sugar beets 467,000, corn (maize) 308,000; livestock (number of live animals) 552,000 pigs, 471,000 cattle; roundwood (1999) 2,133,000 cu m; fish catch (1997) 3,262. *Mining and quarrying* (1998): ferrosilicon 10,000; kaolin 10,000. *Manufacturing* (value added in SIT '000,000; 1997): base and fabricated metals 89,189; food, beverages, and tobacco products 81,998; chemicals and chemical products 81,408. *Energy production (consumption):* electricity (kW-hr; 1999) 12,456,000,000 (10,432,-000,000); coal (metric tons; 1998) 5,200,000 ([1997] 5,456,000); crude petroleum (barrels; 1999) 6,000 ([1996] 3,335,000); petroleum products (metric tons; 1996) 389,000 ([1998] 2,328,-000); natural gas (cu m; 1999) 5,700,000 (996,-000,000). **Land use** (1994): forest 53.2%; pasture 24.8%; agricultural 11.6%; other 10.4%. **Household income and expenditure** (1999). Average household size 2.8; income per household SIT 2,557,500; sources of income: wages 58.8%, transfers 29.7%, self-employment 7.0%, other 4.5%; expenditure: transportation and communications 18.9%, food and beverages 18.6%, housing 11.3%, recreation 8.2%, clothing and footwear 8.1%. **Gross national product** (at current market prices; 1999): $19,862,-000,000 ($10,000 per capita). **Population economically active** (1998): total 967,000; activity rate 49.6% (participation rates: ages 15–64, 89.1%; female 46.3%; unemployed [2000] 12.2%). **Tourism** (2000): receipts $957,000,000; expenditures $517,000,000.

Foreign trade

Imports (2000-c.i.f.): $10,115,000,000 (machinery and transport equipment 34.2%, other manufactured goods 21.9%, chemicals and chemical products 12.4%, mineral fuels 9.1%, food products 5.1%). *Major import sources:* Germany 19.0%; Italy 17.4%; France 10.3%; Austria 8.2%; Croatia 4.4%. **Exports** (2000-f.o.b.): $8,731,000,000 (machinery and transport equipment 36.0%, other manufactured goods 27.3%, chemicals and chemical products 11.2%, food products 2.3%). *Major export destinations:* Germany 27.2%; Italy 13.6%; Croatia 7.9%; Austria 7.5%; France 7.1%.

Transport and communications

Transport. *Railroads* (1999): length 1,201 km; passenger-km 625,000,000; metric ton-km cargo 2,784,000,000. *Roads* (1999): total length 20,128 km (paved 81%). *Vehicles* (1999): passenger cars 829,674; trucks and buses 67,111. *Air transport* (1999): passenger-km 832,000,000; metric ton-km cargo 4,160,000; airports (1999) with scheduled flights 3. **Communications** Total units (units per 1,000 persons). Daily newspaper circulation (1996): 397,000 (199); Radio receivers (1997): 630,000 (317); Television receivers (1998): 710,000 (358); Telephone main lines (1999): 786,229 (399); Cellular telephone subscribers (1999): 613,780 (309); Personal computers (1999): 500,000 (252); Internet users (1999): 250,000 (126).

Education and health

Educational attainment (1991). Percentage of pop. age 25 and over having: no formal schooling 0.7%; incomplete and complete primary education 45.1%; incomplete and complete secondary 42.4%; higher 10.4%; unknown 1.4%. **Literacy** (2000): 99.7%. **Health** (1999): physicians 4,486 (1 per 440 persons); hospital beds 10,050 (1 per 180 persons); infant mortality rate per 1,000 live births 4.5.

Military

Total active duty personnel (2000): 9,000 (army 100%). **Military expenditure as percentage of GNP** (1997): 5.2% (world 2.6%); per capita expenditure $614.

Did you know? The Skocjan Caves in southern Slovenia are one of the world's best sites for the study of karst (limestone) topography. Located about 13 km (8 mi) east of Trieste, Italy, the caves have immense underground caverns and deep chasms. They were designated a UNESCO World Heritage site in 1986.

Background

The Slovenes settled the region in the 6th century AD. In the 8th century it was incorporated into the Frankish empire of Charlemagne, and in the 10th century it came under Germany as part of the Holy Roman Empire. Except for 1809–14, when Napoleon ruled the area, most of the lands belonged to Austria until the formation of the Kingdom of Serbs, Croats, and

Slovenes in 1918. It became a constituent republic of Yugoslavia in 1946 and received a section of the former Italian Adriatic coastline in 1947. In 1990 Slovenia held the first contested multiparty elections in Yugoslavia since before World War II. In 1991 it seceded from Yugoslavia; its independence was internationally recognized in 1992.

Recent Developments

Parliamentary elections held in October 2000 were won by the center-left parties, which took two-thirds of the 90 seats. A four-party center-left coalition government was formed. Slovenia made progress in relations with its immediate neighbors, working to protect the Slovene minority in Italy and define boundaries with Croatia, the latter with limited success. An embassy was opened in Belgrade and relations were normalized with Yugoslavia. Seeking to join both the European Union and NATO, Slovenia made progress in meeting conditions for membership. The leftist government's relations with the dominant Roman Catholic Church, including the return of church property, were mixed, but the nation was cheered by a visit from Pope John Paul II in 1999, during which the first bishop of Maribor, Anton Martin Slomsek, was beatified—the first Slovene so honored.

Internet resources: <www.slovenia-tourism.si>

Solomon Islands

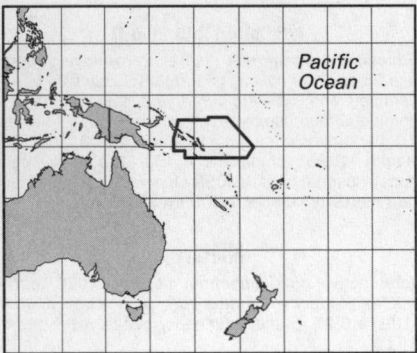

Pacific
Ocean

Official name: Solomon Islands. Form of government: constitutional monarchy with one legislative house (National Parliament [50]). Chief of state: Queen Elizabeth II (from 1952), represented by Governor-General John Lapli (from 1999). Head of government: Prime Minister Allan Kemakeza (from 17 Dec 2001). Capital: Honiara. Official language: English. Official religion: none. Monetary unit: 1 Solomon Islands dollar (SI$) = 100 cents; valuation (28 Jun 2002) US$1 = SI $7.10.

Demography

Area: 10,954 sq mi, 28,370 sq km. Population (2001): 480,000. Density (2001): persons per sq mi 43.9, persons per sq km 16.9. Urban (1999): 19.0%. Sex distribution (1996): male 51.65%; female 48.35%. Age breakdown (1996): under 15, 43.7%; 15–29, 28.7%; 30–44, 15.2%; 45–59, 8.1%; 60–74, 3.6%; 75 and over, 0.7%. Ethnic composition (1986): Melanesian 94.2%; Polynesian 3.7%; other Pacific Islander 1.4%; European 0.4%; Asian 0.2%; other 0.1%. Religious affiliation (1995): Christian 85.6%, of which Protestant 67.1% (including Church of Melanesia [Anglican] 31.0%), Roman Catholic 17.4%; traditional beliefs 3.1%; other 11.3%. Major cities (1986; ward populations): Honiara (1996) 43,643 (urban agglomeration [1999] 68,000); Gizo 3,727; Auki 3,262. Location: southwestern Pacific Ocean, east of Papua New Guinea.

Vital statistics

Birth rate per 1,000 pop. (2001): 38.3 (world avg. 22.5). Death rate per 1,000 pop. (2001): 4.8 (world avg. 9.0). Natural increase rate per 1,000 pop. (2001): 33.5 (world avg. 13.5). Total fertility rate (avg. births per childbearing woman; 2001): 5.4. Life expectancy at birth (2001): male 68.0 years; female 70.0 years.

National economy

Budget (1998). Revenue: SI$557,800,000 (foreign grants 33.0%, taxes on foreign trade 25.8%, income taxes 19.5%, taxes on goods and services 13.1%, nontax revenue 8.6%). Expenditures: SI$558,700,000 (capital expenditure 35.9%, administrative 28.6%, wages and salaries 27.2%, interest payments 8.3%). Tourism: receipts from visitors (1999) US$6,000,000; expenditures by nationals abroad US$7,000,000. Land use (1994): forested 87.5%; meadows and pastures 1.4%; agricultural and under permanent cultivation 2.0%; other 9.1%. Gross national product (at current market prices; 1999): US$320,000,000 (US$750 per capita). Household income and expenditure. Average household size (1996) 5.8; average annual income per household (1983; public-service earnings) SI$1,010; sources of income (1983): wages and salaries 74.1%, self-employment, remittances, gifts, and other assistance 25.9%; expenditure (1992; retail price index components): food 46.8%, housing 11.0%, household operations 10.9%, transportation 9.9%, recreation and health 7.9%, clothing 5.7%, drinks and tobacco 5.0%. Population economically active (1993; persons employed in the monetary sector only): total 29,577; activity rate of total pop. 8.3% (participation rates: ages 15–60 [1986] 98.6%; female 22.6%; unemployed n.a.). Production (metric tons except as noted). Agriculture, forestry, fishing (1999): coconuts 240,000, palm oil fruit 140,000, sweet potatoes 73,000; livestock (number of live animals) 58,000 pigs, 10,000 cattle, 185,000 chickens; roundwood (1998) 872,000 cu m; fish catch (1997) 53,442. Mining and quarrying (1998): gold 33,300 troy oz. Manufacturing (1997): palm oil 30,100, copra 23,500, coconut oil 3,900. Energy production (consumption): electricity (kW-hr; 1996) 32,000,000 (32,000,000); petroleum products (metric tons; 1996) none (52,000). Public debt (external, outstanding; 1999): US$120,400,000.

Foreign trade

Imports (1996-f.o.b.): SI$536,870,000 (machinery and transport equipment 30.3%, basic manufac-

1 metric ton = about 1.1 short tons;   1 kilometer = 0.6 mi (statute);   1 metric ton-km cargo = about 0.68 short ton-mi cargo;   c.i.f.: cost, insurance, and freight;   f.o.b.: free on board

tured goods 22.2%, food and live animals 15.1%, mineral fuels and lubricants 11.3%). *Major import sources*: Australia 44.1%; Japan 12.5%; Singapore 7.0%; US 2.1%; Thailand 1.8%; UK 1.6%. **Exports** (1996): SI$656,300,000 (timber products 60.6%, fish products 18.3%, palm oil products 10.9%, copra 4.1%, cacao beans 2.2%). *Major export destinations*: Japan 40.1%; South Korea 19.4%; UK 18.4%; Thailand 3.8%; Australia 2.3%; Singapore 2.2%.

Transport and communications

Transport. *Roads* (1996): total length 1,360 km (paved 2.5%). *Vehicles* (1993): passenger cars 2,052; trucks and buses 2,574. *Air transport* (1999): passenger-km 47,278,000; metric ton-km cargo 1,250,000; airports (1997) with scheduled flights 21. **Communications** Total units (units per 1,000 persons). Radio receivers (1997): 57,000 (141); Television receivers (1998): 6,000 (14); Telephone main lines (1999): 8,132 (19); Cellular telephone subscribers (1999): 1,093 (2.5); Personal computers (1999): 18 (0.04); Internet users (1999): 2,000 (4.7).

Education and health

Educational attainment (1986; indigenous pop. only). Percentage of pop. age 25 and over having: no schooling 44.4%; primary education 46.2%; secondary 6.8%; higher 2.6%. **Literacy** (1976): total pop. age 15 and over literate 55,500 (54.1%); males 33,600 (62.4%); females 21,900 (44.9%). **Health** (1997): physicians 31 (1 per 13,258 persons); hospital beds 210 (1 per 1,957 persons); infant mortality rate per 1,000 live births (2001) 22.0. **Food** (1999): daily per capita caloric intake 2,222 (vegetable products 92%, animal products 8%); (1997) 97% of FAO recommended minimum requirement.

Military

Total active duty personnel: no military forces are maintained, but a police force of 475 provides internal security.

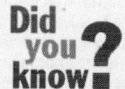 **Did you know?** A common traditional belief about life after death in the Solomon Islands is that a person's spirit lives on for a time in sharks, birds, or reptiles, making these animals sacred. People are thus forbidden to eat these animals. Ancestors are believed to prefer returning as sharks.

Background

The Solomon Islands were probably settled c. 2000 BC by Austronesian people. Visited by the Spanish in 1568, they were subsequently explored and charted by the Dutch, French, and British. They came under British protection in 1893 and became the British Solomon Islands. During World War II, the Japanese invasion of 1942 ignited three years of the most bitter fighting in the Pacific, particularly on Guadalcanal. The protectorate became self-governing in 1976 and fully independent in 1978. (Another island group named Solomon Islands, which includes Bougainville, is part of Papua New Guinea.)

Recent Developments

A peace accord that ended two years of anti-immigrant ethnic conflict was signed in 2000. The conflict had left the country in disarray, with the government virtually unable to function. The countryside was in the hands of the Isatabu Freedom Movement while paramilitary groups controlled the urban area. With the help of an international monitoring group, order was restored and an amnesty granted but some violent incidents continued to occur. Elections for parliament took place in December 2001. The upheaval had serious effects on the economy; as operations were interrupted and foreign companies feared for the safety of their workers.

Internet resources: <www.solomons.com>

Somalia

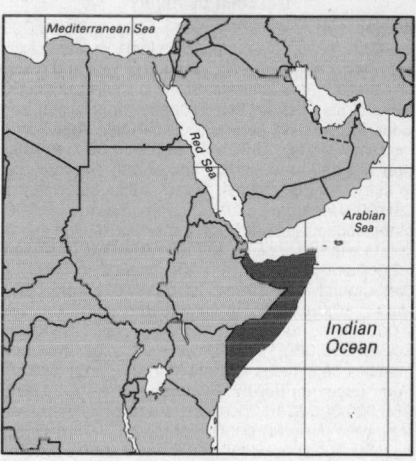

Official name: Soomaaliya (Somali); As-Sumal (Arabic) (Somalia). **Form of government:** Since 1991 there has been no sovereign Somalia, only chaos as numerous warlords vie for whatever resources they can secure from the remnants of what was Somalia. In recent years a number of attempts have been made to establish a legitimate national government; to date none has been recognized by the international community. At present Somalia is partitioned into three "autonomous regions": Somaliland in the northwest, Puntland in the northeast, and "Somalia" in the south. **Chief of state:** Abdikassim Salad Hassan (from 2000). **Head of government:** Hassan Abshir Farah (from 12 Nov 2001). **Capital:** Mogadishu. **Official languages:** Somali; Arabic. **Official religion:** Islam. **Monetary unit:** 1 Somali shilling (So.Sh.) = 100 cents; valuation (28 Jun 2002) $1 = So.Sh. 2,620.00 (in the spring of 2001 the "black market" value was about 17,000 So.Sh = $1).

Demography

Area: 246,000 sq mi, 637,000 sq km. **Population** (2001): 7,489,000. **Density** (2001): persons per sq mi 30.4, persons per sq km 11.8. **Urban** (1999): 27.1%. **Sex distribution** (2000): male 50.18%; female 49.82%. **Age breakdown** (2000): under 15,

44.4%; 15–29, 26.8%; 30–44, 17.9%; 45–59, 6.6%; 60–74, 3.5%; 75 and over, 0.8%. **Ethnic composition** (1983): Somali 98.3%; Arab 1.2%; Bantu 0.4%; other 0.1%. **Religious affiliation** (1995): Sunni Muslim 99.9%; other 0.1%. **Major cities** (1990): Mogadishu 1,162,000 (1999); Hargeysa 90,000; Kismaayo 90,000; Berbera 70,000; Marka 62,000. **Location:** eastern Africa, bordering Djibouti, the Gulf of Aden, the Indian Ocean, Kenya, and Ethiopia.

Vital statistics

Birth rate per 1,000 pop. (2000): 47.7 (world avg. 22.5). **Death rate** per 1,000 pop. (2000): 18.7 (world avg. 9.0). **Natural increase rate** per 1,000 pop. (2000): 29.0 (world avg. 13.5). **Total fertility rate** (avg. births per childbearing woman; 2000): 7.2. **Life expectancy** at birth (2000): male 44.7 years; female 47.9 years.

National economy

Budget (1991). *Revenue:* So.Sh. 151,453,000,000 (domestic revenue sources, principally indirect taxes and import duties 60.4%; external grants and transfers 39.6%). *Expenditures:* So.Sh. 141,141,000,000 (general services 46.9%; economic and social services 31.2%; debt service 7.0%). **Public debt** (external, outstanding; 1999): $1,859,000,000. **Production** (metric tons except as noted). *Agriculture, forestry, fishing* (1999): fruits (excluding melons) 210,000, sugarcane 210,000, corn (maize) 150,000, other products include khat, frankincense, and myrrh; livestock (number of live animals) 13,000,000 sheep, 12,000,000 goats, 6,000,000 camels, 5,000,000 cattle; roundwood (1998) 7,955,000 cu m; fish catch (1998) 16,000. *Mining and quarrying* (1992): salt 2,000 metric tons. *Manufacturing* (value added in So.Sh. '000,000; 1988): food 794; cigarettes and matches 562; hides and skins 420. *Energy production (consumption):* electricity (kW-hr; 1998) 265,000,000 (246,000,000); crude petroleum (barrels; 1991) N/A (806,000); petroleum products (metric tons; 1991) none (59,000). **Population economically active** (1991): total 3,215,000; activity rate of total pop. 40.9% (participation rates [1987] over age 10, 63.1%; female 48.7%; unemployed N/A). **Gross national product** (1996): $706,000,000 ($110 per capita). **Land use** (1994): forest 25.5%; pasture 68.6%; agriculture 1.6%; other 4.3%.

Foreign trade

Imports (1998-c.i.f.): $327,000,000 (1995; agricultural products 38.0%, of which raw sugar 16.1%, rice 7.8%, wheat 5.0%; unspecified 62.0%). *Major import sources* (1997): Djibouti 20%; Kenya 11%; Belarus 11%; India 10%; Saudi Arabia 9%; Brazil 9%. **Exports** (1998-f.o.b.): $187,000,000 (1995; agricultural products 51.4%, of which live sheep and goats 40.0%, bananas 6.9%, live camels and cattle 4.3%; other 48.6%). *Major export destinations* (1997): Saudi Arabia 57%; United Arab Emirates 15%; Italy 12%; Yemen 8%.

Transport and communications

Transport. *Roads* (1996): total length 22,100 km (paved 12%). *Vehicles* (1996): passenger cars 1,020;

trucks and buses 6,440. *Air transport* (1991): passenger-km 131,000,000; metric ton-km cargo 5,000,000; airports (1998) with scheduled flights 1. **Communications** Total units (units per 1,000 persons). Daily newspaper circulation (1996): 10,000 (1.2); Radio receivers (1997): 470,000 (53); Television receivers (1997): 135,000 (15 units); Telephone main lines (1999): 15,000 (2.1).

Education and health

Literacy (1995): percentage of total pop. age 15 and over literate 24%; males literate 36%; females literate 14%. **Health:** physicians (1997) 265 (1 per 25,034 persons); hospital beds (1985) 5,536 (1 per 1,130 persons); infant mortality rate (2000) 125.8. **Food** (1999): daily per capita caloric intake 1,555 (vegetable products 60%, animal products 40%); 67% of FAO recommended minimum.

Military

Total active duty personnel: clan warfare between 1991 and mid-2001. **Military expenditure as percentage of GNP** (1990): 0.9% (world 4.3%); per capita expenditure $1.

Background

Muslim Arabs and Persians first established trading posts along the coasts of Somalia in the 7th–10th centuries. By the 10th century Somali nomads occupied the area inland from the Gulf of Aden, and the south and west were inhabited by various groups of pastoral Oromo peoples. Intensive European exploration began after the British occupation of Aden in 1839, and in the late 19th century Britain and Italy set up protectorates in the region. During World War II the Italians invaded British Somaliland (1940); a year later British troops retook the area, and Britain administered the region until 1950, when Italian Somaliland became a UN trust territory. In 1960 it was united with the former British Somaliland, and the two became the independent Republic of Somalia. Since then it has suffered political and civil strife, including military dictatorship, civil war, drought, and famine. In the 1990s no effective central government existed. In 1991, a proclamation of a Republic of Somaliland, on territory corresponding to the former British Somaliland, was issued by a breakaway group, but it did not receive international recognition. A multinational force intervened from 1992 to 1994 in an unsuccessful attempt to stabilize the region. The country remained in turmoil.

Recent Developments

Hope for peace after decades of interclan fighting was raised in 2000 when a reconciliation conference, backed by regional and international groups, was convened to create a transitional national assembly. The government moved to the capital in October, but outbreaks of fighting continued. The Republic of Somaliland in the north, which had managed to maintain stability and begin economic recovery, rejected the new government even though delegates from the area had taken their seats. The various factions opposed to the new government signed a peace deal in December 2001.

1 metric ton = about 1.1 short tons;　1 kilometer = 0.6 mi (statute);　1 metric ton-km cargo = about 0.68 short ton-mi cargo;　c.i.f.: cost, insurance, and freight;　f.o.b.: free on board

The economy suffered from drought in the north east, floods in the central region, and a ban on cattle exports following an outbreak of Rift Valley fever. A flood of currency caused hyperinflation. A crippling blow was dealt in November 2001 when the US closed down Al Barakat, the company that handled most of the money-transfer and telecommunications services, on the grounds that it supported terrorism. Some areas faced starvation.

Internet resources: <www.somalitalk.com>

South Africa

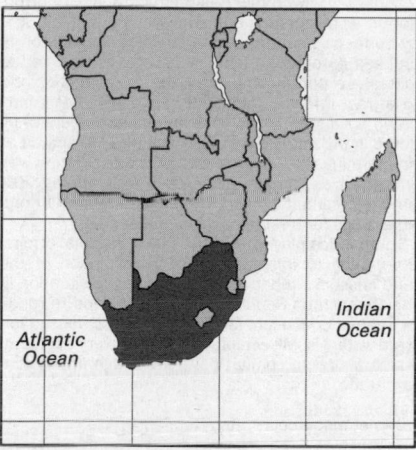

Indian Ocean

Atlantic Ocean

Official name: Republiek van Suid-Afrika (Afrikaans); Republic of South Africa (English). **Form of government:** multiparty republic with two legislative houses (National Council of Provinces [90]; National Assembly [400]). **Head of state and government:** President Thabo Mbeki (from 1999). **Capitals** (de facto): Pretoria/Tshwane (executive); Bloemfontein/Mangaung (judicial); Cape Town (legislative). **Official languages:** Afrikaans; English; Ndebele; Pedi; Sotho; Swazi; Tsonga; Tswana; Venda; Xhosa; Zulu. **Official religion:** none. **Monetary unit:** 1 rand (R) = 100 cents; valuation (28 Jun 2002) $1 = R 10.31.

Demography

Area: 470,693 sq mi, 1,219,090 sq km. **Population** (2001): 43,586,000. **Density** (2001): persons per sq mi 92.6, persons per sq km 35.8. **Urban** (1996): 53.7%. **Sex distribution** (1996): male 47.98%; female 52.02%. **Age breakdown** (1990): under 15, 33.9%; 15–29, 28.6%; 30–44, 19.4%; 45–59, 9.0%; 60–74, 5.3%; 75 and over, 1.7%; unknown, 1.2%. **Ethnic composition** (1999): black 77.2%, of which Zulu c. 22.0%, Xhosa c. 18.0%, Pedi c. 9.0%, Sotho c. 7.0%, Tswana c. 7.0%, Tsonga c. 3.5%, Swazi c. 3.0%; white 10.5%; Coloured 8.8%; Asian 2.5%; other 1.0%. **Religious affiliation** (2000): Christian 83.1%, of which black independent churches 39.1%, Protestant 31.8%, Roman Catholic 7.1%; traditional beliefs 8.4%; Hindu 2.4%; Muslim 2.4%; nonreligious 2.4%; Baha'i 0.6%; Jewish 0.4%; other 0.3%. **Major cities** (1996): Cape Town 2,415,408; Durban 2,117,650;

Johannesburg 1,480,530; Pretoria 1,104,479; Soweto 1,098,094. **Location:** southern Africa, bordering Namibia, Botswana, Zimbabwe, Mozambique, Swaziland, and the southern Atlantic and western Indian Oceans; wholly contained within South Africa is the country of Lesotho.

Vital statistics

Birth rate per 1,000 pop. (2000): 21.6 (world avg. 22.5). **Death rate** per 1,000 pop. (2000): 14.7 (world avg. 9.0). **Natural increase rate** per 1,000 pop. (2000): 6.9 (world avg. 13.5). **Marriage rate** per 1,000 pop. (1996): 3.6. **Total fertility rate** (avg. births per childbearing woman; 2000): 2.5. **Life expectancy** at birth (2000): male 51.4 years; female 54.1 years.

National economy

Budget (1999–2000). *Revenue:* R 196,302,000,000 (personal income taxes 43.9%, value-added taxes 23.7%, company income taxes 11.1%). *Expenditures:* R 223,564,000,000 (education 21.4%, interest on public debt 19.9%, health 13.4%, police and prisons 9.7%, defense 4.8%). **Public debt** (external, outstanding; 1999): $10,627,000,000. **Production** (in R '000,000 except as noted). *Agriculture, forestry, fishing* (in value of production; 1998): poultry 7,987, corn (maize) 4,374, beef 3,201; roundwood (2000) 30,616,000 cu m; fish catch (1999) 592,144 metric tons. *Mining and quarrying* (in value of sales; 1998): gold 24,155; rough diamonds (1995) 16,431; coal 17,878; platinum group metals (1997) 8,511. *Manufacturing* (in $000,000 value added; 1995): food products 3,028; iron and steel 2,700; transport equipment 2,334. *Energy production (consumption):* electricity (kW-hr; 1999) 203,532,000,000 ([1998] 187,517,000,000); coal (metric tons; 1999) 223,357,000 ([1997] 149,076,000); crude petroleum (barrels; 1999) 5,493,000 ([1997] 159,061,000); petroleum products (metric tons; 1997[includes Botswana, Lesotho, Namibia, and Swaziland]) 19,193,000 (17,252,000); natural gas (cu m; 1999 [includes Botswana, Lesotho, Namibia, and Swaziland]): 1,616,500,000 (1,616,500,000). **Tourism** (1999): receipts $2,526,000,000; expenditures $1,806,000,000. **Household income and expenditure.** Average household size (1996) 4.5; average annual disposable income per household (1996) R 47,600; expenditure (1998): food, beverages, and tobacco 31.3%; transportation 14.3%; housing 9.3%; household furnishings and operation 8.9%. **Population economically active** (1999): total 12,553,000; activity rate of total pop. 29.3% (participation rates [1995]: over age 15, c. 53%; female 43.6%; unemployed [1999] 25.2%). **Gross national product** (1999): $133,569,000,000 ($3,170 per capita). **Land use** (1994): forest 6.7%; pasture 66.7%; agriculture 10.8%; other 15.8%.

Foreign trade

Imports (1995): R 98,614,000,000 (machinery and apparatus 31.9%, chemicals and chemical products 12.5%, motor vehicles 11.6%). *Major import sources* (1999): Germany 14.5%; US 13.3%; UK 9.4%; Japan 7.5%; France 4.3%. **Exports** (1995): R 101,397,000,000 (gold 19.9%, base metals and metal products 15.4%, gem diamonds 9.8%, food 7.4%). *Major export destinations* (1999): UK 8.3%; US 8.2%; Germany 7.0%; Japan 5.2%; Italy 4.2%; unspecified 21.8%.

Transport and communications

Transport. *Railroads:* route length (1998) 20,319 km; passenger-km (1997–98) 1,775,000,000; metric ton-km cargo (1997–98) 103,866,000,000. *Roads* (1999): length 331,265 km (paved 41%). *Vehicles* (1996): passenger cars 3,966,252; trucks and buses 1,904,871. *Air transport* (2000 [SAA only]): passenger-km 19,320,000,000; metric ton-km cargo 677,048,000; airports (1996) 24. **Communications** Total units (unit per 1,000 persons). Daily newspaper circulation (1996): 1,288,000 (31); Radio receivers (1997): 13,750,000 (324); Television receivers (1999): 5,450,000 (124); Telephone main lines (1999): 5,493,000 (125); Cellular telephone subscribers (1999): 5,269,000 (120); Personal computers (1999): 2,400,000 (55); Internet users (1999): 1,820,000 (42).

Education and health

Educational attainment (1994). Percentage of pop. age 25 and over having: no formal schooling 14.5%; primary/incomplete secondary 61.6%; secondary/incomplete higher 20.4%; complete higher 3.1%; other/unknown 0.4%. **Literacy** (1995): total pop. age 15 and over literate: 81.8%. **Health:** physicians (1998) 29,020 (1 per 1,476 persons); hospital beds [public hospitals] 99,313 (1 per 431 persons); infant mortality rate per 1,000 live births (2000) 58.9. **Food** (1999): daily per capita caloric intake 2,805 (vegetable products 87%, animal products 13%); 114% of FAO recommended minimum.

Military

Total active duty personnel (2000): 63,389 (army 67.0%, navy 8.2%, air force 15.2%, intraservice medical service 9.6%). **Military expenditure as percentage of GNP** (1997): 1.8% (world 2.6%); per capita expenditure $55.

Background

San and Khoikhoi peoples roamed southern Africa as hunters and gatherers in the Stone Age, and the latter had developed a pastoralist culture by the time of European contact. By the 14th century, Bantu-speaking peoples had settled in the area and developed gold and copper mining and an active East African trade. In 1652 the Dutch established a colony at the Cape of Good Hope; the Dutch settlers became known as Boers and later as Afrikaners, after their Afrikaans language. In 1795 British forces captured the Cape, and in the 1830s, to escape British rule, Dutch settlers began the Great Trek northward and established the independent Boer republics of Orange Free State and the South African Republic (later the Transvaal region), which the British annexed as colonies by 1902. In 1910 the British colonies of Cape Colony, Transvaal, Natal, and Orange River were unified into the new Union of South Africa. It became independent and withdrew from the Commonwealth in 1961. Throughout the 20th century South African politics were dominated by the issue of maintaining white supremacy over the country's black majority, and in 1948 South Africa formally instituted apartheid. Faced by increasing worldwide condemna-

tion, it began dismantling the policy in the 1980s and ended it in 1990. In free elections in 1994, Nelson Mandela became the country's first black president. South Africa also rejoined the Commonwealth in 1994.

Recent Developments

In June 1999, Thabo Mbeki succeeded Nelson Mandela as president at the head of the African National Congress party; he identified crime, lack of jobs, and AIDS as the main challenges facing the nation. While the Truth and Reconciliation Commission continued amnesty hearings and trials for apartheid-era offenses, the government also struck against corruption in all sectors. High unemployment, topping 35% by some calculations, led to strikes and calls for increased government aid. The government worked to increase export income by increasing production and to attract foreign investment capital. Statistics indicated a substantial increase in the black share of income in the mid-1990s. AIDS continued to spread at an alarming rate—at least 10% of the population was HIV positive, a figure that rose to an alarming 20% among pregnant women. The procurement of affordable drugs for treatment was a major goal.

South Africa played an active role in regional affairs, attempting to influence peaceful resolution of the land crisis in Zimbabwe and stabilize the situation in the Democratic Republic of the Congo and Burundi. In international economic forums, Mbeki pressed forward with his Millennium Africa Recovery Program, which aimed to combat poverty through investment and trade.

Internet resources: <http://tourism.org.za>

Spain

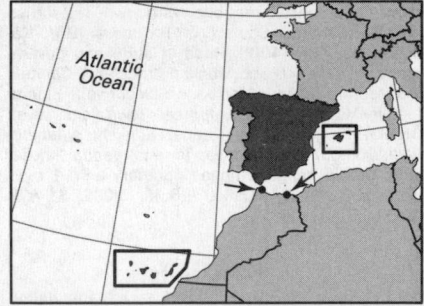

Official name: Reino de España (Kingdom of Spain). **Form of government:** constitutional monarchy with two legislative houses (Senate [259; 208 directly elected, 51 indirectly elected]; Congress of Deputies [350]). **Chief of state:** King Juan Carlos I (from 1975). **Head of government:** Prime Minister José María Aznar López (from 1996). **Capital:** Madrid. **Official languages:** Castilian Spanish. **Official religion:** none. **Monetary unit:** 1 euro (€) = 100 cents; valuation (28 Jun 2002) $1 = €1.01 (at conversion on 1 Jan 2002; €1 = 166.386 pesetas [Ptas]).

1 metric ton = about 1.1 short tons;   1 kilometer = 0.6 mi (statute);   1 metric ton-km cargo = about 0.68 short ton-mi cargo;   c.i.f.: cost, insurance, and freight;   f.o.b.: free on board

Demography

Area: 195,364 sq mi, 505,990 sq km. **Population** (2001): 40,144,000. **Density** (2001): persons per sq mi 205.5, persons per sq km 79.3. **Urban** (1990): 78.4%. **Sex distribution** (2001): male 48.86%; female 51.14%. **Age breakdown** (2001): under 15, 14.9%; 15–29, 22.2%; 30–44, 23.4%; 45–59, 17.8%; 60–74, 14.3%; 75 and over, 7.4%. **Ethnolinguistic composition** (1991): Spanish 74.4%; Catalan 16.9%; other 8.7%. **Religious affiliation** (2000): Roman Catholic 92.0%; Muslim 0.5%; Protestant 0.3%; other 7.2%. **Major cities** (2000): Madrid 2,882,860; Barcelona 1,496,266; Valencia 739,014; Seville 700,716; Zaragoza 604,631. **Location:** southwestern Europe, bordering France, Andorra, the Mediterranean Sea, Gibraltar, the Atlantic Ocean, and Portugal.

Vital statistics

Birth rate per 1,000 pop. (2000): 9.8 (world avg. 22.5). **Death rate** per 1,000 pop. (2000): 9.1 (world avg. 9.0). **Natural increase rate** per 1,000 pop. (2000): 0.7 (world avg. 13.5). **Total fertility rate** (avg. births per childbearing woman; 1999): 1.2. **Life expectancy** at birth (1999): male 74.4 years; female 81.6 years.

National economy

Budget (2000). *Revenue:* Ptas 18,736,200,000,000 (indirect taxes 45.7%, of which value-added tax on products 30.2%; direct taxes 42.7%; other taxes on production 11.6%). *Expenditures:* Ptas 19,762,900,-000,000 (health 21.6%; public debt 14.2%; pensions 5.0%; defense 4.9%; public works 4.8%). **Tourism** (1999): receipts $32,497,000,000; expenditures $5,523,000,000. **Gross national product** (1999): $583,082,000,000 ($14,800 per capita). **Production** (metric tons except as noted). *Agriculture, forestry, fishing* (2000): barley 11,283,100, sugar beets 8,343,800, wheat 7,333,100; livestock (number of live animals) 23,700,000 sheep, 23,682,000 pigs, 6,203,000 cattle; roundwood (1999) 15,113,-000 cu m; fish catch (1997) 1,341,000. *Mining and quarrying* (metal content in metric tons; 1998): zinc 128,000; iron ore 52,000; lead 19,000. *Manufacturing* (value added in $'000; 1994): machinery and transport equipment 20,322,000; food products 11,072,000; chemical products 8,618,000. *Energy production (consumption):* electricity (kW-hr; 1995) 166,380,000,000 (170,866,000,000); coal (metric tons; 1995) 28,403,000 (42,640,000); crude petroleum (barrels; 1995) 6,000,000 (415,000,000); petroleum products (metric tons; 1995) 47,064,000 (42,327,000); natural gas (cu m; 1995) 178,000,-000 (8,879,000,000). **Public debt** (2000): Ptas 51,372,300,000,000 ($335,122,000,000). **Population economically active** (2000): total 16,844,200; activity rate of total pop. 41.6% (participation rates: ages [1995] 16–64, 60.7%; female 38.3%; unemployed 22.9%). **Household income and expenditure.** Average household size (1991) 3.4; income per household (2000) Ptas 3,205,693; expenditure (1995): housing 26.0%, food 24.0%, transportation 12.8%, clothing and footwear 7.4%, household goods and services 6.1%.

Foreign trade

Imports (2000-c.i.f.): Ptas 27,643,097,000,000 (machinery 12.5%; energy products 12.0%; transporta-tion equipment 10.9%; agricultural products 8.1%). *Major import sources:* France 17.1%; Germany 14.9%; Italy 14.3%; UK 7.0%. **Exports** (2000-f.o.b.): Ptas 20,482,039,900,000 (transport equipment 19.5%; agricultural products 12.9%; machinery 7.9%). *Major export destinations:* France 19.4%; Germany 12.4%; Portugal 9.4%; Italy 8.8%; UK 8.3%.

Transport and communications

Transport. *Railroads* (2000; Spanish National Railways [RENFE] only): route length 13,832 km; passenger-km 18,547,000,000; metric ton-km cargo 11,620,000,000. *Roads* (1997): length 346,548 km (paved 99%). *Vehicles* (1999): cars 16,847,000; trucks and buses 3,659,000. *Air transport* (1999): passenger-km 60,696,083,000; metric ton-km cargo 6,406,562,000; airports (1997) with scheduled flights 25. **Communications** Total units (units per 1,000 persons). Daily newspaper circulation (1996): 3,931,000 (99); Radio receivers (1998): 12,000,000 (332); Television receivers (1998): 22,000,000 (553); Telephone main lines (1999): 16,480,000 (412); Cellular telephone subscribers (1999): 12,300,000 (307); Personal computers (1999): 4,800,000 (120); Internet users (1999): 4,652,000 (116).

Education and health

Educational attainment (1997). Percentage of economically active pop. age 16 and over having: no formal schooling 6.4% primary 26.6%; secondary 58.9%; higher 8.1%. **Health** (1995): physicians 162,650 (1 per 241 persons); hospital beds (1999) 164,097 (1 per 244 persons); infant mortality rate (2000) 5.0. **Food** (1999): daily per capita caloric intake 3,353 (vegetable products 72%, animal products 28%); 136% of FAO recommended minimum requirement.

Military

Total active duty personnel (2000): 166,050 (army 60.2%, navy 22.3%, air force 17.5%). **Military expenditure as percentage of GNP** (1997): 1.5% (world 2.6%); per capita expenditure $196.

Did you know? Part of the aqueduct system built by the Romans during the 1st century AD still exists. Stretching for about 16 km (10 mi) from the Frío River to Segovia, this nearly 2,000-year-old aqueduct is still in use.

Background

Romains of Stone Age populations dating back some 35,000 years have been found throughout Spain. Celtic peoples arrived in the 9th century BC followed by the Romans, who dominated Spain from c. 200 BC until the Visigoth invasion in the early 5th century. In the early 8th century most of the peninsula fell to Muslims (Moors) from North Africa and remained under their control until it was gradually reconquered by the Christian kingdoms of Castile, Aragon, and Portugal. Spain was reunited in 1479 following the marriage of Ferdinand II (of Aragon) and Isabella I (of Castile). The last Muslim kingdom, Granada, was reconquered in 1492, and around this time Spain also established a colonial empire in the

Americas. In 1516 the throne passed to the Habsburgs, whose rule ended in 1700 when Philip V became the first Bourbon king of Spain. His ascendancy caused the War of the Spanish Succession, which resulted in the loss of numerous European possessions and sparked revolution within most of Spain's American colonies. It lost its remaining overseas possessions to the U.S. in the Spanish-American War (1898). Spain became a republic in 1931. The Spanish Civil War (1936–39) ended in victory for the Nationalists under General Francisco Franco, who ruled as dictator until his death in 1975. His successor as head of state, Juan Carlos I, restored the monarchy upon his accession to the throne; a new constitution in 1978 established a parliamentary monarchy. Spain joined NATO in 1982 and the European Community in 1986.

Recent Developments

In general elections in March 2000 the right-wing Popular Party (PP) led by Prime Minister José María Aznar López won a majority of the votes, defeating a leftist coalition. The victory was attributed in part to Spain's expanding economy. Domestic issues dominated the PP's agenda, including financial scandals involving the foreign minister and junior finance minister. Serious race riots broke out in Andalusia, where there was a large North African immigrant population.

The most disturbing development was the renewal of terrorist attacks by the Basque separatist organization Euskadi Ta Askatasuna (ETA) after more than a year of calm. Beginning in January 2000, the ETA stepped up a campaign of vandalism, arson, car bombing, and assassination; in 2000–01 at least 33 people were killed by the ETA. In addition to such targets as politicians, military personnel, judges, police, and journalists, many bystanders were killed and injured. The public's outrage kept candidates of the political wing of the ETA out of office in Basque regional elections in May 2001, and the government cracked down on known terrorists. After 11 Sep 2001 11 suspected members of al-Qaeda were arrested in Spain and controls were tightened on the Spanish enclaves in Morocco, exacerbating the deterioriating relations with that country.

Internet resources: <www.tourspain.es>

Sri Lanka

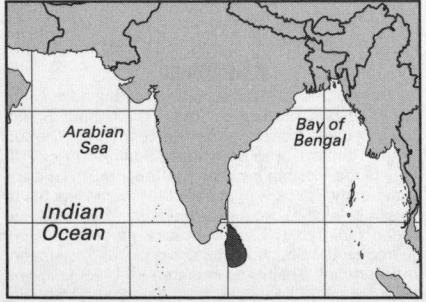

Arabian Sea

Bay of Bengal

Indian Ocean

Official name: Sri Lanka Prajatantrika Samajavadi Janarajaya (Sinhala); Ilangai Jananayaka Socialisa Kudiarasu (Tamil) (Democratic Socialist Republic of Sri Lanka). **Form of government:** unitary multiparty republic with one legislative house (Parliament [225]). **Head of state and government:** President Chandrika Kumaratunga (from 1994) assisted by Prime Minister Ranil Wickremesinghe (from 9 Dec 2001). **Capitals:** Colombo (executive); Sri Jayewardenepura Kotte (Colombo suburb; legislative and judicial). **Official languages:** Sinhala; Tamil. **Official religion:** none. **Monetary unit:** 1 Sri Lanka rupee (SL Rs) = 100 cents; valuation (28 Jun 2002) $1 = SL Rs 96.13.

Demography

Area: 25,332 sq mi, 65,610 sq km. **Population** (2001): 19,399,000. **Density** (2001): persons per sq mi 765.8, persons per sq km 295.7. **Urban** (2000): 24.0%. **Sex distribution** (1998): male 50.97%; female 49.03%. **Age breakdown** (1996): under 15, 28.0%; 15–29, 26.9%; 30–44, 22.5%; 45–59, 13.6%; 60–74, 7.0%; 75 and over, 2.0%. **Ethnic composition** (2000): Sinhalese 72.4%; Tamil 17.8%; Sri Lankan Moor 7.4%; other 2.4%. **Religious affiliation** (2000): Buddhist 68.4%; Hindu 11.3%; Christian 9.4%; Muslim 9.0%; other 1.9%. **Major cities** (1997): Colombo 800,982; Dehiwala–Mount Lavinia 220,780; Moratuwa 213,000; Kandy 150,532; Jaffna 145,600. **Location:** island in the northern Indian Ocean, lying southeast of India.

Vital statistics

Birth rate per 1,000 pop. (2000): 17.5 (world avg. 22.5); (1986) legitimate 96.3%; illegitimate 3.7%. **Death rate** per 1,000 pop. (2000): 5.8 (world avg. 9.0). **Total fertility rate** (avg. births per childbearing woman; 2000): 2.1. **Marriage rate** per 1,000 pop. (1997): 8.9. **Life expectancy** at birth (2000): male 71.0 years; female 76.0 years.

National economy

Budget (2000). *Revenue:* SL Rs 233,974,000,000 (sales and turnover tax 22.8%, excise taxes 19.9%, nontax revenue 13.8%, income taxes 12.5%, import duties 11.5%). *Expenditures:* SL Rs 329,012,000,-000 (interest payments 21.1%, defense 11.7%, transport and communications 11.7%, social welfare 10.5%, education 9.5%, administration 8.5%). **Public debt** (external, outstanding; 1999): $7,649,000,000. **Production** (metric tons except as noted). *Agriculture, forestry, fishing* (2000): rice 2,767,000, coconuts 1,950,000, sugarcane 1,114,000, plantains 600,-000; livestock (number of live animals) 1,616,700 cattle, 727,700 buffalo, 514,400 goats; roundwood (1999) 10,344,000 cu m; fish catch (1998) 266,100. *Mining and quarrying* (1998): limestone 950,000; titanium concentrate 23,000; graphite 5,000; gemstones $63,000,000. *Manufacturing* (value added, in $'000,000; 1995): food, beverages, and tobacco 601; textiles and apparel 391; petrochemicals 116. *Energy production (consumption):* electricity (kW-hr; 1997) 5,148,000,000 ([1996] 4,366,000,000); coal (metric tons, 1996) none (negligible); crude petroleum (barrels; 1996) none (15,063,000); petroleum products (metric tons;

---

1 metric ton = about 1.1 short tons;   1 kilometer = 0.6 mi (statute);   1 metric ton-km cargo = about 0.68 short ton-mi cargo;   c.i.f.: cost, insurance, and freight;   f.o.b.: free on board

1996) 1,908,000 (2,188,000). **Gross national product** (1998): $15,176,000,000 ($810 per capita). **Population economically active:** total (1997) 6,213,086; activity rate 40.2% (participation rates: ages 15 and over, 55.2%; female 32.4%; unemployed [2000] 8.0%). **Household income and expenditure** (1992). Average household size (1994 [excludes area controlled by Tamil rebels]) 4.6; income per household SL Rs 116,100; sources of income: wages 48.5%, property income and self-employment 41.8%, transfers 9.7%; expenditure: food 58.6%, transportation 16.0%, clothing 8.4%. **Tourism** (1999): receipts $275,000,000; expenditures $219,000,000.

Foreign trade

Imports (1999): $5,981,000,000 (textile products 22.1%, machinery and equipment 11.3%, transport equipment 8.7%, petroleum 8.4%, processed foods 6.7%). *Major import sources:* Japan 10.4%; India 9.5%; Singapore 8.4%; UK 4.7%; US 4.0%. **Exports** (1999): $4,600,000,000 (clothing and accessories 52.7%, tea 13.5%, gems 4.7%, coconuts 1.8%). *Major export destinations:* US 39.6%; UK 13.3%; Germany 4.8%; Japan 3.6%; The Netherlands 2.4%.

Transport and communications

Transport. *Railroads* (1998): route length 1,447 km; passenger-km 3,264,000,000; metric ton-km cargo 132,000,000. *Roads* (1996): total length 99,200 km (paved 40%). *Vehicles* (1996): passenger cars 107,000; trucks and buses 150,160. *Air transport* (1999): passenger-km 5,156,000,000; metric ton-km cargo 669,700,000; airports (1996) 1. **Communications** Total units (units per 1,000 persons). Daily newspaper circulation (1996): 530,000 (29); Radio receivers (1997): 3,850,000 (211); Television receivers (1999): 1,900,000 (102); Telephone main lines (1999): 679,207 (36); Cellular telephone subscribers (1999): 227,941 (12); Personal computers (1999): 105,000 (5.6); Internet users (1999): 65,000 (3.6).

Education and health

Educational attainment (1981). Percentage of pop. age 25 and over having: no schooling 15.5%; less than complete primary education 12.1%; complete primary 52.3%; postprimary 14.7%; secondary 3.0%; higher 1.1%; unspecified 1.3%. **Literacy** (1999): percentage of pop. age 15 and over literate 90.2%; males literate 93.4%; females literate 87.2%. **Health** (1999): physicians 6,938 (1 per 2,740 persons); hospital beds (1997) 52,298 (1 per 355 persons); infant mortality rate (2000) 17.0. **Food** (1999): daily per capita caloric intake 2,411 (vegetable products 94%, animal products 6%); (1997) 109% of FAO recommended minimum.

Military

Total active duty personnel (2000): 112,500 (army 82.2%, navy 8.9%, air force 8.9%). **Military expenditure as percentage of GNP** (1997): 5.1% (world 2.6%); per capita expenditure $41.

Background

The Sinhalese people of Sri Lanka (Ceylon) probably originated with aboriginal inhabitants blending with migrating Indo-Aryans from India c. 5th century BC. The Tamils were later immigrants from Dravidian India, migrating over a period from the early centuries AD to c. 1200. Buddhism was introduced during the 3rd century BC. As Buddhism spread, the Sinhalese kingdom extended its political control over Ceylon, but lost it to invaders from southern India in the 10th century AD. Between 1200 and 1505 Sinhalese power gravitated to southwestern Ceylon, while a southern Indian dynasty seized power in the north and established the Tamil kingdom in the 14th century. Foreign invasions from India, China, and Malaya occurred in the 13th–15th centuries. In 1505 the Portuguese arrived, and by 1619 they controlled most of the island. The Sinhalese enlisted the Dutch to help oust the Portuguese and eventually came under the control of the Dutch East India Co., which relinquished power in 1796 to the British. In 1802 Ceylon became a crown colony, gaining independence in 1948. It became the Republic of Sri Lanka in 1972, and was renamed the Democratic Socialist Republic of Sri Lanka in 1978. Civil strife between Tamil and Sinhalese groups has beset the country in recent years, with the Tamils demanding a separate autonomous state in northern Sri Lanka.

Recent Developments

The civil war that had dragged on since the mid-1980s dominated the political life of Sri Lanka and threw obstacles in the path of a generally expansive economy. Bombings and assassinations were frequent, as the Liberation Tigers of Tamil Eelam (LTTE) continued to press their demands for an independent homeland for the country's two million Tamils. In addition to attacks on individuals, including an attempt on the life of Pres. Chandrika Kumaratunga in 1999, the LTTE battled the army and briefly seized the international airport, destroying planes and an oil depot. Kumaratunga's coalition government lacked the necessary majority to effectively fight the LTTE or pass constitutional reforms and she lost support of the Sri Lankan Muslim Congress in 2001. General elections in December 2001 turned control of the government to the opposition United National Party, which declared a cease-fire and pressed forward with Norwegian-brokered peace negotiations with the rebels.

Internet resources: <www.infolanka.com>

The Sudan

Official name: Jumhuriyat as-Sudan (Republic of the Sudan). **Form of government:** federal republic with one legislative body (National Assembly [360; includes 90 seats not elected directly]). **Head of state and government:** President Omar Hassan Ahmad al-Bashir (from 1989). **Capitals:** Khartoum (executive); Omdurman (legislative). **Official language:** Arabic. **Official religion:** Islam. **Monetary unit:** 1 Sudanese dinar (Sd); valuation (28 Jun 2002) $1 = Sd 258.70.

Demography

Area: 2,503,890 sq km (includes about 130,000 sq km of inland water). **Population** (2001): 36,080,000. **Density** (2001): persons per sq mi 37.3, persons per sq km 14.4. **Urban** (1999): 35.2%. **Sex distribution** (2000): male 50.66%; female 49.34%. **Age breakdown** (2000): under 15, 45.0%; 15–29, 27.5%;

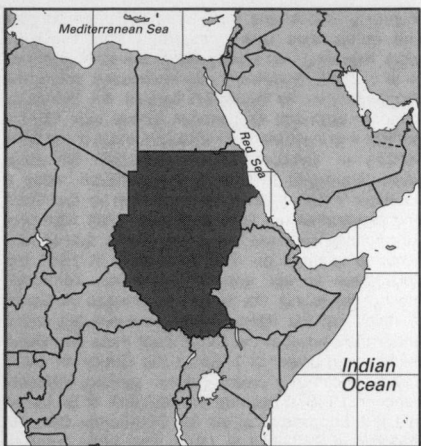

coal, none (none); crude petroleum (barrels; 1999–2000) 60,700,000 ([1996] 7,616,000); petroleum products (metric tons; 1996) 878,000 (1,039,000). **Gross national product** (1999): $9,435,000,000 ($330 per capita). **Population economically active** (1993): total 8,866,000; activity rate of total pop. 32.3% (participation rates: ages 15–64 [1983] 57.4%; female 22.3%; unemployed c. 30.0%). **Household income and expenditure.** Expenditure (1983): food and beverages 63.6%, housing 11.5%, household goods 5.5%, clothing and footwear 5.3%. **Land use** (1994): forested 18.1%; meadows and pastures 46.3%; agricultural and under permanent cultivation 5.5%; desert and other 30.1%.

30–44, 15.4%; 45–59, 8.4%; 60–74, 3.2%; 75 and over, 0.5%. **Ethnic composition** (1983): Sudanese Arab 49.1%; Dinka 11.5%; Nuba 8.1%; Beja 6.4%; Nuer 4.9%; Azande 2.7%; Bari 2.5%; Fur 2.1%; other 12.7%. **Religious affiliation** (2000): Sunni Muslim 70.3%; Christian 16.7%, of which Roman Catholic c. 8%, Anglican c. 6%; traditional beliefs 11.9%; other 1.1%. **Major cities** (1993): Omdurman 1,267,077; Khartoum 924,505; Khartoum North 879,105; Port Sudan 305,385; Kassala 234,270. **Location:** northeastern Africa, bordering Egypt, the Red Sea, Eritrea, Ethiopia, Kenya, Uganda, Democratic Republic of the Congo, Central African Republic, Chad, and Libya.

Vital statistics

Birth rate per 1,000 pop. (2000): 38.6 (world avg. 22.5). **Death rate** per 1,000 pop. (2000): 10.3 (world avg. 9.0). **Natural increase rate** per 1,000 pop. (2000): 28.3 (world avg. 13.5). **Total fertility rate** (avg. births per childbearing woman; 2000): 5.5. **Life expectancy** at birth (2000): male 55.5 years; female 57.7 years.

National economy

Budget (1999–2000). *Revenue:* Sd 206,700,000,-000 (import duties 26.0%, nontax revenue 25.8%, excise duties 11.9%, taxes on business profits 11.1%). *Expenditures:* Sd 227,200,000,000 (current expenditure 85.8%, development expenditure 14.2%). **Public debt** (external, outstanding; 1999): $8,852,000,000. **Tourism** (1999): receipts $2,000,000; expenditures $35,000,000. **Production** (metric tons except as noted). *Agriculture, forestry, fishing* (1999): sugarcane 5,950,000, sorghum 3,045,000, peanuts (groundnuts) 980,000, millet 499,000; livestock (number of live animals) 42,500,000 sheep, 37,500,000 goats, 35,000,000 cattle, 3,150,000 camels; roundwood (1998) 9,486,000 cu m; fish catch (1997) 48,072. *Mining and quarrying* (1998): salt 45,000; gold 161,000 troy oz. *Manufacturing* (1999): raw sugar 622,000; flour 532,000; cement 267,000. *Energy production (consumption):* electricity (kW-hr; 1999) 2,243,000,000 (1,317,000,000);

Foreign trade

Imports (1999-c.i.f.): $1,412,000,000 (machinery and equipment 25.4%; foodstuffs 19.5%, of which wheat and wheat flour 8.7%; petroleum products 13.0%; transport equipment 9.3%). *Major import sources:* Saudi Arabia 11.8%; France 8.6%; Italy 6.3%; UAE 5.5%; Germany 5.4%; UK 5.1%. **Exports** (1999-f.o.b.): $780,000,000 (crude petroleum 35.4%; sesame seeds 16.3%; sheep and lambs 13.0%; gold 7.1%; cotton 5.8%). *Major export destinations:* Saudi Arabia 18.1%; Japan 15.7%; UK 9.2%; South Korea 7.9%; Italy 7.1%.

Transport and communications

Transport. *Railroads:* route length (1998) 4,595 km; (1995–96) passenger-km 161,000,000; (1995–96) metric ton-km cargo 1,965,000,000. *Roads* (1996): total length 11,900 km (paved 36%). *Vehicles* (1996): passenger cars 285,000; trucks and buses 53,000. *Air transport* (1998 [Sudan Airways only]): passenger-km 530,671,000; metric ton-km cargo 20,293,000; airports (1997) with scheduled flights 3. **Communications** Total units (units per 1,000 persons). Daily newspaper circulation (1996): 737,000 (24); Radio receivers (1997): 7,550,000 (235); Television receivers (1999): 5,000,000 (147); Telephone main lines (1999): 251,420 (7.4); Cellular telephone subscribers (1999): 13,000 (0.4); Personal computers (1999): 85,000 (2.5); Internet users (1999): 5,000 (0.1).

Education and health

Educational attainment (1983). Percentage of pop. age 25 and over having: no formal schooling 76.7%; complete secondary 2.0%; higher 0.8%. **Literacy** (1995): total pop. age 15 and over literate 8,720,000 (50.8%); males 5,460,000 (63.5%); females 3,260,000 (38.3%). **Health:** physicians (1994) 2,736 (1 per 10,900 persons); hospital beds (1990) 19,449 (1 per 1,369 persons); infant mortality rate (2000) 70.2. **Food** (1998): daily per capita caloric intake 2,444 (vegetable products 80%, animal products 20%); 104% of FAO recommended minimum.

Military

Total active duty personnel (2000): 104,500 (army 95.7%, navy 1.4%, air force 2.9%). **Military expenditure as percentage of GNP** (1997): 4.6% (world 2.6%); per capita expenditure $13.

1 metric ton = about 1.1 short tons;   1 kilometer = 0.6 mi (statute);   1 metric ton-km cargo = about 0.68 short ton-mi cargo;   c.i.f.: cost, insurance, and freight;   f.o.b.: free on board

Did you know? Since the mid-1980s a civil war has wracked Sudan; the Islamic government in the north has decimated the Christian and animist population in the south. This has resulted in nearly 2,000,000 deaths from famine, disease, and the war itself. At the same time many southern Sudanese have been taken as slaves and hundreds of thousands of refugees have fled to Sudan's neighboring countries.

Background

From the end of the 4th millennium BC Nubia (now northern Sudan) periodically came under Egyptian rule, and it was part of the kingdom of Cush from the 11th century BC to the 4th century AD. Christian missionaries converted the Sudan's three principal kingdoms during the 6th century AD; these black Christian kingdoms coexisted with their Muslim Arab neighbors in Egypt for centuries, until the influx of Arab immigrants brought about their collapse in the 13th–15th century. Egypt had conquered all of the Sudan by 1874 and encouraged British interference in the region; this aroused Muslim opposition and led to the revolt of al-Mahdi, who captured Khartoum in 1885 and established a Muslim theocracy in the Sudan that lasted until 1898, when his forces were defeated by the British. The British ruled the country, generally in partnership with Egypt, until The Sudan achieved independence in 1956. Since then the country has fluctuated between ineffective parliamentary government and unstable military rule. The non-Muslim population of the south has engaged in ongoing rebellion against the Muslim-controlled government of the north, leading to famines and the displacement of some 4 million people.

Recent Developments

Lieut. Omar Hassan al-Bashir, acting as both president and prime minister, declared a state of emergency in The Sudan for all of 2000, which was extended to include 2001. Domestic politics were dominated by power struggles and shifting alliances between the government and its opposition groups, including the National Democratic Alliance, a coalition that had been waging war against government strongholds in the east. Civil war with the Sudanese People's Liberation Army dragged on. Oil revenue, which amounted to $1 million per day for the government, was entirely consumed in defense spending. Millions of people were suffering food shortages caused by drought and warfare; international relief agencies charged that aid was being blocked as a means of subduing the population. The Sudan had some success in mending fences with neighboring countries, UN sanctions were lifted in 2001, and the US attempted to broker a peace agreement with the rebels.

Internet resources: <www.sudan.net>

Suriname

Official name: Republiek Suriname (Republic of Suriname). **Form of government:** multiparty republic with one legislative house (National Assembly [51]). **Head of state and government:** President Runaldo Ronald Venetiaan (from 2000). **Capital:** Paramaribo. **Official**

language: Dutch. **Official religion:** none. **Monetary unit:** 1 Suriname guilder (Sf) = 100 cents; valuation (28 Jun 2002) $1 = Sf 2,178.50.

Demography

Area: 63,251 sq mi, 163,820 sq km. **Population** (2001): 434,000. **Density** (2001): persons per sq mi 6.9, persons per sq km 2.6. **Urban** (1998): 51.0%. **Sex distribution** (2000): male 50.77%; female 49.23%. **Age breakdown** (2000): under 15, 32.1%; 15–29, 27.2%; 30–44, 22.7%; 45–59, 9.9%; 60–74, 6.4%; 75 and over, 1.7%. **Ethnic composition** (1999): Indo-Pakistani 37.0%; Suriname Creole 31.0%; Javanese 15.0%; Bush Negro 10.0%; Amerindian 2.5%; Chinese 2.0%; white 1.0%; other 1.5%. **Religious affiliation** (1995): Hindu 27.4%; Roman Catholic 21.0%; Muslim 19.6%; Protestant (mostly Moravian) 16.4%; other 15.6%. **Major cities** (1996/1997): Paramaribo 222,800 (urban agglomeration 289,000); Lelydorp 15,600; Nieuw Nickerie 11,100; Mungo (Moengo) 6,800; Meerzorg 6,600. **Location:** northern South America, bordering the North Atlantic Ocean, French Guiana, Brazil, and Guyana.

Vital statistics

Birth rate per 1,000 pop. (2000): 21.1 (world avg. 22.5). **Death rate** per 1,000 pop. (2000): 5.7 (world avg. 9.0). **Natural increase rate** per 1,000 pop. (2000): 15.4 (world avg. 13.5). **Total fertility rate** (avg. births per childbearing woman; 2000): 2.5. **Marriage rate** per 1,000 pop. (1991): 4.9. **Divorce rate** per 1,000 pop. (1991): 2.5. **Life expectancy** at birth (2000): male 68.7 years; female 74.1 years.

National economy

Budget (1996). *Revenue:* Sf 90,874,600,000 (direct taxes 42.2%; indirect taxes 32.2%; bauxite levy 25.0%; other 0.6%). *Expenditures:* Sf 96,957,700,-000 (current expenditures 99.6%, of which wages and salaries 28.5%, transfers 13.7%, debt service 1.7%; capital expenditures 0.4%). **Production** (metric tons except as noted). *Agriculture, forestry, fishing* (1999): rice 180,400, sugarcane 90,000, bananas 55,000; livestock (number of live animals) 102,000 cattle, 25,000 pigs, 10,600 sheep; roundwood

(1998) 183,000 cu m; fish catch (1997) 13,000. *Mining and quarrying* (1997): bauxite 3,877,000; gold 6,993 troy oz. *Manufacturing* (value of production at factor cost in Sf; 1993): food products 992,000,000; beverages 558,000,000; tobacco 369,000,000. *Energy production (consumption):* electricity (kW-hr; 1996) 1,621,000,000 (1,621,000,000); crude petroleum (barrels; 1996) 1,519,000 (1,227,000); petroleum products (metric tons; 1996) none (478,000). **Household income and expenditure.** Average household size (1998) 4.8; sources of income (1975): wages and salaries 74.6%, transfer payments 3.2%, other 22.2%; expenditure (1968–69): food and beverages 40.0%, household furnishings 12.3%, clothing and footwear 11.0%, transportation and communications 9.5%, recreation and education 8.4%, energy 6.9%, housing 4.4%, other 7.5%. **Land use** (1994): forested 96.2%; meadows and pastures 0.1%; agricultural and under permanent cultivation 0.4%; other 3.3%. **Gross national product** (at current market prices; 1998): $684,000,000 ($1,660 per capita). **Public debt** (external, outstanding; 1996): $216,500,000. **Population economically active** (1994): total 98,240; activity rate of total pop. 24.3% (participation rates [District of Wanica and Paramaribo only; 1992]: ages 15–64, 56.0%; female 37.5%; unemployed [1996] 10.7%). **Tourism** (1999): receipts from visitors $53,000,000; expenditures by nationals abroad $11,000,000 (1998).

Foreign trade

Imports (1995): Sf 258,916,700,000 (raw materials 36.4%, investment goods 25.2%, fuels and lubricants 11.1%, food and live animals 9.7%, cars and motorcycles 3.8%). *Major import sources:* US 42.1%; The Netherlands 19.8%; Trinidad and Tobago 7.4%; Netherlands Antilles 2.6%; Japan 2.1%. **Exports** (1995): Sf 211,020,600,000 (1994; alumina 63.6%, shrimp and fish 9.7%, rice 9.6%, aluminum 9.3%, petroleum 3.0%, bananas 2.9%). *Major export destinations:* The Netherlands 27.9%; Norway 24.9%; US 22.3%; Japan 6.1%; Brazil 5.2%.

Transport and communications

Transport. *Railroads* (1997-private only): length 301 km. *Roads* (1996): total length 4,530 km (paved 26%). *Vehicles* (1996): passenger cars 46,408; trucks and buses 19,255. *Air transport* (1996): passenger-km 883,347,000; metric ton-km cargo 106,000,000; airports (1998) with scheduled flights 1. **Communications** Total units (units per 1,000 persons). Daily newspaper circulation (1996): 50,000 (122); Radio receivers (1997): 300,000 (728); Television receivers (1999): 98,000 (236); Telephone main lines (1999): 67,308 (163); Cellular telephone subscribers (1999): 18,000 (43); Internet users (1999): 7,236 (17.5).

Education and health

Literacy (1995): total pop. age 15 and over literate 271,000 (93.0%); males literate 137,000 (95.1%); females literate 134,000 (91.0%). **Health:** physicians (1998) 166 (1 per 2,518 persons); hospital beds (1998) 1,449 (1 per 288 persons); infant mortality rate per 1,000 live births (2000) 25.1. **Food** (1999):

daily per capita caloric intake 2,604 (vegetable products 85%, animal products 15%); 116% of FAO recommended minimum.

Military

Total active duty personnel (2000): 2,040 (army 78.4%, navy 11.8%, air force 9.8%). **Military expenditure as percentage of GNP** (1997): 1.2% (world 2.6%); per capita expenditure $43.

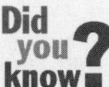 **Did you know?** Suriname is known for its dense rainforest. Located on the equator and receiving a significant amount of rainfall during its wet season, Suriname provides an ideal habitat for monkeys, toucans, and tree frogs.

Background

Suriname was inhabited by various native peoples prior to European settlement. Spanish explorers claimed it in 1593, but the Dutch began to settle there in 1602, followed by the English in 1651. It was ceded to the Dutch in 1667, and in 1682 the Dutch West India Co. introduced coffee and sugarcane plantations and African slaves to cultivate them. Slavery was abolished in 1863, and indentured servants were brought from China, Java, and India to work the plantations, adding to the population mix. Except for brief interludes of British rule (1799–1802, 1804–15), it remained a Dutch colony. It gained internal autonomy in 1954 and independence in 1975. A military coup in 1980 ended civilian control until the electorate approved a new constitution in 1987. Military control resumed after a coup in 1990. Elections were held in 1991, followed by a resumption of democratic government.

Recent Developments

Elections in May 2000 brought in a new majority in the National Assembly for the New Front party, which chose Ronald Venetiaan as president. Suriname was still recovering from the 1986–92 civil conflict that had polarized the interior and coastal regions. He faced a struggling economy, inflation, falling export prices for bauxite and rice, and a host of political and economic problems caused by illegal activities, chiefly drug traffic and unauthorized mining and logging. The former military dictator, Dési Bouterse, had been convicted in 1999 by a court in The Hague of having led an international cocaine-smuggling ring; he was not extradited, however, and he continued to wield considerable political power. However, the country celebrated its return to peace and democratic government under the guidance of the Organization of American States.

Internet resources: <www.surinam.net>

Swaziland

Official name: Umbuso weSwatini (Swazi); Kingdom of Swaziland (English). **Form of government:** monarchy with two legislative houses (Senate [30]; House of

---

1 metric ton = about 1.1 short tons;   1 kilometer = 0.6 mi (statute);   1 metric ton-km cargo = about 0.68 short ton-mi cargo;   c.i.f.: cost, insurance, and freight;   f.o.b.: free on board

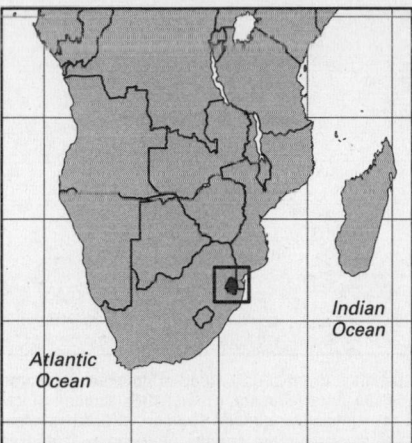

Indian
Ocean

Atlantic
Ocean

Assembly [65]). **Head of state:** King Mswati III (from 1986). **Head of government:** Prime Minister Sibusiso Barnabas Dlamini (from 1996). **Capitals:** Mbabane (administrative and judicial); Lozitha and Ludzidzini (royal); Lobamba (legislative). **Official languages:** Swazi; English. **Official religion:** none. **Monetary unit:** 1 lilangeni (plural emalangeni [E]) = 100 cents; valuation (28 Jun 2002) 1 $ = E 10.31.

Demography

Area: 6,704 sq mi. 17,364 sq km. **Population** (2001): 1,104,000. **Density** (2001): persons per sq mi 164.7; persons per sq km 63.6. **Urban** (1997): 22.6%. **Sex distribution** (1997): male 48.28%; female 51.72%. **Age breakdown** (1997): under 15, 42.5%; 15–29, 29.2%; 30–44, 15.5%; 45–59, 7.8%; 60–74, 3.3%; 75 and over, 1.2%; unknown 0.5%. **Ethnic composition** (2000): Swazi 82.3%; Zulu 9.6%; Tsonga 2.3%; Afrikaner 1.4%; mixed (black-white) 1.0%; other 3.4%. **Religious affiliation** (1995): Christian 66.7%, of which African indigenous 44.7%, Protestant 14.8%, Roman Catholic 5.3%; other (mostly traditional beliefs) 33.3%. **Major cities** (1986): Mbabane 38,290; Manzini 18,084 (urban agglomeration 46,058); Big Bend 9,676; Simunye/Ngomane 9,060; Mhlume 6,509. **Location:** southern Africa, bordering South Africa and Mozambique.

Vital statistics

Birth rate per 1,000 pop. (2000): 40.6 (world avg. 22.5). **Death rate** per 1,000 pop. (2000): 20.4 (world avg. 9.0). **Natural increase rate** per 1,000 pop. (2000): 20.2 (world avg. 13.5). **Total fertility rate** (avg. births per childbearing woman; 2000): 5.9. **Life expectancy at birth** (2000): male 39.5 years; female 41.4 years.

National economy

Budget (1999–2000). *Revenue:* E 2,436,400,000 (receipts from Customs Union of Southern Africa 50.1%; tax on income and profits 25.8%; sales tax 12.0%; foreign-aid grants 3.5%; property income 2.1%; fees, services, and fines 1.1%). *Expenditures:* E 2,630,700,000 (recurrent expenditure 78.2%, of which general administration 28.0%, education 17.3%, economic services 11.2%, justice and police

8.0%, health 6.5%, defense 4.8%). **Gross national product** (1999): $1,379,000,000 ($1,350 per capita). **Population economically active** (1986): total 160,355; activity rate of total pop. 23.5% (participation rates: ages 15 and over, 44.1%; female 34.2%; unemployed 27.0%). **Public debt** (external, outstanding; 1999): $205,500,000. **Production** (metric tons except as noted). *Agriculture, forestry, fishing* (1999): sugarcane 3,700,000, corn (maize) 113,000, oranges 31,200; livestock (number of live animals) 652,000 cattle, 438,000 goats, 31,000 pigs; roundwood (1998) 1,494,000 cu m; fish catch (1998) 60. *Mining and quarrying* (1999): asbestos 22,912; diamonds 64,000 carats (1994). *Manufacturing* (value added in $'000; 1994): food and beverages 244,000, of which beverage processing 153,000; paper and paper products 35,000. *Energy production (consumption):* electricity (kW-hr; 1991) 387,000,000 (815,000,000); coal (metric tons; 1999) 426,299 (1989; 28,454). **Household income and expenditure.** Average household size (1986) 5.7; annual income per household (1985) E 332 ($151); sources of income (1985): wages and salaries 44.4%, self-employment 22.2%, transfers 12.2%, other 21.2%; expenditure (1985): food and beverages 33.5%, rent and fuel 13.4%, household durable goods 12.8%, transportation and communications 8.8%, clothing and footwear 6.0%, recreation 3.3%. **Tourism** (1999): receipts $35,000,000; expenditures $45,000,000.

Foreign trade

Imports (1998): $1,068,000,000 (machinery and transport equipment 26.2%; manufactured items 17.0%; foodstuffs 15.8%; chemicals 13.9%; minerals, fuels, and lubricants 11.8%). *Major import sources* (1997–98): South Africa 82.9%; U.K. 1.7%; U.S. 0.9%; Zimbabwe 0.2%; Spain 0.2%. **Exports** (1998): $921,000,000 (sugar 11.0%; wood and wood products 8.1%; refrigerators 7.5%; cotton yarn 2.3%; paper and paper products 2.0%; canned fruits 1.4%; citrus fruits 1.3%; asbestos 1.0%). *Major export destinations* (1997): South Africa 74.0%; Italy 8.7%; Mozambique 5.2%; U.S. 2.4%; U.K. 2.1%.

Transport and communications

Transport. *Railroads* (1995): length 187 mi, 301 km; passenger-mi 752,000,000 (1988), passenger-km 1,210,000,000 (1988); short ton-mi cargo 1,993,-000,000 (1991), metric ton-km cargo 2,910,-000,000 (1991). *Roads* (1996): total length 2,367 mi, 3,810 km (paved 29%). *Vehicles* (1997): passenger cars 31,882; trucks and buses 32,772. *Air transport* (1995-Royal Swazi National Airways): passenger-mi 30,710,000, passenger-km 49,423,000; short ton-mi cargo 87,000, metric ton-km cargo 127,000; airports (1997) with scheduled flights 1. **Communications.** Total units (units per 1,000 persons). Daily newspaper circulation (1996): 24,000 (24.3); Radio receivers (1997): 155,000 (153); Television receivers (1999): 110,000 (104); Telephone main lines (1999): 30,569 (28.8); Cellular telephone subscribers (1999): 14,000 (13.2); Personal computers (1998): 278 (0.3); Internet users (1999): 5,000 (4.7).

Education and health

Educational attainment (1986). Percentage of pop. age 25 and over having: no formal schooling 42.1%;

some primary education 23.9%; complete primary 10.5%; some secondary 19.2%; complete secondary and higher 4.3%. **Literacy** (1995): total pop. age 15 and over literate 76.7%; males literate 78.0%; females literate 75.6%. **Health:** physicians (1996) 148 (1 per 6,663 persons); hospital beds (1984) 1,608 (1 per 396 persons); infant mortality rate per 1,000 live births (2000) 109.0. **Food** (1999): daily per capita caloric intake 2,698 (vegetable products 87%, animal products 13%); 116% of FAO recommended minimum requirement.

Military

Military expenditure as percentage of GNP (1997): 2.7% (world 2.6%); per capita expenditure $34.

Did you know? Landlocked Swaziland is the smallest country on the continent of Africa.

Background

Stone tools and rock paintings indicate prehistoric habitation in the region, but it was not settled until the Bantu-speaking Swazi people migrated there in the 18th century and established the nucleus of the Swazi nation. The British gained control in the 19th century after the Swazi king sought their aid against the Zulus. Following the South African War, the British governor of Transvaal administered Swaziland; his powers were transferred to the British high commissioner in 1906. In 1949 the British rejected the Union of South Africa's request to control Swaziland. The country gained limited self-government in 1963 and achieved independence in 1968. In the 1970s new constitutions were framed based on the supreme authority of the king and traditional tribal government. During the 1990s forces demanding democracy arose, but the kingdom remained in place.

Recent Developments

The government of Swaziland, the world's last remaining absolute monarchy, had not facilitated efforts of the Constitutional Review Commission (CRC) to create a draft constitution, but in August 2001 the CRC submitted to King Mswati III their report providing a framework for the legal experts who would write the country's constitution. Prodemocracy groups agitated for the establishment of political parties, which according to the CRC were not favored by the majority of the Swazi, and for open participation in government. In 2001, for the first time, local elections were promoted publicly.

Internet resources: <www.swazi.com>

Sweden

Official name: Konungariket Sverige (Kingdom of Sweden). **Form of government:** constitutional monarchy and parliamentary state with one legislative house (Parliament [349]). **Chief of state:** King Carl

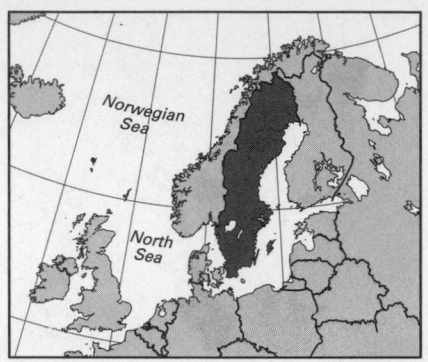

Gustaf XVI (from 1973). **Head of government:** Prime Minister Göran Persson (from 1996). **Capital:** Stockholm. **Official language:** Swedish. **Official religion:** none (formerly the Church of Sweden [Lutheran Church]). **Monetary unit:** 1 Swedish krona (SKr) = 100 ore; valuation (28 Jun 2002) $1 = SKr 9.19.

Demography

Area: 173,732 sq mi, 449,964 sq km. **Population** (2001): 8,888,000. **Density** (2001; land area only): persons per sq mi 51.2, persons per sq km 19.8. **Urban** (1999): 83.3%. **Sex distribution** (2000): male 49.42%; female 50.58%. **Age breakdown** (2000): under 15, 18.5%; 15–29, 18.3%; 30–44, 20.8%; 45–59, 20.3%; 60–74, 13.3%; 75 and over, 8.8%. **Ethnic composition** (1997): Swedish 89.3%; Finnish 2.3%; Yugoslavian 0.8%; Iranian 0.6%; Bosnian 0.5%; other 6.5%. **Religious affiliation** (1999): Church of Sweden 86.5% (nominally; about 30% nonpracticing); Muslim 2.3%; Roman Catholic 1.8%; Pentecostal 1.1%; other 8.3%. **Major cities** (2000): Stockholm 743,703; Göteborg 462,470; Malmö 257,574; Uppsala 188,478; Linköping 132,500. **Location:** northern Europe, bordering Finland, the Gulf of Bothnia, the Baltic Sea, and Norway.

Vital statistics

Birth rate per 1,000 pop. (2000): 9.9 (world avg. 22.5); (1999) legitimate 48.2%; illegitimate 51.8%. **Death rate** per 1,000 pop. (2000): 10.6 (world avg. 9.0). **Natural increase rate** per 1,000 pop. (2000): –0.7 (world avg. 13.5). **Total fertility rate** (avg. births per childbearing woman; 2000): 1.5. **Marriage rate** per 1,000 pop. (1999): 3.6. **Divorce rate** per 1,000 pop. (1999): 2.4. **Life expectancy** at birth (2000): male 77.1 years; female 82.5 years.

National economy

Budget (1999). *Revenue:* SKr 725,104,000,000 (value-added and excise taxes 34.8%, social security 32.1%, income and capital gains taxes 18.8%, property taxes 5.4%). *Expenditures:* SKr 643,147,000,000 (health and social affairs 25.5%, debt service 14.0%, defense 6.9%, education 4.5%). **Public debt** (2000): $61,046,000,000. **Production** (metric tons except as noted). *Agriculture, forestry, fishing* (2001): sugar beets 2,752,600, wheat 2,390,000, barley

1 metric ton = about 1.1 short tons;   1 kilometer = 0.6 mi (statute);   1 metric ton-km cargo = about 0.68 short ton-mi cargo;   c.i.f.: cost, insurance, and freight;   f.o.b.: free on board

1,600,000; livestock (number of live animals) 1,891,456 pigs, 1,713,000 cattle, 451,594 sheep; roundwood (2000) 55,250,000 cu m; fish catch (1999) 357,317. *Mining and quarrying* (1998): iron ore 20,930,000; zinc 297,000; copper 270,000. *Manufacturing* (value added, in SKr '000,000; 1999): transport equipment 76,274; machinery, except electrical 76,133; paper products 46,363; electrical machinery 40,603; food 21,474; wood products 15,825. *Energy production (consumption):* electricity (kW-hr; 1999) 154,663,000,000 (158,882,000,000); coal (metric tons; 1997) none (3,113,000); crude petroleum (barrels; 1997) none (146,382,000). **Tourism** (1999): receipts $3,894,000,000; expenditures $7,557,000,000. **Land use** (1994): forest 68.0%; pasture 1.4%; agriculture 6.8%; other 23.8%. **Gross national product** (1998): $236,940,000 ($26,750 per capita). **Population economically active** (1999): total 4,308,000; activity rate of total pop. 48.6% (participation rates: ages 16–64, 77.2%; female 47.7%; unemployed 5.6%). **Household income and expenditure.** Average household size (1999) 2.2; median income per household (1994) SKr 396,100; sources of income (1992): wages and salaries 58.9%, transfer payments 25.8%, self-employment 15.3%; expenditure (1995): housing and energy 29.6%, food 20.9%, transportation 16.1%, education and recreation 9.2%.

Foreign trade

Imports (1999): SKr 565,950,000,000 (machinery and transport equipment 42.4%; manufactured goods 13.6%; chemicals 10.3%; food 5.7%). *Major import sources* (1998): Germany 19.0%; UK 10.2%; Norway 7.6%; Denmark 6.5%; US 6.2%. **Exports** (1999): SKr 700,853,000,000 (machinery and transport equipment 50.8%, of which electrical machinery 21.1%, road vehicles 12.6%; paper products 8.1%; chemicals 9.6%; iron and steel products 4.6%). *Major export destinations* (1998): Germany 11.2%; UK 9.1%; Norway 8.8%; US 8.8%.

Transport and communications

Transport. *Railroads* (2000): length 10,961 km; (1999) passenger-km 7,638,000,000; metric ton-km cargo 19,088,000,000. *Roads* (2000): total length 210,000 km (paved 74%). *Vehicles* (2000): passenger cars 3,890,159; trucks and buses 352,897. *Air transport* (2000; one-third of SAS): passenger-km 11,261,000; metric ton-km cargo 286,404,000; airports (1996) 48. **Communications** Total units (units per 1,000 persons). Daily newspaper circulation (1996): 3,933,000 (446); Radio receivers (1997): 8,250,000 (932); Television receivers (1999): 4,900,000 (553); Telephone main lines (1999): 5,889,000 (665); Cellular telephone subscribers (1999): 5,165,000 (583); Personal computers (1999): 4,000,000 (451); Internet users (1999): 3,666,000 (414).

Education and health

Educational attainment (2000). Percentage of pop. age 16–64 having: primary education 32.0%; lower secondary education 28.0%; higher secondary 16.0%; some postsecondary 24.0%. **Literacy** (2000): virtually 100%. **Health** (1999): physicians 24,200 (1 per 366 persons); hospital beds 32,755 (1 per 271 persons); infant mortality rate per 1,000 live births (2000) 3.5. **Food** (1999): daily per capita caloric in-

take 3,141 (vegetable 67%, animal 33%) 117% of FAO recommended minimum requirement.

Military

Total active duty personnel (2000): 53,100 (army 66.1%, navy 17.3%, air force 16.6%). **Military expenditure as percentage of GNP** (1997): 2.5% (world 2.6%); per capita expenditure $626.

 **Did you know?** Swedish scholars made many great contributions to the sciences in the 18th century. Anders Celsius, for example, invented the centigrade thermometer scale, and Carolus Linnaeus is credited with the invention of a widely used classification system for plants and animals.

Background

The first inhabitants of Sweden were apparently hunters who crossed the land bridge from Europe c. 9000 BC. During the Viking era (9th–10th centuries), the Swedes controlled river trade in eastern Europe between the Baltic Sea and the Black Sea and also raided western European lands. Sweden was loosely united and Christianized in the 11th–12th centuries. It conquered the Finns in the 12th century and in the 14th united with Norway and Denmark under a single monarchy. It broke away in 1523 under Gustav I Vasa. In the 17th century it emerged as a great European power in the Baltic region, but its dominance declined after its defeat in the Second Northern War (1700–21). It became a constitutional monarchy in 1809 and united with Norway 1814–1905; it acknowledged Norwegian independence in 1905. It maintained its neutrality during both world wars. It was a charter member of the UN but abstained from membership in the European Union (EU) until the 1990s and in NATO altogether. A new constitution drafted in 1975 reduced the monarch's powers to ceremonial head of state. In 1997 it decided to begin the controversial shutdown of its nuclear power industry.

Recent Developments

At the turn of the 21st century Sweden was enjoying a comeback from its troubling economic situation of the mid-1990s. The GDP was growing, inflation was in check, and unemployment rates were falling. In 2000 the economy posted a surplus after years of deficits, allowing for some relief in the form of tax cuts and increases in government spending. One reason for the turnaround was Sweden's embrace of new technologies; there was a high rate of mobile-phone and Internet usage and a strong presence in telecommunications equipment manufacturing. As a center of IT research, Sweden saw a boom in jobs and dot-com start-ups, but it suffered along with many other countries when the technology bubble burst in 2001.

Sweden assumed the rotating presidency of the European Union in 2001 and won praise for its efficient administration and the diplomatic initiatives of Prime Minister Göran Persson. An EU summit held in Göteborg was marred by violent clashes between police and antiglobalization protestors. Although an EU member, Sweden did not adopt the euro as the public was wary of encroachments on national sovereignty.

Internet resources: <www.sverigeturism.se>

Switzerland

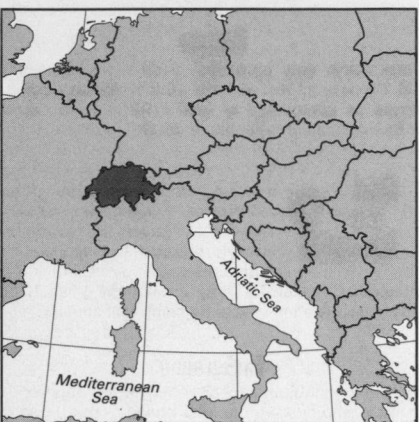

Official name: Confédération Suisse (French); Schweizerische Eidgenossenschaft (German); Confederazione Svizzera (Italian); Confederaziun Helvetica (Romansh) (Swiss Confederation). **Form of government:** federal state with two legislative houses (Council of States [46]; National Council [200]). **Head of state and government:** President of the Federal Council Kaspar Villiger (from 1 Jan 2002). **Capitals:** Bern (administrative); Lausanne (judicial). **Official languages:** French; German; Italian; Romansh (locally). **Official religion:** none. **Monetary unit:** 1 Swiss Franc (Sw F) = 100 centimes; valuation (28 Jun 2002) $1 = Sw F 1.49.

Demography

Area: 15,940 sq mi, 41,284 sq km. **Population** (2001): 7,222,000. **Density** (2001): persons per sq mi 453.1, persons per sq km 174.9. **Urban** (1999): 67.5%. **Sex distribution** (2000): male 48.86%; female 51.14%. **Age breakdown** (2000): under 15, 17.4%; 15–29, 18.3%; 30–44, 24.4%; 45–59, 19.8%; 60–74, 13.0%; 75 and over, 7.1%. **National composition** (2000; includes 1,406,600 resident aliens, excludes 107,010 refugees): Swiss 80.4%; former Yugoslav 4.7%; Italian 4.6%; Portuguese 1.9%; German 1.4%; Spanish 1.2%; other 5.8%. **Religious affiliation** (1990): Roman Catholic 46.2%; Protestant 40.0%; Muslim 2.2%; Orthodox Christian 1.0%; Jewish 0.3%; other 10.3%. **Major urban agglomerations** (2000): Zürich 943,400; Geneva 457,500; Basel 401,600; Bern 319,100; Lausanne 288,100. **Location:** Central Europe, bordering Germany, Austria, Liechtenstein, Italy, and France.

Vital statistics

Birth rate per 1,000 pop. (1999): 11.0 (world avg. 22.5); legitimate 90.0%; illegitimate 10.0%. **Death rate** per 1,000 pop. (1999): 8.7 (world avg. 9.0). **Natural increase rate** per 1,000 pop. (1999): 2.3 (world avg. 13.5). **Total fertility rate** (avg. births per childbearing woman; 1999): 1.5. **Marriage rate** per 1,000 pop. (1999): 5.7. **Life expectancy** at birth (1998–99): male 76.7 years; female 82.6 years.

National economy

Budget (1997; for consolidated central government). *Revenue:* Sw F 99,349,000,000 (social security contributions 46.7%, taxes on goods and services 20.2%, income taxes 11.6%). *Expenditures:* Sw F 103,528,000,000 (social security and welfare 50.5%, health 19.7%, economic affairs 10.4%, defense 5.2%, education 2.3%). **National debt** (end of year; 2000): Sw F 108,108,000,000. **Tourism** (1999): receipts from visitors $7,739,000,000; expenditures by nationals abroad $6,842,000,000. **Production** (metric tons except as noted). *Agriculture, forestry, fishing* (2000): cow's milk 3,910,000, sugar beets 1,410,000, potatoes 584,000, wheat 548,200; livestock (number of live animals) 1,600,000 cattle, 1,450,000 pigs; roundwood (1999) 5,000,000 cu m; fish catch (1998) 1,709. *Mining* (1998): salt 300,000; cut and polished diamond exports $1,340,000,000. *Manufacturing* (value added in Sw F '000,000; 1997): machinery and transport equipment 22,530; chemicals and chemical products 19,414; iron and steel 7,972. *Energy production (consumption):* electricity (kW-hr; 1999) 66,696,000,000 ([1996] 56,117,000,000); coal (metric tons; 1996) none (183,000); crude petroleum (barrels; 1996) none (38,534,000); petroleum products (metric tons; 1996) 5,103,000 (11,738,000); natural gas (cu m; 1996) negligible (2,902,000,000). **Gross national product** (1999): $273,856,000,000 ($38,380 per capita). **Population economically active** (1999): total 3,984,000; activity rate of total pop. 55.6% (participation rates: ages 15 and over, 67.8%; female 44.4%; unemployed [April 2000–March 2001] 1.9%). **Household income and expenditure.** Average household size (1998) 2.4; average gross income per household (1998) Sw F 100,272 ; sources of income (1996): wages 58.5%, transfers 25.6%; expenditure (1998): housing 26.2%, food 13.2%, recreation 11.4%. **Land use** (1994): forested 31.6%; meadows and pastures 29.0%; agricultural and under permanent cultivation 11.0%; other 28.4%.

Foreign trade

Imports (2000-c.i.f.): Sw F 128,615,000,000 (machinery 24.6%, chemical products 17.1%, vehicles 11.6%, food products 7.7%). *Major import sources:* Germany 31.2%; France 10.8%; Italy 10.0%; US 6.8%; the Netherlands 6.1%. **Exports** (2000-f.o.b.): Sw F 126,549,000,000 (machinery 29.3%, chemical products 28.4%, precision instruments, watches, jewelry 16.2%, fabricated metals 8.6%). *Major export destinations:* Germany 22.2%; US 11.6%; France 9.0%; Italy 7.6%; UK 5.4%.

Transport and communications

Transport. *Railroads* (1997): length 5,035 km; passenger-km 14,104,000,000; metric ton-km cargo 8,688,000,000. *Roads* (1998): total length 71,211 km. *Vehicles* (1999): passenger cars 3,467,275; trucks and buses 313,646. *Air transport* (1999; Swissair only): passenger-km 31,767,000,000; metric ton-km cargo 1,776,000,000; airports (1996) with scheduled flights 5. **Communications** Total units (units per 1,000 persons). Daily newspaper circulation (1996): 2,383,000 (337); Radio receivers (1997): 7,100,000 (1,002); Television receivers

1 metric ton = about 1.1 short tons;　1 kilometer = 0.6 mi (statute);　1 metric ton-km cargo = about 0.68 short ton-mi cargo;　c.i.f.: cost, insurance, and freight;　f.o.b.: free on board

(1999): 3,700,000 (518); Telephone main lines (1999): 4,992,000 (699); Cellular telephone subscribers (1999): 2,935,000 (411); Personal computers (1999): 3,300,000 (462); Internet users (1999): 1,427,000 (200).

Education and health

Educational attainment (1997). Percentage of resident Swiss and resident alien pop. age 25–64 having: lower secondary education or less 20%; vocational 50%; upper secondary 7%; higher technical 13%; university 10%. **Health** (1998): physicians 22,950 est. (1 per 310 persons); hospital beds 45,989 (1 per 155 persons); infant mortality rate per 1,000 live births (1999) 3.4. **Food** (1999): daily per capita caloric intake 3,258 (vegetable products 67%, animal products 33%); 121% of FAO recommended minimum.

Military

Total active duty personnel (2000): 3,470 (excludes 361,200 reservists). **Military expenditure as percentage of GNP** (1997): 1.4% (world 2.8%); per capita expenditure $545.

Background

The original inhabitants of Switzerland were the Helvetians, who were conquered by the Romans in the 1st century BC. Germanic tribes penetrated the region from the 3rd–6th centuries AD, and Muslim and Magyar raiders ventured in during the 10th century. It came under the Holy Roman Empire in the 11th century. In 1291 three cantons formed an anti-Habsburg league that became the nucleus of the Swiss Confederation. It was a center of the Reformation, which divided the confederation and led to a period of political and religious conflict. The French organized Switzerland as the Helvetic Republic in 1798. In 1815 the Congress of Vienna recognized Swiss independence and guaranteed its neutrality. A new federal state was formed in 1848 with Bern as the capital. It remained neutral in both world wars and continued to guard this stance. With the formation of the European Union (EU), it took steps toward provisional association with the European economic area.

Recent Developments

Long known for its conservatism and carefully protected neutrality, Switzerland took a major step into the international arena in March 2002 when its voters narrowly approved a referendum in favor of joining the United Nations; it would become the 190th member. Geneva had long been home to UN agencies, and the country had participated in many UN activities. Switzerland remained outside the European Union, in part because of the potential for disruption of the banking industry, which would have to adhere to EU requirements. In 2000 several banks were fined for having accepted $600 million in deposits on behalf of Nigerian dictator Sani Abacha. The assets held in Swiss banks since before World War II, mainly those of Jews, had come under scrutiny in 1999.

Although the economy was generally strong, the national airline Swissair collapsed, the worldwide drop in passengers after 11 Sep 2001 providing the final blow after several years of financial difficulties. Crossair took over 52 of Swissair's planes, bolstered by bankruptcy protection and an influx of capital.

Domestic issues included the scaling back of army personnel by more than 40% and restrictions on immigration. After a year's delay Expo02, the sixth Swiss National Exhibition, opened in May 2002.

Internet resources: <www.myswitzerland.com>

Syria

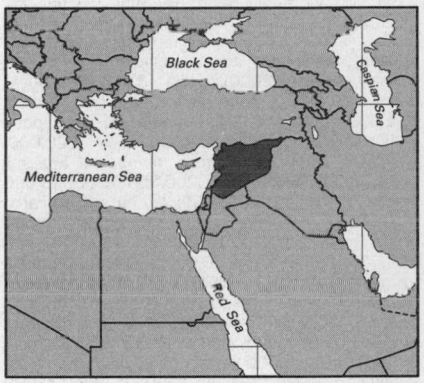

Official name: Al-Jumhuriyah al-'Arabiyah as-Suriyah (Syrian Arab Republic). **Form of government:** unitary multiparty (parties ideologically compatible with the ruling Ba'th Party) republic with one legislative house (People's Council [250]). **Head of state and government:** President Bashar al-Assad, assisted by Prime Minister Muhammad Mustafa Miru (from 2000). **Capital:** Damascus. **Official language:** Arabic. **Official religion:** none; although Islam is the required religion of the head of state and is the basis of the legal system. **Monetary unit:** 1 Syrian pound (LS) = 100 piastres; valuation (28 Jun 2002) $1 = LS 51.40.

Demography

Area (includes territory in the Golan Heights recognized internationally as part of Syria): 71,498 sq mi, 185,180 sq km. **Population** (2001): 16,729,000. **Density** (2001): persons per sq mi 234.0, persons per sq km 90.3. **Urban** (1999): 54.0%. **Sex distribution** (2000): male 51.23%; female 48.77%. **Age breakdown** (2000): under 15, 40.1%; 15–29, 30.6%; 30–44, 16.6%; 45–59, 7.4%; 60–74, 3.8%; 75 and over, 1.5%. **Ethnic composition** (2000): Syrian Arab 74.9%; Bedouin Arab 7.4%; Kurd 7.3%; Palestinian Arab 3.9%; Armenian 2.7%; other 3.8%. **Religious affiliation** (1992): Muslim 86.0%, of which Sunni 74.0%, 'Alawite (Shi'i) 12.0%; Christian 5.5%; Druze 3.0%; other 5.5%. **Major cities** (1994): Aleppo 1,591,400; Damascus 1,549,932; Homs 644,204; Latakia 306,535; Hamah 229,000. **Location:** the Middle East, bordering Turkey, Iraq, Jordan, Israel, Lebanon, and the Mediterranean Sea.

Vital statistics

Birth rate per 1,000 pop. (2000): 31.1 (world avg. 22.5). **Death rate** per 1,000 pop. (2000): 5.3 (world avg. 9.0). **Natural increase rate** per 1,000 pop. (2000): 25.8 (world avg. 13.5). **Total fertility rate** (avg. births per childbearing woman; 2000): 4.1. **Marriage rate** per 1,000 pop. (1995; Syrian Arabs or

8.4. Life expectancy at birth (2000): male 67.4 years; female 69.6 years.

National economy

Budget (1999). *Revenue*: LS 255,300,000,000 (current revenues 85.4%, capital [development] revenues 14.6%). *Expenditures*: LS 255,300,000,000 (current expenditures 56.4%, capital [development] expenditures 43.6%). **Public debt** (external, outstanding; 1999): $16,142,000,000. **Gross national product** (1999): $15,172,000,000 ($970 per capita). **Production** (metric tons except as noted). *Agriculture, forestry, fishing* (2000): wheat 3,104,969, sugar beets 1,300,000, seed cotton 930,000, grapes 451,000, olives 750,000, tomatoes 610,000, potatoes 450,000, oranges 400,000, apples 320,000, eggplants 128,000; livestock (number of live animals) 15,000,000 sheep, 1,200,000 goats, 905,000 cattle; roundwood (2000) 50,400 cu m; fish catch (1999) 14,024. *Mining and quarrying* (1999): phosphate rock 2,127,000; gypsum 232,000; salt 104,000; marble blocks 16,000,000 cu m. *Manufacturing* (1998): cement 5,016,000; refined sugar 89,000; cottonseed cake 226,000; olive oil 145,000; soap 89,000; vegetable oil 65,000; glass and pottery products 57,000; television receivers 150,500 units; refrigerators 136,900 units. *Energy production (consumption)*: electricity (kW-hr; 1999) 21,568,000,000 (21,568,000,000); crude petroleum (barrels; 1996) 189,426,000 (84,083,000); petroleum products (metric tons; 1996) 11,580,000 (10,287,000); natural gas (cu m; 1996) 2,614,000,000 (2,614,000,-000). **Population economically active** (1999): 4,527,258; activity rate of total pop. 28.8% (participation rates: ages 10 and over, 32.9%; female 11.3%; unemployed 9.5%). **Average household size** (1999): 5.0; expenditure (1987; weights of consumer price index components for Damascus only): food 58.8%, rent, fuel, and light 16.0%, clothing 7.5%, household goods 5.8%, transportation 2.4%, education and recreation 2.1%. **Tourism** (1998): receipts $1,360,-000,000; expenditures $630,000,000. **Land use** (1994): steppe and pasture 45.2%; agricultural and under permanent cultivation 30.1%; forested 2.6%; other 22.1%.

Foreign trade

Imports (1999-c.i.f.): LS 43,010,000,000 (basic metals and manufactures 16.9%, food and beverages 13.8%, machinery and transport equipment 13.0%, textiles 9.9%, chemicals and chemical products 8.9%, resins 5.8%). *Major import sources*: Germany 7.0%; France 5.7%; Italy 5.6%; Turkey 4.7%; United States 4.6%; Japan 4.1%; China 3.3%; Belgium 2.9%. **Exports** (1999): LS 38,880,000,000 (crude petroleum and petroleum products 62.9%, fresh vegetables and fruits 12.4%, textiles and fabrics 7.2%, raw cotton 4.5%, live animals and meat 1.3%). *Major export destinations*: Italy 26.6%; France 20.6%; Turkey 9.2%; Saudi Arabia 8.3%; Spain 6.9%; Lebanon 4.0%.

Transport and communications

Transport. Railroads (1998): route length 2,425 km; —r-km 181,575,000; metric ton-km cargo

(1997) 1,364,000,000. Roads (1998): total length 41,451 km (paved 23%). Vehicles (1998): passenger cars 138,900; trucks and buses 282,664. Air transport (2000): passenger-km 1,421,537,000; metric ton-km cargo 20,813,000; airports (1999) with scheduled flights 5. **Communications** Daily newspaper circulation (1996): 287,000 (20 units per 1,000 persons); Radio receivers (1997): 4,150,000 (278 units per 1,000 persons); Television receivers (1999): 1,070,000 (66.4 units per 1,000 persons); Telephones main lines (1999): 1,600,000 (99.3 units per 1,000 persons); Cellular telephones (1999): 4,000 (0.4 units per 1,000 persons); Personal computers (1999): 230,000 (22.7 units per 1,000 persons); Internet users (1999): 20,000 (2.0 per 1,000 persons).

Education and health

Educational attainment (1984). Percentage of population age 10 and over having: no schooling 20.1%; knowledge of reading and writing 26.3%; primary education 29.3%; secondary 18.4%; certificate 3.3%; higher 2.7%. **Literacy** (1995): percentage of population age 15 and over literate 74.4%; males literate 88.3%; females literate 60.4%. **Health** (1998): physicians 22,293 (1 per 694 persons); hospital beds (1995) 17,623 (1 per 832 persons); infant mortality rate (2000) 34.8. **Food** (1999): daily per capita caloric intake 3,272 (vegetable products 88%, animal products 12%); 132% of FAO recommended minimum requirement.

Military

Total active duty personnel (2000): 316,000 (army 68.0%, navy 1.9%, air force 30.1%). **Military expenditure as percentage of GNP** (1997): 5.6% (world 2.6%); per capita expenditure $211.

Did you know?  Syria's Olympic history has been limited to participation in the Summer Games only. It won its first Olympic medal at the 1984 Games—a silver in heavyweight freestyle wrestling—and its first gold medal—in women's javelin—in 1996 in Atlanta.

Background

Syria has been inhabited for several thousand years. From the 3rd millennium BC, it was under the control variously of Sumerians, Akkadians, Amorites, Egyptians, Hittites, Assyrians, and Babylonians. In the 6th century BC it became part of the Persian Achaemenian dynasty, which fell to Alexander the Great in 330 BC. Seleucid rulers governed it 301–c. 164 BC; then Parthians and Nabataean Arabs divided the region. It flourished as a Roman province (64 BC–AD 300) and as part of the Byzantine empire (300–634), until Muslims invaded and established control. It came under the Ottoman empire in 1516, which held it, except for brief rules by Egypt, until the British invaded in World War I. After the war it became a French mandate; it achieved independence in 1945. It united with Egypt in the United Arab Republic (1958–61). During the Six-Day War (1967), it lost the Golan

Heights to Israel. Syrian troops frequently clashed with Israeli troops in Lebanon during the 1980s and '90s. Hafez al-Assad's long and harsh regime was marked also by antagonism toward Syria's neighbors Turkey and Iraq.

Recent Developments

Syria was shocked by Hafez al-Assad's sudden death on 10 Jun 2000, in the second year of his fifth term as president. The age requirement in the constitution was quickly amended to allow Assad's son, Bashar, to qualify for the presidency. In balloting held on 10 July he received 97% of the vote. In his inaugural address he reaffirmed the government's refusal to relinquish any part of the Golan Heights to Israel. He proposed no major changes in the country's political system but pledged to fight corruption and affirmed his commitment to a form of democracy appropriate to Syria. Six hundred political prisoners were set free to mark the 30th anniversary of the senior Assad's rise to power. Cautious criticism of the government and the Ba'th Party began to appear, but by mid-2001 dissidents were being arrested and the state-run media and conservative forces attacked the reform movement.

Syria strengthened ties with neighboring countries, especially Iraq. In 2001 agreements were concluded to phase out tariffs on trade and increase commerce and technological exchange. A mutual defense pact was signed. Iraq agreed to work with Turkey to combat crime and terrorism. Relations with Israel, however, were stalemated. Israel bombed Syrian positions in Lebanon in April and July 2001 in response to Hezbollah operations in the Golan Heights.

Internet resources: <http://syriatourism.org>

Taiwan

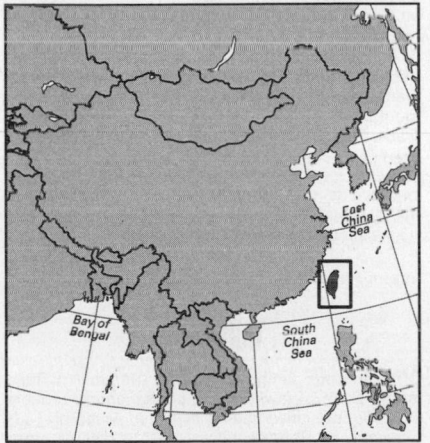

Official name: Chung-hua Min-kuo (Republic of China). **Form of government:** multiparty republic with a Legislature (Legislative Yuan [225]). **Chief of state:** President Chen Shui-bian (from 2000). **Head of government:** Premier Yu Shyi-kun (from 1 Feb 2002). **Capital:** Taipei. **Official language:** Mandarin Chinese. **Official religion:** none. **Monetary unit:** 1 New Taiwan

dollar (NT$) = 100 cents; valuation (28 Jun 2002) US$1 = NT$33.41.

Demography

Area: 36,188 sq km. **Population** (2001): 22,340,000. **Density** (2001): persons per sq mi 1,598.9, persons per sq km 617.3. **Urban** (1991): 74.7%. **Sex distribution** (2001): male 51.10%; female 48.90%. **Age breakdown** (2000): under 15, 21.1%; 15–29, 25.4%; 30–44, 25.4%; 45–59, 16.0%; 60–74, 9.0%; 75 and over, 3.1%. **Ethnic composition** (1997): Han Chinese, Chinese mainland minorities, and others 98.2%; indigenous tribal peoples 1.8%, of which Ami 0.6%. **Religious affiliation** (1997; formal subscribers to religious beliefs [almost all Taiwanese adults engage in religious practices stemming from one or a combination of traditional folk religions]): Buddhism 22.4%; Taoism 20.7%; I-kuan Tao 4.3%; Protestant 1.6%; Roman Catholic 1.4%; other Christian 0.3%; Muslim 0.2%; Baha'i 0.1%; other 49.0%. **Major cities** (2000): Taipei 2,646,753; Kao-hsiung 1,482,899; T'ai-chung 954,177; T'ai-nan 732,241; Chung-ho (1998) 388,174. **Location:** between the East China Sea, the Philippine Sea, and the South China Sea north of the Philippines and southeast of mainland China.

Vital statistics

Birth rate per 1,000 pop. (2000): 13.8 (world avg. 22.5). **Death rate** per 1,000 pop. (2000): 5.7 (world avg. 9.0). **Natural increase rate** per 1,000 pop. (2000): 8.1 (world avg. 13.5). **Total fertility rate** (avg. births per childbearing woman; 2000): 1.8. **Life expectancy** at birth (2000): male 73.6 years; female 79.3 years.

National economy

Budget (1999). *Revenue:* NT$2,218,135,000,000 (income taxes 19.5%, business tax 8.8%, land tax 6.7%, commodity tax 6.6%, customs duties 4.6%). *Expenditures:* NT$2,217,846,000,000 (administration and defense 25.5%, education 15.3%). **Population economically active** (1990): total 10,236,324; activity rate 50.5% (participation rates: ages 15–64, 72.5%; female 38.5%; unemployed [2000] 3.0%). **Production** (metric tons except as noted). *Agriculture, forestry, fishing* (2000): sugarcane 2,894,000, rice 1,559,000, citrus fruits 440,382; livestock (number of live animals) 7,495,000 pigs, 202,000 goats, 161,700 cattle; timber 21,134 cu m; fish catch 1,356,275. *Mining and quarrying* (2000): marble 17,800,000. *Manufacturing* (2000): cement 17,572,303; steel ingots 17,302,396; telephones 4,722,353 units; *Energy production (consumption):* electricity (kW-hr; 2000) 175,165,000,000 ([1996] 111,140,000,000); coal (metric tons; 1996) 147,500 (29,983,000); crude petroleum (barrels; 1996) 335,000 (226,387,000); natural gas (cu m; 1996) 870,000,000 (4,500,000,000). **Tourism** (1999): receipts from visitors US$3,571,000,000; expenditures by nationals abroad US$5,635,000,000. **Gross national product** (2000): US$314,421,000,000 (US$14,220 per capita). **Household income and expenditure** (1999). Average household size (2000) 3.3; income per household NT$1,181,082; expenditure: food, beverage, and tobacco 25.1%, rent, fuel, and power 24.9%, education and recreation 13.0%, transportation 11.1%, health care 11.0%, clothing 4.1%, furniture 2.9%.

Foreign trade

Imports (2000-c.i.f.): US$140,010,600,000 (electronic machinery 19.5%, nonelectrical machinery 12.2%, minerals 10.1%, chemicals 9.3%, metals and metal products 7.9%, transportation equipment 3.4%). *Major import sources:* Japan 27.5%; US 17.9%; South Korea 6.4%; Germany 4.0%; Malaysia 3.8%. **Exports** (2000-f.o.b.): US$148,320,600,000 (electronics and other machinery 55.7%, textile products 10.3%, plastic articles 6.1%, transportation equipment 3.9%). *Major export destinations:* US 23.5%; Hong Kong 21.1%; Japan 11.2%; Singapore 3.7%; Germany 3.3%.

Transport and communications

Transport. *Railroads* (2000): track length 3,879 km; passenger-km 12,606,000,000; metric ton-km cargo 1,179,000,000. *Roads* (2000): total length 20,375 km (paved [1996] 89%). *Vehicles* (2000): passenger cars 4,716,000; trucks and buses 833,000. *Air transport* (1998): passenger-km 39,218,000,000; metric ton-km cargo 4,129,300,000; airports (1996) 13. **Communications** Total units (units per 1,000 persons). Radio receivers (1996): 8,620,000 (402); Television receivers (1999): 9,200,000 (418); Telephone main lines (2000): 12,642,000 (570); Cellular telephone subscribers (2000): 17,874,000 (806); Personal computers (1999): 4,353,000 (198); Internet users (2000): 4,650,000 (210).

Education and health

Educational attainment (1999). Percentage of pop. age 25 and over having: no formal schooling 7.0%; less than complete primary education 6.3%; primary 21.3%; incomplete secondary 25.7%; secondary 21.8%; some college 10.4%; higher 7.5%. **Literacy** (1999): pop. age 15 and over literate 16,414,896 (94.6%); males 8,641,549 (97.6%); females 7,773,347 (91.4%). **Health** (1999): physicians 28,216 (1 per 780 persons); hospital beds 122,937 (1 per 179 persons); infant mortality rate per 1,000 live births (2000) 7.1.

Military

Total active duty personnel (2000): 370,000 (army 64.9%, navy 16.8%, air force 18.4%). **Military expenditure as percentage of GNP** (1997): 4.6% (world 2.6%); per capita expenditure US$606.

Did you know? Taiwan's first national park, Kenting, at Taiwan's southernmost tip was opened in 1984. Encompassing both land and adjacent ocean, the park comprises Taiwan's only tropical area and is known for both its tropical and subtropical flora as well as its coral reefs.

Background

Known to the Chinese as early as the 7th century, Taiwan was widely settled by them early in the 17th ~~...~~ 1646 the Dutch seized control of the is~~...~~ be ousted in 1661 by a large influx of

Chinese Ming-dynasty refugees. Taiwan fell to the Manchus in 1683 and was not open to Europeans again until 1858. In 1895 it was ceded to Japan following the Sino-Japanese War. A Japanese military center in World War II, it was frequently bombed by US planes. After Japan's defeat, it was returned to China, which was then governed by the Nationalists. When the Communists took over mainland China in 1949, the Nationalist government fled to Taiwan and made it their seat of government, with Gen. Chiang Kai-shek as president. In 1954 he and the US signed a mutual defense treaty, and Taiwan received US support for almost three decades, developing its economy in spectacular fashion. It was recognized by many noncommunist countries as the representative of all China until 1971, when it was replaced in the UN by the People's Republic of China. Martial law was lifted in Taiwan in 1987, and travel restrictions with mainland China in 1988. In 1989 opposition parties were legalized. The relationship with the mainland became increasingly close in the 1990s.

Recent Developments

The election of Chen Shui-bian, opposition candidate of the Democratic Progressive Party (DPP) as president of Taiwan in March 2000 marked the termination of 50 years of uninterrupted rule by the Kuomintang. The Kuomintang retained its majority in the legislature, however; this edge was eroded in 2001 parliamentary elections, when its share of the vote fell from 46 to 31%. The DPP victory initiated a spate of new parties and reshuffling in domestic politics. The news of Chen's victory was anything but welcome in Beijing, which regarded him as a dangerous advocate of independence for Taiwan. Overtures to Beijing met with a cool reception, but US-Taiwan ties were strengthened. The Bush administration proved sympathetic to Taiwanese defense concerns, agreeing in 2001 to provide Taiwan with ships, submarines, aircraft, and armaments, a move vehemently protested by Beijing.

Chen bowed to opposition pressure and approved the construction of Taiwan's fourth nuclear power plant, over the objections of the DPP and environmentalists. Taiwan's application to join the World Trade Organization was approved, but the economy, which had been strong in 2000, faltered in 2001 in response to the worldwide downturn in demand for Taiwan's high-tech exports. Unemployment soared to record levels, growth slowed, and the country entered recession for the first time since 1975.

Internet resources: <www.tbroc.gov.tw>

Tajikistan

Official name: Jumhurii Tojikistan (Republic of Tajikistan). **Form of government:** parliamentary republic with two legislative houses (National Assembly [33]; Assembly of Representatives [63]). **Chief of state:** President Imomali Rakhmonov (from 1994). **Head of government:** Prime Minister Akil Akilov (from 1999). **Capital:** Dushanbe. **Official language:** Tajik. **Official religion:** none. **Monetary unit:** 1 somoni = 100 dinar; valuation (28 Jun 2002) $1 = 2.70 somoni.

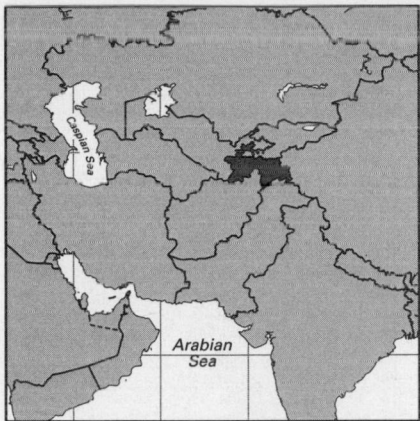

Arabian
Sea

Demography

Area: 55,300 sq mi, 143,100 sq km. **Population** (2001): 6,252,000. **Density** (2001): persons per sq mi 113.1, persons per sq km 43.7. **Urban** (1999): 33.0%. **Sex distribution** (2000): male 49.81%; female 50.19%. **Age breakdown** (2000): under 15, 39.4%; 15–29, 27.7%; 30–44, 18.4%; 45–59, 7.6%; 60–74, 5.4%; 75 and over, 1.5%. **Ethnic composition** (2000): Tajik 64.9%; Uzbek 25.9%; Russian 3.5%; Tatar 1.4%; Kyrgyz 1.3%; other 3.0%. **Religious affiliation** (1995): Sunni Muslim 80.0%; Shi'i Muslim 5.0%; Russian Orthodox 1.5%; Jewish 0.1%; other (mostly nonreligious) 13.4%. **Major cities** (1998 est.): Dushanbe 513,000; Khujand 163,000. **Location:** central Asia, bordering Kyrgyzstan, China, Afghanistan, and Uzbekistan.

Vital statistics

Birth rate per 1,000 pop. (2001): 24.7 (world avg. 22.5); (1994) legitimate 90.8%; illegitimate 9.2%. **Death rate** per 1,000 pop. (2001): 6.4 (world avg. 9.0). **Natural increase rate** per 1,000 pop. (2001): 18.3 (world avg. 13.5). **Total fertility rate** (avg. births per childbearing woman; 2001): 4.4. **Marriage rate** per 1,000 pop. (1994): 6.8. **Divorce rate** per 1,000 pop. (1994): 0.8. **Life expectancy** at birth (2001): male 65.0 years; female 71.0 years.

National economy

Budget (1998). *Revenue:* 115,144,000,000 Tajik rubles (tax revenue 96.6%, of which taxes on aluminum and cotton 35.6%, income and profit taxes 18.4%, value-added tax 17.2%, customs duties 10.7%; nontax revenue 3.4%). *Expenditures:* 153,797,000,000 Tajik rubles (national economy 26.2%, education 14.4%, defense 8.8%, law enforcement 8.3%, health 7.6%, state bodies and administration 5.7%). **Production** (metric tons except as noted). *Agriculture, forestry, fishing* (1999): vegetables and melons 526,300; grain 521,000; milk 302,000; livestock (number of live animals) 2,247,000 sheep and goats, 911,500 cattle, 2,000 pigs; fish catch (1997) 285. *Mining and quarrying* (1998): aluminum 195,630; lead 3,500 (1996); gold 3.2. *Manufacturing* (value of production in '000,000 Tajik rubles; 1996): ferrous and nonferrous metals 80,333; textiles 35,023; grain mill prod-

ucts 23,526. *Energy production (consumption):* electricity (kW-hr; 1996) 15,000,000,000 (15,320,-000,000); coal (metric tons; 1996) 20,000 (120,000); crude petroleum (barrels; 1996) 146,600 (146,600); petroleum products (metric tons; 1996) n.a. (1,116,000); natural gas (cu m; 1996) 54,000,000 (1,276,000). **Public debt** (external, outstanding; 1999): $594,900,000. **Land use** (1994): forest 3.8%; pasture 24.8%; agriculture 6.0%; other 65.4%. **Population economically active** (1998): total 1,855,000; activity rate of total pop. 30.4% (participation rates: ages 16–59 [male], 16–54 [female] 60.3%; female [1996] 46.5%; unemployed 3.0%). **Gross national product** (1999): $1,749,000,000 ($280 per capita). **Household income and expenditure.** Average household size (1989) 6.1; (1995) income per household: 18,744 Tajik rubles; sources of income (1995): wages and salaries 34.5%, self-employment 34.0%, borrowing 2.4%, pension 2.0%, other 27.1%; expenditure: food 81.5%, clothing 10.2%, transport 2.5%, fuel 2.1%, other 3.7%.

Foreign trade

Imports (1998-c.i.f.): $731,000,000 (electricity 16.0%, petroleum products and natural gas 15.6%, alumina 15.0%, grain and flour 5.6%). *Major import sources* (1996): Uzbekistan 29.8%; Switzerland 14.9%; United Kingdom 11.7%; Russia 11.1%; Kazakhstan 7.8%. **Exports** (1998): $586,000,000 (aluminum 39.9%, cotton fiber 19.1%, electricity 17.6%). *Major export destinations* (1996). The Netherlands 28.3%; Uzbekistan 24.8%; Switzerland 10.8%; Russia 10.2%; Kazakhstan 3.2%.

Transport and communications

Transport. *Railroads* (1995): length 294.5 mi, 474.0 km; passenger-mi 77,000,000, passenger-km 124,-000,000; short ton-mi cargo 1,449,000,000, metric ton-km cargo 2,115,000,000. *Roads* (1996): total length 8,500 mi, 13,700 km (paved 83%). *Vehicles* (1996): passenger cars 680,000; trucks and buses, 8,190. *Air transport* (1995): passenger-mi 1,386,-000,000, passenger-km 2,231,000,000; short ton-mi cargo 140,000,000, metric ton-km cargo 205,000,000; airports (1997) with scheduled flights 1. **Communications** Total units (units per 1,000 persons). Daily newspaper circulation (1996): 120,000 (21); Radio receivers (1997): 850,000 (143); Television receivers (1999): 2,000,000 (328); Telephone main lines (1999): 212,500 (35); Cellular phone subscribers (1999): 625 (0.1); Internet users (1999): 2,000 (0.3).

Education and health

Educational attainment (1989). Percentage of pop. age 25 and over having: primary education or no formal schooling 16.3%; some secondary 21.1%; completed secondary and some postsecondary 55.1%; higher 7.5%. **Literacy** (1995): percentage of total pop. age 15 and over literate 98.7%; males literate 99.3%; females literate 98.1%. **Health** (1996): physicians 12,456 (1 per 475 persons); hospital beds 43,400 (1 per 136 persons); infant mortality rate per 1,000 live births (2001) 54.0. **Food** (1999): daily per capita caloric intake 1,927 (vegetable products 93°° animal products 7%); (1997) 75% of FAO recommended minimum requirement.

Military

Total active duty personnel (2000): 6,000 (army 100%); more than 8,200 Russian troops remained in Tajikistan in late 2000. Military expenditure as percentage of GNP (1997): 1.7% (world 2.6%); per capita expenditure $19.

 **Did you know?** Mountains cover about 90% of Tajikistan, and nearly half of its territory is at least 10,000 ft (3,050 m) above sea level. The other 10% consists of valleys where most of the population of the country lives.

Background

Settled by the Persians c. 6th century BC, Tajikistan was part of the empires of the Persians and of Alexander the Great and his successors. In the 7th–8th century AD, it was conquered by the Arabs, who introduced Islam. The Uzbeks controlled the region in the 15th–18th century. In the 1860s Russia took over much of Tajikistan. In 1924 it became an autonomous republic under the administration of the Uzbek Soviet Socialist Republic, and it gained republic status in 1929. It achieved independence with the collapse of the Soviet Union in 1991. Civil war raged through much of the 1990s between government forces and an opposition of mostly Islamic forces. Peace was reached in 1997.

Recent Developments

Although peace had been declared, sporadic outbreaks of violence continued, including assassinations of several prominent members of the government; various forces were blamed. Government troops battled armed gangs in 2001. Relations with neighboring countries were tense. Kyrgyzstan and Uzbekistan both charged that Tajikistan was harboring extremists who were using that country as a base for launching attacks. Uzbekistan mined the border, and numerous Tajik citizens were maimed or killed by stepping on mines. Russia, China, Tajikistan, Kazakhstan, Kyrgyzstan, and Uzbekistan (the Shanghai Cooperation Organization) met to coordinate antiterrorist activities.

The fighting in northern Afghanistan forced thousands of refugees from their homes, and many massed at the Tajik border in desperate straits. Tajikistan, impoverished by civil war and suffering through the third year of a regional drought, refused to accept the refugees, being unable to care for its own people without the help of international humanitarian aid. It also feared the entrance into Tajikistan of armed militants among the refugees. After 11 September the government agreed to provide help to the international antiterrorist coalition.

Internet resources: <www.traveltajikistan.com>

Tanzania

[...]e: Jamhuri ya Muungano wa Tanzania [...]ed Republic of Tanzania (English). Form

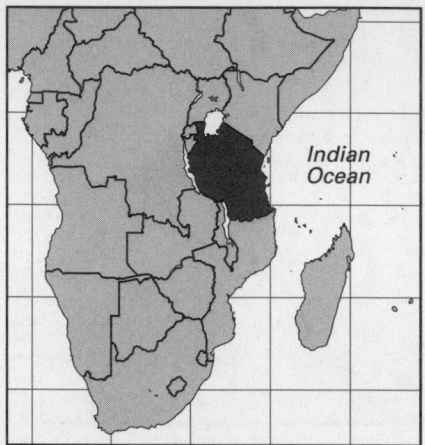
Indian Ocean

of government: unitary multiparty republic with one legislative house (National Assembly [275]). **Head of state and government:** President Benjamin William Mkapa (from 1995), assisted by Prime Minister Frederick Tulway Sumaye (from 1995). **Seat of government:** Dar es Salaam (Capital designate, Dodoma). **Official languages:** Swahili; English. **Official religion:** none. **Monetary unit:** 1 Tanzania shilling (T Sh) = 100 cents; valuation (28 Jun 2002) $1 = T Sh 939.00.

Demography

Area: 942,799 sq km. **Population** (2001): 36,232,000. **Density** (2001): persons per sq mi 99.3, persons per sq km 38.3. **Urban** (1999): 31.7%. **Sex distribution** (2000): male 49.69%; female 50.31%. **Age breakdown** (2000): under 15, 44.9%; 15–29, 28.8%; 30–44, 14.1%; 45–59, 7.7%; 60–74, 3.6%; 75 and over, 0.9%. **Ethnolinguistic composition** (1987): Nyamwezi and Sukuma 21.1%; Swahili 8.8%; Hehet and Bena 6.9%; Haya 5.9%; Makonde 5.9%; Nyakyusa 5.4%; Chagga 4.9%; other 41.1%. **Religious affiliation** (1997): Christian c. 44%; Muslim c. 37%; animist c. 19%. **Location:** eastern Africa, bordering Kenya, the Indian Ocean, Mozambique, Malawi, Zambia, the Dem. Rep. of the Congo, Burundi, Rwanda, and Uganda.

Vital statistics

Birth rate per 1,000 pop. (2000): 40.2 (world avg. 22.5). **Death rate** per 1,000 pop. (2000): 12.9 (world avg. 9.0). **Natural increase rate** per 1,000 pop. (2000): 27.3 (world avg. 13.5). **Total fertility rate** (avg. births per childbearing woman; 2000): 5.5. **Life expectancy** at birth (2000): male 51.3 years; female 53.2 years.

National economy

Budget (1998–99). *Revenue:* T Sh 689,470,000,-000 (import duties 31.7%, sales and excise tax 23.7%, income tax 23.6%). *Expenditures:* T Sh 898,800,000,000 (wages 24.5%, interest payments on debt 12.9%). **Public debt** (external, outstanding;

1999): $6,595,000,000. **Tourism** (1998): receipts from visitors $570,000,000; expenditures by nationals abroad $493,000,000. **Gross national product** (1999-mainland only): $8,515,000,000 ($260 per capita). **Production** (metric tons except as noted). *Agriculture* (1999): cassava 7,181,500, corn (maize) 2,457,745, sugarcane 1,354,999; livestock (number of live animals) 14,350,000 cattle, 9,900,000 goats, 4,150,000 sheep, 28,000,000 chickens; roundwood (1998) 39,022,000 cu m; fish catch (1998) 348,000. *Mining and quarrying* (1994): gemstones (including emeralds, sapphires, and rubies) 33,000 kg; gold 3,370 kg; diamonds 15,700 carats. *Manufacturing* (1999): cement 833,000; petroleum products 287,000; sugar 153,000. *Energy production (consumption):* electricity (kW-hr; 1996) 1,737,000,-000 (1,737,000,000); coal (metric tons; 1995) 5,000 (5,000); crude petroleum (barrels; 1996) none (4,317,000); petroleum products (metric tons; 1996) 583,000 (656,000). **Population economically active** (1994): total 13,852,000; activity rate 48.0% (participation rates [1991]: over age 10, 87.8%; female 40.0%). **Household income and expenditure.** Average household size (1998) 5.4; expenditure (1994): food 64.2%, clothing 9.9%, housing 8.3%, energy 7.6%, transportation 4.1%. **Land use** (1995): forested 37.0%; meadows and pastures 39.6%; agricultural and under permanent cultivation 4.2%; other 19.2%.

Foreign trade

Imports (1999): $1,630,600,000 (consumer goods 33.9%, machinery 20.9%, transport equipment 18.2%, food 10.8%). *Major import sources:* Japan 10.9%; UK 7.8%; US 6.0%; Kenya 5.8%; India 5.6%. **Exports** (1999): $541,000,000 (cashew nuts 18.3%, coffee 14.2%, minerals 13.2%, tobacco 8.0%, cotton 5.2%, tea 4.5%). *Major export destinations:* India 19.5%; UK 17.0%; Japan 8.0%; The Netherlands 5.7%; Singapore 4.5%.

Transport and communications

Transport. *Railroads* (1997): length 3,569 km; passenger-journeys 694,000,000 (Tanzania Railways); metric ton-km cargo 1,354,000,000 (Tanzania Railways). *Roads* (1996): length 88,200 km (paved 4.2%). *Vehicles* (1996): passenger cars 23,760; trucks and buses 115,700. *Air transport* (1995-Air Tanzania): passenger-km 184,383,000; metric ton-km 2,904,000; airports (1998) with scheduled flights 11. **Communications** Total units (units per 1,000 persons). Daily newspaper circulation (1996): 120,000 (3.9); Radio receivers (1997): 8,800,000 (280); Television receivers (1999): 690,000 (20); Telephone main lines (1999): 149,611 (4.4); Cellular telephone subscribers (1999): 50,950 (1.5); Personal computers (1999): 80,000 (2.3); Internet users (1999): 25,000 (0.7 per 1,000 persons).

Education and health

Educational attainment (1978). Percentage of pop. age 10 and over having: no schooling 48.6%; some primary education 40.7%; completed primary 8.7%; secondary and higher 1.9%. **Literacy** (1995): percentage of pop. age 15 and over literate 67.8%; males 79.4%; females 56.8%. **Health** (1993): physicians 1,365 (1 per 20,511 persons); hospital beds 26,820 (1 per 1,000 persons); infant mortality rate (2000) 81.0. **Food** (1999): daily per capita caloric intake

1,940 (vegetable products 94%, animal products 6%); 84% of FAO recommended minimum requirement.

Military

Total active duty personnel (2000): 34,000 (army 88.2%, navy 2.9%, air force 8.9%). **Military expenditure as percentage of GNP** (1997): 1.3% (world 2.6%); per capita expenditure $3.

Did you know? An archaeological site in the eastern Serengeti Plains of Tanzania has yielded evidence of early human existence. The fossils discovered in the area include remains of *Homo habilis*, a hominid that dates back 1.75 million years.

Background

Inhabited from the 1st millennium BC, Tanzania was occupied by Arab and Indian traders and Bantu-speaking peoples by the 10th century AD. The Portuguese gained control of the coastline in the late 15th century, but they were driven out by the Arabs of Oman and Zanzibar in the late 18th century. German colonists entered the area in the 1880s, and in 1891 the Germans declared the region a protectorate as German East Africa. In World War I Britain captured the German holdings, which became a British mandate (1920) under the name Tanganyika. Britain retained control of the region after World War II when it became a UN trust territory (1947). Tanganyika gained independence in 1961 and became a republic in 1962. In 1964 it united with Zanzibar under the name Tanzania. It experienced both political and economic struggles in recent years.

Recent Developments

Mining in Tanzania began to make a substantial contribution to the economy. The first gold was produced in June 2000 in what promised to be East Africa's largest gold field, and the government held a 25% share in the only known mine producing the rare gem tanzanite, which was being worked by a South African company. The economy was still heavily dependent on external grants and loans. External debt servicing was eating up more than a fourth of Tanzania's export earnings, but the International Monetary Fund and World Bank agreed to reduce debt payments substantially in 2002. Revenue from tourism was also increasing.

In October 2000 elections, the ruling Chama Cha Mapinduzi party won a landslide victory, vindicating the economic policies of Pres. Benjamin William Mkapa. However, results in Zanzibar and Pemba were challenged, and in demonstrations demanding a rerun of the elections at least 20 people were killed. Nationalist sentiment on these islands was a cause of continuing concern.

Internet resources: <www.tanzanianews.com>

Thailand

Official name: Muang Thai, or Prathet Thai (Kingdom of Thailand). **Form of government:** constitutional monarchy with two legislative houses (Senate [200];

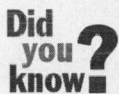

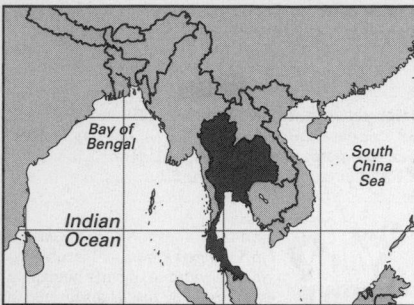

House of Representatives [500]). **Chief of state:** King Bhumibol Adulyadej (from 1946). **Head of government:** Prime Minister Thaksin Shinawatra (from 9 Feb 2001). **Capital:** Bangkok. **Official language:** Thai. **Official religion:** Buddhism. **Monetary unit:** 1 Thai baht (B) = 100 stangs; valuation (28 Jun 2002) $1 = B 41.53.

Demography

Area: 198,115 sq mi, 513,115 sq km. **Population** (2001): 61,251,000. **Density** (2001): persons per sq mi 315.1, persons per sq km 121.7. **Urban** (2001): 22.0%. **Sex distribution** (2000): male 49.24%; female 50.76%. **Age breakdown** (1999): under 15, 26.0%; 15–29, 27.7%; 30–44, 23.3%; 45–59, 14.1%; 60–74, 7.2%; 75 and over, 1.7%. **Ethnic composition** (2000): Tai peoples 81.4%, of which Thai (Siamese) 34.9%, Lao 26.5%; Han Chinese 10.6%; Malay 3.7%; Khmer 1.9%; other 2.4%. **Religious affiliation** (1996): Buddhist 92.6%; Muslim 5.3%; Christian 1.3%; other 0.8%. **Major cities** (1996): Bangkok 5,584,963; Nonthaburi 271,084; Nakhon Ratchasima 180,000; Chiang Mai 170,217; Udon Thani 159,595. **Location:** southeastern Asia, bordering Laos, Cambodia, the Gulf of Thailand, Malaysia, and Myanmar (Burma).

Vital statistics

Birth rate per 1,000 pop. (2001): 16.1 (world avg. 22.5). **Death rate** per 1,000 pop. (2001): 6.0 (world avg. 9.0). **Natural increase rate** per 1,000 pop. (2001): 10.1 (world avg. 13.5). **Total fertility rate** (avg. births per childbearing woman; 2001): 1.8. **Marriage rate** per 1,000 pop. (1998): 5.4. **Divorce rate** per 1,000 pop. (1998): 1.1. **Life expectancy** at birth (2001): male 71.0 years; female 76.0 years.

National economy

Budget (1998). *Revenue:* B 753,569,000,000 (taxes on goods and services 48.6%; income taxes 28.5%; taxes on international trade 9.0%). *Expenditures:* B 854,264,000,000 (education 23.1%; transportation and communications 15.9%; defense 10.3%; health 9.2%; agriculture 7.5%; public order and safety 6.1%; housing 4.8%). **Production** (metric tons except as noted). *Agriculture, forestry, fishing* (2000): sugarcane 51,210,472, rice 23,402,900, cassava 18,508,568; livestock (number of live animals) 7,682,000 pigs, 6,100,000 cattle, 2,100,000 buffalo; roundwood (1999) 36,631,000 cu m; fish catch

(1998) 2,900,320. *Mining and quarrying* (1998): limestone 37,251,000; gypsum 4,334,000; kaolin clay 266,000. *Manufacturing* (1996): cement 38,739,000; refined sugar 6,323,000; crude steel 2,143,000. *Energy production (consumption):* electricity (kW-hr; 1996) 91,467,000,000 (92,183,-000,000); coal (metric tons; 1996) 21,477,000 (24,826,000); crude petroleum (barrels; 1996) 8,900,000 (221,000,000). **Tourism** (1999): receipts from visitors $6,695,000,000; expenditures by nationals abroad $1,843,000,000. **Land use** (1998): meadows and pastures 1.6%; agricultural and under permanent cultivation 39.8%; forested and other 58.6%. **Population economically active** (2000): total 33,973,000; activity rate of total pop. 54.4% (participation rates: over age 13, 69.7%; female 45.0%; unemployed 2.4%). **Gross national product** (1999): $121,051,000,000 ($2,010 per capita). **Public debt** (external, outstanding; 1998): $28,113,000,000. **Household income and expenditure** (1998). Average household size (2000) 3.9; average annual income per household B 149,904; sources of income: wages and salaries 40.1%, self-employment 29.8%, transfer payments 7.9%, other 22.2%; expenditure: food, tobacco, and beverages 37.7%, housing 21.4%, transportation and communications 13.3%, medical and personal care 5.1%, clothing 3.5%, education 2.3%.

Foreign trade

Imports (1998-c.i.f.): B 1,778,564,000,000 (electrical machinery 26.2%, power generating equipment 14.6%, mineral fuels and lubricants 8.0%, iron and steel products 8.0%, plastics 4.2%, organic chemicals 3.3%, aircraft and parts 2.7%). *Major import sources:* Japan 23.6%; US 14.0%; Singapore 5.6%; Taiwan 5.2%; Malaysia 5.1%. **Exports** (1998): B 2,242,579,000,000 (electrical machinery 18.9%, power generating equipment 18.6%, garments 6.1%, rubber products 4.1%, live fish 4.0%, meat and fish preparations 3.9%, cereals 3.9%). *Major export destinations:* US 22.3%; Japan 13.7%; Singapore 8.6%; Hong Kong 5.1%; The Netherlands 4.0%.

Transport and communications

Transport. *Railroads* (1998): route length 4,623 km; passenger-km 10,680,000,000; metric ton-km cargo 2,832,000,000. *Roads* (1996): total length 64,600 km (paved 98%). *Vehicles* (1999): passenger cars 1,661,000; trucks and buses 2,855,000. *Air transport* (1999): passenger-km 38,345,195,000; metric ton-km cargo 1,670,717,000; airports (1996) 25. **Communications** Total units (units per 1,000 persons). Daily newspaper circulation (1996): 3,800,000 (64); Radio receivers (1997): 13,959,000 (234); Television receivers (1999): 17,600,000 (289); Telephone main lines (1999): 5,216,000 (86); Cellular telephone subscribers (1999): 2,339,000 (38); Personal computers (1999): 1,382,000 (23); Internet users (1999): 800,000 (13).

Education and health

Educational attainment (1990). Percentage of pop. age 25 and over having: no formal schooling 11.8%; primary education 71.3%; secondary 9.5%; postsecondary 6.6%; unknown 0.8%. **Literacy** (1995): total

1 metric ton = about 1.1 short tons; 1 kilometer = 0.6 mi (statute); 1 metric ton-km cargo = about 0.68 short ton-mi cargo; c.i.f.: cost, insurance, and freight; f.o.b.: free on board

pop. age 15 and over literate 93.8%; males literate 96.0%; females literate 91.6%. **Health** (1997): physicians 16,569 (1 per 3,553 persons); hospital beds 132,405 (1 per 445 persons); infant mortality rate (2001) 18.0. **Food** (1999): daily per capita caloric intake 2,411 (vegetable products 88%, animal products 12%); (1997) 109% of FAO recommended minimum.

Military

Total active duty personnel (2000): 301,000 (army 63.1%, navy 22.6%, air force 14.3%). **Military expenditure as percentage of GNP** (1997): 2.3% (world 2.6%); per capita expenditure $57.

Background

The region of Thailand has been continuously occupied for 20,000 years. It was part of the Mon and Khmer kingdoms from the 9th century AD. Thai-speaking peoples emigrated from China c. the 10th century. During the 13th century two Thai states emerged: the Sukhothai kingdom, founded c. 1220 after a successful revolt against the Khmer, and Chiang Mai, founded in 1296 after defeating the Mon. In 1350 the Thai kingdom of Ayutthaya succeeded Sukhothai. The Burmese were its most powerful rival, occupying it briefly in the 16th century and destroying it in 1767. The Chakri dynasty came to power in 1782, moving the capital to Bangkok and extending the empire along the Malay Peninsula and into Laos and Cambodia. The country was named Siam in 1856. Though Western influence increased during the 19th century, Siam's rulers avoided colonization by granting concessions to European countries; it was the only southeast Asian nation able to do so. In 1917 it entered World War I on the side of the Allies. It became a constitutional monarchy following a military coup in 1932 and was officially renamed Thailand in 1939. It was occupied by Japan in World War II. It participated in the Korean War as a UN forces member. It was allied with South Vietnam in the Vietnam War. Along with other southeast Asian nations, it suffered from the 1990s regional financial crisis.

Recent Developments

National elections in January 2001 brought a change of government, with the newly formed Thai Rak Thai Party taking a majority of seats in parliament, under the leadership of billionaire telecommunications tycoon Thaksin Shinawatra. A coalition cabinet was sworn in in February. Thaksin had campaigned on a populist platform, pledging to create 70,000 village development funds and provide free health care and debt relief.

There were concerted efforts to stamp out corruption. The national Election Commission rejected the results of 10 seats in the 2000 Senate elections and held new elections in which only 2 of the senators were reelected. They had previously disqualified 78 of the 200 winners for cheating. The National Countercorruption Commission acted against a number of cabinet ministers who had understated their wealth in mandatory disclosures; in 2000 the interior minister was forced to resign. Thaksin was also accused of understating his wealth but was cleared by the Constitutional Court in a split decision. Addiction to methamphetamine drugs became so rampant that death penalties were imposed on large numbers of traffickers. Financial and sexual scandals involving

the Buddhist clergy led to calls for a thorough overhaul of the ecclesiastical hierarchy.

Internet resources: <www.ithailand.com>

Togo

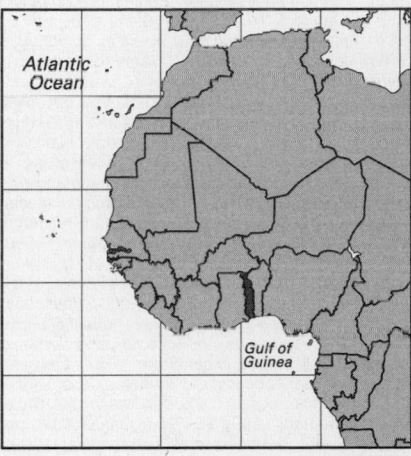

Official name: République Togolaise (Togolese Republic). **Form of government:** multiparty republic with one legislative body (National Assembly [81]). **Chief of state:** President Gnassingbé Eyadéma (from 1967; personal military-supported rule from 1967 continues under constitution approved by referendum in September 1992. **Head of government:** Prime Minister Koffi Sama (from 29 Jun 2002). **Capital:** Lomé. **Official language:** French. **Official religion:** none. **Monetary unit:** 1 CFA franc (CFAF) = 100 centimes; valuation (28 Jun 2002) $1 = CFAF 664.20; the CFAF is pegged to the euro (€) at 1€ = CFAF 655.96 from 1 Jan 2002.

Demography

Area: 21,925 sq mi, 56,785 sq km. **Population** (2001): 5,153,000. **Density** (2001): persons per sq mi 235.0, persons per sq km 90.7. **Urban** (1998): 32.2%. **Sex distribution** (2000): male 49.20%; female 50.80%. **Age breakdown** (2000): under 15, 46.1%; 15–29, 27.8%; 30–44, 14.7%; 45–59, 7.5%; 60 74, 3.2%; 75 and over, 0.7%. **Ethnic composition** (2000): Ewe 22.2%; Kabre 13.4%; Wachi 10.0%; Mina 5.6%; Kotokoli 5.6%; Bimoba 5.2%; Losso 4.0%; Gurma 3.4%; Lamba 3.2%; Adja 3.0%; other 24.4%. **Religious affiliation** (1993): traditional beliefs 50%; Christian 35%, of which Roman Catholic 23%; Muslim 15%. **Major cities** (1997): Lomé 375,000 (urban agglomeration [1999] 790,000); Sokodé 51,000, Kara 35,000; Kpalimé 30,000; Atakpamé 30,000. **Location:** western Africa, bordering Burkina Faso, Benin, the Bight of Benin, and Ghana.

Vital statistics

Birth rate per 1,000 pop. (2000): 38.0 (world avg. 22.5). **Death rate** per 1,000 pop. (2000): 11.2 (world avg. 9.0). **Natural increase rate** per 1,000 pop. (2000): 26.8 (world avg. 13.5). **Total fertility rate** (avg. births per childbearing woman; 2000): 5.5. **Life expectancy** at birth (2000): male 52.8 years; female 56.7 years.

National economy

Budget (1998). *Revenue:* CFAF 142,400,000,000 (tax revenue 81.0%, of which taxes on international trade 40.3%, public enterprise taxes 10.0%, sales tax 9.6%; grants 10.4%; nontax revenue 8.6%). *Expenditures:* CFAF 187,500,000,000 (current expenditure 70.9%, of which wages 31.4%, materials and supplies 20.2%; transfers 14.0%; other 5.4%; debt service 9.6%). **Production** (metric tons except as noted). *Agriculture, forestry, fishing* (1997): yams 696,147, cassava 579,381, corn (maize) 350,484; livestock (number of live animals) 1,110,000 goats, 850,000 pigs, 740,000 sheep; roundwood (1998) 1,182,000 cu m; fish catch (1997) 14,290. *Mining and quarrying* (1996): phosphate rock 2,700,000; limestone is quarried for cement manufacture. *Manufacturing* (value added in CFAF '000,000; 1998): food products, beverages, and tobacco manufactures 41,400; metallic goods 12,000; nonmetallic manufactures 8,500. *Energy production (consumption):* electricity (kW-hr; 1997) 34,700,000 (282,200,000); petroleum products (metric tons; 1998) none (231,000). **Household income and expenditure.** Average household size (1998) 6.0; average annual income per household (1980) CFAF 102,000; expenditure (1987): food and beverages 45.9%, household durable goods 13.9%, clothing 11.4%, housing 5.9%, services 20.5%. **Gross national product** (1999): $6,794,000,000 ($320 per capita). **Public debt** (external, outstanding; 1999): $1,263,000,000. **Population economically active** (1994): total 1,538,000; activity rate of total pop. 33.8% (participation rates over age 10, 50.7%; female 35.6%; unemployed 16–18%). **Tourism** (1999): receipts $6,000,000; expenditures $2,000,000.

Foreign trade

Imports (1998-f.o.b): CFAF 263,400,000,000 (consumer goods 55.8%; capital equipment 18.8%; intermediate goods 18.0%; petroleum products 7.4%). *Major import sources* (1998; est.): Ghana 21%; France 12.7%; China 12.0%; Nigeria 2.1%; Japan 1.8%. **Exports** (1998): CFAF 244,800,000,000 (domestic exports 80.4%, of which cotton 24.5%, phosphates 22.0%, coffee 9.1%, cocoa 4.3%; reexports 19.6%). *Major export destinations* (1998; est.): Canada 12.1%; Bolivia 9.5%; Nigeria 7.4%; France 3.8%; Ghana 3.1%.

Transport and communications

Transport. *Railroads* (1996): route length 395 km; (1996) passenger-km 16,500,000; metric ton-km cargo 49,000,000. *Roads* (1996): total length 7,520 km (paved 32%). *Vehicles* (1996): passenger cars 79,200; trucks and buses 34,240. *Air transport* (1996; represents ¹⁄₁₁ of the traffic of Air Afrique, which is operated by 11 West African states): passenger-km 224,736,000; metric ton-km cargo 16,420,000; airports (1998) 2. **Communications** Total units (units per 1,000 persons). Daily newspaper circulation (1996): 15,000 (3.6); Radio receivers (1998): 720,000 (167); Television receivers (1999): 100,000 (21); Telephone main lines (1999): 38,166 (7.8); Cellular telephone subscribers (1999): 17,000 (3.5); Personal computers (1999): 80,000 (16); Internet users (1999): 15,000 (3.1).

Education and health

Educational attainment (1981). Percentage of pop. age 25 and over having: no formal schooling 76.5%; primary education 13.5%; secondary 8.7%; higher 1.3%. **Literacy** (1995): total pop. age 15 and over literate 51.7%; males 67.0%; females 37.0%. **Health:** physicians (1995) 320 (1 per 13,158 persons); hospital beds (1990) 5,307 (1 per 694 persons); infant mortality rate (2000) 71.6. **Food** (1999): daily per capita caloric intake 2,527 (vegetable products 96%, animal products 4%); 110% of FAO recommended minimum requirement.

Military

Total active duty personnel (2000): 6,950 (army 93.5%, navy 2.9%, air force 3.6%). **Military expenditure as percentage of GNP** (1997): 2.0% (world 2.6%); per capita expenditure $6.

Background

Until 1884 what is now Togo was an intermediate zone between the black African military states of Ashanti and Dahomey, and its various ethnic groups lived in general isolation from each other. In 1884 it became part of the Togoland German protectorate, which was occupied by British and French forces in 1914. In 1922 the League of Nations assigned eastern Togoland to France and the western portion to Britain. In 1946 the British and French governments placed the territories under UN trusteeship. Ten years later British Togoland was incorporated into the Gold Coast, and French Togoland became an autonomous republic within the French Union. Togo gained independence in 1960. It suspended its constitution 1967–80. A multiparty constitution was approved in 1992, but the political situation remained unstable.

Recent Developments

Pres. Gen. Gnassingbé Eyadéma attempted to keep his hold on power despite a rising tide of dissent. In January 2000 laws limiting press freedom had imposed fines and imprisonment for publishing what was judged to be false or defamatory. Security forces broke up protest demonstrations on several occasions. In August the prime minister was forced to resign after his explanations of the government's failure to address long-standing problems met with a no-confidence vote. In January 2001 new parliamentary elections were announced for October; in February a report released by a UN–Organization of African Unity panel found that the government had systematically violated human rights during the 1998 elections. A senior journalist was convicted in June of having published "falsehoods" about killings that were alleged to have taken place during the 1998 election campaign. A proposed constitutional amendment to allow Eyadéma, in power for 34 years, to stand for a third 5-year term met with strong protests; he announced that he would step down at the end of his term. In October the electoral commission announced the postponement of elections.

Internet resources:
<www.republicoftogo.com/english>

---

1 metric ton = about 1.1 short tons;   1 kilometer = 0.6 mi (statute);   1 metric ton-km cargo = about 0.68 short ton-mi cargo;   c.i.f.: cost, insurance, and freight;   f.o.b.: free on board

Tonga

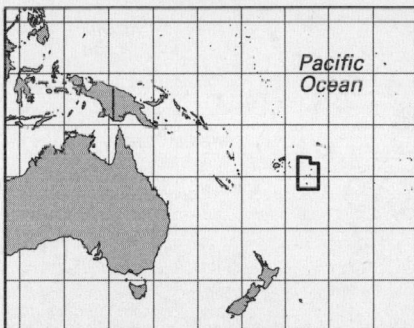

Pacific
Ocean

Official name: Pule'anga Fakatu'i 'o Tonga (Tongan); Kingdom of Tonga (English). **Form of government:** constitutional monarchy with one legislative house (Legislative Assembly [30; includes 12 nonelective seats and 9 nobles elected by the 33 hereditary nobles of Tonga]). **Head of state and government:** King Taufa'ahau Tupou IV (from 1965) assisted by the prime minister of the Privy Council. **Capital:** Nuku'alofa. **Official languages:** Tongan; English. **Official religion:** none. **Monetary unit:** 1 pa'anga (T$) = 100 seniti; valuation (28 Jun 2002) US$1 = T$1.78.

Demography

Area: 289.5 sq mi, 749.9 sq km, of which land area equals 278.1 sq mi, 720.3 sq km. **Population** (2001): 101,000. **Density** (2001; based on land area): persons per sq mi 363.2, persons per sq km 140.2. **Urban** (1999): 45.0%. **Sex distribution** (1996): male 50.74%; female 49.26%. **Age breakdown** (1996): under 15, 39.1%; 15–29, 28.0%; 30–44, 15.1%; 45–59, 10.0%; 60–74, 6.0%; 75 and over, 1.8%. **Ethnic composition** (1996): Tongan and part Tongan 98.2%; other 1.8%. **Religious affiliation** (2000): Protestant 55.9%, of which Methodist 45.2%, Pentecostal 5.5%; Church of Jesus Christ of Latter-day Saints (Mormon) 34.5%; Roman Catholic 9.3%; other 0.3%. **Major city** (1996): Nuku'alofa 22,400. **Location:** archipelago in the South Pacific Ocean between Hawaii and New Zealand.

Vital statistics

Birth rate per 1,000 pop. (2000): 27.2 (world avg. 22.5). **Death rate** per 1,000 pop. (2000): 6.1 (world avg. 9.0). **Natural increase rate** per 1,000 pop. (2000): 21.1 (world avg. 13.5). **Total fertility rate** (avg. births per childbearing woman; 1999): 3.6. **Marriage rate** per 1,000 pop. (1992): 8.2. **Divorce rate** per 1,000 pop. (1992): 1.1. **Life expectancy** at birth (1999): male 67.7 years; female 72.2 years.

National economy

Budget (1997–98). *Revenue:* T$63,000,000 (foreign trade taxes 47.9%, government services revenue 20.0%, direct taxes 13.8%, indirect taxes 11.6%, interest and rent 3.5%). *Expenditures* (excluding amortization of public debt): T$63,000,000 (education 18.4%, general administration 13.8%, health 13.2%, law and order 12.5%, public works and com-

munications 9.2%, agriculture 6.2%). **Production** (metric tons except as noted). *Agriculture, forestry, fishing* (1999): yams 31,000, cassava 28,000, taro 27,200; livestock (number of live animals) 80,853 pigs, 13,939 goats, 266,000 chickens; roundwood (1998) 4,600 cu m; fish catch (1997) 2,739. *Mining and quarrying* (1982): coral 150,000; sand 25,000. *Manufacturing* (output in T$'000,000; 1996): food products and beverages 8,203; paper products 1,055; chemical products 964. *Energy production (consumption):* electricity (kW-hr; 1996) 34,000,000 (34,000,000); petroleum products (metric tons; 1996) n.a. (38,000). **Gross national product** (1999): US$172,000,000 (US$1,730 per capita). **Population economically active** (1996–97): total 33,908; activity rate 34.7% (participation rates: ages 15 and over 57.0%; female 36.0%; unemployed 13.3%). **Public debt** (external, outstanding; 1999): US$63,500,000. **Household income and expenditure.** Average household size (1996) 6.0; expenditure (1991–92): food 43.2%, transportation 15.5%, household 14.2%, housing 6.4%, tobacco and beverages 5.4%, clothing and footwear 4.2%. **Tourism:** receipts (1999) US$9,000,000; expenditures (1997) US$3,000,000. **Land use** (1994): forest 11.1%; pasture 5.6%; agriculture 66.7%; other 16.6%.

Foreign trade

Imports (1998–99-c.i.f.): T$104,900,000 (food and live animals 31.8%, basic manufactures 17.4%, machinery and transport equipment 17.0%, mineral fuels 11.0%, chemicals 7.8%). *Major import sources:* New Zealand 35.0%; Australia 28.6%; US 13.1%; Fiji 8.6%; Japan 4.9%. **Exports** (1998–99): T$12,000,-000 (squash 35.8%, fish 24.2%, vanilla beans 6.7%, root crops 2.5%). *Major export destinations:* Japan 40.8%; US 17.5%; New Zealand 14.2%; Fiji 5.8%; Australia 3.3%.

Transport and communications

Transport. *Roads* (1996): total length 680 km (paved 27%). *Vehicles* (1996): passenger cars 1,140, commercial vehicles 780. *Air transport* (1996): passenger-km 11,000,000; metric ton-km cargo 1,000,000; airports (1996) with scheduled flights 6. **Communications** Total units (units per 1,000 persons). Daily newspaper circulation (1996): 7,000 (72); Radio receivers (1997): 61,000 (619); Television receivers (1997): 2,000 (21); Telephone main lines (1999): 9,100 (93); Cellular telephone subscribers (1999): 140 (1.4).

Education and health

Educational attainment (1996). Percentage of pop. age 25 and over having: primary education 26%; lower secondary 58%; upper secondary 8%; higher 6%; not stated 2%. **Health:** physicians (1997) 43 (1 per 2,279 persons); hospital beds (1992) 307 (1 per 320 persons); infant mortality rate per 1,000 live births (1999) 37.9. **Food** (1992): daily per capita caloric intake 2,946 (vegetable products 82%, animal products 18%); 129% of FAO recommended minimum requirement.

Military

Total active duty personnel (1996): 125-member naval force; an air force was created in 1996. **Military**

expenditure as percentage of GNP (1989): 4.9% (world 4.7%); per capita expenditure US$21.

 **Did you know** Tonga is one of the few countries in the world where observing Sunday as a day of rest receives mention in the constitution. Christian evangelization of Tonga by Methodist missionaries began in the early 19th century and by 1853 all Tongans were at least nominally Christian, nearly all Methodist. Recently many Tongans have been converting to the Church of Jesus Christ of Latter-day Saints (Mormonism).

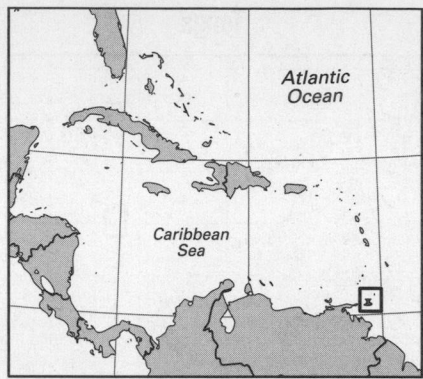

Background
Tonga was inhabited at least 3,000 years ago by people of the Lapita culture. The Tongans developed a stratified social system headed by a paramount ruler whose dominion by the 13th century extended as far as the Hawaiian Islands. The Dutch visited the islands in the 17th century; in 1773, Capt. James Cook arrived and named the archipelago the Friendly Islands. The modern kingdom was established during the reign (1845–93) of King George Tupou I. It became a British protectorate in 1900. This was dissolved in 1970, when Tonga, the only ancient kingdom surviving from the pre-European period in Polynesia, achieved complete independence within the Commonwealth.

Recent Developments
In January 2000 King Taufa'ahau Tupou IV appointed his youngest son, 'Ulukalala Lavaka Ata, prime minister rather than his oldest son, Crown Prince Tupouto'a, who was known to favor constitutional change. The nation's economic situation was acknowledged to be grave. Attempts were made to bolster the fishing and tourism industries.

In 2001 a major political financial scandal broke when it was learned that more than $20 million (an amount equal to about half of the national budget) of Tonga's trust fund, which had been kept in a checking account in the Bank of America in the US, had been lost following investment in a highly questionable Nevada company. The speculator blamed for the loss, a former Bank of America employee, had convinced the king to name him court jester and to allow him to speculate with the fund. The former prime minister, the deputy prime minister, and the minister of education were implicated in the scandal.

Internet resources: <www.vacations.tvb.gov.to>

Trinidad and Tobago

Official name: Republic of Trinidad and Tobago. **Form of government:** multiparty republic with two legislative houses (Senate [31]; House of Representatives [36; excludes speaker]). **Chief of state:** President A.N.R. Robinson (from 1997). **Head of government:** Prime Minister Patrick Manning (from 24 Dec 2001). **Capital:** Port of Spain. **Official language:** English. **Official religion:** none. **Monetary unit:** 1 Trinidad and Tobago dollar (TT$) = 100 cents; valuation (28 Jun 2002) US$1 = TT$6.09.

Demography
Area: 5,128 sq km. **Population** (2001): 1,298,000. **Density** (2001): persons per sq mi 655.6, persons per sq km 253.1. **Urban** (1999): 73.6% **Sex distribution** (1998): male 49.81%; female 50.19%. **Age breakdown** (1995): under 15, 30.3%; 15–29, 26.6%; 30–44, 22.0%; 45–59, 12.3%; 60–74, 6.5%; 75 and over, 2.3%. **Ethnic composition** (2000): black 39.2%; East Indian 38.6%; mixed 16.3%; Chinese 1.6%; white 1.0%; other/not stated 3.3%. **Religious affiliation** (1990): six largest Protestant bodies 29.7%; Roman Catholic 29.4%; Hindu 23.7%; Muslim 5.9%; other 11.3%. **Major cities** (1990): Chaguanas 56,601; Port of Spain (1996) 43,396; San Fernando (1991) 30,115; Arima (1991) 29,483; Point Fortin 20,025. **Location:** islands northeast of Venezuela between the North Atlantic Ocean and the Caribbean Sea.

Vital statistics
Birth rate per 1,000 pop. (1997): 14.5 (world avg. 22.5). **Death rate** per 1,000 pop. (1997): 7.2 (world avg. 9.0). **Natural increase rate** per 1,000 pop. (1997): 7.3 (world avg. 13.5). **Total fertility rate** (avg. births per childbearing woman; 2000): 1.8. **Marriage rate** per 1,000 pop. (1996): 5.6. **Divorce rate** per 1,000 pop. (1996): 1.2. **Life expectancy** at birth (2000): male 65.4 years; female 70.6 years.

National economy
Budget (1999). *Revenue*: TT$9,789,000,000 (company taxes 21.2%, of which petroleum sector 9.2%; individual income taxes 20.3%; value-added taxes 17.0%; nontax revenues 8.3%). *Expenditures*: TT$11,076,000,000 (current expenditures 95.6%; development expenditures 4.4%). **Production** (metric tons except as noted). *Agriculture, forestry, fishing* (1999): sugarcane 1,200,000, coconuts 22,000, oranges 15,000; livestock (number of live animals) 59,000 goats, 8,500,000 chickens; roundwood (1998) 60,000 cu m; fish catch (1997) 15,012. *Mining and quarrying* (1999): natural asphalt 12,600. *Manufacturing* (1999): anhydrous ammonia and urea (nitrogenous fertilizers) 3,946,800; methanol 2,149,800; steel billets 723,900. *Energy production (consumption):* electricity (kW-hr; 1997) 4,848,000,-000 ([1996] 4,541,000,000); crude petroleum (bar-

1 metric ton = about 1.1 short tons; 1 kilometer = 0.6 mi (statute); 1 metric ton-km cargo = about 0.68 short ton-mi cargo; c.i.f.: cost, insurance, and freight; f.o.b.: free on board

rels; 1999) 35,903,000 ([1996] 39,840,000); petroleum products (metric tons; 1996) 5,454,000 (1,448,000); natural gas (cu m; 1999) 9,296,000,-000 ([1996] 7,509,000,000). **Household income and expenditure.** Average household size (1998) 3.8; average income per household (1988) TT$21,760; expenditure (1993): food, beverages, and tobacco 25.5%, housing 21.6%, transportation 15.2%, household furnishings 14.3%, clothing and footwear 10.4%. **Tourism** (1998): receipts from visitors US$201,000,000; expenditures by nationals abroad US$67,000,000. **Land use** (1994): forested 45.8%; meadows and pastures 2.1%; agricultural and under permanent cultivation 23.8%; other 28.3%. **Gross national product** (at current market prices; 1999): US$6,142,000,000 (US$4,750 per capita). **Population economically active** (1998): total 558,700; activity rate of total pop. 43.6% (participation rates: [1995] ages 15–64, 65.4%; female 38.3%; unemployed [1999] 13.1%). **Public debt** (external, outstanding; 1999): US$1,485,000,000.

Foreign trade

Imports (1998-c.i.f.): TT$18,887,000,000 (machinery and apparatus 30.8%, fuels 12.2%, food 7.3%, transport equipment 6.2%). *Major import sources* (1999): US 39.8%; Venezuela 11.9%; Japan 5.1%; Canada 4.9%; UK 4.7%. **Exports** (1998-f.o.b.): TT$14,221,-000,000 (refined petroleum 29.6%, crude petroleum 10.6%, anhydrous ammonia 10.6%, iron and steel 8.8%, reexports 7.1%, methanol 6.3%). *Major export destinations* (1999): US 39.3%; Carlcom 26.1%, of which Jamaica 8.7%, Barbados 5.3%; EC 5.7%.

Transport and communications

Transport. *Roads* (1995): total length 8,320 km (paved 51%). *Vehicles* (1996): passenger cars 122,000; trucks and buses 24,000. *Air transport* (2000; BWIA only): passenger-km 2,869,000,000; metric ton-km cargo 56,021,000; airports (1996) with scheduled flights 2. **Communications** Total units (units per 1,000 persons). Daily newspaper circulation (1996): 156,000 (123); Radio receivers (1997): 680,000 (535); Television receivers (1999): 435,000 (338); Telephone main lines (1999): 279,000 (217); Cellular telephone subscribers (1999): 38,659 (30); Personal computers (1999): 70,000 (54); Internet users (1999): 30,000 (23).

Education and health

Educational attainment (1990). Percentage of pop. age 25 and over having: no formal schooling 4.5%; primary education 56.4%; secondary 32.1%; higher 3.4%; other/not stated 3.6%. **Literacy** (1995): total pop. age 15 and over literate 886,000 (97.9%). **Health:** physicians (1997) 1,074 (1 per 1,183 persons); hospital beds (1996) 6,622 (1 per 191 persons); infant mortality rate (1997) 17.1. **Food** (1998): daily per capita caloric intake 2,711 (vegetable products 85%, animal products 15%); 112% of FAO recommended minimum requirement.

Military

Total active duty personnel (2000). 2,700 (army 74.1%, coast guard 25.9%). **Military expenditure as percentage of GNP** (1997): 1.5% (world 2.6%); per capita expenditure US$65.

Background

When Christopher Columbus visited Trinidad in 1498, it was inhabited by the Arawak Indians; Caribs inhabited Tobago. The islands were settled by the Spanish in the 16th century. In the 17th–18th centuries African slaves were imported for plantation labor to replace the original Indian population, which had been worked to death by the Spanish. Trinidad was surrendered to the British in 1797. The British attempted to settle Tobago in 1721, but the French captured the island in 1781 and transformed it into a sugar-producing colony; the British acquired it in 1802. After slavery ended in the islands 1834–38, immigrants from India were brought in to work the plantations. Trinidad and Tobago were administratively combined in 1889. Granted limited self-government in 1925, the islands became an independent state within the Commonwealth in 1962, and a republic in 1976. Political unrest was followed in 1990 by an attempted Muslim-fundamentalist coup against the government.

Recent Developments

In parliamentary elections held on 10 Dec 2001, the two major parties, the United National Congress (UNC) and the People's National Movement (PNM) each won 18 seats. The voting was largely split on racial lines, as the ruling UNC was backed by those of Indian descent, while the opposition PNM's adherents were mainly of African descent. Pres. Arthur Robinson chose the PNM leader, Patrick Manning, as prime minister, but the UNC leader and former prime minister, Basdeo Panday, refused to accept the decision. When parliament attempted to convene in 2002, neither party would accept the other's nominees for speaker of the house, bringing the government to a standstill, as parliament could not function without a speaker. As the standoff continued, business leaders expressed their concern that the economy was being adversely affected. Panday was adamant and called for new elections immediately; Manning rejected the proposal.

Internet resources: <www.central-bank.org.tt>

Tunisia

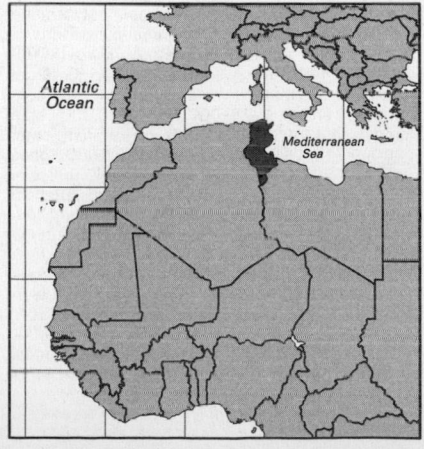

Official name: Al-Jumhuriyah at-Tunisiyah (Republic of Tunisia). **Form of government:** multiparty republic with one legislative house (Chamber of Deputies [182]). **Chief of state:** President Zine El Abidine Ben Ali (from 1987). **Head of government:** Prime Minister Mohamed Ghannouchi (from 1999). **Capital:** Tunis. **Official language:** Arabic. **Official religion:** Islam. **Monetary unit:** 1 dinar (D) = 1,000 millimes; valuation (28 Jun 2002) $1= D 1.38.

Demography

Area: 63,378 sq mi, 164,150 sq km (total includes 3,714 sq mi [9,620 sq km] of territory that is not distributed by governorate). **Population** (2001): 9,828,000. **Density** (2001): persons per sq mi 155.1, persons per sq km 59.9. **Urban** (2000): 62.6%. **Sex distribution** (2000): male 50.40%; female 49.60%. **Age breakdown** (2000): under 15, 29.7%; 15–29, 30.4%; 30–44, 21.2%; 45–59, 10.6%; 60–74, 6.8%; 75 and over, 1.3%. **Ethnic composition** (2000): Tunisian Arab 67.2%; Bedouin Arab 26.6%; Algerian Arab 2.4%; Berber 1.4%; other 2.4%. **Religious affiliation** (2000): Sunni Muslim 98.9%; Christian 0.5%; other 0.6%. **Major cities** (commune; 1994): Tunis 674,100; Safaqis 230,900; Al-Arianah 152,700; Ettadhamen 149,200; Susah 125,000. **Location:** northern Africa, bordering the Mediterranean Sea, Libya, and Algeria.

Vital statistics

Birth rate per 1,000 pop. (2000): 17.1 (world avg. 22.5). **Death rate** per 1,000 pop. (2000): 5.6 (world avg. 9.0). **Natural increase rate** per 1,000 pop. (2000): 11.5 (world avg. 13.5). **Total fertility rate** (avg. births per childbearing woman; 2000): 2.1. **Marriage rate** per 1,000 pop. (1995): 6.0. **Life expectancy** at birth (2000): male 70.1 years; female 74.2 years.

National economy

Budget (2000). *Revenue:* D 7,625,000,000 (tax revenue 91.1%, of which goods and services 39.1%, income tax 20.0%, social security 17.8%, import duties 9.8%; nontax revenue 8.9%). *Expenditures:* D 8,454,000,000 (current expenditure 77.2%, of which interest on public debt 10.3%; development expenditure 22.8%). **Public debt** (external, outstanding; 1999): $9,487,000,000. **Production** (metric tons except as noted). *Agriculture, forestry, fishing* (2000): wheat 1,144,000, olives 1,000,000, tomatoes 905,000; livestock (number of live animals) 6,600,000 sheep, 1,400,000 goats, 790,000 cattle; roundwood (2000) 2,841,800 cu m; fish catch (2000) 90,100. *Mining and quarrying* (2000): phosphate rock 8,301,200; iron ore (1998) 140,000; zinc 28,200. *Manufacturing* (2000): cement 5,398,900; phosphoric acid 845,000; flour 745,500. *Energy production (consumption):* electricity (kW-hr; 2000) 9,221,900,000 (8,150,400,000); coal (metric tons; 1996) 2,000 (2,000); crude petroleum (barrels; 1999) 30,956,000 (1996; 7,097,000); petroleum products (metric tons; 1996) 1,844,000 (3,106,000); natural gas (cu m; 2000) 1,862,500,000 ([1997] 2,107,300,000). **Household income and expenditure.** Average household size (1999) 4.9; ex-

penditure (1995): food and beverages 37.7%, housing and energy 22.2%, health and personal care 9.6%, transportation 8.9%, recreation 8.7%, other 12.9%. **Gross national product** (1999): $19,757,000,000 ($2,090 per capita). **Population economically active** (1997): total 3,502,000; activity rate of total pop. 37.9% (participation rates [1989]: ages 15–64, 42.2%; female [1997] 30.9%; unemployed [2000] 15.9%). **Land use** (1994): forested 4.3%; meadows and pastures 20.0%; agricultural and under permanent cultivation 31.9%; other 43.8%. **Tourism** (1999): receipts $1,560,000,000; expenditures $235,000,000.

Foreign trade

Imports (2000-c.i.f.): D 11,728,000,000 (textiles, clothing, and leather 22.9%, nonelectrical equipment 20.3%, electrical equipment 10.2%, transport equipment 10.2%). *Major import sources:* France 26.3%; Italy 19.1%; Germany 10.0%; US 4.6%; Libya 3.7%. **Exports** (2000): D 8,005,000,000 (textiles, clothing, and leather products 46.6%, mineral fuels and lubricants 12.1%, electrical equipment 10.1%, phosphates and phosphate derivatives 9.0%). *Major export destinations:* France 26.8%; Italy 23.0%; Germany 12.5%; Belgium 5.1%; Libya 3.6%.

Transport and communications

Transport. *Railroads* (2000): route length 2,169 km; passenger-km 1,196,000,000; metric ton-km cargo 2,365,000,000. *Roads* (1997): total length 23,100 km (paved 79%). *Vehicles* (1996): passenger cars 269,000; trucks and buses 312,000. *Air transport* (2000; Tunis Air only): passenger-km 2,694,167,000; metric ton-km cargo 20,821,000; airports (1998) 5. **Communications** Total units (units per 1,000 persons). Daily newspaper circulation (1996): 280,000 (31); Radio receivers (1997): 2,060,000 (224); Television receivers (1999): 1,800,000 (190); Telephone main lines (1999): 850,381 (90); Cellular telephone subscribers (1999) 55,258 (5.8); Personal computers (1999): 145,000 (15); Internet users (1999): 30,000 (3.2).

Education and health

Educational attainment (1989). Percentage of pop. age 25 and over having: no formal schooling 54.9%; primary 26.9%; secondary 14.3%; higher 3.4%; unspecified 0.5%. **Literacy** (2000): total pop. age 10 and over literate 74.4%; males literate 83.5%; females literate 65.3%. **Health** (2000): physicians 7,444 (1 per 1,284 persons); hospital beds (1999) 16,256 (1 per 581 persons); infant mortality rate (2000) 25.8. **Food** (1999): daily per capita caloric intake 3,388 (vegetable products 91%, animal products 9%); 142% of FAO recommended minimum requirement.

Military

Total active duty personnel (2000): 35,000 (army 77.1%, navy 12.9%, air force 10.0%). **Military expenditure as percentage of GNP** (1997): 2.0% (world 2.6%); per capita expenditure $39.

1 metric ton = about 1.1 short tons; 1 kilometer = 0.6 mi (statute); 1 metric ton-km cargo = about 0.68 short ton-mi cargo; c.i.f.: cost, insurance, and freight; f.o.b.: free on board

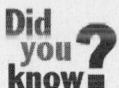

Tunisia has been known as one of the most socially liberal of the Arab countries. Tunisian women may receive custody of children in divorce as well as alimony payments, and family violence against women is punishable by law. Family planning counseling has also been widely available since the 1960s.

Background

From the 12th century BC the Phoenicians had a series of trading posts on the North African coast. By the 6th century BC the Carthaginian kingdom encompassed most of present-day Tunisia. The Romans ruled from 146 BC until the Muslim Arab invasions in the mid-7th century AD. The area was fought over, won, and lost by many, including the Abbasids, the Almohads, the Spanish, and the Ottoman Turks, who finally conquered it in 1574 and held it until the late 19th century. For a time it maintained autonomy as the French, British, and Italians contended for the region. In 1881 it became a French protectorate. In World War II US and British forces captured it (1943) to end a brief German occupation. In 1956 France granted it full independence; Habib Bourguiba assumed power and remained in office until 1987.

Recent Developments

In April 2000, Habib Bourgiba, Tunisia's founding father, died at age 96 at his home, where he had been under house arrest since being deposed by Pres. Gen. Zine al-Abidine Ben Ali in 1987. The government came under continuing criticism for its human rights record. There were more than 1,000 political prisoners, and protestors, journalists, and judges were among those jailed, restricted, and subjected to various forms of harassment. International pressures helped ameliorate their situation.

The economy, however, remained strong, with a boom in tourism and foreign investment. Tunisia's free-trade-area agreement with the European Union came into effect in 1998, and improved trading relationships were sought with other North African nations. A large-scale privatization plan was nearing completion.

Internet resources: <www.tourismtunisia.com>

Turkey

Official name: Turkiye Cumhuriyeti (Republic of Turkey). Form of government: multiparty republic with one legislative house (Turkish Grand National Assembly [550]). Chief of state: President Ahmet Necdet Sezer (from 2000). Head of government: Prime Minister Bulent Ecevit (from 2000). Capital: Ankara. Official language: Turkish. Official religion: none. Monetary unit: 1 Turkish lira (LT) = 100 kurush; valuation (28 Jun 2002) $1 = LT 1,585,500.00.

Demography

Area: 300,948 sq mi, 779,452 sq km. Population (2001): 66,229,000. Density (2001): persons per sq mi 220.1, persons per sq km 85.0. Urban (1997): 64.7%. Sex distribution (2000): male 50.57%; female 49.43%. Age breakdown (2000): under 15,

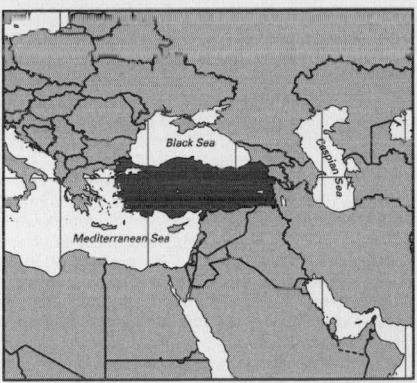

29.1%; 15–29, 20.0%; 30–44, 21.5%; 45–59, 11.8%; 60–74, 6.8%; 75 and over, 2.0%. Ethnic composition (2000; per unofficial source): Turk 65.1%; Kurd 18.9%; Crimean Tatar 7.2%; Arab 1.8%; Azerbaijani 1.0%; Yoruk 1.0%; other 5.0%. Religious affiliation (2000): Muslim 97.2%, of which Sunni c. 67%, Shi'i c. 30% (including nonorthodox Alevi c. 26%); Christian (mostly Eastern Orthodox) 0.6%; other 2.2%. Major cities (1997): Istanbul 8,260,438; Ankara 2,984,099; Izmir 2,081,556; Adana 1,041,509; Bursa 1,066,559. Location: southwestern Asia and a small part in southeastern Europe, bordering the Black Sea, Georgia, Armenia, Azerbaijan, Iran, Iraq, Syria, the Mediterranean Sea, Greece, and Bulgaria.

Vital statistics

Birth rate per 1,000 pop. (2000): 18.7 (world avg. 22.5). Death rate per 1,000 pop. (2000): 6.0 (world avg. 9.0). Natural increase rate per 1,000 pop. (2000): 12.7 (world avg. 13.5). Total fertility rate (avg. births per childbearing woman; 2000): 2.2. Marriage rate per 1,000 pop. (1997): 7.8. Divorce rate per 1,000 pop. (1997): 0.5. Life expectancy at birth (2000): male 68.6 years; female 73.4 years.

National economy

Budget (2000). Revenue: LT 33,756,347,000,000,-000 (tax revenue 78.5%, nontax revenue 10.3%, special funds 9.7%). Expenditures: LT 46,602,627,000,-000,000 (interest payments 38.3%, personnel 24.7%, investments 5.5%). Public debt (external, outstanding; 1999): $50,095,000,000. Production (in metric tons except as noted). Agriculture, forestry, fishing (2000): wheat 21,000,000 barley 8,000,000 grapes 3,550,000; livestock (number of live animals) 29,435,000 sheep, 11,031,000 cattle, (1997) 615,000 angora goats; roundwood (2000) 17,767,-000 cu m; fish catch (1000) 638,007. Mining and quarrying (1999): boron minerals 2,600,000; chromite 770,000; copper ore (metal content) 45,000. Manufacturing (value added in $'000,000; 1995): refined petroleum 4,583; food products 3,044; textiles 3,007. Energy production (consumption): electricity (kW-hr; 1999) 115,424,000,000 ([1997] 80,862,000,000); hard coal (metric tons; 1999) 2,738,000 ([1996] 8,145,000); lignite (metric tons; 1999) 64,896,000 ([1996] 54,961,000); crude petroleum (barrels; 1999) 21,013,000 ([1996] 193,791,000); petroleum products (metric tons;

1996) 22,906,000 (26,183,000); natural gas (cu m; 1997) 250,800,000 ([1996] 8,541,800,000). **Tourism** (1999): receipts from visitors $5,203,-000,000; expenditures by nationals abroad $1,471,-000,000. **Household income and expenditure** (1994). Average household size (1999) 4.6; income per household LT 165,089,000; expenditure: food, tobacco, and café expenditures 38.5%, housing 22.8%, clothing 9.0%. **Population economically active** (1997; civilian population only): total 22,359,000; activity rate of total pop. 35.8% (participation rates: ages 15–64, 53.1%; female 26.8%; unemployed [2000] 6.6%). **Gross national product** (1999): $186,490,000,000 ($2,900 per capita). **Land use** (1994): forested 26.2%; meadows and pastures 16.1%; agricultural and under permanent cultivation 36.1%; other 21.6%.

Foreign trade

Imports (2000-c.i.f.): $53,983,000,000 (mineral fuels 17.6%; nonelectrical machinery 14.3%; electrical machinery 11.2%; transport equipment 10.1%; iron and steel 5.1%; chemicals 3.7%). *Major import sources:* Germany 13.2%; Italy 8.0%; US 7.2%; France 6.5%; UK 5.0%. **Exports** (2000-f.o.b.): $27,324,000,000 (textiles and clothing 22.6%; electrical and electronic machinery 7.1%; vehicles 5.7%; iron and steel 5.7%). *Major export destinations:* Germany 18.8%; US 11.2%; Russia and Eastern Europe 10.8%; UK 7.4%; Italy 6.3%; France 6.0%.

Transport and communications

Transport. *Railroads* (2000): length 8,671 km; passenger-km 6,122,000,000; metric ton-km cargo 10,032,000,000. *Roads* (2000): total length 383,636 km (paved [1997] 25%). *Vehicles* (2000): passenger cars 4,283,080; trucks and buses 1,488,016. *Air transport* (2000; Turkish Airlines only): passenger-km 16,492,416; metric ton-km cargo 379,630,000; airports (1996) 26. **Communications** Total units (units per 1,000 persons). Daily newspaper circulation (1996): 6,845,000 (111); Radio receivers (1997): 11,300,000 (181); Television receivers (1999): 21,500,000 (331); Telephone main lines (1999): 18,054,000 (278); Cellular telephone subscribers (1999): 8,122,000 (125); Personal computers (1999): 2,200,000 (34); Internet users (1999): 1,500,000 (23).

Education and health

Educational attainment (1993). Percentage of pop. age 25 and over having: no formal schooling 30.5%; incomplete primary education 6.6%; complete primary 40.4%; incomplete secondary 3.1%; complete secondary or higher 19.1%; unknown 0.3%. **Literacy** (1995): total pop. age 15 and over literate 33,605,000 (82.3%); males literate 19,191,000 (91.7%); females literate 14,414,000 (72.4%). **Health:** physicians (1997; includes assistant doctors) 73,659 (1 per 853 persons); hospital beds (1997) 144,984 (1 per 431 persons); infant mortality rate (2000) 48.9. **Food** (1999): daily per capita caloric intake 3,469 (vegetable products 89%, animal products 11%); 138% of FAO recommended minimum requirement.

Military

Total **active duty personnel (2000):** 609,700 (army 81.2%, navy 9.0%, air force 9.8%). Military expenditure as percentage of GNP (1997): 4.0% (world 2.6%); per capita expenditure $124.

Background

Turkey's early history corresponds to that of Asia Minor, the Byzantine empire, and the Ottoman empire. Byzantine rule emerged when Constantine the Great made Constantinople (now Istanbul) his capital. The Ottoman empire, begun in the 12th century, dominated for more than 600 years; it ended in 1918 after the Young Turk revolt precipitated its demise. Under the leadership of Mustafa Kemal Ataturk, a republic was proclaimed in 1923, and the caliphate was abolished in 1924. Turkey remained neutral throughout most of World War II, siding with the Allies in 1945. Since the war it has alternated between civil and military governments and has had several conflicts with Greece over Cyprus. The 1990s saw political and civic turmoil between Islamicists and secularists.

Recent Developments

Although the government had been focused since December 1999 on the political and economic reforms that were required for Turkey to become a member of the European Union, Turkey was struck with a financial crisis in November 2000 that deepened throughout the ensuing year. The banking system was hard hit, and the resulting capital flight caused a number of banks to fail. The lira was allowed to float, and it depreciated by more than 100%. The gross national product, industrial production, and imports all were down, and inflation of consumer prices stood at 68% for the year, following a nearly 40% rise the previous year. A World Bank official was appointed minister of state in charge of the economy, and he secured help from the International Monetary Fund as well as from international financial institutions to carry the government through the crisis.

Turkey walked a fine line between control of terrorist and subversive elements and suppression of political dissent. Grounds for banning political parties were narrowed, and sweeping changes to the civil code expanded the rights of women in family matters and divorce. Kurdish separatists, Hezbollah terrorists, and Islamic militants remained sources of anxiety. The only Muslim country in NATO, Turkey responded with immediate offers of aid, troops, and the use of Turkish soil after 11 Sep 2001. Pres. Ahmet Necdet Sezer and Foreign Minister Ismail Cem launched a diplomatic initiative to support the antiterrorist coalition.

Internet resources: <www.turizm.gov.tr>

Turkmenistan

Official name: Turkmenistan. **Form of government:** unitary republic with one legislative body (Majlis [Parliament; 50]). **Head of state and government:** President Saparmurad Niyazov (from 1990) assisted by the People's Council. **Capital:** Ashgabat (formerly

---

1 metric ton = about 1.1 short tons;   1 kilometer = 0.6 mi (statute);   1 metric ton-km cargo = about 0.68 short ton-mi cargo;   c.i.f.: cost, insurance, and freight;   f.o.b.: free on board

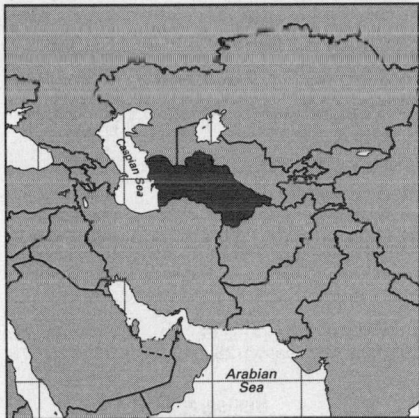

Ashkhabad). **Official language:** Turkmen. **Official religion:** none. **Monetary unit:** manat; valuation (12 Jul 2002) $1 = 5,250.00 manat.

Demography

Area: 188,500 sq mi, 488,100 sq km. **Population** (2001): 5,462,000. **Density** (2001): persons per sq mi 29.0, persons per sq km 11.2. **Urban** (1999): 45.0%. **Sex distribution** (1996): male 49.59%; female 50.41%. **Age breakdown** (1995): under 15, 40.4%; 15–29, 27.6%; 30–44, 18.7%; 45–59, 7.5%; 60–74, 4.7%; 75 and over, 1.1%. **Ethnic composition** (1997): Turkmen 77.0%; Uzbek 9.2%; Russian 6.7%; Kazakh 2.0%; Tatar 0.8%; other 4.3%. **Religious affiliation** (1995): Muslim (mostly Sunni) 87.0%; Russian Orthodox 2.4%; other (mostly nonreligious) 10.6%. **Major cities** (1999 est.): Ashgabat 605,000; Turkmenabad (Charjew) 203,000; Dashhowuz 165,000; Mary 123,000; Nebitdag 119,000. **Location:** central Asia, bordering Kazakhstan, Uzbekistan, Afghanistan, Iran, and the Caspian Sea.

Vital statistics

Birth rate per 1,000 pop. (2000): 28.9 (world avg. 22.5); (1998) legitimate 96.2%; illegitimate 3.8%. **Death rate** per 1,000 pop. (2000): 9.0 (world avg. 9.0). **Natural increase rate** per 1,000 pop. (2000): 19.9 (world avg. 13.5). **Total fertility rate** (avg. births per childbearing woman; 2000): 1.8. **Marriage rate** per 1,000 pop. (1994): 8.7. **Divorce rate** per 1,000 pop. (1994): 1.5. **Life expectancy** at birth (2000): male 57.3 years; female 64.7 years.

National economy

Budget (1999). *Revenue:* 3,693,100,000,000 manat (value-added tax 25.6%, pension and social security fund 22.5%, repayments of scheduled gas 13.0%, excise tax 10.2%, personal income tax 6.1%). *Expenditures:* 3,894,300,000,000 manat (education 26.9%, pension and social security 15.6%, defense and security 14.9%, health 14.1%, agriculture 5.7%). **Public debt** (external, outstanding; 1999): $1,678,-000,000. **Production** (metric tons except as noted). *Agriculture, forestry, fishing* (1999): cereals 1,567,200, seed cotton 1,300,000, vegetables and melons 336,400; livestock (number of live animals)

6,025,000 sheep and goats, 880,000 cattle, 48,000 pigs, roundwood (1990) 4,000,000 cu m; fish catch (1997) 8,828. *Mining and quarrying* (1996): gypsum 169,577, sodium sulphate 30,820, sulfur 8,112. *Manufacturing* (value of production in '000,000 manat; 1994): ferrous and nonferrous metals 278; machinery and metalworks 223; food products 129. *Energy production (consumption):* electricity (kW-hr; 1996) 10,100,000,000 (7,300,000,000); coal (metric tons; 1996) none (100,000); crude petroleum (barrels; 1996) 28,000,000 (29,000,000); petroleum products (metric tons; 1996) 2,223,000 (2,266,000); natural gas (cu m; 1996) 33,991,000,-000 (10,803,000,000). **Household income and expenditure.** Average household size (1998) 5.0; sources of income (1996): wages and salaries 70.6%, pensions and grants 20.9%, self-employment (mainly agricultural income) 2.3%, nonwage income of workers 1.1%; expenditure (1996): goods 26.8%, services 13.5%, taxes and other payments 9.4%. **Land use** (1994): forested 8.2%; meadows and pastures 61.6%; agricultural and under permanent cultivation 3.0%; other 27.2%. **Population economically active** (1996): total 1,680,000; activity rate of total pop. 36.8% (participation rates [1995]: ages 16–59 [male] 16–54 [female] 81.0%; female 41.0%; unemployed 3.0%; all Turkmen citizens guaranteed employment). **Gross national product** (1999): $3,205,-000,000 ($670 per capita). **Tourism:** receipts from visitors (1998) $192,000,000; expenditures (1997) $125,000,000.

Foreign trade

Imports (1998-c.i.f.): $1,137,100,000 (machinery and equipment 39.1%, food products 8.0%, chemicals 5.1%, medicines 1.8%). *Major import sources:* Ukraine 16.1%; Turkey 13.1%; Russia 11.6%; Germany 6.9%; US 6.4%; Uzbekistan 5.2%; Armenia 3.0%. **Exports** (1998): $614,100,000 (natural gas and oil products 54.6%, cotton 22.0%, electricity 5.2%). *Major export destinations:* Iran 24.1%; Turkey 18.3%; Azerbaijan 6.9%; UK 4.9%; Russia 4.7%; Tajikistan 4.5%.

Transport and communications

Transport. *Railroads* (1996): length 2,120 km; passenger-km 2,104,000,000, metric ton-km cargo 6,779,000,000. *Roads* (1996): total length 13,700 km (paved 83%). *Vehicles* (1995): passenger cars 220,000; trucks and buses, 58,200. *Air transport* (1996): passenger-km 1,562,000,000; metric ton-km cargo 143,000,000; airports (1997) with scheduled flights 1. **Communications** Total units (units per 1,000 persons). Radio receivers (1997): 1,225,000 (289); Television receivers (1998): 865,000 (201); Telephone main lines (1999): 359,000 (82); Cellular phone subscribers (1999): 4,000 (0.9); Internet users (1999): 2000 (0.5).

Education and health

Educational attainment (1989). Percentage of pop. age 25 and over having: primary education or no formal schooling 13.6%; some secondary 21.3%; completed secondary and some postsecondary 56.8%; higher 8.3%. **Literacy** (1989): total pop. age 15 and over literate 3,453,000 (97.7%); males literate 1,714,000 (98.8%); females literate 1,739,000 (96.6%). **Health** (1995): physicians 13,500 (1 per

330 persons); hospital beds 46,000 (1 per 97 persons); (2000) infant mortality rate per 1,000 live births 73.3. **Food** (1999): daily per capita caloric intake 2,746 (vegetable products 82%, animal products 18%); (1997) 107% of FAO recommended minimum.

Military

Total active duty personnel (2000): 17,500 (army 82.9%; air force 17.1%). **Military expenditure as percentage of GNP** (1997): 4.6% (world 2.6%); per capita expenditure $71.

Background

The earliest traces of human settlement in Central Asia, dating back to Paleolithic times, have been found in Turkmenistan. The nomadic, tribal Turkmen probably entered the area in the 11th century AD. They were conquered by the Russians in the early 1880s and the region became part of Russian Turkistan. It was organized as the Turkmen Soviet Socialist Republic in 1924 and became a constituent republic of the USSR in 1925. The country gained full independence from the USSR in 1991 under the name Turkmenistan. The next decade was marked by economic struggles.

Recent Developments

In 2001, Pres. Saparmurad Niyazov, both head of state and head of government, kept a tight control on Turkmenistan with the help of the National Security Committee (KNB). There was a rapid turnover of personnel in government posts, and power was concentrated in the hands of the chairman of the KNB, who held a number of important government posts. Dissidents were jailed, small unregistered religious congregations were discouraged from holding services, and religious schools closed except those operated by the state. The clergy of the two registered religions (Sunni Islam and Russian Orthodoxy) were put on the state payroll. Niyazov presented a moral code for the nation to the People's Council. Foreigners were required to pay $50,000 to marry a Turkmen citizen, and requirements for the use of the Turkmen language were stiffened.

In early August 2002 Turkmenistan was in the news when the Turkmen National Council voted to change the names of the months and days. Henceforth, for example, January would be known as "Turkmenbashi," the affectionate nickname by which President Niyazov is known.

Internet resources: <www.turkmenistanembassy.org>

Tuvalu

Official name: Tuvalu. **Form of government:** constitutional monarchy with one legislative house (Parliament [12]). **Chief of state:** British Queen Elizabeth II (from 1952), represented by Governor-General Tomasi Puapua (from 1998). **Head of government:** Prime Minister Saufatu Sopoanga (from 2 Aug 2002). **Capital:** government offices are at Vaiaku, Fongafale islet, on Funafuti Atoll. **Official language:** none. **Official religion:** none. **Monetary units:** 1 Tuvalu dollar =

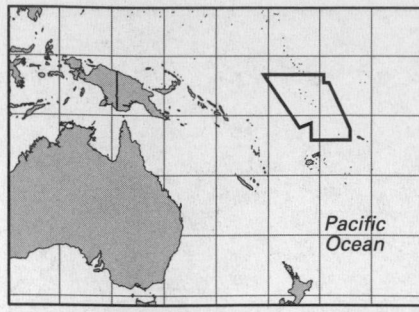

1 Australian dollar ($T = $A) = 100 Tuvalu and Australian cents; valuation (28 Jun 2002) US$1 = $A 1.78.

Demography

Area: 9.90 sq mi, 25.63 sq km. **Population** (2001): 11,000. **Density** (2001): persons per sq mi 1,110, persons per sq km 429. **Urban** (1999): 51.0%. **Sex distribution** (1997): male 48.59%; female 51.41%. **Age breakdown** (1997): under 15, 35.7%; 15–29, 23.2%; 30–44, 23.4%; 45–59, 10.5%; 60–74, 6.1%; 75 and over, 1.1%. **Ethnic composition** (2000): Tuvaluan (Polynesian) 96.3%; mixed (Pacific Islander/European/Asian) 1.0%; Micronesian 1.0%; European 0.5%; other 1.2%. **Religious affiliation** (1995): Church of Tuvalu (Congregational) 85.4%; Seventh-day Adventist 3.6%; Roman Catholic 1.4%; Jehovah's Witness 1.1%; Baha'i 1.0%; other 7.5%. **Major locality** (1995): Fongafale, on Funafuti atoll, 4,000. **Location:** western Pacific Ocean, lying east of Papua New Guinea near the equator.

Vital statistics

Birth rate per 1,000 pop. (2000): 21.4 (world avg. 22.5); (1989) legitimate 82.2%; illegitimate 17.8%. **Death rate** per 1,000 pop. (2000): 7.8 (world avg. 9.0). **Natural increase rate** per 1,000 pop. (2000): 13.6 (world avg. 13.5). **Total fertility rate** (avg. births per childbearing woman; 1998): 3.1. **Life expectancy** at birth (1998): male 62.7 years; female 65.1 years.

National economy

Budget (1996). *Revenue:* $A 7,905,000 (nontax revenues 67.2%; taxes 32.8%). *Expenditures:* $A 8,203,000 (1987; capital [development] expenditures 68.9%, of which marine transport 20.7%, education 13.0%, fisheries 5.6%, health 3.1%; current expenditures 31.1%). **Public debt** (external; 1993): US$6,000,000. **Gross national product** (at current market prices; 1998): US$14,700,000 (US$1,400 per capita). **Production** (metric tons except as noted). *Agriculture, forestry, fishing* (1999): coconuts 1,800, bananas 180, hens' eggs 12, other agricultural products include breadfruit, pulaka (taro), pandanus fruit, sweet potatoes, and pawpaws; livestock (number of live animals) 27,000 chickens; 12,600 pigs, 7,000 ducks; fish catch (1998) 400. *Mining and quarrying* (mineral potential for Tuvalu's maritime economic zone is under exploration): *Manufacturing* (1988): copra 90; handicrafts and baked goods are also im-

1 metric ton = about 1.1 short tons;   1 kilometer = 0.6 mi (statute);   1 metric ton-km cargo = about 0.68 short ton-mi cargo;   c.i.f.: cost, insurance, and freight;   f.o.b.: free on board

portant. *Energy production (consumption):* electricity (kW-hr; 1992) 1,300,000 (1,300,000). **Tourism** (1998): receipts from visitors US$200,000. **Population economically active** (1991): total 5,910; activity rate of total population 65.3% (participation rates: ages 15–64, 85.5%; female [1979] 51.3%; unemployed [1979] 4.0%). **Household income and expenditure.** Average household size (1979) 6.4; average annual income per household $A 2,575; sources of income (1987): agriculture and other 45.0%, cash economy only 38.0%, overseas remittances 17.0%; expenditure (1992): food 45.5%, housing and household operations 11.5%, transportation 10.5%, alcohol and tobacco 10.5%, clothing 7.5%, other 14.5%. **Land use** (1987): agricultural and under permanent cultivation 73.6%; scrub 16.1%; other 10.3%.

Foreign trade

Imports (1998-c.i.f.): $A 11,408,000 (1989; food 29.3%, manufactured goods 28.2%, petroleum and petroleum products 12.8%, machinery and transport equipment 12.2%, chemicals 7.1%, beverages and tobacco 3.9%). *Major import sources* (1995): Fiji 65.8%; Australia 17.1%; New Zealand 3.9%; UK 3.3%; US 2.0%, Germany 1.3%; The Netherlands 1.3%. **Exports** (1998): $A 67,000 (1989; clothing and footwear 29.5%, copra 21.5%, fruits and vegetables 8.0%). *Major export destinations* (1995): South Africa 63.6%; Colombia 9.1%; Belgium-Luxembourg 9.1%.

Transport and communications

Transport. *Roads* (1996): total length 8 km (paved, none). *Air transport* (1977): passenger arrivals (Funafuti) 1,443; airports (1997) with scheduled flights 1. **Communications** Total units (units per 1,000 persons). Radio receivers (1997): 4,000 (384); Television receivers (1996): 100 (13); Telephone main lines (1999): 630 (55).

Education and health

Educational attainment (1991). Percentage of pop. age 25 and over having: no formal schooling 0.8%; primary education 71.4%; secondary 16.2%; higher 7.0%. **Literacy** (1990): total pop. literate in Tuvaluan 8,593 (95.0%); literacy in English estimated at 45.0%. **Health** (1999): physicians 8 (1 per 1,375 persons); hospital beds (1990) 30 (1 per 302 persons); infant mortality rate per 1,000 live births (1998): 26.2.

Military

Total active duty personnel: none; Tuvalu relies on Australian-trained volunteers from Fiji and Papua New Guinea.

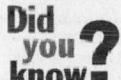 **Did you know?** Lying off the beaten path of the tourist industry, Tuvalu and its culture have remained unscathed by much of the modern world's frenetic activity. If one can get there, Tuvalu provides the ideal getaway for any traveler who just wants to be left alone.

Background

The original Polynesian settlers of Tuvalu probably came mainly from Samoa or Tonga. The islands were sighted by the Spanish in the 16th century. Europeans settled there in the 19th century and intermarried with Tuvaluans. During this period Peruvian slave traders, known as "blackbirders," decimated the population. In 1856 the US claimed the four southern islands for guano mining. Missionaries from Europe arrived in 1865 and rapidly converted the islanders to Christianity. In 1892 Tuvalu joined the British Gilbert Islands, a protectorate that became the Gilbert and Ellice Islands Colony in 1916. Tuvaluans voted in 1974 for separation from the Gilberts (now Kiribati), whose people are Micronesian. Tuvalu gained independence in 1978, and in 1979 the US relinquished its claims. Elections were held in 1981, and a revised constitution was adopted in 1986. In recent decades, the government has tried to find overseas job opportunities for its citizens.

Recent Developments

In 2000 Tuvalu was admitted to the United Nations as the 189th member, and in the same year it achieved full membership status as the 54th state in the Commonwealth of Nations. The country prospered because of some $50 million in revenue realized by the commercialization of its domain name, .tv. Major infrastructure projects were begun to upgrade roads, airport facilities, and electrification of outer islands. The .tv Corp. also became a major shareholder in Air Fiji, which had the exclusive right to provide air service for five years.

Prime Minister Ionatana Ionatana, in office since 1999, died unexpectedly in December 2000; Faimalaga Luka was elected in February 2001 but left office after a no-confidence vote in December, to be replaced by Koloa Talake. Talake in turn was replaced by Saufatu Sopoanga in August 2002.

Internet resources:
<www.tcsp.com/destinations/tuvalu/index.shtml>

Uganda

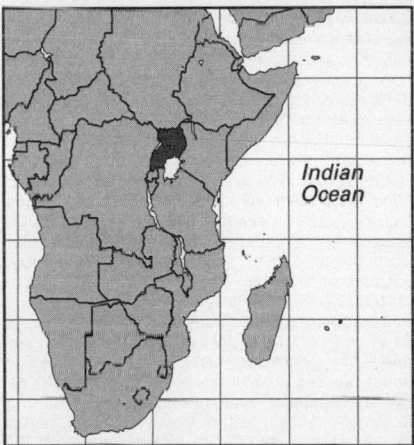

Indian Ocean

Official name: Republic of Uganda. **Form of government:** nonparty republic with one legislative house (Parliament [305; includes 10 unelected members]). **Head of state and government:** President Yoweri Museveni (from 1986). **Capital:** Kampala. **Official language:** English. **Official religion:** none. **Monetary unit:** 1 Uganda shilling (U Sh) = 100 cents; valuation (28 Jun 2002) $1 = U Sh 1,795.50.

Demography

Area: 93,065 sq mi, 241,038 sq km (includes 16,984 sq mi [43,989 sq km] water area). **Population** (2001): 23,986,000. **Density** (2001; for land area only): persons per sq mi 315.3, persons per sq km 121.7. **Urban** (1999–2000): 13.0%. **Sex distribution** (2000): male 49.55%; female 50.45%. **Age breakdown** (2000): under 15, 51.1%; 15–29, 26.2%; 30–44, 13.6%; 45–59, 5.7%; 60–74, 2.9%; 75 and over, 0.5%. **Ethnolinguistic composition** (1991): Ganda 18.1%; Nkole 10.7%; Kiga 8.4%; Soga 8.2%; Lango 5.9%; Lugbara 4.7%; Gisu 4.5%; Acholi 4.4%. **Religious affiliation** (1995): Christian 66%, of which Roman Catholic 33%, Protestant 33% (of which mostly Anglican); traditional beliefs 18%; Muslim 16%. **Major cities** (1991): Kampala 1,154,000 (1998); Jinja 61,000; Mbale 53,600; Masaka 49,100; Gulu 42,800; Entebbe 41,600. **Location:** east Africa, bordering the Sudan, Kenya, Lake Victoria, Tanzania, Rwanda, and the Dem. Rep. of the Congo.

Vital statistics

Birth rate per 1,000 pop. (2000): 48.0 (world avg. 22.5). **Death rate** per 1,000 pop. (2000): 22.4 (world avg. 9.0). **Natural increase rate** per 1,000 pop. (2000): 25.6 (world avg. 13.5). **Total fertility rate** (avg. births per childbearing woman; 2000): 7.0. **Life expectancy** at birth (2000): male 42.2 years; female 43.7 years.

National economy

Budget (1997–98). *Revenue:* U Sh 1,193,100,000,000 (taxes 62.7%, of which customs duties 25.5%, sales taxes 20.2%, income taxes 10.5%; grants 33.3%). *Expenditures:* U Sh 1,239,900,000,000 (current expenditures 58.7%, of which wages and salaries 20.6%, education 16.6%, security 11.0%, health 4.3%; capital expenditures 41.3%). **Public debt** (external, outstanding; 1999): $3,564,000,000. **Production** (metric tons except as noted). *Agriculture, forestry, fishing* (1999): plantains 9,400,000, cassava 3,400,000, sweet potatoes 2,520,000; livestock (number of live animals) 5,700,000 cattle, 3,650,000 goats, 1,970,000 sheep; roundwood (1998) 15,649,000 cu m; fish catch (1998) 220,626. *Mining and quarrying* (1997): gold 3,000 kg. *Manufacturing* (1998): cement 278,800; sugar 93,000; soap 36,100. *Energy production (consumption):* electricity (kW-hr; 1998) 1,282,800,000 (872,000,000); petroleum products (metric tons; 1996) none (319,000). **Tourism** (1999): receipts from visitors $149,000,000; expenditures by nationals abroad $141,000,000. **Land use** (1994): forest 31.5%; pasture 9.1%; agriculture 34.0%; other 25.4%. **Gross national product** (1999): $6,794,000,000 ($330 per capita). **Population economically active** (1991): total 8,365,000; activity rate of total pop. 49.6% (participation rates: ages 15–64, 78.9%; female 35.2%). **Household income and expenditure** (1999–2000). Average household size 5.2; income per household: U

Sh 141,000; sources of income: wages and self-employment 78.0%; transfers 13.0%; rent 9.0%; expenditure: food and beverages 51.0%; rent, energy, and services 17.0%; education 7.0%; household durable goods 6.0%; transportation 5.0%; health 4.0%.

Foreign trade

Imports (1997–98-c.i.f.): $1,411,100,000 (1996; machinery and transport equipment 33.8%, basic manufactures 22.0%, chemicals 15.9%, food and live animals 7.3%). *Major import sources* (1996): Kenya 21.5%; UK 14.2%; Japan 9.1%; United Arab Emirates 6.1%; Germany 4.2%; US 3.1%. **Exports** (1997–98-f.o.b.): $458,400,000 (unroasted coffee 58.7%, tea 7.6%, fish 6.1%, cotton 2.5%). *Major export destinations* (1996): UK 20.8%; Belgium-Luxembourg 12.3%; Spain 9.1%; US 8.1%; France 6.4%; Germany 4.3%.

Transport and communications

Transport. *Railroads* (1998): route length 1,241 km; passenger-km (1996) 27,000,000; metric ton-km cargo (1996) 236,000,000. *Roads* (1996): total length 26,800 km (paved 7.7%). *Vehicles* (1996): passenger cars 35,361; trucks and buses 48,430. *Air transport* (1997): passenger-km 52,117,000; metric ton-km cargo 5,000,000; airports (1998) 1. **Communications** Total units (units per 1,000 persons). Daily newspaper circulation (1997): 40,000 (2.1); Radio receivers (1997): 2,600,000 (130); Television receivers (1998): 580,000 (28.0); Telephone main lines (1999): 57,239 (2.5); Cellular telephone subscribers (1999): 56,358 (2.4); Personal computers (1999): 55,000 (2.4); Internet users (1999): 25,000 (1.1).

Education and health

Educational attainment (1991). Percentage of pop. age 25 and over having: no formal schooling or less than one full year 46.9%; primary education 42.1%; secondary 10.5%; higher 0.5%. **Literacy** (1999–2000): pop. age 10 and over literate 65.0%; males literate 74.0%; females literate 57.0%. **Health** (1993): physicians 840 (1 per 22,399 persons); hospital beds (1989) 20,136 (1 per 817 persons); infant mortality rate (2000) 93.3. **Food** (2000): daily per capita caloric intake 2,238 (vegetable products 94%, animal products 6%); 96% of FAO recommended minimum requirement.

Military

Total active duty personnel (2000): 50,000–60,000. **Military expenditure as percentage of GNP** (1997): 4.2% (world 2.6%); per capita $12.

Background

By the 19th century the region around Uganda comprised several separate kingdoms inhabited by various peoples, including Bantu- and Nilotic-speaking tribes. Arab traders reached the area in the 1840s. The native kingdom of Buganda was visited by the first European explorers in 1862. Protestant and Catholic missionaries arrived in the 1870s, and the development of religious factions led to persecution and civil strife. In 1894 Buganda was formally pro-

1 metric ton = about 1.1 short tons; 1 kilometer = 0.6 mi (statute); 1 metric ton-km cargo = about 0.68 short ton-mi cargo; c.i.f.: cost, insurance, and freight; f.o.b.: free on board

claimed a British protectorate. As Uganda, it gained its independence in 1962, and in 1967 it adopted a republican constitution. The civilian government was overthrown in 1971 and replaced by a military regime under Idi Amin. His invasion of Tanzania in late 1978 resulted in the collapse of his regime. The civilian government was again deposed by the military in 1985, which in turn was overthrown in 1986. A constituent assembly enacted a new constitution in 1995.

Recent Developments

Presidential and parliamentary elections in 2001 confirmed the grip on power by incumbent Pres. Yoweri Museveni, who captured nearly 70% of the vote in a six-way race, and by his National Resistence Movement, which won 230 out of 292 seats in the legislature. A referendum held in 2000 had confirmed the country's "no-party" government system, but the referendum had been boycotted by the opposition. An agreement signed in 1999 between Uganda and The Sudan attempted to end the support each country was giving to rebels acting against the other. Uganda, however, was accused along with Rwanda of interference in the Democratic Republic of the Congo, including committing atrocities and illegally exploiting the Congo's mineral reserves. It was revealed in 2000 that 55% of Uganda's military budget came as "development aid" from external donors.

An outbreak of ebola virus in 2000 in the northern districts claimed 224 lives before it was declared to be at an end in February 2001. Uganda's campaign against HIV/AIDS was considered a model for Africa; an international treatment and training center was planned for Kampala.

Internet resources: <www.visituganda.com>

Ukraine

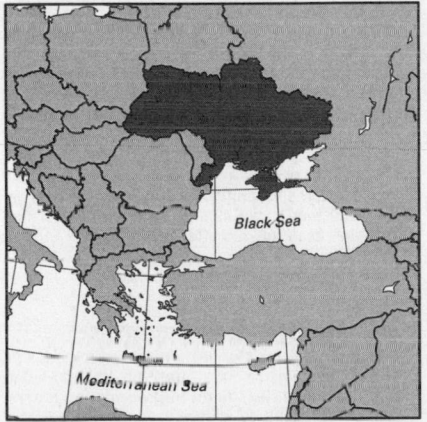

Official name: Ukrayina (Ukraine). Form of government: unitary multiparty republic with a single legislative body (Supreme Council [450]). Head of state: President Leonid Kuchma (from 1994). Head of government: Prime Minister Anatoly Kinakh (from 29 May 2001). Capital: Kiev (Kyyiv). Official language: Ukrainian. Official religion: none. Monetary unit: hryvnya (pl. hryvnyas); valuation (28 Jun 2002) $1 = 5.33 hryvnyas.

Demography

Area: 603,700 sq km. Population (2001): 48,767,000. Density (2001): persons per sq mi 209.2, persons per sq km 80.8. Urban (1999): 67.9%. Sex distribution (1999): male 46.30%; female 53.70%. Age breakdown (1999): under 15, 18.4%; 15–29, 21.7%; 30–44, 21.8%; 45–59, 17.7%; 60–74, 15.6%; 75 and over, 4.8%. Ethnic composition (2000): Ukrainian 70.4%; Russian 20.0%; Polish 2.3%; Rom (Gypsy) 1.3%; Ruthenian 1.1%; other/unspecified 4.9%. Religious affiliation (1995): Ukrainian Orthodox (Russian patriarchy) 19.5%; Ukrainian Orthodox (Kiev patriarchy) 9.7%; Ukrainian Catholic (Uniate) 7.0%; Protestant 3.6%; other Orthodox 1.6%; Roman Catholic 1.2%; Jewish 0.9%; other (mostly nonreligious) 56.5%. Major cities (1998): Kiev 2,629,300; Kharkiv 1,521,400; Dnipropetrovsk 1,122,400; Donetsk 1,065,400; Odessa 1,027,400. Location: Eastern Europe bordering Belarus, Russia, the Black Sea, Romania, Moldova, Hungary, Slovakia, and Poland.

Vital statistics

Birth rate per 1,000 pop. (2000): 7.9 (world avg. 22.5); (1993) legitimate 87.0%; illegitimate 13.0%. Death rate per 1,000 pop. (2000): 13.9 (world avg. 9.0). Natural increase rate per 1,000 pop. (2000): -6.0 (world avg. 13.5). Total fertility rate (avg. births per childbearing woman; 2000): 1.3. Life expectancy at birth (2000): male 60.8 years, female 72.0 years.

National economy

Budget (1998). Revenue: 36,892,000,000 hryvnyas (tax revenue 95.5%, of which taxes on goods and services 31.5%, payroll tax 29.3%, income tax 26.3%; nontax revenue 4.5%). Expenditures: 39,714,000,000 hryvnyas (social security 36.3%; national economy 15.1%; education 11.3%; health 9.1%; defense 3.4%). Public debt (external; 1999): $10,027,000,000. Production (metric tons except as noted). Agriculture, forestry, fishing (1999): potatoes 15,405,100, sugar beets 13,890,000, wheat 13,476,200; livestock (number of live animals) 11,722,000 cattle, 10,083,000 pigs, 2,026,000 sheep and goats; roundwood (1998) 10,052,000 cu m; fish catch (1997) 462,308. Mining and quarrying (1998): iron ore 50,700,000; manganese 2,226,000; uranium 500,000. Manufacturing (value of production in '000,000 hryvnyas; 1997): iron and steel 12,832; food products 12,221; nonelectrical machinery 3,447. Energy production (consumption): electricity (kW-hr; 1999) 172,104,000,000 (146,700,000,000); hard coal (metric tons; 1999) 81,648,000 ([1996] 79,500,000); lignite (metric tons; 1999) 1,188,000 ([1996] 4,300,000); crude petroleum (barrels; 1999) 27,795,000 ([2000] 126,290,000); petroleum products (1996) 11,759,000 (16,168,000); natural gas (cu m; 1999) 15,740,000,000 (78,013,000,000). Population economically active (1997): total 22,598,000; activity rate of total pop. 44.6% (participation rates: ages 16–59 [male] 15–54 [female] 79.7%; female [1994] 51.0%; unemployed [1999–2000] 4.3%). Gross national product (1999): $41,991,000,000 ($840 per capita). Tourism

(1997): receipts $270,000,000; expenditures $305,-000,000. **Household income and expenditure** (1996). Average household size (1998) 3.0; income per household (1996) 4,968 hryvnyas; sources of income (1995): wages and salaries 66.4%, sales of agricultural products 9.3%, subsidies 6.9%, pensions 6.5%, remuneration from abroad 5.3%; expenditures (1995): food and beverages 43.1%, consumer goods 27.5%, services 7.2%, housing 6.7%, taxes 6.2%.

Foreign trade

Imports (1999): $12,945,000,000 (fuel and energy products 39.9%; machinery 17.4%; chemicals and chemical products 11.3%; food and raw materials 7.0%). *Major import sources:* Russia 47.9%; Germany 7.3%; Turkmenistan 3.7%; US 3.1%; Belarus 2.6%. **Exports** (1999): $12,463,000,000 (ferrous and nonferrous metals 39.1%; food and raw materials 11.4%; machinery 11.1%; chemicals and chemical products 11.1%). *Major export destinations:* Russia 19.2%; China 5.9%; Turkey 5.4%; Germany 4.5%; Italy 3.7%.

Transport and communications

Transport. *Railroads* (1998): length 22,564 km; passenger-km 54,500,000,000; metric ton-km cargo (1997) 160,419,000,000. *Roads* (1997): total length 172,378 km (paved 95%). *Vehicles* (1997): passenger cars 4,885,691. *Air transport* (1998): passenger-km 1,972,134,000; (10 Ukrainian airlines only) metric ton-km cargo 27,395,000; airports (1998) with scheduled flights 12. **Communications** Total units (units per 1,000 persons). Daily newspaper circulation (1996): 2,780,000 (54); Radio receivers (1997): 45,050,000 (889); Television receivers (1998): 21,000,000 (418); Telephone main lines (1999): 10,074,000 (202); Cellular telephone subscribers (1999): 216,567 (4.4); Personal computers (1999): 800,000 (16); Internet users (1999): 200,000 (4.0).

Education and health

Educational attainment (1989). Percentage of pop. age 15 and over having: some primary education 6.8%; completed primary 13.8%; some secondary 18.4%; completed secondary 31.1%; some postsecondary 19.5%; higher 10.4%. Literacy (1989): percentage of total pop. age 15 and over literate 98.4%; males literate 99.5%; females literate 97.4%. **Health** (1998): physicians 150,382 (1 per 334 persons); hospital beds 508,030 (1 per 99 persons); infant mortality rate per 1,000 live births (2000) 21.7. **Food** (1999): daily per capita caloric intake 2,809 (vegetable products 78%, animal products 22%); 110% of FAO recommended minimum requirement.

Military

Total active duty personnel (2000): 303,800 (army 49.8%, air force 31.6%, navy 4.3%, headquarters 14.3%). **Military expenditure as percentage of GNP** (1997) 3.7% (world 2.6%); per capita expenditure $85.

Background

The area around Ukraine was invaded and occupied in the first millennium BC by the Cimmerians, Scythi-ans, and Sarmatians, and in the first millennium AD by the Goths, Huns, Bulgars, Avars, Khazars, and Magyars. Slavic tribes settled there after the 4th century. Kiev was its chief town. The Mongol conquest in the mid-13th century decisively ended Kievan power. Ruled by Lithuania in the 14th century and Poland in the 16th century, it fell to Russian rule in the 18th century. The Ukrainian National Republic, established in 1917, declared its independence from Soviet Russia in 1918 but was reconquered in 1919; it was made the Ukrainian Soviet Socialist Republic of the USSR in 1922. The northwestern region was held by Poland from 1919 to 1939. Ukraine suffered a severe famine in 1932–33 under Soviet leader Joseph Stalin; over 5 million Ukrainians died of starvation in an unprecedented peacetime catastrophe. Overrun by Axis armies in 1941 in World War II, it was further devastated before being retaken by the Soviets in 1944. In 1986 it was the site of the Chernobyl accident, at a Soviet-built nuclear power plant. It declared independence in 1991. In recent years it has struggled both politically and economically.

Recent Developments

Political turmoil wracked the Supreme Council of Ukraine, as shifting coalitions of center-rightist and leftist parties jockeyed for power. In a 2000 referendum, voters approved a decrease in the number of legislators and removed their immunity from prosecution; they also approved measures to create a second chamber in the legislature and to expedite its forming of governments and passing of budgets. Pres. Leonid Kuchma faced the fallout from the disappearance of Georgy Gongadze, a dissident journalist; Kuchma had been captured on tape calling for Gongadze's "elimination." The discovery of a body thought to be Gongadze ignited a protest movement, and several officials were dismissed, including the interior minister and the head of the Security Service. The pro-Western prime minister Viktor Yushchenko was replaced by Anatoly Kinakh on a vote of no-confidence called by the Communist bloc over the economic situation.

Nonetheless, the economy was making progress, with the gross domestic product increasing and wages rising, and a good grain harvest in 2001. The Chernobyl nuclear power plant closed at the end of December 2000; the country was desperately short of energy and the coal industry was in dire straits. Relations with Russia remained difficult, and they were not improved when Ukraine had to take responsibility for accidentally shooting down a Russian commercial airliner over the Black Sea in October 2001. The minister of defense resigned after the incident.

Internet resources: <www.ukremb.com>

United Arab Emirates

Official name: Al-Imarat al-'Arabiyah al-Muttahidah (United Arab Emirates). **Form of government:** federation of seven emirates with one appointive advisory body (Federal National Council [40; all appointed seats]). **Chief of state:** President Sheikh Zaid ibn Sultan al-Nahayan (from 1971). **Head of government:** Prime Minister Sheikh Maktum ibn Rashid al-Maktum

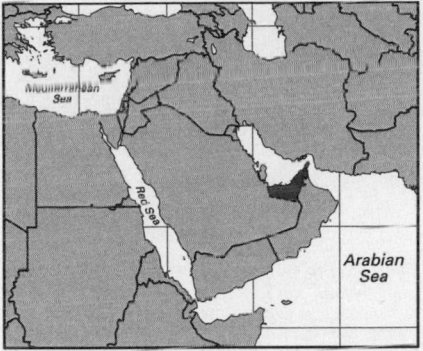

(from 1990). **Capital:** Abu Dhabi. **Official language:** Arabic. **Official religion:** Islam. **Monetary unit:** 1 UAE dirham (Dh) = 100 fils; valuation (28 Jun 2002) $1 = Dh 3.67.

Demography

Area: 32,2803 sq mi, 83,600 sq km. **Population** (2001): 3,108,000. **Density** (2001): persons per sq mi 96.3, persons per sq km 37.2. **Urban** (1998): 85.1%. **Sex distribution** (2001): male 67.54%; female 32.46%. **Age breakdown** (2001): under 15, 26.2%; 15–29, 29.2%; 30–44, 33.4%; 45–59, 9.6%; 60–74, 1.4%; 75 and over, 0.2%. **Ethnic composition** (2000): Arab 48.1%, of which UAE Arab 12.2%, UAE Bedouin 9.4%, Egyptian Arab 6.2%, Omani Arab 4.1%, Saudi Arab 4.0%; South Asian 35.7%, of which Pashtun 7.1%, Balochi 7.1%, Malayali 7.1%; Persian 5.0%; Filipino 3.4%; white 2.4%; other 5.4%. **Religious affiliation** (1995): Muslim 96.0% (Sunni 80.0%, Shi'i 16.0%); other (mostly Christian and Hindu) 4.0%. **Major cities** (1995): Dubai 669,181; Abu Dhabi 398,695; Sharjah 320,095; Al-'Ayn 225,970; 'Ajman 114,395. **Location:** the Middle East, bordering the Persian Gulf, the Gulf of Oman, Oman, Saudia Arabia, and Qatar.

Vital statistics

Birth rate per 1,000 pop. (2000): 18.0 (world avg. 22.5). **Death rate** per 1,000 pop. (2000): 3.7 (world avg. 9.0). **Natural increase rate** per 1,000 pop. (2000): 14.3 (world avg. 13.5). **Total fertility rate** (avg. births per childbearing woman; 2000): 3.3. **Marriage rate** per 1,000 pop. (1999): 3.5. **Divorce rate** per 1,000 pop. (1999): 0.9. **Life expectancy** at birth (1999): male 71.6 years; female 76.6 years.

National economy

Budget (1999). *Revenue:* Dh 52,003,000,000 (oil revenue 54.2%, non-oil revenue 45.8%). *Expenditures:* Dh 77,089,000,000 (current expenditures 66.2%, capital [development] expenditure 33.8%). **Gross national product** (1999): $52,008,000,000 ($17,985 per capita). **Tourism** (1999). total number of tourist arrivals 3,392,000. **Production** (metric tons except as noted). *Agriculture, forestry, fishing* (2000): tomatoes 780,000, dates 318,000, cantaloupes and watermelons 64,000; livestock (number of live animals) 1,200,000 goats, 467,281 sheep, 200,000 camels; fish catch (1999) 117,007. *Mining and quarrying* (1998): sulfur 268,000; gypsum 110,000;

chromite 54,000. *Manufacturing* (value of production in Dh '000,000; 1993): chemical products 13,086; fabricated metal products 2,234; food, beverages, and tobacco 2,122. *Energy production (consumption):* electricity (kW-hr; 1997) 20,571,000,000 (20,571,000,000); crude petroleum (barrels; 2000) 769,000,000 ([1997] 86,000,000); petroleum products (metric tons; 1997) 18,995,000 (7,190,000); natural gas (cu m; 1997) 35,859,000,000 (28,839,-000,000). **Population economically active** (2001): total 1,947,000; activity rate of total pop. 59.2% (participation rates [1995]: over age 15, 55.4%; female 13.2%; unemployment [2000] 2.3%). **Household income and expenditure.** Average household size (1999) 6.1; expenditure (1991): rent, fuel, and light 23.9%, food 22.7%, transportation and communications 14.1%, durable household goods 11.6%, education, recreation, and entertainment 8.6%. **Land use** (1994): forested, virtually none; meadows and pastures 2.4%; agricultural and under permanent cultivation 0.5%; built-on, wasteland, and other 97.1%.

Foreign trade

Imports (1997): Dh 109,100,000,000 (machinery and transport equipment 38.4%, basic manufactures 24.8%, food and live animals 9.7%, chemicals 6.1%, crude minerals 1.6%, mineral fuels 1.4%). *Major import sources:* Japan 10.2%; US 9.4%; UK 8.7%; China 8.0%; Germany 6.9%; India 5.8%; Italy 5.2%; South Korea 5.1%. **Exports** (1997): Dh 139,500,000,000 (crude petroleum 37.6%, natural gas 7.1%, refined petroleum products 4.8%). *Major export destinations:* Japan 36.2%; India 6.6%; Singapore 6.4%; South Korea 6.1%; Iran 3.7%; Oman 3.7%.

Transport and communications

Transport. *Roads* (1999): total length 3,791 km (paved 100%). *Vehicles* (1996): passenger cars 201,000; trucks and buses 56,950. *Air transport* (2000; Emirates Air and one-fourth apportionment of Gulf Air): passenger-km 19,552,500,000; metric ton-km cargo 1,427,500,000; airports (1999) with scheduled flights 6. **Communications** Total units (units per 1,000 persons). Daily newspaper circulation (1996): 384,000 (170); Radio receivers (1997): 820,000 (355); Television receivers (1999): 740,000 (252); Telephones main lines (1999): 975,178 (332); Cellular telephone subscribers (1999): 832,267 (283); Personal computers (1999): 300,000 (102); Internet users (1999): 400,000 (136).

Education and health

Educational attainment (1995). Percentage of pop. age 10 and over having: no formal schooling 47.6%; primary education 27.8%; secondary 16.0%; higher 8.6%. **Literacy** (1995): total pop. age 15 and over literate 79.2%; males literate 78.9%; females literate 79.8%. **Health** (1999): physicians 6,059 (1 per 485 persons); hospital beds 7,448 (1 per 394 persons); infant mortality rate per 1,000 live births (1999) 8.8. **Food** (1999): daily per capita caloric intake 3,182 (vegetable products 75%, animal products 25%); 132% of FAO recommended minimum.

Military

Total active duty personnel (2000): 65,000 (army 90.7%, navy 3.1%, air force 6.2%). **Military expendi-**

ture as percentage of GDP (1997): 6.9% (world 2.6%); per capita expenditure $1,004.

Did you know? The UAE is home to the Dubai World Cup, which, with a total purse of $15,250,000 in 2002, was the world's richest horse race (the American Breeders Cup, at $13,500,000, is second).

Background

In 1820 the British exacted a peace treaty with local rulers along the coast of the eastern Arabian peninsula. The area formerly called the Pirate Coast became known as the Trucial Coast. In 1892 the rulers agreed to restrict foreign relations to Britain. Though the British administered the region from 1853, they never assumed sovereignty; each state maintained full internal control. The states formed the Trucial States Council in 1960. In 1971 the sheiks terminated defense treaties with Britain and established the six-member federation. Ra's al-Khaymah joined it in 1972. The UAE aided coalition forces against Iraq in the Persian Gulf War (1991).

Recent Developments

In 2000 the UAE struck a $6.4 billion deal with US-based Lockheed-Martin to purchase 80 fighter aircraft; in addition, Russia announced that it was selling the UAE $5 billion in antiaircraft equipment. The economy of the UAE, based signficantly on oil, benefited from the world rise in oil prices. In addition, the UAE became the chief trader among Persian Gulf states, owing primarily to the re-export of imported goods. It enjoyed the second highest per capita income (after Qatar) and was the largest importer and second largest exporter among Arab states. In March 2001 a major deal was struck with Qatar to develop Qatar's North Field natural gas and to import it by an undersea pipeline to Abu Dhabi and Dubai. Gas was expected to begin flowing by 2004 or 2005. Diplomatic initiatives strengthened ties with Iran, one of the UAE's main trading partners.

Internet resources: <www.emirates.org>; <www.uae.org.ae>

United Kingdom

Official name: United Kingdom of Great Britain and Northern Ireland. **Form of government:** constitutional monarchy with two legislative houses (House of Lords [695]; House of Commons [659]). **Chief of state:** Queen Elizabeth II (from 1952). **Head of government:** Prime Minister Anthony C.L. Blair (from 1997). **Capital:** London. **Official language:** English. **Official religion:** Churches of England and Scotland "established" (protected by the state, but not "official") in their respective countries; no established church in Northern Ireland or Wales. **Monetary unit:** 1 pound sterling (£) = 100 new pence; valuation (28 Jun 2002) 1£ = $1.52; $1 = £0.66.

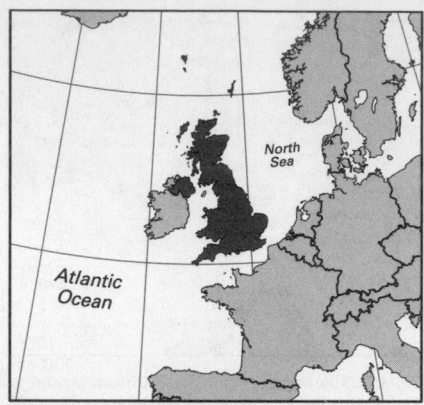

North Sea

Atlantic Ocean

Demography

Population (2001): 59,953,000. **Area:** 94,248 sq mi; 244,101 sq km, of which England 50,351 sq mi, 130,410 sq km; Wales 8,015 sq mi, 20,758 sq km; Scotland 30,421 sq mi, 78,789 sq km; Northern Ireland (figures represent remainder) 5,461 sq mi, 14,144 sq km. **Density** (2001): persons per sq mi 636.1, persons per sq km 245.6. **Urban** (1999): 88.2%. **Age breakdown** (1999): under 15, 20.4%; 15–29, 18.0%; 30–44, 22.8%; 45–59, 18.4%; 60–74, 13.1%; 75 and over, 7.3%. **Ethnic composition** (1998): white 93.2%; black 1.8%; Asian Indian 1.7%; Pakistani 1.2%; Bangladeshi 0.5%; Chinese 0.2%; other and not stated 1.4%. **Sex distribution** (1999): male 49.24%; female 50.76%. **Religious affiliation** (2000): Christian 66.4%, of which Protestant 53.3% (Anglican 45.0%), Roman Catholic 9.6%, Orthodox 0.9%; Muslim 2.0%; Hindu 0.7%; Sikh 0.5%; Jewish 0.4%; other/nonreligious 30.0%. **Major cities** (1999): Greater London 7,285,000; Birmingham 1,013,200; Leeds 726,800; Glasgow 668,100; Sheffield 530,600. **Location:** Western Europe, bordering the North Sea, the English Channel, the Celtic Sea, the Irish Sea, and Ireland. **Dependent territories:** Anguilla, Bermuda, British Virgin Islands, Cayman Islands, Falkland Islands, Gibraltar, Guernsey, Isle of Man, Jersey, Montserrat, Pitcairn Island, Saint Helena and Dependencies, and Turks and Caicos Islands. **Mobility** (1991). Population living in the same residence as 1990: 90.1%; different residence, same country (of Great Britain) 8.1%; different residence, different country of Great Britain 1.2%; from outside Great Britain 0.6%. **Households** (1994). Average household size 2.4; 1 person 27%, 2 persons 34%, 3 persons 16%, 4 persons 15%, 5 persons 6%, 6 or more persons 2%. Family household: 16,900,000 (72.0%), nonfamily 6,600,000 (28.0%, of which 1-person 12.0%). **Immigration** (1998): permanent residents 332,000, from Australia 7.5%, US 5.7%, New Zealand 4.2%, South Africa 3.6%, Bangladesh, India, and Sri Lanka 3.0%, Canada 1.5%, Pakistan 1.2%, other 73.3%, of which EU 8.7%.

Vital statistics

Birth rate per 1,000 pop. (1999): 11.8 (world avg. 22.5); legitimate 61.2%; illegitimate 38.8%. **Death**

1 metric ton = about 1.1 short tons;   1 kilometer = 0.6 mi (statute);   1 metric ton-km cargo = about 0.68 short ton-mi cargo;   c.i.f.: cost, insurance, and freight;   f.o.b.: free on board

rate per 1,000 pop. (1999): 10.6 (world avg. 9.0). **Natural increase rate** per 1,000 pop. (1999): 1.2 (world avg. 13.5). **Total fertility rate** (avg. births per childbearing woman; 1999): 1.7. **Marriage rate** per 1,000 pop. (1999): 5.1. **Divorce rate** per 1,000 pop. (1999): 2.7. **Life expectancy** at birth (1997–99): male 74.9 years; female 79.8 years. **Educational attainment** (1981). Percentage of pop. age 25 and over having: primary or secondary education only 89.7%; some postsecondary 4.8%; bachelor's or equivalent degree 4.9%; higher university degree 0.6%. **Quality of working life** (1999). Average workweek (hours): male 41.4, female 37.5. Annual rate per 100,000 workers for (1996): injury or accident 553.6; death 1.0. Proportion of labor force (employed persons) insured for damages or income loss resulting from: injury 100%; permanent disability 100%; death 100%. Average days lost to labor stoppages per 1,000 employee workdays 1999: 0.04. Principal means of transport to work (1991; London only): public transportation 81%, private automobile 15%, motor or pedal cycle 2%, other 2%. **Access to services** (1991). Proportion of households having access to: bath or shower 98.7%; toilet 99.8%; central heating 81.1%. **Social participation.** Eligible voters participating in last national election (May 1997): 71.4%. Population age 16 and over participating in voluntary work (1987): 22%. Trade union membership in total workforce (1998) 26.7%. **Social deviance** (1998–99). Offense rate per 100,000 pop. for: theft and handling stolen goods 3,574.2; burglary 1,599.8; violence against the person 387.9; fraud and forgery 291.9; robbery 111.3; sexual offense 58.6. **Leisure** (1994). Favorite leisure activities (hours weekly): watching television 17.1; listening to radio 10.3; reading 8.8, of which books 3.8, newspapers 3.3; gardening 2.1. **Material well being** (1999). Households possessing: automobile 71.0%, telephone 95.0%, television receiver 98.3% (color 95% [1995]), refrigerator 98.5%, central heating 90.0%, washing machine 91.0%, video recorder 86.0%.

National economy

Budget (1999). *Revenue:* £328,168,000,000 (income tax 39.3%, customs and excise taxes 32.4%, social security contributions 17.2%). *Expenditures:* £336,930,000,000 (1996–97; social security 24.9%, health 11.0%, debt interest 7.2%, defense 7.2%). **Total national debt** (31 Mar 2000): £421,635,700,000 ($672,551,100,000). **Gross national product** (at current market prices; 1999): $1,403,843,000,000 ($23,590 per capita). **Land use** (1994): forested 10.4%; meadows and pastures 45.9%; agricultural and under permanent cultivation 24.8%; other 18.9%. **Tourism** (1999): receipts from visitors $20,223,000,000; expenditures by nationals abroad $35,631,000,000. **Production** (metric tons except as noted). *Agriculture, forestry, fishing* (2001): wheat 12,060,000, sugar beets 10,000,000, barley 6,690,000, potatoes 6,647,000, rapeseed 1,129,000; livestock (number of live animals) 42,000,000 sheep, 11,000,000 cattle, 6,500,000 pigs; roundwood (1999) 7,451,000 cu m; fish catch (1999) 992,552. *Mining and quarrying* (1999): limestone 91,485,000; lead 1,000. *Manufacturing* (value added in £'000,000; 1998): electrical and optical equipment 19,478; food and beverages 10,337, iron and ferro alloys 17,375; paper, printing, and publishing 17,717; transport equipment 16,968. *Energy production (consumption):* electricity (kW-hr; 1997)

344,955,000,000 (361,529,000,000); coal (metric tons; 1997) 45,895,000 (63,128,000); crude petroleum (barrels; 1997) 892,985,000 (648,791,000); petroleum products (metric tons; 1997) 89,779,000 (72,673,000); natural gas (cu m; 1997) 104,174,000,000 (102,506,000,000). **Population economically active** (2000): total 29,412,000, activity rate of total pop. 49.2% (participation rates: ages 16–64, 74.3%; female 44.5%; unemployed 5.5%). **Household income and expenditure** (1998–99). Average household size 2.4; average annual disposable income per household £19,230; sources of income: wages and salaries 65.7%, social security benefits 12.1%, income from self-employment 9.6%, dividends and interest 4.5%; expenditure: food and beverages 20.8%, transport and vehicles 17.2%, housing 15.8%, household goods 8.5%, clothing 5.8%, energy 3.1%.

Foreign trade

Imports (1999): £194,434,000,000 (machinery and transport equipment 46.0%, of which electrical equipment 21.2%, road vehicles 12.5%; chemicals 9.7%, of which plastics 2.0%, organic chemicals 1.5%; clothing and footwear 4.9%; food 4.7%; petroleum and petroleum products 2.5%, textiles 2.3%; paper and paperboard 2.2%). *Major import sources:* Germany 13.8%; US 12.7%; France 9.3%; The Netherlands 7.0%. **Exports** (1999): £165,667,000,000 (machinery and transport equipment 47.5%, of which electrical equipment 21.6%, road vehicles 9.1%; chemicals 13.9%, of which organic chemicals 3.3%; petroleum and petroleum products 5.5%; professional and scientific 4.1%; food 2.0%; iron and steel products 1.6%). *Major export destinations:* US 14.7%; Germany 12.3%; France 10.1%; The Netherlands 8.2%; Ireland 6.5%; Belgium-Luxembourg 5.5%.

Transport and communications

Transport. *Railroads* (1999–2000): length (1990) 37,849 km; passenger-km 38,300,000,000; metric ton-km cargo 18,400,000,000. *Roads* (1999): total length 371,914 km (paved 100%). *Vehicles* (1999): passenger cars 23,393,000, trucks and buses 2,368,000. *Air transport* (1999): passenger-km 160,336,400,000; metric ton-km cargo 4,924,900,000; airports (1997) 57. **Communications.** Total units (units per 1,000 persons). Daily newspaper circulation (1996): 19,332,000 (332); Radio receivers (1997): 84,500,000 (1,443); Television receivers (1999): 38,800,000 (652); Telephone main lines (1999): 33,750,000 (567); Cellular telephone subscribers (1999): 27,185,000 (457); Personal computers (1999): 18,000,000 (303); Internet users (1999): 12,500,000 (210).

Education and health

Literacy (1990): total pop. literate, virtually 100%. **Health** (1993): physicians 92,474 (1 per 629 persons); hospital beds 283,814 (1 per 205 persons); infant mortality rate per 1,000 live births (1999) 5.8. **Food** (1999): daily per capita caloric intake 3,318 (vegetable products 68%, animal products 32%); 132% of FAO recommended minimum.

Military

Total active duty personnel (2001): 211,430 (army 53.9%, navy 20.6%, air force 25.5%). **Military expen-**

diture as percentage of GNP (1997): 2.7% (world 2.6%); per capita expenditure $600.

Background

The early pre-Roman inhabitants of Britain were Celtic-speaking peoples, including the Brythonic people of Wales, the Picts of Scotland, and the Britons of Britain. Celts also settled in Ireland c. 500 BC. Julius Caesar invaded and took control of the area in 55–54 BC. The Roman province of Britannia endured until the 5th century and included present-day England and Wales. In the 5th century Nordic tribes of Angles, Saxons, and Jutes invaded Britain. The invasions had little effect on the Celtic peoples of Wales and Scotland.

Christianity began to flourish in the 6th century. During the 8th–9th centuries, Vikings, particularly Danes, raided the coasts of Britain. In the late 9th century Alfred the Great repelled a Danish invasion, which helped bring about the unification of England under Athelstan. The Scots attained dominance in Scotland, which was finally unified under Malcolm II (1005–34).

William of Normandy took England in 1066. The Norman kings established a strong central government and feudal state. The French language of the Norman rulers eventually merged with the Anglo-Saxon of the common people to form the English language. From the 11th century, Scotland came under the influence of the English throne. Henry II conquered Ireland in the late 12th century. His sons Richard I and John had conflicts with the clergy and nobles, and eventually John was forced to grant the nobles concessions in Magna Carta (1215). The concept of community of the realm developed during the 13th century, providing the foundation for parliamentary government. During the reign of Edward I, statute law developed to supplement English common law, and the first Parliament was convened. In 1314 Robert Bruce won independence for Scotland.

The Tudors became the ruling family of England following the Wars of the Roses (1455–85). Henry VIII established the Church of England and made Wales part of his realm. The reign of Elizabeth I began a period of colonial expansion; 1588 brought the defeat of the Spanish Armada. In 1603 James VI of Scotland ascended to the English throne, becoming James I, and established a personal union of the two kingdoms.

The English Civil Wars erupted in 1642 between Royalists and Parliamentarians, ending in the execution of Charles I (1649). After eleven years of Puritan rule under Oliver Cromwell and his son (1649–60), the monarchy was restored with Charles II. In 1707 England and Scotland assented to the Act of Union, forming the kingdom of Great Britain. The Hanoverians ascended to the English throne in 1714, when George Louis, elector of Hanover, became George I of Great Britain. During the reign of George III, Great Britain's American colonies won independence (1783). This was followed by a period of war with revolutionary France and later with the empire of Napoleon (1789–1815).

In 1801 legislation united Great Britain with Ireland to create the United Kingdom of Great Britain and Ireland. Britain was the birthplace of the Industrial Revolution in the late 18th century, and it remained the world's foremost economic power until the late 19th century. During the reign of Queen Victoria, Britain's colonial expansion reached its zenith, though the older dominions, including Canada and Australia, were granted independence (1867 and 1901, respectively).

The United Kingdom entered World War I allied with France and Russia in 1914. Following the war, revolutionary disorder erupted in Ireland, and in 1921 the Irish Free State was granted dominion status. The six counties of Ulster, however, remained in the United Kingdom as Northern Ireland. The United Kingdom entered World War II in 1939. Following the war the Irish Free State became the Irish Republic and left the Commonwealth. India gained independence from the United Kingdom in 1947.

Throughout the postwar period and into the 1970s, the United Kingdom continued to grant independence to its overseas colonies and dependencies. With UN forces, it participated in the Korean War (1950–53). In 1956 it intervened militarily in Egypt during the Suez Crisis. In 1982 it defeated Argentina in the Falkland Islands War. As a result of continuing social strife in Northern Ireland, it joined with Ireland in several peace initiatives, which eventually resulted in an agreement to establish an assembly in Northern Ireland. In 1997 referenda approved in Scotland and Wales devolved power to both countries, though both remained part of the United Kingdom.

Recent Developments

British agriculture sustained back-to-back blows when outbreaks of bovine spongiform encephalopathy (BSE; mad cow disease) and foot and mouth (hoof and mouth) disease struck cows, sheep, and pigs. Eating beef tainted with BSE can cause a fatal human brain disease; in the first six months of 2001, there were more than 200 cases of human infection, bringing fears of another boycott of British beef like the one that had crippled the industry in 1996. In February 2001 the first case of foot and mouth disease in 20 years was reported; within weeks England and Wales were in the throes of a major outbreak. Millions of cows, pigs, and sheep on more than 2,000 infected farms were destroyed. Movement between rural areas was curtailed to prevent the spread of the disease.

The economy grew in 2000 for the eighth year in a row, and a budget surplus enabled the government to reduce the national debt, decrease fuel taxes, and increase benefits for retirees. In 2001 the worldwide economic slowdown began to affect Britain but it still posted growth of 2% for the year. Interest rates fell and the pound sterling remained strong, although it was considered overvalued against the euro. The UK had not yet adopted the euro, but that possibility remained open, if the public approved the move in a referendum.

The Labour government of Tony Blair won a landslide victory over the Conservatives in general elections in June, posting one of the strongest showings in 60 years, taking 413 of 659 seats in the House of Commons. The victory was attributed in part to the support of the middle class, responding to the strong economy. The losing Conservative leader, William Hague, resigned and was replaced by Iain Duncan Smith, whom many considered to be anti-European Union (EU) and right-wing. Only 59% of registered electors went to the polls, however, a 12% decrease from the 1997 election that had brought Labour to power.

1 metric ton = about 1.1 short tons;   1 kilometer = 0.6 mi (statute);   1 metric ton-km cargo = about 0.68 short ton-mi cargo;   c.i.f.: cost, insurance, and freight;   f.o.b.: free on board

Real progress was made in Northern Ireland on the decommissioning of arms by the Irish Republican Army (IRA), despite the IRA's foot dragging throughout 2000 and most of 2001. The head of the Northern Ireland Executive, First Minister David Trimble, had threatened to resign in 2000 and did resign in July 2001 and withdrew his party's support over the IRA's inaction, leading the UK's Northern Ireland secretary to suspend the Executive during cooling-off periods. By an October 2001 deadline, an independent international commission verified that the IRA had put a significant amount of arms, ammunition, and explosives beyond use. In November Trimble was reelected first minister.

Blair responded to the terrorist attacks on the US by throwing his full support to the US, pledging British troops and resources, helping to ensure EU and NATO support for military action, and launching a diplomatic initiative that included visits to Russia, Pakistan, India, and several countries of the Middle East.

Internet resources: <www.uktravel.com>

United States

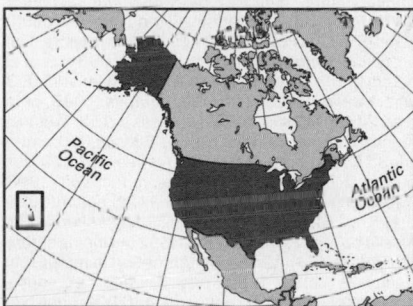

Official name: United States of America. **Form of government:** federal republic with two legislative houses (Senate [100]; House of Representatives [435; excludes 5 delegates having only committee voting rights]). **Head of state and government:** President George W. Bush (from 20 Jan 2001). **Capital:** Washington DC. **Official language:** none. **Official religion:** none. **Monetary unit:** 1 dollar ($) = 100 cents.

Demography

Area: 3,675,031 sq mi, 9,518,323 sq km (total area per most recent official survey equals 3,675,267 sq mi [9,518,898 sq km], of which land area equals 3,536,278 sq mi [9,158,918 sq km], inland water area equals 78,937 sq mi [204,446 sq km], and Great Lakes water area equals 60,052 sq mi [155,534 sq km]). **Population** (2001): 286,067,000 (includes military personnel residing overseas). **Density** (2001; includes military personnel residing overseas): persons per sq mi 77.8, persons per sq km 30.5. **Urban** (2000): 77.2%. **Sex distribution** (2000): male 49.06%; female 50.94%. **Age breakdown** (2000): under 15, 21.4%; 15–29, 20.8%; 30–44, 23.3%; 45–59, 18.2%; 60–74, 10.4%; 75 and over, 5.9%. **Population by race and Hispanic origin** (1999; persons of Hispanic origin may be of any race): non-Hispanic white 71.9%; non-Hispanic black 12.1%; Hispanic 11.6%; Asian and Pacific Islander 3.7%; Ameri-

can Indian and Eskimo 0.7%. **Religious affiliation** (1995): Christian 85.3%, of which Protestant 57.9%, Roman Catholic 21.0%, other Christian 6.4%; Jewish 2.1%; Muslim 1.9%; nonreligious 8.7%, other 2.0%. **Mobility** (1999). Pop. living in the same residence as in 1998: 84.0%; different residence, same county 9.0%; different county, same state 3.0%; different state 3.0%; moved from abroad 1.0%. **Households** (1999). Total households 103,874,000 (married-couple families 54,770,000 [52.7%]). Average household size (1998) 2.6; 1 person 25.6%, 2 persons 32.2%, 3 persons 16.9%, 4 persons 15.0%, 5 or more persons 10.2%. Family households: 71,535,000 (68.9%); nonfamily 32,339,000 (31.1%), of which 1-person 82.2%. **Immigration** (1998; fiscal year ending 30 Sep): permanent immigrants admitted 660,477, from Mexico 19.9%, China 5.6%, India 5.5%, Philippines 5.2%, Dominican Republic 3.1%, Cuba 2.9%, Vietnam 2.7%, Ukraine 2.6%, Jamaica 2.3%, El Salvador 2.2%, South Korea 2.2%, Pakistan 2.0%, Russia 1.7%. Refugee arrivals (1998; fiscal year ending 30 Sep): 54,645. **Major cities** (1999): New York 7,428,162; Los Angeles 3,633,591; Chicago 2,799,050; Houston 1,845,967; Philadelphia 1,417,601; San Diego 1,238,974; Phoenix 1,211,466; San Antonio 1,147,213; Dallas 1,076,214; Detroit 965,084. **Location:** North America, bordering Canada, the Atlantic Ocean, the Gulf of Mexico, Mexico, and the Pacific Ocean. Outlying state of Alaska nearly touches eastern Russia and borders the Arctic Ocean and the Atlantic Ocean; Hawaii is an island group in the Pacific Ocean. **Place of birth** (1999): native-born 245,295,000 (90.3%); foreign-born 26,448,000 (9.7%), of which Mexico 7,197,000, Philippines 1,455,000, China and Hong Kong 985,000, Vietnam 966,000, Cuba 943,000, India 839,000, El Salvador 761,000, South Korea 611,000.

Vital statistics

Birth rate per 1,000 pop. (1999): 14.3 (world avg. 22.5); (1998) legitimate 67.2%; illegitimate 32.8%. **Death rate** per 1,000 pop. (1999): 8.7 (world avg. 9.0). **Natural increase rate** per 1,000 pop. (1999): 5.6 (world avg. 13.5). **Total fertility rate** (avg. births per childbearing woman; 1999): 2.0. **Marriage rate** per 1,000 pop. (1998): 8.3; median age at first marriage (1991): men 26.3 years, women 24.1 years. **Divorce rate** per 1,000 pop. (1998): 3.1. **Life expectancy** at birth (1998): white male 74.8 years, black and other male (1996) 68.9 years; white female 79.9 years, black and other female (1996) 76.1 years. **Morbidity rates of infectious diseases** per 100,000 pop. (1998): chlamydia 223.4; gonorrhea 131.7; chicken pox 30.5; AIDS 17.2; syphilis 14.0; salmonellosis 16.2; shigellosis 8.7; hepatitis A (infectious) 8.6; tuberculosis 6.8; lyme disease 6.2; hepatitis B (serum) 3.8; pertussis 2.7. **Incidence of chronic health conditions** per 1,000 pop. (1990). chronic sinusitis 125.0; arthritis 126.8; deformities or orthopedic impairments 111.2; hypertension 100.8; hay fever 89.4; hearing impairment 83.1; heart conditions 77.9; asthma 55.0; chronic bronchitis 53.4; migraine 43.5.

Social indicators

Educational attainment (1996). Percentage of pop. age 25 and over having: some primary 9.3%; incomplete secondary 16.5%; secondary 35.1%; some postsecondary 25.5%; 4-year higher degree or more

13.6%. Number of earned degrees (1995): bachelor's degree 1,192,000; master's degree 405,000; doctor's degree 43,000; first-professional degrees (in fields such as medicine, theology, and law) 77,000. **Quality of working life** (1999). Average workweek: 39.5 hours. Annual rate per 100,000 workers for (1995): injury or accident 2,720; death 4.0. Proportion of labor force insured for damages or income loss resulting from: injury, permanent disability, and death (1988) 56.6%. Average days per 1,000 workdays lost to labor stoppages (1996): 1.6. Average duration of journey to work (1990): 22.4 minutes (private automobile 94.7%, of which drive alone 80.0%, carpool 14.7%; take public transportation 5.3%). Rate per 1,000 employed workers of discouraged workers (unemployed no longer seeking work; 1992): 6.9. **Access to services** (1995). Proportion of occupied dwellings having access to: electricity, virtually 100.0%; safe public water supply 99.4% (12.6% from wells); public sewage collection 77.0%; septic tanks 22.8%. **Social participation.** Eligible voters participating in last presidential election (2000): 51.2%. Pop. age 18 and over participating in voluntary work (1999): 66.0%. Trade-union membership in total workforce (1996): 14.5%. Practicing religious pop. in total affiliated pop. (church attendance; 1987) once a week 47%; once in six months 67%; once a year 74%. **Social deviance** (1998). Offense rate per 100,000 pop. for: murder 6.3; rape 34.4; robbery 165.2; aggravated assault 360.5; motor-vehicle theft 459.0; burglary and housebreaking 862.0; larceny-theft 2,728.1; drug-abuse violation 434.2 (1995); drunkenness 200.2 (1995). Drug and substance users (pop. age 26 and over; 1994): alcohol 41.2%; tobacco (cigarettes) 33.5%; marijuana 16.0%; cocaine 0.4%; analgesics 1.3%; tranquilizers 0.2%; stimulants 0.4%; hallucinogens 1.2%; Rate per 100,000 pop. of suicide (1997): 11.5. **Leisure** (1997). Favorite leisure activities (percentage of total pop. age 18 and over that undertook activity at least once in the previous year): movie 66.0%, amusement park 57.0%, sports event 41.0%, exercise program 76.0%, home improvement 66.0%; charity work 43.0%, playing sports 45.0%. **Material well-being** (1995). Occupied dwellings with householder possessing: (1988) automobile (1988) 84.9%; telephone 93.9%; radio receiver 99.0%; television receiver 98.3%; air conditioner (1993) 68.4%; washing machine (1993) 77.1%; video-cassette recorder 81.0%; cable television 63.4%. **Recreational expenditures** (1998): $494,700,000,000 (television and radio receivers, computers, and video equipment 18.7%; sports supplies 11.7%; golfing, bowling, and other participatory activities 11.4%; nondurable toys and sports equipment 9.5%; magazines and newspapers 6.4%; books and maps 5.6%; spectator amusements 4.8%, of which theater and opera 1.9%, movies 1.4%, spectator sports 1.5%; flowers, seeds, and potted plants 3.3%).

National economy

Budget (2000). *Revenue:* $2,046,800,000,000 (individual income tax 49.3%, social-insurance taxes and contributions 33.8%, corporation income tax 11.5%, excise taxes 3.4%, customs duties 1.0%, other 1.0%). *Expenditures:* $1,741,000,000,000 (social security and medicare 32.4%, defense 17.4%, interest on debt 15.1%, other 35.1%). **Total national debt** (2000):

$5,686,338,000,000. **Gross national product** (2000): $9,860,800,000,000 ($35,040 per capita). **Business activity** (1997): number of businesses 23,645,000 (sole proprietorships 72.6%, active corporations 19.9%, active partnerships 7.5%), of which services 10,114,000, wholesaling and retailing 4,455,000; business receipts $18,057,000,000,000 (active corporations 88.0%, sole proprietorships 4.8%, active partnerships 7.2%), of which wholesaling and retailing $5,136,000,000,000, services $2,130,-000,000,000; net profit $1,270,000,000,000 (active corporations 72.0%, sole proprietorships 14.7%, partnerships 13.3%), of which services $203,000,-000,000, wholesaling and retailing $10,000,000,-000. New business starts and business failures (1995): total number of new business starts 168,158; total failures 71,194, of which commercial service 21,850, retail trade 12,952; failure rate per 10,000 concerns 90.0; current liabilities of failed concerns $37,507,000,000; average liability $526,830. Business expenditures for new plant and equipment (1995): total $594,465,000,000, of which trade, services, and communications $244,829,000,000, manufacturing businesses $172,308,000,000 (durable goods 53.0%, nondurable goods 47.0%), public utilities $42,816,000,000, transportation $37,021,000,000, mining and construction $35,985,000. **Production.** *Agriculture, forestry, fishing* (value of production/catch in $'000,000 except as noted; 2000): corn (maize) 18,621, soybeans 13,073, wheat 5,970, cotton lint 4,781, grapes 3,063, potatoes 2,539, tobacco 2,056, oranges 1,752; livestock (number of live animals; 2000) 98,048,000 cattle, 59,337,000 pigs, 7,215,000 sheep, 5,320,000 horses, 1,720,000,000 chickens; roundwood (1998) 420,458,000 cu m; fish and shellfish catch (1998) 3,128, of which fish 1,447 (including salmon 257, Alaska pollack 190), shellfish 1,682 (including shrimp 516, crabs 473). *Mining* (metal content in metric tons except as noted; 1996): iron 39,342,000; copper 1,910,000; zinc 620,000; lead 430,000; molybdenum 57,000; vanadium 2,700; mercury 550; silver 1,800,000 kg. *Quarrying* (metric tons; 1996): crushed stone 1,300,000,000; sand and gravel 992,000,000; cement 75,000,000; clay 44,000,000; phosphate rock 43,000,000; common salt 40,000,000; gypsum 17,000,000; lime 18,900,000. *Manufacturing* (1996): motor vehicles 329,155; industrial machinery 135,393; electronic components 127,996; computers and office equipment 103,270; meat products 102,103; aircraft 83,394; commercial printing 67,842; medical instruments 47,406. *Energy production (consumption):* electricity (kW-hr; 1994) 3,268,250,000,000 (3,312,888,000,000); coal (metric tons; 1994) 937,580,000 (843,873,000); crude petroleum (barrels; 1994) 2,464,000,000 (5,024,000,000); petroleum products (metric tons; 1994) 704,201,000 (737,681,000); natural gas (cu m; 1994) 530,014,000,000 (592,209,000,000). Domestic production of energy by source (1994): coal 31.2%, natural gas 27.6%, crude petroleum 19.9%, other (includes hydroelectric, nuclear, and geothermal power) 21.3%. *Energy consumption by source* (1997): petroleum and petroleum products 38.6%, natural gas 24.1%, coal 22.3%, other (includes hydroelectric, nuclear, and geothermal power) 15.0%; *by end use:* industrial 38.0%, residential and commercial 35.5%, transportation 26.5%. **Household income and expen-**

---

1 metric ton = about 1.1 short tons;　1 kilometer = 0.6 mi (statute);　1 metric ton-km cargo = about 0.68 short ton-mi cargo;　c.i.f.: cost, insurance, and freight;　f.o.b.: free on board

diture. Average household size (1997) 2.6; average (median) annual income per household $37,005, of which average white household $35,766, average Hispanic (persons of Hispanic origin may be of any race) household $22,860, average black household $22,393; sources of income: wages and salaries 55.8%, transfer payments 16.5%, self-employment 7.9%, other 19.8%; expenditure: transportation 18.6%, housing 18.4%, food 14.0%, fuel and utilities 6.8%, household furnishings 5.9%, recreation 5.5%, health 5.4%, wearing apparel 5.3%, education 1.5%, other 18.6%. **Average annual expenditure** of "consumer units" (households, plus individuals sharing households or budgets; 1997–98): total $35,535, of which housing $11,713, transportation $6,616, food $4,810, pensions and social security $2,982, health care $1,903, clothing $1,674, other $5,837. **Selected household characteristics** (1996). Total number of households 99,627,000, of which (by race) white 84.8%, black 11.6%, other 3.6%; in central cities (1994) 31.4%, in suburbs (1994) 46.3%, outside metropolitan areas (1994) 22.3%; (by tenure; 1994) owned 64,045,000 (64.7%), rented 34,946,000 (35.3%); family households 69,594,000, of which married couple 76.9%, female head with own children ("own children" includes adopted children and stepchildren) under age 18, 11.0%, female head without own children ("own children" includes adopted children and stepchildren) under 18, 7.0%; nonfamily households 30,033,000, of which female living alone 48.6%, male living alone 34.2%, other 17.2%. **Population economically active** (1999): total (excludes military personnel overseas) 139,368,000; activity rate of total pop. 51.1% (participation rates: ages 15–64, 80.0%; female 46.5%; unemployed 4.2%). **Tourism** (1998): receipts from visitors $91,240,000,000; expenditures by nationals abroad $75,902,000,000; number of foreign visitors 46,395,000 (13,422,000 from Canada, 9,276,000 from Mexico, 10,675,000 from Europe); number of nationals traveling abroad 56,287,000 (18,338,000 to Mexico, 14,880,000 to Canada). **Land use** (1994): forested 32.3%; meadows and pastures 26.1%; agricultural and under permanent cultivation 20.5%; other 21.0%.

Foreign trade

Imports (1999): $1,025,032,000,000 (machinery and transport equipment 41.6%, of which motor vehicles and parts 14.3%; wearing apparel 6.9%; chemicals and chemical products 6.1%; petroleum and petroleum products 6.3%; food and live animals 3.4%). *Major import sources:* Canada 19.3%; Japan 12.8%; Mexico 10.7%; China 8.0%; Germany 5.4%; UK 3.8%; Taiwan 3.4%; South Korea 3.0%; France 2.5%; Italy 2.2%; Malaysia 2.1%; Singapore 1.8%; Thailand 1.4%; Philippines 1.2%; Brazil 1.1%. **Exports** (1999): $695,009,000,000 (machinery and transport equipment 47.1%, of which motor vehicles and parts 7.7%; chemicals and related products 8.1%; scientific and precision equipment 4.5%; food and live animals 5.3%). *Major export destinations:* Canada 23.9%; Mexico 12.2%; Japan 8.3%; UK 5.4%; Germany 3.8%; South Korea 3.3%; Taiwan 2.8%; The Netherlands 2.8%; France 2.7%; Singapore 2.3%; Brazil 1.9%; China 1.9%.

Transport and communications

Transport. *Railroads* (1997): length (1994) 222,000 km; passenger-km 22,500,000,000; metric ton-km cargo 2,075,000,000. *Roads* (1998): total length

6,286,396 km (paved 91.0%). *Vehicles* (1998): passenger cars 131,839,000; trucks and buses 79,778,000. *Air transport* (1998): passenger-km 997,000,000,000; metric ton-km cargo 26,449,000,000; localities (1996) with scheduled flights 834 (includes 292 localities in Alaska). Certified route passenger/cargo air carriers (1992) 77; operating revenue ($'000,000; 1991) 74,942, of which domestic 56,119, international 18,823; operating expenses 76,669, of which domestic 56,596, international 20,073. **Communications** Total units (units per 1,000 persons). Daily newspaper circulation (1996): 57,100,000 (215); Radio receivers (1997): 575,000,000 (2,116); Television receivers (1999): 233,000,000 (843); Telephone main lines (1999): 183,521,000 (664); Cellular telephone subscribers (1999): 86,047,000 (307); Personal computers (1999): 141,000,000 (510); Internet users (1998): 81,000,000 (290).

Education and health

Literacy: studies in the late 1980s indicated that adult "functional" literacy may not exceed 85%. **Food** (1999): daily per capita caloric intake 3,754 (vegetable products 72%, animal products 28%); 142% of FAO recommended minimum. Per capita consumption of major food groups (kilograms annually; 1995): milk 255.7; fresh fruits 123.2; cereal products 114.5; fresh vegetables 110.4; red meat 74.8; sweeteners 69.3; potatoes 58.7; poultry products 43.8; fats and oils 30.8; fish and shellfish 21.8. **Health** (1995): doctors of medicine 720,300 (1 per 365 persons; 646,000 professionally active), of which office based practice 427,300 (including specialties in internal medicine 17.0%, general and family practice 14.0%, pediatrics 7.9%, obstetrics and gynecology 6.8%, general surgery 5.6%, psychiatry 5.4%, anesthesiology 5.6%, orthopedics 4.0%, ophthalmology 4.3%); doctors of osteopathy 35,700; nurses 2,116,000 (1 per 124 persons); dentists 190,000 (1 per 1,385 persons); hospital beds 1,081,000 (1 per 243 persons), of which nonfederal 92.9% (community hospitals 80.8%, psychiatric 10.2%, long-term general and special 1.8%), federal 7.1%; infant mortality rate per 1,000 live births (1997) 7.1.

Military

Total active duty personnel (2000): 1,365,800 (army 34.6%, navy 27.1%, air force 25.9%, marines 12.4%). **Military expenditure as percentage of GNP** (1997): 3.3% (world 2.6%); per capita expenditure $1,024. **Military aid** (1993): total $4,143,000,000 (Middle East 76.2%, of which Israel 43.4%, Egypt 31.4%; Europe 20.8%, of which Turkey 10.9%; Latin America 1.8%).

Background

The territory that is now the US was originally inhabited for several thousand years by numerous American Indian peoples who had probably emigrated from Asia. European exploration and settlement from the 16th century began displacement of the Indians. The first permanent European settlement, by the Spanish, was at St. Augustine FL, in 1565; the British settled Jamestown VA (1607), Plymouth MA (1620), Maryland (1632), and Pennsylvania (1681). They took New York, New Jersey, and Delaware from the Dutch in 1664, a year before the Carolinas had been granted to British noblemen. The British defeat of the French in 1763 assured British political control over the 13 colonies.

Political unrest caused by British colonial policy culminated in the American Revolution (1775–83) and the Declaration of Independence (1776). The US was first organized under the Articles of Confederation (1781), then finally under the Constitution (1787) as a federal republic. Boundaries extended west to the Mississippi River, excluding Spanish Florida. Land acquired from France by the Louisiana Purchase (1803) nearly doubled the country's territory. The US fought the War of 1812 with the British and acquired Florida from Spain in 1819. In 1830 it legalized removal of American Indians to lands west of the Mississippi River. Settlement expanded to the west coast in the mid-19th century, especially after the discovery of gold in California in 1848. Victory in the Mexican War (1846–48) brought the territory of seven more future states (including California and Texas) into US hands. The northwestern boundary was established by treaty with Great Britain in 1846. The US acquired southern Arizona by the Gadsden Purchase (1853). It suffered disunity during the conflict between the slavery-based plantation economy in the South and the free industrial and agricultural economy in the North, culminating in the American Civil War, and the abolition of slavery under the 13th Amendment.

After Reconstruction (1865–77), the US experienced rapid growth, urbanization, industrial development, and European immigration. In 1877 it authorized allotment of Indian reservation land to individual tribesmen, resulting in widespread loss of land to whites. By the beginning of the 20th century, it had acquired outlying territories, including Alaska, the Midway Islands, the Hawaiian Islands, the Philippines, Puerto Rico, Guam, Wake Island, American Samoa, the Panama Canal Zone, and the Virgin Islands.

The US participated in World War I during 1917–18. It granted suffrage to women in 1920 and citizenship to American Indians in 1924. The stock market crash of 1929 led to the Great Depression. The US entered World War II after the Japanese bombing of Pearl Harbor (7 Dec 1941). The explosion of the first atomic bomb on Hiroshima, Japan (6 Aug 1945), brought about the end of the war and made the US the leader of the Western world. After the war the US was involved in the reconstruction of Europe and Japan and embroiled in a rivalry with the Soviet Union that became known as the Cold War. It participated in the Korean War. In 1952 it granted autonomous commonwealth status to Puerto Rico.

Racial segregation in schools was declared unconstitutional in 1954. Alaska and Hawaii were made states in 1959, bringing the total to 50. In 1964 Congress passed the Civil Rights Act and authorized full-scale intervention in the Vietnam War. The mid- to late 1960s were marked by widespread civil disorders, including race riots and antiwar demonstrations. The US accomplished the first manned lunar landing in 1969. All US troops were withdrawn from Vietnam by 1973. The US led a coalition of forces against Iraq in the Persian Gulf War (1991), sent troops to Somalia (1992) to aid starving populations, and participated in NATO air strikes against Serb forces in the former Yugoslavia in 1995 and 1999. Administration of the Panama Canal was turned over to Panama in 1999.

Recent Developments

Few events in US history had the impact of the terrorist attacks of 11 Sep 2001. Two hijacked passenger airliners crashed into the two World Trade Center towers in New York City, causing their collapse; a third plane hit the Pentagon in Washington DC; and a fourth that was apparently intended for a Washington target, whose passengers overcame the hijackers, crashed into a field in Pennsylvania. Everyone on the four planes was killed, along with thousands in the target buildings; the death total topped 3,000. The worldwide reaction was immediate: NATO invoked Article 5 for the first time in its history, in which an attack on one member is viewed as an attack on all; the Organization of American States invoked its mutual defense treaty; and heads of government around the world offered their sympathy and pledged aid. Osama bin Laden, a former Saudi citizen who ran a terrorist training network under the protection of the extreme Islamic fundamentalist Taliban in Afghanistan, was identified as the mastermind. The US closed its airspace and shut down all airports for the first time in history and moved swiftly to promise reprisals, identify the perpetrators, and institute safety measures, creating the Office of Homeland Security to coordinate antiterrorism efforts. Stunned Americans pledged millions in aid to the victims and their families, rallied around the president, and came together in an outpouring of solidarity and patriotic sentiment. Anxiety increased when it was discovered that letters contaminated with anthrax had been sent to individuals in the media and government; five persons had died from anthrax by year's end.

US Pres. George W. Bush took office in January 2001 after one of the closest and most controversial elections in history. Acceptance of his victory over the Democrat Al Gore, who won the popular vote but not the electoral vote, was postponed while votes were recounted until the US Supreme Court stopped the process, in effect declaring Bush the winner. The Republicans and Democrats were evenly split in the Senate (the advantage went to the Democrats when a senator from Vermont changed his party affiliation to Independent in May), while the Republicans enjoyed a slim majority in the House of Representatives. One of Bush's first legislative initiatives involved a 10-year, $1.6 trillion tax cut package. Although Congress was quick to approve antiterrorist appropriations and legislation, through partisan opposition other administration bills failed to pass, affecting many domestic issues that had been debated for years.

World opinion rallied against what was seen as a disturbing trend of the US failing to participate in mutinational treaties and initiatives, including the Kyoto Protocol on global warming and the UN World Conference Against Racism. Some 60 countries, however, including Muslim Pakistan, offered assistance to the US in a military assault against Bin Laden's al-Qaeda network in Afghanistan. After the Taliban refused to turn over Bin Laden, on 7 Oct 2001 air attacks began throughout Afghanistan. By year's end the Taliban had been driven from power, replaced by a UN-brokered coalition. The al-Qaeda leaders for the most part evaded capture, however. Russia's support in the endeavor led to improved relations. The US announced a sharp decrease in nuclear warheads over the next decade and Russia hinted at similar reductions. When the two nations failed to agree over al-

---

1 metric ton = about 1.1 short tons;   1 kilometer = 0.6 mi (statute);   1 metric ton-km cargo = about 0.68 short ton-mi cargo;   c.i.f.: cost, insurance, and freight;   f.o.b.: free on board

lowing the US to test a missile defense system, the US withdrew from the 1972 Anti-Ballistic Missile Treaty.

Riding a decade-long economic expansion, the GDP expanded by 4.2% in 1999 and by 5.6% in the first half of 2000. A healthy budget surplus was recorded in 2000. In the second half of the year the expansion slowed, however, beginning a steady descent. Factors blamed were worldwide oil price increases, anti-inflationary increases in interest rates, a precipitous drop in tech stocks, the collapse of many dubious dot-com enterprises, and the loss of revenues after the terrorist attacks that brought many businesses to a standstill. Widespread layoffs and cutbacks made unemployment figures soar, stock market averages fall steadily, and the budget surplus evaporate. Conditions began to improve somewhat by the end of 2001, when the energy giant Enron Corporation, the seventh largest employer in the US, filed for bankruptcy. The value of its stock evaporated, wiping out thousands of investors, including many of the corporation's employees. It was charged that Enron executives had colluded with their accounting firm, Arthur Andersen, to grossly misrepresent the state of the company's finances and had sold their own stock while prices remained artificially high.

The census of 2000 revealed that over the past decade the US population had grown by 13%. Immigrants constituted 11% of the population, the highest proportion since the 1930s; the Hispanic population rose by 58%. In many cities, non-whites constituted a majority.

Internet resources: <www.tourstates.com>

Uruguay

Atlantic Ocean

Official name: República Oriental del Uruguay (Oriental Republic of Uruguay). Form of government: republic with two legislative houses (Senate [31, includes the vice president who serves as ex-officio presiding officer]; Chamber of Representatives [99]). Head of state and government: President Jorge Batlle (from 2000). Capital: Montevideo. Official language: Spanish. Official religion: none. Monetary unit: 1 peso uruguayo ($U; replaced the Uruguayan peso [Nur$] in 1993) = 100 centésimos; valuation (28 Jun 2002) US$1 = $U 18.73.

Demography

Area: 68,037 sq mi, 176,215 sq km. Population (2001): 3,303,000. Density (2001): persons per sq mi 48.6, persons per sq km 18.7. Urban (1996): 89.0%. Sex distribution (2000): male 48.51%; female 51.49%. Age breakdown (2000): under 15, 24.8%; 15–29, 23.4%; 30–44, 19.4%; 45–59, 15.3%; 60–74, 11.9%; 75 and over, 5.2%. Ethnic composition (1990): white (mostly Spanish, Italian, or mixed Spanish-Italian) 86.0%; mestizo 8.0%; mulatto or black 6.0%. Religious affiliation (1997): Roman Catholic 78.5% (of which about 30-40% are estimated to be nonreligious); Protestant 4.5%; other Christian 3.5%; Jewish 0.9%; other 12.6%. Major cities (1996): Montevideo 1,378,707; Salto 93,113; Paysandú 74,568; Las Piedras 66,584; Rivera 62,859. Location: southern South America, bordering Brazil, the South Atlantic Ocean, and Argentina.

Vital statistics

Birth rate per 1,000 pop. (2000): 17.4 (world avg. 22.5). Death rate per 1,000 pop. (2000): 9.1 (world avg. 9.0). Total fertility rate (avg. births per childbearing woman; 2000): 2.4. Marriage rate per 1,000 pop. (1996): 5.6. Divorce rate per 1,000 pop. (1996): 2.1. Life expectancy at birth (2000): male 71.9 years; female 78.8 years.

National economy

Budget (1998). Revenue: $U 70,664,000,000 (taxes on goods and services 39.4%, social security contributions 28.6%, income taxes 12.6%, nontax revenue 7.1%, receipts from foreign trade 3.7%). Expenditures: $U 72,673,000,000 (social security and welfare 61.4%, general public services 7.4%, education 7.0%, health 5.8%, interest payments 4.7%). Public debt (external, outstanding; 1999): $5,108,000,000. Production (metric tons except as noted). Agriculture, forestry, fishing (1999): rice 1,328,000, wheat 377,000, corn (maize) 243,000; livestock (number of live animals) 15,500,000 sheep, 10,700,000 cattle; roundwood (1998) 6,163,000 cu m; fish catch (1998) 140,609. Mining and quarrying (1997): hydraulic cement 770,000; gypsum 183,000. Manufacturing (value added in $'000,000; 1995): food products 1,012; beverages 426; chemical products 402. Energy production (consumption): electricity (kW-hr; 1996) 6,666,000,000 (6,538,000,000); crude petroleum, none (13,942,000); petroleum products (metric tons; 1996) 1,821,000 (1,626,000). Land use (1998): forested and other 15.2%; meadows and pastures 77.3%; agricultural and under permanent cultivation 7.5%. Household income and expenditure. Avg. household size (1985) 3.3; avg. annual income per household (1985; Uruguayan peso [Nur$ replaced in 1993 by the peso Uruguayo ($U)]) Nur$266,261; sources of income (salaried employees only): wages 53.5%, self employment 17.0%, transfer payments and other 29.5%; expenditure (1982–83; weights of consumer price index components in Montevideo): food 39.9%, housing 17.6%, transportation and communications 10.4%, health care 9.3%, clothing 7.0%. Gross national product (1999): $20,604,000,000 ($6,220 per capita). Population economically active (1998): total 1,239,400; activity rate 47.0% (participation rates: ages 14 and over, 60.4%; female 44.0%). Tourism (1999): receipts $653,000,000; expenditures $280,000,000.

Foreign trade

Imports (1999): $3,356,770,000 (machinery and appliances 22.2%; chemical products 14.6%; mineral products 11.6%; transport equipment 9.1%; processed foods 7.1%; synthetic plastics, resins, and rubber 7.0%; metal products 4.8%). *Major import sources* (1998): Argentina 22.0%; Brazil 20.8%; US 12.1%; France 4.7%; Italy 4.6%; Spain 3.7%. **Exports** (1999): $2,236,848,000 (live animals and live-animal products 30.1%; vegetable products 15.8%; textiles and textile products 11.8%; hides and skins 9.8%; processed foods 5.4%). *Major export destinations* (1998): Brazil 33.8%; Argentina 18.5%; US 5.7%; Germany 4.0%.

Transport and communications

Transport. *Railroads* (1996): route length 2,073 km; metric ton-km cargo 180,000,000. *Roads* (1997; excludes streets under local control): length 8,683 km (paved 30%). *Vehicles* (1997): passenger cars 516,889; trucks and buses 50,264. *Air transport* (1996): passenger-km 640,000,000; metric ton-km cargo 62,000,000; airports (1997) with scheduled flights 1. **Communications** Total units (units per 1,000 persons). Daily newspaper circulation (1996): 950,000 (293); Radio receivers (1997): 1,970,000 (603); Television receivers (1999): 1,760,000 (531); Telephone main lines (1999): 896,849 (271); Cellular telephone subscribers (1999): 316,131 (95); Personal computers (1999): 330,000 (100); Internet users (1999): 330,000 (100).

Education and health

Educational attainment (1996). Percentage of pop. age 25 and over having: no formal schooling 3.4%; primary education 53.6%; secondary 31.7%; higher 10.1%; unknown 1.2%. **Literacy** (1995 est.): pop. age 15 and over literate 97.3%; males 96.9%; females 97.7%. **Health** (1999): physicians 12,357 (1 per 263 persons); hospital beds 6,651 (1 per 488 persons); infant mortality rate (2000) 15.1. **Food** (1999): daily per capita caloric intake 2,862 (vegetable products 61%, animal products 39%); (1997) 107% of FAO recommended minimum.

Military

Total active duty personnel (2000): 23,700 (army 64.1%, navy 23.2%, air force 12.7%). **Military expenditure as percentage of GNP** (1997): 1.4% (world 2.6%); per capita expenditure $88.

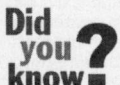

Did you know? Second only to Suriname, Uruguay is the smallest country in South America. It is largely treeless with vegetation consisting mostly of tall prairie grass.

Background

The Spanish navigator Juan Díaz de Solís sailed into the Río de la Plata in 1516. The Portuguese established Colonia in 1680. Subsequently, the Spanish established Montevideo in 1726, driving the Portuguese from their settlement; 50 years later Uruguay became part of the viceroyalty of Río de la Plata. It gained independence from Spain in 1811. The Portuguese regained it in 1821, incorporating it into Brazil as a province. A revolt against Brazil in 1825 led to its being recognized as an independent state in 1828. It battled Paraguay 1865–70. For much of World War II it remained neutral. The presidential office was abolished in 1951 and replaced with a nine-member council. The country adopted a new constitution and restored the presidential system in 1966. A military coup occurred in 1973, but the country returned to civilian rule in 1985. The 1990s brought a general upturn in the economy.

Recent Developments

In March 2000 a new president, Jorge Batlle Ibáñez, took office at the head of the Colorado Party, ruling in a coalition with the Blanco Party. He called for trade and governmental reforms. Departmental elections in May saw power split between party coalitions along rural-urban lines. Batlle established a commission to investigate the fate of some 150–180 Uruguayans who had disappeared during the period when the country was a military dictatorship, 1973–85. The commission revealed that Uruguayan armed forces had taken part in Operation Condor, an antiterrorist campaign. Children of persons detained by the government had been taken from their parents and given to the families of policemen or soldiers. One was the grandchild of Argentine poet Juan Gelman, whose daughter-in-law had been kidnapped in Argentina in 1976.

An outbreak of foot-and-mouth disease in 2001 damaged Uruguay's important meat-export industry. The economy was also hit hard by economic crises in Brazil and Argentina, which adversely affected both exports and tourism. Unemployment rose to 16%, and the GDP rate slid to a negative phase.

Internet resources: <www.uruguay.com>

Uzbekistan

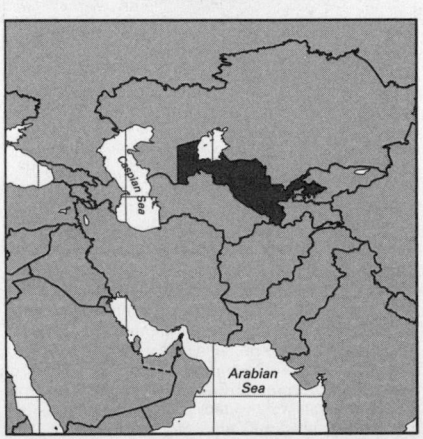

---

1 metric ton = about 1.1 short tons;   1 kilometer = 0.6 mi (statute);   1 metric ton-km cargo = about 0.68 short ton-mi cargo;   c.i.f.: cost, insurance, and freight;   f.o.b.: free on board

Official name: Uzbekiston Respublikasi (Republic of Uzbekistan). **Form of government:** multiparty republic with a single legislative body (Supreme Assembly [250]). **Heads of state and government:** President Islam Karimov (from 1990) assisted by Prime Minister Otkir Sultonov (from 1995). **Capital:** Tashkent (Toshkent). **Official language:** Uzbek. **Official religion:** none. **Monetary unit:** sum (plural sumy); valuation (28 Jun 2002) $1 = 750.05 sumy.

Demography

Area: 172,700 sq mi, 447,400 sq km. **Population** (2001): 25,155,000. **Density** (2001): persons per sq mi 145.7, persons per sq km 56.2. **Urban** (1999): 37.1%. **Sex distribution** (1999): male 49.55%; female 50.45%. **Age breakdown** (1999): under 15, 37.9%; 15–29, 27.7%; 30–44, 19.4%; 45–59, 8.1%; 60–74, 5.5%; 75 and over, 1.4%. **Ethnic composition** (1998): Uzbek 75.8%; Russian 6.0%; Tajik 4.8%; Kazakh 4.1%; Tatar 1.6%; other 7.7%. **Religious affiliation** (2000): Muslim (mostly Sunni) 76.2%; nonreligious 18.1%; Russian Orthodox 0.8%; Jewish 0.2%; other 4.7%. **Major cities** (1998 est.): Tashkent 2,124,000; Samarkand 388,000; Namangan 291,000; Andijon 288,000; Bukhara 220,000. **Location:** Central Asia, bordering Kazakhstan, Kyrgyzstan, Tajikistan, Afghanistan, and Turkmenistan.

Vital statistics

Birth rate per 1,000 pop. (2001): 21.7 (world avg. 22.5); (1994) legitimate 96.5%; illegitimate 3.5%. **Death rate** per 1,000 pop. (2001): 5.9 (world avg. 9.0). **Natural increase rate** per 1,000 pop. (2001): 15.8 (world avg. 13.5). **Total fertility rate** (avg. births per childbearing woman; 2001): 3.1. **Marriage rate** per 1,000 pop. (1994): 7.9. **Divorce rate** per 1,000 pop. (1994): 1.1. **Life expectancy** at birth (2001): male 66.0 years; female 72.0 years.

National economy

Budget (1998). *Revenue:* 440,140,000,000 sumy (taxes on income and profits 31.5%, value-added tax 30.2%, excise taxes 18.9%, property and land taxes 12.5%, other 6.9%). *Expenditures:* 488,297,000,000 sumy (social and cultural affairs 34.2%, investments 19.4%, national economy 11.2%, transfers 9.2%, administration 2.3%, interest on debt 2.0%, other 21.7%). **Household income and expenditure** (1995). Average household size (1998) 5.5; income per household 35,165 sumy; sources of income: wages and salaries 63.0%, subsidies, grants, and nonwage income 34.9%, other 2.1%; expenditure: food and beverages 71%, clothing and footwear 14%, recreation 6%, household durables 4%, housing 3%. **Public debt** (external, outstanding; 1999): $3,421,000,000. *Agriculture, forestry, fishing* (1999): seed cotton 3,680,000, vegetables 2,800,000, fruit (except grapes) and berries 1,350,000; livestock (number of live animals) 8,000,000 sheep, 5,225,200 cattle, 697,900 goats; roundwood (1990) 15,000 cu m; fish catch (1998) 2,798. *Mining and quarrying* (1998): copper 89,930; zinc 38,000; uranium 2,000. *Manufacturing* (metric tons except as noted; 1998): cement 3,358,000; cotton fiber 1,138,000; mineral fertilizer 897,000. *Energy production (consumption):* electricity (kW-hr; 1998) 46,056,000,000 (46,100,000,000), coal (metric tons; 1998) 2,952,000

(2,792,000); crude petroleum (barrels; 1998) 59,400,000 (57,870,000); petroleum products (metric tons; 1998) 8,104,000 (6,934,000); natural gas (cu m; 1998) 51,245,000,000 (44,246,000,000). **Gross national product** (1999): $17,613,000,000 ($720 per capita). **Population economically active** (1999): total 8,831,000; activity rate of total pop. 36.4% (participation rates: ages 16–59 [male], 16–54 [female] 70.4%; female [1994] 43.0%; unemployed 0.6%; official unemployment rate). **Tourism** (1997): receipts $19,000,000. **Land use** (1994): forested 2.9%; meadows and pastures 46.5%; agricultural and under permanent cultivation 10.1%; other 40.5%.

Foreign trade

Imports (1998): $2,717,000,000 (machinery and metalworking products 49.6%, food products 20.9%, other 29.5%). *Major import sources:* Western Europe 30.6%; Russia 20.5%; Asia 14.2%; Kazakhstan 5.2%; Ukraine 3.2%. **Exports** (1998): $2,888,000,000 (cotton fiber 41.5%, energy 22.7%, gold 6.0%, other 29.8%). *Major export destinations:* Western Europe 33.7%; Russia 22.6%; Asia 11.6%; Ukraine 5.4%; Kazakhstan 5.4%; Tajikistan 2.9%; Turkmenistan 2.5%.

Transport and communications

Transport. *Railroads* (1997): length 3,655 km; (1995) passenger-km 2,500,000,000; (1995) metric ton-km cargo 16,907,000,000. *Roads* (1997): total length 84,400 km (paved 87%). *Vehicles* (1994): passenger cars 865,300; buses 14,500. *Air transport* (1996): passenger-km 3,460,000,000; metric ton-km cargo 321,000,000; airports (1998) with scheduled flights 9. **Communications** Total units (units per 1,000 persons). Daily newspaper circulation (1996): 75,000 (3.3); Television receivers (1999): 6,700,000 (276); Telephone main lines (1999): 1,599,000 (66); Cellular telephone subscribers (1999): 40,389 (1.7); Internet users (1999): 7,500 (0.3).

Education and health

Educational attainment (1989). Percentage of pop. age 25 and over having: primary education or no formal schooling 13.3%; some secondary 19.8%; completed secondary and some postsecondary 57.7%; higher 9.2%. **Literacy** (1997): percentage of total pop. age 15 and over literate 99.0%. **Health** (1995): physicians 76,000 (1 per 302 persons); hospital beds 192,000 (1 per 120 persons); infant mortality rate per 1,000 live births (2001) 38.0. **Food** (1999): daily per capita caloric intake 2,870 (vegetable products 85%, animal products 15%); (1997) 112% of FAO recommended minimum requirement.

Military

Total active duty personnel (2000): 78,100 (army 64.0%, air force 11.7%, other 24.3%). **Military expenditure as percentage of GNP** (1996): 2.5% (world 2.6%); per capita expenditure $62.

Background

Genghis Khan's grandson Shibaqan received the territory of Uzbekistan as his inheritance in the 13th century AD. His Mongols ruled over nearly 100 mainly Turkic tribes, who would eventually intermarry with the Mongols to form the Uzbeks and other Turkic peoples of Central Asia. In the early 16th century, a federation of Mongol-Uzbeks invaded and occupied settled regions, including an area called Transoxania that would become the Uzbeks' permanent homeland. By the early 19th century, the region was dominated by the khanates of Khiva, Bukhara, and Quqon, all of which eventually succumbed to Russian domination. The Uzbek Soviet Socialist Republic was created in 1924. In June 1990 Uzbekistan became the first Central Asian republic to declare sovereignty. It achieved full independence from the USSR in 1991. During the 1990s, its economy was considered the strongest in Central Asia, though its political system was deemed harsh.

Recent Developments

Uzbekistan was preoccupied with battling terrorism in recent years. Islamic militants of the Islamic Movement of Uzbekistan, said to be funded by Osama bin Laden, were classified as terrorists and accused of conspiring to set up a radical Islamic state like that of the Taliban in neighboring Afghanistan. The government of Pres. Islam Karimov came down hard on the militants, jailing thousands and restricting the media and religious expression. Critics feared that the harsh repression was fueling the militancy it was meant to repress. International relations deteriorated when, to prevent incursions, Uzbekistan mined its borders, and citizens of adjacent countries began to be killed or maimed. After the 11 Sep 2001 attacks on the US, Uzbekistan joined the antiterrorist coalition and allowed US troops to be stationed in its territory.

International financial aid groups expressed their dissatisfaction with the lack of progress toward economic reforms and threatened to withdraw or curtail their assistance. Economic woes piled up: foreign investors were withdrawing, a drought caused a shortfall in the cotton crop, and, in the aftermath of 11 September, the tourist industry collapsed.

Internet resources:
<www.tashkent.org/uzland/index.html>

Vanuatu

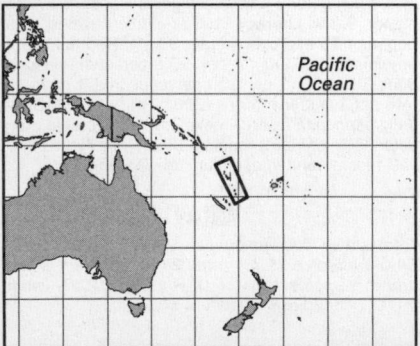

Pacific Ocean

Official name: Ripablik blong Vanuatu (Bislama); République de Vanuatu (French); Republic of Vanuatu (English). **Form of government:** republic with a single legislative house (Parliament [52]). **Chief of state:** President John Bani (from 1999). **Head of government:** Prime Minister Edward Natapei (from 2001). **Capital:** Vila. **Official languages:** Bislama; French; English. **Official religion:** none. **Monetary unit:** vatu (VT); valuation (28 Jun 2002) $1 = VT 134.90.

Demography

Area: 4,707 sq mi, 12,190 sq km. **Population** (2001): 195,000. **Density** (2001): persons per sq mi 41.4, persons per sq km 16.0. **Urban** (1999): 21.5%. **Sex distribution** (1999): male 51.46%; female 48.54%. **Age breakdown** (1999): under 15, 37.8%; 15–29, 29.4%; 30–44, 18.2%; 45–59, 9.7%; 60–74, 4.0%; 75 and over, 0.9%. **Ethnic composition** (1989): Ni-Vanuatu 97.9%; European 1.0%; other Pacific Islanders 0.4%; other 0.7%. **Religious affiliation** (1989): Christian 89.7%, of which Presbyterian 35.8%, Roman Catholic 14.5%, Anglican 14.0%, Seventh-day Adventist 8.2%; Custom (traditional beliefs) 4.6%; unknown 4.0%; nonreligious 1.7%. **Major towns** (1999): Vila (Port-Vila) 30,139; Luganville 11,360. **Location:** Oceania, island group between the South Pacific Ocean and the Coral Sea.

Vital statistics

Birth rate per 1,000 pop. (2001): 32.1 (world avg. 22.5). **Death rate** per 1,000 pop. (2001): 5.6 (world avg. 9.0). **Natural increase rate** per 1,000 pop. (2001): 26.5 (world avg. 13.5). **Total fertility rate** (avg. births per childbearing woman; 2001): 4.4. **Marriage rate** per 1,000 pop. (1985): c. 7.4. **Divorce rate** per 1,000 pop. (1985): less than 0.7. **Life expectancy** at birth (2001): male 67.0 years; female 70.0 years.

National economy

Budget (1998). *Revenue:* VT 8,536,000,000 (taxes on international trade 33.0%; taxes on goods and services 32.0%; foreign grants 20.9%; nontax revenue 10.2%). *Expenditures:* VT 12,611,000,000 (current expenditure 58.0%, of which general public services 17.2%, education 13.2%, public order and safety 8.4%, health 6.6%, economic affairs and services 5.8%; capital expenditure 42.0%). **Public debt** (external, outstanding; 1999): $63,400,000. **Household income and expenditure** (1985; Vila and Luganville only). Average household size (1989) 5.1; income per household $11,299; sources of income: wages and salaries 59.0%, self-employment 33.7%; expenditure (1990; weights of consumer price index components in Vila and Luganville only): food and nonalcoholic beverages 30.5%, housing 20.7%, transportation 13.2%, health and recreation 12.3%, tobacco and alcohol 10.4%. **Production** (metric tons except as noted). *Agriculture, forestry, fishing* (1999): coconuts 339,000, bananas 12,500, vegetables and melons 9,800; livestock (number of live animals) 151,000 cattle, 62,000 pigs, 320,000 chickens; roundwood (1998) 63,200 cu m; fish catch (1997) 2,589. *Mining and quarrying:* small quantities of coral-reef limestone, crushed stone, sand, and gravel. *Manufacturing* (value added in VT '000,000; 1995): food, beverages, and tobacco

---

1 metric ton = about 1.1 short tons;   1 kilometer = 0.6 mi (statute);   1 metric ton-km cargo = about 0.68 short ton-mi cargo;   c.i.f.: cost, insurance, and freight;   f.o.b.: free on board

645; wood products 423; fabricated metal products 377. *Energy production (consumption):* electricity (kW hr; 1996) 30,000,000 (30,000,000); petroleum products (metric tons; 1996) none (20,000). **Land use** (1994): forested 75.0%; meadows and pastures 2.0%; agricultural 11.8%; other 11.2%. **Population economically active** (1989): total 66,957; activity rate of total pop. 47.0% (participation rates: ages 15–64, 85.0%; female 46.3%; unemployed 0.5%). **Gross national product** (1999): $227,000,000 ($1,180 per capita). **Tourism** (1999): receipts from visitors $56,000,000; expenditures by nationals abroad $9,000,000.

Foreign trade

Imports (1997): VT 10,888,000,000 (machinery and transport equipment 25.7%, food and live animals 19.7%, basic manufactures 15.2%, mineral fuels 10.6%, chemical products 6.2%, beverages and tobacco 3.6%). *Major import sources:* Australia 42.1%; France 13.5%; New Zealand 12.2%; Japan 7.3%; Fiji 6.0%. **Exports** (1997): VT 4,087,000,000 (copra 49.0%, timber 12.3%, beef 10.2%, cacao beans 5.9%). *Major export destinations* (destination of domestic exports only): European Union 45.9%; Bangladesh 12.6%; Japan 10.4%; New Caledonia 4.5%; Australia 2.3%.

Transport and communications

Transport. *Roads* (1996): total length 1,070 km (paved 24%). *Vehicles* (1996): passenger cars 4,000; trucks and buses 2,600. *Air transport* (1999): passenger-km 178,316,000; metric ton-km 1,924,000; airports (1996) with scheduled flights 29. **Communications.** Total units (units per 1,000 persons). Radio receivers (1997): 62,000 (350); Television receivers (1997): 2,000 (14); Telephone main lines (1999): 5,500 (30); Cellular telephone subscribers (1999): 300 (1.6).

Education and health

Educational attainment (1989). Percentage of pop. age 6 and over having: no formal schooling or less than one year 22.3%; some primary education 52.6%; lower-level secondary 18.3%; upper-level secondary and higher 4.8%; not stated 2.0%. **Literacy** (1979): total pop. age 15 and over literate 32,120 (52.9%); males 18,550 (57.3%); females 13,570 (47.8%). **Health** (1997): physicians 21 (1 per 8,524 persons); hospital beds 573 (1 per 312 persons); infant mortality rate per 1,000 live births (2001) 30.0. **Food** (1999): daily per capita caloric intake 2,766 (vegetable products 86%, animal products 14%); (1997) 121% of FAO recommended minimum.

Military

Total active duty personnel: Vanuatu has a paramilitary force of about 300.

Did you know? Mt. Yasur, a volcano on Tanna Island, is a favorite among tourists because one can easily descend into its crater—the closest one can safely get to an active volcano anywhere in the world. Black lava-sands blanket the ground around the volcano's crater, creating a lunarlike landscape totally devoid of vegetation.

Background

The islands of Vanuatu were inhabited for at least 3,000 years by Melanesian peoples before being discovered in 1606 by the Portuguese. They were rediscovered by French navigator L.-A. de Bougainville in 1768, then explored by English mariner Capt. James Cook in 1774 and named New Hebrides. Sandalwood merchants and European missionaries arrived in the mid-19th century; they were followed by British and French cotton planters. Control of the islands was sought by both the French and British, who agreed in 1906 to form a condominium government. During World War II a major Allied naval base was on Espíritu Santo; the island group escaped Japanese invasion. New Hebrides became the independent Republic of Vanuatu in 1980. Much of the nation's housing was ravaged by a hurricane in 1987.

Recent Developments

Politics and the economy preoccupied Vanuatu; after a disputed election in 1999, Barak Sopé was chosen prime minister. He faced a national debt of $70 million (the annual GDP was some $245 million, based mainly on agriculture, with some logging, manufacturing, and tourism). The Organization for Economic Cooperation and Development charged in 2000 that Vanuatu was a tax haven engaged in money laundering and questionable tax practices. After a series of confrontations, scandals, and crises, Sopé was forced to step down, replaced by a coalition government led by Prime Minister Edward Natapei. Vanuatu was accepted for membership in the World Trade Organization in 2001.

Internet resources: <vanuatutourism.com>

Vatican City

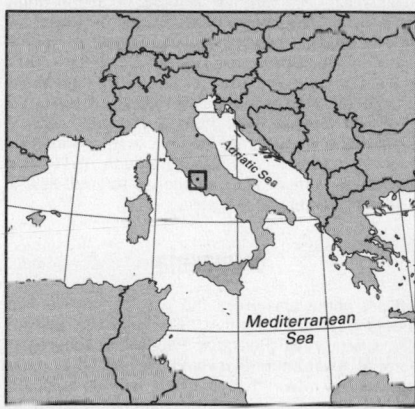

Mediterranean Sea

In full: State of the Vatican City (Holy See). **Form of government:** ecclesiastical. **Chief of state:** Pope John Paul II. **Head of government:** Secretary of State Cardinal Angelo Sodano. **Capital:** Vatican City. **Languages:** Italian, Latin. **Religion:** Roman Catholic. **Monetary unit:** 1 euro (€) = 100 cents; $1 = € 1.01 (28 Jun 2002); at conversion on 1 Jan 2002, € 1 = 1,936.3 lira (Lit).

Demography

Area: 108.7 acres (44 hectares; .44 sq mi). **Population:** (1997 est.): 850. **Density:** (2001): persons per sq mi 0.07, persons per sq km 0.19. **Location:** Southern Europe, within the commune of Rome, Italy. **Annual budget:** $209 million. **Industries:** banking and finance; printing; production of a small amount of mosaics and uniforms; tourism.

Background

Vatican City, the independent papal state, is the smallest independent state in the world. Its medieval and Renaissance walls form its boundaries except on the southeast, at St. Peter's Square. Within the walls is a miniature nation, with its own diplomatic missions, newspaper, post office, radio station, banking system, army of more than 100 Swiss Guards, and publishing house. Extraterritoriality of the state extends to Castel Gandolfo, summer home of the Pope, and to several churches and palaces in Rome proper. Its independent sovereignty was recognized in the Lateran Treaty of 1929. The pope has absolute executive, legislative, and judicial powers within the city. He appoints the members of the Vatican's government organs, which are separate from those of the Holy See. Its many imposing buildings include St. Peter's Basilica, the Vatican Palace, and the Vatican Museums. Frescoes by Michelangelo and Pinturicchio in the Sistine Chapel and Raphael's Stanze are also there. The Vatican Library contains a priceless collection of manuscripts from the pre-Christian and Christian eras.

Recent Developments

The year 2000 was a jubilee year for the Roman Catholic church, marked by observances addressed to the concerns of various segments of society and the church and culminating in World Youth Day in August, which drew two million young people to Rome for a six-day celebration. The status of Jerusalem in light of ongoing peace negotiations was of special concern. The pope visited Israel in December 2000; in 2001 he traced the route of St. Paul through Malta, Greece, and Damascus. He also went to Eastern Europe and Central Asia, making pastoral visits to Ukraine and Kazakhstan. John Paul's travels in 2002 took him to Azerbaijan, Bulgaria, Canada, and Central America, in addition to an emotional "farewell visit" to his Polish homeland in August.

Venezuela

Official name (based on the new constitution approved by referendum in 1999): República Bolivariana de Venezuela (Bolivarian Republic of Venezuela). **Form of government** (based on the new constitution approved by referendum in 1999): federal multiparty republic with a unicameral legislature (National Assembly [165]). **Head of state and government:** President Hugo Chávez Frias (second time, from 14 Apr 2002). **Capital:** Caracas. **Official language:** Spanish. **Official religion:** none. **Monetary unit:** 1 bolívar (B, plural Bs) = 100 céntimos; valuation (28 Jun 2002) $1 = Bs 1,345.51.

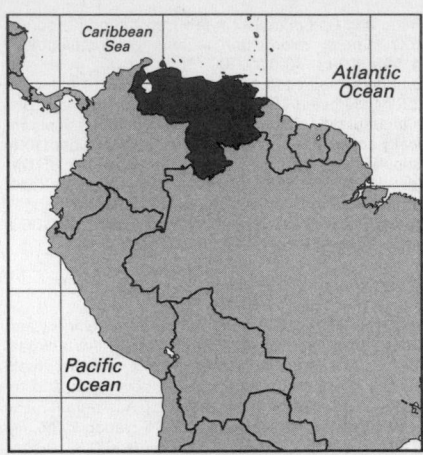

Demography

Area: 353,841 sq mi, 916,445 sq km. **Population** (2001): 24,632,000. **Density** (2001): persons per sq mi 69.6, persons per sq km 26.9. **Urban** (1997): 86.1%. **Sex distribution** (1997): male 50.35%; female 49.65%. **Age breakdown** (1997): under 15, 35.4%; 15–29, 27.6%; 30–44, 19.9%; 45–59, 10.8%; 60–74, 5.0%; 75 and over, 1.3%. **Ethnic composition** (1993): mestizo 67%; white 21%; black 10%; Indian 2%. **Religious affiliation** (2000): Roman Catholic 89.5%; Protestant 2.0%; other Christian 1.4%; Spiritist 1.1%; nonreligious/atheist 2.2%; other 3.8%. **Major cities** (2000 est.): Caracas 1,975,787; Maracaibo 1,764,038; Valencia 1,338,833; Barquisimeto 875,790; Ciudad Guayana 704,168. **Location:** northern South America, bordering the Caribbean Sea, the North Atlantic Ocean, Guyana, Brazil, and Colombia.

Vital statistics

Birth rate per 1,000 pop. (2000): 21.1 (world avg. 22.5); (1974) legitimate 47.0%; illegitimate 53.0%. **Death rate** per 1,000 pop. (2000): 4.9 (world avg. 9.0). **Total fertility rate** (avg. births per childbearing woman; 2000): 2.5. **Marriage rate** per 1,000 pop. (1997): 3.8. **Divorce rate** per 1,000 pop. (1997): 0.9. **Life expectancy** at birth (2000): male 70.1 years; female 76.3 years.

National economy

Budget (1998). *Revenue:* Bs 9,017,475,000,000 (tax revenues 73.6%; non-tax revenues 26.4%, of which oil revenues 24.9%). *Expenditures:* Bs 10,460,235,000,000 (subsidies 43.7%, goods and services 23.9%; capital expenditure 18.9%; debt service 11.8%). **Public debt** (external, outstanding; 1999): $25,216,000,000. **Tourism** (1999): receipts $656,000,000; expenditures $1,646,000,000. **Production** (metric tons except as noted). *Agriculture, forestry, fishing* (1999): sugar cane 6,850,000, corn (maize) 1,024,000, bananas 1,000,394; livestock (number of live animals) 15,992,400 cattle, 4,500,000 pigs, 110,000,000 chickens; roundwood (1998) 2,038,000 cu m; fish catch (1998) 506,177.

1 metric ton = about 1.1 short tons;   1 kilometer = 0.6 mi (statute);   1 metric ton-km cargo = about 0.68 short ton-mi cargo;   c.i.f.: cost, insurance, and freight;   f.o.b.: free on board

Mining and quarrying (1998): iron ore 19,305,000; bauxite 4,633,000; gold 14,046 kg. *Manufacturing* (value added in 1984 Bs '000,000; 1997): ferrous and nonferrous metals 16,355; food products 13,277; chemicals 10,004. *Energy production (consumption)*: electricity (kW-hr; 1996) 74,968,000,000 (74,817,000,000); coal (metric tons; 1996) 3,486,000 (328,000); crude petroleum (barrels; 1996) 1,005,526,000 (370,722,000); petroleum products (metric tons; 1996) 54,847,000 (23,096,000); natural gas (cu m; 1996) 39,411,000,000 (30,411,000,000). **Gross national product** (1999): $87,313,000,000 ($3,680 per capita). **Population economically active** (1997): total 9,507,125; activity rate 41.7% (participation rates: over age 15, 64.6%; female 35.9%; unemployed 10.6%). **Household income and expenditure.** Average household size (1990) 5.1; average annual income per household (1981) Bs 42,492; expenditure (1995): food 40.6%, housing 13.8%, transportation and communications 8.6%, clothing 5.3%, health 3.1%, education and recreation 2.9%. **Land use** (1998): forest and other 75.3%; pasture 20.7%; agriculture 4.0%.

Foreign trade

Imports (1998-f.o.b.; first six months only): $7,794,000,000 (processed industrial supplies 28.0%, machinery 22.1%, transport equipment 22.1%, manufactured consumer goods 17.8%, construction materials 5.4%). *Major import sources*: US 46.0%; Andean Pact countries 7.0%; Japan 5.0%; Germany 4.1%; Italy 3.9%. **Exports** (1998-f.o.b.): $17,534,000,000 (crude petroleum and petroleum products 69.8%, basic and precious metals 6.6%). *Major export destinations*: US 48.5%; Andean Pact countries 11.1%; Canada 2.1%; United Kingdom 2.0%.

Transport and communications

Transport. *Railroads* (1996): length (1994) 627 km; passenger-km 149,905; metric ton-km cargo 54,474,000. *Roads* (1997): total length 95,664 km (paved 36%). *Vehicles* (1997): passenger cars 1,505,000; trucks and buses 542,000. *Air transport* (1996): passenger-km 5,800,000,000; metric ton-km cargo 639,000,000; airports (1997) with scheduled flights 20. **Communications** Total units (units per 1,000 persons). Daily newspaper circulation (1996): 4,600,000 (206); Radio receivers (1997): 10,750,000 (472); Television receivers (1998): 4,300,000 (185); Telephone main lines (1999): 2,586,000 (109); Cellular telephone subscribers (1999): 3,400,000 (143); Personal computers (1999): 1,000,000 (42); Internet users (1999): 525,000 (22).

Education and health

Educational attainment (1993). Percentage of pop. age 25 and over having: no formal schooling 8.0%; primary education or less 43.7%; some secondary 38.3%; postsecondary 10.0%. **Literacy** (1995 est.): total pop. age 15 and over literate 91.1%; males 91.8%; females 90.3%. **Health** (1997): physicians 28,341 (1 per 804 persons); hospital beds 38,924 (1 per 585 persons); infant mortality rate per 1,000 live births (2000) 26.2. **Food** (1999): daily per capita caloric intake 2,229 (vegetable products 84%, animal products 16%); (1997) 90% of FAO recommended minimum.

Military

Total active duty personnel (2000): 79,000 (army 72.1%, navy 19.0%, air force 8.9%). **Military expenditure as percentage of GNP** (1997): 2.2% (world 2.6%); per capita expenditure $82.

Background

In 1498 Christopher Columbus sighted Venezuela; in 1499 the navigators Alonso de Ojeda, Amerigo Vespucci, and Juan de la Cosa traced the coast. A Spanish missionary established the first European settlement at Cumana c. 1520. In 1718 it was included in the viceroyalty of New Granada and was made a captaincy general in 1731. Venezuelan Creoles led by Francisco de Miranda and Simón Bolívar spearheaded the South American independence movement, and though Venezuela declared independence from Spain in 1811, it was not assured until 1821. Military dictators generally ruled the country from 1830 until the overthrow of Marcos Pérez Jiménez in 1958. A new constitution adopted in 1961 marked the beginning of democracy. As a founding member of OPEC (Organization of Petroleum Exporting Countries), it enjoyed relative economic prosperity from oil production during the 1970s, and its economy has remained dependent on the world petroleum market. The government of Hugo Chávez Frías promulgated a new constitution in 1999, the year in which a devastating rainstorm killed thousands in and around Caracas.

Recent Developments

In July 2000, Hugo Chávez Frías was reelected president of Venezuela by a 21% margin. Appealing to the urban poor and the downwardly mobile middle class, his Fifth Republic Movement and its ally, the Movement to Socialism, captured 99 of the 163 legislative seats and won 14 of 23 governorships. Chávez's coalition soon passed legislation to enable him to legislate unilaterally on a broad range of economic and political matters. He affirmed his leftist stance and support for the less developed nations, strengthening ties with Cuba and adding it to the list of Central American countries to which Venezuela agreed to sell oil at a discount. His trip to the Middle East reinforced solidarity with the OPEC nations, urging them not to comply with Western pressure to increase production and lower the price of crude oil.

Venezuela's economy mirrored large-scale world changes, showing improvement fueled by oil-price increases in 2000 but losing momentum in 2001, when the communications and finance sectors failed to make progress. A serious breach developed between Chávez and the powerful trade unions, who balked at attempts by the central government to control them and to implement unpopular economic legislation. The government was also forced to back down after an attempt to increase control over both public and private education met with stiff opposition from parents and the Roman Catholic church.

Matters came to a head in early 2002. Chávez let the bolívar float in February, and the currency promptly dropped 19% in value. In April, business interests and some military officers forced Chávez out of office, but his supporters rallied and he was reinstated after one day.

Internet resources: <www.venezuelatuya.com>

Vietnam

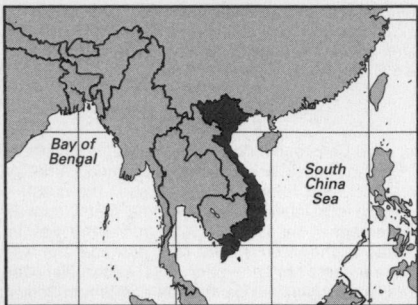

Bay of Bengal

South China Sea

Official name: Cong Hoa Xa Hoi Chu Nghia Viet Nam (Socialist Republic of Vietnam). **Form of government:** socialist republic with one legislative house (National Assembly [450]). **Head of state:** President Tran Duc Luong (from 1997). **Head of government:** Prime Minister Phan Van Khai (from 1997). **Capital:** Hanoi. **Official language:** Vietnamese. **Official religion:** none. **Monetary unit:** 1 dong (D) = 10 hao = 100 xu; valuation (28 Jun 2002) $1 = D 15,272.50.

Demography

Area: 127,816 sq mi, 331,041 sq km. **Population** (2001): 79,939,000. **Density** (2001): persons per sq mi 625.4, persons per sq km 241.5. **Urban** (1999): urban 23.5%. **Sex distribution** (1999): male 49.15%; female 50.85%. **Age breakdown** (2001): under 15, 32.1%; 15–29, 29.4%; 30–44, 21.1%; 45–59, 9.7%; 60–74, 5.8%; 75 and over, 1.9%. **Ethnic composition** (1989): Vietnamese 86.8%; Tho (Tay) 1.9%; Tai 1.6%; Chinese (Hoa) 1.4%; Khmer 1.4%; Muong 1.4%; Nung 1.1%; other 4.4%. **Religious affiliation** (1995): Buddhist 66.7%; Christian 8.7%, of which Roman Catholic 7.7%, Protestant 1.0%; Cao Dai (a New-Religionist group) 3.5%; Hoa Hao (a New-Religionist group) 2.1%; other 19.0%. **Major cities** (1992): Ho Chi Minh City (1999) 4,549,000; Hanoi (1993) 2,154,900; Haiphong 783,133; Da Nang 382,674; Buon Ma Thuot 282,095. **Location:** southeastern Asia, bordering China, the Gulf of Tonkin, the South China Sea, the Gulf of Thailand, Cambodia, and Laos.

Vital statistics

Birth rate per 1,000 pop. (2000): 21.6 (world avg. 22.5). **Death rate** per 1,000 pop. (2000): 6.3 (world avg. 9.0). **Natural increase rate** per 1,000 pop. (2000): 15.3 (world avg. 13.5). **Total fertility rate** (avg. births per childbearing woman; 2000): 2.5. **Life expectancy** at birth (2000): male 66.8 years; female 71.9 years.

National economy

Budget (1998). *Revenue:* D 73,000,000,000,000 (tax revenue 80.8%, of which taxes on trade 20.4%, corporate income taxes 17.9%, turnover taxes 16.2%; nontax revenues 16.3%; grants 2.9%). *Expenditures:* D 80,200,000,000,000 (current expenditures 67.6%, of which social services 30.4%; capital ex-

penditures 25.6%; other 6.8%). **Public debt** (external, outstanding; 1999): $20,529,000,000. **Gross national product** (1999): $28,733,000,000 ($370 per capita). **Tourism** (1997): receipts from visitors $88,000,000. **Production** (metric tons except as noted). *Agriculture, forestry, fishing* (2000): rice 32,554,000, sugarcane 15,145,000, cassava 2,036,000; livestock (number of live animals) 54,500,000 ducks, 20,194,000 pigs, 4,137,000 cattle; roundwood (1999) 36,730,000 cu m, of which fuelwood 32,174,000 cu m, industrial roundwood 4,556,000 cu m; fish catch (1997) 1,546,000, of which marine fish 668,000. *Mining and quarrying* (1998): phosphate rock (gross weight) 860,000; tin (metal content) 5,000. *Manufacturing* (gross value of production in D '000,000,000; 1998): food and beverages 36.5; cement, bricks, pottery, and glass 13.7; textiles 8.4. *Energy production (consumption):* electricity (kW-hr; 1998) 21,847,000,000 ([1996] 16,320,000,000); coal (metric tons; 1998) 10,800,000 ([1996] 5,551,000); crude petroleum (barrels; 1998) 83,000,000 ([1996] 283,300); petroleum products (metric tons; 1996) 38,000 (5,483,000); natural gas (cu m; 1996): 7,700,000 (7,700,000). **Population economically active** (1989): total 30,521,019; activity rate 47.4% (participation rates: ages 15–64, 79.9%; female 51.7%; unemployed [1997] 10.3%). **Household income and expenditure.** Average household size (1989) 4.8; income per household (1990; wage workers and government officials only) D 577,008; expenditure (1990): food 62.4%, clothing 5.0%, household goods 4.6%, education 2.9%, housing 2.5%. **Land use** (1994): forested 29.6%; meadows and pastures 1.0%; agricultural and under permanent cultivation 21.5%; other 47.9%.

Foreign trade

Imports (1998-c.i.f.): $11,527,000,000 (machinery equipment [including aircraft] 17.8%; petroleum products 7.2%; textiles, clothing, and leather 7.1%; iron and steel 4.5%; unspecified 50.1%). *Major import sources:* Singapore 13.4%; South Korea 12.1%; Japan 11.8%; Taiwan 10.8%; China 9.1%. **Exports** (1998-f.o.b.): $9,365,000,000 (garments 14.4%; crude petroleum 13.2%; rice 10.9%; footwear 10.7%; fish, crustaceans, and mollusks 8.7%; coffee 6.3%). *Major export destinations:* Japan 18.0%; Germany 9.2%; US 6.2%; France 5.8%; Australia 5.4%.

Transport and communications

Transport. *Railroads* (1999): route length 3,142 km; passenger-km 2,727,000,000; metric ton-km cargo 1,398,000,000. *Roads* (1996): total length 93,300 km (paved 25%). *Vehicles* (1994): passenger cars, trucks, and buses 200,000. *Air transport* (1999; Vietnam Airlines only): passenger-km 3,831,000,000; metric ton-km cargo 98,455,000; airports (1997) with scheduled flights 12. **Communications** Total units (units per 1,000 persons). Daily newspaper circulation (1996): 300,000 (4.1); Radio receivers (1997): 8,200,000 (109); Television receivers (1999): 14,500,000 (187); Telephone main lines (2000): 2,800,000 (36); Cellular telephone subscribers (1999): 328,671 (4.2); Personal computers (1999): 700,000 (9.0); Internet users (1999): 100,000 (1.3).

1 metric ton = about 1.1 short tons;   1 kilometer = 0.6 mi (statute);   1 metric ton-km cargo = about 0.68 short ton-mi cargo;   c.i.f.: cost, insurance, and freight;   f.o.b.: free on board

Education and health

Educational attainment (1989). Percentage of pop. age 25 and over having: no formal education (illiterate) 16.6%; incomplete and complete primary 69.8%; incomplete and complete secondary 10.6%; higher 2.6%; unknown 0.4%. **Literacy** (2000): percentage of pop. age 15 and over literate 93.3%; males 95.7%; females 91.0%. **Health** (1999): physicians 37,100 (1 per 2,092 persons); hospital beds (1997) 197,900 (1 per 380 persons); infant mortality rate per 1,000 live births (2000) 31.1. **Food** (1999): daily per capita caloric intake 2,564 (vegetable products 89%, animal products 11%); 119% of FAO recommended minimum.

Military

Total active duty personnel (2000): 484,000 (army 85.1%, navy 8.7%, air force 6.2%). **Military expenditure as percentage of GNP** (1997): 2.8% (world 2.6%); per capita expenditure $45.

Background

A distinct Vietnamese group began to emerge c. 200 BC in the independent kingdom of Nam Viet, which was annexed to China in the 1st century BC. The Vietnamese were under continuous Chinese control until the 10th century AD. The southern region was gradually overrun by Vietnamese from the north in the late 15th century. The area was divided into two parts in the early 17th century, with the northern part known as Tonkin, and the southern part as Cochin China. In 1802 the northern and southern parts of Vietnam were unified under a single dynasty.

Following several years of attempted French colonial expansion in the region, the French captured Saigon in 1859 and later the rest of the area, controlling it until World War II. The Japanese occupied Vietnam 1940–45 and declared it independent at the end of World War II, a move the French opposed. The French and Vietnamese fought the First Indochina War until French forces with US financial backing were defeated at Dien Bien Phu in 1954; evacuation of French troops ensued.

Following an international conference at Geneva, Vietnam was partitioned along the 17th parallel, with the northern part under Ho Chi Minh, and the southern part under Bao Dai; the partition was to be temporary, but the reunification elections scheduled for 1956 were never held. Bao Dai declared the independence of South Vietnam (Republic of Vietnam), while the Communists established North Vietnam (Democratic Republic of Vietnam). The activities of North Vietnamese guerrillas and pro-communist rebels in South Vietnam led to US intervention and the Vietnam War. A cease-fire agreement was signed in 1973, and US troops were withdrawn. The civil war soon resumed, and in 1975 North Vietnam invaded South Vietnam and the South Vietnamese government collapsed. In 1976 the two Vietnams were united as the Socialist Republic of Vietnam. From the mid-1980s, the government enacted a series of economic reforms and began to open up to Asian and Western nations. During the 1990s the US moved to normalize relations with it.

Recent Developments

In 2000 Vietnam celebrated the 25th anniversary of the end of the Vietnam War. The degree of improvement in relations with the US was demonstrated by visits from US Sec. of Defense William Cohen, Sen. John McCain, a former prisoner of war, and by Pres. Bill Clinton and his wife Hillary. A landmark US-Vietnam trade agreement was reached in July. The economy also received a highly symbolic boost when Vietnam's first stock exchange opened in July 2000 to an enthusiastic local welcome. Improvement in the economic picture was a focus of the National Congress of the Communist Party of Vietnam, held in April 2001. The new party chairman, Nong Duc Manh, set ambitious goals of doubling the GDP by 2010 and continuing with the reform of state-owned enterprises. A major hydoelectric scheme was planned for the north to supply power for industry.

Relations with Russia, China, and North Korea also underwent improvement. Domestic issues receiving attention were corruption in government and the situation of Vietnam's ethnic minorities, who complained of encroachment on their ancestral lands.

Internet resources: <www.vietnamtourism.com>

Virgin Islands (US)

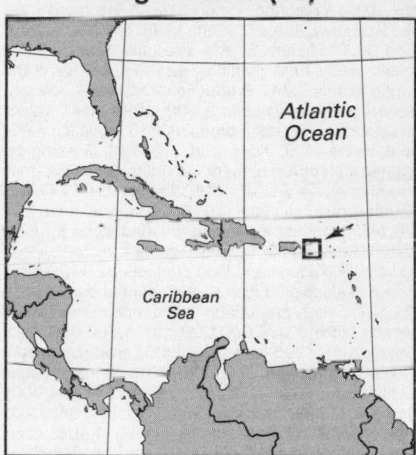

Official name: Virgin Islands of the United States. **Political status:** organized unincorporated territory of the United States with one legislative house (Senate [15]). **Chief of state:** President of the United States George W. Bush (from 20 Jan 2001). **Head of government:** Governor Charles Turnbull (from 1999). **Capital:** Charlotte Amalie. **Official language:** English. **Official religion:** none. **Monetary unit:** 1 US dollar ($) = 100 cents.

Demography

Area: 130 sq mi, 353 sq km. **Population** (2001): 122,000 (de facto estimate not adjusted for 2000 census). **Density** (2001): persons per sq mi 898.6, persons per sq km 346.2. **Urban** (1998): 45.7%. **Sex distribution** (2000): male 46.91%; female 53.09%. **Age breakdown** (2000): under 15, 27.8%; 15–29, 22.4%; 30–44, 17.9%; 45–59, 19.1%; 60–74, 9.7%; 75 and over, 3.1%. **Ethnic composition** (1995): black 76.7%, of which Hispanic 6.7%; white 10.4%, of which Hispanic 1.5%; other 12.9%, of which Hispanic 9.1%.

Religious affiliation (1993): Baptist 42.0%; Roman Catholic 34.0%; Episcopalian 17.0%; other 7.0%. Major towns (2000): Charlotte Amalie 11,004; Christiansted 2,637; Frederiksted 732. Location: northeastern Caribbean, islands between the Caribbean Sea and the North Atlantic Ocean.

Vital statistics

Birth rate per 1,000 pop. (2000): 16.0 (world avg. 22.5); (1998) legitimate 30.2% (percentage of legitimate births may be an underestimation due to the common practice of consensual marriage); illegitimate 69.8%. Death rate per 1,000 pop. (2000): 5.4 (world avg. 9.0). Natural increase rate per 1,000 pop. (2000): 10.6 (world avg. 13.5). Total fertility rate (avg. births per childbearing woman; 2000): 2.3. Marriage rate per 1,000 pop. (1993): 35.1. Divorce rate per 1,000 pop. (1993): 4.5. Life expectancy at birth (2000): male 74.2 years; female 82.5 years.

National economy

Budget Revenue (1998): $459,485,000 (personal income tax 45.7%, gross receipts tax 18.5%, property tax 9.9%, corporate income tax 5.4%, excise tax 3.7%). Expenditures (1998): $398,394,000 (education 30.4%, health 17.8%, executive branch 7.8%, public safety 7.6%, public works 6.3%, College of the Virgin Islands 5.7%). Production Agriculture, forestry, fishing (value of sales in $'000; 1998): milk 1,263, livestock and livestock products 655 (of which cattle and calves 439, hogs and pigs 46), ornamental plants and other nursery products 364; livestock (number of live animals) 3,636 cattle, 3,074 sheep, 2,944 goats; fish catch (1998) 910 metric tons. Mining and quarrying: sand and crushed stone for local use. Manufacturing ($'000 [figures are for value of sales]; 1997): food and food products 31,949; stone, clay, and glass products 21,897; print and publishing 21,127. Energy production (consumption): electricity (kW-hr; 1996) 1,075,000,000 (1,075,000,000); coal (metric tons; 1996) none (250,000); crude petroleum (barrels; 1996) none (119,528,000); petroleum products (metric tons; 1996) 15,096,000 (2,284,000). Tourism (1999): receipts from visitors $940,000,-000; number of hotel rooms (1997) 4,406; occupancy percentage (1993) 61.3%. Household income and expenditure. Average household size (1990) 3.1; average annual income per household (1989) $29,953; sources of income (1984): wages and salaries 65.7%, transfer payments 13.0%, interest, dividends, and rent 12.7%, self-employment 2.6%. Population economically active (1995; excludes armed forces): total 47,810; activity rate of total pop. (1990) 46.6% (participation rates: ages 16–64, [1990] 72.5%; female [1990] 47.8%; unemployed 5.3%). Gross national product (at current market prices; 1997): $2,666,000,000 ($18,287 per capita). Public debt (1999): $1,200,000,000. Land use (1994): forested 5.9%; meadows and pastures 26.5%; agricultural and under permanent cultivation 20.6%; other 47.0%.

Foreign trade

Imports (1995): $3,200,300,000 (breakdown of 1992 imports from US only, totaling $1,768,000,-

000: crude petroleum 60.7%, food and beverages 4.5%, iron and steel [all forms] 4.5%, fuel oils 3.2%). Major import sources: US 32.6%; other countries 67.4%. Exports (1995): $3,026,300,000 (breakdown of 1999 exports to US only, totaling $2,971,899,000: petroleum products 90.4%, chemicals and chemical products 2.4%, antibiotics 0.4%, alcoholic beverages 0.3%). Major export destinations: US 92.7%; other countries 7.3%.

Transport and communications

Transport. Roads (1996): total length 856 km. Vehicles (1993): passenger cars 51,000; trucks and buses 13,300. Air transport (1989; St. Croix and St. Thomas airports only): passenger arrivals and departures 1,897,000; cargo loaded and unloaded 4,600 metric tons; airports (1999) with scheduled flights 2. Communications Total units (units per 1,000 persons). Daily newspaper circulation (1996): 42,000 (364); Radio receivers (1996): 107,000 (927); Television receivers (1996): 67,000 (580); Telephone main lines (1999): 67,229 (562); Cellular telephone subscribers (1998): 25,000 (211).

Education and health

Educational attainment (1997). Percentage of pop. age 25 and over having: incomplete primary education 4.4%; completed lower secondary 18.5%; incomplete upper secondary 27.3%; completed upper secondary 24.0%; incomplete undergraduate 14.0%; completed undergraduate 11.8%. Health (1989): physicians 130 (1 per 780 persons); hospital beds 252 (1 per 402 persons); infant mortality rate per 1,000 live births (2000) 9.6.

Military

Total active duty personnel: no domestic military force is maintained; the US is responsible for defense and external security.

Background

The Virgin Islands of the US probably were originally settled by Arawak Indians, but they were inhabited by the Caribs when Christopher Columbus landed on St. Croix in 1493. St. Croix was occupied by the Dutch, English, French, and Spanish, and at one time owned by the Knights of Malta. Denmark occupied St. Thomas, St. John, and St. Croix and established them as a Danish colony in 1754. The US purchased the Danish West Indies in 1917 for $25 million and changed the name to the Virgin Islands. They were administered by the US Department of the Interior from 1931. In 1954 the Organic Act of the Virgin Islands created the current governmental structure, and in 1970 the first popularly elected governor took office. The area suffered extensive damage by hurricanes in 1995.

Recent Developments

In a 2001 ruling that would have a great impact on the Virgin Islands, the World Trade Organization ruled that a US export tax law violated international trade rules. Businesses known as Foreign Sales Corpora-

---

1 metric ton = about 1.1 short tons;   1 kilometer = 0.6 mi (statute);   1 metric ton-km cargo = about 0.68 short ton-mi cargo;   c.i.f.: cost, insurance, and freight;   f.o.b.: free on board

tions had been allowed to funnel overseas sales through offshore subsidiaries, which are exempt from many US taxes. More than 6,000 companies took advantage of this system.

The US Virgin Islands Coral Reef National Monument off St. Croix island was expanded to more than 18,000 acres in 2001.

Internet resources: <www.usvitourism.vi>

Yemen

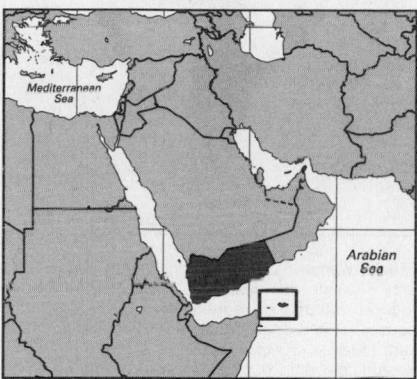

Official name: Al-Jumhuriyah al-Yamaniyah (Republic of Yemen). **Form of government:** multiparty republic with two legislative houses (Consultative Council [111]; House of Representatives [301]). **Head of state:** President Field Marshall Ali Abdallah Salih (from 1990). **Head of government:** Prime Minister Abd al-Qadir Ba Jamal (from 2001). **Capital:** Sana. **Official language:** Arabic. **Official religion:** Islam. **Monetary unit:** 1 Yemeni Rial (YRls) = 100 fils; valuation (28 Jun 2002): $1 = YRls 174.29.

Demography

Area: 182,278 sq mi, 472,099 sq km. **Population** (2001): 18,078,000. **Density** (2000): persons per sq mi 84.4, persons per sq km 32.6. **Urban** (1998): 36.1%. **Sex distribution** (2000): male 50.98%; female 49.02%. **Age breakdown** (2000): under 15, 47.5%; 15–29, 27.8%; 30–44, 13.2%; 45–59, 7.1%; 60–74, 3.3%; 75 and over, 1.1%. **Ethnic composition** (2000): Arab 92.8%; Somali 3.7%; black 1.1%; Indo-Pakistani 1.0%; other 1.4%. **Religious affiliation** (1995): Muslim 99.9%, of which Sunni c. 60%, Shi'i 40%; other 0.1%. **Major cities** (1994): Sana 954,400; Aden 398,300; Ta'izz 317,600; Al-Hudaydah 298,500; Al-Mukalla 122,400. **Location:** the Middle East, bordering Oman, the Arabian Sea, the Gulf of Aden, the Red Sea, and Saudi Arabia.

Vital statistics

Birth rate per 1,000 pop. (2000): 43.4 (world avg. 22.5). **Death rate** per 1,000 pop. (2000): 9.9 (world avg. 9.0). **Natural increase rate** per 1,000 pop. (2000): 33.5 (world avg. 13.5). **Total fertility rate** (avg. births per childbearing woman; 2000): 7.1. **Life expectancy** at birth (2000): male 58.1 years; female 61.6 years.

National economy

Budget (2000). *Revenue:* YRls 388,950,000,000 (1999; tax revenue 90.1%, of which oil revenue 64.1%, taxes on income and profits 9.4%, custom duties 7.8%; nontax revenue 9.9%). *Expenditures:* YRls 422,250,000,000 (1999; wages and salaries 23.0%; defense 18.1%; economic development 17.5%; interest on debt 13.8%; subsidies 7.7%). **Population economically active** (1999): total 4,118,000; activity rate of total pop. 24.3% (participation rates [1994]: age 15 and over, 45.8%; female 18.2%; unemployed [1995] 30%). **Production** (metric tons except as noted). *Agriculture, forestry, fishing* (2000): sorghum 401,212, tomatoes 244,720, potatoes 213,445; livestock (number of live animals) 4,760,389 sheep, 4,214,170 goats, 1,282,975 cattle; roundwood (1998) 324,000 cu m; fish catch (1999) 123,252. *Mining and quarrying* (1999): gypsum 103,000; salt 149,000. *Manufacturing* (value of production in YRls '000,000; 1996): food, beverages, and tobacco 43,927; chemicals and chemical products 42,369; nonmetallic mineral products 8,571. *Energy production (consumption):* electricity (kW-hr; 1999) 2,633,000,000 (2,633,000,000); crude petroleum (barrels; 2000) 160,600,000 ([1996] 40,559,000); petroleum products (metric tons; 1996) 3,494,000 (3,304,000). **Gross national product** (1999): $6,386,000,000 ($360 per capita). **Household income and expenditure.** Average household size (1998) 7.1; income per household YRls 29,035 ($217). **Tourism** (2000): receipts $64,000,000; expenditures $83,000,000. **Public debt** (external, outstanding; 1999): $3,729,000,000. **Land use** (1994): forest 3.8%; pasture 30.4%; agriculture 2.9%; other 62.9%.

Foreign trade

Imports (1999-c.i.f.): $1,535,900,000 (food and live animals 36.2%, of which cereals and related products 17.1%; machinery 15.3%; chemicals and chemical products 8.5%; mineral fuels 7.4%). *Major import sources:* U.A.E. 11.7%; Saudi Arabia 10.2%; US 5.5%; Australia 4.8%; UK 4.7%. **Exports** (1999): $2,435,800,000 (crude petroleum 87.5%; petroleum products 8.0%; coffee 0.5%; fish 0.5%). *Major export destinations:* China 28.8%; Thailand 25.5%; South Korea 14.5%; Singapore 8.6%.

Transport and communications

Transport. *Roads* (1996): total length 64,725 km (paved 8.1%). *Vehicles* (1996): passenger cars 240,567; trucks and buses 291,149. *Air transport* (2000): passenger-km 1,574,000,000; metric ton-km cargo 32,000,000; airports (1998) with scheduled flights 12. **Communications** Total units (units per 1,000 persons). Daily newspaper circulation (1996): 230,000 (15); Radio receivers (1997): 1,050,000 (64); Television receivers (1999): 5,000,000 (286); Telephone main lines (1999): 291,359 (16.7); Cellular telephone subscribers (1999): 27,677 (1.6); Internet users (1999): 10,000 (0.6).

Education and health

Educational attainment (1998). Percentage of pop. age 10 and over having: no formal schooling 49.5%; reading and writing ability 32.2%; primary education 11.0%; secondary education 4.6%; higher 2.7%. Literacy (1998): percentage of total pop. age 10 and over literate 50.5%; males literate 71.8%; females literate 29.1%. **Health** (1998): physicians 3,883 (1 per 4,211 persons); hospital beds 9,143 (1 per 1,788 persons); infant mortality rate per 1,000 live births (2000) 70.3. **Food** (1999): daily per capita caloric intake 2,002 (vegetable products 94%, animal products 6%); 83% of FAO recommended minimum.

Military

Total active duty personnel (2000): 66,300 (army 92.0%, navy 2.7%, air force 5.3%). **Military expenditure as percentage of GNP** (1997): 8.1% (world 2.6%); per capita expenditure $26.

 **Did you know?** Mocha, considered by many to be the best coffee in the world, comes from Yemen. The coffee was originally grown on the hillsides along the Red Sea.

Background

Yemen was the home of ancient Minaean, Sabaean, and Himyarite kingdoms. The Romans invaded the region in the 1st century AD. In the 6th century it was conquered by Ethiopians and Persians. Following conversion to Islam in the 7th century, it was ruled nominally under a caliphate. The Egyptian Ayyubid dynasty ruled there from 1173 to 1229, after which the region passed to the Rasulids. From 1517 through 1918, the Ottoman Empire maintained varying degrees of control, especially in the northwestern section. A boundary agreement was reached in 1934 between the northwestern imam-controlled territory, which subsequently became the Yemen Arab Republic (North Yemen), and the southeastern British-controlled territory, which subsequently became the People's Democratic Republic of Yemen (South Yemen). Relations between the two Yemens remained tense and were marked by conflict throughout the 1970s and 1980s. Reaching an accord, the two officially united as the Republic of Yemen in 1990. Its 1993 elections were the first free, multiparty general elections held in the Arabian Peninsula, and they were the first in which women participated. In 1994, after a two-month civil war, a new constitution was approved.

Recent Developments

In June 2000 the foreign ministers of Yemen and Saudi Arabia reached an agreement demarcating the full extent of their common border; the border had been left officially incomplete since 1934. On 12 Oct 2000 suicide bombers steered a small craft into the *USS Cole*, a destroyer on a visit to the harbor at Aden; 17 sailors were killed and 39 wounded. The damaged ship was eventually returned to service. Yemen cooperated with the US in the investigation of the incident, arresting several suspects and freezing bank accounts. Yemen subsequently asked the US for aid in counterterrorist training.

In February 2001 the first local council elections were held in unified Yemen, in which 7,000 repre-

sentatives were chosen. A cabinet reshuffle brought a new prime minister and Yemen's first woman cabinet minister.

Internet resources: <www.y.net.ye>

Yugoslavia

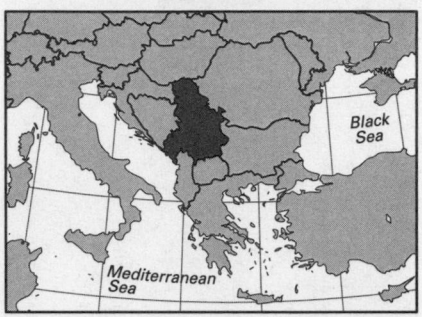

Official name: Savezna Republika Jugoslavija (Federal Republic of Yugoslavia). **Form of government:** federal multiparty republic with two legislative houses (Chamber of Republics [40]; Chamber of Citizens [138]). **Chief of state:** Federal President Vojislav Kostunica (from 2000). **Head of government:** Prime Minister Dragisa Pesic (from 2001). **Capital:** Belgrade. **Official language:** Serbian (Serbo-Croatian). **Official religion:** none. **Monetary unit:** 1 Yugoslav dinar = 100 paras; valuation (28 Jun 2002) $1 = 61.51 Yugoslav dinars (euro widely circulated in Serbia). Beginning in 2002, the euro officially replaced the Deutsche Mark in Montenegro.

Demography

Area: 39,449 sq mi, 102,173 sq km. **Population** (2001): 10,677,000. **Density** (2001): persons per sq mi 270.7, persons per sq km 104.5. **Urban** (1999): 52.0%. **Sex distribution** (1999): male 49.53%; female 50.47%. **Age breakdown** (1991): under 15, 22.8%; 15–29, 21.6%; 30–44, 21.7%; 45–59, 17.1%; 60–74, 12.2%; 75 and over, 3.5%; unknown, 1.1%. **Ethnic composition** (1991): Serb 62.6%; Albanian 16.5%; Montenegrin 5.0%; multi-ethnic 3.4%; Hungarian 3.3%; Sandzak and Bosniak Muslim 3.2%. **Religious affiliation** (1995): Serbian Orthodox 62.6%; Muslim 19.0%; Roman Catholic 5.8%; other, mostly nonreligious 12.6%. **Major cities** (1999): Belgrade 1,168,454; Novi Sad 179,626; Nis 175,391; Kragujevac 147,305; Podgorica 117,875. **Location:** southeastern Europe, bordering Romania, Bulgaria, Macedonia, Albania, the Adriatic Sea, Bosnia and Herzegovina, Croatia, and Hungary.

Vital statistics

Birth rate per 1,000 pop. (1997): 12.4 (world avg. 22.5). **Death rate** per 1,000 pop. (1997): 10.6 (world avg. 9.0). **Natural increase rate** per 1,000 pop. (1997): 1.8 (world avg. 13.5). **Total fertility rate** (avg. births per childbearing woman; 1997): 1.7. **Marriage rate** per 1,000 pop. (1997): 5.3. **Life ex-**

pectancy at birth (1995): male 69.9 years; female 74.7 years.

National economy

Budget (1998). *Revenue:* 44,200,696,000 Yugoslav dinars (turnover tax 30.3%, social security tax 22.1%, income tax 20.6%). *Expenditure:* 44,200,696,000 Yugoslav dinars (government 20.8%, health 20.0%, education 12.2%, other 47.0%). **Public debt** (external, outstanding; 1999): $7,416,000,000. **Production** (metric tons except as noted). *Agriculture, forestry, fishing* (2000): corn (maize) 2,944,302, wheat 1,927,273, sugar beets 1,070,033; livestock (number of live animals) 4,087,000 pigs, 1,917,000 sheep, 1,452,000 cattle; roundwood 1,140,000 cu m; fish catch 9,940. *Mining and quarrying* (1998): copper ore 19,939,000; lead-zinc ore 1,249,000; magnesite 81,000. *Manufacturing* (1998): wheat flour 830,000; crude steel 949,000; pig iron 826,000. *Energy production (consumption):* electricity (kW-hr; 1999) 34,456,000,000 (34,456,000,-000); coal (metric tons; 1999) 40,619,000 (40,619,-000); crude petroleum (barrels; 1999) 5,229,000 (5,229,000); petroleum products (metric tons; 1998) 763,000 (1,383,000); natural gas (cu m; 1998) 731,000,000 (2,935,400,000). **Land use** (1994): forested 17.3%; meadows and pastures 20.7%; agricultural and under permanent cultivation 40.0%; other 22.0%. **Population economically active** (1998): total 4,508,900; activity rate 42.6% (1998; participation rates: over age 15, 58.3%; female [1995] 43.7%; [1999] unemployed 19.8%). **Household income and expenditure.** Average household size (1999) 3.2; income per household (1998) 34,582 Yugoslav dinars; sources of income (1998): wages and salaries 50.3%, pensions 14.8%, self-employment 9.2%, other 25.7%; expenditure (1998): food 52.8%, fuel and light 10.4%, beverages and tobacco 7.3%, clothing and footwear 0.7%, health 5.0%, transportation and communications 4.9%, education 2.1%, housing 1.1%, other 9.1%. **Gross domestic product** (1999): $18,491,-000,000 ($1,742 per capita). **Tourism** (2000): receipts from visitors $17,000,000.

Foreign trade

Imports (1998): Din 44,805,000,000 (manufactured goods 20.8%, machinery and transport equipment 18.4%, chemicals 16.9%, mineral fuels and lubricants 15.0%, food and live animals 8.2%). *Major import sources:* Germany 12.5%; Italy 10.9%; Russia 10.7%; Macedonia 5.2%. **Exports** (1998): Din 26,335,000,000 (manufactured goods 38.5%, machinery and transport equipment 14.2%, chemicals 13.4%, food 8.3%). *Major export destinations:* Italy 11.6%; Macedonia 10.8%; Germany 8.9%; Russia 8.6%; Switzerland 5.3%.

Transport and communications

Transport. *Railroads* (1999): length 4,069 km; passenger-km 1,614,000,000; metric ton-km cargo 2,570,000,000. *Roads* (1998): total length 50,497 km (paved 60%). *Vehicles* (1994): passenger cars 1,400,000; trucks and buses 132,000. *Air transport* (1998): passenger-mi 551,155,000, passenger-km 887,000,000; short ton-mi cargo 3,730,000,000, metric ton-km cargo 6,003,000,000; airports (1999) 5. **Communications** Total units (units per 1,000 persons). Daily newspaper circulation (1995): 1,363,000

(256); Radio receivers (1997): 1,384,000 (131); Television receivers (1999): 2,000,000 (272); Telephone main lines (1999): 2,281,000 (214), Cellular telephone subscribers (1999): 605,697 (57); Personal computers (1999): 220,000 (40); Internet users (1999): 80,000 (7.5).

Education and health

Educational attainment (1991). Percentage of pop. age 15 and over having: less than full primary education 33.5%; primary 25.0%; secondary 32.2%; post-secondary and higher 9.3%. **Literacy** (1991): total pop. age 10 and over literate 93.0%; males literate 97.2%; females literate 88.9%. **Health** (1997): physicians 22,498 (1 per 471 persons); hospital beds 58,576 (1 per 181 persons); infant mortality rate per 1,000 live births 14.3. **Food** (1999): daily per capita caloric intake 2,963 (vegetable products 66%, animal products 34%); 111% of FAO recommended minimum.

Military

Total active duty personnel (2000): 97,700 (army 75.7%, air force 17.1%, navy 7.2%). **Military expenditure as percentage of government expenditure** (1991): 3.9% (world 4.0%); per capita expenditure $167.

Background

The Kingdom of the Serbs, Croats, and Slovenes was created after the collapse of Austria-Hungary at the end of World War I. The country signed treaties with Czechoslovakia and Romania in 1920–21, marking the beginning of the Little Entente. In 1929 an absolute monarchy was established, the country's name was changed to Yugoslavia, and it was divided without regard to ethnic boundaries. Axis powers invaded Yugoslavia in 1941, and German, Italian, Hungarian, and Bulgarian troops occupied it for the rest of World War II. In 1945 the Socialist Federal Republic of Yugoslavia was established; it included the republics of Bosnia and Herzegovina, Croatia, Macedonia, Montenegro, Serbia, and Slovenia. Its independent form of Communism under Josip Broz Tito's leadership provoked the USSR. Internal ethnic tensions flared up in the 1980s, causing the country to collapse. In 1991–92 independence was declared by Croatia, Slovenia, Macedonia, and Bosnia and Herzegovina; the new Federal Republic of Yugoslavia (containing roughly 45% of the population and 40% of the area of its predecessor) was proclaimed by Serbia and Montenegro. Still fueled by long-standing ethnic tensions, hostilities continued into the 1990s. Despite the approval of the Dayton peace accord (1995), sporadic fighting continued and was followed in 1998–99 by Serbian repression and expulsion of ethnic populations in Kosovo.

Recent Developments

In September and October 2000, the battered nation of Yugoslavia ended the autocratic rule of Pres. Slobodan Milosevic, replacing him with opposition candidate Vojislav Kostunica. The September election was nullified by the Constitutional Court, but massive demonstrations forced Milosevic to accept the defeat in October. Opposition parties also swept to victory in parliamentary and municipal elections. The international community welcomed the change of government as hope for stability and rebuilding in the region. Yugoslavia was reinstated into the UN, the Council of Europe, and the Organization for Security and Cooperation in Europe and it reestablished diplomatic relations with many countries, including the US and the independent former republics. Milosevic was reelected head of the Socialist Party of Serbia, but in April 2001 he was arrested and in June extradited to The Hague to stand trial for war crimes, genocide, and crimes against humanity committed during the fighting in Kosovo in 1999.

The nation's economic state, though perilous, began to improve. The tax system was adjusted to European standards, the central bank took over the currency supply, foreign currency exchange stabilized and foreign currency reserves rose, and key privatization legislation was passed. These changes enabled Yugoslavia to rejoin the International Monetary Fund (IMF), the World Bank, and other international bodies. Aid was pledged and a portion of the foreign debt was written off. Day to day life remained a struggle, nonetheless; with about 40% of the population living below the poverty line, many were unable to afford adequate food, fuel, or electricity. In 2001 unemployment stood at almost 30%, and prices of basic commodities jumped 120%.

In 2002 both houses of the federal legislature approved changing the name of the country to Serbia and Montenegro. Montenegro agreed to postpone a referendum on independence for at least three years. Tensions between the country's ethnic groups and political parties remained high, and internal rivalries made reaching consensus on most subjects difficult.

Internet resources: <www.gov.yu>

Zambia

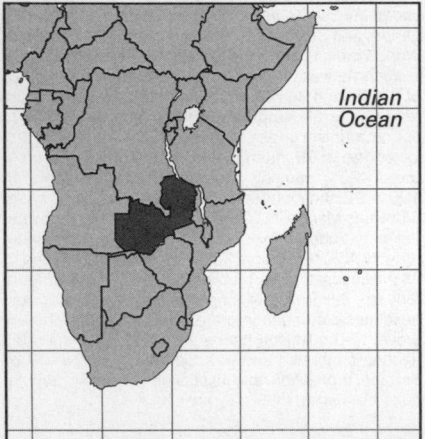

Official name: Republic of Zambia. **Form of government:** multiparty republic with one legislative house (National Assembly [156; includes 5 nonelective seats]). **Head of state and government:** President Levy Mwanawasa (from 2 Jan 2002). **Capital:** Lusaka. **Official language:** English. **Official religion:** none.

Monetary unit: 1 Zambian kwacha (K) = 100 ngwee; valuation (28 Jun 2002) $1 = K 4,467.50.

Demography

Area: 290,586 sq mi, 752,614 sq km. **Population** (2001): 9,770,000. **Density** (2001): persons per sq mi 33.6, persons per sq km 13.0. **Urban** (1998): 43.9%. **Sex distribution** (2000): male 49.73%; female 50.27%. **Age breakdown** (2000): under 15, 47.6%; 15–29, 30.6%; 30–44, 12.4%; 45–59, 5.5%; 60–74, 3.1%; 75 and over, 0.8%. **Ethnolinguistic composition** (1990): Bemba peoples 39.7%; Maravi (Nyanja) peoples 20.1%; Tonga peoples 14.8%; North-Western peoples 8.8%; Barotze peoples 7.5%; Tumbuka peoples 3.7%; Mambwe peoples 3.4%; other 2.0%. **Religious affiliation** (1995): Christian 47.8%, of which Protestant 22.9%, Roman Catholic 16.9%, African Christian 5.6%; traditional beliefs 27.0%; Muslim 1.0%; other 24.2%. **Major cities** (1990): Lusaka 982,362 (urban agglomeration, 1,577,000 [1999 est.]); Ndola 370,000; Kitwe 290,000; Chingola 167,954; Kabwe 159,000. **Location:** southern Africa, bordering Tanzania, Malawi, Mozambique, Zimbabwe, Botswana, Namibia, Angola, and the Dem. Rep. of the Congo.

Vital statistics

Birth rate per 1,000 pop. (2000): 41.9 (world avg. 22.5). **Death rate** per 1,000 pop. (2000): 22.1 (world avg. 9.0). **Natural increase rate** per 1,000 pop. (2000): 19.8 (world avg. 13.5). **Total fertility rate** (avg. births per childbearing woman; 2000): 5.6. **Life expectancy** at birth (2000): male 37.1 years; female 37.4 years.

National economy

Budget (1998). *Revenue:* K 1,529,054,000,000 (tax revenue 71.5%, of which income tax 24.9%, excise taxes 13.8%, value-added tax 13.1%, company income tax 5.9%; grants 26.0%; nontax revenue 2.5%). *Expenditures:* K 1,943,165,000,000 (current expenditures 65.0%, of which debt service 21.7%, education 7.7%, transfers 7.7%, health 5.7%, defense 1.4%; capital expenditures 35.0%). **Public debt** (external, outstanding; 1999): $4,498,000,000. **Production** (metric tons except as noted). *Agriculture, forestry, fishing* (2000): sugarcane 1,600,000, corn (maize) 1,260,000, cassava 1,020,000. *Mining and quarrying* (1999): copper (metal content) 260,000; cobalt (metal content) 4,700; silver 8,000 kg. *Manufacturing* (value added in K '000,000; 1994): food products 39,765.1; beverages 36,596.5; chemicals and pharmaceuticals 32,141.5. *Energy production (consumption):* electricity (kW-hr; 1996) 7,795,000,000 (6,315,000,000); coal (metric tons; 1996) 350,000 (345,000); crude petroleum (barrels; 1996) none (4,178,000). **Household income and expenditure.** Average household size (1997) 5.0; average annual income per household (1981) K 1,041; sources of income (1981): wages and salaries 94.0%, other 6.0%; expenditure (1977): food 37.7%, housing 11.0%, clothing 8.3%, transportation 4.3%, education 2.1%, health 1.0%. **Tourism** (1999): receipts $85,000,000. **Population economically active** (1996): total 3,454,000; activity rate of total pop.

1 metric ton = about 1.1 short tons;   1 kilometer = 0.6 mi (statute);   1 metric ton-km cargo = about 0.68 short ton-mi cargo;   c.i.f.: cost, insurance, and freight;   f.o.b.: free on board

38.2% (participation rates [1991]: over age 10, 52.6%; female 29.6%; unemployed 17.4% [1987]). **Gross national product** (1999): $3,222,000,000 ($330 per capita). **Land use** (1994): forest 43.0%; pasture 40.4%; agriculture 7.1%; other 9.5%.

Foreign trade

Imports (1998): $1,022,000,000 (1995; machinery 24.5%; transport equipment 13.4%; chemicals and chemical products 13.3%; crude petroleum 11.3%; cereals and related products 6.5%). *Major import sources* (1999): South Africa 50.3%; Zimbabwe 9.3%; UK 5.9%; Saudi Arabia 5.7%. **Exports** (1998): $873,600,000 (copper 49.3%; cobalt 17.7%; nonmetal exports 33.0%). *Major export destinations* (1999): Japan 11.3%; UK 8.5%; India 6.6%; Thailand 5.7%; Saudi Arabia 4.8%.

Transport and communications

Transport. *Railroads* (1997): length 1,266 km; passenger-km 267,000,000; metric ton-km cargo 462,000,000. *Roads* (1997): total length 38,898 km (paved 18%). *Vehicles* (1995): passenger cars 157,000; trucks and buses 81,000. *Air transport* (1996; Lusaka airport): passenger arrivals and departures 284,000; metric ton cargo unloaded and loaded 8,800; airports (1998) with scheduled flights 4. **Communications** Total units (units per 1,000 persons). Daily newspaper circulation (1996): 114,000 (14) Radio receivers (1997): 1,030,000 (120); Television receivers (1999): 1,300,000 (156); Telephone main lines (1999): 83,064 (9.3); Cellular telephone subscribers (1999): 28,100 (3.1); Internet users (1999): 15,000 (1.5).

Education and health

Educational attainment (1993). Percentage of pop. age 14 and over having: no formal schooling 18.6%; some primary education 54.8%; some secondary 25.1%; higher 1.5%. **Literacy** (1995): pop. age 15 and over literate 3,890,000 (78.2%); males literate 2,060,000 (85.6%); females literate 1,830,000 (71.3%). **Health:** physicians (1993) 786 (1 per 10,917 persons); hospital beds (1989) 22,461 (1 per 349 persons); infant mortality rate per 1,000 live births (2000) 92.4. **Food** (1999): daily per capita caloric intake 1,934 (vegetable products 95%, animal products 5%); 84% of FAO recommended minimum.

Military

Total active duty personnel (2000): 21,600 (army 92.6%; air force 7.4%). **Military expenditure as percentage of GNP** (1997): 1.1% (world 2.6%); per capita expenditure $4.

Background

Archaeological evidence suggests that early humans roamed present-day Zambia 1–2 million years ago. Ancestors of the modern Tonga tribe reached the region early in the 2nd millennium BC, but other modern peoples from Congo and Angola reached the country only in the 17th–18th centuries. Portuguese trading missions were established early in the 18th century. Emissaries of Cecil Rhodes and the British South Africa Co. concluded treaties with most of the Zambian chiefs during the 1890s. The company adminis-

tered the region known as Northern Rhodesia until 1924, when it became a British protectorate. It was part of the Central African Federation of Rhodesia and Nyasaland in 1953–63. In 1964 Northern Rhodesia became the independent republic of Zambia. A constitutional amendment was passed in 1990 allowing opposition parties; the following years were filled with political tension.

Recent Developments

Zambia was preoccupied with presidential and general elections in 2001. Pres. Frederick Chiluba considered pressing for a constitutional amendment that would allow him to run for a third term, but demonstrations caused him to reconsider, and former vice president Levy Mwanawasa was selected as the candidate of the ruling Movement for Multiparty Democracy (MMD). The splintered opposition fielded 11 candidates, allowing Mwanawasa to be elected; there were widespread allegations of ballot rigging and other improprieties. Disgruntled voters took to the streets, but Mwanawasa was inaugurated as the third president of independent Zambia on 2 Jan 2002. He took over as leader of the MMD in March.

He soon confronted an economic crisis in the copper-mining industry. The prospects of the industry, responsible for nearly half of Zambia's export earnings, had improved in 2000 when the bulk of the country's mining assets were turned over to Anglo American Corp., with Zambia retaining a 20% share of the new Konkola Copper Mines. Deals with other international companies and with the Chinese government promised continued expansion. Optimism prevailed until October 2001, when falling world copper prices began to cause major cutbacks. In January 2002 Anglo American announced it was pulling out of Zambia after 22 months; thousands of jobs would be lost. Zambia appealed to the world community for aid in restoring its infrastructure and in averting famine.

Internet resources: <www.zambia.co.zm>

Zimbabwe

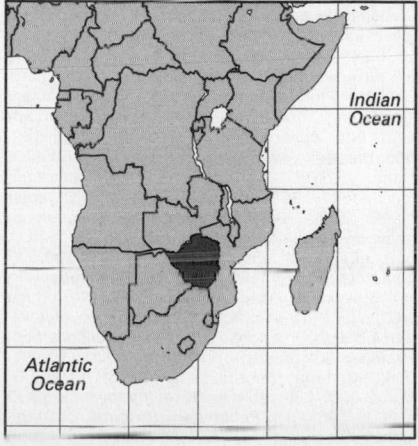

Official name: Republic of Zimbabwe. **Form of government:** multiparty republic with one legislative house (House of Assembly [150; includes 30 non-elective seats]). **Head of state and government:** President Robert Mugabe (from 1987). **Capital:** Harare. **Official language:** English. **Official religion:** none. **Monetary unit:** 1 Zimbabwe dollar (Z$) = 100 cents; valuation (28 Jun 2002) US$1 = Z$55.45.

Demography

Area: 150,872 sq mi, 390,757 sq km. **Population** (2001): 11,365,000. **Density** (2001): persons per sq mi 75.3, persons per sq km 29.1. **Urban** (1998): 33.9%. **Sex distribution** (2001): male 50.52%; female 49.48%. **Age breakdown** (2000): under 15, 39.6%; 15–29, 33.1%; 30–44, 14.8%; 45–59, 7.2%; 60–74, 4.1%; 75 and over, 1.2%. **Ethnic composition** (2000): Shona 67.1%; Ndebele 13.0%; Chewa 4.9%; British 3.5%; other 11.5%. **Religious affiliation** (1995): Christian 45.4%, of which Protestant (including Anglican) 23.5%, African indigenous 13.5%, Roman Catholic 7.0%; animist 40.5%; other 14.1%. **Major cities** (1992): Harare 1,184,169; Bulawayo 620,936; Chitungwiza 274,035; Mutare 131,808; Gweru 124,735. **Location:** southern Africa, bordering Mozambique, South Africa, Botswana, Namibia, and Zambia.

Vital statistics

Birth rate per 1,000 pop. (2000): 25.0 (world avg. 22.5). **Death rate** per 1,000 pop. (2000): 22.4 (world avg. 9.0). **Natural increase rate** per 1,000 pop. (2000): 2.6 (world avg. 13.5). **Total fertility rate** (avg. births per childbearing woman; 2000): 3.3. **Life expectancy** at birth (2000): male 39.2 years; female 36.3 years.

National economy

Budget (1997–98). *Revenue:* Z$57,596,000,000 (tax revenue 93.0%, of which income tax 48.0%, sales tax 20.4%, customs duties 17.3%, excise tax 4.2%; nontax revenue 7.0%). *Expenditures:* Z$70,332,000,000 (recurrent expenditures 92.1%, of which goods and services 48.5%, interest payments 25.0%, transfer payments 18.4%). **Population economically active** (1992): total 3,600,000; activity rate of total pop. 34.6% (participation rates: over age 15, 63.4%; female 39.8%; unemployed 7.2% [1986-87; excludes seasonal unemployment of communal workers]). **Production** (metric tons except as noted). *Agriculture, forestry, fishing* (1999): sugarcane 4,657,000, corn (maize) 1,520,000, wheat 320,-000; livestock (number of live animals) 5,500,000 cattle, 2,770,000 goats, 15,000,000 chickens; roundwood (1998) 8,378,000 cu m; fish catch (1998) 16,386 metric tons. *Mining and quarrying* (value of production in Z$; 1997): gold 3,076,800,-000; nickel 944,500,000; chrome 263,500,000. *Manufacturing* (value in Z$; 1994): foodstuffs 6,746,300,000; metals and metal products 5,662,700,000; chemicals and petroleum products 3,314,800,000. *Energy production (consumption):* electricity (kW-hr; 1996) 7,819,000,000 (10,991,-000,000); coal (metric tons; 1996) 5,247,000 (5,242,000); petroleum products (metric tons; 1996) none (1,375,000). **Public debt** (external, outstanding; 1999): US$3,211,000,000. **Household income**

and expenditure. Average household size (1992) 4.8; income per household Z$1,689; expenditure (1990; based on consumer price index): food, beverages, and tobacco 39.1%, housing 18.7%, clothing and footwear 9.8%, transportation 8.4%, education 7.6%, household durable goods 7.2%, health 2.8%, recreation 2.0%, other 4.4%. **Gross national product** (1999): US$6,302,000,000 (US$530 per capita). **Tourism:** receipts (1999) US$202,000,000; expenditures (1998) US$131,000,000.

Foreign trade

Imports (1998): US$1,968,000,000 (1996; machinery and transport equipment 38.7%, of which transport equipment 9.1%; manufactured goods 16.7%, of which textiles 2.6%, paper and paperboard 1.8%; fuels 10.4%, of which petroleum 9.7%). *Major import sources* (1996): South Africa 38.3%; UK 7.9%; Japan 5.1%; US 5.0%; Germany 4.9%; France 3.1%; Italy 2.5%; The Netherlands 1.8%. **Exports** (1998; excludes reexports): US$2,047,000,000 (1996; domestic exports 86.8%, of which tobacco 30.5%, gold sales 12.3%, ferroalloys 6.7%, nickel metal 3.2%, cotton 2.7%, asbestos 2.6%, cut flowers 1.4%, corn [maize] 1.2%). *Major export destinations* (1996): UK 10.1%; South Africa 9.6%; Germany 7.9%; US 6.7%; Japan 5.1%; Zambia 4.3%; Italy 4.3%; Botswana 4.0%; The Netherlands 3.8%.

Transport and communications

Transport. *Railroads* (1998): route length 2,759 km; passenger-km 408,223,000; metric ton-km cargo 4,603,000. *Roads* (1996): total length 18,338 km (paved 47%). *Vehicles* (1996): passenger cars 323,000; trucks and buses 32,000. *Air transport* (1999; Air Zimbabwe only): passenger-km 874,998,-000; metric ton-km cargo 35,062,000; airports (1997) with scheduled flights 7. **Communications** Total units (units per 1,000 persons). Daily newspaper circulation (1996): 209,000 (19); Radio receivers (1997): 1,140,000 (102); Television receivers (1999): 2,074,000 (183); Telephone main lines (1999): 238,956 (21); Personal computers (1999): 150,000 (13); Internet users (1999): 20,000 (1.8)

Education and health

Educational attainment (1992). Percentage of pop. age 25 and over having: no formal schooling 22.3%; primary 54.3%; secondary 13.1%; higher 3.4%. **Literacy** (1995): percentage of total pop. age 15 and over literate 85.1%; males literate 90.4%; females literate 79.9%. **Health:** physicians (1996) 1,603 (1 per 6,904 persons); hospital beds (1996) 22,975 (1 per 501 persons); infant mortality rate per 1,000 live births (2000) 62.3. **Food** (1999): daily per capita caloric intake 2,076 (vegetable products 95%, animal products 5%); 87% of FAO recommended minimum.

Military

Total active duty personnel (2000): 40,000 (army 87.5%, air force 12.5%). **Military expenditure as percentage of GNP** (1997): 3.8% (world 2.6%); per capita expenditure $29.

1 metric ton = about 1.1 short tons;   1 kilometer = 0.6 mi (statute);   1 metric ton-km cargo = about 0.68 short ton-mi cargo;   c.i.f.: cost, insurance, and freight;   f.o.b.: free on board

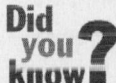

Did you know? Zimbabwe's greatest tourist attraction is Victoria Falls. Located along the Zambezi River, the falls measure 1.7 km (1.1 mi) wide and plunge over a sheer precipice to a maximum drop of 108 m (354 ft) into the Zambezi Gorge. An average of 550,000 cubic m (719,000 cubic yd) of water plummet over the edge every minute. In and around the falls one can go white-water rafting, kayaking, microlighting, parachuting, horse-riding, cycling and even do the world's highest bungee jump.

Background

Remains of Stone Age cultures dating back 500,000 years have been found in the Zimbabwe area. The first Bantu-speaking peoples reached it during the 5th–10th century AD, driving the San (Bushmen) inhabitants into the desert. A second migration of Bantu-speakers began c. 1830. During this period the British and Afrikaners moved up from the south, and the area came under the administration of the British South Africa Co. 1889–1923. Called Southern Rhodesia (1911–64), it became a self-governing British colony in 1923. The colony united in 1953 with Nyasaland (Malawi) and Northern Rhodesia (Zambia) to form the Central African Federation of Rhodesia and Nyasaland. The federation dissolved in 1963, and Southern Rhodesia reverted to its former colonial status. In 1965 it issued a unilateral declaration of independence considered illegal by the British government, which led to economic sanctions against it. The country proclaimed itself a republic in 1970 and called itself Rhodesia 1964–79. In 1979 it instituted limited majority rule and changed its name to Zimbabwe Rhodesia. It was granted independence by Britain in 1980 and became Zimbabwe. A multiparty system was established in 1990. During recent years, there has been increased tension between white farmers and black government leaders as the government has tried to introduce policies offering blacks redress for discrimination suffered during the nation's colonial days.

Recent Developments

Two issues—land reform and the presidential election—have occupied attention in Zimbabwe. Pres. Robert Mugabe was determined to turn over land held by white Zimbabweans to blacks, particularly to veterans of the war for independence, in order to redress past inequities. About 32% of farmland was owned by whites; their holdings included many large and productive farms that employed black farmworkers and produced export crops. After buying some land, the government was moving to seize land without compensation and without providing alternate employment for workers. Squatters moved onto farms, and violent incidents increased. Citing a drop in essential export income from tobacco and other crops and in the face of food shortages following the worst drought in 50 years, analysts feared that the seizures would precipitate a famine and cripple the economy. It was estimated that half the population would require food assistance in 2002. In late June a law goes into effect forcing some 3,000 white farmers to vacate their land by 10 August.

Presidential elections scheduled for March 2002 were preceded by attempts to curtail the opposition and severely restrict the press. The government rejected attempts by international monitoring groups to supervise the elections. Mugabe, in power for 21 years, was reelected in voting characterized by widespread irregularities. In response, Zimbabwe was suspended from the Commonwealth for a year.

The economy continued to deteriorate after entering recession in 1998. The IMF threatened to suspend Zimbabwe if it failed to meet debt obligations. Annual inflation rates were running at over 100%.

Internet resources: <www.rbz.co.zw>

Antarctica

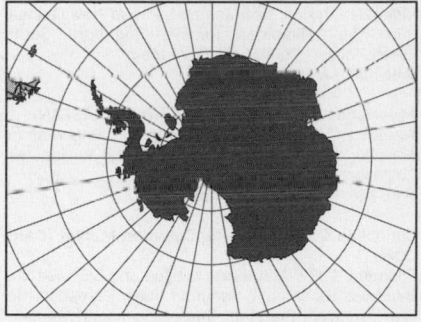

Background

The Russian F.G. von Bellingshausen (1778–1852), the Englishman Edward Bransfield (1795?–1852), and the American Nathaniel Palmer (1799–1877) all claimed first sightings of the continent in 1820. The period from the 1760s to c. 1900 was dominated by the exploration of Antarctic and subantarctic seas. In the early 20th century, the "heroic era" of Antarctic exploration, Robert Scott and later Ernest Shackleton made expeditions deep into the interior. Roald Amundsen reached the South Pole in December 1911, and Scott followed in 1912. The first half of the 20th century was also Antarctica's colonial period. Seven nations claimed sectors of the continent, while many other nations carried out explorations. In 1957–58, 12 nations established over 50 stations on the continent for cooperative study. In 1961 the Antarctic Treaty, which reserved Antarctica for free and nonpolitical scientific study, was enacted. A 1991 agreement imposed a permanent ban on mineral exploitation.

Recent Developments

The Antarctic Treaty had 45 signatories by late 2001. Of the 45 nations, 27 were pursuing programs of Antarctic scientific research. Some 8,000 scientists and supporting personnel in these programs were in Antarctica and aboard ships in the adjacent Southern Ocean.

The National Ice Center reported in March 2002 that a new iceberg—some 85 km (53 mi) long and 65 km (40 mi) wide—was adrift in the waters off Antarctica. The iceberg, designated B 22, had broken off from the Thwaites Ice Tongue, a peninsula of ice extending from the continent's mainland into the Amundsen Sea. The large number of icebergs that have recently calved from Antarctica caused some experts to question whether there was a connection to global warming.

Membership in International Organizations

African Union (AU; formerly [until 2002] Organization for African Unity)
Founded: 1963. Members: 52 countries of Africa, excluding Morocco
Web site: <www.africa-union.org>

Andean Community
Founded: 1969. Members: Bolivia, Colombia, Ecuador, Peru, Venezuela
Web site: <www.comunidadandina.org>

Asia-Pacific Economic Cooperation (APEC)
Founded: 1989. Members: Australia, Brunei, Canada, Chile, China, Hong Kong, Indonesia, Japan, Malaysia, Mexico, New Zealand, Papua New Guinea, Peru, the Philippines, Russia, Singapore, South Korea, Taiwan, Thailand, US, Vietnam
Web site: <www.apec.org>

Association of Southeast Asian Nations (ASEAN)
Founded: 1967. Members: Brunei, Cambodia, Indonesia, Laos, Malaysia, Myanmar, the Philippines, Singapore, Thailand, Vietnam
Web site: <www.aseansec.org>

Caribbean Community and Common Market (CARICOM)
Founded: 1973. Members: Antigua and Barbuda, the Bahamas (Community member only), Barbados, Belize, Dominica, Grenada, Guyana, Jamaica, Montserrat, St. Kitts and Nevis, St. Lucia, St. Vincent and the Grenadines, Suriname, Trinidad and Tobago; also 9 observers and 3 associate members
Web site: <www.caricom.org>

Central American Common Market (CACM)
Founded: 1960. Members: Costa Rica, El Salvador, Guatemala, Honduras, Nicaragua

Common Market for Eastern and Southern Africa (COMESA)
Founded: 1994. Members: Angola, Burundi, Comoros, Democratic Republic of the Congo, Djibouti, Egypt, Eritrea, Ethiopia, Kenya, Madagascar, Malawi, Mauritius, Namibia, Rwanda, Seychelles, the Sudan, Swaziland, Uganda, Zambia, Zimbabwe
Web site: <www.comesa.int>

Commonwealth (also known as the Commonwealth of Nations)
Founded: 1931. Members: United Kingdom and 53 other countries, all of which (except Mozambique) were once under British rule or administratively connected to another member country
Web site: <www.thecommonwealth.org>

Commonwealth of Independent States (CIS)
Founded: 1991. Members: Azerbaijan, Armenia, Belarus, Georgia, Kazakhstan, Kyrgyzstan, Moldova, Russia, Tajikistan, Turkmenistan, Uzbekistan, Ukraine
Web site: <www.cis.minsk.by>

Council of Europe
Founded: 1949. Members: 44 European and former Soviet countries; 6 observer states
Web site: <www.coe.int>

Economic Community of West African States (ECOWAS)
Founded: 1975. Members: Benin, Burkina Faso, Cape Verde, Cote d'Ivoire, the Gambia, Ghana, Guinea, Guinea-Bissau, Liberia, Mali, Niger, Nigeria, Senegal, Sierra Leone, Togo
Web site: <www.ecowas.int>

European Free Trade Association (EFTA)
Founded: 1960. Members: Iceland, Liechtenstein, Norway, Switzerland
Web site: <www.efta.int>

European Union (EU)
Founded: 1950. Members: Austria, Belgium, Denmark, Finland, France, Germany, Greece, Ireland, Italy, Luxembourg, the Netherlands, Portugal, Spain, Sweden, UK; in mid-2002, 13 additional countries in Eastern and southern Europe were undergoing membership preparations
Web site: <europa.eu.int>

Group of Eight (G-8)
Founded: 1975. Members: Canada, France, Germany, Italy, Japan, Russia, UK, US

Gulf Cooperation Council (GCC)
Founded: 1981. Members: Bahrain, Kuwait, Oman, Qatar, Saudi Arabia, United Arab Emirates
Web site: <www.gcc-sg.org/home_e.html>

Latin American Integration Association (ALADI)
Founded: 1980. Members: Argentina, Bolivia, Brazil, Chile, Colombia, Cuba, Ecuador, Mexico, Paraguay, Peru, Uruguay, Venezuela
Web site: <www.aladi.org>

League of Arab States (Arab League)
Founded: 1945. Members: Algeria, Bahrain, Comoros, Djibouti, Egypt, Iraq, Jordan, Kuwait, Lebanon, Libya, Mauritania, Morocco, Oman, Palestine Liberation Organization, Qatar, Saudi Arabia, Somalia, the Sudan, Syria, Tunisia, United Arab Emirates, Yemen
Web site: <www.arableagueonline.org>/arableague/index_en.jsp>

Nordic Council of Ministers
Founded: 1971. Members: Denmark, Finland, Iceland, Norway, Sweden; autonomous regions of Greenland, Faroe Islands, Åland Islands
Web site: <www.norden.org>

North Atlantic Treaty Organization (NATO)
Founded: 1949. Members: Belgium, Canada, Czech Republic, Denmark, France, Germany, Greece, Hungary, Iceland, Italy, Luxembourg, the Netherlands, Norway, Poland, Portugal, Spain, Turkey, UK, US
Web site: <www.nato.int>

Organisation for Economic Co-operation and Development (OECD)
Founded: 1961. Members: Australia, Austria, Belgium, Canada, Czech Republic, Denmark, Finland, France, Germany, Greece, Hungary, Iceland, Ireland, Italy, Japan, Luxembourg, Mexico, the Netherlands, New Zealand, Norway, Poland, Portugal, Slovak Republic, South Korea, Spain, Sweden, Switzerland, Turkey, UK, US
Web site: <www.oecd.org>

Organization for Security and Co-operation in Europe (OSCE)
Founded: 1973. Members: 53 countries of Europe and Central Asia, plus Canada and the US
Web site: <www.osce.org>

Organization of American States (OAS)
Founded: 1948. Members: 35 countries of North, Central, and South America and the Caribbean
Web site: <www.oas.org>

Organization of Petroleum Exporting Countries (OPEC)
Founded: 1960. Members: Algeria, Indonesia, Iran, Iraq, Kuwait, Libya, Nigeria, Qatar, Saudi Arabia, United Arab Emirates, Venezuela
Web site: <www.opec.org>

Organization of the Islamic Conference (OIC)
Founded: 1969. Members: 57 Islamic countries, mainly in Africa and Asia; 3 observer countries
Web site: <www.oic-oci.org>

Pacific Islands Forum (formerly [until 2000] South Pacific Forum)
Founded: 1971. Members: Australia, Cook Islands, Fiji, Kiribati, Marshall Islands, Micronesia, Nauru, New Zealand, Niue, Palau, Papua New Guinea, Samoa, Solomon Islands, Tonga, Tuvalu, Vanuatu
Web site: <www.forumsec.org.fj>

Secretariat of the Pacific Community (SPC; formerly South Pacific Commission)
Founded: 1947. Members: American Samoa, Australia, Cook Islands, Fiji, France, French Polynesia, Guam, Kiribati, Marshall Islands, Micronesia, Nauru, New Caledonia, New Zealand, Niue, Northern Mariana Islands, Palau, Papua New Guinea, Pitcairn Island, Samoa, Solomon Islands, Tokelau, Tonga, Tuvalu, UK, US, Vanuatu, Wallis and Futuna
Web site: <www.spc.org.nc>

South Asian Association for Regional Cooperation (SAARC)
Founded: 1985. Members: Bangladesh, Bhutan, India, Maldives, Nepal, Pakistan, Sri Lanka
Web site: <www.saarc-sec.org>

Southern African Development Community (SADC)
Founded: 1980. Members: Angola, Botswana, Democratic Republic of the Congo, Lesotho, Malawi, Mauritius, Mozambique, Namibia, Seychelles, South Africa, Swaziland, Tanzania, Zambia, Zimbabwe
Web site: <www.sadc.int>

Southern Common Market (MERCOSUR)
Founded: 1991. Members: Argentina, Brazil, Paraguay, Uruguay; associate members Chile, Bolivia
Web site: <www.mercosur.org.uy>

United Nations (UN)
Founded: 1945. Members: 189 countries (nearly all world countries)
Web site: <www.un.org>

World Trade Organization (WTO)
Founded: 1995. Members: 144 member countries worldwide; 32 observer states
Web site: <www.wto.org>

Did you know? Africa's Lake Chad has shrunk from a surface area of about 25,000 sq km (10,000 sq mi) in 1963 to 1,350 sq km (839 sq mi) today, due to devastating droughts and increased human demand for water.

Rulers and Regimes
Europe

Roman Emperors

Overlapping reigns denote co-rulers. Diocletian (284–305) laid the foundation for the Byzantine Empire in the East when he appointed Maximian (286–305) to rule over the Western portion of the empire. Rome thus remained a unified state but was divided administratively. Theodosius I (379–395) was the last emperor to rule over a unified Roman Empire. When he died, Rome split into Eastern and Western empires. For a complete list of the Eastern emperors after the fall of Rome, see "Byzantine Empire."

BYNAME	FULL NAME	REIGN
Augustus	Caesar Augustus	27 BC–AD 14
Tiberius	Tiberius Caesar Augustus	14–37
Caligula	Gaius Caesar Augustus Germanicus	37–41
Claudius	Tiberius Claudius Caesar Augustus Germanicus	41–54
Nero	Nero Claudius Caesar Augustus Germanicus	54–68
Galba	Servius Galba Caesar Augustus	68–69
Otho	Marcus Otho Caesar Augustus	69
Vitellius	Aulus Vitellius Germanicus	69
Vespasian	Caesar Vespasianus Augustus	69–79
Titus	Titus Vespasianus Augustus	79–81
Domitian	Caesar Domitianus Augustus	81–96
Nerva	Nerva Caesar Augustus	96–98
Trajan	Caesar Nerva Traianus Augustus	98–117
Hadrian	Caesar Traianus Hadrianus Augustus	117–138
Antoninus Pius	Caesar Titus Aelius Hadrianus Antoninus Augustus Pius	138–161

Roman Emperors (continued)

BYNAME	FULL NAME	REIGN
Marcus Aurelius	Marcus Aurelius Antoninus	161–180
Lucius Verus	Lucius Aurelius Verus	161–169
Commodus	Lucius Aelius Aurelius Commodus	177–192
Pertinax	Publius Helvius Pertinax	193
Didius Julianus	Marcus Didius Severus Julianus	193
Septimius Severus	Lucius Septimius Severus Pertinax	193–211
Caracalla	Marcus Aurelius Severus Antoninus	198–217
Geta	Publius Septimius Geta	209–212
Macrinus	Marcus Opellius Severus Macrinus	217–218
Elagabalus	Sacerdos dei invicti solis Elagabali Marcus Aurelius Antoninus	218–222
Alexander Severus	Marcus Aurelius Severus Alexander	222–235
Maximin	Gaius Julius Verus Maximinus	235–238
Gordian I	Marcus Antonius Gordianus Sempronianus Romanus Africanus	238
Gordian II	Marcus Antonius Gordianus Sempronianus Romanus Africanus	238
Maximus	Marcus Clodius Pupienus Maximus	238
Balbinus	Decius Caelius Calvinus Balbinus	238
Gordian III	Marcus Antonius Gordianus	238–244
Philip		244–249
Decius	Galus Messius Quintus Trianus Decius	249–251
Hostilian	Gaius Valens Hostilianus Messius Quintus	251
Gallus	Gaius Vibius Trebonianus Gallus	251–253
Aemilian	Marcus Aemilius Aemilianus	253
Valerian	Publius Licinius Valerianus	253–260
Gallienus	Publius Licinius Egnatius Gallienus	253–268
Claudius II Gothicus	Marcus Aurelius Valerius Claudius	268–270
Quintillus	Marcus Aurelius Claudius Quintillus	269–270
Aurelian	Lucius Domitius Aurelianus	270–275
Tacitus	Marcus Claudius Tacitus	275–276
Florian	Marcus Annius Florianus	276
Probus	Marcus Aurelius Probus	276–282
Carus	Marcus Aurelius Carus	282–283
Carinus	Marcus Aurelius Carinus	283–285
Numerian	Marcus Aurelius Numerius Numerianus	283–284
Diocletian	Gaius Aurelius Valerius Diocletianus	284–305[1]
Maximian	Marcus Aurelius Valerius Maximianus Heraclius	286–305[2]
Galerius	Gaius Galerius Valerius Maximianus	305–311[1]
Constantius I Chlorus	Flavius Valerius Constantius	305–306[2]
Severus	Flavius Valerius Severus	306–307[2]
Maxentius	Marcus Aurelius Valerius Maxentius	306–312[2]
Licinius	Valerius Licinianus Licinius	308–324[1]
Constantine I	Flavius Valerius Constantinus	312–337
Constantine II	Flavius Claudius [or Julius] Constantinus	337–340
Constans I	Flavius Julius Constans	337–350
Constantius II	Flavius Julius [or Valerius] Constantius	337–361
Magnentius	Flavius Magnus Magnentius	350–353
Julian	Flavius Claudius Julianus	361–363
Jovian	Flavius Jovianus	363–364
Valentinian I	Flavius Valentinianus	364–375[2]
Valens	Flavius Valens	364–378[1]
Procopius		365–366[1]
Gratian	Flavius Gratianus Augustus	375–383[2]
Valentinian II	Flavius Valentinianus	375–392[2]
Theodosius I	Flavius Theodosius	379–395
Arcadius	Flavius Arcadius	395–408[1]
Honorius	Flavius Honorius	395–423[2]
Theodosius II		408–450[1]
Constantius III		421[2]
Valentinian III	Flavius Placidius Valentinianus	425–455[2]
Marcian	Marcianus	450–457[1]
Petronius Maximus	Flavius Ancius Petronius Maximus	455[2]
Avitus	Flavius Maccilius Eparchus Avitus	455–456[2]
Leo I	Leo Thrax Magnus	457–474[1]
Majorian	Julius Valerius Majorianus	457–461[2]
Libius Severus	Libius Severianus Severus	461–467[2]
Anthemius	Procopius Anthemius	467–472[2]
Olybrius	Anicius Olybrius	472[2]
Glycerius		473–474[2]
Julius Nepos		474–475[2]

Roman Emperors (continued)

BYNAME	FULL NAME	REIGN
Leo II		474[1]
Zeno		474–491[1]
Romulus Augustulus	Flavius Momyllus Romulus Augustulus	475–476[2]

[1]Ruled in the East only. [2]Ruled in the West only.

Sovereigns of Britain

SOVEREIGN	DYNASTY OR HOUSE	REIGN
Kings of Wessex (West Saxons)		
Egbert	Saxon	802–839
Aethelwulf (Ethelwulf)	Saxon	839–856/858
Aethelbald (Ethelbald)	Saxon	855/856–860
Aethelberht (Ethelbert)	Saxon	860–865/866
Aethelred I (Ethelred)	Saxon	865/866–871
Alfred the Great	Saxon	871–899
Edward the Elder	Saxon	899–924
Sovereigns of England		
Athelstan[1]	Saxon	925–939
Edmund I	Saxon	939–946
Eadred (Edred)	Saxon	946–955
Eadwig (Edwy)	Saxon	955–959
Edgar	Saxon	959–975
Edward the Martyr	Saxon	975–978
Ethelred II the Unready (Aethelred)	Saxon	978–1013
Sweyn Forkbeard	Danish	1013–14
Ethelred II the Unready (restored)	Saxon	1014–16
Edmund II Ironside	Saxon	1016
Canute	Danish	1016–35
Harold I Harefoot	Danish	1035–40
Hardecanute	Danish	1040–42
Edward the Confessor	Saxon	1042–66
Harold II	Saxon	1066
William I the Conqueror	Norman	1066–87
William II	Norman	1087–1100
Henry I	Norman	1100–35
Stephen	Blois	1135–54
Henry II	Plantagenet	1154–89
Richard I	Plantagenet	1189–99
John	Plantagenet	1199–1216
Henry III	Plantagenet	1216–72
Edward I	Plantagenet	1272–1307
Edward II	Plantagenet	1307–27
Edward III	Plantagenet	1327–77
Richard II	Plantagenet	1377–99
Henry IV	Plantagenet: Lancaster	1399–1413
Henry V	Plantagenet: Lancaster	1413–22
Henry VI	Plantagenet: Lancaster	1422–61
Edward IV	Plantagenet: York	1461–70

SOVEREIGN	DYNASTY OR HOUSE	REIGN
Sovereigns of England (continued)		
Henry VI (restored)	Plantagenet: Lancaster	1470–71
Edward IV (restored)	Plantagenet: York	1471–83
Edward V	Plantagenet: York	1483
Richard III	Plantagenet: York	1483–85
Henry VII	Tudor	1483–1509
Henry VIII	Tudor	1509–47
Edward VI	Tudor	1547–53
Mary I	Tudor	1553–58
Elizabeth I	Tudor	1558–1603
Sovereigns of Great Britain and the United Kingdom[2, 3]		
James I (VI of Scotland)[2]	Stuart	1603–25
Charles I	Stuart	1625–49
Commonwealth		
Oliver Cromwell, Lord Protector		1653–58
Richard Cromwell, Lord Protector		1658–59
Sovereigns of Great Britain and the United Kingdom (restored)		
Charles II	Stuart	1660–85
James II	Stuart	1685–88
William III and Mary II[4]	Orange/ Stuart	1689–1702
Anne	Stuart	1702–14
George I	Hanover	1714–27
George II	Hanover	1727–60
George III[3]	Hanover	1760–1820
George IV[5]	Hanover	1820–30
William IV	Hanover	1830–37
Victoria	Hanover	1837–1901
Edward VII	Saxe Coburg-Gotha	1901–10
George V[6]	Windsor	1910–36
Edward VIII[7]	Windsor	1936
George VI	Windsor	1936–52
Elizabeth II	Windsor	1952–

[1]Athelstan was king of Wessex and the first king of all England. [2]James VI of Scotland became also James I of England in 1603. Upon accession to the English throne he styled himself "King of Great Britain" and was so proclaimed. Legally, however, he and his successors held separate English and Scottish kingships until the Act of Union of 1707, when the two kingdoms were united as the Kingdom of Great Britain. [3]The United Kingdom was formed on 1 Jan 1801, with the union of Great Britain and Ireland. After 1801 George III was styled "King of the United Kingdom of Great Britain and Ireland." [4]William and Mary, as husband and wife, reigned jointly until Mary's death in 1694. William then reigned alone until his own death in 1702. [5]George IV was regent from 5 Feb 1811. [6]In 1917, during World War I, George V changed the name of his house from Saxe-Coburg-Gotha to Windsor. [7]Edward VIII succeeded upon the death of his father, George V, on 20 Jan 1936, but abdicated on 11 Dec 1936, before coronation.

Rulers of Scotland

Knowledge about the early Scottish kings (until Malcolm II) is slim and is partly based on traditional lists. The dating of reigns is thus inexact.

RULER	REIGN	RULER	REIGN
Kenneth I MacAlpin	843–858	Malcolm IV	1153–65
Donald I	858–862	William I the Lion	1165–1214
Constantine I	862–877	Alexander II	1214–49
Aed (Aodh)	877–878	Alexander III	1249–86
Eochaid (Eocha) and Giric (Ciric)[1]	878–889	Margaret, Maid of Norway	1286–90
Donald II	889–900		
Constantine II	900–943	**Interregnum**	1290–92
Malcolm I	943–954		
Indulf	954–962	John de Balliol	1292–96
Dub	962–966		
Culen	966–971	**Interregnum**	1296–1306
Kenneth II	971–995		
Constantine III	995–997	Robert I the Bruce	1306–29
Kenneth III	997–1005	David II	1329–71
Malcolm II	1005–34		
Duncan I	1034–40	**House of Stewart (Stuart)[2]**	
Macbeth	1040–57	Robert II	1371–90
Lulach	1057–58	Robert III	1390–1406
Malcolm III Canmore	1058–93	James I	1406–37
Donald Bane (Donalbane)	1093–94	James II	1437–60
Duncan II	1093–94	James III	1460–88
Donald Bane (restored)	1094–97	James IV	1488–1513
Edgar	1097–1107	James V	1513–42
Alexander I	1107–24	Mary, Queen of Scots	1542–67
David I	1124–53	James VI[3]	1567–1625

[1]*Eochaid may have been a minor and Giric his guardian, or Giric may have been a usurper. Both appear in the lists of kings for the period.* [2]*"Stewart" was the original spelling for the Scottish family, but during the 16th century French influence led to the adoption of the spelling Stuart (or Steuart), owing to the absence of the letter "w" in the French alphabet.* [3]*James VI of Scotland became also James I of England in 1603. Upon accession to the English throne he styled himself "King of Great Britain" and was so proclaimed. Legally, however, he and his successors held separate English and Scottish kingships until the Act of Union of 1707, when the two kingdoms were united as the Kingdom of Great Britain.*

British Prime Ministers

The origin of the term prime minister and the question to whom it should originally be applied have long been issues of scholarly and political debate. Although the term was used as early as the reign of Queen Anne (1702–14), it acquired wider currency during the reign of George II (1727–60), when it began to be used as a term of reproach toward Robert Walpole. The title prime minister did not become official until 1905, to refer to the leader of a government.

Before the development of the Conservative and Liberal parties in the mid-19th century, parties in Britain were largely simply alliances of prominent groups or aristocratic families. The designations Whig and Tory tend often to be approximate. In all cases, the party designation is that of the prime minister; he might lead a coalition government, as did David Lloyd George and Winston Churchill (in his first term).

PRIME MINISTER	PARTY	TERM	PRIME MINISTER	PARTY	TERM
Robert Walpole	Whig	1721–42	William Pitt	Tory	1783–1801
Spencer Compton	Whig	1742–43	Henry Addington	Tory	1801–04
Henry Pelham	Whig	1743–54	William Pitt	Tory	1804–06
Thomas Pelham-Holles	Whig	1754–56	William Wyndham Gren-		1806–07
William Cavendish	Whig	1756–57	ville		
Thomas Pelham-Holles	Whig	1757–62	William Henry Cavendish-	Whig	1807–09
John Stuart		1762–63	Bentinck		
George Grenville		1763–65	Spencer Perceval	Tory	1809–12
Charles Watson Went-	Whig	1765–66	Robert Banks Jenkinson	Tory	1812–27
worth			George Canning	Tory	1827
William Pitt		1766–68	Frederick John Robinson	Tory	1827–28
Augustus Henry Fitzroy		1768–70	Arthur Wellesley	Tory	1828–30
Frederick North		1770–82	Charles Grey	Whig	1830–34
Charles Watson Went-	Whig	1782	William Lamb	Whig	1834
worth			Arthur Wellesley	Tory	1834
William Petty-Fitzmaurice		1782–83	Robert Peel	Tory	1834–35
William Henry Cavendish-	Whig	1783	William Lamb	Whig	1835–41
Bentinck			Robert Peel	Conservative	1841–46

British Prime Ministers (continued)

PRIME MINISTER	PARTY	TERM
John Russell	Whig-Liberal	1846–52
Edward Geoffrey Stanley	Conservative	1852
George Hamilton-Gordon		1852–55
Henry John Temple	Liberal	1855–58
Edward Geoffrey Stanley	Conservative	1858–59
Henry John Temple	Liberal	1859–65
John Russell	Liberal	1865–66
Edward Geoffrey Stanley	Conservative	1866–68
Benjamin Disraeli	Conservative	1868
William Ewart Gladstone	Liberal	1868–74
Benjamin Disraeli	Conservative	1874–80
William Ewart Gladstone	Liberal	1880–85
Robert Cecil	Conservative	1885–86
William Ewart Gladstone	Liberal	1886
Robert Cecil	Conservative	1886–92
William Ewart Gladstone	Liberal	1892–94
Archibald Philip Primrose	Liberal	1894–95
Robert Cecil	Conservative	1895–1902
Arthur James Balfour	Conservative	1902–05
Henry Campbell-Bannerman	Liberal	1905–08
H.H. Asquith	Liberal	1908–16

PRIME MINISTER	PARTY	TERM
David Lloyd George	Liberal	1916–22
Bonar Law	Conservative	1922–23
Stanley Baldwin	Conservative	1923–24
Ramsay Macdonald	Labour	1924
Stanley Baldwin	Conservative	1924–29
Ramsay Macdonald	Labour	1929–35
Stanley Baldwin	Conservative	1935–37
Neville Chamberlain	Conservative	1937–40
Winston Churchill	Conservative	1940–45
Clement Attlee	Labour	1945–51
Winston Churchill	Conservative	1951–55
Anthony Eden	Conservative	1955–57
Harold Macmillan	Conservative	1957–63
Alec Douglas-Home	Conservative	1963–64
Harold Wilson	Labour	1964–70
Edward Heath	Conservative	1970–74
Harold Wilson	Labour	1974–76
James Callaghan	Labour	1976–79
Margaret Thatcher	Conservative	1979–90
John Major	Conservative	1990–97
Tony Blair	Labour	1997–

Rulers of France

RULER	REIGN
Carolingian dynasty	
Charles I (Charlemagne, Kingdom of the Franks)	768–814
Louis I (Kingdom of the Franks)	840–843
Civil War	
Charles II (Kingdom of the West Franks)	843–877
Louis II (Kingdom of the West Franks)	877–879
Louis III (Kingdom of the West Franks)	879–882
Carloman (Kingdom of the West Franks)	879–884
Charles (III) (Charles III, Holy Roman Empire)	884–887
Robertian (Capetian) dynasty	
Eudes	888–898
Carolingian dynasty	
Charles III	893/898–923
Robertian (Capetian) dynasty	
Robert I	922–923
Rudolf (Raoul, or Rodolphe)	923–936
Carolingian dynasty	
Louis IV	936–954
Lothair (Lothaire)	954–986
Louis V	986–987
Capetian dynasty	
Hugh Capet (Hugues Capet)	987–996
Robert II	996–1031
Henry I (Henri)	1031–60
Philip I (Philippe)	1060–1108
Louis VI	1108–37
Louis VII	1137–80
Philip II (Philippe)	1180–1223
Louis VIII	1223–26
Louis IX (Saint Louis)	1226–70
Philip III (Philippe)	1270–85
Philip IV (Philippe)	1285–1314
Louis X	1314–16

RULER	REIGN
Capetian dynasty (continued)	
John I (Jean)	1316
Philip V (Philippe)	1316–22
Charles IV	1322–28
Valois dynasty	
Philip VI (Philippe)	1328–50
John II (Jean)	1350–64
Charles V	1364–80
Charles VI	1380–1422
Charles VII	1422–61
Louis XI	1461–83
Charles VIII	1483–98
Valois dynasty (Orléans branch)	
Louis XII	1498–1515
Valois dynasty (Angoulême branch)	
Francis I (François)	1515–47
Henry II (Henri)	1547–59
Francis II (François)	1559–60
Charles IX	1560–74
Henry III (Henri)	1574–89
House of Bourbon	
Henry IV (Henri)	1589–1610
Louis XIII	1610–43
Louis XIV	1643–1715
Louis XV	1715–74
Louis XVI	1774–92
Louis (XVII)	1793–95
First Republic	
National Convention	1792–95
Directorate	1795–99
Consulate (Napoléon Bonaparte)	1799–1804
First Empire (emperors)	
Napoleon I (Napoléon Bonaparte)	1804–14, 1815
Napoleon (II)	1815

Rulers of France (continued)

RULER	REIGN	RULER	REIGN
House of Bourbon		**Third Republic (presidents) continued**	
Louis XVIII	1814–24	Raymond Poincaré	1913–20
Charles X	1824–30	Paul Deschanel	1920
		Alexandre Millerand	1920–24
House of Orléans		Gaston Doumergue	1924–31
Louis-Philippe	1830–48	Paul Doumer	1931–32
		Albert Lebrun	1932–40
Second Republic (president)			
Louis-Napoléon Bonaparte	1848–52	**French State (État Français, or Vichy France)**	
		Philippe Pétain	1940–44
Second Empire (emperor)			
Napoleon III (Louis-Napoléon Bonaparte)	1852–70	**Provisional government**	1944–47
Third Republic (presidents)		**Fourth Republic (presidents)**	
Adolphe Thiers	1871–73	Vincent Auriol	1947–54
Marie-Edmé-Patrice-Maurice, comte de Mac-Mahon, duc de Magenta	1873–79	René Coty	1954–58
Jules Grévy	1879–87	**Fifth Republic (presidents)**	
Sadi Carnot	1887–94	Charles de Gaulle	1959–69
Jean Casimir-Périer	1894–95	Georges Pompidou	1969–74
Félix Faure	1895–99	Valéry Giscard d'Estaing	1974–81
Émile Loubet	1899–1906	François Mitterrand	1981–95
Armand Fallières	1906–13	Jacques Chirac	1995–

Rulers of Spain

RULER	REIGN	RULER	REIGN
House of Habsburg		**Interregnum**	1868–70
Charles I (Carlos)	1516–56		
Philip II (Felipe)	1556–98	**House of Savoy**	
Philip III (Felipe)	1598–1621	Amadeus I (Amadeo)	1870–73
Philip IV (Felipe)	1621–65		
Charles II (Carlos)	1665–1700	**Republic**	1873–74
House of Bourbon (Borbón)		**House of Bourbon (Borbón)**	
Philip V (Felipe)	1700–24	Alfonso XII	1874–85
Louis (Luis)	1724	Alfonso XIII	1886–1931
Philip V (2nd time)	1724–46		
Ferdinand VI (Fernando)	1746–59	**Republic**	1931–39
Charles III (Carlos)	1759–88		
Charles IV (Carlos)	1788–1808	**Nationalist Regime**	
Ferdinand VII (Fernando)	1808	Francisco Franco	1939–75
House of Bonaparte		**House of Bourbon (Borbón)**	
Joseph (José)	1808–13	Juan Carlos	1975–
House of Bourbon (Borbón)			
Ferdinand VII (2nd time)	1814–33		
Isabella II (Isabel)	1833–68		

Holy Roman Emperors

The Holy Roman Empire encompassed a varying complex of lands in Western and Central Europe. Ruled over by Frankish and then German kings, the empire officially dissolved on 6 Aug 1806, when Francis II resigned his title.

EMPEROR	REIGN	EMPEROR	REIGN
Carolingian dynasty		**House of Spoleto**	
Charlemagne (Charles I)	800–814	Guy	891–894
Louis I	814–840	Lambert	894–898
Civil War	840–843		
Lothair I	843–855	**Carolingian dynasty**	
Louis II	855–875	Arnulf	896–899
Charles II	875–877	Louis III	901–905
Interregnum	877–881		
Charles III	881–887	**House of Franconia**	
Interregnum	887–891	Conrad I	911–918

Holy Roman Emperors (continued)

EMPEROR	REIGN
Carolingian dynasty	
Berengar	915–924
House of Saxony (Liudolfings)	
Henry I	919–936
Otto I	936–973
Otto II	973–983
Otto III	983–1002
Henry II	1002–24
Salian dynasty	
Conrad II	1024–39
Henry III	1039–56
Henry IV	1056–1106
Rival claimants:	
Rudolf	1077–80
Hermann	1081–93
Conrad	1093–1101
Henry V	1105/06–25
House of Supplinburg	
Lothair II	1125–37
House of Hohenstaufen	
Conrad III	1138–52
Frederick I (Barbarossa)	1152–90
Henry VI	1190–97
Philip	1198–1208
Welf dynasty	
Otto IV	1198–1214
House of Hohenstaufen	
Frederick II	1215–50
Rival claimants:	
Henry (VII)	1220–35
Henry Raspe	1246–47
William of Holland	1247–56
Conrad IV	1250–54
Great Interregnum	1254–73
Richard	1257–72
Alfonso (Alfonso X of Castile)	1257–75
House of Habsburg	
Rudolf I	1273–91
House of Nassau	
Adolf	1292–98

EMPEROR	REIGN
House of Habsburg	
Albert I	1298–1308
House of Luxembourg	
Henry VII	1308–13
House of Habsburg	
Frederick (III)	1314–26
House of Wittelsbach	
Louis IV	1314–46
House of Luxembourg	
Charles IV	1346–78
Wenceslas	1378–1400
House of Wittelsbach	
Rupert	1400–10
House of Luxembourg	
Jobst	1410–11
Sigismund	1410–37
House of Habsburg	
Albert II	1438–39
Frederick III	1440–93
Maximilian I	1493–1519
Charles V	1519–56
Ferdinand I	1556–64
Maximilian II	1564–76
Rudolf II	1576–1612
Matthias	1612–19
Ferdinand II	1619–37
Ferdinand III	1637–57
Leopold I	1658–1705
Joseph I	1705–11
Charles VI	1711–40
House of Wittelsbach	
Charles VII	1742–45
House of Habsburg	
Francis I	1745–65
Joseph II	1765–90
Leopold II	1790–92
Francis II	1792–1806

Rulers of Germany

On 25 Jul 1806 the Confederation of the Rhine was founded, with Carl Theodor Reichsfreiherr von Dalberg as Prince-Primate (1806–13). After the dissolution of the Rhine Confederation, there was no true central power until 1815, when the German Confederation was founded. In 1867 the governing structure became the North German Confederation, and in 1871 the German Reich. For rulers of Germany before the Confederation of the Rhine, see "Holy Roman Emperors."

RULER	REIGN OR TERM
Emperors	
Hohenzollern dynasty	
Wilhelm I	1871–88
Friedrich III	1888
Wilhelm II	1888–1918
Presidents	
Richard Müller	1918
Robert Leinert	1918–19

RULER	REIGN OR TERM
Presidents (continued)	
Wilhelm Pfannkuch	1919
Eduard David	1919
Friedrich Ebert	1919–25
Hans Luther (acting)	1925
Walter Simons (acting)	1925
Paul von Hindenburg	1925–34
Adolf Hitler (Führer)	1934–45
Karl Dönitz	1945

Rulers of Germany (continued)

RULER	REIGN OR TERM	RULER	REIGN OR TERM
Chancellors		**Chairmen of the Council of State**	
Otto Fürst von Bismarck	1871–90	Walter Ulbricht	1960–73
Leo Graf von Caprivi	1890–94	Friedrich Ebert (acting)	1973
Chlodwig Fürst zu Hohenlohe-	1894–1900	Willi Stoph	1973–76
Schillingsfürst		Erich Honecker	1976–89
Bernhard Graf Fürst von Bülow	1900–09	Egon Krenz	1989
Theobald von Bethmann Hollweg	1909–17	Manfred Gerlach (acting)	1989–90
Georg Michaelis	1917	Sabine Bergmann–Pohl[2]	1990
Georg Graf von Hertling	1917–18		
Maximilian Prinz von Baden	1918	**Federal Republic of Germany (West Germany)[1]**	
Friedrich Ebert	1918	**Presidents**	
Philipp Scheidemann	1919	Karl Arnold (acting)	1949
Gustav Bauer	1919–20	Theodor Heuss	1949–59
Wolfgang Kapp (in rebellion)	1920	Heinrich Lübke	1959–69
Hermann Müller	1920	Gustav Heinemann	1969–74
Konstantin Fehrenbach	1920–21	Walter Scheel	1974–79
Joseph Wirth	1921–22	Karl Carstens	1979–84
Wilhelm Cuno	1922–23	Richard von Weizsäcker	1984–94
Gustav Stresemann	1923	Roman Herzog	1994–99
Wilhelm Marx	1923–24	Johannes Rau	1999–
Hans Luther	1925–26		
Wilhelm Marx	1926–28	**Chancellors**	
Hermann Müller	1928–30	Konrad Adenauer	1949–63
Heinrich Brüning	1930–32	Ludwig Erhard	1963–66
Franz von Papen	1932	Kurt Georg Kiesinger	1966–69
Kurt von Schleicher	1932–33	Willy Brandt	1969–74
Adolf Hitler	1933–45	Walter Scheel (acting)	1974
Joseph Goebbels	1945	Helmut Schmidt	1974–82
Lutz Graf Schwerin von Krosigk	1945	Helmut Kohl	1982–98
(chairman of interim government)		Gerhard Schröder	1998–
Allied occupation	1945–49		

German Democratic Republic (East Germany)[1]
Presidents

RULER	REIGN OR TERM
Johannes Dieckmann (acting)	1949
Wilhelm Pieck	1949–60
Johannes Dieckmann (acting)	1960

[1]*After WWII, Germany was split into four occupational zones, governed by the French, British, American, and Soviet powers. The Western zones were merged and, on 23 May 1949, became the independent Federal Republic of Germany. On 7 October of the same year, the Soviet zone was proclaimed the German Democratic Republic. On 3 Oct 1990, the latter was incorporated into the Federal Republic of Germany.*
[2]*Bergmann–Pohl was president of the People's Chamber.*

Rulers of Russia[1]

RULER	REIGN	RULER	REIGN
Princes and Grand Princes of Moscow		**Tsars of Russia: Time of Troubles**	
(Muscovy): Danilovich dynasty[2]		Boris Godunov	1598–1605
Daniel (son of Alexander Nevsky)	c. 1276–1303	Fyodor II	1605
Yury	1303–25	False Dmitry	1605–06
Ivan I	1325–40	Vasily (IV)	1606–10
Semyon (Simeon)	1340–53		
Ivan II	1353–59	**Interregnum**	1610–12
Dmitry Donskoy	1359–89		
Vasily I	1389–1425	**Tsars and Empresses of Russia and the**	
Vasily II	1425–62	**Russian Empire: Romanov dynasty[3]**	
Ivan III	1462–1505	Michael III	1613–45
Vasily III	1505–33	Alexis	1645–76
Ivan IV	1533–47	Fyodor III	1676–82
		Peter I (Ivan V coruler 1682–96)	1682–1725
Tsars of Russia: Danilovich dynasty		Catherine I	1725–27
Ivan IV	1547–84	Peter II	1727–30
Fyodor I	1584–98	Anna	1730–40

Rulers of Russia[1] (continued)

RULER	REIGN	RULER	REIGN
Tsars and Empresses of Russia and the Russian Empire: Romanov dynasty[3] (continued)		**Chairmen (or First Secretaries) of the Communist Party of the Soviet Union**	
Ivan VI	1740–41	Vladimir Lenin	1917–24
Elizabeth	1741–61 (O.S.)	Joseph Stalin	1924–53
Peter III[4]	1761–62 (O.S.)	Georgy Malenkov	1953
Catherine II	1762–96	Nikita Khrushchev	1953–64
Paul	1796–1801	Leonid Brezhnev	1964–82
Alexander I	1801–25	Yury Andropov	1982–84
Nicholas I	1825–55	Konstantin Chernenko	1984–85
Alexander II	1855–81	Mikhail Gorbachev	1985–91
Alexander III	1881–94		
Nicholas II	1894–1917	**Presidents of Russia**	
		Boris Yeltsin	1990–99
Provisional government	1917	Vladimir Putin	2000–

[1]This table includes leaders of Muscovy, Russia, the Russian Empire, and the Soviet Union.   [2]The Danilovich dynasty is a late branch of the Rurik dynasty, named after its progenitor, Daniel.   [3]On 22 (O.S.) Oct 1721, Peter I the Great took the title of "emperor." However, despite the official titling, conventional usage took an odd turn. Every male sovereign continued usually to be called tsar, but every female sovereign was conventionally called empress.   [4]The direct line of the Romanov dynasty came to an end in 1761 with the death of Elizabeth, daughter of Peter I, but subsequent rulers of the "Holstein-Gottorp dynasty" (the first, Peter III, was son of Charles Frederick, duke of Holstein-Gottorp, and Anna, daughter of Peter I) took the family name of Romanov.

Middle East

Byzantine Emperors

The Byzantine Empire was comprised of what was previously the eastern half of the Roman Empire. It survived for nearly 1,000 years after the western half had crumbled into various feudal kingdoms; it finally fell to Ottoman Turkish onslaughts in 1453. For emperors of the Eastern Roman Empire (at Constantinople) before the fall of Rome, see "Roman Emperors."

EMPEROR	REIGN	EMPEROR	REIGN
Zeno	474–491	Basil I	867–886
Anastasius I	491–518	Leo VI	886–912
Justin I	518–527	Alexander	912–913
Justinian I	527–565	Constantine VII Porphyrogenitus	913–959
Justin II	565–578	Romanus I Lecapenus	920–944
Tiberius II Constantine	578–582	Romanus II	959–963
Maurice Tiberius	582–602	Nicephorus II Phocas	963–969
Phocas	602–610	John I Tzimisces	969–976
Heraclius	610–641	Basil II Bulgaroctonus	976–1025
Heraclius Constantine	641	Constantine VIII	1025–28
Heraclonas (or Heraclius)	641	Romanus III Argyrus	1028–34
Constans II (Constantine Pogonatus)	641–668	Michael IV	1034–41
Constantine IV	668–685	Michael V Calaphates	1041–42
Justinian II Rhinotmetus	685–695	Zoe (empress)	1042–56
Leontius	695–698	Constantine IX Monomachus	1042–55
Tiberius III	698–705	Theodora (empress)	1055–56
Justinian II Rhinotmetus (restored)	705–711	Michael VI Stratioticus	1056–57
Philippicus	711–713	Isaac I Comnenus	1057–59
Anastasius II	713–715	Constantine X Ducas	1059–67
Theodosius III	715–717	Romanus IV Diogenes	1067–71
Leo III	717–741	Michael VII Ducas	1071–78
Constantine V Copronymus	741–775	Nicephorus III Botaniates	1078–81
Leo IV	775–780	Alexius I Comnenus	1081–1118
Constantine VI	780–797	John II Comnenus	1118–43
Irene (empress)	797–802	Manuel I Comnenus	1143–80
Nicephorus I	802–811	Alexius II Comnenus	1180–83
Stauracius	811	Andronicus I Comnenus	1183–85
Michael I Rhangabe	811–813	Isaac II Angelus	1185–95
Leo V	813–820	Alexius III Angelus	1195–1203
Michael II Balbus	820–829	Isaac II Angelus (restored) and Alexius IV Angelus (joint ruler)	1203–04
Theophilus	829–842		
Michael III	842–867	Alexius V Ducas Murtzuphlus	1204

Byzantine Emperors (continued)

EMPEROR	REIGN	EMPEROR	REIGN
Latin emperors		**Greek emperors restored**	
Baldwin I	1204–06	Michael VIII Palaeologus	1261–82
Henry	1206–16	Andronicus II Palaeologus	1282–1328
Peter	1217	Andronicus III Palaeologus	1328–41
Yolande (empress)	1217–19	John V Palaeologus	1341–76
Robert	1221–28	John VI Cantacuzenus	1347–54
Baldwin II	1228–61	Andronicus IV Palaeologus	1376–79
John	1231–37	John V Palaeologus (restored)	1379–90
		John VII Palaeologus	1390
Nicaean emperors		John V Palaeologus (restored)	1390–91
Constantine (XI) Lascaris	1204–05?	Manuel II Palaeologus	1391–1425
Theodore I Lascaris	1205?–22	John VIII Palaeologus	1421–48
John III Ducas Vatatzes	1222–54	Constantine XI Palaeologus	1449–53
Theodore II Lascaris	1254–58		
John IV Lascaris	1258–61		

Caliphs

When Muhammad died on 8 Jun 632, Abu Bakr, his father-in-law, succeeded to his political and administrative functions. He and his three immediate successors are known as the "perfect" or "rightly guided" caliphs. After them, the title was borne by the 14 Umayyad caliphs of Damascus (from 661–750) and subsequently by the 38 'Abbasid caliphs of Baghdad (both are named after their clans of origin). The empire of the caliphate grew rapidly through conquest during its first two centuries to include most of southwest Asia, North Africa, and Spain. 'Abbasid power ended in 945,

when the Buyids took Baghdad under their rule. They retained the 'Abbasid caliphs as figureheads; other dynasties in Central Asia and the Ganges River basin acknowledged the 'Abbasid caliphs as spiritual leaders. The Fatimids, however, proclaimed a new caliphate in 920 in their capital of al-Mahdiyah in Tunisia; it lasted until 1171, by which time opposition within the sect caused it to disintegrate. 'Abbasid authority was partially restored in the 12th century, but the caliphate ceased to exist with the Mongol destruction of Baghdad in 1258. Some principal caliphs are listed below.

CALIPH	REIGN	CALIPH	REIGN
"Perfect" caliphs		**Fatimid caliphs (al-Mahdiyah)**	
Abu Bakr	632–634	al-Mahdi	909–934
'Umar I	634–644	al-Qa'im	934–946
'Uthman ibn 'Affan	644–656	al-Mansur	946–953
'Ali	656–661	al-Mu'izz	953–975
		al-Hakim	996–1021
Umayyad caliphs (Damascus)		al-Mustansir	1036–94
Mu'awiyah I	661–680	al-Musta'li	1094–1101
Abd al-Malik	685–705		
al-Walid	705–715		
Hisham	724–743	**'Abbasid caliph (Baghdad)**	
Marwan II	744–750	an-Nasir	1180–1225
'Abbasid caliphs (Baghdad)			
as-Saffah	749–754		
Harun	786–809		
al-Ma'mun	813–833		

Persian Dynasties

Dates given are approximate and may overlap.

DYNASTY/KINGDOM	PERIOD	DYNASTY/KINGDOM	PERIOD
Median	728–550 BC	Seljuqs	1038–1157
Achaemenian	559–330 BC	Mongols[4]	1220–1335
Hellenistic period of Alexander and the Seleucids[1]	330 BC–247 BC	Timurids and Ottoman Turks	1380–1501
Parthian period (Arsacid dynasty)[2]	247 BC–AD 224	Safavid	1502–1736
Sasanian	224–651	Afghan interlude	1723–36
Arab invasion and the advent of Islam	640–829	Nader Shah	1736–47
		Zand	1750–79
Iranian intermezzo[3]	821–1055	Qajars	1794–1925
		Pahlavi	1925–79

[1]*Dates from the death of Darius III, the last Achaemenian king, and the invasion of Alexander the Great.* [2]*Dates from the year in which the Parnian chief Arsaces first battled the Seleucids.* [3]*Includes the Tahirid, Samanid, Ghaznavids, and Buyid dynasties.* [4]*Mainly the Il-Khanid dynasty (1256–1353).*

Did you know? The land boundary between Asia and Europe is a historical and cultural concept. It has changed more than once, and only as a matter of agreement is it tied to a specific borderline.

Asia

Indian Dynasties

Dates given are approximations.

DYNASTY	LOCATION	DATES	DYNASTY	LOCATION	DATES
Nanda	Ganges Valley	400 BC	Pala	Bengal	800–1100
Maurya	India, barring the area south of Mysore (Karnataka)	400–200 BC	Pratihara	western India and upper Ganges Valley	900–1100
Indo-Greeks	northern India	200–100 BC	Rastrakuta	western and central Deccan	800–1100
Sunga	Ganges Valley and parts of central India	200–100 BC	Cola	Tamil Nadu	900–1300
			Candella	Bundelkhand	1000–1200
			Cauhan	Rajasthan	1000–1200
Satavahana	northern Deccan	100 BC–AD 300	Caulukya	Gujarat	1000–1300
Saka	western India	100 BC–AD 400	Paramara	western and central India	1000–1100
Kusana	northern India and Central Asia	AD 100–300	Later Caulukya	western and central Deccan	1000–1200
Gupta	northern India	400–600			
Harsa	northern India	700	Hoysala	central and southern Deccan	1200–1400
Pallava	Tamil Nadu	400–900			
Calukya	western and central Deccan	600–800	Yadava	northern Deccan	1200–1300
			Pandya	Tamil Nadu	1300–1400

Japanese Historical Periods and Rulers

PERIOD	DATES	PERIOD	DATES
Asuka	552–710	Muromachi (or Ashikaga)	1338–1573
Nara	710–784	Azuchi-Momoyama	1574–1600
Heian	794–1185	Edo (or Tokugawa)	1603–1867
Kamakura	1192–1333	Meiji	1868–1912

Reign dates for the first 28 sovereigns (Jimmu through Senka) are taken from the *Nihon shoki* ("Chronicles of Japan"). The first 14 sovereigns are considered legendary, and while the next 14 are known to have existed, their exact reign dates have not been verified historically. When the year of actual accession and year of formal coronation are different, the latter is placed in parenthesis after the former. If the two events took place in the same year, no special notation is used. If only the coronation year is known, it is placed in parenthesis.

EMPEROR	REIGN	EMPEROR	REIGN
Jimmu	(660)–585 BC	Seinei	(480)–484
Suizei	(581)–549 BC	Kenzo	(485)–487
Annei	549–511 BC	Ninken	(488)–498
Itoku	(510)–477 BC	Buretsu	498–506
Kosho	(475)–393 BC	Keitai	(507)–531
Koan	(392)–291 BC	Ankan	531 (534)–535
Korei	(290)–215 BC	Senka	535–539
Kogen	(214)–158 BC	Kimmei	539–571
Kaika	158–98 BC	Bidatsu	(572)–585
Sujin	(97)–30 BC	Yomei	585–587
Suinin	(29 BC)–AD 70	Sushun	587–592
Keiko	(71)–130	Suiko (empress regnant)	593–628
Seimu	(131)–190	Jomei	(629)–641
Chuai	(192)–200	Kogyoku (empress regnant)	(642)–645
Jingu Kogo (regent)	201–269	Kotoku	645–654
Ojin	(270)–310	Saimei (empress regnant: Kogyoku rethroned)	(655)–661
Nintoku	(313)–399		
Richu	(400)–405	Tenji	661 (668)–672
Hanzei	(406)–410	Kobun	672
Ingyo	(412)–453	Temmu	672 (673)–686
Anko	453–456	Jito (empress regnant)	686 (690)–697
Yuryaku	456–479	Mommu	697–707

Japanese Historical Periods and Rulers (continued)

EMPEROR	REIGN	EMPEROR	REIGN
Gemmei (empress regnant)	707–715	Kameyama	1259/60–74
Gensho (empress regnant)	715–724	Gouda	1274–87
Shomu	724–749	Fushimi	1287 (1288)–98
Koken (empress regnant)	749–758	Go–Fushimi	1298–1301
Junnin	758–764	Go–Nijo	1301–08
Shotoku (empress regnant:	764 (765)–770	Hanazono	1308–18
Koken rethroned)		Go–Daigo	1318–39
Konin	770–781	Go–Murakami	1339–68
Kammu	781–806	Chokei	1368–83
Heizei	806–809	Go–Kameyama	1383–92
Saga	809–823		
Junna	823–833	**The Northern court[2]**	
Nimmyo	833–850	Kogon	1331 (1332)–33
Montoku	850–858	Komyo	1336 (1337/38)–48
Seiwa	858–876	Suko	1348 (1349/50)–51
Yozei	876 (877)–884	Go–Kogon	1351 (1353/54)–71
Koko	884–887	Go–Enyu	1371 (1374/75)–82
Uda	887–897	Go–Komatsu	1382–92
Daigo	897–930	Go–Komatsu	1392–1412
Suzaku	930–946	Shoko	1412 (1414)–28
Murakami	946–967	Go–Hanazono	1428 (1429/30)–64
Reizei	967–969	Go–Tsuchimikado	1464 (1465/66)–1500
En'yu	969–984	Go–Kashiwabara	1500 (1521)–26
Kazan	984–986	Go–Nara	1526 (1536)–57
Ichijo	986–1011	Ogimachi	1557 (1560)–86
Sanjo	1011–16	Go–Yozei	1586 (1587)–1611
Go–Ichijo	1016–36	Go–Mizunoo	1611–29
Go–Suzaku	1036–45	Meisho (empress regnant)	1629 (1630)–43
Go–Reizei	1045–68	Go–Komyo	1643–54
Go–Sanjo	1068–72	Go–Sai	1654/55 (1656)–63
Shirakawa	1072–86	Reigen	1663–87
Horikawa	1086–1107	Higashiyama	1687–1709
Toba	1107–23	Nakamikado	1709 (1710)–35
Sutoku	1123–41	Sakuramachi	1735–47
Konoe	1141–55	Momozono	1747–62
Go–Shirakawa	1155–58	Go–Sakuramachi	1762 (1763)–71
Nijo	1158–65	(empress regnant)	
Rokujo	1165–68	Go–Momozono	1771–79
Takakura	1168–80	Kokaku	1780–1817
Antoku	1180–85[1]	Ninko	1817–46
Go–Toba	1183 (1184)–98	Komei	1846 (1847)–66
Tsuchimikado	1198–1210	Meiji (personal name:	1867 (1868)–1912
Juntoku	1210 (1211)–21	Mutsuhito; era name: Meiji)	
Chukyo	1221	Taisho (personal name:	1912 (1915)–26
Goshirakawa	1221 (1222)–32	Yoshihito; era name: Taisho)	
Shijo	1232 (1233)–42	Hirohito (era name: Showa)	1926 (1928)–1989
Go–Saga	1242–46	Akihito (era name: Heisei)	1989 (1990)–
Go–Fukakusa	1246–59/60		

[1]Antoku's reign overlaps that of Go-Toba. Go-Toba was placed on the throne by the Minamoto clan after the rival Taira clan had fled Kyoto with Antoku.   [2]From 1336 until 1392 Japan witnessed the spectacle of two contending Imperial courts—the Southern court of Go-Daigo and his descendants, whose sphere of influence was restricted to the immediate vicinity of the Yoshino Mountains, and the Northern court of Kogon and his descendants, which was under the domination of the Ashikaga family.

Chinese Dynasties

Dates given for early dynasties are approximate and may overlap.

DYNASTY	ALTERNATE NAME	DATES	DYNASTY	ALTERNATE NAME	DATES
Hsia[1]	Xia	c. 2205–1766 BC	Six Dynasties[2]		220–589
Shang		c. 1760–1030 BC	Wu		222–80
Western Zhou	Chou	c. 1050–771 BC	Eastern Jin[2]		317–420
Eastern Zhou	Chou	c. 771–255 BC	Liusong		420–79
Qin	Ch'in	221–206 BC	Southern Qi		479–502
Han		206 BC–AD 220	Southern Liang		502–57
Western Jin	Chin	265–317	Southern Chen		557–89
Eastern Jin[2]	Chin	317–420	Sui		581–618

Chinese Dynasties (continued)

Dates given for early dynasties are approximate and may overlap.

DYNASTY	ALTERNATE NAME	DATES	DYNASTY	ALTERNATE NAME	DATES
T'ang	Tang	618–907	Yüan	Yuan, Mongol	1206–1368
Five Dynasties[3]	Ten Kingdoms[3]	907–960	Ming		1368–1644
Sung	Song	960–1279	Ch'ing	Qing, Manchu	1644–1911/12

[1]*The Hsia Dynasty is mentioned in legends but is of undetermined historicity.*   [2]*Between the fall of the Han and the establishment of the Sui, China was divided into two societies, northern and southern. The Six Dynasties had their capital at Nanjing in the south. The Eastern Jin is considered one of these six dynasties and so is listed twice.*   [3]*Period of time between the fall of the T'ang dynasty and the founding of the Sung dynasty, when five would-be dynasties followed one another in quick succession in North China. The era is also known as the period of the Ten Kingdoms because 10 regimes dominated separate regions of South China during the same period.*

The Americas

Pre-Columbian Civilizations

Various aboriginal American Indian cultures evolved in Meso-America (part of Mexico and Central America) and the Andean region (western South America) prior to Spanish exploration and conquest in the 16th century. These pre-Columbian civilizations were extraordinary developments in human society and culture, characterized by kingdoms and empires, great monuments and cities, and refinements in the arts, metallurgy, and writing. Dates given below are approximations.

CULTURE	LOCATION	DATES
Meso-American civilizations		
Olmec	Gulf coast of southern Mexico	1150 BC–800 BC
Zapotec	Oaxaca, particularly Monte Albán	500 BC–AD 900
Totonac	east-central Mexico	500 BC–AD 900
Teotihuacán	Teotihuacán, in the Valley of Mexico	AD 400–600
Maya	southern Mexico and Guatemala	250–900
Toltec	central Mexico	900–1200
Aztec	central and southern Mexico	1400–early 1500s
Andean civilizations		
Nazca	southern coast of Peru	200 BC–AD 600
Recuay	northern highlands of Peru	200 BC–AD 600
Tiwanaku	Lake Titicaca, Bolivia	200 BC–AD 1000
Moche (Mochica)	northern coast of Peru	AD 1–700
Inca	Pacific coast of South America	1100–1532

Encyclopædia Britannica's Most Influential Leaders of All Time

The 250 persons listed below, in the opinion of Britannica's editors, have had the greatest influence—good and bad—on the course of history and the state of the world as it is in 2002.

'Abbas I (byname 'Abbas the Great; 27 Jan 1571, Herat, Persia [now in Afghanistan]—19 Jan 1629, Mazandaran, Persia [now in Iran]), Persian ruler, shah of Persia from 1588 to 1629, who expelled Ottoman and Uzbek troops from Persia, created a standing army, and fostered commerce and the arts; Persian artistic achievement reached a high point in his reign.

Muhammad 'Abduh (1849, Nile Delta area, Egypt—11 Jul 1905, near Alexandria, Egypt), Egyptian religious scholar, jurist, and liberal reformer who led the late 19th-century movement in Egypt and other Muslim countries to revitalize Islamic teachings and institutions in the modern world.

Abu Bakr (also called As-siddiq [Arabic: "The Upright"]; c. 573, Mecca, Arabia [now in Saudi Arabia]—23 Aug 674, Medina, Arabia [Saudi Arabia]), Muhammad's closest companion and adviser, who succeeded to the Prophet's political and administrative functions, thereby initiating the office of the caliphate.

Dean (Gooderham) Acheson (11 Apr 1893, Middletown CT—12 Oct 1971, Sandy Spring MD), American secretary of state (1949–53) and adviser to four presidents; the principal creator of US foreign policy in the Cold War period.

Jane Addams (6 Sep 1860, Cedarville IL—21 May 1935, Chicago IL), American social reformer and pacifist; cowinner of the Nobel Prize for Peace, 1931.

Konrad Adenauer (5 Jan 1876, Cologne, Prussia [Germany]—19 Apr 1967, Rhöndorf, West Germany), German statesman; first chancellor of the Federal Republic of Germany (West Germany; 1949–63), presiding over its reconstruction after World War II. He supported NATO and worked to reconcile Germany with its former enemies.

Akbar (in full Abu-ul-fath Jalal-ud-din Muhammad Akbar; 15 Oct 1542, Umarkot, Sind [now Sindh province, Pakistan]—16 Oct 1605, Agra, Mughal Empire [India]), Mughal ruler; greatest of the Mughal emperors of India (1556–1605); extended Mughal power over most of the Indian subcontinent, won the loyalty of non-Muslims in his realm, and reformed, strengthened, and centralized its administrative and financial system.

Alexander the Great (also known as Alexander III or Alexander of Macedonia; 356 BC, Pella, Macedonia, [now in Greece]—13 June 323 BC, Babylon [now in Iraq]), Greek ruler and military leader; king of Macedonia (336–323 BC); overthrew the Persian Empire, carried Macedonian arms to India, and laid the foundations for the Hellenistic world of territorial kingdoms.

'Ali (in full 'Ali Ibn Abu Talib; c. 600, Mecca, Arabia [now in Saudi Arabia]—January 661, Kufah, Iraq) religious and secular leader; son-in-law of Muhammad and fourth caliph, reigning 656–661. The question of his right to the caliphate resulted in the only major split in Islam (into Sunnah and Shi'ah branches). Revered by the Shi'ah as the only true successor to the Prophet.

Muhammad 'Ali (1769, Kavala, Macedonia, Ottoman Empire [now in Greece]—2 Aug 1849, Alexandria, Egypt), Egyptian ruler; viceroy and pasha of Egypt (1805–49), founder of the dynasty that ruled Egypt from the beginning of the 19th century to the middle of the 20th. He encouraged the emergence of the modern Egyptian state.

Kofi (Atta) Annan (born 8 Apr 1938, Kumasi, Gold Coast [now Ghana]) Ghanaian diplomat; UN secretary-general from 1997; corecipient of the Nobel Prize for Peace, 2001.

Susan B(rownell) Anthony (15 Feb 1820, Adams MA—13 Mar 1906, Rochester NY), American crusader for the woman suffrage movement in the US.

Thomas Aquinas (also called Aquinas, Italian San Tommaso d'Aquino, byname Doctor Angelicus; 1224/25, Roccasecca, near Aquino, Terra di Lavoro, Kingdom of Sicily [Italy]—7 Mar 1274, Fossanova, near Terracina, Latium, Papal States, [Italy]), Italian Dominican theologian, the foremost medieval Scholasticist, canonized 18 Jul 1323; developed from Aristotelian premises conclusions in the metaphysics of personality, creation, and Providence. Responsible for the classical systematization of Latin theology and for some of the church's most beautiful eucharistic hymns.

Yasir 'Arafat (Muhammad 'Abd ar-Ra'uf al-Qudwah al-Husayni; 24? Aug 1929, Cairo, Egypt?) Palestinian statesman; president (from 1996) of the Palestinian Authority, chairman (from 1969) of the Palestine Liberation Organization (PLO), and leader of Fatah, the largest of the PLO groups. Awarded the Nobel Prize for Peace, 1994.

Aristotle (Greek Aristoteles; 384 BC, Stagira, Chalcidice, [Greece]—322 BC, Chalcis, Euboea [Greece]) ancient Greek philosopher and scientist, third (with Socrates and Plato) of the trio of ancient Greeks who laid the philosophical foundations of Western culture; he surveyed the whole of human knowledge as it was known in the Mediterranean world in his day.

Asoka (or Ashoka; c. 304 BC, India—c. 238? BC, India) last major emperor in the Mauryan dynasty of India. His vigorous patronage of Buddhism during his reign (c. 265–238 BC; also given as c. 273–232 BC) furthered the expansion of that religion throughout India.

Kemal Atatürk (original name Mustafa Kemal, also called Mustafa Kemal Pasa; 1881, Salonika [now Thessaloniki], Greece—10 Nov 1938, Istanbul,

Turkey), Turkish soldier, statesman, and reformer who was the founder and first president (1923–38) of the Republic of Turkey.

Attila (byname Flagellum Dei [Latin: "Scourge of God"]; c. 406–453) Hunnish king (434–453) and military leader; one of the greatest of the barbarian rulers who assailed the Roman Empire, invading the southern Balkan provinces and Greece and then Gaul and Italy.

Augustine (also called Saint Augustine of Hippo, original Latin name Aurelius Augustinus; 13 Nov 354, Tagaste, Numidia, [now Souk Ahras, Algeria]—28 Aug 430, Hippo Regius, [now Annaba, Algeria]), Roman clergyman and theologian, bishop of Hippo (396–430), one of the Latin Fathers of and a Doctor of the Church, and perhaps the most significant Christian thinker after St. Paul; his adaptation of classical thought to Christian teaching created a theological system of great power and lasting influence.

Caesar Augustus (also called [until 27 BC] Octavian, original name Gaius Octavius, adopted name Gaius Julius Caesar Octavianus; 23 Sep 63 BC, Velitrae, near Rome, [now Velletri, Italy]—19 Aug AD 14, Nola, near Naples, [Italy]), Roman emperor, the first following the collapse of the republic. With unlimited patience, skill, and efficiency, he overhauled every aspect of Roman life and brought durable peace and prosperity to the Greco-Roman world.

Averroës (Abu al-Walid Muhammad ibn Ahmad ibn Muhammad ibn Rushd; 1126, Cordoba, [Spain]—1198, Marrakech, Almohad Empire [now in Morocco]) Muslim religious philosopher who integrated Islamic traditions with ancient Greek thought; produced an influential series of summaries and commentaries on Aristotle and Plato and wrote several major treatises in defense of the philosophical study of religion.

Hasan al-Banna' (1906, Egypt—February 1949, Cairo) Egyptian political and religious leader who established a new religious society, the Muslim Brotherhood, and played a central role in Egyptian political and social affairs.

Stephen Báthory (Hungarian István Báthory, Polish Stefan Batory; 27 Sep 1533, Szilagysomlyo, Transylvania [now in Romania]—12 Dec 1586, near Grodno, grand duchy of Lithuania [now Hrodno, Belarus]), Hungarian-Polish ruler; prince of Transylvania (1571–76) and king of Poland (1575–86); opposed the Habsburg candidate for the Polish throne, defended Poland's eastern Baltic provinces against the Russians, and attempted to form a great state from Poland, Muscovy, and Transylvania.

Simone de Beauvoir (in full Simone Lucie-Ernestine-Marie-Bertrand de Beauvoir; 9 Jan 1908, Paris, France—14 Apr 1986, Paris, France), French writer and feminist, among the philosopher-writers who expounded on Existentialism; known primarily for *Le Deuxième sexe* (1949; *The Second Sex*), a classic of feminist literature in which she denounced what she called the myth of the "eternal feminine."

David Ben-Gurion (David Gruen; 16 Oct 1886, Plonsk, Poland, Russian Empire [now in Poland]—1 Dec 1973, Tel Aviv-Yafo, Israel), Israeli statesman and political leader, the first prime minister (1948–53, 1955–63) and defense minister (1948–53; 1955–63) of Israel; delivered Israel's declaration of independence in 1948.

Jeremy Bentham (15 Feb 1748, London, England—6 Jun 1832, London, England), English philosopher, economist, and theoretical jurist, the earliest and chief expounder of Utilitarianism.

Otto von Bismarck (in full Otto Eduard Leopold, Fürst [prince] von Bismarck, Graf [count] von Bismarck-Schönhausen, Herzog [duke] von Lauenburg; 1 Apr 1815, Schönhausen, Altmark, Prussia [Germany]—30 Jul 1898, Friedrichsruh, near Hamburg, Germany), German statesman; prime minister of Prussia (1862–73, 1873–90) and founder and first chancellor (1871–90) of the German Empire. His pacific policies in foreign affairs preserved the peace in Europe for about two decades.

Simón Bolívar (byname The Liberator, Spanish El Libertador; 24 Jul 1783, Caracas, New Granada [now in Venezuela]—17 Dec 1830, near Santa Marta, Colombia), South American soldier and statesman who led the revolutions against Spanish rule in New Granada (Colombia, Venezuela, and Ecuador), Peru, and Upper Peru (Bolivia).

Norman Ernest Borlaug (born 25 Mar 1914, Cresco IA) American agricultural scientist, plant pathologist; the increased yields resulting from Borlaug's new strains of basic crops enabled many developing countries to become agriculturally self-sufficient; Nobel Prize for Peace in 1970.

Willy Brandt (Herbert Ernst Karl Frahm; 18 Dec 1913, Lübeck, Germany—8/9 Oct 1992, Unkel, near Bonn, Germany), German statesman, leader of the Social Democratic Party of Germany and chancellor of the Federal Republic of Germany from 1969 to 1974.

Buddha (original name [Sanskrit] Gautama, or [Pali] Gotama, also called Siddhartha; c. 563 BC, Kapilavastu, Sakya republic, Kosala kingdom [India]) founder of Buddhism, the predominant religious and philosophical system of much of Asia.

Ralph (Johnson) Bunche (7 Aug 1904, Detroit MI—9 Dec 1971, New York NY), American diplomat and scholar, a key member of the UN for more than two decades; winner of the 1950 Nobel Prize for Peace for his role in brokering the 1949 Arab-Israeli truce in Palestine.

Edmund Burke (12 Jan? [1 Jan old style] 1729, Dublin, Ireland—9 Jul 1797, Beaconsfield, England), British statesman, parliamentary orator, and theorist of political Conservatism, among the foremost British political thinkers.

Julius Caesar (in full Gaius Julius Caesar; 12/13 Jul 100 BC?, Rome [Italy]—15 Mar 44 BC, Rome), Roman general and statesman, the conqueror of Gaul (58–50 BC), victor in the Civil War of 49–46 BC, and dictator (46–44 BC).

John C(aldwell) Calhoun (18 Mar 1782, Abbeville district, South Carolina—31 Mar 1850, Washington DC), American statesman; throughout his career as US congressman, secretary of war, vice president (1825–32), senator, and secretary of state, he championed states' rights, slavery, and the values of the Old South.

John Calvin (French Jean Calvin, or Cauvin; 10 Jul 1509, Noyon, Picardy, France—27 May 1564, Geneva, Switzerland), French theologian and ecclesiastical statesman; he was the leading French Protestant Reformer and the most important figure in the second generation of the Protestant Reformation.

Canute (I); in full Canute Sweynsson, byname Canute the Great; died 12 Nov 1035), as king of England (1016–35), of Denmark (as Canute II; 1019–35), and of Norway (1028–35), he was a power in the politics of 11th century Europe, respected by both emperor and pope.

Rachel (Louise) Carson (27 May 1907, Springdale PA—14 Apr 1964, Silver Spring MD). American biologist whose writings on environmental pollution and the natural history of the sea, notably *Silent Spring* (1962), are credited with creating a worldwide awareness of the dangers of environmental pollution.

Fidel Castro (born 13 Aug 1926/27, near Birán, Cuba) Cuban revolutionary and leader of Cuba from 1959, who became a symbol of communist revolution in Latin America.

Catherine II (Russian in full Yekaterina Alekseyevna, byname Catherine The Great, original name Sophie Friederike Auguste, Prinzessin [princess] Von Anhalt-zerbst; 2 May [21 Apr old style] 1729, Stettin, Prussia [now Szczecin, Poland]—17 Nov [6 Nov old style] 1796, Tsarskoye Selo [now Pushkin], near St. Petersburg, Russia), German-born empress of Russia (1762–96); led Russia into full participation in the political and cultural life of Europe and extended Russian territory to include the Crimea and much of Poland.

Camillo Benso, conte di (count of) Cavour (10 Aug 1810, Turin, Piedmont, French Empire [now in Italy]—6 Jun 1861, Turin, Italy), Piedmontese statesman who helped bring about the unification of Italy (1861) under the House of Savoy, with himself as the first prime minister.

Charlemagne (also called Charles I, byname Charles the Great; 2 Apr c. 742—28 Jan 814, Aachen, Austrasia [now in Germany], king of the Franks (768–814) and the Lombards (774–814), and emperor (800–814); conquered the Lombard kingdom in Italy, subdued the Saxons, annexed Bavaria, fought in Spain and Hungary, and, with the exception of areas in Spain, Italy, and the British Isles, united in one state nearly all the Christian lands of western Europe, over which he assumed the title of emperor.

Charles V (24 Feb 1500, Ghent, Flanders [Belgium]—21 Sep 1558, San Jerónimo de Yuste, Spain), Habsburg Holy Roman emperor (1519–56), king of Spain (as Charles I, 1516–56), and archduke of Austria (as Charles I, 1519–21), who inherited a Spanish and Habsburg empire extending across Europe; struggled to hold the empire together against the tide of Protestantism, Turkish and French pressure, and papal hostility, before abdicating to his son Philip II and his brother Ferdinand I.

Chiang Kai-shek (31 Oct 1887, Chekiang province, China—5 Apr 1975, Taipei, Taiwan), Chinese soldier and statesman, head of the Nationalist government in China from 1928 to 1949, and subsequently head of the Chinese Nationalist government in exile on Taiwan.

Sir Winston Churchill (30 Nov 1874, Blenheim Palace, Oxfordshire, England—24 Jan 1965, London, England), British statesman, orator, and author, who as prime minister (1940–45, 1951–55) rallied the British people during World War II and led his country from the brink of defeat to victory.

Henry Clay (byname The Great Pacificator, or The Great Compromiser; 12 Apr 1777, Hanover county, Virginia—29 Jun 1852, Washington DC), American statesman, US congressman (1811–14, 1815–21, 1823–25), secretary of state (1825–29), and senator (1806–07, 1810–11, 1831–42, 1849–52); promoter of the Missouri Compromise (1820), the compromise tariff of 1833, and the Compromise of 1850, all efforts to balance the rights of free and slave states. Twice the Whig candidate for president (1832, 1844).

Cleopatra VII (69 BC, Egypt—30 Aug 30 BC, Alexandria, Egypt) Egyptian ruler; queen of Egypt (51–30 BC), lover of Julius Caesar and later the wife of Mark Antony; after the Roman armies of Octavian defeated their combined forces, Antony and Cleopatra committed suicide, and Egypt fell under Roman domination. She actively influenced Roman politics at a crucial period and came to represent the prototype of the romantic *femme fatale.*

Christopher Columbus (Italian Cristoforo Colombo, Spanish Cristóbal Colón; between 26 Aug and 31 October 1451, Genoa [Italy]—20 May 1506, Valladolid, Spain), Genoese master navigator and admiral whose four transatlantic voyages (1492–93, 1493–96, 1498–1500, and 1502–04) opened the way for the European colonization of the Americas; granted the title "Admiral of the Ocean Sea" (1492) but died disappointed and convinced that the lands he had found were part of Asia.

Confucius (Chinese [Wade-Giles] K'ung-fu-tzu [Master K'ung], or K'ung-tzu, or [pinyin] Kongfuzi, or Kongzi, original name K'ung Ch'iu, literary name Chung-ni; 551 BC, Ch'ü-fu, state of Lu [now in Shantung Province], China—479 BC, Lu, China) Chinese teacher, philosopher, and political theorist, perhaps China's most famous, whose ideas (as Confucianism) have deeply influenced the civilization of East Asia.

Constantine I (byname Constantine the Great; 27 Feb after AD 280?, Naissus, Moesia, Roman Empire [now Nis, Yugoslavia]—22 May 337, Ancyrona, near Nicomedia, Bithynia, Roman Empire [now Izmit, Turkey]), Roman emperor, the first to profess Christianity. He not only initiated the evolution of the empire into a Christian state but also provided the impulse for a distinctively Christian culture that prepared the way for the growth of Byzantine and Western medieval culture.

Oliver Cromwell (25 Apr 1599, Huntingdon, Huntingdonshire, England—3 Sep 1658, London, England), English soldier and statesman who led parliamentary forces in the English Civil Wars; he was lord protector of England, Scotland, and Ireland from 1653 to 1658 during the republican Commonwealth. As lord protector, he raised his country's status once more to that of a leading European power.

Cyrus II (byname Cyrus the Great; c. 600–580 BC, Persis? [now Fars province, Iran]—529 BC?, lower Oxus river [Amu Darya]?, Central Asia), Persian conqueror who founded the Achaemenian empire, centered on Persia and stretching from the Aegean Sea to the Indus River; remembered in legend as an ideal monarch who was called the father of his people by the ancient Persians, and in the Bible as the liberator of the Jews captive in Babylonia.

Dalai Lama (Tenzin Gyatso, the 14th Dalai Lama; in full Jetsun Jamphel Ngawang Lobsang Yeshe Tenzin Gyatso [Holy Lord, Gentle Glory, Compassionate, Defender of the Faith, Ocean of Wisdom]; birth name Lhamo Dhondrub; 6 Jun 1935, Takster, Amdo province, Tibet [now Tsinghai province, China]), Tibetan spiritual leader (enthroned in 1940) and ruler-in-exile; head of the Tibetan Buddhists, who recognize him as a manifestation of the Bodhisattva of Compassion and the reincarnation of the previous Dalai Lama. Until 1959, he was both spiritual and temporal leader of Tibet (invaded by China, 1950); has led the Tibetan government-in-exile from India since 1959, and won the Nobel Prize for Peace, 1989.

Darius I (byname Darius the Great; 550 BC—486 BC) Persian ruler; king of Persia in 522–486 BC, noted for his administrative genius and for his great building projects. Darius attempted several times to conquer Greece; his fleet was destroyed by a storm in 492, and the Athenians defeated his army at Marathon in 490.

Charles Darwin (12 Feb 1809, The Mount, Shrewsbury, Shropshire, England—19 Apr 1882, Down House, Downe, Kent, England), English naturalist renowned for his documentation of evolution and for his theory of its operation, known as Darwinism.

F(rederik) W(illem) de Klerk (18 Mar 1936, Johannesburg, South Africa), politician who as president of South Africa (1989–94) brought apartheid to an end and negotiated a transition to majority rule; shared (with Nelson Mandela) the Nobel Prize for Peace, 1993.

Deng Xiaoping (Wade-Giles Teng Hsiao-p'ing; 22 Aug 1904, Sichuan province, China—19 Feb 1997, Beijing, China), Chinese communist leader, the most powerful figure in the People's Republic of China from the late 1970s until his death; abandoned orthodox communist doctrines and incorporated some elements of the free-enterprise system into the Chinese economy.

John Dewey (20 Oct 1859, Burlington VT—1 Jun 1952, New York NY), American philosopher and educator who was one of the founders of the philosophical school of pragmatism, a pioneer in functional psychology, and a leader of the progressive movement in education in the US.

Diocletian (Latin in full Gaius Aurelius Valerius Diocletianus, original name Diocles; AD 245, Salonae?, Dalmatia, Roman Empire [now Solin, Croatia]—316, Salonae) Roman emperor (284–305) who restored efficient government to the empire. His reorganization of the machinery of the empire laid the foundation for the Byzantine Empire and temporarily shored up the decaying empire of the West; presided over the last great persecution of the Christians.

Benjamin Disraeli (Earl of Beaconsfield, Viscount Hughenden of Hughenden; 21 Dec 1804, London, England—19 Apr 1881, London), British statesman and novelist who was twice prime minister (1868, 1874–80) and who provided the Conservative Party with a twofold policy of Tory democracy and imperialism.

Frederick Douglass (February 1818?, Tuckahoe MD—20 Feb 1895, Washington DC), American writer and human rights leader, an escaped slave whose oratorical and literary brilliance thrust him into the forefront of the US Abolition Movement; the first black citizen to hold high rank in the US government, as a consultant to president Lincoln (1861–65) and minister to Haiti (1889–91).

W(illiam) E(dward) B(urghardt) Du Bois (23 Feb 1868, Great Barrington MA—27 Aug 1963, Accra, Ghana), American sociologist and social activist, the most important black protest leader in the US during the first half of the 20th century; shared in the creation of the National Association for the Advancement of Colored People (NAACP).

Albert Einstein (14 Mar 1879, Ulm, Germany—18 Apr 1955, Princeton NJ), German-born American physicist who developed the special and general theories of relativity; awarded the Nobel Prize for Physics, 1921.

Dwight D(avid) Eisenhower (14 Oct 1890, Denison TX—28 Mar 1969, Washington DC), American general and statesman; 34th president of the US (1953–61) [see full biography at Presidents].

Eleanor of Aquitaine (also called Eleanor of Guyenne; c. 1122–1 Apr 1204, Fontevrault, Anjou, France), French royal; queen consort of both Louis VII of France (in 1137–52) and Henry II of England (in 1152–1204) and mother of Richard I the Lion-Heart and John of England. She was perhaps the most powerful woman in 12th-century Europe.

Elizabeth I (byname The Virgin Queen, or Good Queen Bess; 7 Sep 1533, Greenwich, near London, England—24 Mar 1603, Richmond, Surry, England), English royal; queen of England (1558–1603) during a period, often called the Elizabethan Age, when England asserted itself vigorously as a major European power in politics, commerce, and the arts.

Francis I (8 Dec 1708, Nancy, duchy of Lorraine [France]—18 Aug 1765, Innsbruck, Austria), French-born Holy Roman emperor from 13 Sep 1745; he was duke of Lorraine (as Francis Stephen) from 1729 to 1735 and grand duke of Tuscany from 1737.

Francisco Franco (Francisco Paulino Hermenegildo Teódulo Franco Bahamonde, byname El Caudillo ["The Leader"]; 4 Dec 1892, El Ferrol, Spain—20 Nov 1975, Madrid, Spain), Spanish general and leader of the Nationalist forces that overthrew the Spanish democratic republic in the Spanish Civil War (1936–39); thereafter he was the head of the government of Spain until 1973 and head of state until his death in 1975.

Benjamin Franklin (17 Jan [6 Jan old style] 1706, Boston, Massachusetts Bay Colony—17 Apr 1790, Philadelphia PA), American printer and publisher (including *Poor Richard's Almanack* [Philadelphia, 1732–64]), author, inventor and scientist, and diplomat.

Frederick II (byname Frederick the Great, German Friedrich der Grosse; 24 Jan 1712, Berlin, Prussia [Germany]—17 Aug 1786, Potsdam, Prussia), Prussian royal; king of Prussia (1740–86), a brilliant military campaigner who greatly enlarged Prussia's territories and made Prussia the foremost military power in Europe.

Milton Friedman (31 Jul 1912, Brooklyn NY) American laissez-faire economist, professor at the University of Chicago, and one of the leading conservative economists in the second half of the 20th century. Awarded the Nobel Prize for Economics, 1976.

Galileo (in full Galileo Galilei; 15 Feb 1564, Pisa [Italy]—8 Jan 1642, Arcetri, near Florence [Italy]), Italian natural philosopher, astronomer, and mathematician who made fundamental contributions to the sciences of motion, astronomy, and strength of materials and to the development of the scientific method.

Indira (Priyadarshini) Gandhi (19 Nov 1917, Allahabad, India—31 Oct 1984, New Delhi, India), Indian stateswoman; prime minister of India (1966–77 and 1980–84), assassinated by Sikh extremists

Mohandas Karamchand Gandhi (byname Mahatma ["Great-Souled"] Gandhi; 2 Oct 1869, Porbandar, India—30 Jan 1948, Delhi, India), Indian nationalist leader, head of the Indian nationalist movement against British rule, considered the father of his country; internationally esteemed for his doctrine of nonviolent protest to achieve political and social progress.

Alfonso García Robles (20 Mar 1911, Zamora, Michoacán, Mexico—2 Sep 1991, Mexico City, Mex-

ico), Mexican diplomat and advocate of nuclear disarmament, corecipient with Alva Reimer Myrdal of Sweden of the Nobel Prize for Peace, 1982.

Giuseppe Garibaldi (4 Jul 1807, Nice, French Empire [now in France]—2 Jun 1882, Caprera, Italy), Italian patriot and soldier of the Risorgimento, a republican who, by his conquest of Sicily and Naples with his guerrilla "Redshirts," contributed to the achievement of Italian unification under the royal House of Savoy.

William Lloyd Garrison (10/12 Dec 1805, Newburyport MA—24 May 1879, New York NY), American journalistic crusader who published a newspaper, *The Liberator* (1831–65), and helped lead the successful Abolitionist campaign against slavery in the US.

Bill Gates (in full William Henry Gates III; born 28 Oct 1955, Seattle WA) American computer programmer and businessman who cofounded the Microsoft Corp.

Charles de Gaulle (Charles André Joseph Marie de Gaulle; 22 Nov 1890, Lille, France—9 Nov 1970, Colombey-les-Deux-Églises), French soldier, writer, and statesman; head of two post-World War II provisional governments (1944–46), and architect and first president (1958–69) of France's Fifth Republic.

Genghis Khan (original name Temujin; 1155, 1162, or 1167, near Lake Baikal, Mongolia—18 Aug 1227), Mongolian warrior-ruler who consolidated tribes into a unified Mongolia and then extended his empire across Asia to the Adriatic Sea.

William Ewart Gladstone (29 Dec 1809, Liverpool, England—19 May 1898, Hawarden, Flintshire, Wales), British statesman and four-time prime minister of Great Britain (1868–74, 1880–85, 1886, 1892–94).

Emma Goldman (also known as Red Emma; 27 Jun 1869, Kovno, Lithuania, Russian Empire [now Kaunas, Lithuania]—14 May 1940, Toronto ON), American anarchist, orator, and author who conducted leftist activities in the US from about 1890 to 1917 and wrote and lectured on a variety of social subjects until her death.

Mikhail Sergeyevich Gorbachev (born 2 Mar 1931, Privolye, Stavropol kray, USSR) Soviet Russian official, general secretary of the Communist Party of the Soviet Union (1985–91) and president of the Soviet Union (1990–91); presided over the political and economic liberalization that led to the downfall of Soviet communism and the breakup of the USSR in 1991; was awarded the Nobel Prize for Peace, 1990.

Saint Gregory I (byname Gregory the Great; c. 540, Rome—12 Mar 604, Rome), Roman architect of the medieval papacy (reigned 590–604), a notable theologian who was also an administrative, social, liturgical, and moral reformer.

Saint Gregory VII (original name Hildebrand; c. 1020, near Soana, Papal States [now in Tuscany, Italy]—25 May 1085, Principality of Salerno, [Italy]), Italian pope, one of the great reform popes of the Middle Ages (reigned 1073–85). Mainly a spiritual rather than a political leader, he attacked various abuses in the church. Canonized 1606.

Hugo Grotius (10 Apr 1583, Delft, The Netherlands—28 Aug 1645, Rostock, Mecklenburg-Schwerin [Germany]), Dutch jurist and scholar, whose legal masterpiece, *De Jure Belli ac Pacis* (1625; On the Law of War and Peace), was one of the first great contributions to modern international law.

Che Guevara (Ernesto Guevara de la Serna; 14 Jun 1928, Rosario, Argentina—October 1967, Bolivia)

Argentine-born theoretician and tactician of guerrilla warfare, prominent Communist figure in the Cuban Revolution (1956–59), and later guerrilla leader in South America.

Gustav II Adoph (Latin Gustavus Adolphus; 9 Dec 1594, Stockholm, Sweden—6 Nov 1632, Lützen, Saxony [now in Germany]), king of Sweden (1611–32) who laid the foundations of the modern Swedish state and made it a major European power.

Johannes Gutenberg (in full Johann Gensfleisch Zur Laden Zum Gutenberg; c. 1400, Mainz, [Germany]—3? Feb 1468, Mainz), German craftsman and inventor who originated a method of printing from movable type that was used without important change until the 20th century.

Hadrian (Latin in full Caesar Traianus Hadrianus Augustus, original name [until AD 117] Publius Aelius Hadrianus; 24 Jan 76, Italica, Baetica? [now in Spain]—10 Jul 138, Baiae [Baia], near Naples [Italy]), Roman emperor (AD 117–138), the emperor Trajan's nephew and successor, who was a cultivated admirer of Greek civilization and who unified and consolidated Rome's vast empire.

Haile Selassie I (original name Tafari Makonnen; 23 Jul 1892, near Harer, Ethiopia—26 Aug 1975, Addis Ababa, Ethiopia), Ethiopian ruler; emperor of Ethiopia from 1930 to 1974; sought to modernize his country and steered it into the mainstream of post-World War II African politics. Regarded as the Messiah of the African race by the Rastafarian movement.

Alexander Hamilton (11 Jan 1755/57, Nevis, British West Indies—12 Jul 1804, New York NY), American statesman and political theorist; delegate to the Constitutional Convention (1787), major author of the *Federalist* papers, first secretary of the Treasury of the US (1789–95), and champion of a strong central government for the new US.

Dag Hammarskjöld (in full Dag Hjalmar Agne Carl Hammarskjöld; 29 Jul 1905, Jönköping, Sweden—18 Sep 1961, near Ndola, Northern Rhodesia [now Zambia]), Swedish economist and statesman, second secretary-general of the UN (1953–61), whose leadership enhanced the prestige and effectiveness of the organization; posthumously awarded the Nobel Prize for Peace, 1961.

Hammurabi (born in Babylon [now Iraq]—died c. 1750 BC) Babylonian king, the sixth and best-known ruler of the first (Amorite) dynasty (reigning c. 1792–50 BC), noted for his surviving set of laws, once considered the oldest promulgation of laws in human history.

Harun ar-Rashid (Feb 766/Mar 763, Rayy, Iran—24 Mar 809, T'us [near modern Meshed], Iran), fifth caliph of the 'Abbasid dynasty (786–809), who ruled Islam at the zenith of its empire.

G(eorg) W(ilhelm) F(riedrich) Hegel (27 Aug 1770, Stuttgart, Württemberg [Germany]—14 Nov 1831, Berlin [Germany]), German philosopher who developed a dialectical scheme that emphasized the progress of history and of ideas from thesis to antithesis and thence to a synthesis. His work marks the pinnacle of classical German philosophy.

Henry the Navigator (Portuguese Henrique o Navegador, [prince] de Portugal, Duque [duke] de Viseu, Senhor [lord] da Covilhã, byname of Henrique, Infante; 4 Mar 1394, Porto, Portugal—13 Nov 1460, Vila do Infante, near Sagres, Portugal), Portuguese prince noted for his patronage of voyages of discovery among the Madeira Islands and along the western coast of Africa, his grand strategy—not to

be brought to fulfillment until after his death—whereby Christian Europe outflanked the power of Islam by establishing contact with Africa south of the Sahara and with Asia.

Henry VIII (28 Jun 1491, Greenwich, near London, England—28 Jan 1547, London, England), English king (1509–47), who presided over the beginnings of the English Renaissance and the English Reformation.

Theodor Herzl (2 May 1860, Budapest, Hungary, Austrian Empire [now in Hungary]—3 Jul 1904, Edlach, Austria), Hungarian political organizer; founder of the political form of Zionism. His pamphlet *The Jewish State* (1896) proposed that the Jewish question was a political question to be settled by a world council of nations.

Ito Hirobumi (original name Toshisuke; 14 Oct 1841, Suo province, Japan—26 Oct 1909, Harbin, Manchuria, China), Japanese elder statesman and premier (1885–88, 1892–96, 1898, 1900–01), who played a crucial role in the building of modern Japan. He helped draft the Meiji constitution (1889) and brought about the establishment of a bicameral national Diet (1890).

Hirohito (original name Michinomiya Hirohito, posthumous name Showa; 29 Apr 1901, Tokyo, Japan—7 Jan 1989, Tokyo, Japan), Japanese royal; emperor of Japan from 1926 until his death in 1989, the longest-reigning monarch in Japan's history.

Adolf Hitler (byname Der Führer [German: "The Leader"]; 20 Apr 1889, Braunau am Inn, Austria—30 Apr 1945, Berlin, Germany), Austrian-born German dictator; leader of the National Socialist (Nazi) Party (from 1920–21) and chancellor and Führer of Germany (1933–45). Hitler presided over the aggressive expansion of German territory that sparked World War II in Europe, and he set in motion the confiscation of property, internment, and systematic murder of some six million Jews and other "enemies" of his Aryan German state.

Ho Chi Minh (Nguyen Sinh Cung; 19 May 1890, Hoang Tru, Vietnam, French Indochina—2 Sep 1969, Hanoi, Vietnam), Vietnamese founder of the Indochina Communist Party (1930) and the Viet-Minh (1941), and president (1945–69) of North Vietnam; a prime mover of the post-World War II anticolonial movement in Asia and one of the most influential communist leaders of the 20th century.

Thomas Hobbes (5 Apr 1588, Westport, Wiltshire, England—4 Dec 1679, Hardwick Hall, Derbyshire, England), English philosopher and political theorist, best known for his publications on individual security and the social contract.

Oliver Wendell Holmes, Jr. (byname The Great Dissenter; 8 Mar 1841, Boston MA—6 Mar 1935, Washington DC), American jurist; legal historian and philosopher who advocated judicial restraint. He stated the concept of "clear and present danger" as the only basis for limiting free speech; justice of the Supreme Court, 1902–32.

Félix Houphouët-Boigny (18 Oct 1905, Yamoussoukro, Côte d'Ivoire, French West Africa—7 Dec 1993, Yamoussoukro, Côte d'Ivoire), Ivoirien politician and physician who was president of Côte d'Ivoire from independence in 1960 until his death; under his rule it became one of the most prosperous nations in sub-Saharan Africa.

David Hume (7 May [26 Apr old style] 1711, Edinburgh, Scotland—25 Aug 1776, Edinburgh, Scotland), Scottish philosopher, historian, economist, and essayist, known especially for his philosophical empiricism and skepticism.

Hung Hsiu-ch'üan (pinyin Hong Xiuquan; 1 Jan 1814, Fuyüan-shui, Kwangtung, China—1 Jun 1864, Nanking), Chinese religious prophet and leader of the Taiping Rebellion (1850–64), during which he declared his own new dynasty, which centered on the captured (1853) city of Nanking.

Al-Husayn ibn 'Ali (624, Medina, Arabia [now Saudi Arabia]—10 Oct 680, Medina), Shi'ite Muslim hero, grandson of the prophet Muhammad, and son of 'Ali (the fourth Islamic caliph) and Fatimah, daughter of Muhammad. He is revered by Shi'ite Muslims as the third imam.

Saddam Hussein (in full Saddam Hussein At-Tikriti; 28 Apr 1937, Tikrit district, Iraq) Iraqi military leader and politician; president of Iraq from 1979.

Ibn Khaldun (in full Wali Al-din 'abd Ar-rahman Ibn Muhammad Ibn Muhammad Ibn Abi Bakr Muhammad Ibn Al-hasan Ibn Khaldun; 27 May 1332, Tunis [Tunisia]—17 Mar 1406, Cairo, [Egypt]), Arab historian, who developed one of the earliest nonreligious philosophies of history.

Ibn Sa'ud (in full 'abd Al-'aziz Ibn 'abd Ar-rahman Ibn Faysal Ibn Turki 'abd Allah Ibn Muhammad Al Sa'ud; 1880, Riyadh, Arabia—9 Nov 1953, at-Ta'if, Saudi Arabia), Arabian tribal and Muslim religious leader who formed the modern state of Saudi Arabia and initiated the exploitation of its oil.

Innocent III (1160/61, Gavignano Castle, Campagna di Roma, Papal States [now outside Rome, Italy]—16 July 1216, Perugia [Italy]), Italian clergyman; pope from 1198 to 1216, under whom the medieval papacy reached the height of its prestige and power.

Isabella I (byname Isabella The Catholic; 22 Apr 1451, Madrigal de las Altas Torres, Castile [Spain]—26 Nov 1504, Medina del Campo, Spain), Spanish royal, queen of Castile (1474–1504) and of Aragon (1479–1504), ruling the two kingdoms from 1479 with her husband, Ferdinand II of Aragon (Ferdinand V of Castile). Their reign saw the beginning of an empire in the New World, discovered by Christopher Columbus under Isabella's sponsorship.

Isma'il I (17 Jul 1487, Ardabil?, Azerbaijan—23 May 1524, Ardabil, Safavid Iran), Iranian royal; shah of Iran (1501–24) and religious leader who founded the Safavid dynasty (first native dynasty to rule the kingdom in 800 years) and converted Iran from the Sunni to the Shi'i sect of Islam.

Andrew Jackson (15 Mar 1767, Waxhaws region, South Carolina—8 Jun 1845, the Hermitage, near Nashville TN), American military hero, statesman, and seventh president of the US (1829–37) [see full biography at Presidents].

Ja'far ibn Muhammad (also called Ja'far As-sadiq [Arabic: "Ja'far the Trustworthy"]; 699/700 or 702/703, Medina, Arabia [now Saudi Arabia]—765, Medina, Arabia [now Saudi Arabia]) Islamic leader; sixth imam, or spiritual successor to the Prophet Muhammad, of the Shi'ite branch of Islam and the last to be recognized as imam by all the Shi'ite sects.

Jamal ad-Din al-Afghani (in full Jamal Ad-din Al-afghani As-sayyid Muhammad Ibn Safdar Al Husayn; 1838, Asadabad, Persia [now Iran]—9 Mar 1897, Istanbul, Ottoman Empire [now in Turkey]), Muslim politician, political agitator, and journalist whose belief in the potency of a revived Islamic civilization in the face of European domination significantly influenced the development of Muslim thought in the 19th and early 20th centuries.

John Jay (12 Dec 1745, New York NY—17 May 1829, Bedford NY), American founding father who served the new nation in both law and diplomacy; first chief justice of the US Supreme Court (1789–95).

Thomas Jefferson (2 Apr [13 Apr n.s.] 1743, Shadwell VA—4 July 1826, Monticello VA), American statesman; third president of the US (1801–09) [see full biography at Presidents].

Jesus Christ (also called Jesus of Galilee or Jesus of Nazareth; c. 6–4 BC, Bethlehem, Palestine, Roman Empire [now in Israel]—c. AD 30, Jerusalem, Palestine [now in Israel]) Hebrew prophet, the founder of Christianity, revered by Christians as the son of God.

Saint Joan of Arc (byname The Maid of Orléans, French Sainte Jeanne d'Arc, or La Pucelle d'Orléans; c. 1412, Domrémy, Bar, France—30 May 1431, Rouen, France), French religious visionary and military leader; the national heroine of France, a peasant girl who, believing that she was acting under divine guidance, led the French army in a momentous victory at Orléans that repulsed an English attempt to conquer France during the Hundred Years' War.

John (byname John Lackland; 24 Dec 1167, Oxford, England—18/19 Oct 1216, Newark, Nottinghamshire, England), English king of England from 1199 to 1216; he was forced to seal the Magna Carta (1215).

John XXIII (25 Nov 1881, Sotto il Monte, Italy—3 Jun 1963, Rome, Italy), Italian pope; one of the most popular of all times (reigned 1958–63), who inaugurated a new era in the history of the Roman Catholic Church by his openness to change, shown especially in his convoking of the second Vatican Council.

John Paul II (Latin Johannes Paulus, original name Karol Jozef Wojtyla; 18 May 1920, Wadowice, Poland) Polish-born pope (from 1978); the first non-Italian to serve in that capacity in 455 years and the first ever from a Slavic country. By 2002 he had made almost 100 trips abroad and traveled greater distances than all other popes combined in his efforts at global bridge-building.

Benito (Pablo) Juárez (21 Mar 1806, San Pablo Guelatao, Oaxaca, Mexico—18 Jul 1872, Mexico City, Mexico), Mexican reformer and statesman; a national hero of Mexico, president of Mexico (1861–72), who, for three years (1864–67), fought against foreign occupation under the emperor Maximilian and who sought constitutional reforms to create a democratic federal republic.

Justinian I (Latin in full Flavius Justinianus, original name Petrus Sabbatius; 483, Tauresium, Dardania—14 Nov 565, Constantinople, Byzantium [now Istanbul, Turkey]), Byzantine emperor (527–565), noted for his administrative reorganization of the imperial government and for his sponsorship of a codification of laws known as the Codex Justinianus (534).

K'ang Yu-wei (Pinyin Kang Youwei; 19 Mar 1858, Kwangtung province, China—31 Mar 1927, Tsing tao, Shantung province, China), Chinese scholar, a leader of the Reform Movement of 1898 and a key figure in the intellectual development of modern China; sought to promote Confucianism as an antidote against "moral degeneration" and indiscriminate westernization.

K'ang-hsi (pinyin Kangxi (reign name), personal name (Wade-Giles) Hsüan-yeh, temple name (Ch'ing) Sheng Tsu, posthumous name Jen Ti; 4 May 1654, Beijing, China—20 Dec 1722, Beijing, China), Chinese emperor, second emperor of the Ch'ing dynasty (1661–1722); extended Chinese control over

parts of Russia, Outer Mongolia, and Tibet. Opened ports to foreign trade and encouraged the introduction of Western culture and religion.

Jomo Kenyatta (original name Kamau Ngengi; c. 1894, Ichaweri, British East Africa [now in Kenya]—22 Aug 1978, Mombasa, Kenya), Kenyan statesman and nationalist, the first prime minister (1963–64) and then president (1964–78) of independent Kenya.

John Maynard Keynes (5 Jun 1883, Cambridge, England—21 Apr 1946, Firle, Sussex, England), English economist, journalist, and financier, best known for his revolutionary economic theories (Keynesian economics) on the causes of prolonged unemployment.

Ruhollah Khomeini (original name Ruhollah Musawi; 17 May 1900, Khomeyn, Iran—3 Jun 1989, Tehran, Iran), Iranian Shi'ite cleric who led the revolution that overthrew Mohammad Reza Shah Pahlavi in 1979 and who was Iran's ultimate political and religious authority for the next 10 years.

Nikita (Sergeyevich) Khrushchev (17 Apr 1894, Kalinovka, Ukraine, Russian Empire—11 Sep 1971, Moscow, USSR), Ukrainian-born Soviet politician; first secretary of the Communist Party of the Soviet Union (1953–64) and premier of the Soviet Union (1958–64) whose policy of de-Stalinization had widespread repercussions throughout the Communist Bloc.

Kim Il-sung (original name Kim Song Ju; 5 Apr 1912, Man'gyondae, near P'yongyang, Korea [now in North Korea]—8 Jul 1994, P'yongyang, North Korea), Korean politician; communist leader of North Korea from 1948 until his death. He was the nation's premier from 1948 to 1972, chairman of its dominant Korean Workers (Communist) Party from 1949, and president and head of state from 1972.

Martin Luther King, Jr. (15 Jan 1929, Atlanta GA—4 Apr 1968, Memphis TN), American Baptist minister, a compelling orator who led the civil-rights movement in the US from the mid-1950s until his death by assassination in 1968. His leadership was fundamental to that movement's success in ending the legal segregation of blacks in the US.

W(illiam) L(yon) Mackenzie King (17 Dec 1874, Berlin ON—22 Jul 1950, Kingsmere PQ), Canadian statesman; prime minister of Canada (1921–26, 1926–30, 1935–48) and leader of the Liberal Party, who helped preserve the unity of the English and French populations of Canada.

Henry A(lfred) Kissinger (27 May 1923, Fürth, Germany) German-born Amrican political scientist, adviser for national security affairs, secretary of state from 22 Sep 1973 in the second term cabinet of Pres. Richard Nixon and the cabinet of Pres. Gerald Ford. With Le Duc Tho of North Vietnam, awarded the Nobel Prize for Peace in 1973 for their efforts toward ending the Vietnam War.

Lajos Kossuth (19 Sep 1802, Monok, Hungary—20 Mar 1894, Turin, Italy), Hungarian political reformer who inspired and led Hungary's struggle for independence from Austria.

Peter Alekseyevich Kropotkin (21 Dec 1842 [9 Dec old style], Moscow, Russia—8 Feb 1921, Dmitrov, near Moscow), Russian revolutionary and geographer, the foremost theorist of the anarchist movement.

Kublai Khan (1215—1294) Mongolian general and statesman, grandson of Genghis Khan. He conquered China and became the first emperor of its Yüan, or Mongol, dynasty.

Lao-tzu (Pinyin Laozi [Chinese: "Master Lao," or "Old Master"]; lived 6th century BC) Chinese philosopher of Taoism and the alleged author of the *Tao-te Ching*. Venerated as a philosopher by Confucianists and as a saint or god by some of the common people and was worshiped as an imperial ancestor during the T'ang dynasty.

Vladimir Ilich Lenin (10 Apr [22 Apr n.s.] 1870, Simbirsk, Russia—21 Jan 1924, Gorki [later Gorki Leninskiye], near Moscow, USSR), Russian revolutionary, political theorist, and statesman, founder of the Russian Communist Party (Bolsheviks), inspirer and leader of the Bolshevik Revolution (1917), and the architect, builder, and first head (1917–24) of the Soviet state.

Saint Leo I (byname Leo The Great; 4th century, Tuscany?—10 Nov 461, Rome), Roman pope from 440 to 461, master exponent of papal supremacy.

Leo X (original name Giovanni de' Medici; 11 Dec 1475, Florence—1 Dec 1521, Rome), Italian pope (1513–21), one of the most extravagant of the Renaissance popes; made Rome a center of culture and increased papal political power in Europe. By his response to the Reformation (he excommunicated Martin Luther), contributed to the dissolution of the unified Church.

Abraham Lincoln (12 Feb 1809, near Hodgenville KY—15 Apr 1865, Washington DC), American statesman; 16th president of the US, 1861–65 [see full biography at Presidents].

David Lloyd George (also called [1945] 1st Earl Lloyd-George of Dwyfor, Viscount Gwynedd of Dwyfor; 17 Jan 1863, Manchester, England—26 Mar 1945, Tynewydd, near Llanystumdwy, Caernarvonshire, Wales), British prime minister (1916–22) who dominated the British political scene in the latter part of World War I.

John Locke (29 Aug 1632, Wrington, Somerset, England—28 Oct 1704, Oates, Essex, England), English philosopher who was an initiator of the Enlightenment in England and France, an inspirer of the US Constitution, and the author of, among other works, "An Essay Concerning Human Understanding," his account of human knowledge.

Louis XIV (byname Louis The Great, Louis The Grand Monarch, or The Sun King; 5 Sep 1638, Saint-Germain-en-Laye, France—1 Sep 1715, Versailles, France), French king (1643–1715) who ruled his country during one of its most brilliant periods and who remains the symbol of absolute monarchy of the classical age.

Martin Luther (10 Nov 1483, Eisleben, Saxony [Germany]—18 Feb 1546, Eisleben, Saxony [Germany]), German priest and scholar whose questioning of the Roman Catholic church led to the Protestant Reformation. His actions and writings led to a movement which created one of the three major theological units of Christianity and became a seedbed for social, economic, and political thought.

Seán MacBride (26 Jan 1904, Paris, France—15 Jan 1988, Dublin, Ireland), Irish statesman; was awarded the Nobel Prize for Peace in 1974 for his efforts on behalf of human rights.

Niccolò Machiavelli (3 May 1469, Florence [Italy]—21 Jun 1527, Florence [Italy]), Italian writer and statesman, Florentine patriot, and original political theorist whose principal work, *The Prince*, brought him a reputation of amoral cynicism.

Mahmud (in full Yamin Al-daula Abu'l-qasim Mahmud Ibn Sebüktigin; 971—30? Apr 1030, Ghazna, [Afghanistan]), Islamic sultan of the kingdom of Ghazna (998–1030), originally comprising modern Afghanistan and northeastern modern Iran but, through his conquests, eventually including north-western India and most of Iran.

Malcolm X (original name Malcolm Little, Muslim name el-Hajj Malik el-Shabazz; 19 May 1925, Omaha NE—21 Feb 1965, New York NY), American black militant leader who articulated concepts of race pride and black nationalism in the early 1960s.

Thomas Robert Malthus (14/17 Feb 1766, Rookery, near Dorking, Surrey, England—23 Dec 1834, St. Catherine, near Bath, Somerset, England), English economist and demographer, best known for his theory that population growth will always tend to outrun the food supply and that betterment of the lot of mankind is impossible without stern limits on reproduction.

Nelson Rolihlahla Mandela (18 Jul 1918, Umtata, Cape of Good Hope, South Africa) South African black nationalist leader and statesman; political prisoner 1962–90, president of South Africa (1994–99); co-recipient of the Nobel Prize for Peace, 1993.

Mao Zedong (Wade-Giles Mao Tse-tung; 26 Dec 1893, Shaoshan, Hunan province, China—9 Sep 1976, Beijing, China), Chinese Marxist theorist, soldier, and statesman who led China's communist revolution. Leader of Chinese Communist Party from 1931, chief of state of People's Republic of China (1949–59) and chairman of the party until his death.

Maria Theresa (German Maria Theresia; 13 May 1717, Vienna, Austria, Holy Roman Empire—29 Nov 1780, Vienna, Austria), Habsburg royal; archduchess of Austria and queen of Hungary and Bohemia (1740–80), wife and empress of Holy Roman emperor Francis I (reigned 1745–65), mother of Holy Roman emperor Joseph II (reigned 1765–90). Her accession sparked the War of the Austrian Succession (1740–48), the Seven Years' War (1756–63), and the War of the Bavarian Succession (1778–79), diminishing Austrian power.

George C(atlett) Marshall (31 Dec 1880, Uniontown PA—16 Oct 1959, Washington DC), American general of the army and US Army chief of staff during World War II (1939–45) and later secretary of state (1947–49) and of defense (1950–51). The European Recovery Program he proposed in 1947 became known as the Marshall Plan. He received the Nobel Prize for Peace, 1953.

John Marshall (24 Sep 1755, near Germantown, Virginia—6 Jul 1835, Philadelphia PA), American jurist, the fourth chief justice of the US and principal founder of the US system of constitutional law, including the doctrine of judicial review.

Karl (Heinrich) Marx (5 May 1818, Trier, Rhine province, Prussia [now in Germany]—14 Mar 1883, London, England), German revolutionary, sociologist, historian, and economist. Published (with Friedrich Engels) *The Communist Manifesto* (1848); also the author of socialist movement's most important book, *Das Kapital*.

Tomas (Garrigue) Masaryk (7 Mar 1850, near Göding, Moravia, Austrian Empire [now Hodonin, Czech Republic] 14 Sep 1937, Lany, Czechoslovakia), Czech statesman; chief founder and first president (1918–35) of Czechoslovakia.

Giuseppe Mazzini (22 Jun 1805, Genoa [Italy]—10 Mar 1872, Pisa, Italy), Genoese propagandist and revolutionary, founder of the secret revolutionary society Young Italy (1832), and a champion of the movement for Italian unity known as the Risorgimento.

Lorenzo de' Medici (byname Lorenzo The Magnificent; 1 Jan 1449, Florence [Italy]—9 Apr 1492, Careggi, near Florence), Florentine statesman, ruler, and patron of arts and letters, the most brilliant of the Medici. Ruled Florence (1469–78) with his younger brother, Giuliano, and, after the latter's assassination, was sole ruler (1478–92).

Mehmed II (30 Mar 1432, Adrianople, Thrace, Ottoman Empire [now Edirne, Turkey]—3 May 1481, Hunkarcayiri, near Maltepe, Ottoman Empire [now in Turkey]), Ottoman Turkish sultan (1444–46 and 1451–81). Captured Constantinople and conquered territories in Anatolia and the Balkans that comprised the Ottoman Empire's heartland for the next four centuries.

Meiji (in full Meiji Tenno, personal name Mutsuhito; 3 Nov 1852, Kyoto, Japan—30 Jul 1912, Tokyo, Japan), Japanese royal; emperor of Japan from 1867 to 1912, during whose reign Japan was dramatically transformed from a feudal country into one of the great powers of the modern world.

Klemens, Fürst von Metternich (in full Klemens Wenzel Nepomuk Lothar, Fürst Von Metternich-winneburg-beilstein; 15 May 1773, Coblenz, Archbishopric of Trier—11 Jun 1859, Vienna, Austria), Austrian statesman, minister of foreign affairs (1809–48), and a champion of conservatism, who helped form the victorious alliance against Napoleon I.

John Stuart Mill (20 May 1806, London, England—8 May 1873, Avignon, France), English philosopher, economist, and exponent of Utilitarianism.

Yoritomo Minamoto (1147, Japan—9 Feb 1199, Kamakura, Japan), Japanese founder of the bakufu, or shogunate, a system whereby feudal lords ruled Japan for 700 years.

Daniel Totoitich arap Moi (1924, Sacho, Kenya colony [now in Kenya]) Kenyan politician; president of Kenya from 1978.

Jean Monnet (9 Nov 1888, Cognac, France—16 Mar 1979, Houjarray, France), French political economist and diplomat who, after World War II, initiated comprehensive economic planning in Western Europe. He was the first president (1952–55) of the European Coal and Steel Community, a forerunner of the European Union.

James Monroe (28 Apr 1758, Westmoreland County, Virginia—4 Jul 1831, New York NY), American statesman; fifth president of the US (1817–25) [see full biography at Presidents].

Montesquieu (Charles-Louis de Secondat, baron de La Brede et de Montesquieu; 18 Jan 1689, Château La Brède, near Bordeaux, France—10 Feb 1755, Paris, France), French political philosopher whose major work, *The Spirit of Laws*, was a major contribution to political theory.

Sir Thomas More (7 Feb 1477, London, England—6 Jul 1535, London, England), British humanist and statesman, chancellor of England (1529–32), who was beheaded for refusing to accept King Henry VIII as head of the Church of England. He is recognized as a saint by the Roman Catholic church.

Moses (fl. 14th–13th century BCE), Hebrew prophet, teacher, and leader who delivered his people from Egyptian slavery. He founded the religious community known as Israel and organized of the community's religious and civil traditions. In the Judaic tradition, he is revered as the greatest prophet and teacher.

Muhammad (in full Abu al-Qasim Muhammad ibn 'Abd Allah ibn 'Abd al-Mut talib ibn Hashim; c. 570, Mecca, Arabia [now in Saudi Arabia]—8 Jun 632,

Medina, Arabia [now in Saudi Arabia]), Arabian prophet; founder of the religion of Islam and of the Muslim community.

Benito Mussolini (29 Jul 1883, Predappio, Italy—28 Apr 1945, near Dongo, Italy), Italian prime minister (1922–43) and the first of 20th-century Europe's fascist dictators.

Napoleon I (French in full Napoléon Bonaparte, original Italian Napoleone Buonaparte, byname The Corsican, or The Little Corporal; 15 Aug 1769, Ajaccio, Corsica—5 May 1821, St. Helena Island [South Atlantic Ocean]), Corsican-born French general, first consul (1799–1804), and emperor of the French (1804–14/15). Revolutionized military organization and training; sponsored the Napoleonic Code, the prototype of later civil-law codes; reorganized education; and established the Concordat with the papacy.

Gamal Abdel Nasser (15 Jan 1918, Alexandria, Egypt—28 Sep 1970, Cairo, Egypt), Egyptian army officer, prime minister (1954–56) and then president (1956–70) of Egypt.

Nebuchadrezzar II (c. 630 BC—c. 561 BC) Babylonian ruler; the second and greatest king of the Chaldean dynasty of Babylonia (reigned c. 605–c. 561 BC); known for his military might, the splendor of his capital, Babylon, and his important part in Jewish history.

Jawaharlal Nehru (byname Pandit [Hindi: "pundit," or "teacher"] Nehru; 14 Nov 1889, Allahabad, India—27 May 1964, New Delhi, India), Indian statesman; first prime minister of independent India (1947–64), who established parliamentary government and became noted for his "neutralist" policies in foreign affairs.

Richard Milhous Nixon (9 Jan 1913, Yorba Linda CA—22 Apr 1994, New York NY), American statesman; 37th president of the US (1969–74) [see full biography at Presidents].

Nizam al-Mulk (Arabic "Order of the Kingdom"; original name Abu 'ali Hasan Ibn 'ali; 1018/19, Tus, Khorasan, Iran—14 Oct 1092, near Nehavand, Iran), Persian vizier of the Turkish Seljuq sultans (1063–92), best remembered for his large treatise on kingship, *Seyasat-nameh* (*The Book of Government; or Rules for Kings*).

Kwame Nkrumah (Sep 1909, Nkroful, Gold Coast [now Ghana]—27 Apr 1972, Bucharest, Romania), Ghanaian nationalist leader who led the Gold Coast's drive for independence from Britain and presided over its emergence (1957) as the new nation of Ghana; prime minister 1957–60, president 1960–66.

Julius (Kambarage) Nyerere (also called Mwalimu [Swahili: "teacher"]; March 1922, Butiama, Tanganyika [now Tanzania]—14 Oct 1999, London, England), Tanzanian statesman; first prime minister of independent Tanganyika (1961), first president of the new state of Tanzania (1964), and the major force behind the Organization of African Unity.

Bernardo O'Higgins (20 Aug 1778, Chillán, Chile, viceroyalty of La Plata—October 1842, Peru) Chilean revolutionary leader and first Chilean head of state ("supreme director," 1817–23), who commanded the military forces that won independence from Spain.

Saint Paul the Apostle (original name Saul of Tarsus; c. AD 10?, Tarsus, Cilicia [now in Turkey]—67?, Rome), Jewish Christian missionary and theologian; after first being a bitter enemy of Christianity, later

became an important figure in its history and author of several texts now part the New Testament.

Lester B(owles) Pearson (23 Apr 1897, Toronto ON—27 Dec 1972, Ottawa ON), Canadian politician, diplomat, and prime minister of Canada; was awarded the Nobel Prize for Peace, 1957.

Shimon Peres (original name Shimon Perski; 16 Aug 1923, Wolozyn, Poland [now Valozhyn, Belarus]), Israeli statesman, leader of the Israel Labor Party (1977–92; 1995–97), and prime minister (1984–86, 1995–96); shared the Nobel Prize for Peace, 1994.

Pericles (c. 495 BC, Athens—429 BC, Athens) Athenian statesman largely responsible for the full development, in the later 5th century BC, of both the Athenian democracy and the Athenian empire, making Athens the political and cultural focus of Greece.

Peter I (Russian in full Pyotr Alekseyevich, byname Peter the Great; 9 Jun [30 May old style] 1672, Moscow, Russia—8 Feb [28 Jan old style] 1725, St. Petersburg, Russia), tsar of Russia, who in 1721 was proclaimed emperor; he was one of his country's greatest statesmen, organizers, and reformers.

Saint Peter the Apostle (original name Simeon, or Simon; born in Bethsaida, Galilee, Palestine [now in Israel]—c. AD 64, Rome), Jewish disciple of Jesus Christ, recognized in the early Christian church as the leader of the disciples and by the Roman Catholic church as the first of its unbroken succession of popes.

William Pitt, the Elder (15 Nov 1708, London, England—11 May 1778, Hayes, Kent, England), British statesman, twice virtual prime minister (1756–61, 1766–68), who secured the transformation of his country into an imperial power.

Pius IX (original name Giovanni Maria Mastai-ferretti; 13 May 1792, Senigallia, Papal States—7 Feb 1878, Rome), Italian pontiff whose reign (1846–78) was the longest in history and was marked by a transition from liberalism to conservatism, including the declaration of the dogma of the Immaculate Conception (1854) and the first Vatican Council (1869–70).

Plato (428/427 BC, Athens, or Aegina, Greece—348/347 BC, Athens, Greece) ancient Greek philosopher; building on the teachings of Socrates, he developed an ethical philosophy devoted to the proposition that reason must be followed wherever it leads.

Pol Pot (original name Saloth Sar; 19 May 1925/28, Kompong Thom province, Cambodia—15 Apr 1998, near Anlong Veng, Cambodia), Khmer political leader whose totalitarian regime (1975–79) imposed severe hardships on the people of Cambodia. His radical communist government forced the mass evacuations of cities, killed or displaced millions, and left a legacy of brutality and impoverishment.

Marco Polo (c. 1254, Venice [Italy], or Curzola, Venetian Dalmatia [now Korcula, Croatia]—8 Jan 1324, Venice), Venetian merchant and adventurer who traveled from Europe to Asia in 1271–95, remaining in China for 17 of those years; his written account of his journeys is a classic of travel literature.

Qin Shihuangdi (Pinyin Shi Huangdi, personal name Chao Cheng; c. 259 BC, Ch'in, northwestern China—210/209, China) Chinese emperor of the Ch'in dynasty (221–210/209 BC), creator of the first unified Chinese empire.

Yitzhak Rabin (1 Mar 1922, Jerusalem, Palestine [now in Israel]—4 Nov 1995, Tel Aviv-Yafo, Israel), Israeli statesman and soldier; headed Israeli armed forces during Six-Day War (June 1967), leader of the Israel Labour Party and prime minister of Israel (1974–77, 1992–95); shared the Nobel Prize for Peace, 1994.

Cecil (John) Rhodes (5 Jul 1853, Bishop's Stortford, Hertfordshire, England—26 Mar 1902, Muizenberg, Cape Colony [now Cape Province, South Africa]), British financier, statesman, and empire builder of British South Africa, prime minister of Cape Colony (1890–96); organized diamond-mining company De Beers Consolidated Mines, Ltd. (1888) and established Oxford's Rhodes scholarship (1902).

Cardinal Richelieu (Armand-Jean du Plessis, cardinal et duc de [cardinal and duke of]; byname The Red Eminence; 9 Sep 1585, Richelieu, Poitou, France—4 Dec 1642, Paris, France), French statesman and clergyman, chief minister (1624–42) to King Louis XIII of France; his major goals were the establishment of royal absolutism in France and the end of Spanish-Habsburg hegemony in Europe.

José Rizal (y Alonso; in full José Protasio Rizal Mercado y Alonso Realonda; 19 Jun 1861, Calamba, Philippines—30 Dec 1896, Manila, Philippines), Filipino patriot, physician, and man of letters who was an inspiration to the Philippine nationalist movement.

Robespierre (Maximilien-François-Marie-Isidore de Robespierre; 6 May 1758, Arras, France—28 Jul 1794, Paris, France), French revolutionary; radical Jacobin leader and one of the principal figures in the French Revolution.

Eleanor Roosevelt (née Anna Eleanor Roosevelt; 11 Oct 1884, New York NY—7 Nov 1962, New York NY), American diplomat, humanitarian, and the wife of Pres. Franklin D. Roosevelt; one of the world's most widely admired women.

Franklin Delano Roosevelt (byname FDR; 30 Jan 1882, Hyde Park, NY—12 Apr 1945, Warm Springs GA), American statesman; 32nd president of the US (1933–45) [see full biography at Presidents].

Theodore Roosevelt (bynames Teddy Roosevelt and TR; 27 Oct 1858, New York NY—6 Jan 1919, Oyster Bay NY), American statesman; 26th president of the US (1901–09) [see full biography at Presidents].

Jean-Jacques Rousseau (28 Jun 1712, Geneva, Switzerland—2 July 1778, Ermenonville, France), French philosopher, writer, and political theorist whose treatises and novels inspired the leaders of the French Revolution and the Romantic generation.

Bertrand Russell (in full Bertrand Arthur William Russell, 3rd Earl Russell of Kingston Russell, Viscount Amberley of Amberley and of Ardsalla; 18 May 1872, Trelleck, Monmouthshire, England—2 Feb 1970, near Penrhyndeudraeth, Merioneth, Wales), English logician and philosopher, best known for his work in mathematical logic and for his social and political campaigns, including his advocacy of both pacifism and nuclear disarmament; was awarded the Nobel Prize for Literature, 1950.

Saladin (Arabic in full Salah Ad-din Yusuf Ibn Ayyub ["Righteousness of the Faith, Joseph, Son of Job"]; 1137/38, Tikrit, Mesopotamia—4 Mar 1193, Damascus, [Syria]), Muslim sultan of Egypt, Syria, Yemen, and Palestine, founder of the Ayyubid dynasty, and the most famous of Muslim heroes; he recaptured Jerusalem in 1187, ending an 88-year Christian occupation.

José de San Martín (25 Feb 1778, Yapeyú, viceroyalty of Río de la Plata [now in Argentina]—17 Aug 1850, Boulogne-sur-Mer, France), Argentine soldier, statesman, and national hero who helped lead the revolutions against Spanish rule in Argentina (1812), Chile (1818), and Peru (1821).

Margaret (Higgins) Sanger (14 Sep 1879, Corning NY—6 Sep 1966, Tucson AZ), American founder of the birth-control movement in the US and an international leader in the field; she is credited with originating the term birth control.

Sargon (byname Sargon of Akkad; fl. 23rd century BC), ancient Semitic Mesopotamian ruler (reigned c. 2334–2279 BC), one of the world's earliest empire builders, conquering southern Mesopotamia and parts of Syria, Anatolia, and Iran; considered the founder of the Mesopotamian military tradition.

Sejong (1397–1450), Korean monarch during whose reign (1419–50) cultural achievements in Korea reached their highest point; best known for his development of a phonetic system for writing Korean and for banning all Buddhist monks from Seoul.

Léopold Sédar Senghor (9 Oct 1906, Joal, Senegal, French West Africa [now in Senegal]—20 Dec 2001, Verson, France), Senegalese poet, teacher, and statesman, first president of Senegal, and a major proponent of the concept of Negritude.

Shaka (also spelled Chaka or Tshaka; c. 1787–22 Sep 1828), Zulu chief (1816–28), founder of southern Africa's Zulu Empire, who created a fighting force that devastated the entire region.

Sitting Bull (Indian name Tatanka Iyotake; c. 1831, near Grand River, Dakota Territory, US [now in South Dakota]—15 Dec 1890, on the Grand River, South Dakota), Dakota Sioux chief under whom the Sioux tribes united in their struggle for survival on the North American Great Plains; remembered for his lifelong distrust of white men and determination to resist their domination.

Adam Smith (baptized 5 Jun 1723, Kirkcaldy, Fife, Scotland—17 Jul 1790, Edinburgh, Scotland), Scottish social philosopher and political economist; best known for *An Inquiry into the Nature and Causes of the Wealth of Nations* (1776), the first comprehensive system of political economy, though his economic writings are only part of an overarching view of political and social evolution.

Socrates (c. 470 BC, Athens [Greece]—399, Athens [Greece]), ancient Greek philosopher, first of the trio of ancient Greeks (with Plato and Aristotle) who laid the philosophical foundations of Western culture; he assessed the character and conduct of human life in terms of an original theory of the soul.

Solomon (Hebrew Shlomo; fl. 10th century BC), Hebrew king, traditionally regarded as the greatest king of Israel; maintained his dominions with military strength and established colonies outside Israel. The pinnacle of his vast building program was the famous temple at Jerusalem.

Joseph Stalin (Russian in full Iosif Vissarionovich Stalin, original name (Georgian) Ioseb Dzhugashvili; 21 Dec [9 Dec old style] 1879, Gori, Georgia, Russian Empire—5 Mar 1953, Moscow, Russia, USSR), Georgian-born Soviet leader, secretary-general of the Communist Party of the Soviet Union (1922–53) and premier of the Soviet state (1941–53), who for a quarter of a century dictatorially ruled the Soviet Union and transformed it into a major world power.

Elizabeth Cady Stanton (12 Nov 1815, Johnstown NY—26 Oct 1902, New York NY), American leader in the women's rights movement who in 1848 formulated the first organized demand for woman suffrage in the US.

Stephen I (also called Saint Stephen, Hungarian Szent István, original name Vajk; c. 970–75, Esztergom, Hungary—15 Aug 1038, Esztergom, Hun-

gary), first king of Hungary, considered to be the founder of the Hungarian state and one of the most renowned figures in that country's history.

Sukarno (6 Jun 1901, Surabaja, Java, Dutch East Indies [Indonesia]—21 Jun 1970, Jakarta, Indonesia), leader of the Indonesian independence movement and the country's first president (1949–66).

Süleyman I (byname Süleyman the Magnificent, or The Lawgiver; Nov 1494/Apr 1495–5/6 Sep 1566, near Szigetvár, Hungary), sultan of the Ottoman Empire (1520–1566) who undertook bold military campaigns that enlarged his realm and oversaw the development of the most characteristic achievements of Ottoman civilization in law, literature, art, and architecture.

Sun Yat-sen (12 Nov 1866, Hsiang-shan, Kwangtung province, China—12 Mar 1925, Beijing, China), Chinese leader of the Chinese Kuomintang (Nationalist Party), known as the father of modern China.

Charles-Maurice de Talleyrand(-Périgord), prince de Bénévent (2 Feb 1754, Paris, France—17 May 1838, Paris, France), French statesman and diplomat noted for his capacity for political survival, who held high office during the French Revolution, under Napoleon, at the restoration of the Bourbon monarchy, and under King Louis-Philippe.

Tecumseh (1768, Old Piqua [modern Clark county, Ohio]—5 Oct 1813, near Thames River, Upper Canada [now in Ontario]), Shawnee Indian chief, orator, military leader, and advocate of intertribal Indian alliance who directed Indian resistance to white rule in the Ohio River valley.

Timur (byname Timur Lenk, or Timurlenk [Turkish: "Timur the Lame"], English Tamerlane or Tamburlaine; 1336, Kesh, near Samarkand, Transoxania [now in Uzbekistan]—19 Feb 1405, Otrar, near Chimkent, [now Shymkent, Kazakstan]), Turkic conqueror of Islamic faith, chiefly remembered for the barbarity of his conquests from India and Russia to the Mediterranean Sea and for the cultural achievements of his dynasty.

Josip Broz Tito (7 May 1892, Kumrovec, near Zagreb, Croatia, Austria-Hungary [Croatia]—4 May 1980, Ljubljana, Yugoslavia [Slovenia]), Yugoslav revolutionary and statesman, head of the Communist Party of Yugoslavia (1939–80), the Yugoslav Partisans (1941–45), and the Yugoslav People's Army (1945–80), and marshal (1943–80), premier (1945–53), and president (1953–80) of Yugoslavia; architect of the "second Yugoslavia" (from World War II until 1991) and the first Communist leader to defy the Soviets.

Yoshimune Tokugawa (27 Nov 1684, Kii province, Japan—12 Jul 1751, Edo [Tokyo], Japan), eighth Tokugawa shogun, who is considered one of Japan's greatest rulers. His far-reaching reforms totally reshaped the central administrative structure and temporarily halted the decline of the shogunate.

Toussaint-Louverture (Louverture also spelled L'Ouverture, original name (until c. 1793) François Dominique Toussaint; c. 1743, Bréda, near Cape François, Saint-Domingue [Haiti]—7 Apr 1803, Fort-de-Joux, France), Haitian revolutionary, leader of the Haitian independence movement during the French Revolution, who emancipated the slaves and briefly established Haiti as a black-governed French protectorate.

Leon Trotsky (Lev Davidovich Bronshtein; 7 Nov [26 Oct old style] 1879, Yanovka, Ukraine, Russian Empire—20 Aug 1940, Coyoacán, near Mexico City, Mexico), Ukrainian-born Communist theorist and agitator, leader in Russia's 1917 October Revolution and commissar of foreign affairs and of war in the USSR (1917–24); leader of an anti-Stalinist opposition abroad until his assassination by a Stalinist agent.

Harry S. Truman (8 May 1884, Lamar MO—26 Dec 1972, Kansas City MO), American statesman; 33rd president of the US (1945–53) [see full biography at Presidents].

Harriet Tubman (née Araminta Greene; c. 1820, Dorchester county, Maryland—10 Mar 1913, Auburn, NY), American bondwoman who escaped from slavery in the South to become a leading Abolitionist before the American Civil War; she led hundreds of slaves to freedom in the North along the Underground Railroad.

Desmond (Mpilo) Tutu (7 Oct 1931, Klerksdorp, South Africa), South African bishop and black activist; was awarded the Nobel Prize for Peace, 1984.

'Umar I (in full 'Umar Ibn Al-Khattab; c. 586, Mecca, Arabia [now in Saudi Arabia]—3 Nov 644, Medina, Arabia [now in Saudi Arabia]), Arabian royal; the second Muslim caliph (from 634), under whom Arab armies conquered Mesopotamia and Syria and began the conquest of Iran and Egypt.

Urban II (original name Odo of Châtillon-sur-marne; c. 1035, Châtillon-sur-Marne, or Lagery, or Lagny, Champagne, France—29 July 1099, Rome, [Italy]), French pontiff (1088–99) who developed ecclesiastical reforms begun by Pope Gregory VII, launched the Crusade movement, and strengthened the papacy as a political entity.

'Uthman ibn 'Affan (before 615, Medina?, Arabia [now in Saudi Arabia]—17 Jun 656, Medina, Arabia [now in Saudi Arabia]), third caliph to rule after the death of the Prophet. He centralized the administration of the caliphate and established an official version of the Qur'an.

Victoria (in full Alexandrina Victoria; 24 May 1819, Kensington Palace, London, England—22 Jan 1901, Osborne, near Cowes, Isle of Wight), British queen of the United Kingdom of Great Britain and Ireland (1837–1901) and empress of India (1876–1901). She was the last of the House of Hanover and gave her name to an era, the Victorian Age.

Vladimir I (in full Vladimir Svyatoslavich, byname Saint Vladimir, or Vladimir The Great; c. 956, Kiev, Kievan Rus [now Ukraine]—15 Jul 1015, Berestova near Kiev, Kievan Rus [now Ukraine]), Russian grand prince of Kiev and first Christian ruler in Kievan Rus; consolidated the provinces of Kiev and Novgorod into a single state and determined the course of Christianity in the region with his Byzantine baptism.

Wang Kon (c. 900–c. 949) Korean soldier and king, founder of a unified kingdom on the Korean peninsula, and first ruler of the Koryo dynasty, during the reign of which (935–1392) Korea began to form its own cultural tradition distinct from the rest of East Asia.

Earl Warren (19 Mar 1891, Los Angeles CA—9 Jul 1974, Washington DC), American jurist, the 14th chief justice of the US (1953–69), who presided over the Supreme Court during a period of sweeping changes in US constitutional law, especially in the areas of race relations, criminal procedure, and legislative apportionment.

George Washington (byname Father of His Country; 22 Feb [11 Feb old style] 1732, Westmoreland county, Virginia—14 Dec 1799, Mt. Vernon, Fairfax county, Virginia), American Revolutionary commander-in-chief (1775-83); statesman; and first president of the US (1789-97) [see full biography at Presidents].

Elie Wiesel (Eliezer Wiesel; 30 Sep 1928, Sighet, Romania), Romanian-born American scholar and author whose works provide a sober yet passionate testament of the destruction of European Jewry during World War II. Awarded the Nobel Prize for Peace, 1986.

William I (byname William The Conqueror, or The Bastard, or William of Normandy, French Guillaume Le Conquérant, or Le Bâtard, or Guillaume de Normandie, c. 1028, Falaise, Normandy, [now in France]—9 Sep 1087, Rouen, Normandy [France]), duke of Normandy [as William II] from 1035 and king of England from 1066; Norman soldier and ruler, one of the greatest of the Middle Ages. He made himself the mightiest feudal lord in France and then changed the course of England's history by his conquest of that country.

(Thomas) Woodrow Wilson (28 Dec 1856, Staunton VA—3 Feb 1924, Washington DC), American statesman; 28th president of the US (1913-21) [see full biography at Presidents].

Mary Wollstonecraft (married name Mary Wollstonecraft Godwin; 27 Apr 1759, London, England—10 Sep 1797, London), English writer and passionate advocate of educational and social equality for women, whose works, especially *A Vindication of the Rights of Woman* (1792) were trailblazing works of feminism.

Aritomo Yamagata (3 Aug 1838, Hagi, Japan—1 Feb 1922, Tokyo, Japan), Japanese soldier and statesman who exerted a strong influence in Japan's emergence as a formidable military power at the beginning of the 20th century.

Yi Song-gye (1335, Korea—Hanyang? [now Seoul], Korea—1408) Korean general and Confucian scholar, first ruler (1392-98) of the Choson (Yi) Dynasty, the last and longest-lived imperial dynasty (1392-1910) of Korea.

Emiliano Zapata (8 Aug 1879, Anenecuilco, Mexico—10 Apr 1919, Morelos, Mexico), Mexican revolutionary, champion of agrarianism, who fought in guerrilla actions during and after the Mexican Revolution (1911-17).

Zhou Enlai (Wade-Giles Chou En-lai; 1898, Huaian, Kiangsu province, China—8 Jan 1976, Beijing, China), Chinese statesman, premier (1949-76) and foreign minister (1949-58) of the People's Republic of China; a major player in the Chinese revolution and later in foreign relations. One of the great negotiators of the 20th century and a master of policy implementation, with infinite capacity for details.

Populations

Largest Urban Agglomerations

Agglomerations include a central city and associated neighboring communities.
Source: United Nations, World Urbanization Prospects, the 2001 Revision.

RANK	AGGLOMERATION	COUNTRY	POPULATION (2000)	RANK	AGGLOMERATION	COUNTRY	POPULATION (2000)
1	Tokyo	Japan	26,444,000	17	Manila	Philippines	9,950,000
2	Mexico City	Mexico	18,066,000	18	Seoul	Korea	9,888,000
3	São Paulo	Brazil	17,962,000	19	Paris	France	9,630,000
4	New York City	US	16,732,000	20	Cairo	Egypt	9,462,000
5	Bombay	India	16,086,000	21	Tianjin	China	9,156,000
6	Los Angeles	US	13,213,000	22	Istanbul	Turkey	8,953,000
7	Calcutta	India	13,058,000	23	Lagos	Nigeria	8,665,000
8	Shanghai	China	12,887,000	24	Moscow	Russia	8,367,000
9	Dhaka	Bangladesh	12,519,000	25	London	United Kingdom	7,640,000
10	Delhi	India	12,441,000				
11	Buenos Aires	Argentina	12,024,000	26	Lima	Peru	7,443,000
12	Jakarta	Indonesia	11,018,000	27	Bangkok	Thailand	7,372,000
13	Osaka	Japan	11,013,000	28	Chicago	US	6,989,000
14	Beijing	China	10,839,000	29	Tehran	Iran	6,979,000
15	Rio de Janeiro	Brazil	10,652,000	30	Hong Kong	China	6,860,000
16	Karachi	Pakistan	10,032,000				

Migration of Foreigners Into and Out of Selected Countries

Inflows and outflows of foreign population into selected OECD countries, estimates for 1999. N/A indicates not available. Source: Organisation for Economic Co-operation and Development, Trends in International Migration (2001).

COUNTRY	FOREIGN INFLOW	FOREIGN OUTFLOW	COUNTRY	FOREIGN INFLOW	FOREIGN OUTFLOW
Australia	84,100	47,400	Luxembourg	11,800	6,900
Belgium	57,800	36,400	Netherlands	78,400	20,700
Canada	189,800	N/A	New Zealand	36,200	15,900
France	104,400	N/A	Norway	32,200	12,700
Germany	673,900	555,600	Portugal	10,500	N/A
Hungary	15,000	6,100	Sweden	34,600	13,600
Ireland	21,600	N/A	Switzerland	85,800	58,100
Italy	268,000	N/A	United Kingdom	276,900	130,000
Japan	281,900	198,300	United States	646,600	N/A

Principal Sources of Refugees Worldwide

Estimates as of 31 Dec 2001. Source: US Committee for Refugees: World Refugee Survey 2002

AREA	REFUGEES	AREA	REFUGEES	AREA	REFUGEES
Afghanistan	4,500,000	Eritrea	305,000	Bosnia and Herzegovina	210,000
Palestine	4,123,000	Iraq	300,000	Sierra Leone	185,000
Burma	450,000	Somalia	300,000	China (including Tibet)	151,000
Angola	445,000	Vietnam	295,000	Sri Lanka	144,000
Sudan	440,000	Croatia	272,000	Guatemala	129,000
Burundi	375,000	El Salvador	217,000	Bhutan	126,000
Dem. Rep. of the Congo	355,000	Liberia	215,000	Western Sahara	110,000

Internally Displaced Persons (IDPS)

Estimates of major populations of Internally Displaced Persons (individuals forced to move within their own countries as the result of armed conflict or natural disasters) as of 1 Jan 2002. Source: United Nations High Commissioner for Refugees (UNHCR): The UN Refugee Agency

COUNTRY	IDPS	COUNTRY	IDPS	COUNTRY	IDPS
Afghanistan	1,200,000	Russian Federation	443,300	Yugoslavia	263,600
Colombia	720,000	Bosnia and	438,300	Angola	202,000
Sri Lanka	683,300	Herzegovina		Liberia	196,100
Azerbaijan	573,000	Georgia	264,200		

Areas with High Ratios of Refugee Populations

Ratio of refugees to host-country populations, selected estimates as of 31 Dec 2001. Source: US Committee for Refugees: World Refugee Survey 2002

HOST AREA	RATIO OF REFUGEE POPULATION TO TOTAL POPULATION	NUMBER OF REFUGEES	HOST AREA	RATIO OF REFUGEE POPULATION TO TOTAL POPULATION	NUMBER OF REFUGEES
Gaza Strip	1:2	852,600	Tanzania	1:73	498,000
Jordan	1:3	1,643,900	Sudan	1:104	307,000
West Bank	1:3	607,800	Uganda	1:138	174,000
Lebanon	1:11	389,500	Saudi Arabia	1:168	128,500
Iran	1:26	2,558,000	Dem. Rep. of	1:176	305,000
Djibouti	1:27	22,000	Congo		
Yugoslavia	1:27	400,000	Thailand	1:225	277,000
Rep. of Congo	1:30	102,000	Malaysia	1:395	57,500
Zambia	1:36	270,000	Canada	1:443	70,000
Guinea	1:40	190,000	United States	1:578	492,500
Liberia	1:53	60,000	Germany	1:709	116,000
Pakistan	1:72	2,018,000	United Kingdom	1:972	61,700

Languages of the World

Endangered Languages

Many linguists estimate that of the 6,800 languages currently spoken, only about 3,000 will remain viable by the end of this century. Other linguists feel the decrease could be more severe, leaving only a few hundred languages in use by 2100. A large number of languages have been lost in the past, but linguists are concerned that we may be losing them much more quickly in modern times. Some 95% of the world's population living today learn one of about 100 languages as a first language. Thus, the remaining 6,700 languages are spoken by only 5% of the population.

In the vast majority of instances, languages die because of assimilation. That is, native speakers learn the language of a more dominant culture and teach that dominant language to their children. In certain instances the dominant culture may, for political reasons, make the native language illegal. Such was the case in Ireland, where England outlawed the Gaelic language and promulgated English. Occasionally, the dominant culture does not actually ban the native language but does forbid its being taught in schools. Many Native Americans were forbidden to learn or speak their languages at state-run schools in the US. More often, the reason languages become endangered is economic rather than political. People begin to adopt the language of the dominant culture and teach that language to their children because they believe it may improve their ability to find employment.

Two areas of the world have the largest number of languages (about 300–400 total) that are currently becoming extinct: Australia and North America. Each area has indigenous populations (Aboriginals and Native Americans, respectively) that are rapidly losing their mother tongues. Some 140 languages are thought to be dead or dying in Australia and some 80 to 90 in the US and Canada. Other countries that are home to groups who are losing languages are Indonesia, Brazil, Mexico, Papua New Guinea, Nigeria, Peru, and Taiwan.

Occasionally, moribund or dead languages can be revived, but this reversal process is far less common. One example of such a revival is Hebrew. When the newly formed Israeli government required a lingua franca for a disparate population, an ancient language that had been used only for religious purposes for more than 1,000 years eventually became one of two official languages for the state (Arabic is the other official language). Hebrew is now spoken by the majority of the people living in Israel (though not necessarily as a first language.) Gaelic is again in use in Ireland, but the process of reintroduction of a language has been less successful in other countries.

Most Widely Spoken Languages

Listing the languages spoken by more than 1% of humankind, this table enumerates speakers of each tongue as a primary or secondary language. Figures based on data from Linguasphere 2000. For more information visit <www.linguasphere.org>.

LANGUAGE	NUMBER OF SPEAKERS (MILLIONS)	% OF WORLD POPULATION (APPROXIMATE)	LANGUAGE FAMILY
English	1,000	16	Indo-European (Germanic)
Mandarin	1,000	16	Sino-Tibetan (Chinese)
Hindi/Urdu[1]	900	15	Indo-European (Indo-Aryan)
Spanish	450	7	Indo-European (Romance)
Russian/Belarusian	320	5	Indo-European (Slavic)
Arabic	250	4	Afro-Asiatic (Semitic)
Bengali/Sylhetti	250	4	Indo-European (Indo-Aryan)
Malay/Indonesian	200	3	Austronesian (Malayo-Polynesian)
Portuguese	200	3	Indo-European (Romance)
Japanese	130	2	isolated language
French	125	2	Indo-European (Romance)
German	125	2	Indo-European (Germanic)
Thai/Lao	90	1	Tai
Punjabi	85	1	Indo-European (Indo-Aryan)
Wu	85	1	Sino-Tibetan (Chinese)
Javanese	80	1	Austronesian (Malayo-Polynesian)
Marathi	80	1	Indo-European (Indo-Aryan)
Turkish/Azeri/Turkmen	80	1	Altaic (Turkic)
Korean	75	1	isolated language
Vietnamese	75	1	Mon-Khmer (Victic)
Cantonese	70	1	Sino-Tibetan (Chinese)
Italian	70	1	Indo-European (Romance)
Tamil	70	1	Dravidian
Telugu	70	1	Dravidian
Ukrainian	65	1	Indo-European (Slavic)
Bhojpuri/Maithili	60	1	Indo-European (Indo-Aryan)
Persian/Tajik	60	1	Indo-European (Iranian)
Swahili	60	1	Afro-Asiatic (Niger-Congo)
Tagalog	60	1	Austronesian (Malayo-Polynesian)

[1]*Although Hindi and Urdu use different writing systems, these languages are branches of Hindustani and are orally mutually intelligible.*

Foreign Words and Phrases

à droite [F] : to or on the right hand
à gauche [F] : to or on the left hand
aloha oe [Hawaiian] : love to you : greetings : farewell
amor patriae [L] : love of one's country
amor vincit omnia [L] : love conquers all things
aqua et igni interdictus [L] : forbidden to be furnished with water and fire : outlawed
ars longa, vita brevis [L] : art is long, life is short
à votre santé [F] : to your health—used as a toast
bella figura [It] : fine appearance or impression
bien entendu [F] : well understood : of course
bon appétit [F] : good appetite : enjoy your meal
bonjour [F] : good day : good morning
bonne foi [F] : good faith
bonsoir [F] : good evening
carte d'identité [F] : identity card
c'est la guerre [F] : that's war : it cannot be helped
c'est la vie [F] : that's life : that's how things happen

chacun à son goût [F] : everyone to his taste
cherchez la femme [F] : look for the woman
che sarà, sarà [It] : what will be, will be
cogito, ergo sum [L] : I think, therefore I exist
comédie humaine [F] : human comedy : the whole variety of human life
comme ci, comme ça [F] : so-so
compte rendu [F] : report (as of proceedings in an investigation)
cum grano salis [L] : with a grain of salt
d'accord [F] : in accord : agreed
de gustibus non est disputandum [L] : there is no disputing about tastes
Dei gratia [L] : by the grace of God
de integro [L] : anew : afresh
Deo gratias [L] : thanks (be) to God
de profundis [L] : out of the depths
dies irae [L] : day of wrath—used of the Judgment Day

Dieu et mon droit [F] : God and my right—motto on the British royal arms
Dominus vobiscum [L] : the Lord be with you
d'un certain âge [F] : of a certain age : no longer young
en famille [F] : in or with one's family : at home : informally
en garde [F] : on guard
en plein air [F] : in the open air
e pluribus unum [L] : one out of many—used on the Great Seal of the US and on several US coins
Erin go bragh [Ir go brách or go bráth, lit., till doomsday] : Ireland forever
errare humanum est [L] : to err is human
et tu Brute [L] : thou too, Brutus—exclamation attributed to Julius Caesar on seeing his friend Brutus among his assassins
eureka [Gk] : I have found it—motto of California
excelsior [L] : still higher—motto of New York
ex libris [L] : from the books of—used on bookplates
façon de parler [F] : manner of speaking : figurative or conventional expression
faire suivre [F] : have forwarded : please forward
fils [F] : son—used orig. after French and now also after other family names to distinguish a son from his father
force de frappe [F] : military striking force esp. with nuclear weapons
gardez la foi [F] : keep faith
guten Tag [G] : good day
hasta la vista [Sp] : good-bye
homme d'affaires [F] : man of business : business agent
hors commerce [F] : outside the trade : not offered through regular commercial channels
id est [L] : that is (*i.e.*)
ignorantia juris neminem excusat [L] : ignorance of the law excuses no one
in aeternum [L] : forever
inshallah [Ar] : if Allah wills : God willing
in vino veritas [L] : there is truth in wine
j'accuse [F] : I accuse : bitter denunciation
janius clausis [L] : behind closed doors
le roi est mort, vive le roi [F] : the king is dead, long live the king
l'état, c'est moi [F] : the state, it is I
mal vu [F] : badly regarded : disapproved of
mano a mano [Sp] : hand to hand : in direct competition or confrontation

mens sana in corpore sano [L] : a sound mind in a sound body
nolens volens [L] : unwilling (or) willing : willy-nilly
nuit blanche [F] : white night : a sleepless night
nyet [Russ] : no
omertà [It] : submission : code chiefly among members of the criminal underworld that enjoins private vengeance and the refusal to give information to outsiders (as the police)
ora pro nobis [L] : pray for us
outre-mer [F] : overseas : distant lands
par avion [F] : by airplane—used on airmail
pax vobiscum [L] : peace (be) with you
père [F] : father—used orig. after French and now also after other family names to distinguish a father from his son
pour rire [F] : for laughing : not to be taken seriously
pro bono publico [L] : for the public good
pro hac vice [L] : for this occasion
pro patria [L] : for one's country
quis custodiet ipsos custodes? [L] : who will keep the keepers themselves?
qui s'excuse s'accuse [F] : he who excuses himself accuses himself
quod vide [L] : which see (*q.v.*)
raison d'état [F] : reason of state
répondez s'il vous plaît [F] : reply, if you please (*RSVP*)
requiescat in pace [L] : may he or she rest in peace—used on tombstones (*RIP*)
sans souci [F] : without worry
sayonara [Jp] : good-bye
semper fidelis [L] : always faithful—motto of the US Marine Corps
s'il vous plaît [F] : if you please
tout à fait [F] : altogether : quite
tout de suite [F] : immediately *also* : all at once : consecutively
tout le monde [F] : all the world : everybody
tristesse [F] : melancholy
über alles [G] : above everything else
uebermensch [G] : superman
und so weiter [G] : and so on
urbi et orbi [L] : to the city (Rome) and the world : to everyone
veni, vidi, vici [L] : I came, I saw, I conquered
voilà tout [F] : that's all
wie geht's? [G] : how goes it?

English Neologisms

New entries from Merriam-Webster's Collegiate Dictionary, Tenth Edition *(2002 copyright revision)*

anime (1988): a style of animation originating in Japan that is characterized by stark colorful graphics depicting vibrant characters in action-filled plots often with fantastic or futuristic themes
blunt (1990): a cigar that has been hollowed out and filled with marijuana
booty (1928): buttocks
chipotle (1988): a smoked and usually dried jalapeño
dollarization (1982): the adoption of the US $ as a country's official national currency
e-book (1992): a book composed in or converted to digital format for display on a computer screen or handheld device
e-tail (1997): retail business conducted on-line via the World Wide Web
gearhead (1974): a person who engages in technical or technological pursuits
hottie (1990): a physically attractive person

megapixel (1984): one million pixels
nakfa: currency unit, Eritrea
noogie (1972): the act of rubbing one's knuckles on a person's head so as to produce a mildly painful sensation
road rage (1988): a motorist's uncontrolled anger that is usually incited by an irritating act of another motorist and is expressed in aggressive or violent behavior
toolbar (1983): a strip of icons on a computer display providing quick access to certain functions
tree hugger (1982): environmentalist; especially an advocate for the preservation of woodlands
webcam (1995): a camera used in transmitting live images over the World Wide Web
webcast (1995): a transmission of sound and images (as of an event) via the World Wide Web—**webcasting, webcaster**

NEW SENSES

burn: to record data on (an optical disk) with a laser <*burn* a CD>

chops *slang:* expertise in a particular field or activity <acting *chops*>

hard *of money:* contributed (as by individuals or political action committees) directly to a political candidate or campaign

rave: a large overnight dance party featuring techno music and usually involving the taking of mind-altering drugs

soft *of money:* contributed (as by a corporation) to a political party rather than directly to a particular candidate

---

 **Did you know?** Africa has the greatest number of languages of any continent—more than 2,000. North of the Sahara Desert, Arabic is by far the most widespread language, with some 80 million speakers. Sub-Saharan Africa has an astonishing variety of languages. Nigeria has more than 250 languages within its borders, making the production of newspapers and television shows a challenge. A few languages have been adopted for general communication, such as Swahili in East Africa, Hausa in much of West Africa, and European languages in countries that were formerly European colonies.

Religion

World Religions

At the beginning of the 21st century, one-third of the world's population is Christian, another one-fifth is Muslim, about one-eighth is Hindu, and one-eighth is nonreligious. Most people living in Europe and the Americas are Christian, while the vast majority of Muslims and Hindus are found in Asia. The plurality of Christians are Roman Catholics, of Muslims are Sunni, and of Hindus are Vaishnavites. Africa hosts slightly more Chistians than Muslims, with much of the rest of the population listed as ethnic religionists, which describes followers of local, tribal, animistic, or shamanistic religions.

In addition to the predominant world religions (Christianity, Islam, Hinduism), there are small but noticeable percentages of Chinese folk religionists, Buddhists, other ethnic religionists, atheists, and new-religionists. Among the remaining distinct religions, less than one-half of one percent of religious adherents are Sikhs, Spiritists, Jews, Baha'is, Confucianists, Jains, Shintoists, Taoists, and Zoroastrians.

Christianity

Christianity traces its origins to the 1st century AD and to Jesus of Nazareth, whom it affirms to be the chosen one (Christ) of God. Geographically the most widely diffused of all faiths, it has a constituency of more than two billion people. Its largest groups are the Roman Catholic Church, the Eastern Orthodox churches, and the Protestant churches; in addition, there are several independent churches of Eastern Christianity as well as numerous sects throughout the world.

Christianity's sacred scripture is the Bible, particularly the New Testament. Its principal tenets are that Jesus is the son of God (the second person of the Holy Trinity), that God's love for the world is the essential component of his being, and that Jesus died to redeem humankind.

Christianity was originally a movement of Jews who accepted Jesus as the messiah, but the movement quickly became predominantly gentile. Nearly all Christian churches have an ordained clergy, which lead group worship services and are viewed as intermediaries between the laity and the divine in some churches. Most Christian churches administer at least two sacraments: baptism and the Lord's Supper.

Islam

Islam is a religion that originated in the Middle East and was promulgated by the Prophet Muhammad in Arabia in the 7th century AD. The Arabic term *islam*, literally "surrender," illuminates the fundamental religious idea of Islam—that the believer (called a Muslim, from the active particle of *islam*) accepts "surrender to the will of Allah (Arabic: God)." Allah's will is made known through the sacred scriptures, the Qur'an (Koran), which Allah revealed to his messenger, Muhammad. In Islam, Muhammad is considered the last of a series of prophets (including Adam, Noah, Jesus, and others), and his message simultaneously consummates and abrogates the "revelations" attributed to earlier prophets.

The religious obligations of all Muslims are summed up in the Five Pillars of Islam. The fundamental concept in Islam is the Sharia, or Law, which embraces the total way of life commanded by God. Observant Muslims pray five times a day and join in community worship on Fridays at the mosque, where worship is led by an imam. Every believer is required to make a pilgrimage to Mecca, the holiest city, at least once in a lifetime, barring poverty or physical incapacity. The month of Ramadan is set aside for fasting. Jihad, considered a sixth pillar by some sects, is not accepted by most of the Islamic community as a call to wage physical war against unbelievers.

Divisions occurred early in Islam, brought about by disputes over the succession to the caliphate, resulting in various sects (Sunni, Shiites, Ismailis, Sufis). From the 19th century, the concept of the Islamic community inspired Muslim peoples to cast off Western colonial rule, and in the late 20th century fundamentalist movements toppled a number of secular Middle Eastern governments. A movement of African American Muslims emerged in the 20th century in the US.

Hinduism

Hinduism is the oldest of the world's major religions, dating back more than 3,000 years, though its present forms are of more recent origin. It evolved from Vedism, the religion of the Indo-European peoples who settled in India at the end of the 2nd millennium

World Religions (continued)

BC. The vast majority of the world's Hindus live in India, though significant minorities may be found in Pakistan and Sri Lanka, and smaller numbers live in Myanmar, South Africa, Trinidad, Europe, and the US.

Though the various Hindu sects each rely on their own set of scriptures, they all revere the ancient Vedas, which were brought to India by Aryan invaders after 1200 BC. The philosophical Vedic texts called the Upanishads explored the search for knowledge that would allow mankind to escape the cycle of reincarnation. Fundamental to Hinduism is the belief in a cosmic principle of ultimate reality called brahman, and its identity with the individual soul, or atman. All creatures go through a cycle of rebirth, or samsara, which can only be broken by spiritual self-realization, after which liberation, or moksha, is attained. The principle of karma determines a being's status within the cycle of rebirth.

The greatest Hindu deities are Brahma, Vishnu, and Shiva. The major sources of classical mythology are the Mahabharata (which includes the Bhagavadgita, the most important religious text of Hinduism), the

Worldwide Adherents of All Religions, mid-2001

This table and the US table that follows were prepared by David B. Barrett and Todd M. Johnson, coauthors of World Christian Encyclopedia, *and extracted from* Britannica Book of the Year 2002.

	AFRICA	ASIA	EUROPE	LATIN AMERICA
Christians	368,244,000	317,759,000	559,359,000	486,591,000
Affiliated Christians	342,819,000	312,182,000	536,588,000	481,132,000
Roman Catholics	123,467,000	112,086,000	285,554,000	466,226,000
Protestants	90,989,000	50,718,000	77,497,000	49,008,000
Orthodox	36,038,000	14,219,000	158,375,000	564,000
Anglicans	43,524,000	735,000	26,628,000	1,098,000
Independents	85,476,000	157,605,000	25,850,000	40,357,000
Marginal Christians	2,502,000	2,521,000	3,606,000	6,779,000
Unaffiliated Christians	25,425,000	5,577,000	22,771,000	5,459,000
Baha'is	1,779,000	3,538,000	132,000	893,000
Buddhists	139,000	356,533,000	1,570,000	660,000
Chinese folk religionists	33,100	385,758,000	258,000	197,000
Confucianists	250	6,277,000	10,800	450
Ethnic religionists	97,762,000	129,005,000	1,258,000	1,288,000
Hindus	2,384,000	813,396,000	1,425,000	775,000
Jains	66,900	4,207,000	0	0
Jews	215,000	4,476,000	2,506,000	1,145,000
Muslims	323,556,000	845,341,000	31,724,000	1,702,000
New-Religionists	28,900	101,065,000	160,000	633,000
Shintoists	0	2,669,000	0	6,900
Sikhs	54,400	22,689,000	241,000	0
Spiritists	2,600	2,000	134,000	12,169,000
Taoists	0	2,658,000	0	0
Zoroastrians	910	2,519,000	670	0
Other religionists	67,300	63,100	238,000	99,600
Nonreligious	5,170,000	611,876,000	105,742,000	16,214,000
Atheists	432,000	122,408,000	22,555,000	2,787,000
Total population	**802,150,000**	**3,730,168,000**	**728,270,000**	**525,878,000**

Continents. *These follow current UN demographic terminology, which now divides the world into the six major areas shown above. See United Nations,* World Population Prospects: The 1998 Revision *(New York: UN, 1999), with populations of all continents, regions, and countries covering the period 1950–2050. Note that "Asia" includes the former Soviet Central Asian states and "Europe" includes all of Russia extending eastward to Vladivostok, the Sea of Japan, and the Bering Strait.*

Countries. *The last column enumerates sovereign and nonsovereign countries in which each religion or religious grouping has a numerically significant and organized following.*

Adherents. *As defined in the 1948 Universal Declaration of Human Rights, a person's religion is what he or she says it is. Totals are enumerated for each of the world's 238 countries following the methodology of the* World Christian Encyclopedia, *2nd ed. (2001), using recent censuses, polls, surveys, reports, Web sites, literature, and other data.*

Christians: *Followers of Jesus Christ affiliated with churches, plus persons professing in censuses or polls to be Christians though not so affiliated. Figures for the subgroups of Christians do not add up to the totals in the first line because some Christians adhere to more than one denomination.*

Independents: *Members of churches and networks that regard themselves as postdenominationalist and neoapostolic and thus independent of historic, organized, institutionalized, denominationalist Christianity.*

Marginal Christians: *Members of denominations on the margins of organized mainstream Christianity (e.g., Church of Jesus Christ of Latter-day Saints, Jehovah's Witnesses, and Christian Science).*

World Religions (continued)

Ramayana, and the Puranas. The hierarchical social structure of the caste system is important in Hinduism; it is supported by the principle of dharma. During the 20th century Hinduism was blended with Indian nationalism to become a potent political force.

Other major religions

Buddhism, a religion concentrated in Asia with some representation in North America, was founded by Buddha (Siddhartha Gautama, or Gotama) in northeast India in the 5th century BC. By adhering to Buddha's teachings, the believer can alleviate suffering through an understanding of the transitory nature of existence, in the hopes of achieving enlightenment. Distinct from Buddhism, **Shinto** is the indigenous religion of Japan and has no founder, no sacred scriptures, or fixed dogmas. Also based in Asia, **Chinese folk religionists** are followers of local deities and engage in ancestor worship, univerism, and divination. They also adhere to Confucian ethics, though statistically **Confucianists** are categorized as non-Chinese (mostly Korean) followers of Confucius, a Chinese

NORTHERN AMERICA	OCEANIA	WORLD	%	NUMBER OF COUNTRIES
261,752,000	25,343,000	2,019,052,000	32.9	238
213,038,000	21,600,000	1,907,363,000	31.1	238
71,391,000	8,327,000	1,067,053,000	17.4	235
70,164,000	7,478,000	345,855,000	5.6	232
6,400,000	718,000	216,314,000	3.5	134
3,231,000	5,428,000	80,644,000	1.3	163
81,032,000	1,536,000	391,856,000	6.4	221
10,747,000	468,000	26,623,000	0.4	215
48,714,000	3,743,000	111,689,000	1.8	232
799,000	113,000	7,254,000	0.1	218
2,777,000	307,000	361,985,000	5.9	126
857,000	64,200	387,167,000	6.3	89
0	24,000	6,313,000	0.1	15
446,000	267,000	230,026,000	3.8	140
1,350,000	359,000	819,689,000	13.4	114
7,000	0	4,281,000	0.1	10
6,045,000	97,600	14,484,000	0.2	134
4,518,000	307,000	1,207,148,000	19.7	204
847,000	66,900	102,801,000	1.7	60
56,700	0	2,732,000	0.0	8
535,000	18,500	23,538,000	0.4	34
152,000	7,100	12,400,000	0.2	55
11,200	0	2,670,000	0.0	5
79,100	1,400	2,601,000	0.0	22
605,000	9,500	1,082,000	0.0	78
28,994,000	3,349,000	771,345,000	12.6	236
1,700,000	369,000	150,252,000	2.5	161
311,877,000	30,164,000	6,128,512,000	100.0	238

Buddhists: 56% Mahayana, 38% Theravada (Hinayana), 6% Tantrayana (Lamaism).
Chinese folk-religionists: Followers of traditional Chinese religion (local deities, ancestor veneration, Confucian ethics, Taoism, universism, divination, and some Buddhist elements.)
Confucianists: Non-Chinese followers of Confucius and Confucianism, mostly Koreans in Korea.
Ethnic religionists: Followers of local, tribal, animistic, or shamanistic religions.
Hindus: 70% Vaishnavites, 25% Shaivites, 2% neo-Hindus and reform Hindus.
Jews: Adherents of Judaism. For detailed data on "core" Jewish population, see the annual "World Jewish Populations" article in the American Jewish Committee's American Jewish Year Book.
Muslims: 83% Sunnites, 16% Shi'ites, 1% other schools.
New-Religionists: Followers of Asian 20th-century New Religions, New Religious movements, radical new crisis religions, and non-Christian syncretistic mass religions, all founded since 1800 and most since 1945.
Atheists: Persons professing atheism, skepticism, disbelief, or irreligion, including the antireligious (opposed to all religion).
Total population: UN medium variant figures for mid-2000, as given in World Population Prospects: The 1998 Revision.

World Religions (continued)

philosopher of the 6th century BC. Confucianism is not an organized religion as much as it is a political and social ideology. Also in the Confucian tradition, a **Taoist** seeks the correct path of human conduct and an understanding of the Absolute Tao.

Zoroastrianism is an ancient pre-Islamic religion of Iran that survives there and in India. It was founded by the Iranian prophet Zoroaster in the 6th century BC and has both monotheistic and dualistic features. Also founded in Iran is the **Baha'i** faith, created as a

universal religion in the mid-19th century AD for the worship of Baha' Ullah and his forerunner Bab; it has no priesthood or formal sacraments and is chiefly concerned with social ethics.

Jainism was founded in India in the 6th century BC by Vardhamana, or Mahavira, a monastic reformer in the Vedic, or early Hindu tradition. Jainism emphasizes a path to spiritual purity and enlightenment through a disciplined mode of life founded upon the tradition of ahimsa, nonviolence to all living creatures.

Religious Adherents in the US, 1900–2000

For categories not described below, see notes to "Worldwide Adherents of All Religions," pp. 726–27.

	1900	%	MID-1970	%	MID-1990	%
Christians	73,270,000	96.4	191,182,000	91.0	217,719,000	85.7
Affiliated Christians	54,425,000	71.6	153,299,000	73.0	175,820,000	69.2
Protestants	35,000,000	46.1	58,568,000	27.9	60,216,000	23.7
Roman Catholics	10,775,000	14.2	48,305,000	23.0	56,500,000	22.2
Anglicans	1,600,000	2.1	3,196,000	1.5	2,450,000	1.0
Orthodox	400,000	0.5	4,163,000	2.0	5,150,000	2.0
Multiple affiliation	0	0.0	-2,704,000	-1.3	-24,336,000	-9.6
Independents	5,850,000	7.7	35,645,000	17.0	66,900,000	26.3
Marginal Christians	800,000	1.1	6,126,000	2.9	8,940,000	3.5
Evangelicals	*32,068,000*	*42.2*	*31,516,000*	*15.0*	*37,349,000*	*14.7*
evangelicals	*11,000,000*	*14.5*	*45,500,000*	*21.7*	*87,656,000*	*34.5*
Unaffiliated Christians	18,845,000	24.8	37,883,000	18.0	41,899,000	16.5
Baha'is	2,800	0.0	138,000	0.1	600,000	0.2
Buddhists	30,000	0.0	200,000	0.1	1,880,000	0.7
Chinese folk religionists	70,000	0.1	90,000	0.0	76,000	0.0
Ethnic religionists	100,000	0.1	70,000	0.0	280,000	0.1
Hindus	1,000	0.0	100,000	0.1	750,000	0.3
Jains	0	0.0	0	0.0	5,000	0.0
Jews	1,500,000	2.0	6,700,000	3.2	5,535,000	2.2
Muslims	10,000	0.0	800,000	0.4	3,560,000	1.4
Black Muslims	0	0.0	200,000	0.1	1,250,000	0.5
New-Religionists	0	0.0	110,000	0.1	575,000	0.2
Shintoists	0	0.0	0	0.0	50,000	0.0
Sikhs	0	0.0	1,000	0.0	160,000	0.1
Spiritists	0	0.0	0	0.0	120,000	0.1
Taoists	0	0.0	0	0.0	10,000	0.0
Zoroastrians	0	0.0	0	0.0	42,400	0.0
Other religionists	10,000	0.0	450,000	0.2	530,000	0.2
Nonreligious	1,000,000	1.3	10,070,000	4.8	21,414,000	8.4
Atheists	1,000	0.0	200,000	0.1	770,000	0.3
Total population	**75,995,000**	**100.0**	**210,111,000**	**100.0**	**254,076,000**	**100.0**

Methodology. This table extracts and analyzes a microcosm of the world religion table. It depicts the United States, the country with the largest number of adherents to Christianity, the world's largest religion. Statistics at five points in time across the 20th century are presented. Each religion's Annual Change for 1990–2000 is also analyzed by Natural increase (births minus deaths, plus immigrants minus emigrants) per year and Conversion increase (new converts minus new defectors) per year, which together constitute the Total increase per year. Rate increase is then computed as percentage per year.

Structure. Vertically the table lists 30 major religious categories. The major religions (including nonreligion) in the US are listed with largest (Christians) first. Indented names of groups in the "Adherents" column are subcategories of the groups above them and are also counted in these unindented totals, so they should not be added twice into the column total. Figures in italics draw adherents from all categories of Christians above and so cannot be added together with them. Figures for Christians are built upon detailed head counts by churches, often to the last digit. Totals are then rounded to the nearest 1,000. Because of rounding, the corresponding percentage figures may sometimes not total exactly 100%.

World Religions (continued)

Sikhism is a monotheistic religion founded in the late-15th century AD in India, historically associated with the Punjab region, though it includes representation in Europe and North America.

Judaism, like Christianity and Islam, is monotheistic and maintains the manifestation of God in human events, particulary through Moses in the Torah at Mount Sinai in the 13th century BC. Jews, who come together in both religious and ethnic communities, have worldwide representation, with the greatest concentration in North America and the Middle East. **New-religionists** are followers of New Religious movements and non-Christian syncretistic mass religions.

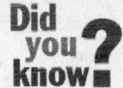

Did you know? In 1870 London, England, was home to more Irish than Dublin, and home to more Catholics than Rome.

MID-1995	%	MID-2000	%	AVERAGE ANNUAL CHANGE, 1990-2000			
				NATURAL	CONVERSION	TOTAL	RATE (%)
227,586,000	85.2	235,742,000	84.7	2,081,000	-278,000	1,802,000	0.80
184,244,000	69.0	191,828,000	68.9	1,680,000	-79,500	1,601,000	0.88
62,525,000	23.4	64,570,000	23.2	575,000	-140,000	435,000	0.70
56,715,000	21.2	58,000,000	20.8	540,000	-390,000	150,000	0.26
2,445,000	0.9	2,400,000	0.9	23,400	-28,400	-5,000	-0.21
5,472,000	2.1	5,762,000	2.1	49,200	12,000	61,200	1.13
-25,360,000	-9.5	-27,534,000	-9.9	-233,000	-87,300	-320,000	1.24
72,943,000	27.3	78,550,000	28.2	639,000	526,000	1,165,000	1.62
9,502,000	3.6	10,080,000	3.6	85,400	28,600	114,000	1.21
39,314,000	14.7	40,640,000	14.6	357,000	-27,800	329,000	0.85
93,457,000	35.0	98,662,000	35.4	838,000	263,000	1,101,000	1.19
43,342,000	16.2	43,914,000	15.8	400,000	-199,000	202,000	0.47
682,000	0.3	753,000	0.3	5,700	9,600	15,300	2.30
2,150,000	0.8	2,450,000	0.9	18,000	39,000	57,000	2.68
77,000	0.0	78,500	0.0	730	-480	250	0.32
387,000	0.1	435,000	0.2	2,700	12,800	15,500	4.50
930,000	0.4	1,032,000	0.4	7,200	21,000	28,200	3.24
6,000	0.0	7,000	0.0	48	150	200	3.36
5,600,000	2.1	5,621,000	2.0	52,900	-44,300	8,600	0.15
3,825,000	1.4	4,132,000	1.5	34,000	23,200	57,200	1.50
1,400,000	0.5	1,650,000	0.6	12,700	17,300	30,000	2.29
690,000	0.3	811,000	0.3	5,500	18,100	23,600	3.50
53,900	0.0	56,200	0.0	480	140	620	1.18
192,000	0.1	234,000	0.1	1,500	5,900	7,400	3.87
133,000	0.1	138,000	0.1	1,100	690	1,800	1.44
10,600	0.0	11,100	0.0	96	17	110	1.08
47,500	0.0	52,700	0.0	410	630	1,000	2.20
550,000	0.2	577,000	0.2	5,100	-390	4,700	0.85
23,150,000	8.7	25,078,000	9.0	205,000	162,000	366,000	1.59
950,000	0.4	1,149,000	0.4	7,400	30,600	37,900	4.09
267,020,000	100.0	278,357,000	100.0	2,428,000	0	2,428,000	0.92

Christians. All persons who profess publicly to follow Jesus Christ as Lord and Savior. This category is subdivided into Affiliated Christians (church members) and Unaffiliated (nominal) Christians (professing Christians not affiliated with any church).

Evangelicals/evangelicals. These two designations cut across all of the six Christian traditions listed above them and should be considered separately from them. Evangelicals are Protestant churches, agencies, and individuals that call themselves by this term. The evangelicals are Christians from all traditions who are committed to the evangel (gospel) and involved in personal witness and mission in the world.

Jews. Core Jewish population relating to Judaism, excluding Jewish persons professing a different religion.
Other categories. Definitions are as given under the world religion table.

THE WORLD—RELIGION

Chronological List of Popes

According to Roman Catholic doctrine, the pope is the successor of **St. Peter**, who was head of the Apostles. The pope thus is seen to have full and supreme power of jurisdiction over the universal church in matters of faith and morals, as well as in church discipline and government. Until the 4th century, the popes were usually known only as bishops of Rome. From 1309–77, the popes' seat was at Avignon, France. In the table, **antipopes**, who opposed the legitimately elected bishop of Rome and endeavored to secure the papal throne, are listed in italics. The elections of several antipopes are greatly obscured by incomplete or biased records, and at times even their contemporaries could not decide who was the true pope. It is impossible, therefore, to establish an absolutely definitive list of antipopes.

POPE	REIGN	POPE	REIGN	POPE	REIGN
Peter	?–c. 64	Anastasius II	496–498	Valentine	827
Linus	c. 67–76/79	Symmachus	498–514	Gregory IV	827–844
Anacletus	76–88 or 79–91	*Laurentius*	498, 501– c. 505/507	*John*	844
Clement I	88–97 or 92–101	Hormisdas	514–523	Sergius II	844–847
		John I	523–526	Leo IV	847–855
Evaristus	c. 97–c. 107	Felix IV (or III)[1]	526–530	Benedict III	855–858
Alexander I	105–115 or 109–119	*Dioscorus*	530	*Anastasius* *(Anastasius the Librarian)*	855
		Boniface II	530–532		
Sixtus I	c. 115–c. 125	John II	533–535	Nicholas I	858–867
Telesphorus	c. 125–c. 136	Agapetus I	535–536	Adrian II	867–872
Hyginus	c. 136–c. 140	Silverius	536–537	John VIII	872–882
Pius I	c. 140–155	Vigilius	537–555	Marinus I	882–884
Anicetus	c. 155–c. 166	Pelagius I	556–561	Adrian III	884–885
Soter	c. 166–c. 175	John III	561–574	Stephen V (or VI)[2]	885–891
Eleutherius	c. 175–189	Benedict I	575–579	Formosus	891–896
Victor I	c. 189–199	Pelagius II	579–590	Boniface VI	896
Zephyrinus	c. 199–217	Gregory I	590–604	Stephen VI (or VII)[2]	896
Calixtus I (Callistus)	217?–222	Sabinian	604–606	Romanus	897
		Boniface III	604	Theodore II	897
Hippolytus	217, 218–235	Boniface IV	608–615	John IX	898–900
Urban I	222–230	Deusdedit (Adeodatus I)	615–618	Benedict IV	900
Pontian	230–235			Leo V	903
Anterus	235–236	Boniface V	619–625	*Christopher*	903–904
Fabian	236–250	Honorius I	625–638	Sergius III	904–911
Cornelius	251–253	Severinus	640	Anastasius III	911–913
Novatian	251	John IV	640–642	Lando	913–914
Lucius I	253–254	Theodore I	642–649	John X	914–928
Stephen I	254–257	Martin I	649–655	Leo VI	928
Sixtus II	257–258	Eugenius I	654–657	Stephen VII (or VIII)[2]	929–931
Dionysius	259–268	Vitalian	657–672	John XI	931–935
Felix I	269–274	Adeodatus II	672–676	Leo VII	936–939
Eutychian	275–283	Donus	676–678	Stephen VIII (or IX)[2]	939–942
Gaius	283–296	Agatho	678–681	Marinus II	942–946
Marcellinus	291/296–304	Leo II	682–683	Agapetus II	946–955
Marcellus I	308–309	Benedict II	684–685	John XII	955–964
Eusebius	309/310	John V	685–686	Leo VIII[3]	963–965
Miltiades (Melchiades)	311–314	Conon	686–687	Benedict V[3]	964–966?
		Sergius I	687–701	John XIII	965–972
Sylvester I	314–335	*Theodore*	687	Benedict VI	973–974
Mark	336	*Paschal*	687	*Boniface VII (1st time)*	974
Julius I	337–352	John VI	701–705		
Liberius	352–366	John VII	705–707	Benedict VII	974–983
Felix (II)	355–358	Sisinnius	708	John XIV	983–984
Damasus I	366–384	Constantine	708–715	*Boniface VII (2nd time)*	984–985
Ursinus	366–367	Gregory II	715–731		
Siricius	384–399	Gregory III	731–741	John XV (or XVI)[4]	985–996
Anastasius I	399–401	Zacharias (Zachary)	741–752	Gregory V	996–999
Innocent I	401–417	Stephen (II)[2]	752	*John XVI (or XVII)[4]*	997–998
Zosimus	417–418	Stephen II (or III)[2]	752–757	Sylvester II	999–1003
Boniface I	418–422	Paul I	757–767	John XVII (or XVIII)[4]	1003
Eulalius	418–419	Constantine (II)	767–768	John XVIII (or XIX)[4]	1004–09
Celestine I	422–432	*Philip*	768	Sergius IV	1009–12
Sixtus III	432–440	Stephen III (or IV)[2]	768–772	*Gregory (VI)*	1012
Leo I	440–461	Adrian I	772–795	Benedict VIII	1012–24
Hilary	461–468	Leo III	795–816	John XIX (or XX)[4]	1024–32
Simplicius	468–483	Stephen IV (or V)[2]	816–817	Benedict IX (1st time)	1032–44
Felix III (or II)[1]	483–492	Paschal I	817–824		
Gelasius I	492–496	Eugenius II	824–827	Sylvester III	1045

Chronological List of Popes (continued)

POPE	REIGN	POPE	REIGN	POPE	REIGN
Benedict IX	1045	Clement IV	1265-68	Innocent VIII	1484-92
(2nd time)		Gregory X	1271-76	Alexander VI	1492-1503
Gregory VI	1045-46	Innocent V	1276	Pius III	1503
Clement II	1046-47	Adrian V	1276	Julius II	1503-13
Benedict IX	1047-48	John XXI[4]	1276-77	Leo X	1513-21
(3rd time)		Nicholas III	1277-80	Adrian VI	1522-23
Damasus II	1048	Martin IV[5]	1281-85	Clement VII	1523-34
Leo IX	1049-54	Honorius IV	1285-87	Paul III	1534-49
Victor II	1055-57	Nicholas IV	1288-92	Julius III	1550-55
Stephen IX (or X)[2]	1057-58	Celestine V	1294	Marcellus II	1555
Benedict X	1058-59	Boniface VIII	1294-1303	Paul IV	1555-59
Nicholas II	1059-61	Benedict XI	1303-04	Pius IV	1559-65
Alexander II	1061-73	Clement V (at	1305-14	Pius V	1566-72
Honorius (II)	1061-72	Avignon from		Gregory XIII	1572-85
Gregory VII	1073-85	1309)		Sixtus V	1585-90
Clement (III)	1080-1100	John XXII[4]	1316-34	Urban VII	1590
Victor III	1086-87	(at Avignon)		Gregory XIV	1590-91
Urban II	1088-99	Nicholas (V)	1328-30	Innocent IX	1591
Paschal II	1099-1118	(at Rome)		Clement VIII	1592-1605
Theodoric	1100-02	Benedict XII	1334-42	Leo XI	1605
Albert (Aleric)	1102	(at Avignon)		Paul V	1605-21
Sylvester (IV)	1105-11	Clement VI	1342-52	Gregory XV	1621-23
Gelasius II	1118-19	(at Avignon)		Urban VIII	1623-44
Gregory (VIII)	1118-21	Innocent VI	1352-62	Innocent X	1644-55
Calixtus II	1119-24	(at Avignon)		Alexander VII	1655-67
(Callixtus)		Urban V	1362-70	Clement IX	1667-69
Honorius II	1124-30	(at Avignon)		Clement X	1670-76
Celestine (II)	1124	Gregory XI	1370-78	Innocent XI	1676-89
Innocent II	1130-43	(at Avignon, then		Alexander VIII	1689-91
Anacletus (II)	1130-38	Rome from 1377)		Innocent XII	1691-1700
Victor (IV)	1138	Urban VI	1378-89	Clement XI	1700-21
Celestine II	1143-44	Clement (VII)	1378-94	Innocent XIII	1721-24
Lucius II	1144-45	(at Avignon)		Benedict XIII	1724-30
Eugenius III	1145-53	Boniface IX	1389-1404	Clement XII	1730-40
Anastasius IV	1153-54	Benedict (XIII)	1394-1423	Benedict XIV	1740-58
Adrian IV	1154-59	(at Avignon)		Clement XIII	1758-69
Alexander III	1159-81	Innocent VII	1404-06	Clement XIV	1769-74
Victor (IV)	1159-64	Gregory XII	1406-15	Pius VI	1775-99
Paschal (III)	1164-68	Alexander (V)	1409-10	Pius VII	1800-23
Calixtus (III)	1168-78	(at Bologna)		Leo XII	1823-29
Innocent (III)	1179-80	John (XXIII)	1410-15	Pius VIII	1829-30
Lucius III	1181-85	(at Bologna)		Gregory XVI	1831-46
Urban III	1185-87	Martin V[5]	1417-31	Pius IX	1846-78
Gregory VIII	1187	Clement (VIII)	1423-29	Leo XIII	1878-1903
Clement III	1187-91	Eugenius IV	1431-47	Pius X	1903-14
Celestine III	1191-98	Felix (V) (Amadeus	1439-49	Benedict XV	1914-22
Innocent III	1198-1216	VIII of Savoy)		Pius XI	1922-39
Honorius III	1216-27	Nicholas V	1447-55	Pius XII	1939-58
Gregory IX	1227-41	Calixtus III	1455-58	John XXIII	1958-63
Celestine IV	1241	(Callistus)		Paul VI	1963-78
Innocent IV	1243-54	Pius II	1458-64	John Paul I	1978
Alexander IV	1254-61	Paul II	1464-71	John Paul II	1978-
Urban IV	1261-64	Sixtus IV	1471-84		

[1]The higher number is used If Felix (II), who reigned from 355 to 358 and is ordinarily classed as an antipope, is counted as a pope.   [2]Though elected on 23 Mar 752, Stephen (II) died two days later before he could be consecrated and thus is ordinarily not counted. The issue has made the numbering of subsequent Stephens somewhat irregular.   [3]Either Leo VIII or Benedict V may be considered an antipope.   [4]A confusion in the numbering of popes named John after John XIV (reigned 983–84) resulted because some 11th-century historians mistakenly believed that there had been a pope named John between antipope Boniface VII and the true John XV (reigned 985–86). Therefore they mistakenly numbered the real popes John XV to XIX as John XVI to XX. These popes have since customarily been renumbered XV to XIX, but John XXI and John XXII continue to bear numbers that they themselves formally adopted on the assumption that there had indeed been 20 Johns before them. In current numbering there thus exists no pope by the name of John XX.   [5]In the 13th century the papal chancery misread the names of the two popes Marinus as Martin, and as a result of this error Simon de Brie in 1281 assumed the name of Pope Martin IV instead of Martin II. The enumeration has not been corrected, and thus there exist no Martin II and Martin III.

Roman Catholic Cardinals

Members of the **Sacred College of Cardinals** elect the pope, act as his principal counselors, and aid in the government of the Roman Catholic church throughout the world. Cardinals serve as chief officials of the **Roman Curia** (the papal administration), as bishops of major dioceses, and often as papal envoys. New cardinals are appointed only by the pope. He calls a secret **consistory** (meeting) of the cardinals and announces to them the names of the new cardinals. The newly named cardinals then receive the red biretta and the ring symbolic of the office in a public consistory. There are three orders of cardinals: bishops, priests, and deacons. These ranks correspond not to a cardinal's rank of ordination but to his position within the College of Cardinals. These distinctions are not made in the table below. The total **number of cardinals** was fixed at 70 by Sixtus V in 1586. John XXIII eliminated the restriction of 70 in 1959, although the number of papal electors was later set at 120. Those aged over 80 no longer serve as papal electors.

The following cardinals hold specific offices within the college. **Dean:** Bernardin Gantin; **Sub-Dean:** Joseph Ratzinger; **Senior Deacon:** Luigi Poggi; **Camerlengo of the Holy Roman Church:** Eduardo Martínez Somalo.

NAME	BIRTH DATE	DATE APPOINTED CARDINAL	BIRTHPLACE
Franz König	3 Aug 1905	15 Dec 1958	Austria
Corrado Ursi	26 Jul 1908	26 Jun 1967	Italy
Eugênio de Araújo Sales	8 Nov 1920	28 Apr 1969	Brazil
Stephen Sou Hwan Kim	8 May 1922	28 Apr 1969	Korea
Johannes Willebrands	4 Sep 1909	28 Apr 1969	The Netherlands
Luis Aponte Martínez	4 Aug 1922	5 Mar 1973	Puerto Rico
Paulo Evaristo Arns	14 Sep 1921	5 Mar 1973	Brazil
Marcelo González Martín	16 Jan 1918	5 Mar 1973	Spain
Maurice Michael Otunga	Jan 1923	5 Mar 1973	Kenya
Salvatore Pappalardo	23 Sep 1918	5 Mar 1973	Italy
Raúl Francisco Primatesta	14 Apr 1919	5 Mar 1973	Argentina
Pio Taofinu'u	8 Dec 1923	5 Mar 1973	Samoa
Juan Carlos Aramburu	11 Feb 1912	24 May 1976	Argentina
Corrado Bafile	4 Jul 1903	24 May 1976	Italy
William Wakefield Baum	21 Nov 1926	24 May 1976	US
Aloísio Lorscheider	8 Oct 1924	24 May 1976	Brazil
Opilio Rossi	14 May 1910	24 May 1976	US
Jaime L. Sin	31 Aug 1928	24 May 1976	Philippines
Hyacinthe Thiandoum	2 Feb 1921	24 May 1976	Senegal
Bernardin Gantin	8 May 1922	27 Jun 1977	Benin
Joseph Ratzinger	16 Apr 1927	27 Jun 1977	Germany
Giuseppe Caprio	15 Nov 1914	30 Jun 1979	Italy
Gerald Emmett Carter	1 Mar 1912	30 Jun 1979	Canada
Marco Cé	8 Jul 1925	30 Jun 1979	Italy
Ernesto Corripio Ahumada	29 Jun 1919	30 Jun 1979	Mexico
Roger Etchegaray	25 Sep 1922	30 Jun 1979	France
Franciszek Macharski	20 May 1927	30 Jun 1979	Poland
Godfried Danneels	4 Jun 1933	2 Feb 1983	Belgium
Alexandre do Nascimento	1 Mar 1925	2 Feb 1983	Angola
Józef Glemp	18 Dec 1929	2 Feb 1983	Poland
Michael Michai Kitbunchu	25 Jan 1929	2 Feb 1983	Thailand
Alfonso López Trujillo	8 Nov 1935	2 Feb 1983	Colombia
Jean-Marie Lustiger	17 Sep 1926	2 Feb 1983	France
Carlo Maria Martini	15 Feb 1927	2 Feb 1983	Italy
Joachim Meisner	25 Dec 1933	2 Feb 1983	Germany (present-day Poland)
Aurelio Sabattani	18 Oct 1912	2 Feb 1983	Italy
Thomas Stafford Williams	20 Mar 1930	2 Feb 1983	New Zealand
Francis Arinze	1 Nov 1932	25 May 1985	Nigeria
Giacomo Biffi	13 Jun 1928	25 May 1985	Italy
Rosalio José Castillo Lara	4 Sep 1922	25 May 1985	Venezuela
Andrzej Maria Deskur	29 Feb 1924	25 May 1985	Poland
Juan Francisco Fresno Larraín	26 Jul 1914	25 May 1985	Chile
Edouard Gagnon	15 Jan 1918	25 May 1985	Canada
Henryk Roman Gulbinowicz	17 Oct 1928	25 May 1985	Poland
Antonio Innocenti	23 Aug 1915	25 May 1985	Italy
Bernard Francis Law	4 Nov 1931	25 May 1985	US
D. Simon Lourdusamy	5 Feb 1924	25 May 1985	India
Paul Augustin Mayer	23 May 1911	25 May 1985	Germany
Miguel Obando Bravo	2 Feb 1926	25 May 1985	Nicaragua
Silvano Piovanelli	21 Feb 1924	25 May 1985	Italy
Paul Poupard	30 Aug 1930	25 May 1985	France

Roman Catholic Cardinals (continued)

NAME	BIRTH DATE	DATE APPOINTED CARDINAL	BIRTHPLACE
Adrianus Johannes Simonis	26 Nov 1931	25 May 1985	The Netherlands
Alfons Maria Stickler	23 Aug 1910	25 May 1985	Austria
Angel Suquía Goicoechea	2 Oct 1916	25 May 1985	Spain
Jozef Tomko	11 Mar 1924	25 May 1985	Slovakia
Paulos Tzadua	25 Aug 1921	25 May 1985	Ethiopia
Louis-Albert Vachon	4 Feb 1912	25 May 1985	Canada
Ricardo Vidal	6 Feb 1931	25 May 1985	Philippines
Friedrich Wetter	20 Feb 1928	25 May 1985	Germany
Giovanni Canestri	30 Sep 1918	28 Jun 1988	Italy
Edward Bede Clancy	13 Dec 1923	28 Jun 1988	Australia
José Freire Falcão	23 Oct 1925	28 Jun 1988	Brazil
Angelo Felici	26 Jul 1919	28 Jun 1988	Italy
Michele Giordano	26 Sep 1930	28 Jun 1988	Italy
Hans Hermann Gröer	13 Oct 1919	28 Jun 1988	Austria
James Aloysius Hickey	11 Oct 1920	28 Jun 1988	US
Antonio María Javierre Ortas	21 Feb 1921	28 Jun 1988	Spain
Jean Margéot	3 Feb 1916	28 Jun 1988	Mauritius
Eduardo Martínez Somalo	31 Mar 1927	28 Jun 1988	Spain
Lucas Moreira Neves	16 Sep 1925	28 Jun 1988	Brazil
László Paskai	8 May 1927	28 Jun 1988	Hungary
Simon Ignatius Pimenta	1 Mar 1920	28 Jun 1988	India
Alexandre José Maria dos Santos	18 Mar 1924	28 Jun 1988	Mozambique
Achille Silvestrini	25 Oct 1923	28 Jun 1988	Italy
Edmund Casimir Szoka	14 Sep 1927	28 Jun 1988	US
Christian Wiyghan Tumi	15 Oct 1930	28 Jun 1988	Cameroon
John Baptist Wu Cheng-Chung	26 Mar 1925	28 Jun 1988	China
Fiorenzo Angelini	1 Aug 1916	28 Jun 1991	Italy
Anthony Joseph Bevilacqua	17 Jun 1923	28 Jun 1991	US
Edward Idris Cassidy	5 Jul 1924	28 Jun 1991	Australia
Cahal Brendan Daly	1 Oct 1917	28 Jun 1991	Ireland
Frédéric Etsou-Nzabi-Bamungwabi	3 Dec 1930	28 Jun 1991	Dem. Rep. of the Congo
Ján Chryzostom Korec	22 Jan 1924	28 Jun 1991	Slovakia
Pio Laghi	21 May 1922	28 Jun 1991	Italy
Nicolás de Jesús López Rodríguez	31 Oct 1936	28 Jun 1991	Dominican Rep.
Roger Michael Mahony	27 Feb 1936	28 Jun 1991	US
Virgilio Noè	30 Mar 1922	28 Jun 1991	Italy
Camillo Ruini	19 Feb 1931	28 Jun 1991	Italy
Giovanni Saldarini	11 Dec 1924	28 Jun 1991	Italy
José T. Sánchez	17 Mar 1920	28 Jun 1991	Philippines
Henri Schwery	14 Jun 1932	28 Jun 1991	Switzerland
Angelo Sodano	23 Nov 1927	28 Jun 1991	Italy
Georg Maximilian Sterzinsky	9 Feb 1936	28 Jun 1991	Germany
Gilberto Agustoni	26 Jul 1922	26 Nov 1994	Switzerland
Ricardo María Carles Gordó	24 Sep 1926	26 Nov 1994	Spain
Julius Riyadi Darmaatmadja	20 Dec 1934	26 Nov 1994	Indonesia
Carlo Furno	2 Dec 1921	26 Nov 1994	Italy
William Henry Keeler	4 Mar 1931	26 Nov 1994	US
Adam Joseph Maida	18 Mar 1930	26 Nov 1994	US
Jaime Lucas Ortega y Alamino	18 Oct 1936	26 Nov 1994	Cuba
Paul Joseph Pham Dinh Tung	15 Jun 1919	26 Nov 1994	Vietnam
Luigi Poggi	25 Nov 1917	26 Nov 1994	Italy
Vinko Puljic	8 Sep 1945	26 Nov 1994	Bosnia-Herzegovina
Armand Gaétan Razafindratandra	7 Aug 1925	26 Nov 1994	Madagascar
Juan Sandoval Iñiguez	28 Mar 1933	26 Nov 1994	Mexico
Jan Pieter Schotte	29 Apr 1928	26 Nov 1994	Belgium
Nasrallah Pierre Sfeir	15 May 1920	26 Nov 1994	Lebanon
Peter Seiichi Shirayanagi	17 Jun 1928	26 Nov 1994	Japan
Adolfo Antonio Suárez Rivera	9 Jan 1927	26 Nov 1994	Mexico
Kazimierz Swiatek	21 Oct 1914	26 Nov 1994	Estonia
Ersilio Tonini	20 Jul 1914	26 Nov 1994	Italy
Jean-Claude Turcotte	26 Jun 1936	26 Nov 1994	Canada
Miloslav Vlk	17 May 1932	26 Nov 1994	Czech Rep.
Emmanuel Wamala	15 Dec 1926	26 Nov 1994	Uganda
Aloysius Matthew Ambrozic	27 Jan 1930	21 Feb 1998	Slovenia
Lorenzo Antonetti	31 Jul 1922	21 Feb 1998	Italy

Roman Catholic Cardinals (continued)

NAME	BIRTH DATE	DATE APPOINTED CARDINAL	BIRTHPLACE
Serafim Fernandes de Araújo	13 Aug 1924	21 Feb 1998	Brazil
Darío Castrillón Hoyos	4 Jul 1929	21 Feb 1998	Colombia
Giovanni Cheli	4 Oct 1918	21 Feb 1998	Italy
Francesco Colasuonno	2 Jan 1925	21 Feb 1998	Italy
Salvatore de Giorgi	6 Sep 1930	21 Feb 1998	Italy
Francis Eugene George	16 Jan 1937	21 Feb 1998	US
Adam Kozlowiecki	1 Apr 1911	21 Feb 1998	Poland
Jorge Arturo Medina Estévez	23 Dec 1926	21 Feb 1998	Chile
Dino Monduzzi	2 Apr 1922	21 Feb 1998	Italy
Polycarp Pengo	5 Aug 1944	21 Feb 1998	Tanzania
Norberto Rivera Carrera	6 Jun 1942	21 Feb 1998	Mexico
Antonio María Rouco Varela	24 Aug 1936	21 Feb 1998	Spain
Christoph Schönborn	22 Jan 1945	21 Feb 1998	Bohemia (present-day Czech Rep.)
Paul Shan Kuo-Hsi	3 Dec 1923	21 Feb 1998	China
James Francis Stafford	26 Jul 1932	21 Feb 1998	US
Dionigi Tettamanzi	14 Mar 1934	21 Feb 1998	Italy
Marian Jaworski[1]	21 Aug 1926	28 Jan 2001	Ukraine
Karl Lehmann	16 May 1936	28 Jan 2001	Germany
Wilfrid Fox Napier	8 Mar 1941	28 Jan 2001	South Africa
Janis Pujats[1]	14 Nov 1930	28 Jan 2001	Latvia
Julio Terrazas Sandoval	7 Mar 1936	28 Jan 2001	Bolivia
Geraldo Majella Agnelo	19 Oct 1933	21 Feb 2001	Brazil
Bernard Agré	2 Mar 1926	21 Feb 2001	Côte d'Ivoire
Francisco Álvarez Martínez	14 Jul 1925	21 Feb 2001	Spain
Audrys Juozas Backis	1 Feb 1937	21 Feb 2001	Lithuania
Jorge Mario Bergoglio	17 Dec 1936	21 Feb 2001	Argentina
Louis-Marie Billé	18 Feb 1938	21 Feb 2001	France
Agostino Cacciavillan	14 Aug 1926	21 Feb 2001	Italy
Juan Luis Cipriani Thorne	28 Dec 1943	21 Feb 2001	Peru
Desmond Connell	24 Mar 1926	21 Feb 2001	Ireland
José da Cruz Policarpo	26 Feb 1936	21 Feb 2001	Portugal
Ignace Moussa I Daoud	18 Sep 1930	21 Feb 2001	Syria
Johannes Joachim Degenhardt	31 Jan 1926	21 Feb 2001	Germany
Ivan Dias	14 Apr 1936	21 Feb 2001	India
Avery Dulles	24 Aug 1918	21 Feb 2001	US
Edward Michael Egan	2 Apr 1932	21 Feb 2001	US
Francisco Javier Errázuriz Ossa	5 Sep 1933	21 Feb 2001	Chile
Stéphanos II Ghattas	16 Jan 1920	21 Feb 2001	Egypt
Antonio José González Zumárraga	18 Mar 1925	21 Feb 2001	Ecuador
Zenon Grocholewski	11 Oct 1939	21 Feb 2001	Poland
Jean Honoré	13 Aug 1920	21 Feb 2001	France
Cláudio Hummes	8 Aug 1934	21 Feb 2001	Brazil
Lubomyr Husar	26 Feb 1933	21 Feb 2001	Ukraine
Walter Kasper	5 Mar 1933	21 Feb 2001	Germany
Theodore Edgar McCarrick	7 Jul 1930	21 Feb 2001	US
Jorge María Mejía	31 Jan 1923	21 Feb 2001	Argentina
Cormac Murphy-O'Connor	24 Aug 1932	21 Feb 2001	UK
François Xavier Nguyên van Thuân	17 Apr 1928	21 Feb 2001	Vietnam
Severino Poletto	18 Mar 1933	21 Feb 2001	Italy
Mario Francesco Pompedda	18 Apr 1929	21 Feb 2001	Italy
Giovanni Battista Re	30 Jan 1934	21 Feb 2001	Italy
Oscar Andrés Rodríguez Maradiaga	29 Dec 1942	21 Feb 2001	Honduras
Pedro Rubiano Sáenz	13 Sep 1932	21 Feb 2001	Colombia
José Saraiva Martins	6 Jan 1932	21 Feb 2001	Portugal
Leo Scheffczyk	21 Feb 1920	21 Feb 2001	Germany
Sergio Sebastiani	11 Apr 1931	21 Feb 2001	Italy
Crescenzio Sepe	2 Jun 1943	21 Feb 2001	Italy
Roberto Tucci	19 Apr 1921	21 Feb 2001	Italy
Ignacio Antonio Velasco García	17 Jan 1929	21 Feb 2001	Venezuela
Varkey Vithayathil	29 May 1927	21 Feb 2001	India

[1]Held in pectore (in secret) from the consistory of 21 Feb 1998; officially announced 28 Jan 2001.

Scholarship

National and Public Libraries of the World

The national and public libraries listed below are generally open to the public. National libraries are usually the primary repository for a nation's printed works. Sources: "National Libraries of the World: an Address List," IFLA Publications. *International Dictionary of Library Histories*, 2001, Fitzroy Dearborn Publishers. *The Bowker Annual Library and Book Trade Almanac 2002*, R.R. Bowker.

LIBRARY	LOCATION	YEAR FOUNDED	NUMBER OF VOLUMES (MILLIONS)	SPECIAL COLLECTIONS, ARCHIVES, PAPERS
national libraries				
Biblioteca Nacional Venezuela	Caracas	1833	5.8	politics and diplomacy, Simón Bolívar
Biblioteca Nazionale Centrale	Florence	1861	5.4	Reformation, Galileo Galilei
Biblioteca Nazionale Centrale Vittorio Emanuele II	Rome	1876	6.0	Jesuit collections, Gabriele D'Annunzio
Bibliothèque nationale de France	Paris	1461	14.0	Denis Diderot, Jean-Paul Sartre
Bibliothèque nationale du Québec	Montreal	1967	0.594	artist's books, musical scores
British Library[1]	London	1973	16.0	Charles Dickens, George B. Shaw
Deutsche Bibliothek	Frankfurt[2]	1947	6.3	bibliographies, exile literature (1933–45)
Deutsche Bücherei	Leipzig	1990	9.2	socialism, Anne-Frank-Shoah-Bibliothek
Jewish National and University Library[3]	Jerusalem	1892	3.0	world Jewish history, Albert Einstein
Library of Congress	Washington DC	1800	27.8	Americana, Irving Berlin, Walt Whitman
National Diet Library[4]	Tokyo	1948	7.3	Japanese culture, Allied occupation
National Library of China[5]	Beijing	1909	20	art, early communism
National Library of India	Calcutta	1903	3.0	rare journals of vernacular languages
National Library of Mexico	Mexico City	1867	3.0	Jesuit works, Mexican printing
National Library of Russia	St. Petersburg	1795	2.0	rare books, Russian history
public libraries				
Biblioteca Luis Angel Arango	Bogotá	1932	0.95	Spanish New World chroniclers
Bibliothèque Mazarine Institut de France	Paris	1643	0.5	French theology, Jansenist materials
Bibliothèque municipale de Lyon	Lyon	1765	2.0	history of the book, occult studies
Bibliothèque publique et universitaire de Genéve	Switzerland	1502	1.9	Reformation, Jean Calvin, Voltaire
Birmingham Central Library	England	1865	1.2	Industrial Revolution, Shakespeare
Boston Public Library	Massachusetts	1848	6.9	music, fine arts, Emily Dickinson
Chetham's Library	Manchester, UK	1653	0.1	religious history, Robert Southey
Chicago Public Library	Illinois	1873	5.8	African American studies, blues music
Enoch Pratt Free Library	Baltimore MD	1886	2.4	Henry L. Mencken, Edgar Allan Poe
Free Library of Philadelphia	Pennsylvania	1891	3.0	Oliver Goldsmith, Edgar Allan Poe
Los Angeles Public Library	California	1872	2.2	Calif. cookbooks, fairy tales, Mexicana
Manchester Central Library	UK	1852	2.1	music, commerce, Samuel T. Coleridge
Mitchell Library	Glasgow	1877	1.2	angling, architecture, Robert Burns
New York Public Library	New York	1895	8.0	gay and lesbian works, theater and music
Öffentliche Bibliothek der Universität Basel	Switzerland	1470	3.1	Swiss Medical Academy, F. Nietzsche[6]
Shanghai Tushu Guang	China	1952	10.0	chronicles, genealogies
Toronto Public Library[7]	Ontario	1884	1.9	science fiction, Arthur Conan Doyle

[1]*Originally founded in 1753 as the British Museum Library.* [2]*Frankfurt am Main, Germany.* [3]*Bet Ha-Sefarim Ha-Leumini Weha-Universitai Giv'at Ram.* [4]*Kokuritsu Kokkai Toshokan.* [5]*Zhongguo Guojia Tushuguan.* [6]*Friedrich Nietzsche.* [7]*Metropolitan Toronto Library Board Reference Library.*

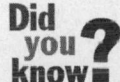

Did you know? The bridges of Florence, Italy, were destroyed by floods in the 12th century and in 1333. In 1557 the Ponte Vecchio held fast, but others were destroyed. Then, in 1944 their replacements were blown up by the retreating German army, which spared the Ponte Vecchio but destroyed antique quarters at either end of it.

Military Affairs

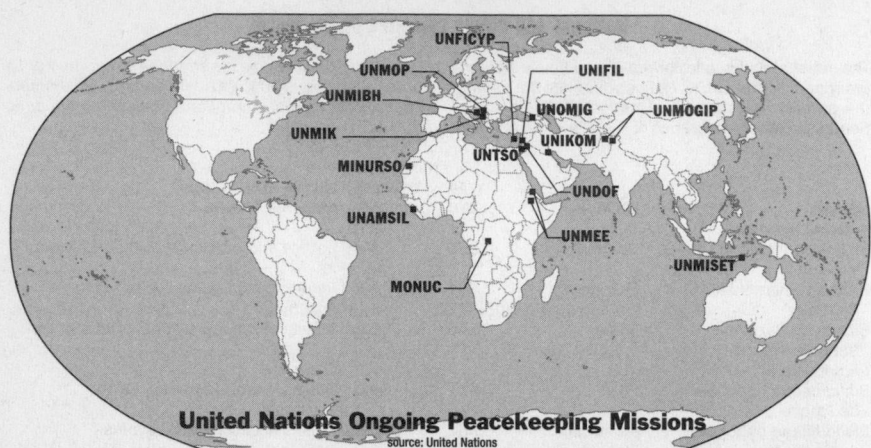

United Nations Ongoing Peacekeeping Missions
Source: United Nations

MINURSO - United Nations Mission for the Referendum in Western Sahara – since April 1991

MONUC - United Nations Organization Mission in the Democratic Republic of the Congo – since December 1999

UNAMSIL - United Nations Mission in Sierra Leone – since October 1999

UNDOF - United Nations Disengagement Observer Force – since June 1974

UNFICYP - United Nations Peacekeeping Force in Cyprus – since March 1964

UNIFIL - United Nations Interim Force in Lebanon – since March 1978

UNIKOM - United Nations Iraq-Kuwait Observation Mission – since April 1991

UNMEE - United Nations Mission in Ethiopia and Eritrea – since July 2000

UNMIBH - United Nations Mission in Bosnia and Herzegovina – since December 1995

UNMIK - United Nations Interim Administration Mission in Kosovo – since June 1999

UNMISET - United Nations Mission of Support in East Timor – since May 2002

UNMOGIP - United Nations Military Observer Group in India and Pakistan – since January 1949

UNMOP - United Nations Mission of Observers in Prevlaka – since January 1996

UNOMIG - United Nations Observer Mission in Georgia – since August 1993

UNTSO - United Nations Truce Supervision Organization – since June 1948

Nations with Largest Armed Forces

Countries with a military strength of at least 200,000 active personnel. Personnel numbers are in thousands ('000). Dollars refer to US currency. Source: The Military Balance, 2001–02, The International Institute of Strategic Studies

| | | | | ARMY | NAVY | | AIR FORCE | |
| | MILITARY PERSONNEL | | DEFENSE SPENDING | MAIN BATTLE | MAJOR WARSHIPS/ | SUB- | COMBAT | STRATEGIC NUCLEAR |
COUNTRY	ACTIVE	RESERVES	($ BILLIONS)	TANKS	CARRIERS	MARINES	AIRCRAFT	WEAPONS
China	2,310.0	>500	42.0	8,000	62/0	69	2,900	yes
US	1,367.7	1,200.6	291.2	7,620	116/12	73	4,147	yes
India	1,263.0	535.0	14.7	3,414	26/1	16	738	
N. Korea	1,082.0	4,700.0	2.1	3,500	3/0	26	621	
Russia	977.1	2,400.0	60.0	21,820	34/1	56	4,380	yes
S. Korea	683.0	4,500.0	12.8	2,330	39/0	19	555	
Pakistan	620.0	513.0	3.7	>2,300	8/0	10	353	
Turkey	515.1	378.7	10.8	4,205	23/0	13	505	
Iran	513.0	350.0	7.5	1,565	3/0	6	283	
Vietnam	484.0	>3,000	1.0	1,315	6/0	2	189	
Myanmar	444.0	0.0	2.1	100	0/0	0	113	
Egypt	443.0	254.0	2.9	3,860	11/0	4	580	
Iraq	424.0	650.0	1.4	2,200	0/0	0	316	
Taiwan	370.0	1,658.0	17.6	>926	32/0	4	482	
Syria	321.0	354.0	0.8	4,700	2/0	0	589	
Germany	308.4	363.5	28.8	2,521	14/0	14	434	
Thailand	306.0	200.0	2.5	333	12/1	0	153	
Ukraine	303.8	1,000.0	1.1	3,937	3/0	1	543	
Indonesia	297.0	400.0	1.5	0	17/0	2	108	
Brazil	287.6	1,115.0	17.9	178	18/1	4	281	

Nations with Largest Armed Forces (continued)

COUNTRY	MILITARY PERSONNEL		DEFENSE SPENDING ($ BILLIONS)	ARMY MAIN BATTLE TANKS	NAVY MAJOR WARSHIPS/ CARRIERS	SUB- MARINES	AIR FORCE COMBAT AIRCRAFT	STRATEGIC NUCLEAR WEAPONS
	ACTIVE	RESERVES						
France	273.7	419.0	35.0	809	34/1	10	473	yes
Ethiopia	252.5	0.0	0.5	>300	0/0	0	51	
Japan	239.8	47.4	45.6	1,050	54/0	16	297	
Italy	230.4	65.2	21.0	1,349	21/1	7	329	
UK	211.4	247.1	34.6	636	31/3	16	427	yes
Poland	206.0	406.0	3.3	1,677	3/0	3	212	

Law & Crime

International Terrorist Organizations

"Terrorism" is a subjective term. The list of organizations included here is that of the US Department of State, issued on 5 Oct 2001. The list is updated every other year.

Abu Nidal Organization (ANO) (Fatah Revolutionary Council, Arab Revolutionary Brigades, Black September, Revolutionary Organization of Socialist Muslims)
Founded in 1974 as splinter group from PLO; led by Sabri al-Banna
country or region of operation: Middle East, primarily Iraq and Lebanon; has also operated in Asia and Europe
primary goals: elimination of Israel, establishment of Palestinian state

Abu Sayyaf Group (ASG)
Founded in early 1990s as splinter group from Moro National Liberation Front by Abdurajak Abubakar Janjalani; nominally led by Khadaffy Janjalani, but mainly made up of semiautonomous factions.
country or region of operation: the Philippines, Malaysia
primary goals: establishment of independent Islamic state in southern Philippines

Armed Islamic Group (GIA)
Founded in 1992; leadership uncertain, but may be led by Rachid Abou Tourab
country or region of operation: Algeria
primary goals: replacement of secular Algerian government with an Islamic state

Aum Shinrikyo (Aum Supreme Truth, Aleph)
Founded in 1987 by Shoko Asahara; led by Fumihiro Joyu.
country or region of operation: Japan
primary goals: takeover of Japan and the world

Basque Fatherland and Liberty (ETA) (Euzkadi Ta Askatasuna)
Founded in 1959; leadership uncertain.
country or region of operation: Basque autonomous regions of northern Spain and south western France
primary goals: establishment of independent Basque state based on Marxism

Al-Gama'a al-Islamiyya (Islamic Group, IG)
Founded late 1970s; loosely organized in two factions led by Mustafa Hamza and Rifa'i Taha Musa; spiritual leader Sheikh Umar Abd al-Rahman.
country or region of operation: Egypt; also operates in several countries worldwide

primary goals: replacement of Egyptian government with an Islamic state

Hamas (Islamic Resistance Movement)
Founded in 1987 by Sheikh Ahmed Yasin as offshoot of Muslim Brotherhood; political leaders include Yasin, Abdel Aziz al-Rantisi, and Khalid Meshal.
country or region of operation: Gaza Strip, West Bank, Israel; also present throughout Middle East
primary goals: elimination of Israel, establishment of Islamic Palestinian state

Harakat ul Mujahidin (HUM) (Movement of Holy Warriors)
Founded mid-1980s or early 1990s, led by Farooq Kashmiri.
country or region of operation: the Kashmir region of Pakistan and India
primary goals: to make Kashmir part of an Islamic state

Hezbollah (Party of God) (Islamic Jihad, Revolutionary Justice Organization, Organization of the Oppressed on Earth, Islamic Jihad for the Liberation of Palestine)
Founded in 1982; governed by the Majlis al-Shura (Consultative Council) headed by Hassan Nasrallah; spiritual leader Sheikh Muhammad Hussein Fadlallah.
country or region of operation: Lebanon; also has cells worldwide
primary goals: establishment of Islamic rule in Lebanon, elimination of Israel, liberation of occupied Arab lands

Islamic Movement of Uzbekistan (IMU)
Founded in 1996; led by Tohir Yoldashev.
country or region of operation: Central and South Asia, primarily Uzbekistan, Tajikistan, Kyrgyzstan, Afghanistan, Iran, and Pakistan
primary goals: replacement of secular Uzbekistan government with an Islamic state

al-Jihad (Egyptian Islamic Jihad, Jihad Group, Islamic Jihad)
Founded late 1970s by Ayman al-Zawahiri; merged with al-Qaeda in 2001.
country or region of operation: Egypt and other countries, including Yemen, Afghanistan, Pakistan,

Lebanon, and Great Britain; activities now centred mainly outside Egypt

primary goals: replacement of Egyptian government with an Islamic state, attacks on US and Israeli interests

Kahane Chai (Kach)

Kach founded in 1971 by Meir Kahane; Kahane Chai founded as follow-up group by Binyamin Kahane after Meir's assassination in 1990; Binyamin assassinated in 2000.

country or region of operation: Israel, West Bank

primary goals: expansion of Israel, removal of Palestinians

Kurdistan Workers' Party (PKK)

Founded in 1974; led by Abdullah Ocalan (imprisoned since 1999).

country or region of operation: Turkey; also operates in Europe and the Middle East

primary goals: establishment of independent Kurdish state

Liberation Tigers of Tamil Eelam (LTTE)

Founded in 1976; led by Velupillai Prabhakaran.

country or region of operation: Sri Lanka

primary goals: establishment of independent Tamil state

Mujahedin-e Khalq Organization (MEK) (National Liberation Army of Iran [NLA, the militant wing], People's Mujahidin of Iran [PMOI], National Council of Resistance [NCR], Muslim Iranian Student's Society [front organization to garner financial support])

Founded 1960s; led by Maryam and Masud Rajavi.

country or region of operation: Iran, Iraq

primary goals: establishment of secular government in Iran

National Liberation Army (ELN)

Founded in 1965; led by Nicolas Rodríguez Bautista.

country or region of operation: Colombia

primary goals: replacement of ruling government with Marxist state

Palestine Islamic Jihad (PIJ)

Founded 1970s; most active faction led by Ramadan Shallah.

country or region of operation: Israel, West Bank, Gaza Strip; also elsewhere in Middle East, primarily Lebanon and Syria

primary goals: elimination of Israel, establishment of Islamic Palestinian state

Palestine Liberation Front (PLF)

Founded mid-1970s as splinter group from PFLP-GC; pro-PLO faction led by Muhammad Abbas (Abu Abbas).

country or region of operation: Israel, Iraq

primary goals: elimination of Israel, establishment of Palestinian state

Popular Front for the Liberation of Palestine (PFLP)

Founded as part of PLO in 1967 by George Habash (discontinued PLO participation in 1993); led by Ahmed Sadat.

country or region of operation: Syria, Lebanon, Israel, West Bank, Gaza Strip

primary goals: promotion of national unity and revitalization of PLO, opposition to peace negotiations with Israel

Popular Front for the Liberation of Palestine–General Command (PFLPGC)

Founded in 1968 as splinter group from PFLP; led by Ahmad Jabril.

country or region of operation: Syria, Lebanon, Israel, West Bank, Gaza Strip

primary goals: opposition to PLO and to peace negotiations with Israel

al-Qaeda

Founded late 1980s; established and led by Osama bin Laden.

country or region of operation: worldwide

primary goals: establishment of worldwide Islamic rule, overthrow of non-Islamic governments, expulsion of Western influences from Muslim states, killing of US citizens

Real IRA (True IRA)

Founded in 1998 as splinter group of Irish Republican Army (IRA); led by Michael "Mickey" McKevitt (imprisoned since 2001).

country or region of operation: Northern Ireland; also elsewhere in Great Britain and in Ireland

primary goals: removal of British forces from Northern Ireland, unification of Ireland

Revolutionary Armed Forces of Colombia (FARC)

Founded in 1964 as military branch of Colombian Communist Party; governed by group led by Manuel Marulanda and including Jorge Briceno and five others.

country or region of operation: Colombia; also some operations in Venezuela, Ecuador, and Panama

primary goals: replacement of ruling government with Marxist state

Revolutionary Nuclei (Revolutionary Cells)

Founded in 1995 as offshoot of or successor to Revolutionary People's Struggle (ELA).

country or region of operation: Greece, primarily Athens

primary goals: elimination of US military bases in Greece, opposition to capitalism and NATO/EU membership

Revolutionary Organization 17 November

Founded in 1975; relatively small group operating secretly.

country or region of operation: Greece, primarily Athens

primary goals: elimination of US military bases in Greece, removal of Turkish forces from Cyprus, opposition to capitalism and NATO/EU membership

Revolutionary People's Liberation Party/Front (DHKP/C) (Devrimci Sol, Revolutionary Left, Dev Sol)

Founded in 1978 as splinter group from Turkish People's Liberation Party/Front; led by Dursun Karatas.

country or region of operation: Turkey, primarily Istanbul

primary goals: promotion of Marxism, opposition to US and NATO

Shining Path (Sendero Luminoso, SL)

Founded late 1960s by Abimael Guzman; led by Macario Ala.

country or region of operation: Peru, primarily rural areas

primary goals: replacement of Peruvian government with communist state, opposition to influence by foreign governments

United Self-Defense Forces of Colombia (AUC-Autodefensas Unidas de Colombia)

Founded in 1997 as umbrella organization of paramilitary groups; led by Carlos Castaño.
country or region of operation: Colombia
primary goals: opposition to and defense against leftist guerilla groups

 **Did you know?** Vatican City is the world's smallest independent state, with a population of 1,000 and a birthrate of zero.

Universal Declaration of Human Rights

Completed by the UN Commission on Human Rights in June 1948 the Declaration was adopted by the General Assembly on 10 Dec 1948 by unanimous vote (with the six members of the Soviet bloc, Saudi Arabia, and the Union of South Africa abstaining). The declaration contained general definitions not only of those principal civil and political rights recognized in democratic constitutions but also of several so-called economic, social, and cultural rights.

Preamble
Whereas recognition of the inherent dignity and of the equal and inalienable rights of all members of the human family is the foundation of freedom, justice and peace in the world,

Whereas disregard and contempt for human rights have resulted in barbarous acts which have outraged the conscience of mankind, and the advent of a world in which human beings shall enjoy freedom of speech and belief and freedom from fear and want has been proclaimed as the highest aspiration of the common people,

Whereas it is essential, if man is not to be compelled to have recourse, as a last resort, to rebellion against tyranny and oppression, that human rights should be protected by the rule of law,

Whereas it is essential to promote the development of friendly relations between nations,

Whereas the peoples of the United Nations have in the Charter reaffirmed their faith in fundamental human rights, in the dignity and worth of the human person and in the equal rights of men and women and have determined to promote social progress and better standards of life in larger freedom,

Whereas Member States have pledged themselves to achieve, in co-operation with the United Nations, the promotion of universal respect for and observance of human rights and fundamental freedoms,

Whereas a common understanding of these rights and freedoms is of the greatest importance for the full realization of this pledge,

Now, therefore,

The General Assembly

Proclaims this Universal Declaration of Human Rights as a common standard of achievement for all peoples and all nations, to the end that every individual and every organ of society, keeping this Declaration constantly in mind, shall strive by teaching and education to promote respect for these rights and freedoms and by progressive measures, na-

tional and international, to secure their universal and effective recognition and observance, both among the peoples of Member States themselves and among the peoples of territories under their jurisdiction.

Article 1
All human beings are born free and equal in dignity and rights. They are endowed with reason and conscience and should act towards one another in a spirit of brotherhood.

Article 2
Everyone is entitled to all the rights and freedoms set forth in this Declaration, without distinction of any kind, such as race, colour, sex, language, religion, political or other opinion, national or social origin, property, birth or other status.

Furthermore, no distinction shall be made on the basis of the political, jurisdictional or international status of the country or territory to which a person belongs, whether it be independent, trust, non-self-governing or under any other limitation of sovereignty.

Article 3
Everyone has the right to life, liberty and the security of person.

Article 4
No one shall be held in slavery or servitude; slavery and the slave trade shall be prohibited in all their forms.

Article 5
No one shall be subjected to torture or to cruel, inhuman or degrading treatment or punishment.

Article 6
Everyone has the right to recognition everywhere as a person before the law.

Article 7
All are equal before the law and are entitled without any discrimination to equal protection of the law. All are entitled to equal protection against any discrimination in violation of this Declaration and against any incitement to such discrimination.

Article 8

Everyone has the right to an effective remedy by the competent national tribunals for acts violating the fundamental rights granted him by the constitution or by law.

Article 9

No one shall be subjected to arbitrary arrest, detention or exile.

Article 10

Everyone is entitled in full equality to a fair and public hearing by an independent and impartial tribunal, in the determination of his rights and obligations and of any criminal charge against him.

Article 11

1. Everyone charged with a penal offence has the right to be presumed innocent until proved guilty according to law in a public trial at which he has had all the guarantees necessary for his defence.

2. No one shall be held guilty of any penal offence on account of any act or omission which did not constitute a penal offence, under national or international law, at the time when it was committed. Nor shall a heavier penalty be imposed than the one that was applicable at the time the penal offence was committed.

Article 12

No one shall be subjected to arbitrary interference with his privacy, family, home or correspondence, nor to attacks upon his honour and reputation. Everyone has the right to the protection of the law against such interference or attacks.

Article 13

1. Everyone has the right to freedom of movement and residence within the borders of each state.

2. Everyone has the right to leave any country, including his own, and to return to his country.

Article 14

1. Everyone has the right to seek and to enjoy in other countries asylum from persecution.

2. This right may not be invoked in the case of prosecutions genuinely arising from non-political crimes or from acts contrary to the purposes and principles of the United Nations.

Article 15

1. Everyone has the right to a nationality.

2. No one shall be arbitrarily deprived of his nationality nor denied the right to change his nationality.

Article 16

1. Men and women of full age, without any limitation due to race, nationality or religion, have the right to marry and to found a family. They are entitled to equal rights as to marriage, during marriage and at its dissolution.

2. Marriage shall be entered into only with the free and full consent of the intending spouses.

3. The family is the natural and fundamental group unit of society and is entitled to protection by society and the State.

Article 17

1. Everyone has the right to own property alone as well as in association with others.

2. No one shall be arbitrarily deprived of his property.

Article 18

Everyone has the right to freedom of thought, conscience and religion; this right includes freedom to change his religion or belief, and freedom, either alone or in community with others and in public or private, to manifest his religion or belief in teaching, practice, worship and observance.

Article 19

Everyone has the right to freedom of opinion and expression; this right includes freedom to hold opinions without interference and to seek, receive and impart information and ideas through any media and regardless of frontiers.

Article 20

1. Everyone has the right to freedom of peaceful assembly and association.

2. No one may be compelled to belong to an association.

Article 21

1. Everyone has the right to take part in the government of his country, directly or through freely chosen representatives.

2. Everyone has the right of equal access to public service in his country.

3. The will of the people shall be the basis of the authority of government; this will shall be expressed in periodic and genuine elections which shall be by universal and equal suffrage and shall be held by secret vote or by equivalent free voting procedures.

Article 22

Everyone, as a member of society, has the right to social security and is entitled to realization, through national effort and international co-operation and in accordance with the organization and resources of each State, of the economic, social and cultural rights indispensable for his dignity and the free development of his personality.

Article 23

1. Everyone has the right to work, to free choice of employment, to just and favourable conditions of work and to protection against unemployment.

2. Everyone, without any discrimination, has the right to equal pay for equal work.

3. Everyone who works has the right to just and favourable remuneration ensuring for himself and his family an existence worthy of human dignity, and supplemented, if necessary, by other means of social protection.

4. Everyone has the right to form and to join trade unions for the protection of his interests.

Article 24

Everyone has the right to rest and leisure, including reasonable limitation of working hours and periodic holidays with pay.

Article 25

1. Everyone has the right to a standard of living adequate for the health and well-being of himself and of his family, including food, clothing, housing and medical care and necessary social services, and the right to security in the event of unemployment, sickness, disability, widowhood, old age or other lack of livelihood in circumstances beyond his control.

2. Motherhood and childhood are entitled to special care and assistance. All children, whether born in or out of wedlock, shall enjoy the same social protection.

Article 26

1. Everyone has the right to education. Education shall be free, at least in the elementary and fundamental stages. Elementary education shall be compulsory. Technical and professional education shall be made generally available and higher education shall be equally accessible to all on the basis of merit.

2. Education shall be directed to the full development of the human personality and to the strengthening of respect for human rights and fundamental freedoms. It shall promote understanding, tolerance and friendship among all nations, racial or religious groups, and shall further the activities of the United Nations for the maintenance of peace.

3. Parents have a prior right to choose the kind of education that shall be given to their children.

Article 27

1. Everyone has the right freely to participate in the cultural life of the community, to enjoy the arts and to share in scientific advancement and its benefits.

2. Everyone has the right to the protection of the moral and material interests resulting from any scientific, literary or artistic production of which he is the author.

Article 28

Everyone is entitled to a social and international order in which the rights and freedoms set forth in this Declaration can be fully realized.

Article 29

1. Everyone has duties to the community in which alone the free and full development of his personality is possible.

2. In the exercise of his rights and freedoms, everyone shall be subject only to such limitations as are determined by law solely for the purpose of securing due recognition and respect for the rights and freedoms of others and of meeting the just requirements of morality, public order and the general welfare in a democratic society.

3. These rights and freedoms may in no case be exercised contrary to the purposes and principles of the United Nations.

Article 30

Nothing in this Declaration may be interpreted as implying for any State, group or person any right to engage in any activity or to perform any act aimed at the destruction of any of the rights and freedoms set forth herein.

The International Court of Justice

The International Court of Justice is the principal judicial organ of the United Nations. Its seat is at the Peace Palace in The Hague (The Netherlands). It began work in 1946, when it replaced the Permanent Court of International Justice which had functioned in the Peace Palace since 1922. It operates under a Statute largely similar to that of its predecessor, which is an integral part of the Charter of the United Nations.

Functions of the Court

The Court has a dual role: to settle in accordance with international law the legal disputes submitted to it by States, and to give advisory opinions on legal questions referred to it by duly authorized international organs and agencies.

Composition

The Court is composed of 15 judges elected to nine-year terms of office by the United Nations General Assembly and Security Council sitting independently of each other. It may not include more than one judge of any nationality. Elections are held every three years for one-third of the seats, and retiring judges may be re-elected. The Members of the Court do not represent their governments but are independent magistrates.

The judges must possess the qualifications required in their respective countries for appointment to the highest judicial offices, or be jurists of recognized competence in international law. The composition of the Court has also to reflect the main forms of civilization and the principal legal systems of the world.

When the Court does not include a judge possessing the nationality of a State party to a case, that State may appoint a person to sit as a judge ad hoc for the purpose of the case.

The present composition of the Court is as follows: President Gilbert Guillaume (France), Vice President Shi Jiuyong (China), Judges Shigeru Oda (Japan), Raymond Ranjeva (Madagascar), Géza Herczegh (Hungary), Carl-August Fleischhauer (Germany), Abdul G. Koroma (Sierra Leone), Vladlen S. Vereshchetin (Russian Federation), Rosalyn Higgins (United Kingdom), Gonzalo Parra-Aranguren (Venezuela), Pieter H. Kooijmans (Netherlands), Francisco Rezek (Brazil), Awn Shawkat Al-Khasawneh (Jordan), Thomas Buergenthal (United States of America) and Nabil Elaraby (Egypt).

The Registrar of the Court is Mr. Philippe Couvreur (Belgium) and Deputy-Registrar of the Court is Mr. Jean-Jacques Arnaldez (France).

Cases between States

The Parties: Only States may apply to and appear before the Court. The States Members of the United Nations (at present numbering 189), and one State which is not a Member of the United Nations but which has become party to the Court's Statute (Switzerland), are so entitled.

Jurisdiction: The Court is competent to entertain a dispute only if the States concerned have accepted its jurisdiction in one or more of the following ways:
1. by the conclusion between them of a special agreement to submit the dispute to the Court;
2. by virtue of a jurisdictional clause, i.e., typically, when they are parties to a treaty containing a provision whereby, in the event of a disagreement over its interpretation or application, one of them may refer the dispute to the Court. Several hundred treaties or conventions contain a clause to such effect;
3. through the reciprocal effect of declarations made by them under the Statute whereby each has accepted the jurisdiction of the Court as compulsory in the event of a dispute with another State having made a similar declaration. The declarations of 64 States are at present in force, a number of them having been made subject to the exclusion of certain categories of dispute.

In cases of doubt as to whether the Court has jurisdiction, it is the Court itself which decides.

Procedure: The procedure followed by the Court in contentious cases is defined in its Statute, and in the Rules of Court adopted by it under the Statute. The latest version of the Rules dates from 5 December 2000. The proceedings include a written phase, in which the parties file and exchange pleadings, and an oral phase consisting of public hearings at which agents and counsel address the Court. As the Court has two official languages (English and French) everything written or said in one is translated into the other.

After the oral proceedings the Court deliberates in camera and then delivers its judgment at a public sitting. The judgment is final and without appeal. Should one of the States involved fail to comply with it, the other party may have recourse to the Security Council of the United Nations.

The Court discharges its duties as a full court but, at the request of the parties, it may also establish a special chamber. The Court constituted such a chamber in 1982 for the first time, formed a second one in 1985 and constituted two more in 1987. A Chamber of Summary Procedure is elected every year by the Court in accordance with its Statute. In July 1993 the Court has also established a seven-member Chamber to deal with any environmental cases falling within its jurisdiction.

Since 1946 the Court has delivered 74 Judgments on disputes concerning inter alia land frontiers and maritime boundaries, territorial sovereignty, the non-use of force, non-interference in the internal affairs of States, diplomatic relations, hostage-taking, the right of asylum, nationality, guardianship, rights of passage and economic rights.

Sources of applicable law: The Court decides in accordance with international treaties and conventions in force, international custom, the general principles of law and, as subsidiary means, judicial decisions and the teachings of the most highly qualified publicists.

Advisory Opinions
The advisory procedure of the Court is open solely to international organizations. The only bodies at present authorized to request advisory opinions of the Court are five organs of the United Nations and 16 specialized agencies of the United Nations family.

On receiving a request, the Court decides which States and organizations might provide useful information and gives them an opportunity of presenting written or oral statements. The Court's advisory procedure is otherwise modelled on that for contentious proceedings, and the sources of applicable law are the same.

In principle the Court's advisory opinions are consultative in character and are therefore not binding as such on the requesting bodies. Certain instruments or regulations can, however, provide in advance that the advisory opinion shall be binding.

Since 1946 the Court has given 24 Advisory Opinions, concerning inter alia admission to United Nations membership, reparation for injuries suffered in the service of the United Nations, territorial status of South-West Africa (Namibia) and Western Sahara, judgments rendered by international administrative tribunals, expenses of certain United Nations operations, applicability of the United Nations Headquarters Agreement, the status of human rights rapporteurs, and the legality of the threat or use of nuclear weapons.

Internet resources: <www.icj-cij.org>

Did you know? The city of Kyoto is the repository of hundreds of designated "national treasures" and "important cultural objects" of Japan. Included among these are individuals who have been named "living national treasures" in recognition of their superior skills in the traditional arts and crafts. During World War II US Secretary of State Henry L. Stimson, recalling his visits to Kyoto, struck the city from the list of targets for aerial bombing.

United States

United States History

United States Chronology

1492 Christopher Columbus, sailing under the Spanish flag, discovers America, 12 October.

1497 John Cabot, representing England, explores Atlantic coast of what is now Canada.

1513 Ponce de León of Spain lands in Florida and gives that region its name.

1519-22 Magellan's Spanish ship—the *Vittoria*—is the first to sail around the world.

1534 France sends out Jacques Cartier to find a route to the Far East; he explores along St. Lawrence River, and France then lays claim to part of North America.

1541 Hernando de Soto of Spain discovers Mississippi River near site of Memphis.

1565 St. Augustine, oldest permanent settlement in the US, founded by Spaniards.

1587 A party under John White lands at Roanoke Island (now North Carolina); when White returns three years later, entire settlement has disappeared.

1607 English make first permanent settlement in New World at Jamestown; Virginia becomes first of 13 English colonies.

1619 First representative assembly in America, the House of Burgesses, meets in Virginia; first blacks land in Virginia.

1620 Pilgrims from ship *Mayflower* found settlement at Plymouth.

1649 Act Concerning Religion passed by Maryland legislature is first law of religious toleration in English colonies.

1682 La Salle explores lower Mississippi Valley and claims entire region for France.

1733 Georgia, 13th and last of English colonies in America, is founded.

1754 Both England and the colonies reject Albany Plan of Union to unite colonies. Decisive French and Indian War between France and England begins in America.

1763 Treaty of Paris ends French and Indian War; Britain wins control of New World; Louisiana ceded to Spain; Florida, to Britain.

1765 Quartering Act and Stamp Act anger Americans; nine colonies represented at Stamp Act Congress.

1770 British troops fire on a crowd, killing five people in the so-called Boston Massacre.

1772 Committees of Correspondence organized in almost all colonies.

1773 Boston Tea Party is first action in chain leading to war with Britain.

1774 First Continental Congress meets at Philadelphia; protests Five Intolerable Acts.

1775 Battles of Lexington and Concord, Bunker Hill; Second Continental Congress meets.

1776 Declaration of Independence is adopted. Washington crosses the Delaware to fight at Trenton.

1777 Americans capture General Burgoyne and large British force at Saratoga, New York.

1778-79 Gen. George Rogers Clark leads victorious expedition into Northwest Territory.

1781 Washington accepts surrender of Cornwallis at Yorktown, Virginia. Articles of Confederation become government of the US.

1783 Treaty of peace with Great Britain signed at Paris, formally ending Revolutionary War.

1786-87 Shays's Rebellion in Massachusetts shows weaknesses of Confederation government.

1787 Northwest Territory organized by Congress. Convention meets to draft new constitution.

1788 US Constitution is ratified by necessary nine states to ensure adoption.

1789 New US government goes into effect; Washington inaugurated president; first Congress meets in New York City.

1791 Bill of Rights added to Constitution. Vermont is first new state admitted to Union.

1793 Eli Whitney invents cotton gin, which leads to large-scale cotton growing in the South.

1800 National capital moved from Philadelphia PA to Washington DC.

1803 Louisiana purchased from France. Supreme Court makes *Marbury* v. *Madison* decision; Congress halts the importation of slaves into the US after 1807.

1804-6 Lewis and Clark blaze overland trail to the Pacific and return.

1807 Robert Fulton's steamboat makes successful journey from New York City to Albany NY.

1812-14 US maintains its independence in conflict with Britain, War of 1812.

1818 US–Canada boundary dispute settled; agree on open border between countries.

1820 Missouri Compromise settles problem of slavery in new states for next 30 years.

1823 Monroe Doctrine warns European nations that US will protect the Americas.

1825 Erie Canal, from Hudson River to Great Lakes, becomes great water highway to Middle West.

1829 Inauguration of Pres. Andrew Jackson introduces era of Jacksonian Democracy.

1836 Texas wins its independence from Mexico.

1843 First great migration begins on Oregon Trail.

1845 Texas annexed and admitted as a state.

1846 Oregon boundary dispute settled with Britain. Mexican War begins.

1847 Brigham Young leads party of Mormons into Salt Lake Valley UT.

1848 Mexican War ends; US gains possession of California and New Mexico regions.

1849 Gold rush to California begins.

1850 Compromise of 1850 admits California as free state; postpones war between North and South.

1853 Gadsden Purchase adds 117,935 sq km (45,535 sq mi) to what is now southern Arizona and New Mexico.

1854 Kansas-Nebraska Act reopens slavery issue, leads to organization of Republican party.

1857 Dred Scott Decision of Supreme Court declares Missouri Compromise illegal.

1860 Lincoln elected president; South Carolina secedes from the Union.

1861 Confederate States of America formed; Civil War begins; Union forces routed at Bull Run VA. Telegraph links New York City with San Francisco CA.

1862 Grant launches Union attack in the West; Confederate invasion of Maryland halted at Antietam. Homestead Act grants 160 acres to each settler.

1863 Federal forces win decisive battles at Gettysburg, Vicksburg, and Chattanooga. Emancipation Proclamation takes effect.

1864 Sherman captures Atlanta and marches across Georgia. Grant closes in on Richmond VA.

1865 Lee surrenders to Grant at Appomattox Court House VA, ending Civil War. Lincoln is assassinated.

1867 Reconstruction acts impose military rule on South. Alaska purchased from Russia.

1869 First transcontinental railroad completed as two lines meet at Promontory UT.

1876 Telephone is invented. Centennial Exposition in Philadelphia PA celebrates 100th birthday of the US.

1877 Withdrawal of last federal troops from South ends reconstruction period. Railroad workers begin first nationwide strike.

1879 First practical electric light is invented by Thomas A. Edison.

1883 Pendleton Civil Service Act provides for examinations as basis of appointment to some government positions.

1884–85 First skyscraper, the Home Insurance Building, is erected in Chicago.

1886 American Federation of Labor is organized; first president is Samuel Gompers.

1887 Interstate Commerce Act adopted to control railroads that cross state lines.

1889–90 First Pan American Conference is held in Washington DC.

1890 Sherman Anti-Trust Act is passed in effort to curb growth of monopolies.

1896 Henry Ford's first car is driven on streets of Detroit MI.

1898 US wins Spanish-American War; gains Philippines, Puerto Rico, and Guam.

1903 Air age begins with successful airplane flight by Wright brothers.

1906 Federal Food and Drug Act passed to protect public from impure food and drugs.

1912 New Mexico and Arizona, 47th and 48th states, admitted to the Union.

1913 Federal income tax authorized by 16th Amendment; 17th Amendment provides for popular election of US senators.

1914 Panama Canal opened. World War I breaks out in Europe; Pres. Woodrow Wilson appeals for neutrality in the US.

1915 German submarine sinks *Lusitania* with loss of 124 American lives. Telephone line established coast to coast.

1917 Germany begins open submarine warfare; US declares war against Germany.

1918 Pres. Wilson proposes "Fourteen Points" as basis for peace. Americans fight at Chateau-Thierry, Belleau Wood, St-Mihiel, Argonne Forest. Armistice ends war.

1918–19 Pres. Wilson attends Paris Peace Conference of victorious nations.

1919 US Senate rejects League of Nations. Navy pilots make first flight across Atlantic. Prohibition established by 18th Amendment.

1920 Right to vote given women by 19th Amendment. Pittsburgh PA radio station, KDKA, begins broadcasting.

1921 Immigration restricted according to national quotas.

1921–22 Washington Conference restricts warship construction among chief naval powers.

1924 Army plane *Chicago* makes first flight around the world.

1927 Charles A. Lindbergh makes first nonstop solo flight across Atlantic.

1928 US signs Kellogg-Briand Pact to outlaw war.

1929 Stock market reaches new high, then crashes. Panic marks beginning of Great Depression; millions of workers are unemployed.

1932 Franklin Delano Roosevelt elected president.

1933 New Deal launched; gold standard suspended; National Recovery Act passed; bank deposits insured; Tennessee Valley Authority organized. 21st Amendment repeals prohibition.

1934 Congress tightens control over securities; passes first Reciprocal Trade Agreement Act; launches federal housing program.

1935 National Labor Relations (Wagner) Act guarantees collective bargaining to labor. Social Security Act passed. CIO founded.

1936 Hoover Dam (Boulder Dam) completed across Colorado River.

1938 Fair Labor Standards Act provides federal yardstick for wages and hours of workers.

1939 Germany invades Poland to start World War II. US declares neutrality.

1940 US begins huge rearmament program; first peacetime draft takes effect. Roosevelt defies tradition and accepts presidential nomination for a third term.

1941 Lend-Lease Act passed. Atlantic Charter signed. Japanese attack on Pearl Harbor brings US into World War II.

1942 Americans launch counteroffensive in Pacific. Allies invade North Africa.

1943 Allied invasion of Italy is first landing on European continent.

1944 Allies launch greatest sea-to-land assault in history in invasion of France. Allies invade Philippines. "GI Bill of Rights" passed.

1945 Germany surrenders, 8 May; atomic bomb dropped on Hiroshima, 6 August; Japan surrenders, 2 September. Cold War begins between US and Soviet Union. United Nations (UN) formally launched on 24 October.

1946 Philippines granted independence by US. Atomic Energy Commission created.

1947 Senate passes Truman Doctrine. Taft-Hartley labor law enacted. Department of Defense consolidates Army, Navy, and Air Force.

1948 European Recovery Program enacted. Truman elected president.

1949 Fair Deal program announced. US and its allies force Soviet Union to lift Berlin blockade. North Atlantic Treaty Organization (NATO) founded.

1950 US and several other members of UN send military forces to aid of Republic of Korea; bitter war develops.

1951 Two-term limit put on presidency by ratification of 22nd Amendment to Constitution.

1952 US and allies end occupation of West Germany. Election of Eisenhower ends 20 years of Democratic rule.

1953 Korean War ends. Department of Health, Education, and Welfare becomes 10th Cabinet post.

1954 Racial segregation of public schools declared illegal by Supreme Court. Southeast Asia Treaty Organization (SEATO) founded.

1955 Two largest labor organizations merge into one group the AFL-CIO. Salk poliomyelitis vaccine is proved successful.

1956 Eisenhower reelected president. Democrats win control of Congress.

1957 Eisenhower Doctrine to strengthen US position in Middle East adopted.

1958 First US artificial Earth satellite launched. US joins the International Atomic Energy Agency.

1959 Alaska becomes 49th state, Hawaii the 50th.

1960 US reconnaissance plane shot down over Soviet Union.

1961 CIA is involved in unsuccessful invasion of Cuba at Bay of Pigs. 23rd Amendment to Constitution gives Washington DC residents right to vote in presidential elections. First American makes space flight. American troops sent to defend West Berlin.

1962 Cuban missile crisis erupts; Soviets remove missiles from Cuba on US urging.

1963 March on Washington takes place. Pres. John F. Kennedy assassinated in Dallas TX. Nuclear test-ban treaty signed.

1964 24th Amendment to Constitution bans poll taxes in federal elections. Civil rights bill passed. Supreme Court makes possible reapportionment.

1965 US combat forces fight in Vietnam. Voting-rights bill and Medicare act signed. Department of Housing and Urban Development becomes 11th Cabinet post.

1966 Department of Transportation becomes 12th Cabinet post.

1967 25th Amendment to Constitution provides for presidential succession.

1968 Assassinations of Martin Luther King, Jr., and Robert F. Kennedy provoke race riots.

1969 US astronauts become the first men to land on the moon.

1970 Four students at Kent State University in Ohio killed by National Guard during anti-Vietnam War protest.

1971 26th Amendment to Constitution gives 18-year-olds right to vote in all elections.

1972 Pres. Richard M. Nixon visits China and Soviet Union.

1973 US withdraws troops from Vietnam. Vice-Pres. Spiro T. Agnew resigns. OPEC raises price of petroleum 400%.

1974 Watergate scandal and threat of impeachment force Nixon to resign.

1977 Department of Energy becomes new Cabinet post. Treaty altered to return Panama Canal to Panama by year 2000.

1978 Pres. Jimmy Carter hosts Camp David talks between Israel's Menachem Begin and Egypt's Anwar el-Sadat.

1979 Strategic Arms Limitation Talks (SALT II) signed by US and Soviet Union. Militants seize 66 American hostages in takeover of US Embassy in Iran.

1980 Department of Health, Education, and Welfare is separated into Department of Health and Human Services and Department of Education.

1981 Pres. Ronald Reagan wounded in assassination attempt. Major tax cut and increased defense spending pass Congress. Sandra Day O'Connor appointed first woman Supreme Court justice.

1983 Reagan announces Star Wars program. US invades Grenada.

1985 Summit conference between Reagan and Soviet leader Mikhail Gorbachev held in Geneva, Switzerland.

1986 Space shuttle *Challenger* explodes shortly after liftoff. US bombs targets in Libya. Summit conference in Iceland fails. Iran-contra affair revealed.

1987 Iran-contra hearings held. Stock market collapses. Reagan and Gorbachev sign Intermediate-Range Nuclear Forces (INF) treaty.

1988 Fourth Reagan-Gorbachev summit held in Moscow. Department of Veterans Affairs approved as Cabinet post.

1989 *Exxon Valdez* supertanker spills 10 million gallons of crude oil off Alaskan coast. US invades Panama. Berlin Wall ceases to divide the two Germanies, signaling the end of the Cold War.

1990 Troops sent to Saudi Arabia in response to Iraq's invasion of Kuwait.

1991 Air and ground war leads to Iraqi surrender and withdrawal from Kuwait. Soviet Union comes apart.

1992 27th Amendment to Constitution bars Congress from giving itself a midterm pay raise. Severe rioting begins in Los Angeles CA after jury fails to convict white policemen accused of beating Rodney King. North American Free Trade Agreement (NAFTA) signed by US, Canada, and Mexico.

1993 Janet Reno becomes the first woman attorney general. World Trade Center in New York City bombed.

1995 Timothy McVeigh detonates a bomb in a terrorist attack on the Alfred P. Murrah Federal Building in Oklahoma City OK, killing 168 people.

1998 Pres. Clinton impeached for perjury and obstruction of justice; he is acquitted by the Senate the following year.

2000 The results of the presidential election are challenged by Vice Pres. Al Gore; US Supreme Court overrules Florida Supreme Court's order for a statewide manual recount of ballots; George W. Bush assumes the presidency.

2001 On 11 September, two hijacked airplanes hit the World Trade Center in New York City; another crashes into the Pentagon outside Washington DC; and a fourth crashes in the southern Pennsylvania countryside. Pres. Bush calls for a global war on terrorism and sends US troops into Afghanistan, eventually helping to displace the Taliban regime.

Did you know? A public competition was held in 1792 to determine the best design for a new residence for the President of the United States. The Irish-American architect James Hoban of Philadelphia won the commission (and a $500 prize) with his plan for a Georgian mansion in the Palladian style. Its original color was the pale grey of the sandstone from which it was built, but it was called the "White House" as early as 1809 because the light sandstone contrasted sharply with the red brick of nearby buildings. It was not until 1902, however, that the building was officially renamed the "White House" by Pres. Theodore Roosevelt.

Important Documents in US History

Mayflower Compact

On 21 Nov 1620 (11 November, Old Style), 41 male passengers on the Mayflower signed the following compact prior to their landing at Plymouth (now Massachusetts). The compact resulted from the fear that some members of the company might leave the group and settle on their own. The Mayflower Compact bound the signers into a body politic for the purpose of forming a government and pledged them to abide by any laws and regulations that would later by established. The document was not a constitution but rather an adaptation of the usual church covenant to a civil situation. It became the foundation of Plymouth's government.

In the name of God, Amen.

We whose names are underwritten, the loyal subjects of our dread sovereign Lord, King James, by the grace of God, of Great Britain, France and Ireland king, defender of the faith, etc., having undertaken, for the glory of God, and advancement of the Christian faith, and honor of our king and country, a voyage to plant the first colony in the Northern parts of Virginia, do by these presents solemnly and mutually in the presence of God, and one of another, covenant and combine ourselves together into a civil body politic, for our better ordering and preservation and furtherance of the ends aforesaid; and by virtue hereof to enact, constitute, and frame such just and equal laws, ordinances, acts, constitutions, and offices, from time to time, as shall be thought most meet and convenient for the general good of the colony, unto which we promise all due submission and obedience.

In witness whereof we have hereunder subscribed our names at Cape-Cod the 11 of November, in the year of the reign of our sovereign lord, King James, of England, France, and Ireland the eighteenth, and of Scotland the fifty-fourth. Anno Domine 1620.

Declaration of Independence

On 4 Jul 1776 the Continental Congress officially adopted the Declaration of Independence. Two days before, the Congress had "unanimously" voted (with New York abstaining) to be free and independent from Britain. The Declaration of Independence was written largely by Thomas Jefferson. After modifications by the Congress, the document was prepared and voted upon. New York delegates voted to accept it on 15 July, and on 19 July the Congress ordered the document to be engrossed as "The Unanimous Declaration of the Thirteen United States of America." It was accordingly put on parchment, and members of the Congress present on 2 August affixed their signatures to this parchment copy on that day, and others later. The last signer was Thomas McKean of Delaware, whose name was not placed on the document before 1777.

The Unanimous Declaration of the Thirteen United States of America

When in the Course of human events, it becomes necessary for one people to dissolve the political bands which have connected them with another, and to assume among the powers of the earth, the separate and equal station to which the Laws of Nature and of Nature's God entitle them, a decent respect to the opinions of mankind requires that they should declare the causes which impel them to the separation.—We hold these truths to be self-evident, that all men are created equal, that they are endowed by their Creator with certain unalienable Rights, that among these are Life, Liberty and the pursuit of Happiness.—That to secure these rights, Governments are instituted among Men, deriving their just powers from the consent of the governed,—That whenever any Form of Government becomes destructive of these ends, it is the Right of the People to alter or to abolish it, and to institute new Government, laying its foundation on such principles and organizing its powers in such form, as to them shall seem most likely to effect their Safety and Happiness.

Prudence, indeed, will dictate that Governments long established should not be changed for light and transient causes; and accordingly all experience hath shown, that mankind are more disposed to suffer, while evils are sufferable, than to right themselves by abolishing the forms to which they are accustomed. But when a long train of abuses and usurpations, pursuing invariably the same Object evinces a design to reduce them under absolute Despotism, it is their right, it is their duty, to throw off such Government, and to provide new Guards for their future security.—Such has been the patient sufferance of these Colonies; and such is now the necessity which constrains them to alter their former Systems of Government. The history of the present King of Great Britain is a history of repeated injuries and usurpations, all having in direct object the establishment of an absolute Tyranny over these States.

To prove this, let Facts be submitted to a candid world.—He has refused his Assent to Laws, the most wholesome and necessary for the public good.—He has forbidden his Governors to pass Laws of immediate and pressing importance, unless suspended in their operation till his Assent should be obtained; and when so suspended, he has utterly neglected to attend to them.—He has refused to pass other Laws for the accommodation of large districts of people, unless those people would relinquish the right of Representation in the Legislature, a right inestimable to them and formidable to tyrants only.—He has called together legislative bodies at places unusual, uncomfortable, and distant from the depository of their public Records, for the sole purpose of fatiguing them into compliance with his measures.—He has dissolved Representative Houses repeatedly, for opposing with manly firmness his invasions on the rights of the people.—He has refused for a long time, after such dissolutions, to cause others to be elected; whereby the Legislative powers, incapable of Annihilation, have returned to the People at large for their exercise; the State remaining in the mean time exposed to all the dangers of invasion from without, and convulsions within.—He has endeavoured to prevent the population of these States; for that purpose obstructing the Laws for Naturalization of Foreigners; refusing to pass others to encourage their migration hither, and raising the conditions of new Appropriations of Lands.—He has obstructed the Administration of Justice, by refusing his Assent to Laws for establishing Judiciary powers.—He has made Judges dependent on his Will alone, for the tenure of their offices, and the amount and payment of their salaries.—He has erected a multitude of New Offices, and sent hither swarms of Officers to harrass our people, and eat out their substance.—He has kept among us, in times of peace, Standing Armies, without the Consent of our legislatures.—He has affected to render the Military independent of and superior to the Civil power.—He has combined with others to subject us to a jurisdiction foreign to our constitution, and unacknowledged by our laws; giving his Assent to their Acts of pretended Legislation:—For quartering large bodies of armed troops among us:—For protecting them, by a mock Trial, from punishment for any Murders which they should commit on the Inhabitants of these States:—For cutting off our Trade with all parts of the world:—For imposing Taxes on us with out our Consent:—For depriving us in many cases, of the benefits of Trial by Jury:—For transporting us beyond Seas to be tried for pretended offences:—For abolishing the free System of English Laws in a neighbouring Province, establishing therein an Arbitrary government, and enlarging its Boundaries so as to render it at once an example and fit instrument for introducing the same absolute rule into these Colonies:—For taking away our Charters, abolishing our most valuable Laws, and altering fundamentally the Forms of our Governments:—For suspending our own Legislatures, and declaring themselves invested with power to legislate for us in all cases whatsoever.—He has abdicated Government here, by declaring us out of his Protection and waging War against us.—He has plundered our seas, ravaged our Coasts, burnt our towns, and destroyed the lives of our people.—He is at this time transporting large Armies of foreign Mercenaries to compleat the works of death, desolation and tyranny, already begun with circumstances of Cruelty & perfidy scarcely paralleled in the most barbarous ages, and totally unworthy the Head

of a civilized nation.—He has constrained our fellow Citizens taken Captive on the high Seas to bear Arms against their Country, to become the executioners of their friends and Brethren, or to fall themselves by their Hands.—He has excited domestic insurrections amongst us, and has endeavoured to bring on the inhabitants of our frontiers, the merciless Indian Savages, whose known rule of warfare, is an undistinguished destruction of all ages, sexes and conditions. In every stage of these Oppressions We have Petitioned for Redress in the most humble terms: Our repeated Petitions have been answered only by repeated injury. A Prince, whose character is thus marked by every act which may define a Tyrant, is unfit to be the ruler of a free people. Nor have We been wanting in attentions to our Brittish brethren. We have warned them from time to time of attempts by their legislature to extend an unwarrantable jurisdiction over us. We have reminded them of the circumstances of our emigration and settlement here. We have appealed to their native justice and magnanimity, and we have conjured them by the ties of our common kindred to disavow these usurpations, which, would inevitably interrupt our connections and correspondence. They too have been deaf to the voice of justice and of consanguinity. We must, therefore, acquiesce in the necessity, which denounces our Separation, and hold them, as we hold the rest of mankind. Enemies in War, in Peace Friends.—

We, therefore, the Representatives of the United States of America, in General Congress, Assembled, appealing to the Supreme Judge of the world for the rectitude of our intentions, do, in the Name, and by Authority of the good People of these Colonies, solemnly publish and declare, That these United Colonies are, and of Right ought to be Free and Independent States; that they are Absolved from all Allegiance to the British Crown, and that all political connection between them and the State of Great Britain, is and ought to be totally dissolved; and that as Free and Independent States, they have full Power to levy War, conclude Peace, contract Alliances, establish Commerce, and to do all other Acts and Things which Independent States may of right do.—And for the support of this Declaration, with a firm reliance on the protection of Divine Providence, we mutually pledge to each other our Lives, our Fortunes and our sacred Honor.

Signers of the Declaration of Independence

	BIRTHPLACE	OCCUPATION
Connecticut		
Samuel Huntington (1731–1796)	Windham CT	lawyer, judge
Roger Sherman (1721–1793)	Newton MA	cobbler, surveyor, lawyer, judge
William Williams (1731–1811)	Lebanon CT	merchant, judge
Oliver Wolcott (1726–1797)	Windsor CT	soldier, sheriff, judge
Delaware		
Thomas McKean (1734–1817)	New London PA	lawyer, judge
George Read (1733–1798)	North East MD	lawyer, judge
Caesar Rodney (1728–1784)	Dover DE	judge
Georgia		
Button Gwinnett (c. 1735–1777)	bapt. Gloucester, England	merchant
Lyman Hall (1724–1790)	Wallingford CT	physician
George Walton (c. 1741–1804)	Farmville VA	lawyer, judge

Signers of the Declaration of Independence (continued)

	BIRTHPLACE	OCCUPATION
Maryland		
Charles Carroll of Carrollton (1737–1832)	Annapolis MD	lawyer
Samuel Chase (1741–1811)	Somerset county MD	lawyer, judge
William Paca (1740–1799)	Abingdon MD	lawyer, judge
Thomas Stone (1743–1787)	Charles county MD	lawyer
Massachusetts		
John Adams (1735–1826)	Braintree (Quincy) MA	lawyer
Samuel Adams (1722–1803)	Boston MA	politician
Elbridge Gerry (1744–1814)	Marblehead MA	merchant
John Hancock (1737–1793)	Braintree (Quincy) MA	merchant
Robert Treat Paine (1731–1814)	Boston MA	lawyer, judge
New Hampshire		
Josiah Bartlett (1729–1795)	Amesbury MA	physician, judge
Matthew Thornton (c. 1714–1803)	Ireland	physician
William Whipple (1730–1785)	Kittery ME	merchant, soldier, judge
New Jersey		
Abraham Clark (1726–1794)	Elizabethtown NJ	surveyor, lawyer, sheriff
John Hart (c. 1711–1779)	Stonington CT	farmer, judge
Francis Hopkinson (1737–1791)	Philadelphia PA	lawyer, judge, author
Richard Stockton (1730–1781)	near Princeton NJ	lawyer
John Witherspoon (1723–1794)	Gifford, Scotland	clergyman, author, educator
New York		
William Floyd (1734–1821)	Brookhaven NY	soldier
Francis Lewis (1713–1802)	Llandaff, Wales	merchant
Philip Livingston (1716–1778)	Albany NY	merchant
Lewis Morris (1726–1798)	Morrisania (Bronx county) NY	farmer, soldier, judge
North Carolina		
Joseph Hewes (1730–1779)	Kingston NJ	merchant
William Hooper (1742–1790)	Boston MA	lawyer, judge
John Penn (1741–1788)	near Port Royal VA	lawyer
Pennsylvania		
George Clymer (1739–1813)	Philadelphia PA	merchant
Benjamin Franklin (1706–1790)	Boston MA	printer, publisher, author, scientist
Robert Morris (1734–1806)	Lancashire, England	merchant
John Morton (1724–1777)	Ridley PA	judge
George Ross (1730–1779)	New Castle DE	lawyer, judge
Benjamin Rush (1746–1813)	Byberry PA	physician
James Smith (c. 1719–1806)	Dublin, Ireland	lawyer
George Taylor (1716–1781)	Ireland	ironmaster
James Wilson (1742–1798)	Fife, Scotland	lawyer, judge
Rhode Island		
William Ellery (1727–1820)	Newport RI	lawyer, judge
Stephen Hopkins (1707–1785)	Providence RI	judge, educator
South Carolina		
Thomas Heyward, Jr. (1746–1809)	St. Helena's (now St. Luke's) parish SC	lawyer, judge
Thomas Lynch, Jr. (1749–1779)	Winyah SC	lawyer
Arthur Middleton (1742–1787)	near Charleston SC	planter, legislator
Edward Rutledge (1749–1800)	Charleston SC	lawyer
Virginia		
Carter Braxton (1736–1797)	Newington Plantation VA	planter
Thomas Jefferson (1743–1826)	Shadwell VA	lawyer, author, educator
Benjamin Harrison (c. 1726–1791)	Berkeley VA	planter, politician
Francis Lightfoot Lee (1734–1797)	Westmoreland county VA	farmer
Richard Henry Lee (1732–1794)	Westmoreland county VA	planter, judge
Thomas Nelson, Jr. (1738–1789)	Yorktown VA	planter
George Wythe (1726–1806)	Elizabeth City county (Hampton) VA	lawyer, educator

The Constitution of the United States

The Constitution was written during the summer of 1787 in Philadelphia by 55 delegates to a Constitutional Convention that was called ostensibly to amend the Articles of Confederation. It was submitted for ratification to the 13 states on 28 Sep 1787. In June 1788, after the Constitution had been ratified by nine states (as required by Article VII), Congress set 4 Mar 1789 as the date for the new government to commence proceedings.

Preamble

We the People of the United States, in Order to form a more perfect Union, establish Justice, insure domestic Tranquility, provide for common defence, promote the general Welfare, and secure the Blessings of Liberty to ourselves and our Posterity, do ordain and establish this Constitution for the United States of America.

Article I

Section 1—

All legislative Powers herein granted shall be vested in a Congress of the United States, which shall consist of a Senate and House of Representatives.

Section 2—

The House of Representatives shall be composed of Members chosen every second Year by the People of the several States, and the Electors in each State shall have the Qualifications requisite for Electors of the most numerous Branch of the State Legislature.

No Person shall be a Representative who shall not have attained to the Age of twenty five Years, and been seven Years a Citizen of the United States, and who shall not, when elected, be an Inhabitant of that State in which he shall be chosen.

Representatives and direct Taxes shall be apportioned among the several States which may be included within this Union, according to their respective Numbers, which shall be determined by adding to the whole Number of free Persons, including those bound to Service for a Term of Years, and excluding Indians not taxed, three fifths of all other Persons. The actual Enumeration shall be made within three Years after the first Meeting of the Congress of the United States, and within every subsequent Term of ten Years, in such Manner as they shall by Law direct. The Number of Representatives shall not exceed one for every thirty Thousand, but each State shall have at Least one Representative; and until such enumeration shall be made, the State of New Hampshire shall be entitled to chuse three, Massachusetts eight, Rhode-Island and Providence Plantations one, Connecticut five, New-York six, New Jersey four, Pennsylvania eight, Delaware one, Maryland six, Virginia ten, North Carolina five, South Carolina five, and Georgia three.

When vacancies happen in the Representation from any State, the Executive Authority thereof shall issue Writs of Election to fill such Vacancies.

The House of Representatives shall chuse their speaker and other Officers; and shall have the sole Power of Impeachment.

Section 3—

The Senate of the United States shall be composed of two Senators from each State, chosen by the Legislature thereof for six Years; and each Senator shall have one Vote.

Immediately after they shall be assembled in Consequence of the first Election, they shall be divided as equally as may be into three Classes. The Seats of the Senators of the first Class shall be vacated at the Expiration of the second Year, of the second Class at the Expiration of the fourth Year, and of the third Class at the Expiration of the sixth Year, so that one third may be chosen every second Year; and if Vacancies happen by Resignation, or otherwise, during the Recess of the Legislature of any State, the Executive thereof may make temporary Appointments until the next Meeting of the Legislature, which shall then fill such Vacancies.

No Person shall be a Senator who shall not have attained to the Age of thirty Years, and been nine Years a Citizen of the United States, and who shall not, when elected, be an Inhabitant of that State for which he shall be chosen.

The Vice President of the United States shall be President of the Senate, but shall have no Vote, unless they be equally divided.

The Senate shall chuse their other Officers, and also a President pro tempore, in the Absence of the Vice President, or when he shall exercise the Office of President of the United States.

The Senate shall have the sole Power to try all Impeachments. When sitting for that Purpose, they shall be on Oath or Affirmation. When the President of the United States is tried, the Chief Justice shall preside: And no Person shall be convicted without the concurrence of two thirds of the Members present. Judgment in Cases of Impeachment shall not extend further than to removal from Office, and disqualification to hold and enjoy any Office of honor, Trust or Profit under the United States: but the Party convicted shall nevertheless be liable and subject to Indictment, Trial, Judgment and Punishment, according to law.

Section 4—

The Times, Places and Manner of holding Elections for Senators and Representatives, shall be prescribed in each State by the Legislature thereof; but the Congress may at any time by Law make or alter such Regulations, except as to the Places of chusing Senators.

The Congress shall assemble at least once in every Year, and such Meeting shall be on the first Monday in December, unless they shall by Law appoint a different Day.

Section 5—

Each House shall be the Judge of the Elections, Returns and Qualifications of its own Members, and a Majority of each shall constitute a Quorum to do business; but a smaller Number may adjourn from day to day, and may be authorized to compel the Attendance of absent Members, in such Manner, and under such Penalties as each House may provide.

Each House may determine the Rules of its Proceedings, punish its Members for disorderly Behaviour, and, with the Concurrence of two thirds, expel a Member.

Each House shall keep a journal of its Proceedings, and from time to time publish the same, excepting such Parts as may in their Judgment require Secrecy; and the yeas and Nays of the Members of either House on any question shall, at the Desire of one fifth of those Present, be entered on the journal.

Neither House, during the Session of Congress, shall, without the Consent of the other, adjourn for more than three days, nor to any other place than that in which the two Houses shall be sitting.

Section 6—

The Senators and Representatives shall receive a Compensation for their Services, to be ascertained by Law, and paid out of the Treasury of the United States. They shall in all Cases, except Treason, Felony and Breach of the Peace, be privileged from Arrest during their Attendance at the Session of their respective Houses, and in going to and returning from the same; and for any Speech or Debate in either House, they shall not be questioned in any other Place.

No Senator or Representative shall, during the Time for which he was elected, be appointed to any civil Office under the Authority of the United States, which shall have been created, or the Emoluments whereof shall have been encreased during such time; and no Person holding any Office under the United States, shall be a Member of either House during his Continuance in Office.

Section 7—

All Bills for raising Revenue shall originate in the House of Representatives; but the Senate may propose or concur with Amendments as on other Bills.

Every Bill which shall have passed the House of Representatives and the Senate, shall, before it become a Law, be presented to the President of the United States; If he approve he shall sign it, but if not he shall return it, with his Objections to that House in which it shall have originated, who shall enter the Objections at large on their Journal, and proceed to reconsider it. If after such Reconsideration two thirds of that House shall agree to pass the Bill, it shall be sent, together with the Objections, to the other House, by which it shall likewise be reconsidered, and if approved by two thirds of that House, it shall become a Law. But in all such Cases the Votes of both Houses shall be determined by yeas and Nays, and the Names of the Persons voting for and against the Bill shall be entered on the Journal of each House respectively. If any Bill shall not be returned by the President within ten Days (Sundays excepted) after it shall have been presented to him, the Same shall be a Law, in like Manner as if he had signed it, unless the Congress by their Adjournment prevent its Return, in which Case it shall not be a Law.

Every Order, Resolution, or Vote to which the Concurrence of the Senate and House of Representatives may be necessary (except on a question of Adjournment) shall be presented to the President of the United States; and before the Same shall take Effect, shall be approved by him, or being disapproved by him, shall be repassed by two thirds of the Senate and House of Representatives, according to the Rules and Limitations prescribed in the Case of a Bill.

Section 8—

The Congress shall have Power To lay and collect Taxes, Duties, Imposts and Excises, to pay the Debts and provide for the common Defence and general Welfare of the United States; but all Duties, Imposts and Excises shall be uniform throughout the United States;

To borrow Money on the credit of the United States;

To regulate Commerce with foreign Nations, and among the several States, and with the Indian Tribes;

To establish an uniform Rule of Naturalization, and uniform Laws on the subject of Bankruptcies throughout the United States;

To coin Money, regulate the Value thereof, and of foreign Coin, and fix the Standard of Weights and Measures;

To provide for the Punishment of counterfeiting the Securities and current Coin of the United States;

To establish Post Offices and post Roads;

To promote the Progress of Science and useful Arts, by securing for limited Times to Authors and Inventors the exclusive Right to their respective Writings and Discoveries;

To constitute Tribunals inferior to the supreme Court;

To define and punish Piracies and Felonies committed on the high Seas, and Offences against the Law of Nations;

To declare War, grant Letters of Marque and Reprisal, and make rules concerning Captures on Land and Water;

To raise and support Armies, but no Appropriation of Money to that Use shall be for a longer Term than two Years;

To provide and maintain a Navy;

To make Rules for the Government and Regulation of the land and naval Forces;

To provide for calling forth the Militia to execute the Laws of the Union, suppress Insurrections and repel Invasions;

To provide for organizing, arming, and disciplining, the Militia, and for governing such Part of them as may be employed in the Service of the United States, reserving to the States respectively, the Appointment of the Officers, and the Authority of training the Militia according to the discipline prescribed by Congress;

To exercise exclusive Legislation in all Cases whatsoever, over such District (not exceeding ten Miles square), as may, by Cession of particular States, and the Acceptance of Congress, become the Seat of the Government of the United States, and to exercise like Authority over all Places purchased by the Consent of the Legislature of the State in which the Same shall be for the Erection of Forts, Magazines, Arsenals, dock-Yards, and other needful Buildings; — And

To make all Laws which shall be necessary and proper for carrying into Execution the foregoing Powers, and all other Powers vested by this Constitution in the Government of the United States, or in any Department or Officer thereof.

Section 9—

The Migration or Importation of such Persons as any of the States now existing shall think proper to admit, shall not be prohibited by the Congress prior to the Year one thousand eight hundred and eight, but a Tax or duty may be imposed on such Importation, not exceeding ten dollars for each Person.

The Privilege of the Writ of Habeas Corpus shall not be suspended, unless when in Cases of Rebellion or Invasion the public Safety may require it.

No Bill of Attainder or ex post facto Law shall be passed.

No Capitation, or other direct, Tax shall be laid, unless in Proportion to the Census or Enumeration herein before directed to be taken.

No Tax or Duty shall be laid on Articles exported from any State.

No Preference shall be given by any Regulation of Commerce or Revenue to the Ports of one State over those of another; nor shall Vessels bound to, or from, one State, be obliged to enter, clear or pay Duties in another.

No money shall be drawn from the Treasury, but in Consequence of Appropriations made by Law; and a regular Statement and Account of the Receipts and Expenditures of all public Money shall be published from time to time.

No Title of Nobility shall be granted by the United States: And no Person holding any Office of Profit or Trust under them, shall, without the Consent of the Congress, accept of any present, Emolument, Office, or Title, of any kind whatever, from any King, Prince, or foreign State.

Section 10—

No State shall enter into any Treaty, Alliance, or Confederation; grant Letters of Marque and Reprisal; coin Money; emit Bills of Credit; make any Thing but gold and silver Coin a Tender in Payment of Debts; pass any Bill of Attainder, ex post facto Law, or Law impairing the Obligation of Contracts, or grant any Title of Nobility.

No State shall, without the Consent of the Congress, lay any Imposts or Duties on Imports or Exports, except what may be absolutely necessary for executing it's Inspection Laws: and the net Produce of all Duties and Imposts, laid by any State on Imports or Exports, shall be for the Use of the Treasury of the United States; and all such Laws shall be subject to the Revision and Controul of the Congress.

No State shall, without the Consent of Congress, lay any Duty of Tonnage, keep Troops, or Ships of War in time of Peace, enter into any Agreement or Compact with another State, or with a foreign Power, or engage in War, unless actually invaded, or in such imminent Danger as will not admit of delay.

Article II
Section 1—

The executive Power shall be vested in a President of the United States of America. He shall hold his Office during the Term of four Years, and, together with the Vice President, chosen for the same Term, be elected, as follows

Each State shall appoint, in such Manner as the Legislature thereof may direct, a Number of Electors, equal to the whole Number of Senators and Representatives to which the State may be entitled in the Congress: but no Senator or Representative, or Person holding an Office of Trust or Profit under the United States, shall be appointed an Elector.

The Electors shall meet in their respective States, and vote by Ballot for two Persons, of whom one at least shall not be an Inhabitant of the same State with themselves. And they shall make a List of all the Persons voted for, and of the Number of Votes for each; which List they shall sign and certify, and transmit sealed to the Seat of the Government of the United States, directed to the President of the Senate. The President of the Senate shall, in the Presence of the Senate and House of Representatives, open all the Certificates, and the Votes shall then be counted. The Person having the greatest Number of Votes shall be the President, if such Number be a Majority of the whole Number of Electors appointed; and if there be more than one who have such Majority, and have an equal Number of Votes, then the House of Representatives shall immediately chuse by Ballot one of them for President; and if no Person have a Majority, then from the five

highest on the List the said House shall in like Manner chuse the President. But in chusing the President, the Votes shall be taken by States, the Representation from each State having one Vote; A quorum for this Purpose shall consist of a Member or Members from two thirds of the States, and a Majority of all the States shall be necessary to a Choice. In every Case, after the Choice of the President, the Person having the greatest Number of Votes of the Electors shall be the Vice President. But if there should remain two or more who have equal Votes, the Senate shall chuse from them by Ballot the Vice President.

The Congress may determine the Time of chusing the Electors, and the Day on which they shall give their Votes; which Day shall be the same throughout the United States.

No Person except a natural born Citizen, or a Citizen of the United States, at the time of the Adoption of this Constitution, shall be eligible to the Office of President; neither shall any Person be eligible to that Office who shall not have attained to the Age of thirty five Years, and been fourteen Years a Resident within the United States.

In Case of the Removal of the President from Office, or of his Death, Resignation, or Inability to discharge the Powers and Duties of the said Office, the Same shall devolve on the Vice President, and the Congress may by Law provide for the Case of Removal, Death, Resignation or Inability, both of the President and Vice President, declaring what Officer shall then act as President, and such Officer shall act accordingly, until the Disability be removed, or a President shall be elected.

The President shall, at stated Times, receive for his Services, a Compensation, which shall neither be encreased nor diminished during the Period for which he shall have been elected, and he shall not receive within that Period any other Emolument from the United States, or any of them.

Before he enter on the Execution of his Office, he shall take the following Oath or Affirmation: "I do solemnly swear (or affirm) that I will faithfully execute the Office of President of the United States, and will to the best of my Ability, preserve, protect and defend the Constitution of the United States."

Section 2—

The President shall be Commander in Chief of the Army and Navy of the United States, and of the Militia of the several States, when called into the actual Service of the United States; he may require the Opinion, in writing, of the principal Officer in each of the executive Departments, upon any Subject relating to the Duties of their respective Offices, and he shall have Power to grant Reprieves and Pardons for Offences against the United States, except in Cases of Impeachment.

He shall have Power, by and with the Advice and Consent of the Senate, to make Treaties, provided two thirds of the Senators present concur; and he shall nominate, and by and with the Advice and Consent of the Senate, shall appoint Ambassadors, other public Ministers and Consuls, Judges of the supreme Court, and all other Officers of the United States, whose Appointments are not herein otherwise provided for, and which shall be established by Law: but the Congress may by Law vest the Appointment of such inferior Officers, as they think proper, in the President alone, in the Courts of Law, or in the Heads of Departments.

The President shall have Power to fill up all Vacancies that may happen during the Recess of the Senate, by granting Commissions which shall expire at the End of their next Session.

Section 3—

He shall from time to time give to the Congress Information of the State of the Union, and recommend to their Consideration such Measures as he shall judge necessary and expedient; he may, on extraordinary Occasions, convene both Houses, or either of them, and in Case of Disagreement between them, with Respect to the Time of Adjournment, he may adjourn them to such Time as he shall think proper; he shall receive Ambassadors and other public Ministers; he shall take Care that the Laws be faithfully executed, and shall Commission all the Officers of the United States.

Section 4—

The President, Vice President and all civil Officers of the United States, shall be removed from Office on Impeachment for, and Conviction of, Treason, Bribery, or other High Crimes and Misdemeanors.

Article III

Section 1—

The judicial Power of the United States, shall be vested in one supreme Court, and in such inferior Courts as the Congress may from time to time ordain and establish. The Judges, both of the supreme and inferior Courts, shall hold their Offices during good Behaviour, and shall, at stated Times, receive for their Services, a Compensation, which shall not be diminished during their Continuance in Office.

Section 2—

The judicial Power shall extend to all Cases, in Law and Equity, arising under this Constitution, the Laws of the United States, and Treaties made, or which shall be made, under their Authority; — to all Cases affecting Ambassadors, other public Ministers and Consuls; — to all Cases of admiralty and maritime jurisdiction; — to Controversies to which the United States shall be a Party; — to Controversies between two or more States;-between a State and Citizens of another State; — between Citizens of different States; — between Citizens of the same State claiming Lands under Grants of different States, and between a State, or the Citizens thereof, and foreign States, Citizens or Subjects.

In all Cases affecting Ambassadors, other public Ministers and Consuls, and those in which a State shall be Party, the supreme Court shall have original Jurisdiction. In all the other Cases before mentioned, the supreme Court shall have appellate Jurisdiction, both as to Law and Fact, with such Exceptions, and under such Regulations as the Congress shall make.

The Trial of all Crimes, except in Cases of Impeachment, shall be by Jury; and such Trial shall be held in the State where the said Crimes shall have been committed; but when not committed within any State, the Trial shall be at such Place or Places as the Congress may by Law have directed.

Section 3—

Treason against the United States, shall consist only in levying War against them, or in adhering to their Enemies, giving them Aid and Comfort. No Person shall be convicted of Treason unless on the Testimony of two Witnesses to the same overt Act, or on Confession in open Court.

The Congress shall have Power to declare the Punishment of Treason, but no Attainder of Treason shall work Corruption of Blood, or Forfeiture except during the Life of the Person attainted.

Article IV

Section 1—

Full Faith and Credit shall be given in each State to the public Acts, Records, and judicial Proceedings of every other State. And the Congress may by general Laws prescribe the Manner in which such Acts, Records and Proceedings shall be proved, and the Effect thereof.

Section 2—

The Citizens of each State shall be entitled to all Privileges and Immunities of Citizens in the several States.

A person charged in any State with Treason, Felony, or other Crime, who shall flee from justice, and be found in another State, shall on Demand of the executive Authority of the State from which he fled, be delivered up, to be removed to the State having Jurisdiction of the Crime.

No Person held to Service or Labour in one State, under the Laws thereof, escaping into another, shall in Consequence of any Law or Regulation therein, be discharged from such Service or Labour, but shall be delivered upon on Claim of the Party to whom such Service or Labour may be due.

Section 3—

New States may be admitted by the Congress into this Union; but no new State shall be formed or erected within the Jurisdiction of any other State; nor any State be formed by the Junction of two or more States, or Parts of States, without the Consent of the Legislatures of the States concerned as well as of the Congress.

The Congress shall have Power to dispose of and make all needful Rules and Regulations respecting the Territory or other Property belonging to the United States; and nothing in this Constitution shall be so construed as to Prejudice any Claims of the United States, or of any particular State.

Section 4—

The United States shall guarantee to every State in this Union a Republican Form of Government, and shall protect each of them against Invasion; and on Application of the Legislature, or of the Executive (when the Legislature cannot be convened) against domestic Violence.

Article V

The Congress, whenever two thirds of both Houses shall deem it necessary, shall propose Amendments to this Constitution, or, on the Application of the Legislatures of two thirds of the several States, shall call a Convention for proposing Amendments, which, in either Case, shall be valid to all Intents and Purposes, as Part of this Constitution, when ratified by the Legislatures of three fourths of the several States, or by Conventions in three fourths thereof, as the one or the other Mode of Ratification may be proposed by the Congress; Provided that no Amendment which may be made prior to the Year One thousand eight hundred and eight shall in any Manner affect the first and fourth Clauses in the Ninth Section of the first Article; and that no State, without its Consent, shall be deprived of its equal Suffrage in the Senate.

Article VI

All Debts contracted and Engagements entered into, before the Adoption of this Constitution, shall be as valid against the United States under this Constitution, as under the Confederation.

This Constitution, and the Laws of the United States which shall be made in Pursuance thereof; and all Treaties made, or which shall be made, under the Authority of the United States, shall be the supreme Law of the Land; and the Judges in every State shall be bound thereby, any Thing in the Constitution or Laws of any State to the Contrary notwithstanding.

The Senators and Representatives before mentioned, and the Members of the several State Legislatures, and all executive and judicial Officers, both of the United States and of the several States, shall be bound by Oath or Affirmation, to support this Constitution; but no religious Test shall ever be required as a Qualification to any Office or public Trust under the United States.

Article VII

The Ratification of the Conventions of nine States, shall be sufficient for the Establishment of this Constitution between the States so ratifying the Same.

Done in Convention by the Unanimous Consent of the States present the Seventeenth Day of September in the Year of our Lord one thousand seven hundred and Eighty seven and of the Independence of the United States of America the Twelfth   IN WITNESS whereof We have hereunto subscribed our Names,

G⁰ Washington—
*Presid*ᵗ. *and deputy from Virginia*

New Hampshire
John Langdon
Nicholas Gilman

Massachusetts
Nathaniel Gorham
Rufus King

Connecticut
Wm. Saml. Johnson
Roger Sherman

New York
Alexander Hamilton

New Jersey
Wil: Livingston
David Brearley
Wm. Paterson
Jona: Dayton

Pennsylvania
B. Franklin
Thomas Mifflin
Robᵗ Morris
Geo. Clymer
Thos. FitzSimons
Jared Ingersoll
James Wilson
Gouv Morris

Delaware
Geo: Read
Gunning Bedford jun
John Dickinson
Richard Bassett
Jaco: Broom

Maryland
James McHenry
Dan of Sᵗ Thos. Jenifer
Danˡ Carroll

Virginia
John Blair—
James Madison Jr.

North Carolina
Wm. Blount
Rich'd Dobbs Spaight
Hu Williamson

South Carolina
J. Rutledge
Charles Cotesworth Pinckney
Charles Pinckney
Pierce Butler

Georgia
William Few
Abr Baldwin

Attest:
William Jackson, *Secretary*

[*Rhode Island and the Providence Plantations*
Rhode Island did not send delegates to the Constitutional Convention.]

Bill of Rights

The first 10 amendments to the Constitution were adopted as a single unit on 15 Dec 1791. Together, they constitute a collection of mutually reinforcing guarantees of individual rights and of limitations on federal and state governments.

Amendment I

Congress shall make no law respecting an establishment of religion, or prohibiting the free exercise thereof; or abridging the freedom of speech, or of the press; or the right of the people peaceably to assemble, and to petition the Government for a redress of grievances.

Amendment II

A well regulated Militia, being necessary to the secu-

rity of a free State, the right of the people to keep and bear Arms, shall not be infringed.

Amendment III

No Soldier shall, in time of peace be quartered in any house, without the consent of the Owner, nor in time of war, but in a manner to be prescribed by law.

Amendment IV

The right of the People to be secure in their persons,

houses, papers, and effects, against unreasonable searches and seizures, shall not be violated, and no Warrants shall issue, but upon probable cause, supported by Oath or affirmation, and particularity describing the place to be searched, and the persons or things to be seized.

Amendment V

No person shall be held to answer for a capital, or otherwise infamous crime, unless on a presentment or indictment of a Grand Jury, except in cases arising in the land or naval forces, or in the Militia, when in actual service in time of War or public danger; nor shall any person be subject for the same offence to be twice put in jeopardy of life or limb; nor shall be compelled in any criminal case to be a witness against himself, nor be deprived of life, liberty, or property, without due process of law; nor shall private property be taken for public use, without just compensation.

Amendment VI

In all criminal prosecutions, the accused shall enjoy the right to a speedy and public trial, by an impartial jury of the State and district wherein the crime shall have been committed, which district shall have been previously ascertained by law, and to be informed of the nature and cause of the accusation; to be confronted with the witnesses against him; to have compulsory process for obtaining witnesses in his favor, and to have Assistance of Counsel for his defence.

Amendment VII

In Suits at common law, where the value in controversy shall exceed twenty dollars, the right of trial by jury shall be preserved, and no fact tried by a jury, shall be otherwise re-examined in any Court of the United States, than according to the rules of the common law.

Amendment VIII

Excessive bail shall not be required, nor excessive fines imposed, nor cruel and unusual punishments inflicted.

Amendment IX

The enumeration in the Constitution, of certain rights, shall not be construed to deny or disparage others retained by the people.

Amendment X

The powers not delegated to the United States by the Constitution, nor prohibited by it to the States, are reserved to the States respectively, or to the people.

Further Amendments

Amendment XI
(ratified 7 Feb 1795)

The Judicial power of the United States shall not be construed to extend to any suit in law or equity, commenced or prosecuted against one of the United States by Citizens of another State, or by Citizens or Subjects of any Foreign State.

Amendment XII
(ratified 15 Jun 1804)

The Electors shall meet in their respective states and vote by ballot for President and Vice-President, one of whom, at least, shall not be an inhabitant of the same state with themselves; they shall name in their ballots the person voted for as President, and in distinct ballots the person voted for as Vice-President, and they shall make distinct lists of all persons voted for as President, and of all persons voted for as Vice-President, and of the number of votes for each, which lists they shall sign and certify, and transmit sealed to the seat of the government of the United States, directed to the President of the Senate; — The President of the Senate shall, in the presence of the Senate and House of Representatives, open all the certificates and the votes shall then be counted; — The person having the greatest number of votes for President, shall be the President, if such number be a majority of the whole number of Electors appointed; and if no person have such majority, then from the persons having the highest numbers not exceeding three on the list of those voted for as President, the House of Representatives shall choose immediately, by ballot, the President. But in choosing the President, the votes shall be taken by states, the representation from each state having one vote; a quorum for this purpose shall consist of a member or members from two-thirds of the states, and a majority of all the states shall be necessary to a choice. And if the House of Representatives shall not choose a President whenever the right of choice shall devolve upon then, before the fourth day of March next following, then the Vice-President shall act as President, as in the case of the death or other constitutional disability of the President. — The person having the greatest number of votes as Vice-President, shall be the Vice-President, if such number be a majority of the whole number of Electors appointed, and if no person have a majority, then from the two highest numbers on the list, the Senate shall choose the Vice-President; a quorum for the purpose shall consist of two-thirds of the whole number of Senators, and a majority of the whole number shall be necessary to a choice. But no person constitutionally ineligible to the office of President shall be eligible to that of Vice-President of the United States.

Amendment XIII
(ratified 6 Dec 1865)

Section 1—

Neither slavery nor involuntary servitude, except as a punishment for crime whereof the party shall have been duly convicted, shall exist within the United States, or any place subject to their jurisdiction.

Section 2—

Congress shall have power to enforce this article by appropriate legislation.

Amendment XIV
(ratified 9 Jul 1868)

Section 1—

All persons born or naturalized in the United States, and subject to the jurisdiction thereof, are citizens of the United States and of the State wherein they reside. No State shall make or enforce any law which shall abridge the privileges or immunities of citizens of the United States; nor shall any State deprive any person of life, liberty, or property, without due process of law; nor deny to any person within its jurisdiction the equal protection of the laws.

Section 2—

Representatives shall be apportioned among the several States according to their respective numbers, counting the whole number of persons in each State, excluding Indians not taxed. But when the right to vote at any election for the choice of electors for President and Vice President of the United States, Representatives in Congress, the Executive and Judicial officers of a State, or the members of the Legislature thereof, is denied to any of the male inhabitants of such State, being twenty-one years of age, and citizens of the United States, or in any way abridged, except for participation in rebellion, or other crime, the basis of representation therein shall be reduced in the proportion which the number of such male citizens shall bear to the whole number of male citizens twenty-one years of age in such State.

Section 3—

No person shall be a Senator or Representative in Congress, or elector of President and Vice President, or hold any office, civil or military, under the United States, or under any State, who, having previously taken an oath, as a member of Congress, or as an officer of the United States, or as a member of any State legislature, or as an executive or judicial officer of any State, to support the Constitution of the United States, shall have engaged in insurrection or rebellion against the same, or given aid or comfort to the enemies thereof. But Congress may by a vote of two-thirds of each House, remove such disability.

Section 4—

The validity of the public debt of the United States, authorized by law, including debts incurred for payment of pensions and bounties for services in suppressing insurrection or rebellion, shall not be questioned. But neither the United States nor any State shall assume or pay any debt or obligation incurred in aid of insurrection or rebellion against the United States, or any claim for the loss or emancipation of any slave; but all such debts, obligations and claims shall be held illegal and void.

Section 5—

The Congress shall have power to enforce, by appropriate legislation, the provisions of this article.

Amendment XV
(ratified 8 Feb 1870)

Section 1—

The right of citizens of the United States to vote shall not be denied or abridged by the United States or by any State on account of race, color, or previous condition of servitude.

Section 2—

The Congress shall have power to enforce this article by appropriate legislation.

Amendment XVI
(ratified 3 Feb 1913)

The Congress shall have power to lay and collect taxes on incomes, from whatever source derived, without apportionment among the several States, and without regard to any census or enumeration.

Amendment XVII
(ratified 13 Feb 1913)

The Senate of the United States shall be composed of two Senators from each State, elected by the people

thereof for six years; and each Senator shall have one vote. The electors in each State shall have the qualifications requisite for electors of the most numerous branch of the State legislatures.

When vacancies happen in the representation of any State in the Senate, the executive authority of such State shall issue writs of election to fill such vacancies: Provided, That the legislature of any State may empower the executive thereof to make temporary appointments until the people fill the vacancies by election as the legislature may direct.

This amendment shall not be so construed as to affect the election or term of any Senator chosen before it becomes valid as part of the Constitution.

Amendment XVIII
(ratified 16 Jan 1919; repealed 5 Dec 1933
by Amendment XXI)

Section 1—

After one year from the ratification of this article the manufacture, sale, or transportation of intoxicating liquors within, the importation thereof into, or the exportation thereof from the United States and all territory subject to the jurisdiction thereof for beverage purposes is hereby prohibited.

Section 2—

The Congress and the several States shall have concurrent power to enforce this article by appropriate legislation.

Section 3—

This article shall be inoperative unless it shall have been ratified as an amendment to the Constitution by the legislatures of the several States as provided in the Constitution, within seven years from the date of the submission hereof to the States by the Congress.

Amendment XIX
(ratified 18 Aug 1920)

The right of citizens of the United States to vote shall not be denied or abridged by the United States or by any State on account of sex.

Congress shall have power to enforce this article by appropriate legislation.

Amendment XX
(ratified 23 Jan 1933)

Section 1—

The terms of the President and Vice President shall end at noon on the 20th day of January, and the terms of Senators and Representatives at noon on the 3d day of January, of the years in which such terms would have ended if this article had not been ratified; and the terms of their successors shall then begin.

Section 2—

The Congress shall assemble at least once in every year, and such meeting shall begin at noon on the 3d day of January, unless they shall by law appoint a different day.

Section 3—

If, at the time fixed for the beginning of the term of the President, the President elect shall have died, the Vice President elect shall become President. If a President shall not have been chosen before the time fixed for the beginning of his term, or if the President elect shall have failed to qualify, then the Vice President elect shall act as President until a President shall have qualified; and the Congress may by law provide for the case wherein neither a President elect nor a Vice President elect shall have qualified, declaring who shall then act as President, or the manner in which one who is to act shall be selected, and such person shall act accordingly until a President or Vice President shall have qualified.

Section 4—

The Congress may by law provide for the case of the death of any of the persons from whom the House of Representatives may choose a President whenever the right of choice shall have devolved upon them, and for the case of the death of any of the persons from whom the Senate may choose a Vice President whenever the right of choice shall have devolved upon them.

Section 5—

Sections 1 and 2 shall take effect on the 15th day of October following the ratification of this article.

Section 6—

This article shall be inoperative unless it shall have been ratified as an amendment to the Constitution by the legislatures of three-fourths of the several States within seven years from the date of its submission.

Amendment XXI
(ratified 5 Dec 1933)

Section 1—

The eighteenth article of amendment to the Constitution of the United States is hereby repealed.

Section 2—

The transportation or importation into any State, Territory, or possession of the United States for delivery or use therein of intoxicating liquors, in violation of the laws thereof, is hereby prohibited.

Section 3—

This article shall be inoperative unless it shall have been ratified as an amendment to the Constitution by conventions in the several States, as provided in the Constitution, within seven years from the date of the submission hereof to the States by the Congress.

Amendment XXII
(ratified 27 Feb 1951)

Section 1—

No person shall be elected to the office of the President more than twice, and no person who has held the office of President, or acted as President, for more than two years of a term to which some other person was elected President shall be elected to the office of the President more than once. But this Article shall not apply to any person holding the office of President when this Article was proposed by the Congress, and shall not prevent any person who may be holding the office of President, or acting as President, during the term within which this Article becomes operative from holding the office of President or acting as President during the remainder of such term.

Section 2—

This Article shall be inoperative unless it shall have been ratified as an amendment to the Constitution by the legislatures of three-fourths of the several States within seven years from the date of its submission to the States by the Congress.

Amendment XXIII
(ratified 29 Mar 1961)

Section 1—

The District constituting the seat of Government of the United States shall appoint in such manner as the Congress may direct:

A number of electors of President and Vice President equal to the whole number of Senators and Representatives in Congress to which the District would be entitled if it were a State, but in no event more than the least populous State; they shall be in addition to those appointed by the States, but they shall be considered, for the purposes of the election of President and Vice President, to be electors appointed by a State; and they shall meet in the District and perform such duties as provided by the twelfth article of amendment.

Section 2—

The Congress shall have power to enforce this article by appropriate legislation.

Amendment XXIV
(ratified 23 Jan 1964)

Section 1—

The right of citizens of the United States to vote in any primary or other election for President or Vice President, for electors for President or Vice President, or for Senator or Representative in Congress, shall not be denied or abridged by the United States or any State by reason of failure to pay any poll tax or other tax.

Section 2—

The Congress shall have power to enforce this article by appropriate legislation.

Amendment XXV
(ratified 23 Jan 1967)

Section 1—

In case of the removal of the President from office or of his death or resignation, the Vice President shall become President.

Section 2—

Whenever there is a vacancy in the office of the Vice President, the President shall nominate a Vice President who shall take office upon confirmation by a majority vote of both Houses of Congress.

Section 3—

Whenever the President transmits to the President pro tempore of the Senate and the Speaker of the House of Representatives his written declaration that he is unable to discharge the powers and duties of his office, and until he transmits to them a written declaration to the contrary, such powers and duties shall be discharged by the Vice President as Acting President.

Section 4—

Whenever the Vice president and a majority of either the principal officers of the executive departments or of such other body as Congress may by law provide, transmit to the President pro tempore of the Senate and the Speaker of the House of Representatives their written declaration that the President is unable to discharge the powers and duties of his office, the Vice President shall immediately assume the powers and duties of the office as Acting President.

Thereafter, when the President transmits to the President pro tempore of the Senate and the Speaker of the House of Representatives his written declaration that no inability exists, he shall resume the powers and duties of his office unless the Vice President and a majority of either the principal officers of the executive department or of such other body as Congress may by law provide, transmit within four days to the President pro tempore of the Senate and the Speaker of the House of Representatives their written declaration that the President is unable to discharge the powers and duties of his office. Thereupon Congress shall decide the issue, assembling within forty-eight hours for that purpose if not in session. If the Congress, within twenty-one days after receipt of the latter written declaration, or, if Congress is not in session, within twenty-one days after Congress is required to assemble, determines by two-thirds vote of both Houses that the President is unable to discharge the powers and duties of his office, the Vice President shall continue to discharge the same as Acting President; otherwise, the President shall resume the powers and duties of his office.

Amendment XXVI
(ratified 1 Jul 1971)

Section 1—
The right of citizens of the United States, who are eighteen years of age or older, to vote shall not be denied or abridged by the United States or by any State on account of age.

Section 2—
The Congress shall have power to enforce this article by appropriate legislation.

Amendment XXVI
(ratified 7 May 1992)
No law, varying the compensation for the services of the Senators and Representatives, shall take effect, until an election of representatives shall have intervened.

Confederate States and Secession Dates

In the months following Abraham Lincoln's election as president in 1860, seven states of the Deep South held conventions and approved secession, thus precipitating the Civil War. After the attack on Fort Sumter SC on 12 Apr 1861, Virginia, Arkansas, North Carolina, and Tennessee also seceded (Tennessee was the only state to hold a popular referendum without a convention on secession). The Confederacy operated as a separate government, with Jefferson Davis as president and Alexander H. Stephens as vice president. Its principal goals were the preservation of states' rights and the institution of slavery. Although it enjoyed a series of military victories in the first two years of fighting, the surrender at Appomattox VA by Gen. Robert E. Lee on 9 Apr 1865 signaled its dissolution.

STATE	DATE	STATE	DATE	STATE	DATE
South Carolina	20 Dec 1860	Georgia	19 Jan 1861	Arkansas	6 May 1861
Mississippi	9 Jan 1861	Louisiana	26 Jan 1861	North Carolina	20 May 1861
Florida	10 Jan 1861	Texas	1 Feb 1861	Tennessee	8 Jun 1861
Alabama	11 Jan 1861	Virginia	17 Apr 1861		

Emancipation Proclamation

The Emancipation Proclamation was issued by Pres. Abraham Lincoln and freed the slaves of the Confederate states in rebellion against the Union. After the Battle of Antietam (17 Sep 1862), Lincoln issued his proclamation calling on the revolted states to return to their allegiance before the next year, otherwise their slaves would be declared free men. No state returned, and the threatened declaration was issued on 1 Jan 1863.

By the President of the United States of America:

A Proclamation.

Whereas, on the twenty-second day of September, in the year of our Lord one thousand eight hundred and sixty-two, a proclamation was issued by the President of the United States, containing, among other things, the following, to wit:

"That on the first day of January, in the year of our Lord one thousand eight hundred and sixty-three, all persons held as slaves within any State or designated part of a State, the people whereof shall then be in rebellion against the United States, shall be then, thenceforward, and forever free; and the Executive Government of the United States, including the military and naval authority thereof, will recognize and maintain the freedom of such persons, and will do no act or acts to repress such persons, or any of them, in any efforts they may make for their actual freedom.

"That the Executive will, on the first day of January aforesaid, by proclamation, designate the States and parts of States, if any, in which the people thereof, respectively, shall then be in rebellion against the United States; and the fact that any State, or the people thereof, shall on that day be, in good faith, represented in the Congress of the United States by members chosen thereto at elections wherein a majority of the qualified voters of such State shall have participated, shall, in the absence of strong countervailing testimony, be deemed conclusive evidence that such State, and the people thereof, are not then in rebellion against the United States."

Now, therefore I, Abraham Lincoln, President of the United States, by virtue of the power in me vested as Commander-in-Chief, of the Army and Navy of the United States in time of actual armed rebellion against the authority and government of the United States, and as a fit and necessary war measure for suppressing said rebellion, do, on this first day of January, in the year of our Lord one thousand eight hundred and sixty-three, and in accordance with my purpose so to do publicly proclaimed for the full period of one hundred days, from the day first above mentioned, order and designate as the States and parts of States wherein the people thereof respectively, are this day in rebellion against the United States, the following, to wit:

Arkansas, Texas, Louisiana, (except the Parishes of St. Bernard, Plaquemines, Jefferson, St. John, St. Charles, St. James Ascension, Assumption, Terrebonne, Lafourche, St. Mary, St. Martin, and Orleans, including the City of New Orleans) Mississippi, Alabama, Florida, Georgia, South Carolina, North Carolina, and Virginia, (except the forty-eight counties designated as West Virginia, and also the counties of Berkley, Accomac, Northampton, Elizabeth City, York, Princess Ann, and Norfolk, including the cities of Norfolk and Portsmouth[)], and which excepted parts, are for the present, left precisely as if this proclamation were not issued.

And by virtue of the power, and for the purpose aforesaid, I do order and declare that all persons held as slaves within said designated States, and parts of States, are, and henceforward shall be free; and that the Executive government of the United States, including the military and naval authorities

thereof, will recognize and maintain the freedom of said persons.

And I hereby enjoin upon the people so declared to be free to abstain from all violence, unless in necessary self-defence; and I recommend to them that, in all cases when allowed, they labor faithfully for reasonable wages.

And I further declare and make known, that such persons of suitable condition, will be received into the armed service of the United States to garrison forts, positions, stations, and other places, and to man vessels of all sorts in said service.

And upon this act, sincerely believed to be an act of justice, warranted by the Constitution, upon military necessity, I invoke the considerate judgment of mankind, and the gracious favor of Almighty God.

In witness whereof, I have hereunto set my hand and caused the seal of the United States to be affixed.

Done at the City of Washington, this first day of January, in the year of our Lord one thousand eight hundred and sixty three, and of the Independence of the United States of America the eighty-seventh.

By the President: Abraham Lincoln.
William H. Seward, Secretary of State.

Gettysburg Address

On 19 Nov 1863 Pres. Abraham Lincoln delivered this speech at the consecration of the National Cemetery at Gettysburg PA, the site of one of the most decisive battles of the American Civil War. The main address at the dedication ceremony was one of two hours, delivered by Edward Everett, the best-known orator of the time. It is Lincoln's short speech, however, which is remembered, not only as a memorial to those who gave their lives on the battlefield, but as a statement of the ideals on which the nation was founded.

Four score and seven years ago our fathers brought forth on this continent a new nation, conceived in Liberty, and dedicated to the proposition that all men are created equal. Now we are engaged in a great civil war, testing whether that nation or any nation so conceived and so dedicated, can long endure. We are met on a great battle-field of that war. We have come to dedicate a portion of that field, as a final resting place for those who here gave their lives that that nation might live. It is altogether fitting and proper that we should do this. But, in a larger sense, we can not dedicate—we can not consecrate—we can not hallow—this ground. The brave men, living and dead, who struggled here, have consecrated it, far above

our poor power to add or detract. The world will little note, nor long remember what we say here, but it can never forget what they did here. It is for us the living, rather, to be dedicated here to the unfinished work which they who fought here have thus far so nobly advanced. It is rather for us to be here dedicated to the great task remaining before us—that from these honored dead we take increased devotion to that cause for which they gave the last full measure of devotion—that we here highly resolve that these dead shall not have died in vain—that this nation, under God, shall have a new birth of freedom—and that government of the people, by the people, for the people, shall not perish from the earth.

United States Government

US Presidents

Party abbreviations: Democratic (Dem); Republican (Rep); Federalist (Fed); Jeffersonian Republican (Jeff Rep); National Republican (Nat Rep)

	NAME	POLITICAL PARTY	TIME IN OFFICE	VICE PRESIDENT
1	George Washington	Fed	1789–97	John Adams
2	John Adams	Fed	1797–1801	Thomas Jefferson
3	Thomas Jefferson	Jeff Rep	1801–09	Aaron Burr
				George Clinton
4	James Madison	Jeff Rep	1809–17	George Clinton
				Elbridge Gerry
5	James Monroe	Jeff Rep	1817–25	Daniel D. Tompkins

US Presidents (continued)

	NAME	POLITICAL PARTY	TIME IN OFFICE	VICE PRESIDENT
6	John Quincy Adams	Nat Rep	1825-29	John C. Calhoun
7	Andrew Jackson	Dem	1829-37	John C. Calhoun
				Martin Van Buren
8	Martin Van Buren	Dem	1837-41	Richard M. Johnson
9	William Henry Harrison*	Whig	4 Mar-4	John Tyler
			Apr 1841	
10	John Tyler	Whig	1841-45	none
11	James K. Polk	Dem	1845-49	George Mifflin Dallas
12	Zachary Taylor*	Whig	1849-50	Millard Fillmore
13	Millard Fillmore	Whig	1850-53	none
14	Franklin Pierce	Dem	1853-57	William Rufus de Vane King
15	James Buchanan	Dem	1857-61	John C. Breckinridge
16	Abraham Lincoln*1	Rep	1861-65	Hannibal Hamlin
				Andrew Johnson
17	Andrew Johnson	Dem (Union)	1865-69	none
18	Ulysses S. Grant	Rep	1869-77	Schuyler Colfax
				Henry Wilson
19	Rutherford B. Hayes	Rep	1877-81	William A. Wheeler
20	James A. Garfield*1	Rep	4 Mar-	Chester A. Arthur
			19 Sep 1881	
21	Chester A. Arthur	Rep	1881-85	none
22	Grover Cleveland	Dem	1885-89	Thomas A. Hendricks
23	Benjamin Harrison	Rep	1889-93	Levi Parsons Morton
24	Grover Cleveland	Dem	1893-97	Adlai E. Stevenson
25	William McKinley*1	Rep	1897-1901	Garret A. Hobart
				Theodore Roosevelt
26	Theodore Roosevelt	Rep	1901-09	Charles Warren Fairbanks
27	William Howard Taft	Rep	1909-13	James Schoolcraft Sherman
28	Woodrow Wilson	Dem	1913-21	Thomas R. Marshall
29	Warren G. Harding*	Rep	1921-23	Calvin Coolidge
30	Calvin Coolidge	Rep	1923-29	Charles G. Dawes
31	Herbert Hoover	Rep	1929-33	Charles Curtis
32	Franklin D. Roosevelt*	Dem	1933-45	John Nance Garner
				Henry A. Wallace
				Harry S. Truman
33	Harry S. Truman	Dem	1945-53	Alben W. Barkley
34	Dwight D. Eisenhower	Rep	1953-61	Richard M. Nixon
35	John F. Kennedy*1	Dem	1961-63	Lyndon B. Johnson
36	Lyndon B. Johnson	Dem	1963-69	Hubert H. Humphrey
37	Richard M. Nixon**	Rep	1969-74	Spiro T. Agnew
				Gerald R. Ford
38	Gerald R. Ford	Rep	1974-77	Nelson A. Rockefeller
39	Jimmy Carter	Dem	1977-81	Walter F. Mondale
40	Ronald Reagan	Rep	1981-89	George H.W. Bush
41	George H.W. Bush	Rep	1989-93	Dan Quayle
42	William J. Clinton	Dem	1993-2001	Albert Gore
43	George W. Bush	Rep	2001-	Richard B. Cheney

*Died in office   **Resigned from office   1Assassinated

Presidential Biographies

George Washington (22 Feb [11 Feb, Old Style] 1732, Westmoreland county VA–14 Dec 1799, Mt. Vernon, in Fairfax county VA), American Revolutionary commander-in-chief (1775-83) and first president of the US (1789-97). Born into a wealthy family, he was educated privately and worked as a surveyor from age 14. In 1752 he inherited his brother's estate at Mount Vernon, including 18 slaves whose ranks grew to 49 by 1760, though he disapproved of slavery. In the French and Indian War he was commissioned a colonel and sent to the Ohio Territory. After Edward Braddock was killed, Washington became commander of all Virginia forces, entrusted with defending the western frontier (1755-58). He resigned to manage his es-

tate and in 1759 married Martha Dandridge Custis (1731-1802), a widow. He served in the House of Burgesses 1759-74, where he supported the colonists' cause, and in the Continental Congress 1774-75. In 1775 he was elected to command the Continental Army. In the ensuing American Revolution, he proved a brilliant commander and stalwart leader despite several defeats. With the war effectively ended by the capture of Yorktown (1781), he resigned his commission and returned to Mount Vernon (1783). He was a delegate to and presiding officer of the Constitutional Convention (1787) and helped secure ratification of the Constitution in Virginia. When the state electors met to select the first president (1789), Washington was the unanimous choice. He formed a cabinet to balance sectional and political differences but was committed to a strong central government. Elected to a second term, he followed a middle course between the political factions that became the Federalist Party and Democratic Party. He proclaimed a policy of neutrality in the war between Britain and France (1793) and sent troops to suppress the Whiskey Rebellion (1794). He declined to serve a third term, setting a 144-year precedent, and retired in 1797 after delivering his "Farewell Address." Known as the "father of his country," he is regarded as one of the greatest figures in US history.

John Adams (30 Oct [19 Oct, Old Style] 1735, Braintree [now in Quincy] MA—4 Jul 1826, Quincy MA), first vice president (1789–97) and second president (1797–1801) of the US. He practiced law in Boston and in 1764 married Abigail Smith. Active in the American independence movement, he was elected to the Massachusetts legislature and served as a delegate to the Continental Congress (1774–78), where he was appointed to several committees, including one with Thomas Jefferson and others to draft the Declaration of Independence. He served as a diplomat in France, The Netherlands, and England (1778–88). In the first US presidential election, he received the second-largest number of votes and became vice president under George Washington. Adams's term as president was marked by controversy over his signing the Alien and Sedition Acts in 1798 and by his alliance with the conservative Federalist Party. In 1800 he was defeated for reelection by Jefferson and retired to live a secluded life in Massachusetts. In 1812 he was reconciled with Jefferson, with whom he began an illuminating correspondence. Both men died on 4 Jul 1826, the Declaration's 50th anniversary. Pres. John Quincy Adams was his son.

Thomas Jefferson (13 Apr [2 Apr, Old Style] 1743, Shadwell VA—4 Jul 1826, Monticello VA), third president of the US (1801–9). He was a planter and lawyer from 1767, as well as a slaveholder who opposed slavery. While a member of the House of Burgesses (1769–75), he initiated the Committee of Correspondence (1773) with Richard Henry Lee and Patrick Henry. In 1774 he wrote the influential *Summary View of the Rights of British America*, stating that the British Parliament had no authority to legislate for the colonies. A delegate to the second Continental Congress, he was appointed to the committee to draft the Declaration of Independence and became its primary author. He was elected governor of Virginia (1779–81) but was unable to organize effective opposition when British forces invaded the colony (1780–81). Criticized for his conduct, he retired, vowing to remain a private citizen. Again a member of the Continental Congress (1783–85), he proposed territorial provisions later incorporated in the Northwest Ordinances. He traveled in Europe on diplomatic missions and became minister to France (1785–89). George Washington made him secretary of state (1790–93). He soon became embroiled in conflict with Alexander Hamilton over their opposing interpretations of the Constitution. This led to the rise of factions and political parties, with Jefferson representing the Democratic-Republicans. He served as vice president (1797–1801) but opposed the Alien and Sedition Acts enacted under Pres. John Adams. As part of this opposition, Jefferson drafted one of the Virginia and Kentucky Resolutions. In 1801 he be-

came president after an electoral-vote tie with Aaron Burr was settled by the House of Representatives. Jefferson initiated frugal fiscal policies and simplicity in the ceremonial role of the president. He oversaw the Louisiana Purchase and authorized the Lewis and Clark Expedition. He sought to avoid involvement in the Napoleonic Wars by signing the Embargo Act. He retired to his plantation, Monticello, where he pursued his many interests in science, philosophy, and architecture. He served as president of the American Philosophical Society 1797–1815, and in 1819 founded and designed the University of Virginia. In January 2000, the Thomas Jefferson Memorial Foundation accepted the conclusion, supported by DNA evidence, that Jefferson had fathered at least one, and perhaps as many as six, children with Sally Hemings, one of his house slaves. After a long estrangement, he and Adams became reconciled in 1813 and exchanged views on national issues. They both died on July 4, 1826, the 50th anniversary of the signing of the Declaration of Independence.

James Madison (16 Mar [5 Mar, Old Style] 1751, Port Conway VA—28 Jun 1836, Montpelier VA), fourth president of the US (1809–17). He served in the state legislature (1776–80, 1784–86). At the Constitutional Convention (1787), his active participation and his careful notes on the debates earned him the title "father of the Constitution." To promote ratification, he collaborated with Alexander Hamilton and John Jay on *The Federalist*. In the House of Representatives (1789–97), he sponsored the Bill of Rights, was a leading Jeffersonian Republican, and split with Hamilton over funding state war debts. In reaction to the Alien and Sedition Acts, he drafted one of the Virginia and Kentucky Resolutions (1798). He was appointed secretary of state (1801–9) by Thomas Jefferson, with whom he developed US foreign policy. Elected president in 1808, he was occupied by the trade and shipping embargo problems caused by France and Britain that led to the War of 1812. He was reelected in 1812; his second term was marked principally by the war, during which he reinvigorated the Army, and also saw approval of the charter of the Second Bank of the US and the first US protective tariff. He retired to his Virginia estate, Montpelier, with his wife, Dolley (1768–1849), whose political acumen he had long prized. He continued to write articles and letters and served as rector of the University of Virginia (1826–36).

James Monroe (28 Apr 1758, Westmoreland county VA—4 Jul 1831, New York NY), fifth president of the US (1817–25). He fought in the American Revolution and studied law under Thomas Jefferson. He served in the Congress (1783–86) and Senate (1790–94), where he opposed George Washington's administration. He nevertheless became minister to France (1794–96), where he misled the French about US politics and was recalled. He served as governor of Virginia 1799–1802. Pres. Jefferson sent him to France, where he helped negotiate the Louisiana Purchase (1803), then named him minister to Britain (1803–7). He returned to Virginia and became governor (1811), but resigned to become US secretary of state (1811–17) and secretary of war (1814–15). He served two terms as president, presiding in a period that became known as the Era of Good Feelings. He oversaw the Seminole War (1817–18) and the acquisition of the Floridas (1819–21), and signed the Missouri Compromise (1820). With secretary of state John Quincy Adams, he developed the principles of US foreign policy later called the Monroe Doctrine.

John Quincy Adams (11 Jul 1767, Braintree [now in Quincy] MA—23 Feb 1848, Washington DC), sixth president of the US (1825–29). He was the eldest son of Pres. John Adams and Abigail. He accompanied his father to Europe on diplomatic missions (1778–80) and was later appointed minister to The Netherlands (1794) and Prussia (1797). In 1801 he returned to Massachusetts and served in the Senate (1803–8). Resuming his diplomatic service, he became minister to Russia (1809–11) and Britain (1815–17). Appointed secretary of state (1817–24), he was instrumental in acquiring Florida from Spain and in drafting the Monroe Doctrine. He was one of three candidates in the 1824 presidential election, in which none received a majority of the electoral votes, though Andrew Jackson received a plurality. The decision went to the House of Representatives, where Adams received crucial support from Henry Clay and the electoral votes necessary to elect him president. He appointed Clay secretary of state, which further angered Jackson. Adams's presidency was unsuccessful; when he ran for reelection, Jackson defeated him. In 1830 he was elected to the House of Representatives, where he served until his death. He was outspoken in his opposition to slavery and in 1839 proposed a constitutional amendment forbidding slavery in any new state admitted to the Union. Southern congressmen prevented discussion of antislavery petitions by passing gag rules (repealed in 1844 as a result of Adams's persistence). In 1841 he successfully defended the slaves in the Amistad Mutiny case.

Andrew Jackson (15 Mar 1767, Waxhaws region SC—8 Jun 1845, the Hermitage, near Nashville TN), seventh president of the US (1829–37). He fought briefly in the American Revolution near his frontier home, where his family was killed. He studied law and in 1788 was appointed prosecuting attorney for western North Carolina. When the region became the state of Tennessee, he was elected to the House of Representatives (1796–97) and Senate (1797–98). He served on the state supreme court (1798–1804) and in 1802 was elected major general of the Tennessee militia. When the War of 1812 began, he offered the US the services of his 50,000-volunteer militia. He was sent to fight the Creek Indians allied with the British in Mississippi Territory. After a lengthy battle (1813–14), he defeated them at the Battle of Horseshoe Bend. After capturing Pensacola FL from the British-allied Spanish, he marched overland to engage the British in Louisiana. A decisive victory at the Battle of New Orleans made him a national hero, dubbed "Old Hickory" by the press. After US acquisition of Florida, he was named governor of the territory (1821). One of four candidates in the 1824 presidential election, he won an electoral-votes plurality but the House gave the election to John Quincy Adams. In 1828 Jackson defeated Adams after a fierce campaign and became the first president elected from west of the Appalachian Mountains. His election was considered a triumph of political democracy. He replaced many federal officeholders with his supporters, a process that became known as the spoils system. He pursued a policy of moving

Native Americans westward with the Indian Removal Acts. He split with his vice president, John C. Calhoun, over the nullification movement. His reelection in 1832 was due in part to support for his anticapitalistic fiscal policies and a controversial veto that affected the Bank of the US. His popularity continued to build throughout his presidency. During his tenure a strong Democratic Party developed that led to a vigorous two-party system.

Martin Van Buren (5 Dec 1782, Kinderhook NY–24 Jul 1862, Kinderhook NY), eighth president of the US (1837–41). He practiced law and served in the NY state senate (1812–20) and as state attorney general (1816–19). He became the leader of an informal group of political supporters, called the Albany Regency because they dominated state politics even while Van Buren was in Washington. He was elected to the US Senate (1821–28), where he supported states' rights and opposed a strong central government. After John Quincy Adams became president, he joined with Andrew Jackson and others to form a group that later became the Democratic Party. He was elected governor of New York (1828) but resigned to become US secretary of state (1829–31). He was nominated for vice president at the first Democratic Party convention (1832) and served under Jackson (1833–37). As Jackson's chosen successor, he defeated William H. Harrison to win the 1836 election. His presidency was marked by an economic depression, the Maine–Canada border dispute, the Seminole War in Florida, and debate over the annexation of Texas. He was defeated in his bid for reelection and failed to win the Democratic nomination in 1844 because of his antislavery views. In 1848 he was nominated for president by the Free Soil Party but failed to win the election and retired.

William Henry Harrison (9 Feb 1773, Charles City county VA–4 Apr 1841, Washington DC), ninth president of the US (1841). Born into a political family, he enlisted in the army at 18 and served under Anthony Wayne at the Battle of Fallen Timbers. In 1798 he became secretary of the Northwest Territories, and in 1800 governor of the new Indiana Territory. In response to pressure from white settlers, he negotiated treaties with the Native Americans that ceded millions of acres of additional land to the US. When Tecumseh organized an uprising in 1811, Harrison led a US force to defeat the Indians at the Battle of Tippecanoe, a victory that largely established his reputation in the public mind. In the War of 1812 he was made a brigadier general and defeated the British and their Indian allies at the Battle of the Thames in Ontario. After the war he moved to Ohio, where he became prominent in the Whig Party. He served in the House of Representatives (1816–19) and Senate (1825–28). As the Whig candidate in the 1836 presidential election, he lost narrowly. In 1840 he and his running mate, John Tyler, won election with a slogan emphasizing Harrison's frontier triumph: "Tippecanoe and Tyler too." The 68-year-old Harrison delivered his inaugural speech without a hat or overcoat in a cold drizzle, contracted pneumonia, and died one month later, the first president to die in office.

John Tyler (29 Mar 1790, Charles City county VA–18 Jan 1862, Richmond VA), 10th president of the US (1841–45). He practiced law before serving in the state legislature (1811–16, 1823–25, 1839) and as governor of Virginia (1825–27). In the House of

Representatives (1817–21) and Senate (1827–36), he was a states-rights supporter. Though a slaveholder, he sought to prohibit the slave trade in the District of Columbia, provided Maryland and Virginia concurred. He resigned from the Senate rather than acquiesce to state instructions to change his vote on a censure of Pres. Andrew Jackson. After breaking with the Democratic Party, he was nominated by the Whig Party for vice president under William H. Harrison. They won the 1840 election, carefully avoiding the issues and stressing party loyalty and the slogan "Tippecanoe and Tyler too!" Harrison died a month after taking office, and Tyler became the first to attain the presidency "by accident." He vetoed a national bank bill supported by the Whigs, and all but one member of the cabinet resigned, leaving him without party support. Nonetheless, he reorganized the navy, settled the second of the Seminole Wars in Florida, and oversaw the annexation of Texas. He was nominated for reelection but withdrew in favor of James Polk and retired to his Virginia plantation. Committed to states' rights but opposed to secession, he organized the Washington Peace Conference (1861) to resolve sectional differences. When the Senate rejected a proposed compromise, Tyler urged Virginia to secede.

James Knox Polk (2 Nov 1795, Mecklenburg county NC—15 Jun 1849, Nashville TN), 11th president of the US (1845–49). He became a lawyer in Tennessee and a friend and supporter of Andrew Jackson, who helped Polk win election to the House of Representatives (1825–39). He left the House to become governor of Tennessee (1839–41). At the deadlocked 1844 Democratic convention Polk was nominated as the compromise candidate; he is considered the first dark-horse presidential candidate. A proponent of western expansion, he campaigned with the slogan "Fifty-four Forty or Fight," to bring a solution to the Oregon Question. Elected at 49, the youngest president to that time, he successfully concluded the Oregon border dispute with Britain (1846) and secured passage of the Walker Tariff Act (1846), which lowered import duties and helped foreign trade. He led the prosecution of the Mexican War, which resulted in large territorial gains but reopened the debate over the extension of slavery. His administration also established the Department of the Interior, the US Naval Academy, and the Smithsonian Institution, oversaw revision of the treasury system, and proclaimed the validity of the Monroe Doctrine. Though an efficient and competent president, deft in his handling of Congress, he was exhausted by his efforts and did not seek reelection; he died three months after leaving office.

Zachary Taylor (24 Nov 1784, Montebello VA—9 Jul 1850, Washington DC), 12th president of the US (1849–50). Born in Virginia, he grew up on the Kentucky frontier. He fought in the War of 1812, the Black Hawk War (1832), and the Seminole War in Florida (1835–42), earning the nickname "Old Rough-and-Ready" for his indifference to hardship. Sent to Texas in anticipation of war with Mexico, he defeated the Mexican invaders at the battles of Palo Alto and Resaca de la Palma (1846). After the Mexican War formally began, he captured Monterrey and granted the Mexican army an eight-week armistice. Displeased, Pres. James Polk moved Taylor's best troops to serve under Winfield Scott in the invasion of Veracruz. Taylor ignored orders to remain in Monterrey and marched south to defeat a large Mexican force at the Battle of Buena Vista (1847). He became a national hero and was nominated as the Whig candidate for president (1848). He defeated Lewis Cass to win the election. His brief term was marked by a controversy over the new territories that produced the Compromise of 1850 and by a scandal involving members of his cabinet. He died, probably of cholera, after only 16 months in office and was succeeded by Millard Fillmore.

Millard Fillmore (7 Jan 1800, Locke Township, NY—8 Mar 1874, Buffalo NY), 13th president of the US (1850–53). Born into poverty, he became an indentured apprentice at 15. He studied law with a local judge and began to practice in Buffalo in 1823. Initially identified with the Anti-Masonic Party (1828–34), he followed his political mentor, Thurlow Weed, to the Whigs and was soon a leader of the party's northern wing. He served in the House of Representatives (1833–35, 1837–43), where he became a follower of Henry Clay. In 1848 the Whigs nominated Fillmore as vice president, and he was elected with Zachary Taylor. He became president on Taylor's death in 1850. Though he abhorred slavery, he supported the Compromise of 1850 and insisted on federal enforcement of the Fugitive Slave Act. His stand, which alienated the North, led to his defeat by Winfield Scott at the Whigs' nominating convention in 1852 and effectively led to the death of the party. Throughout his career he advocated US internal development and was an early champion of expansion in the Pacific. In 1853 he sent Matthew Perry with a US fleet to Japan, forcing its isolationist government to enter into trade and diplomatic relations. He returned to Buffalo and was nominated for president by the third-party Know-Nothing Party in 1856, won by Democrat James Buchanan.

Franklin Pierce (23 Nov 1804, Hillsboro NH—8 Oct 1869, Concord NH), 14th president of the US (1853–57). He practiced law and served in the House of Representatives (1833–37) and Senate (1837–42). He returned to his law practice, serving briefly in the Mexican War. At the deadlocked Democratic convention of 1852, he was nominated as the compromise candidate; though largely unknown nationally, he unexpectedly trounced Winfield Scott in the general election. For the sake of harmony and business prosperity, he was inclined to oppose antislavery agitation so as to placate Southern opinion. He promoted US territorial expansion, resulting in the diplomatic controversy of the Ostend Manifesto. He reorganized the diplomatic and consular service and created the Court of Claims. He encouraged plans for a transcontinental railroad and approved the Gadsden Purchase. To promote northwestern migration and conciliate sectional demands, he approved the Kansas-Nebraska Act but was unable to settle the resultant problems. Defeated for renomination by James Buchanan in 1856, he retired from politics.

James Buchanan (23 Apr 1791, near Mercersburg PA—1 Jun 1868, near Lancaster PA), 15th president of the US (1857–61). He became a lawyer and member of the Pennsylvania legislature before serving in the House of Representatives (1821–31), as minister to Russia (1832–34), and in the Senate (1834–45). He was secretary of state in James Polk's cabinet (1845–49). As minister to Britain (1853–56), he helped draft the Ostend Manifesto. In 1856 he secured the Democratic nomination and election as president, defeating John C. Fremont. Though experienced in government and law, he lacked the moral courage to deal effectively with the slavery crisis and equivocated on the question of Kansas's status as a slaveholding state. The ensuing split within his party allowed Abraham Lincoln to win the election of 1860. He denounced the secession of South Carolina following the election and sent reinforcements to Fort Sumter, but failed to respond further to the mounting crisis.

Abraham Lincoln (12 Feb 1809, near Hodgenville KY—15 Apr 1865, Washington DC), 16th president of the US (1861–65). Born in a Kentucky log cabin, he moved to Indiana in 1816 and to Illinois in 1830. He worked as a storekeeper, rail-splitter, postmaster, and surveyor, then enlisted as a volunteer in the Black Hawk War and became a captain. Though largely self-taught, he practiced law in Springfield IL and served in the state legislature (1834–40). He was elected as a Whig to the House of Representatives (1847–49). As a circuit-riding lawyer from 1849, he became one of the state's most successful lawyers, noted for his shrewdness, common sense, and honesty (earning the nickname "Honest Abe"). In 1856 he joined the Republican Party, which nominated him as its candidate in the 1858 Senate election. In a series of seven debates with Stephen A. Douglas (the Lincoln-Douglas Debates), he argued against the extension of slavery into the territories, though not against slavery itself. Although morally opposed to slavery, he was not an abolitionist. During the campaign, he attempted to rebut Douglas' charge that he was a dangerous radical by reassuring audiences that he did not favor political equality for blacks. Despite his loss in the election, the debates brought him national attention. He again ran against Douglas in the 1860 presidential election, which he won by a large margin. But the South opposed his position on slavery in the territories, and before his inauguration seven Southern states had seceded from the Union. The ensuing American Civil War completely consumed Lincoln's administration. He excelled as a wartime leader, creating a high command for directing all the country's energies and resources toward the war effort and combining statecraft and overall command of the armies with what some have called military genius. However, his abrogation of some civil liberties, especially the writ of habeas corpus, and the closing of several newspapers by his generals disturbed both Democrats and Republicans, including some members of his own cabinet. To unite the North and influence foreign opinion, he issued the Emancipation Proclamation (1863); his Gettysburg Address (1863) further ennobled the war's purpose. The continuing war affected some Northerners' resolve and his reelection was not assured, but strategic battle victories turned the tide and he easily defeated George B. McClellan in 1864. His platform included passage of the 13th Amendment outlawing slavery (ratified 1865). At his second inaugural, with victory in sight, he spoke of moderation in reconstructing the South and building a harmonious Union. On 14 Apr, five days after the war ended, he was shot by John Wilkes Booth and soon after died.

Andrew Johnson (29 Dec 1808, Raleigh NC—31 Jul 1875, near Carter Station TN), 17th president of the US (1865–69). Born in North Carolina and reared in Tennessee, he was self-educated and initially worked as a tailor. He organized a workingman's party and was elected in the state legislature (1835–43), where he became a spokesman for small farmers. He served in the House of Representatives (1843–53) and as governor of Tennessee (1853–57). Elected to the Senate (1857–62), he opposed antislavery agitation, but in 1860 he opposed Southern secession, even after Tennessee seceded in 1861, and during the Civil War he was the only Southern senator who refused to join the Confederacy. In 1862 he was appointed military governor of Tennessee, then under Union control. In 1864 he was selected to run for vice president with Pres. Abraham Lincoln; he assumed the presidency after Lincoln's assassination. During Reconstruction he favored a moderate policy that readmitted former Confederate states to the Union with few provisions for reform or civil rights for freedmen. In 1867 the Radical Republicans in Congress passed civil rights legislation and established the Freedmen's Bureau. His veto angered Congress, which passed the Tenure of Office Act. In 1868 in defiance of the act, Johnson dismissed secretary of war Edwin M. Stanton, an ally of the Radicals. The House responded by impeaching the president for the first time in US history. In the subsequent Senate trial, the charges proved weak and the necessary two-thirds vote needed for conviction failed by one vote. Johnson remained in office until 1869, but his effectiveness had ended. He returned to Tennessee, where he won reelection to the Senate shortly before he died.

Ulysses S. Grant (Hiram Ulysses Grant) (27 Apr 1822, Point Pleasant OH—23 Jul 1885, Mount McGregor NY), 18th president of the US (1869–77). He served in the Mexican War under Zachary Taylor; he resigned his commission in 1854 when he could not afford to bring his family west. Allegations that he became a drunkard in the lonely years in the West and in later life, though never proved, would affect his reputation. He worked unsuccessfully at farming in Missouri and at his family's leather business in Illinois. When the Civil War began (1861), he was appointed brigadier general; his 1862 attack on Fort Donelson TN, produced the first major Union victory. He drove off a Confederate attack at Shiloh but was criticized for heavy Union losses. He devised the campaign to take the stronghold of Vicksburg MS, in 1863, cutting the Confederacy in half from east to west. Following his victory at the Battle of Chattanooga in 1864, he was appointed commander of the Union army. While William T. Sherman made his famous march across Georgia, Grant attacked Robert E. Lee's forces in Virginia, bringing the war to an end in 1865. Grant's administrative ability and innovative strategies were largely responsible for the Union victory. His successful Republican presidential campaign made him, at 46, the youngest man yet elected president. His two terms were marred by administrative inaction and political scandal involving members of his cabinet, including the Crédit Mobilier scandal and the Whiskey Ring operation. He was more successful in foreign affairs, in which he was aided by his secretary of state, Hamilton Fish. He supported amnesty for Confederate leaders and protection for black civil rights. His veto of a bill to increase the amount of legal tender (1874) diminished the currency crisis in the next 25 years. In 1881 he moved to New York; when a partner defrauded an investment firm co-owned by his son, the family was impoverished. His memoirs were published by his friend Mark Twain.

Rutherford Birchard Hayes (4 Oct 1822, Delaware OH—17 Jan 1893, Fremont OH), 19th president of the US (1877–81). He practiced law in Cincinnati, representing defendants in several fugitive-slave cases and becoming associated with the new Republican Party. After fighting in the Union army, he served in the House of Representatives (1865–67). As governor of Ohio (1868–72, 1875–76), he advocated a sound currency backed by gold. In 1876 he won the Republican nomination for president. His opponent, Samuel Tilden, won a larger popular vote, but Hayes's managers contested the electoral-vote returns in four states, and a special Electoral Commission awarded the election to Hayes. As part of a secret compromise reached with Southerners, he withdrew the remaining federal troops from the South, ending Reconstruction, and promised not to interfere with elections there, ensuring the return of white Democratic supremacy. He introduced civil-service reform based on merit, incurring a dispute with Roscoe Conkling and the conservative "stalwart" Republicans. At the request of state governors, he used federal troops against strikers in the railroad strikes of 1877. Declining to run for a second term, he retired to work for humanitarian causes.

James Abram Garfield (19 Nov 1831, near Orange [in Cuyahoga county] OH—19 Sep 1881, Elberon [now in Long Branch] NJ), 20th president of the US (1881). He graduated from Williams College, then returned to Ohio to teach and head an academy that became Hiram College. In the Civil War he led the 42nd Ohio Volunteers and fought at Shiloh and Chickamauga. He resigned as a major general to serve in the House of Representatives (1863–80). A Radical Republican during Reconstruction, he served on the Electoral Commission in the 1876 election, and was the House Republican leader from 1876 to 1880, when he was elected to the Senate. At the 1880 Republican nominating convention, the delegates supporting Ulysses S. Grant and James Blaine became deadlocked. On the 36th ballot Garfield was nominated as a compromise presidential candidate, with Chester Arthur as vice president, and won by a narrow margin. His brief term, less than 150 days, was marked by a dispute with Sen. Roscoe Conkling over patronage. On July 2 he was shot at Washington's railroad station by Charles J. Guiteau, an Arthur supporter. He died on September 19 after 11 weeks of public debate over the ambiguous constitutional conditions for presidential succession (later clarified by the 20th and 25th Amendments).

Chester Alan Arthur (5 Oct 1829, North Fairfield VT—18 Nov 1886, New York NY), 21st president of the US (1881–85). He practiced law in New York City from 1854. He became active in local Republican politics and a close associate of party leader Roscoe Conkling, and was appointed customs collector for the port of New York (1871–78), an office long known for its employment of the spoils system. He conducted the business of the office with integrity but continued to pad its payroll with Conkling loyalists. At the Republican national convention in 1880, Arthur became the compromise choice for vice president on the ticket with James Garfield, and became president on Garfield's assassination. As president, Arthur displayed unexpected independence by vetoing measures that rewarded political patronage. He also signed the Pendleton Act, which created a civil-service system based on merit. He recommended the appropriations that initiated the rebuilding of the Navy toward the strength it later achieved in the Spanish–American War (1898). He failed to win his party's nomination for a second term.

(Stephen) Grover Cleveland (18 Mar 1837, Caldwell NJ—24 Jun 1908, Princeton NJ), 22nd and 24th president of the US (1885–89, 1893–97). He practiced law in Buffalo NY from 1859, where he entered Democratic Party politics. As mayor of Buffalo (1881–82), he was known as a foe of corruption. As governor of New York (1883–85), he earned the hostility of Tammany Hall with his independence, but in 1884 he won the Democratic nomination for president. The first Democratic president since 1856, he supported civil-service reform and opposed high protective tariffs, which became an issue in the 1888 election, when he was narrowly defeated by Benjamin Harrison. In 1892 he was re-elected by a huge popular plurality. In 1893 he attributed the US's severe economic depression to the Sherman Silver Purchase Act of 1890 and strongly urged Congress to repeal the act. The economic unrest resulted in the Pullman Strike in 1894. An isolationist, he opposed territorial expansion. In 1895 he invoked the Monroe Doctrine in the border dispute between Britain and Venezuela. By 1896 supporters of the Free Silver Movement controlled the Democratic Party, which nominated William Jennings Bryan instead of Cleveland for president. He retired to New Jersey, where he lectured at Princeton University.

Benjamin Harrison (20 Aug 1833, North Bend OH—13 Mar 1901, Indianapolis IN), 23rd president of the US (1889–93). The grandson of Pres. William H. Harrison, he practiced law in Indianapolis from the mid-1850s. He served in the Union army in the Civil War, rising to brigadier general. He served a term in the Senate (1881–87) and, even though he lost reelection, was nominated for president by the Republicans. He went on to defeat the incumbent, Grover Cleveland, who lost despite winning more of the popular vote. As president, his domestic policy was marked by passage of the Sherman Antitrust Act. His foreign policy expanded US influence abroad. His secretary of state, James Blaine, presided at the conference that led to the establishment of the Pan-American Union, resisted pressure to abandon US interests in the Samoan Islands (1889), and negotiated a treaty with Britain in the Bering Sea Dispute (1891). Defeated for reelection by Cleveland in 1892, he returned to Indianapolis to practice law. In 1898–99 he was the leading counsel for Venezuela in its boundary dispute with Britain.

William McKinley (29 Jan 1843, Niles OH—14 Sep 1901, Buffalo NY), 25th president of the US (1897–1901). He served in the Civil War as an aide to Col. Rutherford B. Hayes, who later encouraged his political career. He was elected to the House of Representatives (1877–91), where he favored protective tariffs and sponsored the McKinley Tariff of 1890. With the support of Mark Hanna, he was elected governor (1892–96). In 1896 he won the Republican presidential nomination and the general election, defeating William Jennings Bryan. He called a special session of Congress to increase customs duties, but was soon embroiled in events in Cuba and responses to the sinking of the USS

Maine, which led to the Spanish-American War. At the war's end, he advocated US dependency status for the Philippines, Puerto Rico, and other former Spanish territories. He again defeated Bryan by a large majority in 1900, and began a tour to urge control of trusts and commercial reciprocity to boost foreign trade, issues neglected during the war. In Buffalo NY on 6 Sep 1901, he was fatally shot by an anarchist, Leon Czolgosz. He was succeeded by Theodore Roosevelt.

Theodore Roosevelt (27 Oct 1858, New York NY—6 Jan 1919, Oyster Bay NY), 26th president of the US (1901–9). He was elected to the New York legislature in 1882, where he became a Republican leader opposed to the Democratic political machine. After political defeats and the death of his wife, he went to the Dakota Territory to ranch. He returned to New York to serve on the US Civil Service Commission (1889–95) and as head of the city's board of police commissioners (1895–97). A supporter of William McKinley, he served as assistant secretary of the navy (1897–98). When the Spanish-American War was declared, he resigned to organize a cavalry unit, the Rough Riders. He returned to New York a hero and was elected governor in 1899. As the Republican vice-presidential nominee, he took office when McKinley was re-elected, and he became president on McKinley's assassination in 1901. One of his early initiatives was to urge enforcement of the Sherman Antitrust Act against business monopolies. He won election in his own right in 1904, defeating Alton Parker. At his urging, Congress regulated railroad rates and passed the Pure Food and Drug Act and Meat Inspection Act (1906) to provide new consumer protections. He set aside national forests, parks, and mineral, oil, and coal lands for conservation. He and secretary of state Elihu Root announced the Roosevelt corollary to the Monroe Doctrine, which reinforced the US position as defender of the Western Hemisphere. For mediating an end to the Russo-Japanese War, he received the 1906 Nobel Peace Prize. He secured a treaty with Panama for construction of a trans-isthmus canal. Declining to seek reelection, he secured the nomination for William H. Taft. After traveling in Africa and Europe, he tried to win the Republican presidential nomination in 1912; when he was rejected, he organized the Bull Moose Party and ran on a policy of New Nationalism, but failed to win the election. Throughout his life he continued to write, publishing extensively on history, politics, travel, and nature.

William Howard Taft (15 Sep 1857, Cincinnati OH–8 Mar 1930, Washington DC), 27th president of the US (1909–13). He served on the state superior court (1887–90), as US solicitor general (1890–92), and as US appellate judge (1892–1900). He was appointed head of the Philippine Commission to set up a civilian government in the islands and was its first civilian governor (1901–4). He served as US secretary of war (1904–8) under Pres. Theodore Roosevelt, who supported Taft's nomination for president in 1908. He won the election but became allied with the conservative Republicans, causing a rift with party progressives. He was again the nominee in 1912, but the split with Roosevelt and the Bull Moose Party resulted in the electoral victory of Woodrow Wilson. Taft later taught law at Yale University (1913–21), served on the National War Labor Board (1918), and was a supporter of the League of Nations. As chief justice of the Supreme Court (1921–30), he introduced reforms that made it more efficient. He secured passage of the Judges Act of 1925, which gave the Court wider discretion in accepting cases. His important opinion in *Myers* v *US* (1926) upheld the president's authority to remove federal officials. In poor health, he resigned in 1930.

(Thomas) Woodrow Wilson (28 Dec 1856, Staunton VA–3 Feb 1924, Washington DC), 28th president of the US (1913–21). He earned a law degree and later received his doctorate from Johns Hopkins University. He taught political science at Princeton University (1890–1902), and as its president (1902–10), he introduced various reforms. With the support of progressives, he was elected governor of New Jersey. His reform measures attracted national attention, and he became the Democratic presidential nominee in 1912. His campaign emphasized the progressive measures of his New Freedom policy, and he defeated Theodore Roosevelt and William H. Taft to win the presidency. As president, he approved legislation that lowered tariffs, created the Federal Reserve System, established the Federal Trade Commission, and strengthened labor unions. In foreign affairs he promoted self-government for the Philippines and sought to contain the Mexican civil war. From 1914 he maintained US neutrality in World War I, offering to mediate a settlement and initiate peace negotiations. After the sinking of the *Lusitania* (1915) and other unarmed ships, he obtained a pledge from Germany to stop its submarine campaign. Campaigning on the theme that he had "kept us out of war," he was narrowly reelected in 1916, defeating Charles Evans Hughes. Germany's renewed submarine attacks on unarmed passenger ships caused Wilson to ask for a declaration of war in April 1917. In a continuing effort to negotiate a peace agreement, he presented the Fourteen Points (1918). He led the US delegation to the Paris Peace Conference, where he attempted to stand on his original principles but was forced to compromise by the demands of various countries. The Treaty of Versailles faced opposition in the Senate from the Republican majority led by Henry C. Lodge. In search of popular support for the treaty and its League of Nations, Wilson began a cross-country speaking tour, but he collapsed and returned to Washington DC (Sep 1919), where a stroke left him partially paralyzed. He rejected any attempts to compromise his version of the League of Nations and urged his Senate followers to vote against ratification of the treaty, which was defeated in 1920. He was awarded the 1919 Nobel Peace Prize for his work on the League of Nations.

Warren Gamaliel Harding (2 Nov 1865, Caledonia (now Blooming Grove) OH–2 Aug 1923, San Francisco CA), 29th president of the US (1921–23). He became a newspaper publisher in Marion OH, where he was allied with the Republican Party's political machine. He served successively as state senator (1899–1902), lieutenant governor (1903–4), and US senator (1915–21), supporting conservative policies. At the deadlocked 1920 Republican presidential convention, he was chosen as the compromise candidate. Pledging a "return to normalcy" after World War I, he defeated James Cox with over 60% of the popular vote, the largest margin to that time. On his recommendation, Congress established a budget system for the federal government, passed a high protective tariff, revised wartime taxes, and restricted immigration. His administration convened the Washington Conference (1921–22). His ill-advised cabinet and patronage appointments, including Albert Fall, led to the Teapot Dome scandal and characterized his administration as corrupt. While in Alaska, he received word of the corruption about to be exposed and headed back. He arrived in San Francisco exhausted, reportedly suffering from food poisoning and other ills, and died there under unclear circumstances. He was succeeded by his vice president, Calvin Coolidge.

(John) Calvin Coolidge (4 Jul 1872, Plymouth VT—5 Jan 1933, Northampton MA), 30th president of the US (1923–29). He practiced law in Massachusetts from 1897 and served as lieutenant governor before being elected governor in 1918. He gained national attention by calling out the state guard during the Boston police strike in 1919. At the 1920 Republican convention, "Silent Cal" was nominated for vice president on Warren G. Harding's winning ticket. When Harding died in office in 1923, Coolidge became president. He restored confidence in an administration discredited by scandals and won the presidential election in 1924, defeating Robert La Follette. He vetoed measures to provide farm relief and bonuses to World War I veterans. His presidency was marked by apparent prosperity. Congress maintained a high protective tariff and instituted tax reductions that favored capital. Coolidge declined to run for a second term. His conservative policies of domestic and international inaction have come to symbolize the era between World War I and the Great Depression.

Herbert Clark Hoover (10 Aug 1874, West Branch IA—20 Oct 1964, New York NY), 31st president of the US (1929–33). As a mining engineer, he administered engineering projects on four continents (1895–1913). He then headed Allied relief operations in England and Belgium prior to World War I, at which time he was appointed national food administrator (1917–19) and instituted programs that furnished food to the Allies and famine-stricken areas of Europe. Appointed secretary of commerce (1921–27), he reorganized the department, creating divisions to regulate broadcasting and aviation. He oversaw commissions to build Boulder (later Hoover) Dam and the St. Lawrence Seaway. In 1928, as the Republican presidential candidate, he soundly defeated Alfred E. Smith. His hopes for a "New Day" program were quickly overwhelmed by the Great Depression. As a believer in individual freedom, he vetoed bills to create a federal unemployment agency and to fund public-works projects, instead favoring private charity. In 1932 he finally allowed relief to farmers through the Reconstruction Finance Corp. He was overwhelmingly defeated in 1932 by Franklin Roosevelt. He continued to speak out against relief measures and criticized New Deal programs. After World War II he participated in famine-relief work in Europe and was appointed head of the Hoover Commission.

Franklin Delano Roosevelt (30 Jan 1882, Hyde Park NY—12 Apr 1945, Warm Springs GA), 32nd president of the US (1933–45). He was attracted to politics as an admirer of his cousin Pres. Theodore Roosevelt and became active in the Democratic Party. In 1905 he married distant cousin Eleanor Roosevelt, who would become a valued adviser in future years. He served in the state senate (1910–13) and as assistant secretary of the navy

(1913–20). In 1920 he was nominated for vice president. The next year he was stricken with polio; though unable to walk, he remained active in politics. As governor of New York (1929–33), he set up the first state relief agency in the US In 1932 he won the Democratic presidential nomination with the help of James Farley and easily defeated Pres. Herbert Hoover. In his inaugural address to a nation of more than 13 million unemployed, he pronounced that "the only thing we have to fear is fear itself." Congress passed most of the changes he sought in his New Deal program in the first hundred days of his term. He was overwhelmingly reelected in 1936 over Alf Landon. To solve legal challenges to the New Deal, he proposed enlarging the Supreme Court, but his "court-packing" plan aroused strong opposition and had to be abandoned. By the late 1930s economic recovery had slowed, but Roosevelt was more concerned with the growing threat of war. In 1940 he was reelected to an unprecedented third term, defeating Wendell Willkie. He maintained US neutrality toward the war in Europe, but approved the principle of lend-lease and in 1941 met with Winston Churchill to draft the Atlantic Charter. With US entry into World War II, he mobilized industry for military production and formed an alliance with Britain and the Soviet Union; he met with Churchill and Joseph Stalin to form war policy at Tehran (1943) and Yalta (1945). Despite declining health, he won reelection for a fourth term against Thomas Dewey (1944) but served only briefly before his death. His presidency is well regarded in US history.

Harry S. Truman (8 May 1884, Lamar MO—26 Dec 1972, Kansas City MO), 33rd president of the US (1945–53). He worked at various jobs before serving with distinction in World War I. He became a partner in a Kansas City haberdashery; when the business failed, he entered Democratic Party politics with the help of Thomas Pendergast. He was elected county judge (1922–24), and later became presiding judge of the county court (1926–34). His reputation for honesty and good management gained him bipartisan support. In the Senate (1935–45), he led a committee that exposed fraud in defense production. In 1944 he was chosen to replace the incumbent Henry Wallace as vice-presidential nominee and was elected with Pres. Franklin Roosevelt. After only 82 days as vice president, he became president on Roosevelt's death (April 1945). He quickly made final arrangements for the San Francisco charter-writing meeting of the UN, helped arrange Germany's unconditional surrender on 8 May, which ended World War II in Europe, and in July attended the Potsdam Conference. The Pacific war ended officially on 2 Sep, after he ordered atomic bombs dropped on Hiroshima and Nagasaki; his justification was a report that 500,000 US troops would be lost in a conventional invasion of Japan. He announced the Truman Doctrine to aid Greece and Turkey (1947), established the Central Intelligence Agency, and pressed for passage of the Marshall Plan to aid European countries. In 1948 he defeated Thomas Dewey despite widespread expectation of his own defeat. He initiated a foreign policy of containment to restrict the Soviet Union's sphere of influence, pursued his Point Four Program, and initiated the Berlin airlift and the NATO pact of 1949. In the Korean War he sent troops under Gen. Douglas MacArthur to head the UN forces. Problems of pursuing the war occupied his administration until he retired. Though he was often criticized during his presidency, Truman's reputation grew steadily in later years.

Dwight David Eisenhower (14 Oct 1890, Denison TX —28 Mar 1969, Washington DC), 34th president of the US (1953–61). He graduated from West Point (1915), then served in the Panama Canal Zone (1922–24) and in the Philippines under Douglas MacArthur (1935–39). In World War II Gen. George Marshall appointed him to the army's war-plans division (1941), then chose him to command US forces in Europe (1942). After planning the invasions of North Africa, Sicily, and Italy, he was appointed supreme commander of Allied forces (1943). He planned the Normandy Campaign (1944) and the conduct of the war in Europe until the German surrender (1945). He was promoted to five-star general (1944) and was named army chief of staff in 1945. He served as president of Columbia University from 1948 until being appointed supreme commander of NATO in 1951. Both Democrats and Republicans courted Eisenhower as a presidential candidate; in 1952, as the Republican candidate, he defeated Adlai Stevenson with the largest popular vote up to that time. He defeated Stevenson again in 1956 in an even larger landslide. His achievements included efforts to contain Communism with the Eisenhower Doctrine. He sent federal troops to Little Rock AR to enforce integration of a city high school (1957). When the Soviet Union launched Sputnik I (1957), he was criticized for failing to develop the US space program and responded by creating NASA (1958). In his last weeks in office the US broke diplomatic relations with Cuba.

John Fitzgerald Kennedy (29 May 1917, Brookline MA—22 Nov 1963, Dallas TX), 35th president of the US (1961–63). The son of Joseph P. Kennedy, he graduated from Harvard University and joined the Navy in World War II, where he earned medals for heroism. Elected to the House of Representatives (1947–53) and the Senate (1953–60), he supported social legislation and became increasingly committed to civil rights legislation. He supported the policies of Harry Truman but accused the State Department of trying to force Chiang Kai-shek into a coalition with Mao Zedong. In 1960 he won the Democratic nomination for president; after a vigorous campaign, managed by his brother Robert F. Kennedy and aided financially by his father, he narrowly defeated Richard Nixon. He was the youngest person and the first Roman Catholic elected president. In his inaugural address he called on Americans to "ask not what your country can do for you, ask what you can do for your country." He proposed tax-reform and civil rights legislation but received little congressional support. He established the Peace Corps and the Alliance for Progress. His foreign policy began with the abortive Bay of Pigs invasion (1961), which emboldened the Soviet Union to move missiles to Cuba, sparking the Cuban missile crisis. In 1963 he successfully concluded the Nuclear Test-Ban Treaty. In November 1963 he was assassinated while riding in a motorcade in Dallas by a sniper, allegedly Lee Harvey Oswald. The killing is considered the most notorious political murder of the 20th century. Kennedy's youth, energy, and charming family brought him world adulation and sparked the idealism of a generation, for whom the Kennedy White House became known as "Camelot." Details about his powerful family and personal life, especially concerning his extramarital affairs, tainted his image in later years.

Lyndon Baines Johnson (27 Aug 1908, Gillespie county TX—22 Jan 1973, San Antonio TX), 36th president of the US (1963–69). He taught school in Houston before going to Washington DC in 1932 as a congressional aide. There he was befriended by Sam Rayburn and his political career blossomed. He won a seat in the House of Representatives (1937–49) as the New Deal was under conservative attack. His loyalty impressed Pres. Franklin Roosevelt, who made Johnson a protégé. He won election to the Senate in 1949 in a vicious campaign that saw fraud on both sides. As Democratic whip (1951–55) and majority leader (1955–61), he developed a talent for consensus building among dissident factions with methods both tactful and ruthless. He was largely responsible for passage of the civil rights bills of 1957 and 1960, the first in the 20th century. In 1960 he was elected vice president; he became president after the assassination of John F. Kennedy. In his first few months in office he won from Congress passage of a huge quantity of important civil rights, tax-reduction, antipoverty, and conservation legislation. He defeated Barry Goldwater in the 1964 election by the largest popular majority to that time and announced his Great Society program. He was diverted from overseeing its enactment by the escalation of US involvement in the Vietnam War, beginning with the Gulf of Tonkin Resolution. His approval ratings diminished markedly and led to his decision not to seek reelection in 1968. He retired to his Texas ranch.

Richard Milhous Nixon (9 Jan 1913, Yorba Linda CA— 22 Apr 1994, New York NY), 37th president of the US (1969–74). He studied law at Duke University and practiced in California 1937–42. After serving in World War II, he was elected to the House of Representatives in 1947, employing harsh campaign tactics. He came to national attention with the Alger Hiss case, and was elected to the Senate in 1951, again following a bitter campaign. He won the vice presidency in 1952 on a ticket with Dwight D. Eisenhower; they were reelected easily in 1956. As presidential candidate in 1960, he lost narrowly to John F. Kennedy. After failing to win the 1962 California gubernatorial race, he retired from politics and moved to New York to practice law. He reentered politics by running for president in 1968, and he defeated Hubert H. Humphrey with his "southern strategy" of seeking votes from southern and western conservatives in both parties. As president, he began to gradually withdraw US military forces in an effort to end the Vietnam War while ordering the secret bombing of North Vietnamese military centers in Laos and Cambodia. Attacks on North Vietnamese sanctuaries in Cambodia drew widespread protest. Economic problems caused by inflation made the US budget deficit the largest to date, and in 1971 Nixon established unprecedented peacetime controls on wages and prices. He won reelection in 1972 with a landslide victory over George McGovern. Assisted by Henry A. Kissinger, he concluded the Vietnam War. He reopened communications with Communist China and made a state visit there. On his visit to the Soviet Union, the first by a US president, he signed the bilateral SALT agreements. The Watergate scandal overshadowed his second term; his complicity in efforts to cover up his involvement and the likelihood of impeachment led to his becoming, in August 1974, the first president to resign from office. Though never convicted of wrongdoing, he was pardoned by his successor, Gerald Ford. He retired to write his memoirs and books on foreign policy.

Gerald Rudolph Ford, Jr. (Leslie Lynch King, Jr.; 14 Jul 1913, Omaha NE), 38th president of the US (1974–77). He was an infant when his parents divorced, and his mother later married Gerald R. Ford. He attended the University of Michigan and Yale law school, and practiced law in Michigan after World War II. He served in the House of Representative 1948–73, becoming minority leader in 1965. After Spiro Agnew resigned as vice president in 1973, Richard Nixon nominated Ford to fill the vacant post. When the Watergate scandal forced Nixon's departure, Ford became the first president who had not been elected to either the vice presidency or the presidency. A month later he pardoned Nixon; to counter widespread outrage, he voluntarily appeared before a House subcommittee to explain his action. His administration gradually lowered the high inflation rate it inherited. Ford's relations with the Democratic-controlled Congress were typified by his more than 50 vetoes, of which more than 40 were sustained. In the final days of the Vietnam War in 1975, he ordered an airlift of 237,000 anti-Communist Vietnamese refugees, most of whom came to the US. Reaction against Watergate contributed to his defeat by James Earl Carter, Jr., in 1976.

James Earl Carter, Jr. (1 Oct 1924, Plains GA), 39th president of the US (1977–81). He graduated from Annapolis and served in the Navy until 1953, when he left to manage the family peanut business. He served in the state senate 1962–66. Elected governor (1971–75), he opened Georgia's government offices to blacks and women and introduced stricter budgeting procedures for state agencies. In 1976, though lacking a national political base or major backing, he won the Democratic nomination and the presidency, defeating the sitting president, Gerald Ford. As president, he helped negotiate a peace treaty between Egypt and Israel, signed a treaty with Panama to make the Panama Canal a neutral zone after 1999, and established full diplomatic relations with China. In 1979–80 the Iran hostage crisis became a major political liability. He responded more forcefully to the Soviet Union's invasion of Afghanistan in 1979, embargoing the shipment of US grain to that country and leading a boycott of the 1980 Summer Olympics in Moscow. Hampered by high inflation and a recession engineered to tame it, he lost his bid for reelection to Ronald Reagan. He subsequently became involved in numerous international diplomatic negotiations and helped oversee elections in countries with insecure democratic traditions.

Ronald Wilson Reagan (6 Feb 1911, Tampico IL), 40th president of the US (1981–89). He attended Eureka College and worked as a radio sports announcer before going to Hollywood in 1937. In his career as a movie actor, he had roles in 50 films and was twice president of the Screen Actors Guild (1947–52, 1959–60). He became a spokesman for the General Electric Co. and hosted its television theater program 1954–62. Having gradually changed his political affiliation from liberal Democrat to conservative Republican, he was elected governor of California and served 1967–74. In 1980

he defeated incumbent Pres. James Earl Carter, Jr., to become president. Shortly after taking office, he was wounded in an assassination attempt. He adopted supply-side economics to promote rapid economic growth and reduce the federal deficit. Congress approved most of his proposals (1981), which succeeded in lowering inflation but doubled the national debt by 1986. He began the largest peacetime military buildup in US history and in 1983 proposed construction of the Strategic Defense Initiative. His foreign policy included the INF Treaty to restrict intermediate-range nuclear weapons and the invasion of Grenada. In 1984 he defeated Walter Mondale in a landslide for reelection. Details of his administration's involvement in the Iran-Contra Affair emerged in 1986 and significantly weakened his popularity and authority. Though his intellectual capacity for governing was often disparaged, his artful communication skills enabled him to pursue numerous conservative policies with conspicuous success. In 1994 he revealed that he had Alzheimer's disease.

George Herbert Walker Bush (12 Jun 1924, Milton MA), 41st president of the US (1989–93). The son of Prescott Bush, later a Connecticut senator, he served in World War II, graduated from Yale University, and started an oil business in Texas. He served in the House of Representatives 1966–70 as a Republican. He then served as ambassador to the UN (1971–72), chief of liaison to China (1974–76), and head of the CIA (1976–77). In 1980 he ran for president but lost the nomination to Ronald Reagan. He served as vice president with Reagan (1981–88), whom he succeeded as president, defeating Michael Dukakis. He made no dramatic departures from Reagan's policies. In 1989 he ordered a brief military invasion of Panama, which toppled that country's leader, General Manuel Noriega. He helped impose a UN-approved embargo against Iraq in 1990 to force its withdrawal from Kuwait. When Iraq refused, he authorized a US-led air offensive that began the Persian Gulf War. Despite general approval of his foreign policy, an economic recession led to his defeat by William Jefferson Clinton in 1992. His son George W. Bush was elected president in 2000.

William Jefferson Clinton (William Jefferson Blythe III; 19 Aug 1946, Hope, AR), 42nd president of the US (1993–2001). He was adopted, after his father's death in a car crash, by his mother's second husband, Roger Clinton. He attended Georgetown University, Oxford University (as a Rhodes Scholar), and Yale law school, then taught at the University of Arkansas law school. He served as state attorney general (1977–79) and served several terms as governor (1979–81, 1983–92), during which he reformed Arkansas's educational system and encouraged the growth of industry through favorable tax policies. He won the Democratic presidential nomination in 1992 after withstanding charges of personal impropriety, and defeated the incumbent, George H.W. Bush. As president, he obtained approval of the North American Free Trade Agreement in 1993. He and his wife, Hillary Rodham Clinton, strongly advocated their plan to overhaul the US healthcare system, but Congress rejected it. He committed US forces to a peacekeeping initiative in Bosnia and Herzegovina. In 1994 the Democrats lost control of Congress for the first time since 1954. He defeated Robert Dole to win reelection in 1996. He faced renewed charges of personal impropriety, this time involving Monica Lewinsky, and as a result, in 1998 he became the second president in history to be impeached. Charged with perjury and obstruction of justice, he was acquitted at his Senate trial in 1999. His two terms saw sustained economic growth and successive budget surpluses, the first in three decades.

George Walker Bush (6 Jul 1946, New Haven CT), 43rd president of the US (from 2001). The eldest child of Pres. George H.W. Bush, he attended Yale University and Harvard Business School. After spending a decade in the oil business with mixed success, he served as managing general partner of the Texas Rangers baseball franchise. In 1994 he

was elected governor of Texas (1995–2000). Popular for his genial style and his support of education reform, he was reelected by a landslide in 1998. In 1999 he launched his presidential campaign and quickly raised the largest presidential war chest in history. Despite losing the national popular vote to Al Gore by more than 500,000 votes, he gained the presidency when a Supreme Court ruling effectively ended a statewide recount of ballots in Florida, whose 25 electoral votes were needed by both candidates to secure a narrow majority in the electoral college. His response to the terrorist attacks on 11 Sep 2001, which included military retaliation in Afghanistan, gave shape to his administration.

Presidents' Wives and Children

Maiden names of the presidents' wives appear in small caps.

DATE OF MARRIAGE	PRESIDENT AND SPOUSE(S)	CHILDREN
	George Washington	
6 Jan 1759	Martha DANDRIDGE Custis (2 Jun 1731–22 May 1802)	none
	John Adams	
25 Oct 1764	Abigail SMITH (22 Nov 1744–28 Oct 1818)	Abigail Amelia Adams (1765–1813)
		John Quincy Adams (1767–1848)
		Susanna Adams (1768–70)
		Charles Adams (1770–1800)
		Thomas Boylston Adams (1772–1832)
	Thomas Jefferson	
1 Jan 1772	Martha WAYLES Skelton (30 Oct 1748–6 Sep 1782)	Martha Washington Jefferson (1772–1836)
		Jane Randolph Jefferson (1774–75)
		Infant son (1777–77)
		Mary Jefferson (1778–1804)
		Lucy Elizabeth Jefferson (1780–81)
		Lucy Elizabeth Jefferson (1782–85)
	James Madison	
15 Sep 1794	Dolley Dandridge PAYNE Todd (20 May 1768–12 Jul 1849)	none
	James Monroe	
16 Feb 1786	Elizabeth KORTRIGHT (30 Jun 1768–23 Sep 1830)	Eliza Kortright Monroe (1786–1835?)
		James Spence Monroe (1799–1800)
		Maria Hester Monroe (1803–50)
	John Quincy Adams	
26 Jul 1797	Louisa Catherine JOHNSON (12 Feb 1775–15 May 1852)	George Washington Adams (1801–29)
		John Adams (1803–34)
		Charles Francis Adams (1807–86)
		Louisa Catherine Adams (1811–12)
	Andrew Jackson	
Aug 1791	Rachel DONELSON Robards (15? Jun 1767–22 Dec 1828)	none
	Martin Van Buren	
21 Feb 1807	Hannah HOES (8 Mar 1783–5 Feb 1819)	Abraham Van Buren (1807–73)
		John Van Buren (1810–66)
		Martin Van Buren (1812–55)
		Smith Thompson Van Buren (1817–76)
	William Henry Harrison	
25 Nov 1795	Anna Tuthill SYMMES (25 Jul 1775–25 Feb 1864)	Elizabeth Bassett Harrison (1796–1846)
		John Cleves Symmes Harrison (1798–1830)
		Lucy Singleton Harrison (1800–26)
		William Henry Harrison (1802–38)
		John Scott Harrison (1804–78)
		Benjamin Harrison (1806–40)
		Mary Symmes Harrison (1809–42)
		Carter Bassett Harrison (1811–39)
		Anna Tuthill Harrison (1813–65)
		James Findlay Harrison (1814–17)

Presidents' Wives and Children (continued)

DATE OF MARRIAGE	PRESIDENT AND SPOUSE(S)	CHILDREN
	John Tyler	
29 Mar 1813	Letitia CHRISTIAN (12 Nov 1790–10 Sep 1842)	Mary Tyler (1815–48) Robert Tyler (1816–77) John Tyler (1819–96) Letitia Tyler (1821–1907) Anne Contesse Tyler (1825–25) Alice Tyler (1827–54) Tazewell Tyler (1830–74)
26 Jun 1844	Julia GARDINER (4 May 1820–10 Jul 1889)	David Gardiner Tyler (1846–1927) John Alexander Tyler (1848–83) Julia Gardiner Tyler (1849?–71) Lachlan Tyler (1851–1902) Lyon Gardiner Tyler (1853–1935) Robert Fitzwalter Tyler (1856–1927) Pearl Tyler (1860–1947)
	James K. Polk	
1 Jan 1824	Sarah CHILDRESS (4 Sep 1803–14 Aug 1891)	none
	Zachary Taylor	
21 Jun 1810	Margaret Mackall SMITH (21 Sep 1788–14 Aug 1852)	Anne Margaret Mackall Taylor (1811–75) Sarah Knox Taylor (1814–35) Octavia Pannel Taylor (1816–20) Margaret Smith Taylor (1819–20) Mary Elizabeth Taylor (1824–1909) Richard Taylor (1826–79)
	Millard Fillmore	
5 Feb 1826	Abigail POWERS (13 Mar 1798–30 Mar 1853)	Millard Powers Fillmore (1828–89) Mary Abigail Fillmore (1832–54)
10 Feb 1858	Caroline CARMICHAEL McIntosh (21 Oct 1813–11 Aug 1881)	none
	Franklin Pierce	
10 Nov 1834	Jane Means APPLETON (12 Mar 1806–2 Dec 1863)	Franklin Pierce (1836–36) Frank Robert Pierce (1839–43) Benjamin Pierce (1841–53)
	James Buchanan never married	
	Abraham Lincoln	
4 Nov 1842	Mary Ann TODD (13 Dec 1818–16 Jul 1882)	Robert Todd Lincoln (1843–1926) Edward Baker Lincoln (1846–50) William Wallace Lincoln (1850–62) Thomas Lincoln (1853–71)
	Andrew Johnson	
17 May 1827	Eliza McCARDLE (4 Oct 1810–15 Jan 1876)	Martha Johnson (1828–1901) Charles Johnson (1830–63) Mary Johnson (1832–83) Robert Johnson (1834–69) Andrew Johnson (1852–79)
	Ulysses S. Grant	
22 Aug 1848	Julia Boggs DENT (26 Jan 1826–14 Dec 1902)	Frederick Dent Grant (1850–1912) Ulysses Simpson Grant (1852–1929) Ellen Wrenshall Grant (1855–1922) Jesse Root Grant (1858–1934)
	Rutherford B. Hayes	
30 Dec 1852	Lucy Ware WEBB (28 Aug 1831–25 Jun 1889)	Birchard Austin Hayes (1853–1926) James Webb Cook Hayes (1856–1934) Rutherford Platt Hayes (1858–1927) Joseph Thompson Hayes (1861–63) George Crook Hayes (1864–66) Fanny Hayes (1867–1950) Scott Russell Hayes (1871–1923) Manning Force Hayes (1873–74)
	James A. Garfield	
11 Nov 1858	Lucretia RUDOLPH (19 Apr 1832–13 Mar 1918)	Eliza Arabella Garfield (1860–63) Harry Augustus Garfield (1863–1942)

Presidents' Wives and Children (continued)

DATE OF MARRIAGE	PRESIDENT AND SPOUSE(S)	CHILDREN
		James Rudolph Garfield (1865–1950)
		Mary Garfield (1867–1947)
		Irvin McDowell Garfield (1870–1951)
		Abram Garfield (1872–1958)
		Edward Garfield (1874–76)
	Chester A. Arthur	
25 Oct 1859	Ellen Lewis HERNDON (30 Aug 1837–12 Jan 1880)	William Lewis Herndon Arthur (1860–63)
		Chester Alan Arthur (1864–1937)
		Ellen Herndon Arthur (1871–1915)
	Grover Cleveland	
2 Jun 1886	Frances FOLSOM (21 Jul 1864–29 Oct 1947)	Ruth Cleveland (1891–1904)
		Esther Cleveland (1893–1980)
		Marion Cleveland (1895–1977)
		Richard Folsom Cleveland (1897–1974)
		Francis Grover Cleveland (1903–95)
	Benjamin Harrison	
20 Oct 1853	Caroline Lavinia SCOTT (1 Oct 1832–25 Oct 1892)	Russell Benjamin Harrison (1854–1936)
		Mary Scott Harrison (1858–1930)
6 Apr 1896	Mary Scott LORD Dimmick (30 Apr 1858–5 Jan 1948)	Elizabeth Harrison (1897–1955)
	William McKinley	
25 Jan 1871	Ida SAXTON (8 Jun 1847–26 May 1907)	Katherine McKinley (1871–75)
		Ida McKinley (1873–73)
	Theodore Roosevelt	
27 Oct 1880	Alice Hathaway LEE (29 Jul 1861–14 Feb 1884)	Alice Lee Roosevelt (1884–1980)
2 Dec 1886	Edith Kermit CAROW (6 Aug 1861–30 Sep 1948)	Theodore Roosevelt (1887–1944)
		Kermit Roosevelt (1889–1943)
		Ethel Carow Roosevelt (1891–1977)
		Archibald Bulloch Roosevelt (1894–1979)
		Quentin Roosevelt (1897–1918)
	William Howard Taft	
19 Jun 1886	Helen HERRON (2 Jun 1861–22 May 1943)	Robert Alphonso Taft (1889–1953)
		Helen Herron Taft (1891–1987)
		Charles Phelps Taft (1897–1983)
	Woodrow Wilson	
24 Jun 1885	Ellen Louise AXSON (15 May 1860–6 Aug 1914)	Margaret Woodrow Wilson (1886–1944)
		Jessie Woodrow Wilson (1887–1933)
		Eleanor Randolph Wilson (1889–1967)
18 Dec 1915	Edith BOLLING Galt (15 Oct 1872–28 Dec 1961)	none
	Warren G. Harding	
8 Jul 1891	Florence Mabel KLING De Wolf (15 Aug 1860–21 Nov 1924)	none
	Calvin Coolidge	
4 Oct 1905	Grace Anna GOODHUE (3 Jan 1879–8 Jul 1957)	John Coolidge (1906–2000)
		Calvin Coolidge (1908–24)
	Herbert Hoover	
10 Feb 1899	Lou HENRY (29 Mar 1874–7 Jan 1944)	Herbert Clark Hoover (1903–69)
		Allan Henry Hoover (1907–93)
	Franklin D. Roosevelt	
17 Mar 1905	(Anna) Eleanor ROOSEVELT (11 Oct 1884–7 Nov 1962)	Anna Eleanor Roosevelt (1906–75)
		James Roosevelt (1907–91)
		Franklin Roosevelt (1909–09)
		Elliott Roosevelt (1910–90)
		Franklin Delano Roosevelt (1914–88)
		John Aspinwall Roosevelt (1916–81)
	Harry S. Truman	
28 Jun 1919	Elizabeth Virginia (Bess) WALLACE (13 Feb 1885–18 Oct 1982)	Margaret (Mary) Truman (1924–)

Presidents' Wives and Children (continued)

DATE OF MARRIAGE	PRESIDENT AND SPOUSE(S)	CHILDREN
	Dwight D. Eisenhower	
1 Jul 1916	Marie (Mamie) Geneva Doud (14 Nov 1896–1 Nov 1979)	Doud Dwight Eisenhower (1917–21) John Sheldon Doud Eisenhower (1922–)
	John F. Kennedy	
12 Sep 1953	Jacqueline Lee Bouvier (28 Jul 1929–19 May 1994)	Caroline Bouvier Kennedy (1957–) John Fitzgerald Kennedy (1960–99) Patrick Bouvier Kennedy (1963–63)
	Lyndon B. Johnson	
17 Nov 1934	Claudia Alta (Lady Bird) Taylor (22 Dec 1912–)	Lynda Bird Johnson (1944–) Luci Baines Johnson (1947–)
	Richard M. Nixon	
21 Jun 1940	Thelma Catherine (Patricia) Ryan (16 Mar 1912–22 Jun 1993)	Patricia Nixon (1946–) Julie Nixon (1948–)
	Gerald R. Ford	
15 Oct 1948	Elizabeth Ann (Betty) Bloomer Warren (8 Apr 1918–)	Michael Gerald Ford (1950–) John Gardner Ford (1952–) Steven Meigs Ford (1956–) Susan Elizabeth Ford (1957–)
	Jimmy Carter	
7 Jul 1946	(Eleanor) Rosalynn Smith (18 Aug 1927–)	John William Carter (1947–) James Earl Carter (1950–) Donnel Jeffrey Carter (1952–) Amy Lynn Carter (1967–)
	Ronald Reagan	
24 Jan 1940	Jane Wyman (née Sarah Jane Fulks) (4 Jan 1914–)	Maureen Elizabeth Reagan (1941–2001) Michael Edward Reagan (1945–)
4 Mar 1952	Nancy Davis (née Anne Frances Robbins) (6 Jul 1921–)	Patricia Ann Reagan (1952–) Ronald Prescott Reagan (1958–)
	George H.W. Bush	
6 Jan 1945	Barbara Pierce (8 Jun 1925–)	George Walker Bush (1946–) Robin Bush (1949–53) John Ellis (Jeb) Bush (1953–) Neil Mallon Bush (1955–) Marvin Pierce Bush (1956–) Dorothy Walker Bush (1959–)
	William J. Clinton	
11 Oct 1975	Hillary Diane Rodham (26 Oct 1947–)	Chelsea Clinton (1980–)
	George W. Bush	
5 Nov 1977	Laura Lane Welch (4 Nov 1946–)	Barbara Bush (1981–) Jenna Bush (1981–)

Presidential Succession

The president is the chief executive of the US. In contrast to the parliamentary form of government, under which the head of state is mainly ceremonial, the presidential system, such as that in the US, vests the president with great authority. The role of the president—including the process of presidential succession—is outlined in Article II of the Constitution of 1787, the fundamental law of the US federal system of government. Presidential nomination procedures are often recognized as constitutional elements, though they are outside the letter of the Constitution.

The Presidential Succession Act of 1792 established the stages of succession: from the president to the vice president, then to the Senate president pro tempore and next to the speaker of the House of Representatives. In 1886 new legislation removed the latter two from succession, replacing them with cabinet officers. The pattern of presidential succession was again changed in 1947, when the the speaker of the House was placed next in line after the vice president, followed by the Senate president pro tempore, the secretary of state, and finally, the remaining cabinet officers in the order that their departments were first formed.

History

The administration of the first president, George Washington, set the customary precedent of serving only two terms, a tradition maintained until Pres. Franklin D. Roosevelt was elected to a third and fourth term in the 1940s. Congress adopted the 22nd Amendment in 1951, which limits presidents to two terms in office.

In 1841 William Henry Harrison became the first president to die in office and was succeeded by his vice president, John Tyler. In 1850, when Zachary Taylor died after only 16 months in office, he was succeeded by Millard Fillmore. In the same manner, vice president Andrew Johnson assumed the presidency after Pres. Abraham Lincoln's assassination.

When Pres. James Garfield was shot on 2 Jul 1881, he became incapacitated, raising serious constitutional questions over who should perform the functions of the presidency. For 80 days the president lay ill, and it was generally agreed that, in such cases, the vice president (Chester Arthur) was empowered by the Constitution to assume the powers and duties of the office of president. But should Arthur serve merely as acting president until Garfield recovered, or would he receive the office itself and thus displace his predecessor? Because of an ambiguity in the Constitution, opinion was divided, and, because Congress was not in session, the problem could not be debated there. No further action was taken before the death of the president, the result of slow blood poisoning, on 19 Sep. This ambiguity over succession was later clarified by the 20th (1933) and 25th (1967) Amendments. Other vice presidents who succeeded upon the death of presidents included Theodore Roosevelt in 1901; Calvin Coolidge in 1923; Harry S. Truman in 1945; and Lyndon B. Johnson in 1963.

In the 2000 presidential election, Republican George W. Bush lost the popular vote but narrowly defeated Democratic Vice President Al Gore after a divided Supreme Court intervened to halt the manual recounting of disputed ballots in Florida, thereby giving Bush enough electoral votes to capture the presidency.

US Vice Presidents

	NAME	DATES OF BIRTH/DEATH	BIRTHPLACE	TIME IN OFFICE	PRESIDENT
1	John Adams	30 Oct 1735–4 Jul 1826	Braintree (now Quincy) MA	1789–97	George Washington
2	Thomas Jefferson	13 Apr 1743–4 Jul 1826	Shadwell VA	1797–1801	John Adams
3	Aaron Burr	6 Feb 1756–14 Sep 1836	Newark NJ	1801–05	Thomas Jefferson
4	George Clinton*	26 Jul 1739–20 Apr 1812	Little Britain NY	1805–09 1809–12	Thomas Jefferson James Madison
5	Elbridge Gerry	17 Jul 1744–23 Nov 1814	Marblehead MA	1813–14	James Madison
6	Daniel D. Tompkins	21 Jun 1774–11 Jun 1825	Scarsdale NY	1817–25	James Monroe
7	John C. Calhoun**	18 Mar 1782–31 Mar 1850	Abbeville district SC	1825–29 1829–32	John Quincy Adams Andrew Jackson
8	Martin Van Buren	5 Dec 1782–24 Jul 1862	Kinderhook NY	1833–37	Andrew Jackson
9	Richard M. Johnson	17 Oct 1781–19 Nov 1850	Beargrass VA (now Louisville KY)	1837–41	Martin Van Buren
10	John Tyler	29 Mar 1790–18 Jan 1862	Charles City county VA	1841	William Henry Harrison*
11	George Mifflin Dallas	10 Jul 1792–31 Dec 1864	Philadelphia PA	1845–49	James K. Polk
12	Millard Fillmore	7 Jan 1800–8 Mar 1874	Locke township NY	1849–50	Zachary Taylor*
13	William Rufus de Vane King*	7 Apr 1786–18 Apr 1853	Sampson county NC	4 Mar– 18 Apr 1853	Franklin Pierce
14	John C. Breckinridge	21 Jan 1821–17 May 1875	near Lexington KY	1857–61	James Buchanan
15	Hannibal Hamlin	27 Aug 1809–4 Jul 1891	Paris Hill ME	1861–65	Abraham Lincoln*
16	Andrew Johnson	29 Dec 1808–31 Jul 1875	Raleigh NC	1865	
17	Schuyler Colfax	23 Mar 1823–13 Jan 1885	New York NY	1869–73	Ulysses S. Grant
18	Henry Wilson*	16 Feb 1812–22 Nov 1875	Farmington NH	1873–75	Ulysses S. Grant
19	William A. Wheeler	30 Jun 1819–4 Jun 1887	Malone NY	1877–81	Rutherford B. Hayes
20	Chester A. Arthur	5 Oct 1829–18 Nov 1886	North Fairfield VT	1881	James A. Garfield*
21	Thomas A. Hendricks*	7 Sep 1819–25 Nov 1885	Zanesville OH	4 Mar– 25 Nov 1885	Grover Cleveland
22	Levi Parsons Morton	16 May 1824–16 May 1920	Shoreham VT	1889–93	Benjamin Harrison
23	Adlai E. Stevenson	23 Oct 1835–14 Jun 1914	Christian county KY	1893–97	Grover Cleveland
24	Garret A. Hobart*	3 Jun 1844–21 Nov 1899	Long Branch NJ	1897–99	William McKinley*
25	Theodore Roosevelt	27 Oct 1858–6 Jan 1919	New York NY	1901	William McKinley*
26	Charles Warren Fairbanks	11 May 1852–4 Jun 1918	Union county OH	1905–09	Theodore Roosevelt
27	James Schoolcraft Sherman*	24 Oct 1855–30 Oct 1912	Utica NY	1909–12	William Howard Taft
28	Thomas R. Marshall	14 Mar 1854–1 Jun 1925	North Manchester IN	1913–21	Woodrow Wilson
29	Calvin Coolidge	4 Jul 1872–5 Jan 1933	Plymouth VT	1921–23	Warren G. Harding*
30	Charles G. Dawes	27 Aug 1865–23 Apr 1851	Marietta OH	1925–29	Calvin Coolidge
31	Charles Curtis	25 Jan 1860–8 Feb 1936	Kansas Territory	1929–33	Herbert Hoover

US Vice Presidents (continued)

NAME	DATES OF BIRTH/DEATH	BIRTHPLACE	TIME IN OFFICE	PRESIDENT
32 John Nance Garner	22 Nov 1868–7 Nov 1967	Red River county TX	1933–41	Franklin D. Roosevelt*
33 Henry A. Wallace	7 Oct 1888–18 Nov 1965	Adair county IA	1941–45	Franklin D. Roosevelt*
34 Harry S. Truman	8 May 1884–26 Dec 1972	Lamar MO	1945	Franklin D. Roosevelt*
35 Alben W. Barkley	24 Nov 1877–30 Apr 1956	Graves county KY	1949–53	Harry S. Truman
36 Richard M. Nixon	9 Jan 1913–22 Apr 1994	Yorba Linda CA	1953–61	Dwight D. Eisenhower
37 Lyndon B. Johnson	27 Aug 1908–22 Jan 1973	Gillespie county TX	1961–63	John F. Kennedy*
38 Hubert H. Humphrey	27 May 1911–13 Jan 1978	Wallace SD	1965–69	Lyndon B. Johnson
39 Spiro T. Agnew**	9 Nov 1918–17 Sep 1996	Baltimore MD	1969–73	Richard M. Nixon**
40 Gerald R. Ford	14 Jul 1913	Omaha NE	1973–74	Richard M. Nixon**
41 Nelson A. Rockefeller	8 Jul 1908–26 Jan 1979	Bar Harbor ME	1974–77	Gerald R. Ford
42 Walter F. Mondale	5 Jan 1928	Ceylon MN	1977–81	Jimmy Carter
43 George H.W. Bush	12 Jun 1924	Milton MA	1981–89	Ronald Reagan
44 Dan Quayle	4 Feb 1947	Indianapolis IN	1989–93	George H.W. Bush
45 Albert Gore	31 Mar 1948	Washington, D.C.	1993–2001	William J. Clinton
46 Richard B. Cheney	30 Jan 1941	Lincoln NE	2001–	George W. Bush

*Died in office
**Resigned from office

US Presidential Cabinets

The cabinet is composed of the heads of executive departments chosen by the president with the consent of the Senate. Cabinet officials do not hold seats in Congress and are not regulated by the US Constitution, which makes no mention of such a body. The existence of the cabinet is a matter of custom dating back to George Washington, who consulted regularly with his department heads as a group. Original dates of service given for officials appointed midterm and for newly created posts. Ad interim officials not named. Presidencies and new positions indicated in bold.

George Washington

TERM 1 (4 MAR 1789–3 MARCH 1793)

State	Thomas Jefferson
Treasury	Alexander Hamilton
War	Henry Knox
Attorney General	Edmund Randolph

TERM 2 (4 MAR 1793–3 MAR 1797)

State	Thomas Jefferson; Edmund Randolph (2 Jan 1794); Timothy Pickering (20 Aug 1795)
Treasury	Alexander Hamilton; Oliver Wolcott, Jr. (2 Feb 1795)
War	Henry Knox; Timothy Pickering (2 Jan 1795); James McHenry (6 Feb 1796)
Attorney General	Edmund Randolph; William Bradford (29 Jan 1794); Charles Lee (10 Dec 1795)

John Adams

(4 MAR 1797–3 MAR 1801)

State	Timothy Pickering; John Marshall (6 Jun 1800)
Treasury	Oliver Wolcott, Jr.; Samuel Dexter (1 Jan 1801)
War	James McHenry; Samuel Dexter (12 Jun 1800)
Navy	Benjamin Stoddert (18 Jun 1798)
Attorney General	Charles Lee

Thomas Jefferson

TERM 1 (4 MAR 1801–3 MAR 1805)

State	James Madison
Treasury	Samuel Dexter; Albert Gallatin (14 May 1801)
War	Henry Dearborn
Navy	Benjamin Stoddert; Robert Smith (27 Jul 1801)
Attorney General	Levi Lincoln

US Presidential Cabinets (continued)

Thomas Jefferson (continued)

TERM 2 (4 MAR 1805–3 MAR 1809)
State — James Madison
Treasury — Albert Gallatin
War — Henry Dearborn
Navy — Robert Smith
Attorney General — John Breckenridge; Caesar Augustus Rodney (20 Jan 1807)

James Madison

TERM 1 (4 MAR 1809–3 MAR 1813)
State — Robert Smith
Treasury — Albert Gallatin
War — John Smith; William Eustis (8 Apr 1809); John Armstrong (5 Feb 1813)
Navy — Robert Smith; Paul Hamilton (15 May 1809); William Jones (19 Jan 1813)
Attorney General — Caesar Augustus Rodney; William Pinkney (6 Jan 1812)

TERM 2 (4 MAR 1813–3 MAR 1817)
State — James Monroe
Treasury — Albert Gallatin; George Washington Campbell (9 Feb 1814); Alexander James Dallas (14 Oct 1814); William Harris Crawford (22 Oct 1816)
War — John Armstrong; James Monroe (1 Oct 1814); William Harris Crawford (8 Aug 1815)
Navy — William Jones; Benjamin Williams Crowninshield (16 Jan 1815)
Attorney General — William Pinkney; Richard Rush (11 Feb 1814)

James Monroe

TERM 1 (4 MAR 1817–3 MAR 1821)
State — John Quincy Adams
Treasury — William Harris Crawford
War — John C. Calhoun
Navy — Benjamin Williams Crowninshield; Smith Thompson (1 Jan 1819)
Attorney General — Richard Rush; William Wirt (15 Nov 1817)

TERM 2 (4 MAR 1821–3 MAR 1825)
State — John Quincy Adams
Treasury — William Harris Crawford
War — John C. Calhoun
Navy — Smith Thompson; Samuel Lewis Southard (16 Sep 1823)
Attorney General — William Wirt

John Quincy Adams

(4 MAR 1825–3 MAR 1829)
State — Henry Clay
Treasury — Richard Rush
War — James Barbour; Peter Buell Porter (21 Jun 1828)
Navy — Samuel Lewis Southard
Attorney General — William Wirt

Andrew Jackson

TERM 1 (4 MAR 1829–3 MAR 1833)
State — Martin Van Buren; Edward Livingston (24 May 1831)
Treasury — Samuel Delucenna Ingham; Louis McLane (8 Aug 1831)
War — John Henry Eaton; Lewis Cass (8 Aug 1831)
Navy — John Branch; Levi Woodbury (23 May 1831)
Attorney General — John Macpherson Berrien; Roger Brooke Taney (20 Jul 1831)

TERM 2 (4 MAR 1833–3 MAR 1837)
State — Edward Livingston; Louis McLane (29 May 1833); John Forsyth (1 Jul 1834)
Treasury — Louis McLane; William John Duane (1 Jun 1833); Roger Brooke Taney (23 Sep 1833); Levi Woodbury (1 Jul 1834)
War — Lewis Cass
Navy — Levi Woodbury; Mahlon Dickerson (30 Jun 1834)
Attorney General — Roger Brooke Taney; Benjamin Franklin Butler (18 Nov 1833)

US Presidential Cabinets (continued)

Martin Van Buren

(4 MAR 1837–3 MAR 1841)

State	John Forsyth
Treasury	Levi Woodbury
War	Joel Roberts Poinsett
Navy	Mahlon Dickerson; James Kirke Paulding (1 Jul 1838)
Attorney General	Benjamin Franklin Butler; Felix Grundy (1 Sep 1838); Henry Dilworth Gilpin (11 Jan 1840)

William Henry Harrison

(4 MAR 1841–4 APR 1841)

State	Daniel Webster
Treasury	Thomas Ewing
War	John Bell
Navy	George Edmund Badger
Attorney General	John Jordan Crittenden

John Tyler

(6 APR 1841–3 MAR 1845)

State	Daniel Webster; Abel Parker Upshur (24 Jul 1843); John C. Calhoun (1 Apr 1844)
Treasury	Thomas Ewing; Walter Forward (13 Sep 1841); John Canfield Spencer (8 Mar 1843); George Mortimer Bibb (4 Jul 1844)
War	John Bell; John Canfield Spencer (12 Oct 1841); James Madison Porter (8 Mar 1843); William Wilkins (20 Feb 1844)
Navy	George Edmund Badger; Abel Parker Upshur (11 Oct 1841); David Henshaw (24 Jul 1843); Thomas Walker Gilmer (19 Feb 1844); John Young Mason (26 Mar 1844)
Attorney General	John Jordan Crittenden; Hugh Swinton Legaré (20 Sep 1841); John Nelson (1 Jul 1843)

James K. Polk

(4 MAR 1845–3 MAR 1849)

State	James Buchanan
Treasury	Robert James Walker
War	William Learned Marcy
Navy	George Bancroft; John Young Mason (9 Sep 1846)
Attorney General	John Young Mason; Nathan Clifford (17 Oct 1846); Isaac Toucey (29 Jun 1848)

Zachary Taylor

(4 MAR 1849–9 JUL 1850)

State	John Middleton Clayton
Treasury	William Morris Meredith
War	George Washington Crawford
Navy	William Ballard Preston
Attorney General	Reverdy Johnson
Interior	Thomas Ewing (8 Mar 1849)

Millard Fillmore

(10 JUL 1850–3 MAR 1853)

State	Daniel Webster; Edward Everett (6 Nov 1852)
Treasury	Thomas Corwin
War	George Washington Crawford; Charles Magill Conrad (15 Aug 1850)
Navy	William Alexander Graham; John Pendleton Kennedy (26 Jul 1852)
Attorney General	Reverdy Johnson; John Jordan Crittenden (14 Aug 1850)
Interior	Thomas Ewing; Thomas McKean Thompson McKennan (15 Aug 1850); Alexander Hugh Holmes Stuart (16 Sep 1850)

Franklin Pierce

(4 MAR 1853–3 MAR 1857)

State	William Learned Marcy
Treasury	James Guthrie
War	Jefferson Davis
Navy	James Cochran Dobbin
Attorney General	Caleb Cushing
Interior	Robert McClelland

US Presidential Cabinets (continued)

James Buchanan

(4 MAR 1857–3 MAR 1861)
State	Lewis Cass; Jeremiah Sullivan Black (17 Dec 1860)
Treasury	Howell Cobb; Philip Francis Thomas (12 Dec 1860); John Adams Dix (15 Jan 1861)
War	John Buchanan Floyd
Navy	Isaac Toucey
Attorney General	Jeremiah Sullivan Black; Edwin McMasters Stanton (22 Dec 1860)
Interior	Jacob Thompson

Abraham Lincoln

TERM 1 (4 MAR 1861–3 MAR 1865)
State	William Henry Seward
Treasury	Salmon Portland Chase; William Pitt Fessenden (5 Jul 1864)
War	Simon Cameron; Edwin McMasters Stanton (20 Jun 1862)
Navy	Gideon Welles
Attorney General	Edward Bates; James Speed (5 Dec 1864)
Interior	Caleb Blood Smith; John Palmer Usher (8 Jan 1863)

TERM 2 (4 MAR 1865–15 APR 1865)
State	William Henry Seward
Treasury	Hugh McCulloch
War	Edwin McMasters Stanton
Navy	Gideon Welles
Attorney General	James Speed
Interior	John Palmer Usher

Andrew Johnson

(15 APR 1865–3 MAR 1869)
State	William Henry Seward
Treasury	Hugh McCulloch
War	Edwin McMasters Stanton; John McAllister Schofield (1 Jun 1868)
Navy	Gideon Welles
Attorney General	James Speed; Henry Stanbery (23 Jul 1866); William Maxwell Evarts (20 Jul 1808)
Interior	John Palmer Usher; James Harlan (15 May 1865); Orville Hickman Browning (1 Sep 1866)

Ulysses S. Grant

TERM 1 (4 MAR 1869–3 MAR 1873)
State	Elihu Benjamin Washburne; Hamilton Fish (17 Mar 1869)
Treasury	George Sewall Boutwell
War	John Aaron Rawlins; William Tecumseh Sherman (11 Sep 1869); William Worth Belknap (1 Nov 1869)
Navy	Adolph Edward Borie; George Maxwell Robeson (25 Jun 1869)
Attorney General	Ebenezer Rockwood Hoar; Amos Tappan Akerman (8 Jul 1870); George Henry Williams (10 Jan 1872)
Interior	Jacob Dolson Cox; Columbus Delano (1 Nov 1870)

TERM 2 (4 MAR 1873–3 MAR 1877)
State	Hamilton Fish
Treasury	William Adams Richardson; Benjamin Helm Bristow (4 Jun 1874); Lot Myrick Morrill (7 Jul 1876)
War	William Worth Belknap; Alphonso Taft (11 Mar 1876); James Donald Cameron (1 Jun 1876)
Navy	George Maxwell Robeson
Attorney General	George Henry Williams; Edward Pierrepont (15 May 1875); Alphonso Taft (1 Jun 1876)
Interior	Columbus Delano; Zachariah Chandler (19 Oct 1875)

Rutherford B. Hayes

(4 MAR 1877–3 MAR 1881)
State	William Maxwell Evarts
Treasury	John Sherman
War	George Washington McCrary; Alexander Ramsey (12 Dec 1879)
Navy	Richard Wigginton Thompson; Nathan Goff, Jr. (6 Jan 1881)
Attorney General	Charles Devens
Interior	Carl Schurz

US Presidential Cabinets (continued)

James A. Garfield

(4 MAR 1881–19 SEP 1881)
State	James Gillespie Blaine
Treasury	William Windom
War	Robert Todd Lincoln
Attorney General	Wayne McVeagh
Navy	William Henry Hunt
Interior	Samuel Jordan Kirkwood

Chester A. Arthur

(20 SEP 1881–3 MAR 1885)
State	James Gillespie Blaine; Frederick Theodore Frelinghuysen (19 Dec 1881)
Treasury	William Windom; Charles James Folger (14 Nov 1881); Walter Quintin Gresham (24 Sep 1884); Hugh McCulloch (31 Oct 1884)
War	Robert Todd Lincoln
Navy	William Henry Hunt; William Eaton Chandler (17 Apr 1882)
Attorney General	Wayne MacVeagh; Benjamin Harris Brewster (3 Jan 1882)
Interior	Samuel Jordan Kirkwood; Henry Moore Teller (17 Apr 1882)

Grover Cleveland

(4 MAR 1885–3 MAR 1889)
State	Thomas Francis Bayard
Treasury	Daniel Manning; Charles Stebbins Fairchild (1 Apr 1887)
War	Willliam Crowninshield Endicott
Navy	William Collins Whitney
Attorney General	Augustus Hill Garland
Interior	Lucius Quintus Cincinnatus Lamar; William Freeman Vilas (16 Jan 1888)
Agriculture	Norman Jay Colman (13 Feb 1889)

Benjamin Harrison

(4 MAR 1889–3 MAR 1893)
State	James Gillespie Blaine; John Watson Foster (29 Jun 1892)
Treasury	William Windom; Charles Foster (24 Feb 1891)
War	Redfield Proctor; Stephen Benton Elkins (24 Dec 1891)
Navy	Benjamin Franklin Tracy
Attorney General	William Henry Harrison Miller
Interior	John Willock Noble
Agriculture	Jeremiah McLain Rusk

Grover Cleveland

(4 MAR 1893–3 MAR 1897)
State	Walter Quintin Gresham; Richard Olney (10 Jun 1895)
Treasury	John Griffin Carlisle
War	Daniel Scott Lamont
Navy	Hilary Abner Herbert
Attorney General	Richard Olney; Judson Harmon (11 Jun 1895)
Interior	Hoke Smith; David Rowland Francis (4 Sep 1896)
Agriculture	Julius Sterling Morton

William McKinley

TERM 1 (4 MAR 1897–3 MAR 1901)
State	John Sherman; William Rufus Day (28 Apr 1898); John Hay (30 Sep 1898)
Treasury	Lyman Judson
War	Russell Alexander Alger; Elihu Root (1 Aug 1899)
Navy	John Davis Long
Attorney General	Joseph McKenna; John William Griggs (1 Feb 1898)
Interior	Cornelius Newton Bliss; Ethan Allen Hitchcock (20 Feb 1899)
Agriculture	James Wilson

TERM 2 (4 MAR 1901–14 SEP 1901)
State	John Hay
Treasury	Lyman Judson Gage
War	Elihu Root
Navy	John Davis Long
Attorney General	John William Griggs; Philander Chase Knox (10 Apr 1901)
Interior	Ethan Allen Hitchcock
Agriculture	James Wilson

US Presidential Cabinets (continued)

Theodore Roosevelt

TERM 1 (14 SEP 1901 – 3 MAR 1905)

State	John Hay
Treasury	Lyman Judson Gage; Leslie Mortier Shaw (1 Feb 1902)
War	Elihu Root; William Howard Taft (1 Feb 1904)
Navy	John Davis Long; William Henry Moody (1 May 1902); Paul Morton (1 Jul 1904)
Attorney General	Philander Chase Knox; William Henry Moody (1 Jul 1904)
Interior	Ethan Allen Hitchcock
Agriculture	James Wilson
Commerce and Labor	George Bruce Cortelyou (16 Feb 1903); Victor Howard Metcalf (1 Jul 1904)

TERM 2 (4 MAR 1905–3 MAR 1909)

State	John Hay; Elihu Root (19 Jul 1905); Robert Bacon (27 Jan 1909)
Treasury	Leslie Mortier Shaw; George Bruce Cortelyou (4 Mar 1907)
War	William Howard Taft; Luke Edward Wright (1 Jul 1908)
Navy	Paul Morton; Charles Joseph Bonaparte (1 Jul 1905); Victor Howard Metcalf (17 Dec 1906); Truman Handy Newberry (1 Dec 1908)
Attorney General	William Henry Moody; Charles Joseph Bonaparte (17 Dec 1906)
Interior	Ethan Allen Hitchcock; James Rudolph Garfield (4 Mar 1907)
Agriculture	James Wilson
Commerce and Labor	Victor Howard Metcalf; Oscar Solomon Straus (17 Dec 1906)

William Howard Taft

(4 MAR 1909–3 MAR 1913)

State	Philander Chase Knox
Treasury	Franklin MacVeagh
War	Jacob McGavock Dickinson; Henry Lewis Stimson (22 May 1911)
Navy	George von Lengerke Meyer
Attorney General	George Woodward Wickersham
Interior	Richard Achilles Ballinger; Walter Lowrie Fisher (7 Mar 1911)
Agriculture	James Wilson
Commerce and Labor	Charles Nagel

Woodrow Wilson

TERM 1 (4 MAR 1913–3 MAR 1917)

State	William Jennings Bryan; Robert Lansing (23 Jun 1915)
Treasury	William Gibbs McAdoo
War	Lindley Miller Garrison; Newton Diehl Baker (9 Mar 1916)
Navy	Josephus Daniels
Attorney General	James Clark McReynolds; Thomas Watt Gregory (3 Sep 1914)
Interior	Franklin Knight Lane
Agriculture	David Franklin Houston
Commerce	William Cox Redfield (5 Mar 1913)
Labor	William Bauchop Wilson (5 Mar 1913)

TERM 2 (4 MAR 1917–3 MAR 1921)

State	Robert Lansing; Bainbridge Colby (23 Mar 1920)
Treasury	William Gibbs McAdoo; Carter Glass (16 Dec 1918); David Franklin Houston (2 Feb 1920)
War	Newton Diehl Baker
Navy	Josephus Daniels
Attorney General	Thomas Watt Gregory; Alexander Mitchell Palmer (5 Mar 1919)
Interior	Franklin Knight Lane; John Barton Payne (13 Mar 1920)
Agriculture	David Franklin Houston; Edwin Thomas Meredith (2 Feb 1920)
Commerce	William Cox Redfield; Joshua Willis Alexander (16 Dec 1919)
Labor	William Bauchop Wilson

Warren G. Harding

(4 MAR 1921–2 AUG 1923)

State	Charles Evans Hughes
Treasury	Andrew William Mellon
War	John Wingate Weeks
Navy	Edwin Denby
Attorney General	Harry Micaiah Daugherty

US Presidential Cabinets (continued)

Warren G. Harding (continued)

(4 MAR 1921–2 AUG 1923) (CONTINUED)

Interior	Albert Bacon Fall; Hubert Work (5 Mar 1923)
Agriculture	Henry Cantwell Wallace
Commerce	Herbert Hoover
Labor	James John Davis

Calvin Coolidge

TERM 1 (3 AUG 1923–3 MAR 1925)

State	Charles Evans Hughes
Treasury	Andrew William Mellon
War	John Wingate Weeks
Navy	Edwin Denby; Curtis Dwight Wilbur (18 Mar 1924)
Attorney General	Harry Micajah Daugherty; Harlan Fiske Stone (9 Apr 1924)
Interior	Hubert Work
Agriculture	Henry Cantwell Wallace; Howard Mason Gore (21 Nov 1924)
Commerce	Herbert Hoover
Labor	James John Davis

TERM 2 (4 MAR 1925–3 MAR 1929)

State	Frank Billings Kellogg
Treasury	Andrew William Mellon
War	John Wingate Weeks; Dwight Filley Davis (14 Oct 1925)
Navy	Curtis Dwight Wilbur
Attorney General	John Garibaldi Sargent
Interior	Hubert Work; Roy Owen West (21 Jan 1929)
Agriculture	William Marion Jardine
Commerce	Herbert Hoover; William Fairfield Whiting (11 Dec 1928)
Labor	James John Davis

Herbert Hoover

(4 MAR 1929–3 MAR 1933)

State	Henry Lewis Stimson
Treasury	Andrew William Mellon; Ogden Livingston Mills (13 Feb 1932)
War	James William Good; Patrick Jay Hurley (9 Dec 1929)
Navy	Charles Francis Adams
Attorney General	William De Witt Mitchell
Interior	Ray Lyman Wilbur
Agriculture	Arthur Mastick Hyde
Commerce	Robert Patterson Lamont; Roy Dikeman Chapin (14 Dec 1932)
Labor	James John Davis; William Nuckles Doak (9 Dec 1930)

Franklin D. Roosevelt

TERM 1 (4 MAR 1933–20 JAN 1937)

State	Cordell Hull
Treasury	William Hartman Woodin; Henry Morgenthau, Jr. (8 Jan 1934)
War	George Henry Dern
Navy	Claude Augustus Swnason
Attorney General	Homer Stille Cummings
Interior	Harold Le Claire Ickes
Agriculture	Henry Agard Wallace
Commerce	Daniel Calhoun Roper
Labor	Frances Perkins

TERM 2 (20 JAN 1937–20 JAN 1941)

State	Cordell Hull
Treasury	Henry Morgenthau, Jr.
War	Harry Hines Woodring; Henry Lewis Stimson (10 Jul 1940)
Attorney General	Homer Stille Cummings; Frank Murphy (17 Jan 1939); Robert Houghwout Jackson (18 Jan 1940)
Navy	Claude Augustus Swanson; Charles Edison (11 Jan 1940); Frank Knox (10 Jul 1940)
Interior	Harold Le Claire Ickes
Agriculture	Henry Agard Wallace; Claude Raymond Wickard (5 Sep 1940)
Commerce	Daniel Calhoun Roper; Harry Lloyd Hopkins (23 Jan 1939); Jesse Holman Jones (19 Sep 1940)
Labor	Frances Perkins

US Presidential Cabinets (continued)

Franklin D. Roosevelt (continued)

TERM 3 (20 JAN 1941–20 JAN 1945)

State	Cordell Hull; Edward Reilly Stettinius (1 Dec 1944)
Treasury	Henry Morgenthau, Jr.
War	Henry Lewis Stimson
Navy	Frank Knox; James Vincent Forrestal (18 May 1944)
Attorney General	Robert Houghwout Jackson; Francis Biddle (5 Sep 1941)
Interior	Harold Le Claire Ickes
Agriculture	Claude Raymond Wickard
Commerce	Jesse Holman Jones
Labor	Frances Perkins

TERM 4 (20 JAN 1945–12 APR 1945)

State	Edward Reilly Stettinius
Treasury	Henry Morgenthau, Jr.
War	Henry Lewis Stimson
Navy	James Vincent Forrestal
Attorney General	Francis Biddle
Interior	Harold Le Claire Ickes
Agriculture	Claude Raymond Wickard
Commerce	Jesse Holman Jones; Henry Agard Wallace (2 Mar 1945)
Labor	Frances Perkins

Harry S. Truman

TERM 1 (12 APR 1945–20 JAN 1949)

State	Edward Reilly Stettinius; James Francis Byrnes (3 Jul 1945); George Catlett Marshall (21 Jan 1947)
Treasury	Henry Morgenthau, Jr.; Frederick Moore (23 Jul 1945); John Wesley Snyder (25 Jun 1946)
War	Henry Lewis Stimson; Robert Porter Patterson (27 Sep 1945); Kenneth Clairborne Royall (25 Jul 1947)
Defense	James Vincent Forrestal (17 Sep 1947)
Navy	James Vincent Forrestal
Attorney General	Francis Biddle; Thomas Campbell Clark (1 Jul 1945)
Interior	Harold Le Claire Ickes; Julius Albert Krug (18 Mar 1946)
Agriculture	Claude Raymond Wickard; Clinton Presba Anderson (30 Jun 1945); Charles Franklin Brannan (2 Jun 1948)
Commerce	Henry Agard Wallace; William Averell Harriman (28 Jan 1947); Charles Sawyer (6 May 1948)
Labor	Frances Perkins; Lewis Baxter Schwellenbach (1 Jul 1945)

TERM 2 (20 JAN 1949–20 JAN 1953)

State	Dean Gooderham Acheson
Treasury	John Wesley Snyder
Defense	James Vincent Forrestal; Louis Arthur Johnson (28 Mar 1949); George Catlett Marshall (21 Sep 1950); Robert Abercrombie Lovett (17 Sep 1951)
Attorney General	Thomas Campbell Clark; James Howard McGrath (24 Aug 1949)
Interior	Julius Albert Krug; Oscar Littleton Chapman (19 Jan 1950)
Agriculture	Charles Franklin Brannan
Commerce	Charles Sawyer
Labor	Maurice Joseph Tobin

Dwight D. Eisenhower

TERM 1 (20 JAN 1953–20 JAN 1957)

State	John Foster Dulles
Treasury	George Magoffin Humphrey
Defense	Charles Erwin Wilson
Attorney General	Herbert Brownell
Interior	Douglas McKay; Frederick Andrew Seaton (8 Jun 1956)
Agriculture	Ezra Taft Benson
Commerce	Sinclair Weeks
Labor	Martin Patrick Durkin; James Paul Mitchell (9 Oct 1953)
Health, Education, and Welfare	Oveta Culp Hobby (11 Apr 1953); Marion Bayard Folson (1 Aug 1955)

TERM 2 (20 JAN 1957–20 JAN 1961)

State	John Foster Dulles; Christian Archibald Herter (22 Apr 1959)
Treasury	George Magoffin Humphrey; Robert Bernerd Anderson (29 Jul 1957)

US Presidential Cabinets (continued)

Dwight D. Eisenhower (continued)

TERM 2 (20 JAN 1957–20 JAN 1961) (CONTINUED)

Defense	Charles Erwin Wilson; Neil Hosler McElroy (9 Oct 1957); Thomas Sovereign Gates, Jr. (2 Dec 1959)
Attorney General	Herbert Brownell, Jr.; William Pierce Rogers (27 Jan 1958)
Interior	Frederick Andrew Seaton
Agriculture	Ezra Taft Benson
Commerce	Sinclair Weeks; Frederick Henry Mueller (10 Aug 1959)
Labor	James Paul Mitchell
Health, Education, and Welfare	Marion Bayard Folsom; Arthur Sherwood Flemming (1 Aug 1958)

John F. Kennedy

20 JAN 1961–22 NOV 1963

State	(David) Dean Rusk
Treasury	C. (Clarence) Douglas Dillon
Defense	Robert Strange McNamara
Attorney General	Robert F. Kennedy
Interior	Stewart Lee Udall
Agriculture	Orville Lothrop Freeman
Commerce	Luther Hartwell Hodges
Labor	Arthur Joseph Goldberg; W. (William) Willard Wirtz (25 Sep 1962)
Health, Education, and Welfare	Abraham Alexander Ribicoff; Anthony Joseph Celebrezze (31 Jul 1962)

Lyndon B. Johnson

TERM 1 (22 NOV 1963–20 JAN 1965)

State	(David) Dean Rusk
Treasury	C. (Clarence) Douglas Dillon
Defense	Robert Strange McNamara
Attorney General	Robert F. Kennedy
Interior	Stewart Lee Udall
Agriculture	Orville Lothrop Freeman
Commerce	Luther Hartwell Hodges
Labor	W. (William) Willard Wirtz
Health, Education, and Welfare	Anthony Joseph Celebrezze

TERM 2 (20 JAN 1965–20 JAN 1969)

State	(David) Dean Rusk
Treasury	C. (Clarence) Douglas Dillon; Henry Hamill Fowler (1 Apr 1965); Joseph Walker Barr (23 Dec 1968)
Defense	Robert Strange McNamara; Clark McAdams Clifford (1 Mar 1968)
Attorney General	Nicholas deBelleville Katzenbach; William Ramsey Clark (10 Mar 1967)
Interior	Stewart Lee Udall
Agriculture	Orville Lothrop Freeman
Commerce	John Thomas Connor; Alexander Buel Trowbridge (14 Jun 1967); Cyrus Rowlett Smith (6 Mar 1968)
Labor	W. William Willard Wirtz
Health, Education, and Welfare	Anthony Joseph Celebrezze; John William Gardner (18 Aug 1965); Wilbur Joseph Cohen (9 May 1968)
Housing and Urban Development	Robert Clifton Weaver (18 Jan 1966); Robert Coldwell Wood (7 Jan 1969)
Transportation	Alan Stephenson Boyd (16 Jan 1967)

Richard Nixon

TERM 1 (20 JAN 1969–20 JAN 1973)

State	William Pierce Rogers
Treasury	David Matthew Kennedy; John Bowden Connally, Jr. (11 Feb 1971); George Pratt Shultz (12 Jun 1972)
Defense	Melvin Robert Laird
Attorney General	John Newton Mitchell; Richard Gordon Kleindienst (12 Jun 1972)
Interior	Walter Joseph Hickel; Rogers Clark Ballard Morton (29 Jan 1971)
Agriculture	Clifford Morris Hardin; Earl Lauer Butz (2 Dec 1971)
Commerce	Maurice Hubert Stans; Peter George Peterson (21 Feb 1972)
Labor	George Pratt Shultz; James Day Hodgson (2 Jul 1970)
Health, Education, and Welfare	Robert Hutchinson Finch; Elliot Lee Richardson (24 Jun 1970)
Housing and Urban Development	George Wilcken Romney
Transportation	John Anthony Volpe

TERM 2 (20 JAN 1973–9 AUG 1974)

State	William Pierce Rogers; Henry Alfred Kissinger (22 Sep 1973)
Treasury	George Pratt Shultz; William Edward Simon (8 May 1974)

US Presidential Cabinets (continued)

Richard Nixon (continued)

Defense	Elliot Lee Richardson; James Rodney Schlesinger (2 Jul 1973)
Attorney General	Richard Gordon Kleindienst; Elliot Lee Richardson (25 May 1973); William Bart Saxbe (4 Jan 1974)
Interior	Rogers Clark Ballard Morton
Agriculture	Earl Lauer Butz
Commerce	Frederick Baily Dent
Labor	Peter Joseph Brennan
Health, Education, and Welfare	Caspar Willard Weinberger
Housing and Urban Development	James Thomas Lynn
Transportation	Claude Stout Brinegar

Gerald Ford

(9 AUG 1974-20 JAN 1977)

State	Henry Alfred Kissinger
Treasury	William Edward Simon
Defense	James Rodney Schlesinger; Donald Henry Rumsfeld (20 Nov 1975)
Attorney General	William Bart Saxbe; Edward Hirsch Levi (7 Feb 1975)
Interior	Rogers Clark Ballard Morton, Jr.; Stanley Knapp Hathaway (13 Jun 1975); Thomas Savig Kleppe (17 Oct 1975)
Agriculture	Earl Lauer Butz; John Albert Knebel (4 Nov 1976)
Commerce	Frederick Baily Dent; Rogers Clark Ballard Morton, Jr. (1 May 1975); Elliot Lee Richardson (2 Feb 1976)
Labor	Peter Joseph Brennan; John Thomas Dunlop (18 Mar 1975); Willie Julian Usery, Jr (10 Feb 1976)
Health, Education, and Welfare	Caspar Willard Weinberger; Forrest David Matthews (8 Aug 1975)
Housing and Urban Development	James Thomas Lynn; Carla Anderson Hills (10 Mar 1975)
Transportation	Claude Stout Brinegar; William Thaddeus Coleman, Jr. (7 Mar 1975)

Jimmy Carter

20 JAN 1977-20 JAN 1981

State	Cyrus Vance; Edmund Sixtus Muskie (8 May 1980)
Treasury	Werner Michael Blumenthal; George William Miller (6 Aug 1979)
Defense	Harold Brown
Attorney General	Griffin Boyette Bell; Benjamin Richard Civiletti (16 Aug 1979)
Interior	Cecil Dale Andrus
Agriculture	Robert Selmer Bergland
Commerce	Juanita Morris Kreps; Philip Morris Klutznick (9 Jan 1980)
Labor	Fred Ray Marshall
Health, Education, and Welfare	Joseph Anthony Califano, Jr.; Patricia Roberts Harris (3 Aug 1979)
Health and Human Services	Patricia Roberts Harris (27 Sep 1979)
Housing and Urban Development	Patricia Roberts Harris; Moon Landrieu (24 Sep 1979)
Transportation	Brockman Adams; Neil Edward Goldschmidt (24 Sep 1979)
Energy	James Rodney Schlesinger (1 Oct 1977); Charles William Duncan, Jr. (24 Aug 1979)
Education	Shirley Mount Hufstedler (6 Dec 1979)

Ronald Reagan

TERM 1 (20 JAN 1981-20 JAN 1985)

State	Alexander Meigs Haig, Jr.; George Pratt Shultz (16 Jul 1982)
Treasury	Donald Thomas Regan
Defense	Caspar Willard Weinberger
Attorney General	William French Smith
Interior	James Gaius Watt; William Patrick Clark (21 Nov 1983)
Agriculture	John Rusling Block
Commerce	Malcolm Baldrige
Labor	Raymond Joseph Donovan
Health and Human Services	Richard Schultz Schweiker; Margaret Mary O'Shaughnessy Heckler (9 Mar 1983)
Housing and Urban Development	Samuel Riley Pierce, Jr.
Transportation	Drew (Andrew) Lindsay Lewis, Jr.; Elizabeth Hanford Dole (7 Feb 1983)
Energy	James Burrows Edwards; Donald Paul Hodel (8 Dec 1982)
Education	Terrel Howard Bell

TERM 2 (20 JAN 1985-20 JAN 1989)

State	George Pratt Shultz
Treasury	Donald Thomas Regan; James Addison Baker III (25 Feb 1985); Nicholas Frederick Brady (18 Aug 1988)

US Presidential Cabinets (continued)

Ronald Reagan (continued)

TERM 2 (20 JAN 1985–20 JAN 1989) (CONTINUED)

Defense	Caspar Willard Weinberger; Frank Charles Carlucci III (21 Nov 1987)
Attorney General	Edwin Meese III; Richard Lewis (Dick) Thornburgh (11 Aug 1988)
Interior	Donald Paul Hodel
Agriculture	John Rusling Block; Richard Edmund Lyng (7 Mar 1986)
Commerce	Malcolm Baldrige; Calvin William Verity, Jr. (19 Oct 1987)
Labor	Raymond James Donovan; William Emerson (Bill) Brock III (29 Apr 1985); Ann Dore McLaughlin (17 Dec 1987)
Health and Human Services	Margaret Mary O'Shaughnessy Heckler; Otis Ray Bowen (13 Dec 1985)
Housing and Urban Development	Samuel Riley Pierce, Jr.
Transportation	Elizabeth Hanford Dole; James Horace Burnley IV (3 Dec 1987)
Energy	John Stewart Herrington
Education	Terrel Howard Bell; William John Bennett (7 Feb 1985); Lauro Fred Cavazos, Jr. (20 Sep 1988)
Justice	Edward French Smith; Edwin Meese III (25 Feb 1985); Richard Lewis (Dick) Thornburgh (12 Aug 1988)

George H.W. Bush

(20 JAN 1989–20 JAN 1993)

State	James Addison Baker III
Treasury	Nicholas Frederick Brady
Attorney General	Richard Lewis (Dick) Thornburgh; William P. Barr (20 Nov 1991)
Interior	Manuel Lujan, Jr.
Agriculture	Clayton Keith Yeutter; Edward Madigan (7 Mar 1991)
Commerce	Robert Adam Mosbacher
Labor	Elizabeth Hanford Dole
Defense	Richard (Dick) Cheney
Health and Human Services	Louis Wade Sullivan
Housing and Urban Development	Jack F. Kemp
Transportation	Samuel K. Skinner; Andrew H. Card (22 Jan 1992)
Energy	James David Watkins
Education	Lauro Fred Cavazos, Jr.; Lamar Alexander (14 Mar 1991)
Veterans Affairs	Edward Joseph Derwinski (15 Mar 1989)

William J. Clinton

TERM 1 (20 JAN 1993–20 JAN 1997)

State	Warren M. Christopher
Treasury	Lloyd Bentsen, Jr.; Robert E. Rubin (10 Jan 1995)
Interior	Bruce Babbitt
Agriculture	Mike Espy; Dan Glickman (30 Mar 1995)
Commerce	Ronald H. Brown; Mickey Kantor (12 Apr 1996)
Labor	Robert B. Reich
Defense	Les Aspin; William J. Perry (3 Feb 1994)
Health and Human Services	Donna E. Shalala
Housing and Urban Development	Henry G. Cisneros
Transportation	Federico Peña
Energy	Hazel R. O'Leary
Education	Richard W. Riley
Justice	Janet Reno
Veterans Affairs	Jesse Brown

TERM 2 (20 JAN 1997–20 JAN 2001)

State	Madeleine Albright
Treasury	Robert E. Rubin; Lawrence H. Summers (2 Jul 1999)
Attorney General	Janet Reno
Interior	Bruce Babbitt
Commerce	William M. Daley; Norman Mineta (21 Jul 2000)
Labor	Alexis M. Herman
Defense	William Cohen
Health and Human Services	Donna E. Shalala
Housing and Urban Development	Andrew M. Cuomo
Transportation	Rodney Slater
Energy	Federico Peña; Bill Richardson (18 Aug 1998)
Education	Richard Riley
Veterans Affairs	Togo D. West, Jr.; Hershel W. Gober (25 Jul 2000)

US Presidential Cabinets (continued)

George W. Bush

(20 JAN 2001–)	
State	Colin Powell
Treasury	Paul O'Neill
Attorney General	John Ashcroft
Interior	Gale Norton
Commerce	Don Evans
Labor	Elaine Chao
Defense	Donald Rumsfeld
Health and Human Services	Tommy Thompson
Housing and Urban Development	Mel Martinez
Transportation	Norman Mineta
Energy	Spencer Abraham
Education	Rod Paige
Veterans Affairs	Anthony Principi

Did you know? The first woman to hold a cabinet post was Frances Perkins, who in 1933 became Secretary of Labor under President Franklin D. Roosevelt.

Presidential Libraries

The presidential libraries serve as repositories for the papers, records, and materials of the US presidents since Herbert Hoover. Each of the 10 libraries contains a museum and conducts public programs. The network is administered by the the Office of Presi-

dential Libraries, which is itself a division of the US National Archives and Records Administration (NARA). The system also includes the Nixon Presidential Materials Staff and the William J. Clinton Presidential Materials Project.

NAME, ADDRESS, & CONTACT INFORMATION
Herbert Hoover Library
210 Parkside Drive
P.O. Box 488
West Branch IA 52358-0488
Web site: <hoover.nara.gov>

Franklin D. Roosevelt Library
4079 Albany Post Road
Hyde Park NY 12538-1999
Web site: <www.fdrlibrary.marist.edu>

Harry S. Truman Library
500 West US Highway 24
Independence MO 64050-1798
Web site: <www.trumanlibrary.org>

Dwight D. Eisenhower Library
200 SE 4th Street
Abilene KS 67410-2900
Web site: <www.eisenhower.utexas.edu>

John F. Kennedy Library
Columbia Point
Boston MA 02125-3398
Web site: <www.jfklibrary.org>

Lyndon B. Johnson Library
2313 Red River Street
Austin TX 78705-5702
Web site: <www.lbjlib.utexas.edu>

Richard Nixon Library and Birthplace
18001 Yorba Linda Boulevard
Yorba Linda CA 92886-3949
Web site: <www.nixonlibrary.org>

NAME, ADDRESS, & CONTACT INFORMATION
Nixon Presidential Materials Staff
National Archives at College Park
8601 Adelphi Road
College Park MD 20740-6001
Web site: <www.nara.gov/nixon>

Gerald R. Ford Library
1000 Beal Avenue
Ann Arbor MI 48109-2114
Web site: <www.ford.utexas.edu>

Jimmy Carter Library
441 Freedom Parkway
Atlanta GA 30307-1498
Web site: <www.jimmycarterlibrary.org>

Ronald Reagan Library
40 Presidential Drive
Simi Valley CA 93065-0600
Web site: <www.reagan.utexas.edu>

George Bush Library
1000 George Bush Drive West
College Station TX 77845
Web site: <bushlibrary.tamu.edu>

William J. Clinton Presidential Materials Project
1000 LaHarpe Boulevard
Little Rock AR 72201
Web site: <www.clinton.nara.gov>

Office of Presidential Libraries
National Archives at College Park
8601 Adelphi Road
College Park MD 20740-6001
Web site: <www.nara.gov>

Impeachment

The American federal impeachment process is rooted in Art. II sec. 4 of the US Constitution. Impeachment has rarely been employed, largely because it is such a cumbersome process. It can occupy Congress for a lengthy period of time, fill thousands of pages of testimony, and involve conflicting and troublesome political pressures. Repeated attempts in the US Congress to amend the procedure, however, have been unsuccessful, partly because impeachment is regarded as an integral part of the system of checks and balances in the US government.

Andrew Johnson was the first US president ever impeached. In 1868 he was charged with attempting to remove, contrary to statute, the secretary of war, Edwin M. Stanton, with inducing a general of the army to violate an act of Congress, and with contempt of Congress. Johnson was acquitted by a margin of a single vote. In 1974 the Judiciary Committee of the House of Representatives voted three articles of impeachment against Pres. Richard M. Nixon, but he resigned before impeachment proceedings in the full House could begin. In December 1998 the House of Representatives voted to impeach Pres. William J. Clinton, charging him with perjury and obstruction of justice in investigations of his relationship with a White House intern, Monica Lewinsky. In the trial, the Senate voted not guilty on the perjury charge (55–45) and not guilty on the obstruction of justice charge (50–50); since 67 guilty votes are needed for a conviction, President Clinton was acquitted.

Every US state except Oregon provides for the removal of executive and judicial officers by impeachment. Exact procedures vary somewhat from state to state, but they are all similar to federal impeachment.

Executive Departments

Department of Agriculture
Secretary: Ann M. Veneman
Deputy secretary: Jim Moseley
Web site: <www.usda.gov>
Mission: To enhance the quality of life for the American people by supporting production of agriculture.
Divisions and agencies:
Farm and Foreign Agricultural Service
  Farm Service Agency
  Foreign Agricultural Service
  Risk Management Agency
Food Safety
  Food Safety and Inspection Service
Natural Resources and Environment
  Forest Service
  Natural Resources Conservation Service
Rural Development
  Rural Business–Cooperative Service
  Office of Community Development
  Rural Housing Service
  Rural Utilities Service
Food, Nutrition, and Consumer Services
  Food and Nutrition Service
  Center for Nutrition Policy and Promotion
Marketing and Regulatory Programs
  Agricultural Marketing Service
  Animal and Plant Health Inspection Service
  Grain Inspection, Packers and Stockyards Administration
Research, Education, and Economics
  Agricultural Research Service
  Cooperative State Research, Education, and Extension Service
  Economic Research Service
  National Agricultural Statistics Service

Department of Commerce
Secretary: Donald L. Evans
Deputy secretary: Samuel W. Bodman
Web site: <www.commerce.gov>
Mission: To promote job creation, economic growth, sustainable development, and improved living standards for all Americans by working in partnership with business, universities, communities, and workers.
Divisions and agencies:
Economics and Statistics Administration
  Bureau of Economic Analysis
  Bureau of the Census

National Oceanic and Atmospheric Administration
  National Weather Service
Technology Administration
  National Institute of Standards and Technology
  National Technical Information Service
  Office of Technology Policy
Economic Development Administration
Bureau of Industry and Security
International Trade Administration
Minority Business Development Agency
National Telecommunications and Information Administration
Office of the Inspector General
Patent and Trademark Office

Department of Defense
Secretary: Donald H. Rumsfeld
Deputy secretary: Paul Wolfowitz
Web site: <www.defenselink.mil>
Mission: To provide the military forces needed to deter war and to protect the security of the US.
Divisions and agencies:
Army
Navy
  Marine Corps
Air Force
Defense Advanced Research Projects Agency
Defense Commissary Agency
Defense Contract Audit Agency
Defense Contract Management Agency
Defense Finance and Accounting Service
Defense Information Systems Agency
Defense Intelligence Agency
Defense Legal Services Agency
Defense Logistics Agency
Defense Security Cooperation Agency
Defense Security Service
Defense Threat Reduction Agency
Missile Defense Agency
National Imagery and Mapping Agency
National Security Agency

Department of Education
Secretary: Rod Paige
Deputy secretary: William D. Hansen
Web site: <www.ed.gov>
Mission: To establish policies relating to federal financial aid for education, administer distribution of

these funds, and monitor their use; to collect data and oversee research on US schools and disseminate this information; to identify the major issues and problems in education and focus national attention on them, and to enforce federal statutes prohibiting discrimination in programs and activities receiving federal funds and ensure equal access to education for every individual.

Divisions and agencies:
Budget, Policy and Planning
  Budget Service
  Planning and Evaluation Service
External Relations
  Office of Legislation and Congressional Affairs
  Office of Intergovernmental and Interagency Affairs
Decision/Strategy Support
  Executive Management Team
Operations
  Office of Management
  Office of the Chief Financial Officer
  Office of the Chief Information Officer
White House Initiatives
  Faith-Based
  Historically Black Colleges and Universities
  Hispanic Education
  Tribal Colleges and Universities
Office of Elementary and Secondary Education
Office of Postsecondary Education
Office of Educational Research and Improvement
Office of Special Education and Rehabilitative Services
Office of Federal Student Aid
Office of Vocational and Adult Education
Office for Civil Rights
Office of English Language Acquisition
Office of General Counsel
Office of the Inspector General
Office of Public Affairs
Office of Educational Technology

Department of Energy
Secretary: Spencer Abraham
Deputy secretary: vacant
Web site: <www.energy.gov>
Mission: To ensure the integrity and safety of US nuclear weapons; to promote international nuclear safety; to advance nonproliferation; to provide safe, efficient, and effective nuclear power plants for the US Navy; to increase domestic energy production; to revolutionize the approach to energy conservation and efficiency; to promote the development of renewable and alternative energy sources; to ensure that safety legacies of the cold war are addressed and resolved; to dispose of the nation's radioactive wastes safely and permanently; and to sponsor cutting-edge science and technology research and development that revolutionizes the nation's approach to energy.

Divisions and agencies:
National Nuclear Security Administration
  Defense Programs
  Defense Nuclear Nonproliferation
  Naval Reactors
  Office of Emergency Operations
  Facilities and Operations
  Management and Administration
Energy, Science and Environment
  Office of Science
  Office of Civilian Radioactive Waste Management
  Office of Nuclear Energy, Science, and Technology

Office of Worker and Community Transition
Office of Counterintelligence
Office of Intelligence
Office of Security
Office of the Inspector General
Office of Independent Oversight and Performance Assurance
Office of Hearings and Appeals
Office of Energy Assurance
Office of Management, Budget and Evaluation/CFO
Energy Information Administration
Office of Economic Impact and Diversity
Office of Public Affairs

Department of Health and Human Services
Secretary: Tommy G. Thompson
Deputy secretary: Claude A. Allen
Web site: <www.hhs.gov>
Mission: To protect the health of all Americans and provide essential human services, especially for those who are least able to help themselves.

Divisions and agencies:
Administration for Children and Families
Administration on Aging
Centers for Medicare and Medicaid Services
Agency for Healthcare Research and Quality
Centers for Disease Control and Prevention
Agency for Toxic Substances and Disease Registry
Food and Drug Administration
Health Resources and Services Administration
Indian Health Service
National Institutes of Health
Substance Abuse and Mental Health Services Administration
Program Support Center
Office of Public Health Preparedness
Faith Based and Community Initiatives
Office for Civil Rights
Departmental Appeals Board

Department of Housing and Urban Development
Secretary: Mel R. Martinez
Deputy secretary: Alphonso R. Jackson
Web site: <www.hud.gov>
Mission: To create a safe and sanitary living environment for every American by creating opportunities for homeownership; by providing housing assistance for low-income persons; by working to create, rehabilitate, and maintain the nation's affordable housing; by enforcing the nation's fair housing laws; by helping the homeless; by spurring economic growth in distressed neighborhoods; and by helping local communities meet their development needs.

Divisions and agencies:
Housing Office
Community Planning/Development Office
Fair Housing/Equal Opportunity Office
Ginnie Mae Office
Multifamily Housing Assistance Restructuring Office

Department of the Interior
Secretary: Gale A. Norton
Deputy secretary: J. Steven Griles
Web site: <www.doi.gov>
Mission: To protect and provide access to the nation's natural and cultural heritage, and to honor responsibilities to Indian tribes and commitments to island communities.

Divisions and agencies:
Fish and Wildlife and Parks
  National Park Service

US Fish and Wildlife Service
Indian Affairs
  Bureau of Indian Affairs
Land and Minerals Management
  Bureau of Land Management
  Minerals Management Service
  Office of Surface Mining Reclamation and Enforcement
Water and Science
  US Geological Survey
  Bureau of Reclamation

Department of Justice

Attorney General: John Ashcroft
Deputy Attorney General: Larry D. Thompson
Web site: <www.usdoj.gov>
Mission: To enforce the law and defend the interests of the US according to the law; to provide federal leadership in preventing and controlling crime; to seek just punishment for those guilty of unlawful behavior; to administer and enforce the nation's immigration laws fairly and effectively; and to ensure fair and impartial administration of justice for all Americans.
Divisions and agencies:
Office of Legal Policy
Office of Legislative Affairs
Office of Intergovernmental Affairs
Office of Public Affairs
Office of Legal Counsel
Office of the Solicitor General
Office of Justice Programs
Community Oriented Policing Office
Executive Office for United States Trustees
Office of Dispute Resolution
Office of Information and Privacy
Foreign Claims Settlement Commission
Civil Rights Division
Civil Division
Antitrust Division
Environment and Natural Resources Division
Tax Division
Community Relations Service
Federal Bureau of Investigation
Drug Enforcement Administration
Executive Office for United States Attorneys
Immigration and Naturalization Service
United States Attorneys
Criminal Division
Bureau of Prisons
United States Marshals Service
US National Central Bureau—Interpol
Office of the Detention Trustee
Office of the Inspector General
Office of Intelligence Policy and Review
Justice Management Division
Executive Office for Immigration Review
Office of Professional Responsibility
Office of the Pardon Attorney
United States Parole Commission
National Drug Intelligence Center
Professional Responsibility Advisory Office

Department of Labor

Secretary: Elaine L. Chao
Deputy secretary: D. Cameron Findlay
Web site: <www.dol.gov>
Mission: To foster and promote the welfare of the job seekers, wage earners, and retirees of the US by improving their working conditions, advancing their opportunities for profitable employment, protecting their retirement and health care benefits, helping employers find workers, strengthening free collective bargaining, and tracking changes in employment, prices, and other national economic measurements.
Divisions and agencies:
Office of Disability Employment Policy
Occupational Safety and Health Administration
Mine Safety and Health Administration
Pension and Welfare Benefits Administration
Bureau of Labor Statistics
Pension Benefit Guaranty Corporation
Employment and Training Administration
Women's Bureau
Veterans' Employment and Training Service
Bureau of International Labor Affairs
Office of the Assistant Secretary for Policy
Employment Standards Administration
Office of Congressional and Intergovernmental Affairs
Office of Administration and Management and Chief Information Officer
Office of the Chief Financial Officer
Office of the Solicitor
Office of the Inspector General
Office of Public Affairs
Office of Small Business Programs

Department of State

Secretary: Colin L. Powell
Deputy secretary: Richard L. Armitage
Web site: <www.state.gov>
Mission: To promote peace and stability in regions of vital interest; to create jobs in the US by opening markets abroad; to help developing nations establish stable economic environments that provide investment and export opportunities; and to bring nations together to address global problems.
Divisions and agencies:
Political Affairs
  African Affairs
  East Asian and Pacific Affairs
  European and Eurasian Affairs
  Near Eastern Affairs
  South Asian Affairs
  Western Hemisphere Affairs
  International Organization Affairs
Economic, Business, and Agricultural Affairs
  Economic and Business Affairs
Arms Control and International Security
  Arms Control
  Nonproliferation
  Political-Military Affairs
  Verification and Compliance
Public Diplomacy and Public Affairs
  Educational and Cultural Affairs
  Public Affairs
  International Information Programs
Management
  Administration
  Consular Affairs
  Diplomatic Security and Foreign Missions
  Director General of the Foreign Service and Director of Human Resources
  Foreign Service Institute
  Information Resource Management
  Office of White House Liaison
  Overseas Buildings Operations
Global Affairs
  Democracy, Human Rights, and Labor
  International Narcotics and Law Enforcement Affairs

Oceans and International Environmental and Scientific Affairs
Population, Refugees, and Migration
Inspector General
Policy Planning Staff
Office of Civil Rights
Legal Adviser
Legislative Affairs
Intelligence and Research
Chief of Protocol
Counterterrorism
War Crimes Issues
Counselor

Department of Transportation
Secretary: Norman Y. Mineta
Deputy secretary: Michael P. Jackson
Web site: <www.dot.gov>
Mission: To serve the US by ensuring a fast, safe, efficient, accessible, and convenient transportation system that meets vital national interests and enhances the quality of life of the American people.
Divisions and agencies:
Office of Drug and Alcohol Policy and Compliance
Executive Secretariat
Office of Civil Rights
Board of Contract Appeals
Office of Small and Disadvantaged Business Utilization
Office of Intelligence and Security
Office of Public Affairs
Office of the Chief Information Officer
General Counsel
Transportation Policy
Aviation and International Affairs
Budget and Programs/Chief Financial Officer
Governmental Affairs
Administration
Office of the Inspector General
Transportation Administrative Service Center
United States Coast Guard
Federal Aviation Administration
Federal Highway Administration
Federal Railroad Administration
National Highway Traffic Safety Administration
Federal Transit Administration
Saint Lawrence Seaway Development Corporation
Maritime Administration
Research and Special Programs Administration
Bureau of Transportation Statistics
Federal Motor Carrier Safety Administration
Transportation Security Administration

Department of the Treasury
Secretary: Paul H. O'Neill
Deputy secretary: Kenneth W. Dam
Web site: <www.ustreas.gov>
Mission: To promote prosperous and stable US and world economies; to manage the government's finances; to safeguard US financial systems; to protect US leaders; and to secure a safe and drug-free America.
Divisions and agencies:
Domestic Finance Office
Economic Policy Office
Enforcement Office
General Counsel
Inspector General
Treasury Inspector General for Tax Administration
International Affairs Office
Management Office

Public Affairs Office
Tax Policy Office
Treasurer of the United States
Bureau of Alcohol, Tobacco and Firearms
Bureau of Engraving and Printing
Bureau of the Public Debt
Federal Law Enforcement Training Center
Financial Crimes Enforcement Network
Financial Management Service
Internal Revenue Service
Office of the Comptroller of the Currency
Office of Thrift Supervision
US Customs Service
US Mint
US Secret Service

Department of Veterans Affairs
Secretary: Anthony J. Principi
Deputy secretary: Leo S. Mackay, Jr.
Web site: <www.va.gov>
Mission: To serve US veterans and their families with dignity and compassion and be their principal advocate in ensuring that they receive medical care, benefits, social support, and lasting memorials promoting the health, welfare, and dignity of all veterans in recognition of their service.
Divisions and agencies:
Veterans Health Administration
Veterans Benefits Administration
National Cemetery Administration
Board of Contract Appeals
Board of Veterans' Appeals
Center for Minority Veterans
Center for Women Veterans
Office of Acquisition and Materiél Management
Office of Alternate Dispute Resolution and Mediation
Office of Budget
Office of Public and Intergovernmental Affairs
Office of Congressional Affairs
Office of Employment Discrimination Complaint Adjudication
Office of Financial Management
Office of the General Counsel
Office of Human Resources and Administration
Office of Information and Technology
Office of the Inspector General
Office of Occupational Safety and Health
Office of Policy and Planning
Office of Small and Disadvantaged Business Utilization

*Pres. George W. Bush has proposed the creation of a new department, the **Department of Homeland Security.** Currently, Gov. Tom Ridge heads the Office of Homeland Security; its mission is to develop and coordinate the implementation of a comprehensive national strategy to secure the US from terrorist threats or attacks. The proposed department would have four divisions:
Border and Transportation Security
  US Coast Guard
  Immigration and Visa Services
Chemical, Biological, Radiological and Nuclear Countermeasures
  Science and Technology Agenda
Emergency Preparedness and Response
  Federal Emergency Management Administration
  Incident Management
Information Analysis and Infrastructure Protection
  Threat Analysis and Warning
  Critical Infrastructure Protection

United States Congress

The Senate, 107th Congress

According to Article I, Section 3, of the US Constitution, a US senator must be at least 30 years old, must reside in the state he or she represents at the time of the election, and must have been a citizen of the United States for 9 years. Voters elect two senators from each state; terms are for 6 years and begin on 3 January. Senators originally made $6.00 per day; each current senator's salary is $150,000 per year. The majority and minority leaders and the president pro tempore receive $181,400 per year.

US Senate Web site: <www.senate.gov>

Senate leadership

President pro tempore:	Robert C. Byrd
Majority leader:	Tom Daschle
Minority leader:	Trent Lott
Asst. majority leader (Majority whip):	Harry Reid
Asst. minority leader (Minority whip):	Don Nickles

STATE	NAME AND PARTY	SERVICE BEGAN	TERM ENDS
Alabama	Richard Shelby (R)	1987	2005
	Jeff Sessions (R)	1997	2003
Alaska	Ted Stevens (R)	1968[1]	2003
	Frank Murkowski (R)	1981	2005
Arizona	John McCain (R)	1987	2005
	Jon Kyl (R)	1995	2007
Arkansas	Tim Hutchinson (R)	1997	2003
	Blanche Lambert Lincoln (D)	1999	2005
California	Dianne Feinstein (D)	1992[2]	2007
	Barbara Boxer (D)	1993	2005
Colorado	Ben Nighthorse Campbell (R)	1993	2005
	Wayne Allard (R)	1997	2003
Connecticut	Chris Dodd (D)	1981	2005
	Joe Lieberman (D)	1989	2007
Delaware	Joseph R. Biden, Jr. (D)	1973	2003
	Tom Carper (D)	2001	2007
Florida	Bob Graham (D)	1987	2005
	Bill Nelson (D)	2001	2007
Georgia	Max Cleland (D)	1997	2003
	Zell Miller (D)	2000[3]	2005
Hawaii	Daniel K. Inouye (D)	1963	2005
	Daniel Kahikina Akaka (D)	1990[4]	2007
Idaho	Larry Craig (R)	1991	2003
	Mike Crapo (R)	1999	2005
Illinois	Dick Durbin (D)	1997	2003
	Peter G. Fitzgerald (R)	1999	2005
Indiana	Richard G. Lugar (R)	1977	2007
	Evan Bayh (D)	1999	2005
Iowa	Chuck Grassley (R)	1981	2005
	Tom Harkin (D)	1985	2003
Kansas	Sam Brownback (R)	1996[5]	2005
	Pat Roberts (R)	1997	2003
Kentucky	Mitch McConnell (R)	1985	2003
	Jim Bunning (R)	1999	2005
Louisiana	John Breaux (D)	1987	2005
	Mary L. Landrieu (D)	1997	2003
Maine	Olympia J. Snowe (R)	1995	2007
	Susan Collins (R)	1997	2003
Maryland	Paul S. Sarbanes (D)	1977	2007
	Barbara A. Mikulski (D)	1987	2005
Massachusetts	Edward M. Kennedy (D)	1963[6]	2007
	John Kerry (D)	1985	2003
Michigan	Carl Levin (D)	1979	2003
	Debbie Stabenow (D)	2001	2007
Minnesota	Paul D. Wellstone (D)	1991	2003
	Mark Dayton (D)	2001	2007
Mississippi	Thad Cochran (R)	1979	2003
	Trent Lott (R)	1989	2007
Missouri	Kit Bond (R)	1987	2005
	Jean Carnahan (D)	2001[7]	2007
Montana	Max Baucus (D)	1979	2003
	Conrad Burns (R)	1989	2007
Nebraska	Chuck Hagel (R)	1997	2003
	Ben Nelson (D)	2001	2007
Nevada	Harry Reid (D)	1987	2005
	John Ensign (R)	2001	2007

The Senate, 107th Congress (continued)

STATE	NAME AND PARTY	SERVICE BEGAN	TERM ENDS
New Hampshire	Bob Smith (R)	1991	2003
	Judd Gregg (R)	1993	2005
New Jersey	Robert G. Torricelli (D)	1997	2003
	Jon S. Corzine (D)	2001	2007
New Mexico	Pete V. Domenici (R)	1973	2003
	Jeff Bingaman (D)	1983	2007
New York	Charles E. Schumer (D)	1999	2005
	Hillary Rodham Clinton (D)	2001	2007
North Carolina	Jesse Helms (R)	1973	2003
	John Edwards (D)	1999	2005
North Dakota	Kent Conrad (D)	1987	2007
	Byron Dorgan (D)	1993	2005
Ohio	Mike DeWine (R)	1995	2007
	George V. Voinovich (R)	1999	2005
Oklahoma	Don Nickles (R)	1981	2005
	James M. Inhofe (R)	1995[8]	2003
Oregon	Ron Wyden (D)	1996[9]	2005
	Gordon H. Smith (D)	1997	2003
Pennsylvania	Arlen Specter (R)	1981	2005
	Rick Santorum (R)	1995	2007
Rhode Island	Jack Reed (D)	1997	2003
	Lincoln D. Chafee (R)	1999[10]	2007
South Carolina	Strom Thurmond (R)	1954	2003
	Fritz Hollings (D)	1967	2005
South Dakota	Tom Daschle (D)	1987	2005
	Tim Johnson (D)	1997	2003
Tennessee	Fred Thompson (R)	1994[11]	2003
	Bill Frist (R)	1995	2007
Texas	Phil Gramm (R)	1985	2003
	Kay Bailey Hutchison (R)	1993[12]	2007
Utah	Orrin G. Hatch (R)	1977	2007
	Bob Bennett (R)	1993	2005
Vermont	Patrick Leahy (D)	1975	2005
	Jim Jeffords (I)	1989	2007
Virginia	John Warner (R)	1979	2003
	George Allen (R)	2001	2007
Washington	Patty Murray (D)	1993	2005
	Maria Cantwell (D)	2001	2007
West Virginia	Robert C. Byrd (D)	1959	2007
	Jay Rockefeller (D)	1985	2003
Wisconsin	Herb Kohl (D)	1989	2007
	Russ Feingold (D)	1993	2005
Wyoming	Craig Thomas (R)	1995	2007
	Mike Enzi (R)	1997	2003

Democrats: 50; Republicans: 49; Independents: 1

[1]Ted Stevens was appointed in December 1968 to fill the vacancy caused by the death of Edward Lewis (Bob) Bartlett.
[2]Dianne Feinstein was elected in November 1992 to complete the term of Pete Wilson, who resigned in 1991 to become California's governor.
[3]Zell Miller was appointed in July 2000 to fill the vacancy caused by the death of Paul Coverdell.
[4]Daniel Kahikina Akaka was appointed in April 1990 after winning a special election to fill the vacancy caused by the death of Spark M. Matsunaga.
[5]Sam Brownback was elected in November 1996 to complete the term of Bob Dole, who resigned to campaign for the presidency.
[6]Edward M. Kennedy was elected in November 1962 to complete the term of his brother, Pres. John F. Kennedy.
[7]After candidate Mel Carnahan was killed in a plane crash on 16 Oct 2000, his widow agreed to serve in his place should he be elected.
[8]James M. Inhofe was elected in November 1994 to complete the term of David Boren, who resigned to become president of the University of Oklahoma.
[9]Ron Wyden was elected in January 1996 to complete the term of Bob Packwood, who resigned in 1995.
[10]Lincoln D. Chafee was appointed in November 1999 to fill the vacancy caused by the death of his father, John H. Chafee.
[11]Fred Thompson was elected in November 1994 to fill the vacancy left by Albert Gore, Jr., who resigned in 1993 to run for vice president (Harlan Mathews served in the interim).
[12]Kay Bailey Hutchison was elected in June 1993 to fill the vacancy left by the retirement of Lloyd Bentsen, Jr.

Senate Standing Committees

COMMITTEE	CHAIRMAN (STATE)	RANKING REPUBLICAN (STATE)	NUMBER OF MEMBERS: MAJORITY	NUMBER OF MEMBERS: MINORITY	NUMBER OF SUBCOMMITTEES
Agriculture, Nutrition, and Forestry	Tom Harkin (IA)	Richard Lugar (IN)	11	10	4
Appropriations	Robert C. Byrd (WV)	Ted Stevens (AK)	15	14	13
Armed Services	Carl Levin (MI)	John Warner (VA)	13	12	6
Banking, Housing, and Urban Affairs	Paul S. Sarbanes (MD)	Phil Gramm (TX)	11	10	5
Budget	Kent Conrad (ND)	Pete V. Domenici (NM)	12	11	none
Commerce, Science, and Transportation	Ernest Hollings (SC)	John McCain (AZ)	12	11	6
Energy and Natural Resources	Jeff Bingaman (NM)	Frank H. Murkowski (AK)	12	11	4
Environment and Public Works	James M. Jeffords (VT)	Robert Smith (NH)	10	9	4
Finance	Max Baucus (MT)	Chuck Grassley (IA)	11	10	5
Foreign Relations	Joseph R. Biden, Jr. (DE)	Jesse Helms (NC)	10	9	8
Governmental Affairs	Joseph Lieberman (CT)	Fred Thompson (TN)	9	8	3
Health, Education, Labor, and Pensions	Edward M. Kennedy (MA)	Judd Gregg (NH)	11	10	4
Judiciary	Patrick Leahy (VT)	Orrin G. Hatch (UT)	10	9	6
Rules and Administration	Christopher Dodd (CT)	Mitch McConnell (KY)	10	9	none
Small Business and Entrepreneurship	John F. Kerry (MA)	Christopher Bond (MO)	10	9	none
Veterans' Affairs	John D. Rockefeller, IV (WV)	Arlen Specter (PA)	8	7	none

Senate Special, Select, and Other Committees

COMMITTEE	CHAIRMAN (STATE)	RANKING REPUBLICAN (STATE)	NUMBER OF MEMBERS: MAJORITY	NUMBER OF MEMBERS: MINORITY
Special Committee on Aging	John Breaux (LA)	Larry E. Craig (ID)	11	10
Select Committee on Ethics	Harry Reid (NV)	Pat Roberts (KS)	3	3
Committee on Indian Affairs	Daniel K. Inouye (HI)	Ben Nighthorse Campbell (CO)	8	7
Select Committee on Intelligence	Bob Graham (FL)	Richard C. Shelby (AL)	9	8

Joint Committees of Congress

The joint committees of Congress include members from both the Senate and the House of Representatives. They function as overseeing entities but do not have the power to approve appropriations or legislation. Chairmanship of the Joint Economic Committee is determined by seniority and alternates between the Senate and the House every Congress. The Joint Committee on the Library of Congress is evenly made up of members from the House Administration Committee and the Senate Rules and Administration Committees. Chairmanship and vice chairmanship of the Joint Committee on Printing alternates between the House and the Senate every Congress. The Joint Committee on Taxation is composed of five members from the Senate Committee on Finance and five members from the House Committee on Ways and Means (three majority and two minority members from each).

COMMITTEE	CHAIRMAN (PARTY-STATE)	RANKING MEMBER (PARTY-STATE)	NUMBER OF MEMBERS: MAJORITY	NUMBER OF MEMBERS: MINORITY
Economic	Rep. Jim Saxton (R-NJ)	Sen. Jack Reed (D-RI)	11	10
Library	Rep. Vernon J. Ehlers (R-MI)	Sen. Christopher J. Dodd (D-CT)	5	5
Printing	Rep. William M. Thomas (R-CA)	Sen. Mitch McConnell (R-KY)	6	4
Taxation	Sen. Max Baucus (D-MT)	Rep. William M. Thomas (R-CA)	6	4

Did you know? The US was an independent nation for 13 years before the Constitution was signed in 1789, the same year George Washington was elected the country's first president. In 1781, American Revolutionary leader John Hanson was elected by the Continental Congress "President of the United States in Congress Assembled." Hanson is thus referred to by some as the first US president, but he was a congressional presiding officer and had none of the presidential powers that would be granted under the Constitution.

The House of Representatives, 107th Congress

Parties: Democrat (D); Republican (R); Independent (I). Party totals: Democrats 211; Republicans 222; Independents 2.

According to Article I, Section 2, of the US Constitution, a US representative must be at least 25 years old, must reside in the state he or she represents at the time of the election, and must have been a citizen of the United States for 7 years. Each state is entitled to at least one representative, with additional seats apportioned based on population. Each congressperson originally represented 30,000 people; the current range is from 495,304 (Wyoming) to 905,316 (Montana) persons per representative. Terms are for 2 years and begin on 3 January (unless otherwise noted). The current representative's salary is $150,000 per year. The majority and minority leaders receive $166,700 per year; the speaker of the house receives $192,600 per year.

American Samoa, the District of Columbia, Guam, and the Virgin Islands elect delegates; Puerto Rico elects a resident commissioner. Their formal duties are the same, but the resident commissioner serves a 4-year term. They may participate in debate and serve on committees but are not permitted to vote. US House Web site: <www.house.gov>

Numbers preceding the names refer to districts.

House leadership

Speaker of the house:	J. Dennis Hastert
Majority leader:	Dick Armey
Minority leader:	Richard A. Gephardt
Republican whip:	Tom DeLay
Democratic whip:	Nancy Pelosi

STATE	REPRESENTATIVES	SERVICE BEGAN
Alabama	1. Sonny Callahan (R)	Jan 1985
	2. Terry Everett (R)	Jan 1993
	3. Bob Riley (R)	Jan 1997
	4. Robert B. Aderholt (R)	Jan 1997
	5. Robert E. (Bud) Cramer, Jr. (D)	Jan 1991
	6. Spencer Bachus (R)	Jan 1993
	7. Earl F. Hilliard (D)	Jan 1993
Alaska	Don Young (R)	Mar 1973
Arizona	1. Jeff Flake (R)	Jan 2001
	2. Ed Pastor (D)	Jun 1991
	3. Bob Stump (R)	Jan 1977
	4. John B. Shadegg (R)	Jan 1995
	5. Jim Kolbe (R)	Jan 1985
	6. J.D. Hayworth (R)	Jan 1995
Arkansas	1. Marion Berry (D)	Jan 1997
	2. Vic Snyder (D)	Jan 1997
	3. John Boozman (R)[1]	Nov 2001
	4. Mike Ross (D)	Jan 2001
California	1. Mike Thompson (D)	Jan 1999
	2. Wally Herger (R)	Jan 1987
	3. Doug Ose (R)	Jan 1999
	4. John T. Doolittle (R)	Jan 1991
	5. Robert T. Matsui (D)	Jan 1979
	6. Lynn C. Woolsey (D)	Jan 1993
	7. George Miller (D)	Jan 1975
	8. Nancy Pelosi (D)	Jun 1987
	9. Barbara Lee (D)	Jan 1999
	10. Ellen O. Tauscher (D)	Jan 1997
	11. Richard W. Pombo (R)	Jan 1993
	12. Tom Lantos (D)	Jan 1981
	13. Fortney Pete Stark (D)	Jan 1973
	14. Anna G. Eshoo (D)	Jan 1993
	15. Michael M. Honda (D)	Jan 2001
	16. Zoe Lofgren (D)	Jan 1995
	17. Sam Farr (D)	Jun 1993
	18. Gary A. Condit (D)	Sep 1989
	19. George Radanovich (R)	Jan 1995
	20. Calvin M. Dooley (D)	Jan 1991
	21. William M. Thomas (R)	Jan 1979
	22. Lois Capps (D)	Mar 1998
	23. Elton Gallegly (R)	Jan 1987
	24. Brad Sherman (D)	Jan 1997
	25. Howard P. "Buck" McKeon (R)	Jan 1993

STATE	REPRESENTATIVES	SERVICE BEGAN
California (cont.)	26. Howard L. Berman (D)	Jan 1983
	27. Adam B. Schiff (D)	Jan 2001
	28. David Dreier (R)	Jan 1981
	29. Henry A. Waxman (D)	Jan 1975
	30. Xavier Becerra (D)	Jan 1993
	31. Hilda L. Solis (D)	Jan 2001
	32. Diane E. Watson (D)[2]	Jun 2001
	33. Lucille Roybal-Allard (D)	Jan 1993
	34. Grace F. Napolitano (D)	Jan 1999
	35. Maxine Waters (D)	Jan 1991
	36. Jane F. Harman (D)	Jan 1993[3]
	37. Juanita Millender-McDonald (D)	Mar 1996
	38. Stephen Horn (R)	Jan 1993
	39. Edward R. Royce (R)	Jan 1993
	40. Jerry Lewis (R)	Jan 1979
	41. Gary G. Miller (R)	Jan 1999
	42. Joe Baca (D)	Nov 1999
	43. Ken Calvert (R)	Jan 1993
	44. Mary Bono (R)	Apr 1998
	45. Dana Rohrabacher (R)	Jan 1989
	46. Loretta Sanchez (D)	Jan 1997
	47. Christopher Cox (R)	Jan 1989
	48. Darrell E. Issa (R)	Jan 2001
	49. Susan A. Davis (D)	Jan 2001
	50. Bob Filner (D)	Jan 1993
	51. Randy "Duke" Cunningham (R)	Jan 1991
	52. Duncan Hunter (R)	Jan 1981
Colorado	1. Diana DeGette (D)	Jan 1997
	2. Mark Udall (D)	Jan 1999
	3. Scott McInnis (R)	Jan 1993
	4. Bob Schaffer (R)	Jan 1997
	5. Joel Hefley (R)	Jan 1987
	6. Thomas G. Tancredo (R)	Jan 1999
Connecticut	1. John B. Larson (D)	Jan 1999
	2. Rob Simmons (R)	Jan 2001
	3. Rosa L. DeLauro (D)	Jan 1991
	4. Christopher Shays (R)	Aug 1987
	5. James H. Maloney (D)	Jan 1997
	6. Nancy L. Johnson (R)	Jan 1983
Delaware	Michael N. Castle (R)	Jan 1993
Florida	1. Jeff Miller (R)[4]	Oct 2001
	2. Allen Boyd (D)	Jan 1997
	3. Corrine Brown (D)	Jan 1993

The House of Representatives, 107th Congress (continued)

STATE	REPRESENTATIVES	SERVICE BEGAN	STATE	REPRESENTATIVES	SERVICE BEGAN
Florida	4. Ander Crenshaw (R)	Jan 2001	Indiana	9. Baron P. Hill (D)	Jan 1999
(cont.)	5. Karen L. Thurman (D)	Jan 1993	(cont.)	10. Julia Carson (D)	Jan 1997
	6. Cliff Stearns (R)	Jan 1989			
	7. John L. Mica (R)	Jan 1993	Iowa	1. James A. Leach (R)	Jan 1977
	8. Ric Keller (R)	Jan 2001		2. Jim Nussle (R)	Jan 1991
	9. Michael Bilirakis (R)	Jan 1983		3. Leonard L. Boswell (D)	Jan 1997
	10. C.W. Bill Young (R)	Jan 1971		4. Greg Ganske (R)	Jan 1995
	11. Jim Davis (D)	Jan 1997		5. Tom Latham (R)	Jan 1995
	12. Adam H. Putnam (R)	Jan 2001			
	13. Dan Miller (R)	Jan 1993	Kansas	1. Jerry Moran (R)	Jan 1997
	14. Porter J. Goss (R)	Jan 1989		2. Jim Ryun (R)	Nov 1996
	15. Dave Weldon (R)	Jan 1995		3. Dennis Moore (D)	Jan 1999
	16. Mark Foley (R)	Jan 1995		4. Todd Tiahrt (R)	Jan 1995
	17. Carrie P. Meek (D)	Jan 1993			
	18. Ileana Ros-Lehtinen (R)	Jan 1991	Kentucky	1. Ed Whitfield (R)	Jan 1995
	19. Robert Wexler (D)	Jan 1997		2. Ron Lewis (R)	May 1994
	20. Peter Deutsch (D)	Jan 1993		3. Anne M. Northup (R)	Jan 1997
	21. Lincoln Diaz-Balart (R)	Jan 1993		4. Ken Lucas (D)	Jan 1999
	22. E. Clay Shaw, Jr. (R)	Jan 1981		5. Harold Rogers (R)	Jan 1981
	23. Alcee L. Hastings (D)	Jan 1993		6. Ernie Fletcher (R)	Jan 1999
Georgia	1. Jack Kingston (R)	Jan 1993	Louisiana	1. David Vitter (R)	May 1999
	2. Sanford D. Bishop, Jr. (D)	Jan 1993		2. William J. Jefferson (D)	Jan 1991
	3. Mac Collins (R)	Jan 1993			
	4. Cynthia A. McKinney (D)	Jan 1993		3. W.J. (Billy) Tauzin (R)	May 1980
	5. John Lewis (D)	Jan 1987		4. Jim McCrery (R)	Apr 1988
	6. Johnny Isakson (R)	Jan 2001		5. John Cooksey (R)	Jan 1997
	7. Bob Barr (R)	Jan 1995		6. Richard H. Baker (R)	Jan 1987
	8. Saxby Chambliss (R)	Jan 1995		7. Christopher John (D)	Jan 1997
	9. Nathan Deal (R)	Jan 1997			
	10. Charlie Norwood (R)	Jan 1995	Maine	1. Thomas H. Allen (D)	Jan 1997
	11. John Linder (R)	Jan 1993		2. John Elias Baldacci (D)	Jan 1995
Hawaii	1. Neil Abercrombie (D)	Sep 1986[5]			
	2. Patsy T. Mink (D)	Jan 1965[6]	Maryland	1. Wayne T. Gilchrest (R)	Jan 1991
				2. Robert L. Ehrlich, Jr. (R)	Jan 1995
Idaho	1. C.L. "Butch" Otter (R)	Jan 2001			
	2. Michael K. Simpson (R)	Jan 1999		3. Benjamin L. Cardin (D)	Jan 1987
				4. Albert Russell Wynn (D)	Jan 1993
Illinois	1. Bobby L. Rush (D)	Jan 1993		5. Steny H. Hoyer (D)	May 1981
	2. Jesse L. Jackson, Jr. (D)	Jan 1997		6. Roscoe G. Bartlett (R)	Jan 1993
	3. William O. Lipinski (D)	Jan 1983		7. Elijah E. Cummings (D)	Apr 1996
	4. Luis V. Gutierrez (D)	Jan 1993		8. Constance A. Morella (R)	Jan 1987
	5. Rod R. Blagojevich (D)	Jan 1997			
	6. Henry J. Hyde (R)	Jan 1975	Massachusetts	1. John W. Olver (D)	Jun 1991
	7. Danny K. Davis (D)	Jan 1997		2. Richard E. Neal (D)	Jan 1989
	8. Philip M. Crane (R)	Jan 1971		3. James P. McGovern (D)	Jan 1997
	9. Janice D. Schakowsky (D)	Jan 1999		4. Barney Frank (D)	Jan 1981
	10. Mark Steven Kirk (R)	Jan 2001		5. Martin T. Meehan (D)	Jan 1993
	11. Jerry Weller (R)	Jan 1995		6. John F. Tierney (D)	Jan 1997
	12. Jerry F. Costello (D)	Jan 1989		7. Edward J. Markey (D)	Nov 1976
	13. Judy Biggert (R)	Jan 1999		8. Michael E. Capuano (D)	Jan 1999
	14. J. Dennis Hastert (R)	Jan 1987		9. Stephen F. Lynch (D)[7]	Oct 2001
	15. Timothy V. Johnson (R)	Jan 2001		10. William D. Delahunt (D)	Jan 1997
	16. Donald A. Manzullo (R)	Jan 1993			
	17. Lane Evans (D)	Jan 1983			
	18. Ray LaHood (R)	Jan 1995			
	19. David D. Phelps (D)	Jan 1999	Michigan	1. Bart Stupak (D)	Jan 1993
	20. John Shimkus (R)	Jan 1997		2. Peter Hoekstra (R)	Jan 1993
				3. Vernon J. Ehlers (R)	Dec 1993
Indiana	1. Peter J. Visclosky (D)	Jan 1985		4. Dave Camp (R)	Jan 1991
	2. Mike Pence (R)	Jan 2001		5. James A. Barcia (D)	Jan 1993
	3. Tim Roemer (D)	Jan 1991		6. Fred Upton (R)	Jan 1987
	4. Mark E. Souder (R)	Jan 1995		7. Nick Smith (R)	Jan 1993
	5. Steve Buyer (R)	Jan 1993			
	6. Dan Burton (R)	Jan 1983			
	7. Brian D. Kerns (R)	Jan 2001			
	8. John N. Hostettler (R)	Jan 1995			

The House of Representatives, 107th Congress (continued)

STATE	REPRESENTATIVES	SERVICE BEGAN
Michigan (cont.)	8. Mike Rogers (R)	Jan 2001
	9. Dale E. Kildee (D)	Jan 1977
	10. David E. Bonior (D)	Jan 1977
	11. Joe Knollenberg (R)	Jan 1993
	12. Sander M. Levin (D)	Jan 1983
	13. Lynn N. Rivers (D)	Jan 1995
	14. John Conyers, Jr. (D)	Jan 1965
	15. Carolyn C. Kilpatrick (D)	Jan 1997
	16. John D. Dingell (D)	Dec 1955
Minnesota	1. Gil Gutknecht (R)	Jan 1995
	2. Mark R. Kennedy (R)	Jan 2001
	3. Jim Ramstad (R)	Jan 1991
	4. Betty McCollum (D)	Jan 2001
	5. Martin Olav Sabo (D)	Jan 1979
	6. Bill Luther (D)	Jan 1995
	7. Collin C. Peterson (D)	Jan 1991
	8. James L. Oberstar (D)	Jan 1975
Mississippi	1. Roger F. Wicker (R)	Jan 1995
	2. Bennie G. Thompson (D)	Apr 1993
	3. Charles W. "Chip" Pickering (R)	Jan 1997
	4. Ronnie Shows (D)	Jan 1999
	5. Gene Taylor (D)	Oct 1989
Missouri	1. William Lacy Clay (D)	Jan 2001
	2. W. Todd Akin (R)	Jan 2001
	3. Richard A. Gephardt (D)	Jan 1977
	4. Ike Skelton (D)	Jan 1977
	5. Karen McCarthy (D)	Jan 1995
	6. Sam Graves (R)	Jan 2001
	7. Roy Blunt (R)	Jan 1997
	8. Jo Ann Emerson (R)	Jan 1997
	9. Kenny C. Hulshof (R)	Jan 1997
Montana	Dennis R. Rehberg (R)	Jan 2001
Nebraska	1. Doug Bereuter (R)	Jan 1979
	2. Lee Terry (R)	Jan 1999
	3. Tom Osborne (R)	Jan 2001
Nevada	1. Shelley Berkley (D)	Jan 1999
	2. Jim Gibbons (R)	Jan 1997
New Hampshire	1. John E. Sununu (R)	Jan 1997
	2. Charles F. Bass (R)	Jan 1995
New Jersey	1. Robert E. Andrews (D)	Nov 1990
	2. Frank A. LoBiondo (R)	Jan 1995
	3. Jim Saxton (R)	Nov 1984
	4. Christopher H. Smith (R)	Jan 1981
	5. Marge Roukema (R)	Jan 1981
	6. Frank Pallone, Jr. (D)	Nov 1988
	7. Mike Ferguson (R)	Jan 2001
	8. Bill Pascrell, Jr. (D)	Jan 1997
	9. Steven R. Rothman (D)	Jan 1997
	10. Donald M. Payne (D)	Jan 1989
	11. Rodney P. Frelinghuysen (R)	Jan 1995

STATE	REPRESENTATIVES	SERVICE BEGAN
New Jersey (cont.)	12. Rush D. Holt (D)	Jan 1999
	13. Robert Menendez (D)	Jan 1993
New Mexico	1. Heather Wilson (R)	Jun 1998
	2. Joe Skeen (R)	Jan 1981
	3. Tom Udall (D)	Jan 1999
New York	1. Felix J. Grucci, Jr. (R)	Jan 2001
	2. Steve Israel (D)	Jan 2001
	3. Peter T. King (R)	Jan 1993
	4. Carolyn McCarthy (D)	Jan 1997
	5. Gary L. Ackerman (D)	Mar 1983
	6. Gregory W. Meeks (D)	Feb 1998
	7. Joseph Crowley (D)	Jan 1999
	8. Jerrold Nadler (D)	Nov 1992
	9. Anthony D. Weiner (D)	Jan 1999
	10. Edolphus Towns (D)	Jan 1983
	11. Major R. Owens (D)	Jan 1983
	12. Nydia M. Velázquez (D)	Jan 1993
	13. Vito Fossella (R)	Nov 1997
	14. Carolyn B. Maloney (D)	Jan 1993
	15. Charles B. Rangel (D)	Jan 1971
	16. José E. Serrano (D)	Mar 1990
	17. Eliot L. Engel (D)	Jan 1989
	18. Nita M. Lowey (D)	Jan 1989
	19. Sue W. Kelly (R)	Jan 1995
	20. Benjamin A. Gilman (R)	Jan 1973
	21. Michael R. McNulty (D)	Jan 1989
	22. John E. Sweeney (R)	Jan 1999
	23. Sherwood L. Boehlert (R)	Jan 1983
	24. John M. McHugh (R)	Jan 1993
	25. James T. Walsh (R)	Jan 1989
	26. Maurice D. Hinchey (D)	Jan 1993
	27. Thomas M. Reynolds (R)	Jan 1999
	28. Louise McIntosh Slaughter (D)	Jan 1987
	29. John J. LaFalce (D)	Jan 1975
	30. Jack Quinn (R)	Jan 1993
	31. Amo Houghton (R)	Jan 1987
North Carolina	1. Eva M. Clayton (D)	Nov 1992
	2. Bob Etheridge (D)	Jan 1997
	3. Walter B. Jones (R)	Jan 1995
	4. David E. Price (D)	Jan 1997
	5. Richard Burr (R)	Jan 1995
	6. Howard Coble (R)	Jan 1985
	7. Mike McIntyre (D)	Jan 1997
	8. Robin Hayes (R)	Jan 1999
	9. Sue Wilkins Myrick (R)	Jan 1995
	10. Cass Ballenger (R)	Nov 1986
	11. Charles H. Taylor (R)	Jan 1991
	12. Melvin L. Watt (D)	Jan 1993
North Dakota	Earl Pomeroy (D)	Jan 1993
Ohio	1. Steve Chabot (R)	Jan 1995
	2. Rob Portman (R)	May 1993
	3. Tony P. Hall (D)	Jan 1979
	4. Michael G. Oxley (R)	Jun 1981
	5. Paul E. Gillmor (R)	Jan 1989
	6. Ted Strickland (D)	Jan 1997
	7. David L. Hobson (R)	Jan 1991
	8. John A. Boehner (R)	Jan 1991
	9. Marcy Kaptur (D)	Jan 1983
	10. Dennis J. Kucinich (D)	Jan 1997

The House of Representatives, 107th Congress (continued)

STATE	REPRESENTATIVES	SERVICE BEGAN
Ohio (cont.)	11. Stephanie Tubbs Jones (D)	Jan 1999
	12. Patrick J. Tiberi (R)	Jan 2001
	13. Sherrod Brown (D)	Jan 1993
	14. Tom Sawyer (D)	Jan 1987
	15. Deborah Pryce (R)	Jan 1993
	16. Ralph Regula (R)	Jan 1973
	17. James A. Traficant, Jr. (D)	Jan 1985
	18. Robert W. Ney (R)	Jan 1995
	19. Steven C. LaTourette (R)	Jan 1995
Oklahoma	1. John Sullivan (R)[8]	Feb 2002
	2. Brad Carson (D)	Jan 2001
	3. Wes Watkins (R)	Jan 1977[9]
	4. J.C. Watts, Jr. (R)	Jan 1995
	5. Ernest J. Istook, Jr. (R)	Jan 1993
	6. Frank D. Lucas (R)	May 1994
Oregon	1. David Wu (D)	Jan 1999
	2. Greg Walden (R)	Jan 1999
	3. Earl Blumenauer (D)	May 1996
	4. Peter A. DeFazio (D)	Jan 1987
	5. Darlene Hooley (D)	Jan 1997
Pennsylvania	1. Robert A. Brady (D)	May 1998
	2. Chaka Fattah (D)	Jan 1995
	3. Robert A. Borski (D)	Jan 1983
	4. Melissa A. Hart (R)	Jan 2001
	5. John E. Peterson (R)	Jan 1997
	6. Tim Holden (D)	Jan 1993
	7. Curt Weldon (R)	Jan 1987
	8. James C. Greenwood (R)	Jan 1993
	9. Bill Shuster (R)	May 2001
	10. Don Sherwood (R)	Jan 1999
	11. Paul E. Kanjorski (D)	Jan 1985
	12. John P. Murtha (D)	Feb 1974
	13. Joseph M. Hoeffel (D)	Jan 1999
	14. William J. Coyne (D)	Jan 1981
	15. Patrick J. Toomey (R)	Jan 1999
	16. Joseph R. Pitts (R)	Jan 1997
	17. George W. Gekas (R)	Jan 1983
	18. Michael F. Doyle (D)	Jan 1995
	19. Todd Russell Platts (R)	Jan 2001
	20. Frank Mascara (D)	Jan 1995
	21. Phil English (R)	Jan 1995
Rhode Island	1. Patrick J. Kennedy (D)	Jan 1995
	2. James R. Langevin (D)	Jan 2001
South Carolina	1. Henry E. Brown, Jr. (R)	Jan 2001
	2. Joe Wilson (R)[10]	Dec 2001
	3. Lindsey O. Graham (R)	Jan 1995
	4. Jim DeMint (R)	Jan 1999
	5. John M. Spratt, Jr. (D)	Jan 1983
	6. James E. Clyburn (D)	Jan 1993
South Dakota	John R. Thune (R)	Jan 1997
Tennessee	1. William L. Jenkins (R)	Jan 1997
	2. John J. Duncan, Jr. (R)	Nov 1988
	3. Zach Wamp (R)	Jan 1995
	4. Van Hilleary (R)	Jan 1995
	5. Bob Clement (D)	Jan 1988
	6. Bart Gordon (D)	Jan 1985

STATE	REPRESENTATIVES	SERVICE BEGAN
Tennessee (cont.)	7. Ed Bryant (R)	Jan 1995
	8. John S. Tanner (D)	Jan 1989
	9. Harold E. Ford, Jr. (D)	Jan 1997
Texas	1. Max Sandlin (D)	Jan 1997
	2. Jim Turner (D)	Jan 1997
	3. Sam Johnson (R)	May 1991
	4. Ralph M. Hall (D)	Jan 1981
	5. Pete Sessions (R)	Jan 1997
	6. Joe Barton (R)	Jan 1985
	7. John Abney Culberson (R)	Jan 2001
	8. Kevin Brady (R)	Jan 1997
	9. Nick Lampson (D)	Jan 1997
	10. Lloyd Doggett (D)	Jan 1995
	11. Chet Edwards (D)	Jan 1991
	12. Kay Granger (R)	Jan 1997
	13. Mac Thornberry (R)	Jan 1995
	14. Ron Paul (R)	Jan 1997
	15. Rubén Hinojosa (D)	Jan 1997
	16. Silvestre Reyes (D)	Jan 1997
	17. Charles W. Stenholm (D)	Jan 1979
	18. Sheila Jackson-Lee (D)	Jan 1995
	19. Larry Combest (R)	Jan 1985
	20. Charles A. Gonzalez (D)	Jan 1999
	21. Lamar S. Smith (R)	Jan 1987
	22. Tom DeLay (R)	Jan 1985
	23. Henry Bonilla (R)	Jan 1993
	24. Martin Frost (D)	Jan 1979
	25. Ken Bentsen (D)	Jan 1995
	26. Dick Armey (R)	Jan 1985
	27. Solomon P. Ortiz (D)	Jan 1983
	28. Ciro D. Rodriguez (D)	Apr 1997
	29. Gene Green (D)	Jan 1993
	30. Eddie Bernice Johnson (D)	Jan 1993
Utah	1. James V. Hansen (R)	Jan 1981
	2. Jim Matheson (D)	Jan 2001
	3. Chris Cannon (R)	Jan 1997
Vermont	Bernard Sanders (I)	Jan 1991
Virginia	1. Jo Ann Davis (R)	Jan 2001
	2. Edward L. Schrock (R)	Jan 2001
	3. Robert C. Scott (D)	Jan 1993
	4. J. Randy Forbes (R)[11]	Jun 2001
	5. Virgil H. Goode, Jr. (I)	Jan 1997
	6. Bob Goodlatte (R)	Jan 1993
	7. Eric Cantor (R)	Jan 2001
	8. James P. Moran (D)	Jan 1991
	9. Rick Boucher (D)	Jan 1983
	10. Frank R. Wolf (R)	Jan 1981
	11. Tom Davis (R)	Jan 1995
Washington	1. Jay Inslee (D)	Jan 1993[12]
	2. Rick Larsen (D)	Jan 2001
	3. Brian Baird (D)	Jan 1999
	4. Doc Hastings (R)	Jan 1995
	5. George R. Nethercutt, Jr. (R)	Jan 1995
	6. Norman D. Dicks (D)	Jan 1977
	7. Jim McDermott (D)	Jan 1989
	8. Jennifer Dunn (R)	Jan 1993
	9. Adam Smith (D)	Jan 1997

The House of Representatives, 107th Congress (continued)

STATE	REPRESENTATIVES	SERVICE BEGAN	STATE	REPRESENTATIVES	SERVICE BEGAN
West Virginia	1. Alan B. Mollohan (D)	Jan 1983	Wisconsin	5. Thomas M. Barrett (D)	Jan 1993
	2. Shelley Moore Capito (R)	Jan 2001	(cont.)	6. Thomas E. Petri (R)	Apr 1979
	3. Nick J. Rahall II (D)	Jan 1977		7. David R. Obey (D)	Apr 1969
				8. Mark Green (R)	Jan 1999
Wisconsin	1. Paul Ryan (R)	Jan 1999		9. F. James Sensenbrenner, Jr. (R)	Jan 1979
	2. Tammy Baldwin (D)	Jan 1999			
	3. Ron Kind (D)	Jan 1997	Wyoming	Barbara Cubin (R)	Jan 1995
	4. Gerald D. Kleczka (D)	Apr 1984			

TERRITORIES	REPRESENTATIVES	SERVICE BEGAN
American Samoa	(Delegate) Eni F.H. Faleomavaega (D)	Jan 1989
District of Columbia	(Delegate) Eleanor Holmes Norton (D)	Jan 1991
Guam	(Delegate) Robert A. Underwood (D)	Jan 1993
Puerto Rico	(Res. Comm.) Aníbal Acevedo-Vilá (D)	Jan 2001
Virgin Islands	(Delegate) Donna M. Christensen (D)	Jan 1997

[1]John Boozman was elected 20 Nov 2001 following the resignation of Asa Hutchinson. [2]Diane E. Watson was elected 5 Jun 2001 to complete the term of the late Julian C. Dixon. [3]Jane Harman did not serve 3 Jan 1999–3 Jan 2001. [4]Jeff Miller was elected 16 Oct 2001 following the resignation of Joe Scarborough. [5]Neil Abercrombie did not serve 3 Jan 1987–3 Jan 1991. [6]Patsy Mink did not serve 3 Jan 1977–3 Jan 1991. [7]Stephen F. Lynch was elected 16 Oct 2001 to complete the term of the late John Joseph Moakley. [8]John Sullivan was elected 8 Jan 2002 following the resignation of Steve Largent. [9]Wes Watkins did not serve 3 Jan 1991–3 Jan 1997. [10]Joe Wilson was elected 18 Dec 2001 to complete the term of the late Floyd Spence. [11]J. Randy Forbes was elected 19 Jun 2001 to complete the term of the late Norman Sisisky. [12]Jay Inslee did not serve 3 Jan 1995–3 Jan 1999.

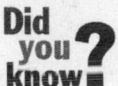

Did you know? Thomas Jefferson enjoyed the study of mathematics and found its precision and certitude a welcome relief from the untidiness of politics and government. An enthusiastic practitioner of scientific farming, he conducted numerous experiments at Monticello and was always on the lookout for new plants or seeds, once going so far as to smuggle a particular variety of rice across the Italian border.

House of Representatives Standing Committees

COMMITTEE	CHAIRMAN (STATE)	RANKING DEMOCRAT (STATE)	NUMBER OF MEMBERS: MAJORITY	MINORITY	NUMBER OF SUBCOMMITTEES
Agriculture	Larry Combest (TX)	Charlie Stenholm (TX)	27	24	5
Appropriations	C.W. Bill Young (FL)	David Obey (WI)	36	29	13
Armed Services	Bob Stump (AZ)	Ike Skelton (MO)	32	28	5
Budget	Jim Nussle (IA)	John Spratt (SC)	24	19	none
Education and the Workforce	John A. Boehner (OH)	George Miller (CA)	27	22	5
Energy and Commerce	W.J. "Billy" Tauzin (LA)	John D. Dingell (MI)	31	26	6
Financial Services	Michael G. Oxley (OH)	John J. LaFalce (NY)	37	33[1]	6
Government Reform	Dan Burton (IN)	Henry A. Waxman (CA)	24	20[1]	7
House Administration	Robert W. Ney (OH)	Steny Hoyer (MD)	6	3	none
International Relations	Henry J. Hyde (IL)	Tom Lantos (CA)	26	23	6
Judiciary	F. James Sensenbrenner (WI)	John Conyers, Jr. (MI)	21	16	5
Resources	James V. Hansen (UT)	Nick J. Rahall, II (WV)	28	24	5
Rules	David Dreier (CA)	Martin Frost (TX)	9	4	2
Science	Sherwood L. Boehlert (NY)	Ralph M. Hall (TX)	25	22	4
Small Business	Donald Manzullo (IL)	Nydia M. Velazquez (NY)	19	17	4
Standards of Official Conduct	Joel Hefley (CO)	Howard L. Berman (CA)	5	5	none
Transportation and Infrastructure	Don Young (AK)	James L. Oberstar (MN)	41	34	6
Veterans' Affairs	Christopher Smith (NJ)	Lane Evans (IL)	17	14	3
Ways and Means	Bill Thomas (CA)	Charles B. Rangel (NY)	24	17	6
Permanent Select Committee on Intelligence	Porter J. Goss (FL)	Nancy Pelosi (CA)	11	10	4

[1]Bernard Sanders (VT) is an independent but caucuses with the Democratic Party.

Congressional Apportionment

The US Constitution requires a decennial census to determine the apportionment of representatives for each state in the House of Representatives. There was no reapportionment based on 1920 census figures.

STATE	representatives										
	1790	1800	1810	1820	1830	1840	1850	1860	1870	1880	1890
Alabama	NA	NA	1[1]	3	5	7	7	6	8	8	9
Alaska	NA	NA	NA	NA	NA	NA	NA	NA	NA	NA	NA
Arizona	NA	NA	NA	NA	NA	NA	NA	NA	NA	NA	NA
Arkansas	NA	NA	NA	NA	1[1]	1	2	3	4	5	6
California	NA	NA	NA	NA	NA	2[1]	2	3	4	6	7
Colorado	NA	NA	NA	NA	NA	NA	NA	NA	1[1]	1	2
Connecticut	7	7	7	6	6	4	4	4	4	4	4
Delaware	1	1	2	1	1	1	1	1	1	1	1
Florida	NA	NA	NA	NA	NA	1[1]	1	1	2	2	2
Georgia	2	4	6	7	9	8	8	7	9	10	11
Hawaii	NA	NA	NA	NA	NA	NA	NA	NA	NA	NA	NA
Idaho	NA	NA	NA	NA	NA	NA	NA	NA	NA	1[1]	1
Illinois	NA	NA	1[1]	1	3	7	9	14	19	20	22
Indiana	NA	NA	1[1]	3	7	10	11	11	13	13	13
Iowa	NA	NA	NA	NA	NA	2[1]	2	6	9	11	11
Kansas	NA	NA	NA	NA	NA	NA	NA	1	3	7	8
Kentucky	2	6	10	12	13	10	10	9	10	11	11
Louisiana	NA	NA	1[1]	3	3	4	4	5	6	6	6
Maine	NA	NA	NA	7	8	7	6	5	5	4	4
Maryland	8	9	9	9	8	6	6	5	6	6	6
Massachusetts	14	17	20	13	12	10	11	10	11	12	13
Michigan	NA	NA	NA	NA	1[1]	3	4	6	9	11	12
Minnesota	NA	NA	NA	NA	NA	NA	2[1]	2	3	5	7
Mississippi	NA	NA	1[1]	1	2	4	5	5	6	7	7
Missouri	NA	NA	NA	1	2	5	7	9	13	14	15
Montana	NA	NA	NA	NA	NA	NA	NA	NA	NA	1[1]	1
Nebraska	NA	NA	NA	NA	NA	NA	NA	1[1]	1	3	6
Nevada	NA	NA	NA	NA	NA	NA	NA	1[1]	1	1	1
New Hampshire	4	5	6	6	5	4	3	3	3	2	2
New Jersey	5	6	6	6	6	5	5	5	7	7	8
New Mexico	NA	NA	NA	NA	NA	NA	NA	NA	NA	NA	NA
New York	10	17	27	34	40	34	33	31	33	34	34
North Carolina	10	12	13	13	13	9	8	7	8	9	9
North Dakota	NA	NA	NA	NA	NA	NA	NA	NA	NA	1[1]	1
Ohio	NA	1[1]	6	14	19	21	21	19	20	21	21
Oklahoma	NA	NA	NA	NA	NA	NA	NA	NA	NA	NA	NA
Oregon	NA	NA	NA	NA	NA	NA	1[1]	1	1	1	2
Pennsylvania	13	18	23	26	28	24	25	24	27	28	30
Rhode Island	2	2	2	2	2	2	2	2	2	2	2
South Carolina	6	8	9	9	9	7	6	4	5	7	7
South Dakota	NA	NA	NA	NA	NA	NA	NA	NA	NA	2[1]	2
Tennessee	1[1]	3	6	9	13	11	10	8	10	10	10
Texas	NA	NA	NA	NA	NA	2[1]	2	4	6	11	13
Utah	NA	NA	NA	NA	NA	NA	NA	NA	NA	NA	1[1]
Vermont	2	4	6	5	5	4	3	3	3	2	2
Virginia	19	22	23	22	21	15	13	11	9	10	10
Washington	NA	NA	NA	NA	NA	NA	NA	NA	NA	1[1]	2
West Virginia	NA	NA	NA	NA	NA	NA	NA	NA	3	4	4
Wisconsin	NA	NA	NA	NA	NA	2[1]	3	6	8	9	10
Wyoming	NA	NA	NA	NA	NA	NA	NA	NA	NA	1[1]	1
Total	106	142	186	213	242	232	237	243	293	332	357

Congressional Apportionment (continued)

STATE	representatives									
	1900	1910	1930	1940	1950	1960	1970	1980	1990	2000
Alabama	9	10	9	9	9	8	7	7	7	7
Alaska	NA	NA	NA	NA	1[1]	1	1	1	1	1
Arizona	NA	1[2]	1	2	2	3	4	5	6	8
Arkansas	7	7	7	7	6	4	4	4	4	4
California	8	11	20	23	30	38	43	45	52	53
Colorado	3	4	4	4	4	4	5	6	6	7
Connecticut	5	5	6	6	6	6	6	6	6	5
Delaware	1	1	1	1	1	1	1	1	1	1
Florida	3	4	5	6	8	12	15	19	23	25
Georgia	11	12	10	10	10	10	10	10	11	13
Hawaii	NA	NA	NA	NA	1[1]	2	2	2	2	2
Idaho	1	2	2	2	2	2	2	2	2	2
Illinois	25	27	27	26	25	24	24	22	20	19
Indiana	13	13	12	11	11	11	11	10	10	9
Iowa	11	11	9	8	8	7	6	6	5	5
Kansas	8	8	7	6	6	5	5	5	4	4
Kentucky	11	11	9	9	8	7	7	7	6	6
Louisiana	7	8	8	8	8	8	8	8	7	7
Maine	4	4	3	3	3	2	2	2	2	2
Maryland	6	6	6	6	7	8	8	8	8	8
Massachusetts	14	16	15	14	14	12	12	11	10	10
Michigan	12	13	17	17	18	19	19	18	16	15
Minnesota	9	10	9	9	9	8	8	8	8	8
Mississippi	8	8	7	7	6	5	5	5	5	4
Missouri	16	16	13	13	11	10	10	9	9	9
Montana	1	2	2	2	2	2	2	2	1	1
Nebraska	6	6	5	4	4	3	3	3	3	3
Nevada	1	1	1	1	1	1	1	2	2	3
New Hampshire	2	2	2	2	2	2	2	2	2	2
New Jersey	10	12	14	14	14	15	15	14	13	13
New Mexico	NA	1[2]	1	2	2	2	2	3	3	3
New York	37	43	45	45	43	41	39	34	31	29
North Carolina	10	10	11	12	12	11	11	11	12	13
North Dakota	2	3	2	2	2	2	1	1	1	1
Ohio	21	22	24	23	23	24	23	21	19	18
Oklahoma	5[1]	8	9	8	6	6	6	6	6	5
Oregon	2	3	3	4	4	4	4	5	5	5
Pennsylvania	32	36	34	33	30	27	25	23	21	19
Rhode Island	2	3	2	2	2	2	2	2	2	2
South Carolina	7	7	6	6	6	6	6	6	6	6
South Dakota	2	3	2	2	2	2	2	1	1	1
Tennessee	10	10	9	10	9	9	8	9	9	9
Texas	16	18	21	21	22	23	24	27	30	32
Utah	1	2	2	2	2	2	2	3	3	3
Vermont	2	2	1	1	1	1	1	1	1	1
Virginia	10	10	9	9	10	10	10	10	11	11
Washington	3	5	6	6	7	7	7	8	9	9
West Virginia	5	6	6	6	6	5	4	4	3	3
Wisconsin	11	11	10	10	10	10	9	9	9	8
Wyoming	1	1	1	1	1	1	1	1	1	1
Total	391	435	435	435	437	435	435	435	435	435

NA: Not applicable   [1]Number assigned after apportionment.   [2]Included in anticipation of statehood.

Electoral Votes by State

Each state receives one electoral vote for each of its representatives and one for each of its two senators, ensuring at least three votes for each state, as the Constitution guarantees at least one representative regardless of population. Allocations are based on the 2000 census and applicable for the 2004 presidential election.

Total: 538; Majority needed to elect president and vice president: 270

STATE	NUMBER OF VOTES	STATE	NUMBER OF VOTES	STATE	NUMBER OF VOTES
Alabama	9	Kentucky	8	North Dakota	3
Alaska	3	Louisiana	9	Ohio	20
Arizona	10	Maine	4	Oklahoma	7
Arkansas	6	Maryland	10	Oregon	7
California	55	Massachusetts	12	Pennsylvania	21
Colorado	9	Michigan	17	Rhode Island	4
Connecticut	7	Minnesota	10	South Carolina	8
Delaware	3	Mississippi	6	South Dakota	3
District of Columbia	3	Missouri	11	Tennessee	11
Florida	27	Montana	3	Texas	34
Georgia	15	Nebraska	5	Utah	5
Hawaii	4	Nevada	5	Vermont	3
Idaho	4	New Hampshire	4	Virginia	13
Illinois	21	New Jersey	15	Washington	11
Indiana	11	New Mexico	5	West Virginia	5
Iowa	7	New York	31	Wisconsin	10
Kansas	6	North Carolina	15	Wyoming	3

Supreme Court

Justices of the Supreme Court of the United States

Listed under presidents who made appointments (bold). Chief Justices names in italics.

NAME	TERM OF SERVICE[1]	NAME	TERM OF SERVICE[1]	NAME	TERM OF SERVICE[1]
George Washington		**Martin Van Buren**		**James Garfield**	
John Jay	1789–95	John Catron	1837–65	Stanley Matthews	1881–89
James Wilson	1789–98	John McKinley	1838–52	**Chester A. Arthur**	
John Rutledge	1790–91	Peter V. Daniel	1842–60	Horace Gray	1882–1902
William Cushing	1790–1810	**John Tyler**		Samuel Blatchford	1882–93
John Blair	1790–96	Samuel Nelson	1845–72	**Grover Cleveland**	
James Iredell	1790–99	**James Polk**		Lucius Q.C. Lamar	1888–93
Thomas Johnson	1792–93	Levi Woodbury	1845–51	*Melville Weston Fuller*	1888–1910
William Paterson	1793–1806	Robert C. Grier	1846–70	**Benjamin Harrison**	
John Rutledge[2]	1795	**Millard Fillmore**		David J. Brewer	1890–1910
Samuel Chase	1796–1811	Benjamin R. Curtis	1851–57	Henry B. Brown	1891–1906
Oliver Ellsworth	1796–1800	**Franklin Pierce**		George Shiras, Jr.	1892–1903
John Adams		John Archibald Campbell	1853–61	Howell E. Jackson	1893–95
Bushrod Washington	1799–1829	**James Buchanan**		**Grover Cleveland**	
Alfred Moore	1800–04	Nathan Clifford	1858–81	Edward Douglass White	1894–1910
John Marshall	1801–35	**Abraham Lincoln**		Rufus Wheeler Peckham	1896–1909
Thomas Jefferson		Noah H. Swayne	1862–81	**William McKinley**	
William Johnson	1804–34	Samuel Freeman Miller	1862–90	Joseph McKenna	1898–1925
Brockholst Livingston	1807–23	David Davis	1862–77	**Theodore Roosevelt**	
Thomas Todd	1807–26	Stephen Johnson Field	1863–97	Oliver Wendell Holmes	1902–32
James Madison		*Salmon P. Chase*	1864–73	William R. Day	1903–22
Gabriel Duvall	1811–35	**Ulysses S. Grant**		William H. Moody	1906–10
Joseph Story	1812–45	William Strong	1870–80	**William H. Taft**	
James Monroe		Joseph P. Bradley	1870–92	Horace H. Lurton	1910–14
Smith Thompson	1823–43	Ward Hunt	1873–82	Charles Evans Hughes	1910–16
John Quincy Adams		*Morrison Remick Waite*	1874–88	Willis Van Devanter	1911–37
Robert Trimble	1826–28	**Rutherford B. Hayes**		Joseph R. Lamar	1911–16
Andrew Jackson		John Marshall Harlan	1877–1911	*Edward Douglass White*	1910–21
John McLean	1830–61	William B. Woods	1881–87	Mahlon Pitney	1912–22
Henry Baldwin	1830–44				
James M. Wayne	1835–67				
Roger Brooke Taney	1836–64				
Philip P. Barbour	1836–41				

Justices of the Supreme Court of the United States (continued)

NAME	TERM OF SERVICE[1]	NAME	TERM OF SERVICE[1]	NAME	TERM OF SERVICE[1]
Woodrow Wilson		William O. Douglas	1939–75	Lyndon B. Johnson	
James C. McReynolds	1914–41	Frank Murphy	1940–49	Abe Fortas	1965–69
Louis Brandeis	1916–39	Harlan Fiske Stone	1941–46	Thurgood Marshall	1967–91
John H. Clarke	1916–22	James F. Byrnes	1941–42	Richard M. Nixon	
Warren G. Harding		Robert H. Jackson	1941–54	Warren E. Burger	1969–86
William Howard Taft	1921–30	Wiley B. Rutledge	1943–49	Harry A. Blackmun	1970–94
George Sutherland	1922–38	Harry S. Truman		Lewis F. Powell, Jr.	1972–87
Pierce Butler	1923–39	Harold H. Burton	1945–58	William H. Rehnquist	1972–86
Edward T. Sanford	1923–30	Fred M. Vinson	1946–53	Gerald Ford	
Calvin Coolidge		Tom C. Clark	1949–67	John Paul Stevens	1975–
Harlan Fiske Stone	1925–41	Sherman Minton	1949–56	Ronald Reagan	
Herbert Hoover		Dwight D. Eisenhower		Sandra Day O'Connor	1981–
Charles Evans Hughes	1930–41	Earl Warren	1953–69	William H. Rehnquist	1986–
Owen Roberts	1930–45	John Marshall Harlan	1955–71	Antonin Scalia	1986–
Benjamin Nathan Cardozo	1932–38	William J. Brennan, Jr.	1956–90	Anthony M. Kennedy	1988–
Franklin D. Roosevelt		Charles E. Whittaker	1957–62	George H.W. Bush	
Hugo L. Black	1937–71	Potter Stewart	1958–81	David H. Souter	1990–
Stanley F. Reed	1938–57	John F. Kennedy		Clarence Thomas	1991–
Felix Frankfurter	1939–62	Byron R. White	1962–93	Bill Clinton	
		Arthur J. Goldberg	1962–65	Ruth Bader Ginsburg	1993–
				Stephen G. Breyer	1994–

[1]The year the justice took the judicial oath is here used as the beginning date of service, for until that oath is taken the justice is not vested with the prerogatives of the office. Justices, however, receive their commissions ("letters patent") before taking their oaths—in some instances, in the preceding year. [2]John Rutledge was acting chief justice; the U.S. Senate refused to confirm him.

Milestones of US Supreme Court Jurisprudence

Information includes cases' short names, year of release, citation, and a short description of the Supreme Court's findings and importance for US law.

Marbury v. Madison, 5 U.S. 137 (1803): the first instance in which the high court declared an act of Congress (the Judiciary Act of 1789, which in part authorized the court to compel action by the executive branch) to be unconstitutional, thus establishing the doctrine of judicial review.

Martin v. Hunter's Lessee, 14 U.S. 304 (1816): asserted the US Supreme Court's power of appellate review of state supreme court decisions.

McCulloch v. Maryland, 17 U.S. 316 (1819): affirmed the constitutional doctrine of the "implied powers" of Congress, determining that Congress had not only the powers expressly conferred upon it by the Constitution but also all authority "appropriate" to carry out such powers.

Dred Scott v. Sandford, 60 U.S. 393 (1857): ruled that blacks, free or enslaved, were not citizens under the Constitution, and further determined that only states, and not Congress or territorial governments, had the power to prohibit slavery, thus overturning the Missouri Compromise of 1820 and legalizing slavery in all US territories. The citizenship of all races was affirmed with the ratification of the Fourteenth Amendment in 1868.

Santa Clara County v. Southern Pacific Railroad Co., 118 U.S. 394 (1886): established that corporations are "persons" within the meaning of the Fourteenth Amendment, extending to them the rights of due process and equal protection.

Plessy v. Ferguson, 163 U.S. 537 (1896): permitted racial segregation in "separate but equal" public facilities.

Lochner v. New York, 198 U.S. 45 (1905): found that a state labor law limiting the number of hours in the work week violated due process because the "right of contract between the employer and employees" is protected under the Fourteenth Amendment.

Standard Oil Co. of New Jersey et al. v. United States, 221 U.S. 1 (1911): ruled that the activities of the Standard Oil Company of New Jersey, a holding company that through its subsidiaries controlled most of the US petroleum industry, constituted an undue restraint of trade, and ordered the company's dissolution under the Sherman Antitrust Act.

Schenck v. United States, 249 U.S. 47 (1919): found, in the case of an American socialist convicted of espionage for distributing antidraft leaflets during wartime, that First Amendment freedom of expression is limited when there exists a "clear and present danger that [the speech] will bring about the substantive evils that Congress has a right to prevent."

Brown v. Board of Education of Topeka, 349 U.S. 294 (1954): ruled that racial segregation in public schools violated the Fourteenth Amendment, overturning the doctrine of "separate but equal" facilities reached in *Plessy v. Ferguson*.

Mapp v. Ohio, 367 U.S. 643 (1961): found that the Fourth Amendment prohibition of unreasonable search and seizure, and the inadmissibility of evidence obtained in violation of it, applied to state as well as to federal government.

Baker v. Carr, 369 U.S. 186 (1962): ruled that, under the equal protection clause of the Fourteenth Amendment, issues relating to the apportionment of congressional districts could be resolved in federal courts.

Gideon v. Wainwright, 372 U.S. 335 (1963): declared that the Sixth Amendment right to counsel applies to defendants in state as well as federal courts.

New York Times Co. v. *Sullivan,* 376 U.S. 254 (1964): protected the press from the prospects of large damage awards in libel cases by requiring that "actual malice" be demonstrated; public officials who sue for damages must prove that a falsehood had been issued with knowledge that it was false or in reckless disregard of whether it was false or not.

Heart of Atlanta Motel v. *United States,* 379 U.S. 241; *Katzenbach* v. *McClung,* 379 U.S. 294 (1964): upheld Title II of the Civil Rights Act of 1964 (which prohibits segregation or discrimination in places of public accommodation involved in interstate commerce) in the cases of an Atlanta motel and a Birmingham AL restaurant, both of which discriminated against blacks. The court ruled that both engaged in transactions affecting interstate commerce and thus were within the purview of congressional regulation, and that the Civil Rights Act itself was constitutional.

Griswold v. *Connecticut,* 381 U.S. 479 (1965): ruled that a state law prohibiting the use of contraceptives (including providing information, advice, or prescriptions for them) violated "the right of marital privacy" implied within the Bill of Rights.

Miranda v. *Arizona,* 384 U.S. 436 (1966): ruled that the prosecution may not use statements made by a person in police custody unless minimum procedural safeguards were followed and established guidelines to guarantee arrested persons' Fifth Amendment right not to be compelled to incriminate themselves. These guidelines included informing arrestees prior to questioning that they have the right to remain silent, that anything they say may be used against them as evidence, and that they have the right to the counsel of an attorney.

Loving v. *Virginia,* 388 U.S. 1 (1967): declared that antimiscegenation laws (prohibitions of interracial marriage) have no legitimate purpose outside of racial discrimination, and thus violate the Fourteenth Amendment.

New York Times Co. v. *United States,* 403 U.S. 713 (1971): in what was known as the "Pentagon Papers" case, the court vacated a US Justice Department injunction that restrained the *New York Times* and *Washington Post* from publishing excerpts of a top-secret report on the Vietnam War, ruling that such prior restraint of the press was subject to a "heavy burden of . . . justification" which the government failed to meet.

Wisconsin v. *Yoder,* 406 U.S. 205 (1972): in the case of members of an Old Order Amish community who refused on religious grounds to keep their children in school past the eighth grade, found that the right to free exercise of religion outweighed the state's interest in universal education.

Roe v. *Wade,* 410 U.S. 113 (1973): held that overly restrictive state regulation of abortion is unconstitutional. In balancing the "compelling state interest[s]" in protecting the health of pregnant women and the potential life of fetuses, the court ruled that regulation of abortion could begin no sooner than about the end of the first trimester, with increasing regulation permissible in the second and third trimesters; the state's interest in protecting the fetus was found to increase with the fetus' "capability for meaningful life outside the mother's womb."

Gregg v. *Georgia,* 428 U.S. 153; *Proffitt* v. *Florida,* 428 U.S. 242; *Jurek* v. *Texas,* 428 U.S. 262 (1976): ruled that the death penalty, in and of itself, does not violate the Eighth Amendment if applied under certain guidelines in first-degree murder cases.

Regents of the University of California v. *Bakke,* 438 U.S. 265 (1978): in a test of the constitutionality of "affirmative action" programs to redress racial iniquities, the court ruled that the admissions policy of the Medical School of the University of California at Davis, which set aside a certain number of places for members of racial minorities, violated the Fourteenth Amendment and the Civil Rights Act of 1964 because it discriminated on the basis of race. The court did, however, permit "consideration of race in admissions decisions under some circumstances."

Bowers v. *Hardwick,* 478 U.S. 186 (1986): ruled that there is "no such thing as a fundamental right to commit homosexual sodomy"; that such behavior, even between two consenting adults, is not protected by a constitutional right to privacy; and refused to strike down state laws proscribing it.

Cruzan by Cruzan v. *Director, Missouri Department of Health,* 497 U.S. 261 (1990): found that, in the absence of "clear and convincing evidence" of a person's desire to refuse medical treatment or not to live on life support, a state could require that such treatment continue. When such evidence exists, however, a patient's wishes must be respected.

Rust v. Sullivan, 500 U.S. 173 (1991): ruled that Congress could prohibit recipients of family-planning funds from providing or discussing abortion as a family planning option. The court held that this did not violate the first amendment because clinics were still free to provide such counseling as a "financially and physically" separate activity.

Planned Parenthood of Southeastern Pennsylvania v. *Casey,* 505 U.S. 833 (1992): softened the ruling in *Roe* v. *Wade* by finding that some state regulation of abortion prior to fetal viability, including a 24-hour waiting period, mandatory counseling, and a parental-consent requirement for minors, is permissible as long as the regulations do not place an "undue burden" on the woman.

Romer v. *Evans,* 517 U.S. 620 (1996): invalidated a Colorado referendum passed by popular vote that prohibited conferral of protected status on the basis of sexual orientation; the court ruled that the referendum was overbroad, bore little relationship to legimate state interests, and violated the Fourteenth Amendment of the US Constitution.

Faragher v. *City of Boca Raton,* 524 U.S. 775; *Burlington Industries, Inc.* v. *Ellerth* 524 U.S. 742 (1998): held that, under by Title VII of the Civil Rights Act of 1964, an employer is responsible for workplace sexual harassment by supervisory employees if the employer does not act to prevent such harassment and to correct it should it occur.

Oncale v. *Sundowner Offshore Services, Inc., et al,* 523 U.S. 75 (1998): found that Title VII's prohibition of workplace sexual discrimination applied equally in cases when the harasser and victim are of the same sex.

Boy Scouts of America v. *Dale,* 530 U.S. 640 (2000): ruled that the Boy Scouts, because they are a private organization, were within their rights when they dismissed a scoutmaster expressly because of his avowed homosexuality. The court reasoned that a state statute banning discrimination on the basis of sexual orientation in places of public accommodation was outweighed by the Scouts' First Amendment right to freedom of association.

Stenberg v. *Carhart,* 530 U.S. 914 (2000): ruled that a state law criminalizing the performance of dilation and extraction—or "partial-birth"—abortions violated the Constitution (because of the same reasoning as in *Roe* v. *Wade*) because it allowed no consideration of the health of the woman in choosing the procedure.

Bush v. *Gore*, 531 U.S. 98 (2000): stopped the manual recounts, then underway in certain Florida counties at the demand of Al Gore, of disputed ballots from the November 2000 presidential election on the grounds that inconsistent vote-counting standards among the several counties involved amounted to a violation of the Fourteenth Amendment's equal protection clause. Because George W. Bush at the time led Al Gore in the number of officially recognized Florida votes, the decision meant that he would win the state and thus the general election, despite having lost the popular vote.

Republican Party of Minnesota v. *White*, **122 S.Ct. 2528** (2002): held that candidates for judicial office may state their views on disputed legal or political issues within the purview of the court for which they are running.

Atkins v. *Virginia*, **122 S.Ct. 2242** (2002): ruled that the death penalty, when applied to mentally retarded individuals, constitutes a "cruel and unusual punishment" prohibited by the Eighth Amendment.

Ring v. *Arizona*, **122 S.Ct. 2428** (2002): ruled that under the Sixth Amendment, a jury, rather than a judge, must indicate those aggravating factors that would subject a convicted criminal to death rather than a lesser sentence.

Military Affairs

US Military Leadership

President, Commander in Chief:	George W. Bush
Secretary of Defense:	Donald Rumsfeld
Chairman, Joint Chiefs of Staff:	Richard B. Myers
Vice Chairman, Joint Chiefs of Staff:	Peter Pace

The Joint Chiefs of Staff include the Chairman, Joint Chiefs of Staff; the Vice Chairman, Joint Chiefs of Staff; the Chief of Staff, US Army; the Chief of Naval Operations; the Commandant, US Marine Corps; and the Chief of Staff, US Air Force.

RANK/POSITION	NAME/DATE ASSUMED POST
Army	
Chief of Staff	Eric K. Shinseki (22 Jun 1999)
Vice Chief of Staff	John M. Keane (22 Jun 1999)
Sergeant Major	Jack L. Tilley (23 Jun 2000)
Sec. of the Army	Thomas E. White (31 May 2001)
Under Sec. of the Army	Les Brownlee (14 Nov 2001)
Navy	
Chief of Naval Operations	Vern Clark (21 Jul 2000)
Vice Chief of Naval Operations	William J. Fallon (11 Oct 2000)
Master Chief Petty Officer	James L. Herdt (27 Mar 1998)
Sec. of the Navy	Gordon R. England (24 May 2001)
Under Sec. of the Navy	Susan Morrisey Livingstone (25 Jul 2001)
Air Force	
Chief of Staff	John P. Jumper (6 Sep 2001)
Vice Chief of Staff	Robert H. Foglesong (5 Nov 2001)

RANK/POSITION	NAME/DATE ASSUMED POST
Air Force (continued)	
Asst. Vice Chief of Staff	Joseph H. Wehrle, Jr (25 Mar 2002)
Chief Master Sergeant	Frederick J. Finch (2 Aug 1999)
Sec. of the Air Force	James G. Roche (1 Jun 2001)
Under Sec. of the Air Force	Peter B. Teets (13 Dec 2001)
Marine Corps	
Commandant	James L. Jones (1 Jul 1999)
Asst. Commandant	Michael J. Williams (9 Sep 2000)
Sergeant Major	Alford L. McMichael (1 Jul 1999)
Coast Guard	
Commandant	James M. Loy (29 May 1998)
Vice Commandant	Thomas H. Collins (9 Jun 2000)
Chief of Staff	Timothy W. Josiah (31 May 1998)
Master Chief Petty Officer	Vincent Patton III (22 May 1998)

Unified Combatant Commands

The Unified Combatant Commands provide operational control of US combat forces and are organized geographically. Commanders in Chief receive orders through the chairman of the Joint Chiefs of Staff. Although the number of commands may vary, each command must be composed of forces from at least two of the armed services. Information is current as of March 2002.

COMMAND	LOCATION	COMMANDER IN CHIEF
US European Command	Stuttgart-Vaihingen, Germany	Gen. Joseph W. Ralston, USAF
US Pacific Command	Honolulu HI	Adm. Dennis C. Blair, USN
US Joint Forces Command	Norfolk VA	Gen. William F. Kernan, USA/US
Southern Command	Miami FL	Maj. Gen. Gary D. Speer, USA (acting)
US Central Command	MacDill Air Force Base, Florida	Gen. Tommy R. Franks, USA

Unified Combatant Commands (continued)

COMMAND	LOCATION	COMMANDER IN CHIEF
US Space Command	Peterson Air Force Base, Colorado	Gen. Ralph E. Eberhart, USAF
US Special Operations Command	MacDill Air Force Base, Florida	Gen. Charles R. Holland, USAF
US Transportation Command	Scott Air Force Base, Illinois	Gen. John W. Handy, USAF
US Strategic Command	Offutt Air Force Base, Nebraska	Adm. James O. Ellis, Jr., USN

North Atlantic Treaty Organization (NATO) International Commands

The NATO military command structure comprises two main strategic commands, Allied Command Europe and Allied Command Atlantic. Their subordinate regional commands are also listed.

ALLIED COMMAND EUROPE (ACE)
Mons, Belgium
Supreme Allied Commander: Gen. Joseph W. Ralston (USAF) (3 May 2000–   )

SUBORDINATE REGIONAL COMMANDS
Allied Forces South Europe (AFSOUTH)
Naples, Italy
Commander-in-Chief: Adm. Gregory G. Johnson (USN) (24 Oct 2001–   )

Allied Forces North Europe (AFNORTH)
Brunssum, The Netherlands
Commander-in-Chief: Gen. Jack Deverell (Royal Army, UK) (23 Mar 2001–   )

ALLIED COMMAND ATLANTIC (ACLANT)
Norfolk VA
Supreme Allied Commander: Gen. William F. Kernan (USA) (5 Sep 2000–   )

SUBORDINATE REGIONAL COMMANDS
Allied Forces East Atlantic (EASTLANT)
Northwood, United Kingdom
Commander-in-Chief: Adm. Alan West (Royal Navy, UK) (30 Nov 2000–   )

Allied Forces West Atlantic (WESTLANT)
Norfolk VA
Commander-in-Chief: Adm. Robert J. Natter (USN) (23 Jun 2000–   )

Allied Forces South Atlantic (SOUTHLANT)
Oeiras, Portugal
Commander-in-Chief: Vice Adm. Américo da Silva Santos (Portuguese Navy) (10 Nov 2000–   )

Did you know? If a new navy were formed from the US ships now serving as memorials, it would constitute the third-largest navy in the world.

Chairmen of the Joint Chiefs of Staff, 1949–2002

The 1949 Amendments to the National Security Act of 1947 created the position of chairman of the Joint Chiefs of Staff. The president appoints the chairman with the advice and consent of the Senate. Terms are for two years. On 1 Oct 1986 the chairman's eligibility for service increased from two to three reappointments. (During wartime, there is no limit on reappointment.) The chairman's term begins on 1 October of odd-numbered years.

NAME	MILITARY BRANCH	DATES OF SERVICE
Gen. of the Army Omar N. Bradley	US Army	16 Aug 1949–15 Aug 1953
Adm. Arthur W. Radford	US Navy	15 Aug 1953–15 Aug 1957
Gen. Nathan F. Twining	US Air Force	15 Aug 1957–30 Sep 1960
Gen. Lyman L. Lemnitzer	US Army	1 Oct 1960–30 Sep 1962
Gen. Maxwell D. Taylor	US Army	1 Oct 1962–1 Jul 1964
Gen. Earle G. Wheeler	US Army	3 Jul 1964–2 Jul 1970
Adm. Thomas H. Moorer	US Navy	2 Jul 1970–1 Jul 1974
Gen. George S. Brown	US Air Force	1 Jul 1974–20 Jun 1978
Gen. David C. Jones	US Air Force	21 Jun 1978–18 Jun 1982
Gen. John W. Vessey, Jr.	US Army	18 Jun 1982–30 Sep 1985
Adm. William J. Crowe, Jr.	US Navy	1 Oct 1985–30 Sep 1989
Gen. Colin L. Powell	US Army	1 Oct 1989–30 Sep 1993
Adm. David E. Jeremiah (acting)	US Navy	1 Oct 1993–24 Oct 1993
Gen. John M. Shalikashvili	US Army	25 Oct 1993–30 Sep 1997
Gen. Harry Shelton	US Army	1 Oct 1997–1 Oct 2001
Gen. Richard B. Myers	US Air Force	1 Oct 2001–

Worldwide Deployment of the US Military

Deployments of 1,000 or more active duty military personnel as of 31 Dec 2001. Regional totals include countries and areas not shown in the table. Source: US Department of Defense

COUNTRY/REGIONAL AREA	TOTAL	ARMY	NAVY	MARINE CORPS	AIR FORCE
continental US	947,955	340,883	199,694	134,248	273,130
Alaska	15,926	6,593	55	27	9,251
Hawaii	33,191	16,100	6,929	5,719	4,443
Guam	3,398	32	1,583	129	1,654
Puerto Rico	2,525	804	1,642	23	56
transients	27,208	10,408	12,385	2,638	1,777
afloat	99,485	0	99,485	0	0
US and territories totals	1,129,747	374,849	321,776	142,784	290,338
Belgium	1,554	871	106	28	549
Bosnia and Herzegovina	3,109	3,090	2	16	1
Germany	71,434	55,565	319	302	15,248
Iceland	1,713	3	993	47	670
Italy	11,854	2,606	5,051	142	4,055
Serbia (including Kosovo)	5,200	5,196	1	1	2
Spain	1,778	45	1,329	147	257
Turkey	2,170	179	25	207	1,759
United Kingdom	11,361	431	1,247	157	9,526
afloat	4,728	0	2,657	2,071	0
European totals	118,149	68,883	12,158	3,485	33,623
Japan	39,691	1,850	5,448	19,265	13,128
South Korea	37,972	28,989	319	150	8,514
afloat	12,503	0	12,307	196	0
East Asian and Pacific totals	90,822	30,946	18,283	19,774	21,819
Bahrain	1,280	21	984	248	27
Kuwait	4,300	2,125	4	161	2,010
Saudi Arabia	4,802	291	27	40	4,444
afloat	13,559	0	13,559	0	0
North African, Near Eastern, and South Asian totals	26,172	2,882	15,141	785	7,364
Western Hemisphere (afloat)	12,013	0	12,013	0	0
foreign country totals	255,065	103,104	58,140	30,588	63,233
ashore	212,262	103,104	17,604	28,321	63,233
afloat	42,803	0	40,536	2,267	0
worldwide totals	1,384,812	477,953	379,916	173,372	353,571
ashore	1,242,524	477,953	239,895	171,105	353,571
afloat	142,288	0	140,021	2,267	0

Military Rank and Monthly Pay Schedules: 1 Jan 2002

Pay given in dollars.

Enlisted personnel

	E-1	E-2	E-3	E-4	E-5
Army	private	private	private first class	corporal	sergeant
Navy	seaman recruit	seaman apprentice	seaman	petty officer third class	petty officer second class
Air Force	airman basic	airman	airman first class	senior airman	staff sergeant
Marine Corps	private	private first class	lance corporal	corporal	sergeant
0–6 years	1,023–1,106	1,239	1,304–1,468	1,444–1,680	1,562–1,828
6–12 years				1,752	1,913–2,110
12–18 years					2,193
18–24 years					
over 24 years					

Military Rank and Monthly Pay Schedules: 1 Jan 2002 (continued)

Enlisted personnel (continued)

	E-6	E-7	E-8	E-9
Army	staff sergeant	sergeant first class	first sergeant	sergeant major
Navy	petty officer first class	chief petty officer	senior chief petty officer	master chief petty officer
Air Force	technical sergeant	master sergeant	senior master sergeant	chief master sergeant
Marine Corps	staff sergeant	gunnery sergeant	master sergeant, first sergeant	master gunnery sergeant, sergeant major, command sergeant major
0–6 years	1,701–2,034	1,987–2,332		
6–12 years	2,117–2,337	2,417–2,645	2,858–2,941	3,424
12–18 years	2,417–2,558	2,726–2,893	3,018–3,210	3,501–3,715
18–24 years	2,603	2,975–3,200	3,315–3,573	3,830–4,098
over 24 years		3,293–3,527	3,725–3,938	4,251–4,467

Warrant officers

	W-1	W-2	W-3	W-4	W-5
Army	warrant officer	chief warrant officer	chief warrant officer	chief warrant officer	chief warrant officer
Navy	"	"	"	"	"
Air Force	"	"	"	"	"
Marine Corps	"	"	"	"	"
0–6 years	2,050–2,403	2,321–2,654	2,639–2,899	2,890–3,286	
6–12 years	2,512–2,738	2,726–2,984	3,017–3,331	3,437–3,738	
12–18 years	2,850–3,077	3,094–3,318	3,440–3,694	3,885–4,184	
18–24 years	3,190–3,275	3,439–3,680	3,829–4,098	4,334–4,633	4,966–5,136
over 24 years		3,801	4,233–4,369	4,782–4,935	5,307–5,479

Officers (with more than 4 years served as as an enlisted or warrant member of the armed services)

	O-1E	O-2E	O-3E
Army	second lieutenant	first lieutenant	captain
Navy	ensign	lieutenant, Jr. grade	lieutenant
Air Force	second lieutenant	first lieutenant	captain
Marine Corps	second lieutenant	first lieutenant	captain
0–6 years	2,638	3,276	3,699
6–12 years	2,818–3,028	3,344–3,630	3,876–4,232
12–18 years	3,133–3,276	3,769–3,872	4,441–4,717
18–24 years			4,855
over 24 years			

Officers

	O-1	O-2	O-3	O-4	O-5
Army	second lieutenant	first lieutenant	captain	major	lieutenant colonel
Navy	ensign	lieutenant, Jr. grade	lieutenant	lieutenant commander	commander
Air Force	second lieutenant	first lieutenant	captain	major	lieutenant colonel
Marine Corps	second lieutenant	first lieutenant	captain	major	lieutenant colonel
0–6 years	2,098–2,638	2,416–3,276	2,797–3,699	3,024–3,982	3,537–4,494
6–12 years		3,344	3,876–4,232	4,211–4,696	4,673–4,813
12–18 years			4,441–4,549	4,930–5,256	5,073–5,756
18–24 years				5,311	5,919–6,263
over 24 years					

Officers (continued)

	O-6	O-7	O-8	O-9	O-10
Army	colonel	brigadier general	major general	lieutenant general	general
Navy	captain	rear admiral (lower half)	rear admiral (upper half)	vice admiral	admiral
Air Force	colonel	brigadier general	major general	lieutenant general	general
Marine Corps	colonel	brigadier general	major general	lieutenant general	general
0–6 years	4,422–5,177	5,966–6,658	7,180–7,615		
6–12 years	5,197–5,449	6,840–7,262	7,809–8,211		
12–18 years	5,629–6,306	7,473–8,695	8,520–8,874		
18–24 years	6,627–7,131	8,695	9,260–9,615	10,148–10,294	11,602–11,659
over 24 years	7,316–7,675	8,739	9,615	10,505–10,874	11,901–12,324

Women in the Armed Forces

Few early American women were soldiers. With the rise of the women's movement in the late 19th century, women gradually made inroads into the US military, most often in auxiliary roles. It wasn't until the late 20th century that they achieved regular combat status in the armed forces. By the 21st century women continued to fight for full equality across all branches of the military, especially in terms of combat duty.

During World War I many women had enlisted as volunteers in the military services; they usually served in clerical roles. When the war ended, they were released from their duties. The same was true during World War II, when an even greater number of women volunteers served in the armed forces. The war did open other employment opportunities for women—as factory workers ("Rosie the Riveter" became an American icon), nurses, and journalists—but these doors of opportunity were largely closed after the war, when women routinely lost their jobs to men discharged from military service.

During World War II several gender-specific military organizations were formed. Never before had women, with the exception of nurses, served within the ranks of the US Army until the advent of the **Women's Army Corps** (WAC), which placed more than 150,000 women in noncombat positions. In anticipation of the expiration of the WAC law in 1948, the leaders of the Army in 1946 requested that the WACs be made a permanent part of their personnel. Following two years of legislative debate, the bill was passed by Congress and signed into law by Pres. Harry S. Truman on 12 Jun 1948, as the **Women's Armed Services Integration Act.** It enabled women to serve as permanent, regular members of not only the army but also the navy, marine corps, and the recently formed air force. The law limited the number of women who could serve in the military to 2% of the total forces in each branch. The WAC remained a separate unit of the Army until 1978, when male and female forces were integrated.

Another group formed during World War II was the **Coast Guard Women's Reserve**, founded in 1942 for the purpose of making more men available to serve at sea by assigning women to onshore duties. Also established in 1942, the military unit **Women Accepted for Volunteer Emergency Service** (WAVES) was the Navy's corps of female members. During the war some 100,000 WAVES served in a wide variety of capacities, ranging from performing essential clerical duties to serving as instructors for male pilots-in-training. Several thousand WAVES later participated in the Korean War. Unlike the WAC, the WAVES was not an auxiliary and were accorded a status comparable to that of male members of the reserve. The navy, however, did come under fire for excluding African American women from the ranks until the final months of the war, when Pres. Franklin D. Roosevelt ordered racial integration. The corps continued its separate existence until 1978.

At the advent of the 21st century, about 200,000 women were listed as active members of the US armed forces, comprising about 15% of the total military balance. The largest representation of women was in the Air Force, where nearly one-fifth were female; though a larger gross number of women were active in the Army. The smallest number and smallest female-to-male proportion were found in the Marine Corps.

Military education

In the late 20th century women made advances in military education. In 1976 they were first admitted to the **US Military Academy, US Naval Academy,** and **US Air Force Academy;** the previous year they were admitted to the **US Coast Guard Academy.** In 1990 the Justice Department ruled that the **Virginia Military Institute's** male-only admissions policy was unconstitutional. In response, the institute established an associated military program for women at **Mary Baldwin College** in Staunton VA, in 1995. Nonetheless, the Supreme Court ruled in 1996 that the admissions policy was unconstitutional, and the school admitted its first women cadets in 1997.

Military figures

Deborah Sampson of Massachusetts assumed a male identity to serve for the Continental Army in the American Revolutionary War in 1782 until her true identity was discovered and she was discharged; her heirs received a full military pension in 1838. **Sarah Emma Evelyn Edmonds** enlisted as a man in the American Civil War and saw military action as a Union soldier and a spy until she deserted in April 1863; she later received a veteran's pension. According to legend, **Lucy Brewer** was the first woman marine, who, perhaps inspired by the story of Deborah Sampson, disguised herself as a man to serve on the USS *Constitution* during the War of 1812. Officially, however, **Opha Mae Johnson** is credited as the first female in the Marine Corps, enrolling in 1918.

Among the female leaders of military outfits during and after World War II were **Florence A. Blanchfield** (Army Nurse Corps), **Sue Sophia Dauser** (Navy Nurse Corps), **Joy Bright Hancock** (WAVES), **Oveta Culp Hobby** and **Mary Agnes Hallaren** (WAC), **Dorothy Constance Stratton** (Coast Guard Women's Reserve), and **Katherine Amelia Towle**, who was director of the women's reserve of the Marine Corps from 1948.

African American Service in US Wars

During the American Civil War the Union Army enlisted some 179,000 soldiers in 166 all-black regiments, but the first official group of African American professional soldiers was not recognized until the war had ended and the US was reunified. A 1866 law authorized the creation of African American cavalry regiments in the Army; though it required their officers to be white. The resulting units were the 9th and 10th cavalries and the 38th through 41st infantries. These **buffalo soldiers**, as they came to be known, patrolled the Western frontier in the late 19th century, helping to pacify Native Americans.

The 9th and 10th cavalries later distinguished themselves by their fighting in the Spanish-American War and in the 1916 Mexican campaign. One of the 10th Cavalry's officers was **John J. Pershing**, afterwards a World War I general, whose nickname "Black Jack" reflected his advocacy of black troops.

The Medal of Honor, which became a permanent military decoration in 1863, was bestowed upon

African Americans in the Civil War, Indian campaigns, Spanish-American War, both World Wars, the Korean conflict, and the Vietnam War. The seven Medals of Honor awarded to black soldiers in World War II were not granted until 1997, after a study revealed there was racial disparity in the awarding process.

More than 1.2 million African Americans served during World War II. Mostly restricted to segregated units, black soldiers not only fought for the Army but first saw combat duty in the Navy, Marines, and Army Air Corps (later Air Force). The **Tuskegee Airmen** of the all-black 99th Pursuit Squadron of the Air Corps were commanded by Lt. Col. **Benjamin Oliver Davis, Jr.**, whose father, **Benjamin O. Davis, Sr.**, was the first African American to become a US general (Army).

In 1948 President Truman integrated all branches of the military, and all-black units were phased out by 1954. In the decades following, the **Civil Rights Movement** continued to erode public racial segregation, and African Americans continued to figure prominently in the military. **Colin Powell** became the first black officer to hold the highest military post in the US when Pres. George Bush nominated him chairman of the Joint Chiefs of Staff in 1989.

Veterans Living by Age[1]

AGE IN YEARS	KOREAN CONFLICT	VIETNAM ERA	GULF WAR	TOTAL WARTIME	TOTAL VETERANS[4]
Under 35	—	—	1,362,000	1,362,000	1,941,000
35–39	—	12,000	274,000	286,000	1,387,000
40–44	—	518,000	222,000	691,000	1,749,000
45–49	—	1,949,000	202,000	1,996,000	2,391,000
50–54	—	3,310,000	99,000	3,330,000	3,546,000
55–59	—	1,485,000	30,000	1,494,000	2,472,000
60–64	583,000	385,000	9,000	899,000	2,363,000
65 and over	3,481,000	455,000	2,000	8,887,000[3]	10,330,000
Total[2]	**4,064,000**	**8,114,000**	**2,200,000**	**18,945,000**	**26,179,000**

[1]As of 1 Jul 1999. Includes Puerto Rico. Estimated.
[2]Veterans who served in more than one wartime period are counted only once.
[3]Includes 3,000 veterans of World war I and 5,940,000 veterans of World War II, all 65 or over.
[4]Includes those serving during periods of armed conflict not listed.

Disabled Veterans Receiving Compensation

Numbers of veterans receiving compensation for service-related disabilities.

TIME OF SERVICE	1980	1990	1995	1996	1997	1998	1999	2000
World War I[1]	30,000	3,000	1,000	—	—	—	—	—
World War II	1,193,000	876,000	692,000	655,000	616,000	578,000	541,000	505,000
Korean Conflict	236,000	209,000	191,000	187,000	182,000	179,000	175,000	171,000
Vietnam Era	553,000	652,000	705,000	714,000	724,000	729,000	736,000	741,000
Gulf War	NA	NA	134,000	168,000	202,000	241,000	282,000	325,000
Peacetime	262,000	444,000	514,000	529,000	539,000	550,000	561,000	567,000
Total[1]	2,274,000	2,184,000	2,237,000	2,253,000	2,263,000	2,277,000	2,295,000	2,309,000

NA: Not applicable
— Fewer than 500

[1]Includes Spanish-American War and Mexican Border service.

US Casualties of War

Data prior to World War I are based on incomplete records. Casualty data exclude personnel captured or missing in action. N/A means not available or unknown. CG stands for Coast Guard.
Sources: US Department of Defense and US Coast Guard

WAR	SERVICE BRANCH	NUMBER OF COMBATANTS	CASUALTIES BATTLE WOUNDED[1]	OTHER DEATHS	TOTAL DEATHS	DEATHS
Revolutionary War	Army	N/A	6,004	4,044	N/A	4,044
(1775–1783)	Navy	N/A	114	342	N/A	342
	Marines	N/A	70	49	N/A	49
	total	184,000–250,000[2]	6,188	4,435	N/A	4,435
War of 1812	Army	N/A	4,000	1,950	N/A	1,950
(1812–1815)	Navy	N/A	439	265	N/A	265
	Marines	N/A	66	45	N/A	45
	CG	100	N/A	0	N/A	0
	total	286,830	4,505	2,260	N/A	2,260

US Casualties of War (continued)

		CASUALTIES				
WAR	SERVICE BRANCH	NUMBER OF COMBATANTS	BATTLE WOUNDED[1]	OTHER DEATHS	TOTAL DEATHS	DEATHS
Mexican War	Army	N/A	4,102	1,721	11,550	13,271
(1846–1848)	Navy	N/A	3	1	N/A	1
	Marines	N/A	47	11	N/A	11
	CG	71	N/A	N/A	N/A	N/A
	total	78,789	4,152	1,733	11,550	13,283
Civil War (1861–1865)						
Union	Army	2,128,948	280,040	138,154	221,374	359,528
	Navy	N/A	1,710	2,112	2,411	4,523
	Marines	84,415	131	148	312	460
	CG	219	N/A	1	N/A	1
	total	2,213,582	281,881	140,415	224,097	364,512
Confederate[3]	total	600,000–1,500,000	N/A	74,524	59,297	133,821
Spanish-American War	Army	280,564	1,594	369	2,061	2,430
(1898)	Navy	22,875	47	10	N/A	10
	Marines	3,321	21	6	N/A	6
	CG	660	N/A	0	N/A	0
	total	307,420	1,662	385	2,061	2,446
World War I	Army[4]	4,057,101	193,663	50,510	55,868	106,378
(1917–1918)	Navy	599,051	819	431	6,856	7,287
	Marines	78,839	9,520	2,461	390	2,851
	CG	8,836	N/A	111	81	192
	total	4,743,826	204,002	53,513	63,195	116,708
World War II	Army[4]	11,260,000	565,861	234,874	83,400	318,274
(1941–1946)	Navy	4,183,466	37,778	36,950	25,664	62,614
	Marines	669,100	68,207	19,733	4,778	24,511
	CG	241,093	N/A	574	1,343	1,917
	total	16,353,659	671,846	292,131	115,185	407,316
Korean War[5]	Army	2,834,000	77,596	27,728	2,133	29,861
(1950–1953)	Navy	1,177,000	1,576	492	155	647
	Marines	424,000	23,744	4,268	242	4,510
	Air Force	1,285,000	368	1,198	300	1,498
	CG	44,143	0	0	N/A	0
	total	5,764,143	103,284	33,686	2,830	36,516
Vietnam War	Army	4,368,000	96,802	30,947	7,265	38,212
(1964–1973)	Navy	1,842,000	4,178	1,629	933	2,562
	Marines	794,000	51,392	13,091	1,749	14,840
	Air Force	1,740,000	931	1,743	841	2,584
	CG	8,000	60	7	N/A	7
	total	8,752,000	153,363[6]	47,417	10,788	58,205
Persian Gulf War[7]	Army	267,000	354	98	126	224
(1990–1991)	Navy	151,000	12	5	50	55
	Marines	91,000	92	24	44	68
	Air Force	71,000	9	20	15	35
	CG	400	0	0	0	0
	total	580,400	467	147	235	382

[1]Data in this column account for the total number of wounds. Marine Corps data for World War II, the Spanish-American War, and earlier wars represent the number of combatants wounded.   [2]Estimate.   [3]Authoritative statistics are not available. In addition to combat deaths, an estimated 26,000–31,000 Confederates died in Union prisons.   [4]Includes air service.   [5]As of 1 Jun 2000. Korean War casualty figures are under review.   [6]Excludes 150,332 wounded that did not require hospital care.   [7]Data for military personnel serving in the theater of operation.

Treaties Regarding Weapons of Mass Destruction

Following the explosion of the first atomic bombs in 1945 during World War II, critics were less concerned about the economic and military inefficacies of an arms build-up than the danger that nuclear weapons threatened the continued existence of civilization itself. During the Cold War the world's two superpowers, the US and the Soviet Union, each developed large arsenals of nuclear weapons. The possibility of both nations' mutual destruction in an intercontinental exchange of nuclear-armed missiles prompted them to undertake increasingly serious efforts to limit first the testing, then the deployment, and finally the possession of these weapons. Often their negotiations were facilitated by the UN.

The US and the Soviet Union sponsored several international agreements of a limited risk character. The first agreement was the Nuclear Test-Ban Treaty (1963), which banned tests of nuclear weapons in the atmosphere, in outer space, and underwater, thus effectively confining nuclear explosions to underground sites. With the Treaty on the Non-proliferation of Nuclear Weapons (1968), the two superpowers agreed not to promote the spread of nuclear weapons to countries that did not already possess them. Per other treaties, nuclear weapons could not be orbited around the Earth (the Outer Space Treaty of 1967) or placed on the seabed (the Seabed Treaty of 1971).

Substantial advances in limiting the nuclear arms race in the 1970s came out of the Strategic Arms Limitation Talks (SALT), which were intended to restrain the continuing buildup in nuclear-armed intercontinental (long-range or strategic) ballistic missiles (ICBMs). Part of SALT, the Anti-Ballistic Missile Treaty (1972), severely limited each nation's future deployment of antiballistic missiles, which could be used to destroy incoming ICBMs; the agreement thus kept both sides subject to the deterrent effect of the other's strategic offensive forces. The SALT II agreement of 1979 set limits on each side's store of multiple independent reentry vehicles (MIRVs), which are strategic missiles equipped with multiple nuclear warheads capable of hitting different targets on the ground.

Arms-control efforts between the two superpowers were facilitated in 1985 by the more liberal Soviet regime under Mikhail Gorbachev and bore their first

fruits in the Intermediate-Range Nuclear Forces Treaty (1987), in which the US and the Soviet Union agreed to eliminate their stocks of intermediate- and medium-range land-based missiles. Also in the 1980s the nations decided to reduce rather than merely limit their arsenals of nuclear warheads and launch platforms (missiles and bombers), during the Strategic Arms Reduction Treaty (START), signed in 1991.

Following the breakup of the Soviet Union in late 1991, a followup agreement, START II (1993), further reduced each nation's strategic nuclear forces. Both START II and the Comprehensive Test Ban Treaty (1996) were ratified by Russia in 2000. The following year, however, the US announced its intention to withdraw from the 1972 Anti-Ballistic Missile Treaty because it presented an obstacle to its proposed National Missile Defense.

There have also been attempts to eliminate other weapons of mass destruction. In 1971 the UN General Assembly approved a convention (in effect in 1975) prohibiting the manufacture, stockpiling, and use of biological weapons, although many states have never acceded to it. In 1993 the Chemical Weapons Convention, prohibiting the development, production, stockpiling, and use of chemical weapons and providing for their destruction, was opened for signature.

Did you know? 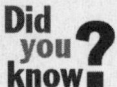 The first sale of a military airplane was made on 8 Feb 1908, when Orville and Wilbur Wright contracted to supply one Wright Model A flyer to the US Army Signal Corps for $25,000, plus a bonus up to $5,000 should it exceed the speed requirement of 65 km (40 miles) per hour. The next year the plane completed its trial flights and met the condition for the bonus.

Leading Department of Defense Contractors

Top 50 Department of Defense contractors listed according to net value of prime contract awards, fiscal year 2000.

RANK	CONTRACTOR	AMOUNT, IN '000 (US$)	RANK	CONTRACTOR	AMOUNT, IN '000 (US$)
1	Lockheed Martin	15,125,846	26	Health Net	550,580
2	Boeing	12,041,420	27	IT Group	493,335
3	Raytheon	6,330,613	28	Rockwell International	473,668
4	General Dynamics	4,195,923	29	Alliant Techsystems	470,397
5	Northrop Grumman	3,079,615	30	Longbow	468,091
6	Litton Industries	2,737,284	31	FedEx	452,385
7	United Technologies	2,071,536	32	Maersk	426,798
8	TRW	2,004,857	33	Stewart & Stevenson Services	424,051
9	General Electric	1,609,329	34	Booz Allen & Hamilton	419,576
10	Science Applications International	1,522,077	35	Mitre	409,217
			36	Federal Republic of Germany	408,004
11	Carlyle Group	1,194,713	37	Raytheon Lockheed Martin	401,584
12	Computer Sciences	1,164,634	38	Jacobs Engineering	387,343
13	Textron	1,164,465	39	Boeing Sikorsky Comanche Team	384,751
14	Marconi	997,339	40	L-3 Communications Holding	377,662
15	Honeywell International	951,255	41	Oshkosh Truck	372,526
16	Newport News Shipbuilding and Dry Dock	789,900	42	AT&T	352,547
			43	Johns Hopkins University	351,776
17	Dyncorp	771,235	44	Massachusetts Institute of Technology	347,197
18	Bechtel Group	694,717			
19	Government of Canada	676,881	45	Triwest Healthcare Alliance	335,878
20	National Amusements	619,696	46	Philipp Holzmann	334,703
21	Morrison Knudsen	596,635	47	Aerospace	334,194
22	Halliburton	595,070	48	Renco Group	330,064
23	BP Amoco	591,953	49	Electronic Data Systems	329,554
24	US Department of Energy	590,631	50	Exxon Mobil	324,816
25	ITT Industries	553,972			

Central Intelligence Agency (CIA) Directors

The National Security Act of 26 Jul 1947 established the CIA on 18 Sep 1947. By authority of a presidential directive of 22 Jan 1946, the director of central intelligence serves as a member of the National Intelligence Authority and head of the Central Intelligence Group. The director coordinates the nation's intelligence activities and informs the president on issues of national security.

NAME	DATES OF SERVICE
Rear Adm. Sidney W. Souers, USNR	23 Jan 1946–10 Jun 1946
Lt. Gen. Hoyt S. Vandenberg, USA	10 Jun 1946–1 May 1947
Rear Adm. Roscoe H. Hillenkoetter, USN	1 May 1947–7 Oct 1950
Gen. Walter Bedell Smith, USA	7 Oct 1950–9 Feb 1953
Allen W. Dulles	26 Feb 1953–29 Nov 1961
John A. McCone	29 Nov 1961–28 Apr 1965
Vice Adm. William F. Raborn, Jr., USN (Ret)	28 Apr 1965–30 Jun 1966

NAME	DATES OF SERVICE
Richard M. Helms	30 Jun 1966–2 Feb 1973
James R. Schlesinger	2 Feb 1973–2 Jul 1973
William E. Colby	4 Sep 1973–30 Jan 1976
George H.W. Bush	30 Jan 1976–20 Jan 1977
Adm. Stansfield Turner, USN (Ret)	9 Mar 1977–20 Jan 1981
William J. Casey	28 Jan 1981–29 Jan 1987
William H. Webster	26 May 1987–31 Aug 1991
Robert M. Gates	6 Nov 1991–20 Jan 1993
R. James Woolsey	5 Feb 1993–10 Jan 1995
John M. Deutch	10 May 1995–15 Dec 1996
George J. Tenet	11 Jul 1997–

The National Security Council (NSC)

The National Security Act of 1947 established the NSC to advise the president on policies relating to national security. In addition to regular attendees, the chief of staff to the president, counsel to the president, and assistant to the president for economic policy are invited to attend all meetings. The attorney general and the director of the office of management and budget are also invited to attend when needed.

chair	George W. Bush (president)
regular attendees	Richard B. Cheney (vice president) Colin L. Powell (sec. of state) Paul H. O'Neill (sec. of the treasury) Donald H. Rumsfeld (sec. of defense) Condoleezza Rice (assistant to the president for national security affairs)
military advisor	Richard B. Myers (chairman of the joint chiefs of staff)
intelligence advisor	George J. Tenet (director of the CIA)
additional participants	Andrew H. Card, Jr. (chief of staff) John B. Bellinger, III (counsel to the president) Lawrence B. Lindsey (assistant to the president for economic policy)

On 23 Mar 1953 President Eisenhower established the office of assistant to the president for national security affairs (commonly referred to as the national security advisor). Former office holders are listed below.

NAME	DATES OF SERVICE
Robert Cutler	23 Mar 1953–2 Apr 1955
Dillon Anderson	2 Apr 1955–1 Sep 1956
Robert Cutler	7 Jan 1957–24 Jun 1958
Gordon Gray	24 Jun 1958–13 Jan 1961
McGeorge Bundy	20 Jan 1961–28 Feb 1966
Walt W. Rostow	1 Apr 1966–2 Dec 1968
Henry A. Kissinger	2 Dec 1968–3 Nov 1975[1]
Brent Scowcroft	3 Nov 1975–20 Jan 1977
Zbigniew Brzezinski	20 Jan 1977–21 Jan 1981

NAME	DATES OF SERVICE
Richard V. Allen	21 Jan 1981–4 Jan 1982
William P. Clark	4 Jan 1982–17 Oct 1983
Robert C. McFarlane	17 Oct 1983–4 Dec 1985
John M. Poindexter	4 Dec 1985–25 Nov 1986
Frank C. Carlucci	2 Dec 1986–23 Nov 1987
Colin L. Powell	23 Nov 1987–20 Jan 1989
Brent Scowcroft	20 Jan 1989–20 Jan 1993
W. Anthony Lake	20 Jan 1993–14 Mar 1997
Samuel R. Berger	14 Mar 1997–20 Jan 2001

[1]Henry A. Kissinger served concurrently as secretary of state from 21 Sep 1973.

Did you know? The tallest monument in the US is the Gateway Arch in St. Louis MO. Although the arch appears to have greater height than width, it is in fact 192 meters (630 feet) at both its tallest and widest points.

United States Population

The Census, History and Gathering

A census enumerates people, houses, firms, or other important items in a country or region at a particular time. Used alone, the term usually refers to a population census and considers population size and density, distribution, and vital statistics. National population censuses, being expensive, are taken only at infrequent intervals: every 10 years in many countries, every 5 years or at irregular intervals in other countries. Specialists such as demographers interpret the statistical results, which are useful to policymakers and businessmen.

Census, a Latin word, was first used by the ancient Romans to describe the counting of the citizenry in order to value their estates for the purpose of taxation. The Domesday Book was an inquest of England in 1086 that was made to acquaint William the Conqueror with the landholders and holdings of his new domain. In 1449, under the threat of siege, the German city of Nürnberg made an almost complete count of its people.

Strictly speaking, though, the modern population census as a complete enumeration of all the people and their characteristics began to evolve only in the 17th century. The United States was the first modern nation to adopt a legal provision for taking a census at regular intervals, which it began in 1790 to establish a basis for representation in Congress. Censuses were taken in England, France, and Canada in 1801, 1836, and 1871, respectively. China was the last major country to report a census, in 1953.

Over time, improvements were made in the administration of census taking and in the compilation of its data. Census information is obtained by using a fixed questionnaire covering such topics as place of residence, sex, age, marital status, occupation, citizenship, language, ethnicity, religious affiliation, and education. From the responses demographers derive data on population distribution, household and family composition, internal migration, labor–force participation, and other topics.

A "de jure" census tallies people according to their regular or legal residence, whereas a "de facto" census allocates them to the place where enumerated—normally where they spend the night of the day enumerated. By either method, the reported territorial distribution is according to where people sleep (nighttime population) rather than where they work (daytime population).

Census 2000—Interpreting the Numbers

The undertaking of a national census every 10 years was mandated in the Constitution of 1787. Since the first census in 1790, each census counts the population of the states, and that population total determines each state's congressional representation. In general, the results of Census 2000 showed states in the Northeast and Midwest losing representatives to states in the West and South.

Twelve seats in the 435-member House of Representatives shifted with the changes in population. Arizona, Florida, Georgia, and Texas each gained two representatives, while California, Colorado, Nevada, and North Carolina each gained one. New York and Pennsylvania each lost two representatives. Connecticut, Illinois, Indiana, Michigan, Mississippi, Ohio, Oklahoma, and Wisconsin all lost one congressional seat.

The Changing Face of America

The population of the United States increased by 32.7 million people between the censuses of 1990 and 2000. That increase represented the largest population growth in census history. Census 2000 revealed a nation with more ethnic and racial diversity. During the 1990s the Hispanic population (Hispanics may be of any race) increased by 58%, the Asian population by 48%. The immigration of these and other groups accounted for about 13.3 million of the country's total population—a number not equaled in United States history. The second largest number of immigrants recorded—10.1 million people—occurred between 1905 and 1914. Of the 281.4 million people residing in the United States on census day, non-Hispanic whites accounted for 69.1% of the population; Hispanics, 12.5%; blacks, 12.3%; and Asians, 3.6%.

The changing face of the United States was reflected in cities, suburbs, and rural areas. For the first time, nearly half of the nation's 100 largest cities were home to more African Americans, Hispanics, Asians, and other minorities than to non-Hispanic whites. While the population of the country's fastest-growing cities, such as Las Vegas and Phoenix, increased in all racial and ethnic categories, the vast majority of cities—71 of the top 100—lost non-His-panic white residents to the suburbs and beyond. The nation's largest cities gained 3.8 million Hispanic residents, a 43% increase from a decade ago. Many cities, including Boston, Los Angeles, and Dallas, would have lost population in the 1990s were it not for large gains in the number of Hispanics.

Even with the arrival of a record number of immigrants (who tend to be relatively young), the United States continued to age as a nation. The median age of the country's population in 2000 was 35.3—five years older than the median age in 1950. (The median age splits the population in half, 50% are over the median age, 50% under it.) This increase in median age was tied to the graying of the post-World War II "Baby Boom" generation. Born from 1946 through 1964, Baby Boomers between 36 and 54 years of age represented 28% of the country's total population. The median age for non-Hispanic whites was 38.6, for Asians 32.7, blacks 30.2, and Hispanics 25.8. Census 2000 revealed that the country's population was 50.9% female and 49.1% male. There were 37.1 million males under the age of 18 as compared to 35.2 million females. By the age of 36, however, there were more females than males. Female senior citizens 65 years and older outnumbered males 20.6 million to 14.4 million.

Although they were not totally comprised of Baby Boomers and their parents, the Northeast and Midwest regions had the country's oldest populations. Median ages for those regions were 36.8 and 35.6, respectively. Interestingly, the Northeast was the only region in the country where all of its states had median ages above the national level. In contrast, the West had the population with the youngest median age, 33.8.

Total US Population and Area, 1790–2000

The total land/water area numbers from 1790 to 1970 were recalculated for the 1980 census. Information for Alaska and Hawaii is included in all censuses after 1940. The entry N/A means not applicable.
Source: US Census Bureau.

CENSUS	POPULATION	POPULATION GROWTH (%)	TOTAL LAND/WATER AREA (SQ MI)	LAND AREA (SQ MI)	PEOPLE/ SQ MI OF LAND AREA
1790	3,929,214	N/A	891,364	864,746	4.5
1800	5,308,483	35.1	891,364	864,746	6.1
1810	7,239,881	36.4	1,722,685	1,681,828	4.3
1820	9,638,453	33.1	1,792,552	1,749,462	5.5
1830	12,866,020	33.5	1,792,552	1,749,462	7.4
1840	17,069,453	32.7	1,792,552	1,749,462	9.8
1850	23,191,876	35.9	2,991,655	2,940,042	7.9
1860	31,443,321	35.6	3,021,295	2,969,640	10.6
1870	39,818,449	26.6	3,021,295	2,969,640	13.4
1880	50,155,783	26.0	3,021,295	2,969,640	16.9
1890	62,947,714	25.5	3,021,295	2,969,040	21.2
1900	75,994,575	20.7	3,021,295	2,969,834	25.6
1910	91,972,266	21.0	3,021,295	2,969,565	31.0
1920	105,710,620	14.9	3,021,295	2,969,451	35.6
1930	122,775,046	16.1	3,021,295	2,977,128	41.2
1940	131,669,275	7.2	3,021,295	2,977,128	44.2
1950	151,325,798	14.5	3,618,770	3,552,206	42.6
1960	179,323,175	18.5	3,618,770	3,540,911	50.6
1970	203,302,031	13.4	3,618,770	3,540,023	57.4
1980	226,542,199	11.4	3,618,770	3,539,289	64.0
1990	248,718,301	9.8	3,717,796	3,536,278	70.3
2000	281,421,906	13.1	3,794,083	3,537,438	79.6

US Population by Race, Sex, Median Age, and Residence

Numbers are in thousands ('000) except for the median age figures and the residency percentages. N/A means not available. Source: US Census Bureau.

YEAR	RACE[1] WHITE	BLACK	OTHER	SEX MALE	FEMALE	MEDIAN AGE	RESIDENCE[2] URBAN (%)	RURAL (%)
1790	3,172	757	N/A	N/A	N/A	N/A	5.1	94.9
1800	4,306	1,002	N/A	N/A	N/A	N/A	6.1	93.9
1810	5,862	1,378	N/A	N/A	N/A	N/A	7.3	92.7
1820	7,867	1,772	N/A	4,897	4,742	16.7	7.2	92.8
1830	10,537	2,329	N/A	6,532	6,334	17.2	8.8	91.2
1840	14,196	2,874	N/A	8,689	8,381	17.8	10.8	89.2
1850	19,553	3,639	N/A	11,838	11,354	18.9	15.4	84.6
1860	26,923	4,442	79	16,085	15,358	19.4	19.8	80.2
1870	34,337	5,392	89	19,494	19,065	20.2	25.7	74.3
1880	43,403	6,581	172	25,519	24,637	20.9	28.2	71.8
1890	55,101	7,489	358	32,237	30,711	22.0	35.1	64.9
1900	66,809	8,834	351	38,816	37,178	22.9	39.6	60.4
1910	81,732	9,828	413	47,332	44,640	24.1	45.6	54.4
1920	94,821	10,463	427	53,900	51,810	25.3	51.2	48.8
1930	110,287	11,891	597	62,137	60,638	26.4	56.1	43.9
1940	118,215	12,866	589	66,062	65,608	29.0	56.5	43.5
1950	134,942	15,042	713	74,833	75,864	30.2	64.0	36.0
1960	158,832	18,872	1,620	88,331	90,992	29.5	69.9	30.1
1970	178,098	22,581	2,557	98,926	104,309	28.0	73.6	26.3
1980	194,713	26,683	5,150	110,053	116,493	30.0	73.7	26.3
1990	199,686	29,986	9,233	121,271	127,494	32.8	75.2	24.8
2000	211,461	34,658	13,118	138,054	143,368	35.3	N/A	N/A

[1]The population in the column heading "other" consists of Asians, Pacific Islanders, American Indians, and Alaska Natives. Alaska and Hawaii are excluded from the population numbers until 1960, the first census after they became states in 1959. [2]The census definitions for urban and rural areas have changed through the decades.

State Populations, 1790–2000

Resident population of the states and the District of Columbia. Numbers are in thousands ('000).
Source: US Census Bureau.

STATE	1790	1800	1810	1820	1830	1840	1850	1860	1870	1880	1890
Alabama		1	9	128	310	591	772	964	997	1,263	1,513
Alaska										33	32
Arizona									10	40	88
Arkansas			1	14	30	98	210	435	484	803	1,128
California							93	380	560	865	1,213
Colorado								34	40	194	413
Connecticut	238	251	262	275	298	310	371	460	537	623	746
Delaware	59	64	73	73	77	78	92	112	125	147	168
Dist. of Columbia		8	15	23	30	34	52	75	132	178	230
Florida					35	54	87	140	188	269	391
Georgia	83	163	252	341	517	691	906	1,057	1,184	1,542	1,837
Hawaii											
Idaho									15	33	89
Illinois			12	55	157	476	851	1,712	2,540	3,078	3,826
Indiana		6	25	147	343	686	988	1,350	1,681	1,978	2,192
Iowa						43	192	675	1,194	1,625	1,912
Kansas								107	364	996	1,428
Kentucky	74	221	407	564	688	780	982	1,156	1,321	1,649	1,859
Louisiana			77	153	216	352	518	708	727	940	1,119
Maine	97	152	229	298	399	502	583	628	627	649	661
Maryland	320	342	381	407	447	470	583	687	781	935	1,042
Massachusetts	379	423	472	523	610	738	995	1,231	1,457	1,783	2,239
Michigan			5	9	32	212	398	749	1,184	1,637	2,094
Minnesota							6	172	440	781	1,310
Mississippi		8	31	75	137	376	607	791	828	1,132	1,290
Missouri			20	67	140	384	682	1,182	1,721	2,168	2,679
Montana									21	39	143
Nebraska								29	123	452	1,063
Nevada								7	42	62	47
New Hampshire	142	184	214	244	269	285	318	326	318	347	377
New Jersey	184	211	246	278	321	373	490	672	906	1,131	1,445
New Mexico							62	94	92	120	160
New York	340	589	959	1,373	1,919	2,429	3,097	3,881	4,383	5,083	6,003
North Carolina	394	478	556	639	738	753	869	993	1,071	1,400	1,618
North Dakota									5	2	37	191
Ohio		45	231	581	938	1,519	1,980	2,340	2,665	3,198	3,672
Oklahoma											259
Oregon							12	52	91	175	318
Pennsylvania	434	602	810	1,049	1,348	1,724	2,312	2,906	3,522	4,283	5,258
Rhode Island	69	69	77	83	97	109	148	175	217	277	346
South Carolina	249	346	415	503	581	594	669	704	706	996	1,151
South Dakota									12	98	349
Tennessee	36	106	262	423	682	829	1,003	1,110	1,259	1,542	1,768
Texas							213	604	819	1,592	2,236
Utah							11	40	87	144	211
Vermont	85	154	218	236	281	292	314	315	331	332	332
Virginia	692	808	878	938	1,044	1,025	1,119	1,220	1,225	1,513	1,656
Washington							1	12	24	75	357
West Virginia	56	79	105	137	177	225	302	377	442	618	763
Wisconsin						31	305	776	1,055	1,315	1,693
Wyoming									9	21	63
US total[1]	3,929	5,308	7,240	9,638	12,866	17,069	23,192	31,443	39,818[2]	50,156	62,948

[1]*Alaska and Hawaii are not included in the US total until 1960, the year after both achieved statehood.*

State Populations, 1790–2000 (continued)

1900	1910	1920	1930	1940	1950	1960	1970	1980	1990	2000
1,829	2,138	2,348	2,646	2,833	3,062	3,267	3,444	3,894	4,040	4,447
64	64	55	59	73	129	226	300	402	550	627
123	204	334	436	499	750	1,302	1,771	2,718	3,665	5,131
1,312	1,574	1,752	1,854	1,949	1,910	1,786	1,923	2,286	2,351	2,673
1,485	2,378	3,427	5,677	6,907	10,586	15,717	19,953	23,668	29,811	33,872
540	799	940	1,036	1,123	1,325	1,754	2,207	2,890	3,294	4,301
908	1,115	1,381	1,607	1,709	2,007	2,535	3,032	3,108	3,287	3,406
185	202	223	238	267	318	446	548	594	666	784
279	331	438	487	663	802	764	757	638	607	572
529	753	968	1,468	1,897	2,771	4,952	6,789	9,746	12,938	15,982
2,216	2,609	2,896	2,909	3,124	3,445	3,943	4,590	5,463	6,478	8,186
154	192	256	368	423	500	633	769	965	1,108	1,212
162	326	432	445	525	589	667	713	944	1,007	1,294
4,822	5,639	6,485	7,631	7,897	8,712	10,081	11,114	11,427	11,431	12,419
2,516	2,701	2,930	3,239	3,428	3,934	4,662	5,194	5,490	5,544	6,080
2,232	2,225	2,404	2,471	2,538	2,621	2,758	2,824	2,914	2,777	2,926
1,470	1,691	1,769	1,881	1,801	1,905	2,179	2,247	2,364	2,478	2,688
2,147	2,290	2,417	2,615	2,846	2,945	3,038	3,219	3,661	3,687	4,042
1,382	1,656	1,799	2,102	2,364	2,684	3,257	3,641	4,206	4,222	4,469
694	742	768	797	847	914	969	992	1,125	1,228	1,275
1,188	1,295	1,450	1,632	1,821	2,343	3,101	3,922	4,217	4,781	5,296
2,805	3,366	3,852	4,250	4,317	4,691	5,149	5,689	5,737	6,016	6,349
2,421	2,810	3,668	4,842	5,256	6,372	7,823	8,875	9,262	9,295	9,938
1,751	2,076	2,387	2,564	2,792	2,982	3,414	3,805	4,076	4,376	4,919
1,551	1,797	1,791	2,010	2,184	2,179	2,178	2,217	2,521	2,575	2,845
3,107	3,293	3,404	3,629	3,785	3,955	4,320	4,677	4,917	5,117	5,595
243	370	549	538	559	591	675	694	787	799	902
1,066	1,192	1,296	1,378	1,316	1,326	1,411	1,483	1,570	1,578	1,711
42	82	77	91	110	160	285	489	800	1,202	1,998
412	431	443	465	492	533	607	738	921	1,109	1,236
1,884	2,537	3,156	4,041	4,160	4,835	6,067	7,168	7,365	7,748	8,414
195	327	360	423	532	681	951	1,010	1,303	1,515	1,819
7,260	9,114	10,385	12,588	13,479	14,830	16,782	18,237	17,558	17,991	18,976
1,894	2,206	2,559	3,170	3,572	4,062	4,556	5,082	5,882	6,632	8,049
319	577	647	681	642	620	632	618	653	639	642
4,158	4,767	5,759	6,647	6,908	7,947	9,706	10,652	10,798	10,847	11,353
790	1,657	2,028	2,396	2,336	2,233	2,328	2,559	3,025	3,146	3,451
414	673	783	954	1,090	1,521	1,769	2,091	2,633	2,842	3,421
6,302	7,665	8,720	9,631	9,900	10,498	11,319	11,794	11,864	11,883	12,281
429	543	604	687	713	792	859	947	947	1,003	1,048
1,340	1,515	1,684	1,739	1,900	2,117	2,383	2,591	3,122	3,486	4,012
402	584	637	693	643	653	681	666	691	696	755
2,021	2,185	2,338	2,617	2,916	3,292	3,567	3,924	4,591	4,877	5,689
3,049	3,897	4,663	5,825	6,415	7,711	9,580	11,197	14,229	16,986	20,852
277	373	449	508	550	689	891	1,059	1,461	1,723	2,233
344	356	352	360	359	378	390	444	511	563	600
1,854	2,062	2,309	2,422	2,678	3,319	3,967	4,648	5,347	6,189	7,079
518	1,142	1,357	1,563	1,736	2,379	2,853	3,409	4,132	4,867	5,894
959	1,221	1,464	1,729	1,902	2,006	1,860	1,744	1,950	1,793	1,808
2,069	2,334	2,632	2,939	3,138	3,435	3,952	4,418	4,706	4,892	5,364
93	146	194	226	251	291	330	332	470	454	494
75,995	91,972	105,711	122,775	131,669	150,697	179,323	203,302[2]	226,540[1]	248,791[1]	281,422

[2]Numbers were revised after the census

US Population by Race and Hispanic Origin

Census 2000 was the first US census in which individuals could report themselves as being of more than one race. For the comparison with the 1990 census results, this table uses the 2000 census information for the population indicating one race. Hispanic or Latino people may be of any race.

N/A: not available.   Source: US Census Bureau.

RACE	1990 CENSUS NUMBER	%	2000 CENSUS NUMBER	%	% DIFFERENCE 1990/2000
White	199,686,070	80.3	211,460,626	75.1	+5.9
Black or African American	29,986,060	12.1	34,658,190	12.3	+15.6
American Indian or Alaska Native	1,959,234	0.8	2,475,956	0.9	+26.4
Asian	6,908,638	2.8	10,242,998	3.6	+48.3
Native Hawaiian/other Pacific Islander	365,024	0.1	398,835	0.1	+9.3
Some other race	9,804,847	3.9	15,359,073	5.5	+56.6
Two or more races	N/A	N/A	6,826,228	2.4	N/A
Total population	**248,709,873**	**100.0**	**281,421,906**	**100.0[1]**	**+13.2**

HISPANIC OR LATINO POPULATION	1990 CENSUS NUMBER	%	2000 CENSUS NUMBER	%	% DIFFERENCE 1990/2000
Hispanic or Latino (of any race)	22,354,059	9.0	35,305,818	12.5	+57.9
Not Hispanic or Latino	226,355,814	91.0	246,116,088	87.5	+8.7
Total population	**248,709,873**	**100.0**	**281,421,906**	**100.0**	**+13.2**

[1]*Totals may not equal 100% due to rounding.*

Foreign-Born Population in the US, 1850–2000

The foreign-born population consists of persons born outside the United States to parents who were not US citizens. Information from 1950 to 1990 was taken from sample data. Year 2000 information was an estimate derived before the decennial census was conducted. Populations of Alaska and Hawaii were included starting in 1960. In 1850 and 1860, information on nativity was not collected for slaves. The data in the table includes the slave population as part of the native-born population. Source: US Census Bureau.

YEAR	POPULATION TOTAL	FOREIGN-BORN	% OF TOTAL	YEAR	POPULATION TOTAL	FOREIGN-BORN	% OF TOTAL
1850	23,191,876	2,244,602	9.7	1930	122,775,046	14,204,149	11.6
1860	31,443,321	4,138,697	13.2	1940	131,669,275	11,594,896	8.8
1870	38,558,371	5,567,229	14.4	1950	150,216,110	10,347,395	6.9
1880	50,155,783	6,679,943	13.3	1960	179,325,671	9,738,091	5.4
1890	62,622,250	9,249,547	14.8	1970	203,210,158	9,619,302	4.7
1900	75,994,575	10,341,276	13.6	1980	226,545,805	14,079,906	6.2
1910	91,972,266	13,515,886	14.7	1990	248,709,873	19,767,316	7.9
1920	105,710,620	13,920,692	13.2	2000	274,087,000	28,379,000	10.4

Total Immigrants Admitted to the US, 1901–2000

Numbers shown include only immigrant aliens admitted for permanent residence and are for fiscal years. Currently the fiscal year begins 1 October and ends 30 September. Prior to 1976, the fiscal year began 1 July and ended 30 June.

YEAR	NUMBER	YEAR	NUMBER	YEAR	NUMBER	YEAR	NUMBER
1901	487,918	1911	878,587	1921	805,228	1931	97,139
1902	648,743	1912	838,172	1922	309,556	1932	35,576
1903	857,046	1913	1,197,892	1923	522,919	1933	23,068
1904	812,870	1914	1,218,480	1924	706,896	1934	29,470
1905	1,026,499	1915	326,700	1925	294,314	1935	34,956
1906	1,100,735	1916	298,826	1926	304,488	1936	36,329
1907	1,285,349	1917	295,403	1927	335,175	1937	50,244
1908	782,870	1918	110,618	1928	307,255	1938	67,895
1909	751,786	1919	141,132	1929	279,678	1939	82,998
1910	1,041,570	1920	430,001	1930	241,700	1940	70,756
Totals 1901–10	**8,795,386**	**1911–20**	**5,735,811**	**1921–30**	**4,107,209**	**1931–40**	**528,431**

Total Immigrants Admitted to the US, 1901–2000 (continued)

YEAR	NUMBER	YEAR	NUMBER	YEAR	NUMBER	YEAR	NUMBER
1941	51,776	1951	205,717	1961	271,344	1971	370,478
1942	28,781	1952	265,520	1962	283,763	1972	384,685
1943	23,725	1953	170,434	1963	306,260	1973	400,063
1944	28,551	1954	208,177	1964	292,248	1974	394,861
1945	38,119	1955	237,790	1965	296,697	1975	386,194
1946	108,721	1956	321,625	1966	323,040	1976	398,613
1947	147,292	1957	326,867	1967	361,972	1976 (TQ)[1]	103,676
1948	170,570	1958	253,265	1968	454,448	1977	462,315
1949	188,317	1959	260,686	1969	358,579	1978	601,442
1950	249,187	1960	265,398	1970	373,326	1979	460,348
Totals 1941–50	1,035,039	1951–60	2,515,479	1961–70	3,321,677	1980	530,639
						1971–80	4,493,314

1981	596,600	1991	1,827,167
1982	594,131	1992	973,977
1983	559,763	1993	904,292
1984	543,903	1994	804,416
1985	570,009	1995	720,461
1986	601,708	1996	915,900
1987	601,516	1997	798,378
1988	643,025	1998	654,451
1989	1,090,924	1999	646,568
1990	1,536,483	2000	849,807
Totals 1981–90	7,338,062	1991–2000	9,095,417

Totals 1901–2000: 46,965,825

[1]Transition quarter (TQ) to new fiscal year, 1 July through 30 September 1976.

Immigrants Admitted to the US by Selected Country of Birth and State of Intended Residence

Fiscal Year 2000. Source: <www.ins.usdoj.gov>

STATE OF INTENDED RESIDENCE	TOTAL IMMIGRANTS	TOP FIVE COUNTRIES OF BIRTH (NUMBER OF IMMIGRANTS)
Alabama	1,094	Mexico (259), India (230), China (172), Russia (95), Vietnam (78)
Alaska	1,374	Philippines (327), Mexico (136), Russia (131), Canada (95), Dominican Rep. (51)
Arizona	11,980	Mexico (6,301), Bosnia-Herzegovina (701), Vietnam (464), India (374), Canada (370)
Arkansas	1,596	Mexico (606), India (124), China (93), El Salvador (89), Vietnam (77)
California	217,753	Mexico (85,551), Philippines (10,773), China (13,232), Vietnam (10,251), El Salvador (9,987)
Colorado	8,216	Mexico (2,915), China (503), Canada (309), India (286), UK (260)
Connecticut	11,346	Jamaica (982), Poland (783), India (594), China (544), Haiti (497)
Delaware	1,570	Mexico (182), India (153), Korea (146), China (117), Haiti (80)
District of Columbia	2,542	El Salvador (544), China (122), Nigeria (96), Nicaragua (79), Philippines (75)
Florida	98,391	Cuba (15,883), Nicaragua (14,400), Haiti (11,044), Colombia (5,739), Jamaica (5,350)
Georgia	14,778	Mexico (2,099), India (1,323), Vietnam (752), China (659), Nigeria (520)
Hawaii	6,056	Philippines (3,053), China (551), Korea (305), Vietnam (196), Canada (106)
Idaho	1,922	Mexico (1,083), Bosnia-Herzegovina (160), China (100), Canada (53), Philippines (41)
Illinois	36,180	Mexico (8,600), Poland (3,635), India (3,239), Philippines (2,738), Bosnia-Herzegovina (1,491)
Indiana	4,128	Mexico (759), China (333), India (328), Philippines (185), Russia (100)
Iowa	3,052	Mexico (699), Bosnia-Herzegovina (692), Vietnam (298), India (145), Russia (94)
Kansas	4,582	Mexico (1,794), Vietnam (350), China (226), India (190), Canada (146)
Kentucky	2,989	Cuba (578), Bosnia-Herzegovina (499), China (176), Mexico (164), India (149)
Louisiana	3,010	Vietnam (335), China (229), India (211), Mexico (194), Nicaragua (154)
Maine	1,133	Canada (199), UK (85), China (81), Russia (62), Vietnam (49)
Maryland	17,705	El Salvador (1,480), India (1,228), China (1,102), Korea (958), Nigeria (888)

Immigrants Admitted to the US by Selected Country of Birth and State of Intended Residence (continued)

STATE OF INTENDED RESIDENCE	TOTAL IMMIGRANTS	TOP FIVE COUNTRIES OF BIRTH (NUMBER OF IMMIGRANTS)
Massachusetts	23,483	China (2,023), Haiti (1,943), India (1,227), Dominican Rep. (1,180), Vietnam (902)
Michigan	16,773	India (1,490), Mexico (935), Canada (842), China (832), Philippines (783)
Minnesota	8,671	Mexico (591), Vietnam (536), China (505), India (441), Russia (441)
Mississippi	1,083	Philippines (163), Mexico (127), India (122), China (109), Vietnam (48)
Missouri	6,053	Mexico (636), Bosnia-Herzegovina (539), China (394), India (359), Vietnam (331)
Montana	493	Canada (112), Mexico (44), Philippines (39), Russia (35), China (25)
Nebraska	2,230	Mexico (834), Vietnam (281), China (86), Bosnia-Herzegovina (81), India (70)
Nevada	7,827	Mexico (3,120), Philippines (859), El Salvador (322), China (283), Nicaragua (278)
New Hampshire	2,001	Canada (228), Philippines (123), China (116), UK (112), India (101)
New Jersey	40,013	India (4,364), Dominican Rep. (2,477), Haiti (2,101), China (1,862), Philippines (1,845)
New Mexico	3,973	Mexico (2,717), Cuba (141), China (139), Vietnam (138), Philippines (82)
New York	106,061	China (8,930), Dominican Rep. (8,543), Jamaica (5,825), Haiti (5,507), Ukraine (4,263)
North Carolina	9,251	Mexico (1,390), India (785), China (514), Canada (499), Philippines (386)
North Dakota	420	Canada (98), Bosnia-Herzegovina (57), India (21), Mexico (15), Germany (12), Vietnam (12)
Ohio	9,263	India (804), China (712), Russia (516), Ukraine (417), Canada (360)
Oklahoma	4,586	Mexico (1,565), Vietnam (365), India (288), China (210), Philippines (174)
Oregon	8,543	Mexico (2,699), China (597), Ukraine (523), Vietnam (511), India (345)
Pennsylvania	18,148	India (1,714), China (1,494), Mexico (1,081), Ukraine (944), Vietnam (879)
Rhode Island	2,526	Dominican Rep. (390), Guatemala (195), Colombia (191), China (85), Nigeria (76)
South Carolina	2,267	India (201), Mexico (191), China (167), Philippines (165), Canada (122)
South Dakota	465	Bosnia-Herzegovina (72), Ukraine (47), Philippines (27), China (26), Mexico (26)
Tennessee	4,882	Mexico (504), Philippines (364), China (326), India (352), Bosnia-Herzegovina (185)
Texas	63,840	Mexico (31,211), India (3,528), El Salvador (2,677), China (2,293), Vietnam (2,275)
Utah	3,710	Mexico (1,036), Bosnia-Herzegovina (317), Vietnam (152), China (146), Canada (140)
Vermont	810	Canada (127), Bosnia-Herzegovina (116), Vietnam (56), China (54), Germany (35)
Virginia	20,087	El Salvador (1,794), India (1,465), Philippines (1,046), Pakistan (1,017), China (868)
Washington	18,486	Mexico (3,256), Ukraine (1,403), Philippines (1,216), Vietnam (1,216), China (1,058)
West Virginia	573	China (47), India (35), Philippines (35), Canada (34), UK (34)
Wisconsin	5,057	Mexico (952), India (308), China (290), Russia (235), Ukraine (149)
Wyoming	248	Mexico (60), China (20), Russia (19), Philippines (18), Canada (15)

Americans 65 and Older, 1900–2000

Data for Hawaii and Alaska are included after 1950. Source: US Census Bureau.

CENSUS YEAR	NUMBER OF PEOPLE 65 AND OLDER	% OF TOTAL POPULATION	CENSUS YEAR	NUMBER OF PEOPLE 65 AND OLDER	% OF TOTAL POPULATION
1900	3,080,498	4.1	1960	16,559,580	9.2
1910	3,949,524	4.3	1970	20,065,502	9.8
1920	4,933,215	4.7	1980	25,549,427	11.3
1930	6,633,805	5.4	1990	31,241,831	12.6
1940	9,019,314	6.8	2000	34,991,753	12.4
1950	12,269,537	8.1			

Poverty Level by State

Source: US Census Bureau. Totals may differ due to rounding. For the definition of poverty, see <www.census.gov/hhes/poverty/povdef.html>.

STATE	% OF PEOPLE IN POVERTY			NUMBER OF PEOPLE IN POVERTY ('000)		
	1980	1990	2000	1980	1990	2000
Alabama	21.2	19.2	14.4	810	779	642
Alaska	9.6	11.4	8.2	36	57	53
Arizona	12.8	13.7	12.0	354	484	590
Arkansas	21.5	19.6	17.8	484	472	467
California	11.0	13.9	12.8	2,619	4,128	4,441
Colorado	8.6	13.7	8.1	247	461	343
Connecticut	8.3	6.0	6.6	255	196	219
Delaware	11.8	6.9	9.1	68	48	72
District of Columbia	20.9	21.1	14.9	131	120	75
Florida	16.7	14.4	10.6	1,692	1,896	1,604
Georgia	13.9	15.8	11.2	727	1,001	869
Hawaii	8.5	11.0	9.9	81	121	115
Idaho	14.7	14.9	12.9	138	157	161
Illinois	12.3	13.7	11.5	1,386	1,606	1,406
Indiana	11.8	13.0	8.7	645	714	504
Iowa	10.8	10.4	7.2	311	289	206
Kansas	9.4	10.3	9.6	215	259	251
Kentucky	19.3	17.3	11.9	701	628	471
Louisiana	20.3	23.6	17.3	868	952	730
Maine	14.6	13.1	8.4	158	162	106
Maryland	9.5	9.9	7.6	389	468	387
Massachusetts	9.5	10.7	10.1	542	626	629
Michigan	12.9	14.3	10.0	1,194	1,315	993
Minnesota	8.7	12.0	6.0	342	524	285
Mississippi	24.3	25.7	12.9	591	684	358
Missouri	13.0	13.4	8.0	625	700	440
Montana	13.2	16.3	15.7	102	134	136
Nebraska	13.0	10.3	9.0	199	167	148
Nevada	8.3	9.8	8.5	70	119	170
New Hampshire	7.0	6.3	5.2	63	68	64
New Jersey	9.0	9.2	8.0	659	711	666
New Mexico	20.6	20.9	16.8	268	319	299
New York	13.8	14.3	13.4	2,391	2,571	2,460
North Carolina	15.0	13.0	12.1	877	829	911
North Dakota	15.5	13.7	10.1	99	87	61
Ohio	9.8	11.5	10.0	1,046	1,256	1,157
Oklahoma	13.9	15.6	15.4	406	481	504
Oregon	11.5	9.2	11.2	309	267	382
Pennsylvania	9.8	11.0	8.9	1,142	1,328	1,062
Rhode Island	10.7	7.5	9.1	97	71	85
South Carolina	16.8	16.2	10.6	534	548	400
South Dakota	18.8	13.3	9.6	127	93	67
Tennessee	19.6	16.9	14.7	884	833	820
Texas	15.7	15.9	14.7	2,247	2,684	3,013
Utah	10.0	8.2	9.6	148	143	212
Vermont	12.0	10.9	11.3	62	61	71
Virginia	12.4	11.1	7.7	647	705	534
Washington	12.7	8.9	10.1	538	434	593
West Virginia	15.2	18.1	14.0	297	328	248
Wisconsin	8.5	9.3	9.6	403	448	518
Wyoming	10.4	11.0	11.0	49	51	54
All US	13.0	13.5	11.3	29,272	33,585	31,139

Population of US Territories

Total midyear population. Source: US Census Bureau.

YEAR	PUERTO RICO	GUAM	VIRGIN ISLANDS	AMERICAN SAMOA	NORTHERN MARIANA ISLANDS
1970	2,721,754	86,470	63,476	27,267	12,359
1975	2,935,124	102,110	94,484	29,640	14,938
1980	3,209,648	106,869	99,636	32,418	16,890
1985	3,382,106	120,615	100,760	38,633	21,386
1990	3,536,910	134,110	104,235	47,199	44,037
1995	3,731,006	143,856	113,896	56,911	58,128
2000	3,915,798	154,623	120,917	65,446	71,912
2001	3,937,316	157,557	122,211	67,084	74,612
2002	3,957,988	160,796	123,498	68,688	77,311

States and Other Areas of the United States

Alabama

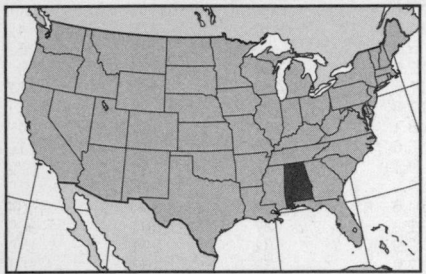

Name: Alabama; derived from the Choctaw language, meaning "thicket clearers." **Nickname:** Heart of Dixie. **Capital:** Montgomery. **Rank:** population: 23rd; area: 28th. **Motto:** *Audemus Jura Nostra Defendere* (We Dare Defend Our Rights). **Song:** "Alabama," words by Julia S. Tutwiler and music by Edna Gockel Gussen. **Amphibian:** Red Hills salamander. **Bird:** yellowhammer. **Fish:** largemouth bass (freshwater); tarpon (saltwater). **Flower:** camellia. **Fossil:** *Basilosaurus cetoides.* **Gemstone:** star blue quartz. **Insect:** monarch butterfly. **Mineral:** hematite. **Reptile:** Alabama red-bellied turtle. **Rock:** marble. **Tree:** southern longleaf pine.

Natural features

Area: 52,237 sq mi, 135,293 sq km. **Mountain ranges:** Appalachians, Raccoon, Lookout. **Highest point:** Cheaha Mountain, 2,407 ft (734 m). **Largest lake:** Lake Guntersville. **Major rivers:** Mobile, Alabama, Tombigbee, Tennessee, Chattahoochee, Conecuh, Pea, Tensaw, Tallapoosa. **Natural regions:** the Appalachian Plateaus, extending across the north central region; interior low plateaus, far north; valley and ridge province and small portion of the Piedmont Province, covering the east; coastal plain, covering the southern half of the state. **Location:** South, bordering Tennessee, Georgia, Florida, Mississippi. **Climate:** temperate, with mild winters and hot, humid summers; temperatures mellowed by altitude in the northern counties and relatively higher in the southern counties; summer heat is often alleviated by winds blowing in from the Gulf of Mexico. **Land use:** forested, 67.5%; agricultural, 13.8%; pasture, 5.7%; other, 13.0%.

People (2000 census)

Population: 4,447,100; 87.6 persons per sq mi (33.8 persons per sq km) (land area only). **Vital statistics** (1998; per 1,000 population): birth rate, 14.2 (1999); death rate, 10.1; marriage rate, 11.5; divorce rate, 6.0. **Major cities:** Birmingham, 242,820; Montgomery, 201,568; Mobile, 198,915; Huntsville, 158,216.

Government

Statehood: entered the Union on 14 Dec 1819 as the 22nd state. **State constitution:** Adopted 1901. **Representation in US Congress:** 2 senators; 7 representatives. **Electoral college:** 9 votes (in the 2004 general elections based on the 2000 census). **Political divisions:** 67 counties.

Economy

Employment: services, 25.2%; trade, 21.6%; manufacturing, 16.9%; government, 16.4%; construction, 6.2%; finance, insurance, real estate, 4.9%; transportation, public utilities, 4.6%; agriculture, forestry, fishing, 3.5%; mining, 0.5%. **Production:** manufacturing, 19.0%; services, 16.9%; trade, 16.9%; government, 15.8%; finance, insurance, real estate, 14.7%; transportation, utilities, 8.7%; construction, 4.7%; agriculture, forestry, fisheries, 2.0%; mining, 1.3%. **Chief agricultural products:** *Crops:* cotton, corn, soybeans, peanuts (groundnuts), potatoes, sweet potatoes, peaches, pecans, fruits and vegetables, winter wheat, hay, honey. *Livestock:* cattle, poultry, hogs. *Fish catch:* marine fish, including red snapper; freshwater fish, including catfish; marine crustaceans, including shrimp, crab; marine mollusks, including mussels, oysters. **Chief manufactured products:** food products, meat products, poultry processing, textiles, apparel, wood products, mobile homes, paper and paperboard, petroleum products, plastics and rubber products, iron and steel, aluminum products, semiconductors, electronic components, motor vehicle parts.

Internet resources: <www.touralabama.org>; <www.state.al.us>.

Alaska

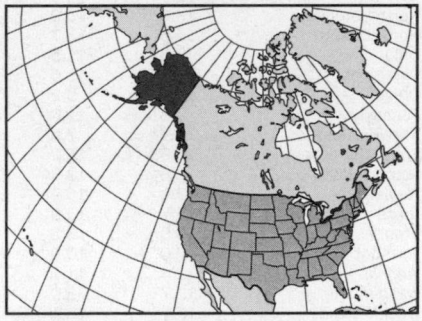

Name: Alaska, from the Aleut word *Alyeska,* meaning "great land." **Nickname:** the Last Frontier. **Capital:** Juneau. **Rank:** population: 48th; area: 1st. **Motto:** North to the Future. **Song:** "Alaska's Flag," words by Marie Drake and music by Elinor Dusenbury. **Bird:** willow ptarmigan. **Fish:** giant king salmon. **Flower:** forget-me-not. **Fossil:** *Mammuthus primigenius* (woolly mammoth). **Gemstone:** jade. **Insect:** four spot skimmer dragonfly. **Mammal:** moose. **Marine mammal:** bowhead whale. **Mineral:** gold. **Tree:** sitka spruce.

Natural features

Area: 615,230 sq mi, 1,593,444 sq km. **Mountain ranges:** Wrangell, Chugach, Alaska, Brooks, Aleutian,

Boundary. **Highest peaks:** Mount McKinley (Denali), 20,320 ft (6,194 m). **Largest lake:** Iliamna. **Major rivers:** Yukon, Porcupine, Tanana, Koyukuk, Noatak, Kuskokwim, Susitna, Copper. **Natural regions:** panhandle, a narrow strip of land that includes portions of the Coast Mountains; coastal archipelago and the Gulf of Alaska islands; the Alaska Peninsula and Aleutian island chain that separates the North Pacific from the Bering Sea; the Alaska Range, extending across south central region; the Interior Plateau, including the basin of the Yukon River, and the central plains and tablelands of the interior, the Seward Peninsula to the west, and the Brooks Range, sometimes called the North Slope, to the north; the Arctic Coastal Plain, a treeless region of tundra lying at the northern-most edge of the state; tundra-covered islands of the Bering Sea. **Location:** bordered by Canada. **Climate:** temperate with much regional variation in temperature and precipitation; *southern coastal and southeastern region, Gulf of and Aleutian islands:* cool summers and moderate winters, with high precipitation; *interior basin:* moderate summers and very cold winters, with low to moderate precipitation; *islands and coast of the Bering Sea:* cool summers and very cold winters; *central plains and uplands:* moderate summers and frigid winters; *North Slope:* moderate summers and frigid winters, though not as severe as interior regions. **Land use:** forested, 24.1 (24)%; pasture, 0.0%; other, 75.6 (76)%.

People (2000 census)

Population: 626,932; 1.1 persons per sq mi (0.4 person per sq km) (land area only). **Vital statistics** (1998; per 1,000 population): birth rate (1999), 16.1; death rate, 4.2; marriage rate, 9.7; divorce rate, 5.2. **Major cities:** Anchorage (metropolitan area), 260,283; Juneau (metropolitan area), 30,711; College, 11,402; Sitka, 8,835.

Government

Statehood: entered the Union on 3 Jan 1959 as the 49th state. **State constitution:** adopted 1956. **Representation in US Congress:** 2 senators; 1 representative. **Electoral college:** 3 votes. **Political divisions:** 16 boroughs.

Economy

Employment: services, 26.9%; government, 24.4%; trade, 18.7%; transportation, public utilities, 7.7%; finance, insurance, real estate, 5.3%; construction, 5.1%; manufacturing, 4.8%; agriculture, forestry, fishing, 4.1%; mining, 3.0%. **Production:** mining, 20.1%; government, 19.4%; transportation, utilities, 16.7%; services, 13.0%; trade, 10.1%; finance, insurance, real estate, 10.1%; construction, 4.6%; manufacturing, 4.2%; agriculture, forestry, fishing, 1.7%. **Chief agricultural products:** *Crops:* hay, milk, potatoes, timber. *Livestock:* cattle, pigs. *Fish catch:* marine fish, salmon, herring, groundfish, shellfish, crab, shrimp. **Chief manufactured products:** processed fish and seafood (fresh, frozen, canned, and cured), lumber and wood products, paper products, transportation products.

Internet resources: <www.travelalaska.com>; <www.state.ak.us>

Arizona

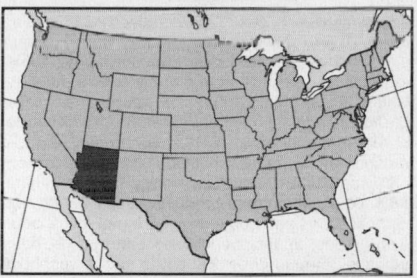

Name: Arizona, from *arizonac,* derived from two Papago Indian words meaning "place of the young spring." **Capital:** Phoenix. **Rank:** population: 20th; area: 6th. **Nickname:** Grand Canyon State. **Motto:** *Ditat Deus* (God Enriches). **Song:** "Arizona March Song," words by Margaret Rowe Clifford and music by Maurice Blumenthal. **Amphibian:** Arizona treefrog. **Bird:** cactus wren. **Fish:** Arizona trout. **Flower:** saguaro blossom. **Fossil:** petrified wood. **Gemstone:** turquoise. **Mammal:** ringtail. **Reptile:** Arizona ridgenose rattlesnake. **Tree:** palo verde.

Natural features

Area: 114,006 sq mi, 295,276 sq km. **Mountain ranges:** Black, Gila Bend, Chuska, Hualapai, San Francisco, White. **Highest point:** Humphreys Peak, 12,633 ft (3,851 m). **Largest lake:** Lake Roosevelt. **Major rivers:** Colorado, Little Colorado, Verde, Salt, Gila. **Natural regions:** the Colorado Plateaus, northeast third of the state, include Grand Canyon and Painted Desert; the basin and range province, south, east, central, and northwest, includes Sonoran Desert in the southwest corner and part of the Great Basin Desert to the northwest. **Location:** Southwest, bordering Utah, Colorado, New Mexico, California, and Nevada; international border with Mexico. **Climate:** varies with location, half of Arizona is semiarid, one-third is arid, and the remainder is humid; *Basin and Range region:* arid and semiarid to subtropical climate; *Colorado Plateau:* cool to cold winters and a semiarid climate; *Transition Zone:* climate ranges widely, from arid to humid. **Land use:** pasture, 55.7%; forested, 22.4%; agricultural, 1.7%; other, 20.2%.

People (2000 census)

Population: 5,130,632; 45.1 persons per sq mi (17.4 persons per sq km) (land area only). **Vital statistics** (1998; per 1,000 population): birth rate, 17.0 (1999); death rate, 8.2; marriage rate, 8.1; divorce rate, 5.5. **Major cities:** Phoenix, 1,321,045; Tucson, 486,699; Mesa, 396,375; Glendale, 218,812; Scottsdale, 202,705; Chandler, 176,581; Tempe, 158,625.

Government

Statehood: entered the Union on 14 Feb 1912 as the 48th state. **State constitution:** adopted 1911. **Representation in US Congress:** 2 senators; 6 representatives. **Electoral college:** 10 votes (in the 2004 general elections based on the 2000 census). **Political divisions:** 15 counties.

Economy

Employment: services, 32.5%; trade, 22.7%; government, 13.4%; manufacturing, 8.8%; finance, insurance, real estate, 8.3%; construction, 6.6%; transportation, public utilities, 4.5%; agriculture, forestry, fishing, 2.6%; mining, 0.6%. **Production:** services, 22.0%; finance, insurance, real estate, 18.7%; trade, 17.4%; manufacturing, 14.4%; government, 12.1%; transportation, public utilities, 7.3%; construction, 5.8%; agriculture, forestry, fishing, 1.5%; mining, 0.8%. **Chief agricultural products:** *Crops*: cotton and cottonseed, wheat, sorghum, hay, barley, corn, potatoes, grapes, apples, vegetables and melons, dairy products, lettuce. *Livestock*: cattle and calves, hogs and pigs, sheep and lambs, angora goats. **Chief manufactured products:** semiconductors, communications equipment, electric and electronic equipment, transportation equipment, soap products, nonferrous metal products.

Internet resources: <www.arizonaguide.com>; <www.state.az.com>.

Arkansas

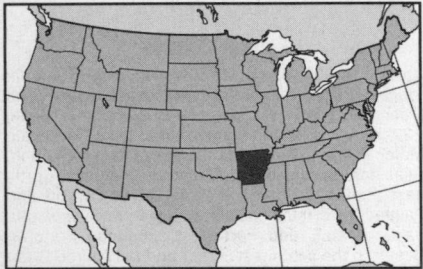

Name: Arkansas, from an unknown Native American word describing the Quapaw tribe (also known as the Arkansaw), meaning "people who live downstream." **Nickname:** The Natural State. **Capital:** Little Rock. **Rank:** population: 33rd; area: 27th. **Motto:** *Regnat Populus* (The People Rule). **Song:** "Arkansas," words and music by Eva Ware Barnett. **Bird:** mockingbird. **Flower:** apple blossom. **Gemstone:** diamond. **Insect:** honeybee. **Mammal:** whitetail deer. **Mineral:** quartz crystal. **Rock:** bauxite. **Tree:** pine tree.

Natural features

Area: 53,182 sq mi, 137,742 sq km. **Mountain ranges:** Ozark, Ouachita. **Highest point:** Mount Magazine, 2,753 ft (839 m). **Largest lake:** Lake Chicot. **Major rivers:** Arkansas, Red, Ouachita, White. **Natural regions:** the Ozark Plateaus, including the Boston Mountains, north and northwest regions; the Ouachita Province, including the Arkansas valley and the Ouachita Mountains, central region; Coastal Plain, extends from southwest to northeast. **Location:** South, bordering Missouri, Tennessee, Mississippi, Louisiana, Texas, and Oklahoma. **Climate:** temperate, with mild winters and hot summers. **Land use:** forested, 55.2%; agricultural, 30.3%; pasture, 6.0%; other, 8.5%.

People (2000 census)

Population: 2,673,400; 51.3 persons per sq mi (19.8 persons per sq km) (land area only). **Vital statistics** (1998; per 1,000 population): birth rate (1999), 14.4; death rate, 6.1; marriage rate, 15.1; divorce rate, 10.8. **Major cities:** Little Rock, 183,133; Fort Smith, 80,268; North Little Rock, 60,433; Fayetteville, 58,047; Jonesboro, 55,515.

Government

Statehood: entered the Union on 15 Jun 1836 as the 25th state. **State constitution:** adopted 1874. **Representation in US Congress:** 2 senators; 4 representatives. **Electoral college:** 6 votes (in the 2004 general elections based on the 2000 census). **Political divisions:** 75 counties.

Economy

Employment: services, 24.4%; trade, 21.3%; manufacturing, 18.3%; government, 13.9%; agriculture, forestry, fishing, 6.6%; construction, 5.8%; transportation, public utilities, 5.5%; finance, insurance, real estate, 4.8%; mining, 0.4%. **Production:** manufacturing, 22.5%; trade, 18.4%; services, 15.6%; government, 12.3%; finance, insurance, real estate, 11.6%; transportation, public utilities, 10.5%; construction, 4.6%; agriculture, forestry, fisheries, 3.7%; mining, 0.8%. **Chief agricultural products:** *Crops*: corn, cotton, hay, rice, sorghum, soybeans, wheat, apples, blueberries, grapes, peaches, pecans, strawberries, tomatoes, watermelon. *Livestock*: cattle and calves, hogs and pigs, poultry. *Aquaculture*: catfish. **Chief manufactured products:** food products, meatpacking, poultry processing, lumber, paper and paper products, refined petroleum, chemical products, plastic and rubber products, iron and steel manufacturing, fabricated metal products, machinery, transportation products.

Internet resources: <www.arkansas.com>; <www.state.ar.us>.

California

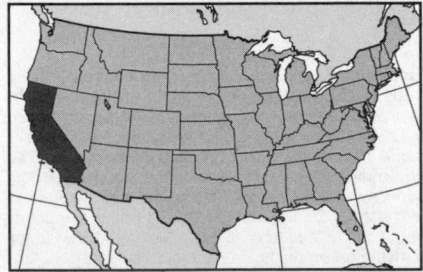

Nickname: Golden State. **Capital:** Sacramento. **Rank:** population: 1st; area: 3rd. **Motto:** *Eureka* (I Have Found It). **Song:** "I Love You, California," words by F.B. Silverwood and music by A.F. Frankenstein. **Bird:** California quail. **Fish:** golden trout (freshwater); garibaldi (saltwater). **Flower:** California poppy. **Fossil:** sabertooth cat. **Gemstone:** benitoite. **Insect:** California dog-

---

For details about state governments, see pages 854–859; for extraction and energy data, see pages 880–884.

face butterfly. **Mammal:** California grizzly bear. **Marine mammal:** California gray whale. **Mineral:** gold. **Reptile:** desert tortoise. **Rock:** serpentine. **Tree:** California redwood.

Natural features

Area: 158,869 sq mi, 411,470 sq km. **Mountain ranges:** Coast Range, Sierra Nevada, Santa Lucia, Cascade Range, Klamath Mountains, Tehachapi Mountains, San Gabriel Mountains, San Bernadino Mountains. **Highest point:** Mount Whitney, 14,494 ft (4,417 m). **Largest lake:** Lake Tahoe. **Major rivers:** Colorado, Sacramento, Pit, San Joaquin. **Natural regions:** Basin and Range Province, northeast corner, also eastern border with Arizona and southern Nevada; Cascade-Sierra Mountains, running from north to south along the east-central region; Pacific Border Province, west, including the Coast Ranges to the west, the Klamath Mountains to the north, the Los Angeles Ranges to the south, and the California Trough (commonly referred to as the Central Valley) to the east; Lower Californian Province, southwest tip. **Location:** Southwest, bordering Oregon, Nevada, and Arizona; international border with Mexico. **Climate:** Mediterranean climate, with moderate temperatures, warm, dry summers, and cool, rainy winters. **Land use:** forested, 32.6%; pasture, 22.4%; agricultural, 10.6%; other, 34.4%.

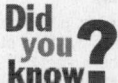

Did you know? It is purely coincidence that Disneyland is in Orange County, California, and Walt Disney World is in Orange County, Florida.

People (2000 census)

Population: 33,871,648; 217.2 persons per sq mi (83.8 persons per sq km) (land area only). **Vital statistics** (1998; per 1,000 population): birth rate, 15.6 (1999); death rate, 6.9; marriage rate, 5.9; divorce rate, N/A. **Major cities:** Los Angeles, 3,694,820; San Diego, 1,223,400; San Jose, 894,043; San Francisco, 776,733; Long Beach, 461,522; Fresno, 427,652; Sacramento, 407,018; Oakland, 399,484.

Government

Statehood: entered the Union on 9 Sep 1850 as the 31st state. **State constitution:** adopted 1879. **Representation in US Congress:** 2 senators; 52 representatives. **Electoral college:** 55 votes (in the 2004 general elections based on the 2000 census). **Political divisions:** 58 counties.

Economy

Employment: services, 33.8%; trade, 20.7%; government, 19.3%; manufacturing, 11.2%; finance, insurance, real estate, 8.0%; construction, 4.6%; transportation, public utilities, 4.5%; agriculture, forestry, fishing, 3.7%; mining, 0.2%. **Production:** services, 23.4%; finance, insurance, real estate, 21.7%; trade, 15.9%; manufacturing, 14.6%; government, 10.7%; transportation, utilities, 7.3%; construction, 3.8%; agriculture, forestry, fishing, 1.9%; mining, 0.6%. **Chief agricultural products:** *Crops:* wheat, oats, rice, grains, apples, apricots, cherries, grapes, olives, peaches, pears, citrus fruits, strawberries, onions, lima beans, artichokes, broccoli, snap beans, vegetables, dairy

products, eggs. *Livestock:* cattle and calves, sheep and lambs. *Fish catch:* bonito, halibut, mackerel, groundfish, rockfish (commonly called Pacific red snapper), sablefish (also called black cod), soles and sanddabs, sardines, white seabass, shark, swordfish, tuna, crab, California spiny lobster, Pacific Ocean (pink) shrimp, prawns, squid. *Extractive products:* timber. **Chief manufactured products:** food products, meat and poultry processing, soft drink products, beer and wine, textiles, apparel, lumber and wood products, paper and paper products, printing, refined petroleum, asphalt, chemical products, pharmaceuticals, plastic and rubber products, glass and glass products, construction materials, steel products, metal products, machinery, communications equipment, semiconductors and computers, electronics, transportation equipment, furniture, medical equipment, sporting goods.

Internet resources: <www.gocalif.com>; <www.state.ca.us>.

Colorado

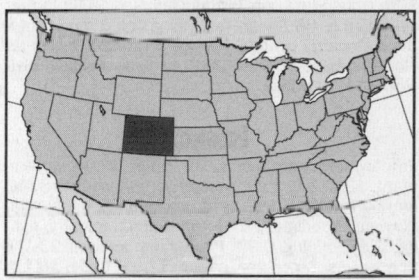

Name: Colorado, derived from a Spanish word meaning red colored earth. **Nickname:** Centennial State. **Capital:** Denver. **Rank:** population: 24th; area: 8th. **Motto:** *Nil Sine Numine* (Nothing Without Providence). **Song:** "Where the Columbines Grow," words and music by A.J. Flynn. **Bird:** lark bunting. **Fish:** greenback cutthroat trout. **Flower:** white and lavender columbine. **Fossil:** stegosaurus. **Gemstone:** aquamarine. **Insect:** Colorado hairstreak butterfly. **Mammal:** Rocky Mountain bighorn sheep. **Tree:** Colorado blue spruce.

Natural features

Area: 104,100 sq mi, 269,618 sq km. **Mountain ranges:** Rocky Mountains, Front, Medicine Bow, Park, Rabbit Ears, San Juan Mountains, Sangre de Cristo Range, Sawatch. **Highest point:** Mount Elbert, 14,433 ft (4,399 m). **Largest lakes:** Blue Mesa Reservoir (man-made); Grand Lake (natural). **Major rivers:** Colorado, Arkansas, South Platte, Rio Grande. **Natural regions:** the Great Plains Province, eastern half of state, includes the High Plains to the east, Colorado Piedmont to the west, and Raton Section to the south; Southern Rocky Mountains, running down the middle of the state; Middle Rocky Mountains and Wyoming Basin, northwest corner; Colorado Plateaus, western and southwestern border, include the Uinta Basin to the north, the Canyon Lands in the middle, and the Navajo Section to the south. **Location:** West, bordering Wyoming, Nebraska, Kansas, Oklahoma, New Mexico, and Utah. **Climate:** *Eastern plains:* with hot summers and dry, cold, windy, and generally harsh winters; *piedmont*: similar to eastern plains, also experiences the Chinook wind, a dry, descending winter airstream from the high mountains that is warmed by compression as it descends; *mountains and high plateaus*: cool summers, cold winters and much increased precipitation; snow may fall during any month of the year, with amounts ranging from about 20 to 50 inches. **Land use:** pasture, 42.0%; forest, 28.3%; agricultural, 17.2%; other, 12.5%.

People (2000 census)

Population: 4,301,261; 41.5 persons per sq mi (16.0 persons per sq km) (land area only). **Vital statistics** (1998; per 1,000 population): birth rate, 15.3 (1999); death rate, 6.7; marriage rate, 7.9; divorce rate, N/A. **Major cities:** Denver, 554,636; Colorado Springs, 360,890; Aurora, 276,393; Lakewood, 144,126; Fort Collins, 118,652.

Government

Statehood: entered the Union on 1 Aug 1876 as the 38th state. **State constitution:** adopted 1876. **Representation in US Congress:** 2 senators; 6 representatives. **Electoral college:** 9 votes (in the 2004 general elections based on the 2000 census). **Political divisions:** 63 counties.

Economy

Employment: services, 32.3%; trade, 22.0%; government, 13.5%; finance, insurance, real estate, 8.4%; manufacturing, 8.2%; construction, 6.5%; transportation, public utilities, 5.4%; agriculture, forestry, fishing, 2.8%; mining, 0.9%. **Production:** services, 23.1%; finance, insurance, real estate, 17.5%; trade, 16.1%; transportation, utilities, 12.2%; government, 11.9%; manufacturing, 10.2%; construction, 6.0%; mining, 1.6%; agriculture, 1.5%. **Chief agricultural products:** *Crops*: millet, corn (maize), hay, potatoes, onions, sugar beets, sunflowers, wheat, dairy products, eggs, greenhouse products. *Livestock*: cattle and calves, hogs and pigs, sheep and lambs. **Chief manufactured products:** meat products, beverages, printing, semiconductors, computer and electronic products.

Internet resources: <www.colorado.com>; <www.state.co.us>.

Connecticut

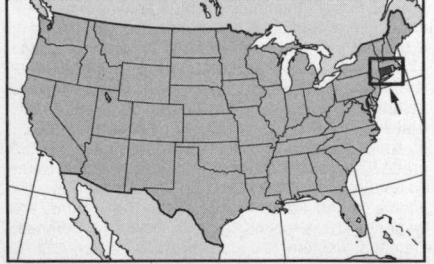

Name: Connecticut, from the Mohegan *Quinnehtukqut,* meaning "Long River Place" or "Beside the Long Tidal River." **Nickname:** Constitution State. **Capital:** Hartford. **Rank:** population: 29th; area: 48th. **Motto:** *Qui Transtulit Sustinet* (He Who Transplanted Still Sustains). **Song:** "Yankee Doodle," words from folk tradition, melody from an English tune, "The World Turned Upside Down." **Bird:** robin. **Flower:** mountain laurel. **Fossil:** *Eubrontes giganteus.* **Insect:** praying mantis. **Mammal:** sperm whale. **Mineral:** garnet. **Shellfish:** eastern oyster. **Tree:** white oak.

Natural features

Area: 5,544 sq mi, 14,358 sq km. **Mountain ranges:** Berkshire Hills. **Highest point:** Mount Frissell, 2,380 ft (725 m). **Largest lake:** Candlewood Lake. **Major rivers:** Connecticut, Housatonic, Thames. **Natural regions:** the New England Province covers the state, divided into the Western Upland, Central Lowland (Connecticut Valley), and Eastern Upland. **Location:** New England, bordering Massachusetts, Rhode Island, and New York. **Climate:** moderate temperate climate; coastal portions have somewhat warmer winters and cooler summers than does the interior; northwestern uplands have cooler and longer winters with heavier falls of snow; occasional hurricanes cause flooding and damage, particularly along the coastline. **Land use:** forest, 54.2%; agricultural, 5.4%; pasture, 1.0%; other, 39.4%.

People (2000 census)

Population: 3,405,565; 702.9 persons per sq mi (271.4 persons per sq km) (land area only). **Vital statistics** (1998; per 1,000 population): birth rate (1999), 13.2; death rate, 9.1; marriage rate, 6.1; divorce rate, 2.9. **Major cities:** Bridgeport, 139,529; New Haven, 123,626; Hartford, 121,578; Stamford, 117,083.

Government

Statehood: entered the Union on 9 Jan 1788 as the 5th state. **State constitution:** adopted 1965. **Representation in US Congress:** 2 senators; 6 representatives. **Electoral college:** 7 votes (in the 2004 general elections based on the 2000 census). **Political divisions:** 8 counties.

Economy

Employment: services, 34.3%; trade, 20.2%; manufacturing, 14.0%; government, 11.2%; finance, insurance, real estate, 9.5%; construction, 4.8%; transportation, public utilities, 4.2%; agriculture, forestry, fishing, 1.5%; mining, 0.1%. **Production:** finance, insurance, real estate, 28.7%; services, 22.0%; manufacturing, 16.5%; trade, 14.5%; government, 8.3%; transportation, utilities, 5.9%; construction, 3.3%; agriculture, 0.7%; mining, 0.1%. **Chief agricultural products:** *Crops*: corn (maize), silage, hay, tobacco, apples, pears, dairy products, eggs. *Livestock*: poultry, cattle, sheep, horses. *Fish catch*: lobster, clams, oysters, shad, marine fish. **Chief manufactured products:** printing, pharmaceutical products, soap and cleaning products, plastics, metal products, machinery, communications equipment, electronics, aerospace products, aircraft engines.

Internet resources: <www.ctbound.org>; <www.state.ct.us>.

For details about state governments, see pages 854–859; for extraction and energy data, see pages 880–884.

Delaware

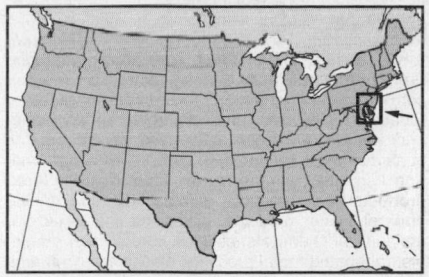

Name: Delaware, from Delaware River and Bay; named in turn for Sir Thomas West, Baron De La Warr. **Nickname:** First State. **Capital:** Dover. **Rank:** population: 45th; area: 49th. **Motto:** Liberty and Independence. **Song:** "Our Delaware," words by George B. Hynson and music by Will M.S. Brown. **Bird:** blue Hen chicken. **Fish:** weakfish. **Flower:** peach blossom. **Insect:** ladybug. **Mineral:** sillimanite. **Tree:** American holly.

Natural features

Area: 2,396 sq mi, 6,206 sq km. **Highest point:** Ebright Road, New Castle County, 442 ft (135 m). **Largest lake:** Red Mill Pond. **Major rivers:** Delaware, Nanticoke, Pocomoke. **Natural regions:** the Piedmont Province, including the Piedmont Upland, covers the northernmost tip of the state; the remainder consists of the Coastal Plain. **Location:** New England, bordering Pennsylvania, New Jersey, and Maryland. **Climate:** temperate, with high humidity, hot summers and cold winters. **Land use:** agricultural, 36.1%; forest, 30.1%; pasture, 0.6%; other, 33.3%.

People (2000 census)

Population: 783,600; 383.2 persons per sq mi (148.0 persons per sq km) (land area only). **Vital statistics** (1998; per 1,000 population): birth rate, 14.2 (1999); death rate, 8.8; marriage rate, 6.8; divorce rate, 4.5. **Major cities:** Wilmington, 72,664; Dover, 32,135; Newark, 28,547.

Government

Statehood: entered the Union on 7 Dec 1787 as the 1st state. **State constitution:** adopted 1897. **Representation in US Congress:** 2 senators; 1 representative. **Electoral college:** 3 votes. **Political divisions:** 3 counties.

Economy

Employment: services, 28.6%; trade, 20.6%; government, 13.5%; finance, insurance, real estate, 12.8%; manufacturing, 12.6%; construction, 6.1%; transportation, public utilities, 3.8%; agriculture, forestry, fishing, 1.9%. **Production:** finance, insurance, real estate, 39.8%; services, 15.5%; manufacturing, 14.2%; trade, 11.1%; government, 9.2%; transportation, utilities, 5.1%; construction, 4.3%; agriculture, 0.8%. **Chief agricultural products:** *Crops:* corn, soybeans, wheat, barley, peas, vegetables, dairy products. *Livestock:* poultry, cattle, hogs. *Fish catch:* crustaceans, crab, clams. **Chief manufactured products:** chemicals, food products, paper products, rubber and plastics products, metal products, printed materials.

Internet resources: <www.visitdelaware.net>; <www.state.de.us>.

District of Columbia

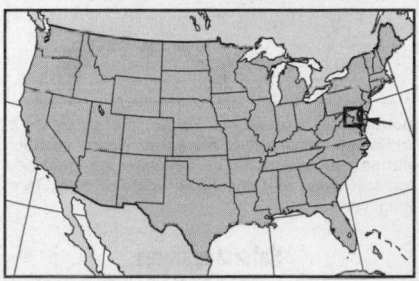

Motto: *Justitia Omnibus* (Justice for All). **Bird:** woodthrush. **Flower:** American Beauty rose. **Tree:** scarlet oak.

Natural features

Area: 68 sq mi, 177 sq km. **Major river:** Potomac. **Location:** Atlantic seaboard, bordered by Maryland and Virginia. **Climate:** humid, subtropical climate.

People (2000 census)

Population: 572,059; 9,378 persons per sq mi (3,620 persons per sq km) (land area only). **Vital statistics:** (1998; per 1,000 population): birth rate (1999), 14.5; death rate, 11.6; marriage rate, 4.6; divorce rate, 3.6.

Government

Representation in US Congress: 1 congressional delegate. **Political divisions:** 8 wards.

Economy

Employment (1997): services, 43.5%; government, 36.0%; trade, 7.3%; finance, insurance, real estate, 5.2%; transportation, public utilities, 3.0%; manufacturing, 1.9%; construction, 1.5%; agricultural service, forestry, fishing, 1.4%. **Production (2000):** services, 38.3%; government, 36.6%; finance, insurance, real estate, 13.5%; transportation, utilities, 5.0%; trade, 4.0%; manufacturing, 1.4%; construction, 1.0%; others, 0.2%. **Chief manufactured products:** printing and publishing products.

Internet resources: <www.washingtondc.gov>.

Florida

Name: Florida, in honor of *Pascua florida* ("feast of the flowers"), Spain's Easter celebration. **Nickname:** Sunshine State. **Capital:** Tallahassee. **Rank:** population: 4th; area: 26th. **Motto:** In God We Trust. **Song:** "Old Folks at Home" ("Swanee River"), words and music by Stephen Foster. **Bird:** mockingbird. **Butterfly:** zebra longwing. **Fish:** sailfish (saltwater); large-

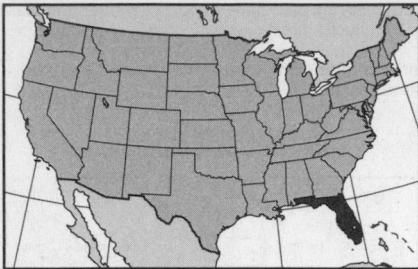

mouth bass (freshwater). **Flower:** orange blossom. **Gemstone:** moonstone. **Mammal:** Florida panther. **Marine mammal:** manatee. **Saltwater mammal:** porpoise. **Reptile:** alligator. **Rock:** agatized coral. **Tree:** sabal palm.

Natural features

Area: 59,928 sq mi, 155,214 sq km. **Highest point:** 345 ft (105 m), in Walton County. **Largest lake:** Lake Okeechobee. **Major rivers:** Kissimmee, Suwannee, St. Johns, Caloosahatchee, Indian, Withlacoochee, Apalachicola, Perdido, St. Marys. **Natural regions:** Western Highlands, a region at the westernmost end of the panhandle; Marianna Lowlands, east of the Western Highlands; Tallahassee Hills, covering the northern border with Georgia; Central Highlands, extending down the middle two thirds of the peninsula; Coastal Lowlands, curving along the east, south, and west coasts of the peninsula; the Everglades, far southern quarter of the peninsula. **Location:** Southeast, bordering Georgia and Alabama. **Climate:** tropical south of a west–east line drawn from Bradenton along the south shore of Lake Okeechobee to Vero Beach, and subtropical north of this line; hot, humid summers and mild, pleasant winters; hurricane season from June to November. **Land use:** forest, 42.3%; pasture, 15.8%; agricultural, 10.6%; other, 31.4%.

People (2000 census)

Population: 15,982,378; 296.0 persons per sq mi (114.3 persons per sq km) (land area only). **Vital statistics** (1998; per 1,000 population): birth rate, 13.0 (1999); death rate, 10.6; marriage rate, 9.4; divorce rate, 5.4. **Major cities:** Jacksonville, 735,617; Miami, 362,470; Tampa, 303,447; St. Petersburg, 248,232; Hialeah, 226,419; Orlando, 185,951; Fort Lauderdale, 152,397; Tallahassee, 150,624.

Government

Statehood: entered the Union on 3 Mar 1845 as the 27th state. **State constitution:** adopted 1968. **Representation in US Congress:** 2 senators; 23 representatives. **Electoral college:** 27 votes (in the 2004 general elections based on the 2000 census). **Political divisions:** 67 counties.

Economy

Employment: services, 35.3%; trade, 23.2%; government, 13.1%; finance, insurance, real estate, 8.2%; manufacturing, 6.4%; construction, 5.7%; transportation, public utilities, 4.8%; agriculture, forestry, fish-

ing, 3.0%; mining, 0.1%. **Production:** services, 24.4%; finance, insurance, real estate, 21.5%; trade, 19.1%; government, 12.2%; transportation, utilities, 8.6%; manufacturing, 7.2%; construction, 5.1%; agriculture, 1.8%; mining, 0.2%. **Chief agricultural products:** *Crops:* citrus fruit, fruits and vegetables, corn (maize), cotton, peanuts (groundnuts), soybeans, sugarcane, tobacco, honey, dairy products, eggs, nursery plants and flowers. *Livestock:* cattle and calves, poultry, hogs and pigs. *Aquaculture:* catfish. *Fish catch:* marine fish, crab, shrimp, oyster. **Chief manufactured products:** food products, meatpacking, soft drinks, apparel, paper products, pesticides and fertilizers, agricultural chemicals, plastics, construction materials, fabricated metal products, machinery, communications equipment, semiconductors, electronics, aerospace products, airplane engines, ships and boats, medical and surgical equipment.

Internet resources: <www.flausa.com>; <www.state.fl.us>.

Georgia

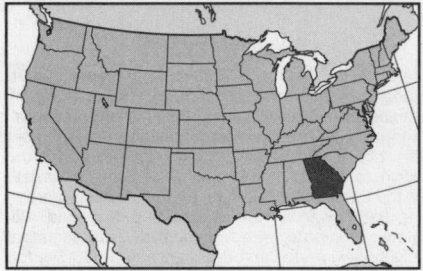

Name: Georgia, named for George II, king of England at the time the colony of Georgia was founded. **Nickname:** Empire State of the South; Peach State. **Capital:** Atlanta. **Rank:** population: 10th; area: 21st. **Mottos:** Wisdom, Justice, and Moderation; Agriculture and Commerce, 1776. **Song:** "Georgia on My Mind," words by Stuart Gorrell and music by Hoagy Carmichael. **Bird:** brown thrasher. **Fish:** largemouth bass. **Flower:** cherokee rose. **Fossil:** shark tooth. **Gemstone:** quartz. **Insect:** honeybee. **Marine mammal:** right whale. **Mineral:** staurolite. **Reptile:** gopher tortoise. **Tree:** live oak.

Natural features

Area: 58,977 sq mi, 152,750 sq km. **Mountain ranges:** Blue Ridge Mountains. **Highest point:** Brasstown Bald, 4,784 ft (1,458 m). **Largest lake:** Lanier. **Major rivers:** Chattahoochee, Flint, Apalachicola, Ocmulgee, Oconee, Altamaha, Savannah. **Natural regions:** Blue Ridge Province, north central edge; Valley and Ridge Province, northwest corner; Piedmont Province, northern half of state; Coastal Plain, southern half of state, divided into the Sea Island Section (southeast) and the East Gulf Coastal Plain (southwest). **Location:** South, bordering North Carolina, South Carolina, Florida, Alabama, and Tennessee. **Climate:** temperate, though maritime tropical air masses dominate the climate in summer; generally hot summers and cool winters; precipitation

For details about state governments, see pages 854–859; for extraction and energy data, see pages 880–884.

somewhat evenly distributed throughout the seasons in the north, whereas the southern and coastal areas have more summer rains; snow seldom occurs outside the mountainous northern counties. **Land use:** forest, 62.1%; agricultural, 19.8%; pasture, 3.6%; other, 14.6%.

People (2000 census)

Population: 8,186,453; 139.0 persons per sq mi (53.7 persons per sq km) (land area only). **Vital statistics** (1998; per 1,000 population): birth rate, 16.0; death rate, 7.9; marriage rate, 7.8; divorce rate, 4.7. **Major cities:** Atlanta, 416,474; Columbus, 186,291; Savannah, 131,510; Macon, 97,255.

Government

Statehood: entered the Union on 2 Jan 1788 as the 4th state. **State constitution:** adopted 1982. **Representation in US Congress:** 2 senators; 11 representatives. **Electoral college:** 15 votes (in the 2004 general elections based on the 2000 census). **Political divisions:** 159 counties.

Economy

Employment: services, 27.7%; trade, 23.1%; government, 14.9%; manufacturing, 13.5%; finance, insurance, real estate, 6.7%; transportation, public utilities, 5.8%; construction, 5.7%; agriculture, forestry, fishing, 2.5%; mining, 0.2%. **Production:** services, 19.2%; trade, 18.4%; manufacturing, 17.0%; finance, insurance, real estate, 15.3%; government, 11.9%; transportation, utilities, 11.4%; construction, 5.0%; agriculture, 1.3%; mining, 0.5%. **Chief agricultural products:** *Crops:* peanuts, pecans, rye, corn, cotton, cottonseed, hay, oats, sorghum, soybeans, tobacco, wheat, peaches, apples, onions, watermelon, snap beans, cabbage, corn, cucumbers, blueberries, grapes, honey, dairy products. *Livestock:* poultry, pigs, cattle. *Aquaculture:* catfish, trout. *Extractive products:* timber. **Chief manufactured products:** food products, soft drinks, textiles, wood products, paper products, chemical products, transportation equipment.

Internet resources: <www.georgia.org>; <www.state.ga.us>.

Hawaii

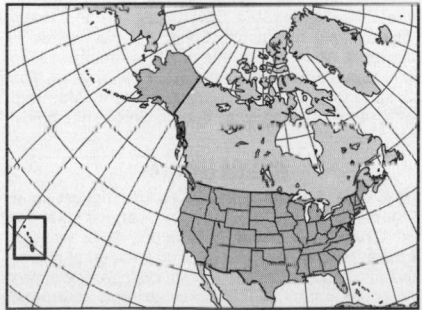

Nickname: Aloha State. **Capital:** Honolulu. **Rank:** population: 42nd; area: 47th. **Motto:** *Ua Mau ke Ea o*

ka Aina i ka Pono (The Life of the Land Is Perpetuated in Righteousness). **Song:** *"Hawaii Ponoi"* ("Our Hawaii"). **Bird:** nene, or Hawaiian goose. **Fish:** rectangular triggerfish (in Hawaiian, *humuhumunukunuku apua'a*). **Flower:** yellow hibiscus (in Hawaiian, *pua ma'o hau hele*). **Gemstone:** black coral. **Marine mammal:** humpback whale. **Tree:** kukui, or candlenut.

Natural features

Area: Total area, 6,459 sq mi, 16,729 sq km; the eight largest islands are: *Hawaii:* 4,028 sq mi, 10,433 sq km; *Maui:* 728 sq mi, 1,886 sq km; *Oahu:* 607 sq mi, 1,574 sq km; *Kauai:* 552 sq mi, 1,430 sq km; *Molokai:* 280 sq mi, 725 sq km; *Lanai:* 140 sq mi, 363 sq km; *Niihau:* 72 sq mi, 186 sq km; *Kahoolawe:* 45 sq mi, 117 sq km. **Highest point:** Mauna Kea, Hawaii, 13,796 ft (4,205 m). **Major rivers:** *Hawaii:* Wailuku; *Kauai:* Waimea, Hanalei. **Natural regions:** The eight major islands at the eastern end of the 1,500-mile-long chain of islands are, from west to east, Niihau, Kauai, Oahu, Molokai, Lanai, Kahoolawe, Maui, and Hawaii; each island contains regions of mountains, deeps, ridges, and wide beaches; active volcanoes are found on the island of Hawaii. **Location:** islands surrounded by the Pacific Ocean. **Climate:** tropical; rainfall variations throughout the state are dramatic, ranging from 8.7 inches (220 mm) a year at Kawaihae on the island of Hawaii, to roughly 444 inches (11,280 mm) at Mount Waialeale on the island of Kauai. **Land use:** forest, 28.9%; pasture, 23.4%; agricultural, 7.1%; other, 40.6%.

People (2000 census)

Population: Total, 1,211,537; 188.6 persons per sq mi (72.8 persons per sq km) (land area only). Populations of the eight largest islands: *Niihau:* 230 (1990 estimate); *Kauai:* 50,947 (1990 estimate); *Maui:* 105,336 (1995 estimate); *Molokai:* 6,838 (1995 estimate); *Lanai:* 2,989 (1995 estimate); *Oahu:* 872,478 (1998 estimate); *Hawaii:* 143,135 (1998 estimate); *Kahoolawe:* uninhabited. **Vital statistics** (1998; per 1,000 population): birth rate, 14.4 (1999); death rate, 6.8; marriage rate, 17.5; divorce rate, 4.0. **Major cities:** Honolulu, 371,657; Hilo, 40,759; Kailua, 36,513; Kaneohe, 34,970; Waipahu, 33,108.

Government

Statehood: entered the Union on 21 Aug 1959 as the 50th state. **State constitution:** adopted 1950. **Representation in US Congress:** 2 senators; 2 representatives. **Electoral college:** 4 votes. **Political divisions:** 5 counties.

Economy

Employment: services, 31.3%; government, 22.3%; trade, 22.0%; finance, insurance, real estate, 8.4%; transportation, public utilities, 6.3%; construction, 4.2%; agriculture, forestry, fishing, 2.8%; manufacturing, 2.7%; mining, 0.1%. **Production:** finance, insurance, real estate, 23.2%; services, 22.1%; government, 21.8%; trade, 14.7%; transportation, utilities, 10.4%; construction, 4.0%; manufacturing, 2.5%; agriculture, 1.2%; mining, 0.1%. **Chief agricultural products:** *Crops:* pineapples, sugarcane, flowers, macadamia nuts, coffee, milk, eggs. *Livestock:*

cattle. *Aquaculture*: fish, shellfish. **Chief manufactured products:** food products, processed sugar, canned pineapple, preserved fruits and vegetables, apparel and textile products, printing and publishing.

Internet resources: <www.gohawaii.com>; <www.state.hi.us>.

Idaho

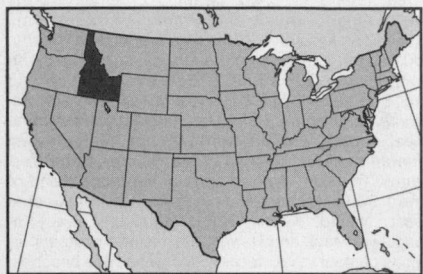

Nickname: Gem State. **Capital:** Boise. **Rank:** population: 39th; area: 11th. **Motto:** *Esto Perpetua* (It Is Forever). **Song:** "Here We Have Idaho," words by McKinley Helm and Albert J. Tompkins, music by Sallie Hume Douglas. **Bird:** mountain bluebird. **Fish:** cutthroat trout. **Flower:** syringa. **Fossil:** Hagerman horse fossil (*Equus simplicidens*). **Gemstone:** star garnet. **Horse:** Appaloosa. **Insect:** monarch butterfly. **Tree:** western white pine.

Natural features

Area: 83,574 sq mi, 216,456 sq km. **Mountain ranges:** Northern Rocky Mountains, Middle Rocky Mountains, Sawtooth, Pioneer, Continental Divide, Beaverhead, Clearwater, Bitterroot, Salmon River, Lost River Range, Lemhi Range. **Highest point:** Borah Peak, 12,662 ft (3,859 m). **Largest lake:** Lake Pend Oreille. **Major rivers:** Snake, Salmon. **Natural regions:** Northern Rocky Mountains, covering most of the northern half of the state; Columbia Plateaus, extending across the south-central and southwestern regions; Great Basin region of the Basin and Range Province, southeast; Middle Rocky Mountains, extreme southeast tip. **Location:** Northwest, bordering Montana, Wyoming, Utah, Nevada, Oregon, and Washington; international border with Canada. **Climate:** continental, with warm wet summers and cold dry winters, but regionally diverse: in general, precipitation increases and mean temperatures drop with increases in altitude. **Land use:** pasture, 40.0%; forest, 32.3%; agricultural, 10.9%; other, 16.8%.

People (2000 census)

Population: 1,293,953; 15.6 persons per sq mi (6.0 persons per sq km) (land area only). **Vital statistics** (1998; per 1,000 population): birth rate, 15.9 (1999); death rate, 7.5; marriage rate, 12.6; divorce rate, 5.7. **Major cities:** Boise, 185,787; Nampa, 51,867; Pocatello, 51,466; Idaho Falls, 50,730; Meridian, 34,919.

Government

Statehood: entered the Union on 3 Jul 1890 as the 43rd state. **State constitution:** adopted 1889. **Representation in US Congress:** 2 senators; 2 representatives. **Electoral college:** 4 votes. **Political divisions:** 44 counties.

Economy

Employment: services, 26.1%; trade, 22.7%; government, 15.0%; manufacturing, 11.4%; agriculture, forestry, fishing, 7.5%; construction, 7.1%; finance, insurance, real estate, 5.4%; transportation, public utilities, 4.4%; mining, 0.5%. **Production:** manufacturing, 21.6%; trade, 16.6%; services, 16.3%; government, 13.4%; finance, insurance, real estate, 11.8%; transportation, utilities, 7.8%; construction, 6.6%; agriculture, 5.2%; mining, 0.6%. **Chief agricultural products:** *Crops*: potatoes, wheat, hay, sugar beets, barley, alfalfa seed, Kentucky Blue Grass seed, hops, beans, onions, lentils, peas, honey, dairy products. *Livestock*: cattle, calves, sheep, lambs. *Extractive products*: timber, trout. **Chief manufactured products:** food processing, lumber and wood products, paper, printing, chemicals, plastics and rubber products, nonmetallic mineral products, fabricated metal products, machinery, computers and electronic products, transportation equipment, furniture.

Internet resources: <www.visitid.org>; <www.state.id.us>.

Illinois

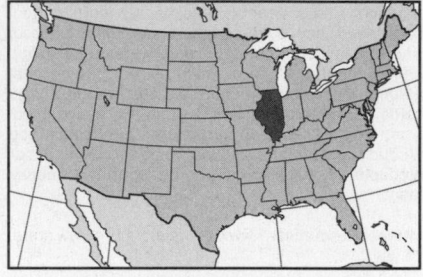

Name: Illinois, derived from a Native American word meaning "tribe of superior men." **Nickname:** Prairie State. **Capital:** Springfield. **Rank:** population: 5th; area: 24th. **Motto:** State Sovereignty, National Union. **Slogan:** Land of Lincoln. **Song:** "Illinois," words by Charles H. Chamberlain and music by Archibald Johnston. **Bird:** cardinal. **Fish:** bluegill. **Flower:** violet. **Fossil:** tully monster. **Insect:** monarch butterfly. **Mammal:** white-tailed deer. **Mineral:** fluorite. **Tree:** white oak.

Natural features

Area: 57,918 sq mi, 150,007 sq km. **Highest point:** Charles Mound, 1,235 ft (376 m). **Largest lake:** Carlyle Lake. **Major rivers:** Mississippi, Ohio, Wabash. **Natural regions:** central Lowland, a region of sloping hills and broad, shallow river valleys covering almost the entire state; Ozark Plateaus, extreme southwest; Interior Low Plateaus and Coastal Plain, extreme southeastern tip. **Location:** Midwest, bordering Wisconsin, Indiana, Kentucky, Missouri, and Iowa. **Climate:** continental, with hot summers and cold, snowy winters; wide seasonal and regional variations. **Land use:** agricultural, 70.1%; forest, 11.4%; pasture, 4.4%; other, 14.2%.

People (2000 census)

Population: 12,419,293; 223.4 persons per sq mi (85.1 persons per sq km) (land area only). **Vital statistics** (1998; per 1,000 population): birth rate, 15.0 (1999); death rate, 8.7; marriage rate, 7.0; divorce rate, 3.4. **Major cities:** Chicago, 2,896,016; Rockford, 150,115; Aurora, 142,990; Naperville, 128,358; Peoria, 112,936; Springfield, 111,454; Joliet, 106,221.

Government

Statehood: entered the Union on 3 Dec 1818 as the 21st state. **State constitution:** adopted 1970. **Representation in US Congress:** 2 senators; 20 representatives. **Electoral college:** 21 votes (in the 2004 general elections based on the 2000 census). **Political divisions:** 102 counties.

Did you know? Cairo IL, which stands on a delta at the confluence of the Mississippi and Ohio rivers, was so named because the site was thought to resemble that of the Egyptian capital.

Economy

Employment: services, 30.9%; trade, 21.2%; manufacturing, 14.0%; government, 12.2%; finance, insurance, real estate, 9.0%; transportation, public utilities, 5.5%; construction, 4.7%; agriculture, forestry, fishing, 2.3%; mining, 0.3%. **Production:** services, 22.6%; finance, insurance, real estate, 20.4%; manufacturing, 16.3%; trade, 16.2%; government, 9.9%; transportation, utilities, 9.2%; construction, 4.5%; agriculture, 0.8%; mining, 0.3%. **Chief agricultural products:** *Crops:* corn (maize), soybeans, wheat, hay, oats, sorghum, apples, peaches, snap beans, sweet corn, potatoes, cabbage, dairy products, eggs. *Livestock:* pigs, cattle, calves, horses, poultry. **Chief manufactured products:** food products, beverages, textiles, leather goods, apparel, wood products, paper products, printing, petroleum and coal products, asphalt paving, chemicals, pharmaceuticals, plastics and rubber products, nonmetallic mineral products, iron and steel products, fabricated metals, machinery, computers and electronics, appliances, and transportation equipment.

Internet resources: <www.enjoyillinois.com>; <www.state.il.us>.

Indiana

Name: Indiana, generally thought to mean "Land of the Indians." **Nickname:** Hoosier State. **Capital:** Indianapolis. **Rank:** population: 14th; area: 38th. **Motto:** The Crossroads of America. **Song:** "On the Banks of the Wabash, Far Away," words and music by Paul Dresser. **Bird:** cardinal. **Flower:** peony. **Rock:** limestone. **Tree:** tulip tree (yellow poplar).

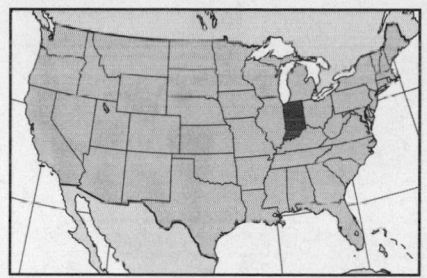

Natural features

Area: 36,420 sq mi, 94,328 sq km. **Highest point:** 1,257 ft (383 m), near Fountain City. **Largest lake:** Lake Monroe. **Major rivers:** Wabash, Ohio. **Natural regions:** Central Lowland comprises most of the state and includes the Eastern Lake section to the north, and the Till Plains in the center; Interior Low Plateaus, including the Highland Rim section, cover the southern quarter of the state. **Location:** Midwest, bordering Michigan, Ohio, Kentucky, and Illinois. **Climate:** continental, with four distinct seasons, hot summers, cold winters, mild spring and fall, with increased risk of tornadoes in spring. **Land use:** agricultural, 59.6%; forest, 18.9%; pasture, 5.0%; other, 16.4%.

People (2000 census)

Population: 6,080,485; 169.5 persons per sq mi (65.4 persons per sq km) (land area only). **Vital statistics** (1998; per 1,000 population): birth rate, 14.5 (1999); death rate, 9.1; marriage rate, 5.9; divorce rate, N/A. **Major cities:** Indianapolis, 791,926; Fort Wayne, 205,727; Evansville, 121,582; South Bend, 107,789; Gary, 102,746; Hammond, 83,048.

Government

Statehood: entered the Union on 11 Dec 1816 as the 19th state. **State constitution:** adopted 1851. **Representation in US Congress:** 2 senators; 10 representatives. **Electoral college:** 11 votes (in the 2004 general elections based on the 2000 census). **Political divisions:** 92 counties.

Economy

Employment: services, 26.2%; trade, 22.7%; manufacturing, 19.7%; government, 11.7%; finance, insurance, real estate, 6.0%; construction, 5.8%; transportation, public utilities, 4.8%; agriculture, forestry, fishing, 3.0%; mining, 0.3%. **Production:** manufacturing, 30.9%; services, 16.6%; trade, 15.4%; finance, insurance, real estate, 13.0%; government, 10.0%; transportation, utilities, 7.6%; construction, 5.1%; agriculture, 1.0%; mining, 0.4%. **Chief agricultural products:** *Crops:* corn (maize), soybeans, wheat, hay, popcorn, tobacco, tomatoes, peppermint, spearmint, watermelon, blueberries, snap beans, cucumbers, apples, milk, eggs. *Livestock:* pigs, cattle, calves, poultry. **Chief manufactured products:** iron and steel, metal products, motor vehicle parts, machinery, food products, dairy products, soft drinks, wood products, paper products, mobile homes, asphalt.

Internet resources: <www.enjoyindiana.com>; <www.state.in.us>.

Iowa

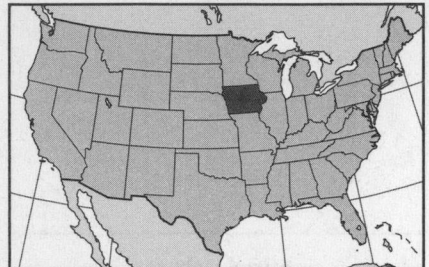

Name: Iowa, named for the Iowa (or Ioway) Indians who once inhabited the area. **Nickname:** Hawkeye State. **Capital:** Des Moines. **Rank:** population: 30th; area: 23rd. **Motto:** Our Liberties We Prize and Our Rights We Will Maintain. **Song:** "The Song of Iowa," words by S.H.M. Byers, to the tune of "O Tannenbaum." **Bird:** eastern goldfinch. **Flower:** wild rose. **Rock:** geode. **Tree:** oak.

Natural features

Area: 56,276 sq mi, 145,754 sq km. **Highest point:** near Sibley, 1,670 ft (509 m). **Largest lake:** Spirit Lake. **Major rivers:** Des Moines, Mississippi, Missouri, Big Sioux. **Natural regions:** overall, Central Lowland, including the Western Lake section, north and central regions; Dissected Till Plains, south; Wisconsin Driftless Section, northeast corner. **Location:** Midwest, bordering Minnesota, Wisconsin, Illinois, Missouri, Nebraska, and South Dakota. **Climate:** continental, with hot summers and cold, snowy winters. **Land use:** agricultural, 78.1%; forest, 5.4%; pasture, 4.1%; other, 12.4%.

People (2000 census)

Population: 2,926,324; 52.4 persons per sq mi (20.2 persons per sq km) (land area only). **Vital statistics** (1998; per 1,000 population): birth rate, 13.1 (1999); death rate, 9.9; marriage rate, 8.2; divorce rate, 3.3. **Major cities:** Des Moines, 198,682; Cedar Rapids, 120,758; Davenport, 98,359; Sioux City, 85,013; Waterloo, 68,747.

Government

Statehood: entered the Union on 28 Dec 1846 as the 29th state. **State constitution:** adopted 1857. **Representation in US Congress:** 2 senators, 5 representatives. **Electoral college:** 7 votes. **Political divisions:** 99 counties.

Economy

Employment: services, 26.8%; trade, 22.4%; manufacturing, 14.0%; government, 13.2%; agriculture, forestry, fishing, 7.7%; finance, insurance, real estate, 6.2%; construction, 5.1%; transportation, public utilities, 4.4%; mining, 0.1%. **Production:** manufacturing, 22.4%; services, 17.0%; trade, 16.9%; finance, insurance, real estate, 15.1%; government, 12.0%; transportation, utilities, 8.5%; construction, 4.4%; agriculture, 3.5%; mining, 0.3%. **Chief agricul-**

tural products: *Crops:* corn, soybeans, hay, oats, grain, milk, eggs, butter, honey, popcorn, sorghum. *Livestock:* poultry, hogs and pigs, beef cattle, sheep. **Chief manufactured products:** food products, dairy products, meatpacking, pesticide, fertilizer, and other agricultural chemicals, farm machinery, construction machinery, household appliances, motor vehicle parts.

Internet resources: <www.traveliowa.com>; <www.state.ia.us>.

Kansas

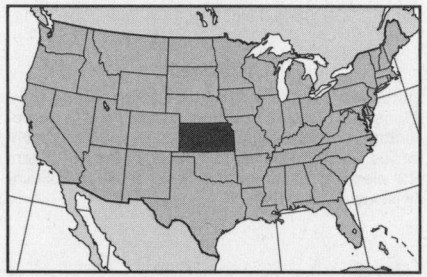

Name: Kansas, derived from the Sioux word *Kansa* ("people of the south wind") for the Native Americans who lived in the region. **Nickname:** Sunflower State. **Capital:** Topeka. **Rank:** population: 32nd; area: 13th. **Motto:** *Ad Astra Per Aspera* (To the Stars Through Difficulties). **Song:** "Home on the Range," words by Brewster Higley and music by Dan Kelly. **Amphibian:** barred tiger salamander. **Bird:** western meadowlark. **Flower:** wild native sunflower. **Insect:** honeybee. **Mammal:** American buffalo. **Reptile:** ornate box turtle. **Tree:** cottonwood.

Natural features

Area: 82,282 sq mi, 213,110 sq km. **Highest point:** Mount Sunflower, 4,039 ft (1,231 m). **Largest lake:** Milford Lake. **Major rivers:** Kansas, Arkansas, Big Blue, Republican, Solomon, Saline, Smoky Hill, Cimarron, Verdigris, Neosho (Grand). **Natural regions:** the Great Plains Province, covering the western half of the state, consists of the High Plains to the west and the Plains Border to the east; the Central Lowland covers the eastern half of the state, and consists of the Dissected Till Plains to the north and the Osage Plains to the south. **Location:** Midwest, bordering Nebraska, Missouri, Oklahoma, and Colorado. **Climate:** temperate but continental, with great extremes between summer and winter temperatures but few long periods of extreme hot or cold. **Land use:** agricultural, 64.4%; pasture, 24.0%; forest, 2.8%; other, 8.8%.

People (2000 census)

Population: 2,688,418; 32.9 persons per sq mi (12.7 persons per sq km) (land area only). **Vital statistics** (1998; per 1,000 population): birth rate, 14.6 (1999); death rate, 9.2; marriage rate, 7.9; divorce rate, 4.1. **Major cities:** Wichita, 344,284; Overland Park, 149,080; Kansas City, 146,866; Topeka, 122,377; Olathe, 92,962.

For details about state governments, see pages 854–859; for extraction and energy data, see pages 880–884.

Government

Statehood: entered the Union on 29 Jan 1861 as the 34th state. **State constitution:** adopted 1859. **Representation in US Congress:** 2 senators; 4 representatives. **Electoral college:** 6 votes. **Political divisions:** 105 counties.

Economy

Employment: services, 26.5%; trade, 22.2%; government, 16.0%; manufacturing, 12.6%; agriculture, forestry, fishing, 5.9%; finance, insurance, real estate, 5.7%; construction, 5.2%; transportation, public utilities, 4.9%; mining, 1.2%. **Production:** trade, 18.2%; services, 17.4%; manufacturing, 16.8%; government, 13.5%; finance, insurance, real estate, 12.9%; transportation, utilities, 12.5%; construction, 4.6%; agriculture, 2.9%; mining, 1.3%. **Chief agricultural products:** *Crops:* wheat, corn (maize), sorghum, hay, soybeans, sunflower seed and oil, apples, peaches, pecans. *Livestock:* beef cattle and calves, hogs, lambs, sheep, dairy cows, horses and other equines. **Chief manufactured products:** food products, grain and oilseed milling, meat products, printing, refined petroleum, soap and cleaning products, plastic products, aerospace products and parts, aircraft.

Internet resources: <www.kansas-travel.com>; <www. state.ks.us>.

Kentucky

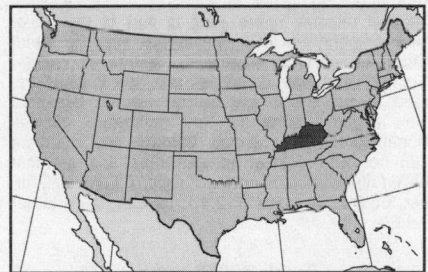

Name: Kentucky, possibly derived from the Iroquois word for "prairie." **Nickname:** Bluegrass State. **Capital:** Frankfort. **Rank:** population: 25th; area: 36th. **Motto:** United We Stand, Divided We Fall. **Song:** "My Old Kentucky Home," words and music by Stephen Foster. **Bird:** cardinal. **Butterfly:** viceroy butterfly. **Fish:** Kentucky bass. **Flower:** goldenrod. **Horse:** thoroughbred. **Tree:** tulip popular. **Wild animal:** gray squirrel.

Natural features

Area: 40,411 sq mi, 104,665 sq km. **Mountain ranges:** Cumberland, Pine. **Highest point:** Black Mountain, 4,145 ft (1,263 m). **Largest lake:** Kentucky Lake. **Major rivers:** Mississippi, Ohio, Big Sandy, Licking, Kentucky, Salt, Green, Tradewater, Cumberland, Tennessee. **Natural regions:** Appalachian Plateaus, eastern third of the state; Interior Low Plateaus, including the Highland Rim section and the Lexington Plain, cover the remainder, with the exception of the Coastal Plain, which covers the extreme southwest tip. **Location:** Midwest, bordering Indiana,

Ohio, West Virginia, Virginia, Tennessee, Missouri, and Illinois. **Climate:** temperate continental climate, with hot, humid summers and cold winters. **Land use:** forest, 48.6%; agricultural, 34.8%; pasture, 5.9%; other, 10.7%.

People (2000 census)

Population: 4,041,769; 101.7 persons per sq mi (39.3 persons per sq km) (land area only). **Vital statistics** (1998; per 1,000 population): birth rate, 13.7 (1999); death rate, 9.6; marriage rate, 11.3; divorce rate, 5.7. **Major cities:** Lexington-Fayette, 260,512; Louisville, 256,231; Owensboro, 54,067; Bowling Green, 49,296; Covington, 43,370.

Government

Statehood: entered the Union on 1 Jun 1792 as the 15th state. **State constitution:** adopted 1891. **Representation in US Congress:** 2 senators; 6 representatives. **Electoral college:** 8 votes. **Political divisions:** 120 counties.

Economy

Employment: services, 25.4%; trade, 21.7%; government, 14.9%; manufacturing, 14.9%; agriculture, forestry, fishing, 6.4%; construction, 5.8%; transportation, public utilities, 5.2%; finance, insurance, real estate, 4.5%; mining, 1.2%. **Production:** manufacturing, 27.5%; services, 16.0%; trade, 15.7%; government, 13.5%; finance, insurance, real estate, 10.9%; transportation, utilities, 8.0%; construction, 4.5%; mining, 2.1%; agriculture, 1.8%. **Chief agricultural products:** *Crops:* tobacco, soybeans, corn, wheat, hay, sorghum, eggs, dairy products. *Livestock:* racing and show horses, beef and dairy cattle, hogs, poultry, sheep. **Chief manufactured products:** food products, meat packing, beverages, tobacco, apparel, paper products, printing, chemical products, paint, resin and synthetic rubber products, plastic products, iron and steel, aluminum, fabricated metal products, machinery, appliances, motor vehicles

Internet resources: <www.kentuckytourism.com>; <www.state.ky.us>.

Louisiana

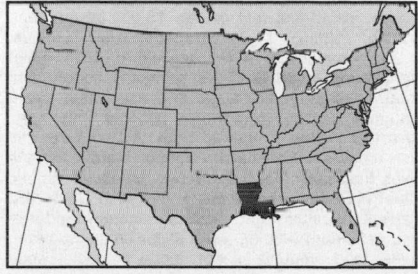

Name: Louisiana, named for Louis XIV, King of France. **Nickname:** Pelican State. **Capital:** Baton Rouge. **Rank:** population: 22nd; area: 33rd. **Motto:** Union, Justice and Confidence. **Songs:** "Give Me Louisiana," words and music by Doralice Fontane, arranged by John W. Schaum; "You Are My Sunshine,"

words and music by Jimmy H. Davis and Charles Mitchell. **Amphibian:** green tree frog. **Bird:** brown pelican. **Crustacean:** crawfish. **Freshwater fish:** white perch. **Flower:** magnolia. **Fossil:** petrified palmwood. **Gemstone:** agate. **Insect:** honeybee. **Mammal:** black bear. **Reptile:** alligator. **Tree:** bald cypress.

Natural features

Area: 49,651 sq mi, 128,595 sq km. **Highest point:** Driskill Mountain, 535 ft (163 m). **Largest lake:** Lake Ponchartrain. **Major rivers:** Mississippi, Red, Sabine. **Natural regions:** the entire state consists of the Coastal Plain and is divided into the West Gulf Coastal Plain to the west, the Mississippi Alluvial Plain to the northeast, and the East Gulf Coastal Plain in the southeast. **Location:** South, bordering Arkansas, Mississippi, and Texas. **Climate:** subtropical, with hot, humid summers, tempered by frequent afternoon thunder showers, alternating with mild winters; subject to tropical storms: the hurricane season extends for six months, from June through November. **Land use:** forest, 49.1%; agricultural, 19.7%; pasture, 5.7%; other, 25.6%.

People (2000 census)

Population: 4,468,976; 102.6 persons per sq mi (39.6 persons per sq km) (land area only). **Vital statistics** (1998; per 1,000 population): birth rate, 15.4 (1999); death rate, 9.2; marriage rate, 9.7; divorce rate, N/A. **Major cities:** New Orleans, 484,674; Baton Rouge, 227,818; Shreveport, 200,145; Lafayette, 110,257; Lake Charles, 71,757.

Government

Statehood: entered the Union on 30 Apr 1812 as the 18th state. **State constitution:** adopted 1974. **Representation in US Congress:** 2 senators; 7 representatives. **Electoral college:** 9 votes. **Political divisions:** 64 parishes.

Economy

Employment: services, 29.2%; trade, 21.6%; government, 17.4%; manufacturing, 8.7%; construction, 6.8%; transportation, public utilities, 5.6%; finance, insurance, real estate, 5.3%; agriculture, forestry, fishing, 2.8%; mining, 2.7%. **Production:** services, 17.6%; manufacturing, 15.2%; trade, 15.1%; finance, insurance, real estate, 13.0%; government, 12.3%; mining, 11.7%; transportation, utilities, 9.2%; construction, 4.9%; agriculture, 1.0%. **Chief agricultural products:** *Crops:* soybeans, cotton, corn (maize), sorghum, hay, sugarcane, rice, wheat, sweet potatoes, pecans, strawberries, peaches, milk, eggs. *Livestock:* cattle, chickens, hogs. *Aquaculture:* catfish, crawfish. *Fish catch:* shrimp, oysters, marine fish, freshwater fish. *Extractive products:* timber. **Chief manufactured products:** industrial chemicals, agricultural chemicals, plastics materials and resins, petroleum refining, cane sugar products, beverages, food products, paper, metal products, wood products, communications equipment, ships and boats.

Internet resources: <www.louisianatravel.com>; <www.state.la.us>.

Maine

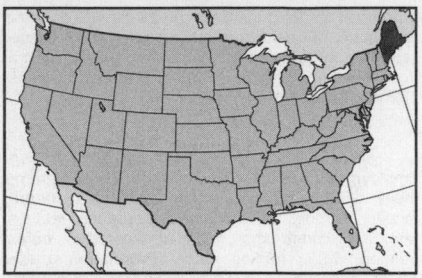

Name: Maine, possibly named for the former French province of Maine, or used to distinguish the mainland portion of the territory from offshore islands. **Nickname:** Pine Tree State. **Capital:** Augusta. **Rank:** population: 40th; area: 39th. **Motto:** *Dirigo* (I Direct). **Song:** "State of Maine Song," words and music by Roger Vinton Snow. **Bird:** chickadee. **Fish:** landlocked salmon. **Flower:** white pine cone and tassel. **Fossil:** *Pertica quadrifaria.* **Gemstone:** tourmaline. **Insect:** honeybee. **Mammal:** moose. **Tree:** white pine.

Natural features

Area: 33,741 sq mi, 87,388 sq km. **Mountain ranges:** Appalachians, Longfellow. **Highest point:** Mount Katahdin, 5,268 ft (1,606 m). **Largest lake:** Moosehead Lake. **Major rivers:** Saco, Androscoggin, Kennebec, Penobscot, St. John's, St. Croix, Allagash. **Natural regions:** entire state is part of the larger New England Province, subdivided into the White Mountain section (southwest), Seaboard Lowland Section (southeast coastline), and New England Upland Section (north and central regions). **Location:** New England, bordering New Hampshire; international border with Canada. **Climate:** cool maritime climate, with coldest temperatures and greatest snowfall occurring in northern regions. **Land use:** forest, 85.8%; agricultural, 2.4%; pasture, 0.2%; other 11.6%.

People (2000 census)

Population: 1,274,923; 41.3 persons per sq mi (15.9 persons per sq km) (land area only). **Vital statistics** (1998; per 1,000 population): birth rate, 10.9 (1999); death rate, 9.8; marriage rate, 8.4; divorce rate, 4.1. **Major cities:** Portland, 64,249; Lewiston, 35,690; Bangor, 31,473; South Portland, 23,324; Auburn, 23,203.

Government

Statehood: entered the Union on 15 Mar 1820 as the 23rd state. **State constitution:** adopted 1819. **Representation in US Congress:** 2 senators; 2 representatives. **Electoral college:** 4 votes. **Political divisions:** 16 counties.

Economy

Employment: services, 30.2%; trade, 23.0%; government, 13.7%; manufacturing, 13.1%; constrution, 6.3%; finance, insurance, real estate, 5.9%; transportation, public utilities, 4.1%; agriculture, forestry, fishing, 3.7%. **Production:** services, 20.1%; finance, insurance, real estate, 18.8%; trade, 18.0%; manufacturing, 15.4%; government, 14.0%; transportation, utilities, 7.0%; construction, 4.6%; agriculture, forestry, fishing 2.0%. **Chief agricultural products:** *Crops:* potatoes, blueberries, hay, apples, cranberries, oats, honey, corn (maize), dairy products, eggs. *Livestock:* poultry, cattle, sheep. *Aquaculture:* salmon, rainbow trout. *Fish catch:* marine fish, lobster, shrimp, crab, clams, haddock, cod, mackerel. *Extractive industries:* timber. **Chief manufactured products:** paper, leather, lumber and wood products, food products, semiconductors, apparel, printing and publishing, plastic products, ships and boats.

Internet resources: <www.visitmaine.com>; <www.state.me.us>.

Maryland

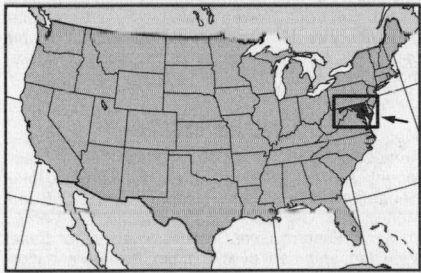

Name: Maryland, in honor of Henrietta Maria (queen of Charles I of England). **Nickname:** Old Line State. **Capital:** Annapolis. **Rank:** population: 19th; area: 42nd. **Motto:** *Fatti Maschii, Parole Femine* (Manly Deeds, Womanly Words). **Song:** "Maryland, My Maryland," words by James Ryder Randall, to the tune of "Lauriger Horatius." **Bird:** Baltimore oriole. **Crustacean:** Maryland blue crab. **Dinosaur:** *Astrodon johnstoni.* **Fish:** rockfish (striped bass). **Flower:** black-eyed Susan. **Insect:** Baltimore checkerspot. **Reptile:** diamondback terrapin. **Tree:** white oak.

Natural features

Area: 12,297 sq mi, 31,849 sq km. **Mountain ranges:** Allegheny Mountains, Appalachians. **Highest point:** Backbone Mountain, 3,360 ft (1,024 m). **Largest lake:** Deep Creek Lake. **Major rivers:** Potomac, Patuxent, Susquehanna. **Natural regions:** Coastal Plain, eastern half of the state, includes the Embayed Section near the southwest corner of the peninsula; Piedmont Province, central, and including the Piedmont Upland to the north and the Piedmont Lowlands to the west; Blue Ridge Province, northwest; Valley and Ridge Province, part of western neck; Appalachian Plateau, extreme western neck. **Location:** East coast, bordering Pennsylvania, Delaware, District of Columbia, Virginia, and West Virginia. **Climate:** continental in the west, but a humid, subtropical climate prevails in the east; hurricanes often bring much rain to eastern regions. **Land use:** forest, 38.7%; agricultural, 24.9%; pasture, 3.3%; other, 33.1%.

People (2000 census)

Population: 5,296,486; 541.8 persons per sq mi (209.2 persons per sq km) (land area only). **Vital statistics** (1998; per 1,000 population): birth rate, 13.9 (1999); death rate, 8.2; marriage rate, 7.3; divorce rate, 3.2. **Major cities:** Baltimore, 651,154; Frederick, 52,767; Gaithersburg, 52,613; Bowie, 50,269; Rockville, 47,388.

Government

Statehood: entered the Union on 28 Apr 1788 as the 7th state. **State constitution:** adopted 1867. **Representation in US Congress:** 2 senators; 8 representatives. **Electoral college:** 10 votes. **Political divisions:** 23 counties.

Economy

Employment: services, 34.4%; trade, 21.1%; government, 17.3%; finance, insurance, real estate, 8.3%; manufacturing, 6.4%; construction, 6.3%; transportation, public utilities, 4.4%; agriculture, forestry, fishing, 1.8%; mining, 0.1%. **Production:** services, 24.2%; finance, insurance, real estate, 21.3%; government, 17.5%; trade, 15.2%; manufacturing, 8.1%; transportation, utilities, 7.5%; construction, 5.4%; agriculture, 0.8%; mining, 0.1%. **Chief agricultural products:** *Crops:* corn, soybeans, wheat, vegetables, potatoes, tobacco, dairy products, eggs. *Livestock:* cattle, pigs, poultry. *Aquaculture:* hybrid striped bass, catfish, tilapia, trout, oysters. *Fish catch:* blue crab, other crustaceans, oysters, mollusks, marine fish. **Chief manufactured products:** primary metals, ships and boats, food products, motor vehicles, chemical products, paper and printing, plastics and rubber, fabricated metal products, machinery, computers and electronics, transportation equipment.

Internet resources: <www.mdisfun.org>; <www.state.md.us>.

Massachusetts

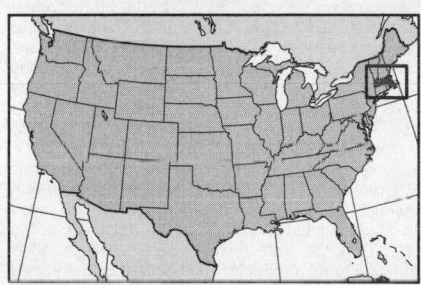

Name: Massachusetts, named for the Massachuset tribe of Native Americans who lived in the Great Blue Hill region south of Boston; the word *Massachuset* means "at or about the great hill." **Nickname:** Bay State. **Capital:** Boston. **Rank:** population: 13th; area: 45th. **Motto:** *Ense Petit Placidam Sub Libertate Quietem* (By the Sword We Seek Peace, but Peace Only Under Liberty). **Song:** "All Hail to Massachusetts," words and music by Arthur J. Marsh. **Bird:** black-capped chickadee. **Fish:** cod. **Flower:** mayflower. **Fossil:** theropod dinosaur tracks. **Gemstone:** rhodonite.

Insect: ladybug. **Marine mammal:** right whale. **Mineral:** babingtonite. **Rock:** Roxbury puddingstone. **Tree:** American elm.

Michigan

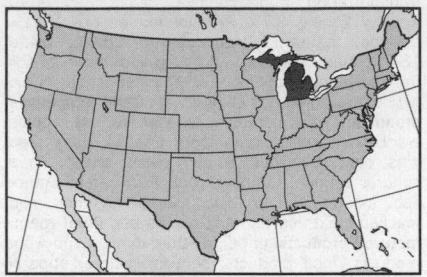

Natural features

Area: 9,241 sq mi, 23,934 sq km. **Mountain ranges:** Berkshire Mountains, Hoosac Range, Taconic Range. **Highest point:** Mount Greylock, 3,491 ft (1,064 m). **Largest lake:** Webster Lake. **Major rivers:** Connecticut, Charles, Merrimack, Housatonic, Taunton. **Natural regions:** the New England Province, comprising most of the state, subdivided into the Taconic Section along the west, the New England Upland Section in the central region, and the Seaboard Lowland Section covering the eastern third of the state; Coastal Plain, comprising the peninsula region. **Location:** New England, bordering New Hampshire, Rhode Island, Connecticut, New York, and Vermont. **Climate:** temperate continental climate, with cold snowy winters and warm, humid summers; climate is colder but drier in western Massachusetts, although its winter snowfalls may be more severe. **Land use:** forest, 53.3%; agricultural, 4.2%; pasture, 0.7%; other, 41.8%.

People (2000 census)

Population: 6,349,097; 810.0 persons per sq mi (312.8 persons per sq km) (land area only). **Vital statistics** (1998; per 1,000 population): birth rate, 13.1 (1999); death rate, 9.0; marriage rate, 6.4; divorce rate, 2.7. **Major cities:** Boston, 589,141; Worcester, 172,648; Springfield, 152,082; Lowell, 105,167; Cambridge, 101,355.

Government

Statehood: entered the Union on 6 Feb 1788 as the 6th state. **State constitution:** adopted 1780. **Representation in US Congress:** 2 senators; 10 representatives. **Electoral college:** 12 votes. **Political divisions:** 14 counties.

Economy

Employment: services, 38.2%; trade, 20.6%; manufacturing, 11.9%; government, 11.2%; finance, insurance, real estate, 8.2%; construction, 4.6%; transportation, public utilities, 4.1%; agriculture, forestry, fishing, 1.3%; mining, 0.1%. **Production:** services, 26.8%; finance, insurance, real estate, 24.5%; trade, 15.3%; manufacturing, 13.9%; government, 9.1%; transportation, utilities, 5.6%; construction, 4.1%; agriculture, 0.5%. **Chief agricultural products:** *Crops:* tobacco, cranberries, hay, potatoes, sweet corn, dairy products, eggs. *Livestock:* cattle, poultry. *Fish catch:* marine fish, lobster, crab, mollusks. *Aquaculture:* oysters, quahogs, soft-shelled clams, scallops. **Chief manufactured products:** Food products, dairy products, soft drinks, textiles, paper products, printing, pharmaceuticals, plastic products, nonferrous metal products, fabricated metal products, machinery, communications equipment, semiconductors and electronics, electrical equipment, software, aerospace equipment, aircraft engines, surgical and medical equipment.

Internet resources: <www.mass-vacation.com>; <www.state.ma.us>.

Name: Michigan, derived from Native American word *Michigana* meaning "great, or, large lake." **Nicknames:** Wolverine State and Great Lake State. **Capital:** Lansing. **Rank:** population: 8th; area: 22nd. **Motto:** *Si Quaeris Peninsulam Amoenam, Circumspice* (If You Seek a Pleasant Peninsula, Look Around You). **Song:** "Michigan, My Michigan," words by Giles Kavanagh and music by H.J. O'Reilly Clint. **Bird:** robin. **Fish:** brook trout. **Flower:** apple blossom. **Gemstone:** chlorastrolite. **Mammal:** white-tailed deer (game mammal). **Reptile:** painted turtle. **Rock:** petoskey stone. **Tree:** white pine.

Natural features

Area: 96,705 sq mi, 250,465 sq km. **Highest point:** Mount Arvon, 1,980 ft (604 m). **Largest lake:** Houghton Lake. **Major rivers:** Montreal, Brule, Menominee, St. Clair. **Natural regions:** the Central Lowland, Eastern Lake Section, covers all of Lower Michigan and part of the Upper Peninsula region; the western half of the Upper Peninsula consists of Superior Upland, as do two small areas at the eastern end. **Location:** Midwest, bordering Ohio, Indiana, and Wisconsin; international border with Canada. **Climate:** continental; the Great Lakes cool the hot winds of summer and warm the cold winds of winter, giving Michigan a milder climate than some other north central states, although the Upper Peninsula is relatively cooler; very high snowfall along the coast of Lake Michigan. **Land use:** forest, 51.3%; agricultural, 22.8%; pasture, 4.4%; other, 21.4%.

People (2000 census)

Population: 9,938,444; 174.9 persons per sq mi (67.5 persons per sq km) (land area only). **Vital statistics** (1998; per 1,000 population): birth rate, 13.5 (1999); death rate, 8.7; marriage rate, 6.7; divorce rate, 4.0. **Major cities:** Detroit, 951,270; Grand Rapids, 197,800; Warren, 138,247; Flint, 124,943; Sterling Heights, 124,471; Lansing, 119,128; Ann Arbor, 114,024; Livonia, 100,545.

Government

Statehood: entered the Union on 26 Jan 1837 as the 26th state. **State constitution:** adopted 1963. **Representation in US Congress:** 2 senators; 16 representatives. **Electoral college:** 17 votes (in the 2004 general elections based on the 2000 census). **Political divisions:** 83 counties.

For details about state governments, see pages 854–859; for extraction and energy data, see pages 880–884.

Economy

Employment: services, 29.2%; trade, 22.2%; manufacturing, 18.4%; government, 12.1%; finance, insurance, real estate, 6.9%; construction, 4.9%; transportation, public utilities, 3.8%; agriculture, forestry, fishing, 2.3%; mining, 0.2%. **Production:** manufacturing, 26.2%; services, 19.6%; trade, 17.1%; finance, insurance, real estate, 14.1%; government, 10.3%; transportation, utilities, 6.6%; construction, 4.8%; agriculture, 0.9%; mining, 0.3%. **Chief agricultural products:** Crops: apples, asparagus, beans, blueberries, carrots, celery, cherries, corn, flowers, grapes and wine, honey, wool, maple syrup, mint, onions, peaches, plums, potatoes, dairy products, eggs, strawberries, sugar, soybeans. Livestock: beef and dairy cattle and calves, pigs, poultry, sheep and lambs. Aquaculture: Rainbow, brook and brown trout, yellow perch, catfish. Extractive industries: Christmas trees. **Chief manufactured products:** Motor vehicles, salt, plastics, pharmaceuticals, soaps and cleansers, milled grain, dry cereals, agricultural machinery, office furniture, dairy products, preserved fruits and vegetables, printed matter, electrical equipment, construction materials, measuring and control devices.

Internet resources: <www.michigan.org>; <www.state.mi.us>.

Minnesota

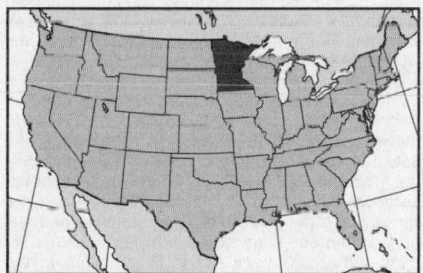

Name: Minnesota, derived from a Dakota word meaning "sky-tinted water." **Nickname:** North Star State. **Capital:** St. Paul. **Rank:** population: 21st; area: 14th. **Motto:** L'Etoile du Nord (The Star of the North). **Song:** "Hail! Minnesota," first verse and music by Truman F. Rickard, second verse by Arthur E. Upson. **Bird:** common loon. **Fish:** walleye pike. **Flower:** pink and white lady slipper. **Gemstone:** Lake Superior agate. **Insect:** monarch butterfly. **Tree:** Norway pine.

Natural features

Area: 86,943 sq mi, 225,182 sq km. **Mountain ranges:** Mesabi, Vermillion, Cuyuna. **Highest point:** Eagle Mountain, 2,301 ft (701 m). **Largest lake:** Red Lake. **Major rivers:** Minnesota, St. Croix, Mississippi. **Natural regions:** Superior Upland, northeast corner; Central Lowland, covering most of the state; Western Lake Section, center; Dissected Till Plains, extreme southwest corner and south-central edge; Wisconsin Driftless Section, extreme southeast. **Location:** Midwest, bordering Wisconsin, Iowa, South Dakota, and North Dakota; international border with Canada. **Climate:** continental, with very cold winters and warm

summers. **Land use:** agricultural, 44.8 (45)%; forest, 29.1 (29)%; pasture, 3.0%; other, 23.1 (23)%.

People (2000 census)

Population: 4,919,479; 61.8 persons per sq mi (23.9 persons per sq km) (land area only). **Vital statistics** (1998; per 1,000 population): birth rate, 13.8 (1999); death rate, 7.9; marriage rate, 6.8; divorce rate, 3.2. **Major cities:** Minneapolis, 382,618; St. Paul, 287,151; Duluth, 86,918; Rochester, 85,806; Bloomington, 85,172.

Government

Statehood: entered the Union on 11 May 1858 as the 32nd state. **State constitution:** adopted 1857. **Representation in US Congress:** 2 senators; 8 representatives. **Electoral college:** 10 votes. **Political divisions:** 87 counties.

Economy

Employment: services, 30.3%; trade, 22.0%; manufacturing, 14.3%; government, 12.0%; finance, insurance, real estate, 7.6%; transportation, public utilities, 4.7%; construction, 4.6%; agriculture, forestry, fishing, 4.2%; mining, 0.3%. **Production:** services, 20.8%; finance, insurance, real estate, 18.5%; manufacturing, 18.1%; trade, 17.6%; government, 10.2%; transportation, utilities, 7.6%; construction, 5.0%; agriculture, 1.7%; mining, 0.5%. **Chief agricultural products:** Crops: corn, green peas, dry beans, onions, carrots, apples, oats, hay, spring wheat, barley, soybeans, potatoes, sugar beets, flaxseed, dairy products, eggs. Livestock: pigs, cattle and calves, poultry, sheep and lambs. **Chief manufactured products:** food processing, beer and malt beverages, dairy products, meatpacking, industrial machinery, computers and office machines, electronics and electric equipment, precision instruments, printing and publishing, call centers and communications, information technology, forest products, medical manufacturing, plastics manufacturing.

Internet resources: <www.exploreminnesota.com>; <www.state.mn.us>.

Mississippi

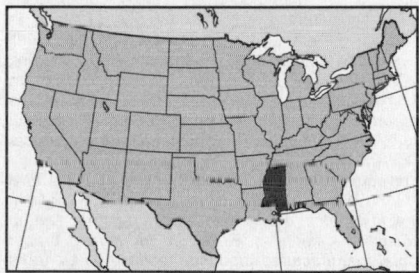

Name: Mississippi, derived from a Native American word meaning "great waters" or "father of waters." **Nickname:** Magnolia State. **Capital:** Jackson. **Rank:** population: 31st; area: 31st. **Motto:** Virtute et Armis (By Valor and Arms). **Song:** "Go, Mississippi," words and music by Houston Davis. **Bird:** mockingbird. **Fish:**

largemouth bass. **Flower:** magnolia. **Fossil:** prehistoric whale. **Insect:** honeybee. **Mammal:** white-tailed deer. **Marine mammal:** bottlenosed dolphin (porpoise). **Rock:** petrified wood. **Tree:** magnolia tree.

Natural features

Area: 48,286 sq mi, 125,060 sq km. **Highest point:** Woodall Mountain, 806 ft (246 m). **Major rivers:** Mississippi, Pearl, Big Black, Yazoo, Tombigbee, Pascagoula, Tennessee. **Natural regions:** the entire state consists of the Coastal Plain, subdivided into the Mississippi Alluvial Plain in the west, and the East Gulf Coastal Plain comprising the central and eastern regions. **Location:** South, bordering Tennessee, Alabama, Louisiana, and Arkansas. **Climate:** mild, with hot, humid summers and mild winters; coastal area is subject to hurricanes from June to October. **Land use:** forest, 61.9%; agricultural, 21.5%; pasture, 6.5%; other, 10.1%.

People (2000 census)

Population: 2,844,658; 60.6 persons per sq mi (23.4 persons per sq km) (land area only). **Vital statistics** (1998; per 1,000 population): birth rate, 15.4 (1999); death rate, 10.1; marriage rate, 7.5; divorce rate, 4.7. **Major cities:** Jackson, 184,256; Gulfport, 71,127; Biloxi, 50,644; Hattiesburg, 44,779; Greenville, 41,633.

Did you know? 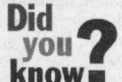 Mississippi ranks highest in the US for deaths by accident (Massachusetts ranks lowest).

Government

Statehood: entered the Union on 10 Dec 1817 as the 20th state. **State constitution:** adopted 1890. **Representation in US Congress:** 2 senators; 5 representatives. **Electoral college:** 6 votes (in the 2004 general elections based on the 2000 census). **Political divisions:** 82 counties.

Economy

Employment: services, 24.5%; trade, 19.7%; government, 17.8%; manufacturing, 17.5%; construction, 5.5%; agriculture, forestry, fishing, 5.2%; finance, insurance, real estate, 4.7%; transportation, public utilities, 4.5%; mining, 0.6%. **Production:** manufacturing, 20.6%; services, 17.4%; trade, 16.8%; government, 16.0%; finance, insurance, real estate, 11.4%; transportation, utilities, 9.5%; construction, 4.7%; agriculture, 2.6%; mining, 1.0%. **Chief agricultural products:** *Crops:* cotton, soybeans, rice, wheat, corn, greenhouse and nursery plants, sweet potatoes, pecans, eggs. *Livestock:* poultry, cattle. *Aquaculture:* catfish, pearl farming. *Fish catch:* marine fish, freshwater fish, shrimp, oysters, crustaceans. *Extractive industries:* timber. **Chief manufactured products:** food products, transportation equipment, apparel, textiles, paper, electrical equipment, rubber products, primary metal products.

Internet resources: <www.visitmississippi.org>; <www.state.ms.us>.

Missouri

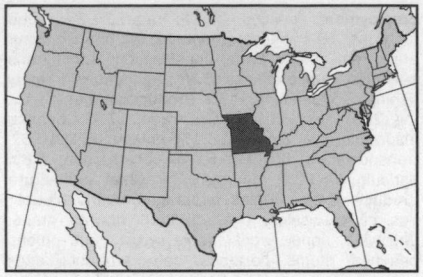

Name: Missouri, named for Native American tribe that lived in the region; the name means "town of the large canoes." **Nickname:** Show Me State. **Capital:** Jefferson City. **Rank:** population: 17th; area: 18th. **Motto:** *Salus Populi Suprema Lex Esto* (The Welfare of the People Shall Be the Supreme Law). **Song:** "Missouri Waltz," words by J.R. Shannon and music by John Valentine Eppel, arrangement by Frederick Knight Logan. **Aquatic animal:** paddlefish. **Bird:** bluebird. **Fish:** channel catfish. **Flower:** white hawthorn blossom. **Fossil:** crinoid. **Insect:** honeybee. **Mammal:** Missouri mule. **Mineral:** galena. **Rock:** mozarkite. **Tree:** flowering dogwood.

Natural features

Area: 69,709 sq mi, 180,546 sq km. **Mountain ranges:** Ozark Plateau, St. Francois Mountains. **Highest point:** Taum Sauk Mountain, 1,772 ft (540 m). **Largest lake:** Truman Lake. **Major rivers:** Missouri, Mississippi, Des Plaines. **Natural regions:** the Central Lowland, northwestern, subdivided into the Dissected Till Plains to the north and the Osage Plains to the west; Ozark Plateaus, including the Springfield-Salem Plateaus, southeast; Coastal Plain, including the Mississippi Alluvial Plain, extreme southeast tip. **Location:** Central, bordering Iowa, Illinois, Kentucky, Tennessee, Arkansas, Oklahoma, Kansas, and Nebraska. **Climate:** continental, with hot, humid summers and cold winters; lies in "Tornado Alley," the zone of maximum tornado occurrence, and has an average of 27 tornadoes annually. **Land use:** agricultural, 45.4%; forest, 30.4%; pasture, 13.6%; other, 10.6%.

People (2000 census)

Population: 5,595,211; 81.2 persons per sq mi (31.4 persons per sq km) (land area only). **Vital statistics** (1998; per 1,000 population): birth rate, 13.8 (1999); death rate, 10.1; marriage rate, 8.1; divorce rate, 4.7. **Major cities:** Kansas City, 441,545; St. Louis, 348,189; Springfield, 151,580; Independence, 113,288; Columbia, 84,531.

Government

Statehood: entered the Union on 10 Aug 1821 as the 24th state. **State constitution:** adopted 1945. **Representation in US Congress:** 2 senators; 9 representatives. **Electoral college:** 11 votes. **Political divisions:** 114 counties.

For details about state governments, see pages 854–859; for extraction and energy data, see pages 880–884.

Economy

Employment: services, 29.3%; trade, 21.8%; government, 13.3%; manufacturing, 12.9%; finance, insurance, real estate, 6.8%; transportation, public utilities, 5.8%; construction, 5.5%; agriculture, forestry, fishing, 4.5%; mining, 0.2%. **Production:** services, 20.5%; manufacturing, 19.3%; trade, 17.1%; finance, insurance, real estate, 15.3%; government, 11.4%; transportation, utilities, 10.1%; construction, 4.9%; agriculture, 1.1%; mining, 0.3%. **Chief agricultural products:** *Crops:* soybeans, corn (maize), cotton, rice, grain sorghum, hay, wheat, fruits and vegetables, dairy products. *Livestock:* cattle, pigs, sheep, poultry. *Extractive industries:* timber. **Chief manufactured products:** industrial machinery, transportation equipment, food processing, malt beverages, soft drinks, meat and poultry products, preserved fruits and vegetables, soaps and detergents, agricultural chemicals, pharmaceuticals, printing and publishing, primary metals, nonelectrical machinery, fabricated metals, petroleum and coal products, electrical equipment, stone, clay and glass products.

Internet resources: <www.missouritourism.org>; <www.state.mo.us>.

Montana

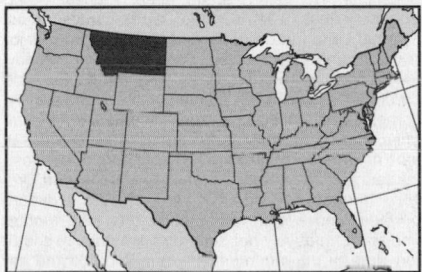

Name: Montana, derived from the Spanish word *montaña* ("mountain," or "mountainous region"). **Nickname:** Treasure State. **Capital:** Helena. **Rank:** population: 44th; area: 4th. **Motto:** *Oro y Plata* (Gold and Silver). **Song:** "Montana," words by Charles C. Cohan and music by Joseph E. Howard. **Bird:** western meadowlark. **Fish:** cutthroat trout. **Flower:** bitterroot. **Fossil:** *Maiasaura*. **Gemstones:** agate and sapphire. **Mammal:** grizzly bear. **Tree:** ponderosa pine.

Natural features

Area: 147,046 sq mi, 380,849 sq km. **Mountain ranges:** Rocky Mountains, Grand Tetons. **Highest point:** Granite Peak, 12,799 ft (3,901 m). **Largest lake:** Flathead Lake. **Major rivers:** Kootenai, Clark Fork, Flathead, Missouri, Yellowstone. **Natural regions:** Northern Rocky Mountains, western two-fifths of the state; Middle Rocky Mountains, small area along the south-central border; Missouri Plateau region of the Great Plains Province, eastern three-fifths of the state. **Location:** Northwest, bordering North Dakota, South Dakota, Wyoming, and Idaho; international border with Canada. **Climate:** continental; most of Great Plains region is semiarid, with warm summers and cold winters; west of the Rocky Mountains

the climate is milder. **Land use:** pasture, 49.4%; forest, 20.6%; agricultural, 19.9%; other, 10.1%.

People (2000 census)

Population: 902,195; 6.2 persons per sq mi (2.4 persons per sq km) (land area only). **Vital statistics** (1998; per 1,000 population): birth rate, 12.2 (1999); death rate, 9.1; marriage rate, 7.2; divorce rate, 3.8. **Major cities:** Billings, 89,847; Missoula, 57,053; Great Falls, 56,690; Butte-Silver Bow, 34,606; Bozeman, 27,509; Helena, 25,780.

Government

Statehood: entered the Union on 8 Nov 1889 as the 41st state. **State constitution:** adopted 1972. **Representation in US Congress:** 2 senators; 1 representative. **Electoral college:** 3 votes. **Political divisions:** 56 counties.

Economy

Employment: services, 30.4%; trade, 23.4%; government, 15.5%; agriculture, forestry, fishing, 6.7%; finance, insurance, real estate, 6.1%; construction, 6.1%; manufacturing, 5.6%; transportation, public utilities, 5.0%; mining, 1.3%. **Production:** services, 20.3%; trade, 16.9%; government, 16.4%; finance, insurance, real estate, 13.7%; transportation, utilities, 11.9%; manufacturing, 7.5%; construction, 5.6%; agriculture, 4.0%; mining, 3.7%. **Chief agricultural products:** *Crops:* wheat, barley, hay, oats, safflowers, sunflowers, mustard, sugar beets, dry beans, grapes, garlic, oil seeds, corn, potatoes, honey, cherries, dairy products. *Livestock:* beef and dairy cattle and calves, sheep and lambs, poultry, horses, llamas. *Extractive industries:* timber, Christmas trees. **Chief manufactured products:** food processing, lumber and wood products, metal processing, petroleum products, chemical manufacturing, cement and concrete products, fabricated metal products, machinery.

Internet resources: <www.visitmt.com>; <www.state.mt.us>.

Nebraska

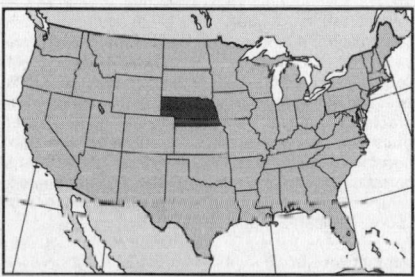

Name: Nebraska, derived from a Native American word meaning "flat water," a reference to the Platte River. **Nickname:** Cornhusker State. **Capital:** Lincoln. **Rank:** population: 38th; area: 15th. **Motto:** Equality Before the Law. **Song:** "Beautiful Nebraska," words and music by Jim Fras. **Bird:** western meadowlark. **Fish:** channel catfish. **Flower:** goldenrod. **Fossil:** mammoth. **Gemstone:** blue agate. **Insect:** honeybee.

Mammal: white-tailed deer. **Rock:** prairie agate. **Tree:** cottonwood.

Natural features

Area: 77,358 sq mi, 200,358 sq km. **Highest point:** 5,424 ft (1,653 m), in Johnson Township, southwestern part of Kimball County. **Largest lake:** Lake McConaughy. **Major rivers:** Missouri, Platte, Elkhorn, Loup, Republican, Big Blue, Niobrara. **Natural regions:** Great Plains Province, western three-quarters of the state; Missouri Plateau at the northern corners; High Plains, central and north-central; Plains Border, south border; Central Lowland, including the Dissected Till Plains, eastern quarter of the state. **Location:** Central, bordering South Dakota, Iowa, Missouri, Kansas, Colorado, and Wyoming. **Climate:** continental, with hot summers and very cold winters; blizzards are not uncommon in winter; western half of state is semiarid. **Land use:** agricultural, 47.9%; pasture, 44.4%; forest, 1.6%; other, 6.1%.

People (2000 census)

Population: 1,711,263; 22.5 persons per sq mi (8.7 persons per sq km) (land area only). **Vital statistics** (1998; per 1,000 population): birth rate, 14.3 (1999); death rate, 9.1; marriage rate, 7.4; divorce rate, 3.8. **Major cities:** Omaha, 390,007; Lincoln, 225,581; Bellevue, 44,382; Grand Island, 42,940; Kearney, 27,431.

Government

Statehood: entered the Union on 1 Mar 1867 as the 37th state. **State constitution:** adopted 1875. **Representation in US Congress:** 2 senators; 3 representatives. **Electoral college:** 5 votes. **Political divisions:** 93 counties.

Economy

Employment: services, 28.1%; trade, 22.2%; government, 14.1%; manufacturing, 10.4%; agriculture, forestry, fishing, 7.3%; finance, insurance, real estate, 7.2%; transportation, public utilities, 5.5%; construction, 5.0%; mining, 0.2%. **Production:** services, 19.1%; trade, 16.7%; finance, insurance, real estate, 15.5%; government, 14.1%; manufacturing, 14.0%; transportation, utilities, 10.8%; agriculture, 4.8%; construction, 4.8%; mining, 0.1%. **Chief agricultural products:** *Crops:* corn, soybeans, hay, wheat, sorghum, dry edible beans, sugar beets. *Livestock:* beef and dairy cattle, pigs, sheep, poultry. **Chief manufactured products:** meatpacking, canned and frozen fruits and vegetables, flour, cereal, grain products, beverages, dairy products, livestock feeds, transportation equipment, motorcycles, small commercial vehicles, printing and publishing, rubber and plastic goods, fabricated metals, primary metals.

Internet resources: <www.visitnebraska.org>; <www.state.ne.us>.

Nevada

Name: Nevada, from the Spanish *nevada* ("snow clad"), a reference to the high mountain scenery of the

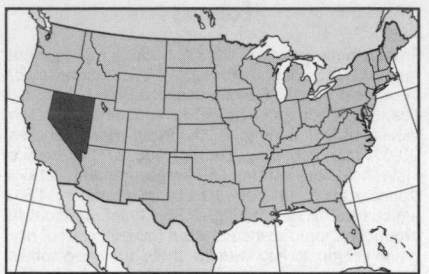

Sierra Nevada on the southwestern border with California. **Nicknames:** Sagebrush State and Silver State. **Capital:** Carson City. **Rank:** population: 35th; area: 7th. **Motto:** All for Our Country. **Song:** "Home Means Nevada," words and music by Bertha Raffeto. **Bird:** mountain bluebird. **Fish:** Lahontan cutthroat trout. **Flower:** sagebrush. **Fossil:** ichthyosaur. **Gemstones:** fire opal, turquoise. **Mammal:** desert bighorn sheep. **Metal:** silver. **Reptile:** desert tortoise. **Rock:** sandstone. **Trees:** single-leaf piñon and bristlecone pine.

Natural features

Area: 110,567 sq mi, 286,367 sq km. **Mountain ranges:** Snake, Schell Creek, Monitor, Toiyabe, Shoshone, Humboldt, Santa Rosa. **Highest point:** Boundary Peak, 13,140 ft (4,005 m). **Largest lakes:** Pyramid Lake (natural), Lake Mead (artificial). **Major rivers:** Humboldt, Truckee, Carson, Walker, Muddy, Virgin. **Natural regions:** Basin and Range Province covers all of the state, except for the southwestern corner, which consists of the Cascade-Sierra Mountains, and the northeastern corner, which comprises part of the Columbia Plateau. **Location:** Southwest, bordering Idaho, Utah, Arizona, California, and Oregon. **Climate:** semiarid but with regional variation: northern and eastern areas have long, cold winters and short, relatively hot summers, whereas in southern Nevada the summers are long and hot and the winters brief and mild. **Land use:** pasture, 65.9%; forest, 11.7%; agricultural, 1.2%; other, 21.2%.

People (2000 census)

Population: 1,998;257; 18.2 persons per sq mi (7.0 persons per sq km) (land area only). **Vital statistics** (1998; per 1,000 population): birth rate, 16.2 (1999); death rate, 8.3; marriage rate, 82.5; divorce rate, 8.5. **Major cities:** Las Vegas, 478,434; Reno, 180,480; Henderson, 175,381; North Las Vegas, 115,488; Sparks, 66,346.

Government

Statehood: entered the Union on 31 Oct 1864 as the 36th state. **State constitution:** adopted 1864. **Representation in US Congress:** 2 senators; 2 representatives. **Electoral college:** 5 votes (in the 2004 general elections based on the 2000 census). **Political divisions:** 16 counties; 1 independent city.

Economy

Employment: services, 42.2%; trade, 19.5%; government, 10.7%; construction, 8.9%; finance, insurance,

For details about state governments, see pages 854–859; for extraction and energy data, see pages 880–884.

real estate, 7.0%; transportation, public utilities, 4.7%; manufacturing, 4.1%; agriculture, forestry, fishing, 1.5%; mining, 1.5%. **Production:** services, 32.5%; finance, insurance, real estate, 16.9%; trade, 15.0%; government, 10.3%; construction, 10.2%; transportation, utilities, 8.0%; manufacturing, 4.1%; mining, 2.2%; agriculture, 0.7%. **Chief agricultural products:** *Crops:* hay, wheat, corn (maize), potatoes, rye, oats, alfalfa, barley, vegetables, dairy products, some fruits. *Livestock:* cattle, horses, sheep, hogs, poultry. **Chief manufactured products:** food processing, candy, frozen desserts, dairy products, soft drinks, paper products, chemical products, plastics, construction materials, industrial machinery, printing and publishing.

Internet resources: <www.travelnevada.com>; <www.state.nv.us>.

New Hampshire

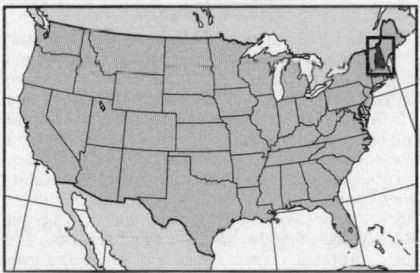

Name: New Hampshire, named for Hampshire, England by Captain John Mason. **Nickname:** Granite State. **Capital:** Concord. **Rank:** population: 41st; area: 44th. **Motto:** Live Free or Die. **Songs:** "Old New Hampshire," words by John F. Holmes and music by Maurice Hoffmann; "New Hampshire, My New Hampshire," words by Julius Richelson and music by Walter P. Smith. **Amphibian:** red-spotted newt. **Bird:** purple finch. **Fish:** brook trout (freshwater); striped bass (saltwater). **Flower:** purple lilac. **Gemstone:** smokey quartz. **Insect:** ladybug. **Mammal:** white-tailed deer. **Mineral:** beryl. **Rock:** granite. **Tree:** white birch.

Natural features

Area: 9,283 sq mi, 24,044 sq km. **Mountain ranges:** White Mountains, Ossipee, Sandwich Range, Presidential Range. **Highest point:** Mount Washington, 6,288 ft (1,917 m). **Largest lake:** Lake Winnipesaukee. **Major rivers:** Merrimack, Salmon Falls, Connecticut, Saco, Piscataqua, Androscoggin. **Natural regions:** the New England Province covers the entire state, and is subdivided into the White Mountain Section occupying the northern third, the New England Upland Section in the south central region, and the Seaboard Lowland Section in the southeast corner. **Location:** New England, bordering Maine, Massachusetts, and Vermont; international border with Canada. **Climate:** temperate, but highly varied: winter temperatures may drop below 0° F (-18° C) for days at a time; summers are relatively cool, and precipitation is rather evenly distributed over the four seasons. **Land use:** forest, 79.3%; agricultural, 2.0%; pasture, 0.7%; other, 18.1%.

People (2000 census)

Population: 1,235,786; 137.8 persons per sq mi (53.2 persons per sq km) (land area only). **Vital statistics** (1998; per 1,000 population): birth rate, 11.7 (1999); death rate, 8.0; marriage rate, 6.2; divorce rate, 5.9. **Major cities:** Manchester, 107,006; Nashua, 86,605; Concord, 40,687; Derry, 34,021; Rochester, 28,461.

Government

Statehood: entered the Union on 21 Jun 1788 as the 9th state. **Representation in US Congress:** 2 senators; 2 representatives. **Electoral college:** 4 votes. **Political divisions:** 10 counties.

Economy

Employment: services, 31.5%; trade, 24.0%; manufacturing, 15.5%; government, 10.9%; finance, insurance, real estate, 0.9%; construction, 6.0%; transportation, public utilities, 3.5%; agriculture, forestry, fishing, 1.6%; mining, 0.1%. **Production:** finance, insurance, real estate, 23.2%; manufacturing, 22.1%; services, 19.6%; trade, 16.5%; government, 7.8%; transportation, utilities, 5.8%; construction, 4.1%; agriculture, 0.7%; mining, 0.1%. **Chief agricultural products:** *Crops:* apples, honey, fruits and vegetables, ornamental horticulture, Christmas trees, dairy products, eggs, herbs, maple syrup, wool. *Livestock:* horses, dairy cattle, sheep. *Fish catch:* marine fish, seafood. *Extractive products:* timber. **Chief manufactured products:** industrial machinery, computers and software, electrical equipment, semiconductors, processed foods, precision instruments, medical and surgical instruments, fabricated metal products, rubber and plastic products, printing and publishing, paper products.

Internet resources: <www.visitnh.gov>; <www.state.nh.us>.

New Jersey

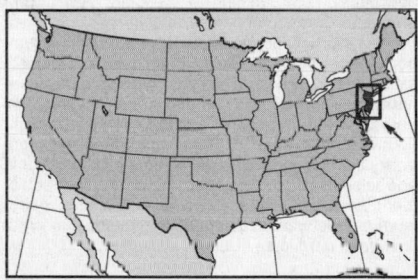

Name: New Jersey, named for the island of Jersey in the English Channel. **Nickname:** Garden State. **Capital:** Trenton. **Rank:** population: 9th; area: 46th. **Motto:** Liberty and Prosperity. **Bird:** eastern goldfinch. **Fish:** brook trout. **Flower:** violet. **Fossil:** *Hadrosaurus foulkii.* **Insect:** honeybee. **Mammal:** horse. **Tree:** red oak.

Natural features

Area: 8,215 sq mi, 21,277 sq km. **Mountain range:** Appalachians. **Highest point:** Kittatinny Mountain,

1,803 ft (550 m). **Largest lake:** Lake Hopatcong. **Major rivers:** Delaware, Hudson, Passaic, Hackensack, Raritan. **Natural regions:** the Valley and Ridge Province, Middle Section, northwest corner; the New England Province, consisting of the New England Upland Section, located east of the Valley and Ridge area; Piedmont Province, including the Piedmont Lowlands, extending from the northeast corner to part of the border with Pennsylvania; the southern half of the state consists of the Coastal Plain, Embayed Section. **Location:** New England, bordering New York, Delaware, and Pennsylvania. **Climate:** continental; relatively colder winters in northwest, milder conditions in the south, and hot summers throughout the state. **Land use:** forest, 31.7%; agricultural, 13.4%; pasture, 0.6%; other, 54.3%.

People (2000 census)

Population: 8,414,350; 1,134.3 persons per sq mi (438.0 persons per sq km) (land area only). **Vital statistics** (1998; per 1,000 population): birth rate, 14.0 (1999); death rate, 8.8; marriage rate, 6.0; divorce rate, 3.1. **Major cities:** Newark, 273,546; Jersey City, 240,055; Paterson, 149,222; Elizabeth, 120,568; Trenton, 85,403.

Government

Statehood: entered the Union on 18 Dec 1787 as the 3rd state. **State constitution:** adopted 1947. **Representation in US Congress:** 2 senators; 13 representatives. **Electoral college:** 15 votes. **Political divisions:** 21 counties.

Economy

Employment: services, 32.8%; trade, 21.6%; government, 13.0%; manufacturing, 11.0%; finance, insurance, real estate, 9.7%; transportation, public utilities, 6.3%; construction, 4.3%; agriculture, forestry, fishing, 1.2%; mining, 0.1%. **Production:** finance, insurance, real estate, 23.7%; services, 23.5%; trade, 17.0%; manufacturing, 11.9%; government, 10.1%; transportation, utilities, 9.5%; construction, 3.8%; agriculture, 0.5%; mining, 0.1%. **Chief agricultural products:** *Crops:* cranberries, blueberries, peaches, asparagus, bell peppers, spinach, lettuce, cucumbers, sweet corn, tomatoes, snap beans, cabbage, escarole and endive, eggplants, nursery and greenhouse products, dairy products, eggs. *Livestock:* horses, cattle, poultry. *Fish catch:* bluefish, tilefish, flounder, hake, shellfish. **Chief manufactured products:** chemical products, pharmaceuticals, electronic and electrical equipment, communications equipment, semiconductors, industrial equipment, petroleum products, fabricated metal products, clay products, food products.

Internet resources: <www.visitnj.org>; <www.state.nj.us>.

New Mexico

Name: New Mexico, named for the country of Mexico. **Nickname:** Land of Enchantment. **Capital:** Santa Fe. **Rank:** population: 36th; area: 5th. **Motto:** *Crescit Eundo* (It Grows as It Goes). **Songs:** "O, Fair New Mex-

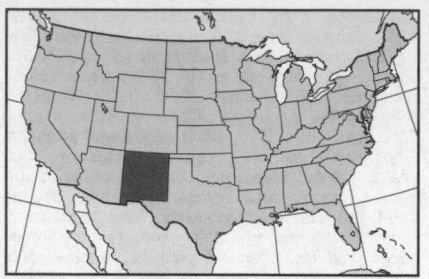

ico," words and music by Elizabeth Garrett; *"Así es Nuevo Mexico,"* words and music by Amadeo Lucero. **Bird:** roadrunner. **Fish:** New Mexico cutthroat trout. **Flower:** yucca. **Fossil:** coelophysis. **Gemstone:** turquoise. **Insect:** tarantula hawk wasp. **Tree:** piñon pine.

Natural features

Area: 121,598 sq mi, 314,939 sq km. **Mountain ranges:** Rocky Mountains, Sangre de Cristo Range. **Highest point:** Wheeler Peak, 13,160 ft (4,011 m). **Largest lake:** Elephant Butte Reservoir. **Major rivers:** Rio Grande, Pecos, Canadian, San Juan, Gila. **Natural regions:** eastern third of the state consists of the Great Plains Province, subdivided into the Raton Section to the north, the High Plains along the eastern edge, and the Pecos Valley to the west; Southern Rocky Mountains, north-central region; Colorado Plateau, including the Navajo Section and Datil Section, northwest corner; Basin and Range Province, central region and southwest corner, with the Sacramento Section to the east and the Mexican Highland to the south. **Location:** Southwest, bordering Colorado, Oklahoma, Texas, and Arizona; international border with Mexico. **Climate:** arid; moderate temperatures but great variation by altitude; temperatures drop dramatically after dark. **Land use:** Pasture, 67.2%; forest, 18.1%; agricultural, 3.1%; other, 11.6%.

People (2000 census)

Population: 1,819,046; 15.0 persons per sq mi (5.8 persons per sq km). **Vital statistics** (1998; per 1,000 population). Birth rate, 15.6 (1999); death rate, 7.4; marriage rate, 7.7; divorce rate, 4.6. **Major cities:** Albuquerque, 448,607; Las Cruces, 74,267; Santa Fe, 62,203; Rio Rancho, 51,765; Roswell, 45,293.

Government

Statehood: entered the Union on 6 Jan 1912 as the 47th state. **State constitution:** adopted 1911. **Representation in US Congress:** 2 senators; 3 representatives. **Electoral college:** 5 votes. **Political divisions:** 33 counties.

Economy

Employment: services, 29.7%; trade, 21.9%; government, 20.4%; construction, 6.4%; finance, insurance, real estate, 6.0%; manufacturing, 5.7%; transportation, public utilities, 4.2%; agriculture, forestry, fishing, 3.6%; mining, 2.1%. **Production:** services, 18.0%;

government, 16.8%; manufacturing, 16.7%; trade, 13.6%; finance, insurance, real estate, 13.1%; mining, 8.4%; transportation, utilities, 7.4%; construction, 4.0%; agriculture, 2.1%. **Chief agricultural products:** *Crops:* pecans, apples, potatoes, onions, dry beans, chile, peanuts (groundnuts), hay, sorghum, corn, wheat, eggs, dairy products, wool. *Livestock:* dairy and beef cattle, poultry, sheep and lambs. *Extractive industries:* timber. **Chief manufactured products:** electronic equipment, semiconductors, printing and publishing, processed foods.

Internet resources: <www.newmexico.org>; <www.state.nm.us>.

New York

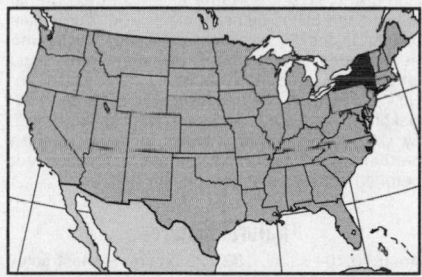

Name: New York, named in honor of the English Duke of York. **Nickname:** Empire State. **Capital:** Albany. **Rank:** population: 3rd; area: 30th. **Motto:** *Excelsior* (Ever Upward). **Song:** "I Love New York," words and music by Steve Karmen. **Bird:** bluebird. **Fish:** brook trout. **Flower:** rose. **Fossil:** *Eurypterus remipes.* **Gemstone:** garnet. **Mammal:** beaver. **Tree:** sugar maple.

Natural features

Area: 53,989 sq mi, 139,833 sq km. **Mountain ranges:** Adirondack, Catskill, Shawangunk, Taconic. **Highest point:** Mount Marcy, 5,344 ft (1,629 m). **Largest lake:** Oneida Lake. **Major rivers:** Hudson, Mohawk, Genesee, Oswego, Delaware, Susquehanna, Allegheny. **Natural regions:** the Central Lowland, Eastern Lake Section, extends along the northern coast of Lake Ontario; St. Lawrence Valley, Northern Section, extends along the northern border with Canada; Adirondack Province, northeast; Appalachian Plateaus, including the Mohawks, Southern New York, and Catskill Sections, extend along southern border with Pennsylvania and up halfway through the state; Valley and Ridge Province, southeastern edge bordering Connecticut and Massachusetts; Coastal Plain, Embayed Section, covering the islands of Manhattan and Long Island. **Location:** northeast, bordering Vermont, Massachusetts, Connecticut, New Jersey, and Pennsylvania, international border with Canada. **Climate:** temperate continental, with hot, humid summers and cold, dry, snowy winters. **Land use:** forest, 56.4%; agricultural, 17.4%; pasture, 8.7%; other, 17.5%.

People (2000 census)

Population: 18,976,457; 401.8 persons per sq mi (155.2 persons per sq km) (land area only). **Vital statistics** (1999; per 1,000 population): birth rate, 14.0 (1999); death rate, 8.5; marriage rate, 7.0; divorce

rate, 3.2. **Major cities:** New York, 8,008,278; Buffalo, 292,648; Rochester, 219,773; Yonkers, 196,086; Syracuse, 147,306, Albany, 95,658.

Government

Statehood: entered the Union on 26 Jul 1788 as the 11th state. **State constitution:** adopted 1894. **Representation in US Congress:** 2 senators; 31 representatives. **Electoral college:** 31 votes (in the 2004 general elections based on the 2000 census). **Political divisions:** 62 counties.

Economy

Employment: services, 35.9%; trade, 19.0%; government, 14.1%; finance, insurance, real estate, 11.1%; manufacturing, 9.7%; transportation, public utilities, 4.9%; construction, 3.9%; agriculture, forestry, fishing, 1.3%; mining, 0.1%. **Production:** finance, insurance, real estate, 32.8%; services, 23.0%; trade, 12.9%; manufacturing, 10.3%; government, 10.2%; transportation, utilities, 7.3%; construction, 3.0%; agriculture, 0.4%; mining, 0.1%. **Chief agricultural products:** *Crops:* apples, cabbage, corn, potatoes, onions, grapes, snap beans, dry beans, grain, hay, cherries, strawberries, maple syrup, horticulture products, milk, eggs, dairy products. *Livestock:* cattle and calves, chickens. **Chief manufactured products:** food processing, chemical products, apparel, primary metals, industrial machinery, computers and software, scientific and measuring instruments, transportation equipment, electric and electronic equipment, industrial machinery, printing and publishing, biotechnology.

Internet resources: <www.iloveny.com>; <www.state.us.ny>.

North Carolina

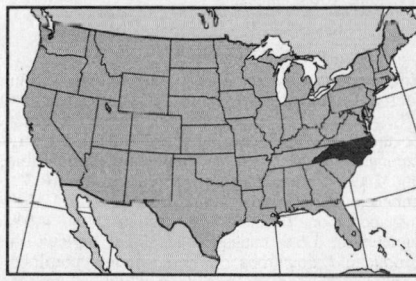

Name: North Carolina, named in honor of Charles I of England. **Nickname:** The Old North State. **Capital:** Raleigh. **Rank:** population: 11th; area: 29th. **Motto:** *Esse Quam Videri* (To Be Rather Than to Seem). **Song:** "The Old North State," words by William Gaston to a German tune. **Bird:** cardinal. **Fish:** channel bass. **Flower:** dogwood. **Gemstone:** emerald. **Insect:** honeybee. **Mammal:** gray squirrel. **Reptile:** eastern box turtle. **Rock:** granite. **Tree:** pine.

Natural features

Area: 52,672 sq mi, 136,421 sq km. **Mountain ranges:** Appalachian, Great Smoky, Blue Ridge. **Highest point:** Mount Mitchell, 6,684 ft (2,037 m).

Largest lake: Lake Mattamuskeet. Major rivers: Roanoke, Yadkin, Pee Dee. Natural regions: Valley and Ridge Province, far western edge; Piedmont Province, consisting of the Piedmont Upland, extends in a southwest to northeast direction through the center of the state; Coastal Plain comprises the eastern third, divided into the Sea Island Section to the south and the Embayed Section to the north. Location: East coast, bordering Virginia, South Carolina, Georgia, and Tennessee. Climate: ranges from medium continental conditions in the mountain region (though summers are cooler and rainfall heavier) to the subtropical conditions of the state's southeastern corner; hurricanes occasionally occur along the coast, and there have been tornadoes inland. Land use: forest, 60%; agricultural, 19%; pasture, 3%; other, 19%.

People (2000 census)

Population: 8,049,313; 165.2 persons per sq mi (63.8 persons per sq km) (land area only). Vital statistics (1998; per 1,000 population): birth rate (1999), 14.9; death rate, 9.0; marriage rate, 8.5; divorce rate, 4.9. Major cities: Charlotte, 540,828; Raleigh, 276,093; Greensboro, 223,891; Durham, 187,035; Winston-Salem, 185,776; Fayetteville, 121,015.

Did you know? The first English child born in the American Colonies was Virginia Dare, born on 18 Aug 1587 in what is now Roanoke Island.

Government

Statehood: entered the Union on 21 Nov 1789 as the 12th state. State constitution: adopted 1970. Representation in US Congress: 2 senators, 12 representatives. Electoral college: 15 votes (in the 2004 general elections based on the 2000 census). Political divisions: 100 counties.

Economy

Employment: services, 25.1%; trade, 21.2%; manufacturing, 18.5%; government, 15.2%; construction, 6.6%; finance, insurance, real estate, 5.9%; transportation, public utilities, 4.3%; agriculture, forestry, fishing, 3.1%; mining, 0.1%. Production: manufacturing, 24.1%; finance, insurance, real estate, 18.3%; services, 16.4%; trade, 15.0%; government, 12.5%; transportation, utilities, 7.1%; construction, 4.9%; agriculture, 1.5%; mining, 0.2%. Chief agricultural products: Crops: tobacco, corn, barley, potatoes, peanuts (groundnuts), apples, blueberries, grapes, peaches, pecans, strawberries, tomatoes, cabbages, watermelons, cucumbers, sweet potatoes, horticultural products, Christmas trees, dairy products, eggs. Livestock: cattle, chickens, pigs, horses. Aquaculture: catfish, trout. Extractive industries: timber. Chief manufactured products: textiles, cotton and synthetic fibers, yarns, threads, knitted goods, cigarettes and tobacco products, chemical products, pharmaceuticals, electronic and electrical equipment, furniture, lumber, paper products, processed foods.

Internet resources: <www.visitnc.com>; <www.state.nc.us>.

North Dakota

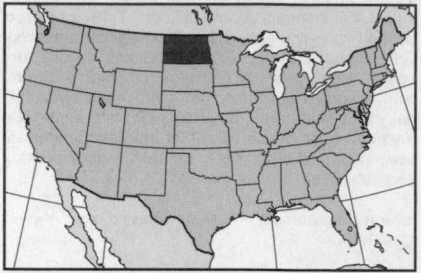

Name: North Dakota, derived from the Dakota division of the Sioux, the Native American tribe who inhabited the plains before the arrival of Europeans; dakota is the Sioux word for "friend." Nickname: Peace Garden State. Capital: Bismarck. Rank: population: 47th; area: 17th. Motto: Liberty and Union Now and Forever, One and Inseparable. Song: "North Dakota Hymn," words by James W. Foley and music by C.S. Putnam. Bird: western meadowlark. Fish: northern pike. Flower: wild prairie rose. Fossil: teredo petrified wood. Tree: American elm.

Natural features

Area: 70,704 sq mi, 183,123 sq km. Highest point: White Butte, 3,506 ft (1,069 m). Largest lake: Devils Lake. Major rivers: Red, Souris, Missouri, Little Missouri, James. Natural regions: central Lowland covers eastern half of the state, with the Western Lake Section lying in the east-central region; Great Plains Province, western half of the state, includes sections of the Missouri Plateau to the north and south. Location: Northwest, bordering Minnesota, South Dakota, and Montana; international border with Canada. Climate: continental climate: hot summers and cold winters, warm days and cool nights in summer, low humidity and low precipitation, and much wind and sunshine. Land use: agricultural, 65.3%; pasture, 25.7%; forest, 1.0%; other, 8.1%.

People (2000 census)

Population: 642,200; 9.3 persons per sq mi (3.6 persons per sq km) (land area only). Vital statistics (1998; per 1,000 population): birth rate (1999), 12.1; death rate, 9.3; marriage rate, 6.6; divorce rate, 3.3. Major cities: Fargo, 90,599; Bismarck, 55,532; Grand Forks, 49,321; Minot, 36,567.

Government

Statehood: entered the Union on 2 Nov 1889 as the 39th state. State constitution: adopted 1889. Representation in US Congress: 2 senators; 1 representative. Electoral college: 3 votes. Political divisions: 53 counties.

Economy

Employment: services, 28.5%; trade, 22.5%; government, 16.4%; agriculture, forestry, fishing, 9.7%; manufacturing, 5.7%; finance, insurance, real estate, 5.6%; transportation, public utilities, 5.3%; construction, 5.2%; mining, 1.1%; **Production:** trade, 19.5%; services, 19.4%; government, 14.4%; finance, insurance, real estate, 14.1%; transportation, utilities, 10.3%; manufacturing, 9.0%; construction, 5.5%; agriculture, 4.1%; mining, 3.6%. **Chief agricultural products:** *Crops:* hard red spring wheat, durum wheat, flaxseed, canola, dry beans, sunflowers, barley, honey, potatoes, dairy products, wool. *Livestock:* cattle, sheep, pigs. *Extractive industries:* timber. **Chief manufactured products:** food processing, wood products, petroleum products, transportation equipment, machinery.

Internet resources: <www.ndtourism.com>; <www.state.nd.us>.

Ohio

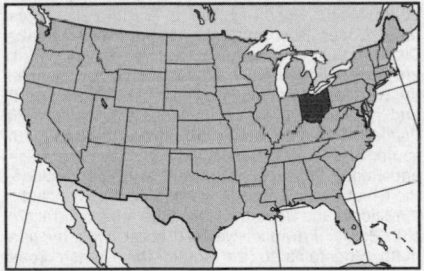

Name: Ohio, derived from an Iroquois word meaning "great river." **Nickname:** Buckeye State. **Capital:** Columbus. **Rank:** population: 7th; area: 35th. **Motto:** With God, All Things Are Possible. **Song:** "Beautiful Ohio," words by Ballad MacDonald and music by Mary Earl. **Bird:** cardinal. **Flower:** red carnation. **Fossil:** *Trilobite isotelus.* **Gemstone:** flint. **Insect:** ladybug. **Mammal:** white-tailed deer. **Reptile:** black racer snake. **Tree:** Ohio buckeye.

Natural features

Area: 44,828 sq mi, 116,103 sq km. **Highest point:** Campbell Hill, 1,550 ft (472 m). **Largest lake:** Grand Lake St. Marys. **Major rivers:** Ohio, Maumee, Cuyahoga, Miami, Scioto, Muskingum. **Natural regions:** the Appalachian Plateau, eastern half of the state, includes the Southern New York Section to the north, and the Kanawha Section to the east; the Central Lowlands, western half of the state, includes the Eastern Lake Section in the northwest corner, the Till Plains in the central region, and the Lexington Plain in the southwest. **Location:** Midwest, bordering Michigan, Pennsylvania, West Virginia, Kentucky, and Indiana. **Climate:** continental, with hot, humid summers and cold, dry winters. **Land use:** agricultural, 45.9%; forest, 28.9%; pasture, 5.3%; other, 20.0%.

People (2000 census)

Population: 11,353,140; 277.2 persons per sq mi (107.0 persons per sq km) (land area only). **Vital statistics** (1998; per 1,000 population): birth rate, 13.6 (1999); death rate, 9.4; marriage rate, 7.6; divorce rate, 4.1. **Major cities:** Columbus, 711,470; Cleveland, 478,403; Cincinnati, 331,285; Toledo, 313,619; Akron, 217,074; Dayton, 166,179.

Government

Statehood: entered the Union on 1 Mar 1803 as the 17th state. **State constitution:** adopted 1851. **Representation in US Congress:** 2 senators; 19 representatives. **Electoral college:** 20 votes (in the 2004 general elections based on the 2000 census). **Political divisions:** 88 counties.

Economy

Employment: services, 29.0%; trade, 22.8%; manufacturing, 17.0%; government, 12.1%; finance, insurance, real estate, 7.2%; construction, 5.1%; transportation, public utilities, 4.3%; agriculture, forestry, fishing, 2.3%; mining, 0.3%. **Production:** manufacturing, 25.8%; services, 18.2%; trade, 16.8%; finance, insurance, real estate, 15.5%; government, 10.7%; transportation, utilities, 7.4%; construction, 4.3%; agriculture, 0.8%; mining, 0.4%. **Chief agricultural products:** *Crops:* corn (maize), soybeans, grapes, apples, vegetables, tobacco, winter wheat, dairy products, eggs, greenhouse and nursery products. *Livestock:* cattle, hogs, poultry, goats. *Extractive industries:* timber. **Chief manufactured products:** Industrial machinery, non-electrical machinery, food processing, transportation equipment, fabricated metals, iron and steel, chemical products and pharmaceuticals, rubber products.

Internet resources: <www.ohiotourism.com>; <www.state.oh.us>.

Oklahoma

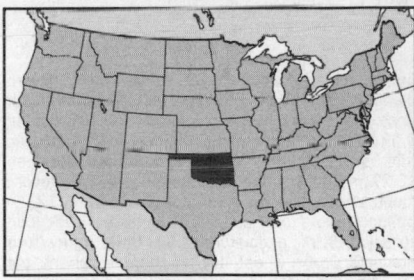

Name: Oklahoma, derived from two Choctaw words: *okla* meaning "people" and *humma* meaning "red." **Nickname:** Sooner State. **Capital:** Oklahoma City. **Rank:** population: 27th; area: 19th. **Motto:** *Labor Omnia Vincit* (Labor Conquers All Things). **Song:** "Oklahoma," words by Richard Rodgers and music by Oscar Hammerstein. **Bird:** scissor-tailed flycatcher. **Fish:** white, or sand, bass. **Flower:** mistletoe. **Insect:** honeybee. **Mammal:** bison. **Reptile:** collared lizard (also know as the mountain boomer). **Rock:** rose rock. **Tree:** redbud.

Natural features

Area: 69,903 sq mi, 181,048 sq km. **Mountain ranges:** Ouachita, Arbuckle, Wichita, Sandstone Hills. **Highest point:** Black Mesa, 4,978 ft (1,517 m). **Largest lake:** Lake Eufaula. **Major rivers:** Arkansas, Red, Canadian. **Natural regions:** Great Plains Province, panhandle region, includes the High Plains to the west and the Plains Border to the east; Central

Lowland, covers most of the state, includes the Osage Plains in the central region; West Gulf Coastal Plain, southeastern corner; Ouachita Province, east-central region, includes the Arkansas Valley in the center and the Ouachita Mountains to the south; Ozark Plateaus, northeast corner, includes the Boston Mountains and Springfield-Salem Plateaus. **Location:** South central, bordering Kansas, Missouri, Arkansas, Texas, New Mexico, and Colorado. **Climate:** variable range: the southern humid belt merges with a colder northern continental one and humid eastern and dry western zones that cut through the state; no region is free from heavy wind; typical sudden rises and falls in temperature cause many heavy thunderstorms, blizzards, and tornadoes. **Land use:** pasture, 39.4%; agricultural, 37.2%; forest, 14.2%; other, 9.3%.

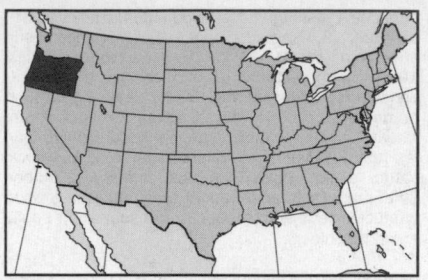

People (2000 census)

Population: 3,450,654; 50.2 persons per sq mi (19.4 persons per sq km) (land area only). **Vital statistics** (1998; per 1,000 population): birth rate, 14.6 (1999); death rate, 10.1; marriage rate, 7.7; divorce rate, 6.0. **Major cities:** Oklahoma City, 506,132; Tulsa, 393,049; Norman, 95,694; Lawton, 92,757; Broken Arrow, 74,859.

Government

Statehood: entered the Union on 16 Nov 1907 as the 46th state. **State constitution:** adopted 1907. **Representation in US Congress:** 2 senators; 6 representatives. **Electoral college:** 7 votes (in the 2004 general elections based on the 2000 census). **Political divisions:** 77 counties.

Economy

Employment: services, 28.3%; trade, 20.9%; government, 16.6%; manufacturing, 10.0%; finance, insurance, real estate, 5.8%; agriculture, forestry, fishing, 5.6%; transportation, public utilities, 5.1%; construction, 4.8%; mining, 3.0%. **Production:** services, 18.2%; manufacturing, 16.9%; trade, 16.5%; government, 15.9%; finance, insurance, real estate, 12.2%; transportation, utilities, 9.2%; mining, 4.9%; construction, 3.8%; agriculture, 2.3%. **Chief agricultural products:** *Crops:* wheat, hay, sorghum, soybeans, cotton, dairy products. *Livestock:* cattle and calves, poultry, hogs and pigs. **Chief manufactured products:** electronics and electrical equipment, communications equipment, transportation equipment, food processing, petroleum products.

Internet resources: <www.travelok.com>; <www.state.ok.us>.

Oregon

Nickname: Beaver State. **Capital:** Salem. **Rank:** population: 28th; area: 10th. **Motto:** *Alis Volat Propiis* (She Flies with Her Own Wings). **Song:** "Oregon, My Oregon," words by J.A. Buchanan and music by Henry B. Murtagh. **Bird:** western meadowlark. **Fish:** Chinook salmon. **Flower:** Oregon grape. **Gemstone:** Oregon sunstone. **Insect:** Oregon swallowtail. **Mammal:** beaver. **Rock:** thunderegg. **Tree:** Douglas fir.

Natural features

Area: 97,132 sq mi, 251,517 sq km. **Mountain ranges:** Coast Range, Klamath Mountains, Cascade Range, Blue Mountains, Wallowa Mountains. **Highest point:** Mount Hood, 11,235 ft (3,424 m). **Largest lake:** Upper Klamath Lake. **Major rivers:** Snake, Owyhee, Columbia, Coquille. **Natural regions:** northern Rocky Mountains, northeastern corner, includes the Blue Mountain Section; Columbia Plateaus, north and north-central region, includes the Walla Walla Plateau in the central section, Harney Section to the south, and Payette Section to the southeast; Basin and Range Province, south-central border, includes the Great Basin; Cascade Sierra Mountains, includes the Middle and Southern Cascades, west-central; Pacific Border Province, western coast, with the Klamath Mountains to the south, the Oregon Coast Range in the center and north, and the Puget Trough to the east. **Location:** Northwest, bordering Washington, Idaho, Nevada, and California. **Climate:** ranges from equable, mild, marine conditions on the coast to continental conditions of dryness and extreme temperature in the interior. **Land use:** forest, 43.4%; pasture, 36.4%; agricultural, 8.7%; other, 11.5%.

People (2000 census)

Population: 3,421,399; 35.6 persons per sq mi (13.8 persons per sq km) (land area only). **Vital statistics** (1998; per 1,000 population): birth rate, 13.6 (1999); death rate, 9.0; marriage rate, 7.9; divorce rate, 4.6. **Major cities:** Portland, 529,121; Eugene, 137,893; Salem, 136,924; Gresham, 90,205; Beaverton, 76,129.

Government

Statehood: entered the Union on 14 Feb 1859 as the 33rd state. **State constitution:** adopted 1857. **Representation in US Congress:** 2 senators; 5 representatives. **Electoral college:** 7 votes. **Political divisions:** 36 counties.

Economy

Employment: services, 29.4%; trade, 22.8%; manufacturing, 13.1%; government, 12.6%; finance, insurance, real estate, 6.6%; construction, 5.7%; agriculture, forestry, fishing, 5.1%; transportation, public utilities, 4.5%; mining, 0.2%. **Production:** manufacturing, 24.8%; services, 17.6%; trade, 16.1%; finance, insurance, real estate, 14.4%; government, 11.8%; transportation, utilities, 7.1%; construction, 5.3%; agriculture, 2.8%; mining, 0.1%. **Chief agricul-**

For details about state governments, see pages 854–859; for extraction and energy data, see pages 880–884.

tural products: *Crops*: horticulture and nursery products, Christmas trees, berries, pears, cherries, apples, hazelnuts, snap beans, peas, onions, carrots, wheat, hay, potatoes, barley, dry beans, mint, hops, corn (maize), sugar beets, dairy products. *Livestock*: cattle and calves, horses, mink, poultry, sheep and lambs. *Fish catch*: marine fish, tuna, salmon, shellfish, crab, shrimp. *Extractive industries*: timber. **Chief manufactured products**: lumber and wood products, food processing, aircraft and spacecraft, electronics, semiconductors, computers.

Internet resources: <www.traveloregon.com>; <www.state.or.us>.

Pennsylvania

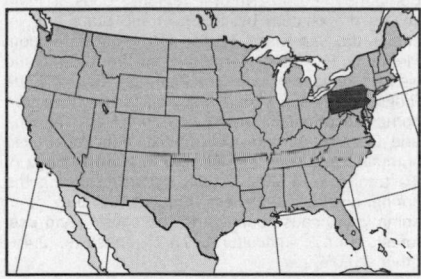

Name: Pennsylvania, named for Admiral Sir William Penn, father of the territory's founder, William Penn, and including also the term *sylvania* ("woodlands"). **Nickname**: Keystone State. **Capital**: Harrisburg. **Rank**: population: 6th; area: 32nd. **Motto**: Virtue, Liberty, and Independence. **Song**: "Pennsylvania," written and composed by Eddie Khoury and Ronnie Bonner. **Bird**: ruffled grouse. **Fish**: brook trout. **Flower**: mountain laurel. **Fossil**: *Phacops rana*. **Insect**: firefly. **Mammal**: white-tailed deer. **Tree**: hemlock.

Natural features

Area: 46,058 sq mi, 119,291 sq km. **Mountain ranges**: Appalachian, Allegheny. **Highest point**: Mount Davis, 3,213 ft (979 m). **Largest lake**: Raystown Lake. **Major rivers**: Delaware, Lehigh, Schuylkill, Susquehanna, Ohio. **Natural regions**: central Lowland, Eastern Lake Section, extreme northwestern edge; Appalachian Plateaus, including the Southern New York, Allegheny Mountain, and Kanawha Sections, western half of state; Valley and Ridge Province, central region, includes portions of the Appalachian Mountains; Piedmont Province, comprising the Piedmont Lowlands and Upland, southeast corner; Coastal Plain, extreme southeast edge; New England Province, with the New England Upland Section, east-central border. **Location**: Northeast, bordering New York, New Jersey, Delaware, Maryland, West Virginia, Ohio. **Climate**: continental, with warm humid summers and cold snowy winters in general, but with wide fluctuations in seasonal temperatures. **Land use**: forest, 55.3%; agricultural, 18.1%; pasture, 3.2%; other, 23.5%.

People (2000 census)

Population: 12,281,054; 274.0 persons per sq mi (105.8 persons per sq km) (land area only). **Vital sta-

tistics (1998; per 1,000 population): birth rate, 12.1 (1999); death rate, 10.6; marriage rate, 6.2; divorce rate, 3.2. **Major cities**: Philadelphia, 1,517,550; Pittsburgh, 334,563; Allentown, 106,632; Erie, 103,717; Reading, 81,207.

Government

Statehood: entered the Union on 12 Dec 1787 as the 2nd state. **State constitution**: adopted 1968. **Representation in US Congress**: 2 senators, 21 representatives. **Electoral college**: 21 votes (in the 2004 general elections based on the 2000 census). **Political divisions**: 67 counties.

Economy

Employment: services, 32.7%; trade, 21.5%; manufacturing, 14.5%; government, 11.4%; finance, insurance, real estate, 7.7%; construction, 5.0%; transportation, public utilities, 4.9%; agriculture, forestry, fishing, 2.0%; mining, 0.4%. **Production**: services, 22.4%; manufacturing, 19.4%; finance, insurance, real estate, 18.4%; trade, 15.2%; government, 10.2%; transportation, utilities, 8.6%; construction, 4.2%; agriculture, 0.9%; mining, 0.7%. **Chief agricultural products**: *Crops*: mushrooms, apples, tobacco, grapes, peaches, cut flowers, dairy products. *Livestock*: cattle, poultry, pigs, horses. **Chief manufactured products**: electronic equipment, communications systems, semiconductors, chemical and pharmaceutical products, food processing, iron and steel, industrial machinery, transportation equipment, paper products, printing and publishing.

Internet resources: <www.experiencepa.com>; <www.state.pa.us>.

Rhode Island

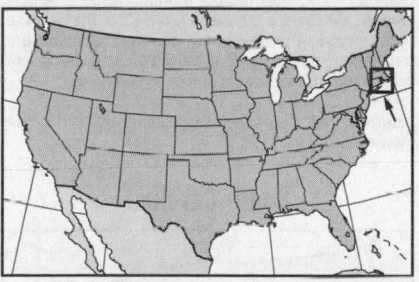

Name: Rhode Island, from the Greek island of Rhodes. **Nicknames**: Little Rhody and Ocean State. **Capital**: Providence. **Rank**: population: 43rd; area: 50th. **Motto**: Hope. **Song**: "Rhode Island," words and music by T. Clarke Brown. **Bird**: Rhode Island red. **Flower**: violet. **Mineral**: bowenite. **Rock**: cumberlandite.

Natural features

Area: 1,231 sq mi, 3,189 sq km, including 168 sq mi, 435 sq km of water surface. **Highest point**: Jerimoth Hill, 812 ft (247 m). **Largest lake**: Scituate Reservoir. **Major rivers**: Blackstone, Pawtuxet, Pawcatuck. **Natural regions**: the entire state is part of the New England Province, subdivided into the New England Upland (western two thirds) and the Seaboard Lowland (eastern third). **Location:** New England, bordering Connecticut and Massachusetts. **Climate:** humid continental climate; marine influences are discernible in differences between coastal and inland location; extreme weather conditions including tropical storms, ice storms, and heavy snow. **Land use:** forest, 53.2%; agricultural, 4.5%; pasture, 0.4%; other, 41.9%.

People (2000 census)

Population: 1,048,319; 864.9 persons per sq mi (334.0 persons per sq km) (land area only). **Vital statistics** (1998; per 1,000 population): birth rate, 12.5 (1999); death rate, 9.7; marriage rate, 7.6; divorce rate, 3.2. **Major cities:** Providence, 173,618; Warwick, 85,808; Cranston, 79,269; Pawtucket, 72,958; East Providence, 48,688.

Government

Statehood: entered the Union on 29 May 1790 as the 13th state. **State constitution:** adopted 1986. **Representation in US Congress:** 2 senators; 2 representatives. **Electoral college:** 4 votes. **Political divisions:** 5 counties.

Economy

Employment: services, 34.7%; trade, 20.3%; manufacturing, 14.8%; government, 13.4%; finance, insurance, real estate, 7.6%; construction, 4.4%; transportation, public utilities, 3.4%; agriculture, forestry, fishing, 1.3%; mining, 0.1%. **Production:** finance, insurance, real estate, 26.7%; services, 21.7%; trade, 14.3%; manufacturing, 12.6%; government, 12.0%; transportation, utilities, 6.7%; construction, 5.3%; agriculture, 0.7%. **Chief agricultural products:** *Crops:* hay, corn, apples, peaches, dairy products, eggs, potatoes. *Livestock:* poultry, cattle, sheep. *Fish catch:* marine fish, shellfish. **Chief manufactured products:** jewelry, silverware, textiles, fabricated metal products, electrical equipment, machinery, surgical and navigation instruments, plastic goods, printing and publishing, primary metals, food processing.

Internet resources: <www.visitrhodeisland.com>; <www.state.ri.us>.

South Carolina

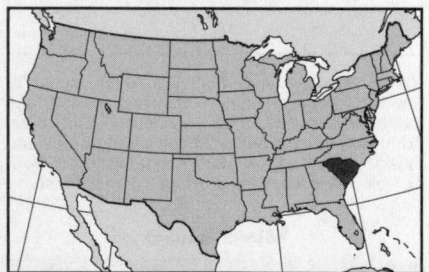

Name: South Carolina, named in honor of Charles I of England. **Nickname:** Palmetto State. **Capital:** Columbia. **Rank:** population: 26th; area: 40th. **Mottoes:** An-

imis Opibusque Parati (Prepared in Mind and Resources); *Dum Spiro Spero* (While I Breathe, I Hope). **Songs:** "Carolina," words by Henry Timrod and music by Anne Custis Burgess; "South Carolina on My Mind," words and music by Hank Martin and Buzz Arledge. **Amphibian:** spotted salamander. **Bird:** Carolina wren. **Fish:** striped bass. **Flower:** Carolina jessamine. **Gemstone:** amethyst. **Insect:** Carolina mantid. **Mammal:** white-tailed deer. **Reptile:** loggerhead turtle. **Rock:** blue granite. **Tree:** palmetto.

Natural features

Area: 31,189 sq mi, 80,779 sq km. **Mountain range:** Blue Ridge Mountains. **Highest point:** Sassafras Mountain, 3,560 ft (1,085 m). **Largest lake:** Lake Marion. **Major rivers:** Pee Dee, Savannah, Ashley, Combahee, Edisto. **Natural regions:** Coastal Plain covers the eastern two-thirds of the state and includes the Sea Island Section in the central region; Piedmont Province extends across the central and western region, includes the Piedmont Upland; Blue Ridge Province, Southern Section, far northwestern corner. **Location:** Southeast, bordering North Carolina and Georgia. **Climate:** subtropical, with hot, humid summers and generally mild winters; an average of 10 tornadoes a year, usually occurring during the spring; hurricanes are less frequent, but they do in some years cause damage to the coast. **Land use:** forest, 64.4%; agricultural, 13.1%; pasture, 2.4%; other, 20.0%.

People (2000 census)

Population: 4,012,012; 133.2 persons per sq mi (51.4 persons per sq km) (land area only). **Vital statistics** (1998; per 1,000 population): birth rate, 14.1 (1999); death rate, 9.1; marriage rate, 10.8; divorce rate, 4.9. **Major cities:** Columbia, 116,278; Charleston, 96,650; North Charleston, 79,641; Greenville, 56,002; Rock Hill, 49,765.

Government

Statehood: entered the Union on 23 May 1788 as the 8th state. **State constitution:** adopted 1895. **Representation in US Congress:** 2 senators; 6 representatives. **Electoral college:** 8 votes. **Political divisions:** 46 counties.

Economy

Employment: services, 24.7%; trade, 22.4%; manufacturing, 17.3%; government, 16.7%; construction, 6.4%; finance, insurance, real estate, 5.9%; transportation, public utilities, 4.1%; agriculture, forestry, fishing, 2.4%; mining, 0.1%. **Production:** manufacturing, 21.4%; trade, 17.4%; services, 16.4%; government, 15.1%; finance, insurance, real estate, 13.7%; transportation, utilities, 8.9%; construction, 5.9%; agriculture, 1.1%; mining, 0.2%. **Chief agricultural products:** *Crops:* tobacco, cotton, barley, corn, peanuts, oats, grains, peaches, apples, pecans, watermelons, sweet potatoes, tomatoes, snap beans, cucumbers, dairy products, eggs. *Livestock:* cattle and calves, chickens, pigs. **Chief extractive products:** timber, marine fish, oysters, clams, shrimp. **Chief manufactured products:** Chemical products, industrial chemicals, pharmaceuticals, and agricultural fer-

For details about state governments, see pages 854–859; for extraction and energy data, see pages 880–884.

tilizers, textiles, apparel, industrial machinery, plastic and rubber products, paper and paperboard, electronics and electrical equipment, motor vehicle parts and accessories, lumber.

Internet resources: <www.travelsc.com>; <www.state.sc.us>.

South Dakota

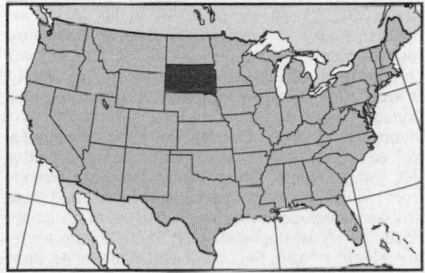

Name: South Dakota, derived from the Dakota division of the Sioux, the Native American tribe who inhabited the plains before the arrival of Europeans; *dakota* is the Sioux word for "friend." Nickname: Mount Rushmore State. Capital: Pierre. Rank: population: 46th; area: 16th. Motto: Under God the People Rule. Song: "Hail! South Dakota," words and music by Deecort Hammitt. Bird: Chinese ring-necked pheasant. Fish: walleye. Flower: pasque. Fossil: triceratops. Gemstone: Fairburn agate. Insect: honeybee. Mammal: coyote. Mineral: rose quartz. Tree: Black Hills spruce.

Natural features

Area: 77,121 sq mi, 199,744 sq km. Mountain range: Black Hills. Highest point: Harney Peak, 7,242 ft (2,207 m). Largest lake: Lake Thompson. Major rivers: Big Sioux, Vermillion, James, Grand, Moreau, Cheyenne, Bad, White. Natural regions: the Central Lowland, eastern third of the state, includes the Dissected Till Plains along the eastern edge and the Western Lake Section at the center; the Great Plains Province, western two thirds of the state; Black Hills, far west; High Plains, southern border; Missouri Plateau, west. Location: Northwest, bordering North Dakota, Minnesota, Iowa, Nebraska, Wyoming, and Montana. Climate: characterized by extremes in temperature, low precipitation, and relatively low humidity; cyclonic storms occur frequently in the east-river section during the spring and summer. Land use: pasture, 46.5%; agricultural, 44.8%; forest, 3.3%; other, 5.4%.

People (2000 census)

Population: 754,844; 9.8 persons per sq mi (3.8 persons per sq km) (land area only). Vital statistics (1998; per 1,000 population): birth rate, 14.4 (1999); death rate, 9.3; marriage rate, 9.2; divorce rate, 3.5. Major cities: Sioux Falls, 123,975; Rapid City, 59,607; Aberdeen, 24,658.

Government

Statehood: entered the Union on 2 Nov 1889 as the 40th state. State constitution: adopted 1889. Repre-

sentation in US Congress: 2 senators; 1 representative. Electoral college: 3 votes. Political divisions: 66 counties.

Economy

Employment: services, 27.5%; trade, 22.3%; government, 13.7%; manufacturing, 10.3%; agriculture, forestry, fishing, 9.1%; finance, insurance, real estate, 7.2%; construction, 5.0%; transportation, public utilities, 4.5%; mining, 0.5%. Production: finance, insurance, real estate, 18.1%; trade, 17.7%; services, 17.6%; manufacturing, 14.0%; government, 12.6%; transportation, utilities, 8.2%; agriculture, 6.9%; construction, 4.1%; mining, 0.6%. Chief agricultural products: Crops: corn, hay, wheat, sunflowers, dairy products, eggs, flaxseed, barley, wool, rye, sorghum, soybeans. Livestock: cattle and calves, pigs, sheep. Chief manufactured products: industrial machinery, office machines, computers, food products, electronics, printing and publishing, lumber mills, fabricated metal products, medical instruments, truck-trailer manufactures, jewelry.

Internet resources: <www.travelsd.com>; <www.state.sd.us>.

Tennessee

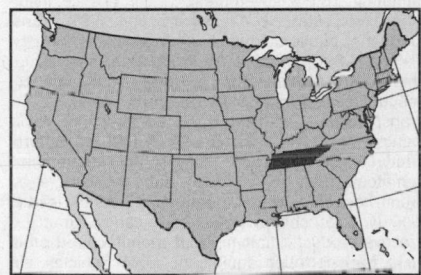

Nickname: Volunteer State. Capital: Nashville. Rank: population: 16th; area: 34th. Motto: Agriculture and Commerce. Songs: "My Homeland, Tennessee," by Nell Grayson Taylor and Roy Lamont Smith; "When It's Iris Time in Tennessee," by Willa Mae Waid; "My Tennessee," by Francis Hannah Tranum; "The Tennessee Waltz," by Redd Stewart and Pee Wee King; "Rocky Top," by Boudleaux and Felice Bryant. Amphibian: cave salamander. Bird: mockingbird. Fish: largemouth bass, channel catfish. Flower: iris. Gemstone: river pearl. Insects: firefly, ladybug. Mammal: raccoon. Reptile: box turtle. Rocks: limestone, agate. Tree: tulip poplar.

Natural features

Area: 42,146 sq mi, 109,168 sq km. Mountain ranges: Unaka Mountains, Great Smoky Mountains. Highest point: Clingmans Dome, 6,642 ft (2,024 m). Largest lake: Reelfoot. Major rivers: Tennessee, Cumberland, Mississippi. Natural regions: Blue Ridge Province, eastern border; Valley and Ridge Province, extends from southwest to northeast; Appalachian Plateau, central, running from south to north, includes the Cumberland Plateau Section in the center and the Cumberland Mountain Section at the northern end; Interior Low Plateau, west-central, includes the Nashville Basin and Highland Rim Section. **Location:** South, bordering Kentucky, Virginia, North Carolina, Georgia, Alabama, Mississippi, Arkansas, and Missouri. **Climate:** moderate continental climate, with cool, but not cold, winters and warm summers. **Land use:** forest, 50.3%; agricultural, 28.4%; pasture, 4.3%; other, 17.1%.

People (2000 census)

Population: 5,689,283; 138.0 persons per sq mi (53.3 persons per sq km) (land area only). **Vital statistics** (1998; per 1,000 population): birth rate, 14.2 (1999); death rate, 9.8; marriage rate, 14.9; divorce rate, 6.4. **Major cities:** Memphis, 650,100; Nashville-Davidson, 569,891; Knoxville, 173,890; Chattanooga, 155,554; Clarksville, 103,455.

Government

Statehood: entered the Union on 1 Jun 1796 as the 16th state. **State constitution:** adopted 1870. **Representation in US Congress:** 2 senators; 9 representatives. **Electoral college:** 11 votes. **Political divisions:** 95 counties.

Economy

Employment: services, 27.8%; trade, 21.8%; manufacturing, 16.2%; government, 12.1%; finance, insurance, real estate, 6.7%; construction, 5.9%; transportation, public utilities, 5.4%; agriculture, forestry, fishing, 3.8%; mining, 0.2%. **Production:** manufacturing, 20.8%; services, 20.6%; trade, 19.1%; finance, insurance, real estate, 14.1%; government, 11.5%; transportation, utilities, 8.3%; construction, 4.4%; agriculture, 0.9%; mining, 0.3%. **Chief agricultural products:** *Crops:* cotton, tobacco, peaches, apples, tomatoes, snap beans, honey, dairy products, eggs, wool, hay, corn, wheat, sorghum. *Livestock:* cattle, poultry, hogs, sheep. *Aquaculture:* catfish, trout. *Extractive products:* timber. **Chief manufactured products:** transportation equipment, motor vehicles, aircraft parts, boats, chemical and pharmaceutical products, printing and publishing, electronics, lumber, paper, apparel, surgical appliances and supplies.

Internet resources: <www.state.tn.us>.

Texas

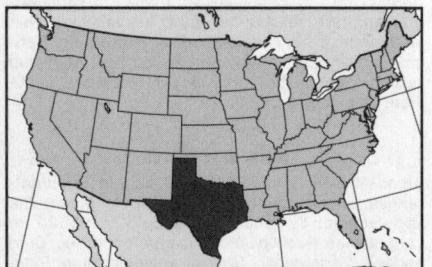

Name: Texas, derived from the Caddo Indian word *teysha,* or *tejas,* which means "hello friend." **Nickname:** Lone Star State. **Capital:** Austin. **Rank:** population: 2nd; area: 2nd. **Motto:** Friendship. **Song:** "Texas, Our Texas," by William J. Marsh and Gladys Yoakum Wright. **Bird:** mockingbird. **Fish:** Guadelupe bass. **Flower:** bluebonnet. **Fossil:** pleurocoelus. **Gemstone:** Texas blue topaz. **Insect:** monarch butterfly. **Mammal:** Mexican free-tailed bat (flying); longhorn (large); armadillo (small). **Reptile:** horned lizard. **Rock:** petrified palmwood. **Tree:** pecan.

Natural features

Area: 267,277 sq mi, 692,248 sq km. **Mountain ranges:** Rocky Mountains, Guadalupe Mountains. **Highest point:** Guadalupe Peak, 8,751 ft (2,667 m). **Largest lake:** Caddo Lake. **Major rivers:** Red, Trinity, Brazos, Colorado, Rio Grande. **Natural regions:** Coastal Plain, southern and eastern regions, includes the West Gulf Coastal Plain near the east-central coast; Central Lowland, north-central, includes the Osage Plains; Great Plains Province, extends from the panhandle across most of central and western Texas, includes the Edwards Plateau to the south, Pecos Valley to the west, High Plains to the north, and Central Texas Section; Basin and Range Province, extreme western region, comprising the Mexican Highland to the south and the Sacramento Section to the north. **Location:** Southwest, bordering Oklahoma, Arkansas, Louisiana, and New Mexico; international border with Mexico. **Climate:** varies by region, though summers are generally very hot and winters are somewhat mild; East Texas is considerably wetter than the very dry West Texas region; tornadoes are a frequent threat between April and November. **Land use:** pasture, 58.5%; agricultural, 23.9%; forest, 7.0%; other, 10.6%.

 **Did you know?** Although the boundary of Texas had been the Nueces River, following the annexation of Texas the US claimed the Rio Grande as the boundary.

People (2000 census)

Population: 20,851,820; 79.6 persons per sq mi (30.7 persons per sq km) (land area only). **Vital statistics** (1998; per 1,000 population): birth rate, 17.4 (1999); death rate, 7.2; marriage rate, 9.6; divorce rate, NA. **Major cities:** Houston, 1,953,631; Dallas, 1,188,580; San Antonio, 1,144,646; Austin, 656,562; El Paso, 563,662; Fort Worth, 534,694; Arlington, 332,969; Corpus Christi, 277,454; Plano, 222,030; Garland, 215,768.

Government

Statehood: entered the Union on 29 Dec 1845 as the 28th state. **State constitution:** adopted 1876. **Representation in US Congress:** 2 senators; 30 representatives. **Electoral college:** 34 votes (in the 2004 general elections based on the 2000 census). **Political divisions:** 254 counties.

Economy

Employment: services, 29.1%; trade, 21.6%; government, 14.5%; manufacturing, 10.1%; finance, insurance, real estate, 7.5%; construction, 6.1%; transportation, public utilities, 5.4%; agriculture, forestry, fishing, 3.5%; mining, 2.2%. **Production:** services, 19.9%; trade, 17.6%; finance, insurance, real estate, 14.7%; manufacturing, 14.0%; government, 11.2%; transportation, utilities, 10.9%; mining, 5.7%; construction, 4.7%; agriculture, 1.3%. **Chief agricultural products:** *Crops:* cotton, apples, greenhouse and nursery products, corn, sorghum, wheat, dairy products, eggs, rice. *Livestock:* cattle, pigs, chickens. *Extractive products:* timber, shrimp. **Chief manufactured products:** Refined petroleum, petroleum products, food products, computers and electronics, chemicals and plastics, apparel, wood and paper products, nonelectrical machinery, fabricated metal products, aerospace products and parts, aircraft parts, motor vehicle parts.

Internet resources: <www.traveltex.com>; <www.state.tx.us>.

Utah

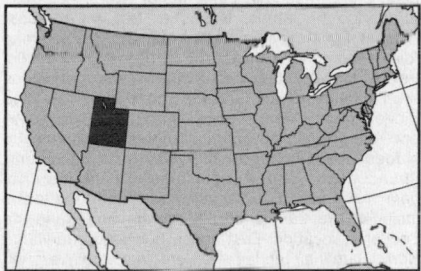

Name: Utah, named for the Ute tribe; the word *ute* means "people of the mountains." **Nickname:** Beehive State. **Capital:** Salt Lake City. **Rank:** population: 34th; area: 12th. **Motto:** Industry. **Song:** "Utah, We Love Thee," by Evan Stephens. **Bird:** California seagull. **Fish:** Bonneville cutthroat trout. **Flower:** sego lily. **Fossil:** allosaurus. **Gemstone:** topaz. **Insect:** honeybee. **Mammal:** Rocky Mountain elk. **Mineral:** copper. **Rock:** coal. **Tree:** blue spruce.

Natural features

Area: 84,904 sq mi, 219,902 sq km. **Mountain ranges:** Uinta Mountains, Wasatch Range, Rocky Mountains. **Highest point:** Kings Peak, 13,528 ft (4,123 m). **Largest lake:** Great Salt Lake. **Major rivers:** Colorado, Green, Sevier. **Natural regions:** Basin and Range Province, western half of the state, includes the Great Salt Lake Desert and Bonneville Salt Flats to the north and the Great Basin to the south; Middle Rocky Mountains, northeast; Colorado Plateaus, east-central and southeast regions, includes the Grand Canyon Section to the south, the High Plateaus of Utah and Canyon Lands in the center, the Navajo Section in the extreme southeast corner, and the Uinta Basin to the north. **Location:** West, bordering Idaho, Wyoming, Colorado, Arizona, and Nevada. **Climate:** primarily arid; southwest has a warm, almost dry, subtropical climate, while the southern part of the Colorado Plateau has cool, dry winters and wet summers. **Land use:** pasture, 45.1%; forest, 26.3%; agricultural, 3.9%; other, 24.7%.

People (2000 census)

Population: 2,233,169; 27.2 persons per sq mi (10.5 persons per sq km) (land area only). **Vital statistics** (1998; per 1,000 population): birth rate, 21.7 (1999); death rate, 5.6; marriage rate, 10.3; divorce rate, 4.2. **Major cities:** Salt Lake City, 181,743; West Valley City, 108,896; Provo, 105,166; Sandy, 88,418; Orem, 84,324.

Government

Statehood: entered the Union on 4 Jan 1896 as the 45th state. **State constitution:** adopted 1895. **Representation in US Congress:** 2 senators; 3 representatives. **Electoral college:** 5 votes. **Political divisions:** 29 counties.

Economy

Employment: services, 29.7%; trade, 22.0%; government, 14.6%; manufacturing, 10.9%; finance, insurance, real estate, 7.8%; construction, 7.0%; transportation, public utilities, 4.9%; agriculture, forestry, fishing, 2.4%; mining, 0.7%. **Production:** services, 20.6%; trade, 18.9%; finance, insurance, real estate, 16.4%; government, 14.4%; manufacturing, 13.3%; transportation, utilities, 8.8%; construction, 6.5%; mining, 1.8%; agriculture, 1.1%. **Chief agricultural products:** *Crops:* hay, grains, peaches, cherries, onions, dairy products. *Livestock:* cattle, sheep, poultry. *Aquaculture:* trout. *Other:* mink. **Chief manufactured products:** industrial machinery, computers, office equipment, transportation equipment, aerospace products, missile parts, motor vehicle parts, surgical tools, electromedical equipment, food processing.

Internet resources: <www.utah.com>; <www.state.ut.us>.

Vermont

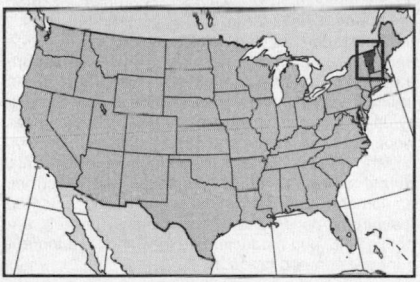

Name: Vermont, derived from the French *vert mont,* meaning "green mountain." **Nickname:** Green Mountain State. **Capital:** Montpelier. **Rank:** population: 49th; area: 43rd. **Motto:** Freedom and Unity. **Song:** "These Green Mountains," by Diane Martin and Rita Burgess Gluck. **Bird:** hermit thrush. **Flower:** red clover. **Insect:** honeybee. **Mammal:** Morgan horse. **Tree:** sugar maple.

Natural features

Area: 9,615 sq mi, 24,903 sq km. **Mountain ranges:** Green Mountains, Appalachian Mountains, Hoosac Range, Taconic Range. **Highest point:** Mount Mansfield, 4,393 ft (1,339 m). **Largest lake:** Lake Champlain. **Major rivers:** Lamoille, Winooski, Otter Creek, Poultney, White, Missisquoi. **Natural regions:** the New England Province, eastern two thirds of the state, includes the Taconic Section to the south, the Green Mountain Section in the center, New England Upland Section along the east-central edge, and the White Mountain Section in the far northeast corner; the St. Lawrence Valley, western edge of the state, with the Champlain Section in the central portion; the Valley and Ridge Province, with the Hudson Valley, small section along the west-central edge. **Location:** Northeast, bordering New Hampshire, Massachusetts, and New York; international border with Canada. **Climate:** cool continental, with very cold, snowy winters and warm, mild summers. **Land use:** forest, 75.4%; agricultural, 8.2%; pasture, 3.6%; other, 12.9%.

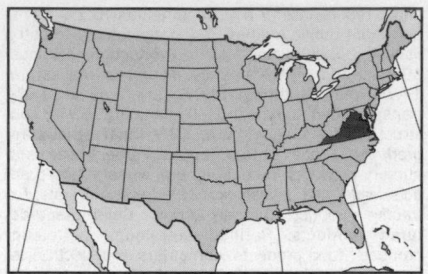

People (2000 census)

Population: 608,827; 65.8 persons per sq mi (25.4 persons per sq km) (land area only). **Vital statistics** (1998; per 1,000 population): birth rate, 11.1 (1999); death rate, 8.4; marriage rate, 9.9; divorce rate, 4.3. **Major city:** Burlington, 38,889.

Government

Statehood: entered the Union on 4 Mar 1791 as the 14th state. **State constitution:** adopted 1793. **Representation in US Congress:** 2 senators; 1 representative. **Electoral college:** 3 votes. **Political divisions:** 14 counties.

Economy

Employment: services, 32.4%; trade, 21.0%; manufacturing, 13.7%; government, 12.8%; construction, 6.5%; finance, insurance, real estate, 5.7%; transportation, public utilities, 4.0%; agriculture, forestry, fishing, 3.7%; mining, 0.2%. **Production:** services, 22.3%; finance, insurance, real estate, 17.7%; manufacturing, 17.5%; trade, 15.7%; government, 12.4%; transportation, utilities, 7.6%; construction, 4.4%; agriculture, 2.2%; mining, 0.3%. **Chief agricultural products:** *Crops:* apples, honey, corn, hay, greenhouse and nursery products, Christmas trees, maple syrup, fruits and vegetables, dairy products, eggs, wool. *Livestock:* cattle and calves, chickens, turkeys, sheep, horses. *Extractive products:* timber. **Chief manufactured products:** electrical and electronic equipment, fabricated metal products, nonelectrical machinery, paper and allied products, printing and publishing, food products, transportation equipment, lumber and wood products.

Internet resources: <www.travel-vermont.com>; <www.state.vt.us>.

Virginia

Name: Virginia, named in honor of Elizabeth I of England, known as the "Virgin Queen." **Nickname:** Old Dominion. **Capital:** Richmond. **Rank:** population: 12th; area: 37th. **Motto:** *Sic Semper Tyrannis* (Thus Ever to Tyrants). **Song:** "Carry Me Back to Old Virginia," words and music by James B. Bland. **Bird:** cardinal. **Fish:** brook trout. **Flower:** dogwood. **Fossil:** *Chesapecten jeffersonius.* **Insect:** tiger swallowtail butterfly. **Tree:** dogwood.

Natural features

Area: 42,326 sq mi, 109,625 sq km. **Mountain ranges:** Blue Ridge, Appalachian Mountains. **Highest point:** Mount Rogers, 5,729 ft (1,746 m). **Largest lake:** Smith Mountain Lake. **Major rivers:** Potomac, Shenandoah, James, Roanoke. **Natural regions:** Coastal Plain, eastern region below the Potomac River; Piedmont Province extends from the south-central border up to the border with Maryland, includes the Piedmont Upland and Piedmont Lowlands; Blue Ridge Province, west of the Piedmont Province; Valley and Ridge region, covers most of western Virginia, includes the Shenandoah Valley and Allegheny, Shenandoah, and Appalachian Mountains; Appalachian Plateau, extreme western tip of the state, includes the Cumberland Mountain and Kanawha Sections. **Location:** East coast, bordering Maryland, North Carolina, Tennessee, Kentucky, and West Virginia. **Climate:** generally mild and equable but varies according to elevation and proximity to Chesapeake Bay and the Atlantic. **Land use:** forest, 60.5%; agricultural, 17.1%; pasture, 6.0%; other, 16.3%.

People (2000 census)

Population: 7,078,515; 178.8 persons per sq mi (69.0 persons per sq km) (land area only). **Vital statistics** (1998; per 1,000 population): birth rate, 13.9 (1999); death rate, 8.0; marriage rate, 9.5; divorce rate, 4.4. **Major cities:** Virginia Beach, 425,257; Norfolk, 234,403; Chesapeake, 199,184; Richmond, 197,790; Newport News, 180,150; Hampton, 146,437; Alexandria, 128,283; Portsmouth, 100,565; Roanoke, 94,911.

Government

Statehood: entered the Union on 26 Jun 1788 as the 10th state. **State constitution:** adopted 1970. **Representation in US Congress:** 2 senators; 11 representatives. **Electoral college:** 13 votes. **Political divisions:** 95 counties.

Economy

Employment: services, 30.1%; trade, 20.1%; government, 18.9%; manufacturing, 10.2%; finance, insurance, real estate, 6.9%; construction, 6.2%; transportation, public utilities, 4.7%; agriculture, forestry, fishing, 2.5%; mining, 0.3%. **Production:** services,

22.6%; government, 17.8%; finance, insurance, real estate, 17.3%; trade, 14.4%; manufacturing, 13.1%; transportation, utilities, 9.0%; construction, 4.6%; agriculture, 0.8%; mining, 0.4%. **Chief agricultural products:** *Crops:* tobacco, soybeans, corn, peanuts, cotton, apples, tomatoes, wheat, hay, potatoes, honey. *Livestock:* chickens, turkeys, pigs, cattle, sheep. *Aquaculture:* clams, soft-shell crabs, oysters, trout, catfish, hybrid striped bass. *Extractive products:* timber, blue crab. **Chief manufactured products:** electronics and electrical equipment, paper products, tobacco products, plastic materials, pharmaceutical and chemical products, food products, printing and publishing.

Internet resources: <www.virginia.org>; <www.state.va.us>.

Washington

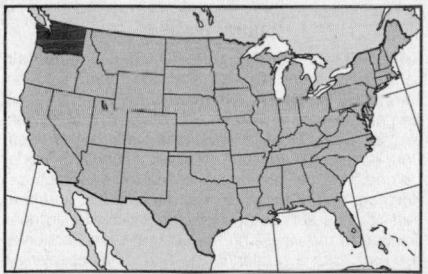

Name: Washington, named in honor of George Washington. **Nickname:** Evergreen State. **Capital:** Olympia. **Rank:** population: 15th; area: 20th. **Motto:** *Alki* (By and By). **Song:** "Washington My Home," words and music by Helen Davis. **Bird:** willow goldfinch. **Fish:** steelhead trout. **Flower:** coast rhododendron. **Fossil:** Columbian mammoth. **Gemstone:** petrified wood. **Insect:** green darner dragonfly. **Tree:** western hemlock.

Natural features

Area: 70,637 sq mi, 182,949 sq km. **Mountain ranges:** Olympic Mountains, Cascade Range, Blue Mountains. **Highest point:** Mount Rainier, 14,410 ft (4,392 m). **Largest lake:** Moses Lake. **Major rivers:** Columbia, Pend Oreille, Snake, Yakima. **Natural regions:** Pacific Border Province, western quarter of the state, includes the Olympic Mountains to the west and the Puget Trough to the east; Cascade-Sierra Mountains, running north to south down center of state, include the Northern and Middle Cascades; Northern Rocky Mountains, northeast corner; Columbia Plateaus, eastern, central and southern regions, include the Walla Walla Plateau in the center and the Blue Mountain Section in the southeast corner. **Location:** Northwest, bordering Idaho and Oregon; international border with Canada. **Climate:** moderate winters and cool summers west of the Cascades; east of the Cascade Range seasonal temperature variations are greater, with cold winters and warm, mild summers; throughout the state precipitation is greatest in the cooler months, with frequent cyclonic storms, some with gale-force winds. **Land use:** forest, 40.9%; agricultural, 19.7%; pasture, 17.4%; other, 22.0%.

People (2000 census)

Population: 5,894,121; 88.5 persons per sq mi (34.2 persons per sq km) (land area only). **Vital statistics** (1998; per 1,000 population): birth rate, 13.8 (1999); death rate, 7.5; marriage rate, 7.2; divorce rate, 5.1. **Major cities:** Seattle, 563,374; Spokane, 195,629; Tacoma, 193,556; Vancouver, 143,560; Bellevue, 109,569; Everett, 91,488.

Government

Statehood: entered the Union on 11 Nov 1889 as the 42nd state. **State constitution:** adopted 1889. **Representation in US Congress:** 2 senators; 9 representatives. **Electoral college:** 11 votes. **Political divisions:** 39 counties.

Economy

Employment: services, 28.7%; trade, 21.9%; government, 15.7%; manufacturing, 11.8%; finance, insurance, real estate, 7.3%; construction, 5.6%; transportation, public utilities, 4.6%; agriculture, forestry, fishing, 4.2%; mining, 0.2%. **Production:** services, 26.0%; finance, insurance, real estate, 17.4%; trade, 16.8%; government, 13.2%; manufacturing, 12.6%; transportation, utilities, 7.9%; construction, 4.9%; agriculture, 2.1%; mining, 0.2%. **Chief agricultural products:** *Crops:* apples, peaches, pears, cherries, grapes, apricots, raspberries dried peas, lentils, asparagus, carrots, sweet corn, green peas, potatoes, mint oil, hops, wheat, hay. *Livestock:* cattle and calves, poultry, horses. *Extractive products:* oysters, clams, mussels, crab, shrimp, geoduck, sea cucumbers, marine fish, salmon, timber. **Chief manufactured products:** aerospace equipment, food processing, forest products, advanced medical and technology products, aluminum products, fish processing.

Internet resources: <www.experiencewashington.com>; <www.state.wa.us>.

West Virginia

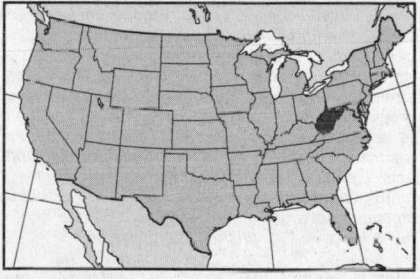

Name: West Virginia, named in honor of Elizabeth I of England, who was also known as the "Virgin Queen." **Nickname:** Mountain State. **Capital:** Charleston. **Rank:** population: 37th; area: 41st. **Motto:** *Montani Semper Liberi* (Mountaineers Are Always Free). **Song:** "This Is My West Virginia," words and music by Iris Bell; "West Virginia, My Home Sweet Home," words and music by Julian G. Hearne, Jr.; "The West Virginia Hills," words by David King and music by H.E. Engle. **Bird:** cardinal. **Fish:** brook trout. **Flower:** rhododendron.

Gemstone: West Virginia fossil coral. **Insect:** monarch butterfly. **Mammal:** black bear. **Tree:** sugar maple.

Natural features

Area: 24,231 sq mi, 62,759 sq km. **Mountain ranges:** Appalachian Mountains, Allegheny Mountains. **Highest point:** Spruce Knob, 4,862 ft (1,482 m). **Largest lake:** Summersville Lake. **Major rivers:** Ohio, Big Sandy, Guyandotte, Great Kanawha, Little Kanawha, Monongahela, Potomac. **Natural regions:** Valley and Ridge Province, eastern edge of the state, includes portions of the Shenandoah Mountains; the remainder of the state consists of the Appalachian Plateaus, and includes the Kanawha Section to the south, the Allegheny Mountains, and the Allegheny Mountains in the northeast. **Location:** East, bordering Pennsylvania, Maryland, Virginia, Kentucky, and Ohio. **Climate:** humid continental, except for a marine modification in the lower panhandle. **Land use:** forest, 77.2%; agricultural, 9.2%; pasture, 3.1%; other, 10.5%.

People (2000 census)

Population: 1,808,344; 75.1 persons per sq mi (29.0 persons per sq km) (land area only). **Vital statistics** (1998; per 1,000 population): birth rate, 11.5 (1999); death rate, 11.5; marriage rate, 6.5; divorce rate, 5.1. **Major cities:** Charleston, 53,421; Huntington, 51,475; Parkersburg, 33,099; Wheeling, 31,419; Morgantown, 26,809.

Government

Statehood: entered the Union on 20 Jun 1863 as the 35th state. **State constitution:** adopted 1872. **Representation in US Congress:** 2 senators; 3 representatives. **Electoral college:** 5 votes. **Political divisions:** 55 counties.

Economy

Employment: services, 28.1%; trade, 22.2%; government, 17.1%; manufacturing, 9.9%; construction, 5.9%; transportation, public utilities, 5.2%; finance, insurance, real estate, 4.8%; agriculture, forestry, fishing, 3.3%; mining, 3.3%. **Production:** services, 17.9%; manufacturing, 16.0%; government, 15.5%; trade, 15.5%; finance, insurance, real estate, 11.3%; transportation, utilities, 11.3%; mining, 7.3%; construction, 4.6%; agriculture, 0.6%. **Chief agricultural products:** *Crops:* hay, apples, corn, tobacco, peaches, dairy products. *Livestock:* cattle, sheep, poultry. *Extractive products:* timber. **Chief manufactured products:** chemical products, automobile parts, primary metal and fabricated metal products, glassware, computer software, wood products, electrical equipment, industrial machinery, pharmaceuticals.

Internet resources: <www.callwva.com>; <www.state. wv.us>.

Wisconsin

Name: Wisconsin, an anglicized version of a French rendering of a Native American name said to mean "the place where we live." **Nickname:** Badger State.

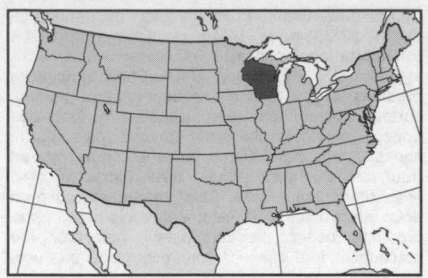

Capital: Madison. **Rank:** population: 18th; area: 25th. **Motto:** Forward. **Song:** "On, Wisconsin," words and music by William T. Purdy. **Bird:** robin. **Fish:** muskellunge (muskie). **Flower:** wood violet. **Fossil:** trilobite. **Insect:** honeybee. **Mammal:** badger. **Mineral:** galena. **Rock:** red granite. **Tree:** sugar maple.

Natural features

Area: 65,499 sq mi, 169,643 sq km. **Mountain ranges:** Baraboo Range, Rib Mountain, Gogebic Range. **Highest point:** Timms Hill, 1,953 ft (595 m). **Largest lake:** Lake Winnebago. **Major rivers:** Wisconsin, St. Croix, Rock, Mississippi, Namekagon, Wolf, Pine-Popple, Brule, Pike. **Natural regions:** Superior Upland, divided into highland and lowland sections, northern half of the state; Central Lowland, southern half of the state, divided into the Wisconsin Driftless Section to the west and the Eastern Lake Section to the east, with a section of the Till Plains occupying a small area at the southern border. **Location:** Midwest, bordering Michigan, Illinois, Iowa, and Minnesota. **Climate:** continental, with long, cold winters and warm, but relatively short, summers. **Land use:** forest, 45.2%; agricultural, 27.5%; pasture, 5.3%; other, 22.0%.

People (2000 census)

Population: 5,363,675; 98.8 persons per sq mi (38.1 persons per sq km). **Vital statistics** (1998; per 1,000 population): birth rate, 13.0 (1999); death rate, 8.8; marriage rate, 6.7; divorce rate, 3.4. **Major cities:** Milwaukee, 596,974; Madison, 208,054; Green Bay, 102,313; Kenosha, 90,352; Racine, 81,855.

Government

Statehood: entered the Union on 29 May 1848 as the 30th state. **State constitution:** adopted 1848. **Representation in US Congress:** 2 senators; 9 representatives. **Electoral college:** 10 votes (in the 2004 general elections based on the 2000 census). **Political divisions:** 72 counties.

Economy

Employment: services, 26.7%; trade, 21.8%; manufacturing, 19.2%; government, 11.9%; finance, insurance, real estate, 6.8%; construction, 4.8%; transportation, public utilities, 4.4%; agriculture, forestry, fishing, 4.2%; mining, 0.1%. **Production:** manufacturing, 26.3%; services, 17.8%; trade, 15.8%; finance, insurance, real estate, 15.6%; government, 10.6%;

For details about state governments, see pages 854–859; for extraction and energy data, see pages 880–884.

transportation, utilities, 7.1%; construction, 4.7%; agriculture, 1.9%; mining, 0.1%. **Chief agricultural products:** *Crops:* Dairy products, corn, honey, maple syrup, oats, hay, snap and green beans, potatoes, strawberries, tart cherries, cranberries, Christmas trees, mint for oil, beets, cabbage, carrots, green peas, cucumbers. *Livestock:* cattle and calves, hogs. *Other:* mink. *Extractive products:* freshwater fish. **Chief manufactured products:** processed foods, beer, industrial machinery, paper and paper products, fabricated metal products, transportation equipment, household appliances.

Internet resources. <www.travelwisconsin.com>; <www.state.wi.us>.

Wyoming

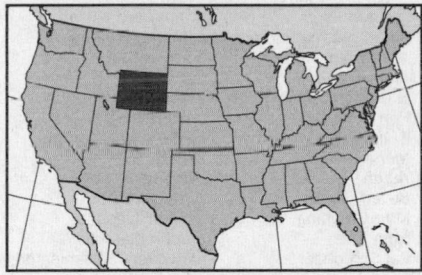

Name: Wyoming, from the Delaware Indian word, meaning "mountains and valleys alternating." **Nicknames:** Equality State and Cowboy State. **Capital:** Cheyenne. **Rank:** population: 50th; area: 9th. **Motto:** Equal Rights. **Song:** "Wyoming," words by Charles E. Winter and music by George E. Knapp. **Bird:** meadowlark. **Fish:** cutthroat trout. **Flower:** Indian paintbrush. **Fossil:** knightia. **Gemstone:** jade. **Mammal:** bison. **Reptile:** horned toad. **Tree:** plains cottonwood.

Natural features

Area: 97,818 sq mi, 253,349 sq km. **Mountain ranges:** Rocky Mountains, Big Horn, Grand Tetons, Wind River Range, Continental Divide, Sierra Madre Range, Washakie Mountains. **Highest point:** Gannett Peak, 13,804 ft (4,207 m). **Largest lake:** Yellowstone Lake. **Major rivers:** Snake, Colorado, Green, Colum-

bia. **Natural regions:** Great Plains Province, eastern third of the state, includes the Black Hills in the northeast corner, the High Plains in the southwest corner, and the Missouri Plateau in the center; Wyoming Basin, central and southern regions; Southern Rocky Mountains, southern border; the Middle Rocky Mountains, northwest third of the state, also cover a small area on the southern border; Northern Rocky Mountains, extreme northwest tip of the state. **Location:** West, bordering Montana, South Dakota, Nebraska, Colorado, Utah, and Idaho. **Climate:** semiarid continental, with long, cold winters and relatively short, warm summers. **Land use:** pasture, 72.2%; forest, 8.2%; agricultural, 5.0%; other, 14.7%.

People (2000 census)

Population: 493,782; 5.1 persons per sq mi (2.0 persons per sq km) (land area only). **Vital statistics** (1998; per 1,000 population): birth rate, 12.8 (1999); death rate, 8.0; marriage rate, 9.7; divorce rate, 5.9. **Major cities:** Cheyenne, 53,011; Casper, 49,644; Laramie, 27,204.

Government

Statehood: entered the Union on 10 Jul 1890 as the 44th state. **State constitution:** adopted 1889. **Representation in US Congress:** 2 senators; 1 representative. **Electoral college:** 3 votes. **Political divisions:** 23 counties.

Economy

Employment: services, 25.0%; trade, 21.3%; government, 19.5%; construction, 6.9%; finance, insurance, real estate, 6.6%; mining, 5.9%; transportation, public utilities, 5.4%; agriculture, forestry, fishing, 5.3%; manufacturing, 4.1%. **Production:** mining, 22.0%; transportation, utilities, 14.8%; government, 14.1%; trade, 11.8%; services, 11.6%; finance, insurance, real estate, 11.3%; manufacturing, 6.6%; construction, 5.4%; agriculture, 2.5%. **Chief agricultural products:** *Crops:* hay, wheat, barley, sugar beets and sugar, corn, wool. *Livestock:* cattle and calves, sheep and lambs. **Chief manufactured products:** refined petroleum, lumber and wood products, food products, fabricated metal products.

Internet resources: <www.wyomingtourism.com>; <www.state.wy.us>.

Famous People from the 50 States, DC, and Puerto Rico

Alabama
Hank Aaron
Hugo Black
Helen Keller
Rosa Parks
Alaska
Charles E. Bunnell
William Egan
Jewel
Hillary Lindh
Arizona
Lynda Carter
Cesar Chavez
Barry Goldwater
Helen Hull Jacobs

Arkansas
Daisy Gatson Bates
Johnny Cash
Joycelyn Elders
Douglas MacArthur
California
Tom Hanks
Marilyn Monroe
Sally Ride
John Steinbeck
Colorado
Tim Allen
Ruth Handler
Florence Sabin
Paul Whiteman

Connecticut
Ethan Allen
Katharine Hepburn
Annie Leibovitz
Noah Webster
Delaware
Annie Jump Cannon
Pierre Samuel du Pont
Henry Heimlich
Elisabeth Shue
District of Columbia
Elgin Baylor
Katie Couric
Duke Ellington
Helen Hayes

Florida
Zora Neale Hurston
Jim Morrison
Sidney Poitier
Janet Reno
Georgia
Jimmy Carter
Otis Redding
Julia Roberts
Joanne Woodward
Hawaii
Hiram Bingham
King Kamehameha I
Queen Liliuokalani
Bette Midler

Famous People from the 50 States, DC, and Puerto Rico (continued)

Idaho
Pappy Boyington
Ezra Pound
Sacagawea
Lana Turner

Illinois
Jane Addams
Hillary Rodham Clinton
Walt Disney
Wild Bill Hickok

Indiana
Anne Baxter
James Dean
David Letterman
Jane Pauley

Iowa
Johnny Carson
Ann Landers
Lillian Russell
John Wayne

Kansas
Annette Bening
Walter Chrysler
Amelia Earhart
Maurice Greene

Kentucky
Muhammad Ali
Kit Carson
bell hooks
Carry Nation

Louisiana
Louis Armstrong
Truman Capote
Ellen DeGeneres
Britney Spears

Maine
Dorothea Dix
Stephen King
Joan Benoit Samuelson
John Hay Whitney

Maryland
Goldie Hawn
Billie Holiday
Johns Hopkins
Babe Ruth

Massachusetts
Clara Barton
Cotton Mather
Dr. Seuss
Barbara Walters

Michigan
Ellen Burstyn
Magic Johnson
Charles Lindbergh
Madonna

Minnesota
Bob Dylan
Judy Garland
Garrison Keillor
Winona Ryder

Mississippi
Jim Henson
Elvis Presley
Eudora Welty
Oprah Winfrey

Missouri
Maya Angelou
Josephine Baker
Yogi Berra
Jesse James

Montana
Gary Cooper
Myrna Loy
David Lynch
Jeannette Rankin

Nebraska
Grace Abbott
Marlon Brando
Malcolm X
Mari Susette Sandoz

Nevada
Andre Agassi
Jack Kramer
Pat Nixon
Sarah Winnemucca

New Hampshire
Mary Baker Eddy
Sarah Josepha Hale
John Irving
Franklin Pierce

New Jersey
Amiri Baraka
Bruce Springsteen
Martha Stewart
Meryl Streep

New Mexico
Paula Allen
John Denver
William Hanna
Linda Wertheimer

New York
Woody Allen
Aaron Copland
Vera Wang
Edith Wharton

North Carolina
John Coltrane
Elizabeth Dole
Ava Gardner
Billy Graham

North Dakota
Angie Dickinson
Louis L'Amour
Peggy Lee
Lawrence Welk

Ohio
Thomas Edison
Toni Morrison
Sarah Jessica Parker
Ted Turner

Oklahoma
L. Gordon Cooper
Ron Howard
Reba McEntire
Maria Tallchief

Oregon
Beverly Cleary
Matt Groening
John Reed
Pat Schroeder

Pennsylvania
Marian Anderson
James Buchanan
Grace Kelly
Andy Warhol

Puerto Rico
Roberto Clemente
Sr. M. Isolina Ferré
Raul Julia
Rita Moreno

Rhode Island
Thomas Wilson Dorr
Gilbert Stuart
Mena Suvari
Jemima Wilkinson

South Carolina
Mary McLeod Bethune
John C. Calhoun
Althea Gibson
Jesse Jackson

South Dakota
Tom Brokaw
Tom Daschle
Mary Hart
Cheryl Ladd

Tennessee
Hattie Caraway
Davy Crockett
Aretha Franklin
Quentin Tarantino

Texas
Joan Crawford
Howard Hughes
Lyndon B. Johnson
Janis Joplin

Utah
Butch Cassidy
J. Willard Marriott
Marie Osmond
Roseanne

Vermont
John Deere
Stephen Douglas
Mary Jane Safford
Patty Sheehan

Virginia
Willa Cather
Ella Fitzgerald
John Marshall
Booker T. Washington

Washington
Gail Devers
Bill Gates
Robert Joffrey
Hilary Swank

West Virginia
Belle Boyd
Anna Jarvis
Cyrus Vance
Chuck Yeager

Wisconsin
Aldrich Ames
Carrie Chapman Catt
John Ringling
Laura Ingalls Wilder

Wyoming
Lynne Cheney
June Etta Downey
Curt Gowdy
Jackson Pollock

State Government

Governors of US States and Territories

Governors of New Hampshire and Vermont serve two-year terms; all others serve four-year terms. Parties: Democrat (D); Republican (R); Independent (I); Minnesota Independent (Minn I); Popular Democrat (PD).

STATE	GOVERNOR	IN OFFICE SINCE	PRESENT TERM EXPIRES
Alabama	Don Siegelman (D)	Jan 1999	Jan 2003*
Alaska	Tony Knowles (D)	Dec 1994	Dec 2002
Arizona	Jane Dee Hull (R)[1]	Sep 1997	Jan 2003
Arkansas	Mike Huckabee (R)[2]	Jul 1996	Jan 2003*
California	Gray Davis (D)	Jan 1999	Jan 2003*
Colorado	Bill Owens (R)	Jan 1999	Jan 2003*
Connecticut	John G. Rowland (R)	Jan 1995	Jan 2003*
Delaware[3]	Ruth Ann Minner (D)	Jan 2001	Jan 2005*

Governors of US States and Territories (continued)

STATE	GOVERNOR	IN OFFICE SINCE	PRESENT TERM EXPIRES
Florida	Jeb Bush (R)	Jan 1999	Jan 2003*
Georgia	Roy Barnes (D)	Jan 1999	Jan 2003*
Hawaii	Benjamin J. Cayetano (D)	Dec 1994	Dec 2002
Idaho	Dirk Kempthorne (R)	Jan 1999	Jan 2003*
Illinois	George H. Ryan (R)	Jan 1999	Jan 2003*
Indiana	Frank O'Bannon (D)	Jan 1997	Jan 2005
Iowa	Tom Vilsack (D)	Jan 1999	Jan 2003*
Kansas	Bill Graves (R)	Jan 1995	Jan 2003
Kentucky	Paul E. Patton (D)	Dec 1995	Dec 2003
Louisiana	M.J. "Mike" Foster, Jr. (R)	Jan 1996	Jan 2004
Maine	Angus S. King, Jr. (I)	Jan 1995	Jan 2003
Maryland	Parris N. Glendening (D)	Jan 1995	Jan 2003
Massachusetts	Jane Swift (R)[4]	Apr 2001	Jan 2003*
Michigan	John Engler (R)[5]	Jan 1991	Jan 2003
Minnesota	Jesse Ventura (Minn I)	Jan 1999	Jan 2003*
Mississippi	Ronnie Musgrove (D)	Jan 2000	Jan 2004*
Missouri	Bob Holden (D)	Jan 2001	Jan 2005*
Montana[6]	Judy Martz (R)	Jan 2001	Jan 2005*
Nebraska	Mike Johanns (R)[7]	Jan 1999	Jan 2003*
Nevada	Kenny C. Guinn (R)	Jan 1999	Jan 2003*
New Hampshire	Jeanne Shaheen (D)	Jan 1997	Jan 2003*
New Jersey	James E. McGreevey (D)	Jan 2002	Jan 2006*
New Mexico	Gary E. Johnson (R)	Jan 1995	Jan 2003
New York	George E. Pataki (R)	Jan 1995	Jan 2003*
North Carolina	Michael F. Easley (D)	Jan 2001	Jan 2005*
North Dakota	John Hoeven (R)	Jan 2001	Jan 2005*
Ohio	Bob Taft (R)	Jan 1999	Jan 2003*
Oklahoma	Frank Keating (R)	Jan 1995	Jan 2003
Oregon	John A. Kitzhaber (D)	Jan 1995	Jan 2003
Pennsylvania	Mark S. Schweiker (R)	Oct 2001[8]	Jan 2003*
Rhode Island	Lincoln Almond (R)	Jan 1995	Jan 2003
South Carolina	Jim Hodges (D)	Jan 1999	Jan 2003*
South Dakota	William J. Janklow (R)[9]	Jan 1995	Jan 2003
Tennessee	Don Sundquist (R)	Jan 1995	Jan 2003
Texas	Rick Perry (R)[10]	Dec 2000	Jan 2003*
Utah	Michael O. Leavitt (R)[11]	Jan 1993	Jan 2005
Vermont	Howard Dean (D)[12]	Aug 1991	Jan 2003*
Virginia[13]	Mark R. Warner (D)	Jan 2002	Jan 2006
Washington	Gary Locke (D)	Jan 1997	Jan 2005*
West Virginia	Bob Wise (D)	Jan 2001	Jan 2005*
Wisconsin	Scott McCallum (R)[14]	Feb 2001	Jan 2003*
Wyoming	Jim Geringer (R)	Jan 1995	Jan 2003

TERRITORIES	GOVERNOR	IN OFFICE SINCE	PRESENT TERM EXPIRES
American Samoa	Tauese P.F. Sunia (D)	Jan 1997	Jan 2005
Guam	Carl T.C. Gutierrez (D)	Jan 1995	Jan 2003
Northern Mariana Islands	Juan N. Babauta (R)	Jan 2002	Jan 2006*
Puerto Rico	Sila M. Calderón (PD)	Jan 2001	Jan 2005*
Virgin Islands	Charles W. Turnbull (D)	Jan 1999	Jan 2003*

*Present governor is eligible for reelection. [1]Sec. of State Jane Dee Hull became governor in September 1997 following Fife Symington's resignation. She was elected to a full term in November 1998 and is not eligible for another term. [2]Lt. Gov. Mike Huckabee became governor in July 1996 following Jim Guy Tucker's resignation. He was elected to a full term in November 1998 and is eligible to serve one more term. [3]Delaware allows two terms, but these need not be served consecutively. [4]Lt. Gov. Jane Swift became governor in April 2001 after Argeo Paul Cellucci was named ambassador to Canada. [5]Michigan limits the term of office to two four-year terms, but because John Engler was elected before this law was enacted, he is grandfathered. [6]Montana allows no more than 8 years of service every 16 years. [7]Nebraska allows the governor to serve two consecutive terms, but the candidate must wait four years before running for a third term. [8]Lt. Gov. Mark S. Schweiker became governor in October 2001 following the appointment of Tom Ridge as secretary of the US Office of Homeland Security. [9]William J. Janklow previously served as governor from 1979 to 1987. [10]Lt. Gov. Rick Perry became governor in December 2000 following George W. Bush's election as President of the United States. [11]During Michael Leavitt's term of service, Utah enacted a provision limiting the governor's term to three consecutive terms. Leavitt was grandfathered and may serve one more term upon completion of his present term. [12]Lt. Gov. Howard Dean became governor in August 1991 following the death of Richard A. Snelling. [13]In Virginia, the governor cannot serve successive terms. [14]Lt. Gov. Scott McCallum became governor in February 2001 following the appointment of Tommy Thompson as secretary of the US Department of Health and Human Services.

State Officers and Legislatures

N/A means not available. Sources: Web sites from the individual states, The Book of the States, vol. 34, and the CSG State Directory, published by The Council of State Governments.

STATE/OFFICE	OFFICEHOLDER	PAY[1]
Alabama		
Governor	Don Siegelman (D)	$94,655
Lt. Gov.	Steve Windom (R)	$48,620
Sec. of State	Jim Bennett (R)	$66,722
Att. Gen.	Bill Pryor (R)	$124,951
Treasurer	Lucy Baxley (D)	$66,722
Legislature		
Senate	Dem: 24; Rep: 11	
House	Dem: 67; Rep: 38	
Alaska		
Governor	Tony Knowles (D)	$83,280
Lt. Gov.	Fran Ulmer (D)	$77,712
Sec. of State[2]		
Att. Gen.	Bruce M. Botelho (D)	$88,548
Treasurer[3]	Neil Slotnick (Deputy Commissioner)	$91,668
Legislature		
Senate	Dem: 6; Rep: 14	
House	Dem: 13; Rep: 27	
Arizona		
Governor	Jane Dee Hull (R)	$95,000
Lt. Gov.[4]		
Sec. of State	Betsey Bayless (R)	$70,000
Att. Gen.	Janet Napolitano (D)	$90,000
Treasurer	Carol Springer (R)	$70,000
Legislature		
Senate	Dem: 15; Rep: 15	
House	Dem: 24; Rep: 36	
Arkansas		
Governor	Mike Huckabee (R)	$71,738
Lt. Gov.	Win Rockefeller (R)	$34,673
Sec. of State	Sharon Priest (D)	$43,000
Att. Gen.	Mark Lunsford Pryor (D)	$59,781
Treasurer	Jimmie Lou Fisher (D)	$44,836
Legislature		
Senate	Dem: 28; Rep: 7	
House	Dem: 70; Rep: 30	
California		
Governor	Gray Davis (D)	$175,000
Lt. Gov.	Cruz M. Bustamante (D)	$131,250
Sec. of State	Bill Jones (R)	$123,750
Att. Gen.	Bill Lockyer (D)	$148,750
Treasurer	Philip Angelides (D)	$140,000
Legislature		
Senate	Dem: 26; Rep: 14	
House	Dem: 50; Rep: 30	
Colorado		
Governor	Bill Owens (R)	$90,000
Lt. Gov.	Joe Rogers (R)	$68,500
Sec. of State	Donetta Davidson (R)	$68,500
Att. Gen.	Ken Salazar (D)	$80,000
Treasurer	Mike Coffman (R)	$68,500
Legislature		
Senate	Dem: 18; Rep: 17	
House	Dem: 27; Rep: 38	
Connecticut		
Governor	John G. Rowland (R)	$150,000
Lt. Gov.	M. Jodi Rell (R)	$77,756
Sec. of State	Susan Bysiewicz (D)	$50,000
Att. Gen.	Richard Blumenthal (D)	$81,562

STATE/OFFICE	OFFICEHOLDER	PAY[1]
Connecticut (continued)		
Treasurer	Denise L. Nappier (D)	$76,125
Legislature		
Senate	Dem: 21; Rep: 15	
House	Dem: 100; Rep: 51	
Delaware		
Governor	Ruth Ann Minner (D)	$114,000
Lt. Gov.	John Carney (D)	$60,000
Sec. of State	Harriet Smith Windsor (D)	$103,900
Att. Gen.	M. Jane Brady (R)	$114,400
Treasurer	Jack Markell (D)	$92,200
Legislature		
Senate	Dem: 13; Rep: 8	
House	Dem: 15; Rep: 26	
Florida		
Governor	Jeb Bush (R)	$120,171
Lt. Gov.	Frank T. Brogan (R)	$115,112
Sec. of State	Katherine Harris (R)	$116,056
Att. Gen.	Robert A. Butterworth (D)	$118,957
Treasurer	Tom Gallagher (R)	$118,957
Legislature		
Senate	Dem: 15; Rep: 25	
House	Dem: 43; Rep: 77	
Georgia		
Governor	Roy Barnes (D)	$127,303
Lt. Gov.	Mark Taylor (D)	$83,148
Sec. of State	Cathy Cox (D)	$89,538
Att. Gen.	Thurbert E. Baker (D)	$125,889
Treasurer	W. Daniel Ebersole	$116,093
Legislature		
Senate	Dem: 33; Rep: 23	
House	Dem: 105; Rep: 75	
Hawaii		
Governor	Benjamin J. Cayetano (D)	$94,780
Lt. Gov.	Mazie K. Hirono (D)	$90,041
Sec. of State[2]		
Att. Gen.	Earl I. Anzai (D)	$85,302
Treasurer[3]	Neal Miyahira (Director of Finance)	$85,302
Legislature		
Senate	Dem: 22; Rep: 3	
House	Dem: 32; Rep: 19	
Idaho		
Governor	Dirk Kempthorne (R)	$98,500
Lt. Gov.	Jack Riggs (R)	$26,000
Sec. of State	Pete T. Cenarrusa (R)	$80,000
Att. Gen.	Alan G. Lance (R)	$88,500
Treasurer	Ron G. Crane (R)	$80,000
Legislature		
Senate	Dem: 3; Rep: 32	
House	Dem: 9; Rep: 61	
Illinois		
Governor	George H. Ryan (R)	$150,691
Lt. Gov.	Corinne Wood (R)	$115,235
Sec. of State	Jesse White (D)	$123,700
Att. Gen.	Jim Ryan (R)	$132,963
Treasurer	Judy Baar Topinka (R)	$115,235
Legislature		
Senate	Dem: 27; Rep: 32	
House	Dem: 62; Rep: 56	

State Officers and Legislatures (continued)

STATE/OFFICE	OFFICEHOLDER	PAY[1]
Indiana		
Governor	Frank O'Bannon (D)	$95,000
Lt. Gov.	Joseph E. Kernan (D)	$76,000
Sec. of State	Sue Anne Gilroy (R)	$66,000
Att. Gen.	Steve Carter (R)	$79,400
Treasurer	Tim Berry (R)	$66,000
Legislature		
Senate	Dem: 18; Rep: 32	
House	Dem: 53; Rep: 47	
Iowa		
Governor	Tom Vilsack (D)	$107,482
Lt. Gov.	Sally Pederson (D)	$76,698
Sec. of State	Chet Culver (D)	$82,940
Att. Gen.	Tom Miller (D)	$105,430
Treasurer	Michael L. Fitzgerald (D)	$87,990
Legislature		
Senate	Dem: 21; Rep: 29	
House	Dem: 44; Rep: 56	
Kansas		
Governor	Bill Graves (R)	$95,446
Lt. Gov.	Gary Sherror (R)	$26,967
Sec. of State	Ron Thornburgh (R)	$74,148
Att. Gen.	Carla J. Stovall (R)	$85,267
Treasurer	Tim Shallenburger (R)	$74,148
Legislature		
Senate	Dem: 10; Rep: 30	
House	Dem: 46; Rep: 79	
Kentucky		
Governor	Paul Patton (D)	$103,018
Lt. Gov.	Stephen L. Henry (D)	$87,580
Sec. of State	John Y. Brown III (D)	$82,521
Att. Gen.	A. B. "Ben" Chandler III (D)	$87,580
Treasurer	Jonathan Miller (D)	$87,580
Legislature		
Senate	Dem: 18; Rep: 20	
House	Dem: 66; Rep: 34	
Louisiana		
Governor	M.J. "Mike" Foster, Jr. (R)	$95,000
Lt. Gov.	Kathleen Babineaux Blanco (D)	$85,000
Sec. of State	Fox McKeithen (R)	$85,000
Att. Gen.	Richard P. Ieyoub (D)	$85,000
Treasurer	John Neely Kennedy (D)	$85,000
Legislature		
Senate	Dem: 25; Rep: 14	
House	Dem: 71; Rep: 34	
Maine		
Governor	Angus S. King, Jr. (Ind[6])	$70,000
Lt. Gov.[5]		
Sec. of State	Dan A. Gwadosky (D)	N/A
Att. Gen.	G. Steven Rowe (D)	$78,062
Treasurer	Dale McCormick (D)	$71,032
Legislature		
Senate	Dem: 18; Rep: 16; Ind: 1	
House	Dem: 81; Rep: 69; Ind: 1	
Maryland		
Governor	Parris N. Glendening (D)	$120,000
Lt. Gov.	Kathleen Kennedy Townsend (D)	$100,000
Sec. of State	John T. Willis (D)	$70,000
Att. Gen.	J. Joseph Curran, Jr. (D)	$100,000
Treasurer	Nancy Kopp	$100,000

STATE/OFFICE	OFFICEHOLDER	PAY[1]
Maryland (continued)		
Legislature		
Senate	Dem: 34; Rep: 13	
House	Dem: 106; Rep: 35	
Massachusetts		
Governor	Jane Swift (R)	$135,000
Lt. Gov.	Vacant	$120,000
Sec. of State	William Francis Galvin (D)	$120,000
Att. Gen.	Tom Reilly (D)	$122,500
Treasurer	Shannon P. O'Brien (D)	$120,000
Legislature		
Senate	Dem: 33; Rep: 6; Vacant: 1	
House	Dem: 134; Rep: 22; Vacant: 4	
Michigan		
Governor	John Engler (R)	$177,000
Lt. Gov.	Dick Posthumus (R)	$123,000
Sec. of State	Candice Miller (R)	$124,900
Att. Gen.	Jennifer Granholm (D)	$124,900
Treasurer	Douglas B. Roberts	$161,000
Legislature		
Senate	Dem: 15; Rep: 23	
House	Dem: 52; Rep: 58	
Minnesota		
Governor	Jesse Ventura (IPM[7])	$120,303
Lt. Gov.	Mae Schunk (IPM)	$62,980
Sec. of State	Mary Kiffmeyer (R)	$66,169
Att. Gen.	Mike Hatch (DFL[8])	$93,000
Treasurer	Carol C. Johnson (DFL)	$71,129
Legislature		
Senate	Dem: 39; Rep: 27; Ind: 1	
House	Dem: 64; Rep: 70	
Mississippi		
Governor	Ronnie Musgrove (D)	$101,800
Lt. Gov.	Amy Tuck (D)	$60,000
Sec. of State	Eric Clark (D)	$75,000
Att. Gen.	Mike Moore (D)	$90,800
Treasurer	Marshall Bennett (D)	$75,000
Legislature		
Senate	Dem: 34; Rep: 18	
House	Dem: 86; Rep: 33; Ind: 3	
Missouri		
Governor	Bob Holden (D)	$120,087
Lt. Gov.	Joe Maxwell (D)	$77,184
Sec. of State	Matt Blunt (R)	$90,471
Att. Gen.	Jeremiah W. Nixon (D)	$104,332
Treasurer	Nancy Farmer (D)	$96,445
Legislature		
Senate	Dem: 16; Rep: 17; Vacant: 1	
House	Dem: 87; Rep: 76	
Montana		
Governor	Judy Martz (R)	$88,190
Lt. Gov.	Karl Ohs (R)	$62,471
Sec. of State	Bob Brown (R)	$67,512
Att. Gen.	Mike McGrath (D)	$75,550
Treasurer[3]	Scott Darkenwald (Dept. of Administration)	$80,704
Legislature		
Senate	Dem: 19; Rep: 31	
House	Dem: 42; Rep: 58	
Nebraska		
Governor	Mike Johanns (R)	$65,000

State Officers and Legislatures (continued)

STATE/OFFICE	OFFICEHOLDER	PAY[1]
Nebraska (continued)		
Lt. Gov.	Dave Heineman (R)	$47,000
Sec. of State	John A. Gale (R)	$52,000
Att. Gen.	Don Stenberg (R)	$64,500
Treasurer	Lorelee Byrd (R)	$49,500
Legislature (unicameral)		
Senate	49 nonpartisan members	
Nevada		
Governor	Kenny C. Guinn (R)	$117,000
Lt. Gov.	Lorraine T. Hunt (R)	$50,000
Sec. of State	Dean Heller (R)	$80,000
Att. Gen.	Frankie Sue Del Papa (D)	$110,000
Treasurer	Brian K. Krolicki (R)	$80,000
Legislature		
Senate	Dem: 9; Rep: 12	
House	Dem: 27; Rep: 15	
New Hampshire		
Governor	Jeanne Shaheen (D)	$100,690
Lt. Gov.[5]		
Sec. of State	William M. Gardner (D)	$65,540
Att. Gen.	Philip T. McLaughlin (D)	$85,753
Treasurer	Georgie A. Thomas	$76,603
Legislature		
Senate	Dem: 11; Rep: 13	
House	Dem: 142; Rep: 255; Libertarian: 1; Vacant: 2	
New Jersey		
Governor	James E. McGreevey (D)	$130,000
Lt. Gov.[5]		
Sec. of State	Regena L. Thomas (D)	$100,225
Att. Gen.	David Samson	$100,225
Treasurer	John E. McCormac	$100,225
Legislature		
Senate	Dem: 20; Rep: 20	
House	Dem: 44; Rep: 36	
New Mexico		
Governor	Gary E. Johnson (R)	$90,000
Lt. Gov.	Walter Bradley (R)	$65,000
Sec. of State	Rebecca Vigil-Giron (D)	$65,000
Att. Gen.	Patricia A. Madrid (D)	$72,500
Treasurer	Michael A. Montoya (D)	$65,000
Legislature		
Senate	Dem: 24; Rep: 18	
House	Dem: 42; Rep: 28	
New York		
Governor	George E. Pataki (R)	$179,000
Lt. Gov.	Mary O. Donohue (R)	$151,500
Sec. of State	Randy A. Daniels (D)	$120,800
Att. Gen.	Eliot Spitzer (D)	$151,500
Treasurer	George H. Gasser	$108,510
Legislature		
Senate	Dem: 25; Rep: 36	
House	Dem: 99; Rep: 51	
North Carolina		
Governor	Michael F. Easley (D)	$118,430
Lt. Gov.	Beverly Perdue (D)	$104,523
Sec. of State	Elaine F. Marshall (D)	$94,552
Att. Gen.	Roy Cooper III (D)	$104,523
Treasurer	Richard H. Moore (D)	$104,523
Legislature		
Senate	Dem: 35; Rep: 15	
House	Dem: 62; Rep: 58	

STATE/OFFICE	OFFICEHOLDER	PAY[1]
North Dakota		
Governor	John Hoeven (R)	$83,013
Lt. Gov.	Jack Dalrymple (R)	$64,452
Sec. of State	Alvin A. Jaeger (R)	$68,000
Att. Gen.	Wayne Stenehjem (R)	$71,076
Treasurer	Kathi Gilmore (D)	$62,976
Legislature		
Senate	Dem: 17; Rep: 32	
House	Dem: 29; Rep: 69	
Ohio		
Governor	Bob Taft (R)	$126,485
Lt. Gov.	Maureen O'Connor (R)	$73,715
Sec. of State	J. Kenneth Blackwell (R)	$90,725
Att. Gen.	Betty D. Montgomery (R)	$93,434
Treasurer	Joseph T. Deters (R)	$93,434
Legislature		
Senate	Dem: 12; Rep: 21	
House	Dem: 40; Rep: 59	
Oklahoma		
Governor	Frank Keating (R)	$101,040
Lt. Gov.	Mary Fallin (R)	$75,530
Sec. of State	Mike Hunter (R)	$65,000
Att. Gen.	W.A. Drew Edmondson (D)	$94,349
Treasurer	Robert Butkin (D)	$82,000
Legislature		
Senate	Dem: 30; Rep: 18	
House	Dem: 52; Rep: 49	
Oregon		
Governor	John A. Kitzhaber (D)	$93,600
Lt. Gov.[4]		
Sec. of State	Bill Bradbury (D)	$67,900
Att. Gen.	Hardy Myers (D)	$77,200
Treasurer	Randall Edwards (D)	$72,000
Legislature		
Senate	Dem: 14; Rep: 16	
House	Dem: 28; Rep: 32	
Pennsylvania		
Governor	Mark Schweiker (R)	$142,000
Lt. Gov.	Robert C. Jubelirer (R)	$116,185
Sec. of State	C. Michael Weaver (R)	$97,603
Att. Gen.	Mike Fisher (R)	$115,041
Treasurer	Barbara Hafer (R)	$115,041
Legislature		
Senate	Dem: 21; Rep: 29	
House	Dem: 98; Rep: 104; Vacant: 1	
Rhode Island		
Governor	Lincoln Almond (R)	$95,000
Lt. Gov.	Charles J. Fogarty (D)	$80,000
Sec. of State	Edward S. Inman III (D)	$80,000
Att. Gen.	Sheldon Whitehouse (D)	$85,000
Treasurer	Paul J. Tavares (D)	$80,000
Legislature		
Senate	Dem: 44; Rep: 6	
House	Dem: 85; Rep: 15	
South Carolina		
Governor	Jim Hodges (D)	$106,078
Lt. Gov.	Bob Peeler (R)	$44,737
Sec. of State	Jim Miles (R)	$92,007
Att. Gen.	Charlie Condon (R)	$92,007
Treasurer	Grady L. Patterson, Jr. (D)	$92,007

State Officers and Legislatures (continued)

STATE/OFFICE	OFFICEHOLDER	PAY[1]
South Carolina (continued)		
Legislature		
Senate	Dem: 21; Rep: 25	
House	Dem: 53; Rep: 69; Vacant: 2	
South Dakota		
Governor	William J. Janklow (R)	$95,389
Lt. Gov.	Carole Hillard (R)	$12,635
Sec. of State	Joyce Hazeltine (R)	$64,812
Att. Gen.	Mark Barnett (R)	$80,995
Treasurer	Richard D. Butler (D)	$64,813
Legislature		
Senate	Dem: 11; Rep: 24	
House	Dem: 20; Rep: 50	
Tennessee		
Governor	Don Sundquist (R)	$87,276
Lt. Gov.	John S. Wilder (D)	$49,500
Sec. of State	Riley Darnell (D)	$120,000
Att. Gen.	Paul G. Summers (D)	$112,068
Treasurer	Steve Adams	$120,000
Legislature		
Senate	Dem: 18; Rep: 15	
House	Dem: 57; Rep: 42	
Texas		
Governor	Rick Perry (R)	$115,345
Lt. Gov.	Bill Ratliff (R)	$99,122
Sec. of State	Gwyn Shea (R)	$117,546
Att. Gen.	John Cornyn (R)	$92,217
Treasurer[3]	Carole Keeton Rylander (Comptroller) (R)	$92,217
Legislature		
Senate	Dem: 15; Rep: 16	
House	Dem: 78; Rep: 72	
Utah		
Governor	Michael O. Leavitt (R)	$100,600
Lt. Gov.	Olene S. Walker (R)	$78,200
Sec. of State[2]		
Att. Gen.	Mark Shurtleff (R)	$84,000
Treasurer	Edward T. Alter (R)	$80,700
Legislature		
Senate	Dem: 9; Rep: 20	
House	Dem: 23; Rep: 52	
Vermont		
Governor	Howard Dean (D)	$88,026
Lt. Gov.	Douglas A. Racine (D)	$50,253
Sec. of State	Deborah L. Markowitz (D)	$75,317
Att. Gen.	William H. Sorrell (D)	$90,272
Treasurer	James H. Douglas (R)	$75,317
Legislature		
Senate	Dem: 16; Rep: 14	
House	Dem: 63; Rep: 82; Ind: 1 Progressive: 4	

STATE/OFFICE	OFFICEHOLDER	PAY[1]
Virginia		
Governor	Mark R. Warner (D)	$125,000
Lt. Gov.	Tim Kaine (D)	$32,000
Sec. of State	Anita A. Rimler (D)	$76,346
Att. Gen.	Jerry Kilgore (R)	$97,500
Treasurer	Jody M. Wagner	$93,573
Legislature		
Senate	Dem: 18; Rep: 22	
House	Dem: 33; Rep: 64; Ind: 2; Vacant: 1	
Washington		
Governor	Gary Locke (D)	$139,087
Lt. Gov.	Brad Owen (D)	$72,705
Sec. of State	Sam Reed (R)	$91,048
Att. Gen.	Christine O. Gregoire (D)	$126,443
Treasurer	Michael J. Murphy (D)	$97,446
Legislature		
Senate	Dem: 25; Rep: 24	
House	Dem: 50; Rep: 48	
West Virginia		
Governor	Bob Wise (D)	$90,000
Lt. Gov.[5]		
Sec. of State	Joe Manchin III (D)	$65,000
Att. Gen.	Darrell V. McGraw, Jr. (D)	$75,000
Treasurer	John D. Perdue (D)	$70,000
Legislature		
Senate	Dem: 28; Rep: 6	
House	Dem: 75; Rep: 25	
Wisconsin		
Governor	Scott McCallum (R)	$122,407
Lt. Gov.	Margaret A. Farrow (R)	$60,182
Sec. of State	Doug LaFollette (D)	$54,610
Att. Gen.	James E. Doyle (D)	$112,274
Treasurer	Jack C. Voight (R)	$54,610
Legislature		
Senate	Dem: 18; Rep: 15	
House	Dem: 43; Rep: 56	
Wyoming		
Governor	Jim Geringer (R)	$95,000
Lt. Gov.[4]		
Sec. of State	Joseph B. Meyer (R)	$77,000
Att. Gen.	Hoke MacMillan (R)	$89,067
Treasurer	Cynthia Lummis (R)	$77,000
Legislature		
Senate	Dem: 10; Rep: 20	
House	Dem: 14; Rep: 46	

[1] In most cases, the salary rates are from January 2002. [2] Lieutenant governor serves as secretary of state. [3] No official state treasurer—official in charge of general treasury performs duties. [4] Secretary of state assumes duties of lieutenant governor. [5] No official lieutenant governor—president of the senate succeeds the governor. [6] Independent (Ind). [7] Independence Party of Minnesota (IPM). [8] Democratic Farm Labor (DFL) party.

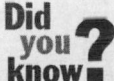
Did you know? Three US state capitals had populations of less than 20,000 in 2000. They were: Augusta, Maine at 18,560; Pierre, South Dakota at 13,876; and tiny Montpelier, Vermont at only 8,035.

Area and Zip Codes Web Sites

US telephone area codes and postal codes change frequently to accommodate telecommunications user patterns and expansions and shifts in patterns of business and residential development. With regard to telephone area codes, in some cases, an area receives an entirely new area code; in others, a new area code "overlays" the preceding one. Check local listings to determine whether to dial "1" before dialing outside of the area code or whether to dial the area code as well as the telephone number when dialing within the area code.

Area codes:
<www.cs.ucsd.edu/users/bsy/area.html#872>
Zip codes:
<www.usps.gov/ncsc/ziplookup/lookupmenu.htm>

Cities of the United States

US Urban Growth, 1850–2000

Source: US Census Bureau.

RANK	CITY	2000	1990	1980	1950	1900	1850
1	New York NY[1]	8,008,278	7,322,564	7,071,639	7,891,957	3,437,202	515,547
2	Los Angeles CA	3,694,820	3,485,398	2,966,850	1,970,358	102,479	1,610
3	Chicago IL	2,896,016	2,783,726	3,005,072	3,620,962	1,698,575	29,963
4	Houston TX	1,953,631	1,630,553	1,595,138	596,163	44,633	2,396
5	Philadelphia PA[1]	1,517,550	1,585,577	1,688,210	2,071,605	1,293,697	121,376
6	Phoenix AZ	1,321,045	983,403	789,704	106,818	5,544	
7	San Diego CA	1,223,400	1,110,549	875,538	334,387	17,700	
8	Dallas TX	1,188,580	1,006,877	904,078	434,462	42,638	
9	San Antonio TX	1,144,646	935,933	785,880	408,442	53,321	3,488
10	Detroit MI	951,270	1,027,974	1,203,339	1,849,568	285,704	21,019
11	San Jose CA	894,943	782,248	629,442	95,280	21,500	
12	Indianapolis IN	791,926	741,952	700,807	427,173	169,164	8,091
13	San Francisco CA[1]	776,733	723,959	678,974	775,357	342,782	34,776
14	Jacksonville FL	735,617	635,230	540,920	204,517	28,429	1,045
15	Columbus OH	711,470	632,910	564,871	375,901	125,560	17,882
16	Austin TX	656,562	465,622	345,496	132,459	22,258	629
17	Baltimore MD	651,154	736,014	786,775	949,708	508,957	169,054
18	Memphis TN	650,100	610,337	646,356	396,000	102,320	8,841
19	Milwaukee WI	596,974	628,088	636,212	637,392	285,315	20,061
20	Boston MA	589,141	574,283	562,994	801,444	560,892	136,881
21	Washington DC[1]	572,059	606,900	638,333	802,178	278,718	40,001
22	Nashville TN[1]	569,891	510,784	455,651	174,307	80,865	10,165
23	El Paso TX	563,662	515,342	425,259	130,485	15,906	
24	Seattle WA	563,374	516,259	493,846	467,591	80,671	
25	Denver CO[1]	554,636	467,610	492,365	415,786	133,859	
26	Charlotte NC	540,828	395,934	314,447	134,042	18,091	1,065
27	Fort Worth TX	534,694	447,619	385,164	278,778	26,688	
28	Portland OR	529,121	437,319	366,383	373,628	90,426	
29	Oklahoma City OK	506,132	444,719	403,213	243,504	10,037	
30	Tucson AZ	486,699	405,390	330,537	45,454	7,531	
31	New Orleans LA	484,674	496,938	557,515	570,445	287,104	116,375
32	Las Vegas NV	478,434	258,295	164,674	24,624		
33	Cleveland OH	478,403	505,616	573,822	914,808	381,768	17,034
34	Long Beach CA	461,522	429,433	361,334	250,767	2,252	
35	Albuquerque NM	448,607	384,736	331,767	96,815	6,238	
36	Kansas City MO	441,545	435,146	448,159	456,622	163,752	
37	Fresno CA	427,652	354,202	218,202	91,669	12,470	
38	Virginia Beach VA	425,257	393,069	262,199	5,390		
39	Atlanta GA	416,474	394,017	425,022	331,314	89,872	2,572
40	Sacramento CA	407,018	369,365	275,741	137,572	29,282	6,820
41	Oakland CA	399,484	372,242	339,337	384,575	66,960	
42	Mesa AZ	396,375	288,091	152,453	16,790	722	
43	Tulsa OK	393,049	367,302	360,919	182,740		
44	Omaha NE	390,007	335,795	314,255	251,117	102,555	
45	Minneapolis MN	382,618	368,383	370,951	521,718	202,718	
46	Honolulu HI[1]	371,657	365,272	365,048	248,034	39,306	
47	Miami FL	362,470	358,548	346,865	249,276	1,681	
48	Colorado Springs CO	360,890	281,140	215,150	45,472	21,085	
49	St. Louis MO	348,189	396,685	453,085	856,796	575,238	77,860
50	Wichita KS	344,284	304,011	279,272	168,279	24,671	
51	Santa Ana CA	337,977	293,742	203,713	45,533	4,933	
52	Pittsburgh PA	334,563	369,879	423,938	676,806	321,616	46,601
53	Arlington TX	332,969	261,721	160,113	7,692	1,079	

US Urban Growth, 1850–2000 (continued)

RANK	CITY	2000	1990	1980	1950	1900	1850
54	Cincinnati OH	331,285	364,040	385,457	503,998	325,902	115,435
55	Anaheim CA	328,014	266,406	219,311	14,556	1,456	
56	Toledo OH	313,619	332,943	354,635	303,616	131,822	3,829
57	Tampa FL	303,447	280,015	271,523	124,681	15,839	
58	Buffalo NY	292,648	328,123	357,870	580,132	352,387	42,261
59	St. Paul MN	287,151	272,235	270,230	311,349	163,065	1,112
60	Corpus Christi TX	277,454	257,453	231,999	108,287	4,703	
61	Aurora CO	276,393	222,103	158,588	11,421	202	
62	Raleigh NC	276,093	207,951	150,255	65,679	13,643	4,518
63	Newark NJ	273,546	275,221	329,248	438,776	246,070	38,894
64	Lexington KY	260,512	225,366	204,165	55,534	26,369	8,159
65	Anchorage AK[1]	260,283	226,338	174,431	11,254		
66	Louisville KY	256,231	269,063	298,451	369,129	204,731	43,194
67	Riverside CA	255,166	226,505	170,876	46,764	7,973	
68	St. Petersburg FL	248,232	238,629	238,647	96,738	1,575	
69	Bakersfield CA	247,057	174,820	105,611	34,784	4,836	
70	Stockton CA	243,771	210,943	149,779	70,853	17,506	
71	Birmingham AL	242,820	265,968	284,413	326,037	38,415	
72	Jersey City NJ	240,055	228,537	223,532	299,017	206,433	6,856
73	Norfolk VA	234,403	261,229	266,979	213,513	46,624	14,326
74	Baton Rouge LA	227,818	219,531	219,419	125,629	11,269	3,905
75	Hialeah FL	226,419	188,004	145,254	19,676		
76	Lincoln NE	225,581	191,972	171,932	98,884	40,169	
77	Greensboro NC	223,891	183,521	155,642	74,389	10,035	
78	Plano TX	222,030	128,713	72,331			
79	Rochester NY	219,773	231,636	241,741	332,488	162,608	36,403
80	Glendale AZ	218,812	148,134	97,172			
81	Akron OH	217,074	223,019	237,177	274,605	42,728	3,266
82	Garland TX	215,768	180,650	138,857	10,571	819	
83	Madison WI	208,054	191,262	170,616	96,056	19,164	1,525
84	Fort Wayne IN	205,727	173,072	172,196	133,607	45,115	4,282
85	Fremont CA	203,413	173,339	131,945			
86	Scottsdale AZ	202,705	130,069	88,412			
87	Montgomery Al	201,568	187,106	177,857	106,525	30,346	8,728
88	Shreveport LA	200,145	198,525	205,820	127,206	16,013	1,728
89	Augusta GA[1]	199,775	44,639	47,532	71,508	39,441	9,448
90	Lubbock TX	199,564	186,206	173,979	71,747		
91	Chesapeake VA	199,184	151,976	114,486			
92	Mobile AL	198,915	196,278	200,452	129,009	38,469	20,515
93	Des Moines IA	198,682	193,187	191,003	177,965	62,139	
94	Grand Rapids MI	197,800	189,126	181,843	176,515	87,565	2,686
95	Richmond VA	197,790	203,056	219,214	230,310	85,050	27,570
96	Yonkers NY	196,086	188,082	195,351	152,798	47,931	
97	Spokane WA	195,629	177,196	171,300	161,721	36,848	
98	Glendale CA	194,973	180,038	139,060	95,702		
99	Tacoma WA	193,556	176,664	158,501	143,673	37,714	
100	Irving TX	191,615	155,037	109,943	2,621		

[1]*The following cities have boundaries that include their respective counties: New York, Philadelphia, San Francisco, Washington (District of Columbia), Nashville-Davidson (Davidson County), Denver, Honolulu, Anchorage, and, since the year 2000, Augusta (Augusta-Richmond County).*

Ten Fastest-Growing Cities in the US

Based on a population of 250,000 or more. Source: US Census Bureau.

CITY	POPULATION		CHANGE (%)
	1 APR 1990	1 APR 2000	
Las Vegas NV	258,295	478,434	+85.2
Austin TX	465,622	656,562	+41.0
Mesa AZ	288,091	396,375	+37.6
Charlotte NC	395,934	540,828	+36.6
Phoenix AZ	983,403	1,321,045	+34.3
Raleigh NC	207,951	276,093	+32.8
Colorado Springs CO	281,140	360,890	+28.4
Arlington TX	261,721	332,969	+27.2
Aurora CO	222,103	276,393	+24.4
Anaheim CA	266,406	328,014	+23.1

Ten Cities with the Greatest Population Losses in the US

Based on a population of 250,000 or more. Source: US Census Bureau.

CITY	CHANGE (%)	POPULATION 1 APR 1990	POPULATION 1 APR 2000	CITY	CHANGE (%)	POPULATION 1 APR 1990	POPULATION 1 APR 2000
St. Louis MO	−12.2	396,685	348,189	Detroit MI	−7.5	1,027,974	951,270
Baltimore MD	−11.5	736,014	651,154	Toledo OH	−5.8	332,943	313,619
Buffalo NY	−10.8	328,123	292,648	Washington DC	−5.7	606,900	572,059
Pittsburgh PA	−9.5	369,879	334,563	Cleveland OH	−5.4	505,616	478,403
Cincinnati OH	−9.0	364,040	331,285	Milwaukee WI	−5.0	628,088	596,974

Racial Makeup of the Ten Largest US Cities

Information is given in percent of the total population. The Hispanic or Latino category is listed for comparative purposes even though Hispanic or Latino people may be of any race, thus the rows of racial percentages will not add up to 100 if the Hispanic or Latino entries are included. Source: US Census Bureau, census 2000.

CITY	WHITE	BLACK OR AFRICAN AMERICAN	AMERICAN INDIAN AND ALASKA NATIVE	ASIAN	NATIVE HAWAIIAN AND OTHER PACIFIC ISLANDER	SOME OTHER RACE	TWO OR MORE RACES	HISPANIC OR LATINO	TOTAL POPULATION
New York NY	44.7	26.6	0.5	9.8	0.1	13.4	4.9	27.0	8,008,278
Los Angeles CA	46.9	11.2	0.8	10.0	0.2	25.7	5.2	46.5	3,694,820
Chicago IL	42.0	36.8	0.4	4.3	0.1	13.6	2.9	26.0	2,896,016
Houston TX	49.3	25.3	0.4	5.3	0.1	16.5	3.1	37.4	1,953,631
Philadelphia PA	45.0	43.2	0.3	4.5	−	4.8	2.2	8.5	1,517,550
Phoenix AZ	71.1	5.1	2.0	2.0	0.1	16.4	3.3	34.1	1,321,045
San Diego CA	60.2	7.9	0.6	13.6	0.5	12.4	4.8	25.4	1,223,400
Dallas TX	50.8	25.9	0.5	2.7	−	17.2	2.7	35.6	1,188,580
San Antonio TX	67.7	6.8	0.8	1.6	0.1	19.3	3.7	58.7	1,144,646
Detroit MI	12.3	81.6	0.3	1.0	−	2.5	2.3	5.0	951,270

— Percent rounds to 0.0.

Law and Crime

US Crime Trends, 2001

The crime trends shown below represent the percent change in crimes reported to police for the first six months of 2001 as compared to the same time period in the year 2000. A negative number indicates that crime has declined. Source: Federal Bureau of Investigation, *Uniform Crime Reports*, January–June 2001.

POPULATION GROUP AND AREA	NUMBER OF AGENCIES[1]	POPULATION ('000)	CRIME INDEX TOTAL	MODIFIED TOTAL[2]	VIOLENT CRIME[3]	PROPERTY CRIME[4]	MURDER
cities							
over 1,000,000	10	23,598	−1.3	−1.3	−2.6	−1.0	+1.8
500,000 to 999,999	21	13,726	+0.1	+0.1	−2.2	+0.6	−9.7
250,000 to 499,999	34	11,721	+1.9	+2.0	−0.5	+2.3	+6.9
100,000 to 249,999	164	24,162	+0.6	+0.5	+1.9	+0.4	+1.3
50,000 to 99,999	294	20,044	−1.7	−1.6	−0.4	−1.9	+10.5
25,000 to 49,999	553	19,085	−0.3	−0.3	+0.7	−0.4	−0.8
10,000 to 24,999	1,238	19,681	−1.3	−1.3	−2.3	−1.3	−9.2
under 10,000	4,263	14,627	+0.1	+0.2	+0.5	+0.1	+11.9
counties							
suburban[5]	898	36,817	−0.6	−0.5	−3.2	−0.3	+7.2
rural[6]	1,749	19,763	−1.9	−1.8	−6.7	−1.3	−11.6
areas							
suburban area[7]	4,540	73,998	−0.4	−0.4	−1.2	−0.3	+4.5
cities outside metropolitan areas	2,412	16,212	−1.0	−1.0	−2.4	−0.9	−1.4
total	9,224	203,224	−0.3	−0.3	−1.3	−0.2	+0.3

US Crime Trends, 2001 (continued)

POPULATION GROUP AND AREA	FORCIBLE RAPE	ROBBERY	AGGRAVATED ASSAULT	BURGLARY	LARCENY/ THEFT	CAR THEFT	ARSON
cities							
over 1,000,000	−0.7	−3.0	−2.5	−4.0	+0.8	−4.0	+4.0
500,000 to 999,999	−8.8	+2.6	−4.4	+1.7	−0.1	+1.8	−9.1
250,000 to 499,999	−1.9	+1.8	−1.8	+0.2	+0.9	+11.5	+7.7
100,000 to 249,999	−2.3	+3.5	+1.5	−1.7	+0.1	+4.9	−1.5
50,000 to 99,999	−3.0	+3.1	−1.8	−2.7	−2.2	+1.5	+10.3
25,000 to 49,999	+3.9	+2.1	−0.2	−0.2	−0.7	+2.3	−1.9
10,000 to 24,999	+1.9	−3.2	−2.5	−0.6	−1.9	+4.1	+3.9
under 10,000	+4.3	+2.8	−0.5	+1.4	−0.5	+3.7	+8.9
counties							
suburban[5]	+2.0	+4.2	−5.6	−1.1	−0.8	+5.3	+5.8
rural[6]	−8.9	−3.5	−6.6	−2.7	−0.6	−0.5	+5.2
areas							
suburban area[7]	+3.6	+3.4	−3.1	−0.2	−1.0	+4.8	+4.5
cities outside metro- politan areas	+0.5	−4.1	−2.4	−1.2	−0.9	+0.3	+3.8
total	**−1.7**	**+0.8**	**−2.4**	**−1.2**	**−0.4**	**+2.6**	**+2.9**

[1]Law enforcement agencies. [2]Modified total is sum of all offenses, including arson. [3]Includes murder, forcible rape, robbery, and aggravated assault. [4]Includes burglary, larceny/theft, and car theft, but excludes data for arson. [5]Includes crimes reported to sheriffs' departments, county police departments, and state police within Metropolitan Statistical Areas. [6]Includes crimes reported to sheriffs' departments, county police departments, and state police outside Metropolitan Statistical Areas. [7]Includes crimes reported to city, county, and state law enforcement agencies within Metropolitan Statistical Areas, but outside the central cities.

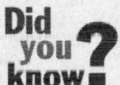

Did you know? Joseph Valachi, who turned informer in 1962, was the first member ever to describe the history, membership, and inner workings of the national crime syndicate popularly called the Mafia.

State Crime Rates, 1997–99

Crimes reported to the police per 100,000 population.

STATE	1997 TOTAL	1998 TOTAL	1999 TOTAL	STATE	1997 TOTAL	1998 TOTAL	1999 TOTAL
Alabama	4,890	4,597	4,412	Nebraska	4,284	4,405	4,108
Alaska	5,273	4,777	4,363	Nevada	6,065	5,281	4,654
Arizona	7,195	6,575	5,897	New Hampshire[4]	2,640	2,420	2,282
Arkansas	4,719	4,283	4,043	New Jersey	4,057	3,654	3,400
California	4,865	4,343	3,805	New Mexico	6,907	6,719	5,962
Colorado	4,650	4,488	4,063	New York	3,911	3,589	3,279
Connecticut	3,984	3,787	3,389	North Carolina	5,492	5,322	5,175
Delaware[2]	5,783	5,363	4,835	North Dakota	2,711	2,681	2,393
District of Columbia[1]	9,839	8,836	8,067	Ohio	4,510	4,328	3,996
Florida	7,272	6,886	6,206	Oklahoma	5,495	5,004	4,684
Georgia	5,792	5,463	5,149	Oregon	6,270	5,647	5,002
Hawaii	6,023	5,333	4,838	Pennsylvania	3,432	3,273	3,114
Idaho	3,925	3,715	3,149	Rhode Island	3,654	3,518	3,582
Illinois[4]	5,141	4,859	4,507	South Carolina	6,134	5,777	5,324
Indiana	4,466	4,169	3,766	South Dakota	3,245	2,024	2,645
Iowa	3,816	3,601	3,224	Tennessee	5,512	6,034	4,694
Kansas[4]	5,152	4,872	4,439	Texas	5,401	5,112	5,032
Kentucky[4]	3,127	3,116	2,878	Utah	5,996	5,506	4,977
Louisiana	6,449	6,098	5,747	Vermont[5]	2,828	3,139	2,817
Maine	3,132	3,041	2,875	Virginia	3,876	3,660	3,374
Maryland	5,653	5,366	4,919	Washington	5,920	5,867	5,256
Massachusetts	3,675	3,436	3,263	West Virginia	2,469	2,547	2,721
Michigan	4,917	4,683	4,325	Wisconsin[6]	3,678	3,543	3,296
Minnesota	4,414	4,047	3,597	Wyoming	4,181	3,808	3,455
Mississippi	4,630	4,384	4,270				
Missouri	4,815	4,826	4,579	**Crime rate US**	**4,930**	**4,619**	**4,267**
Montana[4]	4,409	4,359	4,070				

State Crime Rates, 1997–99 (continued)

1999 CRIME RATES IN DETAIL

| | | VIOLENT CRIMES | | | | | PROPERTY CRIMES | | |
| | | | | | | | | MOTOR | |
STATE	MURDER[1]	FORCIBLE RAPE	AGGRAVATED ASSAULT	ROBBERY	TOTAL	BURGLARY	LARCENY/ THEFT	VEHICLE THEFT	TOTAL
Alabama	7.9	34.6	327	121	490	884	2,737	301	3,922
Alaska	8.6	83.5	448	91	632	612	2,691	429	3,732
Arizona	8.0	28.9	362	153	551	1,034	3,511	801	5,345
Arkansas	5.6	27.8	313	79	425	850	2,506	261	3,618
California	6.0	28.2	412	181	627	675	1,994	508	3,178
Colorado	4.6	41.4	219	75	341	665	2,693	365	3,723
Connecticut	3.3	19.9	199	124	346	588	2,112	344	3,044
Delaware[2]	3.2	70.2	463	198	734	696	3,002	404	4,101
District of Columbia[3]	46.4	47.8	889	644	1,628	976	4,181	1,282	6,439
Florida	5.7	46.3	591	212	854	1,200	3,535	617	5,352
Georgia	7.5	29.8	330	166	534	917	3,182	515	4,615
Hawaii	3.7	29.9	113	88	235	795	3,414	393	4,602
Idaho	2.0	33.3	192	18	245	610	2,143	152	2,904
Illinois[4]	7.7	34.2	471	219	733	712	2,632	430	3,774
Indiana	6.6	27.0	232	109	375	715	2,335	341	3,391
Iowa	1.5	27.2	215	37	280	593	2,172	179	2,944
Kansas[4]	6.0	40.1	260	77	383	824	3,004	228	4,056
Kentucky[4]	5.4	26.3	189	80	301	611	1,749	218	2,578
Louisiana	10.7	33.1	515	174	733	1,093	3,425	496	5,014
Maine	2.2	19.1	72	19	112	601	2,027	135	2,763
Maryland	9.0	30.0	441	264	743	836	2,848	492	4,176
Massachusetts	2.0	26.9	426	96	551	534	1,763	415	2,712
Michigan	7.0	49.2	376	143	575	778	2,396	576	3,750
Minnesota	2.8	42.7	147	82	274	580	2,465	278	3,323
Mississippi	7.7	41.7	188	112	349	1,051	2,381	489	3,921
Missouri	6.6	26.3	337	131	500	777	2,881	420	4,079
Montana[4]	2.6	28.3	150	26	207	429	3,220	215	3,863
Nebraska	3.6	24.8	326	76	430	610	2,742	327	3,678
Nevada	9.1	52.1	276	233	570	974	2,386	724	4,084
New Hampshire[4]	1.5	28.7	45	21	97	308	1,765	113	2,185
New Jersey	3.5	17.3	216	175	412	577	1,977	434	2,988
New Mexico	9.8	54.3	622	148	835	1,235	3,426	467	5,128
New York	5.0	19.6	324	241	589	512	1,858	320	2,691
North Carolina	7.2	28.2	349	158	542	1,287	3,012	334	4,633
North Dakota	1.6	22.4	34	9	67	369	1,794	163	2,326
Ohio	3.5	36.7	148	128	316	773	2,559	348	3,680
Oklahoma	6.9	40.9	378	83	508	1,027	2,788	361	4,176
Oregon	2.7	36.8	249	86	375	807	3,409	411	4,627
Pennsylvania	4.9	27.3	233	156	421	467	1,899	327	2,693
Rhode Island	3.6	39.5	164	80	287	640	2,249	407	3,295
South Carolina	6.6	40.8	651	148	847	1,020	3,086	372	4,477
South Dakota	2.5	45.8	105	14	167	444	1,916	118	2,477
Tennessee	7.1	44.0	487	157	695	937	2,602	461	3,999
Texas	6.1	38.0	370	147	560	950	3,063	459	4,472
Utah	2.1	37.8	181	54	276	685	3,669	347	4,701
Vermont[5]	2.9	22.9	77	11	114	596	1,955	154	2,704
Virginia	5.7	25.0	183	101	315	472	2,326	261	3,059
Washington	3.0	47.1	226	101	377	950	3,342	587	4,878
West Virginia	4.4	18.6	291	37	351	570	1,592	208	2,370
Wisconsin[6]	3.4	20.1	138	85	246	488	2,299	263	3,051
Wyoming	2.3	28.5	186	15	232	489	2,609	124	3,223
Total US	**5.7**	**32.7**	**336**	**150**	**525**	**770**	**2,551**	**421**	**3,742**

[1]Includes nonnegligent manslaughter
[2]Forcible rape count estimated
[3]Includes offenses at the National Zoo
[4]Crime counts estimated for all years shown
[5]Crime count estimated for 1997
[6]Crime count estimated for 1998

Crime in the US, 1980–2001

This table presents the number of crimes reported in the seven categories that make up the FBI's Crime Index. Although the crime totals reported in 2001 were not available at press time, the year's Crime Index trends had been released. The FBI's Crime Index trends reflect the percent change in the offenses reported to law enforcement for the calendar years indicated. Source: Federal Bureau of Investigation.

		VIOLENT CRIME				PROPERTY CRIME		
YEAR	CRIME INDEX TOTAL	MURDER[1]	FORCIBLE RAPE	ROBBERY	AGGRA-VATED ASSAULT	BURGLARY	LARCENY/ THEFT	MOTOR VEHICLE THEFT
1980	13,408,300	23,040	82,990	565,840	672,650	3,795,200	7,136,900	1,131,700
1981	13,423,800	22,520	82,500	592,910	663,900	3,779,700	7,194,400	1,087,800
1982	12,974,400	21,010	78,770	553,130	669,480	3,447,100	7,142,500	1,062,400
1983	12,108,630	19,308	78,918	506,567	653,294	3,129,851	6,712,759	1,007,933
1984	11,881,755	18,692	84,233	485,008	685,349	2,984,434	6,591,874	1,032,165
1985	12,430,357	18,976	87,671	497,874	723,246	3,073,348	6,926,380	1,102,862
1986	13,211,869	20,613	91,459	542,775	834,322	3,241,410	7,257,153	1,224,137
1987	13,508,708	20,096	91,111	517,704	855,088	3,236,184	7,499,851	1,288,674
1988	13,923,086	20,675	92,486	542,968	910,092	3,218,077	7,705,872	1,432,916
1989	14,251,449	21,500	94,504	578,326	951,707	3,168,170	7,872,442	1,564,800
1990	14,475,613	23,438	102,555	639,271	1,054,863	3,073,909	7,945,670	1,635,907
1991	14,872,883	24,703	106,593	687,732	1,092,739	3,157,150	8,142,228	1,661,738
1992	14,438,191	23,760	109,062	672,478	1,126,974	2,979,884	7,915,199	1,610,834
1993	14,144,794	24,526	106,014	659,870	1,135,607	2,834,808	7,820,909	1,563,060
1994	13,989,543	23,326	102,216	618,949	1,113,179	2,712,774	7,879,812	1,539,287
1995	13,862,727	21,606	97,470	580,509	1,099,207	2,593,784	7,997,710	1,472,441
1996	13,493,863	19,645	96,252	535,594	1,037,049	2,506,400	7,904,685	1,394,238
1997	13,194,571	18,208	96,153	498,534	1,023,201	2,460,526	7,743,760	1,354,189
1998	12,485,714	16,974	93,144	447,186	976,583	2,332,735	7,376,311	1,242,781
1999	11,634,378	15,522	89,411	409,371	911,740	2,100,739	6,955,520	1,152,075
2000	11,605,751	15,517	90,186	407,842	910,744	2,049,946	6,965,957	1,165,559

Crime Index trends: percent change in number of offenses[2]

		VIOLENT CRIME				PROPERTY CRIME		
YEARS COM-PARED TO 2000	CRIME INDEX TOTAL	MURDER[1]	FORCIBLE RAPE	ROBBERY	AGGRA-VATED ASSAULT	BURGLARY	LARCENY/ THEFT	MOTOR VEHICLE THEFT
1991	−22.0	−37.2	−15.4	−40.7	−16.7	−35.1	−14.4	−29.9
1996	−14.0	−21.0	−6.3	−23.9	−12.2	−18.2	−11.9	−16.4
1999	−0.2	<0.1	+0.9	−0.4	−0.1	−2.4	+0.2	+1.2
2001	+2.0	+3.1	+0.2	+3.9	−1.4	+2.6	+1.4	+5.9

[1]Includes the crime of nonnegligent manslaughter. [2]A minus sign indicates a decrease in crime; a plus sign indicates an increase.

US Cities with Highest and Lowest Crime Rates

This table ranks cities by the number of violent and property crimes—the crime index total—reported during the first six months of 2001. All cities listed have a population of 100,000 or more. The information in the table is derived from preliminary data provided by the FBI. Source: Federal Bureau of Investigation.

CITIES	CRIME INDEX TOTAL[1]	MURDER	FORCIBLE RAPE	ROBBERY	AGGRAVATED ASSAULT	BURGLARY	LARCENY/ THEFT	CAR THEFT
Highest Crime Rates								
New York NY	126,626	300	788	13,192	19,089	14,738	64,550	13,969
Los Angeles CA	91,426	238	652	7,902	15,644	12,642	39,594	14,754
Chicago IL[2]	90,413	276	N/A	8,180	12,277	11,355	45,642	12,683
Houston TX	66,438	115	494	4,242	5,861	11,767	33,211	10,748
Dallas TX	53,654	109	299	3,923	4,238	9,888	25,981	9,216
Phoenix AZ	50,841	89	186	2,111	2,528	8,059	27,622	10,246
San Antonio TX	46,503	47	225	987	3,343	6,441	32,510	2,950
Philadelphia PA	44,779	129	529	4,427	5,203	5,364	21,786	7,341
Detroit MI	43,228	175	331	3,457	6,187	6,780	14,426	11,872
Baltimore MD	32,484	137	163	2,808	4,266	5,381	15,622	4,107

US Cities with Highest and Lowest Crime Rates (continued)

CITIES	CRIME INDEX TOTAL[1]	MURDER	FORCIBLE RAPE	ROBBERY	AGGRAVATED ASSAULT	BURGLARY	LARCENY/ THEFT	CAR THEFT
Lowest Crime Rates								
Mission Viejo CA	667	2	6	5	32	118	454	50
Simi Valley CA	840	1	5	12	53	175	507	87
Thousand Oaks CA	899	1	4	15	78	159	575	67
Amherst Town NY	984	0	0	11	29	74	813	57
Daly City CA	1,061	3	12	73	71	96	593	213
Sunnyvale CA	1,232	0	10	28	57	136	887	114
Stamford CT	1,439	1	9	44	62	136	1,000	187
Livonia MI	1,556	1	12	35	59	201	1,121	127
Ventura CA	1,568	2	18	46	81	273	1,031	117
Manchester NH	1,591	0	23	50	36	292	1,043	147

N/A stands for not available. [1]*Includes murder, forcible rape, robbery, aggravated assault, burglary, larceny/theft, and car theft.* [2]*Total excludes the crime of forcible rape.*

US Crime Rates by Type of Victim

This table covers rates of violent crime, personal theft, and property crime for the year 2000. The crime rates are based on the reports of victims, thus the table does not include rates for murder and manslaughter. For violent crime and personal theft, each crime rate represents victimizations per 1,000 people of age 12 or older. Property crime rates are related in victimizations per 1,000 households. Source: US Bureau of Justice Statistics.

PROFILE OF VICTIM	VIOLENT CRIME RATES					PERSONAL THEFT RATES
	ALL VIOLENT CRIME	RAPE/ SEXUAL ASSAULT	ROBBERY	ASSAULT AGGRAVATED	SIMPLE	
sex						
male	32.9	0.1[1]	4.5	8.3	19.9	1.0
female	23.2	2.1	2.0	3.2	15.8	1.4
age						
12–15	60.1	2.1	4.2	9.9	43.9	1.8
16–19	64.3	4.3	7.3	14.3	38.3	3.0
20–24	49.4	2.1	6.2	10.9	30.3	1.1[1]
25–34	34.8	1.3	3.9	6.8	22.7	1.5
35–49	21.8	0.8	2.7	4.7	13.7	0.9
50–64	13.7	0.4[1]	2.1	2.8	8.4	0.5[1]
65 or older	3.7	0.1[1]	0.7[1]	0.9	2.0	1.2
race/ethnicity						
white	27.1	1.1	2.7	5.4	17.9	1.1
black	35.3	1.2	7.2	7.7	19.2	1.9
other[2]	20.7	1.1[1]	2.8	5.2	11.5	1.8[1]
Hispanic[3]	28.4	0.5[1]	5.0	5.6	17.4	2.4
household income						
less than $7,500	60.3	5.2	7.1	14.7	33.4	2.3[1]
$7,500–$14,999	37.8	1.7	4.7	9.5	21.8	2.1
$15,000–$24,999	31.8	1.4	3.2	6.1	21.2	1.2
$25,000–$34,999	29.8	1.9	4.2	6.2	17.5	1.4
$35,000–$49,999	28.5	0.8	2.3	6.2	19.2	0.6[1]
$50,000–$74,999	23.7	1.0	3.6	3.8	15.3	1.0
$75,000 or more	22.3	0.2[1]	2.0	4.4	15.7	1.2

PROFILE OF VICTIM	PROPERTY CRIME RATES			
	ALL PROPERTY CRIME	BURGLARY	CAR THEFT	THEFT
race/ethnicity				
white	173.3	29.4	7.9	136.0
black	212.2	47.6	13.2	151.4
other[2]	171.3	32.4	10.4	128.6
Hispanic[3]	227.0	41.7	19.7	165.6

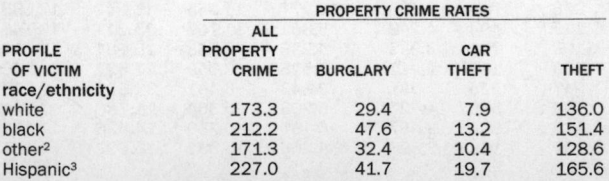

US Crime Rates by Type of Victim (continued)

PROPERTY CRIME RATES (CONTINUED)

PROFILE OF VICTIM	ALL PROPERTY CRIME	BURGLARY	CAR THEFT	THEFT
household income				
less than $7,500	220.9	61.7	7.9	151.2
$7,500–$14,999	167.1	41.1	9.1	116.8
$15,000–$24,999	193.1	39.3	9.9	143.8
$25,000–$34,999	192.2	33.3	9.5	149.4
$35,000–$49,999	192.9	32.0	9.6	151.4
$50,000–$74,999	181.9	24.0	10.0	147.9
$75,000 or more	197.2	27.7	7.0	162.5

[1]Based on 10 or fewer sample cases. [2]Asians, Native Hawaiians, other Pacific Islanders, Alaska Natives, and American Indians. [3]Hispanics may be of any race.

Total Arrests in the US

Estimates for the year 2000. Numbers may not add up to totals because of rounding. Source: Federal Bureau of Investigation, Uniform Crime Reports 2000.

TYPE OF CRIME	NUMBER OF ARRESTS	TYPE OF CRIME	NUMBER OF ARRESTS
violent crime		other crime types (continued)	
aggravated assault	478,417	drunkenness	637,554
robbery	106,130	fraud	345,732
forcible rape	27,469	vandalism	281,305
murder and nonnegligent manslaughter	13,227	weapons (carrying, possessing, etc.)	159,181
violent crime total	625,132	curfew and loitering law violations	154,711
		offenses against the family and children	147,663
property crime		runaways	141,975
larceny/theft	1,166,362	stolen property (buying, receiving, possessing)	118,641
burglary	289,844		
car theft	148,225	forgery and counterfeiting	108,654
arson	16,530	sex offenses (except forcible rape and prostitution)	93,399
property crime total	1,620,928	prostitution and commercialized vice	87,620
other crime types		vagrancy	32,542
drug abuse violations	1,579,566	embezzlement	18,952
driving under the influence	1,471,289	gambling	10,842
other assaults	1,312,169	suspicion (not included in total)	6,682
liquor laws	683,124	all other offenses	3,710,434
disorderly conduct	638,740	total arrests	13,980,297

US State and Federal Prison Population

Source: US Bureau of Justice Statistics.

STATE	NUMBER OF PRISONERS				% CHANGE (31 DEC 2000 TO 30 JUNE 2001)
	31 DEC 1980	31 DEC 1990	31 DEC 2000	30 JUNE 2001	
Alabama	6,543	15,665	26,225	27,286	+4.0
Alaska[1]	822	2,622	4,173	4,197	+0.6
Arizona[2]	4,372	14,261	26,510	27,136	+2.4
Arkansas	2,911	7,322	11,915	12,332	+3.5
California	24,569	97,309	163,001	163,965	+0.6
Colorado	2,620	7,071	16,833	17,122	+1.7
Connecticut[1]	4,308	10,500	18,355	18,875	+2.8
Delaware[1]	1,474	3,471	6,921	7,122	+2.9
District of Columbia[1]	3,145	9,947	7,456	5,388	-27.7
Florida[2]	20,735	44,387	71,319	72,007	+1.0
Georgia[2]	12,178	22,411	44,232	45,363	+2.6
Hawaii[1]	985	2,533	5,053	5,412	+7.1
Idaho	817	1,901	5,535	5,688	+2.8
Illinois	11,899	27,516	45,281	45,629	+0.8
Indiana	6,683	12,736	20,125	20,576	+2.2
Iowa[2]	2,481	3,967	7,955	8,101	+1.8
Kansas	2,494	5,775	8,344	8,543	+2.4
Kentucky	3,588	9,023	14,919	15,400	+3.2

US State and Federal Prison Population (continued)

	NUMBER OF PRISONERS			% CHANGE (31 DEC 2000 TO
STATE	31 DEC 1980	31 DEC 1990	31 DEC 2000	30 JUNE 2001	30 JUNE 2001)
Louisiana	8,889	18,599	35,207	35,494	+0.8
Maine	814	1,523	1,679	1,693	+0.8
Maryland	7,731	17,848	23,538	23,970	+1.8
Massachusetts	3,185	8,345	10,722	10,734	+0.1
Michigan	15,124	34,267	47,718	48,371	+1.4
Minnesota	2,001	3,176	6,238	6,514	+4.4
Mississippi	3,902	8,375	20,241	20,672	+2.1
Missouri	5,726	14,943	27,382	28,167	+2.9
Montana	739	1,425	3,105	3,250	+4.7
Nebraska	1,446	2,403	3,895	3,944	+1.3
Nevada	1,839	5,322	10,063	10,291	+2.3
New Hampshire	326	1,342	2,257	2,323	+2.9
New Jersey	5,884	21,128	29,784	28,108	−5.6
New Mexico	1,279	3,187	5,342	5,288	−1.0
New York	21,815	54,895	70,198	69,158	−1.5
North Carolina	15,513	18,411	31,532	31,142	−1.2
North Dakota	253	483	1,076	1,080	+0.4
Ohio	13,489	31,822	45,833	45,684	−0.3
Oklahoma	4,796	12,285	23,181	23,139	−0.2
Oregon	3,177	6,492	10,580	11,077	+4.7
Pennsylvania	8,171	22,290	36,847	37,105	+0.7
Rhode Island[1]	813	2,392	3,286	3,147	−4.2
South Carolina	7,862	17,319	21,778	22,267	+2.2
South Dakota	635	1,341	2,616	2,673	+2.2
Tennessee	7,022	10,388	22,166	23,168	+4.5
Texas	29,892	50,042	166,719	164,465	−1.4
Utah	932	2,496	5,632	5,440	−3.4
Vermont[1]	480	1,049	1,697	1,782	+5.0
Virginia	8,920	17,593	30,168	30,473	+1.0
Washington	4,399	7,995	14,915	15,242	+2.2
West Virginia	1,257	1,565	3,856	4,130	+7.1
Wisconsin	3,980	7,465	20,612	20,931	+1.5
Wyoming	534	1,110	1,680	1,679	−0.1
state	305,458	708,393	1,245,695	1,252,743	+0.6
federal	24,363	65,526	145,416	152,788	+5.1
US total	329,821	773,919	1,391,111	1,405,531	+1.0

[1]*Jails and prisons are part of an integrated system. Data include total jail and prison population.*   [2]*Population figures are based on custody counts.*

Death Penalty Sentences in the US

This table excludes military and federal sentences and executions. Sources: US Bureau of Justice Statistics; Death Penalty Information Center; NAACP Legal Defense and Educational Fund, Inc.

STATE	EXECUTIONS 1977–2000[1]	2001	PRISONERS UNDER DEATH SENTENCE (AS OF 1 APR 2002)[2]	SOME DEATH PENALTY CRIMES
Alabama	23	0	187	intentional murder[3]
Alaska	—	—	—	no death penalty
Arizona	22	0	129	1st-degree murder[3]
Arkansas	23	1	41	capital murder[3]; treason
California	8	1	606	1st-degree murder[3]; treason; train wrecking
Colorado	1	0	5	1st-degree murder[3]; treason
Connecticut	0	0	7	capital felony (9 types of aggravated murder)
Delaware	11	2	20	1st-degree murder[3]
District of Columbia	—	—	—	no death penalty
Florida	50	1	383	1st-degree murder; felonious murder; capital drug trafficking; capital sexual battery
Georgia	23	4	124	murder; treason; aircraft hijacking; kidnapping[4]
Hawaii	—	—	—	no death penalty
Idaho	1	0	21	1st-degree murder[3]; aggravated kidnapping
Illinois	12	0	175	1st-degree murder[3]
Indiana	7	2	39	murder[3]
Iowa	—	—	—	no death penalty
Kansas	0	0	4	capital murder[3]

Death Penalty Sentences in the US (continued)

STATE	EXECUTIONS 1977-2000[1]	2001	PRISONERS UNDER DEATH SENTENCE (AS OF 1 APR 2002)[2]	SOME DEATH PENALTY CRIMES
Kentucky	2	0	41	murder[3]; aggravated kidnapping
Louisiana	26	0	93	1st-degree murder; treason; rape[5]
Maine	—	—	—	no death penalty
Maryland	3	0	16	1st-degree murder[6]
Massachusetts	—	—	—	no death penalty
Michigan	—	—	—	no death penalty
Minnesota	—	—	—	no death penalty
Mississippi	4	0	68	capital murder; aircraft hijacking
Missouri	46	7	72	1st-degree murder
Montana	2	0	6	capital murder[3]; capital sexual assault
Nebraska	3	0	7	1st-degree murder[3]
Nevada	8	1	88	1st-degree murder[3]
New Hampshire	0	0	0	capital murder (6 types)
New Jersey	0	0	16	murder by one's own conduct; contract murder; solicitation[7]
New Mexico	0	1	4	1st-degree murder[3]
New York	0	0	6	1st-degree murder[3]
North Carolina	16	5	222	1st-degree murder
North Dakota	—	—	—	no death penalty
Ohio	1	1	204	murder[3]
Oklahoma	30	18	119	1st-degree murder[3]
Oregon	2	0	30	murder3
Pennsylvania	3	0	247	1st-degree murder[3]
Rhode Island	—	—	—	no death penalty
South Carolina	25	0	77	murder[3]
South Dakota	0	0	5	1st-degree murder[3]; aggravated kidnapping
Tennessee	1	0	105	1st-degree murder[3]
Texas	239	17	457	criminal homicide[3]
Utah	6	0	11	murder[3]
Vermont	—	—	—	no death penalty
Virginia	81	2	28	1st-degree murder[3]
Washington	3	1	14	1st-degree murder[3]
West Virginia	—	—	—	no death penalty
Wisconsin	—	—	—	no death penalty
Wyoming	1	0	2	1st-degree murder
totals	683	64	3,679	

[1]In 1976 the US Supreme Court ruled that capital punishment was constitutionally legal. [2]In mid-2002 the Supreme Court ruled that juries, not judges, must make decisions determining death penalty cases and that it was unconstitutional to execute mentally retarded offenders. These two decisions could reduce the number of people sentenced to death. [3]With aggravating factors or circumstances. [4]With bodily injury or ransom when the victim dies. [5]Aggravated rape of a victim under 12. [6]Premeditated or committed during the act of a felony, and that meets certain death penalty requirements. [7]By command or threat in the act of a narcotics conspiracy.

Directors of the Federal Bureau of Investigation (FBI)

The FBI evolved from an unnamed force appointed by Attorney General Charles J. Bonaparte on 26 Jul 1908. It is the unit of the Department of Justice responsible for investigating foreign intelligence and terrorist activities and violations of federal criminal law. The president appoints the director of the FBI with confirmation from the Senate. A director's term may not exceed 10 years.

NAME	DATES OF SERVICE
Stanley Finch	26 Jul 1908–30 Apr 1912
Alexander Bruce Bielaski	30 Apr 1912–10 Feb 1919
William E. Allen (acting)	10 Feb 1919–30 Jun 1919
William J. Flynn	1 Jul 1919–21 Aug 1921
William J. Burns	22 Aug 1921–14 Jun 1924
J. Edgar Hoover	10 May 1924–2 May 1972
L. Patrick Gray (acting)	3 May 1972–27 Apr 1973
William D. Ruckelshaus (acting)	30 Apr 1973–9 Jul 1973

NAME	DATES OF SERVICE
Clarence M. Kelley	9 Jul 1973–15 Feb 1978
William H. Webster	23 Feb 1978–25 May 1987
John Otto (acting)	26 May 1987–2 Nov 1987
William S. Sessions	2 Nov 1987–19 Jul 1993
Floyd I. Clarke (acting)	19 Jul 1993–1 Sep 1993
Louis J. Freeh	1 Sep 1993–25 Jun 2001
Thomas J. Pickard (acting)	25 Jun 2001–4 Sep 2001
Robert S. Mueller, III	4 Sep 2001–

Social and Health Statistics

Family

Average Family Size, 1950–2000
Source: US Census Bureau

YEAR	NUMBER OF FAMILIES ('000)	PEOPLE PER FAMILY (AVERAGE)	YEAR	NUMBER OF FAMILIES ('000)	PEOPLE PER FAMILY (AVERAGE)	YEAR	NUMBER OF FAMILIES ('000)	PEOPLE PER FAMILY (AVERAGE)
1950	39,303	3.54	1970	51,586	3.58	1990	66,090	3.17
1955	41,951	3.59	1975	55,712	3.42	1995	69,305	3.19
1960	45,111	3.67	1980	59,550	3.29	2000	72,025	3.17
1965	47,956	3.70	1985	62,706	3.23			

US Population by Age
Source: US Census Bureau decennial census of 1 Apr 2000.

AGE	POPULATION NUMBER	(%)	AGE	POPULATION NUMBER	(%)
under 5 years	19,175,798	6.8	65 to 74 years	18,390,986	6.5
5 to 9 years	20,549,505	7.3	75 to 84 years	12,361,180	4.4
10 to 14 years	20,528,072	7.3	85 years and over	4,239,587	1.5
15 to 19 years	20,219,890	7.2	total population	281,421,906	100.0
20 to 24 years	18,964,001	6.7			
25 to 34 years	39,891,724	14.2	under 18 years	72,293,812	25.7
35 to 44 years	45,148,527	16.0	18 years and over	209,128,094	74.3
45 to 54 years	37,677,952	13.4	21 years and over	196,899,193	70.0
55 to 59 years	13,469,237	4.8	62 years and over	41,256,029	14.7
60 to 64 years	10,805,447	3.8	65 years and over	34,991,753	12.4

Living Arrangements of Children Under 18 in the US
Children under 18 years of age, March 2000. Numbers in thousands ('000). Source: US Census Bureau

	YEARS OF AGE			
LIVING IN HOUSEHOLD WITH:	UNDER 6	6–11	12–17	UNDER 18
both parents	16,590	17,024	16,181	49,795
mother only	5,118	5,774	5,270	16,162
father only	1,020	1,036	1,002	3,058
neither parent	846	922	1,214	2,981
totals	23,580	24,761	23,671	72,012

Children Living Below the Poverty Level

This table covers children under the age of 18 (as of March of the following year). Hispanics may be of any race. All numbers are in thousands ('000). Statistics that are not available are noted N/A. Source: US Census Bureau. For the definition of the poverty level, see <www.census.gov/hhes/poverty/povdef.html>.

	% OF CHILDREN BELOW THE POVERTY LEVEL					NUMBER OF CHILDREN BELOW THE POVERTY LEVEL				
YEAR	ALL	WHITE	BLACK	ASIAN/ PACIFIC ISLANDER	HISPANIC	ALL	WHITE	BLACK	ASIAN/ PACIFIC ISLANDER	HISPANIC
1975	17.1	12.7	41.7	N/A	N/A	11,104	6,927	3,925	N/A	N/A
1976	16.0	11.6	40.6	N/A	30.2	10,273	6,189	3,787	N/A	1,443
1977	16.2	11.6	41.8	N/A	28.3	10,288	6,097	3,888	N/A	1,422
1978	15.9	11.3	41.5	N/A	27.6	9,931	5,831	3,830	N/A	1,384
1979	16.4	11.8	41.2	N/A	28.0	10,377	6,193	3,833	N/A	1,535
1980	18.3	13.9	42.3	N/A	33.2	11,543	7,181	3,961	N/A	1,749
1981	20.0	15.2	45.2	N/A	35.9	12,505	7,785	4,237	N/A	1,925
1982	21.9	17.0	47.6	N/A	39.5	13,647	8,678	4,472	N/A	2,181
1983	22.3	17.5	46.7	N/A	38.1	13,911	8,862	4,398	N/A	2,312
1984	21.5	16.7	46.6	N/A	39.2	13,420	8,472	4,413	N/A	2,376
1985	20.7	16.2	43.6	N/A	40.3	13,010	8,253	4,157	N/A	2,606
1986	20.5	16.1	43.1	N/A	37.7	12,876	8,209	4,148	N/A	2,507
1987	20.3	15.3	45.1	23.5	39.3	12,843	7,788	4,385	455	2,670
1988	19.5	14.5	43.5	24.1	37.6	12,455	7,435	4,296	474	2,631

Children Living Below the Poverty Level (continued)

	% OF CHILDREN BELOW THE POVERTY LEVEL					NUMBER OF CHILDREN BELOW THE POVERTY LEVEL				
YEAR	ALL	WHITE	BLACK	ASIAN/ PACIFIC ISLANDER	HISPANIC	ALL	WHITE	BLACK	ASIAN/ PACIFIC ISLANDER	HISPANIC
1989	19.6	14.8	43.7	19.8	36.2	12,590	7,599	4,375	392	2,603
1990	20.6	15.9	44.8	17.6	38.4	13,431	8,232	4,550	374	2,865
1991	21.8	16.8	45.9	17.5	40.4	14,341	8,848	4,755	360	3,094
1992	22.3	17.4	46.6	16.4	40.0	15,294	9,399	5,106	363	3,637
1993	22.7	17.8	46.1	18.2	40.9	15,727	9,752	5,125	375	3,873
1994	21.8	16.9	43.8	18.3	41.5	15,289	9,346	4,906	318	4,075
1995	20.8	16.2	41.9	19.5	40.0	14,665	8,981	4,761	564	4,080
1996	20.5	16.3	39.9	19.5	40.3	14,463	9,044	4,519	571	4,237
1997	19.9	16.1	37.2	20.3	36.8	14,113	8,990	4,225	628	3,972
1998	18.9	15.1	36.7	18.0	34.4	13,467	8,443	4,151	564	3,837
1999	16.9	13.5	33.1	11.8	30.3	12,109	7,568	3,759	361	3,506
2000	16.1	12.9	30.6	14.4	28.0	11,553	7,283	3,487	447	3,328

Child Care Arrangements in the US

This table is based on sample surveys of households with children 3–5 years old who were not yet in kindergarten. Day care centers, Head Start programs, preschools, prekindergarten, and nursery schools were included as center-based programs. The columns do not add to 100% because some children participated in more than one type of nonparental arrangement. Detail may not add to totals due to rounding. Source: US National Center for Education Statistics.

YEAR OF SURVEY	CHILDREN NUMBER	(%)	UNDER PARENTAL CARE (%)	UNDER A RELATIVE'S CARE (%)	UNDER A NONRELATIVE'S CARE (%)	IN A CENTER-BASED PROGRAM (%)
1991	8,428,000	100.0	31.0	16.9	14.8	52.8
1995	9,232,000	100.0	25.9	19.4	16.9	55.1
1999	8,525,000	100.0	23.1	22.8	16.1	59.7

details from the 1999 survey

FEATURE	CHILDREN NUMBER	(%)	UNDER PARENTAL CARE (%)	UNDER A RELATIVE'S CARE (%)	UNDER A NONRELATIVE'S CARE (%)	IN A CENTER-BASED PROGRAM (%)
age						
3 years old	3,814,000	44.7	30.8	24.4	16.2	45.7
4 years old	3,705,000	43.5	17.7	22.0	15.9	69.6
5 years old	1,006,000	11.8	13.5	20.2	16.1	76.5
race/ethnic group						
white, non-Hispanic	5,389,000	63.2	23.2	18.8	19.4	60.0
black, non-Hispanic	1,214,000	14.2	13.7	33.4	7.4	73.2
Hispanic	1,376,000	16.1	33.4	26.5	12.7	44.2
other	547,000	6.4	16.6	30.2	10.4	66.1
household income						
less than $10,001	1,064,000	12.5	27.5	27.5	13.2	55.9
$10,001–20,000	1,342,000	15.7	27.7	29.4	13.7	51.1
$20,001–30,000	1,333,000	15.6	29.8	27.1	12.5	51.4
$30,001–40,000	1,098,000	12.9	24.8	22.5	14.7	55.4
$40,001–50,000	848,000	9.9	23.1	21.3	13.6	60.2
$50,001–75,000	1,397,000	16.4	17.8	17.3	21.0	66.6
more than $75,000	1,443,000	16.9	13.1	15.9	21.3	74.6

Children in the US Living with Non-Parents

Children under 18 years of age, March 2000. Numbers in thousands ('000). Source: US Census Bureau

LIVING ARRANGEMENT	UNDER 6	6–11	12–17	UNDER 18
		YEARS OF AGE		
with grandparent	394	476	491	1,359
with other relative	228	222	350	799
in foster home	63	61	95	219
with other nonrelative of householder	162	162	278	603
in group quarters	6	4	4	15

US Adoptions of Foreign-Born Children

Adoptions of foreign children by US citizens are tracked by the number of immigrant visas issued to orphans entering the United States. Source: US Department of State

TOP 10 COUNTRIES OF ORIGIN	ADOPTIONS FISCAL YEAR 2001	2000	TOP 10 COUNTRIES OF ORIGIN	ADOPTIONS FISCAL YEAR 2001	2000	TOTAL FOREIGN ADOPTIONS (CALENDAR YEAR)	
1. China	4,681	5,053	6. Romania	782	1,122	1995	8,987
2. Russia	4,279	4,269	7. Vietnam	737	724	1996	10,641
3. South Korea	1,870	1,794	8. Kazakhstan	672	399	1997	12,743
4. Guatemala	1,609	1,518	9. India	543	503	1998	15,774
5. Ukraine	1,246	659	10. Cambodia	407	402	1999	16,363
						2000	17,718
						2001	19,237

US Nursing Home Population

The data in this table were gathered in 1999 through interviews conducted by the National Nursing Home Survey. Residents of more than one race were recorded in the "black and other" category. Numbers may not add to totals because of rounding. N/A indicates that reliable numbers were not available. Source: US National Center for Health Statistics.

AGE AT INTERVIEW	TOTAL RESIDENTS	%	GENDER MALE	%	FEMALE	%
under 65	158,700	9.8	80,000	17.5	78,700	6.7
65–74	194,800	12.0	84,100	18.4	110,700	9.5
75–84	517,600	31.8	149,500	32.7	368,100	31.5
85 and older	757,100	46.5	144,200	31.5	612,900	52.4
total	**1,628,300**	**100.0**	**457,900**	**100.0**	**1,170,400**	**100.0**

	WHITE	%	RACE BLACK AND OTHER	%	BLACK	%	UNKNOWN
under 65	115,400	8.3	39,300	18.2	32,800	18.4	N/A
65–74	157,300	11.3	35,800	16.6	30,300	17.0	N/A
75–84	440,600	31.6	71,100	32.9	58,700	32.8	N/A
85 and older	681,700	48.9	69,700	32.3	56,900	31.8	N/A
total	**1,394,400**	**100.0**	**215,900**	**100.0**	**178,700**	**100.0**	**17,400**

	NORTHWEST	%	RESIDENT LOCATION MIDWEST	%	SOUTH	%	WEST	%
under 65	34,200	8.9	45,000	9.0	51,300	9.7	28,200	13.1
65–74	46,400	12.1	58,900	11.8	63,400	11.9	26,100	12.1
75–84	118,500	30.9	153,200	30.8	179,100	33.7	66,800	31.1
85 and older	184,300	48.1	241,100	48.4	237,700	44.7	94,000	43.7
total	**383,400**	**100.0**	**498,200**	**100.0**	**531,500**	**100.0**	**215,200**	**100.0**

Unmarried-Couple Households in the US

Data based on Current Population Survey except for census years of 1960 and 1970. Census 2000 data shown separately. Numbers in thousands ('000). Source: US Census Bureau

YEAR	TOTAL US HOUSEHOLDS	UNMARRIED-COUPLE HOUSEHOLDS (OPPOSITE SEX)	% OF TOTAL HOUSEHOLDS	NO CHILDREN UNDER 15	WITH CHILDREN UNDER 15
1960 census	52,799	439	0.8	242	197
1970 census	63,401	523	0.8	327	196
1980	80,776	1,589	2.0	1,159	431
1985	86,789	1,983	2.3	1,380	603
1990	93,347	2,856	3.1	1,966	891
1995	98,990	3,668	3.7	2,349	1,319
1996	99,627	3,958	3.9	2,516	1,442
1997	101,018	4,130	4.0	2,660	1,470
1998	102,528	4,236	4.1	2,716	1,520
1999	103,874	4,486	4.3	2,981	1,505
2000	104,705	4,736	4.5	3,061	1,675

Unmarried-Couple Households in the US (continued)

UNMARRIED-COUPLE HOUSEHOLDS	2000 CENSUS
male householder/female partner	2,615
male householder/male partner	301
female householder/female partner	293
female householder/male partner	2,266
unmarried-couple households	**5,475**
total households	105,480

Marriage Statistics, 1960–2001

Beginning in 1996, the collection of detailed data was suspended at the National Center for Health Statistics. Information that is not available is indicated with an N/A. Information is subject to monthly reporting variation and may differ from previously published statistics. Statistics for 1980 and later include nonlicensed marriages registered in California. Source: US National Center for Health Statistics.

			RATE PER 1,000 POPULATION			
		TOTAL	MEN, 15	WOMEN, 15	UNMARRIED WOMEN	
YEAR	NUMBER	POPULATION	AND OVER	AND OVER	15 AND OVER	15 TO 44
1960	1,523,000	8.5	25.4	24.0	73.5	148.0
1965	1,800,000	9.3	27.9	26.0	75.0	144.3
1970	2,158,802	10.6	31.1	28.4	76.5	140.2
1975	2,152,662	10.0	27.9	25.6	66.9	118.5
1980	2,390,252	10.6	28.5	26.1	61.4	102.6
1985	2,412,625	10.1	27.0	24.9	57.0	94.9
1990	2,443,489	9.8	26.0	24.1	54.5	91.3
1995	2,336,000	8.9	N/A	N/A	50.8	83.0
2000	2,398,000	8.7	N/A	N/A	N/A	N/A
2001	2,344,000	8.5	N/A	N/A	N/A	N/A

Divorce Statistics, 1960–2001

Beginning in 1996, the collection of detailed data was suspended at the National Center for Health Statistics. Information that is not available is indicated with an N/A. Since 1998, divorce rates exclude data for California, Colorado, Indiana, and Louisiana. Information is subject to monthly reporting variation and may differ from previously published statistics. Source: US National Center for Health Statistics.

		RATE PER 1,000 POPULATION				RATE PER 1,000 POPULATION	
	DIVORCES		MARRIED		DIVORCES		MARRIED
	AND	TOTAL	WOMEN, 15		AND	TOTAL	WOMEN, 15
YEAR	ANNULMENTS	POPULATION	AND OVER	YEAR	ANNULMENTS	POPULATION	AND OVER
1960	393,000	2.2	9.2	1985	1,190,000	5.0	21.7
1965	479,000	2.5	10.6	1990	1,182,000	4.7	20.9
1970	708,000	3.5	14.9	1995	1,169,000	4.4	19.8
1975	1,036,000	4.8	20.3	2000	N/A	4.1	N/A
1980	1,189,000	5.2	22.6	2001	N/A	4.0	N/A

United States Education

Educational Attainment by Gender and Race

For people 25 years and older. Percentage rates for 1960, 1970, and 1980 are based on sample data from the decennial censuses. Rates for 1990 and 2000 are based on the Current Population Survey. N/A means not available. Source: US Census Bureau.

Percentage who had graduated from high school[1]

	ALL RACES[2]		WHITE		BLACK		HISPANIC[3]		ASIAN/PACIFIC ISLANDER	
CENSUS	MALE	FEMALE	MALE	FEMALE	MALE	FEMALE	MALE	FEMALE	MALE	FEMALE
1960	39.5	42.5	41.6	44.7	18.2	21.8	N/A	N/A	N/A	N/A
1970	51.9	52.8	54.0	55.0	30.1	32.5	37.9	34.2	N/A	N/A
1980	67.3	65.8	69.6	68.1	50.8	51.5	67.3	65.8	N/A	N/A
1990	77.7	77.5	79.1	79.0	65.8	66.5	50.3	51.3	84.0	77.2
2000	84.2	84.0	84.8	85.0	78.7	78.3	56.6	57.5	88.2	83.4

Educational Attainment by Gender and Race (continued)

Percentage who had graduated from college[1]

CENSUS	ALL RACES[2]		WHITE		BLACK		HISPANIC[3]		ASIAN/PACIFIC ISLANDER	
	MALE	FEMALE	MALE	FEMALE	MALE	FEMALE	MALE	FEMALE	MALE	FEMALE
1960	9.7	5.8	10.3	6.0	2.8	3.3	N/A	N/A	N/A	N/A
1970	13.5	8.1	14.4	8.4	4.2	4.6	7.8	4.3	N/A	N/A
1980	20.1	12.8	21.3	13.3	8.4	8.3	9.4	6.0	N/A	N/A
1990	24.4	18.4	25.3	19.0	11.9	10.8	9.8	8.7	44.9	35.4
2000	27.8	23.6	28.5	23.9	16.3	16.7	10.7	10.6	47.6	40.7

[1]Through 1990, finished four years or more of high school and four years or more of college.   [2]Includes races not shown separately in the table.   [3]Hispanics may be of any race.

Libraries and Museums

Public Libraries in the US

Information from public libraries reporting for fiscal year 2000. The number of libraries includes central and branch libraries. Data for operating income and the number of books and serial volumes are given in thousands ('000). The circulation percentages for children's materials are given as a percentage of total circulation. N/A means not available. The totals used at the bottom of the table were those provided by the source. Source: National Center for Education Statistics.

STATE	NUMBER OF LIBRARIES	OPERATING INCOME ($)	TOTAL NUMBER OF BOOKS AND SERIAL VOLUMES	AVERAGE NUMBER OF INTERNET TERMINALS PER LIBRARY	CIRCULATION OF CHILDREN'S MATERIALS (%)
Alabama	275	64,927	8,600	4.2	33.3
Alaska	104	24,458	2,224	5.7	35.7
Arizona	170	110,803	8,723	8.2	35.2
Arkansas	209	38,531	5,408	4.0	27.9
California	1,065	830,267	66,193	7.6	40.2
Colorado	243	158,704	10,863	5.9	37.2
Connecticut	242	137,326	14,238	4.8	37.6
Delaware	35	14,513	1,445	4.5	38.7
District of Columbia	27	25,669	2,385	6.2	32.6
Florida	466	355,388	29,222	10.0	28.8
Georgia	367	143,396	14,869	9.1	39.9
Hawaii	50	22,789	3,194	3.3	32.8
Idaho	142	23,811	3,506	4.1	41.2
Illinois	786	481,279	41,014	3.9	41.1
Indiana	426	224,581	21,730	6.6	36.3
Iowa	559	70,422	11,595	2.3	37.8
Kansas	370	70,936	10,207	4.3	40.8
Kentucky	190	72,818	7,856	6.2	30.5
Louisiana	327	112,091	10,608	5.1	28.7
Maine	278	26,059	5,683	2.4	36.8
Maryland	179	174,458	15,387	11.1	39.2
Massachusetts	489	205,569	30,238	5.5	39.1
Michigan	655	288,142	26,753	5.9	37.4
Minnesota	359	146,199	15,599	5.6	41.5
Mississippi	241	35,998	5,602	4.7	27.2
Missouri	359	146,528	22,697	4.8	37.5
Montana	107	16,021	2,638	3.4	34.1
Nebraska	255	34,635	5,605	2.9	43.1
Nevada	83	63,119	4,136	5.6	32.7
New Hampshire	237	33,217	5,506	2.0	40.5
New Jersey	452	299,426	30,593	6.6	38.0
New Mexico	99	29,416	4,108	5.3	35.2
New York	1,083	834,402	77,571	6.6	34.0
North Carolina	372	145,107	15,609	5.1	35.4
North Dakota	87	8,134	2,145	2.2	39.7
Ohio	716	680,401	47,122	7.1	33.6
Oklahoma	210	61,141	6,110	3.6	34.3
Oregon	206	108,554	8,346	4.8	31.8
Pennsylvania	631	235,416	26,351	6.7	36.8
Rhode Island	72	33,990	4,345	6.1	34.8

Public Libraries in the US (continued)

STATE	NUMBER OF LIBRARIES	OPERATING INCOME ($)	TOTAL NUMBER OF BOOKS AND SERIAL VOLUMES	AVERAGE NUMBER OF INTERNET TERMINALS PER LIBRARY	CIRCULATION OF CHILDREN'S MATERIALS (%)
South Carolina	183	71,918	8,055	6.2	38.9
South Dakota	139	13,618	2,703	2.6	34.8
Tennessee	280	73,891	9,747	7.6	37.1
Texas	816	294,967	35,040	8.0	37.9
Utah	105	54,114	5,756	4.9	41.7
Vermont	193	12,640	2,772	1.7	42.7
Virginia	334	178,385	18,378	4.7	35.8
Washington	322	218,086	16,561	7.5	31.3
West Virginia	175	N/A	4,814	4.7	29.0
Wisconsin	454	156,649	18,294	5.4	38.1
Wyoming	74	14,539	2,375	2.7	34.7
total	16,298	7,702,768	760,513	5.8	36.4

Selected Specialized Libraries in the United States

NAME	LOCATION	TYPE OF COLLECTION	WEB SITE
American Antiquarian Society	Worcester MA	American history	<www.americanantiquarian.org/index.htm>
American Philosophical Society	Philadelphia PA	history of science, medicine, and technology	<www.amphilsoc.org>
The Athenaeum of Philadelphia	Philadelphia PA	architecture, interior design	<www.philaathenaeum.org>
Boston Athenaeum	Boston MA	history, art, literature	<www.bostonathenaeum.org>
Dumbarton Oaks Research Library	Washington DC	Byzantine and pre-Columbian art, gardening	<www.doaks.org>
Folger Shakespeare Library	Washington DC	Shakespeare	<www.folger.edu/Home_02B.html>
Frick Art Reference Library	New York NY	Western art	<www.frick.org>
Hagley Museum and Library	Wilmington DE	American business and technology history	<www.hagley.lib.de.us/index.html>
The Huntington Library, Art Collections, and Botanical Gardens	San Marino CA	history, literature, science	<www.huntington.org>
John Carter Brown Library	Providence RI	history, humanities	<www.brown.edu/Facilities/John_Carter_Brown_Library>
The Library Company of Philadelphia	Philadelphia PA	American history and culture through end of 19th century	<www.librarycompany.org>
Library of Congress	Washington DC	diverse knowledge	<www.loc.gov>
Linda Hall Library	Kansas City MO	science, engineering, technology	<www.lindahall.org>
The Morgan Library	New York NY	rare manuscripts, books, and prints	<www.morganlibrary.org/index.html>
National Agricultural Library	Beltsville MD	agriculture	<www.nal.usda.gov>
National Archives	College Park MD	American history	<www.archives.gov>
National Library of Education	Washington DC	education	<www.ed.gov/NLE>
National Library of Medicine	Bethesda MD	medical science	<www.nlm.nih.gov>
New York Academy of Medicine	New York NY	medical science	<www.nyam.org>
The Newberry Library	Chicago IL	humanities	<www.newberry.org/nl/newberryhome.html>
Smithsonian Institution Libraries	Washington DC	science, history, art, culture	<www.sil.si.edu>
Winterthur Museum, Garden, and Library	Winterthur DE	art, design, American material culture	<www.winterthur.org>
YIVO Institute for Jewish Research	New York NY	Jewish history and culture	<www.yivoinstitute.org>

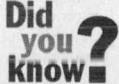

Did you know? Upon the death of Thomas Paine, most US newspapers reprinted the obituary notice from the *New York Citizen*, which read in part: "He had lived long, did some good and much harm." This remained the verdict of history for more than a century following his death, but eventually the tide turned, and on 18 May 1952, Paine's bust was placed in the New York University Hall of Fame.

National Spelling Bee

A spelling bee is a contest or game in which players attempt to spell correctly and aloud words assigned them by an impartial judge. Competition may be individual, with players eliminated when they misspell a word and the last remaining player being the winner, or between teams, the winner being the team with the most players remaining at the close of the contest. The spelling bee is an old custom that was revived in schools in the United States in the late 19th century and enjoyed a great vogue there and in Great Britain. In the US, local, regional, and national competitions continue to be held annually. The US National Spelling Bee was begun by the *Louisville Courier-Journal* newspaper in 1925, and it was taken over by Scripps Howard, Inc., in 1941. The National Spelling Bee was not held in 1943–45. To qualify, spellers must meet nine requirements, including that they have neither reached their 16th birthday nor passed beyond the eighth grade. National Spelling Bee Web site: <www.spellingbee.com>.

YEAR	CHAMPION & SPONSOR	WINNING WORD
1949	Kim Calvin, *Canton Repository* (Ohio)	dulcimer
1950	Diana Reynard, *Cleveland Press* (Ohio)	
	Colquitt Dean, *Atlanta Journal* (Georgia)	meticulosity
1951	Irving Belz, *Memphis Press-Scimitar* (Tennessee)	insouciant
1952	Doris Ann Hall, *Winston-Salem Journal,* (North Carolina)	vignette
1953	Elizabeth Hess, *Arizona Republic* (Phoenix AZ)	soubrette
1954	William Cashore, *Norristown Times Herald* (Pennsylvania)	transept
1955	Sandra Sloss, *St. Louis Globe-Democrat* (Missouri)	crustaceology
1956	Melody Sachko, *The Pittsburgh Press* (Pennsylvania)	condominium
1957	Sandra Owen, *Canton Repository* (Ohio)	
	Dana Bennett, *Rocky Mountain News* (Denver CO)	schappe
1958	Jolitta Schlehuber, *Topeka Daily Capital* (Kansas)	syllepsis
1959	Joel Montgomery, *Rocky Mountain News* (Denver CO)	catamaran
1960	Henry Feldman, *Knoxville News-Sentinel* (Tennessee)	eudaemonic
1961	John Capehart, *Tulsa Tribune* (Oklahoma)	smaragdine
1962	Nettie Crawford, *El Paso Herald-Post* (Texas)	
	Michael Day, *St. Louis Democrat* (Missouri)	esquamulose
1963	Glen Van Slyke III, *The Knoxville News-Sentinel* (Tennessee)	equipage
1964	William Kerek, *Akron Beacon Journal* (Ohio)	sycophant
1965	Michael Kerpan, Jr., *Tulsa Tribune* (Oklahoma)	eczema
1966	Robert A. Wake, *Houston Chronicle* (Texas)	ratoon
1967	Jennifer Reinke, *The Omaha World-Herald* (Nebraska)	chihuahua
1968	Robert L. Walters, *The Topeka Daily Capital* (Kansas)	abalone
1969	Susan Yoachum, *Dallas Morning News* (Texas)	interlocutory
1970	Libby Childress, *Winston-Salem Journal & Sentinel* (North Carolina)	croissant
1971	Jonathan Knisely, *Phildelphia Bulletin* (Pennsylvania)	shalloon
1972	Robin Kral, *Lubbock Avalanche-Journal* (Texas)	màcerate
1973	Barrie Trinkle, *Fort Worth Press* (Texas)	vouchsafe
1974	Julie Ann Junkin, *Birminghan Post-Herald* (Alabama)	hydrophyte
1975	Hugh Tosteson, *San Juan Star* (Puerto Rico)	incisor
1976	Tim Kneale, *Syracuse Herald Journal-American* (New York)	narcolepsy
1977	John Paola, *The Pittsburgh Press* (Pennsylvania)	cambist
1978	Peg McCarthy, *The Topeka Capital-Journal* (Kansas)	deification
1979	Katie Kerwin, *Rocky Mountain News* (Denver CO)	maculature
1980	Jacques Bailly, *Rocky Mountain News* (Denver CO)	elucubrate
1981	Paige Pipkin, *El Paso Herald-Post* (Texas)	sarcophagus
1982	Molly Dieveney, *Rocky Mountain News* (Denver CO)	psoriasis
1983	Blake Giddens, *El Paso Herald-Post* (Texas)	purim
1984	Daniel Greenblatt, *Loudoun Times-Mirror* (Virginia)	luge
1985	Balu Natarajan, *Chicago Tribune* (Illinois)	milieu
1986	Jon Pennington, *The Patriot News* (Harrisburg PA)	odontalgia
1987	Stephanie Petit, *The Pittsburgh Press* (Pennsylvania)	staphylococci
1988	Rageshree Ramachandran, *The Sacramento Bee* (California)	elegiacal
1989	Scott Isaacs, *Rocky Mountain News* (Denver CO)	spoliator
1990	Amy Marie Dimak, *The Seattle Times* (Washington)	fibranne
1991	Joanne Lagatta, *The Wisconsin State Journal* (Madison WI)	antipyretic
1992	Amanda Goad, *The Richmond News Leader* (Virginia)	lyceum
1993	Geoff Hooper, *The Commercial Appeal* (Memphis TN)	kamikaze
1994	Ned G. Andrews, *The Knoxville News-Sentinel* (Tennessee)	antediluvian
1995	Justin Tyler Carroll, *The Commercial Appeal* (Memphis TN)	xanthosis
1996	Wendy Guey, *The Palm Beach Post* (Florida)	vivisepulture
1997	Rebecca Sealfon, *Daily News* (New York NY)	euonym
1998	Jody-Anne Maxwell, Phillips & Phillips Stationery Suppliers, Ltd., (Kingston, Jamaica)	chiaroscurist
1999	Nupur Lala, *The Tampa Tribune* (Florida)	logorrhea
2000	George Abraham Thampy, *St. Louis Post-Dispatch* (Missouri)	demarche
2001	Sean Conley, *Aitkin Independent Age* (Minnesota)	succedaneum
2002	Pratyush Buddiga, *Rocky Mountain News* (Denver CO)	prospicience

Economics & Business

World Economy
Banking

The banking systems of the world share many similarities but have principal differences in the details of organization and technique. Banking systems may be classified in terms of their structure as unit banking, branch banking, or hybrids of the two. For example, unit banking prevails in the United States. In other countries, such as England and Wales, it is more usual to find a small number of large commercial banks, each operating a highly developed network of branches. Examples of hybrid systems include those of France, Germany, and India, where banks that are national in scope are supplemented by regional or local banks.

Unit banking: the United States
In the years following World War II, bank organization in the US was still passing through a phase of structural development that many other countries had completed decades earlier. Because the US Constitution permits both national and state governments to regulate banking, there were particular state mandates against branch banking that contributed to the proliferation of unit banks.

From the 1970s there was an acceleration in the evolution of American banking patterns. New financial institutions moved into traditional banking activities; at the same time, depository institutions began offering a fuller range of financial services. Rapid changes in the industry resulted in legislation to improve monetary control, remove impediments to competition, and to expand the availability of financial services to the public.

Branch banking: the United Kingdom
If the US banks can be taken as representative of a unit banking system, the British system is the prototype of branch banking. Its development was linked to the growth of transportation and communications, for otherwise banks cannot clear checks drawn on other banks and effect remittances speedily and efficiently. The Scots long favored branch banking (the Bank of Scotland was founded in 1695), though they were early hampered by poor communications and inadequate coinage.

As the Industrial Revolution progressed and as the size of businesses increased, the structure of English banking underwent a corresponding change. The growth in size of banks was also greatly encouraged by legislation that encouraged joint-stock ownership, beginning in 1020. The banking system in England and Wales evolved into its modern form before World War I, though there was to be a further degree of concentration in the years after World War II. By these means, British banks were able to attract deposits from all parts of the country and to spread the banking risk over a wide range of industries and areas.

Hybrid systems
A third group of banking systems is characterized by the existence of a small number of banks with branches throughout the country, holding a significant part of total deposits, along with a relatively large number of smaller banks that are regional or local in emphasis. Such systems exist in France, Germany, and India. Japan has a small number of large city banks with branch networks but a larger number of local banks.

France
In the years following World War II, banking activities in France were tightly controlled by the government through the Banque de France. However, deregulation in the last four decades of the century gradually reduced federal controls and led to a substantial increase in branch banking and bank account holders. The advent of the EU in the 1990s allowed the free movement of capital across country borders. In 1993 the Banque de France was granted independent staus, which freed it from state control.

Germany
An even more direct conflict between the forces favoring concentration and those working against it may be seen in Germany, where modern banking developed in the latter part of the 19th century and eventually became concentrated in Berlin. The Berlin banks built up a widespread network of branch offices, which were also used to establish and maintain industrial contacts throughout the country. Each of the big Berlin banks came to be associated with a group of provincial banks more or less under its control. At the same time, all of the banks, Berlin and provincial alike, expanded their business by opening branches.

During World War I the degree of centralization increased and continued during the financial crisis of 1931, resulting in further consolidation until the German banking system was dominated by three giants. Among the countervailing forces were the establishment of publicly owned banking institutions, such as the communal savings banks and their central institutions, the Girozentralen, which became of increasing importance after World War II.

German savings banks offer a wide range of services, especially to lower income groups and smaller businesses, and now compete in wholesale banking as well. The large commercial banks have concerned themselves more with big business and with wealthy individuals. The Big Three (the Deutsche Bank, the Dresdner Bank, and the Commerzbank) remain unchallenged in stock exchange and foreign banking business. Regional and private banks are often within the sphere of influence of the Big Three. While banking in Germany remains a hybrid system, a trend toward greater concentration is evident.

India
Until the 1950s, banking in India was carried on by a large number of banks, many of them quite small. India remains agricultural in parts, with an economic and social structure based on the village, and so banking and credit was handled by the so-called indigenous banker and the village moneylender. Al-

though their influence has been greatly reduced in recent years, the indigenous bankers offer genuine banking services: accepting deposits and remitting funds; making loans quickly and with a minimum of formality; and making use of the *hundi*, a credit instrument in the form of a bill of exchange.

Efforts to eliminate the local moneylender resulted in changes requiring banks to open branches in rural areas. This caused many smaller banks to close down, leaving a few dozen large national and commerical banks by the end of the 20th century. Banking services are also provided by chit funds, which accept and pay interest on monthly deposits against which it is possible to draw only by way of loan, and by Nidhis, mutual loan societies that have developed into semibanking institutions but deal only with their member shareholders.

The main path of banking development in India is the expansion of bank branches into the underbanked rural areas and to increase lending to weak areas of the economy. The ultimate objective is to encourage the mobilization of deposits on a massive scale throughout the country, a formidable challenge in a country of more than 500,000 villages.

Japan

Banking business in Japan is largely concentrated in the hands of the big banks (some of which are specialized), though a number of small banks still survive. The principal classes of banks are city banks and regional banks, but it should be noted that the distinction has no legal basis, though they are separately supervised. Both belong to the Federation of Bankers' Associations of Japan.

Between World War II and the 1990s Japanese banking enjoyed notable stability. The decline in overall economic performance of the past decade, exacerbated by burdensome bad loans and a persistent lack of profitability, led to changes in the Japanese banking system including financial deregulation, increased competition, and greater governmental intervention.

Islamic banking

In contrast to people in the West, many in the Islamic world look askance at some common practices of capitalism, notably giving or receiving interest payments and speculating on futures. The prohibition on collecting interest is based on the teachings of the Qur'an (Koran), the holy book of Islam, which prohibits the practice of *riba*, or usury. In Saudi Arabia, for example, banks charge service fees on loans but are disallowed from charging interest. Islamic alternatives to Western banking include interest-free loans, informal money-changers, and a form of profit-sharing known as *mudarabah*. Islamic banking expanded rapidly in the mid-1970s, fueled by the rise in oil industry revenues as well as growing Muslim conservatism. *Hawala*, like the *hundi* of India at times a facet of the black market economy, is the international movement of capital through a trust-based system of personal contacts, without governmental or institutional oversight.

Economic Performance
Real Gross Domestic Products of Selected Developed Countries
% annual change

COUNTRY	1997	1998	1999	2000	2001
US	4.4	4.3	4.1	4.1	1.2
Japan	1.9	-1.1	0.8	1.5	-0.5[1]
Germany	1.4	2.0	1.8	3.0	0.7
France	1.9	3.5	3.0	3.4	1.8
Italy	2.0	1.8	1.6	2.9	1.8
UK	3.5	2.6	2.3	3.1	2.2
Canada	4.3	3.9	5.1	4.4	1.5
European Union	2.6	2.9	2.7	3.4	1.8[1]
Seven major countries above	3.2	2.8	3.0	3.4	1.1[1]
All developed countries	3.5	2.7	3.4	3.8	1.3[1]

[1]*Estimated.*   *Note: Seasonally adjusted at annual rates.*   *Source: International Monetary Fund,* World Economic Outlook, *October 2001.   International Monetary Fund,* International Financial Statistics, *July 2002.*

Standardized Unemployment Rates in Selected Developed Countries
% of total labor force

COUNTRY	1997	1998	1999	2000	2001[1]
US	4.9	4.5	4.2	4.0	4.8
Japan	3.4	4.1	4.7	4.7	5.0
Germany	9.5	9.3	8.6	7.9	8.1
France	12.2	11.8	11.2	9.5	8.9
Italy	11.8	11.8	11.4	10.5	10.0
UK	6.5	6.3	6.1	5.5	5.1
Canada	9.1	8.3	7.6	6.8	7.3
European Union	11.4	9.9	9.1	8.2	8.5
Seven major countries above	6.4	6.4	6.1	5.7	—
All developed countries	6.8	7.1	6.8	6.4	6.5

[1]*Projected.*   *Source: OECD,* Economic Outlook, *November 2001.*

Changes in Consumer Prices in Less-Developed Countries
% change from preceding year

AREA	1997	1998	1999	2000	2001[1]
All less-developed countries	9.7	10.5	6.8	6.0	5.9
Regional groups					
Africa	14.2	10.8	11.5	13.6	12.6
Asia	4.8	7.7	2.5	1.9	2.8
Middle East, Europe, Malta, & Turkey	27.7	27.6	23.2	19.2	18.9
Western Hemisphere	12.9	9.9	8.8	8.1	6.2

[1]Projected.　Source: International Monetary Fund, World Economic Outlook, October 2001.

Changes in Output in Less-Developed Countries
% annual change in real gross domestic product

AREA	1997	1998	1999	2000	2001[1]
All less-developed countries	5.8	3.5	3.9	5.8	4.3
Regional groups					
Africa	3.1	3.3	2.5	2.8	3.8
Asia	6.5	4.0	6.1	6.8	5.8
Middle East, Europe, Malta, & Turkey	5.1	4.1	1.0	6.0	2.3
Western Hemisphere	5.3	2.3	0.2	4.2	1.7
Countries in transition	1.6	−0.8	3.6	6.3	4.0

[1]Projected.　Source: International Monetary Fund, World Economic Outlook, October 2001.

Did you know? Some early automakers were originally manufacturers of other products including bicycles, sewing machines, washing machines, and sheep-shearing machinery. One American company, Pierce, made birdcages, and another, Buick, made plumbing fixtures, including the first enameled cast-iron bathtub.

US Economy
Banking
The Federal Reserve System

The Federal Reserve System is the central banking authority of the United States. It acts as a fiscal agent for the US government, is custodian of the reserve accounts of commercial banks, makes loans to commercial banks, and issues paper currency. It protects the stability of the nation's financial system by regulating and supervising banking institutions and containing risk in financial markets. Created on 23 Dec 1913, it consists of the Board of Governors, the 12 Federal Reserve banks, and the Federal Open Market Committee. There are also several thousand member banks.

The Board of Governors determines the reserve requirements of the member banks, reviews and determines the discount rates established by the reserve banks, and reviews reserve bank budgets. It has seven members who each serve a single 14-year term (a member who finishes an incomplete term may be reappointed). The chairman and vice chairman are chosen for four-year terms. In mid-2002, the Federal Reserve Board consisted of Alan Greenspan (chairman), Roger W. Ferguson, Jr (vice chairman), Edward M. Gramlich, Susan Schmidt Bies, and Mark W. Olson; two positions were vacant.

Each Federal Reserve bank is governed by nine directors. The banks are located in Boston, New York, Philadelphia, Chicago, San Francisco, Cleveland, Richmond, Atlanta, St. Louis, Minneapolis, Kansas City, and Dallas. The Federal Open Market Committee determines reserve bank policy for securities transactions on the open market. It consists of the Board of Governors, the president of the Federal Reserve Bank of New York, and four other bank presidents serving rotating one-year terms. All national banks are members of the Federal Reserve System, and state banks may qualify to become members. The Federal Advisory Council operates as a general advisory group. The Consumer Advisory Council addresses consumer finance and credit issues. The Thrift Institutions Advisory Council offers input on issues relating to banks, credit unions, and savings and loans.

The Federal Reserve System exercises its regulatory powers in several ways. One method is to adjust the legal reserve ratio (the proportion of deposits a member bank must hold in its reserve account), thus increasing or reducing the amount of new loans a bank can make. Because loans create new deposits, the money supply is expanded or reduced. The money supply is also influenced by manipulating the discount rate (the rate of interest charged by reserve banks on short-term secured loans to member banks). Since these loans are typically sought to maintain reserves at their required level, an increase

in the cost of such loans has an effect similar to that of increasing the reserve requirement. Open-market operations may be employed to make small adjustments in the market. Reserve bank sales or purchases of securities on the open market tend to reduce or increase the size of commercial-bank reserves. The board can also change the margin requirements involved in the purchase of securities.

The US Mint

The US Mint, the world's largest producer of coins and medals, was established by Congress on 2 Apr 1792. It is a bureau of the United States Department of the Treasury. The mint manufactures and distributes coins, protects the country's gold and silver assets, and creates medals, commemorative coins, and coin proof sets for purchase by the public. In 2001 it produced 19,401,459,500 pennies, nickels, dimes, quarters, half dollars, and Golden Dollars. The director of the mint is appointed by the president and serves a five-year term; in mid-2002 the director was Henrietta Holsman Fore.

From its Washington DC headquarters, the mint operates facilities in Philadelphia PA, Denver CO, San Francisco CA, and West Point NY. All designing and engraving of coins is done at the Philadelphia site (established 1792), where general circulation coins, medals, and coin dies are also produced. Denver (1863) manufactures general circulation coins and coin dies and provides storage for gold and silver bullion. San Francisco (1854) produces only commemorative coins and proof sets; West Point (1937) manufactures uncirculated and proof sets of gold, silver, and platinum coins and stores these metals. The mint is also responsible for the storage and protec-

tion of more than 145 million ounces of gold bullion at Fort Knox KY.

Although general circulation coins were once made from gold, silver, and copper, this is no longer the case. Gold coin production was discontinued in 1933, and in 1965 silver ceased to be used in dimes and quarters. Currently, pennies are composed of copper-plated zinc, golden dollar coins of manganese brass, and all other general circulation coins of cupronickel, an alloy of copper and nickel. In early 2000 the mint began circulating the Golden Dollar coin, intended to replace the older Susan B. Anthony dollar coin. The new coin featured the image of Sacagawea, the Shoshone Indian woman who traveled as a guide with the Lewis and Clark Expedition in 1804–06. In 1999 the mint began issuing a series of quarters featuring the 50 states. Over a 10-year period, five quarters were to be issued annually, about 10 weeks apart, each featuring one state's design. State quarters were released in order of the states' ratification of the US Constitution. Introduced in 2002 were Tennessee, Ohio, Louisiana, Indiana, and Mississippi; scheduled for 2003 were Illinois, Alabama, Maine, Missouri, and Arkansas.

US Bureau of Engraving and Printing

The US Bureau of Engraving and Printing is responsible for the printing of paper money and is a part of the United States Department of the Treasury. In addition to Federal Reserve Notes (paper currency), the bureau produces other government security documents and creates postage stamps for the United States Postal Service. Each year it prints billions of bills at a rate of some 37 million per day (valued at nearly $700 million). The bureau operates facilities in Washington DC and Fort Worth TX. A director is appointed by the Secretary of the Treasury; in mid-2002, the director was Thomas A. Ferguson.

The vast majority of bills are printed to replace those already in circulation. Currency is printed on paper made of cotton and linen with red and blue fibers throughout and is produced in denominations of $1, $5, $10, $20, $50, $100, and, occasionally, $2. No currency has been printed in denominations of $500, $1,000, $5,000, or $10,000 since 1946. The greatest number of bills printed are the $1 denomination,

with more than five billion produced in fiscal year 2001.

The bureau was established in 1862 and by 1877 was the only producer of US paper money; previously, private companies had printed currency. In 1894 the bureau began producing postage stamps. By the mid-1980s it was recognized that a western office was needed, and the Fort Worth facility opened in April 1991. To protect against technologically advanced counterfeiting techniques, new currency designs began circulating in 1996 that incorporated enhanced deterrence measures. Since 1990 all paper money except $1 bills has included a security thread and microprinting, components that were improved for later print series. New anticounterfeiting features included watermarks, color-shifting inks, fine-line printing patterns, and enlarged, off-center portraits; elements were also added to help the blind and those with poor vision identify different denominations. Counterfeiting crimes are handled by the US Secret Service.

Production
Mining, Minerals, & Metals

Value of nonfuel mineral production in the US and the principal minerals produced in the year 2000. Data may not add to totals given because of rounding. N/A means not applicable. Source: US Geological Survey.

STATE	($) VALUE IN MILLIONS	RANK	% OF US TOTAL	PRINCIPAL MINERALS IN ORDER OF VALUE
Alabama	930	16	2.36	portland cement, crushed stone, lime, construction sand & gravel, masonry cement
Alaska	1,140	12	2.89	zinc, gold, lead, silver, construction sand & gravel

Mining, Minerals, & Metals (continued)

STATE	($) VALUE IN MILLIONS	RANK	% OF US TOTAL	PRINCIPAL MINERALS IN ORDER OF VALUE
Arizona	2,510	3	6.38	copper, construction sand & gravel, portland cement, molybdenum concentrates, crushed stone
Arkansas	484	30	1.23	bromine, crushed stone, portland cement, construction sand & gravel, gypsum (crude)
California	3,270	1	8.30	construction sand & gravel, portland cement, boron, crushed stone, gold
Colorado	592	26	1.50	construction sand & gravel, portland cement, crushed stone, gold, molybdenum concentrates
Connecticut[1]	112	42	0.29	crushed stone, construction sand & gravel, dimension stone, clays (common), gemstones
Delaware[1]	12.4	50	0.03	construction sand & gravel, magnesium compounds, gemstones
Florida	1,820	5	4.62	phosphate rock, crushed stone, portland cement, construction sand & gravel, masonry cement
Georgia	1,620	7	4.11	clays (kaolin), crushed stone, portland cement, clays (fuller's earth), construction sand & gravel
Hawaii	92	44	0.23	crushed stone, portland cement, construction sand & gravel, masonry cement, gemstones
Idaho	358	33	0.91	phosphate rock, silver, construction sand & gravel, molybdenum concentrates, lead
Illinois	913	17	2.32	crushed stone, portland cement, construction sand & gravel, industrial sand & gravel, lime
Indiana	695	22	1.77	crushed stone, portland cement, construction sand & gravel, lime, masonry cement
Iowa	503	28	1.28	portland cement, crushed stone, construction sand & gravel, gypsum (crude), lime
Kansas	629	23	1.60	portland cement, helium (grade-A), salt, crushed stone, helium (crude)
Kentucky	501	29	1.27	crushed stone, lime, portland cement, construction sand & gravel, clays (ball)
Louisiana	325	35	0.83	salt, sulfur (Frasch), construction sand & gravel, crushed stone, industrial sand & gravel
Maine	95.5	43	0.24	construction sand & gravel, portland cement, crushed stone, masonry cement, peat
Maryland[1]	358	34	0.91	crushed stone, portland cement, construction sand & gravel, masonry cement, dimension stone
Massachusetts[1]	200	39	0.51	crushed stone, construction sand & gravel, dimension stone, lime, clays (common)
Michigan	1,640	6	4.17	portland cement, iron ore (usable), construction sand & gravel, crushed stone, magnesium compounds
Minnesota	1,460	8	3.70	iron ore (usable), construction sand & gravel, crushed stone, dimension stone, industrial sand & gravel
Mississippi	149	41	0.38	construction sand & gravel, clays (fuller's earth), portland cement, crushed stone, industrial sand & gravel
Missouri	1,370	10	3.48	crushed stone, portland cement, lead, lime, zinc
Montana	596	25	1.51	palladium, gold, platinum, portland cement, construction sand & gravel
Nebraska[1]	83.7	45	0.21	portland cement, crushed stone, construction sand & gravel, lime, masonry cement
Nevada	2,980	2	7.56	gold, construction sand & gravel, silver, lime, portland cement
New Hampshire[1]	57.1	47	0.14	construction sand & gravel, crushed stone, dimension stone, gemstones
New Jersey[1]	291	37	0.74	crushed stone, construction sand & gravel, industrial sand & gravel, greensand marl, peat
New Mexico	786	18	2.00	copper, potash, construction sand & gravel, portland cement, crushed stone
New York	1,020	13	2.58	crushed stone, salt, portland cement, construction sand & gravel, zinc
North Carolina	744	19	1.89	crushed stone, phosphate rock, construction sand & gravel, industrial sand & gravel, feldspar
North Dakota	35.2	48	0.09	construction sand & gravel, lime, crushed stone, clays (common), industrial sand & gravel
Ohio	999	14	2.54	crushed stone, construction sand & gravel, salt, lime, portland cement
Oklahoma	473	31	1.20	crushed stone, portland cement, construction sand & gravel, industrial sand & gravel, gypsum (crude)

Mining, Minerals, & Metals (continued)

STATE	($) VALUE IN MILLIONS	RANK	% OF US TOTAL	PRINCIPAL MINERALS IN ORDER OF VALUE
Oregon	299	36	0.76	crushed stone, construction sand & gravel, portland cement, diatomite, lime
Pennsylvania[1]	1,250	11	3.17	crushed stone, portland cement, construction sand & gravel, lime, masonry cement
Rhode Island[1]	20.3	49	0.05	crushed stone, construction sand & gravel, industrial sand & gravel, gemstones
South Carolina	551	27	1.40	portland cement, crushed stone, masonry cement, construction sand & gravel, clays (kaolin)
South Dakota	233	38	0.59	gold, portland cement, construction sand & gravel, crushed stone, dimension stone
Tennessee	737	20	1.87	crushed stone, zinc, portland cement, construction sand & gravel, clays (ball)
Texas	1,950	4	4.95	portland cement, crushed stone, construction sand & gravel, lime, salt
Utah	1,430	9	3.64	copper, gold, portland cement, construction sand & gravel, salt
Vermont[1]	66.9	46	0.17	dimension stone, crushed stone, construction sand & gravel, talc (crude), gemstones
Virginia	710	21	1.80	crushed stone, portland cement, construction sand & gravel, lime, clays (fuller's earth)
Washington	607	24	1.54	construction sand & gravel, crushed stone, magnesium metal, portland cement, gold
West Virginia	172	40	0.44	crushed stone, portland cement, industrial sand & gravel, lime, salt
Wisconsin[1]	372	32	0.94	construction sand & gravel, crushed stone, lime, industrial sand & gravel, dimension stone
Wyoming	978	15	2.48	soda ash, clays (bentonite), helium (grade-A), portland cement, crushed stone
undistributed	157	N/A	0.40	
total	39,400	N/A	100.00	

[1]Partial total—excludes proprietary data that are included, however, in "undistributed."

Energy Consumption by Sector

Figures represent '000,000,000,000 Btu. Source: Britannica World Data 2002.

	TOTAL	RESIDENTIAL	COMMERCIAL	INDUSTRIAL	TRANS-PORTATION	PER CAPITA ('000,000 BTU)
Alabama	1,975.1	353.2	182.6	991.3	448.0	457.3
Alaska	696.8	49.5	66.7	419.2	161.4	1,143.6
Arizona	1,114.9	251.6	238.2	226.8	398.3	244.7
Arkansas	1,012.9	195.3	119.4	430.2	268.0	401.5
California	7,697.1	1,340.4	1,193.5	2,289.7	2,873.5	238.5
Colorado	1,133.5	3255.0	240.2	302.4	335.9	291.2
Connecticut	824.5	254.7	189.9	164.4	215.5	252.2
Delaware	273.2	57.3	42.8	106.0	67.1	373.4
Florida	3,579.4	1,002.7	761.1	582.0	1,233.6	244.3
Georgia	2,634.5	561.8	391.9	835.7	845.1	351.9
Hawaii	241.9	21.5	23.8	76.3	120.3	203.9
Idaho	491.1	91.1	82.9	202.0	115.1	405.8
Illinois	3,897.4	986.5	722.4	1,356.5	832.0	327.6
Indiana	2,663.7	503.5	301.9	1,242.7	615.6	454.2
Iowa	1,090.7	240.5	156.3	417.5	276.4	382.4
Kansas	1,060.0	210.9	183.3	389.3	276.5	408.5
Kentucky	1,776.8	327.7	199.6	848.0	401.5	454.6
Louisiana	3,994.9	326.6	222.0	2,617.3	829.0	918.0
Maine	538.4	102.1	57.8	271.9	106.6	433.5
Maryland	1,349.2	387.6	322.3	277.7	361.6	264.8
Massachusetts	1,533.5	426.4	371.3	312.9	422.9	250.7
Michigan	3,249.2	795.9	577.8	1,099.5	776.0	332.4
Minnesota	1,688.9	377.8	227.5	635.6	448.0	360.4
Mississippi	1,098.4	205.3	117.5	432.4	343.2	402.3
Missouri	1,744.8	459.4	337.1	374.8	573.5	323.0
Montana	395.1	70.4	55.6	167.6	101.5	449.6
Nebraska	604.4	140.5	123.2	160.1	180.6	364.8
Nevada	575.3	108.9	88.8	198.1	179.5	343.2

Energy Consumption by Sector (continued)

Figures represent '000,000,000,000 Btu. Source: Britannica World Data 2002.

	TOTAL	RESIDENTIAL	COMMERCIAL	INDUSTRIAL	TRANS- PORTATION	PER CAPITA ('000,000 BTU)
New Hampshire	302.2	83.9	55.6	78.9	83.8	257.7
New Jersey	2,574.8	565.3	520.4	655.0	834.1	319.8
New Mexico	595.2	87.5	101.8	217.5	188.4	344.1
New York	4,129.6	1,104.7	1,118.9	949.8	956.2	227.7
North Carolina	2,416.5	583.1	414.1	773.3	646.0	325.4
North Dakota	351.9	61.7	46.5	168.2	75.5	549.1
Ohio	4,115.7	930.8	649.2	1,640.5	895.2	367.9
Oklahoma	1,405.6	273.1	196.2	550.3	386.0	423.8
Oregon	1,108.1	234.9	180.0	386.3	306.9	341.8
Pennsylvania	3,927.3	935.8	607.8	1,477.9	905.8	326.7
Rhode Island	235.9	72.1	52.2	52.4	59.2	238.9
South Carolina	1,426.8	291.5	191.0	614.1	330.2	379.4
South Dakota	244.8	61.8	41.1	61.5	80.4	331.6
Tennessee	2,067.8	475.3	139.4	905.1	548.0	385.2
Texas	11,278.2	1,310.2	1,080.4	6,542.3	2,345.3	580.2
Utah	674.4	120.0	106.5	254.2	193.7	327.5
Vermont	162.5	46.1	27.3	36.7	52.4	275.7
Virginia	2,115.3	518.7	451.9	532.5	612.2	314.1
Washington	1,835.3	435.5	321.2	757.8	320.8	380.6
West Virginia	803.4	150.0	97.2	391.1	164.2	412.6
Wisconsin	1,791.6	403.6	278.9	708.8	400.3	346.0
Wyoming	423.1	41.0	44.5	235.3	102.3	882.1
District of Columbia	177.4	38.3	110.0	3.2	25.9	335.4
total/average	93,398.5	18,930.0	14,429.2	35,420.3	24,619.0	349.0

Energy Consumption by Source

Figures represent '000,000,000,000 Btu. Source: Britannica World Data 2002.

	PETROLEUM	NATURAL GAS	COAL	HYDROELECTRIC POWER	NUCLEAR ELECTRIC POWER
Alabama	562.5	336.3	887.5	114.6	315.6
Alaska	224.0	443.6	11.2	13.1	...
Arizona	427.4	121.7	343.2	98.0	306.4
Arkansas	309.7	277.7	260.2	28.9	141.9
California	3,341.9	1,865.1	53.9	487.6	362.2
Colorado	412.2	314.7	340.3	17.6	...
Connecticut	412.5	131.5	24.4	15.7	66.1
Delaware	139.0	55.9	50.8	0.0	...
Florida	1,629.6	510.7	694.5	2.2	270.6
Georgia	1,017.1	392.2	725.6	51.6	317.9
Hawaii	221.4	2.8	3.6	1.1	...
Idaho	159.4	69.0	7.3	138.9	...
Illinois	1,272.8	1,140.6	906.9	1.1	741.2
Indiana	859.2	579.8	1,372.1	4.6	...
Iowa	371.3	274.3	380.5	9.7	41.7
Kansas	379.7	362.0	338.6	0.1	87.2
Kentucky	599.1	248.0	951.8	36.2	...
Louisiana	1,612.2	1,737.7	205.6	10.0	167.5
Maine	253.2	5.8	5.9	76.3	53.8
Maryland	518.2	198.1	292.2	25.4	128.5
Massachusetts	690.7	367.5	113.1	16.8	56.6
Michigan	998.4	1,026.7	789.3	26.2	285.0
Minnesota	638.6	375.1	345.5	92.9	128.5
Mississippi	424.0	277.4	128.1	0.0	98.0
Missouri	721.1	297.5	629.7	12.8	94.4
Montana	175.3	63.2	135.7	143.0	...
Nebraska	235.6	133.8	179.0	16.6	100.5
Nevada	216.1	127.6	169.5	22.4	...
New Hampshire	156.6	19.4	36.2	29.2	104.6
New Jersey	1,228.0	624.6	62.4	0.0	117.1
New Mexico	209.4	228.2	279.2	2.2	...
New York	1,569.3	1,159.9	294.3	343.3	374.2
North Carolina	885.1	220.8	687.0	66.2	358.2
North Dakota	119.8	51.5	404.1	40.8	...

Energy Consumption by Source (continued)

Figures represent '000,000,000,000 Btu. Source: Britannica World Data 2002.

	PETROLEUM	NATURAL GAS	COAL	HYDROELECTRIC POWER	NUCLEAR ELECTRIC POWER
Ohio	1,236.6	972.0	1,448.8	4.1	147.9
Oklahoma	469.6	580.2	349.9	21.5	...Oregon
363.9	175.3	20.3	491.3	...	
Pennsylvania	1,329.3	752.7	1,432.3	23.2	729.5
Rhode Island	97.3	87.7	0.1	9.4	...
South Carolina	445.1	154.1	352.5	23.6	462.9
South Dakota	116.7	37.4	33.2	82.5	...
Tennessee	690.9	289.3	648.6	111.6	243.5
Texas	5,166.4	4,123.0	1,475.4	9.9	379.9
Utah	251.6	167.8	355.0	10.8	...
Vermont	85.2	7.4	...	41.0	40.4
Virginia	792.9	248.4	378.8	6.2	279.2
Washington	842.1	247.5	90.9	1,045.5	59.4
West Virginia	257.6	164.5	898.3	14.8	...
Wisconsin	550.0	408.0	452.8	29.3	107.5
Wyoming	145.5	107.6	473.0	12.7	...
District of Columbia	35.4	34.2	0.6	0.0	...
total	35,886.2	22,598.1	20,519.6	3,881.3	7,167.6

Travel and Tourism

Passports, Visas, and Immunizations

With certain exceptions, a **passport** is required by law for all US citizens, including infants, to travel outside the United States and its territories. Exceptions include travel to Canada, Mexico, some Central American countries, and most Caribbean countries; these usually require a birth certificate or other proof of US citizenship for entry. Passports can be applied for at 4,500 passport acceptance facilities nationwide, including courts, post offices, libraries, and county and city offices. Passport agencies generally accept applications only by appointment, usually from those in need of expedited service (two weeks or less). Passport agencies are located in Boston MA, Chicago IL, Norwalk CT, Honolulu HI, Houston TX, Los Angeles CA, Miami FL, New Orleans LA, New York City NY, Philadelphia PA, San Francisco CA, Seattle WA, and Washington DC. Those age 14 and up must apply in person for new passports, but renewals may be done by mail. Applicants should submit the appropriate paperwork several months in advance of planned travel to allow for processing. New passport fees total $60 for persons age 16 and up ($45 passport fee, $15 execution fee) and $40 for those under 16 ($25 passport fee, $15 execution fee); expedited service is an additional $35. Renewal fees are $40 for all ages. Passports are mailed to applicants in about six weeks, or about two weeks for rush service. The status of a passport application may be checked only by contacting the National Passport Information Center at 1-888-362-8668 (using a credit card; $4.95 per call) or 1-900-225-5674 (an operator-assisted call, required to check status, is $1.05 per minute; service is available weekdays from 8:30 AM to 5:30 PM Eastern Standard Time).

To apply in person for a passport requires submission of an application form; proof of US citizenship, such as a certified birth certificate; proof of identity, such as a driver's license; two identical, recent, 2x2-inch photographs; a social security number; and all applicable fees. Options for proving identity or citizenship are listed on the State Department Web site.

Passports can be renewed by mail if the applicant has received a passport within the past 15 years, was over age 16 when the passport was issued, and has legal documentation to verify any name changes (such as a marriage certificate or divorce decree). To renew by mail requires submission of an application form, the most recent passport, two identical photographs, and applicable fees. Frequent travelers may request a passport with extra pages to minimize renewals. A passport that is lost or stolen in a foreign country must be immediately reported to local police and the nearest US embassy or consulate to allow for the citizen's reentry into the US. Replacing a lost or stolen passport requires completion of a form reporting the loss or theft and an application for a new passport, as well as the usual documentation, photographs, and fees.

Visas. A visa is usually a stamp placed on a US passport by a foreign country's officials allowing the passport owner to visit that country. It is the traveler's responsibility to check visa regulations and obtain visas where necessary before traveling to a foreign country. Visas may be acquired from the embassy or consulate of the intended destination, and can be applied for by mail. Processing fees vary among countries.

Immunizations. Under regulations adopted by the World Health Organization, some countries require International Certificates of Vaccination against yellow fever. Other immunizations, such as those for tetanus and polio, should also be up-to-date. Preventive measures for malaria are recommended for some destinations. There are no immunization requirements for returning to the United States. Many countries require HIV/AIDS testing for work, study, or residence permits or for long-term stays.

For passport information, forms, and office locations, access the State Department Web site at <http://travel.state.gov/passport_services.html>. Entry requirements for foreign countries, including necessity of visas, immunizations, and HIV testing, is available at <http://travel.state.gov/foreignentryreqs.html>. Additional information on required or recommended health care measures can be obtained from the Centers for Disease Control and Prevention ator by calling 1-877-FYI-TRIP; also helpful are local health departments and the Government Printing Office publication *Health Information for International Travel*, available for $25 at <http://bookstore.gpo.gov/index.html>.

US and Overseas Travelers

Preliminary data for 2001 show that overseas travel to the US dropped significantly during 2001, primarily as a response to the terrorist attacks of 11 Sep 2001. Data for US resident travel to specific overseas countries are not yet available, but 2001 data for air travel to the various regions, as well as Mexico and Canada, are presented below. Source: US Department of Commerce, International Trade Administration.

COUNTRY OF ORIGIN OF OVERSEAS VISITORS TO THE US (2001)		% CHANGE FROM 2000
UK	4,199,159	-11.0
Japan	4,124,450	-19.0
Germany	1,346,822	-25.0
France	935,322	-14.0
South Korea	626,669	-5.0
Venezuela	570,521	-1.0
Brazil	569,687	-23.0
Italy	491,330	-20.0
Australia	445,175	-17.0
Argentina	443,134	-17.0
total[1]	22,425,497	-14.0

REGIONAL DESTINATION OF US TRAVELERS ABROAD (2001)		% CHANGE FROM 2000
Europe	11,891,361	-7.0
Caribbean	4,360,958	-5.0
Asia	3,731,139	-3.0
South America	1,841,262	+2.0
Central America	1,574,272	+3.0
Oceania	795,620	4.0
Middle East	326,098	-27.0
Africa	229,611	+3.0
Mexico	4,516,391	-5.0
Canada	3,767,084	-3.0
total	33,014,414[2]	-5.0

Top 10 States and Cities Visited by Overseas Travelers in 2000[3]

STATE	VISITORS/ IN THOUSANDS ('000)	MARKET SHARE (%)	CITY	VISITORS/ IN THOUSANDS ('000)	MARKET SHARE (%)
California	6,364	24.5	New York NY	5,714	22.0
Florida	6,026	23.2	Los Angeles CA	3,533	13.6
New York	5,922	22.8	Orlando FL	3,013	11.6
Hawaii	2,727	10.5	Miami FL	2,935	11.3
Nevada	2,364	9.1	San Francisco CA	2,831	10.9
Massachusetts	1,429	5.5	Las Vegas NV	2,260	8.7
Illinois	1,377	5.3	Oahu/Honolulu HI	2,234	8.6
Guam	1,325	5.1	Washington DC	1,481	5.7
Texas	1,169	4.5	Chicago IL	1,351	5.2
New Jersey	909	3.5	Boston MA	1,325	5.1

[1]*Total includes other countries not listed in the table, but it excludes Mexico and Canada.* [2]*Total provided by the source.* [3]*Excludes Canadian and Mexican visitors to the US. Although it is actually a territory of the US, Guam is included because of the relatively large number of overseas people visiting it. If Guam were excluded from this table, Arizona would rank 10th on the list with about 883,000 overseas visitors and 3.4% of the market share.*

Customs Exemptions

Upon returning to the US from a foreign country, travelers must pay duty on items purchased outside the US. If the value of the items is greater than the allowable exemption, duty must be paid on the excess amount. The general exemption is $400 per person, but can also be $600 or $1,200 in certain situations. Exemptions apply if the items are in the traveler's possession, are for the traveler's own use, and are declared to Customs. The traveler must also have been out of the country for at least 48 hours (unless returning from Mexico or the US Virgin Islands) and must not have used any part of the exemption within the past 30 days; if one or both of these requirements does not apply, the allowable exemption

drops to $200 per person and includes additional restrictions. The general exemption of $400 applies to travelers returning from any country except several in the Caribbean Sea region and from US island possessions. This exemption includes no more than 200 previously exported cigarettes and no more than one liter of alcoholic beverages. Cuban tobacco products purchased in any country other than Cuba are prohibited. Family members may combine their total exemptions in a joint declaration. A $600 exemption applies to travelers returning from any of 24 countries in the Caribbean region and may include two liters of alcoholic beverages, as long as one of the liters was produced in one of those countries. The 24 countries are

Antigua and Barbuda, Aruba, the Bahamas, Barbados, Belize, the British Virgin Islands, Costa Rica, Dominica, the Dominican Republic, El Salvador, Grenada, Guatemala, Guyana, Haiti, Honduras, Jamaica, Montserrat, the Netherlands Antilles, Nicaragua, Panama, St. Kitts and Nevis, St. Lucia, St. Vincent and the Grenadines, and Trinidad and Tobago. A $1,200 exemption applies to travelers returning from a trip that included the US Virgin Islands, American Samoa, or Guam. This exemption includes 1,000 cigarettes and five liters of alcoholic beverages; of this amount, 800 cigarettes and one liter of alcohol must be from one of the US islands. The $1,200 exemption also applies to multi-country travel (such as a cruise) to a US possession and any of the 24 Caribbean region countries, as long as no more than $600 worth of goods was purchased in the Caribbean countries.

Gifts valued at $100 or less may be sent to the US without duty as long as no single person receives more than this value within a single day; the exempt value increases to $200 for gifts sent from American Samoa, Guam, or the US Virgin Islands. Alcoholic beverages may not be sent by mail; tobacco and alcohol-based perfumes worth more than $5 are not included in the exemption. Travelers may ship goods home for personal use without duty if the value of the goods is $200 or less and no single person receives more than this value within a single day. This personal exemption increases to $1,200 for goods purchased and shipped from American Samoa, Guam, or the US Virgin Islands.

Customs information is available from the US Customs Service Web site at <www.customs.gov/travel/travel.htm>. The general-information brochure "Know Before You Go" and other Customs publications can be viewed or ordered online.

US State Department Travel Warnings

The State Department issues travel warnings when it is believed best for Americans to avoid certain countries in the interests of safety. It also releases public announcements of more short-term hazards, such as terrorist threats or political coups, that may endanger American travelers; these include an expiration date when the announcement need no longer be heeded. The department also makes available Consular Information Sheets for all countries, which may discuss safety conditions in that country not severe enough to require a travel warning. Current information can be found at <http://travel.state.gov/travel_warnings. html>, or by phone at 1-888-407-4747 (weekdays 8 AM to 8 PM Eastern Standard Time) or 1-202-647-5225 (all other times).

Travel warnings were in effect on 21 May 2002, for the following: Afghanistan, Albania, Algeria, Angola, Bosnia and Herzegovina, Burundi, Central African Republic, Colombia, Democratic Republic of the Congo, Guinea-Bissau, Indonesia, Iran, Iraq, Israel (including the West Bank and Gaza Strip), Lebanon, Liberia, Libya, Macedonia, Madagascar, Nigeria, Pakistan, Yugoslavia, Sierra Leone, Somalia, The Sudan, Syria, Tajikistan, and Yemen.

Public announcements in effect at various times throughout 2002 included advisories for Argentina, Colombia, Democratic Republic of the Congo, East Timor, Ghana, India, Kyrgyzstan, Malaysia, the Middle East, Nepal, Peru, the Philippines, Rwanda, Turkmenistan, Uzbekistan, Venezuela, and Zimbabwe; a worldwide caution regarding terrorist acts was also in effect from mid-March through mid-August.

Employment and Labor
US Employment by Gender and Occupation, 2001

Numbers may not add up to totals due to rounding. Source: US Bureau of Labor Statistics.

OCCUPATION	16 YEARS AND OLDER (NUMBERS IN '000)		
	MEN	WOMEN	TOTAL
managerial and professional specialty			
officials and administrators, public administration	427	403	830
other executive, administrative, and managerial	8,437	5,932	14,369
management-related occupations	2,125	3,014	5,139
engineers	1,902	221	2,122
mathematical and computer scientists	1,470	633	2,103
natural scientists	382	200	582
health diagnosing occupations	778	312	1,090
health assessment and treating occupations	423	2,629	3,052
teachers, university and college level	568	435	1,003
teachers, except university and college	1,375	4,098	5,473
lawyers and judges	682	283	966
other professional specialty occupations	2,396	2,769	5,164
	20,966	**20,928**	**41,894**
technical, sales, and administrative support			
health technologists and technicians	330	1,477	1,807
engineering and science technicians	958	348	1,306
technicians, except health, engineering, and science	808	576	1,384
supervisors and proprietors	2,846	1,990	4,836
sales representatives, finance and business services	1,611	1,280	2,891

US Employment by Gender and Occupation, 2001 (continued)

OCCUPATION	16 YEARS AND OLDER (NUMBERS IN '000)		
	MEN	WOMEN	TOTAL
technical, sales, and administrative support (continued)			
sales representatives, commodities, except retail	1,157	354	1,511
sales workers, retail and personal services	2,474	4,236	6,711
sales-related occupations	31	65	96
supervisors	244	476	720
computer equipment operators	152	172	324
secretaries, stenographers, and typists	72	3,014	3,086
financial records processing	181	2,024	2,205
mail and message distributing	555	381	936
other administrative support, including clerical	2,746	8,486	11,231
	14,167	24,877	39,044
service occupations			
private household	27	688	715
protective service	1,972	507	2,478
food service	2,685	3,562	6,246
health service	293	2,387	2,680
cleaning and building service	1,682	1,431	3,114
personal service	604	2,522	3,126
	7,263	11,096	18,359
precision production, craft, and repair			
mechanics and repairers	4,571	237	4,807
construction trades	6,099	153	6,253
other precision production, craft, and repair	2,875	897	3,772
	13,545	1,287	14,833
operators, fabricators, and laborers			
machine operators, assemblers, and inspectors	4,286	2,448	6,734
motor vehicle operators	3,827	529	4,356
other transportation and material moving occupations	1,222	60	1,282
construction laborers	988	36	1,024
other handlers, equipment cleaners, helpers, and laborers	3,246	1,055	4,302
	13,569	4,129	17,698
farming, forestry, and fishing			
farm operators and managers	828	281	1,108
other farming, forestry, and fishing occupations	1,742	394	2,136
	2,570	675	3,245
total	72,080	62,992	135,073

US Workers Earning the Minimum Wage

This table refers to wage and salary workers who are paid hourly rates. It excludes the incorporated self-employed. The prevailing federal minimum wage was $5.15/hour in 2001. Workers earning less than $5.15/hour may be working in jobs that are exempted from the minimum wage provision of the Fair Labor Standards Act. Numbers in thousands ('000). Source: US Bureau of Labor Statistics.

WORKER CHARACTERISTICS	TOTAL NUMBER OF WORKERS	BELOW $5.15/HR	AT $5.15/HR	TOTAL NUMBER OF WORKERS AT OR BELOW $5.15/HR	
				NUMBER	%
age					
16–24 years	16,602	830	376	1,206	7.3
25 years and over	55,884	771	260	1,032	1.8
total (16 years and over)	72,486	1,602	636	2,238	3.1
men					
16–24 years	8,491	296	177	473	5.6
25 years and over	27,538	233	78	311	1.1
16 years and over	36,029	529	255	784	2.2
women					
16–24 years	8,111	534	199	733	9.0
25 years and over	28,346	539	182	721	2.5
16 years and over	36,457	1,073	381	1,454	4.0
white (16 years and over)	59,152	1,359	502	1,861	3.1

US Workers Earning the Minimum Wage (continued)

WORKER CHARACTERISTICS	TOTAL NUMBER OF WORKERS	BELOW $5.15/HR	AT $5.15/HR	TOTAL NUMBER OF WORKERS AT OR BELOW $5.15/HR NUMBER	%
women (continued)					
black (16 years and over)	10,014	183	114	297	3.0
Hispanic (16 years and over)	10,030	187	114	302	3.0
full- and part-time workers²					
full-time	55,232	662	191	853	1.5
part-time	17,124	937	441	1,378	8.0

¹Data for racial groups other than the two listed are not included. Hispanics may be of any race and are included in both white and black population groups. For these reasons, data for the race/ethnic group category will not add up to total. ²Full- and part-time workers are distinguished by the number of hours worked. These data will not add up to total because of a small number of multiple jobholders whose full- or part-time status on the principal job is unknown.

Comparative Hourly Compensation Costs

The table shows private-industry employer compensation costs per hour worked by an employee in 2002. Sums may not add to totals due to rounding. Source: US Bureau of Labor Statistics.

COMPENSATION	ALL WORKERS COST ($)	(%)	GOODS-PRODUCING WORKERS¹ COST ($)	(%)	SERVICE WORKERS² COST ($)	(%)
wages and salaries	15.80	72.8	17.47	68.7	15.33	74.2
paid leave	1.44	6.6	1.66	6.5	1.37	6.6
vacation	0.72	3.3	0.86	3.4	0.68	3.3
holiday	0.49	2.3	0.60	2.4	0.46	2.2
sick	0.17	0.8	0.12	0.5	0.18	0.9
other	0.06	0.3	0.08	0.3	0.06	0.3
supplemental pay	0.62	2.9	1.11	4.4	0.48	2.3
premium³	0.24	1.1	0.54	2.1	0.16	0.8
shift differentials	0.06	0.3	0.08	0.3	0.05	0.2
nonproduction bonuses	0.32	1.5	0.49	1.9	0.27	1.3
insurance	1.40	6.4	2.01	7.9	1.22	5.9
life	0.04	0.2	0.06	0.2	0.04	0.2
health	1.29	5.9	1.84	7.2	1.13	5.5
short-term disability	0.04	0.2	0.08	0.3	0.03	0.1
long-term disability	0.03	0.1	0.03	0.1	0.03	0.1
retirement and savings	0.63	2.9	0.88	3.5	0.56	2.7
defined benefit	0.23	1.1	0.42	1.7	0.17	0.8
defined contribution	0.40	1.8	0.46	1.8	0.39	1.9
legally required benefits	1.80	8.3	2.25	8.8	1.67	8.1
Social Security⁴	1.32	6.1	1.49	5.9	1.27	6.1
Old-Age, Survivors, and Disability Insurance (OASDI)	1.06	4.9	1.20	4.7	1.02	4.9
Medicare	0.26	1.2	0.29	1.1	0.25	1.2
ederal unemployment insurance	0.03	0.1	0.03	0.1	0.03	0.1
state unemployment insurance	0.10	0.5	0.12	0.5	0.09	0.4
workers' compensation	0.35	1.6	0.61	2.4	0.28	1.4
other benefits⁵	0.03	0.1	0.05	0.2	0.02	0.1
total benefits	5.90	27.2	7.96	31.3	5.33	25.8
total compensation	21.71	100.0	25.44	100.0	20.66	100.0

¹Includes mining, construction, and manufacturing. ²Includes transportation, communication, and public utilities; wholesale and retail trade; finance, insurance, and real estate; and service industries. ³Pay for overtime, weekends, and holidays. ⁴The total employer cost for Social Security comprises an OASDI portion and a Medicare portion. ⁵Includes severance pay and supplemental unemployment benefits.

Median Income by Educational and Social Variables

Table refers to people 15 years and over as of March of the following year. Source: US Census Bureau, Census 2000.

	median income ($) males		median income ($) females	
	2000	1999	2000	1999
educational level				
less than 9th grade	14,149	13,438	8,404	8,238
9th to 12th grade (no diploma)	18,953	17,707	9,996	9,625
high school graduate	27,666	27,240	15,119	14,695
some college, no degree	33,039	32,724	20,181	19,665
associate degree	37,953	36,632	23,269	21,959
bachelor's degree	49,178	47,325	30,487	28,594
master's degree	59,376	58,933	40,249	39,744
professional degree	81,602	81,934	45,999	45,510
doctorate degree	71,738	70,452	48,894	46,499
race and origin[1]				
white	29,696	28,564	16,218	15,362
white (non-Hispanic)	31,213	30,594	16,805	15,922
black	21,662	20,579	16,081	14,771
Hispanic origin	19,833	18,234	12,255	11,314
age				
15 to 24 years	9,557	8,302	7,746	6,689
25 to 34 years	30,634	29,864	20,937	19,396
35 to 44 years	37,087	36,217	21,861	20,683
45 to 54 years	41,072	40,939	24,196	22,588
55 to 64 years	34,412	33,648	16,465	15,917
65 years and over	19,168	19,079	10,899	10,943
	all males		all females	
	28,272	27,275	16,190	15,311

[1]Hispanic people may be of any race.

The 20 US Metropolitan Areas with the Highest Average Annual Salary

Includes workers covered by two programs, Unemployment Insurance and Unemployment Compensation for Federal Employees. Source: US Bureau of Labor Statistics.

METROPOLITAN AREA	ANNUAL SALARY ($) 1999	2000	SALARY INCREASE (%)	METROPOLITAN AREA	ANNUAL SALARY ($) 1999	2000	SALARY INCREASE (%)
San Jose CA	61,117	76,076	24.5	Seattle WA[5]	43,925	45,171	2.8
San Francisco CA	50,125	59,314	18.3	Trenton NJ	42,445	44,576	5.0
New York NY	52,467	56,377	7.5	Oakland CA	40,994	44,170	7.7
New Haven CT[1]	47,133	50,585	7.3	Bergen-Passaic NJ	41,511	43,789	5.5
Middlesex NJ[2]	46,200	48,977	6.0	Hartford CT	40,059	42,394	5.8
Newark NJ	44,647	48,733	9.2	Detroit MI	40,781	42,303	3.7
Jersey City NJ	43,046	47,514	10.4	Dallas TX	39,259	42,133	7.3
Boulder-Longmont CO	40,002	45,565	13.9	Chicago IL	39,525	41,549	5.1
Washington DC[3]	42,660	45,333	6.3	Denver CO	38,115	41,413	8.7
Boston MA[4]	40,892	45,191	10.5	Austin-San Marcos TX	38,940	41,012	5.3

[1]New Haven area includes Bridgeport, Stamford, Waterbury, and Danbury. [2]Middlesex area includes Somerset and Hunterdon. [3]Washington DC entry includes areas in Maryland, Virginia, and West Virginia. [4]Boston area includes Worcester, Lawrence, Lowell, and Brockton. [5]Seattle area includes Bellevue and Everett.

US Federal Minimum Wage Rates

The table shows the actual minimum wage for the year in question (since 1950) and the value of that minimum wage adjusted for inflation in the year 2002. Source: US Bureau of Labor Statistics.

YEAR	minimum wage DOLLARS	2002 DOLLARS	YEAR	minimum wage DOLLARS	2002 DOLLARS	YEAR	minimum wage DOLLARS	2002 DOLLARS
1950	0.75	5.60	1953	0.75	5.05	1956	1.00	6.61
1951	0.75	5.19	1954	0.75	5.01	1957	1.00	6.40
1952	0.75	5.09	1955	0.75	5.03	1958	1.00	6.22

US Federal Minimum Wage Rates (continued)

YEAR	minimum wage DOLLARS	minimum wage 2002 DOLLARS	YEAR	minimum wage DOLLARS	minimum wage 2002 DOLLARS	YEAR	minimum wage DOLLARS	minimum wage 2002 DOLLARS
1959	1.00	6.18	1974	2.00	7.29	1989	3.35	4.86
1960	1.00	6.07	1975	2.10	7.02	1990	3.80	5.23
1961	1.15	6.92	1976	2.30	7.27	1991	4.25	5.61
1962	1.15	6.85	1977	2.30	6.82	1992	4.25	5.45
1963	1.25	7.34	1978	2.65	7.31	1993	4.25	5.29
1964	1.25	7.25	1979	2.90	7.18	1994	4.25	5.16
1965	1.25	7.13	1980	3.10	6.76	1995	4.25	5.01
1966	1.25	6.94	1981	3.35	6.63	1996	4.75	5.44
1967	1.40	7.54	1982	3.35	6.24	1997	5.15	5.77
1968	1.60	8.27	1983	3.35	6.05	1998	5.15	5.68
1969	1.60	7.84	1984	3.35	5.80	1999	5.15	5.56
1970	1.60	7.41	1985	3.35	5.60	2000	5.15	5.38
1971	1.60	7.10	1986	3.35	5.50	2001	5.15	5.23
1972	1.60	6.88	1987	3.35	5.30	2002	5.15	5.15
1973	1.60	6.48	1988	3.35	5.09			

US Civilian Federal Employment

Source: US Office of Personnel Management.

AGENCY[1]	1970	1980	1990	2000
executive departments	**1,772,363**	**1,716,970**	**2,065,542**	**1,592,200**
State	40,042	23,497	25,288	27,983
Treasury	90,683	124,663	158,655	143,508
Defense	1,169,173	960,116	1,034,152	676,268
Justice	40,075	56,327	83,932	125,970
Interior	71,671	77,357	77,679	73,818
Agriculture	114,309	129,139	122,594	104,466
Commerce	36,124	48,563	69,920	47,652
Labor	10,928	23,400	17,727	16,040
Health & Human Services (HHS)	110,186	155,662	123,959	62,605
Housing & Urban Development	15,046	16,964	13,596	10,319
Transportation	66,970	72,361	67,364	63,598
Energy	7,156	21,557	17,731	15,692
Education	0	7,364	4,771	4,734
Veterans Affairs (formerly Veterans Administration)	169,241	228,285	248,174	219,547
independent agencies[2]				
Armed Forces Retirement Home	N/A	N/A	966	765
Board of Governors of the Federal Reserve System	N/A	N/A	1,525	1,644
Commodity Futures Trading Commission	N/A	N/A	542	574
Consumer Product Safety Commission	N/A	N/A	520	479
Environmental Protection Agency	0	14,715	17,123	18,036
Equal Employment Opportunity Commission	797	3,515	2,880	2,780
Federal Communications Commission	N/A	N/A	1,778	1,965
Federal Deposit Insurance Corporation	2,462	3,520	17,641	6,958
Federal Emergency Management Agency	0	3,427	3,137	4,813
Federal Trade Commission	N/A	N/A	988	1,019
General Services Administration[3]	37,661	37,654	20,277	14,334
International Boundary & Water Commission (US/Mexico)	N/A	N/A	260	268
National Archives & Records Administration	N/A	N/A	3,120	2,702
National Aeronautics & Space Administration	30,674	23,714	24,872	18,819
National Labor Relations Board	N/A	N/A	2,263	2,054
National Science Foundation	N/A	N/A	1,318	1,247
Nuclear Regulatory Commission	0	3,283	3,353	2,858
Office of Personnel Management	5,513	8,280	6,636	3,780
Panama Canal Commission	N/A	N/A	8,240	6
Peace Corps	N/A	N/A	1,178	1,065
Railroad Retirement Board	N/A	N/A	1,772	1,176
Securities & Exchange Commission	N/A	N/A	2,302	2,955
Small Business Administration	4,397	5,804	5,128	4,150
Smithsonian Institution (summary)	2,547	4,403	5,092	5,065
Social Security Administration	N/A	N/A	N/A[4]	64,474
Tennessee Valley Authority	23,785	51,714	28,392	13,145
US Information Agency	10,156	8,138	8,555	2,436
US Postal Service	721,183	660,014	816,886	860,726
executive branch total	2,829,495	2,820,978	3,067,167	2,644,758

US Civilian Federal Employment (continued)

AGENCY[1]	1970	1980	1990	2000
legislative branch total	29,939	39,710	37,495	31,157
Judicial branch	6,879	15,178	23,605	32,186
total, all agencies	**2,866,313**	**2,875,866**	**3,128,267**	**2,708,101**

N/A means not available. [1]*Includes other branches or agencies not shown separately. The Office of Homeland Security was created by an executive order of Pres. George W. Bush after the terrorist attacks of 11 Sep 2001. In mid-2002 the president proposed to Congress the creation of a Department of Homeland Security, a cabinet-level agency within the executive branch of government.* [2]*The Defense Intelligence Agency was excluded as of November 1984, the National Imagery and Mapping Agency as of October 1996. Entries for 1990 and 2000 exclude the Central Intelligence Agency and the National Security Agency.* [3]*Entry for 1980 includes the National Archives and Records Administration, which became an independent agency in 1985.* [4]*Included with HHS.*

Older Americans in the Workforce

All numbers are in thousands ('000). Source: US Census Bureau.

| | TOTAL WORKFORCE 55 AND OVER | | AGE | | | | | |
| | | | 55–59 | | 60–64 | | 65 AND OLDER | |
GENDER AND OCCUPATION TYPE	NUMBER	%	NUMBER	%	NUMBER	%	NUMBER	%
men and women								
managerial and professional	5,908	33.0	2,989	34.7	1,629	32.7	1,291	30.0
technical, sales, and administrative support	5,138	28.7	2,394	27.8	1,384	27.8	1,361	31.7
service occupations	2,406	13.4	1,093	12.7	686	13.8	626	14.6
precision production, craft, and repair	1,584	8.9	935	10.9	403	8.1	246	5.7
operators, fabricators, and laborers	2,113	11.8	998	11.6	652	13.1	463	10.8
farming, forestry, and fishing	737	4.1	198	2.3	227	4.6	312	7.3
total	17,885	100.0	8,606	100.0	4,981	100.0	4,298	100.0
men								
managerial and professional	3,434	35.3	1,621	36.3	954	34.5	859	34.4
technical, sales, and administrative support	1,905	19.6	820	18.4	512	18.5	573	22.9
service occupations	864	8.9	387	8.7	241	8.7	235	9.4
precision production, craft, and repair	1,400	14.4	815	18.3	371	13.4	214	8.6
operators, fabricators, and laborers	1,554	16.0	692	15.5	501	18.1	361	14.4
farming, forestry, and fishing	571	5.9	126	2.8	189	6.8	256	10.2
total	9,728	100.0	4,461	100.0	2,768	100.0	2,499	100.0
women								
managerial and professional	2,474	30.3	1,368	33.0	675	30.5	432	24.0
technical, sales, and administrative support	3,233	39.6	1,574	38.0	872	39.4	788	43.8
service occupations	1,542	18.9	706	17.0	445	20.1	391	21.7
precision production, craft, and repair	184	2.3	120	2.9	33	1.5	31	1.7
operators, fabricators, and laborers	559	6.9	306	7.4	151	6.8	102	5.7
farming, forestry, and fishing	166	2.0	72	1.7	38	1.7	56	3.1
total	8,157	100.0	4,145	100.0	2,213	100.0	1,799	100.0

Strikes and Lockouts in the US

Strikes and lockouts are referred to as work stoppages by the Bureau of Labor Statistics. This table covers work stoppages since 1950 involving 1,000 workers or more. The number of workers and stoppages are for stoppages begun during that year. The number of days out from work pertains to all strikes or lockouts in effect during the year, whether they began in that year or not. The heading for estimated working time includes all workers except those employed in private households, forestry, or fisheries. Source: US Bureau of Labor Statistics.

| | strikes and lockouts | | worktime lost | | | strikes and lockouts | | worktime lost | |
| | | WORKERS INVOLVED | DAYS LOST | % OF WORKING | | | WORKERS INVOLVED | DAYS LOST | % OF WORKING |
YEAR	NUMBER	('000)	('000)	TIME	YEAR	NUMBER	('000)	('000)	TIME
1950	424	1,698	30,390	0.26	1954	265	1,075	16,630	0.13
1951	415	1,462	15,070	0.12	1955	363	2,055	21,180	0.16
1952	470	2,746	48,820	0.38	1956	287	1,370	26,840	0.20
1953	437	1,623	18,130	0.14	1957	279	887	10,340	0.07

Strikes and Lockouts in the US (continued)

	strikes and lockouts		worktime lost			strikes and lockouts		worktime lost	
		WORKERS		% OF			WORKERS		% OF
		INVOLVED	DAYS LOST	WORKING			INVOLVED	DAYS LOST	WORKING
YEAR	NUMBER	('000)	('000)	TIME	YEAR	NUMBER	('000)	('000)	TIME
1958	332	1,587	17,900	0.13	1980	187	795	20,844	0.09
1959	245	1,381	60,850	0.43	1981	145	729	16,908	0.07
1960	222	896	13,260	0.09	1982	96	656	9,061	0.04
1961	195	1,031	10,140	0.07	1983	81	909	17,461	0.08
1962	211	793	11,760	0.08	1984	62	376	8,499	0.04
1963	181	512	10,020	0.07	1985	54	324	7,079	0.03
1964	246	1,183	16,220	0.11	1986	69	533	11,861	0.05
1965	268	999	15,140	0.10	1987	46	174	4,481	0.02
1966	321	1,300	16,000	0.10	1988	40	118	4,381	0.02
1967	381	2,192	31,320	0.18	1989	51	452	16,996	0.07
1968	392	1,855	35,367	0.20	1990	44	185	5,926	0.02
1969	412	1,576	29,397	0.16	1991	40	392	4,584	0.02
1970	381	2,468	52,761	0.29	1992	35	364	3,989	0.01
1971	298	2,516	35,538	0.19	1993	35	182	3,981	0.01
1972	250	975	16,764	0.09	1994	45	322	5,020	0.02
1973	317	1,400	16,260	0.08	1995	31	192	5,771	0.02
1974	424	1,796	31,809	0.16	1996	37	273	4,889	0.02
1975	235	965	17,563	0.09	1997	29	339	4,497	0.01
1976	231	1,519	23,962	0.12	1998	34	387	5,116	0.02
1977	298	1,212	21,258	0.10	1999	17	73	1,996	0.01
1978	219	1,006	23,774	0.11	2000	39	394	20,419	0.06
1979	235	1,021	20,409	0.09	2001	29	99	1,151	<.005

US Trade Union Membership

Numbers are in thousands ('000). N/A means not available. Source: US Bureau of Labor Statistics.

	NUMBER OF UNION MEMBERS	% OF TOTAL LABOR FORCE	YEAR	NUMBER OF UNION MEMBERS	% OF TOTAL LABOR FORCE	YEAR	NUMBER OF UNION MEMBERS	% OF TOTAL LABOR FORCE
YEAR								
1900[1]	791	N/A	1940	8,717	26.9	1980	20,095	23.0
1905	1,918	N/A	1945	14,322	35.5	1985	16,996	18.0
1910	2,116	N/A	1950	14,300[3]	31.5	1990	16,740	16.1
1915	2,560	N/A	1955	16,802	33.2	1995	16,360	14.9
1920	5,034	N/A	1960	17,049	31.4	2000	16,258	13.5
1925	3,566	N/A	1965	17,299	28.4	2001	16,275	13.5
1930[2]	3,401	11.6	1970	19,381	27.4			
1935	3,584	13.2	1977[4]	19,335	23.8			

[1]Data from 1900 to 1925 includes Canadian members whose union headquarters were in the US. [2]Agricultural workers were not included as part of the total labor force for the years from 1930 to 1970. [3]Rounded to nearest hundred thousand. [4]Data for 1975 was not available. Data for 1977 on includes only employed union members.

US Unemployment Rates

Unemployment rates of the civilian labor force 16 years and older. Source: US Bureau of Labor Statistics.

YEAR	UNEMPLOYMENT RATE (%)	YEAR	UNEMPLOYMENT RATE (%)	YEAR	UNEMPLOYMENT RATE (%)	YEAR	UNEMPLOYMENT RATE (%)
1947	3.9	1961	6.7	1975	8.5	1989	5.3
1948	3.8	1962	5.5	1976	7.7	1990	5.6
1949	5.9	1963	5.7	1977	7.1	1991	6.8
1950	5.3	1964	5.2	1978	6.1	1992	7.5
1951	3.3	1965	4.5	1979	5.8	1993	6.9
1952	3.0	1966	3.8	1980	7.1	1994	6.1
1953	2.9	1967	3.8	1981	7.6	1995	5.6
1954	5.5	1968	3.6	1982	9.7	1996	5.4
1955	4.4	1969	3.5	1983	9.6	1997	4.9
1956	4.1	1970	4.9	1984	7.5	1998	4.5
1957	4.3	1971	5.9	1985	7.2	1999	4.2
1958	6.8	1972	5.6	1986	7.0	2000	4.0
1959	5.5	1973	4.9	1987	6.2	2001	4.8
1960	5.5	1974	5.6	1988	5.5		

Social Characteristics of the Unemployed in the US

Unemployment as a percent of the civilian labor force. Source: US Bureau of Labor Statistics.

SOCIAL CHARACTERISTICS	UNEMPLOYMENT RATES BY YEAR (%)						
	1975	1980	1985	1990	1995	2000	2001
age (both sexes)							
16–19	19.9	17.8	18.6	15.5	17.3	13.1	14.7
25 and over	6.0	5.1	5.6	4.4	4.3	3.0	3.7
sex (20 years and older)							
men	6.8	5.9	6.2	5.0	4.8	3.3	4.2
women	8.0	6.4	6.6	4.9	4.9	3.6	4.1
race/ethnicity							
white	7.8	6.3	6.2	4.8	4.9	3.5	4.2
black	14.8	14.3	15.1	11.4	10.4	7.6	8.7
Hispanic[1]	12.2	10.1	10.5	8.2	9.3	5.7	6.6
family							
women who maintain families	10.0	9.2	10.4	8.3	8.0	5.9	6.6
married men, spouse present	5.1	4.2	4.3	3.4	3.3	2.0	2.7
overall unemployment	8.5	7.1	7.2	5.6	5.6	4.0	4.8

[1]*Hispanics may be of any race and are included in both the white and black racial categories in this table.*

US Unemployment Rates by Occupation

Unemployment rates are for the civilian noninstitutional population 16 years and older. Rates represent unemployment as a percent of the labor force for each occupational group. The unemployment rate totals include people without previous work experience and those whose last job was in the military. Data are not strictly comparable across the years. Source: US Bureau of Labor Statistics.

OCCUPATION	UNEMPLOYMENT RATES (%)			
	1990	1995	2000	2001
managerial and professional specialty	2.1	2.4	1.7	2.3
executive, administrative, and managerial	2.3	2.4	1.8	2.4
professional specialty	2.0	2.5	1.7	2.2
technical, sales, and administrative support	4.3	4.5	3.6	4.2
technicians and related support	2.9	2.8	2.2	2.9
sales occupations	4.8	5.0	4.0	4.7
administrative support (including clerical)	4.1	4.3	3.5	4.0
service occupations	6.6	7.5	5.3	5.9
private household	5.6	10.7	6.9	6.9
protective service	3.6	3.7	2.6	2.9
service (except private household and protective)	7.1	7.9	5.6	6.3
precision production, craft, and repair	5.9	6.0	3.6	4.6
mechanics and repairers	3.8	4.0	2.6	3.1
construction trades	8.5	9.0	4.9	5.9
other precision production, craft, and repair	4.7	4.2	2.8	4.2
operators, fabricators, and laborers	8.7	8.2	6.3	7.7
machine operators, assemblers, inspectors	8.1	7.4	5.9	7.8
transportation and material moving occupations	6.3	6.0	4.4	5.0
handlers, equipment cleaners, helpers, and laborers	11.6	11.7	8.7	10.3
construction laborers	18.1	16.7	11.6	13.1
farming, forestry, and fishing	8.4	7.9	6.0	7.4
total	5.6	5.6	4.0	4.8

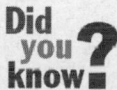

Did you know? Whitcomb L. Judson invented the zipper in the late 1800s; it was further refined by Swedish inventor Gideon Sundback in his 1917 patent, and it was first called a "zipper" when the B.F. Goodrich company began using the device in its rubber boots and galoshes. Most zippers have the letters "YKK" on them, which stands for the Yoshida Kogyo Kabushikikaisha corporation of Japan, the world's leading zipper manufacturer.

Occupational Illnesses and Injuries in the US

This table displays the number of nonfatal work injuries and illnesses recorded in 2000. The injuries and illnesses resulted in days away from work in the private industries listed. Numbers may not add to totals because of rounding and nonclassifiable responses. Numbers are in thousands ('000). N/A means not available. Source: US Bureau of Labor Statistics.

| CHARACTERISTIC | PRIVATE INDUSTRY TOTALS | GOODS PRODUCING | | | |
		AGRICULTURE, FORESTRY, AND FISHING[1]	MINING[2]	CONSTRUCTION	MANU-FACTURING
injury or illness					
sprains, strains	728.2	12.5	5.5	74.7	145.1
bruises, contusions	151.7	3.4	1.6	15.4	32.4
cuts, lacerations	121.3	3.4	1.0	17.5	32.7
fractures	116.7	3.7	1.8	21.5	26.2
heat burns	24.3	0.4	0.2	2.7	6.0
carpal tunnel syndrome	27.7	0.2	0.1	1.0	10.9
tendonitis	14.4	0.1	<50[3]	0.9	5.8
chemical burns	9.4	0.1	<50[3]	1.0	2.8
amputations	9.7	0.7	0.1	1.1	4.5
multiple traumatic injuries	59.2	1.4	0.9	8.2	11.8
body part affected by injury or illness					
head	110.3	3.2	1.2	15.1	28.4
eye	53.8	1.5	0.3	8.1	18.0
neck	28.6	0.4	0.3	2.4	5.6
trunk	618.3	10.9	5.5	67.1	131.1
shoulder	96.1	1.5	0.5	10.5	23.9
back	411.1	7.1	3.2	42.7	79.4
upper extremities	382.7	10.3	3.0	44.5	115.5
wrist	85.2	1.6	0.5	6.9	24.6
hand, except finger	69.5	2.2	0.5	10.3	19.7
finger	138.3	4.2	1.2	16.3	48.2
lower extremities	347.7	8.8	3.0	46.4	66.1
knee	130.1	2.8	1.2	17.9	23.9
foot, except toe	58.1	1.9	0.6	8.1	12.7
toe	18.2	0.3	0.1	2.6	4.2
body systems	21.0	0.5	0.1	1.4	4.5
multiple parts	145.6	2.9	1.0	15.8	23.6
source of injury or illness					
chemicals and chemical products	25.4	0.5	0.8	1.9	7.9
containers	240.1	2.9	0.9	10.3	51.2
furniture and fixtures	56.4	0.2	0.1	3.2	9.8
machinery	111.6	3.4	1.5	11.9	44.8
parts and materials	182.5	3.2	3.3	45.0	67.7
worker motion or position	258.5	5.7	0.7	27.5	70.4
floors, walkways, ground surfaces	278.5	6.1	2.2	37.5	40.5
tools, instruments, and equipment	103.9	2.5	1.5	21.0	24.1
vehicles	138.8	3.0	0.8	11.4	19.8
health care patient	74.6	N/A	N/A	N/A	<50[3]
exposure or event leading to injury or illness					
contact with objects and equipment	443.6	11.6	5.7	62.7	128.5
struck by object	225.0	5.8	3.2	34.5	54.1
struck against object	107.7	2.5	1.0	13.4	28.4
caught in equipment or object	74.8	2.4	1.1	7.5	34.2
fall to lower level	95.3	2.9	1.1	24.4	12.7
fall on same level	198.9	3.7	1.0	14.6	31.3
slip, trip, loss of balance—without fall	52.8	1.3	0.3	5.6	10.0
overexertion	454.7	6.0	4.4	43.0	97.4
overexertion in lifting	256.7	3.5	1.9	23.5	51.2
repetitive motion	68.3	0.5	0.1	2.8	30.6
exposure to harmful substances	69.1	1.8	0.5	6.5	18.3
transportation accidents	73.0	2.1	0.2	8.0	7.6
fires and explosions	3.7	0.2	0.1	1.0	0.8
assaults and violent acts by person	18.4	N/A	N/A	0.3	0.4
total cases	**1,664.0**	**37.3**	**14.1**	**194.4**	**376.6**

Occupational Illnesses and Injuries in the US (continued)

CHARACTERISTIC	SERVICE PRODUCING				
	TRANSPORTATION AND PUBLIC UTILITIES[2]	WHOLE-SALE TRADE	RETAIL TRADE	FINANCE, INSURANCE, REAL ESTATE	SERVICES
injury or illness					
sprains, strains	104.7	56.8	116.9	15.6	196.4
bruises, contusions	21.6	12.1	29.2	2.7	33.4
cuts, lacerations	8.4	8.8	30.8	1.8	17.1
fractures	11.6	10.0	19.1	3.2	19.6
heat burns	0.8	0.9	8.8	0.3	4.1
carpal tunnel syndrome	2.0	1.5	3.8	2.6	5.5
tendonitis	1.1	0.7	1.9	0.6	3.3
chemical burns	0.8	0.5	1.8	0.2	2.1
amputations	0.4	1.0	1.2	0.1	0.5
multiple traumatic injuries	6.8	4.4	10.6	1.4	13.7
body part affected by injury or illness					
head	12.5	7.8	17.6	2.4	22.1
eye	4.5	3.8	7.1	0.9	9.6
neck	5.6	2.0	4.0	0.7	7.6
trunk	82.3	50.6	96.6	12.5	161.7
shoulder	13.8	7.1	14.9	2.2	21.6
back	54.4	34.6	64.6	8.6	116.5
upper extremities	33.2	27.1	71.8	9.6	67.7
wrist	8.4	6.4	14.5	4.1	18.3
hand, except finger	5.4	5.1	14.6	1.2	10.3
finger	9.3	9.1	27.4	2.0	20.7
lower extremities	49.6	26.4	60.9	8.1	78.3
knee	19.1	8.0	22.6	2.3	32.3
foot, except toe	7.0	5.3	11.8	1.4	9.5
toe	2.3	1.7	3.7	0.5	2.8
body systems	2.7	1.2	2.6	1.6	6.4
multiple parts	19.9	9.8	26.5	4.3	41.7
source of injury or illness					
chemicals and chemical products	2.2	1.6	3.7	0.6	6.3
containers	45.6	30.7	59.7	4.8	34.0
furniture and fixtures	4.4	3.3	15.2	2.0	18.3
machinery	5.1	9.4	18.2	2.3	14.9
parts and materials	17.7	13.1	18.5	1.3	12.7
worker motion or position	29.7	17.2	38.0	9.0	60.3
floors, walkways, ground surfaces	34.1	17.7	56.8	9.6	74.1
tools, instruments, and equipment	8.2	5.4	19.4	1.5	20.3
vehicles	37.6	15.6	19.1	2.2	29.3
health care patient	1.5	N/A	0.5	0.5	72.1
exposure or event leading to injury or illness					
contact with objects and equipment	46.2	35.9	80.3	6.7	65.9
struck by object	24.9	19.1	44.1	3.3	35.9
struck against object	11.6	7.9	22.6	2.1	18.1
caught in equipment or object	6.0	6.5	8.9	0.6	7.7
fall to lower level	13.7	7.4	13.1	2.8	17.3
fall on same level	20.7	12.2	47.4	7.1	60.9
slip, trip, loss of balance—without fall	7.6	3.5	9.6	1.7	13.2
overexertion	62.3	37.4	70.8	8.3	125.0
overexertion in lifting	35.2	22.9	48.5	4.6	65.3
repetitive motion	4.5	3.9	8.7	4.6	12.6
exposure to harmful substances	6.7	3.4	13.6	1.8	16.5
transportation accidents	18.5	8.0	7.9	1.7	19.0
fires and explosions	0.2	0.2	0.7	0.1	0.5
assaults and violent acts by person	0.8	0.2	3.4	0.4	12.8
total cases	207.0	125.6	281.3	39.5	388.3

[1]Farms with fewer than 11 employees were not included.   [2]The Mine Safety and Health Administration provided data for mining; the Federal Railroad Administration provided railroad transportation data. The mining category excludes independent mining contractors.   [3]Fewer than 50 cases reported.

US Work-related Fatalities by Cause

Totals for major categories may include some smaller categories not listed in the table. Percentages may not add up to totals because of rounding. Source: US Bureau of Labor Statistics.

CAUSE OF FATALITY	1995–99 NUMBER (AVG.)	2000 NUMBER	(%)
transportation accidents	**2,611**	**2,571**	**43.0**
highway	1,405	1,363	23.0
collision between vehicles, mobile equipment	674	694	12.0
moving in same direction	115	136	2.0
moving in opposite directions, oncoming	248	243	4.0
moving in intersection	140	153	3.0
vehicle struck stationary object or equipment	288	279	5.0
noncollision	371	356	6.0
jack-knifed or overturned—no collision	290	304	5.0
nonhighway (farm, industrial premises)	376	399	7.0
overturned	211	213	4.0
aircraft	264	280	5.0
worker struck by a vehicle	380	370	6.0
water vehicle	106	84	1.0
rail vehicle	73	71	1.0
assaults and violent acts	**1,085**	**929**	**16.0**
homicides	837	677	11.0
shooting	663	533	9.0
stabbing	69	66	1.0
other, including bombing	106	78	1.0
self-inflicted injury	216	220	4.0
contact with objects and equipment	**987**	**1,005**	**17.0**
struck by object	563	570	10.0
struck by falling object	361	357	6.0
struck by flying object	58	61	1.0
caught in or compressed by equipment or objects	286	294	5.0
caught in running equipment or machinery	152	157	3.0
caught in or crushed in collapsing materials	123	123	2.0
falls	**697**	**734**	**12.0**
fall to lower level	620	659	11.0
fall from ladder	103	110	2.0
fall from roof	151	150	3.0
fall from scaffold, staging	89	85	1.0
fall on same level	54	56	1.0
exposure to harmful substances or environments	**561**	**480**	**8.0**
contact with electric current	308	256	4.0
contact with overhead power lines	134	128	2.0
contact with temperature extremes	46	29	<0.5
exposure to caustic, noxious, or allergenic substances	113	100	2.0
inhalation of substance	60	48	1.0
oxygen deficiency	92	93	2.0
drowning, submersion	74	74	1.0
fires and explosions	**202**	**177**	**3.0**
other events or exposures	**21**	**19**	**<0.5**
total	**6,165**	**5,915**	**100.0**

Did you know? Only 10,000 people visited Walt Disney World during its first day of operation in 1971. The massive theme park now attracts visitors at the rate of 10,000 per hour.

Arts, Entertainment, & Leisure

Encyclopædia Britannica's 50 Great Museums of the World

Listed alphabetically by country.

Kunsthistorisches Museum, Vienna, Austria: The Museum of Art History's Picture Gallery was built around the collection of Archduke Leopold Wilhelm, who in the mid-17th century acquired some 1,400 paintings of the Venetian Renaissance (including works by Titian, Veronese, Tintoretto) and of Flemish masters from the 15th–17th century (van Eyck, Rubens, van Dyck). The museum's extensive collections also include ancient Egyptian and Near Eastern art and artifacts, Greek and Roman antiquities, more than 700,000 examples of historical currency, ancient musical instruments, arms and armor, and historical carriages and court uniforms.

National Museum of Australia, Canberra, Australia: The National Museum of Australia houses unique exhibitions that explore all aspects of Australian history and culture. Historical artifacts and interactive exhibits tell the story of the people, land, and symbols of the island nation.

The Bahrain National Museum, Manama, Bahrain: The museum houses a large collection of documents, artifacts, and craftwork relating to Arabic history and Islamic studies.

Museum of Art, São Paulo, Brazil: Known as "MASP" (Museu de Arte de São Paulo), the museum owns one of the world's most prestigious collections of works by European masters, including pieces from the 13th century through the present, with a strong emphasis on Impressionists.

Museum of Art and History, Shanghai, China: Also known as the Shanghai Museum, the institution is primarily devoted to ancient Chinese art. It has more than 120,000 relics on permanent display and is especially renowned for its collections of bronzes, ceramics, paintings, and calligraphy.

Egyptian Museum, Cairo, Egypt: Established by the Egyptian government in 1835, the Egyptian Museum houses more than 120,000 objects from prehistoric civilizations to the Greco-Roman period. Much of the museum is devoted to ancient Egyptian history; permanent exhibits explore the Pharaonic era.

The British Museum, London, England: The British Museum explores the histories of virtually all world cultures, from ancient to contemporary. Nations and their civilizations are represented by displays of art, sciences, cultural and historical artifacts, clothing, and currency.

The National Gallery, London, England: On permanent display at the National Gallery is one of the world's greatest collections of Western European painting, with more than 2,300 works from the 13th–20th century.

Tate Britain (formerly the Tate Gallery), London, England: One of the world's most prestigious art institutions, Tate Britain houses the world's most extensive collection of British art from the 16th century to the present. Branches of the Tate in Liverpool, St. Ives, and Bankside are devoted to modern British and world art.

Victoria and Albert Museum, London, England: Although it boasts a wide array of fine arts and cultural artifacts, the Victoria and Albert Museum is especially devoted to applied and decorative arts. Examples of fashion, sculpture, ceramics, glass, metalwork, jewelry, furniture, photography, and paintings from various nations are on permanent display.

La Cité des Sciences et d'Industrie, Paris, France: The museum is devoted primarily to popular science. It houses its own planetarium as well as permanent exhibits on space, information technology, medicine, mathematics, the ocean, and numerous other topics. Also on display is a French navy submarine.

Musée d'Orsay, Paris, France: The Musée d'Orsay acquired a reputation as a world-class museum soon after it opened in 1986. It is devoted to art of the Western world from 1848 to 1914, and its collection is drawn from three art institutions: the Louvre Museum, the Musée du Jeu de Paume, and France's National Museum of Modern Art.

The Louvre Museum, Paris, France: The Louvre is the most famous and revered museum in the world. The main building served as a medieval fortress and as a palace for the kings of France and has been used as a museum since 1793. The Louvre's collections are divided into seven departments: paintings; sculptures; prints and drawings; objets d'art; Oriental antiquities and Islamic art; Egyptian antiquities; and Greek, Etruscan, and Roman antiquities.

Château de Versailles, Versailles, France: The original château of the Palace of Versailles was built in 1623 as a hunting lodge and retreat for King Louis XIII. The palace was expanded throughout the 17th century, and in 1682 it became the official residence of the king and the Court of France. It is still used as an official national palace when both houses of parliament are convened, although much of the palace—including its many rooms of artistic and architectural masterpieces—is open to the public.

Deutsches Historisches Museum, Berlin, Germany: The German Historical Museum chronicles German history through its vast collection of artwork, historical documents, militaria, and artifacts of German culture.

Gemäldegalerie Alte Meister, Dresden, Germany: Located in historic Zwinger Castle, the Old Masters Picture Gallery houses a large collection of Italian Renaissance, Baroque, and 17th-century Flemish and Dutch paintings, including works by such masters as Rembrandt, Rubens, and Raphael.

Alte Pinakothek, Munich, Germany: The Old Pinakothek is home to one of the world's premier collections of European paintings from the

14th–18th century, including works by Rembrandt, da Vinci, and Raphael.

The Acropolis Museum, Athens, Greece: Located near the ruins of the Acropolis, the museum is the world's main repository of masterpieces of ancient Greek civilization, especially those of the Archaic period.

National Archaeological Museum, Athens, Greece: Considered the most important archaeological museum in Greece, the National Archaeological Museum is home to exhibits representative of all aspects of Greek cultural history. The museum houses one of the largest collections of ancient Greek art in the world.

National Museum, New Delhi, India: The National Museum houses a vast collection of art objects from India and the world. Its major holdings include archaeological objects, jewelry, paintings, decorative arts, and arms and armor.

National Museum of Ireland, Dublin, Ireland: The museum merged several major collections of Irish art and artifacts when it opened in 1890. Its archaeological and artistic exhibits include masterworks from 2000 BC to the 20th century.

Galleria dell'Accademia, Florence, Italy: The Gallery of the Academy houses a collection of 15th- and 16th-century paintings and many Tuscan paintings from the 13th–16th century. The museum is best known, however, for its sculptures by Michelangelo, notably his *David*.

Galleria degli Uffizi, Florence, Italy: The Uffizi is renowned for its world's finest collection of Italian Renaissance painting, particularly of the Florentine school. The gallery was established in the 16th century to house the many art treasures of the Medici family.

Pinacoteca di Brera, Milan, Italy: One of Italy's largest art galleries, founded in 1809 by Napoleon I, the Brera Picture Gallery is especially renowned for its paintings by the Venetian school.

The Vatican Museums, Rome, Italy: The Vatican Museums have housed the art collections of the popes since the beginning of the 15th century. The various galleries contain ancient sculptures and epigraphy, Etruscan and Egyptian artifacts, an outstanding collection of Italian religious paintings, and Russian and Byzantine paintings. A modern art collection was initiated in 1956, and the Vatican's first museum of contemporary art, housed in 65 galleries in the Vatican palace, opened in 1973.

Gallerie dell'Accademia di Venezia, Venice, Italy: The Galleries of the Academy of Venice house an unrivaled collection of paintings from the Venetian masters of the 13th–18th century, including outstanding works by Giovanni Bellini, Giorgione, Titian, Tintoretto, and Canaletto.

Tokugawa Art Museum, Nagoya, Japan: The Tokugawa Art Museum holds a vast collection of objects belonging to the descendants of the Tokugawa family, including weapons and furniture used by the family's feudal lords. One section of the museum is dedicated to the 12th-century picture scrolls of the Tale of Genji.

Tokyo National Museum, Tokyo, Japan: The TNM's collection includes major exhibits of Asian painting, sculpture, calligraphy, decorative art, rare books, photographs, metalwork, lacquerware, ceramics, textiles, and antiquities.

Museo Nacional de Antropología, Mexico City, Mexico: The collection of the National Museum of Anthropology includes anthropological, ethnological, and archaeological materials from Mexico's pre-Hispanic past, including treasures of the Aztecs, Mayas, Zapotecs, Mixtec, Purépechas, and Olmecs.

Rijksmuseum, Amsterdam, The Netherlands: With nearly one million objects, the Rijksmuseum is the largest museum of art and history in The Netherlands. It is perhaps best known for its collection of 17th-century Dutch paintings, including works by Rembrandt, Vermeer, and Jan Steen.

Muzeum Narodowe w Warszawie, Warsaw, Poland: The National Museum in Warsaw houses 780,000 items in its permanent galleries, including one of the richest and most diverse collections of European art in Poland. It is also home to the largest Polish scholarly library of books and documents related to art and world culture.

The Catherine Palace, Moscow, Russia: The immense Catherine Palace, with its extravagantly gilded interior, was originally built in the early 18th century for Catherine I. Visitors have access to several of the palace's suites, the Cameron Gallery, and the rooms of the Agate Pavilion.

The State Hermitage Museum, St. Petersburg, Russia: Occupying six buildings in the heart of St. Petersburg, the Hermitage was founded in 1764 as a private gallery for the art amassed by Empress Catherine the Great. In addition to its many Russian masterpieces, the museum houses works by Renaissance Italian and Baroque Dutch, Flemish, and French painters. Also noteworthy is its collection of Central Asian art.

The State Russian Museum, St. Petersburg, Russia: Housed in the buildings of the former Mikhailovsky Palace, the State Russian Museum is the central museum of Russian art and culture. The main building houses art from the 10th century through the revolution, including a comprehensive collection of painting and sculpture from the 18th and 19th centuries and an excellent collection of early Russian art, with fine icons from the 12th–14th century. In addition, there are collections of late 19th- and early 20th-century paintings, portraits, and applied arts and an ethnographic museum.

Asian Civilisations Museum, Singapore: The Asian Civilisations Museum traces the cultural history of China, Southeast Asia, India, and West Asia through its vast collection of ceramics, sculptures, and other artifacts.

South African Museum, Cape Town, South Africa: The South African Museum documents the natural history and anthropology of southern Africa. Objects dating to the origins of the region's indigenous populations are featured in the collection. The museum also houses a planetarium.

Museo del Prado, Madrid, Spain: The Prado Museum houses the world's richest and most comprehensive collection of Spanish painting, as well as masterpieces of other schools of European painting, especially Italian and Flemish art. The museum contains the world's most complete collections of the works of El Greco, Diego Velázquez, and Francisco de Goya.

Swedish Museum of Natural History, Stockholm, Sweden: Dedicated to the history of natural sciences, the Swedish Museum of Natural History houses millions of specimens within its four main divisions of botany, geology, paleontology, and zoology.

National Palace Museum, Taipei, Taiwan: The National Palace Museum houses several international art masterpieces but is especially known for its collections of porcelain, jade, silk paintings, calligraphy, and other arts of ancient China.

The National Museum, Bangkok, Thailand: In 1874 King Rama V established this first public museum in Bangkok to display the royal art collection. The museum today houses objects of art, archaeology, and culture from prehistoric to modern times. Among the major permanent exhibits are the Gallery of Thai History and the Gallery of Prehistory.

Boston Museum of Fine Arts, Boston MA: One of the world's most comprehensive art museums, the MFA was founded in 1870 with the art holdings of the Boston Athenaeum library as the nucleus of its collection. The museum has a major collection of Asian art from the 3rd millennium BC to modern times. It also has the largest collection outside France of paintings by Claude Monet, the world's foremost collection of 19th-century American art, and one of the world's finest collections of Egyptian Old Kingdom objects.

The Art Institute of Chicago, Chicago IL: The Art Institute's permanent exhibits include European, American, and Oriental sculpture, paintings, prints and drawings, and decorative arts, as well as photography and African and pre-Columbian American art. The museum is noted for its extensive collections of 19th-century French painting (Impressionist works in particular) and of 20th-century painting.

Field Museum of Natural History, Chicago IL: The Field Museum was established in 1893 to display the biological and anthropological artifacts gathered for the World's Colombian Exposition. Permanent exhibits explore the Earth's cultural history and biological and geologic development. A major addition to the museum in 2000 was "Sue," the largest, most complete, and best-preserved *Tyrannosaurus rex* fossil ever discovered.

Los Angeles County Museum of Art, Los Angeles CA: The museum's permanent collections emphasize Asian, Islamic, European, and American art from ancient times to the present. Also important are the exhibits of costumes and textiles, decorative arts, and photography that represent various world cultures.

Guggenheim Museum, New York NY: The museum's permanent collections emphasize modern art, including Impressionist, nonobjective, abstract, surrealist, minimalist, and avant-garde works.

Metropolitan Museum of Art, New York NY: The most prestigious art institution in the United States, the museum houses more than three million objects representing virtually all nations and all periods of human history.

Museum of Modern Art, New York NY: The collection at "MoMA" includes more than 100,000 paintings, sculptures, drawings, prints, photographs, architectural models and drawings, and design objects. Also housed in the museum are more than 14,000 films, 4,000,000 film stills, and an extensive library of books and periodicals.

The National Gallery of Art, Washington DC: The National Gallery, founded by Andrew Mellon in the 1930s, houses many of the world's most renowned examples of European and American painting, sculpture, and graphic arts from the 14th century to the present.

The Smithsonian Institution, Washington DC: One of the world's leading museums and research institutions, the Smithsonian comprises 16 museums (which house more than 140 million artifacts) and several research facilities throughout the world. The museums include the National Museum of American History, the National Zoological Park, the National Air and Space Museum, the Anacostia Museum and Center for African American History and Culture, the National Museum of the American Indian, and the National Portrait Gallery.

United States Holocaust Memorial Museum, Washington DC: The United States' national institution for studying the Holocaust, the museum also serves as a memorial to the millions who died in the Holocaust. Located near the National Mall in Washington DC, the museum uses exhibitions, publications, and public programs to promote awareness of the issues related to the Holocaust.

Encyclopædia Britannica's 25 Global Dance Companies

COMPANY	LOCATION	ARTISTIC DIRECTOR (2002)	FOUNDED
Alvin Ailey American Dance Theater	New York NY	Judith Jamison	1958
American Ballet Theatre	New York NY	Kevin McKenzie	1940
Ballet Folklórico de Mexico	Mexico City, Mexico	Norma Lopez	1952
Ballet Nacional de Cuba	Havana, Cuba	Alicia Alonso	1948
Bat-Dor Dance Company	Tel Aviv, Israel	Jeanette Ordman	1968
Batsheva Dance Company	Tel Aviv, Israel	Ohad Naharin	1964
Bolshoi Ballet	Moscow, Russia	Boris Akimov	1776
Compañía Nacional de Danza	Madrid, Spain	Nacho Duato	1990
Dance Theatre of Harlem	New York NY	Arthur Mitchell	1969
Hubbard Street Dance Chicago	Chicago IL	Jim Vincent	1978
Joffrey Ballet	Chicago IL	Gerald Arpino	1956
José Limón Dance Company	New York NY	Carla Maxwell	1947
Kibbutz Contemporary Dance Company	Tel Aviv, Israel	Rami Be'er	1970
Kirov-Mariinsky Ballet	St. Petersburg, Russia	Valery Gergiev	1738
Martha Graham Center of Contemporary Dance	New York NY	Kenneth Topping	1926
Merce Cunningham Dance	New York NY	Merce Cunningham	1952
Nederlands Dans Theater	The Hague, The Netherlands	Glenn Edgerton	1959
New York City Ballet	New York NY	Peter Martins	1946
Paul Taylor Dance Company	New York NY	Paul Taylor	1954
Paris Opéra Ballet	Paris, France	Brigitte Lefèvre	1661

Encyclopædia Britannica's 25 Global Dance Companies (continued)

COMPANY	LOCATION	ARTISTIC DIRECTOR (2002)	FOUNDED
Rambert Dance Company	London, England	Christopher Bruce*	1926
Royal Ballet	London, England	Ross Stretton	1926
Royal Swedish Ballet	Stockholm, Sweden	Peter Jacobsson	1773
Twyla Tharp Dance	New York NY	Twyla Tharp	1965
White Oak Dance Project	White Oak Plantation; Florida-Georgia border	Mikhail Baryshnikov	1990

*To retire in 2002; no successor yet named.

Encyclopædia Britannica's 25 Notable US Theater Companies

COMPANY	LOCATION	ARTISTIC DIRECTOR (2002)
The Acting Company	New York NY	Gregory Lamont Allen
Actors Theatre	Louisville KY	Marc Masterson
Alley Theatre	Houston TX	Gregory Boyd
American Conservatory Theater	San Francisco CA	Carey Perloff
American Repertory Theatre	Cambridge MA	Robert Woodruff
Arena Stage	Washington DC	Molly Smith
Black Theatre Ensemble	Chicago IL	Jackie Taylor
Center Theatre Group	Los Angeles CA	Gordon Davidson
Circle in the Square	New York NY	Theodore Mann
Cleveland Public Theatre	Cleveland OH	James Levin
Colony Theatre Company	Los Angeles CA	Barbara Beckley
El Teatro Campesino	San Juan Bautista CA	Luis Valdez
Ford's Theatre	Washington DC	Frankie Hewitt
Goodman Theatre	Chicago IL	Robert Falls
Guthrie Theater	Minneapolis MN	Joe Dowling
La Jolla Playhouse	La Jolla CA	Des McAnuff
Long Wharf Theatre	New Haven CT	Gordon Edelstein
National Actors Theatre	New York NY	Tony Randall
Pasadena Playhouse	Pasadena CA	Sheldon Epps
The Public Theater	New York NY	George Wolfe
Seattle Repertory Theatre	Seattle WA	Sharon Ott
Steppenwolf Theatre Company	Chicago IL	Martha Lavey
Studio Arena Theatre	Buffalo NY	Gavin Cameron-Webb
Victory Gardens Theater	Chicago IL	Dennis Zacek
Yale Repertory Theatre	New Haven CT	Stan Wojewodski, Jr.

Longest-Running Broadway Shows

Phantom of the Opera, Beauty and the Beast, Rent, and Chicago are all expected to move up in the standings by the end of 2002.

	SHOW	RUN	TOTAL PERFORMANCES		SHOW	RUN	TOTAL PERFORMANCES
1	Cats	1982–2000	7,485	11	Tobacco Road	1933–41	3,182
2	Les Misérables	1987–		13	Hello, Dolly!	1964–70	2,844
3	A Chorus Line	1975–90	6,137	14	My Fair Lady	1956–62	2,717
4	The Phantom of the Opera	1988–		15	Rent	1996–	
				16	Annie	1977–83	2,377
5	Oh! Calcutta! [revival]	1976–89	5,959	17	Man of La Mancha	1965–71	2,328
				18	Chicago [revival]	1996–	
6	Miss Saigon	1991–2001	4,092	19	Abie's Irish Rose	1922–27	2,327
7	42nd Street	1980–89	3,486	20	Oklahoma!	1943–48	2,212
8	Grease	1972–80	3,338	21	Smokey Joe's Cafe	1995–2000	2,037
9	Beauty and the Beast	1994–		22	Pippin	1972–77	1,944
				23	South Pacific	1949–54	1,925
9	Fiddler on the Roof	1964–72	3,242	24	The Magic Show	1974–78	1,920
10	Life with Father	1939–47	3,224	25	Gemini	1977–81	1,819

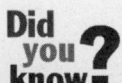

Did you know? Although theater has not flourished as a major art under Islam, mime and shadow-puppet shows have persisted as forms of popular entertainment.

Encyclopædia Britannica's 150 Greatest Films

(Title, director, year of release.)

The Adventure (L'avventura; Michelangelo Antonioni, 1960)
The African Queen (John Huston, 1951)
Aguirre: The Wrath of God (Aguirre, der Zorn Gottes; Werner Herzog, 1972)
All About Eve (Joseph Mankiewicz, 1950)
American Graffiti (George Lucas, 1973)
An American in Paris (Vincente Minelli, 1951)
The Apartment (Billy Wilder, 1960)
Apocalypse Now (Francis Ford Coppola, 1979)
The Apu Trilogy (Satyajit Ray): Pather Panchali (1955), Aparajito (1956), The World of Apu (Apur Sansar; 1959)
Bagdad Café (Out of Rosenheim; Percy Aldon, 1988)
The Band Wagon (Vincente Minnelli, 1953)
The Bank Dick (Edward F. Cline, 1940)
The Battleship Potemkin or Potemkin (Bronenosets Potyomkin; Sergei Eisenstein, 1925)
Beauty and the Beast (La belle et la bête; Jean Cocteau, 1946)
The Bicycle Thief (Ladri di biciclette; Vittorio De Sica, 1948)
The Birth of a Nation (D.W. Griffith, 1915)
Blade Runner (Ridley Scott, 1982)
The Blue Angel (Der blaue Engel; Josef Von Sternberg, 1930)
Blue Velvet (David Lynch, 1986)
Bob the Gambler (Bob le flambeur; Jean-Pierre Melville, 1955)
Brazil (Terry Gilliam, 1985)
Breathless (À bout de souffle; Jean-Luc Godard, 1959)
Bride of Frankenstein (James Whale, 1935)
The Bridge on the River Kwai (David Lean, 1957)
Brief Encounter (David Lean, 1945)
Bringing Up Baby (Howard Hawks, 1938)
By Chance Balthazar (Au hasard, Balthazar; Robert Bresson, 1966)
Cabaret (Bob Fosse, 1972)
The Cabinet of Dr. Caligari (Das Kabinett des Doktor Caligari; Robert Wiene, 1919)
Camille (George Cukor, 1936)
Casablanca (Michael Curtiz, 1942)
Central Station (Walter Salles, Jr., 1988)
Children of Paradise (Les Enfants du paradis; Marcel Carné, 1945)
Chinatown (Roman Polanski, 1974)
Cinema Paradiso (Nuovo Cinema Paradiso; Giuseppe Tornatore, 1988)
Citizen Kane (Orson Welles, 1941)
City Lights (Charlie Chaplin, 1931)
The Conformist (Il conformista; Bernardo Bertolucci, 1970)
The Conversation (Francis Ford Coppola, 1974)
Crimes and Misdemeanors (Woody Allen, 1989)
Day for Night (La Nuit américaine; François Truffaut, 1973)
Days of Heaven (Terence Malick, 1978)
Decalogue (Krzysztof Kieslowski, 1988)
Do the Right Thing (Spike Lee, 1989)
Double Indemnity (Billy Wilder, 1944)
Dr. Strangelove or How I Learned to Stop Worrying and Love the Bomb (Stanley Kubrick, 1964)
Duck Soup (Leo McCarey, 1933)
8½ (Otto e mezzo; Federico Fellini, 1963)
Fargo (Joel Coen, 1996)

The 400 Blows (Le Quatre cents coups; François Truffaut, 1959)
The French Connection (William Friedkin, 1971)
From Here to Eternity (Fred Zinneman, 1953)
The General (Buster Keaton, 1927)
The Godfather and The Godfather Part II (Francis Ford Coppola; 1972, 1974)
The Gold Rush (Charlie Chaplin, 1925)
Gone with the Wind (Victor Fleming, 1939)
The Graduate (Mike Nichols, 1967)
Grand Illusion (Le Grande illusion; Jean Renoir, 1937)
Greed (Erich Von Stroheim, 1924)
A Hard Day's Night (Richard Lester, 1964)
His Girl Friday (Howard Hawks, 1940)
Holiday (George Cukor, 1938)
The Hustler (Robert Rossen, 1961)
Ikiru (Akira Kurosawa, 1952)
Intolerance (D.W. Griffith, 1916)
Invasion of the Body Snatchers (Don Siegel, 1956)
It's a Wonderful Life (Frank Capra, 1946)
Jules and Jim (Jules et Jim; François Truffaut, 1961)
King Kong (Merian C. Cooper and Ernest B. Schoedsack, 1933)
Lancelot of the Lake (Lancelot du lac; Robert Bresson, 1974)
The Last Laugh (Der letze Mann; F.W. Murnau, 1924)
La strada (Federico Fellini, 1954)
The Last Picture Show (Peter Bogdanovich, 1971)
Laura (Otto Preminger, 1944)
Lawrence of Arabia (David Lean, 1962)
The Magnificent Ambersons (Orson Welles, 1942)
The Maltese Falcon (John Huston, 1941)
A Man Escaped (Un condamné à mort s'est echappé; Robert Bresson, 1956)
The Manchurian Candidate (John Frankenheimer, 1962)
M*A*S*H (Robert Altman, 1970)
Mephisto (István Szabó, 1981)
Metropolis (Fritz Lang, 1927)
Mr. Smith Goes to Washington (Frank Capra, 1939)
Nanook of the North (Robert Flaherty, 1922)
Napoléon (Abel Gance, 1927)
Nashville (Robert Altman, 1975)
The Night of the Hunter (Charles Laughton, 1955)
Nights of Cabiria (La notti di Cabiria; Federico Fellini, 1957)
Ninotchka (Ernst Lubitsch, 1939)
North by Northwest (Alfred Hitchcock, 1959)
Nosferatu, the Vampire (Nosferatu—eine Symphonie des Grauens; F.W. Murnau, 1922)
Odd Man Out (Carol Reed, 1947)
On the Waterfront (Elia Kazan, 1954)
Out of the Past (Jacques Tourneur, 1947)
Pandora's Box (Die Büchse der Pandora; G.W. Pabst, 1929)
Passion Fish (John Sayles, 1992)
The Passion of Joan of Arc (La Passion de Jeanne d'Arc; Carl Theodor Dreyer, 1928)
Persona (Ingmar Bergman, 1966)
Pinocchio (Walt Disney, 1940)
The Postman Always Rings Twice (Tay Garnett, 1946)
Psycho (Alfred Hitchcock, 1960)
Public Enemy (William Wellman, 1931)
Pulp Fiction (Quentin Tarantino, 1994)
The Quiet Man (John Ford, 1952)
Raging Bull (Martin Scorsese, 1980)

Raise the Red Lantern (Dahong Denglong Gaogao Gua; Yimou Zhang, 1991)
Rashomon (Akira Kurosawa, 1951)
Rear Window (Alfred Hitchcock, 1954)
Red River (Howard Hawks, 1948)
The Red Shoes (Michael Powell and Emeric Pressburger, 1948)
Rome, Open City or Open City (Roma, città aperta; Roberto Rossellini, 1945)
The Rules of the Game (La Règle du jeu; Jean Renoir, 1939)
Schindler's List (Steven Spielberg, 1993)
The Searchers (John Ford, 1956)
Secrets and Lies (Mike Leigh, 1996)
Seven Samurai (Shichinin no Samurai; Akira Kurosawa, 1954)
The Seventh Seal (Det Sjunde inseglet; Ingmar Bergman, 1957)
Shane (George Stevens, 1953)
Sherlock, Jr. (Buster Keaton, 1924)
Shoah (Claude Lanzmann, 1985)
Shoot the Piano Player (Tirez sur le pianiste; François Truffaut, 1960)
The Silence of the Lambs (Jonathan Demme, 1991)
Singin' in the Rain (Stanley Donen and Gene Kelly, 1952)
Some Like It Hot (Billy Wilder, 1959)
Stagecoach (John Ford, 1939)
The Story of Qui Ju (Qin Ju da Guansi; Yimou Zhang, 1992)

A Streetcar Named Desire (Elia Kazan, 1951)
Sunrise (F.W. Murnau, 1927)
Sunset Boulevard (Billy Wilder, 1950)
Taxi Driver (Martin Scorsese, 1976)
The Third Man (Carol Reed, 1949)
The 39 Steps (Alfred Hitchcock, 1935)
"Three Colors" ("Trois Couleurs"; Krzysztof Kieslowski): Bleu (Blue, 1993); Blanc (White, 1994); Rouge (Red, 1994)
To Have and Have Not (Howard Hawks, 1944)
Top Hat (Mark Sandrich, 1935)
Touch of Evil (Orson Welles, 1958)
The Treasure of the Sierra Madre (John Huston, 1948)
Triumph of the Will (Leni Riefenstahl, 1934)
2001: A Space Odyssey (Stanley Kubrick, 1968)
Umberto D. (Vittorio De Sica, 1952)
Unforgiven (Clint Eastwood, 1992)
Vertigo (Alfred Hitchcock, 1958)
The White Balloon (Badkonak-E Sefid; Jafar Panahi, 1995)
Wild Strawberries (Smultronstället; Ingmar Bergman, 1957)
Wings of Desire (Der Himmel über Berlin; Wim Wenders, 1987)
The Wizard of Oz (Victor Fleming, 1939)
The Year of Living Dangerously (Peter Weir, 1982)
Yojimbo (Akira Kurosawa, 1961)
Young Frankenstein (Mel Brooks, 1974)

100 Top-Grossing Films

As of 30 Apr 2002. Source: The Internet Movie Database: <http://imdb.com>.

1 Titanic	1997	
2 Harry Potter and the Sorcerer's Stone	2001	
3 Star Wars: The Phantom Menace	1999	
4 Jurassic Park	1993	
5 The Lord of the Rings: The Fellowship of the Ring	2001	
6 Independence Day	1996	
7 Star Wars	1977	
8 The Lion King	1994	
9 E.T.	1982	
10 Forrest Gump	1994	
11 The Sixth Sense	1999	
12 Jurassic Park: The Lost World	1997	
13 Men in Black	1997	
14 Star Wars: Return of the Jedi	1983	
15 Armageddon	1998	
16 Mission: Impossible 2	2000	
17 Star Wars: The Empire Strikes Back	1980	
18 Home Alone	1990	
19 Ghost	1990	
20 Terminator 2: Judgment Day	1991	
21 Monsters, Inc.	2001	
22 Aladdin	1992	
23 Indiana Jones and the Last Crusade	1989	
24 Twister	1996	
25 Toy Story 2	1999	
26 Saving Private Ryan	1998	
27 Jaws	1975	
28 The Matrix	1999	
29 Gladiator	2000	
30 Shrek	2001	
31 Mission: Impossible	1996	
32 Pearl Harbor	2001	
33 Ocean's Eleven	2001	
34 Pretty Woman	1990	
35 Tarzan	1999	
36 Dances with Wolves	1990	
37 Cast Away	2000	
38 Mrs. Doubtfire	1993	
39 The Mummy Returns	2001	
40 The Mummy	1999	
41 Batman	1989	
42 Rain Man	1988	
43 The Bodyguard	1992	
44 Gone with the Wind	1939	
45 Robin Hood: Prince of Thieves	1991	
46 Raiders of the Lost Ark	1981	
47 Grease	1978	
48 Godzilla	1998	
49 What Women Want	2000	
50 The Fugitive	1993	
51 True Lies	1994	
52 Die Hard: With a Vengeance	1995	
53 Notting Hill	1999	
54 Jurassic Park III	2001	
55 There's Something About Mary	1998	
56 Planet of the Apes	2001	
57 The Flintstones	1994	
58 Toy Story	1995	
59 A Bug's Life	1998	
60 The Exorcist	1973	
61 Beauty and the Beast	1991	
62 Basic Instinct	1992	
63 The World is Not Enough	1999	
64 Goldeneye	1995	
65 Back to the Future	1985	
66 Seven	1995	
67 Hannibal	2001	
68 Who Framed Roger Rabbit?	1988	
69 Deep Impact	1998	
70 Dinosaur	2000	
71 Pocahontas	1995	

100 Top-Grossing Films (continued)

72	Tomorrow Never Dies	1997	87	Fatal Attraction	1987
73	Top Gun	1986	88	Lethal Weapon 3	1992
74	How the Grinch Stole Christmas	2000	89	Beverly Hills Cop	1984
75	American Beauty	1999	90	Air Force One	1997
76	Batman Forever	1995	91	As Good As It Gets	1997
77	Apollo 13	1995	92	Austin Powers: The Spy Who Shagged Me	1999
78	Indiana Jones and the Temple of Doom	1984			
79	Back to the Future, Part II	1989	93	Ransom	1996
80	The Rock	1996	94	Runaway Bride	1999
81	Rush Hour 2	2001	95	Liar Liar	1997
82	Crocodile Dundee	1986	96	101 Dalmatians	1996
83	The Perfect Storm	2000	97	Mulan	1998
84	The Hunchback of Notre Dame	1996	98	Hook	1991
85	Schindler's List	1993	99	Rocky IV	1985
86	The Mask	1994	100	Rambo: First Blood Part II	1985

Encyclopædia Britannica's Top 25 Opera Companies

COMPANY	LOCATION	GENERAL OR ARTISTIC DIRECTOR (2002)	FOUNDED
Arena di Verona*	Verona, Italy	Mauro Trombetta	1913
Bavarian State Opera	Munich, Germany	Sir Peter Jonas	1653
Bolshoi Theater	Moscow, Russia	Anatoly Iksanov	1776
Boston Lyric Opera	Boston MA	Leon Major	1976
Budapest Opera	Budapest, Hungary	Domokos Moldován	1884
Canadian Opera Company	Toronto ON	Richard Bradshaw	1950
Cleveland Opera	Cleveland OH	David Bamberger	1976
Finnish National Opera	Helsinki, Finland	Erkki Korhonen	1914
Grand Théâtre de Genève	Geneva, Switzerland	Jean-Marie Blanchard	1964
Kirov-Mariinsky Opera	St. Petersburg, Russia	Valery Gergiev	1860
Los Angeles Opera	Los Angeles CA	Plácido Domingo	1986
Lyric Opera	Chicago IL	Matthew A. Epstein	1954
Metropolitan Opera	New York NY	James Levine	1883
Opera Australia	Sydney and Melbourne, Australia	Richard Gill	1996
Teatro dell'Opera di Roma	Rome, Italy	Gianni Tangucci	1880
Royal Opera House at Covent Garden	London, England	Elaine Padmore	1732
Teatro alla Scala (La Scala)	Milan, Italy	Paolo Arcà	1778
San Francisco Opera	San Francisco CA	Pamela Rosenberg	1923
Staatsoper Unter den Linden	Berlin, Germany	Peter Mussbach	1742
Théâtre du Châtelet	Paris, France	Jean-Pierre Brossmann	1862
Opéra National de Paris	Paris, France	Frédéric Chambert	1669
Teatro Massimo	Palermo, Italy	Marco Betta	1897
Teatro di San Carlo	Naples, Italy	Marcello Panni	1737
Vancouver Opera	Vancouver BC	Randy Smith	1958
Vienna State Opera	Vienna, Austria	Seiji Ozawa	1869

*The Arena di Verona was built in the first century AD; it has been primarily an opera venue since 1913.

Britannica's 25 World-Class Orchestras

ORCHESTRA	LOCATION	FOUNDED	CONDUCTOR (2002)
Berlin Philharmonic Orchestra	Berlin, Germany	1882	Claudio Abbado
Boston Symphony Orchestra	Boston MA	1881	James Levine[1]
Chicago Symphony Orchestra	Chicago IL	1891	Daniel Barenboim
Cleveland Orchestra	Cleveland OH	1918	Franz Welser-Möst
Israel Philharmonic Orchestra	Tel Aviv, Israel	1936	Zubin Mehta
Leipzig Gewandhaus Orchestra	Leipzig, Germany	1743	Herbert Blomstedt
London Philharmonic Orchestra	London, England	1932	Kurt Masur
London Symphony Orchestra	London, England	1904	Colin Davis
Los Angeles Philharmonic	Los Angeles CA	1919	Esa-Pekka Salonen
Montreal Symphony Orchestra	Montreal, Quebec, Canada	1934	Charles Dutoit[2]
New York Philharmonic	New York NY	1842	Lorin Maazel[1]
NHK Symphony Orchestra	Tokyo, Japan	1926	Charles Dutoit
Orchestre de la Suisse Romande	Geneva, Switzerland	1918	Fabio Luisi
Orchestre de Paris	Paris, France	1967	Christoph Eschenbach

Britannica's 25 World-Class Orchestras (continued)

ORCHESTRA	LOCATION	FOUNDED	CONDUCTOR (2002)
Orchestre National de France	Paris, France	1934	Charles Dutoit
Oslo Philharmonic Orchestra	Oslo, Norway	1919	Mariss Jansons
Philadelphia Orchestra	Philadelphia PA	1900	Wolfgang Sawallisch
Philharmonia Orchestra	London, England	1945	Christoph von Dohnányi
Pittsburgh Symphony Orchestra	Pittsburgh PA	1896	Mariss Jansons
Royal Concertgebouw Orchestra	Amsterdam, The Netherlands	1888	Riccardo Chailly
Royal Philharmonia Orchestra	London, England	1946	Daniele Gatti
Saint Louis Symphony Orchestra	St. Louis MO	1880	Hans Vonk
St. Petersburg State Symphony Orchestra	St. Petersburg, Russia	1988	Alexander Kantorov
San Francisco Symphony	San Francisco CA	1911	Michael Tilson Thomas
Vienna Philharmonic Orchestra	Vienna, Austria	1842	guest conductors

[1]Maazel and Levine will assume, respectively, the direction of the New York Philharmonic and the Boston Symphony Orchestra in the fall of 2002. Kurt Masur (New York) and Seiji Ozawa (Boston) are in their final seasons of conducting the orchestras.   [2]Charles Dutoit resigned from the Montreal Symphony Orchestra in April 2002.

The Top 50 Best-Selling Albums

As of January 2002. Source: Recording Industry Association of America (RIAA).

	ALBUM	ARTIST	YEAR		ALBUM	ARTIST	YEAR
1	Their Greatest Hits	The Eagles	1976	26	Bat Out of Hell	Meat Loaf	1977
2	Thriller	Michael Jackson	1982	27	Backstreet Boys	Backstreet Boys	1997
3	The Wall	Pink Floyd	1979	28	Double Live	Garth Brooks	1998
4	Untitled ("Led Zeppelin IV")	Led Zeppelin	1971	29	Purple Rain	Prince	1984
				30	Whitney Houston	Whitney Houston	1985
5	Greatest Hits	Billy Joel	1985	31	...Baby One More Time	Britney Spears	1999
6	Back in Black	AC/DC	1980				
7	The Beatles ("The White Album")	The Beatles	1968	32	Millennium	Backstreet Boys	1999
				33	Simon & Garfunkel's Greatest Hits	Simon & Garfunkel	1972
8	Rumours	Fleetwood Mac	1977				
9	Come On Over	Shania Twain	1997	34	Live /1975–85 and the E Street Band	Bruce Springsteen	1986
10	The Bodyguard Soundtrack	Whitney Houston & various artists	1992				
11	Boston	Boston	1976	35	Slippery When Wet	Bon Jovi	1986
12	Jagged Little Pill	Alanis Morissette	1995	36	II	Boyz II Men	1994
13	No Fences	Garth Brooks	1990	37	Greatest Hits	Kenny Rogers	1980
14	Cracked Rear View	Hootie and the Blowfish	1995	38	Breathless	Kenny G	1992
				39	Hysteria	Def Leppard	1987
15	Hotel California	The Eagles	1976	40	Led Zeppelin II	Led Zeppelin	1969
16	The Beatles: 1967–70	The Beatles	1973	41	Metallica	Metallica	1991
				42	The Woman in Me	Shania Twain	1995
17	Born in the U.S.A.	Bruce Springsteen	1984	43	Abbey Road	The Beatles	1969
18	Dark Side of the Moon	Pink Floyd	1973	44	No Jacket Required	Phil Collins	1985
				45	Yourself or Someone Like You	matchbox 20	1996
19	Appetite for Destruction	Guns 'n' Roses	1987				
20	Greatest Hits	Elton John	1974	46	Forest Gump Soundtrack	various artists	1994
21	Saturday Night Fever Soundtrack	The Bee Gees & various artists	1977	47	Dirty Dancing Soundtrack	various artists	1988
22	Physical Graffiti	Led Zeppelin	1975	48	James Taylor's Greatest Hits	James Taylor	1976
23	The Beatles: 1962–66	The Beatles	1973	49	Sgt. Pepper's Lonely Hearts Club Band	The Beatles	1967
24	Ropin' the Wind	Garth Brooks	1991	50	CrazySexyCool	TLC	1994
25	Supernatural	Santana	1999				

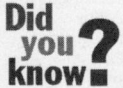

Did you know ❓ Songwriter-composer Randy Newman won his first Academy Award for his score for the film Monsters, Inc. (2001), the 11th film for which he had been nominated. Newman's uncles Alfred and Lionel Newman were also Oscar-winning film composers. Another uncle, Emil, and two cousins, Thomas and David, have also received Oscar nominations for their film scores.

Rock and Roll Hall of Fame Inductees

Music-industry professionals established the Rock and Roll Hall of Fame Foundation in 1983 in order to "recognize the contributions of those who have had a significant impact on the evolution, development and perpetuation of rock and roll." Performers are eligible for induction 25 years after the release of their first record. The Foundation's nominating committee compiles an annual list of eligible artists and distributes this list to about 1,000 rock experts throughout the world. Those performers receiving the highest number of votes, as well as at least 50% of the vote, are inducted. Special committees select inductees in other categories. Those elected to membership receive a statuette depicting an abstract figure holding aloft a gold record.

NAME (YEAR OF INDUCTION)

Paul Ackerman[1] (1995)
Aerosmith (2001)
The Allman Brothers Band (1995)
The Animals (1994)
Louis Armstrong[2] (1990)
Chet Atkins[3] (2002)
LaVern Baker (1991)
Hank Ballard (1990)
The Band (1994)
Dave Bartholomew[1] (1991)
Ralph Bass[1] (1991)
The Beach Boys (1988)
The Beatles (1988)
The Bee Gees (1997)
Chuck Berry (1986)
Chris Blackwell[1] (2001)
Hal Blaine[3] (2000)
Bob Wills and His Texas Playboys[2] (1999)
Bobby "Blue" Bland (1992)
Booker T. and the M.G.'s (1992)
David Bowie (1996)
Charles Brown[3] (1999)
James Brown (1986)
Ruth Brown (1993)
Buffalo Springfield (1997)
Solomon Burke (2001)
James Burton[3] (2001)
The Byrds (1991)
Johnny Cash (1992)
Ray Charles (1986)
Leonard Chess[1] (1987)
Charlie Christian[2] (1990)
Eric Clapton (2000)
Dick Clark[1] (1993)
The Coasters (1987)
Eddie Cochran (1987)
Nat "King" Cole[2] (2000)
Sam Cooke (1986)
Cream (1993)
Creedence Clearwater Revival (1993)
Crosby, Stills & Nash (1997)
King Curtis[3] (2000)
Bobby Darin (1990)
Clive Davis[1] (2000)
Bo Diddley (1987)
Dion (1989)
Willie Dixon[2] (1994)
Fats Domino (1986)
Tom Donahue[1] (1996)
The Doors (1993)
The Drifters (1988)
Bob Dylan (1988)
The Eagles (1998)
Earth, Wind & Fire (2000)
Duane Eddy (1994)
Ahmet Ertegun[1] (1987)
Nesuhi Ertegun[4] (1991)

NAME (YEAR OF INDUCTION)

The Everly Brothers (1986)
Leo Fender[1] (1992)
The Flamingos (2001)
Fleetwood Mac (1998)
The Four Seasons (1990)
The Four Tops (1990)
Frankie Lymon and the Teenagers (1993)
Aretha Franklin (1987)
Alan Freed[1] (1986)
Milt Gabler[1] (1993)
Marvin Gaye (1987)
Gladys Knight and the Pips (1996)
Gerry Goffin and Carole King[1] (1990)
Berry Gordy, Jr.[1] (1988)
Bill Graham[1] (1992)
The Grateful Dead (1994)
Al Green (1995)
Woody Guthrie[2] (1988)
Bill Haley (1987)
John Hammond[4] (1986)
Isaac Hayes (2002)
Billie Holiday[2] (2000)
Holland, Dozier, and Holland[1] (1990)
Buddy Holly (1986)
John Lee Hooker (1991)
The Impressions (1991)
The Inkspots[2] (1989)
The Isley Brothers (1992)
The Jackson Five (1997)
Mahalia Jackson[2] (1997)
Michael Jackson (2001)
James Jamerson[3] (2000)
Elmore James[2] (1992)
Etta James (1993)
Jefferson Airplane (1996)
The Jimi Hendrix Experience (1992)
Billy Joel (1999)
Elton John (1994)
Little Willie John (1996)
Johnnie Johnson[3] (2001)
Robert Johnson[2] (1986)
Janis Joplin (1995)
Louis Jordan[1] (1987)
B.B. King (1987)
The Kinks (1990)
Leadbelly[2] (1988)
Led Zeppelin (1995)
Brenda Lee (2002)
Jerry Leiber and Mike Stoller[1] (1987)
John Lennon (1994)
Jerry Lee Lewis (1986)
Professor Longhair[2] (1992)
The Lovin' Spoonful (2000)

NAME (YEAR OF INDUCTION)

The Mamas and the Papas (1998)
Bob Marley (1994)
Martha and the Vandellas (1995)
George Martin[1] (1999)
Curtis Mayfield (1999)
Paul McCartney (1999)
Clyde McPhatter (1987)
Joni Mitchell (1997)
Bill Monroe[2] (1997)
The Moonglows (2000)
Scotty Moore[3] (2000)
Van Morrison (1993)
Jelly Roll Morton[2] (1998)
Syd Nathan[1] (1997)
Ricky Nelson (1987)
Roy Orbison (1987)
The Orioles[2] (1995)
Johnny Otis[1] (1994)
Earl Palmer[3] (2000)
Parliament - Funkadelic (1997)
Les Paul[2] (1988)
Carl Perkins (1987)
Sam Phillips[1] (1986)
Wilson Pickett (1991)
Pink Floyd (1996)
Gene Pitney (2002)
The Platters (1990)
Doc Pomus[1] (1992)
Elvis Presley (1986)
Lloyd Price (1998)
Queen (2001)
Ma Rainey[2] (1990)
Bonnie Raitt (2000)
Ramones (2002)
Otis Redding (1989)
Jimmy Reed (1991)
Little Richard (1986)
Smokey Robinson (1987)
Jimmie Rodgers[2] (1986)
The Rolling Stones (1989)
Sam and Dave (1992)
Santana (1998)
Pete Seeger[2] (1996)
Del Shannon (1999)
The Shirelles (1996)
Simon and Garfunkel (1990)
Paul Simon (2001)
Sly and the Family Stone (1993)
Bessie Smith[2] (1989)
The Soul Stirrers[2] (1989)
Phil Spector[1] (1989)
Dusty Springfield (1999)
Bruce Springsteen (1999)
The Staple Singers (1999)
Steely Dan (2001)
Jim Stewart[1] (2002)
Rod Stewart (1994)
The Supremes (1988)

Rock and Roll Hall of Fame Inductees (continued)

NAME (YEAR OF INDUCTION)	NAME (YEAR OF INDUCTION)	NAME (YEAR OF INDUCTION)
Talking Heads (2002)	The Velvet Underground (1996)	Howlin' Wolf[2] (1991)
James Taylor (2000)	Gene Vincent (1998)	Stevie Wonder (1989)
The Temptations (1989)	T-Bone Walker[2] (1987)	Jimmy Yancey[2] (1986)
Tom Petty and the Heartbreakers (2002)	Dinah Washington[2] (1993)	The Yardbirds (1992)
	Muddy Waters (1987)	Neil Young (1995)
Allen Toussaint[1] (1998)	Jerry Wexler[1] (1987)	The (Young) Rascals (1997)
Big Joe Turner (1987)	The Who (1990)	Frank Zappa (1995)
Ike and Tina Turner (1991)	Hank Williams[2] (1987)	
Ritchie Valens (2001)	Jackie Wilson (1987)	

[1]Non-performer.　[2]Early Influence.　[3]Sidemen.　[4]Lifetime Achievement.

Bestselling Fiction (Hardcover), 2001

	TITLE (PUBLISHER)	AUTHOR
1	*Desecration (Left Behind #9)* (Tyndale House)	Tim LaHaye, Jerry B. Jenkins
2	*Skipping Christmas* (Random House)	John Grisham
3	*A Painted House* (Doubleday)	John Grisham
4	*Dreamcatcher* (Simon & Schuster)	Stephen King
5	*The Corrections* (Farrar, Straus & Giroux)	Jonathan Franzen
6	*Black House* (Random House)	Stephen King, Peter Straub
7	*The Kiss* (Delacorte Press)	Danielle Steel
8	*Valhalla Rising* (Penguin USA)	Clive Cussler
9	*A Day Late and a Dollar Short* (Viking Penguin)	Terry McMillan
10	*Violets Are Blue* (Little, Brown & Company)	James Patterson

Source: Publisher's Weekly.

Bestselling Nonfiction (Hardcover), 2001

	TITLE (PUBLISHER)	AUTHOR
1	*The Prayer of Jabez* (Multnomah)	Bruce Wilkinson
2	*Secrets of the Vine* (Multnomah)	Bruce Wilkinson
3	*Who Moved My Cheese?* (Putnam)	Spencer Johnson
4	*John Adams* (Simon & Schuster)	David McCullough
5	*Guiness Book of World Records 2002* (Guinness World Records, Ltd.)	Guinness World Records, Ltd.
6	*Prayer of Jabez Devotional* (Multnomah)	Bruce Wilkinson
7	*The No-Spin Zone* (Broadway)	Bill O'Reilly
8	*Body for Life* (HarperCollins)	Bill Phillips
9	*How I Play Golf* (Warner Books)	Tiger Woods
10	*Jack: Straight from the Gut* (Warner Books)	Jack Welch

Source: Publisher's Weekly.

Did you know? Author Ian Fleming desired a simple name, "brief, unromantic, and yet very masculine," when conceiving his secret-agent hero for the novel *Casino Royale* (1953). Fleming, an avid bird watcher living in Jamaica at the time, discovered the perfect name while reading the book *Birds of the West Indies* by James Bond, an ornithologist from Philadelphia. In a letter to Bond's wife in 1961, Fleming wrote, "I must confess that your husband has every reason to sue me....In return, I can only offer your James Bond unlimited use of the name Ian Fleming for any purpose he may think fit."

Encyclopædia Britannica's 200 Greatest Novels

Absalom, Absalom!, by William Faulkner
Ada, by Vladimir Nabokov
The Adventures of Huckleberry Finn, by Mark Twain
The Age of Reason, by Jean-Paul Sartre
Alice's Adventures in Wonderland, by Lewis Carroll
All Quiet on the Western Front, by Erich Maria Remarque

An American Tragedy, by Theodore Dreiser
Angle of Repose, by Wallace Stegner
Animal Farm, by George Orwell
Anna Karenina, by Leo Tolstoy
Aunt Julia and the Scriptwriter, by Mario Vargas Llosa
Babbitt, by Sinclair Lewis
Barchester Towers, by Anthony Trollope

Beloved, by Toni Morrison
A Bend in the River, by V.S. Naipaul
The Betrothed, by Alessandro Manzoni
Billiards at Half-Past Nine, by Heinrich Böll
The Bostonians, by Henry James
Brave New World, by Aldous Huxley
The Bridge on the Drina, by Ivo Andric
The Brothers Karamazov, by Fyodor Dostoyevsky
Buddenbrooks: The Decline of a Family, by Thomas Mann
Burger's Daughter, by Nadine Gordimer
Call It Sleep, by Henry Roth
Candide, by Voltaire
Cane, by Jean Toomer
Catch-22, by Joseph Heller
Charlotte's Web, by E.B. White
The Charterhouse of Parma, by Stendhal
Chéri, by Colette
The Color Purple, by Alice Walker
Confessions of Zeno, by Italo Svevo
Cousin Bette, by Honoré de Balzac
Crime and Punishment, by Fyodor Dostoyevsky
The Crime of Inspector Maigret, by Georges Simenon
Cry, the Beloved Country, by Alan Paton
A Dance to the Music of Time, by Anthony Powell
David Copperfield, by Charles Dickens
The Day of the Locust, by Nathanael West
Dead Souls, by Nikolay Gogol
Death Comes for the Archbishop, by Willa Cather
The Death of Artemio Cruz, by Carlos Fuentes
Don Quixote, by Miguel de Cervantes
Dona Flor and Her Two Husbands, by Jorge Amado
Emma, by Jane Austen
The English Patient, by Michael Ondaatje
Ethan Frome, by Edith Wharton
Evelina, by Fanny Burney
The Expedition of Humphry Clinker, by Tobias Smollett
Fathers and Sons, by Ivan Turgenev
Fifth Business, by Robertson Davies
Frankenstein, by Mary Wollstonecraft Shelley
The French Lieutenant's Woman, by John Fowles
Gargantua and Pantagruel, by François Rabelais
Germinal, by Émile Zola
Go Tell It on the Mountain, by James Baldwin
The Golden Notebook, by Doris Lessing
The Good Soldier, by Ford Madox Ford
The Good Soldier Schweik, by Jaroslav Hasek
The Grapes of Wrath, by John Steinbeck
Gravity's Rainbow, by Thomas Pynchon
Great Expectations, by Charles Dickens
The Great Gatsby, by F. Scott Fitzgerald
Gulliver's Travels, by Jonathan Swift
The Handmaid's Tale, by Margaret Atwood
Heart of Darkness, by Joseph Conrad
A Hero of Our Time, by Mikhail Lermontov
Herzog, by Saul Bellow
The History of Tom Jones, A Foundling, by Henry Fielding
Hopscotch, by Julio Cortázar
The Horse's Mouth, by Joyce Cary
A House for Mr. Biswas, by V.S. Naipaul
The House in Paris, by Elizabeth Bowen
The House of Mirth, by Edith Wharton
Howards End, by E.M. Forster
I, Claudius, by Robert Graves
The Idiot, by Fyodor Dostoyevsky
If on a Winter's Night a Traveler, by Italo Calvino
In Cold Blood, by Truman Capote
Invisible Man, by Ralph Ellison

The Italian, by Ann Radcliffe
Jane Eyre, by Charlotte Brontë
Jealousy, by Alain Robbe-Grillet
Jude the Obscure, by Thomas Hardy
The Jungle, by Upton Sinclair
Kiss of the Spider Woman, by Manuel Puig
La Mare au diable, by George Sand
The Leopard, by Giuseppe Tomasi di Lampedusa
Les Misérables, by Victor-Marie Hugo
The Lonely Passion of Judith Hearne, by Brian Moore
Look Homeward, Angel, by Thomas Wolfe
Lord Jim, by Joseph Conrad
Lord of the Flies, by William Golding
The Lord of the Rings, by J.R.R. Tolkien
Madame Bovary, by Gustave Flaubert
The Magic Mountain, by Thomas Mann
The Magnificent Ambersons, by Booth Tarkington
Main Street, by Sinclair Lewis
The Man Who Was Thursday, by G.K. Chesterton
Man's Fate, by André Malraux
The Master and Margarita, by Mikhail Bulgakov
The Member of the Wedding, by Carson McCullers
Memoirs of Hadrian, by Marguerite Yourcenar
The Metamorphosis, by Franz Kafka
Middlemarch, by George Eliot
Midnight's Children, by Salman Rushdie
The Mill on the Floss, by George Eliot
Moby Dick, by Herman Melville
Moll Flanders, by Daniel Defoe
Mother, by Maxim Gorky
Mrs. Dalloway, by Virginia Woolf
My Ántonia, by Willa Cather
Naked Lunch, by William S. Burroughs
Native Son, by Richard Wright
Neuromancer, by William Gibson
Nineteen Eighty-four, by George Orwell
North and South, by Elizabeth Gaskell
Oblomov, by Ivan Goncharov
Of Human Bondage, by W. Somerset Maugham
Of Mice and Men, by John Steinbeck
The Old Man and the Sea, by Ernest Hemingway
The Old Wives' Tale, by Arnold Bennett
On the Beach, by Nevil Shute
On the Road, by Jack Kerouac
One Hundred Years of Solitude, by Gabriel García Márquez
Palace Walk, by Naguib Mahfouz
Pale Fire, by Vladimir Nabokov
Pamela, by Samuel Richardson
Paradiso, by José Lezama Lima
A Passage to India, by E.M. Forster
A Personal Matter, by Kenzaburo Oe
The Picture of Dorian Gray, by Oscar Wilde
The Pilgrim's Progress, by John Bunyan
The Portrait of a Lady, by Henry James
A Portrait of the Artist as a Young Man, by James Joyce
Possession, by A.S. Byatt
The Postman Always Rings Twice, by James M. Cain
The Power and the Glory, by Graham Greene
Pride and Prejudice, by Jane Austen
The Prime of Miss Jean Brodie, by Muriel Spark
Rasselas, Prince of Abissinia, by Samuel Johnson
The Red and the Black, by Stendhal
The Red Badge of Courage, by Stephen Crane
The Remains of the Day, by Kazuo Ishiguro
Remembrance of Things Past, by Marcel Proust
Robinson Crusoe, by Daniel Defoe
St. Urbain's Horsemen, by Mordecai Richler
Satyricon, by Petronius
The Scarlet Letter, by Nathaniel Hawthorne

The Sea of Fertility, by Yukio Mishima
Second Skin, by John Hawkes
The Serpent and the Rope, by Raja Rao
She, by H. Rider Haggard
The Sheltering Sky, by Paul Bowles
Ship of Fools, by Katherine Anne Porter
The Shipping News, by Annie Proulx
A Single Man, by Christopher Isherwood
Slaughterhouse Five, by Kurt Vonnegut
Sons and Lovers, by D.H. Lawrence
Sophie's Choice, by William Styron
The Sorrows of Young Werther, by Johann Wolfgang von Goethe
The Sound and the Fury, by William Faulkner
Steppenwolf, by Hermann Hesse
Strait Is the Gate, by André Gide
Strange Case of Dr. Jekyll and Mr. Hyde, by Robert Louis Stevenson
The Stranger, by Albert Camus
Sula, by Toni Morrison
The Sun Also Rises, by Ernest Hemingway
The Tale of Genji, by Murasaki Shikibu
Their Eyes Were Watching God, by Zora Neale Hurston
Them, by Joyce Carol Oates
Things Fall Apart, by Chinua Achebe
The Time Machine, by H.G. Wells
To Kill A Mockingbird, by Harper Lee

To the Lighthouse, by Virginia Woolf
Treasure Island, by Robert Louis Stevenson
The Trial, by Franz Kafka
Tristram Shandy, by Laurence Sterne
Tropic of Cancer, by Henry Miller
The True Story of Ah Q, by Lu Hsun
Twenty Thousand Leagues Under the Sea, by Jules Verne
Ulysses, by James Joyce
The Unbearable Lightness of Being, by Milan Kundera
Uncle Tom's Cabin, by Harriet Beecher Stowe
Under the Net, by Iris Murdoch
Under the Volcano, by Malcolm Lowry
The Underdogs, by Mariano Azuela
Underworld, by Don DeLillo
Utopia, by Thomas More
Vanity Fair, by William Makepeace Thackeray
War and Peace, by Leo Tolstoy
Waverley, by Walter Scott
The Way of All Flesh, by Samuel Butler
Where the Red Fern Grows, by Wilson Rawls
Wide Sargasso Sea, by Jean Rhys
The Wind in the Willows, by Kenneth Grahame
Wise Blood, by Flannery O'Connor
Women in Love, by D.H. Lawrence
The Wonderful Wizard of Oz, by L. Frank Baum
Wuthering Heights, by Emily Brontë

The Tale of Genji:

In Celebration of the World's First Novel

One thousand years ago in Heian Japan, a woman of whom little is known was widowed. But for her personal loss, that woman, known as Murasaki Shikibu, might never have written *Genji monogatari* (c. 1010; *The Tale of Genji*), which is considered the greatest work of Japanese literature and the world's first novel.

The details of the author's life are sketchy. Even her actual name is unknown; Murasaki Shikibu was assigned by scholars—who used the name of the book's dominant female character (Murasaki) and the author's father's position (Shikibu) at the Bureau of Rites to identify her. Born into a lesser branch of the noble and highly influential Fujiwara family, she had been well educated, learning Chinese (generally the exclusive sphere of males). She had married a much older distant cousin and borne a daughter by him, and after two years of marriage, he had died. It is not known how, four years later, she came to be summoned to the court. In any case, her new position within what was then a leading literary center enabled her to produce a diary, a collection of poetry, and, most famously, the classic romance *Genji monogatari*.

Because Chinese was the scholarly language of the Japanese court, works written in Japanese (the literary language used by women) were not taken very seriously. Nor was prose considered the equal of poetry. What made Lady Murasaki's work different is this: although it is prose, it is clearly informed by a comprehensive knowledge of Chinese and Japanese poetry; it is a graceful work of imaginative fiction, not a personal account of life at court; it incorporates some 800 *waka*, courtly poems purported to be the writing of the main character; and its supple narrative sustains the story through 54 chapters of one character and his legacy.

At its most basic, *Genji* is an absorbing introduction to the culture of the aristocracy in early Heian Japan, its forms of entertainment, its manner of dress, its daily life, and its moral code. The era is exquisitely re-created through the story of Genji, the handsome, sensitive, gifted courtier, an excellent lover, and a worthy friend.

Eminent British sinologist Arthur Waley was the first to translate *Genji monogatari* into English, completing the last of six volumes in 1933. Waley's was a beautiful and inspiring translation, but it was also very free. Edward Seidensticker's 1976 translation was true to the original in both content and tone, but its notes and reader aids were very sparse, an assessment not lost on *Genji*'s third translator, American scholar Royall Tyler of Australian National University. The publication of Tyler's version in 2001—nearly a millennium after *Genji monogatari* was written—attests to a continuing fascination with early Japanese culture and the durability of one remarkable woman's literary achievement.

Sports

T he tables that follow contain the significant information about the top contests of all the major sports that are international in character, as well as some professional and amateur sports that attract a huge national following—such as baseball in the United States and cricket in the United Kingdom, Australia, India, and the other Test Match countries—and some sports, such as rowing, in which national competition overshadows international events. In many sports the Olympic Games held every four years constitute the world championships; they are included in the listings below.

Sporting Codes for Countries

These codes are used to identify countries in the Sports & Games section of the Britannica Almanac.

Codes of the International Olympic Committee (IOC)

AFG	Afghanistan	COM	Comoros
AHO	Netherlands Antilles	CPV	Cape Verde
ALB	Albania	CRC	Costa Rica
ALG	Algeria	CRO	Croatia
AND	Andorra	CUB	Cuba
ANG	Angola	CYP	Cyprus
ANT	Antigua and Barbuda	CZE	Czech Rep.
ARG	Argentina	DEN	Denmark
ARM	Armenia	DJI	Djibouti
ARU	Aruba	DMA	Dominica
ASA	American Samoa	DOM	Dominican Rep.
AUS	Australia	ECU	Ecuador
AUT	Austria	EGY	Egypt
AZE	Azerbaijan	ERI	Eritrea
BAH	Bahamas	ESA	El Salvador
BAN	Bangladesh	ESP	Spain
BAR	Barbados	EST	Estonia
BDI	Burundi	ETH	Ethiopia
BEL	Belgium	FIJ	Fiji
BEN	Benin	FIN	Finland
BER	Bermuda	FRA	France
BHU	Bhutan	FSM	Micronesia, Fed. States of
BIH	Bosnia and Herzegovina	GAB	Gabon
BIZ	Belize	GAM	Gambia
BLR	Belarus	GBR	Great Britain
BOL	Bolivia	GBS	Guinea-Bissau
BOT	Botswana	GEO	Georgia
BRA	Brazil	GEQ	Equatorial Guinea
BRN	Bahrain	GER	Germany
BRU	Brunei Darussalam	GHA	Ghana
BUL	Bulgaria	GRE	Greece
BUR	Burkina Faso	GRN	Grenada
CAF	Central African Rep.	GUA	Guatemala
CAM	Cambodia	GUI	Guinea
CAN	Canada	GUM	Guam
CAY	Cayman Islands	GUY	Guyana
CGO	Congo	HAI	Haiti
CHA	Chad	HKG	Hong Kong
CHI	Chile	HON	Honduras
CHN	China, People's Rep. of	HUN	Hungary
CIV	Côte d'Ivoire	INA	Indonesia
CMR	Cameroon	IND	India
COD	Congo, Dem. Rep. of the	IRI	Iran
COK	Cook Islands	IRL	Ireland
COL	Colombia	IRQ	Iraq
		ISL	Iceland
		ISR	Israel
		ISV	US Virgin Islands
		ITA	Italy
		IVB	British Virgin Islands

JAM	Jamaica	PLW	Palau
JOR	Jordan	PNG	Papua New Guinea
JPN	Japan	POL	Poland
KAZ	Kazakhstan	POR	Portugal
KEN	Kenya	PRK	Korea, Dem. People's Rep. of (North Korea)
KGZ	Kyrgyzstan		
KOR	Korea, Rep. of (South Korea)	PUR	Puerto Rico
KSA	Saudi Arabia	QAT	Qatar
KUW	Kuwait	ROM	Romania
LAO	Laos	RSA	South Africa
LAT	Latvia	RUS	Russia
LBA	Libya	RWA	Rwanda
LBR	Liberia	SAM	Samoa
LCA	St. Lucia	SEN	Senegal
LES	Lesotho	SEY	Seychelles
LIB	Lebanon	SIN	Singapore
LIE	Liechtenstein	SKN	St. Kitts and Nevis
LTU	Lithuania		
LUX	Luxembourg	SLE	Sierra Leone
MAD	Madagascar	SLO	Slovenia
MAR	Morocco	SMR	San Marino
MAS	Malaysia	SOL	Solomon Islands
MAW	Malawi	SOM	Somalia
MDA	Moldova	SRI	Sri Lanka
MDV	Maldives	STP	São Tomé and Príncipe
MEX	Mexico		
MGL	Mongolia	SUD	Sudan
MKD	Macedonia	SUI	Switzerland
MLI	Mali	SUR	Suriname
MLT	Malta	SVK	Slovakia
MON	Monaco	SWE	Sweden
MOZ	Mozambique	SWZ	Swaziland
MRI	Mauritius	SYR	Syria
MTN	Mauritania	TAN	Tanzania
MYA	Myanmar (Burma)	TGA	Tonga
NAM	Namibia	THA	Thailand
NCA	Nicaragua	TJK	Tajikistan
NED	Netherlands, The	TKM	Turkmenistan
NEP	Nepal	TOG	Togo
NGR	Nigeria	TPE	Taiwan
NIG	Niger	TRI	Trinidad and Tobago
NOR	Norway		
NRU	Nauru	TUN	Tunisia
NZL	New Zealand	TUR	Turkey
OMA	Oman	UAE	United Arab Emirates
PAK	Pakistan		
PAN	Panama	UGA	Uganda
PAR	Paraguay	UKR	Ukraine
PER	Peru	URU	Uruguay
PHI	Philippines	USA	United States
PLE	Palestine		

Sporting Codes for Countries (continued)

Codes of the International Olympic Committee (IOC) (continued)

UZB	Uzbekistan	VIE	Vietnam	YEM	Yemen	ZIM	Zimbabwe
VAN	Vanuatu	VIN	St. Vincent and	YUG	Yugoslavia		
VEN	Venezuela		the Grenadines	ZAM	Zambia		

Continental, Historical, and Other Country Codes

AFR	Africa	DMN	Dominica	MAC	Macao	SKR	Korea, Rep. of
AIA	Anguilla	ENG	England	MAU	Mauritius		(South Korea)
AME	The Americas	EUR	Europe	MOL	Moldova	SPA	Spain
ARS	Saudi Arabia	FRG	Germany, Federal	MOR	Morocco	SWZ	Switzerland
ASI	Asia		Rep. of (West	MSR	Montserrat	TAH	Tahiti
BIR	Burma (Myanmar)		Germany)	NIC	Nicaragua	TAI	Taiwan
BLS	Belarus	FRO	Faroe Islands	NIR	Northern Ireland	TCA	Turks and Caicos
BOH	Bohemia	GDR	German Demo-	NKO	Korea, Dem.		Islands
BOS	Bosnia and		cratic Rep. (East		People's Rep. of	TCH	Czechoslovakia
	Herzegovina		Germany)		(North Korea)	UAR	United Arab Rep.
BUR	Burma	HBR	British Honduras	OCE	Oceania	UCS	Union of the
BWI	British West	HEB	New Hebrides	PAL	Palestine		Czech Rep. and
	Indies	HOL	Holland/The	PDR	Korea, Dem.		Slovakia
CAM	Cameroon		Netherlands		People's Rep. of	UNT	Unified Team
CEY	Ceylon	ICE	Iceland		(North Korea)	UPV	Upper Volta
CIS	Commonwealth of	IHO	Netherlands India	PNG	Papua New	URS	USSR
	Indep. States	IRE	Ireland		Guinea	UVI	US Virgin Islands
CKN	Congo-Kinshasa	IVC	Côte d'Ivoire/Ivory	RHO	Rhodesia	WAL	Wales
COB	Congo-Brazzaville		Coast	ROC	China, People's	ZAI	Zaire
CSV	Czechoslovakia	JAP	Japan		Rep. of		
CUR	Curaçao	KZK	Kazakhstan	SAA	Saarland		
DAH	Dahomey	LIT	Lithuania	SCO	Scotland		

The James E. Sullivan Memorial Trophy

Awarded by the Amateur Athletic Union (AAU) since 1930 to honor an athlete who, "by his or her performance, example and influence as an amateur, has done the most during the year to advance the cause of sportsmanship." The award, named for a past president of the AAU, is usually announced in April of the year after that for which the award is given. Winners receive a replica in bronze of the original trophy.

YEAR	WINNER	SPORT	YEAR	WINNER	SPORT
1930	Bobby Jones	golf	1953	Sammy Lee	diving
1931	Barney Berlinger	track (decathlon)	1954	Mal Whitfield	track (middle distance
1932	Jim Bausch	track (decathlon)			running)
1933	Glenn Cunningham	track (distance running)	1955	Harrison Dillard	track (sprints/hurdles)
1934	Bill Bonthron	track (middle distance	1956	Pat McCormick	diving
		running)	1957	Bobby Morrow	track (sprints)
1935	Lawson Little	golf	1958	Glenn Davis	track (hurdles)
1936	Glenn Morris	track (decathlon)	1959	Parry O'Brien	track (shot put)
1937	Don Budge	tennis	1960	Rafer Johnson	track (decathlon)
1938	Don Lash	track (distance running)	1961	Wilma Rudolph	track (sprints)
1939	Joe Burk	rowing	1962	Jim Beatty	track (distance running)
1940	Greg Rice	track (distance running)	1963	John Pennel	track (pole vault)
1941	Leslie MacMitchell	track (middle distance	1964	Don Schollander	swimming
		running)	1965	Bill Bradley	basketball
1942	Cornelius "Dutch"	track (pole vault)	1966	Jim Ryun	track (middle distance
	Warmerdam				running)
1943	Gilbert Dodds	track (middle distance	1967	Randy Matson	track (shot put/discus)
		running)	1968	Debbie Meyer	swimming
1944	Ann Curtis	swimming	1969	Bill Toomey	track (decathlon)
1945	Doc Blanchard	football	1970	John Kinsella	swimming
1946	Arnold Tucker	football	1971	Mark Spitz	swimming
1947	John B. Kelly, Jr.	rowing	1972	Frank Shorter	track (distance running)
1948	Bob Mathias	track (decathlon)	1973	Bill Walton	basketball
1949	Dick Button	figure skating	1974	Rick Wohlhuter	track (middle distance
1950	Fred Wilt	track (distance running)			running)
1951	Bob Richards	track (pole vault/	1975	Tim Shaw	swimming
		decathlon)	1976	Bruce Jenner	track (decathlon)
1952	Horace Ashenfelter	track (distance running)	1977	John Naber	swimming

The James E. Sullivan Memorial Trophy (continued)

YEAR	WINNER	SPORT	YEAR	WINNER	SPORT
1978	Tracy Caulkins	swimming	1990	John Smith	freestyle wrestling
1979	Kurt Thomas	gymnastics	1991	Mike Powell	track (long jump)
1980	Eric Heiden	speed skating	1992	Bonnie Blair	speed skating
1981	Carl Lewis	track (sprints/long jump)	1993	Charlie Ward	football
			1994	Dan Jansen	speed skating
1982	Mary Decker	track (distance running)	1995	Bruce Baumgartner	freestyle wrestling
1983	Edwin Moses	track (hurdles)	1996	Michael Johnson	track (middle distance running)
1984	Greg Louganis	diving			
1985	Joan Benoit Samuelson	track (marathon)	1997	Peyton Manning	football
			1998	Chamique Holdsclaw	basketball
1986	Jackie Joyner-Kersee	track (heptathlon)			
			1999	Coco and Kelly Miller	basketball
1987	Jim Abbott	baseball (pitcher)			
1988	Florence Griffith Joyner	track (sprints)	2000	Rulon Gardner	Greco-Roman wrestling
			2001	Michelle Kwan	figure skating
1989	Janet Evans	swimming			

Encyclopædia Britannica's Top Figures of Sports History

The athletes named here represent the Encyclopædia Britannica editors' choice of the 250 (counting pairs as one) greatest sports figures of the past. Information includes full name, date and place of birth, date and place of death, and a short sketch indiciating why they were chosen for this list. Sportsmen and sportswomen who are still active in their primary field of excellence are not included here, but see Newsmakers and Celebrities.

Hank Aaron (Henry Louis Aaron; 5 Feb 1934, Mobile AL), American baseball player who, during 23 seasons in the major leagues (1954–76), surpassed batting records set by some of the greatest hitters in the game, including Babe Ruth, Ty Cobb, and Stan Musial. He retired with a .305 career batting average, 3,771 hits, 2,297 runs batted in, and 755 home runs, the latter two were records that remained unbroken in 2001.

Kareem Abdul-Jabbar (called Lew Alcindor [Ferdinand Lewis Alcindor, Jr.] until 1971; 16 Apr 1947, New York NY), American collegiate and professional basketball player, who as a 7-ft 1⅜-in center led UCLA to 3 NCAA titles, then as a pro (1969–89) was the NBA MVP 6 times, leading the Milwaukee Bucks to the 1971 NBA championship and the Los Angeles Lakers to 5 titles in 9 years. He retired with a record 38,387 career points.

Vasily (Ivanovich) Alekseyev (7 Jan 1942, Pokrovo-Shiskino, Russia, USSR), Soviet super-heavyweight weightlifter who between 1970 and 1980 set 81 world records and won 42 world and European championships and 2 Olympic gold medals (1972, 1976).

Grover Cleveland Alexander (26 Feb 1887, Elba NE—4 Nov 1950, St. Paul MN), American baseball player, one of the finest right-handed pitchers in the history of the game, frequently considered the greatest master of control. For 3 consecutive years (1915–17) he won 30 or more games; in 1916, when he achieved 33 victories, 16 were shutouts, a major league record.

Muhammad Ali (called Cassius Clay [Cassius Marcellus Clay, Jr.] until 1964; 17 Jan 1942, Louisville KY), American boxer, the first to win the heavyweight championship 3 separate times. He was the 1960 Olympic gold medalist as a light-heavyweight, and on 25 Feb 1964 he upset heavyweight champion Sonny Liston. Stripped of his title in 1967 for refusing military service, he defeated George Foreman to regain it in 1974; he lost it in 1978, then held it again 1978–79. Ali's quick reflexes and de-

fensive speed in the ring, combined with his engaging (sometimes outrageous) personality and his refusal on religious grounds to be inducted into the army made him a cultural icon during his 20-year career and long after his final retirement.

Phog Allen (Forrest Clare Allen; 15 Nov 1885, Jamesport MO—16 Sep 1974, Lawrence KS), American college basketball coach who was instrumental in making basketball an Olympic sport. During his 49-year coaching career, he compiled a 771–233 record, including a 591–219 record and the 1952 national championship as coach at the University of Kansas (1908, 1909, 1920–56).

Mario Andretti (28 Feb 1940, Montona, Italy), Italian-born American race-car driver whose versatility brought him victories in the NASCAR Daytona 500 (1967), the Indianapolis 500 (1969), and the Formula 1 world drivers' championship (1978); he was the only driver to win races in 5 decades. In 1999 he was voted joint Driver of the Century with A.J. Foyt.

Earl Anthony (27 Apr 1938, Kent WA—found dead 14 Aug 2001, New Berlin WI), American bowler, the winningest player in PBA history, he captured a record 41 tournaments from 1970 to 1983, including 10 majors; he also became the first bowler to earn $1 million in his career and achieved widespread fame during a era when bowling was regularly broadcast on US television.

Eddie Arcaro (George Edward Arcaro; 10 Feb 1916, Cincinnati OH—14 Nov 1997, Miami FL), American jockey who rode 5 Kentucky Derby winners, 6 Preakness Stakes winners, 6 Belmont Stakes winners, and 2 US Triple Crown champions (Whirlaway, 1941; Citation, 1948). In 31 years of riding Thoroughbreds (1931–61), he won 549 stakes events, a total of 4,779 races, and more than $30 million in purses.

Henry Armstrong (original name Henry Jackson; 12 Dec 1912, Columbus MS—24 Oct 1988, Los Angeles CA), American boxer, the only professional boxer to hold 3 world championship titles simultane-

ously—featherweight (1937–38), lightweight (1938–39), and welterweight (1938–40). He defended the welterweight title 19 times and ended his 19-year pro career in 1945 with a record of 151–21–9 (101 knockouts).

Arthur Ashe (10 Jul 1943, Richmond VA—6 Feb 1993, New York NY), American tennis player, the first African American winner of a men's Grand Slam singles title, when he captured the US Open, in 1968, and the first African American to represent the US in Davis Cup competition, in 1963. He eventually won 33 tournament titles and ranked among the men's top 10 players for 12 years.

Evelyn Ashford (15 Apr 1957, Shreveport LA), American sprinter, twice Woman Athlete of the Year and 5-time Olympian, gaining four gold medals and one silver and a record as the oldest American woman to win an Olympic gold medal in track and field (1992, age 35).

Shirley Babashoff (31 Jan 1957, Whittier CA), American swimmer who won 8 Olympic medals and was one of only 2 women to win 5 medals in swimming at one Olympic Games (1972). In her 11-year career she set 6 world records (in the 200-m, 400-m, and 800-m freestyle) and swam on relay teams that set 5 world records.

Roger Bannister (23 Mar 1929, Harrow, Eng.), English neurologist who was the first athlete to run a mile in less than 4 minutes, a feat previously thought impossible.

Sammy Baugh (Samuel Adrian Baugh; 17 Mar 1914, Temple TX), American football player, the first outstanding quarterback in the history of American pro football; he led the NFL in passing in 6 of his 16 seasons (1937–52) with the Washington Redskins. On 2 occasions he passed for 6 touchdowns in a single game.

Elgin Baylor (16 Sep 1934, Washington DC), American pro basketball player (6 ft 5 in; 197 cm) who is regarded as one of the game's greatest forwards and a mainstay of the Minneapolis (later Los Angeles) Lakers. On 15 Nov 1960, Baylor became the first player in NBA history to break the 70-point barrier when he scored 71 against the New York Knicks. He retired in 1972 with 23,149 points, the NBA's third highest.

Bob Beamon (29 Aug 1946, Bronx NY), American long jumper who set a world record of 29 ft 2½ in (8.90 m) at the 1968 Olympic Games. The new record surpassed the existing mark by an astounding 21¾ in (0.55 m) and lasted for 23 years until Mike Powell jumped 29 ft 4½ in (8.95 m) in 1991.

Franz Beckenbauer (11 Sep 1945, Munich, Ger.), German association football (soccer) player who is credited with inventing the modern attacking sweeper and hence "total football." He played 103 international matches for Germany, was voted European Player of the Year twice (1972, 1976), and led Germany to a World Cup title both as the captain (1974) and as the coach (1990).

Boris (Franz) Becker (22 Nov 1967, Leimen, near Heidelberg, W.Ger.), German tennis player who in 1985, at age 17, became the youngest champion in the history of the men's singles at the British (Wimbledon) championship. At the same time, he became the first unseeded player, the first German ever to win the title, and the youngest man ever to win a Grand Slam singles title. He eventually won 3 British, 1 US, and 2 Australian singles titles.

Jean (Arthur) Béliveau ("Le Gros Bill"; 31 Aug 1931, Trois-Rivières PQ), Canadian ice hockey center who

was noted for scoring winning goals in Stanley Cup playoff games. During a 21-year NHL career (1950–71), he was a 10-time all-star and the Montreal Canadiens' all-time leading scorer.

Lyudmila (Yevgeniyevna) Belousova (22 Nov 1935, Ulyanovsk, USSR [now Simbirsk, Russia]), & **Oleg (Alekseyevich) Protopopov** (16 Jul 1932, Leningrad USSR [now St. Petersburg, Russia]), Russian-born figure skaters who twice won gold medals in the pairs championship in the Olympic Winter Games (1964, 1968). The married couple, known for their elegance and grace on the ice, also won the world pairs title 4 consecutive years (1965–68).

Nino Benvenuti (Giovanni Benvenuti; 26 Apr 1938, Trieste, Italy), Italian boxer, 1960 Olympic welterweight gold medalist, world junior middleweight (1965–66) and middleweight (1967–70) champion; a sports legend in his homeland, he retired (1971) with a record of 82–7–1 (35 knockouts).

Patty Berg (Patricia Jane Berg; 13 Feb 1918, Minneapolis MN), American golfer, winner of more than 80 tournaments (57 professional), including the first US Women's Open in 1946; she was also a founder and the first president (1949–52) of the LPGA.

George Best (22 May 1946, Belfast, N.Ire.), British association football (soccer) player who led Manchester United to 2 Football Association championships (1964–65 and 1966–67) and the European Cup (1968). A masterful dribbler, in the latter year he was top scorer and was named European Player of the Year. He represented Northern Ireland on Great Britain's national team in 37 international matches.

Abebe Bikila (7 Aug 1932, Mont, Eth.—25 Oct 1973, Addis Ababa, Eth.), Ethiopian marathon runner who won a gold medal and set an unofficial world record while running barefoot at the 1960 Olympic Games, then bested his own record at the 1964 Olympics. He was the first athlete to win 2 Olympic marathons.

Matt Biondi (8 Oct 1965, Moraga CA), American swimmer, who won a total of 11 medals in 3 successive Olympics (1984, 1988, 1992), including 7 medals (5 gold) and 4 world records in the 1988 Games.

Larry Bird (7 Dec 1956, West Baden IN), American college and professional basketball player and coach; was elected NBA MVP in 3 consecutive seasons (1984–86) and led the Boston Celtics to 13 straight postseason appearances and 3 NBA titles (1981, 1984, 1986).

Bonnie Blair (18 Mar 1964, Cornwall NY), American speed skater who became the most successful American woman athlete in the history of Olympic competition. For 8 years she dominated the sprint events in women's speed skating, and, at 3 Olympic Games (1988, 1992, 1994), she collected 5 gold medals and 1 bronze.

George Blanda (17 Sep 1927, Youngwood PA), American football player, who first as a quarterback and later as a kicker established records for most seasons played (26), most games played (340), most points scored (2,002; later broken), most points after touchdowns (943 of 959 attempted), and most field goals (335 of 638 attempted; broken in 1983).

Fanny Blankers-Koen (Francina Blankers-Koen; 26 Apr 1918, Amsterdam, Neth.), Dutch athlete who was the first woman to win 4 gold medals in a single Olympics, capturing gold in the 100 m, 200 m,

80-m hurdles, and sprint relay at the 1924 Games. During her career, she also set world records in 7 events, including the high and long jumps.

Bjorn Borg (6 Jun 1956, Södertälje, Sweden), Swedish tennis player, the first man to win the Wimbledon singles championship 5 successive times (1976–80), since 1906. Known for his unorthodox baseline stance and cool demeanor, he won the French Open men's singles championship an unprecedented 4 times in a row and 6 times in all (1974–75, 1978–81) and won 33 straight Davis Cup matches, leading Sweden to its first Davis Cup title (1975).

Don Bradman (Sir Donald George Bradman, "The Don"; 27 Aug 1908, Cootamundra, Australia—25 Feb 2001, Adelaide, Australia), Australian cricketer, the most effective batsman in the history of the game and one of the most celebrated Australians of the 20th century; he set records that dwarfed all other cricketers, most notably his international Test average of 99.94 (6,996 runs in 52 Tests) and first-class average of 95.14 (28,067 runs in 234 matches over 20 years). In 1930 he hit more than 300 runs in a single day; his highest first-class score was 452 not out, a record that stood for 30 years.

Jim Brown (James Nathaniel Brown; 17 Feb 1936, St. Simons GA), American football player, an outstanding fullback who was considered one of the game's greatest runners; he led the NFL in rushing for 8 of his 9 seasons and was twice named MVP (1958, 1965). His records for rushing (12,312 yd) and total yardage (15,459 yd) were broken by Walter Payton. After retiring, Brown became a motion-picture actor.

Bear Bryant (Paul William Bryant; 11 Sep 1913, Kingsland AR—26 Jan 1983, Tuscaloosa AL), American college football coach who led the University of Alabama to 28 bowl games and 6 national championships; his career record of 323-85–17 broke Amos Alonzo Stagg's record for the most games won by a collegiate coach. In 1971 Bryant recruited the first black player on the Alabama team; he was credited with helping to stimulate the integration of college football at mostly white Southern universities.

Sergey Bubka (4 Dec 1963, Voroshilovgrad, Ukr., USSR [now Luhansk, Ukr.]), Ukrainian athlete, the first pole vaulter to clear 6.1 m (20 ft), in 1991. He dominated the sport for more than a decade, winning the world championship 6 times (1983–97) and setting 35 world records.

Don Budge (John Donald Budge; 13 Jun 1915, Oakland CA—26 Jan 2000, Scranton PA), American tennis player who was the first to win the 4 Grand Slam events, the Australian, French, US, and British (Wimbledon) titles, in one calendar year (1938). In 1937 he was the first tennis player to be awarded the Sullivan Trophy as the outstanding US amateur athlete of the year. In late 1938 he turned pro, making him ineligible to compete in the Grand Slam events again.

Dick Butkus (Richard J. Butkus; 9 Dec 1942, Chicago IL), American football player, as middle linebacker for the Chicago Bears (1965–73), he was considered one of the best defensive players in pro football; known for his strength, speed, and instinct on the field, he made 22 career interceptions and recovered 25 opposition fumbles.

Dick Button (Richard Totten Button; 18 Jul 1929, Englewood NJ), American figure skater, dominated international amateur competition from 1948 until 1952, when he became a professional. Button, whose innovations included the flying camel, the double axel, and the first triple jump, was the only man to hold the Olympic, World, European, North American, and US championships, and in 1948 he held all those titles simultaneously. He later became an ice skating commentator on television.

Walter Chauncey Camp (7 Apr 1859, New Britain CT—14 Mar 1925, New York NY), American sports authority known as "the father of American football." A rugby football halfback at Yale University, Camp helped to develop the game of football as distinct from rugby; in about 1880 the basic rules he had prepared were accepted by the Intercollegiate Football Association. He also was involved in selecting the earliest All-America football teams.

David Campese (21 Oct 1962, Queanbeyan, Australia), Australian rugby player, who holds that country's record for most appearances (101) and the world record for most Test tries (64) in Rugby Union competition; fast and elusive on the field, he was named player of the tournament in the 1991 World Cup final.

Don Carter (29 Jan 1926, St. Louis MO), American bowler who dominated the professional game from 1951 through 1964. He was named bowler of the year 6 times and led the PBA money-winners list twice.

Vera Caslavska (3 May 1942, Prague, Czech. [now in Czech Rep.]), Czech gymnast who dazzled audiences and won a total of 35 medals, including 22 golds, at the Olympics and in world and European championships in the 1950s and '60s.

Wilt Chamberlain (Wilton N. Chamberlain; 21 Aug 1936, Philadelphia PA—12 Oct 1999, Los Angeles CA), American basketball player, considered to be one of the game's greatest offensive players. In 1961–62 he became the first NBA player to score more than 4,000 points in a regular season, and he was the only NBA player ever to score 100 points in a game (2 Mar 1962). He retired with 31,419 points, second behind Kareem Abdul-Jabbar on the all-time list.

Roberto ("Bob") Clemente (18 Aug 1934, Carolina PR—31 Dec 1972, San Juan PR), American baseball player, who could hit almost every kind of pitch and whose powerful throwing arm as a right fielder helped tag many base runners; he was also a daring base runner and a team leader. During his 17-year major league career (1955–72) he scored 1,416 runs and led the National League in hitting four times.

Ty Cobb (Tyrus Raymond Cobb; "The Georgia Peach"; 18 Dec 1886, Narrows GA—17 Jul 1961, Atlanta GA), American baseball player, frequently considered the greatest offensive player in baseball history and generally regarded as the fiercest competitor in the game. He set records for hits (4,191) and runs scored (2,246) that stood for at least 60 years, and his lifetime batting average (.366) has never been equaled.

Henri Cochet (14 Dec 1901, Lyon, France—1 Apr 1987, Saint-Germain-en-Laye, France), French tennis player who, as one of the 4 Musketeers (with Jean Borotra, René Lacoste, and Jacques Brugnon), helped establish the French domination of world tennis, especially Davis Cup competition, in the mid-1920s. A naturally gifted stylist on the court, Cochet also won 7 Grand Slam singles titles: 4 French, 2 British (Wimbledon), and 1 US.

Nadia Comaneci (12 Nov 1961, Gheorghe Gheor-ghiu-Dej, Rom.), Romanian gymnast, the first to be awarded a perfect score of 10 in an Olympic gymnastic event. A captivating performer, she won 7 perfect scores and 3 gold medals, including the all-around title, at the 1976 Olympic Games, at age 14, and 2 gold medals at the 1980 Games.

Maureen Catherine Connolly ("Little Mo"; 17 Sep 1934, San Diego CA—21 Jun 1969, Dallas TX), American tennis player who dominated the sport in the early 1950s; in 1953 she had a match record of 61–2 and became the first woman to win the Grand Slam, the British (Wimbledon), US, Australian, and French singles titles, in a calendar year. She won 3 British (1952–54), 3 US (1951–53), 1 Australian (1953), and 2 French (1953–54) championships before an accident in 1954 prematurely ended her career.

Jimmy Connors (James Scott Connors; 2 Sep 1952, East St. Louis IL), American left-handed tennis player; often criticized for his fiery temper on the court, he was ranked number one for 268 weeks (160 consecutive), ranked in the top 10 for 16 years (1973–88), and won 109 titles, including 8 Grand Slam singles championships.

James J. Corbett ("Gentleman Jim"; 1 Sep 1866, San Francisco CA—18 Feb 1933, New York NY), American boxer, world heavyweight champion from 7 Sep 1892, when he knocked out John L. Sullivan in 21 rounds, until 17 Mar 1897, when he was knocked out by Robert Fitzsimmons. Known for his finesse in the ring and his elegant style out of it, he was the first "scientific boxer."

Pierre baron de Coubertin (originally Pierre de Frédy; 1 Jan 1863, Paris, France—2 Sep 1937, Geneva, Switz.), French educator who was primarily responsible for the revival of the Olympic Games in 1896. He was a founding member of the IOC and served as its first president (1896–1925).

Bob Cousy (Robert J. Cousy; 9 Aug 1928, New York NY), American professional basketball player and coach and collegiate coach, who, at only 6 ft 1 in (187 cm), was one of the greatest ball-handling guards in the NBA, expert both at scoring and at playmaking.

Buster Crabbe (Clarence Lindon Crabbe; 7 Feb 1910?, Oakland CA—23 Apr 1983, Scottsdale AZ), American swimmer whose Olympic gold medal in 1932 (and 16 world swimming records) led to a long acting career.

Johan Cruyff (Hendrick Johannes Cruijff; 25 Apr 1947, Amsterdam, Neth.), Dutch association football (soccer) center-forward admired for his superb ball control and tactical skills; he was voted European Player of the Year 3 times (1971, 1973, 1974) and World Cup MVP in 1974, despite Holland's loss to West Germany in the final. He also led Ajax Amsterdam to 3 straight European Cups (1971–73) and later was a manager for Ajax and Barcelona.

Bjorn Daehlie (19 Jun 1967, Råholt, Nor.), Norwegian cross-country skier who owns the Winter Olympic records for the most medals won (12) and the most golds (8); beside winning medals in 3 Olympics (1992, 1994, 1998), he won 6 overall World Cup titles and 14 world championship gold medals.

Alfredo De Oro (1862—April 1948) Spanish diplomat who won the pocket billiards championship 16 times beginning in 1887 and, in the period 1909–18 held the 3-cushion title as well; he was the first non-American inducted (1967) into the Billiard Hall of Fame.

Christopher Dean (see Jayne Torvill).

Jack Dempsey (William Harrison Dempsey; "The Manassa Mauler"; 24 Jun 1895, Manassa CO—31 May 1983, New York NY), American world heavyweight boxing champion, regarded by many as the apotheosis of the professional fighter. He held the title from 4 Jul 1919, when he knocked out Jess Willard, until 23 Sep 1926, when he lost a 10-round decision to Gene Tunney. Known for his bob-and-weave style and quick punches, he retired with a record of 60–6–8 (50 knockouts).

Alfredo Di Stéfano (Laulhe; "The Blond Arrow"; 4 Jun (Jul?) 1926, Buenos Aires, Arg.), Argentine-born Spanish association football (soccer) player, considered by many to be the best all-around player ever. He won 8 league titles, one Spanish Cup, 5 consecutive European Champions' Cups (1956–60), and the first ever World Club Cup (1960). He was voted European Player of the Year in 1957 and 1959, the first to receive the award twice.

Klaus Dibiasi (also spelled Di Biasi; 6 Oct 1947, Solbad Hall, Austria), Italian diver who dominated the platform event from the late 1960s to the mid-1970s, winning 5 Olympic medals, including 3 gold (1968, 1972, 1976).

Joe DiMaggio (Joseph Paul DiMaggio; "Joltin' Joe" or "The Yankee Clipper"; 25 Nov 1914, Martinez CA—8 Mar 1999, Hollywood FL), American baseball player who was an outstanding hitter and fielder and one of the best all-round players in the history of the game. Between 1936 and 1951 he helped the New York Yankees win 9 World Series titles and was named American League MVP 3 times; in 1941 he hit safely in a record 54 consecutive games.

Robert L. Douglas (4 Nov 1882, St. Kitts, BWI—16 July 1979, New York NY), American basketball executive and coach, the first African American to be elected to the Basketball Hall of Fame. The New York Renaissance, which Douglas founded in 1922, bested opponents 2,318 times over the 22 years (1922–49) they toured the country; in 1932–33 the Rens had a record of 120–8 (including an 88-game winning streak).

Ken Dryden (Kenneth Wayne Dryden; 8 Aug 1947, Hamilton ON), Canadian ice hockey goaltender, who led the Montreal Canadiens to 6 Stanley Cup titles; he won the Conn Smythe Trophy (1970–71), the Calder Trophy (1971–72), and won or shared 5 Vezina trophies (1972–73, 1975–76 through 1978–79).

Dale Earnhardt (Ralph Dale Earnhardt; "The Intimidator"; 29 Apr 1951, Kannapolis NC—18 Feb 2001, Daytona Beach FL), American stock-car racer who was the dominant driver in NASCAR during the 1980s and '90s, with 76 victories and 7 Winston Cup season championships; he was NASCAR driver of the year twice (1987, 1994) and had an all-time earnings record of more than $41.7 million at the time of his death in a crash during the 2001 Daytona 500.

John Elway (28 Jun 1960, Port Angeles WA), American football player, the winningest starting quarterback in NFL history, was tied for the most seasons (12) with at least 3,000 passing yards, and led the NFL with 45 4th-quarter game-winning drives. He led the Denver Broncos to victory in 2 successive Super Bowls (1998, 1999).

Julius Erving (Julius Winfield Erving II, "Dr. J"; 22 Feb 1950, Roosevelt NY), American collegiate and professional basketball player who was one of the

most colorful and exciting figures in the game during the 1970s and '80s. He played with unprecedented on-court flair and was one of only three pro players to score more than 30,000 points (30,026).

Phil Esposito (Philip Anthony Esposito; 20 Feb 1942, Sault Ste. Marie ON), Canadian-born American ice hockey center (1963–81) who was a leading scorer in his day. He scored 40 or more goals in 7 straight NHL seasons (1968–75), with 50 or more in 5; his record 76-goal season (1970–71) was broken by Wayne Gretzky in 1981–82.

Eusébio (Eusébio da Silva Ferreira; "The Black Pearl"; 25 Jan 1942, Lourenço Marques [now Maputo], Mozambique), Portuguese association football (soccer) player, was the Portuguese League top scorer each year from 1964 to 1973 and led his club to 10 league championships and 5 cups. Known for his powerful running and spectacular shots, he was awarded the 1965 European Player of the Year.

Janet Evans (28 Aug 1971, Placentia CA), American swimmer, known for her exceptional speed in freestyle distance events. She won 4 gold medals in 3 Olympic competitions (1988, 1992, 1996), set world records at 400 m, 800 m, and 1,500 m, and dominated women's swimming in the 1980s and early '90s. She won the Sullivan Trophy as the top US amateur athlete in 1989.

Lee Evans (25 Feb 1947, Madera CA), American sprinter who won 2 gold medals at the 1968 Olympic Games; he set a world record in the 400-m event (43.86 sec) and shared another in the 4 x 400 relay (2 min 56.1 sec), both of which lasted for 2 decades.

Chris Evert (Christine Marie Evert, also called [1979–87] Chris Evert Lloyd; 21 Dec 1954, Fort Lauderdale FL), American tennis player who dominated the sport in the mid- and late 1970s and remained a major competitor into the late 1980s. A slow-court baseline specialist, she won 3 British (Wimbledon), 6 US, 2 Australian, and 7 French singles championships and later was president of the Women's Tennis Association. In 1985 the Women's Sports Foundation named her the "greatest woman athlete of the last 25 years."

Ray C. Ewry (14 Oct 1873, Lafayette IN—29 Sep 1937, Douglaston NY), American track athlete, the only Olympic athlete to win 8 gold medals in individual events; he won 3 in 1900, 3 in 1904, and 2 in 1908.

Juan Manuel Fangio (24 Jun 1911, Balcarce, Arg—17 Jul 1995, Buenos Aires, Arg.), Argentine Formula 1 race-car driver who captured 5 world driving championships (1951, 1954–57). He had won 24 world-championship Grand Prix races when he retired from racing in 1958.

Viacheslav Fetisov (20 Apr 1958, Moscow, USSR), Russian ice hockey player who was regarded as one of the best defensemen in the sport's history. As a member of the Soviet team in the 1980s, he won 2 Olympic gold medals and a silver and 7 world championships (1978–79, 1981–84, 1986). In 1989, nine years after he was drafted into the NHL, he was allowed to leave Russia; he retired from the NHL in 1998.

Bob Fitzsimmons (Ruby Robert Fitzsimmons; 26 May 1863, Helston, Eng.—22 Oct 1917, Chicago IL), British-born New Zealander who was world champion boxer in 3 weight divisions—middleweight, light heavyweight, and heavyweight, despite weighing only 170 lb. He knocked out James Corbett for the heavyweight title on 17 Mar 1897 and lost it to James Jeffries on 9 Jun 1899.

Peggy Fleming (27 Jul 1948, San Jose CA), American ice skater who dominated world women's amateur figure skating competition from 1964 through 1968; beloved for her grace and sheer perfection, she won 3 straight world championships and the 1968 Olympic gold medal.

Doug Flutie (Douglas Richard Flutie; 23 Oct 1962, Manchester MD), American-born Canadian Football League quarterback, who, during an 8-year CFL career, was named the league's top player an unprecedented 6 times; 3 of the teams for which he played won the Grey Cup. In 1998 he moved back to the US and led the NFL Buffalo Bills to a conference championship.

Dick Fosbury (Richard Douglas Fosbury; 6 Mar 1947, Portland OR), American high jumper who revolutionized the sport in 1968 by replacing the traditional approach to jumping with an innovative backward style that became known as the "Fosbury flop."

A.J. Foyt (16 Jan 1935, Houston TX), American race-car driver who dominated Indy car racing for 2 decades, he was the first 4-time winner of the Indianapolis 500 (1961, 1964, 1967, 1977). He also won the NASCAR Daytona 500 (1972) and the Le Mans 24-hour road rally (1967). In 1999 he was named joint Driver of the Century with Mario Andretti.

Dawn Fraser (4 Sep 1937, Balmain, Australia), Australian swimmer, the first to win gold medals in 3 consecutive Olympic Games (1956, 1960, 1964). From 1956 to 1964 she broke 39 world records and the women's world record for the 100-m freestyle race 9 successive times; her final time was not beaten until 1972.

William ("Pop") Gates (30 Aug 1917, Decatur AL—2 (or 1?) Dec 1999, New York NY), American basketball player, was one of the first blacks to play in an organized league. In a 17-year career (1938–55) he played on several barnstorming teams, including the New York Rens, which in 1939 won 68 consecutive games and the World Basketball Championship, and the Washington Bears, which had an undefeated season en route to the world title in 1943. He later played with and coached the Harlem Globetrotters.

Lou Gehrig (Henry Louis Gehrig; 19 Jun 1903, New York NY—2 Jun 1941, New York NY), American baseball player, one of the most durable and one of its great hitters. From 1925 to 1939 he appeared in 2,130 consecutive games, a record finally broken in 1995 by Cal Ripken, Jr. Gehrig retired with 2,721 hits, 493 home runs, and a lifetime batting average of .340.

Althea Gibson (25 Aug 1927, Silver SC), American tennis player who dominated women's competition 1956–58. She was the first black to play in the US championship tournament (1950) and the first to win the British (Wimbledon; 1957, 1958) and US (1957, 1958) singles titles. In 1956 she had won the French singles championship and the French and British doubles titles.

Bob Gibson (9 Nov 1935, Omaha NE), American baseball player, a pitcher who was at his best in crucial games. In 9 World Series games, he won 7 and lost 2.

Josh Gibson (21 Dec 1911, Buena Vista GA—20 Jan 1947, Pittsburgh PA), American baseball player

called the black Babe Ruth, one of the greatest players kept from the major leagues by the unwritten rule (enforced until the year of his death) against black ballplayers. During his 20 years (1927–46) in the Negro National League, he had a career batting average of .347; in 1931 he reportedly hit 75 home runs.

Pancho Gonzales (Richard Alonzo Gonzales, also spelled Gonzalez; 9 May 1928, Los Angeles CA–3 Jul 1995, Las Vegas NV), American tennis player who won the US professional championship in men's singles 8 times, 7 consecutively (1953–59, 1961). He won the US Grand Slam singles event twice (1948, 1949) before turning pro.

W.G. Grace (William Gilbert Grace; 18 Jul 1848, Downend, Eng.–23 Oct 1915, Kent, Eng.), English cricketer whose dominating physical presence, gusto, and inexhaustible energy made him a national figure in Victorian England. He evolved the modern principles of batting and achieved many notable performances on rough and unpredictable wickets, such as are unknown to modern players.

Steffi Graf (Stephanie Maria Graf; 14 Jun 1969, Brühl, W.Ger.), German tennis player who dominated the sport during the late 1980s and '90s with her intensity, speed, and powerful forehand. Between 1987 and her retirement in 1999, she won 7 British (Wimbledon), 5 US, 4 Australian, and 6 French singles titles; in 1988 she captured all 4 Grand Slam events and the gold medal at the Olympic Games.

Otto Graham (Otto Everett Graham, Jr.; "Automatic Otto"; 6 Dec 1921, Waukegan IL), American collegiate and professional football player and coach, best remembered as the quarterback of the Cleveland Browns during a 10-year period (1946–55) in which they won 105 games, lost 17, and tied 5 in regular-season play and won 7 of 10 championship games.

Red Grange (Harold Grange; "Galloping Ghost"; 13 Jun 1903, Forksville PA–28 Jan 1991, Lake Wales FL), American collegiate and professional football player, a great running back and one of the most highly publicized players in American football history. A 3-time All-American at the University of Illinois (1923–25), in 20 varsity games there he scored 31 touchdowns and gained 3,637 yd. On 19 Oct 1924, he scored 5 touchdowns against the University of Michigan, 4 in the first 12 minutes of play.

Harry Greb (Edward Henry Greb; "The Human Windmill"; 6 Jun 1894, Pittsburgh PA–22 Oct 1926, New York NY), American boxer who was one of the cleverest, toughest, and most colorful performers in the ring. From 1913 to 1926 Greb lost only 7 of his 294 bouts; he was world middleweight champion 1923–26, despite being blind in his right eye.

Ralph Greenleaf (c. 1899, Monmouth IL–15 Mar 1950, Philadelphia PA), American world champion pocket-billiards (pool) player from 1919 through 1924 and intermittently from 1926 to 1937. His great skill and colorful personality made him a leading American sports figure of the 1920s.

Wayne (Douglas) Gretzky ("The Great One"; 26 Jan 1961, Brantford ON), Canadian ice hockey player who in polls was consistently voted the greatest player in the history of the NHL. In 20 seasons (1978–99), he broke Bobby Orr's assists record (with 109), Phil Esposito's one-season scoring record (with 92), and Gordie Howe's all-time scoring record (with 894 goals and 1,963 assists). Gretzky

won the Art Ross Trophy (10 times), the Conn Smythe Trophy (2), the Hart Memorial Trophy (10), the Lady Byng Memorial Trophy (5), and the Lester B. Pearson Award (5).

Florence Griffith Joyner (Delorez Florence Griffith Joyner; "FloJo"; 21 Dec 1959, Los Angeles CA–21 Sep 1998, Mission Viejo CA), American sprinter who was considered one of the fastest women in track. Since 1988, the year she won the Sullivan Trophy as the best US amateur athlete, her world records in the 100-m (10.49 sec) and 200-m (21.34 sec) races have remained unbroken.

Michael Gross (17 Jun 1964, Frankfurt am Main, W.Ger.), German swimmer who set 12 world records in the 1980s and won 6 Olympic medals, including 3 golds, in 3 consecutive Olympics (1980, 1984, 1988).

George Stanley Halas (2 Feb 1895, Chicago IL–31 Oct 1983, Chicago IL), American founder and owner of the Chicago Bears pro football team, from its inception as the Decatur Staleys in 1920 until 1983; as head coach he led the team to 324 wins and 6 NFL championships. Halas revolutionized American football strategy in the late 1930s when he revived the T-formation and added to it the man in motion.

Scott Hamilton (28 Aug 1958, Toledo OH), American figure skater who was a 4-time world champion and the 1984 Olympic gold-medal winner in men's figure skating. He has been credited with imbuing men's figure skating with an air of athleticism.

Bob Hayes (Robert Lee Hayes; 20 Dec 1942, Jacksonville FL), American sprinter who was a remarkably powerful runner with as much raw speed as any athlete in history. In 1964 he won 2 Olympic gold medals and set a 100-m record (10.06). He later played professional football.

Marques Haynes (3 Oct 1926, Sand Springs OK), American basketball player, considered the finest dribbler and ball-handler ever, played for the Harlem Globetrotters (1947–53, 1972–79), the Magicians, a team he founded (1953–72, 1983–92), and other teams of the Independent League. He was the first Globetrotter inducted into the Basketball Hall of Fame.

George (Alphonso) Headley (30 May 1909, Colón, Panama–30 Nov 1983, Meadowbridge, Kingston, Jamaica), Jamaican cricketer, one of the best batsman ever and the first black to play for the West Indies in international Test cricket. In 103 first-class matches (1927–54), he scored 9,921 first-class runs (average 69.86), including 33 centuries (100 runs in a single innings) and a career high 344 not out; in 22 Tests he made 2,190 runs (average 60.83) and 10 centuries.

Eric Heiden (14 Jun 1958, Madison WI), American athlete who at the 1980 Winter Olympics became the first skater to win gold medals in all speed-skating events (500, 1,000, 1,500, 5,000, 10,000 m). He set a world record in the 10,000-m and Olympic records in all 5 events.

Sonja Henie (8 Apr 1912, Kristiania [now Oslo], Nor.–12 Oct 1969, in an airplane en route to Oslo, Nor.), Norwegian-born American figure skater who revolutionized the sport for women with her technical athleticism and glamour; she was European champion for a decade (1927–36) and captured 3 consecutive Olympic gold medals (1928, 1932, 1936); she went on to achieve financial success and international stardom as a professional ice skater and motion-picture actress.

(Norman) Graham Hill (15 Feb 1929, London, Eng.—29 Nov 1975, near London, Eng.), British race-car driver who won the Grand Prix world championship (1962, 1968), the Indianapolis 500 (1966), and the Le Mans 24-hour Race (1972).

Phil Hill (Philip Toll Hill; 20 Apr 1927, Miami FL), American race-car driver, the first American to win the world driving championship (1961).

Bernard Hinault (14 Nov 1954, Yffiniac, France), French cyclist whose professional career spanned more than a decade (1975–86), during which he won the Tour de France 5 times (1978, 1979, 1981, 1982, 1985), the Giro d'Italia 3 times (1980, 1982, 1985), and the World Championship in 1980.

Jack Hobbs (Sir John Berry Hobbs; 16 Dec 1882, Cambridge, Eng.—21 Dec 1963, Hove, Sussex, Eng.), English cricketer, was England's most prolific batsman, with 61,237 runs and 197 centuries (100 runs in a single innings), both first-class career records, and a personal-high 316 not out. During his career (1905–34) he played for England in 61 international Test matches and scored 5,410 Test runs, including 15 centuries.

Ben Hogan (William Benjamin Hogan; 13 Aug 1912, Dublin TX—25 Jul 1997, Fort Worth TX), American golfer who reigned supreme in the decade after World War II, despite sustaining permanent leg injuries in a 1949 car accident. With 63 PGA Tour victories, he was only the second man (after Gene Sarazen) to claim a career modern Grand Slam, winning 2 Masters, 2 PGA Championships, 4 US Opens, and the 1953 British Open.

Willie Hoppe (William Frederick Hoppe; 11 Oct 1887, Cornwall-on-the-Hudson NY—1 Feb 1959, Miami FL), American master of carom (balkline and 3-cushion) billiards, was one of the most durable of all sports champions, winning 51 world titles between 1906 and 1952.

Rogers Hornsby (27 Apr 1896, Winters TX—5 Jan 1963, Chicago IL), American baseball player, generally considered the game's greatest right-handed hitter. His major league career batting average of .358 is second only to Ty Cobb's .366.

Gordie Howe (Gordon Howe; 31 Mar 1928, Floral SK), Canadian-born American ice hockey player and administrator. His career record of 1,850 total points (goals and assists) in the NHL stood until it was broken by Wayne Gretzky in 1989. His record of 801 goals in the NHL was broken by Gretzky in 1994.

Bobby Hull (Robert Marvin Hull, Jr.; 3 Jan 1939, Point Anne ON), Canadian ice hockey player (1957–72). His speed on the ice and swinging slap shot, which was reportedly timed at 120 mph, made him one of hockey's dominant scorers in his time. In 1960–61 he led the Chicago Black Hawks to the franchise's first Stanley Cup since 1938.

Don Hutson (Donald Montgomery Hutson; 31 Jan 1913, Pine Bluff AR—26 Jun 1997, Rancho Mirage CA), American football player who, in his 11-year career (1935–45) in the NFL, led the league in pass receptions for a total of 8 seasons, 5 of them consecutive, and made a total of 488 catches for 7,991 yd and 99 touchdowns. He held 18 records when he retired and in 1969 was named the NFL's all-time greatest end.

Miguel Indurain (Larraya) (16 Jul 1964, Villava, Spain), Spanish Basque cyclist, the only man to win the Tour de France 5 times in a row (1991–95); he also won the Giro d'Italia 3 times in succession (1992–94) and set a world hour record (53.040 km [32.959 mi]) in 1994.

Jack Johnson (John Arthur Johnson; 31 Mar 1878, Galveston TX—10 Jun 1946, Raleigh NC), American boxer; the first black to hold the heavyweight boxing championship of the world. A colorful and controversial champion, he won the title by knocking out champion Tommy Burns on 26 Dec 1908, and lost it on a knockout by Jess Willard in 26 rounds on 5 Apr 1915.

Magic Johnson (Earvin Johnson, Jr.; 14 Aug 1959, Lansing MI), American basketball player who led the NBA Los Angeles Lakers to 5 championships. At 6 ft 9 in (208 cm), he was a dangerous inside scorer and a capable rebounder, best known for innovative no-look and bounce passes and expert floor leadership.

Michael Johnson (13 Sep 1967, Dallas TX), American sprinter, perhaps the most eminent figure in track and field in the 1990s. For much of the decade he was virtually unbeaten in 200-m and 400-m races, and he held world records in the indoor 400 m and the outdoor 200 m. At the 1996 Olympic Games, he became the first man to win gold medals at both distances; he also set Olympic marks in both events.

Walter (Perry) Johnson ("Big Barney," "The Big Train"; 6 Nov 1887, Humboldt KS—10 Dec 1946, Washington DC), American baseball pitcher who had perhaps the greatest fastball in the history of the game. He played professionally from 1907 to 1927 and pitched a record 110 career shutouts; his 417 wins is second only to Cy Young's 511.

Bobby Jones (Robert Tyre Jones, Jr.; 17 Mar 1902, Atlanta GA—18 Dec 1971, Atlanta GA), American amateur golfer, the first man to achieve the Grand Slam, winning in a single year the 4 major tournaments of the time. In 1930 he won both the British and US Opens and both Amateur championships. From 1923 through 1930 he won 13 championships in those 4 annual tournaments; in 1934 he helped initiate the annual Masters Tournament.

Jackie Joyner-Kersee (Jacqueline Joyner-Kersee, née Jacqueline Joyner; 3 Mar 1962, East St. Louis IL), American track and field star who became the first Olympian to score more than 7,000 points (7,291) in the heptathlon (in 1988); in 1992, she became the first athlete to win the heptathlon in consecutive Olympics.

Jigoro Kano (28 Oct 1860, Kobe, Japan—4 May 1938, at sea between Europe and Japan), Japanese educator who in the early 1880s incorporated elements of jujitsu and other martial arts to invent the sport of judo. In 1911 he founded the Japan Athletic Association and was named his country's first representative to the IOC.

Aleksandr Karelin (19 Sep 1967, Novosibirsk, USSR [now in Russia]), Russian Greco-Roman wrestler revered for his extraordinary strength and unprecedented success in international competition. Beginning in 1988 he won 12 consecutive world championships and 3 Olympic gold medals until he was defeated in the final at the 2000 Olympics by Rulon Gardner.

Kip Keino (Hezekiah Kipchoge Keino; 17 Jan 1940, Nandi Hills, Kenya), Kenyan distance runner who won 4 Olympic medals (1968, 1972) and set world records at 3,000 m (7 min 39.6 sec) and 5,000 m (13 min 24.2 sec); his achievements inspired a generation of Kenyan athletes.

Jahangir Khan (10 Dec 1963, Karachi, Pak.), Pakistani squash player who holds the longest unbeaten run in any professional sport, racking up 10 successive British Open titles (1982–91), as well as 6 World Opens in the 1980s; he was undefeated in more than 500 straight matches between the 1981 British Open, where he defeated Geoff Hunt, and the 1987 World Open, when he lost to his compatriot Jansher Khan.

Jansher Khan (15 Jun 1969, Peshawar, Pak.), Pakistani squash player who between 1987 and 1997 won the British open 6 consecutive times, and the World Open 8 times, a record comparable only to that of his equally renowned countryman Jahangir Khan.

Jean-Claude Killy (30 Aug 1943, Saint-Cloud, near Paris, France), French skier, a dominant figure in men's international Alpine skiing competitions (1965–68) and a popular sports personage known for his irreverent behavior; he won the first 2 overall World Cups (1967, 1968) and all 3 men's Alpine skiing events at the 1968 Winter Olympics.

Billie Jean King (née Billie Jean Moffitt; 22 Nov 1943, Long Beach CA), American tennis player whose influence and playing style elevated the status of women's professional tennis. In her career (1961–83) she won 39 major titles, competing in both singles and doubles; her records include 20 British (Wimbledon) titles and 27 Grand Slam doubles championships. She was also a founder of the Women's Tennis Association and the World Team Tennis competition.

Franz Klammer (3 Dec 1953, Mooswald, Austria), Austrian Alpine skier who attacked the slopes with what appeared to be reckless abandon yet won 23 World Cup downhill races in his career. He held the World Cup downhill title 1975–78 and 1983 and won the gold medal in the downhill event at the 1976 Winter Olympics by one-third of a second.

Olga Korbut (16 May 1956, Grodno, Belorussia, USSR [now in Belarus]), Soviet gymnast who charmed audiences and won 3 gold medals and a silver at the 1972 Olympics.

Julie Krone (Julieanne Louise Krone; 24 Jul 1963, Benton Harbor MI), American jockey, the first woman to win one of the US Triple Crown races, the 1993 Belmont Stakes. She retired in 1999 with 3,545 victories in 20,470 races over an 18-year career and was the first female jockey elected to thoroughbred racing's hall of fame.

René Lacoste (Jean-René Lacoste, "The Crocodile"; 2 Jul 1904, Paris, France—12 Oct 1996, Saint-Jean-de-Luz, France), French tennis player who was a leading competitor in the late 1920s. As one of the powerful 4 Musketeers (with Jean Borotra, Henri Cochet, and Jacques Brugnon), he helped France win its first Davis Cup in 1927, starting its 6-year domination of the cup. He also won 3 French, 2 US, and 2 British (Wimbledon) singles titles. Later he began a successful sportswear company.

Ron Lancaster (14 Oct 1938, Fairchance PA), American-born Canadian football player, was one of the top passers in CFL history, he retired in 1978 after 18 seasons with a career 50,535 total passing yards, 3,384 pass completions, and a record 333 passing touchdowns, as well as a record 396 interceptions. He was twice Most Outstanding Player (1970, 1976) and twice CFL Coach of the Year (1996, 1998).

Larisa Latynina (27 Dec 1934, Kherson, Ukr., USSR [now in Ukraine]), Soviet gymnast who won the most medals of any athlete in Olympic history, 18 in 3 Olympic Games (1956, 1960, 1964); known for her balletic grace, she was the first woman athlete to win 9 Olympic gold medals.

Rod Laver (9 Aug 1938, Rockhampton, Australia), Australian left-handed tennis player, the second man in the history of the sport (after Don Budge in 1938) to win the 4 major singles championships, the British (Wimbledon), US, Australian, and French, in one calendar year (1962) and the first to repeat this Grand Slam (1969). He ultimately won 17 Grand Slam titles (singles and doubles, not counting mixed doubles) and was ranked in the top 10 for 15 years (1959–75).

Greg LeMond (Gregory James LeMond; 26 Jun 1961, Lakewood CA), American cyclist who was the first non-European rider to win the Tour de France. In his career he won that tour 3 times (1986, 1989, 1990) and twice won the World Road Race Championship (1983, 1989).

Suzanne (Rachel Flore) Lenglen (24 May 1899, Compiègne, France—4 Jul 1938, Paris, France), French tennis player and 6-time British (Wimbledon) champion who dominated women's amateur lawn tennis from 1919 until 1926, when she turned professional; she was also one of the greatest women players of hard-court tennis in her time. Lenglen changed the future of women's tennis with her aggressive play, short-cropped hair, and "scandalous" unstarched clothing that left her ankles and lower arms exposed.

Sugar Ray Leonard (Ray Charles Leonard; 17 May 1956, Rocky Mount NC), American boxer, known for his agility and finesse, who won 36 of 39 professional fights (25 knockouts) and held titles as a welterweight, junior middleweight, middleweight, light heavyweight, and super middleweight. As an amateur he won the light welterweight gold medal at the 1976 Olympics.

Carl Lewis (Frederick Carlton Lewis; 1 Jul 1961, Birmingham AL), American athlete who was one of the greatest Olympians in history; he won 9 Olympic track-and-field gold medals (4 in 1984, 2 in 1988, 2 in 1992, 1 in 1996), and he was only the second athlete (after Al Oerter) to win the same event (long jump) in 4 consecutive Games.

Nancy Lieberman-Cline (1 Jul 1958, Brooklyn NY), American college, Olympic, and professional basketball player; she excelled in the defunct Women's Professional Basketball League and Women's American Basketball Association; was the first woman to play in a men's professional league, in 1986; and played in the inaugural season of the Women's NBA, later coaching as well.

Bobby Locke (Arthur D'arcy Locke; 20 Nov 1917, Germiston, S.Af.—9 Mar 1987, Johannesburg, S.Af.), South African golfer who won the British Open 4 times.

Vince Lombardi (Vincent Thomas Lombardi; 11 Jun 1913, Brooklyn NY—3 Sep 1970, Washington DC), American football coach who became a national symbol of single-minded determination to win. In 9 seasons (1959–67) he led the Green Bay Packers to 5 NFL championships and to victory in the first 2 Super Bowl games. He was voted the NFL man of the decade for the 1960s.

Greg Louganis (Gregory Efthimios Louganis; 29 Jan 1960, San Diego CA), American diver generally considered the greatest in history. After winning a silver at the 1976 Olympic Games, he won 4 Olympic gold medals (he missed the 1980 Games), plus 5 golds

in world championship events, 6 golds at Pan American Games, and 4 golds (and one siver) in FINA Cup competition; 8 times he won both the springboard and platform competition.

Joe Louis (Joseph Louis Barrow, "The Brown Bomber"; 13 May 1914, Lafayette AL—12 Apr 1981, Las Vegas NV), American boxer who was world heavyweight champion from 22 Jun 1937, when he knocked out James J. Braddock in 8 rounds in Chicago, until 1 Mar 1949, when he briefly retired. During his reign, the longest in the heavyweight division's history, he successfully defended the title 25 times, scoring 21 knockouts. He was arguably the most admired African American of the 1940s and retired in 1951 with a career record of 68–3 (54 knockouts).

Sid Luckman (Sidney Luckman; 21 Nov 1916, Brooklyn NY—5 Jul 1998, North Miami Beach FL), American football quarterback who, during his 12 NFL seasons (1939–50), directed the revolutionary T-formation offense of the Chicago Bears. Luckman's accomplishment (14,683 passing yards and 139 touchdowns) terminated a long era in professional football in which offensive systems were based largely on rushing from the single-wing formation.

Hank Luisetti (Angelo Enrico Luisetti; 16 Jun 1916, San Francisco CA), American collegiate basketball player who introduced the one-handed shot. He also combined all skills on both offense and defense, including dribbling and passing behind his back. He was the first college player to score 50 points in a game.

John McEnroe (John Patrick McEnroe, Jr.; 16 Feb 1959, Wiesbaden, W.Ger.), American left-handed tennis player who established himself as a leading competitor in the late 1970s and the '80s. He won 154 professional matches, 77 in singles (including 7 Grand Slam events) and 77 in doubles (9 in Grand Slams) and was ranked in the top 10 for 10 years. He also was noted for his poor behavior on court, which resulted in a number of fines and suspensions.

Mark McGwire (1 Oct 1963, Pomona CA), American baseball player, considered one of the most powerful hitters in the history of the game. In 1998 he set a major league record for most home runs in a season (70), breaking Roger Maris's mark of 61, set in 1961. He retired in 2001 with 583 home runs, sixth on the all-time list.

Mickey (Charles) Mantle (20 Oct 1931, Spavinaw OK—13 Aug 1995, Dallas TX), American baseball player who was an enormously popular member of the dominating NY Yankees (1951–68); he was a powerful switch-hitter who hit 536 home runs, led the American League in runs scored 6 times and home runs 4 times, and was named MVP 3 times.

Diego (Armando) Maradona (30 Oct 1960, Lanes, Buenos Aires, Arg.), Argentine association football (soccer) player considered one of the finest players ever until his career was torpedoed by drug scandals in 1991 and 1994. He led Argentina to a World Cup championship and was elected World Player of the Year in 1986. He played 90 international matches, in which he scored 34 goals, and held the record for World Cup appearances (21).

Rocky Marciano (Rocco Francis Marchegiano; "The Brockton Blockbuster"; 1 Sep 1923, Brockton MA—31 Aug 1969, near Newton IA), American world heavyweight boxing champion from 23 Sep 1952, when he knocked out champion Jersey Joe Walcott in 13 rounds, to 27 Apr 1956, when he retired from

the ring. Marciano was undefeated in 49 professional fights, scoring 43 knockouts.

Roger (Eugene) Maris (10 Sep 1934, Hibbing MN—14 Dec 1985, Houston TX), American baseball player whose 61 home runs (1961) broke Babe Ruth's single-season record (set in 1927). Maris's accomplishment was often denigrated because Ruth's 60 home runs were hit in a season with 8 fewer games, but the new record wasn't broken until 1998 when Mark McGwire hit 70.

Christy Mathewson (Christopher Mathewson; 12 Aug 1880, Factoryville PA—7 Oct 1925, Saranac Lake NY), American baseball pitcher, one of the first 5 players chosen for the Baseball Hall of Fame (1936). He had exceptional control and was a master of the fadeaway, or screwball, pitch; between 1900 and 1916 he won 373 games, including more than 20 games in each of 13 seasons.

Bob Mathias (Robert Bruce Mathias; 17 Nov 1930, Tulare CA), American athlete, the youngest to win a gold medal in the decathlon in Olympic competition. After his victory in 1948, at the age of 17, he returned to win a second Olympic gold medal in 1952.

Willie (Howard) Mays (6 May 1931, Westfield AL), American baseball player who was considered one of the game's finest all-around players, notable for both his batting and his fielding. His 660 career home runs place him third on the all-time list, behind Hank Aaron (755) and Babe Ruth (714).

Aleksandr (Vasilyevich) Medved (16 Sep 1937, Belaya Tserkov, Ukr., USSR [now Bila Tserkva, Ukr.]), Russian wrestler who is considered one of the greatest freestyle competitors of all time. He won gold medals in 3 consecutive Olympics (1964–72).

Eddy Merckx ("The Cannibal"; 17 Jun 1945, Meensel-Kiezegem, Belgium), Belgian cyclist, a formidable competitor with almost 450 victories during 1965–77, he was a 5-time winner of both the Tour de France (1969–72, 1974) and the Giro d'Italia (1968, 1970, 1972–74) and 3-time world champion (1967, 1971, 1974).

George Mikan (18 Jun 1924, Joliet IL), American basketball player and executive who was selected in an Associated Press poll in 1950 as the greatest basketball player of the first half of the 20th century. In 9 pro seasons, he led the league in scoring 6 times and retired with a then-record 11,764 points.

Stan Mikita (Stanislav Gvoth; 20 May 1940, Sokolce, Czech. [now in Slovakia]), Czechoslovak ice hockey player, the first from Czechoslovakia to play for the NHL and the first person in NHL history to capture the Hart Trophy, Art Ross Trophy, and Lady Byng Trophy in the same year (1966–67)—he then repeated the feat the following season. Mikita propelled the Chicago Blackhawks to their first Stanley Cup victory (1960–61) since 1938 and led the NHL in scoring in 4 seasons with a career high 40 goals in 1967–68.

Cheryl Miller (3 Jan 1964, Riverside CA), American high school, college, Olympic, and pro basketball player. She was elected national high school player of the year twice (1981, 1982) and college player of the year for 3 years running (1984–86), led the University of Southern California to the NCAA title (1983, 1984), and set USC records for points (3,018), rebounds, field goals, free throws, steals, and games played. She led the US women to a gold medal in the 1984 Olympics. She later coached and worked as a sports announcer.

Joe Montana (11 Jun 1956, New Eagle PA), American football quarterback who led the San Francisco 49ers to 4 Super Bowl victories and was named Super Bowl MVP 3 times. Known for his league-leading passing performance, he specialized in snatching victory from the jaws of defeat, most memorably the 92-yd drive in the last seconds that won the 49ers Super Bowl XXIII in January 1989.

Archie Moore (Archibald Lee Wright; 13 Dec 1913, Benoit MS—9 Dec 1998, San Diego CA), American boxer, world light-heavyweight champion from 1952, when he defeated Joey Maxim, until 1962, when he lost recognition as champion for failing to meet a challenger. From 1936 to 1963 Moore had 229 bouts, winning 194; he scored more knock-outs (141) than any other pro boxer in history.

Willie Mosconi (William Joseph Mosconi; 27 Jun 1913, Philadelphia PA—16 Sep 1993, Haddon Heights NJ), American pocket billiards player who was men's world champion 15 times between 1941 and 1957. His gentlemanly appearance and demeanor helped to establish pocket billiards as a reputable pastime.

Annemarie Moser-Pröll (née Annemarie Pröll; 27 Mar 1953, Kleinarl, Austria), Austrian Alpine skier who held the all-time record of 6 women's World Cup overall championships, 5 in succession (1971–75, 1979); she also won 2 world championship races in 1979 and the gold medal in the downhill event at the 1980 Winter Olympics.

Edwin Moses (31 Aug 1956, Dayton OH), American hurdler and winner of the gold medal for the 400-m hurdles in the 1976 and 1984 Olympic Games.

Marian Motley (5 Jun 1920, Leesburg GA—27 Jun 1999, Cleveland OH), African American football full-back who helped desegregate professional football in the 1940s. A member of the All-American Football Conference Cleveland Browns from 1946, he led the AAFC in rushing (3,024 yd in 4 seasons); when Cleveland joined the NFL in 1950 he rushed for 810 yd and led the team to the NFL championship.

Stan Musial (Stanley Frank Musial; 21 Nov 1920, Donora PA), American baseball player who, in his 22-year playing career (1941–63) with the St. Louis Cardinals, won 7 National League batting championships and made 3,630 hits, making him fourth on the all-time list.

Bronko Nagurski (Bronislaw Nagurski; 30 Nov 1908, Rainy River ON—7 Jan 1990, International Falls MN), American collegiate and professional football player, who was named All-American (1929) at the University of Minnesota. A legendary fullback for the Chicago Bears in the days before specialization, he was equally powerful on offense and defense and helped the Bears win the NFL title in 1932, 1933, and 1943 (after a 6-year retirement).

James A. Naismith (6 Nov 1861, Almonte ON—28 Nov 1939, Lawrence KS), Canadian-born American physical-education director who, in December 1891, at the International YMCA Training School, afterward Springfield (MA) College, invented the game of basketball.

Joe Namath (Joseph William Namath; "Joe Willie," "Broadway Joe"; 31 May 1943, Beaver Falls PA), American collegiate and professional football quarterback who was one of the best passers in the game and a flamboyant personality off the field. He passed for a record 4,007 yd in his first season with the AFL New York Jets and two years later upset the NFL's highly favored Baltimore Colts

16–7 in Super Bowl III. By the time he retired in 1978, he had passed for 27,663 yd and 173 touchdowns.

Martina Navratilova (18 Oct 1956, Prague, Czech. [now in Czech Rep.]), Czech-born American left-handed tennis player who dominated her sport from 1973 to 1995; she was the most prolific winner of the modern open era, with a career match record of 1,438–212. A serve-and-volley specialist, she won a record 167 titles, including 18 singles and 37 doubles titles in the 4 Grand Slam events, capped by a record 9 singles and 10 doubles at the British (Wimbledon) championship. She also led both Czechoslovakia (1975) and the US (1986) to Federation Cup victories.

Sir Ranjitsinhji Vibhaji, Maharaja Jam Sahib of Nawanagar (also called [until 1907] Kumar Shri Ranjitsinhji Vibhaji; 10 Sep 1872, Sarodar, India—2 Apr 1933, Jamnagar, India), Indian-born English cricketer, one of the world's finest batsmen; he scored 24,692 career runs (average 56.37), including 72 centuries (100 runs in an innings), and made more than 3,000 runs in 1899 and again in 1900. In 15 international Test matches for England, he scored 989 runs (average 44.95).

George Nepia (25 Apr 1905, Wairoa, Hawkes Bay, N.Z.—27 Aug 1986, Ruatoria, N.Z.), New Zealand Maori rugby football player, who, following his masterful performance on "The Invincibles," the All Black (New Zealand) team on the 1924 tour of Great Britain, France, and Canada, was hailed as the greatest fullback in the history of Rugby Union. He later played Rugby League in Great Britain.

Jack (William) Nicklaus ("The Golden Bear"; 21 Jan 1940, Columbus OH), American golfer, a dominating figure in world golf for 30 years. After turning professional in 1962, he won the Masters (1963, 1965, 1966, 1972, 1975, 1986), US Open (1962, 1967, 1972, 1980), PGA Championship (1963, 1971, 1973, 1975, 1980), and British Open (1966, 1970, 1978), only the fourth man to win all 4 Grand Slam tournaments. By 1986 he had won 71 official PGA events. He also designed golf courses, wrote golf books, and, from 1990, played on the PGA Senior Tour.

Paavo (Johannes) Nurmi (13 Jun 1897, Turku, Fin.—2 Oct 1973, Helsinki, Fin.), Finnish athlete who dominated long-distance running in the 1920s, capturing 6 gold medals in 3 Olympic Games (1920, 1924, 1928). For 8 years (1923–31) he held the world record for the mile run: 4 min 10.4 sec.

Al(fred) Oerter (19 Sep 1936, Astoria NY [now part of New York City]), American discus thrower who won 4 consecutive Olympic gold medals (1956, 1960, 1964, 1968). During his career he set new world records 4 times (1962–64). He was the first to throw the discus more than 200 ft.

Sadaharu Oh (20 May 1940, Tokyo, Japan), Japanese baseball player who holds the world record for most professional career home runs (868). Oh led the Tokyo Yomiuri Giants to 9 consecutive Japan League championships, a record unmatched by any other professional team worldwide. He also captured the league home-run title 15 times and holds the Japanese season home-run record (55). He later managed the Fukuoka Daiei Hawks to the 1999 championship.

Barney Oldfield (Berna Eli Oldfield; 29 Jan 1878, near Wauseon OH—4 Oct 1946, Beverly Hills CA), American automobile-racing driver, whose name was synonymous with speed in the first 2 decades of the 20th century.

Bobby Orr (Robert Gordon Orr; 20 Mar 1948, Parry Sound ON), Canadian-American ice hockey player, who was the first defenseman to lead the NHL in scoring, a feat he accomplished twice (1970 and 1975). In 10 seasons he led the Boston Bruins to 8 consecutive play-offs and 2 Stanley Cups. His season record for assists (102, set in 1970–71) was broken by Wayne Gretzky in 1980–81.

Jesse Owens (James Cleveland Owens; 12 Sep 1913, Oakville AL—31 Mar 1980, Phoenix AZ), American athlete who, while a student at Ohio State University, set 4 track-and-field world records in one day (25 May 1935), including a running broad jump record (26 ft 8¼ in) that stood for 25 years; he went on to win a then-record 4 gold medals at the 1936 Olympic Games.

Satchel Paige (Leroy Robert Paige; 7 Jul 1906?, Mobile AL—8 Jun 1982, Kansas City MO), American baseball pitcher who earned legendary fame during his many years in the Negro leagues; he finally was allowed to enter the major leagues in 1948. Paige had considerable pitching speed, developed a comprehensive mactory of slow-breaking deliveries, and was reputed to have won some 2,000 games in his 30-year career.

Arnold Palmer (10 Sep 1929, Youngstown PA), American golfer, the first to win the Masters Tournament 4 times and the first to earn $1 million in tournament prize money. From 1954, when he became a professional, through 1975 he won 61 PGA tournaments.

Walter Payton (Walter Jerry Payton, "Sweetness"; 25 Jul 1954, Columbia MS—1 Nov 1999, Barrington IL), American football player who set the standard of productivity and durability for running backs. The NFL's all-time leader in rushing (16,726 yd) and combined net yards (21,803 yd), he scored 110 touchdowns rushing (125 total), rushed for more than 100 yd in 77 games, and set a single-game rushing record of 275 yd (broken in 2000).

Pelé (Edson Arantes do Nascimento; 23 Oct 1940, Três Corações, Braz.), Brazilian association football (soccer) inside-forward who was revered as much for his sportsmanship as for his extraordinary skill and innovative style; in his time he was probably the most famous and possibly the best paid athlete in the world. Pelé led Brazil to 3 World Cup victories (1958, 1962, 1970) and permanent possession of the trophy. He scored 77 goals in 92 international matches and 1,090 goals in 1,114 club matches for Santos; later he played professionally in the US. He was awarded the FIFA Gold Medal in 1982, named Brazil's minister of sport in 1994, granted an honorary British knighthood in 1997, and voted footballer of the century in 1999.

Willie Pep (Guglielmo Papaleo; "Will o' the Wisp"; 19 Sep 1922, Hartford CT), American boxer known for his defensive tactics and elusiveness; he won his first 62 fights and held the world featherweight championship for 6 years (1942–48), lost it to Sandy Saddler, and regained it for 2 more years (1948–50). His professional record was 230–11–1 with 65 knockouts.

Richard Petty (2 Jul 1937, Level Cross NC), American race-car driver who won 200 NASCAR races including 7 Daytona 500s; he was the NASCAR national champion for 7 years (1964, 1967, 1971–72, 1974–75, 1979) and was the first stock-car driver to win $1 million in his career.

Michel Platini (21 Jun 1955, Joeuf, France), French association football (soccer) midfielder who, in his 15-year professional career (1972–87), scored 224 goals in 429 games, including 41 goals in 72 international matches. He was voted European Player of the Year 3 years in succession (1983–85) and World Player of the Year in 1984 and 1985.

Gary Player (1 Nov 1935, Johannesburg, S.Af.), South African golfer, the third man (after Gene Sarazen and Ben Hogan) to win the 4 tournaments of the modern golf Grand Slam: the Masters (1961, 1974, 1978), US Open (1965), the British Open (1959, 1968, 1974), and PGA Championship (1962, 1972). When he won the Masters in 1978, the span of his major championship victories covered 3 decades, longer than any previous golfer.

Alain Prost (Alain Marie Pascal Prost; "The Calculator"; 24 Feb 1955, St. Chamond, France), French Formula 1 race-car driver known for his meticulous care and attention to details; he tallied 51 wins in Grand Prix contests, won the world driver's championship 4 times (1985, 1986, 1989, 1993), and racked up a record 798.5 career championship points. He was also awarded France's Legion d'Honneur in 1985 and the retired race car drivers' Champion of Champions Trophy in 1988.

Oleg Protopopov (see Lyudmila Belousova).

Ferenc Puskas ("The Galloping Major"; 2 Apr 1927, Budapest, Hung.), Hungarian association football (soccer) player; short, overweight, and unable to head, he seemed an unlikely star, but he led his Kispest Honved team to 4 national championships and Hungary to a gold medal in the 1952 Olympics. After scoring 83 goals in 84 international matches for Hungary, he defected to Spain (1956) where he helped that country win the 1960 World Club Championship and led Real Madrid to 5 straight Spanish league championships (1961–65).

Steven Geoffrey Redgrave (23 Mar 1962, Marlow, Eng.), British rower who dominated his sport in the 1980s and '90s. His Olympic record in pairs and 4s included 5 gold medals (and one bronze) at 5 consecutive Olympic games; he also won 6 world championship golds and 2 silvers, 3 Commonwealth golds, and 20 golds at England's Henley Regatta.

George (Robert) Reed (2 Oct 1939, Mississippi), American-born Canadian football player, the greatest rusher in the annals of Canadian football, played in 4 Grey Cup competitions; upon his retirement in 1975 his many records included the all-time rushing yardage record for professional football anywhere: 16,116 yd (with a record 134 touchdowns) in 13-seasons of CFL play (1963–75).

Wilfred Rhodes (29 Oct 1877, Kirkheaton, near Huddersfield, Eng.—8 Jul 1973, Bournemouth, Eng.), English cricketer who during his career (1898–1930) completed more doubles (1,000 runs and 100 wickets in a single season) than any other player. He appeared in 58 international Test matches and played in his last Test at age 52. Rhodes scored 1,000 runs 21 times, captured 100 wickets 23 times, and set the world record for the most career wickets taken (4,187).

Maurice Richard (Joseph Henri Maurice Richard; "The Rocket"; 4 Aug 1921, Montreal PQ—27 May 2000, Montreal PQ), Canadian ice hockey player who played in 978 regular-season games for the Montreal Canadiens in 1942–60, scoring 544 goals (the first player to score 500) and 421 assists. The Canadiens won 8 Stanley Cup Cham-

pionships in the 1940s and '50s. Richard was awarded the Hart Trophy in 1947.

Bob Richards (Robert Eugene Richards; 20 Feb 1926, Champaign IL), American athlete, the first pole-vaulter to win 2 Olympic gold medals (1952, 1956). Sportswriters called him "the Vaulting Vicar" because he was an ordained minister.

Branch (Wesley) Rickey (20 Dec 1881, Stockdale OH—9 Dec 1965, Columbia MO), American baseball executive who devised the farm system of training ballplayers (1919) and hired the first black players in organized baseball in the 20th century (1945).

Cal Ripken, Jr. (Calvin Edwin Ripken, Jr.; 24 Aug 1960, Havre de Grace MD), American major league baseball player known for breaking (5 Sep 1995) Lou Gehrig's 56-year-old major league record of 2,130 consecutive games played. In 1983 and 1991 he won the American League's MVP award.

Oscar (Palmer) Robertson (24 Nov 1938, Charlotte TN), American collegiate and professional basketball player who redefined the point guard from a mere passer to a powerful offensive scoring position. While playing with the NBA Cincinnati Royals in 1961–62, he averaged double figures in per-game points (30.8), rebounds (12.5), and assists (11.4), a feat unmatched by any other player. He retired in 1974 with 26,710 points and 9,887 assists.

Frank Robinson (31 Aug 1935, Beaumont TX), American baseball player who was the first black manager in major league baseball. As a player he hit .300 in 5 of his first 10 years as a pro (1956–66), and retired in 1976 with 586 home runs (fifth on the all-time list).

Jackie Robinson (Jack Roosevelt Robinson; 31 Jan 1919, Cairo GA—24 Oct 1972, Stamford CT), American baseball player who was the first black player in the major leagues during the 20th century and a symbol of the integration of sports in the US long after his retirement. An infielder and outfielder for the Brooklyn Dodgers (1947–56), he led the National League in stolen bases in 1947 and was chosen rookie of the year. In 1949 he won the batting championship with a .342 average and was voted the league's MVP. His career average was .311.

Sugar Ray Robinson (Walker Smith, Jr.; 3 May 1921, Detroit MI—12 Apr 1989, Culver City CA), American boxer, 6 times a world champion: once as a welterweight (1946–51) and 5 times as a middleweight between 1951 and 1960. In 1951 his record stood at an astounding 129–1–2 (83 knockouts), and he retired at 175–19–6 (109). He is considered by many authorities to have been the best fighter in history.

Knute (Kenneth) Rockne (4 Mar 1888, Voss, Norway—31 Mar 1931, Chase Co. KS), American football coach who built the University of Notre Dame into a major power in US college football. The success of his teams and his humorous, colorful personality captured the public's imagination during the 1920s, the "golden age" of American sports. In 13 seasons Rockne's "Fighting Irish" teams won 105 games, while losing only 12 and tying 5; they were undefeated in 1919, 1920, 1924, 1929, and 1930, and were considered national champion in 1924, 1929, and 1930. Rockne prefigured the modern "platoon system" by substituting complete teams, which he called "shock troops," during games.

Irina (Konstantinovna) Rodnina (12 Sep 1949, Moscow, USSR), Soviet figure skater, was the most successful pairs skater in history; with her partners, Aleksey Ulanov (1969–72) and Aleksandr Zaytsev (from 1973; her husband from 1975), she won 10 successive world championships (1969–78) and 3 straight Olympic gold medals (1972, 1976, 1980).

Pete Rose (14 Apr 1942, Cincinnati OH), American baseball player who was noted for his all-around ability and enthusiasm. In 1985 he exceeded Ty Cobb's record of hits in a career (4,191) and retired in 1986, after 23 years, with 4,256 hits. He was barred from the Hall of Fame because of a gambling scandal.

Wilma Rudolph (Wilma Glodean Rudolph; 23 Jun 1940, St. Bethlehem, near Clarksville TN—12 Nov 1994, Brentwood TN), American sprinter, the first American woman runner to win 3 gold medals at a single Olympics (1964); she was also a world-record holder in the 100 m (11.3) and 200 m (22.9), despite having been crippled as a child. She later worked with underprivileged children.

Bill Russell (William Felton Russell; 12 Feb 1934, Monroe LA), American basketball player regarded in his day as the greatest defensive center in the history of the game; he was NBA MVP 5 times and led the Boston Celtics to 11 national championships in 13 years, including twice (1968, 1969) as player-coach; he was the first black coach of a major professional sports team in the US.

Babe Ruth (George Herman Ruth; 6 Feb 1895, Baltimore MD—16 Aug 1948, New York NY), American baseball player; he was one of the most popular figures in the US in the 1920s and was credited with saving baseball's image after the 1919 "Black Sox" scandal; he was the American League's leading home run hitter 12 times and the longtime holder of a record 60 home runs in a major-league season (1927), broken by Roger Maris in 1961, and a record 714 career home runs, finally broken by Hank Aaron in 1974.

Nolan Ryan (Lynn Nolan Ryan, Jr.; 31 Jan 1947, Refugio TX), American baseball player, who in 1983 became the first pitcher to surpass Walter Johnson's record of 3,508 career strikeouts, set in 1927. He finished his 27-year career (1966–93) with 5,714 strikeouts, including 383 in 1973.

Jim Ryun (James Ronald Ryun; 29 Apr 1947, Wichita KS), American middle-distance runner, was a star in high school and 3-time Olympian (1964–72) in the 1,500-m race, winning a silver medal in 1968. He held world records in the mile, half-mile, 1,500-m, and 800-m distances as well as the medley relay. He was awarded the Sullivan Trophy as the outstanding US amateur athlete of the year in 1966. He later served in the US Congress.

Ulrich Salchow (Karl Emil Julius Ulrich Salchow; 7 Aug 1877—19 Apr 1949, Stockholm, Sweden), Swedish figure skater who established a record by winning 10 world championships for men (1901–05, 1907–11). At the 1908 Games, he won the first Olympic gold medal awarded for men's figure skating.

Gene Sarazen (Eugene Saraceni; 27 Feb 1902, Harrison NY—13 May 1999, Naples FL), American golfer of the 1920s and '30s. His double eagle (3 strokes under par) on the par-5 15th hole in the last round of the 1935 Masters Tournament is one of the most famous shots in the history of the game. That victory, combined with his 2 US Opens (1922,

1932), 3 PGA Championships (1922, 1923, 1933), and the 1932 British Open, made him the first man to win all 4 tournaments in the modern Grand Slam.

Terry Sawchuk (Terrence Gordon Sawchuk; 28 Dec 1929, Winnipeg MB—31 May 1970, New York NY), Canadian ice hockey goaltender, considered one of the greatest in the game; he played 971 games in a 21-year NHL career (1949–70), and his record of 103 shutouts persisted into the mid-1980s.

Ard Schenk (Adrianus Schenk; 16 Sep 1944, Anna Paulowna, Neth.), Dutch speed skater who in 1972 won 3 gold medals in the Winter Olympics. He became the first skater to win the 500-, 1,500-, 5,000- and 10,000-m races at the world championships in a single year (1972).

Ayrton Senna (21 Mar 1960, São Paulo, Braz.—1 May 1994, Imola, Italy), Brazilian Formula 1 race-car driver who was renowned for his ruthless and risky maneuvers on the Grand Prix circuit; he dominated the sport with 41 Grand Prix titles and 3 driver's world championships (1988, 1990, 1991). His death from a collision suffered during the 1994 San Marino Grand Prix triggered national mourning in Brazil.

Bill Shoemaker (William Lee Shoemaker; Willie; 19 Aug 1931, near Fabens TX), American jockey, considered the greatest jockey of the second half of the 20th century. Between 1949 and 1990 he rode 8,833 winners on 40,350 mounts, including 11 US Triple Crown races. He became a trainer in 1990 and continued even after a 1991 car accident left him paralyzed.

Don Shula (Donald Francis Shula, 4 Jan 1930, Grand River OH), American football player and coach, who as head coach of the Baltimore Colts (1963–69) and the Miami Dolphins (1970–95), was the winningest coach in NFL football history, with a 33-year career record of 347 wins, 173 losses, and 6 ties, 20 play-off appearances, 6 Super Bowls, and 2 NFL championships.

O.J. Simpson (Orenthal James Simpson; 9 Jul 1947, San Francisco CA), American collegiate and professional football player who was a premier running back known for his speed and evasiveness. The 1968 Heisman Trophy winner at USC, in his 10-year pro career (1969–79) he rushed for 11,236 yd, and made 203 receptions, 990 yd in kickoff returns, and 14,368 combined yards. His single-game rushing record of 273 yd was broken by Walter Payton. In 1995–97 Simpson was the defendant in highly publicized criminal and civil suits over the murder of Simpson's former wife and her friend.

Sam Snead (Samuel Jackson Snead; "Slammin' Sammy"; 27 May 1912, near Hot Springs VA—23 May 2002, Hot Springs VA), American golfer who won 84 PGA tournaments and, except for the US Open in which he placed second 4 times, every major championship for which he was eligible.

Gary Sobers (Sir Garfield St. Aubrun Sobers; 28 Jul 1936, Bridgetown, Barbados), West Indian cricketer, considered by many authorities the most gifted all-around player of all time. As a batsman he scored 365 not out (against Pakistan in 1958), a record for international Test matches that stood until 1994. He was also exceptional in bowling (1,043 wickets taken, 235 in Tests) and in close-to-the wicket fielding.

Warren Spahn (23 Apr 1921, Buffalo NY), American baseball player whose total of 363 major-league victories established a record for left-handed pitchers. His feat of winning 20 or more games in each of 13 seasons also was a record for left-handers. He set still another mark by striking out at least 100 batters each year for 17 consecutive seasons (1947–63).

Mark (Andrew) Spitz (10 Feb 1950, Modesto CA), American swimmer who was the first athlete to win 7 gold medals in a single Olympic Games (1972); Spitz set world records in the 100-m and 200-m freestyle and the 100-m and 200-m butterfly, he added 3 more gold medals as a member of victorious US men's relay teams, which also set world records.

Amos Alonzo Stagg (16 Aug 1862, West Orange NJ—17 Mar 1965, Stockton CA), American college football coach who had the longest coaching career, 71 years, in the history of the sport. In 1943, at age 81, he was named college coach of the year, and he remained active in coaching until the age of 98. He is the only person selected for the National Football Hall of Fame as both a player and a coach. As a basketball coach for the University of Chicago and founder of five-man basketball, he also was elected to the Basketball Hall of Fame.

Ingemar Stenmark (18 Mar 1956, Josesjö, Sweden), Swedish Alpine skier, a slalom specialist who, in 1976, became the first Scandinavian to win the overall Alpine World Cup. He repeated the victory in 1977–78. At the time of his retirement he had won 86 World Cup races, more than any other skier.

Teofilo Stevenson (29 Mar 1952, Las Tunas, Cuba), Cuban heavyweight boxer who became the first fighter to win 3 Olympic gold medals in one weight class (1972, 1976, 1980) and one of only two to win 3 World Amateur Boxing titles. He remained an amateur throughout his long career.

Louise Suggs (Mae Louise Suggs; 7 Sep 1923, Lithia Springs GA), American golfer who was a founder and 3-time president of the LPGA and winner of 58 professional tournaments, including the US Women's Open (1949, 1952) and the 1957 LPGA Championship.

Naim Suleymanoglu (original name Naim Suleimanov, Bulgarian Naum Shalamanov; "Pocket Hercules"; 23 Jan 1967, Ptichar, Bulg.), Bulgarian-born Turkish weight lifter who went 8½ years without a loss, set numerous world records, and was the first weight lifter to win 3 Olympic gold medals (1988, 1992, 1996).

John L(awrence) Sullivan (15 Oct 1858, Roxbury MA—2 Feb 1918, Abington MA), American boxer, one of the most popular heavyweight champions and a symbol of the bareknuckle era of boxing. He was the first officially recognized world heavyweight champion under the new Marquess of Queensberry's rules from 1889 until he lost to James J. Corbett on 7 Sep 1892.

Madge Syers (or Cave Syers; née Florence Madeleine Cave; 1881, England—September 1917), British ice skater who was the first woman to compete at the highest level of international figure skating. She finished second to Ulrich Salchow at the 1902 world championships, an accomplishment that triggered the creation of a separate women's championship, the first 2 of which she won (1906, 1907). At the 1908 Olympic Games she won the first Olympic gold medal ever awarded in women's figure skating, as well as the bronze medal for pairs with her husband and coach, Edgar Syers.

Lawrence Taylor (4 Feb 1959, Williamsburg VA), American collegiate and professional football player, considered one of the best linebackers in the history of the game. As a member of the NFL New York Giants (1981–93), he recorded 132.5 official quarterback sacks, 1,088 tackles, 33 forced fumbles, 10 fumble recoveries, and 9 interceptions and won 2 Super Bowl championships (1987, 1991). He was only the second defensive player ever chosen league MVP (1986).

Jim Thorpe (James Francis Thorpe; 28 May 1888, near Prague, Indian Territory [now in OK]—28 Mar 1953, Lomita CA), American athlete, one of the most accomplished all-around athletes in history, who in 1950 was selected by American sports writers and broadcasters as the greatest American athlete and the greatest football player of the first half of the 20th century. He won the decathlon and pentathlon at the 1912 Olympic Games but was stripped of his medals when it was revealed that he had played semiprofessional baseball in 1909 and 1910 (they were restored in 1983). Thorpe played pro baseball (1913–19) and football (1919–26) and excelled in basketball, boxing, lacrosse, swimming, and hockey.

Bill Tilden (William Tatem Tilden II; 20 Feb 1893, Philadelphia PA—5 Jun 1953, Hollywood CA), American tennis player who used his speed, endurance, and mastery of spin to dominate the sport from before World War I until the early 1930s; he won 7 US singles and 9 doubles championships, 3 British (Wimbledon) singles and one doubles titles, and 2 professional titles.

Jayne Torvill (7 Oct 1957, Nottingham, Eng.), **& Christopher Dean** (27 Jul 1958, Nottingham), British figure skaters who revolutionized the sport of ice dancing. At the 1984 Winter Olympics, Torvill and Dean's now famous free-dance interpretation of Maurice Ravel's *Boléro* garnered an unprecedented perfect score of 6.0 for artistic impression from all 9 Olympic judges and the gold medal. They also won 4 world championships (1981–84) and a bronze medal at the 1994 Olympics.

Vladislav (Aleksandrovich) Tretyak (25 Apr 1952, Dmitrovo, USSR), Soviet ice hockey player who was considered one of the greatest goaltenders in the history of the sport. As a member of the Central Red Army team and Soviet national squad, he won 10 world championships (1970–71, 1973–75, 1978–79, 1981–83) and 3 Olympic gold medals (1972, 1976, 1984).

Victor (Thomas) Trumper (2 Nov 1877, Darlinghurst, Australia—28 Jun 1915, Darlinghurst, Australia), Australian cricketer who, with Sir Don Bradman, is considered one of that country's finest batsmen. His accomplishments include a famous century (100 runs in an innings) before lunch in 1902, the first in Test history. Between 1894 and 1914 he scored 16,939 runs (average 44.57) and 42 centuries, with a high of 300 not out in 1899; in 48 international Test matches, he made 3,163 runs (average 39.04).

Gene Tunney (James Joseph Tunney; "The Fighting Marine"; 25 May 1898, New York NY—7 Nov 1978, Greenwich CT), American boxer who defeated Jack Dempsey in 1926 to become the world heavyweight boxing champion. The rematch on 22 Sep 1927 gave rise to the lasting controversy of the "long count." In the seventh round Tunney was knocked to the canvas, Dempsey failed to retire immediately to a neutral corner, and the count did not begin until he had done so, several seconds later. Tunney rose on the count of nine and won the 10-round fight by decision. From 1915 to 1928 Tunney fought 77 bouts, winning 65 (43 by knockouts).

Wyomia Tyus (29 Aug 1945, Griffin GA), American sprinter who several times held the world record for the 100-m race and was the first person to win the Olympic gold medal in the event twice (1964, 1968).

Johnny Unitas (John Constantine Unitas; 7 May 1933, Pittsburgh PA—11 Sep 2002, Baltimore MD), American football player who in 1969 was named the greatest all-time NFL quarterback; he steered the Baltimore Colts to 3 NFL titles, including a stunning overtime win over the New York Giants in 1958 and the 1971 Super Bowl. During his NFL career (1957–74), Unitas passed for 40,239 yd and 290 touchdowns, he holds the record for most consecutive games with at least one touchdown pass (47).

Harry Vardon (9 May 1870, Grouville, Jersey, Channel Islands—20 Mar 1937, Totteridge, Eng.), British golfer who pioneered accurate and reliable hitting techniques that are still the basis of the modern golf swing; between 1896 and 1914 he won the British Open a record 6 times and the US Open once.

Honus Wagner (John Peter Wagner, "The Flying Dutchman"; 24 Feb 1874, Mansfield [now Carnegie] PA—6 Dec 1955, Carnegie PA), American baseball player, one of the first 5 men elected to the Baseball Hall of Fame (1936). He was generally considered the greatest shortstop in baseball history and by some was regarded as the finest all-around player in the history of the National League. He retired in 1917, after 21 years, with a 327 batting average and 722 stolen bases.

Cornelius Warmerdam ("Dutch"; 22 Jun 1915, Long Beach CA—13 Nov 2001, Fresno CA), American pole-vaulter, the first to attain 15 ft (4.57 m) and the last to set major records with a bamboo pole; his final records established in 1942 (outdoor) and 1943 (indoor) were broken in 1957 and 1959, respectively, by athletes using more flexible aluminum poles.

Pop Warner (Glenn Scobey Warner; 5 Apr 1871, Springville NY—7 Sep 1954, Palo Alto CA), American college football coach who, in the decade after World War I, perfected the single- and double-wing systems of offense. As coach at the Carlisle (PA) Indian Industrial School, he trained Jim Thorpe.

George Weah (George Manneh Oppong Ousman Weah; 1 Oct 1966, Monrovia, Liberia), Liberian-born association football (soccer) star, played center-forward for several African and European teams and in 1995–96 achieved the triple honor of being elected European, African, and FIFA World Footballer of the Year, the first player ever to win three such titles in one year. At that point he had scored 131 goals in 310 games in France and Italy. In October 1996 Weah was named Commonwealth Sportsman of the Year and in 1999, African Player of the Century.

Dick Weber (23 Dec 1929, Indiana), American bowler who won the PBA Bowler of the Year award in 1961, 1963, and 1965; he was famed for his consistency over a career in professional bowling and seniors bowling that stretched to 5 decades.

Johnny Weissmuller (Peter John Weissmuller, original name Jonas Weissmuller; 2 Jun 1904, Freidorf, Rom.—20 Jan 1984, Acapulco, Mex.), American freestyle swimmer of the 1920s who won 5 Olympic gold medals and set 67 world records. He became even more famous as a motion-picture actor, most notably in the role of Tarzan.

Jerry West (28 May 1938, Chelyan WV), American basketball player, who excelled at the University of West Virginia, led the US to gold medals in the 1959 Pan American Games and the 1960 Olympics, and led the Los Angeles Lakers to an NBA title in 1972. In various coaching and executive positions, West saw the Lakers win the NBA title 7 more times.

Ted Williams (30 Aug 1918, San Diego CA–5 Jul 2002, Inverness FL), American baseball player who compiled a lifetime batting average of .344 as a left-handed hitting outfielder with the Boston Red Sox from 1939 to 1960. He was the last .400 hitter (.406 in 1941) in the 20th century.

Helen Wills (Helen Newington Wills, also called Helen Wills Moody and Helen Roark; 6 Oct 1905, Centerville CA–1 Jan 1998, Carmel CA), American tennis player who was the top female competitor in the world for 8 years (1927–33, 1935). She won 19 of 22 Grand Slam singles events she entered, 7 US, 4 French, and 8 British (Wimbledon), as well as 12 Grand Slam doubles championships and 2 gold medals at the 1924 Olympics.

John Wooden (14 Oct 1910, Hall IN), American collegiate basketball coach who directed UCLA teams to 8 NCAA championships in 9 years (1964–65, 1967–72). In 1932 he was college player of the year and led Purdue University to the national championship; as a coach (from 1946) he amassed a 40-year career record of 885–203. He was the first man enshrined in the Basketball Hall of Fame as a player and as a coach.

Mickey Wright (Mary Kathryn Wright; 14 Feb 1935, San Diego CA), American golfer whose record-setting play made her one of the dominant golfers of her time. She won 82 tournaments (13 majors), including the US Women's Open and the LPGA Championship 4 times each. In 1999 the Associated Press named her Female Golfer of the Century.

Lev (Ivanovich) Yashin ("The Black Panther"; 22 Oct 1929, Moscow, USSR–21 Mar 1990, Moscow USSR), Russian association football (soccer) goalkeeper renowned for his acrobatic skills. He played with Moscow Dynamo (1949–70), which won 5 national titles and the 1960 European championship, represented the Soviet Union in 3 World Cups (1958, 1962, 1966) and the gold medal–winning 1956 Olympics. He was voted European Player of the Year in 1963.

Cy Young (29 Mar 1867, Gilmore OH–4 Nov 1955, Newcomerstown OH), American baseball pitcher, whose record for major league games won (511) still stands. He also holds the record for most games started (815), games completed (749), and innings pitched (7,356). The annual award for best major league pitcher in each league is named after him.

Babe Didrikson Zaharias (Mildred Ella Zaharias, née Mildred Ella Didriksen; 26 Jun 1914, Port Arthur TX–27 Sep 1956, Galveston TX), American sportswoman who was one of the greatest athletes of the 20th century. A 3-time All-American basketball player (1930–32) and winner of 2 gold medals in track and field at the 1932 Olympic Games, she also excelled at baseball, softball, swimming, figure skating, billiards, and football. From 1934 until her death from cancer in 1956, she won 10 major golf championships. She was a cofounder of the LPGA and was named the Associated Press Woman of the Year 6 times.

Emil Zatopek (19 Sep 1922, Koprivnice, Czech. [now in Czech Rep.]–22 Nov 2000, Prague, Czech Rep.), Czech athlete, one of the greatest long-distance runners in history. He won the gold medal in the 10,000-m race at the 1948 Olympics and 3 golds at the 1952 Olympics (5,000 m, 10,000 m, and marathon). During his career he set 18 world records.

Did you know? Sportswriter Grantland Rice's syndicated column, "The Sportlight," was the most influential of its day. He coined the famous phrase that it was not important whether you "won or lost, but how you played the game."

The Olympic Games

By the 6th century BC several sporting festivals had achieved cultural importance in the Greek world, the most prominent among them the Olympic Games at the city of Olympia, first recorded in 776 BC and held at four year intervals thereafter. Those games, comprising many of the sports now included in the Summer Games, were abolished in AD 393 by the Roman emperor Theodosius I.

In 1887 the 24-year-old French aristocrat and educator Pierre, baron de Coubertin, conceived the idea of reviving the Olympic Games and spent seven years gathering support for his plan. At a international congress in 1894, his plan was accepted and the International Olympic Committee (IOC) was founded. The first modern Olympic Games were held in Athens in April 1896, with some 300 representatives from 13 nations competing. The revival led to the formation of international amateur sports organizations and national Olympic committees throughout the world.

The IOC is responsible for maintaining the regular celebration of the games, seeing that the games are carried out in a spirit of peace and intercultural communication, and promoting amateur sport throughout the world. IOC members may not accept from the government of their country, or from any other entity, instructions that compromise their independence.

The Olympic Games have come to be regarded as the world's foremost sports competition. Before the 1970s the Games were officially limited to amateurs, but since that time many events have been opened to professional athletes. In 1924 the Winter Games were created, and in 1986 the IOC voted to alternate the Winter and Summer Games every two years, beginning in 1994.

The games were canceled during the two World Wars (1916, 1940, and 1944) and have frequently served as venues for the expression of political dissent. China refused to participate in the Summer Games from 1956 until 1984 because of Taiwan's participation; 26 nations boycotted in 1976 over the participation of New Zealand, some of whose athletes had competed in apartheid-era South Africa; the United States and some 60 other countries boycotted the 1980 games in Moscow to protest the Soviet invasion of Afghanistan, and the Communist bloc and Cuba in turn boycotted the 1984 Los Angeles games.

In light of the IOC's declared independence from political and financial interests, in 1998 the world was shocked by allegations of widespread corruption within the committee. Several committee members, it was found, had accepted bribes to approve the bid of Salt Lake City UT as the site for the 2002 Winter Games. Impropriety was also alleged for several previous bid committees. The IOC responded by expelling six members, and in 1999 announced a number of wide-ranging reforms.

Sites of the Modern Olympic Games

Summer Games

YEAR	LOCATION	YEAR	LOCATION	YEAR	LOCATION
1896	Athens, Greece	1936	Berlin, Germany	1984	Los Angeles CA
1900	Paris, France	1940–44	*not held*	1988	Seoul, South Korea
1904	St. Louis MO	1948	London, England	1992	Barcelona, Spain
1908	London, England	1952	Helsinki, Finland	1996	Atlanta GA
1912	Stockholm, Sweden	1956	Melbourne, Australia	2000	Sydney, Australia
1916	*not held*	1960	Rome, Italy	2004	*scheduled to be held*
1920	Antwerp, Belgium	1964	Tokyo, Japan		*13–29 August, Athens,*
1924	Paris, France	1968	Mexico City, Mexico		*Greece*
1928	Amsterdam, the Netherlands	1972	Munich, West Germany	2008	*scheduled to be held 25*
		1976	Montreal, Quebec		*July–10 August, Beijing,*
1932	Los Angeles CA	1980	Moscow, USSR		*China*

Winter Games

YEAR	LOCATION	YEAR	LOCATION	YEAR	LOCATION
1924	Chamonix, France	1956	Cortina d'Ampezzo, Italy	1988	Calgary, Alberta
1928	St. Moritz, Switzerland	1960	Squaw Valley CA	1992	Albertville, France
1932	Lake Placid NY	1964	Innsbruck, Austria	1994	Lillehammer, Norway
1936	Garmisch-Partenkirchen, Germany	1968	Grenoble, France	1998	Nagano, Japan
		1972	Sapporo, Japan	2002	Salt Lake City UT
1940–44	*not held*	1976	Innsbruck, Austria	2006	*scheduled to be held*
1948	St. Moritz, Switzerland	1980	Lake Placid NY		*10–26 February, Torino,*
1952	Oslo, Norway	1984	Sarajevo, Yugoslavia		*Italy*

Summer Olympic Games Champions

Gold-medal winners in all Summer Olympic contests since 1896. Note: East and West Germany fielded a joint all-Germany team in 1956, 1960, and 1964, abbreviated here as GER. The Unified Team in 1992 consisted of the Commonwealth of Independent States plus Georgia, and is abbreviated here as UNT.

Archery

MEN'S INDIVIDUAL
1972   John Williams (USA)
1976   Darrell Pace (USA)
1980   Tomi Poikolainen (FIN)
1984   Darrell Pace (USA)
1988   Jay Barrs (USA)
1992   Sebastien Flute (FRA)
1996   Justin Huish (USA)
2000   Simon Fairweather (AUS)

AU CORDON DORÉ (50 METERS)
1900   Henri Herouin (FRA)

AU CORDON DORÉ (33 METERS)
1900   Hubert van Innis (BEL)

AU CHAPELET (50 METERS)
1900   Eugène Mougin (FRA)

SUR LA PERCHE À LA HERSE
1900   Emmanuel Foulon (FRA)

AU CHAPELET (33 METERS)
1900   Hubert van Innis (BEL)

SUR LA PERCHE À LA PYRAMIDE
1900   Émile Grumiaux (FRA)

Archery (continued)

DOUBLE AMERICAN ROUND
1904   George Philipp Bryant (USA)

(DOUBLE) YORK ROUND
1904   George Philipp Bryant (USA)
1908   William Dod (GBR)

CONTINENTAL STYLE
1908   Eugène G. Grizot (FRA)

FIXED BIRD TARGET (SMALL)
1920   Edmond van Moer (BEL)

FIXED BIRD TARGET (LARGE)
1920   Édouard Cloetens (BEL)

MOVING BIRD TARGET (28 M)
1920   Hubert van Innis (BEL)

MOVING BIRD TARGET (33 M)
1920   Hubert van Innis (BEL)

MOVING BIRD TARGET (50 M)
1920   Julien Brulé (FRA)

WOMEN'S INDIVIDUAL
1972   Doreen Wilber (USA)
1976   Luann Ryon (USA)
1980   Ketevan Losaberidze (URS)

Summer Olympic Games Champions (continued)

Archery (continued)

WOMEN'S INDIVIDUAL
1984	Seo Hyang Soon (KOR)
1988	Kim Soo Nyung (KOR)
1992	Cho Youn Jeong (KOR)
1996	Kim Kyung-Wook (KOR)
2000	Yun Mi-Jin (KOR)

DOUBLE COLUMBIA ROUND
1904	Matilda Scott Howell (USA)

(DOUBLE) NATIONAL ROUND
1904	Matilda Scott Howell (USA)
1908	Sybil Fenton "Queenie" Newall (GBR)

MEN'S TEAM
1904	United States
1988	South Korea
1992	Spain
1996	United States
2000	South Korea

WOMEN'S TEAM
1904	United States
1988	South Korea
1992	South Korea
1996	South Korea
2000	South Korea

FIXED TARGET (2 EVENTS)
1920	Belgium

MOVING TARGET (28 M)
1920	The Netherlands

MOVING TARGET (33 M)
1920	Belgium

MOVING TARGET (50 M)
1920	Belgium

Association football (soccer)[1]

MEN
1900	Great Britain
1904	Canada
1908	Great Britain
1912	Great Britain
1920	Belgium
1924	Uruguay
1928	Uruguay
1936	Italy
1948	Sweden
1952	Hungary
1956	USSR
1960	Yugoslavia
1964	Hungary
1968	Hungary
1972	Poland
1976	East Germany
1980	Czechoslovakia
1984	France
1988	USSR
1992	Spain
1996	Nigeria
2000	Cameroon

WOMEN
1996	United States
2000	Norway

Athletics (track-and field) (men)

60 METERS SEC
1900	Alvin Kraenzlein (USA)	7
1904	Archie Hahn (USA)	7

100 METERS SEC
1896	Thomas Burke (USA)	12.0
1900	Francis Jarvis (USA)	11.0
1904	Archie Hahn (USA)	11.0
1908	Reginald Walker (RSA)	10.8
1912	Ralph Craig (USA)	10.8
1920	Charles Paddock (USA)	10.8
1924	Harold Abrahams (GBR)	10.6
1928	Percy Williams (CAN)	10.8
1932	Eddie Tolan (USA)	10.3
1936	Jesse Owens (USA)	10.3
1948	Harrison Dillard (USA)	10.3
1952	Lindy Remigino (USA)	10.4
1956	Robert Morrow (USA)	10.5
1960	Armin Hary (GER)	10.2
1964	Robert Hayes (USA)	10.0
1968	James Hines (USA)	9.9
1972	Valery Borzov (URS)	10.14
1976	Hasely Crawford (TRI)	10.06
1980	Allan Wells (GBR)	10.25
1984	Carl Lewis (USA)	9.99
1988	Carl Lewis (USA)	9.92
1992	Linford Christie (GBR)	9.96
1996	Donovan Bailey (CAN)	9.84
2000	Maurice Greene (USA)	9.87

200 METERS SEC
1900	Walter Tewksbury (USA)	22.2
1904	Archie Hahn (USA)	21.6
1908	Robert Kerr (CAN)	22.6
1912	Ralph Craig (USA)	21.7
1920	Allen Woodring (USA)	22.0
1924	Jackson Scholz (USA)	21.6
1928	Percy Williams (CAN)	21.8
1932	Eddie Tolan (USA)	21.2
1936	Jesse Owens (USA)	20.7
1948	Melvin Patton (USA)	21.1
1952	Andy Stanfield (USA)	20.7
1956	Robert Morrow (USA)	20.6
1960	Livio Berruti (ITA)	20.5
1964	Henry Carr (USA)	20.3
1968	Tommie Smith (USA)	19.8
1972	Valery Borzov (URS)	20.00
1976	Donald Quarrie (JAM)	20.23
1980	Pietro Mennea (ITA)	20.19
1984	Carl Lewis (USA)	19.80
1988	Joe DeLoach (USA)	19.75
1992	Mike Marsh (USA)	20.01
1996	Michael Johnson (USA)	19.32
2000	Konstantinos Kenteris (GRE)	20.09

400 METERS SEC
1896	Thomas Burke (USA)	54.2
1900	Maxwell Long (USA)	49.4
1904	Harry Hillman (USA)	49.2
1908	Wyndham Halswelle (GBR)	50.0
1912	Charles Reidpath (USA)	48.2
1920	Bevil Rudd (RSA)	49.6
1924	Eric Liddell (GBR)	47.6
1928	Raymond Barbuti (USA)	47.8
1932	William Carr (USA)	46.2
1936	Archie Williams (USA)	46.5
1948	Arthur Wint (JAM)	46.2
1952	Vincent George Rhoden (JAM)	45.9

Summer Olympic Games Champions (continued)

Athletics (track-and-field) (men) (continued)

400 METERS		SEC
1956	Charles Jenkins (USA)	46.7
1960	Otis Davis (USA)	44.9
1964	Michael Larrabee (USA)	45.1
1968	Lee Evans (USA)	43.8
1972	Vincent Matthews (USA)	44.66
1976	Alberto Juantorena (CUB)	44.26
1980	Viktor Markin (URS)	44.60
1984	Alonzo Babers (USA)	44.27
1988	Steven Lewis (USA)	43.87
1992	Quincy Watts (USA)	43.50
1996	Michael Johnson (USA)	43.49
2000	Michael Johnson (USA)	43.84

800 METERS		MIN:SEC
1896	Edwin Flack (AUS)	2:11.0
1900	Alfred Tysoe (GBR)	2:01.2
1904	James Lightbody (USA)	1:56.0
1908	Melvin Sheppard (USA)	1:52.8
1912	James Edward Meredith (USA)	1:51.9
1920	Albert Hill (GBR)	1:53.4
1924	Douglas Lowe (GBR)	1:52.4
1928	Douglas Lowe (GBR)	1:51.8
1932	Thomas Hampson (GBR)	1:49.7
1936	John Woodruff (USA)	1:52.9
1948	Malvin Whitfield (USA)	1:49.2
1952	Malvin Whitfield (USA)	1:49.2
1956	Thomas Courtney (USA)	1:47.7
1960	Peter Snell (NZL)	1:46.3
1964	Peter Snell (NZL)	1:45.1
1968	Ralph Doubell (AUS)	1:44.3
1972	David Wottle (USA)	1:45.9
1976	Alberto Juantorena (CUB)	1:43.50
1980	Steven Ovett (GBR)	1:45.40
1984	Joaquim Cruz (BRA)	1:43.00
1988	Paul Ereng (KEN)	1:43.45
1992	William Tanui (KEN)	1:43.66
1996	Vebjoern Rodal (NOR)	1:42.58
2000	Nils Schumann (GER)	1:45.08

1,500 METERS		MIN:SEC
1896	Edwin Flack (AUS)	4:33.2
1900	Charles Bennett (GBR)	4:06.2
1904	James Lightbody (USA)	4:05.4
1908	Melvin Sheppard (USA)	4:03.4
1912	Arnold Jackson (GBR)	3:56.8
1920	Albert Hill (GBR)	4:01.8
1924	Paavo Nurmi (FIN)	3:53.6
1928	Harry Larva (FIN)	3:53.2
1932	Luigi Beccali (ITA)	3:51.2
1936	John Lovelock (NZL)	3:47.8
1948	Henry Eriksson (SWE)	3:49.8
1952	Joseph Barthel (LUX)	3:45.1
1956	Ronald Delany (IRE)	3:41.2
1960	Herbert Elliott (AUS)	3:35.6
1964	Peter Snell (NZL)	3:38.1
1968	Hezekiah Kipchoge ("Kip") Keino (KEN)	3:34.9
1972	Pekka Vasala (FIN)	3:36.3
1976	John Walker (NZL)	3:39.17
1980	Sebastian Coe (GBR)	3:38.40
1984	Sebastian Coe (GBR)	3:32.53
1988	Peter Rono (KEN)	3:35.96
1992	Fermin Cacho Ruiz (ESP)	3:40.12
1996	Noureddine Morceli (ALG)	3:35.78
2000	Noah Ngeny (KEN)	3:32.07

Athletics (track-and-field) (men) (continued)

5,000 METERS		MIN:SEC
1912	Hannes Kolehmainen (FIN)	14:36.6
1920	Joseph Guillemot (FRA)	14:55.6
1924	Paavo Nurmi (FIN)	14:31.2
1928	Vilho Ritola (FIN)	14:38.0
1932	Lauri Lehtinen (FIN)	14:30.0
1936	Gunnar Höckert (FIN)	14:22.2
1948	Gaston Reiff (BEL)	14:17.6
1952	Emil Zatopek (TCH)	14:06.6
1956	Vladimir Kuts (URS)	13:39.6
1960	Murray Halberg (NZL)	13:43.4
1964	Robert Keyser Schul (USA)	13:48.8
1968	Mohamed Gammoudi (TUN)	14:05.0
1972	Lasse Viren (FIN)	13:26.4
1976	Lasse Viren (FIN)	13:24.76
1980	Miruts Yifter (ETH)	13:21.00
1984	Said Aouita (MAR)	13:05.59
1988	John Ngugi (KEN)	13:11.70
1992	Dieter Baumann (GER)	13:12.52
1996	Venuste Niyongabo (BDI)	13:07.97
2000	Millon Wolde (ETH)	13:35.49

5 MILES		MIN:SEC
1908	Emil Voigt (GBR)	25:11.2

10,000 METERS		MIN:SEC
1912	Hannes Kolehmainen (FIN)	31:20.8
1920	Paavo Nurmi (FIN)	31:45.8
1924	Vilho Ritola (FIN)	30:23.2
1928	Paavo Nurmi (FIN)	30:18.8
1932	Janusz Kusocinski (POL)	30:11.4
1936	Ilmari Salminen (FIN)	30:15.4
1948	Emil Zatopek (TCH)	29:59.6
1952	Emil Zatopek (TCH)	29:17.0
1956	Vladimir Kuts (URS)	28:45.6
1960	Pyotr Bolotnikov (URS)	28:32.2
1964	William Mills (USA)	28:24.4
1968	Nabiba Temu (KEN)	29:27.4
1972	Lasse Viren (FIN)	27:38.4
1976	Lasse Viren (FIN)	27:40.38
1980	Miruts Yifter (ETH)	27:42.70
1984	Alberto Cova (ITA)	27:47.54
1988	Brahim Boutaib (MAR)	27:21.46
1992	Khalid Skah (MAR)	27:46.70
1996	Haile Gebrselassie (ETH)	27:07.34
2000	Haile Gebrselassie (ETH)	27:18.20

MARATHON		HR:MIN:SEC
1896	Spiridon Louis (GRE)	2:58:50.0
1900	Michel Theato (FRA)	2:59:45.0
1904	Thomas Hicks (USA)	3:28:53.0
1908	John Hayes (USA)	2:55:18.4
1912	Kenneth McArthur (RSA)	2:36:54.8
1920	Hannes Kolehmainen (FIN)	2:32:35.8
1924	Albin Stenroos (FIN)	2:41:22.6
1928	Boughèra El Ouafi (FRA)	2:32:57.0
1932	Juan Carlos Zabala (ARG)	2:31:36.0
1936	Kitei Son (JPN)	2:29:19.2
1948	Delfo Cabrera (ARG)	2:34:51.6
1952	Emil Zatopek (TCH)	2:23:03.2
1956	Alain Mimoun-O-Kacha (FRA)	2:25:00.0
1960	Abebe Bikila (ETH)	2:15:16.2
1964	Abebe Bikila (ETH)	2:12:11.2
1968	Mamo Wolde (ETH)	2:20:26.4
1972	Frank Shorter (USA)	2:12:19.8
1976	Waldemar Cierpinski (GDR)	2:09:55.0
1980	Waldemar Cierpinski (GDR)	2:11:03.0
1984	Carlos Lopes (POR)	2:09:21.0

Summer Olympic Games Champions (continued)

Athletics (track-and-field) (men) (continued)

MARATHON		HR:MIN:SEC
1988	Gelindo Bordin (ITA)	2:10:32.0
1992	Hwang Young-Cho (KOR)	2:13:23.0
1996	Josia Thugwane (RSA)	2:12:36.0
2000	Gezahgne Abera (ETH)	2:10:11.0

110-METER HURDLES		SEC
1896[2]	Thomas Curtis (USA)	17.6
1900	Alvin Kraenzlein (USA)	15.4
1904	Frederick Schule (USA)	16.0
1908	Forrest Smithson (USA)	15.0
1912	Frederick Kelly (USA)	15.1
1920	Earl Thomson (CAN)	14.8
1924	Daniel Kinsey (USA)	15.0
1928	Sydney Atkinson (RSA)	14.8
1932	George Saling (USA)	14.6
1936	Forrest Towns (USA)	14.2
1948	William Porter (USA)	13.9
1952	Harrison Dillard (USA)	13.7
1956	Lee Calhoun (USA)	13.5
1960	Lee Calhoun (USA)	13.8
1964	Hayes Wendell Jones (USA)	13.6
1968	Willie Davenport (USA)	13.3
1972	Rodney Milburn (USA)	13.24
1976	Guy Drut (FRA)	13.30
1980	Thomas Munkelt (GDR)	13.39
1984	Roger Kingdom (USA)	13.20
1988	Roger Kingdom (USA)	12.98
1992	Mark McKoy (CAN)	13.12
1996	Allen Johnson (USA)	12.95
2000	Anier Garcia (CUB)	13.00

200-METER HURDLES		SEC
1900	Alvin Kraenzlein (USA)	25.4
1904	Harry Hillman (USA)	24.6

400-METER HURDLES		SEC
1900	Walter Tewksbury (USA)	57.6
1904[3]	Harry Hillman (USA)	53.0
1908	Charles Bacon (USA)	55.0
1920	Frank Loomis (USA)	54.0
1924	Frederick Morgan Taylor (USA)	52.6
1928	David George Burghley (GBR)	53.4
1932	Robert Tisdall (IRE)	51.7
1936	Glenn Hardin (USA)	52.4
1948	Roy Cochran (USA)	51.1
1952	Charles Moore (USA)	50.8
1956	Glenn Davis (USA)	50.1
1960	Glenn Davis (USA)	49.3
1964	Warren Cawley (USA)	49.6
1968	David Hemery (GBR)	48.1
1972	John Akii-Bua (UGA)	47.82
1976	Edwin Moses (USA)	47.64
1980	Volker Beck (GDR)	48.70
1984	Edwin Moses (USA)	47.75
1988	Andre Phillips (USA)	47.19
1992	Kevin Young (USA)	46.78
1996	Derrick Adkins (USA)	47.54
2000	Angelo Taylor (USA)	47.50

2,500-METER STEEPLECHASE		MIN:SEC
1900	George Orton (USA)	7:34.4

2,590-METER STEEPLECHASE		MIN:SEC
1904	James Lightbody (USA)	7:39.6

3,000-METER STEEPLECHASE		MIN:SEC
1920	Percy Hodge (GBR)	10:00.4

Athletics (track-and-field) (men) (continued)

3,000-METER STEEPLECHASE		MIN:SEC
1924	Vilho Ritola (FIN)	9:33.6
1928	Toivo Loukola (FIN)	9:21.8
1932	Volmari Iso-Hollo (FIN)	10:33.4[4]
1936	Volmari Iso-Hollo (FIN)	9:03.8
1948	Thore Sjöstrand (SWE)	9:04.6
1952	Horace Ashenfelter (USA)	8:45.4
1956	Christopher Brasher (GBR)	8:41.2
1960	Zdislaw Krzyszkowiak (POL)	8:34.2
1964	Gaston Roelants (BEL)	8:30.8
1968	Amos Biwott (KEN)	8:51.0
1972	Kipchoge Keino (KEN)	8:23.6
1976	Anders Gärderud (SWE)	8:08.02
1980	Bronislaw Malinowski (POL)	8:09.70
1984	Julius Korir (KEN)	8:11.80
1988	Julius Kariuki (KEN)	8:05.51
1992	Mathew Birir (KEN)	8:08.84
1996	Joseph Keter (KEN)	8:07.12
2000	Reuben Kosgei (KEN)	8:21.43

3,200-METER STEEPLECHASE		MIN:SEC
1908	Arthur Russell (GBR)	10:47.8

3,000 METERS (TEAM) (TEAM/INDIVIDUAL WINNER)		MIN:SEC
1912	United States/Tell Berna	8:44.6
1920	United States/Horace Brown	8:45.4
1924	Finland/Paavo Nurmi	8:32

3 MILES (TEAM) (TEAM/INDIVIDUAL WINNER)		MIN:SEC
1908	Great Britain/Joseph Deakin	14:39.6

5,000 METERS (TEAM) (TEAM/INDIVIDUAL WINNER)		MIN:SEC
1900	Great Britain-Australia/Charles Bennett	15:20

4 MILES (TEAM) (TEAM/INDIVIDUAL WINNER)		MIN:SEC
1904	United States/Arthur Newton (USA)	21:17.8

4 × 100 METER RELAY		SEC
1912	Great Britain	42.4
1920	United States	42.2
1924	United States	41.0
1928	United States	41.0
1932	United States	40.0
1936	United States	39.8
1948	United States	40.6
1952	United States	40.1
1956	United States	39.5
1960	Germany	39.5
1964	United States	39.0
1968	United States	38.2
1972	United States	38.19
1976	United States	38.33
1980	USSR	38.26
1984	United States	37.83
1988	USSR	38.19
1992	United States	37.40
1996	Canada	37.69
2000	United States	37.61

4 × 400 METER RELAY		MIN:SEC
1912	United States	3:16.6
1920	Great Britain	3:22.2
1924	United States	3:16.0
1928	United States	3:14.2
1932	United States	3:08.2

Summer Olympic Games Champions (continued)

Athletics (track-and-field) (men) (continued)

4 × 400 METER RELAY

		MIN:SEC
1936	Great Britain	3:09.0
1948	United States	3:10.4
1952	Jamaica	3:03.9
1956	United States	3:04.8
1960	United States	3:02.2
1964	United States	3:00.7
1968	United States	2:56.1
1972	Kenya	2:59.8
1976	United States	2:58.65
1980	USSR	3:01.1
1984	United States	2:57.91
1988	United States	2:56.16
1992	United States	2:55.74
1996	United States	2:55.99
2000	United States	2:56.35

1,600-METER RELAY (200 × 200 × 400 × 800 METERS)

		MIN:SEC
1908	United States	3:29.4

8,000 M CROSS-COUNTRY

		MIN:SEC
1920	Paavo Nurmi (FIN)	27:15

10,000 M CROSS-COUNTRY

		MIN:SEC
1924	Paavo Nurmi (FIN)	32:54.8

12,000 M CROSS-COUNTRY

		MIN:SEC
1912	Hannes Kölehmainen (FIN)	45:11.6

3,000-METER WALK

		MIN:SEC
1920	Ugo Frigerio (ITA)	13:14.2

3,500-METER WALK

		MIN:SEC
1908	George Larner (GBR)	14:55

10,000-METER WALK

		MIN:SEC
1912	George Goulding (CAN)	46:28.4
1920	Ugo Frigerio (ITA)	48:06.2
1924	Ugo Frigerio (ITA)	47:49
1948	John Mikaelsson (SWE)	45:13.2
1952	John Mikaelsson (SWE)	45:02.8

10-MILE WALK

		HR:MIN:SEC
1908	George Larner (GBR)	1:15:57.4

20,000-METER WALK

		HR:MIN:SEC
1956	Leonid Spirin (URS)	1:31:27.4
1960	Vladimir Golubnichy (URS)	1:34:07.2
1964	Kenneth Matthews (GBR)	1:29:34.0
1968	Vladimir Golubnichy (URS)	1:33:58.4
1972	Peter Frenkel (GDR)	1:26:42.6
1976	Daniel Bautista (MEX)	1:24:40.6
1980	Maurizio Damilano (ITA)	1:23:35.5
1984	Ernesto Canto (MEX)	1:23:13.0
1988	Jozef Pribilinec (TCH)	1:19:57.0
1992	Daniel Plaza Montero (ESP)	1:21:45.0
1996	Jefferson Pérez (ECU)	1:20:07.0
2000	Robert Korzeniowski (POL)	1:18:59.0

50,000-METER WALK

		HR:MIN:SEC
1932	Thomas Green (GBR)	4:50:10.0
1936	Harold Whitlock (GBR)	4:30:41.4
1948	John Ljunggren (SWE)	4:41:52.0
1952	Giuseppe Dordoni (ITA)	4:28:07.8
1956	Norman Read (NZL)	4:30:42.8
1960	Donald Thompson (GBR)	4:25:30.0
1964	Abdon Pamich (ITA)	4:11:12.4

Athletics (track-and-field) (men) (continued)

50,000-METER WALK

		HR:MIN:SEC
1968	Christophe Höhne (GDR)	4:20:13.6
1972	Bernd Kannenberg (FRG)	3:56:11.6
1980	Hartwig Gauder (GDR)	3:49:24.0
1984	Raúl Gonzáles (MEX)	3:47:26.0
1988	Vyacheslav Ivanenko (URS)	3:38:29.0
1992	Andrey Perlov (UNT)	3:50:13.0
1996	Robert Korzeniowski (POL)	3:43:03.0
2000	Robert Korzeniowski (POL)	3:42:22.0

HIGH JUMP

		METERS
1896	Ellery Clark (USA)	1.81
1900	Irving Baxter (USA)	1.90
1904	Samuel Jones (USA)	1.80
1908	Harry Porter (USA)	1.90
1912	Alma Richards (USA)	1.93
1920	Richmond Landon (USA)	1.93
1924	Harold Osborn (USA)	1.98
1928	Robert King (USA)	1.94
1932	Duncan McNaughton (CAN)	1.97
1936	Cornelius Johnson (USA)	2.03
1948	John Winter (AUS)	1.98
1952	Walter Davis (USA)	2.04
1956	Charles Dumas (USA)	2.12
1960	Robert Shavlakadze (URS)	2.16
1964	Valery Brumel (URS)	2.18
1968	Richard Fosbury (USA)	2.24
1972	Yury Tarmak (URS)	2.23
1976	Jacek Wszola (POL)	2.25
1980	Gerd Wessig (GDR)	2.36
1984	Dietmar Mögenburg (FRG)	2.35
1988	Gennady Avdeyenko (URS)	2.38
1992	Javier Sotomayor (CUB)	2.34
1996	Charles Austin (USA)	2.39
2000	Sergey Klyugin (RUS)	2.35

STANDING HIGH JUMP

		METERS
1900	Ray Ewry (USA)	1.65
1904	Ray Ewry (USA)	1.6
1908	Ray Ewry (USA)	1.57
1912	Platt Adams (USA)	1.63

POLE VAULT

		METERS
1896	William Welles Hoyt (USA)	3.30
1900	Irving Baxter (USA)	3.30
1904	Charles Dvorak (USA)	3.50
1908	Edward Cooke (USA); Alfred Gilbert (USA) (tied)	3.71
1912	Harry Babcock (USA)	3.95
1920	Frank Foss (USA)	4.09
1924	Lee Barnes (USA)	3.95
1928	Sabin Carr (USA)	4.20
1932	William Miller (USA)	4.31
1936	Earle Meadows (USA)	4.35
1948	Owen Guinn Smith (USA)	4.30
1952	Robert Richards (USA)	4.55
1956	Robert Richards (USA)	4.56
1960	Donald Bragg (USA)	4.70
1964	Fred Hansen (USA)	5.10
1968	Robert Seagren (USA)	5.40
1972	Wolfgang Nordwig (GDR)	5.50
1976	Tadeusz Slusarski (POL)	5.50
1980	Wladyslaw Kozakiewicz (POL)	5.78
1984	Pierre Quinon (FRA)	5.75
1988	Sergey Bubka (URS)	5.90
1992	Maksim Tarasov (UNT)	5.80
1996	Jean Galfione (FRA)	5.92
2000	Nick Hysong (USA)	5.90

Summer Olympic Games Champions (continued)

Athletics (track-and-field) (men) (continued)

LONG JUMP
		METERS
1896	Ellery Clark (USA)	6.35
1900	Alvin Kraenzlein (USA)	7.18
1904	Meyer Prinstein (USA)	7.34
1908	Francis Irons (USA)	7.48
1912	Albert Gutterson (USA)	7.60
1920	William Pettersson (SWE)	7.15
1924	William de Hart-Hubbard (USA)	7.44
1928	Edward Hamm (USA)	7.73
1932	Edward Gordon (USA)	7.64
1936	Jesse Owens (USA)	8.06
1948	Willie Steele (USA)	7.82
1952	Jerome Biffle (USA)	7.57
1956	Gregory Bell (USA)	7.83
1960	Ralph Boston (USA)	8.12
1964	Lynn Davies (GBR)	8.07
1968	Robert Beamon (USA)	8.90
1972	Randy Williams (USA)	8.24
1976	Arnie Robinson (USA)	8.35
1980	Lutz Dombrowski (GDR)	8.54
1984	Carl Lewis (USA)	8.54
1988	Carl Lewis (USA)	8.72
1992	Carl Lewis (USA)	8.67
1996	Carl Lewis (USA)	8.50
2000	Ivan Pedroso (CUB)	8.55

STANDING LONG JUMP
		METERS
1900	Ray Ewry (USA)	3.21
1904	Ray Ewry (USA)	3.47
1908	Ray Ewry (USA)	3.33
1912	Constantinos Tsiklitiras (GRE)	3.37

TRIPLE JUMP
		METERS
1896	James Connolly (USA)	13.71
1900	Myer Prinstein (USA)	14.47
1904	Myer Prinstein (USA)	14.35
1908	Timothy Ahearne (GBR)	14.91
1912	Gustaf Lindblom (SWE)	14.76
1920	Vilho Tuulos (FIN)	14.50
1924	Anthony Winter (AUS)	15.53
1928	Mikio Oda (JPN)	15.21
1932	Chuhei Nambu (JPN)	15.72
1936	Naoto Tajima (JPN)	16.00
1948	Arne Åhman (SWE)	15.40
1952	Adhemar Ferreira da Silva (BRA)	16.22
1956	Adhemar Ferreira da Silva (BRA)	16.35
1960	Josef Szmidt (POL)	16.81
1964	Josef Szmidt (POL)	16.85
1968	Viktor Saneyev (URS)	17.39
1972	Viktor Saneyev (URS)	17.35
1976	Viktor Saneyev (URS)	17.29
1980	Jaak Uudmae (URS)	17.35
1984	Al Joyner (USA)	17.26
1988	Khristo Markov (BUL)	17.61
1992	Michael Conley (USA)	17.63
1996	Kenny Harrison (USA)	18.09
2000	Jonathan Edwards (GBR)	17.71

STANDING TRIPLE JUMP
		METERS
1900	Ray Ewry (USA)	10.58
1904	Ray Ewry (USA)	10.54

SHOT PUT
		METERS
1896	Robert Garrett (USA)	11.22
1900	Richard Sheldon (USA)	14.10
1904	Ralph Rose (USA)	14.81
1908	Ralph Rose (USA)	14.21
1912	Patrick McDonald (USA)	15.34

Athletics (track-and-field) (men) (continued)

SHOT PUT
		METERS
1920	Frans Pörhölä (FIN)	14.81
1924	Lemuel Clarence Houser (USA)	14.99
1928	John Kuck (USA)	15.87
1932	Leo Sexton (USA)	16.00
1936	Hans Woellke (GER)	16.20
1948	Wilbur Thompson (USA)	17.12
1952	William Parry O'Brien (USA)	17.41
1956	William Parry O'Brien (USA)	18.57
1960	William Nieder (USA)	19.68
1964	Dallas Long (USA)	20.33
1968	Randy Matson (USA)	20.54
1972	Wladislaw Komar (POL)	21.18
1976	Udo Beyer (GDR)	21.05
1980	Vladimir Kiselyov (URS)	21.35
1984	Alessandro Andrei (ITA)	21.26
1988	Ulf Timmermann (GDR)	22.47
1992	Michael Stulce (USA)	21.70
1996	Randy Barnes (USA)	21.62
2000	Arsi Harju (FIN)	21.29

SHOT PUT (TWO HANDS)
		METERS
1912	Ralph Rose (USA)	27.7

DISCUS THROW
		METERS
1896	Robert Garrett (USA)	29.15
1900	Rezso Bauer (HUN)	36.04
1904	Martin Sheridan (USA)	39.28
1908	Martin Sheridan (USA)	40.89
1912	Armas Taipale (FIN)	45.21
1920	Elmer Niklander (FIN)	44.68
1924	Lemuel Clarence Houser (USA)	46.15
1928	Lemuel Clarence Houser (USA)	47.32
1932	John Anderson (USA)	49.49
1936	Kenneth Carpenter (USA)	50.48
1948	Adolfo Consolini (ITA)	52.78
1952	Sim Iness (USA)	55.03
1956	Alfred Oerter (USA)	56.36
1960	Alfred Oerter (USA)	59.18
1964	Alfred Oerter (USA)	61.00
1968	Alfred Oerter (USA)	64.78
1972	Ludvig Danek (TCH)	64.40
1976	Mac Wilkins (USA)	67.50
1980	Viktor Rashchupkin (URS)	66.64
1984	Rolf Danneberg (FRG)	66.60
1988	Jürgen Schult (GDR)	68.82
1992	Romas Ubartas (LTU)	65.12
1996	Lars Riedel (GER)	69.40
2000	Virgilijus Alekna (LTU)	69.30

DISCUS (GREEK STYLE)
		METERS
1908	Martin Sheridan (USA)	37.99

DISCUS (TWO HANDS)
		METERS
1912	Armas Taipale (FIN)	82.86

HAMMER THROW
		METERS
1900	John Flanagan (USA)	49.73
1904	John Flanagan (USA)	51.23
1908	John Flanagan (USA)	51.92
1912	Matthew McGrath (USA)	54.74
1920	Patrick Ryan (USA)	52.87
1924	Frederick Tootell (USA)	53.30
1928	Patrick O'Callaghan (IRE)	51.39
1932	Patrick O'Callaghan (IRE)	53.92
1936	Karl Hein (GER)	56.49
1948	Imre Nemeth (HUN)	56.07
1952	Jozsef Csermak (HUN)	60.34

Summer Olympic Games Champions (continued)

Athletics (track-and-field) (men) (continued)

HAMMER THROW		METERS
1956	Harold Connolly (USA)	63.19
1960	Vasily Rudenkov (URS)	67.10
1964	Romuald Klim (URS)	69.74
1968	Gyula Zsivotzky (HUN)	73.36
1972	Anatoly Bondarchuk (URS)	75.50
1976	Yury Sedykh (URS)	77.52
1980	Yury Sedykh (URS)	81.80
1984	Juha Tiainen (FIN)	78.08
1988	Sergey Litvinov (URS)	84.80
1992	Andrey Abduvaliyev (UNT)	82.53
1996	Balazs Kiss (HUN)	81.24
2000	Szymon Ziolkowski (POL)	80.02

JAVELIN THROW		METERS
1908	Eric Lemming (SWE)	54.83
1912	Eric Lemming (SWE)	60.64
1920	Jonni Myyrä (FIN)	65.78
1924	Jonni Myyrä (FIN)	62.96
1928	Erik Lundkvist (SWE)	66.60
1932	Matti Järvinen (FIN)	72.71
1936	Gerhard Stöck (GER)	71.84
1948	Kai Rautavaara (FIN)	69.77
1952	Cy Young (USA)	73.78
1956	Egil Danielson (NOR)	85.71
1960	Viktor Tsybulenko (URS)	84.64
1964	Pauli Nevala (FIN)	82.66
1968	Janis Lusis (URS)	90.10
1972	Klaus Wolfermann (FRG)	90.48
1976	Miklos Nemeth (HUN)	94.58
1980	Dainis Kula (URS)	91.20
1984	Arto Härkönen (FIN)	86.76
1988	Tapio Korjus (FIN)	84.28
1992	Jan Zelezny (TCH)	89.66
1996	Jan Zelezny (CZE)	88.16
2000	Jan Zelezny (CZE)	90.17

JAVELIN (FREESTYLE)		METERS
1908	Eric Lemming (SWE)	54.45

JAVELIN (TWO HANDS)		METERS
1912	Juho Saaristo (FIN)	109.42

THROWING THE 56 LB WEIGHT		METERS
1904	Étienne Desmarteau (CAN)	10.46
1920	Patrick McDonald (USA)	11.26

TUG-OF-WAR
1900	Sweden-Denmark
1904	United States
1908	Great Britain
1912	Sweden
1920	Great Britain

TRIATHLON (LONG JUMP/SHOT PUT/100 YARDS)
1904 Max Emmerich (USA)

PENTATHLON
1912 Jim Thorpe (USA)[5]; Ferdinand Bie (NOR) (cowinners)
1920 Eero Lehtonen (FIN)
1924 Eero Lehtonen (FIN)

DECATHLON
1904 Thomas Kiely (IRL)
1912 Jim Thorpe (USA)[5]; Hugo Wieslander (SWE) (cowinners)
1920 Helge Lövland (NOR)

Athletics (track-and-field) (men) (continued)

DECATHLON	
1924	Harold Osborn (USA)
1928	Paavo Yrjölä (FIN)
1932	James Bausch (USA)
1936	Glenn Morris (USA)
1948	Robert Mathias (USA)
1952	Robert Mathias (USA)
1956	Milton Campbell (USA)
1960	Rafer Johnson (USA)
1964	Willi Holdorf (GER)
1968	William Toomey (USA)
1972	Nikolay Avilov (URS)
1976	Bruce Jenner (USA)
1980	Daley Thompson (GBR)
1984	Daley Thompson (GBR)
1988	Christian Schenk (GDR)
1992	Robert Zmelik (TCH)
1996	Dan O'Brien (USA)
2000	Erki Nool (EST)

Athletics (track-and-field) (women)

100 METERS		SEC
1928	Elizabeth Robinson (USA)	12.2
1932	Stanislawa Walasiewicz (POL)	11.9
1936	Helen Stephens (USA)	11.5
1948	Francina Blankers-Koen (NED)	11.9
1952	Marjorie Jackson (AUS)	11.5
1956	Elizabeth Cuthbert (AUS)	11.5
1960	Wilma Rudolph (USA)	11.0
1964	Wyomia Tyus (USA)	11.4
1968	Wyomia Tyus (USA)	11.0
1972	Renate Stecher (GDR)	11.07
1976	Annegret Richter (FRG)	11.08
1980	Lyudmila Kondratyeva (URS)	11.06
1984	Evelyn Ashford (USA)	10.97
1988	Florence Griffith Joyner (USA)	10.54
1992	Gail Devers (USA)	10.82
1996	Gail Devers (USA)	10.94
2000	Marion Jones (USA)	10.75

200 METERS		SEC
1948	Francina Blankers-Koen (NED)	24.4
1952	Marjorie Jackson (AUS)	23.7
1956	Elizabeth Cuthbert (AUS)	23.4
1960	Wilma Rudolph (USA)	24.0
1964	Edith Marie McGuire (USA)	23.0
1968	Irena Szewinska (POL)	22.5
1972	Renate Stecher (GDR)	22.40
1976	Bärbel Eckert (GDR)	22.37
1980	Bärbel Eckert-Wöckel (GDR)	22.03
1984	Valerie Brisco-Hooks (USA)	21.81
1988	Florence Griffith Joyner (USA)	21.34
1992	Gwen Torrence (USA)	21.81
1996	Marie-Jose Perec (FRA)	22.12
2000	Marion Jones (USA)	21.84

400 METERS		SEC
1964	Elizabeth Cuthbert (AUS)	52.0
1968	Colette Besson (FRA)	52.0
1972	Monika Zehrt (GDR)	51.08
1976	Irena Szewinska (POL)	49.29
1980	Marita Koch (GDR)	48.88
1984	Valerie Brisco-Hooks (USA)	48.83
1988	Olga Bryzgina (URS)	48.65
1992	Marie-Jose Perec (FRA)	48.83
1996	Marie-Jose Perec (FRA)	48.25
2000	Cathy Freeman (AUS)	49.11

Summer Olympic Games Champions (continued)

Athletics (track-and-field) (women) (continued)

800 METERS — MIN:SEC

Year	Name	MIN:SEC
1928	Lina Radke-Batschauer (GER)	2:16.8
1960	Lyudmila Lysenko-Shevtsova (URS)	2:04.3
1964	Ann Packer (GBR)	2:01.1
1968	Madeline Manning (USA)	2:00.9
1972	Hildegard Falck (FRG)	1:58.6
1976	Tatyana Kazankina (URS)	1:54.94
1980	Nadezhda Olizarenko (URS)	1:53.50
1984	Doina Melinte (ROM)	1:57.6
1988	Sigrun Wodars (GDR)	1:56.10
1992	Ellen van Langen (NED)	1:55.54
1996	Svetlana Masterkova (RUS)	1:57.73
2000	Maria Mutola (MOZ)	1:56.15

1,500 METERS — MIN:SEC

Year	Name	MIN:SEC
1972	Lyudmila Bragina (URS)	4:01.4
1976	Tatyana Kazankina (URS)	4:05.48
1980	Tatyana Kazankina (URS)	3:56.6
1984	Gabriella Dorio (ITA)	4:03.25
1988	Paula Ivan (ROM)	3:53.96
1992	Hassiba Boulmerka (ALG)	3:55.30
1996	Svetlana Masterkova (RUS)	4:00.83
2000	Nouria Merah-Benida (ALG)	4:05.10

3,000 METERS — MIN:SEC

Year	Name	MIN:SEC
1984	Maricica Puica (ROM)	8:35.96
1988	Tatyana Samolenko (URS)	8:26.53
1992	Yelena Romanova (UNT)	8:46.04

5,000 METERS — MIN:SEC

Year	Name	MIN:SEC
1996	Wang Junxia (CHN)	14:59.88
2000	Gabriela Szabo (ROM)	14:40.79

10,000 METERS — MIN:SEC

Year	Name	MIN:SEC
1988	Olga Bondarenko (URS)	31:05.21
1992	Derartu Tulu (ETH)	31:06.02
1996	Fernanda Ribeiro (POR)	31:01.63
2000	Derartu Tulu (ETH)	30:17.49

MARATHON — HR:MIN:SEC

Year	Name	HR:MIN:SEC
1984	Joan Benoit (USA)	2:24:52
1988	Rosa Mota (POR)	2:25:40
1992	Valentina Yegorova (UNT)	2:32:41
1996	Fatuma Roba (ETH)	2:26:05
2000	Naoko Takahashi (JPN)	2:23:14

80-METER HURDLES (100 METERS FROM 1972) — SEC

Year	Name	SEC
1932	Mildred Didrikson (USA)	11.7
1936	Trebisonda Valla (ITA)	11.7
1948	Francina Blankers-Koen (NED)	11.2
1952	Shirley Strickland de La Hunty (AUS)	10.9
1956	Shirley Strickland de La Hunty (AUS)	10.7
1960	Irina Press (URS)	10.8
1964	Karin Balzer (GER)	10.5
1968	Maureen Caird (AUS)	10.3
1972	Annelie Ehrhardt (GDR)	12.59
1976	Johanna Schaller (GDR)	12.77
1980	Vera Komisova (URS)	12.56
1984	Benita Fitzgerald-Brown (USA)	12.84
1988	Iordanka Donkova (BUL)	12.38
1992	Paraskevi Patoulidou (GRE)	12.64
1996	Ludmila Engquist (SWE)	12.58
2000	Olga Shishigina (KAZ)	12.65

400-METER HURDLES — SEC

Year	Name	SEC
1984	Nawal el Moutawakel (MAR)	54.61
1988	Debra Flintoff-King (AUS)	53.17
1992	Sally Gunnell (GBR)	53.23
1996	Deon Hemmings (JAM)	52.82
2000	Irina Privalova (RUS)	53.02

Athletics (track-and-field) (women) (continued)

4 × 100-METER RELAY — SEC

Year	Team	SEC
1928	Canada	48.4
1932	United States	47.0
1936	United States	46.9
1948	The Netherlands	47.5
1952	United States	45.9
1956	Australia	44.5
1960	United States	44.5
1964	Poland	43.6
1968	United States	42.8
1972	West Germany	42.81
1976	East Germany	42.55
1980	East Germany	41.60
1984	United States	41.65
1988	United States	41.98
1992	United States	42.11
1996	United States	41.95
2000	The Bahamas	41.95

4 × 400-METER RELAY — MIN:SEC

Year	Team	MIN:SEC
1972	East Germany	3:23.0
1976	East Germany	3:19.23
1980	USSR	3:20.2
1984	United States	3:18.29
1988	USSR	3:15.18
1992	Unified Team	3:20.20
1996	United States	3:20.91
2000	United States	3:22.62

10,000-METER WALK — MIN:SEC

Year	Name	MIN:SEC
1992	Chen Yueling (CHN)	44:32
1996	Yelena Nikolayeva (RUS)	41:49

20,000-METER WALK — MIN:SEC

Year	Name	MIN:SEC
2000	Wang Liping (CHN)	1:29.05

HIGH JUMP — METERS

Year	Name	METERS
1928	Ethel Catherwood (CAN)	1.59
1932	Jean Shiley (USA)	1.66
1936	Ibolya Csak (HUN)	1.60
1948	Alice Coachman (USA)	1.68
1952	Esther Brand (RSA)	1.67
1956	Mildred Louise McDaniel (USA)	1.76
1960	Iolanda Balas (ROM)	1.85
1964	Iolanda Balas (ROM)	1.90
1968	Miloslava Rezkova (TCH)	1.82
1972	Ulrike Meyfarth (FRG)	1.92
1976	Rosemarie Ackermann (GDR)	1.93
1980	Sara Simeoni (ITA)	1.97
1984	Ulrike Meyfarth (FRG)	2.02
1988	Louise Ritter (USA)	2.03
1992	Heike Henkel (GER)	2.02
1996	Stefka Kostadinova (BUL)	2.05
2000	Yelena Yelesina (RUS)	2.01

POLE VAULT — METERS

Year	Name	METERS
2000	Stacy Dragila (USA)	4.60

LONG JUMP — METERS

Year	Name	METERS
1948	Olga Gyarmati (HUN)	5.69
1952	Yvette Williams (NZL)	6.24
1956	Elzbieta Krzesinska (POL)	6.35
1960	Vera Krepkina (URS)	6.37
1964	Mary Rand (GBR)	6.76

Summer Olympic Games Champions (continued)

Athletics (track-and-field) (women) (continued)

LONG JUMP		METERS
1968	Viorica Viscopoleanu (ROM)	6.82
1972	Heidemarie Rosendahl (FRG)	6.78
1976	Angela Voigt (GDR)	6.72
1980	Tatyana Kolpakova (URS)	7.06
1984	Anisoara Stanciu (ROM)	6.96
1988	Jackie Joyner-Kersee (USA)	7.40
1992	Heike Drechsler (GER)	7.14
1996	Chioma Ajunwa (NGR)	7.12
2000	Heike Drechsler (GER)	6.99

TRIPLE JUMP		METERS
1996	Inessa Kravets (UKR)	15.33
2000	Tereza Marinova (BUL)	15.20

SHOT PUT		METERS
1948	Micheline Ostermeyer (FRA)	13.75
1952	Galina Zybina (URS)	15.28
1956	Tamara Tyshkevich (URS)	16.59
1960	Tamara Press (URS)	17.32
1964	Tamara Press (URS)	18.14
1968	Margitta Gummel (GDR)	19.61
1972	Nadezhda Chizhova (URS)	21.03
1976	Ivanka Khristova (BUL)	21.16
1980	Ilona Slupianek (GDR)	22.41
1984	Claudia Losch (FRG)	20.48
1988	Natalya Lisovskaya (URS)	22.24
1992	Svetlana Krivalyova (UNT)	21.06
1996	Astrid Kumbernuss (GER)	20.56
2000	Yanina Korolchik (BLR)	20.56

DISCUS THROW		METERS
1928	Halina Konopacka (POL)	39.62
1932	Lillian Copeland (USA)	40.58
1936	Gisela Mauermayer (GER)	47.63
1948	Micheline Ostermeyer (FRA)	41.92
1952	Nina Romashkova (URS)	51.42
1956	Olga Fikotova (TCH)	53.69
1960	Nina Ponomaryova-Romashkova (URS)	55.10
1964	Tamara Press (URS)	57.27
1968	Lia Manoliu (ROM)	58.28
1972	Faina Melnik (URS)	66.62
1976	Evelin Schlaak (GDR)	69.00
1980	Evelin Schlaak Jahl (GDR)	69.96
1984	Ria Stalman (NED)	65.36
1988	Martina Hellmann (GDR)	72.30
1992	Maritza Marten (CUB)	70.06
1996	Ilke Wyludda (GER)	69.66
2000	Ellina Zvereva (BLR)	68.40

HAMMER THROW		METERS
2000	Kamila Skolimowska (POL)	71.16

JAVELIN THROW		METERS
1932	Mildred Didrikson (USA)	43.68
1936	Tilly Fleischer (GER)	45.18
1948	Hermine Bauma (AUT)	45.57
1952	Dana Zatopkova (TCH)	50.47
1956	Inese Jaunzeme (URS)	53.86
1960	Elvira Ozolina (URS)	55.98
1964	Mihaela Penes (ROM)	60.54
1968	Angela Nemeth (HUN)	60.36
1972	Ruth Fuchs (GDR)	63.88
1976	Ruth Fuchs (GDR)	65.94
1980	María Colón (CUB)	68.40
1984	Tessa Sanderson (GBR)	69.56
1988	Petra Felke (GDR)	74.68
1992	Silke Renk (GER)	68.34

Athletics (track-and-field) (women) (continued)

JAVELIN THROW		METERS
1996	Heli Rantanen (FIN)	67.94
2000	Trine Hattestad (NOR)	68.91

PENTATHLON (HEPTATHLON FROM 1984)	
1964	Irina Press (URS)
1968	Ingrid Becker (FRG)
1972	Mary Peters (GBR)
1976	Siegrun Siegl (GDR)
1980	Nadezhda Tkachenko (URS)
1984	Glynis Nunn (AUS)
1988	Jackie Joyner-Kersee (USA)
1992	Jackie Joyner-Kersee (USA)
1996	Ghada Shouaa (SYR)
2000	Denise Lewis (GBR)

Badminton

MEN'S SINGLES
1992	Allan Budi Kusuma (INA)
1996	Poul-Erik Hoyer-Larsen (DEN)
2000	Ji Xinpeng (CHN)

MEN'S DOUBLES
1992	South Korea
1996	Indonesia
2000	Indonesia

WOMEN'S SINGLES
1992	Susi Susanti (INA)
1996	Bang Soo-Hyun (KOR)
2000	Gong Zhichao (CHN)

WOMEN'S DOUBLES
1992	South Korea
1996	China
2000	China

MIXED DOUBLES
1996	South Korea
2000	China

Baseball

1992	Cuba
1996	Cuba
2000	United States

Basketball

MEN
1936	United States
1948	United States
1952	United States
1956	United States
1960	United States
1964	United States
1968	United States
1972	USSR
1976	United States
1980	Yugoslavia
1984	United States
1988	USSR
1992	United States
1996	United States
2000	United States

WOMEN
1976	USSR
1980	USSR
1984	United States

Summer Olympic Games Champions (continued)

Basketball (continued)

WOMEN

1988	United States
1992	Unified Team
1996	United States
2000	United States

Boxing

LIGHT FLYWEIGHT (48 KG; 106 LB)

1968	Francisco Rodríguez (VEN)
1972	Gyorgy Gedo (HUN)
1976	Jorge Hernández (CUB)
1980	Shamil Sabyrov (URS)
1984	Paul Gonzales (USA)
1988	Ivailo Khristov (BUL)
1992	Rogelio Marcelo (CUB)
1996	Daniel Petrov Bojilov (BUL)
2000	Brahim Asloum (FRA)

FLYWEIGHT (51 KG; 112 LB)

1904	George Finnegan (USA)
1920	Frank di Genaro (USA)
1924	Fidel La Barba (USA)
1928	Antal Kocsis (HUN)
1932	Istvan Enekes (HUN)
1936	Willi Kaiser (GER)
1948	Pascual Pérez (ARG)
1952	Nate Brooks (USA)
1956	Terence Spinks (GBR)
1960	Gyula Torok (HUN)
1964	Fernando Atzori (ITA)
1968	Ricardo Delgado (MEX)
1972	Georgi Kostadinov (BUL)
1976	Leo Randolph (USA)
1980	Petar Lesov (BUL)
1984	Steven McCrory (USA)
1988	Kim Kwang Sun (KOR)
1992	Chol Choi Su (PRK)
1996	Maikro Romero (CUB)
2000	Wijan Ponlid (THA)

BANTAMWEIGHT (54 KG; 119 LB)

1904	Oliver Kirk (USA)
1908	Henry Thomas (GBR)
1920	Clarence Walker (RSA)
1924	William Smith (RSA)
1928	Vittorio Tamagnini (ITA)
1932	Horace Gwynne (CAN)
1936	Ulderico Sergo (ITA)
1948	Tibor Csik (HUN)
1952	Pentti Hämäläinen (FIN)
1956	Wolfgang Behrendt (GER)
1960	Oleg Grigoryev (URS)
1964	Takao Sakurai (JPN)
1968	Valery Sokolov (URS)
1972	Orlando Martínez (CUB)
1976	Gu Yong Jo (PRK)
1980	Juan Hernández (CUB)
1984	Maurizio Stecca (ITA)
1988	Kennedy McKinney (USA)
1992	Joel Casamayor (CUB)
1996	Istvan Kovacs (HUN)
2000	Guillermo Rigondeaux (CUB)

FEATHERWEIGHT (57 KG; 125 LB)

1904	Oliver Kirk (USA)
1908	Richard Gunn (GBR)
1920	Paul Fritsch (FRA)
1924	John Fields (USA)

Boxing (continued)

FEATHERWEIGHT (57 KG; 125 LB)

1928	Lambertus van Kleveren (NED)
1932	Carmelo Robledo (ARG)
1936	Oscar Casanovas (ARG)
1948	Ernesto Formenti (ITA)
1952	Jan Zachara (TCH)
1956	Vladimir Safronov (URS)
1960	Francesco Musso (ITA)
1964	Stanislav Stepashkin (URS)
1968	Antonio Roldan (MEX)
1972	Boris Kuznetsov (URS)
1976	Angel Herrera (CUB)
1980	Rudi Fink (GDR)
1984	Meldrick Taylor (USA)
1988	Giovanni Parisi (ITA)
1992	Andreas Tews (GER)
1996	Somluck Kamsing (THA)
2000	Bekzat Sattarkhanov (KAZ)

LIGHTWEIGHT (60 KG; 132 LB)

1904	Harry Spanger (USA)
1908	Frederick Grace (GBR)
1920	Samuel Mosberg (USA)
1924	Hans Nielsen (DEN)
1928	Carlo Orlandi (ITA)
1932	Lawrence Stevens (RSA)
1936	Imre Harangi (HUN)
1948	Gerald Dreyer (RSA)
1952	Aureliano Bolognesi (ITA)
1956	Richard McTaggart (GBR)
1960	Kazimierz Pazdzior (POL)
1964	Jozef Grudzien (POL)
1968	Ronnie Harris (USA)
1972	Jan Szczepanski (POL)
1976	Howard Davis (USA)
1980	Angel Herrera (CUB)
1984	Pernell Whitaker (USA)
1988	Andreas Zuelow (GDR)
1992	Oscar De La Hoya (USA)
1996	Hocine Soltani (ALG)
2000	Mario Kindelan (CUB)

LIGHT WELTERWEIGHT (63.5 KG; 140 LB)

1952	Charles Adkins (USA)
1956	Vladimir Engibaryan (URS)
1960	Bohumil Nemecek (TCH)
1964	Jerzy Kulej (POL)
1968	Jerzy Kulej (POL)
1972	Ray Seales (USA)
1976	Ray Leonard (USA)
1980	Patrizio Oliva (ITA)
1984	Jerry Page (USA)
1988	Vyacheslav Yanovsky (URS)
1992	Héctor Vinent (CUB)
1996	Héctor Vinent (CUB)
2000	Mahamadkadyz Abdullayev (UZB)

WELTERWEIGHT (67 KG; 147 LB)

1904	Albert Young (USA)
1920	Julius Schneider (CAN)
1924	Jean Delarge (BEL)
1928	Edward Morgan (NZL)
1932	Edward Flynn (USA)
1936	Sten Suvio (FIN)
1948	Julius Torma (TCH)
1952	Zygmunt Chychla (POL)
1956	Nicolae Linca (ROM)
1960	Giovanni Benvenuti (ITA)

Summer Olympic Games Champions (continued)

Boxing (continued)

WELTERWEIGHT (67 KG; 147 LB)

1964	Marian Kasprzyk (POL)
1968	Manfred Wolke (GDR)
1972	Emilio Correa (CUB)
1976	Jochen Bachfeld (GDR)
1980	Andres Aldama (CUB)
1984	Mark Breland (USA)
1988	Robert Wangila (KEN)
1992	Michael Carruth (IRL)
1996	Oleg Saytov (RUS)
2000	Oleg Saytov (RUS)

LIGHT MIDDLEWEIGHT (71 KG; 156 LB)

1952	Laszlo Papp (HUN)
1956	Laszlo Papp (HUN)
1960	Wilbert McClure (USA)
1964	Boris Lagutin (URS)
1968	Boris Lagutin (URS)
1972	Dieter Kottysch (FRG)
1976	Jerzy Rybicki (POL)
1980	Armando Martínez (CUB)
1984	Frank Tate (USA)
1988	Park Si Hun (KOR)
1992	Juan Lemus (CUB)
1996	David Reid (USA)
2000	Yermakhan Ibraimov (KAZ)

MIDDLEWEIGHT (75 KG; 165 LB)

1904	Charles Mayer (USA)
1908	John Douglas (GBR)
1920	Harry Mallin (GBR)
1924	Harry Mallin (GBR)
1928	Piero Toscani (ITA)
1932	Carmen Barth (USA)
1936	Jean Despeaux (FRA)
1948	Laszlo Papp (HUN)
1952	Floyd Patterson (USA)
1956	Gennady Shatkov (URS)
1960	Edward Crook (USA)
1964	Valery Popenchenko (URS)
1968	Christopher Finnegan (GBR)
1972	Vyatcheslav Lemeshev (URS)
1976	Michael Spinks (USA)
1980	Jose Gómez (CUB)
1984	Shin Joon Sup (KOR)
1988	Henry Maske (GDR)
1992	Ariel Hernández (CUB)
1996	Ariel Hernández (CUB)
2000	Jorge Gutiérrez (CUB)

LIGHT HEAVYWEIGHT (81 KG; 178 LB)

1920	Edward Eagan (USA)
1924	Harry Mitchell (GBR)
1928	Viktor Avendano (ARG)
1932	David Carstens (RSA)
1936	Roger Michelot (FRA)
1948	George Hunter (RSA)
1952	Norvel Lee (USA)
1956	James Boyd (USA)
1960	Cassius Clay (USA)
1964	Cosimo Pinto (ITA)
1968	Dan Poznyak (URS)
1972	Mate Parlov (YUG)
1976	Leon Spinks (USA)
1980	Slobodan Kacar (YUG)
1984	Anton Josipovic (YUG)
1988	Andrew Maynard (USA)
1992	Torsten May (GER)

Boxing (continued)

LIGHT HEAVYWEIGHT (81 KG; 178 LB)

1996	Vasily Zhirov (KAZ)
2000	Aleksandr Lebzyak (RUS)

HEAVYWEIGHT (OVER 81 KG; 179 LB) (91 KG; 200 LB FROM 1984)

1904	Samuel Berger (USA)
1908	Albert Oldman (GBR)
1920	Ronald Rawson (GBR)
1924	Otto Von Porat (NOR)
1928	Arturo Rodriguez (ARG)
1932	Alberto Santiago Lovell (ARG)
1936	Herbert Runge (GER)
1948	Rafael Iglesias (ARG)
1952	Edward Sanders (USA)
1956	Peter Rademacher (USA)
1960	Franco de Piccoli (ITA)
1964	Joseph Frazier (USA)
1968	George Foreman (USA)
1972	Teofilo Stevenson (CUB)
1976	Teofilo Stevenson (CUB)
1980	Teofilo Stevenson (CUB)
1984	Henry Tillman (USA)
1988	Ray Mercer (USA)
1992	Félix Savon (CUB)
1996	Félix Savon (CUB)
2000	Félix Savon (CUB)

SUPERHEAVYWEIGHT (OVER 91 KG; 200 LB)

1984	Tyrell Biggs (USA)
1988	Lennox Lewis (CAN)
1992	Roberto Balado (CUB)
1996	Vladimir Klichko (UKR)
2000	Audley Harrison (GBR)

Canoeing (men)

KAYAK SINGLES (500 METERS)

		MIN:SEC
1976	Vasile Diba (ROM)	1:46.41
1980	Vladimir Parfenovich (URS)	1:43.43
1984	Ian Ferguson (NZL)	1:47.84
1988	Zsolt Gyulay (HUN)	1:44.82
1992	Mikko Kolehmainen (FIN)	1:40.34
1996	Antonio Rossi (ITA)	1:37.423
2000	Knut Holmann (NOR)	1:57.84

KAYAK PAIRS (500 METERS)

		MIN:SEC
1976	East Germany	1:35.87
1980	USSR	1:32.38
1984	New Zealand	1:34.21
1988	New Zealand	1:33.98
1992	Germany	1:29.84
1996	Germany	1:28.697
2000	Hungary	1:47.05

KAYAK SINGLES (1,000 METERS)

		MIN:SEC
1936	Gregor Hradetzky (AUT)	4:22.90
1948	Gert Fredriksson (SWE)	4:33.20
1952	Gert Fredriksson (SWE)	4:07.90
1956	Gert Fredriksson (SWE)	4:12.80
1960	Erik Hansen (DEN)	3:53.00
1964	Rolf Peterson (SWE)	3:57.13
1968	Mihaly Hesz (HUN)	4:03.58
1972	Aleksandr Shaparenko (URS)	3:48.06
1976	Rüdiger Helm (GDR)	3:48.20
1980	Rüdiger Helm (GDR)	3:48.77
1984	Alan Thompson (NZL)	3:45.73
1988	Gregory Barton (USA)	3:55.27
1992	Clint Robinson (AUS)	3:37.26

Summer Olympic Games Champions (continued)

Canoeing (men) (continued)

KAYAK SINGLES (1,000 METERS)	MIN:SEC
1996 Knut Holmann (NOR)	3:25.785
2000 Knut Holmann (NOR)	3:33.26

KAYAK PAIRS (1,000 METERS)	MIN:SEC
1936 Austria	4:03.80
1948 Sweden	4:07.30
1952 Finland	3:51.10
1956 Germany	3:49.60
1960 Sweden	3:34.70
1964 Sweden	3:38.54
1968 USSR	3:37.54
1972 USSR	3:31.23
1976 USSR	3:29.01
1980 USSR	3:26.72
1984 Canada	3:24.22
1988 United States	3:32.42
1992 Germany	3:16.10
1996 Italy	3:09.190
2000 Italy	3:14.46

KAYAK FOURS (1,000 METERS)	MIN:SEC
1964 USSR	3:14.67
1968 Norway	3:14.38
1972 USSR	3:14.02
1976 USSR	3:08.69
1980 East Germany	3:13.76
1984 New Zealand	3:02.28
1988 Hungary	3:00.20
1992 Germany	2:54.18
1996 Germany	2:51.528
2000 Hungary	2:55.18

KAYAK SINGLES (10,000 METERS)	MIN:SEC
1936 Ernst Krebs (GER)	46:01.6
1948 Gert Fredriksson (SWE)	50:47.7
1952 Thorvald Strömberg (FIN)	47:22.8
1956 Gert Fredriksson (SWE)	47:43.4

KAYAK PAIRS (10,000 METERS)	MIN:SEC
1936 Germany	41:45
1948 Sweden	46:09.4
1952 Finland	44:21.3
1956 Hungary	43:37

COLLAPSIBLE KAYAK SINGLES (10,000 METERS)	MIN:SEC
1936 Gregor Hradetzky (AUT)	50:01.2

COLLAPSIBLE KAYAK PAIRS (10,000 METERS)	MIN:SEC
1936 Sweden	45:48.9

KAYAK SINGLES RELAY (1,500 METERS)	MIN:SEC
1960 Germany	7:39.43

SLALOM KAYAK SINGLES	
1972 Siegbert Horn (GDR)	
1992 Pierpaolo Ferrazzi (ITA)	
1996 Oliver Fix (GER)	
2000 Thomas Schmidt (GER)	

CANADIAN SINGLES (500 METERS)	MIN:SEC
1976 Aleksandr Rogov (URS)	1:59.23
1980 Sergey Postrekin (URS)	1:53.37
1984 Larry Cain (CAN)	1:57.01
1988 Olaf Heukrodt (GDR)	1:56.42
1992 Nikolay Bukhalov (BUL)	1:51.15
1996 Martin Doktor (CZE)	1:49.934
2000 Gyorgy Kolonics (HUN)	2:24.81

Canoeing (men) (continued)

CANADIAN PAIRS (500 METERS)	MIN:SEC
1976 USSR	1:45.81
1980 Hungary	1:43.39
1984 Yugoslavia	1:43.67
1988 USSR	1:41.77
1992 Unified Team	1:41.54
1996 Hungary	1:40.420
2000 Hungary	1:51.28

CANADIAN SINGLES (1,000 METERS)	MIN:SEC
1936 Francis Amyot (CAN)	5:32.10
1948 Josef Holecek (TCH)	5:42.00
1952 Josef Holecek (TCH)	4:56.30
1956 Leon Rottman (ROM)	5:05.30
1960 Janos Parti (HUN)	4:33.03
1964 Jürgen Eschert (GER)	4:35.14
1968 Tibor Tatai (HUN)	4:36.14
1972 Ivan Patzaichin (ROM)	4:08.94
1976 Matija Ljubek (YUG)	4:09.51
1980 Lyubomir Lyubenov (BUL)	4:12.38
1984 Ulrich Eicke (FRG)	4:06.32
1988 Ivans Klementyev (URS)	4:12.78
1992 Nikolay Bukhalov (BUL)	4:05.92
1996 Martin Doktor (CZE)	3:54.418
2000 Andreas Dittmer (GER)	3:54.37

CANADIAN PAIRS (1,000 METERS)	MIN:SEC
1936 Czechoslovakia	4:50.10
1948 Czechoslovakia	5:07.10
1952 Denmark	4:38.30
1956 Romania	4:47.40
1960 USSR	4:17.04
1964 USSR	4:04.65
1968 Romania	4:07.18
1972 USSR	3:52.60
1976 USSR	3:52.76
1980 Romania	3:47.65
1984 Romania	3:40.60
1988 USSR	3:48.36
1992 Germany	3:37.42
1996 Germany	3:31.870
2000 Romania	3:37.35

CANADIAN SINGLES (10,000 METERS)	MIN:SEC
1948 Frantisek Capek (TCH)	62:05.2
1952 Frank Havens (USA)	57:41.1
1956 Leon Rottman (ROM)	56:41.0

CANADIAN PAIRS (10,000 METERS)	MIN:SEC
1936 Czechoslovakia	50:35.5
1948 United States	55:55.4
1952 France	54:08.3
1956 USSR	54:02.4

SLALOM CANADIAN SINGLES	
1972 Reinhard Eiben (GDR)	
1992 Lukas Pollert (TCH)	
1996 Michal Martikan (SVK)	
2000 Tony Estanguet (FRA)	

SLALOM CANADIAN PAIRS	
1972 East Germany	
1992 United States	
1996 France	
2000 Slovakia	

Summer Olympic Games Champions (continued)

Canoeing (women)

KAYAK SINGLES (500 METERS)   MIN:SEC
1948 Karen Hoff (DEN)   2:31.90
1952 Sylvi Saimo (FIN)   2:18.40
1956 Yelizaveta Dementyeva (URS)   2:18.90
1960 Antonina Seredina (URS)   2:08.08
1964 Lyudmila Khvedosyuk (URS)   2:12.87
1968 Lyudmila Pinayeva-Khvedosyuk   2:11.09
      (URS)
1972 Yuliya Ryabchinskaya (URS)   2:03.17
1976 Carola Zirzow (GDR)   2:01.05
1980 Birgit Fischer (GDR)   1:57.96
1984 Agneta Andersson (SWE)   1:58.72
1988 Vanya Gecheva (BUL)   1:55.19
1992 Birgit Fischer Schmidt (GER)   1:51.60
1996 Rita Koban (HUN)   1:47.655
2000 Josefa Idem Guerrini (ITA)   2:13.84

KAYAK PAIRS (500 METERS)   MIN:SEC
1960 USSR   1:54.76
1964 Germany   1:56.95
1968 West Germany   1:56.44
1972 USSR   1:53.50
1976 USSR   1:51.15
1980 East Germany   1:43.88
1984 Sweden   1:45.25
1988 East Germany   1:43.46
1992 Germany   1:40.29
1996 Sweden   1:39.329
2000 Germany   1:56.99

KAYAK FOURS (500 METERS)   MIN:SEC
1984 Romania   1:38.34
1988 East Germany   1:40.78
1992 Hungary   1:38.32
1996 Germany   1:31.077
2000 Germany   1:34.53

SLALOM KAYAK SINGLES
1972 Angelika Bahmann (GDR)
1992 Elisabeth Micheler (GER)
1996 Stepanka Hilgertova (CZE)
2000 Stepanka Hilgertova (CZE)

Cricket
1900 Great Britain

Croquet
SINGLES (ONE BALL)
1900 Aumoitte (FRA)

SINGLES (TWO BALLS)
1900 Waydelick (FRA)

DOUBLES
1900 France

Cycling (men)
1,000-METER SPRINT
1896[6] Paul Masson (FRA)
1900[6] Georges Taillandier (FRA)
1920 Mauritius Peeters (NED)
1924 Lucien Michard (FRA)
1928 Roger Beaufrand (FRA)
1932 Jacobus Van Egmond (NED)
1936 Toni Merkens (GER)
1948 Mario Ghella (ITA)
1952 Enzo Sacchi (ITA)
1956 Michel Rousseau (FRA)

Cycling (men) (continued)
1,000-METER SPRINT
1960 Sante Gaiardoni (ITA)
1964 Giovanni Pettenella (ITA)
1968 Daniel Morelon (FRA)
1972 Daniel Morelon (FRA)
1976 Anton Tkac (TCH)
1980 Lutz Hesslich (GDR)
1984 Mark Gorski (USA)
1988 Lutz Hesslich (GDR)
1992 Jens Fiedler (GER)
1996 Jens Fiedler (GER)
2000 Marty Nothstein (USA)

1,000-METER TIME TRIAL   MIN:SEC
1896[7] Paul Masson (FRA)   24.0
1928 Willy Falck-Hansen (DEN)   1:14.4
1932 Edgar Gray (AUS)   1:13.0
1936 Arie van Vliet (NED)   1:12.0
1948 Jacques Dupont (FRA)   1:13.5
1952 Russell Mockridge (AUS)   1:11.1
1956 Leandro Faggin (ITA)   1:09.8
1960 Sante Gaiardoni (ITA)   1:07.27
1964 Patrick Sercu (BEL)   1:09.59
1968 Pierre Trentin (FRA)   1:03.91
1972 Niels Fredborg (DEN)   1:06.44
1976 Klaus-Jürgen Grünke (GDR)   1:05.927
1980 Lothar Thoms (GDR)   1:02.955
1984 Fredy Schmidtke (FRG)   1:06.104
1988 Aleksandr Kirichenko (URS)   1:04.499
1992 José Moreno (ESP)   1:03.342
1996 Florian Rousseau (FRA)   1:02.712
2000 Jason Queally (GBR)   1:01.609

1,500-METER TEAM PURSUIT
1900 United States

2,000 METERS
1904 Marcus Hurley (USA)

2,000-METER TANDEM
1908 France
1920 Great Britain
1924 France
1928 The Netherlands
1932 France
1936 Germany
1948 Italy
1952 Australia
1956 Australia
1960 Italy
1964 Italy
1968 France
1972 USSR

4,000-METER INDIVIDUAL PURSUIT
1964 Jiri Daler (TCH)
1968 Daniel Rebillard (FRA)
1972 Knut Knudsen (NOR)
1976 Gregor Braun (FRG)
1980 Robert Dill-Bondi (SUI)
1984 Steve Hegg (USA)
1988 Gintaoutas Umaras (URS)
1992 Christopher Boardman (GBR)
1996 Andrea Collinelli (ITA)
2000 Robert Bartko (GER)

4,000-METER TEAM PURSUIT
1908 Great Britain

Summer Olympic Games Champions (continued)

Cycling (men) (continued)

4,000-METER TEAM PURSUIT

1920	Italy
1924	Italy
1928	Italy
1932	Italy
1936	France
1948	France
1952	Italy
1956	Italy
1960	Italy
1964	Germany
1968	Denmark
1972	West Germany
1976	West Germany
1980	USSR
1984	Australia
1988	USSR
1992	Germany
1996	France
2000	Germany

5,000 METERS — MIN:SEC
1908	Benjamin Jones (GBR)	8:36.2

10,000 METERS — MIN:SEC
1896	Paul Masson (FRA)	17:54.2

20,000 METERS — MIN:SEC
1908	Charles Kingsbury (GBR)	34:13.6

50,000 METERS — HR:MIN:SEC
1920	Henry George (BEL)	1:16:43.2
1924	Jacobus Willems (NED)	1:18:24.0

100,000 METERS — HR:MIN:SEC
1896	Léon Flameng (FRA)	3:08:19.2
1908	Charles Bartlett (GBR)	2:41:48.6

ONE-QUARTER MILE (440 YARDS) — SEC
1904	Marcus Hurley (USA)	31.8

ONE-THIRD MILE (586⅔ YARDS) — SEC
1904	Marcus Hurley (USA)	43.8

ONE-LAP TIME TRIAL (660 YARDS) — SEC
1908	Victor Johnson (GBR)	51.2

ONE-HALF MILE (880 YARDS) — MIN:SEC
1904	Marcus Hurley (USA)	1:09.0

1 MILE — MIN:SEC
1904	Marcus Hurley (USA)	2:41.6

1 MILE 1 FURLONG (1,980 YARDS) TEAM PURSUIT
1908	Great Britain

2 MILES — MIN:SEC
1904	Burton Downing (USA)	4:58.0

5 MILES — MIN:SEC
1904	Charles Schlee (USA)	13:08.2

25 MILES
1904	Burton Downing (USA)

12 HOURS
1896	Adolf Schmal (AUT)

Cycling (men) (continued)

POINTS RACE
1984	Roger Ilegems (BEL)
1988	Dan Frost (DEN)
1992	Giovanni Lombardi (ITA)
1996	Silvio Martinello (ITA)
2000	Juan Llaneras (ESP)

KEIRIN — SEC
2000	Florian Rousseau (FRA)	11.020

MADISON
2000	Australia

OLYMPIC SPRINT — SEC
2000	France	44.233

ROAD RACE (INDIVIDUAL)[8] — HR:MIN:SEC
1896	Aristidis Konstantinidis (GRE)	3:22:31.0
1912	Rudolph Lewis (RSA)	10:42:39.0
1920	Harry Stenqvist (SWE)	4:40:01.8
1924	Armand Blanchonnet (FRA)	6:20:48.0
1928	Henry Hansen (DEN)	4:47.18.0
1932	Attilio Pavesi (ITA)	2:28:05.6
1936	Robert Charpentier (FRA)	2:33:05.0
1948	Jose Beyaert (FRA)	5:18:12.6
1952	Andre Noyelle (BEL)	5:06:03.4
1956	Ercole Baldini (ITA)	5:21:17.0
1960	Viktor Kapitonov (URS)	4:20:37.0
1964	Mario Zanin (ITA)	4:39:51.63
1968	Pierfranco Vianelli (ITA)	4:41:25.24
1972	Hennie Kuiper (NED)	4:14:37.0
1976	Bernt Johansson (SWE)	4:46:52.0
1980	Sergey Sukhoruchenkov (URS)	4.48.28.90
1984	Alexei Grewal (USA)	4:59:57.0
1988	Olaf Ludwig (GDR)	4:32:22.0
1992	Fabio Casartelli (ITA)	4:35:21.0
1996	Pascal Richard (SUI)	4:53:56.0
2000	Jan Ullrich (GER)	5:29:08

ROAD RACE (TEAM) — HR:MIN:SEC
1912	Sweden	44:35:33.6
1920	France	19:16:43.2
1924	France	19:30:14
1928	Denmark	15:09:14
1932	Italy	7:27:15.2
1936	France	7:39:16.2
1948	Belgium	15:58:17.4
1952	Belgium	15:20:46.6
1956	France	5:21:17

ROAD TIME TRIAL (INDIVIDUAL) — HR:MIN:SEC
1996	Miguel Indurain (ESP)	1:04:05
2000	Vyacheslav Yekimov (RUS)	57:40.420

ROAD TIME TRIAL (TEAM) — HR:MIN:SEC
1960	Italy	2:14:33.53
1964	The Netherlands	2.26:31.19
1968	The Netherlands	2:07:49.06
1972	USSR	2:11:17.8
1976	USSR	2:08:53
1980	USSR	2:01:21.7
1984	Italy	1:58:28
1988	East Germany	1:57:47.7
1992	Germany	2:01:39

CROSS COUNTRY (MOUNTAIN BIKE) — HR:MIN:SEC
1996	Bart Jan Brentjens (NED)	2:17:38
2000	Miguel Martinez (FRA)	2:09:2.50

Summer Olympic Games Champions (continued)

Cycling (women)

500-METER TIME TRIAL   HR:MIN:SEC
2000 Felicia Ballanger (FRA)   34.140

1,000-METER SPRINT
1988 Erika Salumae (URS)
1992 Erika Salumae (EST)
1996 Felicia Ballanger (FRA)
2000 Felicia Ballanger (FRA)

3,000-METER INDIVIDUAL PURSUIT
1992 Petra Rossner (GER)
1996 Antonella Bellutti (ITA)
2000 Leontien Zijlaard-van Moorsel
     (NED)

POINTS RACE
1996 Nathalie Lancien (FRA)
2000 Antonella Bellutti (ITA)

ROAD RACE (INDIVIDUAL)   HR:MIN:SEC
1984 Connie Carpenter-Phinney (USA)   2:11:14.0
1988 Monique Knol (NED)   2:00:52.0
1992 Kathryn Watt (AUS)   2:04:42.0
1996 Jeannie Longo-Ciprelli (FRA)   2:36:13.0
2000 Leontien Zijlaard-van Moorsel   3:06:31
     (NED)

ROAD TIME TRIAL (INDIVIDUAL)   MIN:SEC
1996 Zulfiya Zabirova (RUS)   36:40
2000 Leontien Zijlaard-van Moorsel   42:00.781
     (NED)

CROSS COUNTRY (MOUNTAIN BIKE)   HR:MIN:SEC
1996 Paola Pezzo (ITA)   1:50:51
2000 Paola Pezzo (ITA)   1:49:24.38

Diving (men)

3-METER SPRINGBOARD
1908 Albert Zürner (GER)
1912 Paul Günther (GER)
1920 Louis Kuehn (USA)
1924 Albert White (USA)
1928 Peter Desjardins (USA)
1932 Michael Galitzen (USA)
1936 Richard Degener (USA)
1948 Bruce Harlan (USA)
1952 David Browning (USA)
1956 Robert Clotworthy (USA)
1960 Gary Tobian (USA)
1964 Kenneth Sitzberger (USA)
1968 Bernie Wrightson (USA)
1972 Vladimir Vasin (URS)
1976 Philip Boggs (USA)
1980 Aleksandr Portnov (URS)
1984 Gregory Louganis (USA)
1988 Gregory Louganis (USA)
1992 Mark Edward Lenzi (USA)
1996 Xiong Ni (CHN)
2000 Xiong Ni (CHN)

10-METER PLATFORM (HIGH) DIVING
1904 George Sheldon (USA)
1908 Hjalmar Johansson (SWE)
1912 Erik Adlerz (SWE)
1920 Clarence Pinkston (USA)
1924 Albert White (USA)
1928 Peter Desjardins (USA)
1932 Harold Smith (USA)

Diving (men) (continued)

10-METER PLATFORM (HIGH) DIVING
1936 Marshall Wayne (USA)
1948 Samuel Lee (USA)
1952 Samuel Lee (USA)
1956 Joaquin Capilla Perez (MEX)
1960 Robert Webster (USA)
1964 Robert Webster (USA)
1968 Klaus DiBiasi (ITA)
1972 Klaus DiBiasi (ITA)
1976 Klaus DiBiasi (ITA)
1980 Falk Hoffman (GDR)
1984 Gregory Louganis (USA)
1988 Gregory Louganis (USA)
1992 Sun Shuwei (CHN)
1996 Dmitry Sautin (RUS)
2000 Tian Liang (CHN)

3-METER SYNCHRONIZED SPRINGBOARD DIVING
2000 China

10-METER SYNCHRONIZED PLATFORM (HIGH) DIVING
2000 Russia

PLUNGE FOR DISTANCE
1904 William Paul Dickey (USA)

PLAIN HIGH DIVING
1912 Erik Adlerz (SWE)
1920 Arvid Wallman (SWE)
1924 Richmond Eve (AUS)

Diving (women)

3-METER SPRINGBOARD
1920 Aileen Riggin (USA)
1924 Elizabeth Becker-Pinkton (USA)
1928 Helen Meany (USA)
1932 Georgia Coleman (USA)
1936 Marjorie Gestring (USA)
1948 Victoria Draves (USA)
1952 Patricia McCormick (USA)
1956 Patricia McCormick (USA)
1960 Ingrid Krämer-Engel-Gulbin (GER)
1964 Ingrid Krämer-Engel-Gulbin (GER)
1968 Sue Gossick (USA)
1972 Micki King (USA)
1976 Jennifer Chandler (USA)
1980 Irina Kalinina (URS)
1984 Sylvie Bernier (CAN)
1988 Gao Min (CHN)
1992 Gao Min (CHN)
1996 Fu Mingxia (CHN)
2000 Fu Mingxia (CHN)

10-METER PLATFORM (HIGH) DIVING
1912 Greta Johansson (SWE)
1920 Stefani Fryland Clausen (DEN)
1924 Caroline Smith (USA)
1928 Elizabeth Anna Becker-Pinkston (USA)
1932 Dorothy Poynton (USA)
1936 Dorothy Poynton-Hill (USA)
1948 Victoria Draves (USA)
1952 Patricia McCormick (USA)
1956 Patricia McCormick (USA)
1960 Ingrid Krämer-Engel-Gulbin (GER)
1964 Lesley Leigh Bush (USA)
1968 Milena Duchkova (TCH)
1972 Ulrika Knape (SWE)
1976 Yelena Vaytsekhovskaya (URS)

Summer Olympic Games Champions (continued)

Diving (women) (continued)

10-METER PLATFORM (HIGH) DIVING
1980	Martina Jäschke (GDR)	
1984	Zhou Ji-Hong (CHN)	
1988	Xu Yan-Mei (CHN)	
1992	Fu Mingxia (CHN)	
1996	Fu Mingxia (CHN)	
2000	Laura Wilkinson (USA)	

3-METER SYNCHRONIZED SPRINGBOARD DIVING
2000	Russia

10-METER SYNCHRONIZED PLATFORM (HIGH) DIVING
2000	China

Equestrian sports

GRAND PRIX (DRESSAGE) INDIVIDUAL
		MOUNT
1912	Carl Bonde (SWE)	Emperor
1920	Janne Lundblad (SWE)	Uno
1924	Ernst Linder (SWE)	Piccolomini
1928	Carl Friedrich Freiherr von Langen-Parow (GER)	Draufgänger
1932	Xavier Lesage (FRA)	Taine
1936	Heinz Pollay (GER)	Kronos
1948	Hans Moser (SUI)	Hummer
1952	Henri St. Cyr (SWE)	Master Rufus
1956	Henri St. Cyr (SWE)	Juli
1960	Sergey Filatov (URS)	Absent
1964	Henri Chammartin (SUI)	Woermann
1968	Ivan Kizimov (URS)	Ikhor
1972	Liselott Linsenhoff (FRG)	Piaff
1976	Christine Stückelberger (SUI)	Granat
1980	Elisabeth Theurer (AUT)	Mon Cherie
1984	Reiner Klimke (FRG)	Ahlerich
1988	Nicole Uphoff (FRG)	Rembrandt 24
1992	Nicole Uphoff (GER)	Rembrandt 24
1996	Isabell Werth (GER)	Gigolo
2000	Anky van Grunsven (NED)	Bonfire

GRAND PRIX (DRESSAGE) TEAM
1928	Germany
1932	France
1936	Germany
1948	France
1952	Sweden
1956	Sweden
1964	Germany
1968	West Germany
1972	USSR
1976	West Germany
1980	USSR
1984	West Germany
1988	West Germany
1992	Germany
1996	Germany
2000	Germany

GRAND PRIX (JUMPING) INDIVIDUAL
		MOUNT
1900	Aimé Haegeman (BEL)	Denton II
1912	Jean Cariou (FRA)	Mignon
1920	Tommaso Lequio di Assaba (ITA)	Trebecco
1924	Alphonse Gemuseus (SUI)	Lucette
1928	Frantisek Ventura (TCH)	Eliot
1932	Takeichi Nishi (JPN)	Uranus
1936	Kurt Hasse (GER)	Tora
1948	Humberto Mariles Cortés (MEX)	Arete
1952	Pierre Jonquères d'Oriola (FRA)	Ali Baba
1956	Hans-Günter Winkler (GER)	Halla
1960	Raimondo d'Inzeo (ITA)	Posillipo

Equestrian sports (continued)

GRAND PRIX (JUMPING) INDIVIDUAL
		MOUNT
1964	Pierre Jonquères d'Oriola (FRA)	Lutteur
1968	William Steinkraus (USA)	Snowbound
1972	Graziano Mancinelli (ITA)	Ambassador
1976	Alwin Schockemöhle (FRG)	Warwick Rex
1980	Jan Kowalczyk (POL)	Artemor
1984	Joe Fargis (USA)	Touch of Class
1988	Pierre Durand (FRA)	Jappeloup
1992	Ludger Beerbaum (GER)	Classic Touch
1996	Ulrich Kirchhoff (GER)	Jus des Pommes
2000	Jeroen Dubbeldam (NED)	Sjiem

GRAND PRIX (JUMPING) TEAM
1912	Sweden
1920	Sweden
1924	Sweden
1928	Spain
1936	Germany
1948	Mexico
1952	Great Britain
1956	Germany
1960	Germany
1964	Germany
1968	Canada
1972	West Germany
1976	France
1980	USSR
1984	United States
1988	West Germany
1992	The Netherlands
1996	Germany
2000	Germany

THREE-DAY EVENT (INDIVIDUAL)
		MOUNT
1912	Axel Nordlander (SWE)	Lady Artist
1920	Helmer Mörner (SWE)	Germania
1924	Adolph van der Voort van Zijp (NED)	Silver Piece
1928	Charles Pahud de Mortanges (NED)	Marcroix
1932	Charles Pahud de Mortanges (NED)	Marcroix
1936	Ludwig Stubbendorff (GER)	Nurmi
1948	Bernard Chevallier (FRA)	Aiglonne
1952	Hans von Blixen-Finecke, Jr. (SWE)	Jubal
1956	Petrus Kastenman (SWE)	Iluster
1960	Lawrence Morgan (AUS)	Salad Days
1964	Mauro Checcoli (ITA)	Surbean
1968	Jean-Jacques Goyon (FRA)	Pitou
1972	Richard Meade (GBR)	Laurieston
1976	Edmund Coffin (USA)	Bally-Cor
1980	Federico Euro Roman (ITA)	Rossinan
1984	Mark Todd (NZL)	Charisma
1988	Mark Todd (NZL)	Charisma
1992	Matthew Ryan (AUS)	Kibah Tic Toc
1996	Robert Blyth Tait (NZL)	Ready Teddy
2000	David O'Connor (USA)	Custom Made

THREE-DAY EVENT (TEAM)
1912	Sweden
1920	Sweden
1924	The Netherlands
1928	The Netherlands
1932	United States
1936	Germany
1948	United States
1952	Sweden

Summer Olympic Games Champions (continued)

Equestrian sports (continued)

THREE-DAY EVENT (TEAM)
1956   Great Britain
1960   Australia
1964   Italy
1968   Great Britain
1972   Great Britain
1976   United States
1980   USSR
1984   United States
1988   West Germany
1992   Australia
1996   Australia
2000   Australia

HIGH JUMP		MOUNT
1900	Dominique Maximien Gardéres (FRA); Gian Giorgio Trissino (ITA) (*tied*)	Canela; Oreste

LONG JUMP		MOUNT
1900	Constant van Langhendonck (BEL)	Extra Dry

FIGURE RIDING (INDIVIDUAL)
1920   T. Bouckaert (BEL)

FIGURE RIDING (TEAM)
1920   Belgium

Fencing (men)

FOIL (INDIVIDUAL)
1896   Eugène-Henri Gravelotte (FRA)
1900   Émile Coste (FRA)
1904   Ramón Fonst (CUB)
1912   Nedo Nadi (ITA)
1920   Nedo Nadi (ITA)
1924   Roger Ducret (FRA)
1928   Lucien Gaudin (FRA)
1932   Gustavo Marzi (ITA)
1936   Giulio Gaudini (ITA)
1948   Jehan Buhan (FRA)
1952   Christian d'Oriola (FRA)
1956   Christian d'Oriola (FRA)
1960   Viktor Zhdanovich (URS)
1964   Egon Franke (POL)
1968   Ion Drimba (ROM)
1972   Witold Woyda (POL)
1976   Fabio dal Zotto (ITA)
1980   Vladimir Smirnov (URS)
1984   Mauro Numa (ITA)
1988   Stefano Cerioni (ITA)
1992   Philippe Omnes (FRA)
1996   Alessandro Puccini (ITA)
2000   Kim Young Ho (KOR)

FOIL (TEAM)
1904   Cuba
1920   Italy
1924   France
1928   Italy
1932   France
1936   Italy
1948   France
1952   France
1956   Italy
1960   USSR
1964   USSR
1968   France

Fencing (men) (continued)

FOIL (TEAM)
1972   Poland
1976   West Germany
1980   France
1984   Italy
1988   USSR
1992   Germany
1996   Russia
2000   France

INDIVIDUAL FOIL, PROFESSIONAL (MASTERS)
1896   Leon Pyrgos (GRE)
1900   Lucien Mérignac (FRA)

INDIVIDUAL FOIL, JUNIOR
1904   Arthur Fox (USA)

ÉPÉE (INDIVIDUAL)
1900   Ramón Fonst (CUB)
1904   Ramón Fonst (CUB)
1908   Gaston Alibert (FRA)
1912   Paul Anspach (BEL)
1920   Armand Massard (FRA)
1924   Charles Delporte (BEL)
1928   Lucien Gaudin (FRA)
1932   Giancarlo Cornaggia-Medici (ITA)
1936   Franco Riccardi (ITA)
1948   Luigi Cantone (ITA)
1952   Edoardo Mangiarotti (ITA)
1956   Carlo Pavesi (ITA)
1960   Giuseppe Delfino (ITA)
1964   Grigory Kriss (URS)
1968   Gyoso Kulcsar (HUN)
1972   Csaba Fenyvesi (HUN)
1976   Alexander Pusch (FRG)
1980   Johan Harmenberg (SWE)
1984   Philippe Boisse (FRA)
1988   Arnd Schmitt (FRG)
1992   Eric Srecki (FRA)
1996   Aleksandr Beketov (RUS)
2000   Pavel Kolobkov (RUS)

ÉPÉE (TEAM)
1908   France
1912   Belgium
1920   Italy
1924   France
1928   Italy
1932   France
1936   Italy
1948   France
1952   Italy
1956   Italy
1960   Italy
1964   Hungary
1968   Hungary
1972   Hungary
1976   Sweden
1980   France
1984   West Germany
1988   France
1992   Germany
1996   Italy
2000   Italy

INDIVIDUAL ÉPÉE, PROFESSIONAL (MASTERS)
1900   Albert Ayat (FRA)

Summer Olympic Games Champions (continued)

Fencing (men) (continued)

INDIVIDUAL ÉPÉE, OPEN (AMATEUR AND MASTERS)
1900   Albert Ayat (FRA)

SABRE (INDIVIDUAL)
1896   Ioannis Georgiadis (GRE)
1900   Georges de la Falaise (FRA)
1904   Manuel Díaz (CUB)
1908   Jeno Fuchs (HUN)
1912   Jeno Fuchs (HUN)
1920   Nedo Nadi (ITA)
1924   Sandor Posta (HUN)
1928   Odon Vitez Tersztyanszky (HUN)
1932   Gyorgy Piller (HUN)
1936   Endre Kabos (HUN)
1948   Aladar Gerevich (HUN)
1952   Pal Kovacs (HUN)
1956   Rudolph Karpati (HUN)
1960   Rudolph Karpati (HUN)
1964   Tibor Pezsa (HUN)
1968   Jerzy Pawlowski (POL)
1972   Viktor Sidyak (URS)
1976   Viktor Krovopuskov (URS)
1980   Viktor Krovopuskov (URS)
1984   Jean-François Lamour (FRA)
1988   Jean-François Lamour (FRA)
1992   Bence Szabo (HUN)
1996   Stanislav Pozdnyakov (RUS)
2000   Mihai Claudiu Covaliu (ROM)

SABRE (TEAM)
1908   Hungary
1912   Hungary
1920   Italy
1924   Italy
1928   Hungary
1932   Hungary
1936   Hungary
1948   Hungary
1952   Hungary
1956   Hungary
1960   Hungary
1964   USSR
1968   USSR
1972   Italy
1976   USSR
1980   USSR
1984   Italy
1988   Hungary
1992   Unified Team
1996   Russia
2000   Russia

INDIVIDUAL SABRE, PROFESSIONAL (MASTERS)
1900   Antonio Conte (ITA)

THREE-CORNERED SABRE
1906   Gustav Casmir (GER)

SINGLE STICK
1904   Albertson Van Zo Post (CUB)

Fencing (women)

FOIL (INDIVIDUAL)
1924   Ellen Osiier (DEN)
1928   Helene Mayer (GER)
1932   Ellen Preis (AUT)
1936   Ilona Schacherer-Elek (HUN)
1948   Ilona Elek (HUN)

Fencing (women) (continued)

FOIL (INDIVIDUAL)
1952   Irene Camber (ITA)
1956   Gillian Sheen (GBR)
1960   Adelheid Schmid (GER)
1964   Ildiko Ujlaki-Rejto (HUN)
1968   Yelena Novikova (URS)
1972   Antonella Ragno Lonzi (ITA)
1976   Ildiko Schwarczenberger (HUN)
1980   Pascale Trinquet (FRA)
1984   Jujie Luan (CHN)
1988   Anja Fichtel (FRG)
1992   Giovanna Trillini (ITA)
1996   Laura Gabriela Badea (ROM)
2000   Valentina Vezzali (ITA)

FOIL (TEAM)
1960   USSR
1964   Hungary
1968   USSR
1972   USSR
1976   USSR
1980   France
1984   West Germany
1988   West Germany
1992   Italy
1996   Italy
2000   Italy

ÉPÉE (INDIVIDUAL)
1996   Laura Flessel (FRA)
2000   Timea Nagy (HUN)

ÉPÉE (TEAM)
1996   France
2000   Russia

Field hockey

MEN
1908   Great Britain
1920   Great Britain
1928   India
1932   India
1936   India
1948   India
1952   India
1956   India
1960   Pakistan
1964   India
1968   Pakistan
1972   West Germany
1976   New Zealand
1980   India
1984   Pakistan
1988   Great Britain
1992   Germany
1996   The Netherlands
2000   The Netherlands

WOMEN
1980   Zimbabwe
1984   The Netherlands
1988   Australia
1992   Spain
1996   Australia
2000   Australia

Summer Olympic Games Champions (continued)

Golf

MEN, INDIVIDUAL
1900   Charles Sands (USA)
1904   George Lyon (CAN)

MEN, TEAM
1904   United States

WOMEN
1900   Margaret Abbott (USA)

Gymnastics (men)

COMBINED, OR ALL-AROUND (INDIVIDUAL)
1900   Gustave Sandras (FRA)
1904   Julius Lenhardt (USA)
1908   G. Alberto Braglia (ITA)
1912   G. Alberto Braglia (ITA)
1920   Giorgio Zampori (ITA)
1924   Leon Stukelj (YUG)
1928   Georges Miez (SUI)
1932   Romeo Neri (ITA)
1936   Karl-Alfred Schwarzmann (GER)
1948   Veikko Huhtanen (FIN)
1952   Viktor Chukarin (URS)
1956   Viktor Chukarin (URS)
1960   Boris Shakhlin (URS)
1964   Yukio Endo (JPN)
1968   Sawao Kato (JPN)
1972   Sawao Kato (JPN)
1976   Nikolay Andrianov (URS)
1980   Aleksandr Dityatin (URS)
1984   Koji Gushiken (JPN)
1988   Vladimir Artyomov (URS)
1992   Vitaly Shcherbo (UNT)
1996   Li Xiaosahuang (CHN)
2000   Aleksey Nemov (RUS)

COMBINED, OR ALL-AROUND (TEAM)
1920   Italy
1924   Italy
1928   Switzerland
1932   Italy
1936   Germany
1948   Finland
1952   USSR
1956   USSR
1960   Japan
1964   Japan
1968   Japan
1972   Japan
1976   Japan
1980   USSR
1984   United States
1988   USSR
1992   Unified Team
1996   Russia
2000   China

FLOOR EXERCISE
1932   Istvan Pelle (HUN)
1936   Georges Miez (SUI)
1948   Ferenc Pataki (HUN)
1952   William Thoresson (SWE)
1956   Valentin Muratov (URS)
1960   Nobuyuki Aihara (JPN)
1964   Franco Menichelli (ITA)
1968   Sawao Kato (JPN)
1972   Nikolay Andrianov (URS)
1976   Nikolay Andrianov (URS)

Gymnastics (men) (continued)

FLOOR EXERCISE
1980   Roland Brückner (GDR)
1984   Li Ning (CHN)
1988   Sergey Kharikov (URS)
1992   Li Xiaosahuang (CHN)
1996   Ioannis Melissanidis (GRE)
2000   Igors Vihrovs (LAT)

HORIZONTAL BAR
1896   Hermann Weingärtner (GER)
1904   Anton Heida (USA); Edward Henning (USA)
         (tied)
1924   Leon Stukelj (YUG)
1928   Georges Miez (SUI)
1932   Dallas Bixler (USA)
1936   Aleksanteri Saarvala (FIN)
1948   Josef Stalder (SUI)
1952   Jack Günthard (SUI)
1956   Takashi Ono (JPN)
1960   Takashi Ono (JPN)
1964   Boris Shakhlin (URS)
1968   Mikhail Voronin (URS); Akinori Nakayama
         (JPN) (tied)
1972   Mitsuo Tsukahara (JPN)
1976   Mitsuo Tsukahara (JPN)
1980   Stoyan Delchev (BUL)
1984   Shinji Morisue (JPN)
1988   Vladimir Artyomov (URS); Valery Lyukin (URS)
         (tied)
1992   Trent Dimas (USA)
1996   Andreas Wecker (GER)
2000   Aleksey Nemov (RUS)

PARALLEL BARS
1896   Alfred Flatow (GER)
1904   George Eyser (USA)
1924   August Güttinger (SUI)
1928   Ladislav Vacha (TCH)
1932   Romeo Neri (ITA)
1936   Konrad Frey (GER)
1948   Michael Reusch (SUI)
1952   Hans Eugster (SUI)
1956   Viktor Chukarin (URS)
1960   Boris Shakhlin (URS)
1964   Yukio Endo (JPN)
1968   Akinori Nakayama (JPN)
1972   Sawao Kato (JPN)
1976   Sawao Kato (JPN)
1980   Aleksandr Tkachyov (URS)
1984   Bart Conner (USA)
1988   Vladimir Artyomov (URS)
1992   Vitaly Shcherbo (UNT)
1996   Rustam Sharipov (UKR)
2000   Li Xiaopeng (CHN)

SIDE, OR POMMEL, HORSE
1896   Louis Zutter (SUI)
1904   Anton Heida (USA)
1924   Josef Wilhelm (SUI)
1928   Hermann Hänggi (SUI)
1932   Istvan Pelle (HUN)
1936   Konrad Frey (GER)
1948   Paavo Aaltonen (FIN); Veikko Huhtanen (FIN);
         Heikki Savolainen (FIN) (tied)
1952   Viktor Chukarin (URS)
1956   Boris Shakhlin (URS)
1960   Boris Shakhlin (URS); Eugen Ekman (FIN)
         (tied)

Summer Olympic Games Champions (continued)

Gymnastics (men) (continued)

SIDE, OR POMMEL, HORSE
1964 Miroslav Cerar (YUG)
1968 Miroslav Cerar (YUG)
1972 Viktor Klimenko (URS)
1976 Zoltan Magyar (HUN)
1980 Zoltan Magyar (HUN)
1984 Li Ning (CHN); Peter Vidmar (USA) (tied)
1988 Lyubomir Geraskov (BUL); Zsolt Borkai (HUN); Dmitry Bilozerchev (URS) (tied)
1992 Vitaly Shcherbo (UNT); Pae Gil-su (PRK) (tied)
1996 Li Donghua (SUI)
2000 Marius Urzica (ROM)

LONG, OR VAULTING, HORSE
1896 Karl Schuhmann (GER)
1904 Anton Heida (USA); George Eyser (USA) (tied)
1924 Frank Kriz (USA)
1928 Eugen Mack (SUI)
1932 Savino Guglielmetti (ITA)
1936 Karl-Alfred Schnorzmann (GER)
1948 Paavo Johannes Aaltonen (FIN)
1952 Viktor Chukarin (URS)
1956 Valentin Muratov (URS); Helmut Bantz (GER) (tied)
1960 Takashi Ono (JPN); Boris Shakhlin (URS) (tied)
1964 Haruhiro Yamashita (JPN)
1968 Mikhail Voronin (URS)
1972 Klaus Köste (GDR)
1976 Nikolay Andrianov (URS)
1980 Nikolay Andrianov (URS)
1984 Lou Yun (CHN)
1988 Lou Yun (CHN)
1992 Vitaly Shcherbo (UNT)
1996 Aleksey Nemov (RUS)
2000 Gervasio Deferr (ESP)

RINGS
1896 Ioannis Mitropoulos (GRE)
1904 Hermann Glass (USA)
1924 Francesco Martino (ITA)
1928 Leon Stukelj (YUG)
1932 George Gulack (USA)
1936 Alois Hudec (TCH)
1948 Karl Frei (SUI)
1952 Grant Shaginyan (URS)
1956 Albert Azaryan (URS)
1960 Albert Azaryan (URS)
1964 Takuji Hayata (JPN)
1968 Akinori Nakayama (JPN)
1972 Akinori Nakayama (JPN)
1976 Nikolay Andrianov (URS)
1980 Aleksandr Dityatin (URS)
1984 Li Ning (CHN); Koji Gushiken (JPN) (tied)
1988 Holger Behrendt (GDR); Dmitry Bilozerchev (URS) (tied)
1992 Vitaly Shcherbo (UNT)
1996 Yury Chechi (ITA)
2000 Szilveszter Csollany (HUN)

ROPE CLIMBING
1896 Nicolaos Andriakopoulos (GRE)
1904 George Eyser (USA)
1924 Bedrich Supcik (TCH)
1932 Raymond Bass (USA)

SWEDISH EXERCISES (TEAM)
1912 Sweden

Gymnastics (men) (continued)

SWEDISH EXERCISES (TEAM)
1920 Sweden

OPTIONAL EXERCISES (TEAM)
1912 Norway
1920 Denmark
1932 United States

PARALLEL BARS (TEAM)
1896 Germany

HORIZONTAL BARS (TEAM)
1896 Germany

CLUB SWINGING
1904 Edward Hennig (USA)
1932 George Roth (USA)

TUMBLING
1932 Rowland Wolfe (USA)

COMBINED COMPETITION (7 APPARATUS)
1904 Anton Heida (USA)

COMBINED COMPETITION (9 EVENTS)
1904 Adolf Spinnler (SUI)

PRESCRIBED APPARATUS (TEAM)
1904 United States
1908 Sweden
1912 Italy
1952 Sweden
1956 Hungary

MASS EXERCISES (TEAM)
1952 Finland

SIDE HORSE (VAULTS)
1924 Albert Séguin (FRA)

Gymnastics (women)

COMBINED, OR ALL-AROUND (INDIVIDUAL)
1952 Mariya Gorokhovskaya (URS)
1956 Larisa Latynina (URS)
1960 Larisa Latynina (URS)
1964 Vera Caslavska (TCH)
1968 Vera Caslavska (TCH)
1972 Lyudmila Turishcheva (URS)
1976 Nadia Comaneci (ROM)
1980 Yelena Davydova (URS)
1984 Mary-Lou Retton (USA)
1988 Yelena Shushunova (URS)
1992 Tatyana Gutsu (UNT)
1996 Liliya Podkopayeva (UKR)
2000 Simona Amanar (ROM)

COMBINED, OR ALL-AROUND (TEAM)
1928 The Netherlands
1936 Germany
1948 Czechoslovakia
1952 USSR
1956 USSR
1960 USSR
1964 USSR
1968 USSR
1972 USSR
1976 USSR
1980 USSR

Summer Olympic Games Champions (continued)

Gymnastics (women) (continued)

COMBINED, OR ALL-AROUND (TEAM)
1984 Romania
1988 USSR
1992 Unified Team
1996 United States
2000 Romania

BALANCE BEAM
1952 Nina Bocharova (URS)
1956 Agnes Keleti (HUN)
1960 Eva Bosakova (TCH)
1964 Vera Caslavska (TCH)
1968 Natalya Kuchinskaya (URS)
1972 Olga Korbut (URS)
1976 Nadia Comaneci (ROM)
1980 Nadia Comaneci (ROM)
1984 Ecaterina Szabo (ROM); Simona Pauca
     (ROM) *(tied)*
1988 Daniela Silivas (ROM)
1992 Tatyana Lysenko (UNT)
1996 Shannon Miller (USA)
2000 Liu Xuan (CHN)

UNEVEN PARALLEL BARS
1952 Margit Korondi (HUN)
1956 Agnes Keleti (HUN)
1960 Polina Astakhova (URS)
1964 Polina Astakhova (URS)
1968 Vera Caslavska (TCH)
1972 Karin Janz (GDR)
1976 Nadia Comaneci (ROM)
1980 Maxi Gnauck (GDR)
1984 Julianne McNamara (USA); Ma Yanhong
     (CHN) *(tied)*
1988 Daniela Silivas (ROM)
1992 Li Lu (CHN)
1996 Svetlana Khorkina (RUS)
2000 Svetlana Khorkina (RUS)

VAULTING HORSE
1952 Yekaterina Kalinchuk (URS)
1956 Larisa Latynina (URS)
1960 Margarita Nikolayeva (URS)
1964 Vera Caslavska (TCH)
1968 Vera Caslavska (TCH)
1972 Karin Janz (GDR)
1976 Nelli Kim (URS)
1980 Natalya Shaposhnikova (URS)
1984 Ecaterina Szabo (ROM)
1988 Svetlana Boginskaya (URS)
1992 Henrietta Onodi (HUN); Lavinia Milosovici
     (ROM) *(tied)*
1996 Simona Amanar (ROM)
2000 Yelena Zamolodchikova (RUS)

FLOOR EXERCISE
1952 Agnes Keleti (HUN)
1956 Larisa Latynina (URS); Agnes Keleti (HUN)
     (tied)
1960 Larisa Latynina (URS)
1964 Larisa Latynina (URS)
1968 Vera Caslavska (TCH); Larissa Petrik (URS)
     (tied)
1972 Olga Korbut (URS)
1976 Nelli Kim (URS)
1980 Nadia Comaneci (ROM); Nelli Kim (URS) *(tied)*
1984 Ecaterina Szabo (ROM)
1988 Daniela Silivas (ROM)

Gymnastics (women) (continued)

FLOOR EXERCISE
1992 Lavinia Milosovici (ROM)
1996 Liliya Podkopayeva (UKR)
2000 Yelena Zamolodchikova (RUS)

RHYTHMIC GYMNASTICS (INDIVIDUAL)
1984 Lori Fung (CAN)
1988 Marina Lobatch (URS)
1992 Aleksandra Timoshenko (UNT)
1996 Yekaterina Serebryanskaya (UKR)
2000 Yuliya Barsukova (RUS)

RHYTHMIC GYMNASTICS (TEAM)
1996 Spain
2000 Russia

HAND APPARATUS (TEAM)
1952 Sweden
1956 Hungary

Handball (team) (outdoors to 1972)

MEN
1936 Germany
1952 Sweden (demonstration)
1972 Yugoslavia
1976 USSR
1980 East Germany
1984 Yugoslavia
1988 USSR
1992 Unified Team
1996 Croatia
2000 Russia

WOMEN
1976 USSR
1980 USSR
1984 Yugoslavia
1988 South Korea
1992 South Korea
1996 Denmark
2000 Denmark

JEU DE PAUME (ROYAL TENNIS)
1908 Jay Gould (USA)

Judo (men)[9]

60 KG; 132.5 LB (EXTRA LIGHTWEIGHT)
1964 Takehide Nakatani (JPN)
1972 Takao Kawaguchi (JPN)
1976 Héctor Rodríguez (CUB)
1980 Thierry Rey (FRA)
1984 Shinji Hosokawa (JPN)
1988 Kim Jae-Yup (KOR)
1992 Nazim Guseynov (UNT)
1996 Tadahiro Nomura (JPN)
2000 Tadahiro Nomura (JPN)

66 KG; 145.5 LB (HALF-LIGHTWEIGHT)
1980 Nikolay Solodukhin (URS)
1984 Yoshiyuki Matsuoka (JPN)
1988 Lee Kyung Ken (KOR)
1992 Rogerio Sampaio Cardoso (BRA)
1996 Udo Quellmalz (GER)
2000 Huseyin Ozkan (TUR)

73 KG; 161 LB (LIGHTWEIGHT)
1972 Takao Kawaguchi (JPN)
1976 Héctor Rodríguez Torres (CUB)

Summer Olympic Games Champions (continued)

Judo (men)[9] (continued)

73 KG; 161 LB (LIGHTWEIGHT)
1980 Ezio Gamba (ITA)
1984 Ahn Byeong Keun (KOR)
1988 Marc Alexandre (FRA)
1992 Toshihiko Koga (JPN)
1996 Kenzo Nakamura (JPN)
2000 Giuseppe Maddaloni (ITA)

81 KG; 178.5 LB (HALF-MIDDLEWEIGHT)
1972 Toyojazu Nomura (JPN)
1976 Vladimir Nevzorov (URS)
1980 Shota Khabareli (URS)
1984 Frank Wieneke (FRG)
1988 Waldemar Legien (POL)
1992 Hidehiko Yoshida (JPN)
1996 Djamel Bouras (FRA)
2000 Makoto Takimoto (JPN)

90 KG; 198 LB (MIDDLEWEIGHT)
1964 Isao Okano (JPN)
1972 Shinobu Sekine (JPN)
1976 Isamu Sonoda (JPN)
1980 Jürg Röthlisberger (SUI)
1984 Peter Seisenbacher (AUT)
1988 Peter Seisenbacher (AUT)
1992 Waldemar Legien (POL)
1996 Jeon Ki-Young (KOR)
2000 Mark Huizinga (NED)

100 KG; 220.5 LB (HALF-HEAVYWEIGHT)
1972 Shota Chochoshvili (URS)
1976 Kazuhiro Ninomiya (JPN)
1980 Robert van de Walle (BEL)
1984 Ha Young Zoo (KOR)
1988 Aurelio Miguel (BRA)
1992 Antal Kovacs (HUN)
1996 Pawel Nastula (POL)
2000 Kosei Inoue (JPN)

OVER 100 KG; 220.5 LB (HEAVYWEIGHT)
1964 Isao Inokuma (JPN)
1972 Willem Ruska (NED)
1976 Sergey Novikov (URS)
1980 Angelo Parisi (FRA)
1984 Hitoshi Saito (JPN)
1988 Hitoshi Saito (JPN)
1992 David Khakhaleishvili (UNT)
1996 David Douillet (FRA)
2000 David Douillet (FRA)

OPEN (NO WEIGHT LIMIT)
1964 Antonius Johannes Geesink (NED)
1972 Willem Ruska (NED)
1976 Haruki Uemura (JPN)
1980 Dietmar Lorenz (GDR)
1984 Yasuhiro Yamashita (JPN)

Judo (women)[10]

48 KG; 106 LB (EXTRA LIGHTWEIGHT)
1992 Cecile Nowak (FRA)
1996 Kye Sun-Hi (PRK)
2000 Ryoko Tamura (JPN)

52 KG; 114.5 LB (HALF-LIGHTWEIGHT)
1992 Almudena Muñoz Martínez (ESP)
1996 Marie-Claire Restoux (FRA)
2000 Legna Verdecia (CUB)

Judo (women)[10] (continued)

57 KG; 125.5 LB (LIGHTWEIGHT)
1992 Miriam Blasco Soto (ESP)
1996 Driulis González Morales (CUB)
2000 Isabel Fernández (ESP)

63 KG; 139 LB (HALF-MIDDLEWEIGHT)
1992 Catherine Fleury-Vachon (FRA)
1996 Yuko Emoto (JPN)
2000 Severine Vandenhende (FRA)

70 KG; 154.5 LB (MIDDLEWEIGHT)
1992 Odalis Reve Jiménez (CUB)
1996 Cho Min-Sun (KOR)
2000 Sibelis Veranes (CUB)

78 KG; 172 LB (HALF-HEAVYWEIGHT)
1992 Kim Mi-Jung (KOR)
1996 Ulla Werbrouck (BEL)
2000 Tang Lin (CHN)

OVER 78 KG; 172 LB (HEAVYWEIGHT)
1992 Zhuang Xiaoyan (CHN)
1996 Sun Fuming (CHN)
2000 Yuan Hua (CHN)

Lacrosse
1904 Canada
1908 Canada

Modern pentathlon

INDIVIDUAL (MEN)
1912 Gösta Lilliehöök (SWE)
1920 Gustaf Dyrssen (SWE)
1924 Bo Lindman (SWE)
1928 Sven Thofelt (SWE)
1932 Johan Oxenstierna (SWE)
1936 Gotthardt Handrick (GER)
1948 William Grut (SWE)
1952 Lars-Goran Hall (SWE)
1956 Lars-Goran Hall (SWE)
1960 Ferenc Nemeth (HUN)
1964 Ferenc Torok (HUN)
1968 Björn Ferm (SWE)
1972 Andras Balczo (HUN)
1976 Janusz Pyciak-Peciak (POL)
1980 Anatoly Starostin (URS)
1984 Daniele Masala (ITA)
1988 Janos Martinek (HUN)
1992 Arkadiusz Skrzypaszek (POL)
1996 Aleksandr Parygin (KAZ)
2000 Dmitry Svatkovsky (RUS)

INDIVIDUAL (WOMEN)
2000 Stephanie Cook (GBR)

TEAM (MEN)
1952 Hungary
1956 USSR
1960 Hungary
1964 USSR
1968 Hungary
1972 USSR
1976 Great Britain
1980 USSR
1984 Italy
1988 Hungary
1992 Poland

Summer Olympic Games Champions (continued)

Motorboat racing

OPEN CLASS, 40 NAUTICAL MILES — **BOAT**
1908　Émile Thubron (FRA)　　*Camille*

8-METER CLASS, 40 NAUTICAL MILES
1908　Thomas Thornycroft, Bernard　　*Cyrinus*
　　　　Redwood (GBR)

UNDER 60-FOOT CLASS, 40 NAUTICAL MILES
1908　Thomas Thornycroft, Bernard　　*Cyrinus*
　　　　Redwood (GBR)

Polo
1900　team comprising members from Great
　　　　Britain and the United States
1908　Great Britain
1920　Great Britain
1924　Argentina
1936　Argentina

Rackets
SINGLES
1908　Evan Noel (GBR)

DOUBLES
1908　Vane Pennell, John Jacob Astor (GBR)

Roque
1904　Charles Jacobus (USA)

Rowing (men)[11]

SINGLE SCULLS		MIN:SEC
1900	Henri Barrelet (FRA)	7:35.6
1904	Frank Greer (USA)	10:08.5
1908	Harry Blackstaffe (GBR)	9:26.0
1912	William Kinnear (GBR)	7:47.6
1920	John Kelly, Sr. (USA)	7:35.0
1924	Jack Beresford (GBR)	7:49.2
1928	Henry Pearce (AUS)	7:11.0
1932	Henry Pearce (AUS)	7:44.4
1936	Gustav Schäfer (GER)	8:21.5
1948	Mervyn Wood (AUS)	7:24.4
1952	Yury Tyukalov (URS)	8:12.8
1956	Vyacheslav Ivanov (URS)	8:02.5
1960	Vyacheslav Ivanov (URS)	7:13.96
1964	Vyacheslav Ivanov (URS)	8:22.51
1968	Henri-Jan Wienese (NED)	7:47.80
1972	Yury Malyshev (URS)	7:10.12
1976	Pertti Karppinen (FIN)	7:29.03
1980	Pertti Karppinen (FIN)	7:09.61
1984	Pertti Karppinen (FIN)	7:00.24
1988	Thomas Lange (GDR)	6:49.86
1992	Thomas Lange (GER)	6:51.40
1996	Xeno Mueller (SUI)	6:44.85
2000	Robert Waddell (NZL)	6:48.90

DOUBLE SCULLS		MIN:SEC
1904	United States	10:03.2
1920	United States	7:09.0
1924	United States	6:34.0
1928	United States	6:41.4
1932	United States	7:17.4
1936	Great Britain	7:20.8
1948	Great Britain	6:51.3
1952	Argentina	7:32.2
1956	USSR	7:24.0
1960	Czechoslovakia	6:47.50
1964	USSR	7:10.66
1968	USSR	6:51.82

Rowing (men)[11] (continued)

DOUBLE SCULLS		MIN:SEC
1972	USSR	7:01.77
1976	Norway	7:13.20
1980	East Germany	6:24.33
1984	United States	6:36.87
1988	The Netherlands	6:21.13
1992	Australia	6:17.32
1996	Italy	6:16.98
2000	Slovenia	6:16.63

FOUR SCULLS		MIN:SEC
1976	East Germany	6:18.65
1980	East Germany	5:49.81
1984	West Germany	5:57.55
1988	Italy	5:53.37
1992	Germany	5:45.17
1996	Germany	5:56.93
2000	Italy	5:45.56

LIGHTWEIGHT DOUBLE SCULLS		MIN:SEC
1996	Switzerland	6:23.47
2000	Poland	6:21.75

PAIRS (WITHOUT COXSWAIN)		MIN:SEC
1904	United States	10:57.0
1908	Great Britain	9:41.0
1924	The Netherlands	8:19.4
1928	Germany	7:06.4
1932	Great Britain	8:00.0
1936	Germany	8:16.1
1948	Great Britain	7:21.1
1952	United States	8:20.7
1956	United States	7:55.4
1960	USSR	7:02.01
1964	Canada	7:32.94
1968	East Germany	7:26.56
1972	East Germany	6:53.16
1976	East Germany	7:23.31
1980	East Germany	6:48.01
1984	Romania	6:45.39
1988	Great Britain	6:36.84
1992	Great Britain	6:27.72
1996	Great Britain	6:20.09
2000	France	6:32.97

PAIRS (WITH COXSWAIN)		MIN:SEC
1900	The Netherlands/France	7:34.2
1920	Italy	7:56.0
1924	Switzerland	8:39.0
1928	Switzerland	7:42.6
1932	United States	8:25.8
1936	Germany	8:36.9
1948	Denmark	8:00.5
1952	France	8:28.6
1956	United States	8:26.1
1960	Germany	7:29.14
1964	United States	8:21.23
1968	Italy	8:04.81
1972	East Germany	7:17.25
1976	East Germany	7:58.99
1980	East Germany	7:02.54
1984	Italy	7:05.99
1988	Italy	6:58.79
1992	Great Britain	6:49.83

LIGHTWEIGHT FOURS (WITHOUT COXSWAIN)		MIN:SEC
1996	Denmark	6:09.58
2000	France	6:01.68

Summer Olympic Games Champions (continued)

Rowing (men)[11] (continued)

FOURS (WITHOUT COXSWAIN)

		MIN:SEC
1900	France	7:11.0
1904	United States	9:53.8
1908	Great Britain	8:34.0
1920	Great Britain	7:08.6
1928	Great Britain	6:36.0
1932	Great Britain	6:58.2
1936	Germany	7:01.8
1948	Italy	6:39.0
1952	Yugoslavia	7:16.0
1956	Canada	7:08.8
1960	United States	6:26.26
1964	Denmark	6:59.30
1968	East Germany	6:39.18
1972	East Germany	6:24.27
1976	East Germany	6:37.42
1980	East Germany	6:08.17
1984	New Zealand	6:03.48
1988	East Germany	6:03.11
1992	Australia	5:55.04
1996	Australia	6:06.37
2000	Great Britain	5:56.24

FOURS (WITH COXSWAIN)

		MIN:SEC
1900	Germany	5:59.0
1912	Germany	6:59.4
1920	Switzerland	6:54.0
1924	Switzerland	7:18.4
1928	Italy	6:47.8
1932	Germany	7.19.0
1936	Germany	7:16.2
1948	United States	6:50.3
1952	Czechoslovakia	7:33.4
1956	Italy	7:19.4
1960	Germany	6:39.12
1964	Germany	7:00.44
1968	New Zealand	6:45.62
1972	West Germany	6:31.85
1976	USSR	6:40.22
1980	East Germany	6:14.51
1984	Great Britain	6:18.64
1988	East Germany	6:10.74
1992	Romania	5:59.37

FOURS, INRIGGERS (WITH COXSWAIN)

		MIN:SEC
1912	Denmark	7:47.0

EIGHTS (WITH COXSWAIN)

		MIN:SEC
1900	United States	6:09.8
1904	United States	7:50.0
1908	Great Britain	7:52.0
1912	Great Britain	6:15.0
1920	United States	6:02.6
1924	United States	6:33.4
1928	United States	6:03.2
1932	United States	6:37.6
1936	United States	6:25.4
1948	United States	5:56.7
1952	United States	6:25.9
1956	United States	6:35.2
1960	Germany	5:57.18
1964	United States	6:18.23
1968	West Germany	6:07.00
1972	New Zealand	6:08.94
1976	East Germany	5:58.29
1980	East Germany	5:49.05
1984	Canada	5:41.32
1988	West Germany	5:46.05

Rowing (men)[11] (continued)

EIGHTS (WITH COXSWAIN)

		MIN:SEC
1992	Canada	5:29.53
1996	The Netherlands	5:42.74
2000	Great Britain	5:33.08

SIX-MAN NAVAL ROWING BOATS (2,000 METERS)

		MIN:SEC
1906	Italy	10:45.0

SIXTEEN-MAN NAVAL ROWING BOATS (3,000 METERS)

		MIN:SEC
1906	Greece	16:35.0

Rowing (women)[12]

SINGLE SCULLS

		MIN:SEC
1976	Christine Scheiblich (GDR)	4:05.56
1980	Sanda Toma (ROM)	3:40.69
1984	Valeria Racila (ROM)	3:40.68
1988	Jutta Behrendt (GDR)	7:47.19
1992	Elisabeta Lipa (ROM)	7:25.54
1996	Yekaterina Khodotovich (BLR)	7:32.21
2000	Yekaterina Khodotovich Karsten (BLR)	7:28.14

DOUBLE SCULLS

		MIN:SEC
1976	Bulgaria	3:44.36
1980	USSR	3:16.27
1984	Romania	3:26.75
1988	East Germany	7:00.48
1992	Germany	6:49.00
1996	Canada	6:56.84
2000	Germany	6:55.44

LIGHTWEIGHT DOUBLE SCULLS

		MIN:SEC
1996	Romania	7:12.78
2000	Romania	7:02.64

FOUR SCULLS

		MIN:SEC
1976	East Germany	3:29.99
1980	East Germany	3:15.32
1984	Romania	3:14.11
1988	East Germany	6:21.06
1992	Germany	6:20.18
1996	Germany	6:27.44
2000	Germany	6:19.58

PAIRS (WITHOUT COXSWAIN)

		MIN:SEC
1976	Bulgaria	4:01.22
1980	East Germany	3:30.49
1984	Romania	3:32.60
1988	Romania	7:28.13
1992	Canada	7:06.22
1996	Australia	7:01.39
2000	Romania	7:11.00

FOURS (WITH COXSWAIN [WITHOUT IN 1992])

		MIN:SEC
1976	East Germany	3:45.08
1980	East Germany	3:19.27
1984	Romania	3:19.3
1988	East Germany	6:56.0
1992	Canada	6:30.85

EIGHTS (WITH COXSWAIN)

		MIN:SEC
1976	East Germany	3:33.32
1980	East Germany	3:03.32
1984	United States	2:59.80
1988	East Germany	6:15.17
1992	Canada	6:02.62
1996	Romania	6:19.73

Summer Olympic Games Champions (continued)

Rowing (women)[12] (continued)

EIGHTS (WITH COXSWAIN)		**MIN:SEC**
2000	Romania	6:06.44

Rugby football

1900 | France |
1908 | Australia |
1920 | United States |
1924 | United States |

Sailing (yachting)

BOARDSAILING (WINDGLIDER/DIVISION II) (OPEN)
1984 | Stephan van den Berg (NED) |
1988 | Anthony Bruce Kendall (NZL) |

BOARDSAILING (MISTRAL FROM 1996) (MEN)
1992 | Franck David (FRA) |
1996 | Nikolaos Kaklamanakis (GRE) |
2000 | Christoph Sieber (AUT) |

BOARDSAILING (MISTRAL FROM 1996) (WOMEN)
1992 | Barbara Anne Kendall (NZL) |
1996 | Lee Lai Shan (HKG) |
2000 | Alessandra Sensini (ITA) |

SINGLE-HANDED DINGHY (EUROPE) (WOMEN)
1992 | Linda Andersen (NOR) |
1996 | Kristine Roug (DEN) |
2000 | Shirley Anne Robertson (GBR) |

SINGLE-HANDED DINGHY (LASER) (OPEN)
1996 | Robert Scheidt (BRA) |
2000 | Ben Ainslie (GBR) |

SINGLE-HANDED DINGHY (FINN FROM 1952) (MEN; OPEN UNTIL 1992)
1924 | Léon Huybrechts (BEL) |
1928 | Sven Thorell (SWE) |
1932 | Jacques Lebrun (FRA) |
1936 | Daniel Kagchelland (NED) |
1948 | Paul Elvström (DEN) |
1952 | Paul Elvström (DEN) |
1956 | Paul Elvström (DEN) |
1960 | Paul Elvström (DEN) |
1964 | Wilhelm Kuhweide (GER) |
1968 | Valentin Mankin (URS) |
1972 | Serge Maury (FRA) |
1976 | Jochen Schümann (GDR) |
1980 | Esko Rechardt (FIN) |
1984 | Russell Coutts (NZL) |
1988 | José Luis Doreste (ESP) |
1992 | José van der Ploeg (ESP) |
1996 | Mateusz Kusznierewicz (POL) |
2000 | Iain Percy (GBR) |

DOUBLE-HANDED DINGHY (470) (MEN)
1976 | West Germany |
1980 | Brazil |
1984 | Spain |
1988 | France |
1992 | Spain |
1996 | Ukraine |
2000 | Australia |

DOUBLE-HANDED DINGHY (470) (WOMEN)
1988 | United States |
1992 | Spain |
1996 | Spain |
2000 | Australia |

Sailing (yachting) (continued)

HIGH-PERFORMANCE DINGHY (49ER) (OPEN)
2000 | Finland |

MULTIHULL (TORNADO) (OPEN)
1976 | Great Britain |
1980 | Brazil |
1984 | New Zealand |
1988 | France |
1992 | France |
1996 | Spain |
2000 | Austria |

FLEET/MATCH RACE KEELBOAT (SOLING) (OPEN)
1972 | United States |
1976 | Denmark |
1980 | Denmark |
1984 | United States |
1988 | East Germany |
1992 | Denmark |
1996 | Germany |
2000 | Denmark |

TWO-PERSON KEELBOAT (STAR) (OPEN)
1932 | United States |
1936 | Germany |
1948 | United States |
1952 | Italy |
1956 | United States |
1960 | USSR |
1964 | The Bahamas |
1968 | United States |
1972 | Australia |
1980 | USSR |
1984 | United States |
1988 | Great Britain |
1992 | United States |
1996 | Brazil |
2000 | United States |

40-METER CLASS
1920 | Sweden |

30-METER CLASS
1920 | Sweden |

12-METER CLASS
1920 (old) | Norway |
1920 (new) | Norway |

OVER-10-METER CLASS
1900 | France |
1908 | Great Britain |
1912 | Norway |

10-METER CLASS
1900 | Germany |
1912 | Sweden |
1920 (old) | Norway |
1920 (new) | Norway |

8-METER CLASS
1900 | Great Britain |
1908 | Great Britain |
1912 | Norway |
1920 (old) | Norway |
1920 (new) | Norway |
1924 | Norway |
1928 | France |

Summer Olympic Games Champions (continued)

Sailing (yachting) (continued)

8-METER CLASS
1932   United States
1936   Italy

7-METER CLASS
1908   Great Britain
1920 (old) Great Britain

6.5-METER CLASS
1920 (new) The Netherlands

6-METER CLASS
1900   Switzerland
1908   Great Britain
1912   France
1920 (old) Belgium
1920 (new) Norway
1924   Norway
1928   Norway
1932   Sweden
1936   Great Britain
1948   United States
1952   United States

5.5-METER CLASS
1952   United States
1956   Sweden
1960   United States
1964   Australia
1968   Sweden

18-FOOT CENTERBOARD BOAT
1920   Great Britain

12-FOOT CENTERBOARD BOAT
1920   The Netherlands
1924   Belgium

12-FOOT DINGHY
1928   Sweden

MONOTYPE CLASS
1932   France

MONOTYPE CLASS "NÜRNBERG"
1936   The Netherlands

SWALLOW
1948   Great Britain

FIREFLY
1948   Denmark

SHARPIE
1956   New Zealand

DRAGON
1948   Norway
1952   Norway
1956   Sweden
1960   Greece
1964   Denmark
1968   United States
1972   Australia

TEMPEST
1972   USSR
1976   Sweden

Sailing (yachting) (continued)

FLYING DUTCHMAN
1960   Norway
1964   New Zealand
1968   Great Britain
1972   Great Britain
1976   West Germany
1980   Spain
1984   United States
1988   Denmark
1992   Spain

Shooting (men)

individual

TRAP (CLAY PIGEON) (OPEN 1968–92)
1900   Roger de Barbarin (FRA)
1908   Walter Ewing (CAN)
1912   James Graham (USA)
1920   Mark Arie (USA)
1924   Gyula Halasy (HUN)
1952   George Généreux (CAN)
1956   Galliano Rossini (ITA)
1960   Ion Dumitrescu (ROM)
1964   Ennio Mattarelli (ITA)
1968   John Braithwaite (GBR)
1972   Angelo Scalzone (ITA)
1976   Donald Haldeman (USA)
1980   Luciano Giovannetti (ITA)
1984   Luciano Giovannetti (ITA)
1988   Donald Monakov (URS)
1992   Petr Hrdlicka (TCH)
1996   Michael Constantine Diamond (AUS)
2000   Michael Constantine Diamond (AUS)

DOUBLE TRAP
1996   Russell Andrew Mark (AUS)
2000   Richard Faulds (GBR)

SKEET (OPEN UNTIL 1996)
1968   Yevgeny Petrov (URS)
1972   Konrad Wirnhier (FRG)
1976   Josef Panacek (TCH)
1980   Hans Kjeld Rasmussen (DEN)
1984   Matthew Dryke (USA)
1988   Axel Wegner (GDR)
1992   Zhang Shan (CHN)
1996   Ennio Falco (ITA)
2000   Mykola Milchev (UKR)

FREE PISTOL
1896   Sumner Paine (USA)
1900   Karl Konrad Röderer (SUI)
1912   Alfred Lane (USA)
1920   Carl Frederick (USA)
1936   Torsten Ullmann (SWE)
1948   Edwin Vásquez Cam (PER)
1952   Huelet Benner (USA)
1956   Pentti Tapio Linnosvuo (FIN)
1960   Aleksey Gushchin (URS)
1964   Väinö Johannes Markkanen (FIN)
1968   Grigory Kosykh (URS)
1976   Uwe Potteck (GDR)
1980   Aleksandr Melentev (URS)
1984   Xu Haifeng (CHN)
1988   Sorin Babii (ROM)
1992   Konstantin Lukachik (UNT)
1996   Boris Kokorev (RUS)
2000   Tanyu Kiryakov (BUL)

Summer Olympic Games Champions (continued)

Shooting (men) (continued)
individual (continued)

RAPID-FIRE PISTOL
1896	Joannis Phrangudis (GRE)
1900	Maurice Larrouy (FRA)
1908	Paul van Asbrock (BEL)
1912	Alfred Lane (USA)
1920	Guilherme Paraense (BRA)
1924	Henry Bailey (USA)
1932	Renzo Morigi (ITA)
1936	Cornelius van Oyen (GER)
1948	Karoly Takacs (HUN)
1952	Karoly Takacs (HUN)
1956	Stefan Petrescu (ROM)
1960	William McMillan (USA)
1964	Pentti Tapio Linnosvuo (FIN)
1968	Jozef Zapedzki (POL)
1972	Jozef Zapedzki (POL)
1976	Norbert Klaar (GDR)
1980	Corneliu Ion (ROM)
1984	Takeo Kamachi (JPN)
1988	Afanasy Kuzmin (URS)
1992	Ralf Schumann (GER)
1996	Ralf Schumann (GER)
2000	Sergey Alifirenko (RUS)

SMALL-BORE RIFLE (PRONE)
1908	Arthur Ashton Carnell (GBR)
1912	Frederick Hird (USA)
1920	Lawrence Nuesslein (USA)
1924	Pierre Coquelin de Lisle (FRA)
1932	Bertil Rönnmark (SWE)
1936	Willy Røgeberg (NOR)
1948	Arthur Cook (USA)
1952	Iosif Sarbu (ROM)
1956	Gerald Ouellette (CAN)
1960	Peter Kohnke (GER)
1964	Laszlo Hammerl (HUN)
1968	Jan Kurka (TCH)
1972	Ho Jun Li (PRK)
1976	Karlheinz Smieszek (FRG)
1980	Karoly Varga (HUN)
1984	Edward Etzel (USA)
1988	Miroslav Varga (TCH)
1992	Lee Eun Chul (KOR)
1996	Christian Klees (GER)
2000	Jonas Edman (SWE)

SMALL-BORE RIFLE (3 POSITIONS)
1952	Erling Kongshaug (NOR)
1956	Anatoly Bogdanov (URS)
1960	Viktor Shamburkin (URS)
1964	Lones Wesley Wigger (USA)
1968	Bernd Klingner (FRG)
1972	John Writer (USA)
1976	Lanny Bassham (USA)
1980	Viktor Vlasov (URS)
1984	Malcolm Cooper (GBR)
1988	Malcolm Cooper (GBR)
1992	Gratchia Petikian (UNT)
1996	Jean-Pierre Amat (FRA)
2000	Rajmond Debevec (SLO)

MOVING TARGET (RUNNING BOAR)
1900	Louis Debray (FRA)
1972	Yakov Zheleznyak (URS)
1976	Aleksandr Gazov (URS)
1980	Igor Sokolov (URS)
1984	Li Yuwei (CHN)

Shooting (men) (continued)
individual (continued)

MOVING TARGET (RUNNING BOAR)
1988	Tor Heiestad (NOR)
1992	Michael Jakosits (GER)
1996	Yang Ling (CHN)
2000	Yang Ling (CHN)

AIR RIFLE
1984	Philippe Heberle (FRA)
1988	Goran Maksimovic (YUG)
1992	Yury Fedkin (UNT)
1996	Artyom Khadzhibekov (RUS)
2000	Cai Yalin (CHN)

AIR PISTOL
1988	Tanyu Kiryakov (BUL)
1992	Wang Yifu (CHN)
1996	Roberto di Donna (ITA)
2000	Franck Dumoulin (FRA)

FREE RIFLE (300 M, 3 POSITIONS)
1908	Albert Helgerud (NOR)
1912	Paul René Colas (FRA)
1920	Morris Fisher (USA)
1924	Morris Fisher (USA)
1948	Emil Grünig (SUI)
1952	Anatoly Bogdanov (URS)
1956	Vasily Borisov (URS)
1960	Hubert Hammerer (AUT)
1964	Gary Lee Anderson (USA)
1968	Gary Lee Anderson (USA)
1972	Lones Wesley Wigger (USA)

ARMY RIFLE (300 M, 3 POSITIONS)
1896	Georgios Orphanidis (GRE)
1900	Emil Kellenberger (SUI)
1912	Sandor Prokop (HUN)

ARMY RIFLE (200 M)
1896	Pantelis Karasevdas (GRE)

FREE RIFLE (1,000 YD PRONE)
1908	Joshua Millner (GBR)

FULL-BORE RIFLE (300 M STANDING)
1900	Lars Madsen (DEN)

FULL-BORE RIFLE (300 M KNEELING)
1900	Konrad Staeheli (SUI)

FULL-BORE RIFLE (300 M PRONE)
1900	Achille Paroche (FRA)

FULL-BORE RIFLE (300 M)
1900	Emil Kellenberger (SUI)

RIFLE (300 M, 2 POSITIONS)
1920	Morris Fisher (USA)

RIFLE (300 M STANDING)
1920	Carl Osburn (USA)

RIFLE (600 M PRONE)
1920	Hugo Johansson (SWE)

RIFLE (300 M PRONE)
1920	Otto Olsen (NOR)

Summer Olympic Games Champions (continued)

Shooting (men) (continued)

individual (continued)

6-MILLIMETER SMALL GUN (OPEN REAR SIGHT)
1900 C. Grosett (FRA)

SMALL-BORE RIFLE (VANISHING TARGET)
1908 William Styles (GBR)
1912 Wilhelm Carlberg (SWE)

SMALL-BORE RIFLE (MOVING TARGET)
1908 John Francis Fleming (GBR)

RUNNING DEER (100 M SINGLE SHOT)
1908 Oscar Swahn (SWE)
1912 Alfred Swahn (SWE)
1920 Otto Olsen (NOR)
1924 John Boles (USA)

RUNNING DEER (100 M DOUBLE SHOT)
1908 Walter Winans (USA)
1912 Ake Lundeberg (SWE)
1920 Ole Andreas Lilloe-Olsen (NOR)
1924 Ole Andreas Lilloe-Olsen (NOR)

RUNNING DEER (100 M SINGLE AND DOUBLE SHOT)
1952 John Larsen (NOR)
1956 Vitaly Romanenko (URS)

LIVE PIGEON
1900 Léon de Lunden (BEL)

GAME SHOOTING
1900 Donald Mackintosh (AUS)

MILITARY REVOLVER (25 M)
1896 John Paine (USA)

MILITARY REVOLVER (20 M)
1906 Louis Richardet (SUI)
1906 (model 1873-74) Jean Fouconnier (FRA)

REVOLVER AND PISTOL
1900 Paul van Asbrock (BEL)
1908 Paul van Asbrock (BEL)
1912 Alfred Lane (USA)

DUELING PISTOL
1906 (20 m) Léon Moreaux (FRA)
1906 (25 m) Konstantinos Skarlatos (GRE)
1912 Alfred Lane (USA)

team
FREE RIFLE (300 M)
1908 Norway
1912 Sweden

ARMY RIFLE (300 M)
1900 Norway

ARMY RIFLE (ALL-AROUND)
1900 United States
1908 United States
1912 United States

FULL-BORE RIFLE (300 M)
1900 Switzerland

SMALL-BORE RIFLE
1900 Great Britain

Shooting (men) (continued)

team (continued)
SMALL-BORE RIFLE
1908 Great Britain
1920 United States
1924 France

SMALL-BORE RIFLE (VANISHING TARGET)
1912 Sweden

RIFLE (600 M PRONE)
1920 United States

RIFLE (300 M, 2 POSITIONS)
1920 United States

RIFLE (300 M STANDING)
1920 Denmark

RIFLE (300 M PRONE)
1920 United States

RIFLE (ALL-AROUND)
1920 United States
1924 United States

RUNNING DEER (SINGLE SHOT)
1908 Sweden
1912 Sweden
1920 Norway
1924 Norway

RUNNING DEER (DOUBLE SHOT)
1920 Norway
1924 Great Britain

CLAY PIGEON
1900 Great Britain
1908 Great Britain
1912 United States
1920 United States
1924 United States

REVOLVER
1900 Switzerland

PISTOL
1920 United States
1924 United States

REVOLVER AND PISTOL
1900 United States
1908 United States
1912 United States
1920 United States

DUELING PISTOL
1912 Sweden

Shooting (women)
TRAP (CLAY PIGEON)
2000 Daina Gudzineviciute (LTU)

DOUBLE TRAP
1996 Kim Rhode (USA)
2000 Pia Hansen (SWE)

SKEET
2000 Zemfira Meftakhetdinova (AZE)

Summer Olympic Games Champions (continued)

Shooting (women) (continued)

SPORT PISTOL

1984	Linda Thom (CAN)	
1988	Nino Salukvadze (URS)	
1992	Marina Logvinenko (UNT)	
1996	Li Duihong (CHN)	
2000	Maria Zdravkova Grozdeva (BUL)	

SMALL-BORE RIFLE (3 POSITIONS)

1984	Wu Xiao-Xuan (CHN)
1988	Silvia Sperber (FRG)
1992	Launi Meili (USA)
1996	Aleksandra Ivosev (YUG)
2000	Renata Mauer (POL)

AIR RIFLE

1984	Pat Spurgin (USA)
1988	Irina Chilova (URS)
1992	Yeo Kab Soon (KOR)
1996	Renata Mauer (POL)
2000	Nancy Johnson (USA)

AIR PISTOL

1988	Jasna Sekaric (YUG)
1992	Marina Logvinenko (UNT)
1996	Olga Klochneva (RUS)
2000	Tao Luna (CHN)

Softball

1996	United States
2000	United States

Swimming (men)

50-METER FREESTYLE — SEC

1988	Matthew Biondi (USA)	22.14
1992	Aleksandr Popov (RUS)	21.91
1996	Aleksandr Popov (RUS)	22.13
2000	Anthony Ervin (USA); Gary Hall, Jr. (USA) *(tied)*	21.98

100-METER FREESTYLE — MIN:SEC

1896	Alfred Hajos (HUN)	1:22.2
1904	Zoltan Halmay (HUN)	1:02.8[13]
1908	Charles Daniels (USA)	1:05.6
1912	Duke Paoa Kahanamoku (USA)	1:03.4
1920	Duke Paoa Kahanamoku (USA)	1:00.4
1924	Johnny Weissmuller (USA)	59.0
1928	Johnny Weissmuller (USA)	58.6
1932	Yasuji Miyazaki (JPN)	58.2
1936	Ferenc Csik (HUN)	57.6
1948	Walter Ris (USA)	57.3
1952	Clark Scholes (USA)	57.4
1956	Jon Henricks (AUS)	55.4
1960	John Devitt (AUS)	55.2
1964	Donald Schollander (USA)	53.4
1968	Michael Wenden (AUS)	52.2
1972	Mark Spitz (USA)	51.22
1976	Jim Montgomery (USA)	49.99
1980	Jörg Wöithe (GDR)	50.40
1984	Ambrose Gaines (USA)	49.80
1988	Matthew Biondi (USA)	48.63
1992	Aleksandr Popov (UNT)	49.02
1996	Aleksandr Popov (RUS)	48.74
2000	Pieter Van den Hoogenband (NED)	48.30

100 METER FREESTYLE FOR SAILORS — MIN:SEC

1896	Ioannis Malokinis (GRE)	2:20.4

Swimming (men) (continued)

200-METER FREESTYLE — MIN:SEC

1900	Fred Lane (AUS)	2:25.2
1904	Charles Daniels (USA)	2:44.2[14]
1968	Michael Wenden (AUS)	1:55.2
1972	Mark Spitz (USA)	1:52.78
1976	Bruce Furniss (USA)	1:50.29
1980	Sergey Koplyakov (URS)	1:49.81
1984	Michael Gross (FRG)	1:47.44
1988	Duncan Armstrong (AUS)	1:47.25
1992	Yevgeny Sadovy (UNT)	1:46.70
1996	Danyon Loader (NZL)	1:47.63
2000	Pieter Van den Hoogenband (NED)	1:45.35

400-METER FREESTYLE — MIN:SEC

1896	Paul Neumann (AUT)	8:12.6[15]
1904	Charles Daniels (USA)	6:16.2[16]
1908	Henry Taylor (GBR)	5:36.8
1912	George Hodgson (CAN)	5:24.4
1920	Norman Ross (USA)	5:26.8
1924	Johnny Weissmuller (USA)	5:04.2
1928	Victoriano Zorilla (ARG)	5:01.6
1932	Clarence Crabbe (USA)	4:48.4
1936	Jack Medica (USA)	4:44.5
1948	William Smith (USA)	4:41.0
1952	Jean Boiteux (FRA)	4:30.7
1956	Murray Rose (AUS)	4:27.3
1960	Murray Rose (AUS)	4:18.3
1964	Donald Schollander (USA)	4:12.2
1968	Michael Burton (USA)	4:09.0
1972	Bradford Cooper (AUS)	4:00.27
1976	Brian Goodell (USA)	3:51.93
1980	Vladimir Salnikov (URS)	3:51.31
1984	George DiCarlo (USA)	3:51.23
1988	Uwe Dassler (GDR)	3:46.95
1992	Yevgeny Sadovy (UNT)	3:45.00
1996	Danyon Loader (NZL)	3:47.97
2000	Ian Thorpe (AUS)	3:40.59

1,500-METER FREESTYLE — MIN:SEC

1896	Alfred Hajos (HUN)	18:22.2[17]
1900	Johnny Arthur Jarvis (GBR)	13:40.2[18]
1904	Emil Rausch (GER)	27:18.2[19]
1908	Henry Taylor (GBR)	22:48.4
1912	George Hodgson (CAN)	22:00.0
1920	Norman Ross (USA)	22:23.2
1924	Andrew Charlton (AUS)	20:06.6
1928	Arne Borg (SWE)	19:51.8
1932	Kusuo Kitamura (JPN)	19:12.4
1936	Noboru Terada (JPN)	19:13.7
1948	James McLane (USA)	19:18.5
1952	Ford Konno (USA)	18:30:0
1956	Murray Rose (AUS)	17:58.9
1960	John Konrads (AUS)	17:19.6
1964	Robert Windle (AUS)	17:01.7
1968	Michael Burton (USA)	16:38.9
1972	Michael Burton (USA)	15:52.58
1976	Brian Goodell (USA)	15:02.40
1980	Vladimir Salnikov (URS)	14:58.27
1984	Michael O'Brien (USA)	15:05.20
1988	Vladimir Salnikov (URS)	15:00.40
1992	Kieren Perkins (AUS)	14:43.48
1996	Kieren Perkins (AUS)	14:56.40
2000	Grant Hackett (AUS)	14:48.33

4,000-METER FREESTYLE — MIN:SEC

1900	Johnny Arthur Jarvis (GBR)	58:24

Summer Olympic Games Champions (continued)

Swimming (men) (continued)

880-YARD FREESTYLE		MIN:SEC
1904	Emil Rausch (GER)	13:11.4

1-MILE FREESTYLE		MIN:SEC
1904	Emil Rausch (GER)	27:18.2

100-METER BUTTERFLY		SEC
1968	Douglas Russell (USA)	55.9
1972	Mark Spitz (USA)	54.27
1976	Matt Vogel (USA)	54.35
1980	Pär Arvidsson (SWE)	54.92
1984	Michael Gross (FRG)	53.08
1988	Anthony Nesty (SUR)	53.00
1992	Pablo Morales (USA)	53.32
1996	Denis Pankratov (RUS)	52.27
2000	Lars Frölander (SWE)	52.00

200-METER BUTTERFLY		MIN
1956	William Yorzyk (USA)	2:19.3
1960	Michael Troy (USA)	2:12.8
1964	Kevin Berry (AUS)	2:06.6
1968	Carl Roble (USA)	2:08.7
1972	Mark Spitz (USA)	2:00.70
1976	Mike Bruner (USA)	1:59.23
1980	Sergey Fesenko (URS)	1:59.76
1984	Jonathan Sieben (AUS)	1:57.04
1988	Michael Gross (FRG)	1:56.94
1992	Mel Stewart (USA)	1:56.26
1996	Denis Pankratov (RUS)	1:56.51
2000	Tom Malchow (USA)	1:55.35

100-METER BACKSTROKE		MIN:SEC
1904	Walter Brack (GER)	1:16.8[20]
1908	Arno Bieberstein (GER)	1:24.6
1912	Harry Hebner (USA)	1:21.2
1920	Warren Paoa Kealoha (USA)	1:15.2
1924	Warren Paoa Kealoha (USA)	1:13.2
1928	George Kojac (USA)	1:08.2
1932	Masaji Kiynkawa (JPN)	1:08.6
1936	Adolph Kiefer (USA)	1:05.9
1948	Allen Stack (USA)	1:06.4
1952	Yoshinobu Oyakawa (JPN)	1:05.4
1956	David Theile (AUS)	1:02.2
1960	David Theile (AUS)	1:01.9
1968	Roland Matthes (GDR)	58.7
1972	Roland Matthes (GDR)	56.58
1976	John Naber (USA)	55.49
1980	Bengt Baron (SWE)	56.53
1984	Richard Carey (USA)	55.79
1988	Daichi Suzuki (JPN)	55.05
1992	Mark Tewksbury (CAN)	53.98
1996	Jeff Rouse (USA)	54.10
2000	Lenny Krayzelburg (USA)	53.72

200-METER BACKSTROKE		MIN:SEC
1900	Ernst Hoppenberg (GER)	2:47.0
1964	Jed Graef (USA)	2.10.3
1968	Roland Matthes (GDR)	2:09.6
1972	Roland Matthes (GDR)	2:02.82
1976	John Naber (USA)	1:59.19
1980	Sandor Wladar (HUN)	2:01.93
1984	Richard Carey (USA)	2:00.23
1988	Igor Polyansky (URS)	1:59.37
1992	Martin López-Zubero (ESP)	1:58.47
1996	Brad Bridgewater (USA)	1:58.54
2000	Lenny Krayzelburg (USA)	1:56.76

Swimming (men) (continued)

100-METER BREASTSTROKE		MIN:SEC
1968	Donald McKenzie (USA)	1:07.7
1972	Nobutaka Tagushi (JPN)	1:04.94
1976	John Hencken (USA)	1:03.11
1980	Duncan Goodhew (GBR)	1:03.34
1984	Steve Lundquist (USA)	1:01.65
1988	Adrian Moorhouse (GBR)	1:02.04
1992	Nelson Diebel (USA)	1:01.50
1996	Frederick Deburghgraeve (BEL)	1:00.65
2000	Domenico Fioravanti (ITA)	1:00.46

200-METER BREASTSTROKE		MIN:SEC
1908	Frederick Holman (GBR)	3:09.2
1912	Walter Bathe (GER)	3:01.8
1920	Hakan Malmroth (SWE)	3:04.4
1924	Robert Skelton (USA)	2:56.6
1928	Yoshiyuki Tsuruta (JPN)	2:48.8
1932	Yoshiyuki Tsuruta (JPN)	2:45.4
1936	Tetsuo Hamuro (JPN)	2:42.5
1948	Joseph Verdeur (USA)	2:39.3
1952	John Davies (AUS)	2:34.4
1956	Masaru Furukawa (JPN)	2:34.7
1960	William Mulliken (USA)	2:37.4
1964	Ian O'Brien (AUS)	2:27.8
1968	Felipe Muñoz (MEX)	2:28.7
1972	John Hencken (USA)	2:21.55
1976	David Wilkie (GBR)	2:15.11
1980	Robertas Zulpa (URS)	2:15.85
1984	Victor Davis (CAN)	2:13.34
1988	Jozsef Szabo (HUN)	2:13.52
1992	Mike Barrowman (USA)	2:10.16
1996	Norbert Rozsa (HUN)	2:12.57
2000	Domenico Fioravanti (ITA)	2:10.87

400-METER BREASTSTROKE		MIN:SEC
1904	Georg Zacharias (GER)	7:23.6[21]
1912	Walter Bathe (GER)	6:29.6
1920	Hakan Malmroth (SWE)	6:31.8

200-YARD RELAY		MIN:SEC
1904	United States	2:04.6

200-METER MEDLEY		MIN:SEC
1968	Charles Hickcox (USA)	2:12.0
1972	Gunnar Larsson (SWE)	2:07.17
1984	Alex Baumann (CAN)	2:01.42
1988	Tamas Darnyi (HUN)	2:00.17
1992	Tamas Darnyi (HUN)	2:00.76
1996	Attila Czene (HUN)	1:59.91
2000	Massimiliano Rosolino (ITA)	1:58.98

400-METER MEDLEY		MIN:SEC
1964	Richard William Roth (USA)	4:45.4
1968	Charles Hickcox (USA)	4:48.4
1972	Gunnar Larsson (SWE)	4:31.98
1976	Rod Strachan (USA)	4:23.68
1980	Aleksandr Sidorenko (URS)	4:22.89
1984	Alex Baumann (CAN)	4:17.41
1988	Tamas Darnyi (HUN)	4:14.75
1992	Tamas Darnyi (HUN)	4:14.23
1996	Tom Dolan (USA)	4:14.90
2000	Tom Dolan (USA)	4:11.76

4 × 100-METER MEDLEY RELAY		MIN:SEC
1960	United States	4:05.4
1964	United States	3:58.4
1968	United States	3:54.9
1972	United States	3:48.16

Summer Olympic Games Champions (continued)

Swimming (men) (continued)

4 × 100-METER MEDLEY RELAY

		MIN:SEC
1976	United States	3:42.22
1980	Australia	3:45.70
1984	United States	3:39.30
1988	United States	3:36.93
1992	United States	3:36.93
1996	United States	3:34.84
2000	United States	3:33.73

4 × 100-METER FREESTYLE RELAY

		MIN:SEC
1964	United States	3:33.2
1968	United States	3:31.7
1972	United States	3:26.42
1984	United States	3:19.03
1988	United States	3:16.53
1992	United States	3:16.74
1996	United States	3:15.41
2000	Australia	3:13.67

4 × 200-METER FREESTYLE RELAY

		MIN:SEC
1908	Great Britain	10:55.6
1912	Australia	10:11.2
1920	United States	10:04.4
1924	United States	9:53.4
1928	United States	9:36.2
1932	Japan	8:58.4
1936	Japan	8:51.5
1948	United States	8:46.0
1952	United States	8:31.1
1956	Australia	8:23.6
1960	United States	8:10.2
1964	United States	7:52.1
1968	United States	7:52.3
1972	United States	7:35.78
1976	United States	7:23.22
1980	USSR	7:23.50
1984	United States	7:15.69
1988	United States	7:12.51
1992	Unified Team	7:11.95
1996	United States	7:14.84
2000	Australia	7:07.05

60-METER UNDERWATER

		MIN:SEC (UNDERWATER)
1900	Charles de Vendeville (FRA)	1:08.4

200-METER OBSTACLE

		MIN:SEC
1900	Frederick Lane (AUS)	2:38.4

Swimming (women)

50-METER FREESTYLE

		SEC
1988	Kristin Otto (GDR)	25.49
1992	Yang Wenyi (CHN)	24.79
1996	Amy Van Dyken (USA)	24.87
2000	Inge de Bruijn (NED)	24.32

100-METER FREESTYLE

		MIN:SEC
1912	Fanny Durack (AUS)	1:22.2
1920	Ethelda Bleibtrey (USA)	1:13.6
1924	Ethel Lackie (USA)	1:12.4
1928	Albina Osipowich (USA)	1:11.0
1932	Helene Madison (USA)	1:06.8
1936	Hendrika Mastenbroek (NED)	1:05.9
1948	Greta Andersen (DEN)	1:06.3
1952	Katalin Szoke (HUN)	1:06.8
1956	Dawn Fraser (AUS)	1:02.0
1960	Dawn Fraser (AUS)	1:01.2
1964	Dawn Fraser (AUS)	59.5

Swimming (women) (continued)

100-METER FREESTYLE

		MIN:SEC
1968	Jan Henne (USA)	1:00.0
1972	Sandra Neilson (USA)	58.59
1976	Kornelia Ender (GDR)	55.65
1980	Barbara Krause (GDR)	54.79
1984	Carrie Steinseifer (USA); Nancy Hogshead (USA) (tied)	55.92
1988	Kristin Otto (GDR)	54.93
1992	Zhuang Yong (CHN)	54.64
1996	Le Jingyi (CHN)	54.50
2000	Inge de Bruijn (NED)	53.83

200-METER FREESTYLE

		MIN:SEC
1968	Debbie Meyer (USA)	2:10.5
1972	Shane Gould (AUS)	2:03.56
1976	Kornelia Ender (GDR)	1:59.26
1980	Barbara Krause (GDR)	1:58.33
1984	Mary Wayte (USA)	1:59.23
1988	Heike Friedrich (GDR)	1:57.65
1992	Nicole Haislett (USA)	1:57.90
1996	Claudia Poll (CRC)	1:58.16
2000	Susie O'Neill (AUS)	1:58.24

400-METER FREESTYLE

		MIN:SEC
1920	Ethelda Bleibtrey (USA)	4:34.0[22]
1924	Martha Norelius (USA)	6:02.2
1928	Martha Norelius (USA)	5:42.8
1932	Helene Madison (USA)	5:28.5
1936	Hendrika Mastenbroek (NED)	5:26.4
1948	Ann Curtis (USA)	5:17.8
1952	Valeria Gyenge (HUN)	5:12.1
1956	Lorraine Crapp (AUS)	4:54.6
1960	Susan Christina von Saltza (USA)	4:50.6
1964	Virginia Duenkel (USA)	4:43.3
1968	Debbie Meyer (USA)	4:31.8
1972	Shane Gould (AUS)	4:19.04
1976	Petra Thümer (GDR)	4:09.89
1980	Ines Diers (GDR)	4:08.76
1984	Tiffany Cohen (USA)	4:07.10
1988	Janet Evans (USA)	4:03.85
1992	Dagmar Hase (GER)	4:07.18
1996	Michelle Smith (IRE)	4:07.25
2000	Brooke Bennett (USA)	4:05.80

800-METER FREESTYLE

		MIN:SEC
1968	Debbie Meyer (USA)	9:24.0
1972	Keena Rothhammer (USA)	8:53.68
1976	Petra Thümer (GDR)	8:37.14
1980	Michelle Ford (AUS)	8:28.90
1984	Tiffany Cohen (USA)	8:24.95
1988	Janet Evans (USA)	8:20.20
1992	Janet Evans (USA)	8:25.52
1996	Brooke Bennett (USA)	8:27.89
2000	Brooke Bennett (USA)	8:19.67

100-METER BUTTERFLY

		MIN:SEC
1956	Shelley Mann (USA)	1:11.0
1960	Carolyn Schuler (USA)	1:09.5
1964	Sharon Stouder (USA)	1:04.7
1968	Lynette McClements (AUS)	1:05.5
1972	Mayumi Aoki (JPN)	1:03.34
1976	Kornelia Ender (GDR)	1:00.13
1980	Caren Metschuck (GDR)	1:00.42
1984	Mary Meagher (USA)	59.26
1988	Kristin Otto (GDR)	59.00
1992	Qian Hong (CHN)	58.62
1996	Amy Van Dyken (USA)	59.13
2000	Inge de Bruijn (NED)	56.61

Summer Olympic Games Champions (continued)

Swimming (women) (continued)

200-METER BUTTERFLY		MIN:SEC
1968	Aagje Kok (NED)	2:24.7
1972	Karen Moe (USA)	2:15.57
1976	Andrea Pollack (GDR)	2:11.41
1980	Ines Geissler (GDR)	2:10.44
1984	Mary Meagher (USA)	2:06.90
1988	Kathleen Nord (GDR)	2:09.51
1992	Summer Sanders (USA)	2:08.67
1996	Susie O'Neill (AUS)	2:07.76
2000	Misty Hyman (USA)	2:05.88

100-METER BACKSTROKE		MIN:SEC
1924	Sybil Bauer (USA)	1:23.2
1928	Maria Braun (NED)	1:22.0
1932	Eleanor Holm (USA)	1:19.4
1936	Dina Senff (NED)	1:18.9
1948	Karen-Margrete Harup (DEN)	1:14.4
1952	Joan Harrison (RSA)	1:14.3
1956	Judith Grinham (GBR)	1:12.9
1960	Lynn Burke (USA)	1:09.3
1964	Cathy Ferguson (USA)	1:07.7
1968	Kaye Hall (USA)	1:06.2
1972	Melissa Belote (USA)	1:05.78
1976	Urike Richter (GDR)	1:01.83
1980	Rica Reinisch (GDR)	1:00.86
1984	Theresa Andrews (USA)	1:02.55
1988	Kristin Otto (GDR)	1:00.89
1992	Krisztina Egerszegi (HUN)	1:00.68
1996	Beth Botsford (USA)	1:01.19
2000	Diana Mocanu (ROM)	1:00.21

200-METER BACKSTROKE		MIN:SEC
1968	Pokey Watson (USA)	2:24.8
1972	Melissa Belote (USA)	2:19.19
1976	Ulrike Richter (GDR)	2:13.43
1980	Rica Reinisch (GDR)	2:11.77
1984	Jolanda De Rover (NED)	2:12.38
1988	Krisztina Egerszegi (HUN)	2:09.29
1992	Krisztina Egerszegi (HUN)	2:07.06
1996	Krisztina Egerszegi (HUN)	2:07.83
2000	Diana Mocanu (ROM)	2:08.16

100-METER BREASTSTROKE		MIN:SEC
1968	Djurdjica Bjedov (YUG)	1:15.8
1972	Cathy Carr (USA)	1:13.58
1976	Hannelore Anke (GDR)	1:11.16
1980	Ute Geveniger (GDR)	1:10.22
1984	Petra van Staveren (NED)	1:09.88
1988	Tanya Dangalakova (BUL)	1:07.95
1992	Yelena Rudkovskaya (UNT)	1:08.00
1996	Penelope Heyns (RSA)	1:07.73
2000	Megan Quann (USA)	1:07.05

200-METER BREASTSTROKE		MIN:SEC
1924	Lucy Morton (GBR)	3:33.2
1928	Hilde Schrader (GER)	3:12.6
1932	Claire Dennis (AUS)	3:06.3
1936	Hideko Maehata (JPN)	3:03.6
1948	Petronella van Vliet (NED)	2:57.2
1952	Eva Szekely (HUN)	2:51.7
1956	Ursula Happe (GER)	2:53.1
1960	Anita Lonebrough (GBR)	2:49.5
1964	Galina Prozumenshchikova-Stepanova (URS)	2:46.4
1968	Sharon Wichman (USA)	2:44.4
1972	Beverley Whitfield (AUS)	2:41.71
1976	Marina Koshevaya (URS)	2:33.35
1980	Lina Kachushite (URS)	2:29.54

200-METER BREASTSTROKE		MIN:SEC
1984	Anne Ottenbrite (CAN)	2:30.38
1988	Silke Hörner (GDR)	2:26.71
1992	Kyoko Iwasaki (JPN)	2:26.65
1996	Penelope Heyns (RSA)	2:25.41
2000	Agnes Kovacs (HUN)	2:24.35

200-METER MEDLEY		MIN:SEC
1968	Claudia Kolb (USA)	2:24.7
1972	Shane Gould (AUS)	2:23.07
1984	Tracy Caulkins (USA)	2:12.64
1988	Daniela Hunger (GDR)	2:12.59
1992	Li Lin (CHN)	2:11.65
1996	Michelle Smith (IRE)	2:13.93
2000	Yana Klochkova (UKR)	2:10.68

400-METER MEDLEY		MIN:SEC
1964	Donna De Varona (USA)	5:18.7
1968	Claudia Kolb (USA)	5:08.5
1972	Gail Neall (AUS)	5:02.97
1976	Ulrike Tauber (GDR)	4:42.77
1980	Petra Schneider (GDR)	4:36.29
1984	Tracy Caulkins (USA)	4:39.24
1988	Janet Evans (USA)	4:37.76
1992	Krisztina Egerszegi (HUN)	4:36.54
1996	Michelle Smith (IRE)	4:39.18
2000	Yana Klochkova (UKR)	4:33.59

4 × 100-METER MEDLEY RELAY		MIN:SEC
1960	United States	4:41.1
1964	United States	4:33.9
1968	United States	4:28.3
1972	United States	4:20.75
1976	East Germany	4:07.95
1980	East Germany	4:06.67
1984	United States	4:08.34
1988	East Germany	4:03.74
1992	United States	4:02.54
1996	United States	4:02.88
2000	United States	3:58.30

4 × 200-METER FREESTYLE RELAY		MIN:SEC
1996	United States	7:59.87
2000	United States	7:57.80

4 × 100-METER FREESTYLE RELAY		MIN:SEC
1912	Great Britain	5:52.8
1920	United States	5:11.6
1924	United States	4:58.8
1928	United States	4:47.6
1932	United States	4:38.0
1936	The Netherlands	4:36.0
1948	United States	4:29.2
1952	Hungary	4:24.4
1956	Australia	4:17.1
1960	United States	4:08.9
1964	United States	4:03.8
1968	United States	4:02.5
1972	United States	3:55.19
1976	United States	3:44.82
1980	East Germany	3:42.71
1984	United States	3:43.43
1988	East Germany	3:40.63
1992	United States	3:39.46
1996	United States	3:39.29
2000	United States	3:36.61

Summer Olympic Games Champions (continued)

Swimming (women) (continued)

SYNCHRONIZED SWIMMING (INDIVIDUAL)
1984   Tracie Ruiz (USA)
1988   Carolyn Waldo (CAN)
1992   Kristen Babb-Sprague (USA);
         Sylvie Fréchette (CAN)[23]

SYNCHRONIZED SWIMMING (DUET)
1984   United States
1988   Canada
1992   United States
2000   Russia

SYNCHRONIZED SWIMMING (TEAM)
1996   United States
2000   Russia

Table tennis (men)

SINGLES
1988   Yoo Nam Kyu (KOR)
1992   Jan-Ove Waldner (SWE)
1996   Liu Guoliang (CHN)
2000   Kong Linghui (CHN)

DOUBLES
1988   China
1992   China
1996   China
2000   China

Table tennis (women)

SINGLES
1988   Chen Jing (CHN)
1992   Deng Yaping (CHN)
1996   Deng Yaping (CHN)
2000   Wang Nan (CHN)

DOUBLES
1988   South Korea
1992   China
1996   China
2000   China

Taekwondo (men)

58 KG (128 LBS)
2000   Michail Mouroutsos (GRE)

68 KG (150 LBS)
2000   Steven Lopez (USA)

80 KG (176.5 LBS)
2000   Angel Valodia Matos (CUB)

OVER 80 KG (176.5 LBS)
2000   Kim Kyong-Hun (KOR)

Taekwondo (women)

49 KG (108 LBS)
2000   Lauren Burns (AUS)

57 KG (125.5 LBS)
2000   Jung Jae-Eun (KOR)

67 KG (147.5 LBS)
2000   Lee Sun-Hee (KOR)

OVER 67 KG (147.5 LBS)
2000   Chen Zhong (CHN)

Tennis (men)

SINGLES
1896   John Pius Boland (GBR)
1900   Hugh (Laurie) Doherty (GBR)
1904   Beals Wright (USA)
1908   Josiah Ritchie (GBR)
1912   Charles Winslow (RSA)
1920   Louis Raymond (RSA)
1924   Vincent Richards (USA)
1988   Miloslav Mecir (TCH)
1992   Marc Rosset (SUI)
1996   Andre Agassi (USA)
2000   Yevgeny Kafelnikov (RUS)

DOUBLES
1896   John Pius Boland (GBR), Friedrich Thraun
         (GER)
1900   Hugh (Laurie) Doherty, Reginald Doherty
         (GBR)
1904   Edgar Leonard, Beals Wright (USA)
1908   George Hillyard, Reginald Doherty (GBR)
1912   Harold Kitson, Charles Winslow (RSA)
1920   Oswald Noel Turnbull, Maxwell Woosnam
         (GBR)
1924   Francis Hunter, Vincent Richards (USA)
1988   Kenneth Flach, Robert Seguso (USA)
1992   Boris Becker, Michael Stich (GER)
1996   Todd Woodbridge, Mark Woodforde (AUS)
2000   Sebastien Lareau, Daniel Nestor (CAN)

MIXED DOUBLES
1900   Charlotte Cooper, Reginald Doherty (GBR)
1912   Dora Köring, Heinrich Schomburgk (GER)
1920   Suzanne Lenglen, Max Décugis (FRA)
1924   Hazel Wightman, R. Norris Williams (USA)

Tennis (women)

SINGLES
1900   Charlotte Cooper (GBR)
1908   Dorothy Chambers-Lambert (GBR)
1912   Marguerite Broquedis (FRA)
1920   Suzanne Lenglen (FRA)
1924   Helen Wills-Moody (USA)
1988   Steffi Graf (FRG)
1992   Jennifer Capriati (USA)
1996   Lindsay Davenport (USA)
2000   Venus Williams (USA)

DOUBLES
1920   Winifred Margaret McNair, Kathleen McKane
         (GBR)
1924   Helen Wills-Moody, Hazel Wightman (USA)
1988   Zina Garrison, Pamela Shriver (USA)
1992   Gigi Fernandez, Mary Joe Fernandez (USA)
1996   Gigi Fernandez, Mary Joe Fernandez (USA)
2000   Serena Williams, Venus Williams (USA)

Tennis—Covered Courts (indoor tennis)

MEN'S SINGLES
1908   Arthur Gore (GBR)
1912   André Gobert (FRA)

MEN'S DOUBLES
1908   Arthur Gore, Herbert Roper-Barrett (GBR)
1912   Maurice Germot, André Gobert (FRA)

WOMEN'S SINGLES
1908   Gladys Eastlake-Smith (GBR)
1912   Edith Hannam (GBR)

Summer Olympic Games Champions (continued)

Tennis—Covered Courts (indoor tennis)
(continued)

MIXED DOUBLES
1912 Edith Hannam, Charles Dixon (GBR)

Triathlon (swim/bike/run) (men)
2000 Simon Whitfield (CAN)

Triathlon (swim/bike/run) (women)
2000 Brigitte McMahon (SUI)

Volleyball (men)
INDOOR
1964 USSR
1968 USSR
1972 Japan
1976 Poland
1980 USSR
1984 United States
1988 United States
1992 Brazil
1996 The Netherlands
2000 Yugoslavia

BEACH
1996 United States
2000 United States

Volleyball (women)
INDOOR
1964 Japan
1968 USSR
1972 USSR
1976 Japan
1980 USSR
1984 China
1988 USSR
1992 Cuba
1996 Cuba
2000 Cuba

BEACH
1996 Brazil
2000 Australia

Water polo (men)
1900 Great Britain
1904 United States
1908 Great Britain
1912 Great Britain
1920 Great Britain
1924 France
1928 Germany
1932 Hungary
1936 Hungary
1948 Italy
1952 Hungary
1956 Hungary
1960 Italy
1964 Hungary
1968 Yugoslavia
1972 USSR
1976 Hungary
1980 USSR
1984 Yugoslavia
1988 Yugoslavia
1992 Italy
1996 Spain
2000 Hungary

Water polo (women)
2000 Australia

Weight lifting (men)[24, 25]

		KG
56 KG (123.5 LB)		
1972	Zygmunt Smalcerz (POL)	337.5
1976	Aleksandr Varonin (URS)	242.5
1980	Kanybek Osmanaliyev (URS)	245.0
1984	Zeng Guoqiang (CHN)	235.0
1988	Sevdalin Marinov (BUL)	270.0
1992	Ivan Ivanov (BUL)	265.0
1996	Halil Mutlu (TUR)	287.5
2000	Halil Mutlu (TUR)	305.0
62 KG (136.5 LB)		**KG**
1948	Joseph de Pietro (USA)	307.5
1952	Ivan Udodov (URS)	315.0
1956	Charles Vinci (USA)	342.5
1960	Charles Vinci (USA)	345.0
1964	Aleksey Vakhonin (URS)	357.5
1968	Mohammad Nassiri (IRI)	367.5
1972	Imre Foldi (HUN)	377.5
1976	Norair Nurikian (BUL)	262.5
1980	Daniel Núñez (CUB)	275.0
1984	Wu Shude (CHN)	267.5
1988	Oksen Mirzoyan (URS)	292.5
1992	Chun Byung Kwan (KOR)	287.5
1996	Tang Ningsheng (CHN)	307.5
2000	Nikolay Pechalov (CRO)	325.0
69 KG (152 LB)		**KG**
1920	Frans de Haes (BEL)	220.0
1924	Pierino Gabetti (ITA)	402.5[26]
1928	Franz Andrysek (AUT)	287.5
1932	Raymond Suvigny (FRA)	287.5
1936	Anthony Terlazzo (USA)	312.5
1948	Mahmoud Fayad (EGY)	332.5
1952	Rafael Chimishkyan (URS)	337.5
1956	Isaac Berger (USA)	352.5
1960	Yevgeny Minayev (URS)	372.5
1964	Yoshinobu Miyake (JPN)	397.5
1968	Yoshinobu Miyake (JPN)	392.5
1972	Norair Nurikian (BUL)	402.5
1976	Nikolay Kolesnikov (URS)	285.0
1980	Viktor Mazin (URS)	290.0
1984	Chen Weiqiang (CHN)	282.5
1988	Naim Suleymanoglu (TUR)	342.5
1992	Naim Suleymanoglu (TUR)	320.0
1996	Naim Suleymanoglu (TUR)	335.0
2000	Galabin Bocvski (BUL)	357.5
70 KG (154.5 LB)		**KG**
1920	Alfred Neyland (EST)	257.5
1924	Edmond Décottignies (FRA)	440.0[26]
1928	Kurt Helbig (GER); Hans Haas (AUT) (tied)	322.5
1932	René Duverger (FRA)	325.0
1936	Mohamed Ahmed Mesbah (EGY); Robert Fein (AUT) (tied)	342.5
1948	Ibrahim Shams (EGY)	360.0
1952	Tommy Kono (USA)	362.5
1956	Igor Rybak (URS)	380.0
1960	Viktor Bushuyev (URS)	397.5
1964	Waldemar Baszanowski (POL)	432.5
1968	Waldemar Baszanowski (POL)	437.5
1972	Mukharbi Kirzhinov (URS)	460.0
1976	Pyotr Korol (URS)	305.0
1980	Yanko Rusev (BUL)	342.5
1984	Yao Jingyuan (CHN)	320.0

Summer Olympic Games Champions (continued)

Weight lifting (men)[24, 25] (continued)

70 KG (154.5 LB)   KG
1988	Joachim Kunz (GDR)	340.0
1992	Israil Militosyan (UNT)	337.5
1996	Zhan Xugang (CHN)	357.5

77 KG (170 LB)   KG
1920	Henri Gance (FRA)	245.0
1924	Carlo Galimberti (ITA)	492.5[26]
1928	François Roger (FRA)	335.0
1932	Rudolf Ismayr (GER)	345.0
1936	Khadr el Thouni (EGY)	387.5
1948	Frank Spellman (USA)	390.0
1952	Peter George (USA)	400.0
1956	Fyodor Bogdanovsky (URS)	420.0
1960	Aleksandr Kurynov (URS)	437.5
1964	Hans Zdrazila (TCH)	445.0
1968	Viktor Kurentsov (URS)	475.0
1972	Iordan Bikov (BUL)	485.0
1976	Iordan Mitkov (BUL)	335.0
1980	Asen Zlatev (BUL)	360.0
1984	Karl-Heinz Radschinsky (FRG)	340.0
1988	Borislav Gidikov (BUL)	375.0
1992	Fyodor Kassapu (UNT)	357.5
1996	Pablo Lara (CUB)	367.5
2000	Zhan Xugang (CHN)	367.5

85 KG (187.5 LB)   KG
1920	Ernest Cadine (FRA)	290.0
1924	Charles Rigoulot (FRA)	502.5[26]
1928	El Sayed Nosseir (EGY)	355.0
1932	Louis Hostin (FRA)	365.0
1936	Louis Hostin (FRA)	372.5
1948	Stanley Stanczyk (USA)	417.5
1952	Trofim Lomakin (URS)	417.5
1956	Tommy Kono (USA)	447.5
1960	Ireneusz Palinski (POL)	442.5
1964	Rudolph Plyukfelder (URS)	475.0
1968	Boris Selitsky (URS)	485.0
1972	Leif Jenssen (NOR)	507.5
1976	Valery Shary (URS)	365.0
1980	Yury Vardanyan (URS)	400.0
1984	Petre Becheru (ROM)	355.0
1988	Israil Arsamakov (URS)	377.5
1992	Pyrros Dimas (GRE)	370.0
1996	Pyrros Dimas (GRE)	392.5
2000	Pyrros Dimas (GRE)	390.0

94 KG (207 LB)   KG
1952	Norbert Schemansky (USA)	445.0
1956	Arkady Vorobyev (URS)	462.5
1960	Arkady Vorobyev (URS)	472.5
1964	Vladimir Golovanov (URS)	487.5
1968	Kaarlo Kangasniemi (FIN)	517.5
1972	Andon Nikolov (BUL)	525.0
1976	David Rigert (URS)	382.5
1980	Peter Baczako (HUN)	377.5
1984	Nicu Vlad (ROM)	392.5
1988	Anatoly Khrapaty (URS)	412.5
1992	Kakhi Kakhiashvili (UNT)	412.5
1996	Aleksey Petrov (RUS)	402.5
2000	Akakios Kakhiashvilis (GRE)	405.0

99 KG (218.5 LB)   KG
1980	Ota Zaremba (TCH)	395.0
1984	Rolf Milser (FRG)	385.0
1988	Pavel Kuznetsov (URS)	425.0
1992	Viktor Tregubov (UNT)	410.0
1996	Akakios Kakhiashvilis (GRE)	420.0

Weight lifting (men)[24, 25] (continued)

105 KG (231.5 LB)   KG
1972	Jan Talts (URS)	580.0
1976	Yury Zaytsev (URS)	385.0
1980	Leonid Taranenko (URS)	422.5
1984	Norberto Oberburger (ITA)	390.0
1988	Yury Zakharevitch (URS)	455.0
1992	Ronny Weller (GER)	432.5
1996	Timur Taymazov (UKR)	430.0
2000	Hossein Tavakoli (IRI)	425.0

OVER 105 KG (231.5 LB)   KG
1920	Filippo Bottino (ITA)	265.5
1924	Giuseppe Tonani (ITA)	517.5[26]
1928	Josef Strassberger (GER)	372.5
1932	Jaroslav Skobia (TCH)	380.0
1936	Josef Manger (GER)	410.0
1948	John Davis (USA)	452.5
1952	John Davis (USA)	460.0
1956	Paul Anderson (USA)	500.0
1960	Yury Vlasov (URS)	537.5
1964	Leonid Zhabotinsky (URS)	572.5
1968	Leonid Zhabotinsky (URS)	572.5
1972	Vasily Alekseyev (URS)	640.0
1976	Vasily Alekseyev (URS)	440.0
1980	Sultan Rakhmanov (URS)	440.0
1984	Dinko Lukin (AUS)	412.5
1988	Aleksandr Kurlovich (URS)	462.5
1992	Aleksandr Kurlovich (UNT)	450.0
1996	Andrey Chemerkin (RUS)	457.5
2000	Hossein Rezazadeh (IRI)	472.5

ONE-HAND LIFT (UNLIMITED CLASS)   KG
1896	Launceston Elliot (GBR)	71.0
1906	Josef Steinbach (AUT)	76.55

TWO-HAND LIFT (UNLIMITED CLASS)   KG
1896	Viggo Jensen (DEN)	111.5
1904	Perikles Kakousis (GRE)	111.7
1906	Dimitrios Tofalos (GRE)	142.4

ALL-AROUND DUMBBELLS (UNLIMITED CLASS)
1904	Oscar Osthoff (USA)

Weight lifting (women)

48 KG (106 LB)   KG
2000	Tara Nott (USA)	185.0

53 KG (117 LB)   KG
2000	Yang Xia (CHN)	225.0

58 KG (128 LB)   KG
2000	Soraya Jiménez Mendívil (MEX)	222.5

63 KG (139 LB)   KG
2000	Chen Xiaomin (CHN)	242.5

69 KG (152 LB)   KG
2000	Lin Weining (CHN)	242.5

75 KG (165.5 LB)   KG
2000	Maria Isabel Urrutia (COL)	245.0

OVER 75 KG (165.5 LB)   KG
2000	Ding Meiyuan (CHN)	300.0

Wrestling—Freestyle[24]

48 KG (106 LB)
1904	Robert Curry (USA)

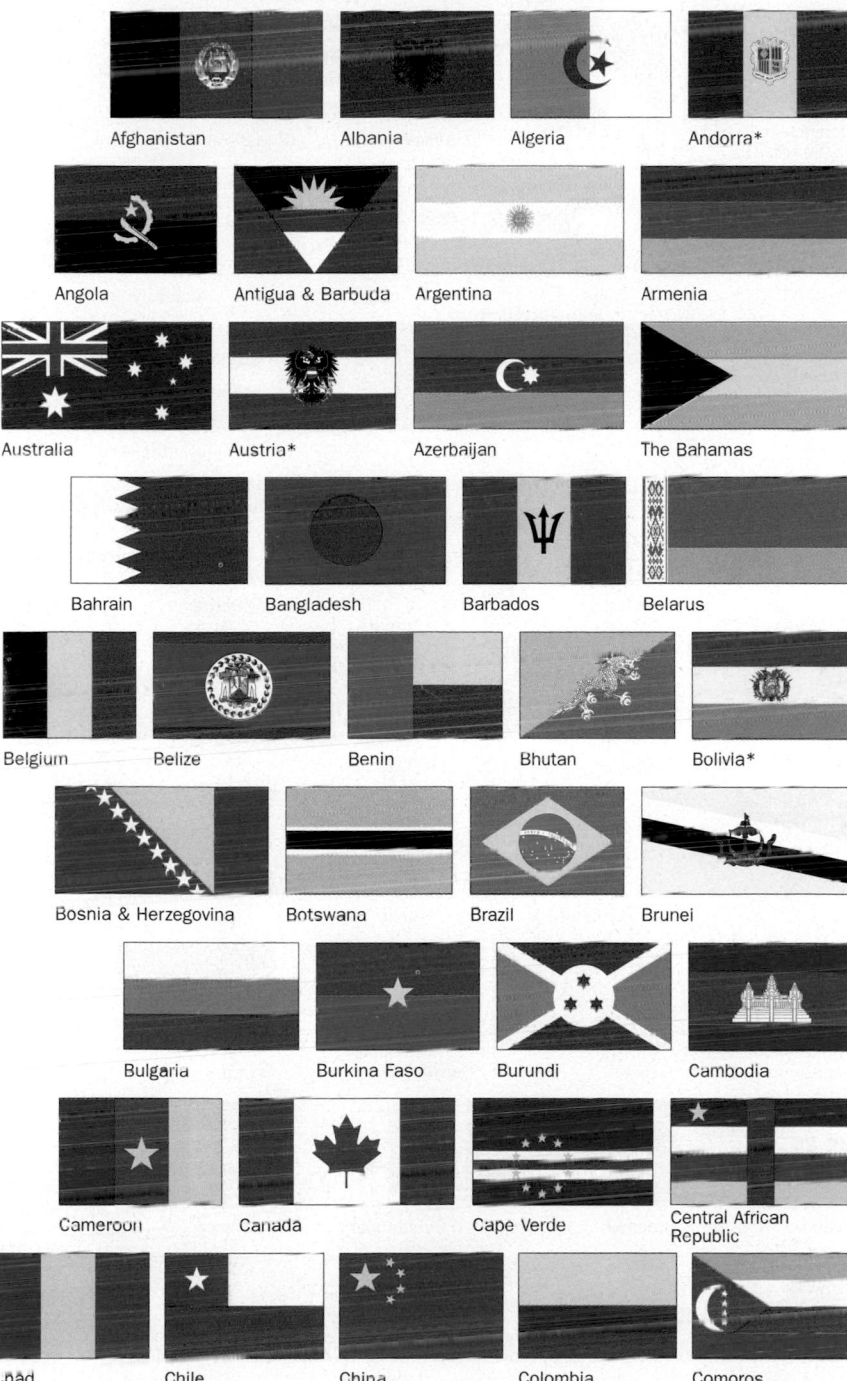

Afghanistan · Albania · Algeria · Andorra*

Angola · Antigua & Barbuda · Argentina · Armenia

Australia · Austria* · Azerbaijan · The Bahamas

Bahrain · Bangladesh · Barbados · Belarus

Belgium · Belize · Benin · Bhutan · Bolivia*

Bosnia & Herzegovina · Botswana · Brazil · Brunei

Bulgaria · Burkina Faso · Burundi · Cambodia

Cameroon · Canada · Cape Verde · Central African Republic

Chad · Chile · China · Colombia · Comoros

Civil flags are shown except where marked thus(*); in these cases, government flags are shown in order to illustrate emblems. Both styles are official national flags.

Plate 2   FLAGS OF THE WORLD

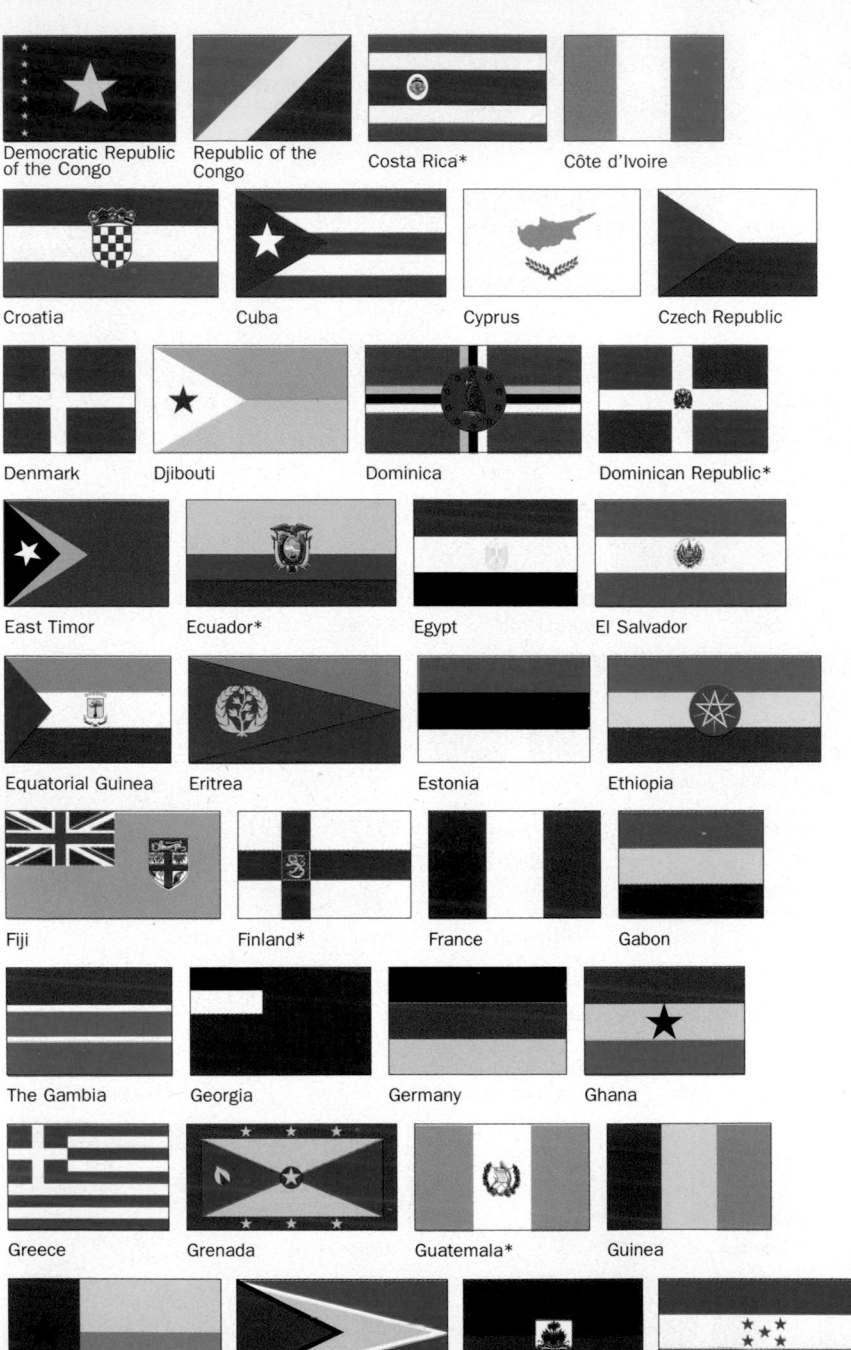

Democratic Republic of the Congo

Republic of the Congo

Costa Rica*

Côte d'Ivoire

Croatia

Cuba

Cyprus

Czech Republic

Denmark

Djibouti

Dominica

Dominican Republic*

East Timor

Ecuador*

Egypt

El Salvador

Equatorial Guinea

Eritrea

Estonia

Ethiopia

Fiji

Finland*

France

Gabon

The Gambia

Georgia

Germany

Ghana

Greece

Grenada

Guatemala*

Guinea

Guinea-Bissau

Guyana

Haiti*

Honduras

Civil flags are shown except where marked thus(*); in these cases, government flags are shown in order to illustrate emblems. Both styles are official national flags.

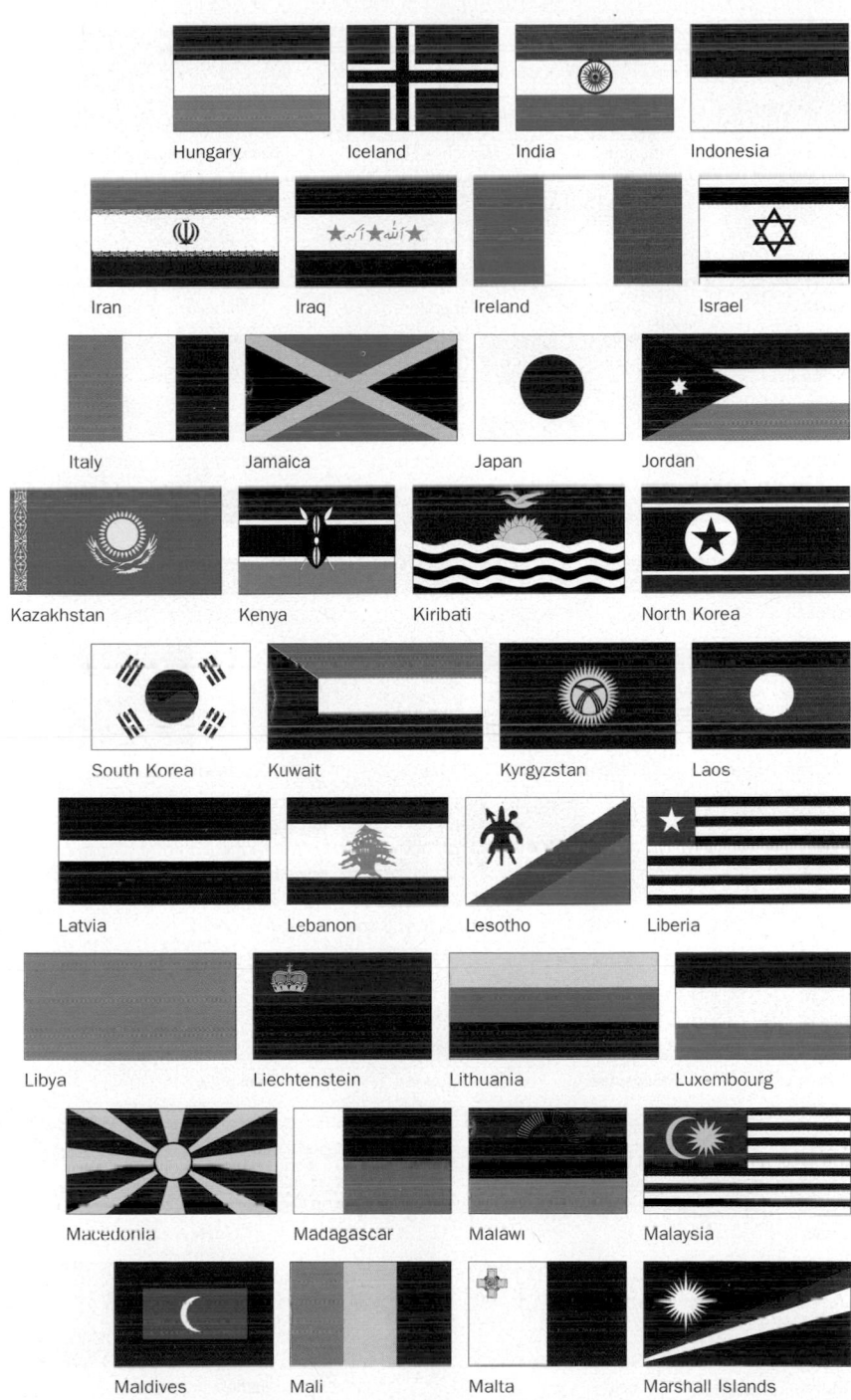

Hungary   Iceland   India   Indonesia

Iran   Iraq   Ireland   Israel

Italy   Jamaica   Japan   Jordan

Kazakhstan   Kenya   Kiribati   North Korea

South Korea   Kuwait   Kyrgyzstan   Laos

Latvia   Lebanon   Lesotho   Liberia

Libya   Liechtenstein   Lithuania   Luxembourg

Macedonia   Madagascar   Malawi   Malaysia

Maldives   Mali   Malta   Marshall Islands

Civil flags are shown except where marked thus(*); in these cases, government flags are shown in order to illustrate emblems. Both styles are official national flags.

Plate 4 — FLAGS OF THE WORLD

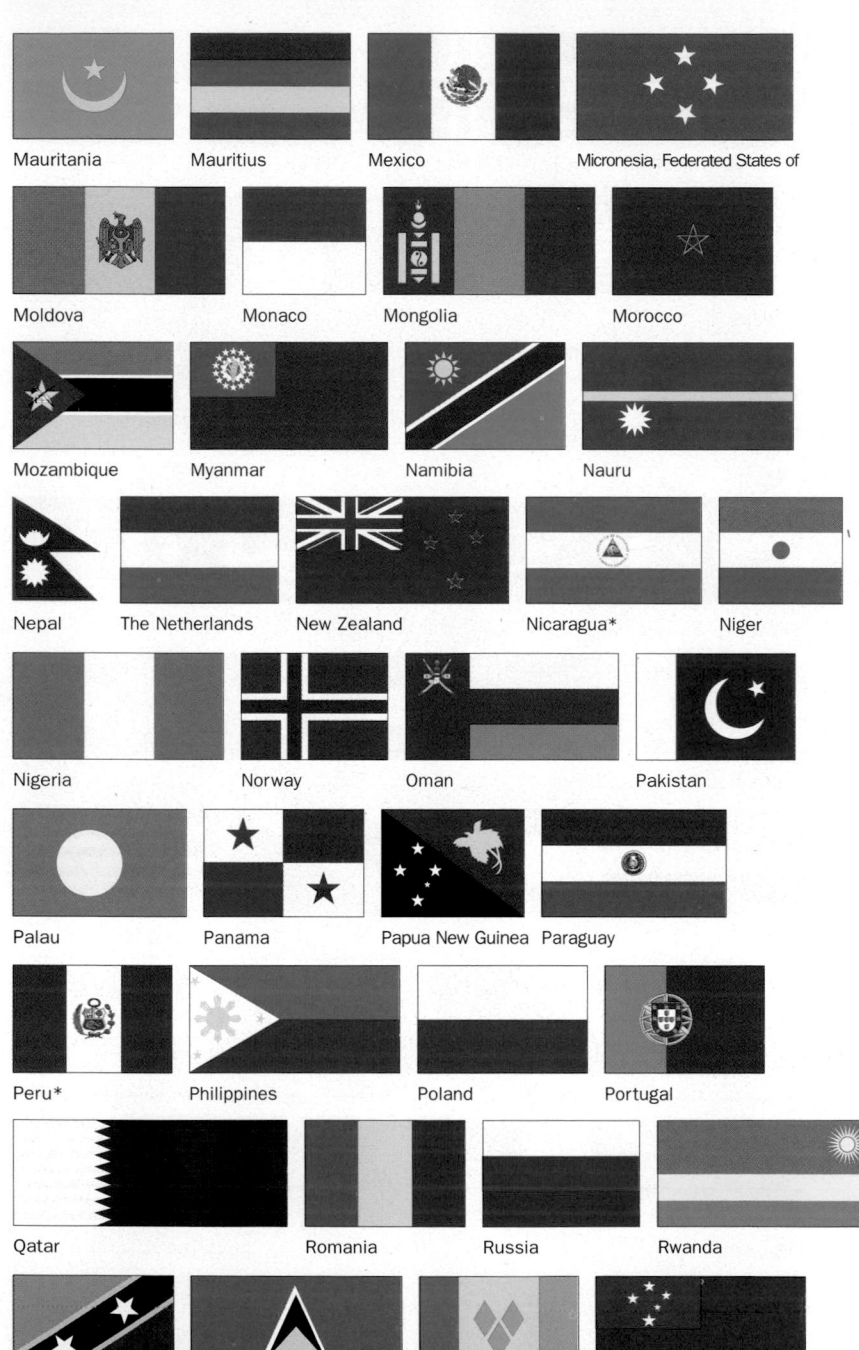

Mauritania   Mauritius   Mexico   Micronesia, Federated States of

Moldova   Monaco   Mongolia   Morocco

Mozambique   Myanmar   Namibia   Nauru

Nepal   The Netherlands   New Zealand   Nicaragua*   Niger

Nigeria   Norway   Oman   Pakistan

Palau   Panama   Papua New Guinea   Paraguay

Peru*   Philippines   Poland   Portugal

Qatar   Romania   Russia   Rwanda

St. Kitts & Nevis   St. Lucia   St. Vincent & the Grenadines   Samoa

Civil flags are shown except where marked thus(*); in these cases, government flags are shown in order to illustrate emblems. Both styles are official national flags.

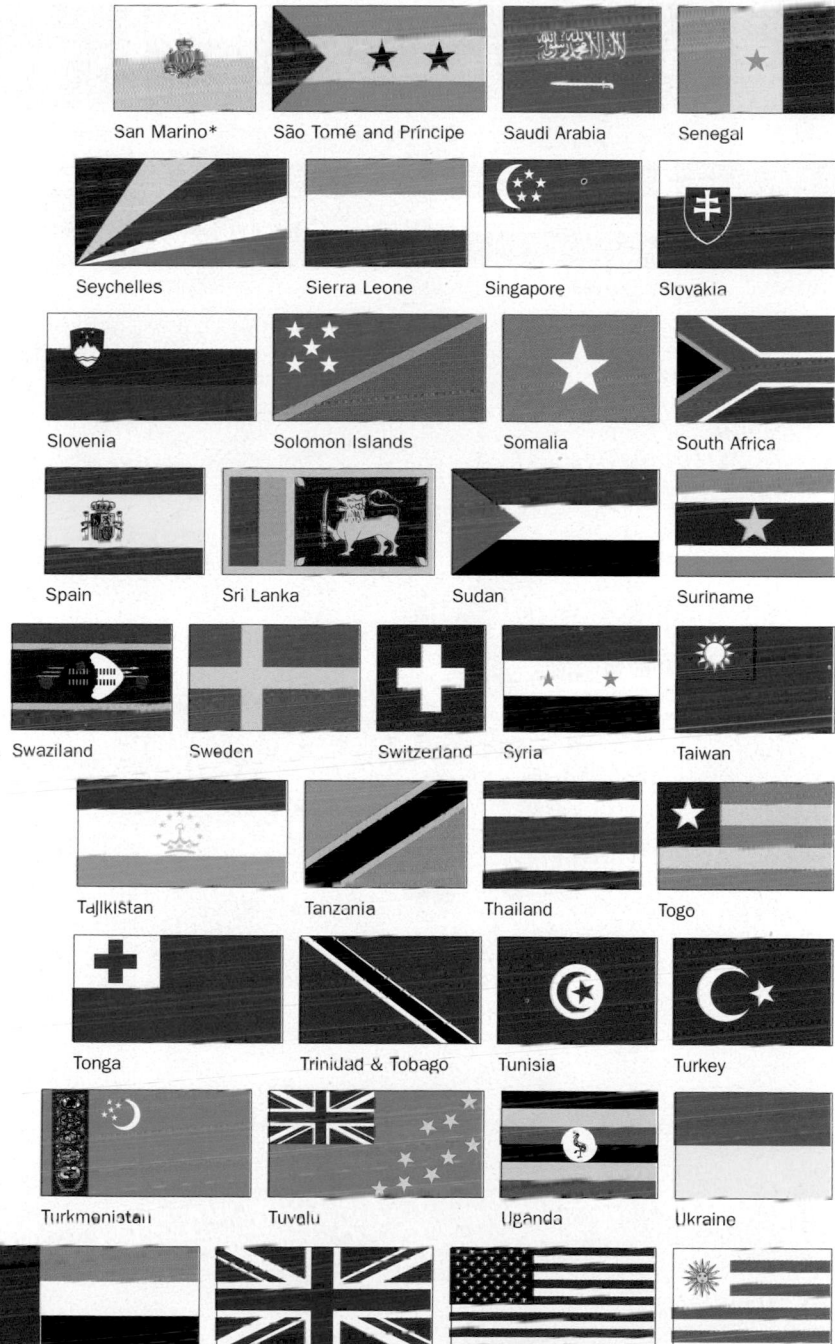

San Marino*   São Tomé and Príncipe   Saudi Arabia   Senegal

Seychelles   Sierra Leone   Singapore   Slovakia

Slovenia   Solomon Islands   Somalia   South Africa

Spain   Sri Lanka   Sudan   Suriname

Swaziland   Sweden   Switzerland   Syria   Taiwan

Tajikistan   Tanzania   Thailand   Togo

Tonga   Trinidad & Tobago   Tunisia   Turkey

Turkmenistan   Tuvalu   Uganda   Ukraine

United Arab Emirates   United Kingdom   United States   Uruguay

Civil flags are shown except where marked thus(*); in these cases, government flags are shown in order to illustrate emblems. Both styles are official national flags.

Plate 6 FLAGS OF THE WORLD/WORLD MAPS

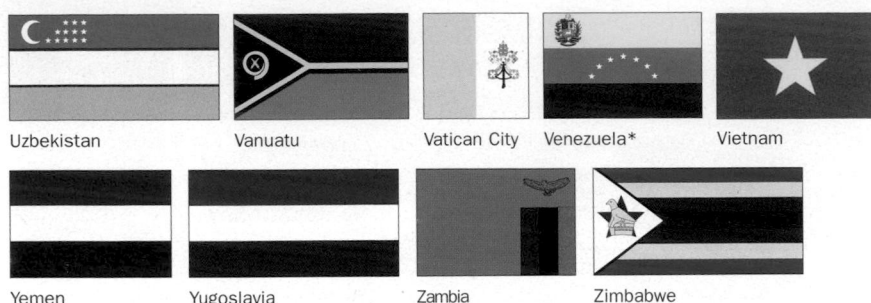

Uzbekistan Vanuatu Vatican City Venezuela* Vietnam

Yemen Yugoslavia Zambia Zimbabwe

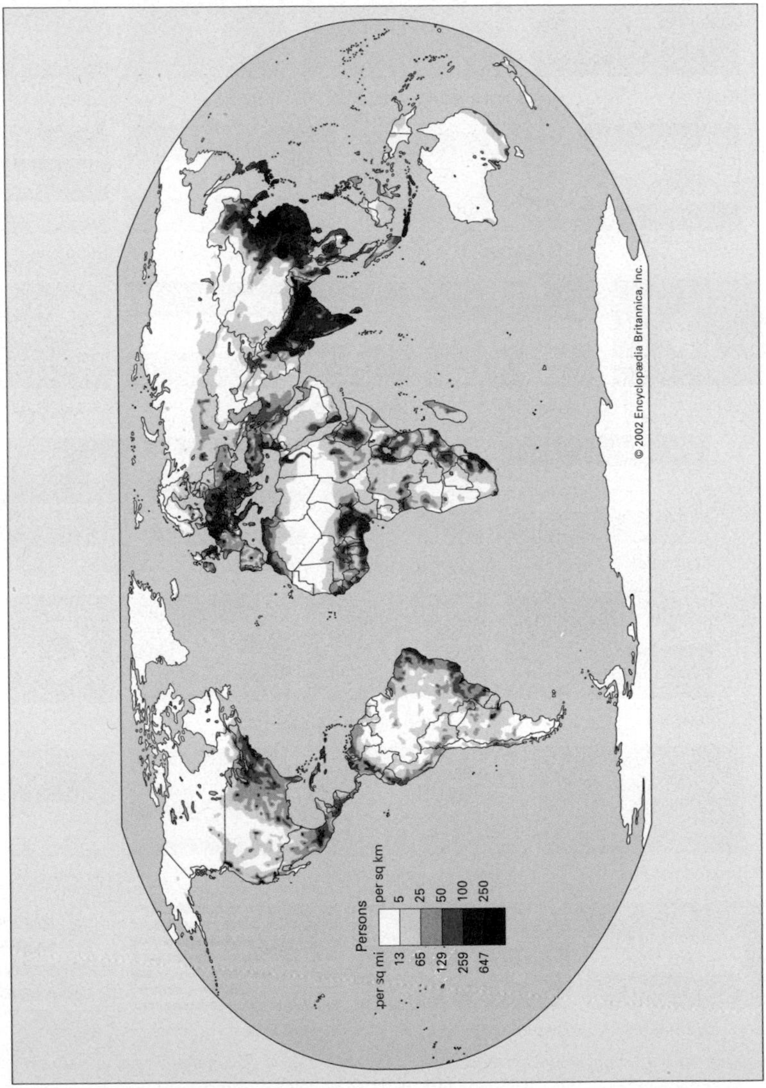

© 2002 Encyclopædia Britannica, Inc.

World Population Density

Persons

per sq mi — per sq km

13 — 5

65 — 25

129 — 50

259 — 100

647 — 250

World Religions

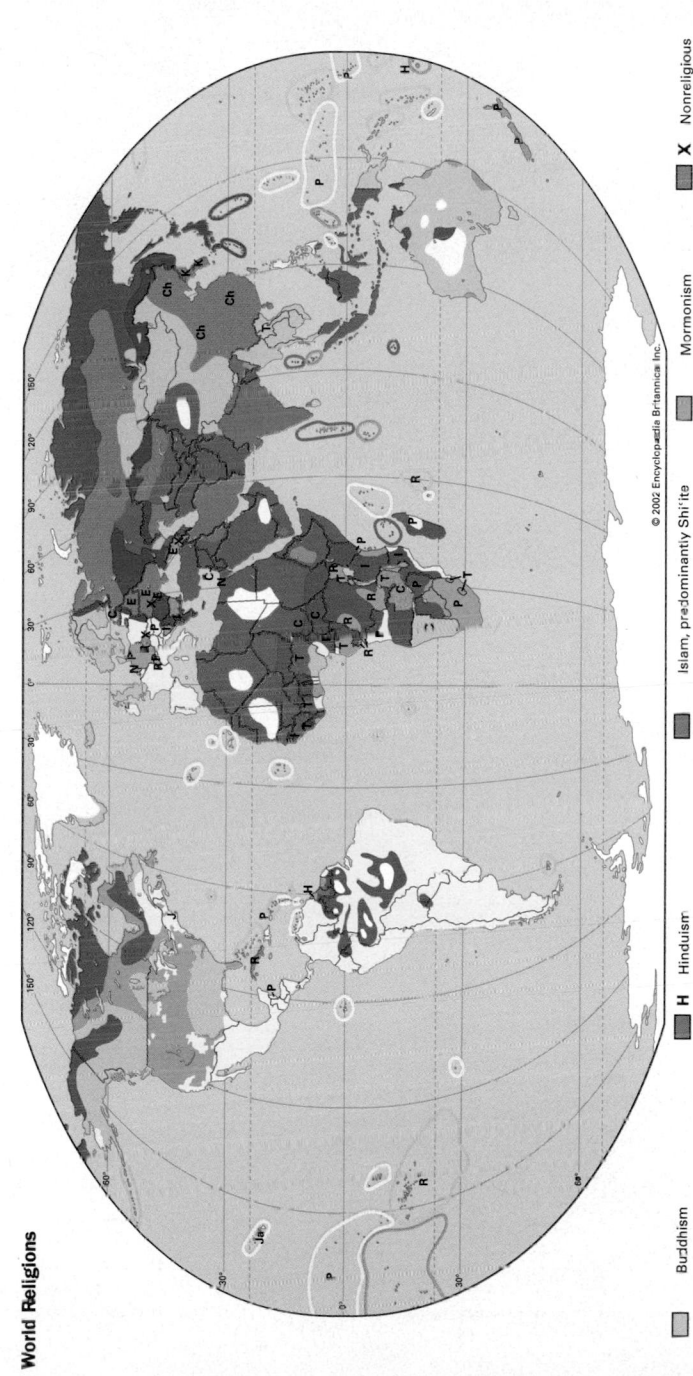

© 2002 Encyclopaedia Britannica Inc.

Buddhism

Ch Chinese religions[1]

C Christianity, undifferentiated by branch[2]

E Eastern Orthodoxy[3]

H Hinduism

N Independent churches of Eastern Christianity[4]

T Indigenous (tribal) religions

I Islam, predominantly Sunni

Islam, predominantly Shi'ite

Ja Japanese religions[1]

J Judaism

K Korean religions[1]

Mormonism

Sikhism

P Protestantism

R Roman Catholicism

X Nonreligious

No dominant religion

Uninhabited

Note:
The majority of the inhabitants in each of the areas colored on the map share the religious tradition indicated. Letter symbols show religious traditions shared by at least 25 percent of the inhabitants within areas no smaller than 1,000 square miles. Therefore minority religions or city dwellers have generally not been represented.

Footnotes:
[1] In certain eastern Asian areas, many of the people have plural religious affiliations. Chinese and Korean religions include Buddhism, Taoism, Confucianism, and folk cults. The Japanese religions include Shinto and Buddhism, neither predominant.
[2] Chiefly mingled Protestantism and Roman Catholicism.
[3] Including Greek and Russian Orthodox Christianity.
[4] Including Armenian, Coptic, Ethiopian, East and West Syrian.

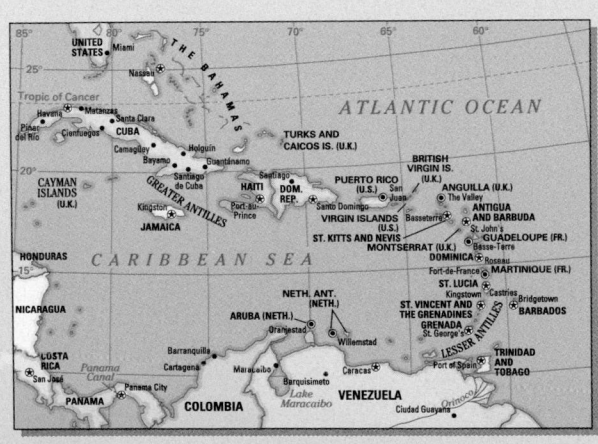
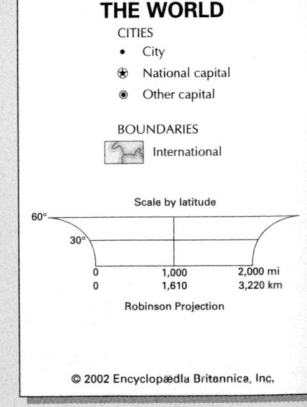

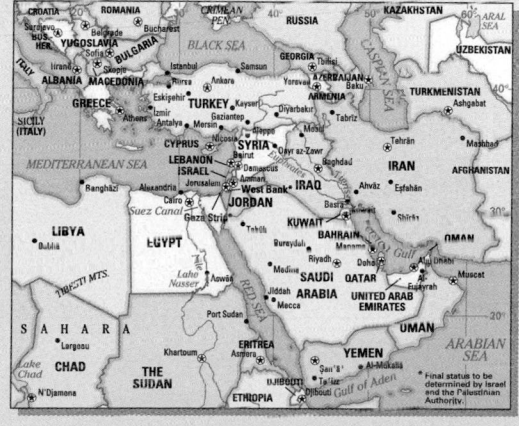

Plate 10   **WORLD MAPS**

Africa

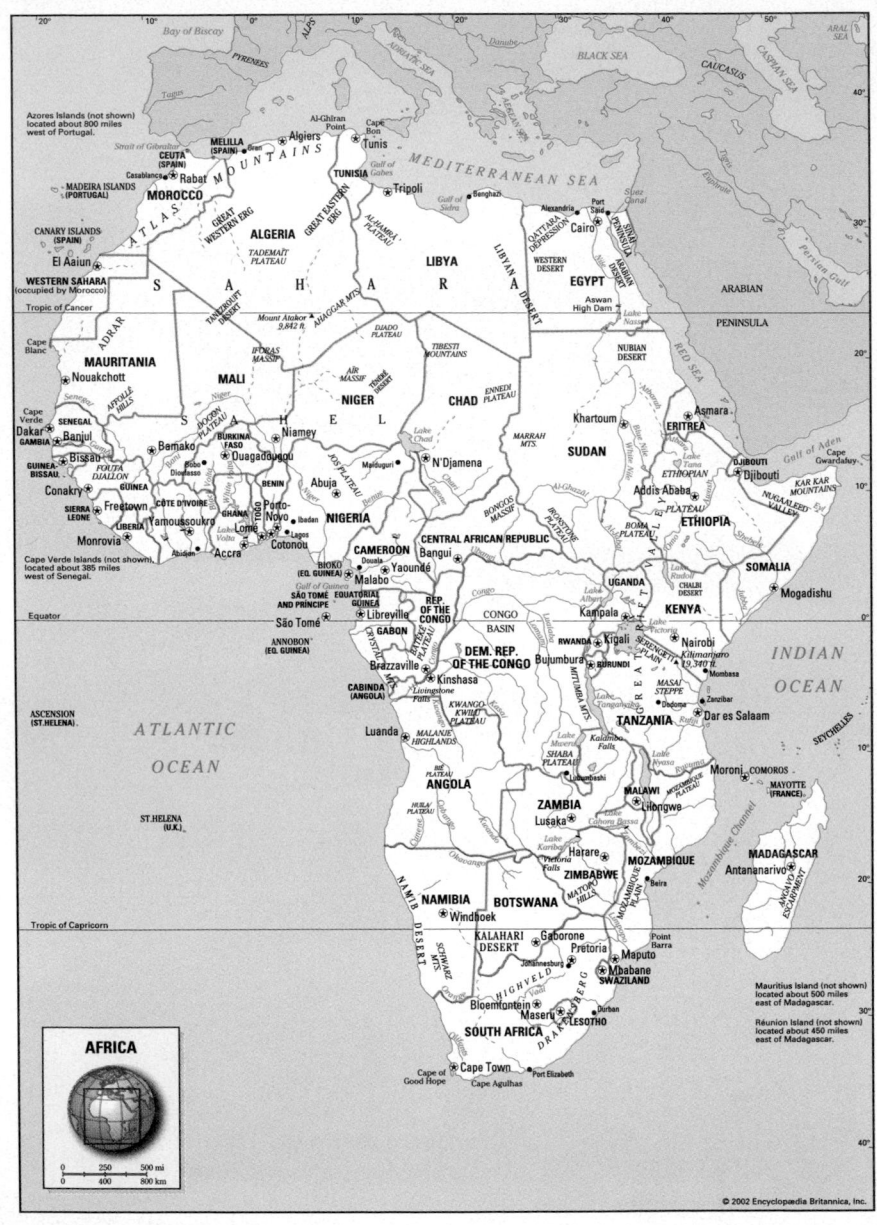

© 2002 Encyclopædia Britannica, Inc.

Asia

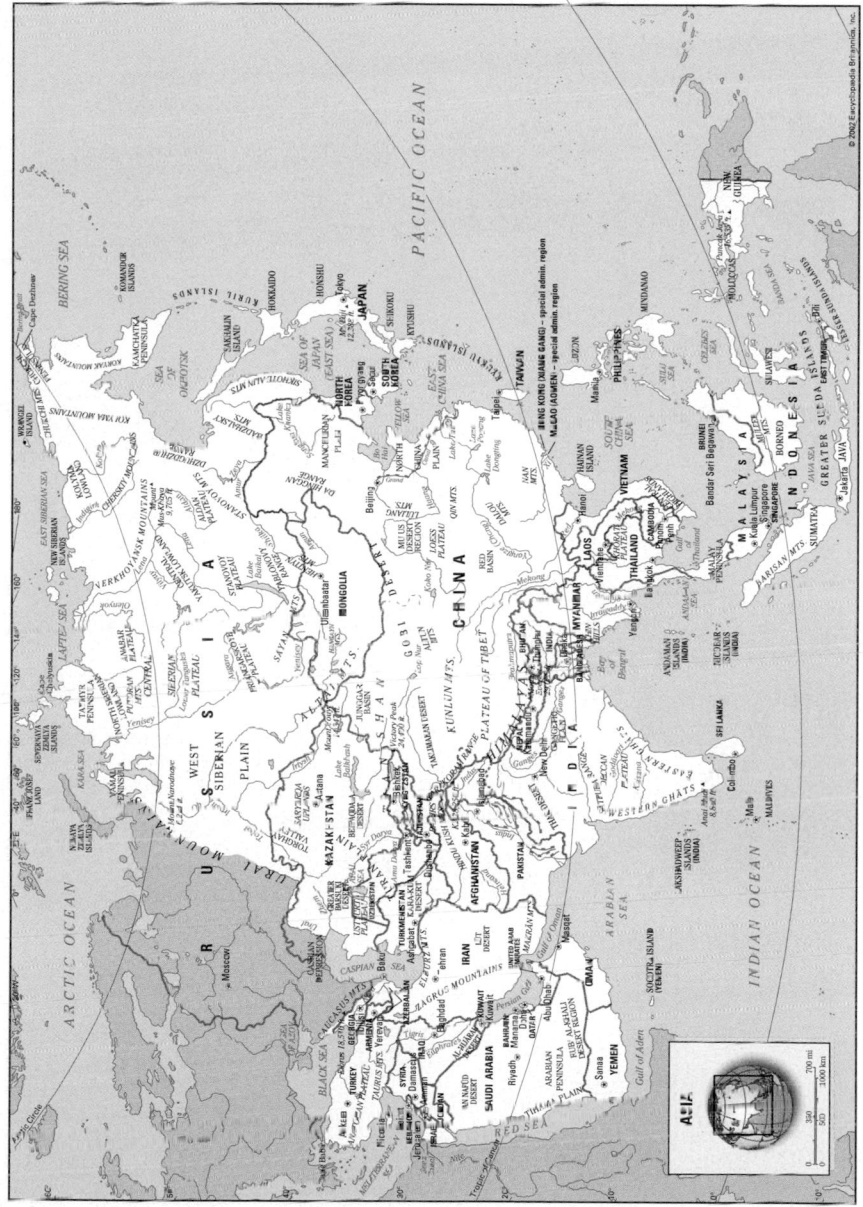

Plate 12

WORLD MAPS

Europe

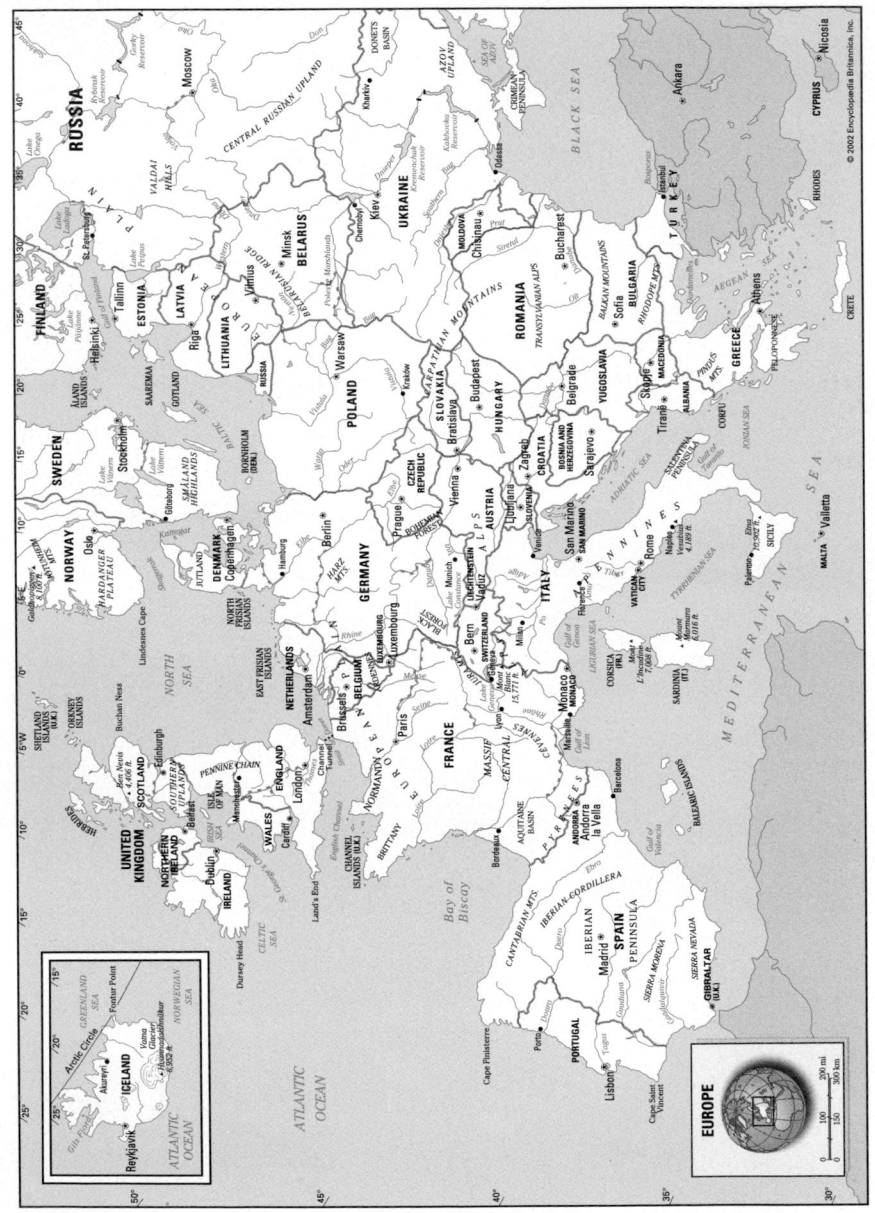

North America

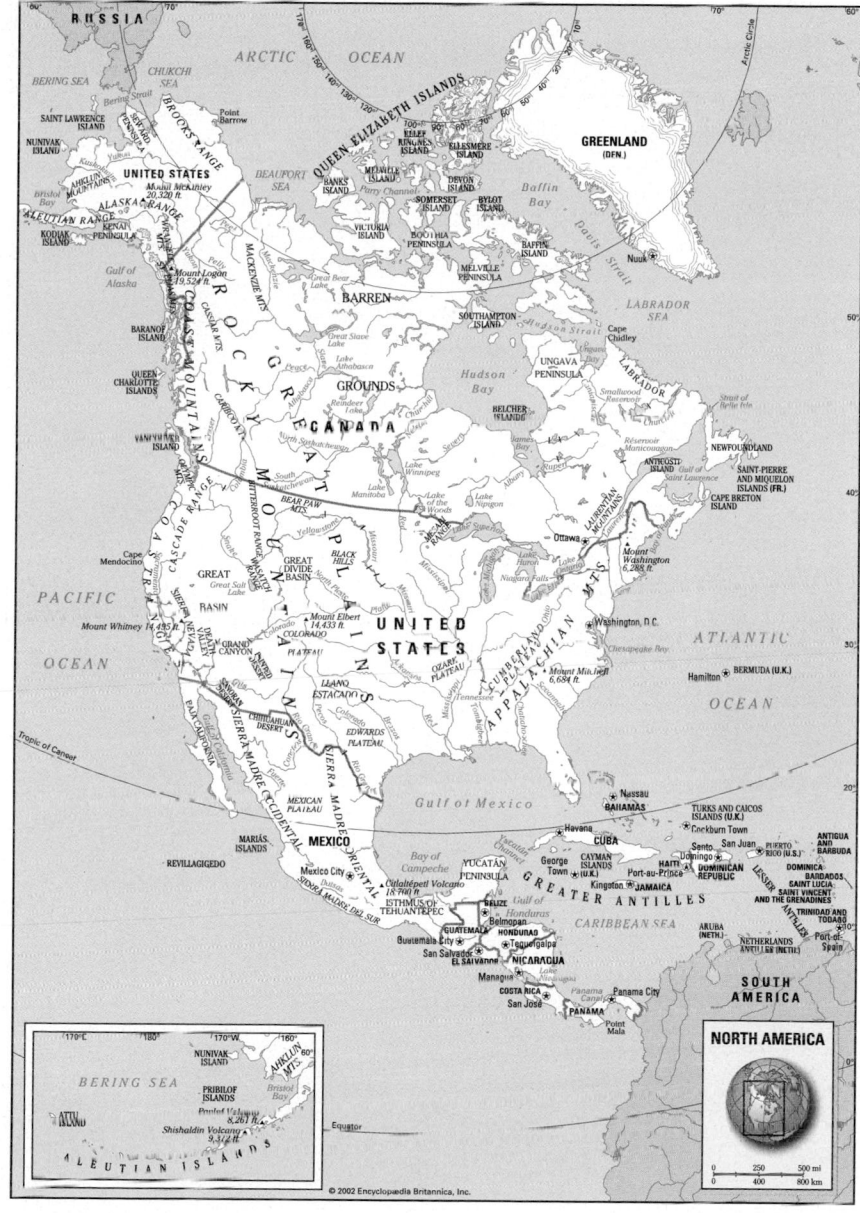

© 2002 Encyclopædia Britannica, Inc.

Plate 14   WORLD MAPS

South America

CARIBBEAN SEA

ATLANTIC OCEAN

PACIFIC OCEAN

ATLANTIC OCEAN

VENEZUELA

COLOMBIA

ECUADOR

PERU

BOLIVIA

BRAZIL

PARAGUAY

CHILE

URUGUAY

ARGENTINA

SURINAME

GUYANA

FRENCH GUIANA

AMAZON BASIN

BRAZILIAN HIGHLANDS

Caracas

Bogotá

Quito

Lima

La Paz

Sucre

Asunción

Santiago

Buenos Aires

Montevideo

Brasília

Georgetown

Paramaribo

Cayenne

Equator 0°

Tropic of Capricorn

SOUTH AMERICA

FALKLAND ISLANDS
(ISLAS MALVINAS)
(Administered by U.K.,
claimed by Argentina)

Stanley

TIERRA DEL FUEGO

SOUTH GEORGIA
(U.K.)

0   200   400 mi
0   300   600 km

© 2002 Encyclopædia Britannica, Inc.

Australia

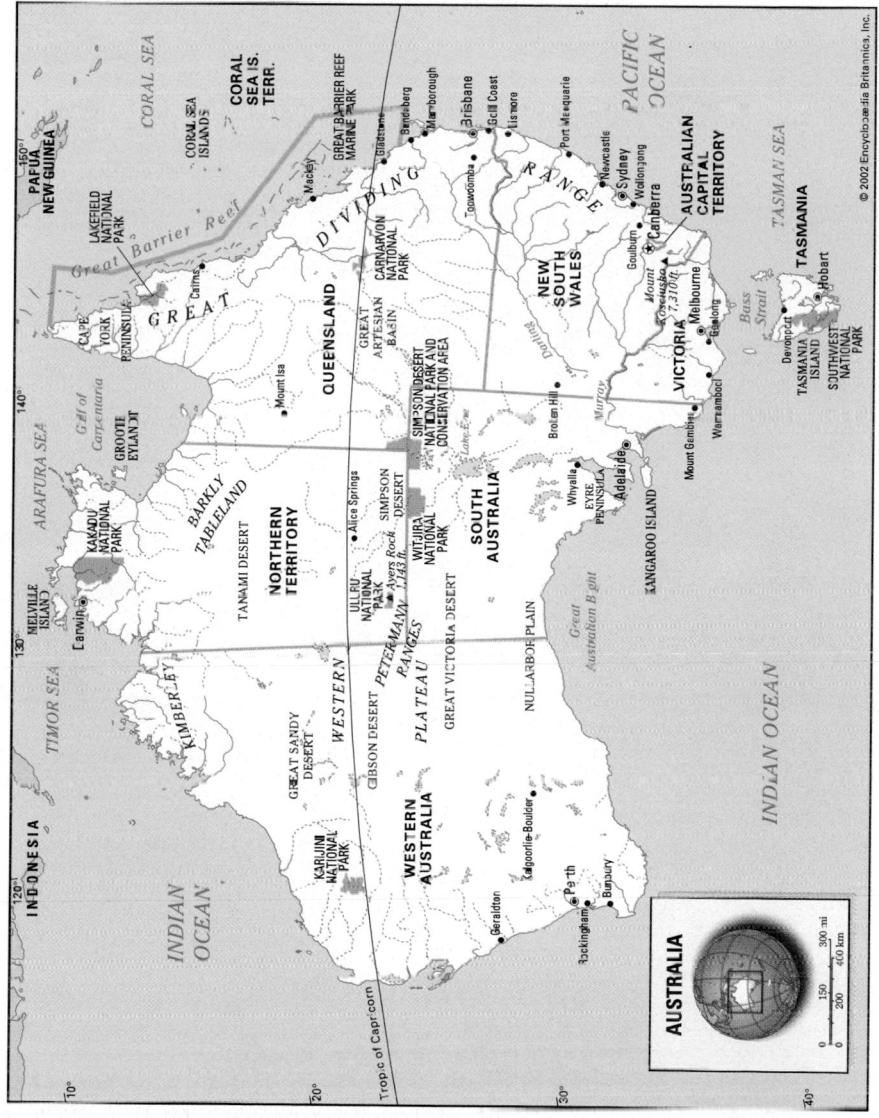

© 2002 Encyclopædia Britannica, Inc.

Plate 16   WORLD MAPS

Oceania/Pacific Islands

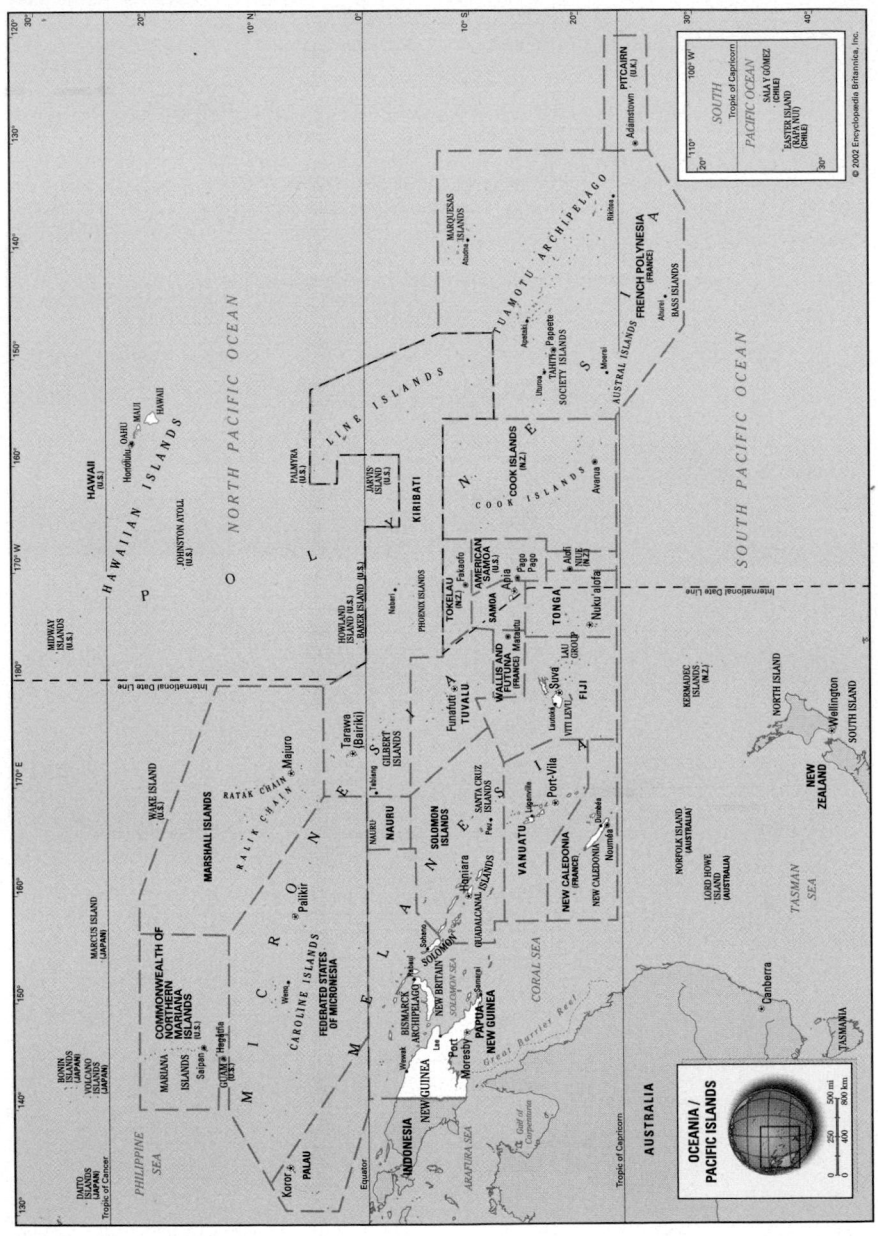

Summer Olympic Games Champions (continued)

Wrestling—Freestyle[24] (continued)

48 KG (106 LB)

1972 Roman Dmitriyev (URS)
1976 Khassan Issaev (BUL)
1980 Claudio Pollio (ITA)
1984 Robert Weaver (USA)
1988 Takashi Kobayashi (JPN)
1992 Kim Il (PRK)
1996 Kim Il (PRK)

54 KG (119 LB)

1904 George Mehnert (USA)
1948 Lennart Viitala (FIN)
1952 Hasan Gemici (TUR)
1956 Mirian Tsalkalamanidze (URS)
1960 Ahmet Bilek (TUR)
1964 Yoshikatsu Yoshida (JPN)
1968 Shigeo Nakata (JPN)
1972 Kiyomi Kato (JPN)
1976 Yuji Takada (JPN)
1980 Anatoly Beloglazov (URS)
1984 Saban Trstena (YUG)
1988 Mitsuru Sato (JPN)
1992 Li Hak-son (PRK)
1996 Valentin Iordanov (BUL)
2000 Namig Amdullayev (AZE)

58 KG (128 LB)

1904 Isidor "Jack" Niflot (USA)
1908 George Mehnert (USA)
1924 Kustaa Pihlajamäki (FIN)
1928 Kaarlo Maakinen (FIN)
1932 Robert Pearce (USA)
1936 Odon Zombory (HUN)
1948 Nasuh Akar (TUR)
1952 Shohachi Ishii (JPN)
1956 Mustafa Dagistanli (TUR)
1960 Terence McCann (USA)
1964 Yojiro Uetake (JPN)
1968 Yojiro Uetake (JPN)
1972 Hideaki Yanagida (JPN)
1976 Vladimir Yumin (URS)
1980 Sergey Beloglazov (URS)
1984 Hideaki Tomiyama (JPN)
1988 Sergey Beloglazov (URS)
1992 Alejandro Puerto Diaz (CUB)
1996 Kendall Cross (USA)
2000 Alireza Dabir (IRI)

63 KG (139 LB)

1904 Benjamin Bradshaw (USA)
1908 George Dole (USA)
1920 Charles Ackerly (USA)
1924 Robin Reed (USA)
1928 Allie Morrison (USA)
1932 Hermanni Pihlajamäki (FIN)
1936 Kustaa Pihlajamäki (FIN)
1948 Gazanfer Bilge (TUR)
1952 Bayram Sit (TUR)
1956 Shozo Sasahara (JPN)
1960 Mustafa Dagistanli (TUR)
1964 Osamu Watanabe (JPN)
1968 Masaaki Kaneko (JPN)
1972 Zagalav Abdulbekov (URS)
1976 Yang Jung Mo (KOR)
1980 Magomedgasan Abushev (URS)
1984 Randy Lewis (USA)
1988 John Smith (USA)
1992 John Smith (USA)

Wrestling—Freestyle[24] (continued)

63 KG (139 LB)

1996 Tom Brands (USA)
2000 Murad Umakhanov (RUS)

69 KG (152 LB)

1904 Otto Roehm (USA)
1908 George de Relwyskow (GBR)
1920 Kaarlo "Kalle" Anttila (FIN)
1924 Russell Vis (USA)
1928 Osvald Käpp (EST)
1932 Charles Pacome (FRA)
1936 Karoly Karpati (HUN)
1948 Celal Atik (TUR)
1952 Olle Anderberg (SWE)
1956 Emamali Habibi (IRI)
1960 Shelby Wilson (USA)
1964 Enio Valchev Dimov (BUL)
1968 Abdollah Movahed (IRI)
1972 Dan Gable (USA)
1976 Pavel Pinigin (URS)
1980 Saipulla Absaidov (URS)
1984 You In Tak (KOR)
1988 Arsen Fadzayev (URS)
1992 Arsen Fadzayev (UNT)
1996 Vadim Bogiyev (RUS)
2000 Daniel Igali (CAN)

76 KG (167.5 LB)

1904 Charles Eriksen (USA)
1924 Hermann Gehri (SUI)
1928 Arvo Haavisto (FIN)
1932 Jack van Bebber (USA)
1936 Frank Lewis (USA)
1948 Yasar Dogu (TUR)
1952 William Smith (USA)
1956 Mitsuo Ikeda (JPN)
1960 Douglas Blubaugh (USA)
1964 Ismail Ogan (TUR)
1968 Mahmut Atalay (TUR)
1972 Wayne Wells (USA)
1976 Jiichiro Date (JPN)
1980 Valentin Raychev (BUL)
1984 David Schultz (USA)
1988 Kenneth Monday (USA)
1992 Park Jang Soon (KOR)
1996 Buvaisa Saytyev (RUS)
2000 Brandon Slay (USA)

85 KG (187.5 LB)

1908 Stanley Bacon (GBR)
1920 Eino Leino (FIN)
1924 Fritz Haggmann (SUI)
1928 Ernst Kyburz (SUI)
1932 Ivar Johansson (SWE)
1936 Émile Poilvé (FRA)
1948 Glen Brand (USA)
1952 David Tsimakuridze (URS)
1956 Nikola Stanchev (BUL)
1960 Hasan Gungor (TUR)
1964 Prodan Stoyanov Gardchev (BUL)
1968 Boris Gurevich (URS)
1972 Levan Tediashvili (URS)
1976 John Peterson (USA)
1980 Ismail Abilov (BUL)
1984 Mark Schultz (USA)
1988 Han Myung Woo (KOR)
1992 Kevin Jackson (USA)
1996 Khadshimurad Magomedov (RUS)

Summer Olympic Games Champions (continued)

Wrestling—Freestyle[24] (continued)

85 KG (187.5 LB)
2000 Adam Saytev (RUS)

90 KG (198.5 LB)
1920 Anders Larsson (SWE)
1924 John Franklin Spellman (USA)
1928 Thure Sjöstedt (SWE)
1932 Peter Mehringer (USA)
1936 Knut Fridell (SWE)
1948 Henry Wittenberg (USA)
1952 Bror Wiking Palm (SWE)
1956 Gholam-Reza Takhti (IRI)
1960 Ismet Atli (TUR)
1964 Aleksandr Medved (URS)
1968 Ahmet Ayuk (TUR)
1972 Ben Peterson (USA)
1976 Levan Tediashvili (URS)
1980 Sanasar Oganesyan (URS)
1984 Ed Banach (USA)
1988 Macharbek Khadartsev (URS)
1992 Macharbek Khadartsev (UNT)
1996 Rasul Khadem Azghadi (IRI)

97 KG (214 LB)
1896 Karl Schumann (GER)
1904 Bernhuff Hansen (USA)
1908 George O'Kelly (GBR)
1920 Robert Rothe (SUI)
1924 Harry Steele (USA)
1928 Johan Richthoff (SWE)
1932 Johan Richthoff (SWE)
1936 Kristjan Palusalu (EST)
1948 Gyula Bobis (HUN)
1952 Arsen Mekokishvili (URS)
1956 Hamit Kaplan (TUR)
1960 Wilfried Dietrich (GER)
1964 Aleksandr Ivanitsky (URS)
1968 Aleksandr Medved (URS)
1972 Ivan Yarygin (URS)
1976 Ivan Yarygin (URS)
1980 Ilya Mate (URS)
1984 Lou Banach (USA)
1988 Vasile Puscasu (ROM)
1992 Leri Khabelov (UNT)
1996 Kurt Angle (USA)
2000 Sagid Murtasaliyev (RUS)

OVER 130 KG (286.5 LB)
1972 Aleksandr Medved (URS)
1976 Soslan Andiyev (URS)
1980 Soslan Andiyev (URS)
1984 Bruce Baumgartner (USA)
1988 David Gobedishvili (URS)
1992 Bruce Baumgartner (USA)
1996 Mahmut Demir (TUR)
2000 David Musulbes (RUS)

Wrestling—Greco-Roman[24]

48 KG (106 LB)
1972 Gheorghe Berceanu (ROM)
1976 Aleksey Shumakov (URS)
1980 Zhaksylyk Ushkcmpirov (URS)
1984 Vincenzo Maenza (ITA)
1988 Vincenzo Maenza (ITA)
1992 Oleg Kucherenko (UNT)
1996 Sim Kwon-Ho (KOR)

Wrestling—Greco-Roman[24] (continued)

54 KG (119 LB)
1948 Pietro Lombardi (ITA)
1952 Boris Gurevich (URS)
1956 Nikolay Solovyev (URS)
1960 Dumitru Pirvulescu (ROM)
1964 Tsutomu Hanahara (JPN)
1968 Petar Kirov (BUL)
1972 Petar Kirov (BUL)
1976 Vitaly Konstantinov (URS)
1980 Vakhtang Blagidze (URS)
1984 Atsuji Miyahara (JPN)
1988 Jon Ronningen (NOR)
1992 Jon Ronningen (NOR)
1996 Armen Nazaryan (ARM)
2000 Sim Kwon-Ho (KOR)

58 KG (128 LB)
1924 Eduard Pütsep (EST)
1928 Kurt Leucht (GER)
1932 Jakob Brendel (GER)
1936 Marton Lorincz (HUN)
1948 Kurt Pettersen (SWE)
1952 Imre Hodos (HUN)
1956 Konstantin Vyrupayev (URS)
1960 Oleg Karavayev (URS)
1964 Masamitsu Ichiguchi (JPN)
1968 Janos Varga (HUN)
1972 Rustem Kazakov (URS)
1976 Pertti Ukkola (FIN)
1980 Shamil Serikov (URS)
1984 Pasquale Passarelli (FRG)
1988 Andras Sike (HUN)
1992 An Han Bong (KOR)
1996 Yury Melnichenko (KAZ)
2000 Armen Nazarian (BUL)

63 KG (139 LB)
1912 Kaarlo Koskelo (FIN)
1920 Oskar Friman (FIN)
1924 Kalle Anttila (FIN)
1928 Voldemar Väli (EST)
1932 Giovanni Gozzi (ITA)
1936 Yasar Erkan (TUR)
1948 Mehmet Oktav (TUR)
1952 Yakov Punkin (URS)
1956 Rauno Leonard Mäkinen (FIN)
1960 Muzahir Sille (TUR)
1964 Imre Polyak (HUN)
1968 Roman Rurua (URS)
1972 Georgi Markov (BUL)
1976 Kazimierz Lipien (POL)
1980 Stilianos Migiakis (GRE)
1984 Kim Weon Kee (KOR)
1988 Kamandar Madzhidov (URS)
1992 Akif Pirim (TUR)
1996 Wlodzimierz Zawadzki (POL)
2000 Varteres Samurgashev (RUS)

69 KG (152 LB)
1908 Enrico Porro (ITA)
1912 Eemil Väre (FIN)
1920 Eemil Väre (FIN)
1924 Oskar Friman (FIN)
1928 Lajos Keresztes (HUN)
1932 Erik Malmberg (SWE)
1936 Lauri Koskela (FIN)
1948 Karl Freij (SWE)
1952 Shazam Safin (URS)

Summer Olympic Games Champions (continued)

Wrestling—Greco-Roman[24] (continued)

69 KG (152 LB)

1956	Kyösti Emil Lehtonen (FIN)
1960	Avtandil Koridze (URS)
1964	Kazim Ayvaz (TUR)
1968	Munji Mumemura (JPN)
1972	Shamil Khisamutdinov (URS)
1976	Suren Nalbandyan (URS)
1980	Stefan Rusu (ROM)
1984	Vlado Lisjak (YUG)
1988	Levon Dzhulfalakyan (URS)
1992	Attila Repka (HUN)
1996	Ryszard Wolny (POL)
2000	Filiberto Ascuy Aguilera (CUB)

76 KG (167.5 LB)

1932	Ivar Johansson (SWE)
1936	Rudolf Svedberg (SWE)
1948	Erik Gösta Andersson (SWE)
1952	Miklos Szilvasi (HUN)
1956	Mithat Bayrak (TUR)
1960	Mithat Bayrak (TUR)
1964	Anatoly Kolesov (URS)
1968	Rudolf Vesper (GDR)
1972	Viteslav Macha (TCH)
1976	Anatoly Bykov (URS)
1980	Ferenc Kocsis (HUN)
1984	Jouko Salomaki (FIN)
1988	Kim Young Nam (KOR)
1992	Mnatsakan Iskandaryan (UNT)
1996	Filiberto Ascuy Aguilera (CUB)
2000	Murat Kardanov (URS)

85 KG (187.5 LB)

1908	Frithiof Martenson (SWE)
1912	Claes Johansson (SWE)
1920	Carl Westergren (SWE)
1924	Edward Westerlund (FIN)
1928	Väinö Kokkinen (FIN)
1932	Väinö Kokkinen (FIN)
1936	Ivar Johansson (SWE)
1948	Axel Grönberg (SWE)
1952	Axel Grönberg (SWE)
1956	Givi Kartoziya (URS)
1960	Dimitar Dobrev (BUL)
1964	Branislav Simic (YUG)
1968	Lothar Metz (GDR)
1972	Csaba Hegedus (HUN)
1976	Momir Petkovic (YUG)
1980	Gennady Korban (URS)
1984	Ion Draica (ROM)
1988	Mikhail Mamiashvili (URS)
1992	Peter Farkas (HUN)
1996	Hamza Yerlikaya (TUR)
2000	Hamza Yerlikaya (TUR)

Wrestling—Greco-Roman[24] (continued)

90 KG (198.5 LB)

1908	Verner Weckman (FIN)
1912	Anders Ahlgren (SWE)
1920	Claes Johansson (SWE)
1924	Carl Westergren (SWE)
1928	Ibrahim Moustafa (EGY)
1932	Rudolf Svensson (SWE)
1936	Axel Cadier (SWE)
1948	Karl-Erik Nilsson (SWE)
1952	Kelpo Olavi Gröndahl (FIN)
1956	Valentin Nikolayev (URS)
1960	Tevfik Kis (TUR)
1964	Boyan Radev (BUL)
1968	Boyan Radev (BUL)
1972	Valery Rezantsev (URS)
1976	Valery Rezantsev (URS)
1980	Norbert Nottny (HUN)
1984	Steven Fraser (USA)
1988	Atanas Komchev (BUL)
1992	Maik Bullmann (GER)
1996	Vyatsheslav Oleynyk (UKR)

97 KG (214 LB)

1896	Karl Schumann (GER)
1908	Richard Weisz (HUN)
1912	Yrjö Saarela (FIN)
1920	Adolf Lindfors (FIN)
1924	Henri Deglane (FRA)
1928	Rudolf Svensson (SWE)
1932	Carl Westergren (SWE)
1936	Kristjan Palusalu (EST)
1948	Ahmet Kirecci (TUR)
1952	Johannes Kotkas (URS)
1956	Anatoly Parfenov (URS)
1960	Ivan Bogdan (URS)
1964	Istvan Kozma (HUN)
1968	Istvan Kozma (HUN)
1972	Nicolae Martinescu (ROM)
1976	Nikolay Balboshin (URS)
1980	Georgi Raikov-Petkov (BUL)
1984	Vasile Andrei (ROM)
1988	Andrzej Wronski (POL)
1992	Héctor Milian (CUB)
1996	Andrzej Wronski (POL)
2000	Mikael Ljungberg (SWE)

130 KG (286.5 LB)

1972	Anatoly Roshchin (URS)
1976	Aleksandr Kolchinsky (URS)
1980	Aleksandr Kolchinsky (URS)
1984	Jeffrey Blatnick (USA)
1988	Aleksandr Karelin (URS)
1992	Aleksandr Karelin (UNT)
1996	Aleksandr Karelin (RUS)
2000	Rulon Gardner (USA)

[1]The competitions in 1900 and 1904 are said to be unofficial. [2]100-meter event. [3]Hurdles were 2′ 6″ high, not 3′. [4]An extra lap of 460 meters was run in error. [5]Jim Thorpe was stripped of his gold medals in 1913 when it was discovered he had briefly competed as a professional athlete; in 1982 his gold medals were restored, and he was declared "cowinner" of the events. [6]2,000-meter event. [7]333.3-meter event. [8]Distance varied from 87 to 320 km. [9]Weight classifications were changed in 1980 and 1996. [10]Weight classifications were changed in 2000. [11]The distances in men's rowing events have varied from time to time. In 1904 it was 2 miles; in 1908, 1.5 miles; from 1912 to 1936, 2,000 m; in 1948, 1 mile 350 yards; and since 1952, 2,000 m (1 mile 427 yards). [12]The distance in women's rowing events was 1,000 m until 1988, at which time it became 2,000 m. [13]100 yards. [14]220 yards. [15]500 meters. [16]440 yards. [17]1,200 meters. [18]1,000 meters. [19]One mile. [20]100 yards. [21]440 yards. [22]300 meters. [23]Fréchette's gold medal awarded in 1993 on basis of error in scoring. [24]Weight classifications have been revised numerous times, most recently after the 1996 Games. [25]In 1976 the press lift was removed, weights given thereafter being the total for the clean and jerk and the snatch. [26]Total of five lifts.

Winter Olympic Games Champions

Gold medalists in all events, 1908–2002 (separate Winter Games were not held until 1924).

Biathlon

MEN

10 KILOMETER
		MIN:SEC
1980	Frank Ullrich (GDR)	32:10.69
1984	Eirik Kvalfoss (NOR)	30:53.8
1988	Frank-Peter Rötsch (GDR)	25:08.1
1992	Mark Kirchner (GER)	26:02.3
1994	Sergey Chepikov (RUS)	28:07.0
1998	Ole Einar Bjørndalen (NOR)	27:16.2
2002	Ole Einar Bjørndalen (NOR)	24:51.3

12.5 KILOMETER PURSUIT
		MIN:SEC
2002	Ole Einar Bjørndalen (NOR)	32:34.6

20 KILOMETER
		HR:MIN:SEC
1960	Klas Lestander (SWE)	1:33:21.6
1964	Vladimir Melanin (URS)	1:20:26.8
1968	Magnar Solberg (NOR)	1:13:45.9
1972	Magnar Solberg (NOR)	1:15:55.50[1]
1976	Nikolay Kruglov (URS)	1:14:12.26
1980	Anatoly Alyabyev (URS)	1:08:16.31
1984	Peter Angerer (FRG)	1:11:52.70
1988	Frank-Peter Rötsch (GDR)	56:33.3
1992	Yevgeny Redkin (UNT)[2]	57:34.4
1994	Sergey Tarasov (RUS)	57:25.3
1998	Halvard Hanevold (NOR)	56:16.4
2002	Ole Einar Bjørndalen (NOR)	51:03.3

4 × 7.5-KILOMETER RELAY
		HR:MIN:SEC
1968	USSR	2:13:02.4
1972	USSR	1:51:44.92[1]
1976	USSR	1:57:55.64
1980	USSR	1:34:03.27
1984	USSR	1:38:51.70
1988	USSR	1:22:30.00
1992	Germany	1:24:43.5
1994	Germany	1:30:22.1
1998	Germany	1:19:43.3
2002	Norway	1:23:42.3

MILITARY SKI PATROL
1924	Switzerland
1928	Norway
1936	Italy
1948	Switzerland

DISTANCE SHOOTING
1936	Georg Edenhauser (AUT)

ICE SHOOTING (TEAM)
1936	Austria

TARGET SHOOTING
1936	Ignaz Reiterer (AUT)

WOMEN

7.5 KILOMETER
		MIN:SEC
1992	Anfisa Restsova (UNT)[2]	24:29.2
1994	Myriam Bédard (CAN)	26:08.8
1998	Galina Kukleva (RUS)	23:08.0
2002	Kati Wilhelm (GER)	20:41.4

10 KILOMETER PURSUIT
		MIN:SEC
2002	Olga Pyleva (RUS)	31:07.7

15 KILOMETER
		MIN:SEC
1992	Antje Misersky (GER)	51:47.2

Biathlon (continued)

15 KILOMETER
		MIN:SEC
1994	Myriam Bédard (CAN)	52:06.6
1998	Ekaterina Dafovska (BUL)	54:52.0
2002	Andrea Henkel (GER)	47:29.1

4 × 7.5-KILOMETER RELAY
		HR:MIN:SEC
1992	France (3 × 7.5-meter event)	1:15:55.6
1994	Russia	1:47:19.5
1998	Germany	1:40:13.6
2002	Germany	1:27:55.0

Bobsled

TWO-MAN BOBSLED
		MIN:SEC
1932	United States	8:14.74
1936	United States	5:29.29
1948	Switzerland	5:29.2
1952	West Germany	5:24.54
1956	Italy	5:30.14
1964	Great Britain	4:21.90
1968	Italy	4:41.54
1972	West Germany	4:57.07
1976	East Germany	3:44.42
1980	Switzerland	4:09.36
1984	East Germany	3:25.56
1988	USSR	3:53.48
1992	Switzerland	4:03.26
1994	Switzerland	3:30.81
1998	Canada, Italy (tied)	3:37.24
2002	Germany	3:10.11

FOUR-MAN BOBSLED
		MIN:SEC
1924	Switzerland	5:45.54
1928	United States	3:20.5[3]
1932	United States	7:53.68
1936	Switzerland	5:19.85
1948	United States	5:20.1
1952	West Germany	5:07.84
1956	Switzerland	5:10.44
1964	Canada	4:14.46
1968	Italy	2:17.39
1972	Switzerland	4:43.07
1976	East Germany	3:40.43
1980	East Germany	3:59.92
1984	East Germany	3:20.22
1988	Switzerland	3:47.51
1992	Austria	3:53.90
1994	Germany	3:27.78
1998	Germany	2:39.41
2002	Germany	3:07.51

TWO-WOMAN BOBSLED
		MIN:SEC
2002	United States	1:37.76

Curling

MEN
1924	Great Britain
1998	Switzerland
2002	Norway

WOMEN
1998	Canada
2002	Great Britain

Figure Skating

MEN'S SINGLES
1908	Ulrich Salchow (SWE)

Winter Olympic Games Champions (continued)

Figure Skating (continued)

MEN'S SINGLES

1920	Gillis Gräfström (SWE)
1924	Gillis Gräfström (SWE)
1928	Gillis Gräfström (SWE)
1932	Karl Schäfer (AUT)
1936	Karl Schäfer (AUT)
1948	Richard Button (USA)
1952	Richard Button (USA)
1956	Hayes Alan Jenkins (USA)
1960	David Jenkins (USA)
1964	Manfred Schnelldorfer (GER)[4]
1968	Wolfgang Schwarz (AUT)
1972	Ondrej Nepela (TCH)
1976	John Curry (GBR)
1980	Robin Cousins (GBR)
1984	Scott Hamilton (USA)
1988	Brian Boitano (USA)
1992	Viktor Petrenko (UNT)[2]
1994	Aleksey Urmanov (RUS)
1998	Ilia Kulik (RUS)
2002	Aleksey Yagudin (RUS)

WOMEN'S SINGLES

1908	Madge Syers (GBR)
1920	Magda Julin-Mauroy (SWE)
1924	Herma Planck-Szabo (AUT)
1928	Sonja Henie (NOR)
1932	Sonja Henie (NOR)
1936	Sonja Henie (NOR)
1948	Barbara Ann Scott (CAN)
1952	Jeannette Altwegg (GBR)
1956	Tenley Albright (USA)
1964	Sjoukje Dijkstra (NED)
1968	Peggy Fleming (USA)
1972	Beatrix Schuba (AUT)
1976	Dorothy Hamill (USA)
1980	Annett Potzsch (GDR)
1984	Katarina Witt (GDR)
1988	Katarina Witt (GDR)
1992	Kristi Yamaguchi (USA)
1994	Oksana Bayul (UKR)
1998	Tara Lipinski (USA)
2002	Sarah Hughes (USA)

PAIRS

1908	Anna Hübler, Heinrich Burger (GER)
1920	Ludoviga Jakobsson-Eilers, Walter Jakobsson (FIN)
1924	Helene Engelmann, Alfred Berger (AUT)
1928	Andrée Joly, Pierre Brunet (FRA)
1932	Andrée Brunet-Joly, Pierre Brunet (FRA)
1936	Maxi Herber, Ernst Baier (GER)
1948	Micheline Lannoy, Pierre Baugniet (BEL)
1952	Ria Falk, Paul Falk (FRG)
1956	Elisabeth Schwarz, Kurt Oppelt (AUT)
1960	Barbara Wagner, Robert Paul (CAN)
1964	Lyudmila Belousova, Oleg Protopopov (URS)
1968	Lyudmila Belousova, Oleg Protopopov (URS)
1972	Irina Rodnina, Aleksey Ulanov (URS)
1976	Irina Rodnina, Aleksandr Zaytsev (URS)
1980	Irina Rodnina, Aleksandr Zaytsev (URS)
1984	Yelena Valova, Oleg Vasilyev (URS)

PAIRS

1988	Yekaterina Gordeyeva, Sergey Grinkov (URS)
1992	Natalya Mishkutyonok, Artur Dmitriyev (UNT)[2]
1994	Yekaterina Gordeyeva, Sergey Grinkov (RUS)

Figure Skating (continued)

PAIRS

1998	Oksana Kazakova, Artur Dmitriyev (RUS)
2002	Yelena Berezhnaya, Anton Sikharulidze (RUS); Jamie Sale, David Pelletier (CAN) (shared)

ICE DANCING

1976	Lyudmila Pakhomova, Aleksandr Gorshkov (URS)
1980	Natalya Linichuk, Gennady Karponosov (URS)
1984	Jayne Torvill, Christopher Dean (GBR)
1988	Natalya Bestemyanova, Andrey Bukin (URS)
1992	Marina Klimova, Sergey Ponomarenko (UNT)[2]
1994	Oksana Grishchuk, Yevgeny Platov (RUS)
1998	Oksana Grishchuk, Yevgeny Platov (RUS)
2002	Marina Anissina, Gwendal Peizerat (FRA)

Ice Hockey

MEN

1920	Canada
1924	Canada
1928	Canada
1932	Canada
1936	Great Britain
1948	Canada
1952	Canada
1956	USSR
1960	United States
1964	USSR
1968	USSR
1972	USSR
1976	USSR
1980	United States
1984	USSR
1988	USSR
1992	Unified Team[2]
1994	Sweden
1998	Czech Republic
2002	Canada

WOMEN

1998	United States
2002	Canada

Luge

MEN'S SINGLES

		MIN:SEC
1964	Thomas Köhler (GER)[4]	3:26.77
1968	Manfred Schmid (AUT)	2:52.48
1972	Wolfgang Schneidel (GDR)	3:27.58
1976	Detlef Guenther (GDR)	3:27.688[5]
1980	Bernhard Glass (GDR)	2:54.796
1984	Paul Hildgartner (ITA)	3:04.258
1988	Jens Müller (GDR)	3:05.548
1992	Georg Hackl (GER)	3:02.363
1994	Georg Hackl (GER)	3:21.571
1998	Georg Hackl (GER)	3:18.436
2002	Armin Zöggeler (ITA)	2:57.941

MEN'S PAIRS

		MIN:SEC
1964	Austria	1:41.62
1968	East Germany	1:35.85
1972	Italy; East Germany (tied)	1:28.35
1976	East Germany	1:25.604[5]
1980	East Germany	1:19.331
1984	West Germany	1:23.620
1988	East Germany	1:31.940

Winter Olympic Games Champions (continued)

Luge (continued)

MEN'S PAIRS		MIN:SEC
1992	Germany	1:32.053
1994	Italy	1:36.720
1998	Germany	1:41.105
2002	Germany	1:26.082

WOMEN'S SINGLES		MIN:SEC
1964	Ortrun Enderlein (GER)[4]	3:24.67
1968	Erica Lechner (ITA)	2:29.37
1972	Anna-Maria Müller (GDR)	2:59.18
1976	Margit Schumann (GDR)	2:50.621[5]
1980	Vera Zozulya (URS)	2:36.537
1984	Steffi Martin (GDR)	2:46.570
1988	Steffi Walter-Martin (GDR)	3:03.973
1992	Doris Neuner (AUT)	3:06.696
1994	Gerda Weissensteiner (ITA)	3:15.517
1998	Silke Kraushaar (GER)	3:23.779
2002	Sylke Otto (GER)	2:52.464

Skeleton

MEN		MIN:SEC
1928	Jennison Heaton (USA)	3:01.8
1948	Nino Bibbia (ITA)	5:23.2
2002	Jim Shea (USA)	1:41.96

WOMEN		MIN:SEC
2002	Tristan Gale (USA)	1:45.11

Alpine Skiing (men)

DOWNHILL		MIN:SEC
1948	Henri Oreiller (FRA)	2:55.0
1952	Zeno Colò (ITA)	2:30.8
1956	Toni Sailer (AUT)	2:52.2
1960	Jean Vuarnet (FRA)	2:06.0
1964	Egon Zimmermann (AUT)	2:18.16[1]
1968	Jean-Claude Killy (FRA)	1:59.85
1972	Bernhard Russi (SUI)	1:51.43
1976	Franz Klammer (AUT)	1:45.73
1980	Leonhard Stock (AUT)	1:45.50
1984	Bill Johnson (USA)	1:45.59
1988	Pirmin Zurbriggen (SUI)	1:59.63
1992	Patrick Ortlieb (AUT)	1:50.37
1994	Tommy Moe (USA)	1:45.75
1998	Jean-Luc Cretier (FRA)	1:50.11
2002	Fritz Strobl (AUT)	1:39.13

SLALOM		MIN:SEC
1948	Edy Reinalter (SUI)	2:10.3
1952	Othmar Schneider (AUT)	2:00.0
1956	Toni Sailer (AUT)	3:14.7
1960	Ernst Hinterseer (AUT)	2:08.9
1964	Josef Stiegler (AUT)	2:21.13[1]
1968	Jean-Claude Killy (FRA)	1:39.73
1972	Francisco Ochoa (ESP)	1:49.27
1976	Piero Gros (ITA)	2:03.29
1980	Ingemar Stenmark (SWE)	1:44.26
1984	Phil Mahre (USA)	1:39.41
1988	Alberto Tomba (ITA)	1:39.47
1992	Finn Christian Jagge (NOR)	1:44.39
1994	Thomas Stangassinger (AUT)	2:02.02
1998	Hans-Petter Buraas (NOR)	1:49.31
2002	Jean-Pierre Vidal (FRA)	1:41.06

GIANT SLALOM		MIN:SEC
1952	Stein Eriksen (NOR)	2:25.0
1956	Toni Sailer (AUT)	3:00.1
1960	Roger Staub (SUI)	1:48.3
1964	François Bonlieu (FRA)	1:46.71[1]

Alpine Skiing (men) (continued)

GIANT SLALOM		MIN:SEC
1968	Jean-Claude Killy (FRA)	3:29.28
1972	Gustavo Thöni (ITA)	3:09.62
1976	Heini Hemmi (SUI)	3:26.97
1980	Ingemar Stenmark (SWE)	2:40.74
1984	Max Julen (SUI)	2:41.18
1988	Alberto Tomba (ITA)	2:06.37
1992	Alberto Tomba (ITA)	2:06.98
1994	Markus Wasmeier (GER)	2:52.46
1998	Hermann Maier (AUT)	2:38.51
2002	Stephan Eberharter (AUT)	2:23.28

SUPERGIANT SLALOM		MIN:SEC
1988	Franck Piccard (FRA)	1:39.66
1992	Kjetil-Andre Aamodt (NOR)	1:13.04
1994	Markus Wasmeier (GER)	1:32.53
1998	Hermann Maier (AUT)	1:34.82
2002	Kjetil Andre Aamodt (NOR)	1:21.58

ALPINE COMBINED		MIN:SEC
1936	Franz Pfnür (GER)	
1948	Henri Oreiller (FRA)	
1972	Gustavo Thoeni (ITA)	
1976	Gustavo Thoeni (ITA)	
1988	Hubert Strolz (AUT)	
1992	Josef Polig (ITA)	
1994	Lasse Kjus (NOR)	3:17.53[6]
1998	Mario Reiter (AUT)	3:08.06
2002	Kjetil-Andre Aamodt (NOR)	3:17.56

Alpine Skiing (women)

DOWNHILL		MIN:SEC
1948	Hedy Schlunegger (SUI)	2:28.3
1952	Trude Jochom-Beiser (AUT)	1:47.1
1956	Madeleine Berthod (SUI)	1:40.7
1960	Heidi Beibl (GER)[4]	1:37.6
1964	Christl Haas (AUT)	1:55.39[1]
1968	Olga Pall (AUT)	1:40.87
1972	Marie-Therèse Nadig (SUI)	1:36.68
1976	Rosi Mittermaier (FRG)	1:46.16
1980	Annemarie Moser-Pröll (AUT)	1:37.52
1984	Michael Figini (SUI)	1:13.36
1988	Marina Kiehl (FRG)	1:25.86
1992	Kerrin Lee-Gartner (CAN)	1:52.55
1994	Katja Seizinger (GER)	1:35.93
1998	Katja Seizinger (GER)	1:28.29
2002	Carole Montillet (FRA)	1:39.56

SLALOM		MIN:SEC
1948	Gretchen Fraser (USA)	1:57.2
1952	Andrea Lawrence-Mead (USA)	2:10.6
1956	Renée Colliard (SUI)	1:52.3
1960	Anne Heggtveit (CAN)	1:49.6
1964	Christine Goitschel (FRA)	1:29.86[1]
1968	Marielle Goitschel (FRA)	1:59.85
1972	Barbara Cochran (USA)	1:31.24
1976	Rosi Mittermaier (FRG)	1:30.54
1980	Hanni Wenzel (LIE)	1:25.09
1984	Paoletta Magoni (ITA)	1:36.47
1988	Vreni Schneider (SUI)	1:36.69
1992	Petra Kronberger (AUT)	1:32.68
1994	Vreni Schneider (SUI)	1:56.01
1998	Hilde Gerg (GER)	1:32.40
2002	Janica Kostelic (CRO)	1:46.10

GIANT SLALOM		MIN:SEC
1952	Andrea Lawrence-Mead (USA)	2:06.8
1956	Ossi Reichert (GER)[4]	1:56.5

Winter Olympic Games Champions (continued)

Alpine Skiing (women) (continued)

GIANT SLALOM — **MIN:SEC**

1960	Yvonne Rüegg (SUI)	1:39.9
1964	Marielle Goitschel (FRA)	1:52.24[1]
1968	Nancy Greene (CAN)	1:51.97
1972	Marie-Therèse Nadig (SUI)	1:29.90
1976	Kathy Kreiner (CAN)	1:29.13
1980	Hanni Wenzel (LIE)	2:41.66
1984	Debbie Armstrong (USA)	2:20.98
1988	Vreni Schneider (SUI)	2:06.49
1992	Pernilla Wiberg (SWE)	2:12.74
1994	Deborah Compagnoni (ITA)	2:30.97
1998	Deborah Compagnoni (ITA)	2:50.59
2002	Janica Kostelic (CRO)	2:30.01

SUPERGIANT SLALOM — **MIN:SEC**

1988	Sigrid Wolf (AUT)	1:19.03
1992	Deborah Compagnoni (ITA)	1:21.22
1994	Diann Roffe-Steinrotter (USA)	1:22.15
1998	Picabo Street (USA)	1:18.02
2002	Daniela Ceccarelli (ITA)	1:13.59

ALPINE COMBINED — **MIN:SEC**

1936	Chrislt Cranz (GER)	
1948	Trude Beiser (AUT)	
1972	Annemarie Pröll (AUT)	
1976	Rosi Mittermaier (FRG)	
1988	Anita Wachter (AUT)	
1992	Petra Kronberger (AUT)	
1994	Pernilla Wiberg (SWE)	3:05.16[6]
1998	Katja Seizinger (GER)	2:40.74
2002	Janica Kostelic (CRO)	2:43.28

Freestyle Skiing

MEN'S MOGULS

1992	Edgar Grospiron (FRA)
1994	Jean-Luc Brassard (CAN)
1998	Jonny Moseley (USA)
2002	Janne Lahtela (FIN)

MEN'S AERIALS

1994	Andreas Schönbächler (SUI)
1998	Eric Bergoust (USA)
2002	Ales Valenta (CZE)

WOMEN'S MOGULS

1992	Donna Weinbrecht (USA)
1994	Stine Lise Hattestad (NOR)
1998	Tae Satoya (JPN)
2002	Kari Traa (NOR)

WOMEN'S AERIALS

1994	Lina Cheryazova (UZB)
1998	Nikki Stone (USA)
2002	Alisa Camplin (AUS)

Nordic Skiing (men)

1.5-KILOMETER CROSS-COUNTRY SPRINT — **MIN:SEC**

2002	Tor Arne Hetland (NOR)	2:56.9

10-KILOMETER CROSS-COUNTRY — **MIN:SEC**

1992	Vegard Ulvang (NOR)	27:36.0
1994	Bjørn Daehlie (NOR)	24:20.1
1998	Bjørn Daehlie (NOR)	27:24.5

15-KILOMETER CROSS-COUNTRY[7] — **HR:MIN:SEC**

1924	Thorleif Haug (NOR)	1:14:31.0
1928	Johan Gröttumsbraaten (NOR)	1:37:01.0
1932	Sven Utterström (SWE)	1:23:07.0

Nordic Skiing (men) (continued)

15-KILOMETER CROSS-COUNTRY[7] — **HR:MIN:SEC**

1936	Erik-August Larsson (SWE)	1:14:38.0
1948	Martin Lundström (SWE)	1:13:50.0
1952	Hallgeir Brenden (NOR)	1:01:34.0
1956	Hallgeir Brenden (NOR)	49:39.0
1960	Hakkon Brusveen (NOR)	51:55.5
1964	Eero Mäntyranta (FIN)	50:54.1
1968	Harald Grönningen (NOR)	47:54.2
1972	Sven-Ake Lundbäck (SWE)	45:28.24[1]
1976	Nikolay Bazhukov (URS)	43:58.47
1980	Thomas Wassberg (SWE)	41:57.63
1984	Gunde Svan (SWE)	41:25.60
1988	Mikhail Devyatyarov (URS)	41:18.9
1998	Thomas Alsgaard (NOR)	39:13.7
2002	Andrus Veerpalu (EST)	37:07.4

COMBINED PURSUIT[8] — **HR:MIN:SEC**

1992	Bjørn Daehlie (NOR)	1:05:37.9
1994	Bjørn Daehlie (NOR)	1:00:08.8
1998	Thomas Alsgaard (NOR)	1:07:01.7
2002	Johann Mühlegg (ESP)	49:20.4

30-KILOMETER CROSS-COUNTRY — **HR:MIN:SEC**

1956	Veikko Hakulinen (FIN)	1:44:06.0
1960	Sixten Jernberg (SWE)	1:51:03.9
1964	Eero Mäntyranta (FIN)	1:30:50.7
1968	Franco Nones (ITA)	1:35:39.2
1972	Vyacheslav Vedenin (URS)	1:36:31.15[1]
1976	Sergey Savelyev (URS)	1:30:29.38
1980	Nikolay Zimyatov (URS)	1:27:02.80
1984	Nikolay Zimyatov (URS)	1:28:56.30
1988	Aleksey Prokourorov (URS)	1:24:26.3
1992	Vegard Ulvang (NOR)	1:22:27.8
1994	Thomas Alsgaard (NOR)	1:12:26.4
1998	Mika Myllylä (FIN)	1:33:56.0
2002	Johann Mühlegg (ESP)	1:09:28.9

50-KILOMETER CROSS-COUNTRY — **HR:MIN:SEC**

1924	Thorleif Haug (NOR)	3:44:32.0
1928	Per Erik Hedlund (SWE)	4:52:03.3
1932	Veli Saarinen (FIN)	4:28:00.0
1936	Elis Viklund (SWE)	3:30:11.0
1948	Nils Karlsson (SWE)	3:47:48.0
1952	Veikko Hakulinen (FIN)	3:33:33.0
1956	Sixten Jernberg (SWE)	2:50:27.0
1960	Kalevi Hämäläinen (FIN)	2:59:06.3
1964	Sixten Jernberg (SWE)	2:43:52.6
1968	Olle Ellefsäter (NOR)	2:28:45.8
1972	Pål Tyldum (NOR)	2:43:14.75[1]
1976	Ivar Formo (NOR)	2:37:30.05
1980	Nikolay Zimyatov (URS)	2:27:24.60
1984	Thomas Wassberg (SWE)	2:15:55.80
1988	Gunde Svan (SWE)	2:04:30.9
1992	Bjørn Daehlie (NOR)	2:03:41.5
1994	Vladimir Smirnov (KAZ)	2:07:20.3
1998	Bjørn Daehlie (NOR)	2:05:08.2
2002	Mikhail Ivanov (RUS)[9]	2:06:20.8

4 × 10-KILOMETER RELAY — **HR:MIN:SEC**

1936	Finland	2:41:33.0
1948	Sweden	2:32:08.0
1952	Finland	2:20:16.0
1956	USSR	2:15:30.0
1960	Finland	2:18:45.6
1964	Sweden	2:18:34.6
1968	Norway	2:08:33.5
1972	USSR	2:04:47.94[1]
1976	Finland	2:07:59.72

Winter Olympic Games Champions (continued)

Nordic Skiing (men) (continued)

4 × 10-KILOMETER RELAY		HR:MIN:SEC
1980	USSR	1:57:03.46
1984	Sweden	1:55:06.30
1988	Sweden	1:43:58.6
1992	Norway	1:39:26.0
1994	Italy	1:41:15.0
1998	Norway	1:40:55.7
2002	Norway	1:32:45.5

SKI JUMPING (70 M)[10]
1924	Jacob Tullin Thams (NOR)
1928	Alf Andersen (NOR)
1932	Birger Ruud (NOR)
1936	Birger Ruud (NOR)
1948	Petter Hugsted (NOR)
1952	Arnfinn Bergmann (NOR)
1956	Antti Hyvärinen (FIN)
1960	Helmut Recknagel (GER)[4]
1964	Veikko Kankkonen (FIN)
1968	Jiri Raska (TCH)
1972	Yukio Kasaya (JPN)
1976	Hans-Georg Aschenbach (GDR)
1980	Toni Innauer (AUT)
1984	Jens Weissflog (GDR)
1988	Matti Nykänen (FIN)

SKI JUMPING (90 M)[10]
1964	Toralf Engan (NOR)
1968	Vladimir Belousov (URS)
1972	Wojciech Fortuna (POL)
1976	Karl Schnabl (AUT)
1980	Jens Tormanen (FIN)
1984	Matti Nykänen (FIN)
1988	Matti Nykänen (FIN)
1992	Ernst Vettori (AUT)
1994	Espen Bredesen (NOR)
1998	Jani Soininen (FIN)
2002	Simon Ammann (SUI)

SKI JUMPING (120 M)[10]
1992	Toni Nieminen (FIN)
1994	Jens Weissflog (GER)
1998	Kazuyoshi Funaki (JPN)
2002	Simon Ammann (SUI)

NORDIC COMBINED SPRINT (7.5 KILOMETERS) AND JUMPING
2002	Samppa Lajunen (FIN)

NORDIC COMBINED 15 KILOMETERS AND JUMPING
1924	Thorleif Haug (NOR)
1928	Johan Gröttumsbraaten (NOR)
1932	Johan Gröttumsbraaten (NOR)
1936	Oddbjörn Hagen (NOR)
1948	Heikki Hasu (NOR)
1952	Simon Slåttvik (NOR)
1956	Sverre Stenersen (NOR)
1960	Georg Thoma (GER)[4]
1964	Tormod Knutsen (NOR)
1968	Franz Keller (FRG)
1972	Ulrich Wehling (GDR)
1976	Ulrich Wehling (GDR)
1980	Ulrich Wehling (GDR)
1984	Tom Sandberg (NOR)
1988	Hippolyt Kempf (SUI)
1992	Fabrice Guy (FRA)
1994	Fred Börre Lundberg (NOR)
1998	Bjarte Engen Vik (NOR)
2002	Samppa Lajunen (FIN)

Nordic Skiing (men) (continued)

TEAM SKI JUMPING (120 M)
1988	Finland (90-m event)
1992	Finland
1994	Germany
1998	Japan
2002	Germany

NORDIC COMBINED 30-KILOMETER RELAY AND JUMPING (TEAM)
1988	West Germany
1992	Japan
1994	Japan
1998	Norway
2002	Finland

Nordic Skiing (women)

1.5-KILOMETER CROSS-COUNTRY SPRINT		MIN:SEC
2002	Yuliya Chepalova (RUS)	3:10.6

5-KILOMETER CROSS-COUNTRY		MIN:SEC
1964	Klavdia Boyarskikh (URS)	17:50.5
1968	Toini Gustafsson (SWE)	16:45.2
1972	Galina Kulakova (URS)	17:00.50[1]
1976	Helena Takalo (FIN)	15:48.69
1980	Raisa Smetanina (URS)	15:06.92
1984	Marja-Liisa Hämäläinen (FIN)	17:04.00
1988	Marjo Matikainen (FIN)	15:04.00
1992	Marjut Lukkarinen (FIN)	14:13.8
1994	Lyubov Yegorova (RUS)	14:08.8
1998	Larisa Lazutina (RUS)	17:39.9

10-KILOMETER CROSS-COUNTRY		MIN:SEC
1952	Lydia Wideman (FIN)	41:40.0
1956	Lyubov Kozyreva (URS)	38:11.0
1960	Mariya Gusakova (URS)	39:46.6
1964	Klavdia Boyarskikh (URS)	40:24.3
1968	Toini Gustafsson (SWE)	36:46.5
1972	Galina Kulakova (URS)	34:17.82[1]
1976	Raisa Smetanina (URS)	30:13.41
1980	Barbara Petzold (GDR)	30:31.54
1984	Marja-Liisa Hämäläinen (FIN)	31:44.20
1988	Vida Ventsene (URS)	30:08.30
1998	Larisa Lazutina (RUS)	46:06.9
2002	Bente Skari (NOR)	28:05.6

COMBINED PURSUIT[11]		MIN:SEC
1992	Lyubov Yegorova (UNT)[2]	40:08.4
1994	Lyubov Yegorova (RUS)	41:38.1
1998	Larisa Lazutina (RUS)	46:06.9
2002	Olga Danilova (RUS)	24:52.1

15-KILOMETER CROSS-COUNTRY		MIN:SEC
1992	Lyubov Yegorova (UNT)[2]	42:20.8
1994	Manuela di Centa (ITA)	39:44.5
1998	Olga Danilova (RUS)	46:55.40
2002	Stefania Belmondo (ITA)	39:54.4

20-KILOMETER CROSS-COUNTRY		HR:MIN:SEC
1984	Marja-Liisa Hämäläinen (FIN)	1:01:45.0
1988	Tamara Tikhonova (URS)	55:53.6

30-KILOMETER CROSS-COUNTRY		HR:MIN:SEC
1992	Stefania Belmondo (ITA)	1:22:30.1
1994	Manuela di Centa (ITA)	1:25:41.6
1998	Yuliya Chepalova (RUS)	1:22:01.5
2002	Gabriella Paruzzi (ITA)[9]	1:30:57.1

Winter Olympic Games Champions (continued)

Nordic Skiing (women) (continued)

4 × 5-KILOMETER RELAY — HR:MIN:SEC
2002	Germany	49:30.6

Sled-dog Race
1932	Emile St.Goddard (CAN)	

Snowboarding

GIANT SLALOM—MEN
1998	Ross Rebagliati (CAN)
2002	Philipp Schoch (SUI)

GIANT SLALOM—WOMEN
1998	Karine Ruby (FRA)
2002	Isabelle Blanc (FRA)

HALFPIPE—MEN
1998	Gian Simmen (SUI)
2002	Ross Powers (USA)

HALFPIPE—WOMEN
1998	Nicola Thost (GER)
2002	Kelly Clark (USA)

Speed Skating (men)

4 × 5-KILOMETER RELAY[12] — HR:MIN:SEC
1956	Finland	1:09:01.0
1960	Sweden	1:04:21.4
1964	USSR	59:20.2
1968	Norway	57:30.0
1972	USSR	48:46.15[1]
1976	USSR	1:07:49.75
1980	East Germany	1:02:11.10
1984	Norway	1:06:49.70
1988	USSR	59:51.10
1992	Unified Team[2]	59:34.8
1994	Russia	57:12.5

500 METERS — SEC
1924	Charles Jewtraw (USA)	44.0
1928	Clas Thunberg, Bernt Evensen (tied) (FIN; NOR)	43.4
1932	John Shea (USA)	43.4
1936	Ivar Ballangrud (NOR)	43.4
1948	Finn Helgesen (NOR)	43.1
1952	Kenneth Henry (USA)	43.2
1956	Yevgeny Grishin (URS)	40.2
1960	Yevgeny Grishin (URS)	40.2
1964	Richard McDermott (USA)	40.1
1968	Erhard Keller (FRG)	40.3
1972	Erhard Keller (FRG)	39.44[1]
1976	Yevgeny Kulikov (URS)	39.17
1980	Eric Heiden (USA)	38.03
1984	Sergey Fokichev (URS)	38.19
1988	Uew-Jens Mey (GDR)	36.45
1992	Uew-Jens Mey (GER)	37.14
1994	Aleksandr Golubyov (RUS)	36.33
1998	Hiroyasu Shimizu (JPN)	71.35[13]
2002	Casey Fitzrandolph (USA)	69.23[13]

1,000 METERS — MIN:SEC
1976	Peter Mueller (USA)	1:19.32[1]
1980	Eric Heiden (USA)	1:15.18
1984	Gaetan Boucher (CAN)	1:15.80
1988	Nikolay Gulyayev (URS)	1:13.03
1992	Olaf Zinke (GER)	1:14.85
1994	Dan Jansen (USA)	1:12.43
1998	Ids Postma (NED)	1:10.71
2002	Gerard van Velde (NED)	1:07.18

Speed Skating (men) (continued)

1,500 METERS — MIN:SEC
1924	Clas Thunberg (FIN)	2:20.8
1928	Clas Thunberg (FIN)	2:21.1
1932	John Shea (USA)	2:57.5
1936	Charles Mathisen (NOR)	2:19.2
1948	Sverre Farstad (NOR)	2:17.6
1952	Hjalmar Andersen (NOR)	2:20.4
1956	Yury Mikhaylov; Yevgeny Grishin (tied) (URS; URS)	2:08.6
1960	Yevgeny Grishin; Roald Aas (tied) (URS; NOR)	2:10.4
1964	Ants Antson (URS)	2:10.3
1968	Cornelis Verkerk (NED)	2:03.4
1972	Ard Schenk (NED)	2:02.96[1]
1976	Jan Egil Storholt (NOR)	1:59.38
1980	Eric Heiden (USA)	1:55.44
1984	Gaetan Boucher (CAN)	1:58.36
1988	André Hoffmann (GDR)	1:52.06
1992	Johann Olav Koss (NOR)	1:54.81
1994	Johann Olav Koss (NOR)	1:51.29
1998	Aadne Sondral (NOR)	1:47.87
2002	Derek Parra (USA)	1:43.95

5,000 METERS — MIN:SEC
1924	Clas Thunberg (FIN)	8:39.0
1928	Ivar Ballangrud (NOR)	8:50.5
1932	Irving Jaffee (USA)	9:40.8
1936	Ivar Ballangrud (NOR)	8:19.6
1948	Reidar Liaklev (NOR)	8:29.4
1952	Hjalmar Andersen (NOR)	8:10.6
1956	Boris Shilkov (URS)	7:48.7
1960	Viktor Kosichkin (URS)	7:51.3
1964	Knut Johannesen (NOR)	7:38.4
1968	Fred Anton Maier (NOR)	7:22.4
1972	Ard Schenk (NED)	7:23.61[1]
1976	Sten Stensen (NOR)	7:24.48
1980	Eric Heiden (USA)	7:02.29
1984	Thomas Gustafson (SWE)	7:12.28
1988	Thomas Gustafson (SWE)	6:44.63
1992	Geir Karlstad (NOR)	6:59.97
1994	Johann Olav Koss (NOR)	6:34.96
1998	Gianni Romme (NED)	6:22.20
2002	Jochem Uytdehaage (NED)	6:14.66

10,000 METERS — MIN:SEC
1924	Julius Skutnabb (FIN)	18:04.8
1932	Irving Jaffee (USA)	19:13.6
1936	Ivar Ballangrud (NOR)	17:24.3
1948	Ake Seyffarth (SWE)	17:26.3
1952	Hjalmar Andersen (NOR)	16:45.8
1956	Sigvard Ericsson (SWE)	16:35.9
1960	Knut Johannesen (NOR)	15:46.6
1964	Jonny Nilsson (SWE)	15:50.1
1968	Johnny Höglin (SWE)	15:23.6
1972	Ard Schenk (NED)	15:01.35[1]
1976	Piet Kleine (NED)	14:50.59
1980	Eric Heiden (USA)	14:28.13
1984	Igor Malkov (URS)	14:39.90
1988	Thomas Gustafson (SWE)	13:48.20
1992	Bart Veldkamp (NED)	14:12.12
1994	Johann Olav Koss (NOR)	13:30.55
1998	Gianni Romme (NED)	13:15.33
2002	Jochem Uytdehaage (NED)	12:58.92

COMBINED SPEED SKATING (MEN)
1922	Clas Thunberg (FIN)

Winter Olympic Games Champions (continued)

Speed Skating (women)

500 METERS

		SEC
1960	Helga Haase (GER)[4]	45.9
1964	Lidiya Skoblikova (URS)	45.0
1968	Lyudmila Titova (URS)	46.1
1972	Anne Henning (USA)	43.33[1]
1976	Sheila Young (USA)	42.76
1980	Karin Enke (GDR)	41.78
1984	Christa Rothenburger (GDR)	41.02
1988	Bonnie Blair (USA)	39.10
1992	Bonnie Blair (USA)	40.33
1994	Bonnie Blair (USA)	39.25
1998	Catriona LeMay Doan (CAN)	76.60[13]
2002	Catriona LeMay Doan (CAN)	74.75[13]

1,000 METERS

		MIN:SEC
1960	Klara Guseva (URS)	1:34.1
1964	Lidiya Skoblikova (URS)	1:32.6
1968	Carolina Geijssen (NED)	1:32.6
1972	Monika Pflug (FRG)	1:31.40[1]
1976	Tatyana Averina (URS)	1:28.43
1980	Natalya Petruseva (URS)	1:24.10
1984	Karin Enke (GDR)	1:21.61
1988	Christa Rothenburger (GDR)	1:17.65
1992	Bonnie Blair (USA)	1:21.90
1994	Bonnie Blair (USA)	1:18.74
1998	Marianne Timmer (NED)	1:16.51
2002	Chris Witty (USA)	1:13.83

1,500 METERS

		MIN:SEC
1960	Lidiya Skoblikova (URS)	2:25.2
1964	Lidiya Skoblikova (URS)	2:22.6
1968	Kaija Mustonen (FIN)	2:22.4
1972	Dianne Holum (USA)	2:20.85[1]
1976	Galina Stepanskaya (URS)	2:16.58
1980	Annie Borckink (NED)	2:10.95
1984	Karin Enke (GDR)	2:03.42
1988	Yvonne van Gennip (NED)	2:00.68
1992	Jacqueline Börner (GER)	2:05.87
1994	Emese Hunyady (AUT)	2:02.19
1998	Marianne Timmer (NED)	1:57.58
2002	Anni Friesinger (GER)	1:54.02

3,000 METERS

		MIN:SEC
1960	Lidiya Skoblikova (URS)	5:14.3
1964	Lidiya Skoblikova (URS)	5:14.9
1968	Johanna Schut (NED)	4:56.2
1972	Christina Baas-Kaiser (NED)	4:52.14[1]
1976	Tatyana Averina (URS)	4:45.19
1980	Björg Eva Jensen (NOR)	4:32.13
1984	Andrea Schöne (GDR)	4:24.79
1988	Yvonne van Gennip (NED)	4:11.94
1992	Gunda Niemann (GER)	4:19.90
1994	Svetlana Bazhanova (RUS)	4:17.43
1998	Gunda Niemann-Stirnemann (GER)	4:07.29
2002	Claudia Pechstein (GER)	3:57.70

Speed Skating (women) (continued)

5,000 METERS

		MIN:SEC
1988	Yvonne van Gennip (NED)	7:14.13
1992	Gunda Niemann (GER)	7:31.57
1994	Claudia Pechstein (GER)	7:14.37
1998	Claudia Pechstein (GER)	6:59.61
2002	Claudia Pechstein (GER)	6:46.91

Short-track Speed Skating (men)

500 METERS

		SEC
1994	Chae Ji-Hoon (KOR)	43.45
1998	Takafumi Nishitani (JPN)	42.862[5]
2002	Marc Gagnon (CAN)	41.802

1,000 METERS

		MIN:SEC
1992	Kim Ki-Hoon (KOR)	1:30.76
1994	Kim Ki-Hoon (KOR)	1:34.57
1998	Kim Dong Sung (KOR)	1:32.428[5]
2002	Steven Bradbury (AUS)	1:29.109

1,500 METERS

		MIN:SEC
2002	Apolo Anton Ohno (USA)	2:18.541

5000-METER RELAY

		MIN:SEC
1992	South Korea	7:14.02
1994	Italy	7:11.74
1998	Canada	7:06.075[5]
2002	Canada	6:51.579

Short-track Speed Skating (women)

500 METERS

		SEC
1992	Cathy Turner (USA)	47.04
1994	Cathy Turner (USA)	45.98
1998	Annie Perreault (CAN)	46.568[5]
2002	Yang Yang (A) (CHN)	44.187

1,000 METERS

		MIN:SEC
1994	Chun Lee-Kyung (KOR)	1:36.87
1998	Chun Lee-Kyung (KOR)	1:42.776[5]
2002	Yang Yang (A) (CHN)	1:36.391

1,500 METERS

		MIN:SEC
2002	Ko Gi-Hyun (KOR)	2:31.581

3000-METER RELAY

		MIN:SEC
1992	Canada	4:36.62
1994	South Korea	4:26.64
1998	South Korea	4:16.260[5]
2002	South Korea	4:12.793

Winter Pentathlon[14]

1948	Gustav Lindh (SWE)

---

[1]Race first timed in hundredths of a second.　[2]Unified Team, consisting of athletes from the Commonwealth of Independent States plus Georgia.　[3]Five men.　[4]Joint East-West German team.　[5]Race first timed in thousandths of a second.　[6]Competition scored on points until 1994.　[7]1924–52, 18 km.　[8]Results of a 10-km classical leg determine the starting order of a 10- or 15-km freestyle leg, the first finisher of which is the overall winner; the freestyle leg was shortened from 15 to 10 km in the 2002 games.　[9]Winner after disqualification of top finisher for drug use.　[10]From 1924 to 1960 the jumping was held on one hill. In 1964 there were two events, one on a 70-m and the other on an 80-m hill; from 1968 to 1988 there were 70-m and 90-m events. From 1992 there were 90-m and 120-m events.　[11]Results of a 5-km classical leg determine the starting order of a 5- or 10-km freestyle leg, the first finisher of which is the overall winner; the freestyle leg was shortened from 10 to 5 km in the 2002 games.　[12]3 × 5-km relay until 1976.　[13]Combined time for two runs.　[14]Includes elements of cross-country skiing, downhill skiing, shooting, fencing, and horse riding.

Olympic Medal Winners — XXVII Summer Games

The XXVII Summer Games were held in Sydney, Australia, 15 Sep–1 Oct 2000.

EVENT	GOLD MEDALIST	PERFORMANCE	SILVER MEDALIST	BRONZE MEDALIST
Archery				
Men's individual	Simon Fairweather (AUS)	113–106	Victor Wunderle (USA)	Wietse van Alten (NED)
Men's team	Korea	255–247	Italy	United States
Women's individual	Yun Mi-Jin (KOR)	107–106	Kim Nam-Soon (KOR)	Kim Soo-Nyung (KOR)
Women's team	Korea	251–239	Ukraine	Germany
Badminton				
Men's singles	Ji Xinpeng (CHN)	15–4, 15–13	Hendrawan (INA)	Xia Xuanze (CHN)
Men's doubles	Indonesia	15–10, 9–15, 15–7	Korea	Korea
Women's singles	Gong Zhichao (CHN)	13–10 11–3	Camilla Martin (DEN)	Ye Zhaoying (CHN)
Women's doubles	China	15–5, 15–5	China	China
Mixed doubles	China	1–15, 15–13, 15–11	Indonesia	Great Britain
Baseball	United States	4–0	Cuba	Korea
Basketball				
Men	United States	85–75	France	Lithuania
Women	United States	76–54	Australia	Brazil
Boxing*				
48 kg (light flyweight)	Brahim Asloum (FRA)		Rafael Lozano Muñoz (ESP)	Kim Un Chol (PRK); Maikro Romero Esquirol (CUB)
51 kg (flyweight)	Wijan Ponlid (THA)		Bulat Jumadilov (KAZ)	Vladimir Sidorenko (UKR); Jerome Thomas (FRA)
54 kg (bantamweight)	Guillermo Ortiz (CUB)		Raimkul Malakh-bekov (RUS)	Clarence Vinson (USA); Sergy Danylchenko (UKR)
57 kg (featherweight)	Bekzat Sattarkhanov (KAZ)		Ricardo Juárez (USA)	Kamil Dzamalut-dinov (RUS); Tahar Tamsamani (MAR)
60 kg (lightweight)	Mario Kindelan (CUB)		Andry Kotelnyk (UKR)	Aleksandr Maletin (RUS); Cristian Benitez (MEX)
63.5 kg (light welter-weight)	Mahamadkadyz Abdullayev (UZB)		Ricardo Williams (USA)	Mohamed Allalou (ALG); Diogenes Luna Martínez (CUB)
67 kg (welterweight)	Oleg Saytov (RUS)		Sergy Dotsenko (UKR)	Dorel Simion (ROM); Vitalii Grusac (MDA)
71 kg (light middle-weight)	Yermakhan Ibraimov (KAZ)		Marin Simion (ROM)	Jermaine Taylor (USA); Pornchai Thongburan (THA)
75 kg (middleweight)	Jorge Gutiérrez (CUB)		Gaidarbek Gaidar-bekov (RUS)	Vugar Alekperov (AZE); Zsolt Erdei (HUN)
81 kg (light heavy-weight)	Aleksandr Lebzyak (RUS)		Rudolf Kraj (CZE)	Sergey Mikhaylov (UZB); Andry Fedchuk (UKR)
91 kg (heavyweight)	Félix Savon Fabré (CUB)		Sultanahmed Ibzagi-mov (RUS)	Sebastian Kober (GER); Vladimir Chanturia (GEO)
91+ kg (super heavy-weight)	Audley Harrison (GBR)		Mukhatarkhan Dilda-bekov (KAZ)	Rustam Saidov (UZB); Paolo Vidoz (ITA)
Canoeing				
Men				
500-m kayak singles	Knut Holman (NOR)	1 min 57.84 sec	Petar Merkov (BUL)	Michael Kolganov (ISR)
1,000-m kayak singles	Knut Holman (NOR)	3 min 33.26 sec	Petar Merkov (BUL)	Tim Brabants (GBR)
500-m kayak pairs	Hungary	1 min 47.05 sec	Australia	Germany
1,000-m kayak pairs	Italy	3 min 14.46 sec	Sweden	Hungary
1,000-m kayak fours	Hungary	2 min 55.18 sec	Germany	Poland

Olympic Medal Winners—XXVII Summer Games (continued)

EVENT	GOLD MEDALIST	PERFORMANCE	SILVER MEDALIST	BRONZE MEDALIST
Canoeing (continued)				
Men				
Slalom kayak singles	Thomas Schmidt (GER)	217.25 pt	Paul Ratcliffe (GBR)	Pierpaolo Ferrazzi (ITA)
500-m Canadian singles	Gyorgy Kolonics (HUN)	2 min 24.81 sec	Maksim Opalev (RUS)	Andreas Dittmer (GER)
1,000-m Canadian singles	Andreas Dittmer (GER)	3 min 54.37 sec	Ledys Frank Balceiro (CUB)	Steve Giles (CAN)
500-m Canadian pairs	Hungary	1 min 51.28 sec	Poland	Romania
1,000-m Canadian pairs	Romania	3 min 37.35 sec	Cuba	Germany
Slalom Canadian singles	Tony Estanguet (FRA)	231.87 pt	Michal Martikan (SVK)	Juraj Mincik (SVK)
Slalom Canadian pairs	Slovakia	237.74 pt	Poland	Czech Rep.
Women				
500-m kayak singles	Josefa Idem Guerrini (ITA)	2 min 13.84 sec	Caroline Brunet (CAN)	Katrin Borchert (AUS)
500-m kayak pairs	Germany	1 min 56.99 sec	Hungary	Poland
500-m kayak fours	Germany	1 min 34.53 sec	Hungary	Romania
Slalom kayak singles	Stepanka Hilgertova (CZE)	247.04 pt	Brigitte Guibal (FRA)	Anne-Lise Bardet (FRA)
Cycling				
Men				
Road race	Jan Ullrich (GER)	5 hr 29 min 08 sec	Aleksandr Vinokourov (KAZ)	Andreas Kloeden (GER)
Individual road time trial	Vyacheslav Yekimov (RUS)	57 min 40.420 sec	Jan Ullrich (GER)	Lance Armstrong (USA)
1-km time trial	Jason Queally (GBR)	1 min 1.609 sec	Stefan Nimke (GER)	Shane Kelly (AUS)
4,000-m individual pursuit	Robert Bartko (GER)	4 min 18.515 sec†	Jens Lehmann (GER)	Brad McGee (AUS)
4,000-m team pursuit	Germany	3 min 59.710 sec‡	Ukraine	Great Britain
Individual match sprint	Marty Nothstein (USA)		Florian Rousseau (FRA)	Jens Fiedler (GER)
Olympic sprint	France	44.233 sec	Great Britain	Australia
Individual points race	Juan Llaneras (ESP)		Milton Wynants (URU)	Aleksey Markov (RUS)
Madison	Australia		Belgium	Italy
Keirin	Florian Rousseau (FRA)	11.020 sec	Gary Neiwand (AUS)	Jens Fiedler (GER)
Mountain bike	Miguel Martinez (FRA)	2 hr 9 min 2.50 sec	Filip Meirhaeghe (BEL)	Christoph Sauser (SUI)
Women				
Road race	Leontien Zijlaard–van Moorsel (NED)	3 hr 6 min 31 sec	Hanka Kupfernagel (GER)	Diana Ziliute (LTU)
Individual road time trial	Leontien Zijlaard–van Moorsel (NED)	42 min 0.781 sec	Mari Holden (USA)	Jeannie Longo-Ciprelli (FRA)
500-m time trial	Felicia Ballanger (FRA)	34.140 sec	Michelle Ferris (AUS)	Jiang Cuihua (CHN)
Individual pursuit	Leontien Zijlaard–van Moorsel (NED)	3 min 33.360 sec	Marion Clignet (FRA)	Yvonne McGregor (GBR)
Individual sprint	Felicia Ballanger (FRA)		Oksana Grishina (RUS)	Iryna Yanovych (UKR)
Individual points race	Antonella Bellutti (ITA)		Leontin Zijlaard–van Moorsel (NED)	Olga Slyusareva (RUS)
Mountain bike	Paola Pezzo (ITA)	1 hr 49 min 24.38 sec	Barbara Blatter (SUI)	Margarita Fullana (ESP)
Diving				
Men				
3-m springboard	Xiong Ni (CHN)	708.72 pt	Fernando Platas (MEX)	Dmitry Sautin (RUS)
10-m platform	Tian Liang (CHN)	724.53 pt	Hu Jia (CHN)	Dmitry Sautin (RUS)
3-m synchronized springboard	China	365.58 pt	Russia	Australia

Olympic Medal Winners—XXVII Summer Games (continued)

EVENT	GOLD MEDALIST	PERFORMANCE	SILVER MEDALIST	BRONZE MEDALIST
Diving (continued)				
Men				
10-m synchronized platform	Russia	365.04 pt	China	Germany
Women				
3-m springboard	Fu Mingxia (CHN)	609.42 pt	Guo Jingjing (CHN)	Doerte Lindner (GER)
10-m platform	Laura Wilkinson (USA)	543.75 pt	Li Na (CHN)	Anne Montminy (CAN)
3-m synchronized springboard	Russia	332.64 pt	China	Ukraine
10-m synchronized platform	China	345.12 pt	Canada	Australia
Equestrian				
Individual 3-day event	David O'Connor (USA)		Andrew Hoy (AUS)	Mark Todd (NZL)
Team 3-day event	Australia		Great Britain	United States
Individual dressage	Anky van Grunsven (NED)		Isabell Werth (GER)	Ulla Salzgeber (GER)
Team dressage	Germany		The Netherlands	United States
Individual show jumping	Jeroen Dubbeldam (NED)		Albert Voorn (NED)	Khaled al Eid (SAU)
Team show jumping	Germany		Switzerland	Brazil
Fencing				
Men				
Individual foil	Kim Young Ho (KOR)		Ralf Bissdorf (GER)	Dmitry Shevchenko (RUS)
Team foil	France		China	Italy
Individual épée	Pavel Kolobkov (RUS)		Hugues Obry (FRA)	Lee Sang-Ki (KOR)
Team épée	Italy		France	Cuba
Individual sabre	Mihai Claudiu Covaliu (ROM)		Mathieu Gourdain (FRA)	Wiradech Kothny (GER)
Team sabre	Russia		France	Germany
Women				
Individual foil	Valentina Vezzali (ITA)		Rita Koenig (GER)	Giovanna Trillini (ITA)
Team foil	Italy		Poland	Germany
Individual épée	Timea Nagy (HUN)		Gianna Buerki (SUI)	Laura Flessel-Colovic (FRA)
Team épée	Russia		Switzerland	China
Field Hockey				
Men	The Netherlands	8–7	Korea	Australia
Women	Australia	3–1	Argentina	The Netherlands
Gymnastics				
Men				
Team	China	231.919 pt	Ukraine	Russia
All-around	Aleksey Nemov (RUS)	58.474 pt	Yang Wei (CHN)	Oleksandr Beresh (UKR)
Floor exercise	Igors Vihrovs (LAT)	9.812 pt	Aleksey Nemov (RUS)	Iordan Iovchev (BUL)
Vault	Gervasio Deferr (ESP)	9.712 pt	Aleksey Bondarenko (RUS)	Leszek Blanik (POL)
Pommel horse	Marius Urzica (ROM)	9.862 pt	Eric Poujade (FRA)	Aleksey Nemov (RUS)
Rings	Szilveszter Csollany (HUN)	9.850 pt	Dimosthenis Tampakos (GRE)	Iordan Iovchev (BUL)
Parallel bars	Li Xiaopeng (CHN)	9.825 pt	Lee Joo Hyung (KOR)	Aleksey Nemov (RUS)
Horizontal bar	Aleksey Nemov (RUS)	9.787 pt	Benjamin Varonian (FRA)	Lee Joo Hyung (KOR)
Trampoline	Aleksandr Moskalenko (RUS)	41.70 pt	Ji Wallace (AUS)	Mathieu Turgeon (CAN)
Women				
Team	Romania	154.608 pt	Russia	China
All-around	Simona Amanar (ROM)	38.642 pt	Maria Olaru (ROM)	Liu Xuan (CHN)

Olympic Medal Winners—XXVII Summer Games (continued)

EVENT	GOLD MEDALIST	PERFORMANCE	SILVER MEDALIST	BRONZE MEDALIST
Gymnastics (continued)				
Women				
Floor exercise	Yelena Zamolodchikova (RUS)	9.850 pt	Svetlana Khorkina (RUS)	Simona Amanar (ROM)
Vault	Yelena Zamolodchikova (RUS)	9.731 pt	Andreea Raducan (ROM)	Yekaterina Lobaznyuk (RUS)
Uneven bars	Svetlana Khorkina (RUS)	9.862 pt	Ling Jie (CHN)	Yang Yun (CHN)
Balance beam	Liu Xuan (CHN)	9.825 pt	Yekaterina Lobaznyuk (RUS)	Yelena Produnova (RUS)
Trampoline	Irina Karavayeva (RUS)	38.90 pt	Oksana Tsyhuleva (UKR)	Karen Cockburn (CAN)
Individual rhythmic	Yuliya Barsukova (RUS)	39.632 pt	Yuliya Raskina (BLR)	Alina Kabayeva (RUS)
Team rhythmic	Russia	39.500 pt	Belarus	Greece
Handball (Team)				
Men	Russia	28–26	Sweden	Spain
Women	Denmark	31–27	Hungary	Norway
Judo*§				
Men				
60 kg (extra light-weight)	Tadahiro Nomura (JPN)		Jung Bu-Kyung (KOR)	Manolo Poulot (CUB); Aidyn Smagulov (KGZ)
66 kg (half light-weight)	Huseyein Ozkan (TUR)		Larbi Benboudaoud (FRA)	Girolamo Giovinazzo (ITA); Giorgi Vazagasvili (GEO)
73 kg (lightweight)	Giuseppe Maddaloni (ITA)		Tiago Camilo (BRA)	Vsevolods Zelonijs (LAT); Anatoly Laryukov (BLR)
81 kg (half middle-weight)	Makoto Takimoto (JPN)		Cho In-Chul (KOR)	Nuno Delgado (POR); Aleksy Budolin (EST)
90 kg (middleweight)	Mark Huizinga (NED)		Carlos Honorato (BRA)	Ruslan Mashurenko (UKR); Frederic Demontfaucon (FRA)
100 kg (half heavy-weight)	Kosei Inoue (JPN)		Nicolas Gill (CAN)	Yury Stepkin (RUS); Stephane Traineau (FRA)
100+ kg (heavy-weight)	David Douillet (FRA)		Shinichi Shinohara (JPN)	Tamerlan Tmenov (RUS); Indrek Pertelson (EST)
Women				
48 kg (extra light-weight)	Ryoko Tamura (JPN)		Lyubov Bruletova (RUS)	Anna-Maria Gradante (GER); Ann Simons (BEL)
52 kg (half light-weight)	Legna Verdecia (CUB)		Noriko Narazaki (JPN)	Kye Sun Hui (PRK); Liu Yuxiang (CHN)
57 kg (lightweight)	Isabel Fernández (ESP)		Driulys González (CUB)	Kie Kusakabe (JPN); Maria Pekli (AUS)
63 kg (half middle-weight)	Severine Vandenhende (FRA)		Li Shufang (CHN)	Jung Sung-Sook (KOR); Gella Vandecaveye (BEL)
70 kg (middleweight)	Sibelis Veranes (CUB)		Kate Howey (GBR)	Cho Min-Sun (KOR); Ylenia Scapin (ITA)
78 kg (half heavy-weight)	Tang Lin (CHN)		Celine Lebrun (FRA)	Simona Marcela Richter (ROM); Emanuela Pierantozzi (ITA)
78+ kg (heavyweight)	Yuan Hua (CHN)		Daima Mayelis Beltran (CUB)	Kim Seon-Young (KOR); Mayumi Yamashita (JPN)
Modern Pentathlon				
Men	Dmitry Svatkovsky (RUS)		Gabor Balogh (HUN)	Pavel Dovgal (BLR)
Women	Stephanie Cook (GBR)		Emily de Riel (USA)	Kate Allenby (GBR)

Olympic Medal Winners—XXVII Summer Games (continued)

EVENT	GOLD MEDALIST	PERFORMANCE	SILVER MEDALIST	BRONZE MEDALIST
Rowing				
Men				
Single sculls	Rob Waddell (NZL)	6 min 48.90 sec	Xeno Mueller (SUI)	Marcel Hacker (GER)
Double sculls	Slovenia	6 min 16.63 sec	Norway	Italy
Quadruple sculls	Italy	5 min 45.56 sec	The Netherlands	Germany
Coxless pairs (oars)	France	6 min 32.97 sec	United States	Australia
Coxless fours (oars)	Great Britain	5 min 56.24 sec	Italy	Australia
Eights	Great Britain	5 min 33.08 sec	Australia	Croatia
Lightweight double sculls	Poland	6 min 21.75 sec	Italy	France
Lightweight fours	France	6 min 1.68 sec	Australia	Denmark
Women				
Single sculls	Yekaterina Karsten (BLR)	7 min 28.14 sec	Rumyana Neykova (BUL)	Katrin Rutschow (GER)
Double sculls	Germany	6 min 55.44 sec	The Netherlands	Lithuania
Quadruple sculls	Germany	6 min 19.58 sec	Great Britain	Russia
Coxless pairs (oars)	Romania	7 min 11.00 sec	Australia	United States
Eights	Romania	6 min 6.44 sec	The Netherlands	Canada
Lightweight double sculls	Romania	7 min 2.64 sec	Germany	United States
Sailing				
Men's 470	Australia		United States	Argentina
Women's 470	Australia		United States	Ukraine
Men's Mistral	Christoph Sieber (AUT)		Carlos Espíñola (ARG)	Aaron McIntosh (NZL)
Women's Mistral	Alessandra Sensini (ITA)		Amelie Lux (GER)	Barbara Kendall (NZL)
Men's Finn	Iain Percy (GBR)		Luca Devoti (ITA)	Fredrik Loof (SWE)
Women's Europe	Shirley Robertson (GBR)		Margriet Matthysse (NED)	Serena Amato (ARG)
Mixed 49er	Finland		Great Britain	United States
Mixed Laser	Ben Ainslie (GBR)		Robert Scheidt (BRA)	Michael Blackburn (AUS)
Mixed Soling	Denmark		Germany	Norway
Mixed Star	United States		Great Britain	Brazil
Mixed Tornado	Austria		Australia	Germany
Shooting				
Men				
Rapid-fire pistol	Sergey Alifirenko (RUS)	687.6 pt	Michal Ansermet (SUI)	Iulian Raicea (ROM)
Free pistol	Tanyu Kiriakov (BUL)	666.0 pt	Igor Basinsky (BLR)	Martin Tenk (CZE)
Air pistol	Franck Dumoulin (FRA)	688.9 pt†	Wang Yifu (CHN)	Igor Basinsky (BLR)
10-m running (game) target	Yang Ling (CHN)	681.1 pt	Oleg Moldovan (MDA)	Niu Zhiyuan (CHN)
Small-bore (sport) rifle, 3 positions	Rajmond Debevec (SLO)	1,275.1 pt†	Juha Hirvi (FIN)	Harald Stenvaag (NOR)
Small-bore (sport) rifle, prone	Jonas Edman (SWE)	701.3 pt	Torben Grimmel (DEN)	Sergey Martynov (BLR)
Air rifle	Cai Yalin (CHN)	696.4 pt†	Artyom Khadjibekov (RUS)	Yevgeny Aleynikov (RUS)
Trap	Michael Diamond (AUS)	147.0 pt	Ian Peel (GBR)	Giovani Pellielo (ITA)
Double trap	Richard Faulds (GBR)	187.0 pt	Russell Mark (AUS)	Fehaid al Deehani (KUW)
Skeet	Mykola Milchev (UKR)	150.0 pt†	Petr Malek (CZE)	James Graves (USA)
Women				
Sport pistol	Maria Grozdeva (BUL)	690.3 pt†	Tao Luna (CHN)	Lolita Yevglevskaya (BLR)
Air pistol	Tao Luna (CHN)	488.2 pt	Jasna Sekaric (YUG)	Annemarie Forder (AUS)
Small-bore (sport) rifle	Renata Mauer–Rozanska (POL)	684.6 pt	Tatyana Goldobina (RUS)	Mariya Feklisova (RUS)
Air rifle	Nancy Johnson (USA)	497.7 pt	Kang Cho-Hyun (KOR)	Gao Jing (CHN)

Olympic Medal Winners—XXVII Summer Games (continued)

EVENT	GOLD MEDALIST	PERFORMANCE	SILVER MEDALIST	BRONZE MEDALIST
Shooting (continued)				
Women				
Trap	Daina Gudzineviciute (LTU)	93.0 pt	Delphine Racinet (FRA)	Gao E (CHN)
Double trap	Pia Hansen (SWE)	148.0 pt†	Deborah Gelisio (ITA)	Kimberly Rhode (USA)
Skeet	Zemfira Meftakhetdinova (AZE)	98.0 pt†	Svetlana Demina (RUS)	Diana Igaly (HUN)
Soccer (Association Football)				
Men	Cameroon	2–2 (5–3 on PKs)	Spain	Chile
Women	Norway	3–2 (overtime)	United States	Germany
Softball	United States	2–1	Japan	Australia
Swimming				
Men				
50-m freestyle	Gary Hall, Jr. (USA); Anthony Ervin (USA)¶	21.98 sec	N/A	Pieter Van den Hoogenband (NED)
100-m freestyle	Pieter Van den Hoogenband (NED)	48.30 sec	Aleksandr Popov (RUS)	Gary Hall, Jr. (USA)
200-m freestyle	Pieter Van den Hoogenband (NED)	1 min 45.35 sec‡	Ian Thorpe (AUS)	Massimiliano Rosolino (ITA)
400-m freestyle	Ian Thorpe (AUS)	3 min 40.59 sec‡	Massimiliano Rosolino (ITA)	Klete Keller (USA)
1,500-m freestyle	Grant Hackett (AUS)	14 min 48.33 sec	Kieren Perkins (AUS)	Chris Thompson (USA)
100-m backstroke	Lenny Krayzelburg (USA)	53.72 sec†	Matthew Welsh (AUS)	Stev Theloke (GER)
200-m backstroke	Lenny Krayzelburg (USA)	1 min 56.76 sec†	Aaron Peirsol (USA)	Matthew Welsh (AUS)
100-m breaststroke	Domenico Fioravanti (ITA)	1 min 0.46 sec†	Ed Moses (USA)	Roman Sludnov (RUS)
200-m breaststroke	Domenico Fioravanti (ITA)	2 min 10.87 sec	Terence Parkin (RSA)	Davide Rummolo (ITA)
100-m butterfly	Lars Froelander (SWE)	52.00 sec	Michael Klim (AUS)	Geoff Huegill (AUS)
200-m butterfly	Tom Malchow (USA)	1 min 55.35 sec†	Denys Sylantyev (UKR)	Justin Norris (AUS)
200-m individual medley	Massimiliano Rosolino (ITA)	1 min 58.98 sec†	Tom Dolan (USA)	Tom Wilkens (USA)
400-m individual medley	Tom Dolan (USA)	4 min 11.76 sec‡	Erik Vendt (USA)	Curtis Myden (CAN)
4 x 100-m freestyle relay	Australia	3 min 13.67 sec‡	United States	Brazil
4 x 200-m freestyle relay	Australia	7 min 7.05 sec‡	United States	The Netherlands
4 x 100-m medley relay	United States	3 min 33.73 sec‡	Australia	Germany
Women				
50-m freestyle	Inge de Bruijn (NED)	24.32 sec	Therese Alshammar (SWE)	Dara Torres (USA)
100-m freestyle	Inge de Bruijn (NED)	53.83 sec	Therese Alshammar (SWE)	Jenny Thomspon (USA); Dara Torres (USA)¶
200-m freestyle	Susie O'Neill (AUS)	1 min 58.24 sec	Martina Moravcova (SVK)	Claudia Poll (CRC)
400-m freestyle	Brooke Bennett (USA)	4 min 5.80 sec	Diana Munz (USA)	Claudia Poll (CRC)
800-m freestyle	Brooke Bennett (USA)	8 min 19.67 sec†	Yana Klochkova (UKR)	Kaitlin Sandeno (USA)
100-m backstroke	Diana Mocanu (ROM)	1 min 0.21 sec†	Mai Nakamura (JPN)	Nina Zhivanevskaya (ESP)
200-m backstroke	Diana Mocanu (ROM)	2 min 8.16 sec	Roxana Maracineanu (FRA)	Miki Nakao (JPN)
100-m breaststroke	Megan Quann (USA)	1 min 7.05 sec	Leisel Jones (AUS)	Penny Heyns (RSA)
200-m breaststroke	Agnes Kovacs (HUN)	2 min 24.35 sec	Kristy Kowal (USA)	Amanda Beard (USA)
100-m butterfly	Inge de Bruijn (NED)	56.61 sec‡	Martina Moravcova (SVK)	Dara Torres (USA)

Olympic Medal Winners—XXVII Summer Games (continued)

EVENT	GOLD MEDALIST	PERFORMANCE	SILVER MEDALIST	BRONZE MEDALIST
Swimming (continued)				
Women				
200-m butterfly	Misty Hyman (USA)	2 min 5.88 sec†	Susie O'Neill (AUS)	Petria Thomas (AUS)
200-m individual medley	Yana Klochkova (UKR)	2 min 10.68 sec†	Beatrice Caslaru (ROM)	Cristina Teuscher (USA)
400-m individual medley	Yana Klochkova (UKR)	4 min 33.59 sec‡	Yasuko Tajima (JPN)	Beatrice Caslaru (ROM)
4 x 100-m freestyle relay	United States	3 min 36.61 sec‡	The Netherlands	Sweden
4 x 200-m freestyle relay	United States	7 min 57.80 sec†	Australia	Germany
4 x 100-m medley relay	United States	3 min 58.30 sec‡	Australia	Japan
Synchronized Swimming				
Duet	Russia	99.580 pt	Japan	France
Team	Russia	99.146 pt	Japan	Canada
Table Tennis				
Men's singles	Kong Linghui (CHN)	21-16, 21-19, 17-21, 14-21, 21-13	Jan-Ove Waldner (SWE)	Liu Guoliang (CHN)
Men's doubles	China	22-20, 17-21, 21-19, 21-18	China	France
Women's singles	Wang Nan (CHN)	21-12, 12-21, 19-21, 21-17, 21-18	Li Ju (CHN)	Chen Jing (TPE)
Women's doubles	China	21-18, 21-11, 21-11	China	Korea
Taekwondo				
Men				
58 kg (flyweight)	Michail Mouroutsis (GRE)		Gabriel Esparaza (ESP)	Huang Chih-Hsiung (TPE)
68 kg (featherweight)	Steven Lopez (USA)		Sin Joon-Sik (KOR)	Hadi Saeiboneh-kohal (IRI)
80 kg (welterweight)	Angel Matos Fuentes (CUB)		Faissal Ebnoutalib (GER)	Victor Estrada-Garibay (MEX)
80+ kg (heavyweight)	Kim Kyong Hun (KOR)		Daniel Trenton (AUS)	Pascal Gentil (FRA)
Women				
49 kg (flyweight)	Lauren Burns (AUS)		Urbia Rodríguez (CUB)	Chi Shu-Ji (TPE)
57 kg (featherweight)	Jung Jae-Eun (KOR)		Hieu Ngan Tran (VIE)	Hamide Bikcin (TUR)
67 kg (welterweight)	Lee Sun-Hee (KOR)		Trude Gundersen (NOR)	Yoriko Okamoto (JPN)
67+ kg (heavyweight)	Chen Zhong (CHN)		Natalya Ivanova (RUS)	Dominique Bosshart (CAN)
Tennis				
Men's singles	Yevgeny Kafelnikov (RUS)	7-6 (7-4), 3-6, 6-2, 4-6, 6-3	Tommy Haas (GER)	Arnaud Di Pasquale (FRA)
Men's doubles	Canada	5-7, 6-3, 6-4, 7-6 (7-2)	Australia	Spain
Women's singles	Venus Williams (USA)	6-2, 6-4	Yelena Dementyeva (RUS)	Monica Seles (USA)
Women's doubles	United States	6-1, 6-1	The Netherlands	Belgium
Track and Field (Athletics)				
Men				
100 m	Maurice Greene (USA)	9.87 sec	Ato Boldon (TRI)	Obadele Thompson (BAR)
200 m	Konstantinos Kenteris (GRE)	20.09 sec	Darren Campbell (GBR)	Ato Boldon (TRI)
400 m	Michael Johnson (USA)	43.84 sec	Alvin Harrison (USA)	Gregory Haughton (JAM)
4 x 100-m relay	United States	37.61 sec	Brazil	Cuba
4 x 400-m relay	United States	2 min 56.35 sec	Nigeria	Jamaica
800 m	Nils Schumann (GER)	1 min 45.08 sec	Wilson Kipketer (DEN)	Aissa Said Guerni (ALG)
1,500 m	Noah Ngeny (KEN)	3 min 32.07 sec†	Hicham El Guerrouj (MAR)	Bernard Lagat (KEN)

Olympic Medal Winners—XXVII Summer Games (continued)

Track and Field (Athletics) (continued)

EVENT	GOLD MEDALIST	PERFORMANCE	SILVER MEDALIST	BRONZE MEDALIST
Men				
5,000 m	Millon Wolde (ETH)	13 min 35.49 sec	Ali Saidi-Sief (ALG)	Brahim Lahlafi (MAR)
10,000 m	Haile Gebrselassie (ETH)	27 min 18.20 sec	Paul Tergat (KEN)	Assefa Mezgebu (ETH)
Marathon	Gezahgne Abera (ETH)	2 hr 10 min 11 sec	Eric Wainaina (KEN)	Tesfaye Tola (ETH)
110-m hurdles	Anier Garcia (CUB)	13.00 sec	Terrence Trammell (USA)	Mark Crear (USA)
400-m hurdles	Angelo Taylor (USA)	47.50 sec	Hadi Souan Somayli (SAU)	Llewellyn Herbert (RSA)
3,000-m steeple-chase	Reuben Kosgei (KEN)	8 min 21.43 sec	Wilson Bolt Kipketer (KEN)	Ali Ezzine (MAR)
20-km walk	Robert Korzeniow-ski (POL)	1 hr 18 min 59 sec†	Noe Hernández (MEX)	Vladimir Andreyev (RUS)
50-km walk	Robert Korzeniow-ski (POL)	3 hr 42 min 22 sec	Aigars Fadejevs (LAT)	Joel Sánchez (MEX)
High jump	Sergey Klyugin (RUS)	2.35 m	Javier Sotomayor (CUB)	Abderrahmane Hammad (ALG)
Long jump	Ivan Pedroso (CUB)	8.55 m	Jai Taurima (AUS)	Roman Shchurenko (UKR)
Triple jump	Jonathan Edwards (GBR)	17.71 m	Yoel Garcia (CUB)	Denis Kapustin (RUS)
Pole vault	Nick Hysong (USA)	5.90 m	Lawrence Johnson (USA)	Maksim Tarasov (RUS)
Shot put	Arsi Harju (FIN)	21.29 m	Adam Nelson (USA)	John Godina (USA)
Discus throw	Virgilijus Alekna (LTU)	69.30 m	Lars Riedel (GER)	Frantz Kruger (RSA)
Javelin throw	Jan Zelezny (CZE)	90.17 m†	Steve Backley (GBR)	Sergey Makarov (RUS)
Hammer throw	Szymon Ziolkowski (POL)	80.02 m	Nicola Vizzoni (ITA)	Igor Astapkovich (BLR)
Decathlon	Erki Nool (EST)	8,641 pt	Roman Sebrle (CZE)	Chris Huffins (USA)
Women				
100 m	Marion Jones (USA)	10.75 sec	Ekaterini Thanou (GRE)	Tanya Lawrence (JAM)
200 m	Marion Jones (USA)	21.84 sec	Pauline Davis-Thompson (BAH)	Susanthika Jayasinghe (SRI)
400 m	Cathy Freeman (AUS)	49.11 sec	Lorraine Graham (JAM)	Katharine Merry (GBR)
4 x 100-m relay	The Bahamas	41.95 sec	Jamaica	United States
4 x 400-m relay	United States	3 min 22.62 sec	Jamaica	Russia
800 m	Maria Mutola (MOZ)	1 min 56.15 sec	Stephanie Graf (AUT)	Kelly Holmes (GBR)
1,500 m	Nouria Mérah-Benida (ALG)	4 min 5.10 sec	Violeta Szekely (ROM)	Gabriela Szabo (ROM)
5,000 m	Gabriela Szabo (ROM)	14 min 40.79 sec†	Sonia O'Sullivan (IRL)	Gete Wami (ETH)
10,000 m	Derartu Tulu (ETH)	30 min 17.49 sec†	Gete Wami (ETH)	Fernanda Ribeiro (POR)
Marathon	Naoko Takahashi (JPN)	2 hr 23 min 14 sec†	Lidia Simon (ROM)	Joyce Chepchumba (KEN)
100-m hurdles	Olga Shishigina (KAZ)	12.65 sec	Glory Alozie (NGR)	Melissa Morrison (USA)
400-m hurdles	Irina Privalova (RUS)	53.02 sec	Deon Hemmings (JAM)	Nouzha Bidouane (MAR)
20-km walk	Wang Liping (CHN)	1 hr 29 min 5 sec	Kjersti Plätzer (NOR)	Maria Vasco (ESP)
High jump	Yelena Yelesina (RUS)	2.01 m	Hestrie Cloete (RSA)	Kajsa Bergqvist (SWE)
Long jump	Heike Drechsler (GER)	6.99 m	Fiona May (ITA)	Marion Jones (USA)
Triple jump	Tereza Marinova (BUL)	15.20 m	Tatyana Lebedeva (RUS)	Olena Hovorova (UKR)
Pole vault	Stacy Dragila (USA)	4.60 m	Tatyana Grigoryeva (AUS)	Vala Flosadottir (ISL)
Shot put	Yanina Korolchik (BLR)	20.56 m	Larisa Peleshenko (RUS)	Astrid Kumbernuss (GER)
Discus throw	Ellina Zvereva (BLR)	68.40 m	Anastasia Kelesidou (GRE)	Irina Yachenko (BLR)

Olympic Medal Winners—XXVII Summer Games (continued)

EVENT	GOLD MEDALIST	PERFORMANCE	SILVER MEDALIST	BRONZE MEDALIST
Track and Field (Athletics) (continued)				
Women				
Javelin throw	Trine Hattestad (NOR)	68.91 m	Mirella Maniani-Tzelli (GRE)	Osleidys Menéndez (CUB)
Hammer throw	Kamila Skolimowska (POL)	71.16 m	Olga Kuzenkova (RUS)	Kirsten Muenchow (GER)
Heptathlon	Denise Lewis (GBR)	6,584 pt	Yelena Prokhorova (RUS)	Natalya Sazanovich (BLR)
Triathlon				
Men	Simon Whitfield (CAN)	1 hr 48 min 24 sec	Stefan Vuckovic (GER)	Jan Rehula (CZE)
Women	Brigitte McMahon (SUI)	2 hr 40 sec	Michellie Jones (AUS)	Magali Messmer (SUI)
Volleyball				
Men's 12-team tournament	Yugoslavia	25–22, 25–22, 25–20	Russia	Italy
Women's 12-team tournament	Cuba	25–27, 32–34, 25–19, 25–18, 15–7	Russia	Brazil
Men's beach	United States	12–11, 12–9	Brazil	Germany
Women's beach	Australia	12–11, 12–10	Brazil	Brazil
Water Polo				
Men	Hungary	13–6	Russia	Yugoslavia
Women	Australia	4–3	United States	Russia
Weightlifting§				
Men				
56 kg (bantamweight)	Halil Mutlu (TUR)	305.0 kg‡	Wu Wenxiong (CHN)	Zhang Xiangxiang (CHN)
62 kg (featherweight)	Nikolay Pechalov (CRO)	325.0 kg†	Leonidas Sabanis (GRE)	Gennady Oleschchuk (BLR)
69 kg (lightweight)	Galabin Boevski (BUL)	357.5 kg†	Georgi Markov (BUL)	Sergey Lavrenov (BLR)
77 kg (middleweight)	Zhan Xugang (CHN)	367.5 kg	Viktor Mitrou (GRE)	Arsen Melikyan (ARM)
85 kg (light heavyweight)	Pyrros Dimas (GRE)	390.0 kg	Marc Huster (GER)	George Asanidze (GEO)
94 kg (middle heavyweight)	Akakios Kakiasvilis (GRE)	405.0 kg	Szymon Kolecki (POL)	Aleksey Petrov (RUS)
105 kg (heavyweight)	Hossein Tavakoli (IRI)	425.0 kg	Alan Tsagayev (BUL)	Said Saif Asaad (QAT)
105+ kg (super heavyweight)	Hossein Rezazadeh (IRI)	472.5 kg‡	Ronny Weller (GER)	Andrey Chemerkin (RUS)
Women				
48 kg (flyweight)	Tara Nott (USA)	185.0 kg	Raema Lisa Rumbewas (INA)	Sri Indriyani (INA)
53 kg (featherweight)	Yang Xia (CHN)	225.0 kg‡	Li Feng-Ying (TPE)	Winarni Binti Slamet (INA)
58 kg (lightweight)	Soraya Mendivil (MEX)	222.5 kg	Ri Song Hui (PRK)	Khassaraporn Suta (THA)
63 kg (middleweight)	Chen Xiaomin (CHN)	242.5 kg‡	Valentina Popova (RUS)	Ioanna Chatziioannou (GRE)
69 kg (light heavyweight)	Lin Weining (CHN)	242.5 kg	Erzsébet Markus (HUN)	Kamam Malleswari (IND)
75 kg (heavyweight)	Maria Isabel Urrutia (COL)	245.0 kg	Ruth Ogbeifo (NGR)	Kuo Yi Hang (TPE)
75+ kg (super heavyweight)	Ding Meiyuan (CHN)	300.0 kg‡	Agata Wrobel (POL)	Cheryl Haworth (USA)
Wrestling§				
Freestyle				
54 kg (flyweight)	Namig Abdullayev (AZE)		Samuel Henson (USA)	Amiran Karntanov (GRE)
58 kg (bantamweight)	Alireza Dabir (IRI)		Yevgen Buslovych (UKR)	Terry Brands (USA)

Olympic Medal Winners—XXVII Summer Games (continued)

EVENT	GOLD MEDALIST	PERFORMANCE	SILVER MEDALIST	BRONZE MEDALIST
Wrestling (continued)				
Freestyle				
63 kg (featherweight)	Murad Umakhanov (RUS)		Serafim Barzakov (BUL)	Jang Jae Sung (KOR)
69 kg (lightweight)	Daniel Igali (CAN)		Arsen Gitinov (RUS)	Lincoln McIlravy (USA)
76 kg (welterweight)	Brandon Slay (USA)		Moon Eui Jae (KOR)	Adem Bereket (TUR)
85 kg (middleweight)	Adam Saytyev (RUS)		Yoel Romero (CUB)	Mogamed Ibragimov (MKD)
97 kg (light heavy-weight)	Saghid Murtasaliyev (RUS)		Islam Bayramukov (KAZ)	Eldar Kurtanidze (GEO)
130+ kg (super heavyweight)	David Musulbes (RUS)		Artur Taymazov (UZB)	Alexis Rodriguez (CUB)
Greco-Roman				
54 kg (flyweight)	Sim Kwon Ho (KOR)		Lazaro Rivas (CUB)	Kang Young Gyun (PRK)
58 kg (bantamweight)	Armen Nazaryan (BUL)		Kim In Sub (KOR)	Sheng Zetian (CHN)
63 kg (featherweight)	Varteres Samurgashev (RUS)		Juan Luis Maren (CUB)	Akaki Chachua (GEO)
69 kg (lightweight)	Filiberto Azcuy (CUB)		Katsuhiko Nagata (JPN)	Aleksey Glushkov (RUS)
76 kg (welterweight)	Murat Kardanov (RUS)		Matt James Lindland (USA)	Marko Yli-Hannuksela (FIN)
85 kg (middleweight)	Hamza Yerlikaya (TUR)		Sandor Istvan Bardosi (HUN)	Mukran Vaktang-adze (GEO)
97 kg (light heavy-weight)	Mikael Ljungberg (SWE)		Davyd Saldadze (UKR)	Garrett Lowney (USA)
130+ kg (super heavyweight)	Rulon Gardner (USA)		Aleksandr Karelin (RUS)	Dmitry Debelka (BLR)

*Two bronze medals awarded in each weight division. †Olympic record. ‡World record. §New weight classes introduced for 2000 games. ¶Tie.

Did you know? In the Olympic stadium and its immediate surroundings, the Olympic flag is flown with the flags of the nations taking part in the games. The Olympic flag presented by Baron Coubertin in 1914 is the prototype: it has a white background and in the center are five interlaced rings of blue, yellow, black, green, and red. The blue ring is on the left next to the pole. These rings represent the five continents joined together in the Olympic Movement.

Olympic Medal Winners—XIX Winter Games (2002)
The XIX Winter Games were held in Salt Lake City UT, 8–24 Feb 2002.

EVENT	GOLD MEDALIST	PERFORMANCE	SILVER MEDALIST	BRONZE MEDALIST
Alpine Skiing				
Men				
Downhill	Fritz Strobl (AUT)	1 min 39.13 sec	Lasse Kjus (NOR)	Stephan Eberharter (AUT)
Slalom	Jean-Pierre Vidal (FRA)	1 min 41.06 sec	Sebastien Amiez (FRA)	Benjamin Raich (AUT)
Giant slalom	Stephan Eberharter (AUT)	2 min 23.28 sec	Bode Miller (USA)	Lasse Kjus (NOR)
Super G	Kjetil Andre Aamodt (NOR)	1 min 21.58 sec	Stephan Eberharter (AUT)	Andreas Schifferer (AUT)
Combined event	Kjetil Andre Aamodt (NOR)	3 min 17.56 sec	Bode Miller (USA)	Benjamin Raich (AUT)
Women				
Downhill	Carole Montillet (FRA)	1 min 39.56 sec	Isolde Kostner (ITA)	Renate Götschl (AUT)
Slalom	Janica Kostelic (CRO)	1 min 46.10 sec	Laure Pequegnot (FRA)	Anja Pärson (SWE)
Giant slalom	Janica Kostelic (CRO)	2 min 30.01 sec	Anja Pärson (SWE)	Sonja Nef (SUI)
Super G	Daniela Ceccarelli (ITA)	1 min 13.59 sec	Janica Kostelic (CRO)	Karen Putzer (ITA)
Combined event	Janica Kostelic (CRO)	2 min 43.28 sec	Renate Götschl (AUT)	Martina Ertl (GER)

Olympic Medal Winners—XIX Winter Games (2002) (continued)

EVENT	GOLD MEDALIST	PERFORMANCE	SILVER MEDALIST	BRONZE MEDALIST
Nordic Skiing				
Men				
1.5-km sprint	Tor Arne Hetland (NOR)	2 min 56.9 sec	Peter Schlickenrieder (GER)	Cristian Zorzi (ITA)
10-km freestyle pursuit	Johann Mühlegg (ESP)	49 min 20.4 sec	Thomas Alsgaard (NOR)*; Frode Estil (NOR)*	
15-km classical	Andrus Veerpalu (EST)	37 min 7.4 sec	Frode Estil (NOR)	Jaak Mae (EST)
30-km freestyle mass start	Johann Mühlegg (ESP)	1 hr 9 min 28.9 sec	Christian Hoffmann (AUT)	Mikhail Botvinov (AUT)
50-km classical	Mikhail Ivanov (RUS)	2 hr 6 min 20.8 sec	Andrus Veerpalu (EST)	Odd-Björn Hjelmeset (NOR)
4 x 10-km relay	Norway	1 hr 32 min 45.5 sec	Italy	Germany
90-m ski jump	Simon Ammann (SUI)	269.0 pt	Sven Hannawald (GER)	Adam Malysz (POL)
120-m ski jump	Simon Ammann (SUI)	281.4 pt	Adam Malysz (POL)	Matti Hautamäki (FIN)
120-m team ski jump	Germany	974.1 pt	Finland	Slovenia
Nordic combined sprint (7.5-km)	Samppa Lajunen (FIN)	16 min 40.1 sec	Ronny Ackermann (GER)	Felix Gottwald (AUT)
Nordic combined 15-km	Samppa Lajunen (FIN)	39 min 11.76cc	Jaakko Tallus (FIN)	Felix Gottwald (AUT)
Nordic combined team relay	Finland	48 min 42.2 sec	Germany	Austria
Women				
1.5-km sprint	Yuliya Chepalova (RUS)	3 min 10.6 sec	Evi Sachenbacher (GER)	Anita Moen (NOR)
5-km freestyle pursuit	Olga Danilova (RUS)	24 min 52.1 sec	Larisa Lazutina (RUS)	Beckie Scott (CAN)
10-km classical	Bente Skari (NOR)	28 min 5.6 sec	Olga Danilova (RUS)	Yuliya Chepalova (RUS)
15-km freestyle mass start	Stefania Belmondo (ITA)	39 min 54.4 sec	Larisa Lazutina (RUS)	Katerina Neumannova (CZE)
30-km classical	Gabriella Paruzzi (ITA)	1 hr 30 min 57.1 sec	Stefania Belmondo (ITA)	Bente Skari (NOR)
4 x 5-km relay	Germany	49 min 30.6 sec	Norway	Switzerland
Biathlon				
Men				
10-km sprint	Ole Einar Björndalen (NOR)	24 min 51.3 sec	Sven Fischer (GER)	Wolfgang Perner (AUT)
12.5-km pursuit	Ole Einar Björndalen (NOR)	32 min 34.6 sec	Raphael Poiree (FRA)	Ricco Gross (GER)
20 km	Ole Einar Björndalen (NOR)	51 min 3.3 sec	Frank Luck (GER)	Viktor Maygourov (RUS)
4 x 7.5-km relay	Norway	1 hr 23 min 42.3 sec	Germany	France
Women				
7.5-km sprint	Kati Wilhelm (GER)	20 min 41.4 sec	Uschi Disl (GER)	Magdalena Forsberg (SWE)
10-km pursuit	Olga Pyleva (RUS)	31 min 7.7 sec	Kati Wilhelm (GER)	Irina Nikulchina (RUS)
15 km	Andrea Henkel (GER)	47 min 29.1 sec	Liv Grete Poiree (NOR)	Magdalena Forsberg (SWE)
4 x 7.5-km relay	Germany	1 hr 27 min 55.0 sec	Norway	Russia
Freestyle Skiing				
Men				
Moguls	Janne Lahtela (FIN)	27.97 pt	Travis Mayer (USA)	Richard Gay (FRA)
Aerials	Ales Valenta (CZE)	257.02 pt	Joe Pack (USA)	Aleksey Grishin (BLR)
Women				
Moguls	Kari Traa (NOR)	25.94 pt	Shannon Bahrke (USA)	Tae Satoya (JPN)
Aerials	Alisa Camplin (AUS)	193.47 pt	Veronica Brenner (CAN)	Deidra Dionne (CAN)

Olympic Medal Winners—XIX Winter Games (2002) (continued)

EVENT	GOLD MEDALIST	PERFORMANCE	SILVER MEDALIST	BRONZE MEDALIST
Snowboarding				
Men				
Parallel giant slalom	Philipp Schoch (SUI)		Richard Richardsson (SWE)	Chris Klug (USA)
Halfpipe	Ross Powers (USA)	46.1 pt	Danny Kass (USA)	Jarret Thomas (USA)
Women				
Parallel giant slalom	Isabelle Blanc (FRA)		Karine Ruby (FRA)	Lidia Trettel (ITA)
Halfpipe	Kelly Clark (USA)	47.9 pt	Doriane Vidal (FRA)	Fabienne Reuteler (SUI)
Figure skating				
Men	Aleksey Yagudin (RUS)	1.5 pt	Yevgeny Plushchenko (RUS)	Timothy Goebel (USA)
Women	Sarah Hughes (USA)	3.0 pt	Irina Slutskaya (RUS)	Michelle Kwan (USA)
Pairs	Yelena Berezhnaya, Anton Sikharulidze (RUS)*; Jamie Salé, David Pelletier (CAN)*			Shen Xue, Zhao Hongbo (CHN)
Ice dancing	Marina Anissina, Gwendal Peizerat (FRA)	2.0 pt	Irina Lobacheva, Ilya Averbukh (RUS)	Barbara Fusar Poli, Maurizio Margaglio (ITA)
Speed Skating				
Men				
500 m	Casey FitzRandolph (USA)	1 min 9.23 sec	Hiroyasu Shimizu (JPN)	Kip Carpenter (USA)
1,000 m	Gerard van Velde (NED)	1 min 7.18 sec†	Jan Bos (NED)	Joey Cheek (USA)
1,500 m	Derek Parra (USA)	1 min 43.95 sec†	Jochem Uytdehaage (NED)	Adne Sondral (NOR)
5,000 m	Jochem Uytdehaage (NED)	6 min 14.66 sec†	Derek Parra (USA)	Jens Boden (GER)
10,000 m	Jochem Uytdehaage (NED)	12 min 58.92 sec†	Gianni Romme (NED)	Lasse Saetre (NOR)
Women				
500 m	Catriona LeMay Doan (CAN)	1 min 14.75 sec	Monique Garbrecht-Enfeldt (GER)	Sabine Völker (GER)
1,000 m	Chris Witty (USA)	1 min 13.83 sec†	Sabine Völker (GER)	Jennifer Rodriguez (USA)
1,500 m	Anni Friesinger (GER)	1 min 54.02 sec†	Sabine Völker (GER)	Jennifer Rodriguez (USA)
3,000 m	Claudia Pechstein (GER)	3 min 57.70 sec†	Renate Groenewold (NED)	Cindy Klassen (CAN)
5,000 m	Claudia Pechstein (GER)	6 min 46.91 sec†	Gretha Smit (NED)	Clara Hughes (CAN)
Short-Track Speed Skating				
Men				
500 m	Marc Gagnon (CAN)	41.802 sec‡	Jonathan Guilmette (CAN)	Rusty Smith (USA)
1,000 m	Steven Bradbury (AUS)	1 min 29.109 sec	Apolo Anton Ohno (USA)	Mathieu Turcotte (CAN)
1,500 m	Apolo Anton Ohno (USA)	2 min 18.541 sec	Li Jiajun (CHN)	Marc Gagnon (CAN)
5,000-m relay	Canada	6 min 51.579 sec	Italy	China
Women				
500 m	Yang Yang (A) (CHN)	44.187 sec	Evgeniya Radanova (BUL)	Wang Chunlu (CHN)
1,000 m	Yang Yang (A) (CHN)	1 min 36.391 sec	Ko Gi Hyun (KOR)	Yang Yang (S) (CHN)
1,500 m	Ko Gi Hyun (KOR)	2 min 31.581 sec	Choi Eun Kyung (KOR)	Evgeniya Radanova (BUL)
3,000-m relay	South Korea	4 min 12.793 sec†	China	Canada
Ice Hockey				
Men (winning team)	Canada	4-1-1	United States	Russia
Women (winning team)	Canada	5-0-0	United States	Sweden

Olympic Medal Winners—XIX Winter Games (2002) (continued)

EVENT	GOLD MEDALIST	PERFORMANCE	SILVER MEDALIST	BRONZE MEDALIST
Curling				
Men (winning team)	Norway	9-2-0	Canada	Switzerland
Women (winning team)	Great Britain	9-4-0	Switzerland	Canada
Bobsleigh (Bobsled)				
Two man	Christoph Langen, Markus Zimmermann (GER 1)	3 min 10.11 sec	Steve Anderhub, Christian Reich (SUI 1)	Martin Annen, Beat Hefti (SUI 2)
Four man	Germany 2	3 min 7.51 sec	United States 1	United States 2
Women	Jill Bakken, Vonetta Flowers (USA 2)	1 min 37.76 sec	Sandra Prokoff, Ulrike Holzner (GER 1)	Susi-Lisa Erdmann, Nicole Herschmann (GER 2)
Luge				
Men (singles)	Armin Zöggeler (ITA)	2 min 57.941 sec	Georg Hackl (GER)	Markus Prock (AUT)
Men (doubles)	Patric-Fritz Leitner, Alexander Resch (GER)	1 min 26.082 sec	Brian Martin, Mark Grimmette (USA)	Chris Thorpe, Clay Ives (USA)
Women (singles)	Sylke Otto (GER)	2 min 52.464 sec	Barbara Niedernhuber (GER)	Silke Kraushaar (GER)
Skeleton				
Men	Jim Shea (USA)	1 min 41.96 sec	Martin Rettl (AUT)	Gregor Staehli (SUI)
Women	Tristan Gale (USA)	1 min 45.11 sec	Lea Ann Parsley (USA)	Alex Coomber (GBR)

*Two medals awarded. †World record. ‡Olympic record.

Special Olympics

The Special Olympics is an international program to provide retarded persons (8 years of age or older) with year-round sports training and athletic competition in a variety of Olympic-type summer and winter sports. Inaugurated in 1968, the Special Olympics was officially recognized by the International Olympic Committee on 15 Feb 1988. **International headquarters** are in Washington DC.

In June 1963, with support from the Joseph P. Kennedy, Jr., Foundation, **Eunice Kennedy Shriver** (sister of Pres. John F Kennedy) started a summer day-camp for retarded children at her home in Rockville MD. Between 1963 and 1968, the Kennedy Foundation promoted the creation of dozens of similar camps in the United States and Canada. Special awards were developed for physical achievements, and by 1968 Shriver had persuaded the Chicago Park District to join with the Kennedy Foundation in sponsoring a "Special Olympics," held at Soldier Field on 19-20 July. About 1,000 athletes from 26 US states and Canada participated. The games were such a success that, in December, Special Olympics, Inc. (now **Special Olympics International**), was founded, with chapters in the United States, Canada, and France. The first International Winter Special Olympics Games were held on **5-11 Feb 1977** (in Steamboat Springs CO). The number of participating countries proliferated so that by the 1990s there were chapters in some 90 countries. Over 15,000 meets and tournaments are held worldwide each year, culminating in the International Special Olympics Games every two years, alternating between winter and summer sports and each lasting for nine days.

Special Olympics Web site: <www.specialolympics.org>

Did you know? More than 11,500 people ran in the 2002 Olympic Torch Relay, which began in Atlanta GA on 4 Dec 2001, and ended in Salt Lake City UT on 8 Feb 2002.

Archery

The international governing body for archery, the **Fédération Internationale de Tir à l'Arc (FITA)**, instituted world championships in 1931. Between 1931 and 1957 a variety of scoring rounds were used. In 1957, however, FITA established its own competition standard—two FITA rounds shot over four days. A single FITA **round** consists of 36 arrows shot from each of four distances; different distances are used for men's and women's competition. From 1987 to 1991 the grand FITA round was used. The Olympic round was used for the 1992 Olympic Games and the 1993 world championships; under this system the highest possible individual score in the finals round was 120. Since 1959 championships have been held biennially. Olympic competition is held with the **recurve style** of bow in which the limbs of the bow curve in one direction, then "recurve" in the other.

FITA Web site: <www.archery.org>

FITA Outdoor World Target Archery Championships

Competition dates from 1931. Table includes data from 1983 in the Olympic (recurve) division only.

	men's				women's			
YEAR	INDIVIDUAL	POINTS	TEAM	POINTS	INDIVIDUAL	POINTS	TEAM	POINTS
1983	Rick McKinney (USA)	2,617	USA	7,812	Kim Jin Ho (KOR)	2,616	KOR	7,704
1985	Rick McKinney (USA)	2,601	KOR	7,660	Irina Soldatova (URS)	2,595	URS	7,721
1987	Vladimir Yesheyev (URS)	329	FRG	891	Ma Xiangjun (CHN)	330	URS	884
1989	Stanislav Zabrodsky (URS)	332	URS	985	Kim Soo Nyung (KOR)	338	KOR	995
1991	Simon Fairweather (AUS)	334	KOR	998	Kim Soo Nyung (KOR)	333	KOR	1,030
1993	Park Kyung Mo (KOR)	113	FRA	249	Kim Soo Nyung (KOR)	104	KOR	236
1995	Lee Kyung Chul (KOR)	109	KOR	255	Natalya Valeyeva (MDA)	113	KOR	247
1997	Kim Kyung Ho (KOR)	108	KOR	254	Kim Du Ri (KOR)	105	KOR	242
1999	Hong Sung Chil (KOR)	115	ITA	252	Lee Eun Kyung (KOR)	115	ITA	240
2001	Yeon Jung Ki (KOR)	115	KOR	247	Park Sung Hyun (KOR)	111	CHN	232

Did you know? It is generally agreed that the worst team in NFL history was the Dallas Texans during their one year of existence in 1952. Their play was so bad, the Texans' owner relinquished the team to the NFL halfway through the season, whereupon they were without a home and traveled as an itinerant road team. Head coach Jim Phelan and his players disliked practicing so much, they often spent practice time playing volleyball over the goalposts or going to the local racetrack. The Texans' only victory during that season came when Chicago Bears head coach George Halas fielded his second-string players in a display of overconfidence. Attendance was so sparse at some Texans games, Coach Phelan once commented, "Instead of running under the goal posts for introductions, let's just go up and shake hands with everybody. It would be faster. It won't take more than a minute or two."

Automobile Racing

O f the various types of automobile races, the closed-circuit, or speedway, course was largely developed in the United States. The Indianapolis 500—[now] the premiere Indy car event—was first run in 1911. A low-slung, fenderless (open-wheel) car—called an Indy car—is essential for this race; its suspension (i.e., its ability to hold the track) is as important to a car's performance as its turbocharged engine. Often the chassis manufacturer is different from the engine manufacturer, resulting in cars identified, for example, as a Brabham/Repco. In such cases the chassis-maker is listed first, and the chassis-maker receives any money or awards that the car may win.

Indy car racing began in 1909, when the American Automobile Association (AAA) began sponsoring a 24-race championship series, including three races at the newly opened Indianapolis Motor Speedway (IMS). In 1956 the AAA gave up its involvement with auto racing, and the United States Auto Club (**USAC**) was organized as the sport's governing body. In 1978 two race-car owners broke away from USAC to form a new organization, Championship Auto Racing Teams, Inc. (**CART**), which sponsored its own series of races. In 1980 CART and USAC joined to form the Championship Racing League, which dissolved after five races. In 1994 the IMS announced a new Indy Racing League (IRL) to oversee the Indianapolis 500 beginning in 1996 and a new series of IRL races (leading to an annual drivers' championship) separate from those sponsored by CART.

The standard cars used for Grand Prix road (i.e., closed highway) racing are known as Formula One (or F-1) cars because they are built according to an evolving formula that was established after World War I by the Fédération Internationale de l'Automobile (**FIA**). Like the Indy car, the Formula One racer is open-

wheeled and low-slung, but the F-1 is slightly smaller and more maneuverable.

There are approximately 17 Grand Prix events held worldwide throughout the year. Drivers compete for the **World Championship of Drivers** (inaugurated in 1950), receiving a total number of points based on their placement in each of the official Grand Prix events.

Many Grand Prix drivers participate in various endurance races, the most famous of which is the **Le Mans Grand Prix d'Endurance**, held on the 13.4-km (8.3-mi) Sarthe circuit, Le Mans, France.

Another type of popular racing event is the rally, which was established in 1907. More than 35 such competitions, raced over a specified route on public roads, take place yearly throughout the world. The classic occasion for rally racing is the **Rallye Automobile Monte-Carlo**, now started in various European cities with Monaco as its terminal point.

Stock car racing, which began in the United States in the first half of the 20th century, involves the racing of commercial cars that have been altered to increase their speed and maneuverability. The National Association for Stock Car Auto Racing (**NASCAR**) was founded in 1947 and awards the Winston Cup to the driver who has achieved the greatest number of points earned in a series of official NASCAR Winston Cup events over the stock car racing season. The **Daytona 500** is the premiere stock car event.

Related Internet sites: CART: <www.cart.com>; USAC: <www.usacracing.com>; IRL: <www.indyracingleague. com>; FIA (English and French): <www.fia.com>; Automobile Club de Monaco (rallye—English and French) <www.acm.mc/acm/acm-intro.php>; NASCAR: <www. nascar.com>

Formula One Grand Prix Race Results, 2001–02

The following 17 races comprise the Formula One circuit. The season is March–October.
The United States Grand Prix, held at the Indianapolis Motor Speedway, was added in 2000.

RACE	DATE	LOCALE	DRIVER (COUNTRY)	WINNER'S TIME (HR:MIN:SEC)
Hungarian Grand Prix	19 Aug 2001	Budapest	Michael Schumacher (GER)	1:41:49.675
Belgian Grand Prix	2 Sep 2001	Spa-Francorchamps	Michael Schumacher (GER)	1:08:05.002
Italian Grand Prix	16 Sep 2001	Monza	Juan Pablo Montoya (COL)	1:16:58.493
United States Grand Prix	30 Sep 2001	Indianapolis	Mika Häkkinen (FIN)	1:32:42.840
Japanese Grand Prix	14 Oct 2001	Suzuka	Michael Schumacher (GER)	1:27:33.298
Australian Grand Prix	3 Mar 2002	Albert Park, Melbourne	Michael Schumacher (GFR)	1:35:36.792
Malaysian Grand Prix	17 Mar 2002	Kuala Lumpur	Ralf Schumacher (GER)	1:34:12.912
Brazilian Grand Prix	31 Mar 2002	São Paulo	Michael Schumacher (GER)	1:31:43.663
San Marino Grand Prix	14 Apr 2002	Imola	Michael Schumacher (GER)	1:29:10.789
Spanish Grand Prix	28 Apr 2002	Barcelona	Michael Schumacher (GER)	1:30:29.981
Austrian Grand Prix	12 May 2002	A1-Ring	Michael Schumacher (GER)	1:33:51.562
Monaco Grand Prix	26 May 2002	Monaco	David Coulthard (GBR)	1:45:39.055
Canadian Grand Prix	9 Jun 2002	Montreal	Michael Schumacher (GER)	1:33:36.111
European Grand Prix	23 Jun 2002	Nurburgring, Ger.	Rubens Barrichello (BRA)	1:35:07.426
British Grand Prix	7 Jul 2002	Silverstone	Michael Schumacher (GER)	1:31:45.015
French Grand Prix	21 Jul 2002	Magny-Cours	Michael Schumacher (GER)	1:32:09.837
German Grand Prix	28 Jul 2002	Hockenheim	Michael Schumacher (GER)	1:27:52.078

World Championship of Drivers

Points are awarded to the top-finishing drivers in each race on the Grand Prix circuit and totaled at the end of the season to determine the championship. In 2001 the top three were: Michael Schumacher (GER) 123 points, David Coulthard (GBR) 65 points, Rubens Barrichello (BRA) 56 points. Where chassis and engine are made by different manufacturers, the chassis is given first and separated from the engine name by a slash.

YEAR	DRIVER (NATIONALITY)	CONSTRUCTOR
1950	Giuseppe Farina (ITA)	Alfa Romeo
1951	Juan Manuel Fangio (ARG)	Alfa Romeo
1952	Alberto Ascari (ITA)	Ferrari
1953	Alberto Ascari (ITA)	Ferrari
1954	Juan Manuel Fangio (ARG)	Mercedes & Maserati
1955	Juan Manuel Fangio (ARG)	Mercedes
1956	Juan Manuel Fangio (ARG)	Lancia/Ferrari
1957	Juan Manuel Fangio (ARG)	Maserati
1958	Mike Hawthorn (GBR)	Ferrari
1959	Jack Brabham (AUS)	Cooper/Climax
1960	Jack Brabham (AUS)	Cooper/Climax
1961	Phil Hill (USA)	Ferrari
1962	Graham Hill (GBR)	BRM
1963	Jim Clark (GBR)	Lotus/Climax
1964	John Surtees (GBR)	Ferrari
1965	Jim Clark (GBR)	Lotus/Climax
1966	Jack Brabham (AUS)	Brabham/Repco
1967	Denny Hulme (NZL)	Brabham/Repco
1968	Graham Hill (GBR)	Lotus/Ford
1969	Jackie Stewart (GBR)	Matra/Ford
1970	Jochen Rindt (AUT)	Lotus/Ford
1971	Jackie Stewart (GBR)	Tyrrell/Ford
1972	Emerson Fittipaldi (BRA)	John Player Special/Ford
1973	Jackie Stewart (GBR)	Tyrrell/Ford
1974	Emerson Fittipaldi (BRA)	McLaren/Ford
1975	Niki Lauda (AUT)	Ferrari
1976	James Hunt (GBR)	McLaren/Ford
1977	Niki Lauda (AUT)	Ferrari

YEAR	DRIVER (NATIONALITY)	CONSTRUCTOR
1978	Mario Andretti (USA)	Lotus
1979	Jody Scheckter (RSA)	Ferrari
1980	Alan Jones (AUS)	Williams
1981	Nelson Piquet (BRA)	Brabham
1982	Keke Rosberg (FIN)	Williams
1983	Nelson Piquet (BRA)	Brabham
1984	Niki Lauda (AUT)	McLaren/Porsche-TAG
1985	Alain Prost (FRA)	McLaren/Porsche-TAG
1986	Alain Prost (FRA)	McLaren/Porsche-TAG
1987	Nelson Piquet (BRA)	Williams/Honda
1988	Ayrton Senna (BRA)	McLaren/Honda
1989	Alain Prost (FRA)	McLaren/Honda
1990	Ayrton Senna (BRA)	McLaren/Honda
1991	Ayrton Senna (BRA)	McLaren/Honda
1992	Nigel Mansell (GBR)	Williams/Renault
1993	Alain Prost (FRA)	Williams/Renault
1994	Michael Schumacher (GER)	Benetton/Ford
1995	Michael Schumacher (GER)	Benetton/Renault
1996	Damon Hill (GBR)	Williams/Renault
1997	Jacques Villeneuve (CAN)	Williams/Renault
1998	Mika Häkkinen (FIN)	McLaren/Mercedes
1999	Mika Häkkinen (FIN)	McLaren/Mercedes
2000	Michael Schumacher (GER)	Ferrari
2001	Michael Schumacher (GER)	Ferrari

 **Did you know?** Race car is a palindrome.

Constructors' Championship

Points are awarded to the constructors of the top-finishing autos in each race on the Grand Prix circuit and totaled at the end of the season to determine the Constructors' Championship. In 2001 the top three were: Ferrari 179 points, McLaren/Mercedes 102 points, Williams/BMW 80 points.

YEAR	CONSTRUCTOR	YEAR	CONSTRUCTOR	YEAR	CONSTRUCTOR	YEAR	CONSTRUCTOR
1958	Vanwall	1969	Matra	1980	Williams	1991	McLaren/Honda
1959	Cooper	1970	Lotus	1981	Williams	1992	Williams/Renault
1960	Cooper	1971	Tyrrell	1982	Ferrari	1993	Williams/Renault
1961	Ferrari	1972	Lotus	1983	Ferrari	1994	Williams/Renault
1962	BRM	1973	Lotus	1984	McLaren	1995	Benetton/Renault
1963	Lotus	1974	McLaren	1985	McLaren	1996	Williams/Renault
1964	Ferrari	1975	Ferrari	1986	Williams/Honda	1997	Williams/Renault
1965	Lotus	1976	Ferrari	1987	Williams/Honda	1998	McLaren/Mercedes
1966	Brabham	1977	Ferrari	1988	McLaren/Honda	1999	Ferrari
1967	Brabham	1978	Lotus	1989	McLaren/Honda	2000	Ferrari
1968	Lotus	1979	Ferrari	1990	McLaren/Honda	2001	Ferrari

Indy Car Champions

Between 1909 and 1955 called the AAA National Champions; called the USAC National Champions from 1956 to 1978. There was no competition 1942–45. The title was won by an American racer except as indicated. Indianapolis Motor Speedway Web site: <http://my.brickyard.com/500>.

YEAR	DRIVER	YEAR	DRIVER	YEAR	DRIVER
1909	George Robertson	1940	Rex Mays	1975	A.J. Foyt, Jr.
1910	Ray Harroun	1941	Rex Mays	1976	Gordon Johncock
1911	Ralph Mulford	1946	Ted Horn	1977	Tom Sneva
1912	Ralph DePalma	1947	Ted Horn	1978	Tom Sneva
1913	Earl Cooper	1948	Ted Horn	1979	A.J. Foyt, Jr.*; Rick
1914	Ralph DePalma	1949	Johnnie Parsons		Mears†
1915	Earl Cooper	1950	Henry Banks	1980	Johnny Rutherford
1916	Dario Resta (FRA)	1951	Tony Bettenhausen, Sr.	1981	Rick Mears
1917	Earl Cooper	1952	Chuck Stevenson	1982	Rick Mears
1918	Ralph Mulford	1953	Sam Hanks	1983	Al Unser
1919	Howard ("Howdy") Wilcox	1954	Jimmy Bryan	1984	Mario Andretti
1920	Tommy Milton	1955	Robert Sweikert	1985	Al Unser
1921	Tommy Milton	1956	Jimmy Bryan	1986	Bobby Rahal
1922	Jimmy Murphy	1957	Jimmy Bryan	1987	Bobby Rahal
1923	Eddie Hearne	1958	Tony Bettenhausen, Sr.	1988	Danny Sullivan
1924	Jimmy Murphy	1959	Rodger Ward	1989	Emerson Fittipaldi (BRA)
1925	Peter DePaolo	1960	A.J. Foyt, Jr.	1990	Al Unser, Jr.
1926	Harry Hartz	1961	A.J. Foyt, Jr.	1991	Michael Andretti
1927	Peter DePaolo	1962	Rodger Ward	1992	Bobby Rahal
1928	Louie Meyer	1963	A.J. Foyt, Jr.	1993	Nigel Mansell (GBR)
1929	Louie Meyer	1964	A.J. Foyt, Jr.	1994	Al Unser, Jr.
1930	Billy Arnold	1965	Mario Andretti	1995	Jacques Villeneuve (CAN)
1931	Louis Schneider	1966	Mario Andretti	1996	Jimmy Vasser
1932	Bob Carey	1967	A.J. Foyt, Jr.	1997	Alessandro (Alex) Zanardi
1933	Louie Meyer	1968	Bobby Unser		(ITA)
1934	Bill Cummings	1969	Mario Andretti	1998	Alessandro (Alex) Zanardi
1935	Kelly Petillo	1970	Al Unser		(ITA)
1936	Mauri Rose	1971	Joe Leonard	1999	Juan Montoya (COL)
1937	Wilbur Shaw	1972	Joe Leonard	2000	Gil de Ferran (FRA)
1938	Floyd Roberts	1973	Roger McCluskey	2001	Gil de Ferran (FRA)
1939	Wilbur Shaw	1974	Bobby Unser		

*USAC champion.   †CART champion from 1980.

Indianapolis 500

There was no competition 1917–18; 1942–45.
The race was won by an American racer unless otherwise noted.

YEAR	WINNER	AVG. SPEED (MPH)	YEAR	WINNER	AVG. SPEED (MPH)	YEAR	WINNER	AVG. SPEED (MPH)
1911	Ray Harroun	74.602	1914	René Thomas (FRA)	82.474	1916*	Dario Resta (FRA)	84.001
1912	Joe Dawson	78.719				1919	Howdy Wilcox	88.050
1913	Jules Goux (FRA)	75.933	1915	Ralph DePalma	89.840	1920	Gaston Chevrolet	88.618

Indianapolis 500 (continued)

YEAR	WINNER	AVG. SPEED (MPH)	YEAR	WINNER	AVG. SPEED (MPH)	YEAR	WINNER	AVG. SPEED (MPH)
1921	Tommy Milton	89.621	1955	Robert Sweikert	128.209	1982	Gordon John- cock	162.029
1922	Jimmy Murphy	94.484	1956	Pat Flaherty	128.490			
1923	Tommy Milton	90.954	1957	Sam Hanks	135.601	1983	Tom Sneva	162.117
1924	L.L. Corum, Joe Boyer	98.234	1958	Jimmy Bryan	133.791	1984	Rick Mears	163.612
			1959	Rodger Ward	135.857	1985	Danny Sullivan	152.982
1925	Peter DePaolo	101.127	1960	Jim Rathmann	138.767	1986	Bobby Rahal	170.722
1926†	Frank Lockhart	95.904	1961	A.J. Foyt, Jr.	139.131	1987	Al Unser	162.175
1927	George Souders	97.545	1962	Rodger Ward	140.293	1988	Rick Mears	144.809
1928	Louie Meyer	99.482	1963	Parnelli Jones	143.137	1989	Emerson Fitti- paldi (BRA)	167.581
1929	Ray Keech	97.585	1964	A.J. Foyt, Jr.	147.350			
1930	Billy Arnold	100.448	1965	Jim Clark (GBR)	150.686	1990	Arie Luyendyk (NED)	185.984
1931	Louis Schneider	96.629	1966	Graham Hill (GBR)	144.317			
1932	Fred Frame	104.144				1991	Rick Mears	176.457
1933	Louie Meyer	104.162	1967	A.J. Foyt, Jr.	151.207	1992	Al Unser, Jr.	134.479
1934	Bill Cummings	104.863	1968	Bobby Unser	152.882	1993	Emerson Fitti- paldi (BRA)	157.207
1935	Kelly Petillo	106.240	1969	Mario Andretti	156.867			
1936	Louie Meyer	109.069	1970	Al Unser	155.749	1994	Al Unser, Jr.	160.872
1937	Wilbur Shaw	113.580	1971	Al Unser	157.735	1995	Jacques Ville- neuve (CAN)	153.616
1938	Floyd Roberts	117.200	1972	Mark Donohue	162.962			
1939	Wilbur Shaw	115.035	1973†	Gordon John- cock	159.036	1996	Buddy Lazier	147.956
1940	Wilbur Shaw	114.277				1997	Arie Luyendyk (NED)	145.827
1941	Floyd Davis, Mauri Rose	115.117	1974	Johnny Ruther- ford	158.589			
						1998	Eddie Cheever, Jr.	145.155
1946	George Robson	114.820	1975†	Bobby Unser	149.213			
1947	Mauri Rose	116.338	1976†	Johnny Ruther- ford	148.725	1999	Kenny Brack (SWE)	153.176
1948	Mauri Rose	119.814						
1949	Bill Holland	121.327	1977	A.J. Foyt, Jr.	161.331	2000	Juan Montoya (COL)	167.607
1950†	Johnnie Parsons	124.002	1978	Al Unser	161.363			
1951	Lee Wallard	126.244	1979	Rick Mears	158.899	2001	Helio Castro- neves (BRA)	153.601
1952	Troy Ruttman	128.922	1980	Johnny Ruther- ford	142.802			
1953	Bill Vukovich	128.740				2002	Helio Castro- neves (BRA)	166.499
1954	Bill Vukovich	130.840	1981	Bobby Unser	139.084			

*Scheduled 300-mile race. †Race stopped because of rain (in 1926 after 400 miles, in 1950 after 345 miles, in 1973 after 332.5 miles, in 1975 after 435 miles, in 1976 after 255 miles).

Le Mans Grand Prix d'Endurance
Also called Le Mans 24-hour Race.

YEAR	CAR	DRIVERS
1923	Chenard & Walcker	André Lagache, René Léonard
1924	Bentley	John Duff, Frank Clément
1925	Lorraine-Dietrich	Gérard de Courcelles, André Rossignol
1926	Lorraine-Dietrich	Robert Bloch, André Rossignol
1927	Bentley	John Benjafield, Sammy Davis
1928	Bentley	Woolf Barnato, Bernard Rubin
1929	Bentley	Woolf Barnato, Henry Birkin
1930	Bentley	Woolf Barnato, Glen Kidston
1931	Alfa Romeo	Lord Howe, Henry Birkin
1932	Alfa Romeo	Raymond Sommer, Luigi Chinetti
1933	Alfa Romeo	Raymond Sommer, Tazio Nuvolari
1934	Alfa Romeo	Luigi Chinetti, Philippe Etancelin
1935	Lagonda	John Hindmarsh, Luis Fontés
1936	no competition	
1937	Bugatti	Jean-Pierre Wimille, Robert Benoist
1938	Delahaye	Eugene Chaboud, Jean Trémoulet
1939	Bugatti	Jean-Pierre Wimille, Pierre Veyron
1940–48	no competition	
1949	Ferrari	Luigi Chinetti, Lord Selsdon
1950	Talbot	Louis Rosier, Jean-Louis Rosier
1951	Jaguar	Peter Walker, Peter Whitehead
1952	Mercedes-Benz	Hermann Lang, Fritz Riess
1953	Jaguar C-type	Tony Rolt, Duncan Hamilton
1954	Ferrari 375	Froilan Gonzalez, Maurice Trintignant
1955	Jaguar D-type	Mike Hawthorn, Ivor Bueb
1956	Jaguar D-type	Ron Flockhart, Ninian Sanderson

Le Mans Grand Prix d'Endurance (continued)

YEAR	CAR	DRIVERS
1957	Jaguar D-type	Ivor Bueb, Ron Flockhart
1958	Ferrari	Phil Hill, Olivier Gendebien
1959	Aston Martin	Roy Salvadori, Carroll Shelby
1960	Ferrari	Paul Frère, Olivier Gendebien
1961	Ferrari	Phil Hill, Olivier Gendebien
1962	Ferrari	Phil Hill, Olivier Gendebien
1963	Ferrari	Lodovico Scarfiotti, Lorenzo Bandini
1964	Ferrari	Jean Guichet, Nino Vaccarella
1965	Ferrari	Masten Gregory, Jochen Rindt
1966	Ford Mk II	Bruce McLaren, Chris Amon
1967	Ford Mk IV	A.J. Foyt, Dan Gurney
1968	Ford G.T. 40	Pedro Rodriguez, Lucien Bianchi
1969	Ford G.T. 40	Jacky Ickx, Jackie Oliver
1970	Porsche	Richard Attwood, Hans Hermann
1971	Porsche	Helmut Marko, Gijs van Lennep
1972	Matra-Simca	Henri Pescarolo, Graham Hill
1973	Matra-Simca	Henri Pescarolo, Gérard Larrousse
1974	Matra-Simca	Henri Pescarolo, Gérard Larrousse
1975	Gulf-Ford	Jacky Ickx, Derek Bell
1976	Porsche	Jacky Ickx, Gijs van Lennep
1977	Porsche	Jacky Ickx, Jurgen Barth, Hurley Haywood
1978	Renault-Alpine	Jean-Pierre Jaussaud, Didier Pironi
1979	Porsche	Klaus Ludwig, Don Whittington, Bill Whittington
1980	Porsche	Jean Rondeau, Jean-Pierre Jaussaud
1981	Porsche	Derek Bell, Jacky Ickx
1982	Porsche 956	Derek Bell, Jacky Ickx
1983	Porsche 956	Al Holbert, Hurley Hayward, Vern Schuppan
1984	Porsche 956	Henri Pescarolo, Klaus Ludwig
1985	Porsche 956	Klaus Ludwig, John Winter, Paulo Barilla
1986	Porsche 962 C	Derek Bell, Hans Stuck, Al Holbert
1987	Porsche 962 C	Hans Stuck, Derek Bell, Al Holbert
1988	Jaguar XJR 9 LM	Jan Lammers, Johnny Dumfries, Andy Wallace
1989	Sauber Mercedes-Benz C9	Jochen Mass, Manuel Reuter, Stanley Dickens
1990	Jaguar XJR 12	John Nielsen, Price Cobb, Martin Brundle
1991	Mazda 787 B	Volker Weidler, Johnny Herbert, Bertrand Gachot
1992	Peugeot 905	Yannick Dalmas, Mark Blundell, Derek Warwick
1993	Peugeot 905	Geoff Brabham, Christophe Bouchut, Eric Helary
1994	Dauer Porsche 962 LM	Yannick Dalmas, Hurley Haywood, Mauro Baldi
1995	McLaren F1 GTR	Yannick Dalmas, J.J. Lehto, Masanori Sekiya
1996	TWR-Porsche WSC 95	Manuel Reuter, Davy Jones, Alex Wurz
1997	TWR-Porsche WSC 95	Michele Alboreto, Stefan Johansson, Tom Kristensen
1998	Porsche 911 GT1	Alan McNish, Laurent Aiello, Stephane Ortelli
1999	BMW V12 LMR	Yannick Dalmas, Pierluigi Martini, Joachim Winkelhock
2000	Audi R8	Frank Biela, Tom Kristensen, Emanuele Pirro
2001	Audi 3596 T	Frank Biela, Tom Kristensen, Emanuele Pirro
2002	Audi R8 2002	Frank Biela, Tom Kristensen, Emanuele Pirro

Monte-Carlo Rally

YEAR	CAR	DRIVER, CODRIVER
1911	Turcat Méry	Henri Rougier (FRA)
1912	Berliet	Julius Beutler (GER)
1913–23	*no competition*	
1924	Bignan	Jean Ledure (FRA)
1925	Renault 40CV	François Repusseau (FRA)
1926	A.C. Bristol	Victor Bruce (GBR)
1927	Amilcar	Lefèbvre (FRA), Despeaux (FRA)
1928	Fiat	Jacques Bignan (FRA)
1929	Graham-Paige	Dr. Sprenger van Eijk (NED)
1930	Licorne	Hector Petit (FRA)
1931	Invicta	Donald Healey (GBR)
1932	Hotchkiss	M. Vasselle (FRA)
	Peugeot	G. de Lavelette, C. de Cortanze
1933	Hotchkiss	M. Vasselle (FRA)
1934	Hotchkiss	Gas (FRA), Jean Trevoux (FRA)
1935	Renault Nervasport	Christian Lahaye (FRA), R. Quatresous (FRA)
1936	Ford	Lionel Samfirescu (ROM), Petre Cristea (ROM)

Monte-Carlo Rally (continued)

YEAR	CAR	DRIVER, CODRIVER
1937	Delahaye	Rene Le Begue (FRA), J. Quinlin (FRA)
1938	Ford	G. Baker Schut (NED), Karelton (NED)
1939	Hotchkiss	Jean Trevoux (FRA), Marcel Lesurque (FRA)
	Delahaye	Joseph Paul, Marcel Contet (FRA)
1940–48	no competition	
1949	Hotchkiss	Jean Trevoux (FRA), Marcel Lesurque (FRA)
1950	Hotchkiss	Marcel Becquart (FRA), H. Secret (FRA)
1951	Delahaye	Jean Trevoux (FRA), Roger Crovetto (FRA)
1952	Allard P-1	Sydney Allard (GBR), Guy Warburton (GBR), Tom Lush (GBR)
1953	Ford Zephyr	Maurice Gatsonides (NED), P. Worledge (GBR)
1954	Lancia Aurelia	Louis Chiron (FRA), Giro Basadonna (SPA)
1955	Sunbeam Talbot	Per Malling (NOR), Gunnar Fadum (NOR)
1956	Jaguar Mk VII	Ronnie Adams (GBR), Frank Bigger (GBR)
1957	no competition	
1958	Renault Dauphine	Guy Monraisse (FRA), Jacques Feret (FRA)
1959	Citroën ID19	Paul Coltelloni (FRA), Pierre Alexandre (FRA)
1960	Mercedes 220SE	Walter Schock (FRG), Rolf Moll (FRG)
1961	Panhard PL17	M. Martin (FRA), Roger Bateau (FRA)
1962	Saab 96	Erik Carlsson (SWE), Gunnar Häggbom (SWE)
1963	Saab 96	Erik Carlsson (SWE), Gunnar Palm (SWE)
1964	Mini-Cooper S	Paddy Hopkirk (GBR), Henry Liddon (GBR)
1965	Mini-Cooper S	Timo Makinen (FIN), Paul Easter (GBR)
1966	Citroen ID19	Pauli Toivonen (FIN), Ensio Mikkander (FIN)
1967	Mini-Cooper S	Rauno Aaltonen (FIN), Henry Liddon (GBR)
1968	Porsche 911T	Vic Elford (GBR), David Stone (GBR)
1969	Porsche 911S	Bjorn Waldegaard (SWE), Lars Helmer (SWE)
1970	Porsche 911S	Bjorn Waldegaard (SWE), Lars Helmer (SWE)
1971	Alpine-Renault A110	Ove Andersson (SWE), David Stone (GBR)
1972	Lancia Fulvia 1.6HF	Sandro Munari (ITA), Mario Mannucci (ITA)
1973	Alpine-Renault A110	Jean-Claude Andruet (FRA), Michèle "Biche" Petit (FRA)
1974	no competition	
1975	Lancia Stratos HF	Sandro Munari (ITA), Mario Mannucci (ITA)
1976	Lancia Stratos HF	Sandro Munari (ITA), Mario Mannucci (ITA)
1977	Lancia Stratos HF	Sandro Munari (ITA), Silvio Maiga (ITA)
1978	Porsche 911 Carrera	Jean-Pierre Nicolas (FRA), Vincent Laverne (FRA)
1979	Lancia Stratos HF	Bernard Darniche (FRA), Alain Mahé (FRA)
1980	Fiat 131 Abarth	Walter Röhrl (FRG), Christian Geistdorfer (FRG)
1981	Renault 5 Turbo	Jean Ragnotti (FRA), Jean-Marc Andrie (FRA)
1982	Opel Ascona 400	Walter Röhrl (FRG), Christian Geistdorfer (FRG)
1983	Lancia Rally 037	Walter Röhrl (FRG), Christian Geistdorfer (FRG)
1984	Audi Quattro	Walter Röhrl (FRG), Christian Geistdorfer (FRG)
1985	Peugeot 205 Turbo	Ari Vatanen (FIN), Terry Harryman (GBR)
1986	Lancia Delta S4	Henri Toivonen (FIN), Sergio Cresto (USA)
1987	Lancia Delta HF 4WD	Mickey Biasion (ITA), Tiziano Siviero (ITA)
1988	Lancia Delta HF 4WD	Bruno Saby (FRA), Jean-François Fauchille (FRA)
1989	Lancia Delta HF Integrale	Mickey Biasion (ITA), Tiziano Siviero (ITA)
1990	Lancia Delta HF Integrale	Didier Auriol (FRA), Bernard Occelli (FRA)
1991	Toyota Celica GT4	Carlos Sainz (ESP), Luis Moya (ESP)
1992	Lancia Delta HF Integrale	Didier Auriol (FRA), Bernard Occelli (FRA)
1993	Toyota Celica Turbo 4WD	Didier Auriol (FRA), Bernard Occelli (FRA)
1994	Ford Escort RS Cosworth	François Delecour (FRA), Daniel Grataloup (FRA)
1995	Subaru Impreza 555	Carlos Sainz (ESP), Luis Moya (ESP)
1996	Ford Escort RS Cosworth	Patrick Bernardini (FRA), Bernard Occelli (FRA)
1997	Subaru Impreza WRC97	Piero Liatti (ITA), Fabrizia Pons (ITA)
1998	Toyota Corolla WRC	Carlos Sainz (ESP), Luis Moya (ESP)
1999	Mitsubishi Lancer Evo VI	Tommi Mäkinen (FIN), Risto Mannisenmaki (FIN)
2000	Mitsubishi Lancer Evo VI	Tommi Mäkinen (FIN), Risto Mannisenmaki (FIN)
2001	Mitsubishi Lancer Evo VI	Tommi Mäkinen (FIN), Risto Mannisenmaki (FIN)
2002	Subaru Impreza	Tommi Mäkinen (FIN), Kaj Lindstrom (FIN)
2003	Scheduled to be held January 2003	

Did you know? A football player ranks fourth (behind firefighter, race-car driver, and astronaut) on the list of America's most dangerous occupations.

NASCAR Winston Cup Champions

YEAR	WINNER	YEAR	WINNER	YEAR	WINNER	YEAR	WINNER
1949	Red Byron	1963	Joe Weatherly	1977	Cale Yarborough	1991	Dale Earnhardt
1950	Bill Rexford	1964	Richard Petty	1978	Cale Yarborough	1992	Alan Kulwicki
1951	Herb Thomas	1965	Ned Jarrett	1979	Richard Petty	1993	Dale Earnhardt
1952	Tim Flock	1966	David Pearson	1980	Dale Earnhardt	1994	Dale Earnhardt
1953	Herb Thomas	1967	Richard Petty	1981	Darrell Waltrip	1995	Jeff Gordon
1954	Lee Petty	1968	David Pearson	1982	Darrell Waltrip	1996	Terry Labonte
1955	Tim Flock	1969	David Pearson	1983	Bobby Allison	1997	Jeff Gordon
1956	Buck Baker	1970	Bobby Isaac	1984	Terry Labonte	1998	Jeff Gordon
1957	Buck Baker	1971	Richard Petty	1985	Darrell Waltrip	1999	Dale Jarrett
1958	Lee Petty	1972	Richard Petty	1986	Dale Earnhardt	2000	Bobby Labonte
1959	Lee Petty	1973	Benny Parsons	1987	Dale Earnhardt	2001	Jeff Gordon
1960	Rex White	1974	Richard Petty	1988	Bill Elliott	2002	*Season ends*
1961	Ned Jarrett	1975	Richard Petty	1989	Rusty Wallace		*17 Nov 2002 in*
1962	Joe Weatherly	1976	Cale Yarborough	1990	Dale Earnhardt		*Homestead FL*

Daytona 500 Winners, 1959–2002

The most recent race was held at Daytona International Speedway, Daytona Beach FL, 17 Feb 2002. Daytona 500 Web site: <www.daytona500.com>.

YEAR	WINNER	YEAR	WINNER	YEAR	WINNER
1959	Lee Petty	1972	A.J. Foyt	1988	Bobby Allison
1960	Junior Johnson	1973	Richard Petty	1989	Darrell Waltrip
1961	Marvin Panch	1974	Richard Petty	1990	Derrike Cope
1962	Edward Glen ("Fireball") Roberts	1975	Benny Parsons	1991	Ernie Irvan
		1976	David Pearson	1992	David Carl ("Davey") Allison
1963	DeWayne Louis ("Tiny") Lund	1977	Cale Yarborough		
		1978	Bobby Allison	1993	Dale Jarrett
1964	Richard Petty	1979	Richard Petty	1994	Sterling Marlin
1965	Fred Lorenzen	1980	Wylie ("Buddy") Baker, Jr.	1995	Sterling Marlin
1966	Richard Petty	1981	Richard Petty	1996	Dale Jarrett
1967	Mario Andretti	1982	Bobby Allison	1997	Jeff Gordon
1968	William Caleb ("Cale") Yarborough	1983	Cale Yarborough	1998	Dale Earnhardt, Sr.
		1984	Cale Yarborough	1999	Jeff Gordon
1969	Lee Roy Yarbrough	1985	Bill Elliott	2000	Dale Jarrett
1970	Pete Hamilton	1986	Geoff Bodine	2001	Michael Waltrip
1971	Richard Petty	1987	Bill Elliott	2002	Ward Burton

Badminton

The oldest, and still the classic, tournament for badminton is the All-England Badminton Championships, which have been held annually since 1900. An international governing body, the International Badminton Federation (**IBF**), was established in 1934. It first proposed international team badminton for men in 1939, but actual tournament play for the **Thomas Cup** did not begin until 1948–49. A similar contest for women's teams, the **Uber Cup**, was inaugurated in 1956–57. Competition for the biennial team championships (held in even years since 1982) consists of three singles matches and two doubles matches.

Official **world badminton championships** were first held in 1977. The program for this biennial event (held in odd years) includes mixed doubles and individual and doubles competition for men and for women.

International Badminton Federation Web site: <www.intbadfed.org>

Uber Cup

YEAR	WINNER	RUNNER-UP	YEAR	WINNER	RUNNER-UP
1956–57	United States	Denmark	1985–86	China	Indonesia
1959–60	United States	Denmark	1987–88	China	South Korea
1962–63	United States	England	1989–90	China	South Korea
1965–66	Japan	United States	1991–92	China	South Korea
1968–69	Japan	Indonesia	1993–94	Indonesia	China
1971–72	Japan	Indonesia	1995–96	Indonesia	China
1974–75	Indonesia	Japan	1997–98	China	Indonesia
1977–78	Japan	Indonesia	1999–2000	China	Denmark
1980–81	Japan	Indonesia	2001–02	China	South Korea
1983–84	China	England			

All-England Championships—Singles

Held since 1900. No competition 1915-19; 1940-46. Table shows results for past 20 years.

YEAR	MEN	WOMEN	YEAR	MEN	WOMEN
1982	Morten Frost (DEN)	Zhang Ailing (CHN)	1996	Poul-Erik Hoyer-	Bang Soo Hyun (KOR)
1983	Luan Jin (CHN)	Zhang Ailing (CHN)		Larsen (DEN)	
1984	Morten Frost (DEN)	Li Lingwei (CHN)	1997	Dong Jiong (CHN)	Ye Zhaoying (CHN)
1985	Zhao Jianhua (CHN)	Han Aiping (CHN)	1998	Sun Jun (CHN)	Ye Zhaoying (CHN)
1986	Morten Frost (DEN)	Kim Yun Ja (KOR)	1999	Peter Gade Christen-	Ye Zhaoying (CHN)
1987	Morten Frost (DEN)	Kirsten Larsen (DEN)		sen (DEN)	
1988	Ib Frederiksen (DEN)	Gu Jiaming (CHN)	2000	Xia Xuanze (CHN)	Gong Zhichao (CHN)
1989	Yang Yang (CHN)	Li Lingwei (CHN)	2001	Pulella Gopichand	Gong Zhichao (CHN)
1990	Zhao Jianhua (CHN)	Susi Susanti (INA)		(IND)	
1991	Ardy Wiranata (INA)	Susi Susanti (INA)	2002	Chen Hong (CHN)	Camilla Martin (DEN)
1992	Liu Jun (CHN)	Tang Jiuhong (CHN)	2003	*Scheduled to be held 11-16 Feb 2003,*	
1993	Heryanto Arbi (INA)	Susi Susanti (INA)		*Birmingham, Eng.*	
1994	Heryanto Arbi (INA)	Susi Susanti (INA)			
1995	Poul-Erik Hoyer-	Lim Xiao Qing (SWE)			
	Larsen (DEN)				

Thomas Cup

YEAR	WINNER	RUNNER-UP	YEAR	WINNER	RUNNER-UP
1948-49	Malaya	Denmark	1981-82	China	Indonesia
1951-52	Malaya	United States	1983-84	Indonesia	China
1954-55	Malaya	Denmark	1985-86	China	Indonesia
1957-58	Indonesia	Malaya	1987-88	China	Malaysia
1960-61	Indonesia	Thailand	1989-90	China	Malaysia
1963-64	Indonesia	Denmark	1991-92	Malaysia	Indonesia
1966-67	Malaysia	Indonesia	1993-94	Indonesia	Malaysia
	(by default)		1995-96	Indonesia	Denmark
1969-70	Indonesia	Malaysia	1997-98	Indonesia	Malaysia
1972-73	Indonesia	Denmark	1999-2000	Indonesia	China
1975-76	Indonesia	Malaysia	2001-02	Indonesia	Malaysia
1978-79	Indonesia	Denmark			

World Badminton Championships

YEAR	MEN'S SINGLES	WOMEN'S SINGLES	MEN'S DOUBLES
1977	Flemming Delfs (DEN)	Lene Köppen (DEN)	Tjun Tjun, Johan Wahjudi (INA)
1980	Rudy Hartono (INA)	Verawaty Wiharjo (INA)	Ado Chandra, Christian Hadinata (INA)
1983	Icuk Sugiarto (INA)	Li Lingwei (CHN)	Steen Fladberg, Jasper Helledie (DEN)
1985	Han Jian (CHN)	Han Aiping (CHN)	Park Joo Bong, Kim Moon Soo (KOR)
1987	Yang Yang (CHN)	Han Aiping (CHN)	Li Yongbo, Tian Bingyi (CHN)
1989	Yang Yang (CHN)	Li Lingwei (CHN)	Li Yongbo, Tian Bingyi (CHN)
1991	Zhao Jianhua (CHN)	Tang Jiuhong (CHN)	Park Joo Bong, Kim Moon Soo (KOR)
1993	Joko Suprianto (INA)	Susi Susanti (INA)	Ricky Subagja, Rudy Gunawan (INA)
1995	Heryanto Arbi (INA)	Ye Zhaoying (CHN)	Ricky Subagja, Rexy Mainaky (INA)
1997	Peter Rasmussen (DEN)	Ye Zhaoying (CHN)	Budiarto Sigit, Candra Wijaya (INA)
1999	Sun Jun (CHN)	Camilla Martin (DEN)	Kim Dong Moon, Ha Tae Kwon (KOR)
2001	Hendrawan (INA)	Gong Ruina (CHN)	Tony Gunawan, Halim Haryanto (INA)
2003	*Scheduled to be held 12-19 May 2003, Birmingham, Eng.*		

YEAR	WOMEN'S DOUBLES	MIXED DOUBLES
1977	Etsuko Toganu, Emiko Ueno (JPN)	Steen Skovgaard, Lene Köppen (DEN)
1980	Nora Perry, Jane Webster (ENG)	Christian Hadinata, Imelda Wiguno (INA)
1983	Lin Ying, Wu Dixi (CHN)	Thomas Kihlström, Nora Perry (SWE, ENG)
1985	Han Aiping, Li Lingwei (CHN)	Park Joo Bong, Yoo Sang Hee (KOR)
1987	Lin Ying, Guan Weizhen (CHN)	Wang Pengren, Shi Fangjing (CHN)
1989	Lin Ying, Guan Weizhen (CHN)	Park Joo Bong, Chung Myung Hee (KOR)
1991	Guan Weizhen, Nong Qunhua (CHN)	Park Joo Bong, Chung Myung Hee (KOR)
1993	Nong Qunhua, Zhou Lei (CHN)	Thomas Lund, Catrine Bengtsson (DEN, SWE)
1995	Gil Young Ah, Jang Hye Ock (KOR)	Thomas Lund, Marlene Thomsen (DEN)
1997	Ge Fei, Gu Jun (CHN)	Liu Yong, Ge Fei (CHN)
1999	Ge Fei, Gu Jun (CHN)	Kim Dong Moon, Ra Kyung Min (KOR)
2001	Gao Ling, Huang Sui (CHN)	Zhang Jun, Gao Ling (CHN)
2003	*Scheduled to be held 12-19 May 2003, Birmingham, Eng.*	

Baseball

The sport of baseball—given its definitive form in the United States in the late 19th century—is popular throughout the world, though it is not organized internationally except at the **Little League** (for children ages 5–18) level. Little League Baseball was founded in Pennsylvania in 1939. The first Little League World Series was in 1947, and the first Little League outside the US was organized in British Columbia in 1951. Baseball is especially popular in Japan and Latin America; it is also one of the national sports of the US.

On a **professional** level, the premier event of baseball in the US is the **World Series** of **Major League Baseball**, in which the first team to win four games wins the Series. In fact, the Series is not contested on an international level, but rather it is played between the leading team of the **National League** (NL; formed 1876 and including, from 1969, one Canadian team) and the leading team of the **American League** (AL; formed 1900 and also including, from 1977, one Canadian team).

Professional baseball began in Japan in 1936. Teams are organized into two leagues of six teams each. The seven-game **Japan Series**, first played in 1950, is contested between the leading team of the Central League (CL) and the leading team of the Pacific League (PL). The modern **Caribbean Series** began in 1970 with the winning team from each league in the Dominican Republic, Mexico, Puerto Rico, and Venezuela.

Related Web sites: Major League: <mlb.mlb.com>; Little League: <www.littleleague.org>

Final Major League Standings, 2001

American League

East Division

CLUB	WON	LOST	GAMES BACK
New York*	95	65	—
Boston	82	79	13½
Toronto	80	82	16
Baltimore	63	98	32½
Tampa Bay	62	100	34

Central Division

CLUB	WON	LOST	GAMES BACK
Cleveland*	91	71	—
Minnesota	85	77	6
Chicago	83	79	8
Detroit	66	96	25
Kansas City	65	97	26

West Division

CLUB	WON	LOST	GAMES BACK
Seattle*	116	46	—
Oakland*	102	60	14
Anaheim	75	87	41
Texas	73	89	43

National League

East Division

CLUB	WON	LOST	GAMES BACK
Atlanta*	88	74	—
Philadephia	86	76	2
New York	82	80	6
Florida	76	86	12
Montreal	68	94	20

Central Division

CLUB	WON	LOST	GAMES BACK
Houston*	93	69	—
St. Louis*	93	69	—
Chicago	88	74	5
Milwaukee	68	94	25
Cincinnati	66	96	27
Pittsburgh	62	100	31

West Division

CLUB	WON	LOST	GAMES BACK
Arizona*	92	70	—
San Francisco	90	72	2
Los Angeles	86	76	6
San Diego	79	83	13
Colorado	73	89	19

Gained play-off berth.

World Series

AL—American League; NL—National League.

YEAR	WINNING TEAM	LOSING TEAM	RESULTS
1903	Boston Pilgrims (AL)	Pittsburgh Pirates (NL)	5–3
1904	*not held*		
1905	New York Giants (NL)	Philadelphia Athletics (AL)	4–1
1906	Chicago White Sox (AL)	Chicago Cubs (NL)	4–2
1907*	Chicago Cubs (NL)	Detroit Tigers (AL)	4–0
1908	Chicago Cubs (NL)	Detroit Tigers (AL)	4–1
1909	Pittsburgh Pirates (NL)	Detroit Tigers (AL)	4–3
1910	Philadelphia Athletics (AL)	Chicago Cubs (NL)	4–1
1911	Philadelphia Athletics (AL)	New York Giants (NL)	4–2
1912*	Boston Red Sox (AL)	New York Giants (NL)	4–3
1913	Philadelphia Athletics (AL)	New York Giants (NL)	4–1
1914	Boston Braves (NL)	Philadelphia Athletics (AL)	4–0
1915	Boston Red Sox (AL)	Philadelphia Phillies (NL)	4–1
1916	Boston Red Sox (AL)	Brooklyn Robins (NL)	4–1
1917	Chicago White Sox (AL)	New York Giants (NL)	4–2
1918	Boston Red Sox (AL)	Chicago Cubs (NL)	4–2
1919	Cincinnati Reds (NL)	Chicago White Sox (AL)	5–3
1920	Cleveland Indians (AL)	Brooklyn Robins (NL)	5–2
1921	New York Giants (NL)	New York Yankees (AL)	5–3
1922*	New York Giants (NL)	New York Yankees (AL)	4–0
1923	New York Yankees (AL)	New York Giants (NL)	4–2

World Series (continued)

YEAR	WINNING TEAM	LOSING TEAM	RESULTS
1924	Washington Senators (AL)	New York Giants (NL)	4-3
1925	Pittsburgh Pirates (NL)	Washington Senators (AL)	4-3
1926	St. Louis Cardinals (NL)	New York Yankees (AL)	4-3
1927	New York Yankees (AL)	Pittsburgh Pirates (NL)	4-0
1928	New York Yankees (AL)	St. Louis Cardinals (NL)	4-0
1929	Philadelphia Athletics (AL)	Chicago Cubs (NL)	4-1
1930	Philadelphia Athletics (AL)	St. Louis Cardinals (NL)	4-2
1931	St. Louis Cardinals (NL)	Philadelphia Athletics (AL)	4-3
1932	New York Yankees (AL)	Chicago Cubs (NL)	4-0
1933	New York Giants (NL)	Washington Senators (AL)	4-1
1934	St. Louis Cardinals (NL)	Detroit Tigers (AL)	4-3
1935	Detroit Tigers (AL)	Chicago Cubs (NL)	4-2
1936	New York Yankees (AL)	New York Giants (NL)	4-2
1937	New York Yankees (AL)	New York Giants (NL)	4-1
1938	New York Yankees (AL)	Chicago Cubs (NL)	4-0
1939	New York Yankees (AL)	Cincinnati Reds (NL)	4-0
1940	Cincinnati Reds (NL)	Detroit Tigers (AL)	4-3
1941	New York Yankees (AL)	Brooklyn Dodgers (NL)	4-1
1942	St. Louis Cardinals (NL)	New York Yankees (AL)	4-1
1943	New York Yankees (AL)	St. Louis Cardinals (NL)	4-1
1944	St. Louis Cardinals (NL)	St. Louis Browns (AL)	4-2
1945	Detroit Tigers (AL)	Chicago Cubs (NL)	4-3
1946	St. Louis Cardinals (NL)	Boston Red Sox (AL)	4-3
1947	New York Yankees (AL)	Brooklyn Dodgers (NL)	4-3
1948	Cleveland Indians (AL)	Boston Braves (NL)	4-2
1949	New York Yankees (AL)	Brooklyn Dodgers (NL)	4-1
1950	New York Yankees (AL)	Philadelphia Phillies (NL)	4-0
1951	New York Yankees (AL)	New York Giants (NL)	4-2
1952	New York Yankees (AL)	Brooklyn Dodgers (NL)	4-3
1953	New York Yankees (AL)	Brooklyn Dodgers (NL)	4-2
1954	New York Giants (NL)	Cleveland Indians (AL)	4-0
1955	Brooklyn Dodgers (NL)	New York Yankees (AL)	4-3
1956	New York Yankees (AL)	Brooklyn Dodgers (NL)	4-3
1957	Milwaukee Braves (NL)	New York Yankees (AL)	4-3
1958	New York Yankees (AL)	Milwaukee Braves (NL)	4-3
1959	Los Angeles Dodgers (NL)	Chicago White Sox (AL)	4-2
1960	Pittsburgh Pirates (NL)	New York Yankees (AL)	4-3
1961	New York Yankees (AL)	Cincinnati Reds (NL)	4-1
1962	New York Yankees (AL)	San Francisco Giants (NL)	4-3
1963	Los Angeles Dodgers (NL)	New York Yankees (AL)	4-0
1964	St. Louis Cardinals (NL)	New York Yankees (AL)	4-3
1965	Los Angeles Dodgers (NL)	Minnesota Twins (AL)	4-3
1966	Baltimore Orioles (AL)	Los Angeles Dodgers (NL)	4-0
1967	St. Louis Cardinals (NL)	Boston Red Sox (AL)	4-3
1968	Detroit Tigers (AL)	St. Louis Cardinals (NL)	4-3
1969	New York Mets (NL)	Baltimore Orioles (AL)	4-1
1970	Baltimore Orioles (AL)	Cincinnati Reds (NL)	4-1
1971	Pittsburgh Pirates (NL)	Baltimore Orioles (AL)	4-3
1972	Oakland Athletics (AL)	Cincinnati Reds (NL)	4-3
1973	Oakland Athletics (AL)	New York Mets (NL)	4-3
1974	Oakland Athletics (AL)	Los Angeles Dodgers (NL)	4-1
1975	Cincinnati Reds (NL)	Boston Red Sox (AL)	4-3
1976	Cincinnati Reds (NL)	New York Yankees (AL)	4-0
1977	New York Yankees (AL)	Los Angeles Dodgers (NL)	4-2
1978	New York Yankees (AL)	Los Angeles Dodgers (NL)	4-2
1979	Pittsburgh Pirates (NL)	Baltimore Orioles (AL)	4-3
1980	Philadelphia Phillies (NL)	Kansas City Royals (AL)	4-2
1981	Los Angeles Dodgers (NL)	New York Yankees (AL)	4-2
1982	St. Louis Cardinals (NL)	Milwaukee Brewers (AL)	4-3
1983	Baltimore Orioles (AL)	Philadelphia Phillies (NL)	4-1
1984	Detroit Tigers (AL)	San Diego Padres (NL)	4-1
1985	Kansas City Royals (AL)	St. Louis Cardinals (NL)	4-3
1986	New York Mets (NL)	Boston Red Sox (AL)	4-3
1987	Minnesota Twins (AL)	St. Louis Cardinals (NL)	4-3
1988	Los Angeles Dodgers (NL)	Oakland Athletics (AL)	4-1
1989	Oakland Athletics (AL)	San Francisco Giants (NL)	4-0
1990	Cincinnati Reds (NL)	Oakland Athletics (AL)	4-0
1991	Minnesota Twins (AL)	Atlanta Braves (NL)	4-3

World Series (continued)

YEAR	WINNING TEAM	LOSING TEAM	RESULTS
1992	Toronto Blue Jays (AL)	Atlanta Braves (NL)	4-2
1993	Toronto Blue Jays (AL)	Philadelphia Phillies (NL)	4-2
1994	*not held*		
1995	Atlanta Braves (NL)	Cleveland Indians (AL)	4-2
1996	New York Yankees (AL)	Atlanta Braves (NL)	4-2
1997	Florida Marlins (NL)	Cleveland Indians (AL)	4-3
1998	New York Yankees (AL)	San Diego Padres (NL)	4-0
1999	New York Yankees (AL)	Atlanta Braves (NL)	4-0
2000	New York Yankees (AL)	New York Mets (NL)	4-1
2001	Arizona Diamondbacks (NL)	New York Yankees (AL)	4-3

*One tied game.

Major League Baseball All-Time Records[1]

	PLAYERS (TEAMS)	NUMBER	SEASON/DATE
Individual career records			
Games played	Pete Rose	3,562	1963-1986
World Series games played	Yogi Berra	75	14 series 1947-1963
At bats	Pete Rose	14,053	1963-1986
Batting average[2]	Ty Cobb	.366	1905-1928
Earned run average[3]	Ed Walsh	1.82	1904-1917
Home runs	Hank Aaron	755	1954-1976
Runs	Rickey Henderson[4]	2,248	1979-2002
Runs batted in	Hank Aaron	2,297	1954-1976
Doubles	Tris Speaker	792	1907-1928
Triples	Sam Crawford	309	1899-1917
Walks (batting)	Rickey Henderson[4]	2,141	1979-2002
Stolen bases (batting)	Rickey Henderson[4]	1,395	1979-2002
Strikeouts (pitching)	Nolan Ryan	5,714	1966-1993
Wins	Cy Young	511	1890-1911
Saves	Lee Smith	478	1980-1997
No-hitters	Nolan Ryan	7	1966-1993
Shutouts	Walter Johnson	110	1907-1927
Losses	Cy Young	316	1890-1911
Individual season records			
At bats	Willie Wilson	705	1980
Batting average[5]	Hugh Duffy	.440	1894
Earned run average[6]	Tim Keefe	0.86	1880
Home runs	Barry Bonds[4]	73	2001
Runs	Billy Hamilton	192	1894
Runs batted in	Hack Wilson	191	1930
Doubles	Earl Webb	67	1931
Triples	Chief Wilson	36	1912
Walks (batting)	Barry Bonds[4]	177	2001
Stolen bases (batting)	Hugh Nicol	138	1887
Strikeouts (pitching)	Charlie Buffinton	417	1884
Wins	Al Spalding	54	1875
Saves	Bobby Thigpen	57	1990
Shutouts	Grover Alexander	16	1916
Losses	John Coleman	48	1883
Individual game records[7]			
Home runs	*11 players hold record*	4	N/A
Runs	*14 players hold record*	6	N/A
Runs batted in	Jim Bottomley; Mark Whiten	12	16 Sep 1924; 7 Sep 1993
Doubles	*too numerous to list*	4	N/A
Triples	George Strief; Bill Joyce	4	25 Jun 1885; 18 May 1897
Walks (batting)	Jimmie Fox; Walt Wilmot	6	16 Jun 1938; 22 Aug 1891
Stolen bases (batting)	George Gore; Billy Hamilton	7	25 Jun 1881; 31 Aug 1894
Strikeouts (pitching)	Roger Clemens (twice); Kerry Wood	20	29 Apr 1986 and 18 Sep 1996; 6 May 1998

Major League Baseball All-Time Records[1] (continued)

	PLAYERS (TEAMS)	NUMBER	SEASON/DATE
Team season records			
Games won (percentage)	Chicago Cubs	116–36 (.763)	1906
Home runs	Seattle Mariners	264	1997
Runs	Boston Braves	1,220	1894
Runs batted in	Boston Braves	1,043	1894
Doubles	Boston Red Sox; St. Louis Cardinals	373	1997; 1930
Triples	Philadelphia Phillies	131	1894
Walks (batting)	Boston Red Sox	835	1949
Stolen bases (batting)	St. Louis Cardinals	581	1887
Strikeouts (pitching)	Chicago Cubs	1,344	2001
Game records			
Highest total score	Chicago Cubs v. Philadelphia Phillies	26 to 23 (total 49)	25 Aug 1922
Longest nine-inning game	Los Angeles Dodgers v. San Francisco Giants	4 hr 27 min	5 Oct 2001
Longest extra-innings game (time)	Chicago White Sox v. Milwaukee Brewers	8 hr 6 min	9 May 1984
Longest extra-innings game (innings)	Brooklyn Dodgers v. Boston Braves	26 innings	1 May 1920

[1]As of 30 Jun 2002.   [2]Minimum of 5,000 at-bats.   [3]Minimum of 2,000 innings pitched.   [4]Active in 2002.
[5]Minimum of 3.1 plate appearances per game played.   [6]Minimum of one inning pitched per game played.
[7]Nine-inning games only.

Caribbean Series

YEAR	WINNING TEAM	COUNTRY	YEAR	WINNING TEAM	COUNTRY
1970	Magallanes Navigators	VEN	1987	Caguas Creoles	PUR
1971	Licey Tigers	DOM	1988	Escogido Lions	DOM
1972	Ponce Lions	PUR	1989	Zulia Eagles	VEN
1973	Licey Tigers	DOM	1990	Escogido Lions	DOM
1974	Caguas Creoles	PUR	1991	Licey Tigers	DOM
1975	Bayamon Cowboys	PUR	1992	Mayagüez Indians	PUR
1976	Hermosillo Orange Growers	MEX	1993	Santurce Crabbers	PUR
1977	Licey Tigers	DOM	1994	Licey Tigers	DOM
1978	Mayagüez Indians	PUR	1995	San Juan Senators	PUR
1979	Magallanes Navigatoro	VEN	1996	Culiacán Tomato Growers	MEX
1980	Licey Tigers	DOM	1997	Northern Eagles	DOM
1981	not held		1998	Northern Eagles	DOM
1982	Caracas Lions	VEN	1999	Licey Tigers	DOM
1983	Arecibo Wolves	PUR	2000	Santurce Crabbers	PUR
1984	Zulia Eagles	VEN	2001	Cibao Eagles	DOM
1985	Licey Tigers	DOM	2002	Culiacán Tomato Growers	MEX
1986	Mexicali Eagles	MEX			

Japan Series

CI—Central League; PL—Pacific League.

YEAR	WINNING TEAM	LOSING TEAM	RESULTS
1992	Seibu Lions (PL)	Yakult Swallows (CL)	4–3
1993	Yakult Swallows (CL)	Seibu Lions (PL)	4–3
1994	Yomiuri Giants (CL)	Seibu Lions (PL)	4–2
1995	Yakult Swallows (CL)	Orix BlueWave (PL)	4–1
1996	Orix BlueWave (PL)	Yomiuri Giants (CL)	4–1
1997	Yakult Swallows (CL)	Seibu Lions (PL)	4–1
1998	Yokohama BayStars (CL)	Seibu Lions (PL)	4–2
1999	Fukuoka Daiei Hawks (PL)	Chunichi Dragons (CL)	4–1
2000	Yomiuri Giants (CL)	Fukuoka Daiei Hawks (PL)	4–2
2001	Yakult Swallows (CL)	Osaka Kintetsu Buffaloes (PL)	4–1

Little League World Series

The Little League World Series, first called the National Little League Tournament, was established in 1947. The table shows the Series winners for the past 10 years. Winners are Americans unless otherwise stated.

YEAR	WINNING TEAM/HOME	RUNNER-UP	SCORE
1992	Long Beach/Long Beach CA*	Zamboanga City (PHI)*	6–0
1993	Long Beach/Long Beach CA	David Doleguita/Chiriquí (PAN)	3–2
1994	Coquivacoa/Maracaibo (VEN)	Northridge City/Northridge CA	4–3
1995	Shan-Hua/Tainan county (TAI)	Northwest 45/Spring TX	17–3
1996	Fu-Hsing/Kao-Hsuing (TAI)	Cranston/Cranston RI	13–3
1997	Linda Vista/Guadalupe (MEX)	South Mission Viejo/Mission Viejo CA	5–4
1998	Toms River/Toms River NJ	Kashima/Ibaraki (JAP)	12–9
1999	Hirakata/Osaka (JAP)	Phenix City National/Phenix City AL	5–0
2000	Sierra Maestra/Maracaibo (VEN)	Bellaire/Bellaire TX	3–2
2001	Kitasuna/Tokyo (JAP)	Apopka National/Apopka FL	2–1

*Zamboanga City won but was later disqualified.

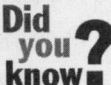

Did you know? At the start of the 2002 season, 33 players in baseball history had hit more than 400 career home runs, including 17 players at more than 500. When Babe Ruth retired in 1935 after hitting 714 home runs, only 2 other players had as many as 300 lifetime homers: Lou Gehrig (378) and Rogers Hornsby (300).

Basketball

American professional basketball is directed by the **National Basketball Association** (NBA; formed 1949). The NBA is divided into two conferences, the top-ranking teams of which compete yearly for the championship. The NBA began a **women's professional league**, known as the WNBA, in 1997.

As an **amateur** sport, basketball is organized on an international level. Since the inclusion of basketball as an **Olympic sport** in 1936, the winners of the Olympic tournament have been considered the world champions. The **Fédération Internationale de Basketball Amateur** (FIBA; founded 1932) instituted separate world championships in 1950 for men and in 1953 for women. (Women's basketball was not admitted to the Olympics until 1976.) Amateur basketball in the United States is most closely followed at the **collegiate** level, where the most important event of the season is the **National Collegiate Athletic Association (NCAA) Championship**. The NCAA tournament was first contested in 1939 (by men's teams only). Women's college basketball was first played on a national level in 1972, under the auspices of the Association for Intercollegiate Athletics for Women (AIAW), which gave way in 1982 to the NCAA's first tournament for women.

Related Web sites: NBA: <www.nba.com>; WNBA: <www.wnba.com>; NCAA: <www.ncaa.org>; FIBA: <www.fiba.com>

National Basketball Association Final Standings, 2001–02

EASTERN CONFERENCE

Atlantic Division	WON	LOST	GAMES BACK
TEAM			
*New Jersey Nets	52	30	—
*Boston Celtics	49	33	3
*Orlando Magic	44	38	8
*Philadelphia 76ers	43	39	9
Washington Wizards	37	45	15
Miami Heat	36	46	16
New York Knicks	30	52	22

Central Division	WON	LOST	GAMES BACK
TEAM			
*Detroit Pistons	50	32	—
*Charlotte Hornets	44	38	6
*Toronto Raptors	42	40	8
*Indiana Pacers	42	40	8
Milwaukee Bucks	41	41	9
Atlanta Hawks	33	49	17
Cleveland Cavaliers	29	53	21
Chicago Bulls	21	61	29

WESTERN CONFERENCE

Midwest Division	WON	LOST	GAMES BACK
TEAM			
*San Antonio Spurs	58	24	—
*Dallas Mavericks	57	25	1
*Minnesota Timberwolves	50	32	8
*Utah Jazz	44	38	14
Houston Rockets	28	54	30
Denver Nuggets	27	55	31
Memphis Grizzlies	23	59	35

*Gained play-off berth.

Pacific Division	WON	LOST	GAMES BACK
TEAM			
*Sacramento Kings	61	21	—
*Los Angeles Lakers	58	24	3
*Portland Trail Blazers	49	33	12
*Seattle Supersonics	45	37	16
Los Angeles Clippers	39	43	22
Phoenix Suns	36	46	25
Golden State Warriors	21	61	40

National Basketball Association All-Time Records

	PLAYERS (TEAMS)	NUMBER	SEASON/DATE
Individual career records			
Games played	Robert Parish	1,611	1976-77—1996-97
Points scored	Kareem Abdul-Jabbar	38,387	1969-70—1988-89
Field goals attempted	Kareem Abdul-Jabbar	28,307	1969-70—1988-89
Field goals made	Kareem Abdul-Jabbar	15,837	1969-70—1988-89
Field-goal percentage[1]	Artis Gilmore	.599	1976-77—1987-88
Three-point field goals attempted	Reggie Miller[3]	5,536	1987-88—2001-02
Three-point field goals made	Reggie Miller[3]	2,217	1987-88—2001-02
Three-point field goal percentage[2]	Steve Kerr[3]	.459	1988-89—2001-02
Free throws attempted	Karl Malone[3]	12,342	1985-86—2001-02
Free throws made	Karl Malone[3]	9,145	1985-86—2001-02
Free-throw percentage[4]	Mark Price	.904	1986-87—1997-98
Assists	John Stockton[3]	15,177	1984-85—2001-02
Rebounds	Wilt Chamberlain	23,924	1959-60—1972-73
Coaching total wins (losses)	Lenny Wilkens[3]	1,268 (1,056)	1969-70—2001-02
Coaching winning percentage[5]	Phil Jackson[3]	.738	1989-90—2001-02
Individual season records			
Points scored	Wilt Chamberlain (Philadelphia Warriors)	4,029	1961-62
Field goals attempted	Wilt Chamberlain (Philadelphia Warriors)	3,159	1961-62
Field goals made	Wilt Chamberlain (Philadelphia Warriors)	1,597	1961-62
Field-goal percentage	Wilt Chamberlain (Los Angeles Lakers)	.727	1972-73
Three-point field goals attempted	George McCloud (Dallas Mavericks)	678	1995-96
Three-point field goals made	Dennis Scott (Orlando Magic)	267	1995-96
Three-point field-goal percentage	Steve Kerr (Chicago Bulls)	.524	1994-95
Free throws attempted	Wilt Chamberlain (Philadelphia Warriors)	1,363	1961-62
Free throws made	Jerry West (Los Angeles Lakers)	840	1965-66
Free-throw percentage	Calvin Murphy (Houston Rockets)	.958	1980-81
Assists	John Stockton (Utah Jazz)	1,164	1990-91
Rebounds	Wilt Chamberlain (Philadelphia Warriors)	2,149	1960-61
Individual game records			
Points scored	Wilt Chamberlain (Philadelphia Warriors)	100	2 Mar 1962
Field goals attempted	Wilt Chamberlain (Philadelphia Warriors)	63	2 Mar 1962
Field goals made	Wilt Chamberlain (Philadelphia Warriors)	36	2 Mar 1962
Field goals, none missed	Wilt Chamberlain (Philadelphia 76ers)	18	24 Feb 1967
Three-point field goals attempted	Michael Adams (Denver Nuggets); George McCloud (Dallas Mavericks)	20	12 Apr 1991; 5 Mar 1996
Three-point field goals made	Dennis Scott (Orlando Magic)	11	18 Apr 1996
Three-point field goals, none missed	Jeff Hornacek (Utah Jazz); Sam Perkins (Seattle Supersonics)	8	23 Nov 1994; 15 Jan 1997
Free throws attempted	Wilt Chamberlain (Philadelphia Warriors)	34	22 Feb 1962
Free throws made	Wilt Chamberlain (Philadelphia Warriors); Adrian Dantley (Utah Jazz)	28	2 Mar 1962; 4 Jan 1984
Free throws made, none missed	Dominique Wilkins (Atlanta Hawks)	23	8 Dec 1992
Assists	Scott Skiles (Orlando Magic)	30	30 Dec 1990
Rebounds	Wilt Chamberlain (Philadelphia Warriors)	55	24 Nov 1960
Team records			
Highest winning pct., one season	Chicago Bulls	.878 (72-10)	1995-96
Highest winning pct., all time	Los Angeles Lakers (Minneapolis Lakers to 1960-61)	.619 (2,621-1,616)	1948-49—2001-02
Highest winning pct., one playoff series	Los Angeles Lakers	.938 (15-1)	2000-01
Most championships won	Boston Celtics	16	
Most championships won consecutively	Boston Celtics	8	1959-66
Most consecutive wins, one season	Los Angeles Lakers	33	5 Nov 1971- 7 Jan 1972
Most consecutive losses, one season	Vancouver Grizzlies; Denver Nuggets	23	16 Feb-2 Apr 1996; 9 Dec 1997- 23 Jan 1998
Game records			
Highest combined score	Detroit Pistons v. Denver Nuggets	370 (186-184)	13 Dec 1983

National Basketball Association All-Time Records (continued)

PLAYERS (TEAMS)		NUMBER	SEASON/DATE
Game records (continued)			
Largest margin of victory	Cleveland Cavaliers v. Miami Heat	68 (148–80)	17 Dec 1991
Longest game (overtime periods)	Indianapolis Olympians v. Rochester Royals	6	6 Jan 1951

¹Minimum 2,000 made.   *²Minimum 250 made.*   *³Active in 2002–03.*   *⁴Minimum 1,200 made.*   *⁵Minimum 400 games.*

National Basketball Association (NBA) Championship

SEASON	WINNER	RUNNER-UP	RESULTS
1946–47	Philadelphia Warriors	Chicago Stags	4–1
1947–48	Baltimore Bullets	Philadelphia Warriors	4–2
1948–49	Minneapolis Lakers	Washington Capitols	4–2
1949–50	Minneapolis Lakers	Syracuse Nationals	4–2
1950–51	Rochester Royals	New York Knickerbockers	4–3
1951–52	Minneapolis Lakers	New York Knickerbockers	4–3
1952–53	Minneapolis Lakers	New York Knickerbockers	4–1
1953–54	Minneapolis Lakers	Syracuse Nationals	4–3
1954–55	Syracuse Nationals	Fort Wayne Pistons	4–3
1955–56	Philadelphia Warriors	Fort Wayne Pistons	4–1
1956–57	Boston Celtics	St. Louis Hawks	4–3
1957–58	St. Louis Hawks	Boston Celtics	4–2
1958–59	Boston Celtics	Minneapolis Lakers	4–0
1959–60	Boston Celtics	St. Louis Hawks	4–3
1960–61	Boston Celtics	St. Louis Hawks	4–1
1961–62	Boston Celtics	Los Angeles Lakers	4–3
1962–63	Boston Celtics	Los Angeles Lakers	4–2
1963–64	Boston Celtics	San Francisco Warriors	4–1
1964–65	Boston Celtics	Los Angeles Lakers	4–1
1965–66	Boston Celtics	Los Angeles Lakers	4–3
1966–67	Philadelphia 76ers	San Francisco Warriors	4–2
1967–68	Boston Celtics	Los Angeles Lakers	4–2
1968–69	Boston Celtics	Los Angeles Lakers	4–3
1969–70	New York Knickerbockers	Los Angeles Lakers	4–3
1970–71	Milwaukee Bucks	Baltimore Bullets	4–0
1971–72	Los Angeles Lakers	New York Knickerbockers	4–1
1972–73	New York Knickerbockers	Los Angeles Lakers	4–1
1973–74	Boston Celtics	Milwaukee Bucks	4–3
1974–75	Golden State Warriors	Washington Bullets	4–0
1975–76	Boston Celtics	Phoenix Suns	4–2
1976–77	Portland Trail Blazers	Philadelphia 76ers	4–2
1977–78	Washington Bullets	Seattle SuperSonics	4–3
1978–79	Seattle SuperSonics	Washington Bullets	4–1
1979–80	Los Angeles Lakers	Philadelphia 76ers	4–2
1980–81	Boston Celtics	Houston Rockets	4–2
1981–82	Los Angeles Lakers	Philadelphia 76ers	4–2
1982–83	Philadelphia 76ers	Los Angeles Lakers	4–0
1983–84	Boston Celtics	Los Angeles Lakers	4–3
1984–85	Los Angeles Lakers	Boston Celtics	4–2
1985–86	Boston Celtics	Houston Rockets	4–2
1986–87	Los Angeles Lakers	Boston Celtics	4–2
1987–88	Los Angeles Lakers	Detroit Pistons	4–3
1988–89	Detroit Pistons	Los Angeles Lakers	4–0
1989–90	Detroit Pistons	Portland Trail Blazers	4–1
1990–91	Chicago Bulls	Los Angeles Lakers	4–1
1991–92	Chicago Bulls	Portland Trail Blazers	4–2
1992–93	Chicago Bulls	Phoenix Suns	4–2
1993–94	Houston Rockets	New York Knickerbockers	4–3
1994–95	Houston Rockets	Orlando Magic	4–0
1995–96	Chicago Bulls	Seattle SuperSonics	4–2
1996–97	Chicago Bulls	Utah Jazz	4–2
1997–98	Chicago Bulls	Utah Jazz	4–2
1998–99	San Antonio Spurs	New York Knickerbockers	4–1
1999–2000	Los Angeles Lakers	Indiana Pacers	4–2
2000–01	Los Angeles Lakers	Philadelphia 76ers	4–1
2001–02	Los Angeles Lakers	New Jersey Nets	4–0

Women's National Basketball Association (WNBA) Championship

SEASON	WINNER	RUNNER-UP	RESULTS
1996–97	Houston Comets	New York Liberty	1–0
1997–98	Houston Comets	Phoenix Mercury	2–1
1998–99	Houston Comets	New York Liberty	2–1
1999–2000	Houston Comets	New York Liberty	2–0
2000–01	Los Angeles Sparks	Charlotte Sting	2–0
2001–02	*scheduled to be held September 2002*		

Division I National Collegiate Athletic Association (NCAA) Championship—Men

YEAR	WINNER	RUNNER-UP	SCORE	YEAR	WINNER	RUNNER-UP	SCORE
1939	Oregon	Ohio State	46–43	1971	UCLA	Villanova	68–62
1940	Indiana	Kansas	60–42	1972	UCLA	Florida State	81–76
1941	Wisconsin	Washington State	39–34	1973	UCLA	Memphis State	87–66
1942	Stanford	Dartmouth	53–38	1974	North Carolina State	Marquette	76–64
1943	Wyoming	Georgetown	46–34				
1944	Utah	Dartmouth	42–40	1975	UCLA	Kentucky	92–85
1945	Oklahoma A & M	New York	49–45	1976	Indiana	Michigan	86–68
1946	Oklahoma A & M	North Carolina	43–40	1977	Marquette	North Carolina	67–59
1947	Holy Cross	Oklahoma	58–47	1978	Kentucky	Duke	94–88
1948	Kentucky	Baylor	58–42	1979	Michigan State	Indiana State	75–64
1949	Kentucky	Oklahoma State	46–36	1980	Louisville	UCLA	59–54
1950	CCNY	Bradley	71–68	1981	Indiana	North Carolina	63–50
1951	Kentucky	Kansas State	68–58	1982	North Carolina	Georgetown	63–62
1952	Kansas	St. John's (NY)	80–63	1983	North Carolina State	Houston	54–52
1953	Indiana	Kansas	69–68				
1954	La Salle	Bradley	92–76	1984	Georgetown	Houston	84–75
1955	San Francisco	La Salle	77–63	1985	Villanova	Georgetown	66–64
1956	San Francisco	Iowa	83–71	1986	Louisville	Duke	72–69
1957	North Carolina	Kansas	54–53	1987	Indiana	Syracuse	74–73
1958	Kentucky	Seattle	84–72	1988	Kansas	Oklahoma	83–79
1959	California (Berkeley)	West Virginia	71–70	1989	Michigan	Seton Hall	80–79
				1990	UNLV	Duke	103–73
1960	Ohio State	California (Berkeley)	75–55	1991	Duke	Kansas	72–65
				1992	Duke	Michigan	71–51
1961	Cincinnati	Ohio State	70–65	1993	North Carolina	Michigan	77–71
1962	Cincinnati	Ohio State	71–59	1994	Arkansas	Duke	76–72
1963	Loyola (IL)	Cincinnati	60–58	1995	UCLA	Arkansas	89–78
1964	UCLA	Duke	98–83	1996	Kentucky	Syracuse	76–67
1965	UCLA	Michigan	91–80	1997	Arizona	Kentucky	84–79
1966	Texas Western	Kentucky	72–65	1998	Kentucky	Utah	78–69
1967	UCLA	Dayton	79–64	1999	Connecticut	Duke	77–74
1968	UCLA	North Carolina	78–55	2000	Michigan State	Florida	89–76
1969	UCLA	Purdue	92–72	2001	Duke	Arizona	82–72
1970	UCLA	Jacksonville	80–69	2002	Maryland	Indiana	64–52

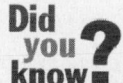

Did you know? On 12 Jan 1998, the Harlem Globetrotters played their 20,000th career game—more games than any other American professional sports team.

Division I National Collegiate Athletic Association (NCAA) Championship—Women

YEAR	WINNER	RUNNER-UP	SCORE	YEAR	WINNER	RUNNER-UP	SCORE
1982	Louisiana Tech	Cheney (PA)	76–62	1993	Texas Tech	Ohio State	84–82
1983	Southern California	Louisiana Tech	69–67	1994	North Carolina	Louisiana Tech	60–59
1984	Southern California	Tennessee	72–61	1995	Connecticut	Tennessee	70–64
1985	Old Dominion	Georgia	70–65	1996	Tennessee	Georgia	83–65
1986	Texas	Southern California	97–81	1997	Tennessee	Old Dominion	68–59
1987	Tennessee	Louisiana Tech	67–44	1998	Tennessee	Louisiana Tech	93–75
1988	Louisiana Tech	Auburn	56–54	1999	Purdue	Duke	62–45
1989	Tennessee	Auburn	76–60	2000	Connecticut	Tennessee	71–52
1990	Stanford	Auburn	88–81	2001	Notre Dame	Purdue	68–66
1991	Tennessee	Virginia	70–67	2002	Connecticut	Oklahoma	82–70
1992	Stanford	Western Kentucky	78–62				

World Amateur Basketball Championship—Men

YEAR	WINNER	RUNNER-UP	YEAR	WINNER	RUNNER-UP
1936*	United States	Canada	1976*	United States	Yugoslavia
1948*	United States	France	1978	Yugoslavia	USSR
1950	Argentina	United States	1980*	Yugoslavia	Italy
1952*	United States	USSR	1982	USSR	United States
1954	United States	Brazil	1984*	United States	Spain
1956*	United States	USSR	1986	United States	USSR
1959	Brazil†	United States	1988*	USSR	Yugoslavia
1960*	United States	USSR	1990	Yugoslavia	USSR
1963	Brazil	Yugoslavia	1992*	United States	Croatia
1964*	United States	USSR	1994	United States	Russia
1967	USSR	Yugoslavia	1996*	United States	Yugoslavia
1968*	United States	Yugoslavia	1998	Yugoslavia	Russia
1970	Yugoslavia	Brazil	2000*	United States	France
1972*	USSR	United States	2002	final is scheduled to be held on	
1974	USSR	Yugoslavia		8 Sep 2002 in Indianapolis IN	

*Olympic championships, recognized as world championships.   †By default.

World Amateur Basketball Championship—Women

YEAR	WINNER	RUNNER-UP	YEAR	WINNER	RUNNER-UP
1953	United States	Chile	1984*	United States	South Korea
1957	United States	USSR	1986	United States	USSR
1959	USSR	Bulgaria	1988*	United States	Yugoslavia
1964	USSR	Czechoslovakia	1990	United States	Yugoslavia
1967	USSR	South Korea	1992*	Unified Team†	China
1971	USSR	Czechoslovakia	1994	Brazil	China
1975	USSR	Japan	1996*	United States	Brazil
1976*	USSR	United States	1998	United States	Russia
1979	United States	South Korea	2000*	United States	Australia
1980*	USSR	Bulgaria	2002	final is scheduled to be held	
1983	USSR	United States		25 Sep 2002 in China	

*Olympic championships, recognized as world championships.   †Athletes from the Commonwealth of Independent States plus Georgia.

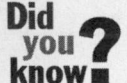

The Los Angeles Lakers' Shaquille O'Neal wears size 22EEE shoes. He wears a new pair for every game.

Billiard Games

The game of billiards has a surprising number of **varieties** throughout the world. Factors in that variety include the number and appearance of the billiard balls, the size of the table, the existence of side and corner pockets, and the object of play. The classic form of the game—**three-cushion billiards**—is played on a pocketless table with one red ball and two white balls, one of which is marked with a spot; it is often known as French billiards, carom, or (simply) billiards.

Pocket billiards, which embraces both **snooker** and the game sometimes known (for the sake of clarity) as **English billiards,** is the prevalent form of billiards in the United Kingdom. The world professional snooker championship was first held in 1927; until 1947 it was won each year by Joe Davis (championships were not held during World War II). The championship was discontinued during the 1950s; it was revived during the 1960s, and in 1969 it became a knockout event. The results that are given in the table below begin with that year. Competition is open to both men and women.

The American form of pocket billiards, usually known as **pool,** differs markedly from the British game. Its most popular variations are **eight-ball, nine-ball,** and **straight (or 14.1) pool.** Though earlier straight pool tournaments were held with regularity, the game has largely fallen into abeyance for national competition, and few national tournaments are held. Since the 1970s nine-ball and eight-ball pool have surpassed straight pool in popularity in the United States, and **nine-ball** has gained some prominence internationally. In 1990 the **World Pool-Billiard Association** (WPA; founded 1987) inaugurated the nine-ball world championship.

WPA Web site: <www.wpa-pool.com>

World Three-Cushion Championship

Competition has been held since 1928; table shows champions for the past 20 years.

YEAR	WINNER	YEAR	WINNER	YEAR	WINNER
1982	Rini van Bracht (NED)	1990	Ludo Dielis (BEL)	1998	Torbjörn Blomdahl (SWE)
1983	Raymond Ceulemans (BEL)	1991	Raymond Ceulemans (BEL)	1999	Dick Jaspers (NED)
1984	Kobayashi Nobuaki (JAP)	1992	Torbjörn Blomdahl (SWE)	2000	Dick Jaspers (NED)
1985	Raymond Ceulemans (BEL)	1993	Sang Chun Lee (USA)	2001	Raymond Ceulemans (BEL)
1986	Avelino Rico (SPA)	1994	Torbjörn Blomdahl (SWE)	2002	scheduled to be held 2–6
1987	Torbjörn Blomdahl (SWE)	1995	Torbjörn Blomdahl (SWE)		October, Randers, Den-
1988	Torbjörn Blomdahl (SWE)	1996	Torbjörn Blomdahl (SWE)		mark
1989	Torbjörn Blomdahl (SWE)	1997	Dick Jaspers (NED)		

World Professional Snooker Championship

Won by a British player unless otherwise noted.

YEAR	WINNER	YEAR	WINNER	YEAR	WINNER	YEAR	WINNER
1969	John Spencer	1978	Ray Reardon	1987	Steve Davis	1996	Stephen Hendry
1970	Ray Reardon	1979	Terry Griffiths	1988	Steve Davis	1997	Ken Doherty (IRE)
1971	John Spencer	1980	Cliff Thorburn (CAN)	1989	Steve Davis	1998	John Higgins
1972	Alex Higgins	1981	Steve Davis	1990	Stephen Hendry	1999	Stephen Hendry
1973	Ray Reardon	1982	Alex Higgins	1991	John Parrott	2000	Mark Williams
1974	Ray Reardon	1983	Steve Davis	1992	Stephen Hendry	2001	Ronnie O'Sullivan
1975	Ray Reardon	1984	Steve Davis	1993	Stephen Hendry	2002	Peter Ebdon
1976	Ray Reardon	1985	Dennis Taylor	1994	Stephen Hendry		
1977	John Spencer	1986	Joe Johnson	1995	Stephen Hendry		

WPA World Nine-Ball Championships

YEAR	MEN'S CHAMPION	WOMEN'S CHAMPION	YEAR	MEN'S CHAMPION	WOMEN'S CHAMPION
1990	Earl Strickland (USA)	Robin Bell (USA)	1996	Ralf Souquet (GER)	Allison Fisher (GBR)
1991	Earl Strickland (USA)	Robin Bell (USA)	1997	Johnny Archer (USA)	Allison Fisher (GBR)
1992	Johnny Archer (USA)	Franziska Stark (FRG)	1998	Kunihiko Takahashi (JPN)	Allison Fisher (GBR)
1993	Chao Fong-Pang (TPE)	Loree Jon Jones (USA)	1999	Nick Varner (USA)	Liu Shin-Mei (TPE)
			2000	Chao Fong-Pang (TPE)	Julie Kelly (IRE)
1994	Takeshi Okumura (JPN)	Ewa Mataya-Laurance (USA)	2001	Mika Immonen (FIN)	Allison Fisher (GBR)
1995	Oliver Ortmann (GER)	Gerda Hofstatter (AUT)	2002	Earl Strickland (USA)	Liu Shin-Mei (TPE)

Did you know? Crossword puzzles were first printed in 19th-century England in books of general puzzles for children. Later these developed into a popular adult pastime in the US. The first modern crossword puzzle appeared in a New York newspaper on Sunday, 21 Dec 1913. By the early 1920s most leading newspapers in the US had at least one crossword.

Bowling

The world governing body for bowling is the **Fédération Internationale des Quilleurs (FIQ).** Since 1954 it has sponsored world bowling championships, with seven countries participating. In 1979 the FIQ discontinued the eights for men and fours for women and introduced the triples competition for men and for women.

In the **United States** men's bowling is governed by the **American Bowling Congress (ABC),** which was founded in 1895. Six years later the first national championship was organized; in 1961 the yearly competition was split into two divisions—regular (for those with a combined average score of 851 or higher) and classic for professionals. The classic division was discontinued in 1980. The **Women's International Bowling Congress (WIBC)** was organized in 1916 and has since sponsored an annual women's championship. The women's open division is for those with a combined average score of 851 or higher, but the highest score in the tournament wins, regardless of division. In both the ABC tournament and the WIBC tournament, competition takes place between teams, doubles, and singles. The all-events category is won by the individual who has the best score of nine games—three team, three doubles, and three singles scores. The **Professional Bowlers Association (PBA)** was established in 1958. One of its major tournaments is the annual Tournament of Champions.

Related Web sites: FIQ: <www.fiq.org>; WBC: <www.bowl.com>; WIBC: <www.bowl.com/bowl/wibc>; PBA: <www.pba.com>

Professional Bowlers Association (PBA) Tournament of Champions

YEAR	CHAMPION	YEAR	CHAMPION	YEAR	CHAMPION
1965	Billy Hardwick	1979	George Pappas	1993	George Branham III
1966	Wayne Zahn	1980	Wayne Webb	1994	Norm Duke
1967	Jim Stefanich	1981	Steve Cook	1995	Mike Aulby
1968	Dave Davis	1982	Mike Durbin	1996	Dave D'Entremont
1969	Jim Godman	1983	Joe Berardi	1997	John Gant
1970	Don Johnson	1984	Mike Durbin	1998	Bryan Goebel
1971	Johnny Petraglia	1985	Mark Williams	1999	Jason Couch
1972	Mike Durbin	1986	Marshall Holman	2000	Jason Couch
1973	Jim Godman	1987	Pete Weber	2001	not held
1974	Earl Anthony	1988	Mark Williams	2002	not held; tournament scheduled to be reinstated in 2003
1975	Dave Davis	1989	Del Ballard, Jr.		
1976	Marshall Holman	1990	Dave Ferraro		
1977	Mike Berlin	1991	David Ozio		
1978	Earl Anthony	1992	Marc McDowell		

American Bowling Congress (ABC) Bowling Championships—Regular Division

The championships have been held since 1901. This table shows results only for the past 20 years.

YEAR	SINGLES	SCORE	ALL-EVENTS	SCORE
1983	Rickey Kendrick	735	Tony Cariello	2,059
1984	Bob Antczak & Neal Young (tied)	764	Bob Goike	2,142
1985	Glenn Harbison	774	Barry Asher	2,033
1986	Jeff Mackey	774	Ed Marzka	2,116
1987	Terry Taylor	749	Ryan Shafer	2,044
1988	Steve Hutkowski	774	Rick Steelsmith	2,053
1989	Paul Tetreault	813	George Hall	2,227
1990	Robert Hochrein	791	Mike Neumann	2,168
1991	Ed Deines	826	Tom Howery	2,216
1992	Gary Blatchford & Bob Youker, Jr. (tied)	801	Mike Tucker	2,158
1993	Dan Bock	798	Jeff Nimke	2,254
1994	John Weltzien	810	Thomas Holt	2,190
1995	Matt Surina	826	Jeff Kwiatkowski	2,191
1996	Don Scudder, Jr.	823	Scott Kurtz	2,224
1997	John Socha	847	Jeff Richgels	2,241
1998	John Gaines	814	Chris Barnes	2,151
1999	Dan Winter	825	Thomas Jones	2,158
2000	Garran Hein	811	Roy Daniels	2,181
2001	Nicholas Hoagland	798	D.J. Archer	2,219
2002	Mark Millsap	823	Stephen A. Hardy	2,279

Women's International Bowling Congress (WIBC) Bowling Championships—Open Division

The championships have been held since 1916. The table shows results for the past 20 years.

YEAR	SINGLES	SCORE	ALL-EVENTS	SCORE
1983	Aleta (Rzepecki) Sill	726	Virginia Norton	1,922
1984	Frieda Gate	712	Shigeo Saito (JPN)	1,921
1985	Polly Schwarzel	694	Aleta (Rzepecki) Sill	1,900
1986	Dana Stewart	698	Robin Romeo & Maria Lewis (tied)	1,877
1987	Regi Jonak	728	Leanne Barrette	1,972
1988	Michelle Meyer-Welty	690	Lisa Wagner	1,988
1989	Laura Anderson	683	Nancy Fehr	1,911
1990	Paula Carter & Dana Miller-Mackie (tied)	705	Carol Norman	1,984
1991	Debbie Kuhn	773	Debbie Kuhn	2,036
1992	Patty Ann	680	Mitsuko Tokimoto (JPN)	1,928
1993	Karen Collura (CAN) & Kari Murph (tied)	747	Anne Marie Duggan	1,990
1994	Vicki Fifield	716	Wendy Macpherson-Papanos	1,940
1995	Beth Owen	749	Beth Owen	1,983
1996	Cindy Berlanga	723	Lorrie Nichols	1,985
1997	Jan Schmidt	765	Kendra Cameron	2,039
1998	Nellie Glandon	714	Liz Johnson	1,989
1999	Nikki Gianulias	746	Hidemi Mizobuchi	2,065
2000	Cathy Krasner	729	Carolyn Dorin-Ballard	2,147
2001	Lisa Wagner	756	Jonquay Armon	2,044
2002	Theresa Smith	752	Cara Honeychurch	2,150

FIQ World Bowling Championships—Men

In 1979 the singles category was added; previously, the masters had been the only individual event. Also in that year, eights were discontinued and triples were introduced.

YEAR	SINGLES	MASTERS	PAIRS	TRIPLES	FIVES	EIGHTS
1954		Gösta Algeskog (SWE)	FIN		SWE	SWE
1955		Nisse Backstrom (SWE)	SWE		FRG	FIN
1958		Kalle Asukas (FIN)	SWE		FIN	SWE
1960		Tito Reynolds (MEX)	MEX		VEN	MEX
1963		Les Zikes (USA)	USA		USA	USA
1967		David Pond (GBR)	GBR		FIN	USA
1971		Ed Luther (USA)	PUR		USA	USA
1975		Bud Stoudt (USA)	GBR		FIN	FRG
1979	Ollie Ongtawco (PHI)	Gary Bugden (GBR)	AUS	MAS	AUS	
1983	Armando Marino (COL)	Tony Cariello (USA)	AUS	SWE	FIN	
1987	Patrick Rolland (FRA)	Roger Pieters (BEL)	SWE	USA	SWE	
1991	Ying Chieh Ma (TAI)	Mika Koivuniemi (FIN)	USA	USA	TAI	
1995	Marc Doi (CAN)	Chen-Min Yang (TPE)	SWE	NED	NED	
1999	Gery Verbruggen (BEL)	Ahmed Shaheen (QAT)	SWE	FIN	SWE	
2003	*TBA*					

FIQ World Bowling Championships—Women

In 1963 fives was played as a four-woman team, European style (either the entire game on one lane or half of game on one lane, balance on accompanying lane). In 1979 fours were discontinued altogether and triples were introduced. Also in that year, the singles category was added; previously, the masters had been the only individual event.

YEAR	MASTERS	SINGLES	PAIRS	TRIPLES	FOURS	FIVES
1963	Helen Shablis (USA)		USA		MEX	USA
1967	Helen Weston (USA)		MEX		FIN	FIN
1971	Ashie Gonzalez (PUR)		JPN		USA	USA
1975	Anne Haefker (FRG)		SWE		IPN	JPN
1979	Lita de la Rosa (PHI)	Lita de la Rosa (PHI)	PHI	USA		USA
1983	Lena Sulkanen (SWE)	Lena Sulkanen (SWE)	DEN	FRG		SWE
1987	Annette Hägre (SWE)	Edda Piccini (MEX)	USA	USA		USA
1991	Catherine Willis (CAN)	Martina Beckel (GER)	JPN	CAN		KOR
1995	Celia Flores (MEX)	Debby Ship (CAN)	THA	AUS		FIN
1999	Ann-Maree Putney (AUS)	Kelly Kulick (USA)	AUS	KOR		KOR
2003	*TBA*					

Boxing

Modern boxing is dated to about the 1880s, when the **Marquess of Queensberry**'s rules (or rules derived from them) became more or less standard. John L. Sullivan (USA) was the last of the **bare-knuckles** heavyweight champions and one of the first recognized champions to fight by the "new" rules. Despite an early trend toward some kind of organization, there is no single recognized world governing body in professional boxing. Europe, the Commonwealth, and Great Britain—not to mention a number of Asian boxing federations—all have championships. The **World Boxing Association (WBA)**, formed under a different name in 1920, is basically an American organization, though its headquarters are currently situated in Venezuela. It was once the largely undisputed governing body for the Americas. Since 1963 it has had some competition from the **World Boxing Council (WBC)**, which includes British and European countries as well as Latin American and Asian countries. In 1983 another organization, the **International Boxing Federation (IBF**; called the United States Boxing Association International from 1983 to 1984) was born of dissatisfaction with the WBA and the WBC. Other feder-

ations, such as the World Boxing Organization (WBO; formed in 1988), have not received international recognition.

The tables below contain the names of the **undisputed champions** in each weight class, their nationalities, and the dates of title bouts when titles changed hands, followed by the champions recognized by the three sanctioning bodies. Each organization (or sanctioning body) ranks boxers according to its own criteria and sanctions fights according to its own rules. Only a ranked boxer who wins a sanctioned fight is recognized as champion. Unless otherwise indicated, a champion retains his title until he is defeated. In the early 1990s the WBA, WBC, and IBF all recognized 17 weight divisions. In the tables below the primary name given for each division is that used by the WBA. If a different name is used by the WBC or the IBF, or by both, that name is given as an alternate.

Related Web sites: WBA: <www.wbaonline.com>; WBC: <www.wbcboxing.com>; IBF-USBA: <www.ibf-usba-boxing.com>

World Heavyweight Champions
No weight limit.

CHAMPION (NATIONALITY)	DATE OF TITLE
Undisputed champions	
John L. Sullivan (USA)	29 Aug 1885
James J. Corbett (USA)	7 Sep 1892
Bob Fitzsimmons (USA—formerly a	17 Mar 1897
British subject)	
James J. Jeffries (USA)	9 Jun 1899
retired in 1905	
Marvin Hart (USA)	3 Jul 1905
Tommy Burns (CAN)	23 Feb 1906
Jack Johnson (USA)	26 Dec 1908
Jess Willard (USA)	5 Apr 1915
Jack Dempsey (USA)	4 Jul 1919
Gene Tunney (USA)	23 Sep 1926
retired in 1928	
Max Schmeling (GER)	12 Jun 1930
Jack Sharkey (USA)	21 Jun 1932
Primo Carnera (ITA)	29 Jun 1933
Max Baer (USA)	14 Jun 1934
James J. Braddock (USA)	13 Jun 1935
Joe Louis (USA)	22 Jun 1937
retired in 1949	
Ezzard Charles (USA)	27 Sep 1950
Jersey Joe Walcott (USA)	18 Jul 1951
Rocky Marciano (USA)	23 Sep 1952
Floyd Patterson (USA)	30 Nov 1956
Ingemar Johansson (SWE)	26 Jun 1959
Floyd Patterson (USA)	20 Jun 1960
Sonny Liston (USA)	25 Sep 1962
Cassius Clay (later Muhammad Ali)	25 Feb 1964
(USA)	
stripped of WBA title in 1965; stripped of WBC	
title in 1967; title in dispute	

CHAMPION (NATIONALITY)	DATE OF TITLE
WBA	
Ernest Terrell (USA)	5 Mar 1965
defeated by Ali 6 Feb 1967; gave up title	
Jimmy Ellis (USA)	27 Apr 1968
Joe Frazier (USA)	16 Feb 1970
George Foreman (USA)	22 Jan 1973
Muhammad Ali (USA)	30 Oct 1974
Leon Spinks (USA)	15 Feb 1978
Muhammad Ali (USA)	15 Sep 1978
retired in 1979	
John Tate (USA)	20 Oct 1979
Mike Weaver (USA)	21 Mar 1980
Michael Dokes (USA)	10 Dec 1982
Gerrie Coetzee (RSA)	23 Sep 1983
Greg Page (USA)	1 Dec 1984
Tony Tubbs (USA)	29 Apr 1985
Tim Witherspoon (USA)	17 Jan 1986
James Smith (USA)	12 Dec 1986
Mike Tyson (USA)	7 Mar 1987
James Douglas (USA)	11 Feb 1990
Evander Holyfield (USA)	26 Oct 1990
Riddick Bowe (USA)	13 Nov 1992
Evander Holyfield (USA)	6 Nov 1993
Michael Moorer (USA)	22 Apr 1994

CHAMPION (NATIONALITY)	DATE OF TITLE
WBA (continued)	
George Foreman (USA)	5 Nov 1994
stripped of title in 1995	
Bruce Seldon (USA)	8 Apr 1995
Mike Tyson (USA)	7 Sep 1996
Evander Holyfield (USA)	9 Nov 1996
Lennox Lewis (GBR)	13 Nov 1999
stripped of title in 2000	
Evander Holyfield (USA)	12 Aug 2000
John Ruiz (PUR)	3 Mar 2001
WBC	
Joe Frazier (USA)	16 Feb 1970
George Foreman (USA)	22 Jan 1973
Muhammad Ali (USA)	30 Oct 1974
stripped of title in 1978	
Ken Norton (USA)	18 Mar 1978
Larry Holmes (USA)	9 Jun 1978
gave up title in 1983	
Tim Witherspoon (USA)	9 Mar 1984
Pinklon Thomas (USA)	31 Aug 1984
Trevor Berbick (CAN)	22 Mar 1986
Mike Tyson (USA)	22 Nov 1986
James Douglas (USA)	11 Feb 1990
Evander Holyfield (USA)	26 Oct 1990
Riddick Bowe (USA)	13 Nov 1992
stripped of title in 1992	
Lennox Lewis (GBR)	14 Dec 1992
Oliver McCall (USA)	24 Sep 1994
Frank Bruno (GBR)	2 Sep 1995
Mike Tyson (USA)	16 Mar 1996
gave up title in 1996	
Lennox Lewis (GBR)	7 Feb 1997
Hasim Rahman (USA)	22 Apr 2001
Lennox Lewis (GBR)	17 Nov 2001
IBF	
Larry Holmes (USA)	25 Nov 1983
recognized as champion in November 1983	
Michael Spinks (USA)	21 Sep 1985
stripped of title in 1987	
Tony Tucker (USA)	30 May 1987
Mike Tyson (USA)	1 Aug 1987
James Douglas (USA)	11 Feb 1990
Evander Holyfield (USA)	25 Oct 1990
Riddick Bowe (USA)	13 Nov 1992
Evander Holyfield (USA)	6 Nov 1993
Michael Moorer (USA)	22 Apr 1994
George Foreman (USA)	5 Nov 1994
gave up title in 1995	
François Botha (RSA)	9 Dec 1995
stripped of title in 1996	
Michael Moorer (USA)	22 Jun 1996
Evander Holyfield (USA)	8 Nov 1997
Lennox Lewis (GBR)	13 Nov 1999
Hasim Rahman (USA)	22 Apr 2001
Lennox Lewis (GBR)	17 Nov 2001

World Cruiserweight Champions
Top weight 195 pounds; until 1982 not over 182 pounds. Division first recognized by WBA in 1982.

CHAMPION (NATIONALITY)	DATE OF TITLE
WBA	
Ossie Ocasio (PUR)	13 Feb 1982
Piet Crous (RSA)	1 Dec 1984
Dwight Muhammad Qawi (USA)	27 Jul 1985

CHAMPION (NATIONALITY)	DATE OF TITLE
WBA (continued)	
Evander Holyfield (USA)	12 Jul 1986
gave up title in 1988	

World Cruiserweight Champions (continued)

CHAMPION (NATIONALITY)	DATE OF TITLE
WBA (continued)	
Taoufik Belbouli (FRA)	25 Mar 1989
declared vacant in 1989	
Robert Daniels (USA)	28 Nov 1989
Bobby Czyz (USA)	8 Mar 1991
vacant	
Orlin Norris (USA)	6 Nov 1993
Nate Miller (USA)	22 Jul 1995
Fabrice Tiozzo (FRA)	8 Nov 1997
Virgil Hill (USA)	9 Dec 2000
WBC	
Marvin Camel (USA)	31 Mar 1980
Carlos de León (PUR)	25 Nov 1980
S.T. Gordon (USA)	27 Jun 1982
Carlos de León (PUR)	17 Jul 1983
Alfonso Ratliff (USA)	6 Jun 1985
Bernard Benton (USA)	21 Sep 1985
Carlos de León (PUR)	22 Mar 1986
Evander Holyfield (USA)	9 Apr 1988
gave up title in 1988	
Carlos de León (PUR)	17 May 1989
Massimiliano Duran (ITA)	27 Jul 1990

CHAMPION (NATIONALITY)	DATE OF TITLE
WBC (continued)	
Anaclet Wamba (FRA)	20 Jul 1991
Marcelo Domínguez (ARG)	19 Apr 1996
Juan Carlos Gómez (GER—formerly a	21 Feb 1998
Cuban citizen)	
IBF	
Marvin Camel (USA)	13 Dec 1983
Lee Roy Murphy (USA)	6 Oct 1984
Rickey Parkey (USA)	25 Oct 1986
Evander Holyfield (USA)	15 May 1987
Glenn McCrory (GBR)	3 Jun 1989
Jeff Lampkin (USA)	22 Mar 1990
gave up title in 1991	
James Warring (USA)	7 Sep 1991
Alfred Cole (USA)	30 Jul 1992
gave up title in 1996	
Adolpho Washington (USA)	31 Aug 1996
Uriah Grant (USA)	21 Jun 1997
Imamu Mayfield (USA)	8 Nov 1997
Arthur Williams (USA)	30 Oct 1998
Vassily Jirov (KAZ)	5 Jun 1999

World Light Heavyweight Champions
Top weight 175 pounds.

CHAMPION (NATIONALITY)	DATE OF TITLE
Undisputed champions	
Jack Root (AUT)	22 Apr 1903
George Gardner (IRE)	4 Jul 1903
Bob Fitzsimmons (USA—formerly a	25 Nov 1903
British subject)	
Philadelphia Jack O'Brien (USA)	20 Dec 1905
retired in 1912	
Jack Dillon (USA)	28 Apr 1914
Battling Levinsky (USA)	24 Oct 1916
Georges Carpentier (FRA)	12 Oct 1920
Battling Siki (Louis Phal) (SEN)	24 Sep 1922
Mike McTigue (IRF)	17 Mar 1923
Paul Berlenbach (USA)	30 May 1925
Jack Delaney (CAN)	16 Jul 1926
gave up title in 1927	
Tommy Loughran (USA)	12 Dec 1927
gave up title in 1929	
Maxie Rosenbloom (USA)	14 Jul 1932
Bob Olin (USA)	16 Nov 1934
John Henry Lewis (USA)	31 Oct 1935
retired in 1939	
Melio Bettina (USA)	3 Feb 1939
Billy Conn (USA)	13 Jul 1939
gave up title in 1941	
Gus Lesnevich (USA)	14 May 1946
Freddie Mills (GBR)	26 Jul 1948
Joey Maxim (USA)	24 Jan 1950
Archie Moore (USA)	17 Dec 1952
stripped of title in 1962	
Harold Johnson (USA)	12 May 1962
Willie Pastrano (USA)	1 Jun 1963
José Torres (PUR)	30 Mar 1965
Dick Tiger (NGR)	16 Dec 1966
Bob Foster (USA)	24 May 1968
stripped of WBA title in 1970	
WBA	
Vicente Rondon (VEN)	27 Feb 1971

CHAMPION (NATIONALITY)	DATE OF TITLE
WBA (continued)	
Bob Foster (USA)	7 Apr 1972
retired in 1974	
Víctor Galíndez (ARG)	7 Dec 1974
Mike Rossman (USA)	15 Sep 1978
Víctor Galíndez (ARG)	14 Apr 1979
Marvin Johnson (USA)	30 Nov 1979
Eddie Gregory (later Eddie	31 Mar 1980
Mustafa Muhammad) (USA)	
Michael Spinks (USA)	18 Jul 1981
gave up title in 1985	
Marvin Johnson (USA)	9 Feb 1986
Leslie Stewart (TRI)	23 May 1987
Virgil Hill (USA)	5 Sep 1987
Thomas Hearns (USA)	3 Jun 1991
Iran Barkley (USA)	21 Mar 1992
gave up title in 1992	
Virgil Hill (USA)	29 Sep 1992
Darlusz Michalczewski (GER)	13 Jun 1997
stripped of title in 1997	
Lou Del Valle (USA)	20 Sep 1997
Roy Jones, Jr. (USA)	18 Jul 1998
declared super champion in 2001	
Bruno Girard (FRA)	22 Dec 2001
WBC	
Bob Foster (USA)	24 May 1968
retired in 1974	
John Conteh (GBR)	1 Oct 1974
stripped of title in 1977	
Miguel Cuello (ARG)	21 May 1977
Mate Parlov (YUG)	7 Jan 1978
Marvin Johnson (USA)	2 Dec 1978
Matthew Franklin (later Matthew	22 Apr 1979
Saad Muhammad) (USA)	
Dwight Braxton (later Dwight	19 Dec 1981
Muhammad Qawi) (USA)	
Michael Spinks (USA)	18 Mar 1983
gave up title in 1985	

World Light Heavyweight Champions (continued)

CHAMPION (NATIONALITY)	DATE OF TITLE
WBC (continued)	
J.B. Williamson (USA)	10 Dec 1985
Dennis Andries (GBR)	30 Apr 1986
Thomas Hearns (USA)	7 Mar 1987
gave up title in 1987	
Don Lalonde (CAN)	27 Nov 1987
Sugar Ray Leonard (USA)	7 Nov 1988
gave up title in 1988	
Dennis Andries (GBR)	2 Feb 1989
Jeff Harding (AUS)	24 Jun 1989
Dennis Andries (GBR)	28 Jul 1990
Jeff Harding (AUS)	11 Sep 1991
Mike McCallum (JAM)	23 Jul 1994
Fabrice Tiozzo (FRA)	16 Jun 1995
Roy Jones, Jr. (USA)	23 Nov 1996

CHAMPION (NATIONALITY)	DATE OF TITLE
WBC (continued)	
Montell Griffin (USA)	21 Mar 1997
Roy Jones, Jr. (USA)	7 Aug 1997
IBF	
Slobodan Kacar (YUG)	21 Dec 1985
Bobby Czyz (USA)	6 Sep 1986
Charles Williams (USA)	29 Oct 1987
Henry Maske (GER)	20 Mar 1993
Virgil Hill (USA)	23 Nov 1996
Dariusz Michalczewski (GER)	13 Jun 1997
gave up title in 1997	
William Guthrie (USA)	19 Jul 1997
Reggie Johnson (USA)	6 Feb 1998
Roy Jones, Jr. (USA)	5 Jun 1999

World Super Middleweight Champions

Top weight 168 pounds. Super middleweight division first recognized by WBA in 1987 and by WBC in 1988.

CHAMPION (NATIONALITY)	DATE OF TITLE
WBA	
Park Chong-Pal (KOR)	6 Dec 1987
Fulgencio Obelmejias (VEN)	23 May 1988
Baek In-chul (KOR)	27 May 1989
Christophe Tiozzo (FRA)	30 Mar 1990
Víctor Cordoba (PAN)	5 Apr 1991
Michael Nunn (USA)	12 Sep 1992
Steve Little (USA)	26 Feb 1994
Frank Liles (USA)	12 Aug 1994
Byron Mitchell (USA)	12 Jun 1999
Bruno Girard (FRA)	8 Apr 2000
stripped of title in 2001	
Byron Mitchell (USA)	3 Mar 2001
WBC	
Sugar Ray Leonard (USA)	7 Nov 1988
gave up title in 1990	
Mauro Galvano (ITA)	15 Dec 1990
Nigel Benn (GBR)	3 Oct 1992
Thulane Malinga (RSA)	2 Mar 1996
Vincenzo Nardiello (ITA)	6 Jul 1996
Robin Reid (GBR)	12 Oct 1996
Thulane Malinga (RSA)	19 Dec 1997

CHAMPION (NATIONALITY)	DATE OF TITLE
WBC (continued)	
Richie Woodhall (GBR)	27 Mar 1998
Markus Beyer (GER)	23 Oct 1999
Glenn Catley (GBR)	6 May 2000
Dingaan Thobela (RSA)	1 Sep 2000
Davey Hilton (CAN)	15 Dec 2000
stripped of title in 2001	
Eric Lucas (CAN)	10 Jul 2001
IBF	
Murray Sutherland (GBR)	28 Mar 1984
Park Chong-Pal (KOR)	22 Jul 1984
gave up title in 1987	
Graciano Rocchigiani (GER)	12 Mar 1988
gave up title in 1989	
Lindell Holmes (USA)	27 Jan 1990
Darrin Van Horn (USA)	18 May 1991
Iran Barkley (USA)	10 Jan 1992
James Toney (USA)	13 Feb 1993
Roy Jones, Jr. (USA)	18 Nov 1994
gave up title in 1997	
Charles Brewer (USA)	21 Jun 1997
Sven Ottke (GER)	24 Oct 1998

World Middleweight Champions

Top weight 160 pounds; until 1915 not over 158 pounds.

CHAMPION (NATIONALITY)	DATE OF TITLE
Undisputed champions	
Jack ("the Nonpareil") Dempsey (USA)	30 Jul 1884
Bob Fitzsimmons (GBR—later	14 Jan 1891
became US citizen)	
gave up title in 1895	
Tommy Ryan (USA)	24 Oct 1898
retired in 1907	
Stanley Ketchel (USA)	9 May 1908
Billy Papke (USA)	7 Sep 1908
Stanley Ketchel (USA)	26 Nov 1908
died in 1910	
George Chip (USA)	11 Oct 1913
Al McCoy (USA)	6 Apr 1914
Mike O'Dowd (USA)	14 Nov 1917
Johnny Wilson (USA)	6 May 1920
Harry Greb (USA)	31 Aug 1923
Tiger Flowers (USA)	26 Feb 1926

CHAMPION (NATIONALITY)	DATE OF TITLE
Undisputed champions (continued)	
Mickey Walker (USA)	3 Dec 1926
gave up title in 1931; title in dispute	
Tony Zale (USA)	28 Nov 1941
Rocky Graziano (USA)	16 Jul 1947
Tony Zale (USA)	10 Jun 1948
Marcel Cerdan (FRA)	21 Sep 1948
Jake La Motta (USA)	16 Jun 1949
Sugar Ray Robinson (USA)	14 Feb 1951
Randy Turpin (GBR)	10 Jul 1951
Sugar Ray Robinson (USA)	12 Sep 1951
retired 1952–54	
Carl Olson (USA)	21 Oct 1953
Sugar Ray Robinson (USA)	9 Dec 1955
Gene Fullmer (USA)	2 Jan 1957
Sugar Ray Robinson (USA)	1 May 1957
Carmen Basilio (USA)	23 Sep 1957

World Middleweight Champions (continued)

CHAMPION (NATIONALITY)	DATE OF TITLE	CHAMPION (NATIONALITY)	DATE OF TITLE
Undisputed champions (continued)		**WBC**	
Sugar Ray Robinson (USA)	25 Mar 1958	Rodrigo Valdés (COL)	24 May 1974
stripped of NBA (later WBA) title in 1959		Carlos Monzón (ARG)	26 Jun 1976
Dick Tiger (Richard Ihetu) (NGR)	10 Aug 1963	gave up title in 1977	
Joey Giardello (USA)	7 Dec 1963	Rodrigo Valdés (COL)	5 Nov 1977
Dick Tiger (NGR)	21 Oct 1965	Hugo Corro (ARG)	22 Apr 1978
Emile Griffith (USA)	25 Apr 1966	Vito Antuofermo (ITA)	30 Jun 1979
Nino Benvenuti (ITA)	17 Apr 1967	Alan Minter (GBR)	16 Mar 1980
Emile Griffith (USA)	29 Sep 1967	Marvin Hagler (USA)	27 Sep 1980
Nino Benvenuti (ITA)	4 Mar 1968	Sugar Ray Leonard (USA)	6 Apr 1987
Carlos Monzón (ARG)	7 Nov 1970	gave up title in 1987	
stripped of WBC title in 1974		Thomas Hearns (USA)	29 Oct 1987
		Iran Barkley (USA)	6 Jun 1988
WBA		Roberto Durán (PAN)	24 Feb 1989
Carlos Monzón (ARG)	5 Oct 1974	stripped of title in 1990	
gave up title in 1977		Julian Jackson (USA)	24 Nov 1990
Rodrigo Valdés (COL)	5 Nov 1977	Gerald McClellan (USA)	8 May 1993
Hugo Corro (ARG)	22 Apr 1978	vacant	
Vito Antuofermo (ITA)	30 Jun 1979	Julian Jackson (USA)	17 Mar 1995
Alan Minter (GBR)	16 Mar 1980	Quincy Taylor (USA)	19 Aug 1995
Marvin Hagler (USA)	27 Sep 1980	Keith Holmes (USA)	16 Mar 1996
stripped of title in 1987		Hassine Cherifi (FRA)	2 May 1998
Sumbu Kalambay (ITA)	23 Oct 1987	Keith Holmes (USA)	24 Apr 1999
stripped of title in 1989		Bernard Hopkins (USA)	14 Apr 2001
Mike McCallum (JAM)	13 May 1989		
stripped of title in 1991		**IBF**	
Reggie Johnson (USA)	22 Apr 1992	Marvin Hagler (USA)	27 May 1983
John David Jackson (USA)	2 Oct 1993	relinquished title in 1987	
stripped of title in 1994		Frank Tate (USA)	10 Oct 1987
Jorge Castro (ARG)	12 Aug 1994	Michael Nunn (USA)	28 Jul 1988
Shinji Takehara (JPN)	19 Dec 1995	James Toney (USA)	10 May 1991
William Joppy (USA)	24 Jun 1996	gave up title in 1993	
Julio César Green (DOM)	23 Aug 1997	Roy Jones, Jr. (USA)	22 May 1993
William Joppy (USA)	31 Jan 1998	gave up title in 1994	
Félix Trinidad (PUR)	12 May 2001	Bernard Hopkins (USA)	29 Apr 1995
Bernard Hopkins (USA)	29 Sep 2001		
declared super champion in 2001			
William Joppy (USA)	17 Nov 2001		

World Junior Middleweight Champions

Top weight 154 pounds. Also called super welterweight.

CHAMPION (NATIONALITY)	DATE OF TITLE	CHAMPION (NATIONALITY)	DATE OF TITLE
WBA		**WBA (continued)**	
Dennis Moyer (USA)	20 Oct 1962	Roberto Durán (PAN)	16 Jun 1983
Ralph Dupas (USA)	29 Apr 1963	gave up title in 1984	
Sandro Mazzinghi (ITA)	7 Sep 1963	Mike McCallum (JAM)	19 Oct 1984
Nino Benvenuti (ITA)	18 Jun 1965	gave up title in 1987	
Kim Ki Soo (KOR)	25 Jun 1966	Julian Jackson (USA)	21 Nov 1987
Sandro Mazzinghi (ITA)	25 May 1968	gave up title in 1990	
stripped of title in 1969		Gilbert Dele (FRA)	23 Feb 1991
Freddie Little (USA)	17 Mar 1969	Vinny Pazienza (USA)	11 Oct 1991
Carmelo Bossi (ITA)	9 Jul 1970	gave up title in 1992	
Koichi Wajima (JPN)	31 Oct 1971	Julio César Vásquez (ARG)	22 Dec 1992
Oscar Albarado (USA)	3 Jun 1974	Pernell Whitaker (USA)	4 Mar 1995
Koichi Wajima (JPN)	21 Jun 1975	gave up title in 1995	
Yuh Jae Do (KOR)	7 Jun 1975	Carl Daniels (USA)	16 Jun 1995
Koichi Wajima (JPN)	17 Feb 1976	Julio César Vásquez (ARG)	16 Dec 1995
José Durán (ESP)	18 May 1976	Laurent Boudouani (FRA)	21 Aug 1996
Miguel Castellini (ARG)	8 Oct 1976	David Reid (USA)	6 Mar 1999
Eddie Gazo (NCA)	5 Mar 1977	Félix Trinidad (PUR)	3 Mar 2000
Kudo Masashi (JPN)	9 Aug 1978	gave up title in 2001	
Ayub Kalule (DEN)	24 Oct 1979	Fernando Vargas (USA)	22 Sep 2001
Sugar Ray Leonard (USA)	25 Jun 1981		
gave up title in 1981		**WBC**	
Tadashi Mihara (JPN)	7 Nov 1981	Miguel de Oliveira (BRA)	7 May 1975
Davey Moore (USA)	2 Feb 1982	Elisha Obed (BAH)	13 Nov 1975

World Junior Middleweight Champions (continued)

CHAMPION (NATIONALITY) WBC (continued)	DATE OF TITLE	CHAMPION (NATIONALITY) IBF	DATE OF TITLE
Eckhard Dagge (FRG)	18 Jun 1976	Mark Medal (USA)	11 Mar 1984
Rocco Mattioli (ITA)	6 Aug 1977	Carlos Santos (PUR)	2 Nov 1984
Maurice Hope (GBR)	4 Mar 1979	Buster Drayton (USA)	4 Jun 1986
Wilfred Benítez (PUR)	3 May 1981	Matthew Hilton (CAN)	27 Jun 1987
Thomas Hearns (USA)	3 Dec 1982	Robert Hines (USA)	4 Nov 1988
gave up title in 1986		Darrin Van Horn (USA)	4 Feb 1989
Duane Thomas (USA)	5 Dec 1986	Gianfranco Rosi (ITA)	16 Jul 1989
Lupe Aquino (MEX)	12 Jul 1987	Vincent Pettway (USA)	17 Sep 1994
Gianfranco Rosi (ITA)	2 Oct 1987	Paul Vaden (USA)	12 Aug 1995
Donald Curry (USA)	8 Jul 1988	Terry Norris (USA)	16 Dec 1995
René Jacquot (FRA)	11 Feb 1989	gave up title in 1997	
John Mugabi (UGA)	8 Jul 1989	Raul Marquez (USA)	12 Apr 1997
Terry Norris (USA)	31 Mar 1990	Yory Boy Campas (MEX)	6 Dec 1997
Simon Brown (USA)	18 Dec 1993	Fernando Vargas (USA)	12 Dec 1998
Terry Norris (USA)	7 May 1994	Félix Trinidad (PUR)	2 Dec 2000
Luis Santana (DOM)	12 Nov 1994	gave up title in 2001	
Terry Norris (USA)	19 Aug 1995	Ronald Wright (USA)	12 Oct 2001
Keith Mullings (USA)	6 Dec 1997		
Javier Castillejo (ESP)	29 Jan 1999		
Oscar de la Hoya (USA)	23 Jun 2001		

World Welterweight Champions

Top weight 147 pounds; until about 1909 not over 145 pounds.

CHAMPION (NATIONALITY) Undisputed champions	DATE OF TITLE	CHAMPION (NATIONALITY) Undisputed champions (continued)	DATE OF TITLE
Paddy Duffy (USA)	30 Oct 1888	Tony DeMarco (USA)	1 Apr 1955
died in 1890		Carmen Basilio (USA)	10 Jun 1955
Mysterious Billy Smith (USA)	14 Dec 1892	Johnny Saxton (USA)	14 Mar 1956
Tommy Ryan (USA)	26 Jul 1894	Carmen Basilio (USA)	12 Sep 1956
gave up title in 1898		gave up title in 1957	
Mysterious Billy Smith (USA)	25 Aug 1898	Virgil Akins (USA)	6 Jun 1958
Jim ("Rube") Ferns (USA)	15 Jan 1900	Don Jordan (USA)	5 Dec 1958
Matty Matthews (USA)	16 Oct 1900	Benny ("Kid") Paret (CUB)	27 May 1960
Jim ("Rube") Ferns (USA)	24 May 1901	Emile Griffith (USA)	1 Apr 1961
Joe Walcott (BAR)	18 Dec 1901	Benny ("Kid") Paret (CUB)	3 Sep 1961
title in dispute from 1904		Emile Griffith (USA)	24 Mar 1962
Ted ("Kid") Lewis (GBR)	31 Aug 1915	Luis Rodríguez (CUB)	21 Mar 1963
Jack Britton (USA)	24 Apr 1916	Emile Griffith (USA)	8 Jun 1963
Ted ("Kid") Lewis (GBR)	25 Jun 1917	gave up title in 1966	
Jack Britton (USA)	17 Mar 1919	Curtis Cokes (USA)	28 Nov 1966
Mickey Walker (USA)	1 Nov 1922	José Nápoles (MEX)	18 Apr 1969
Pete Latzo (USA)	20 May 1926	Billy Backus (USA)	3 Dec 1970
Joe Dundee (USA)	3 Jun 1927	José Nápoles (MEX)	4 Jun 1971
stripped of NBA (later WBA) title in 1928		stripped of WBA title in 1975	
Jackie Fields (USA)	25 Jul 1929		
Young Jack Thompson (USA)	9 May 1930	**WBA**	
Tommy Freeman (USA)	5 Sep 1930	Ángel Espada (PUR)	28 Jun 1975
Young Jack Thompson (USA)	14 Apr 1931	Pipino Cuevas (MEX)	17 Jul 1976
Lou Brouillard (CAN)	23 Oct 1931	Thomas Hearns (USA)	2 Aug 1980
Jackie Fields (USA)	28 Jan 1932	Sugar Ray Leonard (USA)	16 Sep 1981
Young Corbett III (Rafelle Giordano) (USA)	22 Feb 1933	retired in 1982	
Jimmy McLarnin (CAN)	29 May 1933	Donald Curry (USA)	13 Feb 1983
Barney Ross (USA)	28 May 1934	Lloyd Honeyghan (GBR)	27 Sep 1986
Jimmy McLarnin (CAN)	17 Sep 1934	gave up title in 1986	
Barney Ross (USA)	28 May 1935	Mark Breland (USA)	6 Feb 1987
Henry Armstrong (USA)	31 May 1938	Marlon Starling (USA)	22 Aug 1987
Fritzie Zivic (USA)	4 Oct 1940	Tomás Molinares (COL)	29 Jul 1988
Freddie ("Red") Cochrane (USA)	29 Jul 1941	gave up title in 1988	
Marty Servo (USA)	1 Feb 1946	Mark Breland (USA)	4 Feb 1989
retired in 1946		Aaron Davis (USA)	8 Jul 1990
Sugar Ray Robinson (USA)	20 Dec 1946	Meldrick Taylor (USA)	19 Jan 1991
gave up title in 1951		Crisanto España (VEN)	31 Oct 1992
Kid Gavilan (CUB)	18 May 1951	Ike Quartey (GHA)	4 Jun 1994
Johnny Saxton (USA)	20 Oct 1954	stripped of title in 1998	

World Welterweight Champions (continued)

CHAMPION (NATIONALITY)	DATE OF TITLE
WBA (continued)	
James Page (USA)	10 Oct 1998
stripped of title in 2000	
Andrew Lewis (GUY)	17 Feb 2001
WBC	
John Stracey (GBR)	6 Dec 1975
Carlos Palomino (USA)	22 Jun 1976
Wilfred Benítez (PUR)	14 Jan 1979
Sugar Ray Leonard (USA)	30 Nov 1979
Roberto Durán (PAN)	20 Jun 1980
Sugar Ray Leonard (USA)	25 Nov 1980
retired in 1982	
Milton McCrory (USA)	13 Aug 1983
Donald Curry (USA)	6 Dec 1985
Lloyd Honeyghan (GBR)	27 Sep 1986
Jorge Vaca (MEX)	28 Oct 1987
Lloyd Honeyghan (GBR)	29 Mar 1988
Marlon Starling (USA)	4 Feb 1989
Maurice Blocker (USA)	19 Aug 1990
Simon Brown (JAM)	18 Mar 1991

CHAMPION (NATIONALITY)	DATE OF TITLE
WBC (continued)	
James McGirt (USA)	29 Nov 1991
Pernell Whitaker (USA)	6 Mar 1993
Oscar de la Hoya (USA)	12 Apr 1997
Félix Trinidad (PUR)	18 Sep 1999
gave up title in 2000	
Oscar de la Hoya (USA)	20 Mar 2000
Shane Mosley (USA)	17 Jun 2000
IBF	
Donald Curry (USA)	4 Feb 1984
Lloyd Honeyghan (GBR)	27 Sep 1986
stripped of title in 1987	
Simon Brown (JAM)	23 Apr 1988
gave up title in 1991	
Maurice Blocker (USA)	4 Oct 1991
Félix Trinidad (PUR)	19 Jun 1993
gave up title in 2000	
Vernon Forrest (USA)	12 May 2001
stripped of title in 2001	

World Junior Welterweight Champions
Top weight 140 pounds. Also called super lightweight.

CHAMPION (NATIONALITY)	DATE OF TITLE
Undisputed champions	
Myron Mitchell (USA)	15 Nov 1922
proclaimed champion as the result of a poll taken	
by *The Boxing Blade*	
Mushy Callahan (USA)	21 Sep 1926
Jack ("Kid") Berg (GBR)	18 Feb 1930
Tony Canzoneri (USA)	24 Apr 1931
Johnny Jadick (USA)	18 Jan 1932
Battling Shaw (MEX)	20 Feb 1933
Tony Canzoneri (USA)	21 May 1933
Barney Ross (USA)	23 Jun 1933
gave up title in 1935; title vacant	
Tippy Larkin (USA)	29 Apr 1946
title vacant from 1946	
Carlos Ortíz (PUR)	12 Jun 1959
Duilio Loi (ITA)	1 Sep 1960
Eddie Perkins (USA)	14 Sep 1962
Duilio Loi (ITA)	15 Dec 1962
retired in 1963	
Eddie Perkins (USA)	15 Jun 1963
Carlos Hernández (VEN)	18 Jan 1965
Sandro Lopopolo (ITA)	29 Apr 1966
Paul Takeshi Fujii (USA)	30 Apr 1967
WBA	
Nicolino Loche (ARG)	12 Dec 1968
Alfonso Frazer (PAN)	10 Mar 1972
Antonio Cervantes (COL)	28 Oct 1972
Wilfred Benítez (PUR)	6 Mar 1976
stripped of title in 1976	
Antonio Cervantes (COL)	25 Jun 1977
Aaron Pryor (USA)	2 Aug 1980
retired in 1983	
Johnny Bumphus (USA)	22 Jan 1984
Gene Hatcher (USA)	1 Jun 1984
Ubaldo Sacco (ARG)	21 Jul 1985
Patrizio Oliva (ITA)	15 Mar 1986
Juan Martín Coggi (ARG)	4 Jul 1987
Loreto Garza (USA)	17 Aug 1990
Edwin Rosario (PUR)	15 Jun 1991
Akinobu Hiranaka (JPN)	10 Apr 1992

CHAMPION (NATIONALITY)	DATE OF TITLE
WBA (continued)	
Morris East (PHI)	9 Sep 1992
Juan Martín Coggi (ARG)	12 Jan 1993
Frankie Randall (USA)	17 Sep 1994
Juan Martín Coggi (ARG)	13 Jan 1996
Frankie Randall (USA)	16 Aug 1996
Khalid Rahilou (FRA)	11 Jan 1997
Sharmba Mitchell (USA)	10 Oct 1998
Kostya Tszyu (AUS)	3 Feb 2001
declared super champion in 2001	
WBC	
Pedro Adigue (PHI)	14 Dec 1968
Bruno Arcari (ITA)	31 Jan 1970
gave up title in 1974	
Perico Fernández (ESP)	21 Sep 1974
Saensak Muangsurin (THA)	15 Jul 1975
Miguel Velásquez (ESP)	30 Jun 1976
Saensak Muangsurin (THA)	29 Oct 1976
Kim Sang Hyun (KOR)	30 Dec 1978
Saoul Mamby (USA)	23 Feb 1980
Leroy Haley (USA)	26 Jun 1982
Bruce Curry (USA)	18 May 1983
Bill Costello (USA)	29 Jan 1984
Lonnie Smith (USA)	21 Aug 1985
René Arredondo (MEX)	6 May 1986
Tsuyoshi Hamada (JPN)	24 Jul 1986
René Arredondo (MEX)	22 Jul 1987
Roger Mayweather (USA)	12 Nov 1987
Julio César Chávez (MEX)	13 May 1989
Frankie Randall (USA)	29 Jan 1994
Julio César Chávez (MEX)	7 May 1994
Oscar de la Hoya (USA)	7 Jun 1996
gave up title in 1997	
Kostya Tszyu (AUS)	21 Aug 1999
IBF	
Aaron Pryor (USA)	December 1984
recognized as champion by the IBF; stripped of	
title in 1985	
Gary Hinton (USA)	26 Apr 1986

World Junior Welterweight Champions (continued)

CHAMPION (NATIONALITY)	DATE OF TITLE
IBF (continued)	
Joe Louis Manley (USA)	30 Oct 1986
Terry Marsh (GBR)	4 Mar 1987
gave up title in 1987	
James McGirt (USA)	14 Feb 1988
Meldrick Taylor (USA)	3 Sep 1988
Julio César Chávez (MEX)	17 Mar 1990
gave up title in 1991	
Rafael Pineda (COL)	7 Dec 1991
Pernell Whitaker (USA)	18 Jul 1992
gave up title in 1993	

CHAMPION (NATIONALITY)	DATE OF TITLE
IBF (continued)	
Charles Murray (USA)	15 May 1993
Jake Rodriguez (PUR)	13 Feb 1994
Kostya Tszyu (AUS)	28 Jan 1995
Vince Phillips (USA)	31 May 1997
Terronn Millett (USA)	20 Feb 1999
stripped of title in 2000	
Zab Judah (USA)	12 Feb 2000
Kostya Tszyu (AUS)	3 Nov 2001

World Lightweight Champions

Top weight 135 pounds; until 1912 usually 133 pounds, but sometimes as high as 140 pounds.

CHAMPION (NATIONALITY)	DATE OF TITLE
Undisputed champions	
George ("Kid") Lavigne (USA)	1 Jun 1896
Frank Erne (USA)	3 Jul 1899
Joe Gans (USA)	12 May 1902
Battling Nelson (USA)	4 Jul 1908
Ad Wolgast (USA)	22 Feb 1910
Willie Ritchie (USA)	28 Nov 1912
Freddie Welsh (GBR)	7 Jul 1914
Benny Leonard (USA)	28 May 1917
retired in 1925	
Jimmy Goodrich (USA)	13 Jul 1925
Rocky Kansas (USA)	7 Dec 1925
Sammy Mandell (USA)	3 Jul 1926
Al Singer (USA)	17 Jul 1930
Tony Canzoneri (USA)	14 Nov 1930
Barney Ross (USA)	23 Jun 1933
gave up title in 1933	
Tony Canzoneri (USA)	10 May 1935
Lou Ambers (USA)	3 Sep 1936
Henry Armstrong (USA)	17 Aug 1938
Lou Ambers (USA)	22 Aug 1939
Lew Jenkins (USA)	10 May 1940
Sammy Angott (USA)	19 Dec 1941
retired in 1942	
Ike Williams (USA)	4 Aug 1947
Jimmy Carter (USA)	25 May 1951
Lauro Salas (MEX)	14 May 1952
Jimmy Carter (USA)	15 Oct 1952
Paddy DeMarco (USA)	5 Mar 1954
Jimmy Carter (USA)	17 Nov 1954
Wallace ("Bud") Smith (USA)	29 Jun 1955
Joe Brown (USA)	24 Aug 1956
Carlos Ortíz (PUR)	21 Apr 1962
Ismael Laguna (PAN)	10 Apr 1965
Carlos Ortíz (PUR)	13 Nov 1965
Carlos Teo Cruz (DOM)	29 Jun 1968
Armando Ramos (USA)	18 Feb 1969
Ismael Laguna (PAN)	3 Mar 1970
stripped of WBC title in 1970	
WBA	
Ken Buchanan (GBR)	26 Sep 1970
Roberto Durán (PAN)	26 Jun 1972
gave up title in 1979	
Ernesto España (VEN)	16 Jun 1979
Hilmer Kenty (USA)	2 Mar 1980
Sean O'Grady (USA)	12 Apr 1981
stripped of title in 1981	
Claude Noel (TRI)	12 Sep 1981
Arturo Frias (USA)	5 Dec 1981
Ray Mancini (USA)	8 May 1982

CHAMPION (NATIONALITY)	DATE OF TITLE
WBA (continued)	
Livingstone Bramble (ISV)	1 Jun 1984
Edwin Rosario (PUR)	26 Sep 1986
Julio César Chávez (MEX)	21 Nov 1987
gave up title in 1989	
Edwin Rosario (PUR)	9 Jul 1989
Juan Nazario (PUR)	4 Apr 1990
Pernell Whitaker (USA)	11 Aug 1990
gave up title in 1992	
Joey Gamache (USA)	13 Jun 1992
Tony Lopez (USA)	24 Oct 1992
Dingaan Thobela (RSA)	26 Jun 1993
Olzubek Nazarov (RUS)	30 Oct 1993
Jean-Baptiste Mendy (FRA)	16 May 1998
Julien Lorcy (FRA)	10 Apr 1999
Stefano Zoff (ITA)	7 Aug 1999
Gilberto Serrano (VEN)	13 Nov 1999
Takanori Hatakeyama (JPN)	11 Jun 2000
Julien Lorcy (FRA)	1 Jul 2001
Raul Balbi (ARG)	8 Oct 2001
WBC	
Rodolfo Gonzáles (MEX)	10 Nov 1972
Ishimatsu Suzuki (JPN)	11 Apr 1974
Esteban de Jesus (PUR)	8 May 1976
Roberto Durán (PAN)	21 Jan 1978
gave up title in 1979	
Jim Watt (GBR)	17 Apr 1979
Alexis Argüello (NCA)	20 Jun 1981
gave up title in 1983	
Edwin Rosario (PUR)	1 May 1983
José Luis Ramírez (MEX)	3 Nov 1984
Hector Camacho (PUR)	10 Aug 1985
stripped of title in 1987	
José Luis Ramírez (MEX)	19 Jul 1987
Julio César Chávez (MEX)	29 Oct 1988
gave up title in 1989	
Pernell Whitaker (USA)	20 Aug 1989
gave up title in 1992	
Miguel González (MEX)	24 Aug 1992
gave up title in 1996	
Jean-Baptiste Mendy (FRA)	20 Apr 1996
Steve Johnston (USA)	1 Mar 1997
César Bazan (MEX)	13 Jun 1998
Steve Johnston (USA)	27 Feb 1999
José Luis Castillo (MEX)	17 Jun 2000
IBF	
Charlie Brown (USA)	30 Jan 1984
Harry Arroyo (USA)	15 Apr 1984
Jimmy Paul (USA)	6 Apr 1985

World Lightweight Champions (continued)

CHAMPION (NATIONALITY)	DATE OF TITLE
IBF (continued)	
Greg Haugen (USA)	6 Dec 1986
Vinny Pazienza (USA)	7 Jun 1987
Greg Haugen (USA)	6 Feb 1988
Pernell Whitaker (USA)	20 Feb 1989
gave up title in 1992	
Fred Pendleton (USA)	10 Jan 1993
Rafael Ruelas (USA)	19 Feb 1994

CHAMPION (NATIONALITY)	DATE OF TITLE
IBF (continued)	
Oscar de la Hoya (USA)	6 May 1995
gave up title in 1995	
Philip Holiday (RSA)	19 Aug 1995
Shane Mosley (USA)	2 Aug 1997
gave up title in 1999	
Paul Spadafora (USA)	20 Aug 1999

World Junior Lightweight Champions

Top weight 130 pounds. Also called super featherweight.

CHAMPION (NATIONALITY)	DATE OF TITLE
Undisputed champions	
Johnny Dundee (USA)	18 Nov 1921
Jack Bernstein (USA)	30 May 1923
Johnny Dundee (USA)	17 Dec 1923
Steve ("Kid") Sullivan (USA)	20 Jun 1924
Mike Ballerino (USA)	1 Apr 1925
Tod Morgan (USA)	2 Dec 1925
Benny Bass (USA)	20 Dec 1929
Kid Chocolate (Eligio Sardiniao) (CUB)	15 Jul 1931
Frankie Klick (USA)	25 Dec 1933
title vacant from 1934	
Sandy Saddler (USA)	6 Dec 1949
title vacant from 1951	
Harold Gomes (USA)	20 Jul 1959
Gabriel ("Flash") Elorde (PHI)	16 Mar 1960
Yoshiaki Numata (JPN)	15 Jun 1967
Hiroshi Kobayashi (JPN)	14 Dec 1967
stripped of WBO title in 1969	
WBA	
Alfredo Marcano (VEN)	29 Jul 1971
Ben Villaflor (PHI)	25 Apr 1972
Kuniaki Shibata (JPN)	12 Mar 1973
Ben Villaflor (PHI)	17 Oct 1973
Samuel Serrano (PUR)	16 Oct 1976
Yasutsune Uehara (JPN)	2 Aug 1980
Samuel Serrano (PUR)	9 Apr 1981
Roger Mayweather (USA)	19 Jan 1983
Rocky Lockridge (USA)	26 Feb 1984
Wilfredo Gómez (PUR)	19 May 1985
Alfredo Layne (PAN)	24 May 1986
Brian Mitchell (RSA)	27 Sep 1986
gave up title in 1991	
Joey Gamache (USA)	28 Jun 1991
gave up title in 1991	
Genaro Hernandez (USA)	22 Nov 1991
gave up title in 1995	
Choi Yong Soo (KOR)	21 Oct 1995
Takanori Hatakeyama (JPN)	5 Sep 1998
Lakva Sim (MGL)	27 Jun 1999
Jong Kwon Baek (KOR)	31 Oct 1999
Joel Casamayor (CUB)	21 May 2000

CHAMPION (NATIONALITY)	DATE OF TITLE
WBC	
Rene Barrientos (PHI)	15 Feb 1969
Yoshiaki Numata (JPN)	5 Apr 1970
Ricardo Arredondo (MEX)	10 Oct 1971
Kuniaki Shibata (JPN)	28 Feb 1974
Alfredo Escalera (PUR)	5 Jul 1975
Alexis Argüello (NCA)	28 Jan 1978
gave up title in 1980	
Rafael Limón (MEX)	11 Dec 1980
Cornelius Boza-Edwards (UGA)	8 Mar 1981
Rolando Navarrete (PHI)	29 Aug 1981
Rafael Limón (MEX)	29 May 1982
Bobby Chacon (USA)	11 Dec 1982
stripped of title in 1983	
Hector Camacho (USA)	7 Aug 1983
gave up title in 1984	
Julio César Chávez (MEX)	13 Sep 1984
vacant	
Azumah Nelson (GHA)	29 Feb 1988
Jesse James Leija (USA)	7 May 1994
Gabriel Ruelas (USA)	17 Sep 1994
Azumah Nelson (GHA)	1 Dec 1995
Genaro Hernandez (USA)	22 Mar 1997
Floyd Mayweather, Jr. (USA)	3 Oct 1998
IBF	
Yuh Hwan-Kil (KOR)	2 Apr 1984
Lester Ellis (AUS)	15 Feb 1985
Barry Michael (AUS)	12 Jul 1985
Rocky Lockridge (USA)	9 Aug 1987
Tony Lopez (USA)	27 Jul 1988
Juan Molina (PUR)	7 Oct 1989
Tony Lopez (USA)	20 May 1990
Brian Mitchell (RSA)	13 Sep 1991
gave up title in 1992	
Juan Molina (PUR)	22 Feb 1992
vacant	
Eddie Hopson (USA)	22 Apr 1995
Tracy Patterson (USA)	9 Jul 1995
Arturo Gatti (USA)	15 Dec 1995
gave up title in 1998	
Roberto Garcia (USA)	13 Mar 1998
Diego Corrales (USA)	23 Oct 1999
gave up title in 2000	
Steve Forbes (USA)	3 Dec 2000

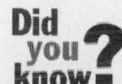

Did you know? Sophocles reported that dice were invented by a Greek named Palamedes during the siege of Troy, whereas Herodotus maintained that they were invented by the Lydians in the days of King Atys. Actually, numerous archaeological finds have demonstrated that dice were used in many earlier societies. They were originally magical devices used for the casting of lots to divine the future.

World Featherweight Champions

Top weight 126 pounds; until 1901 weight varied between 115 and 122 pounds.

CHAMPION (NATIONALITY)	DATE OF TITLE
Undisputed champions	
Billy Murphy (NZL)	13 Jan 1890
Young Griffo (AUS)	2 Feb 1890
vacant	
George Dixon (CAN)	27 Jun 1892
Solly Smith (USA)	4 Oct 1897
Dave Sullivan (GBR)	26 Sep 1898
George Dixon (CAN)	11 Nov 1898
Terry McGovern (USA)	19 Jan 1900
Young Corbett (USA)	28 Nov 1901
Jimmy Britt (USA)	25 Mar 1904
title vacant in 1904	
Tommy Sullivan (USA)	13 Oct 1904
title vacant from 1905	
Abe Atell (USA)	22 Feb 1906
Johnny Kilbane (USA)	22 Feb 1912
Eugène Criqui (FRA)	2 Jun 1923
Johnny Dundee (USA)	26 Jul 1923
gave up title in 1924	
Louis ("Kid") Kaplan (USA)	2 Jan 1925
gave up title in 1926	
Tony Canzoneri (USA)	24 Oct 1927
André Routis (FRA)	28 Sep 1928
Battling Battalino (USA)	23 Sep 1929
gave up title in 1932	
Henry Armstrong (USA)	29 Oct 1937
gave up title in 1938	
Joey Archibald (USA)	18 Apr 1939
Harry Jeffra (USA)	20 May 1940
Joey Archibald (USA)	12 May 1941
Chalky Wright (USA)	11 Sep 1941
Willie Pep (USA)	20 Nov 1942
Sandy Saddler (USA)	29 Oct 1948
Willie Pep (USA)	11 Feb 1949
Sandy Saddler (USA)	8 Sep 1950
retired in 1957	
Hogan Bassey (NGR)	24 Jun 1957
Davey Moore (USA)	18 Mar 1959
Sugar Ramos (CUB)	21 Mar 1963
Vicente Saldivar (MEX)	26 Sep 1964
retired 1967-70	
WBA	
Raoul Rojas (USA)	28 Mar 1968
Shozo Saijo (JPN)	28 Sep 1968
Antonio Gómez (VEN)	2 Sep 1971
Ernesto Marcel (PAN)	19 Aug 1972
retired in 1974	
Rubén Olivares (MEX)	9 Jul 1974
Alexis Argüello (NCA)	23 Nov 1974
gave up title in 1976	
Rafael Ortega (PAN)	15 Jan 1977
Cecilio Lastra (ESP)	17 Dec 1977
Eusebio Pedroza (PAN)	15 Apr 1978
Barry McGuigan (NIR)	8 Jun 1985
Steve Cruz (USA)	23 Jun 1986
Antonio Esparragoza (VEN)	6 Mar 1987
Park Yung Kyun (KOR)	30 Mar 1991
Eloy Rojas (VEN)	4 Dec 1993
Wilfredo Vásquez (PUR)	18 May 1996
gave up title in 1998	

CHAMPION (NATIONALITY)	DATE OF TITLE
WBA (continued)	
Freddie Norwood (USA)	3 Apr 1998
stripped of title in 1998	
Antonio Cermeño (VEN)	3 Oct 1998
Freddie Norwood (USA)	29 May 1999
Derrick Gainer (USA)	9 Sep 2000
WBC	
José Legra (CUB)	24 Jul 1968
Johnny Famechon (AUS)	21 Jan 1969
Vicente Saldivar (MEX)	9 May 1970
Kuniaki Shibata (JPN)	11 Dec 1970
Clemente Sánchez (MEX)	19 May 1972
José Legra (ESP)	16 Dec 1972
Eder Jofre (BRA)	5 May 1973
stripped of title in 1974	
Bobby Chacon (USA)	7 Sep 1974
Rubén Olivares (MEX)	20 Jun 1975
David Kotey (GHA)	20 Sep 1975
Danny López (USA)	5 Nov 1976
Salvador Sánchez (MEX)	2 Feb 1980
died in 1982	
Juan LaPorte (PUR)	15 Sep 1982
Wilfredo Gómez (PUR)	31 Mar 1984
Azumah Nelson (GHA)	8 Dec 1984
gave up title in 1988	
Jeff Fenech (AUS)	7 Mar 1988
gave up title in 1990	
Marcos Villasana (MEX)	2 Jun 1990
Paul Hodkinson (GBR)	13 Nov 1991
Gregorio Vargas (MEX)	28 Apr 1993
Kevin Kelley (USA)	4 Dec 1993
Alejandro González (MEX)	7 Jan 1995
Manuel Medina (MEX)	23 Sep 1995
Luisito Espinosa (PHI)	11 Dec 1995
César Soto (MEX)	15 May 1999
Naseem Hamed (GBR)	22 Oct 1999
stripped of title in 1999	
Gustavo Espadas (MEX)	14 Apr 2000
Erik Morales (MEX)	17 Feb 2001
IBF	
Oh Min-kuem (KOR)	4 Mar 1984
Chung Ki-yung (KOR)	29 Nov 1985
Antonio Rivera (PUR)	30 Aug 1986
Calvin Grove (USA)	23 Jan 1988
Jorge Paez (MEX)	4 Aug 1988
gave up title in 1991	
Troy Dorsey (USA)	3 Jun 1991
Manuel Medina (MEX)	12 Aug 1991
Tom Johnson (USA)	26 Feb 1993
Naseem Hamed (GBR)	8 Feb 1997
gave up title in 1997	
Hector Lizarraga (USA)	13 Dec 1997
Manuel Medina (MEX)	24 Apr 1998
Paul Ingle (GBR)	13 Nov 1999
Mbulelo Botile (RSA)	16 Dec 2000
Frankie Toledo (USA)	6 Apr 2001
Manuel Medina (MEX)	16 Nov 2001

World Junior Featherweight Champions

Top weight 122 pounds. Also called super bantamweight. Weight division at first recognized only by WBC.

CHAMPION (NATIONALITY)	DATE OF TITLE	CHAMPION (NATIONALITY)	DATE OF TITLE
WBA		**WBC (continued)**	
Hong Soo Hwan (KOR)	26 Nov 1977	Juan Meza (MEX)	3 Nov 1984
Ricardo Cardona (COL)	7 May 1978	Guadalupe Pintor (MEX)	18 Aug 1985
Leo Randolph (USA)	4 May 1980	Samart Payakaroon (THA)	18 Jan 1986
Sergio Palma (ARG)	9 Aug 1980	Jeff Fenech (AUS)	8 May 1987
Leonardo Cruz (DOM)	12 Jun 1982	gave up title in 1990	
Loris Stecca (ITA)	22 Feb 1984	Daniel Zaragoza (MEX)	29 Feb 1988
Víctor Callejas (PUR)	26 May 1984	Paul Banke (USA)	23 Apr 1990
stripped of title in 1986		Pedro Decima (ARG)	5 Nov 1990
Louie Espinoza (USA)	16 Jan 1987	Kiyoshi Hatanaka (JPN)	3 Feb 1991
Julio Gervacio (DOM)	28 Nov 1987	Daniel Zaragoza (MEX)	14 Jun 1991
Bernardo Pinango (VEN)	5 Mar 1988	Thierry Jacob (FRA)	20 Mar 1992
Juan José Estrada (MEX)	28 May 1988	Tracy Patterson (USA)	23 Jun 1992
Jesus Salud (USA)	11 Dec 1989	Hector Acero-Sánchez (USA)	26 Aug 1994
stripped of title in 1990		Daniel Zaragoza (MEX)	6 Nov 1995
Luís Mendoza (COL)	11 Sep 1990	Erik Morales (MEX)	6 Sep 1997
Raul Pérez (MEX)	7 Oct 1991	gave up title in 2000	
Wilfredo Vásquez (PUR)	27 Mar 1992	Willie Jorrin (USA)	9 Sep 2000
Antonio Cermeño (VEN)	13 May 1995		
gave up title in 1997		**IBF**	
Enrique Sanchez (MEX)	8 Feb 1998	Bobby Berna (PHI)	4 Dec 1983
vacant		Suh Seung-il (KOR)	15 Apr 1984
Néstor Garza (MEX)	12 Dec 1998	Kim Ji-won (KOR)	3 Jan 1985
Clarence Adams (USA)	4 Mar 2000	vacant	
stripped of title in 2001		Lee Seung-hoon (KOR)	18 Jan 1987
Yober Ortega (VEN)	17 Nov 2001	gave up title in 1988	
		José Sanabria (VEN)	21 May 1988
WBC		Fabrice Benichou (FRA)	10 Mar 1989
Rigoberto Riasco (PAN)	3 Apr 1976	Welcome Ncita (RSA)	10 Mar 1990
Kazuo Kobayashi (JPN)	10 Oct 1976	Kennedy McKinney (USA)	2 Dec 1992
Yum Dong Kyun (KOR)	24 Nov 1976	Vuyani Bungu (RSA)	20 Aug 1994
Wilfredo Gómez (PUR)	21 May 1977	gave up title in 1999	
gave up title in 1983		Lehlohonolo Ledwaba (RSA)	29 May 1999
Jaime Garza (USA)	15 Jun 1983	Manny Pacquiao (PHI)	23 Jun 2001

World Bantamweight Champions

Top weight 118 pounds; until 1920 weight limits varied between 105 and 116 pounds.

CHAMPION (NATIONALITY)	DATE OF TITLE	CHAMPION (NATIONALITY)	DATE OF TITLE
Undisputed champions		**Undisputed champions (continued)**	
Terry McGovern (USA)	12 Sep 1899	Manuel Ortiz (USA)	7 Aug 1942
gave up title in 1900		Harold Dade (USA)	6 Jan 1947
Harry Harris (USA)	18 Mar 1901	Manuel Ortiz (USA)	11 Mar 1947
gave up title in 1901		Vic Toweel (RSA)	31 May 1950
Harry Forbes (USA)	2 Apr 1901	Jimmy Carruthers (AUS)	15 Nov 1952
Frankie Neil (USA)	13 Aug 1903	retired in 1954; title in dispute	
Joe Bowker (GBR)	17 Oct 1904	Alphonse Halimi (ALG)	6 Nov 1957
gave up title in 1905; title in dispute		José Becerra (MEX)	8 Jul 1959
Kid Williams (USA)	9 Jun 1914	retired in 1961	
Pete Herman (USA)	9 Jan 1917	Eder Jofre (BRA)	18 Jan 1962
Joe Lynch (USA)	22 Dec 1920	Masahiko Harada (JPN)	17 May 1965
Pete Herman (USA)	25 Jul 1921	Lionel Rose (AUS)	26 Feb 1968
Johnny Buff (USA)	23 Sep 1921	Rubén Olivares (MEX)	22 Aug 1969
Joe Lynch (USA)	10 Jul 1922	Chucho Castillo (MEX)	16 Oct 1970
Abe Goldstein (USA)	21 Mar 1924	Rubén Olivares (MEX)	3 Apr 1971
Eddie Martin (USA)	19 Dec 1924	Rafael Herrera (MEX)	19 Mar 1972
Charlie Rosenberg (USA)	20 Mar 1925	Enrique Pinder (PAN)	30 Jul 1972
stripped of title in 1927; title in dispute		stripped of WBC title in 1972	
Panama Al Brown (PAN)	18 Jun 1929		
stripped of NBA (later WBA) title in 1934; title in dispute		**WBA**	
		Romeo Anaya (MEX)	20 Jan 1973
Sixto Escobar (PUR)	31 Aug 1936	Arnold Taylor (RSA)	3 Nov 1973
Harry Jeffra (USA)	23 Sep 1937	Hong Soo Hwan (KOR)	3 Jul 1974
Sixto Escobar (PUR)	20 Feb 1938	Alfonso Zamora (MEX)	14 Mar 1975
gave up title in 1939		Jorge Luján (PAN)	19 Nov 1977
Lou Salica (USA)	13 Jan 1941	Julian Solís (PUR)	29 Aug 1980

World Bantamweight Champions (continued)

CHAMPION (NATIONALITY)	DATE OF TITLE	CHAMPION (NATIONALITY)	DATE OF TITLE
WBA (continued)		**WBC (continued)**	
Jeff Chandler (USA)	14 Nov 1980	Carlos Zárate (MEX)	8 May 1976
Richie Sandoval (USA)	7 Apr 1984	Guadalupe Pintor (MEX)	3 Jun 1979
Gaby Canizales (USA)	10 Mar 1986	stripped of title in 1983	
Bernardo Pinango (VEN)	4 Jun 1986	Alberto Davila (USA)	1 Sep 1983
gave up title in 1987		stripped of title in 1985	
Takuyama Muguruma (JPN)	29 Mar 1987	Daniel Zaragoza (MEX)	4 May 1985
Park Chang Young (KOR)	24 May 1987	Miguel Lora (COL)	9 Aug 1985
Wilfredo Vásquez (PUR)	4 Oct 1987	Raul Pérez (MEX)	29 Oct 1988
Khaokor Galaxy (THA)	9 May 1988	Greg Richardson (USA)	25 Feb 1991
Moon Sung Kil (KOR)	14 Aug 1988	Joichiro Tatsuyoshi (JPN)	19 Sep 1991
Khaokor Galaxy (THA)	9 Jul 1989	vacant	
Luisito Espinosa (PHI)	18 Oct 1989	Victor Rabañales (MEX)	30 Mar 1992
Israel Contreras (VEN)	19 Oct 1991	Byun Jong-il (KOR)	28 Mar 1993
Eddie Cook (USA)	15 Mar 1992	Yasuei Yakushiji (JPN)	22 Dec 1993
Eliecer Julio (COL)	10 Oct 1992	Wayne McCullough (NIR)	30 Jul 1995
Junior Jones (USA)	23 Oct 1993	Sirimongkol Singmanassuk (THA)	10 Aug 1996
John Michael Johnson (USA)	22 Apr 1994	Joichiro Tatsuyoshi (JPN)	22 Nov 1997
Daorung Chuvatana Siriwat (THA)	16 Jul 1994	Veeraphol Sahaprom (THA)	29 Dec 1998
Veeraphol Sahaprom (THA)	17 Sep 1995		
Nana Konadu (GHA)	28 Jan 1996	**IBF**	
Daorung Chuvatana Siriwat (THA)	26 Oct 1996	Satoshi Shingaki (JPN)	15 Apr 1984
Nana Konadu (GHA)	21 Jun 1997	Jeff Fenech (AUS)	26 Apr 1985
Johnny Tapia (USA)	6 Dec 1998	vacant	
Paulie Ayala (USA)	26 Jun 1999	Kelvin Seabrooks (USA)	16 May 1987
stripped of title in 2001		Orlando Canizales (USA)	9 Jul 1988
Eidy Moya (VEN)	14 Oct 2001	gave up title in 1994	
		Harold Mestre (COL)	21 Jan 1995
WBC		Mbulelo Botile (RSA)	29 Apr 1995
Rafael Herrera (MEX)	15 Apr 1973	Tim Austin (USA)	19 Jul 1997
Rudolfo Martínez (MEX)	7 Dec 1974		

World Junior Bantamweight Champions

Top weight 115 pounds. Also called super flyweight.

CHAMPION (NATIONALITY)	DATE OF TITLE	CHAMPION (NATIONALITY)	DATE OF TITLE
WBA		**WBC (continued)**	
Gustavo Ballas (ARG)	12 Sep 1981	Moon Sung Kil (KOR)	20 Jan 1990
Rafael Pedroza (PAN)	5 Dec 1981	José Luis Bueno (MEX)	13 Nov 1993
Watanabe Jiro (JPN)	8 Apr 1982	Hiroshi Kawashima (JPN)	4 May 1994
stripped of title in 1984		Gerry Peñalosa (PHI)	20 Feb 1997
Khaosai Galaxy (THA)	21 Nov 1984	Cho In Joo (KOR)	29 Aug 1998
gave up title in 1991		Masanori Tokuyama (JPN)	27 Aug 2000
Katsuya Onizuka (JPN)	10 Apr 1992		
Lee Hyung Chul (KOR)	18 Sep 1994	**IBF**	
Alima Goitia (VEN)	22 Jul 1995	Chun Joo-do (KOR)	10 Dec 1983
Yokthai Sithoar (THA)	24 Aug 1996	Ellyas Pical (INA)	3 May 1985
Satoshi Iida (JPN)	23 Dec 1997	César Polanco (DOM)	15 Feb 1986
Jesús Rojas (VEN)	23 Dec 1998	Ellyas Pical (INA)	6 Jul 1986
Hideki Todaka (JPN)	31 Jul 1999	vacant	
Leo Gámez (VEN)	9 Oct 2000	Chang Tae-il (KOR)	17 May 1987
Shoji Kobayashi (JPN)	11 Mar 2001	Ellyas Pical (INA)	17 Oct 1987
		Juan Polo Pérez (COL)	14 Oct 1989
WBC		Robert Quiroga (USA)	21 Apr 1990
Rafael Oroño (VEN)	1 Feb 1980	Julio Borboa (MEX)	16 Jan 1993
Kim Chul Ho (KOR)	24 Jan 1981	Harold Grey (COL)	29 Aug 1994
Rafael Oroño (VEN)	28 Nov 1982	Carlos Salazar (ARG)	7 Oct 1995
Payao Poontarat (THA)	27 Nov 1983	Harold Grey (COL)	27 Apr 1996
Watanabe Jiro (JPN)	5 Jul 1984	Danny Romero (USA)	24 Aug 1996
Gilberto Román (MEX)	30 Mar 1986	Johnny Tapia (USA)	18 Jul 1997
Santos Laciar (ARG)	16 May 1987	gave up title in 1998	
Jesús Rojas (COL)	9 Aug 1987	Mark Johnson (USA)	24 Apr 1999
Gilberto Román (MEX)	8 Apr 1988	stripped of title in 2000	
Nana Konadu (GHA)	7 Nov 1989	Félix Machado (VEN)	22 Jul 2000

World Flyweight Champions
Top weight 112 pounds.

CHAMPION (NATIONALITY)	DATE OF TITLE
Undisputed champions	
Jimmy Wilde (GBR)	18 Dec 1916
Pancho Villa (Francisco Guilledo) (PHI)	18 Jun 1923
died in 1925	
Fidel La Barba (USA)	21 Jan 1927
retired in 1927; title in dispute	
Benny Lynch (GBR)	19 Jan 1937
gave up title in 1938	
Peter Kane (GBR)	22 Sep 1938
Jackie Paterson (GBR)	19 Jun 1943
title in dispute from 1947	
Rinty Monaghan (IRE)	23 Mar 1948
retired in 1950	
Terry Allen (GBR)	25 Apr 1950
Dado Marino (Hawaii)	1 Aug 1950
Yoshio Shirai (JPN)	19 May 1952
Pascual Pérez (ARG)	26 Nov 1954
Pone Kingpetch (THA)	16 Apr 1960
Masahiko Harada (JPN)	10 Oct 1962
Pone Kingpetch (THA)	12 Jan 1963
Hiroyuki Ebihara (JPN)	18 Sep 1963
Pone Kingpetch (THA)	23 Jan 1964
Salvatore Burruni (ITA)	23 Apr 1965
title in dispute from 1965	
WBA	
Horacio Accavallo (ARG)	1 Mar 1966
retired in 1968	
Hiroyuki Ebihara (JPN)	30 Mar 1969
Bernabe Villacampo (PHI)	19 Oct 1969
Berkrerk Chartvanchai (THA)	14 Apr 1970
Ohba Masao (JPN)	22 Oct 1970
died in 1973	
Chartchai Chionoi (THA)	17 May 1973
Susumu Hanagata (JPN)	18 Oct 1974
Erbito Salavarria (PHI)	1 Apr 1975
Alfonso López (PAN)	27 Feb 1976
Gustavo Espadas (MEX)	2 Oct 1976
Betulio González (VEN)	12 Aug 1978
Luis Ibarra (PAN)	17 Nov 1979
Kim Tae Shik (KOR)	16 Feb 1980
Peter Mathebula (RSA)	13 Dec 1980
Santos Laciar (ARG)	28 Mar 1981
Luis Ibarra (PAN)	6 Jun 1981
Juan Herrera (MEX)	26 Sep 1981
Santos Laciar (ARG)	1 May 1982
gave up title in 1985	
Hilario Zapata (PAN)	5 Oct 1985
Fidel Bassa (COL)	13 Feb 1987
Jesús Rojas (VEN)	30 Sep 1989
Lee Yul Woo (KOR)	10 Mar 1990
Leopard Tamakuma (JPN)	29 Jul 1990
Elvis Álvarez (COL)	14 Mar 1991
Kim Yong Kang (KOR)	1 Jun 1991
Aquiles Guzmán (VEN)	26 Sep 1992
David Griman (VEN)	15 Dec 1992
Saen Sow Ploenchit (THA)	13 Feb 1994
José Bonilla (VEN)	14 Nov 1996
Hugo Soto (ARG)	29 May 1998

CHAMPION (NATIONALITY)	DATE OF TITLE
WBA (continued)	
Leo Gámez (VEN)	13 Mar 1999
Sornpichai Kratchingdaeng (THA)	3 Sep 1999
Eric Morel (USA)	5 Aug 2000
WBC	
Walter McGowan (GBR)	14 Jun 1966
Chartchai Chionoi (THA)	30 Dec 1966
Efren Torres (MEX)	23 Feb 1969
Chartchai Chionoi (THA)	20 Mar 1970
Erbito Salavarria (PHI)	7 Dec 1970
stripped of title in 1971	
Betulio González (VEN)	20 Nov 1971
Venice Borkorsor (THA)	29 Sep 1972
gave up title in 1973	
Betulio González (VEN)	4 Aug 1973
Shoji Oguma (JPN)	1 Oct 1974
Miguel Canto (MEX)	8 Jan 1975
Park Chan Hee (KOR)	18 Mar 1979
Shoji Oguma (JPN)	18 May 1980
Antonio Avelar (MEX)	12 May 1981
Prudencio Cardona (COL)	20 Mar 1982
Freddie Castillo (MEX)	24 Jul 1982
Eleoncio Mercedes (DOM)	6 Nov 1982
Charlie Magri (GBR)	15 Mar 1983
Frank Cedeno (PHI)	27 Sep 1983
Koji Kobayashi (JPN)	18 Jan 1984
Gabriel Bernal (MEX)	9 Apr 1984
Sot Chitalada (THA)	8 Oct 1984
Kim Yong Kang (KOR)	24 Jul 1988
Sot Chitalada (THA)	3 Jun 1989
Muangchai Kittikasem (THA)	15 Feb 1991
Yury Arbachakov (RUS)	23 Jun 1992
Chatchai Dutchboygym (Sasakul) (THA)	9 May 1997
Manny Pacquiao (PHI)	4 Dec 1998
stripped of title in 1999	
Medgeon Singsurat (THA)	17 Sep 1999
Malcolm Tunacao (PHI)	19 May 2000
Pongsaklek Wongjongkam (THA)	2 Mar 2001
IBF	
Kwon Soon Chun (KOR)	24 Dec 1983
Chung Chong Kwan (KOR)	20 Dec 1985
Chung Bi Won (KOR)	27 Apr 1986
Shin Hi Sup (KOR)	2 Aug 1986
Dodie Penalosa (PHI)	22 Feb 1987
Choi Chang Ho (KOR)	5 Sep 1987
Rolando Bohol (PHI)	16 Jan 1988
Duke McKenzie (GBR)	5 Oct 1988
Dave McAuley (GBR)	7 Jun 1989
Rodolfo Blanco (COL)	11 Jun 1992
Phichit Sithbangprachan (THA)	29 Nov 1992
vacant	
Francisco Tejedor (COL)	18 Feb 1995
Danny Romero (USA)	22 Apr 1995
gave up title in 1996	
Mark Johnson (USA)	4 May 1996
gave up title in 1999	
Irene Pacheco (COL)	10 Apr 1999

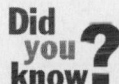

World Junior Flyweight Champions

Top weight 108 pounds. Also called light flyweight.

CHAMPION (NATIONALITY)	DATE OF TITLE
WBA	
Jaime Ríos (PAN)	23 Aug 1975
Juan Guzmán (DOM)	1 Jul 1976
Yoko Gushiken (JPN)	10 Oct 1976
Pedro Flores (MEX)	8 Mar 1981
Kim Hwan Jin (KOR)	19 Jul 1981
Katsuo Tokashiki (JPN)	16 Dec 1981
Lupe Madera (MEX)	10 Jul 1983
Francisco Quiroz (DOM)	19 May 1984
Joey Olivo (USA)	29 Mar 1985
Yuh Myung Woo (KOR)	8 Dec 1985
Hiroki Ioka (JPN)	17 Dec 1991
Yuh Myung Woo (KOR)	18 Nov 1992
gave up title in 1993	
Leo Gámez (VEN)	21 Oct 1993
Choi Hi Yong (KOR)	4 Feb 1995
Carlos Murillo (PAN)	13 Jan 1996
Keiji Yamaguchi (JPN)	21 May 1996
Pichitnoi Siriwat (THA)	3 Dec 1996
vacant	
Bebis Mendoza (COL)	12 Aug 2000
Rosendo Álvarez (NCA)	3 Mar 2001
WBC	
Franco Udella (ITA)	4 Apr 1975
stripped of title in 1975	
Luis Alberto Estaba (VEN)	13 Sep 1975
Freddie Castillo (MEX)	19 Feb 1978
Netrnoi Sor Vorasingh (THA)	6 May 1978
Kim Sung Jun (KOR)	30 Sep 1978
Shigeo Nakajima (JPN)	3 Jan 1980
Hilario Zapata (PAN)	24 Mar 1980
Amado Ursua (MEX)	6 Feb 1982

CHAMPION (NATIONALITY)	DATE OF TITLE
WBC (continued)	
Tadashi Tomori (JPN)	13 Apr 1982
Hilario Zapata (PAN)	20 Jul 1982
Chang Jung Koo (KOR)	26 Mar 1983
gave up title in 1988	
German Torres (MEX)	11 Dec 1988
Lee Yul Woo (KOR)	19 Mar 1989
Humberto González (MEX)	25 Jun 1989
Rolando Pascua (PHI)	19 Dec 1990
Melchor Cob Castro (MEX)	25 Mar 1991
Humberto González (MEX)	4 Jun 1991
Michael Carbajal (USA)	13 Mar 1993
Chiquita González (MEX)	19 Feb 1994
Saman Sorjaturong (THA)	15 Jul 1995
Choi Yo Sam (KOR)	17 Oct 1999
IBF	
Dodie Penalosa (PHI)	10 Dec 1983
stripped of title in 1986	
Choi Chong Hwon (KOR)	7 Dec 1986
Tacy Macalos (PHI)	6 Nov 1988
Muangchai Kittikasem (THA)	2 May 1989
Michael Carbajal (USA)	29 Jul 1990
Chiquita González (MEX)	19 Feb 1994
Saman Sorjaturong (THA)	15 Jul 1995
vacant	
Michael Carbajal (USA)	16 Mar 1996
Mauricio Pastrana (COL)	18 Jan 1997
stripped of title in 1997	
Mauricio Pastrana (COL)	13 Dec 1997
stripped of title in 1998	
Will Grigsby (USA)	18 Dec 1998
Ricardo López (MEX)	2 Oct 1999

World Mini-Flyweight Champions

Top weight 105 pounds. Also called strawweight. Division first recognized by WBA in 1988 and by WBC and IBF in 1987.

CHAMPION (NATIONALITY)	DATE OF TITLE
WBA	
Leo Gámez (VEN)	10 Jan 1988
vacant	
Kim Bong Jun (KOR)	16 Apr 1989
Choi Hi Yong (KOR)	2 Feb 1991
Hideyuki Ohashi (JPN)	14 Oct 1992
Chana Porpaoin (THA)	10 Feb 1993
Rosendo Álvarez (NCA)	2 Dec 1995
Ricardo López (MEX)	13 Nov 1998
gave up title in 1999	
Noel Arambulet (VEN)	9 Oct 1999
stripped of title in 2000	
Joma Gamboa (PHI)	20 Aug 2000
Hoshino Keitaro (JPN)	6 Dec 2000
Chana Porpaoin (THA)	16 Apr 2001
Yutaka Niida (JPN)	25 Aug 2001
gave up title in 2001	
WBC	
Ioka Hiroki (JPN)	18 Oct 1987
Napa Kiatwanchai (THA)	13 Nov 1988
Choi Jum Hwan (KOR)	12 Nov 1989

CHAMPION (NATIONALITY)	DATE OF TITLE
WBC (continued)	
Hideyuki Ohashi (JPN)	7 Feb 1990
Ricardo López (MEX)	25 Oct 1990
gave up title in 1999	
Wande Chareon (THA)	4 May 1999
José Antonio Aguirre (MEX)	11 Feb 2000
IBF	
Lee Kyung Yun (KOR)	14 Jun 1987
vacant	
Samuth Sithnaruepol (THA)	24 Mar 1988
Nico Thomas (INA)	17 Jun 1989
Eric Chávez (PHI)	21 Sep 1989
Falan Lookmingkwan (THA)	21 Feb 1990
Manny Melchor (PHI)	6 Sep 1992
Ratanapol Vorapin (THA)	10 Dec 1992
stripped of title in 1996	
Ratanapol Vorapin (THA)	16 May 1996
Zolani Petelo (RSA)	27 Dec 1997
gave up title in 2000	
Roberto Leyva (MEX)	29 Apr 2001

Chess

William Steinitz is generally recognized as the first official chess world champion, although dates for his 19th-century reign vary. With a few notable exceptions, each successive champion defeated his predecessor in match play. The first exception followed the death of the incumbent **Alexander Alekhine** in 1946. The **Fédération Internationale des Échecs** (FIDE; founded 1924) stepped into the vacancy and arranged a tournament among leading contenders to determine a new champion in 1948. FIDE continued to oversee regular tournaments and matches to determine challengers—although another exception occurred in 1975, when **Robert (Bobby) Fischer** refused to defend his crown and retired. In 1993 **Garry Kasparov** pulled out of FIDE to defend his title under rival organizations (Professional Chess Association and later Braingames). Without a universally recognized champion, FIDE struggled to obtain funding for its multiyear system of tournaments and matches leading to a title match. So, in 1999 FIDE began to hold annual "**knockout**" **tournaments**, with very fast game play, to determine their champion. Few chess players recognize the FIDE champion as legitimate, however.

FIDE began organizing the **women's chess championship** in 1953. Controversy also has afflicted this title, with **Zsuzsa Polgar** refusing to accept FIDE's terms for her title defense in 1999. In 2000, FIDE adopted a knockout tournament format for the women's championship, similar to the open tournament.

The **Olympiads** are held biennially. Competition is open to both men and women, but since 1957 there has been a separate Olympiad that is restricted to women.

FIDE Web site: <www.fide.com>

World Chess Champions—Men
Generally recognized (see head note)

REIGN	NAME	NATIONALITY	REIGN	NAME	NATIONALITY
1866–94	Wilhelm Steinitz	Austrian American	1960–61	Mikhail Tal	Soviet Russian
1894–1921	Emanuel Lasker	German	1961–63	Mikhail Botvinnik	Soviet Russian
1921–27	José Raúl Capablanca	Cuban	1963–69	Tigran Petrosyan	Soviet Georgian-born Armenian
1927–35	Alexander Alekhine	Russian-born French	1969–72	Boris Spassky	Soviet Russian
1935–37	Max Euwe	Dutch	1972–75	Robert (Bobby) Fischer	American
1937–46	Alexander Alekhine	Russian-born French	1975–85	Anatoly Karpov	Soviet Russian
1948–57	Mikhail Botvinnik	Soviet Russian	1985–2000	Garry Kasparov	Azerbaijani-born Russian
1957–58	Vasily Smyslov	Soviet Russian	2000–	Vladimir Kramnik	Russian
1958–60	Mikhail Botvinnik	Soviet Russian			

World Chess Champions—Women

REIGN	NAME	NATIONALITY	REIGN	NAME	NATIONALITY
1927–44	Vera Menchik*	Soviet Russian	1978–91	Maya Chiburdanidze	Soviet Georgian
1949–53	Lyudmila Rudenko	Soviet Russian	1991–96	Xie Jun	Chinese
1953–56	Yelizaveta Bykova	Soviet Russian	1996–99	Zsuzsa Polgar†	Hungarian
1956–58	Olga Rubtsova	Soviet Russian	1999–2001	Xie Jun	Chinese
1958–62	Yelizaveta Bykova	Soviet Russian	2001–	Zhu Chen	Chinese
1962–78	Nona Gaprindashvili	Soviet Georgian			

*Killed in an air raid on London in 1944; title left vacant. †Rejected conditions for title defense; title regained by Xie.

Chess Olympiads
The table lists the competitions for the past 20 years only.
The next Olympiads are scheduled for 25 Oct–11 Nov 2002 in Bled, Slovenia.

YEAR	Open		Women		YEAR	Open		Women	
	WINNER	RUNNER-UP	WINNER	RUNNER-UP		WINNER	RUNNER-UP	WINNER	RUNNER-UP
1982	USSR	Czechoslovakia	USSR	Rumania	1992	Russia	Uzbekistan	Georgia	Ukraine
1984	USSR	Great Britain	USSR	Bulgaria	1994	Russia	Bosnia	Georgia	Hungary
1986	USSR	Great Britain	USSR	Hungary	1996	Russia	Ukraine	Georgia	China
1988	USSR	Great Britain	Hungary	USSR	1998	Russia	United States	China	Russia
1990	USSR	United States	Hungary	USSR	2000	Russia	Germany	China	Georgia

Contract Bridge

The world team contract bridge championships were instituted in 1950 with what was then an annual and zonal competition called the **Bermuda Bowl**. When the **World Team Olympiad**, held quadrennially, was instituted in 1960, it represented the world team championship. The only exception to this rule occurred in 1976, when both events were held. The Bermuda Bowl is organized by the **World Bridge Federation** (WBF; founded 1958), and since 1977 it has been held in odd-numbered years (the 1999 competition took place in January 2000). Among women's teams the major competition is the World Team Olympiad, although another team competition, the **Venice Trophy**, was inaugurated in 1974. In pairs competition the quadrennial **World Bridge Championships** (inaugurated in 1962, it features open and women's sections) is the premiere international event.

WBF Web site: <www.worldbridge.org>

Bermuda Bowl

YEAR	WINNER	RUNNER-UP	YEAR	WINNER	RUNNER-UP
1950	United States	United Kingdom	1971	United States	France
1951	United States	Italy	1972	*not held**	
1952	*postponed*		1973	Italy	United States
1953	United States	Sweden	1974	Italy	North America
1954	United States	France	1975	Italy	North America
1955	United Kingdom	United States	1976	North America	Italy
1956	France	United States	1977	North American	North American
1957	Italy	United States		Defenders	Challengers
1958	Italy	United States	1979	North America	Italy
1959	Italy	United States	1981	United States	Pakistan
1960	*not held**		1983	United States	Italy
1961	Italy	North America	1985	United States	Austria
1962	Italy	North America	1987	United States	United Kingdom
1963	Italy	North America	1989	Brazil	United States
1964	*not held**		1991	Iceland	Poland
1965	Italy	United States	1993	The Netherlands	Norway
1966	Italy	North America	1995	United States	Canada
1967	Italy	North America	1997	France	United States
1968	*not held**		2000	United States	Brazil
1969	Italy	Taiwan	2001	United States II	Norway
1970	North America	Taiwan	2003	*tentatively scheduled for October*	

*not held because of World Team Olympiad

World Contract Bridge Team Olympiad

	open		women's	
YEAR	WINNER	RUNNER-UP	WINNER	RUNNER-UP
1960	France	United Kingdom	United Arab Republic	France
1964	Italy	United States	Great Britain	United States
1968	Italy	United States	Sweden	South Africa
1972	Italy	United States	Italy	South Africa
1976	Brazil	Italy	Italy	United Kingdom
1980	France	United States	United States	Italy
1984	Poland	France	United States	United Kingdom
1988	United States	Austria	Denmark	United Kingdom
1992	France	United States	Austria	United Kingdom
1996	France	Indonesia	United States	China
2000	Italy	Poland	United States	Canada
2004	*will possibly be held in Istanbul, Turkey*			

World Contract Bridge Pair Championships

YEAR	OPEN WINNERS	WOMEN'S WINNERS	MIXED WINNERS
1962	Pierre Jais, Roger Trézel (FRA)	Rixi Markus, Fritzi Gordon (GBR)	*
1966	Bob Slavenburg, Hans Kreyns (NED)	Joan Durran, Jane Juan (GBR)	Mary Jane Ferell, Ivan Erdos (USA)
1970	Fritz Babsch, Peter Manhardt (AUT)	Mary Jane Farell, Marilyn Johnson (USA)	Barbara Brier, Waldemar von Zedtwitz (USA)
1974	Robert Hamman, Bobby Wolff (USA)	Fritzi Gordon, Rixi Markus (GBR)	Loula Gordon, Tony Trad (SUI)

World Contract Bridge Pair Championships (continued)

YEAR	OPEN WINNERS	WOMEN'S WINNERS	MIXED WINNERS
1978	Marcelo Branco, Gabino Cintra (BRA)	Kathie Wei, Judi Radin (USA)	Barry Crane, Kerri Shuman (USA)
1982	Chip Martel, Lew Stansby (USA)	Carol Saders, Betty Ann Kennedy (USA)	Dianna Gordon, George Mittelman (CAN)
1986	Jeff Mecksroth, Eric Rodwell (USA)	Jacqui Mitchell, Amalya Kearse (USA)	Pam Wittes, John Wittes (USA)
1990	Marcelo Branco, Gabriel Chagas (BRA)	Kerri Shuman, Karen McCallum (USA)	Peter Wechsel, Juanita Chambers (USA)
1994	Martin Lesniewski, Marek Szymanowski (POL)	Carla Arnolds, Bep Vriend (NED)	Danuta Hocheker, Apolinare Kowalski (POL)
1998	Michal Kwiecien, Jacek Pszczola (POL)	Jill Meyers, Shawn Quinn (USA)	Enza Rossano, Antonio Vivaldi (ITA)
2002	scheduled to be held 16–31 August, Montreal		

*A mixed team competition, won by a team from the United Kingdom, was held in 1962.

Cricket

Cricket is one of the **national sports** of England, and consequently it is played in nearly all the countries with which England has been associated. The world governing body is the **International Cricket Council** (ICC; founded as the Imperial Cricket Conference in 1909). The most important international cricket matches are the **Test matches**, which have been played since 1877. The Test-playing countries are England, Australia, South Africa (banned from international competition between about 1970 and 1992), West Indies (representing Barbados, Guyana, Jamaica, Trinidad and Tobago, and the Leeward and Windward islands), New Zealand, India,

Pakistan, Sri Lanka, Zimbabwe (since 1992), and Bangladesh (since 2001).

The Test table is designed to be read from left to right across the columns. This will indicate, for example, that in Test match play against England, South Africa has won 23 games, has had 47 drawn matches, and has lost 50 games.

The **World Cup** is a quadrennial one-day, limited-overs competition. It was first held in 1975.

Related Web sites: CricInfo: <www.cricket.org>; John Wisden & Co Ltd: <www.wisden.com>

All-Time First-Class Test Cricket Standings (as of 30 Sep 2001)

	England			Australia			South Africa			West Indies			New Zealand		
	WINS	DRAWS	LOSSES	W	D	L	W	D	L	W	D	L	W	D	L
England v.	—	—	—	94	86	121	50	47	23	31	43^	52	37	39	6
Australia v.	121	80	94	—	—	—	34	17	14	42	22†	31	18	12	7
South Africa v.	23	47	50	14	17	34	—	—	—	7	2	2	15	9	3
West Indies v.	52	43*	31	31	22†	42	2	2	7	—	—	—	10	14	6
New Zealand v.	6	39	37	7	12	18	3	9	15	6	14	10	—	—	—
India v.	14	38	32	13	18†	29	2	4	6	7	35	28	14	20*	7
Pakistan v.	10	34	16	11	17	18	1	1	2	10	14	13	19	17	6
Sri Lanka v.	3	1	5	1	5	7	1	4	6	0	2	1	4	7	7
Zimbabwe v.	0	3	1	0	0	1	0	1	4	0	1	3	0	6	5
Bangladesh v.	‡	‡	‡	‡	‡	‡	‡	†	‡	‡	‡	‡	‡	‡	‡

	India			Pakistan			Sri Lanka			Zimbabwe			Bangladesh		
	W	D	L	W	D	L	W	D	L	W	D	L	W	D	L
England v.	32	38	14	16	34	10	5	1	3	1	3	0	‡	‡	‡
Australia v.	29	18†	13	18	17	11	7	5	1	1	0	0	‡	‡	‡
South Africa v.	6	4	2	2	1	1	6	4	1	4	1	0	‡	‡	‡
West Indies v.	28	35	7	13	14	10	1	2	0	3	1	0	‡	‡	‡
New Zealand v.	7	20*	14	6	17	19	7	7	4	5	6	0	†	‡	‡
India v.	—	—	—	5	33	9	8	12	3	3	2	2	1	0	0
Pakistan v.	9	33	5	—	—	—	13	9^	5	6	5*	2	1	0	0
Sri Lanka v.	3	12	8	5	9*	13	—	—	—	5	5	0	1	0	0
Zimbabwe v.	2	2	3	2	5*	6	0	5	5	—	—	—	2	0	0
Bangladesh v.	0	0	1	0	0	1	0	0	1	0	0	2	—	—	—

^Including one match abandoned.   †Including one tie.   ‡No matches.

Cricket World Cup

YEAR	RESULT				YEAR	RESULT			
1975	West Indies	291–8	Australia	274	1992	Pakistan	249–6	England	227
1979	West Indies	286–9	England	194	1996	Sri Lanka	245–3	Australia	241
1983	India	183	West Indies	140	1999	Australia	133–2	Pakistan	132
1987	Australia	253–5	England	246–8	2003	*Date and place to be announced.*			

Curling

The game of curling, played on ice and somewhat akin to bowls or shuffleboard, varies little from country to country. The maximum permitted weight of the curling stones is 44 lb (19.9 kg). The top international **men's competition** was instituted in 1959 (called the Scotch Whisky Cup from 1959 to 1967; the Silver Broom from 1968 to 1985; and the World Curling Championship since 1986). Although curling has been played among women of many countries since at least the mid-20th century, the first **women's world curling championship** was not held until 1979.

World Curling Federation Web site: <www.world-curlingfederation.org>

World Curling Championships—Men

The championship was called the Scotch Whisky Cup (unofficial) 1959–67, the Silver Broom 1968–85; the IOC President's Cup 1986–2000; and the World Curling Championships since 2001.

YEAR	WINNER	RUNNER-UP	YEAR	WINNER	RUNNER-UP
1959	Canada	Scotland	1981	Switzerland	United States
1960	Canada	Scotland	1982	Canada	Switzerland
1961	Canada	Scotland	1983	Canada	West Germany
1962	Canada	Scotland	1984	Norway	Switzerland
1963	Canada	Scotland	1985	Canada	Sweden
1964	Canada	Scotland	1986	Canada	Scotland
1965	United States	Canada	1987	Canada	West Germany
1966	Canada	Scotland	1988	Norway	Canada
1967	Scotland	Canada	1989	Canada	Switzerland
1968	Canada	Scotland	1990	Canada	Scotland
1969	Canada	Scotland	1991	Scotland	Canada
1970	Canada	Scotland	1992	Switzerland	Scotland
1971	Canada	Scotland	1993	Canada	Scotland
1972	Canada	United States	1994	Canada	Sweden
1973	Sweden	Canada	1995	Canada	Scotland
1974	United States	Canada	1996	Canada	Scotland
1975	Switzerland	Canada	1997	Sweden	Germany
1976	United States	Scotland	1998	Canada	Sweden
1977	Sweden	Canada	1999	Scotland	Canada
1978	United States	Canada	2000	Canada	Sweden
1979	Norway	Switzerland	2001	Sweden	Switzerland
1980	Canada	Norway	2002	Canada	Norway

World Curling Championships—Women

YEAR	WINNER	RUNNER-UP	YEAR	WINNER	RUNNER-UP
1979	Switzerland	Sweden	1991	Norway	Canada
1980	Canada	Sweden	1992	Sweden	United States
1981	Sweden	Canada	1993	Canada	Germany
1982	Denmark	Sweden	1994	Canada	Scotland
1983	Switzerland	Norway	1995	Sweden	Canada
1984	Canada	Switzerland	1996	Canada	United States
1985	Canada	Scotland	1997	Canada	Norway
1986	Canada	West Germany	1998	Sweden	Denmark
1987	Canada	West Germany	1999	Sweden	United States
1988	West Germany	Canada	2000	Canada	Switzerland
1989	Canada	Norway	2001	Canada	Sweden
1990	Norway	Scotland	2002	Scotland	Sweden

Cycling

By all accounts, the greatest cycling event of all is the annual **Tour de France** road race (founded 1903). It is raced in several stages over distances exceeding 3,500 km (2,175 mi). From 1911 to 1929 distances exceeded 5,300 km. A Tour de France for women was first held, over an 18-stage course of 991 km, in 1984. In addition to this and a great number of other road races held yearly, there are yearly **road racing world championships.**

Track racing championships are also held. The oldest events of track racing are the **sprint** (in which only the last part of the race can actually be considered sprinting) and the **pursuit** (both a team and individual event in which contestants start the race on opposite sides of the track and attempt to catch each other). **Mountain bike racing** and **cyclo-cross,** a cross-country bicycle race that requires cyclists to carry their bikes over parts of the course, developed in the latter part of the 20th century. World championships were established for these sports in 1997.

International Cycling Union (Union Cycliste Internationale—UCI) Web site: <www.uci.ch>

Cycling Champions, 2001–02
In the case of multiday events, the concluding date is given.

EVENT	WINNER (COUNTRY)	DATE
world champions—mountain bikes		**16 Sep 2001**
men		
Cross-country	Roland Green (CAN)	
Downhill	Nicolas Vouilloz (FRA)	
women		
Cross-country	Alison Dunlap (USA)	
Downhill	Anne-Caroline Chausson (FRA)	
world champions—track		**30 Sep 2001**
men		
Sprint	Arnaud Tournant (FRA)	
Individual pursuit	Oleksandr Symonenko (UKR)	
Kilometre time trial	Arnaud Tournant (FRA)	
40-km points	Bruno Risi (SUI)	
Team pursuit	Sergy Chernyavsky, Oleksandr Fedenko, Oleksandr Symonenko, Lyubamyr Polotayko (UKR)	
Keirin	Ryan Bayley (AUS)	
Olympic sprint	Laurent Gané, Florian Rousseau, Arnaud Tournant (FRA)	
60-km Madison	Jérôme Neuville, Robert Sassone (FRA)	
women		
Sprint	Svetlana Grankovskaya (RUS)	
Individual pursuit	Leontien Zijlaard-Van Moorsel (NED)	
500-m time trial	Nancy Contreras Reyes (MEX)	
24-km points	Olga Slyusareva (RUS)	
world champions—road		**14 Oct 2001**
men		
Individual road race	Oscar Freire Gómez (ESP)	
Individual time trial	Jan Ullrich (GER)	
women		
Individual road race	Rasa Polikeviciute (LTU)	
Individual time trial	Jeannie Longo-Ciprelli (FRA)	
world champions—cyclo-cross		**3 Feb 2002**
Men	Mario De Clercq (BEL)	
Women	Laurence Leboucher (FRA)	
major elite road-race winners (starred races comprise the World Cup)		
^HEW-Cyclassics Cup	Erik Zabel (GER)	31 Aug 2001
*San Sebastian Classic (Klasika Ciclista San Sebastian)	Laurent Jalabert (FRA)	11 Aug 2001
*Zürich Championship (Meisterschaft von Zürich)	Paolo Bettini (ITA)	26 Aug 2001
Tour of Spain (Vuelta a España)	Angel Casero Moreno (ESP)	30 Sep 2001
*Paris–Tours	Richard Virenque (FRA)	7 Oct 2001
*Tour of Lombardy (Giro di Lombardia)	Danilo Di Luca (ITA)	20 Oct 2001
Paris–Nice	Aleksandr Vinokurov (KAZ)	17 Mar 2002
Tirreno–Adriatico	Erik Dekker (NED)	20 Mar 2002
*Milan–San Remo	Mario Cipollini (ITA)	23 Mar 2002
*Tour of Flanders (Ronde van Vlaanderen)	Andrea Tafi (ITA)	7 Apr 2002

Cycling Champions, 2001–02 (continued)

EVENT	WINNER (COUNTRY)	DATE
major elite road-race winners (starred races comprise the World Cup) (continued)		
Ghent–Wevelgem	Mario Cipollini (ITA)	10 Apr 2002
*Paris–Roubaix	Johan Museeuw (BEL)	14 Apr 2002
La Flèche Wallonne	Mario Aerts (BEL)	17 Apr 2002
*Liège–Bastogne–Liège	Paolo Bettini (ITA)	21 Apr 2002
*Amstel Gold	Michele Bartoli (ITA)	28 Apr 2002
Tour of Romandie (Tour de Romandie)	Dario Frigo (ITA)	5 May 2002
Tour of Italy (Giro d'Italia)	Paolo Savoldelli (ITA)	2 Jun 2002
Critérium de Dauphiné Libéré	Lance Armstrong (USA)	16 Jun 2002
Tour of Switzerland (Tour de Suisse)	Alex Zulle (SUI)	27 Jun 2002
Tour de France	Lance Armstrong (USA)	28 Jul 2002

Tour de France

YEAR	WINNER (COUNTRY)	LENGTH OF ROUTE (KM)	YEAR	WINNER (COUNTRY)	LENGTH OF ROUTE (KM)
1903	Maurice Garin (FRA)	2,428	1958	Charly Gaul (LUX)	4,319
1904	Henri Cornet (FRA)	2,388	1959	Federico Bahamontes (ESP)	4,355
1905	Louis Trousselier (FRA)	2,975	1960	Gastone Nencini (ITA)	4,173
1906	René Pottier (FRA)	4,637	1961	Jacques Anquetil (FRA)	4,397
1907	Lucien Petit-Breton (FRA)	4,488	1962	Jacques Anquetil (FRA)	4,274
1908	Lucien Petit-Breton (FRA)	4,487	1963	Jacques Anquetil (FRA)	4,137
1909	François Faber (LUX)	4,507	1964	Jacques Anquetil (FRA)	4,504
1910	Octave Lapize (FRA)	4,474	1965	Felice Gimondi (ITA)	4,183
1911	Gustave Garrigou (FRA)	5,344	1966	Lucien Aimar (FRA)	4,303
1912	Odile Defraye (BEL)	5,319	1967	Roger Pingeon (FRA)	4,780
1913	Philippe Thys (BEL)	5,387	1968	Jan Janssen (NED)	4,662
1914	Philippe Thys (BEL)	5,405	1969	Eddy Merckx (BEL)	4,110
1915–18	not held		1970	Eddy Merckx (BEL)	4,366
1919	Firmin Lambot (BEL)	5,560	1971	Eddy Merckx (BEL)	3,689
1920	Philippe Thys (BEL)	5,519	1972	Eddy Merckx (BEL)	3,846
1921	Léon Scieur (BEL)	5,484	1973	Luis Ocaña (ESP)	4,140
1922	Firmin Lambot (BEL)	5,375	1974	Eddy Merckx (BEL)	4,098
1923	Henri Pélissier (FRA)	5,386	1975	Bernard Thévenet (FRA)	4,000
1924	Ottavio Bottecchia (ITA)	5,425	1976	Lucien Van Impe (BEL)	4,050
1925	Ottavio Bottecchia (ITA)	5,430	1977	Bernard Thévenet (FRA)	4,098
1926	Lucien Buysse (BEL)	5,745	1978	Bernard Hinault (FRA)	3,920
1927	Nicolas Frantz (LUX)	5,341	1979	Bernard Hinault (FRA)	3,719
1928	Nicolas Frantz (LUX)	5,377	1980	Joop Zoetemelk (NED)	3,948
1929	Maurice De Waele (BEL)	5,286	1981	Bernard Hinault (FRA)	3,765
1930	André Leducq (FRA)	4,818	1982	Bernard Hinault (FRA)	3,489
1931	Antonin Magne (FRA)	5,095	1983	Laurent Fignon (FRA)	3,568
1932	André Leducq (FRA)	4,520	1984	Laurent Fignon (FRA)	3,880
1933	Georges Speicher (FRA)	4,395	1985	Bernard Hinault (FRA)	4,100
1934	Antonin Magne (FRA)	4,363	1986	Greg LeMond (USA)	4,091
1935	Romain Maes (BEL)	4,338	1987	Stephen Roche (IRL)	4,100
1936	Romain Maes (BEL)	4,442	1988	Pedro Delgado (ESP)	3,300
1937	Roger Lapébie (FRA)	4,415	1989	Greg LeMond (USA)	3,215
1938	Gino Bartali (ITA)	4,694	1990	Greg LeMond (USA)	3,399
1939	Sylvere Maes (BEL)	4,224	1991	Miguel Indurain (ESP)	3,935
1940–46	not held		1992	Miguel Indurain (ESP)	3,983
1947	Jean Robic (FRA)	4,640	1993	Miguel Indurain (ESP)	3,700
1948	Gino Bartali (ITA)	4,922	1994	Miguel Indurain (ESP)	3,978
1949	Fausto Coppi (ITA)	4,808	1995	Miguel Indurain (ESP)	3,635
1950	Ferdi Kubler (SUI)	4,775	1996	Bjarne Riis (DEN)	3,764
1951	Hugo Koblet (SUI)	4,697	1997	Jan Ullrich (GER)	3,944
1952	Fausto Coppi (ITA)	4,807	1998	Marco Pantani (ITA)	3,831
1953	Louison Bobet (FRA)	4,479	1999	Lance Armstrong (USA)	3,687
1954	Louison Bobet (FRA)	4,469	2000	Lance Armstrong (USA)	3,663
1955	Louison Bobet (FRA)	4,855	2001	Lance Armstrong (USA)	3,454
1956	Roger Walkowiak (FRA)	4,496	2002	Lance Armstrong (USA)	3,272
1957	Jacques Anquetil (FRA)	4,686			

Fencing

What had been the European fencing championship from 1921 to 1935 was officially recognized as the **world fencing** championship at the Olympic Games of 1936. The only event that does not reflect Olympics winners in the designated years is the women's team foil competition, which was not an Olympic event until 1960. Traditionally **women** competed only in the foil; women's épée competition has been part of the world championships since 1989 and sabre since 1999.

Men's fencing bouts last about six minutes, and the first man to score five hits with the designated portion of the weapon (for foil and épée, only hits made with the point of the weapon are scored) is the winner. Women's bouts last about five minutes, and only four hits must be scored.

Each **weapon** has a different target area: for the **foil**, it is the torso; for the **épée**, the entire body; and for the **sabre**, roughly the upper half of the body (including the head and arms).

Related Web sites: Fédération Internationale d'Escrime (FIE): <www.fie.ch>; US Fencing Association (USFA): <www.usfencing.org>

World Fencing Championships—Men

Competition has been held since 1936. Table shows results for the past 20 years.
The 2002 championships are scheduled to be concluded 18 August in Lisbon.

	Foil			Épée	
YEAR	INDIVIDUAL	TEAM	YEAR	INDIVIDUAL	TEAM
1982	Aleksandr Romankov (URS)	USSR	1982	Jeno Pap (HUN)	France
1983	Aleksandr Romankov (URS)	West Germany	1983	Elmar Bormann (FRG)	France
1984*	Mauro Numa (ITA)	Italy	1984*	Philippe Boisse (FRA)	West Germany
1985	Mauro Numa (ITA)	Italy	1985	Philippe Boisse (FRA)	West Germany
1986	Andrea Borella (ITA)	Italy	1986	Philippe Riboud (FRA)	West Germany
1987	Mathias Gey (FRG)	West Germany	1987	Volker Fischer (FRG)	USSR
1988*	Stefano Cerioni (ITA)	USSR	1988*	Arnd Schmitt (FRG)	France
1989	Alexander Koch (FRG)	USSR	1989	Manuel Pereira (SPA)	Italy
1990	Philippe Omnès (FRA)	Italy	1990	Thomas Gerull (FRG)	Italy
1991	Ingo Weissenborn (GER)	Cuba	1991	Andrey Shuvalov (URS)	USSR
1992*	Philippe Omnès (FRA)	Germany	1992*	Eric Srecki (FRA)	Germany
1993	Alexander Koch (GER)	Germany	1993	Pavel Kolobkov (RUS)	Italy
1994	Rolando Tucker (CUB)	Germany	1994	Pavel Kolobkov (RUS)	France
1995	Dmitry Shevchenko (RUS)	Cuba	1995	Eric Srecki (FRA)	Germany
1996	Alessandro Puccini (ITA)	Russia	1996	Aleksandr Beketov (RUS)	Italy
1997	Sergey Golubitsky (UKR)	France	1997	Eric Srecki (FRA)	Cuba
1998	Sergey Golubitsky (UKR)	Poland	1998	Hugues Obry (FRA)	Hungary
1999	Sergey Golubitsky (UKR)	France	1999	Arnd Schmitt (GER)	France
2000	Kim Young Ho (KOR)	France	2000	Pavel Kolobkov (RUS)	Italy
2001	Salvatore Sanzo (ITA)	France	2001	Paolo Milanoli (ITA)	Hungary

	Sabre			Sabre	
YEAR	INDIVIDUAL	TEAM	YEAR	INDIVIDUAL	TEAM
1982	Viktor Krovopuskov (URS)	Hungary	1993	Grigory Kiriyenko (URS)	Hungary
1983	Vassil Etropolski (BUL)	USSR	1994	Felix Becker (GER)	Russia
1984*	Jean-François Lamour (FRA)	Italy	1995	Grigory Kiriyenko (URS)	Italy
1985	Gyorgy Nebald (HUN)	USSR	1996	Stanislav Pozdnyakov (RUS)	Russia
1986	Sergey Mindirgasov (URS)	USSR	1997	Stanislav Pozdnyakov (RUS)	France
1987	Jean-François Lamour (FRA)	USSR	1998	Luigi Tarantino (ITA)	Hungary
1988*	Jean-François Lamour (FRA)	Hungary	1999	Damien Touya (FRA)	France
1989	Grigory Kiriyenko (URS)	USSR	2000	Mihai Claudiu Covaliu (ROM)	Russia
1990	Gyorgy Nebald (HUN)	USSR	2001	Stanislav Pozdnyakov (RUS)	Russia
1991	Grigory Kiriyenko (URS)	Hungary			
1992*	Bence Szabo (HUN)	Unified Team†			

*Olympic titles are recognized as world championships.   †Consisting of athletes from the Commonwealth of
Independent States and Georgia.

Did you know In a shell game the conjurer places a bead or ball under one of three inverted cups. As the cups are rearranged on a flat surface, the ball is made to "jump" invisibly from one cup to another. The basis for the illusion is a secret additional ball that, by skilled manipulation, is put under one cup while the known ball is removed as secretly from another cup.

World Fencing Championships—Women

Foil competition has been held since 1936. Table shows results for the past 20 years.
The 2002 championships are scheduled to be concluded 18 August in Lisbon.

	Foil				Épée	
YEAR	INDIVIDUAL	TEAM		YEAR	INDIVIDUAL	TEAM
1982	Nailya Gilyazova (URS)	Italy		1989	Anja Straub (SUI)	Hungary
1983	Dorina Vaccaroni (ITA)	Italy		1990	Taymi Chappe (CUB)	West Germany
1984*	Luan Jujie (CHN)	West Germany		1991	Mariann Horvath (HUN)	Hungary
1985	Cornelia Hanisch (FRG)	West Germany		1992	not held	
1986	Anja Fichtel (FRG)	USSR		1993	Oksana Jermakova (EST)	Hungary
1987	Elisabeta Tufan (ROM)	Hungary		1994	Laura Chiesa (ITA)	Spain
1988*	Anja Fichtel (FRG)	West Germany		1995	Joanna Jakimiuk (POL)	Hungary
1989	Olga Velichko (URS)	West Germany		1996	Laura Flessel (FRA)	France
1990	Anja Fichtel (FRG)	Italy		1997	Mirayda Garcia-Soto (CUB)	Hungary
1991	Giovanna Trillini (ITA)	Italy		1998	Laura Flessel (FRA)	France
1992*	Giovanna Trillini (ITA)	Italy		1999	Laura Flessel-Colovic (FRA)	Hungary
1993	Francesca Bortolozzi (ITA)	Germany		2000	Timea Nagy (HUN)	Russia
1994	Reka Szabo (ROM)	Romania		2001	Claudia Bokel (GER)	Russia
1995	Laura Badea (ROM)	Italy				
1996	Laura Badea (ROM)	Italy			Sabre	
1997	Giovanna Trillini (ITA)	Italy		YEAR	INDIVIDUAL	TEAM
1998	Sabine Bau (GER)	Italy		1999	Yelena Yemayeva (AZE)	Italy
1999	Valentina Vezzali (ITA)	Germany		2000	Yelena Yemayeva (AZE)	United States
2000	Valentina Vezzali (ITA)	Italy		2001	Anne-Lise Touya (FRA)	Russia
2001	Valentina Vezzali (ITA)	Italy				

*Olympic titles are recognized as world championships.

 Athletic pursuits of U.S. Presidents: George Washington was an avid fox hunter.

Field Hockey

The sport of **field hockey** is quite popular in the United Kingdom, India, Pakistan, and much of Europe. Curiously, the sport was not seriously promoted among American men, and, in the United States, field hockey has been largely regarded as a sport for women. Despite its recognizable origins in the mid-19th century the game was not organized on an **international** level until the mid-20th century. One of a number of international tournaments is the **World Cup**, which is organized by the **International Hockey Federation** (Fédération Internationale de Hockey, FIH; founded 1924).

FIH Web site: <www.fihockey.org>

World Cup Field Hockey Championship

The 2002 championship for women is scheduled to be concluded 8 December in Perth, Australia.

	men				women	
YEAR	WINNER	RUNNER-UP		YEAR	WINNER	RUNNER-UP
1971	Pakistan	India		1974	The Netherlands	Argentina
1973	The Netherlands	India		1976	West Germany	Argentina
1975	India	Pakistan		1978	The Netherlands	West Germany
1978	Pakistan	The Netherlands		1981	West Germany	The Netherlands
1982	Pakistan	West Germany		1983	The Netherlands	Canada
1986	Australia	England		1986	The Netherlands	West Germany
1990	The Netherlands	Pakistan		1990	The Netherlands	Australia
1994	Pakistan	The Netherlands		1994	Australia	Argentina
1998	The Netherlands	Spain		1998	Australia	The Netherlands
2002	Germany	Australia				

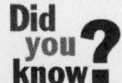 Yogi Berra's Words of Wisdom: "It was impossible to get a conversation going, everybody was talking too much."

Football

Many types of games are known as football, among them association football (also called soccer), gridiron football (also called American football and known in the United States as, simply, football), Canadian football (also called rugby football), Australian Rules Football (also called footy), and Rugby Union and Rugby League football (also known as rugby, or rugger). Each of these games is unique, although some—such as US football and Canadian football—bear more than a little resemblance, and each has its own distinct following.

American Football—professional. The National Football League (NFL) championship play-offs were organized in 1933. The American Football League (founded 1959) was a rival organization until 1970, when it merged with the NFL. The resulting reorganization added a few new teams (1976) and divided the reconstituted NFL into two conferences, the American Football Conference and the National Football Conference. The play-off winner in each conference becomes that conference's representative in the Super Bowl, the final game of the professional football season.

American Football—college. Historically the national champion of college football has been informally selected by two rival opinion polls—one based on a survey of collegiate football coaches (currently conducted by USA Today/ESPN) and the other by sports writers (conducted by the Associated Press [AP]). The AP sports writers' poll began in 1936. The coaches' poll was begun in 1950 by the United Press (now United Press International [UPI]). Where polls designated different teams, both are listed. Desire for a clear-cut national champion led to the creation of the Bowl Championship Series (BCS) in 1999. The BCS uses a formula involving team records, strength of schedule, and rankings to determine the top two teams, who then meet in a national championship game. The site of the game annually shifts between the four major Bowls—Fiesta, Orange, Rose, and Sugar. The first of the Bowl games, the Rose Bowl, was played in 1902 during the 12th annual Tournament of Roses festival in Pasadena CA. In 1935 the Sugar Bowl (played in New Orleans) and the Orange Bowl (played in Miami) were inaugurated. The Fiesta Bowl (played in Phoenix) began play in 1971.

Canadian football—professional. The rules and organization of professional football in Canada have evolved gradually for well over 100 years based on the Canadian Rugby Union (formed in 1891). Until 1936 the game included intercollegiate teams. Since 1959, the Canadian Football League has been divided into two conferences, Eastern and Western. The two teams that win the division championships meet for the championship of the League, the Grey Cup (instituted in 1909). The intercollegiate teams withdrew from the Grey Cup competition in 1936, but the league did not become strictly professional until the mid-1950s.

Australian football. Australian Rules Football, originally called Melbourne Rules Football, emerged in the state of Victoria in the late 1850s as a sporting alternative during the southern winter when cricket was not played. The Victorian Football Association (formed in 1877) was supplanted by the Victorian Football League (formed in 1896), which was renamed the Australian Football League (AFL) in 1990 after two teams from outside Victoria were admitted in 1987. Currently, the eight AFL teams with the best records at the end of a 22-week season qualify for the play-offs. The first premiership Grand Final was played in 1886.

Association football. The game of association football is governed by the Fédération Internationale de Football Association (FIFA; founded 1904). The quadrennial FIFA World Cup (organized as the World Cup in 1930) was the first official internationally contested association football match. The popularity of the World Cup and the even earlier Copa América (1916) in South America led to the development of several regional cup competitions, including the European Champion Clubs' Cup (1955; discontinued after the 1992–93 season and superseded by the UEFA Champions League), the Asian Cup (1956), the African Cup of Nations (1957), and the Libertadores de América Cup (1960). Competition for the FIFA Women's World Cup began in 1991. The Major League Soccer Cup in the US was launched in 1996.

Rugby Union football. Rugby Union football was open to amateurs only until 1995. The Six Nations Championship was first played in 1882 (as the Four Nations) and is now contested by England, Scotland, Wales, Ireland, France (since 1910), and Italy (since 2000). The international Test matches further include South Africa, New Zealand, and Australia. The International Rugby Football League (now FIRA-AER) oversees rugby in 39 other (i.e., non-Test) countries. The chief international competition between Rugby Union clubs in the southern hemisphere is the tri-nation Super 12 (Super 10 from 1993 until 1996). Teams from Australia (three), South Africa (four), and New Zealand (five) play in a round-robin tournament; the four teams with the best records qualify for the semifinals. The World Cup, sponsored by the International Rugby Board (IRB; founded 1886), was inaugurated in 1987. The competition is held every four years.

Rugby League football. Rugby League World Cup competition began in 1954 between professionals from Australia, France, Great Britain, and New Zealand. In 1975 it was renamed the International Championship. Competition was discontinued after 1977 but revived during the 1980s. The match has been held irregularly every few years.

Related Web sites: National Football League (NFL): <www.nfl.com>; Canadian Football League (CFL): <www.cfl.ca>; Australian Football League (AFL): <www.afl.com.au>; Fédération Internationale de Football Association (FIFA): <www.fifa.com>; Union des Associations Européennes de Football (UEFA): <www.uefa.com>; Major League Soccer (MLS): <www.majorleaguesoccer.com>; International Rugby Board (Rugby Union): <www.irb.org> or <www.irfb.com>; International Rugby League: <www.world.rleague.com>, (Super 12) <www.super12.rugby.com.au>

National Football League (NFL) Final Standings, 2001–02

AMERICAN CONFERENCE

Eastern Division				Central Division				Western Division			
TEAM	WON	LOST	TIED	TEAM	WON	LOST	TIED	TEAM	WON	LOST	TIED
*New England Patri-ots	11	5	0	*Pittsburgh Steelers	13	3	0	*Oakland Raiders	10	6	0
*Miami Dolphins	11	5	0	*Baltimore Ravens	10	6	0	Seattle Seahawks	9	7	0
*New York Jets	10	6	0	Cleveland Browns	7	9	0	Denver Broncos	8	8	0
Indianapolis Colts	6	10	0	Tennessee Titans	7	9	0	Kansas City Chiefs	6	10	0
Buffalo Bills	3	13	0	Jacksonville Jaguars	6	10	0	San Diego Chargers	5	11	0
				Cincinnati Bengals	6	10	0				

NATIONAL CONFERENCE

Eastern Division				Central Division				Western Division			
TEAM	WON	LOST	TIED	TEAM	WON	LOST	TIED	TEAM	WON	LOST	TIED
*Philadelphia Eagles	11	5	0	*Chicago Bears	13	3	0	*St. Louis Rams	14	2	0
Washington Red-skins	8	8	0	*Green Bay Packers	12	4	0	*San Francisco 49ers	12	4	0
New York Giants	7	9	0	*Tampa Bay Bucca-neers	9	7	0	New Orleans Saints	7	9	0
Arizona Cardinals	7	9	0	Minnesota Vikings	5	11	0	Atlanta Falcons	7	9	0
Dallas Cowboys	5	11	0	Detroit Lions	2	14	0	Carolina Panthers	1	15	0

Gained play-off berth.

American Pro Football All-Time Records

	PLAYERS (TEAMS)	NUMBER	SEASON/DATE
Individual career records			
Total appearances	George Blanda	340	1949–1975, except 1959
Total Super Bowl appearances	Mike Lodish	6	1991, '92, '93, '94, '98, '99
Total points scored	Gary Anderson*	2,133	1982–2001
TDs scored, total	Jerry Rice*	196	1985–2001
TDs scored by passer	Dan Marino	420	1983–1999
TDs scored by receiver	Jerry Rice*	185	1985–2001
TDs scored by rusher	Emmit Smith*	145	1990–2001
FGs scored	Gary Anderson*	476	1982–2001
Extra points scored (kicked)	George Blanda	943	1949–1975, except 1959
Passing yardage	Dan Marino	61,361	1983–1999
Passing completions (attempts)	Dan Marino	4,967 (8,358)	1983–1999
Receiving yardage	Jerry Rice*	20,386	1985–2001
Rushing yardage	Walter Payton	16,726	1975–1987
Interceptions (defense)	Paul Krause	81	1964–1979
Sacks (defense)†	Reggie White	198	1985–2000, except 1999
Coaching total wins	Don Shula	328-156-6	1963–1995
Coaching winning percentage	Vince Lombardi	.740	1959–1969
Individual season records			
Total points scored	Paul Hornung (Green Bay Packers)	176	1960
TDs scored, total	Marshall Faulk* (St. Louis Rams)	26	2000
TDs scored by passer	Dan Marino (Miami Dolphins)	48	1984
TDs scored by receiver	Jerry Rice* (San Francisco 49ers)	22	1987
TDs scored by rusher	Emmit Smith* (Dallas Cowboys)	25	1995
FGs scored	Olindo Mare* (Miami Dolphins)	39	1999
Extra points scored (kicked)	Uwe von Schamann (Miami Dolphins)	66	1984
Passing yardage	Dan Marino (Miami Dolphins)	5,084	1984
Passing completions (attempts)	Warren Moon (Houston Oilers)	404 (655)	1991
Receiving yardage	Jerry Rice* (San Francisco 49ers)	1,848	1995
Rushing yardage	Eric Dickerson (Los Angeles Rams)	2,105	1984
Interceptions (defense)	Dick "Night Train" Lane (Los Angeles Rams)	14	1952
Sacks (defense)†	Mark Gastineau (New York Jets)	22	1984

American Pro Football All-Time Records (continued)

Individual game records

PLAYERS (TEAMS)		NUMBER	SEASON/DATE
Total points scored	Ernie Nevers (Chicago Cardinals v. Chicago Bears)	40	28 Nov 1929
TDs scored, total	Ernie Nevers (Chicago Cardinals v. Chicago Bears); Dub Jones (Cleveland Browns v. Chicago Bears); Gale Sayers (Chicago Bears v. San Francisco 49ers)	6	28 Nov 1929; 25 Nov 1951; 12 Dec 1965
TDs scored by passer	Sid Luckman (Chicago Bears v. New York Giants); Adrian Burk (Philadelphia Eagles v. Washington Redskins); George Blanda (Houston Oilers v. New York Titans); Y.A. Tittle (New York Giants v. Washington Redskins); Joe Kapp (Minnesota Vikings v. Baltimore Colts) (tied)	7	14 Nov 1943; 17 Oct 1954; 19 Nov 1961; 28 Oct 1962; 28 Sept 1969
TDs scored by receiver	Bob Shaw (Chicago Cardinals v. Baltimore Colts); Kellen Winslow (San Diego Chargers v. Oakland Raiders); Jerry Rice* (San Francisco 49ers v. Atlanta Hawks)	5	2 Oct 1950; 22 Nov 1981; 14 Oct 1990
TDs scored by rusher	Ernie Nevers (Chicago Cardinals v. Chicago Bears)	6	28 Nov 1929
FGs scored	Jim Bakken (St. Louis Cardinals v. Pittsburgh Steelers); Rich Karlis (Minnesota Vikings v. Los Angeles Rams); Chris Boniol (Dallas Cowboys v. Green Bay Packers)	7	24 Sep 1967; 5 Nov 1989 (OT); 18 Nov 1996
Longest FG	Tom Dempsey (New Orleans Saints); Jason Elam (Denver Broncos)	63 yd	8 Nov 1970; 25 Oct 1998
Extra points scored (kicked)	Pat Harder (Chicago Cardinals v. New York Giants); Bob Waterfield (Los Angeles Rams v. Baltimore Colts); Charlie Gogolak (Washington Redskins v. New York Giants)	9	17 Oct 1948; 22 Oct 1950; 27 Nov 1966
Passing yardage	Norm Van Brocklin (Los Angeles Rams v. New York Yanks)	554	28 Sep 1951
Passing completions (non-overtime game)	Richard Todd (New York Jets v. San Francisco 49ers)	42	21 Sep 1980
Receiving yardage (non-overtime game)	Stephone Paige (Kansas City Chiefs v. San Diego Chargers)	309	22 Dec 1985
Rushing yardage	Corey Dillon* (Cincinnati Bengals v. Denver Broncos)	278	22 Oct 2000
Longest run from scrimmage	Tony Dorsett (Dallas Cowboys v. Minnesota Vikings)	99 yd	3 Jan 1983
Interceptions (defense)	*too numerous to list*	4	
Sacks (defense)†	Derrick Thomas (Kansas City Chiefs v. Seattle Seahawks)	7	11 Nov 1990

Team season records

Total points scored	Minnesota Vikings	556	1998
Total TDs scored	Miami Dolphins	70	1984
Passing TDs scored	Miami Dolphins	49	1984
Rushing TDs scored	Green Bay Packers	36	1962
Total FGs scored	Miami Dolphins	39	1999
Passing yardage	St. Louis Rams	5,232	2000
Passing completions (attempts)	San Francisco 49ers	432 (644)	1995
Rushing yardage	New England Patriots	3,165	1978

Game records

Highest total score	Washington Redskins v. New York Giants	113 (72–41)	27 Nov 1966
Widest margin of victory in a shutout	Philadelphia Eagles v. Cincinnati Reds	64–0	6 Nov 1934
Longest game	Miami Dolphins v. Kansas City Chiefs	82:40 (two overtimes)	25 Dec 1971

*Active in 2002; as of 30 Jun 2002 Gary Anderson had not signed with any team.   †Since 1982; before that year sacks were not officially recorded by the NFL.

Super Bowl

NFL-AFL championship 1966–70; NFL championship from 1971–72 season.

	SEASON	WINNER	RUNNER-UP	SCORE
I	1966–67	Green Bay Packers (NFL)	Kansas City Chiefs (AFL)	35–10
II	1967–68	Green Bay Packers (NFL)	Oakland Raiders (AFL)	33–14
III	1968–69	New York Jets (AFL)	Baltimore Colts (NFL)	16–7
IV	1969–70	Kansas City Chiefs (AFL)	Minnesota Vikings (NFL)	23–7
V	1970–71	Baltimore Colts (AFC)	Dallas Cowboys (NFC)	16–13
VI	1971–72	Dallas Cowboys (NFC)	Miami Dolphins (AFC)	24–3
VII	1972–73	Miami Dolphins (AFC)	Washington Redskins (NFC)	14–7
VIII	1973–74	Miami Dolphins (AFC)	Minnesota Vikings (NFC)	24–7
IX	1974–75	Pittsburgh Steelers (AFC)	Minnesota Vikings (NFC)	16–6

Super Bowl (continued)

	SEASON	WINNER	RUNNER-UP	SCORE
X	1975-76	Pittsburgh Steelers (AFC)	Dallas Cowboys (NFC)	21-17
XI	1976-77	Oakland Raiders (AFC)	Minnesota Vikings (NFC)	32-14
XII	1977-78	Dallas Cowboys (NFC)	Denver Broncos (AFC)	27-10
XIII	1978-79	Pittsburgh Steelers (AFC)	Dallas Cowboys (NFC)	35-31
XIV	1979-80	Pittsburgh Steelers (AFC)	Los Angeles Rams (NFC)	31-19
XV	1980-81	Oakland Raiders (AFC)	Philadelphia Eagles (NFC)	27-10
XVI	1981-82	San Francisco 49ers (NFC)	Cincinnati Bengals (AFC)	26-21
XVII	1982-83	Washington Redskins (NFC)	Miami Dolphins (AFC)	27-17
XVIII	1983-84	Los Angeles Raiders (AFC)	Washington Redskins (NFC)	38-9
XIX	1984-85	San Francisco 49ers (NFC)	Miami Dolphins (AFC)	38-16
XX	1985-86	Chicago Bears (NFC)	New England Patriots (AFC)	46-10
XXI	1986-87	New York Giants (NFC)	Denver Broncos (AFC)	39-20
XXII	1987-88	Washington Redskins (NFC)	Denver Broncos (AFC)	42-10
XXIII	1988-89	San Francisco 49ers (NFC)	Cincinnati Bengals (AFC)	20-16
XXIV	1989-90	San Francisco 49ers (NFC)	Denver Broncos (AFC)	55-10
XXV	1990-91	New York Giants (NFC)	Buffalo Bills (AFC)	20-19
XXVI	1991-92	Washington Redskins (NFC)	Buffalo Bills (AFC)	37-24
XXVII	1992-93	Dallas Cowboys (NFC)	Buffalo Bills (AFC)	52-17
XXVIII	1993-94	Dallas Cowboys (NFC)	Buffalo Bills (AFC)	30-13
XXIX	1994-95	San Francisco 49ers (NFC)	San Diego Chargers (AFC)	49-26
XXX	1995-96	Dallas Cowboys (NFC)	Pittsburgh Steelers (AFC)	27-17
XXXI	1996-97	Green Bay Packers (NFC)	New England Patriots (AFC)	35-21
XXXII	1997-98	Denver Broncos (AFC)	Green Bay Packers (NFC)	31-24
XXXIII	1998-99	Denver Broncos (AFC)	Atlanta Falcons (NFC)	34-19
XXXIV	1999-2000	St. Louis Rams (NFC)	Tennessee Titans (AFC)	23-16
XXXV	2000-01	Baltimore Ravens (AFC)	New York Giants (NFC)	34-7
XXXVI	2001-02	New England Patriots (AFC)	St. Louis Rams (NFC)	20-17

College Football National Champion

SEASON	CHAMPION	SEASON	CHAMPION	SEASON	CHAMPION
1924	Notre Dame	1952	Michigan State	1977	Notre Dame
1925	Dartmouth	1953	Maryland	1978	Alabama (AP), Southern California (UPI)
1926	Stanford	1954	Ohio State (AP), UCLA (UP)		
1927	Illinois	1955	Oklahoma	1979	Alabama
1928	Southern California	1956	Oklahoma	1980	Georgia
1929	Notre Dame	1957	Auburn (AP), Ohio State (UP)	1981	Clemson
1930	Notre Dame	1958	Louisiana State	1982	Penn State
1931	Southern California	1959	Syracuse	1983	Miami (FL)
1932	Michigan	1960	Minnesota	1984	Brigham Young
1933	Michigan	1961	Alabama	1985	Oklahoma
1934	Minnesota	1962	Southern California	1986	Penn State
1935	Southern Methodist	1963	Texas	1987	Miami (FL)
1936	Minnesota	1964	Alabama	1988	Notre Dame
1937	Pittsburgh	1965	Alabama (AP), Michigan State (UPI)	1989	Miami (FL)
1938	Texas Christian			1990	Colorado (AP), Georgia Tech (UPI)
1939	Texas A&M	1966	Notre Dame		
1940	Minnesota	1967	Southern California	1991	Miami (FL; AP), Washington (UPI)
1941	Minnesota	1968	Ohio State		
1942	Ohio State	1969	Texas	1992	Alabama
1943	Notre Dame	1970	Nebraska (AP), Texas (UPI)	1993-94	Florida State
1944	Army	1971	Nebraska	1994-95	Nebraska
1945	Army	1972	Southern California	1995-96	Nebraska
1946	Notre Dame	1973	Notre Dame (AP), Alabama (UPI)	1996-97	Florida
1947	Notre Dame			1997-98	Michigan/Nebraska*
1948	Michigan	1974	Oklahoma (AP), Southern California (UPI)	1998-99	Tennessee
1949	Notre Dame			1999-2000	Florida State
1950	Oklahoma	1975	Oklahoma	2000-01	Oklahoma
1951	Tennessee	1976	Pittsburgh	2001-02	Miami (FL)

*Tied.

Rose Bowl

SEASON	WINNER	RUNNER-UP	SCORE	SEASON	WINNER	RUNNER-UP	SCORE
1901–02	Michigan	Stanford	49–0	1959–60	Washington	Wisconsin	44–8
1915–16	Washington State	Brown	14–0	1960–61	Washington	Minnesota	17–7
1916–17	Oregon	Pennsylvania	14–0	1961–62	Minnesota	UCLA	21–3
1917–18	Mare Island	Camp Lewis	19–7	1962–63	Southern California	Wisconsin	42–37
1918–19	Great Lakes	Mare Island	17–0	1963–64	Illinois	Washington	17–7
1919–20	Harvard	Oregon	7–6	1964–65	Michigan	Oregon State	34–7
1920–21	California	Ohio State	28–0	1965–66	UCLA	Michigan State	14–12
1921–22	California	Washington & Jefferson	0–0	1966–67	Purdue	Southern California	14–13
1922–23	Southern California	Penn State	14–3	1967–68	Southern California	Indiana	14–3
1923–24	Washington	Navy	14–14	1968–69	Ohio State	Southern California	27–16
1924–25	Notre Dame	Stanford	27–10	1969–70	Southern California	Michigan	10–3
1925–26	Alabama	Washington	20–19				
1926–27	Alabama	Stanford	7–7	1970–71	Stanford	Ohio State	27–17
1927–28	Stanford	Pittsburgh	7–6	1971–72	Stanford	Michigan	13–12
1928–29	Georgia Tech	California	8–7	1972–73	Southern California	Ohio State	42–17
1929–30	Southern California	Pittsburgh	47–14	1973–74	Ohio State	Southern California	42–21
1930–31	Alabama	Washington State	24–0	1974–75	Southern California	Ohio State	18–17
1931–32	Southern California	Tulane	21–12	1975–76	UCLA	Ohio State	23–10
1932–33	Southern California	Pittsburgh	35–0	1976–77	Southern California	Michigan	14–6
1933–34	Columbia	Stanford	7–0	1977–78	Washington	Michigan	27–20
1934–35	Alabama	Stanford	29–13	1978–79	Southern California	Michigan	17–10
1935–36	Stanford	Southern Methodist	7–0	1979–80	Southern California	Ohio State	17–16
1936–37	Pittsburgh	Washington	21–0	1980–81	Michigan	Washington	23–6
1937–38	California	Alabama	13–0	1981–82	Washington	Iowa	28–0
1938–39	Southern California	Duke	7–3	1982–83	UCLA	Michigan	24–14
1939–40	Southern California	Tennessee	14–0	1983–84	UCLA	Illinois	45–9
1940–41	Stanford	Nebraska	21–13	1984–85	Southern California	Ohio State	20–17
1941–42	Oregon State	Duke	20–16	1985–86	UCLA	Iowa	45–28
1942–43	Georgia	UCLA	9–0	1986–87	Arizona State	Michigan	22–15
1943–44	Southern California	Washington	29–0	1987–88	Michigan State	Southern California	20–17
1944–45	Southern California	Tennessee	25–0	1988–89	Michigan	Southern California	22–14
1945–46	Alabama	Southern California	34–14	1989–90	Southern California	Michigan	17–10
1946–47	Illinois	UCLA	45–14	1990–91	Washington	Iowa	46–34
1947–48	Michigan	Southern California	49–0	1991–92	Washington	Michigan	34–14
1948–49	Northwestern	California	20–14	1992–93	Michigan	Washington	38–31
1949–50	Ohio State	California	17–14	1993–94	Wisconsin	UCLA	21–16
1950–51	Michigan	California	14–6	1994–95	Penn State	Oregon	38–20
1951–52	Illinois	Stanford	40–7	1995–96	Southern California	Northwestern	41–32
1952–53	Southern California	Wisconsin	7–0	1996–97	Ohio State	Arizona State	20–17
1953–54	Michigan State	UCLA	28–20	1997–98	Michigan	Washington State	21–16
1954–55	Ohio State	Southern California	20–7	1998–99	Wisconsin	UCLA	38–31
1955–56	Michigan State	UCLA	17–14	1999–2000	Wisconsin	Stanford	17–9
1956–57	Iowa	Oregon State	35–19	2000–01	Washington	Purdue	34–24
1957–58	Ohio State	Oregon	10–7	2001–02	Miami (FL)	Nebraska	37–14
1958–59	Iowa	California	38–12				

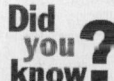

Did you know? In the 1930s radio announcers would often describe a football field as being divided into squares, thus aiding listeners in the visualization of the game. The area just in front of the goal posts was known as "square one." From this usage comes the modern expression "back to square one."

Orange Bowl

SEASON	WINNER	RUNNER-UP	SCORE	SEASON	WINNER	RUNNER-UP	SCORE
1934-35	Bucknell	Miami (FL)	26-0	1967-68	Oklahoma	Tennessee	26-24
1935-36	Catholic	Mississippi	20-19	1968-69	Penn State	Kansas	15-14
1936-37	Duquesne	Mississippi State	13-12	1969-70	Penn State	Missouri	10-3
1937-38	Auburn	Michigan State	6-0	1970-71	Nebraska	Louisiana State	17-12
1938-39	Tennessee	Oklahoma	17-0	1971-72	Nebraska	Alabama	38-6
1939-40	Georgia Tech	Missouri	21-7	1972-73	Nebraska	Notre Dame	40-6
1940-41	Mississippi State	Georgetown	14-7	1973-74	Penn State	Louisiana State	16-9
1941-42	Georgia	Texas Christian	40-26	1974-75	Notre Dame	Alabama	13-11
1942-43	Alabama	Boston College	37-21	1975-76	Oklahoma	Michigan	14-6
1943-44	Louisiana State	Texas A&M	19-14	1976-77	Ohio State	Colorado	27-10
1944-45	Tulsa	Georgia Tech	26-12	1977-78	Arkansas	Oklahoma	31-6
1945-46	Miami (FL)	Holy Cross	13-6	1978-79	Oklahoma	Nebraska	31-24
1946-47	Rice	Tennessee	8-0	1979-80	Oklahoma	Florida State	24-7
1947-48	Georgia Tech	Kansas	20-14	1980-81	Oklahoma	Florida State	18-17
1948-49	Texas	Georgia	41-28	1981-82	Clemson	Nebraska	22-15
1949-50	Santa Clara	Kentucky	21-13	1982-83	Nebraska	Louisiana State	21-20
1950-51	Clemson	Miami (FL)	15-14	1983-84	Miami (FL)	Nebraska	31-30
1951-52	Georgia Tech	Baylor	17-14	1984-85	Washington	Oklahoma	28-17
1952-53	Alabama	Syracuse	61-6	1985-86	Oklahoma	Penn State	25-10
1953-54	Oklahoma	Maryland	7-0	1986-87	Oklahoma	Arkansas	42-8
1954-55	Duke	Nebraska	34-7	1987-88	Miami (FL)	Oklahoma	20-14
1955-56	Oklahoma	Maryland	20-6	1988-89	Miami (FL)	Nebraska	23-3
1956-57	Colorado	Clemson	27-21	1989-90	Notre Dame	Colorado	21-6
1957-58	Oklahoma	Duke	48-21	1990-91	Colorado	Notre Dame	10-9
1958-59	Oklahoma	Syracuse	21-6	1991-92	Miami (FL)	Nebraska	22-0
1959-60	Georgia	Missouri	14-0	1992-93	Florida State	Nebraska	27-14
1960-61	Missouri	Navy	21-14	1993-94	Florida State	Nebraska	18-16
1961-62	Louisiana State	Colorado	25-7	1994-95	Nebraska	Miami	24-17
1962-63	Alabama	Oklahoma	17-0	1995-96	Florida State	Notre Dame	31-26
1963-64	Nebraska	Auburn	13-7	1996-97	Nebraska	Virginia Tech	41-21
1964-65	Texas	Alabama	21-17	1997-98	Nebraska	Tennessee	42-17
1965-66	Alabama	Nebraska	39-28	1998-99	Florida	Syracuse	31-10
1966-67	Florida	Georgia Tech	27-12	1999-2000	Michigan	Alabama	35-34
				2000-01	Oklahoma	Florida State	13-2
				2001-02	Florida	Maryland	56-23

Sugar Bowl

SEASON	WINNER	RUNNER-UP	SCORE	SEASON	WINNER	RUNNER-UP	SCORE
1934-35	Tulane	Temple	20-14	1962-63	Mississippi	Arkansas	17-13
1935-36	Texas Christian	Louisiana State	3-2	1963-64	Alabama	Mississippi	12-7
1936-37	Santa Clara	Louisiana State	21-14	1964-65	Louisiana State	Syracuse	13-10
1937-38	Santa Clara	Louisiana State	6-0	1965-66	Missouri	Florida	20-18
1938-39	Texas Christian	Carnegie Tech	15-7	1966-67	Alabama	Nebraska	34-7
1939-40	Texas A&M	Tulane	14-13	1967-68	Louisiana State	Wyoming	20-13
1940-41	Boston College	Tennessee	19-13	1968-69	Arkansas	Georgia	16-2
1941-42	Fordham	Missouri	2-0	1969-70	Mississippi	Arkansas	27-22
1942-43	Tennessee	Tulsa	14-7	1970-71	Tennessee	Air Force	34-13
1943-44	Georgia Tech	Tulsa	20-18	1971-72	Oklahoma	Auburn	40-22
1944-45	Duke	Alabama	29-26	1972-73	Oklahoma	Penn State	14-0
1945-46	Oklahoma A&M	St. Mary's	33-13	1973-74	Notre Dame	Alabama	24-23
1946-47	Georgia	North Carolina	20-10	1974-75	Nebraska	Florida	13-10
1947-48	Texas	Alabama	27-7	1975-76	Alabama	Penn State	13-6
1948-49	Oklahoma	North Carolina	14-6	1976-77	Pittsburgh	Georgia	27-3
1949-50	Oklahoma	Louisiana State	35-0	1977-78	Alabama	Ohio State	35-6
1950-51	Kentucky	Oklahoma	13-7	1978-79	Alabama	Penn State	14-7
1951-52	Maryland	Tennessee	28-13	1979-80	Alabama	Arkansas	24-9
1952-53	Georgia Tech	Mississippi	24-7	1980-81	Georgia	Notre Dame	17-10
1953-54	Georgia Tech	West Virginia	42-19	1981-82	Pittsburgh	Georgia	24-20
1954-55	Navy	Mississippi	21-0	1982-83	Penn State	Georgia	27-23
1955-56	Georgia Tech	Pittsburgh	7-0	1983-84	Auburn	Michigan	9-7
1956-57	Baylor	Tennessee	13-7	1984-85	Nebraska	Louisiana State	28-10
1957-58	Mississippi	Texas	39-7	1985-86	Tennessee	Miami (FL)	35-7
1958-59	Louisiana State	Clemson	7-0	1986-87	Nebraska	Louisiana State	30-15
1959-60	Mississippi	Louisiana State	21-0	1987-88	Auburn	Syracuse	16-16
1960-61	Mississippi	Rice	14-6	1988-89	Florida State	Auburn	13-7
1961-62	Alabama	Arkansas	10-3	1989-90	Miami (FL)	Alabama	33-25

Sugar Bowl (continued)

SEASON	WINNER	RUNNER-UP	SCORE	SEASON	WINNER	RUNNER-UP	SCORE
1990-91	Tennessee	Virginia	23-22	1996-97	Florida	Florida State	52-20
1991-92	Notre Dame	Florida	39-28	1997-98	Florida State	Ohio State	31-14
1992-93	Alabama	Miami (FL)	34-13	1998-99	Ohio State	Texas A&M	24-14
1993-94	Florida	West Virginia	41-7	1999-2000	Florida State	Virginia Tech	46-29
1994-95	Florida State	Florida	23-17	2000-01	Miami (FL)	Florida	37-20
1995-96	Virginia Tech	Texas	28-10	2001-02	Louisiana State	Illinois	47-34

Fiesta Bowl

SEASON	WINNER	RUNNER-UP	SCORE	SEASON	WINNER	RUNNER-UP	SCORE
1971-72	Arizona State	Florida State	45-38	1986-87	Penn State	Miami (FL)	14-10
1972-73	Arizona State	Missouri	49-35	1987-88	Florida State	Nebraska	31-28
1973-74	Arizona State	Pittsburgh	28-7	1988-89	Notre Dame	West Virginia	34-21
1974-75	Oklahoma State	Brigham Young	16-6	1989-90	Florida State	Nebraska	41-17
1975-76	Arizona State	Nebraska	17-14	1990-91	Louisville	Alabama	34-7
1976-77	Oklahoma	Wyoming	41-7	1991-92	Penn State	Tennessee	42-17
1977-78	Penn State	Arizona State	42-30	1992-93	Syracuse	Colorado	26-22
1978-79	Arkansas	UCLA	10-10	1993-94	Arizona	Miami (FL)	29-0
1979-80	Pittsburgh	Arizona	16-10	1994-95	Colorado	Notre Dame	41-24
1980-81	Penn State	Ohio State	31-19	1995-96	Nebraska	Florida	62-24
1981-82	Penn State	Southern California	26-10	1996-97	Penn State	Texas	38-15
				1997-98	Kansas State	Syracuse	35-18
1982-83	Arizona State	Oklahoma	32-21	1998-99	Tennessee	Florida State	23-16
1983-84	Ohio State	Pittsburgh	28-23	1999-2000	Nebraska	Tennessee	31-21
1984-85	UCLA	Miami (FL)	39-37	2000-01	Oregon State	Notre Dame	41-9
1985-86	Michigan	Nebraska	27-23	2001-02	Oregon	Colorado	38-16

Cotton Bowl

SEASON	WINNER	RUNNER-UP	SCORE	SEASON	WINNER	RUNNER-UP	SCORE
1936-37	Texas Christian	Marquette	16-6	1969-70	Texas	Notre Dame	21-17
1937-38	Rice	Colorado	28-14	1970-71	Notre Dame	Texas	24-11
1938-39	St. Mary's	Texas Tech	20-13	1971-72	Penn State	Texas	30-6
1939-40	Clemson	Boston College	6-3	1972-73	Texas	Alabama	17-13
1940-41	Texas A&M	Fordham	13-12	1973-74	Nebraska	Texas	19-3
1941-42	Alabama	Texas A&M	29-21	1974-75	Penn State	Baylor	41-20
1942-43	Texas	Georgia Tech	14-7	1975-76	Arkansas	Georgia	31-10
1943-44	Texas	Randolph Field	7-7	1976-77	Houston	Maryland	30-21
1944-45	Oklahoma A&M	Texas Christian	34-0	1977-78	Notre Dame	Texas	38-10
1945-46	Texas	Missouri	40-27	1978-79	Notre Dame	Houston	35-34
1946-47	Arkansas	Louisiana State	0-0	1979-80	Houston	Nebraska	17-14
1947-48	Southern Methodist	Penn State	13-13	1980-81	Alabama	Baylor	30-2
				1981-82	Texas	Alabama	14-12
1948-49	Southern Methodist	Oregon	21-13	1982-83	Southern Methodist	Pittsburgh	7-3
1949-50	Rice	North Carolina	27-13	1983-84	Georgia	Texas	10-9
1950-51	Tennessee	Texas	20-14	1984-85	Boston College	Houston	45-28
1951-52	Kentucky	Texas Christian	20-7	1985-86	Texas A&M	Auburn	36-16
1952-53	Texas	Tennessee	16-0	1986-87	Ohio State	Texas A&M	28-12
1953-54	Rice	Alabama	28-6	1987-88	Texas A&M	Notre Dame	35-10
1954-55	Georgia Tech	Arkansas	14-6	1988-89	UCLA	Arkansas	17-3
1955-56	Mississippi	Texas Christian	14-13	1989-90	Tennessee	Arkansas	31-27
1956-57	Texas Christian	Syracuse	28-27	1990-91	Miami (FL)	Texas	46-3
1957-58	Navy	Rice	20-7	1991-92	Florida State	Texas A&M	10-2
1958-59	Air Force	Texas Christian	0-0	1992-93	Notre Dame	Texas A&M	28-3
1959-60	Syracuse	Texas	23-14	1993-94	Notre Dame	Texas A&M	24-21
1960-61	Duke	Arkansas	7-6	1994-95	Southern California	Texas Tech	55-14
1961-62	Texas	Mississippi	12-7				
1962-63	Louisiana State	Texas	13-0	1995-96	Colorado	Oregon	38-6
1963-64	Texas	Navy	28-6	1996-97	Brigham Young	Kansas State	19-15
1964-65	Arkansas	Nebraska	10-7	1997-98	UCLA	Texas A&M	29-23
1965-66	Louisiana State	Arkansas	14-7	1998-99	Texas	Mississippi State	38-11
1966-67	Georgia	Southern Methodist	24-9	1999-2000	Arkansas	Texas	27-6
1967-68	Texas A&M	Alabama	20-16	2000-01	Kansas State	Tennessee	35-21
1968-69	Texas	Tennessee	36-13	2001-02	Oklahoma A&M	Arkansas	10-3

Canadian Football League Grey Cup

YEAR	WINNER	RUNNER-UP	SCORE
1982	Edmonton Eskimos (WFC)	Toronto Argonauts (EFC)	32–16
1983	Toronto Argonauts (EFC)	British Columbia Lions (WFC)	18–17
1984	Winnipeg Blue Bombers (WFC)	Hamilton Tiger-Cats (EFC)	47–17
1985	British Columbia Lions (WFC)	Hamilton Tiger-Cats (EFC)	37–24
1986	Hamilton Tiger-Cats (EFC)	Edmonton Eskimos (WFC)	39–15
1987	Edmonton Eskimos (WFC)	Toronto Argonauts (EFC)	38–36
1988	Winnipeg Blue Bombers (EFC)	British Columbia Lions (WFC)	22–21
1989	Saskatchewan Roughriders (WFC)	Hamilton Tiger-Cats (EFC)	43–40
1990	Winnipeg Blue Bombers (EFC)	Edmonton Eskimos (WFC)	50–11
1991	Toronto Argonauts (EFC)	Calgary Stampeders (WFC)	36–21
1992	Calgary Stampeders (WFC)	Winnipeg Blue Bombers (EFC)	24–10
1993	Edmonton Eskimos (WFC)	Winnipeg Blue Bombers (EFC)	33–23
1994	British Columbia Lions (WFC)	Baltimore Stallions (EFC)	26–23
1995	Baltimore Stallions (SD)	Calgary Stampeders (ND)	37–20
1996	Toronto Argonauts (ED)	Edmonton Eskimos (WD)	43–37
1997	Toronto Argonauts (ED)	Saskatchewan Roughriders (WD)	47–23
1998	Calgary Stampeders (WD)	Hamilton Tiger-Cats (ED)	26–24
1999	Hamilton Tiger-Cats (ED)	Calgary Stampeders (WD)	32–21
2000	British Columbia Lions (WD)	Montreal Alouettes (ED)	28–26
2001	Calgary Stampeders (WD)	Winnipeg Blue Bombers (EFC)	27–19

Did you know? Perhaps the roughest game in NFL history was the contest between the Cleveland Browns and the Chicago Bears on 25 Nov 1951. More penalties were called during this game than in any other in history, with the referees throwing flags an average of every 96 seconds. Cleveland was penalized 209 yards in 21 infractions, whereas Chicago had 16 infractions for total penalties of 165 yards. According to one sportswriter, "The only combatants who quit punching, kicking, and cheating were the ones ejected from the game or carted off on stretchers."

Australian Football League Final Standings, 2001

League ladder after round 22; teams that qualified for play-offs only.

TEAM	WON	LOST	TIED	POINTS	TEAM	WON	LOST	TIED	POINTS
Essendon Bombers	17	5	0	68	Carlton Blues	14	8	0	56
Brisbane Lions	17	5	0	68	Hawthorn Hawks	13	9	0	53
Port Adelaide Power	16	6	0	64	Sydney Swans	12	10	0	48
Richmond Tigers	15	7	0	60	Adelaide Crows	12	10	0	48

Super 12 Rugby Championship

Four points are awarded for a win, two for a draw, one bonus point for a loss by seven points or fewer, and one bonus point for a team that scores four or more tries. Final match held 25 May 2002, Christchurch, New Zealand.

TEAMS (COUNTRY)	POINTS	W	L	D	BONUS	TEAMS (COUNTRY)	POINTS	W	L	D	BONUS
Canterbury Crusaders (NZL)	51	11	0	0	7	Stormers (RSA)	27	5	6	0	7
NSW Waratahs (AUS)	39	8	3	0	7	Waikato Chiefs (NZL)	24	4	7	0	8
ACT Brumbies (AUS)	38	7	4	0	10	Wellington Hurricanes (NZL)	23	5	6	0	3
Otago Highlanders (NZL)	38	8	3	0	6	Sharks (RSA)	20	4	7	0	4
Queensland Reds (AUS)	34	7	4	0	6	Cats (RSA)	6	1	10	0	2
Auckland Blues (NZL)	29	6	5	0	5	Northern Bulls (RSA)	4	0	11	0	4

Six Nations Championship

Five Nations until 2000. Round-robin tournament, usually ending in April.

YEAR	WINNER	YEAR	WINNER	YEAR	WINNER
1947	England, Wales*	1955	France, Wales*	1963	England
1948	Ireland†	1956	Wales	1964	Scotland, Wales*
1949	Ireland‡	1957	England†	1965	Wales‡
1950	Wales†	1958	England	1966	Wales
1951	Ireland	1959	France	1967	France
1952	Wales†	1960	England‡, France*	1968	France§
1953	England	1961	France	1969	Wales‡
1954	England‡, France, Wales*	1962	France	1970	France, Wales*

Six Nations Championship (continued)

YEAR	WINNER	YEAR	WINNER	YEAR	WINNER
1971	Wales†	1982	Ireland‡	1993	France
1972	not completed	1983	France, Ireland*	1994	Wales
1973	quintuple tie	1984	Scotland†	1995	England§
1974	Ireland	1985	Ireland†	1996	England
1975	Wales	1986	France, Scotland*	1997	France§
1976	Wales†	1987	France§	1998	France§
1977	France§ ‖	1988	Wales†	1999	Scotland
1978	Wales†	1989	France	2000	England
1979	Wales‡	1990	Scotland§	2001	England
1980	England†	1991	England§	2002	France§
1981	France§	1992	England§		

*Tied. †Triple Crown (all three matches, excluding France) and Grand Slam (all four matches) winner.
‡Triple Crown winner. §Grand Slam winner. ‖Triple Crown won by Wales.

Rugby Union World Cup

YEAR	WINNER	RUNNER-UP	SCORE	YEAR	WINNER	RUNNER-UP	SCORE
1987	New Zealand	France	29–9	1999	Australia	France	35–12
1991	Australia	England	12–6	2003	scheduled to be held in November 2003 in		
1995	South Africa	New Zealand	15–12		Australia		

Rugby League World Cup

YEAR	WINNER	RUNNER-UP	SCORE	YEAR	WINNER	RUNNER-UP	SCORE
1954	Great Britain	France	16–12	1977†	Australia	Great Britain	13–12
1957	Australia	Great Britain	29–21	1988	Australia	New Zealand	25–12
1960	Great Britain	Australia	66–37	1992	Australia	Great Britain	10–6
1968	Australia	France	20–2	1995	Australia	England	16–8
1970	Australia	Great Britain	12–7	2000	Australia	New Zealand	40–12
1972	Great Britain	Australia	10–10*	2005	scheduled to be held in England		
1975†	Australia‡						

*Great Britain won on match points. †Called International Championship from 1975 to 1977. ‡Championships played without a grand final match; England was the runner up.

FIFA World Cup—Men

YEAR	WINNER	RUNNER-UP	SCORE	YEAR	WINNER	RUNNER-UP	SCORE
1930	Uruguay	Argentina	4–2	1974	West Germany	The Netherlands	2–1
1934	Italy	Czechoslovakia	2–1	1978	Argentina	The Netherlands	3–1
1938	Italy	Hungary	4–2	1982	Italy	West Germany	3–1
1950	Uruguay	Brazil	2–1	1986	Argentina	West Germany	3–2
1954	West Germany	Hungary	3–2	1990	West Germany	Argentina	1–0
1958	Brazil	Sweden	5–2	1994	Brazil	Italy	0–0 (3–2*)
1962	Brazil	Czechoslovakia	3–1	1998	France	Brazil	3–0
1966	England	West Germany	4–2	2002	Brazil	Germany	2–0
1970	Brazil	Italy	4–1				

*Penalty kick shoot-out.

FIFA World Cup—Women

YEAR	WINNER	RUNNER-UP	SCORE	YEAR	WINNER	RUNNER-UP	SCORE
1991	United States	Norway	2–1	2003	scheduled to be held 24 Sep–11 Oct 2003		
1995	Norway	Germany	2–0		in China		
1999	United States*	China	0–0				

*Won on penalty kicks.

Association Football (Soccer) National Champions, 2002

Selected countries

COUNTRY	LEAGUE CHAMPION	CUP WINNER	COUNTRY	LEAGUE CHAMPION	CUP WINNER
Albania	Dinamo Tiranë	Sportklub Tiranë	Japan	Kashima Antlers	Shimizu S-Pulse
Andorra	Encamp Dicoansa		Luxembourg	F91 Dudelange	Avenir Peggen
Argentina	Racing (Opening)	River Plate (Closing)	Mexico	Pachuca	
Australia	Perth Glory		Morocco	Hassania	
Austria	Innsbruck	Graz AK	Netherlands	Ajax	Ajax
Azerbaijan		Neftchi Baku	Nigeria	Enyimba	Dolphin
Belgium	Genk	FC Brugge	Northern Ireland	Portadown	Linfield
Bolivia	Oriente		Norway	Rosenborg	Viking
Bosnia and Herzegovina	NK Zeljeznicar Sarajevo	FK Sarajevo	Paraguay	Cerro Porteno	
Brazil	Atletico Paranaense	Corinthians	Peru	Alianza	
Bulgaria	Levski	Levski	Poland	Legia	Wisla
Cameroon	Cotonsport	Fovu	Portugal	Sporting	Sporting
Chile	Santiago Wanderers		Romania	Dinamo	Rapid
China	Dalian Shide	Dalian Shide	Russia	Spartak Moscow	CSKA Moscow
Colombia	America Cali		Saudi Arabia	Al-Hilal	Al-Ahli
Costa Rica	Alajuelense		Scotland	Celtic	Rangers
Croatia	Zagreb	Dynamo Zagreb	Senegal	Jeanne d'Arc	AS Douanes
			Slovakia	Zilina	Koba
Cyprus	Nicosia	Anorthosis Famagusta	Slovenia	Maribor	Gorica
			South Africa	Santos	
Czech Republic	Slovan Liberec	Slavia Prague	South Korea	Songnam	Taejon Citizens
Denmark	Brondby	Odense	Spain	Valencia	La Coruna
Ecuador	Emelec		Sweden	Hammarby	
England	Arsenal	Arsenal	Switzerland	Basle	Basle
Faroe Islands		NSÍ Runavík	Tunisia	Esperance	Hammam-Lif
Finland	Tampere U	Atlantis			
France	Lyon	Lorient	Turkey	Galatasaray	Kocaeli
Georgia	Torpedo Kutaisi	Lokomotiv Tbilisi	Ukraine	Shakhtjor Donetsk	Shakhtjor Donetsk
Germany	Borussia Dortmund	Schalke	United States (MLS)	San Jose Earthquake	
Greece	Olympiakos	AEK Athens	Uruguay	Nacional	
Hungary	Zalaegerszeg	Ujpest	Venezuela	Nacional	
Ireland	Shelbourne	Dundalk	Wales	Barry Town	Barry Town
Israel	Maccabi Haifa	Maccabi Tel Aviv	Yugoslavia	Partizan Belgrade	Red Star Belgrade
Italy	Juventus	Parma			

UEFA Champions League

Known until 1992–93 as the European Champion Clubs' Cup; played on a knockout basis until 1992–93 and a combination of group, knockout, and quarter-finals, semifinals, and finals since then.

SEASON	WINNING TEAM (COUNTRY)	RUNNER-UP (COUNTRY)	SCORE
1955–56	Real Madrid CF (ESP)	Stade de Reims (FRA)	4–3
1956–57	Real Madrid CF (ESP)	AC Fiorentina (ITA)	2–0
1957–58	Real Madrid CF (ESP)	AC Milano (ITA)	3–2
1958–59	Real Madrid CF (ESP)	Stade de Reims (FRA)	2–0
1959–60	Real Madrid CF (ESP)	Eintracht Frankfurt (FRG)	7–3
1960–61	SL Benfica (POR)	FC Barcelona (ESP)	3–2
1961–62	SL Benfica (POR)	Real Madrid CF (ESP)	5–3
1962–63	AC Milano (ITA)	SL Benfica (POR)	2–1
1963–64	Internazionale FC (ITA)	Real Madrid CF (ESP)	3–1
1964–65	Internazionale FC (ITA)	SL Benfica (POR)	1–0
1965–66	Real Madrid CF (ESP)	FK Partizan (YUG)	2–1
1966–67	Celtic FC (SCO)	Internazionale FC (ITA)	2–1
1967–68	Manchester United (ENG)	SL Benfica (POR)	4–1
1968–69	AC Milano (ITA)	AFC Ajax (NED)	4–1
1969–70	Feyenoord (NED)	Celtic FC (SCO)	2–1
1970–71	AFC Ajax (NED)	Panathinaikos FC (GRE)	2–0
1971–72	AFC Ajax (NED)	Internazionale FC (ITA)	2–0
1972–73	AFC Ajax (NED)	Juventus FC (ITA)	1–0
1973–74	Bayern München (FRG)	Club Atlético de Madrid (ESP)	1–1, 4–0†
1974–75	Bayern München (FRG)	Leeds United AFC (ENG)	2–0

UEFA Champions League (continued)

SEASON	WINNING TEAM (COUNTRY)	RUNNER-UP (COUNTRY)	SCORE
1975–76	Bayern München (FRG)	AS Saint-Etienne (FRA)	1–0
1976–77	Liverpool FC (ENG)	VfL Borussia Mönchengladbach (FRG)	3–1
1977–78	Liverpool FC (ENG)	Club Brugge KV (BEL)	1–0
1978–79	Nottingham Forest FC (ENG)	Malmö FF (SWE)	1–0
1979–80	Nottingham Forest FC (ENG)	Hamburger SV (FRG)	1–0
1980–81	Liverpool FC (ENG)	Real Madrid CF (ESP)	1–0
1981–82	Aston Villa FC (ENG)	Bayern München (FRG)	1–0
1982–83	Hamburger SV (FRG)	Juventus FC (ITA)	1–0
1983–84	Liverpool FC (ENG)	AS Roma (ITA)	1–1*
1984–85	Juventus FC (ITA)	Liverpool FC (ENG)	1–0
1985–86	FC Steaua Bucuresti (ROM)	FC Barcelona (ESP)	0–0*
1986–87	FC Porto (POR)	Bayern München (FRG)	2–1
1987–88	PSV Eindhoven (NED)	SL Benfica (POR)	0–0*
1988–89	AC Milan (ITA)	FC Steaua Bucuresti (ROM)	4–0
1989–90	AC Milan (ITA)	SL Benfica (POR)	1–0
1990–91	FK Crvena Zvezda Beograd (YUG)	Olympique de Marseille (FRA)	0–0*
1991–92	FC Barcelona (ESP)	Sampdoria UC (ITA)	1–0
1992–93	Olympique de Marseille (FRA)	AC Milan (ITA)	1–0
1993–94	AC Milan (ITA)	FC Barcelona (ESP)	4–0
1994–95	AFC Ajax (NED)	AC Milan (ITA)	1–0
1995–96	Juventus FC (ITA)	AFC Ajax (NED)	1–1*
1996–97	BV Borussia Dortmund (GER)	Juventus FC (ITA)	3–1
1997–98	Real Madrid CF (ESP)	Juventus FC (ITA)	1–0
1998–99	Manchester United (ENG)	Bayern München (GER)	2–1
1999–2000	Real Madrid CF (ESP)	Valencia CF (ESP)	3–0
2000–01	Bayern München (GER)	Valencia CF (ESP)	1–1*
2001–02	Real Madrid CF (ESP)	Bayer 04 Leverkusen (GER)	2–1

*Won on penalty kicks.   †Match replayed.

UEFA Cup

The UEFA Cup is considered Europe's second most important football competition. Established in the 1971–72 season, the Cup was restructured after the UEFA Cup Winners' Cup was abolished in 1998–99. Originally played on a knockout basis, since 1998 the competition has concluded with a single match. The Cup competition is open to top- and second-ranked teams in each country's league as well as winners of domestic cups.

SEASON	WINNING TEAM (COUNTRY)	RUNNER-UP (COUNTRY)	SCORE
1971–72	Tottenham Hotspur FC (ENG)	Wolverhampton Wanderers FC (ENG)	2–1; 1–1
1972–73	Liverpool FC (ENG)	VfL Borussia Mönchengladbach (FRG)	3–0; 0–2
1973–74	Feyenoord (NED)	Tottenham Hotspur FC (ENG)	2–2; 2–0
1974–75	VfL Borussia Mönchengladbach (FRG)	FC Twente (NED)	0–0; 5–1
1975–76	Liverpool FC (ENG)	Club Brugge KV (BEL)	3–2; 1–1
1976–77	Juventus FC (ITA)	Athletic Club Bilbao (ESP)	1–0; 1–2
1977–78	PSV Eindhoven (NED)	SC Bastia (FRA)	0–0; 3–0
1978–79	VfL Borussia Mönchengladbach (FRG)	FK Crvena Zvezda Beograd (YUG)	1–1; 1–0
1979–80	Eintracht Frankfurt (FRG)	VfL Borussia Mönchengladbach (FRG)	2–3; 1–0
1980–81	Ipswich Town FC (ENG)	AZ Alkmaar (NED)	3–0; 2–4
1981–82	IFK Göteborg (SWE)	Hamburger SV (FRG)	1–0; 3–0
1982–83	RSC Anderlecht (BEL)	SL Benfica (POR)	1–0; 1–1
1983–84	Tottenham Hotspur FC (ENG)*	RSC Anderlecht (BEL)	1–1; 1–1
1984–85	Real Madrid CF (ESP)	Videoton FCF (HUN)	3–0; 0–1
1985–86	Real Madrid CF (ESP)	1. FC Köln (FRG)	5–1; 0–2
1986–87	IFK Göteborg (SWE)	Dundee United FC (SCO)	1–0; 1–1
1987–88	Bayer 04 Leverkusen (FRG)*	RCD Espanyol (ESP)	0–3; 3–0
1988–89	SSC Napoli (ITA)	VfB Stuttgart (FRG)	2–1; 3–3
1989–90	Juventus FC (ITA)	AC Fiorentina (ITA)	3–1; 0–0
1990–91	Internazionale FC (ITA)	AS Roma (ITA)	2–0; 0–1
1991–92	AFC Ajax (NED)	Torino Calcio (ITA)	2–2; 0–0
1992–93	Juventus FC (ITA)	BV Borussia Dortmund (FRG)	3–1; 3–0
1993–94	Internazionale FC (ITA)	SV Austria Salzburg (AUT)	1–0; 1–0
1994–95	Parma AC (ITA)	Juventus FC (ITA)	1–0; 1–1
1995–96	FC Bayern München (GER)	FC Girondins de Bordeaux (FRA)	2–0; 3–1
1996–97	FC Schalke 04 (GER)*	Internazionale FC (ITA)	1–0; 0–1
1997–98	Internazionale FC (ITA)	S.S. Lazio (ITA)	3–0
1998–99	Parma AC (ITA)	Olympique de Marseille (FRA)	3–0

UEFA Cup (continued)

SEASON	WINNING TEAM (COUNTRY)	RUNNER-UP (COUNTRY)	SCORE
1999–2000	Galatasaray SK (TUR)*	Arsenal FC (ENG)	0–0
2000–01	Liverpool FC (ENG)	Deportivo Alavés (ESP)	5–4
2001–02	Feyenoord (NED)	BV Borussia Dortmund (GER)	3–2

Won on penalty kicks.

Libertadores de América Cup

Contested since 1960. Table shows results for the past 20 years.

YEAR	WINNER (COUNTRY)	RUNNER-UP (COUNTRY)	SCORES
1983	Grêmio (BRA)	Peñarol (URU)	1–1, 2–1
1984	Independiente (ARG)	Grêmio (BRA)	1–0, 0–0
1985	Argentinos Juniors (ARG)	América de Cali (COL)	1–0, 0–1, 1–1*
1986	River Plate (ARG)	América de Cali (COL)	2–1, 1–0
1987	Peñarol (URU)	América de Cali (COL)	0–2, 2–1, 1–0*
1988	Nacional (URU)	Newell's Old Boys (ARG)	0–1, 3–0
1989	Atlético Nacional (COL)	Olimpia (PAR)	0–2, 2–0, 5–4*
1990	Olímpia (PAR)	Barcelona (ECU)	2–0, 1–1
1991	Colo Colo (CHI)	Olimpia (PAR)	0–0, 3–0
1992	São Paulo (BRA)	Newell's Old Boys (ARG)	0–1, 1–0, 3–2*
1993	São Paulo (BRA)	Universidad Católica (CHI)	5–1, 0–2
1994	Vélez Sarsfield (ARG)	São Paulo (BRA)	1–0, 0–1, 5–4*
1995	Grêmio (BRA)	Atlético Nacional (COL)	3–1, 1–1
1996	River Plate (ARG)	América de Cali (COL)	0–1, 2–0
1997	Cruzeiro (BRA)	Sporting Cristal (PER)	0–0, 1–0
1998	Vasco da Gama (BRA)	Barcelona (ECU)	2–0, 2–1
1999	Palmeiras (BRA)	Deportiva Cali (COL)	0–1, 2–1, 4–3*
2000	Boca Juniors (ARG)	Palmeiras (BRA)	2–2, 0–4, 4–2*
2001	Boca Juniors (ARG)	Cruz Azul (MEX)	1–0, 0–1, 3–1*
2002	Olimpia (PAR)	São Caetano (BRA)	0–1, 2–1, 4–2*

Winner determined in penalty shoot-out after tiebreaking game.

Copa América

Held since 1916. Table shows results for past 20 years. The cup was contested by a best-of-series in 1983, by rounds in 1989 and 1991 (scores are shown here as winner's wins/losses/draws in final round), and by a final championship match in 1987 and from 1993.

YEAR	WINNER	RUNNER-UP	SCORE	YEAR	WINNER	RUNNER-UP	SCORE
1983	Uruguay	Brazil	1/0/1	1995	Uruguay*	Brazil	1–1
1987	Uruguay	Chile	1–0	1997	Brazil	Bolivia	3–1
1989	Brazil	Uruguay	3/0/0	1999	Brazil	Uruguay	3–0
1991	Argentina	Brazil	4/0/0	2001	Colombia	Mexico	1–0
1993	Argentina	Mexico	2–1	2003	scheduled to be held in July in Peru		

Uruguay won penalty shoot-out 5–3.

Asian Cup

Scored on a points (percentage of wins) system until 1972.

YEAR	WINNER	RUNNER-UP	SCORE	YEAR	WINNER	RUNNER-UP	SCORE
1956	South Korea	Israel	83.3	1984	Saudi Arabia	China	2–0
1960	South Korea	Israel	100	1988	Saudi Arabia	South Korea	0–0 (4–3*)
1964	Israel	India	100	1992	Japan	Saudi Arabia	1–0
1968	Iran	Burma	100	1996	Saudi Arabia	United Arab Emirates	0–0 (4–2*)
1972	Iran	South Korea	2–1	2000	Japan	Saudi Arabia	1–0
1976	Iran	Kuwait	1–0	2004	scheduled to be held in China		
1980	Kuwait	South Korea	3–0				

Penalty kick shoot-out.

African Cup of Nations

YEAR	WINNER	RUNNER-UP	SCORE	YEAR	WINNER	RUNNER-UP	SCORE
1957	Egypt	Ethiopia	4-0	1982	Ghana	Libya	1-1 (7-6‡)
1959	Egypt	The Sudan	2-1	1984	Cameroon	Nigeria	3-1
1962	Ethiopia	Egypt	4-2	1986	Egypt	Cameroon	0-0 (5-4‡)
1963	Ghana	The Sudan	3-0	1988	Cameroon	Nigeria	1-0
1965	Ghana	Tunisia	3-2	1990	Algeria	Nigeria	1-0
1968	Congo (Kinshasa)	Ghana	1-0	1992	Côte d'Ivoire	Ghana	0-0 (11-10‡)
1970	The Sudan	Ghana	1-0	1994	Nigeria	Zambia	2-1
1972	Congo (Brazzaville)	Mali	3-2	1996	South Africa	Tunisia	2-0
1974	Zaire	Zambia	2-2, 2-0*	1998	Egypt	South Africa	2-0
1976	Morocco	Guinea	1-1†	2000	Cameroon	Nigeria	2-2 (4-3‡)
1978	Ghana	Uganda	2-0	2002	Cameroon	Senegal	0-0 (3-2‡)
1980	Nigeria	Algeria	3-0	2004	final game scheduled to be played in Tunisia		

*Game replayed.   †Group format.   ‡Penalty kick shoot-out.

Major League Soccer Cup

YEAR	WINNER	RUNNER-UP	SCORE	YEAR	WINNER	RUNNER-UP	SCORE
1996	DC United	Los Angeles Galaxy	3-2*	2000	Kansas City Wizards	Chicago Fire	1-0
1997	DC United	Colorado Rapids	2-1	2001	San Jose Earthquakes	Los Angeles Galaxy	2-1*
1998	Chicago Fire	DC United	2-0	2002	final match scheduled to be held		
1999	DC United	Los Angeles Galaxy	2-0		20 October, Foxboro MA		

*In overtime.

Golf

Individual events. Two of the major men's golf championships, the British and US Open tournaments, are played annually at a variety of golf courses in their respective countries. Each is played over 72 holes, and each is preceded by qualifying rounds. The **Professional Golfers' Association championship** and the invitational **Masters Tournament** (which is held annually at the Augusta [GA] National Golf Course) are also top tournaments. Events for amateurs include the **US and British Amateur championships.**

Women's golf has been around nearly as long as men's golf, but until the late 1940s, it was limited to amateurs. Thus, for women, the **British and US Amateur championships** were the major tournaments. The **US Women's Open Championship** was started in 1946, and the **Ladies' Professional Golf Association** (LPGA) was formed in 1950. Since that time, women's professional golf has flourished. In 1976 the **Women's British Open Championship** was added to the golf calendar.

Team events. The **Ryder Cup** was originally a biennial match between the United States and Great Britain, but, beginning in 1979, it was expanded into a biennial match between the United States and Europe. The **World Cup**, formerly known as the Canada Cup, is a men's tournament for two-man professional teams. Teams of British and US women golfers compete every two years for the **Curtis Cup**, which since 1964 has involved two days' play of three 18-hole foursomes and six 18-hole singles. The **Solheim Cup**, the women's professional team tournament, has been played in even-numbered years since 1990, but has been moved to odd-numbered years (beginning in 2003) following the rescheduling of the Ryder Cup because of the events of 11 September.

Related Web sites: United States Golf Association: <www.usga.org>; Professional Golf Association: <www.pgatour.com>; Ladies Professional Golf Association:<www.lpga.com>

Masters Tournament

Won by an American golfer except as indicated.

YEAR	WINNER	YEAR	WINNER	YEAR	WINNER
1934	Horton Smith	1948	Claude Harmon	1960	Arnold Palmer
1935	Gene Sarazen	1949	Sam Snead	1961	Gary Player (RSA)
1936	Horton Smith	1950	Jimmy Demaret	1962	Arnold Palmer
1937	Byron Nelson	1951	Ben Hogan	1963	Jack Nicklaus
1938	Henry Picard	1952	Sam Snead	1964	Arnold Palmer
1939	Ralph Guldahl	1953	Ben Hogan	1965	Jack Nicklaus
1940	Jimmy Demaret	1954	Sam Snead	1966	Jack Nicklaus
1941	Craig Wood	1955	Cary Middlecoff	1967	Gay Brewer
1942	Byron Nelson	1956	Jack Burke	1968	Bob Goalby*
1943-45	not held	1957	Doug Ford	1969	George Archer
1946	Herman Keiser	1958	Arnold Palmer	1970	Billy Casper
1947	Jimmy Demaret	1959	Art Wall	1971	Charles Coody

Masters Tournament (continued)

YEAR	WINNER	YEAR	WINNER	YEAR	WINNER
1972	Jack Nicklaus	1984	Ben Crenshaw	1996	Nick Faldo (GBR)
1973	Tommy Aaron	1985	Bernhard Langer (FRG)	1997	Tiger Woods
1974	Gary Player (RSA)	1986	Jack Nicklaus	1998	Mark O'Meara
1975	Jack Nicklaus	1987	Larry Mize	1999	José María Olazábal (ESP)
1976	Raymond Floyd	1988	Sandy Lyle (SCO)	2000	Vijay Singh (FIJ)
1977	Tom Watson	1989	Nick Faldo (GBR)	2001	Tiger Woods
1978	Gary Player (RSA)	1990	Nick Faldo (GBR)	2002	Tiger Woods
1979	Fuzzy Zoeller†	1991	Ian Woosnam (GBR)	2003	scheduled to be held
1980	Seve Ballesteros (ESP)	1992	Fred Couples		7–13 Apr 2003,
1981	Tom Watson	1993	Bernhard Langer (GER)		Augusta GA
1982	Craig Stadler‡	1994	José María Olazábal (ESP)		
1983	Seve Ballesteros (ESP)	1995	Ben Crenshaw		

*Play-off averted when R. de Vicenzo was penalized for signing an incorrect scorecard.　†Sudden death play-off against T. Watson and E. Sneed.　‡Won on the first hole of a play-off against D. Pohl.

United States Open Championship—Men
Won by an American golfer except as indicated.

YEAR	WINNER	YEAR	WINNER	YEAR	WINNER
1895	Horace Rawlins	1932	Gene Sarazen	1971	Lee Trevino
1896	James Foulis	1933	John Goodman	1972	Jack Nicklaus
1897	Joe Lloyd	1934	Olin Dutra	1973	Johnny Miller
1898	Fred Herd	1935	Sam Parks, Jr.	1974	Hale Irwin
1899	Willie Smith	1936	Tony Manero	1975	Lou Graham
1900	Harry Vardon (GBR)	1937	Ralph Guldahl	1976	Jerry Pate
1901	Willie Anderson	1938	Ralph Guldahl	1977	Hubert Green
1902	Laurence Auchterlonie	1939	Byron Nelson	1978	Andy North
1903	Willie Anderson	1940	Lawson Little	1979	Hale Irwin
1904	Willie Anderson	1941	Craig Wood	1980	Jack Nicklaus
1905	Willie Anderson	1942–45 not held		1981	David Graham (AUS)
1906	Alex Smith	1946	Lloyd Mangrum	1982	Tom Watson
1907	Alex Ross	1947	Lew Worsham	1983	Larry Nelson
1908	Fred McLeod	1948	Ben Hogan	1984	Fuzzy Zoeller
1909	George Sargent	1949	Cary Middlecoff	1985	Andy North
1910	Alex Smith	1950	Ben Hogan	1986	Raymond Floyd
1911	John J. McDermott	1951	Ben Hogan	1987	Scott Simpson
1912	John J. McDermott	1952	Julius Boros	1988	Curtis Strange
1913	Francis Ouimet	1953	Ben Hogan	1989	Curtis Strange
1914	Walter Hagen	1954	Ed Furgol	1990	Hale Irwin
1915	Jerome D. Travers	1955	Jack Fleck	1991	Payne Stewart
1916	Chick Evans	1956	Cary Middlecoff	1992	Tom Kite
1917–18 not held		1957	Dick Mayer	1993	Lee Janzen
1919	Walter Hagen	1958	Tommy Bolt	1994	Ernie Els (RSA)
1920	Edward Ray (GBR)	1959	Billy Casper	1995	Corey Pavin
1921	James M. Barnes	1960	Arnold Palmer	1996	Steve Jones
1922	Gene Sarazen	1961	Gene Littler	1997	Ernie Els (RSA)
1923	Bobby Jones	1962	Jack Nicklaus	1998	Lee Janzen
1924	Cyril Walker	1963	Julius Boros	1999	Payne Stewart
1925	Willie MacFarlane, Jr.	1964	Ken Venturi	2000	Tiger Woods
1926	Bobby Jones	1965	Gary Player (RSA)	2001	Retief Goosen (RSA)
1927	Tommy Armour	1966	Billy Casper	2002	Tiger Woods
1928	Johnny Farrell	1967	Jack Nicklaus	2003	scheduled to be held
1929	Bobby Jones	1968	Lee Trevino		12–15 Jun 2003,
1930	Bobby Jones	1969	Orville Moody		Olympia Fields IL
1931	Billy Burke	1970	Tony Jacklin (GBR)		

British Open Tournament—Men
Won by a British golfer unless otherwise indicated.

YEAR	WINNER	YEAR	WINNER	YEAR	WINNER
1860	Willie Park, Sr.	1865	Andrew Strath	1870	Tom Morris, Jr.
1861	Tom Morris, Sr.	1866	Willie Park, Sr.	1871	not held
1862	Tom Morris, Sr.	1867	Tom Morris, Sr.	1872	Tom Morris, Jr.
1863	Willie Park, Sr.	1868	Tom Morris, Jr.	1873	Tom Kidd
1864	Tom Morris, Sr.	1869	Tom Morris, Jr.	1874	Mungo Park

British Open Tournament——Men (continued)

YEAR	WINNER	YEAR	WINNER	YEAR	WINNER
1875	Willie Park, Jr.	1920	George Duncan	1966	Jack Nicklaus (USA)
1876	Bob Martin	1921	Jock Hutchison (USA)	1967	Roberto de Vicenzo (ARG)
1877	Jamie Anderson	1922	Walter Hagen (USA)	1968	Gary Player (RSA)
1878	Jamie Anderson	1923	Arthur Havers	1969	Tony Jacklin
1879	Jamie Anderson	1924	Walter Hagen (USA)	1970	Jack Nicklaus (USA)
1880	Robert Ferguson	1925	James Barnes (USA)	1971	Lee Trevino (USA)
1881	Robert Ferguson	1926	Bobby Jones (USA)	1972	Lee Trevino (USA)
1882	Robert Ferguson	1927	Bobby Jones (USA)	1973	Tom Weiskopf (USA)
1883	Willie Fernie	1928	Walter Hagen (USA)	1974	Gary Player (RSA)
1884	Jack Simpson	1929	Walter Hagen (USA)	1975	Tom Watson (USA)
1885	Bob Martin	1930	Bobby Jones (USA)	1976	Johnny Miller (USA)
1886	David Brown	1931	Tommy Armour (USA)	1977	Tom Watson (USA)
1887	Willie Park, Jr.	1932	Gene Sarazen (USA)	1978	Jack Nicklaus (USA)
1888	Jack Burns	1933	Denny Shute (USA)	1979	Seve Ballesteros (ESP)
1889	Willie Park, Jr.	1934	Henry Cotton	1980	Tom Watson (USA)
1890	John Ball	1935	Alfred Perry	1981	Bill Rogers (USA)
1891	Hugh Kirkaldy	1936	Alfred Padgham	1982	Tom Watson (USA)
1892	Harold Hilton	1937	Henry Cotton	1983	Tom Watson (USA)
1893	William Auchterlonie	1938	Reg A. Whitcombe	1984	Seve Ballesteros (ESP)
1894	John H. Taylor	1939	Richard Burton	1985	Sandy Lyle (SCO)
1895	John H. Taylor	1940–45 not held		1986	Greg Norman (AUS)
1896	Harry Vardon	1946	Sam Snead (USA)	1987	Nick Faldo
1897	Harold Hilton	1947	Fred Daly (IRE)	1988	Seve Ballesteros (ESP)
1898	Harry Vardon	1948	Henry Cotton	1989	Mark Calcavecchia (USA)
1899	Harry Vardon	1949	Bobby Locke (RSA)	1990	Nick Faldo
1900	John H. Taylor	1950	Bobby Locke (RSA)	1991	Ian Baker-Finch (AUS)
1901	James Braid	1951	Max Faulkner	1992	Nick Faldo
1902	Sandy Herd	1952	Bobby Locke (RSA)	1993	Greg Norman (AUS)
1903	Harry Vardon	1953	Ben Hogan (USA)	1994	Nick Price (ZIM)
1904	Jack White	1954	Peter Thomson (AUS)	1995	John Daly (USA)
1905	James Braid	1955	Peter Thomson (AUS)	1996	Tom Lehman (USA)
1906	James Braid	1956	Peter Thomson (AUS)	1997	Justin Leonard (USA)
1907	Arnaud Massy (FRA)	1957	Bobby Locke (RSA)	1998	Mark O'Meara (USA)
1908	James Braid	1958	Peter Thomson (AUS)	1999	Paul Lawrie (SCO)
1909	John H. Taylor	1959	Gary Player (RSA)	2000	Tiger Woods (USA)
1910	James Braid	1960	Kel Nagle (AUS)	2001	David Duval (USA)
1911	Harry Vardon	1961	Arnold Palmer (USA)	2002	Ernie Els (RSA)
1912	Ted Ray	1962	Arnold Palmer (USA)	2003	scheduled to be held
1913	John H. Taylor	1963	Bob Charles (NZL)		17–20 Jul 2003, Royal
1914	Harry Vardon	1964	Tony Lema (USA)		St George's, Kent
1915–19 not held		1965	Peter Thomson (AUS)		

US Professional Golfers' Association (PGA) Championship

Won by an American golfer except as indicated.

YEAR	WINNER	YEAR	WINNER	YEAR	WINNER
1916	James M. Barnes	1938	Paul Runyan	1959	Bob Rosburg
1917–18 not held		1939	Henry Picard	1960	Jay Hebert
1919	James M. Barnes	1940	Byron Nelson	1961	Jerry Barber*
1920	Jock Hutchison	1941	Vic Ghezzi	1962	Gary Player (RSA)
1921	Walter Hagen	1942	Sam Snead	1963	Jack Nicklaus
1922	Gene Sarazen	1943	not held	1964	Bobby Nichols
1923	Gene Sarazen	1944	Bob Hamilton	1965	Dave Marr
1924	Walter Hagen	1945	Byron Nelson	1966	Al Geiberger
1925	Walter Hagen	1946	Ben Hogan	1967	Don January*
1926	Walter Hagen	1947	Jim Ferrier	1968	Julius Boros
1927	Walter Hagen	1948	Ben Hogan	1969	Raymond Floyd
1928	Leo Diegel	1949	Sam Snead	1970	Dave Stockton
1929	Leo Diegel	1950	Chandler Harper	1971	Jack Nicklaus
1930	Tommy Armour	1951	Sam Snead	1972	Gary Player (RSA)
1931	Tom Creavy	1952	Jim Turnesa	1973	Jack Nicklaus
1932	Olin Dutra	1953	Walter Burkemo	1974	Lee Trevino
1933	Gene Sarazen	1954	Chick Harbert	1975	Jack Nicklaus
1934	Paul Runyan	1955	Doug Ford	1976	Dave Stockton
1935	Johnny Revolta	1956	Jack Burke	1977	Lanny Wadkins
1936	Denny Shute	1957	Lionel Hebert	1978	John Mahaffey*
1937	Denny Shute	1958	Dow Finsterwald	1979	David Graham (AUS)*

US Professional Golfers' Association (PGA) Championship (continued)

YEAR	WINNER	YEAR	WINNER	YEAR	WINNER
1980	Jack Nicklaus	1990	Wayne Grady (AUS)	2000	Tiger Woods
1981	Larry Nelson	1991	John Daly	2001	David Toms
1982	Raymond Floyd	1992	Nick Price (ZIM)	2002	*scheduled to be held*
1983	Hal Sutton	1993	Paul Azinger		*15–18 Aug 2002,*
1984	Lee Trevino	1994	Nick Price (ZIM)		*Hazeltine National Golf*
1985	Hubert Green	1995	Steve Elkington (AUS)		*Club, Chaska, MN*
1986	Bob Tway	1996	Mark Brooks	2003	*scheduled to be held*
1987	Larry Nelson	1997	Davis Love III		*14–17 Aug 2003,*
1988	Jeff Sluman	1998	Vijay Singh (FIJ)		*Oak Hill Country Club,*
1989	Payne Stewart	1999	Tiger Woods		*Rochester NY*

*Winner by play-off.

Ladies' Professional Golf Association (LPGA) Champions
Won by an American golfer except as indicated.

YEAR	WINNER	YEAR	WINNER	YEAR	WINNER
1955	Beverly Hanson	1972	Kathy Ahern	1989	Nancy Lopez
1956	Marlene Hagge	1973	Mary Mills	1990	Beth Daniel
1957	Louise Suggs	1974	Sandra Haynie	1991	Meg Mallon
1958	Mickey Wright	1975	Kathy Whitworth	1992	Betsy King
1959	Betsy Rawls	1976	Betty Burfeindt	1993	Patty Sheehan
1960	Mickey Wright	1977	Chako Higuchi	1994	Laura Davies (GBR)
1961	Mickey Wright	1978	Nancy Lopez	1995	Kelly Robbins
1962	Judy Kimball	1979	Donna Caponi	1996	Laura Davies (GBR)
1963	Mickey Wright	1980	Sally Little	1997	Chris Johnson
1964	Mary Mills	1981	Donna Caponi	1998	Se Ri Pak (KOR)
1965	Sandra Haynie	1982	Jan Stephenson (AUS)	1999	Juli Inkster
1966	Gloria Ehret	1983	Patty Sheehan	2000	Juli Inkster
1967	Kathy Whitworth	1984	Patty Sheehan	2001	Karrie Webb (AUS)
1968	Sandra Post	1985	Nancy Lopez	2002	Se Ri Pak (KOR)
1969	Betsy Rawls	1986	Pat Bradley		
1970	Shirley Englehorn	1987	Jane Geddes		
1971	Kathy Whitworth	1988	Sherri Turner		

United States Women's Open Champions
Won by an American golfer except as indicated.

YEAR	WINNER	YEAR	WINNER	YEAR	WINNER
1946	Patty Berg	1967	Catherine Lacoste (FRA)*	1988	Liselotte Neumann (SWE)
1947	Betty Jameson	1968	Susie Berning	1989	Betsy King
1948	Babe Didrikson Zaharias	1969	Donna Caponi	1990	Betsy King
1949	Louise Suggs	1970	Donna Caponi	1991	Meg Mallon
1950	Babe Didrikson Zaharias	1971	JoAnne Carner	1992	Patty Sheehan
1951	Betsy Rawls	1972	Susie Berning	1993	Lauri Merten
1952	Louise Suggs	1973	Susie Berning	1994	Patty Sheehan
1953	Betsy Rawls	1974	Sandra Haynie	1995	Annika Sörenstam (SWE)
1954	Babe Didrikson Zaharias	1975	Sandra Palmer	1996	Annika Sörenstam (SWE)
1955	Fay Crocker	1976	JoAnne Carner	1997	Alison Nicholas (GBR)
1956	Kathy Cornelius	1977	Hollis Stacy	1998	Se Ri Pak (KOR)
1957	Betsy Rawls	1978	Hollis Stacy	1999	Juli Inkster
1958	Mickey Wright	1979	Jerilyn Britz	2000	Karrie Webb (AUS)
1959	Mickey Wright	1980	Amy Alcott	2001	Karrie Webb (AUS)
1960	Betsy Rawls	1981	Pat Bradley	2002	Juli Inkster
1961	Mickey Wright	1982	Janet Anderson	2003	*scheduled to be held in*
1962	Murle Breer	1983	Jan Stephenson (AUS)		*July 2003 at the*
1963	Mary Mills	1984	Hollis Stacy		*Pumpkin Ridge Golf*
1964	Mickey Wright	1985	Kathy Baker		*Club, Oregon*
1965	Carol Mann	1986	Jane Geddes		
1966	Sandra Spuzich	1987	Laura Davies (GBR)		

*Amateur.

Ryder Cup

YEAR	RESULT	YEAR	RESULT
1927	United States 9½, Great Britain 2½	1969	United States 16, Great Britain 16
1929	Great Britain 7, United States 5	1971	United States 18½, Great Britain 13½
1931	United States 9, Great Britain 3	1973	United States 19, Great Britain 13
1933	Great Britain 6½, United States 5½	1975	United States 21, Great Britain 11
1935	United States 9, Great Britain 3	1977	United States 12½, Great Britain 7½
1937	United States 8, Great Britain 4	1979	United States 17, Europe 11
1939–45	*not held*	1981	United States 18½, Europe 9½
1947	United States 11, Great Britain 1	1983	United States 14½, Europe 13½
1949	United States 7, Great Britain 5	1985	Europe 16½, United States 11½
1951	United States 9½, Great Britain 2½	1987	Europe 15, United States 13
1953	United States 6½, Great Britain 5½	1989	Europe 14, United States 14
1955	United States 8, Great Britain 4	1991	United States 14½, Europe 13½
1957	Great Britain 7½, United States 4½	1993	United States 15, Europe 13
1959	United States 8½, Great Britain 3½	1995	Europe 14½, United States 13½
1961	United States 14½, Great Britain 9½	1997	Europe 14½, United States 13½
1963	United States 23, Great Britain 9	1999	United States 14½, Europe 13½
1965	United States 19½, Great Britain 12½	2001	*Postponed until 27–29 Sep 2002*
1967	United States 23½, Great Britain 8½		

British Amateur Championship—Men
Won by a British golfer except as indicated.

YEAR	WINNER	YEAR	WINNER	YEAR	WINNER
1885	Allen MacFie	1927	William Tweddell	1970	Michael Bonallack
1886	Horace Hutchinson	1928	Thomas Perkins	1971	Steve Melnyk (USA)
1887	Horace Hutchinson	1929	Cyril Tolley	1972	Trevor Homer
1888	John Ball	1930	Bobby Jones (USA)	1973	Richard Siderowf (USA)
1889	Johnny Laidlay	1931	Eric Smith	1974	Trevor Homer
1890	John Ball	1932	John de Forest	1975	Vinny Giles (USA)
1891	Johnny Laidlay	1933	Michael Scott	1976	Richard Siderowf (USA)
1892	John Ball	1934	Lawson Little (USA)	1977	Peter McEvoy
1893	Peter Anderson	1935	Lawson Little (USA)	1978	Peter McEvoy
1894	John Ball	1936	Hector Thomson	1979	Jay Sigel (USA)
1895	Leslie Balfour-Melville	1937	Robert Sweeny, Jr. (USA)	1980	Duncan Evans
1896	Freddie Tait	1938	Charles Yates (USA)	1981	Phillipe Ploujoux (FRA)
1897	Jack Allan	1939	Alexander Kyle	1982	Martin Thompson
1898	Freddie Tait	1940–45	*not held*	1983	Philip Parkin
1899	John Ball	1946	James Bruen	1984	José María Olazábal
1900	Harold Hilton	1947	William Turnesa		(ESP)
1901	Harold Hilton	1948	Frank Stranahan (USA)	1985	Garth McGimpsey (IRL)
1902	Charles Hutchings	1949	Samuel McCready	1986	David Curry
1903	Robert Maxwell	1950	Frank Stranahan (USA)	1987	Paul Mayo
1904	Walter Travis (USA)	1951	Richard Chapman (USA)	1988	Christian Hardin (SWE)
1905	Arthur Barry	1952	Harvie Ward (USA)	1989	Stephen Dodd
1906	James Robb	1953	Joe Carr (IRL)	1990	Rolf Muntz (NED)
1907	John Ball	1954	Douglas Bachli	1991	Gary Wolstenholme
1908	E.A. Lassen	1955	Joe Conrad (USA)	1992	Stephen Dundas
1909	Robert Maxwell	1956	John Beharrell	1993	Ian Pyman
1910	John Ball	1957	Reid Jack	1994	Lee James
1911	Harold Hilton	1958	Joe Carr (IRL)	1995	Gordon Sherry
1912	John Ball	1959	Deane Beman (USA)	1996	Warren Bledon
1913	Harold Hilton	1960	Joe Carr (IRL)	1997	Craig Watson
1914	J.L.C. Jenkins	1961	Michael Bonallack	1998	Sergio Garcia (ESP)
1915–19	*not held*	1962	Richard Davies (USA)	1999	Graeme Storm
1920	Cyril Tolley	1963	Michael Lunt	2000	Mikko Ilonen (FIN)
1921	William Hunter	1964	Gordon Clark	2001	Michael Hoey (IRL)
1922	Ernest Holderness	1965	Michael Bonallack	2002	Martin Sell
1923	Roger Wethered	1966	Bobby Cole (RSA)		
1924	Ernest Holderness	1967	Bob Dickson (USA)		
1925	Robert Harris	1968	Michael Bonallack		
1926	Jesse Sweetser (USA)	1969	Michael Bonallack		

United States Amateur Championship—Men

Won by an American golfer except as indicated.

YEAR	WINNER	YEAR	WINNER	YEAR	WINNER
1895	Charles Macdonald	1932	Ross Somerville	1971	Gary Cowan (CAN)
1896	H.J. Whigham	1933	George Dunlap	1972	Vinny Giles
1897	H.J. Whigham	1934	Lawson Little	1973	Craig Stadler
1898	Findlay Douglas	1935	Lawson Little	1974	Jerry Pate
1899	H.M. Harriman	1936	John Fischer	1975	Fred Ridley
1900	Walter Travis	1937	John Goodman	1976	Bill Sander
1901	Walter Travis	1938	William Turnesa	1977	John Fought
1902	Louis James	1939	Bud Ward	1978	John Cook
1903	Walter Travis	1940	Richard Chapman	1979	Mark O'Meara
1904	H.Chandler Egan	1941	Bud Ward	1980	Hal Sutton
1905	H.Chandler Egan	1942–45	*not held*	1981	Nathaniel Crosby
1906	Eben Byers	1946	Ted Bishop	1982	Jay Sigel
1907	Jerry Travers	1947	Skee Riegel	1983	Jay Sigel
1908	Jerry Travers	1948	William Turnesa	1984	Scott Verplank
1909	Robert Gardner	1949	Charles Coe	1985	Sam Randolph
1910	W.C. Fownes, Jr.	1950	Sam Urzetta	1986	Buddy Alexander
1911	Harold Hilton	1951	Billy Maxwell	1987	Billy Mayfair
1912	Jerry Travers	1952	Jack Westland	1988	Eric Meeks
1913	Jerry Travers	1953	Gene Littler	1989	Chris Patton
1914	Francis Ouimet	1954	Arnold Palmer	1990	Phil Mickelson
1915	Robert Gardner	1955	Harvie Ward	1991	Mitch Voges
1916	Chick Evans	1956	Harvie Ward	1992	Justin Leonard
1917–18	*not held*	1957	Hillman Robbins	1993	John Harris
1919	Davidson Herron	1958	Charles Coe	1994	Tiger Woods
1920	Chick Evans	1959	Jack Nicklaus	1995	Tiger Woods
1921	Jesse Guildford	1960	Deane Beman	1996	Tiger Woods
1922	Jess Sweetser	1961	Jack Nicklaus	1997	Matt Kuchar
1923	Max Marston	1962	Labron Harris, Jr.	1998	Hank Kuehne
1924	Bobby Jones	1963	Deane Beman	1999	David Gossett
1925	Bobby Jones	1964	Bill Campbell	2000	Jeff Quinney
1926	George von Elm	1965	Bob Murphy	2001	Ben Dickerson
1927	Bobby Jones	1966	Gary Cowan (CAN)	2002	*Scheduled to be held*
1928	Bobby Jones	1967	Bob Dickson		*19–25 Aug 2002,*
1929	Harrison Johnston	1968	Bruce Fleisher		*Bloomfield Hills MI*
1930	Bobby Jones	1969	Steve Melnyk		
1931	Francis Ouimet	1970	Lanny Wadkins		

Women's British Open Championship

YEAR	WINNER	YEAR	WINNER	YEAR	WINNER
1976	J. Lee Smith (GBR)	1986	Laura Davies (GBR)	1995	Karrie Webb (AUS)
1977	Vivien Saunders (GBR)	1987	Alison Nicholas (GBR)	1996	Emilee Klein (USA)
1978	Janet Melville (GBR)	1988	Corinne Dibnah (AUS)	1997	Karrie Webb (AUS)
1979	Alison Sheard (RSA)	1989	Jane Geddes (USA)	1998	Sherri Steinhauer (USA)
1980	Debbie Massey (USA)	1990	Helen Alfredsson (SWE)	1999	Sherri Steinhauer (USA)
1981	Debbie Massey (USA)	1991	Penny Grice-Whittaker	2000	Sophie Gustafson (SWE)
1982	Marta Figueras-Dotti (SPA)		(GBR)	2001	Se Ri Pak (KOR)
1983	*not held*	1992	Patty Sheehan (USA)	2002	Karrie Webb (AUS)
1984	Okamoto Ayako (JAP)	1993	Mardi Lunn (AUS)		
1985	Betsy King (USA)	1994	Liselotte Neumann (SWE)		

Ladies' British Amateur Championship

Won by a British golfer except as indicated.

YEAR	WINNER	YEAR	WINNER	YEAR	WINNER
1893	Lady Margaret Scott	1903	Rhona Adair	1913	Muriel Dodd
1894	Lady Margaret Scott	1904	Lottie Dod	1914	Cecil Leitch
1895	Lady Margaret Scott	1905	Bertha Thompson	1915–19	*not held*
1896	Amy Pascoe	1906	Mrs. W. Kennion	1920	Cecil Leitch
1897	Edith Orr	1907	May Hezlet	1921	Cecil Leitch
1898	Lena Thomson	1908	Maud Titterton	1922	Joyce Wethered
1899	May Hezlet	1909	Dorothy Campbell	1923	Doris Chambers
1900	Rhona Adair	1910	Elsie Grant-Suttie	1924	Joyce Wethered
1901	Mary Graham	1911	Dorothy Campbell	1925	Joyce Wethered
1902	May Hezlet	1912	Gladys Ravenscroft	1926	Cecil Leitch

Ladies' British Amateur Championship (continued)

YEAR	WINNER	YEAR	WINNER	YEAR	WINNER
1927	Simone de la Chaume (FRA)	1956	Wiffi Smith (USA)	1981	Belle Robertson
1928	Nanette le Blan (FRA)	1957	Philomena Garvey	1982	Kitrina Douglas
1929	Joyce Wethered	1958	Jessie Valentine	1983	Jill Thornhill
1930	Diana Fishwick	1959	Elizabeth Price	1984	Jody Rosenthal (USA)
1931	Enid Wilson	1960	Barbara McIntire (USA)	1985	Lillian Behan (IRE)
1932	Enid Wilson	1961	Marley Spearman	1986	Marnie McGuire
1933	Enid Wilson	1962	Marley Spearman	1987	Janet Collingham
1934	Helen Holm	1963	Brigitte Varangot (FRA)	1988	Joanne Furby
1935	Wanda Morgan	1964	Carol Sorenson (USA)	1989	Helen Dobson
1936	Pam Barton	1965	Brigitte Varangot (FRA)	1990	Julie Wade Hall
1937	Jessie Anderson	1966	Elizabeth Chadwick	1991	Valerie Michaud
1938	Helen Holm	1967	Elizabeth Chadwick	1992	Bernille Pedersen (DEN)
1939	Pam Barton	1968	Brigitte Varangot (FRA)	1993	Catriona Lambert
1940–45	not held	1969	Catherine Lacoste (FRA)	1994	Emma Duggleby
1946	Jean Hetherington	1970	Dinah Oxley	1995	Julie Wade Hall
1947	Babe Didrikson Zaharias	1971	Michelle Walker	1996	Kelli Kuehne (USA)
	(USA)	1972	Michelle Walker	1997	Alison Rose
1948	Louise Suggs (USA)	1973	Ann Irvin	1998	Kim Rostron
1949	Frances Stephens	1974	Carol Semple (USA)	1999	Marine Monnet (FRA)
1950	Lally de Saint Sauveur (FRA)	1975	Nancy Roth Syms (USA)	2000	Rebecca Hudson
1951	Catherine MacCann	1976	Cathy Panton	2001	Marta Prieto (ESP)
1952	Moira Paterson	1977	Angela Uzielli	2002	Rebecca Hudson
1953	Marlene Stewart (CAN)	1978	Edwina Kennedy (AUS)		
1954	Frances Stephens	1979	Maureen Madill		
1955	Jessie Valentine	1980	Anne Quast Sander (USA)		

United States Women's Amateur Championship

Won by an American golfer except as indicated.

YEAR	WINNER	YEAR	WINNER	YEAR	WINNER
1895	Mrs. C.S. Brown	1933	Virginia Van Wie	1973	Carol Semple
1896	Beatrix Hoyt	1934	Virginia Van Wie	1974	Cynthia Hill
1897	Beatrix Hoyt	1935	Glenna Collett Vare	1975	Beth Daniel
1898	Beatrix Hoyt	1936	Pamela Barton (GBR)	1976	Donna Horton
1899	Ruth Underhill	1937	Estelle Lawson Page	1977	Beth Daniel
1900	Frances C. Griscom	1938	Patty Berg	1978	Cathy Sherk (CAN)
1901	Genevieve Hecker	1939	Betty Jameson	1979	Cynthia Hill
1902	Genevieve Hecker	1940	Betty Jameson	1980	Juli Inkster
1903	Bessie Anthony	1941	Elizabeth Hicks	1981	Juli Inkster
1904	Georgianna M. Bishop	1942–45	not held	1982	Juli Inkster
1905	Pauline Mackay	1946	Babe Didrikson Zaharias	1983	Joanne Pacillo
1906	Harriot S. Curtis	1947	Louise Suggs	1984	Deb Richard
1907	Margaret Curtis	1948	Grace Lenczyk	1985	Michiko Hattori (JPN)
1908	Katherine Harley	1949	Dorothy Porter	1986	Kay Cockerill
1909	Dorothy I. Campbell	1950	Beverly Hanson	1987	Kay Cockerill
1910	Dorothy I. Campbell	1951	Dorothy Kirby	1988	Pearl Sinn
1911	Margaret Curtis	1952	Jacqueline Pung	1989	Vicki Goetze
1912	Margaret Curtis	1953	Mary Lena Faulk	1990	Pat Hurst
1913	Gladys Ravenscroft	1954	Barbara Romack	1991	Amy Fruhwirth
1914	Katherine Harley Jackson	1955	Patricia Lesser	1992	Vicki Goetze
1915	Florence Vanderbeck	1956	Marlene Stewart (CAN)	1993	Jill McGill
1916	Alexa Stirling	1957	JoAnne Gunderson	1994	Wendy Ward
1917–18	not held	1958	Anne Quast	1995	Kelli Kuehne
1919	Alexa Stirling	1959	Barbara McIntire	1996	Kelli Kuehne
1920	Alexa Stirling	1960	JoAnne Gunderson	1997	Silvia Cavalleri (ITA)
1921	Marion Hollins	1961	Anne Quast Sander	1998	Grace Park
1922	Glenna Collett	1962	JoAnne Gunderson	1999	Dorothy Delasin
1923	Edith Cummings	1963	Anne Quast Sander	2000	Marcy Newton
1924	Dorothy Campbell Hurd	1964	Barbara McIntire	2001	Meredith Duncan
1925	Glenna Collett	1965	Jean Ashley	2002	scheduled to be held
1926	Helen Stetson	1966	JoAnne Gunderson Carner		12–17 August, Scar-
1927	Miriam Burns Horn	1967	Mary Lou Dill		borough NY
1928	Glenna Collett	1968	JoAnne Gunderson Carner	2003	scheduled to be held
1929	Glenna Collett	1969	Catherine Lacoste (FRA)		4–9 August, Philadel-
1930	Glenna Collett	1970	Martha Wilkinson		phia Country Club,
1931	Helen Hicks	1971	Laura Baugh		Gladwyne PA
1932	Virginia Van Wie	1972	Mary Budke		

World Cup

YEAR	WINNER
1953	Argentina (Antonio Cerda and Roberto de Vicenzo)
1954	Australia (Peter Thomson and Kel Nagle)
1955	United States (Chick Harbert and Ed Furgol)
1956	United States (Ben Hogan and Sam Snead)
1957	Japan (Torakichi Nakamura and Koichi Ono)
1958	Ireland (Harry Bradshaw and Christy O'Connor)
1959	Australia (Peter Thomson and Kel Nagle)
1960	United States (Sam Snead and Arnold Palmer)
1961	United States (Sam Snead and Jimmy Demaret)
1962	United States (Sam Snead and Arnold Palmer)
1963	United States (Arnold Palmer and Jack Nicklaus)
1964	United States (Arnold Palmer and Jack Nicklaus)
1965	South Africa (Gary Player and Harold Henning)
1966	United States (Arnold Palmer and Jack Nicklaus)
1967	United States (Arnold Palmer and Jack Nicklaus)
1968	Canada (Al Balding and George Knudson)
1969	United States (Orville Moody and Lee Trevino)
1970	Australia (David Graham and Bruce Devlin)
1971	United States (Jack Nicklaus and Lee Trevino)
1972	Taiwan (Hsieh Min-nan and Lu Liang-huan)
1973	United States (Johnny Miller and Jack Nicklaus)

YEAR	WINNER
1974	South Africa (Bobby Cole and Dale Hayes)
1975	United States (Johnny Miller and Lou Graham)
1976	Spain (Seve Ballesteros and Manuel Piñero)
1977	Spain (Seve Ballesteros and Antonio Garrido)
1978	United States (John Mahaffey and Andy North)
1979	United States (Hale Irwin and John Mahaffey)
1980	Canada (Dan Halldorson and Jim Nelford)
1981	*not held*
1982	Spain (Manuel Piñero and Jose-Maria Cañizares)
1983	United States (Rex Caldwell and John Cook)
1984	Spain (Jose-Maria Cañizares and Jose Rivero)
1985	Canada (Dan Halldorson and Dave Barr)
1986	*not held*
1987	Wales (Ian Woosnam and David Llewellyn)
1988	United States (Ben Crenshaw and Mark McCumber)
1989	Australia (Peter Fowler and Wayne Grady)
1990	Germany (Bernhard Langer and Torsten Giedeon)
1991	Sweden (Anders Forsbrand and Per-Ulrik Johansson)
1992	United States (Fred Couples and Davis Love III)
1993	United States (Fred Couples and Davis Love III)
1994	United States (Fred Couples and Davis Love III)
1995	United States (Fred Couples and Davis Love III)
1996	South Africa (Ernie Els and Wayne Westner)
1997	Ireland (Padraig Harrington and Paul McGinley)
1998	England (Nick Faldo and David Carter)
1999	United States (Tiger Woods and Mark O'Meara)
2000	United States (Tiger Woods and David Duval)
2001	South Africa (Ernie Els and Retief Goosen)
2002	*scheduled to be held 10–15 Dec 2002, Puerto Vallarta, Mexico*

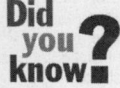

Did you know? Before the mid-19th century, golf balls were made of leather and stuffed with feathers. Making a "featherie" was an exacting art, requiring ballmakers to stuff a "top hat full" of wet feathers into a leather shell. The shell was hammered into a round shape as it dried and hardened. A well-struck featherie could travel some 180–200 yards.

Curtis Cup

YEAR	RESULT
1932	United States 5½, Britain 3½
1934	United States 6½, Britain and Ireland 2½
1936	United States* 4½, Britain and Ireland 4½
1938	United States 5½, Britain and Ireland 3½
1940–46	not held
1948	United States 6½, Britain and Ireland 2½
1950	United States 7½, Britain and Ireland 2½
1952	Britain and Ireland 5, United States 4
1954	United States 6, Britain and Ireland 3
1956	Britain and Ireland 5, United States 4
1958	Britain and Ireland* 4½, United States 4½
1960	United States 6½, Britain and Ireland 2½
1962	United States 8, Britain and Ireland 1
1964	United States 10½, Britain and Ireland 7½
1966	United States 13, Britain and Ireland 5
1968	United States 10½, Britain and Ireland 7½
1970	United States 11½, Britain and Ireland 6½

YEAR	RESULT
1972	United States 10, Britain and Ireland 8
1974	United States 13, Britain and Ireland 5
1976	United States 11½, Britain and Ireland 6½
1978	United States 12, Britain and Ireland 6
1980	United States 13, Britain and Ireland 5
1982	United States 14½, Britain and Ireland 3½
1984	United States 9½, Britain and Ireland 8½
1986	Britain and Ireland 13, United States 5
1988	Britain and Ireland 11, United States 7
1990	United States 14, Britain and Ireland 4
1992	Britain and Ireland 10, United States 8
1994	Britain and Ireland 9, United States 9
1996	Britain and Ireland 11½, United States 6½
1998	United States 10, Britain and Ireland 8
2000	United States 10, Britain and Ireland 8
2002	United States 11, Britain and Ireland 7

In case of a tie the defenders retain the cup.

Gymnastics

Aside from the gymnastics events in **Olympic Games**, the most popular venue for gymnastics competition is the **world championship games**. Men's events are six in number with all-around individual and all-around team awards in addition. The latter two awards are given on a cumulative points basis. Women also have all-around team and individual awards, determined by their performance in four individual events.

International Gymnastics Federation Web site: <www.fig-gymnastics.com>

World Gymnastics Championships—Men

YEAR	ALL-AROUND TEAM	ALL-AROUND INDIVIDUAL	HORIZONTAL BAR	PARALLEL BARS
1950	Switzerland	Walter Lehmann (SUI)	Paavo Aaltonen (FIN)	Hans Eugster (SUI)
1952*	USSR	Viktor Chukarin (URS)	Jack Günthard (SUI)	Hans Eugster (SUI)
1954	USSR	Valentin Muratov (URS)	Valentin Muratov (URS)	Viktor Chukarin (URS)
1956*	USSR	Viktor Chukarin (URS)	Takashi Ono (JPN)	Viktor Chukarin (URS)
1958	USSR	Boris Shakhlin (URS)	Boris Shakhlin (URS)	Boris Shakhlin (URS)
1960*	Japan	Boris Shakhlin (URS)	Takashi Ono (JPN)	Boris Shakhlin (URS)
1962	Japan	Yury Titov (URS)	Takashi Ono (JPN)	Miroslav Cerar (YUG)
1964*	Japan	Yukio Endo (JPN)	Boris Shakhlin (URS)	Yukio Endo (JPN)
1966	Japan	Mikhail Voronin (URS)	Akinori Nakayama (JPN)	Sergey Diomidov (URS)
1968*	Japan	Sawao Kato (JPN)	Mikhail Voronin (URS), Akinori Nakayama (JPN)†	Akinori Nakayama (JPN)
1970	Japan	Eizo Kenmotsu (JPN)	Eizo Kenmotsu (JPN)	Akinori Nakayama (JPN)
1972*	Japan	Sawao Kato (JPN)	Mitsuo Tsukahara (JPN)	Sawao Kato (JPN)
1974	Japan	Shigeru Kasamatsu (JPN)	Eberhard Gienger (FRG)	Eizo Kenmotsu (JPN)
1976*	Japan	Nikolay Andrianov (URS)	Mitsuo Tsukahara (JPN)	Sawao Kato (JPN)
1978	Japan	Nikolay Andrianov (URS)	Shigeru Kasamatsu (JPN)	Eizo Kenmotsu (JPN)
1979	USSR	Aleksandr Dityatin (URS)	Kurt Thomas (USA)	Bart Conner (USA)
1980*	USSR	Aleksandr Dityatin (URS)	Stoyan Delchev (BUL)	Aleksandr Tkachyov (URS)
1981	USSR	Yury Korolyov (URS)	Aleksandr Tkachyov (URS)	Aleksandr Dityatin (URS), Koji Gushiken (JPN)†
1983	China	Dmitry Bilozerchev (URS)	Dmitry Bilozerchev (URS)	Lou Yun (CHN), Vladimir Artyomov (URS)†
1984*	United States	Koji Gushiken (JPN)	Shinji Morisue (JPN)	Bart Conner (USA)
1985	USSR	Yury Korolyov (URS)	Tong Fei (CHN)	Sylvio Kroll (GDR), Valentin Mogilny (URS)†
1987	USSR	Dmitry Bilozerchev (URS)	Dmitry Bilozerchev (URS)	Vladimir Artyomov (URS)
1988*	USSR	Vladimir Artyomov (URS)	Vladimir Artyomov (URS), Valery Lyukin (URS)†	Vladimir Artyomov (URS)
1989	USSR	Igor Korobchinsky (URS)	Li Chunyang (CHN)	Vladimir Artyomov (URS), Li Jing (CHN)†
1991	USSR	Grigory Misutin (URS)	Ralf Buechner (GER), Li Chunyang (CHN)†	Li Jing (CHN)
1992	‡	‡	Grigory Misutin (CIS)	Li Jing (CHN), Aleksey Voropayev (CIS)†
1993	‡	Vitaly Sherbo (BLR)	Sergey Charkov (RUS)	Vitaly Sherbo (BLR)
1994	China	Ivan Ivankov (BLR)	Vitaly Sherbo (BLR)	Liping Huang (CHN)
1995	China	Li Xiaoshuang (CHN)	Andreas Wecker (GER)	Vitaly Sherbo (BLR)
1996	‡	‡	Jesús Carballo (ESP)	Rustam Charipov (UKR)
1997	China	Ivan Ivankov (BLR)	Jani Tanskanen (FIN)	Zhang Jinjing (CHN)
1999	China	Nikolay Krukov (RUS)	Jesús Carballo (ESP)	Lee Joo Hyung (KOR)
2000*	China	Aleksey Nemov (RUS)	Aleksey Nemov (RUS)	Li Xiaopeng (CHN)
2001	Belarus	Feng Jing (CHN)	Vlasios Maras (GRE)	Sean Townsend (USA)
2003	*The competition is scheduled to be held 16–24 Aug 2003, Anaheim CA.*			

YEAR	POMMEL HORSE	RINGS	VAULT	FLOOR EXERCISE
1950	Josef Stalder (SUI)	Walter Lehmann (SUI)	Ernst Gebendinger (SUI)	Josef Stalder (SUI)
1952*	Viktor Chukarin (URS)	Grant Shaginyan (URS)	Viktor Chukarin (URS)	Karl Thoresson (SWE)
1954	Grant Shaginyan (URS)	Albert Azaryan (URS)	Leo Sotornik (TCH)	Valetin Muratov (URS), Masao Takemoto (JPN)†
1956*	Boris Shakhlin (URS)	Albert Azaryan (URS)	Valentin Muratov (URS), Helmut Bantz (FRG)†	Valentin Muratov (URS)
1958	Boris Shakhlin (URS)	Albert Azaryan (URS)	Yury Titov (URS)	Masao Takemoto (JPN)
1960*	Boris Shakhlin (URS), Eugen Ekman (FIN)†	Albert Azaryan (URS)	Takashi Ono (JPN), Boris Shakhlin (URS)†	Nobuyuki Aihara (JPN)
1962	Miroslav Cerar (YUG)	Yury Titov (URS)	Premysel Krbec (TCH)	Nobuyuki Aihara (JPN), Yukio Endo (JPN)†
1964*	Miroslav Cerar (YUG)	Takuji Hayata (JPN)	Haruhiro Yamasita (JPN)	Franco Menichelli (ITA)

World Gymnastics Championships—Men (continued)

YEAR	POMMEL HORSE	RINGS	VAULT	FLOOR EXERCISE
1966	Miroslav Cerar (YUG)	Mikhail Voronin (URS)	Haruhiro Matsuda (JPN)	Akinori Nakayama (JPN)
1968*	Miroslav Cerar (YUG)	Akinori Nakayama (JPN)	Mikhail Voronin (URS)	Sawao Kato (JPN)
1970	Miroslav Cerar (YUG)	Akinori Nakayama (JPN)	Mitsuo Tsukahara (JPN)	Akinori Nakayama (JPN)
1972*	Viktor Klimenko (URS)	Akinori Nakayama (JPN)	Klaus Koeste (GDR)	Nikolay Andrianov (URS)
1974	Zoltan Magyar (HUN)	Danut Grecu (ROM), Nikolay Andrianov (URS)†	Shigeru Kasamatsu (JPN)	Shigeru Kasamatsu (JPN)
1976*	Zoltan Magyar (HUN)	Nikolay Andrianov (URS)	Nikolay Andrianov (URS)	Nikolay Andrianov (URS)
1978	Zoltan Magyar (HUN)	Nikolay Andrianov (URS)	Junichi Shimizu (JPN)	Kurt Thomas (USA)
1979	Zoltan Magyar (HUN)	Aleksandr Dityatin (URS)	Alexandr Dityatin (URS)	Kurt Thomas (USA), Roland Bruckner (GDR)†
1980*	Zoltan Magyar (HUN)	Aleksandr Dityatin (URS)	Nikolay Andrianov (URS)	Roland Bruckner (GDR)
1981	Li Xiaoping (CHN), Michael Nikolay (GDR)†	Aleksandr Dityatin (URS)	Ralf-Peter Hemmann (GDR)	Li Yuijiu (CHN), Yury Korolyov (URS)†
1983	Dmitry Bilozerchev (URS)	Dmitry Bilozerchev (URS), Koji Gushiken (JPN)†	Arthur Akopyan (URS)	Tong Fei (CHN)
1984*	Li Ning (CHN), Peter Vidmar (USA)†	Koji Gushiken (JPN), Li Ning (CHN)†	Lou Yun (CHN)	Li Ning (CHN)
1985	Valentin Mogilny (URS)	Li Ning (CHN), Yury Korolyov (URS)†	Yury Korolyov (URS)	Tong Fei (CHN)
1987	Dmitry Bilozerchev (URS), Zsolt Borkai (HUN)†	Yury Korolyov (URS)	Sylvio Kroll (GDR), Lou Yun (CHN)†	Lou Yun (CHN)
1988*	Dmitry Bilozerchev (URS), Zsolt Borkai (HUN), Lyubomir Geraskov (BUL)†	Holger Behrendt (GDR), Dmitri Bilozerchev (URS)†	Lou Yun (CHN)	Sergey Kharkov (URS)
1989	Valentin Mogilny (URS)	Andreas Aguilar (FRG)	Joerg Behrend (GDR)	Igor Korobchinsky (URS)
1991	Valery Belenky (URS)	Grigory Misutin (URS)	You Ok Youl (KOR)	Igor Korobchinsky (URS)
1992	Pae Gil Su (PRK), Vitaly Sherbo (CIS), Li Jing (CHN)†	Vitaly Sherbo (CIS)	You Ok Youl (KOR)	Igor Korobchinsky (CIS)
1993	Pae Gil Su (PRK)	Yury Chechi (ITA)	Vitaly Sherbo (BLR)	Grigory Misutin (UKR)
1994	Marius Urzica (ROM)	Yury Chechi (ITA)	Vitaly Sherbo (BLR)	Vitaly Sherbo (BLR)
1995	Li Donghua (SUI)	Yury Chechi (ITA)	Aleksey Nemov (RUS), Grigory Misutin (UKR)†	Vitaly Sherbo (BLR)
1996	Pae Gil Su (PRK)	Yury Chechi (ITA)	Aleksey Nemov (RUS)	Vitaly Sherbo (BLR)
1997	Valery Belenki (GER)	Yury Chechi (ITA)	Sergey Fedorchenko (KAZ)	Aleksey Nemov (RUS)
1999	Aleksey Nemov (RUS)	Dong Zhen (CHN)	Li Xiaopeng (CHN)	Aleksey Nemov (RUS)
2000*	Marius Urzica (ROM)	Szilveszter Csollany (HUN)	Gervasio Deferr (ESP)	Igor Vihrons (LAT)
2001	Marius Urzica (ROM)	Jordan Jovtchev (BUL)	Marian Dragulescu (ROM)	Jordan Jovtchev (BUL), Marian Dragulescu (ROM)†
2003	The competition is scheduled to be held 16–24 Aug 2003, Anaheim CA.			

*Olympic championships, recognized as world championships (for Olympic results 1896–1948, and from 1992, see Olympic Games). †Tied. ‡Not held.

World Gymnastics Championships—Women

YEAR	ALL-AROUND TEAM	ALL-AROUND INDIVIDUAL	BALANCE BEAM	UNEVEN PARALLEL BARS
1950	Sweden	Helena Rakoczy (POL)	Helena Rakoczy (POL)	Gertchen Kolar (AUT), Anna Pettersson (SWE)*
1952†	USSR	Mariya Gorokhovskaya (URS)	Nina Bocharova (URS)	Margit Korondi (HUN)
1954	USSR	Galina Rudiko (URS)	Keiko Tanaka (JPN)	Agnes Keleti (HUN)
1956†	USSR	Larisa Latynina (URS)	Agnes Keleti (HUN)	Agnes Keleti (HUN)
1958	USSR	Larisa Latynina (URS)	Larisa Latynina (URS)	Larisa Latynina (URS)
1960†	USSR	Larisa Latynina (URS)	Eva Bosakova (TCH)	Polina Astakhova (URS)

World Gymnastics Championships—Women (continued)

YEAR	ALL-AROUND TEAM	ALL-AROUND INDIVIDUAL	BALANCE BEAM	UNEVEN PARALLEL BARS
1962	USSR	Larisa Latynina (URS)	Eva Bosakova (TCH)	Irina Pervushina (URS)
1964†	USSR	Vera Caslavska (TCH)	Vera Caslavska (TCH)	Polina Astakhova (URS)
1966	Czechoslovakia	Vera Caslavska (TCH)	Natalya Kuchinskaya (URS)	Natalya Kuchinskaya (URS)
1968†	USSR	Vera Caslavska (TCH)	Natalya Kuchinskaya (URS)	Vera Caslavska (TCH)
1970	USSR	Lyudmila Turishcheva (URS)	Erika Zuchold (GDR)	Karin Janz (GDR)
1972†	USSR	Lyudmila Turishcheva (URS)	Olga Korbut (URS)	Karin Janz (GDR)
1974	USSR	Lyudmila Turishcheva (URS)	Lyudmila Turishcheva (URS)	Annelore Zinke (GDR)
1976†	USSR	Nadia Comaneci (ROM)	Nadia Comaneci (ROM)	Nadia Comaneci (ROM)
1978	USSR	Yelena Mukhina (URS)	Nadia Comaneci (ROM)	Marcia Frederick (USA)
1979	Romania	Nelli Kim (URS)	Vera Cerna (TCH)	Ma Yanhong (CHN), Maxi Gnauck (GDR)*
1980†	USSR	Yelena Davydova (URS)	Nadia Comaneci (ROM)	Maxi Gnauck (GDR)
1981	USSR	Olga Bicherova (URS)	Maxi Gnauck (GDR)	Maxi Gnauck (GDR)
1983	USSR	Natalya Yurchenko (URS)	Olga Mostepanova (URS)	Maxi Gnauck (GDR)
1984†	Romania	Mary Lou Retton (USA)	Ecaterina Szabo (ROM), Simona Pauca (ROM)*	Julianne McNamara (USA), Ma Yanhong (CHN)*
1985	USSR	Yelena Shushunova (URS), Oksana Omelyanchik (URS)*	Daniela Silivas (ROM)	Gabriele Fahrnich (GDR)
1987	Romania	Aurelia Dobre (ROM)	Aurelia Dobre (ROM)	Daniela Silivas (ROM), Doerte Thuemmler (GDR)*
1988†	USSR	Yelena Shushunova (URS)	Daniela Silivas (ROM)	Daniela Silivas (ROM)
1989	USSR	Svetlana Boginskaya (URS)	Daniela Silivas (ROM)	Fan Di (CHN), Daniela Silivas (ROM)*
1991	USSR	Kim Zmeskal (USA)	Svetlana Boginskaya (URS)	Kim Gwang Suk (PRK)
1992	‡	‡	Kim Zmeskal (USA)	Lavinia Milosovici (ROM)
1993	‡	Shannon Miller (USA)	Lavinia Milosovici (ROM)	Shannon Miller (USA)
1994	Romania	Shannon Miller (USA)	Shannon Miller (USA)	Li Luo (CHN)
1995	Romania	Liliya Podkopayeva (UKR)	Mo Huilan (CHN)	Svetlana Khorkina (RUS)
1996	‡	‡	Dina Kochetkova (RUS)	Svetlana Khorkina (RUS), Yelena Piskun (BLR)*
1997	Romania	Svetlana Khorkina (RUS)	Gina Gogean (ROM)	Svetlana Khorkina (RUS)
1999	Romania	Maria Olaru (ROM)	Ling Jie (CHN)	Svetlana Khorkina (RUS)
2000†	Romania	Simona Amanar (ROM)	Liu Xuan (CHN)	Svetlana Khorkina (RUS)
2001	Romania	Svetlana Khorkina (RUS)	Andreea Raducan (ROM)	Svetlana Khorkina (RUS)
2003	The competition is scheduled to be held 16–24 Aug 2003, Anaheim CA.			

YEAR	VAULT	FLOOR EXERCISE
1950	Helena Rakoczy (POL)	Helena Rakoczy (POL)
1952†	Yekaterina Kalinchuk (URS)	Agnes Keleti (HUN)
1954	Anna Pettersson (SWE), Tamara Manina (URS)†	Tamara Manina (URS)
1956†	Larisa Latynina (URS)	Larissa Latynina (URS), Agnes Keleti (HUN)*
1958	Larisa Latynina (URS)	Eva Bosakova (TCH)
1960†	Margarita Nikolayeva (URS)	Larisa Latynina (URS)
1962	Vera Caslavska (TCH)	Larisa Latynina (URS)
1964†	Vera Caslavska (TCH)	Larisa Latynina (URS)
1966	Vera Caslavska (TCH)	Natalya Kuchinskaya (URS)
1968†	Vera Caslavska (TCH)	Vera Caslavska (TCH), Larisa Petrik (URS)*
1970	Erika Zuchold (GDR)	Lyudmila Turishcheva (URS)
1972†	Karin Janz (GDR)	Olga Korbut (URS)
1974	Olga Korbut (URS)	Lyudmila Turishcheva (URS)
1976†	Nelli Kim (URS)	Nelli Kim (URS)
1978	Nelli Kim (URS)	Yelena Mukhina (URS), Nelli Kim (URS)*
1979	Dumitrita Turner (ROM)	Emilia Eberle (ROM)
1980†	Natalya Shaposhnikova (URS)	Nadia Comaneci (ROM), Nelli Kim (URS)*
1981	Maxi Gnauck (GDR)	Natalya Ilenko (URS)
1983	Boriana Stoyanova (BUL)	Ecaterina Szabo (ROM)
1984†	Ecaterina Szabo (ROM)	Ecaterina Szabo (ROM)
1985	Yelena Shushunova (URS)	Oksana Omelyanchik (URS)

World Gymnastics Championships—Women (continued)

YEAR	VAULT	FLOOR EXERCISE
1987	Yelena Shushunova (URS)	Yelena Shushunova (URS), Daniela Silivas (ROM)*
1988†	Svetlana Boginskaya (URS)	Daniela Silivas (ROM)
1989	Olesia Dudnik (URS)	Svetlana Boginskaya (URS), Daniela Silivas (ROM)*
1991	Lavinia Milosovici (ROM)	Cristina Bontas (ROM), Oksana Chusovitina (URS)*
1992	Henrietta Onodi (HUN)	Kim Zmeskal (USA)
1993	Yelena Piskun (BLR)	Shannon Miller (USA)
1994	Gina Gogean (ROM)	Dina Kochetkova (RUS)
1995	Simona Amanar (ROM), Liliya Podkopayeva (UKR)*	Gina Gogean (ROM)
1996	Gina Gogean (ROM)	Gina Gogean (ROM), Kui Yuanyuan (CHN)*
1997	Simona Amanar (ROM)	Gina Gogean (ROM)
1999	Yelena Zamolodchikova (RUS)	Andreea Raducan (ROM)
2000†	Yelena Zamolodchikova (RUS)	Yelena Zamolodchikova (RUS)
2001	Svetlana Khorkina (RUS)	Andreea Raducan (ROM)
2003	The competition is scheduled to be held 16–24 Aug 2003, Anaheim CA.	

*Tied. †Olympic championships, recognized as world championships (for 1896–1952 Olympics, see Olympic Games). ‡Not held.

Horse Racing

In the **oldest type** of horse racing, the rider sits astride the horse; in the other type of race, best known as **harness racing**, the driver sits in a sulky— a two-wheeled vehicle attached by shafts and traces to the horse. In the former type, a **Thoroughbred** horse is raced over either a track or over a course of jumps and turns (**steeplechase**). Harness horses can be trotters or pacers and are Standardbred horses raced on a track.

The English Thoroughbred classics. The races are run by 3-year-old colts and fillies. **The Derby**, first run in 1780, is run at Epsom Downs, Surrey, over 1½ miles. **The Oaks** (for fillies only), also run at Epsom Downs, was first run in 1779; the oldest of the English races, however, is the **St. Leger** (1776). It is run over 1 mile 6½ furlongs at Doncaster, South Yorkshire. The **2,000 Guineas** (1809) is run over 1 mile at Newmarket, Suffolk. A horse that wins the 2,000 Guineas, the Derby, and the St. Leger all in one year is said to have won the **British Triple Crown**.

The American Thoroughbred classics. The **Kentucky Derby**, a **Triple Crown** event first run in 1875 and perhaps the best known of American horse races, is raced at Churchill Downs in Louisville KY, over a 10-furlong (1¼-mile) track. Another of the Triple Crown classics, the **Preakness Stakes**, was instituted in 1873; it is run over 9½ furlongs (1³⁄₁₆ miles) at Pimlico Race Track in Baltimore MD. The third Triple Crown event is the 12-furlong (1½-mile) **Belmont Stakes**, established in 1867. It is run at Belmont Park Race Track, Long Island NY. All three events are for 3-year-old horses.

Australian Thoroughbred racing. The Victoria Racing Club's **Melbourne Cup**, first run in 1861, is one of the world's great handicap races. The day on which it is held (the first Tuesday in November) is a public holiday in Melbourne.

Dubai World Cup, first run in 1996, is the world's richest horse race ($6 million in 2002). The 2,000-m (about 1¼-mi) race is held on the dirt track at the Nad Al Sheba Racecourse in Dubai, United Arab Emirates, and is open to four-year-old and older Thoroughbred horses.

The **Grand National**, the world's most significant and widely followed **steeplechase** race, has been run annually at Aintree Racecourse near Liverpool, England, since 1839. The race includes 30 jumps over a traditional distance of 4 miles 4 furlongs.

Harness racing. In the United States, the **Hambletonian Trot** is probably the most prestigious of harness races. It was established in 1926, was raced in New York, Kentucky, and Illinois, and is now run at The Meadowlands in New Jersey.

Related Web sites: US National Thoroughbred Racing Association: <www.ntra.com>; Fédération Equestre Internationale: <www.horsesport.org>; the magazine Thoroughbred Times: <www.thoroughbred times.com>; and <www.racingpost.co.uk>.

Major Thoroughbred Race Winners 2001–02

United States

DATE	RACE	WINNER	JOCKEY
1 Jul 2001	United Nations Handicap	Senure	Robbie G. Davis
1 Jul 2001	Hollywood Gold Cup	Aptitude	Laffit Pincay, Jr.
1 Jul 2001	Suburban Handicap	Albert the Great	Jorge F. Chávez
15 Jul 2001	Swaps Stakes	Congaree	Gary Stevens
21 Jul 2001	Coaching Club American Oaks	Tweedside	John R. Velazquez
28 Jul 2001	Test Stakes	Victory Ride	Edgar S. Prado
28 Jul 2001	Eddie Read Handicap	Redattore	Alex O. Solis
28 Jul 2001	Whitney Handicap	Lido Palace	Jerry D. Bailey
29 Jul 2001	Go for Wand Handicap	Serra Lake	Edgar S. Prado

Major Thoroughbred Race Winners (continued)

United States (continued)

DATE	RACE	WINNER	JOCKEY
4 Aug 2001	Jim Dandy Stakes	Scorpion	Jerry D. Bailey
5 Aug 2001	Haskell Invitational	Point Given	Gary Stevens
11 Aug 2001	Sword Dancer Invitational Handicap	With Anticipation	Pat Day
18 Aug 2001	Secretariat Stakes	Startac	Alex O. Solis
18 Aug 2001	Arlington Million*	Silvano	Andreas Suborics
18 Aug 2001	Beverly D. Stakes	England's Legend	Corey Nakatani
18 Aug 2001	Alabama Stakes	Flute	Edgar S. Prado
19 Aug 2001	Pacific Classic	Skimming	Garrett Gomez
24 Aug 2001	Personal Ensign Handicap	Pompeii	Richard Migliore
25 Aug 2001	King's Bishop Stakes	Squirtle Squirt	Jerry D. Bailey
25 Aug 2001	Travers Stakes	Point Given	Gary Stevens
26 Aug 2001	Ballerina Handicap	Shine Again	Jean-Luc Samyn
26 Aug 2001	Del Mar Debutante Stakes	Habibti	Victor Espinoza
31 Aug 2001	Spinaway Stakes	Cashier's Dream	Donnie Meche
1 Sep 2001	Hopeful Stakes	Came Home	Chris J. McCarron
1 Sep 2001	Forego Handicap	Delaware Township	Jerry D. Bailey
8 Sep 2001	Gazelle Handicap	Exogenous	Javier Castellano
8 Sep 2001	Man o' War Stakes	With Anticipation	Pat Day
8 Sep 2001	Woodward Stakes	Lido Palace	Jerry D. Bailey
15 Sep 2001	Ruffian Handicap	canceled	
16 Sep 2001	Futurity Stakes	canceled	
16 Sep 2001	Matron Stakes	canceled	
22 Sep 2001	Vosburgh Stakes	Left Bank	John R. Velazquez
22 Sep 2001	Kentucky Cup Classic	Guided Tour	Larry Melancon
23 Sep 2001	Super Derby XXII	Outofthebox	Lonnie Meche
29 Sep 2001	Yellow Ribbon Stakes	Janet	David Romero Flores
29 Sep 2001	Turf Classic Invitational	Timboroa	Edgar S. Prado
29 Sep 2001	Flower Bowl Invitational	Lailani	Jerry D. Bailey
30 Sep 2001	Oak Leaf Stakes	Tali'sluckybusride	José Valdivia, Jr.
30 Sep 2001	Clement L. Hirsch Memorial Turf Championship	Senure	Alex O. Solis
6 Oct 2001	Ancient Title Breeders' Cup Handicap	Swept Overboard	Eddie J. Delahoussaye
6 Oct 2001	Frizette Stakes	You	Edgar S. Prado
6 Oct 2001	Champagne Stakes	Officer	Victor Espinoza
6 Oct 2001	Beldame Stakes	Exogenous	Javier Castellano
6 Oct 2001	Jockey Club Gold Cup	Aptitude	Jerry D. Bailey
7 Oct 2001	Overbrook Spinster Stakes	Miss Linda	Richard Migliore
13 Oct 2001	Queen Elizabeth II Challenge Cup	Affluent	Eddie J. Delahoussaye
27 Oct 2001	Breeders' Cup Juvenile Fillies	Tempera	David Romero Flores
27 Oct 2001	Breeders' Cup Sprint	Squirtle Squirt	Jerry D. Bailey
27 Oct 2001	Breeders' Cup Juvenile	Johannesburg	Mick Kinane
27 Oct 2001	Breeders' Cup Mile	Val Royal	José Valdivia, Jr.
27 Oct 2001	Breeders' Cup Filly and Mare Turf	Banks Hill	Olivier Peslier
27 Oct 2001	Breeders' Cup Turf*	Fantastic Light	Frankie Dettori
27 Oct 2001	Breeders' Cup Distaff	Unbridled Elaine	Pat Day
27 Oct 2001	Breeders' Cup Classic*	Tiznow	Chris J. McCarron
17 Nov 2001	Frank J. DeFrancis Memorial	Delaware Township	Jerry D. Bailey
24 Nov 2001	Cigar Mile Handicap	Left Bank	John R. Velazquez
25 Nov 2001	Hollywood Derby	Denon	Chris J. McCarron
25 Nov 2001	Matriarch Stakes	Starine	John R. Velazquez
1 Dec 2001	Hollywood Turf Cup	Super Quercus	Alex O. Solis
16 Dec 2001	Hollywood Futurity	Siphonic	Jerry D. Bailey
2 Feb 2002	Charles H. Strub Stakes	Mizzen Mast	Kent J. Desormeaux
9 Feb 2002	Donn Handicap	Mongoose	Edgar S. Prado
16 Feb 2002	Fountain of Youth Stakes	Booklet	Jorge F. Chavez
2 Mar 2002	Santa Anita Handicap	Milwaukee Brew	Kent J. Desormeaux
9 Mar 2002	Santa Anita Oaks	You	Jerry D. Bailey
10 Mar 2002	Louisiana Derby	Repent	Jerry D. Bailey
16 Mar 2002	Florida Derby	Harlan's Holiday	Edgar S. Prado
23 Mar 2002	Lane's End Spiral Stakes	Perfect Drift	Eddie J. Delahoussaye
30 Mar 2002	Gulfstream Park Handicap	Hal's Hope	Roger I. Velez
6 Apr 2002	Ashland Stakes	Take Charge Lady	Tony D'Amico
6 Apr 2002	Santa Anita Derby	Came Home	Chris J. McCarron
6 Apr 2002	Illinois Derby	War Emblem	Larry J. Sterling, Jr.
6 Apr 2002	Oaklawn Handicap	Kudos	Eddie J. Delahoussaye
6 Apr 2002	Apple Blossom Handicap	Azeri	Mike E. Smith
13 Apr 2002	Blue Grass Stakes	Harlan's Holiday	Edgar S. Prado

Major Thoroughbred Race Winners (continued)

United States (continued)

DATE	RACE	WINNER	JOCKEY
13 Apr 2002	Arkansas Derby	Private Emblem	Donnie J. Meche
13 Apr 2002	Wood Memorial Stakes	Buddha	Pat Day
21 Apr 2002	San Juan Capistrano Invitational Handicap	Ringaskiddy	Eddie J. Delahoussaye
3 May 2002	Kentucky Oaks	Farda Amiga	Chris J. McCarron
4 May 2002	Kentucky Derby†	War Emblem	Victor Espinoza
11 May 2002	Lone Star Derby	Wiseman's Ferry	Jorge F. Chávez
18 May 2002	Hawthorne Gold Cup Handicap	Hail the Chief	Jorge F. Chávez
18 May 2002	Preakness Stakes†	War Emblem	Victor Espinoza
27 May 2002	Gamely Breeders' Cup Handicap	Astra	Kent J. Desormeaux
27 May 2002	Metropolitan Mile Handicap	Swept Overboard	Jorge F. Chávez
27 May 2002	Shoemaker Breeders' Cup Mile Stakes	Ladies Din	Patrick Valenzuela
1 Jun 2002	Massachusetts Handicap	Macho Uno	Gary Stevens
7 Jun 2002	Acorn Stakes	You	Jerry D. Bailey
8 Jun 2002	Belmont Stakes†	Sarava	Edgar S. Prado
15 Jun 2002	Charles Whittingham Memorial Handicap	Denon	Garrett K. Gomez
15 Jun 2002	Californian Stakes	Milwaukee Brew	Kent J. Desormeaux
29 Jun 2002	Mother Goose Stakes	Nonsuch Bay	Jerry D. Bailey
6 Jul 2002	Suburban Handicap	Albert the Great	Jorge F. Chávez
6 Jul 2002	United Nations Handicap	With Anticipation	Pat Day
14 Jul 2002	Hollywood Gold Cup	Aptitude	Laffit Pincay, Jr.

Canada

DATE	RACE	WINNER	JOCKEY
22 Jul 2001	Prince of Wales Stakes‡	Win City	Constant Montpellier
11 Aug 2001	Breeders' Stakes‡	Sweetest Thing	Jim McAleney
9 Sep 2001	Atto Mile Stakes	Numerous Times	Patrick Husbands
22 Sep 2001	Mazarine Breeders' Cup Stakes	Lady Shari	Constant Montpellier
30 Sep 2001	Canadian International Stakes*	Mutamam	Richard Hills
23 Jun 2002	Queen's Plate Stakes‡	TJ's Lucky Moon	Steve Bahen

England

DATE	RACE	WINNER	JOCKEY
7 Jul 2001	Coral-Eclipse Stakes	Medicean	Kieren Fallon
12 Jul 2001	Darley July Cup	Mozart	Mick Kinane
28 Jul 2001	King George VI and Queen Elizabeth Diamond Stakes*	Galileo	Mick Kinane
1 Aug 2001	Sussex Stakes	Noverre	Frankie Dettori
21 Aug 2001	Juddmonte International Stakes	Sakhee	Frankie Dettori
23 Aug 2001	Nunthorpe Stakes	Mozart	Mick Kinane
15 Sep 2001	St. Leger	Milan	Mick Kinane
29 Sep 2001	Queen Elizabeth II Stakes	Summoner	Richard Hills
20 Oct 2001	Dubai Champion Stakes	Nayef	Richard Hills
4 May 2002	Two Thousand Guineas	Rock of Gibraltar	Johnny Murtagh
5 May 2002	One Thousand Guineas	Kazzia	Frankie Dettori
7 Jun 2002	Oaks	Kazzia	Frankie Dettori
20 Jun 2002	Ascot Gold Cup	Royal Rebel	Johnny Murtagh

Ireland

DATE	RACE	WINNER	JOCKEY
1 Jul 2001	Irish Derby	Galileo	Mick Kinane
15 Jul 2001	Irish Oaks	Lailani	Frankie Dettori
8 Sep 2001	Irish Champion Stakes*	Fantastic Light	Frankie Dettori
15 Sep 2001	Irish St. Leger	Vinnie Roe	Pat Smullen
25 May 2002	Irish Two Thousand Guineas	Rock of Gibraltar	Mick Kinane
26 May 2002	Irish One Thousand Guineas	Gossamer	Jamie Spencer
30 Jun 2002	Irish Derby		

France

DATE	RACE	WINNER	JOCKEY
1 Jul 2001	Grand Prix de Saint-Cloud	Mirio	Christophe Soumillon
19 Aug 2001	Prix du Haras de Fresnay-le-Buffard Jacques le Marois	Vahorimix	Olivier Peslier
16 Sep 2001	Prix Vermeille	Aquarelliste	Dominique Boeuf
7 Oct 2001	Prix de l'Arc de Triomphe*	Sakhee	Frankie Dettori
7 Oct 2001	Grand Criterium	Rock of Gibraltar	Mick Kinane
28 Oct 2001	Prix Royal-Oak	Vinnie Roe	Pat Smullen
28 Apr 2002	Prix Ganay	Aquarelliste	Dominique Boeuf
12 May 2002	Poule d'Essai des Poulains	Landseer	Mick Kinane

Major Thoroughbred Race Winners (continued)

France (continued)

DATE	RACE	WINNER	JOCKEY
12 May 2002	Poule d'Essai des Pouliches	Zenda	Richard Hughes
2 Jun 2002	Prix du Jockey-Club	Sulamani	Thierry Thulliez
9 Jun 2002	Prix de Diane	Bright Sky	Dominique Boeuf
23 Jun 2002	Grand Prix de Paris		
30 Jun 2002	Grand Prix de Saint-Cloud		

Germany

DATE	RACE	WINNER	JOCKEY
2 Sep 2001	Grosser Preis von Baden*	Morshdi	Philip Robinson
23 Sep 2001	Preis von Europa	Kutub	Frankie Dettori
7 Jul 2002	Deutsches Derby		

Italy

DATE	RACE	WINNER	JOCKEY
21 Oct 2001	Gran Premio del Jockey Club	Kutub	Frankie Dettori
26 May 2002	Derby Italiano	Rakti	Mirco Demuro

Australia

DATE	RACE	WINNER	JOCKEY
27 Oct 2001	Cox Plate*	Northerly	Damien Oliver
6 Nov 2001	Melbourne Cup	Ethereal	Scott Seamer
6 Nov 2001	Caulfield Cup	Ethereal	Scott Seamer

United Arab Emirates

DATE	RACE	WINNER	JOCKEY
23 Mar 2002	Godolphin Mile	Grey Memo	Gary Stevens
23 Mar 2002	UAE Derby	Essence of Dubai	Frankie Dettori
23 Mar 2002	Dubai Sheema Classic	Nayef	Richard Hills
23 Mar 2002	Dubai Golden Shaheen	Caller One	Gary Stevens
23 Mar 2002	Dubai Duty Free	Terre a Terre	Christophe Soumillon
23 Mar 2002	Dubai World Cup*	Street Cry	Jerry D. Bailey

Japan

DATE	RACE	WINNER	JOCKEY
25 Nov 2001	Japan Cup*	Jungle Pocket	Olivier Peslier

Hong Kong

DATE	RACE	WINNER	JOCKEY
16 Dec 2001	Hong Kong Cup*	Agnes Digital	Hirofumi Shii
21 Apr 2002	Queen Elizabeth II Cup*	Eishin Preston	Yuichi Fukunaga

Singapore

DATE	RACE	WINNER	JOCKEY
11 May 2002	International Cup*	Grandera	Frankie Dettori

*World Series race (14 races in 11 countries).   †American Triple Crown race.   ‡Canadian Triple Crown race.

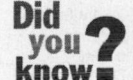 **Did you know?** Frank Hayes was the only deceased jockey to win a horse race. Hayes suffered a heart attack and died while riding in a race in 1923. Nevertheless, his horse, Sweet Kiss, was the first to cross the finish line.

Triple Crown Champions—United States

YEAR	HORSE	YEAR	HORSE	YEAR	HORSE	YEAR	HORSE
1919	Sir Barton	1937	War Admiral	1946	Assault	1977	Seattle Slew
1930	Gallant Fox	1941	Whirlaway	1948	Citation	1978	Affirmed
1935	Omaha	1943	Count Fleet	1973	Secretariat		

The Kentucky Derby

YEAR	HORSE	JOCKEY	YEAR	HORSE	JOCKEY
1875	Aristides	Oliver Lewis	1939	Johnstown	James Stout
1876	Vagrant	Bobby Swim	1940	Gallahadion	Carroll Bierman
1877	Baden-Baden	William Walker	1941	Whirlaway	Eddie Arcaro
1878	Day Star	Jimmy Carter	1942	Shut Out	Wayne D. Wright
1879	Lord Murphy	Charlie Shauer	1943	Count Fleet	John Longden
1880	Fonso	George Garret Lewis	1944	Pensive	Conn McCreary
1881	Hindoo	James McLaughlin	1945	Hoop Jr.	Eddie Arcaro
1882	Apollo	Babe Hurd	1946	Assault	Warren Mehrtens
1883	Leonatus	William Donohue	1947	Jet Pilot	Eric Guerin
1884	Buchanan	Isaac Murphy	1948	Citation	Eddie Arcaro
1885	Joe Cotton	Erskine Henderson	1949	Ponder	Steve Brooks
1886	Ben Ali	Paul Duffy	1950	Middleground	William Boland
1887	Montrose	Isaac Lewis	1951	Count Turf	Conn McCreary
1888	Macbeth II	George Covington	1952	Hill Gail	Eddie Arcaro
1889	Spokane	Thomas Kiley	1953	Dark Star	Henry Moreno
1890	Riley	Isaac Murphy	1954	Determine	Raymond York
1891	Kingman	Isaac Murphy	1955	Swaps	William Shoemaker
1892	Azra	Alonzo Clayton	1956	Needles	David Erb
1893	Lookout	Eddie Kunze	1957	Iron Liege	William Hartack
1894	Chant	Frank Goodale	1958	Tim Tam	Ismael Valenzuela
1895	Halma	James Perkins	1959	Tomy Lee	William Shoemaker
1896	Ben Brush	Willie Simms	1960	Venetian Way	William Hartack
1897	Typhoon II	Fred Garner	1961	Carry Back	John Sellers
1898	Plaudit	Willie Simms	1962	Decidedly	William Hartack
1899	Manuel	Fred Taral	1963	Chateaugay	Braulio Baeza
1900	Lieut. Gibson	Jimmy Boland	1964	Northern Dancer	William Hartack
1901	His Eminence	James Winkfield	1965	Lucky Debonair	William Shoemaker
1902	Alan-a-Dale	James Winkfield	1966	Kauai King	Don Brumfield
1903	Judge Himes	Harold Booker	1967	Proud Clarion	Robert Ussery
1904	Elwood	Frank Prior	1968	Forward Pass	Ismael Valenzuela
1905	Agile	Jack Martin	1969	Majestic Prince	William Hartack
1906	Sir Huon	Roscoe Troxler	1970	Dust Commander	Mike Manganello
1907	Pink Star	Andy Minder	1971	Canonero II	Gustavo Avila
1908	Stone Street	Arthur Pickens	1972	Riva Ridge	Ron Turcotte
1909	Wintergreen	Vincent Powers	1973*	Secretariat	Ron Turcotte
1910	Donau	Fred Herbert	1974	Cannonade	Angel Cordero, Jr.
1911	Meridian	George Archibald	1975	Foolish Pleasure	Jacinto Vasquez
1912	Worth	Carroll Hugh Shilling	1976	Bold Forbes	Angel Cordero, Jr.
1913	Donerail	Roscoe Goose	1977	Seattle Slew	Jean Cruguet
1914	Old Rosebud	John McCabe	1978	Affirmed	Steve Cauthen
1915	Regret	Joe Notter	1979	Spectacular Bid	Ronnie Franklin
1916	George Smith	John Loftus	1980	Genuine Risk	Jacinto Vasquez
1917	Omar Khayyam	Charles Borel	1981	Pleasant Colony	Jorge Velasquez
1918	Exterminator	William Knapp	1982	Gato del Sol	Eddie Delahoussaye
1919	Sir Barton	John Loftus	1983	Sunny's Halo	Eddie Delahoussaye
1920	Paul Jones	Ted Rice	1984	Swale	Laffit Pincay, Jr.
1921	Behave Yourself	Charles Thompson	1985	Spend a Buck	Angel Cordero, Jr.
1922	Morvich	Albert Johnson	1986	Ferdinand	William Shoemaker
1923	Zev	Earl Sande	1987	Alysheba	Chris McCarron
1924	Black Gold	John D. Mooney	1988	Winning Colors	Gary Stevens
1925	Flying Ebony	Earl Sande	1989	Sunday Silence	Patrick Valenzuela
1926	Bubbling Over	Albert Johnson	1990	Unbridled	Craig Perret
1927	Whiskery	Linus McAtee	1991	Strike the Gold	Chris Antley
1928	Reigh Count	Charles Lang	1992	Lil E. Tee	Pat Day
1929	Clyde Van Dusen	Linus McAtee	1993	Sea Hero	Jerry Bailey
1930	Gallant Fox	Earl Sande	1994	Go for Gin	Chris McCarron
1931	Twenty Grand	Charles Kurtsinger	1995	Thunder Gulch	Gary Stevens
1932	Burgoo King	Eugene James	1996	Grindstone	Jerry Bailey
1933	Brokers Tip	Don Meade	1997	Silver Charm	Gary Stevens
1934	Cavalcade	Mack Garner	1998	Real Quiet	Kent Desormeaux
1935	Omaha	William Saunders	1999	Charismatic	Chris Antley
1936	Bold Venture	Ira Hanford	2000	Fusaichi Pegasus	Kent Desormeaux
1937	War Admiral	Charles Kurtsinger	2001	Monarchos	Jorge Chávez
1938	Lawrin	Eddie Arcaro	2002	War Emblem	Victor Espinoza

Fastest time—1 min 59⅖ sec. No other horse has raced the Derby in less than 2 min.

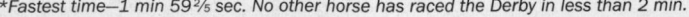

The Preakness Stakes

YEAR	HORSE	JOCKEY	YEAR	HORSE	JOCKEY
1873	Survivor	George Barbee	1939	Challedon	George Seabo
1874	Culpepper	William Donohue	1940	Bimelech	Fred A. Smith
1875	Tom Ochiltree	Lloyd Hughes	1941	Whirlaway	Eddie Arcaro
1876	Shirley	George Barbee	1942	Alsab	Basil James
1877	Cloverbrook	Cyrus Holloway	1943	Count Fleet	John Longden
1878	Duke of Magenta	Cyrus Holloway	1944	Pensive	Conn McCreary
1879	Harold	Lloyd Hughes	1945	Polynesian	Wayne D. Wright
1880	Grenada	Lloyd Hughes	1946	Assault	Warren Mehrtens
1881	Saunterer	T. Costello	1947	Faultless	Doug Dodson
1882	Vanguard	T. Costello	1948	Citation	Eddie Arcaro
1883	Jacobus	George Barbee	1949	Capot	Ted Atkinson
1884	Knight of Ellerslie	S. Fisher	1950	Hill Prince	Eddie Arcaro
1885	Tecumseh	James McLaughlin	1951	Bold	Eddie Arcaro
1886	The Bard	S. Fisher	1952	Blue Man	Conn McCreary
1887	Dunboyne	William Donohue	1953	Native Dancer	Eric Guerin
1888	Refund	F. Littlefield	1954	Hasty Road	Johnny Adams
1889	Buddhist	George Anderson	1955	Nashua	Eddie Arcaro
1890	Montague	W. Martin	1956	Fabius	William Hartack
1894*	Assignee	Fred Taral	1957	Bold Ruler	Eddie Arcaro
1895	Belmar	Fred Taral	1958	Tim Tam	Ismael Valenzuela
1896	Margrave	Henry Griffin	1959	Royal Orbit	William Harmatz
1897	Paul Kauvar	T. Thorpe	1960	Bally Ache	Robert Ussery
1898	Sly Fox	Willie Simms	1961	Carry Back	John Sellers
1899	Half Time	R. Clawson	1962	Greek Money	John L. Rotz
1900	Hindus	H. Spencer	1963	Candy Spots	William Shoemaker
1901	The Parader	Fred Landry	1964	Northern Dancer	William Hartack
1902	Old England	L. Jackson	1965	Tom Rolfe	Ron Turcotte
1903	Flocarline	W. Gannon	1966	Kauai King	Don Brumfield
1904	Bryn Mawr	Eugene Hildebrand	1967	Damascus	William Shoemaker
1905	Cairngorm	W. Davis	1968	Forward Pass	Ismael Valenzuela
1906	Whimsical	Walter Miller	1969	Majestic Prince	William Hartack
1907	Don Enrique	G. Mountain	1970	Personality	Eddie Belmonte
1908	Royal Tourist	Eddie Dugan	1971	Canonero II	Gustavo Avila
1909	Effendi	Willie Doyle	1972	Bee Bee Bee	Eldon Nelson
1910	Layminster	R. Estep	1973	Secretariat	Ron Turcotte
1911	Watervale	Eddie Dugan	1974	Little Current	Miguel Rivera
1912	Colonel Holloway	C. Turner	1975	Master Derby	Darrel McHargue
1913	Buskin	James Butwell	1976	Elocutionist	John Lively
1914	Holiday	Andy Schuttinger	1977	Seattle Slew	Jean Cruguet
1915	Rhine Maiden	Douglas Hoffman	1978	Affirmed	Steve Cauthen
1916	Damrosch	Linus McAtee	1979	Spectacular Bid	Ron Franklin
1917	Kalitan	E. Haynes	1980	Codex	Angel Cordero, Jr.
1918†	War Cloud	John Loftus	1981	Pleasant Colony	Jorge Velasquez
	Jack Hare, Jr.	Charles Peak	1982	Aloma's Ruler	Jack Kaenel
1919	Sir Barton	John Loftus	1983	Deputed Testamony	Donald Miller
1920	Man o' War	Clarence Kummer	1984	Gate Dancer	Angel Cordero, Jr.
1921	Broomspun	Frank Coltiletti	1985‡	Tank's Prospect	Pat Day
1922	Pillory	L. Morris	1986	Snow Chief	Alex Solis
1923	Vigil	Benny Marinelli	1987	Alysheba	Chris McCarron
1924	Nellie Morse	John Merimee	1988	Risen Star	Eddie Delahoussaye
1925	Coventry	Clarence Kummer	1989	Sunday Silence	Patrick Valenzuela
1926	Display	John Maiben	1990	Summer Squall	Pat Day
1927	Bostonian	A. Abel	1991	Hansel	Jerry Bailey
1928	Victorian	Raymond Workman	1992	Pine Bluff	Chris McCarron
1929	Dr. Freeland	Louis Schaefer	1993	Prairie Bayou	Mike Smith
1930	Gallant Fox	Earl Sande	1994	Tabasco Cat	Pat Day
1931	Mate	George Ellis	1995	Timber Country	Pat Day
1932	Burgoo King	Eugene James	1996	Louis Quatorze	Pat Day
1933	Head Play	Charles Kurtsinger	1997	Silver Charm	Gary Stevens
1934	High Quest	Robert Jones	1998	Real Quiet	Kent Desormeaux
1935	Omaha	Willie Saunders	1999	Charismatic	Chris Antley
1936	Bold Venture	George Woolf	2000	Red Bullet	Jerry Bailey
1937	War Admiral	Charles Kurtsinger	2001	Point Given	Gary Stevens
1938	Dauber	Maurice Peters	2002	War Emblem	Victor Espinoza

*No competition 1891–93.   †Run in two divisions in 1918 because of the large number of starters.
‡Fastest time—1 min 53⅖ sec.

The Belmont Stakes

YEAR	HORSE	JOCKEY	YEAR	HORSE	JOCKEY
1867	Ruthless	Gilbert Patrick	1936	Granville	James Stout
1868	General Duke	Bobby Swim	1937	War Admiral	Charles Kurtsinger
1869	Fenian	Charley Miller	1938	Pasteurized	James Stout
1870	Kingfisher	Edward Brown	1939	Johnstown	James Stout
1871	Harry Bassett	W. Miller	1940	Bimelech	Fred A. Smith
1872	Joe Daniels	James Rowe	1941	Whirlaway	Eddie Arcaro
1873	Springbok	James Rowe	1942	Shut Out	Eddie Arcaro
1874	Saxon	George Barbee	1943	Count Fleet	John Longden
1875	Calvin	Bobby Swim	1944	Bounding Home	Gayle L. Smith
1876	Algerine	Billy Donohue	1945	Pavot	Eddie Arcaro
1877	Cloverbrook	Cyrus Holloway	1946	Assault	Warren Mehrtens
1878	Duke of Magenta	Lloyd Hughes	1947	Phalanx	Ruperto Donoso
1879	Spendthrift	George Evans	1948	Citation	Eddie Arcaro
1880	Grenada	Lloyd Hughes	1949	Capot	Ted Atkinson
1881	Saunterer	T. Costello	1950	Middleground	William Boland
1882	Forester	James McLaughlin	1951	Counterpoint	David Gorman
1883	George Kinney	James McLaughlin	1952	One Count	Eddie Arcaro
1884	Panique	James McLaughlin	1953	Native Dancer	Eric Guerin
1885	Tyrant	Paul Duffy	1954	High Gun	Eric Guerin
1886	Inspector B	James McLaughlin	1955	Nashua	Eddie Arcaro
1887	Hanover	James McLaughlin	1956	Needles	David Erb
1888	Sir Dixon	James McLaughlin	1957	Gallant Man	William Shoemaker
1889	Eric	W. Hayward	1958	Cavan	Pete Anderson
1890	Burlington	Shelby Barnes	1959	Sword Dancer	William Shoemaker
1891	Foxford	Edward Garrison	1960	Celtic Ash	William Hartack
1892	Patron	W. Hayward	1961	Sherluck	Braulio Baeza
1893	Comanche	Willie Simms	1962	Jaipur	William Shoemaker
1894	Henry of Navarre	Willie Simms	1963	Chateaugay	Braulio Baeza
1895	Belmar	Fred Taral	1964	Quadrangle	Manuel Ycaza
1896	Hastings	Henry Griffin	1965	Hail to All	John Sellers
1897	Scottish Chieftain	J. Scherrer	1966	Amberoid	William Boland
1898	Bowling Brook	F. Littlefield	1967	Damascus	William Shoemaker
1899	Jean Bereaud	R. Clawson	1968	Stage Door Johnny	Heliodoro Gustines
1900	Ildrim	Nash Turner	1969	Arts and Letters	Braulio Baeza
1901	Commando	H. Spencer	1970	High Echelon	John Rotz
1902	Masterman	John Bullman	1971	Pass Catcher	Walter Blum
1903	Africander	John Bullman	1972	Riva Ridge	Ron Turcotte
1904	Delhi	George Odom	1973†	Secretariat	Ron Turcotte
1905	Tanya	Eugene Hildebrand	1974	Little Current	Miguel Rivera
1906	Burgomaster	Lucien Lyne	1975	Avatar	William Shoemaker
1907	Peter Pan	G. Mountain	1976	Bold Forbes	Angel Cordero, Jr.
1908	Colin	Joe Notter	1977	Seattle Slew	Jean Cruguet
1909	Joe Madden	Eddie Dugan	1978	Affirmed	Steve Cauthen
1910	Sweep	James Butwell	1979	Coastal	Ruben Hernandez
1913*	Prince Eugene	Roscoe Troxler	1980	Temperence Hill	Eddie Maple
1914	Luke McLuke	Merritt Buxton	1981	Summing	George Martens
1915	The Finn	George Byrne	1982	Conquistador Cielo	Laffit Pincay, Jr.
1916	Friar Rock	E. Haynes	1983	Caveat	Laffit Pincay, Jr.
1917	Hourless	James Butwell	1984	Swale	Laffit Pincay, Jr.
1918	Johren	Frank Robinson	1985	Creme Fraiche	Eddie Maple
1919	Sir Barton	John Loftus	1986	Danzig Connection	Chris McCarron
1920	Man o' War	Clarence Kummer	1987	Bet Twice	Craig Perret
1921	Grey Lag	Earl Sande	1988	Risen Star	Eddie Delahoussaye
1922	Pillory	C.H. Miller	1989	Easy Goer	Pat Day
1923	Zev	Earl Sande	1990	Go and Go	Michael Kinane
1924	Mad Play	Earl Sande	1991	Hansel	Jerry Bailey
1925	American Flag	Albert Johnson	1992	A.P. Indy	Eddie Delahoussaye
1926	Crusader	Albert Johnson	1993	Colonial Affair	Julie Krone
1927	Chance Shot	Earl Sande	1994	Tabasco Cat	Pat Day
1928	Vito	Clarence Kummer	1995	Thunder Gulch	Gary Stevens
1929	Blue Larkspur	Mack Garner	1996	Editor's Note	Rene Douglas
1930	Gallant Fox	Earl Sande	1997	Touch Gold	Chris McCarron
1931	Twenty Grand	Charles Kurtsinger	1998	Victory Gallop	Gary Stevens
1932	Faireno	Tom Malley	1999	Lemon Drop Kid	Jose Santos
1933	Hurryoff	Mack Garner	2000	Commendable	Pat Day
1934	Peace Chance	Wayne D. Wright	2001	Point Given	Gary Stevens
1935	Omaha	Willie Saunders	2002	Sarava	Edgar S. Prado

*No competition 1911–12.   †Fastest time—2 min 24 sec.

Horse of the Year

A Horse of the Year was selected by the *Daily Racing Form* from 1936 to 1970 and independently by the Thoroughbred Racing Association beginning in 1950. From 1971 these two organizations, plus the Na- tional Turf Writers Association, founded the Eclipse Awards, of which the Horse of the Year is the top among the 22 prizes.

YEAR	HORSE	YEAR	HORSE	YEAR	HORSE	YEAR	HORSE
1936	Granville	1953	Tom Fool	1970	Fort Marcy;*	1987	Ferdinand
1937	War Admiral	1954	Native Dancer		Personality†	1988	Alysheba
1938	Seabiscuit	1955	Nashua	1971	Ack Ack	1989	Sunday Silence
1939	Challedon	1956	Swaps	1972	Secretariat	1990	Criminal Type
1940	Challedon	1957	Bold Ruler;*	1973	Secretariat	1991	Black Tie Affair
1941	Whirlaway		Dedicate†	1974	Forego	1992	A.P. Indy
1942	Whirlaway	1958	Round Table	1975	Forego	1993	Kotashaan
1943	Count Fleet	1959	Sword Dancer	1976	Forego	1994	Holy Bull
1944	Twilight Tear	1960	Kelso	1977	Seattle Slew	1995	Cigar
1945	Busher	1961	Kelso	1978	Affirmed	1996	Cigar
1946	Assault	1962	Kelso	1979	Affirmed	1997	Favorite Trick
1947	Armed	1963	Kelso	1980	Spectacular Bid	1998	Skip Away
1948	Citation	1964	Kelso	1981	John Henry	1999	Charismatic
1949	Capot;* Coal-	1965	Roman Brother;*	1982	Conquistador	2000	Tiznow
	town†		Moccasin†		Cielo	2001	Point Given
1950	Hill Prince	1966	Buckpasser	1983	All Along		
1951	Counterpoint	1967	Damascus	1984	John Henry		
1952	One Count;* Na-	1968	Dr. Fager	1985	Spend a Buck		
	tive Dancer†	1969	Arts and Letters	1986	Lady's Secret		

Daily Racing Form. †Throughbred Racing Association.

2,000 Guineas

The 2,000 Guineas has been run since 1809. The table shows the winners for the past 20 years.

YEAR	HORSE	JOCKEY	YEAR	HORSE	JOCKEY
1983	Lomond	Pat Eddery	1993	Zafonic	Pat Eddery
1984	El Gran Señor	Pat Eddery	1994	Mister Baileys	Jason Weaver
1985	Shadeed	Lester Piggott	1995	Pennekamp	Thierry Jarnet
1986	Dancing Brave	Greville Starkey	1996	Mark of Esteem	Frankie Dettori
1987	Don't Forget Me	Willie Carson	1997	Entrepreneur	Michael Kinane
1988	Doyoun	Walter R. Swinburn	1998	King of Kings	Michael Kinane
1989	Nashwan	Willie Carson	1999	Island Sands	Frankie Dettori
1990	Tirol	Michael Kinane	2000	King's Best	Kieren Fallon
1991	Mystiko	Michael Roberts	2001	Golan	Kieren Fallon
1992	Rodrigo de Triano	Lester Piggott	2002	Rock of Gibraltar	Johnny Murtagh

The Derby

The Derby has been run since 1780. The table shows the winners for the past 20 years.

YEAR	HORSE	JOCKEY	YEAR	HORSE	JOCKEY
1983	Teenoso	Lester Piggott	1993	Commander in Chief	Michael Kinane
1984*	Secreto	Christy Roche	1994	Erhaab	Willie Carson
1985	Slip Anchor	Steve Cauthen	1995	Lammtarra	Walter R. Swinburn
1986	Shahrastani	Walter R. Swinburn	1996	Shaamit	Michael Hills
1987	Reference Point	Steve Cauthen	1997	Benny the Dip	Willie Ryan
1988	Kahyasi	Ray Cochrane	1998	High Rise	Olivier Peslier
1989	Nashwan	Willie Carson	1999	Oath	Kieren Fallon
1990	Quest for Fame	Pat Eddery	2000	Sinndar	Johnny Murtaugh
1991	Generous	Alan Munro	2001	Galileo	Michael Kinane
1992	Dr Devious	John Reid	2002	High Chaparral	Johnny Murtagh

Record time—2 min 12 sec.

The St. Leger

The St. Leger has been run since 1776. The table shows the winners for the past 20 years.

YEAR	HORSE	JOCKEY	YEAR	HORSE	JOCKEY
1982	Touching Wood	Peter Cook	1993	Bob's Return	Philip Robinson
1983	Sun Princess	Willie Carson	1994	Moonax	Pat Eddery
1984	Comanche Run	Lester Piggott	1995	Classic Cliché	Frankie Dettori
1985	Oh So Sharp	Steve Cauthen	1996	Shantou	Frankie Dettori
1986	Moon Madness	Pat Eddery	1997	Silver Patriarch	Pat Eddery
1987	Reference Point	Steve Cauthen	1998	Nedawi	John Reid
1988	Minster Son	Willie Carson	1999	Mutafaweq	Richard Hills
1989	Michelozzo	Steve Cauthen	2000	Millenary	Richard Quinn
1990	Snurge	Richard Quinn	2001	Milan	Michael Kinane
1991	Toulon	Pat Eddery	2002	*scheduled to be held 14 Sep 2002,*	
1992	User Friendly	George Duffield		*Doncaster, England*	

Triple Crown Champions—British

YEAR	WINNER	YEAR	WINNER	YEAR	WINNER	YEAR	WINNER
1853	West Australian	1891	Common	1900	Diamond Jubilee	1918	Gainsborough
1865	Gladiateur	1893	Isinglass	1903	Rock Sand	1935	Bahram
1866	Lord Lyon	1897	Galtee More	1915	Pommern	1970	Nijinsky
1886	Ormonde	1899	Flying Fox	1917	Gay Crusader		

Melbourne Cup

The Melbourne Cup race has been run since 1861. The table shows the winners for the past 20 years.

YEAR	HORSE	JOCKEY	YEAR	HORSE	JOCKEY
1982	Gurner's Lane	Mick Dittman	1993	Vintage Crop	Michael Kinane
1983	Kiwi	Jim Cassidy	1994	Jeune	Wayne Harris
1984	Black Knight	Peter Cook	1995	Doriemus	Damien Oliver
1985	What a Nuisance	Pat Hyland	1996	Saintly	Darren Beadman
1986	At Talaq	Michael Clarke	1997	Might and Power	Jim Cassidy
1987	Kensei	Larry Olsen	1998	Jezabeel	Chris Munce
1988	Empire Rose	Tony Allan	1999	Rogan Josh	John Marshall
1989	Tawrrific	Shane Dye	2000	Brew	Kerrin McEvoy
1990	Kingston Rule	Darren Beadman	2001	Ethereal	Scott Seamer
1991	Let's Elope	Steven King	2002	*scheduled to be held 5 Nov 2002,*	
1992	Subzero	Greg Hall		*Melbourne, Australia*	

The Hambletonian Trot

YEAR	HORSE	DRIVER	YEAR	HORSE	DRIVER
1926	Guy McKinney	Nat Ray	1951	Mainliner	Guy Crippen
1927	Iosola's Worthy	Marvin Childs	1952	Sharp Note	Bion Shively
1928	Spencer	William H. Leese	1953	Helicopter	Harry Harvey
1929	Walter Dear	Walter Cox	1954	Newport Dream	Adelbert Cameron
1930	Hanover's Bertha	Thomas Berry	1955	Scott Frost	Joseph O'Brien
1931	Calumet Butler	Richard D. McMahon	1956	The Intruder	Ned Bower
1932	The Marchioness	William Caton	1957	Hickory Smoke	John Simpson, Sr.
1933	Mary Reynolds	Ben White	1958	Emily's Pride	Flave Nipe
1934	Lord Jim	Hugh M. Parshall	1959	Diller Hanover	Frank Ervin
1935	Greyhound	Scepter F. Palin	1960	Blaze Hanover	Joseph O'Brien
1936	Rosalind	Ben White	1961	Harlan Dean	James Arthur
1937	Shirley Hanover	Henry Thomas	1962	A.C.'s Viking	Sanders Russell
1938	McLin Hanover	Henry Thomas	1963	Speedy Scot	Ralph Baldwin
1939	Peter Astra	Hugh M. Parshall	1964	Ayres	John Simpson, Sr.
1940	Spencer Scott	Fred Egan	1965	Egyptian Candor	Adelbert Cameron
1941	Bill Gallon	Lee Smith	1966	Kerry Way	Frank Ervin
1942	The Ambassador	Ben White	1967	Speedy Streak	Adelbert Cameron
1943	Volo Song	Ben White	1968	Nevele Pride	Stanley Dancer
1944	Yankee Maid	Henry Thomas	1969	Lindy's Pride	Howard Beissinger
1945	Titan Hanover	Harry Pownall, Sr.	1970	Timothy T.	John Simpson, Sr.
1946	Chestertown	Thomas Berry	1971	Speedy Crown	Howard Beissinger
1947	Hoot Mon	Scepter F. Palin	1972	Super Bowl	Stanley Dancer
1948	Demon Hanover	Harrison Hoyt	1973	Flirth	Ralph Baldwin
1949	Miss Tilly	Fred Egan	1974	Christopher T.	William Haughton
1950	Lusty Song	Delvin Miller	1975	Bonefish	Stanley Dancer

The Hambletonian Trot (continued)

YEAR	HORSE	DRIVER	YEAR	HORSE	DRIVER
1976	Steve Lobell	William Haughton	1990	Harmonious	John Campbell
1977	Green Speed	William Haughton	1991	Giant Victory	Jack Moiseyev
1978	Speedy Somolli	Howard Beissinger	1992	Alf Palema	Mickey McNichol
1979	Legend Hanover	George Sholty	1993	American Winner	Ron Pierce
1980	Burgomeister	William Haughton	1994	Victory Dream	Michel Lachance
1981	Shiaway St. Pat	Ray Remmen	1995	Tagliabue	John Campbell
1982	Speed Bowl	Tom Haughton	1996	Continentalvictory	Michel Lachance
1983	Duenna	Stanley Dancer	1997	Malabar Man	Malvern Burroughs
1984	Historic Freight	Ben Webster	1998	Muscles Yankee	John Campbell
1985	Prakas	William O'Donnell	1999	Self Possessed	Michel Lachance
1986	Nuclear Kosmos	Ulf Thoresen	2000	Yankee Paco	Trevor Ritchie
1987	Mack Lobell	John Campbell	2001	Scarlet Knight	Stefan Melander
1988	Armbro Goal	John Campbell	2002	Chip Chip Hooray	Eric Ledford
1989*	Park Avenue Joe	Ronald Waples			
	Probe	William Fahy			

*Tied.

The Dubai World Cup

YEAR	HORSE	JOCKEY	YEAR	HORSE	JOCKEY
1996	Cigar	Jerry Bailey	2000	Dubai Millennium	Lanfranco Dotorri
1997	Singspiel	Jerry Bailey	2001	Captain Steve	Jerry Bailey
1998	Silver Charm	Gary Stevens	2002	Street Cry	Jerry Bailey
1999	Almutawakel	Richard Hills	2003	scheduled to be held in March, Dubai	

Ice Hockey

The **National Hockey League** (NHL), which was organized in Canada in 1917 with five professional teams, welcomed the first US team, the Boston Bruins, in 1924. Since 1926 the symbol of supremacy in professional hockey has been the **Stanley Cup**, which is awarded to the winner of a play-off that concludes the season of the National Hockey League. The Stanley Cup was presented to amateur champions from 1893 to 1925. The **World Hockey Champi-**onships, contested by national teams and sponsored by the **International Ice Hockey Federation** (IIHF; founded 1908), has been held since 1930 for men and 1990 for women.

Related Web sites: National Hockey League: <www.nhl.com>; International Ice Hockey Federation: <www.iihf.com>

World Hockey Championship—Men

YEAR	WINNER	YEAR	WINNER	YEAR	WINNER	YEAR	WINNER
1930	Canada	1954	USSR	1972†	Czechoslovakia	1990	Sweden
1931	Canada	1955	Canada	1973	USSR	1991	Sweden
1932*	Canada	1956*	USSR	1974	USSR	1992	Sweden
1933	United States	1957	Sweden	1975	USSR	1993	Russia
1934	Canada	1958	Canada	1976	Czechoslovakia	1994	Canada
1935	Canada	1959	Canada	1977	Czechoslovakia	1995	Finland
1936*	Great Britain	1960*	United States	1978	USSR	1996	Czech Republic
1937	Canada	1961	Canada	1979	USSR	1997	Canada
1938	Canada	1962	Sweden	1980*	United States	1998	Sweden
1939	Canada	1963	USSR	1981	USSR	1999	Czech Republic
1940–46	not held	1964*	USSR	1982	USSR	2000	Czech Republic
1947	Czechoslovakia	1965	USSR	1983	USSR	2001	Czech Republic
1948*	Canada	1966	USSR	1984*	USSR	2002	Slovakia
1949	Czechoslovakia	1967	USSR	1985	Czechoslovakia		
1950	Canada	1968*	USSR	1986	USSR		
1951	Canada	1969	USSR	1987	Sweden		
1952*	Canada	1970	USSR	1988	USSR		
1953	Sweden	1971	USSR	1989	USSR		

*Olympic champions, recognized as world champions (for earlier Olympics, see Olympic Games).
†In 1972 a separate world championship was held for the first time.

World Hockey Championship—Women

YEAR	WINNER	YEAR	WINNER	YEAR	WINNER
1990	Canada	1998*	United States	2002*	Canada
1992	Canada	1999	Canada	2003	*scheduled to be held 1–7 Apr 2003, Beijing*
1994	Canada	2000	Canada		
1997	Canada	2001	Canada		

Olympic champion; separate world championships have not been held in Olympic years. Olympic gold medalists are sometimes considered world champions.

National Hockey League (NHL) Final Standings, 2002

EASTERN CONFERENCE

Northeast Division	W	L	T	OTL*	Atlantic Division	W	L	T	OTL*	Southeast Division	W	L	T	OTL*
†Boston Bruins	43	24	6	9	†Philadelphia Flyers	42	27	10	3	†Carolina Hurricanes	35	26	16	5
†Toronto Maple Leafs	43	25	10	4	†New York Islanders	42	28	8	4	Washington Capitals	36	33	11	2
†Ottawa Senators	39	27	9	7	†New Jersey Devils	41	28	9	4	Tampa Bay Lightning	27	40	11	4
†Montreal Canadiens	36	31	12	3	New York Rangers	36	38	4	4	Florida Panthers	22	44	10	6
Buffalo Sabres	35	35	11	1	Pittsburgh Penguins	28	41	8	5	Atlanta Thrashers	19	47	11	5

WESTERN CONFERENCE

Central Division	W	L	T	OTL*	Northwest Division	W	L	T	OTL*	Pacific Division	W	L	T	OTL*
†Detroit Red Wings	51	17	10	4	†Colorado Avalanche	45	28	8	1	†San Jose Sharks	44	27	8	3
†St. Louis Blues	43	27	8	4	†Vancouver Canucks	42	30	7	3	†Los Angeles Kings	40	27	11	4
†Chicago Blackhawks	41	27	13	1	Edmonton Oilers	38	28	12	4	†Phoenix Coyotes	40	27	9	6
Nashville Predators	28	41	13	0	Calgary Flames	32	35	12	3	Dallas Stars	36	28	13	5
Columbus Blue Jackets	22	47	8	5	Minnesota Wild	26	35	12	9	Anaheim Mighty Ducks	29	42	8	3

*Overtime losses, worth one point.   †Qualified for play-offs.

The Stanley Cup

SEASON	WINNER	RUNNER-UP	GAMES
1892–93	Montreal Amateur Athletic Association	*no challengers*	
1893–94	Montreal Amateur Athletic Association	Ottawa Generals	2–0
1894–95	Montreal Victorias	*no challengers*	
1895–96	Winnipeg Victorias (Feb.), Montreal Victorias (Dec.)	Montreal Victorias (Feb.), Winnipeg Victorias (Dec.)	1–0, 1–0
1896–97	Montreal Victorias	Ottawa Capitals	1–0
1897–98	Montreal Victorias	*no challengers*	
1898–99	Montreal Victorias (Feb.), Montreal Shamrocks (March)	Winnipeg Victorias (Feb.), Queen's University (March)	2–0, 1–0
1899–1900	Montreal Shamrocks	Winnipeg Victorias, Halifax Crescents	2–1, 2–0
1900–01	Winnipeg Victorias	Montreal Shamrocks	2–0
1901–02	Winnipeg Victorias (Jan.), Montreal Amateur Athletic Association (March)	Toronto Wellingtons (Jan.), Winnipeg Victorias (March)	2–0, 2–1
1902–03	Montreal Amateur Athletic Association (Feb.), Ottawa Silver Seven (March)	Winnipeg Victorias (Feb.), Montreal Victorias (March), Rat Portage Thistles (March)	2–1, 1–0, 2–0
1903–04	Ottawa Silver Seven	Winnipeg Rowing Club, Toronto Marlboros, Montreal Wanderers, Brandon Wheat Kings	2–1, 2–0, tie, 2–0
1904–05	Ottawa Silver Seven	Dawson City Nuggets, Rat Portage Thistles	2–0, 2–1

The Stanley Cup (continued)

SEASON	WINNER	RUNNER-UP	GAMES
1905–06	Ottawa Silver Seven (Feb.), Montreal Wanderers (March, Dec.)	Queen's University (Feb.), Smiths Falls (Feb.), Ottawa Silver Seven (March), New Glasgow Cubs (Dec.)	2–0, 2–0, 1–1, 2–0
1906–07	Kenora Thistles (Jan.), Montreal Wanderers (March)	Montreal Wanderers (Jan.), Kenora Thistles (March)	2–0, 1–1
1907–08	Montreal Wanderers	Ottawa Victorias, Winnipeg Maple Leafs, Toronto Trolley Leaguers, Edmonton Eskimos	2–0, 2–0, 1–0, 1–1
1908–09	Ottawa Senators	no challengers	
1909–10	Montreal Wanderers, Ottawa Senators	Berlin Union Jacks, Edmonton Eskimos, Galt	1–0, 2–0, 2–0
1910–11	Ottawa Senators	Port Arthur Bearcats, Galt	1–0, 1–0
1911–12	Quebec Bulldogs	Moncton Victories	2–0
1912–13*	Quebec Bulldogs	Sydney Miners	2–0
1913–14	Toronto Blueshirts	Victoria Cougars, Montreal Canadiens	3–0, 1–1
1914–15	Vancouver Millionaires	Ottawa Senators	3–0
1915–16	Montreal Canadiens	Portland Rosebuds	3–2
1916–17	Seattle Metropolitans	Montreal Canadiens	3–1
1917–18	Toronto Arenas	Vancouver Millionaires	3–2
1918–19	no decision†		
1919–20	Ottawa Senators	Seattle Metropolitans	3–2
1920–21	Ottawa Senators	Vancouver Millionaires	3–2
1921–22	Toronto St. Pats	Vancouver Millionaires	3–2
1922–23	Ottawa Senators	Edmonton Eskimos, Vancouver Maroons	2–0, 3–1
1923–24	Montreal Canadiens	Calgary Tigers, Vancouver Maroons	2–0, 2–0
1924–25	Victoria Cougars	Montreal Canadiens	3–1
1925–26	Montreal Maroons	Victoria Cougars	3–1
1926–27	Ottawa Senators	Boston Bruins	2–0
1927–28	New York Rangers	Montreal Maroons	3–2
1928–29	Boston Bruins	New York Rangers	2–0
1929–30	Montreal Canadiens	Boston Bruins	2–0
1930–31	Montreal Canadiens	Chicago Black Hawks	3–2
1931–32	Toronto Maple Leafs	New York Rangers	3–0
1932–33	New York Rangers	Toronto Maple Leafs	3–1
1933–34	Chicago Black Hawks	Detroit Red Wings	3–1
1934–35	Montreal Maroons	Toronto Maple Leafs	3–0
1935–36	Detroit Red Wings	Toronto Maple Leafs	3–1
1936–37	Detroit Red Wings	New York Rangers	3–2
1937–38	Chicago Black Hawks	Toronto Maple Leafs	3–1
1938–39	Boston Bruins	Toronto Maple Leafs	4–1
1939–40	New York Rangers	Toronto Maple Leafs	4–2
1940–41	Boston Bruins	Detroit Red Wings	4–0
1941–42	Toronto Maple Leafs	Detroit Red Wings	4–3
1942–43	Detroit Red Wings	Boston Bruins	4–0
1943–44	Montreal Canadiens	Chicago Black Hawks	4–0
1944–45	Toronto Maple Leafs	Detroit Red Wings	4–3
1945–46	Montreal Canadiens	Boston Bruins	4–1
1946–47	Toronto Maple Leafs	Montreal Canadiens	4–2
1947–48	Toronto Maple Leafs	Detroit Red Wings	4–0
1948–49	Toronto Maple Leafs	Detroit Red Wings	4–0
1949–50	Detroit Red Wings	New York Rangers	4–3
1950–51	Toronto Maple Leafs	Montreal Canadiens	4–1
1951–52	Detroit Red Wings	Montreal Canadiens	4–0
1952–53	Montreal Canadiens	Boston Bruins	4–1
1953–54	Detroit Red Wings	Montreal Canadiens	4–3
1954–55	Detroit Red Wings	Montreal Canadiens	4–3
1955–56	Montreal Canadiens	Detroit Red Wings	4–1
1956–57	Montreal Canadiens	Boston Bruins	4–1
1957–58	Montreal Canadiens	Boston Bruins	4–2
1958–59	Montreal Canadiens	Toronto Maple Leafs	4–1
1959–60	Montreal Canadiens	Toronto Maple Leafs	4–0
1960–61	Chicago Black Hawks	Detroit Red Wings	4–2
1961–62	Toronto Maple Leafs	Chicago Black Hawks	4–2
1962–63	Toronto Maple Leafs	Detroit Red Wings	4–1
1963–64	Toronto Maple Leafs	Detroit Red Wings	4–3
1964–65	Montreal Canadiens	Chicago Black Hawks	4–3
1965–66	Montreal Canadiens	Detroit Red Wings	4–2

The Stanley Cup (continued)

SEASON	WINNER	RUNNER-UP	GAMES
1966–67	Toronto Maple Leafs	Montreal Canadiens	4–2
1967–68	Montreal Canadiens	St. Louis Blues	4–0
1968–69	Montreal Canadiens	St. Louis Blues	4–0
1969–70	Boston Bruins	St. Louis Blues	4–0
1970–71	Montreal Canadiens	Chicago Black Hawks	4–3
1971–72	Boston Bruins	New York Rangers	4–2
1972–73	Montreal Canadiens	Chicago Black Hawks	4–2
1973–74	Philadelphia Flyers	Boston Bruins	4–2
1974–75	Philadelphia Flyers	Buffalo Sabres	4–2
1975–76	Montreal Canadiens	Philadelphia Flyers	4–0
1976–77	Montreal Canadiens	Boston Bruins	4–0
1977–78	Montreal Canadiens	Boston Bruins	4–2
1978–79	Montreal Canadiens	New York Rangers	4–1
1979–80	New York Islanders	Philadelphia Flyers	4–2
1980–81	New York Islanders	Minnesota North Stars	4–1
1981–82	New York Islanders	Vancouver Canucks	4–0
1982–83	New York Islanders	Edmonton Oilers	4–0
1983–84	Edmonton Oilers	New York Islanders	4–1
1984–85	Edmonton Oilers	Philadelphia Flyers	4–1
1985–86	Montreal Canadiens	Calgary Flames	4–1
1986–87	Edmonton Oilers	Philadelphia Flyers	4–3
1987–88	Edmonton Oilers	Boston Bruins	4–0
1988–89	Calgary Flames	Montreal Canadiens	4–2
1989–90	Edmonton Oilers	Boston Bruins	4–1
1990–91	Pittsburgh Penguins	Minnesota North Stars	4–2
1991–92	Pittsburgh Penguins	Chicago Black Hawks	4–0
1992–93	Montreal Canadiens	Los Angeles Kings	4–1
1993–94	New York Rangers	Vancouver Canucks	4–3
1994–95	New Jersey Devils	Detroit Red Wings	4–0
1995–96	Colorado Avalanche	Florida Panthers	4–0
1996–97	Detroit Red Wings	Philadelphia Flyers	4–0
1997–98	Detroit Red Wings	Washington Capitals	4–0
1998–99	Dallas Stars	Buffalo Sabres	4–2
1999–2000	New Jersey Devils	Dallas Stars	4–2
2000–01	Colorado Avalanche	New Jersey Devils	4–3
2001–02	Detroit Red Wings	Carolina Hurricanes	4–1
2002–03	*will be held in May or June 2003*		

*Though Victoria defeated Quebec in challenge games, Victoria's win was not officially recognized.
†Series called because of flu epidemic.

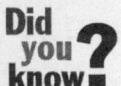 **Did you know?** The standard hockey puck is three inches in diameter and one inch thick. It is made of hard, vulcanized rubber and frozen before games to minimize bounce.

Ice Skating

The world governing body for ice skating, the **International Skating Union** (ISU; founded 1892), held the first world **figure skating competition** in 1896. Women's figure skating was not a separate event until 1906, and pairs championships were first held in 1908. Until 1991, individual competitors were judged on a set of **compulsory figures** as well as programs of **freestyle** moves. In 1991 the compulsory figures portion of the competition was eliminated, and judging was based on a short technical program and a long freestyle program. **Ice dancing**, officially introduced in 1950, is based on compulsory and freestyle movements—in this case, dances.

In contrast to figure skating and ice dancing, **speed skating** involves only two factors—speed and endurance. **Men** compete over distances of 500 m, 1,000 m, 1,500 m, 5,000 m, and 10,000 m. **Women**, who entered the sport several decades after men, compete over 500 m, 1,000 m, 1,500 m, 3,000 m, and 5,000 m. **World speed-skating sprint** championships for both men and women were inaugurated in 1972. **Short-track speed skating**—very different from distance skating in strategy and skill—is held indoors over distances of 500 m, 1,000 m, 1,500 m, and 3,000 m. The skater having the best combined results is the overall winner. Championships were held annually from 1978 to 1980 before being recognized by the ISU in 1981.

International Skating Union Web site: <www.isu.org>

World Figure Skating Championship—Men

YEAR	WINNER	YEAR	WINNER	YEAR	WINNER
1896	Gilbert Fuchs (GER)	1935	Karl Schäfer (AUT)	1974	Jan Hoffmann (GDR)
1897	Gustav Hügel (AUT)	1936	Karl Schäfer (AUT)	1975	Sergey Volkov (URS)
1898	Henning Grenander	1937	Felix Kaspar (AUT)	1976	John Curry (GBR)
	(SWE)	1938	Felix Kaspar (AUT)	1977	Vladimir Kovalev (URS)
1899	Gustav Hügel (AUT)	1939	Graham Sharp (GBR)	1978	Charles Tickner (USA)
1900	Gustav Hügel (AUT)	1940–46 not held		1979	Vladimir Kovalev (URS)
1901	Ulrich Salchow (SWE)	1947	Hans Gerschwiler (SUI)	1980	Jan Hoffmann (GDR)
1902	Ulrich Salchow (SWE)	1948	Richard Button (USA)	1981	Scott Hamilton (USA)
1903	Ulrich Salchow (SWE)	1949	Richard Button (USA)	1982	Scott Hamilton (USA)
1904	Ulrich Salchow (SWE)	1950	Richard Button (USA)	1983	Scott Hamilton (USA)
1905	Ulrich Salchow (SWE)	1951	Richard Button (USA)	1984	Scott Hamilton (USA)
1906	Gilbert Fuchs (GER)	1952	Richard Button (USA)	1985	Aleksandr Fadeyev (URS)
1907	Ulrich Salchow (SWE)	1953	Hayes Alan Jenkins (USA)	1986	Brian Boitano (USA)
1908	Ulrich Salchow (SWE)	1954	Hayes Alan Jenkins (USA)	1987	Brian Orser (CAN)
1909	Ulrich Salchow (SWE)	1955	Hayes Alan Jenkins (USA)	1988	Brian Boitano (USA)
1910	Ulrich Salchow (SWE)	1956	Hayes Alan Jenkins (USA)	1989	Kurt Browning (CAN)
1911	Ulrich Salchow (SWE)	1957	David Jenkins (USA)	1990	Kurt Browning (CAN)
1912	Fritz Kachler (AUT)	1958	David Jenkins (USA)	1991	Kurt Browning (CAN)
1913	Fritz Kachler (AUT)	1959	David Jenkins (USA)	1992	Viktor Petrenko (UNT†)
1914	Gösta Sandahl (SWE)	1960	Alain Giletti (FRA)	1993	Kurt Browning (CAN)
1915–21 not held		1961	not held*	1994	Elvis Stojko (CAN)
1922	Gillis Grafström (SWE)	1962	Donald Jackson (CAN)	1995	Elvis Stojko (CAN)
1923	Fritz Kachler (AUT)	1963	Donald McPherson (CAN)	1996	Todd Eldredge (USA)
1924	Gillis Grafström (SWE)	1964	Manfred Schnelldorfer	1997	Elvis Stojko (CAN)
1925	Willy Böckl (AUT)		(FRG)	1998	Aleksey Yagudin (RUS)
1926	Willy Böckl (AUT)	1965	Alain Calmat (FRA)	1999	Aleksey Yagudin (RUS)
1927	Willy Böckl (AUT)	1966	Emmerich Danzer (AUT)	2000	Aleksey Yagudin (RUS)
1928	Willy Böckl (AUT)	1967	Emmerich Danzer (AUT)	2001	Yevgeny Plushchenko
1929	Gillis Grafström (SWE)	1968	Emmerich Danzer (AUT)		(RUS)
1930	Karl Schäfer (AUT)	1969	Tim Wood (USA)	2002	Aleksey Yagudin (RUS)
1931	Karl Schäfer (AUT)	1970	Tim Wood (USA)	2003	scheduled to be held
1932	Karl Schäfer (AUT)	1971	Ondrej Nepela (TCH)		24–30 Mar 2003,
1933	Karl Schäfer (AUT)	1972	Ondrej Nepela (TCH)		Washington DC
1934	Karl Schäfer (AUT)	1973	Ondrej Nepela (TCH)		

*The entire US team died in an airplane crash, and the championships were canceled.
†Unified Team, consisting of athletes from the Commonwealth of Independent States plus Georgia.

World Figure Skating Championship—Women

YEAR	WINNER	YEAR	WINNER	YEAR	WINNER
1906	Madge Syers (GBR)	1937	Cecilia Colledge (GBR)	1969	Gabriele Seyfert (GDR)
1907	Madge Syers (GBR)	1938	Megan Taylor (GBR)	1970	Gabriele Seyfert (GDR)
1908	Lily Kronberger (HUN)	1939	Megan Taylor (GBR)	1971	Beatrix Schuba (AUT)
1909	Lily Kronberger (HUN)	1940–46 not held		1972	Beatrix Schuba (AUT)
1910	Lily Kronberger (HUN)	1947	Barbara Ann Scott (CAN)	1973	Karen Magnussen (CAN)
1911	Lily Kronberger (HUN)	1948	Barbara Ann Scott (CAN)	1974	Christine Errath (GDR)
1912	Opika von Meray Horvath	1949	Alena Vrzanova (TCH)	1975	Dianne de Leeuw (NED)
	(HUN)	1950	Alena Vrzanova (TCH)	1976	Dorothy Hamill (USA)
1913	Opika von M. Horvath (HUN)	1951	Jeannette Altwegg (GBR)	1977	Linda Fratianne (USA)
1914	Opika von M. Horvath (HUN)	1952	Jacqueline du Bief (FRA)	1978	Anett Pötzsch (GDR)
1915–21 not held		1953	Tenley Albright (USA)	1979	Linda Fratianne (USA)
1922	Herma Planck-Szabo (AUT)	1954	Gundi Busch (GER)	1980	Anett Pötzsch (GDR)
1923	Herma Planck-Szabo (AUT)	1955	Tenley Albright (USA)	1981	Denise Biellmann (SUI)
1924	Herma Planck-Szabo (AUT)	1956	Carol Heiss (USA)	1982	Elaine Zayak (USA)
1925	Herma Planck-Szabo (AUT)	1957	Carol Heiss (USA)	1983	Rosalynn Sumners (USA)
1926	Herma Planck-Szabo (AUT)	1958	Carol Heiss (USA)	1984	Katarina Witt (GDR)
1927	Sonja Henie (NOR)	1959	Carol Heiss (USA)	1985	Katarina Witt (GDR)
1928	Sonja Henie (NOR)	1960	Carol Heiss (USA)	1986	Debi Thomas (USA)
1929	Sonja Henie (NOR)	1961	not held*	1987	Katarina Witt (GDR)
1930	Sonja Henie (NOR)	1962	Sjoukje Dijkstra (NED)	1988	Katarina Witt (GDR)
1931	Sonja Henie (NOR)	1963	Sjoukje Dijkstra (NED)	1989	Midori Ito (JPN)
1932	Sonja Henie (NOR)	1964	Sjoukje Dijkstra (NED)	1990	Jill Trenary (USA)
1933	Sonja Henie (NOR)	1965	Petra Burka (CAN)	1991	Kristi Yamaguchi (USA)
1934	Sonja Henie (NOR)	1966	Peggy Fleming (USA)	1992	Kristi Yamaguchi (USA)
1935	Sonja Henie (NOR)	1967	Peggy Fleming (USA)	1993	Oksana Baiul (UKR)
1936	Sonja Henie (NOR)	1968	Peggy Fleming (USA)	1994	Yuka Sato (JPN)

World Figure Skating Championship—Women (continued)

YEAR	WINNER	YEAR	WINNER	YEAR	WINNER
1995	Chen Lu (CHN)	1999	Maria Butyrskaya (RUS)	2003	scheduled to be held
1996	Michelle Kwan (USA)	2000	Michelle Kwan (USA)		24–30 Mar 2003,
1997	Tara Lipinski (USA)	2001	Michelle Kwan (USA)		Washington DC
1998	Michelle Kwan (USA)	2002	Irina Slutskaya (RUS)		

*The entire US team died in an airplane crash, and the championships were canceled.

World Figure Skating Championship—Pairs

YEAR	WINNERS	YEAR	WINNERS
1908	Anna Hübler, Heinrich Burger (GER)	1964	Marika Kilius, Hans-Jürgen Bäumler (FRG)
1909	Phyllis Johnson, James Johnson (GBR)	1965	Lyudmila Belousova, Oleg Protopopov (URS)
1910	Anna Hübler, Heinrich Burger (GER)	1966	Lyudmila Belousova, Oleg Protopopov (URS)
1911	Ludowika Eilers, Walter Jakobsson (FIN)	1967	Lyudmila Belousova, Oleg Protopopov (URS)
1912	Phyllis Johnson, James Johnson (GBR)	1968	Lyudmila Belousova, Oleg Protopopov (URS)
1913	Helene Engelmann, Karl Mejstrik (AUT)	1969	Irina Rodnina, Aleksey Ulanov (URS)
1914	Ludowika Jakobsson, Walter Jakobsson (FIN)	1970	Irina Rodnina, Aleksey Ulanov (URS)
1915–21 not held		1971	Irina Rodnina, Aleksey Ulanov (URS)
1922	Helene Engelmann, Alfred Berger (AUT)	1972	Irina Rodnina, Aleksey Ulanov (URS)
1923	Ludowika Jakobsson, Walter Jakobsson (FIN)	1973	Irina Rodnina, Aleksandr Zaytsev (URS)
1924	Helene Engelmann, Alfred Berger (AUT)	1974	Irina Rodnina, Aleksandr Zaytsev (URS)
1925	Herma Planck-Szabo, Ludwig Wrede (AUT)	1975	Irina Rodnina, Aleksandr Zaytsev (URS)
1926	Andrée Joly, Pierre Brunet (FRA)	1976	Irina Rodnina, Aleksandr Zaytsev (URS)
1927	Herma Planck-Szabo, Ludwig Wrede (AUT)	1977	Irina Rodnina, Aleksandr Zaytsev (URS)
1928	Andrée Joly, Pierre Brunet (FRA)	1978	Irina Rodnina, Aleksandr Zaytsev (URS)
1929	Lily Scholz, Otto Kaiser (AUT)	1979	Tai Babilonia, Randy Gardner (USA)
1930	Andrée Brunet, Pierre Brunet (FRA)	1980	Marina Cherkasova, Sergey Shakhray (URS)
1931	Emilia Rotter, Laszlo Szollas (HUN)	1981	Irina Vorobyova, Igor Lisovsky (URS)
1932	Andrée Brunet, Pierre Brunet (FRA)	1982	Sabine Baess, Tassilo Thierbach (GDR)
1933	Emilia Rotter, Laszlo Szollas (HUN)	1983	Yelena Valova, Oleg Vasilyev (URS)
1934	Emilia Rotter, Laszlo Szollas (HUN)	1984	Barbara Underhill, Paul Martini (CAN)
1935	Emilia Rotter, Laszlo Szollas (HUN)	1985	Yelena Valova, Oleg Vasilyev (URS)
1936	Maxi Herber, Ernst Baier (GER)	1986	Yekaterina Gordeyeva, Sergey Grinkov (URS)
1937	Maxi Herber, Ernst Baier (GER)	1987	Yekaterina Gordeyeva, Sergey Grinkov (URS)
1938	Maxi Herber, Ernst Baier (GER)	1988	Yelena Valova, Oleg Vasilyev (URS)
1939	Maxi Herber, Ernst Baier (GER)	1989	Yekaterina Gordeyeva, Sergey Grinkov (URS)
1940–46 not held		1990	Yekaterina Gordeyeva, Sergey Grinkov (URS)
1947	Micheline Lannoy, Pierre Baugniet (BEL)	1991	Natalya Mishkutyonok, Artur Dmitriyev (URS)
1948	Micheline Lannoy, Pierre Baugniet (BEL)	1992	Natalya Mishkutyonok, Artur Dmitriyev (UNT†)
1949	Andrea Kekessy, Ede Kiraly (HUN)	1993	Isabelle Brasseur, Lloyd Eisler (CAN)
1950	Karol Kennedy, Peter Kennedy (USA)	1994	Yevgeniya Shishkova, Vadim Naumov (RUS)
1951	Ria Baran, Paul Falk (FRG)	1995	Radka Kovarikova, René Novotny (CZE)
1952	Ria Falk, Paul Falk (FRG)	1996	Marina Yeltsova, Andrey Bushkov (RUS)
1953	Jennifer Nicks, John Nicks (GBR)	1997	Mandy Wötzel, Ingo Steur (GER)
1954	Frances Dafoe, Norris Bowden (CAN)	1998	Yelena Berezhnaya, Anton Sikharulidze (RUS)
1955	Frances Dafoe, Norris Bowden (CAN)	1999	Yelena Berezhnaya, Anton Sikharulidze (RUS)
1956	Elisabeth Schwarz, Kurt Oppelt (AUT)	2000	Maria Petrova, Aleksey Tikhonov (RUS)
1957	Barbara Wagner, Robert Paul (CAN)	2001	Jamie Sale, David Pelletier (CAN)
1958	Barbara Wagner, Robert Paul (CAN)	2002	Xue Shen, Hongbo Zhao (CHN)
1959	Barbara Wagner, Robert Paul (CAN)	2003	scheduled to be held 24–30 Mar 2003, Washington DC
1960	Barbara Wagner, Robert Paul (CAN)		
1961	not held*		
1962	Maria Jelinek, Otto Jelinek (CAN)		
1963	Marika Kilius, Hans-Jürgen Bäumler (FRG)		

*The entire US team died in an airplane crash, and the championships were canceled.   †Unified Team, consisting of athletes from the Commonwealth of Independent States plus Georgia.

World Ice Dancing Championships

YEAR	WINNERS	YEAR	WINNERS
1950	Lois Waring, Michael McGean (USA)	1953	Jean Westwood, Lawrence Demmy (GBR)
1951	Jean Westwood, Lawrence Demmy (GBR)	1954	Jean Westwood, Lawrence Demmy (GBR)
1952	Jean Westwood, Lawrence Demmy (GBR)	1955	Jean Westwood, Lawrence Demmy (GBR)

World Ice Dancing Championships (continued)

YEAR	WINNERS	YEAR	WINNERS
1956	Pamela Weight, Paul Thomas (GBR)	1980	Krisztina Regöczy, Andras Sallay (HUN)
1957	June Markham, Courtney Jones (GBR)	1981	Jayne Torvill, Christopher Dean (GBR)
1958	June Markham, Courtney Jones (GBR)	1982	Jayne Torvill, Christopher Dean (GBR)
1959	Doreen Denny, Courtney Jones (GBR)	1983	Jayne Torvill, Christopher Dean (GBR)
1960	Doreen Denny, Courtney Jones (GBR)	1984	Jayne Torvill, Christopher Dean (GBR)
1961	*not held**	1985	Natalya Bestemyanova, Andrey Bukin (URS)
1962	Eve Romanova, Pavel Roman (TCH)	1986	Natalya Bestemyanova, Andrey Bukin (URS)
1963	Eve Romanova, Pavel Roman (TCH)	1987	Natalya Bestemyanova, Andrey Bukin (URS)
1964	Eve Romanova, Pavel Roman (TCH)	1988	Natalya Bestemyanova, Andrey Bukin (URS)
1965	Eve Romanova, Pavel Roman (TCH)	1989	Marina Klimova, Sergey Ponomarenko (URS)
1966	Diane Towler, Bernard Ford (GBR)	1990	Marina Klimova, Sergey Ponomarenko (URS)
1967	Diane Towler, Bernard Ford (GBR)	1991	Isabelle Duchesnay, Paul Duchesnay (FRA)
1968	Diane Towler, Bernard Ford (GBR)	1992	Marina Klimova, Sergey Ponomarenko
1969	Diane Towler, Bernard Ford (GBR)		(UNT†)
1970	Lyudmila Pakhomova, Aleksandr Gorshkov	1993	Maya Usova, Aleksandr Zhulin (RUS)
	(URS)	1994	Oksana Grichuk, Yevgeny Platov (RUS)
1971	L. Pakhomova, A. Gorshkov (URS)	1995	Oksana Grichuk, Yevgeny Platov (RUS)
1972	L. Pakhomova, A. Gorshkov (URS)	1996	Oksana Grichuk, Yevgeny Platov (RUS)
1973	L. Pakhomova, A. Gorshkov (URS)	1997	Oksana Grichuk, Yevgeny Platov (RUS)
1974	L. Pakhomova, A. Gorshkov (URS)	1998	Angelika Krylova, Oleg Ovsyannikov (RUS)
1975	Irina Moiseyeva, Andrey Minenkov (URS)	1999	Angelika Krylova, Oleg Ovsyannikov (RUS)
1976	L. Pakhomova, A. Gorshkov (URS)	2000	Marina Anissina, Gwendal Peizerat (FRA)
1977	Irina Moiseyeva, Andrey Minenkov (URS)	2001	Barbara Fusar-Poli, Maurizio Margaglio (ITA)
1978	Natalya Linichuk, Gennady Karponosov	2002	Irina Lobachyova, Ilya Averbukh (RUS)
	(URS)	2003	*scheduled to be held 24–30 Mar 2003,*
1979	N. Linichuk, G. Karponosov (URS)		*Washington DC*

*The entire US team died in an airplane crash, and the championships were canceled.
†Unified Team, consisting of athletes from the Commonwealth of Independent States plus Georgia.

Speed Skating World Records (Major Tracks)

men

EVENT	RECORD HOLDER (NATIONALITY)	PERFORMANCE	DATE
500 m	Hiroyasu Shimizu (JPN)	34.32 sec	10 Mar 2001
1,000 m	Gerard van Velde (NED)	1 min 7.18 sec	16 Feb 2002
1,500 m	Derek Parra (USA)	1 min 43.95 sec	19 Feb 2002
3,000 m	Gianni Romme (NED)	3 min 42.75 sec	11 Aug 2000
5,000 m	Jochem Uytdehaage (NED)	6 min 14.66 sec	9 Feb 2002
10,000 m	Jochem Uytdehaage (NED)	12 min 58.92 sec	22 Feb 2002

women

EVENT	RECORD HOLDER (NATIONALITY)	PERFORMANCE	DATE
500 m	Catriona LeMay Doan (CAN)	37.22 sec	9 Dec 2001
1,000 m	Christine Witty (USA)	1 min 13.83 sec	17 Feb 2002
1,500 m	Anni Friesinger (GER)	1 min 54.02 sec	20 Feb 2002
3,000 m	Claudia Pechstein (GER)	3 min 57.70 sec	10 Feb 2002
5,000 m	Claudia Pechstein (GER)	6 min 46.91 sec	23 Feb 2002

Speed Skating World Records (Short Tracks)

men

EVENT	RECORD HOLDER (NATIONALITY)	PERFORMANCE	DATE
500 m	Jeffrey Scholten (CAN)	41.514 sec	13 Oct 2001
1,000 m	Steve Robillard (CAN)	1 min 26.005 sec	14 Oct 2001
1,500 m	Apolo Anton Ohno (USA)	2 min 13.728 sec	15 Dec 2001
3,000 m	Kim Dong Sung (KOR)	4 min 46.727 sec	8 Nov 1998
5,000-m relay	Canada National Team	6 min 43.730 sec	14 Oct 2001

women

EVENT	RECORD HOLDER (NATIONALITY)	PERFORMANCE	DATE
500 m	Evgenia Radanova (BUL)	43.671 sec	19 Oct 2001
1,000 m	Yang Yang (A) (CHN)	1 min 31.191 sec	3 Feb 2002
1,500 m	Choi Eun Kyung (KOR)	2 min 21.069 sec	13 Feb 2002
3,000 m	Choi Eun Kyung (KOR)	5 min 01.976 sec	22 Oct 2000
3,000-m relay	South Korea National Team	4 min 12.793 sec	20 Feb 2002

World All-Around Speed-Skating Championship—Men

There was no winner in 1894, 1902, 1903, 1906, and 1907. Before the points system was established, only a contestant who had won at least three of the four events was considered the all-around champion.

YEAR	WINNER	YEAR	WINNER	YEAR	WINNER
1893	Jaap Eden (NED)	1935	Michael Staksrud (NOR)	1973	Göran Claeson (SWE)
1895	Jaap Eden (NED)	1936	Ivar Ballangrud (NOR)	1974	Sten Stensen (NOR)
1896	Jaap Eden (NED)	1937	Michael Staksrud (NOR)	1975	Harm Kuipers (NED)
1897	Jack K. McCullock (CAN)	1938	Ivar Ballangrud (NOR)	1976	Piet Kleine (NED)
1898	Peder Østlund (NOR)	1939	Birger Wasenius (FIN)	1977	Eric Heiden (USA)
1899	Peder Østlund (NOR)	1940–	no competition	1978	Eric Heiden (USA)
1900	Edvard Engelsaas (NOR)	46		1979	Eric Heiden (USA)
1901	Franz Wathen (FIN)	1947	Lassi Parkkinnen (FIN)	1980	Hilbert van der Duim
1904	Sigurd Mathisen (NOR)	1948	Odd Lundberg (NOR)		(NED)
1905	C. Coen de Koning (NED)	1949	Kornel Pajor (HUN)	1981	Amund Sjøbrend (NOR)
1908	Oscar Mathisen (NOR)	1950	Hjalmar Andersen (NOR)	1982	Hilbert van der Duim
1909	Oscar Mathisen (NOR)	1951	Hjalmar Andersen (NOR)		(NED)
1910	Nikolay Strunnikov (RUS)	1952	Hjalmar Andersen (NOR)	1983	Rolf Falk-Larssen (NOR)
1911	Nikolay Strunnikov (RUS)	1953	Oleg Goncharenko (URS)	1984	Oleg Bozhyev (URS)
1912	Oscar Mathisen (NOR)	1954	Boris Shilkov (URS)	1985	Hein Vergeer (NED)
1913	Oscar Mathisen (NOR)	1955	Sigvard Ericsson (SWE)	1986	Hein Vergeer (NED)
1914	Oscar Mathisen (NOR)	1956	Oleg Goncharenko (URS)	1987	Nikolai Gulyaev (URS)
1915–	no competition	1957	Knut Johannesen (NOR)	1988	Eric Flaim (USA)
21		1958	Oleg Goncharenko (URS)	1989	Leo Visser (NED)
1922	Harald Strom (NOR)	1959	Juhani Jäevinen (FIN)	1990	Johann Olav Koss (NOR)
1923	Clas Thunberg (FIN)	1960	Boris Stenin (URS)	1991	Johann Olav Koss (NOR)
1924	Roald Larsen (NOR)	1961	Henk van der Grift (NED)	1992	Roberto Sighel (ITA)
1925	Clas Thunberg (FIN)	1962	Viktor Kosichkin (URS)	1993	Falko Zandstra (NED)
1926	Ivar Ballangrud (NOR)	1963	Jonny Nilsson (SWE)	1994	Johann Olav Koss (NOR)
1927	Bernt Evensen (NOR)	1964	Knut Johannesen (NOR)	1995	Rintje Ritsma (NED)
1928	Clas Thunberg (FIN)	1965	Per Ivar Moe (NOR)	1996	Rintje Ritsma (NED)
1929	Clas Thunberg (FIN)	1966	Kees Verkerk (NED)	1997	Ids Postma (NED)
1930	Michael Staksrud (NOR)	1967	Kees Verkerk (NED)	1998	Ids Postma (NED)
1931	Clas Thunberg (FIN)	1968	Fred Anton Maier (NOR)	1999	Rintje Ritsma (NED)
1932	Ivar Ballangrud (NOR)	1969	Dag Fornaess (NOR)	2000	Gianni Romme (NED)
1933	Hans Engnestangen	1970	Ard Schenk (NED)	2001	Rintje Ritsma (NED)
	(NOR)	1971	Ard Schenk (NED)	2002	Jochem Uytdehaage
1934	Bernt Evensen (NOR)	1972	Ard Schenk (NED)		(NED)

World All-Around Speed-Skating Championship—Women

YEAR	WINNER	YEAR	WINNER	YEAR	WINNER
1936	Kit Klein (USA)	1964	Lidiya Skoblikova (URS)	1983	Andrea Schöne (GDR)
1937	Laila Schou Nilsen (NOR)	1965	Inga Artamonova (URS)	1984	Karin Enke (GDR)
1938	Laila Schou Nilsen (NOR)	1966	Valentina Stenina (URS)	1985	Andrea Schöne (GDR)
1939	Verné Lesche (FIN)	1967	Stien Kaiser (NED)	1986	Karin Kania (GDR)
1940–46	not held	1968	Stien Kaiser (NED)	1987	Karin Kania (GDR)
1947	Verné Lesche (FIN)	1969	Lasma Kauniste (URS)	1988	Karin Kania (GDR)
1948	Mariya Isakova (URS)	1970	Atje Keulen-Deelstra	1989	Constance Moser (GDR)
1949	Mariya Isakova (URS)		(NED)	1990	Jacqueline Börner (GDR)
1950	Mariya Isakova (URS)	1971	Nina Statkevich (URS)	1991	Gunda Kleeman (GER)
1951	Eevi Huttunen (FIN)	1972	Atje Keulen-Deelstra	1992	Gunda Kleeman (GER)
1952	Lidiya Selikhova (URS)		(NED)	1993	Gunda Kleeman (GER)
1953	Khalida Shchegoleva	1973	Atje Keulen-Deelstra	1994	Emese Hunyady (AUT)
	(URS)		(NED)	1995	Gunda Niemann (GER)
1954	Lidiya Selikhova (URS)	1974	Atje Keulen-Deelstra	1996	Gunda Niemann (GER)
1955	Rimma Zhukova (URS)		(NED)	1997	Gunda Niemann (GER)
1956	Sofiya Kondakova (URS)	1975	Karin Kessow (GDR)	1998	Gunda Niemann-
1957	Inga Artamonova (URS)	1976	Sylvia Burka (CAN)		Stirnemann (GER)
1958	Inga Artamonova (URS)	1977	Vera Bryndzey (URS)	1999	Gunda Niemann-
1959	Tamara Rylova (URS)	1978	Tatyana Averina (URS)		Stirnemann (GER)
1960	Valentina Stenina (URS)	1979	Beth Heiden (USA)	2000	Claudia Pechstein (GER)
1961	Valentina Stenina (URS)	1980	Nataliya Petruseva (URS)	2001	Anni Friesinger (GER)
1962	Inga Artamonova (URS)	1981	Nataliya Petruseva (URS)	2002	Anni Friesinger (GER)
1963	Lidiya Skoblikova (URS)	1982	Karin Busch (GDR)		

World Speed-Skating Sprint Championships

YEAR	MEN	WOMEN	YEAR	MEN	WOMEN
1970	Valery Muratov (URS)	Lyudmila Titova (URS)	1988	Dan Jansen (USA)	Christa Rothenburger (GDR)
1971	Erhard Keller (FRG)	Ruth Schleiermacher (GDR)	1989	Igor Zhelezovsky (URS)	Bonnie Blair (USA)
1972	Leo Linkovesi (FIN)	Monica Pflug (FRG)	1990	Ki-Tae Bae (KOR)	Angela Hauck (GDR)
1973	Valery Muratov (URS)	Sheila Young (USA)	1991	Igor Zhelezovsky (URS)	Monique Garbrecht (GER)
1974	Per Bjørang (NOR)	Leah Poulos (USA)	1992	Igor Zhelezovsky (UNT*)	Ye Qiaobo (CHN)
1975	Aleksandr Safronov (URS)	Sheila Young (USA)	1993	Igor Zhelezovsky (URS)	Ye Qiaobo (CHN)
1976	Johan Granath (SWE)	Sheila Young (USA)	1994	Dan Jansen (USA)	Bonnie Blair (USA)
1977	Eric Heiden (USA)	Sylvia Burka (CAN)	1995	Kim Yoon Man (KOR)	Bonnie Blair (USA)
1978	Eric Heiden (USA)	Lyubov Sadchikova (URS)	1996	Sergey Klevchenya (RUS)	Christine Witty (USA)
1979	Eric Heiden (USA)	Leah Poulos-Mueller (USA)	1997	Sergey Klevchenya (RUS)	Franziska Schenk (GER)
1980	Eric Heiden (USA)	Karin Enke (GDR)	1998	Jan Bos (NED)	Catriona LeMay Doan (CAN)
1981	Frode Ronning (NOR)	Karin Enke (GDR)	1999	Jeremy Wotherspoon (CAN)	Monique Garbrecht (GER)
1982	Sergey Khlebnikov (URS)	Nataliya Petruseva (URS)	2000	Jeremy Wotherspoon (CAN)	Monique Garbrecht (GER)
1983	Akira Kuroiwa (JPN)	Karin Enke (GDR)	2001	Michael Ireland (CAN)	Monique Garbrecht-Enteldt (GER)
1984	Gaetan Boucher (CAN)	Karin Enke (GDR)	2002	Jeremy Wotherspoon (CAN)	Catriona LeMay Doan (CAN)
1985	Igor Zhelezovsky (URS)	Christa Rothenburger (GDR)			
1986	Igor Zhelezovsky (URS)	Karin Kania (GDR)			
1987	Akira Kuroiwa (JPN)	Karin Kania (GDR)			

*Unified Team, consisting of athletes from the Commonwealth of Independent States plus Georgia.

World Short-Track Speed-Skating Championships—Overall Winners

YEAR	MEN	WOMEN	YEAR	MEN	WOMEN
1976	Alan Rattray (USA)	Celeste Chlapaty (USA)	1988	Peter van der Velde (NED)	Sylvie Daigle (CAN)
1977	Gaetan Boucher (CAN)	Brenda Webster (CAN)	1989	Michel Daignault (CAN)	Sylvie Daigle (CAN)
1978	James Lynch (AUS)	Sarah Docter (CAN)	1990	Joon-ho Lee (KOR)	Sylvie Daigle (CAN)
1979	Hiroshi Toda (JPN)	Sylvie Daigle (CAN)	1991	Wilfred O'Reilly (GBR)	Nathalie Lambert (CAN)
1980	Gaetan Boucher (CAN)	Miyoshi Kato (JPN)	1992	Ki Hoon Kim (KOR)	So He Kim (KOR)
1981	Benoît Baril (CAN)	Miyoshi Kato (JPN)	1993	Marc Gagnon (CAN)	Nathalie Lambert (CAN)
1982	Guy Daigneault (CAN)	Maryse Perreault (CAN)	1994	Marc Gagnon (CAN)	Nathalie Lambert (CAN)
1983	Louis Grenier (CAN)	Sylvie Daigle (CAN)	1995	Chae Ji Hoon (KOR)	Chun Lee Kyung (KOR)
1984	Guy Daigneault (CAN)	Mariko Kinoshita (JPN)	1996	Marc Gagnon (CAN)	Chun Lee Kyung (KOR)
1985	Toshinobu Kawai (JPN)	Eiko Shishii (JPN)	1997	Kim Dong Sung (KOR)	Chun Lee Kyung (KOR), Yang Yang (A) (CHN)*
1986	Tatsuyoshi Isihara (JPN)	Bonnie Blair (USA)	1998	Marc Gagnon (CAN)	Yang Yang (A) (CHN)
1987	Michel Daignault (CAN), Toshinobu Kawai (JPN)*	Eiko Shishii (JPN)	1999	Li Jianjun (CHN)	Yang Yang (A) (CHN)
			2000	Min Ryung (KOR)	Yang Yang (A) (CHN)
			2001	Li Jianjun (CHN)	Yang Yang (A) (CHN)
			2002	Kim Dong Sung (KOR)	Yang Yang (A) (CHN)

*Tied.

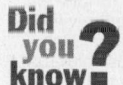

Did you know? Ice for pro hockey games is usually ¾″ thick and kept at a temperature of 16 °F. Thicker, warmer ice is typically a bit slower; such ice is used for figure skating and ice shows.

Judis

World championships for judo were first held in 1956 under the auspices of the **International Judo Federation** (IJF; founded 1951). At that time all contestants participated on an equal basis. At the fourth world championship match, 65 kg, 78 kg, and 95 kg classes were added to the open weight division; at the next championship match, two more weight classes were added, and in 1979 two of the classes were divided once more and assigned weight values. World championships for **women** were first held in 1980; they are contested biennially in eight weight classes. New weight classes were established in 1999.

International Judo Federation Web site: <www.ijf.org>

World Judo Championships—Men

Figures in parentheses represent weight classes before 1999. The 2003 championship is scheduled to be held in Osaka, Japan.

YEAR	OPEN WEIGHTS
1956*	Shokichi Natsui (JPN)
1958*	Koji Sone (JPN)
1961*	Anton Geesink (NED)
1965†	Isao Inokuma (JPN)
1967‡	Mitsuo Matsunaga (JPN)
1969‡	Masatoshi Shinomaki (JPN)
1971‡	Masatoshi Shinomaki (JPN)
1973‡	Kasuhiro Ninomiya (JPN)
1975‡	Haruki Uemura (JPN)
1979	Sumio Endo (JPN)
1981	Yasuhiro Yamashita (JPN)
1983	Hitoshi Saito (JPN)
1985	Y. Masaki (JPN)
1987	Naoya Ogawa (JPN)
1989	Naoya Ogawa (JPN)
1991	Naoya Ogawa (JPN)
1993	Rafael Kubacki (POL)
1995	David Douillet (FRA)
1997	Rafael Kubacki (POL)
1999	Shinichi Shinohara (JPN)
2001	Aleksandr Mikhaylin (RUS)

YEAR	60 KG
1979	Thierry Rey (FRA)
1981	Yasuhiro Moriwaki (JPN)
1983	Khazret Tletseri (URS)
1985	Shinji Hosokawa (JPN)
1987	Kim Jae Yup (KOR)
1989	Amiran Totikashvili (URS)
1991	Tadanori Koshino (JPN)
1993	Ryoji Sonada (JPN)
1995	Nikolay Ozhegin (RUS)
1997	Tadahiro Nomura (JPN)
1999	Manuelo Poulot (CUB)
2001	Anis Lounifi (TUN)

YEAR	66 KG (65 KG)
1965†	Hirofumi Matsuda (JPN)
1967‡	Takafumi Shigeoka (JPN)
1969‡	Yoshio Sonoda (JPN)
1971‡	Takao Kawaguchi (JPN)
1973‡	Yoshiharu Minami (JPN)
1975‡	Yoshiharu Minami (JPN)
1979	Nikolay Solodukhin (URS)
1981	Katsuhito Kashiwazaki (JPN)
1983	Nicolai Solodukhin (URS)
1985	Yuri Sokolov (URS)
1987	Yosuke Yamamoto (JPN)

YEAR	66 KG (65 KG) (CONTINUED)
1989	Dragomir Becanovic (YUG)
1991	Udo Quellmalz (GER)
1993	Yukimasa Nakamura (JPN)
1995	Udo Quellmalz (GER)
1997	Kim Hyuk (KOR)
1999	Larbi Benboudaoud (FRA)
2001	Arash Miresmaeili (IRI)

YEAR	73 KG (71 KG)
1967‡	Hiroshi Minatoya (JPN)
1969‡	Hiroshi Minatoya (JPN)
1971‡	Hisashi Tsuzawa (JPN)
1973‡	Toyokazu Nomura (JPN)
1975‡	Vladimir Nevzorov (URS)
1979	Kyoto Katsuki (JPN)
1981	Park Chong Hak (KOR)
1983	Hidetoshi Nakanishi (JPN)
1985	Keun Ahn Byung (KOR)
1987	Mike Swain (USA)
1989	Toshihigo Koga (JPN)
1991	Toshihigo Koga (JPN)
1993	Yung Chung Hoon (KOR)
1995	Daisuke Hideshima (JPN)
1997	Kenzo Nakamura (JPN)
1999	Jimmy Pedro (USA)
2001	Vitaly Makarov (RUS)

YEAR	81 KG (78 KG)
1965†	Isao Okano (JPN)
1967‡	Eijii Maruki (JPN)
1969‡	Isamu Sonoda (JPN)
1971‡	Shozo Fujii (JPN)
1973‡	Shozo Fujii (JPN)
1975‡	Shozo Fujii (JPN)
1979	Shozo Fujii (JPN)
1981	Neil Adams (GBR)
1983	Nobutoshi Hikage (JPN)
1985	Nobutoshi Hikage (JPN)
1987	Hirotaka Okada (JPN)
1989	Kim Bying Ju (KOR)
1991	Daniel Lascau (GER)
1993	Chun Ki Young (KOR)
1995	Toshihigo Koga (JPN)
1997	Cho In Chul (KOR)
1999	Graeme Randall (GBR)
2001	Cho In Chul (KOR)

YEAR	90 KG (86 KG)
1967‡	Nobuyuki Sato (JPN)
1969‡	Fumio Sasahara (JPN)

YEAR	90 KG (86 KG) (CONTINUED)
1971‡	Fumio Sasahara (JPN)
1973‡	Nobuyuki Sato (JPN)
1975‡	Jean-Louc Rouge (FRA)
1979	Detlef Ultsch (GDR)
1981	Bernard Tchoullouyan (FRA)
1983	Detlef Ultsch (GDR)
1985	Peter Seisenbacher (AUT)
1987	Fabien Canu (FRA)
1989	Fabien Canu (FRA)
1991	Hirotaka Okada (JPN)
1993	Yoshio Nakamura (JPN)
1995	Chun Ki Young (KOR)
1997	Jeon Ki Young (KOR)
1999	Hidehiko Yoshida (JPN)
2001	Frédéric Demontfaucon (FRA)

YEAR	100 KG (95 KG)
1965†	Anton Geesink (NED)
1967‡	Wilhem Ruska (NED)
1969‡	Shuji Suma (JPN)
1971‡	Wilhem Ruska (NED)
1973‡	Chonosuke Takagi (JPN)
1975‡	Sumio Endo (JPN)
1979	Tengiz Khubuluri (URS)
1981	Tengiz Khubuluri (URS)
1983	Andreas Preschel (GDR)
1985	Hitoshi Sugai (JPN)
1987	Hitoshi Sugai (JPN)
1989	Koba Kurtanidze (URS)
1991	Stéphane Traineau (FRA)
1993	Antal Kovacs (HUN)
1995	Pawel Nastula (POL)
1997	Pawel Nastula (POL)
1999	Kosei Inoue (JPN)
2001	Kosei Inoue (JPN)

YEAR	+100 KG (+95 KG)
1979	Yasuhiro Yamashita (JPN)
1981	Yasuhiro Yamashita (JPN)
1983	Yasuhiro Yamashita (JPN)
1985	Chul Cho Yong (KOR)
1987	Grigory Verichev (URS)
1989	Naoya Ogawa (JPN)
1991	Sergey Kosorotov (URS)
1993	David Douillet (FRA)
1995	David Douillet (FRA)
1997	David Douillet (FRA)
1999	Shinichi Shinohara (JPN)
2001	Aleksandr Mikhaylin (RUS)

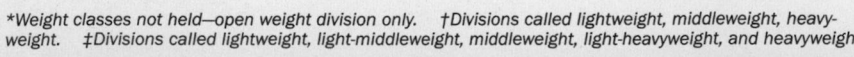

Weight classes not held—open weight division only. †Divisions called lightweight, middleweight, heavyweight. ‡Divisions called lightweight, light-middleweight, middleweight, light-heavyweight, and heavyweight.

World Judo Championships—Women

Figures in parentheses represent weight classes before 1999. The 2003 championship is scheduled to be held in Osaka, Japan.

YEAR	OPEN WEIGHTS
1980	Ingrid Berghmans (BEL)
1982	Ingrid Berghmans (BEL)
1984	Ingrid Berghmans (BEL)
1986	Ingrid Berghmans (BEL)
1987	Fengliang Gao (CHN)
1989	Estela Rodriguez (CUB)
1991	Zhuang Xiaoyan (CHN)
1993	Beata Maksymow (POL)
1995	Monique van der Lee (NED)
1997	Daina Beltran (CUB)
1999	Daina Beltran (CUB)
2001	Celine Lebrun (FRA)

YEAR	48 KG
1980	Jane Bridge (GBR)
1982	Karen Briggs (GBR)
1984	Karen Briggs (GBR)
1986	Karen Briggs (GBR)
1987	Zhang Yun Li (CHN)
1989	Karen Briggs (GBR)
1991	Cecile Nowak (FRA)
1993	Ryoko Tamura (JPN)
1995	Ryoko Tamura (JPN)
1997	Ryoko Tamura (JPN)
1999	Ryoko Tamura (JPN)
2001	Ryoko Tamura (JPN)

YEAR	52 KG
1980	Edith Hrovat (AUT)
1982	Loretta Doyle (GBR)
1984	Kaori Yamaguchi (JPN)
1986	Dominique Brun (FRA)
1987	Sharon Rendle (GBR)
1989	Sharon Rendle (GBR)
1991	Alessandra Giungi (ITA)
1993	Legna Verdecia Rodríguez (CUB)
1995	Marie-Claire Restoux (FRA)

YEAR	52 KG (CONTINUED)
1997	Marie-Claire Restoux (FRA)
1999	Noriko Narasaki (JPN)
2001	Kye Sun Hui (KOR)

YEAR	57 KG (56 KG)
1980	Gerda Winklbauer (AUT)
1982	Béatrice Rodriguez (FRA)
1984	Anne-Marie Burns (USA)
1986	Ann Hughes (GBR)
1987	Catherine Arnaud (FRA)
1989	Catherine Arnaud (FRA)
1991	Miriam Blasco (ESP)
1993	Nicola Fairbrother (GBR)
1995	Driulis González (CUB)
1997	Isabel Fernández (ESP)
1999	Driulis González (CUB)
2001	Yurisleidis Lupetey (CUB)

YEAR	63 KG (61 KG)
1980	Anita Staps (NED)
1982	Martine Rottier (FRA)
1984	Natasha Hernández (VEN)
1986	Diane Bell (GBR)
1987	Diane Bell (GBR)
1989	Catherine Fleury (FRA)
1991	Frauke Eickhoff (GER)
1993	Gella van de Cavaye (BEL)
1995	Jung Sung Sook (KOR)
1997	Severin Vandenhende (FRA)
1999	Keiko Maeda (JPN)
2001	Gella van de Cavaye (BEL)

YEAR	70 KG (66 KG)
1980	Edith Simon (AUT)
1982	Brigitte Deydier (FRA)
1984	Brigitte Deydier (FRA)
1986	Brigitte Deydier (FRA)
1987	Alexandra Schreiber (FRG)

YEAR	70 KG (66 KG) (CONTINUED)
1989	Emanuela Pierantozzi (ITA)
1991	Emanuela Pierantozzi (ITA)
1993	Cho Min Sun (KOR)
1995	Cho Min Sun (KOR)
1997	Kate Howey (GBR)
1999	Sibelis Veranes (CUB)
2001	Masae Ueno (JPN)

YEAR	78 KG (72 KG)
1980	Jocelyne Triadou (FRA)
1982	Barbara Classen (FRG)
1984	Ingrid Berghmans (BEL)
1986	Irene de Kok (NED)
1987	Irene de Kok (NED)
1989	Ingrid Berghmans (BEL)
1991	Kim Mi Jong (KOR)
1993	Leng Chin Hui (CHN)
1995	Cactoliano Diaz Luna (CUB)
1997	Noriko Anno (JPN)
1999	Noriko Anno (JPN)
2001	Noriko Anno (JPN)

YEAR	+78 KG (+72 KG)
1980	Margerita de Cal (ITA)
1982	Natalina Lupino (FRA)
1984	Maria-Theresa Motta (ITA)
1986	Fengliang Gao (CHN)
1987	Fengliang Gao (CHN)
1989	Fengliang Gao (CHN)
1991	Moon Ji Yoon (KOR)
1993	Johanna Hagn (GER)
1995	Angelique Seriese (NED)
1997	Christine Cicot (FRA)
1999	Beata Maksymow (POL)
2001	Yuan Hua (CHN)

 **Did you know?** It is generally agreed that softball developed from a game called indoor baseball, first played in Chicago in 1887. The official softball is 12 inches in circumference; one variation, popular especially in Chicago, is played with a ball that is 16 inches in circumference.

Marathon

The marathon is a long-distance footrace first held at the revival of the Olympic Games at Athens, Greece, in 1896. It commemorates the legendary feat of a Greek soldier who, in 490 BC, is supposed to have run from Marathon to Athens, a distance of about 40 km (25 mi), to bring news of the Athenian victory over the Persians. Appropriately, the first modern marathon winner in 1896 was a Greek, Spyridon Louis. In 1924 the **Olympic marathon distance** was standardized at 42,195 m, or 26 mi 385 yd. This was based on a decision of the British Olympic Committee to start the 1908 Olympic race from Windsor Castle and finish it in front of the royal box in the stadium at London. The marathon was added to the **women's Olympic program** in 1984. Because marathon courses are not of equal difficulty, the International Amateur Athletic Federation does not list a world record for the event. After the Olympic Games championship, one of the most coveted honors in marathon running is victory in the **Boston Marathon**, held annually since 1897. It draws athletes from all parts of the world and in 1972 became the first marathon to officially allow women to compete. The **New York Marathon** also attracts participants from many countries. Other popular marathons are held in London, Berlin, Rotterdam (Neth.), and Chicago.

Boston Marathon

Won by an American runner except as indicated.

men

YEAR	WINNER	TIME	YEAR	WINNER	TIME
1897	John J. McDermott	2:55:10	1950	Ham Kee Yong (KOR)	2:32:39
1898	Ronald J. McDonald (CAN)	2:42:00	1951	Tanaka Shigeki (JPN)	2:27:45
1899	Lawrence J. Brignoli	2:54:38	1952	Doroteo Flores (GUA)	2:31:53
1900	John J. Caffrey (CAN)	2:39:44	1953	Yamada Keizo (JPN)	2:18:51
1901	John J. Caffrey (CAN)	2:29:23	1954	Veikko L. Karanen (FIN)	2:20:39
1902	Sammy A. Mellor	2:43:12	1955	Hamamura Hideo (JPN)	2:18:22
1903	John C. Lorden	2:41:29	1956	Antti Viskari (FIN)	2:14:14
1904	Michael Spring	2:39:04	1957	John J. Kelley	2:20:05
1905	Frederick Lorz	2:38:25	1958	Franjo Mihalic (YUG)	2:25:54
1906	Tim Ford	2:45:45	1959	Eino Oksanen (FIN)	2:22:42
1907	Thomas Longboat (CAN)	2:24:24	1960	Paavo Kotila (FIN)	2:20:54
1908	Thomas P. Morrissey	2:25:43	1961	Eino Oksanen (FIN)	2:23:39
1909	Henri Renaud	2:53:36	1962	Eino Oksanen (FIN)	2:23:48
1910	Fred L. Cameron (CAN)	2:28:52	1963	Aurele Vandendriessche (BEL)	2:18:58
1911	Clarence H. DeMar	2:21:39	1964	Aurele Vandendriessche (BEL)	2:19:59
1912	Michael J. Ryan	2:21:18	1965	Shigematsu Morio (JPN)	2:16:33
1913	Fritz Carlson	2:25:14	1966	Kimihara Kenji (JPN)	2:17:11
1914	James Duffy (CAN)	2:25:01	1967	David McKenzie (NZL)	2:15:45
1915	Edouard Fabre (CAN)	2:31:41	1968	Amby Burfoot	2:22:17
1916	Arthur V. Roth	2:27:16	1969	Unetani Yoshiaki (JPN)	2:13:49
1917	William K. Kennedy	2:28:37	1970	Ron Hill (ENG)	2:10:30
1918	*no regular competition*		1971	Alvaro Mejia (COL)	2:18:45
1919	Carl W.A. Linder	2:29:13	1972	Olavi Suomalainen (FIN)	2:15:30
1920	Peter Trivoulides (GRE)	2:29:31	1973	Jon Anderson	2:16:03
1921	Frank Zuna	2:18:57	1974	Neil Cusack	2:13:39
1922	Clarence H. DeMar	2:18:10	1975	Bill Rodgers	2:09:55
1923	Clarence H. DeMar	2:23:47	1976	Jack Fultz	2:20:19
1924	Clarence H. DeMar	2:29:40	1977	Jerome Drayton (CAN)	2:14:46
1925	Charles L. Mellor	2:33:06	1978	Bill Rodgers	2:10:13
1926	John C. Miles (CAN)	2:25:40	1979	Bill Rodgers	2:09:27
1927	Clarence H. DeMar	2:40:22	1980	Bill Rodgers	2:12:11
1928	Clarence H. DeMar	2:37:07	1981	Seko Toshihiko (JPN)	2:09:26
1929	John C. Miles (CAN)	2:33:08	1982	Alberto Salazar	2:08:51
1930	Clarence H. DeMar	2:34:48	1983	Greg A. Meyer	2:09:00
1931	James P. Hennigan	2:46:45	1984	Geoff Smith (ENG)	2:10:34
1932	Paul deBruyn	2:33:36	1985	Geoff Smith (ENG)	2:14:05
1933	Leslie S. Pawson	2:31:01	1986	Robert de Castella (AUS)	2:07:51
1934	Dave Komonen (CAN)	2:32:53	1987	Seko Toshihiko (JPN)	2:11:50
1935	John A. Kelley	2:32:07	1988	Ibrahim Hussein (KEN)	2:08:43
1936	Ellison M. Brown	2:33:40	1989	Abebe Mekonnen (ETH)	2:09:06
1937	Walter Young (CAN)	2:33:20	1990	Gelindo Bordin (ITA)	2:08:19
1938	Leslie S. Pawson	2:35:34	1991	Ibrahim Hussein (KEN)	2:11:06
1939	Ellison M. Brown	2:28:51	1992	Ibrahim Hussein (KEN)	2:08:14
1940	Gerard Cote (CAN)	2:28:28	1993	Cosmas N'Deti (KEN)	2:09:33
1941	Leslie S. Pawson	2:30:38	1994	Cosmas N'Deti (KEN)	2:07:15
1942	Joe Smith	2:26:51	1995	Cosmas N'Deti (KEN)	2:09:22
1943	Gerard Cote (CAN)	2:28:25	1996	Moses Tanui (KEN)	2:09:16
1944	Gerard Cote (CAN)	2:31:50	1997	Lameck Aguta (KEN)	2:10:34
1945	John A. Kelley	2:30:40	1998	Moses Tanui (KEN)	2:07:34
1946	Stylianos Kyriakides (GRE)	2:29:27	1999	Joseph Chebet (KEN)	2:09:52
1947	Suh Yun Bok (KOR)	2:25:39	2000	Elijah Lagat (KEN)	2:09:47
1948	Gerard Cote (CAN)	2:31:02	2001	Bong-Ju Lee (KOR)	2:09:43
1949	Karl G. Leandersson (SWE)	2:31:50	2002	Rodgers Rop (KEN)	2:09:02

women

YEAR	WINNER	TIME	YEAR	WINNER	TIME
1972	Nina Kuscsik	3:10:26	1978	Gayle S. Barron	2:44:52
1973	Jacqueline Hansen	3:05:59	1979	Joan Benoit	2:35:15
1974	Michiko Gorman	2:47:11	1980	Jacqueline Gareau (CAN)	2:34:28
1975	Liane Winter (FRG)	2:42:24	1981	Allison Roe (NZL)	2:26:46
1976	Kim Merritt	2:47:10	1982	Charlotte Teske (FRG)	2:29:33
1977	Michiko Gorman	2:46:22	1983	Joan Benoit	2:22:42

Boston Marathon (continued)

women (continued)

YEAR	WINNER	TIME	YEAR	WINNER	TIME
1984	Lorraine Moller (NZL)	2:29:28	1994	Uta Pippig (GER)	2:21:45
1985	Lisa Larsen	2:34:06	1995	Uta Pippig (GER)	2:25:11
1986	Ingrid Kristiansen (NOR)	2:24:55	1996	Uta Pippig (GER)	2:27:12
1987	Rosa Mota (POR)	2:25:21	1997	Fatuma Roba (ETH)	2:26:23
1988	Rosa Mota (POR)	2:24:30	1998	Fatuma Roba (ETH)	2:23:21
1989	Ingrid Kristiansen (NOR)	2:24:33	1999	Fatuma Roba (ETH)	2:23:25
1990	Rosa Mota (POR)	2:25:23	2000	Catherine Ndereba (KEN)	2:26:11
1991	Wanda Panfil (POL)	2:24:18	2001	Catherine Ndereba (KEN)	2:23:53
1992	Olga Markova (RUS)	2:23:43	2002	Margaret Okayo (KEN)	2:20:43
1993	Olga Markova (RUS)	2:25:27			

New York City Marathon

Won by an American runner except as indicated.

YEAR	MEN	H:MIN:SEC	WOMEN	H:MIN:SEC
1970	Gary Muhrcke	2:31:38	no finisher	
1971	Norm Higgins	2:22:54	Beth Bonner	2:55:22
1972	Robert Karlin	2:27:52	Nina Kuscsik	3:08:41
1973	Tom Fleming	2:21:54	Nina Kuscsik	2:57:07
1974	Norbert Sander	2:26:30	Katherine Switzer	3:07:29
1975	Tom Fleming	2:19:27	Kim Merritt	2:46:14
1976	Bill Rodgers	2:10:09	Michiko Gorman	2:39:11
1977	Bill Rodgers	2:11:28	Michiko Gorman	2:43:10
1978	Bill Rodgers	2:12:12	Grete Waitz (NOR)	2:32:30
1979	Bill Rodgers	2:11:42	Grete Waitz (NOR)	2:27:33
1980	Alberto Salazar	2:09:41	Grete Waitz (NOR)	2:25:41
1981	Alberto Salazar	2:08:13	Allison Roe (NZL)	2:25:29
1982	Alberto Salazar	2:09:29	Grete Waitz (NOR)	2:27:14
1983	Rod Dixon	2:08:59	Grete Waitz (NOR)	2:27:00
1984	Orlando Pizzolato	2:14:53	Grete Waitz (NOR)	2:29:30
1985	Orlando Pizzolato	2:11:34	Grete Waitz (NOR)	2:28:34
1986	Gianni Poli (ITA)	2:11:06	Grete Waitz (NOR)	2:28:06
1987	Ibrahim Hussein (KEN)	2:11:01	Priscilla Welch (GBR)	2:30:17
1988	Steve Jones (WAL)	2:08:20	Grete Waitz (NOR)	2:28:07
1989	Juma Ikangaa (TAN)	2:08:01	Ingrid Kristiansen (NOR)	2:25:30
1990	Douglas Wakiihuri (KEN)	2:12:39	Wanda Panfil (POL)	2:30:45
1991	Salvador Garcia (MEX)	2:09:28	Liz McColgan (SCO)	2:27:23
1992	Willie Mtolo (RSA)	2:09:29	Lisa Ondieki (AUS)	2:24:40
1993	Andrés Espinosa (MEX)	2:10:04	Uta Pippig (GER)	2:26:24
1994	German Silva (MEX)	2:11:21	Tegla Loroupe (KEN)	2:27:37
1995	German Silva (MEX)	2:11:00	Tegla Loroupe (KEN)	2:28:06
1996	Giacomo Leone (ITA)	2:09:54	Anuta Catuna (ROM)	2:28:18
1997	John Kagwe (KEN)	2:08:12	Franziska Rochat-Moser (SUI)	2:28:43
1998	John Kagwe (KEN)	2:08:45	Franca Fiacconi (ITA)	2:25:17
1999	Joseph Chebet (KEN)	2:09:14	Adriana Fernández (MEX)	2:25:06
2000	Abdelkhader El Mouaziz (MAR)	2:10:09	Lyudmila Petrova (RUS)	2:25:45
2001	Tesfaye Jifar (ETH)	2:07:43	Margaret Okayo (KEN)	2:24:21
2002	scheduled to be run 3 Nov 2002, New York City			

Rodeo

A uniquely **North American** competition, the rodeo has been held on a more or less formal basic since the late 1920s. From 1929 to 1944 the men's world all-around rodeo champion was named by the **Rodeo Association of America**. Since 1944 the all-around champion has been the leading money-winner of the year—with the exception of the years 1976–78, when the champion was the cowboy who won the most money at the National Finals Rodeo. The Rodeo Association of America changed its name several times, but has been known as the **Professional Rodeo Cowboys Association** (PRCA)

since 1975. Among other rodeo sanctioning activities, the PRCA qualifies cowboys for the **National Finals Rodeo**, a contest held in early December in Las Vegas NV among the top competitors in each of several events including bronc riding (bareback and saddle), bull riding, calf roping, and steer wrestling (individual and team). Women compete in one event only, barrel racing.

Professional Rodeo Cowboys Association Web site: <www.prorodeo.com>

Men's World All-Around Rodeo Champions

Awarded since 1929. Table shows champions for the past 20 years.

YEAR	WINNER	YEAR	WINNER	YEAR	WINNER	YEAR	WINNER
1982	Chris Lybbert	1987	Lewis Feild	1992	Ty Murray	1997	Dan Mortensen
1983	Roy Cooper	1988	Dave Appleton	1993	Ty Murray	1998	Ty Murray
1984	Dee Pickett	1989	Ty Murray	1994	Ty Murray	1999	Fred Whitfield
1985	Lewis Feild	1990	Ty Murray	1995	Joe Beaver	2000	Joe Beaver
1986	Lewis Feild	1991	Ty Murray	1996	Joe Beaver	2001	Cody Ohl

Rowing

World championship rowing was established in 1962 by the **Fédération Internationale des Sociétés d'Aviron** (FISA; founded 1892). Events are contested over a 2,000-meter course and include single, double, and quadruple sculls; pairs (with and without coxswain); fours (with and without coxswain); and eights (with coxswain). **Women's world championships**, held since 1974, include single, double, and coxed quadruple sculls; coxless pairs; fours; and eights, raced over a 1,000-meter course until 1985 (2,000-meter course thereafter).

The most famous and historic of rowing courses is the 2,112-meter course at Henley-on-Thames, Oxfordshire, England. Two events of the **Henley Regatta** are open to the world, the **Diamond Challenge Sculls** for single sculls and the **Grand Challenge Cup** for eights. Unless otherwise mentioned, the clubs listed in the Henley Regatta events are English.

Another historic event is the annual University Boat Race between Eights from Oxford and Cambridge universities, which was instituted on 10 Jun 1829. The record time for the course of 4 mi 374 yd (6,779 m) from Putney to Mortlake on the River Thames is 16 min 19 sec by Cambridge in 1998.

International Federation of Rowing Associations Web site: <www.fisa.org>

World Rowing Championships—Men

The competition has been held since 1962. The table shows only the past 20 years.
Results are for heavyweight events only. Times are given in minutes:seconds.
The next championship is scheduled to be held in August 2002.

YEAR	SINGLE SCULLS	TIME	DOUBLE SCULLS	TIME
1982	Rudiger Reiche (GDR)	7:00.67	Ron Thorsen, Alf Hansen (NOR)	6:23.66
1983	Peter-Michael Kolbe (FRG)	6:49.88	Tom Lange, Uwe Heppner (GDR)	6:20.17
1984*	Pertti Karppinen (FIN)	7:00.24	Bradley Lewis, Paul Enquist (USA)	6:36.87
1985	Pertti Karppinen (FIN)	6:48.08	Uwe Heppner, Thomas Lange (GDR)	6:15.49
1986	Peter-Michael Kolbe (FRG)	6:54.09	Alberto Belgeri, Igor Pescialli (ITA)	6:33.64
1987	Thomas Lange (GDR)	7:36.41	D. Iordanov, V. Dadev (BUL)	7:03.33
1988*	Thomas Lange (GDR)	6:49.86	Ronald Florijan, Nicolaas Rienks (NED)	6:21.13
1989	Thomas Lange (GDR)	6:58.14	Rolf Thorsen, Lars Bjoenness (NOR)	6:23.40
1990	Yury Jensen (URS)	7:22.15	Christoph Zerbst, Arnold Jonke (AUT)	6:56.37
1991	Thomas Lange (GDR)	6:41.29	Henk-Jan Zwolle, Nicolaas Rienks (NED)	6:06.14
1992*	Thomas Lange (GDR)	6:51.40	Stephen Hawkins, Peter Antonie (AUT)	6:17.32
1993	Derek Porter (CAN)	6:59.03	Yves Lamarque, Samuel Barathay (FRA)	6:24.69
1994	André Willims (GER)	6:46.33	Rolf Thorsen, Lars Bjoenness (NOR)	6:08.33
1995	Iztok Cop (SLO)	6:52.93	Lars Christensen, Martin Haldbo-Hansen (DEN)	6:17.01
1996	Xeno Müller (SUI)	6:44.85	Davide Tizzano, Agostino Abbagnale (ITA)	6:16.90
1997	James Koven (USA)	6:44.86	Stephan Volkert, Andreas Hajek (GER)	6:13.35
1998	Robert Waddell (NZL)	6:39.65	Stephan Volkert, Andreas Hajek (GER)	6:13.20
1999	Robert Waddell (NZL)	6:36.68	Luka Spik, Iztok Cop (SLO)	6:04.37
2000	Robert Waddell (NZL)	6:48.90	Luka Spik, Iztok Cop (SLO)	6:16.63
2001	Olaf Tufte (NOR)	6:43.04	Akos Haller, Tibor Peto (HUN)	6:14.16

YEAR	COXED PAIRS	TIME	COXLESS PAIRS	MIN:S
1982	Guiseppe Abbagnale, Carmine Abbagnale (ITA)	6:59.63	Magnus Grepperud, Sverre Loken (NOR)	6:41.98
1983	Thoman Greiner, Ullrich Diessner (GDR)	6:49.75	C. Ertel, Ulf Sauerbrey (GDR)	6:35.85
1984*	G. Abbagnale, C. Abbagnale (ITA)	7:05.99	Petru Iosub, Valer Toma (ROM)	6:45.39
1985	G. Abbagnale, C. Abbagnale (ITA)	6:53.40	Nikolay Pimenov, Yury Pimenov (URS)	6:38.39
1986	Andy Holmes, Steve Redgrave (GBR)	6:51.66	Nikolay Pimenov, Yury Pimenov (URS)	6:42.37
1987	G. Abbagnale, C. Abbagnale (ITA)	7:40.81	Steve Redgrave, Andrew Holmes (GBR)	7:11.20
1988*	G. Abbagnale, C. Abbagnale (ITA)	6:58.79	Steve Redgrave, Andrew Holmes (GBR)	6:36.84
1989	G. Abbagnale, C. Abbagnale (ITA)	6:54.81	Thomas Jung, Uwe Kellner (GDR)	6:39.95
1990	G. Abbagnale, C. Abbagnale (ITA)	6:48.30	Thomas Jung, Uwe Kellner (GDR)	7:07.91
1991	G. Abbagnale, C. Abbagnale (ITA)	7:34.49	Steve Redgrave, Matthew Pinsent (GBR)	6:21.35
1992*	Jonny Searle, Greg Searle (GBR)	6:49.83	Steve Redgrave, Matthew Pinsent (GBR)	6:27.72
1993	Jonny Searle, Greg Searle (GBR)	7:01.50	Steve Redgrave, Matthew Pinsent (GBR)	6:37.11

World Rowing Championships—Men (continued)

YEAR	COXED PAIRS	TIME	COXLESS PAIRS	MIN:S
1994	Tihomir Frankovic, Igor Boraska (CRO)	6:42.16	Steve Redgrave, Matthew Pinsent (GBR)	6:18.65
1995	Luca Sartori, Giuliano DeStabile (ITA)	7:35.11	Steve Redgrave, Matthew Pinsent (GBR)	6:28.11
1996	Yannick Schulte, Luc Prevot (FRA)	7:18.26	Steve Redgrave, Matthew Pinsent (GBR)	6:20.09
1997	Scott Fentress, Jordan Irving (USA)	6:56.30	Michel Andrieux, Jean-Christophe Rolland (FRA)	6:27.69
1998	Nick Green, James Tomkins (AUS)	6:45.01	Robert Sens, Detlef Kirchhoff (GER)	6:22.32
1999	James Neil, Phil Henry (USA)	6:48.56	Drew Ginn, James Tomkins (AUS)	6:19.00
2000	Kurt Borcherding, Matt Guerrieri (USA)	7:07.15	Michel Andrieux, Jean-Christophe Rolland (FRA)	6:32.97
2001	James Cracknell, Matthew Pinsent (GBR)	6:49.33	James Cracknell, Matthew Pinsent (GBR)	6:27.57

YEAR	COXED FOURS	TIME	YEAR	COXLESS FOURS	TIME	YEAR	EIGHTS	TIME
1982	East Germany	6:19.04	1982	Switzerland	6:10.41	1982	New Zealand	5:36.99
1983	New Zealand	6:13.89	1983	West Germany	5:57.02	1983	New Zealand	5:34.39
1984*	Great Britain	6:18.64	1984*	New Zealand	6:03.48	1984*	Canada	5:41.32
1985	USSR	6:07.23	1985	West Germany	6:00.19	1985	USSR	5:33.71
1986	East Germany	6:03.81	1986	United States	6:03.53	1986	Australia	5:33.54
1987	East Germany	6:41.74	1987	East Germany	6:39.70	1987	United States	5:58.83
1988*	East Germany	6:10.74	1988*	East Germany	6:03.11	1988*	West Germany	5:46.05
1989	Romania	6:14.90	1989	East Germany	6:06.94	1989	West Germany	5:43.88
1990	East Germany	6:46.73	1990	Australia	6:52.20	1990	West Germany	5:26.62
1991	Germany	5:58.96	1991	Australia	6:29.69	1991	Germany	5:50.98
1992*	Romania	5:59.37	1992*	Australia	5:55.04	1992*	Canada	5:29.53
1993	Romania	6:14.64	1993	France	6:04.54	1993	Germany	5:37.08
1994	Romania	6:06.69	1994	Italy	5:48.44	1994	United States	5:24.50
1995	United States	6:37.50	1995	Italy	5:58.28	1995	Germany	5:53.40
1996	Romania	6:25.74	1996	Australia	6:06.37	1996	Netherlands	5:42.74
1997	France	6:04.17	1997	Great Britain	5:52.40	1997	United States	5:27.20
1998	Australia	6:09.43	1998	Great Britain	5:48.06	1998	United States	5:38.78
1999	United States	6:38.31	1999	Great Britain	5:40.57	1999	United States	6:01.58
2000	Great Britain	6:16.82	2000	Great Britain	5:56.24	2000	Great Britain	5:33.08
2001	France	6:08.25	2001	Great Britain	5:48.98	2001	Romania	5:27.48

*Olympic champions, recognized as world champions.

World Rowing Championships—Women

The competition has been held since 1974. The table shows only the past 20 years. Results are for heavyweight events only. Times are given in minutes:seconds.

YEAR	SINGLE SCULLS	TIME	DOUBLE SCULLS	TIME
1982	I. Fetisova (URS)	3:42.83	Antonina Makhina, E. Bratishko (URS)	3:19.47
1983	Jutta Behrendt-Hampe (GDR)	3:36.51	J. Schenk, Martina Schröter (GDR)	3:13.44
1984*	Valeria Racila (ROM)	3:40.68	Marioara Popescu, Elisabeta Oleniuc (ROM)	3:26.75
1985	Cornelia Linse (GDR)	7:40.37	Sylvia Schwabe, Martina Schröter (GDR)	6:58.80
1986	Jutta Behrendt-Hampe (GDR)	7:29.60	Sylvia Schwabe, Martina Schröter (GDR)	6:57.71
1987	Magdalena Georgieva (BUL)	8:59.26	Stefka Madina, Violeta Ninova (BUL)	7:47.89
1988*	Jutta Behrendt-Hampe (GDR)	7:47.19	Birgit Peter, Martina Schröter (GDR)	7:00.48
1989	Elisabeth Lipa (ROM)	7:27.96	Jana Sorges, Beate Schramm (GDR)	7:01.71
1990	Birgit Peter (GDR)	7:24.10	Kathrin Boron, Beate Schramm (GDR)	8:18.63
1991	Silken Laumann (CAN)	8:17.58	Kathrin Boron, Beate Schramm (GER)	6:44.71
1992*	Elisabeth Lipa (ROM)	7:25.54	Kathrin Boron, Kerstin Köppen (GER)	6:49.00
1993	Jana Thieme (GER)	7:26.00	Philippa Baker, Brenda Lawson (NZL)	7:03.42
1994	Trine Hansen (DEN)	7:23.96	Philippa Baker, Brenda Lawson (NZL)	6:45.30
1995	Maria Brandin (SWE)	7:26.00	Marnie McBean, Kathleen Heddle (CAN)	6:55.76
1996	Yekaterina Khodotovich (BLR)	7:32.21	Marnie McBean, Kathleen Heddle (CAN)	6:56.84
1997	Yekaterina Khodotovich (BLR)	7:29.30	Meike Evers, Kathrin Boron (GER)	6:51.07
1998	Irina Fedotova (RUS)	7:25.09	Miriam Batten, Gillian Lindsay (GBR)	6:48.85
1999	Yekaterina Khodotovich-Karsten (BLR)	7:11.68	Jana Thieme, Kathrin Boron (GER)	6:41.98
2000	Yekaterina Khodotovich-Karsten (BLR)	7:28.14	Jana Thieme, Kathrin Boron (GER)	6:55.44
2001	Katrin Rutschow-Stomporowski (GER)	7:19.25	Kathrin Boron, Kerstin Kowalski (GER)	6:50.20
2002	*the 2002 competition will be held in August*			

World Rowing Championships—Women (continued)

YEAR	QUADRUPLE SCULLS	TIME	YEAR	QUADRUPLE SCULLS	TIME
1982	USSR	3:07.58	1993	China	6:21.07
1983	USSR	3:02.48	1994	Germany	6:11.73
1984*	Romania	3:14.11	1995	Germany	6:40.80
1985	East Germany	6:22.47	1996	Germany	6:27.44
1986	East Germany	6:13.91	1997	Germany	6:16.15
1987	East Germany	6:58.42	1998	Germany	6:24.38
1988*	East Germany	6:21.06	1999	Germany	7:06.53
1989	East Germany	6:16.62	2000	Germany	6:19.58
1990	East Germany	6:14.08	2001	Germany	6:12.95
1991	Germany	6:55.85	2002	the 2002 competition will be held in August	
1992*	Germany	6:20.18			

YEAR	COXLESS PAIRS	TIME	YEAR	COXLESS PAIRS	TIME
1982	M. Sandig, S. Fruhlich (GDR)	03:32.4	1992*	Marnie McBean, Kathleen Heddle (CAN)	07:06.2
1983	Marita Gasch, S. Fruhlich (GDR)	03:26.7			
1984*	Rodica Arba, Elena Horvat (ROM)	03:32.6	1993	Christine Gosse, Helene Cortin (FRA)	07:24.7
1985	Rodica Arba, Elena Horvat-Florea (ROM)	07:25.1	1994	Christine Gosse, Helene Cortin (FRA)	07:01.8
			1995	Megan Still, Kate Slatter (AUS)	07:12.7
1986	Rodica Arba, Olga Homeghi (ROM)	07:12.2	1996	Megan Still, Kate Slatter (AUS)	07:01.4
1987	Rodica Arba, Olga Homeghi (ROM)	08:00.7	1997	Emma Robinson, Alison Korn (CAN)	07:08.1
1988*	Rodica Arba, Olga Homeghi (ROM)	07:28.1	1998	Emma Robinson, Alison Korn (CAN)	07:05.2
1989	K. Haaker, Judith Zeidler (GDR)	07:27.0	1999	Emma Robinson, Theresa Luke (CAN)	07:00.9
1990	Stefani Werremeier, Ingeburg Althoff (FRG)	08:28.4	2000	Georgeta Damian, Doina Ignat (ROM)	07:11.0
			2001	Georgeta Damian, Vlorica Susanu (ROM)	07:01.2
1991	Marnie McBean, Kathleen Heddle (CAN)	06:57.4	2002	the 2002 competition will be held in August	

YEAR	FOURS‡	TIME	YEAR	FOURS‡	TIME	YEAR	EIGHTS	TIME
1982	USSR	3:17.16	1998	Ukraine	6:30.63	1990	Romania	5:59.26
1983	East Germany	3:11.18	1999	Belarus	6:26.25	1991	Canada	6:28.20
1984*	Romania	3:19.30	2000	Belarus	6:44.90	1992*	Canada	6:02.62
1985	East Germany	6:50.08	2001	Australia	6:27.23	1993	Romania	6:18.88
1986	Romania	6:43.86	2002	the 2002 competition will be held in August		1994	Germany	6:07.42
1987	Romania	7:30.12				1995	United States	6:50.73
1988*	East Germany	6:56.00				1996	Romania	6:19.73
1989	East Germany	6:45.81	YEAR	EIGHTS	TIME	1997	Romania	6:02.40
1990	Romania	7:51.68	1982	USSR	2:57.97	1998	Romania	6:14.62
1991	Canada	6:25.43	1983	USSR	2:56.22	1999	Romania	6:47.66
1992*	Canada	6:30.85	1984*	United States	2:59.80	2000	Romania	6:44.00
1993	China	6:42.06	1985	USSR	6:14.00	2001	Australia	6:03.66
1994	Netherlands	6:30.76	1986	USSR	6:08.76	2002	the 2002 competition will be held in August	
1995	United States	7:03.53	1987	Romania	6:55.61			
1996	United States	6:49.48	1988*	East Germany	6:15.17			
1997	Great Britain	6:40.30	1989	Romania	6:07.92			

Olympic champions, recognized as world champions. ‡With coxswain until 1989; coxless since then.

Grand Challenge Cup

Cup has been contested since 1839. Table shows results for the past 20 years. Winners are British except as indicated.

YEAR	WINNER	MIN:SEC	YEAR	WINNER	MIN:SEC
1983	London R.C. and University of London	6:26	1994	Charles River and San Diego (USA)	6:13
			1995	San Diego Training Center (USA)	5:59
1984	Leander Club and London R.C.	6:22	1996	Imperial College and Queens Tower	6:11
1985	Harvard University (USA)	6:27	1997	Institutes of Sport (AUS)	6:03
1986	Nautilus R.C.	6:18	1998	Hansa Dortmund and Berlin (GER)	6:18
1987	Soviet Army (URS)	6:11	1999	Hansa Dortmund and Berlin (GER)	6:15
1988	Leander-University of London	6:17	2000	Institutes of Sport (AUS)	6:19
1989	Hansa Dortmund (FRG)	5:58	2001	H.A.V.K. Mladost and V.K. Croatia (CRO)	6:29
1990	Hansa Dortmund (FRG)	6:36			
1991	Leander and Star R.C.	6:22	2002	Victoria C.R.C. and University of Victoria (CAN)	
1992	University of London	6:04			
1993	Dortmund (GER)	6:11	2003	scheduled to be held in July	

R.C.—Rowing Club.

The Diamond Challenge Sculls

The race has been rowed since 1844. The table shows the winners for the past 20 years. Winners are British except as indicated.

YEAR	WINNER (CLUB, COUNTRY)	MIN:SEC	YEAR	WINNER (CLUB, COUNTRY)	MIN:SEC
1983	Steve Redgrave (Marlow R.C.)	8:23	1993	Tomas Lange (GER)	7:39
1984	Chris Baillieu (Leander Club)	7:57	1994	Xeno Müller (Grasshopper, SUI)	7:35
1985	Steve Redgrave (Marlow R.C.)	8:28	1995	Juri Jaanson (Parnu, EST)	7:24
1986	B. Eltang (DEN)	8:08*	1996	Merlin Vervoorn (Delft, NED)	7:42
1987	Peter-Michael Kolbe (Ruder-Club Hamburg)	7:52	1997	Greg Searle (Molesey B.C.)	7:38
1988	Hamish McGlashan (Melbourne Univ.)	7:43	1998	James Koven (USA)	7:56
			1999	Marcel Hacker (GER)	7:59
1989	Vaclav Chalupa (Dukla Praha, TCH)	7:23†	2000	Aquil Abdullah (USA)	8:12
1990	Eric Verdonk (Koru, NZL)	8:21	2001	Duncan Free (AUS)	8:18
1991	W. Van Belleghem (BEL)	8:14*	2002	P.J.C. Wells (Univ. of London)	8:30
1992	R.G.F. Henderson (Leander Club)	7:44	2003	*scheduled to be held in July*	

B.C.—Boating Club.   R.C.—Rowing Club.   *Not rowed out.   †Record.

Sailing (Yachting)

One of the classic sailing events is the race that was first proposed by the Royal Yacht Squadron (RYS), best known as the **America's Cup**. This cup, open to challenge since 1870, was originally the Hundred-Guinea Cup, presented by the RYS for a race around the Isle of Wight, UK, and won handily by the American yacht *America*. The most graceful of the yachts entered for the America's Cup are generally considered to have been the J-class yachts raced between 1930 and 1937. The cost of maintenance, however, was prohibitive, and since 1958, both winning and challenging vessels have been 12-m (39-ft).

The **Transpacific Race** was inaugurated in 1906 and usually was raced over 3,580 km (2,225 mi) between San Pedro CA, and Diamond Head Light, Oahu, HI. It was made biennial in 1939, alternating with the Bermuda Race.

The **Bermuda Race**, from 1906 to 1910, was an annual race between Gravesend Bay NY (in 1908 the starting point was Marblehead MA), and Bermuda. Six races from New London CT, and one from Montauk Point NY (1932), were held in 1923–34. Since 1936 it has been raced biennially from Newport RI over a 1,022-km (635-mi) course. In 1982 it was divided into two classes—one for cruiser/racers and one for grand prix racers—with the craft winning its race by the greatest margin as overall winner. Since 1986 two equal awards have been offered.

The **Admiral's Cup** is awarded biennially to the national team accumulating the most total points in a series of six races (five until 1987) held off the southern coast of England.

Related Internet resources: America's Cup: <www.americascupnews.com>; Transpacific Race: <www.transpacificyc.org>; Bermuda Race: <www.bermudarace.com>; Admiral's Cup (Royal Ocean Racing Club Web site): <www.rorc.org>

World-Class Boat Champions, 2001

CLASS	WINNER	COUNTRY	CLASS	WINNER	COUNTRY
Etchells 22	Stuart Childerley	Great Britain	Laser	Robert Scheidt	Brazil
Europe	Sari Multala	Finland	Mistral (men)	Nikos Kaklamanakis	Greece
Finn	Sebastien Godefroid	Belgium	Mistral (women)	Lee Lai Shan	Hong Kong
2.4 Meter	Heiko Kroger	Germany	J/24	Kazuyuki Hyodo	Japan
470 (men)	Yevgeny Braslavets/ Igor Matviyenko	Ukraine	Optimist	Lucas Calabrese	Argentina
			Star	Fredrik Lööf/Christian Finnsgård	Sweden
470 (women)	Sofia Bekatorou/ Emilia Tsoulfa	Greece			
			Tornado	Darren Bundock/John Forbes	Australia
49er	Jonathan McKee/ Charlie McKee	United States	Yngling	Christoph Skolaut	Austria

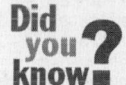

Athletic pursuits of US Presidents: John F. Kennedy was an avid sailor.

America's Cup

YEAR	WINNING YACHT	OWNER	SKIPPER	LOSING YACHT	OWNER
1851	*America* (USA)	John Cox Stevens	Richard Brown	*Aurora* (GBR)	Thomas Le Marchant
1870	*Magic* (USA)	Franklin Osgood	Andrew Comstock	*Cambria* (GBR)	James Ashbury
1871	*Columbia* (USA)	Franklin Osgood	Nelson Comstock	*Livonia* (GBR)	James Ashbury
	Sappho (USA)	William P. Douglas	Sam Greenwood		
1876	*Madeleine* (USA)	John S. Dickerson	Josephus Williams	*Countess of Dufferin* (CAN)	Charles Gifford and syndicate
1881	*Mischief* (USA)	Joseph R. Busk	Nathaniel Clock	*Atalanta* (CAN)	Alexander Cuthbert
1885	*Puritan* (USA)	J. Malcolm Forbes, Charles J. Paine and syndicate	Aubrey Crocker	*Genesta* (GBR)	Sir Richard Sutton
1886	*Mayflower* (USA)	Charles J. Paine	Martin V.B. Stone	*Galatea* (GBR)	William Henn
1887	*Volunteer* (USA)	Charles J. Paine	Henry C. Haff	*Thistle* (GBR)	James Bell and syndicate
1893	*Vigilant* (USA)	C. Oliver Iselin and syndicate	William Hansen	*Valkyrie II* (GBR)	Lord Dunraven
1895	*Defender* (USA)	William K. Vanderbilt, C. Oliver Iselin, Edwin D. Morgan	Henry C. Haff	*Valkyrie III* (GBR)	Lord Dunraven, Lord Lonsdale, Lord Wolverton, H. McCalmont
1899	*Columbia* (USA)	J.P. Morgan, C. Oliver Iselin, Edwin D. Morgan	Charles Barr	*Shamrock* (GBR)	Sir Thomas Lipton
1901	*Columbia* (USA)	J.P. Morgan, Edwin D. Morgan	Charles Barr	*Shamrock II* (GBR)	Sir Thomas Lipton
1903	*Reliance* (USA)	C. Oliver Iselin and syndicate	Charles Barr	*Shamrock III* (GBR)	Sir Thomas Lipton
1920	*Resolute* (USA)	Henry Walters and syndicate	Charles Francis Adams II	*Shamrock IV* (GBR)	Sir Thomas Lipton
1930	*Enterprise* (USA)	Winthrop Aldrich and syndicate	Harold S. Vanderbilt	*Shamrock V* (GBR)	Sir Thomas Lipton
1934	*Rainbow* (USA)	Harold S. Vanderbilt and syndicate	Harold S. Vanderbilt	*Endeavour* (GBR)	Thomas Octave Murdoch Sopwith
1937	*Ranger* (USA)	Harold S. Vanderbilt	Harold S. Vanderbilt	*Endeavour II* (GBR)	Thomas Octave Murdoch Sopwith
1958	*Columbia* (USA)	Henry Sears and syndicate	Briggs S. Cunningham	*Sceptre* (GBR)	Hugh L. Goodson and syndicate
1962	*Weatherly* (USA)	Henry D. Mercer, Arnold D. Frese, Cornelius S. Walsh	Emil Mosbacher, Jr.	*Gretel* (AUS)	Sir Frank Packer and syndicate
1964	*Constellation* (USA)	Walter S. Gubelmann, Eric Ridder and syndicate	Robert N. Bavier, Jr., Eric Ridder	*Sovereign* (GBR)	J. Anthony Boyden
1967	*Intrepid* (USA)	Intrepid syndicate	Emil Mosbacher, Jr.	*Dame Pattie* (GBR)	Emil Christensen and 15 commercial firms
1970	*Intrepid* (USA)	Intrepid syndicate	William Ficker	*Gretel II* (AUS)	Sir Frank Packer and syndicate
1974	*Courageous* (USA)	Courageous syndicate	Ted Hood	*Southern Cross* (AUS)	Alan Bond
1977	*Courageous* (USA)	Courageous syndicate	Ted Turner	*Australia* (AUS)	Alan Bond and syndicate
1980	*Freedom* (USA)	Maritime College at Ft. Schuyler Foundation, Inc.	Dennis Conner	*Australia* (AUS)	Alan Bond and syndicate
1983	*Australia II* (AUS)	Alan Bond and syndicate	John Bertrand	*Liberty* (USA)	Maritime Col. at Ft. Schuyler Foundation, Inc.
1987	*Stars & Stripes* (USA)	Sail America syndicate	Dennis Conner	*Kookaburra III* (AUS)	Kevin Parry and syndicate
1988	*Stars & Stripes* (USA)	Sail America syndicate	Dennis Conner	*New Zealand* (NZL)	Michael Fay
1992	*America³* (USA)	America³ Foundation	William Koch	*Il Moro di Venezia* (ITA)	Compagnia della Vela di Venezia
1995	*Black Magic* (NZL)	Peter Blake and Team New Zealand	Russell Coutts	*Young America* (USA)	Pact 95 syndicate
2000	*Black Magic* (NZL)	Team New Zealand	Russell Coutts	*Luna Rossa* (ITA)	Prada Challenge
2003	*scheduled to be held 15 February–1 March, Auckland, New Zealand*				

Transpacific Race

YEAR	WINNING YACHT	OWNER	YEAR	WINNING YACHT	OWNER
1906	*Lurline*	Harold H. Sinclair	1961	*Nam Sang*	A.B. Robbs, Jr.
1908	*Lurline*	Harold H. Sinclair	1963	*Islander*	Earl Corkett
1910	*Hawaii*	Honolulu Yachting Club	1965	*Psyche*	Don Salisbury
1912	*Lurline*	A.E. Davis	1967	*Holiday Too*	Robert Allan
1923	*Diablo*	A.R. Pedder	1969	*Argonaut*	Jon Andron
1925	*Mariner*	L.A. Norris	1971	*Windward Passage*	Robert Johnson
1926	*Invader*	Don M. Lee	1973	*Chutzpah*	Stuart Cowan
1928	*Teva*	Clem W. Stose	1975	*Chutzpah*	Stuart Cowan
1930	*Enchantress*	Morgan Adams	1977	*Merlin*	Bill Lee
1932	*Fayth*	William S. McNutt	1979	*Arriba*	Dennis Choate
1934	*Manulwa*	Harold Dillingham	1981	*Sweet Okole*	Dean Treadway
1936	*Dorade*	James Flood	1983	*Bravura*	Irving Loube
1939	*Blitzen*	T.J. Reynolds	1985	*Montgomery Street*	James Denning
1941	*Escapade*	D.W. Elliott	1987	*Merlin*	Don Campion
1943–45	not held		1989	*Silver Bullet*	John DeLaura
1947	*Dolphin*	Frank Morgan	1991	*Chance*	Robert McNulty
1949	*Kitten*	Fred W. Lyon	1993	*Silver Bullet*	John DeLaura
1951	*Sea Witch*	A.L. McCormick	1995	*Merlin*	Dan Sinclair
1953	*Staghound*	Ira P. Fulmor	1997	*Ralphie*	Jerry Montgomery
1955	*Staghound*	Ira P. Fulmor	1999	*Grand Illusion*	James McDowell
1957	*Legend*	Charles Ullman	2001	*Bull*	Seth Radow
1959	*Nalu II*	Peter Grant	2003	scheduled to be held July, Los Angeles	

Bermuda Race

YEAR	WINNING YACHT	OWNER	YEAR	WINNING YACHT	OWNER
1906	*Tamerlane*	Frank Maier	1962	*Nina*	DeCoursey Fales
1907	*Dervish*	Henry A. Morss	1964	*Burgoo*	Milton Ernstof
1908	*Venona*	Elmer J. Bliss	1966	*Thunderbird*	T.V. Learson
1909	*Margaret*	George S. Runk	1968	*Robin*	Ted Hood
1910	*Vagrant*	Harold S. Vanderbilt	1970	*Carina*	Richard S. Nye
1923*	*Malabar IV*	John G. Alden	1972	*Noryema*	Ron Amey
1924	*Memory*	Robert N. Bavier	1974	*Scaramouche*	Charles Kirsch
1926	*Malabar VII*	John G. Alden	1976	*Running Tide*	Al Van Metre
1928	*Rugosa II*	Russell Grinnell	1978	*Babe*	Arnie Gay
1930	*Malay*	Raymond W. Ferris	1980	*Holger Danske*	Rich Wilson
1932	*Malabar X*	John G. Alden and R.I. Gale	1982†	*Brigadoon III*	Robert Morton
1934	*Edlu*	Rudolph J. Schaefer	1984	*Pamir*	Francis H. Curren, Jr.
1936	*Kirawan*	Robert P. Baruch	1986‡	*Silver Star*	David H. Clarke
1938	*Baruna*	Henry C. Taylor		*Puritan*	Donald P. Robinson
1946*	*Gesture*	Howard Fuller	1988	*Congere*	Bevin Koeppel
1948	*Baruna*	Henry C. Taylor	1990	*Denali*	Lawrence S. Huntington
1950	*Argyll*	William T. Moore	1992	*Constellation*	US Naval Academy
1952	*Carina*	Richard S. Nye	1994	*Gaylark*	Kaighn Smith
1954	*Malay*	D.D. Strohmeier	1996	*Boomerang*	George Coumantaros
1956	*Finisterre*	Carleton Mitchell	1998	*Kodiak*	Llwyd Ecclestone
1958	*Finisterre*	Carleton Mitchell	2000	*Restless*	Eric Crawford
1960	*Finisterre*	Carleton Mitchell	2002	*Pyewacket*	Roy Disney

*No competition 1911–22; 1940–44.   †Overall winner under new measurement rules.   ‡First listed is IOR (International Offshore Rule) winner; second is IMS (International Measurement System) winner.

Admiral's Cup

YEAR	WINNING TEAM	YEAR	WINNING TEAM	YEAR	WINNING TEAM	YEAR	WINNING TEAM
1957	United Kingdom	1971	United Kingdom	1985	West Germany	1999	The Netherlands
1959	United Kingdom	1973	West Germany	1987	New Zealand	2001	canceled
1961	United States	1975	United Kingdom	1989	United Kingdom	2003	scheduled to be
1963	United Kingdom	1977	United Kingdom	1991	France		held 12–26 Jul
1965	United Kingdom	1979	Australia	1993	Germany		2003, Dublin
1967	Australia	1981	United Kingdom	1995	Italy		
1969	United States	1983	West Germany	1997	United States		

Skiing

Although most of the events had been contested at the regional level since the mid-19th century, the first internationally organized **skiing championships** did not take place until 1924. From 1924 to 1931 only **Nordic** competition was involved; **Alpine** championship events were added to world competition in 1931 and to the Olympics in 1936. Except for Olympic years, the Nordic and Alpine championships are held separately and at different locations. **Events** include cross-country races, ski-jumping, biathlon, and relay races (Nordic) and downhill and slalom skiing (Alpine). Since 1967, an **Alpine World Cup** has been presented to the competitor with the best combined downhill, slalom, supergiant slalom (super-G), and giant slalom performance over a series of major contests. A **Nordic World Cup** for cross-country events has been awarded since 1979.

International Ski Federation Web site: <www.fis-ski.com>

Alpine Skiing World Championships—Men

Next championships are scheduled to be held 1–16 Feb 2003, St. Moritz, Switz.

DOWNHILL

1931	Walter Prager (SUI)
1932	*not held*
1933	Walter Prager (SUI), Hans Hauser (AUT)*
1934	David Zogg (SUI)
1935	Franz Zingerle (AUT)
1936†	*not held*
1937	Emile Allais (FRA)
1938	James Couttet (FRA)
1939	Hermuth Lantschner (GER)
1940–47	*not held*
1948†	Henri Oreiller (FRA)
1950	Zeno Colo (ITA)
1952†	Zeno Colo (ITA)
1954	Christian Pravda (AUT)
1956†	Anton (Toni) Sailer (AUT)
1958	Anton (Toni) Sailer (AUT)
1960†	Jean Vuarnet (FRA)
1962	Karl Schranz (AUT)
1964†	Egon Zimmermann (AUT)
1966	Jean-Claude Killy (FRA)
1968†	Jean-Claude Killy (FRA)
1970	Bernhard Russi (SUI)
1972†	Bernhard Russi (SUI)
1974	David Zwilling (AUT)
1976†	Franz Klammer (AUT)
1978	Josef Walcher (AUT)
1980†	Leonhard Stock (AUT)
1982	Harti Weirather (AUT)
1984†	Bill Johnson (USA)
1985	Permin Zurbriggen (SUI)
1987	Peter Müller (SUI)
1988†	Permin Zurbriggen (SUI)
1989	Hansjorg Tauscher (FRG)
1991	Franz Heinzer (SUI)
1992†	Patrick Ortlieb (AUS)
1993	Urs Lehmann (SUI)
1994†	Tommy Moe (USA)
1995	*not held*
1996	Patrick Ortlieb (AUS)
1997	Bruno Kernen (SUI)
1998†	Jean-Luc Cretier (FRA)
1999	Hermann Maier (AUT)
2000	*not held*
2001	Hannes Trinkl (AUT)
2002†	Fritz Strobl (AUT)

COMBINED

1933	Anton Seelos (AUT)
1934	David Zogg (SUI)
1935	Anton Seelos (AUT)
1936†	Franz Pfnür (GER)

COMBINED (CONTINUED)

1937	Emile Allais (FRA)
1938	Emile Allais (FRA)
1939	Josef Jennewein (GER)
1940–47	*not held*
1948†	Henri Oreiller (FRA)
1950	*not held*
1952†	*not held*
1954	Stein Eriksen (NOR)
1956†	*not held*
1958	Anton (Toni) Sailer (AUT)
1960†	*not held*
1962	Karl Schranz (AUT)
1964†	*not held*
1966	Jean-Claude Killy (FRA)
1968†	*not held*
1970	Bill Kidd (USA)
1972†	Gustavo Thoeni (ITA)
1974	Franz Klammer (AUT)
1976†	Gustavo Thoeni (ITA)
1978	Andreas Wenzel (LIE)
1980†	*not held*
1982	Michel Vion (FRA)
1984†	*not held*
1985	Pirmin Zurbriggen (SUI)
1986	*not held*
1987	Marc Girardelli (LUX)
1988†	Hubert Strolz (AUT)
1989	Marc Girardelli (LUX)
1991	Stefan Eberharter (AUT)
1992†	Josef Polig (ITA)
1993	Lasse Kjus (NOR)
1994†	Lasse Kjus (NOR)
1995	*not held*
1996	Marc Girardelli (LUX)
1997	Kjetil Andre Aamodt (NOR)
1998†	Mario Reiter (AUT)
1999	Kjetil Andre Aamodt (NOR)
2000	*not held*
2001	Kjetil Andre Aamodt (NOR)
2002†	Kjetil Andre Aamodt (NOR)

SLALOM

1931	David Zogg (SUI)
1932	*not held*
1933	Anton Seelos (AUT)
1934	Franz Pfnür (GER)
1935	Anton Seelos (AUT)
1936†	*not held*
1937	Emile Allais (FRA)

SLALOM (CONTINUED)

1938	Rudi Rominger (SUI)
1939	Rudi Rominger (SUI)
1940–47	*not held*
1948†	Edi Reinalter (SUI)
1950	Georges Schneider (SUI)
1952†	Othmar Schneider (AUT)
1954	Stein Eriksen (NOR)
1956†	Anton (Toni) Sailer (AUT)
1958	Josi Rieder (AUT)
1960†	Ernst Hinterseer (AUT)
1962	Charles Bozon (FRA)‡
1964†	Josef Stiegler (AUT)
1966	Carlo Senoner (ITA)‡
1968†	Jean-Claude Killy (FRA)
1970	Jean-Noël Augert (FRA)
1972†	Francisco Ochoa (ESP)
1974	Gustavo Thoeni (ITA)
1976†	Piero Gros (ITA)
1978	Ingemar Stenmark (SWE)
1980†	Ingemar Stenmark (SWE)
1982	Ingemar Stenmark (SWE)
1984†	Phil Mahre (USA)
1985	Jonas Nilsson (SWE)
1987	Frank Woerndl (FRG)
1988†	Alberto Tomba (ITA)
1989	Rudolf Nierlich (AUT)
1991	Marc Girardelli (LUX)
1992†	Finn Christian Jagge (NOR)
1993	Kjetil Andre Aamodt (NOR)
1994†	Thomas Stangassinger (AUT)
1995	*not held*
1996	Alberto Tomba (ITA)
1997	Tom Stiansen (NOR)
1998†	Hans-Petter Buraas (NOR)
1999	Kalle Palander (FIN)
2000	*not held*
2001	Mario Matt (AUT)
2002†	Jean-Pierre Vidal (FRA)

GIANT SLALOM

1950	Zeno Colo (ITA)
1952†	Stein Eriksen (NOR)
1954	Stein Eriksen (NOR)
1956†	Anton (Toni) Sailer (AUT)
1958	Anton (Toni) Sailer (AUT)
1960†	Roger Staub (SUI)
1962	Egon Zimmermann (AUT)
1964†	François Bonlieu (FRA)
1966	Guy Perillat (FRA)

Alpine Skiing World Championships—Men (continued)

GIANT SLALOM (CONTINUED)
1968† Jean-Claude Killy (FRA)
1970 Karl Schranz (AUT)
1972† Gustavo Thoeni (ITA)
1974 Gustavo Thoeni (ITA)
1976† Heini Hemmi (SUI)
1978 Ingemar Stenmark (SWE)
1980‡ Ingemar Stenmark (SWE)
1982 Steve Mahre (USA)
1984† Max Julen (SUI)
1985 Markus Wasmeier (FRG)
1987 Pirmin Zurbriggen (SUI)
1988† Alberto Tomba (ITA)
1989 Rudolf Nierlich (AUT)
1991 Rudolf Nierlich (AUT)
1992† Alberto Tomba (ITA)
1993 Kjetil Andre Aamodt (NOR)

GIANT SLALOM (CONTINUED)
1994† Markus Wasmeier (GER)
1995 not held
1996 Alberto Tomba (ITA)
1997 Michael von Grünigen (SUI)
1998† Hermann Maier (AUT)
1999 Lasse Kjus (NOR)
2000 not held
2001 Michael von Grünigen (SUI)
2002† Stephan Eberharter (AUT)

SUPERGIANT SLALOM
1987 Pirmin Zurbriggen (SUI)
1988† Franck Piccard (FRA)
1989 Martin Hangl (SUI)

SUPERGIANT SLALOM (CONTINUED)
1991 Stephan Eberharter (AUT)
1992† Kjetil Andre Aamodt (NOR)
1993 not held
1994† Markus Wasmeier (GER)
1995 not held
1996 Atle Skaardal (NOR)
1997 Atle Skaardal (NOR)
1998† Hermann Maier (AUT)
1999 Lasse Kjus (NOR), Hermann Maier (AUT)§
2000 not held
2001 Daron Rahlves (USA)
2002† Kjetil Andre Aamodt (NOR)

*Special downhill champion.   †Olympic champions, recognized as world champions.
‡Special slalom.   §Tie.

Alpine Skiing World Championships—Women
The next championships are scheduled to be held 11–16 Feb 2003, St. Moritz, Switz.

DOWNHILL
1931 Esme Mackinnon (GBR)
1932 Paula Wiesinger (ITA)
1933 Inge Wersin-Lantschner (AUT)
1934 Anny Rüegg (SUI)
1935 Christl Cranz (GER)
1936 Evelyn Pinching (GBR)
1937 Christl Cranz (GER)
1938 Lisa Resch (GER)
1939 Christl Cranz (GER)
1940–47 not held
1948* Hedy Schlunegger (SUI)
1950 Trude Jochum-Beiser (AUT)
1952* Trude Jochum-Beiser (AUT)
1954 Ida Schöpfer (SUI)
1956ᴬ Madeleine Berthod (SUI)
1958 Lucille Wheeler (CAN)
1960* Heidi Beibl (GER†)
1962 Christl Hass (AUT)
1964* Christl Hass (AUT)
1966 Marielle Goitschel (FRA)‡
1968* Olga Pall (AUT)
1970 Annerösli Zryd (SUI)
1972* Marie-Thérèse Nadig (SUI)
1974 Annemarie Moser-Pröll (AUT)
1976ᴬ Rosi Mittermaier (FRG)
1978 Annemarie Moser-Pröll (AUT)
1980* Annemarie Moser-Pröll (AUT)
1982 Gerry Sorensen (CAN)
1984+ Michela Figini (SUI)
1985 Michela Figini (SUI)
1987 Maria Walliser (SUI)
1988* Marina Kiehl (FRG)
1989 Maria Walliser (SUI)
1991 Petra Kronberger (AUT)
1992* Kerrin Lee-Gartner (CAN)

DOWNHILL (CONTINUED)
1993 Kate Pace (CAN)
1994* Katja Seizinger (GER)
1995 not held
1996 Picabo Street (USA)
1997 Hilary Lindh (USA)
1998* Katja Seizinger (GER)
1999 Renate Götschl (AUT)
2000 not held
2001 Michaela Dorfmeister (AUT)
2002* Carole Montillet (FRA)

COMBINED
1932 Rösli Streiff (SUI)
1933 Inge Wersin-Lantschner (AUT)
1934 Christl Cranz (GER)
1935 Christl Cranz (GER)
1936 Evelyn Pinching (GBR)
1937 Christl Cranz (GER)
1938 Christl Cranz (GER)
1939 Christl Cranz (GER)
1940–47 not held
1948* Trude Beiser (AUT)
1950 not held
1952 not held
1954 Ida Schöpfer (SUI)
1956 Madeleine Berthod (SUI)
1958 Frida Dänzer (SUI)
1960 Anne Heggveit (CAN)
1962 Marielle Goitschel (FRA)
1964 Marielle Goitschel (FRA)
1966 Marielle Goitschel (FRA)
1968 Nancy Greene (CAN)
1970 Michèle Jacot (FRA)
1972 Toril Forland (NOR)
1974 Fabienne Serrat (FRA)
1976 Rosi Mittermaier (FRG)
1978 Annemarie Moser-Pröll (AUT)
1980 Hanni Wenzel (LIE)
1982 Erika Hess (SUI)

COMBINED (CONTINUED)
1984* not held
1985 Erika Hess (SUI)
1987 Erika Hess (SUI)
1988* Anita Wachter (AUT)
1989 Tamara McKinney (USA)
1991 Chantal Bournissen (SUI)
1992* Petra Kronberger (AUT)
1993 Miriam Vogt (GER)
1994* Pernilla Wiberg (SWE)
1995 not held
1996 Pernilla Wiberg (SWE)
1997 Renate Götschl (AUT)
1998* Katja Seizinger (GER)
1999 Pernilla Wiberg (SWE)
2000 not held
2001 Martina Ertl (GER)
2002* Janica Kostelic (CRO)

SLALOM
1931 Esme Mackinnon (GBR)
1932 Rösli Streiff (SUI)
1933 Inge Wersin-Lantschner (AUT)
1934 Christl Cranz (GER)
1935 Anny Rüegg (SUI)
1936 Gerda Paumgarten (AUT)
1937 Christl Cranz (GER)
1938 Christl Cranz (GER)
1939 Christl Cranz (GER)
1940–47 not held
1948* Gretchen Fraser (USA)
1950 Dagmar Rom (AUT)
1952* Andrea Mead Lawrence (USA)
1954 Trude Klecker (AUT)
1956* Renée Colliard (SUI)
1958 Inge Björnbakken (NOR)
1960* Anne Heggtveit (CAN)
1962 Marianne Jahn (Austria)§
1964* Christine Goitschel (FRA)
1966 Annie Famose (FRA)‡
1968* Marielle Goitschel (FRA)

Alpine Skiing World Championships—Women (continued)

SLALOM (CONTINUED)

1970	Ingrid Lafforgue (FRA)
1972*	Barbara Cochran (USA)
1974	Hanni Wenzel (LIE)
1976*	Rosi Mittermaier (FRG)
1978	Lea Sölkner (AUT)
1980*	Hanni Wenzel (LIE)
1982	Erika Hess (SUI)
1984*	Paoletta Magoni (ITA)
1985	Perrine Pelen (FRA)
1987	Erika Hess (SUI)
1988*	Vreni Schneider (SUI)
1989	Mateja Svet (YUG)
1991	Vreni Schneider (SUI)
1992*	Petra Kronberger (AUT)
1993	Karin Buder (AUT)
1994*	Vreni Schneider (SUI)
1995	not held
1996	Pernilla Wiberg (SWE)
1997	Deborah Compagnoni (ITA)
1998*	Hilde Gerg (GER)
1999	Zali Steggall (AUS)
2000	not held
2001	Anja Paerson (SWE)
2002*	Janica Kostelic (CRO)

GIANT SLALOM

1950	Dagmar Rom (AUT)
1952*	Andrea Mead Lawrence (USA)

GIANT SLALOM (CONTINUED)

1954	Lucienne Schmidt-Couttet (FRA)
1956*	Ossi Reichert (FRG)
1958	Lucille Wheeler (CAN)
1960*	Yvonne Rüegg (SUI)
1962	Marianne Jahn (AUT)
1964*	Marielle Goitschel (FRA)
1966	Marielle Goitschel (FRA)
1968*	Nancy Greene (CAN)
1970	Betsy Clifford (CAN)
1972*	Marie-Therese Nadig (SUI)
1974	Fabienne Serrat (FRA)
1976*	Kathy Kreiner (CAN)
1978	Maria Epple (FRG)
1980*	Hanni Wenzel (LIE)
1982	Erika Hess (SUI)
1984*	Debbie Armstrong (USA)
1985	Diann Roffe (USA)
1987	Vreni Schneider (SUI)
1988*	Vreni Schneider (SUI)
1989	Vreni Schneider (SUI)
1991	Pernilla Wiberg (SWE)
1992*	Pernilla Wiberg (SWE)
1993	Carole Merle (FRA)
1994*	Deborah Compagnoni (ITA)
1995	not held
1996	Deborah Compagnoni (ITA)

GIANT SLALOM (CONTINUED)

1997	Deborah Compagnoni (ITA)
1998*	Deborah Compagnoni (ITA)
1999	Alexandra Meissnitzner (AUT)
2000	not held
2001	Sonja Nef (SUI)
2002*	Janica Kostelic (CRO)

SUPERGIANT SLALOM

1987	Maria Walliser (SUI)
1988*	Sigrid Wolf (AUT)
1989	Ulrike Maier (AUT)
1991	Ulrike Maier (AUT)
1992*	Deborah Compagnoni (ITA)
1993	Katja Seizinger (GER)
1994*	Diann Roffe-Steinrotter (USA)
1995	not held
1996	Isolde Kostner (ITA)
1997	Isolde Kostner (ITA)
1998*	Picabo Street (USA)
1999	Alexandra Meissnitzner (AUT)
2000	not held
2001	Régine Cavagnoud (FRA)
2002*	Daniela Ceccarelli (ITA)

*Olympic champions, recognized as world champions.   †Joint East-West German team.   ‡Originally won by Erika Schinegger (AUT), who renounced the medal after a sex test performed for a later Olympic game determined she was actually a man.   §Special slalom.

Alpine World Cup

The winner is determined by the number of points awarded for various wins during the season.

YEAR	MEN	WOMEN	YEAR	MEN	WOMEN
1967	Jean-Claude Killy (FRA)	Nancy Greene (CAN)	1984	Pirmin Zurbriggen (SUI)	Erika Hess (SUI)
1968	Jean-Claude Killy (FRA)	Nancy Greene (CAN)	1985	Marc Girardelli (LUX)	Michela Figini (SUI)
			1986	Marc Girardelli (LUX)	Maria Walliser (SUI)
1969	Karl Schranz (AUT)	Gertrude Gabl (AUT)	1987	Pirmin Zurbriggen (SUI)	Maria Walliser (SUI)
1970	Karl Schranz (AUT)	Michele Jacot (FRA)			
1971	Gustavo Thoeni (ITA)	Annemarie Pröll (AUT)	1988	Pirmin Zurbriggen (SUI)	Michela Figini (SUI)
1972	Gustavo Thoeni (ITA)	Annemarie Pröll (AUT)			
1973	Gustavo Thoeni (ITA)	Annemarie Pröll (AUT)	1989	Marc Girardelli (LUX)	Vreni Schneider (SUI)
1974	Piero Gros (ITA)	Annemarie Moser-Pröll (AUT)	1990	Pirmin Zurbriggen (SUI)	Petra Kronberger (AUT)
1975	Gustavo Thoeni (ITA)	Annemarie Moser-Pröll (AUT)	1991	Marc Girardelli (LUX)	Petra Kronberger (AUT)
1976	Ingemar Stenmark (SWE)	Rosi Mittermaier (FRG)	1992	Paul Accola (SUI)	Petra Kronberger (AUT)
1977	Ingemar Stenmark (SWE)	Lise-Marie Morerod (SUI)	1993	Marc Girardelli (LUX)	Anita Wachter (AUT)
1978	Ingemar Stenmark (SWE)	Hanni Wenzel (LIE)	1994	Kjetil Andre Aamodt (NOR)	Vreni Schneider (SUI)
1979	Peter Luescher (SUI)	Annemarie Moser-Pröll (AUT)	1995	Alberto Tomba (ITA)	Vreni Schneider (SUI)
1980	Andreas Wenzel (LIE)	Hanni Wenzel (LIE)	1996	Lasse Kjus (NOR)	Katja Seizinger (GER)
1981	Phil Mahre (USA)	Marie-Therese Nadig (SUI)	1997	Luc Alphand (FRA)	Pernilla Wiberg (SWE)
			1998	Hermann Maier (AUT)	Katja Seizinger (GER)
1982	Phil Mahre (USA)	Erika Hess (SUI)	1999	Lasse Kjus (NOR)	Alexandra Meissnitzer (AUT)
1983	Phil Mahre (USA)	Tamara McKinney (USA)	2000	Hermann Maier (AUT)	Renate Götschl (AUT)
			2001	Hermann Maier (AUT)	Janica Kostelic (CRO)
			2002	Stephan Eberharter (AUT)	Michaela Dorfmeister (AUT)

Nordic Skiing World Championships   Men

Championships in some events have been held since 1924. The table shows results for the past 20 years. Next championships are scheduled to be held 17 Feb–1 Mar 2003, Val di Fiemme, Italy.

SPRINT
2001	Tor Arne Hetland (NOR)
2002*	Samppa Lajunen (FIN)

10-KM CROSS-COUNTRY
1991	Terje Langli (NOR)
1992*	Vegard Ulvang (NOR)
1993	Sture Sivertsen (NOR)
1994*	Bjørn Daehlie (NOR)
1995	Vladimir Smirnov (KAZ)
1996	not held
1997	Bjørn Daehlie (NOR)
1998*	Bjørn Daehlie (NOR)
1999	Mika Myllyla (FIN)
2000	not held
2001†	Per Elofsson (SWE)
2002*†	Johann Mühlegg (ESP)

15-KM CROSS-COUNTRY‡
1982	Oddvar Braa (NOR)
1984*	Gunde Svan (SWE)
1985	Kari Härkönen (FIN)
1987	Marco Albarello (ITA)
1988*	Mikhail Devyatyarov (URS)
1989	Gunde Svan (SWE)
1991	Bjørn Daehlie (NOR)
1992*	Bjørn Daehlie (NOR)
1993	Bjørn Daehlie (NOR)
1994*	Bjørn Daehlie (NOR)
1995	Vladimir Smirnov (KAZ)
1996	not held
1997	Bjørn Daehlie (NOR)
1998*	Thomas Alsgaard (NOR)

15-KM CROSS-COUNTRY‡ (CONTINUED)
1999	Thomas Alsgaard (NOR)
2000	not held
2001†	Per Elofsson (SWE)
2002*†	Andrus Veerpalu (EST)

30-KM CROSS-COUNTRY
1982	Thomas Eriksson (SWE)
1984*	Nikolay Zimyatov (URS)
1985	Gunde Svan (SWE)
1987	Thomas Wassberg (SWE)
1988*	Aleksey Prokurorov (URS)
1989	Vladimir Smirnov (URS)
1991	Gunde Svan (SWE)
1992*	Vegard Ulvang (NOR)
1993	Bjørn Daehlie (NOR)
1994*	Thomas Alsgaard (NOR)
1995	Vladimir Smirnov (KAZ)
1996	not held
1997	Aleksey Prokurorov (RUS)
1998*	Mika Myllyla (FIN)
1999	Mika Myllyla (FIN)
2000	not held
2001	Andrus Veerpalu (EST)
2002*	Johann Mühlegg (ESP)

50-KM CROSS-COUNTRY
1982	Thomas Wassberg (SWE)
1984*	Thomas Wassberg (SWE)
1985	Gunde Svan (SWE)
1987	Maurilio DeZolt (ITA)
1988*	Gunde Svan (SWE)
1989	Gunde Svan (SWE)

50-KM CROSS-COUNTRY (CONTINUED)
1991	Torgny Mogren (SWE)
1992*	Bjørn Daehlie (NOR)
1993	Torgny Mogren (SWE)
1994	Vladimir Smirnov (KAZ)
1995	Silvio Fauner (ITA)
1996	not held
1997	Mika Myllyla (FIN)
1998*	Bjørn Daehlie (NOR)
1999	Mika Myllyla (FIN)
2000	not held
2001	Johann Mühlegg (ESP)
2002*	Mikhail Ivanov (RUS)

RELAYS§
1982	Norway; USSR (tied)
1984*	Sweden
1987	Sweden
1988*	Sweden
1989	Sweden
1991	Norway
1992*	Norway
1993	Norway
1994*	Italy
1995	Norway
1996	not held
1997	Norway
1998*	Norway
1999	Austria
2001	Norway
2002*	Norway

*Olympic champions, recognized as world champions. †From 1991–2000, the 10-km event was held in tandem with the 15-km event, one event would feature classical and the other freestyle technique. Medals were awarded for both races. Beginning in 2001 this pursuit race instead led to one medal being awarded upon winning. In 2002 the pursuit race featured two 10-km races and the 15-km was a stand-alone event featuring classical technique. ‡18-km cross-country until 1952; 15 km in 1954 and thereafter. §Military relay until 1939; 40-km relay in 1948 and thereafter.

Nordic Skiing World Championships—Nordic Combined

The Nordic combined involves a 15-km cross country race and ski jumping; the sprint is a 7.5-km race plus ski jumping. The next championships are scheduled to be held 18 Feb–1 Mar 2003, Val di Fiemme, Italy.

YEAR	COMBINED
1924*	Thorleif Haug (NOR)
1925	Ottokar Nemecky (TCH)
1926	Johan Gröttumsbraaten (NOR)
1927	Rudolf Purkert (TCH)
1928*	Johan Gröttumsbraaten (NOR)
1929	Hans Vinjarengen (NOR)
1930	Hans Vinjarengen (NOR)
1931	Johan Gröttumsbraaten (NOR)
1932*	Johan Gröttumsbraaten (NOR)
1933	Sven Eriksson (SWE)
1934	Oddbjørn Hagen (NOR)
1935	Oddbjørn Hagen (NOR)
1936*	Oddbjørn Hagen (NOR)
1937	Sigurd Røen (NOR)
1938	Olaf Hoffsbakken (NOR)

YEAR	COMBINED (CONTINUED)
1939	Gustl Berauer (TCH)
1940–47	not held
1948*	Heikki Hasu (FIN)
1950	Heikki Hasu (FIN)
1952*	Simon Slåttvik (NOR)
1954	Sverre Stenersen (NOR)
1956*	Sverre Stenersen (NOR)
1958	Paavo Korhonen (FIN)
1960*	Georg Thoma (GER†)
1962	Arne Larsen (NOR)
1964*	Tormod Knutsen (NOR)
1966	Georg Thoma (FRG)
1968*	Franz Keller (FRG)
1970	Ladislav Rygl (TCH)
1972*	Ulrich Wehling (GDR)
1974	Ulrich Wehling (GDR)
1976*	Ulrich Wehling (GDR)
1978	Konrad Winkler (GDR)
1980*	Ulrich Wehling (GDR)

YEAR	COMBINED (CONTINUED)
1982	Tom Sandberg (NOR)
1984*	Tom Sandberg (NOR)
1985	Herman Weinbach (FRG)
1987	Torbjørn Løkken (NOR)
1988*	Hippolyt Kempf (SUI)
1989	Trond Einar Elden (NOR)
1991	Fred Børre Lundberg (NOR)
1992*	Fabrice Guy (FRA)
1993	Kenji Ogiwara (JPN)
1994*	Fred Børre Lundberg (NOR)
1995	Fred Børre Lundberg (NOR)
1996	not held
1997	Kenji Ogiwara (JPN)
1998*	Bjarte Engen Vik (NOR)
1999	Bjarte Engen Vik (NOR)
2001	Bjarte Engen Vik (NOR)
2002*	Samppa Lajunen (FIN)

Nordic Skiing World Championships—Nordic Combined (continued)

YEAR	SPRINT	YEAR	TEAM (CONTINUED)	YEAR	TEAM (CONTINUED)
1999	Bjarte Engen Vik (NOR)	1987	West Germany	1996	*not held*
2001	Marco Baacke (GER)	1988*	West Germany	1997	Norway
2002*	Samppa Lajunen (FIN)	1989	Norway	1998*	Norway
		1991	Austria	1999	Finland
	TEAM	1992*	Japan	2001	Norway
1982	East Germany	1993	Japan	2002*	Finland
1984*	Norway	1994*	Japan		
1985	West Germany	1995	Japan		

*Olympic champions, recognized as world champions.   †Combined East-West German team.

Nordic Skiing World Championships—Ski Jump

The next championships are scheduled to be held 18 Feb–1 Mar 2003, Val di Fiemme, Italy.

YEAR	NORMAL HILL*	YEAR	NORMAL HILL* (CONTINUED)		LARGE HILL§ (CONTINUED)
1924†	Jacob Tullin-Thams (NOR)	1982	Armin Kogler (AUT)	1991	Franci Petek (YUG)
1925	Willem Dick (TCH)	1984†	Jens Weissflog (GDR)	1992†	Toni Nieminen (FIN)
1926	Jacob Tullin-Thams (NOR)	1985	Jens Weissflog (GDR)	1993	Espen Bredesen (NOR)
1927	Tore Edman (SWE)	1987	Jiri Parma (TCH)	1994†	Jens Weissflog (GER)
1928†	Alf Gunnar Andersen (NOR)	1988†	Matti Nykänen (FIN)	1995	Tommy Ingebrigtsen (NOR)
1929	Sigmund Ruud (NOR)	1989	Jens Weissflog (GDR)		
1930	Gunnar Andersen (NOR)	1991	Heinz Kuttin (AUT)	1996	*not held*
1931	Birger Ruud (NOR)	1992†	Ernst Vettori (AUT)	1997	Masahiko Harada (JPN)
1932†	Birger Ruud (NOR)	1993	Masahiko Harada (JPN)	1998†	Kazuyoshi Funaki (JPN)
1933	Marcel Reymond (SUI)	1994†	Espen Bredesen (NOR)	1999	Martin Schmitt (GER)
1934	Kristian Johansson (NOR)	1995	Takanobu Okabe (JPN)	2001	Martin Schmitt (GER)
1935	Birger Ruud (NOR)	1996	*not held*	2002†	Simon Ammann (SUI)
1936†	Birger Ruud (NOR)	1997	Janne Ahonen (FIN)		
1937	Birger Ruud (NOR)	1998†	Jani Soininen (FIN)		TEAM JUMP (NORMAL HILL)
1938	Asbjørn Ruud (NOR)	1999	Kazuyoshi Funaki (JPN)	2001	Austria
1939	Josef Bradl (AUS)	2001	Adam Malysz (POL)	2002†	*not held*
1940–47	*not held*	2002†	Simon Ammann (SUI)		
1948†	Petter Hugsted (NOR)				TEAM JUMP (LARGE HILL)
1950	Hans Bjørnstad (NOR)		LARGE HILL§	1982	Norway
1952†	Arnfinn Bergmann (NOR)	1962	Helmut Recknagel (GDR)	1984†	*not held*
1954	Matti Pietikäinen (FIN)	1964†	Toralf Engan (NOR)	1985	Finland
1956†	Antti Hyvärinen (FIN)	1966	Bjørn Wirkola (NOR)	1987	Finland
1958	Juhani Kärkinen (FIN)	1968†	Vladimir Belousov (URS)	1988†	Finland
1960†	Helmut Recknagel (GER‡)	1970	Gary Napalkov (URS)	1989	Finland
1962	Toralf Engan (NOR)	1972†	Wojciech Fortuna (POL)	1991	Austria
1964†	Veikko Kankkonen (FIN)	1974	Hans-Georg Aschenbach (GDR)	1992†	Finland
1966	Bjørn Wirkola (NOR)			1993	Norway
1968†	Jiri Raška (TCH)	1976†	Karl Schnabl (AUT)	1994†	Germany
1970	Gary Napalkov (URS)	1978	Tapio Räisänen (FIN)	1995	Finland
1972†	Yukio Kasaya (JPN)	1980†	Jouko Törmänen (FIN)	1996	*not held*
1974	Hans-Georg Aschenbach (GDR)	1982	Matti Nykänen (FIN)	1997	Finland
		1984†	Matti Nykänen (FIN)	1998†	Japan
1976†	Hans-Georg Aschenbach (GDR)	1985	Per Bergerud (NOR)	1999	Germany
		1987	Andreas Felder (AUT)	2001	Germany
1978	Mathias Buse (GDR)	1988†	Matti Nykänen (FIN)	2002†	Germany
1980†	Toni Innauer (AUT)	1989	Jari Puikkonen (FIN)		

*The distance of the jump in the normal hill competition has varied over time; as of 1992 it was set at 90 meters.   †Olympic champions, recognized as world champions.   ‡Combined East-West German team.   §The distance of the jump in the large hill competition has varied over time; it was set at 120 meters in 1992.

Yogi Berra's Words of Wisdom: I always thought that record would stand until it was broken.

Nordic Skiing World Championships—Women

Championships in some events have been held since 1952. The table shows results for the past 20 years. Next championship will be held 17 Feb–1 Mar 2003 in Val di Fiemme, Italy.

SPRINT
2001 Pirjo Manninen (FIN)
2002* Yuliya Chepalova (RUS)

5-KM CROSS-COUNTRY†
1982 Berit Aunli (NOR)
1984* Marja-Liisa Hämäläinen (FIN)
1985 *not held*
1987 Marjo Matikainen (FIN)
1988* Marjo Matikainen (FIN)
1989 *not held*
1991 Trude Dybendahl (NOR)
1992* Marjut Lukkarinen (FIN)
1993 Larisa Lazutina (RUS)
1994* Lyubov Yegorova (RUS)
1995 Larisa Lazutina (RUS)
1997 Yelena Vyalbe (RUS)
1998* Larisa Lazutina (RUS)
1999 Bente Martinsen (NOR)
2001 Virpi Kuitunen (FIN)
2002* Olga Danilova (RUS)

10-KM CROSS-COUNTRY†
1982 Berit Aunli (NOR)
1984* Marja-Liisa Hämäläinen (FIN)
1985 Anette Böe (NOR)
1987 Anne Jahren (NOR)
1988* Vida Ventsene (URS)
1989 Marja-Liisa Kirvesniemi (FIN–classical); Yelena Vyalbe (URS–freestyle)
1991 Yelena Vyalbe (URS)
1992* Lyubov Yegorova (UNT‡)

10-KM CROSS-COUNTRY† (CONT.)
1993 Stefania Belmondo (ITA)
1994* Lyubov Yegorova (RUS)
1995 Larisa Lazutina (RUS)
1997 Stefania Belmondo (ITA)
1998* Larisa Lazutina (RUS)
1999 Stefania Belmondo (ITA)
2001 Bente Skari-Martinsen (NOR)
2002* Bente Skari (NOR)

15-KM CROSS-COUNTRY
1989 Marjo Matikainen (FIN)
1991 Yelena Vyalbe (URS)
1992* Lyubov Egorova (URS)
1993 Yelena Vyalbe (RUS)
1994* Manuela Di Centa (ITA)
1995 Larissa Lazutina (RUS)
1997 Yelena Vyalbe (RUS)
1998* Olga Danilova (RUS)
1999 Stefania Belmondo (ITA)
2001 Bente Skari-Martinsen (NOR)
2002* Stefania Belmondo (ITA)

20-KM CROSS-COUNTRY
1982 Raisa Smetanina (URS)
1984* Marja-Liisa Hämäläinen (FIN)
1985 Grete Nykelmo (NOR)
1987 Marie Helene Oestlund (SWE)
1988* Tamara Tikhonova (URS)
1989 *discontinued*

30-KM CROSS-COUNTRY
1989 Yelena Vyalbe (URS)
1991 Lyubov Yegorova (URS)
1992* Stefania Belmondo (ITA)
1993 Stefania Belmondo (ITA)
1994* Manuela Di Centa (ITA)
1995 Yelena Vyalbe (RUS)
1997 Yelena Vyalbe (RUS)
1998* Yulia Chepalova (RUS)
1999 Larisa Lazutina (RUS)
2001 *canceled*
2002* Gabriella Paruzzi (ITA)

RELAYS§
1982 Norway
1984* Norway
1985 USSR
1987 USSR
1988* USSR
1989 Finland
1991 USSR
1992* Unified Team
1993 Russia
1994* Russia
1995 Russia
1997 Russia
1998* Russia
1999 Russia
2001 Russia
2002* Germany

*Olympic champions, recognized as world champions.   †From 1991–2001, the 5-km event was held in tandem with the 10 km event, one event would feature classical and the other freestyle technique. Medals were awarded for both races. Beginning in 2001 this pursuit race instead led to one medal being awarded upon winning. In 2001 and 2002 the pursuit race featured two 5-km races and the 10-km was a stand-alone event featuring classical technique.   ‡Unified Team, consisting of athletes from the Commonwealth of Independent States plus Georgia.   §15-km relay until 1974; 20-km in 1976 and thereafter.

Nordic World Cup

YEAR	MEN	WOMEN	YEAR	MEN	WOMEN
1979	Oddvar Braa (NOR)	Galina Kulakova (URS)	1991	Vladimir Smirnov (URS)	Yelena Vyalbe (URS)
1981	Aleksandr Zavyalov (URS)	Raisa Smetanina (URS)	1992	Bjørn Daehlie (NOR)	Yelena Vyalbe (URS)
1982	Bill Koch (USA)	Berit Aunli (NOR)	1993	Bjørn Daehlie (NOR)	Lyudmila Yegorova (RUS)
1983	Aleksandr Zavyalov (URS)	Marja-Liisa Hämäläinen (FIN)	1994	Vladimir Smirnov (KAZ)	Manuela Di Centa (ITA)
1984	Gunde Svan (SWE)	Marja-Liisa Hämäläinen (FIN)	1995	Bjørn Daehlie (NOR)	Yelena Vyalbe (RUS)
1985	Gunde Svan (SWE)	Anette Böe (NOR)	1996	Bjørn Daehlie (NOR)	Manuela Di Centa (ITA)
1986	Gunde Svan (SWE)	Marjo Matikainen (FIN)	1997	Bjørn Daehlie (NOR)	Yelena Vyalbe (RUS)
1987	Torgny Mogren (SWE)	Marjo Matikainen (FIN)	1998	Thomas Alsgaard (NOR)	Larisa Lazutina (RUS)
1988	Gunde Svan (SWE)	Marjo Matikainen (FIN)	1999	Bjørn Daehlie (NOR)	Bente Martinsen (NOR)
1989	Gunde Svan (SWE)	Yelena Vyalbe (URS)	2000	Johann Mühlegg (ESP)	Bente Skari-Martinsen (NOR)
1990	Vegard Ulvang (NOR)	Larisa Lazutina (URS)	2001	Per Elofsson (SWE)	Yuliya Chepalova (RUS)
			2002	Per Elofsson (SWE)	Bente Skari (NOR)

Sled Dog Racing

Sled Dog racing (or dogsled racing) is the sport of racing sleds pulled by sled dogs over snow-covered cross-country courses; it was developed from a principal **Eskimo** method of transportation. Dogsleds are still used for transportation and working purposes in some northern areas, although they largely have been replaced by aircraft and snowmobiles. The modern, lightweight **racing sled** weighs about 30 lb (13.5 kg). Its ash frame is lashed together with leather and its runners sheathed with steel or aluminum. **Dogs** usually are especially bred and trained Eskimo dogs, Siberian huskies, Samoyeds, or Alaskan Malamutes. The **teams** typically consist of 4–10 dogs, with more being used for longer races. They are driven in pairs in a gang hitch.

Control of the team is by voice, although drivers may carry whips of limited length. In open country, point-to-point races are held. In more populated areas, back roads form the course, with races usually varying in **length** from 12–30 mi (19–48 km). A team of 6–8 dogs can pull the sled and its driver, called a **musher**, at speeds of more than 20 mph (32 km/hr). Teams start at intervals and race for time. Usually, all dogs must finish in the order they start, and an injured dog must be carried on the sled.

A dogsled-racing event was included in the 1932 **Winter Olympics** program. The sport is popular in Norway, Canada, Alaska, and the northern states of the contiguous United States. The **Iditarod Trail Sled Dog Race** has been held in Alaska since 1973.

Iditarod Trail Sled Dog Race

Both men and women compete together in this annual dogsled race held in March between Anchorage and Nome AK. A short race of 56 mi (90 km) organized in 1967 evolved in 1973 into the current race. The course, roughly 1,100 mi (1,770 km) long, partially follows the old Iditarod Trail dogsled mail route blazed from Knik to Nome in 1910. The course length and route vary slightly from year to year, and the middle third takes alternate routes in odd and even years. In 1976 the US Congress designated the original Iditarod Trail as a National Historic Trail.

YEAR	WINNER	TIME	YEAR	WINNER	TIME
1973	Dick Wilmarth	20 days 49 min 41 sec	1988	Susan Butcher	11 days 11 hr 41 min 40 sec
1974	Carl Huntington	20 days 15 hr 2 min 7 sec	1989	Joe Runyan	11 days 5 hr 24 min 34 sec
1975	Emmitt Peters	14 days 14 hr 43 min 45 sec	1990	Susan Butcher	11 days 1 hr 53 min 23 sec
1976	Gerald Riley	18 days 22 hr 58 min 17 sec	1991	Rick Swenson	12 days 16 hr 34 min 39 sec
1977	Rick Swenson	16 days 16 hr 27 min 13 sec	1992	Martin Buser	10 days 19 hr 17 min 15 sec
1978	Dick Mackey	14 days 18 hr 52 min 24 sec	1993	Jeff King	10 days 15 hr 38 min 15 sec
1979	Rick Swenson	15 days 10 hr 37 min 47 sec	1994	Martin Buser	10 days 13 hr 5 min 39 sec
1980	Joe May	14 days 7 hr 11 min 51 sec	1995	Doug Swingley	10 days 13 hr 2 min 39 sec
1981	Rick Swenson	12 days 8 hr 45 min 2 sec	1996	Jeff King	9 days 5 hr 43 min 13 sec
1982	Rick Swenson	16 days 4 hr 40 min 10 sec	1997	Martin Buser	9 days 8 hr 30 min 45 sec
1983	Rick Mackey	12 days 14 hr 10 min 44 sec	1998	Jeff King	9 days 5 hr 52 min 26 sec
1984	Dean Osmar	12 days 15 hr 7 min 33 sec	1999	Doug Swingley	9 days 14 hr 31 min 7 sec
1985	Libby Riddles	18 days 20 min 17 sec	2000	Doug Swingley	9 days 58 min 6 sec
1986	Susan Butcher	11 days 15 hr 6 min 0 sec	2001	Doug Swingley	9 days 19 hr 55 min 50 sec
1987	Susan Butcher	11 days 2 hr 5 min 13 sec	2002	Martin Buser	8 days 22 hr 46 min 2 sec

Squash

The oldest professional squash rackets tournament recognized as such is the **British Open**, inaugurated in 1930. Both men's amateur and women's squash rackets championships had been held since 1922. The International **Squash Rackets Federation** (ISRF; founded 1967) instituted **world open championships** in 1974 (men) and 1976 (women). The game as played in Great Britain and the rest of the world is quite different in a number of ways from that played in the United States, Canada, and Mexico.

World Squash Federation Web site: <www.world-squash.org>

World Open Championship

men					
YEAR	WINNER (NATIONALITY)	YEAR	WINNER (NATIONALITY)	YEAR	WINNER (NATIONALITY)
1975	Geoff B. Hunt (AUS)	1987	Jansher Khan (PAK)	1997	Rodney Eyles (AUS)
1977	Geoff B. Hunt (AUS)	1988	Jahangir Khan (PAK)	1998	Jonathon Power (CAN)
1979	Geoff B. Hunt (AUS)	1989	Jansher Khan (PAK)	1999	Peter Nicol (SCO)
1980	Geoff B. Hunt (AUS)	1990	Jansher Khan (PAK)	2000	not held
1981	Jahangir Khan (PAK)	1991	Rodney Martin (AUS)	2001	canceled
1982	Jahangir Khan (PAK)	1992	Jansher Khan (PAK)	2002	final match scheduled
1983	Jahangir Khan (PAK)	1993	Jansher Khan (PAK)		for 14 December, Antwerp, Belgium
1984	Jahangir Khan (PAK)	1994	Jansher Khan (PAK)		
1985	Jahangir Khan (PAK)	1995	Jansher Khan (PAK)		
1986	Ross Norman (NZL)	1996	Jansher Khan (PAK)		

World Open Championship (continued)

women

YEAR	WINNER (NATIONALITY)	YEAR	WINNER (NATIONALITY)	YEAR	WINNER (NATIONALITY)
1976	Heather P. Blundell McKay (AUS)	1989	Martine LeMoignan (GBR)	1996	Sarah Fitz-Gerald (AUS)
				1997	Sarah Fitz-Gerald (AUS)
1979	Heather McKay (AUS)	1990	Susan Devoy (NZL)	1998	Sarah Fitz-Gerald (AUS)
1981	Rhonda Thorne (AUS)	1991	*not held*	1999	Cassie Campion (ENG)
1983	Vicki Hoffman Cardwell (AUS)	1992	Susan Devoy (NZL)	2000	Carol Owens (AUS)
		1993	Michelle Martin (AUS)	2001	Sarah Fitz-Gerald (AUS)
1985	Susan Devoy (NZL)	1994	Michelle Martin (AUS)	2002	*final match scheduled for 2 October, Doha, Qatar*
1987	Susan Devoy (NZL)	1995	Michelle Martin (AUS)		

British Open Championship

The championships have been held since 1921–22 (women's) and 1930–31 (men's). The table shows the results for the past 20 years.

men		women	
YEAR	WINNER (NATIONALITY)	YEAR	WINNER (NATIONALITY)
1982–83	Jahangir Khan (PAK)	1982–83	Vicki Hoffman Cardwell (AUS)
1983–84	Jahangir Khan (PAK)	1983–84	Susan Devoy (NZL)
1984–85	Jahangir Khan (PAK)	1984–85	Susan Devoy (NZL)
1985–86	Jahangir Khan (PAK)	1985–86	Susan Devoy (NZL)
1986–87	Jahangir Khan (PAK)	1986–87	Susan Devoy (NZL)
1987–88	Jahangir Khan (PAK)	1987–88	Susan Devoy (NZL)
1988–89	Jahangir Khan (PAK)	1988–89	Susan Devoy (NZL)
1989–90	Jahangir Khan (PAK)	1989–90	Susan Devoy (NZL)
1990–91	Jahangir Khan (PAK)	1990–91	Liz Opie (GBR)
1991–92	Jansher Khan (PAK)	1991–92	Susan Devoy (NZL)
1992–93	Jansher Khan (PAK)	1992–93	Michelle Martin (AUS)
1993–94	Jansher Khan (PAK)	1993–04	Michelle Martin (AUS)
1994–95	Jansher Khan (PAK)	1994–95	Michelle Martin (AUS)
1995–96	Jansher Khan (PAK)	1995–96	Michelle Martin (AUS)
1996–97	Jansher Khan (PAK)	1996–97	Michelle Martin (AUS)
1997–98	Peter Nicol (SCO)	1997–98	Michelle Martin (AUS)
1998–99	Jonathon Power (CAN)	1998–99	Leilani Joyce (NZL)
1999–2000	David Evans (WAL)	1999–2000	Leilani Joyce (NZL)
2000–01	David Palmer (AUS)	2000–01	Sarah Fitz-Gerald (AUS)
2001–02	Peter Nicol (GBR)	2001–02	Sarah Fitz-Gerald (AUS)

Swimming

The **Fédération Internationale de Natation** (International Swimming Federation, still known by its French acronym that includes an "a" for "Amateur," FINA; founded 1908) is the world governing body for amateur swimming. It held the first world swimming championships in 1973. After 1975 the FINA championships were held in non-Olympic, even-numbered years. (An exception was the championship held in Australia, which took place during the summer month of January 1991.) Diving, synchronized (or synchro) swimming, and water polo events are included in the competition.

A distinction is made between **long-course** (50-m) and **short-course** (25-m) pools for purposes of record-setting; world championships and other major contests were long held in 50-m pools, but there is now a separate World Championship and World Cup for 25-m pools.

International Swimming Federation Web site: <www.fina.org>

Did you know? Athletic pursuits of U.S. Presidents: Franklin D. Roosevelt was an avid swimmer.

World Swimming & Diving Championships—Men

The next competition is scheduled to be held 15–19 Jul 2003 in Barcelona, Spain.

swimming

50 M FREESTYLE		100 M FREESTYLE		100 M FREESTYLE (CONTINUED)	
1986	Tom Jager (USA)	1973	Jim Montgomery (USA)	1991	Matt Biondi (USA)
1991	Tom Jager (USA)	1975	Andy Coan (USA)	1994	Aleksandr Popov (RUS)
1994	Aleksandr Popov (RUS)	1978	David McCagg (USA)	1998	Aleksandr Popov (RUS)
1998	Bill Pilczuk (USA)	1982	Jorg Woithe (GDR)	2001	Anthony Ervin (USA)
2001	Anthony Ervin (USA)	1986	Matt Biondi (USA)		

World Swimming & Diving Championships—Men (continued)

swimming

200 M FREESTYLE
1973   Jim Montgomery (USA)
1975   Tim Shaw (USA)
1978   Bill Forrester (USA)
1982   Michael Gross (FRG)
1986   Michael Gross (FRG)
1991   Giorgio Lamberti (ITA)
1994   Antti Kasvio (FIN)
1998   Michael Klim (AUS)
2001   Ian Thorpe (AUS)

400 M FREESTYLE
1973   Rick DeMont (USA)
1975   Tim Shaw (USA)
1978   Vladimir Salnikov (URS)
1982   Vladimir Salnikov (URS)
1986   Rainer Henkel (FRG)
1991   Jörg Hoffmann (GER)
1994   Kieren Perkins (AUS)
1998   Ian Thorpe (AUS)
2001   Ian Thorpe (AUS)

800 M FREESTYLE
2001   Ian Thorpe (AUS)

1,500 M FREESTYLE
1973   Steve Holland (AUS)
1975   Tim Shaw (USA)
1978   Vladimir Salnikov (URS)
1982   Vladimir Salnikov (URS)
1986   Rainer Henkel (FRG)
1991   Jörg Hoffmann (GER)
1994   Kieren Perkins (AUS)
1998   Grant Hackett (AUS)
2001   Grant Hackett (AUS)

50 M BACKSTROKE
2001   Randall Bal (USA)

100 M BACKSTROKE
1973   Roland Matthes (GDR)
1975   Roland Matthes (GDR)
1978   Bob Jackson (USA)
1982   Dirk Richter (GDR)
1986   Igor Polyansky (URS)
1991   Jeff Rouse (USA)
1994   Martín Lopez-Zubero (ESP)
1998   Lenny Krayzelburg (USA)
2001   Matt Welsh (AUS)

200 M BACKSTROKE
1973   Roland Matthes (GDR)
1975   Zoltan Verraszto (HUN)
1978   Jesse Vassallo (USA)
1982   Rick Carey (USA)
1986   Igor Polyansky (URS)

200 M BACKSTROKE (CONTINUED)
1991   Martín Lopez-Zubero (ESP)
1994   Vladimir Selkov (RUS)
1998   Lenny Krayzelburg (USA)
2001   Aaron Peirsol (USA)

50 M BREASTSTROKE
2001   Oleg Lisogor (UKR)

100 M BREASTSTROKE
1973   John Hencken (USA)
1975   David Wilkie (GBR)
1978   Walter Kusch (FRG)
1982   Steve Lundquist (USA)
1986   Victor Davis (CAN)
1991   Norbert Rozsa (HUN)
1994   Norbert Rozsa (HUN)
1998   Fred De Burghgraeve (BEL)
2001   Roman Sloudnov (RUS)

200 M BREASTSTROKE
1973   David Wilkie (GBR)
1975   David Wilkie (GBR)
1978   Nick Nevid (USA)
1982   Victor Davis (CAN)
1986   Joszef Szabo (HUN)
1991   Mike Barrowman (USA)
1994   Norbert Rozsa (HUN)
1998   Kurt Grote (USA)
2001   Brendan Hansen (USA)

50 M BUTTERFLY
2001   Geoff Huegill (AUS)

100 M BUTTERFLY
1973   Bruce Robertson (CAN)
1975   Greg Jagenburg (USA)
1978   Joseph Bottom (USA)
1982   Matt Gribble (USA)
1986   Pablo Morales (USA)
1991   Anthony Nesty (SUR)
1994   Rafal Szukala (POL)
1998   Michael Klim (AUS)
2001   Lars Frolander (SWE)

200 M BUTTERFLY
1973   Robin Backhaus (USA)
1975   Bill Forrester (USA)
1978   Mike Bruner (USA)
1982   Michael Gross (FRG)
1986   Michael Gross (FRG)
1991   Melvin Stewart (USA)
1994   Denis Pankratov (RUS)
1998   Denys Silantyev (UKR)
2001   Michael Phelps (USA)

200 M INDIVIDUAL MEDLEY
1973   Gunnar Larsson (SWE)
1975   Andras Hargitay (HUN)
1978   Graham Smith (CAN)
1982   Aleksandr Sidorenko (URS)
1986   Tamas Darnyi (HUN)
1991   Tamas Darnyi (HUN)
1994   Jani Sievinen (FIN)
1998   Marcel Wouda (NED)
2001   Massimiliano Rosolino (ITA)

400 M INDIVIDUAL MEDLEY
1973   Andras Hargitay (HUN)
1975   Andras Hargitay (HUN)
1978   Jesse Vassallo (USA)
1982   Ricardo Prado (BRA)
1986   Tamas Darnyi (HUN)
1991   Tamas Darnyi (HUN)
1994   Tom Dolan (USA)
1998   Tom Dolan (USA)
2001   Alessio Boggiatto (ITA)

4 X 100-M FREESTYLE RELAY
1973   United States
1975   United States
1978   United States
1982   United States
1986   United States
1991   United States
1994   United States
1998   United States
2001   Australia

4 X 200-M FREESTYLE RELAY
1973   United States
1975   West Germany
1978   United States
1982   United States
1986   East Germany
1991   Germany
1994   Sweden
1998   Australia
2001   Australia

4 X 100-M MEDLEY RELAY
1973   United States
1975   United States
1978   United States
1982   United States
1986   United States
1991   United States
1994   United States
1998   Australia
2001   Australia

diving

1-M SPRINGBOARD
1991   Edwin Jongejans (NED)
1994   Evan Stewart (ZIM)
1998   Yu Zhuocheng (CHN)
2001   Wang Feng (CHN)

3-M SPRINGBOARD
1973   Phil Boggs (USA)
1975   Phil Boggs (USA)
1978   Phil Boggs (USA)
1982   Greg Louganis (USA)
1986   Greg Louganis (USA)
1991   Kent Ferguson (USA)
1994   Yu Zhuocheng (CHN)
1998   Dmitry Sautin (RUS)
2001   Dmitry Sautin (RUS)

PLATFORM
1973   Klaus Dibiasi (ITA)
1975   Klaus Dibiasi (ITA)
1978   Greg Louganis (USA)
1982   Greg Louganis (USA)
1986   Greg Louganis (USA)
1991   Sun Shuwei (CHN)
1994   Dmitry Sautin (RUS)
1998   Dmitry Sautin (RUS)
2001   Tian Liang (CHN)

World Swimming & Diving Championships— Women

The next competition is scheduled to be held 15–19 Jul 2003 In Barcelona, Spain.

swimming

50 M FREESTYLE
1986	Tamara Costache (ROM)
1991	Zhuang Yong (CHN)
1994	Le Jingyi (CHN)
1998	Amy Van Dyken (USA)
2001	Inge De Bruljn (NED)

100 M FREESTYLE
1973	Kornelia Ender (GDR)
1975	Kornelia Ender (GDR)
1978	Barbara Krause (GDR)
1982	Birgit Meineke (GDR)
1986	Kristin Otto (GDR)
1991	Nicole Haislett (USA)
1994	Le Jingyi (CHN)
1998	Jenny Thompson (USA)
2001	Inge De Bruijn (NED)

200 M FREESTYLE
1973	Keena Rothhammer (USA)
1975	Shirley Babashoff (USA)
1978	Cynthia Woodhead (USA)
1982	Annemarie Verstappen (NED)
1986	Heike Friedrich (GDR)
1991	Hayley Lewis (AUS)
1994	Franziska van Almsick (GER)
1998	Claudia Poll (CRC)
2001	Giaan Rooney (AUS)

400 M FREESTYLE
1973	Heather Greenwood (USA)
1975	Shirley Babashoff (USA)
1978	Tracey Wickham (AUS)
1982	Carmela Schmidt (GDR)
1986	Heike Friedrich (GDR)
1991	Janet Evans (USA)
1994	Yang Aihua (CHN)
1998	Chen Yan (CHN)
2001	Yana Klochkova (UKR)

800 M FREESTYLE
1973	Novella Calligaris (ITA)
1975	Jenny Turrall (AUS)
1978	Tracey Wickham (AUS)
1982	Kim Linehan (USA)
1986	Astrid Strauss (GDR)
1991	Janet Evans (USA)
1994	Janet Evans (USA)
1998	Brooke Bennett (USA)
2001	Hannah Stockbauer (GER)

1,500 M FREESTYLE
2001	Hannah Stockbauer (GER)

50 M BREASTSTROKE
2001	Luo Xuejuan (CHN)

100 M BREASTSTROKE
1973	Renate Vogel (GDR)
1975	Hannelore Anke (GDR)
1978	Yuliya Bogdanova (URS)
1982	Ute Geweniger (GDR)
1986	Sylvia Gerasch (GDR)
1991	Linley Frame (AUS)
1994	Samantha Riley (AUS)
1998	Kristy Kowal (USA)
2001	Luo Xuejuan (CHN)

200 M BREASTSTROKE
1973	Renate Vogel (GDR)
1975	Hannelore Anke (GDR)
1978	Lina Kachushite (URS)
1982	Svetlana Varganova (URS)
1986	Silke Hörner (GDR)
1991	Yelena Volkova (URS)
1994	Samantha Riley (AUS)
1998	Agnes Kovacs (HUN)
2001	Agnes Kovacs (HUN)

50 M BUTTERFLY
2001	Inge De Bruijn (NED)

100 M BUTTERFLY
1973	Kornelia Ender (GDR)
1975	Kornelia Ender (GDR)
1978	Joan Pennington (USA)
1982	Mary T. Meagher (USA)
1986	Kornelia Gressler (GDR)
1991	Qian Hong (CHN)
1994	Liu Limin (CHN)
1998	Jenny Thompson (USA)
2001	Petria Thomas (AUS)

200 M BUTTERFLY
1973	Rosemarie Kother (GDR)
1975	Rosemarie Kother (GDR)
1978	Tracy Caulkins (USA)
1982	Ines Geissler (GDR)
1986	Mary T. Meagher (USA)
1991	Summer Sanders (USA)
1994	Liu Limin (CHN)
1998	Susle O'Neill (AUS)
2001	Petria Thomas (AUS)

50 M BACKSTROKE
2001	Haley Cope (USA)

100 M BACKSTROKE
1973	Ulrike Richter (GDR)
1975	Ulrike Richter (GDR)
1978	Linda Jezek (USA)
1982	Kristin Otto (GDR)
1986	Betsy Mitchell (USA)
1991	Krisztina Egerszegi (HUN)
1994	He Cihong (CHN)
1998	Lea Maurer (USA)
2001	Natalie Coughlin (USA)

200 M BACKSTROKE
1973	Melissa Belote (USA)
1975	Birgit Treiber (GDR)
1978	Linda Jezek (USA)
1982	Cornelia Sirch (GDR)
1986	Cornelia Sirch (GDR)
1991	Krisztina Egerszegi (HUN)
1994	He Cihong (CHN)
1998	Roxanna Maracineanu (FRA)
2001	Diana Mocanu (ROM)

200 M INDIVIDUAL MEDLEY
1973	Andrea Hubner (GDR)
1975	Kathy Heddy (USA)
1978	Tracy Caulkins (USA)
1982	Petra Schneider (GDR)
1986	Kristin Otto (GDR)
1991	Lin Li (CHN)
1994	Lu Bin (CHN)
1998	Wu Yanyan (CHN)
2001	Martha Bowen (USA)

400 M INDIVIDUAL MEDLEY
1973	Gudrun Wegner (GDR)
1975	Ulrika Tauber (GDR)
1978	Tracy Caulkins (USA)
1982	Petra Schneider (GDR)
1986	Kathleen Nord (GDR)
1991	Lin Li (CHN)
1994	Dai Guohong (CHN)
1998	Chen Yan (CHN)
2001	Yana Klochkova (UKR)

4 X 100-M FREESTYLE RELAY
1973	East Germany
1975	East Germany
1978	United States
1982	East Germany
1986	East Germany
1991	United States
1994	China
1998	United States
2001	Germany

4 X 200-M FREESTYLE RELAY
1986	East Germany
1991	Germany
1994	China
1998	Germany
2001	Great Britain

4 X 100-M MEDLEY RELAY
1973	East Germany
1975	East Germany
1978	United States
1982	East Germany
1986	East Germany
1991	United States
1994	China
1998	United States
2001	Australia

World Swimming & Diving Championships—Women (continued)

diving

1-M SPRINGBOARD		3-M SPRINGBOARD		PLATFORM	
1991	Gao Min (CHN)	1973	Christa Kohler (GDR)	1973	Ulrika Knape (SWE)
1994	Chen Lixia (CHN)	1975	Irina Kalinina (URS)	1975	Janet Ely (USA)
1998	Irina Lashko (RUS)	1978	Irina Kalinina (URS)	1978	Irina Kalinina (URS)
2001	Blythe Hartley (CAN)	1982	Megan Neyer (USA)	1982	Wendy Wyland (USA)
		1986	Gao Min (CHN)	1986	Chen Lin (CHN)
		1991	Gao Min (CHN)	1991	Fu Mingxia (CHN)
		1994	Tan Shuping (CHN)	1994	Fu Mingxia (CHN)
		1998	Yulia Pakhalina (RUS)	1998	Olena Zhupina (UKR)
		2001	Guo Jingjing (CHN)	2001	Xu Mian (CHN)

Swimming World Records—Long Course (50-m)

men

EVENT	RECORD HOLDER (NATIONALITY)	PERFORMANCE	DATE
50-m freestyle	Aleksandr Popov (RUS)	21.64 sec	16 Jun 2000
100-m freestyle	Pieter van den Hoogenband (NED)	47.84 sec	19 Sep 2000
200-m freestyle	Ian Thorpe (AUS)	1 min 44.06 sec	25 Jul 2001
400-m freestyle	Ian Thorpe (AUS)	3 min 40.17 sec	22 Jul 2001
800-m freestyle	Ian Thorpe (AUS)	7 min 39.16 sec	24 Jul 2001
1,500-m freestyle	Grant Hackett (AUS)	14 min 34.56 sec	29 Jul 2001
50-m backstroke	Lenny Krayzelburg (USA)	24.99 sec	28 Aug 1999
100-m backstroke	Lenny Krayzelburg (USA)	53.60 sec	24 Aug 1999
200-m backstroke	Aaron Peirsol (USA)	1 min 55.15 sec	20 Mar 2002
50-m breaststroke	Ed Moses (USA)	27.39 sec	31 Mar 2001
100-m breaststroke	Roman Sludnov (RUS)	59.94 sec	23 Jul 2001
200-m breaststroke	Mike Barrowman (USA)	2 min 10.16 sec	29 Jul 1992
50-m butterfly	Geoffrey Huegill (AUS)	23.44 sec	27 Jul 2001
100-m butterfly	Michael Klim (AUS)	51.81 sec	12 Dec 1999
200-m butterfly	Michael Phelps (USA)	1 min 54.58 sec	24 Jul 2001
200-m individual medley	Jani Sievinen (FIN)	1 min 58.16 sec	11 Sep 1994
400-m individual medley	Tom Dolan (USA)	4 min 11.76 sec	17 Sep 2000
4 × 100 free relay	Australia (Michael Klim, Chris Fydler, Ashley Callus, Ian Thorpe)	3 min 13.67 sec	16 Sep 2000
4 × 200 free relay	Australia (Grant Hackett, Michael Klim, William Kirby, Ian Thorpe)	7 min 4.66 sec	27 Jul 2001
4 × 100 medley relay	United States (Lenny Krayzelburg, Ed Moses, Ian Crocker, Gary Hall, Jr.)	3 min 33.73 sec	23 Sep 2000

women

EVENT	RECORD HOLDER (NATIONALITY)	PERFORMANCE	DATE
50-m freestyle	Inge de Bruijn (NED)	24.13 sec	22 Sep 2000
100-m freestyle	Inge de Bruijn (NED)	53.77 sec	20 Sep 2000
200-m freestyle	Franziska Van Almsick (GER)	1 min 56.78 sec	6 Sep 1994
400-m freestyle	Janet Evans (USA)	4 min 3.85 sec	22 Sep 1988
800-m freestyle	Janet Evans (USA)	8 min 16.22 sec	20 Aug 1989
1,500-m freestyle	Janet Evans (USA)	15 min 52.10 sec	26 Mar 1988
50-m backstroke	Sandra Völker (GER)	28.25 sec	17 Jun 2000
100-m backstroke	He Chihong (CHN)	1 min 0.16 sec	10 Sep 1994
200-m backstroke	Kristina Egerszegi (HUN)	2 min 6.62 sec	25 Aug 1991
50-m breaststroke	Penelope Heyns (RSA)	30.83 sec	28 Aug 1999
100-m breaststroke	Penelope Heyns (RSA)	1 min 6.52 sec	23 Aug 1999
200-m breaststroke	Qi Hui (CHN)	2 min 22.99 sec	13 Apr 2001
50-m butterfly	Inge de Bruijn (NED)	25.64 sec	26 May 2000
100-m butterfly	Inge de Bruijn (NED)	56.61 sec	17 Sep 2000
200-m butterfly	Susan O'Neill (AUS)	2 min 5.81 sec	17 May 2000
200-m individual medley	Wu Yanyan (CHN)	2 min 9.72 sec	17 Oct 1997
400-m individual medley	Yana Klochkova (UKR)	4 min 33.59 sec	16 Sep 2000
4 × 100 free relay	United States (Amy Van Dyken, Dara Torres, Courtney Shealy, Jenny Thompson)	3 min 36.61 sec	16 Sep 2000
4 × 200 free relay	East Germany (Manuela Stellmach, Astrid Strauss, Anke Möhring, Heike Friedrich)	7 min 55.47 sec	18 Aug 1987
4 × 100 medley relay	United States (B.J. Bedford, Megan Quann, Jenny Thompson, Dara Torres)	3 min 58.30 sec	23 Sep 2000

Swimming World Records—Short Course (25-m)

men

EVENT	RECORD HOLDER (NATIONALITY)	PERFORMANCE	DATE
50-m freestyle	Mark Foster (GBR)	21.13 sec	28 Jan 2001
100-m freestyle	Aleksandr Popov (RUS)	46.74 sec	19 Mar 1994
200-m freestyle	Ian Thorpe (AUS)	1 min 41.10 sec	6 Feb 2000
400-m freestyle	Grant Hackett (AUS)	3 min 35.01 sec	2 Apr 1999
800-m freestyle	Grant Hackett (AUS)	7 min 25.28 sec	3 Aug 2001
1,500 m freestyle	Grant Hackett (AUS)	14 min 10.10 sec	7 Aug 2001
50-m backstroke	Neil Walker (USA)	23.42 sec	16 Mar 2000
100-m backstroke	Neil Walker (USA)	50.75 sec	19 Mar 2000
200-m backstroke	Aaron Peirsol (USA)	1 min 51.17 sec	7 Apr 2002
50-m breaststroke	Oleg Lisogor (UKR)	26.20 sec	26 Jan 2002
100 m breaststroke	Ed Moses (USA)	57.47 sec	23 Jan 2002
200-m breaststroke	Ed Moses (USA)	2 min 3.17 sec	26 Jan 2002
50-m butterfly	Geoffrey Huegill (AUS)	22.74 sec	26 Jan 2002
100-m butterfly	Thomas Rupprath (GER)	50.10 sec	27 Jan 2002
200-m butterfly	Thomas Rupprath (GER)	1 min 51.21 sec	1 Dec 2001
100-m individual medley	Peter Mankoc (SLO)	52.65 sec	15 Dec 2001
200 m individual medley	Jani Sievinen (FIN)	1 min 54.65 sec	21 Apr 1994
	Atila Czene (HUN)	tied record	23 Mar 2000
400-m individual medley	Matthew Dunn (AUS)	4 min 4.24 sec	24 Sep 1998
4 × 100 free relay	Sweden (Johan Nystrom, Lars Frölander, Mattias Öhlin, Stefan Nystrand)	3 min 9.57 sec	16 Mar 2000
4 × 200 free relay	Australia (William Kirby, Ian Thorpe, Michael Kim, Grant Hackett)	6 min 56.41 sec	7 Aug 2001
4 × 100 medley relay	United States (Aaron Peirsol, David Denniston, Peter Marshall, Jason Lezak)	3 min 29.00 sec	7 Apr 2002

women

EVENT	RECORD HOLDER (NATIONALITY)	PERFORMANCE	DATE
50-m freestyle	Therese Alshammar (SWE)	23.59 sec	18 Mar 2000
100-m freestyle	Therese Alshammar (SWE)	52.17 sec	17 Mar 2000
200-m freestyle	Lindsay Benko (USA)	1 min 54.04 sec	7 Apr 2002
400-m freestyle	Claudia Poll (CRC)	4 min 0.03 sec	19 Apr 1997
800-m freestyle	Sachiko Yamada (JPN)	8 min 14.35 sec	2 Apr 2002
50-m backstroke	Li Hui (CHN)	26.83 sec	2 Dec 2001
100-m backstroke	Natalie Coughlin (USA)	57.08 sec	28 Nov 2001
200-m backstroke	Natalie Coughlin (USA)	2 min 3.62 sec	27 Nov 2001
50-m breaststroke	Emma Igelström (SWE)	29.96 sec	4 Apr 2002
100-m breaststroke	Emma Igelström (SWE)	1 min 5.38 sec	6 Apr 2002
200-m breaststroke	Qi Hui (CHN)	2 min 19.25 sec	28 Jan 2001
50-m butterfly	Anna-Karin Kammerling (SWE)	25.36 sec	25 Jan 2001
100-m butterfly	Martina Moravcova (SVK)	56.55 sec	26 Jan 2002
200-m butterfly	Susan O'Neill (AUS)	2 min 4.16 sec	18 Jan 2000
100-m individual medley	Jenny Thompson (USA)	59.30 sec	2 Apr 1999
200-m individual medley	Allison Wagner (USA)	2 min 7.79 sec	5 Dec 1993
400-m individual medley	Yana Klochkova (UKR)	4 min 27.83 sec	19 Jan 2002
4 × 100 free relay	China (Le Jingyi, Na Chao, Shang Ying, Nian Yin)	3 min 34.55 sec	19 Apr 1997
4 × 200 free relay	China (Xu Yanvei, Zhu Yingven, Tang Jingzhi, Yang Yu)	7 min 46.30 sec	3 Apr 2002
4 × 100 medley relay	Sweden (Therese Alshammar, Emma Igelström, Anna-Karin Kammerling, Johanna Sjöberg)	3 min 55.78 sec	5 Apr 2002

Table Tennis

Official world table tennis championships were first held in 1927 under the auspices of the International Table Tennis Federation (ITTF; founded 1926). Women's doubles competition was added in 1928 and women's team competition in 1934. In 1980 the ITTF first sponsored a men's World Cup competition for the top 16 ranking players; it has been held annually since then.

At world championships, held biennially since 1957, players compete for: the Swaythling Cup (men's team event; best of nine singles matches); the Marcel Corbillon Cup (women's team event; best of four singles and one doubles matches); the St. Bride's Vase (men's singles); the G. Geist Prize (women's singles); the Iran Cup (men's doubles championships); the W.J. Pope Trophy (women's doubles championships); and the Heydusek Prize (mixed doubles championships).

International Table Tennis Federation Web site: <www.ittf.com>

Table Tennis World Rankings

ITTF rankings as of 1 Aug 2002

MEN (NATIONALITY)		WOMEN (NATIONALITY)	
1	Wang Liqin (CHN)	1	Wang Nan (CHN)
2	Ma Lin (CHN)	2	Zhang Yining (CHN)
3	Vladimir Samsonov (BLR)	3	Tamara Boros (CRO)
4	Werner Schlager (AUT)	4	Ryu Ji Hae (KOR)
5	Timo Boll (GER)	5	Niu Jianfeng (CHN)

World Table Tennis Championships—Men

Competition has been held annually beginning in 1927 and normally every other year since 1957. Table shows results for the past 20 years.

YEAR	ST. BRIDE'S VASE	IRAN CUP	YEAR	SWAYTHLING CUP
1983	Guo Yuehua (CHN)	Dragutin Surbek, Zoran Kalinic (YUG)	1983	China
1985	Jiang Jialiang (CHN)	Mikael Appelgren, Ulf Carlsson (SWE)	1985	China
1987	Jiang Jialiang (CHN)	Chen Longcan, Wei Qingguang (CHN)	1987	China
1989	Jan-Ove Waldner (SWE)	Jorg Rosskopf, Steffen Fetzner (FRG)	1989	Sweden
1991	Jorgen Persson (SWE)	Peter Karlsson, Thomas Von Scheele (SWE)	1991	Sweden
1993	Jean-Philippe Gatien (FRA)	Wang Tao, Lu Lin (CHN)	1993	Sweden
1995	Kong Linghui (CHN)	Wang Tao, Lu Lin (CHN)	1995	China
1997	Jan-Ove Waldner (SWE)	Kong Linghui, Liu Guoliang (CHN)	1997	China
1999	Liu Guoliang (CHN)	Kong Linghui, Liu Guoliang (CHN)	2000	Sweden
2001	Wang Liqin (CHN)	Wang Liqin, Yan Sen (CHN)	2001	China
2003	*scheduled to be held 19–25 May, Paris*		2004	*scheduled to be held 1–8 March, Doha, Qatar*

World Table Tennis Championships—Women

Competition has been held annually beginning in 1927 (Geist Prize), 1928 (Pope Trophy), and 1934 (Corbillon Cup) and normally every other year since 1957. Table shows the results for the past 20 years.

YEAR	G. GEIST PRIZE	W.J. POPE TROPHY	YEAR	CORBILLON CUP
1983	Cao Yanhua (CHN)	Shen Jianping, Dai Lili (CHN)	1983	China
1985	Cao Yanhua (CHN)	Dai Lili, Geng Lijuan (CHN)	1985	China
1987	He Zhili (CHN)	Hyun Jung Hwa, Yang Young Ja (KOR)	1987	China
1989	Qiao Hong (CHN)	Qiao Hong, Deng Yaping (CHN)	1989	China
1991	Deng Yaping (CHN)	Gao Jun, Chen Zihe (CHN)	1991	Korea
1993	Hyun Jung Hwa (KOR)	Liu Wei, Qiao Yunping (CHN)	1993	China
1995	Deng Yaping (CHN)	Deng Yaping, Qiao Hong (CHN)	1995	China
1997	Deng Yaping (CHN)	Deng Yaping, Yang Ying (CHN)	1997	China
1999	Wang Nan (CHN)	Wang Nan, Li Ju (CHN)	2000	China
2001	Wang Nan (CHN)	Wang Nan, Li Ju (CHN)	2001	China
2003	*scheduled to be held 19–25 May, Paris*		2004	*scheduled to be held 1–8 March, Doha, Qatar*

World Table Tennis Championships—Mixed

Competition has been held since 1927–28. Table shows results for the past 20 years.

YEAR	HEYDUSEK PRIZE	YEAR	HEYDUSEK PRIZE
1983	Guo Yuehua, Ni Xialian (CHN)	1995	Wang Tao, Liu Wei (CHN)
1985	Cai Zhenhua, Cao Yanhua (CHN)	1997	Liu Guoliang, Wu Na (CHN)
1987	Hui Jun, Geng Lijuan (CHN)	1999	Ma Lin, Zhang Yingying (CHN)
1989	Yoo Nam Kyu, Hyung Jung Hwa (KOR)	2001	Qin Zhijian, Yang Ying (CHN)
1991	Wang Tao, Liu Wei (CHN)	2003	*scheduled to be held May, Paris*
1993	Wang Tao, Liu Wei (CHN)		

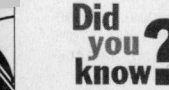

Did you know? In 1900 tennis champion Charlotte Cooper became the first woman to win an Olympic Gold Medal.

Table Tennis World Cup

	men				women	
YEAR	WINNER	YEAR	WINNER	YEAR	WINNER
1980	Guo Yuehua (CHN)	1992	Ma Wenge (CHN)	1996	Deng Yaping (CHN)
1981	Tibor Klampar (HUN)	1993	Zoran Primorac (CRO)	1997	Wang Nan (CHN)
1982	Guo Yuehua (CHN)	1994	Jean-Phillippe Gatien (FRA)	1998	Wang Nan (CHN)
1983	Mikael Appelgren (SWE)	1995	Kong Linghui (CHN)	1999	Wang Nan (CHN)
1984	Jiang Jialiang (CHN)	1996	Liu Guoliang (CHN)	2000	Li Ju (CHN)
1985	Chen Xinhua (CHN)	1997	Zoran Primorac (CRO)	2001	Zhang Yining (CHN)
1986	Chen Longcan (CHN)	1998	Jorg Rosskopf (GER)	2002	*scheduled to be held*
1987	Tong Yi (CHN)	1999	Vladimir Samsonov (BLR)		*September, Singapore*
1988	Andrzej Grubba (POL)	2000	Ma Lin (CHN)		
1989	Ma Wenge (CHN)	2001	Vladimir Samsonov (BLR)		
1990	Jan-Ove Waldner (SWE)	2002	*scheduled to be held 31*		
1991	Jörgen Persson (SWE)		*October–3 November,*		
1992	Ma Wenge (CHN)		*Suzhou, China*		

Tennis

Four events dominate world championship tennis. The first of the traditional "Big Four," or "Grand Slam," events was the All-England Lawn Tennis Championships (better known as the Wimbledon Championships), founded in 1877. Its only event the first year was the men's singles championships; women first competed in 1884. Major tennis tournaments also sprang up in the United States (1881 for men; women's singles competition first contested 1887, added officially 1889), France (1891 for men; women's singles competition added 1897), and Australia (1905 for men; women's singles competition added 1922). Open tennis (open, that is, both to professionals and to amateurs) became the rule in the Big Four tournaments in 1968.

International team tennis was organized in 1900 with the institution of the Davis Cup. Competing men's teams play four singles matches and one doubles match for the trophy. The Wightman Cup was contested yearly between British and American women's teams from 1923 to 1989. The International Tennis Federation (ITF, formerly the International Lawn Tennis Federation; founded 1913) established the Federation Cup in 1963 (called the Fed Cup since 1994) for international women's team competition. It is decided by elimination rounds of two singles and one doubles contest.

Related Web sites: International Tennis Federation: <www.itftennis.com>; Association of Tennis Professionals: <www.atptour.com>; Women's Tennis Association: <www.wtatour.com>

Australian Open Tennis Championships—Singles

YEAR	MEN	WOMEN
1905	Rodney Heath (AUS)	
1906	Tony Wilding (NZL)	
1907	Horace Rice (AUS)	
1908	Fred Alexander (USA)	
1909	Tony Wilding (NZL)	
1910	Rodney Heath (AUS)	
1911	Norman Brookes (AUS)	
1912	J. Cecil Parke (GBR)	
1913	E.F. Parker (AUS)	
1914	Pat O'Hara Wood (AUS)	
1915	Francis Lowe (GBR)	
1916–18	*not held*	
1919	A.R.F. Kingscote (GBR)	
1920	Pat O'Hara Wood (AUS)	
1921	Rhys Gemmell (AUS)	
1922	James Anderson (AUS)	Margaret Molesworth (AUS)
1923	Pat O'Hara Wood (AUS)	Margaret Molesworth (AUS)
1924	James Anderson (AUS)	Sylvia Lance (AUS)
1925	James Anderson (AUS)	Daphne Akhurst (AUS)
1926	John Hawkes (AUS)	Daphne Akhurst (AUS)
1927	Gerald Patterson (AUS)	Esna Boyd (AUS)
1928	Jean Borotra (FRA)	Daphne Akhurst (AUS)
1929	John Gregory (GBR)	Daphne Akhurst (AUS)
1930	Gar Moon (AUS)	Daphne Akhurst (AUS)
1931	Jack Crawford (AUS)	Coral Buttsworth (AUS)
1932	Jack Crawford (AUS)	Coral Buttsworth (AUS)
1933	Jack Crawford (AUS)	Joan Hartigan (AUS)
1934	Fred Perry (GBR)	Joan Hartigan (AUS)
1935	Jack Crawford (AUS)	Dorothy Round (GBR)

Australian Open Tennis Championships—Singles (continued)

YEAR	MEN	WOMEN
1936	Adrian Quist (AUS)	Joan Hartigan (AUS)
1937	Vivian McGrath (AUS)	Nancye Wynne (AUS)
1938	Don Budge (USA)	Dorothy Bundy (USA)
1939	John Bromwich (AUS)	Emily Westacott (AUS)
1940	Adrian Quist (AUS)	Nancye Wynne (AUS)
1941–45	*not held*	
1946	John Bromwich (AUS)	Nancye Wynne Bolton (AUS)
1947	Dinny Pails (AUS)	Nancye Wynne Bolton (AUS)
1948	Adrian Quist (AUS)	Nancye Wynne Bolton (AUS)
1949	Frank Sedgman (AUS)	Doris Hart (USA)
1950	Frank Sedgman (AUS)	Louise Brough (USA)
1951	Dick Savitt (USA)	Nancye Wynne Bolton (AUS)
1952	Ken McGregor (AUS)	Thelma Long (AUS)
1953	Ken Rosewall (AUS)	Maureen Connolly (USA)
1954	Mervyn Rose (AUS)	Thelma Long (AUS)
1955	Ken Rosewall (AUS)	Beryl Penrose (AUS)
1956	Lew Hoad (AUS)	Mary Carter (AUS)
1957	Ashley Cooper (AUS)	Shirley Fry (USA)
1958	Ashley Cooper (AUS)	Angela Mortimer (GBR)
1959	Alex Olmedo (PER)	Mary Carter-Reitano (AUS)
1960	Rod Laver (AUS)	Margaret Smith (AUS)
1961	Roy Emerson (AUS)	Margaret Smith (AUS)
1962	Rod Laver (AUS)	Margaret Smith (AUS)
1963	Roy Emerson (AUS)	Margaret Smith (AUS)
1964	Roy Emerson (AUS)	Margaret Smith (AUS)
1965	Roy Emerson (AUS)	Margaret Smith (AUS)
1966	Roy Emerson (AUS)	Margaret Smith (AUS)
1967	Roy Emerson (AUS)	Nancy Richey (USA)
1968	Bill Bowrey (AUS)	Billie Jean King (USA)
1969	Rod Laver (AUS)	Margaret Smith Court (AUS)
1970	Arthur Ashe (USA)	Margaret Smith Court (AUS)
1971	Ken Rosewall (AUS)	Margaret Smith Court (AUS)
1972	Ken Rosewall (AUS)	Virginia Wade (GBR)
1973	John Newcombe (AUS)	Margaret Smith Court (AUS)
1974	Jimmy Connors (USA)	Evonne Goolagong (AUS)
1975	John Newcombe (AUS)	Evonne Goolagong (AUS)
1976	Mark Edmondson (AUS)	Evonne Goolagong Cawley (AUS)
1977	Roscoe Tanner (USA)	Kerry Reid (AUS)
1978*	Vitas Gerulaitis (USA)	Evonne Goolagong Cawley (AUS)
1979	Guillermo Vilas (ARG)	Chris O'Neill (AUS)
1980	Guillermo Vilas (ARG)	Barbara Jordan (USA)
1981	Brian Teacher (USA)	Hana Mandlikova (TCH)
1982	Johan Kriek (RSA)	Martina Navratilova (USA)
1983	Johan Kriek (RSA)	Chris Evert Lloyd (USA)
1984	Mats Wilander (SWE)	Martina Navratilova (USA)
1985	Mats Wilander (SWE)	Chris Evert Lloyd (USA)
1986	Stefan Edberg (SWE)	Martina Navratilova (USA)
1987	Stefan Edberg (SWE)	Hana Mandlikova (TCH)
1988	Mats Wilander (SWE)	Steffi Graf (FRG)
1989	Ivan Lendl (TCH)	Steffi Graf (FRG)
1990	Ivan Lendl (TCH)	Steffi Graf (FRG)
1991	Boris Becker (GER)	Monica Seles (YUG)
1992	Jim Courier (USA)	Monica Seles (YUG)
1993	Jim Courier (USA)	Monica Seles (YUG)
1994	Pete Sampras (USA)	Steffi Graf (GER)
1995	Andre Agassi (USA)	Mary Pierce (FRA)
1996	Boris Becker (GER)	Monica Seles (YUG)
1997	Pete Sampras (USA)	Martina Hingis (SUI)
1998	Petr Korda (TCH)	Martina Hingis (SUI)
1999	Yevgeny Kafelnikov (RUS)	Martina Hingis (SUI)
2000	Andre Agassi (USA)	Lindsay Davenport (USA)
2001	Andre Agassi (USA)	Jennifer Capriati (USA)
2002	Thomas Johansson (SWE)	Jennifer Capriati (USA)
2003	*Scheduled to be held 13–16 Jan 2003*	

*Tournaments (since December 1977) held in December rather than January.

Australian Open Tennis Championships—Doubles

YEAR	MEN	WOMEN
1905	Tom Tachell, Randolph Lycett	
1906	Tony Wilding, Rodney Heath	
1907	Harry Parker, William Gregg	
1908	Fred Alexander, Alfred Dunlop	
1909	Ernie F. Parker, J.P. Keane	
1910	Horace Rice, Ashley Campbell	
1911	Rodney Heath, Randolph Lycett	
1912	J. Cecil Parke, Charles Dixon	
1913	Ernie F. Parker, Alf Hedemann	
1914	Ashley Campbell, Gerald Patterson	
1915	Horace Rice, Clarrie Todd	
1916–18	*not held*	
1919	Pat O'Hara Wood, Ron Thomas	
1920	Pat O'Hara Wood, Ron Thomas	
1921	S.H. Eaton-Rice, Rhys Gemmell	
1922	Gerald Patterson, John Hawkes	Esne Boyd, Marjorie Mountain
1923	Pat O'Hara Wood, Bert St. John	Esne Boyd, Sylvia Lance
1924	Norman Brookes, James Anderson	Daphne Akhurst, Sylvia Lance
1925	Gerald Patterson, Pat O'Hara Wood	Daphne Akhurst, Sylvia Lance Harper
1926	Gerald Patterson, John Hawkes	Meryl O'Hara Wood, Esne Boyd
1927	Gerald Patterson, John Hawkes	Meryl O'Hara Wood, Louise Bickerton
1928	Jean Borotra, Jacques Brugnon	Daphne Akhurst, Esne Boyd
1929	Jack Crawford, Harry Hopman	Daphne Akhurst, Louise Bickerton
1930	Jack Crawford, Harry Hopman	Margaret Molesworth, Emily Hood
1931	Charles Donohoe, Ray Dunlop	Daphne Akhurst Cozens, Louise Bickerton
1932	Jack Crawford, Gar Moon	Coral Buttsworth, Marjorie Cox Crawford
1933	Ellsworth Vines, Keith Gledhill	Margaret Molesworth, Emily Hood Westacott
1934	Fred Perry, George Hughes	Margaret Molesworth, Emily Hood Westacott
1935	Jack Crawford, Vivian McGrath	Evelyn Dearman, Nancye Wynne Lyle
1936	Adrian Quist, D.P. Turnbull	Thelma Coyne, Nancye Wynne
1937	Adrian Quist, D.P. Turnbull	Thelma Coyne, Nancye Wynne
1938	Adrian Quist, John Bromwich	Thelma Coyne, Nancye Wynne
1939	Adrian Quist, John Bromwich	Thelma Coyne, Nancye Wynne
1940	Adrian Quist, John Bromwich	Thelma Coyne, Nancye Wynne Bolton
1941–45	*not held*	
1946	Adrian Quist, John Bromwich	Joyce Fitch, Mary Bevis
1947	Adrian Quist, John Bromwich	Thelma Coyne Long, Nancye Wynne Bolton
1948	Adrian Quist, John Bromwich	Thelma Coyne Long, Nancye Wynne Bolton
1949	Adrian Quist, John Bromwich	Thelma Coyne Long, Nancye Wynne Bolton
1950	Adrian Quist, John Bromwich	Louise Brough, Doris Hart
1951	Frank Sedgman, Ken McGregor	Thelma Coyne Long, Nancye Wynne Bolton
1952	Frank Sedgman, Ken McGregor	Thelma Coyne Long, Nancye Wynne Bolton
1953	Lew Hoad, Ken Rosewall	Mareuen Connolly, Julia Sampson
1954	Rex Hartwig, Mervyn Rose	Mary Bevis Hawton, Beryl Penrose
1955	Vic Selxas, Tony Trabert	Mary Bevis Hawton, Beryl Penrose
1956	Lew Hoad, Ken Rosewall	Mary Bevis Hawton, Thelma Coyne Long
1957	Lew Hoad, Neale Fraser	Althea Gibson, Shirley Fry
1958	Ashley Cooper, Neale Fraser	Mary Bevis Hawton, Thelma Coyne Long
1959	Rod Laver, Robert Mark	Renee Schuurman, Sandra Reynolds
1960	Rod Laver, Robert Mark	Maria Bueno, Christine Truman
1961	Rod Laver, Robert Mark	Mary Reitano, Margaret Smith
1962	Roy Emerson, Neale Fraser	Margaret Smith, Robyn Ebbern
1963	Bob Hewitt, Fred Stolle	Margaret Smith, Robyn Ebbern
1964	Bob Hewitt, Fred Stolle	Judy Tegart, Lesley Turner
1965	John Newcombe, Tony Roche	Margaret Smith, Lesley Turner
1966	Roy Emerson, Fred Stolle	Carole Graebner, Nancy Richey
1967	John Newcombe, Tony Roche	Judy Tegart, Lesley Turner
1968	Dick Crealy, Allan Stone	Karen Krantzcke, Karrie Melville
1969	Roy Emerson, Rod Laver	Margaret Smith Court, Judy Tegart
1970	Bob Lutz, Stan Smith	Margaret Smith Court, Judy Tegart
1971	John Newcombe, Tony Roche	Margaret Smith Court, Evonne Goolagong
1972	Owen Davidson, Ken Rosewall	Kerry Harris, Helen Gourlay
1973	Mal Anderson, John Newcombe	Margaret Smith Court, Virginia Wade
1974	Ross Case, Geoff Masters	Evonne Goolagong, Peggy Michel
1975	John Alexander, Phil Dent	Evonne Goolagong, Peggy Michel
1976	John Newcombe, Tony Roche	Evonne Goolagong Cawley, Helen Gourlay
1977	Arthur Ashe, Tony Roche	Dianne Fromholtz, Helen Gourlay

Australian Open Tennis Championships—Doubles (continued)

YEAR	MEN	WOMEN
1978*	Allan Stone, Ray Ruffels	Evonne Goolagong Cawley, Helen Gourlay Cawley; Mona Guerrant, Kerry Reld†
1979	Wojtek Fibak, Kim Warwick	Renata Tomanova, Betsy Nagelsen
1980	Peter McNamara, Paul McNamee	Judy Chaloner, Dianne Evers
1981	Kim Warwick, Mark Edmondson	Martina Navratilova, Betsy Nagelsen
1982	Kim Warwick, Mark Edmondson	Kathy Jordan, Anne Smith
1983	J. Alexander, J. Fitzgerald	Martina Navratilova, Pam Shriver
1984	Mark Edmondson, Paul McNamee	Martina Navratilova, Pam Shriver
1985	Mark Edmondson, Sherwood Stewart	Martina Navratilova, Pam Shriver
1986	Paul Annacone, Christo van Rensburg	Martina Navratilova, Pam Shriver
1987	Stefan Edberg, Anders Jarryd	Martina Navratilova, Pam Shriver
1988	Rick Leach, Jim Pugh	Martina Navratilova, Pam Shriver
1989	Rick Leach, Jim Pugh	Martina Navratilova, Pam Shriver
1990	Pieter Aldrich, Danie Visser	Jana Novotna, Helena Sukova
1991	Scott Davis, David Pate	Patty Fendick, Mary Joe Fernandez
1992	Todd Woodbridge, Mark Woodforde	Arantxa Sánchez Vicario, Helena Sukova
1993	Danie Visser, Laurie Warder	Gigi Fernandez, Natasha Zvereva
1994	Paul Haarhuis, Jacco Eltingh	Gigi Fernandez, Natasha Zvereva
1995	Jared Palmer, Richey Reneberg	Arantxa Sánchez Vicario, Jana Novotna
1996	Stefan Edberg, Petr Korda	Arantxa Sánchez Vicario, Chanda Rubin
1997	Todd Woodbridge, Mark Woodforde	Martina Hingis, Natasha Zvereva
1998	Jonas Bjorkman, Jacco Eltingh	Martina Hingis, Mirjana Lucic
1999	Jonas Bjorkman, Patrick Rafter	Martina Hingis, Anna Kournikova
2000	Ellis Ferreira, Rick Leach	Lisa Raymond, Rennae Stubbs
2001	Jonas Bjorkman, Todd Woodbridge	Serena Williams, Venus Williams
2002	Michael Llodra, Fabrice Santoro	Martina Hingis, Anna Kournikova
2003	*Scheduled to be held in Jan 2003*	

Tournaments (since December 1977) held in December rather than January.   †Tie; finals rained out.

French Open Tennis Championships—Singles

From 1891 to 1924, only members of French tennis clubs were eligible to play in the French Open. The table shows the winners only since 1925, when the tournament was opened to international competition.

YEAR	MEN	WOMEN
1925	René Lacoste (FRA)	Suzanne Lenglen (FRA)
1926	Henri Cochet (FRA)	Suzanne Lenglen (FRA)
1927	René Lacoste (FRA)	Kornelia Bouman (NED)
1928	Henri Cochet (FRA)	Helen Wills (USA)
1929	René Lacoste (FRA)	Helen Wills (USA)
1930	Henri Cochet (FRA)	Helen Wills Moody (USA)
1931	Jean Borotra (FRA)	Cilly Aussem (GER)
1932	Henri Cochet (FRA)	Helen Wills Moody (USA)
1933	John Crawford (AUS)	Margaret Scriven (GBR)
1934	Gottfried von Cramm (GER)	Margaret Scriven (GBR)
1935	Fred Perry (GBR)	Hilde Sperling (DEN)
1936	Gottfried von Cramm (GER)	Hilde Sperling (DEN)
1937	Henner Henkel (GER)	Hilde Sperling (DEN)
1938	Don Budge (USA)	Simone Mathieu (FRA)
1939	Don McNeill (USA)	Simone Mathieu (FRA)
1940	*not held*	*not held*
1941	Bernard Destremau (FRA)	*not held*
1942	Bernard Destremau (FRA)	*not held*
1943	Yvon Petra (FRA)	*not held*
1944	Yvon Petra (FRA)	*not held*
1945	Yvon Petra (FRA)	*not held*
1946	Marcel Bernard (FRA)	Margaret Osborne (USA)
1947	Joseph Asboth (HUN)	Patricia Todd (USA)
1948	Frank Parker (USA)	Nelly Landry (BEL)
1949	Frank Parker (USA)	Margaret Osborne du Pont (USA)
1950	Budge Patty (USA)	Doris Hart (USA)
1951	Jaroslav Drobny (TCH)	Shirley Fry (USA)
1952	Jaroslav Drobny (TCH)	Doris Hart (USA)
1953	Ken Rosewall (AUS)	Maureen Connolly (USA)
1954	Tony Trabert (USA)	Maureen Connolly (USA)
1955	Tony Trabert (USA)	Angela Mortimer (GBR)
1956	Lew Hoad (AUS)	Althea Gibson (USA)

French Open Tennis Championships—Singles (continued)

YEAR	MEN	WOMEN
1957	Sven Davidson (SWE)	Shirley Bloomer (GBR)
1958	Mervyn Rose (AUS)	Zsuzsi Kormoczi (HUN)
1959	Nicola Pietrangeli (ITA)	Christine Truman (GBR)
1960	Nicola Pietrangeli (ITA)	Darlene Hard (USA)
1961	Manuel Santana (ESP)	Ann Haydon (GBR)
1962	Rod Laver (AUS)	Margaret Smith (AUS)
1963	Roy Emerson (AUS)	Lesley Turner (Austl.)
1964	Manuel Santana (ESP)	Margaret Smith (AUS)
1965	Fred Stolle (AUS)	Lesley Turner (Austl.)
1966	Tony Roche (AUS)	Ann Haydon Jones (GBR)
1967	Roy Emerson (AUS)	Francoise Durr (FRA)
1968	Ken Rosewall (AUS)	Nancy Richey (USA)
1969	Rod Laver (AUS)	Margaret Smith Court (AUS)
1970	Jan Kodes (TCH)	Margaret Smith Court (AUS)
1971	Jan Kodes (TCH)	Evonne Goolagong (AUS)
1972	Andres Gimeno (ESP)	Billie Jean King (USA)
1973	Ilie Nastase (ROM)	Margaret Smith Court (AUS)
1974	Bjorn Borg (SWE)	Chris Evert (USA)
1975	Bjorn Borg (SWE)	Chris Evert (USA)
1976	Adriano Panatta (ITA)	Sue Barker (USA)
1977	Guillermo Vilas (ARG)	Mima Jausovec (YUG)
1978	Bjorn Borg (SWE)	Virginia Ruzici (ROM)
1979	Bjorn Borg (SWE)	Chris Evert Lloyd (USA)
1980	Bjorn Borg (SWE)	Chris Evert Lloyd (USA)
1981	Bjorn Borg (SWE)	Hana Mandlikova (TCH)
1982	Mats Wilander (SWE)	Martina Navratilova (USA)
1983	Yannick Noah (FRA)	Chris Evert Lloyd (USA)
1984	Ivan Lendl (TCH)	Martina Navratilova (USA)
1985	Mats Wilander (SWE)	Chris Evert Lloyd (USA)
1986	Ivan Lendl (TCH)	Chris Evert Lloyd (USA)
1987	Ivan Lendl (TCH)	Steffi Graf (FRG)
1988	Mats Wilander (SWE)	Steffi Graf (FRG)
1989	Michael Chang (USA)	Arantxa Sánchez Vicario (ESP)
1990	Andres Gomez (ECU)	Monica Seles (YUG)
1991	Jim Courier (USA)	Monica Seles (YUG)
1992	Jim Courier (USA)	Monica Seles (YUG)
1993	Sergi Bruguera (ESP)	Steffi Graf (GER)
1994	Sergi Bruguera (ESP)	Arantxa Sánchez Vicario (ESP)
1995	Thomas Muster (AUT)	Steffi Graf (GER)
1996	Yevgeny Kafelnikov (RUS)	Steffi Graf (GER)
1997	Gustavo Kuerten (BRA)	Iva Majoli (CRO)
1998	Carlos Moya (ESP)	Arantxa Sánchez Vicario (ESP)
1999	Andre Agassi (USA)	Steffi Graf (GER)
2000	Gustavo Kuerten (BRA)	Mary Pierce (FRA)
2001	Gustavo Kuerten (BRA)	Jennifer Capriati (USA)
2002	Albert Costa (ESP)	Serena Williams (USA)

French Open Tennis Championships—Doubles

YEAR	MEN	WOMEN
1925	Jean Borotra, René Lacoste	Suzanne Lenglen, Didi Vlasto
1926	Vinnie Richards, Howard Kinsey	Suzanne Lenglen, Didi Vlasto
1927	Henri Cochet, Jacques Brugnon	Irene Peacock, Bobby Heine
1928	Jean Borotra, Jacques Brugnon	Phoebe Watson, Eileen Bennett
1929	Jean Borotra, René Lacoste	Lili de Alvarez, Kea Bouman
1930	Henri Cochet, Jacques Brugnon	Helen Wills Moody, Elizabeth Ryan
1931	George Lott, John Van Ryn	Eileen Whittingstall, Betty Nuthall
1932	Henri Cochet, Jacques Brugnon	Helen Wills Moody, Elizabeth Ryan
1933	Pat Hughes, Fred Perry	Simone Mathieu, Elizabeth Ryan
1934	Jean Borotra, Jacques Brugnon	Simone Mathieu, Elizabeth Ryan
1935	Jack Crawford, Adrian Quist	Margaret Scriven, Kay Stammers
1936	Jean Borotra, Marcel Bernard	Simone Mathieu, Billy Yorke
1937	Gottfried von Cramm, Henner Henkel	Simone Mathieu, Billy Yorke
1938	Bernard Destremau, Yvon Petra	Simone Mathieu, Billy Yorke
1939	Don McNeill, Charles Harris	Simone Mathieu, Jadwiga Jedrzejowska
1940–45	not held	
1946	Marcel Bernard, Yvon Petra	Louise Brough, Margaret Osborne

French Open Tennis Championships—Doubles (continued)

YEAR	MEN	WOMEN
1947	Eustace Fannin, Eric Sturgess	Louise Brough, Margaret Osborne
1948	Lennart Bergelin, Jaroslav Drobny	Doris Hart, Patricia Todd
1949	Pancho Gonzales, Frank Parker	Louise Brough, Margaret Osborne du Pont
1950	Billy Talbert, Tony Trabert	Doris Hart, Shirley Fry
1951	Ken McGregor, Frank Sedgman	Doris Hart, Shirley Fry
1952	Ken McGregor, Frank Sedgman	Doris Hart, Shirley Fry
1953	Lew Hoad, Ken Rosewall	Doris Hart, Shirley Fry
1954	Vic Seixas, Tony Trabert	Maureen Connolly, Nell Hopman
1955	Vic Seixas, Tony Trabert	Beverly Fleitz, Darlene Hard
1956	Don Candy, Robert Perry	Angela Buxton, Althea Gibson
1957	Mal Anderson, Ashley Cooper	Shirley Bloomer, Darlene Hard
1958	Ashley Cooper, Neale Fraser	Rosie Reyes, Yola Ramirez
1959	Nicola Pietrangeli, Orlando Sirola	Sandra Reynolds, Renee Schuurman
1960	Roy Emerson, Neale Fraser	Maria Bueno, Darlene Hard
1961	Roy Emerson, Rod Laver	Sandra Reynolds, Renee Schuurman
1962	Roy Emerson, Neale Fraser	Sandra Reynolds Price, Renee Schuurman
1963	Roy Emerson, Manuel Santana	Ann Haydon Jones, Renee Schuurman
1964	Roy Emerson, Ken Fletcher	Margaret Smith, Leslie Turner
1965	Roy Emerson, Fred Stolle	Margaret Smith, Leslie Turner
1966	Clark Graebner, Dennis Ralston	Margaret Smith, Judy Tegart
1967	John Newcombe, Tony Roche	Françoise Durr, Gail Sheriff
1968	Ken Rosewall, Fred Stolle	Françoise Durr, Ann Haydon Jones
1969	John Newcombe, Tony Roche	Françoise Durr, Ann Haydon Jones
1970	Ilie Nastase, Ion Tiriac	Françoise Durr, Gail Chanfreau
1971	Arthur Ashe, Marty Riessen	Françoise Durr, Gail Chanfreau
1972	Bob Hewitt, Frew McMillan	Billie Jean King, Betty Stove
1973	John Newcombe, Tom Okker	Margaret Smith Court, Virginia Wade
1974	Dick Crealy, Onny Parun	Chris Evert, Olga Morozova
1975	Brian Gottfried, Raul Ramirez	Chris Evert, Martina Navratilova
1976	Fred McNair, Sherwood Stewart	Fiorella Bonicelli, Gail Chanfreau Lovera
1977	Brian Gottfried, Raul Ramirez	Regina Marsikova, Pam Teeguarden
1978	Hank Pfister, Gene Mayer	Mimi Jausovec, Virginia Ruzici
1979	Sandy Mayer, Gene Mayer	Betty Stove, Wendy Turnbull
1980	Victor Amaya, Hank Pfister	Kathy Jordan, Anne Smith
1981	Heinz Gunthardt, Balazs Taroczy	Rosalyn Fairbank, Tanya Harford
1982	Sherwood Stewart, Ferdi Taygan	Martina Navratilova, Anne Smith
1983	Anders Jarryd, Hans Simonsson	Rosalyn Fairbank, Candy Reynolds
1984	Henri Leconte, Yannick Noah	Martina Navratilova, Pam Shriver
1985	Mark Edmondson, Kim Warwick	Martina Navratilova, Pam Shriver
1986	John Fitzgerald, Tomas Smid	Martina Navratilova, Andrea Temesvari
1987	Robert Seguso, Anders Jarryd	Martina Navratilova, Pam Shriver
1988	Emilio Sánchez, Andres Gomez	Martina Navratilova, Pam Shriver
1989	Jim Grabb, Patrick McEnroe	Larisa Savchenko, Natasha Zvereva
1990	Sergio Casal, Emilio Sánchez	Jana Novotna, Helena Sukova
1991	John Fitzgerald, Anders Jarryd	Gigi Fernandez, Jana Novotna
1992	Jacob Hlasek, Marc Rosset	Gigi Fernandez, Natasha Zvereva
1993	Luke Jensen, Murphy Jensen	Gigi Fernandez, Natasha Zvereva
1994	Byron Black, Jonathan Stark	Gigi Fernandez, Natasha Zvereva
1995	Jacco Eltingh, Paul Haarhuis	Gigi Fernandez, Natasha Zvereva
1996	Yevgeny Kafelnikov, Daniel Vacek	Lindsay Davenport, Mary Joe Fernandez
1997	Yevgeny Kafelnikov, Daniel Vacek	Gigi Fernandez, Natasha Zvereva
1998	Jacco Eltingh, Paul Haarhuis	Martina Hingis, Jana Novotna
1999	Mahesh Bhupathi, Leander Paes	Serena Williams, Venus Williams
2000	Todd Woodbridge, Mark Woodforde	Martina Hingis, Mary Pierce
2001	Mahesh Bhupathi, Leander Paes	Virginia Ruano-Pascal, Paola Suarez
2002	Yevgeny Kafelnikov, Paul Haarhuis	Virginia Ruano-Pascal, Paola Suarez

All-England (Wimbledon) Tennis Championships—Singles

YEAR	MEN	WOMEN
1877	Spencer Gore (GBR)	
1878	Frank Hadow (GBR)	
1879	John Hartley (GBR)	
1880	John Hartley (GBR)	
1881	Willie Renshaw (GBR)	
1882	Willie Renshaw (GBR)	
1883	Willie Renshaw (GBR)	

All-England (Wimbledon) Tennis Championships—Singles (continued)

YEAR	MEN	WOMEN
1884	Willie Renshaw (GBR)	Maud Watson (GBR)
1885	Willie Renshaw (GBR)	Maud Watson (GBR)
1886	Willie Renshaw (GBR)	Blanche Bingley (GBR)
1887	Herbert Lawford (GBR)	Lottie Dod (GBR)
1888	Ernest Renshaw (GBR)	Lottie Dod (GBR)
1889	Willie Renshaw (GBR)	Blanche Bingley Hillyard (GBR)
1890	William Hamilton (GBR)	Lena Rice (GBR)
1891	Wilfred Baddeley (GBR)	Lottie Dod (GBR)
1892	Wilfred Baddeley (GBR)	Lottie Dod (GBR)
1893	Joshua Pim (GBR)	Lottie Dod (GBR)
1894	Joshua Pim (GBR)	Blanche Bingley Hillyard (GBR)
1895	Wilfred Baddeley (GBR)	Charlotte Cooper (GBR)
1896	Harold Mahony (GBR)	Charlotte Cooper (GBR)
1897	Reggie Doherty (GBR)	Blanche Bingley Hillyard (GBR)
1898	Reggie Doherty (GBR)	Charlotte Cooper (GBR)
1899	Reggie Doherty (GBR)	Blanche Bingley Hillyard (GBR)
1900	Reggie Doherty (GBR)	Blanche Bingley Hillyard (GBR)
1901	Arthur Gore (GBR)	Charlotte Cooper Sterry (GBR)
1902	Laurie Doherty (GBR)	Muriel Robb (GBR)
1903	Laurie Doherty (GBR)	Dorothea Douglass (GBR)
1904	Laurie Doherty (GBR)	Dorothea Douglass (GBR)
1905	Laurie Doherty (GBR)	May Sutton (USA)
1906	Laurie Doherty (GBR)	Dorothea Douglass (GBR)
1907	Norman Brookes (AUS)	May Sutton (USA)
1908	Arthur Gore (GBR)	Charlotte Cooper Sterry (GBR)
1909	Arthur Gore (GBR)	Dora Boothby (GBR)
1910	Tony Wilding (NZL)	Dorothea Douglass Lambert Chambers (GBR)
1911	Tony Wilding (NZL)	Dorothea Douglass Lambert Chambers (GBR)
1912	Tony Wilding (NZL)	Ethel Larcombe (GBR)
1913	Tony Wilding (NZL)	Dorothea Douglass Lambert Chambers (GBR)
1914	Norman Brookes (AUS)	Dorothea Douglass Lambert Chambers (GBR)
1915–18	*not held*	
1919	Gerald Patterson (AUS)	Suzanne Lenglen (FRA)
1920	Bill Tilden (USA)	Suzanne Lenglen (FRA)
1921	Bill Tilden (USA)	Suzanne Lenglen (FRA)
1922	Gerald Patterson (AUS)	Suzanne Lenglen (FRA)
1923	Bill Johnston (USA)	Suzanne Lenglen (FRA)
1924	Jean Borotra (FRA)	Kathleen McKane (GBR)
1925	René Lacoste (FRA)	Suzanne Lenglen (FRA)
1926	Jean Borotra (FRA)	Kathleen McKane Godfree (GBR)
1927	Henri Cochet (FRA)	Helen Wills (USA)
1928	René Lacoste (FRA)	Helen Wills (USA)
1929	Henri Cochet (FRA)	Helen Wills (USA)
1930	Bill Tilden (USA)	Helen Wills Moody (USA)
1931	Sidney Wood (USA)	Cilly Aussem (GER)
1932	Ellsworth Vines (USA)	Helen Wills Moody (USA)
1933	Jack Crawford (AUS)	Helen Wills Moody (USA)
1934	Fred Perry (GBR)	Dorothy Round (GBR)
1935	Fred Perry (GBR)	Helen Wills Moody (USA)
1936	Fred Perry (GBR)	Helen Jacobs (USA)
1937	Don Budge (USA)	Dorothy Round (GBR)
1938	Don Budge (USA)	Helen Wills Moody (USA)
1939	Bobby Riggs (USA)	Alice Marble (USA)
1940–45	*not held*	
1946	Yvon Petra (FRA)	Pauline Betz (USA)
1947	Jack Kramer (USA)	Margaret Osborne (USA)
1948	Bob Falkenburg (USA)	Louise Brough (USA)
1949	Ted Schroeder (USA)	Louise Brough (USA)
1950	Budge Patty (USA)	Louise Brough (USA)
1951	Dick Savitt (USA)	Doris Hart (USA)
1952	Frank Sedgman (AUS)	Maureen Connolly (USA)
1953	Vic Seixas (USA)	Maureen Connolly (USA)
1954	Jaroslav Drobny (TCH)	Maureen Connolly (USA)
1955	Tony Trabert (USA)	Louise Brough (USA)
1956	Lew Hoad (AUS)	Shirley Fry (USA)
1957	Lew Hoad (AUS)	Althea Gibson (USA)
1958	Ashley Cooper (AUS)	Althea Gibson (USA)
1959	Alex Olmedo (PER)	Maria Bueno (BRA)

All-England (Wimbledon) Tennis Championships—Singles (continued)

YEAR	MEN	WOMEN
1960	Neale Fraser (AUS)	Maria Bueno (BRA)
1961	Rod Laver (AUS)	Angela Mortimer (GBR)
1962	Rod Laver (AUS)	Karen Susman (USA)
1963	Chuck McKinley (USA)	Margaret Smith (AUS)
1964	Roy Emerson (AUS)	Maria Bueno (BRA)
1965	Roy Emerson (AUS)	Margaret Smith (AUS)
1966	Manuel Santana (ESP)	Billie Jean King (USA)
1967	John Newcombe (AUS)	Billie Jean King (USA)
1968*	Rod Laver (AUS)	Billie Jean King (USA)
1969	Rod Laver (AUS)	Ann Jones (GBR)
1970	John Newcombe (AUS)	Margaret Smith Court (AUS)
1971	John Newcombe (AUS)	Evonne Goolagong (AUS)
1972	Stan Smith (USA)	Billie Jean King (USA)
1973	Jan Kodes (TCH)	Billie Jean King (USA)
1974	Jimmy Connors (USA)	Chris Evert (USA)
1975	Arthur Ashe (USA)	Billie Jean King (USA)
1976	Björn Borg (SWE)	Chris Evert (USA)
1977	Björn Borg (SWE)	Virginia Wade (GBR)
1978	Björn Borg (SWE)	Martina Navratilova (TCH)
1979	Björn Borg (SWE)	Martina Navratilova (USA)
1980	Björn Borg (SWE)	Evonne Goolagong Cawley (AUS)
1981	John McEnroe (USA)	Chris Evert Lloyd (USA)
1982	Jimmy Connors (USA)	Martina Navratilova (USA)
1983	John McEnroe (USA)	Martina Navratilova (USA)
1984	John McEnroe (USA)	Martina Navratilova (USA)
1985	Boris Becker (FRG)	Martina Navratilova (USA)
1986	Boris Becker (FRG)	Martina Navratilova (USA)
1987	Pat Cash (AUS)	Martina Navratilova (USA)
1988	Stefan Edberg (SWE)	Steffi Graf (GDR)
1989	Boris Becker (FRG)	Steffi Graf (GDR)
1990	Stefan Edberg (SWE)	Martina Navratilova (USA)
1991	Michael Stich (GER)	Steffi Graf (GER)
1992	Andre Agassi (USA)	Steffi Graf (GER)
1993	Pete Sampras (USA)	Steffi Graf (GER)
1994	Pete Sampras (USA)	Conchita Martínez (ESP)
1995	Pete Sampras (USA)	Steffi Graf (GER)
1996	Richard Krajicek (NED)	Steffi Graf (GER)
1997	Pete Sampras (USA)	Martina Hingis (SUI)
1998	Pete Sampras (USA)	Jana Novotna (CZE)
1999	Pete Sampras (USA)	Lindsay Davenport (USA)
2000	Pete Sampras (USA)	Venus Williams (USA)
2001	Goran Ivanisevic (CRO)	Venus Williams (USA)
2002	Lleyton Hewitt (AUS)	Serena Williams (USA)

*Open since 1968.

All-England (Wimbledon) Tennis Championships—Doubles

YEAR	MEN	WOMEN
1879	L.R. Erskine, H. Lawford	
1880	William Renshaw, Ernest Renshaw	
1881	William Renshaw, Ernest Renshaw	
1882	J.T. Hartley, R.T. Richardson	
1883	C.W. Grinstead, C.E. Welldon	
1884	William Renshaw, Ernest Renshaw	
1885	William Renshaw, Ernest Renshaw	
1886	William Renshaw, Ernest Renshaw	
1887	Herbert Wilberforce, P.B. Lyon	
1888	William Renshaw, Ernest Renshaw	
1889	William Renshaw, Ernest Renshaw	
1890	Joshua Pim, F.O. Stoker	
1891	Wilfred Baddeley, Herbert Baddeley	
1892	E.W. Lewis, H.S. Barlow	
1893	Joshua Pim, F.O. Stoker	
1894	Wilfred Baddeley, Herbert Baddeley	
1895	Wilfred Baddeley, Herbert Baddeley	
1896	Wilfred Baddeley, Herbert Baddeley	

All-England (Wimbledon) Tennis Championships—Doubles (continued)

YEAR	MEN	WOMEN
1897	Reggie Doherty, Laurie Doherty	
1898	Reggie Doherty, Laurie Doherty	
1899	Reggie Doherty, Laurie Doherty	
1900	Reggie Doherty, Laurie Doherty	
1901	Reggie Doherty, Laurie Doherty	
1902	Sidney Smith, Frank Riseley	
1903	Reggie Doherty, Laurie Doherty	
1904	Reggie Doherty, Laurie Doherty	
1905	Reggie Doherty, Laurie Doherty	
1906	Sidney Smith, Frank Riseley	
1907	Norman Brookes, Anthony Wilding	
1908	Anthony Wilding, M.J.G. Ritchie	
1909	Arthur Gore, H. Roper Barrett	
1910	Anthony Wilding, M.J.G. Ritchie	
1911	Andre Gobert, Max Decugis	
1912	H. Roper Barrett, Charles Dixon	
1913	H. Roper Barrett, Charles Dixon	Winifred McNair, Dora Boothby
1914	Norman Brookes, Anthony Wilding	Elizabeth Ryan, Agatha Morton
1915-18	*not held*	
1919	R.V. Thomas, Pat O'Hara Wood	Suzanne Lenglen, Elizabeth Ryan
1920	Richard Williams, Chuck Garland	Suzanne Lenglen, Elizabeth Ryan
1921	Randolph Lycett, Max Woosnam	Suzanne Lenglen, Elizabeth Ryan
1922	James Anderson, Randolph Lycett	Suzanne Lenglen, Elizabeth Ryan
1923	Leslie Godfree, Randolph Lycett	Suzanne Lenglen, Elizabeth Ryan
1924	Frank Hunter, Vincent Richards	Hazel Wightman, Helen Wills
1925	Jean Borotra, René Lacoste	Suzanne Lenglen, Elizabeth Ryan
1926	Jacques Brugnon, Henri Cochet	Mary Browne, Elizabeth Ryan
1927	Bill Tilden, Frank Hunter	Helen Wills, Elizabeth Ryan
1928	Jacques Brugnon, Henri Cochet	Peggy Saunders, Phoebe Watson
1929	Wilmer Allison, John Van Ryn	Peggy Saunders Michell, Phoebe Watson
1930	Wilmer Allison, John Van Ryn	Helen Wills Moody, Elizabeth Ryan
1931	George Lott, John Van Ryn	Phyllis Mudford, Dorothy Barron
1932	Jean Borotra, Jacques Brugnon	Doris Metaxa, Josane Sigart
1933	Jean Borotra, Jacques Brugnon	Elizabeth Ryan, Simone Mathieu
1934	George Lott, Lester Stoefen	Elizabeth Ryan, Simone Mathieu
1935	Jack Crawford, Adrian Quist	Freda James, Kay Stammers
1936	Pat Hughes, Raymond Tuckey	Freda James, Kay Stammers
1937	Don Budge, Gene Mako	Simone Mathieu, Billie Yorke
1938	Don Budge, Gene Mako	Sarah Palfrey Fabyan, Alice Marble
1939	Bobby Riggs, Elwood Cooke	Sarah Palfrey Fabyan, Alice Marble
1940-45	*not held*	
1946	Jack Kramer, Tom Brown	Louise Brough, Margaret Osborne
1947	Jack Kramer, Bob Falkenburg	Patricia Todd, Doris Hart
1948	John Bromwich, Frank Sedgman	Louise Brough, Margaret Osborne du Pont
1949	Pancho Gonzales, Frank Parker	Louise Brough, Margaret Osborne du Pont
1950	John Bromwich, Adrian Quist	Louise Brough, Margaret Osborne du Pont
1951	Ken McGregor, Frank Sedgman	Doris Hart, Shirley Fry
1952	Ken McGregor, Frank Sedgman	Doris Hart, Shirley Fry
1953	Ken Rosewall, Lew Hoad	Doris Hart, Shirley Fry
1954	Rex Hartwig, Mervyn Rose	Louise Brough, Margaret Osborne du Pont
1955	Rex Hartwig, Lew Hoad	Angela Mortimer, Anne Shilcock
1956	Ken Rosewall, Lew Hoad	Angela Buxton, Althea Gibson
1957	Budge Patty, Gardnar Mulloy	Althea Gibson, Darlene Hard
1958	Sven Davidson, Ulf Schmidt	Maria Bueno, Althea Gibson
1959	Roy Emerson, Neale Fraser	Jeanne Arth, Darlene Hard
1960	Rafael Osuna, Dennis Ralston	Maria Bueno, Darlene Hard
1961	Roy Emerson, Neale Fraser	Karen Hantze, Billie Jean Moffitt
1962	Bob Hewitt, Fred Stolle	Karen Hantze Susman, Billie Jean Moffitt
1963	Rafael Osuna, Antonio Palafox	Maria Bueno, Darlene Hard
1964	Bob Hewitt, Fred Stolle	Margaret Smith, Leslie Turner
1965	John Newcombe, Tony Roche	Maria Bueno, Billie Jean Moffitt
1966	John Newcombe, Ken Fletcher	Maria Bueno, Nancy Richey
1967	Bob Hewitt, Frew McMillan	Rosemary Casals, Billie Jean Moffitt King
1968	John Newcombe, Tony Roche	Rosemary Casals, Billie Jean King
1969	John Newcombe, Tony Roche	Margaret Smith Court, Judy Tegart
1970	John Newcombe, Tony Roche	Rosemary Casals, Billie Jean King
1971	Rod Laver, Roy Emerson	Rosemary Casals, Billie Jean King
1972	Bob Hewitt, Frew McMillan	Billie Jean King, Betty Stove

All-England (Wimbledon) Tennis Championships—Doubles (continued)

YEAR	MEN	WOMEN
1973	Jimmy Connors, Ilie Nastase	Rosemary Casals, Billie Jean King
1974	John Newcombe, Tony Roche	Evonne Goolagong, Peggy Michel
1975	Vitas Gerulaitis, Sandy Mayer	Ann Kiyomura, Kazuko Sawamatsu
1976	Brian Gottfried, Raul Ramirez	Chris Evert, Martina Navratilova
1977	Ross Case, Geoff Masters	Helen Gourlay Cawley, Joanne Russell
1978	Bob Hewitt, Frew McMillan	Kerry Reid, Wendy Turnbull
1979	John McEnroe, Peter Fleming	Billie Jean King, Martina Navratilova
1980	Peter McNamara, Paul McNamee	Kathy Jordan, Anne Smith
1981	John McEnroe, Peter Fleming	Martina Navratilova, Pam Shriver
1982	Peter McNamara, Paul McNamee	Martina Navratilova, Pam Shriver
1983	John McEnroe, Peter Fleming	Martina Navratilova, Pam Shriver
1984	John McEnroe, Peter Fleming	Martina Navratilova, Pam Shriver
1985	Heinz Gunthardt, Balazs Taroczy	Kathy Jordan, Elizabeth Smylie
1986	Joakim Nystrom, Mats Wilander	Martina Navratilova, Pam Shriver
1987	Robert Seguso, Ken Flach	Claudia Kohde-Kilsche, Helena Sukova
1988	Robert Seguso, Ken Flach	Steffi Graf, Gabriela Sabatini
1989	John Fitzgerald, Anders Jarryd	Jana Novotna, Helena Sukova
1990	Rick Leach, Jim Pugh	Jana Novotna, Helena Sukova
1991	John Fitzgerald, Anders Jarryd	Larisa Savchenko, Natasha Zvereva
1992	John McEnroe, Michael Stich	Gigi Fernandez, Natasha Zvereva
1993	Todd Woodbridge, Mark Woodforde	Gigi Fernandez, Natasha Zvereva
1994	Todd Woodbridge, Mark Woodforde	Gigi Fernandez, Natasha Zvereva
1995	Todd Woodbridge, Mark Woodforde	Arantxa Sánchez Vicario, Jana Novotna
1996	Todd Woodbridge, Mark Woodforde	Helena Sukova, Martina Hingis
1997	Todd Woodbridge, Mark Woodforde	Gigi Fernandez, Natasha Zvereva
1998	Jacco Eltingh, Paul Haarhuis	Martina Hingis, Jana Novotna
1999	Mahesh Bhupathi, Leander Paes	Lindsay Davenport, Corina Morariu
2000	Todd Woodbridge, Mark Woodforde	Venus Williams, Serena Williams
2001	Donald Johnson, Jared Palmer	Lisa Raymond, Rennae Stubbs
2002	Todd Woodbridge, Jonas Bjorkman	Venus Williams, Serena Williams

United States Open Tennis Championships—Singles

YEAR	MEN	WOMEN
1881	Richard Sears (USA)	
1882	Richard Sears (USA)	
1883	Richard Sears (USA)	
1884	Richard Sears (USA)	
1885	Richard Sears (USA)	
1886	Richard Sears (USA)	
1887	Richard Sears (USA)	Ellen Hansell (USA)
1888	Henry Slocum, Jr. (USA)	Bertha Townsend (USA)
1889	Henry Slocum, Jr. (USA)	Bertha Townsend (USA)
1890	Oliver Campbell (USA)	Ellen Roosevelt (USA)
1891	Oliver Campbell (USA)	Mabel Cahill (USA)
1892	Oliver Campbell (USA)	Mabel Cahill (USA)
1893	Robert Wrenn (USA)	Aline Terry (USA)
1894	Robert Wrenn (USA)	Helen Helwig (USA)
1895	Fred Hovey (USA)	Juliette Atkinson (USA)
1896	Robert Wrenn (USA)	Elisabeth Moore (USA)
1897	Robert Wrenn (USA)	Juliette Atkinson (USA)
1898	Malcom Whitman (USA)	Juliette Atkinson (USA)
1899	Malcom Whitman (USA)	Marion Jones (USA)
1900	Malcom Whitman (USA)	Myrtle McAteer (USA)
1901	William Larned (USA)	Elisabeth Moore (USA)
1902	William Larned (USA)	Marion Jones (USA)
1903	Laurie Doherty (GBR)	Elisabeth Moore (USA)
1904	Holcombe Ward (USA)	May Sutton (USA)
1905	Beals Wright (USA)	Elisabeth Moore (USA)
1906	Bill Clothier (USA)	Helen Homans (USA)
1907	William Larned (USA)	Evelyn Sears (USA)
1908	William Larned (USA)	Maud Barger-Wallach (USA)
1909	William Larned (USA)	Hazel Hotchkiss (USA)
1910	William Larned (USA)	Hazel Hotchkiss (USA)
1911	William Larned (USA)	Hazel Hotchkiss (USA)
1912	Maurice McLoughlin (USA)	Mary Browne (USA)
1913	Maurice McLoughlin (USA)	Mary Browne (USA)

United States Open Tennis Championships—Singles (continued)

YEAR	MEN	WOMEN
1914	R. Norris Williams (USA)	Mary Browne (USA)
1915	Bill Johnston (USA)	Molla Bjurstedt (NOR)
1916	R. Norris Williams (USA)	Molla Bjurstedt (NOR)
1917	Lindley Murray (USA)	Molla Bjurstedt (NOR)
1918	Lindley Murray (USA)	Molla Bjurstedt (NOR)
1919	Bill Johnston (USA)	Hazel Hotchkiss Wightman (USA)
1920	Bill Tilden (USA)	Molla Bjurstedt Mallory (USA)
1921	Bill Tilden (USA)	Molla Bjurstedt Mallory (USA)
1922	Bill Tilden (USA)	Molla Bjurstedt Mallory (USA)
1923	Bill Tilden (USA)	Helen Wills (USA)
1924	Bill Tilden (USA)	Helen Wills (USA)
1925	Bill Tilden (USA)	Helen Wills (USA)
1926	René Lacoste (FRA)	Molla Bjurstedt Mallory (USA)
1927	René Lacoste (FRA)	Helen Wills (USA)
1928	Henri Cochet (FRA)	Helen Wills (USA)
1929	Bill Tilden (USA)	Helen Wills (USA)
1930	John Doeg (USA)	Betty Nuthall (GBR)
1931	Ellsworth Vines (USA)	Helen Wills Moody (USA)
1932	Ellsworth Vines (USA)	Helen Jacobs (USA)
1933	Fred Perry (GBR)	Helen Jacobs (USA)
1934	Fred Perry (GBR)	Helen Jacobs (USA)
1935	Wilmer Allison (USA)	Helen Jacobs (USA)
1936	Fred Perry (GBR)	Alice Marble (USA)
1937	Don Budge (USA)	Anita Lizana (CHI)
1938	Don Budge (USA)	Alice Marble (USA)
1939	Bobby Riggs (USA)	Alice Marble (USA)
1940	Don McNeill (USA)	Alice Marble (USA)
1941	Bobby Riggs (USA)	Sarah Palfrey Cooke (USA)
1942	Ted Schroeder (USA)	Pauline Betz (USA)
1943	Joe Hunt (USA)	Pauline Betz (USA)
1944	Frank Parker (USA)	Pauline Betz (USA)
1945	Frank Parker (USA)	Sarah Palfrey Cooke (USA)
1946	Jack Kramer (USA)	Pauline Betz (USA)
1947	Jack Kramer (USA)	Louise Brough (USA)
1948	Pancho Gonzales (USA)	Margaret du Pont (USA)
1949	Pancho Gonzales (USA)	Margaret du Pont (USA)
1950	Arthur Larsen (USA)	Margaret du Pont (USA)
1951	Frank Sedgman (AUS)	Maureen Connolly (USA)
1952	Frank Sedgman (AUS)	Maureen Connolly (USA)
1953	Tony Trabert (USA)	Maureen Connolly (USA)
1954	Vic Seixas (USA)	Doris Hart (USA)
1955	Tony Trabert (USA)	Doris Hart (USA)
1956	Ken Rosewall (AUS)	Shirley Fry (USA)
1957	Mal Anderson (AUS)	Althea Gibson (USA)
1958	Ashley Cooper (AUS)	Althea Gibson (USA)
1959	Neale Fraser (AUS)	Maria Bueno (BRA)
1960	Neale Fraser (AUS)	Darlene Hard (USA)
1961	Roy Emerson (AUS)	Darlene Hard (USA)
1962	Rod Laver (AUS)	Margaret Smith (AUS)
1963	Rafael Osuna (MEX)	Maria Bueno (BRA)
1964	Roy Emerson (AUS)	Maria Bueno (BRA)
1965	Manuel Santana (SPA)	Margaret Smith (AUS)
1966	Fred Stolle (AUS)	Maria Bueno (BRA)
1967	John Newcombe (AUS)	Billie Jean King (USA)
1968*	Arthur Ashe (USA)	Virginia Wade (GBR); Margaret Smith Court (AUS)
1969*	Rod Laver (AUS); Stan Smith (USA)	Margaret Smith Court (AUS)
1970	Ken Rosewall (AUS)	Margaret Smith Court (AUS)
1971	Stan Smith (USA)	Billie Jean King (USA)
1972	Ilie Nastase (ROM)	Billie Jean King (USA)
1973	John Newcombe (AUS)	Margaret Smith Court (AUS)
1974	Jimmy Connors (USA)	Billie Jean King (USA)
1975	Manuel Orantes (SPA)	Chris Evert (USA)
1976	Jimmy Connors (USA)	Chris Evert (USA)
1977	Guillermo Vilas (ARG)	Chris Evert (USA)
1978	Jimmy Connors (USA)	Chris Evert (USA)
1979	John McEnroe (USA)	Tracy Austin (USA)
1980	John McEnroe (USA)	Chris Evert Lloyd (USA)
1981	John McEnroe (USA)	Tracy Austin (USA)

United States Open Tennis Championships—Singles (continued)

YEAR	MEN	WOMEN
1982	Jimmy Connors (USA)	Chris Evert Lloyd (USA)
1983	Jimmy Connors (USA)	Martina Navratilova (USA)
1984	John McEnroe (USA)	Martina Navratilova (USA)
1985	Ivan Lendl (TCH)	Hana Mandlikova (TCH)
1986	Ivan Lendl (TCH)	Martina Navratilova (USA)
1987	Ivan Lendl (TCH)	Martina Navratilova (USA)
1988	Mats Wilander (SWE)	Steffi Graf (FRG)
1989	Boris Becker (FRG)	Steffi Graf (FRG)
1990	Pete Sampras (USA)	Gabriela Sabatini (ARG)
1991	Stefan Edberg (SWE)	Monica Seles (YUG)
1992	Stefan Edberg (SWE)	Monica Seles (YUG)
1993	Pete Sampras (USA)	Steffi Graf (GER)
1994	Andre Agassi (USA)	Arantxa Sánchez Vicario (SPA)
1995	Pete Sampras (USA)	Steffi Graf (GER)
1996	Pete Sampras (USA)	Steffi Graf (GER)
1997	Patrick Rafter (AUS)	Martina Hingis (SUI)
1998	Patrick Rafter (AUS)	Lindsay Davenport (USA)
1999	Andre Agassi (USA)	Serena Williams (USA)
2000	Marat Safin (RUS)	Venus Williams (USA)
2001	Lleyton Hewitt (AUS)	Venus Williams (USA)
2002	scheduled to be held in August and September	

In 1968 and 1969 both amateur and open championships were held. Ashe won both men's competitions in 1968; Smith won the amateur championship in 1969. Court won the women's amateur competition in 1968 and both championships in 1969. Thereafter the championships were open.

United States Open Tennis Championships—Doubles

YEAR	MEN	WOMEN
1881	Clarence Clark, Fred Taylor	
1882	Richard Sears, James Dwight	
1883	Richard Sears, James Dwight	
1884	Richard Sears, James Dwight	
1885	Richard Sears, Joseph Clark	
1886	Richard Sears, James Dwight	
1887	Richard Sears, James Dwight	
1888	Oliver Campbell, Valentine Hall	
1889	Henry Slocum, Howard Taylor	Bertha Townsend, Margarette Ballard
1890	Valentine Hall, Clarence Hobart	Ellen Roosevelt, Grace Roosevelt
1891	Oliver Campbell, Robert Huntington	Mabel Cahill, Mrs. W. Fellowes Morgan
1892	Oliver Campbell, Robert Huntington	Mabel Cahill, Adeline McKinley
1893	Clarence Hobart, Fred Hovey	Aline Terry, Hattie Butler
1894	Clarence Hobart, Fred Hovey	Helen Helwig, Juliette Atkinson
1895	Malcom Chace, Robert Wrenn	Helen Helwig, Juliette Atkinson
1896	Carr Neel, Samuel Neel	Elisabeth Moore, Juliette Atkinson
1897	Leo Ware, George Sheldon	Juliette Atkinson, Kathleen Atkinson
1898	Leo Ware, George Sheldon	Juliette Atkinson, Kathleen Atkinson
1899	Holcombe Ward, Dwight Davis	Jane Craven, Myrtle McAteer
1900	Holcombe Ward, Dwight Davis	Edith Parker, Hallie Champlin
1901	Holcombe Ward, Dwight Davis	Juliette Atkinson, Myrtle McAteer
1902	Reginald Doherty, Hugh Doherty	Juliette Atkinson, Marion Jones
1903	Reginald Doherty, Hugh Doherty	Elisabeth Moore, Carrie Neely
1904	Holcombe Ward, Beals Wright	Mary Sutton, Miriam Hall
1905	Holcombe Ward, Beals Wright	Helen Homans, Carrie Neely
1906	Holcombe Ward, Beals Wright	Mrs. L.S. Coe, Mrs. D.S. Platt
1907	Fred Alexander, Harold Hackett	Marie Weimer, Carrie Neely
1908	Fred Alexander, Harold Hackett	Evelyn Sears, Margaret Curtis
1909	Fred Alexander, Harold Hackett	Hazel Hotchkiss, Edith Rotch
1910	Fred Alexander, Harold Hackett	Hazel Hotchkiss, Edith Rotch
1911	Raymond Little, Gustave Touchard	Hazel Hotchkiss, Eleanora Sears
1912	Maurice McLoughlin, Thomas Bundy	Dorothy Green, Mary Browne
1913	Maurice McLoughlin, Thomas Bundy	Mary Browne, Mrs. R.H. Williams
1914	Maurice McLoughlin, Thomas Bundy	Mary Browne, Mrs. R.H. Williams
1915	William Johnston, Clarence Griffin	Hazel Hotchkiss Wightman, Eleanora Sears
1916	William Johnston, Clarence Griffin	Molla Bjurstedt, Eleanora Sears
1917	Fred Alexander, Harold Throckmorton	Molla Bjurstedt, Eleanora Sears
1918	Bill Tilden, Vincent Richards	Marion Zinderstein, Eleanor Goss

United States Open Tennis Championships—Doubles (continued)

YEAR	MEN	WOMEN
1919	Norman Brookes, Gerald Patterson	Marion Zinderstein, Eleanor Goss
1920	William Johnston, Clarence Griffin	Marion Zinderstein, Eleanor Goss
1921	Bill Tilden, Vincent Richards	Mary Browne, Mrs. R.H. Williams
1922	Bill Tilden, Vincent Richards	Marion Zinderstein Jessup, Helen Wills
1923	Bill Tilden, Brian Norton	Kathleen McKane, Phyllis Covell
1924	Howard Kinsey, Robert Kinsey	Hazel Hotchkiss Wightman, Helen Wills
1925	Richard Williams, Vincent Richards	Mary Browne, Helen Wills
1926	Richard Williams, Vincent Richards	Elizabeth Ryan, Eleanor Goss
1927	Bill Tilden, Frank Hunter	Kathleen McKane Godfree, Ermyntrude Harvey
1928	George Lott, John Hennessey	Hazel Hotchkiss Wightman, Helen Wills
1929	George Lott, John Doeg	Phoebe Watson, Peggy Michell
1930	George Lott, John Doeg	Betty Nuthall, Sarah Palfrey
1931	Wilmer Allison, John Van Ryn	Betty Nuthall, Eileen Whittingstall
1932	Elsworth Vines, Keith Gledhill	Helen Jacobs, Sarah Palfrey
1933	George Lott, Lester Stoefen	Betty Nuthall, Freda James
1934	George Lott, Lester Stoefen	Helen Jacobs, Sarah Palfrey
1935	Wilmer Allison, John Van Ryn	Helen Jacobs, Sarah Palfrey Fabyan
1936	Don Budge, Gene Mako	Marjorie Van Ryn, Carolin Babcock
1937	Gottfried von Cramm, Henner Henkel	Sarah Palfrey Fabyan, Alice Marble
1938	Don Budge, Gene Mako	Sarah Palfrey Fabyan, Alice Marble
1939	Adrian Quist, John Bromwich	Sarah Palfrey Fabyan, Alice Marble
1940	Jack Kramer, Ted Schroeder	Sarah Palfrey Fabyan, Alice Marble
1941	Jack Kramer, Ted Schroeder	Sarah Palfrey Fabyan, Margaret Osborne
1942	Gardnar Mulloy, Billy Talbert	Louise Brough, Margaret Osborne
1943	Jack Kramer, Frank Parker	Louise Brough, Margaret Osborne
1944	Don McNeill, Bob Falkenburg	Louise Brough, Margaret Osborne
1945	Gardnar Mulloy, Billy Talbert	Louise Brough, Margaret Osborne
1946	Gardnar Mulloy, Billy Talbert	Louise Brough, Margaret Osborne
1947	Jack Kramer, Ted Schroeder	Louise Brough, Margaret Osborne
1948	Gardnar Mulloy, Billy Talbert	Louise Brough, Margaret Osborne du Pont
1949	John Bromwich, Billy Sidwell	Louise Brough, Margaret Osborne du Pont
1950	John Bromwich, Frank Sedgman	Louise Brough, Margaret Osborne du Pont
1951	Ken McGregor, Frank Sedgman	Shirley Fry, Doris Hart
1952	Mervyn Rose, Vic Seixas	Shirley Fry, Doris Hart
1953	Mervyn Rose, Rex Hartwig	Shirley Fry, Doris Hart
1954	Vic Seixas, Tony Trabert	Shirley Fry, Doris Hart
1955	Kosei Kamo, Atushi Miyagi	Louise Brough, Margaret Osborne du Pont
1956	Lew Hoad, Ken Rosewall	Louise Brough, Margaret Osborne du Pont
1957	Ashley Cooper, Neale Fraser	Louise Brough, Margaret Osborne du Pont
1958	Alex Olmedo, Hamilton Richardson	Jeanne Arth, Darlene Hard
1959	Neale Fraser, Roy Emerson	Jeanne Arth, Darlene Hard
1960	Neale Fraser, Roy Emerson	Darlene Hard, Maria Bueno
1961	Charles McKinley, Dennis Ralston	Darlene Hard, Lesley Turner
1962	Rafael Osuna, Antonio Palafox	Darlene Hard, Maria Bueno
1963	Charles McKinley, Dennis Ralston	Robyn Ebbern, Margaret Smith
1964	Charles McKinley, Dennis Ralston	Billie Jean Moffitt, Karen Susman
1965	Roy Emerson, Fred Stolle	Carole Caldwell Graebner, Nancy Richey
1966	Roy Emerson, Fred Stolle	Maria Bueno, Nancy Richey
1967	John Newcombe, Tony Roche	Billie Jean Moffitt King, Rosemary Casals
1968*	Robert Lutz, Stan Smith	Maria Bueno, Margaret Smith Court
1969*	Ken Rosewall, Fred Stolle; Dick Crealy, Allan Stone	Françoise Durr, Darlene Hard; Margaret Smith Court, Virginia Wade
1970	Pierre Barthes, Nikki Pilic	Margaret Smith Court, Judy Dalton
1971	John Newcombe, Roger Taylor	Rosemary Casals, Judy Dalton
1972	Cliff Drysdale, Roger Taylor	Françoise Durr, Betty Stove
1973	Owen Davidson, John Newcombe	Margaret Smith Court, Virginia Wade
1974	Robert Lutz, Stan Smith	Billie Jean King, Rosemary Casals
1975	Jimmy Connors, Ilie Nastase	Margaret Smith Court, Virginia Wade
1976	Tom Okker, Marty Riessen	Delina Boshoff, Ilana Kloss
1977	Bob Hewitt, Frew McMillan	Martina Navratilova, Betty Stove
1978	Robert Lutz, Stan Smith	Martina Navratilova, Billie Jean King
1979	John McEnroe, Peter Fleming	Wendy Turnbull, Betty Stove
1980	Robert Lutz, Stan Smith	Martina Navratilova, Billie Jean King
1981	John McEnroe, Peter Fleming	Kathy Jordan, Anne Smith
1982	Kevin Curren, Steve Denton	Rosemary Casals, Wendy Turnbull
1983	John McEnroe, Peter Fleming	Martina Navratilova, Pam Shriver
1984	John Fitzgerald, Tomas Smid	Martina Navratilova, Pam Shriver
1985	Ken Flach, Robert Seguso	Claudia Kohde-Kilsch, Helena Sukova

United States Open Tennis Championships—Doubles (continued)

YEAR	MEN	WOMEN
1986	Andres Gómez, Slobodan Zivojinovic	Martina Navratilova, Pam Shriver
1987	Stefan Edberg, Anders Jarryd	Martina Navratilova, Pam Shriver
1988	Sergio Casal, Emilio Sánchez	Gigi Fernandez, Robin White
1989	John McEnroe, Mark Woodforde	Martina Navratilova, Hana Mandlikova
1990	Pieter Aldrich, Danie Visser	Martina Navratilova, Gigi Fernandez
1991	John Fitzgerald, Anders Jarryd	Pam Shriver, Natasha Zvereva
1992	Jim Grabb, Richey Reneberg	Gigi Fernandez, Natasha Zvereva
1993	Ken Flach, Rick Leach	Arantxa Sánchez Vicario, Helena Sukova
1994	Paul Haarhuis, Jacco Eltingh	Arantxa Sánchez Vicario, Jana Novotna
1995	Todd Woodbridge, Mark Woodforde	Gigi Fernandez, Natasha Zvereva
1996	Todd Woodbridge, Mark Woodforde	Gigi Fernandez, Natasha Zvereva
1997	Yevgeny Kafelnikov, Daniel Vacek	Lindsay Davenport, Jana Novotna
1998	Sandon Stolle, Cyril Suk	Martina Hingis, Jana Novotna
1999	Sebastian Lareau, Alex O'Brien	Venus Williams, Serena Williams
2000	Lleyton Hewitt, Max Mirnyi	Julie Halard-Decugis, Ai Sugiyama
2001	Wayne Black, Kevin Ullyet	Lisa Raymond, Rennae Stubbs
2002	scheduled to be held in August and September	

*In 1968 and 1969 both amateur and open championships were held. Lutz and Smith won both men's com-petitions in 1968; Crealy and Stone took the men's amateur championships in 1969. Bueno and Court won both women's competitions in 1968; Court and Wade took the women's amateur championships in 1969. Thereafter the championships were open.

Davis Cup

YEAR	WINNER	RUNNER-UP	RESULTS	YEAR	WINNER	RUNNER-UP	RESULTS
1900	United States	British Isles	3–0	1949	United States	Australia	4–1
1901	not held			1950	Australia	United States	4–1
1902	United States	British Isles	3–2	1951	Australia	United States	3–2
1903	British Isles*	United States	4–1	1952	Australia	United States	4–1
1904	British Isles	Belgium	5–0	1953	Australia	United States	3–2
1905	British Isles	United States	5–0	1954	United States	Australia	3–2
1906	British Isles	United States	5–0	1955	Australia	United States	5–0
1907	Australasia†	British Isles	3–2	1956	Australia	United States	5–0
1908	Australasia	United States	3–2	1957	Australia	United States	3–2
1909	Australasia	United States	5–0	1958	United States	Australia	3–2
1910	not held			1959	Australia	United States	3–2
1911	Australasia	United States	5–0	1960	Australia	Italy	4–1
1912	British Isles	Australia	3–2	1961	Australia	Italy	5–0
1913	United States	British Isles	3–2	1962	Australia	Mexico	5–0
1914	Australasia	United States	3–2	1963	United States	Australia	3–2
1915–18	not held			1964	Australia	United States	3–2
1919	Australasia	British Isles	4–1	1965	Australia	Spain	4–1
1920	United States	Australasia	5–0	1966	Australia	India	4–1
1921	United States	Japan	5–0	1967	Australia	Spain	4–1
1922	United States	Australasia	4–1	1968	United States	Australia	4–1
1923	United States	Australasia	4–1	1969	United States	Romania	5–0
1924	United States	Australasia	5–0	1970	United States	West Germany	5–0
1925	United States	France	5–0	1971	United States	Romania	3–2
1926	United States	France	4–1	1972	United States	Romania	3–2
1927	France	United States	3–2	1973	Australia	United States	5–0
1928	France	United States	4–1	1974	South Africa‡	India	
1929	France	United States	3–2	1975	Sweden	Czechoslovakia	3–2
1930	France	United States	4–1	1976	Italy	Chile	4–1
1931	France	United Kingdom	3–2	1977	Australia	Italy	3–1
1932	France	United States	3–2	1978	United States	United Kingdom	4–1
1933	United Kingdom	France	3–2	1979	United States	Italy	5–0
1934	United Kingdom	United States	4–1	1980	Czechoslovakia	Italy	4–1
1935	United Kingdom	United States	5–0	1981	United States	Argentina	3–1
1936	United Kingdom	Australia	3–2	1982	United States	France	4–1
1937	United States	United Kingdom	4–1	1983	Australia	Sweden	3–2
1938	United States	Australia	3–2	1984	Sweden	United States	4–1
1939	Australia	United States	3–2	1985	Sweden	West Germany	3–2
1940–45	not held			1986	Australia	Sweden	3–2
1946	United States	Australia	5–0	1987	Sweden	India	5–0
1947	United States	Australia	4–1	1988	West Germany	Sweden	4–1
1948	United States	Australia	5–0	1989	West Germany	Sweden	3–2

Davis Cup (continued)

YEAR	WINNER	RUNNER-UP	RESULTS	YEAR	WINNER	RUNNER-UP	RESULTS
1990	United States	Australia	3–2	1997	Sweden	United States	5–0
1991	France	United States	3–1	1998	Sweden	Italy	4–1
1992	United States	Switzerland	3–1	1999	Australia	France	3–2
1993	Germany	Australia	4–1	2000	Spain	Australia	3–1
1994	Sweden	Russia	4–1	2001	France	Australia	3–2
1995	United States	Russia	3–2	2002	final round is scheduled to be played in		
1996	France	Sweden	3–2		November		

*Included Ireland up to 1922.   †Included New Zealand up to 1923.   ‡Forfeit; India withdrew from final.

Federation Cup

YEAR	WINNER	RUNNER-UP	RESULTS	YEAR	WINNER	RUNNER-UP	RESULTS
1963	United States	Australia	2–1	1984	Czechoslovakia	Australia	2–1
1964	Australia	United States	2–1	1985	Czechoslovakia	United States	2–1
1965	Australia	United States	2–1	1986	United States	Czechoslovakia	3–0
1966	United States	West Germany	3–0	1987	West Germany	United States	2–1
1967	United States	United Kingdom	2–0	1988	Czechoslovakia	USSR	2–1
1968	Australia	The Netherlands	3–0	1989	United States	Spain	3–0
1969	United States	Australia	2–1	1990	United States	USSR	2–1
1970	Australia	West Germany	3–0	1991	Spain	United States	2–1
1971	Australia	United Kingdom	3–0	1992	Germany	Spain	2–1
1972	South Africa	United Kingdom	2–1	1993	Spain	Australia	3–0
1973	Australia	South Africa	3–0	1994	Spain	United States	3–0
1974	Australia	United States	2–1	1995	Spain	United States	3–2
1975	Czechoslovakia	Australia	3–0	1996	United States	Spain	5–0
1976	United States	Australia	2–1	1997	France	The Netherlands	4–1
1977	United States	Australia	2–1	1998	Spain	Switzerland	3–2
1978	United States	Australia	2–1	1999	United States	Russia	4–1
1979	United States	Australia	3–0	2000	United States	Spain	5–0
1980	United States	Australia	3–0	2001	Belgium	Russia	2–1
1981	United States	United Kingdom	3–0	2002	Semifinals begin 28 October; dates		
1982	United States	West Germany	3–0		of finals TBA		
1983	Czechoslovakia	West Germany	2–1				

Track & Field

The world governing body for track-and-field, or athletics, is the International Association of Athletics Federations (IAAF), founded in 1912. The sport includes relay running, a number of individual running, jumping, and throwing events, and one event (the decathlon for men and the heptathlon for women) that includes all three activities. The best-known occasion for most track-and-field athletics is the Olympic Games held every four years. The World Cup (inaugurated 1977) is a finals-only competition for national, hemispheric, and continental teams. In 1983, however, the first officially recognized non-Olympic world athletics championships were held.

A long-distance event that has special status is the marathon race. The standard distance for marathons is 42,195 m (26 mi 385 yd), but they are run over routes of varying severity and under a wide array of weather conditions. One of the most renowned marathon races is held in Boston. Except for 1918, it has been held every year since 1897; women's competition officially began in 1972. The New York City Marathon began in 1970.

Related Web sites: IAAF: <www.iaaf.org>; Boston Marathon: <www.bostonmarathon.org>; New York City Marathon <www.nyrrc.org>

Outdoor Track & Field World Records

men			
EVENT	RECORD HOLDER (NATIONALITY)	PERFORMANCE	DATE
100 m	Maurice Greene (USA)	9.79 sec	16 Jun 1999
200 m	Michael Johnson (USA)	19.32 sec	1 Aug 1996
400 m	Michael Johnson (USA)	43.18 sec	26 Aug 1999
800 m	Wilson Kipketer (DEN)	1 min 41.11 sec	24 Aug 1997
1,000 m	Noah Ngeny (KEN)	2 min 11.96 sec	5 Sep 1999
1,500 m	Hicham El Guerrouj (MAR)	3 min 26.00 sec	14 Jul 1998
1 mile	Hicham El Guerrouj (MAR)	3 min 43.13 sec	7 Jul 1999
steeplechase	Brahim Boulami (MAR)	7 min 55.28 sec	24 Aug 2001
3,000 m	Daniel Komen (KEN)	7 min 20.67 sec	1 Sep 1996
5,000 m	Haile Gebrselassie (ETH)	12 min 39.36 sec	13 Jun 1998

Outdoor Track & Field World Records (continued)

men (continued)

EVENT	RECORD HOLDER (NATIONALITY)	PERFORMANCE	DATE
10,000 m	Haile Gebrselassie (ETH)	26 min 22.75 sec	1 Jun 1998
marathon*	Khalid Khannouchi (USA)	2 h 5 min 38 sec	14 Apr 2002
110-m hurdles	Colin Jackson (GBR)	12.91 sec	20 Aug 1993
400-m hurdles	Kevin Young (USA)	46.78 sec	6 Aug 1992
20-km walk	Bernardo Segura (MEX)	1 h 17 min 25.6 sec	7 May 1994
50-km walk	Thierry Toutain (FRA)	3 h 40 min 57.9 sec	29 Sep 1996
4 × 100-m relay	United States	37.40 sec	8 Aug 1992
4 × 400-m relay	United States	2 min 54.20 sec	22 Jul 1998
high jump	Javier Sotomayor (CUB)	2.45 m (8 ft ½ in)	27 Jul 1993
long jump	Mike Powell (USA)	8.95 m (29 ft 4½ in)	30 Aug 1991
triple jump	Jonathan Edwards (GBR)	18.29 m (60 ft ¼ in)	7 Aug 1995
pole vault	Sergey Bubka (UKR)	6.14 m (20 ft 1¾ in)	31 Jul 1994
shot put	Randy Barnes (USA)	23.12 m (75 ft 10¼ in)	20 May 1990
discus throw	Jürgen Schult (GDR)	74.08 m (243 ft)	6 Jun 1986
hammer throw	Yury Sedykh (URS)	86.74 m (284 ft 7 in)	30 Aug 1986
javelin throw	Jan Zelezny (CZE)	98.48 m (323 ft 1 in)	25 May 1996
decathlon	Roman Sebrle (CZE)	9,026 pt	27 May 2001

women

EVENT	RECORD HOLDER (NATIONALITY)	PERFORMANCE	DATE
100 m	Florence Griffith-Joyner (USA)	10.49 sec	16 Jul 1988
200 m	Florence Griffith-Joyner (USA)	21.34 sec	29 Sep 1988
400 m	Marita Koch (GDR)	47.60 sec	6 Oct 1985
800 m	Jarmila Kratochvilova (TCH)	1 min 53.28 sec	26 Jul 1983
1,000 m	Svetlana Masterkova (RUS)	2 min 28.98 sec	23 Aug 1996
1,500 m	Qu Yunxia (CHN)	3 min 50.46 sec	11 Sep 1993
1 mile	Svetlana Masterkova (RUS)	4 min 12.56 sec	14 Aug 1996
steeplechase	Justyna Bak (POL)	9 min 25.31 sec	9 Jul 2001
3,000 m	Wang Junxia (CHN)	8 min 6.11 sec	13 Sep 1993
5,000 m	Jiang Bo (CHN)	14 min 28.09 sec	23 Oct 1997
10,000 m	Wang Junxia (CHN)	29 min 31.78 sec	8 Sep 1993
marathon*	Catherine Ndereba (KEN)	2 h 18 min 47 sec	7 Oct 2001
100-m hurdles	Yordanka Donkova (BUL)	12.21 sec	20 Aug 1988
400-m hurdles	Kim Batten (USA)	52.61 sec	11 Aug 1995
20-km walk	Olimpiada Ivanova (RUS)	1 h 26 min 52.3 sec	6 Sep 2001
4 × 100-m relay	East Germany	41.37 sec	6 Oct 1985
4 × 400-m relay	USSR	3 min 15.17 sec	1 Oct 1988
high jump	Stefka Kostadinova (BUL)	2.09 m (6 ft 10¼ in)	30 Aug 1987
long jump	Galina Chistyakova (URS)	7.52 m (24 ft 8¼ in)	11 Jun 1988
triple jump	Inessa Kravets (UKR)	15.50 m (50 ft 10¼ in)	10 Aug 1995
pole vault	Stacy Dragila (USA)	4.81 m (15 ft 9¼ in)	9 Jun 2001
shot put	Natalya Lisovskaya (URS)	22.63 m (74 ft 3 in)	7 Jun 1987
discus throw	Gabriele Reinsch (GDR)	76.80 m (252 ft)	9 Jul 1988
hammer throw	Mihaela Melinte (ROM)	76.07 m (249 ft 7 in)	29 Aug 1999
javelin throw	Osleidys Menéndez (CUB)	71.54 m (234 ft 8 in)	1 Jul 2001
heptathlon	Jackie Joyner-Kersee (USA)	7,291 pt	24 Sep 1988

*Not an officially ratified event; best performance on record.

Indoor Track & Field World Records

men

EVENT	RECORD HOLDER (NATIONALITY)	PERFORMANCE	DATE
50 m	Donovan Bailey (CAN)	5.56 sec	9 Feb 1996
60 m	Maurice Greene (USA)	6.39 sec	3 Feb 1998
200 m	Frank Fredericks (NAM)	19.92 sec	18 Feb 1996
400 m	Michael Johnson (USA)	44.63 sec	4 Mar 1995
800 m	Wilson Kipketer (DEN)	1 min 42.67 sec	9 Mar 1997
1,000 m	Wilson Kipketer (DEN)	2 min 14.96 sec	20 Feb 2000
1,500 m	Hicham El Guerrouj (MAR)	3 min 31.18 sec	2 Feb 1997
1 mile	Hicham El Guerrouj (MAR)	3 min 48.45 sec	12 Feb 1997
3,000 m	Daniel Komen (KEN)	7 min 24.90 sec	6 Feb 1998
5,000 m	Haile Gebrselassie (ETH)	12 min 50.38 sec	14 Feb 1999
50-m hurdles	Mark McKoy (CAN)	6.25 sec	5 Mar 1986
60-m hurdles	Colin Jackson (GBR)	7.30 sec	6 Mar 1994
5-km walk	Mikhail Shchennikov (RUS)	18 min 7.08 sec	14 Feb 1995

Indoor Track & Field World Records (continued)

men (continued)

EVENT	RECORD HOLDER (NATIONALITY)	PERFORMANCE	DATE
4 × 200-m relay	Great Britain	1 min 22.11 sec	3 Mar 1991
4 × 400-m relay	United States	3 min 2.83 sec	7 Mar 1999
4 × 800-m relay	United States	7 min 13.94 sec	6 Feb 2000
high jump	Javier Sotomayor (CUB)	2.43 m (7 ft 11½ in)	4 Mar 1989
long jump	Carl Lewis (USA)	8.79 m (28 ft 10¼ in)	27 Jan 1984
triple jump	Aliecer Urrutia (CUB)	17.83 m (58 ft 6 in)	1 Mar 1997
pole vault	Sergey Bubka (UKR)	6.15 m (20 ft 2 in)	21 Feb 1993
shot put	Randy Barnes (USA)	22.66 m (74 ft 4¼ in)	20 Jan 1989
heptathlon	Dan O'Brien (USA)	6,476 pt	14 Mar 1993

women

EVENT	RECORD HOLDER (NATIONALITY)	PERFORMANCE	DATE
50 m	Irina Privalova (RUS)	5.96 sec	9 Feb 1995
60 m	Irina Privalova (RUS)	6.92 sec	11 Feb 1993
200 m	Merlene Ottey (JAM)	21.87 sec	13 Feb 1993
400 m	Jarmila Kratochvilova (TCH)	49.59 sec	7 Mar 1982
800 m	Jolanda Ceplak (SLO)	1 min 55.82 sec	3 Mar 2002
1,000 m	Maria Mutola (MOZ)	2 min 30.94 sec	25 Feb 1999
1,500 m	Doina Melinte (ROM)	4 min 0.27 sec	9 Feb 1990
1 mile	Doina Melinte (ROM)	4 min 17.14 sec	9 Feb 1990
3,000 m	Berhane Adero (ETH)	8 min 29.15 sec	3 Feb 2002
5,000 m	Gabriela Szabo (ROM)	14 min 47.35 sec	13 Feb 1999
50-m hurdles	Cornelia Oschkenat (GDR)	6.58 sec	20 Feb 1988
60-m hurdles	Lyudmila Engquist (URS)	7.69 sec	4 Feb 1990
3-km walk	Claudia Iovan (ROM)	11 min 40.33 sec	30 Jan 1999
4 × 200-m relay	West Germany	1 min 32.55 sec	20 Feb 1988
4 × 400-m relay	Russia	3 min 24.25 sec	7 Mar 1999
4 × 800-m relay	Russia	8 min 18.71 sec	4 Feb 1994
high jump	Heike Henkel (GER)	2.07 m (6 ft 9½ in)	8 Feb 1992
long jump	Heike Drechsler (GDR)	7.37 m (24 ft 2¼ in)	13 Feb 1988
triple jump	Ashia Hansen (GBR)	15.16 m (49 ft 9 in)	28 Feb 1998
pole vault	Svetlana Feofanova (RUS)	4.75 m (15 ft 7 in)	3 Mar 2002
shot put	Helena Fibingerova (TCH)	22.50 m (73 ft 10 in)	19 Feb 1977
pentathlon	Irina Belova (EUN)	4,991 pt	15 Feb 1992

World Track & Field Championships—Men

The next championships are scheduled to be held 22–31 Aug 2003, Paris.

100 M
1983 Carl Lewis (USA)
1987 Carl Lewis (USA)
1991 Carl Lewis (USA)
1993 Linford Christie (GBR)
1995 Donovan Bailey (CAN)
1997 Maurice Greene (USA)
1999 Maurice Greene (USA)
2001 Maurice Greene (USA)

200 M
1983 Calvin Smith (USA)
1987 Calvin Smith (USA)
1991 Michael Johnson (USA)
1993 Frank Fredericks (NAM)
1995 Michael Johnson (USA)
1997 Ato Boldon (TRI)
1999 Maurice Greene (USA)
2001 Konstadinos Kederis (GRE)

400 M
1983 Bert Cameron (JAM)
1987 Thomas Schoenlebe (GDR)
1991 Antonio Pettigrew (USA)
1993 Michael Johnson (USA)
1995 Michael Johnson (USA)

400 M (CONTINUED)
1997 Michael Johnson (USA)
1999 Michael Johnson (USA)
2001 Avard Moncur (BAH)

800 M
1983 Willi Wülbeck (FRG)
1987 Billy Konchellah (KEN)
1991 Billy Konchellah (KEN)
1993 Paul Ruto (KEN)
1995 Wilson Kipketer (DEN)
1997 Wilson Kipketer (DEN)
1999 Wilson Kipketer (DEN)
2001 André Bucher (SUI)

1,500 M
1983 Steve Cram (GBR)
1987 Abdi Bile (SOM)
1991 Noureddine Morceli (ALG)
1993 Noureddine Morceli (ALG)
1995 Noureddine Morceli (ALG)
1997 Hicham El Guerrouj (MAR)
1999 Hicham El Guerrouj (MAR)
2001 Hicham El Guerrouj (MAR)

5,000 M
1983 Eamonn Coghlan (IRL)
1987 Said Aouita (MAR)

5,000 M (CONTINUED)
1991 Yobes Ondieki (KEN)
1993 Ismael Kirui (KEN)
1995 Ismael Kirui (KEN)
1997 Daniel Komen (KEN)
1999 Salah Hissou (MAR)
2001 Richard Limo (KEN)

10,000 M
1983 Alberto Cova (ITA)
1987 Paul Kipkoech (KEN)
1991 Moses Tanui (KEN)
1993 Haile Gebrselassie (ETH)
1995 Haile Gebrselassie (ETH)
1997 Haile Gebrselassie (ETH)
1000 Haile Gebrselassie (ETH)
2001 Charles Kamathi (KEN)

STEEPLECHASE
1983 Patriz Ilg (FRG)
1987 Francesco Panetta (ITA)
1991 Moses Kiptanui (KEN)
1993 Moses Kiptanui (KEN)
1995 Moses Kiptanui (KEN)
1997 Wilson Boit Kipketer (KEN)
1999 Christopher Koskei (KEN)
2001 Reuben Kosgei (KEN)

World Track & Field Championships—Men (continued)

110-M HURDLES
1983 Greg Foster (USA)
1987 Greg Foster (USA)
1991 Greg Foster (USA)
1993 Colin Jackson (GBR)
1995 Allen Johnson (USA)
1997 Allen Johnson (USA)
1999 Colin Jackson (GBR)
2001 Allen Johnson (USA)

400-M HURDLES
1983 Edwin Moses (USA)
1987 Edwin Moses (USA)
1991 Samuel Matete (ZAM)
1993 Kevin Young (USA)
1995 Derrick Adkins (USA)
1997 Stéphane Diagana (FRA)
1999 Fabrizio Mori (ITA)
2001 Felix Sánchez (DOM)

MARATHON
1983 Robert de Castella (AUS)
1987 Douglas Wakiihuri (KEN)
1991 Hiromi Taniguchi (JPN)
1993 Mark Plaatjes (USA)
1995 Martín Fiz (ESP)
1997 Abel Antón (ESP)
1999 Abel Antón (ESP)
2001 Gezahegne Abera (ETH)

20-KM WALK
1983 Ernesto Canto (MEX)
1987 Maurizio Damilano (ITA)
1991 Maurizio Damilano (ITA)
1993 Valentí Massana (ESP)
1995 Michele Didoni (ITA)
1997 Daniel García (MEX)
1999 Ilya Markov (RUS)
2001 Roman Rasskazov (RUS)

50-KM WALK
1983 Ronald Weigel (GDR)
1987 Hartwig Gauder (GDR)
1991 Aleksandr Potashov (URS)
1993 Jesús Angel García (ESP)
1995 Valentin Kononen (FIN)
1997 Robert Korzeniowski (POL)
1999 Ivano Brugnetti (ITA)
2001 Robert Korzeniowski (POL)

4 X 100-M RELAY
1983 United States
1987 United States
1991 United States

4 X 100-M RELAY (CONTINUED)
1993 United States
1995 Canada
1997 Canada
1999 United States
2001 United States

4 X 400-M RELAY
1983 USSR
1987 United States
1991 United Kingdom
1993 United States
1995 United States
1997 United States
1999 United States
2001 United States

HIGH JUMP
1983 Gennady Avdeyenko (URS)
1987 Patrik Sjöberg (SWE)
1991 Charles Austin (USA)
1993 Javier Sotomayor (CUB)
1995 Troy Kemp (BAH)
1997 Javier Sotomayor (CUB)
1999 Vyacheslav Voronin (RUS)
2001 Martin Buss (GER)

POLE VAULT
1983 Sergey Bubka (URS)
1987 Sergey Bubka (URS)
1991 Sergey Bubka (URS)
1993 Sergey Bubka (UKR)
1995 Sergey Bubka (UKR)
1997 Sergey Bubka (UKR)
1999 Maksim Tarasov (RUS)
2001 Dmitri Markov (AUS)

LONG JUMP
1983 Carl Lewis (USA)
1987 Carl Lewis (USA)
1991 Mike Powell (USA)
1993 Mike Powell (USA)
1995 Iván Pedroso (CUB)
1997 Iván Pedroso (CUB)
1999 Iván Pedroso (CUB)
2001 Iván Pedroso (CUB)

TRIPLE JUMP
1983 Zdzislaw Hoffman (POL)
1987 Khristo Markov (BUL)
1991 Kenny Harrison (USA)
1993 Mike Conley (USA)
1995 Jonathan Edwards (GBR)
1997 Yoelbi Quesada (CUB)

TRIPLE JUMP (CONTINUED)
1999 Charles Michael Friedek (GER)
2001 Jonathan Edwards (GBR)

SHOT PUT
1983 Edward Sarul (POL)
1987 Werner Günthör (SUI)
1991 Werner Günthör (SUI)
1993 Werner Günthör (SUI)
1995 John Godina (USA)
1997 John Godina (USA)
1999 C.J. Hunter (USA)
2001 John Godina (USA)

DISCUS THROW
1983 Imrich Bugar (TCH)
1987 Jürgen Schult (GDR)
1991 Lars Riedel (GER)
1993 Lars Riedel (GER)
1995 Lars Riedel (GER)
1997 Lars Riedel (GER)
1999 Anthony Washington (USA)
2001 Lars Riedel (GER)

HAMMER THROW
1983 Sergey Litvinov (URS)
1987 Sergey Litvinov (URS)
1991 Yury Sedykh (URS)
1993 Andrey Abduvaliyev (TJK)
1995 Andrey Abduvaliyev (TJK)
1997 Heinz Weis (GER)
1999 Karsten Kobs (GER)
2001 Szymon Ziolkowski (POL)

JAVELIN THROW
1983 Detlef Michel (GDR)
1987 Seppo Räty (FIN)
1991 Kimmo Kinnunen (FIN)
1993 Jan Zelezny (CZE)
1995 Jan Zelezny (CZE)
1997 Marius Corbett (RSA)
1999 Aki Parviainen (FIN)
2001 Jan Zelezny (CZE)

DECATHLON
1983 Daley Thompson (GBR)
1987 Torsten Voss (GDR)
1991 Dan O'Brien (USA)
1993 Dan O'Brien (USA)
1995 Dan O'Brien (USA)
1997 Tomas Dvorak (CZE)
1999 Tomas Dvorak (CZE)
2001 Tomas Dvorak (CZE)

World Track & Field Championships—Women
The next championships are scheduled for 22–31 Aug 2003, Paris.

100 M
1983 Marlies Göhr (GDR)
1987 Silke Gladisch (GDR)
1991 Katrin Krabbe (GER)
1993 Gail Devers (USA)
1995 Gwen Torrence (USA)
1997 Marion Jones (USA)
1999 Marion Jones (USA)
2001 Zhanna Pintusevich (UKR)

200 M
1983 Marita Koch (GDR)
1987 Silke Gladisch (GDR)
1991 Katrin Krabbe (GER)
1993 Merlene Ottey (JAM)
1995 Merlene Ottey (JAM)
1997 Zhanna Pintusevich (UKR)
1999 Inger Miller (USA)
2001 Marion Jones (USA)

400 M
1983 Jarmila Kratochvilova (TCH)
1987 Olga Bryzgina (URS)
1991 Marie-José Pérec (FRA)
1993 Jearl Miles (USA)
1995 Marie-José Pérec (FRA)
1997 Cathy Freeman (AUS)
1999 Cathy Freeman (AUS)
2001 Amy Mbacke Thiam (SEN)

World Track & Field Championships—Women (continued)

800 M
1983 Jarmila Kratochvilova
(TCH)
1987 Sigrun Wodars (GDR)
1991 Liliya Nurutdinova (URS)
1993 Maria Mutola (MOZ)
1995 Ana Quirot (CUB)
1997 Ana Quirot (CUB)
1999 Ludmila Formanova (CZE)
2001 Maria Mutola (MOZ)

1,500 M
1983 Mary Decker (USA)
1987 Tatyana Samolenko (URS)
1991 Hassiba Boulmerka (ALG)
1993 Liu Dong (CHN)
1995 Hassiba Boulmerka (ALG)
1997 Carla Sacramento (POR)
1999 Svetlana Masterkova
(RUS)
2001 Gabriela Szabo (ROM)

3,000 M§
1983 Mary Decker (USA)
1987 Tatyana Samolenko (URS)
1991 Tatyana Dorovskikh (URS)
1993 Qu Yunxia (CHN)
1995 Sonia O'Sullivan (IRL)
1997 Gabriela Szabo (ROM)
1999 Gabriela Szabo (ROM)
2001 Olga Yegorova (RUS)

10,000 M*
1987 Ingrid Kristiansen (NOR)
1991 Liz McColgan (GBR)
1993 Wang Junxia (CHN)
1995 Fernanda Ribeiro (POR)
1997 Sally Barsosio (KEN)
1999 Gete Wami (ETH)
2001 Derartu Tulu (ETH)

100-M HURDLES
1983 Bettine Jahn (GDR)
1987 Ginka Zagorcheva (BUL)
1991 Ludmila Narozhilenko
(URS)
1993 Gail Devers (USA)
1995 Gail Devers (USA)
1997 Ludmila Engquist (SWE)
1999 Gail Devers (USA)
2001 Anjanette Kirkland (USA)

400-M HURDLES
1983 Yekaterina Fesenko (URS)
1987 Sabine Busch (GDR)
1991 Tatyana Ledovskaya (URS)
1993 Sally Gunnell (GBR)
1995 Kim Batten (USA)
1997 Nezha Bidouane (MAR)
1999 Daimi Pernía (CUB)
2001 Nezha Bidouane (MAR)

MARATHON
1983 Grete Waitz (NOR)
1987 Rosa Mota (POR)
1991 Wanda Panfil (POL)
1993 Asari Junko (JPN)
1995 Maria Machado (POR)
1997 Hiromi Suzuki (JPN)
1999 Jong Song Ok (PRK)
2001 Lidia Simon (ROM)

10-KM WALK*
1987 Irina Strakhova (URS)
1991 Alina Ivanova (URS)
1993 Sari Essayeh (FIN)
1995 Irina Stankina (RUS)
1997 Annarita Sidoti (ITA)

20-KM WALK‡
1999 Liu Hongyu (CHN)
2001 Olimpiada Ivanova (RUS)

4 X 100-M RELAY
1983 East Germany
1987 United States
1991 Jamaica
1993 Russia
1995 United States
1997 United States
1999 Bahamas
2001 United States

4 X 400-M RELAY
1983 East Germany
1987 East Germany
1991 USSR
1993 United States
1995 United States
1997 Germany
1999 Russia
2001 Jamaica

HIGH JUMP
1983 Tamara Bykova (URS)
1987 Stefka Kostadinova (BUL)
1991 Heike Henkel (GER)
1993 Ioamnet Quintero (CUB)
1995 Stefka Kostadinova (BUL)
1997 Hanne Haugland (NOR)
1999 Inga Babakova (UKR)
2001 Hestrie Cloete (RSA)

POLE VAULT‡
1999 Stacy Dragila (USA)
2001 Stacy Dragila (USA)

LONG JUMP
1983 Heike Daute (GDR)
1987 Jackie Joyner-Kersee
(USA)
1991 Jackie Joyner-Kersee
(USA)

LONG JUMP (CONTINUED)
1993 Heike Drechsler (GER)
1995 Fiona May (ITA)
1997 Ludmila Galkina (RUS)
1999 Niurka Montalvo (ESP)
2001 Fiona May (ITA)

TRIPLE JUMP†
1993 Anna Biryukova (RUS)
1995 Inessa Kravets (UKR)
1997 Sarka Kasparkova (CZE)
1999 Paraskevi Tsiamita (GRE)
2001 Tatyana Lebedeva (RUS)

SHOT PUT
1983 Helena Fibingerova (TCH)
1987 Natalya Lisovskaya (URS)
1991 Huang Zhihong (CHN)
1993 Huang Zhihong (CHN)
1995 Astrid Kumbernuss (GER)
1997 Astrid Kumbernuss (GER)
1999 Astrid Kumbernuss (GER)
2001 Yanina Korolchik (BLR)

DISCUS THROW
1983 Martina Opitz (GDR)
1987 Martina Hellmann (GDR)
1991 Tsvetanka Khristova (BUL)
1993 Olga Burova (RUS)
1995 Ellina Zvereva (BLR)
1997 Beatrice Faumuina (NZL)
1999 Franka Dietzsch (GER)
2001 Natalya Sadova (RUS)

HAMMER THROW‡
1999 Mihaela Melinte (ROM)
2001 Yipsi Moreno (CUB)

JAVELIN THROW
1983 Tiina Lillak (FIN)
1987 Fatima Whitbread (GBR)
1991 Xu Demei (CHN)
1993 Trine Hattestad (NOR)
1995 Natalya Shikolenko (BLR)
1997 Trine Hattestad (NOR)
1999 Mirela Tzelili (GRE)
2001 Osleidys Menéndez (CUB)

HEPTATHLON
1983 Ramona Neubert (GDR)
1987 Jackie Joyner-Kersee
(USA)
1991 Sabine Braun (GER)
1993 Jackie Joyner-Kersee
(USA)
1995 Ghada Shouaa (SYR)
1997 Sabine Braun (GER)
1999 Eunice Barber (FRA)
2001 Yelena Prokhorova (RUS)

*Event added in 1987. |Event added in 1993.   ‡Event added in 1999.   §Became 5,000 m in 1995.

IAAF World Cup—Men

Next competition is scheduled to be held 20–21 Sep 2002, Madrid.

100 m

YEAR	WINNER
1977	Steve Williams (USA)
1979	James Sanford (USA)
1981	Allan Wells (EUR)
1985	Ben Johnson (AME)
1989	Linford Christie (GBR)
1992	Linford Christie (GBR)
1994	Linford Christie (GBR)
1998	Obadele Thompson (AME)

200 m

1977	Clancy Edwards (USA)
1979	Silvio Leonard (AME)
1981	Melvin Lattany (USA)
1985	Robson Caetano da Silva (AME)
1989	Robson Caetano da Silva (AME)
1992	Robson Caetano da Silva (AME)
1994	John Regis (GBR)
1998	Frank Fredericks (AFR)

400 m

1977	Alberto Juantorena (AME)
1979	Kashief Hassan (AFR)
1981	Cliff Wiley (USA)
1985	Mike Franks (USA)
1989	Roberto Hernández (AME)
1992	Sunday Bada (AFR)
1994	Antonio Pettigrew (USA)
1998	Iwan Thomas (GBR)

800 m

1977	Alberto Juantorena (AME)
1979	James Maina (AFR)
1981	Sebastian Coe (EUR)
1985	Sammy Koskei (AFR)
1989	Tom McKean (GBR)
1992	David Sharpe (GBR)
1994	Mark Everett (USA)
1998	Nils Schumann (GER)

1,500 m

1977	Steve Ovett (EUR)
1979	Thomas Wessinghage (EUR)
1981	Steve Ovett (EUR)
1985	Omer Khalifa (AFR)
1989	Abdi Bile (AFR)
1992	Mohammed Suleiman (ASI)
1994	Noureddine Morceli (AFR)
1998	Laban Rotich (AFR)

3,000 m

1998	Dieter Baumann (GER)

5,000 m

1977	Miruts Yifter (AFR)
1979	Miruts Yifter (AFR)
1981	Eamonn Coghlan (EUR)
1985	Doug Padilla (USA)
1989	Said Aouita (AFR)
1992	Fita Bayesa (AFR)
1994	Brahim Lahlafi (AFR)
1998	Daniel Komen (AFR)

10,000 m

YEAR	WINNER
1977	Miruts Yifter (AFR)
1979	Miruts Yifter (AFR)
1981	Werner Schildhauer (GDR)
1985	Wodajo Bulti (AFR)
1989	Salvatore Antibo (EUR)
1992	Addis Abebe (AFR)
1994	Khalid Skah (AFR)

Steeplechase

1977	Michael Karst (FRG)
1979	Henry Rono (AFR)
1981	Boguslaw Maminski (EUR)
1985	Julius Kariuki (AFR)
1989	Julius Kariuki (AFR)
1992	Philip Barkutwo (AFR)
1994	Moses Kiptanui (AFR)
1998	Damian Kallabis (GER)

110-m hurdles

1977	Thomas Munkelt (GDR)
1979	Reynaldo Nehemiah (USA)
1981	Greg Foster (USA)
1985	Tony Campbell (USA)
1989	Roger Kingdom (USA)
1992	Colin Jackson (GBR)
1994	Tony Jarrett (GBR)
1998	Falk Balzer (GER)

400-m hurdles

1977	Edwin Moses (USA)
1979	Edwin Moses (USA)
1981	Edwin Moses (USA)
1985	Andre Phillips (USA)
1989	David Patrick (USA)
1992	Samuel Matete (AFR)
1994	Samuel Matete (AFR)
1998	Samuel Matete (AFR)

4 x 100-m relays

1977	United States
1979	Americas
1981	Europe
1985	United States
1989	United States
1992	United States
1994	Great Britain
1998	Great Britain

4 x 400-m relays

1977	West Germany
1979	United States
1981	United States
1985	United States
1989	Americas
1992	Africa
1994	Great Britain
1998	United States

Triple jump

1977	João de Oliveira (AME)
1979	João de Oliveira (AME)
1981	João de Oliveira (AME)
1985	Willie Banks (USA)
1989	Mike Conley (USA)
1992	Jonathan Edwards (GBR)

Triple jump (continued)

YEAR	WINNER
1994	Yoelbi Quesada (AME)
1998	Charles Friedek (GER)

High jump

1977	Rolf Beilschmidt (GDR)
1979	Franklin Jacobs (USA)
1981	Tyke Peacock (USA)
1985	Patrik Sjöberg (EUR)
1989	Patrik Sjöberg (EUR)
1992	Yury Sergeyenko (UNT*)
1994	Javier Sotomayor (AME)
1998	Charles Austin (USA)

Pole vault

1977	Mike Tully (USA)
1979	Mike Tully (USA)
1981	Konstantin Volkov (URS)
1985	Sergey Bubka (URS)
1989	Philippe Collet (EUR)
1992	Igor Potapovich (UNT*)
1994	Okkert Brits (AFR)
1998	Maksim Tarasov (EUR)

Long jump

1977	Arnie Robinson (USA)
1979	Larry Myricks (USA)
1981	Carl Lewis (USA)
1985	Mike Conley (USA)
1989	Larry Myricks (USA)
1992	Iván Pedroso (AME)
1994	Fred Salle (GBR)
1998	Iván Pedroso (AME)

Shot put

1977	Udo Beyer (GDR)
1979	Udo Beyer (GDR)
1981	Udo Beyer (GDR)
1985	Ulf Timmermann (GDR)
1989	Ulf Timmermann (GDR)
1992	Mike Stulce (USA)
1994	C.J. Hunter (USA)
1998	John Godina (USA)

Discus throw

1977	Wolfgang Schmidt (GDR)
1979	Wolfgang Schmidt (GDR)
1981	Armin Lemme (GDR)
1985	Gennady Kolnootchenko (URS)
1989	Jürgen Schult (GDR)
1992	Anthony Washington (USA)
1994	Vladimir Dubrovshchik (EUR)
1998	Virgilijus Alekna (EUR)

Hammer throw

1977	Karl-Hans Riehm (FRG)
1979	Sergey Litvinov (URS)
1981	Yury Sedykh (URS)
1985	Yury Tamm (URS)
1989	Heinz Weis (EUR)
1992	Tibor Gecsek (EUR)
1994	Andrey Abduvaliyev (ASI)
1998	Tibor Gecsek (EUR)

IAAF World Cup—Men (continued)

YEAR	WINNER	YEAR	WINNER	YEAR	WINNER
Javelin throw		**Javelin throw (continued)**		**Team (continued)**	
1977	Michael Wessing (FRG)	1994	Steve Backley (GBR)	1981	Europe
1979	Wolfgang Hanisch (FRG)	1998	Steve Backley (GBR)	1985	United States
1981	Dainis Kula (URS)			1989	United States
1985	Uwe Hohn (GDR)	**Team**		1992	Africa
1989	Steve Backley (GBR)	1977	East Germany	1994	Africa
1992	Jan Zelezny (EUR)	1979	United States	1998	Africa

*Unified Team, consisting of athletes from the Commonwealth of Independent States plus Georgia.

IAAF World Cup—Women

Next competition is scheduled to be held 20–21 Sep 2002, Madrid.

YEAR	WINNER	YEAR	WINNER	YEAR	WINNER
100 m		**3,000 m**		**4 x 400-m relays (continued)**	
1977	Marlies Oelsner (GDR)	1977	Grete Waitz (EUR)	1979	East Germany
1979	Evelyn Ashford (USA)	1979	Svetlana Ulmasova (URS)	1981	East Germany
1981	Evelyn Ashford (USA)	1981	Angelika Zauber (GDR)	1985	East Germany
1985	Marlies Göhr (GDR)	1985	Ulrike Bruns (GDR)	1989	Americas
1989	Sheila Echols (USA)	1989	Yvonne Murray (EUR)	1992	Americas
1992	Natalya Voronova (UNT*)	1992	Derartu Tulu (AFR)	1994	Great Britain
1994	Irina Privalova (EUR)	1994	Yvonne Murray (GBR)	1998	Germany
1998	Marion Jones (USA)	1998	Gabriela Szabo (EUR)		
				Triple jump	
200 m		**5,000 m**		1994	Anna Biryukova (EUR)
1977	Irina Szewinska (EUR)	1998	Sonia O'Sullivan (EUR)	1998	Olga Vasdeki (EUR)
1979	Evelyn Ashford (USA)				
1981	Evelyn Ashford (USA)	**10,000 m**		**High jump**	
1985	Marita Koch (GDR)	1985	Aurora Cunha (EUR)	1977	Rosemarie Ackermann
1989	Silke Möller (GDR)	1989	Kathrin Ullrich (GDR)		(GDR)
1992	Marie-José Pérec (EUR)	1992	Derartu Tulu (AFR)	1979	Debbie Brill (AME)
1994	Merlene Ottey (AME)	1994	Elana Meyer (AFR)	1981	Ulrike Meyfarth (EUR)
1998	Marion Jones (USA)			1985	Stefka Kostadinova (URS)
		100-m hurdles		1989	Silvia Costa (AME)
400 m		1977	Grazyna Rabsztyn (EUR)	1992	Ioamnet Quintero (AME)
1977	Irina Szewinska (EUR)	1979	Grazyna Rabsztyn (EUR)	1994	Britta Bilac (EUR)
1979	Marita Koch (GDR)	1981	Tatyana Anisimova (URS)	1998	Monica Iagar-Dinescu
1981	Jarmila Kratochvilova	1985	Cornelia Oschkenat (GDR)		(EUR)
	(EUR)	1989	Cornelia Oschkenat (GDR)		
1985	Marita Koch (GDR)	1992	Aliuska López (AME)	**Long jump**	
1989	Ana Quirot (AME)	1994	Aliuska López (AME)	1977	Lyn Jacenko (OCE)
1992	Jearl Miles (USA)	1998	Glory Alozie (AFR)	1979	Anita Stukane (URS)
1994	Irina Privalova (EUR)			1981	Sigrid Ulbricht (GDR)
1998	Falilat Ogunkoya (AFR)	**400-m hurdles**		1985	Heike Daute Drechsler
		1977	not held		(GDR)
800 m		1979	Bärbel Klepp (GDR)	1989	Galina Chistyakova (URS)
1977	Totka Petrova (EUR)	1981	Ellen Neumann (GDR)	1992	Heike Drechsler (GER)
1979	Nikolina Shtereva (EUR)	1985	Sabine Busch (GDR)	1994	Inessa Kravets (EUR)
1981	Lyudmila Veselkova (URS)	1989	Sandra Farmer-Patrick	1998	Heike Drechsler (GER)
1985	Christine Wachtel (GDR)		(USA)		
1989	Ana Quirot (AME)	1992	Sandra Farmer-Patrick	**Shot put**	
1992	Maria Mutola (AFR)		(USA)	1977	Helena Fibingerova (EUR)
1994	Maria Mutola (AFR)	1994	Sally Gunnell (GBR)	1979	Ilona Slupianek (GDR)
1998	Maria Mutola (AFR)	1998	Nezha Bidouane (AFR)	1981	Ilona Slupianek (GDR)
				1985	Natalya Lisovskaya (URS)
1,500 m		**4 x 100-m relays**		1989	Zhihong Huang (ASI)
1977	Tatyana Kazankina (URS)	1977	Europe Select	1992	Belsis Laza (AME)
1979	Christiane Wartenburg	1979	Europe Select	1994	Zhihong Huang (ASI)
	(GDR)	1981	East Germany	1998	Vita Pavlysh (EUR)
1981	Tamara Sorokina (URS)	1985	East Germany		
1985	Hildegard Körner (GDR)	1989	East Germany	**Discus throw**	
1989	Paula Ivan (EUR)	1992	Asia	1977	Faina Melnik (URS)
1992	Yekaterina Podkopayeva	1994	Africa	1979	Evelin Jahl (GDR)
	(UNT*)	1998	United States	1981	Evelin Jahl (GDR)
1994	Hassiba Boulmerka (AFR)			1985	Martina Optiz (GDR)
1998	Svetlana Masterkova	**4 x 400-m relays**		1989	Ilke Wyludda (GDR)
	(RUS)	1977	East Germany	1992	Maritza Marten (AME)

IAAF World Cup—Women (continued)

YEAR	WINNER
Discus throw (continued)	
1994	Ilke Wyludda (EUR)
1998	Franka Dietzsch (GER)
Javelin throw	
1977	Ruth Fuchs (GDR)
1979	Ruth Fuchs (GDR)
1981	Antoaneta Todorova (EUR)
1985	Olga Gavrilova (URS)

YEAR	WINNER
Javelin throw (continued)	
1989	Petra Felke (GDR)
1992	Tessa Sanderson (GBR)
1994	Trine Hattestad (EUR)
1998	Joanna Stone (OCE)
Team	
1977	Europe Select
1979	East Germany

YEAR	WINNER
Team (continued)	
1981	East Germany
1985	East Germany
1989	East Germany
1992	Unified Team*
1994	Europe
1998	United States

*Unified Team, consisting of athletes from the Commonwealth of Independent States plus Georgia.

World Cross Country Championships

Men's competition held since 1903, women's since 1967. Table shows results from the past 20 years.

men (12,000 meters)

YEAR	INDIVIDUAL (NATIONALITY)	TEAM
1983	Bekele Debele (ETH)	Ethiopia
1984	Carlos Lopes (POR)	Ethiopia
1985	Carlos Lopes (POR)	Ethiopia
1986	John Ngugi (KEN)	Kenya
1987	John Ngugi (KEN)	Kenya
1988	John Ngugi (KEN)	Kenya
1989	John Ngugi (KEN)	Kenya
1990	Khalid Skah (MAR)	Kenya
1991	Khalid Skah (MAR)	Kenya
1992	John Ngugi (KEN)	Kenya
1993	William Sigei (KEN)	Kenya
1994	William Sigei (KEN)	Kenya
1995	Paul Tergat (KEN)	Kenya
1996	Paul Tergat (KEN)	Kenya
1997	Paul Tergat (KEN)	Kenya
1998	Paul Tergat (KEN)	Kenya
1999	Paul Tergat (KEN)	Kenya
2000	Mohammed Mourhit (BEL)	Kenya
2001	Mohammed Mourhit (BEL)	Kenya
2002	Kenenisa Bekele (ETH)	Kenya

women (8,000 meters)

YEAR	INDIVIDUAL (NATIONALITY)	TEAM
1983	Grete Waitz (NOR)	United States
1984	Maricica Puica (ROM)	United States
1985	Zola Budd (GBR)	United States
1986	Zola Budd (GBR)	England
1987	Annette Sargent (FRA)	United States
1988	Ingrid Kristiansen (NOR)	USSR
1989	Annette Sargent (FRA)	USSR
1990	Lynn Jennings (USA)	USSR
1991	Lynn Jennings (USA)	Kenya
1992	Lynn Jennings (USA)	Kenya
1993	Albertina Dias (POR)	Kenya
1994	Hellen Chepngeno (KEN)	Portugal
1995	Derartu Tulu (ETH)	Kenya
1996	Gete Wami (ETH)	Kenya
1997	Derartu Tulu (ETH)	Ethiopia
1998	Sonia O'Sullivan (IRE)	Kenya
1999	Gete Wami (ETH)	Ethiopia
2000	Derartu Tulu (ETH)	Ethiopia
2001	Paula Radcliffe (GBR)	Kenya
2002	Paula Radcliffe (GBR)	Ethiopia

Volleyball

World volleyball championships for men were inaugurated in 1949. **Women's** competition began in 1952. These biennial championships are organized by the **Fédération Internationale de Volleyball** (FIVB; founded 1947). Indoor volleyball has been included in the Olympic Games from 1964, and beach volleyball from 1996.

FIVB Web site: <www.fivb.ch>

World Volleyball Championships

YEAR	MEN	WOMEN
1949	USSR	
1952	USSR	USSR
1956	Czechoslovakia	USSR
1960	USSR	USSR
1962	USSR	Japan
1964*	USSR	Japan
1966	Czechoslovakia	Japan
1967	*not held*	Japan
1968*	USSR	USSR
1970	East Germany	USSR
1972*	Japan	USSR
1974	Poland	Japan
1976*	Poland	Japan
1978	USSR	Cuba

YEAR	MEN	WOMEN
1980*	USSR	USSR
1982	USSR	China
1984*	United States	China
1986	United States	China
1988*	United States	USSR
1990	Italy	USSR
1992*	Brazil	Cuba
1994	Italy	Cuba
1996*	The Netherlands	Cuba
1998	Italy	Cuba
2000*	Yugoslavia	Cuba
2002	*scheduled for 13 October, Buenos Aires*	*scheduled for 15 September, Berlin*

*Olympic champions, considered world champions.

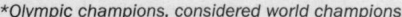

Weight Lifting

World weight lifting is overseen by the International Weightlifting Federation (IWF; founded 1905). The first men's international weight lifting competition was held in London in 1891; the sport was also included in the first modern Olympic Games in 1896. By the 1930s championship events consisted of the snatch, clean and jerk, and press, which was eliminated in 1972. Women's world championships have been held since 1987, and women's competition was added to the Olympics in 2000. In 1998 the IWF established new weight classes (eight for men and seven for women) as well as a new world standard for each class in determining world records.

IWF Web site: <www.iwf.net>

Weight Lifting World Records

Total weight for snatch and clean & jerk. World standards were reset on 1 Jan 1998 and have not been achieved in some men's events.

men

WEIGHT CLASS	WINNER (NATIONALITY)	PERFORMANCE	DATE
56 kg (123 lb)	Halil Mutlu (TUR)	305 kg (671 lb)	16 Sep 2000
62 kg (136.5 lb)	*world standard*	325 kg (715 lb)	1 Jan 1998
69 kg (152 lb)	Galabin Boevski (BUL)	357.5 kg (786.5 lb)	24 Nov 1999
77 kg (169.5 lb)	Plamen Zhelyazkov (BUL)	377.5 kg (830.5 lb)	27 Mar 2002
85 kg (187 lb)	*world standard*	395 kg (869 lb)	1 Jan 1998
94 kg (207 lb)	*world standard*	417.5 kg (918.5 lb)	1 Jan 1998
105 kg (231 lb)	*world standard*	440 kg (968 lb)	1 Jan 1998
+105 kg (+231 lb)	Hossein Rezazadeh (IRI)	472.5 kg (1039.5 lb)	26 Sep 2000

women

WEIGHT CLASS	WINNER (NATIONALITY)	PERFORMANCE	DATE
48 kg (105.5 lb)	Liu Xiuhua (CHN)	197.5 kg (435 lb)	6 Sep 1999
53 kg (116.5 lb)	Yang Xia (CHN)	225 kg (496 lb)	18 Sep 2000
58 kg (127.5 lb)	Chen Yanqing (CHN)	235 kg (518 lb)	22 Nov 1999
63 kg (138.5 lb)	Chen Xiaomin (CHN)	242.5 kg (534.5 lb)	19 Sep 2000
69 kg (152 lb)	Valentina Popova (RUS)	257.5 kg (567.5 lb)	8 Nov 2001
75 kg (165 lb)	Sun Tianni (CHN)	257.5 kg (567.5 lb)	6 May 2000
+75 kg (+165 lb)	Ding Meiyuan (CHN)	300 kg (661 lb)	22 Sep 2000

World Weight Lifting Champions, 2001

Next competition scheduled to be held 17–24 Nov 2002 in Warsaw, Poland.

men

WEIGHT CLASS	WINNER (NATIONALITY)	PERFORMANCE
56 kg (123 lb)	Halil Mutlu (TUR)	300 kg (660 lb)
62 kg (136.5 lb)	Henadzy Alyashchuk (BLR)	317.5 kg (698.5 lb)
69 kg (152 lb)	Galabin Boevski (BUL)	340 kg (748 lb)
77 kg (169.5 lb)	Abbas Nader (QAT)	365 kg (803 lb)
85 kg (187 lb)	George Asanidze (GEO)	390 kg (861.9 lb)
94 kg (207 lb)	Kouroush Bagheri (IRI)	407.5 kg (896.5 lb)
105 kg (231 lb)	Vladimir Smorchkov (RUS)	422.5 kg (929.5 lb)
+105 kg (+231 lb)	Saeed Salem Jaber (QAT)	460 kg (1,012 lb)

women

WEIGHT CLASS	WINNER (NATIONALITY)	PERFORMANCE
48 kg (105.5 lb)	Wei Gao (CHN)	190 kg (418 lb)
53 kg (116.5 lb)	Li Feng-ying (TPE)	210 kg (462 lb)
58 kg (127.5 lb)	Aleksandra Klejnowska (POL)	215 kg (473 lb)
63 kg (138.5 lb)	Xiao Ying (CHN)	230 kg (506 lb)
69 kg (152 lb)	Valentina Popova (RUS)	257.5 kg (566.5 lb)
75 kg (165 lb)	Gyongyi Likerecz (HUN)	255 kg (561 lb)
+75 kg (+165 lb)	Albina Khomitch (RUS)	282.5 kg (621.5 lb)

Did you know? Athletic pursuits of US presidents: Abraham Lincoln was an avid wrestler.

Wrestling

Greco-Roman wrestling involves holds made only above the waist and forbids wrapping the legs about an opponent when the wrestlers go down. **Freestyle (catch-as-catch-can)**, permits holds above the waist and leg grips and is won by a pin-fall (the opponent must be held down for a measurable length of time). In Japanese **sumo** the object is to propel the opponent out of a ring about 4.6 m (15 ft) in diameter or to force him to touch the ground with any part of his body other than the soles of his feet. The wrestlers wear only loincloths and grip each other by the belt.

The first official amateur wrestling **world championship** was organized by the Fédération Interna-

tionale des Lutte Amateur (FILA; founded 1913, reconstituted 1921; and now called the **International Federation of Associated Wrestling Styles**). Although Greco-Roman style wrestling championships were held in 1910 and 1920–22, they were in effect (like the championships of 1923–49 in fact) open European championships, and the first actual world Greco-Roman wrestling championships were not held until 1950. World amateur **freestyle wrestling championships** were first held in 1951.

Related Web sites: International Federation of Associated Wrestling Styles <www.fila-wrestling.org>; sumo <www.sumoweb.com>

World Wrestling Championships—Greco-Roman Style

The maximum weight in some classes was revised in 1962, 1969, 1985, and 1997. The 2002 competition is scheduled to be held 19–22 Sep 2002 in Moscow.

YEAR	WINNER (NATIONALITY)	YEAR	WINNER (NATIONALITY)	YEAR	WINNER (NATIONALITY)
48 kg		**54 kg (continued)**		**58 kg**	
1969	Gheorghe Berceanu (ROM)	1960*	Dumitru Pirvulescu (ROM)	1950	Ali Mahmoud Hassan (EGY)
1970	Gheorghe Berceanu (ROM)	1961	Armais Sayadov (URS)	1952*	Imre Hodos (HUN)
1971	Vladimir Zubkov (URS)	1962	Sergey Rybalko (URS)	1953	Artyom Teryan (URS)
1972*	Gheorghe Berceanu (ROM)	1963	Borivoje Vukov (YUG)	1955	Vladimir Stashkevich (URS)
1973	Vladimir Zubkov (URS)	1964*	Tsutomu Hanahara (JPN)		
1974	Vladimir Zubkov (URS)	1965	Sergey Rybalko (URS)	1956*	Konstantin Vyrupayev (URS)
1975	Vladimir Zubkov (URS)	1966	Angel Keresov (BUL)		
1976*	Aleksey Shumakov (URS)	1967	Vladimir Bakulin (URS)	1958	Oleg Karavayev (URS)
1977	Aleksey Shumakov (URS)	1968*	Petar Kirov (BUL)	1960*	Oleg Karavayev (URS)
1978	Constantin Alexandru (ROM)	1969	Feerooz Aluzadeh (IRI)	1961	Oleg Karavayev (URS)
		1970	Petar Kirov (BUL)	1962	Masamitsu Ichiguchi (JPN)
1979	Constantin Alexandru (ROM)	1971	Petar Kirov (BUL)		
		1972*	Petar Kirov (BUL)	1963	Janos Varga (HUN)
1980*	Saksylik Ushkempirov (URS)	1973	Nicu Ginga (ROM)	1964*	Masamitsu Ichiguchi (JPN)
		1974	Petar Kirov (BUL)		
1981	Saksylik Ushkempirov (URS)	1975	Vitaly Konstantinov (URS)	1965	Ion Chernya (ROM)
		1976*	Vitaly Konstantinov (URS)	1966	Fritz Stange (FRG)
1982	Temo Kazarashvili (URS)	1977	Nicu Ginga (ROM)	1967	Ion Baciu (ROM)
1983	Bratan Tsenov (BUL)	1978	Vakhtang Blagidze (URS)	1968*	Janos Varga (HUN)
1984*	Vincenzo Maenza (ITA)	1979	Lajos Racz (HUN)	1969	Rustam Kazakov (URS)
1985	Magyatdin Allakhverdiyev (URS)	1980*	Vakhtang Blagidze (URS)	1970	Janos Varga (HUN)
		1981	Vakhtang Blagidze (URS)	1971	Rustam Kazakov (URS)
1986	Magyatdin Allakhverdiyev (URS)	1982	Benur Pashayan (URS)	1972*	Rustam Kazakov (URS)
		1983	Benur Pashayan (URS)	1973	Jozef Lipien (POL)
1987	Magyatdin Allakhverdiyev (URS)	1984*	Atsuji Miyahara (JPN)	1974	Farhat Mustafin (URS)
		1985	Jon Ronningen (NOR)	1975	Farhat Mustafin (URS)
		1986	Sergey Dudayev (URS)	1976*	Pertti Olavi Ukkola (FIN)
1988*	Vincenzo Maenza (ITA)	1987	Pedro Favier Roque (CUB)	1977	Pertti Olavi Ukkola (FIN)
1989	Oleg Kucherenko (URS)	1988*	Jon Ronningen (NOR)	1978	Shamil Serikov (URS)
1990	Oleg Kucherenko (URS)	1989	Aleksandr Ignatenko (URS)	1979	Shamil Serikov (URS)
1991	Gooun Duk-Yong (KOR)			1980*	Shamil Serikov (URS)
1992*	Oleg Kucherenko (UNT)†	1990	Aleksandr Ignatenko (URS)	1981	Pasquale Passarelli (FRG)
1993	Wilber Sánchez (CUB)			1982	Piotr Michalik (POL)
1994	Wilber Sánchez (CUB)	1991	Raul Martínez (CUB)	1983	Masaki Ito (JPN)
1995	Sim Kwon Ho (KOR)	1992*	Jon Ronningen (NOR)	1984*	Pasquale Passarelli (FRG)
1996*	Sim Kwon Ho (KOR)	1993	Raul Martínez (CUB)	1985	Stoyan Balov (BUL)
1997	*discontinued*	1994	Alfred Ter-Mkrtchyan (GER)	1986	Emil Ivanov (BUL)
		1995	Samvel Danielane (RUS)	1987	Patrice Mourier (FRA)
54 kg		1996*	Armen Nazaryan (ARM)	1988*	Andras Sike (HUN)
1950	Bengt Johansson (SWE)	1997	Ercan Yildiz (TUR)	1989	Emil Ivanov (BUL)
1952*	Boris Gurevich (URS)	1998	Sim Kwon Ho (KOR)	1990	Rifat Yildiz (GER)
1953	Boris Gurevich (URS)	1999	Lazaro Rivas (CUB)	1991	Rifat Yildiz (GER)
1955	Ignazio Fabra (ITA)	2000*	Sim Kwon Ho (KOR)	1992*	An Han-Bong (KOR)
1956*	Nikolay Solovyov (URS)	2001	Hassan Rangraz (IRI)	1993	Agazi Manukyan (ARM)
1958	Boris Gurevich (URS)			1994	Yury Melnichenko (KAZ)
				1995	Dennis Hall (USA)

World Wrestling Championships—Greco-Roman Style (continued)

YEAR	WINNER (NATIONALITY)
58 kg (continued)	
1996*	Yury Melnichenko (KAZ)
1997	Yury Melnichenko (KAZ)
1998	Kim In Sub (KOR)
1999	Kim In Sub (KOR)
2000*	Armen Nazaryan (BUL)
2001	Dilshod Aripov (UZB)
63 kg	
1950	Olle Anderberg (SWE)
1952*	Yakov Punkin (URS)
1953	Olle Anderberg (SWE)
1955	Imre Polyak (HUN)
1956*	Rauno Leonhard Mäkinen (FIN)
1958	Imre Polyak (HUN)
1960*	Muzahir Sille (TUR)
1961	Hamid Mansour Mustafa (EGY)
1962	Imre Polyak (HUN)
1963	Gennady Sapunov (URS)
1964*	Imre Polyak (HUN)
1965	Yury Grigoryev (URS)
1966	Roman Rurua (URS)
1967	Roman Rurua (URS)
1968*	Roman Rurua (URS)
1969	Roman Rurua (URS)
1970	Hideo Fujimoto (JPN)
1971	Georgi Markov (BUL)
1972*	Georgi Markov (BUL)
1973	Kazimiorz Lipien (POL)
1974	Kazimierz Lipien (POL)
1975	Nelson Davidyan (URS)
1976*	Kazimierz Lipien (POL)
1977	Laszlo Reczi (HUN)
1978	Boris Kramarenko (URS)
1979	Istvan Toth (HUN)
1980*	Stylianos Migiakis (GRE)
1981	Istvan Toth (HUN)
1982	Ryszard Swierad (POL)
1983	Hannu Lahtinen (FIN)
1984*	Kim Weon-Kee (KOR)
1985	Zhivko Vangelov Atanasov (BUL)
1986	Komandar Madshidov (URS)
1987	Zhivko Vangelov Atanasov (BUL)
1988*	Komandar Madshidov (URS)
1989	Komandar Madshidov (URS)
1990	Mario Olivera (CUB)
1991	Sergey Martinov (URS)
1992*	Akif Mehmet Pirim (TUR)
1993	Sergey Martinov (RUS)
1994	Sergey Martinov (RUS)
1995	Sergey Martinov (RUS)
1996*	Wlodzimierz Zawadzki (POL)
1997	Seref Eroglu (TUR)
1998	Makhidar Manukyan (KAZ)
1999	Makhidar Manukyan (KAZ)
2000*	Varteres Samurgashev (RUS)

YEAR	WINNER (NATIONALITY)
63 kg (continued)	
2001	Vaghinak Galustyan (ARM)
69 kg	
1950	Jozsef Gal (HUN)
1952*	Shazam Safin (URS)
1953	Gustav Freij (SWE)
1955	Grigory Gamarnik (URS)
1956*	Kyösti Emil Lehtonen (FIN)
1958	Riza Dogan (TUR)
1960*	Avtandil Koridze (URS)
1961	Avtandil Koridze (URS)
1962	Kazim Ayvaz (TUR)
1963	Stevan Horvat (YUG)
1964*	Kazim Ayvaz (TUR)
1965	Gennady Sapunov (URS)
1966	Stevan Horvat (YUG)
1967	Eero Tapio (FIN)
1968*	Muneji Mumemura (JPN)
1969	Simion Popescu (ROM)
1970	Roman Rurua (URS)
1971	Sreten Damjanovic (YUG)
1972*	Shamil Khisamutdinov (URS)
1973	Shamil Khisamutdinov (URS)
1974	Nelson Davidyan (URS)
1975	Shamil Khisamutdinov (URS)
1976*	Suren Nalbandyan (URS)
1977	Heinz-Helmut Wehling (GDR)
1978	Stefan Rusu (ROM)
1979	Andrzej Supron (POL)
1980*	Stefan Rusu (ROM)
1981	Gennady Yermilov (URS)
1982	Gennady Yermilov (URS)
1983	Tapio Sipila (FIN)
1984*	Vlado Lisjak (YUG)
1985	Stefan Negrisan (ROM)
1986	Levon Dzulfalakyan (URS)
1987	Aslaudin Abayev (URS)
1988*	Levon Dzulfalakyan (URS)
1989	Claudio Passarelli (FRG)
1990	Islam Doguchiyev (RUS)
1991	Islam Doguchiyev (RUS)
1992*	Attila Repka (HUN)
1993	Islam Doguchiyev (RUS)
1994	Islam Doguchiyev (RUS)
1995	Rustam Adzhy (UKR)
1996*	Ryszard Wolny (POL)
1997	Son Sang-Pil (KOR)
1998	Aleksandr Tretyakov (RUS)
1999	Son Sang-Pil (KOR)
2000*	Filiberto Ascuy Aguilera (CUB)
2001	Filiberto Ascuy Aguilera (CUB)
76 kg	
1950	Matti Siimanainen (FIN)
1952*	Miklos Szilvasi (HUN)
1953	Georgy Chatvorglan (URS)
1955	Vladimir Maneyev (URS)
1956*	Mithat Bayrak (TUR)

YEAR	WINNER (NATIONALITY)
76 kg (continued)	
1958	Kazim Ayvaz (TUR)
1960*	Mithat Bayrak (TUR)
1961	Valeriu Bularca (ROM)
1962	Anatoly Kolesov (URS)
1963	Anatoly Kolesov (URS)
1964*	Anatoly Kolesov (URS)
1965	Anatoly Kolesov (URS)
1966	Viktor Igumenov (URS)
1967	Viktor Igumenov (URS)
1968*	Rudolph Vesper (GDR)
1969	Viktor Igumenov (URS)
1970	Viktor Igumenov (URS)
1971	Viktor Igumenov (URS)
1972*	Viteslav Macha (TCH)
1973	Ivan Kolev (BUL)
1974	Viteslav Macha (TCH)
1975	Anatoly Bykov (URS)
1976*	Anatoly Bykov (URS)
1977	Viteslav Macha (TCH)
1978	Arif Niftulayev (URS)
1979	Ferenc Kocsis (HUN), Iyanko Chopov (BUL)‡
1980*	Ferenc Kocsis (HUN)
1981	Aleksandr Kudryavtsev (URS)
1982	Stefan Rusa (ROM)
1983	Mikhail Mamiashvili (URS)
1984*	Jouko Johann Salomaki (FIN)
1985	Mikhail Mamiashvili (URS)
1986	Mikhail Mamiashvili (URS)
1987	Jouko Johann Salomaki (FIN)
1988*	Kim Young-Nam (KOR)
1989	Daulet Turlykhanov (URS)
1990	Mnazakan Iskandaryan (RUS)
1991	Mnazakan Iskandaryan (RUS)
1992*	Mnazakan Iskandaryan (UNT)†
1993	Nestor Alamanza (CUB)
1994	Mnazakan Iskandaryan (RUS)
1995	Yvon Riemer (FRA)
1996*	Filiberto Ascuy Aguilera (CUB)
1997	Marko Yli-Hannuksela (FIN)
1998	Bakhtiar Bayseytov (KAZ)
1999	Nazmi Avluca (TUR)
2000*	Murat Kardanov (RUS)
2001	Ara Abrahamian (SWE)
85 kg	
1950	Axel Grönberg (SWE)
1952*	Axel Grönberg (SWE)
1953	Givi Kartoziya (URS)
1955	Givi Kartoziya (URS)
1956*	Givi Kartoziya (URS)
1958	Givi Kartoziya (URS)
1960*	Dimitar Dobrev (BUL)
1961	Vasily Zenin (URS)
1962	Tevfik Kis (TUR)

World Wrestling Championships—Greco-Roman Style (continued)

YEAR	WINNER (NATIONALITY)
85 kg (continued)	
1963	Tevfik Kis (TUR)
1964*	Branislav Simic (YUG)
1965	Rimantes Bogdanas (URS)
1966	Valentin Olenik (URS)
1967	Laszlo Sillai (HUN)
1968*	Lothar Metz (GDR)
1969	Petar Krumov (BUL)
1970	Anatoly Nazarenko (URS)
1971	Csaba Hegedus (HUN)
1972*	Csaba Hegedus (HUN)
1973	Leonid Liberman (URS)
1974	Anatoly Nazarenko (URS)
1975	Anatoly Nazarenko (URS)
1976*	Momir Petkovic (YUG)
1977	Vladimir Cheboksarov (URS)
1978	Ion Draica (ROM)
1979	Gennady Korban (URS)
1980*	Gennady Korban (URS)
1981	Gennady Korban (URS)
1982	Taymuraz Abkhasava (URS)
1983	Taymuraz Abkhasava (URS)
1984*	Ion Draica (ROM)
1985	Bogdan Daras (POL)
1986	no award
1987	Tibor Komaromi (HUN)
1988*	Mikhail Mamiashvili (URS)
1989	Tibor Komaromi (HUN)
1990	Peter Farkas (HUN)
1991	Peter Farkas (HUN)
1992*	Peter Farkas (HUN)
1993	Hamza Yerlikaya (TUR)
1994	Thomas Zander (GER)
1995	Hamza Yerlikaya (TUR)
1996*	Hamza Yerlikaya (TUR)
1997	Sergey Tsvir (RUS)
1998	Aleksandr Menshikov (RUS)
1999	Luiz Enrique Mendez Lazo (CUB)
2000*	Hamza Yerlikaya (TUR)
2001	Muhran Vakhtangadze (GEO)
90 kg	
1950	Muharrem Candas (TUR)
1952*	Kelpo Olavi Gröndahl (FIN)
1953	August Englas (URS)
1955	Valentin Nikolayev (URS)
1956*	Valentin Nikolayev (URS)
1958	Rostom Abashidze (URS)
1960*	Tevfik Kis (TUR)
1961	Gyorgy Gurics (HUN)
1962	Rostom Abashidze (URS)
1963	Rostom Abashidze (URS)
1964*	Boyan Radev (BUL)
1965	Valery Anisimov (URS)
1966	Boyan Radev (BUL)
1967	Nikolay Yakovenko (URS)

YEAR	WINNER (NATIONALITY)
90 kg (continued)	
1968*	Boyan Radev (BUL)
1969	Aleksandr Yurkevich (URS)
1970	Valery Rezantsev (URS)
1971	Valery Rezantsev (URS)
1972*	Valery Rezantsev (URS)
1973	Valery Rezantsev (URS)
1974	Valery Rezantsev (URS)
1975	Valery Rezantsev (URS)
1976*	Valery Rezantsev (URS)
1977	Frank Andersson (SWE)
1978	Stoyan Nikolov Ivanov (BUL)
1979	Frank Andersson (SWE)
1980*	Norbert Nottny (HUN)
1981	Igor Kanygin (URS)
1982	Frank Andersson (SWE)
1983	Igor Kanygin (URS)
1984*	Steven Fraser (USA)
1985	Michael Houck (USA)
1986	Andrzej Malina (POL)
1987	Vladimir Popov (URS)
1988*	Atanas Komchev (BUL)
1989	Maik Bullmann (GDR)
1990	Maik Bullmann (GER)
1991	Maik Bullmann (GER)
1992*	Maik Bullmann (GER)
1993	Georgy Koguchavilli (RUS)
1994	Georgy Koguchavilli (RUS)
1995	Hakki Basar (TUR)
1996*	Vyatsheslav Oleynyk (UKR)
1997	*discontinued*
97 kg	
1950	Bertil Antonsson (SWE)
1952*	Johannes Kotkas (URS)
1953	Bertil Antonsson (SWE)
1955	Aleksandr Mazur (URS)
1956*	Anatoly Parfenov (URS)
1958	Ivan Bogdan (URS)
1960*	Ivan Bogdan (URS)
1961	Ivan Bogdan (URS)
1962	Istvan Kozma (HUN)
1963	Anatoly Roshchin (URS)
1964*	Istvan Kozma (HUN)
1965	Nikolay Shmakov (URS)
1966	Istvan Kozma (HUN)
1967	Istvan Kozma (HUN)
1968*	Istvan Kozma (HUN)
1969	Nikolay Yakovenko (URS)
1970	Per Oskar Svensson (SWE)
1971	Per Oskar Svensson (SWE)
1972*	Nicolae Martinescu (ROM)
1973	Nikolay Balboshin (URS)
1974	Nikolay Balboshin (URS)
1975	Kamen Losanov (BUL)
1976*	Nikolay Balboshin (URS)
1977	Nikolay Balboshin (URS)
1978	Nikolay Balboshin (URS)
1979	Nikolay Balboshin (URS)

YEAR	WINNER (NATIONALITY)
97 kg (continued)	
1980*	Georgi Raykov-Petkov (BUL)
1981	Michail Saladze (URS)
1982	Roman Wroclawski (POL)
1983	Andrey Dimitrov (BUL)
1984*	Vasile Andrei (ROM)
1985	Andrey Dimitrov (BUL)
1986	Tamas Gaspar (HUN)
1987	Guram Guedekhaorui (URS)
1988*	Andrzej Wronski (POL)
1989	Gerhard Himmel (FRG)
1990	Sergey Demyashkevich (URS)
1991	Hector Milian (CUB)
1992*	Hector Milian (CUB)
1993	Mikael Ljungberg (SWE)
1994	Andrzej Wronski (POL)
1995	Mikael Ljungberg (SWE)
1996*	Andrzej Wronski (POL)
1997	Georgy Koguchavilli (RUS)
1998	Georgy Koguchavilli (RUS)
1999	Georgy Koguchavilli (RUS)
2000*	Mikael Ljungberg (SWE)
2001	Aleksandr Bezruchkin (RUS)
130 kg	
1969	Anatoly Roshchin (URS)
1970	Anatoly Roshchin (URS)
1971	Aleksandar Tomov (BUL)
1972*	Anatoly Roshchin (URS)
1973	Aleksandar Tomov (BUL)
1974	Aleksandar Tomov (BUL)
1975	Aleksandar Tomov (BUL)
1976*	Aleksandar Kolchinsky (URS)
1977	Nikola Dinev (BUL)
1978	Aleksandr Kolchinsky (URS)
1979	Aleksandar Tomov (BUL)
1980*	Aleksandr Kolchinsky (URS)
1981	Refik Memisevic (YUG)
1982	Nikola Dinev (BUL)
1983	Yevgeny Artyukhin (URS)
1984*	Jeffrey Blatnick (USA)
1985	Igor Rostorotsky (URS)
1986	Tomas Johansson (SWE)
1987	Igor Rostorotsky (URS)
1988*	Aleksandr Karelin (URS)
1989	Aleksandr Karelin (URS)
1990	Aleksandr Karelin (URS)
1991	Aleksandr Karelin (URS)
1992*	Aleksandr Karelin (UNT)†
1993	Aleksandr Karelin (RUS)
1994	Aleksandr Karelin (RUS)
1995	Aleksandr Karelin (RUS)
1996*	Aleksandr Karelin (RUS)
1997	Aleksandr Karelin (RUS)
1998	Aleksandr Karelin (RUS)
1999	Aleksandr Karelin (RUS)
2000*	Rulon Gardner (USA)
2001	Rulon Gardner (USA)

*Olympic champions, recognized as world champions (for earlier Olympic champions, see Olympic Games).
†Unified Team, consisting of athletes from the Commonwealth of Independent States plus Georgia. ‡Tied.

World Wrestling Championships—Freestyle

The maximum weight in some classes was revised in 1962, 1969, 1985, and 1997. The 2002 competition is scheduled for 4–7 Sep 2002, Tehran, Iran.

YEAR	WINNER (NATIONALITY)
48 kg	
1969	Ibrahim Javadi (IRI)
1970	Ibrahim Javadi (IRI)
1971	Ibrahim Javadi (IRI)
1972*	Roman Dmitriyev (URS)
1973	Roman Dmitriyev (URS)
1974	Hassan Issaev (Murselov) (BUL)
1975	Hassan Issaev (BUL)
1976*	Hassan Issaev (BUL)
1977	Anatoly Beloglazov (URS)
1978	Sergey Kornilayev (URS)
1979	Sergey Kornilayev (URS)
1980*	Claudio Pollio (ITA)
1981	Sergey Kornilayev (URS)
1982	Sergey Kornilayev (URS)
1983	Kim Hwan Cher (PRK)
1984*	Robert Weaver (USA)
1985	Kim Chol Hwan (PRK)
1986	Li Yae-sik (PRK)
1987	Li Yae-sik (PRK)
1988*	Takashi Kobayashi (JPN)
1989	Kim Jong-shin (KOR)
1990	Aldo Martínez (CUB)
1991	Vugar Orudzhev (URS)
1992*	Kim Il (PRK)
1993	Alexis Vila (CUB)
1994	Alexis Vila (CUB)
1995	Vugar Orudzhev (RUS)
1996*	Kim Il (PRK)
1997	*discontinued*
54 kg	
1951	Ali Yucel (TUR)
1952*	Hasan Gemici (TUR)
1954	Huseyin Akbas (TUR)
1956*	Mirian Tsalkalamanidze (URS)
1957	Mehmet Kartal (TUR)
1959	Ali Aliyev (URS)
1960*	Ahmet Bilek (TUR)
1961	Ali Aliyev (URS)
1962	Ali Aliyev (URS)
1963	Cemal Yanilmaz (TUR)
1964*	Yoshikatsu Yoshida (JPN)
1965	Yoshikatsu Yoshida (JPN)
1966	Chang-Sun Chang (KOR)
1967	Shigeo Nakata (JPN)
1968*	Shigeo Nakata (JPN)
1969	Richard Joseph Sanders (USA)
1970	Ali Riza Alan (TUR)
1971	Mohammad Ghorbani (IRI)
1972*	Kiyomi Kato (JPN)
1973	Ibrahim Javadi (IRI)
1974	Yuji Takada (JPN)
1975	Yuji Takada (JPN)
1976*	Yuji Takada (JPN)
1977	Yuji Takada (JPN)
1978	Anatoly Beloglazov (URS)
1979	Yuji Takada (JPN)
1980*	Anatoly Beloglazov (URS)
1981	Toshio Asakura (JPN)
1982	Hartmut Reich (GDR)
1983	Valentin Iordanov (BUL)

YEAR	WINNER (NATIONALITY)
54 kg (continued)	
1984*	Saban Trstena (YUG)
1985	Valentin Iordanov (BUL)
1986	Kim Yong-sik (PRK)
1987	Valentin Iordanov (BUL)
1988*	Mitsuru Sato (JPN)
1989	Valentin Iordanov (BUL)
1990	Majid Torkan (IRI)
1991	Larry Zeke Jones (USA)
1992*	Li Hak-Son (PRK)
1993	Valentin Iordanov (BUL)
1994	Valentin Iordanov (BUL)
1995	Valentin Iordanov (BUL)
1996*	Valentin Iordanov (BUL)
1997	Wilfredo Garcia Quintana (CUB)
1998	Samuel Henson (USA)
1999	Kim Woo Yong (KOR)
2000*	Namik Abdullayev (AZE)
2001	Herman Kontoyev (BLR)
58 kg	
1951	Nasuh Akar (TUR)
1952*	Shohachi Ishii (JPN)
1954	Mustafa Dagistanli (TUR)
1956*	Mustafa Dagistanli (TUR)
1957	Huseyin Akbas (TUR)
1959	Huseyin Akbas (TUR)
1960*	Terrence McCann (USA)
1961	Mohamad Ebrahim Saif-pour Saidabadi (IRI)
1962	Huseyin Akbas (TUR)
1963	Aydyn Ibragimov (URS)
1964*	Yojiro Uetake (JPN)
1965	Tomiaki Fukuda (JPN)
1966	Ali Aliyev (URS)
1967	Ali Aliyev (URS)
1968*	Yojiro Uetake (JPN)
1969	Tadamichi Tanaka (JPN)
1970	Hideaki Yanagida (JPN)
1971	Hideaki Yanagida (JPN)
1972*	Hideaki Yanagida (JPN)
1973	Moshen Faravashi (IRI)
1974	Vladimir Yumin (URS)
1975	Masao Arai (JPN)
1976*	Vladmir Yumin (URS)
1977	Tadashi Sasaki (JPN)
1978	Hideaki Tomiyama (JPN)
1979	Hideaki Tomiyama (JPN)
1980*	Sergey Beloglazov (URS)
1981	Sergey Beloglazov (URS)
1982	Anatoly Beloglazov (URS)
1983	Sergey Beloglazov (URS)
1984*	Hideaki Tomiyama (JPN)
1985	Sergey Beloglazov (URS)
1986	Sergey Beloglazov (URS)
1987	Sergey Beloglazov (URS)
1988*	Sergey Beloglazov (URS)
1989	Kim Sik-seung (PRK)
1990	Alejandro Puerto (CUB)
1991	Sergey Smal (URS)
1992*	Alejandro Puerto (CUB)
1993	Terry Brands (USA)
1994	Alejandro Puerto (CUB)
1995	Terry Brands (USA)
1996*	Kendall Cross (USA)

YEAR	WINNER (NATIONALITY)
58 kg (continued)	
1997	Mohammad Talaee (IRI)
1998	Ali Reza Dabir (IRI)
1999	Harun Dogan (TUR)
2000*	Ali Reza Dabir (IRI)
2001	Guivi Sissaouri (CAN)
63 kg	
1951	Nurettin Zafer (TUR)
1952*	Bayram Sit (TUR)
1954	Shozo Sasahara (JPN)
1956*	Shozo Sasahara (JPN)
1957	Mustafa Dagistanli (TUR)
1959	Mustafa Dagistanli (TUR)
1960*	Mustafa Dagistanli (TUR)
1961	Vladimir Rubashvili (URS)
1962	Osamu Watanabe (JPN)
1963	Osamu Watanabe (JPN)
1964*	Osamu Watanabe (JPN)
1965	Mohamad Ebrahim Saif-pour Saidabadi (IRI)
1966	Masaaki Kaneko (JPN)
1967	Masaaki Kaneko (JPN)
1968*	Masaaki Kaneko (JPN)
1969	Takeo Morita (JPN)
1970	Shamseddin Seyed-Abbassi (IRI)
1971	Sagalav Abdulbekov (URS)
1972*	Sagalav Abdulbekov (URS)
1973	Sagalav Abdulbekov (URS)
1974	Zeveg Oydov (MGL)
1975	Zeveg Oydov (MGL)
1976*	Yang Jung-Mo (KOR)
1977	Vladimir Yumin (URS)
1978	Vladimir Yumin (URS)
1979	Vladimir Yumin (URS)
1980*	Magomedgasan Abushev (URS)
1981	Simeon Sterev (BUL)
1982	Sergey Beloglazov (URS)
1983	Viktor Alekseyev (URS)
1984*	Randy Lewis (USA)
1985	Viktor Alekseyev (URS)
1986	Hassar Issayev (URS)
1987	John Smith (USA)
1988*	John Smith (USA)
1989	John Smith (USA)
1990	John Smith (USA)
1991	John Smith (USA)
1992*	John Smith (USA)
1993	Thomas Brands (USA)
1994	Magomed Azizov (RUS)
1995	Elbrus Tedeyev (UKR)
1996*	Thomas Brands (USA)
1997	Abbas Hajd Kenari (IRI)
1998	Serafim Barzakov (BUL)
1999	Elbrus Tedeyev (UKR)
2000*	Murad Umakhanov (RUS)
2001	Serafim Barzakov (BUL)
69 kg	
1951	Olle Anderberg (SWE)
1952*	Olle Anderberg (SWE)

World Wrestling Championships—Freestyle (continued)

YEAR	WINNER (NATIONALITY)
69 kg (continued)	
1954	Djahanbakte Tovfighe (IRI)
1956*	Emam Goudarzi Habibi (IRI)
1957	Alimbeg Bestayev (URS)
1959	Vladimir Sinyavsky (URS)
1960*	Shelby Wilson (USA)
1961	Mohammad Sanatkaran (IRI)
1962	Eniu Valchev-Dimov (BUL)
1963	Iwao Horiuchi (JPN)
1964*	Eniu Valchev-Dimov (BUL)
1965	Abdullah Movahed Ard-abili (IRI)
1966	Abdullah Movahed Ard-abili (IRI)
1967	Abdullah Movahed Ard-abili (IRI)
1968*	Abdullah Movahed Ard-abili (IRI)
1969	Abdullah Movahed Ard-abili (IRI)
1970	Abdullah Movahed Ard-abili (IRI)
1971	Danny Mack Gable (USA)
1972*	Danny Mack Gable (USA)
1973	Lloyd Keaser (USA)
1974	Nasrula Nasrullayev (URS)
1975	Pavel Pinigin (URS)
1976*	Pavel Pinigin (URS)
1977	Pavel Pinigin (URS)
1978	Pavel Pinigin (URS)
1979	Mikhail Kharachura (URS)
1980*	Saipulla Absaidov (URS)
1981	Saipulla Absaidov (URS)
1982	Mikhail Kharachura (URS)
1983	Arsen Fadzayev (URS)
1984*	You In-Tak (KOR)
1985	Arsen Fadzayev (URS)
1986	Arsen Fadzayev (URS)
1987	Arsen Fadzayev (URS)
1988*	Arsen Fadzayev (URS)
1989	Boris Bovdayev (URS)
1990	Arsen Fadzayev (URS)
1991	Arsen Fadzayev (URS)
1992*	Arsen Fadzayev (UNT)†
1993	Akbar Fallah (IRI)
1994	Alexander Leipold (GER)
1995	Araik Gevorkian (ARM)
1996*	Vadim Bogiyev (RUS)
1997	Araik Gevorkian (ARM)
1998	Araik Gevorkian (ARM)
1999	Daniel Igali (CAN)
2000*	Daniel Igali (CAN)
2001	Nikolay Paslari (BUL)
76 kg	
1951	Celal Atik (TUR)
1952*	William Thomas Smith (USA)
1954	Vakhtang Balavadze (URS)
1956*	Mitsuo Ikeda (JPN)

YEAR	WINNER (NATIONALITY)
76 kg (continued)	
1957	Vakhtang Balavadze (URS)
1959	Emam Goudarzi Habibi (IRI)
1960*	Douglas Blubaugh (USA)
1961	Emam Goudarzi Habibi (IRI)
1962	Emam Goudarzi Habibi (IRI)
1963	Guliko Sagaradze (URS)
1964*	Ismail Ogan (TUR)
1965	Guliko Sagaradze (URS)
1966	Mahmut Atalay (TUR)
1967	Daniel Sauton-Robin (FRA)
1968*	Mahmut Atalay (TUR)
1969	Zarbeg Beriashvili (URS)
1970	Wayne Wells (USA)
1971	Yury Gusov (URS)
1972*	Wayne Turner Wells (USA)
1973	Mansoor Barzegar (IRI)
1974	Ruslan Ashuraliyev (URS)
1975	Ruslan Ashuraliyev (URS)
1976*	Jiichiro Date (JPN)
1977	Stanley Dziedzic (USA)
1978	Leroy Kemp (USA)
1979	Leroy Kemp (USA)
1980*	Valentin Raychev (BUL)
1981	Martin Knosp (FRG)
1982	Leroy Kemp (USA)
1983	David Schultz (USA)
1984*	David Schultz (USA)
1985	Raul Cascaret Fonseca (CUB)
1986	Raul Cascaret Fonseca (CUB)
1987	Adlan Varayev (URS)
1988*	Kenneth Monday (USA)
1989	Kenneth Monday (USA)
1990	Rahmat Sukra (BUL)
1991	Amir Reza Khadem Azghadi (IRI)
1992*	Park Jang-Soon (KOR)
1993	Park Jang-Soon (KOR)
1994	Turan Ceylan (TUR)
1995	Buvaysa Saytev (RUS)
1996*	Buvaysa Saytev (RUS)
1997	Buvaysa Saytev (RUS)
1998	Buvaysa Saytev (RUS)
1999	Adam Saytev (RUS)
2000*	Brandon Slay (USA)
2001	Buvaysa Saytev (RUS)
85 kg	
1951	Haydar Zafer (TUR)
1952*	David Tsimakurdze (URS)
1954	Abbas Zandi (IRI)
1956*	Nikola Stanchev (BUL)
1957	Nabi Soruri (IRI)
1959	Georgy Skhirtladze (URS)
1960*	Hassan Gungor (TUR)
1961	Mansoor Mehdizadeh (IRI)
1962	Mansoor Mehdizadeh (IRI)
1963	Prodan Gardzhev (BUL)
1964*	Prodan Gardzhev (BUL)

YEAR	WINNER (NATIONALITY)
85 kg (continued)	
1965	Mansoor Mehdizadeh (IRI)
1966	Prodan Gardzhev (BUL)
1967	Boris Gurevich (URS)
1968*	Boris Gurevich (URS)
1969	Fred Fozzard (USA)
1970	Yury Shakhmuradov (URS)
1971	Levan Tediashvili (URS)
1972*	Levan Tediashvili (URS)
1973	Vasily Syulzhin (URS)
1974	Viktor Novozhilov (URS)
1975	Adolf Seger (FRG)
1976*	John Allan Peterson (USA)
1977	Adolf Seger (FRG)
1978	Magomed Aratsilov (URS)
1979	Istvan Kovacs (HUN)
1980*	Ismail Abilov (BUL)
1981	Christopher Campbell (USA)
1982	Tajmuraz Dzgoyev (URS)
1983	Tajmuraz Dzgoyev (URS)
1984*	Mark Schultz (USA)
1985	Mark Schultz (USA)
1986	Vladimir Modozyan (URS)
1987	Mark Schultz (USA)
1988*	Han Myung-Woo (KOR)
1989	Elmadi Jabrailov (URS)
1990	Jozef Lohyna (TCH)
1991	Kevin Jackson (USA)
1992*	Kevin Jackson (USA)
1993	Sabahattin Ozturk (TUR)
1994	Lukman Jabrailov (MDA)
1995	Kevin Jackson (USA)
1996*	Khadshimurad Magome-dov (RUS)
1997	Leslie Gutches (USA)
1998	Ali Reza Heydari (IRI)
1999	Yoel Romero Palacio (CUB)
2000*	Adam Saytev (RUS)
2001	Khadshimurad Magome-dov (RUS)
90 kg	
1951	Yasar Dogu (TUR)
1952*	Viking Palm (SWE)
1954	Arsen Englas (URS)
1956*	Gholamreza Takhti (IRI)
1957	Petko Sirakov Atanasov (BUL)
1959	Gholamreza Takhti (IRI)
1960*	Ismet Atli (TUR)
1961	Gholamreza Takhti (IRI)
1962	Aleksandr Medved (URS)
1963	Aleksandr Medved (URS)
1964*	Aleksandr Medved (URS)
1965	Ahmet Ayik (TUR)
1966	Aleksandr Medved (URS)
1967	Ahmet Ayik (TUR)
1968*	Ahmet Ayik (TUR)
1969	Boris Gurevich (URS)
1970	Gennady Strakhov (URS)
1971	Rusi Petrov (BUL)
1972*	Benjamin Lee Peterson (USA)

World Wrestling Championships—Freestyle (continued)

YEAR	WINNER (NATIONALITY)	YEAR	WINNER (NATIONALITY)	YEAR	WINNER (NATIONALITY)
90 kg (continued)		**97 kg (continued)**		**130 kg**	
1973	Levan Tediashvili (URS)	1961	Wilfried Dietrich (FRG)	1969	Aleksandr Medved (URS)
1974	Levan Tediashvili (URS)	1962	Aleksandr Ivanitsky (URS)	1970	Aleksandr Medved (URS)
1975	Levan Tediashvili (URS)	1963	Aleksandr Ivanitsky (URS)	1971	Aleksandr Medved (URS)
1976*	Levan Tediashvili (URS)	1964*	Aleksandr Ivanitsky (URS)	1972*	Aleksandr Medved (URS)
1977	Anatoly Prokopchuk	1965	Aleksandr Ivanitsky (URS)	1973	Soslan Andiyev (URS)
	(URS)	1966	Aleksandr Ivanitsky (URS)	1974	Simon Ladislav (ROM)
1978	Uwe Neupert (GDR)	1967	Aleksandr Medved (URS)	1975	Soslan Andiyev (URS)
1979	Khasan Ortsuyev (URS)	1968*	Aleksandr Medved (URS)	1976*	Soslan Andiyev (URS)
1980*	Sanasar Oganisyan (URS)	1969	Shota Lomidze (URS)	1977	Soslan Andiyev (URS)
1981	Sanasar Oganisyan (URS)	1970	Vladimir Gulyutkin (URS)	1978	Soslan Andiyev (URS)
1982	Uwe Neupert (GDR)	1971	Shota Lomidze (URS)	1979	Salman Khasimikov
1983	Pyotr Naniyev (URS)	1972*	Ivan Yarygin (URS)		(URS)
1984*	Edward Banach (USA)	1973	Ivan Yarygin (URS)	1980*	Soslan Andiyev (URS)
1985	William Scherr (USA)	1974	Vladimir Gulyutkin (URS)	1981	Salman Khasimikov
1986	Macharbek Khadartsev	1975	Khorloo Bayanmunkh		(URS)
	(URS)		(MGL)	1982	Salman Khasimikov
1987	Macharbek Khadartsev	1976*	Ivan Yarygin (URS)		(URS)
	(URS)	1977	Aslanbek Bisultanov	1983	Salman Khasimikov
1988*	Macharbek Khadartsev		(URS)		(URS)
	(URS)	1978	Harald Buettner (GDR)	1984*	Bruce Baumgartner (USA)
1989	Macharbek Khadartsev	1979	Ilya Mate (URS)	1985	David Gobedzhishvili
	(URS)	1980*	Ilya Mate (URS)		(URS)
1990	Macharbek Khadartsev	1981	Roland Gehrke (GDR)	1986	Bruce Baumgartner (USA)
	(URS)	1982	Ilya Mate (URS)	1987	Aslan Khadartzev (URS)
1991	Macharbek Khadartsev	1983	Aslan Khadartzev (URS)	1988*	David Gobedzhishvili
	(URS)	1984*	Louis Banach (USA)		(URS)
1992*	Macharbek Khadartsev	1985	Leri Khabelov (URS)	1989	Ali Reza Soleimani (IRI)
	(UNT)†	1986	Aslan Khadartzev (URS)	1990	David Gobedzhishvili
1993	Melvin Douglas (USA)	1987	Leri Khabelov (URS)		(URS)
1994	Rasul Khadem Azghadi	1988*	Vasile Puscasu (ROM)	1991	Andreas Schröder (GER)
	(IRI)	1989	Ahmed Atavov (URS)	1992*	Bruce Baumgartner (USA)
1995	Rasul Khadem Azghadi	1990	Leri Khabelov (URS)	1993	Bruce Baumgartner (USA)
	(IRI)	1991	Leri Khabelov (URS)	1994	Mahmut Demir (TUR)
1996*	Rasul Khadem Azghadi	1992*	Leri Khabelov (UNT)†	1995	Bruce Baumgartner (USA)
	(IRI)	1993	Leri Khabelov (RUS)	1996+	Mahmut Demir (TUR)
1997	*discontinued*	1994	Arawat Sabejew (GER)	1997	Zekeriya Guclu (TUR)
		1995	Kurt Angle (USA)	1998	Alexis Rodríguez Valera
97 kg		1996*	Kurt Angle (USA)		(CUB)
1951	Bertil Antonsson (SWE)	1997	Kuramagomed Kuram-	1999	Stephen Neal (USA)
1952*	Arsen Mekokishvili (URS)		agomedov (RUS)	2000*	David Musulbes (RUS)
1954	Arsen Mekokishvili (URS)	1998	Abbas Jadidi (IRI)	2001	David Musulbes (RUS)
1956*	Hamit Kaplan (TUR)	1999	Sagid Murtasaliyev (RUS)		
1957	Hamit Kaplan (TUR)	2000*	Sagid Murtasaliyev (RUS)		
1959	Lyutvi Akhmedov (BUL)	2001	Georgy Gogchelidze		
1960*	Wilfried Dietrich (FRG)		(RUS)		

Olympic champions, recognized as world champions (for earlier Olympic champions, see Olympic Games).
†Unified Team, consisting of athletes from the Commonwealth of Independent States plus Georgia.

2001–02 Sumo Tournament Champions

TOURNAMENT	LOCATION	DATE	WINNER	WINNER'S RECORD
Nagoya Basho (Nagoya tournament)	Nagoya	8–22 Jul 2001	Kaio	13–2
Aki Basho (autumn tournament)	Tokyo	9–23 Sep 2001	Kotomitsuki	13–2
Kyushu Basho (Kyushu tournament)	Fukuoka	11–25 Nov 2001	Musashimaru	13–2
Hatsu Basho (New Year's tournament)	Tokyo	13–27 Jan 2002	Tochiazuma	13–2
Haru Basho (spring tournament)	Osaka	10–24 Mar 2002	Musashimaru	13–2
Natsu Basho (summer tournament)	Tokyo	12–26 May 2002	Musashimaru	13–2
Nagoya Basho (Nagoya tournament)	Nagoya	7–21 Jul 2002	Dilettante	12–3
Aki Basho (autumn tournament)	Tokyo	8–22 Sep 2002		
Kyushu Basho (Kyushu tournament)	Fukuoka	10–24 Nov 2002		
Hatsu Basho (New Year's tournament)	Tokyo	12–26 Jan 2003		
Haru Basho (spring tournament)	Osaka	9–23 Mar 2003		
Natsu Basho (summer tournament)	Tokyo	11–25 May 2003		

Page numbers in **boldface** indicate main subject references; references in *italics* indicate illustrations. Photographs are on the plates after page 192; flags and maps of the world are on the plates after page 960.

death penalty
sentences in the US 868
Decker, Alonzo Galloway, Jr.
106
decimal
equivalents of common
fractions 245
Declaration of Independence
746
signers 747
Defense, Department of
executive departments 786
military affairs 803
defense contractor 810
Defoe, Daniel 175
Deimos 223
Delaware 825
congressional apportionment
798
death penalty sentences
868
electoral votes 800
energy consumption 882
governors of US states and
territories 854
immigration 817
libraries 874
minerals 881
poverty level 819
signers of the Declaration of
Independence 747
state crime rates 863
state officers and legislatures
856
state population 814
US House 793
US prison population 867
US Senate 790
DeLay, Dorothy 106
DeLay, Tom 793
dementia
Alzheimer's disease 316
Demme, Edward 106
democratization
September 11 attack 7
Dempsey, Jack 914
Deneb (star) 209
Deng Xiaoping 712
Denmark 450
flags of the world Plate 2
density 253
Department of: see under
substantive word
dependent personality disorder
324
depression 322
bipolar disorder 322
Derby, The 1055
Dertouzos, Michael Leonidas
106
desert 300
Desio, Ardito 106
Deutsches Historisches Museum
(Berlin, Germany) 897
Dovi, Phoolan 106
photographs Plate 10
Devine, Daniel John 106
Devonian Period 294
Dewey, John 712
Di Stéfano, Alfredo 914
diabetes 314

Diagnostic and Statistical
Manual of Mental
Disorders, or DSM 320
Diamond Challenge Sculls 1073
Diana, Princess of Wales 59
Díaz, Jésus 106
Dibiasi, Klaus 914
dice
chances 240
Dick, Philip K. 175
Dickens, Charles 175
Dickinson, Emily 175
diet, or nutrition 327
body mass index 336
fat intake in US diet 329
FDA 327
food consumption 329
food pyramid 328
dietary guidelines 330
nutrient composition of fruits
and vegetables 330
nutritional value 331
reading food labels 334
vitamins 327
see also health; fitness
Dillard, William T., Jr. 106
DiMaggio, Joe 914
Diocletian 712
disaster 39, 268
chronology 39
geologic 268
avalanches 270
earthquakes 208, 209
tsunami 270
volcanoes 270
weather 271
floods 271
hurricanes 272, 273
storms 271
wildfires 272
Discovery 17
disease 312
AIDS 317
allergies 317
Alzheimer's disease 316
arthritis 316
asthma 317
autoimmune diseases 312,
313
cancer 315
cardiovascular diseases 313
causes of death 310
diabetes 314
HIV 317
infectious diseases 312
STDs 318
stroke 314
disorderly conduct
arrests in the US 867
disorganized schizophrenia, or
hebephrenic schizophrenia
325
Disraeli, Benjamin 712
District of Columbia: see
Washington, DC
diving
championships 1083, 1085
Olympic champions 940
2000 Summer Olympic Games
medal winners 972
divorce

statistics 873
Djibouti 451
flags of the world Plate 2
dodo 562
dogsled racing
Iditarod Trail Sled Dog Race
1082
domestic violence
arrests in the US 867
Dominica 453
flags of the world Plate 2
Dominican Republic 454
flags of the world Plate 2
Donahue, Troy 106
Dönhoff, Marion 106
Donne, John 175
Dostoyevsky, Fyodor 175
Douglas, Robert L. 914
Douglass, Frederick 712
Doyle, Sir Arthur Conan 175
drama, or play
Pulitzer Prize 156
Dred Scott v. Sandford 801
Dreiser, Theodore 175
driving under the influence
arrests in the US 867
drug abuse: see substance
abuse
drunkenness
arrests in the US 867
Dryden, John 175
Dryden, Ken 914
DSM, see Diagnostic and
Statistical Manual of
Mental Disorders
Du Bois, W. E. B. 712
Duarte Cancino, Isaías 106
Dubai World Cup 1057
Dudley, Jane 106
Dumbarton Oaks Research
Library 875
Dunst, Kirsten
photographs Plate 9
Duong Van Minh 106
Dynegy Inc. 9

E

Earnhardt, Dale 914
Earth 220
astronomical constants 204
celestial bodies 216
geologic time scale 294
geology 295
meteorology 262
earthquake 39
historical earthquakes 268
measuring earthquakes 269
East Timor 456
chronology 15, 18 , 33, 36
flags of the world Plate 2
eating disorders 323
eclipse 215
ecology
timelines 338
see also environment
Economic Committee, Joint
US Congress 792
economics 877
Nobel Prize winners 132

worldwide adherents to all
religions 726
island 295
Isle of Man 512
Isma'il 715
Israel 513
chronology 19, 22, 25, 26, 31,
33, 34, 35, 36, 38, 39
flags of the world Plate 3
Italy 515
chronology 37
flags of the world Plate 3
Roman emperors 697

J

Jackson, Andrew 761
influential leaders 715
presidential cabinets 775
Supreme Court appointments
800
US presidents 759
wives and children 769
Jackson, Henry: *see* Armstrong,
Henry
Jackson, John 110
Ja'far ibn Muhammad 715
Jagger, Mick 38
Jahiz, al- 177
Jainism 726, 728
Jamaica 517
flags of the world Plate 3
Jamal ad-Din al-Afghani 715
James, Henry 177
**James E. Sullivan Memorial
Trophy 910**
Jammu and Kashmir
chronology 21
Japan 519
banking 878
chronology 22, 25, 29, 30, 35,
37
flags of the world Plate 3
historical periods and rulers
707
holidays 201
photographs Plate 8
World Cup 14
Japan Series 995
Java Sea
disasters 41
Jay, John 715
Jefferson, Thomas 760
approach to farming 797
influential leaders 715
presidential cabinets 774
Supreme Court appointments
800
US presidents 758
US vice presidents 773
wives and children 769
Jenin 34
Jennings, Elizabeth Joan 110
Jennings, Waylon 110
Jersey 521
Jerusalem
Jerusalem Prize 171
photographs Plate 16
Jerusalem Prize 171
Jesus Christ 715

jeu de paume (royal tennis)
Olympic champions 946
Jewett, Sarah Orne 177
Jewish calendar 199
Jia Lanpo 110
Joan of Arc, Saint 715
John (king of England) 715
John XXIII 715
John Carter Brown Library 875
John Paul II (pope) 71, 715
chronology 22, 24, 25, 28, 31,
34, 36, 38
Johnson, Andrew 763
presidential cabinets 777
US presidents 759
US vice presidents 773
wives and children 770
Johnson, Jack 917
Johnson, Lyndon B. 767
presidential cabinets 782
presidential libraries 785
Supreme Court appointments
801
US presidents 759
US vice presidents 774
wives and children 772
Johnson, Magic 917
Johnson, Michael 917
Johnson, Richard M. 773
Johnson, Samuel 177
Johnson, Walter 917
Joint Chief of Staff 804
Joint Economic Committee: *see*
Economic Committee,
Joint
Jones, Bobby 917
Jones, Chuck 110
Jordan 522
flags of the world Plate 3
Jordan, June 110
Jordan, Michael 71
journalism
Pulitzer Prize 154
Jovanovich, William 110
Joyce, James 177
Joyner-Kersee, Jackie 917
Juárez, Benito 715
Judaism 729
holidays 200
Jewish calendar 199
worldwide religious adherents
726
Judiciary, Committee on the
US House 797
Judiciary Committee
US Senate 792
judo 1066
Olympic champions 946
2000 Summer Olympic Games
medal winners 974
world championships 1066,
1067
Julian calendar 197
Junge, Traudl 110
Jupiter 224
celestial bodies 217
moons 225
morning and evening stars
214
rings 226
Jurassic Period 294

Jurek v. Texas 802
Justice, Department of
executive departments 788
Justinian I 715

K

Kabul 23, 25, 27, 34
Kadare, Ismail 177
Kael, Pauline 110
Kafka, Franz 177
Kahn, Oliver 14
K'ang-hsi 715
K'ang Yu-wei 715
Kano, Jigoro 917
Kansas 830
congressional apportionment
798
death penalty sentences 868
electoral votes 800
energy consumption 882
governors of US states and
territories 855
immigration 817
libraries 874
minerals 881
poverty level 819
state crime rates 863
state officers and legislatures
857
state population 814
US House 794
US prison population 867
US Senate 790
Karelin, Aleksandr 917
Karzai, Hamid 25, 28, 72
photographs Plate 16
Kashmir 10
chronology 15, 36, 37, 38
map 10
Kato, Shizue Hirota 110
Katzenbach v. McClung 802
Kawabata, Yasunari 177
Kawakami, Genichi 110
Kazakhstan 524
adoptions of foreign-born
children 872
flags of the world Plate 3
Kazantzidis, Stelios 110
Keane, John B. 110
Keats, John 177
Keino, Kip 917
Keïta, Seydou 110
Kelly, Thomas Joseph 110
Kelvin 238
Kemal, Yashar 177
Kennedy, John F. 767
presidential cabinets 782
presidential libraries 785
Supreme Court appointments
801
US presidents 759
wives and children 772
Kennedy Center Honors 183
Kentucky 831
congressional apportionment
798
death penalty sentences 869
electoral votes 800
energy consumption 882

Vonnegut, Kurt, Jr. 182
Vostok 258
Voulkos, Peter 117

W

wage
  comparative hourly compensation costs 888
  US military pay scale 805
Wagner, Honus 924
Walcott, Derek 182
Walker, John 24
Wallace, Henry A. 774
Walter, Fritz 117
Walters, Vernon Anthony 117
waltz 393
Wand, Günter 117
Wang, Vera 100
Wang Kon 720
war casualties 808
Warmerdam, Dutch 117, 924
Warner, Pop 924
Warren, Earl 720
Washington 851
  congressional apportionment 798
  death penalty sentences 869
  electoral votes 800
  energy consumption 883
  governors of US states and territories 855
  immigration 818
  libraries 875
  minerals 882
  poverty level 819
  state crime rates 863
  state officers and legislatures 859
  state population 814
  US House 796
  US prison population 868
  US Senate 791
Washington, DC, or District of Columbia 825
  electoral votes 800
  energy consumption 883
  immigration 817
  poverty level 819
  September 11 attack 5
  state crime rates 863
  state population 814
  US House 797
  US prison population 867
Washington, Denzel 32, 100
  photographs Plate 9
Washington, George 759
  influential leaders 720
  presidential cabinets 774
  Supreme Court appointments 800
  US presidents 758
  wives and children 769
Wasserman, Lew 117
water 240
  pollution 268
  worldwide health indicators 307
water polo
  Olympic champions 959

2000 Summer Olympic Games
  medal winners 979
water-soluble vitamin 327
Watkins, Sherron 9
watt 238
Ways and Means, Committee on
  US House 797
Weah, George 924
weapons violation
  arrests in the US 867
weather: see climate;
  meteorology
Weaver, Pat 117
web site 255
  most visited 254
  see also Internet; World Wide
    Web; and specific subjects
    for relevant web sites
Weber, Dick 924
weight
  body mass index 336
  weight, mass, and density 253
weight driven mechanical clock
  measuring time 195
weight lifting 1111
  Olympic champions 959
  2000 Summer Olympic Games
    medal winners 979
  world champions 1111
  world records 1111
Weisskopf, Victor Frederick 117
Weissmuller, Johnny 924
Wells, H. G. 182
Welty, Eudora 117, 182
Werner, Pierre 118
West, Jerry 925
West Bank
  chronology 27, 32, 34
West Virginia 851
  congressional apportionment 798
  electoral votes 800
  energy consumption 883
  governors of US states and territories 855
  immigration 818
  libraries 875
  minerals 882
  poverty level 819
  state crime rates 863
  state officers and legislatures 859
  state population 814
  US House 797
  US prison population 868
  US Senate 791
Weston, Garry 118
Wharton, Edith 182
Wheeler, William A. 773
Whitbread Book Awards 169
White, Byron 118
White, E. B. 182
White House (Washington, DC) 745
Whitehead, Robert 118
Whitehouse, Mary Hutcheson 118
Whitman, Walt 182
WHO: see World Health
  Organization

WIBC Bowling Championships 1002
Wiesel, Elie 721
Wild 2 Comet 217
Wilde, Oscar 182
Wildenstein, Daniel Leopold 118
Wilder, Billy 118
wildfire 39, 272
Willey, Gordon Randolph 118
William I 721
William of Wales, Prince 101
Williams, Harrison Arlington, Jr. 118
Williams, Robin 101
Williams, Serena 19, 38, 101
Williams, Ted 925
Williams, Tennessee 182
Williams, Venus 15, 19, 38, 101
Williams, William Carlos 182
Wills, Helen 925
Wilson, August 182
Wilson, Henry 773
Wilson, Woodrow 765
  influential leaders 721
  presidential cabinets 779
  Supreme Court appointments 801
  US presidents 759
  wives and children 771
Wimbledon: see All-England
  Tennis Championships
Winbergh, Gösta 118
wind
  hurricane and tornado classifications 263
  weather warnings 265
wind chill 264
  weather warnings 266
wind speed
  hurricane and tornado classifications 263
Winship, Thomas 118
Winston Cup 990
Winter Olympic Games 8
  champions 964
  photographs Plate 6
  sites 926
  2002 Games medal winners 980
winter pentathlon
  Olympic champions 970
Winterbottom, Sir Walter 118
Winterthur Museum, Garden, and Library 875
Wisconsin 852
  congressional apportionment 798
  electoral votes 800
  energy consumption 883
  governors of US states and territories 855
  immigration 818
  libraries 875
  minerals 882
  poverty level 819
  state crime rates 863
  state officers and legislatures 859
  state population 814
  US House 797
  US prison population 868

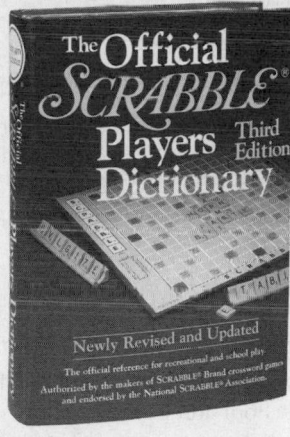

Consider these other fine products from Britannica:

The Encyclopædia Britannica

The reference standard of the world since 1768, the 32-volume *Britannica* is better than ever. More than 4,000 contributors, including many Nobel Prize winners, provide comprehensive and up-to-date entries written for today's world. The *Encyclopædia Britannica* is your gateway to understanding, and underscores Britannica's reputation as a leader in making knowledge accessible to all.

Encyclopædia Britannica 2003 Ultimate Reference Suite

The 2003 Ultimate Reference Suite includes THREE complete reference libraries — Elementary, Student, and Adult — for use from grade school to graduate school and beyond. Every user has just the right encyclopedia, dictionary, atlas, thesaurus, and timeline. Users have access to the authoritative *Encyclopædia Britannica* plus the *Britannica Student Encyclopedia*, the *Britannica Elementary Encyclopedia*, two dictionaries and two thesauruses from Merriam-Webster, three atlases, 25 timelines, and much more. Also includes FREE updates for one year.

Britannica Premium Service

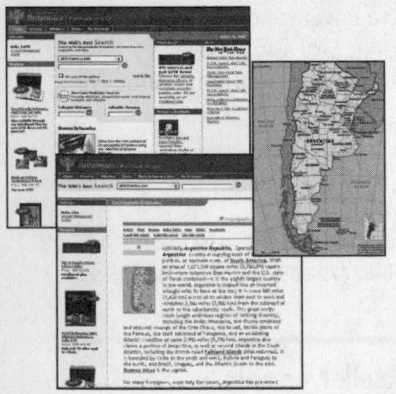

Combining the authority of Britannica with the power of the Web, *Britannica Premium Service* is built for easy, everyday use. This vast online source of information at www.britannica.com contains three encyclopedias, including the famous *Encyclopædia Britannica*. Users can also access a Merriam-Webster dictionary and thesaurus, atlas, Internet guide, and more — all in an advertising-free environment.

ENCYCLOPÆDIA
Britannica

For these and other award-winning reference and learning products, contact Britannica today.
WEB: http://store.britannica.com
PHONE: 1-800-323-1229

OCTOBER 2002–DECEMBER 2003

OCTOBER 2002

Sun	Mon	Tue	Wed	Thu	Fri	Sat
		1	2	3	4	5
6	7	8	9	10	11	12
13	14	15	16	17	18	19
20	21	22	23	24	25	26
27	28	29	30	31		

NOVEMBER 2002

Sun	Mon	Tue	Wed	Thu	Fri	Sat
					1	2
3	4	5	6	7	8	9
10	11	12	13	14	15	16
17	18	19	20	21	22	23
24	25	26	27	28	29	30

DECEMBER 2002

Sun	Mon	Tue	Wed	Thu	Fri	Sat
1	2	3	4	5	6	7
8	9	10	11	12	13	14
15	16	17	18	19	20	21
22	23	24	25	26	27	28
29	30	31				

JANUARY 2003

Sun	Mon	Tue	Wed	Thu	Fri	Sat
			1	2	3	4
5	6	7	8	9	10	11
12	13	14	15	16	17	18
19	20	21	22	23	24	25
26	27	28	29	30	31	

FEBRUARY 2003

Sun	Mon	Tue	Wed	Thu	Fri	Sat
						1
2	3	4	5	6	7	8
9	10	11	12	13	14	15
16	17	18	19	20	21	22
23	24	25	26	27	28	

MARCH 2003

Sun	Mon	Tue	Wed	Thu	Fri	Sat
						1
2	3	4	5	6	7	8
9	10	11	12	13	14	15
16	17	18	19	20	21	22
23	24	25	26	27	28	29
30	31					

APRIL 2003

Sun	Mon	Tue	Wed	Thu	Fri	Sat
		1	2	3	4	5
6	7	8	9	10	11	12
13	14	15	16	17	18	19
20	21	22	23	24	25	26
27	28	29	30			

MAY 2003

Sun	Mon	Tue	Wed	Thu	Fri	Sat
				1	2	3
4	5	6	7	8	9	10
11	12	13	14	15	16	17
18	19	20	21	22	23	24
25	26	27	28	29	30	31

JUNE 2003

Sun	Mon	Tue	Wed	Thu	Fri	Sat
1	2	3	4	5	6	7
8	9	10	11	12	13	14
15	16	17	18	19	20	21
22	23	24	25	26	27	28
29	30					

JULY 2003

Sun	Mon	Tue	Wed	Thu	Fri	Sat
		1	2	3	4	5
6	7	8	9	10	11	12
13	14	15	16	17	18	19
20	21	22	23	24	25	26
27	28	29	30	31		

AUGUST 2003

Sun	Mon	Tue	Wed	Thu	Fri	Sat
					1	2
3	4	5	6	7	8	9
10	11	12	13	14	15	16
17	18	19	20	21	22	23
24	25	26	27	28	29	30
31						

SEPTEMBER 2003

Sun	Mon	Tue	Wed	Thu	Fri	Sat
	1	2	3	4	5	6
7	8	9	10	11	12	13
14	15	16	17	18	19	20
21	22	23	24	25	26	27
28	29	30				

OCTOBER 2003

Sun	Mon	Tue	Wed	Thu	Fri	Sat
			1	2	3	4
5	6	7	8	9	10	11
12	13	14	15	16	17	18
19	20	21	22	23	24	25
26	27	28	29	30	31	

NOVEMBER 2003

Sun	Mon	Tue	Wed	Thu	Fri	Sat
						1
2	3	4	5	6	7	8
9	10	11	12	13	14	15
16	17	18	19	20	21	22
23	24	25	26	27	28	29
30						

DECEMBER 2003

Sun	Mon	Tue	Wed	Thu	Fri	Sat
	1	2	3	4	5	6
7	8	9	10	11	12	13
14	15	16	17	18	19	20
21	22	23	24	25	26	27
28	29	30	31			

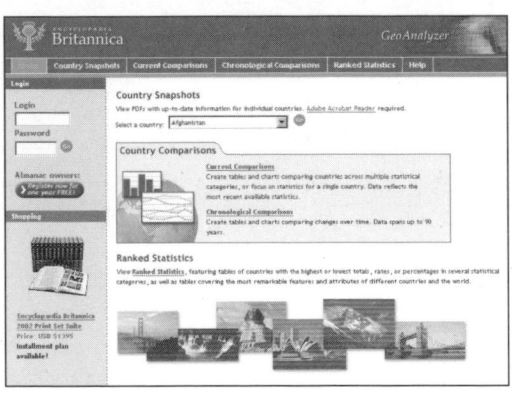